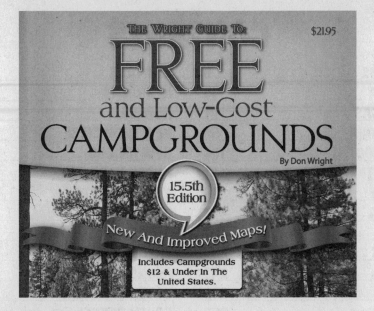

THE WRIGHT GUIDE To:
$21.95

FREE
and Low-Cost
CAMPGROUNDS
By Don Wright

15.5th Edition

New And Improved Maps!

Includes Campgrounds
$12 & Under In The
United States.

Printed in the United States of America

ISBN - 0-937877-55-5

W9-AYB-433

THE WRIGHT GUIDE

P.O. Box 2832
Elkhart, IN 46515-2832
1-800-272-5518
by Don Wright and Joyce Wright

The Wright Guide makes every effort possible to ensure accuracy of
listings, including directions, fees, services and facilities.
Information, including map locations, has been obtained from sources
regarded as reliable. No responsibility is assumed for
inadvertent errors or changes that occur before or after publication.
No representation is made of accuracy, completeness and
interpretation due to map scale.

Note: Camping locations denoted by map numbers represent the
closest proximity to each campground, if not exact location, due to
map size and/or number of campgrounds in a condensed area.

Visit our website at: www.rverbookstore.com
e-mail us at: rverbookstore@gmail.com

00555

6 00419 02195 7

CONTENTS

ABBREVIATIONS

approx	approximately	hrs	hours
ave	avenue	jct	junction
bldg	building	L	Launch (boat)
blk	block	LD	Labor Day
BLM	Bureau of Land Mgmt.	MD	Memorial Day
cfga	campfire - grill area	mi	miles
co	county	N	north
d	dock	Prim	primitive
drkg wtr	drinking water	r	rental
E	east	S	south
elec	electric	st	street
elev	elevation	tbls	tables
FH or FR	forest road	W	west
Hwy	highway	wtr	water

INTRODUCTION

This is not just another ordinary campground guide. This is the only guide that lists thousands of campgrounds across the USA where you can stay absolutely FREE. In addition, to make your travels easier, we have added thousands more campgrounds with overnight fees of <u>$12 or less</u>.

By listing nearly 12,000 $12-and-under campsites, we are providing an enormous collection of camping places not available in any other campground directory. They include city and county parks, national forest and Bureau of Land Management campgrounds, public campgrounds operated by utility firms and lumber companies, overnight stops created by Lions and Kiwanis clubs, state-operated fishing camps, low-cost off-season campgrounds, fairground camping areas and even some small mom-and-pop private campgrounds.

Our listings of state-operated fishing lakes, hunting areas and wildlife management areas where primitive camping is allowed continues to increase. Experienced users of Guide to Free Campgrounds will notice new entries that include dispersed national forest camps, fairgrounds, wildlife area camps, coyote camps and even a few private campgrounds where no fees are charged.

Federal campgrounds that were deleted from previous editions because of higher camping fees are back in this book if fees of $12 or less are charged to holders of the federal Golden Age Passport OR its successor, the America The Beautiful Senior Pass. Holders of those passes pay half prices at nearly all campgrounds operated by the National Park Service, National Forest Service, Bureau of Land Management, Bureau of Reclamation, the Tennessee Valley Authority and the U.S. Army Corps of Engineers.

Each campground in this book is carefully researched, and the information is updated at least bi-annually. We make every effort to keep this continually changing information as accurate as possible by means of field researchers, government sources, reader feedback and, in many cases, personal site visits.

Public campgrounds remain the heart of this book, whether they are free or have fees that must be paid. Those parks offer incredible savings to budget-conscious travelers, but they also have other advantages. They are generally found in peaceful and scenic settings. They are commonly located by a lake, river or ocean and offer numerous recreational opportunities, such as boating, fishing, swimming or waterskiing. Public campgrounds often have hiking trails, and almost all have easy access to nature.

Significantly, most campers today spend the majority of their nights in campgrounds where overnight fees are charged, where they have access to a wide variety of facilities (such as electricity and water hookups) or services (swimming pools, rec halls, etc.). Now, we're providing information about the least expensive of those campgrounds along with the free ones.

The campgrounds in this book are listed alphabetically by state and by towns within each state. Locations of all towns are pinpointed with numbered black dots on the maps at the beginning of each state section.

At the beginning of each state section, we've listed sources for general tourist information and additional camping data. You'll find many valuable suggestions for locating additional campgrounds from these sources.

Although we've listed thousands of free campgrounds in this guide, we've by no means exhausted all the possibilities. Here are a few suggestions for places to check if there isn't a free campground listed in the area you want to stay.

NATIONAL FORESTS AND BUREAU OF LAND MANAGEMENT

You can legally camp anywhere on national forest land, and most places on BLM property. Most state and national forests and BLM lands have so-called "dispersed" sites that may be utilized free. Thousands of those dispersed locations are available throughout the west and in the national forests of Maine, Minnesota and Michigan. Dispersed sites are basically locations where boondock camping has occurred often enough that the sites almost appear to be semi-developed camping locations. Frequently, the government agencies responsible for developing campsites begin to add facilities such as pit toilets, picnic tables and campfire grill areas to the dispersed areas, and formal development of official sites begins to take shape.

Some of the best dispersed sites that are popular among traveling campers are in Arizona around the rim of the Grand Canyon. Others are on the shores of lakes throughout the Upper Peninsula of Michigan and off the dirt roads in northern Minnesota. Our plans for future editions of this guide are to add even more dispersed locations.

CITY PARKS
We have listed numerous city parks in this guide that allow camping, but there are still many to be discovered. Stop at a service station, the local Chamber of Commerce or the police station and ask if there is a park or other free or low-cost place to spend the night.

FACILITIES AT LOW-COST CAMPGROUNDS
You'll be surprised at how many facilities low-cost campgrounds offer -- from drinking water to hot showers and full hookups. Our readers frequently tell us low-cost sites are valuable for them because they like to search out inexpensive places where they can either just park for the night or spend a few days while they economize.

A WORD ABOUT "RV SIZE LIMITS"
Throughout this book, you will see references to RV size limits at campgrounds. Please do not interpret this to mean those sites are not open to larger RVs. The "limits" are really general recommendations on the length of RVs that either fit easily on the sites or can maneuver on the grounds without scraping trees. No one is going to ask you to leave a campground because you have a 30-foot motorhome and the "size limit" is 16 feet.

LONG-TERM VISITOR AREAS (LTVAs)
The Bureau of Land Management (BLM) established nine LTVAs in 1983 in the California desert and along the lower Colorado River where visitors may camp for the entire winter. Winter visitors who wish to stay in an LTVA may do so by purchasing a long-term visitor permit and selecting a location in one of the designated Long-Term Visitor Areas. The permit covers the long-term season from October 1 to May 31. Permit holders may move from one LTVA to another without incurring additional user fees. Guests are allowed to stay with permit holders for short stays during the season at no charge.

STATE PARKS
Many state part systems include campgrounds that offer sites for $12 or less. However, many of those states also charge daily entry fees which sometimes cause overall fees to be higher than our $12 guidelines. In cases when the overnight fees are under $12 when the entry fees are disregarded, we have elected to include those state park facilities in this book. If you intend to camp several times in a particular state's parks, we suggest you invest in the annual entry permits which most states offer.

CORPS OF ENGINEERS
Users of our best-selling CAMPING WITH THE CORPS OF ENGINEERS probably already are aware that the U.S. Army Corps of Engineers eliminated many of its cost-free camping facilities during 1994. Low fees are now charged at most of those sites, and so they are included in this book.

NATIONAL FORESTS
Campgrounds at national forests have become favorite overnight spots of campers who want to reduce their travel costs. As a consequence, many national forest sites are experiencing heavy daily usage, and forest administrators are hard pressed to maintain those sites and keep them both attractive and rustic. Almost across the board, campsite fees at national forest areas have been increased dramatically during the past three years; in some cases, fees have more than doubled. In addition, the forest service is tending toward hiring professional concessionaires to operate the campgrounds, and that tendency also has resulted in higher camping fees.

UPDATED FEES
At various points within the text of this book, you will find references to "fee status uncertain" or "at last report." In these cases, the campgrounds have been listed in this edition even though we were uncertain, at press time, of exact fee amounts. In each case, we verified that the campground offered low-fee sites, but exact fees either were unavailable to us or had not yet been set for the upcoming camping season.

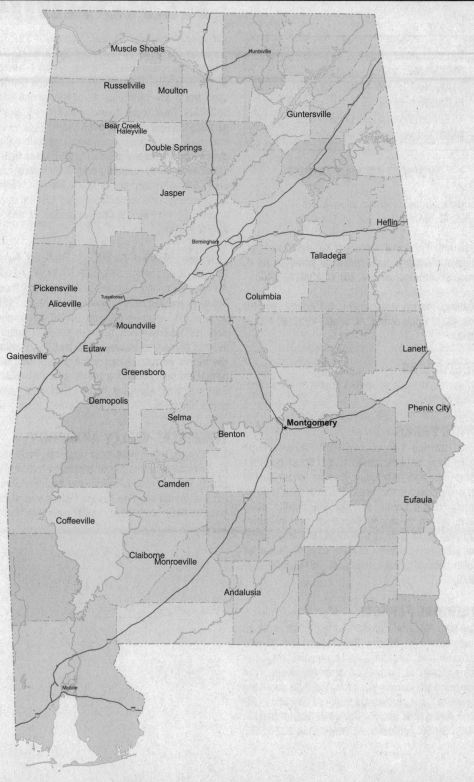

Muscle Shoals

Huntsville

Russellville

Moulton

Guntersville

Bear Creek
Haleyville

Double Springs

Jasper

Heflin

Birmingham

Talladega

Pickensville

Tuscaloosa

Aliceville

Columbia

Moundville

Lanett

Eutaw

Gainesville

Greensboro

Demopolis

Phenix City

Selma

Montgomery

Benton

Camden

Eufaula

Coffeeville

Claiborne
Monroeville

Andalusia

Mobile

ALABAMA

CAPITAL: Montgomery
NICKNAME: Yellowhammer State
STATEHOOD: 1819 – 22nd State
FLOWER: Camelia
TREE: Southern Longleaf Pine
BIRD: Yellowhammer

WWW.ALABAMA.TRAVEL

Toll-free number for travel information:
1-800-ALABAMA.

Department of Conservation and Natural Resources, Division of Wildlife and Freshwater fisheries, 64 N. Union St., Montgomery, AL 36130 (334/242-3465).

Alabama Tourism Department, 401 Adams Ave, PO Box 4927, Montgomery, AL 36103-4927. 334-242-4169.

REST AREAS
No overnight stops permitted in rest areas or welcome centers.

STATE PARKS
Base camping fees at nearly all Alabama state parks have been increased to $17.50 at primitive campsites, and as a result, they no longer qualify for being listed in this book. The exception is Town Creek Fishing Center at Lake Guntersville State Park, where in-season boondock and primitive camping at 13 sites is $14. Dept. of Conservation and Natural Resources, Division of State Parks, 64 North Union St, Montgomery, AL 36130. 800-252-7275.

NATIONAL FORESTS
Conecuh National Forest. Nearly 84,000 acres on Alabama-Florida border. Backpacking on 20-mile Conecuh Trail. Alligator & wild turkey present. Low-fee camping at Open Pond near Andalusia. Free dispersed site camping is permitted throughout the forest, but free permits are required for safety reasons during deer season (Nov-Jan). District Ranger, 24481 SR 55, Andalusia, AL 36420. 334/222-2555.

Talladega National Forest. Includes 392,567 acres at the southern edge of the Appalachian Mountains. Shoal Creek District, SR 46 E, Heflin, AL 36264, phone 256-463-2272; Talladega District, 1001 North St., Talladega, AL 35160, phone 256-362-2909; Oakmulgee District, 9901 Hwy 5, Brent, AL 35034, phone 205-926-9765.

Bankhead National Forest. 179,655 acres in NW of state. Features a natural bridge, limestone canyons, Sipsey Wilderness & Black Warrior Wildlife Management Area. Hunting for deer, squirrel, quail, wild turkey. PO Box 278, Double Springs, AL 35553; 205/489-5111.

Tuskegee National Forest. 125 National Forest Rd 949, Tuskegee, AL 36083-9801; 334-727-2652. A region of rolling hills and slow-moving streams between the mountains and coastal plains. 125-acre wildlife viewing area on US 80 three miles north of Tuskegee and 12 miles south of Auburn. 16-mile horse trail between I-85 and US 29 within the forest. Bartram Trail commemorates the journeys more than 200 years ago of naturalist William Bartram, who identified many species of native plants and trees.

TENNESSEE VALLEY AUTHORITY
The TVA operates more than 80 public recreation areas throughout the South (including two in Alabama). Holders of the America the Beautiful Senior Pass or the Golden Age Passport can camp at half price at sites which have regular overnight fees of $17 to $26 for RVs.

ALICEVILLE
Cochrane Recreation Area　　　　　　　　　$8
Corps of Engineers
Gainesvile Lake
Tennessee-Tombigbee Waterway
10 mi S of Aliceville on SR 17; 2 mi W of Huyck Bridge, following signs; right, then 2 mi on access rd. $8 base at 60 wtr/elec sites with federal senior pass; others pay $16, $18 at premium waterfront locations ($9 with senior pass). All year; 14-day limit. RV limit in excess of 65 ft. Tbls, flush toilets, cfga, drkg wtr, 30-amp elec, dump, showers, playground, fish cleaning station, coin laundry, picnic shelter, handicap fishing area. Boating(l), fishing, basketball, hiking trail. Non-campers pay $3 boat launch.

ANDALUSIA
Open Pond　　　　　　　　　　　　　　　$8
Conecuh National Forest
10 mi SW of Andalusia on US 29; 5 mi S on SR 137; half mi E on CR 24; 1 mi SE on CR 28. $8 base. All year; 14-day limit. Base fee for 9 sites without hookups; 65 sites with wtr/elec, $16 ($12 with federal senior pass). Tbls, flush toilets, cfga, drkg wtr, showers, dump. Swimming, boating (l, no motors), fishing, biking, picnic area. 1.5 mi loop of 20-mi Conecuh Trail; scenic 3-mile loop trail from pond to natural Blue Springs. Group shelter built in 1930s by CCC.

BEAR CREEK
Twin Forks City Park　　　　　　　　　　$10
City of Bear Creek
On CR 79 E in Bear Creek. 3/15-10/15. Sites $10 at primitive sites, $25 with wtr/elec ($275 monthly). 137 sites. Tbls, flush toilets, cfga, drkg wtr, playground, dump, showers. Swimming, boating, fishing, biking.

BENTON
Prairie Creek　　　　　　　　　　　　　$11
Corps of Engineers
Woodruff Lake
From jct with US 80 just E of Benton, 5 mi N on Benton Rd; at 3-way split just S of Edsons, take center rd 0.8 mi N; right (E) on Jones Buff Rd, then left on Prairie Creek Rd into campground; at E shore of river. $11 base for seniors with federal senior pass at 55 elec/wtr sites; others pay $22 base, $24 at premium waterfront locations ($12 with senior pass). 7 tent sites $18 ($9 with senior pass). 35-ft RV limit; 2 pull-through. All year; 14-day limit. Tbls, pavilion, flush toilets, cfga, drkg wtr, showers, dump, playground, picnic shelter, fish cleaning station, coin laundry. Hiking trail, fishing, boating(l), basketball, canoeing.

CAMDEN
Chilatchee Creek　　　　　　　　　　　$7
Corps of Engineers
William Dannelly Lake
From Camden, about 20 mi NW on SR 28; 4 mi NE on SR 5 to

Alberta; 9 mi SE on CR 29, then E on park access rd. $14 at 6 primitive sites; $22 at 33 elec/wtr sites, $24 at waterfront sites ($7, $11 & $12 with federal senior pass); 14-day limit; only primitive camping available 11/1-3/1. RV limit 65 ft; 3 pull-through sites, handicap sites with 50-amp elec/wtr. Tbls, flush toilets, cfga, drkg wtr, showers, dump, picnic shelter, fish cleaning station, playground. Hiking trails, picnicking, fishing, boating(l). Non-campers pay day use fee.

Elm Bluff　　　　　　　　　　　　　　FREE
Corps of Engineers
Bill Dannelly Reservoir
18 mi NE of Camden on SR 41 to near town of Elm Bluff, then 2 mi NW on CR 407; right (N) on access rd; at S shore of Alabama River/Majors Creek. Free. All year; 14-day limit. 10 primitive sites. Tbls, toilets, cfga, drkg wtr. Boating(l), fishing, picnicking.

Millers Ferry　　　　　　　　　　　　$11
Corps of Engineers
William Dannelly Lake
From Camden, 12 mi NW on SR 28 through town of Millers Ferry, then right (NE) before Lee Long Bridge on access rd to campground (also called East Bank Park); at E shore of reservoir. $11 base for seniors with federal senior pass at 42 elec/wtr sites; others pay $22 base, $24 at 29 waterfront sites ($12 with senior pass). RV limit in excess of 65 ft; 6 pull-through sites, 12 handicap sites. All year; 14-day limit. Tbls, flush toilets, cfga, drkg wtr, showers, dump, playground, beach, shelter, multi-use courts, coin laundry. Horseshoes, hiking trails, fishing, boating(ld), swimming.

CLAIBORNE
Damsite West Bank　　　　　　　　　FREE
Corps of Engineers
Claiborne Lake
5 mi NW of Claiborne on SR 48; 3 mi N, on W side of dam. Free. All year; 14-day limit. 2 primitive sites. Tbls, toilets, cfga, drkg wtr. Hiking trails, boating, fishing.

Silver Creek Recreation Area　　　　　FREE
Corps of Engineers
Claiborne Lake
From Claiborne, 8 mi NW on US 84 to just S of Whatley; 5 mi N on CRF 35 to town of Vashti; 0.25 mi E on CR 39, then E on Silver Creek Rd, folowing signs SE to park; at E shore of lake/Majors Creek. All year; 14-day limit. 45 acres. 8 free primitive sites for self-contained RVs under 21 ft. Group camping. Tbls, firewoodtoilets, cfga, no drkg wtr. Fishing, boating(l), hiking trails.

COFFEEVILLE
Lenoir Landing Park　　　　　　　　　FREE
Corps of Engineers
Coffeeville Lake
Black Warrior and Tombigbee River Waterway
From jct with US 84 about 5 mi E of Silas (W of Coffeeville),

3 mi N on CR 21; 3 mi NW on CR 14 to town of Womack Hill; 0.5 mi N on CR 25; 3 mi N on CR 23, then 2 mi S on paved rd to landing, following signs; at W shore of river. Free primitive sites. All year; 14-day limit. Tbls, pit toilets, cfga, drkg wtr, picnic shelter. ORVs prohibited. Boating(l), fishing.

Old Lock 1 Park FREE
Corps of Engineers
Coffeeville Lake
Black Warrior and Tombigbee River Waterway
From jct with US 43 at Jackson, about 7 mi N on SR 69 to town of Mays Crossing, then left (SW) about 5 mi on access rd to park at Tombigbee River oxbow. 10 free primitive sites, primarily for tents. All year; 14-day limit. Tbls, flush toilets, cfga, drkg wtr, picnic shelter. ORVs prohibited.

Service Park $11
Corps of Engineers
Coffeeville Lake
Black Warrior and Tombigbee River Waterway
4 mi W of Coffeeville on US 84, across bridge, then access right following signs. $11 for seniors with federal senior pass at 50-amp elec/wtr RV sites; others pay $22. RV limit in excess of 65 ft; 10 pull-through sites, 1 handicap site. ORVs prohibited. All year; 14-day limit. Flush toilets, cfga, drkg wtr, dump, playground, showers, coin laundry. Non-campers pay $5 dump fee. Boating(l), fishing.

COLUMBIA (12)
Coheelee Creek FREE
Blakely-Early County Park
George W. Andrews Lake
10 mi N of Columbia, in Georgia on county rd. Free. 3/1-11/30; 14-day limit. 28 primitive sites (RVs under 19 ft). Tbls, toilets, cfga, hand-pumped wtr. Boating (l), picnicking, fishing. Former Corps of Engineers park now leased to the county.

DEMOPOLIS
Belmont Park FREE
Corps of Engineers
Demopolis Lake
From about 10 mi W of Demopolis on US 80 at jct with SR 28, about 3 mi N on SR 28 to village of Coatopa; right (E) on CR 23 about 15 mi to village of Belmont; E on CR 22, then NE on Belmont Park access rd; near W shore of Tombigbee River; site inaccessible from E shore except by boat. Free. All year; 14-day limit. Primitive sites with pit toilets, cfga, tbls, drkg wtr, lantern pole. Picnic shelter, $25. Non-campers pay $3 for boat ramp. Boating(l), fishing.

Forkland Campground $10
McConnico Creek
Corps of Engineers
Demopolis Lake
Black Warrior and Tombigbee River Waterway
From Demopolis, 9 mi N on US 43; at Forkland, 1 mi SW (left) on unpaved co rd rd, following signs. $10 with federal senior pass at 10 30-amp elec/wtr sites (others pay $20; $11 with senior pass at 10 50-amp elec/wtr sites (others pay $22). All year; 14-day limit. RV limit in excess of 65 ft; 13 pull-through sites. Tbls, flush toilets, cfga, drkg wtr, dump, showers, coin laundry, fishing pier, hiking trail, playground, shelter with elec ($25), nature trail. Boating(l), fishing, nature trail. ORVs prohibited. Non-campersd pay $3 entry & boat ramp fee ($30 annual).

Foscue Creek Park $11
McConnico Creek
Corps of Engineers
Demopolis Lake
Black Warrior and Tombigbee River Waterway
3 mi W of Demopolis on US 80, following signs; 2 mi N (right) on Maria Ave; S of confluence of Black Warrior & Tombigbee Rivers. $11 base with federal senior pass at 5 elec/wtr 50-amp sites; others pay $22; $24 at 48 full-hookup 50-amp sites ($12 with senior pass). RV limit in excess of 65 ft; 2 pull-through sites, 9 handicap sites with full hookups. 3 group shelters, $25-$35. All year; 14-day limit. Non-campers pay $5 for dump station, $3 for entry & boat ramp. Flush toilets, drkg wtr, cfga, tbls, showers, dump, playground, coin laundry, elec, amphitheater, sewer. Boating(l), fishing, hiking trail, ball field.

Runaway Branch II Park FREE
Corps of Engineers
Demopolis Lake
From Birdeye at jct with CR 25, S on US 43 (Demopolis Hwy) toward Demopolis; 1 mi W on CR 11; S on Runaway II Park access rd. Free. All year; 14-day limit. Primitive sites with picnic shelter, tbls, toilets, cfga, drkg wtr, lantern posts. ORVs prohibited. Boating(l), fishing.

DOUBLE SPRINGS
Corinth Recreation Area $8.50
William Bankhead National Forest
3.9 mi E of Double Springs on US 278; right at Corinth sign for 2.5 mi; at Lake Lewis Smith; 2 camping loops. $8.50 for seniors with federal senior pass at elec sites; others pay $17; full hookups, $14 with senior pass (others pay $28). 3/11-10/31; 14-day limit. 52 sites. Tbls, flush toilets, cfga, drkg wtr, showers, dump, beach, interpretive programs. Swimming, fishing, boating(l), hiking, waterskiing. Picnic shelter, $30. Non-campers pay $6 for day use parking & dump station.

Houston Recreation Area CLOSED
William Bankhead National Forest
10 mi E of Double Springs on US 278; 2 mi S on CR 63; 2 mi SW on CR 64; 1 mi W on FR 118. Campground closed temporarily; check with forest for current status.

EUFAULA
White Oak Creek $12
Corps of Engineers
Walter F. George Lake
8 mi S of Eufaula on US 431; 2 mi SE (left) on SR 95; E (left)
at sign prior to White Oak Creek bridge. $12 for seniors
with federal senior pass at 129 elec/wtr sites; others pay
$24. All year; 14-day limit. 40-ft RV limit; 5 pull-through
sites. Tbls, flush toilets, showers, cfga, drkg wtr, dump,
beach, playground, fishing pier, coin laundry, fish cleaning station. Swimming, boating(ld), fishing, hiking trails,
swimming.

EUTAW
Jennings Ferry $11
Corps of Engineers
Warrior Lake
Black Warrior & Tombigbee Waterway
From Eutaw, 5.7 mi E on SR 14, across Warrior River Bridge.
$11 for seniors with federal senior pass at 52 elec/wtr
50-amp sites; others pay $22. All year; 14-day limit. RV limit
in excess of 65 ft; 8 pull-through sites. Tbls, flush toilets,
showers, cfga, drkg wtr, coin laundry. Bank fishing, boating
(concrete ramp), picnicking. Non-campers pay $5 for dump
station, $3 for boat ramp ($30 annually).

FORT GAINES (GEORGIA)
Hardridge Creek $12
Corps of Engineers
Walter F. George Lake
From Ft. Gaines, Georgia (S of Eufaula, AL), 3 mi W on SR
37 (becoming AL 10) across river; 1 mi W on CR 46; 3 mi
N on CR 97; E at sign. $12 base for seniors with federal
senior pass at 55 elec/wtr sites; others pay $24. 15 full
hookup sites, $26 ($13 with senior pass). RV limit 30 ft. All
year; 14-day limit. Tbls, flush toilets, cfga, drkg wtr, showers, dump, fishing pier, playground, beach, coin laundry,
shelter. Fishing, boating(l), swimming.

GAINESVILLE
Sumter Recreation Area   FREE
Gainesville Lake
Corps of Engineers
Tennessee-Tombigbee Waterway
From Gainesville, SW on SR 116; N on CR 85; E on access
rd to W shore of lake. All year; 14-day limit. Free primitive
undesignated sites; day use fee may be charged. Pit toi-
lets, cfga, drkg wtr, tbls. Fishing boating(l).

GREENSBORO
Lock 5 Park   FREE
Corps of Engineers
Demopolis Lake
From Greensboro, about 3 mi S on SR 69 to village of
Cedarville, then 2 mi W on CR 16 to split with Owl Rd;
continue SW to park; on Big German arm of lake. Free. All

year; 14-day limit. Primitive sites with toilets, tbls, cfga,
drkg wtr, lantern poles, picnic shelter. ORVs prohibited.
Boating(l), fishing.

Payne Lake East Side $5
Payne Lake Recreation Area
Talladega National Forest
16 mi NE of Greensboro on SR 25; 1 mi NE on FR 747. $5
at primitive sites, $12 for wtr with federal senior pass);
($2.50 & $6 with federal senior pass). All year; 14-day
limit. 37 sites (22-ft RV limit). Tbls, toilets, cfga, drkg wtr,
dump. Boating(l, no motors), fishing, swimming, hiking
trails. 49 acres at 110-acre lake. Non-campers pay $3
day use fee.

Payne Lake Spillway $5
Payne Lake Recreation Area
Talladega National Forest
16 mi NE of Greensboro on SR 25; 1 mi NE on CR 714. $5
at primitive sites, $12 for wtr ($2.50 & $6 with federal
senior pass). All year; 14-day limit. 14 sites (32-ft RV limit).
Tbls, toilets, cfga, drkg wtr, dump. Fishing, boating(l, no
motors), swimming. 3 acres. Non-campers pay $3 day
use fee.

Payne Lake West Side $12
Payne Lake Recreation Area
Talladega National Forest
16 mi NE of Greensboro on SR 25; 2 mi NE on CR 714. $12
with wtr, $18 with elec/wtr ($8 & $14 for seniors with fed-
eral senior pass). All year; 14-day limit. 56 modern sites
with elec/wtr. Tbls, flush toilets, cfga, drkg wtr, showers,
dump. Boating(l, no motors), fishing, swimming. 10 acres.
Non-campers pay $3 day use fee.

GUNTERSVILLE (23)
Town Creek Fishing Center $14
Lake Guntersville State Park
From I-59 exit at Guntersville, follow N Frontage Rd about
1 mi; left on US 278 W about 1 mi; left on US 11 for 1 mi;
bear right on US 278 about 1 mi; follow US 431 N past
access to state park lodge to just N of bridge over Town
Creek. $14 for tents & RVs at boondock camping section
(generators allowed) and primitive camping section (no
generators). 13 sites. 3/1-12/1; 14-day limit. Tbls, fire
rings, access to main bath house in improved camping
area. Park admission fee charged. Fishing, boating(l),
hiking, swimming.

HALEYVILLE
Wolfpen Hunters Camp   FREE
William B. Bankhead National Forest
On FR 95. 1.2 mi N on CR 23; 3.8 mi E on CR 60. Free. All
year; 14-day limit. 9 sites. No toilets. Picnicking, hiking.
Elev 600 ft. 10 acres, rolling hills.

HEFLIN

Coleman Lake Recreation Area $12
Talladega National Forest
1 mi N of Heflin on US 78; 2.5 mi NW on CR 61; 4.5 mi NW on FR 553; 1.5 mi NE on FR 5004. $8 base without hook-ups, $16 for elec/wtr ($12 with federal senior pass). Newly renovated campground open 3/1-11/30; 14-day limit. 39 hookup sites (35-ft RV limit). Tbls, flush toilets, cfga, drkg wtr, dump, showers. Picnic shelter, $15. Fishing, boating(l, no motors), swimming, hiking trails. 5 acres in Choccolocco Wildlife Management Area. 21-acre lake. Non-campers pay $3 day use fee.

Pine Glen Recreation Area $3
Talladega National Forest
2.5 mi W of Heflin on US 78; 8 mi N on FR 500, in Choccolocco Wildlife Management Area. $3. All year; 14-day limit. 21 sites (22-ft RV limit). Tbls, toilets, cfga, drkg wtr. Boating, fishing, hiking trails, swimming. 5 acres.

Turnipseed Campground $5
Talladega National Forest
From 2 mi W of Heflin on US 78, about 13 mi S on SR 281 to campground on right. $5 at primitive sites. 3/1-12/1; 14-day limit. 10 sites. Tbls, pit toilets, cfga, no drkg wtr. Hiking, hunting.

Warden Station $6
Hunter-Horse Camp
Talladega National Forest
5.7 mi E of Heflin on US 78; 6.7 mi N on CR 61 following Coleman Lake sign; right for qtr mi on FR 500. $6. All year; 14-day limit. 45 primitive sites, small RVs & tents. Tbls, toilets, cfga, drkg wtr. Hiking. Primarily used as horse camp & hunting camp. Dump at Coleman Lake camp on FR 500.

LANETT

Amity Campground $12
Corps of Engineers
West Point Lake
7 mi N of Lanett on CR 212; half mi E on CR 393, following signs. $12 for seniors with federal senior pass at 93 elec/wtr sites; others pay $24. 3 tent sites, $16 ($8 with senior pass). All year; 14-day limit. Tbls, flush toilets, cfga, drkg wtr, showers, dump, coin laundry, playground, amphitheater. Boating(l), fishing, basketball, tennis, ball field, hiking trail.

JASPER

Clear Creek Recreation Area $12
William B. Bankhead National Forest
From Jasper, 5 mi N on SR 195 to village of Manchester, then 8.1 mi N on CR 27; right on access rd; at S shore of Lake Lewis Smith. $12-13 for seniors with federal senior pass at elec/wt sites; others pay $24-$26. 3/13-12/1; 14-day limit. 102 sites. Tbls, flush toilets, cfga, drkg wtr,

showers, beach, interpretive programs. Non-campers pay $4 day use fee. Hiking, swimming, fishing, boating(l).

MONROEVILLE

Haines Island   FREE
Corps of Engineers
Claiborne Lake
From Monroeville, 8 mi N on SR 41, 10 mi W on CR 17, then 2 mi on gravel rd following signs; secluded, along S shore of Majors Creek/Alabama River. Free. All year; 14-day limit. 12 primitive sites; 40-ft RV limit. Toilets, no drkg wtr, cfga, picnic shelter, playground. Swimming, boating(l), fishing, nature trails. Pets. 390 acres; 5,900-acre lake.

Isaac Creek $11
Corps of Engineers
Claiborne Lake
8 mi N of Monroeville on SR 41; 10 mi W on CR 17 following signs. $10 base with federal senior pass at 50-amp elec sites; others pay $22; $12 base with senior pass at premium waterfront sites; others pay $24. RV limit in excess of 65 ft; 4 pull-through sites. All year; 14-day limit. Tbls, flush toilets, cfga, drkg wtr, fish cleaning station, picnic shelter, multi-use court, showers, playground, coin laundry, dump. Boating(l), hiking, fishing, multi-use court.

MONTGOMERY

Gunter Hill Campground $9
Corps of Engineers
Woodruff Lake
From Montgomery at I-65 exit 167, 9 mi W on SR 80; 4 mi N (right) on CR 7, following signs. $9 for seniors with federal senior pass at 142 elec/wtr sites; others pay $18, $26 at premium sites ($13 with senior pass). All year; 14-day limit. RV limit in excess of 65 ft; 10 handicap sites. Primitive sites available. Tbls, flush toilets, cfga, drkg wtr, hot showers, coin laundry, dump, 4 playgrounds, 2 group shelters, beach, store. Boating(l), fishing, basketball, hiking, tennis.

MOULTON

Brushy Lake Recreation Area $5
William B. Bankhead National Forest
15 mi S of Moulton on SR 33; 5 mi E on FR 245. $5. All year; 14-day limit. Free 11/1-4/1, but no drkg wtr. 13 sites (22-ft RV limit). Tbls, flush & pit toilets, cfga, piped drkg wtr. Fishing, swimming, boating (elec motors), hiking. 33-acre lake. Non-campers pay $3 day use fee.

McDougle Hunter Camp   FREE
William B. Bankhead National Forest
11 mi S on AL 33. Free. All year; 14-day limit. 9 sites (RVs under 22 ft). Toilets, cfga, drkg wtr. Picnicking, hiking. 10 acres. Rolling hills. Hardwood forest. Boat ramp, nature trails at nearby Brushy Lake camp.

Owl Creek Horse Camp　　　　$5
William B. Bankhead National Forest
15 mi S on AL 33; half mi S on AL 63; 6 mi E on FR 245; 1.5 mi NE on FR 262. $5. All year; 14-day limit. 6 sites (RVs under 22 ft). Toilets. Picnicking, horse & hiking trails. Non-campers pay $3 day use fee.

MOUNDVILLE
Moundville Archaeological Park　　　　$12
15 mi S of US 82 on Hwy 69. $12. All year; 14-day limit. 32 sites. Tbls, flush toilets, showers, cfga, drkg wtr, hookups, dump. Fishing. 320-acre park preserves 26 prehistoric Indian mounds.

MUSCLE SHOALS
Lower Rockpile Campground　　　　$8.50
Tennessee Valley Authority
Wilson Reservoir
From S side of Wilson Dam, half mi W on TVA Hwy 133, then half mi N, following signs. $8.50 for seniors with federal senior pass at 23 sites without hookups; others pay $17. 3/15-11/15; 21-day limit. Showers, tbls, drkg wtr, flush toilets, cfga, pay phone. Fishing, hiking, biking, boating(l), walking trail, natural area.

PHENIX CITY
Bluff Creek　　　　$12
Corps of Engineers
Walter F. George Lake
From Phenix City, 18 mi S on US 431; 2 mi S on SR 165; E (left, following signs) across RR to park. $12 for seniors with federal senior pass at 71 elec/wtr sites; others pay $24. All year; 14-day limit. 40-ft RV limit; 6 pull-through sites. Tbls, flush toilets, cfga, drkg wtr, showers, coin laundry, fishing pier, playground, fish cleaning station, shelter. Boating(l), fishing.

PICKENSVILLE
Pickensville　　　　$10
Corps of Engineers
Aliceville Lake
Tennessee-Tombigbee Waterway
From SR 14 at Pickensville, 2.6 mi W on SR 86; across waterway bridge, on right at Aliceville Lake. $10 base for seniors with federal senior pass at 176 elec/wtr sites; others pay $20. Premium waterfront sites $24 ($12 with senior pass); some 50-amp, 29 full hookup. All year; 14-day limit. RV limit in excess of 65 ft. Tbls, flush toilets, showers, cfga, drkg wtr, coin laundry, fishing pier, playground, fish cleaning station, handicap accessible fishing area, beach, visitor center. Boating(l), fishing, swimming, waterskiing, basketball, hiking, multi-use court.

RUSSELLVILLE
Williams Hollow　　　　$10
Bear Creek Development Authority
8 mi W of Russellville on SR 24; 5 mi S on SR 187. $10

without hookups; $17 with elec/wtr ($200-$250 monthly). 3/15-10/15; 14-day limit. 46 sites. Tbls, toilets, cfga, drkg wtr, elec($), showers, dump. Swimming, fishing. Annual or daily user's permit required to use BCDA parks. Other BCDA parks now have camping fees of $14-$17.

SELMA
Six Mile Creek　　　　$11
Corps of Engineers
William Dannelly Lake
From US 80 at Selma, 9 mi S on SR 41; 1.6 mi W (right) on CR 139; 0.7 mi N on CR 77. 31 elec/wtr sites, $22 ($11 with federal senior pass). About 4/1-9/5; 14-day limit. RV limit in excess of 65 ft; 3 handicap sites. Tbls, flush toilets, cfga, drkg wtr, playground, showers, dump, coin laundry, 2 picnic shelters, fishing pier. Basketball, fishing, boating(l), tennis.

TALLADEGA
Lake Chinnabee　　　　CLOSED
Talladega National Forest
6.7 mi NE of Talladega on SR 21; 4 mi E on CR 398; 8 mi E on CR 385 (Cheaha Rd); 1.3 mi SW on FR 646. Closed to camping; day use only following storm damage.

TUSCALOOSA
Blue Creek Park　　　　FREE
Corps of Engineers
Holt Lake
Black Warrior & Tombigbee Waterway
From Tuscaloosa, N 13 mi on SR 69; just S of Windham Springs, 7.5 mi E & SE on CR 38; 1 mi S on GoodwaterRd; 2 mi S on Blue Creek Rd; at W shore of Holt Lake near confluence with Blue Creek. Free. All year; 14-day limit. 18 sites. Toilets, drkg wtr (well pump), tbls, cfga. Boating(l), fishing, picnicking.

Burchfield Branch (Old Lock 16)　　　　$11
Corps of Engineers
Holt Lake
Black Warrior & Tombigbee Waterway
Follow I-20 exit 86 at Tuscaloosa to Brookwood, then 1 mi E on SR 16; 16.6 mi NW on CR 59; veer left 0.1 mi on Ground Hog Rd; 1.2 mi left at stop sign on Lock 16 Rd; 3.9 mi left at grocery store to park. $11 base for seniors with federal senior pass at 36 elec/wtr 50-amp sites; others pay $22. 8 premium waterview sites $24 ($12 with senior pass). All year; 14-day limit. RV limit in excess of 65 ft; 2 pull-through sites, 24 handicap sites. Tbls, flush toilets, cfga, drkg wtr, showers, coin laundry, dump, playground, beach. Picnic shelter $35. Non-campers pay $4 day use fee, $5 for dump station, $3 for boat ramp ($30 annually), $1 per person for beach. Biking, boating(l), swimming, fishing.

ALABAMA

Deerlick Creek Campground $11
Corps of Engineers
Holt Lake
Black Warrior & Tombigbee Waterway
12 mi NE of US 82 near Tuscaloosa on Rice Mountain Rd.
$11 base for seniors with federal senior pass at 40 elec/
wtr 50-amp sites; others pay $22 base. Premium locations
$24 ($12 with senior pass). RV limit 40 ft; several pull-
through sites, 1 handicap site. Picnic shelter with elec,
$25. 3/1-11/29; 14-day limit. Tbls, flush toilets, showers,
cfga, drkg wtr, dump, pavilion, beach, coin laundry, playground, fishing piersm horseshoe pits, paved bike trail,
amphitheater. Non-campers pay $4 day use fee, $3 for
boat ramp, $5 for dump station. Fishing, hiking, boating(l),
swimming.

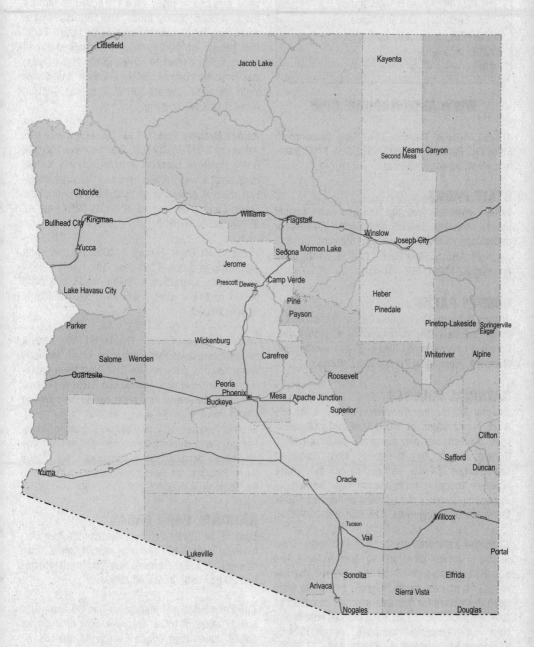

ARIZONA

CAPITAL: Phoenix
NICKNAME: Grand Canyon State
STATEHOOD: 1912 – 48th State
FLOWER: Flower of Saguaro Cactus
TREE: Palo Verde
BIRD: Cactus Wren

WWW.ARIZONAGUIDE.COM

Arizona Office of Tourism, 1110 West Washington, Suite 155, Phoenix, AZ 85007; 602-364-3700. Internet: www.arizonaguide.com.

STATE PARKS

Vehicle entrance fees are charged, with annual passes available. Several parks offer primitive or undeveloped campsites without hookups for $15 per night. Arizona State Parks, 1300 W. Washington, Phoenix, AZ 85007; 602-542-4174.

COUNTY PARKS

Arizona has only 15 counties, but more than half of those operate public campgrounds at their parks. Counties with overnight fees of $12 or less include Maricopa, Pima, Pinal, Navajo and LaPaz.

NATIONAL FORESTS

Apache-Sitgreaves National Forest. 2,003,525 acres in elevations of 5,000-11,500 ft. 48 developed campgrounds and numerous dispersed sites. Normal season: April-November. Most developed campgrounds are now managed by concessionaires -- either Thousand Trails Management Services or Recreation Resource Management of America. 30 S. Chiricahua Dr, Springerville, AZ 85938; 928-333-4301.

Coconino National Forest. 1,821,496 acres. Trout fishing in several lakes and streams. In 2014, two popular campgrounds were converted into day use areas. 14 parcels along Freidlein Praire Rd have been designated for free interspersed camping; no facilities except fire rings; areas marked with brown post and "Designated Campsite" decal. 1824 S. Thompson St., Flagstaff, AZ 86001. 928-527-3600.

Coronado National Forest. 1,780,196 acres, partly in New Mexico. Elevation 3,000-10,720 feet. 39 developed campgrounds. Starting in 2012, day passes of $5 per day, $10 per week or $20 annually were required in many area for activities outside the developed campgrounds. The passes also are necessary for dispersed camping at Lizard Rock. Day passes of $8-$10 also are required of all non-camping visitors to campgrounds in the Douglas, Nogales, Safford, Santa Catalina and Sierra Vista Recreation Areas. 300 W. Congress, Tucson, AZ 85701; 520/388-8300.

Kaibab National Forest. 1,557,274 acres, with elevations of 3,000-10,418 feet. Grand Canyon National Game Preserve contains a famous North Kaibab deer herd, a wild buffalo herd and the unique Kaibab squirrel. Access to north and south rims of the Grand Canyon. 800 South Sixth St., Williams, AZ 86046; 928-635-8200.

Prescott National Forest. 1,237,061 acres, with elevations of 3,000-8,000 feet. The forest has 14 developed campgrounds. Some roads are quite primitive. 344 S. Cortez St., Prescott, AZ 86303; 928-443-8000.

Tonto National Forest. The forest has several dispersed, undeveloped campsites which formerly were free, but daily vehicle fees have been implemented for those near Apache and Roosevelt Lakes. Visitors to those area now must pay $8 daily vehicle (Tonto Pass) fees ($4 with a federal senior pass). Boating fees are now charged in the same areas. Campgrounds where fees are charged are not free off-season because the campgrounds are closed when fees are not collected. 2324 East McDowell Rd., Phoenix, AZ 85006; 602-225-5200.

NATIONAL PARK AREAS

Canyon de Chelly National Monument's free Cottonwood campsite is one mile east of Chinle. Open all year, but water available only from April to October. PO Box 588, Chinle, AZ 86503.

Chiricahua National Monument has 30 campsites and 17 miles of trails. Entry fee now charged for adults. 13063 East Bonita Canyon Rd, Willcox, AZ 85643. 530-824-3560.

Glen Canyon National Recreation Area has 178 campsites and good hiking, but no developed hiking trails. Vehicle pass for 1-7 days is $25; annual pass $50; Boating fees, $30 for 1-7 days; $50 annual vessel permit. PO Box 1507, Page, AZ 86040. 928-608-6200.

NATIONAL PARK AREAS

Grand Canyon National Park. Backcountry camping allowed all year throughout much of the park. Backcountry permit charged. RV camping at Mather and Desert View Campgrounds on South Rim, North Rim Campground on the North Rim (reservations required at 877-4446777) and Tuweep Campground on the remote Northwest Rim.

Lake Mead National Recreation Area, 32 miles west of Kingman on SR 68, has both developed and primitive campsites. Entrance fees are $10 per vehicle for 1-5 days or $30 annually; free entry with America the Beautiful passes. Numerous areas can be reached by boat, vehicle or backpack. Primitive camping, accessible by boat along the shoreline, permitted anywhere outside developed areas or areas marked with no-camping signs, with a 15-day or 30-day limit. Vehicle camping allowed only in designated areas of the backcountry. Campground fees are $10 per site; maximum stay 90 days; after 15 days backcountry, campers must change sites. Sites with full hookups are available at concessioner-operated locations. 601 Nevada Highway, Boulder City, NV 89005. 702-293-8906.

Navajo National Monument is southwest of Keyenta. 30 free primitive campsites and preserved ruins of three villages left behind by prehistoric Pueblo Indians. HC 71, Box 3, Tonalea, AZ 86044.

Organ Pipe Cactus National Monument, south of Ajo, has 174 RV sites. Primitive backcountry camping for $5 per person is available at nine areas. A $12 vehicle entrance fee (good for seven days) also is required. Box 100, Ajo, AZ 85321.

Petrified Forest National Park permits wilderness backpacking & camping, but there are no developed campsites. Backpacking permits are free, but a 7-day $10 park entry fee is charged ($20 annually).

BUREAU OF LAND MANAGEMENT

The BLM manages several developed campgrounds and picnic areas in Arizona. Most campgrounds have fees of $4 to $10 per night, but several popular areas are free.

Long-Term Visitor Areas. Probably the ultimate in low-cost camping is available from the Yuma office of BLM at its LaPosa and Imperial Dam Long-Term Visitor Area (LTVA) sites. Although Imperial Dam LTVA is actually in California, it is close in proximity to Quartzsite and Yuma. To meet the long-term needs of winter visitors while, as the same time, protecting the desert environment, in 1983 the BLM established eight LTVAs where visitors may camp the entire winter.

Currently, a winter-long visit (Sept. 15-April 15) to any of the LTVAs is available to holders of a special $180 permit. Short-term 14-day permits are $40. From April 16 to Sept. 14, fees are $15 per day ($7.50 for holders of federal senior passes) or $75 for the season. Day use is $10 per vehicle.

Permit holders may move from one LTVA to another at no cost. Golden Age and Golden Access Passports as well as America the Beautiful discounts do not apply to the long-term LTVA areas.

Campers who wish to stay on the desert outside of an LTVA may camp free in one location on undeveloped public land for up to 14 days in any 28-day period. Short-term camping in the Quartzsite area is limited, but there are two designated camping areas at milemarkers 99 and 112 adjoining US 95.

Annual permits are available at the bureau's Yuma office. An LTVA permit also allows the holder access to day use facilities at Senator Wash and Squaw Lake recreation areas.

Popular BLMA sites. North of Parker, Empire Landing Campground is on the California side of the Colorado River in the Parker Dam Recreation Area. It has primitive sites without hookups for $15 and electric/water sites for $30 ($7.50 and $15 with federal senior passes). Oxbow Campground, at an old river channel oxbow in both Arizona and California, also has $15 primitive sites. Burro Creek, southeast of Wickiup, offers 30 sites for $14 ($7 with federal senior pass).

ALPINE

Alpine Divide $10
Apache-Sitgreaves National Forest
4 mi N of Alpine on US 191. $10 May-Sept; free approx 10/1-11/15 and 4/15-5/15; 14-day limit. Free off-season, but no services. 12 sites (tents & very small RVs). Tbls, pit toilets, cfga, drkg wtr (no wtr, toilets or trash services after 10/15), dump ($6 non-campers). Picnicking, nearby fishing. Elev 8550 ft; 5 acres, adjacent to highway at foot of Escdilla Mtn. Non-campers pay $5 picnicking, $6 dump.

Aspen Campground $12
East Fork Recreation Area
Apache-Sitgreaves National Forest
2 mi N of Alpine on US 191; 5 mi W on FR 249; 6 mi S on FR 276; at bend in Black River canyon. $12. 5/1-11/1; 14-day limit. Free off-season, but no services. 6 sites. Tbls, toilets, cfga, drkg wtr. Elev 7780 ft. Fishing, hiking.

Blue Crossing FREE
Apache-Sitgreaves National Forest
On FR 281/Apache CR 2104 to Blue River unbridged crossing; just south of Upper Blue Campground. Free. May-Oct; 14-day limit. 4 sites (RVs under 22 ft; no tents). Tbls, toilet, cfga, firewood, no drkg wtr or trash service. Hiking, picnicking, fishing. Elev 6200 ft. 1 acre. Scenic. River. Adjacent to Blue Range Primitive Area.

Blue River FREE
Apache-Sitgreaves National Forest
3 mi E of Alpine on US 191; S on FR 281 (Blue River Rd) along Blue River. Free. Undesignated primitive sites. No facilities, no drkg wtr, no trash service. Camp 100 ft from river. Hiking, horseback riding, fishing.

Buckalou FREE
Apache-Sitgreaves National Forest
9 mi S of Alpine on US 191 & Buckalou Rd. Free. All year; 14-day limit. Primitive undesignated sites; no facilities, no drkg wtr.

Buffalo Crossing $12
East Fork Recreation Area
Apache-Sitgreaves National Forest
1.9 mi NW of Alpine on US 191; 5 mi W on FR 249; 6 mi SW on FR 276. $12 during 5/1-10/30; free rest of year with limited services; 14-day limit. 16 sites (lots of RV space). Tbls, toilets, cfga, drkg wtr. Picnicking, fishing. Elev 7540 ft. Stream. Scenic. On East Fork of Black River.

Butterfly Cienega FREE
and Ackre Lake
Apache-Sitgreaves National Forest
22 mi S of Alpine on US 191 to Hannagan Meadow; 2 mi S on FR 24. Free. All year; 14-day limit. Tbls, toilets, cfga, no drkg wtr. Fishing, boating.

Deer Creek $12
East Fork Recreation Area
Apache-Sitgreaves National Forest
1.9 mi N of Alpine on US 191; 5 mi W on gravel FR 249; 6 mi S on FR 276. $12 during 5/1-10/30; free rest of year but reduced services; 14-day limit. 6 sites. Tbls, toilets, cfga, drkg wtr. Hiking, fishing. On East Fork of Black River; rustic.

Diamond Rock $12
East Fork Recreation Area
Apache-Sitgreaves National Forest
1.9 mi NW of Alpine on US 191; 5 mi W on FR 249; 5.9 mi SW on FR 276. $12 during 5/1-10/30; free rest of year but reduced services; 14-day limit. 12 sites (RVs under 22 ft). Tbls, toilets, cfga, piped drkg wtr. Picnicking, fishing. Elev 7900 ft. 6 acres. Stream. Scenic. On East Fork of Black River. Camp features CCC-era 3-sided Adirondack shelters. Note: Temporarily closed in 2016 due to hazardous conditions.

Double Cienega FREE
Apache-Sitgreaves National Forest
About 27 mi S of Alpine on US 191; 3 mi W on FR 25; right for qtr mi in FR 25B; right on short loop rd (very poor rds, impassable when wet). Free. 5/15-11/15; 14-day limit. Primitive undesignated sites. No facilities, no drkg wtr, no trash service. Hiking, hunting.

FR 54 Road Dispersed Sites FREE
Apache-Sitgreaves National Forest
23 mi SW of Alpine on US 191 to Hannagan Meadow; 5 mi S of Hannagan Meadow. Free. All year; 14-day limit. Primitive undesignated sites. No facilities, no drkg wtr.

Hannagan Donations
Hannagan Meadow Recreation Area
Apache-Sitgreaves National Forest
23 mi SW of Alpine on US 191. 5/1-9/15; 14-day limit. 8 sites (RVs under 17 ft). Free, but donations accepted. Tbls, toilets, cfga, drkg wtr. Picnicking, hiking, fishing (4 mi). Elev 9100 ft. 3 acres. Scenic. Jump off point to Blue Range Primitive Area. Pack out trash.

Horse Springs $7
East Fork Recreation Area
Apache-Sitgreaves National Forest
2 mi N of Alpine on US 191; 5 mi W on gravel FR 249; 6 mi S on FR 276. $7 with federal senior pass; others pay $14. 5/1-10/30; 14-day limit. 27 sites. Tbls, toilets, cfga, drkg wtr, picnic area, dump($6), showers($5). Free off-season, but no wtr, toilets or trash service after 10/15. Equestrian group camping available. Trout fishing in East Fork of Black River. Non-campers pay $3 for picnicking, $6 for dump station.

K.P. Cienega   FREE
Hannagan Meadow Recreation Area
Apache-Sitgreaves National Forest
28 mi SW of Alpine on AZ 191; 1.3 mi SE on FR 155. 5/1-9/15; 14-day limit. Free, but donations accepted. 5 sites (RVs under 17 ft). Tbls, toilets, cfga, piped drkg wtr, horse corrals. Picnicking, hiking, fishing (2 mi). Elev 9000 ft. 2 acres. Scenic. Access point to Blue Range Primitive Area. Pack out trash. Popular among horsemen on trail rides.

Luna Lake $7
Luna Lake Recreation Area
Apache-Sitgreaves National Forest
5 mi SE of Alpine on US 180; 1 mi N on FR 570. $7 with federal senior pass; others pay $14. 5/1-9/15; 14-day limit. 51 sites (32-ft RV limit). Tbls, toilets, cfga, drkg wtr, dump($6). Group sites available by reservation. 2 handicap-accessible toilets at group area; 2 at lake. Boating(rl), fishing (trout), nearby mountain biking trails, hiking, tackle shop. Elev 8000 ft; 8 acres. Non-campers pay $3 day use fee for picnicking, $6 for dump station.

Lost Cienega   FREE
Apache-Sitgreaves National Forest
21 mi S of Alpine on US 191; 1 mi N of Hannagan Meadow. Free. All year; 14-day limit. Primitive undesignated sites; no facilities, no drkg wtr.

Raccoon Campground $12
East Fork Recreation Area
Apache-Sitgreaves National Forest
2 mi N of Alpine on US 191; 5 mi W on FR 249; 6 mi S on FR 276 to East Fork camping area. Raccoon is a relatively new area developed to replace campsites too close to the creek. $12. 5/1-10/31; 14-day limit. Free off-season but reduced services. 10 sites. Tbls, toilets, cfga, drkg wtr. Fishing, hiking.

Round Cienega   FREE
Apache-Sitgreaves National Forest
1.9 mi NW of Alpine on US 180; W on FR 249 toward Big Lake; 3 mi E of Big Lake. Free. All year; 14-day limit. Primitive undesignated sites; no facilities, no drkg wtr. Hiking.

Terry Flat   FREE
Apache-Sitgreaves National Forest
5 mi N of Alpine on US 191, then FR 56 to Terry Flat Loop Rd. Free. All year; 14-day limit. Camp along loop rd at pullout areas. No facilities; no trash service. Hunting, hiking, picnicking. Elev 9600 ft.

Upper Blue   FREE
Apache-Sitgreaves National Forest
4.5 mi SE of Alpine on US 180, then 20 mi S on Apache CR 2104. Free. 4/1-12/1; 14-day limit. 3 sites (RVs under 16 ft); 2 acres. Toilet, no drkg wtr, cfga, tbls, 2 camp shelters.

Picnicking, hiking, fishing. No trash service. Elev 6,200 ft.

West Fork   FREE
Apache-Sitgreaves National Forest
6 mi W & N of Buffalo Crossing (see that entry) on West Fork of the Black River. Free. May-Oct; 14-day limit. 70 undesignated sites along river for RVs or tents; some tbls & toilets, cfga; no drkg wtr. Biking, hiking.

Wildcat Point   FREE
Apache-Sitgreaves National Forest
About 27 mi S of Alpine on US 191; 3 mi W on FR 25; camp where FR 25 crosses the Black River. Free. All year; 14-day limit. Primitive undesignated sites; no facilities, no drkg wtr. Fishing.

APACHE JUNCTION
Tortilla Campground $12
Tonto National Forest
18 mi NE of Apache Junction on SR 88. $12. 10/1-4/30; 14-day limit. 77 sites (30-ft RV limit). Tbls, flush toilets, cfga, drkg wtr & sewerhookups, dump, store. Nearby fishing, boating. Elev 1800 ft; 25 acres.

ARIVACA
Arivaca Lake   FREE
Coronado National Forest
1 mi S of Arivaca on FR 216; 5 mi E on FR 39; E to 90-acre lake. Free. All year; 14-day limit. Primitive undesignated sites. Tbls, toilet, cfga, no drkg wtr, no trash service. Boating(l - elec mtrs), fishing, birdwatching. Summer temperatures around 100.

BOWIE
Indian Bread Rocks   FREE
Picnic Area and Camping
Safford Field Office, Bureau of Land Management
S of Bowie on Apache Pass Rd, then W on dirt rd to Happy Camp Canyon. Free. Primitive, undeveloped sites. 5 tbls, 1 toilet, cfga, no drkg wtr. Hiking, picnicking, hunting, rock climbing.

BUCKEYE
Buckeye Hills Regional Park $12
Maricopa County Parks
From Buckeye, 1 mi W of Pierce about 7 mi SW on SR 85. $12 at primitive camping areas. Tbls, toilets, cfga, no drkg wtr or elec. Picnic sites, shooting range.

Joy Valley Rockhound Area   FREE
Safford Field Office, Bureau of Land Management
16 mi NE of Bowie. From Texaco service station in Bowie, N half mi; right at graded dirt rd; approx 8.5 mi; E (right) again; follow directional signs after crossing the San Simon River (rds may be impassable in July, Aug or Sept due to thunderstorms and flash floods). Free. All year;

14-day limit. No designated sites. Tbls, cfga. Hiking, hunting, picnicking, rockhounding. Elev 3650 ft.

BULLHEAD CITY

Katherine Landing $10
Lake Mead National Recreation Area
3 mi N of Bullhead City on SR 95; 1 mi W on SR 68; 3.4 mi NW on access rd. $10 with federal senior pass; others pay $20. All year; 30-day limit. 157 sites. Tbls, toilets, flush toilets, cfga, drkg wtr, dump, coin laundry. Boating(I), waterskiing, fishing, swimming, Hoover Dam tours & visitor center. On SE shore of Lake Mojave.

CAMP VERDE

Beaver Creek
Coconino National Forest
12 mi N of Camp Verde on I-17; 2 mi E on FR 618; at Wet beaver Creek. Converted to day use area; no camping.

Clear Creek Campground $9
Coconino National Forest
6.5 mi SE of Camp Verde on Alt SR 260; 1 mi E on FR 626; at West Clear Creek. $8 with federal senior pass; others pay $18. All year; 7-day limit. 18 sites & 2 group camping sites. 32-ft RV limit. Tbls, toilets, cfga, drkg wtr. Swimming, fishing, hiking. Elev 3200 ft; 6 acres.

CAREFREE

Bartlett Flat $8
Bartlett Lake Recreation Area
Tonto National Forest
7 mi E of Carefree on FR 24; 6 mi on FR 205; 7 mi on FR 19; 3.5 mi on FR 459. $8 Tonto Pass vehicle fee. All year; 14-day limit; no services off-season. Primitive undesignated sites; RVs under 16 ft. Toilets, no drkg wtr. Fishing, boating (I - $4) on Bartlett Lake. Not recommended for trailers.

CCC Campground $8
Seven Springs Recreation Area
Tonto National Forest
20.5 mi NE of Carefree on FR 24 (Bloody Basin Rd); gravel portion narrow with blind curves. $8 Tonto Pass ($12 onsite). All year; 14-day limit. 10 sites (16-ft RV limit). Tbls, toilets, cfga, no drkg wtr. Picnicking, hiking. Elev 3300 ft. 3 acres. Serves as trailhead for Cave Creek Trail #4. Minimum development facility. On former site of Civilian Conservation Corps camp.

Fisherman's Point $8
Horseshoe Lake Recreation Area
Tonto National Forest
7 mi E of Carefree on FR 24; 17 mi on FR 205. $8 Tonto Pass required. All year; 14-day limit. Primitive undesignated sites (no trailers). Toilets, cfga, no drkg wtr. Minimum-development site. Fishing, boating; access point to Verde River.

Horseshoe   FREE
Horseshoe Lake Recreation Area
Tonto National Forest
6.5 mi E of Carefree on FR 24 (Bloody Basin Rd.); 15.5 mi NE on FR 205; half mi NE on FR 205A. Free. 10/1-5/15; 14-day limit. 12 sites (RVs under 16 ft). Tbls, toilets, cfga, no drkg wtr or trash service. Picnicking, fishing, boating. Elev 1900 ft. 4 acres. Access to Verde River; just downstream from Horseshoe Dam. Steep grades and/or sharp turns; space too tight for large RVs.

Jojoba Boating Camp $8
Bartlett Lake Recreation Area
Tonto National Forest
7 mi E of Carefree on FR 24; 6 mi on FR 205; 7 mi on FR 19. $8 Tonto Pass required. All year; 14-day limit; no services off-season. Undesignated primitive sites (RVs under 16 ft). Toilets, cfga, no drkg wtr. Paved boat launch to Bartlett Lake ($4). Fishing, boating. Elev 1800 ft.

Mesquite Campground   FREE
Horseshoe Lake Recreation Area
Tonto National Forest
6.6 mi E on FR 22; 15.2 mi NE on FR 205. Free. All year; 14-day limit. About 12 undesignated primitive sites. Toilets, cfga, no drkg wtr, no trash service. Fishing, boating, picnicking, hiking. Access to Verde River. Elev 1900 ft.

Ocotillo Boating Camp   FREE
Horseshoe Lake Recreation Area
Tonto National Forest
7 mi E of Carefree on FR 24; 17 mi on FR 205; .4 mi on FR 2100. On Horseshoe Reservoir at Cave Creek. Free. All year; 14-day limit. Undesignated primitive (RVs under 40 ft). No toilets, cfga, drkg wtr or trash service. Fishing, boating (steep paved ramp; 25 hp limit). Elev 1950 ft.

Rattlesnake Cove $8
Bartlett Lake Recreation Area
Tonto National Forest
6.6 mi E of Carefree on CR 21; 6.3 mi E on FR 205; 7 mi E on FR 19; 1 mi on FR 459. $8 Tonto Pass required. All year; 14-day limit. Undesignated primitive sites; RVs under 16 ft. Toilets, cfga, no drkg wtr o. Fishing, picnicking, boating, hiking. Minimum-development site. On Bartlett Lake.

Riverside $8
Bartlett Lake Recreation Area
Tonto National Forest
6.5 mi E of Carefree on FR 24; 6 mi E on FR 205; 9 mi SE on FR 19; 1 mi SW on FR 162. $8 Tonto Pass online or from vendors, $12 onsite. All year; 14-day limit. 12 sites (RVs not recommended). Toilets, tbls, cfga, no drkg wtr, no trash service. Fishing, boating/waterskiing (3 mi); picnicking. Elev 1600 ft. 1 acre. Access to Verde River for canoeing, rafting, tubing. Steep grades and/or sharp turns.

Seven Springs $8
Seven Springs Recreation Area
Tonto National Forest
20 mi NE of Carefree on FR 24 (Bloody Basin Rd) in chaparral desert. $8 Tonto Pass required. All year; 14-day limit. 23 sites. Tbls, toilets, cfga, no drkg wtr. Picnicking, nature trail. Elev 3400 ft. 3 acres above small stream. Access rds have steep grades or sharp turns and aren't recommended for RVs longer than 16 feet.

Sheep Bridge FREE
Tonto National Forest
6.6 mi E of Carefree on CR 51; 30 mi N on FR 24; 11.7 mi SE on FR 269. Free. All year; 14-day limit. Undesignated site. Cfga, no drkg wtr, toilets or trash service. Picnicking, fishing, hiking. Minimum-development site.

SB Cove $8
Bartlett Lake Recreation Area
Tonto National Forest
6.6 mi E of Carefree on CR 17; 6.3 mi E on FR 205; 7.2 mi E on FR 19; .1 mi E on FR 185. $8 Tonto Pass required. All year; 14-day limit. Undesignated sites. Portable toilets, cfga, no drkg wtr except at marina. Picnicking, fishing, hiking.

CHLORIDE
Chloride Municipal Park FREE
21 mi N of Kingman via US 93, then 4 mi E on paved rd. Go into town, turn right at Union 76 station, go one block & turn left. Go about a block to ballfield. Free. All year. Overnight parking while in town. No facilities. Sightseeing. Old 1800s mining town. Murals on rocks 1.3 mi from town.

CLIFTON
Black Jack Campground FREE
Apache-Sitgreaves National Forest
15 mi S of Clifton on US 191; 19 mi SE on SR 78 (10 mi E of state line in New Mexico). Free. All year; 14-day limit. About 10 primitive sites; 16-ft RV limit. Few facilities. Tbls, 1 toilet, cfga, no drkg wtr, no trash service. Hinting, hiking. Elev 6300 ft.

Cherry Lodge FREE
Apache-Sitgreaves National Forest
16 mi N of Clifton on US 191. Free. All year; 1-day limit. Primitive undesignated sites; 32-ft RV limit. 4 picnic sites. Drkg wtr, tbls, toilets, cfga. Elev 6500 ft.

Coal Creek FREE
Apache-Sitgreaves National Forest
15 mi S of Clifton on US 191; 15 mi S on SR 78. Free. All year; 14-day limit. 5 primitive sites; 16-ft RV limit. Tbls, toilets, cfga, no drkg wtr, no trash service. Hunting, picnicking, hiking. Popular among Hwy 78 travelers.

FR 217 Dispersed Sites FREE
Apache-Sitgreaves National Forest
26 mi N of Clifton on US 191; NW on FR 217 (very narrow after 20 mi); numerous pull-out sites on FR 217 & US 191. Free. All year; 14-day limit. No facilities, no drkg wtr. Fishing, hiking.

FR 475 Dispersed Sites FREE
Apache-Sitgreaves National Forest
25.5 mi N of Clifton on US 191; E on FR 475; numerous pull-out sites on FR 475 & US 191 offer free primitive camping; no facilities, no drkg wtr. Fishing, hiking.

Granville FREE
Apache-Sitgreaves National Forest
16 mi N of Clifton on US 191. Free. All year; 14-day limit. 11 sites; 16-ft RV limit. Tbls, toilets, cfga, piped drkg wtr (available only Apr-Nov). 5 acres. Horse corrals. Picnicking, horseback riding. Trash service only in summer.

Honeymoon FREE
Apache-Sitgreaves National Forest
26 mi N of Clifton on US 191; 24 mi NW on FR 217 (very narrow last 5 mi); at Eagle Creek. Under the rim on Eagle Creek. Free. All year; 14-day limit. 4 sites (RVs under 16 ft). Tbls, cfga, toilets. No wtr. Picnicking, fishing, horseback riding, hiking. Elev 5600 ft. 5 acres. Self-clean up area; pack out trash.

Lower Juan Miller FREE
Apache-Sitgreaves National Forest
25.5 mi N of Clifton on US 191; 1.5 mi E on FR 475 (qtr mi from Upper Juan Miller CG. Free. All year; 14-day limit. 4 sites (RVs under 16 ft). Tbls, pit toilet, cfga, no drkg wtr, trash service only in summer. Hiking. 2 acres.

Strayhorse FREE
Apache-Sitgreaves National Forest
54 mi N of Clifton on AZ 191. Free. 5/1-11/30; 14-day limit. 7 sites (RVs under 17 ft). Tbls, toilets, cfga, seasonal piped drkg wtr. Picnicking, horseback riding, hunting. Elev 8200 ft. 2 acres. Horse corrals. Trash service only in summer.

CROWN KING
Coal Camp Trailhead FREE
Prescott National Forest
7 mi SE of Crown King on FR 52 (four-wheel-drive, high-clearance vehicles). Free dispersed camping; poor parking conditions. All year; 14-day limit. 1 site; no facilities. Hiking, mountain biking. Elev 6500 ft.

Hazlett Hollow Patch $10
Prescott National Forest
Half mi S of Crown King on FR 259; 7 mi SE on FR 52 (unimproved dirt road). $10. 5/1-10/31; 14- day limit. 15 sites (40-ft RV limit). Tbls, toilets, cfga, drkg wtr, shelters.

Fishing, hiking trails. Elev 6000 ft; 5 acres. Most walls & walkways were built by the Civilian Conservation Corps in the 1930s.

Kentuck Springs   FREE
Horsethief Basin Recreation Area
Prescott National Forest
Half mi S of Crown King on FR 259; 6.8 mi SE on FR 52 (Horsethief Rd). Free. 5/1-11/30; 14-day limit. 27 sites; 7 acres (RVs under 32 ft). No facilities or trash service. Picnicking, hiking, fishing (2 mi). Elev 6000 ft.

DEWEY
Powell Springs   FREE
Prescott National Forest
8.3 mi NE of Dewey on AZ 169; 5 m N on dirt FR 372 (Cherry Rd); far off the beaten path. Free. All year; 14-day limit. 11 sites; 40-ft RV limit. Tbls, toilets, cfga, no drkg wtr. Picnicking. Elev 5300 ft. 3 acres. No trash service.

DOUGLAS
Camp Rucker $10
Douglas Recreation Area
Coronado National Forest
N of Douglas on Leslie Canyon Rd; N on FR 74 & FR 74E (27 mi E of Elfrida); high-clearance vehicles suggested. $10. All year; 14-day limit. 8 sites (16-ft RV limit). Available to individuals if not being used by groups. Free 12/1-4/1. Tbls, toilets, cfga, no drkg wtr. Excellent trout fishing, hiking. Elev 6100 ft; 50 acres.

Cypress Park $10
Douglas Recreation Area
Coronado National Forest
N of Douglas on Leslie Canyon Rd; N on FR 74 and FR 74E; high-clearance vehicles suggested. $10. 4/1-11/31; 14-day limit. Free during off-season. 16-ft RV limit; 7 sites; 22-ft RV limit. Tbls, toilets, cfga, no drkg wtr. Fishing, hiking nearby. Elev 6200 ft; 30 acres.

Rucker Forest Camp $10
Douglas Recreation Area
Coronado National Forest
N of Douglas on Leslie Canyon Rd; N on FR 74 and FR 74E. $10. All year; 14-day limit; free 12/1-4/1. 13 sites (22-ft RV limit). Tbls, toilets, cfga, no drkg wtr. Fishing, picnicking, hiking. Non-campers pay $10 day use fee. Elev 6500 ft; 50 acres.

DRAKE
Bear Siding   FREE
Prescott National Forest
SW of Drake at the end of FR 492A (on the Verde River); rough/rocky access rd; impassable during wet/winter weather. Free. All year (weather permitting); 14-day limit. Undesignated sites, primitive camping. No drkg wtr or other facilities. Fishing (AZ fishing license required; bass, catfish, carp); hiking. 10 acres. Quiet, beautiful spot; very popular on weekends. Patrolled regularly by Forest Service personnel and Yavapai County Sheriff's Dept. No shooting allowed.

DUNCAN
Round Mountain Rockhound Area   FREE
Safford Field Office, Bureau of Land Management
Approx 10 mi S of Duncan; US 70 S of Duncan into New Mexico; W (right) about 4.5 mi from state line; approx 7 mi on graded dirt rd to BLM sign that gives further directions. Just past milepost 5, right on dirt rd about 12 mi, following signs. Rds may be impassable during summer rainy season. Free. All year. 4 sites. Tbls, toilets, cfga. No drkg wtr. Elev 4100 ft. Hunting, hiking, rockhounding, picnicking. Prize find: fire agates.

EAGAR
Water Canyon   FREE
Apache-Sitgreaves National Forest
2 mi S of Eagar on FR 285 (Water Canyon Rd). Free. All year; 14-day limit. Dispersed primitive camping at numerous pullouts along rd. No facilities; no trash service. Hiking, fishing, picnicking, hunting.

ELFRIDA
Sycamore Campground   FREE
Douglas Recreation Area
Coronado National Forest
14.7 mi N of Elfrida on US 191; 12 mi E on AZ 181; 10.5 mi W on FR 41. Free. All year; 14-day limit. 5 sites (16-ft RV limit). Tbls, toilets, cfga, no drkg wtr. Picnicking. Elev 6200 ft. 35 acres. Stream. Scenic. Hiking. Cluster of dispersed sites.

FLAGSTAFF
Ashurst Lake Campground $9
Coconino National Forest
17.3 mi SE of Flagstaff on FR 3 (Lake Mary Rd); 4 mi E on FR 82E. $9 with federal senior pass during about 5/1-10/15; others pay $18. Free rest of yr, but no wtr & only 1 toilet at boat launch. 14-day limit. 25 sites (35-ft RV limit). Tbls, toilets, cfga, drkg wtr store. Boating(l--8 hp limit), fishing, windsurfing. Elev 7000 ft; 20 acres. Concessionaire operated. Non-campers pay $8 day use fees.

Bonito Campground $12
Coconino National Forest
12 mi NE of Flagstaff on US 89; 2 mi E on FR 545. $12 with federal senior pass; others pay $24. About 5/1-10/15; 14-day limit. 44 sites; 42-ft RV limit. Tbls, flush toilets, cfga, drkg wtr. Nature programs, interpretive programs, lava flows, hiking. Non-campers pay $8 day use fee.

Canyon Vista $10
Coconino National Forest

6 mi SE of Flagstaff on FR 3 (Lake Mary Rd); near Walnut Canyon and Lower Lake Mary. $10 with federal senior pass; others pay $20. About 5/7-10/15; 14-day limit. 11 sites; 22-ft RV limit. Tbls, toilets, cfga, drkg wtr. Hiking, rock climbing, horseback riding. Day use $8.

Cinder Hills OHV Area   FREE
Coconino National Forest
7 mi NE of Flagstaff on US 89; E on FR 776; camp at posted areas along rd. Free. All year; 14-day limit. No facilities. Hiking, picnicking, OHV activities. 13,500 acres. No glass containers.

Dairy Springs $10
Coconino National Forest
20 mi S of Flagstaff on FR 3 (Lake Mary Rd); 3.5 mi W on FR 90. $10 with federal senior pass; others pay $20. About 5/1-10/15; 14-day limit. 30 sites (35-ft RV limit). Tbls, toilets, cfga, drkg wtr, store, coin laundry. Boating, fishing, hiking, nature trail, windsurfing, horseback riding. Elev 7000 ft; 17 acres. Concessionaire-operated. Non-campers pay $8 day use fee.

Double Springs $9
Coconino National Forest
13.5 mi SE of Flagstaff on FR 3 (Lake Mary Rd); 5 mi SW on FR 90. $9 with federal senior pass; others pay $18. 5/1-10/15; 14-day limit. 15 sites (35-ft RV limit). Tbls, toilets, cfga, drkg wtr, store, coin laundry. Boating, fishing, hiking, windsurfing, campfire program. Elev 7000 ft; 9 acres. Concessionaire-operated. Day use $8.

Forked Pine Campground $9
Coconino National Forest
17.3 mi SE of Flagstaff on FR 3 (Lake Mary Rd); 4 mi E on FR 82E. $9 with federal senior pass; others pay $18 during 5/1-10/15; free rest of yr, but no wtr & no toilets except 1 at boat launch. 14-day limit. 25 sites (35-ft RV limit). Tbls, toilets, cfga, drkg wtr. Boating(l), fishing, hiking, windsurfing. Ashurst Lake. Elev 7100 ft; 20 acres. Concessionaire-operated. Non-campers pay $8 day use fees.

Lakeview $11
Coconino National Forest
13.2 mi SE of Flagstaff on FR 3 (Lake Mary Rd). $11 with federal senior pass; others pay $22. Open about 5/1-10/15; 14-day limit. 30 sites; 28-ft RV limit. Tbls, toilets, cfga, drkg wtr. Boating(l), fishing, waterskiing, windsurfing. Elev 6900 ft; 15 acres. Concessionaire operated. Day use $8.

Little Elden Spring Horse Camp $11
Coconino National Forest
5 mi N of Flagstaff on US 89; 2 mi W on FR 556; N on FR 556A. $11 with federal senior pass; others pay $22. About 5/1-10/15; 14-day limit. 15 pull-through sites; 35-ft RV limit. Limited to horsemen. Tbls, toilets, cfga, drkg wtr.

Bridle trails, hiking. Non-campers pay $8 day use fee. Elev 7200 ft.

Lockett Meadow $8
Coconino National Forest
12.5 mi NE of Flagstaff on US 89 to FR 420 (directly across from Sunset Crater turnoff); 1 mi W on FR 420; right on FR 552 at Lockett Meadow sign; dirt rd closed early spring & late fall due to snow. $8 with federal senior pass; others pay $16. 5/15-10/1; 14-day limit. Free off-season when rd is open, but no services & maybe no toilets. 17 sites; RVs larger than 20 ft discouraged. Tbls, toilets, cfga, no drkg wtr. Hiking, mountain biking. Trail to an ancient volcano. Elev 8600 ft.

Marshall Lake   FREE
Coconino National Forest
From Flagstaff, 9 mi S on FR 3 (Lake Mary Rd); 3 mi E on FR 128 to the lake; last mi unpaved & might be impassable with mud or snow. Free. 5/1-10/15; 14-day limit. Primitive undesignated sites near E side of lake. Fishing, hiking, boating(l).

Mather Campground $9
Grand Canyon National Park
National Park Service
From Flagstaff, about 25 mi N on US 180 to park's S entrance; continue about 3 mi N, then left on Center Rd about qtr mi; right on Market Plaza Rd for 1 mi. $9 with federal senior pass at 297 sites without hookups (38 for RVs, 94 RV/tents, 165 tents); others pay $18. All year; 14-day limit. Tbls, flush toilets, cfga, drkg wtr, store, dump, coin laundry, showers. Hiking, sightseeing. GPS: 36.0302, -112.0716

Pinegrove Campground $12
Coconino National Forest
19 mi S of Flagstaff on Hwy 3 (Lake Mary Rd). $12 with federal senior pass; others pay $24. About 5/1-10/15; 14-day limit. 46 sites; 33-ft RV limit. Tbls, flush toilets, cfga, drkg wtr, coin showers($3), dump ($6 for non-campers). Fishing, boating(l), biking, hiking. $6 day use fee for non-campers.

Rest Area #2   FREE
Unmarked; about 5 mi S of Flagstaff on Alt US 89 on east side of hwy. Free. Open area near small stream. All year; 1 night limit. Piped spring wtr. Picnicking.

FOREST LAKES
Al Fulton/Mosquito Lake   FREE
Apache-Sitgreaves National Forest
4 mi W of Forest Lakes on SR 260, along FRs 181, 171, 79. Free. All year; 14-day limit. 57 primitive dispersed sites on FR 171 & numerous undesignated spaces along other rds such as FR 195, FR 9350, FR 509V, FR 84 and FR 9354. No facilities; no trash service. Fishing, boating

at Woods Canyon Lake & Willow Springs Lake. Hiking, hunting, picnicking.

Baca Meadow FREE
Apache-Sitgreaves National Forest
5 mi E of Forest Lakes on SR 260; 2 mi on FR 300, then 4 mi On FR 86. Free. All year; 14-day limit. Primitive dispersed camping area; no facilities; no trash service. Hiking, picnicking. Black Canyon & Willow Springs Lakes nearby.

Rim Lakes Recreation Area FREE
Apache-Sitgreaves National Forest
4 mi W of Forest Lakes on SR 260; camp at numbered sites along FRs 180, 181, 9512E and 79. Free. 75 primitive sites. No facilities, cfga, no drkg wtr. Fire restrictions may apply. Popular sites for OHV use.

GILA BEND

Painted Rock/Petroglyph Site $8
Bureau of Land Management
Lower Sonoran Field Office
20 mi W of Gila Bend on I-8 to exit 102; 11 mi N on Painted Rocks Rd; half mi on Painted Rock Point Rd. $8 (day use $2). All year; 14-day limit. 30 sites. Tbls, toilets, cfga, sun shelters, no drkg wtr. Many examples of Indian petroglyphs. Rockhounding, hiking. No public access to Painted Rocks dam. Host Oct-Apr.

GLOBE

Cholla Campground $8
Tonto National Forest
N of Globe on Hwy 88 to Roosevelt Lake, then N on Hwy 188; E at campground sign. $8 Tonto Pass online or from vendors, $12 onsite. All year; 14-day limit during Apr-Sept, 6-month limit Oct-Mar. America's largest solar-powered campground. 206 sites; 32-ft RV limit. Tbls, toilets, cfga, drkg wtr, showers, free dump across hwy (open Thurs-Fri 12-2pm), fish cleaning station, shade ramadas. Boating(l - $4), fishing, waterskiing, hiking, playgrounds, visitor center.

Grapevine Bay $8
Tonto National Forest
21 mi N of Globe on Hwy 88; 2 mi E on FR 84. $8 Tonto Pass required. All year; 16-day limit. Primitive undesignated sites; 24-ft RV limit. Toilets, cfga, no drkg wtr. Fishing, hiking.

Indian Point $8
Tonto National Forest
30.2 mi N of Globe on SR 88; 11.2 mi N on SR 188; right at A+ Crossing sign (milepost 255) for 2.4 mi to campground sign, then follow sign 1.3 mi (includes ford over Tonto Creek). At N end of Roosevelt Lake. $8 Tonto Pass. All year; 14-day limit. 54 sites; 16-ft RV limit. Tbls, toilets, cfga, drkg wtr, fish cleaning stations. Boating(l - $4), fishing, sailing, waterskiing. 19,200-acre lake.

Jones Water FREE
Tonto National Forest
17.2 mi NE of Globe on US 60. Free. All year; 14-day limit. 12 sites; 7 acres (RVs under 20 ft) & space for self-contained RVs. Tbls, toilets, cfga, piped drkg wtr, no trash service. Picnicking. Elev 4500 ft.

Pinal & Upper Pinal Campgrounds FREE
Tonto National Forest
2.5 mi SW of Globe on FR 112; 2.5 mi SW on FR 55; 9.5 mi SW on FR 651; large RVs might have problems on the narrow, winding rd. Free. 4/15-10/31; 14-day limit. 16 sites; 6 acres (RVs under 20 ft). Tbls, toilets, cfga, no drkg wtr or trash service. Elev 7500 ft.

Pioneer Pass FREE
Tonto National Forest
8.6 mi S of Globe on FR 112. Free. 4/1-12/31; 14-day limit. 23 sites (RVs under 18 ft). Tbls, toilets, cfga, no drkg wtr or trash service. Elev 6000 ft. 18 acres. Steep grades and/or sharp turns.

Sulphide Del Rey FREE
Tonto National Forest
2.5 mi SW on FR 112; 2.5 mi SW on FR 55, then 5 mi SW on FR 651. Free. All year; 14-day limit. 10 primitive sites (RVs under 20 ft). Tbls, toilets, no drkg wtr or trash service. Picnicking. Developed by Boy Scouts.

Timber Camp $8
Tonto National Forest
27 mi NE of Globe on US 60. Free. All year; 14-day limit. $8 Tonto Pass required. Primitive undesignated sites for equestrians when not reserved for group use; 45-ft RV limit. Toilets, tbls, cfga, no drkg wtr or trash service. Hiking, picnicking, hunting, horseback riding.

Windy Hill $8
Tonto National Forest
23 mi N of Globe on Hwy 88; right for 2 mi on FR 82. $8 Tonto Pass online or from vendors, $12 onsite. All year; 14-day limit. 346 sites with shade ramadas, tbls; 32-ft RV limit. Tbls, flush toilets, cfga, drkg wtr, showers, playgrounds, amphitheater, dump (near Cholla Campground). Fishing, boating(l - $4), hiking. Visitor center.

Note: Just 20 miles east of Globe on US70 is the SAN CARLOS APACHE RESERVATION, 1.8 million acres of pristine desert, mountains and lakes. Once the home of Geronimo, the Apache warrior who terrorized settlers, miners and cattlemen in the 1870s and 1880s, the Reservation is now a prime attraction for hunters, fishermen, hikers, and nature lovers. There are plenty of dry camping areas that are $10 daily per vehicle. Daily boating fees are $5; annual fishing/boating permits, $125. A per-person fee is charged for boating and fishing on San Carlos Lake, the largest body of water in southeastern Arizona. At the lake headquarters are 12 RV sites with full hookups; in the near future, the tribe plans to expand its services to RVers. For now, there are boat ramps, a marina, a store for groceries and fishing supplies. Trout fishing may be found in a number of ponds, or "tanks" scattered throughout the Reservation.

GREER

Benny Creek Campground $10
Apache-Sitgreaves National Forest
2 mi N of Greer on SR 373; on N shore of Bunch Reservoir. $10. 5/1-9/30; free rest of year when gate is unlocked; 14-day limit. 24 sites (24-ft RV limit; no tents). Tbls, toilets, cfga, drkg wtr. Fishing, hiking, boating(l), swimming. Elev 8300 ft; 4 acres. Non-campers pay $3 day use fee. Dump station at Hoyer Campground, $6.

Bunch Boat Launch FREE
Apache-Sitgreaves National Forest
2 mi N of Greer on AZ 373. Free. Open May-Nov. Primitive undesignated area; 22-ft RV limit. Pit toilets, no drkg wtr. Fishing, boating(l), Elev 8300 ft.

Ditch Camp & North Fork $8
White Mountain Apache Reservation
W of Greer on SR 260; S on SR 473 (Hawley Lake Rd) past Cyclone Lake (closed to the public). $8. Apr-Nov; 10-day limit. 15 sites. Tbls, toilets, cfga, drkg wtr. Fishing.

Drift Fence Lake Campground $8
White Mountain Apache Reservation
W of Greer on SR 260; S on SR 273 (Sunrise Lake Turnoff); 3 mi S of Reservation Lake to Drift Fence Lake; access difficult. $8. May-Oct; 10-day limit. 10 sites. Tbls, toilets, cfga, no drkg wtr. Fishing, boating. 16-acre lake. Elev 9000 ft.

Gabaldon Campground FREE
Lee Valley Recreation Area
Apache-Sitgreaves National Forest
2 mi N of Greer on AZ 373; 6 mi SE on FR 87; 4 mi SE on AZ 273. Free. 6/1-9/10; 14-day limit. 5 sites (RVs under 16 ft). Tbls, toilets, cfga, no drkg wtr. Mountain climbing, picnicking, fishing, boating. Elev 8500 ft. 3 acres. Botanical. Stream. Campground only for horse users of the Mt. Baldy Wilderness Area; limited corral facilities. Self-cleanup area; no wtr for horses at site. Note: Closed temporarily in 2016.

Government Springs FREE
Apache-Sitgreaves National Forest
1 mi S of Greer on AZ 373. May-Nov. Free. Primitive undesignated area; 16-ft RV limit. No facilities. Fishing, boating. Pack out trash. 3 picnic sites. Elev 8500 ft. Hiking trail.

Horseshoe Cienega $8
White Mountain Apache Reservation
W of Greer on SR 260; S on access rd to Horseshoe Cienega Lake. $8. Apr-Nov; 10-day limit. Numerous sites. Tbls, toilets, cfga, drkg wtr, store. Fishing, boating(rl). At 121 acres, it is the reservation's 4th largest lake.

McCoy's Bridge Campground $8
White Mountain Apache Reservation
W of Greer on SR 260; S on SR 473 (Hawley Lake Turnoff); at North Fork of White River. $8. Apr-Nov; 10-day limit. 10 sites. Tbls, toilets, cfga, drkg wtr. Fishing.

Pacheta Lake Campground $8
White Mountain Apache Reservation
W of Greer on SR 260; S on SR 273 (Sunrise Turnoff) & Rd Y-20 to Pacheta Lake; rough & narrow rd. $8. Apr-Nov; 10-day limit. 15 sites. Tbls, toilets, cfga, no drkg wtr. Fishing, boating.

Reservation Lake $8
White Mountain Apache Reservation
W of Greer on SR 260; S on SR 273 (Sunrise Turnoff) to Reservation Lake; last 25 mi rough (high-clearance vehicles suggested); at foot of Mount Baldy. $8. Apr-Nov; 10-day limit. 60 sites at several camping areas around lake. Tbls, toilets, cfga, drkg wtr, store. Fishing, boating(lr). 280-acre lake, elev 9000 ft.

River Boat Launch FREE
Apache-Sitgreaves National Forest
2 mi N of Greer on AZ 373. Free. May-Nov. Primitive undesignated area; no facilities; 22-ft RV limit. Fishing, boating. Elev 8300 ft.

Rolfe C. Hoyer $10
Apache-Sitgreaves National Forest
2 mi N of Greer on AZ 373, across from Greer Lakes. $10 with federal senior pass; others pay $20. 5/15-9/30; 14-day limit. 91 sites; 32-ft RV limit. Tbls, flush toilets, cfga, drkg wtr, dump, showers. Fishing, hiking, nature walks, interpretive programs, amphitheater. Elev 8300 ft. Non-campers pay $3 day use fees, $5 for showers, $6 dump.

SU Knolls FREE
Apache-Sitgreaves National Forest
SW of Greer on SR 273; 1.5 mi N of Crescent Lake. Free primitive undesignated camping; no facilities, no drkg wtr. Hiking, fishing.

Tunnel Boat Launch FREE
Apache-Sitgreaves National Forest
2 mi N of Greer on AZ 373. Free. May-Nov; 14-day limit. Primitive undesignated area; 22-ft RV limit. No facilities. Fishing, boating. Elev 8300 ft.

Winn Campground $7
Apache-Sitgreaves National Forest
2 mi N of Greer on SR 373; 6 mi SW on FR 87; 3 mi S on SR 273; 1 mi NE on FR 554. $7 with federal senior pass; others pay $14. Fees 5/15-10/15; free rest of year but reduced services; 14-day limit. 63 sites; 45-ft RV limit. 2 group sites. Tbls, pit toilets, cfga, drkg wtr dump($6), showers($6). Fishing, hiking nearby. Elev 9300 ft; 25 acres. Concessionaire-operated. Non-campers pay $3 for picnicking, $6 dump station at Hoyer Campground.

HEBER

Bear Canyon Lake FREE
Apache-Sitgreaves National Forest
38 mi SW of Heber on AZ 260, FR 300 & FR 89 (2.6-mi primitive dirt rd). Free. 5/1-10/15; 14-day limit. Primitive undesignated sites around 60-acre lake. Toilets, cfga, no drkg wtr, no trash service. Artificial lure fishing, boating. Elev 7800 ft.

Black Canyon Dispersed FREE
Apache-Sitgreaves National Forest
18 mi SW of Heber on SR 260 and FR 86 to lake; half mi S of lake to dispersed area. Free. Primitive undesignated sites. No facilities, no drkg wtr. Fishing, boating.

Black Canyon Rim $8
Rim Lakes Recreation Area
Apache-Sitgreaves National Forest
22 mi SW of Heber on SR 260; 3 mi S on FR 300; N on FR 86. $8 with federal senior pass; others pay $16. 5/20-10/10; free rest of year; 14-day limit. 21 sites; 16-ft RV limit. Tbls, toilets, cfga, drkg wtr (no wtr, toilets or trash service during free period). Hiking; nearby fishing & boating. Elev 7600 ft; 20 acres. Pack out trash; self-service area. Concessionaire operated.

Brookbank/Nelson Lake FREE
Apache-Sitgreaves National Forest
13 mi W of Heber on SR 260; half mi S on FR 300; W of Black Canyon Lake. Free. May-Oct; 14-day limit. Primitive undesignated sites along rd. No facilities; no drkg wtr. Hiking, horseback riding, fishing, boating(l - elec mtrs only).

Chevelon Canyon Lake FREE
Apache-Sitgreaves National Forest
38 mi SW of Heber on AZ 260; FR 300 to FR 169; FR 169 to FR 169B; E to campground; rds may be muddy. Free. 5/1-10/31; 14-day limit. Primitive designated, undeveloped campsites. Toilet. Trophy fishing; artificial lures & special size rules (check state fish regs). Elev 6500 ft. No trash service.

Chevelon Crossing FREE
Apache-Sitgreaves National Forest
1.5 mi W of Heber on AZ 260; 16.5 mi NW on FR 504. Free. All year; 14-day limit. 7 sites; RVs under 16 ft; 6 acres. Toilet, tbls, cfga, no drkg wtr, no trash service. Picnicking, fishing, rockhounding. Elev 6300 ft. 5 acres. Stream. Geological. On Chevelon Creek.

Crook Campground $8
Woods Canyon Lake Recreation Area
Apache-Sitgreaves National Forest
22 mi SW of Heber on SR 260; 3.5 mi NW on FR 300; qtr mi on FR 105. $8 with federal senior pass during 5/1-10/31; others pay $16; sites available only when not reserved by group. Some sites may be open & free off-season, but no wtr or services; 14-day limit. 26 sites; 32-ft RV limit. Group camping, $240. Tbls, toilets, cfga, drkg wtr, dump($7). Fishing, boating(l), summer ranger programs. Elev 7500 ft; 15 acres.

Durfee Crossing FREE
Apache-Sitgreaves National Forest
1.5 mi W of Heber on AZ 260; 16.5 mi NW on FR 504 to Chevelon Crossing campground; Durfee is just S of Chevelon. Free. Primitive undesignated sites; no facilities. Fishing, hiking.

FR 169 Dispersed Sites FREE
Apache-Sitgreaves National Forest
38 mi SW of Heber on AZ 260; FR 300 to FR 169. Camp within 50 feet of marked posts along FR 159; road signs indicate if camping is allowed within 300 ft of the road or at a numbered post. Free. All year; 14-day limit. No facilities. Hiking, fishing.

Gentry Campground $11
Rim Lakes Recreation Area
Apache-Sitgreaves National Forest
2.5 mi E of Heber on SR 260; nearly 4 mi SE on FR 300. $11 during 5/15-10/15; free rest of year. 14-day limit. 6 sites; RVs under 16 ft, available only when not reserved by group ($80 group fee). Toilet, cfga, tbls, no drkg wtr or trash service. Picnicking, hiking. Elev 7,725 ft.

Horseshoe Lake FREE
Apache-Sitgreaves National Forest
22 mi SW of Heber on SR 260; NW on FR 300 to FR 76; about 2 mi N of the Promontory Butte area of Mogollon Rim. Free. All year; 14-day limit. Primitive undesignated sites; no facilities. Fishing, hiking.

Mogollon Campground $8
Woods Canyon Lake Recreation Area
Apache-Sitgreaves National Forest
22 mi SW of Heber on SR 260; 4.5 mi NW on FR 300. $8 with federal senior pass; others pay $16. 5/1-10/30; free rest of yr, weather permitting; 14-day limit. 26 sites (32-ft RV limit). Tbls, toilets, cfga, drkg wtr. Fishing, boating(l), hiking. Elev 7500 ft; 15 acres.

Rim Campground　　　　　　　　　　　$8
Rim Lakes Recreation Area
Apache-Sitgreaves National Forest
6 mi W of Heber on SR 260; qtr mi NW on FR 300. $8 with federal senior pass; others pay $16. 5/1-9/15; 14-day limit. 26 sites (32-ft RV limit). Tbls, toilets, cfga, drkg wtr. Hiking, picnicking; nearby boating & fishing. Elev 7600 ft; 15 acres. Near visitor center.

Sinkhole Campground　　　　　　　　　$8
Rim Lakes Recreation Area
Apache-Sitgreaves National Forest
27 mi W of Heber on SR 260; half mi N on FR 149 toward Willow Springs Lake. $8 for seniors with federal senior pass; others pay $16. 5/1-10/30; free rest of year, weather permitting; 14-day limit. 26 sites (32-ft RV limit). Toilets, cfga, drkg wtr, tbls. Hiking, fishing, boating (I - 8 hp limit), mountain biking. Elev 7600 ft; 15 acres.

Twin Springs　　　　　　　　　　　FREE
Apache-Sitgreaves National Forest
12 mi S of Heber on SR 260, then N on FRs 99, 122, 210. Free. All year; 14-day limit. Primitive dispersed RV sites throughout area. No facilities, no trash service. Boating & fishing at Black Canyon Lake; hiking, picnicking, hunting.

Willow Springs Lake　　　　　　　　FREE
Recreation Area
Apache-Sitgreaves National Forest
1.5 mi E of Heber on AZ 260. 5/15-10/15; 14-day limit. Free. Undesignated sites half mi from lake. Toilet, cfga, tbls, no drkg wtr. RVs under 22 ft. Fishing, boating, picnicking. Boating (I - mtrs 8 hp limit).

JACOB LAKE

Buck Farm Overlook　　　　　　　　FREE
Backcountry Camping Area
Kaibab National Forest
20 mi E of North Kaibab Visitor Center at Jacob Lake on US 89A to FR 445 (Buffalo Ranch Headquarters turnoff); then 23.5 mi S to FR 445's fork; 2 mi on left fork to FR 445H, then 3 mi to end of rd. Free. All year; 14-day limit. Undesignated primitive sites; no facilities. Suggested use: early fall to early summer to avoid summer heat.

Crazy Jug Point　　　　　　　　　FREE
Backcountry Camping Area
Kaibab National Forest
From North Kaibab Visitor Center at Jacob Lake, S one-qtr mi on AZ 67 to FR 461; then 9 mi W on FR 461 & FR 462 to FR 422; then 11.5 mi S (5 miles beyond Big Springs) to FR 425; turn right on FR 425 for 10 mi to Big Saddle Point; turn S onto FR 292; 1.5 mi on FR 292 & FR 292B to end of rd. 32 mi of good gravel rd. Free. All year; 14-day limit. Undesignated primitive sites; no facilities. Sightseeing, hiking, picnicking. Wildlife viewing. Elev 7450 ft.

Demotte Campground　　　　　　　　$9
Kaibab National Forest
24 mi S of Jacob Lake on SR 67; qtr mi W on US 616. $9 with federal senior pass; others pay $18. Free 11/1-5/14; fee rest of year; 14-day limit. 38 sites (32-ft RV limit). Tbls, pit toilets, cfga, drkg wtr, store. No wtr, trash pickup during free period. Elev 8700 ft; 14 acres.

East Rim Viewpoint　　　　　　　　FREE
Backcountry Camping Area
Kaibab National Forest
26.5 mi S of Jacob Lake on AZ 67 (.7 mi beyond DeMotte camp entrance); turn left (E) onto FR 611; about 1.4 mi E of AZ 67, FR 611 intersects FR 610; continue E on FR 611 3 more mi. Last 4.5 mi gravel rd, okay for RVs in dry weather. Free. All year; 14-day limit. Late spring to late fall best period. Undesignated sites. Toilets, cfga. No tbls or drkg wtr. Hiking, picnicking, wildlife viewing, bird-watching.

Indian Hollow　　　　　　　　　　FREE
Kaibab National Forest
25.9 mi S of Jacob Lake on AZ 67; 17.8 mi NW on FR 422; 7.8 mi SW on FR 425; 4.7 mi W on FR 232. Rough rds last 4.5 mi. Free. All year; 14-day limit. 3 primitive sites (RVs under 32 ft). Tbls, toilet, cfga, no drkg wtr. Picnicking, rockhounding, hiking. Elev 6300 ft. 2 acres. Scenic. Trailhead for Thunder River Trail into Grand Canyon. Snow blocks access in winter. Rare bighorn sheep seen regularly.

Jacob Lake　　　　　　　　　　　$9
Kaibab National Forest
1 mi N of Jacob Lake on US 89A; qtr mi E on US 89A. $9 with federal senior sass; others pay $18. 5/15-10/15; 14-day limit. 51 sites (32-ft RV limit); 2 handicap sites; 2 group sites. Tbls, pit toilets, cfga, drkg wtr, store, dump nearby ($10 to dump, 50 cents per gallon wtr). Hiking (nature trails), visitor center, picnicking, boating (8-hp limit), horseback riding, chuckwagon rides, guided forest tours, nature programs, nature trails. 44 mi N of N rim of Grand Canyon. 27 acres; elev 7900 ft.

Parissawampitts Point　　　　　　FREE
Backcountry Camping Area
Kaibab National Forest
From quarter mi S of visitor center on AZ 67, take FRs 461 & 462 W 9 mi to FR 422, then S 19 mi (12.3 mi beyond Big Springs) to FR 206; then S 3.5 mi and W on FR 214 8 mi to end of road. Good gravel roads. Free. All year; 14-day limit. Be prepared for summer thunderstorms. Undesignated primitive sites; no facilities. Hiking, sightseeing, picnicking. Elev 7570 ft. Panoramic view of Grand Canyon.

Quaking Aspen Spring　　　　　　　FREE
Backcountry Camping Area
Kaibab National Forest
S on AZ 67 from North Kaibab Visitor at Jacob Lake (.7

mi past Demotte camp entrance) to FR 422; 2 mi W to FR 270; 1 mi S to FR 222; 5 mi W to FR 206; 4 mi S. Last 12 mi good gravel & dirt rds. Free. All year; 14-day limit. Sightseeing, wildlife viewing, hiking. Elem 7800 ft. Scenic, cool meadow along bottom of Quaking Aspen Canyon makes camping attractive in fringes of aspen/spruce trees. Fall colors spectacular. GPS: 36.37859, -112.2824.

Sowats Point   FREE
Backcountry Camping Area
Kaibab National Forest
W on FR 461 off AZ 67 just S of forest visitor center in Jacob Lake; 9 mi W on FRs 461 7 462 to FR 422; 11.5 mi S (5 mi beyond Big Springs) to FR 425; 8 mi S to FR 233; 9.5 mi W to end of rd. Mostly good gravel rds, but last 2-3 mi are rough; high-clearance vehicles recommended. See Crazy Jug Point entry for alternate RV or auto route. Free. All year; 14-day limit. Undesignated primitive sites; no facilities. Sightseeing, wildlife viewing, hiking. Canyonland panoramic view; Mount Trumbull on western horizon; Powell Plateau & Grand Canyon Nat. Park on the S. GPS: 36.5094, -112.5385.

Timp Point   FREE
Backcountry Camping Area
Kaibab National Forest
26.5 mi S of Jacob Lake on AZ 67 (.7 mi beyond DeMotte camp entrance), then W 2 mi on FR 422 to FR 270; S 1 mi, then W 5 mi on FR 222; W one-qtr mi to FR 271; follow FR 271 8 mi to its end. Last 16.5 mi on good gravel rds. Free. All year; 14-day limit. Undesignated prim camping; no facilities. Hiking, sightseeing, picnicking. Elev 7600 ft. Wildlife viewing. Point has panoramic view of Grand Canyon and tributary canyons. Only known, easily accessible point on the Kaibab Plateau where it is possible (with binoculars) to see Thunder River emerge from N wall of Tapeats Canyon. GPS: 36.3819, -112.3563.

JEROME

Mingus Mountain Campground $10
Prescott National Forest
6.6 mi SW of Jerome on US 89A; 2.5 mi SE on FR 104. Located on top of Mingus Mtn. Tough rd for RVs. $10 without hookups, $15 with elec, $6 tents. 5/1-10/31; 14-day limit. 6 primitive sites, 19 with elec. RV limit 40 ft. Tbls, toilets, cfga, no drkg wtr (wtr system being built). Horseback riding, hiking, picnicking, hunting. 10 acres. Pack out trash. Panoramic view of Verde Valley. Access to North Mingus Trail. Elev 7500 ft. Note: Elec system knocked out by lightning in 2012; repairs not finished in 2017; check with rangers for status before arriving (928-567-4121).

Potato Patch $7
Prescott National Forest
6.5 mi SW of Jerome on US 89A, then follow FR 106 to camp; on Mingus Mtn. $7 for seniors with federal senior

pass at 27 non-elec sites (including 3 handicap sites); others pay $14. 12 elec sites, $18 ($11 with senior pass). Group camping area for 4 vehicles, $28. 5/1-10/31; 14-day limit. 40-ft RV limit. Tbls, toilets, cfga, drkg wtr. Hiking, picnicking. 4 acres. Access to Woodchute Trail 102 & Woodchute Wilderness. Elev 7000 ft.

JOSEPH CITY

Cholla Lake County Park $11
Navajo County Park
From I-40 exit 27 E of Joseph City, 1 mi E on South Service Rd. to SE shore of lake. $11 base at 20 non-elec sites, $13 with elec; 50-ft RV limit. All year; 14-day limit. Tbls, drkg wtr, toilets, cfga, showers, playground. Largest lake in state. Swimming, boating(l), fishing.

KAYENTA

Canyon View Campground   FREE
Navajo National Monument
22 mi SW of Kayenta on US 160; 9 mi N/NW on AZ 564 to the monument headquarters; campground on unpaved rd 0.1 mi from visitor center. Free. May-Oct; 7-day limit. 17 sites (3 good for groups). Pit toilets, tbls, cfga, no drkg wtr.

Sunset View Campground   FREE
Navajo National Monument
22 mi SW of Kayenta on US 160; 9 mi N/NW on AZ 564 to the monument headquarters; campground is just beyond visitor center. Free. May-Oct.; 7-day limit. 30 sites (RVs under 28 ft). Tbls, flush toilets, cfga, dump, wtr in restrooms. Picnicking, hiking. In the summer, campfire programs are given on the archeology, history, and natural history of the monument. Elev 7300 ft. No wood fires allowed; only charcoal or propane. Sites quite close. No entry fee to park. In summer, overflow space available at a more primitive campground 1 mi N.

KEAMS CANYON

Keams Canyon   FREE
Hopi Indian Reservation
On Hwy 264 opposite trading post. Free. All year; 2-day limit. About 12 unspecified sites (RVs under 24 ft). Toilets, showers, cfga, tbls. Elev 5500 ft.

KINGMAN

Bonelli Landing   FREE
Lake Mead National Recreation Area
75 mi NW of Kingman on US 93 & Bonelli Landing access. Camp free, but $20 entry fee ($40 annually); enter free with federal senior pass. All year; 15-day limit. Undesignated sites. Tbls, toilets, cfga, no drkg wtr. Fishing, swimming, picnicking, boating(l). Elev 1230 ft.

Gregg's Hideout   FREE
Lake Mead National Recreation Area
70 mi N of Kingman; on SE shore, E of Temple Bar. Camp free, but $20 entry fee ($40 annually); enter free with

federal senior pass. All year; 15-day limit. Undesignated sites. Undeveloped.

Monkey Cove   FREE
Lake Mead National Recreation Area
70 mi N of Kingman. Camp free, but $20 entry fee ($40 annually); enter free with federal senior pass. All year; 15-day limit. Undesignated sites. Undeveloped.

Packsaddle Recreation Site $8
Kingman Field Office, Bureau of Land Management
15 mi NW of Kingman on US 93, then 6 mi NE on Chloride-Big Wash Rd. $8. All year; 14-day limit. 7 sites. Tbls, toilets, cfga, no drkg wtr. Hiking, picnicking, rockhounding. Elev 6200 ft.

Pearce Ferry   FREE
Lake Mead National Recreation Area
77 mi N of Kingman off US 93. Free. All year; 15-day limit. Elev 1300 ft. Primitive sites. Fishing, boating.

Temple Bar Campground $10
Lake Mead National Recreation Area
80 mi N of Kingman on US 93. $10 with federal senior pass; others pay $20. All year; 30-day limit. 153 sites. Tbls, flush toilets, cfga, drkg wtr, coin laundry, dump. Fishing, hiking, boating(l), swimming, waterskiing.

Wild Cow Springs Recreation Site $8
Kingman Field Office, Bureau of Land Management
Approx 12 mi SE of Kingman on Hualapai Mtn Rd to Hualapai Mt Co Pk; approx 5 mi S on winding dirt rd through co pk, to campground. $8 ($4 with federal senior pass); group camping $20 ($10 with senior pass). All year; 14-day limit. 24 sites. Toilets, cfga, no tbls, no drkg wtr. Hunting, hiking. Elev 7200 ft. 10 acres. High-clearance vehicles recommended; large RVs discouraged.

Windy Point Recreation Site $8
Kingman Field office, Bureau of Land Management
21 mi N of Kingman on US 93; right on dirt rd located 2 mi N of AZ 62 (Chloride Rd) for approx 10.2 mi to campground. $8. All year; 14-day limit. 7 primitive sites (RVs under 20 ft). 13 acres. Tbls, flush toilets, cfga, no drkg wtr. Dump at nearby rest area. Hunting, hiking, picnicking, rockhounding. Elev 6100 ft.

LAKE HAVASU CITY
Havasu National   FREE
Wildlife Refuge
N of Lake Havasu City and S of Topock on Arizona shoreline of Lake Havasu for 2 mi S of Topock Gorge. Free. All year. Undesignated camping area; no facilities. Hiking, fishing, boating, wildlife watching. Refuge is home of the Harris hawk, one of America's rarest birds of prey.

LITTLEFIELD
Virgin River Canyon Recreation Area $8
Bureau of Land Management
Arizona Strip Field Office
16 mi N of Littlefield on I-15 at Little Pockets interchange. Adjacent to the Virgin River and Cedar Pockets Rest Area. $8 ($90 monthly). All year; no time limit. 75 sites, several pull-through. Tbls, flush toilets, cfga, drkg wtr, dump. Scenic overlook, interpretive trail, 2 river access trails. Fishing, hiking, picnicking. Elev 2250 ft. Non-campers pay $2 day use fee.

LUKEVILLE
Twin Peaks Campground
Organ Pipe Cactus $8
National Monument
5 mi N of Lukeville on Hwy 85. $8 with federal senior pass; others pay $16. All year; 14-day limit. $12 entry fee also charged, good for 7 days; free with senior pass. 174 RV sites (35-ft RV limit). Tbls, flush toilets, cfga, drkg wtr, dump, visitor center. Hiking, picnicking, sightseeing. 330,000 acres.

MESA
Coon Bluff Recreation Area $8
Lower Salt River Recreation Area
Tonto National Forest
7 mi from Mesa on US 60/70; 12 mi N on FR 204 (Power Rd/Bush Hwy); left for 1 mi on FR 204E. $8 Tonto Pass required. Winter camping Fri, Sat, Sun nights before Columbus Day, Martin Luterh King Jr's birthday, Presidents Day and during Thanksgiving through Saturday night; reduced services 10/1-3/31; 1-day limit in summer; day use rest of year. About 4 primitive sites; 40-ft RV limit. Tbls, toilets, cfga, no drkg wtr. Swimming, fishing, rafting, tubing.

Goldfield Recreation Site $8
Lower Salt River Recreation Area
Tonto National Forest
7 mi from Mesa on US 60/70; 11 mi on FR 204; 1 mi on FR 204E. $8 Tonto Pass required. All year; 1-day limit. 40-ft RV limit. Undesignated primitive sites; toilets 4/15-10/14, no drkg wtr. Fishing, boating.

Phon D. Sutton Recreation Site $8
Lower Salt River Recreation Area
Tonto National Forest
7 mi NE of Mesa on US 60 (Superstition Hwy); 11 mi N on FR 204 (Power Rd/Bush Hwy); left on FR 169 (Phon D. Sutton Rd) for 1 mi. $8 Tonto Pass required. Camp only during 10/15-4/15; 1-day limit; day use rest of year. 2 large, level paved areas, each the size of a football field, for about 15 sites; 44-ft RV limit. Tbls, cfga, toilets, no drkg wtr. Fishing, hiking, tubing, rafting, swimming. River access point.

MORMON LAKE
Kinnikinick
Coconino National Forest
2 mi S of Mormon Lake on FR 90; 2.1 mi SE on CR FH3; 4.8 mi E on FR 125; 4.6 mi SE on FR 82. In 2013, this campground was converted to a day use area; camping prohibited within 1 mi of lake.

NEEDLES, (CA.)
Beale Slough   FREE
Bureau of Land Management
From I-40 S of Needles, take the Five-Mile Rd exit E toward Colorado River; follow dirt rd under the railroad bridge; turn right (S) for 1 mi to interpretive sign. Free. Primitive undesignated sites at slough created during channelization of river. Also follow dirt rd N or S along river to unmarked turnouts available for camping. No facilities. No vehicles on beach. Fishing, boating, hiking, OHV use.

NEW ORAIBI
Oraibi Wash Campground   FREE
Hopi Indian Reservation
1 mi E of New Oraibi on SR 264; at sandy beach. Free. All year; 7-day limit. 7 sites; RVs under 24 ft. 1 acre. Tbls, toilets, cfga, no drkg wtr.

NOGALES
White Rock $10
Nogales Recreation Area
Coronado National Forest
7 mi N of Nogales on I-19; 9 mi W on Hwy 289 (Ruby Rd). $10. All year; 14-day limit. 15 sites; RVs under 23 ft. Tbls, flush toilets, cfga, no drkg wtr. Handicapped facilities. Boating(I--elec mtrs only), fishing, hiking. Elev 4000 ft; 28 acres. Non-campers pay $10 day use fee. No firewood.

ORACLE
Peppersauce $10
Santa Catalina Recreation Area
Coronado National Forest
15 mi SE of Oracle on FR 382; qtr mi W on FR 29. $10. All year; 14-day limit. 17 small sites (RVs under 22 ft; sites quite small). Tbls, toilets, cfga, firewood, piped drkg wtr. Rockhounding, picnicking. Elev 4700 ft. 10 acres. Scenic. Many large sycamore. Only campground on N side of Mt. Lemmon. Reader says entry rd very poor. Base for 4WD use. Non-campers pay $10 day use fee.

PAGE
Lee's Ferry Campground $10
Glen Canyon National Recreation Area
25 mi S of Page on US 89; 14 mi N (right) on Hwy 89A; cross Colorado River & pass Navajo Bridge Interpretive Center (right); NRA entrance on right. $10 with federal senior pass; others pay $20 plus $20 vehicle entry fee for 1-7 days or $50 annual pass. All year; 14-day limit.

55 developed sites with toilets, cfga, drkg wtr. Fishing, boating, picnicking.

Lone Rock Campground $17
Glen Canyon National Recreation Area
13 mi N of Page on US 89. $7 with federal senior pass; others pay $14 plus $20 vehicle entry fee for 1-7 days or $50 annual pass. All year; 14-day limit. Undesignated primitive sites (RVs under 20 ft). 25 acres. Tbls, toilets, cfga, outdoor cold shower, dump. Swimming, fishing, picnicking.

Stateline Campground   FREE
Bureau of Land Management
Arizona Strip Field Office
34 mi W of Page on US 89; pass BLM ranger station & rd to White House trailhead; left on House Rock Valley Rd (dirt) for 9.3 mi. Free. All year; 14-day limit. 4 sites (1 for tents). Tbls, toilets, cfga, no drkg wtr or trash service.

PALO VERDE (CA)
Oxbow Campground $7.50
Yuma Field Office, Bureau of Land Management
3 mi S of Palo Verde on SR 78; 1 mi E on gravel rd from sign marked "Colorado River." Camp is at old river channel oxbow in both Arizona & California. $7.50 for seniors with federal senior pass; others pay $15 ($75 annually). Non-campers pay $10 day use fee. All year; 14-day limit. Undesignated, unmarked primitive sites. No facilities. Boating(l), fishing, hiking, swimming, picnicking. Near popular OHV trails & Cibola National Wildlife Refuge. Free use permit required. No open fires; use charcoal grills or propane stoves.

PARKER
Crossroads Campground $5
Lake Havasu Field Office, Bureau of Land Management
8 mi NW of Parker (in California) on Parker Dam Rd. All year. $5. All year; 14-day limit. 12 undeveloped sites. Tbls, toilets, cfga, no drkg wtr. Along Colorado River. Nearby Empire Landing Campground now privately operated.

PAYSON
Aspen Campground $10
Rim Lakes Recreation Area
Apache-Sitgreaves National Forest
N of Payson on SR 260 toward Heber; 5 mi W on FR 300; right at unmarked, paved Woods Canyon Lake Rd for 0.75 mi; near Rim Visitor Center. $10 with federal senior pass; others pay $20. 5/1-10/31; 14-day limit. 136 sites; 32-ft RV limit. Tbls, toilets, cfga, drkg wtr, dump nearby, picnic area. Boating(I), fishing, interpretive trail.

Blue Ridge $8
Coconino National Forest
51 mi N of Payson on SR 87; 1 mi on FR 138; on Blue Ridge Reservoir. $8. About 4/15-9/30; 14-day limit. 10

sites (22-ft RV limit). Tbls, toilets, cfga, drkg wtr. Fishing, hiking, picnicking, boating. Elev 7300 ft; 5 acres. Renovations included new toilets, faucets, tbls, fire rings, grills, improved sites.

Camp Bonito   FREE
Apache-Sitgreaves National Forest
E of Payson on SR 260; NW on FR 300; 1 mi E on FR 115; 2 mi on FR 91; 1.5 mi E of Ohaco Lookout on FR 40. All year; 14-day limit. Undesignated primitive sites; no facilities; no trash pickup. Picnicking, hiking, horseback riding.

Canyon Point Campground $11.50
Rim Lakes Recreation Area
Apache-Sitgreaves National Forest
NW of Payson on SR 260; at milepost 287. $11.50 base with federal senior pass; others pay $23 (elec hookups, $5). 5/11-10/30; 14-day limit. 106 sites (32 with elec). 75-ft RV limit. Tbls, flush toilets, cfga, drkg wtr, showers ($3 for non-campers), dump ($7 non-campers), public phone. Hiking trails, interpretive programs, fishing.

Christopher Creek $9
Tonto National Forest
21 mi NE of Payson on SR 260; S at milepost 271. $9 with federal senior pass; others pay $18. 4/1-10/31; 14-day limit. 43 sites; 22-ft RV limit. Tbls, toilets, cfga, drkg wtr. Campfire program, fishing, hiking, horseback riding. Elev 5100 ft. Non-campers pay $8 day use fee. Concessionaire.

Deer Lake   FREE
Apache-Sitgreaves National Forest
E of Payson on SR 260; 7 mi NW on FR 300; 2.3 mi N on FR 169; qtr mi E on access rd. Free. All year; 14-day limit. Undesignated primitive sites; camp anywhere except on lakeshore. No facilities except cfga; no trash service. Fishing, hiking, picnicking.

Double Cabin   FREE
Apache-Sitgreaves National Forest
E of Payson on SR 260; 16 mi NW on FR 300; 4 mi N on FR 115; 1 mi E of Ohaco Lookout on FR 40. Free. All year; 14-day limit. Undesignated primitive sites; no facilities except cfga; no trash service. Hiking, picnicking. Ruins of old cabin nearby.

First Crossing   FREE
Tonto National Forest
2 mi N of Payson on SR 87; 7 mi on FR 199; on East Verde River. Free. All year; 14-day limit. Undeveloped primitive sites on 10 acres (16-ft RV limit). Tbls, no toilets, cfga, no drkg wtr. Trout fishing, boating, hiking.

Flowing Spring   FREE
Tonto National Forest
3.5 mi N of Payson via AZ 87; & FR 272. Free. All year; 14-day limit. Undesignated camping area on 20 acres;

20-ft RV limit. Toilet, no drkg wtr, no trash service, no tbls, no cfga. Trout fishing. East Verde River access. Elev 4600 ft.

FR 34 Dispersed Sites   FREE
Apache-Sitgreaves National Forest
E of Payson on SR 260; 16 mi NW on FR 300; 4 mi N on FR 115 to Ohaco Lookout; pick up FR 56, follow it to FR 225; follow FR 225 to FR 34. Free primitive camping within 300 feet of FR 34. No facilities. Hiking, fishing.

Houston Mesa Campground $11
Tonto National Forest
Half mi N of Payson on US 87; right at campground sign for qtr mi; left into campground. $11 with federal senior pass; others pay $22. 2/1-11/30; 14-day limit. 75 sites; 40-ft RV limit. Tbls, flush toilets, cfga, drkg wtr, dump ($10), coin showers($3), water refill, $5. Hiking, horseback riding, half-mi interpretive trail. 30 equestrian sites, $14, $95 at 2 group areas. Non-campers pay $6 day use fee. Concessionaire.

Knoll Lake $7
Coconino National Forest
29 mi NE of Payson on SR 260; 19 mi NW on FR 300; 4 mi E on FR 295E. $7 with federal senior pass; others pay $14. MD-10/31; 14-day limit. 33 sites (32-ft RV limit). Tbls, toilets, cfga, drkg wtr. Boating(l), hiking, fishing. Elev 7400 ft; 20 acres.

Lower Tonto Creek $8
Tonto National Forest
17 mi NE of Payson on SR 260; qtr mi N on FR 289 from near milepost 269. $8 with federal senior pass (double site $15); others pay $16 (double site $30). 4/1-10/31; 14-day limit. Small sites. Tbls, toilets, cfga, drkg wtr at Upper Tonto Creek. Fishing, hiking trails. Nearby trout hatchery. Non-campers pay $8. Concessionaire.

Ponderosa Campground $8
Tonto National Forest
15 mi NE of Payson on SR 260; S to site. $8 with federal senior pass; others pay $16. 4/15-10/31; 14-day limit. 61 sites; 35-ft RV limit. Tbls, toilets, cfga, drkg wtr, dump ($10); day use fee $8. Self-guided Abert Nature Trail, campfire programs.

Second Crossing   FREE
Tonto National Forest
2 mi N of Payson on AZ 87; 8.5 mi on FR 199. Free. May-Sep; 14-day limit. Undeveloped primitive sites on 2 acres (RVs under 16 ft). No toilets, cfga, no drkg wtr, no trash service. Fishing, swimming. East Verde River access point. Elev 5100 ft.

Sharp Creek $11
Tonto National Forest
23 mi NE of Payson on S side of SR 260; about 1.5 mi E of Christopher Creek. $11 with federal senior pass; others pay $22. 4/15-10/31; 14-day limit. 28 sites; 40-ft RV limit. Some pull-through. Tbls, toilets, cfga, drkg wtr. Hiking. Non-campers pay $8 day use fee.

Spillway Campground $11.50
Rim Lakes Recreation Area
Apache-Sitgreaves National Forest
N of Payson on SR 260 toward Heber; 5 mi W on FR 300; right at Woods Canyon Lake Rd for 0.75 mi; across from Rim Visitor Center. $11.50 with federal senior pass; others pay $23. Group camping $140. 5/15-9/30; 14-day limit. 26 sites; 16-ft RV limit. Tbls, toilets, cfga, drkg wtr, picnic area, dump nearby. Boating(l - elec mtrs), fishing, interpretive nature trail. Elev 7500 ft.

Third Crossing FREE
Tonto National Forest
2 mi N of Payson on AZ 87; 9.5 mi on FR 199. Free. May-Sep; 14-day limit. Undeveloped primitive sites on 5 acres (RVs under 17 ft). No toilets, cfga, no drkg wtr. Fishing. East Verde River access point. Minimum-development site.

Upper Tonto Creek $8
Tonto National Forest
17 mi NE of Payson on SR 260; 1 mi N on CR 289; at confluence of Tonto Creek & Horton Creek. $8 with federal senior pass; others pay $16. 4/1-10/30; free rest of year, but no drkg wtr; 14-day limit. 9 small sites (RVs under 17 ft). Tbls, toilets, cfga, drkg wtr, dump nearby($), nature trails. Hiking, fishing, swimming. Elev 5600 ft; 7 acres. Non-campers pay $8 day use fee.

Verde Glen FREE
Tonto National Forest
2 mi N of Payson on AZ 87; 10.5 mi on FR 199; half mi E on FR 64. Free. 5/15-10/15; 14-day limit. Undeveloped primitive sites on 20 acres (RVs under 17 ft). No facilities, no drkg wtr, no trash service; portable toilet or self-contained small RV (van or pickup camper) suggested. Fishing, hiking. River access point.

Water Wheel FREE
Tonto National Forest
2 mi N of Payson on AZ 87; 8 mi on FR 199. Free. Apr-Nov; 14-day limit. Undeveloped primitive sites (RVs under 16 ft). Toilets, cfga, no drkg wtr. Fishing. River access point. Minimum-development site. Elev 5000 ft.

PEORIA
Desert Tortoise Campground $12
Lake Pleasant Regional Park
Maricopa County Park
From I-17 exit 232 at New River, 6 mi SW on N. Lake Pleasant Rd; 3 mi W on SR 74; 1 mi N on Castle Springs Rd; 0.5 mi E on park entrance rd, then follow signs to campground; at NW shore of Lake Pleasant. $12 base. All year; 14-day limit. Base fee for primitive shoreline camping without amenities; $20 for semi-developed non-elec sites with restrooms, tbls, cfga; $30 for developed sites with elec/wtr, dump station access, tbls, cfga. 76 sites (25 developed, 41 non-elec, 10 for tents). Tbls, toilets, cfga, drkg wtr, site ramadas, elec, showers. Boating(l), fishing, hiking. Part of 23,662-acre park.

Main Entrance Camping $12
Lake Pleasant Regional Park
Maricopa County Park
Follow directions for Desert Tortoise Campground to park entrance; primitive shoreline camping at Lake Pleasant near park's main entrance. $12. All year; 14-day limit. Several primitive sites (no RV size limit); no facilities, no drkg wtr. Boating(l), fishing, hiking. 23,662-acre park.

North Entrance Camping $12
Lake Pleasant Regional Park
Maricopa County Park
Follow directions to Desert Tortoise Campground, but continue 2 mi past the main entrance, then right on Castle Creek Rd; primitive shoreline camping on Lake Pleasant. $12. All year; 14-day limit. Several sites; no facilities, no drkg wtr. Boating(l), fishing, hiking. 23,662-acre park.

PHOENIX
Ben Avery Shooting Range $12
Arizona Game & Fish Dept.
25 mi N of Phoenix on I-17. $12 base. All year; 14-day limit. Base fee without hookups ($50 weekly); $25 with wtr/elec ($100 weekly). 96 sites at Shooter's Campground East, 54 with 30/50-amp wtr/elec; 42 primitive for self-contained RVs or tents. New Central Shooter's Campground has 22 full-hookup sites. Tbls, flush toilets, cfga, drkg wtr, showers, playground. Shooting range, archery range, hiking trails. Camping only for registered shooters.

Black Canyon Trailhead $12
Maricopa County Park
25 mi N of Phoenix on I-17; on Carefree Hwy (SR 74). $12. All year; 14-day limit. 100 sites (36-ft RV limit). Tbls, toilets, cfga, drkg wtr, elec/wtr. Camping by reservation only. Shooting ranges, archery range; 5 mi of trails & practice area.

PINE
Clints Well FREE
Coconino National Forest
21.9 mi N of Pine on AZ 87; quarter mi N on FR FH3. Free. All year; 14-day limit. 7 sites (RVs under 23 ft), plus space in trees for several self-contained RVs. Tbls, toilets, cfga, firewood, no drkg wtr. Picnicking. Elev 7000 ft. 3 acres.

Kehl Springs   FREE
Coconino National Forest
13 mi N of Pine on AZ 87; 7.1 mi E on FR 300. Free. All year; 14-day limit. 8 sites (RVs under 23 ft). Tbls, toilets, cfga, firewood, no drkg wtr. Picnicking, mountain biking, fishing, boating. Elev 7500 ft. 6 acres.

Rock Crossing $8
Coconino National Forest
3 mi SW of Blue Ridge Ranger Station; 25 mi on FR 751. $8; double sites $16. About 5/15-10/1; 14-day limit. 35 sites (32-ft RV limit). Toilets, tbls, cfga, drkg wtr. Boating(l), fishing. Elev 7500 ft; 25 acres. Renovated with new toilets, faucets, tbls, fire rings, grills, improved sites.

PINEDALE
Hub Point   FREE
Apache-Sitgreaves National Forest
S of Pinedale on FR 130, past Lons Canyon turnoff; E on FR 219; right on FR 139 for qtr mi, then take Hub Point turnoff on FR 919 for qtr mi. Free. All year; 14-day limit. Primitive undesignated camping area. Hiking, picnicking, hunting.

Lons Canyon   FREE
and Lons Spring
Apache-Sitgreaves National Forest
S of Pinedale on FR 130 (off SR 260) to Lons Canyon cutoff, follow signs. Free. All year; 14-day limit. Primitive undesignated camping areas scattered throughout the canyon. No facilities; no trash service. Picnicking, hiking, horseback riding.

PINETOP-LAKESIDE
A-One Lake Campground $8
White Mountain Apache Reservation
22 mi E of Pinetop on SR 260. $8. 5/15-9/15; 10-day limit. 4 sites. Tbls, toilets, cfga, no drkg wtr. Site can be muddy in snow or rain. Fishing, boating(l), hiking. Lake named for an Apache chief who was called A-1 by soldiers who thought his name was too hard to pronounce. 24-acre lake; elec 8900 ft.

Alchesay Springs Campground $8
White Mountain Apache Reservation
S of Pinetop-Lakeside on Hwy 73. $8. Apr-Nov; 10-day limit. 10 RV sites. Tbls, toilets, cfga, drkg wtr. Fishing. Alchesay Fish Hatchery nearby.

Bog Creek Campground $8
White Mountain Apache Reservation
E of Pinetop via SR 260 (just E of McNary) on reservation rd. $8. Apr-Nov; 10-day limit. 5 sites. Tbls, toilets, cfga, drkg wtr. Fishing. Elev 7500 ft.

Bog Tank Campground $8
White Mountain Apache Reservation
E of Pinetop via SR 260; right on reservation rd past Bog Creek & Shush-B-Zazhe camps to Bog Tank Lake; across Hwy 260 from Horseshoe Cienega Lake. $8. All year; 10-day limit. 10 sites. Tbls, toilets, cfga, drkg wtr. Fishing, boating. 12-acre lake.

Brown Spring Dispersed Area   FREE
Apache-Sitgreaves National Forest
From Pinetop-Lakeside, follow SR 260 to McNary, then NE on FR 224 toward Vernon, following signs to Lake Mountain fire lookout; then 1.5 mi N of lookout. Free primitive undesignated sites. No facilities.

Cooley Lake Campground $8
White Mountain Apache Reservation
S of Pinetop-Lakeside via SR 260; 1 mi S of Hon-Dah just off SR 73. $8. Apr-Nov; 10-day limit. 10 sites. Tbls, toilets, cfga, drkg wtr. Fishing, boating.

East Fork Campground $8
White Mountain Apache Reservation
S of Pinetop-Lakeside on SR 73; NE on R-25; at East Fork of White River. $8. Apr-Nov; 10-day limit. 15 sites. Tbls, toilets, cfga, drkg wtr. Fishing, birdwatching.

Hawley Lake Campground $8
Hawley Lake Recreation Area
White Mountain Apache Reservation
From Pinetop-Lakeside, about 6 mi SE to McNary, then continue 16 mi E on SR 260; about 11 mi S on SR 473 to lake (last 2 mi gravel). Lake office at Cabin C-79 about 0.75 mi off main rd, following signs. $8 at primitive sites, $25 at RV sites with elec/wtr. All year. 125 shoreline sites. Tbls, flush toilets, cfga, drkg wtr. Fishing, boating (l - elec mtrs). Store, boat rentals. Elev 8000 ft.

Los Burros Campground   FREE
Apache-Sitgreaves National Forest
E of Pinetop-Lakeside to McNary; 8 mi NE of McNary on FR 224. Free. 5/15-10/15; 14-day limit. 10 sites (RVs under 23 ft). 12 acres. Tbls, 1 toilet, cfga, firewood, no drkg wtr. Picnicking, hiking. Elev 7900 ft. No trash service.

Lower Log Road Campsites $8
White Mountain Apache Reservation
About 10 mi SE of Pinetop-Lakeside on SR 260; about 100 primitive sites scattered along Lower Log Rd. $8. Apr-Nov; 10-day limit. Tbls, toilets, cfga, no drkg wtr. Fishing. Sites get heavy use.

Pierce Spring   FREE
Apache-Sitgreaves National Forest
E of Pinetop-Lakeside on SR 260 to McNary; about 10 mi NE of McNary on FR 224; right on FR 96 for 1 mi; right on unmarked access rd. Free. All year; 14-day limit. Primitive dispersed camping area; no facilities; no trash service. Horseback riding, picnicking.

Porter Spring/Lons Canyon   FREE
Apache-Sitgreaves National Forest
E of Pinetop-Lakeside on SR 260 to McNary; 13 mi NE of McNary on FR 224. Free. All year; 14-day limit. Primitive undesignated sites; no facilities, no drkg wtr. Fishing, hiking.

Reservation Flat   FREE
Apache-Sitgreaves National Forest
E of Pinetop-Lakeside on SR 260 to McNary; 6 mi N of McNary on FR 224; 1.5 mi on FR 9. All year; 14-day limit. Free primitive dispersed camping area; no facilities; no trash service. Picnicking, hiking.

Ryan Ranch Campground $8
White Mountain Apache Reservation
About 14 mi E of Pinetop-Lakeside on SR 260, then S past Horseshoe Cienega Lake; at North Fork of the White River. $8. Apr-Nov; 10-day limit. 5 sites. Tbls, toilets, cfga, drkg wtr. Fishing, hiking.

Scott Reservoir   FREE
Apache-Sitgreaves National Forest
S of Pinetop-Lakeside on SR 260; 1.5 mi E on FR 45 (Porter Mountain Rd), following signs to lake. Free. All year; 5-day limit. 12 primitive designated sites. Toilets, cfga, tbls, no drkg wtr. Fishing, picnicking, hiking, boating(l).

Shush-Be-Tou Lake Camp $8
White Mountain Apache Reservation
15 mi SE of Pinetop via SR 260; right on reservation rd past Bog Creek & Shush-Be Zazhe Campgrounds. $8. May-Nov; 10-day limit. 10 sites. Tbls, toilets, cfga, drkg wtr. Fishing, boating. Elev 7600 ft.

Shush-Be Zazhe Campground $8
White Mountain Apache Reservation
E of Pinetop via SR 260; right on reservation rd past Bog Creek Campground. $8. May-Oct; 10-day limit. 6 sites. Tbls, toilets, cfga, drkg wtr. Fishing, boating.

PORTAL
Idlewilde Campground $10
Douglas Recreation Area
Coronado National Forest
2 mi W of Portal on FR 42 (or access from Rodeo, NM); must ford stream, which is impassable in wet weather. $10. About 4/1-10/1; free rest of year when open, but usually closed & no wtr Nov-Mar; 14 day limit. 9 sites; 16-ft RV limit (best for vans, pickup campers). Tbls, toilets, cfga, drkg wtr Apr-Sept. Hiking, picnicking. Nature trails. Cave Creek Canyon Visitor Center nearby. Elev 5000 ft; 50 acres. Non-campers pay $10 day use fee.

Pinery Canyon/Cave Creek   FREE
Coronado National Forest
2 mi W of Portal on CR 42; 16 mi W on FR 42; high-clear-ance vehicle suggested. Free. All year; 14-day limit. 4 sites (16-ft RV limit). Tbls, toilets, cfga, no drkg wtr, no trash service. Picnicking, hiking trails. Elev 7000 ft. 30 acres. Scenic.

Rustler Park Campground $10
Douglas Recreation Area
Coronado National Forest
13 mi W of Portal on FR 42 to Onion Saddle; 3 mi SW on FR 42D (or access from Rodeo, NM). $10. Open 4/1-10/31; 14-day limit. 25 sites (22-ft RV limit). Tbls, toilets, cfga, no drkg wtr. Pack out trash; no service. Hiking trails, picnicking. Elev 8300 ft; 200 acres. Non-campers pay $10 day use fee. Rebuilt following 2011 fire.

Stewart Campground $10
Douglas Recreation Area
Coronado National Forest
2.3 mi W of Portal on FR 42. $10. 4/15-10/31; 14-day limit. 6 sites (16-ft RV limit). Tbls, toilets, cfga, drkg wtr Apr-Oct, no trash service. Hiking, picnicking. Non-campers pay $10 day use fee.

Sunny Flat Campground $10
Douglas Recreation Area
Coronado National Forest
3 mi SW of Portal on FR 42. $10 during 4/1-10/31; free rest of year, but no wtr. All year; 14-day limit. 13 sites (28-ft RV limit). Tbls, toilets, cfga, drkg wtr (wtr purification recommended). Picnicking, hiking. Elev 5200 ft; 70 acres.

PRESCOTT
Groom Creek Horse Camp $9
Prescott National Forest
6.5 mi S of Prescott on Mt. Vernon Ave (FR 52) to Groom Creek, then three-fourths mi S. $9 for seniors with federal senior pass at 37 equestrian-only sites; others pay $18. 5/1-10/31; 14-day limit. Redeveloped campground a joint venture with Desert Saddlebag Club of Phoenix; sites can handle large RVs & horse trailers. Tbls, toilets, cfga, drkg wtr, horse tethers, 30 corrals. Horseback riding, hiking trails. Non-campers pay $5 day use fee.

Hilltop Campground $9
Lynx Lake Recreation Area
Prescott National Forest
4.9 mi E on Hwy 69 from Prescott to 1.8 mi past Bradshaw Ranger District office; 3.5 mi on Walker Rd, then left at campground sign about half mi. $9 for seniors with federal senior pass; others pay $18. 4/1-10/31; 7-day limit. 38 sites (40-ft RV limit). Tbls, toilets, cfga, drkg wtr. Boating (elec motors only), fishing, hiking, gold panning, no swimming. Short walk to 55-acre Lynx Lake.

Indian Creek   CLOSED
Prescott National Forest
4 mi SW of Prescott on US 89; half mi S on FR 63. Nestled

along Indian Creek between the White Spar Hwy & the Groom Creek cutoff #97. Now closed to camping.

Lower Wolf Creek $10
Prescott National Forest
7.6 mi S of Prescott on CR 52; 0.9 mi W on FR 97. $10. 5/1-10/31; 14-day limit. 20 sites (40-ft RV limit). Tbls, toilets, cfga, no drkg wtr. Hiking, hunting. 7 acres.

Lynx Lake Campground $9
Lynx Lake Recreation Area
Prescott National Forest
4.9 mi E on Hwy 69; left for 3 mi on Walker Rd (FR 197) to campground sign; left on access rd; on W shore of 55-acre Lynx Lake. $9 for seniors with federal senior pass; others pay $18. 4/1-10/31; 7-day limit. 36 sites (40-ft RV limit). Tbls, flush toilets, cfga, drkg wtr. Boating (elec motors only), fishing, hiking, gold panning, no swimming. Elev 5500 ft.

White Spar $7
Prescott National Forest
2.5 mi S of Prescott on US 89; CG is just off FR 62. $7 for seniors with federal senior pass; others pay $14 during 5/1-10/31. Off-season without wtr, $10 ($5 with senior pass). All year (12 sites open all year); 14-day limit. 57 sites (40-ft RV limit). Tbls, toilets, cfga, drkg wtr. Hiking, picnicking. Elev 5700 ft; 20 acres.

Yavapai Campground $9
Granite Basin Lake Recreation Area
Prescott National Forest
In Prescott, follow Grove Ave N from Gurley St to 4th traffic light, bearing left through the light, then 3.2 mi on Iron Springs Rd to Granite Basin Lake; left on FR 374 about 4 mi. $9 for seniors with federal senior pass; others pay $18; double sites $36. All year; 14-day limit. 21 sites; 40-ft RV limit. Tbls, toilets, cfga, drkg wtr. Boating (l - no mtrs), hiking, fishing, no swimming.

<u>**QUARTZSITE**</u>
Kofa National National Wildlife Refuge FREE
15 mi S of Quartzite off SR 95. Free. All year. Undesignated sites; no facilities; no drkg wtr. Hiking, picnicking, sightseeing. Excellent backpacking. Primitive terrain. Scenic, rugged. Camping not for first-timers.

LaPosa Long-Term Visitor Area $180
Yuma Field Office Bureau of Land Management
1 mi S on SR 95 from I-10 exit 6 mi S of Quartzsite. $180 for whole winter season of 9/15-4/15; $40 for 14 days. $15 daily or $75 for the summer season. 2,000 sites on 11,400 acres. Drkg wtr (8 faucets), trash pickup, dump, cfga, 10 toilets, dance floor, ramada. Rockhounding, picnicking, hiking, sightseeing.

<u>**ROOSEVELT**</u>
Bachelor Cove $8
Tonto National Forest
1.6 mi NW of Roosevelt on AZ 88; 7.3 mi NW on AZ 188. $8 Tonto Pass required. All year; 14-day limit. Approx 10 sites; 16-ft RV limit. No toilets, tbls, drkg wtr or trash service. Swimming, boating ($6 boat fee), fishing, water-skiing, picnicking. Elev 2100 ft. 5 acres. Roosevelt Lake, paved launch area.

Bermuda Flat Recreation Site $8
Tonto National Forest
1.6 mi NW of Roosevelt on AZ 88; 8.9 mi NW on AZ 188. $8 Tonto Pass required. 2/16-11/14; 14-day limit. About 25 primitive sites for tents & self-contained RVs; 32-ft RV limit. Portable toilets, no tbls, no drkg wtr. Swimming, boating(rl - $6 boat fee), fishing, waterskiing. Elev 2100 ft; 18 acres. Roosevelt Lake. Minimum development site. Formerly named Horse Pasture.

Schoolhouse Campground $8
Tonto National Forest
7.3 mi SE of Roosevelt on AZ 88; 3.5 mi NE on FR 447; 11 mi S of dam at Upper Salt River. $8 Tonto Pass online or from vendor, $12 onsite. All year; 14-day limit. 211 sites; 32-ft RV limit. Toilets, tbls, drkg wtr, amphitheater, fish cleaning stations. Swimming, boating (l - $4), fishing, picnicking, waterskiing. Elev 2100 ft. 35 acres. Small boats can be launched.

Upper Burnt Corral Recreation Site $8
Tonto National Forest
17 mi W of Roosevelt on SR 188; qtr mi W on FR 183; on Apache Lake 6 mi S of dam. $8 Tonto Pass required. 3/1-11/15; 14-day limit. 82 sites; 22-ft RV limit due to narrow, winding rd. Tbls, toilets, cfga, drkg wtr. Swimming, boating(l - $4 boat fee), fishing, waterskiing, campfire programs, interpretive programs, fish cleaning station. 38 acres.

<u>**SAFFORD**</u>
Arcadia Campground $10
Safford Recreation Area
Coronado National Forest
7.5 mi S of Safford on US 191; 11 mi SW on SR 366; long RVs have difficulty negotiating SR 366 switchbacks. $10. All year, but closed when snow closes SR 366; 14-day limit. 19 sites (22-ft RV limit). Tbls, toilets, cfga, no drkg wtr. Hiking trails, picnicking. Elev 6700 ft; 10 acres. Non-campers pay $10 day use fee.

Black Hills Rockhound Area FREE
Gila Box Riparian National Conservation Area
Safford Field Office, Bureau of Land Management
17 mi NE of Safford, just off US 191; access rd from AZ 666; approx 1 mi to parking area. Free. All year. No des-

ignated sites. Tbls, toilets, cfga, drkg wtr. Trash pickup. Hunting, hiking, picnicking, fishing, fire agate hunting.

Bonita Creek   FREE
Gila Box Riparian National Conservation Area
Safford Field Office, Bureau of Land Management
From 8th Ave near Safford airport, follow signs NE on Sanchez Rd to Bonita Creek. Free. All year; 14-day limit. Primitive undesignated sites along the creek. No facilities, no wtr or trash service. Hiking, bird-watching.

Clark Peak Corrals   FREE
Safford Recreation Area
Coronado National Forest
7.5 mi S of Safford on US 191; 28 mi SW on SR 366; 7 mi on FR 803. Free. May-Oct; 14-day limit. 2 sites (22-ft RV limit). Tbls, toilet, cfga, no drkg wtr. Horse corrals. Horseback riding, hiking, picnicking. Elev 9000 ft.

Columbine Corrals $10
Safford Recreation Area
Coronado National Forest
7.5 mi S of Safford on US 191; 28 mi SW on SR 366; across from visitor information station. $10. 5/15-11/15; 14-day limit. 6 sites (22-ft RV limit). Tbls, toilets, cfga, drkg wtr; corrals & wtr for horses. Horseback riding, hiking & riding trails, picnicking. Elev 9500 ft. Visitor center open 4/15-9/15.

Cunningham Campground $10
Safford Recreation Area
Coronado National Forest
8 mi S of Safford on US 191; 26 mi SW on Hwy 366; switchbacks too tight for large RVs. $10. 4/15-11/15; 14-day limit. 10 sites (22-ft RV limit due to rd switchbacks). Tbls, toilets, cfga, no drkg wtr. Horse feed & wtr no longer furnished. 2 vehicles per site. Pipe corral, bridle trails. Horseback riding, mountain biking, hiking. Non-campers pay $10 day use fee.

Fourmile Canyon $5
Safford Field Office, Bureau of Land Management
15 mi NW of Safford on Hwy 70 to Aravaipa-Klondyke Rd; 30 mi W on graded gravel rd to Klondyke; 1 mi W on Fourmile Canyon Rd. $5. All year. 10 dirt pull-through sites (30 ft RV limit). Toilets, tbls, drkg wtr, cfga. Elev 3500 ft. Picnicking, hiking. Permit needed to travel in Aravaipa Canyon.

Hot Well Dunes Recreation Area $3
Safford Field Office, Bureau of Land Management
7 mi E of Safford on Hwy 70; 25 mi S on Haekel Rd. $3 (or $30 annually). All year; 14-day limit. 10 sites. Tbls, toilets, cfga, no drkg wtr. 2 natural artesian hot tubs with wtr at 106 degrees. Fishing, hiking. Heavily used weekends.

Owl Creek Campground $5
Bureau of Land Management
Gila Box Riparian National Conservation Area
10 mi E of Safford on US 70; N on US 191 to milepost 160 (4 mi S of Clifton); left on Black Hills Back Country Byway to campground, about 10 mi S of Clifton. $5. All year; 14-day limit. 7 sites. Tbls, cfga, shad ramadas, toilets, drkg wtr. Boating, fishing, hiking, hunting.

Riggs Flat Campground $10
Safford Recreation Area
Coronado National Forest
7.5 mi S of Safford on US 191; 27.5 mi SW on SR 366; 4 mi W on FR 803; 1 mi S on FR 287; on Riggs Flat Lake. Large vehicles have difficulty negotiating SR 366 switchbacks. $10 11/15-4/15; 14-day limit. 31 sites (22-ft RV limit). Tbls, toilets, cfga, no drkg wtr. Boating (l--elec motors only), fishing, hiking trails. Elev 8600 ft; 50 acres. Non-campers pay $10 day use fee.

Riverview Campground $5
Safford Field Office, Bureau of Land Management
Gila Box Riparian National Conservation Area
5 mi E of Safford on US 70 to town of Solomon; left on Sanchez Rd; after crossing Gila River bride, continue 7 mi to Bonita Creek and Gila Box RNCA sign; turn left for 2.5 mi on dirt rd to Gila Box Riparian National Conservation Area. $5. All year; 14-day limit. 13 sites. Tbls, toilets, cfga, drkg wtr, shade ramadas, volleyball court. Fishing, boating, hiking, river floating, hunting.

Shannon $10
Safford Recreation Area
Coronado National Forest
7.5 mi S of Safford on US 191; 21.5 mi SW on SR 366; half mi N on FR 137; large RVs have difficulty negotiating SR 366 switchbacks. $10. 4/15-11/14; 14-day limit. 11 sites (RVs under 23 ft). Tbls, toilets, cfga, no drkg wtr. Hiking, nature trails (including to top of 10,000-ft Heliograph Peak. Elev 9100 ft; 10 acres. Non-campers pay $10 day use fee.

Soldier Creek $10
Safford Recreation Area
Coronado National Forest
7.5 mi S of Safford on US 191; 29.2 mi SW on SR 366; half mi W on FR 34; qtr mi E on FR 656. $10. 4/15-11/15; 14-day limit. 12 sites (RVs under 23 ft). Tbls, flush toilets, cfga, no drkg wtr. Hiking, nature trails. Elev 9300 ft; 7 acres. Non-campers pay $10 day use fee.

Spring Canyon Picnic Area   FREE
Bureau of Land Management
From 8th Ave near Safford airport, follow signs to Bonita Creek NE on Sanchez Rd; area is about 3 mi past first sign along River. Free. All year; 14-day limit. Primitive

sites with 2 tbls, cfga, no other facilities, no wtr, no trash service. Hiking, canoeing, fishing.

Stockton Pass Campground   FREE
Safford Recreation Area
Coronado National Forest
16.5 mi S of Safford on US 191; 12 mi W on AZ 266; half mi NE on FR 198. Free. All year; 14-day limit. 7 sites; RVs under 23 ft. 11 picnic sites; 10 acres. Tbls, toilets, cfga, firewood, no drkg wtr. Picnicking, horseback riding (1 mi). Elev 5600 ft.

Turkey Creek   FREE
Safford Field Office, Bureau of Land Management
13 mi W of Safford on US 70; 32 mi SW on dirt Aravaipa-Klondyke Rd; at Klondyke, follow signs 10 mi to Aravaipa Canyon Wilderness; Turkey Creek at E end of wilderness. Free. Primitive undesignated sites. No facilities except cfga, but toilets at wilderness parking lot. No drkg wtr. Free permit needed to use wilderness. Primarily a hiker camp for those going into the canyon. Nearby Aravaipa Canyon camp is $5 per person.

ST. GEORGE (UTAH)
Arizona Strip   FREE
Arizona Strip Field Office, Bureau of Land Management
E from Bloomington exit of I-15, then S on River Rd to Arizona state line; follow signs on dirt rd; start at Black Rock Mountain. Primitive, undeveloped campsites on 3.2 million acres N of Grand Canyon & S of Utah line, includes 8 wilderness areas. Free. All year; 14-day limit. Undeveloped, few amenities. RVs not recommended off-highway (Vermilion Cliffs highway suggested). Wildlife viewing (antelope, deer, bighorn`, coyotes, mountain lions); hiking, backpacking, mountain biking, rockhounding, boating. Interagency visitor information center in St. George. Attractions include Dominguez-Escalante Interpretive Site on US 89A, 21 mi E of Jacob Lake; Virgin River Canyon's towering multi-colored cliffs, 20 mi SW of St. George; historic one-room Mount Trumbull Schoolhouse; Nampaweap Petroglyph Site; Sawmill Historic Site/Uinkaret Pueblo; Little Black Mountain Petroglyph Site.

SALOME
Centennial Park $8
La Paz County Park
1.5 mi SE of Salome on Salome Rd; 1 mi N on Centennial Park Rd. $8 at 26 primitives sites ($40 weekly, $100 monthly); $14 with elec/wtr ($70 weekly; $160 monthly plus kw charge)). Tbls, toilets, cfga, drkg wtr, playground, dump ($5 campers, $10 non-campers), showers $2 ($8 for non-campers). Picnicking, hiking, tennis, horseshoes, basketball, volleyball, rockhounding. Greasewood Desert Golf Course at N end of park.

SAN CARLOS
Cassadore Springs $10
San Carlos Apache Recreation & Wildlife Department
San Carlos Apache Indian Reservation
From Globe, 5 mi E on US 70; 5 mi NE on SR 170 to San Carlos; 12 mi N of town. $10 at primitive sites. Tbls, toilets, cfga, drkg wtr. Fishing.

Soda Canyon Point Campground $10
San Carlos Apache Recreation & Wildlife Department
San Carlos Apache Indian Reservation
From Globe, 25 mi E on US 70; 9.5 mi S on Coolidge Dam Rd to campground turnoff; then 1 mi to camp on NW shore of lake (2 mi N of dam). $10 daily camping permit for primitive sites. All year. Tbls, toilets, cfga, drkg wtr. Fishing (with $10 daily permit), boating (l - $5 permit). 19,500-acre lake with 158 mi of shoreline.

SECOND MESA
Second Mesa Campground   FREE
and Trailer Park
Hopi Indian Reservation
Jct Hwys 264 & 87, 5 mi NW on Hwy 264; on top of Second Mesa next to Cultural Center. Free. All year; 2-day limit. 6 sites; 10 acres. Tbls, flush toilets, pay showers, laundry. Picnicking. Elev 6000 ft.

SEDONA
Cave Springs Campground $11
Coconino National Forest
13 mi N of Sedona (14 mi S of Flagstaff) on US 89A in Oak Creek Canyon. $11 with federal senior pass; others pay $22. 4/1-11/15; 7-day limit. 82 sites; 35-ft RV limit. Tbls, toilets, cfga, drkg wtr, coin showers ($4). Fishing, swimming, hiking. Crowded on weekends. Non-campers pay $8 day use fee.

Manzanita Campground $11
Coconino National Forest
6 mi N of Sedona (21 mi S of Flagstaff) on US 89A in Oak Creek Canyon. $11 with federal senior pass; others pay $22. All year; 7-day limit. 18 sites for tents & small sleep-in vehicles; no trailers. Tbls, toilets, cfga, drkg wtr. Fishing, swimming, hiking. Non-campers pay $8 day use fee.

Pine Flat Campground $11
Coconino National Forest
12 mi N of Sedona (14 mi S of Flagstaff) on US 89A in Oak Creek Canyon. $11 with federal senior pass; others pay $22. 4/1-10/31; 7-day limit. 56 sites; 30-ft RV limit. Tbls, toilets, cfga, drkg wtr, coin showers ($4). Fishing, swimming, hiking. Non-campers pay $8 day use fee.

SHOW LOW
Cibecue Creek Campground $8
White Mountain Apache Reservation
About 25 mi S of Show Low on US 60; NW on access rd to

town of Cibeque, then N of Cibeque on service rds 12 and O-20; at Cibeque Creek. $8. All year; 14-day limit. 10 sites. Tbls, toilets, cfga, drkg wtr. Fishing. Elev 6000 ft. Closed due to fire at last report. GPS: 34.138599, -110.508

Fence Tank   FREE
Apache-Sitgreaves National Forest
3 mi S of Show Low on SR 260; left on FR 136 at sign marked Joe Tank Rd; after 1.8 mi, left on FR 140 for 2.2 mi; accessible only to high-clearance vehicles. Free. May-Oct; 14-day limit. Primitive undesignated sites. No facilities, no drkg wtr, no trash service. Hiking, wildlife viewing.

Lakeside
Apache-Sitgreaves National Forest
10 mi SE of Show Low on SR 260; just across highway from ranger station. Closed permanently.

Salt River Canyon Campground $10
White Mountain Apache Reservation
SW of Show Low (past Carrizo) on US 60 at Salt River. $10 per person. All year; 10-day limit. 8 sites. Tbls, toilets, cfga, drkg wtr. Fishing, whitewater rafting, boating, kayaking.

Sunrise Lake Campground $8
White Mountain Apache Reservation
SE of Show Low on SR 260 past McNary; S on SR 273 at milepost 377; right 3 mi to entrance of Sunrise Ski Resort. $8. All year. 150 primitive sites. Tbls, portable toilets, cfga, drkg wtr; showers at the lodge. Fishing, boating (10-hp motor limit), store, boat rental. 891-acre lake. Elev 8700 ft.

Sunrise RV Park $9
White Mountain Apache Reservation
SE of Show Low on SR 260 past McNary, then right on Hwy 273; at Sunrise General Store. $9. All year; 10-day limit. 20 RV sites with elec. Tbls, cfga. Flush toilets, showers, coin laundry at the resort; no wtr, but available at nearby general store. Fishing, boating (elec mtrs).

SIERRA VISTA
Ramsey Vista $10
Sierra Vista Recreation Area
Coronado National Forest
8 mi S of Sierra Vista on SR 92; 7 mi W on Carr Canyon Rd (FR 368); sharp switchbacks cannot be negotiated by trailers & motorhomes. $10. All year; 14-day limit. 8 sites for tents, vans, pickup campers or tiny trailers. Tbls, toilets, cfga, no drkg wtr. Handicap-accessible toilet; handicap accessible campsite with accessible picnic table, pedestal grill, hard tent pad. Hiking, sightseeing, picnicking, horseback trails & corrals. Non-campers pay $10 day use fee.

Reef Townsite $10
Sierra Vista Recreation Area
Coronado National Forest
8 mi S of Sierra Vista on SR 92; 5 mi W on Carr Canyon Rd (FR 368); sharp switchbacks cannot be negotiated by trailers & motorhomes. $10 during 5/15-10/30; free 11/1-5/14 but no wtr; 14-day limit. 14 sites for tents, vans, pickup campers, tiny trailers. Tbls, toilets, cfga, no drkg wtr, food prep areas. 2 handicap-accessible campsites with trails to toilets; both with pedestal grill, wheelchair-designed tbl, hard tent pad. Hiking, sightseeing, picnicking, horseback trails. Elev 7200 ft; 20 acres. Group camping area has 16 sites on 10 acres. Built on site for old mining town. Non-campers pay $10 day use fee.

San Pedro $2
Riparian National Conservation Area
Bureau of Land Management
E of Sierra Vista in vast 58,000-acre area of Cochise County between St. David and the Mexican border. $2 per person. Primitive camping permitted in backcountry areas, but not in parking areas. Permit required, available from self-service pay stations at all visitor parking areas. 7-day limit each location. No facilities. Bird watching, hiking, picnicking, horseback riding.

SONOITA
Lakeview $10
Sierra Vista Recreation Area
Coronado National Forest
30 mi SE of Sonoita on SR 83. $10. All year; 14-day limit. 65 sites (32-ft RV limit). Tbls, toilets, cfga, drkg wtr, store, dump, fishing pier. 3 handicap-accessible toilets with paved entry ramps; 3 tbls accessible by paved trail; 2 tbls accessible by compacted soil trail. Hiking, fishing, boating(rl--8 hp limit). Parker Canyon Lake. Concessionaire-operated. Elev 5400 ft; 50 acres. Non-campers pay $10 day-use fee.

SPRINGERVILLE
Burro Mountain   FREE
Apache-Sitgreaves National Forest
4 mi SW of Springerville on SR 260; 23 mi S on SR 261; 4 mi W of Crescent Lake. Free. All year; 14-day limit. Primitive undesignated sites; no facilities, no drkg wtr.

Carnero Lake   FREE
Apache-Sitgreaves National Forest
About 11 mi W of Springerville on SR 260; 5 mi N to Carnero Lake. Free. All year; 14-day limit. Primitive undesignated sites; no facilities, no drkg wtr. Fishing.

CC Cabin   FREE
Apache-Sitgreaves National Forest
About 11 mi W of Springerville on SR 260; 6 mi N. Free. All year; 14-day limit. Primitive undesignated sites; no facilities, no drkg wtr.

Grayling Campground $10
Big Lake Recreation Area
Apache-Sitgreaves National Forest
4 mi SW of Springerville on SR 260; 23 mi S on SR 261; left
at stop sign near Crescent Lake; 2.5 mi to Big Lake Recreation Area. Grayling is in the RA past the visitor's center
and Rainbow CG. $10 with federal senior pass; others pay
$20. 5/15-10/15, free off-season; 14-day limit. 23 sites;
22-ft RV limit. Tbls, flush toilets, cfga, drkg wtr, tackle
shop, visitor center, store, dump($6), showers ($6). Fishing, boating(lr), hiking & biking trails, horseback riding(r),
mountain biking. Elev 9200 ft; 15-acres. Non-campers pay
$5 day use fee for picnicking ($50 annual day use pass).

Mexican Hay Lake   FREE
Apache-Sitgreaves National Forest
About 3 mi SW of Springerville on SR 260; 3 mi S on SR
261. Free. All year; 14-day limit. Primitive undesignated
sites; no facilities, no drkg wtr. Fishing.

Mineral Creek   FREE
Apache-Sitgreaves National Forest
W of Springerville on SR 260 (about 5 mi SE of Vernon),
then just S. Free. All year; 14-day limit. Primitive undesignated sites; no facilities, no drkg wtr. Fishing, hiking.

Rainbow Campground $9
Big Lake Recreation Area
Apache-Sitgreaves National Forest
4 mi SW of Springerville on SR 260; 23 mi S on SR 261; left
at stop sign near Crescent Lake; 2.5 mi to Big Lake Recreation Area. Rainbow is in the RA past the visitor's center.
$9 with federal senior pass, $10 at pull-through sites;
others pay $18 & $20. 5/15-9/30; 14-day limit. 152 sites
(32 ft RV limit). Tbls, flush toilets, cfga, drkg wtr, visitor
center, store, dump($6), showers($6). Boating(lr), fishing,
hiking & biking trails, nature trail, horseback riding(r). Elev
9200 ft; 46 acres. Non-campers pay $5 for picnicking, $6
for dump station, $6 showers ($50 annual day use pass).

South Fork Camp   DAY USE
Apache-Sitgreaves National Forest
5 mi W of Springerville via AZ 260 and AZ 560 at end of FR
4124 south of AZ 260; along South Fork of Little Colorado
River. Now day use area following forest fire.

SUPERIOR
Devils Canyon   FREE
Tonto National Forest
6 mi E of Superior on US 60-70. Free. All year; 1-day limit.
5 sites (no RV size limit, but trailers not recommended).
Tbls, toilets, cfga, no drkg wtr. Hiking, rock climbing. Elev
4000 ft.

Oak Flat   FREE
Tonto National Forest
4 mi NE of Superior on US 60. Free. All year; 14-day limit.

16 sites (RVs under 30 ft). Tbls, toilets, cfga, no drkg wtr,
no trash service. Rockhounding, picnicking. Elev 4200 ft.
20 acres. Steep grades and/or sharp curves.

TUCSON
Bog Springs $10
Nogales Recreation Area
Coronado National Forest
S of Tucson on I-19 to Continental; follow Madera Canyon
signs 7 mi SE on FR 62 and 6 mi S on FR 70. $10. All year;
14-day limit. 13 sites (22-ft RV limit). Tbls, toilets, cfga,
drkg wtr. Hiking, picnicking. Elev 5600 ft; 15 acres. Excellent birdwatching. Non-campers pay $10 day use fee.

Catalina State Park $15
From town of Oro Valley (N of Tucson), NW on SR 77
(Oracle Rd). $15 for non-elec sites at 30-site Ringtail
Campground during 11/1-4/30 & 13 non-elec sites at
Campground A during 5/1-10/31. 14-day limit. Tbls, flush
toilets, cfga, drkg wtr, showers, dump ($15 for non-camp-
ers). Elec sites $25-$30. No RV size limit. Biking, hiking
trails. $7 vehicle entry fee.

Gordon Hirabayashi Camp $10
Santa Catalina Recreation Area
Coronado National Forest
From jct with Tanque Verde Rd in Tucson, 4.2 mi on Catalina Hwy to forest, then 7 mi to campground (on the right on
mtn route). $10. 11/1-4/30; 14-day limit. 12 sites; 22-ft RV
limit. Tbls, toilets, cfga, no drkg wtr. Corral. Hiking, horseback riding. Formerly named Prison Camp. Non-campers
pay $10 day use fee.

Molino Basin $10
Santa Catalina Recreation Area
Coronado National Forest
21.3 mi NE on FR 33; .1 mi NW on FR 5. 11/1-4/30; 14-day
limit. $10. 37 sites (RVs under 23 ft). Tbls, toilets, cfga, no
drkg wtr. Picnicking, hiking. Elev 4400 ft. 65 acres. Mountains. Grassy terrain. Non-campers pay $10 day use fee.

Rose Canyon $11
Santa Catalina Recreation Area
Coronado National Forest
NE of Tucson on Catalina Hwy between mileposts 17 &
18; at Rose Canyon Lake. $11 with federal senior pass;
others pay $22. 4/15-10/31; 14-day limit. 74 sites; 22-ft
RV limit. Tbls, toilets, cfga, drkg wtr. Fishing (6-acre mtn
lake), hiking. Elev 7000 ft. Non-campers pay day use fee.
Concessionaire.

Spencer Canyon $11
Santa Catalina Recreation Area
Coronado National Forest
From Tanque Verde rd in Tucson, 25.7 mi N on Hitchcock
Hwy (milepost 22). $11 with federal senior pass; others
pay $22. 4/15-10/15; 14-day limit. 60 sites; 22-ft RV

limit. Tbls, toilets, cfga, drkg wtr. Hiking, sightseeing. Elev 8000 ft; 65 acres. Non-campers pay $9 day use fee. Concessionaire.

VAIL
Colossal Cave Mountain Park $7.50
Pima County Parks Department
Pima County Parklands Foundation
From I-10 exit 279, 1 mi NE to Vail, then about 5 mi E on E. Colossal Cave Rd, following signs; 1 mi S on E. Old Spanish Trail to park; in Sonaran Desert. $7.50 plus park use fees. Overnight camping in the picnic areas; no hookups; tbls, toilets, cfga, drkg wtr, playground. Butterfly garden, desert tortoise exhibit, gem sluice. Cave tours($).

WENDEN
Alamo Lake State Park $15
From US 60 at Wenden, about 32 mi N & NW on 2nd St (becoming Alamo Rd); use left fork at New Alamo Rd; right on Lakeview Dr to park office. $15 for undeveloped sites with pit & chemical toilets and nearby wtr, $15 base at 36 developed sites with nearby bathhouse (elec/wtr $22, full hookups $25). All year; long-term camping at 15 sites during 1/1-4/30, by reservation; 28-day minimum, 84-night limit. Tbls, dump, cfga. Fishing, swimming, boating(l), interpretive exhibits, store.

WHITERIVER
Lower Big Bonito Creek $8
White Mountain Apache Reservation
S & E of Whiteriver (and Fort Apache) on SR 73; S on Reservation Rd Y-70. $8. Apr-Nov; 10-day limit. 2 sites. Tbls, toilets, cfga, drkg wtr. Fishing.

Rock Creek Campground $8
White Mountain Apache Reservation
SE of Whiteriver on SR 73, E of East Fork crossing. $8. Apr-Nov; 10-day limit. 2 sites. Tbls, toilets, cfga, drkg wtr. Fishing.

Upper Big Bonita Creek $8
White Mountain Apache Reservation
SE of Whiteriver on SR 73; S on reservation rd Y-70 to Big Bonita Creek. $8. Apr-Nov; 10-day limit. 6 sites. Tbls, toilets, cfga, drkg wtr. Fishing.

WHY
Coyote Howls East $9
City Park
Several primitive sites are located along US 85 (north of Organ Pipe Cactus National Monument). $9 daily; $40 weekly; $130 monthly. Group sites available. 600 sites Tbls, flush toilets, cfga, showers, drkg wtr, library, card room, community building, dump. No hookups. 200 acres. West Park has elec sites, $20.

WICKENBURG
Constellation City Park $8
Everett Bowman Rodeo Grounds
From just E of Wickenburg from US 60, turn N on either Jack Burden Rd or El Recreo Rd, then follow Constellation RD NE about 1 mi; right (S) into camping area across rd from park. $8 at 35 self-contained RV sites; no facilities, no drkg wtr, no tents; $12 with horse stall. All year; 7-day limit. Regular rodeo events. City dump near community center on Valentine St, $10.

WIKIEUP
Burro Creek Campground $7
Kingman Field Office, Bureau of Land Management
14 mi SE of Wikieup on US 93; half mi W on Burro Creek Rd. $7 for seniors with federal senior pass; others pay $14 (group camping $50). All year; 21-day limit. 30 sites. Tbls, flush toilets, cfga, drkg wtr, dump ($10 non-campers), picnic area, desert garden. Rockhounding, hiking, fishing.

WILLCOX
Bonita Canyon $12
Chiricahua National Monument
31 mi SE on SR 186; 3.1 mi E on Hwy 181E. $12. All year; 14-day limit. $5 per adult entry fee also charged (free with federal senior pass). 25 sites (29-ft RV limit); group camping area. Tbls, flush toilets, cfga, drkg wtr, visitor center, museum, grey wtr dump. Hiking trails, campfire programs, sightseeing. Elev 5400 ft; 12,000 acres.

Cochise Stronghold $10
Douglas Recreation Area
Coronado National Forest
SW of Willcox on I-10 to US 191; 18 mi S on US 191; 9.5 mi W on Ironwood Rd/FR 84. $10. 9/1-6/31; 14-day limit. 10 sites (22-ft RV limit), plus 8 walk-in tent sites; group sites $20. Tbls, toilets, cfga, no drkg wtr; some handicap sites & facilities. Hiking, picnicking. Cochise Trail and Stronghold Nature Trail. Elev 5000 ft; 30 acres, Non-campers pay $10 day use if parked at campsite.

WILLIAMS
Cataract Lake
Kaibab National Forest
One-third mi W of Williams on I-40; qtr mi W on CR 749. Closed to camping; day use only.

Cataract Lake
Coconino County Park
City of Williams Parks & Recreation
2 mi NW of Williams just off I-40 at Country Club Rd exit. 5/1-10/31; 14-day limit. 30 sites. Tbls, toilets, cfga, drkg wtr, central kitchen ramadas. Boating (6 hp limit), fishing. Elev 6800 ft; 15 acres. Group sites $4 per unit. Now managed by City of Williams. Note: Camping no longer offered here due to budget constraints; day use only for 2017.

Dogtown Lake $10
Kaibab National Forest
3 mi SE of Williams on SR 173; 2 mi E on FR 140; 1 mi N
on FR 132. $10 with federal senior pass; others pay $20;
double sites $32. 5/1-9/30; sometimes free or reduced
fees rest of year, but no wtr or services. 51 sites; 35-ft
RV limit. Group camping area. Tbls, toilets, cfga, drkg wtr,
group ramada by reservation, no dump, firewood ($5).
Boating (l--elec mtrs), fishing, hiking, nature trails. Elev
7000 ft; 60 acres.

Kaibab Lake Campground $10
Kaibab National Forest
2 mi E of Williams on I-40; 2 mi N on SR 64; half mi NW
on FR 747. $10 with federal senior pass; others pay $20;
double site $32. 5/1-9/30; 14-day limit. 73 sites; 40-ft
RV limit). Group camping area. Tbls, toilets, cfga, drkg
wtr, group shelter ($30). Handicap-accessible toilet with
paved path to 2 paved sites. Boating(l--8 hp limit), fishing,
hiking, interpretive programs, no swimming. Filling RV
water tanks prohibited due to wtr shortage. Dump fee
$10 for campers, $13 visitors. Concessionaire-operated.
Elev 6800 ft; 36 acres. Non-campers pay $5 day use fees.

Ten-X Campground $10
Kaibab National Forest
47 mi N of Williams on SR 64/US 180. $10. 5/1-10/15;
14-day limit. 70 sites (40-ft RV limit). Group sites available. Tbls, toilets, cfga, drkg wtr. Nature trail, campfire
programs, picnicking. Camp is 8 mi from Grand Canyon
NP. Elev 6600 ft; 46 acres.

White Horse Lake $10
Kaibab National Forest
8 mi S of Williams on FR 173; 9 mi E on FR 110; 3 mi E on
FR 109. $10 with federal senior pass; others pay $20; double sites $32. 5/1-10/1; free rest of year but no services;
14-day limit. 94 sites; 38-ft RV limit. Tbls, toilets, cfga,
drkg wtr, store. Dump fee $10 for campers, $13 for visitors; firewood $6. Boating(rl--elec motors only), fishing,
hiking, mountain biking, canoeing. Elev 7000 ft; 44 acres.
Concessionaire-operated. Filling RV wtr tank prohibited
due to wtr shortage.

WINSLOW

Jack's Canyon Dispersed Area FREE
Coconino National Forest
From I-40 near Winslow, 30 mi S on SR 87 to milepost 314;
continue 0.3 mi to dirt rd on right; close gate behind you,
then drive 0.3 mi, turning left at fork for 0.2 mi; then right &
continue 0.7 mi to trailhead & campground. Free. All year;
14-day limit. Nearby rock climbing area. Toilet, cfga, no
drkg wtr, no trash service.

Homolovi State Park $15
From I-40 exit 257 just E of Winslow, 2 mi N on SR 87 to
park. $15 at non-elec sites during 11/1-4/14 ($18 rest of

year). 83-ft RV limit. Elec sites $25 all year. 14-day limit.
Tbls, flush toilets, cfga, drkg wtr, dump ($15 non-camp-
ers). Hiking trails, petroglyph walks, pottery talks, Hopi
cemetery. $7 day use fee.

WINTERHAVEN (CA.)

Senator Wash North Shore $7.50
Yuma Field Office, Bureau of Land Management
From Winterhaven exit of I-8, go N 22 mi on CR S-24;
follow Senator Wash Rd 2 mi to South Mesa Campground;
proceed through campground & follow signs to North
Shore. $7.50 for seniors with federal senior pass; others
pay $15 (or $75 annually). Holders of Long-Term Visitor
Area permits also may use the day-use facilities. All year;
14-day limit. Primitive undesignated sites on about 60
acres. Tbls, toilets, cfga, no drkg wtr; dump at South Mesa
(fee charged 9/15-4/15). Boating(l), fishing, swimming,
hiking, waterskiing. Free permit required. No trash service. Fires restricted about MD-LD; cook on charcoal grills
or propane stoves. Non-campers pay $10 day use fee.

Senator Wash South Shore $7.50
Bureau of Land Management
From I-8 exit at Winterhaven, follow CR S-24 about 22
mi N; follow Senator Wash Rd 2 mi to South Mesa Campground, then left about 200 yds; turn right on reservoir
access rd. $7.50 for seniors with federal senior pass;
others pay $15 (or $75 annually). Holders of Long-Term
Visitor Area permits also may use the day-use facilities.
All year; 14-day limit. Primitive undesignated sites on 50
acres. Tbls, flush toilets, outdoor showers, drkg wtr, gravel beach; dump at South Mesa (fee 9/15-4/15); no trash
service. Boating(l), fishing, swimming, hiking. Non-campers pay $10 day use fee.

YOUNG

Airplane Flat FREE
Tonto National Forest
23 mi NE of Young on unpaved SR 288/FR 512; right on FR
33 for 5 mi. Free. Apr-Nov; 14-day limit. Undeveloped tent/
RV sites (RVs under 16 ft). Toilets, cfga, tbls, no drkg wtr,
no trash service. Fishing, picnicking. Elev 6600 ft. Stream
for artificial lure & fly fishing only (1 mi). FR 12 & SR 288
unpaved. Near Canyon Creek.

Alderwood FREE
Tonto National Forest
11 mi N of Young on SR 288; right on FR 200 for 7 mi; left
on FR 200A for half mi; at Haigler Creek. Free. 5/15-10/15;
14-day limit. Undesignated, undeveloped sites; 16-ft RV
limit. Tbls, toilets, cfga, no drkg wtr, no trash service.
Fishing, picnicking. Elev 5200 ft.

Colcord Ridge FREE
Tonto National Forest
23 mi NE of Young on FR 12 & FR 33. Free. Apr-Nov; 14-day
limit. Undeveloped tent & RV sites (RVs under 32 ft). Toilets, cfga, tbls, no drkg wtr, no trash service. Picnicking,

hiking. Elev 7600 ft. FR 12 unpaved. Minimum-development site.

Haigler Canyon Recreation Site $8
Tonto National Forest
3 mi NW of Young on AZ 288; 9 mi on unpaved FR 200. $8 Tonto Pass required; day use free. 5/15-10/15; 14-day limit. 14 sites at 2 areas (RVs under 20 ft). Tbls, toilets, cfga, no drkg wtr or trash service. Picnicking, fishing. Wtr cold for swimming; rocky. Elev 5300 ft.

Lower Canyon Creek FREE
Tonto National Forest
22 mi NE of Young on FR 12 & FR 188. Free. May-Nov. 1-day limit. Facilities: Undeveloped. RVs under 16 ft. Toilets, cfga, no drkg wtr. Fly & lure fishing only. Picnicking. Elev 6400 ft. SR 288 & FR 12 unpaved.

Rose Creek FREE
Tonto National Forest
23.4 mi S of Young on AZ 288. Free. 5/15-10/15; 14-day limit. 5 sites (16-ft RV limit). Tbls, toilets, cfga, piped drkg wtr, no trash service. Picnicking, fly & lure fishing only. Elev 5400 ft. 5 acres. Temporarily closed at last report; check current status with rangers before arrival.

Upper Canyon Creek FREE
Tonto National Forest
31 mi NE of Young. Free. 5/15-10/15; 14-day limit. 10 primitive sites (RVs under 16 ft). Tbls, toilets, no drkg wtr, no trash service. Fly fishing, picnicking. Elev 6700 ft.

Valentine Ridge FREE
Tonto National Forest
3 mi NE on AZ SR 288; 17 mi NE on unpaved FR 512; 3 mi NE on unpaved FR 188. Free. 5/15-10/15; 14-day limit. 10 sites (RVs under 16 ft). Tbls, toilets, cfga, firewood, no drkg wtr, no trash service. Picnicking, hiking, fly & lure fishing only, 9-mi bike loop trail. Elev 6900 ft. 5 acres.

Workman Creek FREE
Tonto National Forest
22 mi N of SR 88 on SR 288, then along Workman Creek on FR 487, past Workman Creek Falls. High-clearance vehicles advised; RVs discouraged. Free. Apr-Nov; 14-day limit. 3 sites at Cascade and Falls Recreation Sites. Tbls, cfga, toilets, no drkg wtr. Fishing, hiking, no trash service. Elev 5400-7748 ft.

YUMA

Imperial Dam $180
Long-Term Visitor Area
Bureau of Land Management
From I-8 Winterhaven exit, 24 mi N of Yuma on CR S-24 in California; follow Senator Wash Rd 2 mi. $180 for whole winter season of 9/15-4/15 or $40 for 14 days. During 4/16-9/14, $15 daily or $75 for summer season. About

2,000 sites on 3,500 acres. Toilets, cfga, drkg wtr, grey & black wtr dumps, outdoor showers, ramadas; limited facilities in winter. Rockhounding, hiking, fishing, boating, swimming.

Mittry Lake Wildlife Area FREE
Yuma Field Office, Bureau of Land Management
7 mi E of Yuma on SR 95; 9.5 mi N on Avenue 7E to 600-acre Mittry Lake. Free. All year; 10 days for the calendar year. Numerous undesignated sites.. Toilet, cfga, no drkg wtr. Fishing jetty. Boating(l), hiking, fishing, swimming, duck hunting. About 2,400 acres of marshland managed jointly by BLM, BOR & state game & fish department. Free permit required. Large fishing jetties.

Rest Area FREE
21 mi N of Yuma on W side of US 95 at big brick gate & sign to US Army Proving Grounds. Free. All year; 1 night limit. Spaces for self-contained RVs (no tent camping). Tbls, toilets, cfga. Picnicking.

Squaw Lake Campground $7.50
Yuma Field Office, Bureau of Land Management
24 mi NE of Yuma on CR S-24 in California (or exit CR S-24 from I-8 at Winterhaven; go N 20 mi; left on Ferguson Lake Rd, then follow signs 4 mi). $7.50 for seniors with federal senior pass; others pay $15 (or $75 annually). Non-campers pay $10 day use fee. All year; 14-day limit. 125 RV sites (30-ft RV limit) & numerous dispersed tent sites. Tbls, flush toilets, cold outdoor showers, cfga, drkg wtr, gray water dump (dump station at nearby South Mesa), beach. Boating(l), fishing, swimming, hiking. 15 acres. No open fires MD-LD.

YUCCA

Havasu Backcountry North FREE
Bureau of Land Management
Access N side of Mohave Mountains off I-40 at Franconia Wash. Or try the El Paso Natural Gas Pipeline area from I-40's Gem Acres exit. For the eastern portion of the Havasu backcountry north, drive S on Alamo Rd from I-40 in Yucca; rd continues to Rawhide Mountains & N shore of Alamo Lake. Free. All year; 14-day limit. Primitive dispersed camping; no facilities. Get access guide from BLM office in Havasu City. Favorite areas for dune buggies, OHV, motorcycles, mountain biking, rockhounding.

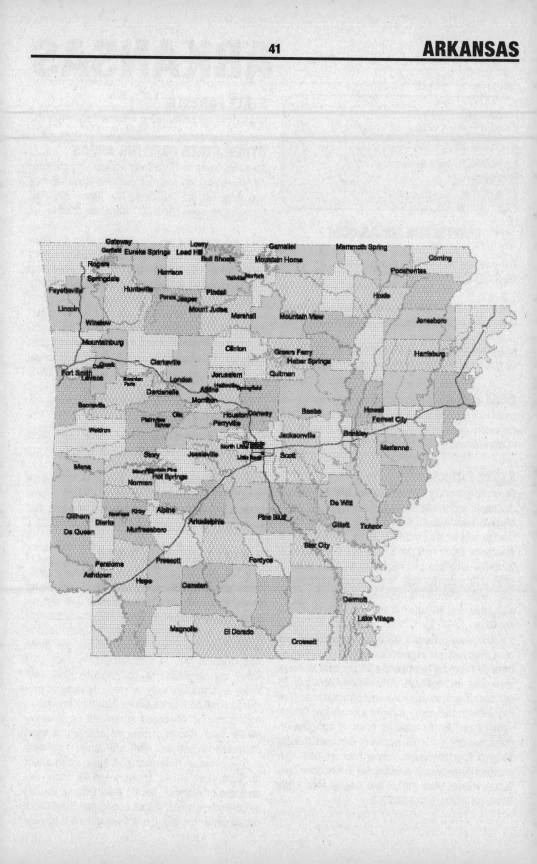

ARKANSAS

CAPITAL: Little Rock
NICKNAME: The Natural State
STATEHOOD: 1836 – 25th State
FLOWER: Apple Blossom
TREE: Pine
BIRD: Mocking Bird

WWW.ARKANSAS.COM

Toll-free numbers for travel information:
1-800-NATURAL.

Division of State Parks, Dept of Parks and Tourism, One Capitol Mall, Little Rock, AR 72201; 888-287-2757.

Game and Fish Commission, No. 2 National Resources Drive, Little Rock, AR 72205; 501/223-6300.

REST AREAS
Overnight parking in self-contained RVs is permitted for safety reasons only. Camping is not allowed. RV dump stations are not provided at state rest areas.

STATE PARKS
Fees are generally $12 to $32 per night, although discounts are available for campers 62 and older. Class D sites without hookups are $12, and Class C sites with either electric or water are $16 before discounts. Other fees are $20 at Class B sites with water/30-amp electric hookups; $25 at Class A sites with water/50-amp hookups; $28 at Class AA sites with 30-amp full hookups, and $32 at Class AAA sites with 50-amp full hookups. Overflow sites are $11.

Arkansas residents 62 or older get a 50 per cent discount off regular campsite fees Sunday through Thursday nights and a 25 per cent discount weekends and holidays. Arkansas seniors pay 25 per cent less than everyone else on weekends (Friday through Saturday). A driver's license or federal senior pass can be used as proof of age. Out-of-state seniors get a 25 per cent discount Sunday through Thursday nights. Lower fees are no longer charged during winter months. For information contact Arkansas State Parks, One Capitol Mall, Little Rock, AR 72201; 888-287-2757.

STATE FORESTS.
Camping is not permitted in Arkansas state forests.

OTHER STATE CAMPING AREAS
Arkansas Game and Fish Commission Campgrounds. All Arkansas Game and Fish camping areas are free and primitive (no facilities). The Game and Fish Commission owns about 300,000 acres of state land and manages wildlife on more than 1 million acres of national forest land, all of which is open for camping. Those properties consist of more than 100 fishing lake Public Access Areas and Wildlife Management Areas. The commission publishes free area fishing guides, which indicate roads and portage points and provide information about the areas. For further information and a map pinpointing each campground, contact: Game and Fish Commission, #2 Natural Resources Dr., Little Rock, AR 72205; 501-223 6300.

NATIONAL FORESTS
Ozark-St. Frances National Forests. 605 West Main, Russellville, AR 72801; 479-964-7200.

Ouachita National Forest. This 1.6-million-acre forest is the nation's oldest national forest. It provides camping at some two dozen campgrounds. 100 Reserve St, Hot Springs, AR 71902. 501/321-5202.

BUFFALO NATIONAL RIVER
The 135-mile Buffalo River passes massive sandstone and limestone bluffs and offers whitewater canoeing (usually floatable in spring and winter). Kyles Landing and Steel Creek are accessible only via steep, winding gravel roads; the park recommends that buses and large RVs not use these campgrounds. All 14 campgrounds except Lost Valley are accessible by boat and by road; Lost Valley is accessible only by road. Camping is permitted on all park lands except historic sites, within half a mile of developed areas and on privately owned land. Camping fees are charged at most campgrounds between April and October; camping is free between November and April, when water hookups, flush toilets, showers and RV dump stations are unavailable. During peak floating periods on spring weekends, Kyles Landing and Steel Creek can be quite crowded. Ozark Campground is popular

throughout the spring and summer, and with the exception of Erbie, campgrounds in the upper river are filled to capacity over Memorial Day weekend. Tyler Bend (now $16 overnight) fills only during holiday weekends; Buffalo Point (now $22 overnight), most weekends in the summer. 402 N. Walnut, Suite 136, Harrison, AR 72601. 870-439-2502 for information; headquarters, 870-365-2700.

WHITE RIVER NATIONAL WILDLIFE REFUGE
Camping is permitted March 16-October 31 in the more than 20 designated areas; there is a 14-day limit. The refuge can be reached from the east or north via US 70 from Little Rock or Memphis; near Hazen, take AR 11 to Stuttgart and follow this route to DeWitt; then take AR 1 to St. Charles. Traveling from the south, take US 65 to Pine Bluff and then to Stuttgart. Campers should ask directions and road conditions at the St. Charles headquarters since the roads are often impassable even in summer. For a map that pinpoints the other camping areas contact: White River National Wildlife Refuge, P.O. Box 308, 704 Jefferson St, DeWitt, AR 72042; 870-282-8234.

Hot Springs National Park. 101 Reserve St, Hot Springs, AR 71901; visitor center: 501-620-6715.

ALPINE

Alpine Ridge $9
Corps of Engineers
DeGray Lake
From Alpine at jct with SR 8, 10 mi E through Fendley on SR 346; follow signs to lake. During 5/1-11/30, $9 with federal senior pass at 49 elec RV/tent sites; others pay $18. Fees $14 before & after regular season. 14-day limit; 40-ft RV limit, all back-in. Tbls, flush toilets, cfga, drkg wtr, playground, dump, showers, beach. Fishing, swimming, boating (l), waterskiing, picnicking. 175 acres.

Ozan Point $10
Corps of Engineers
DeGray Lake
Near Alpine, 12 mi E of through Fendley on SR 346; 1.5 mi E on gravel rd. $10. About 3/1-10/31; 14-day limit. 50 small, primitive sites (15-ft RV limit, limited to pickup campers & van campers; no trailers). Tbls, toilets, cfga, drkg wtr. Boating(l), fishing, picnicking, waterskiing, swimming.

ARKADELPHIA

Arlie Moore $9
Corps of Engineers
DeGray Lake
14 mi N of Arkadelphia on US 7; 2 mi W from Gibson's Store to lake. During about 5/1-9/5, $9 with federal senior pass at 38 RV/tent elec sites & 30 RV elec sites; others pay $18. During 9/5-4/30, fees are $14 ($7 with senior pass). All year; 14-day limit. 30-ft RV limit, all back-in. Tbls, flush toilets, cfga, drkg wtr, elec, showers, dump, playground, beach, shelter, amphitheater. Boating (l), fishing, nature trails, waterskiing, picnicking, swimming. 161 acres.

Iron Mountain $7
Corps of Engineers
DeGray Lake
2 mi W of dam on Skyline Drive to lake. $7 with federal senior pass at 69 elec sites; others pay $14. 3/1-11/30; 14-day limit. 2 pull-through sites. Tbls, flush toilets, cfga, drkg wtr, elec, playground, showers, dump. Boating(l), fishing, picnicking, swimming, waterskiing. 240 acres.

Lenox Marcus FREE
Corps of Engineers
DeGray Lake
3 mi S of Lambert off SR 84; 17 mi N of Arkadelphia on SR 7; 3 mi W on SR 84; 4 mi S on gravel rd. Free. 3/1-11/30; 14-day limit. Open camping on 200 remote acres. Drkg wtr, 30 picnic sites, toilets, cfga. Boating (r), fishing, hiking, picnicking.

Point Cedar $10
Corps of Engineers
DeGray Lake
15 mi N of Arkadelphia on SR 7; 8 mi W on SR 84;

$10. 3/1-11/30; 14-day limit. 62 sites (40-ft RV limit). Tbls, flush toilets, cfga, drkg wtr. Fishing, boating(l), swimming. 50 acres.

Shouse Ford $7
Corps of Engineers
DeGray Lake
15 mi N of Arkadelphia on SR 7; 3.5 mi SE on SR 84, then E on Shouse Ford Rd. During 5/1-9/4, 81 RV/tent elec sites & 19 RV elec sites, $7 with federal senior pass; others pay $14. Some sites open before & after regular season. 40-ft RV limit, all back-in. Tbls, flush toilets, cfga, drkg wtr, beach, playground, dump, showers. Boating (l), fishing, swimming.

ASHDOWN

Beard's Bluff Campground $12
Corps of Engineers
Millwood Lake
13 mi E of Ashdown on SR 32; half mi S on access rd between the road & lake, upstream from dam's E embankment (signs). $12 at non-elec site ($6 with federal senior pass). 24 paved elec/wtr sites, $15 base, $18 for full hookup site all year ($7.50 & $9 with senior pass); 1 buddy site $21 ($10.50 with senior pass). 14-day limit. Tbls, flush toilets, cfga, dump, playground, beach, drkg wtr. Horseback riding, boating(l), picnicking, fishing, swimming. 30 acres. Picnic shelter, reservable outdoor wedding chapel, amphitheater.

Beard's Lake Campground $10
Corps of Engineers
Millwood Lake
9.5 mi E of Ashdown on SR 32; 1.5 mi W on access rd; below dam. During 3/1-10/31, $10 at non-elec RV/tent sites & 3 shoreline tent sites; $13 at 5 elec/wtr sites ($5 & $6.50 with federal senior pass). Lower fees off-season. Tbls, pit toilets, cfga, drkg wtr, fishing pier. Use dump, showers, playground, beach at Beard's Bluff. Fishing, boating(l), hiking trail with boardwalk. 50 acres. Warning: Alligators present. No reservations.

Cottonshed Park $7.50
Corps of Engineers
Millwood Lake
From Ashdown, 20 mi E on SR 32; N on SR 355 to Tollette; 8 mi W on CR 234 to Schaal; 2 mi S on access rd. During 3/1-10/31, $7.50 base with federal senior pass at 43 paved elec/wtr sites. All year; 14-day limit. Tbls, flush toilets, showers, cfga, dump, playground, fish cleaning station, coin laundry. Boating(l), fishing, hiking.

Millwood State Park $10
From Ashdown at jct with US 71, 9 mi E on SR 32 to park at S shore of 29,500-acre Millwood Lake. 13 Class B 30-amp elec/wtr sites, $10 for AR seniors on weekdays, $15 for AR seniors on weekends and for non-resident seniors on

weekdays; others pay $20. All year; 14-day limit. Tbls, flush toilets, showers, cfga, drkg wtr, dump. Visitor center. Fishing, boating(l), 1.5-mi hiking trail, 4-mi wilderness hiking/biking trail, interpretive programs.

River Run East $8
Corps of Engineers
Millwood Lake
12 mi E of Ashdown on SR 32; below dam on shore of Little River outlet channel. $8 ($4 with federal senior pass). All year; 14-day limit. 8 gravel sites. Tbls, pit toilets, cfga, drkg wtr. Fishing, hiking.

River Run West $8
Corps of Engineers
Millwood Lake
9.5 mi E of Ashdown on SR 32; half mi E on access rd, below Millwood Dam on shore of Little River outlet channel. $8 ($4 with federal senior pass). All year; 14-day limit. 4 gravel sites. Tbls, pit toilets, cfga, drkg wtr. Fishing, boating(l), picnicking.

Saratoga Landing $6.50
Corps of Engineers
Millwood Lake
18 mi SE of Ashdown on SR 32; 1 mi W on access rd. $6.50 with federal senior pass at 17 paved elec/wtr sites; others pay $13. All year; 14-day limit. Tbls, flush toilets, cfga, drkg wtr, showers, fishing pier, rock dike, shelter, playground. Boating(l), fishing. Park temporarily closed in 2017.

White Cliffs Park $7.50
Corps of Engineers
Millwood Lake
10 mi N of Ashdown on SR 71; 5 mi E on SR 27; 6 mi S on gravel SR 317; at E shore of Little River. $7.50 with federal senior pass at 25 paved elec/wtr sites; others pay $15. All year; 14-day limit. Tbls, flush toilets, cfga, drkg wtr, pavilion, playground, fish cleaning station. Swimming, fishing, boating(l); hiking trails & ATV activity on adjacent land.

ATKINS
Lake Atkins   FREE
State Fishing Access Site
Just S of Atkins on gravel rd; follow shoreline rd W to one camping area or pick up SR 105 S of spillway , then W on SR 324 to SW & NW shore areas. Free. All year; 14-day limit. Primitive designated camping areas. No facilities, no drkg wtr. Fishing, boating(l). Courtesy dock, fishing pier, bait shop.

Sweeden Island $8
Corps of Engineers
Ormand Lock and Dam #9
J. W. Rockefeller Lake
8.3 mi SW of Atkins on SR 105; near Lock & Dam 9,

Rockefeller Lake, on bluff overlooking Arkansas River. $8 with federal senior pass at 22 elec sites; others pay $16. Tents $10. All year; 14-day limit. Tbls, toilets, cfga, drkg wtr, dump. Boating(l), picnicking, fishing, group shelter($), playground. McClellan-Kerr Arkansas River Navigation System.

BEEBE
Cypress Bayou   FREE
Wildlife Management Area
1.9 mi S of Beebe on gravel rd; on White/Lonoke County line at Cypress Bayou. All year; 14-day limit. Primitive undesignated camping. No facilities, no drkg wtr. Fishing, hunting, hiking, canoeing. Pond.

Lake Barnett State Fishing Access Site   FREE
From jct with US 64 at Beebe, about 3.5 mi NW on SR 31, then N on access rd to S shore of 245-acre lake. Free. All year; 14-day limit. Primitive undesignated sites. No facilities, no drkg wtr. Boating(l), fishing, hiking, swimming.

BISMARCK
Caddo Drive Campground $7
Corps of Engineers
DeGray Lake
3.5 mi SE of Bismarck on SR 7; 2.7 mi W on gravel Edgewood Rd. 15 RV elec sites & 30 RV/tent sites, $7 with federal senior pass; others pay $14. 5/1-9/4; some sites open before & after regular season; 14-day limit. 40-ft RV limit, 8 pull-through. Tbls, flush toilets, cfga, drkg wtr, elec, dump, showers, playground, coin laundry, beach. Fishing, boating(l), swimming, horseback riding.

DeGray Lake Resort State Park $10
From Bismarck, 4 mi S on SR 7; S on Caddo Dr, then follow signs S to park at N shore of 13,800-acre DeGray Lake. 113 Class B 30-amp elec/wtr sites, $10 for AR & LA seniors on weekdays, $15 for AR seniors on weekends and for non-resident seniors on weekdays; others pay $20. All year; 14-day limit. All year; 14-day limit. Tbls, flush toilets, dump, cfga, flush toilets, showers. Fishing, golf, boating, biking, tennis, basketball, swimming, guided horseback riding, interpretive nature programs, guided hikes, lake cruises, hayrides.

Edgewood Campground $7
Corps of Engineers
DeGray Lake
4.8 mi SE of Bismarck on SR 7; 3 mi W on Edgewood Rd (S of Caddo Drive Park). During 5/1-9/4, $9 base with federal senior pass at 47 elec RV sites; others pay $18 base, $22 at premium locations ($11 with senior pass). Elec sites open before & after regular season are $14 ($7 with senior pass). 30-ft RV limit; 9 pull-through sites. Tbls, flush toilets, cfga, drkg wtr, dump, beach, playground, coin laundry. Swimming, horseback riding, golf.

BOONEVILLE

Jack Creek Recreation Area   FREE
Ouachita National Forest
2 mi S of Booneville on SR 23; 1 mi E on SR 116; S at sign on paved county rd for 4 mi; 1 mi S on FR 19; 1 mi E on FR 141. Free camping; no day use fee. 4/1-11/30; 14-day limit. 5 sites. Tbls, toilets, cfga, no drkg wtr. Fishing, hiking, swimming. Natural pool in creek.

Knoppers Ford   FREE
Ouachita National Forest
2 mi S of Booneville on AR 23; 1 mi E on AR 116; S at sign on paved county rd for 4 mi; 3 mi SE on gravel FR 19. Free. All year; 14-day limit. 6 sites (RVs under 22 ft). Tbls, toilets, cfga, firewood, no drkg wtr, shelter. Swimming, fishing, hunting. Stream. Natural pool in Sugar Creek.

Outlet Area $9
Corps of Engineers
Blue Mountain Lake
From jct with SR 23 at Booneville, 10 mi E on SR 10 to Waveland; 1.8 mi S on SR 309 across & below dam; on Petit Jean River (signs). During 3/15-10/31, $9 base with federal senior pass at 30-amp elec/wtr sites; others pay $18 base, $20 for 50-amp elec/wtr ($10 with senior pass). During 11/1-2/28, 30-amp elec/wtr is $15, 50-amp elec/wtr $17 ($7.50 & $8.50 with senior pass). No showers off-season. 36 sites; RV limit in excess of 65 ft; 1 pull-through. Tbls, toilets, cfga, drkg wtr, showers, dump, elec, playground, beach, fish cleaning station. Boating (rl), fishing, swimming.

Primitive Camping   FREE
Corps of Engineers
Blue Mountain Lake
7 free primitive camping areas are available by permits from the lake office at 1052 Outlet Park Rd, Havana, AR 72842 (phone 479-947-2372), located W of Waveland off SR 10. They include Big Island Primitive Camping Area -- boat-in access from Waveland Park boat ramp to Big Island (GPS: 35.106, -93676); Persimmon Point Camping Area 1 -- at NW shore of lake, S end of Persimmon Point Rd (GPS: 35.093, -93.736); Persimmon Point Camping Area 2 -- just S of Hog Thief Rd on Persimmon Point Rd, then E to lake on access rd (GPS: 35.105, -93.74); Persimmon Point Camping Area 3 -- just S of Hog Thief Rd on Persimmon Point Rd, camp on the left (GPS: 35.108, -93.743); Persimmon Point Camping Area 4 -- just S of Hog Thief Rd on Persimmon Point Rd, camp on the right (GPS: 35.107, -93.746); Lease Three Primitive Camping Area -- S & W of Waveland on Hwy 309, then S on CR 28, W on CR 31, N on County Line Rd & E on access rd to area across bay from Lick Creek boat ramp (GPS: 35.09, -93.698); The Slide Primitive Camping Area -- S & W of Waveland on Hwy 309, then N on Mountain View Lane to S shore of lake, or boat-in from lake (GPS: 35.101, -93.675).

Waveland Park $9
Corps of Engineers
Blue Mountain Lake
From jct with SR 23 at Booneville, 10 mi E on SR 10 to Waveland; half mi S on SR 309, then left (W) on CR 32, becoming gravel Waveland Park Rd to park just upstream from dam. During 3/1-10/31, $9 base with federal senior pass at 30-amp elec/wtr sites; others pay $18 base, $20 for 50-amp elec/wtr ($10 with senior pass). During 11/1-2/28, 30-amp elec/wtr $15; 50-amp elec/wtr $17 ($7.50 & $8.50 with senior pass). 51 sites; 40 ft RV limit; all back-in. Tbls, flush toilets, cfga, drkg wtr, showers, dump, beach, playground, shelter, fish cleaning station, change shelter. Swimming, fishing, boating(l).

BRINKLEY

Dagmar   FREE
Wildlife Management Area
About 5 mi SW of Brinkley on US 70; N on gravel rd across railroad track to check station, then N on dirt rds along E side of Big Robe Bayou; campsites along rd N of Gator Pond boat ramp & NE near Hickson Lake. Free. All year; 14-day limit. 14 primitive designated camping areas. No facilities, no drkg wtr. Fishing, boating(l), canoeing, hiking, hunting, birdwatching. Numerous lakes, ponds, bayous. 7,976 acres.

BULL SHOALS

Bull Shoals Lake Boat Dock $10
From Hwy 178 in Bull Shoals, turn on Shorecrest Dr at the Country Inn, then take first left to the dock. $10 base; $15 for site & a marina boat stall. All year. 5 sites with elec/wtr; no dump or showers. Boating(ldr), fishing.

Dam Site Park
Bull Shoals Lake
From Bull Shoals, 1 mi SW on SR 178, following signs; on bluff overlooking lake. Park was closed by Corps of Engineers in 2014, now operated by City of Bull Shoals with overnight fees of $20-$25.

CAMDEN

Rest Area   FREE
5 mi S of Camden on US 79. All year; 1 night limit. Spaces for self-contained RVs; no tent camping. Tbls, toilets, cfga. Picnicking.

CECIL

Citadel Bluff   CLOSED
Corps of Engineers
Ozark Lake
1 mi N of Cecil on SR 41. Closed in 2013 by budget cuts, still closed 2017. Boat ramp open all year.

CLARKSVILLE

Haw Creek Falls Recreation Area $4
Ozark National Forest
From Clarksville, 3 mi E on US 64 toward Lamar; left (N) on SR 123 for about 10 mi (through Hagarville), then right (SE) on FR 1837 gravel access rd; at S shore of Haw Creek. Rough rd negotiable by RVs with caution. $4. All year; 14-day limit. 9 sites (RVs under 22 ft). Tbls, toilets, cfga, no drkg wtr. Hiking, canoeing on nearby Big Piney Creek, fishing. Access to Ozark Highlands Trail. Picturesque falls, rocks, bluffs.

Horsehead Lake Recreation Area $10
Ozark National Forest
8 mi NW of Clarksville on SR 103; 4 mi W on SR 164; 3 mi N on FR 1408 (gravel). $10. All year; 14-day limit. Sites may be free 11/15-3/1, but no wtr service. 10 sites (22-ft RV limit). $15 group site. Tbls, flush toilets, cfga, drkg wtr, cold showers, beach. Fishing, swimming, boating (l--10-hp limit), hiking. 4 acres. Non-campers pay $3 day use fee.

Ozone Recreation Area $3
Ozark National Forest
18 mi N of Clarksville on SR 21. $3. All year; 14-day limit. 8 sites. Tbls, toilets, cfga, drkg wtr. Hiking; access to Ozark Highlands Trail. Site of old Ozone CCC Camp. Donations for picnic, shelter.

Spadra Park $7
Corps of Engineers
Dardanelle Lake
3.6 mi S of US 64 at Clarksville on SR 103 (through Jamestown); on bluff overlooking Arkansas River. $7 base with federal senior pass at 24 elec RV/tent sites; others pay $14, $18 for wtr/elec ($9 with senior pass). All year; 14-day limit. Tbls, flush toilets, cfga, drkg wtr, showers, dump, playground, pavilion, restaurant, marina. Fishing, boating (ldr), waterskiing, hiking trail.

Wolf Pen Recreation Area $3
Ozark National Forest
22 mi N of Clarksville on SR 103; W on SR 215 & FR 1003; at Mulberry River. Free camping, but $3 day use fee charged. All year; 14-day limit. 6 sites (small RVs). Tbls, toilets, cfga, no drkg wtr. Fishing, canoeing.

CLINTON

Choctaw Campground $7
Corps of Engineers
Greers Ferry Lake
5 mi S of Clinton on US 65 to Choctaw; 3.8 mi E on SR 330, following signs; on W end of upper lake. $7 with federal senior pass at 55 non-elec sites, $8.50 base at 91 elec sites, $9.50 at prime locations, $10 for wtr hookup or 50-amp elec (others pay $14, $17, $19 & $20). All year; 14-day limit. 65-ft RV limit. Flush toilets, cfga, drkg wtr,

showers, dump, beach, amphitheater, elec($), shelter, playground. Boating(l), fishing, swimming. Gulf Mountain FREE
Wildlife Management Area
12 mi SW of Clinton on SR 95 to Scotland; 2 mi W of Scotland on SR 389, then N on gravel rd to WMA headquarters; camping areas on gravel rds W & N of headquarters. Free. All year; 14-day limit. 117 sites t 6 primitive designated camping areas. No facilities, no drkg wtr.. Fishing, hunting, hiking. West Fork Point Remove Creek; Little Red River & Cedar Creek.

CONWAY

Toad Suck Ferry $9
Corps of Engineers
Arkansas River
7 mi W of Conway on SR 60 from jct I-40 exit 129 near Conway; half mi E on access rd. $9 with federal senior pass at 30-amp elec sites (otherss pay $18); $10 at 50-amp elec sites (others pay $20). All year; 14-day limit. 48 sites; RV limit in excess of 65 ft; all back-in. Tbls, flush toilets, cfga, drkg wtr, showers, playground, elec, dump. Boating(l), fishing.

Woolly Hollow State Park $12
From I-40 exit 125 at Conway, 12 mi N on US 65, through Greenbrier, then 6 mi E on SR 285; at W shore of 40-acre Bennett Lake. $12 at 10 Class D primitive sites ($6 for AR seniors on weekdays, $9 for AR seniors on weekends and for non-resident seniors on weekdays). Tbls, flush toilets, cfga, drkg wtr, showers, dump, fishing pier, beach. Swimming, boating(lr), fishing, interpretive programs MD-LD, nature trail.

CORNING

Rest Area   FREE
5 mi N of Corning on US 67. All year; 1 night limit. Spaces for self-contained RVs (no tent camping). Tbls, toilets, cfga. Picnicking.

CROSSETT

Crossett Harbor RV Park $10
Crossett Harbor Port Authority
Felsenthal National Wildlife Refuge
8 mi W of Crossett on US 82. $10 for seniors; all others, $14. All year. 117 sites with 30-amp elec plus tent area. Tbls, flush toilets, cfga, drkg wtr, showers, dump, playground, store, wtr/elec, shelter. Hiking trails, fishing, boating(ld). On Ouachita River. Refuge visitor center 5 mi W of Crossett on US 82.

Felsenthal National Wildlife Refuge   FREE
8 mi W of Crossett on US 82. Free. All year; 14-day limit. 11 primitive camping areas. No facilities, no drkg wtr. Fishing, boating, hiking. World's largest green-tree reservoir; 15,000 acres. Visitor center.

DAISY
Daisy State Park $10
From town of Daisy at US 70, qtr mi S on W. Park Rd; at shore of 7,000-acre Lake Greeson. 55 Class B 30-amp elec/wtr sites, $10 for AR seniors on weekdays, $15 for AR seniors on weekends and for non-resident seniors on weekdays; 20 Class D non-elc sites, $12 ($6 for AR seniors on weekdays, $9 for AR seniors on weekends and for non-resident seniors on weekdays. All year; 14-day limit. Tbl, flush toilets, cfga, drkg wtr, showers, dump, playground. Boating(l), fishing, waterskiing, swimming. Visitor center, interpretive center with interpretive programs, guided hikes, nature talks. 276 acres.

DARDANELLE
Dardanelle Campground $10
Lake Dardanelle State Park
From jct with SR 155 at Dardanelle, about 3.5 mi NW on SR 22; N on CR 908 into park at cove of 34,000-acre Lake Dardanelle. 18 Class B 30-amp wtr/elec sites, $10 for AR LA seniors on weekdays, $15 for AR seniors on weekends and for non-resident seniors on weekdays (others pay $20). All year; 14-day limit. Tbls, flush toilets, cfga, drkg wtr, showers, dump, playground. Fishing, boating(l), swimming beach.

Mt. Nebo State Park $10
From jct with SR 22 at Dardanelle, about 4 mi W on SR 155 up mountain. 24 Class B 30-amp elec/wtr sites, $10 for AR seniors on weekdays, $15 for AR seniors on weekends and for non-resident seniors on weekdays (others pay $20). All year; 14-day limit. Tbls, flush toilets, cfga, drkg wtr, showers (Apr-Nov), playground. Swimming pool, tennis courts, ball field, horseshoe pits, interpretive programs, evening programs, guided hikes. Visitor center. Dump station at Lake Dardanelle SP.

Riverview Park $12
Corps of Engineers
Dardanelle Lake
1 mi N of Dardanelle on paved rd to dam; camp is immediately below dam on the Arkansas River. $12 at 10 non-elec sites ($6 with federal senior pass); $18 at 8 elec sites ($9 with senior pass). 3/1-10/31; 14-day limit. Tbls, pit toilets, cfga, drkg wtr, group shelter. Dump at Old Post Rd Park across river from campground. Picnicking, boating (l), fishing. 73 acres. Scenic overlook below dam.

Shoal Bay $8
Corps of Engineers
Dardanelle Lake
From Dardanelle at jct with SR 27, 14 mi W on SR 22 to New Blaine, then about 2 mi N on SR 197, following signs; at Shoal Bay arm of lake. $8 base with federal senior pass at 82 elec sites, $10 with elec/wtr; others pay $16 & $20. All year; 14-day limit. RV limit 50 ft; 1 pull-through site.

Showers, flush toilets, cfga, drkg wtr, dump, playground, beach, elec. Boating(l), waterskiing, swimming, hiking, fishing.

Spring Lake Recreation Area $9
Ozark National Forest
9 mi from Dardanelle on SR 27; 3 mi W on SR 307; 4 mi on FR 1602. $9. MD-LD; 14-day limit. 13 sites. Tbls, flush toilets, cfga, drkg wtr, showers, beach. Boating(l), fishing, swimming, hiking. 82-acre lake; 10-hp boat mtr limit. Non-campers pay $5 day use.

DE QUEEN
Bellah Mine $7
Corps of Engineers
De Queen Lake
7 mi N of De Queen on U.S. 71, then 5 mi W on Bellah Mine Rd, following signs. During 3/1-10/31, $7 base with federal senior pass at 24 elec/wtr sites, $8 at premium locations; others pay $14 & $16. During off-season, sites $10 ($5 with senior pass); no wtr hookups, showers or flush toilets off-season. 14-day limit. RV limit in excess of 65 ft; 8 pull-through. Tbls, toilets, dump, cfga, showers, drkg wtr, elec. Boating (l), fishing, picnicking, hiking.

Oak Grove $7
Corps of Engineers
De Queen Lake
3 mi N of De Queen on US 71; 5.5 mi W on project access rd, then qtr mi N on co rd, following signs. All year; 14-day limit. During 3/1-10/31, $7 base with federal senior pass at 17 elec/wtr sites, $7 for premium locations (others pay $14 & $16). Off-season, sites are $10 ($5 with senior pass); no wtr hookups, showers or flush toilets off-season. RVs in excess of 65 ft; 7 pull-through. Toilets, elec, drkg wtr, cfga, tbls, hot showers, beach, amphitheater, picnic shelter, dump, fish cleaning station. 8 picnic sites. Fishing, swimming, boating(l), hiking.

Pine Ridge $7
Corps of Engineers
De Queen Lake
3 mi N of De Queen on US 71; 5.5 mi W on project access rd, then 2 mi N on co rd, following signs. All year; 14-day limit. $7 with federal senior pass at 18 non-elec sites; others pay $14. During 3/1-10/31, 26 elec/wtr sites, $14 base, $16 at premium locations ($7 & $8 with senior pass). $10 rest of year ($5 with senior pass); no wtr hookups, showers or flush toilets off-season. RV limit in excess of 65 ft; 4 pull-through. Flush toilets, drkg wtr, showers, dump, cfga, tbls, fish cleaning station (no showers or flush toilets off-season). Fishing, hiking, boating(l).

DERMOTT
Cut-Off Creek   FREE
Wildlife Management Area
7 mi E of Dermott on SR 35 to Collins, then S on gravel rd

about 3 mi to W side of WMA; take gravel & dirt rd E & S to camping areas; at Cut-Off Creek. Free. All year; 14-day limit 4 designated primitive camping areas. Capacities: Campsite 1, 200 people; Campsite 2, 100 people; Campsite 3, 30 people; Campsite 4, 30 people. Toilets, cfga, drkg wtr (at Campsite 1 & 2), no trash service. Hiking, fishing, hunting, canoeing.

Lake Wallace   FREE
State Fishing Access Site
About 4 mi S of Dermott on US 165. Lake access 0.1 mi W* via paved rd to NW shore of horseshoe lake; or follow that access rd W, then S along western lakeshore to spillway. Free. All year; 14-day limit. Primitive undesignated camping. No facilities, no drkg wtr. Boating(l), fishing.

DE WITT
Jacks Bay Landing   FREE
White River National Wildlife Refuge
10 mi S of De Witt on AR 1; 9 mi E on AR 44; E on co rd. Free. 3/15-10/31; 14-day limit. Undesignated sites; 10 acres. Tbls, toilets, cfga, no drkg wtr. Boating(l), picnicking, fishing. Free primitive camping also is available in various areas of the refuge's North Unit and at other campgrounds in the South Unit: Moon Lake, Hudson's Landing, Prairie Lakes, Smokehouse Hill and Floodgate.

DIERKS
Blue Ridge Campground $7
Corps of Engineers
Dierks Lake
3 mi N of Dierks on US 70; 4 mi NW on SR 4; 2.6 mi W on paved Blude Ridge Rd. $7 federal senior pass at 22 wtr/elec 30-amp sites; others pay $14. All year; 14-day limit. 45-ft RV limit. Tbls, flush toilets, cfga, drkg wtr, showers, beach. Fishing, boating(l), swimming. Fish cleaning station.

Horseshoe Bend $7
Corps of Engineers
Dierks Lake
2 mi W of Dierks on U.S. 70; 4 mi NW on Lake Rd, then right on access rd, following signs; below dam. $7 with federal senior pass; others pay $14. All year; 14-day limit. 11 sites with 30-amp wtr/elec. Tbls, flush toilets, showers, cfga, drkg wtr, playground, picnic shelter. Fishing, hiking, swimming (beach, change house), picnicking.

Jefferson Ridge $7
Corps of Engineers
Dierks Lake
2 mi W of Dierks on US 70; 7 mi N; access E on W side of dam. During 3/1-10/31, $7 base with federal senior pass at 85 elec/wtr sites, $8 at premium locations (others pay $14 & $16). Most sites have 50-amp elec. Reduced fees rest of year but limited facilities. 14-day limit. RV limit in excess of 65 ft; 33 pull-through sites. Tbls, flush toilets, cfga,

drkg wtr, showers, playground, amphitheater, pavilion, beach, dump, fish cleaning stations. Fishing, swimming, boating(l), basketball.

DOVER
Long Pool Recreation Area $7
Ozark National Forest
6 mi N of Dover on SR 7; 3 mi W on SR 164; 3 mi NE on FR 1801; 2 mi NW on FR 1804. $7 primitive sites during 4/1-11/1 (free rest of year at Loop C, but no wtr); $13 with elec during 4/30-11/1 ($9 with federal senior pass); double sites $20. 14-day limit. 19 sites. Tbls, chemical toilets, cold showers, cfga, drkg wtr, dump. Swimming, hunting, hiking, canoeing(l). 15 acres. On Big Piney Creek. Non-campers pay $3 day use fee. Picnic shelter, $35.

Moccasin Gap Horse Trail and Camp   FREE
Ozark National Forest
14 mi N of Dover on AR 7; turn left, qtr mi uphill to trailhead & horse camp. Free. All year. 17 parking spurs for day use & overnight camping. Toilets, tbls, cfga, drkg wtr. Rugged mountain scenery on 28 mi of horse trails with four different loops; varying degrees of difficulty. Waterfalls, bluff lines.

EL DORADO
Calion Lake   FREE
State Fishing Access Site
8 mi N of El Dorado on US 167; at town of Calion. Free. All year; 14-day limit. Primitive undesignated camping. No facilities, no drkg wtr. Fishing, boating(l).

Moro Bay State Park $10
From jct with US 167 just E of El Dorado, 22 mi NE on US 63; on lower Ouachita River at Morrow Bay & Raymond Lake. 15 Class B 30-amp elec/wtr sites, $10 for AR seniors on weekdays, $15 for AR seniors on weekends and for non-resident seniors on weekdays (others pay $20). All year; 14-day limit. Tbls, flush toilets, cfga, drkg wtr, dump, showers. Boating(l), fishing, hiking trails. Historic ferry, visitor center, marina.

EUREKA SPRINGS
Dam Site Lake Campground $10
Corps of Engineers
Beaver Lake
From Eureka Springs, 4.5 mi W on US 62, following signs; 3 mi S (left) on SR 187. $10 with federal senior pass; others pay $20 at 11 sites with 30-amp elec, $23 at 37 sites with 50-amp elec ($22.50 with senior pass). 4/1-10/31; 14-day limit. 65-ft RV limit, 4 pull-through. Tbls, flush toilets, cfga, drkg wtr, elec, beach, dump, showers. Boating(l), fishing, waterskiing, swimming, hiking.

Dam Site River Campground $10
Corps of Engineers
Beaver Lake
4.3 mi NW of Eureka Springs on US 62, following signs; 2.5 mi SW (left) on SR 187 across & below dam. $10 with federal senior pass; others pay $20 at 47 sites with 30-amp elec; 12 sites with 50-amp elec/wtr, $23 ($11.50 with senior pass). Fees apply 4/1-10/31; 14-day limit. Off-season camping $14 for 30-amp elec, $16 for 50-amp elec/wtr ($7 & $8 with senior pass); showers, wtr & dump available. RVs in excess of 65 ft; all back-in. Tbls, flush toilets, showers, cfga, drkg wtr, beach, elec, playground, dump. Hiking trails, fishing, boating(l). Non-campers pay day use fee for boat ramp, picnicking, dump station, beach.

Kings River Outfitters $10
2 mi E of Eureka Springs on Hwy 62; just after the Eureka Springs recycling facility, 7 mi S on CR 302 (Rockhouse Rd); bear left at fork to SR 221 & follow signs to Kings River; right on gravel CR 539, then left at bottom of hill. $10 per person. Primitive sites with tbls, portable toilets, cfga, drkg wtr. Fishing, kayaking(r), canoeing(r).

Starkey Campground $10
Corps of Engineers
Beaver Lake
4 mi W of Eureka Springs on US 62; 4 mi SW on paved AR 187; 4.3 mi W (right) on CR 2176 (Mundell Rd, signs). $10 with federal senior pass at 16 elec 30-amp sites (others pay $20); $25 for 7 full hookups with 30-amp ($12.50 with senior pass). 5/1-LD; 14-day limit; no off-season camping; 3 pull-through sites. Tbls, flush toilets, shelter, cfga, drkg wtr, playground, dump, showers, elec, beach. Boating(rld), swimming, fishing, waterskiing.

FAYETTEVILLE
Lake Wedington Recreation Area $10
Ozark National Forest
University of Arkansas
13 mi W of Fayetteville on SR 16. $10. All year; 14-day limit. $10 ($5 with federal senior pass). 18 sites. Tbls, flush toilets, cfga, drkg wtr, playground, showers, beach. Swimming, fishing, hiking, boating (10-hp limit), canoeing(r), volleyball, horseshoes. Managed by the University of Arkansas. On National Register of Historic Places. Non-campers pay $5 day use fee.

FORDYCE
Tri-County Lake   FREE
State Fishing Access Site
3 mi SE of Fordyce on SR 8; 2 mi N on SR 205; follow SR 205 around E shore, then NW on gravel rds to S shore of lake. Free. All year; 14-day limit. Primitive designated camping area. No facilities, no drkg wtr. Boating(l), fishing, hiking, picnicking.

FORREST CITY
Burnt Cane Lake   FREE
State Fishing Access Site
8 mi E of Forrest City on I-40; 2 mi S on SR 38 to Widener; 2 mi SE of Widener on gravel rd, then S on St. Francis River Lakes Rd to W shore of Burnt Cane Lake. Free. All year; 14-day limit. Primitive undesignated camping. No facilities, no drkg wtr. Boating(l), fishing.

Village Creek State Park $10
From I-40 exit 242 N of Forrest City, 13 mi N on SR 284 to 7,000-acre park. 67 Class B 30-amp elec/wtr sites, $10 for AR seniors on weekdays, $15 for AR seniors on weekends and for non-resident seniors on weekdays (others pay $20). All year; 14-day limit. Tbls, flush toilets, cfga, drkg wtr, showers, dump, beach, playground, store. Boating(lr), fishing, guided hikes, nature trail, hiking trails. Visitor center with historical exhibits.

FORT SMITH
Clear Creek $10
Corps of Engineers
Ozark Lake
From NE edge of Fort Smith at Arkansas River bridge, 1 mi N on US 64 into Van Buren; right (E) on SR 162 (Kibler Rd) for 5 mi through Kibler onto Clear Creek Rd for 3.6 mi, following signs to Clark Creek arm of lake. $10 at 11 sites without hookups ($5 with federal senior pass). 25 elec sites, $18 ($9 with federal senior pass). All year; 14-day limit. RV limit in excess of 65 ft; 4-pull-through sites. Some sites may be free 11/1-2/28. Tbls, flush toilets, showers, elec($), cfga, drkg wtr, dump, pavilion. Fishing, boating(l). Day use fees for picnicking, boat ramp, dump station.

Rest Area   FREE
On I-40, E edge of Fort Smith. Free. All year; 1 night limit. Spaces for self-contained RVs (no tent camping). Tbls. Picnicking.

Springhill Park $10
Corps of Engineers
Lock & Dam 13, Arkansas River
Ozark Lake
From Ft. Smith at jct with I-540 exit 3, 7.3 mi S on SR 59 (signs); at S shore of river. $10 at 3 sites without hookups ($5 with federal senior pass). 15 sites with 30-amp elec/wtr, $18 ($9 with senior pass); 5 sites with 50-amp elec, no wtr hookups, $18 ($9) with senior pass); 22 sites with 50-amp elec/wtr, $20 ($10 with senior pass). All year; 14-day limit. Some sites may have reduced fees & reduced services in winter. RV limit in excess of 65 ft. Group camping area. 5 picnic shelters ($50). Tbls, flush toilets, cfga, drkg wtr, dump, playground, fishing pier. Biking, hiking, fishing, boating(l). Non-campers pay day use fees.

FORUM

Madison County   FREE
Wildlife Management Area

2 mi N of Forum on SR 23, then E on either CR 407 or CR 30. Series of gravel rds lead to more than 2 dozen designated-camping areas. Northern access via gravel rds from Rockhouse. Free. All year; 14-day limit. Primitive designated sites; no facilities, no drkg wtr. Hiking, hunting, fishing, wildlife study, horseback riding, biking. Rockhouse Creek.

GAMALIEL

Gamaliel Campground $9
Corps of Engineers
Norfork Lake

Half mi S of Gamaliel on SR 101; 2 mi SE on CR 42; at Bennetts Bayou section of lake. $9 with federal senior pass at 30-amp elec/wtr sites, $9.50 at 50-amp elec/wtr sites; others pay $18 & $19. 4/1-10/31; 14-day limit. 64 elec sites; RV limit 40 ft; 3 pull-through. Tbls, flush toilets, cfga, drkg wtr, showers, elec, dump, beach, playground, shelter, playground, marina, amphitheater. Boating (l), fishing, swimming, nature trail, nature trail, marina.

GARFIELD

Lost Bridge North Park $10
Corps of Engineers
Beaver Lake

6.2 mi SE of Garfield on SR 127; follow signs turning on 127 Spur, then left on Marina Rd. During 4/1-9/30, $10 with federal senior pass at 48 elec 30-amp sites; others pay $20. During 10/1-3/31, sites open for $14 (elec, wtr services, dump, no showers; $7 with senior pass). 60-ft RV limit; 9 pull-through sites. Tbls, flush toilets, cfga, drkg wtr, pavilion, beach, playground, showers, dump. Hiking trails, boating(l), fishing, swimming beach.

Lost Bridge South Park $10
Corps of Engineers
Beaver Lake

5 mi SE of Garfield on SR 127, following signs; left on Marina Rd. $10 with federal senior pass at 13 sites with 30/50-amp elec, no wtr hookup (others pay $20); $11.50 with senior pass at 24 sites with 30/50-amp elec/wtr. 5/1-9/30; 14-day limit; no off-season camping. RV limit 55 ft, all back-in. Showers, flush toilets, cfga, drkg wtr, playground, dump, beach. Swimming, boating(l), fishing, hiking, waterskiing.

GATEWAY

Indian Creek $10
Corps of Engineers
Beaver Lake

2 mi E of Gateway on US 62; 4 mi S (right) on Indian Creek Rd (CR 89), following signs. $10 with federal senior pass at 33 elec 30-amp sites; others pay $20; 7 pull-through. 5/1-9/30; 14-day limit; no winter camping. Tbls, flush toilets, cfga, drkg wtr, elec, beach, shelter, dump, playground. Swimming, fishing, waterskiing, boating(l).

GILLETT

Pendleton Bend Park $8
Corps of Engineers
Arkansas River

7.9 mi S of Gillett on US 165; 1 mi E on SR 212; on S shore of river. With federal senior pass, $8 base with for 13 sites with 20/30-amp elec, $9 for prime locations; $9.50 with senior pass at 18 sites with 20/30/50-amp elec sites (others pay $16, $18 or $19). All year; 14-day limit. 31 total sites; RV limit in excess of 65 ft; 2 pull-through sites. Tbls, flush toilets, cfga, drkg wtr, showers, dump, playground. Boating(l), fishing.

Wilbur D. Mills Park $8
Corps of Engineers
Arkansas River

7.9 mi S of Gillett on US 165; about 5 mi E on SR 212; on S shore of river. $8 with federal senior pass at 21 sites with 20/30-amp wtr/elec; others pay $16. 3/1-10/31; 14-day limit. 60-ft RV limit, all back-in. Showers, drkg wtr, tbls, cfga, dump. Fishing, boating(l).

GILLHAM

Big Coon Creek Park $7
Corps of Engineers
Gillham Lake

6 mi NE of Gillham on county rd, then half mi NE to dam; 1 mi NW; NE on access rd. All year; 14-day limit. 31 elec/wtr sites. During 3/1-10/31, $14 base, $16 at premium locations ($7 & $8 with federal senior pass); $10 rest of year ($5 with federal pass). RV limit in excess of 65 ft; 2 pull-through sites. Tbls, flush toilets, cfga, drkg wtr, beach, showers, amphitheater, dump, playground. Fishing, boating(l), swimming, hiking trails, nature trails, canoeing.

Cossatot Reefs $7
Corps of Engineers
Gillham Lake

6 mi NE of Gillham, past project office, near dam at Cossatot River. All year; 14-day limit. 28 elec/wtr sites During 3/1-10/31, $14 base, $16 at premium locations ($7 & $8 with federal senior pass); $10 during 11/1-12/31 ($5 with senior pass). RV limit in excess of 65 ft. Tbls, flush toilets, cfga, drkg wtr, showers, shelter, amphitheater, playground, fish cleaning station, dump, hiking trail. No wtr hookups, showers or flush toilets during 11/1-12/31. Boating(l), swimming, fishing.

Little Coon Creek $7
Corps of Engineers
Gillham Lake
6 mi NE of Gillham, past project office & 1 mi NW past Big Coon Creek Campground on county rd. All year; 14-day limit. 10 elec/wtr (30/50-amp) sites, all back-in. During 3/1-10/31, $14 ($7 with federal senior pass); $10 rest of year ($5 with senior pass). Tbls, flush toilets, showers, cfga, drkg wtr. Boating(l), fishing.

GREERS FERRY

Cherokee Park $7
Corps of Engineers
Greers Ferry Lake
From Greers Ferry at jct with SR 16, 6.5 mi NW on SR 92 (Greers Ferry Rd); 4 mi S on Brownsville Rd, through town of Brownsville; veer left onto Cherokee Park Rd to campground on N side of lower lake just W of Silver Ridge Peninsula. 5/15-9/15; 14-day limit. 16 sites without hookups, $14 base ($7 with federal senior pass); 17 elec sites $17 ($8.50 with senior pass). Tbls, pit toilets, cfga, drkg wtr, dump. Boating(l), fishing. No reservations.

Devils Fork $8.50
Corps of Engineers
Greers Ferry Lake
From jct of SR 92, half mi N on SR 19 at Greers Ferry; qtr mi N on SR 16, following signs. With federal senior pass, $8.50 base for elec at 55 elec sites, $10 for wtr or 50-amp, $11 for wtr & 50-amp (others pay $17, $20 & $22). All year; 14-day limit. RV limit in excess of 65 ft. Tbls, flush toilets, cfga, drkg wtr, dump, showers, playground, beach, pavilion. Fishing, boating(l), swimming.

Hill Creek Park $7
Corps of Engineers
Greers Ferry Lake
From Greers Ferry at jct with SR 16, 2 mi NW on SR 92 (Greers Ferry Rd); 3 mi NW on SR 225, following signs 2 mi S on access rd; on N shore of upper lake. $7 with federal senior pass at 10 non-elec sites, $8.50 at 30 elec sites (others pay $14 & $17). 5/15-9/15; 14-day limit. RV limit in excess of 65 ft. Tbls, flush toilets, cfga, drkg wtr, elec($), beach. Swimming boating(rdl), fishing. 38 acres. Camping season reduced due to budget cuts.

Mill Creek Campground $7
Corps of Engineers
Greers Ferry Lake
7 mi W of Greers Ferry on SR 92 (about 2 mi S of Higden); 3 mi N on Mill Creek Rd, following signs; at S shore of upper lake. 5/15-9/15. 39 sites without hookups, $14 ($7 with federal senior pass). following signs; on shore of upper lake. Tbls, pit toilets, cfga, no drkg wtr. Boating(l), fishing, swimming.

Narrows Campground $8.50
Corps of Engineers
Greers Ferry Lake
2.5 mi SE of Greers Ferry on SR 92; across bridge, on N side near center of lake. $8.50 base with federal senior pass at 60 elec sites ($9.50 at premium locations); others pay $17 & $19. 5/15-9/15; 14-day limit. RV limit in excess of 65 ft. Overflow area. Tbls, flush toilets, cfga, drkg wtr, showers, dump, beach, shelters. Boating(ld), fishing, swimming.

Shiloh Park $7
Corps of Engineers
Greers Ferry Lake
3.5 mi SE of Greers Ferry on SR 110, following signs; on mid-lake shore. $7 with federal senior pass at 56 non-elec sites, $8.50 base at 60 elec sites, $9.50 at prime locations (others pay $14, $17 & $19). 5/15-9/15; 14-day limit. RV limit in excess of 65 ft. Tbls, flush toilets, cfga, drkg wtr, showers, dump, playground, elec($), beach, 2 pavilions, group camp area with 17 sites, $150. Marina; marine dump. Laundry nearby. Swimming, picnicking, fishing, boating(l). Season reduced by budget cuts.

Sugar Loaf Park $7
Corps of Engineers
Greers Ferry Lake
2.2 mi SW of Greers Ferry on SR 16, then 2 mi W on SR 92, following signs; 2 .7 mi W on SR 337; on upper lake. $7 with federal senior pass at 36 non-elec sites, $8.50 base at 57 elec sites, $9.50 at prime locations (others pay $14 & $19). 5/15-9/15; 14-day limit. RV limit in excess of 65 ft. Tbls, flush toilets, cfga, drkg wtr, beach & change shelter, pavilion, dump, marina. Swimming, picnicking, fishing, boating(rld). National nature trail on nearby Sugar Loaf Mountain.

HARRISBURG

Lake Poinsett State Park $10
From Harrisburg, 1 mi E on SR 14; 3 mi S on SR 163 to park at W shore of 640-acre Lake Poinsett. 22 Class B 30-amp elec/wtr sites, $10 for AR seniors on weekdays, $15 for AR seniors on weekends and for non-resident seniors on weekdays; others pay $20. Tbls, flush toilets, cfga, drkg wtr, showers (except in winter), dump, store. Fishing, boating(lr). Visitor center.

HARRISON

Mount Hersey FREE
Buffalo National River
17 mi S of Harrison on U.S. 65; 6 mi on dirt rd. Free. All year; 14-day limit. Open camping. Toilet, tbls. River access. GPS: 36.0137, -92.9501

HATTIEVILLE
Lake Cargile   FREE
State Fishing Access Site
Ed Gordon/Point Remove
Wildlife Management Area
1.2 mi W of Hattieville on CR 26; S on access rd to N shore of lake. Free. All year; 14-day limit. Primitive undesignated camping. No facilities, no drkg wtr. Boating(l), fishing.

HEBER SPRINGS
Dam Site Park $7
Corps of Engineers
Greers Ferry Lake
3.4 mi N of Heber Springs on SR 25, following signs; on W side of dam. All year; 14-day limit. $7 with federal senior pass at 93 non-elec sites, $8.50 base at 148 elec sites, $9.50 at prime locations, $10 for elec/wtr, $11 for 50-amp elec/wtr (others pay $14, $17, $19, $20 & $22). RV limit in excess of 65 ft. 110 acres. Tbls, flush toilets, cfga, drkg wtr, showers, elec($), amphitheater, playground, beaches & change house, dump. Laundry nearby. Swimming, picnicking, fishing, boating(rld). Marine dump at marina.

Heber Springs Park $7
Corps of Engineers
Greers Ferry Lake
2 mi W of Heber Springs on SR 110; half mi N, following signs. $7 with federal senior pass at 20 non-elec sites, $8.50 base at 98 elec sites, $20 for wtr/elec & 50-amp elec (others pay $14, $17 & $20). 5/15-9/15; 14-day limit. RV limit in excess of 65 ft. Tbls, flush toilets, cfga, drkg wtr, elec ($), dump, cold showers, marina, store, playground, marine dump station, beaches, shelter. Picnicking, boating(l), swimming, fishing.

John F. Kennedy $8.50
Corps of Engineers
Greers Ferry Lake
4.4 mi N of Heber Springs on SR 25; 1 mi E across dam, following signs; on S side below dam at Little Red River. $8.50 base with federal senior pass at 68 elec sites, $9.50 at prime locations, $10 with wtr or 50-amp elc, $11 with 50-amp & wtr (others pay $17, $19, $20 & $22). All year; 14-day limit. RV limit in excess of 65 ft. Tbls, flush toilets, cfga, drkg wtr, showers, playground, dump. Boating (l), fishing.

Old Highway 25 Park $7
Corps of Engineers
Greers Ferry Lake
6.3 mi N of Heber Springs on SR 25; 2.8 mi W on old SR 25, following signs; on lakeshore 1 mi from dam. $7 with federal senior pass at 37 non-elec sites, $8.50 base at 79 elec sites, $9.50 at prime locations, $10 for 40-amp (others pay $14, $17, $19 & $20). Group camping area with 16 sites, $150. 5/15-9/15; 14-day limit. RV limit in excess of 65 ft. 47 acres. Tbls, flush toilets, cfga, drkg wtr, showers, dump, playground, 2 beaches, pavilion, elec($). Swimming, picnicking, fishing, boating(l). Camping season reduced by budget cuts.

HECTOR
Bayou Bluff Recreation Area $7
Ozark National Forest
3.1 mi N of Hector on SR 27; 2.4 mi NE on FR 1303. $7 during 4/1-11/1; 14-day limit. 7 sites (22-ft RV limit). Tbls, toilets, cfga, drkg wtr. Fishing, hiking. Large RVs not recommended.

HOPE
Grandview Prairie Wildlife Management Area   FREE
From Hope, drive 10 mi NW on SR 73 to town of Columbus, then N on CR 35. Free. All year; 14-day limit. Primitive undesignated camping. No facilities, no drkg wtr. Hiking, hunting, fishing. Ponds, South Fork Ozan Creek.

Bois D'Arc Lake   FREE
State Fishing Access
& Wildlife Management Area
6 mi SW of Hope on SR 174 to Spring Hill; 2 mi W of Spring Hill on SR 355; on E shore of lake or swing N & W on gravel rd to NE shore. Free. All year; 14 day limit. Primitive designated camping areas around the lake & on W side of the WMA. No facilities, no drkg wtr. Fishing, boating(l), no swimming. Courtesy dock, fishing pier. 13,626 acres.

HOT SPRINGS
Brady Mountain $8
Corps of Engineers
Lake Ouachita
13 mi W of Hot Springs on US 270; 6.1 mi N through Bear on Brady Mtn access rd. During 5/1-9/25, $8 base with federal senior pass at 57 elec RV sites; others pay $16 base, $18 for premium locations, 50-amp elec ($9 with senior pass). Lower fees off-season but reduced services, no wtr in winter until about 3/1. All year; 14-day limit. 55-ft RV limit, all back-in. Tbls, flush toilets, showers, drkg wtr, dump, restaurant, store, marina, group picnic pavilion, cfga, beaches, fish cleaning station, interpretive trail. Boating(l), picnicking, swimming, fishing, bridle trail, hiking trails.

Buckville   FREE
Corps of Engineers
Lake Ouachita
10 mi NE of Hot Springs on SR 7; W for 18 mi on SR 298; 3.5 mi S through Avant & 3.6 mi on gravel Buckville Rd, following signs; at N end of lake. Free. All year; 14-day limit. 5 primitive sites (20-ft RV limit). Concrete tbls, cfga, toilets, no drkg wtr. Boating(l), swimming, fishing, picnicking.

Cedar Fourche Campground — FREE
Corps of Engineers
Lake Ouachita
10 mi NE of Hot Springs; 11 mi W on SR 298 to Lena; 1.1 mi S on gravel Rock Springs Rd; at split with Lena Landing access rd, continue W on Rock Springs Rd; right, then W on Cedar Fourche Rd. Free. All year; 14-day limit. Primitive camping. No facilities except showers, toilets.

Charlton Recreation Area — $10
Ouachita National Forest
13 mi W of Hot Springs on US 270; at Walnut Creek. $10 base for non-elec sites; $16 for 9 sites with elec/wtr, $17 full hookups ($8 & $8.50 with federal senior pass); double elec/wtr sites $23. 4/1-11/1; 14-day limit. 58 sites (22-ft RVimit). Group camping $35. Non-campers pay $3 day use fee. Tbls, flush toilets, cfga, drkg wtr, cold showers, dump. Swimming, fishing, nature trail, hiking trail to Lake Ouachita. Summer outdoor theater programs.

Crystal Springs — $9
Corps of Engineers
Lake Ouachita
15 mi W of Hot Springs on US 270; 2 mi N on Crystal Springs Rd. During 5/1-9/30 $9 base with federal senior pass at 67 elec sites ($11 at premium locations); others pay $18 & $22). Off-season, some fees lower, but reduced services. 14-day limit. 55-ft RV limit. Tbls, flush toilets, hot showers, drkg wtr, dump, group picnic pavilions, playground, store, marina, restaurant, fish cleaning station. Picnicking, boating(l), swimming. Beach with change house & playground.

Lake Catherine State Park — $10
From jct with US 270 just E of Hot Springs, about 2 mi S on SR 128 (Carpenter Dam Rd); about 4 mi E on SR 171 to park entrance at 2,240-acre lake. 25 Class B 30-amp elec/wtr sites, $10 for AR seniors on weekdays, $15 for AR seniors on weekends & for non-resident seniors on weekdays (others pay $20). All year; 14-day limit. Tbls, flush toilets, showers, cfga, drkg wtr, dump. Fishing, boating(l), canoeing(r), waterskiing, swimming beach, guided hikes, nature talks, hiking trails. Visitor center.

Lake Ouachita State Park — $12
3 mi W of Hot Springs on US 270; 12 mi N on SR 227; at 40,000-acre Lake Ouachita. 23 Class D RV sites without hookups, $12 ($6 for AR seniors on weekdays, $9 for AR seniors on weekends & for non-resident seniors on weekdays). All year; 14-day limit. Tbls, flush toilets, cfga, drkg wtr, dump, hookups($), showers, playground, marina, store. Swimming, waterskiing, fishing, boating(ldr), hiking trails, pedal boats(lr), nature program. Springhouse with exhibits, visitor center. 370 acres.

HOUSTON
Cypress Creek — CLOSED
Corps of Engineers
Toad Suck Ferry Lock
2 mi N of Houston on AR 113; 15 mi W of Conway. Closed in 2013 by budget cuts; still closed 2017.

HOWELL
Rex Hancock — FREE
& Black Swamp
Wildlife Management Area
Follow gravel Rd W & S of Howell to WMA. Access to northern section off SR 33 S of Augusta; at Cache River. Free. All year; 14-day limit. Primitive undesignated camping. No facilities, no drkg wtr. Swamp area. Hiking, fishing.

HOXIE
Lake Charles — FREE
State Fishing Access Site
8 mi NW of Hoxie on US 63; 6 mi S on SR 25; near Lake Charles State Park; accesses on gravel rds, all sides of lake. Free. All year; 14-day limit. Primitive undesignated camping. No facilities, no drkg wtr. Boating(l), fishing, hiking, swimming. Courtesy dock, fishing pier at dam. Bait shop.

Lake Charles State Park — $10
From US 67 at Hoxie, 8 mi N on US 63 to Black Rock, then 6 mi S on SR 25 to 645-acre lake. 35 Class B 30-amp elec/wtr sites, $10 for AR seniors on weekdays, $15 for AR & LA seniors on weekends and for non-resident seniors on weekdays (others pay $20). All year; 14-day limit. Tbls, flush toilets, cfga, drkg wtr, showers, dump. 3 walking trails, boating(l), fishing, swimming beach. Bike & kayak rentals. Nature center with nature programs.

JACKSONVILLE
Holland Bottoms — FREE
Wildlife Management Area
Just NE of Jacksonville on US 67, then E on access service rd. Free. All year; 14 day limit. 2 primitive designated camping areas on gravel rd S of Lake Pickthorne. No facilities, no drkg wtr. Fishing, hunting, hiking, boating(l).

JASPER
Carver Campground — $12
Buffalo National River
10 mi E of Jasper on AR 74; then 2.5 mi N on AR 123 to bridge. $12 during 3/15-11/15; free rest of year but no wtr. 8 sites. Toilets, cfga, drkg wtr. Swimming, fishing, picnicking. River access.

Kyles Landing — $12
Buffalo National River
Off AR 74, 5 mi W of Jasper; turn-off is marked for Boy Scout Camp Orr; 3 mi on steep, rough access not recom-

mended for large RVs. $12 during 3/15-11/15; free rest of year but no drkg wtr; 14-day limit. About 33 undesignated sites. Toilets, cfga, flush toilets, drkg wtr. Canoeing, swimming (no diving), hiking, fishing. Designated primarily for floaters. Access to floating by canoe down Buffalo River. Scenic. Trailhead for wilderness area hiking, including Hemmed-in-Hollow and Indian Creek.

Ozark Campground $10
Buffalo National River
5 mi N of Jasper; 1 mi S of Pruitt, turn N for 3 mi on unmarked but graded gravel SR 129 gravel rd; inquire at Pruitt Ranger Station for specific directions. $10 during 3/15-11/15; free rest of year; but no wtr 14-day limit. 31 sites (tents & RVs). Toilets, cfga. Drkg wtr (Apr-Nov). Hiking swimming (no diving), canoeing, picnicking (free pavilion), fishing. Scenic. Access to floating by canoe down Buffalo River. Trailhead for 2.5-mi Ozark-Pruitt trail. Highly recommended by readers.

JERUSALEM
Brock Creek Lake Recreation Area   FREE
Ozark National Forest
5.9 mi N of Jerusalem on gravel FR 1305; 0.1 mi E on gravel FR 1309; 1 mi NE on gravel FR 1331. Free. 4/1-12/1; 14-day limit. 6 sites (RVs under 22 ft). Tbls, toilets, cfga, firewood, no drkg wtr, no trash service. Swimming, picnicking, fishing, boating (primitive ramps), hunting. 35-acre lake, 10-hp limit.

JESSIEVILLE
Iron Springs   FREE
Ouachita National Forest
4.5 mi N on SR 7. Free. All year; 14-day limit. 7 sites; 21-ft RV limit. Tbls, toilets, cfga, no drkg wtr. Fishing, swimming. Hiking trails, small wading area. Hunts Trail connects to Lake Ouachita Vista area. Formerly a fee park, the fee was eliminated at this not-so-popular park. Primarily a day use area.

South Fourche $5
Ouachita National Forest
17 mi SE of Jessieville on AR 7. Conveniently located highway campground. $5. All year; 14-day limit. 6 sites (RVs under 16 ft). Tbls, toilets, cfga, firewood, well drkg wtr. Picnicking, fishing, boating, hiking, hunting. Elev 500 ft. 4 acres. Mountains. Floating access to Fourche River.

JONESBORO
Craighead Forest Park $10
Jonesboro Parks & Recreation Department
3.5 mi S of Jonesboro on SR 141 (2.5 mi S of US 63). $10 for seniors at RV sites with 50-amp elec/wtr; others pay $20. Weekly senior fee $60. Fees during Dec, Jan & Feb also $10 & $60. Tent sites $10 in-season. All year; 14-day limit. 26 RV sites, 5 tent sites, primitive area. Tbls, flush toilets, drkg wtr, showers, dump, playground,

pavilions. Boating(l), ball fields, basketball, volleyball, swimming, fishing, paddleboats(r). 612 acres; 100-acre lake. Non-campers pay $20 for dump station.

Crowley's Ridge State Park $10
From Jonesboro, 15 mi N on SR 141 to Walcott, or off US 63, Southwest Dr to SR 141. 18 Class B 30-amp wtr/elec sites, $10 for AR seniors on weekdays, $15 for AR seniors on weekends and for non-resident seniors on weekdays (others pay $20). All year; 14-day limit. Tbls, flush toilets, cfga, drkg wtr, showers, beach. Swimming, fishing, 4.5 mi hiking trails, interpretive & historic programs, fishing pier. Visitor center. Park built by CCC in 1933, one of 6 original state parks.

Lake Frierson State Park $12
10 mi N of Jonesboro on SR 141. $12 at 3 Class D sites without hookups ($6 for AR seniors on weekdays, $9 for AR seniors on weekends and for non-resident seniors on weekdays); $10 for AR seniors on weekdays at 4 Class B wtr/30-amp elec sites ($9 for AR seniors on weekends and for non-resident seniors on weekdays (others pay $20). All year; 14-day limit. Tbls, flush toilets, cfga, drkg wtr, elec, showers, playground, visitor center, fishing pier. Boating(lr), fishing, hiking.

KIRBY
Arrowhead Point $6
Corps of Engineers
Lake Greeson
9 mi W of Kirby on US 70; qtr mi S on access rd. $6; free 11/1-3/1 but reduced amenities & no wtr; 14-day limit. 23 sites (35-ft RV limit). Tbls, toilets, cfga, drkg wtr. Boating(l), fishing, swimming beach.

Bear Creek $5
Corps of Engineers
Lake Greeson
1.5 mi S of Kirby on SR 27; 1.4 mi W. $5 during 3/1-11/1; free rest of year but no wtr & reduced amenities; 14-day limit. 19 primitive sites (35-ft RV limit). Tbls, pit toilets, cfga, drkg wtr. Boating(l), fishing, waterskiing, hiking, motorcycling.

Cowhide Cove $9
Corps of Engineers
Lake Greeson
From Kirby at jct with US 70, 5.9 mi S on SR 27; 2.7 mi W on access rd. During 3/1-12/15, $9 base with federal senior pass at 9 sites with 50-amp elec/wtr (others pay $18); $10 with senior pass at 34 premium 50-amp elec/wtr sites and 7 full-hookup 50-amp sites (others pay $20). Closed off-season. 40-ft RV limit; 8 pull-through. Flush toilets, drkg wtr, showers, cfga, tbls, dump, playground. Boating(dl), fishing, hiking trails, 5 picnic sites, interpretive trail.

Kirby Landing $9
Corps of Engineers
Lake Greeson
From Kirby at jct with SR 27, 2.2 mi SW on US 70, then 1.2 mi S on access rd. During 3/1-12/15, $9 base with federal senior pass at 20/30/50-amp elec/wtr sites (others pay $18); $14 off-season ($7 with senior pass), but reduced amenities. 14-day limit. 105 sites; 45-ft RV limit; 21 pull-through. Tbls, flush toilets, cfga, drkg wtr, dump. Boating(ld), interpretive trail, hiking trails, cycle trails, swimming (bathhouse), fishing.

Laurel Creek $5
Corps of Engineers
Lake Greeson 4 mi S of Kirby on SR 27, then W on gravel rd. $5 during 3/1-11/1; free rest of year but no wtr; 14-day limit. 24 sites (20-ft RV limit). Tbls, toilets, cfga, drkg wtr. Boating(l), fishing, hiking, hunting, motorcycle trail. 230 acres.

Self Creek/Jim Wylie Campground $7
Corps of Engineers
Lake Greeson
7 mi W of Kirby on US 70 (1 mi W of Daisy), across bridge. All year; 14-day limit. Non-elec sites, $7 with federal senior pass during 3/1-10/31 (others pay $14); 20/30-amp elec sites, $18 ($9 with senior pass), $14 rest of year ($7 with senior pass); 1 full hookup $20 ($10 with senior pass). 76 total sites; 45-ft RV limit; 23 pull-through. Tbls, flush toilets, cfga, drkg wtr, dump, playground, shelter. Wtr may be turned off during winter. Boating(ldr), swimming, fishing, 14 picnic sites.

LAKE VILLAGE
Lake Chicot FREE
State Fishing Access Site
From Lake Village, follow paved rds along both shores of Horseshoe Lake. Free. All year; 14-day limit. Primitive undesignated camping. No facilities, no drkg wtr. Picnic areas at Ditch Bayou dam & Connerly Bayou. Fishing, boating(l), hiking, swimming. Chicot County Park & Lake Chicot State Park both offer developed campsites.

Lake Chicot State Park $10
From US 65 at Lake Village, 8 mi NE on N. Lakeshore Dr to park; at NE shore of oxbow lake. 67 Class B 30-amp elec/wtr sites, $10 for AR seniors on weekdays, $15 for AR seniors on weekends and for non-resident seniors on weekdays (others pay $20). All year; 14-day limit. Tbls, flush toilets, cfga, drkg wtr, dump, showers. Marina/store. Biking(r), hiking, fishing, boating(lr), fishing pier, swimming pool, interpretive programs, guided walks, nature talks. Visitor center exhibits.

LAVACA
River Ridge FREE
Corps of Engineers
Ozark Lake
3 mi E of Lavaca on AR 255 to AR 96; 9 mi NE , then right 1.5 mi on unpaved Hoover's Ferry Rd. Free. 5/1-9/30; 14-day limit. 18 primitive sites. Toilets, drkg wtr, tbls, cfga. Boating(l), fishing, picnicking.

LEAD HILL
Lead Hill Campground $9
Corps of Engineers
Bull Shoals Lake
From Lead Hill at jct with SR 14, 3.5 mi N on SR 7, following signs. $9 base with federal senior pass at 75 elec sites (others pay $18 base), $20 at premium locations ($10 with senior pass). 4/1-10/31; 14-day limit. 40-ft RV limit; 2 pull-through. 55 acres. Tbls, flush toilets, cfga, drkg wtr, dump, showers, beach, playground, marine dump, change shelter, marine dump station, group shelters. Swimming, picnicking, fishing (heated fishing dock), boating(rld).

Tucker Hollow Park $10
Corps of Engineers
Bull Shoals Lake
From Lead Hill at jct with SR 7, 7 mi NW on SR 14 (sign); 3 mi N on SR 281, then E; on bluff overlooking lake. $10 with federal senior pass at 30/50-amp elec/wtr sites, others pay $20. 5/1-10/31; 14-day limit. 30 sites; 40-ft RV limit; 1 pull-through. Tbls, flush toilets, cfga, drkg wtr, dump, showers, elec, beach, playground, change shelter, picnic shelters. Swimming, picnicking, fishing, boating(rld).

West Sugarloaf Recreation Area FREE
Corps of Engineers
Bull Shoals Lake
Near Lead Hill campground where West Sugar Loaf Creek empties into White River arm of lake; access from Diamond City or Lead Hill, AR. Free primitive camping by permit from lake office. Pit toilets, campfire areas, no drkg wtr.

LINCOLN
Lake Bob Kidd FREE
State Fishing Access Site
1 mi E of Lincoln on US 62; N on paved rd, past bait shop & dam to N shore. Free. All year; 14-day limit. Primitive undesignated camping. No facilities, no drkg wtr. Fishing, boating(l). Picnic area, fishing pier.

LINWOOD
Rising Star Park $9.50
Corps of Engineers
Arkansas River
From jct with I-530 at Pine Bluff, 6 mi SE on US 65 to just past town of Linwood; left (E) 4.7 mi on Blankenship Rd, then follow signs; at river by Pool 3 Lock & Dam. $9.50 with federal senior pass at 24 sites with 30/50-amp elec/wtr; others pay $19. 3/1-10/31; 14-day limit. RV limit in excess of 65 ft; all back-in. Tbls, flush toilets, cfga, drkg

wtr, showers, dump, playground. 6 picnic sites, shelter($).
Fishing, boating(l), picnicking, softball.

LONDON
Piney Bay $8
Corps of Engineers
Dardanelle Lake
4 mi W of London on US 64; 3.5 mi N on SR 359, following
signs. 91 sites, 85 with elec, 70 with wtr/elec. $8 with
federal senior pass at 6 non-elec sites; others pay $16. $9
with senior pass at elec sites, $10 for elec/wtr; others pay
$18 & $20. 3/1-10/31; 14-day limit. RV limit in excess of 65
ft. Tbls, flush toilets, cfga, drkg wtr, dump, pavilion, group
picnic area, playground, amphitheater. Boating(l), fishing,
waterskiing, swimming, ranger programs.

LOWRY
Lowry Park   FREE
Corps of Engineers
Bull Shoals Lake
From Lowry, E on Shoals Lake Dr; just W of Tucker Hollow
Park at lake. Free primitive sites with permit from lake
office. Pit toilets, campfire areas, no drkg wtr. Fishing,
boating.

MAGNOLIA
Lake Columbia   FREE
State Fishing Access Site
4 mi W of Columbia on SR 132; 8 mi NW on SR 344; follow
access rds to reach N & S shores of lake. Free. Primitive
undesignated camping. No facilities, no drkg wtr. Fishing,
boating(l). Courtesy docks, fishing pier (S shore), picnic
area (S shore), bait shop.

MAMMOTH SPRING
Many Islands Camp (Priv) $10
7 mi S of Mammoth Spring (8 mi N of Hardy), 2.7 mi SW
of Hwy 63, following signs. $10 base. 4/1-10/1. Base fee
per person ($8 for children 6-11); $10 extra for elec. 200
primitive sites; 100 with elec. Tbls, flush toilets, cfga, drkg
wtr, showers($), elec($), store. Boating(r), canoeing(r), kay-
aking(r), swimming, picnicking, fishing, float trips on Spring
River. 40 acres.

Southfork Resort $8.50
14 mi S of Mammoth Spring on Hwy 289; at South Fork of
Spring River. $8.50 per person; $8.50 extra for elec, $11
elec/wtr. All year. Tbls, flush toilets, cfga, showers, drkg
wtr. Fishing, canoeing(r).

Spring River Oaks
Camp & Canoe Rental $10
8 mi S of Mammoth Spring on US 63; right on county rd
& follow signs to 1868 River Oaks Trail; at Spring River.
$10 per person ($5 children); $10 extra for hookups. All
year. Tbls, flush toilets, cfga, showers, drkg wtr. Fishing,
canoeing(r).

MARIANNA
Lone Pine Campground $11
Mississippi River State Park
St. Francis National Forest
7 mi SE of Marianna on SR 44; 1 mi NE on FR 1913. 14
primitive sites, $11 ($5.50 for AR seniors on weekays,
$8.25 for AR seniors on weekends and for non-resident
seniors on weekdays. 3 Class D non-elec sites, $12 ($6
for AR seniors on weekdays, $8 for AR seniors on week-
ends and for non-resident seniors on weekdays. About
3/15-11/30; 14-day limit. 22-ft RV limit. Tbls, pit toilets,
cfga, drkg wtr. Swimming, hiking trail, fishing, boating(l).
Formerly within the national forest's Bear Creek Recreation Area, Lone Pine is now administered by Arkansas
State Parks as part of creation of 550-acre Mississippi
River State Park at different sites within the St. Francis
National Forest.

MENA
Billy Creek Recreation Area $8
Ouachita National Forest
6 mi W of Big Cedar, Oklahoma (W of Mena, Arkansas);
N at sign on FR 22 for 2 mi. $8. All year; 14-day limit. 11
sites (small RVs). Toilets, cfga, drkg wtr, tbls, hiking trail.
Picnicking, fishing, hiking.

Lake Wilhelmina   FREE
State Fishing Access Site
4.5 mi W of Mena on SR 8; N on gravel rd to camping area.
All year; 14-day limit. Primitive designated camping area.
No facilities, no drkg wtr. Boating(l), fishing, fishing pier.

MORNING STAR
Loafer's Glory Wildlife Management Area   FREE
From jct with US 65 at Marshall, 8 mi NE on SR 27 (past
town of Morning Star to Harriet; left (N) on SR 14, then E
on gravel rd from Pine Grove Church. Access to northern
section from 13 mi SE of Yellville on SR 14. Free. All year;
14-day limit. Primitive undesignated camping in parking
areas. No facilities, no drkg wtr. Fishing, hiking, hunting.
Near E section of Buffalo National River.

Maumee South   FREE
Buffalo National River
From jct with US 65 at Marshall, 5 mi N on SR 27 to town of
Morning Star; 6 mi NW on CR 52 (the only paved rd off SR
27); rd turns to gravel and becomes steep but is well graded to river. Free. All year; 14-day limit. Undesignated open
sites (tents & small RVs). Toilets, cfga. Hiking, canoeing,
swimming (no diving), picnicking, fishing. Scenic. Access
to floating by canoe down Buffalo River.

MORRILTON
Cherokee Lock & Dam #9 Park $9
Corps of Engineers
Arkansas River
From Morrilton, 0.7 mi S on Cherokee St; 0.7 mi S on

ARKANSAS

Quincy Rd, following signs. $9 base with federal senior pass at 30-amp elec/wtr sites (others pay $18); $10 with senior pass at 50-amp elec/wtr (others pay $20). 3/1-10/31; 14-day limit; closed off-season. 33 elec sites. Tbls, flush toilets, cfga, drkg wtr, showers, dump, playground, 2 shelters($). Fishing, boating(l).

Petit Jean State Park $10
From jct with US 64 just E of Morrilton, 4 mi S on SR 9, about 7 mi E on SR 154. 4 campground & group areas. 90 Class B 30-amp elec/wtr sites, $10 for AR seniors on weekdays, $15 for AR seniors on weekends and for non-resident seniors on weekdays (others pay $10). All year; 14-day limit. Tbls, flush toilets, cfga, drkg wtr, showers, dump. Interpretive programs, hiking trails, waterfall.

Point Remove Park   FREE
Corps of Engineers
Arkansas River
From Morrilton, 0.7 mi S on Cherokee St. Free. 3/1-10/31; 14-day limit. 16 primitive sites. Tbls, toilets, cfga, drkg wtr.

Sequoyah Campground $7
Corps of Engineers
Arkansas River
From Morrilton, 4 mi S on SR 9; 2 mi W on River View Rd. $7 for seniors with federal senior pass at 14 elec sites; others pay $14. All year; 14-day limit. Tbls, toilets, cfga, drkg wtr, dump, showers, picnic shelter ($50). Fishing, boating(l). Closed in 2013 for budget cuts; still closed in 2017.

MOUNT IDA

Big Brushy   FREE
Ouachita National Forest
From Mount Ida, 12 mi NW (through Pencil Bluff) on US 270. Free. (formerly $8, but no wtr supply currently). All year; 14-day limit. 9 sites (RVs under 22 ft). Tbls, toilets, cfga, firewood, no drkg wtr, playground. Hunting, hiking, picnic shelter, fishing. Elev 800 ft. 3 acres.

Big Fir Campground   FREE
Corps of Engineers
Lake Ouachita
From Mount Ida at jct with US 270, 5.1 mi NE on SR 27; 6.6 mi E on SR 188, then 4.5 mi E on gravel rd and 1 mi on paved access rd; at W end of lake. Free primitive sies. All year; 14-day limit. 20-ft RV limit; 44 acres. Toilets, tbls, cfga, no drkg wtr. Swimming, fishing, boating(l).

Denby Point $9
Corps of Engineers
Lake Ouachita
8 mi E of Mount Ida on US 270; 0.8 mi N on Denby Rd. $9 base with federal senior pass at 71 elec sites

(up to $11 at premium locations); others pay $18 up to $22). Some 50-amp elec. 5/1-9/25; 14-day limit. Fees lower off-season, but reduced services. 55-ft RV limit. 2 group camping areas with elec, $55 & $65. Tbls, flush toilets, showers, dump, amphitheater, restaurant, marina, nature & interpretive trails, beach, fish cleaning station. Boating(l), hiking. Boat rentals nearby.

Dragover Float Camp   DAY USE
Ouachita National Forest
About 10 mi N of Mount Ida on US 270, past Pencil Bluff to SR 88, then E 3 mi o co rd turnoff and 1 mi S. Day use only for 2017; no camping.

Fulton Branch Flat Camp   DAY USE
Ouachita National Forest
4.8 mi NW of Mount Ida on US 270; half mi N on SR 298; 1.6 mi NE on FR 568; .3 mi N on FR 1437 (gravel access rd). Day use only for 2017; no camping.

Iron Forks   FREE
Corps of Engineers
Lake Ouachita
13 mi NE of Mount Ida on SR 27; 8.3 mi E on SR 298; 1.3 mi S on partially paved access rd. Free all year; 14-day limit. 45 primitive sites. Tbls, pit toilets, cfga, drkg wtr. Boating(l), fishing, swimming beach.

Joplin Campground $7
Corps of Engineers
Lake Ouachita
11 mi E of Mt. Ida on U.S. 270; 2.4 mi N on Mountain Harbor Rd, turning left at campground sign. $7 base at 36 elec RV/tent sites with federal senior pass ($8 at premium locations; others pay $14 & $16. Lower fees 9/26-4/30 but reduced amenities. All year; 14-day limit. 30-ft RV limit, but recommended for small RVs such as fold-outs, truck & van campers, no slideouts (sites not level or paved); all back-in. Drkg wtr, flush toilets, cfga, elec, showers (closed 1/1-2/28), dump, tbls, beach, fish cleaning station, coin laundry; restaurant, boat rentals & marina nearby. Fishing, boating(ldr), swimming, hiking & bridle trails.

Little Fir View $7
Corps of Engineers
Lake Ouachita
From SR 27 W of Rubie (NE of Mount Ida), 3 mi E on SR 188; 2.2 mi N; turn right at campground sign. $7 with federal senior pass at 29 non-elec sites; others pay $14. Free camping 11/1-2/28, but no amenities. Group camping area, $30. All year; 14-day limit. 55-ft RV limit. Tbls, flush toilets, cfga, drkg wtr, marina, dump,.Swimming, boating(rl)

River Bluff Float Camp   DAY USE
Ouachita National Forest
One-third mi NW of Mount Ida on US 270; half mi NE on AR 27; 3.7 mi on CR 59; 2.8 mi NW on FR 138. Day use only for 2017; no camping.

Rocky Shoals Float Camp   DAY USE
Ouachita National Forest
5.4 mi NW of Mount Ida on US 270; right (N) before crossing Ouachita River bridge; on E side of river. Day use only for 2017; no camping.

Tompkins Bend (Shangri La) $7
Corps of Engineers
Lake Ouachita
10 mi E of Mount Ida on US 270; 2.4 mi N on Shangri-La Rd. $7 base with federal senior pass at non-elec sites (others pay $14); 63 elec sites, $9 base with senior pass, $11 at premium locations; others pay $18 & $22); some 50-amp elec, wtr hookups at 15 sites. All year; 14-day limit. 55-ft RV limit. Tbls, toilets, showers (closed 1/1-3/31), drkg wtr, dump, amphitheater, fish cleaning station, restaurant, marina. Boating(ld), fishing, waterskiing.

Shirley Creek Float Camp   DAY USE
Ouachita National Forest
From Mount Ida, 3 mi NW on US 270; right (N) for 2 mi on SR 298; right (W) about 5 mi on SR 88; half mi SE on CR 7991; at Ouachita River. Day use only for 2017; no camping.

Twin Creek $12
Corps of Engineers
Lake Ouachita
11 mi E of Mount Ida on US 270; 1 mi N on gravel access rd, following signs. During 3/1-10/31, $12 at 15 non-elec sites ($6 with federal senior pass). Free during 11/1-2/28, but no amenities. Overflow camping offered on major holidays. 14-day limit. 20-ft RV limit; 41 acres. Tbls, flush toilets except off-season, cfga, drkg wtr (except in winter), dump. Fishing, boating(l), waterskiing. Boat rentals nearby.

MOUNTAIN HOME
Bidwell Point Park $9
Corps of Engineers
Norfolk Lake
From jct with SR 201 at Mountain Home, 9 mi NE on US 62; 2 mi N across bridge on SR 101; on NE side (right). $9 with federal senior pass at 30-amp wtr/elec sites; others pay $18. 50-amp wtr/elec $20 ($10 with senior pass). 48 sites; 35-ft RV limit; 3 pull-through. 5/1-9/30; 14-day limit. Tbls, showers, cfga, drkg wtr, beach, playground, dump, picnic shelter. Fishing, boating(l), swimming.

Bull Shoals-White River State Park $10
From Mountain Home, 6 mi NW on SR 5; 8 mi W on SR 178 to park just SE of Bull Shoals Lake below dam on White River. $10 for AR seniors on weekdays at 44 Class B elec/wtr 30-amp sites, $15 for AR seniors on weekends and for non-resident seniors on weekdays; others pay $20. All year; 14-day limit. Tbls, flush toilets, showers, cfga, drkg wtr, dump, store. Boating(lrd), fishing, hiking trails, 3-mi mountain biking/hiking trail, interpretive programs, fishing workshops, fishing pier. Visitor center with observation tower, exhibits, audiovisual theater.

Calamity Beach Park   FREE
Corps of Engineers
Norfork Lake
From Mountain Home at jct with US 412, about 12 mi N on SR 201 to just N of Clarkridge, then right (E) for 3 mi on CR 37; 2 mi SE on CR 22 & CR 24 (Calamity Beach access rd). Free. All year; 14-day limit. Primitive undesignated sites. Pit toilets, no drkg wtr. Get free camping permit from lake office. Boating(l).

Cranfield Park $9
Corps of Engineers
Norfork Lake
From jct with SR 201 at Mountain Home, 5.5 mi E on US 62; following signs; 1.6 mi N (left) on CR 34. $9 with federal senior pass at 8 sites with 30-amp elec; $10 at 61 sites with 50-amp elec (others pay $18 & $20). 4/1-10/31; 14-day limit; closed off-season. RV limit 35 ft; 6 pull-through. Tbls, flush toilets, cfga, drkg wtr, playground, showers, dump, beach, amphitheater, change shelter, marina. Swimming, fishing, boating(l), canoeing.

George's Cove   FREE
Baxter County Parks
Norfork Lake
6.5 mi SE of Mountain Home on AR 5; 3.5 mi E on paved AR 342. Free (donations accepted). All year; 14-day limit. 12 sites; 20 acres. Tbls, pit toilets, cfga, drkg wtr, dump, beach. Swimming, picnicking, fishing, boating(rl). Note: This campground was closed by the Corps of Engineers and leased to Baxter County.

Henderson Park $9
Corps of Engineers
Norfork Lake
From Mountain Home at jct with SR 201, 8.7 mi E on US 62; cross lake bridge; E side (left, signs); on a peninsula in central area of lake. $9 base with federal senior pass at 36 elec sites (30-amp); others pay $18. 5/1-9/30; 14-day limit. 30-ft RV limit.; 4 pull-through sites. Tbls, toilets, cfga, drkg wtr, dump, beach, marina, marine dump station, shelter. Fishing, boating(l), swimming.

Kerley Point Park   FREE
Corps of Engineers
Norfork Lake
From Mountain Home, about 12 mi E on US 62; 4 mi SE on SR 87 (Elizabeth Rd) to town of Elizabeth; continue S for 1 mi through town on Elizabeth Rd (CR 2); right (S) for 1 mi on Pine Ridge Rd; 3 mi W on Kerley Point Rd (CR 15). On E shore of lake's Big Creek arm. Free. All year; 14-day limit. Primitive camping at undesignated sites. No facilities, no drkg wtr. Get free camping permit from lake office.

Lakeview Park $9
Corps of Engineers
Bull Shoals Lake
6 mi W of Mountain Home on AR 5; 7.1 mi W on AR 178, following signs; N on Boat Dock Rd; on bluff overlooking lake. $9 with federal senior pass at 30-amp elec sites (others pay $18); $10 with senior pass at 50-amp elec/wtr sites (others pay $20). All year; 14-day limit. 186 acres. 78 sites; 40-ft RV limit; 2 pull-through. Tbls, flush toilets, cfga, drkg wtr, dump, showers, playground, nature trail, coin laundry, beach, elec, 2 shelters, group camping. Swimming, picnicking, fishing, boating(l), hiking.

Oakland Park $7.50
Corps of Engineers
Bull Shoals Lake
14 mi N of Mountain Home on SR 5; 10 mi W on SR 202. $7.50 with federal senior pass at 3 nonelec sites (others pay $15); $9 with senior pass at 28 elec sites (others pay $18). 4/1-9/30; 14-day limit. 40-ft RV limit Tbls, flush toilets, cfga, drkg wtr, elec, playground, dump, shelter, change shelter at beach, showers. Fishing, swimming, picnicking, boating(rld).

Ozark Isle $10
Oakland Marina
Bull Shoals Lake
14 mi N of Mountain Home on AR 5; 10.5 mi W on AR 202 (4.5 mi SW of Oakland). $10 without hookups; $17 with wtr/elec. Camp has been leased to Oakland Marina by Corps of Engineers. 51 sites. Tbls, flush toilets, cfga, drkg wtr, showers, beach, playground, coin laundry, elec($). Boating(l), fishing, swimming.

Panther Bay $9
Corps of Engineers
Norfork Lake
From Mountain Home at jct with SR 201, 8.6 mi E on US 62; 1 mi N on SR 101; right on 1st access rd (signs). $9 with federal senior pass at 15 elec sites; others pay $18. 5/1-9/30; 14-day limit. Tbls, flush toilets, cfga, shelter, marine dump station, drkg wtr, dump, beach. Boating(drl), fishing, swimming. 52 acres.

Robinson Point Park $9
Corps of Engineers
Norfork Lake
From jct with SR 201 at Mountain Home, 9 mi E on US 62; 2.5 mi S (right) on CR 279, following signs. $9 with federal senior pass at 30-amp elec/wtr sites, $10 for 50-amp elec/wtr (others pay $18 & $20). 4/1-10/31; 14-day limit. 99 sites; 40-ft RV limit; 3 pull-through sites. Showers, flush toilets, cfga, dump, playground, beach, amphitheater, shelter. Boating(l), swimming, fishing.

Woods Point Landing   FREE
Baxter County Park
Norfork Lake
16 mi E of Mountain Home on US 62; cross lake; 4 mi S on CR 91, then 3 mi on CR 93. Free (donations accepted). Former Corps of Engineers campground has been leased to Baxter county. 11 sites; 10 acres. Tbls, toilets, cfga, drkg wtr, dump. Boating(l), picnicking, fishing.

MOUNT JUDEA

Sam's Throne   FREE
Ozark National Forest
3.5 mi S of Mount Judea on Hwy 123 (steep & sharp switchbacks), no signs; at rock barn, turn left into large open parking area. Free, but donations accepted. All year; 14-day limit. Primitive open camping; about 20 spaces; no facilities, no drkg wtr. Hiking, rock climbing.

MOUNTAIN PINE

Stephens Park $7
Corps of Engineers
Lake Ouachita
From Mountain Pine, 1 mi W on Blakely Dam Rd past school, below dam. $7 with federal senior pass at 9 elec RV/tent sites (others pay $14). All year; 14-day limit. 35-ft RV limit. Tbls, flush toilets & showers (in season), cfga, drkg wtr, playground, shelter. Fish cleaning station nearby. Boat ramp at Avery Park. Boating(l), fishing, waterskiing.

MOUNTAIN VIEW

Barkshed Recreation Area $3
Ozark National Forest
7 mi N of Mountain View on SR 9; 12 mi W on SR 14 (paved); 3 mi NE on FR 1112 (gravel). Rds okay for small RVs. $3. All year; 14-day limit. 6 sites, including 4 picnic sites that may be used for primitive camping. Tbls, toilets, cfga, drkg wtr, shelter. Swimming, picnicking, fishing, hunting, hiking. Clear mountain stream. 3 acres. Note: Closed in 2017 until further notice; storm damage. Check current status before arrival; 870-757-2211.

Blanchard Springs Recreation Area $10
Ozark National Forest
From Mountain View, 12.1 mi W on SR 14; right (N) at Blanchard Springs Cavern sign, follow signs. $10. All year; 5-day limit 4/1-10/31, 14-day limit rest of year. 31 sites. Tbls, flush toilets, cfga, drkg wtr, dump, showers. Swimming, hiking, fishing, Historic gate house built by CCC in 1935. Non-campers pay $3 day use fee. Group camping areas, picnic shelters.

Gunner Pool Recreation Area $7
Ozark National Forest
16 mi NW of Mountain View on SRs 9 & 14; 3 mi N on FR 1102 (not negotiable by large RVs). $7. All year; 14-day limit. 27 sites (16-ft RV limit). Tbls, toilets, cfga, drkg wtr. Hiking, swimming beach, fishing, hunting. On North Sycamore Creek near Blanchard Springs Caverns. 10 acres.

MOUNTAINBURG
Lake Fort Smith State Park $10
From Mountainburg, 1 mi N on US 71; 2 mi N into park on Shepherd Springs Rd; at S shore of Lake Ft. Smith. 10 Class B 30-amp elec/wtr sites, $10 for AR seniors on weekdays, $15 for AR seniors on weekends and for non-resident seniors on weekdays (others pay $20). All year; 14-day limit. Tbls, flush toilets, cfga, drkg wtr, showers, playground. Visitor center with interactive exhibits. Boating(lr), fishing, swimming pool, hiking trails (trailhead for 165-mi Ozark Highlands Trail).

MULBERRY
Shores Lake Recreation Area $8
Ozark National Forest
15 mi N of Mulberry on SR 215; 1 mi on FR 1505. $8 base without hookups during 4/1-11/1; $6 rest of year but no wtr. Elec sites $12 in-season, $10 off-season but no wtr ($8 & with federal senior pass). Double sites with elec, $18 in-season, $15 off-season but no wtr. All year; 14-day limit. 19 sites. Tbls, pit toilets, cfga, drkg wtr, showers, pavilion($). Boating(l), fishing, picnicking, swimming, hiking. On 82-acre lake; access to Ozark Highlands Trail. 10-hp boat mtr limit. Reduced services during off-season.

Vine Prairie Park $10
Ozark Lake
City of Mulberry Parks & Recreation Department
From Mulberry, 1.7 mi S on SR 917; at jct of Little Mulberry River & Vine Prairie Creek. $10 at 10 sites without hookups. 13 elec sites, $20 (discount for seniors). Picnic shelter $50. All year; 14-day limit. Tbls, toilets, cfga, drkg wtr, dump. Boating(l), fishing. $5 day use fee. 479-997-8122. Former Corps of Engineers park now leased by city.

White Rock Mountain Recreation Area $10
Ozark National Forest
15 mi N of Mulberry on SR 215; half mi on FR 1505; 2.5 mi W on FR 1003. $10. All year; 14-day limit. 8 sites. Tbls, toilets, cfga, drkg wtr. Hiking, fishing. Concession operated.

MURFREESBORO
Buckhorn Campground $5
Corps of Engineers
Lake Greeson
From Murfreesboro at jct with SR 27, 6 mi N on SR 19 to the dam and then NW 3 mi and 2 mi E over gravel rd, following signs. $5 ($2.50 with federal senior pass). Free 10/1-3/31 but no wtr & reduced amenities; 14-day limit. 9 primitive sites (30-ft RV limit). Tbls, toilets, cfga, drkg wtr, cfga. Boating(l), fishing.

Dam Area Campground $7
Corps of Engineers
Lake Greeson
6 mi N of Murfreesboro on SR 19; at the dam on E side. During 3/1-10/31, $7 with federal senior pass at 6 non-elec sites (others pay $14); $9 with senior pass at 16 elec sites, 20/30-amp (others pay $18); $10 with senior pass at 2 full hookups (others pay $20). Off-season, $14 ($7 with senior pass) but reduced amenities & no wtr services. 214-day limit. 60-ft RV limit. Tbls, flush toilets, cfga, drkg wtr, dump, playground, shelter. Boating(ldr), hiking trails, fishing, swimming, 34 picnic sites.

Parker Creek $7
Corps of Engineers
Lake Greeson
6 mi N of Murfreesboro on SR 19; 3 mi NW of dam on gravel access rd. 8 primitive RV/tent sites & 3 tent-only sites, $7 with federal senior pass at 8 non-elec RV/tent sites & 3 tent-only sites; (others pay $14); $9 base with senior pass at 49 elec sites (20/30-amp); others pay $18 base, $20 for premium locations ($10 with senior pass). 3/1-12/15; 14-day limit; closed off-seaon. 35-Ft RV limit; all back-in. Tbls, flush toilets, cfga, drkg wtr, showers. Tbls, flush toilets, cfga, drkg wtr, showers, dump, beach, playground. Boating(l), fishing, swimming, hiking, interpretive trails.

Pikeville Campground $5
Corps of Engineers
Lake Greeson
6 mi N of Murfreesboro on SR 19; 2 mi NW of dam, then 2 mi E on gravel rd. $5 at 12 basic sites during 3/1-10/31 ($2.50 with federal senior pass); free rest of year but no wtr & reduced amenities. 14-day limit. 30-ft RV limit. Tbls, pit toilets, cfga, drkg wtr. Boating(l), fishing, waterskiing.

Rock Creek FREE
Corps of Engineers
Lake Greeson
From dam, 6.7 mi NW around W side of dam on gravel rds, following signs. Free. All year; 14-day limit. 14 primitive RV/tent sites. Toilet, cfga, no drkg wtr or tbls. Boating (hand launch), fishing, no waterskiing in area.

ARKANSAS

NEWHOPE

Shady Lake (Loop A and C) $10
Ouachita National Forest
From Athens (about 14 NW of Newhope), drive 2 mi NW on CR 64 (Shady Lake Rd); 0.5 mi S on access rd; at N side of lake. $10 (one site with elec/wtr, $15; one full-hookup sites $17). 3//1-12/1; 14-day limit. 28 sites (22-ft RV limit). Tbls, flush toilets, cfga, drkg wtr, showers, dump (bathhouse open 4/12-11/4). Boating (d, no motors), picnicking, fishing. Group camping or picnicking sites may be reserved for nonrefundable registration fee. $3 day use fee. Recreation area developed by CCC in 1937. Shady Lake hiking & mountain biking trail.

Shady Lake (Loops B & D) $10
Ouachita National Forest
Follow directions to Shady Lake Loop A & B. $10 base for tent sites; $15 for RVs with elec; 1 site full hookups $17; double site with elec/wtr $21. 4/15-11/1; 14-day limit. 44 sites (22-ft RV limit). Tbls, flush toilets, cfga, drkg wtr, showers, dump. Boating(l), swimming, fishing, picnicking.

Star of the West $5
Corps of Engineers
Lake Greeson
2.7 mi E of Newhope on US 70, then SW; along Little Missouri River. $5 during 3/1-10/31 ($2.50 with federal senior pass); free rest of year but no wtr; 14-day limit. 21 sites, 8 for tents; 50-ft RV limit; some pull-through sites. Tbls, toilets, cfga, drkg wtr. Fishing, swimming, picnicking, waterskiing.

NORFORK

Dam - Quarry Cove Park $9
Corps of Engineers
Norfork Lake
2.9 mi NE of Norfork to Salesville on SR 5; 2 mi E on SR 177, following signs. $9 with federal senior pass at 30-amp elec/wtr sites, $10 for 50-amp wtr/elec (others pay $18 & $20). Group camping, $65. All year; 14-day limit. 68 sites; RV limit 60 ft; 1 pull-through. Tbls, flush toilets, cfga, drkg wtr, showers, dump, beach, playground, elec, shelters. Swimming, boating(l), fishing. Handicap accessible fishing area.

Jordan Cove Park FREE
Corps of Engineers
Norfork Lake
From Jordan (about 4 mi NE of Norfork on SR 177), drive 2.5 mi N on CR 64; just W of Jordan Campground. Free. All year; 14-day limit. Primitive camping at undesignated sites. No facilities, no drkg wtr. Get free camping permit from lake office.

NORMAN

Crystal Recreation Area FREE
Ouachita National Forest
1 mi N of Norman on AR 27; 3 mi NE on FR 177 (gravel access rd). Free. Formerly $8, but no wtr services any longer. All year; 14 day limit. 9 sites (RVs under 22 ft). Tbls, toilets, cfga, picnic shelter. Swimming, fishing, hiking, hunting, rockhounding. Elev 1000 ft. 4 acres. Stream. Interpretive trail on soil formation. Scenic drives. Wooded site.

NORTH LITTLE ROCK

Bell Slough Wildlife Management Area FREE
N on US 40 to Mayflower exit, then E to S shore of Lake Conway to Grassy Lake. Free. All year; 14-day limit. Primitive undesignated camping. No facilities, no drkg wtr. Fishing, swimming, boating, hunting.

OLA

River Road Campground $8.50
Corps of Engineers
Nimrod Lake
9 mi SE of Ola on SR 60; 1 mi SE on SR 7; 0.5 mi S on Nimrod Dam Rd; below dam at N shore of Fourche Lefavre River. Continue W & NW 1 mi to Project Point loop (formerly Project Point Park). $8.50 base with federal senior pass at 21 sites with 30-amp elec/wtr at River Road loop & 6 elec sites at Project Point loop; others pay $17 base. Higher fees for 4 sites with 50-amp elec & 2 multi-family sites. All year; 14-day limit. 45-ft RV limit; 2 pull-through sites. Tbls, flush toilets, cfga, drkg wtr, dump, elec, playground, pavilion, showers. nature trail, fishing, boating(l).

OZARK

Byrd's Adventure Center $7
12 mi N of Ozark on Hwy 23; 6 mi W on Hwy 215; at Mulberry River. $7 per person at primitive sites, $10 with elec. 45 sites. Tbls, flush toilets, showers, cfga, drkg wtr, elec($). Hiking & biking trails, canoeing(r).

Aux Arc Park $10
Corps of Engineers
Ozark Lake
1.3 mi S of Ozark on SR 23; 1 mi E on Hwy 309; left at Aux Arc access rd. $10 at 4 basic sites ($5 with federal senior pass). 88 total sites some with 50-amp, $18 base for elec, $20 at premium locations ($9 & $10 with senior pass). All year; 14-day limit. Flush toilets, showers, cfga, drkg wtr, tbls, playground, 3 shelters ($50). Boating(l), fishing.

Redding Recreation Area $10
Ozark National Forest
18 mi N of Ozark on SR 23; 3 mi E on FR 1003; on Mulberry River. $10. All year; 14-day limit. 27 sites (22-ft RV limit). Tbls, flush toilets, showers (except during freezing weather), drkg wtr, cfga. Canoeing(l), fishing, hiking. Trailhead parking for Ozark Highlands Trail.

Turner Bend Campground (Private) $10
N of Ozark on Hwy 23 at Mulberry River. $10 per person.
14 primitive sites (most with shelters), no hookups. Tbls,
pit toilet, cfga, drkg wtr, showers. Fishing, canoeing(r).

PARALOMA
Paraloma Landing $6.50
Corps of Engineers
Millwood Lake
From Brownstown at jct with SR 317, 4 mi SE through
Paraloma on SR 234, then 1.5 mi S on county rd. During
3/1-10/31, $6.50 with federal senior pass at 34 paved
elec/wtr sites (others pay $13). Some pull-through sites.
14-day limit. Tbls, vault toilets, cfga, playground, fish
cleaning station. Horseback riding, fishing, playground,
boating(rl).

PARIS
Cove Lake Recreation Area $10
Ozark National Forest
1 mi S of Paris on SR 109; 9 mi SE on SR 309. $10 during
5/1-10/31; $7 rest of year but no wtr; 14-day limit; 36
sites (22-ft RV limit). Tbls, flush toilets, showers, cfga,
drkg wtr, beach. Fishing, hiking trail (Magazine Trail),
swimming($), boating(l), waterskiing on weekdays, ranger
programs. 8 acres.

Sorghum Hollow Horse Camp $5
Ozark National Forest
E of Paris on SR 22 (or W from Dardanelle); 4.7 mi S on
Sorghum Hollow Rd. $5. All year; 14-day limit. 15 sites.
Tbls, toilets, cfga, no drkg wtr. Pond for watering horses.
Trailhead camp for Huckleberry Mountain Horse Trail; also
open to ATV, hiking, mountain bikes.

PERRYVILLE
Lake Sylvia Recreation Area $10
Ouachita National Forest
9 mi S of Perryville on SR 9; 4 mi SW on SR 324. $10 base
($15 at 19 sites with elec/wtr; $12.50 with federal senior
pass). About 5/15-10/15; 14-day limit. 28 sites; 30-ft RV
limit. Group camping $25. Tbls, flush toilets, showers,
dump, elec($), cfga, drkg wtr. Hiking (Trees of the Forest
Interpretive Trail & Wildlife Trail), outdoor theater programs,
volleyball, swimming, boating(l -- no mtrs), fishing, mountain biking.

PINDALL
Woolum Campground   FREE
Buffalo National River
Access 8.5 mi on unmarked gravel rd from Pindall or
St. Joe; inquire locally. Also 26 mi S of Harrison & 7 mi
from St. Joe. Free. All year; 14-day limit. Undesignated
open sites (tents, small RVs). Toilets, cfga. Swimming (no
diving), hiking, picnicking, fishing, canoeing. Access to
floating by canoe down Buffalo River. Hikers connect to
Ozark Highlands Trail.

PINNACLE
Maumelle Park $11
Corps of Engineers
Arkansas River
From Pinnacle, 2 mi N on SR 300; 4 mi E on Pinnacle Valley
Rd to W shore of Arkansas River & mouth of Maumelle
River. $11 with federal senior pass at 30-amp elec/wtr
sites (others pay $22); $12 with senior pass at 50-amp
elec/wtr sites (others pay $24); $13 with senior pass at
50-amp elec/wtr waterfront sites (thers pay $26). All year;
14-day limit. 129 sites; RV limit in excess of 65 ft; 3 pull-
through sites, 1 handicap site. 8 picnic shelters, $50. Tbls,
flush toilets, cfga, drkg wtr, showers, playground, dump.
Boating(l), fishing, hiking.

PLAINVIEW
Carter Cove $9
Corps of Engineers
Nimrod Lake
3.4 mi S of Plainview on SR 60, following signs; 1.5 mi SE on
CR 229, following signs; 0.5 mi S on CR 233 access rd. $9
base with federal senior pass at 34 sites with 30-amp elec/
wtr; others pay $18 base. Higher fees for six 50-amp sites
& 3 multi-family sites. All year; 14-day limit. 40-ft RV limit;
1 pull-through. Tbls, flush toilets, cfga, drkg wtr, showers,
dump, beach, playground, fish cleaning station, shelter.
Swimming, fishing, boating(l).

County Line   CLOSED
Corps of Engineers
Nimrod Lake
7 mi E of Plainview on SR 60. This campground has been
closed due to budget cuts. Check current status with lake
office before arrival.

Quarry Cove $9
Corps of Engineers
Nimrod Lake
8 mi E of Plainview on SR 60; S on access rd; at NE shore
of lake. $9 base with federal senior pass at 31 sites with
30-amp elec/wtr; others pay $18 base; higher fees for six
50-amp sites. All year; 14-day limit. 45-ft RV limit; 1 pull-
through. Tbls, flush toilets, cfga, showers (closed in winter),
dump, playground, beach, fish cleaning station, amphitheater, shelter. Boating (l), fishing, hiking.

Sunlight Bay $9
Corps of Engineers
Nimrod Lake
0.1 mi W of Plainview on SR 28; 1.5 mi SW on CR 9; 1 mi SE
on gravel Sunlight Bay Rd; S on CR 317 to campground at
N shore of Porter Creek. $9 base with federal senior pass
at 29 sites with 30-amp wtr/elec; others pay $18 base;
higher fees for 4 sites with 50-amp elec & 2 multi-family
sites. All year; 14-day limit. 45-ft RV limit; all back-in.
Tbls, flush toilets, cfga, drkg wtr, elec, dump, playground,

pavilion, fish cleaning station, showers (closed in winter), beach, shelter. Boating(l), fishing, waterskiing. 17 acres.

POCAHONTAS

Lake Ashbaugh Fishing Access Site   FREE
Black River Wildlife Management Area
14 mi SE of Pocahontas on SR 304; N on WMA gravel access rd; at SW edge of lake. Free. All year; 14-day limit. Primitive designated camping area. No facilities, no drkg wtr. Fishing, boating(l), hiking, hunting. Concrete boat ramp on NE shore; bait shop near camping area.

PONCA

Steel Creek $12
Buffalo National River
Easy but steep access off AR 74 (13 mi W of Jasper); 2 mi E of Ponca on steep, winding gravel rd. Not recommended for large RVs. $12 during 3/15-11/15; free rest of year but no wtr; 14-day limit. 24 sites (tents & small RVs); 14 hors sites available. Toilets, cfga. Drkg wtr (Apr-Nov). Swimming (no diving), hiking, canoeing, picnicking, fishing Scenic bluffs. Access to floating by canoe down Buffalo River. Trailhead for wilderness area hiking, featuring Hemmed-in Hollow.

PRESCOTT

White Oak Lake   FREE
State Fishing Access Site
2 mi SE of Bluff City on SR 287 to White Oak Lake State Park; continue S to camping area on SW shore of White Oak Lake. Free. All year; 14-day limit. Primitive designated camping area. No facilities, no drkg wtr. Boating(l), fishing, hiking, picnicking. Fishing pier. Bait shop nearby.

White Oak Lake State Park $10
From I-30 at Prescott, 20 mi E on SR 24 to Bluff City; 100 yds S on SR 299, then 2 mi SE on SR 287 to park at NW shore of lake. 37 Class B 30-amp elec/wtr sites, $10 for AR seniors on weekdays, $15 for AR seniors on weekends and for non-resident seniors on weekdays (others pay $20). All year; 14-day limit. Tbls, flush toilets, cfga, drkg wtr, showers, dump, playground, store. Boating(l), fishing, interpretive programs (MD-LD), 4 nature trails.

PROTEM (MISSOURI)

Buck Creek $7
Corps of Engineers
Bull Shoals Lake
5.5 mi SE of Protem, Missouri, on MO 125; in Arkansas. $7 with federal senior pass at 2 non-elec sites; $9.50 with senior pass at 36 elec (30/50-amp) sites (others pay $14 & $19). 5/1-9/15; 14-day limit. 40-ft RV limit. Tbls, flush toilets, cfga, drkg wtr, dump, showers, playground, shelter, marine dump station, change shelter. Swimming, picnicking, fishing, boating(ld).

QUITMAN

Cove Creek Campground $7
Corps of Engineers
Greers Ferry Lake
6.5 mi NE of Quitman on AR 25; 13.5 mi N on AR 16; 1.2 mi NE on paved co rd following signs; on S end of lower lake. $7 with federal senior pass at 32 non-elec sites; $8.50 base at 31 elec sites, $9.50 for premium locations (others pay $14, $18 & $19). 5/1-9/15; 14-day limit. RV limit in excess of 65 ft. 35 acres. Tbls, flush toilets, cfga, drkg wtr, dump, elec($), pavilion. Swimming, boating(l), fishing.

REDFIELD

Tar Camp Park $9.50
Corps of Engineers
Arkansas River Lock & Dam #5
From Redfield at jct with SR 365/SR 46, 6 mi E on River Rd, following signs (20 mi S of Little Rock on US 65). $9.50 with federal senior pass at 45 sites with 30/50-amp elec/wtr (others pay $19). 3/1-10/31; 14-day limit. RV limit in excess of 65 ft; all back-in. Tbls, flush toilets, cfga, drkg wtr, showers, playground, dump, 2 shelters ($60 reservation). Boating (rl), picnicking, fishing (handicap area), nature trails. 100 acres. McClellan-Kerr Arkansas River Navigation System.

RIDGEDALE (MISSOURI)

Cricket Creek Campground $7
Corps of Engineers
Table Rock Lake
5.3 mi SW of Ridgedale on AR 14 in Arkansas. $7 for seniors with federal senior pass at sites without hookups; others pay $14. Elec sites $21 ($11 with federal senior pass); elec/wtr sites $23 ($11.50 with senior pass). 4/1-9/15; 14-day limit. RV limit in excess of 65 ft; 4 pull-through sites. Tbls, flush toilets, cfga, drkg wtr, elec($), showers, dump, beach, marine dump, sand volleyball. Boating(ldr), fishing, swimming.

ROGERS

Horseshoe Bend Park A & B $10
Corps of Engineers
Beaver Lake
From Rogers at jct with US 71, 5 mi E on SR 94, following signs. During 4/1-10/31, $10 with federal senior pass at 51 Park B sites with 30-amp elec (others pay $20); $12.50 with senior pass at 8 Park B & 67 Park A 30/50-amp elec sites (others pay $25). 3 tent sites, 7 double sites, 1 triple site also available. During 11/1-3/31, 30-amp elec sites open for $14, 50-amp for $16; dump, elec, wtr services but no showers off-season, $7 & $8 with senior pass). RV limit in excess of 65 ft; 2 pull-through. Picnic shelters, $75 plus $4 vehicle day use fee. Non-campers pay day use fee for boat ramp, beach, dump station.

Prairie Creek $10
Corps of Engineers
Beaver Lake
3.3 mi E of Rogers on AR 12; 1 mi N on North Park Rd. During 4/1-10/31, $10 base with federal senior pass at 112 elec 30-amp sites; others pay $20 base (double sites $38), $22 for 50-amp elec no wtr, $24 for 50-amp & wtr ($11 & $12 with senior pass). During 11/1-3/31, elec sites $15 for 30 amp sites, $16 for 50-amp (dump, wtr services no showers; $7.50 & $8 with senior pass). RV limit in excess of 65 ft; 2 pull-through sites. Tbls, toilets, cfga, drkg wtr, ice, store, food, elec, solar showers, dump, 6 shelters, playground, beach. Hiking trail, swimming, picnicking, fishing, boating(ldr). 118 acres.

Rocky Branch $10
Corps of Engineers
Beaver Lake
11 mi E of Rogers on AR 12; 4.5 mi NE on AR 303 to paved access rd. $10 base with federal senior pass at 35 sites with 30-amp elec (others pay $20 base; $10.50 with senior pass for 6 sites with 50-amp elec (othes pay $21). 4/1-LD; 14-day limit; no off-season camping. 44 elec sites; 5 pull-through. Tbls, toilets, cfga, dump, drkg wtr, solar-heated showers, store, ice, food, 2 shelters ($75 plus $4 vehicle day use fee), dump, playground, coin laundry. Swimming beach, boating(ld), picnicking, fishing.

ROVER
Fourche Mountain Recreation Area FREE
Ouachita National Forest
5 mi S of Rover on AR 27. Free. All year; 14-day limit. 5 sites. Toilets, cfga, tbls, no drkg wtr, picnic sites. Picnicking, hiking.

RUSSELLVILLE
Fairview Recreation Area
Ozark National Forest
From Russellville, 37 mi N on SR 7 to Sand Gap (formerly Pelsor; 1.2 mi N on Hwy 7. Decommissioned as campground; trailhead to Ozark Highlands Trail.

Galla Creek Wildlife Management Area FREE
4 mi E of Russellville on I-40 to Pottsville; 1.3 mi S of Pottsville on SR 247 until it turns W, then S on River Rd & E on access rd to WMA headquarters. Dispersed primitive camping or follow directions to camping areas on shore of Lake Atkins (see Atkins entry). Free. All year; 14-day limit. 3 primitive designated camping areas & dispersed open camping. No facilities, no drkg wtr. Fishing, boating(l), hiking, swimming, hunting. Primary WMA area just N of Arkansas River.

Main Campground $10
Lake Dardanelle State Park
From I-40 exit 81 at Russellville, about 3 mi S on SR 7; 4 mi W on SR 326 to park at E shore of 34,000-acre Lake Dardanelle on Arkansas River. 26 Class B 30-amp elec/wtr sites, $10 for AR seniors on weekdays, $15 for AR seniors on weekends and for non-resident seniors on weekdays (others pay $20). All year; 14-day limit. Tbls, flush toilets, cfga, drkg wtr, showers, dump, playground. Fishing, boating(l), swimming beach. Visitor center with 7,000-gallong aquarium, honeybee hive, river darter tank, aquatic turtle table, interactive kiosks, educational programs. Interpretive programs, guided hikes, nature talks See Dardanelle entry.

Old Post Road Campground $10
Corps of Engineers
Dardanelle Lake
From Russellville at jct with US 64, 2.2 mi S on SR 7; 1 mi W on Lock & Dam Rd, following signs; overlooks N bank of Arkansas River. $10 with federal senior pass at 40 elec/wtr sites; others pay $20. All year; 14-day limit. RV limit in excess of 65 ft; all back-in. Tbls, showers, flush toilets, cfga, drkg wtr, playground, dump, 8 picnic shelters. Basketball, soccer, tennis, volleyball, fishing, boating(l), waterskiing. No day use fees.

Richland Creek Recreation Area FREE
Ozark National Forest
From Russellville, 37 mi N on SR 7 to Sand Gap (formerly Pelsor); 6 mi E on SR 16 to Ben Hur & continue on SR 16, turning S for 1.5 mi, then left (N) on gravel FR 1205 for 9 mi to S shore of Richland Creek (left into campground). Rough roads; trailers not encouraged. All year; 14-day limit. Camp free, but donations accepted. 11 sites. Tbls, toilets, cfga, no drkg wtr. Hiking, picnicking, fishing, swimming, backpacking nearby. Elev 1000 ft. 4 acres. Because of rough roads, RVs not recommended. Clear mtn stream. Adjacent to Richland Creek Wilderness Area.

SCOTT
Willow Beach Park $9.50
Corps of Engineers
Willow Beach Lake
Arkansas River
From town of Scott (SE of Little Rock), 2 mi N on US 165, then sharp right for 1 mi S on CR 85 along W shore of Willow Beach Lake (an oxbow lake formed when the Arkansas River changed directions); veer right onto secondary Willow Beach Rd, following signs on Blue Heron Pkwy to SW shore of lake & W shore of river. $9.50 with federal senior pass at 21 sites with 30/50-amp elec/wtr; others pay $19. All year; 14-day limit. 60-ft RV limit; all back-in. Tbls, flush toilets, showers, cfga, drkg wtr, playground, dump, 2 shelters ($50 & $60 reserved). Boating(l), fishing (handicap fishing area).

SCRANTON

Cane Creek   FREE
Corps of Engineers
Dardanelle Lake
3.5 mi NE of Scranton on SR 197; 2 mi N on paved rd. Free. All year; 14 day limit. 16 primitive sites. Tbls, pit toilet, cfga, drkg wtr, pavilion. Closed in 2013 for budget reasons, now operated by Arkansas Wildlife Federation.

SPRINGDALE

Hickory Creek Park $10.50
Corps of Engineers
Beaver Lake
4 mi N of Springdale on US 71; 7 mi E on SR 264; 1 mi N (right) on Cow Face Rd (CR 6602), following signs; E (left) on Hickory Creek Rd. During 4/1-10/31, $10.50 for seniors with federal senior pass at 61 30/50-amp elec sites; others pay $21. During 11/1-3/31, elec sites open for $15 (dump, elec, wtr services but no showers; $7.50 with senior pass). 50-ft RV limit; all back-in. Tbls, flush toilets, cfga, drkg wtr, 2 pavilions ($75 plus $4 vehicle day use fee), beach, playground, showers, dump. Boating(l), fishing, swimming, picnicking, waterskiing.

War Eagle $10
Corps of Engineers
Beaver Lake12 mi NE of Springdale on AR 68 to Nob; 3 mi NW on paved access rd. $10 with federal senior pass at 26 elec 30-amp sites; others pay $20. 5/1-LD; 14-day limit; no off-season camping. 29 acres. Tbls, toilets, cfga, showers, dump, drkg wtr, picnic shelter ($75 plus $4 vehicle day use fee). Swimming, picnicking, boating (rld), fishing.

SPRINGFIELD

Brewer Lake State Fishing Access Site   FREE
SW of Springfield on SR 92; access rds to N & S shores of lake. Free. All year; 14-day limit. Primitive undesignated camping. No facilities, no drkg wtr. Fishing, boating(l).

STAR CITY

Cane Creek Lake State Fishing Access Site   FREE
2 mi E of Star City on SR 11; S & E on gravel access rds. Free. All year; 14-day limit. Primitive undesignated camping. No facilities, no drkg wtr. Fishing, boating(l), swimming. Courtesy dock, fishing pier. Near Cane Creek State Park.

STORY

Avant Campground   FREE
Corps of Engineers
Lake Ouachita
From Story, 12 mi E on SR 298 past village of Mount Tabor; 4 mi S on Buckville Rd to Avant; W on Camp Story Rd, continuing on Avant Campground access rd to N shore of lake. Free. All year; 14-day limit. Primitive camping at undesignated sites; no facilities, no drkg wtr.

Rabbit Tail Campground   FREE
Corps of Engineers
Lake Ouachita
From Story, 12 mi E on SR 298 past village of Mount Tabor; 5 mi S on Buckville Rd through Avant, then E on access rd to park at N shore of lake. Free. All year; 14-day limit. Primitive camping at undesignated sites. No facilities, no drkg wtr.

Washita Campground   FREE
Corps of Engineers
Lake Ouachita
From Story at jct with SR 298, S on US 27 to campground; on Muddy Creek arm of lake at confluence with Ouachita River. Free. All year; 14-day limit. Primitive camping at undesignated sites. No facilities, no drkg wtr.

THEODOSIA (MISSOURI)

Theodosia Park $7
Corps of Engineers
Bull Shoals Lake
1 mi E of Theodosia, Missouri, on MO 160. $7 with federal senior pass at 2 non-elec sites; others pay $14. 26 elec sites, $18 ($9 with senior pass). RV limit 45 ft; all back-in. 4/1-10/31; 14-day limit. 170 acres. Tbls, flush toilets, cfga, drkg wtr, dump, playground, showers, beach, coin laundry. Swimming, picnicking, boating(rld), fishing.

TICHNOR

Merrisach Lake Park $11
Corps of Engineers
Arkansas River Lock #2
8.2 mi SE of SR 44 at Tichnor; exit NW near project office. $11 base at 5 sites without elec; $12 at premium locations ($5.50 & $6 with federal senior pass). 43 sites with 20/30-amp elec, $16 base ($18 at premium locations); 19 sites with 20/30/50-amp elec, $19 ($5.50, $6, $8, $9 & $9.50 with federal senior pass). All year; 14-day limit. 67 total sites; RV limit in excess of 65 ft. Tbls, flush toilets, elec($), cfga, drkg wtr, showers, dump, playground, shelters. Boating(l), fishing, hiking, softball, interpretive trail.

Notrebes Bend Park $9.50
Corps of Engineers
Wilbur D. Mills Dam
From SR 44 at Tichnor, 8.2 mi S across canal W of project office, then 5.5 mi W; on E side of dam. $9.50 for seniors with federal senior pass at 30 sites with 20/30/50-amp elec/wtr; others pay $19. 3/1-10/30; 14-day limit. 50-ft RV limit. Tbls, toilets, cfga, drkg wtr, dump, coin laundry. Boating(l), fishing.

WALDRON

Little Pines $8
Ouachita National Forest
4 mi W of Waldron on SR 248; 7 mi W on co rd; at 1,000-

acre Lake Hinkle. $8 for seniors with federal senior pass for 9 sites with elec; others pay $16. All year; 14-day limit. Suitable for 9 small RVs. Tbls, flush toilets, cfga, drkg wtr, showers, store, dump. Hunting, hiking, fishing, boating(l), swimming. 30 acres. Non-campers pay $3 for day use.

Truman Baker Lake   FREE
State Fishing Access Site
Qtr mi SE of Waldron on US 71 (4.5 mi NW of Needmore). Free. All year; 14-day limit. Primitive undesignated camping. No facilities except picnic area. Hiking, fishing.

WINSLOW
Devil's Den State Park $12
From US 71 at Winslow, 13 mi W on SR 74 (mountainous rd tough climb for large RVs). 24 Class D sites without hookups, $12 ($6 for AR seniors on weekdays, $9 for AR seniors on weekends and for non-resident seniors on weekdays); 13 Class C elec sites, $15 ($7.50 for AR seniors on weekdays, $11.25 for AR seniors on weekends and for non-resident seniors on weekdays); 12 Class B wtr/30-amp elec sites, $20 ($10 for AR seniors on weekdays, $15 for AR seniors on weekends and for non-resident seniors on weekdays). Also 42 equestrian sites, $16. All year; 14-day limit. Tbls, flush toilets, cfga, drkg wtr, dump, showers, cafe, store, pool, group camp, pavilion, playground, coin laundry. Mountain biking(r), canoeing(r), pedal boating(r), swimming($), interpretive hiking trails, ranger programs, horseback riding trails. 1.927 acres.

YELLVILLE
Highway 14   FREE
Buffalo National River
16 mi S of Yellville where SR 14 crosses Buffalo River. Free. All year; 14-day limit. Undesignated sites. Toilets, cfga. Swimming and fishing. Access to floating by canoe down Buffalo River.

Highway 125 Park $9.50
Corps of Engineers
Bull Shoals Lake
14 mi NW of Yellville on SR 14, then 13 mi N on SR 125. $9.50 base with federal senior pass at 38 elec sites; others pay $19 base, $20 for premium locations ($10 with senior pass). 4/1-10/31; 14-day limit. 45-ft RV limit; all back-in. Tbls, flush toilets, drkg wtr, hookups, showers, dump, beach, fishing pier, playground, marine dump station, shelter. Boating(l), fishing, swimming, ball field.

Rush Campground   FREE
Lower Buffalo Wilderness
Buffalo National River
8 mi access on marked paved rd off AR 14 and about 10 mi S of Yellville. Free, but no wtr in winter; 14-day limit. 12 sites (tents & small RVs). Toilets, cfga, drkg wtr (Apr-Nov). Hiking, swimming (no diving), fishing, canoeing. Scenic.

Access to floating by canoe down Buffalo River. Mining ghost town.

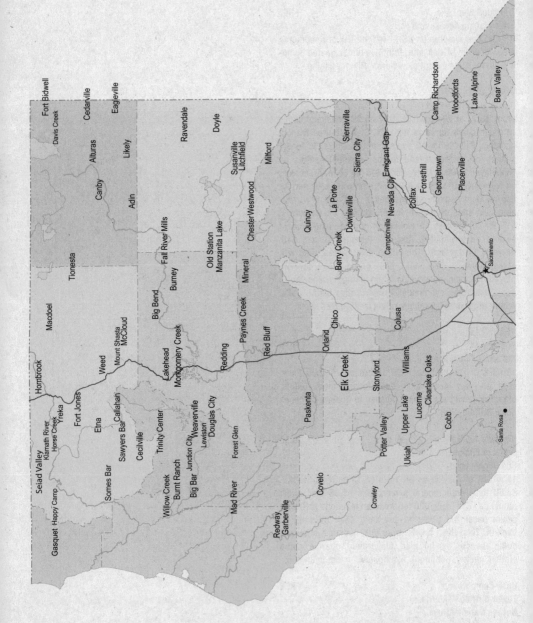

Fort Bidwell
Davis Creek
Cedarville
Eagleville
Ravendale
Doyle
Susanville
Litchfield
Milford
Sierraville
Sierra City
Camp Richardson
Woodfords
Lake Alpine
Bear Valley
Alturas
Canby
Likely
Adin
Chester Westwood
La Porte
Downieville
Emigrant Gap
Foresthill
Georgetown
Placerville
Quincy
Camptonville
Nevada City
Colfax
Tionesta
Old Station
Manzanita Lake
Mineral
Berry Creek
Sacramento
Fall River Mills
Burney
Paynes Creek
Macdoel
Big Bend
Chico
Colusa
Mount Shasta
McCloud
Redding
Red Bluff
Orland
Hornbrook
Weed
Lakehead
Montgomery Creek
Elk Creek
Stonyford
Williams
Clearlake Oaks
Klamath River
Horse Creek
Yreka
Fort Jones
Callahan
Weaverville
Douglas City
Paskenta
Cobb
Seiad Valley
Etna
Sawyers Bar
Trinity Center
Lewiston
Big Bar Junction City
Forest Glen
Potter Valley
Upper Lake
Lucerne
Santa Rosa
Gasquet Happy Camp
Ceciliville
Willow Creek
Burnt Ranch
Mad River
Crowley
Ukiah
Somes Bar
Covelo
Redway
Garberville

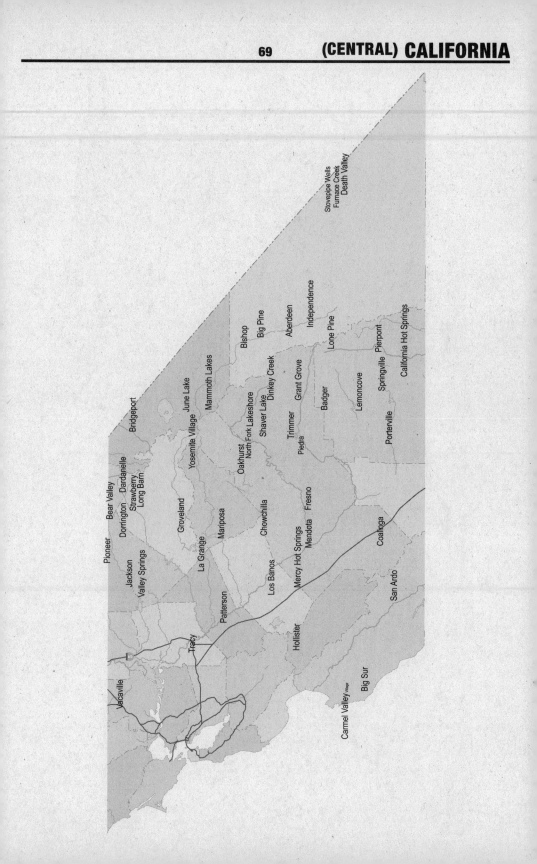

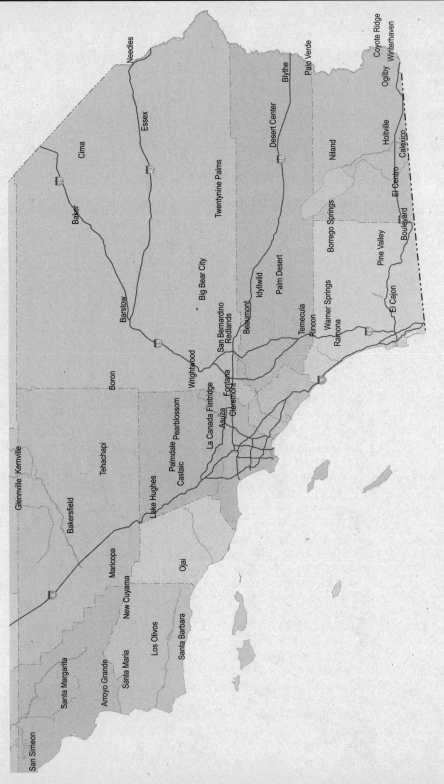

CALIFORNIA

> **CAPITAL:** Sacramento
> **NICKNAME:** The Golden State
> **STATEHOOD:** 1850 – 31st State
> **FLOWER:** Golden Poppy
> **TREE:** California Redwood
> **BIRD:** Valley Quail

WWW.VISITCALIFORNIA.COM

California Division of Tourism, 555 Capitol Mall, Suite 1100, Sacramento, CA 95814. 916-444-4429.

Dept of Parks and Recreation; 1416 9th St, Sacramento, CA 95814. 916/653-6995.

Dept of Fish and Wildlife, 1416 Ninth St., 12th Floor, Sacramento, CA 95814. 916/445-0411.

Department of Forestry & Fire Protection, 1416 9th ST., Sacramento, CA 95814. 916/653-5123.

REST AREAS
Overnight stops are not permitted. RV sanitary dump stations are located at several rest areas.

STATE PARKS
Fees at developed sites are now $15-45 per night, so most state park camping areas have been deleted from this edition.

STATE FORESTS
Camping facilities are quite rustic. Most campgrounds have pit toilets or none at all, and some have no drinking water. No fees are charged for camping at the rustic facilities. Campfire and special use permits are required, available free from the forest headquarters.
Mountain Home Demonstration State Forest. Reached via SR 190 to Springville, then the Balch Park Road and Bear Creek Road northeast of town. Twenty miles of maintained trails in the forest provide a superior opportunity to experience giant sequoias at close range. P.O. Box 517, Springville, CA 93265. Phone 209/539-2321 (summer) or 539-2855.

DEATH VALLEY NATIONAL PARK
Camping fees for RV travelers are $14-$22 per night at the park's campgrounds in addition to entry fees. PO Box 579 Death Valley, CA 92328; 760-786-3200.

JOSHUA TREE NATIONAL PARK
Two deserts merge in the park--the Mohave and the Colorado--and camping areas are located in both. Fees are charged at eight campgrounds and at the group campsites. A park entry fee for 7 days (or annual pass) is charged. Among the free campgrounds, Hidden Valley is open all year, the others from about October through May. RVs up to 32 feet long permitted. Drinking water available only at Cottonwood and Black Rock Canyon campgrounds, visitor center, Oasis visitor center and Indian Cove ranger station. Evening ranger programs at Cottonwood. Summer temperatures commonly exceed 100 degrees.

BUREAU OF LAND MANAGEMENT
The BLM manages 15.2 million acres of public land -- nearly 15% of the state's land area.

LONG-TERM VISITOR AREAS. To meet long-term needs of winter visitors and protect fragile desert resources elsewhere, the BLM established eight Long-Term Visitor Areas (LTVAs) in the California desert and along the lower Colorado River where visitors may camp for the entire winter. Winter visitors who wish to stay in an LTVA may do so by purchasing a long-term visitor permit for $180 and selecting a location in one of the designated LTVAs. The permit covers the long-term use season from Sept. 15 to April 15. Permit holders may move from one LTVA to another without incurring additional user fees. Short-term fees are $40 for 14 days in the winter. Within the Mule Mountain LTVA, long-term visitor permits are not required of campers who stay for less than 14 days. Four additional LTVAs are managed by the El Centro office of the BLM; their seasonal fee is $300. In most cases, drinking water, showers and bathrooms are not available onsite. Garbage and sewage must be transported to the nearest dump site. Obtain permits at LTVA host and entrance stations, visitor information centers, from uniformed BLM employees in the field or by contacting BLM offices in Arizona in southern California. Permits are not available through the mail.

DESERT CAMPING. Campers who wish to stay on the desert outside of an LTVA may camp on undeveloped public lands for up to 14 days in any 28-day period in one location at no charge unless otherwise posted. After 14-days, short-term campers must move to a new site outside a 25-mile radius of their original campsite. Visitors must arrive in a self-contained camping unit wit a permanently affixed waste water holding tank of at least 10 gallons capacity. Units not self-contained are allowed only at Mule Mountain, Imperial and LaPosa LTVAs. Short-term camping in the Quartzsite area is limited, but there are two designated camping areas, at Mile Marker 99 and Mile Marker 112 adjoining Highway 95.

CORPS OF ENGINEERS

Campgrounds built and managed by the U.S. Army Corps of Engineers are regrded as the nation's best federal overnight facilities. In California, camping is available at 12 lakes. Facilities and overnight fees are avilable in our book, Camping With the Corps of Engineers ($17.95 online or call 800-272-5518).

NATIONAL FORESTS

Unless otherwise posted, camping outside developed campgrounds is permitted on national forest lands. Holders of federal senior passes such as America the Beautiful and Golden Age passes pay half rates for the charges levied. In southern California, four national forests now require visitors to purchase $5 daily or $30 annual "Adventure Passes." Those forests are Angeles, Cleveland, Los Padres and San Bernardino.

Angeles National Forest. Free off-season camping permitted at several campgrounds, but water supplies are shut off and trash service is halted. Some roads into the campgrounds are closed during snow periods. Charges daily/annual Adventure Pass fees for vehicles of $5 daily or $30 annually. Campfire permits required all year for any type of campfire at all trail camps and at any area outside developed forest service recreation sites.

Cleveland National Forest. This forest has only 16 campgrounds and also charges $5 daily and $30 annual Adventure Pass fees for vehicles.

Eldorado National Forest. Offers free off-season camping at some fee sites, but snow often prevents access during free periods because most forest roads are not plowed. No fees when all services such as water are not available. California campfire permits are required when camping outside maintained campgrounds.

Inyo National Forest. No free off-season camping in parks where seasonal fees are charged. Campgrounds are closed off-season.

Klamath National Forest. The forest straddles the California/Oregon border and both sides of I-5. Although most campgrounds close in winter, some are open all year without water or services. At those, fees are collected only between May or June and the end of October.

Lake Tahoe Basin Management Unit. Operated by California Land Management, all but two campgrounds are priced above the parameters for inclusion in this book.

Lassen National Forest. Forest surrounds Lassen Volcanic National Park and is famous both for its volcanic exploration and outstanding fly-fishing for trout at Hat Creek. Most campgrounds are $8-$18; some are free in winter, but no water or services; virtually all campgrounds open until Nov 1, even if services ended earlier by concessionaires. Transient occupancy taxes are charged at fee-campgrounds in Plumas County.

Los Padres National Forest. Charges $5 daily and $30 annual fees for vehicles at many of its rustic camping areas.

Mendocino National Forest. Substantial number of its 40 developed campgrounds are free, as are several dispersed sites. Campfire permits required outside developed campgrounds.

Modoc National Forest. Campsites available for free camping (without water available) before Memorial Day and after Labor Day, weather permitting. Numerous primitive, undeveloped free sites as well as 20 developed campground. The most remote of California's national forests; secluded, uncrowded camping and recreational opportunities.

Plumas National Forest. Generally, fee campgrounds open April-October; higher elevations sites open in mid to late May. Fees of $22-$25 are charged at most campgrounds having water systems, maintained restrooms and trash collection. Self-serve campground often charge no fees and depend upon users to pack out trash and keep toilets clean.

San Bernardino National Forest. Numerous primitive, undeveloped sites available by permit, but campers must purchase either daily or annual Adventure Passes in order to park and use the forest's recreational facilities. Cost: $5 or $30 annually. Some of the most highly developed camps are $28-$30. Free off-season camping not permitted at campgrounds where fees are charged; forest campgrounds are closed 10/16-4/14, and no camping is permitted during the closed period. Camping allowed in designated dispersed areas and at Yellow Post sites; no fees are charged, but no services are provided, and campers must have Adventure Passes.

Sequoia National Forest. Offers free camping at its numerous primitive, dispersed areas; camp outside its 50 developed campgrounds anywhere on forest land with a campfire permit. More than 30 groves of giant sequoia trees with diameters of up to 30 feet.

Shasta-Trinity National Forest. Generally, dispersed camping allowed outside developed sites; exceptions are within the Trinity National Recreation Area, at Claire Engle (Trinity) Lake, and at Lewiston Lake, where camping is prohibited within a quarter mile of the high-water mark. Some formerly free dispersed sites now have camping fees, but more free dispersed sites have been added to this book. Shasta-Trinity charges daily parking fees at various sites. Free campfire permits are required outside designated campsites May-October. Most campgrounds are open 5/15-9/15, although some sites are open off-season, as weather permits, with reduced services and no water. Concessioner-managed campgrounds now have higher fees of $20 or more.

Sierra National Forest. This forest has several cost-free campgrounds, but most camps are now $20-$28.

Six Rivers National Forest. Dispersed camping free except in Aikens Creek West and is limited to 30 days per year. Campfire permit required for all use of fires, gas lanterns, barbecues and camp stoves outside developed campgrounds. Six Rivers has several cost-free campgrounds.

Stanislaus National Forest has 47 developed campgrounds, most with fees of $20-$25. They fill quickly on holiday weekends. Some accommodate all size RVs. Campfire permits required for building fires or using camp stoves outside an RV away from a developed campground. Dispersed camping not allowed within boundaries of forest's recreation areas -- Brightman, Clark Fork, Lake Alpine, Pinecrest or Tuolumne-Lumsden.

Tahoe National Forest. California Land Management is now operating most of the forest's 56 developed campgrounds. Base overnight fees are $24 with $30 charged at some premium locations.

ABERDEEN (C)
Goodale Creek $5
Bureau of Land Management
2 mi W of Aberdeen off US 395 on Aberdeen Cutoff Rd. $5 daily during about 4/15-11/30. 30-day permits now available for Tuttle, Horton Creek, Goodale Creek & Crowley for $100. 90-day use permits now replace 8-month seasonal Long-Term Visitor (LTVA) permits at Goodale, Crowley, Horton & Tuttle campgrounds. These permits still cost $300. Day use only 12/1-4/14; no services. 43 sites; pull-through RV spaces. Pit toilets, tbls, cfga, no drkg wtr or trash service. Fishing, mountain biking, hiking, hunting. 40 acres; elev 4,100 ft. Donations accepted. Beware of snakes.

ADIN (N)
Ash Creek FREE
Modoc National Forest
1/10 mi S of Adin on CA 299, 8.3 mi SE on CR 527 (Ash Valley Rd); left (N) on CR 22 (Ash Creek Campground Rd) for half mi. Free. 5/1-10/15. 14-day limit. 5 sites, RVs under 23 ft. Tbls, toilets, cfga, no drkg wtr, no trash service. Rockhounding, picnicking, fishing. Elev 4,800 ft; 7 acres.

Howard's Gulch $12
Modoc National Forest
25 mi E of Adin on SR 299; 6 mi NW on Hwy 139. $12. 6/15-10/30; 14-day limit. 6 sites; 27-ft RV limit. Tbls, toilets, cfga, drkg wtr. Fishing, hiking. Elev 4700 ft.

Lava Camp FREE
Modoc National Forest
10 mi N of Adin on CR 87; 19 mi N on CR 91; 11 mi W on FR 56; 7 mi S on FR 42N23. 6/1-10/30. 12 dispersed sites in isolated, rocky area (RVs under 33 ft). Free. Tbls, toilets, cfga, no drkg wtr, no trash service. Rockhounding, picnicking. Elev 4400 ft; 9 acres. Scenic.

Lower Rush Creek FREE
Modoc National Forest
7.5 mi NE of Adin on CA 299; qtr mi NE on CR 198; left on Rush Creek/Lower Rush Creek Rd for half mi; rd not recommended for trailers. Free. All year, but inaccessible during inclement weather; 14-day limit. 10 sites (RVs under 22 ft). Tbls, toilets, cfga, no drkg wtr. Picnicking, fishing. Elev 4400 ft; 5 acres. Mountains. Lower Rush Creek.

Upper Rush Creek FREE
Modoc National Forest
7.5 mi NE of Adin on CA 299; 2.3 mi NE on FR 40N39 (Rush Creek Rd); rd not recommended for trailers. Free. 5/1-10/31; 14-day limit. 13 sites (RVs under 22 ft). Tbls, toilets, cfga, no drkg wtr. Picnicking, fishing. Elev 5200 ft; 4 acres.

Willow Creek $12
Modoc National Forest
1 mi S of Adin on CA 299; 14.5 mi SE on CA 139. $12. 5/15-10/31; 14-day limit. 8 sites (RVs under 33 ft). Used heavily by travelers to Reno. 5 acres, flat terrain. Tbls, toilets, cfga, no potable drkg wtr. Picnicking, trout fishing. Elev 5200 ft.

ALTURAS (N)
Big Sage Reservoir FREE
Modoc National Forest
3 mi W of Alturas on Hwy 299; 6 mi N on Crowder Flat Rd (CR 73); right on CR 180 for 3.5 mi. Free. 5/15-10/15; 14-day limit. 11 primitive sites (22-ft RV limit). Tbls, toilets, cfga, no drkg wtr or trash service. Fishing, hiking, boating(l). On Big Sage Reservoir. Elev 5100 ft.

Jane's Reservoir FREE
Modoc National Forest
3 mi W of Alturas on Hwy 299; about 26 mi N on Crowder Flat Rd, past Big Sage Reservoir; W for qtr mi on Jane's Reservoir turn-off; at SE shore. Free. 5/15-10/31; 14-day limit. 8 primitive sites; 22-ft RV limit. Tbls, toilets, cfga, no drkg wtr, no trash service. Fishing, boating(l). Devil's Garden wild horse herd nearby.

Pepperdine FREE
Modoc National Forest
13 mi SE of Alturas on CR 56; 6 mi E on FR 31 (Parker Creek Rd); 1 mi S on Pepperdine Rd. Free. 6/1-10/15. 5 off-level sites (RVs under 17 ft). Tbls, toilet, cfga, piped drkg wtr. Picnicking, fishing (4 mi), hiking, horseback riding. Elev 6800 ft. Trailhead to South Warner Wilderness. Corrals & horse facilities moved to nearby Pepperdine Equestrian Campground.

Reservoir C FREE
Modoc National Forest
1 mi W of Alturas on Hwy 299; 9.5 mi N on CR 73 (Crowder Flat Rd); left 7 mi on Triangle Ranch Rd. Free. 5/15-10/15; 14-day limit. 6 primitive sites; 22-ft RV limit. Tbls, toilet, cfga, no drkg wtr. Fishing, hiking, 4-wheeling, boating(l).

ARROYO GRAND (S)
Oceano Dunes $10
State Vehicular Recreation Area
Just SW of Arroyo Grande, off Hwy 1. $10 plus entry fee. All year; by reservation 5/15-9/15 & on holidays. Primitive camping on 1,500 acres. Tbls, toilets, cfga, drkg wtr. Beach, sand dunes, off-road vehicle activities.

AZUSA (S)
Coldbrook $12
Angeles National Forest
18 mi N on SR 39 (San Gabriel Canyon Rd) from I-210 (Azusa Canyon exit) at Azusa. $12. All year; 14-day limit. 20 sites (22-ft RV limit). Tbls, toilets, cfga, no drkg wtr.

Fishing, hiking. On North Fork of San Gabriel River. Elev 3350 ft.

Crystal Lake Recreation Area $12
Angeles National Forest
From I-210 at Azusa, 26 mi N on SR 39 (San Gabriel Canyon Rd). $12. All year (winter walk-in access); 14-day limit. 257 sites, most 20-35 ft. Tbls, flush & portable toilets, cfga, drkg wtr (except in winter). Hiking, fishing. Elev 5800 ft. Non-campers pay $5 day use fee.

BADGER (C)
Eshom Campground $11.50
Giant Sequoia National Monument
Sequoia National Forest
From SR 245 at Badger, N on Hogback Rd, then about 8 mi N on Whitaker Forest Rd (CR 465); at Eshom Creek. $11.50 with federal senior pass; others pay $23. 17 sites (4 for equestrians); 25-ft RV limit due to sharp curves. Tbls, toilets, cfga, drkg wtr. Camping with OHVs okay; pasture for horses. Trails to Redwood Mountain/Whitaker Forest sequoia grove. Fishing, hiking, mountain biking.

BAKER (S)
Little Dunes Camping $15
Dumont Dunes OHV Area
Bureau of Land Management
About 31 mi N of Baker on Hwy 127 to OHV area E of hwy & S of Amargosa River; camping area is directly off Hwy 127 1 mi S of Dumont Rd. $15 weekly with federal senior pass; others pay $30 (or $90-$120 seasonally) for use permit. Primitive camping anywhere within the riding area; 14-day limit. No facilities except pit toilets. ATV use, motorcycling, 4WD touring, hiking, rockhounding.

BAKERSFIELD (S)
Evans Flat FREE
Sequoia National Forest
45 mi NE of Bakersfield via Rancheria Rd. (Road 25S15 -- dirt rd). Free. 5/1-10/31; 14-day limit. 20 sites. Toilets, tbls, cfga, no drkg wtr. 20-ft RV limit. Large-group camping. No trash pickup. Elev 6,200 ft. Suitable for horse camping; fenced pasture adjacent to camp.

Kern River Campground $12
Kern County Parks & Recreation Department
From jct of SRs 178 & 184 just E of Bakersfield, 1 mi NE on SR 178; 2 mi N & W on Alfred Harrell Hwy; exit N on Lake Ming Rd, then follow signs to campground at W shore of Lake Ming. During 10/16-3/15, $12 at 50 non-elec sites ($10 for seniors); in-season fee $24 ($22 for seniors). 10-day limit; 28-ft RV limit. Tbls, flush toilets, coin showers, cfga, drkg wtr, dump.

Walker Pass Campground FREE
Bureau of Land Management
14 mi E of Onyx on Hwy 178 or 15 mi W of Hwy 14 on Hwy 178. Free but donations accepted. All year, but may be inaccessible in winter; 14-day limit. 13 primitive sites (4 RV sites). Tbls, toilets, cfga, drkg wtr nearby. Apr-Oct. Horse corral. Hiking, horseback riding, hunting. On Pacific Crest National Scenic Trail. Elev 5000 ft. Donations accepted.

BARSTOW (S)
Afton Canyon Campground $12
Bureau of Land Management
From I-5 exit, S 3 mi following signs on Afton Canyon Rd; 38 mi E of Barstow. $12 ($6 with federal senior pass). All year; 14-day limit. 22 sites. Tbls, toilets, cold showers, drkg wtr (limited). Scenic cliffs, wildlife area. Mojave River. East Mojave National Preserve. Equestrian camp by permit.

Owl Canyon Campground $6
Rainbow Basin Natural Area
Bureau of Land Management
8 mi N of Barstow via Camp Irwin Rd; 2 mi W on Fossil Beds Rd. (Exit I-15 or I-40 at E Main; W to Yucca St railroad bridge on Ft Irwin Rd to Fossil Bed Rd; right on Rainbow Basin Rd. $6 ($3 with federal senior pass). All year; 14-day limit. 31 sites. Tbls, toilets, cold showers, drkg wtr (limited), cfga. Rockhounding, gold panning, hiking, horseback riding. Scenic cliffs. Adjacent to Rainbow Basin Natural Landmark. Elev 3000 ft; 40 acres.

BEAR VALLEY(C)
Hermit Valley Campground FREE
Stanislaus National Forest
12.1 mi NE of Bear Valley on CA 4; qtr mi S on FR 8N22. Free. 6/15-10/1; 14-day limit. Dispersed sites in lower valley & NE upper valley at Grouse Flat. 50 acres, about 25 spaces for large RVs. Tbls, toilets, cfga, no drkg wtr. River. Swimming, picnicking, fishing, deer hunting. Campfire permit required. Elev 7500 ft. RV dump station at Calaveras Big Trees State Park on Hwy 4 NE of Arnold; use fee.

Highland Lakes $12
Stanislaus National Forest
16 mi NE of Bear Valley on SR 4; 4.5 mi SE on FR 8N01; half mi SW on FR 8N33. $12. 6/1-9/30; 14-day limit; route not recommended for RVs over 25 ft. 35 sites. Tbls, toilets, cfga, drkg wtr. Hiking, swimming, fishing, hunting. No trash service. Elev 8600 ft; 5 acres near top of Ebbetts Pass.

Pacific Valley Campground $10
Stanislaus National Forest
10 mi NE of Bear Valley on SR 4; 1 mi S on FR 8N12 (6 mi W of Ebbetts Pass); along Mokelumne River. $10 during 6/15-10/1, $5 off-season but no wtr. All year, weather permitting; 14-day limit. 15 designated sites (RVs under

16 ft); not recommended for trailers. Tbls, toilets, cfga, no drkg wtr. Fishing, picnicking. Elev 7600 ft. Good early season deer camp. Campfire permit required. Equestrians camp at S end of site.

BEAUMONT (S)

Bogart Park $12
Riverside County Park
From I-10 at Beaumont, 4.5 mi N on Beaumont Ave; at N end of Cherry Valley Ave. $12 for primitive sites; $15 developed sites; some wtr hookups. All year; 14-day limit. 26 sites. Tbls, flush toilets, cfga, drkg wtr, playground. Hiking & equestrian trails, horseback riding, no fishing. 11 corrals, watering trough. Non-campers pay $10 day use fee (or $100 annual county parks pass). 414 acres.

BERRY CREEK (N)

Little North Fork   FREE
Plumas National Forest
14 mi N on CR 27562 (Oroville-Bucks Lake Rd); 5 mi NE on FR 23N60; half mi N on FR 23N15. Not recommended for large trailers/motorhomes; narrow access rd, few turn-arounds; better for pickup & van campers. Free. 5/15-10/15; 14-day limit. 6 sites (RVs under 16 ft); tbls, toilets, cfga, no drkg wtr or trash service. Fishing, hiking. Elev 4000 ft; 3 acres. On Little North Fork of Feather River.

Milsap Bar   FREE
Plumas National Forest
9 mi NE of Berry Creek on CR 27562; half mi S on CR 44603; 7 mi E on FR 22NG2. Free. 5/1-11/1; 14-day limit. 20 sites (RVs under 17 ft). Toilet, tbls, cfga, no drkg wtr or trash service. Elev 1600 ft. No access in early 2017; FR 22N62 closed for repairs; check current status before arrival.

Rogers Cow Camp   FREE
Plumas National Forest
15 mi NE on CR 27562; half mi W on FR 23N15; off Oroville-Bucks Lake Rd. Half mi W of Merrimac. Free. 5/15-11/30 (but open when accessible); 14-day limit. 5 RV/tent sites. Elev 4100 ft; 1 acre. Tbls, toilet, cfga, drkg wtr, no trash service. Stream.

BIG BAR (N)

Big Flat $12
Shasta-Trinity National Forest
3.7 mi E of Big Bar on Hwy 299 past town of Big Flat; right on Wheel Gulch Rd. $12. All year; 14-day limit; 10 sites (22-ft RV limit). Tbls, toilets, cfga, drkg wtr. Hiking, fishing, swimming.

Hayden Flat $12
Shasta-Trinity National Forest
6.2 mi NW of Big Bar on SR 299; one camping area on N side of rd just past town of Del Loma, other area just E on S side of rd. $12. 14-day limit. 35 sites (RVs under 26 ft). Tbls, toilets, cfga, drkg wtr, beach. Swimming, fishing. 8 acres. Self-registration.

BIG BEAR CITY (S)

Big Pine Flat Campground $11.50
San Bernardino National Forest
From N of Big Bear City at jct with SR 38, about 3 mi W on SR 38 through Fawnskin; veer right on Rim of the World Dr, past fire station, continuing after pavement ends, becoming FR 3N14 for 7 mi to campgrounds just past jct with FR 3N16. $11.50 with federal senior pass; others pay $23. 5/1-10/15; 14-day limit. 19 sites; 30-ft RV limit. Tbls, toilets, cfga, drkg wtr. Elev 6820 ft.

Horse Springs $10
San Bernardino National Forest
From N of Big Bear City at jct with SR 18, about 3 mi W on SR 38 to Fawnskin; veer right on Rim of the World Dr, past fire station, then 4 mi NW on FR 3N14. $10. All year; 14-day limit. 11 sites. Tbls, toilets, cfga, no drkg wtr.

South Fork Campground $11.50
San Bernardino National Forest
From jct with Big Bear Blvd in town of Big Bear Lake, 17.7 mi SW on SR 38; left at sign. $11.50 with federal senior pass; others pay $23. 5/15-10/1; 14-day limit. 24 sites: 30-ft RV limit. Tbls, pit toilets, cfga, drkg wtr. Dump($) at nearby Barton Flats. Fishing.

BIG BEND (N)

Deadlun Campground   FREE
Shasta-Trinity National Forest
5.5 mi W of Big Bend on FR 38N11 to 500-acre Iron Canyon Reservoir. Free. All year; 14-day limit. 25 sites; 24-ft RV limit. Tbls, pit toilets, cfga, no drkg wtr. Boating (ramp for small boats), fishing, hiking. Elev 2665 ft. Nearby Hawkins Landing Campground ($10) managed by PG&E.

BIG PINE (C)

Big Pine Creek $11.50
Inyo National Forest
From Big Pine, 8 mi W on Crocker St (road paved but narrow & winding); cross creek at road's end & follow signs. $11.50 with federal senior pass; others pay $23. 6/1-9/30; 14-day limit. 30 sites for small RVs. Tbls, flush toilets, cfga, drkg wtr, bear lockers. Fishing.

Grandview Campground $5
Inyo National Forest
Half mi N on US 395; 13 mi NE on SR 168; 5.5 mi N on CR 4S01 (White Mountain Rd); primitive rds. $5 maintenance donations requested. 5/1-10/31; 14-day limit. 23 sites (RVs under 45 ft). Tbls, toilets, cfga, firewood, no drkg wtr. Picnicking, hiking. Elev 8600 ft; 2 acres. Botanical. Serves Ancient Bristlecone Pine Forest. Nature trails 5 mi.

Sage Flat Campground $11.50
Inyo National Forest
From Big Pine, 8 mi W on Crocker St (road paved but narrow & winding); on left in forested area. $11.50 with federal senior pass; others pay $23. 6/1-9/30; 14-day limit. 28 sites (small RVs). Tbls, flush toilets, cfga, drkg wtr, bear locker.

Upper Sage Flat $11.50
Inyo National Forest
From Big Pine, 8 mi W on Crocker St (road paved but narrow & winding); on the left. $11.50 with federal senior pass; others pay $23. 6/1-9/30; 14-day limit. 21 sites. Tbls, flush toilets, cfga, drkg wtr, bear lockers.

BIG SUR (C)
Bottchers Gap Campground $7.50
Los Padres National Forest
From about 10 mi N of Big Sur on SR 1, 8 mi SE on Palo Colorado Rd (FR 18S05). $7.50 with federal senior pass; others pay $15. 12 sites. Tbls, toilets, cfga, drkg wtr. Trail access to Ventana Wilderness. Horseback riding, hiking. Elev 2100 ft. Non-campers pay $10 day use or trailhead parking. Temporarily closed early 2017 by Soberanes fire; check current status before arrival.

Ponderosa Campground $10
Los Padres National Forest
From Big Sur, about 25 mi S on SR 1; 10 mi E on Nacimiento-Fergusson Rd. $10 with federal senior pass; others pay $20. 23 sites; 35-ft RV limit. All year; 14-day limit. Tbls, toilets, cfga, drkg wtr (Mar-Nov).

BISHOP (C)
Four Jeffrey $11.50
Inyo National Forest
16 mi W of Bishop on SR 168 (West Line St); left on South Lake Rd about 1 mi; at South Fork of Bishop Creek. $11.50 with federal senior pass; others pay $23. 7/1-8/30; 14-day limit. 104 sites; 35-ft RV limit. Tbls, flush toilets, cfga, drkg wtr, bear lockers. Fishing.

Horton Creek Campground $8
Bureau of Land Management
8.5 mi NW of Bishop on US 395; W on Sawmill Rd; 3 mi W on Round Valley Rd. $8 ($4 with federal senior pass). About 5/1-10/31; 14-day limit. Day use only rest of year. 49 primitive sites; pull-through RV spaces. Tbls, pit toilets, cfga, no drkg wtr. Fishing, hiking. Near Tungsten Hills for mountain biking, horseback riding, OHV use Elev 4975 ft. 30-day permits now available for Tuttle, Horton Creek, Goodale Creek & Crowley for $100. 90-day use permits now replace 8-month seasonal Long-Term Visitor (LTVA) permits at Goodale, Crowley, Horton & Tuttle campgrounds. These permits still cost $300.

Pleasant Valley Pit Campground $5
Bureau of Land Management
5.5 mi N of Bishop on US 395; 0.5 mi NE on Pleasant Valley Rd, then left on dirt rd to campground. $5. LD-5/15; 60-day limit. 75 sites. Tbls, toilets, cfga, no drkg wtr. Boulder exploring.

BLYTHE (S)
Coon Hollow $180
Bureau of Land Management
Mule Mountain Long-Term Visitor Area
14 mi W of Blythe on I-10 to Wiley Well Rd; 13 mi S of I-10 via graded dirt Wiley Well Rd. $180 permit for season 9/15-4/15; $40 for 14-days; free up to 14 days during 4/16-9/14. 29 primitive RV sites. Tbls, toilets, cfga, no wtr, no firewood. Dump at Wiley Well rest area on I-10 at Wiley Well Rd. Excellent geode-hunting at nearby geode beds. Pick up map at rock shop in Blythe. Federal senior pass discounts do not apply to LTVA fees.

Midland $180
Bureau of Land Management
Long Term Visitor Area
From I-10 at Lovekin Blvd exit, N 6 blocks, then NW 4 mi on Midland Rd. $180 seasonal permit for 9/15-4/15; $40 for 14 days; free up to 14 days during 4/16-9/14. Undesignated sites. Dump. No toilets, no drkg wtr. Geode hunting nearby. Pick up map at rock shop in Blythe. Federal senior pass discounts do not apply to LTVA fees.

Miller Park   FREE
Riverside County
Regional Park and Open-Space District
12 mi SW of Blythe at Hwy 78 & 38th Ave; on Colorado River. Free. Primitive undesignated sites on 5 undeveloped acres. No facilities, no wtr. Boating, fishing.-

Mule Mountain $5
Bureau of Land Management
Long-Term Visitor Area
From I-10 at Wiley's Well Rd exit, S 9 mi; or, from Hwy 78, N 25 mi on Milpitas Wash Rd. Camping area on both sides of rd from Wiley's Well Camp to Coon Hollow Camp. $5 daily during 4/16-9/14. $180 seasonal permit for 9/15-4/15; $40 for 14 days; free up to 14 days during 4/16-9/14. Undesignated primitive sites. Toilets, trash pickup at Wiley's Well and Coon Hollow Camps; dump, drkg wtr, toilets and trash pickup at Wiley's Well Rest Stop on I-10. Federal Senior Pass discounts do not apply to LTVA fees.

Wiley's Well $5
Bureau of Land Management
Long-Term Visitor Area
14 mi W of Blythe on I-10 to Wiley's Well Rd; 9 mi S of I-10. Free 14 days. $5 daily during 4/16-9/14; $180 permit for season during 9/15-4/15; $40 for 14 days. 14-day limit. Day use off-season but no services. 14 primitive sites.

Tbls, cfga, toilets, no drkg wtr. Dump at Wiley Well rest area on I-10 at Wiley Well Rd. Excellent geode-hunting at nearby geode beds. Pick up map at rock shop in Blythe. Federal senior pass discounts do not apply to LTVA fees.

BORON (S)

Boondock Area	FREE

SR 58 W of 4-Corners near Mojave and Edwards AFB. Free. All year. Many dry washes accessible from the road 100-500 yds for self-contained RVs. In case of Columbia landings or major air events, plan on arriving a day early.

BORREGO SPRINGS (S)

Arroyo Salado Primitive Campground	$10

Anza-Borrego Desert State Park
16 mi E of Borrego Springs on CR 522. $10 daily pass. All year; 15-day limit. Primitive open camping. Tbls, toilets, cfga, no drkg wtr. No open fires. Fishing, rockhounding, hiking.

Backcountry Camping	$10

Anza-Borrego Desert State Park
From Borrego Springs, follow Palm Canyon Dr & Montezuma Valley Rd. $10 daily pass. Camp throughout the park, boondocking without facilities. Fishing, hiking, rockhounding. 600,000 acres of open area.

Culp Valley Primitive Area	$10

Anza-Borrego Desert State Park
10 mi SW of Borrego Springs on CR S22, just inside W park entrance. $10 daily pass. All year; 15-day limit Primitive open camping. Tbls, toilets, cfga, no drkg wtr. No open fires. Rockhounding, hiking.

Ocotillo Wells State Vehicle Recreation Area	FREE

About 12 mi E of Borrego Springs (near town of Ocotillo Wells) on Borrego Springs Rd & SR 78. Free. All year. Primitive sites with tbls, cfga, shade ramadas, toilets, no drkg wtr, dump. Primarily an OHV use area for all-terrain vehicles, 4WD and motorcycles.

Sheep Canyon	$10

Anza-Borrego Desert State Park
NW of Borrego Palm Canyon Campground. $10 daily pass. All year; 15-day limit. Small number of primitive undesignated sites. Tbls, toilets, cfga, no drkg wtr. Hiking, rockhounding.

Yaqui Pass Primitive Area	$10

Anza Borrego Desert State Park
5 mi S of Borrego Springs on CR 53; right on Yaqui Pass Rd for 4 mi. $10 daily pass. All year; 15-day limit. Tbls, toilets, cfga, no drkg wtr. No open fires. Rockhounding, hiking.

Yaqui Well Primitive Campground	$10

Anza-Borrego Desert State Park
5 mi S of Borrego Springs on CR 53; right for 6 mi on CR 53 (Yaqui Pass Rd). $10 daily pass. All year; 15-day limit.

10 numbered primitive sites & numerous undesignated sites. Tbls, toilets, cfga, no drkg wtr. No open fires. Hiking, rockhounding.

BOULEVARD (S)

Cottonwood Campground	$6

McCain Valley Recreation Area
Bureau of Land Management
2 mi E of Boulevard on co rd; 7 mi NW on very rough McCain Valley Rd. $6. All year; 14-day limit. 25 sites. Tbls, toilets, cfga, no drkg wtr. On W edge of McCain Valley national Cooperative Land and Wildlife Management Area. Picnicking, hiking, biking, horseback riding. No OHV. Elev 3000-4500 ft.

Lark Canyon Off-Highway Vehicle Area	$6

McCain Valley Recreation Area
Bureau of Land Management
2 mi E of Boulevard on co rd; 7 mi NW on McCain Valley Rd. $6. 15 sites. All year; 14-day limit. Tbls, toilets, cfga, no drkg wtr. Popular OHV area. Within the McCain Valley National Cooperative Land and Wildlife Management Area. Picnicking, biking, mountain biking. Elev 4000 ft.

BRIDGEPORT (C)

Desert Creek	FREE

Toiyabe National Forest
From jct with US 395 in Bridgeport, 11 mi N on SR 182, becoming SR 338 in Nevada; continue on SR 338 for 10 mi, then left for 7 mi on FR 50 (Risue Canyon Rd); veer right at Desert Creek Rd (FR 027) for 2 mi to campground. Free. About 5/1-11/1; 14-day limit. 13 sites. Tbls, toilets, cfga, no drkg wtr or trash service. Fishing. Elev 6300 ft.

Green Creek	$10

Toiyabe National Forest
4 mi S of Bridgeport on US 395; 11 mi W on Green Creek Rd (FR 142); rd ends at campground. $10 with federal senior pass; others pay $20. About 5/15-10/5; 14-day limit. 11 sites (22-ft RV limit). Tbls, toilet, cfga, drkg wtr. Hiking, fishing. Elev 7500 ft.

Obsidian	$12

Toiyabe National Forest
16 mi N of Bridgeport on US 395; 4 mi W on rough, dirt FR 66 (Little Walker Rd). $12. About 6/15-10/15; 14-day limit. 11 sites (35-ft RV limit). Tbls, toilets, cfga, no drkg wtr, no trash service. Hiking, fishing. Elev 7800 ft. Poorly maintained at last report.

BURNEY (N)

Big Pine	$12

Hat Creek Recreation Area
Lassen National Forest
5 mi NE of Burney on SR 299; 28 mi S on SR 89 (4 mi S of Old Station). $12. 4/15-10/31; 14-day limit. 19 sites (22-

ft RV limit); limited turnaround. Tbls, toilets, cfga, drkg wtr. Fishing at Hat Creek. Lassen Volcanic National Park nearby. Hiking Pacific Crest Trail. Elev 4600 ft; 3 acres. Dump($) behind national park visitor center at jct of SR 89/SR44.

Bridge Campground $10
Lassen National Forest
From jct with SR 299 NE of Burney, 8 mi S on SR 89 toward Hat Creek. $10. 4/1-10/31; 14-day limit. 25 sites; 48-ft RV limit; pull-throughs. Tbls, toilets, cfga, no drkg wtr. Fishing, hiking.

Butte Creek   FREE
Lassen National Forest
5 mi NE of Burney on Hwy 299; 23 mi SE on CA 89; 10 mi E on CA 44; 2.5 mi S on FR 32N21 (off CA 44, 2 mi S on rd to Butte Lane and NE part of Lassen Volcanic National Park). Free. All year, but not maintained in winter; 14-day limit. 10 sites (RVs under 22 ft). 2 acres. Tbls, toilets, cfga, no drkg wtr. Fishing.

Cave Campground $8
Lassen National Forest
From jct with SR 299 NE of Burney, about 15 mi S on US 89; at Hat Creek, across rd from Subway Cave. $8 with federal senior pass during 4/1-10/15; others pay $16. 17 sites open off-season for $10 ($5 with senior pass), but no wtr. 45 sites. Tbls, flush & pit toilets, cfga, drkg wtr. Fishing, hiking. Nearby lava tube.

Dusty Campground $8
Pacific Gas & Electric
Lassen National Forest
5 mi E of Burney on SR 299; 7 mi N on Hwy 89; 7.5 mi W on Clark Creek Rd; 1 mi E on access rd; on N shore of Lake Britton. $8 with federal senior pass; others pay $16. 6/1-10/15; 14 day limit. 6 primitive sites; 20-ft RV limit. Tbls, toilets, cfga, no drkg wtr. Fishing, boating. Managed by PG&E.

Hat Creek Campground $8
Lassen National Forest
From jct with SR 299 NE of Burney, about 20 mi S on US 89 (1 mi N of Old Station, 12 mi E of NW entrance to Lassen Volcanic National Park). $8 with federal senior pass; others pay $16. 4/15-10/15; 14-day limit. 72 sites. Tbls, flush & pit toilets, cfga, drkg wtr. Fishing, hiking. Visitor center at Old Station.

Honn Campground $10
Lassen National Forest
5 mi NE of Burney on Hat Creek; 14 mi S on Hwy 89. $10. 5/1-10/30; 14-day limit. 6 sites. Tbls, toilets, cfga, no drkg wtr. Dump across from Hat Creek Camp on Hwy 89. Hiking. Elev 3400 ft. Limited turn-around space for RVs.

Rocky Campground $10
Lassen National Forest
From jct with SR 299 NE of Burney, about 18 mi S on US 89 (9 mi N of Old Station); along Hat Creek. $10. 4/1-10/15; 14-day limit. 8 sites. Tbl, toilets, cfga, no drkg wtr. Fishing, hiking. Tight turn-around, not recommended for trailers.

BURNT RANCH (N)
Burnt Ranch $12
Shasta-Trinity National Forest
Half mi W of Burnt Ranch on Hwy 299; N to camp; just above Trinity River. $12. 5/15-10/31; 14-day limit. 16 sites (25-ft RV limit). Tbls, toilets, cfga, drkg wtr. Small waterfall, fishing. Elev 1000 ft.

Denny   FREE
Shasta-Trinity National Forest
7 mi W on Hwy 299; 19 mi NE on FR 7N01 (Denny Rd.). Free. All year; 14-day limit. 16 sites (RVs under 23 ft). Tbls, toilets, cfga, no drkg wtr. Camp is self-service 7/1-10/30. Rockhounding, picnicking. Fishing & swimming 1 mi. Elev 1400 ft; 5 acres. Difficult access for RVs. Requires careful driving. On New River.

CALEXICO (S)
Tamarisk LTVA $180
Bureau of Land Management
22.5 mi E of Calexico on SR 98; access via a gravel rd from hwy. All year. $180 seasonal fee during 9/15-4/15; $40 for 14 days. Day use off-season but no services. Undesignated sites. No tbls, toilets, drkg wtr. Dump at Holtville City Dump Station on Holt Rd (S-32), 2 blocks S of Evan Hewes Hwy (S-80); no charge. Hiking, rockhounding. Federal senior pass discounts do not apply to LTVA fees.

CALIF. HOT SPRINGS (C)
Leavis Flat $7.50
Sequoia National Forest
Giant Sequoia National Monument
Just W of California Hot Springs on Hot Springs Rd (0.25 mi inside national forest). $7.50 with federal senior pass; others pay $15. 5/15-11/15; 14-day limit. 9 sites; 16-ft RV limit. Tbls, pit toilets, cfga, no drkg wtr. Fishing. Operated by volunteers.

White River Campground $11.50
Sequoia National Forest
Giant Sequoia National Monument
E of California Hot Springs on Hot Springs Rd about 2 mi to T intersection; right (S) on gravel M56 Rd, through Pine Flat, then 3 mi to river; cross bridge & turn right for 0.25 mi. $11.50 base with federal senior pass; others pay $23 base, $25 for premium locations ($12.50 with senior pass). 5/13-10/2; 14-day limit. 12 sites; 16-ft RV limit. Tbls, pit toilets, cfga, drkg wtr. Fishing. Concession-managed.

CALIFORNIA 80

CALLAHAN (N)
East Fork   FREE
Klamath National Forest
27 mi SW of Callahan on FR 93; at confluence of East & South forks of Salmon River. All year; 14-day limit. 6 sites (50-ft RV limit). Tbls, pit toilet, cfga, no drkg wtr or trash service. Scenic. Fishing, hiking, picnicking, swimming. Elev 2600 ft.

Hidden Horse $10
Klamath National Forest
11 mi S of Callahan on Callahan-Cecilville Rd; 0.5 mi below summit, access rd on right. $10 during May-Oct; free rest of year, but no wtr or trash service. 6 sites (one accessible); 40-ft RV limit. Tbls, toilets, cfga, drkg wtr, 4 corral stalls at each site, horse mounting ramp. Horseback riding, hiking.

Hotelling Campground   FREE
Klamath National Forest
43 mi S of Callahan on Callahan-Cecil Rd; on South Fork of Salmon River. Free. All year; 14-day limit. 4 rustic sites with toilet, cfga, no drkg wtr or trash service.

Kangaroo Lake $7.50
Klamath National Forest
2 mi E of Callahan on SR F1089; 9.5 mi NE on Callahan-Gazelle Rd; 6.7 mi S on Rail Creek Rd; E on access rd. Free 10/16-5/15 when open, but no wtr or services; $15 rest of yr ($7.50 with federal senior pass). 18 sites (30-ft RV limit). Tbls, toilets, cfga, drkg wtr. Swimming, boating (no motors), fishing, hiking trails. Elev 6000 ft; 3 acres. Sites for handicapped & elderly. Elev 6500 ft. 25-acre lake.

Trail Creek $10
Klamath National Forest
16.6 mi SW of Callahan on Callahan-Cecilville Rd; .3 mi S on FR 39N08. $10 MD-10/15; free rest of year but no wtr or trash service. 14-day limit. 12 sites (20-ft RV limit). Tbls, cfga, toilets, no drkg wtr or trash service. Swimming, fishing, nature trails. Elev 4700 ft; 4 shaded acres.

CAMP RICHARDSON (N)
Bayview Campground $8.50
Lake Tahoe Basin Management Unit
5.3 mi NW on Hwy 89. $8.50 with federal senior pass; others pay $17. About 5/1-10/15; 1-day limit. 13 sites (20-ft RV limit); 4 acres. Toilets, cfga, tbls, no drkg wtr. Dump 5 mi. Hiking trails. Elev 6800 ft.

CAMPTONVILLE (N)
Cal Ida Campground $12
Tahoe National Forest
8.5 mi NE of Camptonville on SR 49; on Cal Ida Rd behind Indian Valley Outpost. $12 with federal senior pass at 19 sites (up to 40 ft) without hookups; others pay $24.

4/15-10/15; 14-day limit. Some sites free off-season, but no services or wtr. Tbls, toilets, cfga, drkg wtr. Fishing, hiking, canoeing, gold panning, kayaking, swimming.

Carlton Flat Campground $12
Tahoe National Forest
9 mi NE of Camptonville on SR 49; N on access rd; at North Yuba River. $12 with federal senior pass; others pay $24. Some sites free off-season, but no services or wtr. 4/25-10/15; 14-day limit. 17 small sites, typically 15 ft. Hiking, fishing, kayaking, rafting, swimming, canoeing.

Indian Valley $12
Tahoe National Forest
3 mi S of Camptonville on SR 49; at Middle Yuba River. $12 with federal senior pass; others pay $24. Some sites free off-season, but no services or wtr. 4/15-10/15; 14-day limit. 19 sites; 40-ft RV limit. Tbls, toilets, cfga, drkg wtr, bear boxes. Fishing, hiking, swimming.

Ramshorn Camp $12
Tahoe National Forest
15 mi NE of Camptonville on SR 49 just past Convict Flat picnic area on Ramshorn Creek. $12 with federal senior pass; others pay $24. 4/15-10/15; 14-day limit. 16 sites; 20-ft RV limit. Tbls, toilets, cfga, drkg wtr. Fishing, hiking (trailhead at picnic area). Elev 2600 ft.

CANBY (N)
Cottonwood Flat   FREE
Modoc National Forest
4 mi SE of Canby on CA 299; 4.1 mi W on CR 84; 3.5 mi W on FR 41N44; half mi NW on FR 42N10. Free. MD-10/15; 14-day limit. 10 sites (RVs under 22 ft). No amenities, no drkg wtr. Rockhounding, picnicking; primarily a fall hunter camp. Elev 4700 ft; 6 acres. Historic. Hulbert Creek and Pit River 4 mi.

Lassen Creek Campground   FREE
Modoc National Forest
5 mi N of Canby on Hwy 139. Free. May-Oct; 21-day limit. Primitive undesignated sites. Tbls, toilets, cfga, no drkg wtr. Hiking, no fishing in Lassen Creek. Rockhounding nearby. Elev 4700 ft. May be decommissioned as campground.

Reservoir F Campground   FREE
Modoc National Forest
6 mi N of Canby on Hwy 139; 4 mi N on Mowitz Rd 46 to Reservoir F jct, then E on FR 43N36 for 6 mi. Free. 5/15-10/31; 14-day limit. 6 primitive, spacious sites close to shore; 22-ft RV limit. Tbls, toilet, cfga, no drkg wtr or trash service. Fishing, boating, hiking.

CARMEL VALLEY (C)

White Oaks　　FREE
Los Padres National Forest
22 mi SE of Carmel Valley on Carmel Valley Rd; 8 mi S on Tassajara Rd. Free. 7 sites; 20-ft RV limit. All year; 14-day limit. Tbls, toilets, cfga, no drkg wtr. Hiking, fishing at Anastasia Creek. Elev 4200 ft. Temporarily closed early 2017 by Soberanes fire.

CASTAIC (S)

Frenchman's Flat　　$5
Angeles National Forest
10 mi N of Castaic on I-5, then N on Pyramid Lake Rd. $5 daily or $30 annually. All year; 14-day limit. Primitive undesignated sites; 32-ft RV limit. Tbls, toilets, cfga, no drkg wtr.

Oak Flat Campground　　$5
Angeles National Forest
10 mi N of Castaic on I-5; 3 mi NW on Templin Hwy; qtr mi N on FR 6N46. $5 daily or $30 annually. All year; 14-day limit. 27 sites (18-ft RV limit). Tbls, pit toilets, cfga, drkg wtr. Fishing, hiking trails, biking. 7 acres; elev 2800 ft.

CECILVILLE (N)

Matthews Creek　　$10
Klamath National Forest
8.5 mi NW of Cecilville on CR FH93 (narrow, single-lane rd). $10 during 6/1-10/31; may be free rest of year but no wtr or trash service; 14-day limit. 5 sites; 24-ft RV limit. Tbls, toilets, cfga, drkg wtr; no wtr or trash service during free period. Swimming, fishing. 11 acres on South Fork Salmon River.

Shadow Creek　　FREE
Klamath National Forest
7.2 mi NE of Cecilville on Callahan-Cecilville Rd. Free. All year; 14-day limit. 5 dispersed sites (RVs under 50 ft). No toilets, drkg wtr or trash service. Swimming, fishing, hiking. On Shadow Creek (no fishing) and E Fork Salmon River. Elev 2900 ft.

CEDARVILLE (N)

Cedar Pass　　FREE
Modoc National Forest
8 mi W of Cedarville on CA 299. Free. 5/30-10/15; 14-day limit. 17 sites (RVs under 23 ft). Tbls, toilets, cfga, no drkg wtr, no trash service. Picnicking, fishing. Elev 5900 ft; 10 acres. Mountains. Dense forest. Stream.

Stough Reservoir Campground　　FREE
Modoc National Forest
5.1 mi W of Cedarville on CA 299; half mi N on FR 45N07. Free. 5/15-10/15. 14 sites (22-ft RV limit). Tbls, toilet, cfga, drkg wtr. Rockhounding, picnicking. Elev 6300 ft; 3 acres.

CHESTER (N)

Almanor Campground　　$9
Lassen National Forest
Just W of Chester at jct with SR 36, 5.4 mi S on SR 89 to Almanor West Shore sign; left at sign on Almanor Dr, then 0.7 mi to camp entrances. $9 with federal senior pass; others pay $18. 5/1-10/31; 14-day limit. 104 sites; RV limits 25 & 40 ft. Tbls, pit toilets, cfga, drkg wtr. Boating(l), fishing, hiking trail.

Domingo Springs　　$7
Lassen National Forest
From Chester at SR 36, 6.1 mi N on Feather River Dr to "Y"; bear left 2.3 mi. $7 with federal senior pass; others pay $14. 5/1-10/1; 14-day limit. 18 sites (typically 35 ft). Tbls, pit toilets, cfga, drkg wtr. Hiking.

Elam Campground　　$7
Lassen National Forest
11.5 mi W of Chester on SR 36; 3.4 mi SW on SR 32; on right at Elam Creek. $7 with federal senior pass; others pay $14. 5/1-10/31; 14-day limit. 15 sites (typically 35 ft). Tbls, pit toilets, cfga, drkg wtr. Trout fishing.

Gurnsey Campground　　$7
Lassen National Forest
13.8 mi W of Chester on SR 36; on right. $7 with federal senior pass; others pay $14. 5/1-10/31; 14-day limit. 52 sites (typically 40 ft). Tbls, pit toilets, cfga, drkg wtr. Trout fishing.

Hamilton Beach Dispersed　　FREE
Pacific Gas & Electric
Lassen National Forest
About 30 mi SW of Chester near Hamilton Beach fishing access sites on Lake Almanor. Free. All year; 14-day limit. Toilets, cfga, tbls, no drkg wtr. Primarily a site for hunters & fishermen. Fishing, hunting, hiking, boating(l).

High Bridge Campground　　$7
Lassen National Forest
From Chester at jct with SR 36; 5.5 mi N on Feather River Dr to sign; left for 0.2 mi; campground in two sections on Feather River & Warner Creek. $7 with federal senior pass; others pay $14. 5/1-10/31; 14-day limit. 12 sites. Tbls, toilets, cfga, drkg wtr. Fishing.

Potato Patch Campground　　$7
Lassen National Forest
11.5 mi W of Chester on SR 36; 10 mi SW on SR 32; on left at Deer Creek. $7 with federal senior pass; others pay $14. 5/1-10/31; 14-day limit. 32 paved sites (typically 45 ft). Fishing.

Warner Valley $12
Lassen Volcanic National Park
Off Hwy 36, 16 mi NW on oil and dirt rd; 1 mi W of Warner ranger station; rough gravel rd, trailers not recommended. $12 during 9/12-10/24; $16 during 6/9-9/11 ($8 with federal senior pass); 14-day limit. Also $20 entry fee to park for 7 days. 18 tent/RV sites. Tbls, drkg wtr, toilets, cfga bear lockers. Hiking trail to lakes & Devil's Kitchen Geothermal Area, fishing. Elev 5600 ft.

CHICO (N)
Cherry Hill Campground $7
Lassen National Forest
NE of Chico on SR 32 to Butte Meadows turnoff (sign); right on unmarked Humboldt Rd for 8.7 mi; on right at Butte Creek. $7 with federal senior pass; others pay $14. 5/1-10/31; 14-day limit. 26 sites (typically 30 ft, not level). Tbls, toilets, cfga, drkg wtr.

CHOWCHILLA (C)
Codorniz Recreation Area $10
Eastman Lake
Corps of Engineers
From Raymond (NE of Chowchilla) on SR 99, E on 26th Ave; N on Hwy 29 (signs). All year; 14-day limit. $10 with federal senior pass at 42 non-elec RV/tent sites (others pay $20). Elec/wtr sites & full hookup sites, $30 ($15 with senior pass). Primitive equestrian sites $20, may be reserved by equestrian groups & non-profit organizations. RV limit in excess of 65 ft; 14 pull-through sites. Tbls, flush toilets, cfga, drkg wtr, dump, showers, playground, beach, picnic shelter, amphitheater, fish cleaning station, visitor center. Boating(l), fishing, swimming, bike/hiking/bridle trails, canoeing, disc golf, horseshoe pits, volleyball court, free wireless Internet service.

Hidden View Campground $10
Hensley Lake
Corps of Engineers
From jct with Hwy 99 at Chowchilla, follow signs on Avenue 26. $10 with federal senior pass at 40 non-elec sites; others pay $20. 15 elec sites, $30 ($15 with senior pass). All year; 14-day limit. RV limit in excess of 65-ft; 17 pull-through sites. 2 group camping areas. Tbls, flush toilets, cfga, drkg wtr, dump, showers, beach, playground, fish cleaning station. Fishing, hiking, swimming, water-skiing, boating (l), biking, self-guided nature trail. Evening nature shows Fri & Sat. 3-night minimum stay on holiday weekends.

CIMA (S)
Camp Rock Springs   FREE
Providence Mountains
Bureau of Land Management
35 mi NW of Essex off I-40 via Essex & Black Canyon Rd, then N through outcroppings to Cedar Canyon, E on Cedar Canyon Rd, 5 mi past Black Canyon Rd., right onto dirt track to Camp Rock Springs. Free. Undesignated sites. Drkg wtr from spring fo the W. Hiking, rockhounding. Petroglyphs in rocks above campsite.

CISCO GROVE (N)
Hampshire Rocks $12
Tahoe National Forest
From E of Cisco Grove at Big Bend exit of I-80, left on frontage rd & E 0.25 mi. $12 with federal senior pass; others pay $24. 31 sites: 22-ft RV limit. About 5/15-10/1; 14-day limit. Tbls, toilets, cfga, drkg wtr. Fishing, biking, hiking, swimming.

Indian Springs $12
Tahoe National Forest
From I-80 exit 164 at Cisco Grove, N & then W on Eagle Lakes Rd about 1.5 mi; at South Fork Yuba River. $12 with federal senior pass; others pay $24. b About 5/15-9/30; 14-day limit. 35 sites; 30-ft RV limit. Tbls, toilets, cfga, drkg wtr. Fishing, swimming. Elev 6500 ft.

CLAREMONT (S)
Manker Campground $7
Angeles National Forest
From Foothill Blvd in Claremont, take Mills Ave (Mt. Baldy Rd) 9 mi N (reach Foothill via Mountain Ave N from I-10). $7 with federal senior pass; others pay $14 ($4 discount for those with Adventure Pass). May-Oct; 14-day limit. 21 sites; 16-ft RV limit. Tbls, flush toilets, cfga, drkg wtr. Hiking to San Antonio Falls. $4 day use fee (free with Adventure Pass).

CLEARLAKE OAKS (N)
Blue Oaks Campground   FREE
Indian Valley Recreation Area
Bureau of Land Management
E of Clearlake Oaks 15.5 mi on SR 20; N on Walker Ridge Rd (narrow, dirt) to Reservoir Access Rd., left 2.4 mi to camp, 1.5 mi farther to lake. Free. All year; 14-day limit. 6 sites. Toilets, cfga, drkg wtr. Fishing, boating, hunting, off-road vehicles, hiking, swimming, horseback riding, biking. Marina & store at dam.

Lower Hunting Creek   FREE
Knoxville Recreation Area
Bureau of Land Management
From Hwy 29 at Lower Lake (near Clear Lake), 15 mi SE on Morgan Valley Rd. (Berryessa-Knoxville Rd); 2 mi S on Devilhead Rd. Free. 5 sites. All year; 14-day limit. 5 sites. Tbls, toilet, cfga, no drkg wtr, shade structure. Hunting.

Walker Ridge   FREE
Indian Valley Reservoir
Bureau of Land Management
E of Clearlake Oaks, off SR 20; N on Walker Ridge Rd to reservoir (steep, winding narrow dirt rds; large RVs not

recommended; some rds impassable during wet weather). Free. All year; 14-day limit (Sept-May best time). Undesignated offroad sites; 17,000 acres; 4,000-acre lake. No facilities except at Blue Oak and Wintun locations. Fishing, 10 mph boating, hunting, off-road vehicles, hiking, swimming. Marina & store near dam. Cross dam to access 2.5-mi Kowalski hiking trail.

COALINGA (C)

Coalinga Mineral Springs $9
Fresno County Parks Division
Bureau of Land Management
14 mi W of Coalinga on Hwy 198; right on Coalinga Mineral Springs Rd for 5 mi. $25 ($9 for seniors). All year; 14-day limit. 20 undesignated sites; no facilities, no drkg wtr. Horseback riding, hunting, birdwatching, hiking. Operated by Fresno County. No longer any running wtr at park. Campground is closed, used mainly by hunters; written permission from county parks required for camping. 209-488-3004.

Condon Peak Recreation Area $5
Clear Creek Management Area
Bureau of Land Management
From SR 198 about 2 mi N of Coalinga, 2 mi W on Gale Ave; right (N) on Derrick Ave for 1 mi, then left (W) on Los Gatos Rd to recreation area on left at county line. Camp free, but $5 weekly. Clear Creek vehicle access pass required. Newly built campsites with RV pads, cfga, shade structure, tbls, pit toilets, no drkg wtr or trash service. All year; 14-day limit in 28-day period. Also primitive dispersed camping within the recreation area within 15 ft of roadways. Hiking trail, hunting.

Los Gatos Creek Park   CLOSED
Fresno County Parks Division
2 mi N of Coalinga on SR 33/198; 1 mi W on W. Gale Ave; 1 mi N on S. Monterey Ave; about 15 mi NW on W. Tornado Ave, becoming Los Gatos Creek Rd, to park. Campground closed; day use only.

Upper Sweetwater Campground   FREE
Laguna Mountain Recreation Area
Bureau of Land Management
From SR 198 about 2 mi N of Coalinga, 2 mi W on Gale Ave; right (N) on Derrick Ave for 1 mi, then left (W) on Los Gatos Rd/Coalinga Rd to Condon Peak & county line, then continue on Coalinga Rd, past Lugana Campground to Sweetwater trailhead access. Free camping at new sites with RV pads, cfga, shade structures, tbls, pit toilets, no drkg wtr or trash service. Also dispersed camping within 15 ft of roadways. All year; 14-day limit in 28-day period. Hiking, mountain biking, horseback riding, hunting. Waterfalls.

COBB (N)

Boggs Mountain   FREE
Demonstration State Forest
1 mi N of Cobb on Hwy 175; turn at sign for fire station. All

year; 14-day limit. 15 primitive sites at Calso Ridge Camp; 2 sites at Ridge Camp; no toilets, cfga, no drkg wtr except at Houghton Springs and Big Springs camping areas. Picnicking, hiking, horseback riding. Camp in designated areas only. Campfire & camping permit required; acquire from ranger station. 3,453 acres. Note: Closed in 2016 until further notice due to fire hazards.

COLFAX (N)

Bear River Park and Campground $10
Inland Fishing Access
Placer County Parks & Grounds Division
2 mi N of Colfax off I-80 on Weimar rd; 3 mi E on Placer Hills Rd; 1 mi N on Plum Tree Rd on Milk Ranch Rd. $10. 4/1-10/31; 14-day limit. 23 primitive sites; 35-ft RV limit. Tbls, pit toilets, cfga, no drkg wtr; no hookups. Swimming, hiking trails, canoeing, fishing, horseback riding, gold panning.

COLUSA (N)

Colusa County Fairgrounds $10
From jct with SR 45 in Colusa, half mi S on SR 20 to fairgrounds. $10 without hookups, $20 full hookups. All year. 147 sites; 25 pull-through. 70 sites without hookups; 65-ft RV limit. Tbls, dump, showers, flush toilets.

COVELO (N)

Atchison Dispersed Camp   FREE
Mendocino National Forest
From just N Covelo, 11 mi E on SR 162 to Eel River Work Center, then SE on FR 7, S on FR 21N1. Free. MD-11/1; 14-day limit. 6 sites; 22-ft RV limit. Tbls, toilet, cfga, no drkg wtr, no trash service. Elev 4300 ft.

Eel River Campground $8
Mendocino National Forest
1.5 mi N of Covelo on CR 162; 11.1 mi E on CR 338; .2 mi S on FR 1N02 (next to Eel River Work Center). $8. 4/1-12/1; 14-day limit. 15 sites on 6 acres (30-ft RV limit). Tbls, toilets, cfga, stoves, no drkg wtr. Swimming, fishing, picnicking, boating. Elev 1500 ft.

Georges Valley Dispersed Camp   FREE
Mendocino National Forest
E of Covelo at NE terminus of Indian Dick Rd (CR M1). Free. All year; 14-day limit. Primitive undesignated sites; no facilities, no drkg wtr. Hiking. Trailhead.

Green Springs Campground   FREE
Mendocino National Forest
E of Covelo at Yolla-Bolly Middle Eel Wilderness. Free. All year; 14-day limit. 4 primitive sites. Tbls, pit toilet, cfga, no drkg wtr or trash service. Corrals. Popular trailhead & mountain biking camp.

Hammerhorn Lake $8
Mendocino National Forest
2.6 mi N of Covelo on Hwy 162; 11.1 mi E on CR 338; 22.4 mi N on FR 1N02; half mi E on FR 23N01 (18 mi N of Eel River Work Center via CR 1, Indian Dick Rd. $8. MD-11/1; 14-day limit. 9 sites (30-ft RV limit). Tbls, toilets, cfga, drkg wtr, fishing piers, no trash service. 1 disability site with adjoining toilet. Hiking, fishing, boating(l). 2 accessible fishing piers. 5 acres.

Howard Lake Campground $6
Howard Lake Basin Recreation Area
Mendocino National Forest
2.6 mi E of Covelo on CA 162; 11.1 mi E on CR 38; 17.5 mi N on FR 1N02 (12 mi N of Eel River Work Center via CR M1, Indian Dick Rd; take rd to the left of the Little Doe Campground for 4 mi; bear left at three-point jct; at 20-acre Howard Lake. $6. MD-11/1; 14-day limit. 10 primitive sites. Toilets, cfga, tbls, no drkg wtr, no trash service. High-clearance vehicles suggested. Fishing, boating(l).

Little Doe $6
Mendocino National Forest
2.6 mi E of Covelo on CA 162; 11.1 mi E on CR 38; 17.5 mi N on FR 1N02 (12 mi N of Eel River Work Center via CR M1, Indian Dick Rd. $6. MD-11/1; 14-day limit. 13 sites (RVs under 22 ft). Tbls, toilets, cfga, stoves, no wtr or trash service. Hiking. Elev 3600 ft; 8 acres.

Rock Cabin Trailhead FREE
Mendocino National Forest
About 30 mi NE of Eel River Station at N end of Indian Dick Rd. Free. All year; 14-day limit. 3 primitive sites (24-ft RV limit); no facilities, no drkg wtr, no trash service. Trailhead for Yolla-Bolly Middle Eel Wilderness. Hiking, horseback riding. Elev 6250 ft.

Soldier Ridge Trailhead FREE
Mendocino National Forest
E of Covelo at NE terminus of Indian Dick Rd (RD M-1). Free. All year; 14-day limit. Primitive undesignated sites; no facilities, no drkg wtr.

Surveyors Dispersed Camp FREE
Mendocino National Forest
E of Covelo off FR 7, about 7 mi E of Eel River Station. Free. MD-12/1; 14-day limit. 3 primitive sites. Tbl, cfga, no drkg wtr or trash service.

Y Campground FREE
Mendocino National Forest
From Covelo, follow directions to Atchison Camp & continue 2.4 mi; sign at turnoff says to Keller Place -- campground is half mi on the right. Free. All year; 14-day limit. Primitive undesignated sites; no facilities, no drkg wtr, no trash service. Scenic.

COYOTE RIDGE (S)

Boondock Area FREE
Bureau of Land Management
On Colorado River between Imperial and Laguna Dams. W on old Senator Wash Rd from SR 524. Free. All year. Dry camp in rugged landscape; level spaces for all size rigs. No desert septic tanks allowed. Drkg water, dump nearby. CB Channel 23 monitored.

CROWLEY (N)

Crowley Lake Campground $8
Bureau of Land Management
From Crowley and US 395, 5.5 mi N and W of Tom's Place overlooking Crowley Lake & Long Valley on Crowley Lake Dr. $8 daily. About 4/25-10/30; 14-day limit. 30-day permits now available for Tuttle, Horton Creek, Goodale Creek & Crowley for $100. 90-day use permits now replace 8-month seasonal Long-Term Visitor (LTVA) permits at Goodale, Crowley, Horton & Tuttle campgrounds. These permits still cost $300. Free camping off-season up to 14 days. 47 sites (upgraded in 2012); pull-through RV spaces. Tbls, toilets, cfga, no drkg wtr, dump ($5), group camping. Fishing (3 mi to lake), boating(lr), OHV use. Elev 7000 ft.

DARDANELLE (C)

Baker Campground $10
Stanislaus National Forest
Brightman Recreation Area
From Dardanelle, 4 mi E on SR 108 (Sonora Pass Hwy); S short distance on Kennedy Meadow Rd; at Middle Fork Stanislaus River near Kennedy Meadow trailhead. $10 with federal senior pass; others pay $20. 4/15-10/15; 14-day limit. 44 sites, typically 40 ft. Tbls, toilets, cfga, drkg wtr. Fishing. Managed by Kennedy Meadows Resort.

Beardsley Dam $10
Stanislaus National Forest
From SR 108 near Dardanelle, 7 mi on Beardsley Rd; at shore of Beardsley Reservoir. $10 with federal senior pass; others pay $20. About 5/1-10/10; 14-day limit. 16 sites (including 10 at day-use area); 22-ft RV limit. Toilets, cfga, drkg wtr, bls. Fishing, hiking, boating(l), swimming. Elev 3400 ft.

Boulder Flat Campground $8.50
Brightman Recreation Area
Stanislaus National Forest
From Dardanelle, 2 mi W on SR 108 (Sonora Pass Hwy); on right at bluff above Middle Fork Stanislaus River. $8.50 with federal senior pass; others pay $17. MD-LD; 14-day limit. 20 sites, typically 45 ft. Tbls, toilets, cfga, drkg wtr. Fishing. Managed by Dodge Ridge Corp.

Brightman Flat $7.50
Stanislaus National Forest
Brightman Recreation Area

1.2 mi NW of Dardanelle on SR 108. $7.50 with federal senior pass; others pay $15. 4/15-10/15; 14-day limit. 33 sites (RVs under 23 ft). Tbls, toilets, cfga, no drkg wtr. Mountain climbing, hiking, picnicking, fishing. Elev 5600 ft; 5 acres. Middle fork of Stanislaus River. Nature trails 3 mi. Columns of the Giants 2.5 mi. Geological. Managed by Dodge Ridge Corp.

Clark Fork $10
Stanislaus National Forest
Clark Fork Recreation Area
3 mi W of Dardanelle on SR 108; 6 mi NE on Clark Fork Rd; qtr mi SE on FR 7N40Y. $10 with federal senior pass; others pay $20. Lower fees spring & fall, but no wtr or services. May-Sept; 14-day limit. 88 sites; 50-ft RV limit. Tbls, flush & pit toilets, cfga, drkg wtr, dump. Fishing, hiking, boating(l). Managed by Dodge Ridge Corp.

Clark Fork Horse Camp $9
Stanislaus National Forest
Clark Fork Recreation Area
3 mi W of Dardanelle on SR 108; 6 mi NE on Clark Fork Rd; qtr mi SE on FR 7N40Y; near Clark Fork Campground at Clark Fork River. $9 with federal senior pass; others pay $18. 5/1-12/31; 14-day limit. 13 sites; 22-ft RV limit. Tbls, toilets, cfga, no drkg wtr. Fishing, horseback riding. Elev 6200 ft. Dump station at Clark Fork Campground.

Dardanelle Campground $9.50
Brightman Recreation Area
Stanislaus National Forest
From Dardanelle, 6 mi W on SR 108 (Sonora Pass Hwy). $9.50 with federal senior pass; others pay $19 ($34 double site). MD-LD; 14-day limit. 28 sites, typically 40 ft. Tbls, toilets, cfga, drkg wtr. Fishing. Managed by Dodge Ridge Corp.

Deadman Campground
Brightman Recreation Area
Stanislaus National Forest
From Dardanelle, 4 mi E on SR 108 (Sonora Pass Hwy); 0.5 mi S on Kennedy Meadow Rd; along Middle Fork Stanislaus River. $10 with federal senior pass; others pay $20. About 5/1-10/15. 17 sites, typically 45 ft. Tbls, toilets, cfga, drkg wtr. Hiking, horseback riding, fishing. Managed by Kennedy Meadows Resort.

Eureka Valley Campground $9
Brightman Recreation Area
Stanislaus National Forest
From Dardanelle, 5.5 mi W on SR 108 (Sonora Pass Hwy); left at campground sign; on bluff above Middle Fork Stanislaus River. $9 with federal senior pass; others pay $18. About 5/1-10/10; 14-day limit. 28 sites. Tbls, toilets, cfga, drkg wtr. Fishing. Managed by Dodge Ridge Corp.

Fence Creek Campground $10
Stanislaus National Forest
Clark Fork Recreation Area
21 mi E of Pinecrest on Fence Creek Rd, just off Clark Fork Rd. $10. 5/25-10/10; 14-day limit. 38 sites; 22-ft RV limit. Tbls, toilets, cfga, no drkg wtr. Elev 6100 ft.

Niagara Creek Campground $10
Stanislaus National Forest
7.5 mi SW of Dardanelle on SR 108; qtr mi NE on FR 5N011; half mi NE on FR 6N24. $10. 5/1-9/30; 14-day limit. 10 sites (RVs under 23 ft). Tbls, toilets, cfga, no drkg wtr. Mountain climbing (elev 6600 ft). Nature trails. Trail of Ancient Dwarfs, half mi. Fishing.

Pigeon Flat Campground $11
Brightman Recreation Area
Stanislaus National Forest
From Dardanelle, about 5 mi W on SR 108 (Sonora Pass Hwy); along Middle Fork Stanislaus River. $11. 4/15-11/15; 14-day limit. 7 sites. Tbls, toilet, cfga, no drkg wtr. Fishing, hiking (Column of the Giants interpretive walk). Managed by Dodge Ridge Corp.

Sand Flat $9.50
Stanislaus National Forest
Clark Fork Recreation Area
2.7 mi NW of Dardanelle on SR 108; 7 mi NE on FR 7N83. $9.50 with federal senior pass; others pay $19. 5/15-10/15; 14-day limit. 68 sites; 40-ft RV length limit. Tbls, toilets, cfga, drkg wtr. Fishing. Elev 300 ft. Managed by Sand Flat Corp.

DAVIS CREEK (N)
Plum Valley   FREE
Modoc National Forest
2.4 mi SE of Davis Creek on CR 11. Free. 5/1-10/15. 7 sites (RVs under 16 ft). Tbls, toilets, cfga, no drkg wtr. Picnicking, rockhounding, fishing, boating. Elev 5600 ft; 4 acres. South fork of Davis Creek.

DEATH VALLEY (C)
Furnace Creek $11
Death Valley National Park
N of Wildrose ranger station near Furnace Creek visitor center. $11 with federal senior pass at sites without hookups; others pay $22. Hookup sites $36 ($18 with senior pass). All year; 14-day limit. 136 sites. Tbls, flush toilets, cfga, drkg wtr, dump.

DESERT CENTER (S)
Corn Springs $6
Bureau of Land Management
8 mi E of Desert Center via I-10 & US 60. Half mi SE on Chuckwalla Rd; 6 mi W on Corn Springs Rd (very rough). $6. All year; 14-day limit. 9 sites next to palm tree oasis. Tbls, toilets, cfga, drkg wtr, cold showers. 50 acres.

DINKEY CREEK (C)

Gigantea Campground $11
Dinkey Creek Recreation Area
Sierra National Forest
1.6 mi S on CR PN44 (Dinkey Creek Rd); 6 mi SE on McKinley Grove Rd. 6/1-10/31; 14-day limit. $11 with federal senior pass; others pay $22. 10 sites (RVs under 36 ft). Tbls, toilet, cfga, no drkg wtr. Picnicking, hiking. Elev 6500 ft. Botanical. Half mi from McKinley Grove of giant sequoias.

Sawmill Flat FREE
Patterson Mountain Recreation Area
Sierra National Forest
12.9 mi SE of Dinkey Creek on FR 11S40 (McKinley Grove Rd); 3.1 mi S on FR 11S12. Free. 6/1-10/31; 14-day limit. 15 sites (22-ft RV limit). Tbls, toilets, no drkg wtr or trash service. Fishing, swimming, hiking, hunting. Elev 6700 ft.

DORRINGTON (C)

Wa Ka Luu Hep Yoo Campground $10
Sourgrass Recreation Area
Stanislaus National Forest
From SR 4 at Dorrington, 5 mi E on Boards Crossing Rd; on bluff above North Fork Stanislaus River. $10 with federal senior pass; others pay $20. MD-10/30; 14-day limit. 49 sites; 50-ft RV limit. Tbls, flush toilets, cfga, drkg wtr, showers. Fishing, rafting.

DOUGLAS CITY (N)

Douglas City Campground $10
Bureau of Land Management
Half mi W of Douglas City on SR 299 & Steiner Flat Rd. Free 11/1-5/1; rest of year, $10; 14-day per year limit. 20 sites; 28-ft RV limit. Tbls, flush & pit toilets, cfga, drkg wtr (no wtr during free period), beach. Fishing, boating, hiking, swimming, rockhounding, gold panning. Elev 1500 ft. Along Trinity River. Non-campers pay $2 day use fee.

Steel Bridge $5
Trinity River Recreation Area
Bureau of Land Management
41 mi W of Redding on US 299 to Steelbridge Rd, just 3 mi E of Douglas City; 2 mi to campground at Trinity River. $5. All year; 14-day limit. 12 sites (20-ft RV limit). Toilets, no drkg wtr (wtr at Junction City sites 1.5 mi W of Junction City). Fishing, hunting, rafting, canoeing. 3,500 acres of recreation area along 40 miles of Trinity River. High winds through steep, forested mountains from Lewiston to Helena. Rds easily accessible. Elev 1500-3500 ft.

Steiner Flat FREE
Bureau of Land Management
W of Douglas City on SR 299 & Steiner Flat Rd, just beyond Douglas City Campground. Free. All year; 14-day limit. 8 primitive sites. Tbls, toilets, cfga, no drkg wtr. Hiking, fishing, boating, swimming. Elev 1500 ft.

DOWNIEVILLE (N)

Rocky Rest $12
Tahoe National Forest
10.5 mi S of Downieville on SR 49; left side of rd. $12 with federal senior pass; others pay $24. 10 sites; 30-ft RV limit. About 4/15-10/31; 14-day limit. Free off-season but no services or wtr. Tbls, toilets, cfga, drkg wtr. Fishing, canoeing, hiking, swimming.

Union Flat $12
Tahoe National Forest
5.9 mi N of Downieville on SR 49; left side of rd at North Yuba River. $12 with federal senior pass; others pay $24. About 4/15-10/31; 14-day limit. Free off-season, but no services or wtr. 14 sites; 30-ft RV limit. Tbls, toilets, cfga, drkg wtr. Goldpanning, swimming, canoeing.

DOYLE (N)

Fort Sage OHV Area FREE
Bureau of Land Management
2 mi N of Doyle on US 395 to Laver Crossing, then follow signs. Free. All year; 14-day limit. 5 primitive sites; cfga, toilets, no drkg wtr, OHV staging facilities, no trash service. Trail system for motorcyclists of all abilities. Nearby horseback riding, mountain biking, hiking, wild horse viewing.

Meadow View FREE
Plumas National Forest
6.6 mi W of Doyle on CR 331 (Doyle Grade Rd); .9 mi NW on CR 101. Free. 4/25-10/15; 14-day limit. 6 sites (RVs under 22 ft). Tbls, toilet, cfga, no drkg wtr or trash service. Equestrian camp with corrals. Elev 6100 ft; 2 acres. Dump nearby. Last Chance Creek.

EAGLEVILLE (N)

Emerson Campground FREE
Modoc National Forest
1.1 mi S on CR 1 (Surprise Valley Rd); 3 mi SW on CR 40; access very steep for RVs; poor roads. Free. 7/1-10/15; 14-day limit. 4 sites (16-ft RV limit). Tbls, toilets, cfga, no drkg wtr or trash service. Picnicking, fishing, hiking. Elev 6000 ft; 2 acres. Mountains. Dense forest area. Trailhead to South Warner Wilderness. Very good fishing (also swimming) at nearby Emerson Lake (3.5 mi).

EL CAJON (S)

Boulder Oaks $7
Cleveland National Forest
About 30 mi E of El Cajon on I-8; exit S at Kitchen Creek-Cameron Station jct; right on southern frontage rd for 1 mi. $7 base with federal senior pass; others pay $14, $16 for premium locations. All year; 14-day limit. 30 sites (17 equestrian); 27-ft RV limit. Tbls, toilets, cfga, drkg wtr. Nearby hiking, fishing. Elev 3500 ft. Fires may be forbidden. Closed 3/1-6/15 during arroyo toad breeding season.

Cibbets Flat $7
Cleveland National Forest
About 35 mi E of El Cajon on I-8; 4.5 mi N on Kitchen Creek Rd. $7 with federal senior pass; others pay $14. All year; 14-day limit. 25 sites; 27-ft RV limit. Tbls, toilets, cfga, drkg wtr. Fishing.

EL CENTRO (S)
Hot Spring $180
Bureau of Land Management
Long-Term Visitor Area
From I-8, E of El Centro 12.5 mi, take Hwy 114 N. east on Old Hwy 80 (front-age rd) for 1 mi to site. $180 seasonal fee for period 9/15-4/15; $40 for 14 days. No toilets, no drkg wtr. Dump at Holtville City Dump Station on Holt Rd (S-32), 2 blocks S of Evan Hewes Hwy (S-80); no charge. Federal senior pass discounts do not apply to LTVA fees.

Plaster City Open Area FREE
Bureau of Land Management
17 mi W of El Centro. Exit I-8 on Dunnaway Rd. Free. All year; 14-day limit. Primitive undesignated camping in 41,000-acre open desert area. No facilities, no drkg wtr. OHV activities, photography.

Superstition Mtn Open Area FREE
Bureau of Land Management
From Hwy S-80 to Huff Rd to Wheeler Rd. Follow Wheeler to one of several popular primitive camping areas or to the base of Superstition Mountains. Free. All year; 14-day limit. Primitive undesignated camping; no facilities, no drkg wtr. OHV activities.

ELK CREEK (N)
Plaskett Meadows Campground $10
Mendocino National Forest
4.5 mi N on CR 306; 30 mi NW on Alder Springs Rd (SR 162). $10 (free about 11/1-MD but no wtr or trash service. All year; 14-day limit. 31 sites (RVs under 27 ft). Tbls, toilets, cfga, drkg wtr. Swimming, boating, fishing, hiking. Nature trails. No boat motors. Elev 6000 ft. 2 small trout fishing lakes.

EMIGRANT GAP (N)
Grouse Ridge FREE
Tahoe National Forest
4.8 mi E of Emigrant Gap on I-80; 4.6 mi W on CA 20; 6.4 mi N on FR 18N18; 4.6 mi NE on FR 18N14 (Grouse Ridge Rd); near Grouse Ridge Lookout. Free. 6/15-9/30; 14-day limit; closed in winter. 9 sites (RVs under 16 ft). Tbls, toilet, cfga, no drkg wtr, no trash service. Picnicking; fishing & swimming 1 mi. Elev 7400 ft; 3 acres. Many small lakes nearby in the Grouse Lakes area. Milk Lake and Sanford Lake, quarter mi. Elev 7400 ft.

North Fork $12
Tahoe National Forest
From I-80 at Emigrant Gap, 0.7 mi S on Emigrant Gap Rd, becoming Texas Hill Rd; continue 6 mi; on the right; at Little North Fork of North Fork American River. $12 with federal senior pass; others pay $24 during 4/15-10/15; free off-season but no wtr or services. 17 sites; 45-ft RV limit. Tbls, toilets, cfga, drkg wtr. Gold panning, swimming, fishing, hiking.

ESSEX (S)
Hole-in-the-Wall $12
National Park Service
Mojave National Preserve
16 mi NW of Essex on Essex Rd; 12 mi N on Black Canyon Rd. $12. All year; 14-day limit. 35 RV/tent sites & 2 walk-in sites. Tbls, toilets, cfga, drkg wtr, dump. Scenic volcanic rock walls & formations. Iron rings set in rock for climb down to Wildhorse Canyon. Ramadas. Group camping area. New campground designed particularly for motorhomes. Free primitive camping allowed on disturbed areas adjacent to roads; backpackers may camp at any previously disturbed site. Elev 4400 ft.

Mid Hills Campground $12
Mojave National Preserve
16 mi NW of Essex on Essex Rd; 19 mi N on Black Canyon Rd; 2 mi on unpaved Wild Horse Canyon Rd. $12. All year; 14-day limit. 26 sites. Tbls, toilets, cfga, drkg wtr. Hiking, sightseeing. Motorhomes longer than 26 ft might have trouble maneuvering. Free primitive camping allowed on disturbed areas adjacent to roads; backpackers may camp at any previously disturbed site. Elev 5600 ft.

Primitive Camping FREE
Bureau of Land Management
Mojave National Preserve
16 mi NW of Essex on Essex Rd; 12 mi N on Black Canyon Rd. Free primitive camping allowed on disturbed areas adjacent to roads; backpackers may camp at any previously disturbed sites. No facilities. Elev 4200 ft. Here are the primary roadside camping areas for RVs:
  Kelso Dunes -- near the gate and end of the access road to the dunes (2-3 sites).
  Black Canyon Rd -- 5.2 mi S of Hole-in-the-Wall visitor center on E side of Black Canyon Rd (3-4 sites).
  Powerline Site -- 11.8 mi N of Kelso on Kelbaker Rd, where powerlines cross the rd (2-3 sites).
  Caruthers Canyon -- 5.5 mi W of Ivanpah Rd on New York's Mountains Rd; 1.5-2.7 mi N of New York's Mtns Rd to sites; no RVs (3-4 sites).
  Sunrise Rock -- 10.4 mi S of I-15 on E side of Cima Rd; trailhead for Teutina Peak is nearby on opposite side of Cima Rd.

Providence Mountain $12
State Recreation Area
Bureau of Land Management
N 16 mi from I-40 interchange at Essex to Providence Mountains. $12. All year; 14-day limit. Dry camping permitted throughout area. Park no farther than 300 ft from rd. Limestone caves nearby ($), tours daily mid-Sept to mid-June. Nature trails, canyons, petroglyphs.

ETNA (N)
Red Bank Campground   FREE
Klamath National Forest
33 mi W of Etna on Etna/Somes Bar Rd. Free. All year; 14-day limit. 5 rustic sites. Toilets, cfga, no drkg wtr or trash service. At North Fork of Salmon River.

FALL RIVER MILLS (N)
Cinder Cone   FREE
Wilderness Study Area
Bureau of Land Management
From Fall River Mills, follow directions (below) to Popcorn Cave, but instead of turning left after 3.6 mi, continue another 2.4 mi, then turn right on unnamed rd. Free. About 13 sites, abandoned by BLM. Campfire rings, no drkg wtr, no tbls. Suitable only for small RVs, about 26 ft maximum. Hunting. Elev 3500 ft. Boil wtr before using. Very scenic area. Mountain biking, hiking, birdwatching, fishing.

Pit River Recreation Area $8
Bureau of Land Management
Alturas Field Office
5 mi W on US 299, then follow Campground Rd. On Pit River. $8. 5/1-1/15; 14-day limit. 8 sites. Group site, $12. Tbls, bbq, toilets, cfga, no drkg wtr. Fishing, swimming, birdwatching, hiking, mountain biking. 40 mi N of Lassen Volcanic National Park. Elev 3000 ft; 10 acres.

Popcorn Cave Campground   FREE
Cinder Cone Wilderness Study Area
From Fall River Mills at jct with SR 299 in town, turn onto Main St for 0.4 mi, across Pitt River bridge; 3.3 mi S on Cassel Fall River Rd to an unnamed, unpaved rd, crossing cattle guard; proceed 3.6 mi, then left on another unnamed rd to camping area. Free. All year; 14-day limit. Undeveloped primitive site is access to the wilderness study area, with its extensive lava flows and numerous caves. No facilities, no drkg wtr, no trash service. Campground gets few visitors; suitable only for small RVs such as truck or van campers. Hiking, cave exploring, hunting, birdwatching.

FONTANA (S)
Applewhite $10
San Bernardino National Forest
N of Fontana on Sierra Ave to I-5; 9 mi N on Lytle Creek Rd. $10 (double site $15). All year; 14-day limit. 44 sites (30 ft RV limit). Tbls, flush toilets, cfga, drkg wtr. Fishing. Elev 3300 ft. Closed in 2017 by Blue Cut fire.

FOREST GLEN (N)
Forest Glen $12
Shasta-Trinity National Forest
Qtr mi W of Forest Glen on SR 36. $12. 5/20-11/1; 14-day limit. 15 sites (RVs under 17 ft); 2 picnic sites. Tbls, toilets, cfga, drkg wtr. Fishing, swimming, hiking. Near S fork of Trinity River. Elev 2300 ft.

Hells Gate $12
Shasta-Trinity National Forest
1 mi E of Forest Glen on FR 29N58. $12; free if wtr is shut off. 5/20-11/1; 14-day limit. 17 sites (RVs under 17 ft). Tbls, toilets, cfga, drkg wtr. Fishing, swimming, hiking, birdwatching. Groceries. 10 more sites for tents & RVs half mi beyond camp on dirt rd. South Ford National Recreation Trail. Elev 2300 ft; 4 acres. On S fork of Trinity River.

Scotts Flat   FREE
Shasta-Trinity National Forest
3 mi S of Forest Glen SR 36; 0.5 mi S on FR 1S25. Free. MD-11/1; 14-day limit. 10 sites (20-ft RV limit). Tbls, toilets, cfga, no drkg wtr. Swimming, fishing, hiking. South Fork Trinity River National Recreation Trail.

FORESTHILL (N)
Ahart $10
Tahoe National Forest
36 mi E of Foresthill on Mosquito Ridge Rd, just past French Meadows Reservoir; at Middle Fork American River. $10 with federal senior pass; others pay $20. 5/15-10/15. 14-day limit. 12 sites (22-ft RV limit). Tbls, toilets, cfga, no drkg wtr. Fishing. Elev 5300 ft.

French Meadows $12
Tahoe National Forest
36 mi E of Foresthill on Mosquito Ridge Rd. to French Meadows Reservoir's Anderson Dam, then along S shore 4 mi. $12 with federal senior pass; others pay $24 during 5/15-10/16; free off-season but no wtr or services. 14-day limit. 75 sites; 40-ft RV limit. Tbls, flush toilets, cfga, drkg wtr, bear boxes, dump. Boating, fishing, hiking trail, canoeing, swimming. Boat ramp 1 mi.

Giant Gap $12
Tahoe National Forest
From Foresthill, about 9 mi NE on Forest Hill Rd; 7 mi NW (left) on FR 10 (Sugar Pine Rd); left at fork for 1 mi to rd's end; on W shore of Sugar Pine Lake. $12 with federal senior pass; others pay $24. About 4/15-10/15; 14-day limit. 30 sites; 30-ft RV limit. Tbls, toilets, cfga, drkg wtr, bear boxes. Dump on S shore $6 Sundays 11-1pm. Boating, fishing, canoeing, biking, swimming, hiking. Boating(l).

Lewis Campground $10
Tahoe National Forest
34 mi E of Foresthill on Mosquito Ridge Rd. to French Meadows Reservoir's Anderson Dam, then along S shore 5 mi; left at fork, then 0.5 mi to access rd. $10 with federal senior pass; others pay $20. About 5/15-9/15; 14-day limit. 40 sites; 40-ft RV limit. Tbls, toilets, cfga, drkg wtr, bear boxes. Fishing, biking, hiking, boating(l).

Parker Flat FREE
Tahoe National Forest
15 mi NE of Foresthill on Sugar Pine Rd past Sugar Pines Campground, then left on dirt rd; at Sugar Pine Reservoir. Free. May-Oct; 14-day limit. 7 sites primarily for OHV users, but okay for small RVs & tenters. Tbls, toilets, cfga, drkg wtr in summer. Fishing, hiking, boating.

Shirttail Creek $12
Tahoe National Forest
From Foresthill, about 9 mi NE on Forest Hill Rd; 7 mi NW (left) on FR 10 (Sugar Pine Rd); left at ford for 1 mi to rd's end; on the right. $12 with federal senior pass; others pay $24. About 5/15-10/1; 14-day limit. 30 sites; 40-ft RV limit. Tbls, toilets, cfga, drkg wtr, dump $6. Boating(l), fishing, biking, hiking. Elev 3600 ft.

Sugar Pine FREE
OHV Staging Area
Tahoe National Forest
8 mi N of Foresthill on Foresthill Rd; about 8 mi W on Sugar Pine Rd. Free. All year; 14-day limit. Open undesignated sites for RVs only; no tents. Tbls, toilet, cfga, no drkg wtr. Staging area for off-highway vehicles & motorcycles; loading ramp. Boating(l), swimming, fishing, hiking. Dump nearby. Sugar Pine Trail open for both foot and bike traffic; a pleasant 3.5-mi trail around lake, accessed from campground or boat ramp.

FORT BIDWELL (N)

Fee Reservoir FREE
Bureau of Land Management
Surprise District
7 mi E of Fort Bidwell. From Cedarville, 20-30 mi N on Surprise Valley Rd; right (E) on Fee Reservoir Rd for 6-8 mi. All year; 14-day limit. 7 sites; 24-ft RV limit. Tbls, toilets, cfga, no drkg wtr, no trash service. Boating, fishing, mountain biking.

FORT JONES (N)

Bridge Flat River Access FREE
Klamath National Forest
21.2 mi W of Fort Jones on Scott River Rd. Free. May-Oct; 14-day limit. 4 dispersed sites; 32-ft RV limit. Tbls, toilets, cfga, no drkg wtr or trash service. Swimming, boating, fishing, hiking, whitewater rafting. Primarily a backpacker camp for nearby Marble Mountain Wilderness. Scott River, Kelsey Trail. Elev 2000 ft.

Indian Scotty $10
Klamath National Forest
17.7 mi W of Fort Jones on Scott River Rd; qtr mi SW on FR 44N45; on Scott River. Free 10/15-5/15; $10 rest of year; 14-day limit. 28 sites (RVs under 31 ft) & 1 group site ($50 by reservation). Tbls, toilets, cfga, no drkg wtr during free period. Swimming, fishing, horseshoes. 18 acres.

Mt. Ashland Campground FREE
Klamath National Forest
Atop Mt. Ashland 1 mi W of Mt. Ashland Ski Resort, 10.5 mi off I-5 on FR 20 (narrow & winding). Free. May-Oct; 14-day limit. 9 sites; 28-ft RV limit. Tbls, toilets, cfga, no drkg wtr or trash service. Access to Pacific Coast Trail.

Scott Mountain FREE
Klamath National Forest
33 mi S of Fort Jones on Hwy 3. Free. All year; 14-day limit. 5 sites. Tbls, toilet, cfga, no drkg wtr, no trash service. Hiking. Pacific Crest Trail passes nearby, making this camp a nice resting place for hikers.

FRAZIER PARK (S)

Chuchupate Campground $10
Los Padres National Forest
3 mi from the Chuchupate ranger station off Frazier Mountain Rd (FR 8N04). Previous fee $5 Adventure Pass; now $10 with federal senior pass; others pay $20. May-Oct; 14-day limit. 30 sites; 24-ft RV limit. Tbls, toilets, cfga, no drkg wtr. Hiking, hunting. Elev 6000 ft.

Chula Vista Campground FREE
Los Padres National Forest
17 mi W on CR FH95 (Mt. Pinos Hwy) to parking lot on Mt. Pinos. Free. All year; 14-day limit. Spaces for 12 self-contained RVs in parking lot; 4 acres. Tbls, toilets, cfga, drkg wtr. Picnicking. Elev 8300 ft. No campfires in parking lot. Lots of star-gazing at this campground.

Halfmoon Campground $5
Los Padres National Forest
3.4 mi W of Frazier Park on CR FG95; 20.4 mi SW on CR 9N03 (Lockwood Valley Rd); 8.8 mi SE on FR 7N03 (Grade Valley Mutau Rd) to its end. $5 daily or $30 annually. 5/1-11/30; 14-day limit. 10 sites on 10 acres (RVs under 22 ft). Tbls, cfga, firewood, no drkg wtr. Picnicking. Elev 4700 ft. Usually accessible by 2WD; not accessible in wet weather. Along Little Piru Creek.

McGill Campground $10
Los Padres National Forest
W of Frazier Park on Frazier Mountain & Cutty Valley Rd; left for 6 mi on Mt Pinos Rd. $10 with federal senior pass; others pay $20. About 5/15-11/15; 14-day limit. 78 sites (30-ft RV limit). Tbls, toilets, cfga, no drkg wtr. Hiking, interpretive trail. Elev 7400 ft; 25 acres. Non-campers pay $10 day use fees.

Mount Pinos $10
Los Padres National Forest
W of Frazier Park on Frazier Mountain & Cutty Valley Rd; left for 4 mi on Mt. Pinos Rd. $10 with federal senior pass; others pay $20. 5/15-10/1; 14-day limit. 19 sites (26 ft RV limit). Tbls, toilets, cfga, no drkg wtr. Elev 7800 ft. 12 acres. Adventure pass charged outside campground. Concession.

Pine Springs $5
Los Padres National Forest
3.4 mi W of Frazier Park on CR FH95 (Frazier Mountain Park Rd); 10.4 mi SW on CR 9N03 (Lockwood Valley Rd); 2.8 mi S on FR 7N03 (Grade Valley Rd); 1 mi W on FR 7N03A; a limited area for RVs because of narrow dirt rd; not accessible during wet weather. $5 daily or $30 annually. 5/15-11/1; 14-day limit. 12 sites on 10 acres (RVs under 22 ft). Tbls, toilets, cfga, no drkg wtr. Picnicking. Elev 5800 ft.

FRESNO (C)

Lost Lake Recreation Area $9
Fresno County Park
19 mi N of Fresno below Friant Dam. Seniors pay $9; others, $25. All year; 14-day limit. 42 sites; 36-ft RV limit. Tbls, toilets, cfga, drkg wtr. Fishing, hiking, birdwatching, nature study, softball field, playground, beach ball facility. 70-Acre primitive nature study area; 38-acre lake.

FURNACE CREEK (C)

Mesquite Spring $7
Death Valley National Park
NW of Furnace Creek on SR 190 to 5 mi S of Scotty's Castle. on Grapevine Rd. $7 with federal senior pass; others pay $14. All year; 30-day limit. 30 sites. Tbls, flush toilets, cfga, drkg wtr, dump.

Sunset $7
Death Valley National Park
In town near visitor center. $7 with federal senior pass; others pay $14. 10/15-4/15; 30-day limit. 270 sites (no RV size limit). Tbls, flush toilets, no cfga, drkg wtr, dump. Nature programs, hiking. Visitor center nearby.

Texas Spring $8
Death Valley National Park
1.5 mi S of Furnace Creek visitor center. $8 with federal senior pass; others pay $16. 10/15-5/10; 30-day limit. 92 sites Tbls, flush toilets, cfga, drkg wtr, dump. Nature programs, hiking, exploring.

GARBERVILLE (N)

Watts Lake Primitive Area   FREE
Six Rivers National Forest
9.5 mi E of Garberville on CR 229 toward Zenia Guard Station, then 17.3 me E on CR 516 and 4 mi N on FR 2S08. Free. June-Oct; 30-day limit. Undesignated primitive

camping area. Space for 2 tents, 3 small RVs. Toilet, no other facilities. Fishing, picnicking.

GASQUET (N)

Big Flat $8
Six Rivers National Forest
Smith River National Recreation Area
8.2 mi SW of Gasquet on US 199; 17.2 mi SE on CR 427; qtr mi N on CR 405; at Hurdygurdy Creek (11 mi NE of Crescent City). $8. MD-9/30; 14-day limit. 23 sites on 8 acres; sites up to 68 ft; 2 pull-through of 90 & 120 ft. Tbls, toilets, cfga, firewood, no drkg wtr or trash service. Swimming, hunting, picnicking, fishing.

Grassy Flat $10
Six Rivers National Forest
Smith River National Recreation Area
4.5 mi E of Gasquet on US 199; above N shore of Middle Fork Smith River. $10. About 6/15-9/30; 14-day limit. 19 sites; 30-ft RV limit. Tbls, toilets, cfga, no drkg wtr. Fishing, kayaking. 3 acres.

North Fork $8
Smith River National Recreation Area
Six Rivers National Forest
2.6 mi W of visitor center in Gasquet on US 199; right on FR 17N49 for 7.7 mi; right (E) on CR 305 for 15 mi, past North Fork bride; follow FR 18N28 to campground; long trip over rocky gravel rds. $8. All year; 14-day limit. 5 sites; 22-ft RV limit. Tbls & toilets, cfga, no drkg wtr or trash service.

Panther Flat $7.50
Smith River National Recreation Area
Six Rivers National Forest
About 3 mi E of Gasquet on US 199; at a flat above Middle Fork of Smith River. $7.50 with federal senior pass; others pay $15. All year; 14-day limit. 39 sites; 40-ft RV limit. Tbls, flush toilets, cfga, drkg wtr, showers. Swimming, fishing.

Patrick Creek $7
Smith River National Recreation Area
Six Rivers National Forest
About 5.6 mi E of Gasquet on US 199; right on rd across from Patrick Creek Lodge; on flat above Middle Fork Smith River. $7 with federal senior pass; others pay $14. About 5/15-9/15; 14-day limit. 13 sites; 35-ft RV limit. Tbls, flush toilets, cfga, drkg wtr. Accessible hiking trail with wheelchair access to river for fishing. Campfire circle built by CCC in 1930s.

Sanger Lake Primitive Area   FREE
Six Rivers National Forest
E of US 199, between Sanger and Young's Peaks on FR 18N07. Free. All year; 30-day limit. Undesignated primitive camping area. No facilities. Fishing, hunting, hiking.

GEORGETOWN (N)

Big Meadows $10
Eldorado National Forest
22 mi E of Georgetown on Wentworth Springs Rd; 27 mi NE on FR 2; camp is 1.5 mi NW of Hell Hole Reservoir. $10. 5/15-10/31; 14-day limit. 54 sites. Tbls, flush & pit toilets, cfga, drkg wtr. Fishing, swimming, boating, hiking, 4WD. Elev 5300 ft.

Dru Barner Campground $8
Eldorado National Forest
7.5 mi E of Georgetown on Wentworth Springs Rd; left (NE) on gravel Bypass Rd (FR 13N16 for 1 mi; 0.5 mi NW on FR 13N58. $8. All year; 14-day limit. 47 sites. Flush toilets, cfga, drkg wtr, tbls. Primarily an equestrian camp; water troughs. Bridle trail nearby. Biking. No motorcycles. Elev 3000 ft. Non-campers pay $3 (or $20 annually).

Stumpy Meadows $12
Eldorado National Forest
17 mi E of Georgetown on Wentworth Springs Rd; at Stumpy Meadows Lake. $12 with federal senior pass; others pay $24. 4/15-11/1; 14-day limit. 40 sites (typically 45 ft). Tbls, toilets, cfga, drkg wtr. Boating(l), fishing, swimming. Elev 4400 ft. Dump near Ponderosa Cove overflow camp($6).

GLENNVILLE (S)

Alder Creek FREE
Sequoia National Forest
Giant Sequoia National Monument
8 mi E of Glennville on SR 155; 3 mi S on FR 25S04 (Alder Creek Rd); paved and dirt rds. Free. 5/1-10/31; 14-day limit. 13 sites (20-ft RV limit). Tbls, cfga, no drkg wtr, toilets or trash service. Fishing, picnicking. Elev 3900 ft; 5 acres. Alder Creek and Cedar Creek.

Frog Meadow FREE
Sequoia National Forest
Giant Sequoia National Monument
26 mi NE of Glennville via SR 155 and FR 90 (paved but narrow road). Free. 6/16-10/15; 14-day limit. 10 sites (RVs under 17 ft). Tbls, toilets, cfga, no drkg wtr or trash service. Elev 7500 ft; 4 acres. Used mostly as fall hunt camp. Mountain biking, hiking.

GORMAN (S)

Dutchman Campground $5
Los Padres National Forest
23 mi S from I-5 on Hungry Valley Rd & Alamo Rd (FR 7N01--rough dirt rd). $5 daily or $30 annually. 5/1-10/15; 14-day limit. 8 sites (16-ft RV limit). Tbls, toilets, cfga, no drkg wtr. Pack out trash. Elev 4800 ft. OHV area.

Goldhill Camping Area $5
Los Padres National Forest
10 mi Se of Gorman (about 6 mi from Hungry Valley SVRA)

on FR 8N01 (Gold Hill Rd); next to Piru Creek. $5 daily or $30 annually. All year; 14-day limit. About 17 sites; 26-ft RV limit. Dispersed cfga, sometimes portable toilets, no other facilities, no tbls, no drkg wtr. Primarily used by motorcyclists. Elev 4000 ft. W of Hungry Valley State Vehicular Recreation Area.

Hungry Valley $10
State Vehicular Recreation Area
1 mi N of Gorman on Peace Valley Rd. $10 plus entry fee. All year; 15-day limit. 150 primitive sites on 2,000 acres. Tbls, toilets, cfga, no drkg wtr, shade ramadas. Off road vehicle area. Hiking. 19,000 acres.

Kings Campground $5
Los Padres National Forest
8 mi SE of Gorman on FR 8N01; qtr mi S on access rd. $5 daily or $30 annually. 5/1-11/15; 14-day limit. 7 RV sites; 3 tent sites. Tbls, toilets, cfga, no drkg wtr. Swimming. Hungry Valley State Vehicular Recreation Area (4WD area) nearby. Elev 4200 ft.

Los Alamos Campground $10
Angeles National Forest
8 mi S of Gorman on I-5; W at Smokey Bear Rd exit, follow signs; near Pyramid Lake. $10 with federal senior pass; others pay $20. All year; 14-day limit. 93 sites; some group sites; 26-ft RV limit. Tbls, flush toilets, cfga, drkg wtr, dump. Boating(l), fishing. Launch at Emigrant Landing. Elev 3600 ft. Non-campers pay day use fees. Concession-managed.

GRANT GROVE (C)

Big Meadows FREE
Sequoia National Forest
Giant Sequoia National Monument
1.4 mi S of Grant Grove on SR 180; 6.5 mi SE on US FH78 (General's Hwy); 4.4 mi NE on FR 14S11 (Horse Corral Rd). Paved access rds. Free. 5/15-10/1; 14-day limit. 45 sites (big RV rigs okay at some). Tbls, toilets, cfga, no drkg wtr. Wtr available at Big Meadow Guard Station, 1.5 mi W. Fishing. Elev 7600 ft; 15 acres. Big Meadow Creek.

Buck Rock FREE
Sequoia National Forest
Giant Sequoia National Monument
1.4 mi S of Grant Grove on SR 180; 6.5 mi SE on US FH78 (General's Hwy); 3.2 mi NE on FR 14S01 (Horse Corral Rd); .2 mi N on FR 13S04 (Buck Rock Rd). Paved and dirt rds. Free. 5/15-10/1; 14-day limit. 5 sites on 2 acres (RVs under 16 ft). Tbls, toilets, cfga, no drkg wtr. Wtr available, public phone at Big Meadow Guard Station, 1 mi E. Fishing.

Landslide Campground $9
Sequoia National Forest
6 mi NE of Grant Grove on SR 180; 7 mi S on Hume Rd (FR 13S09) past Hume Lake, then up Tenmile Rd, 1.5 mi past

Tenmile Campground. $9 with federal senior pass; others pay $18. 5/15-10/1; 14-day limit. 9 sites (RVs under 16 ft). Tbls, toilets, cfga, nondrinkable spring wtr. Elev 5800 ft; 2 acres.

Tenmile Campground $10
Sequoia National Forest
Giant Sequoia National Monument
6 mi NE of Grant Grove on SR 180; 7 mi S on Hume Rd (FR 13S09), around Hume Lake and up Tenmile Rd. $10 with federal senior pass; others pay $20. About 5/10-9/15; 14-day limit. Sites free off-season, but 4x4 needed during snow conditions; closed during winter of 2016-17. 13 sites (RVs under 23 ft). Tbls, toilets, cfga, no drkg wtr.

Upper Stony Creek $10.50
Sequoia National Forest
Giant Sequoia National Monument
13 mi SE of Grant Grove on General's Hwy. $10.50 base with federal senior pass; others pay $21 base, $23 for premium locations ($11.50 with senior pass). MD-LD; 14-day limit. 23 sites; 22-ft RV limit. Tbls, flush toilets, cfga, drkg wtr. Hiking, horseback riding, biking in Jennie Lakes Wilderness.

GROVELAND (C)
Cherry Valley $11
Stanislaus National Forest
5 mi E of Groveland on SR 120; left on Cherry Lake Rd for 20 mi to Cherry Lake. $11 with federal senior pass; others pay $22. About 5/15-9/15; 14-day limit 45 sites; 22-ft RV limit. Tbls, pit toilets, cfga, drkg wtr. Fishing, hiking. Note: Closed in 2014 due to fire damages; due to re-open 2017; check current status with rangers or concessioner (American Land & Leisure) before arrival.

Dimond O Campground $12
Stanislaus National Forest
16 mi E of Groveland on SR 120; left on Evergreen Rd for 4 mi; on left at Middle Fork Tuolumne River. $12 with federal senior pass; others pay $24. About 5/1-9/30; 14-day limit. 36 sites (typically 45 ft). Tbls, pit toilets, cfga, drkg wtr. Fishing. Managed by American Land & Leisure.

Lost Claim $9.50
Stanislaus National Forest
12 mi E of Groveland on SR 120. $9.50 with federal senior pass; others pay $19. 5/15-9/15; 14-day limit. 10 sites (22-ft RV limit, but not recommended for RVs). Tbls, toilets, cfga, drkg wtr, cold showers. Elev 3100 ft; 5 acres. Managed by American Land & Leisure.

Lumsden Campground   FREE
Stanislaus National Forest
7.5 mi E of Groveland on SR 120; .9 mi N on CR 6210 (CR A36210, Ferretti Rd); 4.3 mi E on FR 1N10. Free. All year; 14-day limit. 10 sites; RVs not recommended on FR 1N10. Tbls, toilets, cfga, no drkg wtr, no trash service. Swimming, picnicking, fishing, hiking. Elev 1500 ft; 4 acres. 5 mi of dirt rd (one lane); very steep, not advised for trailers or large motorhomes; use extreme caution. 12 mi from Groveland Ranger Station. On Tuolumne River.

Lumsden Bridge   FREE
Stanislaus National Forest
7.5 mi E of Groveland on SR 120; .9 mi N on CR 6210 (CR A3610, Ferretti Rd); 5.5 mi E on FR 1N10. Free. 4/15-12/15; 14-day limit. 9 sites; RVs not recommended on FR 1N10. Tbls, toilets, cfga, no drkg wtr or trash service. Swimming, hiking, picnicking, fishing. Elev 1500 ft; 2 acres. 16 mi from Groveland Ranger station. 5 mi of one-lane dirt rd, very steep, not advisable for trailers or large motorhomes. Tuolumne River. RV dump station at Naco West, S of Hwy 120, 19 mi E of Groveland; $5 use fee.

South Fork   FREE
Stanislaus National Forest
7.5 mi E of Groveland on SR 120; .9 mi N on CR 6210 (CR A36210, Ferretti Rd); 4.6 mi E on FR 1N10 (RVs not recommended. Free. 4/15-12/15; 14-day limit. 8 sites. Tbls, toilets, cfga, no drkg wtr. Hiking, swimming, picnicking, fishing. Elev 1500 ft; 2 acres. River; rafting. Lumsden Rd not suitable for large RVs. Note: Closed by fire in 2014; check current status before arrival.

Sweetwater Campground $12
Stanislaus National Forest
15 mi W of Groveland on SR 120. $12-$13 with federal senior pass; others pay $24-26. About 5/1-LD; 14-day limit. 12 sites; 32-ft RV limit. Tbls, portable toilets, cfga, drkg wtr. Managed by American Land & Leisure.

The Pines $9.50
Stanislaus National Forest
9 mi E of Groveland on SR 120. $9.50 with federal senior pass; others pay $19. All year; 14-day limit (sites free during Oct-Apr, but no wtr). 12 sites; 32-ft RV limit. Tbls, toilets, cfga, drkg wtr. Elev 3200 ft. Managed in-season by American Land & Leisure.

HAPPY CAMP (N)
Curly Jack $7.50
Klamath National Forest
In Happy Camp, 1 mi S of SR 96 on Curly Jack Rd; at Klamath River. $7.50 with federal senior pass; others pay $15. 5/15-10/15; 14-day limit. 16 sites (42-ft RV limit at most sites; 60-ft at 2 sites). Tbls, toilets, cfga, drkg wtr. Fishing, swimming. Group camping $50.

Norcross Campground   FREE
Klamath National Forest
14 mi S of Happy Camp on Elk Creek Rd (FR 16N605), following signs. Free. All year; 14-day limit. 4 sites. Tbls,

toilets, cfga, no drkg wtr (except for horses), no trash service. Hiking, horseback riding. Camp is staging area for various trails into Marble Mountain Wilderness. Elev 2400 ft. Reconstructed after fire in 2008; now has 4 large corrals, horse trailer parking, new sites & toilets.

West Branch   FREE
Klamath National Forest
12 mi N of Happy Camp on Indian Creek Rd (FR 48); at West Branch Indian Creek. Free. All year; 14-day limit. 10 sites on 15 acres (RVs under 29 ft). Tbls, toilets, no drkg wtr or trash service.

HOLLISTER (C)
Hollister Hills $10
State Vehicular Recreation Area
6 mi S of Hollister on SR 156; 6 mi on Cienega Rd, then 4 mi S on Union Rd. $10 plus entry fee. All year; 14-day limit. 125 primitive sites. Tbls, flush toilets, cfga, drkg wtr, showers. Off-road vehicle area; motorcycle & 4WD trails. 6,627 acres.

HOLTVILLE (S)
Walker Park   FREE
Imperial County park
W edge of Holtville on SR 115 off I-80. Free. All year; 3-day limit. 50 sites on 5 acres; pull-through spaces. Tbls, toilets, cfga, drkg wtr. Picnicking, fishing. Golf nearby.

HORNBROOK (N)
Camp Creek Campground   FREE
Pacific Power
Bureau of Land Management
From I-5 exit 789 near Hornbrook, 12.5 mi E on Copco Cr; pass fish hatchery & Iron Gate reservoir dam; last half mi very steep & winding; along Klamath River. All year; 14-day limit. 22 RV sites; 30-ft RV limit. Toilets, cfga, drkg wtr, dump. Boating (dl), fishing, swimming beach.

Juniper Point Camp   FREE
Pacific Power
Bureau of Land Management
11.5 mi NE of Hornbrook on co rd (Hornbrook is 12 mi N of Yreka on I-5); last half mi steep & winding; at Iron Gate Reservoir. Free. May-Oct; 14-day limit. 9 sites. Toilets, tbls, cfga, no drkg wtr. Swimming. Klamath River. Fishing. Half mi from Mirror Cove Camp.

Mirror Cove Camp   FREE
Pacific Power
Bureau of Land Management
11 mi E of Hornbrook on co rd (Hornbrook is 12 mi N of Yreka on I-5); at W side of Iron Gate Reservoir. Free. May-Oct. 10 sites. Toilets, tbls, cfga, no drkg wtr. Swimming; fishing, boating (l). Half mi from Juniper Point.

HORSE CREEK (N)
Sarah Totten $10
Klamath National Forest
6 mi SW of Horse Creek on SR 96 (qtr mi E of Hamburg); on Klamath River. $10. All year; 14-day limit; free during 10/16-5/14 but no wtr or trash service. 8 sites (28-ft RV limit at most sites; 2 sites, 45-ft). Tbls, toilets, cfga, drkg wtr. Group camping ($50) by reservation. Fishing. 5 acres.

IDYLLWILD (S)
Boulder Basin $10
San Bernardino National Forest
9 mi N of Idyllwild on Hwy 243; 6 mi E on unpaved FR 4S01 (Black Mountain Rd). $10. 5/15-11/15; 14-day limit. 34 sites (22-ft RV limit). Tbls, toilets, cfga, drkg wtr. Hiking trails. Elev 7300 ft.

Dark Canyon $12
San Bernardino National Forest
8 mi N of Idyllwild on Hwy 243; 3 mi on FR 4S02 (Stone Creek Campground Rd); at North Fork San Jacinto River. $12. 4/15-10/15; 14-day limit. 17 sites (22-ft RV limit). Tbls, toilets, cfga, drkg wtr. Hiking trails, no fishing access.

Fern Basin $10
San Bernardino National Forest
8 mi N of Idyllwild on Hwy 243; 1 mi on FR 4S02 past Stone Creek Campground. $10. 5/15-10/15; 14-day limit. 22 sites (15-ft RV limit). Tbls, toilets, cfga, drkg wtr. Hiking trails. Elev 5300 ft.

Marion Mountain $10
San Bernardino National Forest
8 mi N of Idyllwild on Hwy 243; 2 mi on FR 4S02 past Stone Creek Campground & Fern Basin Camp. $10. 5/15-10/15; 14-day limit. 24 sites (15-ft RV limit). Tbls, toilets, cfga, drkg wtr. Hiking trails. Elev 6600 ft.

INDEPENDENCE (C)
Lower Gray's Meadow $10.50
Inyo National Forest
5 mi W of Independence on CR 13S02 (Onion Valley Rd). $10.50 with federal senior pass; others pay $21. About 3/15-10/15; 14-day limit. 52 sites; 32-ft RV limit. Tbls, flush toilets, cfga, drkg wtr, bear boxes. Fishing, swimming. Elev 6000 ft. 15 acres.

Oak Creek   CLOSED
Inyo National Forest
1.5 mi NW of Independence on US 395; 2.5 mi W on CR 13S04 (North Oak Creek Dr). Permanently decommissioned as campground.

Onion Valley Campground $10.50
Inyo National Forest
13 mi W of Independence on CR 13S02 (Onion Valley Rd).

$10.50 with federal senior pass; others pay $21. About 6/1-10/1; 14-day limit. 29 sites; 25-ft RV limit. Tbls, pit toilets, cfga, drkg wtr, bear lockers. Fishing, hiking. Elev 9200 ft. 8 acres.

Upper Gray's Meadow $10.50
Inyo National Forest
6 mi W of Independence on CR 13S02 (Onion Valley Rd). $10.50 with federal senior pass; others pay $21. 3/15-10/15; 14-day limit. 35 sites; 40-ft RV limit. Tbls, flush toilets, cfga, drkg wtr, bear lockers.

INYOKERN (S)

Chimney Creek   FREE
Bureau of Land Management
15 mi N of Inyokern on US 395; 13 mi W on CR 152 (Nine Mile Canyon-Kennedy Meadow Rd). Free; donations accepted. All year; 14-day limit; may be inaccessible in winter. 32 sites on 40 acres (25-ft RV limit). Tbls, no drkg wtr, cfga; limited facilities in winter. Elev 5700 ft. Pack out trash. Pacific Crest Trail 2 mi. Horses & pets welcome. Host Apr-Sept.

Fossil Falls Campground $6
Bureau of Land Management
About 50 mi N of Inyokern on E side of US 395; use Cinder Rd exit; in Mojave Desert at foot of eastern Sierra Nevada. $6. All year; 14-day limit. 11 sites. Tbls, toilets, cfga, drkg wtr, no trash service. Hiking, exhibits, rockhounding. Hike to 40-ft waterfall, best viewed late fall, winter, early spring.

Kennedy Meadows   DONATION
Inyo National Forest
Giant Sequoia National Monument
3 mi NW of Inyokern on US 395; 26 mi NW on Nine Mile Canyon Rd, becoming Kennedy Meadows Rd (paved and dirt rd sometimes steep). Formerly $17, now free with donations requestede. All year; 14-day limit. 39 sites; 30-ft RV limit. Tbls, toilets, cfga, firewood, no drkg wtr or trash service. Swimming, fishing. Elev 6100 ft; 15 acres. S fork Kern River. Administered by Sequoia National Forest. Poor cell phone service.

Long Valley   FREE
Bureau of Land Management
15 mi N of Inyokern on US 395; 26 mi NW on CR 152 (Nine Mile Canyon Rd). Free; donations accepted. All year; 14-day limit; may be inaccessible in winter. 13 sites on 15 acres. Toilets, tbls, cfga, no drkg wtr. Limited facilities in winter. Fishing, hiking, horseback riding/rental. Elev 9000 ft. Nature trails. Long Valley Creek. Located in Lamont Meadows-Long Valley Recreation Area. Small pets. Pack out trash. Trailhead for 3-mile trail down South Fork of Kern River. Elev 5200 ft. Note: in early 2014, a portion of the Chimney Peak Back Country Byway N of campground was washed out & closed.

Short Canyon   FREE
Bureau of Land Management
NW of Inyokern on US 395 to Leliter Rd exit (1 mi past SR 14 jct); on W side of hwy, follow Short Canyon signs, taking graded dirt rd W to Powerline Rd, then half mi S to jct with BLM Route SE138; follow that graded rd to Short Canyon parking lot & trailhead. Free dispersed primitive camping; no facilities, no drkg wtr, no trash service. Hiking, horseback riding, birdwatching, photography. Spectacular wildflower displays in spring -- bright yellow coreopsis, orange California poppies, white buckwheats, purple gilias, blue phacelias.

Spangler Hills   FREE
Off-Highway Use Area
Bureau of Land Management
E of Inyokern on SR 178 into Ridgecrest, then S on College Heights Blvd to OHV area's N boundary. Free. All year; 14-day limit. Primitive undesignated sites on 57,000-acre public area designated for OHV activities. No facilities; no drkg wtr. Hiking, horseback riding. Area is home to protected desert tortoise. Most popular OHV staging area is E of Trona-Red Mountain Rd on BLM Rt RM143; large camping area available there.

Troy Meadow $8.50
Sequoia National Forest
Giant Sequoia National Monument
3 mi NW on Inyokern on US 395; 32 mi NW on Nine Mile Canyon Rd, becoming Kennedy Meadows Rd (paved and dirt rd sometimes steep). $8.50 with federal senior pass; others pay $17. 6/1-11/15; 14-day limit. 73 sites (24-ft RV limit due to rds). Tbls, toilets, cfga, piped drkg wtr available 5/15-9/30. Fishing (in season with barbless flies only). Elev 7800 ft; 15 acres. No trash pickup.

JACKSON (C)

Middle Fork Consumnes $8
Eldorado National Forest
32 mi E of Jackson on Hwy 88; 10 mi N on Cat Creek Rd (FR 63). $8 with federal senior pass; others pay $15. 5/1-11/15; 14-day limit. 19 sites (4 for RVs, typically 45 ft). Toilets, cfga, no drkg wtr. Swimming, fishing. Elev 5600 ft.

Pardoes Point $11
Eldorado National Forest
40 mi E of Jackson on Hwy 88; right on Bear River Reservoir Rd for 5 mi; on SE shore of Lower Bear River Reservoir. $11 with federal senior pass; others pay $22. 5/1-11/15; 14-day limit. 10 sites, typically 25 ft. Tbls, toilets, cfga, drkg wtr. Fishing, boating (cartop boat launch), picnicking, 4WD.

JUNCTION CITY (N)

Junction City $10
Bureau of Land Management
Shasta-Trinity National Forest
1.5 mi W of Junction City on Hwy 299; on Trinity River. $10

during 5/1-11/1; 14-day limit. 22 sites (40-ft RV limit). Tbls, toilets, cfga, drkg wtr. Fishing. Elev 1500 ft. Non-campers pay $2 day use fee.

JUNE LAKE (C)

Aerie Crag $10
Inyo National Forest
5.9 mi W of June Lake on SR 158; right at RV Campground sign; on ridge above Rush Creek; RV camping only. $10 with federal senior pass; others pay $20. About 4/15-10/31; 3-day limit. 10 RV sites. Tbls, flush toilets, cfga, no drkg wtr. Dump stations at Mobile station in June Lake ($5) and nearby Fern Creek Lodge (free). Overflow camping area open only when other campgrounds are full.

Glass Creek FREE
Inyo National Forest
2.4 mi NE of June Lake on SR 158 (June Lake Loop Rd); 6 mi SE on US 395; .2 mi W on FR 2S24. Free. 5/15-11/1; 21-day limit. 66 sites (RVs under 46 ft). Tbls, pit toilets, cfga, no drkg wtr, bear boxes. Hiking, fishing. Elev 7600 ft; 15 acres. Glass Creek.

Gull Lake Campground $11.50
Inyo National Forest
Just W of June Lake on SR 158; on S side of Gull Lake. $11.50 with federal senior pass; others pay $23. About 4/15-11/1; 14-day limit. 11 sites; 30-ft RV limit. Tbls, flush toilets, cfga, drkg wtr, bear locker. Dump($) at Shell station, jct of US 395 & SR 158.

Hartley Springs FREE
Inyo National Forest
2 mi NE of June Lake on SR 158; 2 mi SE on US 395; right at Hartley Springs sign, then bear right at Y onto FR 2548 for nearly 1 mi; final leg of rd is rough. Free. 6/1-10/1; 21-day limit. 25 sites; 45-ft RV limit. Tbls, toilets, cfga, no drkg wtr. Elev 8400 ft.

June Lake Campground $11.50
Inyo National Forest
In town of June Lake just W of fire station. $11.50 with federal senior pass; others pay $23. About 4/15-10/31; 14-day limit. 28 sites; 25-ft RV limit. Tbls, flush toilets, cfga, drkg wtr, bear lockers. Fishing.

Reversed Creek $11.50
Inyo National Forest
From June Lake, E on SR 158 about 2 mi. $11.50 with federal senior pass; others pay $22. About 5/15-10/31; 14-day limit. 17 sites; 30-ft RV limit. Tbls, flush toilets, cfga, drkg wtr, bear lockers.

Silver Lake $11.50
Inyo National Forest
About 4 mi W of June Lake on SR 158; at S end of lake. $11.50 with federal senior pass; others pay $22. About

4/15-11/15; 14-day limit. 63 sites; 40-ft RV limit. Tbls, flush toilets, cfga, drkg wtr, bear lockers, interpretive programs, amphitheater. Boating(l), fishing, biking, hiking trail.

KERNVILLE (S)

Brush Creek Campground FREE
Sequoia National Forest
20 mi N of Kernville on CR PM99 (Sierra Hwy--along Kern River). Paved rd. Free. All year; 14-day limit. About 6 undeveloped sites (RVs under 22 ft). Toilets, cfga, firewood, no tbls, no drkg wtr, no trash service. Fishing (in Brush Creek using only barbless flies). Elev 3800 ft; 3 acres. Campfire permit required. Well suited for self-contained RVs.

Camp 9 Recreation Area $8.50
Sequoia National Forest
Giant Sequoia National Monument
5 mi S of Kernville on Sierra Way Rd (SR 99); on E shore of 11,000-acre Lake Isabella. $8.50 for seniors with federal senior pass; others pay $17. All year; 14-day limit. 109 primitive sites; no RV size limit. Tbls, flush toilets, cfga, drkg wtr, dump ($10 per use), beach, fish cleaning station. Boating(ld), fishing.

Chico Flat Campground FREE
Sequoia National Forest
From Kernville, N on CR 521, becoming M-99; at Kern River. Free. All year; 14-day limit. Undeveloped campsites with portable toilets (summer), cfga, no drkg wtr. Campfire permit required. Fishing, hiking.

Corral Creek FREE
Sequoia National Forest
8.9 mi N of Kernville on CR PM99; along the Kern River. Free. All year; 14-day limit. Undeveloped sites (RVs under 22 ft); suited for self-contained RVs. Tbls, portable toilets, cfga, firewood, no drkg wtr. Picnicking, swimming, fishing. Elev 3000 ft; 5 acres. Campfire permit required.

Fish Creek Campground $11
Sequoia National Forest
From Kernville, 54 mi NE on Mtn Rd 99; E on Sherman Pass Rd (FR 22S05); at Crag Peak. $11 with federal senior pass; others pay $22. 6/1-11/30; 14-day limit. 40 sites (12 for RVs up to 27 ft). Tbls, pit toilets, cfga, piped spring drkg wtr, no trash service. Horseback riding; picnicking; fishing (in season with barbless flies only). Elev 7400 ft; 2 acres. Fish Creek.

Greenhorn Mountain Park $12
Kern County Parks & Recreation Department
About 9 mi E of Kernville on SR 155; within Sequoia National Forest. $12 for seniors at 70 non-elec sites; others pay $18. May-Oct; 21-day limit; closed in winter by snow. Tbls, flush & pit toilets, cfga, drkg wtr, showers. Hiking. Amphitheater.

Horse Meadow Campground $8.50
Sequoia National Forest
Giant Sequoia National Monument
20 mi N of Kernville on Sierra Way; right on Sherman Pass Rd for 6.5 mi; right for 4 mi at sign for Horse Meadow; follow signs 3 mi on dirt rd. $8.50 with federal senior pass; others pay $17. 6/1-11/30; 14-day limit. 41 sites (22-ft RV limit). Tbls, toilets, cfga, drkg wtr, no trash service. Horseback riding, hiking, fishing. Bear storage rules.

Limestone Campground $10.50
Sequoia National Forest
Giant Sequoia National Monument
19 mi NW of Kernville on Sierra Way Rd. $10.50 with federal senior pass; others pay $21, or $23 on holiday weekends ($11.50 with senior pass). 4/1-11/30; 14-day limit. 22 sites (30-ft RV limit). Tbls, toilets, cfga, no drkg wtr. Fishing, hiking. Along the Kern River. Elev 3800 ft.

South Fork Recreation Area $10
Sequoia National Forest
From Kernville, S on CR 521 (Sierra Way); W on SR 178 to access rd; near mouth of South Fork of Kern River on S side of Lake Isabella. $10 day use pass required. Tbls, flush toilets, cfga, drkg wtr, information station. Boating(ld), fishing.

KLAMATH RIVER (N)
Beaver Creek   FREE
Klamath National Forest
Half mi E of Klamath River on SR 96; 5 mi N on FR 11 (Beaver Creek Rd). Free. May-Oct; 14-day limit. 8 sites; 28-ft RV limit. Tbls, toilets, cfga, no drkg wtr or trash service. Fishing, hiking. Elev 2400 ft.

LA CANADA-FLINTRIDGE (S)
Buckhorn Campground $12
Angeles National Forest
From I-210 at La Canada, 35 mi N from Angeles Crest Hwy exit (Hwy 2). $12. 4/1-11/15; 14-day limit. 38 sites; 18-ft RV limit. Tbls, toilets, cfga, drkg wtr. High Desert National Recreation Trail to backcountry; Cooper Canyon 1.5-mi hike. Elev 6300 ft.

Chilao Recreation Area $12
Angeles National Forest
From I-210 at La Canada, 26 mi N from Angeles Crest Hwy exit (Hwy 2). $12. 4/1-11/15; 14-day limit. 84 sites; 40-ft RV limit. Tbls, toilets, cfga, limited drkg wtr. Elev 5300 ft. Visitor center closed indefinitely.

Horse Flats Campground $12
Angeles National Forest
From I-210 at La Canada, 29 mi N from Angeles Crest Hwy exit (Hwy 2); left at Santa Clara Divide Rd at Three Points for 3 mi. $12. Apr-Nov; 14-day limit. 26 sites (20-ft RV limit). Tbls, toilets, cfga, no drkg wtr. 2 corrals, hitching rails, water trough. Bridle trails. Elev 5700 ft.

Messenger Flats Campground
Angeles National Forest
From I-210 exit 20 at La Canada, 9 mi N on Angeles Crest Hwy (SR 2); left on Angeles Forest Hwy (CR N3) for 12 mi to Mill Creek Summit; turn left on Santa Clara Divide Rd for 9 mi. $12. All year; 14-day limit. 10 sites. Tbls, toilets, cfga, no drkg wtr, 2 horse corrals. Hiking, horseback riding; adjacent to Pacific Crest Trail.

Monte Cristo Campground $12
Angeles National Forest
From I-210 at La Canada, 9 mi N from Angeles Crest Hwy exit (Hwy 2); left on CR N3 (Angeles Forest Highway) for 9 mi. $12. All year 14-day limit. 19 sites (30-ft RV limit). Tbls, toilets, cfga, drkg wtr. Elev 3600 ft.

LA GRANGE (C)
LaGrange OHV Regional Park $10
Stanislaus County Dept. of Parks & Recreation
From LaGrange at SR 132 (about 18 mi E of Modesto), N on N. LaGrange Rd to park; at S shore of Tuolumne River. $10 for seniors at sites without hookups ($25 non-seniors). All year; 15-day limit. Tbls, flush toilets, cfga, drkg wtr, no showers. 126 acres devoted to OHV activities -- motorcycles, mini-bikes, ATVs, 4WD trucks, dune buggies. Motocross track, under-80cc training area.

LAKE ALPINE (N)
Mosquito Lakes Campground $8
Stanislaus National Forest
6.6 mi NE of Lake Alpine on SR 4; across rd from Mosquito Lakes. $8. 6/1-11/1; 48-hr limit. 11 sites; 40-ft RV limit. Toilets tbls, cfga, no drkg wtr. Fishing, boating. Elev 8260 ft. Campfire permit required. Primarily day-use area, but limited camping.

Stanislaus River Campground $12
Stanislaus National Forest
7 mi S of Lake Alpine on Hwy 4, pass Tamarack; 4 mi S on Spicer Reservoir Rd. $12 ($6 when water shut off). 6/1-10/31; 14-day limit. 25 sites (35-ft RV limit). Tbls, toilets, cfga, drkg wtr. Fishing, boating; on North Fork of Stanislaus River.

Utica/Union Reservoirs Campgrounds $8
Stanislaus National Forest
From Lake Alpine, mi S on SR 4; 3 mi SE on FR 7N01; 2 mi E on FR 7N38 (Spicer Reservoir Rd), then either NE on FR 7N75 to Union Reservoir or N on FR 7N17 to Utica Reservoir. $8 with federal senior pass at lakefront sites; others pay $16. Near Utica Reservoir, 11 sites at Sandy Flats, 12 sites at Rocky Point; near Union Reservoir, 18 sites at Union West, 11 sites at Union East. No facilities except cfga, toilets, but campgrounds under development.

LAKE ELSINORE (S)

Blue Jay Campground $10
Cleveland National Forest
5.7 SW of Lake Elsinore on SR 74, then about 5 mi NW on North Main Divide Rd following signs. $10 with federal senior pass; others pay $20. All year; 14-day limit. 50 sites; 20-ft RV limit. Tbls, toilets, cfga, drkg wtr. Biking, hiking. Elev 3400 ft.

El Cariso Campground $7.50
Cleveland National Forest
5.9 mi SW of Lake Elsinore on SR 74. $7.50 with federal senior pass; others pay $15. May-Oct; 14-day limit. 24 sites; 22-ft RV limit. Tbls, toilets, cfga, drkg wtr. Hiking.

Upper San Juan Camp $9
Cleveland National Forest
About 10 mi SW of Lake Elsinore on SR 74. $9 with federal Senior Pass; others pay $18. May-Nov; 14-day limit. 18 sites; 32-ft RV limit. Tbls, toilets, cfga, drkg wtr. Biking, hiking, horseback riding.

Wildomar Campground $7.50
Cleveland National Forest
5.7 mi SW of Lake Elsinore on SR 74; 10 mi E on Killen Trail Rd. (narrow last half mi). $7.50 with federal senior pass; others pay $15. All year; 14-day limit. 11 sites; 22-ft RV limit. Tbls, toilets, cfga, well drkg wtr. Hiking, OHV trails. Elev 2400 ft.

LAKE HUGHES (S)

Cottonwood Campground $5
Angeles National Forest
1.5 mi S of Lake Hughes on Lake Hughes Rd. $5 daily or $30 annually. All year; 14-day limit. 22 sites. Tbls, toilets, cfga, no drkg wtr. OHV trails in area. Closed in early 2017; call 661-269-2808 for current status.

Sawmill Campground $5
Angeles National Forest
5.4 mi W of Lake Hughes on CR N2 (Elizabeth Lake-Pine Canyon Rd); 4.6 mi W on FR 7N23. $5 daily or $30 annually. All year; 14-day limit. 8 sites (RVs under 16 ft). Tbls, toilet, cfga, firewood, no drkg wtr, no trash service. Picnicking. Elev 5200 ft; 4 acres.

Upper Shake $5
Angeles National Forest
5.8 mi W of Lake Hughes on CR N2; 1.8 mi w on FR 7N23; .8 mi SE on FR 7N230. $5 daily or $30 annually. 5/1-11/30; 14-day limit. 17 sites (22-ft RV limit). Tbls, toilet, cfga, no drkg wtr. Picnicking, hiking. Elev 4300 ft; 4 acres. Closed in early 2017; call 661-269-2808 for current status.

LAKEHEAD (N)

Beehive Point
Shasta-Trinity National Forest
4 mi SE of Lakehead on I-5; 3.7 mi E on gravel rd; on Shasta Lake shoreline. Camping no longer permitted. Concessionaire.

Gregory Beach
Shasta-Trinity National Forest
4.5 mi S of Lakehead on I-5; 2.5 mi SW on CR 7H01 (Salt Creek Rd). On Shasta Lake shore next to Gregory Creek Campground. Camping no longer permitted. Concessionaire.

Gregory Creek $10
Shasta-Trinity National Forest
4.5 mi S of Lakehead on I-5; 2.5 mi SW on CR 7H01 (Salt Creek Rd); adjacent to Gregory Beach dispersed area along Upper Sacramento Arm of Shasta Lake. $10. 6/1-9/30; 14-day limit. 18 sites; 16-ft RV limit. Tbls, flush toilets, cfga, drkg wtr, bear lockers. Fishing, boating.

Lower Salt Creek
Shasta-Trinity National Forest
4.5 mi S of Lakehead on I-5; 2 mi SW on CR 7H01 (Salt Creek Rd); on Shasta Lake. Camping no longer permitted. Concessionaire.

LAKE ISABELLA (S)

Auxiliary Dam Recreation Area $10
Sequoia National Forest
Giant Sequoia National Monument
On NW side of Lake Isabella, NE on SR 155 to turnoff for auxiliary dam; follow signs 300 yds NE to camp. $10 vehicle fee or $50 annual Southern Sierra Pass from forest offices or vendors. All year; 14-day limit. Open camping; no RV limit. Tbls, flush toilets, cfga, drkg wtr, dump($10), showers. Fishing.

Hobo Campground $11.50
Sequoia National Forest
From Lake Isabella, SW on Lake Isabella Blvd & Kern River Canyon Rd; at shore of Kern River. $11.50 with federal senior pass; others pay $23, $25 on holiday weekends. 5/15-10/31; 14-day limit. 25 sites; 22-ft RV limit (unsuitable for trailers). Tbls, toilets, cfga, drkg wtr. Fishing, boating, nature trail.

Live Oak North $12
Sequoia National Forest
Giant Sequoia National Monument
6 mi NW of Lake Isabella on SR 155; on W side of lake. $12 with federal senior pass; others pay $24, $26 on holiday weekends. All year; 14-day limit. 60 sites; 30-ft RV limit. Tbls, flush toilets, cfga, drkg wtr, metered showers. Fishing, boating. Live Oak South Camp has only tent sites.

Main Dam Campground   CLOSED
Sequoia National Forest
In Lake Isabella, follow Wofford Heights Blvd (SR 155) N about 1 mi; at SW end of lake. Closed permanently.

Sandy Flat $11.50
Sequoia National Forest
Giant Sequoia National Monument
4 mi E of Lake Isabella on SR 178; right on Borel Rd; right on Old Canyon Rd for about 2 mi; on Lower Kern River. $11.50 with federal senior pass; others pay $23. All year; 14-day limit. 35 sites. Tbls, pit toilets, cfga, drkg wtr. Fishing.

Stine Cove Recreation Area   FREE
Sequoia National Forest
On E side of Lake Isabella off Sierra Way. Free. All year; 14-day limit. Open camping; no RV length limit. Chemical toilets, tbls, cfga, no drkg wtr. Fishing, boating.

LAKESHORE (C)

Badger Flat $11
Huntington Lake Recreation Area
Sierra National Forest
7 mi E of Lakeshore on Kaiser Pass Rd along Rancheria Creek above Huntington Lake. $11 with federal senior pass; others pay $22. 6/15-10/15; 14-day limit. 15 sites (25-ft RV limit). Tbls, toilets, cfga, no drkg wtr; horse facilities. Fishing, hiking, horseback riding. Elev 8200 ft. Note for all Sierra NF sites: Half of Kaiser Pass Rd is rough, narrow, with blind curves; large RVs not recommended.

Portal Forebay $11
High Sierra Recreation Area
Sierra National Forest
13.5 mi NE of Lakeshore on Kaiser Pass Rd; on N shore of Portal Forebay Lake. $11 with federal senior pass; others pay $22. 5/15-10/1; 14-day limit. 11 sites (16-ft RV limit). Tbls, toilets, cfga, bear locker, no drkg wtr. Hiking, fishing.

Sample Meadow Campground   FREE
High Sierra Recreation Area
Sierra National Forest
14 mi E of Lakeshore on CR M2710; 9.8 mi NE on FR 5S80 (Kaiser Pass Rd); 3 mi NW on FR 7S05 (Low Standard access rd); along Kaiser Creek. Free. 5/15-10/1; 14-day limit. 16 sites (RVs under 16 ft). Tbls, toilets, cfga, no drkg wtr or trash service. Fishing, picnicking. Elev 7800 ft.

West Kaiser   FREE
Huntington Lake Recreation Area
Sierra National Forest
Follow directions to Sample Meadows Camp; beyond Sample Meadows, rd becomes a maintained, graded dirt rd for 10 mi; West Kaiser is at turnoff for Kaiser Diggings. Free. 6/1-9/15; 14-day limit. 10 sites; 26-ft RV limit. Tbls, toilets, cfga, no drkg wtr or trash service. Fishing, hiking. Some sites on West Kaiser Creek.

LA PORTE (N)

Black Rock Campground $11.50
Little Grass Valley Recreation Area
Plumas National Forest
8.8 mi N of LaPorte on LaPorte-Quincy Rd; on right. $11.50 with federal senior pass; others pay $23. About MD-10/1; 14-day limit. 21 walk-in tent sites; overnight RV camping in parking lot. Tbls, pit toilets, cfga, drkg wtr. Dump at Little Beaver Campground. Boating(l), fishing, swimming, hiking trail.

Horse Campground $11.50
Little Grass Valley Recreation Area
Plumas National Forest
From LaPorte, 3.7 mi NW on LaPorte-Quincy Rd to South Fork sign at "Y"; bear left, then right at next Y, following signs 3 mi to campground on shore of Little Grass Reservoir. $11.50 for seniors with federal senior pass; others pay $23. 6/15-LD; 14-day limit. 10 gravel equestrian sites. Tbls, pit toilets, cfga, dump, amphitheater, no drkg wtr. Interpretive programs, fishing, boating(l).

Little Beaver $11.50
Little Grass Valley Recreation Area
Plumas National Forest
From LaPorte, 3.7 mi NW on LaPorte-Quincy Rd to South Fork sign at "Y"; bear left, then right at next Y, following signs 0.2 mi. $11.50 base with federal senior pass; others pay $23 base, $25 for lakeside sites. 5/1-10/31; 14-day limit. 120 sites. Tbls, flush toilets, cfga, drkg wtr, dump. Fishing, swimming, boating(l).

Red Feather $11.50
Little Grass Valley Recreation Area
Plumas National Forest
From LaPorte, 3.7 mi NW on LaPorte-Quincy Rd to South Fork sign at "Y"; bear left, then right at next Y, following signs 2.8 mi to campground. $11.50 base with federal senior pass; others pay $23 base, $25 for lakeside sites ($12.50 with senior pass). MD-LD; 14-day limit. 60 paved sites (most 25-35 ft). Tbls, flush toilets, cfga, drkg wtr, amphitheater. Boating(l), fishing, hiking trail, campfire programs.

Running Deer $11.50
Little Grass Valley Recreation Area
Plumas National Forest
From LaPorte, 3.7 mi NW on LaPorte-Quincy Rd to South Fork sign at "Y"; bear left, then right at next Y, following signs 3.3 mi to campground. $11.50 base with federal senior pass; others pay $23 base, $25 for 6 lakeside sites. About MD-10/31; 14-day limit. 40 paved sites (most 30 ft). Tbls, flush toilets, cfga, drkg wtr, amphitheater, dump. Fishing, boating, hiking.

Sly Creek Campground $10
Sly Creek Recreation Area
Plumas National Forest
Following Main St. (LaPorte Rd) in LaPorte, S 13.6 mi to
Sly Creek Recreation Area sign; right on Barton Hill Rd
for 4 mi. $10 with federal senior pass; others pay $20. 23
sites. MD-10/15; 14-day limit. Boat ramp camping only
after 10/15. Tbls, pit toilets, cfga, drkg wtr. Boating(l),
fishing. Managed by South Feather Water & Power.

Strawberry Campground $10
Sly Creek Recreation Area
Plumas National Forest
Following Main St. (LaPorte Rd) in LaPorte, S 10.4 mi;
right at sign 1.7 mi. $10 with federal senior pass; others
pay $20. About 5/15-10/15; 14-day limit. 17 sites. Tbls,
pit toilets, cfga, drkg wtr. Fishing, boating(l), swimming,
waterskiing. Elev 4000 ft; 2 acres. At Sly Creek Reservoir.
Managed by South Feather Water & Power.

Wyandotte Campground $11.50
Little Grass Valley Recreation Area
Plumas National Forest
4.3 mi N of LaPorte; right at Peninsula sign to T intersection and campground sign; right for 0.2 mi. $11.50 with
federal senior pass; others pay $23 ($38 for double sites).
MD-LD; 14-day limit. 28 sites (2 double). Tbls, flush toilets, cfga, drkg wtr, dump (at the T intersection). Fishing,
boating(l), hiking trail.

LEE VINING (C)
Aspen Grove Campground $7
Inyo National Forest
7 mi W of Lee Vining on SR 120. $7 for seniors with federal
senior pass; others pay $14. 5/15-10/1. 45 sites; RV limit
40 ft. Tbls, toilet, cfga, drkg wtr, bear lockers. Fishing.
Elev 7490 ft. Lee Vining Creek.

Big Bend Campground $11
Inyo National Forest
About 12 mi W of Lee Vining on SR 120; near Tuolumne
Meadows entrance to Yosemite National Park. $11 with
federal senior pass; others pay $22. About 6/1-9/10;
14-day limit. 17 sites; 30-ft RV limit. Tbls, toilets, cfga,
drkg wtr, bear lockers.

Cattleguard $7
Inyo National Forest
Just S of Lee Vining on US 395; 3 mi W on SR 120. $7 with
federal senior pass; others pay $14. 5/1-10/15. 16 sites;
30-ft RV limit. Tbls, portable toilets, cfga, no drkg wtr.
Elev 7500 ft. Closed in 2009 for renovations. Check current status before arrival. New amenities & fee increase
to $16 proposed.

Ellery Lake Campground $11
Inyo National Forest
About 9 mi W of Lee Vining on SR 120, at the top of the
Tioga Pass; W side of Ellery Lake. $11 with federal senior
pass; others pay $22. About 6/1-9/10; 14-day limit. 21
sites; 30-ft RV limit. Tbls, pit toilets, cfga, drkg wtr, bear
lockers. Fishing, boating.

Hartley Springs   FREE
Inyo National Forest
11.3 mi N of Lee Vining on US 395; left at Hartley Springs
sign, then bear right at Y onto FR 2548 for nearly 1 mi;
final leg of rd is rough. Free. 6/1-10/1; 14-day limit. 20
sites; 45-ft RV limit. Tbls, toilets, cfga, no drkg wtr, no
bear lockers.

Junction $8.50
Inyo National Forest
10 mi W of Lee Vining on SR 120; .1 N on FR 1N04. $8.50
with federal senior pass; others pay $17. 6/1-10/15;
14-day limit. 13 sites (RVs under 30 ft). Tbls, toilets, cfga,
no drkg wtr, bear lockers. Mountain climbing, fishing,
hiking, boating (ld--1 mi). Elev 9600 ft; 5 acres. Stream.
Scenic. Tioga Lake. E of Yosemite National Park entrance.

Lower Lee Vining Creek $7
Inyo National Forest
5 mi W of Lee Vining on SR 120; N on FR 4 (Saddlebag
Lake Rd). $7 with federal senior pass; others pay $14.
5/1-10/15; 14-day limit. 54 sites (RVs under 25 ft). Tbls, pit
toilet, cfga, bear lockers, no drkg wtr. Fishing, hiking. New
amenities & fee increase to $16 proposed. Elev 7000 ft.

Moraine Overflow Campground $7
Inyo National Forest
From jct with US 395 at Lee Vining, W on SR 120 to site.
$7 with federal senior pass; others pay $14 (new amenities & fee increase to $16 proposed). 27 sites. Not open
unless needed for overflow. Tbls, toilet, cfga, no drkg
wtr. Fishing.

Saddlebag Lake $11
Inyo National Forest
5 mi W of Lee Vining on SR 120; 2 mi N on FR 4 (Saddlebag
Lake Rd). $11 with federal senior pass; others pay $22.
5/15-10/1; 14-day limit. 19 sites for small RVs, 1 group
area. Tbls, pit toilets, cfga, drkg wtr, bear lockers. Fishing,
boating(l).

Tioga Lake $11
Inyo National Forest
About 9 mi W of Lee Vining on SR 120; at NW shore of Tioga
Lake. $11 with federal senior pass; others pay $22. 5/15-
10/1; 14-day limit. 13 sites for small RVs. Tbls, pit toilet,
cfga, drkg wtr, bear lockers. Fishing, boating. Elev 9700 ft.

LEMONCOVE (C)

Horse Creek Campground $10
Kaweah Lake
Corps of Engineers
From dam just NE of Lemoncove, 3 mi E on SR 198; left side, following signs. $10 with federal senior pass at 80 non-elec sites; others pay $20. 4 non-elec equestrian sites, $20-$25. All year; 14-day limit. 35-ft RV limit; 35 pull-through sites. Tbls, flush toilets, cfga, drkg wtr, showers, dump ($5 for non-campers), fish cleaning stations, playground. Hiking, fishing, boating(l), waterskiing, summer campfire programs, interpretive trails.

LEWISTON (N)

Ackerman Campground $8
Shasta-Trinity National Forest
8 mi N of Lewiston on Trinity Dam Blvd, then right on Ackerman Camp Rd; at NW shore of Lewiston Lake. $8 during 4/1-10/31 with federal senior pass; others pay $16. Half fees rest of year, but no wtr services. 14-day limit. 50 sites (40-ft RV limit). Tbls, toilets, flush toilets, cfga, drkg wtr, dump. Fishing, hiking, canoeing, boating (ramps nearby). 20 acres. Managed by Shasta Recreation Co.

Cooper Gulch $6.50
Shasta-Trinity National Forest
4.2 mi N of Lewiston on Trinity Dam Blvd (CR 105); at S side of Lewiston Lake. $6.50 with federal senior pass during 4/1-10/31; others pay $13 (free 11/1-11/15 but no wtr); 14-day limit. 5 sites (16-ft RV limit). Tbls, pit toilets, cfga, drkg wtr. Swimming, boating(l), fishing, canoeing, hiking. 6 acres. Non-campers pay $5 day use.

Tunnel Rock $10
Shasta-Trinity National Forest
7.2 mi N on Trinity Dam Blvd (CR 105); at NW side of Lewiston Lake. $10 when wtr available; $8 without wtr. All year; 14-day limit. 6 sites (2 for small RVs such as fold-out or truck camper). Tbls, toilets, cfga, drkg wtr. Fishing, boating, hiking. Boat launch 1 mi. Elev 1900 ft; 2 acres.

LIKELY (N)

Blue Lake Campground $7
Modoc National Forest
3.2 mi E of Likely on CR 64; right on Blue Lake Rd following signs for 8.5 mi. Free about 10/15-5/15, weather permitting; $7 with federal senior pass rest of year (others pay $14). 14-day limit. 48 sites on 24 acres (32-ft RV limit). Tbls, toilets, cfga, drkg wtr, fishing pier. No wtr during free period. Swimming, fishing, boating(l), hiking & nature trails. Elev 6000 ft. Site sometimes closed due to nesting bald eagles.

Mill Creek Falls Campground $12
Modoc National Forest
3.2 mi E of Likely on CR 64 (Jess Valley Rd); 2.4 mi NE on W. Warner Rd; 2 mi E on Mill Creek access rd. $6 with federal senior pass; others pay $12. Free about 10/15-6/15, weather permitting; 14-day limit. 19 sites (22-ft RV limit). Tbls, toilets, cfga, drkg wtr (no wtr during free period). Picnicking, hiking, fishing, swimming. Elev 5700 ft; 6 acres. Mountains. Dense forest. Trailhead to Mill Creek Falls, Clear Lake and South Warner Wilderness.

Patterson Campground   FREE
Modoc National Forest
3.2 mi E of Likely on CR 64; right on Blue Lake Rd for 7 mi to turnoff to Blue Lake; left, staying on CR 64 for 8 mi to campground. Free. 5/15-10/15; 14-day limit. 6 sites (RVs under 17 ft). Tbls, toilets, cfga, piped drkg wtr. Hiking, picnicking. Elev 7200 ft; 6 acres. Nature trails. Fishing in East Creek.

Soup Springs Campground $12
Modoc National Forest
3.2 mi E of Likely on CR 64; 5 mi NE on Blue Lake Rd/CR 64; 1 mi N on FR 42N24. $12 (or $6 with federal senior pass). 6/15-10/15; free off-season but no wtr. 14 sites on 2 acres (RVs under 22 ft). Tbls, toilets, cfga, piped drkg wtr. Horseback riding; fishing (2 mi). Elev 6800 ft. Near trailheads to South Warner Wilderness. Corrals available.

LITCHFIELD (N)

Belfast Petroglyph Site   FREE
Bureau of Land Management
W of Litchfield on Hwy 395, then 4 mi W on Center Rd; 4.5 mi N on Belfast Rd; no camping within qtr mi of archaeological sites. Free. All year; 14-day limit. Undesignated sites; no facilities, no drkg wtr. Fishing, hiking, hunting, petroglyph viewing.

LONE PINE (C)

Lone Pine $11
Inyo National Forest
6 mi W of Lone Pine on CR 15S02 (Whitney Portal Rd). $11 with federal senior pass; others pay $22. About 4/15-10/15; 14-day limit. 43 sites (32-ft RV limit). Tbls, toilets, cfga, drkg wtr, bearbox. Hiking, fishing, swimming. Elev 6000 ft.

Tuttle Creek $8
Bureau of Land Management
3 mi W of Lone Pine on Whitney Portal Rd; 1.5 mi S on Horseshoe Meadow Rd; W on winding dirt rd. $8. All year; 14-day limit. 30-day permits now available for Tuttle, Horton Creek, Goodale Creek & Crowley for $100. 90-day use permits now replace 8-month seasonal Long-Term Visitor (LTVA) permits at Goodale, Crowley, Horton & Tuttle campgrounds. These permits still cost $300. 83 sites on 50 acres (27 sites for winter season); pull-throughs. Tbls, toilets, cfga, no drkg wtr, dump ($5). Fishing, picnicking, horseback riding (2 horse corrals). Elev 5120 ft. Interagency visitor center at S end of Lone Pine.

Whitney Portal Campground $12
Inyo National Forest
From center of Lone Pine, W at stop light, then 12.5 mi W
on CR15S02 (Whitney Portal Rd). $12 with federal senior
pass; others pay $24. About 4/15-10/15; 14-day limit. 43
sites, typically 30-35 ft. Tbls, toilets, cfga, drkg wtr, bear
lockers. Hiking, fishing.

LONG BARN (C)

Fraser Flat $9.50
Stanislaus National Forest
6 mi NE of Long Barn on SR 108; from Spring Gap turnoff,
3 mi N on FR 4N14 (Fraser Flat Rd), a steep, winding rd for
20-30 mph travel. $9.50 with federal senior pass; others
pay $19. 5/1-10/15; 14-day limit. 38 sites; 22-ft RV limit.
Tbls, toilets, cfga, drkg wtr, accessible fishing piers. Fishing, hunting, hiking trail. Elev 4800; 13 acres. On South
Fork of Stanislaus River. Non-campers pay $5 day use fee.
Managed by Dodge Ridge Corp.

Hull Creek $12
Stanislaus National Forest
12 mi SE of Long Barn on FR 3N01. $12. Fee 6/1-11/1;
14-day limit. 18 sites; 22-ft RV limit. Tbls, toilets, cfga,
drkg wtr. Ranger station (11 mi). Hiking, picnicking, trout
fishing. Secluded meadow with small stream. Elev 5600
ft; 5 acres. Hull Creek (dry in summer).

Sand Bar Flat $12
Stanislaus National Forest
6 mi NE of Long Barn on SR 108; 6 mi N on FR 4N01; 3 mi
NE on FR 4N88; 3 mi N on FR 4N85; on Middle Fork (Lower)
Stanislaus River. Rd not recommended for large RVs. $12.
5/15-11/15 (free until 12/15 but no wtr or service); 14-day
limit. 10 sites (22-ft RV limit). Tbls, toilets, cfga, drkg wtr.
Swimming, fishing. Elev 5400 ft; 6 acres.

Trout Creek Camp $6
Stanislaus National Forest
15 mi E of Long Barn on Rd 3N01; adjacent to Hull Creek.
$6. All year; 14-day limit. Primitive dispersed sites suit-
able for pickup campers, tents, small trailers. Some tbls,
cfga; toilets & trash service seasonally, drkg wtr. Okay to
camp overnight with horses. Campfire permit required.
OHV area.

LOS BANOS (C)

Cottonwood Creek   FREE
State Wildlife Area
About 20 mi W of Los Banos on SR 152, past N shore of
San Luis Lake; wildlife area at county line, accessible
via Dinosaur Point Rd. Free. All year; 14-day limit. Free
primitive camping only in parking lot of Upper Cottonwood
Creek unit. No facilities. Hunting, hiking.

Los Banos   FREE
State Wildlife Area
About 2 mi N of Los Banos on SR 165; half mi E on Henry
Miller Ave. Free. All year; 14-day limit. Primitive camping
on 6,217 acres. Drkg wtr, cfga, toilets. Hike or drive along
levees. Hunting, fishing, hiking, boating.

North Grasslands   FREE
State Wildlife Area
About 5 mi N of Los Banos on Hwy 168; NE on Wolfsen Rd
to Salt Slough Unit; for China Island Unit, continue N on
Hwy 168 about 10 mi, then W on Hwy 140. Free. Primitive
camping on 7,069 acres of restored & created wetlands.
No facilities. Hunting, fishing, boating.

O'Neill Forebay   FREE
State Wildlife Area
12 mi W of Los Banos on SR 152; N on SR 33 to O'Neill
Forebay Lake. Free. All year; 14-day limit. Primitive camping on 700 acres. Fishing, hunting, hiking.

San Luis Reservoir   FREE
State Wildlife Area
About 15 mi W of Los Banos on SR 152 to San Luis Lake.
Access to W side of area from Dinosaur Point Rd. Free. All
year; 14-day limit. Primitive camping on 902 acres at San
Luis and O'Neill Forebay Lakes. Drkg wtr, toilets. Fishing,
boating, hiking, hunting.

Tumey Hills   FREE
Bureau of Land Management
Between Los Banos & Coalinga on I-5, take Panoche Rd
exit W about 1.5 mi to graded dirt access; a second access
point 5 mi farther on S side of rd. Free. All year; 14-day
limit. Primitive undesignated camping on 36,000 acres of
public land in San Benito & Fresno Counties. No facilities,
no drkg wtr. Camp within 15 feet of existing roads. Biking,
hiking, horseback riding, hunting.

Volta State Wildlife Area   FREE
About 9 mi W of Los Banos on SR 152; 2 mi N on Volta Rd;
half mi NW on Ingomar Grade Rd. Free primitive camping
allowed only at check station during waterfowl season. No
facilities. 2,891 acres.

LOS OLIVOS (S)

Davy Brown Campground $10
Figueroa Mountain Recreation Area
Los Padres National Forest
20.6 mi NE of Los Olivos on Figueroa Mountain Rd; 3.8 mi
N on Sunset Valley Rd to campground sign (on left). No lon-
ger $5 daily Adventure Pass; now $10 with federal senior
pass; others pay $20. All year; 14-day limit. 13 sites; 25-ft
RV limit. Tbls, toilets, cfga, drkg wtr (shut off in winter).
Hiking, horseback riding, mountain biking, no fishing
allowed. In early 2017, 4WD or high clearance needed on
Happy Canyon Rd due to thick mud.

Figueroa Campground $10
Figueroa Mountain Recreation Area
Los Padres National Forest
13 mi NE of Los Olivos on Fugueroa Mountain Rd. No longer $5 daily Adventure Pass; now $10 with federal senior pass; others pay $20. All year; 14-day limit. 33 sites (25-ft RV limit). Tbls, toilets, cfga, no drkg wtr. Hiking trails; scenic; wheelchair access.

LUCERNE (N)
Lakeview Dispersed Site FREE
Mendocino National Forest
2 mi NW of Lucerne on SR 20; 5 mi NE on FR 8; 3 mi SE on FR 15N09. Free. All year; 14-day limit. 9 sites (RVs under 16 ft). No amenities, no trash service. Picnicking. Elev 3400 ft; 3 acres.

MACDOEL (N)
Juanita Lake $7.50
Klamath National Forest
From qtr mi SW of Macdoel at jct with US 97, 6.5 mi W on Meiss Lake-Sam's Neck Rd; 1.2 mi S on FR 46N04 (Butte Valley Rd). Free 11/1-5/15; $7.50 rest of yr with federal senior pass; others pay $15 (double site $20). 14-day limit. 23 sites; average site 42 ft, some 60 ft. Tbls, toilets, cfga, drkg wtr; no wtr or trash service during free period. Swimming, boating (l--no motors), fishing, hiking, interpretive site. Elev 5100 ft; 20 acres; Group site ($50) by reservation. Trail, piers for handicapped. Winter access mainly by snowmobile.

Martins Dairy $10
Klamath National Forest
From jct with US 97 3.8 m S of Macdoel, 6.4 mi W on Ball Mtn Rd; 4.1 mi N (right) on FR 70; left 2 mi on FR 46N12. $10 during MD-10/31; free rest of year but no wtr or trash service. 14-day limit. 6 sites (RVs under 31 ft). Tbls, toilets, cfga, piped drkg wtr. At headwaters of Little Shasta River. Elev 6000 ft.

Shafter Campground $10
Klamath National Forest
From jct with US 97 at Macdoel, 9 mi S on Old State Hwy. $10. May-Oct; 14-day limit. 10 sites (RVs under 40 ft). Tbls, toilets, cfga, drkg wtr. Swimming, boating, fishing. Elev 4400 ft; 11 acres.

MAD RIVER (N)
Bailey Canyon $12
Six Rivers National Forest
13 mi SE of Mad River on Lower Mad River Rd; at Ruth Lake. $12. MD-10/15; 14-day limit. 25 sites (22-ft RV limit). Tbls, toilets, cfga, drkg wtr. Boating, fishing, hiking, waterskiing.

Fir Cove Campground $12
Six Rivers National Forest
12 mi SE of Mad River on Lower Mad River Rd; at Ruth Lake. $12. MD-9/30; 14-day limit. 19 sites (22-ft RV limit). Tbls, toilets, cfga, drkg wtr. Boating(l), fishing, hiking, waterskiing.

Mad River Campground $12
Six Rivers National Forest
5 mi SE of Mad River on SR 36; 3 mi N of dam. $12. MD-9/15; 14-day limit. 40 sites (22-ft RV limit). Tbls, toilets, cfga, drkg wtr. Hunting, hiking, fishing, picnicking, swimming. Elev 2500 ft.

MAMMOTH LAKES (C)
Agnew Meadows Campground $11.50
Inyo National Forest
From Mammoth Springs, about 6 mi W on SR 203, past Mammoth Mtn lodge to Minaret Vista; continue 2.5 mi on Reds Meadow Rd to campground turnoff; narrow, single lane rd, accessible only in summer. $11.50 with federal senior pass; others pay $23. About 6/1-9/10; 14-day limit. 21 sites. Horse camp has 3 sites for horsemen. Tbls, toilets, cfga, drkg wtr, bear lockers. Valley access fee charged non-campers. Closed in 2014 due to wind damage; work progressing in 2017. Check current status before arrival.

Big Springs FREE
Inyo National Forest
From E of Mammoth Lakes at jct with SR 203, 6 mi NW on US 395; 2.1 mi E on Owens River Rd. Free. About 4/15-11/15; 21-day limit. 26 sites. Tbls, toilets, cfga, bear lockers, no drkg wtr. Trout fishing base camp for Deadman Creek, groomed snowmobile trails in winter. Elev 7300 ft.

Coldwater Campground $11
Inyo National Forest
W on Main St in Mammoth Lakes; it becomes Lake Mary Rd; past the first lake, take 2nd left; Coldwater is 2nd camp on left; at Coldwater Creek. $11 base with federal senior pass; others pay $22 base, $23 for premium locations. 5.15-10/31; 14-day limit. 77 sites; 36-ft RV limit. Tbls, flush toilets, cfga, drkg wtr, bear boxes. Hiking, biking & bridle trails, swimming, fishing.

Deadman Campground FREE
Inyo National Forest
1 mi E of Mammoth Lakes on SR 203; 8.1 mi N on US 395; left at Deadman Creek Rd for 1.2 mi; bear left at "Y," for 1.6 mi to lower section and 1.8 mi to upper section; on both sides of creek. 30 sites for tents, fold-outs, truck campers. Free. 6/1-10/15; 14-day limit. Tbls, toilets, cfga, no drkg wtr. Hiking, fishing, OHV activities.

Lake George　　　　　　　　　　　　　$12
Inyo National Forest
W on Main St in Mammoth Lakes; it becomes Lake Mary
Rd; past the first lake, take 3nd left, then cross bridge &
turn right up the hill. $12 with federal senior pass; others
pay $24. 15 sites. Tbls, flush toilets, cfga, drkg wtr, bear
boxes. Boating, fishing, hiking, horseback riding. Elev
9000 ft.

Lake Mary Campground　　　　　　　　$10.50
Inyo National Forest
W on Main St in Mammoth Lakes; it becomes Lake Mary
Rd; past the first lake, take 3rd left; both sides of rd.
$10.50 base for seniors with federal senior pass; others
pay $21 base, $23 for premium locations ($11.50 with
senior pass). 6/1-9/10; 14-day limit. 46 sites. Tbls, toilets,
cfga, drkg wtr, bear lockers. Boating, fishing, hiking,
horseback riding.

Lower Deadman　　　　　　　　　　　FREE
Inyo National Forest
1 mi E of Mammoth Lakes on SR 203; 8.1 mi N on US 395;
W (left) at Deadman Creek Rd. Free. All year; 14-day limit.
15 sites; 45-ft RV limit. Tbls, toilets, cfga, no drkg wtr; no
bear lockers.

McGee Creek　　　　　　　　　　　$11.50
Inyo National Forest
From Mammoth Lakes at jct with SR 203, 8 mi S on US
395; 2 mi S on McGee Creek Rd; on the left. $11.50 with
federal senior pass; others pay $23. 4/27-10/31; 14-day
limit. 28 sites; 35-ft RV limit. Tbls (shaded pavilions), pit
toilets, cfga, drkg wtr, bear lockers. Fishing.

Mineret Falls　　　　　　　　　　　$11.50
Inyo National Forest
From Mammoth Lakes, about 6 mi W on SR 203, past
Mammoth Mtn lodge to Minaret Vista; continue 2.5 mi on
Reds Meadow Rd, passing Agnew Meadows turnoff, then
S about 3 mi on Mineret Summit Rd; narrow, single lane
rd, accessible only in summer. Valley access fee charged.
Campsites $11.50 with federal senior pass; others pay
$23. 6/1-9/10; 14-day limit. 27 sites. Tbls, toilets, cfga,
drkg wtr, bear lockers.

New Shady Rest　　　　　　　　　　$10
Inyo National Forest
E of Mammoth Lakes on SR 203; 0.1 mi N on Sawmill Cut-
off Rd. $10 base with federal senior pass; others pay $20
base, $22 for premium locations ($11 with senior pass).
92 sites; 35-ft RV limit. 5/1-11/12; 14-day limit. Tbls, flush
toilets, cfga, drkg wtr, dump, interpretive programs, bear
boxes.

Old Shady Rest　　　　　　　　　　$10
Inyo National Forest
E of Mammoth Lakes on SR 203; N on Old Sawmill Rd,

then 3rd left into camp. $10 base with federal senior
pass; others pay $20 base, $22 for premium locations ($11
with senior pass). 6/1-9/10; 14-day limit. 47 sites; 50-ft
RV limit. Tbls, flush toilets, cfga, drkg wtr, playground,
amphitheater, dump($7), phone, coin laundry, bear lock-
ers. Mountain biking, golf, bike rental.

Pine City Campground　　　　　　　$12
Inyo National Forest
E on Main St. in Mammoth Lakes; it becomes Lake Mary
Rd; past the 1st lake, take the 2nd left; first campground
on the left. $12 with federal senior pass; others pay $24.
About 5/15-9/30; 14-day limit. 10 sites. Tbls, flush toilet,
cfga, drkg wtr. Hiking, horseback riding.

Pumice Flat Campground　　　　　　$11.50
Inyo National Forest
From Mammoth Lakes, about 6 mi W on SR 203, past
Mammoth Mtn lodge to Minaret Vista; continue 2.5 mi on
Reds Meadow Rd, passing Agnew Meadows turnoff, then
S about 5 mi on Mineret Summit Rd; 0.25 mi E on access
rd; narrow, single lane rds, accessible only in summer. $7
valley access fee charged. Campsites $11.50 with federal
senior pass; others pay $23. About 6/1-9/10; 14-day limit.
17 sites. Tbls, toilets, cfga, drkg wtr, bear lockers.

Reds Meadow　　　　　　　　　　　$11.50
Inyo National Forest
From Mammoth Lakes, about 6 mi W on SR 203, past
Mammoth Mtn lodge to Minaret Vista; continue 2.5 mi on
Reds Meadow Rd, passing Agnew Meadows turnoff, then S
about 2.5 mi on Mineret Summit Rd; narrow, single lane rd,
accessible only in summer. $7 valley access fee charged.
Campsites $11.50 with federal senior pass; others pay $23.
6/1-9/10; 14-day limit. 56 sites. Tbls, toilets, cfga, drkg
wtr, bear lockers.

Sherwin Creek　　　　　　　　　　$10
Inyo National Forest
From Main St. in Mammoth Lakes, S at first traffic light;
0.9 mi onto Old Mammoth Rd; left for 1.5 mi on Sherwin
Creek Rd. $10 base with federal senior pass; others pay
$20 base, $22 for premium locations ($11 with senior
pass). About 5/1-9/10; 21-day limit. 85 sites; 50-ft RV
limit. Tbls, flush toilets, cfga, drkg wtr. Hiking, bridle,
biking & ATV trails.

Tuff Campground　　　　　　　　　$11.50
Inyo National Forest
E From Mammoth Lakes at jct with SR 203, 10 mi S to
Toms Place; 200 yds S on Rock Creek Rd; 0.25 mi on gravel
rd (signs); at Rock Creek. $11.50 with federal senior pass;
others pay $23. 4/27-10/31; 21-day limit. 34 sites; 35-ft RV
limit. Tbls, pit toilets, cfga, drkg wtr, bear lockers. Fishing.

Twin Lakes　　　　　　　　　　　$10.50
Inyo National Forest

W on Main St. in Mammoth Lakes; it becomes Lake Mary Rd, then follow Twin Lakes cutoff. $10.50 base with federal senior pass; others pay $21.24 base, $23.01 for premium locations ($11.50 with senior pass). About 5/15-10/31; 7-day limit. 93 sites; 35-ft RV limit. Tbls, flush toilets, cfga, drkg wtr, bear boxes, coin laundry, showers, phone. Boating(lr), biking, hiking.

MANZANITA LAKE (N)

Crags Campground $12
Lassen Volcanic National Park
N of Manzanita Lake on main park rd. $12. 5/27-9/12; 14-day limit. 45 sites. Tbls, pit toilets, cfga, drkg wtr, bear lockers. Park entry fee charged. GPS: 40.5632148, -121.5199811.

Manzanita Lake Campground $12
Lassen Volcanic National Park
Just S of Manzanita Lake on main park rd. $12 with federal senior pass during 5/27-10/25; others pay $24; dry camping $15 ($7.50 with senior pass). Fee $15 after 10/25 until closed by snow. Park entry fee. 179 sites. Tbls, flush toilets, cfga, drkg wtr, shower, coin laundry, bear lockers, dump, interpretive programs. Fishing, swimming, boating(l), kayaking(r).

Summit Lake North $10
Lassen Volcanic National Park
14 mi S of park entrance on main park rd. $10 with federal senior pass; others pay $20. 7/1-10/24; 14-day limit. Park entry fee. 48 sites. Tbls, pit toilets, cfga, drkg wtr, bear lockers. Swimming, hiking trail, fishing.

MARICOPA (S)

Caballo Campground   FREE
Los Padres National Forest
9 mi S of Maricopa on SR 166; 27 mi SE on CR FH95; half mi N on FR 9N27 (3 mi W of town of Pine Mountain Club). Free. 5/1-11/15; 14-day limit. 5 sites. Tbls, toilets, cfga, no drkg wtr. Swimming. Elev 5800. Rd has ruts; 4WD may be needed.

Campo Alto Campground $10
Los Padres National Forest
9 mi S of Maricopa on SR 166; 27 mi SE on FR 9N27 (Cerro Noroeste Rd) to its end. Previously $5 daily Adventure Pass; now $10 with federal senior pass; others pay $20. 5/15-11/15; 14-day limit. Open for winter sports when rd is plowed. About 12 sites; 30-ft RV limit. Tbls, toilets, cfga, no drkg wtr. Hiking, picnicking, mountain climbing. Elev 8200 ft; 10 acres. At summit of Cerro Noroeste Mountain, Mount Abel. Managed by Parks Management Co.

Toad Springs   FREE
Los Padres National Forest
9 mi S of Maricopa on SR 166; 15 mi SE on CR FH95 (Mill Potrero Hwy); half mi SW on FR 9N09 (Quatal Canyon Rd).

Free. 5/1-11/15; 14-day limit. 5 sites on 2 acres (RVs under 16 ft). Tbls, toilets, cfga, firewood, no drkg wtr. Picnicking. Elev 5700 ft.

Valle Vista $5
Los Padres National Forest
9 mi S of Maricopa on SR 166; 12 mi S on CR FH95 (Mt. Abel Rd). Suitable for small RVs. $5 daily or $30 annually. All year; 14-day limit. 7 sites on 4 acres (RVs under 32 ft). Tbls, toilets, cfga, no drkg wtr. Picnicking. Elev 4800 ft. Operated by Kern County.

MARIPOSA (C)

Jerseydale   FREE
Merced River Recreation Area
Sierra National Forest
5 mi NE of Mariposa on Hwy 140; left for 4.9 mi on Darrah Rd (becoming Jerseydale Rd); 2.2 mi on Jerseydale, then left on FR 4S82 just past fire station. 10ree. 5/1-11/30; 14-day limit. 8 sites (most not level); 24-ft RV limit. Tbls, toilets, cfga, drkg wtr, hitching posts.

McCabe Flat $10
Merced River Recreation Area
Sierra National Forest
Bureau of Land Management
Hwy 140 to Briceville, turn left & follow dirt river rd 2.5 mi W; RVs over 18 ft not recommended on bridge. $10. 4/30-9/5; 14-day limit. 11 walk-in tent sites; 3 RV sites; 18-ft RV limit. Tbls, toilets, cfga, no drkg wtr. Whitewater rafting, trout fishing, rockhounding, prospecting, horseback riding, swimming, gold panning. Managed by BLM.

Railroad Flat Campground $10
Merced River Recreation Area
Sierra National Forest
Bureau of Land Management
Hwy 140 to Briceville, turn left & follow dirt river rd 4.8 mi W; RVs over 18 ft not recommended on bridge. $10. 4/30-9/5; 14-day limit. 6 RV sites; 18-ft RV limit. Tbls, toilets, cfga, no drkg wtr. Whitewater rafting, trout fishing, rockhounding, prospecting, horseback riding, swimming, gold panning. Managed by BLM.

MARKLEEVILLE (N)

Centerville Flat   FREE
Toiyabe National Forest
2 mi E of Markleeville on SR 4; E on Hwy 89, then N on forest service rd. Free. Open June-Sept; 14-day limit. Undeveloped primitive area; about 10 undesignated sites. Tbls, toilets, cfga, no drkg wtr. Hiking, picnicking. Elev 6000 ft.

Wolf Creek Campground   FREE
Toiyabe National Forest
7 mi E of Markleeville on SR 4; about 5 mi E on Wolf Creek Rd (FR 032). Free. Open Apr-Sept; 14-day limit. Undeveloped primitive area; about 10 undesignated sites. Tbls,

toilets, cfga, no drkg wtr. Hiking, fishing, picnicking. Elev 6400 ft. Frequent bear activity.

MARYSVILLE (N)

Spencerville   FREE
State Wildlife Area
E of Spencerville on Erle Rd, then NE on Spencerville Rd. Free. All year; 14-day limit. Primitive camping on 11,448 acres. Hunting, fishing.

MCCLOUD (N)

Algoma Campground   FREE
Shasta-Trinity National Forest
13 mi E on SR 89; half mi S on FR 39N06. Free. 5/1-11/1; 14-day limit. 8 undeveloped user-created sites (RVs under 32 ft). Tbls, toilet, cfga, no drkg wtr. Picnicking, fishing. Elev 3900 ft; 5 acres. Flat terrain.

Blanche Lake Campground   FREE
Modoc National Forest
From McCloud, 16 mi E on US 89; left on FR 15 (Harris Spring Rd) for 4.4 mi; follow FR 49 (Medicine Lake Rd) 24 mi toward Medicine Lake, turning right on FR 43N17 & follow signs. Free. Jul-Oct; 14-day limit. About 6 primitive undesignated sites; tbls, cfga, toilets, no drkg wtr, no trash service. Near Modoc Volcanic Scenic Byway and Lava Beds National Monument. Elev 6500 ft.

Bullseye Lake Campground   FREE
Modoc National Forest
From McCloud, 16 mi E on US 89; left on FR 15 for 4.4 mi; follow FR 49 (Medicine Lake Rd) 24 mi toward Medicine Lake, turning right on FR 43N17 & follow signs. Free. July-Oct; 14-day limit. Undesignated primitive sites; tbls, cfga, no toilets or drkg wtr. 22-ft RV limit. Fishing, swimming, hiking, ice caves.

Cattle Camp $7.50
Shasta-Trinity National Forest
9.5 mi E of McCloud on SR 89; half mi S on FR 40N44; at Upper McCloud River. $7.50 for seniors with federal senior pass; others pay $15. 5/1-11/1; 14-day limit. 27 paved sites (RVs under 32 ft). Tbls, toilets, cfga, drkg wtr, bear boxes. Fishing, swimming, hiking trails. Elev 3700 ft; 7 acres.

Fowlers Camp $7.50
Shasta-Trinity National Forest
6 mi E of McCloud on SR 89; at Upper McCloud River. $7.50 with federal senior pass; others pay $15. 5/15-10/15; 14-day limit. 39 sites, but 29 reservations only; 30-ft RV limit. Tbls, toilets, cfga, drkg wtr, bear boxes. Fishing (poor), hiking, swimming. Easy hike to 2 waterfalls. Elev 3400 ft.

Harris Springs   FREE
Shasta-Trinity National Forest

16 mi E of McCloud on SR 89; 17 mi N on FR 43N15. 8/15-11/1. 15 user-created sites; 32-ft RV limit. Tbls, pit toilet, cfga, firewood, no drkg wtr. Picnicking, hiking. Elev 4800 ft.

Headquarters $7
Modoc National Forest
From McCloud, 16 mi E on US 89; left on FR 15 for 4.4 mi; follow FR 49 (Medicine Lake Rd) 27.5 mi to campground at Medicine Lake. $7 with federal senior pass; others pay $14. About MD-10/15, weather permitting; 14-day limit; free when open off-season, but no wtr or trash service. 16 sites (18-ft RV limit). Tbls, toilets, cfga, drkg wtr, beach, dump. Boating, fishing, picnicking, swimming. On Medicine Lake.

Hemlock Campground $7
Modoc National Forest
From McCloud, 16 mi E on US 89; left on FR 15 (Harris Springs Rd) for 4.4 mi; follow signs on FR 49 (Medicine Lake Rd) to campground at Medicine Lake. $7 with federal senior pass. About 5/15-10/31; 14-day limit. Free off-season, but no wtr or trash service. 19 sites on 10 acres (RVs under 23 ft). Tbls, toilet, cfga, drkg wtr, beach. Swimming, boating(l), fishing, water skiing.

Medicine Campground $7
Modoc National Forest
From McCloud, 16 mi E on US 89; left on FR 15 (Harris Spring Rd) for 4.4 mi; turn on FR 49 (Medicine Lake Rd), following signs to campground at Medicine Lake. $7 with federal senior pass; others pay $14. About 7/1-10/31; 14-day limit. Free when open off-season, but no wtr or trash service. 22 sites on 21 acres (22-ft RV limit). Tbls, toilet, cfga, no drkg wtr, beach. Swimming, boating(l), fishing, waterskiing.

Payne Springs Campground   FREE
Modoc National Forest
From McCloud, 16 mi E on US 89; left for 4.4 mi on FR 15 (Harris Spring Rd), then follow signs on FR 49 (Medicine Lake Rd) 24 mi to Medicine Lake; right on FR 43N17 & follow signs to Payne Springs. Free. July-Oct; 14-day limit. Primitive sites; 20-ft limit. Tbls, toilets, cfga, no drkg wtr. In Medicine Lake Highlands. Near Lava Beds National Monument.

Trout Creek Campground   FREE
Shasta-Trinity National Forest
17 mi N of SR 89 on Pilgrim Creek Rd. Free. June-Oct; 14-day limit. About 10 undesignated sites; 30-ft RV limit. Toilets, cfga, no drkg wtr, no trash service, no tbls. Fishing, swimming.

MENDOTA (C)

Mendota State Wildlife Area   FREE
Half mi S of Mendota on SR 180; 1 mi E on Panoche Rd. Free. All year; 14-day limit. Primitive camping on 11,882

acres at Fresno Slough; no facilities. Hunting, fishing, hiking.

MERCY HOT SPRINGS (C)

Little Panoche Reservoir   FREE
State Wildlife Area
Access from various roads N, W & S of Mercy Hot Springs; four units of wildlife area; lake accessible via Hwy J1 (Little Panoche Rd) NE of town. Free. All year; 14-day limit. Primitive camping on 828 acres; undeveloped. Fishing, hunting.

MILFORD (N)

Conklin Park Campground   FREE
Plumas National Forest
5.5 mi SE of Milford on CR 336; 6 mi S on FR 26N70; .2 mi NE on FR 26N91, on Willow Creek. Free. 5/1-10/15; 14-day limit. 9 sites on 2 acres (RVs under 22 ft). Tbls, toilets, cfga, no drkg wtr or trash service. Hiking. Elev 5900 ft.

Laufman Campground   FREE
Plumas National Forest
From US 395 at Milford, 3 mi SE on Milford Grade Rd. Free. 5/1-10/15; 14-day limit. 6 sites (22-ft RV limit). Tbls, toilets, cfga, no drkg wtr or trash service. Hiking, picnicking. Elev 5100 ft.

MINERAL (N)

Battle Creek $9
Lassen National Forest
2 mi W of Mineral on SR 36. $9 with federal senior pass; others pay $18. 5/1-10/31; 14-day limit. 50 paved sites (many 45 ft). Tbls, flush toilets, cfga, drkg wtr. Trout fishing.

Hole-in-the-Ground Camp $12
Lassen National Forest
From Mineral at jct with SR 36, 5.5 mi E on SR 172; right on gravel, narrow FR 28N06 for 2.8 mi; left on unmarked access rd; at Mill Creek. $12. 5/1-10/31; 14-day limit. 13 sites (typically 35 ft). Tbls, toilets, cfga, drkg wtr. Fishing.

MONTGOMERY CREEK (N)

Madrone Campground   FREE
Shasta-Trinity National Forest
2 mi SW of Montgomery City on US 299; 2.5 mi W on CR 7 (Fender Ferry Rd); 17 mi NW on FR N8G01. Free. 4/15-11/15; 21-day limit. 10 sites; 16-ft RV limit. Tbls, toilets, cfga, no drkg wtr. Fishing; picnicking. Elev 1200 ft; 6 acres. On Squaw Creek. Unit of Whiskeytown-Shasta-Trinity National Recreation area; mainly a backpacker & hunter camp.

MOUNT SHASTA (N)

Castle Lake   FREE
Shasta-Trinity National Forest
11.6 mi SW on CR 2M002 (Castle Lake Rd); half mi below lake. Free. 6/1-10/15; 3-night limit. 6 sites (16-ft RV limit). Tbls, toilets, cfga, no drkg wtr, bear boxes. Picnicking, hiking. Elev 5400 ft; 5 acres. Mountains. Stream. Castle Lake is half mi from campsites; fishing not very good. Popular dispersed campsites along Castle Lake Rd.

Gumboot Lake Campground   FREE
Shasta-Trinity National Forest
3.5 mi SE of Mount Shasta on CR 2M002; 11.1 mi SW on FR 40N30; half mi S on FR 40N37; N side of lake. Free. 6/1-10/30; 7-day limit. 6 undeveloped sites (RVs under 30 ft). Toilets, cfga, no tbls, no drkg wtr. Swimming, picnicking, fishing. Elev 6200 ft. Campfire permit required.

McBride Springs $10
Shasta-Trinity National Forest
4.5 mi NE of Mount Shasta on CR FH98; on lower slope of Mt. Shasta. $10. MD-10/31; 7-day limit. 10 sites on 2 acres; 16-ft RV limit. Tbls, toilets, cfga, drkg wtr. Elev 5000 ft.

Toad Lake Cabin   FREE
Shasta-Trinity National Forest
3.5 mi SE of Mount Shasta on CR 2M002; qtr mi N on FR 41N53; 12 mi W on FR 40N64. Next to Toad Lake Campground tent sites. Free. Undesignated sites, not maintained. Tbls, toilet, cfga, no drkg wtr or trash services. Hiking, fishing.

NEEDLES (S)

Beale Slough   FREE
Bureau of Land Management
From I-40 S of Needles, take the Five-Mile Rd exit E toward Colorado River; follow dirt rd under the railroad bridge; turn right (S) for 1 mi to interpretive sign. Free. Primitive undesignated sites at slough created during channelization of river. Also follow dirt rd N or S along river to unmarked turnouts available for camping. No facilities. No vehicles on beach. Fishing, boating, hiking, OHV use.

Bigelow Cholla Garden   FREE
Bureau of Land Management
From I-40 W of Needles, exit US 95 & follow dirt rd S about 200 ft; right to access the Four Corners Pipeline, then W along area's S boundary. Free primitive undesignated sites; no facilities; no drkg wtr. All year, but very high temperatures in summer; 14-day limit. This area contains the state's largest concentration of Bigelow cholla cactus.

Chemehuevi Wash   FREE
Recreation Area
Bureau of Land Management
20 mi S of Needles on US 95; E of Havasu Lake Rd to Havasu Landing; 17 mi to the recreation area via 3 routes. Free. All year; 14-day limit. Summer temperatures very hot. Dispersed primitive camping; no facilities, no drkg wtr.

Rockhounding, gold panning, fishing, hiking, horseback riding, OHV use.

NEVADA CITY (N)

Bowman Lake   FREE
Tahoe National Forest
23.2 mi E of Nevada City on SR 20; 16.2 mi N on FR 18. RV access from Graniteville Rd recommended. Free. 6/15-9/30; 14-day limit. 7 sites (RVs under 22 ft). Tbls, toilets, cfga, no drkg wtr. Swimming, boating (d), waterskiing, picnicking, trout fishing. Elev 5600 ft; 3 acres. GPS: 39.459317, -120.612392

Canyon Creek   FREE
Tahoe National Forest
23.2 mi E of Nevada City on SR 20; 13.2 mi N on FR 18; 2.3 mi SE on FR 18N13. RV access from Graniteville Rd recommended. Free. 6/15-9/30; 14-day limit. 16 sites (RVs under 22 ft). Tbls, toilets, cfga, no drkg wtr, no trash service. Picnicking, fishing, boating (l), swimming (1 mi). Elev 6000 ft; 5 acres. On Canyon Creek 1 mi below Faucherie Reservoir.

Jackson Creek   FREE
Tahoe National Forest
23.2 mi E of Nevada City on SR 20; 13.2 mi N on FR 18; 4 mi E on CR 843. 6/15-9/30; 14-day limit. RV access from Graniteville Rd recommended. Free. 14 sites (RVs under 22 ft). Tbls, toilets, cfga, bear boxes, no drkg wtr, no trash service. Picnicking. Swimming, waterskiing, boating (d), fishing (1 mi). Elev 5600 ft; 7 acres. On Jackson Creek, 1 mi above Bowman Lake.

South Yuba River Campground $5
Bureau of Land Management
10 mi N of Nevada City on North Bloomfield Rd; 1.5 mi on dirt/gravel rd from bridge at Edwards Crossing. $5. 4/1-10/15; 14-day limit. 16 sites (30-ft RV limit). Toilets, drkg wtr, tbls, cfga. Hiking, hunting, fishing, horseback riding, gold panning. Elev 2500 ft. 12 mi hiking/riding & bridle trail, swimming, mountain biking, trout fishing, rockhounding. South Yuba River. Malakoff Diggins State Historical Park nearby.

White Cloud $12
Tahoe National Forest
12 mi NE of Nevada City on SR 20. $12 with federal senior pass; others pay $24. Free off-season, but no wtr or trash service. About 5/15-9/15; 14-day limit. 46 site; 22-ft RV limit. Tbls, flush toilets, cfga, drkg wtr, dump, phone. Hiking trail, mountain biking trail. Elev 4200 ft.

NEW CUYAMA (S)

Aliso Park $5
Los Padres National Forest
3 mi W of New Cuyama on SR 166; 4 mi S on FR 10N04 (Aliso Canyon Rd); 1 mi S on FR 11N02. $5 daily or $30

annually. All year; 14 day limit. 10 sites; 28-ft RV limit. Tbls, toilets, cfga, no drkg wtr. Boil well wtr before drkg. Horseback riding, hiking. Elev 3200 ft; 3 acres. Elev 3200 ft. Popular camp during deer season.

Ballinger Campground $10
Los Padres National Forest
10 mi E of New Cuyama on SR 166; 4 mi S on SR 33; 3 mi E to end of FR 9N10 (Ballinger Canyon Rd); at Ballinger Canyon OHV Area. Formerly $5 daily Adventure Pass; now $10 with federal senior pass; others pay $20. All year; 14-day limit. 20 sites (RVs under 32 ft). Tbls, toilets, cfga, no drkg wtr. Elev 3000 ft; 8 acres. Mainly used by motorcycles & 4WD, but RVs okay. Hungry Valley Recreation Area nearby for ORV enthusiasts. Nearby Ozena Campground closed indefinitely.

Bates Canyon $5
Los Padres National Forest
10 mi W of New Cuyama on SR 166; 8 mi S on FR 11N01. $5 daily or $30 annually. All year; 14-day limit. 6 sites (RVs under 16 ft). Tbls, toilets, cfga, no drkg wtr. Elev 2900 ft; 1 acre. Entrance into San Rafael Wilderness.

NILAND (S)

Hazard Unit   FREE
Imperial State Wildlife Area
About 2 mi NW of Niland on SR 111; W on McDonald Rd to smallest section of wildlife area. Free. All year; 14-day limit. Toilets, cfga, drkg wtr. Hunting, fishing, boating.

Ramer Unit   FREE
Imperial State Wildlife Area
About 8 mi S of Niland on SR 111, S of Calipatria at Ramer Lake. Free. All year; 14-day limit. Primitive camping. Toilets, cfga, drkg wtr. Hunting, fishing, boating.

Slab City   FREE
Boondock Camp
4 mi E of Niland on Beal Rd. Free desert camping at former Marine Corps training camp where concrete slab foundations are all that's left. Register at Christian Center in mobile bldg on main street. Free. No facilities; pack out trash, haul in wtr from Niland; dump in Niland. Swap meets on weekends. Large population of Loners on Wheels members during winter.

Wister Unit   FREE
Imperial State Wildlife Area
About 3 mi NW of Niland on SR 111; on E shore of Salton Sea. Free. All year; 14-day limit. Primitive camping. Toilets, cfga, drkg wtr. Hunting, fishing, boating.

NORTH FORK (C)

Clover Meadow   FREE
Mammoth Pool Recreation Area
Sierra National Forest
4.6 mi S of North Fork on CR 225; 38 mi NE on FR 4S81

(Minarets Rd); 1.4 mi N on FR 5S30. Free. 6/15-10/15; 14 day limit. 7 sites (20-ft RV limit). Tbls, toilet, cfga, drkg wtr. Hiking, backpacking. Trailhead parking for Ansel Adams Wilderness. Elev 7000 ft.

Granite Creek   FREE
Mammoth Pool Recreation Area
Sierra National Forest
4.6 mi SE of North Fork on CR 225; 50.6 mi NE on FR 4S81; 1.4 mi N on FR 5S30; 3.4 mi NE on FR 5S071. Free. 6/1-10/31; 14-day limit. 20 sites; 20-ft RV limit. Tbls, toilets, cfga, no drkg wtr. Hiking, fishing. Elev 6900 ft. Upper loop has horse corrals; no horses in lower loop.

Little Jackass   FREE
Mammoth Pool Recreation Area
Sierra National Forest
4.6 mi SE on CR 225; 35 mi NE on FR 4S81; 1.5 mi SE on FR 6S22; along Fish Creek. Free. 5/1-10/15; 14-day limit. 5 sites (RVs under 21 ft). Tbls, toilet, cfga, no drkg wtr. Picnicking, fishing, swimming, hiking. Elev 4800 ft.

Redinger Lake   FREE
San Joaquin River Recreation Area
Sierra National Forest
From post office in North Fork, 4.3 mi E on Hwy 41; right on Italian Bar Rd (FR 225) for 3.8 mi; right on FR 235 for 2.1 mi to paved parking area at spillway. Free. All year; 14-day limit. Undeveloped pavement camping; 25-ft RV limit. No tbls, cfga, trash service or drkg wtr; pit toilets. Fishing, hiking, boating (l), waterskiing. No campfires or charcoal grills or hibachis; gas stoves only. No camping on beaches or either side of lake.

Upper Chiquito Campground   FREE
Mammoth Pool Recreation Area
Sierra National Forest
Half mi E of North Fork on CR 225; 9 mi NE on CR 274; 23 mi NE on FR 5S07. Free. 6/1-10/31; 14-day limit. 20 sites (RVs under 21 ft). Toilets, cfga, no drkg wtr. Fishing. Elev 6800 ft; 6 acres. Chiquito Creek. Near Chiquito Trailhead accessing Ansel Adams Wilderness & Yosemite.

Whisky Falls Campground   FREE
Mammoth Pool Recreation Area
Sierra National Forest
1.5 mi E on CR 225; 7 mi NE on FR 8S09; 1.5 mi E on FR 8S70. Free. 6/1-11/15; 14-day limit. 14 sites (RVs under 22 ft). Tbls, toilets, cfga, no drkg wtr. Fishing, swimming.

OAKHURST (C)
Bowler Group Camp   FREE
Sierra National Forest
While driving N from Oakhurst on SR 41, turn right on FR 222 for 5.5 mi, then left on Beasore Rd (FR 7) for about 20 mi. Free. July-Oct; 14-day limit. 12 group sites (20-ft RV limit). Tbls, toilet, cfga, no drkg wtr. Horses allowed.

Nelder Grove   FREE
Yosemite South Recreation Area
Sierra National Forest
.2 mi N of Oakhurst on CR 426; 4 mi N on SR 41; 8.1 mi NE on FR 6S10; 10.3 mi NW on FR 4S04 (steep, narrow entrance rd); along Willow Creek. Free. 5/21-9/30; 14-day limit. 7 sites (RVs under 22 ft). Tbls, toilets, cfga, no drkg wtr. Hiking, picnicking, fishing. Elev 5300 ft; 3 acres. Nature trails. Within Nelder Grove of giant sequoias. Interpretive display.

OGILBY (S)
North Dunes Campgrounds $40/week
Imperial Sand Dunes Recreation Area
Bureau of Land Management
From Ogilby (NW of Winterhaven), 22 mi N on Ogilby Rd (CR S34); 9 mi W on SR 78 to Glamis. 18 primitive camping areas in vicinity, all with paved or gravel RV surfaces, some not maintained. $40 for 14-day short-term permit when purchased off-site; $50 purchased on-site; $180 for season 10/1-4/15. Free camping off-season up to 14 days. All year; 14-day limit. Toilets, cfga, no tbls, no drkg wtr. Glamis Flats Campground at jct of SR 78 & Wash Rd (GPS 32.5932, -114.0445); SE on Wash Rd to Wash 4 site (GPS 32.5927, -115.0341), Wash 6 (GPS 32.5917, -115.0325), Wash 10 (GPS 32.5848, -115.0246) & Wash 20 (GPS 32.5717, -115.0051). Palo Verde Flats just W of Glamis on SR 78 (GPS 32.5938, -115.0526). Cement Flats near jct of SR 78 & Gecko Rd (GPS 32.5829, -115.1035). Roadrunner Campground S on Gecko Rd to its end (GPS 32.5442, -115.0704); Pads 1, 1.5, 2, 2.5, 3, 4, 5 Gecko Loop & Keyhole are along Gecko Rd between Cement Flats & Roadrunner. Osborn Overlook site just off SR 78 between Glamis & Cement Flats (GPS 32.5859, -115.0759). 160,000 acres. Largest sand dunes recreation area in America; 40 mi long, 5 mi wide. Popular ORV area. Visitor center.

South Dunes Campgrounds $40/week
Imperial Sand Dunes Recreation Area
Bureau of Land Management
From I-8 exit 159, qtr mi N on Ogilby Rd (CR S34) to Dunes Vista Campground on left; or continue N on Ogilby Rd, then left (W) on Sidewinder Rd to Ogilby Campground. From I-8 exit 156 (Grays Well Rd), E to Buttercup Campground; or SW to Midway Campground near historic Plank Road; farther SW to Grays Well and Dunebuggy Flats campgrounds. 6 primitive, mostly unmaintained camping areas in desert outside LTVAs; most gravel or paved surfaces for RVs. $40 for 14-day short-term permit when purchased off-site; $50 purchased on-site; $180 for season 10/1-4/15. Free off-season for up to 14 days. All year; 14-day limit. Pit toilets, cfga, no drkg wtr. Dump at RV Dump A Tank, Ave 3E exit off I-8 at Yuma. GPS: Dunes Vista, 32.4553, -114.5014; Buttercup, 32.433, -114.5331; Dunebuggy Flats, 32.4249, -114.5633; Grays Well, 32.4237, -114.5527; Midway, 32.4257, -114.5453; Ogilby, 32.4839, -114.5320. 160,000

acres. Largest sand dunes recreation area in America; 40 mi long, 5 mi wide. Popular ORV area. Visitor center.

OJAI (S)

Middle Lion $10
Los Padres National Forest
Rose Valley Recreation Area
1 mi W of Ojai on SR 150; 14.8 mi NW on SR 33; 5.4 mi E on FR 7N03 (Sespe River Rd); 1 mi S on FR 22W06. Formerly $5 daily Adventure Pass, now $10 with federal senior pass; others pay $20. All year; 14-day limit. 8 sites (RVs under 31 ft). Tbls, toilets, cfga, no drkg wtr. Hiking, picnicking, fishing, mountain biking, horseback riding. Elev 3300 ft.

Reyes Creek Campground $10
Los Padres National Forest
36 mi N of Ojai on SR 33; 3 mi E on CR 9N03; 2 mi S on FR 7N11. Formerly $5 daily Adventure Pass; now $10 with federal senior pass; others pay $20. All year; 14-day limit. 30 sites (22-ft RV limit). Tbls, toilets, cfga, drkg wtr. Fishing, hiking. Concession-managed.

Reyes Peak Campground $10
Los Padres National Forest
1 mi W of Ojai on SR 150; 29.2 mi NW on SR 33; 6 mi E on FR 6N06. Formerly $5 daily Adventure Pass, now $10 with federal senior pass; others pay $20. May-Nov; 14-day limit. 6 sites on 15 acres; 16-ft RV limit. Tbls, cfga, toilet, no drkg wtr. Horseback riding, hiking. Scenic. Concession-managed.

Rose Valley Campground $10
Los Padres National Forest
Rose Valley Recreation Area
15 mi N of Ojai on Hwy 33; 5.5 mi E on Sespe River Rd. Formerly $5 daily Adventure Pass, now $10 with federal senior pass; others pay $20. All year; 14-day limit. 9 sites (30-ft RV limit). Tbls, toilets, cfga, no drkg wtr. Swimming, fishing. Non-campers pay $10 day use fee. Elev 3400 ft. Concession-managed.

OLD STATION (N)

Butte Lake Campground $10
Lassen Volcanic National Park
From Old Station at jct with SR 89, 11 mi E on SR 44, watching for campground signs; right (S) on rough dirt rd. $10 with federal senior pass during 6/3-9/12; others pay $20. During 9/13-10/24, sites are $15 ($7.50 with senior pass) but no wtr. Park entry fee also charged. 101 sites, most 45-ft pull-through. Tbls, flush toilets, cfga, drkg wtr, amphitheater, bear lockers. Boating(l), fishing, hiking.

ORLAND (N)

Buckhorn Campground $9
Black Butte Lake
Corps of Engineers
From Orland at the Black Butte Lake exit of I-5, 14 mi W on CR 200 (Newville Rd), following signs past dam; half mi SW of jct with Black Butte Rd; at N end of lake. $9 base with federal senior pass at 65 non-elec sites; $10 at premium locations during 4/1-10/31, $9 rest of year (others pay $18, $20, $18). Group camping area by reservation. All year; 14-day limit. Tbls, flush toilets, cfga, drkg wtr, showers, playground, beach, amphitheater, dump, fish cleaning station, interpretive trail, shelters. Boating(l), fishing, hiking, swimming. Non-campers pay $5 day use fee.

Orland Buttes Campground $9
Black Butte Lake
Corps of Engineers
From Orland at the Black Butte Lake exit of I-5, 6 mi W on CR 200; 3.3 mi SW on CR 206; half mi W. $9 with federal senior pass at 35 non-elec sites; others pay $18. Group camping by reservation. 4/1-9/30; 14-day limit. 18 pull-through sites, 35-ft RV limit. Tbls, flush toilets, cfga, drkg wtr, dump, beach, fish cleaning station, amphitheater. Horseback riding, swimming, waterskiing, fishing.

ORLEANS (N)

Aikens Creek West   FREE
Six Rivers National Forest
10.5 mi SW of Orleans on SR 96 (5 mi E of Weitchpec); on Klamath River. Free. All year; 14-day limit. 29 sites (35-ft RV limit). Toilet, cfga, no drkg wtr; reduced services in winter. Wheelchair access. Fishing, swimming. Multi-family sites available.

Beans Camp Campground   FREE
Klamath National Forest
From Hwy 96 at S end of Orleans, follow FR 15N01 (Eyesee Rd) 17 mi; right on FR 12N22 for half mi for first two sites; four other sites down the hill. Free. All year; 14-day limit. 6 sites. Tbls, toilets, cfga, no drkg wtr, no trash service. Secluded at 4000-ft elev. Managed by Six Rivers NF.

E-Ne-Nuck $10
Six Rivers National Forest
10.2 mi SW of Orleans on SR 96; next to Bluff Creek camp at Klamath River. $10. 6/1-10/15; 14-day limit. 10 sites (30-ft RV limit). Tbls, toilets, cfga, drkg wtr. Swimming, boating, fishing.

Fish Lake Campground $10
Six Rivers National Forest
10.7 mi SW of Orleans on SR 96; 4 mi NW on FR 16N01 (Bluff Creek Rd); right on Fish Lake Rd (FR 10N12) for 3 mi. $10. MD-10/15; 14-day limit. 24 sites; 12 acres; 20-ft RV limit. Toilets, tbls, drkg wtr. Dump at nearby Aikens Creek Campground. Hiking, fishing, picnicking, swimming.

Frog Pond Campground   FREE
Klamath National Forest
24 mi N of Orleans on SR 96; just past bridge over Klamath River & qtr mi before Dillon Creek Campground, turn on FR

14N69; at 3-way jct, veer left onto FR 14N21 for several miles, then onto dirt rd FR 13N13 to camp. Free. May-Oct; 14-day limit. 3 sites. Tbls, toilet, cfga, no drkg wtr, no trash service. Fishing in Frog Pond, also named Lake Oogarmomtok. Managed by Six Rivers NF.

Nordheimer $8
Klamath National Forest
About 7 mi N of Orleans on SR 96; 14 mi E on Hwy 93; on Salmon River. $8 during 5/1-10/31; free rest of year; 14-day limit. 12 sites. Toilets, cfga, drkg wtr. No wtr or trash service during free period. Boating(l), fishing, whitewater rafting. Secluded. Administered by Six Rivers NF. Not recommended for large RVs due to narrow, one-lane rd.

Pearch Creek Campground $10
Six Rivers National Forest
1 mi NE of Orleans on SR 96. $10. 4/15-10/30; 14-day limit. 10 sites (30-ft RV limit). Toilets, tbls, cfga, drkg wtr, dump. Hiking, fishing, picnicking, swimming.

OROVILLE (N)

Feather Falls   FREE
Plumas National Forest
Follow Oro Dam Blvd NE of Oroville; right on Olive Hwy for 8 mi; right on Forbestown Rd for 7 mi; left on Lumpkin Rd for 10 mi to trailhead turnoff; left for 1.5 mi; at Feather Falls trailhead. Free. All year; 14-day limit. 5 sites, primarily for tents. Tbls, toilets, cfga, piped drkg wtr (no wtr in early 2017). Hiking, fishing. Elev 2500 ft.

Oroville State Wildlife Area   FREE
Just SW of Oroville off SR 70 & S of SR 162. Free. All year; 14-day limit. Primitive camping on 11,870 acres bordered by 12 mi of river channels. Fishing, hunting, hiking, canoeing.

PALMDALE (S)

Southfork Campground $5
Angeles National Forest
From Palmdale, follow 156th St (Valyermo Rd) to Big Rock Creek Rd, then 2 mi. $5 daily or $30 annually. May-Nov (or weather permitting); 14-day limit. 21 sites; 16-ft RV limit. Tbls, toilets, cfga, no drkg wtr. Picnicking, hiking trails. Stocked trout in Big Rock Creek. Elev 4500 ft.

PALM DESERT (S)

Pinyon Flat $8
San Bernardino National Forest
14 mi SW of Palm Desert on SR 74, crossing Santa Rosa Indian Reservation. $8. All year; 14-day limit. 18 sites (15-ft RV limit). Tbls, toilets, cfga, drkg wtr. Hiking. Nearby Santa Rosa Wilderness contains bighorn sheep.

Santa Rosa   FREE
State Wildlife Area
SE and SW of Palm Desert, access from SR 74. Free. All

year; 14-day limit. Primitive camping on 103,862 acres; no facilities. Hiking, hunting. Area contains nation's largest herd of penninsular bighorn sheep.

Santa Rosa Springs   FREE
San Bernardino National Forest
SW of Palm Desert on SR 74, then S on unpaved Santa Rosa Mountain Truck Trail (FR 7S02). Free. All year; 14-day limit. 3 sites. Tbls, toilet, cfga, drkg wtr. Hiking, horseback riding, OHV activities, mountain biking.

Toolbox Springs Campground
San Bernardino National Forest
SW of Palm Desert on SR 74, then W on unpaved FR 6S13 (Thomas Mountain Rd). Free dispersed camping at about 6 primitive sites. Toilet, cfga, no drkg wtr. Hiking, mountain biking, hunting.

PALO VERDE (S)

Oxbow Campground $7.50
Bureau of Land Management
Lake Havasu District
3 mi S of Palo Verde on SR 78; 1 mi E on gravel rd from sign marked "Colorado River." Camp is at old river channel oxbow in both Arizona & California. $7.50 for seniors with federal senior pass; others pay $15 (or $75 annually). Non-campers pay $10 day use fee except holders of LTVA passes. All year; 14-day limit. Undesignated, unmarked primitive sites. No facilities. Boating(l), fishing, hiking, swimming, picnicking. Near popular OHV trails & Cibola National Wildlife Refuge. Free use permit required. No open fires; use charcoal grills or propane stoves.

PARKER (ARIZONA)

Crossroads $5
Bureau of Land Management
8 mi NW of Parker (in California) on Parker Dam Rd. $5. All year; 14-day limit. 12 undeveloped sites. Tbls, toilets, cfga, no drkg wtr. Along Colorado River. Boat trailer fees expected to be levied.

Empire Landing $7.50
Bureau of Land Management
9 mi N of Parker on Parker Dam Rd, on California side of the Colorado River in the Parker Dam Recreation Area (7 mi N of Earp). $7.50 for seniors with federal senior pass at sites without hookups; others pay $15. Elec/wtr sites $30 ($15 with senior pass). All year; 14-day limit. 48 RV sites, 16 elec/wtr, 20 tent sites. Tbls, flush toilets, cfga, drkg wtr, coin showers, dump($5). Fishing, hiking, rockhounding, boating. 20 acres. Non-campers pay $3 for day use.

PASKENTA (N)

Dead Mule   FREE
Mendocino National Forest
28 mi W of Paskenta. S on RD 23N02, right on RD 23N50;

left on Rd 23N54 to campground. Free. 6/1-11/1. 2 RV/tent sites. Tbls, toilets, cfga, no trash service. Wtr W of camp. Elev 5000 ft.

Del Harleson Camp   FREE
Mendocino National Forest
21 mi SW of Paskenta. S on RD 23N02; left on RD 23N69; left on RD 23N03; left on RD 23N74 to campground. Free. 5/15-11/15. 4 sites. Tbls, toilets, cfga, no drkg wtr. Elev 4200 ft.

Kingsley Glade   FREE
Mendocino National Forest
22 mi W of Paskenta on RD 23N01; left on RD 24N01 to campground. Free. 6/1-11/1. 6 sites, edge of meadow. Toilets, cfga, tbls, no drkg wtr. Hitching posts, corral. Riding trails. Elev 4500 ft.

Sugar Spring   FREE
Mendocino National Forest
35 mi W of Paskenta. S on RD 23N02; right on Rd 23N69; right on Rd 23N41 to campground; at N side of Thomas Creek. Free. 6/1-11/1. 3 sites. Tbls, toilets, cfga, no drkg wtr or trash service. Wtr W of camp. Hiking, picnicking. Elev 5400 ft.

Sugarfoot Glade   FREE
Mendocino National Forest
24 mi W of Paskenta on FR 24N01. Free. Open about 6/1-11/15; 14-day limit. 6 primitive sites; 16-ft RV limit. Tbls, cfga, toilet, no wtr (creek dry in summer), no trash service.

Three Prong   FREE
Mendocino National Forest
25 mi W of Paskenta on RD 23N01; left on Rd 24N13 to campground. Dirt rds. Free. 6/1-11/1. 6 sites; 24-ft RV limit. Tbls, toilet, cfga, no trash service. Hiking. Elev 4800 ft.

PATTERSON (C)
Deer Creek Campground $10
Frank Raines OHV Regional Park
Stanislaus County Dept. of Parks & Recreation
From I-5 exit 434 at Patterson, about 0.5 mi W on Diablo Grade Pkwy; right (NW) for 17 mi on Del Puerto Canyon Rd to park. $10 for seniors at 20 non-elec sites (non-seniors pay $25); $15 for seniors at 34 full hookups (non-seniors pay $30). All year; 15-day limit. 850-acre OHV area open about 10/25-6/1; closed during fire season. Tbls, flush toilets, cfga, drkg wtr, showers, rec hall with kitchen. Nature & hiking trails, volleyball, horseshoes pits, OHV activities for dune buggies, ATVs, dirt bikes (including mud bog). No reservations. Non-campers pay $15 day use fee ($5 for seniors).

PAYNES CREEK (N)
Black Rock   FREE
Lassen National Forest
8.5 mi SE of Paynes Creek on CR 202; 22 mi SE on CR 28N29. Free. 5/1-10/31; 14-day limit. 6 dispersed sites; 1 acre. Tbls, toilets, cfga, no drkg wtr. Stream. Hiking, picnicking, fishing.

Paynes Creek   FREE
Bureau of Land Management
Redding Field Office
Near Paynes Creek, follow Jelly Ferry Rd 3 mi N of I-5 to Bend, then 2 mi NE on Bend Ferry Rd. Free. All year; 14-day limit. Primitive undesignated sites. Tbls, toilets, cfga, no drkg wtr. Parking for horse trailers. No camping near mouth of Inks Creek. Fishing, horseback riding, hiking. Mouth of Inks Creek & areas near it are closed to camping.

PEARBLOSSOM (S)
Sycamore Flats Campground $5
Angeles National Forest
S of Pearblossom on Longview Rd; left on Valyermo Rd, pass ranger station; right on Big Rock Rd for 2 mi. $5 daily or $30 annually Adventure Pass. All year; 14-day limit. 12 sites (18-ft RV limit). Tbls, toilet, cfga, drkg wtr.

PIEDRA (C)
Choinumni Park $9
Fresno County Parks Division
From Piedra (30 mi E of Fresno), 0.5 mi N on N. Piedra Rd; 1 mi E on Trimmer Springs Rd; 1 mi E on Pine Flat Rd (toward Pine Flat Lake); at N shore of Kings River. $9 for seniors at 75 primitive sites (non-seniors pay $25). Tbls, pit toilets, cfga, drkg wtr, dump, playground. Fishing, hiking trail. $5 per vehicle entry fee (or $40 annual county pass). 170 acres.

Island Park Campground $10
Pine Flat Lake
Corps of Engineers
9.5 mi NE of Piedra on Trimmer Springs Rd, then S following signs. $10 base with federal senior pass at 54 non-elec sites; others pay $20. 25 elec sites (30-amp), $30 ($15 with senior pass). All year; 14-day limit. 65-ft RV limit. Tbls, flush toilets, coin showers, dump, cfga, drkg wtr, fishing pier, fish cleaning station. Fishing, boating (l), hiking. Non-campers pay $5 day use fee.

PIERPOINT (C)
Upper Peppermint   FREE
Sequoia National Forest
Giant Sequoia National Monument
26.5 mi E of Pierpoint on SR 190; 3 mi S on FR 90; half mi E on FR 21S07. Free. 5/17-9/30; 14-day limit. About 19 dispersed sites on 10 acres; 22-ft RV limit. Tbls, toilets, cfga, no drkg wtr. Picnicking, swimming, stream fishing, horseback riding & rental (2 mi). Elev 7100 ft.

PINE VALLEY (S)

Bobcat Meadows $5
Cleveland National Forest
6.3 mi E of Pine Valley on I-8; follow Buckman Springs Rd
3.3 mi; right on Corral Canyon Rd (FR17S04) at ORV sign
for 5.9 mi (rd quite narrow in places); bear left at "Y" onto
Skye Valley Rd for 2 mi; next to ORV area. $5. All year;
14-day limit. $5 daily pass fee or $30 annually. 20 sites;
27-ft RV limit. Tbls, toilets, cfga, no drkg wtr, no trash
service. Hiking, ORV use.

Burnt Rancheria $12
Cleveland National Forest
E of Pine Valley on I-8, then 9.4 mi N on Sunrise Hwy (Hwy
S1). $12 with federal senior pass; others pay $24. 4/15-
10/1; 14-day limit. 109 sites; 49-ft RV limit. Tbls, flush
& pit toilets, cfga, drkg wtr, amphitheater, coin showers.
Hiking, fishing, biking, horseback riding. $7 day use fee
for non-campers.

Corral Canyon $5
Cleveland National Forest
6.3 mi E of Pine Valley on I-8; follow Buckman Springs Rd
3.3 mi; right on Corral Canyon Rd (FR 17S04) at ORV sign
for 5.9 mi (rd quite narrow in places); bear right at "Y" for
1.4 mi. Next to ORV area. $5. All year; 14-day limit. $5 daily
pass fee or $30 annually. 20 sites; 27-ft RV limit. Tbls,
toilets, cfga, no drkg wtr. Hiking, ORV use. Elev 3500 ft.

Laguna Campground $12
Cleveland National Forest
E of Pine Valley on I-8, then 13 mi N on Sunrise Hwy (Hwy
S1) to just past 26-mile marker. $12 with federal senior
pass; others pay $24. All year; 14-day limit. 104 sites;
45-ft RV limit. Tbls, flush & pit toilets, cfga, drkg wtr, coin
showers, amphitheater. Interpretive programs, biking,
fishing, hiking. Butterfly habitat. Showers/flush toilets
closed 2017 due to water shortage.

PIONEER (C)

Caples Lake $12
Eldorado National Forest
42 mi E of Pioneer on SR 88. $12 with federal senior pass;
others pay $24. MD-10/15; 14-day limit. 34 sites; 35-ft RV
limit. Tbls, toilets, cfga, drkg wtr. Boating, fishing, hiking.
Elev 7800 ft.

Kirkwood Lake $11
Eldorado National Forest
40 mi E of Pioneer on SR 88 to half mi W of town of Kirkwood; left at sign for Kirkwood Ski Resort for half mi.
$11 with federal senior pass; others pay $22. 6/15-10/15;
14-day limit. 12 sites with short parking spurs. Tbls, toilets, cfga, drkg wtr, bear lockers. Boating, fishing, hiking
(rainbow trout). Elev 7600 ft.

Lumberyard   FREE
Eldorado National Forest
19.9 mi NE of Pioneer on SR 88; .1 mi SW on Ellis Rd. Free.
6/1 11/1; 14-day limit. 5 sites (RVs under 16 ft). Tbls, cfga,
no drkg wtr, toilets. Boating (rl), picnicking; swimming,
fishing. Elev 6200 ft; 2 acres.

Mokelumne   FREE
Eldorado National Forest
19.9 mi NE of Pioneer on SR 88; 8.5 mi S on Ellis Rd (FR
92; 2.5 mi E on FR 8N50 (Salt Springs Rd). Free. 5/1-11/16;
14-day limit. 8 RV sites (typically 45 ft). Toilets, cfga, no
drkg wtr, some tbls, no trash service. Swimming; picnicking; fishing; boating. Elev 3200 ft; 2 acres. On Mokelumne
River. Salt Springs Rd. closed early 2017 by storm damage; check current status before arrival.

Moore Creek   FREE
Eldorado National Forest
19 mi NE of Pioneer on SR 88; 8.5 mi S on Ellis Rd; 2.5 mi E
on FR 8N50 (Salt Springs Rd). Free. 5/1-11/15. 8 sites (RVs
under 16 ft). Toilets, cfga, no drkg wtr, some tbls, no trash
service. Swimming, fishing,, boating(l-4 mi). Swimming
holes nearby. Elev 3200 ft; 5 acres. On Mokelumne River.
Salt Sprngs Rd. closed early 2017 by storm damage; check
current status before arrival.

Pipi Campground $11
Eldorado National Forest
11 mi E of Pioneer on SR 88; 0.8 mi NW on Omo Ranch Rd;
5.9 mi N on North/South Rd. $11 with federal senior pass;
others pay $22. About 5/1-11/15; 14-day limit. 51 sites;
35-ft RV limit. Tbls, toilets, cfga, drkg wtr, fishing piers.
Fishing, OHV use.

Silver Lake East $12
Eldorado National Forest
36 mi E of Pioneer on SR 88. $12 with federal senior pass;
others pay $24. About 6/1-10/15; 14-day limit. 24 sites;
35-ft RV limit. Tbls, toilets, cfga, drkg wtr. Fishing, hiking,
boating. Elev 7200 ft.

South Shore $11
Eldorado National Forest
19.9 mi NE of Pioneer on SR 88; 3.5 mi N on Bear River
Rd. $11 with federal senior pass; others pay $22. About
MD-10/15; 14-day limit. 22 sites; 35-ft RV limit. Tbls,
toilets, cfga, drkg wtr. Fishing, hiking.

White Azalea   FREE
Eldorado National Forest
19.9 mi NE of Pioneer on SR 88; 8.5 mi S on Ellis Rd; 3 mi
E on FR 8N50. Free. 5/15-11/15; 14-day limit. 6 RV/tent
sites (RV limit, 16 ft). Toilets, cfga, no drkg wtr, no tbls.
Swimming; picnicking; fishing; boating (ld--3 mi). Elev
3500 ft; 2 acres. On Mokelumne River.

Woods Lake $12
Eldorado National Forest
45 mi NE of Pioneer on SR 88; 1.5 S at sign for Woods Lake Recreation Area. Rd unsuitable for large RVs. $12 with federal senior pass; others pay $24. 7/1-10/15; 14-day limit. 25 small sites. Boating, fishing, hiking. Elev 8200 ft.

PLACERVILLE (N)
Airport Flat   FREE
Eldorado National Forest
23 mi E of Placerville on US 50; 24 mi N on Ice House-Loon Lake Rd; where rd forks for Gerle Creek Campground or Loon Lake, take Gerle Creek branch for 3 mi. Free. All year; 14-day limit. 16 sites. Tbls, toilets, cfga, bear lockers, no drkg wtr, bear boxes. Fishing, swimming, motorcycling, ATV, 4WD, hiking trails. Elev 5300 ft.

Camino Cove   FREE
Eldorado National Forest
Crystal Basin Recreation Area
Sacramento Municipal Utility District
23 mi E of Placerville on US 50; 7 mi N on Ice House-Loon Lake Rd; 3 mi W on Peavine Ridge Rd; 5 mi N on Bryant Springs Rd past West Point boat ramp, then 1.5 mi E to campground turnoff on the right; on NW shore of Union Valley Lake. Free. MD-LD; 14-day limit. 32 sites. Toilets, cfga, no tbls, no drkg wtr. Fishing, boating, hiking. Elev 4875. Lake owned by utility district.

Capps Crossing $10
Eldorado National Forest
15 mi E of Placerville on US 50; 6 mi S on Sly Park Rd; 10 mi NE on Mormon Emigrant Trail; 6 mi S on North/South Rd. $10 with federal senior pass; others pay $20. 5/15-9/15; 14-day limit. 4 RV sites, typically 45 ft. Tbls, toilets, cfga, drkg wtr. Fishing at North Fork of Consumnes River. Hiking, swimming. Elev 5200 ft. Single sites available when not reserved by groups.

China Flat $10
Eldorado National Forest
32.5 mi E of Placerville on US 50; from Kyburz, 4.5 mi S on Silver Fork Rd. $10 with federal senior pass; others pay $20. MD-LD; 14-day limit. 10 RV sites, typically 40-60 ft. Tbls, toilets, cfga, drkg wtr. Swimming, fishing, motorcycling, biking, 4WD, hiking. On Silver Fork of American River. Elev 4800 ft.

Jones Fork $10
Crystal Basin Recreation Area
Eldorado National Forest
Sacramento Municipal Utility District
23 mi E of Placerville on US 50; 13.5 mi N on Ice House Rd; near Jones Fork of Silver Creek at Union Valley Reservoir in the Crystal Basin. $10. MD-9/4; 14-day limit. 10 sites; 35-ft RV limit. Tbls, toilets, bear lockers, cfga, no drkg wtr.

Fishing, hiking, boating, swimming, biking. Elev 4900 ft. Utility district owns lake.

Northshore Campground $10
Crystal Basin Recreation Area
Eldorado National Forest
Sacramento Municipal Water District
23 mi E of Placerville on US 50; 31 mi N on Ice House Rd; take the Loon Lake fork; on NW shore of Loon Lake. $10. 6/15-10/15; 14 day limit. 15 sites. Tbls, toilets, cfga, no drkg wtr. Fishing, boating, swimming, hiking, biking. Elev 6378 ft. Lake owned by utility district.

Northwind Campground $10
Eldorado National Forest
23 mi W of Placerville on US 50; 11 mi N on Ice House Rd; E (right) on FR 32; on N shore of Ice House Reservoir. $10. MD-LD; 14-day limit. 9 sites for self-contained RVs & tents. Tbls, toilets, cfga, drkg wtr. Fishing, boating, swimming, biking, hiking. Elev 5500 ft.

Sand Flat $10
Eldorado National Forest
28 mi E of Placerville on US 50 at South Fork of American River. $10 with federal senior pass; others pay $20. MD-LD; 14-day limit. 29 sites; 60-ft RV limit. Tbls, toilets, cfga, drkg wtr. Fishing, swimming, hiking.

Silver Fork $10
Eldorado National Forest
32 mi E of Placerville on US 50; from Kyburz, 8 mi S on Silver Fork Rd. $10 with federal senior pass; others pay $20. MD-LD weekends; 14-day limit. 35 sites; 45-ft RV limit. Tbls, toilets, cfga, drkg wtr. Fishing, swimming, hiking. Elev 5600 ft.

Strawberry Point $10
Eldorado National Forest
23 mi E of Placervile on Hwy 50; 11 mi N on Ice House Rd (FR 3); right 3 mi on Ice House/Wright Lake Tie Rd (FR 32. On N shore of Ice House Reservoir. $10. MD-10/1; 14-day limit. 10 sites. Tbls, toilets, cfga, no drkg wtr. Swimming, boating, fishing. Boat ramp at Ice House Camp.

West Point   FREE
Crystal Basin Recreation Area
Eldorado National Forest
Sacramento Municipal Utility District
23 mi W of Placerville on US 50; 7 mi N on Ice House Rd; 3 mi E on Peavine Ridge Rd; 5 mi N on Bryant Springs Rd to just past the boat ramp on NW shore of Union Valley Lake. Free. Apr-Nov; 14-day limit. 8 primitive sites. Toilet, cfga, no tbls, no drkg wtr. Boating(l), fishing, hiking. Elev 4875 ft. Lake owned by utility district.

Wrights Lake $10
Crystal Basin Recreation Area
Eldorado National Forest
Sacramento Municipal Utility District
23 mi E of Placerville on US 50; 11 mi N on Ice House Rd (FR 3); right on Wrights Lake Tie Rd for 9 mi; left for 2 mi on Wrights Lake Rd; at S shore of Wrights Lake. $10 with federal senior pass; others pay $20. About 7/1-10/1; 14-day limit. 82 sites (including 15 for equestrians); 35-ft RV limit. Tbls, toilets, cfga, drkg wtr. Boating (no mtrs), fishing, hiking, horseback riding, biking. Elev 7000 ft. Lake owned by utility district.

PORTERVILLE (C)
Tule Recreation Area $10
Success Lake
Corps of Engineers
From dam near Porterville, 2 mi E on SR 190, then N following signs. $10 with federal senior pass at 74 non-elec sites; others pay $20. 29 elec sites, $30 ($15 with senior pass). All year; 14-day limit. 103 sites; 65-ft RV limit; 27 pull-through. Tbls, flush toilets, showers, fish cleaning station, dump, playground. Boating(l), fishing, hiking, golf, Saturday campfire programs MD-LD. 3-day minimum stay on holiday weekends.

PORTOLA (N)
Crocker Campground FREE
Plumas National Forest
5 mi E of Portola on SR 70 to Beckwourth; 10 mi N on CR 111 (Beckwourth-Genessee Rd.); qtr mi W on FR 24N36. Free. 5/15-10/15; 14-day limit. 10 sites (RVs under 32 ft). Tbls, toilets, no drkg wtr or trash service. Elev 5800 ft; 1 acre.

Gold Lake Campground $10
Lakes Basin Recreation Area
Plumas National Forest
6 mi SW of Portola on Rd A15 to jct with SR 89; 3 mi NW on SR 89 to Graegle; 10 mi S on Gold Lake Rd to sign. $10 during 5/1-10/31; free rest of year, but no services or flush toilets. 37 sites. Pit & portable toilets, cfga, tbls, no drkg wtr. Fishing, boating, hiking.

Goose Lake Campground $10
Lakes Basin Recreation Area
Plumas National Forest
6 mi SW of Portola on Rd A15 to jct with SR 89; 3 mi NW on SR 89 to Graegle; 12 mi S on Gold Lake Rd to camp. $10 during 5/15-9/30, free rest of year; 14-day limit. 13 sites. Toilets, cfga, tbls, no drkg wtr. Fishing, boating.

Lakes Basin Campground $11
Lakes Basin Recreation Area
Plumas National Forest
6 mi SW of Portola on Rd A15 to jct with SR 89; 3 mi NW on SR 89 to Graegle; 6.9 mi S on Gold Lake Rd to sign; right on

narrow access rd for 0.3 mi. $11 with federal senior pass; others pay $22; free 9/15-MD, but no wtr or services. All year; 14-day limit. 23 sites; 26-ft RV limit. Tbls, pit toilets, cfga, drkg wtr. Fishing, boating, hiking, interpretive site. Elev 6300 ft.

POTTER VALLEY (N)
Oak Flat $10
Mendocino National Forest
Pacific Gas & Electric
18.1 mi NE of Potter Valley on CR 240; 3 mi NE on FR 20N01. $10 during 5/15-9/30; $5 rest of year when wtr is off; 14-day limit. 12 sites (RVs under 26 ft). Tbls, toilets, cfga, drkg wtr, stoves. Swimming, fishing, sailing, boating (rld), hiking, waterskiing. Elev 1800 ft; 4 acres. Lake. Plenty of overflow space; primarily a motorcycle camp & weekend overflow site on heavy weekends.

QUARTZSITE (ARIZONA)
La Posa LTVA $180
Bureau of Land Management
From I-10 at Quartzsite, take US 95 S 1 mi; site on four graded roads on both sides of US 95. $180 permit for season or $40 for 14 days during 9/15-4/15; $15 per day or $75 seasonal during 4/16-9/14; camp free up to 14 days off-season. 2,000 sites on 11,400 acres. Sanitary dump 2 mi N of Quartzite. Toilets, drkg wtr (8 faucets), telephone, trash pickup, cfga, dance floor, ramada. Federal senior pass discounts do not apply to LTVA fees. Rockhounding, picnicking, hiking, sightseeing.

Short-Term Boondock Area FREE
Bureau of Land Management
Near Quartzsite at Milepost 99 and Milepost 112 adjoining Hwy 95. Free. Undesignated primitive camping areas; no facilities. 14-day limit. Self-contained RVs of any length may be parked in these areas but must move to new sites outside of a 25-mile radius after the 14-day period. RVers use these sites primarily while taking part in events and activities in Quartzsite.

QUINCY (N)
Boulder Creek $11.50
Antelope Lake Recreation Area
Plumas National Forest
About 6 mi N of Quincy on SR 89/70 to split; follow SR 89 about 4 mi NE; 7 mi W on Rd A22 though Taylorsville to "T" at rodeo grounds, then right (NE) for 30 mi on Genesee-Antelope Lake Rd to Antelope Lake & Boulder Creek. $11.50 with federal senior pass; others pay $23. MD-LD; 14-day limit. 35 sites. Tbls, pit toilets, cfga, drkg wtr, bear lockers, amphitheater with campfire programs. Boating(l - $7), fishing, dump (closed at last report).

Deanes Valley FREE
Plumas National Forest
5.4 mi W of Quincy on CR 414 (Quincy Spanish Ranch Rd); 4 mi S on FR 24N29; 1 mi S on FR 24N28. Free. 4/1-10/31; 14-day limit. 7 sites (RVs under 22 ft). Tbls, toilet, cfga, no drkg wtr. Swimming, picnicking, fishing, horseback riding, hiking. Elev 4400 ft; 7 acres. Nature trails. S fork of Rock Creek.

Greenville Campground $10
Plumas National Forest
25 mi N of Quincy on SR 89; 1 mi N of Greenville. $10 with federal senior pass; others pay $20. MD-9/30; 14-day limit. 19 sites. Tbls, new pit toilets, new cfga, drkg wtr, horseshoe pits. Fishing, hiking.

Grizzly Creek $10
Bucks Lake Recreation Area
Plumas National Forest
17 mi SW of Quincy on Bucks Lake Rd; 2 mi W of Bucks Lake on Quincy-Oroville Rd (Hwy 162). $10 with federal senior pass; others pay $20. 5/1-9/30; 14-day limit. Camp often open later; regular fees prevail. 8 sites. Tbls, pit toilets, cfga, no drkg wtr. Elev 5400 ft.

Lower Bucks $10
Bucks Lake Recreation Area
Plumas National Forest
18 mi SW of Quincy on CR PL414; 4 mi NW on FR 24N33; 2 mi w on FR 24N24. $10 with federal senior pass; others pay $20. MD-10/9; 14-day limit. 7 RV sites (RVs under 22 ft). Tbls, toilets, cfga, firewood, no drkg wtr. Dump. Picnicking; boating (rld--5 mi); swimming, fishing, hiking. Elev 5200 ft; 6 acres. Mountains. Self-contained RVs only on Lower Bucks Lake.

Plumas-Sierra County Fairgrounds $10
From SR 89/70 (E. Main St) E of downtown Quincy, N on Fairgrounds Rd at Pioneer Park into fairgrounds. $10 at about 200 sites without hookups; $20 at 147 elec/wtr sites; $30 at 5 full hookups. Flush toilets, showers, drkg wtr, dump.

Silver Lake FREE
Bucks Lake Recreation Area
Plumas National Forest
5.7 mi W of Quincy on CR 414 (Quincy Spanish Ranch Rd); 8.4 mi W on FR 24N30. Free. 5/1-10/31 (no services off-season); 14-day limit. 8 sites (not recommended for RVs except van & pickup campers). Tbls, toilets, cfga, no drkg wtr. Horseback riding, picnicking, fishing, boating (ld), hiking. Elev 5800 ft; 5 acres. Lake trailhead. Entrance to Bucks Lake Wilderness.

Taylor Lake FREE
Plumas National Forest
18 mi N of Quincy on Hwy 89; 5 mi E on CR 214 to Taylors-

ville; 2 mi N on CR 214; 10 mi E on FR 27N10; 1 mi on FR 27N57. Free. Undesignated primitive sites; no facilities, no drkg wtr. Hiking, trout fishing.

Whitehorse Campground $11.50
Bucks Lake Recreation Area
Plumas National Forest
About 14 mi SW of Quincy on Bucks Lake Rd (3 mi E of lake). $11.50 with federal senior pass; others pay $23. 4/15-9/15; 14-day limit. 20 sites. Tbls, pit toilets, cfga, drkg wtr. Concession-managed.

RAMONA (S)

Arroyo Salado $10
Primitive Camp Area
Anza-Borrego Desert State Park
16 mi E on CR S22 from Borrego Springs. $10 daily permit ($8 off-season) All year. Open camping; no facilities, no drkg wtr. Open fires prohibited.

Fish Creek $10
Anza-Borrego Desert State Park
12 mi S of Hwy 78 in Ocotillo Wells on Split Mountain Rd. $10 daily permit ($8 off-season). All year. 15 sites. Tbls, toilets, cfga, no drkg wtr. Scenic "Erosion Road" drive is on dirt & paved roads, directed by markers at 1-mi intervals. Sites include Font's Point Wash, Palo Verde Wash and Borrego Badlands.

Mountain Palm Springs $10
Primitive Camp Area
Anza-Borrego Desert State Park
15 mi N on CR S2 from I-8 at Ocotillo. $10 daily permit ($8 off-season). All year. Open RV or tent camping; no designated sites. Toilets, no drkg wtr, no cfga. Hiking trails nearby.

RAVENDALE (N)

Dodge Reservoir Campground FREE
Bureau of Land Management
From Ravendale, 12 mi NE on CR 502; right (NE) on unimproved dirt CR 506 for 11 mi; at shore of 480-acre irrigation lake. Free. All year; 14-day limit. 11 sites. Tbls, pit toilet, cfga, no drkg wtr or trash service. Trout fishing.

RED BLUFF (N)

Alder Creek $10
Lassen National Forest
44 mi E of Red Bluff on SR 36, then E on SR 36/89; 8 mi S on Hey 32; at Deer Creek. $10 during 4/1-11/1; free rest of year. 6 sites (trailers discouraged). Tbls, toilets, cfga, no drkg wtr. Trout fishing.

Sycamore Grove $8
Red Bluff Recreational Area
Mendocino National Forest
From I-5 at Red Bluff, 100 yds E on SR 36; half mi S on Sale

Lane; on Sacramento River. $8 base with federal senior pass; others pay $16 base, $25 at 10 sites with elec ($17 with senior pass). 1 large family site, $30 by reservation. All year; 14-day limit. 40 sites; 45-ft RV limit. Tbls, flush toilets, cfga, drkg wtr, showers($). Boating(l), swimming, waterskiing, mountain biking. No wtr during winter. 488 acres. 4 mi of trails. Sacramento River Discovery Center.

Tehama   FREE
State Wildlife Area
E of Red Bluff on SR 99, then NE on Hogsback Rd into refuge; or, about 15 mi NE of Red Bluff on Hwy 36, then S on Plum Creek Rd. Free. All year; 14-day limit. Primitive camping, no facilities. 46,862 acres. Hiking, hunting (turkey, deer, wild pigs).

Toomes Camp   FREE
Mendocino National Forest
65 mi W of Red Bluff; near Yolla Bolly Wilderness. Free. 6/1-10/31; 14-day limit. 2 sites. Tbls, toilet, cfga, no drkg wtr, no trash service.

Willow Lake   FREE
Lassen National Forest
55 mi E of Red Bluff on Hwy 36; left for 3 mi on Willow Lake Rd (FR 29N19). Free. Late May-11/1; 14-day limit. Dispersed undesignated sites; no facilities except toilet. Fishing, hiking.

REDLANDS (S)
Heart Bar Campground $11.50
San Bernardino National Forest
From I-10 exit 80 at Redlands, left (N) on University St for about 0.5 mi; right (E) on E. Lugonia Ave (SR 38) for about 30 mi; right on FR 1N02 for qtr mi. $11.50 with federal senior pass; others pay $23. 89 sites; 50-ft RV limit. About 5/15-9/30; 14-day limit. Tbls, toilets, cfga, drkg wtr, dump ($10). 2-day minimum stay required on weekends, 3-days holiday weekends. Hiking, mountain biking.

REDDING (N)
Antlers Campground $10
Shasta-Trinity National Forest
25 mi N of Redding on I-5; after crossing Shasta Lake twice, E toward Lakehead at Lakeshore Dr/Antlers Rd exit; E at end of ramp, then right on Antlers Rd about 1 mi; on Sacramento arm of lake. $10 with federal senior pass; others pay $20 (double sites $35). About 3/15-10/31; 14-day limit. 41 sites; 30-ft RV limit. Tbls, flush toilets, cfga, drkg wtr, bear lockers, amphitheater. Weekend interpretive programs, boating(l - $8 for non-campers), fishing.

Bailey Cove Campground $10
Shasta-Trinity National Forest
19 mi N of Redding on I-5; to O'Brien at Shasta Caverns exit; right at end of ramp for 0.4 mi to campground access;

right for 0.6 mi. $10 with federal senior pass; others pay $20. All year; 14-day limit. 7 sites; 45-ft RV limit (typically 30-ft). Tbls, flush toilets, cfga, drkg wtr, bear lockers. Non-campers pay $6 day use.

Brandy Creek $7.50
Whiskeytown National Recreation Area
11 mi NW of Redding on SR 299; 5 mi W on S Shore Rd (JFK Dr). $7.50 with federal senior pass; others pay $15. All year; 14-day limit. 46 sites for self-contained RVs under 34 ft. Tbls, cfga, drkg wtr, dump, ice. Swimming, picnicking, fishing, deer hunting, boating (rld), horseback riding, waterskiing. Ranger program. Elev 1210 ft; 20 acres. On Whiskeytown Lake. $10 for 7-day entry pass ($40 annual).

Ellery Creek $10
Shasta-Trinity National Forest
About 21 mi N of Redding on I-5; exit at Salt Creek/Gilman Rd, then 16 mi E on Gilman; on the right between Moore Creek & Pine Point Campgrounds; at McCloud arm of Shasta Lake. $10 with federal senior pass; others pay $20. 4/1-9/15; 14-day limit. 19 sites; 30-ft RV limit. Tbls, pit toilets, cfga, drkg wtr, bear lockers. Fishing, boating.

Hirz Bay Campground $10
Shasta-Trinity National Forest
About 21 mi N of Redding on I-5; exit at Salt Creek/Gilman Rd, then 11 mi E on Gilman; on Sacramento arm of Shasta Lake. $10 with federal senior pass; others pay $20 (double sties $35). All year; 14-day limit. 48 sites; 30-ft RV limit. Tbls, flush toilets, cfga, drkg wtr, bear lockers, phone, dump ($8 for non-campers). Fishing, boating.

Jones Inlet $10
Shasta-Trinity National Forest
7.5 mi E of Redding on Hwy 299; 9 mi N on Dry Creek Rd from Bella Vista. $10 during 3/1-10/31; 14-day limit. Portable toilets, cfga, drkg wtr. Undesignated primitive sites (30-ft RV limit). Boating, swimming, fishing on Shasta Lake. Concessionaire.

Lakeshore East $10
Shasta-Trinity National Forest
25 mi N of Redding on I-5; after crossing Shasta Lake twice, take Antlers Rd/Lakeshore Dr exit; W under I-5 overpass, then left 2.5 mi on Lakeshore Dr; on Sacramento arm of Shasta Lake. $10 with federal senior pass; others pay $20. All year; 14-day limit. 17 sites; 30-ft RV limit. Tbls, flush toilets, cfga, drkg wtr, bear lockers. Fishing, boating.

Lower Jones Valley $9
Shasta-Trinity National Forest
About 9 mi N of Redding on I-5 to exit 687 near Mountain Gate; 3 mi E on Old Oregon Tr; left on Bear Mountain Rd for 8.5 mi to jct with Dry Creek Rd; left about 2 mi, then left at

campground sign. $9 with federal senior pass; others pay $18 (double site $30). All year; 14-day limit. Tbls, pit toilets, cfga, drkg wtr, bear lockers. Hiking, boating, fishing.

Mariners Point Shoreline
Shasta-Trinity National Forest
7.5 mi E of Redding on Hwy 299; at Dry Creek Rd, pick up CR 5J050 for 4 mi. Camping no longer permitted; day use only.

McCloud Bridge $10
Shasta-Trinity National Forest
About 21 mi N of Redding on I-5; exit at Salt Creek/Gilman Rd, then 20 mi E on Gilman Rd. $10 with federal senior pass; others pay $20 (double site $35). 4/1-10/24; 14-day limit. 14 sites; 16-ft RV limit. Tbls, pit toilets, cfga, drkg wtr, bear lockers. Hiking, swimming.

Moore Creek Campground $10
Shasta-Trinity National Forest
About 21 mi N of Redding on I-5; exit at Salt Creek/Gilman Rd, then 20 mi E on Gilman Rd. $10 with federal senior pass; others pay $20. Camp basically for groups, but single sites available. 5/15-9/6; 14-day limit. 16 sites; 16-ft RV limit. Tbls, pit toilets, cfga, drkg wtr, bear lockers. Hiking, swimming. Managed by Shasta Recreation Co.

Nelson Point Campground $10
Shasta-Trinity National Forest
About 21 mi N of Redding on I-5; exit at Salt Creek/Gilman Rd, then N to Conflict Point Rd about 0.5 mi; along Salt Creek inlet. $10. 6/3-9/10; 14-day limit. 8 sites; 16-ft RV limit. Tbls, pit toilets, cfga, bear lockers, no drkg wtr. Fishing, boating.

Old Cow Creek FREE
Latour Demonstration State Forest
50 mi E of Redding. Free. June-Oct, depending on snow. 2 sites (RVs under 16 ft). Tbls, cfga, no drkg wtr. Picnicking, fishing, swimming, hiking, horseback riding (corral avail). Elev 5600 ft.

Old Station FREE
Latour Demonstration State Forest
50 mi E of Redding. Free. June-Oct, depending on snow. 1 site (RV under 16 ft). Picnicking, fishing, swimming, hiking, horseback riding. Thousand Lakes Wilderness Area.

Pine Point Campground $10
Shasta-Trinity National Forest
About 21 mi N of Redding on I-5; exit at Salt Creek/Gilman Rd, then 18 mi E on Gilman; on Upper McCloud arm of lake. $10 with federal senior pass; others pay $20. 6/1-9/10; 14-day limit. 14 sites; 24-ft RV limit. Tbls, pit toilets, cfga, drkg wtr, bear lockers. Fishing, boating.

Shasta OHV Area $10
Shasta-Trinity National Forest
Bureau of Land Management
7 mi N of Redding on I-5; 4 mi W on Shasta Dam Blvd; 2 mi N on Lake Blvd to Keswick Reservoir below Shasta Dam. $10. All year; 14-day limit. 27 sites (30-ft RV limit); 4 picnic sites. Tbls, toilets, cfga, drkg wtr. Biking, horseback riding, fishing. Next to Chappe-Shasta off-highway vehicle staging area. Permit needed for access across Shasta Dam; acquire 72 hrs in advance.

Sims Flat $7.50
Shasta-Trinity National Forest
40 mi N of Redding on I-5; 1 mi S on Sims Rd; on Sacramento River. $7.50 with federal senior pass; others pay $15; free when no wtr available. 4/15-11/27; 14-day limit. 19 sites (24-ft RV limit). Tbls, flush toilets, cfga, drkg wtr. Trout fishing, boating, hiking. Site of 1930s CCC camp.

South Cow Creek FREE
Latour Demonstration State Forest
50 mi E of Redding. Free. June-Oct, depending on snow. 2 sites. Tbls, drkg wtr, cfga. Picnicking, fishing, swimming, hiking, horseback riding. Thousand Lakes Wilderness Area.

REDWAY (N)

Honeydew Creek $8
King Range National Conservation Area
Bureau of Land Management
From US 101 at South Fork/Honeydew exit, follow signs to Honeydew, then follow Wilder Ridge Rd 2 mi toward Ettersburg. $8. All year; 14-day limit. 5 sites; 25-ft RV limit. Tbls, toilets, cfga, no drkg wtr. Hunting, fishing, hiking. Creek is an important salmon spawning stream; do not use soap in it.

Horse Mountain $5
King Range National Conservation Area
Bureau of Land Management
17.5 mi W of Redway on Shelter Cove Rd; 6 mi N on Kings Peak Rd. $5. All year; 14-day limit. 9 sites (20-ft RV limit). Tbls, toilets, cfga, no drkg wtr. Hiking, 4WD, mountain biking, fishing, surfing, horseback riding, swimming, boating. Water-based service available at Shelter Cove, about 30 minutes away at ocean.

Mattole Beach $8
King Range National Conservation Area
Bureau of Land Management
US 101 to Redway from Garberville; W about 30 mi; through Honeydew for 15 mi, then left to end of Lighthouse Rd. $8. Large RVs not recommended. All year; 14-day limit. 14 sites; 25-ft RV limit. Portable toilets, no drkg wtr, cfga, beach. Hunting, fishing, hiking, swimming. Steep, winding dirt rds; some impassable during wet weather. Crowded & noisy in summer.

Tolkan Campground $8
King Range National Conservation Area
Bureau of Land Management
17.5 mi W of Redway on Shelter Cove Rd; 3.5 mi N on Kings Peak Rd. $8. All year; 14-day limit. 9 sites (25-ft RV limit). Tbls, toilets, cfga, drkg wtr, cold showers. Wheelchair access. Fishing. No pets. Elev 1800 ft; 50 acres.

Wailaki $8
King Range National Conservation Area
Bureau of Land Management
17 mi W of Redway on Shelter Cove Rd; 2 mi S on Chemise Mtn Rd. $8. All year; 14-day limit. 13 sites (25-ft RV limit). Tbls, toilets, cfga, drkg wtr. Hiking, 4WD trails, biking, hiking, birdwatching, exhibits.

RENO (NEVADA)
Lookout Campground $6
Toiyabe National Forest
NW of Reno on I-80 to Verdi exit; 11 mi on Old Dog Valley Rd. $6. 6/1-9/30; 14-day limit. 22 sites (22-ft RV limit). Tbls, toilets, cfga, no drkg wtr. Rockhounding (limit 1 bucket of crystals at nearby mine), hiking. Elev 6700 ft.

RINCON (S)
Fry Creek $7.50
Cleveland National Forest
From Rincon (20 mi E of I-15 on SR 76), 8.5 mi N on CR S6; across rd from Observatory camp. $7.50 with federal senior pass; others pay $15. 5/1-11/30. 15 sites (15-ft RV limit; no trailers). Tbls, toilets, cfga, drkg wtr. Near Palomar Observatory. Elev 4800 ft.

Observatory Campground $7.50
Cleveland National Forest
From Rincon (20 mi E of I-15 on SR 76), 8.5 mi N on CR S6. $7.50 with federal senior pass; others pay $15. 4/1-11/30; 14-day limit. 42 sites; 32-ft RV limit. Tbls, flush & pit toilets, cfga, drkg wtr, coin showers, amphitheater, pads for telescopes. Near Palomar Observatory. Elev 4800 ft.

SAN ARDO (C)
Williams Hill Recreation Area   FREE
Bureau of Land Management
From San Ardo at the US 101 exit, W onto Paris Valley Rd, then left on Lockwood-San Ardo Rd about 5 mi to the public lands boundary; left on Rd W1 to campground. 7 free new primitive sites with RV pads, cfga, shade structures, tbls, pit toilets, no drkg wtr or trash service. Also dispersed camping within 15 ft of roadways. All year; 14-day limit within 28-day period. Hunting; OHV activities.

SAN BERNARDINO (S)
Crab Flat Campground $10.50
San Bernardino National Forest
From San Bernardino at jct with SR 30, 5.5 mi NE on SR 330 through Arrowbear; 4 mi N on Green Valley Lake Rd to Crab Flat Campground sign at forestry dirt rd; 4.5 mi N; near Crab Creek. $10.50 with federal senior pass; others pay $21. 5/1-10/31; 14-day limit. 29 sites; small RVs. Tbls, pit toilets, cfga, drkg wtr. Camp is ORV oriented.

Green Valley Campground $11.50
San Bernardino National Forest
From San Bernardino at jct with SR 30, 5.5 mi NE on SR 330 through Arrowbear; 6 mi N on Green Valley Lake Rd to its end. $11.50 with federal senior pass; others pay $23. 5/1-10/31; 14-day limit. 37 sites (26 by reservation); 40-ft RV limit. Tbls, flush toilets, cfga, drkg wtr. Hiking trails.

Holcomb Valley $10.50
San Bernardino National Forest
Follow Hwy 30 from San Bernardino to Hwy 330, then 35 mi on Hwy 330 to Big Bear Lake dam; at fork, bear left on Hwy 38 for 10 mi; left on FR 3N09 (Van Dusen Canyon Rd) for 3 mi; left on FR 3N16. $10.50 with federal senior pass; others pay $21. All year; 14-day limit; may be inaccessible in winter. 19 sites; 25-ft RV limit. Tbls, toilets, cfga, no drkg wtr. Elev 7400 ft.

North Shore Campground $11.50
San Bernardino National Forest
From San Bernardino, 20 mi N & E on SR 18 to Lake Arrowhead cutoff; 5 mi N on SR 173 to N side of lake; right on Hospital Rd. $11.50 with federal senior pass; others pay $23. 5/1-9/30; 14-day limit. 28 sites; 35-ft RV limit. Tbls, flush toilets, cfga, drkg wtr. Hiking trail.

SAN SIMEON (S)
Nacimiento Camp $7.50
Los Padres National Forest
35 mi N of San Simeon on SR 1; 8 mi E on Nacimiento-to-Ferguson Rd. $7.50 with federal senior pass; others pay $15. All year; 14-day limit. 8 sites; 25-ft RV limit. Tbls, toilets, cfga, no drkg wtr. Fishing, hiking, hunting. Concession-managed.

SANTA BARBARA (S)
Lower Caliente Campground $5
Upper Santa Ynez Recreation Area
Los Padres National Forest
8 mi NW of Santa Barbara on SR 154; 25 mi E on East Camino Cielo to the old Pendola Station; right on Big Caliente Rd for 2 mi. $5 daily or $30 annually. All year; 14-day limit. 2 sites. Toilet, cfga, no drkg wtr, no trash service. Swimming, hiking, biking, horseback riding. Campground usually full on weekends during deer season. Campground closed in early 2017 due to damage of E. Caminino Cielo Rd. Check current status before arrival.

Middle Santa Ynez $5
Upper Santa Ynez Recreation Area
Los Padres National Forest
8 mi N of Santa Barbara on SR 154; 22 mi E on FR 5NI12;

8.8 mi N on dirt FR 5N15. $5 daily or $30 annually. All year; 14-day limit. 13 sites. Tbls, toilets, cfga, no drkg wtr, limited cell phone service. Hiking, picnicking, mountain biking, swimming, fishing, horseback riding. Elev 1800 ft; 3 acres. Quarter mi W of Pendola Guard Station. Travel via San Marcos Pass Rd. Rd not advisable in wet weather or for travel trailers; okay for motorhomes. Stream. Site usually full on weekends during deer season mid-Aug to late Sept. Closed early 2017 by landslides; check current status before arrival.

SANTA MARIA (S)
Baja Campground   FREE
Los Padres National Forest
25 mi E of Santa Maria on Hwy 166; 3 mi N on Branch Creek Rd; At Alder Creek. Free. All year; 14-day limit. 1 site. Tbl, toilet, cfga, no drkg wtr. Hunting, mountain biking, OHV activities. Temporarily closed early 2017; check current status before arrival.

Brookshire Springs $5
Los Padres National Forest
3 mi N of Santa Maria on US 101; 15 mi E on SR 166; 6 mi E on Miranda Pines Rd. $5 daily or $30 annually. All year; 14-day limit. 2 sites (RVs under 16 ft). Tbls, toilet, cfga, no drkg wtr. Hiking, picnicking. Temporarily closed early 2017; check current status before arrival.

Buck Spring $5
Los Padres National Forest
E of Santa Maria on SR 166; 2 mi on FR 30S022. $5 daily or $30 annually. All year; 14-day limit. 1 site. Tbl, toilet, cfga, no drkg wtr. OHV activities, hunting. Elev 1500 ft. Closed temporarily early 2017; check current status before arrival.

Horseshoe Springs $5
Los Padres National Forest
7 mi E of Santa Maria on Betteravia Rd; 4.5 mi E on Mesa Rd; 4.5 mi N on Tepusquet Canyon Rd; 17.5 mi NE on Colson Canyon Rd. $5 daily or $30 annually. 3 sites. May-Oct; 14-day limit. Tbls, toilet, cfga, no drkg wtr. Hiking, OHV activities. Elev 1600 ft. Closed temporarily early 2017; check current status before arrival.

Miranda Pine Campground $5
Los Padres National Forest
3 mi N of Santa Maria on US 101; 15 mi E on SR 166; 8 mi E on FR 11N04; 10 mi E on FR 11N03. $5 daily or $30 annually. All year; 14-day limit. 3 primitive sites. Tbls, toilet, cfga, no drkg wtr. Hiking, picnicking. Elev 4000 ft.

Wagon Flat Campground $5
Los Padres National Forest
3 mi N on US 101; 15 mi E on SR 166; 8.5 mi S on CR 554; 10.5 mi NE on FR 11N04. $5 daily or $30 annually. All year; 14-day limit. 3 sites (RVs under 16 ft). Tbls, toilets,

cfga, no drkg wtr. Picnicking, hiking. Elev 1400 ft; 1 acre. Mountains. On North Fork of La Brea Creek. Scenic drive; rd impassable in wet weather. Closed in early 2017; check current status before arrival.

SANTA MARGARITA (S)
American Canyon $5
Los Padres National Forest
1.1 mi E of Santa Margarita on SR 58; 17.2 mi E on CR 21 (Pozo Rd); 7 mi SE on FR 30S02; 2.1 mi NE on FR 30S04. $5 daily or $30 annually. Open only during deer season, about 8/10-9/22; 14-day limit. 14 sites; limited RV space (25 ft RV limit). Tbls, toilets, cfga, piped spring drkg wtr. Deer hunting, horseback riding, hiking. Elev 1700 ft.

KCL Campground   FREE
Carrizo Plain National Monument
Bureau of Land Management
From Hwy 58 E of Santa Margarita & W of McKittrick, 13 mi S on Soda Lake Rd; right on Selby Rd for qtr mi. Free, donations accepted. All year; 14-day limit. 12 sites. Tbls, cfga, portable toilets, no drkg wtr, no trash service. Archaeological exploring, birdwatching, hiking, horseback riding, hunting, wild horse viewing. Camp was formerly owned by Kern County Land Company. Very remote location.

Friis Campground $5
Los Padres National Forest
22.5 mi E of Santa Margarita on Pozo-Santa Margarita Rd (#21); 4 mi NE on FR 29S02; 1 mi N on undesignated FS rd. $5 daily or $30 annually. All year; 14-day limit. 3 sites. Toilets, cfga, no drkg wtr. Hiking.

La Panza $10
Los Padres National Forest
1.1 mi E of San Margarita on Hwy 58; 26 mi E on W. Pozo Rd; 1.5 mi E on FR 29S18. All year; 14-day limit. Formerly $5 daily Adventure Pass, now $10 with federal senior pass; others pay $20. 15 sites (RVs under 16 ft). Tbls, toilets, cfga, no drkg wtr; limited facilities in winter. Elev 2400 ft. Concession-managed.

Selby Campground   FREE
Carrizo Plain National Monument
Bureau of Land Management
From Hwy 58 E of Santa Margarita & W of McKittrick, 13 mi S on Soda Lake Rd; right on Selby Rd for two mi. Free, donations accepted. All year; 14-day limit. 13 primitive sites. Tbls, portable toilets, cfga, no drkg wtr, no trash service. Archaeological study, hiking, horseback riding, birdwatching.

SAWYERS BAR (S)
Big Flat Campground   FREE
Klamath National Forest
20 mi W of Coffee Creek Guard Station on Coffee Creek Rd.

Free. June-Oct; 14-day limit. 9 rustic sites; 24-ft RV limit. No drkg wtr or trash service; toilets, cfga. Starting point for hikes to Preachers Peak to Caribou Mountains ridge lines & lakes. Within Shasta-Trinity National Forest, but administered by Klamath NF. Corral.

Idlewild Campground $10
Klamath National Forest
6.2 mi NE of Sawyers Bar on Sawyers Bar Rd & FR 2E01 (narrow, but with turnouts); along North Fork of Salmon River. $10. All year; 14-day limit. 11 sites (24-ft RV limit). Tbls, toilets, cfga, drkg wtr. Trailhead camp for backpackers. Fishing. Elev 2600 ft; 11 acres.

Mulebridge Campground FREE
Klamath National Forest
2 mi upstream by dirt rd from Idlewild campground (see directions above). Free. All year; 14-day limit. 4 small rustic sites with tbls, cfga, toilet, no drkg wtr (except for horses) or trash service; 24-ft RV limit. Stock corral with area for group camping. Trailhead for North Fork Trail into Marble Mountain Wilderness.

SEIAD VALLEY (N)
Grider Creek FREE
Klamath National Forest
1.5 mi E of Seiad Valley on Hwy 96; right on Walker Creek Rd, then right on Grider Creek Rd for 6 mi. Along Grider Creek. Free. 10 sites (28-ft RV limit). Tbls, toilets, cfga, no drkg wtr, no trash service. All year; 14-day limit. Elev 1400 ft. Corrals, loading ramp. Trailhead for Pacific Crest Trail into Marble Mountain Wilderness.

O'Neil Creek CLOSED
Klamath National Forest
5.1 mi SE of Seiad Valley on SR 96. Campground closed until further notice due to wtr system problems.

SHAVER LAKE (C)
Bear Wallow Dispersed Camp FREE
Kings River Special Management Area
Sierra National Forest
19 mi SE of Shaver Lake on FR 40, then follow FR 11S12 S past Teakettle Experimental Area & Black Rock Lake; pass Kirch Flat Campground, crossing Kings River; continue 1 mi to end of pavement at Bailey Bridge; cross bridge & turn right up Garnet Dike Rd for 2.5 mi; on large sandy flat area. Free. All year; 14-day limit. 1 large group site; 25-ft RV limit. Tbls, toilet, cfga, no drkg wtr, no trash service. Hiking, fishing. Nearby Gravel Flat Dispersed Camp also has 1 large free site.

Buck Meadow Campground $11
Dinkey Creek Recreation Area
Sierra National Forest
From Shaver Lake, 0.5 mi S on SR 168; 11.7 mi E on Dinkey Creek Rd, past Dinkey Creek Campground; right on

McKinley Grove Rd for 9.6 mi toward Wishon Reservoir; at confluence of Snow Corral & Deer Creeks. $11 with federal senior pass; others pay $22. 5/15-9/15; 14-day limit. 10 sites; 35-ft RV limit. Tbls, toilets, cfga, no drkg wtr. Fishing.

Kirch Flat Campground FREE
Kings River Special Management Area
Sierra National Forest
19 mi SE of Shaver Lake on FR 40; then follow FR 11S12 south past Teakettle Experimental Area & Black Rock Lake; camp is E of Pine Reservoir on N side of Kings River. Free. All year; 14-day limit. 17 sites; 30-ft RV limit. Tbls, toilets, cfga, no drkg wtr. Fishing, rafting, hiking, rafting. Elev 1100 ft. No boat trailer parking.

Lily Pad Campground $12
Courtwright/Wishon Recreation Area
Sierra National Forest
Pacific Gas & Electric
From Shaver Lake, 0.5 mi S on SR 168; 11.7 mi E on Dinkey Creek Rd, past Dinkey Creek Campground; right on McKinley Grove Rd toward Wishon Reservoir; campground just before dam on SW shore of lake. $12 with federal senior pass; others pay $24. 5/15-9/15; 14-day limit. 15 sites; 35-ft RV limit. Tbls, toilets, cfga, drkg wtr. Fishing, boating. Managed by PG&E.

Swanson Campground $22
Shaver Lake Recreation Area
Sierra National Forest
From Shaver Lake, 0.5 mi S on SR 168; 3 mi E on Dinkey Creek Rd. $11 with federal senior pass; others pay $22. 5/15-9/15; 14-day limit. 8 sites; 25-ft RV limit. Tbls, toilet, cfga, no drkg wtr. Boating, fishing, hiking nearby.

Trapper Springs Campground $12
Courtwright/Wishon Recreation Area
Sierra National Forest
Pacific Gas & Electric
From Shaver Lake, 0.5 mi S on SR 168; 11.7 mi E on Dinkey Creek Rd, past Dinkey Creek Campground; right on McKinley Grove Rd for 13.6 mi; left (N) at Courtwright Reservoir turnoff for 7.5 mi to Courtwright Lake, then 1.5 mi around W side of lake. $12 with federal senior pass; others pay $24. 5/15-9/15; 14-day limit. 70 sites; 35-ft RV limit. Tbls, toilets, cfga, drkg wtr. Fishing, boating. Managed by PG&E.

Ward Lake $11
High Sierra Recreation Area
Sierra National Forest
From Shaver Lake, 12 mi N on SR 168 to its end at NE side of Huntington Lake; near Eastwood Visitor Center, right (NE) on rough, narrow, winding, 1-lane Kaiser Pass Rd for 17 mi (large RVs not recommended), connecting to

Florence Lake Rd for 3.7 mi to site. $11 with federal senior pass; others pay $22. 6/1-10/31; 14-day limit. 17 sites; 25-ft RV limit. Tbls, toilets, cfga, bear boxes, no drkg wtr. Swimming, fishing. Elev 7400 ft; 3 acres. Scenic.

SIERRA CITY (N)

Berger Campground $9
Tahoe National Forest
5 mi NE of Sierra City on SR 49; 1.3 mi NW on CR F424 (Gold Lake Rd); 2.4 mi NW on CR 20N16. $9 with federal senior pass; others pay $18. About 5/1-10/15; 14-day limit. Free off-season, but no services. 9 sites (RVs under 22 ft). Tbls, toilets, cfga, no drkg wtr. Fishing, picnicking, boating (dr--2 mi), swimming (3 mi). Elev 5900 ft; 5 acres. Packer Lake.

Diablo Campground $10
Tahoe National Forest
5 mi NE of Sierra City on SR 49; 1.3 mi NW on CR F424; 2.9 mi NW on FR 20N16; across rd from North Yuba River. $10 with federal senior pass; others pay $20. 5/15-10/31; 14-day limit. Free off-season, but no services. 18 undeveloped sites; tents & self-contained RVs. Tbls, cfga, toilets, no drkg wtr. Gold panning. Fishing & swimming at Packer Lake (2 mi).

Loganville Campground $12
Tahoe National Forest
2 mi W of Sierra City on SR 49; at North Yuba River. $12 with federal senior pass; others pay $24 during 4/15-10/15; free off-season but no services or wtr. 14-day limit. 19 sites; 25-ft RV limit. Tbls, toilets, cfga, drkg wtr. Fishing, gold panning.

Sierra Campground $9
Tahoe National Forest
7 mi NE of Sierra City on SR 49; at North Yuba River. $9 with federal senior pass; others pay $18. 16 sites; 40-ft RV limit. About 5/15-10/15; 14-day limit. May be free off-season, but no services. Tbls, toilets, cfga, no drkg wtr. Swimming, canoeing, fishing, boating (rld--5 mi). Elev 5600 ft; 5 acres. Sardine Lakes (5 mi).

Snag Lake FREE
Tahoe National Forest
5 mi NE of Sierra City on SR 49; 5.3 mi N on CR FH24 (Gold Lake Rd). Free. 6/1-10/1; 14-day limit. 12 undesignated sites (RVs under 22 ft). Tbls, toilets, cfga, no drkg wtr. Swimming, picnicking, trout fishing, waterskiing, boating (rld--2 mi at Gold Lake); no motor boats; hand launch). Elev 6600 ft; 5 acres.

Wild Plum $12
Tahoe National Forest
From Sierra City at jct with SR 49, 1.2 mi S (right) on Wild Plum Rd; at Haypress Creek. $12 with federal senior pass; others pay $24. during about 5/1-10/15; 14-day limit. Free

off-season, but no services or wtr. 47 sites; 30-ft RV limit. Tbls, toilets, cfga, drkg wtr. Canoeing, hiking, fishing, hunting, horseback riding, gold panning. Hike to waterfalls.

SIERRAVILLE (N)

Antelope Valley FREE
State Wildlife Area
About 10 mi NE of Sierraville on SR 49 (Loyalton Rd) to Loyalton, then S on Antelope Valley Rd into refuge. Free. All year; 14-day limit. Primitive camping in 5,616-acre refuge. No facilities. Hunting, hiking. Refuge surrounded by Tahoe National Forest.

Chapman Creek $12
Tahoe National Forest
14.8 mi S of Sierraville on SR 49; on right side of rd at Chapman Creek & North Yuba River. $12 with federal senior pass; others pay $24 about 5/1-10/14; 14-day limit. Free off-season, but no services or wtr. 27 sites; 35-ft RV limit. Tbls, toilets, cfga, drkg wtr, bear lockers. Hiking, fishing.

Haven Lake $5
Lakes Basin Recreation Area
Plumas National Forest
20 mi W of Sierraville on SR 49; 5 mi N on Gold Lake Rd. $5 during 5/15-10/30; free off-season; 14-day limit. 4 primitive sites; portable toilet June-Sept, trash service, tbls, no drkg wtr. Hiking, fishing.

Packsaddle $12
Tahoe National Forest
18 mi S of Sierraville on SR 49; at Bassett store, 1.5 mi N (right) on Gold Lake Rd; left on Packer Lake Rd (FR 93), then right at fork for 2.5 mi. $12 with federal senior pass; others pay $24 during about 5/1-10/15; 14-day limit; some sites may be free rest of year, but no services or wtr. 14 sites; 30-ft RV limit. Tbls, toilets, cfga, drkg wtr. Horses permitted. Hitch rails, corrals. Horseback riding, mountain biking, hiking.

Salmon Creek $12
Tahoe National Forest
18 mi S of Sierraville on SR 49; at Bassett store, 2 mi N (right) on Gold Lake Rd; access on left side of rd at confluence of Salmon & Packer Creeks. $12 with federal senior pass; others pay $24 during about 5/1-10/15; 14-day limit. Free off-season, but no services or wtr. 31 sites; 22-ft RV limit. Tbls, toilets, cfga, drkg wtr, bear boxes. Fishing, hiking, canoeing, gold panning.

Yuba Pass $12
Tahoe National Forest
11 mi S of Sierraville on SR 49; left at ski park entrance for 1 mi; on right side of rd; at Yuba Pass. $12 with federal senior pass; others pay $24 during about 5/1-10/15;

14-day limit. Free off-season, but no services or wtr. 19 sites; 45-ft RV limit. Tbls, toilets, cfga, drkg wtr. Hiking.

SOMES BAR (N)

Dillon Creek $10
Klamath National Forest
Six Rivers National Forest
15 mi N of Somesbar on SR 96. $10. About 5/20-10/15; 14-day limit (free during winter, depending on weather). 21 sites (RVs under 23 ft). Tbls, toilets, cfga, drkg wtr. No wtr or trash service during free period. Biking, swimming, boating(l), hiking, good bank fishing. Nature trails. Administered by Six Rivers NF.

Oak Bottom $10
Klamath National Forest
Six Rivers National Forest
12 mi E of Somesbar on SR 96; 2.5 mi E on FR 93. $10 during 4/15-10/31; free during winter when wtr shut off. 14-day limit. 26 sites (RVs under 31 ft). Tbls, toilets, cfga, drkg wtr. Boating, fishing, biking, swimming, whitewater rafting. Near Salmon River. Administered by Six Rivers NF.

Ti-Bar Flat   FREE
Klamath National Forest
Six Rivers National Forest
7 mi N of Somes Bar on SR 96. Free. All year; 14-day limit. 5 rustic sites. Toilet, cfga, no trash service; drkg wtr at Ti-Bar fire station E of campground. Boating(l), fishing, drifting, rafting. Large, flat dispersed area. Administered by Six Rivers NF.

SPRINGVILLE (C)

Balch County Park $12
Mountain Home State Forest
Sequoia National Forest
Tulare County Park
21 mi NE of Springville on Balch Park Rd & Bear Creek Rd. $12 for seniors; $24 all others. 5/1-11/1; 14-day limit. 80 sites (30-ft RV size limit). Tbls, toilets, cfga, drkg wtr. Fishing. Elev 6500 ft. Managed by Tulare County; within the Mountain Home Demonstration State Forest.

Coy Flat Campground $11.50
Sequoia National Forest
Giant Sequoia National Monument
20 mi E of Springville near Camp Nelson via SR 190. $11.50 with federal senior pass; others pay $23; double site $46. 5/13-11/15; 14-day limit. 19 sites; 24-ft RV limit. Tbls, toilets, cfga, drkg wtr. Hiking trails through groves.

Frasier Mill   FREE
Mountain Home State Forest
23 mi NE of Springville via Bear Creek Rd. Difficult access for RVs. Free. 6/1-10/31; 14-day limit. 46 sites (RVs under 20 ft). Tbls, drkg wtr, firewood, cfga, toilets. Horseback riding, picnicking, fishing, hiking, hunting.

Hedrick Pond   FREE
Mountain Home State Forest
19 mi NE of Springville via Bear Creek Rd. Free. 6/1-10/31; 14-day limit. 15 sites (RVs under 20 ft). Tbls, drkg wtr, cfga, toilets. Picnicking, fishing, hunting, hiking, horseback riding (pack station) and backcountry trails. Elev 6300 ft.

Moses Gulch   FREE
Mountain Home State Forest
3 mi N of Springville on SR 190; 22 mi E on Bear Creek Rd, Summit Rd and River Rd. Free. 6/1-10/31; 14-day limit. 6 sites (RVs under 16 ft). 20 acres. Tbls, toilets, firewood, drkg wtr. Hiking, picnicking.

Shake Camp Campground   FREE
Mountain Home State Forest
18 mi NE of Springville via Bear Creek, Summit and River Rds. Free. 6/1-10/31, weather permitting; 14-day limit. 11 sites (RVs under 16 ft). Tbls, drkg wtr, cfga, toilets. Picnicking, fishing nearby, hiking, horseback riding (rentals & corrals nearby), hunting. Trailhead to Golden Trout Wilderness nearby. Pack station nearby.

Sunset Point Campground   FREE
Mountain Home State Forest
22 mi NE of Springville via Bear Creek Rd. Free. 6/1-10/31, weather permitting; 14-day limit. 4 sites (RVs under 20 ft). Tbls, drkg wtr, cfga, toilets. Picnicking, fishing nearby, hiking, horseback riding (corrals nearby), hunting. Trailhead to Golden Trout Wilderness nearby.

Wishon Campground $11.50
Sequoia National Forest
Giant Sequoia National Monument
About 10 mi E of Springville on SR 190; 4 mi N on M208 (Wishon Dr); on right where rd curves to Doyle Springs; at North Fork of Middle Fork Tule River. $11.50 with federal senior pass; others pay $23. All year; 14-day limit. 31 sites plus 4 double sites ($48); 22-ft RV limit. Tbls, pit toilets, cfga, drkg wtr, phone. Hiking trail, fishing.

STONYFORD (N)

Davis Flat $5
Mendocino National Forest
9.5 mi W of Stonyford on FR 18N03. $5. All year; 14-day limit. 70 dispersed sites. 20 Tbls, toilets, cfga, no drkg wtr. In designated ORV area. Hiking, motorcycling.

Dixie Glade $5
Stonyford Recreation Area
Mendocino National Forest
13 mi W of Stonyford on FR M10 just above Fouts Springs OHV area. $5. All year; 14-day limit. 8 sites. Tbls, toilets, cfga, drkg wtr except in winter, no trash service. Equestrian camping; hitching posts, corrals, watering troughs. Fishing, hiking. Elev 3700 ft.

Fouts Campground $5
Stonyford Recreation Area
Mendocino National Forest
8.8 mi W of Stonyford on CR 18N01 (Fouts Spring Rd); .3 mi N on CR 18N03. $5. All year; 14-day limit. 11 sites; 16-ft RV limit. Tbls, toilets, cfga, drkg wtr. Swimming, picnicking, fishing, rockhounding. Elev 1600 ft; 7 acres. Stony Creek. Snow Mountain Jasper (5 mi). Digger pine trees in N end of camp. Heavy ORV use 10/1-6/1.

Letts Lake Complex $12
Stonyford Recreation Area
Mendocino National Forest
8 mi W of Stonyford on Fouts Springs Rd; 6 mi SW on FR 18N01; 3 mi SE on FR 17N02. $12. 4/15-11/1; 14-day limit. Open later if weather permits; $5 when wtr is off. 42-site complex consists of three camps -- Main Letts, Saddle, Stirrup and Spillway. 24-ft RV limit. Tbls, toilets, cfga, drkg wtr. Fishing, boating(elec mtrs), canoeing on 35-acre lake, 1-mi hiking trail, accessible fishing pier. Historic landmark. Elev 4500 ft.

Mill Creek $5
Stonyford Recreation Area
Mendocino National Forest
8.7 mi W of Stonyford at Mill Creek on CR 18N01 (Fouts Spring Rd). $5. All year; 14-day limit. 6 sites (RVs under 22 ft). Tbls, toilets, cfga, no drkg wtr. Rockhounding, swimming, picnicking, fishing. Elev 1600 ft; 2 acres. Small roadside campground. In winter and early spring stream flow is up. Snow Mountain Jasper is at the site. Heavy ORV use 10/1-6/1.

Mill Valley $10
Stonyford Recreation Area
Mendocino National Forest
9 mi W of Stonyford on Fouts Springs Rd; 6 mi SW on FR 18N01; 1.5 mi S on FR 17N02. $10. 4/15-11/1; 14-day limit. 15 sites (RVs under 16 ft). Tbls, toilet, cfga, drkg wtr. Lily Pond lake. Hiking, fishing. Letts Lake 1 mi. Elev 4200 ft; 5 acres.

North Fork $5
Mendocino National Forest
9 mi W of Stonyford on CR 18N01 (Fouts Spring Rd); 2.3 mi N on CR 18N03. $5. All year; 14-day limit. 6 sites (RVs under 16 ft). Tbls, toilet, cfga, no drkg wtr, no trash service. Swimming, picnicking, fishing, rockhounding. Elev 1700 ft; 3 acres. Adjacent to year-long stream (Stony Creek). Camp is located in open grove of oak trees. Snow Mountain Jasper is at the site. High OHV use between Oct & June.

Old Mill Campground FREE
Mendocino National Forest
6.5 mi W of Stonyford on CR 18N01 (Fouts Spring RD); 7.1 mi S on FR 18N07 (John Smith Rd). Free. 5/1-11/1; 14-day limit. 10 sites (RVs under 16 ft). Tbls, toilet, cfga, gravity piped drkg wtr, no trash service. Rockhounding, picnicking. Fishing (5 mi). Elev 3600 ft; 3 acres. Located in mature stand of mixed pine and fir. Small RVs can use the site, but main access rd up Trough Ridge is narrow. Horseback riding, mountain biking.

South Fork $5
Mendocino National Forest
9.5 mi W of Stonyford on FR 18N03. $5. All year; 14-day limit. 5 sites in two large open areas. Tbls, toilet, cfga, no drkg wtr. Fishing, hiking, horseback riding, mountain biking. On South Fork of Stony Creek.

STOVEPIPE WELLS (C)
Stovepipe Wells $7
Death Valley National Park
In Stovepipe Wells on CR 190. $7 plus entry fee with federal senior pass; others pay $14. 9/15-5/10; 30-day limit. 190 sites (30-ft RV limit). Tbls, flush toilets, cfga, drkg wtr, dump.

STRAWBERRY (C)
Cascade Creek $8
Stanislaus National Forest
9.1 mi NE of Strawberry on SR 108; quarter mi NE on FR 5N28. $8. 5/1-10/15; 14-day limit. 14 sites (RVs under 22 ft). 12 sites. Tbls, toilets, cfga, no drkg wtr. Hiking, mountain climbing, picnicking. Elev 6000 ft; 3 acres. Cascade Creek. Trail of the Ancient Dwarfs (4.6 mi).

Herring Creek FREE
Stanislaus National Forest
1.1 mi N of Strawberry on SR 108; 7 mi NE on FR 4N12 (Herring Creek Rd). 5/15-10/15; 14-day limit. 7 sites (RVs under 22 ft). Tbls, toilets, cfga, no drkg wtr. Hiking, picnicking, fishing. Elev 7300 ft.

Herring Reservoir Campground FREE
Stanislaus National Forest
1.1 mi N of Strawberry on SR 108; 7 mi NE on FR 4N12 (Herring Creek Rd). Free. 6/15-12/15; 14-day limit. 9 sites. Tbls, toilets, cfga, no drkg wtr. Fishing, hiking, horseback riding.

Meadowview Campground $11.50
Pinecrest Recreation Area
Stanislaus National Forest
About 2 mi S of Strawberry on SR 108; 0.5 mi E on Pinecrest Lake Rd; 0.5 mi S on Dodge Ridge Rd. $11.50 with federal senior pass; others pay $23. 5/1-10/15; 14-day limit. About 100 sites, typically 35 ft. Tbls, flush toilets, cfga, drkg wtr. Swimming, boating(l), fishing.

Mill Creek $10
Stanislaus National Forest
11.2 mi NE on SR 108; half mi NE on FR 5N21; half mi N on FR 5N26. $10. MD-10/15; 14-day limit. 17 sites (RVs under 23 ft). Tbls, toilets, cfga, firewood, no drkg wtr. Hiking, mountain climbing, picnicking, fishing. Elev 6200 ft; 3 acres. Donnell Vista (3.6 mi). Rock Garden Nature Trail (2.8 mi). Trail of the Ancient Dwarfs (2.8 mi).

SUSANVILLE (N)

Biscar Reservoir   FREE
Bureau of Land Management
34 mi N of Susanville on Hwy 395; 6 mi W on Karlo Rd to Lower Biscar Reservoir. Free. About 4/15-11/15; 14-day limit. Primitive undesignated sites; no facilities, no drkg wtr. Fishing, hunting, birdwatching. Pack out trash.

Bogard Campground $7
Lassen National Forest
From Susanville, 4 mi W on SR 36; 20 mi W on SR 44; 1.5 mi S on FR 31N26. $7 with federal senior pass; others pay $14; free in winter but no wtr. 14-day limit. 10 sites; 25-ft RV limit. Tbls, toilets, cfga, drkg wtr. Biking, hiking.

Christie Campground $10
Eagle Lake Recreation Area
Lassen National Forest
2.1 mi W of Susanville on SR 36; 16 mi N on CR A1 (Eagle Lake Rd); at Eagle Lake. $10 with federal senior pass; others pay $20. 5/15-11/1 (or through first hard freeze). 69 sites (44 for reservation); 30 pull-through; 45-ft average site. Tbls, flush toilets, cfga, drkg wtr. Dump at Merrill Campground($). Boating(l), swimming, fishing, hiking trail. Eagle Lake Recreation Area managed by the Lassen College Foundation.

Crater Lake Campground $10
Lassen National Forest
2.1 mi W of Susanville on SR 36; 16 mi N on CR A1 (Eagle Lake Rd); at Eagle Lake. $10. 5/15-11/1 (or through first hard freeze). 17 gravel sites (up to 40 ft long). Tbls, pit toilets, cfga, drkg wtr. Boating(l), fishing.

Eagle Campground $10
Eagle Lake Recreation Area
Lassen National Forest
2.1 mi W of Susanville on SR 36; 13 mi N on CR A1 (Eagle Lake Rd); right at sign on Gallatin Rd for 0.7 mi; near Eagle Lake. $10 with federal senior pass; others pay $20. 5/15-12/31 (or through first hard freeze). 50 sites (30 for reservation); 40-ft typical length. Tbls, flush toilets, cfga, drkg wtr. Dump at Merrill Campground ($).

Goumaz Campground $7
Lassen National Forest
From Susanville, W on SR 37 to Devils Corral area, then N on FR 30N03 to site. $7 with federal senior pass during 5/15-10/31; others pay $14. Free off-season, but no wtr. All year; 14-day limit. 5 primitive sites. Tbls, toilets, cfga, drkg wtr.

Lassen County Fairgrounds $10
From jct with SR 139 in downtown Susanville, about 8 blocks E on SR 36; 0.5 mi NE on Fair Dr to fairgrounds. $10 without hookups, $25 for elec/wtr; $10 per person for tents. All year. Tbls, flush toilets, cfga, drkg wtr, showers.

Merrill Campground $10
Eagle Lake Recreation Area
Lassen National Forest
2.1 mi W of Susanville on SR 36; 14 mi N on CR A1 (Eagle Lake Rd); at Eagle Lake. $10 base with federal senior pass; others pay $20 base, $30 elec/wtr (seniors get $10 discount for elec sites), $35 full hookups ($25 with senior pass). 5/15-11/1 (or through first hard freeze). 173 sites (typically 55 ft). Tbls, flush toilets, cfga, drkg wtr, grey wtr dumps. Dump($) just outside campground. Boating(l), fishing, swimming, hiking trail.

North Eagle Lake $8
Bureau of Land Management
29 mi N of Susanville on SR 139; 0.5 mi W on CR A1, then right (N) into campground. $8 (group camping $11). 5/15-11/15; 14-day limit. 20 sites; 35-ft RV limit. Tbls, toilets, cfga, drkg wtr. Biking, boating, fishing, hiking. Elev 5200 ft; 3 acres.

Ramhorn Springs Campground   FREE
Bureau of Land Management
From Susanville, about 45 mi N on US 395; about 2.4 mi N of state rest area, turn right (E) on unimproved dirt BLM Rd 26000 for 2.5 mi to campground on left. Free, but donations requested for maintenance. 10 sites. All year; 14-day limit. Tbls, toilets, cfga, no drkg wtr except for animals. Horse corral.

Rocky Point East   FREE
Bureau of Land Management
29 mi N of Susanville on SR 139; 5 mi W on CR A1; left (S) on Lakeside Dr in Bucks Bay subdivision; follow signs on dirt Rocky Point access rd. Free, but donations requested. All year; 14-day limit. Undeveloped area for self-contained RVs. Toilet, cfga, no drkg wtr or trash service. Boating, fishing.

Rocky Point West   FREE
Bureau of Land Management
229 mi N of Susanville on SR 139; 6 mi W on CR A1; S at bottom of mile-long grade; at W shore of Rocky Point. Free. All year; 14-day limit. Undeveloped sites for self-contained RVs. Pit toilet, cfga, no drkg wtr or trash service. Dispersed RV camping also available around lake; portable toilets provided in some areas. Boating, fishing. Boat launches at Stones Landing, Spalding, Gallatin Marina at S end of lake.

Willow Creek Canyon FREE
Bureau of Land Management
11 mi E of Susanville on Hwy A27; just before Willow Creek, turn N on Belfast Rd for 3-5 mi. Free. All year; 14-day limit. Primitive undesignated camping in remote canyon area. No facilities; no drkg wtr. Hiking, fishing, archaeological exploring. Petroglyph area nearby.

TEHACHAPI (S)

Tehachapi Mountain Park $12
Kern County Parks & Recreation Department
8 mi SW of Tehachapi from SR 58; route complicated, so inquire locally about best directions. $12 for seniors at 61 primitive RV/tent sites ($18 non-seniors). All year, but snow may force road closure. Tbls, toilets, cfga, drkg wtr. Hiking, equestrian trail, nature trail. 10-horse corral at Horseshoe equestrian camp.

TEMECULA (S)

Dripping Springs $7.50
Cleveland National Forest
11 mi E of Temecula on SR 79. $7.50 with federal senior pass; others pay $15. All year; 14-day limit. 18 sites (22-ft RV limit). Tbls, toilets, cfga, drkg wtr. Agua Tibia Wilderness nearby. Hiking (Dripping Springs Trail). This is primarily an equestrian campground; bridle trails, corrals, horse staging area. To protect endangered Arroyo Toad, campground closes about 4/4-5/15.

Oak Grove Campground $7.50
Cleveland National Forest
About 25 mi SE of Temecula on SR 79. $7.50 with federal Senior Pass; others pay $15. All year; 14-day limit. 81 sites; 32-ft RV limit. Tbls, flush & pit toilets, cfga, drkg wtr. Hiking trails, interpretive programs.

TIONESTA (N)

A.H. Hogue $7
Modoc National Forest
About 17 mi W of Tionesta on CR 97 (Tionesta Rd), becoming FR 97; right for 1 mi on Medicine Lake Rd, following signs to campground at Medicine Lake. $7 with federal senior pass; others pay $14. MD-10/15; free rest of yr, but no wtr or trash service; 14-day limit. 24 sites; 30-ft RV limit. Tbls, toilets, cfga, drkg wtr, beach. Fishing, swimming, boating. Elev 6700 ft.

Indian Well $10
Lava Beds National Monument
From Tionesta at jct with CR 97, about 12 mi NW on Lave Beds National Monument Rd to park headquarters; Indian Well is 0.75 mi from park headquarters. $10 ($6 in winter); wtr available at headquarters in winter. Also $10 entry fee for 7 days. Winter temperatures 20-40 degrees. 43 sites for tents & small RVs. Tbls, toilets, cfga, drkg wtr. Elev 4770 ft; 80 acres.

TRACY (C)

Carnegie $10
State Vehicular Recreation Area
6 mi W of I-580, between Tracy & Livermore at 18600 Corral Hollow Rd. $10. All year; 14-day limit. 50 sites. Tbls, flush toilets, cfga, drkg wtr. Off-road vehicle activities. Daily or annual entry fee also charged. 1,500 acres.

TRIMMER (C)

Black Rock $7
Patterson Mountain Recreation Area
Sierra National Forest
Pacific Gas & Electric Company
20 mi E of Trimmer on Trimmer Springs Rd (FR 40); 10 mi NW on Black Rock Rd (FR 11S12). Route not recommended for large RVs. $7 with federal senior pass; others pay $14. All year; 14-day limit. Free in winter, but limited facilities. 10 sites. Tbls, toilets, cfga, drkg wtr, no trash service. Fishing, hiking, kayaking, rafting. Managed by PG&E.

Bretz Mill FREE
Shaver Lake Recreation Area
Sierra National Forest
9 mi E of Trimmer on Trimmer Springs Rd; 15 mi N on Big Creek Rd. Free. All year; 14-day limit. 10 sites (24-ft RV limit). Tbls, toilets, cfga, no drkg wtr or trash service. Fishing, swimming, hiking, OHV activities. Elev 3300 ft.

Trimmer Recreation Area $10
Pine Flat Lake
Corps of Engineers
From Trimmer, 2 mi E on Trimmer Springs Rd, then follow signs to NW shore of lake. $10 with federal senior pass at 10 non-elec sites; others pay $20. All year; 14-day limit. 30-ft RV limit. Tbls, flush toilets, showers, cfga, drkg wtr. Hiking, boating(l), fishing.

TRINITY CENTER (N)

Clear Creek FREE
Shasta-Trinity National Forest
5 mi N on SR 3; 11.2 mi SE on CR 106; 2 mi SE on FR 36N65; at Clear Creek. Free. All year; 14-day limit. 6 sites (RVs under 23 ft). Tbls, toilet, cfga, no drkg wtr. Picnicking, fishing, hiking. Elev 3500 ft; 7 acres. Hunter camp in fall.

Eagle Creek $10
Shasta-Trinity National Forest
12.2 mi N of Trinity Center on SR 3; 3.7 mi NE on CR 1089. $10. All year; free but no wtr 11/1-4/30; 14-day limit. 17 sites (35-ft RV limit). Tbls, toilets, cfga, drkg wtr. On Trinity River. Swimming, fishing. Elev 2800 ft; 10 acres.

Goldfield Campground FREE
Shasta-Trinity National Forest
7 mi N on SR 3; 4 mi W on CR 104 (Coffee Creek Rd). Free. 5/16-9/10; 14-day limit. Open all year. 6 sites on 4 acres;

16-ft RV limit. Tbls, toilets, cfga, no drkg wtr. Picnicking, fishing, swimming, hiking. Boulder Creek trailhead. Elev 3000 ft.

Horse Flat Campground   FREE
Shasta-Trinity National Forest
12.2 mi N of Trinity Center on SR 3; 1.5 mi N on CR 1089; 2.8 mi NW on FR 38N27. Free. 5/26-9/10; 14-day limit. Open until 10/31 with no services. 10 sites; 16-ft RV limit. Tbls, toilets, cfga, no drkg wtr. Hiking, picnicking, fishing, berry-picking, horseback riding; corral. Elev 3000 ft; 12 acres. On Eagle Creek. Trailhead to Salmon Trinity Alps Primitive Area. 7 mi N of Coffee Creek Ranger Station.

Jackass Springs   FREE
Shasta-Trinity National Forest
5.8 mi N on SR 3; 19.9 mi SE on CR 106; 4.5 mi W on CR 119. Free. All year; 14-day limit. 10 sites; 32-ft RV limit. Tbls, toilets, cfga, no drkg wtr. Picnicking, hiking, boating, swimming, fishing, waterskiing. Elev 2400 ft; 7 acres. Mountains. Open all year; snow in winter. Unpaved access rd.

Preacher Meadow $12
Shasta-Trinity National Forest
1.5 mi SW of Trinity Center on SR 3; qtr mi SW on FR 36N98; along Swift Creek. $12. 5/15-10/15; 14-day limit. 45 sites (40-ft RV limit). Tbls, toilets, cfga, drkg wtr. Hiking, fishing. Elev 2900 ft; 6 acres.

Scott Mountain   FREE
Shasta-Trinity National Forest
16 mi N of Coffee Creek on Hwy 3. Free. All year; 14-day limit. 7 sites; 15-ft RV limit. Tbls, toilets cfga, no drkg wtr. Hiking trail camp (Pacific Crest Trail) leading into Trinity Alp Wilderness. Elev 5,400 ft.

Trinity River $10
Shasta-Trinity National Forest
9.5 mi N of Trinity Center on SR 3; on the Trinity River. $10 during 5/15-10/31; $5 rest of year but no wtr; 14-day limit. 7 sites (35-ft RV limit). Tbls, toilets, cfga, drkg wtr. Fishing, gold panning. Elev 2500 ft.

TRUCKEE (N)

Alpine Meadows $10
Martis Creek Lake
Corps of Engineers
On N side of dam, 4 mi NE of SR 267. $10 with federal senior pass at 25 non-elec sites; others pay $20. 5/15-10/15; 14-day limit. 30-ft RV limit; 6 pull-through sites. Tbls, toilets, cfga, drkg wtr, amphitheater. Fishing.

Annie McCloud   CLOSED
Tahoe National Forest
From E of Truckee at jct with I-80, 0.5 mi N on SR 89; right on Prosser Dam Rd for 4.5 mi; cross damp; on the left; on E shore of Prosser Lake. Closed, decommissioned.

Boca Campground $10
Tahoe National Forest
From 10 mi E of Truckee at Boca-Hirschdale Rd exit of I-80, 1 mi N on Hirschdale Rd; right at Boca Dam, then 1 mi to campground; at Boca Reservoir. $10 with federal senior pass; others pay $20. About 5/15-10/10; 14-day limit. 20 sites; 36-ft RV limit. Tbls, toilets, cfga, drkg wtr. Canoeing, boating, fishing.

Boca Rest $10
Tahoe National Forest
From 10 mi E of Truckee at Boca-Hirschdale Rd exit of I-80, 2.5 mi N on CR 270; right side of rd; on NE shore of Boca Lake. $10 with federal senior pass; others pay $20. About 5/15-10/10; 14-day limit. Free off-season, weather permitting, but no services or wtr. 25 sites; 40-ft RV limit. Tbls, toilets, cfga, drkg wtr. Boating (hand launch), fishing, hiking, mountain biking, waterskiing, windsurfing, swimming.

Boca Springs $10
Tahoe National Forest
From 10 mi E of Truckee at Boca-Hirschdale Rd exit, N to CR 73, then 1 mi; right side of rd. $10 with federal senior pass; others pay $20. About 5/15-10/15; 14-day limit. Free off-season, weather permitting, but no services or wtr. 20 sites; 16-ft RV limit. Tbls, toilets, cfga, drkg wtr. Hiking, mountain biking, horseback riding.

Boyington Mill $10
Tahoe National Forest
7 mi E of Truckee on I-80; 3.1 mi N on CR 21N03; at Little Truckee River. $10 with federal senior pass; others pay $20. 5/15-10/10; 14-day limit. Free off-season but no services. 12 sites on 3 acres (RVs under 32 ft). Tbls, toilets, cfga, firewood, no drkg wtr. Swimming, river fishing. Boating (I--4 mi). Elev 5700 ft.

Cold Creek $8
Tahoe National Forest
From NE of Truckee at jct with I-80, 16 mi N on SR 89; on W side of rd. $8 with federal senior pass; others pay $16. About 4/15-10/31; 14-day limit. About 10 sites; 22-ft RV limit. Tbls, toilets, cfga, drkg wtr. Fishing, swimming.

Davies Creek   CLOSED
Tahoe National Forest
7 mi E of Truckee on US 80; 9 mi N on CR 21N03 (Stampede Dam Rd); 2 mi W on CR 19N03 (Henness Pass Rd). Closed & decommissioned.

East Meadow $12
Tahoe National Forest
From E of Truckee at jct with I-80, 17 mi N on SR 89

to Jackson Meadows turnoff; 15 mi W on FR 7 toward Jackson Meadows Lake; access rd on left; at NE shore of lake. $12 with federal senior pass; others pay $24. About MD-10/1; 14-day limit. 46 sites; 40-ft RV limit. Tbls, flush toilets, cfga, drkg wtr, dump, bear lockers. Hiking, fishing, boating(l), swimming.

Findley Campground　　　　　　　　　　　**$12**
Tahoe National Forest
From E of Truckee at jct with I-80, 17 mi N on SR 89 to Jackson Meadows turnoff; 18 mi W on FR 7 to Jackson Meadows Lake, continuing to W side of lake just past the Fir Top entrance; access on left at W shore of lake. $12 with federal senior pass; others pay $24. 15 sites; 45-ft RV limit. About MD-9/25; 14-day limit. Tbls, flush toilets, cfga, drkg wtr. Boat ramp 0.5 mi at Woodcamp.

Fir Top Campground　　　　　　　　　　　**$12**
Tahoe National Forest
From E of Truckee at jct with I-80, 17 mi N on SR 89 to Jackson Meadows turnoff; 18 mi W on FR 7, across the dam at Jackson Meadows Lake, continuing 4 mi around W side of lake on gravel rd; on left side. $12 with federal senior pass; others pay $24. About MD-9/25; 14-day limit. 12 sites; 30-ft RV limit. Tbls, toilets, cfga, drkg wtr, beach, store, bear lockers. Dump across rd from Pass Creek Campground($). Boating(l), fishing, swimming.

Goose Meadows　　　　　　　　　　　　　　**$11**
Tahoe National Forest
From E of Truckee at jct with I-80, 5 mi S on SR 89; on the left above Truckee River. $11 with federal senior pass; others pay $22. About 5/15-10/10; 14-day limit. 24 sites; 45-ft RV limit. Tbls, toilets, cfga, drkg wtr (hand pump), bear boxes. Fishing, rafting, swimming.

Granite Flat　　　　　　　　　　　　　　　**$11**
Tahoe National Forest
From E of Truckee at jct with I-80, 1.5 mi S of Truckee on SR 89; on the right at Truckee River. $11 with federal senior pass; others pay $22. About 5/15-10/1; 14-day limit. 70 sites up to 65 ft. Tbls, toilets, cfga, drkg wtr. Fishing, rafting, swimming.

Lakeside Campground　　　　　　　　　　　**$10**
Tahoe National Forest
From E of Truckee at jct with I-80, 4.5 mi N on SR 89; right at Prosser sign about 1 mi; at cove on W shore of Prosser Reservoir. $10 with federal senior pass; others pay $20. About 5/15-10/10; 14-day limit. 30 sites; 40-ft RV limit. Tbls, toilets, cfga, drkg wtr. Trout fishing, biking, hiking, boating (10mph limit).

Logger Campground　　　　　　　　　　　**$11.50**
Tahoe National Forest
10 mi E of Truckee on Hwy 89 N to Hobart Mills Rd, then

onto newly renovated Dog Valley Rd (Stamped Dam Rd closed in 2017 season). $11.50 with federal senior pass; others pay $23. About 5/15-10/10; 14-day limit. One loop free off-season for RVs if access possible, but no services or wtr. 240 sites; 32-ft RV limit. Tbls, flush toilets, cfga, drkg wtr, dump. Fishing, boating(l), hiking, OHV trails, swimming.

Lower Little Truckee　　　　　　　　　　　**$10**
Tahoe National Forest
From E of Truckee at jct with I-80, 11 mi N on SR 89 to campground on left side of rd; at shore of Little Truckee River. $10 with federal senior pass; others pay $20. About 4/15-10/31; 14-day limit. 15 sites; 22-ft RV limit. Tbls, toilets, cfga, drkg wtr. Elev 6000 ft. Fishing, biking, hiking.

Pass Creek　　　　　　　　　　　　　　　　**$12**
Tahoe National Forest
Jackson Meadow Recreation Area
From E of Truckee at jct with I-80, 17 mi N on SR 89 to Jackson Meadows turnoff; 18 mi W on FR 7 to NE shore of Jackson Meadows Lake. $12 with federal senior pass; others pay $24. About MD-10/15; 14-day limit. 30 sites; 35-ft RV limit. Tbls, flush toilets, cfga, drkg wtr questionable in 2017, beach. Trout fishing, boating(l), swimming, hiking, mountain biking, waterskiing. Elev 6100 ft.

Prosser Campground　　　　　　　　　　　**$10**
Tahoe National Forest
From E of Truckee at jct with I-80, 4.5 mi N on SR 89; right at Prosser Campground sign, then 1.5 mi on access rd; at W shore of Prosser Lake. $10 with federal senior pass; others pay $20. About 5/15-10/1; 14-day limit. 29 sites; 40-ft RV limit. Tbls, toilets, cfga, drkg wtr. Hiking trail, mountain biking, boating(l), fishing, swimming, horseback riding trails.

Sagehen Creek　　　　　　　　　　　　　**FREE**
Tahoe National Forest
From E of Truckee at jct with I-80, 9 mi N on SR 89; 1.5 mi SW on FR 18N11 (Sagehen Summit Rd); rough surface rds. Free. All year, weather permitting. 14-day limit annually. 10 undeveloped sites on 10 acres (22-ft RV limit). Tbls, toilets, cfga, no drkg wtr, no trash service. Fishing. Elev 6500 ft.

Silver Creek　　　　　　　　　　　　　　　**$9**
Tahoe National Forest
From E of Truckee at jct with I-80, 7 mi S on SR 89; along Truckee River. $9 with federal senior pass; others pay $18. About 6/15-9/10; 14-day limit. 27 sites (7 for tents); 40-ft RV limit. Tbls, toilets, cfga, limited drkg wtr, bear boxes. Trout fishing, hiking.

Upper Little Truckee　　　　　　　　　　　**$11**
Tahoe National Forest
From E of Truckee at jct with I-80, 11 mi N on SR 89 just

past Lower Little Truckee campground at Little Truckee River. $11 with federal senior pass; others pay $22. About 4/15-10/31; 14-day limit. 26 sites; 40-ft RV limit. Tbls, toilets, cfga, drkg wtr. Trout fishing, biking, hiking, mountain biking.

Woodcamp Campground $12
Tahoe National Forest
From E of Truckee at jct with I-80, 17 mi N on SR 89 to Jackson Meadows turnoff; 16 mi W on FR 7 to Jackson Meadows Lake, following the W shoreline to campground access rd; on SW shore. $12 with federal senior pass; others pay $24. About MD-9/25; 14-day limit. Tbls, flush & pit toilets, cfga, limited drkg wtr, beach. 20 sites; 35-ft RV limit. Trout fishing, boating(l), swimming, biking, hiking. Interpretive trail nearby.

TWENTYNINE PALMS (S)
Belle Campground $7.50
Joshua Tree National Park
Half mi E of Twentynine Palms on SR 62; 9 mi S on Utah Trail. $7.50 with federal senior pass; others pay $15. All year; 14-day limit 10/1-6/1; rest of year, 30-day limit. 7-day entry fee also charged (free with senior pass). 18 sites, among rock formations (32 ft RV limit). Tbls, toilets, cfga, no drkg wtr. Hiking, picnicking. Elev 3800 ft.

Black Rock Canyon $10
Joshua Tree National Park
12 mi W of Twentynine Palms on SR 62; 5 mi S of Yucca Valley on Joshua Lane. $10 with federal senior pass; others pay $20 plus entry fee. 10/1-5/31; 14-day limit. 100 sites (32-ft RV limit). Tbls, flush toilets, cfga, drkg wtr, dump. Wheelchair access. Hiking, ranger talks, wayside exhibits, horseback riding, mountain biking. Horse owners must provide wtr. Elev 4000 ft.

Cottonwood Campground $10
Joshua Tree National Park
At south entrance to park. $10 with federal senior pass; others pay $20 plus entry fee. All year; 14-day limit 10/1-6/1; rest of year, 30-day limit. 62 sites. Tbls, flush toilets, cfga, drkg wtr, dump.

Hidden Valley Campground $7.50
Joshua Tree National Park
12 me SE of Joshua Tree. $7.50 with federal senior pass; others pay $15. All year; 14-day limit 10/1-6/1; 30 days rest of year. 7-day entry fee also charged (free with senior pass). 39 sites (RVs under 33 ft). Tbls, toilets, cfga, no drkg wtr. Hiking, picnicking; nature program (Nov-May). Elev 4200 ft. Magnificent rock formations in the Wonderland of Rocks. Drkg wtr at Cottonwood Campground & Visitor Center, Oasis Visitor Center, Indian Cove Ranger Station. Summer temperatures above 100 degrees.

Indian Cove $10
Joshua Tree National Park
4.8 mi W of Twentynine Palms on Twentynine Palms Hwy (SR 62); 2.5 mi S on Indian Cove Rd. $10 with federal senior pass; others pay $20 plus entry fee. All year; 14-day limit (30-day limit during 6/1-10/1). 101 sites. Tbls, toilets, cfga, no drkg wtr (wtr at Indian Cove ranger station).

Jumbo Rocks $7.50
Joshua Tree National Park
1 mi E of Twentynine Palms on SR 62; 11 mi S on Utah Trail. $7.50 with federal senior pass; others pay $15. All year; 14-day limit 10/1-6/1; rest of year, 30-day limit. 7-day entry fee also charged (free with senior pass). 124 sites (32-foot RV limit). Tbls, toilets, cfga, no drkg wtr. Hiking trails, picnicking, nature program May-Nov. Elev 4400 ft.

Ryan Campground $7.50
Joshua Tree National Park
16 mi SE of Joshua Tree on Park Blvd-Quail Springs Rd. $7.50 with federal senior pass. All year; 14-day limit 10/1-6/1; 30 days limit rest of year. 7-day entry fee also charged (free with senior pass). 31 sites (RVs under 33 ft). Tbls, toilets, cfga, no drkg wtr. Hiking, horseback riding. Elev 4300 ft. Only monument campground allowing horses. Trails. Drkg wtr at Cottonwood Campground & Visitor Center, Oasis Visitor Center, Indian Cove Ranger Station. Summer temperatures above 100 degrees. Beautiful campground, but toilets often odoriforous. No fee for horses.

White Tank $7.50
Joshua Tree National Park
Half mi E of Twentynine Palms on SR 62; 10 mi S on Utah Trail. $7.50 with federal senior pass; others pay $15. All year; 14-day limit 10/1-6/1; rest of year, 30-day limit. 7-day entry fee also charged (free with senior pass). 15 very small sites (small RVs only). Tbls, toilets, cfga, no drkg wtr. Hiking trails, picnicking. Elev 3800 ft. Sites among rock formations.

UKIAH (N)
Chekaka Recreation Area $20
Lake Mendocino
Corps of Engineers
2 mi N of Ukiah on US 101; N (left) at N. State St; E (right) to Lake Mendocino Dr. to top of hill, following signs; at S end of lake near Coyote Valley Dam. $10 with federal senior pass at 20 non-elec sites; others pay $20. All year;l; 14-day limit. 42-ft RV limit. Tbls, toilets, cfga, drkg wtr, playground, beach, 2 shelters (no showers or flush toilets). Boating(l), fishing, hiking trail, swimming, waterskiing, disc golf, biking, horse staging area.

Fuller Grove Campground $8
Mendocino National Forest
Pacific Gas & Electric
6 mi N of Ukiah on US 101; 5 mi E on SR 20; 26 mi NW on

CR 250 (Potter Valley-Lake Pillsbury Rd). $8 with federal senior pass; others pay $16 (double sites $32). 4/1-12/1; 4-day limit. 24 single sites, 6 double; 22-ft RV limit. Tbls, toilets, cfga, drkg wtr. Boating(l), fishing.

Navy Camp Campground $8
Mendocino National Forest
Pacific Gas & Electric
6 mi N of Ukiah on US 101; 5 mi E on SR 20; 26 mi NW on CR 240 (Potter Valley-Lake Pillsbury Rd). $8 with federal senior pass; others pay $16. 4/1-12/1; 14-day limit. 20 sites; 25-ft RV limit. Tbls, toilets, cfga, drkg wtr. Fishing, boating.

Pogie Point Campground $8
Mendocino National Forest
Pacific Gas & Electric
6 mi N of Ukiah on US 101; 5 mi E on SR 20; 26 mi NW on CR 240 (Potter Valley-Lake Pillsbury Rd). $8 with federal senior pass; others pay $16. All year; 14-day limit. 50 sites; 25-ft RV limit. Fishing, boating.

Sunset Campground $8
Mendocino National Forest
Pacific Gas & Electric
6 mi N of Ukiah on US 101; 5 mi E on SR 20; 26 mi NW on CR 240 (Potter Valley-Lake Pillsbury Rd). $8 with federal senior pass; others pay $16. All year; 14-day limit. 54 sites; 25-ft RV limit. Boating, fishing.

UPPER LAKE (N)

Bear Creek FREE
Upper Lake Recreation Area
Mendocino National Forest
17 mi N of Upper Lake on CR 301 (FR M-1); 6 mi E on CR 18N01; 1.5 mi E on FR 17N33. Free. 5/1-10/15; 14-day limit. 16 sites (RVs under 16 ft). Tbls, toilets, cfga, stoves, no drkg wtr, no trash service. Swimming, picnicking, fishing. Elev 2300 ft; 6 acres. Creek. Check at Upper Lake Ranger Station for info on Rice Fork crossing; closed when creek too high to ford.

Deer Valley $6
Upper Lake Recreation Area
Mendocino National Forest
12 mi N of Upper Lake on CR 301 (FR M-1); 4.5 mi E on FR 16N01. $6. All year; 14-day limit. 13 sites on 4 acres. Tbls, toilets, cfga, no drkg wtr or trash service. Picnicking. Elev 3700 ft. Primarily a deer hunting camp.

Lower Nye Campground FREE
Upper Lake Recreation Ara
Mendocino National Forest
17 mi N of Upper Lake on CR 301 (FR M-1); 6 mi E on CR 18N01 (Rice Creek Rd); 14 mi N on FR 18N04. Free. All year, but closed when creek too high to ford; 14-day limit. 6 sites. No tbls, cfga, wtr or services. Picnicking, hiking.

On Skeleton Creek. Elev 3300 ft; 2 acres. Check at Upper Lake Ranger Station for info on creek crossing.

Middle Creek $8
Upper Lake Recreation Area
Mendocino National Forest
8 mi N of Upper Lake on CR 301 (FR M-1). $8; double sites $12. All year; 21-day limit. 23 sites, typically 40-ft. Tbls, toilets, cfga, drkg wtr. Nature trails; motorcycle trails nearby. Elev 2000 ft. Adjoining picnic area absorbed into campground.

Sunset Point $8
Upper Lake Recreation Area
Mendocino National Forest
Pacific Gas & Electric Corp.
27.1 mi N of Upper Lake on CR 301 (FR M-1) to "T" jct; continue on FR M-1 4.9 mi to campground sign, then right. $8 with federal senior pass; others pay $16. MD-LD; 14-day limit. 53 sites (typically 40 ft). Tbls, pit toilets, cfga, drkg wtr. Boating(l), fishing, hiking trails.

VACAVILLE (C)

Lake Solano $11
Solano County Park
Bureau of Reclamation
11 mi N of Vacaville on I-505; 5 mi W on Hwy 128; left on Pleasant Valley Rd. $11 for seniors at non-hookup sites; others pay $21 ($30-35 for hookups; seniors pay $18). All year; 14-day limit. 90 sites (40 with hookups); 35-ft RV limit. Tbls, flush toilets, cfga, drkg wtr, dump, showers, hookups ($). Boating (lr), fishing. Administered by county.

VALLEY SPRINGS (S)

Acorn Campground $10
New Hogan Lake
Corps of Engineers
Half mi S of Valley Springs on SR 26; 1 mi S (left) on Hogan Dam Rd (signs); three-fourths mi E on Hogan Pkwy. $10 with federal senior pass; others pay $20. All year; 14-day limit. Off-season discounts no longer available. 128 non-elec sites; 65-ft RV limit; 30 pull-through sites. Tbls, flush toilets, cfga, drkg wtr, coin showers, amphitheater, campfire programs, fish cleaning station, dump. Boating(l), fishing, hiking.

Oak Knoll Campground $10
New Hogan Lake
Corps of Engineers
Half mi from Valley Springs on SR 26; 1.8 mi E on Lime Rd; 1.4 mi S on Petersburg Rd. $10 with federal senior pass at 50 primitive sites; others pay $20. 4/1-9/30; 14-day limit. 65-ft RV limit; 8 pull-through. Tbls, toilets, cfga, drkg wtr. Dump, coin showers, fish cleaning station at Acorn Campground. Amphitheater. Fishing.

WARNER SPRINGS (S)

Indian Flats $12

Cleveland National Forest

2 mi NW of Warner Springs on SR 79; 6 mi N on FR 9S05. $12 ($6 with federal senior pass). June-Feb; 14-day limit. 17 sites; 15-ft RV limit. Tbls, toilets, cfga, no drkg wtr. Hiking. Elev 3600 ft.

WEAVERVILLE (N)

Alpine View $10

Shasta-Trinity National Forest

22.5 mi N of Weaverville on SR 3; 2.4 mi W on Guy Covington Rd. $10 with federal senior pass; others pay $20. Double sites $35. About 5/20-9/15; 14-day limit. 54 sites; 32-ft RV limit. Tbls, flush toilets, cfga, drkg wtr, bear lockers. Fishing, boating.

Bridge Camp $12

Shasta-Trinity National Forest

13 mi N of Weaverville on SR 3; cross Stuart Fork bridge, then right on Trinity Alps Rd; dirt rd ends at campground; on North Fork of Stuart Fork Creek. $12. All year (no wtr 11/1-4/1); 14-day limit. 20 sites; 20-ft RV limit. Tbls, flush toilets, cfga, drkg wtr (4/1-10/31). Boating, fishing, hiking, horseback riding.

Bushytail Campground $8

Shasta-Trinity National Forest

16.3 mi N of Weaverville on SR 3 (14 mi S of Trinity Center); follow directional signs; 0.5 mi from Trinity Lake. $8 base in 2017 at 2 no-hookup sites, 4 elec hookup sites $20 (less with federal senior pass). Also double, triple, quad sites. About 5/15-10/31; 14-day limit. 11 sites; 40-ft RV limit. Tbls, flush toilets, cfga, drkg wtr, bear lockers. Note for 2017: Until new well opens, no wtr/flush toilets; fees half price. Managed by Shasta Recreation Co.

Clark Springs $12

Shasta-Trinity National Forest

18 mi N of Weaverville on SR 3; at Mule Creek Station. $12 with federal senior pass; others pay $12 during 2017 until wtr service available. 4/1-10/30 but may be closed. 21 sites (25-ft RV limit). Tbls, flush toilets, cfga, drkg wtr, beach. Swimming, boating(dl), fishing. On Stuart Fork arm in Whiskeytown-Shasta-Trinity National Recreation Area.

East Weaver $11

Shasta-Trinity National Forest

2 mi NE of Weaverville on SR 3; 1.5 mi N on CR 228 (East Weaver Rd); along East Weaver Creek. $11 during 4/1-10/31; less rest of year but no wtr; 14-day limit. 10 sites (25-ft RV limit). Tbls, toilets, cfga, drkg wtr. Hiking, fishing. Elev 2800 ft; 5 acres.

Hayward Flat $10

Shasta-Trinity National Forest

17.5 mi N of Weaverville on SR 3; 2 mi E on Hayward Flat Rd; on W shore of Trinity Lake (9 mi S of Trinity Center). $10 with federal senior pass; others pay $20. About 5/15-9/15; 14-day limit. 76 sites; 40-ft RV limit. Tbls, flush toilets, cfga, drkg wtr, amphitheater, bear lockers. Fishing, boating(l), hiking, swimming.

Minersville Campground $8

Shasta-Trinity National Forest

15 mi NE of Weaverville on SR 3; 1 mi SE on Minersville/Bushytail Rd. During peak season, $8 at 3 RV/tent sites without hookups ($4 with federal senior pass); 1 elec RV site, $16 in-season with senior pass ($20 others). Lower rates charged off-season. 35-ft RV limit. Tbls, flush toilets, cfga, drkg wtr. Boating(l), fishing, swimming, waterskiing. Near Clair Engle Lake on Stuart Fork arm in Whiskeytown-Shasta-Trinity National Recreation Area. 11 acres. During 2017, no wtr or flush toilets available until new well operational; half fees charged.

Pigeon Point $12

Shasta-Trinity National Forest

15 mi W of Weaverville on Hwy 299. $12. May-Oct; 14-day limit. 7 sites (22-ft RV limit). Tbls, toilets, cfga, no drkg wtr. Swimming beach, fishing. Trinity River.

Rush Creek $10

Shasta-Trinity National Forest

8 mi N of Weaverville on SR 3; left at camp sign for qtr mi. $10. About 5/15-9/30; 14-day limit. 10 primitive RV & tent sites; 20-ft RV limit. Tbls, toilets, cfga, no drkg wtr, no trash service. Primarily an overflow camp. Hiking, fishing, swimming, gold panning.

Tannery Gulch $9

Shasta-Trinity National Forest

10.5 mi N of Weaverville on SR 3; 1 mi E on Tannery Gulch Rd. $9 with federal senior pass; others pay $18. About 5/15-10/31; 14-day limit. 82 sites; 40-ft RV limit. Tbls, flush toilets, cfga, drkg wtr, bear lockers. Hiking, fishing, swimming, boating.

WEED (N)

Lake Shastina FREE

Public Access Camping

Siskiyou County Public Works Department

2.5 mi NE of Weed on Hwy 97; 9.5 mi N on Edgewood-Big Springs Rd; 1 mi W on Jackson Ranch Rd; 1 mi SW on Dwinnell Way (public access rd) to lake. Free. 5/1-9/30; 14-day limit. 10-15 undesignated primitive campsites; portable toilet, cfga, drkg wtr. Fishing, boating(l). Lake dries up in mid-July.

WESTWOOD (N)

Echo Lake FREE

Lassen National Forest

From SR 36, N on FR 10 & FR 30N64; near Silver Lake.

Free. May-Nov; 14-day limit. Dispersed undesignated sites, toilets, no tbls, no cfga, no drkg wtr. Fishing, hiking.

Rocky Knoll Campground $12
Silver Lake Recreation Area
Lassen National Forest
From Westwood at jct with SR 36, 14 mi N on CR A21; 5 mi W on Silver Lake Rd to just past North Shore sign; on right. $12. 5/10-10/31; 14-day limit. 18 sites, typically 40 ft. Tbls, toilets, cfga, drkg wtr. Boating(l), fishing.

Silver Bowl Campground $12
Silver Lake Recreation Area
Lassen National Forest
From Westwood at jct with SR 36, 14 mi N on CR A21; 5 mi W on Silver Lake Rd to North Shore sign; right on FR 10 for half mi past 2nd North Shore sign; at T intersection, turn right for 0.2 mi to campground at 2nd right. $12 during 5/1-10/31; free off-season but no services; 14-day limit. 18 sites (typically 45 ft). Tbls, toilets, cfga, drkg wtr. Fishing, boating(l).

WILLIAMS (N)
Cache Creek FREE
State Wildlife Area
About 18 mi SW of Williams on Hwy 20; at main & N fork of Cache Creek. Public access S of Hwy 20 on Hwy 16. Free. All year; 14-day limit. Primitive camping on 2,632 acres. Hunting, hiking, fishing.

Cowboy Camp FREE
State Wildlife Area
20 mi SW of Williams on Hwy 20, then 4 mi S on Hwy 16. Free. All year; 14-dya limit. Primitive camping. Pit toilets, tbls, cfga, no drkg wtr.

Indian Valley FREE
State Wildlife Area
About 17 mi SW of Williams on Hwy 20; 8 mi N on Bear Valley Rd; W on Bartlett Springs Rd to N shore of Indian Valley Lake; follow signs. Free. All year; 14-day limit. Primitive camping on 4,990 acres surrounding the lake. Hunting, fishing, boating, canoeing.

WILLOW CREEK (N)
Boise Creek Campground $10
Six Rivers National Forest
1 mi W of Willow Creek on Hwy 299. $10 during 5/22-10/15; $8 off-seson, but no wtr; 14-day limit. 17 sites (35-ft RV limit). Toilets, tbls, drkg wtr, cfga. Hiking, fishing.

East Fork Willow Creek $8
Six Rivers National Forest
6 mi W of Willow Creek on SR 299. $8. Forest entry information site. 6/1-9/30; limit 7 days in calendar yr; free off-season. 13 primitive sites; 20-ft RV limit. Information display, toilets, tbls, no drkg wtr or trash service. Hunting, hiking.

Horse Linto Primitive Area FREE
Six Rivers National Forest
7 mi NE of Willow Creek on FR 10N02. Free. All year; limit 7 days in calendar yr. 3 undeveloped primitive sites; 20-ft RV limit. Fire pits, toilets, tbls, trash cans, no drkg wtr. Fishing, swimming.

WINTERHAVEN (S)
Imperial Dam $180
Long-Term Visitor Area
Bureau of Land Management
From I-8 at Winterhaven, NE 20 mi on Imperial County Hwy (S-24), then W on Senator Wash Rd. $180 for winter season or $40 for 14 days during 9/15-4/15; during 4/16-9/14, $15 per day or $75 for summer season. About 2,000 sites on 3,500 acres. Toilets, cfga, drkg wtr, grey & black wtr dumps, outdoor showers, ramadas; limited facilities in winter. Rockhounding, hiking, fishing, boating, swimming. Federal senior pass discounts do not apply to LTVA fees.

Pilot Knob $180
Long-Term Visitor Area
Bureau of Land Management
From I-8 at Winterhaven's Sidewinder Rd exit, qtr mi S on Sidewinder Rd. Site on gravel terrace on both sides of rd. $180 for winter season or $40 for 14 days during 9/15-4/15. Free day use off-season, but no services. Undesignated sites. No facilities. Dump($) and water fills($) at Tank and Mobile Wash, I-8 at Ave 3E in Yuma. Federal senior pass discounts do not apply to LTVA fees.

Senator Wash North Shore $7.50
Bureau of Land Management
From Winterhaven exit of I-8, go N 22 mi on CR S24; follow Senator Wash Rd 2 mi to South Mesa Campground; proceed through campground & follow signs to North Shore. $7.50 daily for seniors with federal senior pass; others pay $15 (or $75 annually). Holders of Long-Term Visitor Area permits also may use the day-use facilities; other non-campers pay $10 use fee. All year; 14-day limit. Undesignated primitive sites on 60 acres. Tbls, flush toilets, cfga, no drkg wtr; dump at South Mesa (fee 9/15-4/15). Boating(l), fishing, OHV activities, hiking, swimming.

Senator Wash South Shore $7.50
Bureau of Land Management
From I-8 exit at Winterhaven, follow CR S24 about 22 mi N; follow Senator Wash Rd 2 mi to South Mesa Campground, then left about 200 yds; turn right on reservoir access rd. $7.50 for seniors with federal senior pass; others pay $15 (or $75 annually). Holders of Long-Term Visitor Area permits also may use the day-use facilities. All year; 14-day limit. Primitive undesignated sites on 50 acres. Tbls, flush toilets, outdoor showers, drkg wtr, gravel beach; dump at South Mesa (fee 9/15-4/15); no trash service. Boating(l),

fishing, swimming, hiking. Non-campers pay $10 day use fee.

Squaw Lake Campground $7.50
Bureau of Land Management
From I-8 near Winterhaven, 20 mi N on CR S-24 to sign for Senator Wash & Squaw Lake. $7.50 daily with federal senior pass; others pay $15 (or $75 annually). All year; 14-day limit. 125 RV sites (30-ft RV limit) & numerous dispersed tent sites. Tbls, flush toilets, cfga, cold outdoor showers, drkg wtr, gray water dump (dump station at nearby South Mesa). Boating(l), fishing, swimming, hiking. No open fires MD-LD.

WOODFORDS (N)
Crystal Springs $9
Toiyabe National Forest
1 mi W of Woodfords on SR 88. $9 with federal senior pass; others pay $18. About 4/15-9/30; 14-day limit. 19 sites (35-ft RV limit). Tbls, toilets, cfga, drkg wtr. Fishing, hiking. West Fork of Carson River. Elev 6000 ft. Concession-managed.

Hope Valley $11
Toiyabe National Forest
About 10 mi W of Woodfords on SR 88; 1.5 mi S on Blue Lakes Rd. $11 with federal senior pass; others pay $22. About 6/15-9/30; 14-day limit. 20 sites (40-ft RV limit). Tbls, toilets, cfga, drkg wtr. Fishing, hiking. Elev 7300 ft.

Kit Carson $9
Toiyabe National Forest
5 mi W of Woodfords on SR 88; at W fork of Carson River. $9 with federal senior pass; others pay $18. About 5/15-9/15; 14-day limit. 12 sites (30-ft RV limit). Tbls, toilets, cfga, drkg wtr. Fishing, hiking. Elev 6900 ft.

Markleeville Campground $9
Toiyabe National Forest
About 10.5 mi S of Woodfords on Hwy 89 (half mi S of Markleeville). $9 with federal senior pass; others pay $18. About 4/15-10/15; 14-day limit. 10 sites (24-ft RV limit). Tbls, toilets, cfga, drkg wtr. Fishing at Markleeville Creek. Elev 5500 ft.

Silver Creek $18
Toiyabe National Forest
About 10 mi S of Woodfords on Hwy 89 to Markleeville; 16 mi S on SR 4. $9 with federal senior pass; others pay $18. 6/15-LD; 14-day limit. 22 sites (35-ft RV limit). Tbls, toilets, cfga, drkg wtr. Fishing. Elev 6800 ft.

Turtle Rock $10
Alpine County Public Works Department
3.5 mi S of Woodfords on SR 89. $10 for seniors; others pay $15 at RV sites. 5/1-10/15 (depending upon weather). 26 RV sites (34-ft RV limit). Seniors $250 monthly, others

$350. Tbls, flush toilets, cfga, drkg wtr, coin showers. Tennis, basketball, disc golf, horseshoes. Elev 6000 ft.

WRIGHTWOOD (S)
Blue Ridge Campground $5
Angeles National Forest
5.6 mi W of Wrightwood on SR 2 (Angeles Crest Hwy); 3.8 mi SE on FR 3N06. $5 daily or $30 annually. 5/1-10/31; 14-day limit (walk-in during winter). 8 sites (RVs under 21 ft). Tbls, toilets, cfga, no drkg wtr. Hiking, picnicking. Elev 7900 ft; 3 acres. Snow closes access rd Dec-April. Nature trails (on Pacific Crest Trail).

Lake Campground $10
Angeles National Forest
3 mi from Wrightwood on Angeles Crest Hwy to Big Pines; bear right on Big Pines Hwy (CR N4) for 2.5 mi. $10 with federal senior pass. About 5/1-11/1; 14-day limit. 8 sites (18-ft RV limit). Tbls, toilets, cfga, drkg wtr. Fishing. On Jackson Lake. Elev 6100 ft. Concession-managed.

Mountain Oak $11.50
Angeles National Forest
3 mi from Wrightwood on Angeles Crest Hwy to Big Pines; bear right on Big Pines Hwy (CR N4) for 3 mi. $11.50 with federal senior pass; others pay $23. 4/1-11/1; 4-day limit. 17 sites (18-ft RV limit). Tbls, toilets, cfga, drkg wtr. Elev 6200 ft. Concession-operated.

Table Mountain Camp $11.50
Angeles National Forest
2.4 mi W of Wrightwood to Table Mountain sign; right for 1 mi on Table Mountain Rd. $11.50 with federal senior pass; others pay $23. About 4/20-11/1; 14-day limit. 111 sites; 32-ft RV limit. Tbls, toilets, cfga, drkg wtr. Visitor center. OHV activities. Concession-operated.

YOSEMITE VILLAGE (C)
Bridalveil Creek $9
Yosemite National Park
About 8 mi E of Wawona Rd (Hwy 41) on Glacier Point Rd (S of Yosemite Village). $9 with federal senior ass; others pay $18. 8/1-9/15; 14-day limit. 110 sites; 35-ft motorhome limit, 24-ft trailer limit. Tbls, cfga, drkg wtr, flush toilets, food lockers.

Porcupine Flat $12
Yosemite National Park
30 mi NE of Yosemite Village on Old Big Oak Flat Rd. Just N of Tioga Rd. $12 plus entry fee. About 7/1-10/15; 14-day limit. 52 sites; 24-ft trailer limit, 35-ft motorhome limit. Tbls, toilets, cfga, no drkg wtr. Fishing. Trails to Yosemite Creek & Snow Creek. Elev 8100 ft.

White Wolf $9
Yosemite National Park
20 mi E of Yosemite Buck Meadows on Big Oak Flat Rd

(SR 120), 1 mi Off Tioga Rd. $9 with federal senior pass; others pay $18. 6/1-9/15; 14-day limit. 74 sites (27-ft RV limit). Tbls, flush toilets, cfga, drkg wtr. Fishing, ranger programs, hiking. Elev 8000 ft; 18 acres.

YREKA (N)

Mallard Cove Campground   FREE
Copco Lake Recreation Area
Bureau of Land Management
33 mi NE on Yreka on US 99 (N Central Valley). 6.5 mi E of Hornbrook on Ager Rd, then 15 mi N on Copco Lake Rd. Free. May-Nov. Undesignated sites for 6 RVs. Tbls, cfga, toilet, no drkg wtr. Boating(l), hunting, fishing. Elev 2500 ft. On Klamath River. Cooperative area; Bureau of Land Management & Pacific Power & Light Co.

Tree of Heaven $7.50
Klamath National Forest
8 mi N of Yreka on SR 263; 4 mi W on SR 96. $7.50 with federal senior pass; others pay $15. 5/15-10/15; 14-day limit. 20 sites (30-ft RV limit). Tbls, toilets, cfga, drkg wtr. Swimming, fishing, boating(l), hiking, horseshoes, volleyball. On Klamath River. Elev 2100 ft; 6 acres. Paved birding nature trail with interpretive signs.

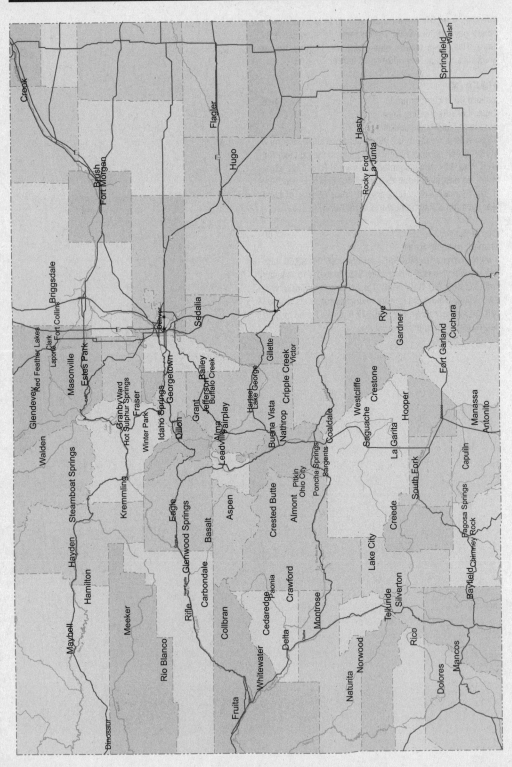

COLORADO

CAPITAL: Denver
NICKNAME: Centennial State
STATEHOOD: 1876 – 38th State
FLOWER: Rocky Mountain Columbine
TREE: Colorado Blue Spruce
BIRD: Lark Bunting

WWW.COLORADO.COM

Colorado Tourism Board, 1675 Broadway, Suite 320, Denver, CO 80202; 800/COLORADO.

Department of Natural Resources, 1313 Sherman St., Room 718, Denver, CO 80203; 866-3311.

REST AREAS
Overnight stops are not permitted.

STATE PARKS
Nearly all state park campgrounds are missing from this edition due to rather dramatic increases in fees. For information about state parks, contact the Department of Natural Resources, Division of Parks and Outdoor Recreation, 1313 Sherman St., Room 618, Denver, CO 80203. Phone 303/866-3437.

COLORADO DIVISION OF WILDLIFE PROPERTIES.
Free camping is permitted for up to 14 days in any 45-day period on most Division of Wildlife properties. 6060 Broadway, Denver, CO 80216; 303/297-1192.

Arapaho and Roosevelt National Forests, 2150 Centre Ave, Building E, Fort Collins, CO 80526-8119; 970-295-6600.

Grand Mesa, Uncompahgre and Gunnison National Forests, 2250 U.S. Highway 50, Delta, CO 81416. 970-874-6600.

Pike and San Isabel National Forests, 2840 Kachina Drive, Pueblo, CO 81008. 719-553-1400.

Rio Grande National Forest, 1803 W. Highway 160, Monte Vista, CO 81144.

Routt National Forest, 2468 Jackson St, Laramie, WY 82070.

San Juan National Forest, 15 Burnett Court, Durango, CO 81301.

White River National Forest, 900 Grand Ave., Box 948, Glenwood Springs, CO 81602. 970-945-2421.

BLACK CANYON OF THE GUNNISON NATIONAL PARK
A vehicle entry fee (or annual pass) is charged, and $16 overnight fees are charged at campgrounds. 102 Elk Creek, Gunnison, CO 81230. 970-641-2337.

COLORADO NATIONAL MONUMENT
A vehicle entry fee (or annual fee) is charged. Evening ranger programs and a visitor center are available at Saddlehorn Campground. Facilities there include drinking water and flush toilets. Colorado National Monument, Fruita, CO 81521.

CURECANTI NATIONAL RECREATION AREA
Fees are charged at all campgrounds in the recreation area except the boat-in backcountry campsites. Most campgrounds are open from May to October, with exact dates depending upon snow and road conditions. No camping fees are collected at developed campgrounds from Oct 1 to mid May. 102 Elk Creek, Gunnison, CO 81230.

DINOSAUR NATIONAL MONUMENT
Free camping is permitted at all back-country locations, but entry fees of $10 per vehicle for 7 days are charged ($20 annually). Camping is $10-18 per night at the monument's campgrounds. 4545 E. Hwy 40, Dinosaur, CO 81610. 970-374-3000.

BUREAU OF LAND MANAGEMENT
Although camping outside improved campsites is not prohibited, it is not encouraged except in designated primitive areas because of sanitary, fire, litter and surface damage problems. Except where specifically prohibited, camping is allowed outside of developed areas. Fees are charged for camping in some of BLM's developed sites in Colorado. Fees vary widely. Bureau of Land Management, 2850 Youngfield St., Lakewood, CO 80215 7076. 303-239-3600.

AGUILAR

Spanish Peaks State Wildlife Area   FREE
18 mi SW of Aguilar on co rd. Free. All year; 14-day limit during 45-day period. Primitive campsites. Toilets, drkg wtr, cfga, tbls. Big game, small game & turnkey hunting. Hiking, picnicking. Elev 6500 ft; 5500 acres. Camping, fires only in designated areas.

ALAMOSA

Pinon Flats $10
Great Sand Dunes National Park
15 mi E of Alamosa on US 160; 16 mi N on CR 150; 1 mi N of visitor center. $10 with federal senior pass; others pay $20. 4/1-10/30; 14-day limit. 88 sites; 35-ft RV limit. Tbls, flush toilets, cfga, drkg wtr, dump (no wtr during winter). Sightseeing, hiking, backpacking. $3 per person entry fee (or $15 annual) also charged.

ALLENSPARK

Peaceful Valley $10.50
Roosevelt National Forest
3 mi SE of Allenspark on SR 7; 4 mi SW on SR 72; 0.25 mi W on Middle Saint Vrain Rd (CR 92). $10.50 with federal senior pass; others pay $21. 5/20-11/20; 14-day limit. 17 sites; 45-ft RV limit. Tbls, pit toilets, cfga, drkg wtr. Biking, hiking trails.

Olive Ridge $10.50
Roosevelt National Forest
N of Allenspark at milepost 14 on SR 7; on SE edge of Rocky Mtn National Park . $10.50 with federal senior pass. 5/15-9/30; 14-day limit. Lower fees when wtr off. 56 sites; 40-ft RV limit. Tbls, toilets, cfga, drkg wtr, playground. Hiking trail, fishing.

Twin Sisters State Wildlife Area   FREE
4 mi N of Allenspark on Hwy 7 to Meeker Park; 2.5 mi N on FR 119; 1 mi W on FR 325. Free. All year; 14-day limit in 45-day period. Primitive camping; no facilities. Hiking, hunting.

ALMA

Alma State Wildlife Area   FREE
1.5 mi N of Alma on Hwy 9; qtr mi NW on CR 4. Free. All year; 14-day limit during a 45-day period. Primitive campsites. Tbls, toilets, cfga. Fishing, picnicking. Elev 10,000 ft; 240 acres. 7 mi of stream.

ALMONT

Almont Campground $10
Gunnison National Forest
1 mi SW of Almont on SR 135. $10 during 5/15-10/15; free off-season but no wtr or services. 14-day limit). 10 sites; 28-ft RV limit Tbls toilets, cfga, drkg wtr. Fishing, mountain biking, kayaking, 4x4 activity.

Cold Spring $10
Gunnison National Forest
16.1 mi NE of Almont on FR 742 (Taylor River Rd). MD-10/30; 14-day limit. $10. 5/15-9/30; 16-day limit. 6 sites (RVs under 16 ft). 2 acres. Tbls, toilet, cfga, no drkg wtr. Fishing, picnicking. Elev 9000 ft.

Dinner Station $8
Gunnison National Forest
32.5 mi NE of Almont on FR 742. $8 with federal senior pass; others pay $16. 5/15-10/1; 14-day limit. 22 sites (35-ft RV limit). Tbls, toilets, cfga, drkg wtr. Fishing (Taylor River). Taylor Park Reservoir nearby. Elev 9600 ft; 12 acres. Primarily used by off-roaders & trail bikers.

Dorchester   FREE
Gunnison National Forest
39.5 mi NE of Almont on FR 742. Free, but donations accepted. Open MD through hunting season; 14-day limit. 10 sites (28-ft RV limit). Tbls, toilets, cfga, no drkg wtr. Hiking, fishing, off-roading.

Lodgepole $8
Gunnison National Forest
14.6 mi NE of Almont on FR 742. $8 with federal senior pass; others pay $16. 5/15-9/30; 14-day limit. 16 sites (35-ft RV limit). Tbls, toilets, cfga, drkg wtr. Hiking, fishing (Taylor River). Elev 8800 ft; 4 acres.

Lottis Creek $9
Gunnison National Forest
17.5 mi NE of Almont on FR 742 (Taylor Canyon Rd). $9 base with federal senior pass; others pay $18 base during 5/15-9/30; center loop free about 10/1-12/1. $6 elec surcharge. 14-day limit. 45 sites (38 with elec); 35-ft RV limit. Tbls, toilets, cfga. drkg wtr. Fishing (Taylor River & Lottis Creek), hiking. Non-campers pay $4 day use fee.

Mirror Lake $12
Gunnison National Forest
26.6 mi NE of Almont on FR 742; 7.6 mi SE on FR 765; 3.1 mi E on FR 211; at East Willow Creek & 36-acre Mirror Lake. $12. About 5/25-9/30; 14-day limit. 10 sites; 32-ft RV limit. Tbls, toilet, cfga, no drkg wtr. Fishing, boating (no mtrs), hiking trails. Elev 11,000 ft. Historic Tincup townsite (2 mi E).

Mosca $7
Gunnison National Forest
7.2 mi NE of Almont on FR 742; 12 mi N on FR 744; on SE shore of Spring Creek Reservoir. $7 with federal senior pass; others pay $14. About 5/23-10/15; 14-day limit. 16 sites (35-ft RV limit). Tbls, toilet, cfga, no drkg wtr. Boating(ld), fishing, hiking, 4x4 activty.

North Bank $7
Gunnison National Forest
7.7 mi NE of Almont on FR 742. $7 with federal senior pass; others pay $14 during 5/15-10/15; free about 10/15-12/1. 16-day limit. 17 sites (35-ft RV limit). Tbls, toilets, cfga, drkg wtr. Fishing (Taylor River), hiking, mountain biking. Elev 8800 ft; 6 acres.

Rivers End $7
Gunnison National Forest
28.3 mi NE of Almont on FR 742; on NE shore of Taylor Park Reservoir. $7 with federal senior pass; others pay $14. 5/15-10/15; 14-day limit. 15 sites (35-ft RV limit). Tbls, toilets, cfga, drkg wtr. Fishing, boating(ld), 4x4, mountain biking, horseback riding.

Rosy Lane $9
Gunnison National Forest
10 mi NE of Almont on FR 742. $9 base with federal senior pass; others pay $18. $6 elec surcharge for elec. 5/15-9/15; 16-day limit. 20 sites (35-ft RV limit). Tbls, toilets, cfga, drkg wtr. Fishing, horseback riding.

Spring Creek $7
Gunnison National Forest
7.2 mi NE of Almont on FR 742; 2 mi N on FR 744. $7 with federal senior pass; others pay $14. 5/15-10/15; 14-day limit. 12 sites (35-ft RV limit). Tbls, toilets, cfga, drkg wtr. Fishing (Spring Creek). Elev 8600 ft; 4 acres.

ANTONITO
Conejos   CLOSED
Rio Grande National Forest
23 mi W of Antonito on SR 17; 7 mi NW on FR 250. Decommissioned and closed.

Cumbres Pass Dispersed   FREE
Rio Grande National Forest
At the top of Cumbres Pass just off SR 17; behind old Cumbres & Toltec Scenic Railroad station. Free. MD-LD; 14-day limit. Primitive undesignated sites; cfga, toilet nearby, no drkg wtr, no trash service. Hiking. Elev 10,000 ft.

La Manga Creek   FREE
Dispersed Camping Area
Rio Grande National Forest
24 mi W of Antonito on SR 17; 1 mi N on FR 114; at La Manga Creek. Free. MD-LD; 14-day limit. No facilities, no drkg wtr, no trash service. Hiking, fishing. Elev 10,300 ft.

Lake Fork $9
Rio Grande National Forest
23 mi W of Antonito on SR 17; 7.5 mi NW on scenic FR 250, then left on access rd; at E shore of Conejos River. $9 with federal senior pass; others pay $18. MD-LD; 14-day limit. 18 sites; 8 pull-through (45-ft RV limit). Tbls, toilets,

cfga, no drkg wtr. Fishing, hiking. Elev 10,100 ft; 10 acres. Reduced services after Labor Day for big game hunting.

Mix Lake $8
Rio Grande National Forest
23 mi W of Antonito on SR 17; 21.5 mi NW on scenic FR 250; .7 mi W on FR 2506B. $8 with federal senior pass; others pay $16. MD-LD; 14-day limit. 22 sites; 40-ft RV limit. Tbls, toilets, cfga, drkg wtr. Hiking, fishing. Elev 10,100 ft; 10 acres.

Old La Manga Dispersed Camping Area   FREE
Rio Grande National Forest
24 mi W of Antonito on SR 17; half mi W on FR 250 to Elk Creek Campground, then half mi SW on FR 128. Free. MD-LD; 14-day limit. Primitive undesignated sites, no facilities, no drkg wtr or trash service. Hiking, fishing.

South Fork Dispersed Camping Area   FREE
Rio Grande National Forest
3 mi N of Rocky Mountain Lodge, W of FR 250 between the road and the Conejos River at the South Fork trailhead. Free. MD-LD; 14-day limit. Primitive undesignated sites. 1 pit toilet, parking for horse trailers; no drkg wtr or trash service. Hiking, horseback riding, fishing at Conejos River. Elev 9100 ft.

Spectacle Lake $8.50
Rio Grande National Forest
24 mi W of Antonito on SR 17; 6 mi NW on FR 250. $8.50 with federal senior pass; others pay $17. MD-LD; 14-day limit. 24 sites; 13 pull-through; 40-ft RV limit. Tbls, toilets, cfga, drkg wtr. Fishing, hiking, no boating. Elev 8700 ft; 17 acres. This camp alternates with Conejos Camp in staying open with reduced services until 11/15 for big game hunting & fall color viewing.

Trail Creek Dispersed Camping Area   FREE
Rio Grande National Forest
23 mi W of Antonito on SR 17; 10 mi NW on scenic FR 250, past access rd to Lake Fork Camp, W side, E of Conejos River. Free. MD-LD; 14-day limit. Designated undeveloped camping area. No facilities, no drkg wtr, no trash service. Fishing, hiking.

Trujillo Meadows $10
Rio Grande National Forest
34 mi W of Antonito on SR 17; SW to FR 118; 3 mi NW to Trujillo Meadows Rd 7 FR 118.1B. $10 with federal senior pass; others pay $20. MD-LD; 14-day limit. 50 sites (40-ft RV limit). Tbls, toilets, cfga, drkg wtr. Fishing, boating(l). 60 acres. Hazardous trees removed.

ASPEN
Difficult Campground $12
White River National Forest
5 mi SE of Aspen on SR 82 (RVs over 35 ft prohibited over

Independence Pass). $12 base with federal senior pass; others pay $24 base, $26 for premium locations. About 5/23-10/10; 5-day limit. 47 sites (plus group area); 40-ft RV limit. Tbls, toilets, cfga, drkg wtr. Hiking trails, fishing. Elev 8180 ft.

Lincoln Gulch $10
White River National Forest
10.5 mi SE of Aspen on SR 82 toward Independeence Pass (no RVs over 35 ft at pass); half mi SW on FR 106 (rough gravel); qtr mi W on access rd. $10 with federal senior pass; others pay $20. 5/20-9/18; 5-day limit. 7 sites; 30-ft RV limit. Tbls, toilets, cfga, drkg wtr. Fishing, hiking, biking, 4WD. At Lincoln Creek & Roaring Fork River. Secluded. Elev 9700 ft.

Lost Man Campground $10
White River National Forest
14.2 mi SE of Aspen on SR 82 toward Independence Pass (no RVs over 35 ft at pass). $10 with federal senior pass; others pay $20. 6/10-9/20; 5-day limit. 10 sites (30-ft RV limit). Tbls, toilets, cfga, drkg wtr. Fishing, hiking. At Lostman Creek & Roaring Fork River. Elev 10,700 ft.

Portal Campground DONATIONS
White River National Forest
11.9 mi SE of Aspen on SR 82 (no RVs over 35 ft on Hwy 82); 7 mi on Lincoln Creek Rd (high-clearance vehicles; 4x4 recommended). At Grizzly Reservoir. Camp free, but donations suggested. All year; 5-day limit. 5 sites (RVs under 21 ft). Tbls, toilets, cfga, firewood, no drkg wtr or trash service; pack it out. Hiking, boating(d), fishing. Elev 10,700 ft; 3 acres. Near Lostman Reservoir.

Silver Bell Campground $7.50
Maroon Bells Scenic Area
White River National Forest
From Aspen, 1 mi W on SR 82 to Maroon Creek Rd exit at roundabout; 5 mi S on Maroon Creek Rd to 0.5 mi past Maroon Bells welcome station. $7.50 with federal senior pass; others pay $15. Visitors also must buy 5-day vehicle pass ($5) at welcome center. 5/20-9/25; 5-day limit. 14 sites; 30-ft RV limit. Tbls, toilets, cfga, drkg wtr. Fishing, hiking.

Silver Queen $7.50
Maroon Bells Scenic Area
White River National Forest
From Aspen, 1 mi W on SR 82 to Maroon Creek Rd exit at roundabout; 5 mi S on Maron Creek Rd to welcome station, then to campground. $7.50 with federal senior pass; others pay $15. Visitors also must buy 5-day vehicle pass ($5) at welcome center. 5/20-9/25; 5-day limit. 6 sites; 30-ft RV limit. Tbls, toilets, cfga, drkg wtr. Fishing, hiking.

Weller Lake $10.50
White River National Forest
11.4 mi SE of Aspen on SR 82; .1 mi S on FR 104. 5/21-9/26; 5-day limit. $10.50 with federal senior pass; others pay $21. 5/20/9/25; 5-day limit. 11 sites (RVs under 30 ft). Tbls, toilets, cfga, firewood, drkg wtr. Hiking, fishing. Elev 9400 ft; 3 acres. Scenic. Nature trails, fishing. Adjacent to Roaring Fork River.

BAILEY
Deer Creek $9
Pike National Forest
2.5 mi N on US 285; 8 mi NW on FR 100. $9 with federal senior pass; others pay $18 during MD-LD. All year; 14-day limit. 13 sites (30-ft RV limit). Tbls, toilets, cfga, no drkg wtr. Fishing, hiking. Elev 9000 ft; 5 acres.

Kelsey Campground $9
Pike National Forest
6.8 mi N of Bailey on US 295; 16.5 mi S on CR 126; right at campground sign. $9 with federal senior pass; others pay $18. 5/1-9/30; 14-day limit. 17 sites; 30-ft RV limit. Tbls, toilets, cfga, drkg wtr.

Meridian Campground $9
Pike National Forest
2.3 mi N of Bailey on US 285; 6.5 mi NW on FR 100; 1 mi N on FR 102. $9 with federal senior pass; others pay $16. On Elk Creek. MD-LD; 14-day limit. 18 sites (RVs under 30 ft). Drkg wtr, toilets, cfga, tbls. Trailhead; wilderness access. Fishing, hiking. Elev 9000ft.

BASALT
Basalt State Wildlife Area FREE
3.2 mi E of Basalt on FR 105 (Frying Pan Rd) to signs; N to site. For Christine Unit, half mi W of Basalt on Hwy 82; dirt access rd N to site. Watson Divide Unit, 6 mi S of Basalt on Hwy 82; N on dirt access rd. Free. Camp only during big-game hunting season, 3 days before & 3 days after. Primitive campsites. Toilets, cfga, drkg wtr. Hunting, fishing, shooting range. No boating. No camping within qtr mi of Fryingpan River. Elev 5800 ft; 4170 acres; 3 acres of wtr.

Chapman Campground $12
White River National Forest
24.5 mi E of Basalt on CR 105 (Frying Pan Rd). $12 with federal senior pass; others pay $24. 5/5-10/15; 14-day limit. May be free before & after fee season, but no services or wtr; Chapman South open about 6/10-9/15. 84 sites, including 13 walk-in sites; 50-ft RV limit. Tbls, toilets, cfga, drkg wtr, dump($) at Mollie B Camp. Hiking trail, fishing, canoeing, swimming, horseshoes; boating at Chapman Reservoir; ball field; interpretive trail. At Frying Pan River. Elev 8800 ft; 13 acres.

Coke Oven State Wildlife Area   FREE
33 mi E of Basalt on FR 105 (Fryingpan River Rd). Free. All year; 14-day limit. Primitive undesignated sites; no facilities, no drkg wtr. About 300 acres for hunting, hiking, fishing.

Dearhamer Campground $12
White River National Forest
23.5 mi E of Basalt on CR 105. $12 with federal senior pass; others pay $24. May be free before & after fee season, but no wtr or services; 5/20-10/23; 14-day limit. 12 sites; 35-ft RV limit. Tbls, toilets, cfga, drkg wtr. Swimming, boating(l), fishing, waterskiing, mountain biking. Ruedi Reservoir.

Elk Wallow $6.50
White River National Forest
23 mi E of Basalt on CR 105 at Ruedi Reservior; 3.3 mi E on FR 501. $6.50 with federal senior pass; others pay $13. About 5/15-10/25; 14-day limit. 7 sites (RVs under 30 ft). Tbls, pit toilet, cfga, no drkg wtr or trash service. Fishing. Elev 9000 ft; 2 acres. North Fork of Fryingpan River.

Little Mattie Campground $10.50
White River National Forest
From Basalt, 16 mi E on CR 104 (Fryingpan River Rd); about 1 mi past Ruedi Reservoir dam, right into Little Maud, Little Mattie & Mollie B Campgrounds. $10.50 with federal senior pass; others pay $21. 18 sites; 22-ft RV limit. About 5/15-10/23; 14-day limit. Tbls, toilets, cfa, drkg wtr. Fishing, boating(l).

Ruedi Marina Campground $11.50
White River National Forest
From Basalt, 15 mi E on CR 104 (Fryingpan River Rd); at Ruidi Reservoir. $11.50 base with federal senior pass; others pay $23, $25 for premium sites. About 5/15-10/23; 14-day liit. 8 sites; 45-ft RV limit. Tbls, toilets, cfga, drkg wtr. Fishing, boating(l).

BAYFIELD

Graham Creek $10
San Juan National Forest
N on CR 501/FR 600 from US 160 at Bayfield for 15 mi to Vallecito Dam; 3.5 mi NW on FR 603; on Vallecito Reservoir about 2 mi N of Old Timers Camp. $10 with federal senior pass; others pay $20. 5/5-9/10; 14-day limit. 25 sites; 35-ft RV limit. Tbls, toilets, cfga, drkg wtr. Boating(l), fishing, horseback riding.

Middle Mountain $10
San Juan National Forest
N on CR 501/FR 600 from US 160 at Bayfield for 15 mi to Vallecito Dam; qtr mi W on FR 602; on Vallecito Reservoir. $10 with federal senior pass; others pay $20. Riverfront sites my cost more. 5/5-9/30; 14-day limit. 24 sites; 40-ft RV limit. Tbls, toilets, cfga, drkg wtr. Boating(l), fishing.

North Canyon $8
San Juan National Forest
N on CR 501/FR 600 from US 160 at Bayfield for 15 mi to Vallecito Dam; 4 mi NW on FR 603; on Vallecito Reservoir. $8 with federal senior pass; others pay $16. 5/5-9/10; 14-day limit. 21 sites; 35-ft RV limit. Tbls, toilets, cfga, drkg wtr. Boating(l), fishing.

Pine Point Campground $10
San Juan National Forest
N on CR 501/FR 600 from US 160 at Bayfield for 15 mi to Vallecito Dam; 4.5 mi NW on FR 603; on Vallecito Reservoir. $10 base with federal senior pass; others pay $20 base, $24 for lakefront sites ($12 with senior pass). About 5/5-9/30; 14-day limit. 30 sites; 35-ft RV limit. Tbls, toilets, cfga, drkg wtr. Fishing, boating(l).

Pine River Campground $10
San Juan National Forest
N on CR 501/FR 600 from US 160 at Bayfield for 15 mi to Vallecito Dam; 4.5 mi NW on FR 603; mi E on FR 602. $10 during MD-LD; free rest of yr, but no trash service. 6 sites; 20-ft RV limit. Tbls, toilets, cfga, no drkg wtr. Hiking, horseback riding. Hitching posts, no corral.

BRIGGSDALE

Crow Valley $6.50
Pawnee National Grassland
Roosevelt National Forest
Half mi W of Briggsdale on SR 14; half mi N on CR 77. $6.50 with federal senior pass; otehrs pay $13 (double sites, $18); half price during winter, but no wtr. About 4/7-11/19 with wtr; 14-day limit. 10 sites (35-ft RV limit). Tbls, toilets, cfga, drkg wtr. Handicap trail, farm equipment museum. Elev 4800 ft.

BRUSH

Memorial Park   FREE
Municipal V.F.W. Park
In Brush, 2 blocks S of traffic light on Clayton St. 4/1-10/31; 7-day limit. 60 sites; 18 for RVs, 12 with hookups. Tbls, flush toilets, cfga, drkg wtr, dump, showers, elect, shelter, playground. First night free; $20 per night thereafter; $17.50 for more than 7 nights. Swimming, picnicking. Golf & tennis nearby. Elev 4300 ft; Register at police station; $10 deposit.

Prewitt Reservoir State Wildlife Area   FREE
15 mi NE of Brush on US 6; 1 mi E on access rd. Free. All year; 14-day limit. Undesignated primitive sites. Tbls, toilets, cfga, no drkg wtr. Fishing, hunting, boating(l). 2400-acre lake.

BUENA VISTA

Collegiate Peaks Campground $10
San Isabel National Forest
10.5 mi W of Buena Vista on SR 306; on Cottonwood Creek.

$10 with federal senior pass; others pay $20. 5/19-LD; 14-day limit. 56 sites (50-ft RV limit). Tbls, pit toilets, cfga, drkg wtr (limited). Fishing, hiking trails, OHV trail.

Cottonwood Lake Campground $10
San Isabel National Forest
7 mi SW of Buena Vista on SR 306; 3.5 mi SW on FR 210. $10 with federal senior pass; others pay $20. 5/19-9/30; 7-day limit. 25 RV sites (35-ft RV limit). Tbls, toilets, cfga, drkg wtr, solar water heating system & wtr pump. No RV wtr tank refills. Fishing. Elev 9600 ft. Very busy site; dispersed camping nearly 1 mi W.

BUFFALO CREEK
Buffalo Campground $9
Pike National Forest
Half mi SE of Buffalo Creek on CR 126; 5.6 mi SW on FR 543; qtr mi E on FR 550. $9 with federal senior pass; others pay $18. MD-LD; 14-day limit. 36 sites (30-ft RV limit). Tbls, toilets, cfga, drkg wtr. Fishing, hiking, mountain biking. Elev 7400 ft.

CANON CITY
Oak Creek Campground   FREE
San Isabel National Forest
12.3 mi SW of Canon City on CR 143 (Oak Creek Grade Rd). Free. All year; 10-day limit. 15 sites; 9 acres. 25-ft RV limit; 4 pull-through. Tbls, toilets, cfga, drkg wtr at well within qtr mi, no trash service. Hiking, fishing, biking, ATV. Elev 7600 ft.

CAPULIN
La Jara Reservoir State Wildlife Area   FREE
15 mi W of Capulin on co rd. Free. MD-11/31; 14-day limit during 45-day period. 50 primitive sites; 100 acres. Primitive. Tbls, toilets, cfga, drkg wtr, no trash service. Boating(l), hunting, picnicking, fishing. Camp within 300 ft of reservoir & W of dam, as posted. 1,241-acre lake. Elev 9700 ft.

CARBONDALE
Avalanche Campground   DONATIONS
White River National Forest
13.5 mi S of Carbondale on SR 133; 2.6 mi E on FR 310. Donations accepted while campground being renovated (sites previously $17). 6 sites currently open about 5/15-10/31; 25-ft RV limit. Limited service. 14-day limit. Fishing, hiking. Along Avalanche Creek. Elev 7400 ft.

Bogan Flats Campground $11.50
White River National Forest
22.5 mi S of Carbondale on SR 133; 1.5 mi E on CR 314. $11.50 with federal senior pass; others pay $23. Free after regular season ends, but no wtr or services. MD-10/7; 14-day limit. 37 sites; 40-ft RV limit. Tbls, composting & pit toilets, cfga, drkg wtr. Fishing, hiking, biking,

horseback riding. Crystal River. Yule Creek marble quarry nearby. Elev 7600 ft.

Thompson Creek Recreation Site   FREE
Bureau of Land Management
Grand Junction District
From Carbondale, about 5 mi W & S on paved CR 108, then 2 mi E on FR 305. Camping area before the trailhead. Free. 4/1-8/31, 8-day limit; 9/1-3/32, 14-day limit. Primitive undesignated campsites. Toilets (May-Sept), no drkg wtr or trash service. Hiking/biking trail, fishing, horseback riding. Very scenic. Environmental education opportunities. Dinosaur footprints reported here.

CEDAREDGE
Cobbett Creek (Carp Lake) $8
Grand Mesa National Forest
15.7 mi N of Cedaredge on SR 65; right at N end of Cobbett Lake. $8 with federal senior pass; others pay $16. 6/15-10/1; 16-day limit. 20 sites (40-ft RV limit). Tbls, toilets, cfga, no drkg wtr. Fishing, hiking, boating. Elev 10,300 ft.

Island Lake $9
Grand Mesa National Forest
15.7 mi N of Cedaredge on SR 65; 1.4 mi W on FR 116. $9 with federal senior pass; others pay $18. $6 elec surcharge. About 6/15-LD; 16-day limit. 41 sites (45-ft RV limit). Tbls, toilets, cfga, drkg wtr. Fishing, boating (l), hiking. 144-acre lake.

Little Bear $8
Grand Mesa National Forest
15.7 mi N of Cedaredge on SR 65; half mi W on FR 116; at shore of Idland Lake. $8 with federal senior pass; others pay $16. 5/15-10/1; 16-day limit. 36 sites (45-ft RV limit). Tbls, flush & pit toilets, cfga, drkg wtr. Boating(lr), fishing, hiking. Elev 10,200 ft; 30 acres. Visitor center.

Ward Lake $8
Grand Mesa National Forest
15.6 mi N of Cedaredge on SR 65; 0.5 mi E on FR 121, right into campground; at Ward Lake. $8 with federal senior pass; others pay $16. 7/1-10/30; 14-day limit. 27 sites (30-ft RV limit). Tbls, toilets, cfga, drkg wtr. Fishing, boating(dr), hiking. Elev 10,200 ft; 30 acres.

Weir & Johnson $7
Grand Mesa National Forest
15.6 mi N of Cedaredge on SR 65; 10 mi E on FR 121; 3 mi E on FR 126; between Weir & Johnson and Sackett Reservoirs. $7 with federal senior pass; others pay $14. 5/1-9/30; 16-day limit. 12 sites; 22 ft. RV limit. Tbls, toilet, cfga, no drkg wtr. Boating, fishing, hiking. Between Weir Lake & Johnson Lake. Elev 10,500 ft.

CENTRAL CITY

Cold Springs $10
Arapaho National Forest
5 mi N of Central City-Blackhawk on Hwy 119. $10 with federal senior pass; others pay $20. 5/12-LD; 14-day limit. 37 sites; 50-ft RV limit. Tbls, toilets, cfga, drkg wtr. Hiking, fishing, mountain biking, gold panning. Elev 9200 ft.

Columbine $9.50
Arapaho National Forest
2 mi NW of Central City on CR 279. $9.50 with federal senior pass; others pay $19. 5/12-9/24; 14-day limit. 46 RV sites (20-ft RV limit). Tbls, toilets, cfga, drkg wtr. Hiking, fishing, mountain biking. Elev 9200 ft; 4 acres.

CHIMNEY ROCK

Lower Piedra Campground $10
San Juan National Forest
19 mi N of Chimney Rock on FR 621; on W bank of Piedra River. $10 with federal senior pass; others pay $20. 5/5-11/15; 14-day limit. 17 sites; 35-ft RV limit. Tbls, toilets, cfga, no drkg wtr. Horseback riding, fishing, hiking. Elev 6000 ft; 6 acres.

Ute Campground $10
San Juan National Forest
5.5 mi SE of Chimney Rock on US 160. $10 with federal senior pass; others pay $20. 5/5-9/15; 14-day limit. 26 sites (RVs under 36 ft). Tbls, toilets, cfga, firewood, piped drkg wtr. Fishing, hunting. Elev 6900 ft; 60 acres.

CLARK

Hahns Peak Lake Campground $12
Routt National Forest
10.6 mi N of Clark on CR 129; 2.5 mi W on FR 486. $12 (double sites $20). 6/15-10/31; 14-day limit. 23 sites (RVs under 40 ft). Tbls, toilets, cfga, no drkg wtr. Boating(l), fishing. Elec mtrs only. Elev 8500 ft; 11 acres.

Hinman Park Campground $12
Routt National Forest
1 mi N of Clark on CR 129; 6 mi NE on FR 400. $12. 6/10-10/15; 14-day limit. 13 sites (RVs under 23 ft). Tbls, toilets, cfga, no drkg wtr. Fishing, hiking, biking, bridle trails. Elev 7600 ft; 6 acres.

Seedhouse Campground $12
Routt National Forest
1 mi N of Clark on CR 129; 9.5 mi NE on FR 400; at Elk River. $12. 6/15-10/31; 14-day limit. 24 sites (RVs under 22 ft). Tbls, toilets, cfga, drkg wtr. Fishing. Elev 8000 ft; 10 acres.

COALDALE

Coaldale $7.50
San Isabel National Forest
4.1 mi SW of Coaldale on FR 249; at Hayden Creek. $7.50 with federal senior pass; others pay $15. 5/19-LD; 14-day limit; free after LD if accessible. 5 RV sites (others for tents); RVs under 26 ft. Tbls, toilets, cfga, no drkg wtr, no trash service. Hiking, fishing. Elev 7800 ft; 4 acres. Note: closed temporarily in 2017 due to forest fire.

Hayden Creek Campground $7.50
San Isabel National Forest
5.2 mi SW of Coaldale on CR 6. $7.50 with federal senior pass; others pay $15 during MD-LD; free off-season when accessible, but no services; 14-day limit. 11 sites (RVs under 31 ft). Tbls, toilets, cfga, no drkg wtr. Hiking, fishing. Elev 8000 ft; 4 acres. Hayden Creek. Hiking trail. Open to motorcycles. Closed temporarily in 2017 due to forest fire.

COLLBRAN

Big Creek Campground $7
Grand Mesa National Forest
14 mi S of Collbran on FR 121. $7 with federal senior pass; others pay $14. 7/1-9/30; 14-day limit. 26 sites; 30-ft RV limit. Tbls, toilets, cfga, drkg wtr. Trout fishing, boating(l).

Cottonwood Lake Campground $7
Grand Mesa National Forest
12 mi S of Collbran on FR 121; 4 mi W on FR 257. $7 with federal senior pass; others pay $14. 6/15-9/15; 14-day limit. 36 sites; 40-ft RV limit. Tbls, toilets, cfga, no drkg wtr. Fishing, boating(l), hunting, hiking. Elev 10,100 ft.

Crag Crest Campground $12
Grand Mesa National Forest
From Collbran, 1.9 mi S on CR 58.5; turn left at "T" intersection, staying on CR 58.5, becoming 59 Rd for 5.8 mi, then veer W on gravel FR 121 (Lakeshore Dr) 12 mi; right into campground at Eggleston Lake. $12. 6/15-LD; 16-day limit. 11 sites; 25-ft RV limit. Tbls, toilets, cfga, no drkg wtr. Hiking, fishing. Elev 10,300 ft.

Fish Hawk Campground FREE
Grand Mesa National Forest
From Collbran, 1.9 mi S on CR 58.5; turn left ato "T" intersection, staying on CR 58.5, becoming 59 Rd for 5.8 mi, then veer W on gravel FR 121 (Lakeshore Dr) to campground; at E shore of Eggleston Lake. Free. 6/20-9/30; 14-day limit. 5 sites (RVs under 16 ft). Tbls, toilets, cfga, no drkg wtr. Fishing, boating (1 mi; r--2 mi), horseback riding. Elev 10,200 ft; 1 acre.

Plateau Creek State Wildlife Area FREE
3.5 mi W of Collbran on Hwy 330; quarter mi N on Sunnyside Rd. Free. Camping during big-game season only. Vehicles prohibited 12/1-8/1; 14-day limit during 45-day period. 1,347 acres. Primitive campsites. No facilities, no campfires. Picnicking, hiking. Elev 6200 ft; 1,350 acres.

CRAIG

Duffy Mountain Access $10
Yampa River State Park River Access Site
Bureau of Land Management
19 mi W of Craig on US 40; 6.5 mi S on CR 17 to Government Bridge at Yampa River, then N to river on BLM Rd 1593 just before cattle guard (stay left at all intersections). $10. All year; 14-day limit. 5 primitive sites. Toilet, cfga, no drkg wtr. Boating(l), fishing.

Freeman Reservoir Campground $12
Routt National Forest
13.2 mi NE of Craig on SR 13; 9 mi NE on FR 112. $12. 6/15-10/31; 14-day limit. 18 sites; RVs under 26 ft. Tbls, toilets, cfga, drkg wtr; some handicap facilities. Fishing, hiking, mountain biking, hiking & bridle trails. Elev 8800 ft; 9 acres. At Freeman Reservoir.

Juniper Canyon $10
Yampa River State Park River Access Site
Bureau of Land Management
About 20 mi W of Craig on US 40; 3.5 mi S on CR 53; left on CR 74 for 8 mi to Yampa River. $10 All year; 14-day limit. 12 primitive sites. Toilet, cfga, no drkg wtr. Boating(l), fishing, rafting.

Sawmill Creek Campground   FREE
Routt National Forest
13 mi N of Craig on SR 13; 12.6 mi NE on FR 110. Free. 7/1-10/31; 14-day limit. 6 undeveloped dispersed sites (RVs under 22 ft). No facilities, drkg wtr or trash service. Mountain climbing, fishing. Elev 9000 ft; 4 acres.

South Beach $10
Yampa River State Park
Yampa Project Pump Station State Parks River Access Site
Bureau of Land Management
About 3 mi S of Craig on SR 13 at Yampa River bridge; large graveled pull-off area; park on W side of pump station near toilet. $10. 2-night limit. Primitive undesignated camping. Toilet, cfga, no drkg wtr. Fishing but no boat or canoe launching at water intake channel.

CRAWFORD

North Rim $8
Black Canyon of Gunnison National Park
From Crawford on Hwy 92, follow signs to North Rim Rd (closed in winter). $8 with federal senior pass; others pay $16. About 4/15-11/15; 14-day limit. 13 sites. Tbls, toilets, cfga, drkg wtr (during 5/15-9/15). Hiking, sightseeing, fishing, rafting. No entry fee to North Rim.

Smith Fork Dispersed Sites   FREE
Gunnison National Forest
6.5 mi E of Crawford on FR 712. Free. 5/15-11/15; 14-day limit. 5 sites. Tbls, toilets, cfga, piped drkg wtr. Picnicking, fishing, hiking. Elev 7500 ft; 2 acres. Foothills. Stream. Crawford Reservoir (7 mi).

CREEDE

Bristol Head Campground $8
Rio Grande National Forest
22 mi SW of Creede on SR 149; qtr mi on FR 510; at South Clear Creek. $8 with federal senior pass; others pay $16. MD-LD; 14-day limit. 15 sites; 11 pull-through (40-ft RV limit). Tbls, toilets, cfga, drkg wtr. Fishing, hiking. Scenic qtr-mi trail to waterfall overlook. Elev 9600 ft; 15 acres.

Crooked Creek Dispersed   FREE
Rio Grande National Forest
20.1 mi S of Creede on Sr 149; 1.8 mi W on FR 520 (Rio Grande Reservoir Rd). Free. 5/1-11/31; 14-day limit. 4 rough, primitive pull-out areas; no facilities; toilet across the road. Elev 9200 ft.

Hanson's Mill Dispersed   FREE
Rio Grande National Forest
7.3 mi SE of Creede on SR 149; 9.5 mi NW on FR 600 (Pool Table Rd). Free. MD-Dec; 14-day limit. Primitive undesignated sites. No wtr or trash service; 1 pit toilet. Hiking & 4WD trails; fishing at East Bellows Creek. Elev 10,800 ft.

Ivy Creek   FREE
Rio Grande National Forest
6.5 mi SW of Creede on SR 149; 4 mi SW on FR 523; 2.7 mi SW on FR 528; 2 mi SW on FR 526 (rough, narrow rd). Free. All year when accessible; 14-day limit. 4 sites (1 developed with tbl & cfga). Most suitable for tents, pickups, fold-outs. Toilet, no drkg wtr, no trash collection. Rockhounding, picnicking, fishing, hiking. Elev 9200 ft; 9 acres. Stream. Trailhead to Weminuche Wilderness Area via Ivy Creek Trail at camp.

Lost Trail Campground   FREE
Rio Grande National Forest
20.5 mi SW of Creede on SR 149; 18.1 mi SW on FR 520 (Rio Grande Reservoir Rd). Free; donations accepted. MD-LD; 14-day limit. 7 sites (RVs under 32 ft; 3 pull-through). Tbls, toilet, cfga, no drkg wtr, no trash service. Hiking, fishing. Primitive boat ramp (elec mtrs). Elev 9500 ft; 3 acres. Scenic. Stream. Limited space for RV maneuvering. Camp usually full mid-June through Aug.

Marshall Park $9
Rio Grande National Forest
7 mi SW of Creede on SR 149; qtr mi on FR 5231A at Rio Grande River. $9 with federal senior pass; others pay $18. 5/15-9/15; 14-day limit. 16 sites; 7 pull-through (40-ft RV limit). Tbls, toilets, cfga, grey water sump, no drkg wtr. Fishing, ATV trails, biking/hiking trails. Summer campfire programs. 12 acres. Elev 8800 ft. Full mid-June through Aug.

North Clear Creek $8
Rio Grande National Forest
23 mi SW of Creede on SR 149; 2 mi N on FR 510. $8 with federal senior pass; others pay $16. MD-9/7; 14-day limit. 21 sites; 30-ft RV limit. Tbls, toilets, cfga, drkg wtr. Fishing. Elev 9600 ft; 15 acres.

Rio Grande Dispersed Area FREE
Rio Grande National Forest
10 mi SW of Creede on SR 149; sign says "Rio Grande Fisherman's Area"; through gated fence, 1 mi S on FR 529 (rd too narrow & steep for big RVs). On Rio Grande River. Free. All year when accessible; 14-day limit. 7 sites (RVs under 32 ft). 8 acres. Tbls, toilet, cfga, firewood, no drkg wtr, no trash service. Fishing, picnicking. Elev 8900 ft.

Rito Hondo Reservoir FREE
Dispersed Camping Area
Rio Grande National Forest
27.3 mi W of Creede on SR 149; 3.3 mi NW on FR 513. Free. MD-LD; 14-day limit. 35 primitive sites; no facilities except 1 toilet; no drkg wtr, no trash service. Boating(l), fishing, hiking. Elev 10,200 ft.

Rito Hondo Reservoir FREE
State Wildlife Area
27.3 mi W of Creede on Hwy 149; 2 mi NW on FR 513 (Rito Hondo Rd) to fork; take right fork 200 yds to lake. Free. All year; 14-day limit during 45-day period. Primitive camp area. Toilets, cfga, no drkg wtr. Fishing (41-acre Rito Hondo Lake) for wild brook trout & stocked rainbows.

River Hill Campground $10
Rio Grande National Forest
18 mi SW of Creede on SR 149; 9 mi W on FR 520 (Rio Grande Reservoir Rd) to FR 520.2D (River Hill Rd); at Rio Grande River just below Rio Grande Reservoir. $10 with federal senior pass; others pay $20. MD-LD; 14-day limit. 20 sites; 6 pull-through (40-ft RV limit). Tbls, toilets, cfga, drkg wtr, gray water sump. Fishing, campfire interpretive program some weekend nights. 15 acres. Elev 9300 ft. Camp usually full mid-June through Aug.

Road Canyon FREE
Rio Grande National Forest
20.5 mi SW of Creede on SR 149; 6 mi SW on FR 520; at Road Canyon Reservoir. Free. 5/1-9/15 or until weather closes access. 6 sites (RVs under 32 ft). 14-day limit. Tbls, toilets, cfga, no drkg wtr. No trash service after LD. Horseback riding, boating (ld), fishing. Elev 9300 ft; 9 acres. Undeveloped overflow camping area across the rd.

Silver Thread $9
Rio Grande National Forest
24.5 mi SW of Creede on SR 149. $9 with federal senior pass; others pay $18 during MD-LD; free later in fall until access closed by weather, but no wtr or trash service; 14-day limit. 11 sites (6 gravel pull-through); 30-ft RV

limit. Tbls, toilet, cfga, drkg wtr. Fishing, hiking. Trail to South Clear Creek Falls. Elev 9500 ft; 18 acres.

Thirty Mile $10
Rio Grande National Forest
18 mi SW of Creede on SR 149; 12 mi on FR 520 to FR 520.2C; at Rio Grande River. $10 with federal senior pass; others pay $20 during MD-LD; free later in fall but no wtr or trash service. 14-day limit. 35 sites (9 pull-through); 40-ft RV limit. Tbls, toilets, cfga, drkg wtr, gray water dump, amphitheater. Fishing, hiking, campfire programs. 30 acres. Elev 9300 ft. Full mid-June through Aug.

CRESTED BUTTE

Cement Creek $7
Gunnison National Forest
7.5 mi SE of Crested Butte on SR 135; 4 mi NE on FR 740. $7 with federal senior pass; others pay $14. 5/15-10/15; 14-day limit. 13 sites (26-ft RV limit). Tbls, toilets, cfga, no drkg wtr. Fishing (Cement Creek), hot springs nearby, hiking.

Gothic Campground $12
Gunnison National Forest
11.4 mi N of Crested Butte on FR 317; rd very rough last qtr mi. $12 during 6/15-9/15; 14-day limit. 4 sites for tents or short RVs. Tbls, toilet, cfga, firewood, no drkg wtr. Fishing, hiking. Elev 9600 ft; 3 acres. 2 mi NW of Rocky Mountain Biological Laboratory and Gothic townsite. 1 mi SE of Gothic Natural Area.

Lake Irwin Campground $8
Gunnison National Forest
7 mi W of Crested Butte on Hwy 2; N on FR 826 from Lake Irwin turnoff. $8 with federal senior pass; others pay $16. 6/15-9/15; 14-day limit. 32 sites; 35-ft RV limit. Tbls, toilets, cfga, drkg wtr. Fishing, hiking, boating(l).

CRESTONE

North Crestone Creek $7
Rio Grande National Forest
1.2 mi N of Crestone on FR 950. $7 during 5/18-11/25; free off-season but no services; 14-day limit. 13 sites; 25-ft RV limit. Tbls, toilets, cfga, no drkg wtr or trash service. Horse loading facilities. Horseback riding, hiking, fishing. Elev 8300 ft; 8 acres.

CRIPPLE CREEK

Sand Gulch Campground $4
Shelf Road Recreation Site
Bureau of Land Management
From Cripple Creek, qtr mi S on Second St; angle right onto CR 88. From N side of Canon City, follow Fields Ave north; it becomes Shelf Rd (CR 9). Off old toll rd behind red BLM gate. $7 (group sites $14). All year; 14-day limit. 16 primitive undesignated sites. Toilets, tbls, no drkg wtr, cfga. Hiking, rock climbing. Plans include 10-15 more sites.

The Banks Campground $4
Shelf Road Recreation Site
Bureau of Land Management
From Cripple Creek, qtr mi S on Second St; angle right onto CR 88. From N side of Canon City, follow Fields Ave north; it becomes Shelf Rd (CR 9). Off old toll rd; continue down Shelf rd from Sand Gulch Camp. $7 (group sites $14). All year; 14-day limit. 13 primitive undesignated sites. Toilets, tbls, no drkg wtr, cfga. Hiking, rock climbing. plans include 10-15 more sites.

CROOK

Jumbo Reservoir State Wildlife Area   FREE
NE of Crook on US 138 to Red Lion Station; 2 mi N on CR 95. Free. All year. Undesignated sites near Jumbo Lake. Toilets, cfga, no drkg wtr. Fishing, boating, hiking, waterskiing, hunting, boating(l).

CUCHARA

Bear Lake Campground $8.50
San Isabel National Forest
3.5 mi S of Cuchara on SR 12; 4.2 mi W on FR 422 (good rd). $8.50 with federal senior pass; others pay $17. 5/19-9/25; 14-day limit. 15 sites (40-ft RV limit). Tbls, toilets, cfga, drkg wtr. Fishing, multi-use trail. Elev 10,700 ft; 5 acres.

Blue Lake Campground $8.50
San Isabel National Forest
3.5 mi S of Cuchara on SR 12; 3.5 mi W on FR 422. $8.50 with federal senior pass; others pay $17. 5/19-9/25; 14-day limit. 15 sites (40-ft RV limit). Tbls, toilets, cfga, drkg wtr. Hiking, fishing. Elev 10,500 ft; 8 acres.

DELTA

Columbine   FREE
Uncompahgre National Forest
30 mi SW of Delta on CR 2214; 2.5 mi S on FR 402. Free. 6/10-9/30. 6 sites; 32-ft RV limit. Toilets, tbls, cfga, no drkg wtr or trash service. Hiking, ATV riding, horseback riding, mountain biking. Secluded.

Escalante State Wildlife Area   FREE
4 mi W of Delta on 5th St. Other tracts 12 mi W of Delta from Hwy 50 (8 separate units). Free. 8/1-3/14 on 2 tracts; all year on others; 14-day limit during 45-day period. Primitive campsites. Hunting, some fishing. Elev 7800 ft; 7598 acres; 5 acres of water; 5 mi of streams.

Gunnison Gorge $10
National Conservation Area
Bureau of Land Management
About 10 mi E of Delta on SR 92 near Austin; follow signs to Peach Valley Rd. $10. All year. $5 per day combination day use/camping fee, so overnight equals 2 days; $15 for 2 nights; annual day use pass $15. Tbls, toilets, cfga, no drkg wtr. Fishing, hiking, rock climbing. Area established by Congress in 1999. 57,700 acres.

Paonia State Park $10
E of Delta on Hwy 92 to Hotchkiss, then N on Hwy 133 through Paonia and 16 mi to park; Spruce Campground (8 sites) is on upper end of the lake along SR 133; Hawsapple Campground (5 sites) is across Muddy Creek, then right on CR 2 for half mi. $10 ($7 for holders of CO Aspen Leaf Pass). Primitive sites. Tbls, toilets, cfga, no drkg wtr. Fishing, boating (l), waterskiing, horseback riding. Entry fee.

DILLON

Heaton Bay Campground $11.25
White River National Forest
From I-70 exit 203 SW of Dillon, left on Dillon Dam Rd (CR 7) to campground on left; at W shore of Dillon Reservoir. $11.25 base with federal senior pass; others pay $22.50 base, $24.30 for premium locations ($12.15 with senior pass). $5 elec surcharge. 5/20-10/1; 14-day limit. 81 sites; 70-ft RV limit. Tbls, toilets, cfga, drkg wtr.

McDonald Flats $6.50
White River National Forest
19 mi NW of Dillon on SR 9; 5 mi NW on CR 30 (Heeney Rd) on W side of Green Mountain Reservoir. $6.50 with federal senior pass; others pay $13 (or $65 season pass). About 5/15-LD; 14-day limit; free when wtr is shut off in fall. 13 sites (21-ft RV limit). Tbls, toilets, cfga, no drkg wtr. Swimming, boating(l), fishing, hiking. Elev 8200 ft.11

Peak One Campground $11
White River National Forest
From I-70 exit 203 SW of Dillon, 1 mi S on SR 9 through town of Frisco to Peninsula Recreation Area; turn left to campground; at S shore of Dillon Reservoir. $11 base with federal senior pass; others pay $22 base, $24 for premium locations ($12 with senior pass). 5/15-9/30; 14-day limit. 79 sites; 50-ft RV limit. Fishing, biking, hiking boating(l), no swimming or water contact activities.

Pine Cove Campground $10
White River National Forest
From I-70 exit 203 SW of Dillon, 1 mi S on SR 9 through town of Frisco to Peninsula Recreation Area; turn left to campground; at S shore of Dillon Reservoir. $10 with federal senior pass; others pay $20. 5/15-9/30; 14-day limit. 56 sites; 40-ft RV limit. Tbls, toilets, cfga, drkg wtr. Biking, hiking, boating, fishing, no swimming or water contact activities.

Prairie Point Campground $6.50
White River National Forest
22 mi NW of Dillon on SR 9. $6.50 with federal senior pass; others pay $13. LD-MD; 14-day limit. 33 sites; 20-ft RV limit). Tbls, toilets, cfga, no drkg wtr. Boating(d), fishing, waterskiing, swimming. Near upper end of Green Mountain Reservoir. Elev 9100 ft; 25 acres.

Prospector Campground $11
White River National Forest
3.5 mi SE of Dillon on US 6; 3 mi W on CR 1. $11 base with
federal senior pass; others pay $22 base, $23 for premium
locations ($11.50 with senior pass). MD-LD; 14-day limit.
107 sites (32-ft RV limit). Tbls, toilets, cfga, drkg wtr.
Boating(dl), fishing, hiking. Elev 9100 ft; 25 acres.

Sugarloaf $8.50
Arapaho National Forest
9 mi N of Dillon on Hwy 9; 5 mi SE on CR 30; 1 mi on FR 138.
$8.50 with federal senior pass; others pay $17. All year;
14-day limit. 11 sites (23-ft RV limit). Tbls, toilets, cfga,
no drkg wtr (available at nearby South Fork Campground).
Fishing, hiking, mountain biking & OHV trails. Elev 9000
ft; 8 acres.

Willows Campground $6.50
White River National Forest
30.2 mi NW of Dillon on SR 9; 1 mi SW on CR 30. $6.50 with
federal senior pass; others pay $13. 5/11-10/15; 14-day
limit. 35 sites (RVs under 32 ft). Tbls, toilets, no drkg
wtr. Fishing, boating, waterskiing. Elev 8200 ft; 18 acres.
Mountains, grassy terrain. Adjacent to Green Mountain
Reservoir.

DINOSAUR
Green River Campground $9
Dinosaur National Monument
5 mi E of Dinosaur Quarry. $9 with federal senior pass;
others pay $18. 4/1-10/31; 14-day limit. 79 sites. Tbls,
flush toilets, cfga, drkg wtr but no wtr tank fill. Fishing,
hiking, ranger talks.Elev 4795 ft. Dinosaur quarry 5 mi.

Rainbow Park $6
Dinosaur National Monument
Located N of Dinosaur on a series of unmarked gravel
co rds; inquire directly from a park ranger. From Jensen,
3 mi N on SR 149; 5 mi NW on Brush Creek Rd; 4 mi N
on gravel rd along Brush Creek; 12 mi E on Island Park
Rd (rough, impassable when wet); RVs discouraged due
to sharp turns. Formerly free, now $6 plus entry fee. All
year; 15-day limit. About 4 undesignated primitive sites.
Tbls, toilets, cfga, no drkg wtr. Whitewater rafting (special
permit required); no swimming (unexpected currents).
Stop at headquarters, 2 mi E of Dinosaur; free audiovi-
sual program & exhibits about the park; get backcountry
permits there.

DOLORES
Bradfield Campground $8
San Juan National Forest
Bureau of Land Management
2 mi W of Dolores on Hwy 145; right on Hwy 184 for 8 mi;
right on US 666 for 13 mi, then right for 1 mi on FR 505.
$8. MD-LD (free off-season but no wtr or services); 14-day

limit. 22 sites; 45-ft RV limit. Tbls, toilets, cfga, drkg wtr.
Boating(l), fishing.

Burro Bridge Campground $9
San Juan National Forest
12.5 mi NE of Dolores on Hwy 145; 23 mi NE on FR 535;
on West Dolores River. $9 with federal senior pass; others
pay $18. MD-11/15 (if demand indicates); 14-day limit. 12
sites (40-ft RV limit). Tbls, toilets, cfga, drkg wtr. Fishing,
hiking, horseback riding (corrals). Elev 9000 ft.

Cabin Canyon Campground $10
San Juan National Forest
7 mi NW of US 666 on FR 505; 34 mi E on FR 504; on
Dolores River at Lone Dome. $10. 5/15-LD; 30-day limit. 11
sites (45-ft RV limit). Tbls, toilets, cfga, no drkg wtr. Fishing, picnicking, concrete barrier-free trail along river. 4WD
& mountain biking nearby on FR 475. Elev 6300 ft; 5 acres.

Ferris Canyon Campground $10
San Juan National Forest
10 mi from US 666 on FR 504. $10 ($5 off-season). 5/15-
11/15; 14-day limit. 7 sites; 45-ft RV limit. Tbls, toilets,
cfga, no drkg wtr, dump. Fishing (catch & release). Elev
6300 ft.

House Creek Campground $10
San Juan National Forest
From 11th St in Dolores, 6 mi N on Dolores-Norwood Rd
(FR 526); 5.4 mi SE on House Creek Rd (FR 528); at McPhee
Reservoir. $10 base with federal senior pass; others pay
$20 base; $5 elec surcharge. 5/5-10/15; 14-day limit. 45
sites; 50-ft RV limit. Tbls, compost toilets, cfga, drkg wtr,
dump. Hiking trail, fishing, boating(l). Elev 7000 ft.

Mavreeso Campground $11
San Juan National Forest
13 mi NE of Dolores on SR 145; 6 mi NE on FR 535. $11
base with federal senior pass; others pay $20 base; $5
elec surcharge. 5/15-9/15; 30-day limit. 19 sites (50-ft
RV limit). Tbls, toilets, cfga, drkg wtr, dump. Fishing. Elev
7600 ft; 9 acres.

McPhee Campground $10
San Juan National Forest
7 mi S of Dolores on Hwy 145 & W on Hwy 184; N on CR
25, then on FR 271. $10 base with federal senior pass at
RV sites without hookups; others pay $20 base; $6 elec
surcharge, $8 full-hookup surcharge. 5/5-10/15; 30-day
limit. 72 sites; 50-ft RV limit. Tbls, flush toilets, drkg wtr,
showers($4), dump, fish cleaning station. Boating(rl),
hiking, fishing.

West Dolores Campground $11
San Juan National Forest
13 mi NE of Dolores on SR 145; 7.5 mi NE on FR 535. $11
base with federal senior pass; others pay $22 base; $6

elec surcharge. 5/5-9/30; 30-day limit. 18 sites, 7 with elec (35-ft RV limit). Tbls, compost toilets, cfga, drkg wtr. Fishing. Elev 7800 ft; 10 acres.

DOVE CREEK

Mountain Sheep Point Recreation Site   FREE
Bureau of Land Management
From E end of town, follow Dolores River access rd 5 mi to river; follow signs to site. Free. 4/1-10/31; 14-day limit. 3 sites (30-ft RV limit). Tbls, toilets, cfga, no drkg wtr. Fishing, boating(l), hiking, hunting, mountain biking. Elev 6100 ft; 7 acres.

DURANGO

Florida Campground $9.50
San Juan National Forest
15 mi E of Durango on CR 240 (Florida Rd); 7 mi N on FR 596; on Florida River. $9.50 with federal senior pass; others pay $19. 5/5-9/15 or until weather forces closing. Full fee required off-season unless wtr is off, then $9.50. 20 sites; 35-ft RV limit. Tbls, toilets, cfga, drkg wtr. Fishing, hiking.

Haviland Lake Campground $11
San Juan National Forest
18 mi N of Durango on US 550; 1 mi on FR 671 across dam. $11 base with federal senior pass; others pay $22 base; higher fees for lakeside locations & 15 elec sites. 5/5-9/30; 14-day limit. 43 sites, typically 35-45 ft. Tbls, pit toilets, cfga, drkg wtr. Fishing, boating (no mtrs), hiking.

Junction Creek Campground $11
San Juan National Forest
5 mi NW of Durango on FRs 171 & 573; on Junction Creek Rd. $11 base with federal senior pass; others pay $22 base (surcharge for 14 elec sites). 5/5-11/15 ($11 without hookups after 10/1); 14-day limit. 44 sites; 50-ft RV limit. Tbls, toilets, cfga, drkg wtr, Fishing, hiking trail, horseshoe pits, volleyball. Elev 7300 ft; 38 acres.

Kroeger Campground $8
San Juan National Forest
12 mi W of Durango on US 160; 6 mi N on CR 124. $8 with federal senior pass; others pay $16. 5/5-9/15; 14-day limit. 11 small sites; 35-ft RV limit at 1 site. Tbls, toilets, cfga, drkg wtr, no trash service. Fishing, mountain biking, hiking. Elev 9000 ft; 2 acres.

Miller Creek Campground $10
San Juan National Forest
15 mi E of Durango on CR 240 (Florida Rd); 3 mi N on FR 596 (2 mi N of dam). $10 with federal senior pass; others pay $20 during 5/5-9/15. 14-day limit. When wtr is off after LD, fee is half price but no services. 12 sites; 35-ft RV limit. Tbls, toilets, cfga, drkg wtr. Fishing, boating(l).

Snowslide Campground $7.50
San Juan National Forest
11 mi W of Durango on US 160; 5 mi N on CR 124 (LaPlata Canyon Rd). $7.50 with federal senior pass; others pay $15 during 5/5-9/15; half price fee after 9/15, but no services. 13 sites; 35-ft RV limit. Tbls, cfga, toilets, no drkg wtr, no trash service. Drkg wtr available at nearby Kroeger Campground. Fishing at La Plata River.

Transfer Park Campground $8.50
San Juan National Forest
15 mi E of Durango on CR 240 (Florida Rd); 8 mi N on CR 243. $8.50 with federal senior pass; others pay $17. 5/5-9/30; 14-day limit (half price fee but no services off-season). 25 sites; 35-ft RV limit. Tbls, toilets, cfga, drkg wtr. Hiking, backpacking, fishing, horseback riding; horse unloading area. Site was once used for transferring ore and supples between pack mules and wagons.

EAGLE

Fulford Cave Campground $8
White River National Forest
12.1 mi S on CR 307; 6 mi E on FR 415 (lat mi narrow & rocky); at East Brush Creek. $8. About 5/15-10/15; 14-day limit. 7 small sites (25-ft RV limit at 1 site). Tbls, 1 toilet, cfga, no drkg wtr. Hiking, fishing. Visitors can explore cave or visit historic mining town of Fulford. "Food storage order" in effect for 2017 due to bear activity.

Yeoman Park Campground $8
White River National Forest
12.1 mi S of Eagle on CR 307; 6 mi SE on FR 154; .1 mi S on FR 15416; near Brush Creek. $8. About 5/20-10/15; 14-day limit. 24 sites typically 30 ft. Tbls, toilets, cfga, firewood, no drkg wtr. Hiking, fishing, mountain climbing, horseback riding. Elev 9000 ft; 20 acres. Geological. Nature trails. Extensive beaver colony nearby. "Food storage order" in effect for 2017 due to bear activity.

ESTES PARK

Meeker Park Overflow $12
Roosevelt National Forest
13 mi S of Estes Park on SR 7 at milemarker 11. $12 during MD-LD; closed off-season. 29 sites; 40-ft RV limit. Portable toilets, cfga, tbls, no drkg wtr. Tends to be full due to proximity to Rocky Mountain NP. Unpaved rds, steep hills, short pull-ins. Elev 8600 ft.

FAIRPLAY

Buffalo Springs $8
Pike National Forest
14.5 mi S of Fairplay on US 285; half mi W on FR 431. $8 with federal senior pass; others pay $16. 5/19-10/9; 14-day limit. Free off-season but no services or wtr. 18 sites; 30-ft RV limit. 9 acres. Tbls, toilets, cfga, well drkg wtr. Rockhounding, hiking trails, biking. Elev 9000 ft.

Fourmile Campground $8
Pike National Forest
1.3 mi S of Fairplay on US 285; W on CR 18. $8 with federal senior pass; others pay $16. MD-10/15; 14-day limit. 14 sites (22-ft RV limit). Tbls, toilets, cfga, drkg wtr. Hiking, fishing (Fourmile Creek). Near 1,000-year-old trees. Elev 10,762 ft.

Horseshoe Campground $8
Pike National Forest
1.3 mi S of Fairplay on US 285; 5.5 mi W on CR 18. $8 with federal senior pass; others pay $16. 5/1-10/1; 14-day limit. 2-night minimum stay required on weekends. 19 sites (25-ft RV limit). Tbls, toilets, cfga, drkg wtr. Hiking, fishing. Elev 10,800 ft; 8 acres.

Selkirk Campground $7
Pike National Forest
About 8 mi Ne of Fairplay on US 285 to Como; NW on CR 33 to CR 50; right on FR 33 for 4 mi, then left on FR 33.3A for 0.3 mi. $7 with federal senior pass; others pay $14. 5/1-10/1; 14-day limit. 15 sites (25-ft RV limit). Tbls, toilets, cfga, no drkg wtr or trash service. Fishing (Tarryall Creek).

Weston Pass Campground $7.50
Pike National Forest
5 mi S of Fairplay on US 285; 7 mi SW on CR 5; 4.1 mi SW on CR 22. $7.50 with federal senior pass; others pay $15. 5/25-9/10; 14-day limit; 2-night minimum stay required on weekends. 14 sites; 25-ft RV limit. Tbls, toilets, cfga, no drkg wtr or trash service. Fishing. Elev 10,200 ft; 6 acres. Nearby Weston Pass Rd was former historic toll rd.

FLAGLER

Flagler Reservoir State Wildlife Area FREE
E on Rd 4 at Flagler City Park (1 block off I-70), 3 mi to lake. Free. All year; 14-day limit during 45-day period. 5 separate, multiple sites. Some with tbls. Pit toilets, no drkg wtr. Fishing, small-game hunting. Elev 5000 ft; 568 acres; 160 acres of water. Reservoir mostly dried up, swampy; boating questionable.

FORT COLLINS

Ansel Watrous $10.50
Roosevelt National Forest
11 mi N of Fort Collins on US 287; left (W) on SR 14 for 13 mi. $10.50 with federal senior pass; others pay $21 (fee discount when wtr is off). All year; 14-day limit. 19 sites; 30-ft RV limit. Tbls, pit toilets, cfga, drkg wtr. Fishing, rafting, hiking.

Bellaire Lake $11
Roosevelt National Forest
21 mi N of Fort Collins on US 287; left (W) on REd Feather Lakes Rd (CR 74E) for 24 mi; left (S) on CR 152 for 2.5 mi; W side of rd. $11 with federal senior pass; others pay $22 (fee discount when wtr is off). $5 surcharge for elec. Peak season 6/1-9/30; 14-day limit. 26 sites; 50-ft RV limit. Tbls, flush & pit toilets, cfga, drkg wtr, elec($). Fishing, hiking, boating.

Bliss State Wildlife Area FREE
60 mi W of Fort Collins on Hwy 14. Free. All year; 14-day limit. Undesignated primitive sites. Toilet, cfga, no tbls, no drkg wtr. Fishing, hunting. No boating.

Chambers Lake $11
Roosevelt National Forest
10 mi N of Fort Collins on US 287; left (W) on SR 14 for 51 mi; about 1 mi past turnoff for Laramie River Rd right (N) following signs. $11 with federal senior pass; others pay $22 (fee discount when wtr is off). Peak season about 6/30-9/30; 14-day limit. 52 sites; 30-ft RV limit. Tbls, toilets, cfga, drkg wtr, playground. Boating(I), fishing, biking/hiking trail.

Dutch George Flats $10.50
Roosevelt National Forest
11 mi N of Fort Collins on Hwy 287; 17 mi W on Hwy 14 (Poudre Canyon Hwy). $10.50 with federal senior pass; others pay $21 (50% fee discount during off-season when water is off). 20 sites; 33-ft RV limit. Fees about MD-9/24; 14-day limit. Tbls, toilets, cfga, drkg wtr. Hiking, fishing. Elev 6500 ft.

Jack's Gulch $11
Roosevelt National Forest
11 mi N of Fort Collins on Hwy 287; 22 mi W on Hwy 14 (Poudre Canyon Hwy). $11 with federal senior pass; others pay $22 during about MD-11/5 (50% fee discount during off-season when wtr turned off). $5 surcharge for elec. Equestrian sites $34 ($17 with senior pass). 70 sites 30-80 ft. All year; 14-day limit. Tbls, toilets, cfga, drkg wtr, elec($). Hiking, fishing, horseback riding, mountain biking. Elev 8100 ft.

Kelly Flats $11
Roosevelt National Forest
11 mi N of Fort Collins on Hwy 287; 22 mi W on Hwy 14 (Poudre Canyon Hwy). $11 with federal senior pass; others pay $22 during about MD-9/24 (25% fee discount when wtr is off); 14-day limit. 29 sites; 40-ft RV limit. Tbls, toilets, cfga, drkg wtr. Hiking, fishing, mountain biking. Elev 6600 ft.

Middle Unit FREE
Cherokee State Wildlife Area
22 mi N from Fort Collins on US 287; W 8 mi on Cherokee Park Rd. Vehicles prohibited from day after Labor Day through day before Memorial Day. Free. All year; 14-day limit during 45-day period. Primitive campsites. Toilets, tbls, cfga. Hunting, fishing, hiking. Elev 6,500-8,000 ft. Camp only in designated areas. Fires only in designated areas.

Mountain Park $11
Roosevelt National Forest
11 mi N of Fort Collins on Hwy 287; 19 mi W on Hwy 14 (Poudre Canyon Hwy). $11 with federal senior pass; others pay $22 during about MD-9/24 (25% fee discount when wtr is off); 14-day limit. $5 surcharge for elec. 55 sites; 45-ft RV limit. Tbls, toilets, cfga, drkg wtr, coin showers, elec($), playground. Hiking, fishing, mountain biking, 4WD, horseshoe pits, rafting, volleyball, basketball. Elev 6500 ft.

Narrows $10.50
Roosevelt National Forest
11 mi N of Fort Collins on Hwy 287; 16 mi W on Hwy 14 (Poudre Canyon Hwy). $10.50 with federal senior pass; others pay $21 (25% fee discount off-season when wtr not available). Peak season MD-LD; 14-day limit. 15 sites; 30-ft RV limit. Tbls, toilets, cfga, drkg wtr. Tents only in lower section. Hiking, fishing, rafting, 4WD.

Stove Prairie $10.50
Roosevelt National Forest
11 mi N of Fort Collins on Hwy 287; 25 mi W on Hwy 14 (Poudre Canyon Hwy). $10.50 with federal senior pass; others pay $21 during about 5/5-10/15; 14-day limit. 9 sites; 30 ft RV limit. Tbls, toilets, cfga, drkg wtr. Hiking, fishing, mountain biking, rafting, 4WD. Elev 6000 ft.

Upper Unit FREE
Cherokee State Wildlife Area
22 mi N from Fort Collins on US 287; 22 mi W on Cherokee Park Rd 80C. Vehicles prohibited from day after Labor Day through day before Memorial Day. Free. All year; 14-day limit during 45-day period. Primitive sites. Toilets, tbls, cfga. Hunting, fishing, hiking. Camp & fires only in designated areas.

FORT GARLAND
Mountain Home Reservoir FREE
State Wildlife Area
2.5 mi E of Fort Garland on Hwy 160 to Trinchera Rd; 2 mi to Icehouse Rd; 1 mi W. Free. Primitive camping. Toilets, no other facilities, no trash service. All year; 14-day limit in 45-day period. Fishing, boating(l), toilets, cfga. Elev 8145 ft; 1,120 acres.

FORT MORGAN
Riverside City Park FREE
Fort Morgan Recreation Department
From I-76 exit 80 at Fort Morgan, drive to 1600 N. Man St at the South Platte River. Free. All year; 3-5 day limit. About 12 sites at 240-acre park. Tbls, toilets, cfga, drkg wtr, elec($), pool. Showers ($3) at pool & recreation dept. Playgrounds, swimming, horseshoes, fitness trails, fishing, volleyball, tennis, disc golf, in-line skating rink.

FRASER
Byers Creek Campground $7
Arapaho National Forest
6.5 mi SW of Fraser on FR 160. $7 with federal senior pass; others pay $14. MD-LD; 14-day limit. 6 sites (32-ft RV limit). Tbls, toilets, cfga, drkg wtr. Fishing, hiking, biking. At St. Louis & Byers Creeks in Fraser Experimental Forest. Elev 9360 ft. Closed in 2010; still closed 2017; trees down; check status before arrival.

St. Louis Creek Campground $10
Arapaho National Forest
3 mi SW of Fraser on CR 73 (St. Louis Creek Rd). $10 with federal senior pass; others pay $20. MD-10/23; 14-day limit. 17 sites (25-ft RV limit). Tbls, toilets, cfga, drkg wtr. Fishing, hiking, mountain biking. Elev 8900 ft; 6 acres. In Fraser Experimental Forest. Operated by Fraser Valley Lions Club.

FRUITA
Saddlehorn Campground $10
Colorado National Monument
3.5 mi S of Fruita on SR 340. $10 with federal senior pass; others pay $20. All year; 14-day limit. 80 sites; 40-ft RV limit. Flush toilets, drkg wtr (except in winter), charcoal grills, tbls. Dump station in Fruita. Hiking. Wood fires prohibited. Visitor center 4 mi from Fruita entrance open all year. Pets on leash, not permitted on trails or in backcountry. Daily entry fee charged Apr-Sept.

GARDNER
Huerfano State Wildlife Area FREE
13 mi SW of Gardner on CR 580. Area both sides of Huerfano River NW of Walsenburg. Free. All year; 14-day limit during 45-day period. Primitive campsites. Toilets, cfga, tbls. No drkg wtr. Hiking, boating(l), fishing, hunting, backpacking. Elev 7600 ft; 544 acres. 343 water acres.

Mt. Evans State Wildlife Area FREE
W on I-70 from to El Rancho Rd. exit; S to Hwy 74 to Evergreen Lake; 6.4 mi W on Upper Bear Creek Rd; 3 mi W on CR 480. Free. 5-day limit during 45-day period except during big-game season in designated campgrounds. Vehicles prohibited day after Labor Day through June 14 except during regular rifle deer and elk seasons. Public access prohibited 1/1-6/14. 15 primitive sites. Tbls, cfga, toilets, no drkg wtr. Big game, small game hunting, swimming, fishing. 4,846 acres. Small streams contain trout.

GEORGETOWN
Clear Lake Campground $8.50
Arapaho National Forest
4 mi S of Georgetown on CR 118 (Guanella Pass Rd). $8.50 with federal senior pass; others pay $17. 6/9-9/4; 14-day limit. 8 sites (15-ft RV limit). Tbls, toilets, cfga, drkg wtr. Fishing, hiking. Elev 10,000 ft. South Clear Creek.

Travelers on US 285 can access only through Grant; no Georgetown access from the highway.

Guanella Pass Campground $9.50
Arapaho National Forest
5 mi S of Georgetown on CR 118 (Guanella Pass Rd). $9.50 with federal senior pass; others pay $19. 6/9-9/4; 14-day limit. 17 sites; 35-ft RV limit. Tbls, toilets, cfga, drkg wtr. Fishing, hiking, mountain biking. Elev 10,900 ft. Travelers on US 85 can access only through Grant; no Georgetown access from the highway.

GILLETTE

Pikes Peak (Bison) State Wildlife Area FREE
2 mi S of Gillette on dirt rd; 1.5 mi E to Bison Reservoir, then NE of reservoir. Free. 7/15-3/31; 14-day limit in 45-day period. Primitive camping; no facilities. Bighorn sheep hunting, photography.

GLENDEVEY

Hohnholz Lakes State Wildlife Area FREE
5 mi N from Glendevey on Laramie River Rd; W at sign. Scenic drive. Free. All year; 14-day limit during 45-day period. Primitive camping only at Laramie River camping area. Toilets, cfga, tbls. Fishing, hiking, picnicking. Hunting. 111 acres of water among 3 lakes. Access to Forrester Creek, Grace Creek.

GLENWOOD SPRINGS

Bison Lake FREE
White River National Forest
16.9 mi E of Glenwood Springs on US 6/24; 2 mi N on CR 301; 25.5 mi NW on FR 600; W on FR 601 past former Klines Folly Camp, then take left fork for 8 mi; right on FR 640 for 2 mi; at Bison Lake. Free. July-Sept; 14-day limit. Undesignated primitive sites. No toilet, no other facilities, no drkg wtr, no trash service. No fishing at Bison Lake; brook trout at nearby Heart Lake.

Coffee Pot Spring Campground $6
White River National Forest
18 mi E of Glenwood Springs on US 6/24; 2 mi N on CR 301; 20.6 mi NW on FR 600; at French Creek. Free before & after regular season of 6/8-10/30, when $6 fee is charged. 14-day limit. 10 sites (RVs under 30 ft). 20 acres. Tbls, toilets, cfga, firewood, piped drkg wtr. Horseback riding; fishing (5 mi). Elev 10,100 ft. "Food storage order" in effect for 2017 due to bear activity.

Deep Lake Campground $6
White River National Forest
16.9 mi E of Glenwood Springs on US 6/24; 2 mi N on CR 301; 26.5 mi NW on FR 600; on E side of Deep Lake. $6 during 7/1-9/30; free rest of year, but no services; 14-day limit. 37 sites (RVs under 36 ft). Tbls, toilets, cfga, firewood, no drkg wtr. Boating (ld); picnicking, fishing. Elev 10,500 ft; 8 acres. "Food storage order" in effect for 2017

due to bear activity.

Supply Basin CLOSED
White River National Forest
16.9 mi E of Glenwood Springs on I-70; 2 mi N on CR 301; 25.5 mi NW on FR 600; left on FR 640, half mi past Klines Folly camp, on Heart Lake. Decommissioned and permanently closed.

Sweetwater Lake Campground $8
White River National Forest
18 mi E of Glenwood Springs on I-70; 7 mi N of Dotsero on CR 37; 10 mi NW on CR 17; S on FR 607. $8. About 5/21-9/30; 14-day limit. 9 sites (30-ft RV limit). Tbls, toilets, cfga, no drkg wtr (but at resort nearby). On S end of Sweetwater Lake. Fishing, hiking, horseback riding, canoeing. Elev 7700 ft. No trash service after mid-Sept. "Food storage order" issued for 2017 due to bear activity.

White Owl Campground $6
White River National Forest
16.9 mi E of Glenwood Springs on US 6/24; 2 mi N on CR 301; 24 mi NW on FR 15600; .8 mi W on FR 6002D; on 21-acre White Owl Lake. $6. 7/1-9/30; 14-day limit. Free off-season, but no trash service. 11 sites (RVs under 20 ft). Tbls, toilets, cfga, firewood, no drkg wtr or trash service. Fishing, boating. Elev 10,600 ft; 1 acre. Scenic. "Food storage order" issued for 2017 due to bear activity.

GRANBY

Arapaho Bay $10.50
Arapaho National Recreation Area
Arapaho National Forest
6 mi NW of Granby on US 34; 9 mi E on CR 6 (FR 125, Arapaho Bay Rd); at SE end of Lake Granby. $10.50 with federal senior pass; others pay $21; double sites $42. Fees MD-10/15; free at 7 sites off-season but no services. 84 sites; 35-ft RV limit. Tbls, toilets, cfga, drkg wtr, interpretive site. Boating(l), fishing. Arapaho NRA pass required.

Denver Creek $10.50
Arapaho National Forest
3 mi NW of Granby on US 40; 12 mi NW on SR 125. $10.50 with federal senior pass; others pay $21. MD-9/24 (free later in fall, but no wtr); 14-day limit. 22 sites (45-ft RV limit). Tbls, toilets, cfga, drkg wtr. Fishing, OHV trails. Elev 8800 ft; 9 acres.

Green Ridge Campground $9.50
Arapaho National Recreation Area
Arapaho National Forest
From Granby at jct with US 40, 12 mi N on Hwy 34; 1 mi E on CR 66; at Shadow Mountain Reservoir. $9.50 with federal senior pass; others pay $19. Arapaho NRA pass fee also required ($5 daily, $10 for 3 days, $15 weekly, $30 annually); senior discounts apply. 5/12-9/24; some sites free 9/25-10/15; 14-day limit. 77 sites; 35-ft RV limit.

Tbls, flush & pit toilets, cfga, drkg wtr. Boating(d), fishing, hiking trail.

Sawmill Gulch CLOSED
Arapaho National Forest
3 mi NW of Granby on US 40; 10 mi NW on SR 125. Closed for 2013; closed indefinitely in 2017.

Stillwater Campground $12
Arapaho National Recreation Area
Arapaho National Forest
8 mi N of Granby on US 34; on right at Lake Granby. $12 base with federal senior pass; others pay $24 base, $28 for waterfront sites, $31 with wtr/elec. Arapaho NRA use fees also charged (free to senior pass holders). 5/12-10/15; 14-day limit; some sites free in winter but no services or wtr; elec surcharge applies off-season. 129 sites; 46-ft RV limit at 3 sites. Tbls, flush & pit toilets, cfga, drkg wtr, showers, dump. Fishing, boating(l), hiking trail, interpretive programs, mountain biking.

Willow Creek $10.50
Arapaho National Recreation Area
Arapaho National Forest
6 mi N of Granby on US 34; 3 mi W on CR 40; at Willow Creek Reservoir. $10.50 with federal senior pass; others pay $21. 5/25-10/15; 14-day limit. 35 sites; 40-ft RV limit. Tbls, toilets, cfga, drkg wtr. Also group camping. Tbls, toilets, cfga, drkg wtr. Boating(l), fishing, hiking.

GRAND JUNCTION

Hay Press FREE
Grand Mesa National Forest
10 mi SW of Grand Junction on SR 340; 20 mi S on CR 400. At Little Fruita Reservoir No. 3. Free. MD-11/15; 16-day limit. 11 sites (RVs under 16 ft). No amenities, no drkg wtr. Elev 9300 ft; 2 acres. Hay Press Creek.

Mud Springs Recreation Site $10
Bureau of Land Management
1 mi from Grand Junction on SR 340; left to Colorado National Monument for 7.5 mi past monument's east entrance; left at Glade Park store sign for 5 mi; S on 16.5 Rd for 6.6 mi. $10 family & group sites. 5/15-10/1; 14-day limit. 14 family sites (RVs under 30 ft), 2 group sites; small RVs. 8 acres. Toilets, cfga, firewood, tbls, drkg wtr. Hiking, rockhounding. Elev 8100 ft.

GRANT

Burning Bear Campground $9
Pike National Forest
5.2 mi NW of Grant on CR 62 (Guanella Pass Rd). $9 with federal senior pass; others pay $18. About MD-LD; 14-day limit. No wtr & reduced services off-season. 30-ft RV limit. Tbls, toilets, cfga, well drkg wtr. River, stream, fishing, trailhead, wilderness area, hiking. Elev 9500 ft; 6 acres. At jct of Bear Creek & Scott Gomer Creek.

Geneva Park Campground $9
Pike National Forest
7 mi NW of Grant on CR 62 Guanalla Pass Rd); qtr mi NW on FR 119. $9 with federal senior pass; others pay $18. MD-LD; 14-day limit. 2-night minimum stay required on weekends. 26 sites (RVs under 21 ft). Tbls, toilets, cfga, drkg wtr. Fishing, stream, hiking, trailhead. Scenic drive. Elev 9800 ft. On Geneva Creek.

GUNNISON

Cochetopa Canyon FREE
Special Recreation Management Area
Bureau of Land Management
SE of Gunnison on SR 114 along Cochetopa River. Access by co rds. Free. Apr-Nov; 14-day limit. 14 primitive sites at 7 roadside pull-offs along Cochetopa Creek; 35-ft RV limit. 3 have toilets, no tbls, trash service or drkg wtr. Limited scattered facilities. Swimming, fishing, hunting, hiking, backpacking. Small, rugged canyon.

Commissary Gulch Campground FREE
Gunnison National Forest
26.1 mi W of Gunnison on US 50; half mi NW on SR 92; 9.2 mi N on FR 721. At Soap Creek. 5/27-10/23; 16-day limit. 7 sites (RVs under 16 ft). Tbls, toilets, cfga, no drkg wtr. Fishing. Elev 7900 ft; 2 acres. Stream. Curecanti National Recreation Area approx 10 mi S.

Dry Gulch Campground $8
Curecanti National Recreation Area
Just N of US 50, 17 mi W of Gunnison; on Blue Mesa Lake. $8 with federal senior pass; others pay $16. All year; 14-day limit. 9 sites; mid-size RVs. Tbls, cfga, toilets, drkg wtr (5/15-9/15), horse corrals. Burn driftwood only. Drkg wtr during winter available at Elk Creek picnic area. Area may be closed by snow or freezing temperatures. Blue Mesa Lake boat fees. Boating, fishing.

Elk Creek $8
Curecanti National Recreation Area
16 mi W of Gunnison on US 50; on Blue Mesa Lake. $8 base with federal senior pass; others pay $16 base ($6 elec surcharge). All year, depending on weather (heavy snowfalls generally close the campground from Dec to March); 14-day limit. 160 sites (no RV size limit). Flush toilets (5/15-9/15), pit toilets, drkg wtr, dump, cfga, hot showers in-season, dump. No wtr or flush toilets in winter. Boating (rld), swimming, fishing. In winter, snowmobiling. Elev 7480 ft. Evening ranger programs. Sites usually accessible all year. During winter, wtr available at picnic area.

Gateview Campground FREE
Curecanti National Recreation Area
7 mi W of Powderhorn on SR 149, then 6 mi N on improved gravel rd. Free. 5/15-11/15; 14-day limit. 6 sites suitable for vans, pickup campers. Tbls, cfga, pit toilets, drkg wtr.

Boating, fishing, hiking. Campground may be closed in winter by snow or freezing temperatures. Obtain drkg wtr in winter at Elk Creek picnic area.

Lake Fork Campground $8
Curecanti National Recreation Area
27 mi W of Gunnison on US 50; near Blue Mesa Dam. $8 with federal senior pass; others pay $16. 4/15-10/15; 14-day limit. 90 sites (limited number available for tents); no RV size limit. Tbls, cfga, flush toilets & showers (5/15-9/15), dump, fish cleaning station, drkg wtr. Boating (l); fishing. Elev 7580 ft. During cold weather, get wtr at Elk Creek picnic area. Evening ranger program.

Ponderosa Campground $8
Curecanti National Recreation Area
Half mi W of Blue Mesa Dam via the Soap Creek Rd off US 50. RVs can make that 6-mi drive, but rd can be very muddy and hazardous when wet. $8 with federal senior pass; others pay $16. About 5/1-10/15; 14-day limit. 28 sites; 22-ft RV limit. Tbls, toilets, cfga, drkg wtr. Boating(l), fishing, hiking. Sites among pine trees at shoreline of Soap Creek arm of Blue Mesa Lake. Elev 8000 ft; 1,000 acres.

Red Bridge Campground $5
Curecanti National Recreation Area
7 mi W of Powderhorn on SR 149; watch for sign on the right that says "Red Bridge and Gateview"; exit on good travel rd for 2 mi. $5. 5/15-10/15; 14-day limit. Primitive clear sites along river. Tbls, toilets, cfga, no drkg wtr or trash service. Boating, fishing.

Red Creek Campground $8
Curecanti National Recreation Area
19 mi W of Gunnison on US 50. $8 with federal senior pass; others pay $16. 5/1-10/15; 14-day limit. Boating, picnicking, fishing, hiking. 1 family site, 1 group site by reservation $28; 22-ft RV limit. Tbls, cfga, toilets, drkg wtr through 9/15. Burn driftwood only. Obtain drkg wtr in winter at Elk Creek picnic area.

Red Creek Dispersed Sites FREE
Curecanti National Recreation Area
19 mi W of Gunnison on US 50. All year; 14-day limit. Primitive dispersed sites along dirt rd around Red Creek Campground, where fee is charged. Free. Obtain drkg wtr in winter at Elk Creek picnic area and Cimarron campground.

Soap Creek Campground $12
Gunnison National Forest
26.1 mi W of Gunnison on US 50; half mi NW on SR 92; 7.2 mi N on FR 721; half mi NE on FR 824. $12. 6/14-9/30; 16-day limit. 21 sites (RVs under 35 ft). Tbls, toilets, cfga, piped drkg wtr. Fishing, picnicking. Elev 7700 ft; 8 acres. Curecanti National Recreation Area approx 9 mi S. On-site

horse corrals, bins & unloading ramp. Non-campers pay $4 day use fee; also trash & firewod fees.

Stevens Creek $8
Curecanti National Recreation Area
12 mi W of Gunnison on US 50. $8 with federal senior pass; others pay $16. About MD-10/15; 14-day limit 53 sites; no RV size limit. Tbls, toilets, cfga, camp store, fish cleaning station. Boating(l), fishing, hiking, evening ranger programs on summer weekends. Elev 7540 ft.

GYPSUM
Community Recreation Site FREE
Eagle River Recreation Area
Bureau of Land Management
2 mi W of Gypsum on US 6 & 24 to Gypsum Recreation Site, then W; on Eagle River. Free. All year; 7-day limit (14 days off-season). Primitive undesignated sites; no facilities. Fishing, river-running, hiking. Elev 6200 ft.

Deep Creek FREE
Bureau of Land Management
Grand Junction District
About 6 mi W of Gypsum on US 6/24; 1 mi N on CR 301 (Colorado River Rd) along Colorado River; 2 mi W on Coffee Pot Rd. Free. 5/1-10/1; 14-day limit. Primitive camping area; roadside & walk-in camping. Toilets (May-Sept), cfga. No drkg wtr or trash service. Very scenic, good fishing, wildlife viewing, rafting, hiking, horseback riding, OHVs, hunting, spelunking. Visitor information.

Gypsum Recreation Site $10
Eagle River Recreation Area
Bureau of Land Management
From I-70 exit 140 at Gypsum, follow frontage rd (Old Hwy 6) on S side of interchange westward along Eagle River about 2 mi; camp between the road & river. $10. 7-day limit during 4/1-8/31; 14 days 9/1-3/31. 6 primitive sites. Tbls, toilets, cfga, no drkg wtr. Trash service only in summer. Fishing, boating(l), hiking.

Lava Flow Recreation Site FREE
Eagle River Recreation Area
Bureau of Land Management
W of Gypsum on US 6 & 24, past Gypsum, Community and Horse Pasture sites. Free. All year; 7-day limit (14 days off-season). Primitive undesignated sites; no facilities, no drkg wtr. Fishing, river-running, hiking.

Lede Reservoir FREE
White River National Forest
17.1 mi SE of Gypsum on FR 412 (last mile narrow & rough). Free. 6/1-10/1; 14-day limit. About 3 undesignated sites (RVs under 22 ft). Toilet, cfga, no drkg wtr or no trash service. Boating(l), canoeing, fishing. Elev 9500 ft; 3 acres. 27-acre Lede Reservoir.

HAMILTON (ROUTT CO)

Indian Run State Wildlife Area   FREE
12 mi E of Hamilton on Hwy 317; 6 mi S of Pagoda on CR 67. Free. All year; 14-day limit during a 45-day period. Primitive undeveloped campsites, designated areas only. Toilets, tbls, no drkg wtr, cfga. Hunting on 2,039 acres. Horse corral. Elev 6700 ft.

HARTSEL

Antero Reservoir State Wildlife Area   FREE
5 mi SW of Hartsel on Hwy 24. Free. All year; 14-day limit during a 45-day period. About 60 primitive campsites; 1,000 acres. Tbls, toilets, drkg wtr; fires prohibited. Fishing (4,000-acre lake), boating(l). Elev 9000 ft.

HASTY

John Martin Reservoir   FREE
State Wildlife Area
4 mi N of Hasty on CR 40. Free. All year except during waterfowl season; 14-day limit during 45-day period. Primitive camping. Toilets, cfga, no drkg wtr. Boating(l), fishing, hiking, hunting. Elev 3700 ft.

HAYDEN

Elkhead Reservoir Area $10
Yampa River State Park
About 10 mi W of Hayden on US 40, then NE on 29 Rd to reservoir. $10 for dispersed camping at the East Beach area; $10 for 25 primitive sites at Elks Campground ($7 for CO seniors with Aspen Leaf pass). All year. Toilets, tbls, cfga, no drkg wtr. Fishing, boating(l).

HOOPER

UFO Watchtower Camground $10
2.5 mi N of Hooper on Hwy 17; at gift shop devoted to alien themes. $10. All year. 24 sites; 45-ft RVs. Tbls, toilets, cfga, drkg wtr.

HOT SULPHUR SPRINGS

Hot Sulphur Springs   FREE
State Wildlife Area
3 mi W of Hot Sulphur Springs on US 40, then along Colorado River through Byers Canyon; short dirt rd leads to primitive camping area beside river. Four individual sections allow camping. Free. All year; 14-day limit. 50 sites. Tbls, toilets, cfga, drkg wtr. Along river are pullouts for overnight parking & fishing. Fishing, big-game hunting. Elev 7600 ft; 5 acres. Part of 1,173-acre area.

HUGO

Hugo State Wildlife Area   FREE
Kinny Lake tract: 12 mi S of Hugo on CR 109;; 2.5 mi E on CR 2G; 1 mi E on CR 2. Clingingsmith tract: 14 mi S on CR 102; 2.2 mi E on CR 2G. Free. All year; 14-day limit during 45-day period. Primitive campsites. Toilets, cfga, tbls. Hunting, fishing, hiking. Elev 4800 ft; 3600 acres.

26 water acres. Boating on Kinney Lake (no motors); no boating in Clingingsmith area.

IDAHO SPRINGS

Echo Lake Campground $9.50
Arapaho National Forest
14 mi SW of Idaho Springs on SR 103. $9.50 with federal senior pass; others pay $19. 6/9-LD; 14-day limit. 17 sites (typically 30 ft). Tbls, toilets, cfga, drkg wtr. Fishing, hiking. Elev 10,600 ft; 4 acres.

West Chicago Creek Campground $9
Arapaho National Forest
6 mi SW of Idaho Springs on SR 103; 4 mi SW on FR 188. $9 with federal senior pass; others pay $18. 5/26-9/3; 14-day limit. 15 sites, typically 40 ft. Tbls, toilets, cfga, drkg wtr. Fishing, hiking. Elev 9600 ft; 3 acres.

JEFFERSON

Aspen Campground $8
Jefferson Lake Recreation Area
Pike National Forest
2 mi W of Jefferson on CR 35; 1 mi N on CR 37; 1.7 mi NW on FR 401. $8 with federal senior pass; others pay $16. One-time $6 fee to enter recreation area. LD-MD; 14-day limit. 12 sites (25-ft RV limit). Tbls, toilets, cfga, drkg wtr. Boating(l), fishing, hiking. Elev 9900 ft; 5 acres.

Jefferson Creek Campground $8
Jefferson Lake Recreation Area
Pike National Forest
2 mi NW of Jefferson on CR 35; 1 mi Non CR 37; 3 mi NW on FR 401. $8 with federal senior pass; others pay $16. One-time $6 fee to enter recreation area. MD-LD; 14-day limit. 17 sites (25-ft RV limit). Tbls, toilets, cfga, drkg wtr. Fishing, hiking. Elev 10,000 ft; 28 acres.

Kenosha Pass Campground $9
Pike National Forest
4 mi NE of Jefferson on US 285 at top of Kenosah Pass. $9 with federal senior pass; others pay $18. MD-LD; 14-day limit. 25 sites (24-ft RV limit). Tbls, toilets, cfga, drkg wtr, information center. Hiking, horseback riding, biking. Elev 10,000 ft; 11 acres.

Lodgepole Campground $8
Jefferson Lake Recreation Area
Pike National Forest
2 mi NW of Jefferson on CR 35; 1 mi N on CR 37; 1.2 mi NW on FR 401. $8 with federal senior pass; others pay $16. MD-LD; 14-day limit. Free but reduced services when open off-season. 34 sites (30-ft RV limit). Tbls, toilets, cfga, drkg wtr. Hiking, fishing. Elev 9900 ft; 15 acres.

Lost Park Campground $7
Pike National Forest
1.2 mi NE of Jefferson on US 285; 19.7 mi E on FR 127; 4

mi E on FR 134. $7 with federal senior pass; others pay $14. Elev 10,000 ft. About MD-9/30 when accessible; 14-day limit. 12 sites on 4 acres (RVs under 23 ft). Tbls, toilets, cfga, firewood, drkg wtr, no trash service. Fishing, picnicking. Elev 10,000 ft.

Michigan Creek Campground $7
Pike National Forest
3 mi NW of Jefferson on CR 35; 2 mi NW on CR 54; 1 mi NW on FR 400. $7 with federal senior pass; others pay $14 (double site $20). 5/10-10/1; 14-day limit. 13 sites (25-ft RV limit). Tbls, toilets, cfga, no drkg wtr, no trash service. Fishing, hiking. Fourmile Creek. Elev 10,000 ft; 6 acres.

Tarryall Reservoir   FREE
State Wildlife Area
15 mi SE of Jefferson on CR 77 to reservoir. Free. All year; 14-day limit during a 45-day period. Primitive campsites. Toilets, cfga, no drkg wtr, fishing jettys. Hunting, fishing, picnicking. Elev 9000 ft; 886 acres. Water 175 acres. Boat ramp.

Karval Reservoir State Wildlife Area   FREE
From Hwys 94/109 jct, S 10 mi on Hwy 109. Free. All year; 14-day limit during 45-day period. Primitive campsites. Toilets (except in winter), cfga, drkg wtr, tbls, shelters. Hunting, fishing, hiking, boating (no motors). Elev 5100 ft; 235 acres. 22-acre lake.

KREMMLING
Cataract Creek $6.50
White River National Forest
Quarter mi E of Kremmling on US 40; 12.3 mi SE on SR 9; 4.7 mi SE on CR 30 (at Green Mountain Lake); 2.1 mi SW on CR 1725 near Lower Cataract Lake. Access rd not recommended for low-clearance vehicles. $6.50 with federal senior pass; others pay $13. 5/1-10/1; 14-day limit. 5 primitive undeveloped sites; 21-ft RV limit. Tbls, toilets, cfga, no drkg wtr. Hiking, fishing, boating (rld--3 mi). Elev 8600 ft; 4 acres. Nature trails. Trailhead to Gore Range Eagles Nest Primitive Area.

Cow Creek North Campground $6.50
White River National Forest
Qtr mi E of Kremmling on US 40; about 14.5 mi SE on SR 9; SW on access rd to NE shore of Green Mountain Lake. $6.50 with federal senior pass; others pay $13. 5/15-11/1; 14-day limit. 15 primitive undeveloped sites. Tbls, toilets, cfga, no drkg wtr or trash service. Fishing, boating, swimming, canoeing. Part of Arapaho National Forest.

Cow Creek South Campground $6.50
White River National Forest
Qtr mi E of Kremmling on US 40; about 14.5 mi SE on SR 9; SW on access rd to NE shore of Green Mountain Lake. $6.50 with federal senior pass; others pay $13. 5/15-11/1; 14-day limit. Free during early spring & late fall. 44 primitive undeveloped sites. Toilets, cfga, no drkg wtr. Fishing, boating, swimming, canoeing. Part of Arapaho National Forest.

Elliott Creek $6.50
White River National Forest
Qtr mi E of Kremmling on US 40; 12 mi SE on SR 9; 3 mi SW on CR 30. At Elliott Creek near NW shore of Green Mountain Lake. $6.50 with federal senior pass; others pay $13. 5/11-10/15; 14-day limit. About 24 primitive undeveloped sites (RVs under 25 ft). Tbls, pit toilets, cfga, no drkg wtr. Fishing, boating (rld--2 mi); swimming, waterskiing. Elev 8000 ft; 13 acres. Part of Arapaho National Forest.

Pumphouse Recreation Site $10
Upper Colorado Recreation Area
Bureau of Land Management
On Upper Colorado River S of Kremmling 1 mi on SR 9; W on CR 1 (Trough Rd) 14 mi; pass Inspiration Point; right on access rd; 2 mi to site. $10. 6/1-LD; 14-day limit. 20 sites; limited RV space (30-ft limit); 2 group sites $30. Toilets, tbls, cfga, drkg wtr. Whitewater float trips, fishing, hiking, sightseeing. Raft launching. Primary raft launch area. Float trip map, $1 from BLM, Kremmling Resource Area Office, P.O. Box 68, Kremmling 80459. Elev 7000 ft.

Radium $10
Upper Colorado Recreation Area
Bureau of Land Management
1 mi S of Kremmling on SR 9; 14 mi W on CR 1 (Trough Rd); then 25 mi, past Inspiration Point & Pumphouse site. $10. 4/1-10/30; 14-day limit. 6 sites (30-ft RV limit); 2 group sites $30. Tbls, toilets, cfga, no drkg wtr. River rafting, fishing, mountain biking.

Radium State Wildlife Area   FREE
2.5 mi S of Kremmling on Hwy 9 to CR 1; SW 12 mi along Colorado River on Trough Rd to State Bridge. Area surrounds town of Radium on both sides of river. Free. All year; 14-day limit during a 45-day period. Primitive scattered sites plus developed campground E of Radium near confluence of Colorado River & Sheephorn Creek. Tbls, toilets, cfga, no drkg wtr. Fishing, boating, hiking, hunting. Vehicles limited to established rds. 11,483 acres; quarter mile of Blacktail Creek; 1.5 mi of Colorado River.

Rock Creek State Wildlife Area   FREE
6 mi NW of Kremmling on US 40; left for 12 mi on Hwy 134; left on Fr 206 for 2.5 mi. Free. All year; 14-day limit. Primitive undesignated camping. Toilets, cfga, no tbls, no drkg wtr. Fishing, birdwatching.

State Bridge   FREE
Bureau of Land Management
S of Kremmling on Hwy 131 to bridge. Or hiking trail from BLM Pumphouse Recreation Site, 11.1 mi downstream from Kremmling (see Pumphouse entry); downstream

----

primitive undeveloped sites. Toilets, cfga, no drkg wtr. Fishing, boating, swimming, canoeing. Part of Arapaho National Forest.

COLORADO

from Radium Camp. Float Colorado River to half mi below SR 131 bridge. Free. No facilities, no drkg wtr or trash service. May-Sept. Rafting, kayaking, canoeing. Relatively easy stretch of whitewater. Class II or III rapids.

LA GARITA

Poso Campground $5
Rio Grande National Forest
6.3 mi NW of La Garita on CR 41G; 1.5 mi W on FR 690; 1.1 mi SW on FR 675. $5 during MD-11/25; free off-season but no services; 14-day limit. 4 acres. 11 sites (RVs under 25 ft). Tbls, toilets, cfga, firewood, no drkg wtr, trash collection. Rockhounding, stream fishing. Elev 9000 ft. On South Fork of Carnero Creek; near Cave Creek.

Storm King Campground $5
Rio Grande National Forest
10 mi NW of La Garita on CR G; 4.5 mi N on CR 41G (after 3.5 mi, becomes dirt & narrows to 1 lane). $5 during 5/20-LD; free off-season, but no services; 14-day limit. 3 tent sites, 8 RV sites (RVs under 26 ft). Tbls, toilets, cfga, firewood, no drkg wtr, trash collection. Rockhounding, 4WD nearby on FR 786. Elev 9200 ft; 4 acres. Middle Fork of Carnero Creek.

LA JUNTA

Carrizo Canyon Picnic Area FREE
Comanche National Grassland
58 mi S of LaJunta on Hwy 109; 18 mi E on Hwy 160; 7 mi S on CR 3; 3 mi E on CR P; 2 mi S on CR 6; 1.5 mi W on CR M; 1.9 mi S on FR 539. Free. All year; 14-day limit. Dispersed camping. Tbls, toilets, cfga, no drkg wtr or trash service. Fishing, hiking, rock art exploration.

Vogel Canyon Picnic Area FREE
Comanche National Grassland
13 mi S of LaJunta on Hwy 109; 1 mi W on CR 802 to sign for Vogel Canyon; 2 mi S. Free. All year; 14-day limit. Dispersed camping allowed at parking area, not on hiking trails. Tbls, toilet, cfga, no drkg wtr. Hiking, horseback riding (2 hitching rails & bridle trails), birdwatching. Ancient rock art nearby.

LAKE CITY

Deer Lakes Campground $12
Gunnison National Forest
9 mi SE of Lake City on SR 149; 3 mi NE on FR 788. $12. About 5/23-9/15; 16-day limit. Free off-season, but no wtr or trash service. 12 sites (30-ft RV limit). Tbls, toilets, cfga, drkg wtr. Fishing. Elev 10,900 ft; 5 acres.

Mill Creek Campground $7
Bureau of Land Management
Gunnison Field Office
2.5 mi S of Lake City on SR 149; 10 mi W on rd to Lake San Cristobal. $7. MD-LD; free off-season, but no drkg wtr.

22 sites (35-ft RV limit). Tbls, toilets, cfga, drkg wtr, bear lockers. Fishing, mountain biking, hiking, rockhounding, off-roading. Nearby ghost towns. Elev 9,500 ft.

Slumgullion Campground $10
Gunnison National Forest
9 mi SE of Lake City on SR 149; NE on FR 788. $10 during about 5/15-10/15; free 10/15-12/1. 14-day limit. 21 sites (40-ft RV limit). Tbls, toilets, cfga, drkg wtr. Hiking. Elev 11,500 ft; 7 acres.

Spruce Campground FREE
Gunnison National Forest
9 mi SE of Lake City on SR 149; 8 mi NE on FR 788. Free, but maintained by donations. 5/1-10/31; 14-day limit. Open in fall through hunting season. 9 sites (22-ft RV limit). Tbls, toilet, cfga, drkg wtr. Fishing (Cebolla Creek), hiking.

Williams Creek Campground $7
Gunnison National Forest
2 mi S of Lake City on SR 149; 6 mi SW on FR 907. $7 with federal senior pass; others pay $14. 5/15-10/15; 16-day limit. 23 sites; 40-ft RV limit. Tbls, toilets, cfga, drkg wtr. Fishing. Elev 9200 ft; 10 acres.

LAKE GEORGE

Blue Mountain Campground $8
Pike National Forest
1.3 mi SW of Lake George on FR 245; half mi S on FR 240. $8 with federal senior pass; others pay $16. 4/27-9/22; 14-day limit. 21 sites (25-ft RV limit). Tbls, toilets, cfga, no drkg wtr. Fishing, hiking. Elev 8200 ft.

Cove Campground $8
Eleven Mile Canyon Recreation Area
Pike National Forest
1 mi SW of Lake George on CR 61; 8.3 mi SW on FR 96. $8 with federal senior pass; others pay $16. 5/19-10/9; 14-day limit. No wtr & reduced services off-season. 4 sites (16-ft RV limit). Tbls, toilets, cfga, drkg wtr. Secluded. Elev 8400 ft.

Happy Meadows Campground $8
Pike National Forest
1.2 mi NW of Lake George on US 24; 1.2 mi N on CR 77; .7 mi NE on CR 112. $8 with federal senior pass; others pay $16. 5/19-10/9; 14-day limit. Open later & earlier without services or wtr. 8 sites (20-ft RV limit). Tbls, toilets, cfga, drkg wtr. Fishing, boating (South Platte River). 7900 ft.

Riverside Campground $8
Eleven Mile Canyon Recreation Area
Pike National Forest
2.5 mi SW of Lake George on FR 245. $8 with federal senior pass; others pay $16. 5/19-10/9; 14-day limit. Free off-season but no wtr & reduced services. 19 sites (30-ft

RV limit). Tbls, toilets, cfga, drkg wtr. Fishing. Elev 8000 ft; 6 acres.

Round Mountain Campground $7
Pike National Forest
5.2 mi NW of Lake George on US 24. $7 with federal senior pass; others pay $14. 5/19-10/9; 14-day limit. Free earlier & later but reduced services. 16 sites (35-ft RV limit). Tbls, toilets, cfga, no drkg wtr, no trash service. Near Eleven-mile Reservoir. Elev 8500 ft. Wtr system was turned off in 2010 due to health concerns; still off in 2017.

Spillway Campground $8
Eleven Mile Canyon Recreation Area
Pike National Forest
9.5 mi SW of Lake George on FR 246. $8 with federal senior pass; others pay $16. 5/19-10/9; 14-day limit. Free off-season if accessible, but no wtr or services. 23 sites (25-ft RV limit). Tbls, toilets, cfga, drkg wtr. Hiking, fishing. Elev 8500 ft.

Springer Gulch Campground $8
Eleven Mile Canyon Recreation Area
Pike National Forest
6.5 mi S of Lake George on FR 245. $8 with federal senior pass; others pay $16. 5/1-10/1; 14-day limit. Free off-season if accessible but no wtr or services. 15 sites (25-ft RV limit). Tbls, toilets, cfga, drkg wtr. Fishing, hiking trails, rock climbing.

Spruce Grove Campground $8
Lost Creek Wilderness Area
Pike National Forest
1.2 mi NW of Lake George on US 24; 12.2 mi SW on CR 77 (road work on CR 77 in 2017 will slow traffic to hourly passage). $8 with federal senior pass; others pay $16. 5/19-10/9; 14-day limit. 27 sites (35-ft RV limit). Tbls, toilets, cfga, drkg wtr. Fishing (Tarryall Creek), hiking. Elev 8600 ft.

Twin Eagles Campground $7
Lost Creek Wilderness Area
Pike National Forest
1.2 mi NW of Lake George on US 24; 11.2 mi SW on CR 77. $7 during 5/1-10/1; free rest of year. 14-day limit. 9 sites; 22-ft RV limit. Tbls, toilets, cfga, no drkg wtr or trash service. Fishing, hiking (Twin Eagles Trail). Elev 8600 ft.

LAMAR
Mike Higbee State Wildlife Area   FREE
4 mi E of Lamar on Hwy 50. Free. All year; 14-day limit in 45-day period. Primitive camping; no facilities. Hunting, pond fishing, archery & rifle ranges.

Queens State Wildlife Area   FREE
5 mi W of Lamar on US 50; 16 mi n on Hwy 287; 1 mi E on co rd. Follow signs. Free. All year except 12/1 through

waterfowl season on Lower (south) Queens and Nee Noshe Lakes; 11/1 through waterfowl season on Upper (north) Queen (including the channel), Nee Grande and Sweetwater (Nee So Pah) Lakes. Primitive campsites with toilets, picnic tables, cfga. 1900 acres. Waterfowl hunting, fishing for northern pike, walleye, bass, catfish. Boating(l). Waterskiing on Upper Queens and Nee Noshe Reservoirs. Elev 3800 ft.

LAPORTE
Aspen Glen $8.50
Roosevelt National Forest
4 mi N of Laporte on US 287; 51 mi W on Hwy 14. $8.50 with federal senior pass during MD-9/24; others pay $17 (25% fee discount off-season if no water available). All year; 14-day limit. 9 sites (30-ft RV limit). Tbls, toilets, cfga, drkg wtr. Boating, fishing, hiking trails, biking. On Joe Wright Creek; 3 lakes within 2 mi -- Chambers, Lost & Barnes Meadow. Elev 8660 ft.

Big Bend $8.50
Roosevelt National Forest
4 mi N of Laporte on US 287; 41 mi W on SR 14. $8.50 with federal senior pass during 5/19-9/24; others pay $17 (25% fee discount off-season, but no wtr). All year; 14-day limit. 6 sites (typically 35-45 ft). Tbls, toilets, cfga, drkg wtr. Hiking, fishing. On Cache La Poudre River. Bighorn sheep viewing station nearby. Elev 7700 ft.

Big South $8.50
Roosevelt National Forest
4 mi N of Laporte on US 287; 51 mi W on SR 14. $8.50 with federal senior pass; others pay $17 during about MD-9/24; 14-day limit. 4 sites; 25-ft RV limit. Tbls, toilets, cfga, no drkg wtr. Fishing, swimming, boating (l-4 mi). Elev 8400 ft; 1 acre. Lake. Scenic. Confluence of Big South Poudre River and Joe Wright Creek.

Browns Park $8
Roosevelt National Forest
4 mi N of Laporte on US 287; 55 mi W on SR 14; 21 mi N on CR 103. $8 with federal senior pass; others pay $16. About 6/23-11/15; 14-day limit. 28 sites; 30-ft RV limit. Tbls, toilets, cfga, no drkg wtr. Hiking, fishing. Elev 8400 ft; 10 acres. Stream. Trailhead to Rawah Wilderness. McIntyre and Link Trailhead. Beside Jinks Creek. Scenic.

Long Draw $9
Roosevelt National Forest
4 mi N of Laporte on US 287; 61 mi W on SR 14; 9 mi SE on FR 156 (Long Draw Rd). $9 with federal senior pass during 6/15-11/30; others pay $18 during about 6/30-11/5 (25% fee discount off-season, but no wtr); 14-day limit. 25 sites; 30-ft RV limit. Tbls, toilets, cfga, drkg wtr. Hiking, fishing. Elev 10,000 ft; 6 acres. Mountains, dense forest. Half mi N of Long Draw Reservoir.

Skyline   FREE
Roosevelt National Forest
4 mi N of Laporte on US 287; 55 mi W on SR 14; 4 mi N
on FR 190. Free. All year; 14-day limit. Flat, dispersed
camping in area of former 8-site campground; 2 acres.
No facilities except cfga; no drkg wtr. Fishing. Elev 8600.

Sleeping Elephant $8.50
Roosevelt National Forest
4 mi N of Laporte on US 287; 46 mi W on SR 14. $8.50 with
federal senior pass during MD-9/24; others pay $17 (25%
fee discount off-season when wtr not available); 14-day
limit. 15 sites (20-ft RV limit). Tbls, toilets, cfga, drkg wtr.
Fishing, hiking, mountain biking. Elev 7800 ft; 6 acres.

Tom Bennett $7
Roosevelt National Forest
4 mi N of Laporte on US 287; 27 mi W on SR 14; 11 mi S
on CR 131; 5 mi W on FR 145. $7 with federal senior pass;
others pay $14. 5/15-10/31; 14-day limit. 12 sites (RVs
under 21 ft). Tbls, toilets, cfga, no drkg wtr. Fishing, hiking, mountain biking. Elev 9000 ft; 3 acres. Poudre River.
Near Pin Gree Park.

Tunnel $10
Roosevelt National Forest
4 mi N of Laporte on US 287; 59 mi W on SR 14; 21 mi N on
CR 103. $10 with federal senior pass during about 6/23-
9/24; others pay $20 (25% fee discount in winter when
wtr not available); 14-day limit. 49 sites (40-ft RV limit).
Tbls, toilets, cfga, drkg wtr. Fishing, hiking, biking. Elev
8600 ft; 18 acres.

LEADVILLE

Baby Doe Campground $10
Turquoise Lake Recreation Area
San Isabel National Forest
About 5 mi W of Leadville on CR 4, following signs to
recreation area. $10 base with federal senior pass; others
pay $20 base, $22 for premium locations ($11 with senior
pass). About MD-LD; 14-day limit. 50 sites; 40-ft RV limit.
Tbls, flush toilets, cfga, drkg wtr (no wtr tank refills).
Fishing, hiking, canoeing, boating(l), interpretive trails.

Elbert Creek Campground $8.50
Halfmoon Recreation Area
San Isabel National Forest
3.6 mi SW of Leadville on US 24; .7 mi W on SR 300; 6.5 mi
SW on CR 11. $8.50 with federal senior pass; others pay
$17. About MD-LD; 14-day limit. 17 sites (typically 35 ft).
Tbls, toilets, cfga, drkg wtr. Fishing, hiking. Elev 10,000 ft;
12 acres. At Elbert Creek & Halfmoon Creek.

Camp Hale Memorial Campground $10
White River National Forest
17 mi N of Leadville on US 24; qtr mi E on FR 729; 1 mi S

on FR 716. $10 base with federal senior pass; others pay
$20 base, $22 at premium sites ($11 with senior pass).
MD-10/1. 10-day limit. 21 sites (60-ft RV limit). Tbls, toilets,cfga, drkg wtr. On East Fork of Eagle River. Fishing,
mountain biking, hiking, rock climbing. "Food Storage
Order" issued for 2017 due to bear activity.

Father Dyer Campground $10
Turquoise Lake Recreation Area
San Isabel National Forest
About 5 mi W of Leadville on CR 4, following signs to
recreation area; near E shore of Turquoise Lake. $10 with
federal senior pass; others pay $20. 26 sites; 30-ft RV
limit. About MD-LD; 14-day limit. Tbls, flush toilets, cfga,
drkg wtr. Boating(l), fishing, hiking.

Halfmoon East Campground $8.50
Halfmoon Recreationa Area
San Isabel National Forest
3.6 mi SW of Leadville on US 24; .7 mi W (right) on SR 300;
5.5 mi SW on FR 11; near Elbert Creek. $8.50 with federal
senior pass; others pay $17. About MD-LD; 14 day limit. 22
sites (typically 35 ft). Tbls, toilets, cfga, drkg wtr. Fishing,
hiking. Elev 9800 ft; 14 acres.

Halfmoon West Campground $8.50
San Isabel National Forest
From I-70 exit 171 (Leadville/Minturn), 3.6 mi SW on US
24; immediately before crossing Eagle River, turn right on
Tigiwon Rd (FR 707) for 8 mi. (Note: reader says this rd is
also called Notch Mountain Rd.) $8.50 with federal senior
pass; others pay $17. About MD-LD; 14-day limit. 7 prim-
itive undesignated sites; 16-ft RV limit. Tbls, toilets, cfga,
drkg wtr. Hiking, fishing. Two trailheads for Holy Cross
Wilderness Area. "Food storage order" issued for 2017
due to bear activity.

Lakeview Campground $9.50
San Isabel National Forest
From Leadville, 15 mi S on US 24; right (W) 4 mi on SR
82; right on CR 24, then 1 mi to campground overlooking
Twin Lakes Reservoir. $9.50 with federal senior pass;
others pay $19. About MD-LD; 14-day limit. 33 sites; 45-ft
RV limit. Tbls, toilets, cfga, drkg wtr (no RV tank refill).
Boating, fishing, hiking.

May Queen Campground $10
Turqoise Lake Recreation Area
San Isabel National Forest
About 5 mi W of Leadville on CR 4, following signs to
recreation area; at W end of lake. $10 with federal senior
pass; others pay $20. About MD-LD; 14-day limit. 23 sites,
typically 35-ft RV limit. Tbls, toilets, cfga, drkg wtr. Boat-
ing(l), fishing, hiking, swimming.

Molly Brown Campground $10
Turquoise Lake Recreation Area
San Isabel National Forest
About 5 mi W of Leadville on CR 4, following signs to recreation area; on E shore of lake. $10 base with federal senior pass; others pay $20 base, $22 for premium locations. About MD-LD; 14-day limit. 48 sites; 35-ft RV limit. Tbls, flush toilets, cfga, drkg wtr. Fishing, boating(l), hiking, swimming.

Parry Peak Campground $8.50
San Isabel National Forest
From Leadville, 15 mi S on US 24; right (W) on SR 82 about 1 mi past Twin Lakes Reservoir & 2.7 mi W of Twin Lakes Village; along Lake Creek. $8.50 with federal senior pass; others pay $17. 25 sites; 32-ft RV limit. About MD-LD; 14-day limit. Boating(l), fishing, hiking.

Tabor Campground $10
San Isabel National Forest
2 mi W of Leadville on CR 37; 2.5 mi W on CR 4; 3 mi W on CR 9C. $10 with federal senior pass; others pay $20. About MD-LD; 14-day limit. 35 RV sites; 37-ft RV limit. Tbls, toilets, cfga, drkg wtr, dump. Hiking, fishing.

Twin Peaks Campground $9.50
San Isabel National Forest
From Leadville, 15 mi S on US 24; right (W) on SR 82 to campground just W of Twin Lakes Reservoir; at Lake Creek. $9.50 with federal senior pass; others pay $19. About MD-LD; 14-day limit. 36 sites; 32-ft RV limit. Tbls, toilets, cfga, drkg wtr. Boating, fishing, hiking.

MANASSA

Sego Springs   FREE
State Wildlife Area
3 mi E of Manassa on Hwy 142; half mi N on access rd. Free. 7/15-2/15; 14-day limit in 45-day period. Primitive camping. No facilities. Fishing. No fires.

MANCOS

Target Tree Campground $9
San Juan National Forest
7 mi E of Mancos on US 160. $9 with federal senior pass; others pay $18. 5/5-9/30; 14-day limit. 25 sites (45-ft RV limit). Tbls, toilets, cfga, drkg wtr. Fishing, interpretive trail. Elev 7800 ft. Indians once used the site's trees for for target practice, and many are still scarred from arrows and bullets.

MASONVILLE

Buckhorn Canyon   FREE
Roosevelt National Forest
4 mi N of Masonville on US 287; 15 mi W on SR 14; 10 mi S on CR 27. Free. 5/1-10/31; 14-day limit. 17 acres. 10 sites (RVs under 32 ft). Individual sites along rd. Tbls, toilets, cfga, no drkg wtr. Fishing, picnicking. Elev 8300 ft.

MAYBELL

Browns Park State Wildlife Area   FREE
Quarter mi W of Maybell on US 40 from Maybell; NW on CR 318 to CR 10; W to Beaver Creek Unit. To reach Cold Spring Mountain Unit, continue on CR 318 to CR 110; W to access rd; S to property. Free. All year; 14-day limit during 45-day period. Primitive campsites. No facilities. Big-game hunting, fishing, picnicking. Elev 8700 ft. 2 mi of Beaver Creek.

Bull Canyon, Willow Creek,   FREE
Skull Creek Wilderness Study Areas
Bureau of Land Management
W of Maybell on US 40; N on co rds. Areas N of highway, S of Dinosaur National Monument. Free. All year; 14-day limit. Accessible earlier and later in spring & fall than higher-elevation areas. Primitive backcountry camping; no facilities. Scenic viewing, hiking, backpacking, viewing wildlife, photography, horseback riding. 39,000 acres in the three areas. Colorful canyons, sandstone cliffs, rock outcrops. Archaeological sites (protected by law). Bull Canyon WSA can be viewed from Dinosaur Monument's Plug Hat picnic area.

Cold Spring Mountain Area   FREE
State Wildlife Area
NW of Maybell in NW corner of state, off SR 318 to CR 10N and CR 72. Lower portion of mountain accessible in Browns Park. Follow signs to camping areas. Free. All year; 14-day limit. Primitive camping at 5 camp areas. Pit toilets; 3 areas have fire rings; no drkg wtr. Hunting, hiking, backpacking, photography, fishing in Beaver Creek. Top of mountain wet until mid-June, restricting vehicle use.

Crook Campground   FREE
Browns Park National Wildlife Refuge
50 mi NW of Maybell on SR 318, past access rd to Lodore Hall Nat'll Historic Site, leftbr on gravel tour rd 1 mi. Free. All yr; 14-day limit during 45-day period. 20 sites for tents or self-contained RVs. No facilities or drkg wtr. Wtr nearby at Subheadquarters and refuge headqtrs. Hiking, hunting, fishing, sightseeing. Swing bridge across Green River. Bridge under capacity for RVs; OK for cars, light trucks.

Diamond Breaks Wilderness Study Area   FREE
Bureau of Land Management
NW of Maybell on SR 318 and W of Browns Park National Wildlife Refuge. Free. All year; 14-day limit. Primitive camping; no facilities. Photography, nature study, viewing wildlife, day hikes, backpacking. Scenic mountainous area. Solitude. Adjacent to north end of Dinosaur National Monument. Spectacular views into Canyon of Lodore. 36,000 acres.

East Cross Mountain $10
Yampa River State Park River Access Site
Bureau of Land Management
13.6 mi W of Maybell on US 40; 2.4 mi N on CR 85; turn

on BLM Rd 1551 for about 1.5 mi to fork, then bear left to Yampa River. $10. All year; 14-day limit. 4 primitive sites. Toilets, tbls, cfga, no drkg wtr. Boating(l), fishing.

Gates of Lodore $10
Dinosaur National Monument
41 mi NW of Maybell on SR 318; 4 mi SW on unpaved rds. $10 plus entry fee during 5/15-10/15; 15-day limit. $6 off-season, but no wtr. 19 sites (30-ft RV limit). Tbls, toilets, cfga, wtr faucets, bear lockers. Boating (concrete launch -- whitewater running craft only; special rafting permit required); fishing; picnicking; no swimming (cold water & dangerous currents). Elev 5600 ft; 6 acres. N portal to Lodore Canyon. Pets on leash. Spectacular scenery where the Green River created the 2,300-foot-deep Lodore Canyon. River runs wild.

Irish Canyon FREE
Bureau of Land Management
About 40 mi NW of Maybell on SR 318, then 4 mi N through Irish Canyon on Moffat County Rd 10N (gravel rd) for 8 mi. 4/15-10/30; 14-day limit. 6 sites (30-ft RV limit). Tbls, cfga, toilet, no drkg wtr or trash service. Mountain biking, wildlife viewing, hunting, hiking, sightseeing.

Little Snake State Wildlife Area FREE
State Wildlife Area
20 mi N of Maybell on CR 19. Free. Camping period from 3 days before big game hunting seasons until 3 days after in self-contained RVs. Primitive camping, undesignated sites. No facilities, no drkg wtr. Big-game hunting camp on 4860 acres.

Maybell Bridge $10
Yampa River State Park River Access Site
Bureau of Land Management
3 mi E of Maybell on US 40; just E of Yampa River. $10. All year; 14-day limit. 6 primitive sites. Toilets, cfga, no drkg wtr. Boating(l), fishing.

Rocky Reservoir Recreation Site FREE
Bureau of Land Management
Little Snake Field Office
NW of Maybell on SR 318 about 45 mi; right on SR 10N for about 15 mi; left (W) on CR 72; follow signs. Free. 6/1-11/1; 14-day limit. 5 primitive RV sites. Toilet, tbl, fire rings, no drkg wtr, no trash service. Hunting, hiking, sightseeing.

Sand Wash Basin Recreation Area FREE
Bureau of Land Management
NW of Maybell, accessible from SR 318. Dirt rds hazardous when wet. Free. All year; 14-day limit. Primitive camping, undesignated sites. No facilities. Hunting, rockhounding, trail bike riding, OHV use. Home of wild mustang herd.

Swinging Bridge Camp FREE
Browns Park National Wildlife Refuge
58 mi NW of Maybell on SR 318, past access to Lodore Hall National Historic Site and past access rd to Crook campground, then left on gravel rd for 2 mi. Free. All year. 15 sites for tents or self-contained RVs. Cfga, shade trees; no drkg wtr or other facilities. Wtr nearby at Subheadquarters and refuge headquarters. Hiking, hunting, fishing, sightseeing. Next to swinging bridge across Green River. Bridge under capacity for RVs, okay for cars & trucks. Boating on Butch Cassidy pond (no motors) & Green River.

West Cold Spring Wilderness Study Area FREE
Bureau of Land Management
NW of Maybell on SR 318 to N side of Browns Park. Free. All year; 14-day limit. Primitive undesignated camping. No facilities. Hunting, backpacking, scenic viewing, fishing, trail hiking. Beaver Creek Canyon. 17,000 acres.

MEEKER
Bel Aire Unit FREE
Oak Ridge State Wildlife Area
2 mi E of Meeker on Hwy 13; 18 mi E on CR 8; 1.5 mi S on CR 17 (S of Buford), then W on dirt rd. Free. 7/15-10/30; 14-day limit during 45-day period. Primitive undesignated sites. Tbls, toilets, cfga, drkg wtr. Hunting, fishing.

Bucks Campground $7.50
Trappers Lake
White River National Forest
2 mi E of Meeker on SR 13; 39 mi SE on CR 8, becoming FR 8; 10 mi S on Trappers Lake Rd (FR 205) to just past Trappers Outlet Trailhead. 6/15-9/15; 14-day limit. $7.50 with federal senior pass; others pay $15. 10 sites; 36-ft RV limit. Tbls, toilets, cfga, drkg wtr. Fishing, boating, hiking.

Cutthroat Campground $9.50
Trapper Lake
White River National Forest
2 mi E of Meeker on SR 13; 39 mi SE on CR 8, becoming FR 8; 10 mi S on Trappers Lake Rd (FR 205) to just past Trappers Outlet Trailhead. $9.50 with federal senior pass; others pay $19. 6/10-10/9; 14-day limit. 14 sites; 36-ft RV limit. Tbls, toilets, cfga, drkg wtr. Fishing, boating, hiking.

East Marvine Campground $7.50
White River National Forest
2 mi E of Meeker on SR 13; 29 mi E on CR 8; 6.5 mi SE on FR 12 (Marvine Creek Rd). $7.50 with federal senior pass; others pay $15. 5/21-10/23; 14-day limit (fees may be reduced if closing is extended and services reduced; horse sites, $10 for corral use. 50-ft RV limit. Tbls, toilets, cfga, no drkg wtr (wtr stock in stream). Fishing, hiking, horseback riding. Elev 8200 ft. Overflow camping on left side of rd; fees apply.

Himes Peak Campground $8
White River National Forest
2 mi E of Meeker on SR 13; 41 mi E on CR 8; 5 mi SE on FR 205 (Trappers Lake Rd). $8 with federal senior pass; others pay $16. Fees may be less if services are reduced. 5/21-11/11; 14-day limit. 11 sites; 36-ft RV limit. Tbls, toilets, cfga, drkg wtr. Hiking, fishing, horseback riding, hiking. Elev 9500 ft.

Jensen State Wildlife Area   FREE
9 mi NE of Meeker on Hwy 13; access via CR 30 at top of Nine-mile Gap. Free. 7/15-12/1; 14-day limit during 45-day period. Primitive camping, only in 3 designated undeveloped areas; no facilities, no drkg wtr. Big-game hunting on 5955 acres.

Marvine Campground $10.50
White River National Forest
2 mi E of Meeker on SR 13; 29 mi E on CR 8; 4.5 mi SE on FR 12 (Marvine Creek Rd). $10.50 with federal senior pass; others pay $21 ($25 for 4 corral sites). 5/21-10/23; 14-day limit. 24 sites (60-ft RV limit); horse camping okay at 4 sites, $5 for corral use. Tbls, toilets, cfga, drkg wtr. Fishing, hiking, horseback riding. Marvine Creek & Marvine Lakes; trailhead to lakes. Elev 8100 ft; 5 acres.

North Fork Campground $11
White River National Forest
2 mi E of Meeker on SR 13; 34 mi E on CR 8 (becoming FR 8); at North Fork of White River. $11 base with federal senior pass; others pay $22 base, $23 for premium locations ($11.50 with senior pass). About 5/15-10/20; 14-day limit. 28 sites; 60-ft RV limit. Tbls, toilets, cfga, drkg wtr. Fishing, hiking.

Oak Ridge   FREE
State Wildlife Area
2 mi N of Meeker on Hwy 13 to CR 8; E 25 mi. Camping at Lake Avery and at area's north and south access points. On White River at 260-acre Lake Avery. Also sites at end of a short access rd from SR 132 about 2 mi E of the lake and from CR 6 on the N side. Free. 7/16-10/30; 14-day limit during 45-day period. 50 primitive lakeside campsites (camp only in designated areas). Toilets, tbls, cfga, drkg wtr. Hunting, hiking, lake trout fishing, horseback riding. Elev 6200 ft; 11,765 acres. Lake Avery Wildlife Area. White River. Eagles, rattlesnakes, marmots, porcupine. Boat ramp at Lake Avery. Horse corrals & loading ramps.

Shepherds Rim Campground $11.50
Trappers Lake
White River National Forest
2 mi E of Meeker on SR 13; 39 mi E on CR 8, becoming FR 8; 10 mi S on Trappers Lake Rd (FR 205) to just past Trappers Outlet Trailhead. $11.50 with federal senior pass; others pay $23. 6/10-10/23; 14-day limit. 16 sites; 36-ft RV limit. Tbls, toilets, cfga, drkg wtr. Boating, fishng.

South Fork Campground $10
White River National Forest
2 mi E of Meeker on SR 13; 23 mi E on CR 8; 9.5 mi S on CR 10; half mi SE on FR 200. $10 with federal senior pass; others pay $20. 5/21-10/23; 14-day limit. 16 sites (36-ft RV limit). Tbls, toilets, cfga, no drkg wtr. Fishing, swimming, hiking. Elev 8000 ft; 6 acres. Season may be extended with reduced services.

Trapline Campground $11.50
Trappers Lake
White River National Forest
2 mi E of Meeker on SR 13; 39 mi E on CR 8 (becoming FR 8); 10 mi S on Trappers Lake Rd (FR 205) to just past Trappers Outlet Trailhead. $11.50 with federal senior pass; others pay $23. 6/10-9/11; 14-day limit. 13 sites; 36-ft RV limit. Tbls, toilets, cfga, drkg wtr. Fishing, boating, hiking.

MESA
Jumbo Campground $9
Grand Mesa National Forest
13 mi S of Mesa on SR 64; S on FR 252. $9 base with federal senior pass; others pay $18 base; $6 surcharge for elec. MD-LD; 14-day limit. 21 elec sites, 5 non-elec (60-ft RV limit). Tbls, toilets, cfga, drkg wtr. Boating(l), fishing, hiking, bike trails. Between Junbo & Sunset Lakes; Mesa Lakes nearby. Elev 9800 ft; 10 acres.

Spruce Grove $12
Grand Mesa National Forest
15 mi S of Mesa on SR 65. $12. 6/15-10/1; 14-day limit; 16 sites; 45-ft RV limit. Tbls, toilets, cfga, drkg wtr. Hiking, picnicking, fishing. Elev 10,000 ft.

MONTE VISTA
Alamosa   FREE
Rio Grande National Forest
12 mi S of Monte Vista on SR 15; 17.4 mi W on FR 250 (Alamosa-Conejos River Rd). Free. MD-LD or until snow closes access; 14-day limit. 5 sites; 1 pull-through (RVs under 26 ft). 3 acres. Tbls, toilet, cfga, firewood, no drkg wtr or trash collection. Horseback riding, no fishing in the Alamosa River.

Comstock   FREE
Rio Grande National Forest
2 mi S of Monte Vista on SR 15; 16.5 mi SW on FR 265 (Rock Creek Rd); very rough road. Free. 4/15-12/15 or until snow closes access; 14-day limit. 7 sites; 40-ft RV limit. 3 acres. Tbls, toilet, cfga, firewood, no drkg wtr or trash collection. Stream fishing, horseback riding. Elev 9600 ft.

Hot Creek   FREE
State Wildlife Area
20 mi S of Monte Vista on Hwy 15; where highway turns E, turn right on gravel rd marked for Hot Creek and La Jara Reservoir; 3 mi to wildlife area. Free. 4/30-12/1; 14-day

limit in 45-day period. No snowmobiles. Primitive unrestricted camping. Toilets at La Jara Reservoir. Hunting, no fishing. 3,494 acres; elev 9000 ft. Solitude. Desert bighorn sheep.

Rock Creek   FREE
Rio Grande National Forest
2 mi S of Monte Vista on SR 15; 13.5 mi SW on FR 265 (Rock Creek Rd; gravel to within 1 mi of campground). Free. Md-11/15 or until snow closes access (no trash service after LD); 14-day limit. 10 sites; 3 pull-through (RVs under 31 ft). 6 acres on Rock Creek. Tbls, toilets, cfga, no wtr. Fishing, horseback riding. Elev 9400 ft.

Stunner Campground   FREE
Rio Grande National Forest
12 mi S of Monte Vista on SR 15; 33.7 mi W on FR 250; quarter mi SW on FR 380. (Approx 14 mi W of Alamosa Campground). On Alamosa River. Free 6/15-LD or unless snow closes access; 14-day limit. 5 sites (RVs under 26 ft). 3 acres. Tbls, toilets, cfga, firewood, no drkg wtr or trash collection. Horseback riding, stream fishing. Elev 9700 ft.

Terrace Reservoir State Wildlife Area   FREE
12 mi S of Monte Vista on Hwy 15; 9 mi W on FR 250. Free. All year; 14-day limit during 45-day period. Primitive camping; no facilities. Fishing. Elev 8525 acres.

MONTROSE

Beaver Lake $12
Uncompahgre National Forest
20 mi E of Montrose on US 50; 20.5 mi S on FR 858 (Big Cimarron Rd). $12. MD-10/1; 14-day limit. 11 sites; 25-ft RV limit. Tbls, toilets, cfga, no drkg wtr (available 1 mi S at Silver Jack Camp). Fishing, hiking.

Big Cimarron Campground $12
Uncompahgre National Forest
20 mi E of Montrose on US 50; 20 mi S on CR 69. At Big Cimarron River. $12 during MD-LD; free LD-11/15. 16-day limit. 10 sites (RVs under 23 ft). Tbls, toilet, cfga, no drkg wtr (available 2 mi S at Silver Jack Camp). Fishing. Elev 8600 ft.

Billy Creek   FREE
State Wildlife Area
16 mi SE from Montrose on Hwy 550 to Billy Creek, then half mi E on CR 2. Three other tracts with different entrances. Free. All year; 14-day limit during 45-day period. Primitive camping. No facilities. Big-game hunting, river fishing. Elev 6000-8000 ft; 5591 acres.

Cimarron Creek Campground $8
Curecanti National Recreation Area
20 mi E of Montrose on US 50. $8 with federal senior pass; otehrs pay $16. Apr-Dec; 14-day limit. 21 sites (no RV size limit). Individual sites indicated by tbls & firepits.

Drkg wtr, dump, flush toilets, store. Intermittent evening campfire programs.

East Portal Campground $8
Curecanti National Recreation Area
8 mi E of Montrose on US 50; 7 mi on SR 347; 6 mi on East Portal access rd. (Buses, trailers and motorhomes larger than 22 feet are prohibited on the last 6 mi. This portion is steep, narrow, hazardous descent into the Black Canyon of the Gunnison.) $8 with federal senior pass; others pay $16. 4/15-11/15; 14-day limit. Campground may be closed by snow or freezing temperatures. 15 shaded sites. Toilets, cfga, tbls, drkg wtr. During cold weather, drkg wtr available at Elk Creek picnic area. Near historic Gunnison River Diversion Tunnel.

Iron Springs Campground   FREE
Uncompahgre National Forest
24 mi SW of Montrose on SR 90. MD-11/15;16-day limit. Free. Jun-Oct; 14-day limit. 8 sites (small RVs). 4 acres. Tbls, toilet, cfga, no drkg wtr. Elev 9500 ft. Hiking.

Silver Jack Campground $7
Uncompahgre National Forest
10 mi E of Montrose on US 50; 20 mi S on FR 858 (Big Cimarron Rd). $7 with federal senior pass; others pay $14. MD-LD; 16-day limit. 60 sites; 30-ft RV limit. Tbls, toilets, cfga, drkg wtr. Fishing, boating (no mtrs), hiking.

South Rim Campground $8
Black Canyon of Gunnison National Park
6 mi E of Montrose on US 50; 5 mi N on Hwy 37. $8 base with federal senior pass), others pay $16 base. $6 surcharge for elec. 5/15-10/15; 14-day limit. 88 sites; 22-ft RV limit. Tbls, toilets, cfga, drkg wtr, visitor center. Hiking, sightseeing, rafting, fishing.

NATHROP

Cascade Campground $10
San Isabel National Forest
Half mi S of Nathrop on US 285; 5.5 mi W on CR 162; 3.2 mi W on FR 212; along Chalk Creek near Chalk Cliffs. $10 with federal senior pass; others pay $20. 5/19-9/30; 7-day limit. 21 sites (35-ft RV limit). Tbls, flush & pit toilets, cfga, drkg wtr. Fishing, hiking trails, swimming, horseback riding. Elev 9700 ft; 8 acres.

Chalk Lake Campground $10
San Isabel National Forest
Half mi S of Nathrop on US 285; 5.5 mi W on CR 162; 3 mi SW on FR 212; along Chalk Creek. $10 with federal senior pass; others pay $20. 5/19-LD; 7-day limit. 18 sites (50-ft RV limit). Tbls, toilets, cfga, no drkg wtr. Fishing, hiking, swimming, horseback riding. Elev 8700 ft; 4 acres.

Iron City Campground　　　　　　　　　$8
San Isabel National Forest
Half mi S of Nathrop on US 285; 15 mi W on CR 162; half mi NE on FR 212. $8 with federal senior pass; others pay $16 during 5/19-9/5; 7-day limit. Free off-season when accessible, but no wtr, toilets or services. 15 sites (25-ft RV limit). Tbls, toilet, cfga, drkg wtr. Fishing, hiking. Elev 9900 ft; 21 acres.

Mount Princeton Campground　　　　　　$10
San Isabel National Forest
Half mi S of Nathrop on US 285; 5.5 mi W on CR 162; 2.5 mi W on FR 212; at Chalk Creek. $10 with federal senior pass; others pay $20. 5/19-9/5; 7-day limit. 19 sites (45-ft RV limit). Tbls, toilets, cfga, drkg wtr. Hiking, fishing, horseback riding, swimming. Elev 8900 ft.

NATURITA

Dry Creek Basin State Wildlife Area　　　FREE
17 mi SE of Naturita on Hwy 141. Free. All year; 14-day limit during 45-day period. Restricted primitive camping. No facilities; 7,833 acres plus 17,000 BLM property & 1,280 acres of leased state land. Hunting, picnicking, fishing in 11 stocked ponds. Elev 7000-8000 ft.

NEDERLAND

Kelly Dahl Campground　　　　　　　　$10.50
Roosevelt National Forest
4 mi S of Nederland on SR 119; on E side at milepost 22 (2 mi N of Rollinsville). $10.50 with federal senior pass; others pay $21 during about 5/19-9/24 (lower fees off-season when wtr is off); 14-day limit. 46 sites; 45-ft RV limit. Tbls, pit toilets, cfga, drkg wtr, playground.

Rainbow Lakes　　　　　　　　　　　$7.50
Roosevelt National Forest
6.5 mi N of Nederland on SR 72; 5 mi W on CR 116. Extremely rough rd leading to site. $7.50 with federal senior pass; others pay $15. 6/15-9/24; 7-day limit. 16 sites up to 50 ft. Toilets, tbls, cfga, no drkg wtr, no trash service. Fishing, hiking, cross-country skiing. Elev 10,000 ft; 10 acres.

NEW CASTLE

Garfield Creek　　　　　　　　　　　FREE
State Wildlife Area
2 mi SW of New Castle on CR 312; S along Garfield Creek. Free. Camping only during elk and deer seasons, 3 days before season & 3 days after. Primitive designated campsites. Toilets, cfga. 4,804 acres. Hunting.

Meadow Lake Campground　　　　　　　$10
White River National Forest
9 mi NW of New Castle on CR 245; 20.5 mi N on FR 244; 3.5 mi E on FR 601; 3 mi S on FR 823. $10 with federal senior pass; others pay $20. MD-10/23; 14-day limit. 10 sites

(16-ft RV limit). Tbls, toilets, cfga, drkg wtr, fishing pier. Fishing, hiking, mountain biking, boating(l), fishing pier.

Meadow Ridge Campground　　　　　　$10
White River National Forest
From I-70 exit 105 just E of New Castle, turn left & follow signs into town; right at 7th St (CR 245 or Buford-New Castle Rd; 22 mi N to Hiner Spring; right (E) on FR 601, then S on FDR 823 to campground. $10 with federal senior pass; others pay $20. MD-10/23; 14-day limit. 20 sites; 50-ft RV limit. Tbls, toilets, cfga, drkg wtr. Fishing, boating, mountain biking.

NORWOOD

Miramonte Reservoir　　　　　　　　　FREE
State Wildlife Area
1 mi E on Hwy 145 (Lone Cone Rd), then 17 mi S on FR 610 (Dolores-Norwood Rd); at NW base of Lone Coune Mountain. Access limited to snowmobiles after Dec. 1. Free. All year; 14-day limit within 45-day period. 50 RV sites; 510 acres. Camp only in designated areas along NE, SW & SE portions of river. Tbls, cfga, toilets, dump, drkg wtr, shelter. Fishing, hiking, firewood, waterfowl hunting, boating (l).

OHIO CITY

Comanche Campground　　　　　　　　FREE
Gunnison National Forest
From northbound SR 76 at Ohio City, left on FR 771.1 (Gold Creek Rd) for 2.5 mi. Free. 5/15-9/15; 14-day limit. 4 small sites. Tbls, toilets, cfga, no drkg wtr, no services. Hiking, fishing.

Gold Creek　　　　　　　　　　　　FREE
Gunnison National Forest
8 mi NE of Ohio City on FR 771. Free but donations accepted. 5/15-10/15; 14-day limit. 6 small sites. Tbls, toilet, cfga, no drkg wtr, no services. Mountain climbing, hiking, fishing. Elev 10,000 ft; 2 acres. Scenic. Trails to high country lakes begin across access rd.

PAGOSA SPRINGS

Bridge Campground　　　　　　　　　$10
San Juan National Forest
2.5 mi W of Pagosa Springs on US 160; 17 mi N on FR 631 (Piedra Rd); at Williams Creek. $10 with federal senior pass; others pay $20. 5/5-10/1; 30-day limit. 19 sites; 50-ft RV limit. Tbls, toilets, cfga, drkg wtr. Fishing.

Cimarrona Campground　　　　　　　　$10
San Juan National Forest
2.5 mi W of Pagosa Springs on US 160; 20 mi N on FR 631 (Piedra Rd); 3 mi N on FR 640; at Cimarrona Creek. $10 with federal senior pass; others pay $20. 5/5-11/15; 30-day limit (half price but no wtr or services after 9/30). 21 sites; 35-ft RV limit. Tbls, toilets, cfga, drkg wtr. Fishing, hiking, horseback riding.

East Fork Campground $10
San Juan National Forest

10 mi E of Pagosa Springs on US 160; left for 0.7 mi on FR 667 (East Fork Rd); on East Fork of San Juan River. $10 with federal senior pass; others pay $20. 5/5-LD; 30-day limit. 26 sites; 35-ft RV limit. Tbls, toilets, cfga, drkg wtr. Fishing, hiking; OHV use nearby. Elev 7600 ft; 20 acres.

Navajo State Park $10

17 mi W of Pagosa Springs on US 160; 18 mi SW on CR 151; 2 mi S on CR 982; at Navajo Lake. $10 base ($7 for CO seniors with Aspen Leaf pass). All year. Base fee at 19 primitive sites with cfga & tbls (reduced fees off-season at Windsurf Beach & Arbles Point); $20 at developed non-elec sites; $30 full hookups. 138 sites. Tbls, toilets, cfga, drkg wtr, hookups($), showers, dump. Visitor center, interpretive programs, snack bar, boating(ldr), waterskiing, sailboarding, fishing, hiking trails, hunting, mountain biking trails, winter sports. Elev 6100 ft; 2,672 acres. Entry fee.

Teal Campground $11
San Juan National Forest

2.5 mi W of Pagosa Springs on US 160; 20 mi N on FR 631 (Piedra Rd); 1.5 mi N on FR 640; on Williams Creek Reservoir. $11 with federal senior pass; others pay $22. 5/5-11/15; 14-day limit. No wtr & limited services after 9/15 (fee half price). 16 sites; 35-ft RV limit. Tbls, toilets, cfga, drkg wtr. Fishing, boating (l). 10 acres; elev 8300 ft.

West Fork Campground $10
San Juan National Forest

14 mi E of Pagosa Springs on US 160; left for 1.5 mi on FR 648 (West Fork Rd); on West Fork of San Juan River. $10 with federal senior pass; others pay $20. 5/5-9/15; 30-day limit. 28 sites; 35-ft RV limit. Tbls, toilets, cfga, drkg wtr. Fishing, hiking. Elev 8000 ft; 10 acres.

Williams Creek Campground $11
San Juan National Forest

2/5 mi W of Pagosa Springs on US 160; 20 mi N on FR 631 (Piedra Rd); half mi N on FR 640; near Williams Creek Reservoir (4 mi N of Bridge Campground). $11 with federal senior pass; others pay $22. 5/5-9/15; 14-day limit. 67 sites; 45-ft RV limit. Tbls, toilets, cfga, drkg wtr, some wtr & sewer hookups, free dump nearby at Piedra & Williams Creek Rds. Fishing. Elev 8300 ft; 12 acres.

PAONIA
Erikson Springs $7
Gunnison National Forest

About 18 mi NE of Paonia on SR 133; 7 mi E on CR 12. $7 with federal senior pass; others pay $14 during about 5/23-9/30; free 10/1-11/15 but no wtr or services. 14-day limit. 18 sites up to 35 ft. Tbls, toilets, cfga, drkg wtr. Fishing (Anthracite Creek), hiking, ATV & horseback riding. Paonia State Recreation Area nearby. Elev 6800 ft.

Lost Lake Campground $9
Gunnison National Forest

16 mi E of Paonia on SR 133; right on CR 12 (Kebler Pass Rd for 16 mi,, then right on FR 706 for 2 mi to its end at Lost Lake. $9 with federal senior pass; others pay $18. 6/15-9/30; 16-day limit. 18 sites 21-28 ft. Tbls, toilets, cfga, drkg wtr. 5 new equestrian sites. Fishing platform added; trails improved. Boating (d), picnicking, fishing, hiking. Elev 9600 ft; 3 acres. Non-campers pay $4 day use fee.

McClure Campground   FREE
Gunnison National Forest

30 mi NE of Paonia on US 133; on S side; at Lee Creek. Free. MD-10/15; 14-day limit. 17 sites (35-ft RV limit). Tbls, toilets, cfga, no drkg wtr or trash service. Hiking, fishing. McClure Pass nearby. Elev 8000 ft; 5 acres. Joint project of forest service & Oxbow Mine.

PARSHALL
Hot Sulphur Springs State Wildlife Area   FREE

2 mi E of Parshall on US 40. Free. All year; 14-day limit. Camp only at Lone Buck Campground, Pioneer Park or Beaver Creek area. 50 sites (RVs under 16 ft). Tbls, toilets, cfga, no drkg wtr except at E end of Pioneer Park bridge. Fishing, big-game hunting, shooting range, birdwatching. Elev 7600 ft.

Horseshoe Campground $8
Roosevelt National Forest

About 18 mi S of Parshall on CR 3, then onto FR 139; at Williams Fork River. $8 with federal senior pass; others pay $16. 6/1-10/15; 14-day limit. 7 sites; 50-ft RV limit. Tbls, toilets, cfga, no drkg wtr. Hiking, fishing.

South Fork $8.50
Roosevelt National Forest

25 mi S of Parshal on US 40, in Williams Fork Valley, off CR 3 on FR 138. $8.50 with federal senior pass; others pay $17. About 6/1-10/15. 21 sites; 23-ft RV limit. Tbls, toilets, cfga, drkg wtr, corral, accessible boardwalk. Hiking, horseback riding, OHV trails. Elev 8970 ft.

PITKIN
Middle Quartz Campground   FREE
Gunnison National Forest

1.5 mi NE of Pitkin on FR 765; 5.5 mi NE on FR 767. Free but donations accepted. About 6/1-LD; 14-day limit. Sites open through hunting season, but no trash services. 7 sites; 16-ft RV limit. Tbls, toilet, cfga, no drkg wtr. Mountain climbing, fishing, 4x4 activity. Elev 10,200 ft; 3 acres. Stream. Historic.

Pitkin Campground $8
Gunnison National Forest

1 mi E of Pitkin on FR 765. $8 with federal senior pass; others pay $16. 5/15-9/30; 14-day limit. 22 sites (35-ft RV

limit). Tbls, toilets, cfga, drkg wtr. Fishing (Quartz Creek), 4WD trails. Elev 9400 ft; 8 acres.

Quartz Campground $10
Gunnison National Forest

4 mi N of Pitkin on FR 765. $10. About 5/23-LD; 14-day limit. 10 sites (16-ft RV limit). Tbls, toilet, cfga, drkg wtr. Fishing (North Quartz Creek), rockhounding.

PONCHA SPRINGS
Monarch Park $9
San Isabel National Forest

14.5 mi W of Poncha Springs on US 50; .7 mi E on FR 231; at South Fork of Arkansas River. $9 with federal senior pass; others pay $18. 6/9-LD; 14-day limit. 36 sites (45-ft RV limit). Tbls, toilets, cfga, drkg wtr (limited), fishing dock. Hiking & mountain biking trails, fishing, 4x4 activities. Elev 10,500 ft; 17 acres.

North Fork Reservoir Campground $9
San Isabel National Forest

6 mi W of Poncha Springs on US 50; 10.2 mi N on CR 240 (very rough, not recommended for vehicles towing trailers; high clearance necessary). $9 with federal senior pass; others pay $18. 6/9-LD; 14-day limit. Free pre-season & post-season but no services or toilets. 9 sites (RVs under 26 ft). Tbls, toilets, cfga, no drkg wtr, no trash service. Boating, fishing (no mtrs). Elev 11,000 ft.

O'Haver Lake Campground $10
San Isabel National Forest

4.5 mi S of Poncha Springs on US 285; 2.3 mi SW on CR 200; 1.5 mi W on CR 202; rd has several sharp curves. $10 with federal senior pass; others pay $20. 5/19-9/30; 14-day limit. 28 sites (45-ft RV limit). Tbls, toilets, cfga, drkg wtr. Fishing, hiking & biking trails, fishing pier, weekend interpretive programs. Elev 9200 ft. 15-acre lake.

POWDERHORN
Cebolla Creek Recreation Site $8
Bureau of Land Management
Gunnison Field Office

S from SR 149 at Powderhorn turnoff; S on CR 27 along Cebolla Creek for 8 mi; right to area marked "Cebolla Campground." $8. MD-LD; 14-day limit. 5 sites (30 ft RV limit) in Cebolla Creek Wildlife Area. Tbls, toilet, cfga, no drkg wtr or trash service. Fishing, swimming. Elev 9500 ft.

RED CLIFF
Gold Park Campground $10.50
White River National Forest

3 mi S of Red Cliff on US 24; 9 no SW on FR 703. $10.50 with federal senior pass; others pay $21. MD-10/1; 10-day limit. 12 sites (40-ft RV limit). Tbls, toilets, cfga, drkg wtr. Fishing, hiking. Elev 9300 ft; 4 acres. Homestake Creek nearby. "Food storage order" issued for 2017 due to bear activity.

Homestake Road FREE
Dispersed Camping Area
White River National Forest

3 mi S of Red Cliff on US 24; SW on FR 703 (Homestake Rd) between former Blodgett (now closed) and Gold Park Campgrounds. Free. Primitive undesignated sites along the road near Homestake Creek. No facilities, no drkg wtr.

Hornsilver Campground $9.50
White River National Forest

2.5 mi S of Red Cliff on US 24; at Homestake Creek. $9.50 with federal senior pass; others pay $19. About 5/15-10/2; 10-day limit; free rest of year if accessible, but no wtr or trash service. 12 sites (30-ft RV limit). Tbls, toilets, cfga, drkg wtr. Fishing, hiking. Eagle River. Elev 8800 ft; 5 acres. "Food storage order" issued in 2017 due to bear activity.

RED FEATHER LAKES
Dowdy Lake $11
Roosevelt National Forest

1 mi E of Red Feather Lakes on CR 74E; half mi N on FR 218 (gravel). $11 with federal senior pass; others pay $22 during MD-9/24; 25% fee discount when wtr off. $5 surcharge for elec. All year; 10-day limit. 62 sites (40-ft RV limit). Tbls, toilets, cfga, drkg wtr. Picnicking, boating(l), fishing, hiking, biking. Elev 8100 ft.

North Fork Poudre $7
Roosevelt National Forest

1 mi S of Red Feather Lakes on CR 4; 7 mi W on FR 162. $7 with federal senior pass; others pay $14. 6/15-10/29; 14-day limit. 9 sites (RVs under 31 ft). Tbls, toilets, cfga, drkg wtr except after 10/16. Fishing, horseback riding. Elev 9200 ft. Stream. Beside north fork of Poudre River.

West Lake Campground $11
Roosevelt National Forest

S of Red Feather Lakes to CR 75, then E to campground. $11 with federal senior pass; others pay $22. $5 surcharge for elec. MD-9/24; 14-day limit. 35 sites; 50-ft RV limit. Tbls, toilets, cfga, drkg wtr. Fishing, boating, hiking trail.

RICO
Cayton Campground $11
San Juan National Forest

6 mi NE of Rico on SR 145; half mi E on FR 578. $1 base with federal senior pass; others pay $22 base (surcharge for 30/50-amp elec). MD-9/15; 30-day limit. 27 sites; 50-ft RV limit. Tbls, toilets, cfga, drkg wtr, dump ($5). Fishing, hiking. Elev 9400 ft; 11 acres. Popular in summer.

RIFLE
West Rifle Creek State Wildlife Area FREE
4 mi NE of Rifle on Hwy 13; 6 mi on Hwy 325; 1 mi NW

on CR 252. Free. Camping LD-12/31 (deer & elk seasons); 14-day limit during 45-day period. 6 primitive campsites. Toilets, cfga, tbls, drkg wtr. Hiking, hunting, fishing. Elev 7700 ft; 320 acres; 2 mi of water.

RIO BLANCO
Piceance State Wildlife Area   FREE
20 mi N of Rio Blanco on Hwy 13; then follow signs on CR 5 (4 different entrances). Free. All year; 14-day limit during 45-day period. Primitive campsites. Toilets, cfga, tbls, drkg wtr. Fishing, hunting on 29,000 acres; elev 6200 ft. Campfires only in designated areas.

ROCKY FORD
Rocky Ford West State Wildlife Area   FREE
3 mi N of Rocky Ford on Hwy 17; 1 mi E on CR 805. Free. Primitive campsites; no facilities. Fishing in Arkansas River, hiking, hunting.

Timpas Creek State Wildlife Area   FREE
4 mi S of Rocky Ford on Hwy 71; 2 mi NE on Hwy 266, across river bridge; 1 mi S on CR 21; 1 mi W on CR Z. Free. All year; 14-day limit during 45-day period. Primitive camping. No facilities. Hunting, fishing. Lots of water pot-holes; 141 acres; elev 4000 ft. Fires prohibited.

RYE
St. Charles Campground $9
San Isabel National Forest
10 mi NW of Rye on SR 165; 1 mi W on FR 308; at St. Charles Creek. $9 with federal senior pass; others pay $18. Reservations required at 10 of 15 sites, adding $9 fee to the cost during MD-LD; open without reservations until 10/16; 14-day limit. 15 sites (35-ft RV limit). Tbls, cfga, drkg wtr, toilets. Hiking, fishing, boating(l). Elev 8400 ft; 10 acres. With reservations, 2-day minimum stay on weekends. Nearby LaVista Campground $24 plus reservation fee.

Southside Campground $8.50
San Isabel National Forest
10 mi NW of Rye on SR 165; half mi W on FR 308. $8.50 with federal senior pass; others pay $17. 5/19-9/25; 14-day limit. 8 RV sites (30-ft RV limit). Tbls, toilets, cfga, limited drkg wtr. Boating(ld), fishing, hiking trail. Elev 8400 ft.

SAGUACHE
Buffalo Pass $5
Rio Grande National Forest
27.6 mi NW of Saguache on SR 114; 1.7 mi S on FR 775. $5 during 5/20-11/25; 14-day limit. 19 sites; 4 pull-through (RVs under 32 ft). Tbls, toilets, cfga, firewood, no drkg wtr or trash collection. Elev 9100 ft; 37 acres. At old Indian camp site & on old stage route.

Horse Canyon Road Area   FREE
Rio Grande National Forest
33 mi NW of Saguache on SR 114; 4 mi S on county rd, then 1.5 mi E on county rd to Saguache Park Rd 787; 8 mi S on Rd 787 to N end of Saguache Park, at jct with Middle Fork Saguache Rd (FR 744) about 1.5 mi W of Stone Cellar Campground. Find several good primitive sites along the roads in this area, including North Ford Rd 766, FR 745 and FR 744. Free. All year; 14-day limit. No facilities; no drkg wtr. Hiking, fishing.

Luders Creek $5
Rio Grande National Forest
22 mi NW of Saguache on SR 114; 11 mi NW on FR 750 (CR NN 14). $5. 5/20-11/25 or when accessible; 14-day limit. 5 sites; 3 pull-through (RVs under 26 ft). Tbls, toilets, cfga, firewood, no drkg wtr or trash service. Elev 9200 ft; 2 acres. Near old Cochetopa Pass on Ute Trail. FR 750 was one of the famous toll roads leading west built by Otto Mears in 1876. 4WD rds 2 mi E.

Stone Cellar $5
Rio Grande National Forest
22 mi NW of Saguache on SR 114; 18.7 mi NW on FR 750; 16.4 mi S on FR 787. $5. MD-11/25; 14-day limit. 6 sites (RVs under 26 ft). Tbls, toilets, cfga, firewood, well drkg wtr, no trash service. Fishing. Elev 9500 ft; 3 acres. Roll-ing hills, grassy terrain. Stream. Near Indian and Soldier Battleground. Pets on leash. On middle fork of Saguache Creek. 4WD activities nearby on FRs 774 & 776.

Trickle Mountain Wildlife Habitat Area   FREE
Bureau of Land Management
From Saguache on US 285, W 15 mi on SR 114. Area is N of highway. Free. All year; 14-day limit. No established campsites; undesignated camping. 52,565 acres. One of few places where bighorn sheep, elk, mule deer, prong-horn use same area; large pronghorn herd.

SALIDA
Angel of Shavano Campground $9
San Isabel National Forest
10 mi W of Salida on US 50; 4 mi N on CR 240; 1 mi on gravel rd; access rd rough, so high-clearance vehicles recommended; near North Fork of South Arkansas River. $9 with federal senior pass; others pay $18. 5/19-LD; 14-day limit. 20 sites; 30-ft RV limit. Tbls, toilets, cfga, limited drkg wtr. Hiking, fishing. Elev 9200 ft; 10 acres.

Salida East   FREE
Bureau of Land Management
Just E of Salida on N side of US 50. Free. Primitive undes-ignated camping; no facilities.

SAN ISABEL
Ophir Creek Campground $8.50
San Isabel National Forest
6 mi N of San Isabel on SR 165; left (W) on FR 360 about 100 ft, then left (E) on FR 361 to its end. $8.50 with federal senior pass; others pay $17. MD-LD (free through 10/15 with reduced services); 10-day limit. 12 RV sites (30-ft RV limit). Tbls, toilets, cfga, drkg wtr. Hiking, fishing, biking. Elev 8900 ft; 14-acres.

SARGENTS
Snowblind Campground $12
Gunnison National Forest
1.1 mi NE of Sargents on US 50; 6.9 mi N on FR 888. $12. 5/15-9/15; 16-day limit. 23 sites (RVs under 22 ft). Tbls, toilets, cfga, drkg wtr. Mountain climbing, fishing, off-roading. Elev 9800 ft; 10 acres. Stream. Scenic. Old mining town of Whitepine is 2 mi N. Canyon Creek Trailhead 1 mi SW.

SEDALIA
Devils Head $9
Pike National Forest
10 mi W of Sedalia on SR 67; 9 mi SE on FR 300; half mi SE on FR 3008C. $9 with federal senior pass; others pay $18. 5/22-9/8; free later when weather permits access, but reduced services. 14-day limit. 21 sites (22-ft RV limit). Tbls, toilets, cfga, no drkg wtr. Hiking, dirt biking. Elev 8800 ft; 10 acres. Fire lookout trail open to visitors.

Flat Rocks Campground $9
Pike National Forest
10 mi SW of Sedalia on SR 67; 4.7 mi S on FR 300. $9 with federal senior pass; others pay $18. 5/15-9/5; free off-season when weather permits access but no wtr & reduced services. 14-day limit. 19 sites (30-ft RV limit). Tbls, toilets, cfga, drkg wtr. Elev 8200 ft; 8 acres. Primarily an OHV campground.

Indian Creek Campground $8
Pike National Forest
10 mi SW of Sedalia on SR 67; .3 mi W on CR 67. $8 with federal senior pass; others pay $16. MD-LD; 14-day limit. 11 sites; 20-ft RV limit. Tbls, toilets, cfga, drkg wtr. Mountain biking, hiking, bridle trail, fishing. Equestrian campground nearby. Elev 7500 ft.

SILVERTHORNE
Blue River Campground $8.50
White River National Forest
From I-70 exit 205 at Silverthorne, 6 mi N on Hwy 9. $8.50 with federal senior pass; others pay $17. 5/20-10/2; 10-day limit (services & fees reduced after LD). 24 sites; 25-ft RV limit. Tbls, toilets, cfga, drkg wtr. Fishing, biking. Camp closed periodically due to bear problems. Traffic noises. "Food storage order" issues for 2017 due to bear activity.

Lowry Campground $11
White River National Forest
About 4 mi E of Silverthorne on Hwy 6; right on Swan Mountain Rd. $11 base with federal senior pass; others pay $22 base ($5 surcharge for elec). MD-LD; 14-day limit. Fee & services may be reduced in fall. 24 sites; 32-ft RV limit. Tbls, toilets, cfga, drkg wtr, elec($), dump. Fishing, boating, hiking. Elev 9300 ft.

SILVERTON
Sig Creek Campground $10
San Juan National Forest
21 mi SW of Silverton on US 550; 6 mi W on FR 578 (Hermosa Park Rd). $10 during MD-LD ($5 off-season, but no wtr or services); 14-day limit. 9 sites (30-ft RV limit). Tbls, toilets, cfga, drkg wtr. Fishing, hiking. 4 acres.

South Mineral Dispersed Camping Area   FREE
San Juan National Forest
4 mi NW of Silverton on US 550; 1-5 mi W on FR 585. Free. All year; 14-day limit. Primitive, designated open sites along FR 585 on way to South Mineral Campground, where fee is charged. No facilities. Fishing, hiking.

SOUTH FORK
Cathedral   FREE
Rio Grande National Forest
5 mi E of South Fork on US 160; 1.6 mi N on CR 18; 3.1 mi N on FR 650; 7 mi NW on FR 640; at Embargo Creek. Free about 4/15-11/15 or when not accessible by snow; 14-day limit. 22 sites; 5 pull-through; sites up to 45 ft. Tbls, toilet, cfga, firewood, no drkg wtr or trash service. Fishing, hiking. Elev 9500 ft; 16 acres.

Cross Creek $8.50
Rio Grande National Forest
2 mi S of South Fork on US 160; from jct of FR 360 (Beaver Creek Rd), E to campground. $8.50 with federal senior pass; others pay $17 during MD-LD; free off-season, but no wtr or trash service; 14-day limit. 12 sites; 25-ft RV limit. Tbls, toilets, cfga, drkg wtr. Boating(l), fishing. Beaver Reservoir qtr mi N. Elev 8840 ft.

Highway Springs Camp $6.50
Rio Grande National Forest
5.2 mi SW of South Fork on US 160. On South Fork of Rio Grande. $6.50 with federal senior pass; others pay $13 during MD-LD; 14-day limit. 13 sites, 3 pull-through (RVs under 36 ft). 4 acres. Tbls, toilets, cfga, firewood, no drkg wtr. Fishing. Elev 8400 ft.

Lower Beaver Creek Camp $8.50
Rio Grande National Forest
2.4 mi SW of South Fork on US 160; 3 mi S on FR 360. $8.50 with federal senior pass; others pay $17 during MD-LD. 4 sites open outside gate in fall but no wtr or ser-

vices. 14-day limit. 18 sites (RVs under 36 ft). Firewood, drkg wtr. Elev 8400 ft. Boating(d), horseback riding.

Palisade Campgound $9
Rio Grande National Forest
9.5 mi N of South Fork on Hwy 149. $9 with federal senior pass; others pay $18 during MD-LD; free until snow prevents access, but no wtr or trash service; 14-day limit. 12 sites (30-ft RV limit). Tbls, toilets, cfga, drkg wtr. Fishing. This is the only campground between South Fork & Creede; it is usually full mid-June through Aug.

Park Creek $8.50
Rio Grande National Forest
9 mi SW of South Fork on US 160. $8.50 with federal senior pass; others pay $17. MD-LD; 14-day limit. 13 gravel sites; 35-ft RV limit. Tbls, toilets, cfga, drkg wtr. Fishing. Elev 8500 ft.

Tucker Ponds Camp $8
Rio Grande National Forest
Approx 11 mi W of South Fork on US 160; 3 mi S on FR 390. $8 with federal senior pass; others pay $16 during MD-LD; 14-day limit. Not open off-season. 19 sites (RVs under 35 ft). 16 acres. Tbls, toilets, cfga, firewood, drkg wtr. Berry picking, lake fishing. Elev 9700 ft.

Upper Beaver Camp $8.50
Rio Grande National Forest
2.4 mi SW of South Fork on US 160; 4 mi S on FR 360. (1 mi farther S of FR 360 past Beaver Creek campground.) $8.50 with federal senior pass during MD-LD; others pay $17. 14-day limit. Not open off-season. 14 sites (RVs under 36 ft). 5 acres. Firewood, drkg wtr. Boating(d), horseback riding, fishing. Elev 8400 ft.

SPRINGFIELD
Two Buttes Reservoir State Wildlife Area FREE
18 mi N of Springfield on US 385/287; 3 mi E on CR B5. Free. 5/1-10/31. 75 sites. Tbls, toilets, cfga, drkg wtr, dump. Store (1 mi). Boating (rl); picnicking, swimming, fishing; waterfowl, small game hunting. Pets on leash. 4,995 land acres; 1,798 water acres. Water level varies. Elev 4400 ft.

STEAMBOAT SPRINGS
Dry Lake Campground $10
Routt National Forest
4 mi N of Steamboat Springs on CR 36 (Strawberry Park Rd); 3 mi E on FR 60 (Buffalo Pass Rd). $10. 6/10-11/1; 14-day limit. 8 sites; 20-ft RV limit. Tbls, toilets, cfga, no drkg wtr. Fishing nearby. Elev 8000 ft.

Dumont Lake Campground $12
Routt National Forest
22.3 mi SE of Steamboat Springs on US 40; 1.5 mi NE on FR 311; half mi N on FR 312. $12. 6/15-10/1; 14-day

limit. 22 sites; 40-ft RV limit. Tbls, toilets, cfga, drkg wtr. Boating(l), fishing, mountain biking, hiking trail. Elev 9500 ft; 5 acres.

Granite Campground $10
Routt National Forest
4 mi S of Buffalo Pass on FR 310; high-clearance vehicles suggested. $10. 6/15-10/1; 14-day limit. 8 sites (4 walk-in); 22-ft RV limit. Tbls, toilets, cfga, no drkg wtr or trash service. Fishing, boating (no mtrs). On shore of recently enlarged Fish Creek Reservoir.

Meadows Campground $10
Routt National Forest
15 mi SE of Steamboat Springs on US 40. $10. 7/1-9/15; 14-day limit. 30 sites; 40-ft RV limit. Tbls, toilets, cfga, no drkg wtr. Fishing, hiking, mountain biking. Elev 9300 ft; 7 acres.

Stagecoach State Park $10
4 mi E of Steamboat Springs on US 40; 5 mi S on SR 131; 7 mi S on CR 14; in Yampa Valley. $10 base ($7 for CO senios with Aspen Leaf pass). All year. 92 sites. Base fee for 9 primitive sites at McKindley Campground; $20 for 18 basic sites at Harding Spur Camp; higher fees at other campgrounds. Tbls, toilets, cfga, drkg wtr, dump, showers, elec($). Interpretive programs, swimming, snack bar, boating(ldr), waterskiing, sailboarding(r), fishing, hiking trails, biking trails, winter sports. Elev 7250 ft; 866 acres. Entry fee.

Summit Lake Campground $10
Routt National Forest
4 mi N of Steamboat Springs on CR 36; 11.6 mi E on FR 60. $10. 7/10-9/30; 14-day limit. 9 back-in RV sites; 22-ft RV limit. All year; 14-day limit. Tbls, toilets, cfga, drkg wtr (no wtr after LD). Fishing, mountain biking, hiking, ATV use. Elev 10,300 ft. 1 mi S of Mt Zirkel Wilderness.

TELLURIDE
Alta Lakes Dispersed Sites FREE
Uncompahgre National Forest
S on SR 145 from Telluride to Boomerang Rd (FR 632), the 3 mi E to lakes. Free. About 16 undesignated primitive campsites for tents or self-contained RVs; about 7 sites. Toilet, cfga, no drkg wtr or trash service. Fishing, hiking.

Illum Valley Dispersed Sites FREE
Uncompahgre National Forest
5 mi W of Telluride on SR 145; S on FR 625 (Illium Valley Rd). Free. Undesignated primitive sites along road next to South Fork of San Miguel River. Hiking, fishing.

Matterhorn $11
Uncompahgre National Forest
12 mi SW of Telluride on Hwy 145. $11 base with federal senior pass without hookups ($10 surcharge for elec/

sewer); others pay $22 base. 5/151-9/30; 7-day limit. 28 sites (4 with elec); 35-ft RV limit. Tbls, flush toilets, cfga, drkg wtr, showers, hookups($). Fishing, hiking.

Priest Lake Dispersed Sites FREE
Uncompahgre National Forest
14 mi S of Telluride on SR 145. All year; 14-day limit. Primitive undesignated sites, best for pop-up campers & vans. No facilities except toilet, cfga. Fishing, hiking.

TRINIDAD
James M. John FREE
and Lake Dorothey State Wildlife Area
S on I-25 17 mi from Trinidad to Folsom exit at Raton, NM; then NM Hwys 526 and 72 up Sugarite Canyon 12 mi; area begins at state line. Access limited to foot or horseback from parking areas. Free. All year; 14-day limit during 45-day period. Primitive tent camping. Toilets, cfga, tbls. Camping prohibited within 200 yards of lake or 100 feet of stream except in designated areas. Fishing; small game, deer, turkey hunting. 4800 acres. 4-acre lake.

VAIL
Gore Creek Campground $11
White River National Forest
From I-70 exit 180 E of Vail, turn right on S frontage rd (Bighorn Rd), then E about 2 mi to its closure gate; camp on left before gate; along Gore Creek near Eagle's Nest Wilderness. $11 base with federal senior pass; others pay $22 base, $24 for premium locations ($12 with senior pass). 5/15-10/1; 14-day limit. 25 sites; 35-ft RV limit. Tbls, toilets, cfga, no drkg wtr. Hiking trails, fishing, horseback riding. Bear food storage order issued in 2017 due to bear activity.

VICTOR
Skagway Reservoir FREE
and Beaver Creek State Wildlife Area
Half mi E of Victor on CR 67; 6.5 mi S on CR 441. Free. All year; 14-day limit during 45-day period. Primitive camping for self-contained RVs; 90 acres. Toilets, cfga. Boating(l), fishing, picnicking. Elev 9000 ft.

WALDEN
Aspen Campground $10
Routt National Forest
22 mi SE of Walden on SR 14; at Gould, 1 mi S on FR 740 (CR 14); qtr mi W on FR 741; at S fork of Michigan River. May be closed as developed campground, but free dispersed camping. MD-LD; 14-day limit. 7 sites; 22-ft RV limit. Tbls, toilets, cfga, no drkg wtr. Fishing. Elev 8900 ft. Near Colorado State Forest.

Big Creek Lakes Campground $10
Routt National Forest
7 mi N of Walden on SR 125; 18.2 mi NW of Cowdrey on CR 6; 5.7 mi SW on FR 600. $10. 6/15-LD; 14-day limit.

Free for dispersed camping off-season, but no services; no drkg wtr after about 8/15. 54 sites; 45-ft RV limit. Tbls, toilets, cfga, drkg wtr. Swimming, boating(l), fishing, waterskiing, hiking trails. Elev 9000 ft; 17 acres.

Colorado State Forest $10
21 mi E of Walden on SR 14. $10 ($7 for CO seniors with Aspen Leaf pass). All year. 158 basic sites plus backcountry areas. Tbls, toilets, cfga, drkg wtr, dump (at Ranger Lakes parking lot). Boating(l), fishing, hiking trails, biking trails, bridle trails, horse facilities, winter sports. Elev 10,000 ft; 70,000 acres (50,000 in backcountry). Entry fee. The following are campground and camping areas within Colorado State Forest:

Ranger Lakes. Accessible directly from Hwy 14, about 6 mi W of Cameron Pass; camp within short walk of lakes. 32 sites, some newly renovated. Tbls, toilets, cfga, drkg wtr, dump. Fishing, nature trail, summer interpretive programs weekend evenings. No boats.

The Crags. Access steep, narrow & winding; not recommended for large RVs. 26 sites. Tbls, toilets, cfga, drkg wtr. Access rd steep, narrow, winding; not recommended for RVs.

North Michigan Reservoir. 48 sites around the lake. Drkg wtr, cfga, toilets, tbls. Fishing, but no swimming; no-wake boating. 2 boat ramps. Sites on S side newly renovated.

Bochman. 1 mi N of North Michigan Reservoir. Toilets, cfga, drkg wtr 52 sites, most undesignated.

Ruby Jewel Lake. Access via Ruby Jewel Rd. Backcountry camping. Artificial lures only for lake's cutthroat trout.

Delaney Butte Lakes State Wildlife Area FREE
Half mi W of Walden on SR 14 to CR 18; 4.5 mi W to CR 5; 1 mi N. Follow signs. Free. All year; 14-day limit during 45-day period. 150 primitive sites. Tbls, toilets, cfga, drkg wtr, shelters. Boating (rl), waterskiing, fishing, small-game hunting. Elev 8100 ft; 300 acres. Pets. 150 water acres. Bleak terrain, few trees. Gusty winds.

Hidden Lakes Campground $10
Routt National Forest
13 mi SW of Walden on SR 14; 10.5 mi N on CR 234; 1.2 mi W on FR 60. $10. 6/15-LD; 14-day limit; free dispersed camping off-season but no services or wtr. 9 sites (RVs under 20 ft). Tbls, toilets, cfga, drkg wtr. Fishing, boating(no mtrs).

Murphy State Wildlife Area FREE
1 mi E of Walden on CR 12. Free. All year; 14-day limit in 45-day period. Primitive camping; no facilities. Fishing, photography. No hunting.

Owl Mountain FREE
State Wildlife Area
13 mi E of Walden on Hwy 14; 6 mi S on CR 25. Free.

8/15-3/1; 14-day limit. Primitive undesignated camping at 920-acre wildlife area. Hunting, hiking.

Pines Campground $10
Routt National Forest
22 mi SE of Walden on SR 14; at Gould, 3.5 mi S on FR 740 (CR 14); at South Fork of Michigan River. $10. MD-LD; 14-day limit; free dispersed camping off-season, but no services or wtr. 11 sites (RVs under 20 ft). Tbls, toilets, cfga, drkg wtr. Fishing. Elev 9200 ft; 5 acres.

Seymour Lake State Wildlife Area FREE
From jct of SR 14 & SR 125, 16.2 mi W on SR 14 to CR 28; 1 mi on CR 28; 1 mi on CR 28 to CR 11; 4 mi on CR 11. Free. All year; 14-day limit during 45-day period. Undesignated primitive campsites. Toilets, cfga, tbls, no drkg wtr. Boating(l).

Teal Lake Campground $10
Routt National Forest
13 mi SW of Walden on SR 14; 10.5 mi W on CR 24; 1 mi E on FR 60. $10. 6/1-LD; 14-day limit; free dispersed camping off-season, but no services or wtr. 17 sites; 22-ft RV limit. Tbls, toilets, cfga, drkg wtr. Fishing, hiking, boating (no gas mtrs).

WALSH

Burchfield State Wildlife Area FREE
11 mi E of Walsh on CR DD. Free. All year. 14-day limit in 45-day period. Camping space near dry lake; 117 acres. No facilities. Small-game hunting. Elev 4000 ft.

WARD

Camp Dick Campground $10.50
Roosevelt National Forest
6.5 mi N of Ward on SR 72; following signs W on Middle Saint Vrain Rd (CR 92 & FR 114) for 1 mi; along Middle Saint Vrain Creek. $10.50 with federal senior pass; others pay $21. About 5/15-11/20; 14-day limit. 41 sites; 45-ft RV limit. Tbls, toilets, cfga, drkg wtr. Fishing, hiking, horseback riding.

Pawnee Campground $10.50
Brainard Lake Recreation Area
Roosevelt National Forest
From Ward at SR 72, follow signs W to Brainard Lake Recreation Area. $10.50 with federal senior pass during 6/10-9/10; others pay $21. Day use fee also charged. 14-day limit. 47 sites; no RV size limit. Tbls, pit toilets, cfga, drkg wtr. Biking, fishing, hiking. Elev 10,500 ft.

WESTCLIFFE

Alvarado Campground $9
San Isabel National Forest
3.5 mi S of Westcliffe on SR 69; 5.2 mi W on CR 302; 1.3 mi SW on FR 302. $9 with federal senior pass; others pay $18. 5/19-9/25; 14-day limit; reservations required

during peak June-Aug period. 50 sites (typically 35 ft). Tbls, toilets, cfga, drkg wtr. Hiking, fishing. Secluded. 3 equestrian sites.

DeWeese Reservoir State Wildlife Area FREE
5 mi NW of Westcliffe on Hwy 69; 1.5 mi N on Copper Gulch Rd, then follow signs. Free. All year; 14-day limit in 45-day period. Primitive undesignated sites. Tbls, toilets, cfga, no drkg wtr. Boating(l), fishing, hunting.

Lake Creek Campground $8.50
San Isabel National Forest
About 12 mi NW of Westcliffe on SR 69 to Hillside; 3 mi W on FR 300. $8.50 with federal senior pass; others pay $17. 5/19-9/25; 14-day limit. 11 sites (small RVs). Tbls, toilets, cfga, drkg wtr. Fishing, hiking. Secluded. Closed temporarily in 2017 due to forest fire.

Middle Taylor Creek State Wildlife Areaa FREE
8 mi W of Westcliff on Hermit Lakes Rd. Free. All year; 14-day limit during 45-day period. Primitive campsites. Toilets, cfga, tbls. Hunting, fishing. Elev 11,000 ft; 486 acres. Small stream. National forest access.

WHITEWATER

Divide Forks Campground FREE
Uncompahgre National Forest
13 mi SW of Whitewater on SR 141; 15 mi SW on FR 402. Free. 5/20-11/1. 11 sites; 20-ft RV limit. Tbls, toilet, cfga, no drkg wtr. Elev 9200 ft; 4 acres.

WINTER PARK

Idlewild Campground $10
Arapaho National Forest
1 mi S of Winter Park on US 40. $10 with federal senior pass; others pay $20. MD-9/25; 14-day limit. 26 sites (30-ft RV limit). Tbls, toilets, cfga, drkg wtr. Fishing, mountain biking, hiking. Elev 9000 ft; 10 acres.

Robbers Roost $10
Roosevelt National Forest
5 mi N of Ward on SR 72 (signs); 1 mi W on Middle Saint Vrain Rd (CR 92 & FR 114); at Middle Saint Vrain Creek. $10 with federal senior pass; others pay $20. About 6/1-LD; 14-day limit. 11 sites; 25-ft RV limit. Tbls, pit toilets, cfga, drkg wtr. Biking & hiking trail, horseback riding. Operated by Fraser Valley Lions Club.

WOLCOTT

Castle Peak Wilderness Study Area FREE
Bureau of Land Management
N on SR 131 from Wolcott several mi, left on dirt rd labeled "Milk Creek." Follow signs to Horse Mountain. Free. All year; 14-day limit. Undesignated sites. No facilities. Fishing, hunting, hiking, backpacking, horse trails. Elev from 8000 ft. Streams, lakes.

Wolcott Recreation Site $10
Eagle River Recreation Area
Bureau of Land Management
From I-70 exit 157 at Wolcott, 1.7 mi W on Hwy 6; at Eagle River. $10. All year; 7-day limit during 4/1-8/31; 14 days 9/1-3/31. 6 primitive sites. Toilets, cfga, tbls, no drkg wtr; no trash in summer. Boating(l), fishing, rock climbing.

WOODLAND PARK
Lone Rock Campground $9
Pike National Forest
20.6 mi N of Woodland Park on SR 67; at Decker, bear left at "Y" onto CR 126 for 0.7 mi to campground sign; right into camp; on South Platte River. All year; 14-day limit. During MD-LD, $9 with federal senior pass; others pay $18; free or lower rates rest of year, but no wtr. Reservations nearly always required; with reservations, 2-night minimum stay required. 18 sites; 30-ft RV limit. Tbls, toilets, cfga, drkg wtr. Boating, fishing.

Springdale Campground $8
Pike National Forest
4 mi E on FR 22 from US 24 to Woodland Park; 1.7 mi E on FR 300 (Rampart Range Rd). $8 with federal senior pass; others pay $16. About MD-LD; 14-day limit. 13 sites; 16-ft RV limit. Tbls, toilets, cfga, no drkg wtr. Rampart Range Lake nearby. Elev 9100 ft.

The Crags Campground $8
Pike National Forest
6 mi W of Woodland Park on US 24; 4.5 mi S of Divide on SR 67; 3.5 mi E on FR 383; narrow, steep access rd. $8 with federal senior pass; others pay $16. About MD-LD; 14-day limit; no camping off-season. 17 sites (RVs under 22 ft). Toilets, cfga, tbls, drkg wtr, no trash service. Fishing, hiking. Elev 10,100 ft; 7 acres. Nature trails. Camp has problems with bears.

YAMPA
Bear Lake Campground $10
Routt National Forest
13 mi SW of Yampa on CR 7. $10. About MD-10/1; 14-day limit. 43 sites (4 double, 1 triple); 30-ft RV limit. Tbls, toilets, cfga, drkg wtr. Boating(l), fishing, hiking trails. Elev 9700 ft; 20 acres.

Bear River Dispersed Sites $5
Routt National Forest
10-20 mi SW of Yampa on FR 900; along Bear River. $5. About MD-11/30; 14-day limit. 32 dispersed numbered sites; 30-ft RV limit. Tbls, fire grates. Toilets & trash deposit at Yamcolo Reservoir boat ramp nearby; drkg wtr & toilets at nearby Bear Lake, Horseshoe & Coldsprings campgrounds. Fishing, hiking, mountain biking. Elev 9300 ft-10,200 ft.

Blacktail Creek Campground $10
Routt National Forest
6 mi S of Yampa on SR131 past Toponas; 13 mi E on SR 134. $10. 6/1-11/15; 14-day limit. 8 RV sites (RVs under 23 ft). Tbls, toilets, cfga, drkg wtr (temporarily unavailable in 2017). Fishing, mountain biking, hiking. Elev 9100 ft.

Chapman Reservoir Campground $10
Routt National Forest
5 mi W/NW of Yampa on CR 17; left on CR 132 (FR 16) for 7 mi; 1 mi S on FR 940. $10. About MD-11/1; 14-day limit. 12 sites; 35-ft RV limit. Tbls, toilets, cfga, no drkg wtr. Fishing, boating, hiking, canoeing, swimming.

Cold Springs Campground $10
Routt National Forest
7 mi SW of Yampa on CR 7; 8.6 mi SW on FR 900. At Stillwater Reservoir. $10. About MD-10/15; 14-day limit. 5 sites; 22-ft RV limit. Tbls, toilets, cfga, no drkg wtr. Boating, fishing. Small waterfall, pond. Elev 10,500 ft.

Crosho Lake Recreation Area   FREE
Routt National Forest
4 mi N/NW of Yampa on CR 17; 6 mi W on CR 15; at S end of Crosho Lake. Free. 6/15-11/15; 14-day limit. 10 dispersed primitive sites; 25-ft RV limit. Toilet, cfga, no drkg wtr, tbls or trash service. Fishing, hiking, mountain biking. Closed in 2017 for dam repair; check current status before arrival. 970-638-4516.

Gardner Park Reservoir Recreation Area   FREE
Routt National Forest
About 7 mi S/SW of Yampa on CR 7; 3 mi on FR 900; left on FR 910 for 2 mi (rd has extensive weather damage in 2017); at Gardner Park Reservoir. Free. About 6/15-11/15; 14-day limit. Primitive dispersed sites. Toilet, cfga, no drkg wtr, no tbls or trash service. Interpretive trail, boating, hiking, fishing.

Horseshoe Campground $10
Routt National Forest
7 mi S/SW of Yampa on CR 7; continue for 9 mi on FR 900; on right. 6/1-11/15; 14-day limit. 7 sites; 25-ft RV limit. Tbls, toilets, cfga, drkg wtr except after 10/1. Fishing, mountain biking, hiking & OHV trails. Elev 10,000 ft.

Lagunita Lake Recreation Area   FREE
Routt National Forest
20 mi SW of Yampa on SR 134; 3 mi N on FR 270; just before Lynx Pass Campground. Free. Primitive dispersed sites. Toilet, cfga, no drkg wtr or trash service. Fishing, hiking, biking. Elev 8900 ft. Wtr at nearby Lynx Pass campground.

Lynx Pass Campground $10
Routt National Forest
6 mi S of Yampa past Toponas on SR 131; 9 mi E on SR 134;

2.5 mi N on FR 270. $10. MD-10/30; 14-day limit. 11 sites; 18-ft RV limit. Tbls, toilets, cfga, drkg wtr (except after 10/1), nature trails. Fishing, hiking, biking. Elev 9000 ft.

Red Dirt Reservoir Recreation Area   FREE
Routt National Forest
11 mi S of Yampa on Hwy 131; 20 mi E on FR 134; 8 mi N on FR 100; 2 mi N on FR 101. Free. About 6/15-11/15; 14-day limit. Primitive dispersed sites around lake. Toilet, tbls, cfga, no drkg wtr, no trash service. Fishing, mountain biking, hiking.

Sheriff Reservoir Campground $10
Routt National Forest
W of Yampa on CR 16, then S on FR 959. $10. About 6/1-10/31; 14-day limit. 6 sites (20-ft RV limit). Tbls, toilet, cfga, no drkg wtr. Boating(l), fishing, hiking trails, horseback riding. Elev 9800 ft.

Trout Creek Recreation Area   FREE
Routt National Forest
About 5 mi N/NW of Yampa on CR 17; left on CR 132 for about 4 mi; 5 mi N/NW on FR 925; at Trout Creek. Free. June-Nov; 14-day limit. Primitive undesignated sites. Toilet, cfga, no drkg wtr, no trash service. Fishing.

Vaughn Lake Campground $10
Routt National Forest
5 mi N of Yampa on SR 131; 18.2 mi W on FR 16. $10. 6/15-10/31; 14-day limit. 6 sites (22-ft RV limit). Tbls, toilets, cfga, no drkg wtr. Boating(ld - elec mtrs), fishing, hunting. Elev 9500 ft; Trailhead nearby to Flat Tops Wilderness.

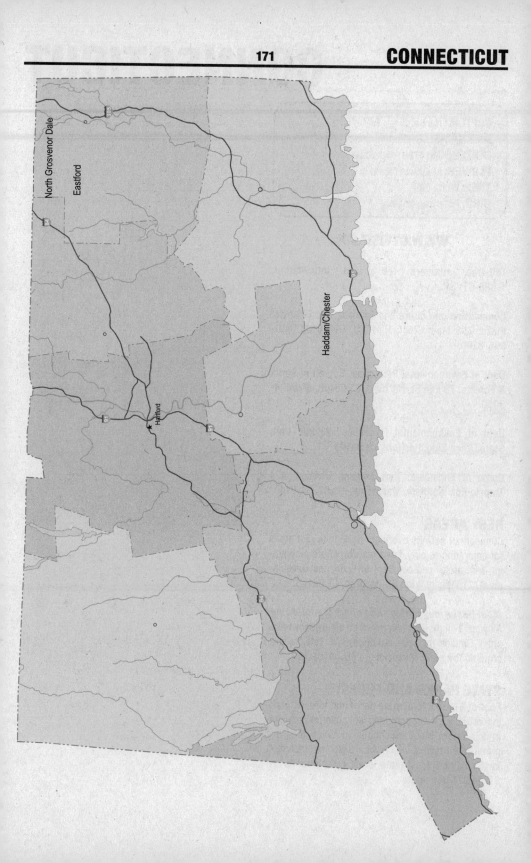

CONNECTICUT

CAPITAL: Hartford
NICKNAME: Constitution State
STATEHOOD: 1788 – 5th State
FLOWER: Mountain Laurel
TREE: White Oak
BIRD: American Robin

WWW.CTVISIT.COM

Toll-free numbers for travel information: 1-888-CTVisit.

Commission on Culture and Tourism, One Financial Plaza, 755 Main Steet, Hartford, CT 06103. 860-256-8200.

Dept of Environmental Protection, Bureau of Parks & Forests, 79 Elm St, Hartford, CT 06106. 860/424-3000.

Dept of Environmental Protection, Wildlife Unit, State Office Bldg, Hartford, CT 06106.

Corps of Engineers, New England Division, 424 Trapelo Rd., Waltham, Massachusetts 02254-9149.

REST AREAS

Connecticut permits overnight parking in rest areas for emergencies only. For a map/brochure pinpointing rest areas contact Dept of Economic Development, 210 Washington St, Hartford, CT 06106.

Most Rest Areas in this state offers the following: All year; 1-night limit (overnight on emergency basis only). Spaces for self-contained RVs. Tbls, toilets, cfga, no drkg wtr. Picnicking. Pets on leash.

STATE PARKS AND FORESTS

Fees of $14 to $40 at state parks and forests, making virtually all campgrounds ineligible for inclusion in this book. Most exceptions to those fees are primitive tent sites, which we are also not including in this edition. Most state forest campgrounds are $17 to $27 per night.

EASTFORD

Silvermine Horse Camp   FREE
Natchaug State Forest
On Pilfershire Rd near Eastford. Free. All year; 14-day limit. 15 wooded primitive sites plus free backpack camping. Tbls, toilets, cfga, drkg wtr. Primarily for equestrian use. No trash service. Fishing, horseback riding, picnicking. 1 pet on leash.

HADDAM/CHESTER

Filley Rd. Campsite   FREE
Cockaponset State Forest
3 mi W of Chester on Hwy 148. Free. All year;14-day limit. 16 primitive sites. Toilets, cfga. Fishing, picnicking, swimming, snowmobiling, hiking, cross-country skiing, hunting. State's second-largest forest.

NORTH GROSVENORDALE

West Thompson $7.50
Corps of Engineers
West Thompson Lake
From North Grosvenordale at I-395 exit 99, 1 mi E on SR 200; 2 mi S (right) on SR 193 (signs); cross SR 12 at traffic light; first right 0.5 mi on Reardon Rd; left 0.2 mi on recreation road. 5/20-9/20; 14-day limit. 11 basic sites without hookups, $15 ($7.50 with federal senior pass). 11 elec/wtr sites, $30 ($15 with federal senior pass). RV limit 45 ft. 1 handicap site with wtr/elec. Flush toilets, showers, cfga, drkg wtr, tbls, beach, playground, dump. Picnic shelters($), horseshoe pits, amphitheater, hiking trails, weekend nature programs, boating(l), fishing. Alcohol prohibited. Checkout time noon. No swimming, no waterfront sites. Firewood($). No day use fees. (860) 923-3121. NRRS. GPS: 41.945, -71.91

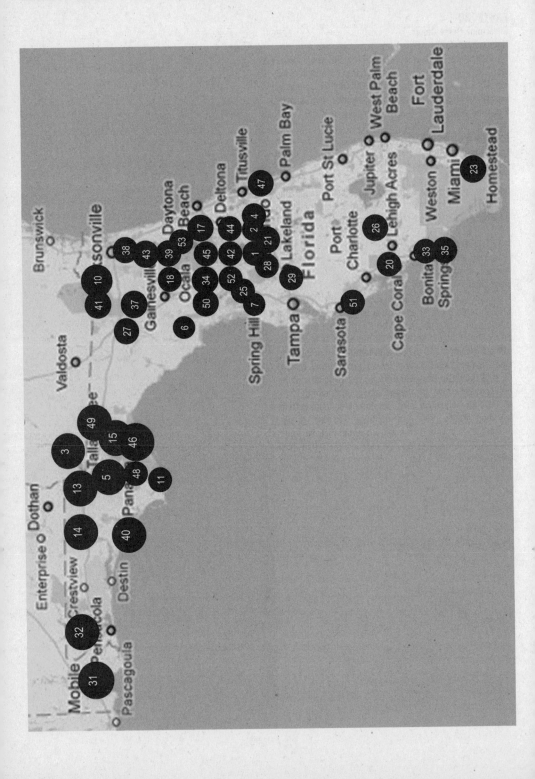

FLORIDA

CAPITAL: Tallahassee
NICKNAME: Sunshine State
STATEHOOD: 1845 – 27th State
FLOWER: Orange Blossom
TREE: Cabbage Palmetto
BIRD: Mockingbird

WWW.VISITFLORIDA.COM

VISITFLORIDA.org, Visitor Inquiry, 866-972-5280.

Florida Fish and Wildlife Conservation Commission, 620 S Meridian, Tallahassee, FL 32399-1600; 850-488-4676.

REST AREAS
Overnight stops are not permitted.

STATE PARKS
Base camping fees are $15-$20; extra fees may be charged for waterfront sites. Lower off-season rates are no longer available. We hear numerous complaints about the inhospitality of Florida's state parks.

STATE FORESTS
Camping fees at most state forests are $10 for primitive sites, $15 for non- electric sites ($8 for Florida seniors/disabled) and $20 for sites with electricity ($10 for Florida seniors/disabled). Some forests require a free permit for primitive sites. RV limits are generally 20 feet; length of stay, 14 days. Camping on open forest property is discouraged because adequate primitive campsites are available. Free hunt maps from the Florida Game and Fresh Water Fish Commission that indicate hunters-only campsites are available during hunting season. A free Wildlife Management Areas map indicates 30 additional free campgrounds. Some hunt camps are now $4 per night or an annual pass.

Apalachicola National Forest. During deer hunting season, about 11/15-2/15, camping is allowed at designated hunt camps and 5 designated campgrounds. Most hunt camps are equipped with portable toilets but do not have drinking water.

Ocala National Forest. Camping fees vary, but are generally $5-12. Camping at primitive and dispersed sites is free. Visitor centers are at 14100 North US 19, Salt Springs, and 45631 US 19, Altoona.

Osceola National Forest. The Osceola contains 187,000 acres and is located in the northeastern part of the State approximately 50 miles west of Jacksonville.

FLORIDA

ALTOONA (1)

Big Bass Lake $10
Ocala National Forest
9 mi W of Altoona on SR 42; half mi N on FR 13; 0.5 mi E
on FR 13-0.158. $10. 10/15-4/15; 120-day limit. 19 sites
(32-ft RV limit). Tbls, flush toilets, cfga, drkg wtr, dump
($3 non-campers), phone. No fishing. GPS: 28.98667,
-81.784103.

Big Scrub $12
Ocala National Forest
8.5 mi N of Altoona on SR 19; 7 mi W on FR 14 (unimproved,
soft sand in places). $12. All year; 14-day limit. 62 sites on
9 acres (typically 40 ft). Tbls, toilets, cfga, piped drkg wtr,
showers. Picnicking. ORV trail; permit required. Dump at
Big Bass Lake($). GPS: 29.050538, -81.7556342

South Tower Hunt Camp   FREE
Ocala National Forest
9 mi W of Altoona on SR 42; 1 mi N on FR 588. Free. All
year; 14-day limit. Primitive undesignated sites; no facilities, no drkg wtr. Fishing, hiking. Limited to hunters during
hunting season. GPS: 28.99967, -81.77797

ASTOR PARK (2)

Alexander Springs $10.50
Ocala National Forest
About 8 mi S of Astor Park on CR 445. $10.50 with federal
senior pass; others pay $21. All year; 14-day limit during
4/16-10/14; 180 days 10/15-4/15. 67 sites; 35-ft RV limit.
Tbls, flush toilets, cfga, showers, drkg wtr, dump. Swimming, scuba diving, canoeing(r), hiking trails, snorkel-
ing(r). Concessionaire. GPS: 29.07889, -81.58

Bluffton Recreation Area
Dexter/Mary Farms Unit   FREE
Lake George Wildlife Management Area
About 3 mi E of Astor Park on SR 40; just across the St.
Johns River bridge, turn S on St. Johns River Rd into
WMA for about 2 mi. Free. All year; 14-day limit. Camp at
designated sites during special-opportunity turkey hunts
& other times by free state forest use permit (386-329-
4404). Tbls, toilets, cfga, no drkg wtr. Hiking trail, fishing,
boating, canoeing, biking, hunting. Fishing also at nearby
Jenkins Pond.

Farles Prairie Recreation Area $5
Ocala National Forest
9 mi SW of Astor Park on SR 445A; 3 mi W on FR 22; at S
shore of Falres Lake. $5 daily use fee. 10 Primitive sites.
Tbls, toilets, cfga, drkg wtr. Boating(l), fishing, hiking
trails, swimming, ORV trail (permit required). Camping
permit required ($30 for 30 days); camping during hunting
season only. GPS: 29.103379, -81.674319

Little Grasshopper Lake   FREE
Ocala National Forest
About 3.5 mi SW of Astor Park on CR 445A; NW on access
rd to lake. Free. All year; 14-day limit. Primitive undesignated sites; no facilities, no drkg wtr. Fishing, hiking.

Sellers Lake North   FREE
Ocala National Forest
About 8 mi SW of Astor Park on CR 445A; half mi N on
SR 19; half mi W on FR 599; qtr mi S on access rd; on N
shore of Sellers Lake. Free. All year; 14-day limit. Primitive
undesignated sites; no facilities, no drkg wtr. Fishing,
boating, hiking. Lake GPS: 29.124, -81.620.

Sellers Lake South   FREE
Ocala National Forest
About 9 mi SW of Astor Park on CR 445A; half mi W on
FR 595; on S shore of Sellers Lake. Free. All year; 14-day
limit. Primitive undesignated sites; no facilities, no drkg
wtr. Fishing, boating.

BAINBRIDGE, (GEORGIA) (3)

Hale's Landing $9
Corps of Engineers
Lake Seminole
SW of Bainbridge on GA 253; S on county's Ten Mile Still
Rd, following signs, then S. $9 with federal senior pass;
others pay $18. All year; 14-day limit. 25 elec/wtr (30/50-
amp) sites; 40-ft RV limit Tbls, flush toilets, showers, cfga,
50-amp elec/wtr, shelter. Boating(l), fishing, picnicking,
canoeing, hunting. Adjoins wildlife management area.
GPS: 30.8477, -84.6599

BARBERVILLE (4)

Deep Creek Camp
Lake George   FREE
Wildlife Management Area
Lake George State Forest
From Barberville, 1 mi S on SR 11, then E on Deep Creek
Rd (4WD trail). Free with state forest use permit (386-329-
4404). All year; 14-day limit (no camping during hunting
seasons). No facilities, no drkg wtr. Hunting, fishing,
hiking, horseback riding. Forest GPS: 39.1011, -81.3049

BRISTOL (5)

Big Gully Landing   FREE
Apalachicola National Forest
12.8 mi S of Bristol on SR 12; veer right on SR 379 at
Orange for 1 mi, then 1 mi W on FR 133; at Equaloxic
Creek. Free. All year; 14-day limit. Primitive undesignated
sites. Portable toilet, cfga, no drkg wtr. Fishing, hiking,
hunting, boating(l). GPS: 30.2407533, -85.0293599.

Camel Lake Recreation Area $10
Apalachicola National Forest
12.1 mi S of Bristol on SR 12; 2 mi E on FR 105. $10 ($5
surcharge for elec/wtr). All year; 14-day limit. 10 sites

(32-ft RV limit). Tbls, flush toilets, cfga, drkg wtr, showers. Swimming beach, fishing, boating(l - elec mtrs), hiking. Non-campers pay $3 day use fee. GPS: 30.2760307, -84.9907487

Cotton Landing Hunt Camp   FREE
Apalachicola National Forest
12 mi S of Bristol on FL 12; 16.2 mi S on FL 379; 2.8 mi S on FL 379; 2.8 mi SW on FR 123; .7 mi W on FR 123B; campground on E bank of Kennedy Creek. Free. All year; 14-day limit. 4 sites on 7 acres (RVs under 31 ft). Tbls, toilets, cfga, well drkg wtr. Boating(ld), picnicking, fishing. Access to Apalachicola River. GPS: 30.0524238, -85.0715812

Hickory Landing $3
Apalachicola National Forest
12.8 mi S of Bristol on FL 12; 22 mi S on FL 379; 2 mi S on FL 65; 1.8 mi SW on FR 101; campground on E bank of Owl Creek. $3. All year; 14-day limit. 10 sites on 2 acres (RVs under 33 ft). Tbls, toilets, piped drkg wtr. Boating(ld), picnicking, fishing, swimming (1 mi). Access to Apalachicola River. Day use fee eliminated. Designated hunt camp during gun season. GPS: 29.98884, -85.01307

Hitchcock Lake   FREE
Apalachicola National Forest
11.4 mi E of Bristol on FL 20; 3.2 mi S on FL 65; 22.8 mi SE on FL 67; 1.5 mi E on FR 125B. Free. All year; 14-day limit. 10 sites (RVs under 33 ft). Tbls, toilets, cfga, no drkg wtr. Boating(ld), picnicking, fishing. No swimming allowed. Elev 100 ft. 3 acres. On Hitchcock Lake, a backwater of the Ochlockonee River. Scenic. GPS: 30.08048, -84.6504622

Porter Lake $3
Apalachicola National Forest
11.4 mi E of Bristol on FL 20; 3.2 mi S on FL 65; 16.9 mi SW on FL 67; 2.9 mi E on FR 13; on W bank of Ochlockonee River. $3 for camping or day use. All year; 14-day limit. 6 sites; 2 acres. Tbls, toilets, cfga, well drkg wtr. Boating, picnicking, fishing. Designated hunt camp during gun season. Trailhead for Florida Trail. GPS: 30.1627007, -84.6749081

White Oak Landing   FREE
Apalachicola National Forest
12.8 mi S of Bristol on CR 12; 9 mi SW on CR 379; 3 mi W on FR 115. Free. All year; 14-day limit. Undesignated primitive sites. Portable toilet, cfga, tbls, no drkg wtr. Boating(l), fishing. Primarily a hunt camp during fall & early winter. GPS: 30.0977007, -85.112693

BRONSON (6)
Goethe State Forest   FREE
Goethe Wildlife Management Area
About 10-20 mi S of Bronson on Hwy 337, then to various sections of forest on Hwys 121 &, 336, 326 & 328. Free camping with special permit from division of forestry (352-

465-8585). Primitive undesignated camping; no facilities, no drkg wtr. No camping during hunting seasons. Hunting, fishing, hiking trail, horseback riding. Forest 15,000 acres; WMA 45,000 acres. GPS: 2919918, -82.57918

BROOKSVILLE (7)
Buttgenbach Mine Campground $10
Croom Motorcycle Recreation Area
Withlacoochee State Forest
N of Brooksville on US 41; E on Croom Rd. $10 at primitive sites plus $2 per person entry fee or $30 annual vehicle pass. All year; 14-day limit. Developed non-elec sites $15 ($8 for Florida seniors); $20 with elec ($10 for Florida seniors). 51 developed sites with 30/50-amp elec). Tbls, flush toilets, cfga, drkg wtr, showers, dump. Motorcycle camping area with motorcycle trails. Amphitheater. GPS: 28.526773, -82.23807

Silver Lake Recreation Area $10
Withlacoochee State Forest
N of Brooksville on US 41; E & S on Croom Rd. $1 at primitive sites plus $2 per person entry fee or $30 annual vehicle pass. All year; 14-day limit. Developed sites $15 ($8 for Florida seniors); $20 with elec ($10 for Florida seniors). Winter rate at elec sites, $24 ($12 for Florida seniors). Three camping areas (Silver Lake, Cypress Glen & Crooked River) with total of 91 sites (57 with elec). Tbls, flush toilets, cfga, drkg wtr, showers, dump, shelter. Fishing, boating, canoeing(l), hiking. GPS: 30.2413, -84.2430

BRYCEVILLE (10)
Cary State Forest $10
On US 301, qtr mi N of Bryceville fire station; right on gravel rd to parking area & kiosk. $10 plus $2 per person entry fee or $30 annual vehicle pass. All year; 14-day limit. 3 primitive group camping areas. Tbls, flush toilets, showers, cfga, drkg wtr. Free forest use permit required (call 904-266-5021). Hiking, horseback riding, wildlife viewing, hunting, nature trail with boardwalk. GPS: 30.405, -81.9123

CARRABELLE (11)
Borrow Pit Camp $10
Tate's Hell Wildlife Management Area
Tate's Hell State Forest
From Hwy 379 SW of Carrabelle, 2.2 mi NW on River Rd; 3.5 mi N on County Rd; on W shore of New River. $10. All year; 14-day limit. Tbls, toilets, cfga, no drkg wtr. Fishing, hiking, canoeing, boating. Free camping permit required. GPS: 30.4580, -82.9432

Bus Stop Camp $10
Tate's Hell Wildlife Management Area
Tate's Hell State Forest
8 mi N of Carrabelle on CR 67; 1.5 mi W on Rock Landing Rd nearly to jct with Pine Log Rd; S on access rd. $10. All year; 14-day limit. Primitive sites. Tbls, toilets, cfga, no drkg wtr. Hiking, hunting. Free camping permit required.

Boundary Road Camp $10
Tate's Hell Wildlife Management Area
Tate's Hell State Forest
About 8 mi N of Carrabelle on SR 67; 5 mi W on Boundary Rd; at New River crossing. $10. All year; 14-day limit. Tbls, toilets, cfga, no drkg wtr. Fishing, hiking, canoeing, boating. Free camping permit required.

Dew Drop Camp $10
Tate's Hell Wildlife Management Area
Tate's Hell State Forest
From Hwy 379 SW of Carrabelle, 2.2 mi NW on River Rd; 5 mi N on County Rd; on W shore of New River. $10. All year; 14-day limit. Tbls, toilets, cfga, no drkg wtr. Fishing, hiking, canoeing(l), boating. Free camping permit required.

Doyle Creek $10
Tate's Hell Wildlife Management Area
Tate's Hell State Forest
From Hwy 376 just SW of Carrabelle,10 mi W on Buck Siding Rd; 2.5 mi S on Tower Rd, bearing right at the "Y"; at N shore of Doyle Creek. $10. All year; 14-day limit. Primitive sites. Tbls, toilets, cfga, no drkg wtr. Fishing, canoeing, hiking. Free camping permit required. Vicinity GPS: 29.4924, -84.5408

Dry Bridge Camp $10
Tate's Hell Wildlife Management Area
Tate's Hell State Forest
From Hwy 376 just SW of Carrabelle, 10 mi W on Dry Bridge Rd to its end at Whisky George Creek. $10. All year; 14-day limit. Primitive sites. Tbls, toilets, cfga, no drkg wtr. Fishing, canoeing, hiking. Free camping permit required.

Log Cabin Camps $10
Womack Creek Unit
Tate's Hell Wildlife Management Area
Tate's Hell State Forest
11 mi N of Carrabelle on CR 67; 2 mi E on Short Rd; S on Log Cabin Rd; along W shore of Ochlockonee River. $10. All year; 14-day limit. 4 primitive camping areas. Tbls, toilets, cfga, no drkg wtr. Fishing, canoeing, boating(l), hiking.

Loop Road Camp $10
Womack Creek Unit
Tate's Hell Wildlife Management Area
Tate's Hell State Forest
8 mi N of Carrabelle on CR 67; 1.7 mi E on Rock Landing Rd; 1 mi N on Jeff Sanders Rd; 1.5 mi E on Loop Rd; at Crooked River. $10. All year; 14-day limit. Primitive sites. Tbls, toilets, cfga, no drkg wtr. Fishing, canoeing, hiking, boating(l).

New River Camp #1 $10
Tate's Hell Wildlife Management Area
Tate's Hell State Forest
From Hwy 379 SW of Carrabelle, 2.2 mi NW on River Rd; 4.5 mi N on County Rd; on W shore of New River. $10. All year; 14-day limit. Tbls, toilets, cfga, no drkg wtr. Fishing, hiking, canoeing(l), boating. Free camping permit required.

New River Camp #2 $10
Tate's Hell Wildlife Management Area
Tate's Hell State Forest
From Hwy 379 SW of Carrabelle, 2.2 mi NW on River Rd; N on County Rd to Guffy Branch Rd; E on Guffy Branch across river, then half mi N on River Rd; on E shore of New River. $10. All year; 14-day limit. Tbls, toilets, cfga, no drkg wtr. Fishing, hiking, canoeing(l), boating. Free camping permit required.

New River Camp #3 $10
Tate's Hell Wildlife Management Area
Tate's Hell State Forest
From Hwy 379 SW of Carrabelle, 2.2 mi NW on River Rd; N on County Rd to Guffy Branch Rd; E on Guffy Branch across river, then 1.5 mi N on River Rd; on E shore of New River. $10. All year; 14-day limit. Tbls, toilets, cfga, no drkg wtr. Fishing, hiking, canoeing(l), boating. Free camping permit required.

New River Camp #4 $10
Tate's Hell Wildlife Management Area
Tate's Hell State Forest
From Hwy 379 SW of Carrabelle, 2.2 mi NW on River Rd; N on County Rd to Guffy Branch Rd; E on Guffy Branch across river, then 2.5 mi N on River Rd; on E shore of New River. $10. All year; 14-day limit. Tbls, toilets, cfga, no drkg wtr. Fishing, hiking, canoeing(l), boating. Free camping permit required.

New River Camp #5 $10
Tate's Hell Wildlife Management Area
Tate's Hell State Forest
From Hwy 379 SW of Carrabelle, 2.2 mi NW on River Rd; N on County Rd to Guffy Branch Rd; E on Guffy Branch across river, then 3.5 mi N on River Rd; on E shore of New River. $10. All year; 14-day limit. Tbls, toilets, cfga, no drkg wtr. Fishing, hiking, canoeing(l), boating. Free camping permit required.

New River Camp #6 $10
Tate's Hell Wildlife Management Area
Tate's Hell State Forest
From Hwy 379 SW of Carrabelle, 2.2 mi NW on River Rd; N on County Rd to Guffy Branch Rd; E on Guffy Branch across river, then 4.5 mi N on River Rd; on E shore of New River. $10. All year; 14-day limit. Tbls, toilets, cfga, no drkg wtr. Fishing, hiking, canoeing(l), boating. Free camping permit required.

New River Camp #7 $10
Tate's Hell Wildlife Management Area
Tate's Hell State Forest
From Hwy 379 SW of Carrabelle, 2.2 mi NW on River Rd;
N on County Rd to Guffy Branch Rd; E on Guffy Branch
across river, then 5 mi N on River Rd; on E shore of New
River. $10. All year; 14-day limit. Tbls, toilets, cfga, no
drkg wtr. Fishing, hiking, canoeing(l), boating. Free camp-
ing permit required.

Nick's Road Camp $10
Womack Creek Unit
Tate's Hell Wildlife Management Area
Tate's Hell State Forest
8 mi N of Carrabelle on CR 67; 1.7 mi E on Rock Landing
Rd; 1.5 mi N on Jeff Sanders Rd; 2 mi NW on Nick's Rd;
at Womack Creek. $10. All year; 14-day limit. Primitive
sites. Tbls, toilets, cfga, no drkg wtr. Fishing, canoeing(l),
hiking. GPS: 30.0139, -84.577499

North Road Camp $10
Tate's Hell Wildlife Management Area
Tate's Hell State Forest
From Hwy 379 SW of Carrabelle, 3.2 mi NW on River Rd
& Five Points Rd; 1.5 mi SW on Trout Creek Rd; 2 mi W
on Buck Siding Rd; about 8 mi N on North Rd to its end;
on S shore of New River. $10. All year; 14-day limit. Tbls,
toilets, cfga, no drkg wtr. Fishing, hiking, canoeing(l),
boating. Free camping permit required.

Parker Place Recreation Site $10
Tate's Hell Wildlife Management Area
Tate's Hell State Forest
From Hwy 379 SW of Carrabelle, 2.2 mi NW on River Rd; 3
mi N on County Rd; on W shore of New River. $10. All year;
14-day limit. Tbls, toilets, cfga, no drkg wtr. Fishing, hiking, canoeing, boating (I). Free camping permit required.

Pope Place Camp $10
Tate's Hell Wildlife Management Area
Tate's Hell State Forest
From Hwy 379 SW of Carrabelle, 2.2 mi NW on River Rd; 2
mi N on County Rd; on W shore of New River. $10. All year;
14-day limit. Tbls, toilets, cfga, no drkg wtr. Fishing, hik-
ing, canoeing, boating (I). Free camping permit required.
GPS: 29.8962, -84.733902

Rock Landing Recreation Site $10
Womack Creek Unit
Tate's Hell Wildlife Management Area
Tate's Hell State Forest
8 mi N of Carrabelle on CR 67; 2 mi E on Rock Landing Rd;
at Crooked River. $10. All year; 14-day limit. 3 primitive
sites. Tbls, toilets, cfga, no drkg wtr. Fishing, canoeing,
hiking. GPS: 29.5849, -84.3406

Roke Creek Camp $10
Tate's Hell Wildlife Management Area
Tate's Hell State Forest
10 mi SW of Carrabelle on US 98; 5 mi N on CR 65; just
across Cash Bayou bridge, turn N on access rd. $10. All
year; 14-day limit. Primitive sites. Tbls, toilets, cfga, no
drkg wtr. Fishing, hiking, canoeing(l). Free camping permit
required.

Sunday Rollaway Camp $10
Tate's Hell Wildlife Management Area
Tate's Hell State Forest
5 mi N of Carrabelle on CR 67; 1 mi W on Guffy Branch
Rd; 1.5 mi S on Warren Bluff Rd; qtr mi E on access rd; at
Crooked River. $10. All year; 14-daylimit. Primitive sites.
Tbls, toilets, cfga, no drkg wtr. Fishing, canoeing(l), hik-
ing, fishing, boating. Free camping permit required. GPS:
29.54174, -84.39102

Warren Bluff Camp $10
Tate's Hell Wildlife Management Area
Tate's Hell State Forest
From Hwy 379 SW of Carrabelle, 2 mi NW on River Rd; qtr
mi N on Burnt Bridge Rd; 1.5 mi E on Warren Bluff Rd; S
on access rd to Crooked River. $10. All year; 14-day limit.
Primitive sites. Tbls, toilets, cfga, no drkg wtr. Fishing,
canoeing, hiking. Free camping permit required.

Whiskey George Camp $10
Tate's Hell Wildlife Management Area
Tate's Hell State Forest
From Carrabelle, about 8 mi W on Buck Siding Rd; 1 mi N
on access rd to SW shore of Whisky George Creek. $10.
All year; 14-day limit. Primitive sites. Tbls, toilets, cfga, no
drkg wtr. Fishing, canoeing, hiking. Free camping permit
required. Vicinity GPS: 29.80632, -84.894353

Womack Creek Rec. Site $10
Womack Creek Unit
Tate's Hell Wildlife Management Area
Tate's Hell State Forest
8 mi N of Carrabelle on CR 67; 1.7 mi E on Rock Landing
Rd; 5 mi N on Jeff Sanders Rd. $10. All year; 14-day
limit. 12 primitive sites. Tbls, toilets, cfga, no drkg wtr.
Fishing, canoeing, hiking, boating(l). Vicinity GPS: 30.001,
-84.3236

CHATTAHOOCHEE (13)

Eastbank Campground $10
Corps of Engineers
Lake Seminole
From Chattahoochee at jct with US 90, 1.5 mi N on Boli-
var St (Booster Club Rd); left on East Bank Rd; near Jim
Woodruff Dam in Georgia. $10 with federal senior pass at
63 elec/wtr sites (30/50-amp); others pay $20. All year;
14-day limit. RV limit in excess of 65 ft. Tbls, flush toilets,

cfga, drkg wtr, showers, coin laundry. Boating(l), fishing, horseshoe pits, courtesy dock. Near Jim Woodruff dam. GPS: 30.71806, -84.86111

Faceville Landing $8
Corps of Engineers
Lake Seminole
From Bainbridge, Georgia, 14 mi S on SR 97, then N on Faceville Landing Rd; between Bainbridge and Chatta-hoochee, FL. $8. All year; 14-day limit. 7 primitive sites (40-ft RV limit). Tbls, drkg wtr, cfga, pit toilets. Picnic shelter located in the area. Picnicking, fishing, swimming, boating, canoeing, courtesy dock. Maintained by Florida Game and Fresh Water Commission. GPS: 30.77, -84.84

River Junction $9
Corps of Engineers
Lake Seminole
4 mi N of Chattahoochee, across state line into Georgia on SR 386, following signs. $9 with federal senior pass; others pay $18. All year; 14-day limit. 11 elec/wtr sites (30/50-amp). 40-ft RV limit. Tbls, flush toilets, cfga, drkg wtr, show-ers, coin laundry. Fishing, boating(l). GPS: 30.75, -84.84

CHIPLEY (14)

Blue Lake FREE
Washington County Park
S of Chipley on SR 77 at Blue Lake (just S of Crow commu-nity). Free. All year; 21-day limit. Undesignated primitive sites. Tbls, cfga, drkg wtr, toilets. Boating(l), fishing, swimming. GPS: 30.4669, -85.7458

Gap Lake FREE
Washington County Park
S of Chipley on SR 77 to S end of Wausau community; fol-low signs E on co rd from Wausau, then 5 mi S on unpaved rd to southbound turnoff for lake. Free. All year; 30-day limit. Primitive undesignated sites on N shore. Tbls, cfga, no drkg wtr or toilets. Fishing, boating(l), waterskiing. GPS: 30.55019, -85.5707619

Gin Lake FREE
Washington County Park
S of Chipley on SR 77 to S end of Wausau community; fol-low signs E on co rd from Wausau, then 5 mi S on unpaved rd to eastbound turnoff for lake. Free. Primitive undesig-nated sites on NW shore. Tbls, cfga, no drkg wtr or toilets. Fishing, boating(l), picnicking. GPS: 30.573707, -85.55084

Lucas Lake FREE
Washington County Park
About 13 mi S of Chipley on SR 77; 4 mi NE on SR 279 to eastbound co rd turnoff for Lucas Lake. Free. All year; 14-day limit. Undesignated primitive sites. Tbls, cfga, no drkg wtr, no toilets. Boating(l), fishing, waterskiing. No trash service. GPS: 30.545937, -85.6941141

Porter Lake FREE
Washington County Park
S of Chipley on SR 77 to S end of Wausau community; follow signs to Gap Lake & Porter Lake E on co rd from Wausau, then about 8 mi S on unpaved rd (1 mi SE of Grantham). Free All year; 30-day limit. 3 primitive sites. Tbls, cfga, no drkg wtr, no toilets, no trash service. Boating(l), fishing, swim-ming, waterskiing. GPS: 30.512035, -85.53876

Rattlesnake Lake FREE
Washington County Park
S of Chipley on SR 77 to S end of Wausau community; follow signs to Porter Lake E on co rd from Wausau, then about 13 mi S on unpaved Rd (5 mi SE of Grantham) past Porter Lake access. Free. All year; 30-day limit. 4 primitive open sites. Tbls, cfga, no drkg wtr, no toilets, no trash service. Boating, swimming, fishing.

CRAWFORDVILLE (15)

Brown Horse Hunt Camp FREE
Apalachicola National Forest
6.5 mi N of Crawfordville on US 319; 8 mi NW on SR 267; 3 mi E on FR 309. Free. All year; 14-day limit. Primitive sites. Tbls, portable toilet, cfga, no drkg wtr. Hunting, hiking. Hunt camp during gun season. GPS: 30.3029773, -84.5093507

Buckhorn Hunt Camp FREE
Apalachicola National Forest
6.4 mi N of Crawfordville on US 319; 12 mi NW on SR 267; 1 mi S on FR 360. Free. 11/1-2/31 (hunting season). 10 sites (RVs under 22 ft). Toilets, well drkg wtr. Hunting, hiking. Elev 100 ft; 8 acres. Primarily a hunting camp. GPS: 30.3338101, -845343517

Otter Hunt Camp FREE
Apalachicola National Forest
6.5 mi N of Crawfordville on US 319; 8 mi NW on SR 267; 7 mi E on FR 309; 1 mi N on FR 344. Free. All year; 14-day limit. Tbls, portable toilet, cfga, no drkg wtr. Hunting. GPS: 30.3079764, -84.6168532

Pope Still Hunt Camp FREE
Apalachicola National Forest
2 mi W of Crawfordville on Bay Ave (Hwy 368); continue E on FR 13 about 5 mi to jct with FR 312; at Pope Still tower. Free. All year; 14-day limit. Primitive sites. Portable toilet, cfga, no drkg wtr. Hunting, hiking. GPS: 30.2238119, -84.4754598

DELAND (17)

Rima Ridge Unit $10
Tiger Bay State Forest
Tiger Bay Wildlife Management Area
11 mi E of Deland on US 92; 1.7 mi N on Indian Lake Rd; 2 mi N on Rima Ridge Rd. $10. All year; 14-day limit. Primi-tive sites, including 5 new equestrian sites with corrals &

non-potable wtr. Tbls, toilets, cfga, no drkg wtr. Hiking, canoeing, horseback riding, biking. Forest use permit required (386-226-0250). GPS: 29.1936, -81.1712

FLORAHOME (18)

Etoniah Creek State Forest $10
Etoniah Wildlife Management Area
From Florahome, 2 mi E on Hwy 100; 2.6 mi N on Holloway Rd; right on 2nd rd (Fieldhouse Rd) for half mi; at Etoniah Creek & George's Lake. $10. All year; 14-day limit. Primitive undesignated camping. No facilities, no drkg wtr. Hunting, fishing, hiking, biking, canoeing, bridle trails. Biking trails planned. Managed by state fish & wildlife commission. 8,679 acres. GPS: 29.445894, -81.504186

FORT MYERS (20)

W.P Franklin North $12
Okeechobee Waterway
Corps of Engineers
From N of Fort Myers at jct with I-75 exit 25, 10 mi E on US 80; 4 mi N on SR 31; 3 mi E on SR 78; N on N. Franklin Rd (signs); at Caloosahatchee River. $12 with federal senior pass at 30 elec/wtr sites (30/50-amp); others pay $24. 8 sleep-onboard elec/wtr boat sites, $24 ($12 with senior pass). 35-ft RV limit. Tbls, flush toilets, cfga. Handicap accessible fishing area. Fishing, hiking, boating(l). GPS: 26.72417, -81.69278

FROSTPROOF (21)

Lake Arbuckle $10
Polk County Park
E of Frostproof on SR 630; right for 4 mi on Lake Reedy Blvd; left at sign for 8 mi. $10 without hookups for non-residents; $23 with hookups. All year; 28-day limit.40 sites. $2 for using A/C. Tbls, flush toilets, cfga, drkg wtr, showers, dump ($5; $10 non-campers), shelter. Boating(l), fishing. Lake GPS: 27.695, -81.39611.

Reedy Creek Campground $10
Lake Wales Ridge State Forest
5 mi S of Frostproof on Lake Arbuckle Rd. $5. All year; 14-day limit. Primitive camping at the Arbuckle tract) and Blue Jordan Primitive Campground (on the Walk in the Water tract). Both open during hunting seasons or with state forest use permit. Also tent camping at 2 sites along the Florida Hiking Trail. $10. Toilets, cfga, no drkg wtr. Fish at Lake Godwin in the forest or at adjoining Lake Arbuckle & Lake Weohyakapka. 20,283 acres. Lake GPS: 27.695, -81.39611

HOMESTEAD (23)

Long Pine Key Campground $8
Everglades National Park
7 mi W of park headquarters on Hwy 27. $8 with federal senior pass; others pay $16. All year; 14-day limit. No fees during June-Aug. 108 sites. Tbls, flush toilets, cfga, drkg wtr, showers, dump, no hookups. Fishing pond, hiking trails. Park entry fee. GPS: 25.409, -80.6862

INVERNESS (25)

Mutual Mine Recreation Area $10
Withlacoochee State Forest
S of Inverness on CR 471; E on TR-14. $10 base. All year; 14-day limit. Base fee for primitive sites; $15 for 13 developed sites ($8 for Florida seniors). Tbls, flush toilets, cfga, drkg wtr, no showers. Fishing, hiking.

LABELLE (26)

Okaloacoochee Slough   FREE
Wildlife Management Area
About 10 mi S of Labelle on SR 29; 3.5 mi E on CR 832; 2-3 mi S on Wild Cow Rd. 3 free primitive camping areas along Wild Cow Rd; one is operated all year by Okaloacoochee Slough State Forest; 2 are open only during as hunter camps during hunting seasons and by state forest use permit other times (863-674-4679). Primitive designated tent/RV sites; tbls, cfga, no drkg wtr. Hiking, hunting, fishing in ponds & canals, biking. 32,039 acres.

Ortona Lock & Dam South $12
Corps of Engineers
Okeechobee Waterway
8 mi E of Labelle on SR 80, then N (left) on Dalton Lane, following signs. $12 with federal senior pass; others pay $24. All year; 14-day limit. 51 elec/wtr sites (30/50-amp); 40-ft RV limit; 4 pull-through sites. Tbls, flush toilets, cfga, showers, dump, fishing pier. Fishing, boating(l), watch manatees travel the waterway. GPS: 26.78722, -81.30861

LAKE CITY (27)

Big Camp Hunt Camp   FREE
Osceola National Forest
8 mi NE of Lake City on Hwy 250; 2 mi N on FR 233; 5.5 mi NE on FR 232 (Old Sand Rd); qtr mi W on FR 212; at N edge of Big Gum Swamp Wilderness. Free. All year; 14-day limit. Primitive undesignated sites. Toilet during hunting season, cfga, no drkg wtr. Hunting, hiking. GPS: 30.3955054, -82.4373437

Sandhill Hunt Camp   FREE
Osceola National Forest
17.1 mi NE of Lake City on FR 237. Free. 11/1-1/15; 14-day limit. Undesignated sites (RVs under 22 ft). 5 acres. Toilets during hunting season, firewood, no drkg wtr. Hunting, picnicking, fishing. GPS: 30.3816153, -82.5101231

West Tower Hunt Camp $4
Osceola National Forest
12.5 mi NE of Lake City on FR 233. $4. 11/1-1/15 (hunting season); 14-day limit. 15 sites on 5 acres (RVs under 22 ft). Flush toilets, firewood, piped drkg wtr. Picnicking, fishing, hunting. GPS: 30.3071731, -82.5573454

Wiggins Hunt Camp   FREE
Osceola National Forest
9.3 mi NE of Lake City on FL 250. Free. 11/1-1/15 (hunting

season); 14-day limit. Undesignated sites; 5 acres. Toilets, firewood, no drkg wtr. Swimming, hunting, hiking, picnicking. GPS: 30.2449539, -82.508177

LAKE WALES (28)

Lake Rosalie $10
Polk County Park
E of Lake Wales on SR 60 past Nalcrest/Fedhaven; 2 mi N on Tiger Lake Rd. $10 for non-residents at sites without hookups; $23 with hookups. All year; 28-day limit. 20 sites. Tbls, flush toilets, cfga, drkg wtr, showers, dump, $5 ($10 non-campers). $2 for using A/C. Boating(l), fishing. GPS: 27.935, -81.4026.

LAKELAND (29)

Saddle Creek $10
Polk County Park
About 8 mi E of Lakeland on US 92; N on Fish Hatchery Rd, follow signs. $10 fir non-residents at sites without hookups; $23 with elec/wtr. All year; 28-day limit. $2 for using A/C. 40 sites. Tbls, flush toilets, cfga, drkg wtr, showers, beach, dump($). Nature trail, swimming. GPS: 28.0545, -81.884.

MILTON (31)

Hutton Unit FREE
Blackwater Wildlife Management Area
Blackwater River State Forest
Florida Fish & Wildlife Commission
5 mi E of Milton on Hwy 90; half mi NW on Pond Rd to check station. Primitive camping in designated areas of forest S of Black River. No facilities, no drkg wtr. Hiking, fishing, hunting.

MUNSON (32)

Bear Lake Recreation Area $10
Blackwater River State Forest
2 mi E of SR 4 & CR 191. $10 base. All year; 14-day limit. Base fee for primitive sites; developed sites $15 (Florida seniors pay $8); $20 with elec (Florida seniors pay $10). 40 RV sites; 5 tent sites. Tbls, flush toilets, drkg wtr, showers, elec($), dump, beach. Fishing, boating (ld--elec mtrs only), swimming, hiking, nature & mountain biking trails. 107-acre lake. Trail GPS: 30.8621, -86.8330

Coldwater Recreation Area $10
Blackwater River State Forest
2.5 mi S of state forest HQ in Munson on CR 191; W on Spanish Trail Rd (FR 64). $10 base. All year; 14-day limit. Base fee for primitive sites; developed sites $15 (Florida seniors pay $8); $20 with elec (Florida seniors pay $10). 63 sites. Tbls, flush toilets, cfga, drkg wtr, showers, elec($), dump, amphitheater, group barbecue pit, pavilion, stables, horse stalls, kennels. Swimming, canoeing(l), bridle trails.

Krul Recreation Area $10
Blackwater River State Forest
1.3 mi W of Munson on SR 4; N on access rd. $10 base. All year; 14-day limit. Base fee for primitive sites; developed sites $15 (Florida seniors pay $8); $20 with elec (Florida seniors pay $10). 50 RV sites; 5 tent sites. Tbls, flush toilets, showers, cfga, drkg wtr, elec($), dump, beach. Swimming, hiking. Beginning of Sweetheart Trail with boardwalk. GPS: 30.8621, -86.8522

South Hurricane Lake $10
Blackwater River State Forest
3.5 mi E of SR 4 & 191. $10. All year. Primitive sites. Toilets, cfga, drkg wtr, tbls. Boating(l), fishing. Lake GPS: 30.9432, -86.7513

NAPLES (33)

Picayune Strand State Forest $10
and Wildlife Management Area
18 mi SE of Naples on Tamiami Trail (US 41), just past Collier-Seminole SP, then 2 mi N. $10. All year; 14-day limit. Two other primitive camping areas are on the N side of the WMA, one on Everglades Blvd (Alligator Alley), the other S of Alligator Alley on dirt Kirkland Rd. Tbls, toilets, cfga, no drkg wtr. Hiking & bridle trails. 69,975-acre state forest; 76,000-acre WMA. 22-mi bridle trail, 3.2-0mi hiking trail State forest camping permit required in some areas. GPS: 26.0370418, -8165039.

OCALA (34)

Hopkins Prairie $10
Ocala National Forest
33 mi E of Ocala on SR 40; 8 mi N on SR 19; 3 mi W on FR 50; 1 mi N on FR 86F. $10. 10/1-7/1; 14-day limit. 21 primitive sites (typically 40 ft). Tbls, toilets, cfga, drkg wtr. Boating (cartop launch), fishing, hiking. GPS: 29.27553, -81.69369.

Juniper Springs Campground $10.26
Juniper Springs Recreation Area
Ocala National Forest
28.3 mi E of Ocala on SR 40 to campground sign; left into camp. $10.26 with federal senior pass; others pay $20.52. All year; 14-day limit 4/16-10/14; 30-day limit 10/15-4/15. 79 sites; 35-ft RV limit. Tbls, flush toilets, cfga, drkg wtr, store, dump, showers, pool, interpretive site, dump, Internet access. Boating, swimming, kayaking, canoeing(r), hiking trail. CCC-era shelters. GPS: 29.1822001, -81.7089675

Lake Delancy East $12
Ocala National Forest
11 mi E of Ocala on SR 40; 19.8 mi NE on SR 314; 5.7 mi N on SR 19; 8.5 mi W on FR 66; 2 mi E on FR 11-18.4. $10. 10/1-5/30; 14-day limit. 29 sites; 32-ft RV limit. Tbls, toilets, cfga, drkg wtr. Boating, fishing. Dump at Salt Springs Camp($). GPS: 29.429716, -81.786478

Lake Delancy West $12
Ocala National Forest
11 mi E of Ocala on FL 40; 19.8 mi NE on FL 314; 5.7 mi N on FL 19; 6.4 mi W on FR 66. $12. 10/1-5/30; 14-day limit. 30 sites (RVs under 32 ft). Tbls, toilets, cfga, well drkg wtr. Boating (dlr 2 mi), picnicking, fishing, OHV trails (permit required). Dump at Salt Springs camp ($). Non-campers pay $6 day use fee. GPS: 29.4311, -81.7856

Lake Eaton $8
Ocala National Forest
17 mi E of Ocala on SR 40; 5 mi N on CR 314A; half mi E on gravel FR 96 & FR 96A. $8 (double site $10). 10/1-5/30; 14-day limit. 14 sites. Tbls, toilets, cfga, drkg wtr (hand pump). Dump($) at nearby Salt Springs, Fore Lake & Juniper Springs campgrounds. Showers at nearby Fore Lake. Boating(l), fishing. Non-campers pay $2 fee at boat ramp & for day use. GPS: 29.254142, -81.8645285

OCHOPEE (35)
Bear Island Campground $10
Big Cypress National Preserve
2 mi E of Ochopee on US 41 (Tamiami Trail); 18 mi N on SR 839 (Turner River Rd) to camp at East Hinson Marsh. $10 ($5 with federal senior pass). All year; 10-day limit in preserve 1/1-4/15; 14-day rest of year. 40 primitive sites. No facilities, no drkg wtr. Dump station ($6) at Dona Drive camp in Ochopee. Canoeing, fishing, hunting, hiking, OHV use. Visitor center at preserve headquarters about 15 mi E of Ochopee. GPS: 26.10893, -81.14483

Burns Lake Campground $12
Big Cypress National Preserve
5 mi E of Ochopee on US 41 (Tamiami Trail); N on unpaved Burns Rd. $12 with federal senior pass; others pay $24. 8/29-1/26; 10-day limit in preserve 1/1-4/15; 14-day rest of year. 10 primitive sites RV sites. No facilities, no drkg wtr. Dump station ($6) at Dona Drive camp in Ochopee. Canoeing, fishing, hunting, hiking, OHV use. Visitor center at preserve headquarters about 10 mi E of Burns Rd. Open all year for day use and backcountry access parking.

Fifty-Mile Bend Camp   FREE
Big Cypress National Preserve
About 22 mi E of Ochopee on US 41 (Tamiami Trail). Free. All year; 10-day limit in preserve 1/1-4/15; 14-day rest of year. No facilities, no drkg wtr. Canoeing, fishing, hunting, hiking, OHV use. Visitor center at preserve headquarters about 7 mi W on US 41.

Loop Road Campground   FREE
Big Cypress National Preserve
About 12 mi E of Ochopee on US 41 (Tamiami Trail) to Monroe Station; S on SR 94 (Loop Rd) to camp. Free. All year; 10-day limit in preserve 1/1-4/15; 14-day rest of year. Open primitive sites. No facilities, no drkg wtr.

Canoeing, fishing, hunting, hiking, OHV use. Visitor center at preserve headquarters 5 mi E of Loop Rd jct with US 41.

OLUSTEE (37)
Boat Basin Hunt Camp   FREE
Osceola National Forest
5.4 mi NE on FR 241. 11/1-1/15; 14-day limit. Undesignated sites; 5 acres. Toilets, firewood, no drkg wtr. Boating, swimming, picnicking, fishing, waterskiing, hunting. GPS: 302388437, -82.4490089

Cobb Hunt Camp   FREE
Osceola National Forest
Just E of Olustee on Hwy 90; 2.5 mi N on Hwy 250A; qtr mi NE on FR 235. Free. All year; 14-day limit. Primitive undesignated sites; no facilities, no drkg wtr. Hunting, hiking. GPS: 30.2482884, -82.4090081

Hog Pen Landing $4
Osceola National Forest
Just W of Olustee on Hwy 90; N on FR 241; E on FR 241A; on N shore of Ocean Pond. $4 daily or $40 annually. All year; 14-day limit. Primitive sites. Chemical toilet, cfga, no drkg wtr. Boating(l), fishing. GPS: 30.2401, -8244568

Ocean Pond $6
Osceola National Forest
1 mi E of Olustee on US 90; 4 mi N on CR 250A; 1.3 mi S on FR 268. $6 without hookups; $12 with wtr hookups; $18 at 19 wtr/elec (seniors with federal senior pass pay $3, $6 & $12). All year; 30-day limit. 67 sites (22-ft RV limit). Tbls, flush toilets, showers, cfga, drkg wtr, dump ($3 non-campers), beach. Boating(l), swimming, hiking, fishing, waterskiing. Used as hunt camp in season. Phone. GPS: 30.2402327, -82.4326196

ORANGE PARK (38)
Jennings State Forest $10
5 mi SW of Orange Park on SR 21; 3 mi W on CR 220A. $10. Forest use permit required (904-291-5530). Primitive undesignated camping at 24,000-acre forest. Tbls, toilets, cfga, no drkg wtr. No camping during hunting seasons. Hiking trails, biking, canoeing, horseback riding, hunting, swimming. Free camping permit required. GPS: 30.1566, -81.8693.

PALATKA (39)
Kenwood Recreation Area $12
State of Florida
Marjorie Harris Carr Cross Florida Greenway
9 m S of Palatka on FR 19; 8 mi to FL 315; left 1 mi to Kenwood sign. $12 (Florida seniors pay $6). All year; 7-day limit. 15 undesignated sites. Tbls, toilets, cfga, no drkg wtr. Boating(l), picnicking, fishing, birdwatching. Formerly Cross Florida Barge Canal. GPS: 29.5261, -81.8775

PANAMA CITY (40)

Pine Log State Forest $10
NW of Panama City on SR 79. $10 base. All year; 14-day limit. Base fee for 3 primitive sites without restrooms or showers; $15 for developed non-elec sites with wtr ($8 for Florida seniors); $20 with elec/wtr ($10 for Florida seniors). 20 developed sites. Tbls, flush toilets, cfga, drkg wtr, elec($), showers, dump. Group camping area. Swimming, fishing, boating (l), nature trail, hiking trails, horseback riding. GPS: 30.4051973, -85.8610451

ST. GEORGE (41)

Friendly Hunt Camp   FREE
Osceola Wildlife Management Area
About 13 mi W of St. George on Hwy 2/94; half mi SE on Eddy Grade Rd; half mi S on FR 8. Free. All year; 14-day limit. Primitive undesignated sites; no facilities, no drkg wtr. Hunting, hiking.

Friendly Hunt Camp   FREE
Osceola Wildlife Management Area
About 7 mi W of St. George on Hwy 2/94 to Baxter; 5 mi SW of Baxter on Hwy 250; 11 mi W on Sand Hill Rd; 1 mi Non FR 36; half mi W on FR 28. Free. All year; 14-day limit. Primitive undesignated sites; no facilities, no drkg wtr. Hunting, hiking.

SALT SPRINGS (42)

Davenport Landing #1   FREE
Ocala National Forest
8 mi N of Salt Springs on SR 19; 1 mi W on FR 77; on S shore of Oklawaha River. Free. All year; 14-day limit. 3 primitive undesignated sites; no facilities, no drkg wtr. Fishing, boating. GPS: 29.47117, -81.77550.

Davenport Landing #3   FREE
Ocala National Forest
8 mi N of Salt Springs on SR 19; 2 mi W on FR 77; on S shore of Oklawaha River. Free. All year; 14-day limit. Primitive undesignated sites; no facilities, no drkg wtr. Fishing, boating.

Davenport Landing #4   FREE
Ocala National Forest
8 mi N of Salt Springs on SR 19; 5 mi W on FR 77; on S shore of Oklawaha River. Free. All year; 14-day limit. Primitive undesignated sites; no facilities, no drkg wtr. Fishing, boating.

Shanty Pond Campground $8
Ocala National Forest
Half mi SE of Salt Springs on SR 19; S on access rd to Shanty Pond. $8. 10/15-4/15; 120-day limit. Toilet, cfga, drkg wtr (hand pump). Hunting, fishing, hiking. Base camp for hunters, equestrians. No tents or soft-sided RVs due to bears. GPS: 29.33256, -81.73139

SANDERSON (43)

East Tower Hunt Camp $4
Osceola National Forest
10.1 mi NW of Sanderson on FL 229. $4. Open all year; hunters only during 11/1-1/15 (hunting season); 14-day limit. 15 sites; 5 acres. Flush toilets, firewood, piped drkg wtr. Store/ice/gas. Fishing, hunting, swimming, hiking. GPS: 30.3838417, -82.330952

Seventeen Mile Hunt Camp   FREE
Osceola National Forest
10.7 mi NW of Sanderson on FL 229. Free. 11/1-1/15; 14-day limit. Undesignated sites (RVs under 22 ft). Toilets, firewood, no drkg wtr. Hunting, hiking, fishing, picnicking. Elev 200 ft. 5 acres. River. GPS: 30.3363417, -82.3820639

SEVILLE (44)

Barrs Road Camp   FREE
Lake George Conservation Area
St. John River
Water Management District
Lake George Wildlife Management Area
2 mi W of Seville on SR 305 (Lake George Rd); 2 mi N on Truck Trail 2; 1 mi W on Barrs Rd to E shore of Lake George. Free with state forest use permit (386-329-4404). Part of 19,000-acre Lake George State Forest & 35,000-acre Lake George WMA, co-managed with St. John River WMD. All year; 14-day limit (no camping during hunting seasons). No facilities, no drkg wtr. Hunting, fishing, boating.

Denver Road Camp   FREE
Lake George Conservation Area
St. John River
Water Management District
Lake George Wildlife Management Area
2 mi W of Seville on SR 305 (Lake George Rd); 4 mi N on Truck Trail 2 to jct with Denver Rd. Free with state forest use permit (386-329-4404). Part of 19,000-acre Lake George State Forest & 35,000-acre Lake George WMA, co-managed with St. John River WMD. All year; 14-day limit (no camping during hunting seasons). No facilities, no drkg wtr. Hunting, fishing, boating.

Willow Point   FREE
Lake George Conservation Area
St. John River
Water Management District
Lake George Wildlife Management Area
2 mi W of Seville on SR 305 (Lake George Rd); near E shore of Lake George. Free with state forest use permit (386-329-4404). Part of 19,000-acre Lake George State Forest & 35,000-acre Lake George WMA, co-managed with St. John River WMD. All year; 14-day limit (no camping during hunting seasons). Toilets, cfga, no drkg wtr. Hunting, fishing, boating(l).

SILVER SPRINGS (45)

Fore Lake　　　　　　　　　　　　　　　　$12
Ocala National Forest
5 mi E of Silver Springs on SR 40; 6 mi NE on SR 314. $12. All year; 14-day limit 4/15-10/14; 30-day limit 10/15-4/14. 31 sites (typically 45 ft). Tbls, flush toilets, cfga, drkg wtr, store, dump. Swimming, fishing, boating (l - no mtrs), canoeing. Non-campers pay $3 for dump station, $2 day use fee. GPS: 29.2746973. -81.91703.

SOPCHOPPY (46)

Mack Landing　　　　　　　　　　　　　　$3
Apalachicola National Forest
10.1 mi NW of Sopchoppy on Hwy 375; 1 mi W on FR 375D. On E bank of Ochlocknee River. $3 for camping or day use. All year; 14-day limit. 3 sites (RVs under 22 ft); 3 acres. Tbls, toilets, cfga, well drkg wtr. Boating(l), picnicking, fishing. Hunt camp during gun season. GPS: 30.0932576, -846449066.

Pine Creek Landing　　　　　　　　　　FREE
Apalachicola National Forest
23 mi NW of Sopchoppy on Hwy 375; 1.5 mi W on FR 335; at Ochlockonee River. Free. All year; 14-day limit. Primitive sites. Tbls, portable toilet, cfga, no drkg wtr. Hunting, fishing, hiking, boating(l). Hunt camp during gun season. GPS: 30.2463101, -846965764

Wood Lake　　　　　　　　　　　　　　FREE
Apalachicola National Forest
12 mi W on SR 375; 2.9 mi S on SR 299; 10 mi W on FR 345; 2.1 mi S on FR 345B. Free. All year. 4 sites. Toilets, tbls, cfga, drkg wtr. Boating, picnicking, fishing. Oxbow lake of Ochlockonee River. Hunt camp during gun season. GPS: 30.02389, -84.56528

STUART (47)

St. Lucie Lock & Dam South　　　　　　$12
Corps of Engineers
Okeechobee Waterway
From Stuart at jct with I-95 exit 101, 0.5 mi W on SR 76; right on Locks Rd, following signs. $12 with federal senior pass at 39 wtr/elec RV/tent sites; others pay $24. 4 sleep-aboard elec/wtr boat sites, $24 ($12 with senior pass). 45-ft RV limit. All year; 14-day limit. Tbls, flush toilets, cfga, drkg wtr, showers, playground, dump. Boating(l), fishing. GPS: 27.11028, -80.285

SUMATRA (48)

Cliff Lake Hunt Camp　　　　　　　　FREE
Apalachicola National Forest
About 8 mi N of Sumatra on SR 65; just past hamlet of Wilma, turn SE on FR 13 for 1 mi. Free. All year; 14-day limit. Tbls, portable toilet, cfga, no drkg wtr. Hunting, hiking. GPS: 30.14504, -84.944075

Smith Creek Landing　　　　　　　　FREE
Apalachicola National Forest
About 3 mi S of Sumatra on SR 65; half mi E on FR 124; at Apalachicola River. Free. All year; 14-day limit. Tbls, portable toilet, cfga, no drkg wtr. Hunting, hiking, fishing. GPS: 29.918195, -85.01476

Twin Poles Hunt Camp　　　　　　　　FREE
Apalachicola National Forest
About 8 mi N of Sumatra on SR 65; just past hamlet of Wilma, turn SE on FR 13 for 10 mi. Free. All year; 14-day limit. Tbls, portable toilet, cfga, no drkg wtr. Hiking, hunting. GPS: 30.12627, -84.85446

Wright Lake　　　　　　　　　　　　　　$10
Apalachicola National Forest
2 mi S of Sumatra on SR 65; 2 mi W on FR 101. $10. All year; 14-day limit. 18 sites (22-ft RV limit). Tbls, flush toilets, cfga, drkg wtr, dump. Swimming, hiking, fishing, boating (no mtrs), hunting. Used as hunt camp in season. Non-campers pay $3 day use fee. GPS: 33.9357, -95.2411

TALLAHASSEE (49)

High Bluff Campground　　　　　　　　$10
Lake Talquin State Forest
Joe Budd Wildlife Management Area
W of Tallahassee on I-10 to exit 192, then 2.1 mi W on US 90; left on Hwy 268 for 2.4 mi, then left for 1.2 mi on Peters Rd; S on High Bluff Rd into Joe Budd WMA; primitive camping on N Shore of Lake Talquin. $10. All year; 14-day limit. Tbls, toilets, cfga, no drkg wtr. Hunting, fishing, wildlife viewing, hiking, biking, horseback riding, boating(l). GPS: 30.272063, -84.241325

Whitehead Landing　　　　　　　　　　$3
Apalachicola National Forest
W of Tallahassee on SR 20; left on CR 375, then right on FR 13 & left at sign for Hickory Landing; campground at end of rd. $3. All year; 14-day limit. 6 sites. Tbls, toilets, cfga, drkg wtr. Boating(l), fishing, hiking, hunting. GPS: 30.165085, -84.67545

Williams Landing　　　　　　　　　　$10
Leon County Park
12 mi W of Tallahassee on SR 20; at Lake Talquin. Free. All year; 10-day limit. 18 primitive sites. Tbls, flush toilets, cfga, drkg wtr, showers. Boating(l), fishing, recreation area, hiking. Fish cleaning stations, picnic shelters, fishing piers. GPS: 30.4484, -84.52110

UMATILLA (50)

Clearwater Lake　　　　　　　　　　$9.25
Ocala National Forest
6.3 mi E of Umatilla on SR 42. $9.25 with federal senior pass; others pay $18.50. All year; 14-day limit (180 days 10/15-4/15). 42 sites (typically 50 ft). Tbls, flush toilets, showers, cfga, drkg wtr, dump, beach, store, coin laundry,

phone, interpretive trail. Boating (no mtrs), fishing, swimming, hiking, bike trail, canoeing(r). Non-campers pay day use fee. GPS: 28.97944, -81.5535

Lake Dorr Recreation Area $12
Ocala National Forest
3 mi N of Umatilla on SR 19; at NW shore of lake. $12. All year; 120-day RV limit. 34 sites (22-ft RV limit). Tbls, flush toilets, cfga, drkg wtr, cold showers, phone, beach, dump. Swimming, boating(l), fishing, waterskiing. 1700-Acre lake. Non-campers pay $2 day use fee, $2 boat launch. GPS: 29.01239, -81.637

VENICE (51)

Myakka State Forest $10
About 5 mi E of Venice on Venice Ave; S on River Rd. $10. All year; 14-day limit. Primitive undesignated sites within 8,593-acre state forest, most of which is within city limits of North Port. Tbls, toilets, cfga, no drkg wtr. Hiking, fishing, horseback riding. GPS: 26.584823, -82.165187

WALDENA (52)

Bear Hole Camp FREE
Ocala National Forest
About 5 mi E of Waldena on Hwy 40; S on forest rd to site. Free. All year; 14-day limit. Primitive undesignated camping area; no facilities, no drkg wtr. Fishing, hiking. GPS: 29.1008, -81.4941.

Clear Pond FREE
Ocala National Forest
1.5 mi E of Waldena on Hwy 40; 2 mi S on Hwy 314A; left on access rd. Free. All year; 14-day limit. Primitive undesignated sites; no facilities, no drkg wtr. Fishing, hiking. GPS: 29.754, -81.3712

Lake Mary FREE
Ocala National Forest
1.5 mi E of Waldena on Hwy 40; about 6 mi S on SR 314A; 2 mi S on CR 95; 4.75 mi S on CR 192; qtr mi E on FR 14; 4.75 mi N on FR 14-0 to boat ramp. Free. All year; 14-day limit. Primitive undesignated sites; no facilities, no drkg wtr. Fishing, hiking. GPS: 29.0511, -818240

Little Lake Bryant FREE
Ocala National Forest
1.5 mi E of Waldena on SR 40; 6 mi S on SR 314A; 0.5 mi E on FR 314A-5.8; right on access rd. Free. All year; 4-day limit. 6 primitive sites; no facilities, no drkg wtr, no trash service. Fishing, hiking. GPS: 29.1478, -81899.

Trout Lake FREE
Ocala National Forest
1.5 mi E of Waldena on Hwy 40; about 6 mi S on Hwy 314A to jct with Blue Rd; bear right for about 3 mi, then 3 mi S on forest boundary rd; qtr mi E on FR 573; 1 mi N on Lake Catherine access rd to NW shore of Trout Lake. Free. All

year; 4-day limit. 2 primitive designated sites; no facilities, no drkg wtr, no trash service. Fishing, hiking. GPS: 29.011, -81.8240

WELAKA (53)

Welaka State Forest $10
1 mi S of Welaka on SR 309. $10. All year; 14-day limit. Primitive sites. Tbls, toilets, cfga, no drkg wtr, horse stables & facilities. Hiking, horseback riding, nature trail. GPS: 29.451, -81.672997

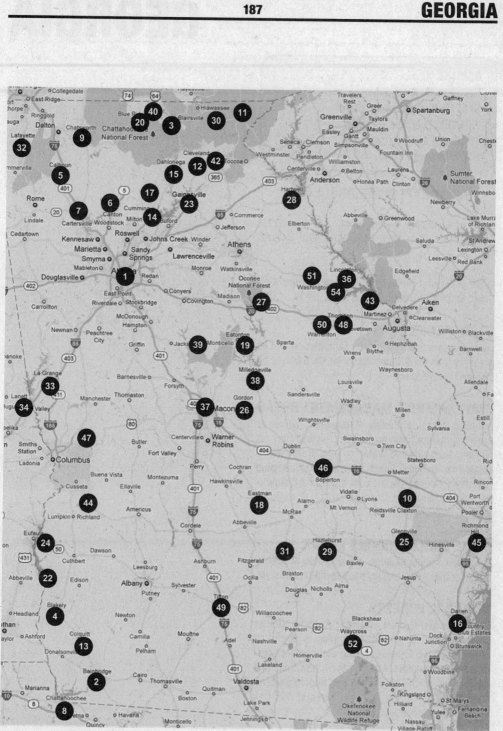

GEORGIA

CAPITAL: Atlanta
NICKNAME: Peach State
STATEHOOD: 1788 – 4th State
FLOWER: Cherokee Rose
TREE: Live Oak
BIRD: Brown Thrasher

WWW.EXPLOREGEORGIA.ORG

Dept. of Economic Development, P.O. Box 1776, Atlanta, GA 30301-1776. 404/656-3590 or 800/VISITGA.

Dept. of Natural Resources, 2 Martin Luther King Drive, Suite 1252, Atlanta, GA 30334.

STATE PARKS
Overnight camping fees vary by campground, but all are more than the $12 necessary for the parks to be included in this book.

STATE WILDLIFE MANAGEMENT AREAS
Although Georgia's Wildlife Management Areas do not have modern camping facilities, visitors may set up camp in designated WMA camping areas. WMAs located on National Forest lands permit camping anywhere. Georgia Department of Natural Resources, Wildlife Resources Division, 2070 U.S. Highway 278, SE, Social Circle, GA 30279.

STATE PUBLIC FISHING AREAS
Primitive camping facilities are available at several areas for those who a enjoy back-to-nature lifestyle.

NATIONAL FORESTS
Chattahoochee-Oconee National Forests. Unless otherwise posted, primitive camping is permitted anywhere in the forest. Camping and campfire permits are not required. Maps of the forest trails and roads are available for a small fee. Superintendent, Chattahoochee-Oconee National Forests, 508 Oak Street NW, Gainesville, GA 30501.

U.S. Army Corps of Engineers, South Atlantic Division, 510 Title Building, 30 Pryor Street, SW, Atlanta, GA 30335-6801.

ATLANTA (1)

Clark Creek South   CLOSED
Corps of Engineers
Allatoona Lake
From I-75 exit 278 N of Atlanta, 2 mi N on Glade Rd, following signs; turn right before lake bridge. This campground was closed in 2011 & not scheduled for reopening. GPS: 34.1031543, -84.6824351

Payne $10
Corps of Engineers
Allatoona Lake
From Atlanta, N on I-75 to exit 277; 2 mi E on SR 92; N (left) on Kellogg Creek Rd, following signs. $11 with federal senior pass at 11 non-elec sites; others pay $20. 49 elec/wtr 30/50-amp sites, $26 base, $30 full hookups ($13 & $15 with senior pass). About 3/25-9/6; 14-day limit. 40-ft RV limit. Tbls, flush toilets, cfga, drkg wtr, showers, dump, coin laundry, playground, beach. Waterskiing, boating(l), fishing, swimming, baseball. GPS: 34.12083, -84.57917

BAINBRIDGE (2)

Faceville Landing $8
Corps of Engineers
Lake Seminole
From Bainbridge, 14 mi S on SR 97, then N on Faceville Landing Rd; between Bainbridge and Chattahoochee, Florida. $8 at 7 primitive sites; 40-ft RV limit. All year; 14-day limit. Tbls, drkg wtr, pit toilets, cfga, picnic shelter, courtesy dock. Fishing, swimming, boating, canoeing, fishing pier. Maintained by Florida Game and Fresh Water Commission. GPS: 30.77, -84.84

Hale's Landing $9
Corps of Engineers
Lake Seminole
SW of Bainbridge on GA 253; S on county's (Ten Mile Still Rd, following signs; in Florida. $9 with federal senior pass at 25 elec/wtr sites (30/50-amp); others pay $18. All year; 14-day limit. Tbls, flush toilets, cfga, drkg wtr, showers, shelter, courtesy dock. Boating(l), fishing, picnicking, canoeing, hunting. GPS: 30.88, -84.66

BLAIRSVILLE (3)

Cooper's Creek Wildlife Management Area   FREE
State Game & Fish Division
5 mi W of Blairsville on US 76 to Mulkey Gap Rd (FR 4); left 8.5 mi to check station. Within Chattahoochee Nat'l Forest. Free. All year; 14-day limit. Primitive dispersed campsites; no facilities. Picnicking, hunting, fishing, hiking. Scenic natural area. GPS: 34.7726, -84.0382.

Lake Winfield Scott $7.50
Chattahoochee National Forest
10 mi S of Blairsville on US 19; 7 mi W on SR 180. $7.50 with federal senior pass; others pay $15 during 4/21-9/30; $7.50 rest of year but no wtr or flush toilets. Non-campers

pay $5 day use fee. 14-day limit. 31 sites (22-ft RV limit). Tbls, flush toilets, cfga, drkg wtr, showers. Swimming, boating, hiking, fishing, hiking trails. Non-campers pay $5 day use fee. GPS: 34.7392585, -83.8879638.

BLAKELY (4)

Coheelee Creek   FREE
Blakely-Earky County Park
George W. Andrews Lake
10 mi SW of Blakely on GA 62 to Hilton; turn N, follow signs approx 2 mi. Free. 3/1-11/30; 14-day limit. 7 primitive sites; 18-ft RV limit. Tbls, toilets, cfga, hand-pumped wtr. Boating(l), fishing. Former Corps of Engineers park now leased to the county. GPS: 31.3043, -85.0852.

BUFORD (14)

Van Pugh South Campground $11
Corps of Engineers
Lake Sidney Lanier
From just NE of Buford from I-985 exit 8, left on SR 347/Friendship Rd; right on McEver Rd; left on Gaines Ferry Rd, following signs. $11 with federal senior pass at 18 non-elec sites; others pay $22. 37 elec/wtr sites, $30 & $32 ($15 & $16 with senior pass). Tbls, flush toilets, cfga, drkg wtr, dump, showers, coin laundry. Fishing, boating. Former day use park now operated as a campground. GPS: 34.18444, -83.9056

CALHOUN (5)

John's Mountain Wildlife Management Area   FREE
State Game & Fish Division
6 mi N of Calhoun on SR 136C to Sugar Valley; left 6 mi to Lake Marvin; check station is at The Pocket. Free. In Chattahoochee National Forest. Primitive dispersed campsites; no facilities. Hunting, hiking. GPS: 34.5334, -850666.

CANTON (6)

Sweetwater Campground $10
Allatoona Lake
Corps of Engineers
From S of Canton at SR 5, 5 mi W on SR 20, across Knox Bridge, then 2 mi S. $10 with federal senior pass at 41 non-elec sites; others pay $20. 118 elec/wtr RV sites (30/50-amp), $26; 2 full hookups $30 ($13 & $15 with senior pass). 23 pull-through sites. 42 tent sites & group camping also available. 3/22-9/3; 14-day limit. During 8/5-8/27, open only Fri & Sat nights; during 8/28-9/3, closed to camping (day use only). RV limit in excess of 65 ft. Tbls, flush toilets, cfga, drkg wtr, dump, coin laundry, playground, beach, showers. Boating(l), fishing, swimming beach. GPS: 34.19444, -84.57889

CARTERSVILLE (7)

Allatoona Wildlife Management Area   FREE
State Game & Fish Division
5 mi e of Cartersville. Hunting, fishing, hiking, birdwatching, field trial access.

Upper Stamp Creek $10
Allatoona Lake
Corps of Engineers
From I-75 exit 290 at Cartersville, 4 mi E on SR 20; 1.3 mi S on Wilderness Rd, following signs; dirt rd to left. $10 with federal senior pass at 2 non-elec sites; others pay $20. 18 elec/wtr 50-amp sites, $26 base, $30 at premium locations ($13 & $15 with senior pass). 5/17-9/3; 14-day limit. 30-ft RV limit. Tbls, flush toilets, cfga, drkg wtr, showers, dump, beach. Swimming, fishing, boating(l). GPS: 34.20278, -84.67667

CHATTAHOOCHEE (FLORIDA) (8)

Eastbank Campground $10
Corps of Engineers
Lake Seminole
From Chattahoochee at jct with US 90, 1.5 mi N on Bolivar St (Booster Club Rd); left on East Bank Rd; near Jim Woodruff Dam. $10 with federal senior pass at 63 elec/wtr 30/50-amp sites; others pay $20. All year; 14-day limit. RV limit over 65 ft. Pavilion, tbls, flush toilets, cfga, drkg wtr, coin laundry, playground, showers, dump, fish cleaning station. Hiking trails, fishing, boating(l), horseshoes, volleyball, dock. Beach nearby. GPS: 30.71806, -84.86111

River Junction $9
Corps of Engineers
Lake Seminole
4 mi N of Chattahoochee, Florida, across state line on SR 386, following signs. $9 with federal senior pass at 11 wtr/elec 30/50-amp sites; others pay $18. All year; 14-day limit. 40-ft RV limit. Tbls, flush toilets, cfga, drkg wtr, showers, coin laundry. Boating(l), fishing. GPS: 30.75, -84.84

CHATSWORTH (9)

Coosawattee FREE
Wildlife Management Area
State Game & Fish Division
12 mi southeast of Chatsworth. Hunting, fishing, hiking, birdwatching, boat ramps, canoe access, picnicking.

Hickey Gap Campground FREE
Chattahoochee National Forest
6 mi N of Chatsworth on US 411; right on Grassy St (narrows to 2 lanes); at "T" jct, turn right for 100 ft, then left on Mill Creek Rd (FR 630) for 6.5 mi; right into camp; at Mill creek. Free. All year; 14-day limit. 5 sites; 24-ft RV limit. Tbls, toilets, cfga, drkg wtr. Fishing. Gap GPS: 34.8942, -84673.

Lake Conasauga $10
Chattahoochee National Forest
4 mi N of Chatsworth on US 411; 10 mi E on FR 18; 10 mi NE on FR 68. $10. About 4/15-10/31; 14-day limit. 31 sites (22-ft RV limit). Tbls, flush toilets, cfga, drkg wtr. Fishing, hiking, boating(l -- elec mtrs), swimming. Elev 3100 ft; 6 acres. GPS: 34.8603581, -84.6493787.

CLAXTON (10)

Evans County Public Fishing Area FREE
State Game & Fish Division
8.5 mi E of Claxton on US 280; right on Old Reidsville-Savanna Rd 1 mi; left on dirt Old Sunbury Rd qtr mi; area marked by Game & Fish sign. Free. 3/1-10/31. Primitive undesignated sites. Tbls, toilets, cfga. Concrete boat ramps, fishing piers. Fishing, hiking, swimming, boating.

CLAYTON (11)

Coleman River Wildlife Management Area FREE
State Game & Fish Division
8 mi W of Clayton on US 76 to Persimmon Rd; right 4.5 mi; left 1.2 mi on Coleman River Rd (gravel) to check station. Very steep mountains; 4WD recommended. Within Chattahoochee National Forest. Free. All year; 14-day limit. Primitive dispersed campsites (several on the Tallulah River); no facilities. Hiking, hunting, fishing. GPS: 34.96676, -83.48988.

Lake Burton Wildlife Management Area FREE
State Game & Fish Division
21 mi N of Clayton on SR 197 to Lake Burton Fish Hatchery on Moccasin Creek; qtr mi on rd opposite hatchery to check station. Free. Within Chattahoochee National Forest. All year; 14-day limit. Primitive dispersed campsites; no facilities. Picnicking, hunting, hiking, fishing, boating. Lake GPS: 34.831075, -83.553652.

Lake Seed Campground FREE
Georgia Power & Light
S of Clayton on US 441; W on Lake Rabun Rd on W side of Lake Seed. Free. 4/1-11/1. 12 primitive sites; no facilities. Beach, picnic area. Boating(l), fishing, swimming. 240-acre lake. Lake GPS: 34.753418, -83.502355

Lake Rabun Beach Recreation Area $7
Chattahoochee National Forest
7 mi S of Clayton on US 441; W on unnumbered county rd, then 2 mi S on SR 15; 5 mi W on CR 10. $7 with federal senior pass for 52 non-elec sites; others pay $14. $9 surcharge for elec/wtr at 21 sites. 4/15-10/31; 21-day limit. Sites typically 50 ft. Tbls, flush toilets, cfga, drkg wtr, dump, showers, store, fishing pier. Swimming, boating(l), hiking, waterskiing. 934-acre Lake Rabun. 34.75708, -83.481934

Sandy Bottoms Recreation Area $7
Chattahoochee National Forest
8 mi W of Clayton on US 76; N on county rd; 5 mi on FR 70; along Tallulah River. $7 with federal senior pass; others pay $14. About 3/15-11/1; 21-day limit. 14 sites (typically 35 ft). Tbls, flush toilets, cfga, drkg wtr. Fishing, hiking. GPS: 34.963867, -83.560303.

Tallulah River Recreation Area $7
Chattahoochee National Forest
8 mi W of Clayton on US 76; 4 mi N on county rd; 1 mi NW

on FR 70. $7 with federal senior pass; others pay $14. About 4/1-11/1; 21-day limit. 17 sites; 45-ft RV limit. Tbls, flush toilets, cfga, drkg wtr. Fishing, hiking trail. GPS: 34.9275627, -835432176.

Tate Branch Recreation Area $7
Chattahoochee National Forest
8 mi W of Clayton on US 76; N on county rd; 4 mi on FR 70; at jct of Tate Branch & Tallulah River. $7 with federal senior pass; others pay $14. About 3/15-10/1; 21-day limit. 19 sites, most small. Tbls, flush toilets, cfga, drkg wtr. Fishing, hiking trail. If camp isn't open, got to Sandy Bottoms. GPS: 34.9550925, -83.5521057.

Warwoman Wildlife Management Area FREE
State Game & Fish Division
Off US 441 N, turn right at Heart of Rabun Motel onto Warwoman Rd for 3.5 mi; left on Finney Creek Rd qtr mi to check station. Within Chattahootchee National Forest. Free. All year; 14-day limit. Primitive undeveloped dispersed sites; no facilities. Hunting, hiking; very rugged terrain. Deer, turkey, wild pigs. GPS: 34.5552, -0831805.

Wildcat Creek #1 $10
Chattahoochee National Forest
9.7 mi W of Clayton on US 76; 5.1 mi S on SR 197; right on FR 26 (Wildcat Rd) for 2.8 mi. $10. All year; 21-day limit. 16 small sites (3 walk-in). Tbls, toilets, cfga, no drkg wtr. Fishing, hiking. Creek GPS: 33.8132, -83.3068.

Wildcat Creek #2 $10
Chattahoochee National Forest
9.7 mi W of Clayton on US 76; 5.1 mi S on SR 197; right on FR 26 (Wildcat Rd) for 4.4 mi. $10. All year; 21-day limit. 16 sites, typically 35 ft. Tbls, toilets, cfga, no drkg wtr. Hiking, fishing.

CLEVELAND (12)

Chattahoochee Wildlife Management Area FREE
State Game & Fish Division
SR 75 from Cleveland to Robertstown; continue qtr mi to first bridge; left on Alt US 75, then right at first rd for 2.8 mi to check station. Free. All year. Primitive dispersed camping; no facilities. In Chattahoochee NF. Hiking.

Chestatee Wildlife Management Area FREE
State Game & Fish Division
10.5 mi N of Cleveland on US 129 to Turner's Corner; left at jct with US 19 for half mi; right on first rd; check station across from campground. Free. Primitive undeveloped camping area. No facilities. In Chattahoochee National Forest. Hunting, hiking. GPS: 34.4253, -083.5515.

Desoto Falls $12
Chattahoochee National Forest
15 mi N of Cleveland on US 129. $12 during 4/3-11/8; $6 with reduced services & no wtr during 1/1-4/2 and 11/9-

12/3. Non-campers pay $3 day use fee. 14-day limit. 24 sites (22-ft RV limit). Chemical flush toilets, cfga, drkg wtr, tbls, showers. Hiking, fishing trail. GPS: 34.710938, -83.912598.

Swallow Creek Wildlife Management Area FREE
State Game & Fish Division
N from Cleveland on SR 75 to Robertstown; continue on to jct with SR 180; 1 mi past jct, follow sign to check station on left. Within Chattahootchee National Forest. Free. All year; 14-day limit. Dispersed sites; no facilities. Hunting, hiking; very rugged. GPS: 34.8625931, 83.6854498.

COLQUITT (13)

Mayhaw Wildlife Management Area FREE
State Game & Fish Division
3 mi northwest of Colquitt. Free. Primitive undesignated camping; no facilities, no drkg wtr. Hunting, hiking, bird-watching, archer and firearm range.

CUMMING (14)

Sawnee Campground $9
Corps of Engineers
Lake Sidney Lanier
From Cumming at jct with SR 400N exit 14, E (left) on Hwy 20; left on Sanders Rd; at 1st stop sign, 3.5 mi right on Buford Dam Rd; on left. $9 with federal senior pass at 11 non-elec sites; others pay $18. 41 elec/wtr RV sites, $30 & $32 ($15 & $16 with senior pass). RV limit 40 ft. Typically open 4/11-9/8, but open all year in 2013; 14-day limit. Tbls, flush toilets, cfga, drkg wtr, showers, dump, coin laundry, beach, playground. Fishing, boating(l), swimming. GPS: 34.17667, -84.07528

Toto Creek $11
Corps of Engineers
Lake Sidney Lanier
From Cumming, N on SR 4009; right on SR 136; right at stop sign; left before crossing bridge. $11 with federal senior pass at 10 primitive sites; others pay $22. About 4/1-9/15; 14-day limit. Tbls, toilets, cfga, drkg wtr, beach. Boating(l), fishing, swimming. Campground may be turned into a county park (probably Dawson County). Most Lanier Corps campgrounds have either been closed, leased out or had their camping fees increased above the levels qualifying them for inclusion here. GPS: 34.16, -84.07

DAHLONEGA (15)

Blue Ridge Wildlife Management Area FREE
State Game & Fish Division
9.3 mi N of Dahlonega on US 19 to Stone Pile Gap; left on SR 60 for 18.7 mi to jct with FR 69; left 2.8 mi. Or, 9 mi W on SR 52 to Grizzle's Store; right for 2.4 mi; right again for 2.4 mi to check station. In Chattahoochee National Forest. Free. Primitive dispersed campsites; no facilities. Hunting, picnicking, hiking. GPS: 34.3941, -84.0912.

Cooper Creek $8-10
Chattahoochee National Forest
26 mi N of Dahlonega on SR 60; 4 mi N on FR 4. $8 base, $10 for waterfront sites during 3/15-10/20; $4 & $5 rest of year but no wtr services. 14-day limit. 15 sites (22-ft RV limit). Tbls, flush toilets, cfga, drkg wtr. Hiking, trout fishing. GPS: 34.763916, -84.066895.

Deep Hole $8-10
Chattahoochee National Forest
27 mi N of Dahlonega on SR 60; at Toccoa River. $8 base, $10 for waterfront sites. All year; 14-day limit. Non-campers pay $3 day use fee. 14-day limit. 8 sites. Tbls, flush toilets, cfga, no drkg wtr. Fishing, hiking, canoeing(l). GPS: 34.74029, -84.14061.

Dockery Lake Recreation Area $8
Chattahoochee National Forest
12 mi N of Dahlonega on SR 60; 1 mi E on FR 654. $8 during 3/20-10/20; $4 off-season but no wtr (restroom open at day use area). 14-day limit. 11 sites (22-ft RV limit). Tbls, flush toilets, cfga, drkg wtr. Fishing, hiking (lakeshore trail to fishing pier), picnicking. 6-acre lake. Carry-down boat access; elec motors. GPS: 34.674805, -83.974609.

Frank Gross Campground $8
Chattahoochee National Forest
27 mi N of Dahlonega on SR 60; 5 mi S on FR 69; at Rock Creek. $8. All year; 14-day limit. 9 sites; 22-ft RV limit. Tbls, flush toilets, cfga, drkg wtr. Fishing, hiking. Fish hatchery nearby. GPS: 34.6739802, -83.9754674.

Mulky Campground $6
Chattahoochee National Forest
26 mi N of Dahlonega on SR 60; 5 mi NE on FR 4; at Cooper Creek. $6. All year;14-day limit; limited service & no wtr 10/21-3/15. 11 sites (22-ft RV limit). Tbls, flush toilets, cfga, drkg wtr. Fishing, hiking. GPS: 34.762451, -87.074463.

DAWSONVILLE (17)
Dawson Forest Wildlife Management Area   FREE
State Game & Fish Division
6 mi w of Dawsonville on GA Hwy 53. Free. Undesignated sites; no facilities. Hunting, interpretive trails, fishing, hiking, birdwatching, canoe access, picnicking, horseback riding. GPS: 34.4501, -84.2274.

EASTMAN (18)
Dodge County Public Fishing Area   FREE
State Game & Fish Division
3 mi S of Eastman on US 23/341; left on CR 49 for .6 mi to lake. All year. Undesignated primitive sites. Tbls, toilets (handicap accessible), cfga. Concrete boat ramps & fishing pier. Fishing, hiking, hunting preserve.

EATONTON (19)
Lake Sinclair Recreation Area $9
Oconee National Forest
10 mi S of Eatonton on US 129; 1 mi E on SR 212; 2 mi E on CR 1062. $9 base; $15 with elec/wtr hookups ($4.50 & $10.50 with federal senior pass). 4/15-12/15; 14-day limit. 44 sites (5 with hookups); 22-ft RV limit. Tbls, flush toilets, cfga, drkg wtr, dump, showers, playground. Boating(l), fishing, swimming, hiking (Twin Bridges Trail). Non-campers pay $3 day use fee. GPS: 33.20639, -83.39778.

ELLIJAY (20)
Rich Mountain Wildlife Management Area   FREE
State Game & Fish Division
7 mi N of Ellijay on SR 5; right for 4 mi on Rock Creek Rd to Stanley Creek check station. Within Chattahootchee National Forest. Free. All year; 14-day limit. Primitive dispersed camping; no facilities. Hunting, hiking, picnicking. GPS: 34.7295, -84.3508.

Ridgeway Campground $10
Corps of Engineers
Carters Lake
From Ellijay, approximately 5 mi W on SR 282; access on left. $10 self-register ($5 with federal senior pass). All year; 14-day limit. 20 primitive sites. Tbls, toilets, cfga, drkg wtr (hand pump). Boating(l), fishing, hiking & mountain biking trails. GPS: 34.63, -8467

Woodring Branch $10
Carters Lake
Corps of Engineers
From Ellijay, 11 mi W on SR 282/US 76, following signs; on N side of lake. $10 at 12 non-elec sites in separate primitive area; $5 with federal senior pass. Main campground, 31 elec/wtr sites, $20 & $22 ($10 & $11 with senior pass). About 5/1-10/30; 14-day limit. RV limit 40 ft. Tbls, flush toilets, cfga, drkg wtr, dump, coin laundry, playground. Fishing, boating(l), picnicking, swimming, hiking. GPS: 34.67056, -84.55

FORT GAINES (22)
Cotton Hill $12
Walter F. George Lake
Corps of Engineers
7 mi N of Fort Gaines on SR 39, then W following signs. $12 with federal senior pass at 91 full-hookup sites; others pay $24. All year; 14-day limit. 40-ft RV limit. Tbls, flush toilets, cfga, drkg wtr, dump, showers, fish cleaning station, beach, playgrounds, coin laundry. Hiking, boating(l), swimming, fishing, waterskiing. GPS: 31.67444, -85.06417

Hardridge Creek $12
Corps of Engineers
Walter F. George Lake
From Ft. Gaines, 3 mi W across river into Alabama; 1 mi W on SR 46; 3 mi N on SR 97; E at sign. $12 with federal senior

pass at 55 elec/wtr sites; others pay $24. 15 full hookups, $26 ($13 with senior pass). RV limit 30 ft. All year; 14-day limit. Tbls, flush toilets, cfga, drkg wtr, showers, dump, fishing pier, playground, beach, coin laundry, shelter. Fishing, boating(l), swimming. GPS: 31.64056, -85.10222

GAINESVILLE (23)

Lake Russell Wildlife Management Area   FREE
State Game & Fish Division
SR 365 N from Gainesville; right on Rock Rd for .7 mi; left for 2.4 mi on Old Hwy 123; right on Ayersville Rd by Milliken plant for 1 mi; left on Check Station Rd for half mi. Within Chattahoochee National Forest. Free. Primitive dispersed campsites; no facilities. Hiking, fishing, hunting. 18 mi of hiking & bridle trails. GPS: 34.5315, -83.4374.

Wilson Shoals Wildlife Management Area   FREE
State Game & Fish Division
14 mi northeast of Gainesville. Free. Undesignated sites; no facilities. Hunting, fishing, hiking, birdwatching, picnicking, horseback riding.

GEORGETOWN (24)

Rood Creek   FREE
Walter F. George Lake
Corps of Engineers
9.5 mi N of Georgetown on SR 39, across Rood Creek, then W. Free. All year; 14-day day limit. Undesignated primitive sites. Tbls, toilets, lantern poles, cfga, drkg wtr. Boating(l), fishing. Boat landing GPS: 32.0257, -85.0424

GLENNVILLE (25)

Big Hammock Public Fishing Area   FREE
State Game & Fish Division
12 mi S of Glennville on US 144 to Altamaha River bridge; area delineated by yellow boundary signs. Free. Access limited during wet weather, closed during flood periods; special access point off CR 441 to Bluff & Cedar Lakes open only 4/1-9/30; remainder of area open all year. Primitive undesignated camping; no facilities. Fishing, hiking, boating (primitive ramps), hunting.

GORDON (26)

Doll Mountain Campground $10
Corps of Engineers
Carters Lake
5.5 mi E of Gordon on SR 136; 3.2 mi E on SR 382, then W; on S side of lake. Caution: Steep downhill grade to campground. $10 base with federal senior pass at 39 elec/wtr sites; others pay $20 base, $22 at premium locations ($11 with senior pass). 4/1-10/30; 14-day limit. RV limit 40 ft; 5 pull-through sites. Tbls, flush toilets, cfga, drkg wtr, pavilion, playground, dump, showers, coin laundry, amphitheater, shelter. Boating(l), fishing, hiking. GPS: 34.51333, -84.62389

Harris Branch Campground   CLOSED
Corps of Engineers
Carters Lake
5.5 mi E of Gordon on SR 136; .7 mi E on SR 382, then NW; on S side of lake. Group camping only; individual sites closed in 2013; check current status with lake office before arrival. GPS: 34.602783, -34.602783, -84.623779

GREENSBORO (27)

Oconee River $5
Oconee National Forest
12 mi N of Greensboro on SR 15. $5. All year; 14-day limit; at Oconee River. 5 sites. Tbls, pit toilets, cfga, no drkg wtr. Hiking, boating(l), fishing. Sites being upgraded (new pads & tbls). 33.7212338, -83.28988.

Redlands Wildlife Management Area   FREE
State Game & Fish Division
4 mi N of Greensboro on SR 15; check station on left. Within Oconee National Forest. Free. All year; 14-day limit. Primitive dispersed campsites; no facilities. Picnicking, hiking, hunting, fishing.

HARTWELL (28)

Georgia River Recreation Area $6
Hartwell Lake
Corps of Engineers
6.5 mi N of Hartwell on US 29 (between Hartwell, GA, and Anderson, SC); on Savannah River just below dam. $6 at 15 primitive sites during 5/1-9/8; some sites may be open & free off-season. 14-day limit. Small RVs welcome, but sites most suitable for folding trailers, pickup campers & tents. Register at lake visitor center on Hwy 29. Tbls, flush toilets, cfga, central drkg wtr spigot, fishing piers. Dump nearby. Fishing, picnicking. 35 acres. GPS: 34.40, -82.70

Hart County Wildlife Management Area   FREE
State Game & Fish Division
5 mi southeast of Hartwell on GA Hwy 77 Alt. E. Free. Undesignated sites; no facilities; no drkg wtr. Hunting, birdwatching, picnicking.

Milltown   CLOSED
Hartwell Lake
Corps of Engineers
From Hartwell, 4 mi N SR 51; 4 mi E on New Prospect Rd, following signs; S of Reed Creek. Individual campsites were closed during 2013 & 2014 due to budget cuts and leased to Hart County. GPS: 34.40972, -82.87583

Paynes Creek $12
Hartwell Lake
Corps of Engineers
10 mi N of Hartwell on SR 51, following signs; on Tugaloo arm of lake. $12 base with federal senior pass at 44 elec/wtr sites (30/50-amp); others pay $24 base, $26 at pre-

mium locations ($13 with senior pass). 5/1-9/8; 14-day limit. 60-ft RV limit. Tbls, flush toilets, cfga, drkg wtr, dump, beach, playground, showers. Swimming, fishing, boating(l). New 7.2-mi hiking/biking trail GPS: 34.47927, -82.97528

HAZELHURST (29)
Bullard Creek Wildlife Management Area   FREE
State Game & Fish Division
6.5 mi N of Hazelhurst on US 221; right at entrance sign to Philadelphia Church; left onto dirt rd 1 mi to check station. Free. All year. Primitive designated camping area; no facilities. Hunting, hiking. Continental Can timberland, S bank of Altamaha River. GPS: 31.9501901, -82.4665193.

HELEN (30)
Andrews Cove $12
Chattahoochee National Forest
6 mi N of Helen on SR 75. $12. About 5/10-11/15; 21-day limit. 10 sites (22-ft RV limit). Tbls, chemical flush toilets, cfga, drkg wtr. Hiking, fishing, picnicking($3). Anna Falls, Appalachian Trail, High Shoals Scenic Area nearby. Elev 2000 ft; 3 acres. GPS: 34.7773163, -83.739344.

Upper Chattahoochee River $12
Chattahoochee National Forest
8 mi N of Helen on SR 75; just past milepost 15, turn left on gravel Chattahoochee River Rd for 5 mi; at headwaters of Chattahoochee River. $12 (groups $35). About 3/15-10/31; 21-day limit. 34 sites; 35-ft RV limit. Tbls, chemical flush toilets, cfga, drkg wtr, lantern posts. Fishing, hiking. Anna Ruby Falls nearby. GPS: 34.78659, -83.68297.

Low Gap Campground $12
Chattahoochee National Forest
1.4 mi N of Helen on SR 75; left on SR 75 Alt. for short distance, then right on Myra Branch Rd for half mi; continue on Poplar Stump Rd for 3.1 mi; at Low Gap Creek. $12. About 3/15-10/31; 21-day limit 13 sites; 28-ft RV limit due to narrow, curving rds. Tbls, chemical flush toilets, cfga, drkg wtr. Hiking, fishing. GPS: 34.7509, -83.782909

JACKSONVILLE (31)
Horse Creek Wildlife Management Area   FREE
State Game & Fish Division
5 mi southeast of Jacksonville along GA 117. Free. Undesignated dispersed camping; no facilities, no drkg wtr. Hunting, fishing, birdwatching, hiking, canoe access.

LAFAYETTE (32)
Crockford-Pigeon Mountain   FREE
Wildlife Management Area
State Game & Fish Division
5 mi southwest of Lafayette. Free. Primitive dispersed camping; no facilities. Hunting, fishing, hiking, birdwatching, field trial access, picnicking, horseback riding.

The Pocket Recreation Area $10
Chattahoochee National Forest
13.5 mi E of Lafayette on SR 136; 8 mi S on FR 203. $10. 4/1-11/1; 14-day limit. 27 sites. Tbls, flush toilets, cfga, drkg wtr. Fishing, hiking. GPS: 34.586426, -85.082275. GPS: 34.58475, -85.0853

LAGRANGE (33)
Holiday Campground $12
Corps of Engineers
West Point Lake
From LaGrange, 7 mi W on SR 109; 2.3 mi S on Thompson Rd. $12 with federal senior pass at 92 elec/wtr sites; others pay $24. About 2/22-9/29; 14-day limit. 65-ft RV limit. 3 group camping areas. Tbls, flush toilets, cfga, drkg wtr, showers, coin laundry, beach, dump. Baseball, basketball, tennis, swimming, hiking, waterskiing, fishing, boating(l). GPS: 33.02611, -85.17889

Ringer Campground   CLOSED
Corps of Engineers
West Point Lake
From LaGrange, 8.7 mi N on US 27, then W. All year; 14-day limit. 37 sites (20-ft RV limit). Free. Tbls, toilets, cfga, drkg wtr (hand pumped). Fishing, waterskiing, boating(l), nature trail. This is the only free camping area at West Point Lake. GPS: 32.91, -85.19. Note: This campground was closed in 2013 by budget cuts; check current status with lake office before arrival.

Whitetail Ridge $12
West Point Lake
Corps of Engineers
7 mi W of LaGrange on SR 109; 0.8 mi S on Thompson Rd; on left. $12 with federal senior pass at 58 elec/wtr sites; others pay $24. 3/18-11/27; 14-day limit. 4 pull-through. RV limit in excess of 65 ft. Flush toilets, cfga, tbls, drkg wtr, coin laundry, playground, dump, showers. Waterskiing, fishing, boating(l), hiking. GPS: 33.02222, -85.19167

LANETT (ALABAMA) (34)
Amity Campground $12
West Point Lake
Corps of Engineers
7 mi N of Lanett, AL, on CR 212; 0.5 mi E on CR 393, following signs. $12 with federal senior pass at 93 elec/wtr sites; others pay $24. Tents $16 ($8 with senior pass). About 3/8-9/8; 14-day limit. Tbls, flush toilets, cfga, drkg wtr, showers, dump, amphitheater, interpretive trail. Basketball, tennis, boating(l), playground, fishing. GPS: 32.97083, -85.22222

LINCOLNTON (36)
Broad River   CLOSED
J. Strom Thurmond Lake
Corps of Engineers
From US 378 at Lincolnton, 14 mi N on SR 79 to access rd; cross bridge; on S shore of Broad River at confluence

with Savannah River. In 2014, campground was leased to Lincoln County. GPS: 33.9616, -83575

Bussy Point $6
J. Strom Thurmond Lake
Corps of Engineers
From Lincolnton, on SR 47 to SR 220 NE; exit S at Kenna on gravel rd; at entrance to Bussy Point Wilderness Area, a peninsula on the lake. $6 self-registration. All year; 14-day limit. 10 primitive sites plus 4 equestrian sites. Tbls, pit toilets, cfga, drkg wtr. 12.5-mi trail for hiking, biking, horseback riding; boating(l), fishing. Note: This campground is scheduled for $25,000 in improvements, primarily for equestrian camping. GPS: 33.42, -82.18

Hester's Ferry CLOSED
Corps of Engineers
J. Strom Thurmond Lake
10 mi N on SR 79 from US 378 at Lincolnton; on Fishing Creek. In 2014, campground was leased to Lincoln County. GPS: 33.9425, -82.55028

MACON (37)
Ocmulgee River Wildlife Management Area FREE
State Game & Fish Division
S of Macon on US 23 to SR 96; continue on 1 mi, then turn right on first paved rd, follow signs to check station. Free. All year. Primitive undeveloped camping area; no facilities. Fishing, hiking, hunting, picnicking, boating.

Rum Creek (Lake Julette) FREE
Public Fishing Area and
Wildlife Management Area
State Game & Fish Division
15 mi N of Macon off US 23 (on W side of rd); located 7 mi E of Forsyth. Free. All year. Primitive undesignated camping. Toilets, tbls, cfga. Concrete boat ramps. Fishing, hunting, picnicking, boating, hiking. 20-hp boat motor limit. 8,100 acres, habitat for one of the most varied bird populations in the Southeast. Hunting. GPS: 33.0546, -83.8055.

MILLEDGEVILLE (38)
Baldwin Forest Public Fishing Area FREE
State Game & Fish Division
4 mi S of Milledgeville on US 441; entrance on E side of rd, marked by Fish & Game sign. Free. 3/1-10/31 on Wed, weekends. Undesignated primitive sites. Toilets, no other facilities. Fishing. GPS: 33.0637, -83.1813.

MONTICELLO (39)
Cedar Creek Wildlife Management Area FREE
State Game & Fish Division
Three-fourths mi E of Monticello on SR 16; take right fork on SR 212 for 12 mi to check station sign; follow arrow half mi to check station. Free. All year. Primitive dispersed camping; no facilities. In Oconee National Forest. Hunting, hiking, picnicking. GPS: 33.221, -83.516.

Hillsboro Hunt Camp FREE
Oconee National Forest
From town of Hillsboro on Hwy 11 just S of Monticello, follow paved county rd 3 mi SE to camp. Free. All year; 14-day limit. 7 sites. Tbls, toilets, cfga, no drkg wtr. Fishing, hiking. GPS: 33.1684634, -83.6629512.

MORGANTON (40)
Morganton Point $7.50
Chattahoochee National Forest
1 mi W of Morganton on CR 616; on Blue Ridge Lake. $7.50 with federal senior pass; others pay $15. About 4/15-10/31; 14-day limit. 43 sites (28-ft RV limit). Tbls, flush toilets, cfga, drkg wtr, hot showers, store. Boating(l), fishing, swimming, waterskiing. GPS: 34.870361, -84.244629.

MOUNT AIRY (42)
Lake Russell $12
Chattahoochee National Forest
1.5 mi N of Mount Airy on US 123; 2 mi E on FR 59. $12 ($14 for picnic/swim sites); seniors with federal senior pass pay $6 & $7. 4/10-10/31; 14-day limit. 41 sites (22-ft RV limit). Tbls, flush toilets, showers, cfga, drkg wtr, dump. Swimming, boating(l), fishing, hiking. Group camping available. 100-acre lake. GPS: 34.494385, -83.494873.

POLLARDS CORNER (43)
Petersburg Campground $9
J. Strom Thurmond Lake
Corps of Engineers
2 mi N of Pollards Corner on US 221, then E. $9 with federal senior pass at 8 non-elec sites; others pay $18. 85 elec/wtr sites (most 50-amp), $24 base for 30-amp, $26 for 50-amp elec/wtr ($12 & $13 with senior pass). All year; 14-day limit. Tbls, flush toilets, cfga, drkg wtr, fish cleaning station, 2 beaches, pond, shelters, fishing dock. Boating(l), fishing, hiking trail, swimming. GPS: 33.66194, -82.26083

Ridge Road Campground $9
J. Strom Thurmond Lake
Corps of Engineers
From Hwy 221 at Pollards Corner, 4 mi W on SR 47 toward Lincolnton, then 4 mi E on Ridge Rd to lake. $9 base with federal senior pass at 6 non-elec sites; $12 at 63 elec/wtr 50-amp site (others pay $18 & $24. Double sites up to $52. 4/1-9/30; 14-day limit. 50-ft RV limit; 27 pull-through. Tbls, flush toilets, cfga, drkg wtr, dump, showers, beach, fish cleaning station, fishing pier. Hiking, boating(l), fishing, swimming. GPS: 33.68, -82.25861

RICHLAND (44)
Hannahatchee Creek FREE
Wildlife Management Area
State Game & Fish Division
9 mi southwest of Richland. Free. Primitive undesignated sites; no facilities. Hunting, hiking, birdwatching. GPS: 32.129197, -84.768112.

RICHMOND HILL (45)

Richmond Hill Wildlife Management Area   FREE
State Game & Fish Division
5 mi southeast of Richmond Hill. Free. All year. Primitive undesignated sites; no facilities. Hunting, fishing, hiking, birdwatching, boating(l).

SOPERTON (46)

Treutlen County Public Fishing Area   FREE
State Game & Fish Division
4.5 mi N of Soperton on CR 166; right at Game & Fish sign onto dirt rd. Free. All year. Primitive undesignated camping; no facilities. Boating(l), fishing, hiking.

TALBOTTON (47)

Big Lazer Creek Pubic Fishing Area   FREE
State Game & Fish Division
4 mi E of Talbotton on US 80; left on Po Biddy Rd 6.4 mi to Bunkham Rd; left into area. Free. All year. Primitive undesignated sites. Toilets, tbls, cfga. Boating(l), fishing pier, hikng, hunting.

THOMSON (48)

Big Hart Campground $12
J. Strom Thurmond Lake
Corps of Engineers
3 mi N of Thomson on US 78, past jct with SR 43, then 4 mi E (right) on Russell Landing Rd, following signs; at confluence of Big Creek & Hart Creek on W end of lake. $12 base for 31 wtr/elec 30/50-amp sites; others pay $24 base, $26 at premium locations ($13 with senior pass). 4/1-10/31; 14-day limit. RV limit 60 ft. Group camping available. Tbls, flush toilets, cfga, drkg wtr, showers, dump, playground, beach, fishing pier, fish cleaning station. Hiking, fishing, boating(l), swimming. GPS: 33.61458, -82.50875

Clark Hill/Thurmond Lake   FREE
Wildlife Management Area
State Game & Fish Division
10 mi N of Thomson on US 78; right on dirt rd at WMA sign for 2.5 mi to check station. Free. All year. Primitive undeveloped campsites; camp only in designated areas. Hunting, picnicking, fishing.

McDuffie Wildlife Management Area   FREE
State Game & Fish Division
8 mi e of Thomson on Fish Hatchery Rd. Free. Hunting, fishing (WMA stamp required to fish), birdwatching, archery range, boating(l), canoe access.

TIFTON (49)

Paradise Public Fishing Area   FREE
State Game & Fish Division
8 mi E of Tifton on Hwy 82 to Brookfield-Nashville Rd near Brookfield; follow signs to the area. Free. All year. Primitive undesignated camping. Toilets (handicap-accessible), tbls, cfga. Boating(ld), fishing pier.

WARRENTON (50)

Ogeechee Wildlife Management Area   FREE
State Game & Fish Division
SW of Warrenton on SR 16 to Jewell; follow signs to check station from Ogeechee River. Free. Primitive undeveloped tent camping 1 day prior to hunting; camp must be cleared by noon on day following hunt.

WASHINGTON (51)

Holiday Campground   FREE
Wilkes County Park
About 20 mi E of Washington on US 378, then SE at park sign. Free. All year. 30 undesignated sites. Tbls, toilets, cfga, dump, no drkg wtr. Boating(l), fishing, swimming, waterskiing. On remote section of Strom Thurmond Lake.

WAYCROSS (52)

Dixon Memorial Wildlife Management Area   FREE
State Game & Fish Division
6 mi southeast of Waycross. Free. All year. Primitive undesignated sites; no facilities. Hunting, fishing, hiking, field trial access, firing range, canoe access.

WEST POINT (53)

R. Shaefer Heard $12
West Point Lake
Corps of Engineers
From West Point, 4 mi N on US 29 to dam rd, then left at signs. $12 with federal senior pass at 117 elec/wtr RV sites; others pay $24; 10 sites with decks; 7 pull-through). About 2/25-9/25; 14-day limit. RV limit in excess of 65 ft. Tbls, flush toilets, cfga, drkg wtr, showers, dump, coin laundry, beach. Hiking, boating(l), fishing, swimming, tennis, baseball. GPS: 39.92722, -85.16389

WOODLAWN (54)

Clay Hill   CLOSED
Corps of Engineers
J. Strom Thurmond Lake
3 mi S of Woodlawn on SR 43; on the E side, N shore of Little River. In 2014, campground was leased to Lincoln County. GPS: 33.3956, -82.670

Eastport

Bonners Ferry

Coolin

Newport

Sandpoint

Priest River   Clark Fork

Athol

Hayden

Coeur d'Alene

Kingston

Plummer   Saint Maries   Calder

Avery

Tensed

Clarkia

Harvard

Deary

Moscow

Headquarters

Orofino   Pierce

Lewiston

Winchester   Kamiah

Kooskia   Lowell

Cottonwood

Grangeville

White Bird   Elk City   Red River Hot Springs

Riggins

Shoup

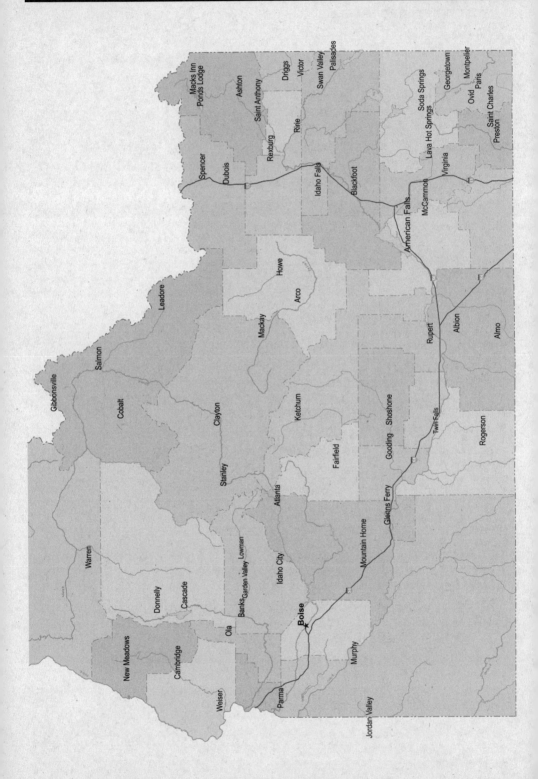

IDAHO

> **CAPITAL:** Boise
> **NICKNAME:** Gem State
> **STATEHOOD:** 1890 – 43rd State
> **FLOWER:** Syringa
> **TREE:** White Pine
> **BIRD:** Mountain Bluebird

WWW.VISITIDAHO.ORG

Idaho Division of Tourism Development, 700 West State St, PO Box 83720, Boise, ID 83720-0093; 208-334-0093; 800/VISIT-ID.

Dept of Fish and Game, 600 S. Walnut St., Boise, ID 83707. 208/334-3700.

REST AREAS
Overnight stops at most state rest areas are not permitted.

STATE PARKS
Campsites $10 to $31 per night, depending upon amenities. Primitive sites without amenities are $10-$13; standard sites (table, grill, campspur, vault toilet, no water) are $12-$21; "serviced" sites (with water OR electric hookups) are $20-$25; serviced sites with water and electric are $24-$29; full hookups, $26-$31 Maximum length of stay, 15 days in any 30-day period. Seniors (62 or older) may camp for half price at nine parks during Monday and Thursday. Day-use fees are no longer charged in addition to camping fees. Monthly rates for campsites are available. Pets on leashes are permitted in campgrounds. RV size restrictions range from 22 feet to 35 feet. Handicapped camping sites area available in each campground. Non-campers pay $3 for showers. For more information, write Idaho Department of Parks and Recreation, PO Box 83720, Boise, ID 83720-0065; 208/334-4199.

NATIONAL FORESTS
Bitterroot National Forest. No fees are charged for camping at the forest's five recreation sites in Idaho. 316 N. 3rd St., Hamilton, MT 59840. 406/363-7161.

Boise National Forest. At 2.6 million acres, it is one of the nation's largest. It has 70 developed campgrounds. Boise National Forest, 1249 S. Vinnell Way, Suite 200, Boise, ID 83709. 208/373-4100.

Caribou National Forest and Curlew National Grasslands. Camping in any unimproved site is regulated only by a 16-day limit. The forest has several developed campgrounds. Caribou-Targhee National Forest, 1405 Hollipark Dr, Idaho Falls, ID 83401; 208-524-7500.

Challis National Forest. The Middle Fork of the Salmon Wild and Scenic River flows 106 miles through the Idaho Primitive Area. Free campsites are along the river, and a primitive trail parallels it. For a free guide and map that pinpoint river campsites and campgrounds accessible by vehicle, contact Forest Service, Intermountain Region, 324-25th St., Ogden, UT 84401. Salmon-Challis National Forest, 1206 S. Challis St., Salmon, ID 83467. 208/756-5100.

Clearwater National Forest. Campgrounds which are not closed by accessibility may be used without charge during the off-season. Camping elsewhere in the forest is permitted unless otherwise posted. Numerous attractive roadside campsites are available. Of special interest to readers of this book: The forest's two main rivers, the North Fork of the Clearwater and the Lochsa, are paralleled by road -- Forest Roads 247 and 250 on the North Fork and Highway 12 along the Lochsa. Numerous no-cost "dispersed" campsites are along both roads. 12730 Highway 12, Orofino, ID 83544; 208/476-4541.

Nez Perce National Forest. It has 29 campgrounds. 1005 Highway 13, Grangeville, ID 83530. 208/983-1950.

Payette National Forest. It has 25 developed campgrounds and more than 2,400 miles of trails. 800 W. Lakeside Avel, PO Box 1026, McCall, ID 83638. 208/634-0700.

St. Joe, Kaniksu and Coeur D'Alene National Forests. The forests do not have free off-season periods; fees are charged the entire time the campgrounds are open. 3815 Schreiber Way, Coeur d'Alene, ID 83815. 208/765-7223.

Salmon National Forest. All sites for which fees are charged are free during the off-season. Weather may prevent access, however. 1206 S. Challis St., Salmon, ID 83467. 208/756-5100.

Bighorn Crags Area--Idaho Primitive Area. Primitive campsites with toilet facilities are Crags Camp (main trailhead), Big Clear Lake, Birdbill Lake, Heart Lake, Terrace Lake and Welcome Lake.

Sawtooth National Forest. Many campgrounds are available without charge before and after the "managed" season. Fees are charged only if all standardly available services, such as drinking water and toilets, are still offered. Water supplies are shut off during free periods. 2647 Kimberly Road East, Twin Falls, ID 83301. 208/737-3200.

Targhee National Forest. This 1.8 million-acre area has 31 developed campgrounds as well as numerous undeveloped, dispersed camping areas that are open to camping without charge. Some campgrounds are open to free dry camping until access is blocked by snow; water and trash service are not provided during free periods. 1405 Hollipark Dr, Idaho Falls, ID 83401; 208-524-7500.

CRATERS OF THE MOON NATIONAL MONUMENT

There are no backcountry campsites, but camping is permitted anywhere in the 68-square-mile wilderness so long as it is one mile within the wilderness boundary. Entrance fees are for 7 days; $15 per vehicle, $7 per person or $10 per motorcycle. Entrance fees are not collected when the park road is closed because of snow (usually mid-October to late April). . Camping fees of $8 are collected at Lava Flow Campground when the water supply is turned off (usually mid-October to late April). Otherwise camping fees at the 42-site facility are $15; no hookups are available. No wood fires; dump stations and showers are not available. A wilderness permit is required for camping in the wilderness.

ALBION (S)

Bennett Springs   FREE
Sawtooth National Forest
5.5 mi SE of Albion on SR 77; 4.9 mi SW on FR 549. 5/30-
10/31; 14-day limit. 6 sites. Tbls, toilets, cfga, no drkg wtr.
Picnicking, hiking, fishing (2 mi). Elev 8000 ft; 5 acres.
Mountains. Streams.

Lake Cleveland $10
Sawtooth National Forest
5.5 mi SE of Albion on SR 77; 10 mi W on FR 549 (very
rough). $10. 7/10-10/31; 14-day limit. 26 sites (17 sites
in E camp, best for RV's, 9 in W camp RV & trailer not
reccommended). Tbls, toilets, cfga, no drkg wtr. Fishing,
hiking, mountain bike trails, bridle trails.

Thompson Flat $8
Sawtooth National Forest
From Albion, 5.6 mi E & S on SR 77; 7.9 mi W on FR 549
(Howell Canyon Rd). $8. 7/1-10/31; 14-day limit. 20 sites;
30-ft RV limit (tight turn-arounds). Tbl, toilets, cfga, no
drkg wtr, no trash service. Biking, hiking, fishing, horseback riding. Elev 8400 ft.

ALMO (S)

City of Rocks National Reserve $12
Idaho Parks & Recreation
3 mi SW of Almo on Elba Almo Rd. $12. 4/1-11/1; 15-day
limit. Managed jointly by National Park Service and Idaho
Department of Parks & Recreation. 65 Standard sites Tbls,
toilets, cfga, no drkg wtr. Mountain biking, rock climbing,
horseback riding. 14,300-acre scenic geologic area.

ALPINE (WYOMING)

Alpine Campground $12
Targhee National Forest
3 mi NW of Alpine on US 26; at SE shore of Palisades Reservoir. $12 during MD-LD; 14-day limit. 19 sites (32-ft RV
limit). Tbls, toilets, cfga, drkg wtr. Fishing, hiking, horseback riding. Palisades Reservoir. Snake River; Yellowstone
and Grand Teton National Parks. Elev 5600 ft

McCoy Creek $10
Targhee National Forest
5 mi S of Alpine on US 89; 7 mi NW on FR 087; at S end
of Palisades Reservoir. $10 during MD-LD; free LD-10/31,
but no wtr or services; 14-day limit. 17 sites (32-ft RV size
limit). Tbls, flush toilets, cfga, drkg wtr. Boating(l), canoeing, swimming, fishing, waterskiing. Elev 5800 ft; 4 acres.

AMERICAN FALLS (S)

Great Rift Backcountry   FREE
Bureau of Land Management
From I-86 exit 40 N of American Falls, NE on SR 39 past
American Falls dam, then left on Center Pleasant Valley
Rd (Rd 2600-S) for 7 mi; 6 mi N on Lava Bed Rd; 6 mi on
dirt Crystal Cave Rd to vicinity called "The Frying Pan."

Free. 4/1-11/31; 14-day limit. Primitive undesignated
camping; no facilities. The 635-square-mile Great Rift is
the largest, deepest and most recent volcanic rift system
in continental U.S. Explore lava caves, spatter caves, ice
tubes, cinder cones.

Massacre Rocks State Park $12
10 mi SW of American Falls on I-86, exit 28. Seniors
receive 50% discount Mon-Thurs. Base Rates, Std site
$12-$21, w/wtr or elec $20-$25. wtr and elec $24-$29
wtr, elec & sewer $26-$29.. All year; 15-day limit. 40 sites
(55-ft RV limit). Tbls, toilets, cfga, drkg wtr, dump, showers. Limited facilities in winter. Boating(ld), fishing, hiking
trails, nature program, mountain biking, horseshoes, visitor center, disc golf, basketball. Elev 4400 ft; 990 acres.
Register Rock from Oregon Trail pioneers.

Pipeline Recreation Site   FREE
Bureau of Land Management
Pocatello Field Office
1 mi W on N Frontage Rd; N toward river. Free. 4/15-10/31;
14-day limit. 8 sites, 25-ft RV limit. Toilets, cfga, tbls.
Boating, fishing, picnicking.

ARCO (S)

Lava Flow $7.50
Craters of the Moon National Monument
18 mi S of Arco on US 20. $7.50 with federal senior pass
others pay $15 plus entry fee; All year; 7-day limit. 42 sites
(35-ft RV limit). Tbls, toilets, cfga, drkg wtr. Hiking, winter
sports, visitor center, interpretive programs. Monument

ASHTON (S)

Cave Falls $10
Targhee National Forest
5.7 mi NE of Ashton on SR 47; 17.6 mi E on E 1400 N Rd
(Cave Falls Rd, 12 mi dirt); half mi S of Yellowstone National Park at Fall River IN WYOMING. $10. 6/1-10/1; 16-day
limit. 23 sites (22-ft RV limit). Tbls, toilets, cfga, drkg wtr.
Swimming, fishing, hiking trails. Elev 6200 ft; 16 acres.

Pole Bridge Camping Area   FREE
Targhee National Forest
15.8 mi NE of Ashton on SR 47; right for 3.5 mi on FR 150,
then left 5 mi; at Warm River. Free. 6/1-10/31. 14-day limit.
Undesignated primitive sites. Pit toilet, cfga, no other facilities. Fishing, picnicking.

Riverside $7.50
Targhee National Forest
16.5 mi N of Ashton on US 20; 1.2 mi SE on Riverside
Campground Rd; at Henry's Fork River. $7.50 with federal
senior pass; others pay $15. MD-9/15; 16-day limit. 55
sites (40-ft RV limit). Tbls, toilets, cfga, drkg wtr. Fishing,
boating. Elev 6200 ft; 24 acres.

Warm River $7.50
Targhee National Forest
10 mi NE of Ashton on SR 47; right on Fish Creek Rd (FR 082) for qtr mi; near confluence of Warm River & Henrys Fork. $7.50 with federal senior pass; others pay $15. 5/15-9/26; 16-day limit. 13 RV/tent sites (40-ft RV limit). Flush toilets, cfga, drkg wtr, Fishing, hiking, floating, biking, horseback riding. Handicap access. Non-campers pay $7.50 day use fee. Elev 5200 ft; 7 acres.

West End FREE
Targhee National Forest
18 mi N of Ashton on US 20; 15 mi NW on FR 167; on Island Park Reservoir. Free. MD-10/15; 16-day limit. 19 dispersed, unmaintained sites (RVs under 23 ft). Toilets, cfga, no drkg wtr.. Swimming, boating (ld), picnicking, fishing, waterskiing, berry picking, horseback riding. Elev 6200 ft.

ASOTIN, WASHINGTON
Heller Bar Campground FREE
Bureau of Land Management
Cottonwood Field Office
21 mi SE of Asotin, WA, on Lower Snake River Rd. Free. Primitive camping. All year; 14-day limit. Tbls, toilets, cfga, no drkg wtr. Boating(l), fishing. Primary take-out spot for rafters & primary launch site for power boats into Hells Canyon.

ATHOL (N)
Farragut State Park $12
Ward Primitive Camping Area
4 mi E of Athol on SR 54; off US 95. $12 at dispersed primitive sites along road edge for self-contained RVs; no services; dump station with fresh wtr nearby. Late Mar to early Nov. Off-season primitive sites open at Thimbleberry area; no services, no wtr, pit toilets.

Standard sites without hookups at Whitetail Campground, $12-21. Late March-early Nov; 15-day limit. Central shower, wtr, restrooms.

Serviced sites with wtr/elec at Waldon Campground, Snowberry Campground, Gilmore Campground, $24-$29; central shower & restroom.

217 sites (60-ft RV limit). Tbls, flush toilets, cfga, drkg wtr, dump, elec($), showers, fish cleaning station. Limited facilities in winter. Swimming, boating(l), fishing, ski trails, snowmobiling, hiking trails, horseback riding, mountain biking, playground, horseshoes, volleyball, nature walks, waterskiing, interpretive programs, visitor center, shooting range, volleyball, disc golf. 3,923 acres. Lake Pend Oreille.

ATLANTA (S)
Neinmeyer Campground FREE
Boise National Forest
27 mi W of Atlanta on FR 268; at Middle Fork Boise River. Free. 6/1-10/31; 14-day limit. 8 sites (RVs under 22 ft). Tbls, toilets, no drk wtr, cfga, fire restrictins may apply,

firewood. Fishing, horseback riding. Minimum-maintenance site.

Power Plant $7.50
Boise National Forest
2.5 mi NE of Atlanta on FR 268; near headwaters of Middle Fork of Boise River. $7.50 with federal senior pass; others pay $15. Elev 5500 ft. 6/1-10/1; 14-day limit. 24 sites; 21-ft RV limit. Tbls, toilets, cfga, drkg wtr. Horseback riding, hiking, fishing. Gateway to Sawtooth Wilderness Area.

AVERY (N)
Conrad Crossing FREE
St. Joe National Forest
29 mi E of Avery on FR 50 (St. Joe River Rd). Free. 6/1-10/30; 14-day limit. 8 sites (3 on river, 5 above hwy); RVs under 16 ft. Tbls, toilets, cfga, well drkg wtr June-Oct. Fishing (cutthroat trout), picnicking, swimming. Elev 3600 ft; 5 acres. Historic Montana trail. On St. Joe Wild & Scenic River, trout waters.

Fly Flat FREE
St. Joe National Forest
29 mi E of Avery on FR 50 (St. Joe River Rd); 4 mi S on FR 218. Camp free, but donations accepted. About 6/1-10/31; 14-day limit. 14 sites (RVs under 32 ft). Tbls, toilets, cfga, firewood, drkg wtr June-Oct. Picnicking, fishing, hiking, swimming. Elev 3500 ft; 6 acres. 5 mi N of Red Ives Ranger Station. On St. Joe River, wild trout waters.

Heller Creek FREE
St. Joe National Forest
29 mi E of Avery on FR 50; 10 mi S on FR 218; 13.7 mi E on FR 320. Free. Elev 4700 ft. 6/15-10/31; 14-day limit. 4 sites on 4 acres (RVs under 22 ft). Tbls, toilets, cfga, no drkg wtr. Memorial. Rd 320 is very rough. Alternative route from Superior, MT, better for low-clearance vehicles. Heller grave site.

Line Creek Stock Camp FREE
St. Joe National Forest
29 mi E of Avery on St. Joe River Rd (FR 50); 10 mi S on Red Ives Rd (FR 218). Free. All year; 14-day limit. 9 pull-through sites for stock trailers. Tbls, toilets, cfga, no drkg wtr. Feed bunks, hitching posts, trailhead parking. Hiking, horseback riding.

Mammoth Springs FREE
St. Joe National Forest
22 mi E of Avery on FR 50; 14 mi S on FR 509; 2.5 mi S on FR 201. Free. 6/15-10/15; 14-day limit. 8 sites (RVs under 23 ft). Tbls, toilets, cfga, drkg wtr Jul-Oct. Picnicking, berry picking. 1 mi to Dismal Lake. Elev 5700 ft.

Packsaddle FREE
St. Joe National Forest
5 mi E of Avery on FR 50; at St. Joe River. Free donations

accepted. 6/1-10/31; 14-day limit. 4 sites. Tbls, toilet, cfga, no drkg wtr, no trash service. Fishing, hiking, horseback riding. Trailhead for Packsaddle Nelson Ridge National Recreation Trail.

Spruce Tree   FREE
St. Joe National Forest
29 mi E of Avery on FR 50 (St. Joe River Rd); 12 mi S on FR 218 (Red Ives Rd). Free. 6/1-10/31; 14-day limit. 9 sites (35-ft RV limit). Tbls, toilets, cfga, drkg wtr June-Oct, no trash service. Swimming, fishing, hiking to virgin backcountry.

Tin Can Flat $8
St. Joe National Forest
11 mi E of Avery on FR 50 (St. Joe River Rd); at St. Joe River. $6. About 5/15-10/31; 14-day limit. 11 sites (32-ft RV limit). Tbls, toilets, drkg wtr, cfga, no trash service. Hiking, fishing.

Turner Flat $8
St. Joe National Forest
8 me E of Avery on FR 50; at St. Joe River. $6. About 5/15-10/31; 14-day limit. 11 sites (32-ft RV limit). Tbls, toilets, drkg wtr, cfga, no trash service. Hiking, fishing.

BANKS (S)
Big Eddy $7.50
Boise National Forest
15 mi N of Banks on SR 55; on North Fork of Payette River. $7.50 with federal senior pass; others pay $15. 4/20-10/20; 14-day limit. 4 sites (30-ft RV limit). Non-campers pay $8 day use fee. Tbls, toilet, cfga, no drkg wtr. Picnicking, fishing, swimming, boating. Elev 4091 ft.

Canyon Creek $12
Boise National Forest
8.2 mi N of Banks on SR 55; in narrow canyon formed by North Fork of Payette River. $12. 4/15-10/15; 14-day limit. 6 sites (30-ft RV limit). Non-campers pay $6 day use fee. Tbls, toilets, cfga, drkg wtr. Trout fishing, whitewater rafting. Elev 3828 ft.

Swinging Bridge $7.50
Boise National Forest
10 mi N of Banks on SR 55; at North Fork of Payette River. $7.50 with federal senior pass; others pay $15. Non-campers pay $8. MD-LD; 14-day limit. 11 sites (25-ft RV limit). Tbls, toilets, cfga, drkg wtr. Fishing, boating. Elev 4000; 6 acres.

BLACKFOOT (S)
Cutthroat Trout   FREE
Bureau of Land Management
Pocatello Field Office
7 mi N of Blackfoot on Hwy 91; 10 mi E on Wolverine rd; right on Cedar Creek Rd for 13 mi; right on Trail Creek

Bridge Rd for 6 mi; road turns into Lincoln Creek Rd; 1 mi to camp. Free. 5/1-10/31; 14-day limit. 3 primitive sites, 15-ft RV limit. Tbls, toilets, cfga, no drkg wtr. Fishing.

Graves Creek   FREE
Bureau of Land Management
Pocatello Field Office
7 mi N of Blackfoot on Hwy 91; 10 mi E on Wolverine Rd; right on Cedar Creek Rd for 13 mi; right on Trail Creek Bridge Rd for 6 mi; road turns into Lincoln Creek Rd; 1 mi to camp. Free. 5/1-10/31; 14-day limit. 5 sites, 15-ft RV limit. Tbls, toilets, cfga, no drkg wtr. Fishing.

McTucker Ponds   FREE
Bingham County Park
13 mi W of Blackfoot on Hwy 39; left for 3 mi at sign for McTucker Ponds; near upper end of American Falls Reservoir. Free. All year. Primitive undesignated sites near 8 small gravel pits. No facilities except cfga; no drkg wtr. Fishing, hiking, birdwatching.

Sagehen Flat   FREE
Bureau of Land Management
Pocatello Field Office
7 mi N of Blackfoot on Hwy 91; 10 mi E on Wolverine Rd; right on Cedar Creek Rd for 13 mi; right on Trail Creek Bridge Rd for 6 mi; rd turns into Lincoln Creek Rd; 6 mi to camp. Free. 5/1-10/31; 14-day limit. 5 sites, 15-ft RV limit. Tbls, pit toilet, cfga, no drkg wtr. Fishing.

BOISE (S)
Badger Creek   FREE
Boise National Forest
16 mi E of Boise on SR 21; at Lucky Peak Nursery, go 21 mi E on FR 268. Road can be rough. Free. Elev 3200 ft. 4/15-10/15; 14-day limit. 5 sites; 1 acre. Tbls, toilets, cfga, firewood, no drkg wtr or trash service. Fishing, horseback riding. On Middle Fork of Boise River.

Cove Recreation Site $12
Snake River Birds of Prey National Conservation Area
Bureau of Land Management
35 mi S of Boise. From I-84 exit 44, follow SR 69 S 8 mi; e mi S on Swan Falls Rd to boundary of conservation area. $12 for RVs, $5 tents. All year; 14-day limit. Developed sites at campground & free dispersed camping throughout the area ($2 day use fee). Toilets, tbls, cfga, drkg wtr. Educational programs, interpretive displays, fishing, hiking, horseback riding, biking, boating(l). Area contains largest concentration of nesting birds in North America; about 800 pairs of falcons, eagles, hawks & owls.

Macks Creek Park $10
Corps of Engineers
Lucky Peak Lake
From Boise, 18 mi SE on SR 21; 4.5 mi E on Arrowrock

Dam Rd; at Boise River arm of Lucky Peak Lake. Free. All year; 3-day limit. 5 primitive RV sites; 45-ft RV limit; tent camping in picnic area. Tbls, toilets, cfga, drkg wtr. Boating(ld), fishing.

Riverside Campground $7.50
Boise National Forest
16 mi N of Boise on SR 21; from Lucky Peak Nursery, go 62 mi E on FR 268 (narrow and rough); on Middle Fork of Boise River. $7.50 with federal senior pass; others pay $15. 6/1-9/30; 14-day limit. 11 sites. Tbls, toilets, cfga, drkg wtr. Hiking (trailhead from Power Plant Camp 1 mi E), fishing, horseback riding. Elev 5400 ft.

Shafer Butte $10
Boise National Forest
16 mi NE of Boise on Bogus Basin Rd; 3 mi N on FR 374; 1.5 mi E on Shafer Butte Rd. $10. 6/15-LD; 14-day limit. 7 sites 22-ft RV limit. Tbls, toilets, cfga, drkg wtr. Hiking. Non-campers pay $5 day use fee.

Troutdale FREE
Boise National Forest
16 mi E of Boise on SR 68; 28 mi NE on FR 268 (narrow and rough). Free. Elev 3600 ft. 4/15-10/31; 14-day limit. 5 sites on 2 acres 21-ft RV limit. Tbls, toilets, cfga, firewood, no drkg wtr. Fishing, horseback riding. On Middle Fork of Boise River. Minimum maintenance.

BONNERS FERRY (N)
Meadow Creek $6
Kaniksu National Forest
From US 2, N of Bonners Ferry, 11 mi N on Meadow Creek Rd (CR 34); at Moyi River. $6. 5/15-9/15; 14-day limit. 22 sites; 35-ft RV limit. Tbls, toilets, cfga, drkg wtr. Fishing (brook & cutthroat trout), berry-picking, boating.

Smith Lake Campground FREE
Kaniksu National Forest
5 mi N of Bonners Ferry on US 95; 2 mi N CR 35. Free. 5/15-9/15; 14-day limit. 7 small sites. Tbls, toilets, cfga, drkg wtr. Hiking, fishing, boating(l), swimming. On an isolated patch of forest, so get permission from landowner for access.

BURLEY (S)
Mill Flat Campground FREE
Sawtooth National Forest
From E of Burley at I-84 exit 228, 8.5 mi E on Yale Rd; 16 mi E on Haigler Canyon Rd. 7 sites. 6/1-10/31; 14-day limit. Tbls, toilets, cfga, no drkg wtr. Biking, hiking, fishing.

Milner Recreation Area $5
Bureau of Land Management
Burley Field Office
7 mi W of Burley on US 30; 1 mi N at the Milner Historic/Recreation Area sign; 3 mi W on gravel rd. $5 (Sept-March sportsman pass, $15; annual pass $25). 5/1-10/31; 14-day limit. Several sites along 4 mi of Snake River shoreline. Tbls, toilets, cfga. Boating(l), fishing, hiking. Non-campers pay $3 day use fee.

CALDER (NN)
Big Creek FREE
St. Joe National Forest
6 mi E on CR 347; 3 mi NW on FR 537. Free. 6/1-10/31; 14-day limit. 9 sites; 30-ft RV limit. Toilets, cfga, drkg wtr, tbls. Hiking, fishing, horseback riding. Site of former CCC camp.

Donkey Creek FREE
St. Joe National Forest
11 mi E of Calder on FR 50; 8 mi S on FR 321; at Marble Creek. Elev 2800 ft. 4 sites 21-Ft RV limit, no drkg wtr. Berry picking, fishing. Historic site.

CAMBRIDGE (S)
Brownlee $10
Payette National Forest
16.5 mi NW of Cambridge on SR 71; 1 mi E on FR 044; at Brownlee Creek. $10 during MD-10/15 (lower fee before & after peak season, but no wtr. 14-day limit. 11 sites 16-ft RV limit. Tbls, toilets, cfga, drkg wtr. Horseback riding, picnicking, fishing. Elev 4200 ft. Closest forest campground to Brownlee Reservoir, perhaps the best fishing lake in Idaho.

Copperfield Park $8
Idaho Power Company
Hwy 71 from Cambridge to Oxbow, Oregon; right on OR 86. $8 for RVs during Nov-March; sites $16 in-season. All year; 14-day limit. 62 sites (50-ft RV limit). Tbls, flush toilets, cfga, drkg wtr, dump, elec($), showers. Hiking, fishing.

Hells Canyon Park $8
Idaho Power Company
Hwy 71 from Cambridge toward Brownlee Dam; right just before crossing Snake River Bridge; half mi N. $8 for RVs during Nov-March; sites $16 in-season. All year; 14-day limit. 24 sites (40-ft RV limit). Tbls, flush toilets, showers, drkg wtr, dump, elec($). Handicap access. Fishing, hiking, boating(ld), hunting.

McCormick Park $8
Idaho Power Company
28 mi N of Cambridge on Hwy 71 to Snake River; follow signs (on Idaho side of Oxbow Reservoir). $8 for RVs during Nov-March; $16 in-season. All year; 14-day limit. 34 sites (30-ft RV limit). Tbls, flush toilets, showers, drkg wtr, cfga, elec/wtr, dump. Fishing, swimming, boating (ld). 12 acres.

Woodhead Park $8
Idaho Power Company
Hwy 71 from Cambridge toward Brownlee Dam; half mi
before reaching dam. $8 for RVs during Nov-March; sites
$16 & $10 in-season. All year; 14-day limit. 124 sites; 40-ft
RV limit. Tbls, flush toilets, drkg wtr, elec, showers, cfga,
dump. Handicap access. Hiking, fishing, boating. 65 acres.

CAREY (S)

Fish Creek Reservoir   FREE
Bureau of Land Management
Shoshone Field Office
Turn N on Hwy 93 about 6 mi E of Carey; proceed about
5 mi; signed. May be difficult access in winter. Free. 5/1-
10/31; 14-day limit. Designated primitive sites (RVs under
30 ft) on N shore; dispersed sites around the lake. Toilets,
cfga, no drkg wtr. Trout fishing, boating (ld), picnicking,
sightseeing.

High-Five Campground   FREE
Bureau of Reclamation
Little Wood River Reservoir
10 mi NW of Carey on Durfee Lane, Dry Creek Rd & Hunt
Lane. Free. 5/15-9/30; 14-day limit. 4 sites (60-ft RV
limit). Tbls, toilets, cfga, drkg wtr. Fishing, picnicking,
boating(l). River

Silver Creek   FREE
Bureau of Land Management
Shoshone Field Office
7 mi S on Hwys 20/26/93, then follow signs 2 mi N. May be
difficult access in winter. Free. 4/15-11/30; 14-day limit.
Silver Creek North has 1 site with pit toilet, cfga, tbls;
Silver Creek South has 2 sites with pit toilet, cfga, tbls. No
drkg wtr. Fishing, picnicking, bird hunting.

CASCADE (S)

Van Wyck Campground $12
Lake Cascade State Park
2.2 mi S of Cascade on Cascade Reservoir. $10 base,
more at premium locations, at standard no-hookup sites;
seniors pay $5 Mon-Thurs. 5/1-10/31; 15-day limit. Unde-
veloped, undefined primitive sites in open area for RVs or
tents. Pit toilets, cfga, drkg wtr.

   Blue Heron Campground, $12 base, more for premium
locations (seniors pay $6 base Mon-Thurs). Open area
with undefined RV/tent sites. Tbls, pit toilets, cfga, drkg
wtr.

   Sugarloaf Campground, $7 base for seniors Mon-Thurs;
others pay $14 base, $16 for premium locations (seniors
pay $8 Mon-Thurs). Pit toilets, central wtr, boat launch.

   Huckleberry Campground, $7 base for seniors Mon-
Thurs; others pay $14 base, $16 for premium locations
(seniors pay $8 Mon-Thurs). Central wtr, pit toilets.

   Ridgeview & Poison Creek Campgrounds, seniors get
no mid-week discounts.

   Sage Bluff Campground, $9 for seniors Mon-Thurs;

others pay $18. Wtr hookups, pit toilets.

   Big Sage Campground, $9 base for seniors Mon-Thurs
for sites with wtr hookup; others pay $18 base, $24 with
wtr/elec (seniors pay $12 Mon-Thurs). Pit toilets.

   Buttercup Campground, $7 base for seniors weekdays;
others pay $14 base, $16 for premium locations (seniors
pay $8 weekdays). Pit toilets, central wtr, boat launch.

   West Mountain Campground, $7 base for seniors Mon-
Thurs; others pay $14 base, $18 for premium locations
(seniors pay $9 Mon-Thurs). Central wtr, flush toilets.

   Crown Point Campground, $7 base for seniors Mon-
Thurs; others pay $14 base, $18 for premium locations
(seniors pay $9 Mon-Thurs). Central wtr, pit toilets.

   55-ft maximum sites. Dump, summer programs, interpretive display. Boating(l), fishing, hiking, swimming,
horseshoes, biking, canoeing.

Buck Mountain   FREE
Boise National Forest
35 mi E of Cascade on Warm Lake Rd; 2 mi N on Johnson
Creek Rd. Free. 6/15-10/30; 14-day limit. 4 sites (RVs
under 16 ft). Tbls, toilets, cfga, firewood. Fishing, hiking.
Elev 6500 ft; 1 acre. Johnson Creek.

French Creek $10
McCall Recreation Area
Boise National Forest
4 mi S of Cascade on CR 10422; 1 mi W on CR 10922;
4 mi N on FR 10922. $10 - $15. 5/15-9/15; 14-day limit.
21 sites; 45-ft RV limit. Tbls, toilets, cfga, drkg wtr.
Boating(l), fishing, swimming, waterskiing. On Cascade
Reservoir. Elev 4800 ft; 49 acres.

Golden Gate   FREE
Boise National Forest
35 mi E of Cascade on Warm Lake Rd; 23 mi N on Johnson
Creek Rd; at South Fork of Salmon River. Free. 5/1-10/30;
14-day limit. 9 sites (RVs under 22 ft). Tbls, toilets, cfga,
no drkg wtr or trash service. Fishing, swimming, hiking,
ATV activities, horseback riding, mountain biking.

Ice Hole   FREE
Boise National Forest
35 mi E of Cascade on Warm Lake Rd; 19 mi N on Johnson
Creek Rd; near South Fork of Salmon River. Free. 5/1-
10/31; 14-day limit. 10 sites (RVs under 16 ft). Tbls, cfga,
toilets, no drkg wtr or trash service. Fishing, swimming,
hiking, ATV activities, horseback riding, mountain biking.
Elev 5200 ft; 6 acres.

Penn Basin   FREE
Boise National Forest
1 mi N of Cascade on SR 55; 35 mi NE on FR 22 (Warm
Lake Rd); 2.5 mi SE on FR 579; near Johnson Creek. Free.
Elev 6700 ft. 6/1-10/30; 14-day limit. 6 sites (RVs under
22 ft). Tbls, toilets, cfga, no drkg wtr. Horseback riding,
fishing, hiking.

Penny Springs   FREE
Boise National Forest
1 mi N of Cascade on SR 55; 23 mi E on FR 2; 4 mi N on FR 474. Free, May - Oct, 14-day limit, 4 sites. Tbls, toilets, cfga, no drkg wtr. Fishing, hiking, picking berries. Elev 5000 ft.

Shoreline $10
Boise National Forest
1 mi N of Cascade on SR 55; 24 mi NE on FR 22; 1 mi SW on FR 489. $10 to $30 most are accessible. 5/15-MD; 14-day limit. 31 sites (45-ft RV limit). Tbls, toilets, cfga, drkg wtr. Boating(l), fishing, swimming, waterskiing, hiking trail, volleyball, horseshoes. Elev 5300 ft.

South Fork Salmon River $7.50
Boise National Forest
1 mi N of Cascade on SR 55; 23 mi NE on FR 22 (Warm Lake Rd). $7.50 with federal senior pass; others pay $15. 5/15-9/15; 14-day limit (camp may be closed during spawning season, 7/1-9/15, to protect salmon). 14 sites (RVs under 23 ft). Tbls, toilets, cfga, drkg wtr. Fishing, swimming. 10 acres. Chinook travel 700 miles from Pacific Ocean to spawn here. Elev 5100 ft.

Summit Lake   FREE
Boise National Forest
1 mi N of Cascade on SR 15; 32 mi NE on FR 22 (Warm Lake Rd); 7 mi SE on FR 579. Free. Elev 7000 ft. 6/1-10/30; 14-day limit. 3 sites (RVs under 16 ft). Tbls, toilets, cfga, no drkg wtr or trash service. Fishing boating(l), hiking. Between Warm Lake Creek and Summit Lake. :

Trout Creek   FREE
Boise National Forest
35 mi E of Cascade on Warm Lake Rd; 8 mi N on Johnson Creek Rd; at Trout Creek. Free. 6/1-10/30; 14-day limit. 8 sites (RVs under 16 ft). Tbls, toilets, cfga, no drkg wtr or trash service. Horseback riding, hiking, picnicking, fishing. Elev 6300 ft; 2 acres.

Warm Lake $10
Boise National Forest
1 mi N of Cascade on SR 55; 26 mi NE on FR 22; qtr mi SE on FR 579RA; at Chipmunk Creek. $10 - $30. 5/15-LD; 14-day limit. 12 sites (30-ft RV limit). Tbls, toilets, cfga, drkg wtr. Boating, fishing, swimming.

Yellow Pine   FREE
Boise National Forest
35 mi E of Cascade on Warm Lake Rd; 25 mi N on Johnson Creek Rd; at South Fork of Salmon River. Free. 5/1-10/30; 14-day limit. 14 sites (RVs under 25 ft). Tbls, toilets, cfga, drkg wtr, no trash service. Fishing, hiking. Elev 5000 ft; 12 acres. Adjacent to Johnson Creek. Historic pioneer cemetery nearby.

CHALLIS (S)

Bayhorse Recreation Site $10
Bureau of Land Management
Challis Field Office
8 mi SW of Challis on SR 75; at Salmon River. $10. All year; 14-day limit. 11 sites, 28-ft RV limit. Tbls, toilets, drkg wtr. Hiking, boating, fishing, picnicking. Elev 5200 ft; 4 acres.

Big Bayhorse Campground   FREE
Challis National Forest
10 mi S of Challis on US 93; 7.5 mi N on FR 051; between Bayhorse & Little Bayhorse Lakes. Free. 7/1-10/15. 7 sites on 12 acres 32-ft RV limit. Tbls, toilets, cfga, firewood, no drkg wtr. Horseback riding, picnicking, fishing, rockhounding, OHV activity, biking, hiking. Trailers not advised; steep, narrow rds. Elev 8600 ft. Historic brickyard at Little Bayhorse Lake.

Big Creek   FREE
Challis National Forest
17 mi N of Challis on US 93 to Ellis; 28 mi S on Farm-to-Market Rd; about 4 mi E on FR 097; at confluence of North & South Forks of Big Creek. Free. 5/15-10/15; 14-day limit. 3 sites; 16-ft RV limit. Tbls, toilets, cfga, no drkg wtr or trash service. Fishing, hiking, horseback riding, OHV use, biking.

Cottonwood Recreation Site $10
Bureau of Land Management
Challis Field Office
15 mi N of Challis on Hwy 93. $10. All year; 16-day limit. 13 sites; 30-ft RV limit. Tbls, toilets, cfga, drkg wtr, dump. Hiking, fishing, boating(l), horseshoe pits. Elev 5000 ft.

Deadman Hole Recreation Site   FREE
Bureau of Land Management
Challis Field Office
2 mi S of Challis on Hwy 93; 12 mi W on Hwy 75; on river side of hwy. Free. All year; 14-day limit. Undesignated sites. Toilet, cfga, drkg wtr, no trash service. Access & interior rds are rough dirt.

Little Bayhorse Lake   FREE
Challis National Forest
10 mi S of Challis on US 75; 7 mi W on FR 051; on Little Bayhorse Lake. Free. 7/1-9/15; 16-day limit. 3 dispersed sites. Tbls, toilets, cfga, firewood, no drkg wtr. Picnicking, fishing, boating. Elev 8400 ft. Trailers not advised; steep, narrow rd. Lake

Little Boulder Recreation Site   FREE
Bureau of Land Management
Challis Field Office
2 mi S of Challis on Hwy 93; right on Hwy 75 for 17 mi; left on East Fork Salmon River Rd for about 20 mi. Free. All year; 14-day limit. 4 sites. Toilet, cfga, drkg wtr. Hiking, horseback riding. Site used as staging area for horsemen.

Mill Creek $10
Challis National Forest
4.5 mi W of Challis on CR 70; 11 mi W on FR 70 (narrow rd); on Yankee Fork of Salmon River. $10. 6/15-9/30; 1-day limit. 8 sites 34-ft RV limit. Tbls, toilets, cfga, firewood, piped drkg wtr. Rockhounding, picnicking, fishing, horseback riding. Elev 7500 ft; 3 acres. Trailers over 22 ft not advised. Historic Custer Adventure Motorway.

Morgan Creek FREE
Recreation Site
Bureau of Land Management
Challis Field Office
10 mi NW of Challis on US 93; W on FR 057 (Morgan Creek Rd). Free. All year. 4 sites. Tbls, toilet, cfga, drkg wtr. Rockhounding, fishing, hiking. No trash service.

Morse Creek Campground FREE
Challis National Forest
17 mi N of Challis on US 93 to Ellis; 10 mi SE on Farm-to-Market Rd; 6 mi E on FR 094. Free. 6/15-9/15; 14-day limit. 3 sites; 16-ft RV limit. Tbls, toilet, cfga, no drkg wtr. Trout fishing, hiking, horseback riding, nature trail, biking. Elev 6500 ft.

Mosquito Flat FREE
Challis National Forest
13 mi W of Challis on FR 070; 4 mi N on FR 080; at shore of Mosquito Flat Reservoir. Free. 6/1-10/15; 14-day limit. 11 sites; 32-ft RV limit. Tbls, toilets, cfga, no drkg wtr. Fishing, hiking, biking, horseback riding, boating(l).

West Fork Morgan Creek FREE
Challis National Forest
8 mi N of Challis on US 93; 6 mi NW on FR 055; 4 mi W on FR 057; at West Fork of Morgan Creek. Free. 6/1-9/30; 14-day limit. 1 site. Toilet, tbl, cfga, no drkg wtr. Fishing, hiking, biking, horseback riding. Elev 6400 ft.

CLARK FORK (N)

Johnson Creek Access Area FREE
Idaho Dept. of Fish & Game
Lake Pend Oreille
1 mi SW of Clark Fork on SR 200 (11 mi E of Trestle Creek day use area). Free. Primitive undesignated sites. 2 toilets, cfga, tbls,no drkg wtr. All year; 3-day limit within 5-day period. Boating(l), fishing.

Whiskey Rock Bay FREE
Kaniksu National Forest
30 mi SW on FR 278; or 10 mi S by boat from Garfield Bay. On Lake Pend Oreille W shore. Free. 5/1-11/30; 14-day limit. 9 sites (15-ft RV limit). Toilets, tbls, cfga, drkg wtr. Swimming, boating(d), fishing, picnicking. Elev 2000 ft.

CLARKIA (N)

Crater Lake FREE
Backcountry Camp
Bureau of Land Management
Coeur d'Alene Field Office
24 mi E of Clarkia on FR 301; on S side of Grandmother Mountain WSA. Free. Crater Lake nearby; no trail. 7/1-9/30; 14-day limit. Primitive campsites along rd. Tbl, cfga, toilet, no drkg wtr, no trash service.

Crater Peak FREE
Backcountry Camp
Bureau of Land Management
Coeur d'Alene Field Office
23 mi E of Clarkia on FR 301; on S side of Grandmother Mountain WSA. Free. 7/1-9/30; 14-day limit. Primitive campsites along rd. Tbl, cfga, toilet, no drkg wtr, no trash service.

Emerald Creek $12
St. Joe National Forest
5.3 mi NW of Clarkia on SR 3; 5.5 mi S on FR 447. $12 base Seniors receive 50% discount Mon-Thurs. Base Rates, Std site $12-$21, w/wtr or elec $20-$25. wtr and elec $24-$29 wtr, elec & sewer $26-$29. Tbls, toilets, cfga, drkg wtr. Fishing, rockhounding (garnets). 10 acres.

Orphan Point Saddle Camp FREE
Bureau of Land Management
Coeur d'Alene Field Office
From Hwy 3 at Clarkia, 26 mi E on FR 301. Roadside sites on S side of Grandmother Mountain WSA. Free. 7/1-9/30; 14-day limit. Tbl, toilet, cfga, no drkg wtr, no trash service. Trailhead for Lookout Mountain & Delaney Creek trails.

CLAYTON (S)

East Fork Recreation Site $10
Bureau of Land Management
Challis Field Office
4 mi E of Clayton on US 93; at confluence of East Fork & Salmon Rivers. $10. 14-day limit. 8 RV sites, 25-ft RV limit. Some pull-through spaces. Tbls, toilets, cfga, piped drkg wtr. Hiking, mountain biking, picnicking, fishing, hunting, horseback riding. Elev 5500 ft; 5 acres.

Herd Lake Recreation Site FREE
Bureau of Land Management
Challis Field Office
5 mi E of Clayton on SR 75; S on East Fork Rd to Herd Lake Rd; 10 mi SE on Herd Lake Rd. Free. All year. 1 dispersed site. Toilet, tbls, cfga, no drkg wtr. Fishing, canoeing.

Holman Creek $8
Sawtooth National Forest
Sawtooth National Recreation Area
7 mi W of Clayton on SR 75; near Salmon River. $8 during

MD-10/15; free rest of season, but no wtr or services; 10-day limit. 10 sites, some 49 ft; no RV turnaround at sites 7-10). Tbls, toilets, drkg wtr, cfga. Fishing, hiking, boating.

COBALT (S)

Deep Creek   FREE
Salmon National Forest
3.5 mi N of Cobalt on FR 055 (Panther Creek Rd). Free. 5/15-10/15. 5 sites on 2 acres, 16-ft RV limit. Tbls, toilet, cfga, no drkg wtr. Fishing, horseback riding. Panther Creek polluted by mine waste, but trout in Deep Creek. Elev 3500 ft.

McDonald Flat   FREE
Salmon National Forest
5 mi SW of Cobalt on FR 055 (Panther Creek Rd). Free. MD-10/15. 6 sites,21 ft R limit. Tbls, toilets, cfga, no drkg wtr. Fishing, horseback riding. Elev 5400 ft; 6 acres.

COEUR D'ALENE (N)

Beauty Creek $10
Coeur d'Alene National Forest
7 mi E of Coeur d'Alene on I-90; exit 22, then 3 mi W on SR 97; 1 mi SE on FR 438. $10 with federal senior pass; others pay $20. 5/15-9/15; 14-day limit. 20 sites, not all suitable for RVs (32-ft RV limit). Tbls, toilets, cfga, drkg wtr. Boating(l), fishing, waterskiing, hiking. Elev 2100 ft.

Bell Bay $9
Coeur d'Alene National Forest
12 mi NE of Coeur d'Alene on FR 268; 11 mi E on FR 612 (6 mi NW of Harrison). $9 with federal senior pass; others pay $18. MD-LD; 14-day limit. 27 sites; not all suitable for RVs. 30-ft RV limit. Toilets, tbls, cfga, drkg wtr. Boating(lr), fishing, swimming, waterskiing, recreational program. Overlooks Canada Lake on E side of Coeur D'Alene Lake.

Honeysuckle $9
Coeur d'Alene National Forest
11 mi NE of Coeur d'Alene on FR 268 (Fernan Lake Rd); 11 mi E on FR 612; at Little North Fork of Coeur d'Alene River. $9 with federal senior pass; others pay $18. MD-LD; 14-day limit. 7, RV Limit 30 ft. Tbls, toilets, cfga, drkg wtr. Fishing, hunting, hiking, rafting, OHV activity, mountain biking.

Killarney Lake Boat Launch $10
Bureau of Land Management
Coeur d'Alene Field Office
I-90 at Coeur D'Alene to Rose Lake Exit; 4 mi S on Hwy 3; 3.5 mi W on Killarney Lake Rd. $10. All year; 14-day limit. 12 sites, 22-ft RV limit. Tbls, toilets, cfga, drkg wtr. Hiking, boating (ld), fishing, picnicking. 500-acre Lake Killarney.

Sheep Springs Recreation Site   FREE
Bureau of Land Management
Coeur d'Alene Field Office
21 mi S of Coeur d'Alene via Latour Creek and Rochat Divide Rds or from St. Maries 11 mi E on St. Joe River Rd & 12 mi N on Rochat Divide Rd. Rough rds & mountainous terrain. Free. 6/1-9/30; 14-day limit. 3 primitive sites (21-ft RV limit). Tbl, toilets, cfga, no drkg wtr, no trash service. Hiking, fishing, picnicking. Primarily for hunters, fishermen. Trail leads to Crystal Lake, where primitive tent camping is permitted.

Tingley Springs   FREE
Bureau of Land Management
Coeur d'Alene Field Office
25 mi E of Coeur d'Alene on I-90 to Cataldo exit 40; 30 mi S on Latour Creek-Rochat Divide Rd; 1 mi W on Phillips Draw Rd. Free. 6/1-9/30; 14-day limit. 6 primitive sites. Tbls, toilet, cfga, no drkg wtr, no trash service.

COOLIN (N)

Dickensheet Campground $12
Priest Lake State Park
11 mi N of Coolin on E shore of Priest Lake. $12-$21 at standard non-hookup sites. Central pit toilet.
     Lionhead Campground, $12-$21 at std sites. Central wtr, pit toilets.
     Indian Creek Campground, $24-$31 at sites with wtr/elec hookups, full hookups, central showers, restrooms; swimming area access, horseshoe pits, basketball court, boat launch. All year; 15-day limit. Limited facilities in winter. 151 sites (50-ft RV limit). Tbls, flush toilets, cfga, drkg wtr, dump, elec($), showers. Beach, swimming, boating (ld), fishing, tobogganing, snowmobiling, hiking trails, nature program, horseshoes, volleyball, rafting, canoeing. 463 acres.

COTTONWOOD (N)

Pine Bar Recreation Site $7
Bureau of Land Management
Cottonwood Field Office
11 mi S of Cottonwood on Graves Creek Rd; 4 mi E on Salmon River Rd; at Lower Salmon River. $7. All year; 14-day limit. 6 sites. 30 acres. Tbls, cfga, toilets, drkg wtr, trash collection, beaches. Boating(l), swimming, picnicking, fishing, hunting. Put-in spot for floaters.

COUNCIL (S)

Big Flat $10
Payette National Forest
12 mi S of Council on US 95; 14 mi SE & E on FR 206. $10 during MD-10/15; lower fee off-season, but no wtr; 14-day limit. 9 single sites, 3 double sites ($15); RVs under 36 ft. Tbls, toilets, cfga, no drkg wtr. Horseback riding, fishing, berry-picking. Elev 4050 ft. Adjacent to Little Weiser River.

Cabin Creek $10
Payette National Forest
4 mi S of Council on US 95; 10 mi E on FR 186, along Middle Fork of Weiser River. $10 during MD-10/15 ($15 double sites); free off-season, but no wtr. 14-day limit. 12 sites; 16-ft RV limit. Tbls, toilets, cfga, piped drkg wtr. Horseback riding, fishing. Elev 4150 ft.

Evergreen $10
Payette National Forest
14 mi N of Council on US 95; on Weiser River. $10 (double sites $15). 6/1-9/10; 16-day limit. 12 sites; 35-ft RV limit. Tbls, toilets, cfga, drkg wtr. Fishing. Elev 3650 ft.

Huckleberry $10
Payette National Forest
30 mi NW of Council on FR 002; 5 mi NE on FR 105; 1 mi E on FR 110; at Bear Creek. $10 during 6/10-9/10; free off-season, but no wtr. 14-day limit. 8 single sites, 1 double site (RVs under 45 ft). Tbls, toilet, cfga, no drkg wtr. Horseback riding, fishing. Elev 4950 ft. Near Hells Canyon/Seven Devils Scenic Area. Stream.

Lafferty Camp $10
Payette National Forest
24 mi NW of Council on FR 002. $10. All year; 14-day limit. Free off-season if wtr is shut off. 16-day limit. 8 sites (16-ft RV limit). Tbls, toilets, cfga, drkg wtr. Horseback riding, hiking, fishing for Crooked River rainbow trout. Elev 4300 ft.

DARBY (MONTANA))

Indian Creek FREE
Bitterroot National Forest
4 mi S of Darby on US 93; 14 mi W on CR 473; 37 mi W on FR 468; 5 mi N on FR 6223; at Selway River. Free. 6/15-9/15; 10-day limit. 6 sites (includes 4 hunter camps); 25-ft RV limit. Tbls, toilets, cfga, no drkg wtr. Hiking, hunting, fishing, biking.

Indian Trees $10
Bitterroot National Forest
4 mi S on US 93; 14 mi SW on CR 473; 37 mi W on FR 468; 5 mi N on FR 6223. $10. 5/20-9/30; 14-day limit. 16 sites (50-ft RV limit). Tbls, toilets, cfga, drkg wtr. Hiking.

Magruder Crossing FREE
Bitterroot National Forest
4 mi S of Darby on US 93; 14 mi SW on CR 423; 37 mi W on FR 468; at Selway River. Free. 6/15-11/1; 10-day limit. 4 sites; 30-ft RV limit. Toilet, tbls, cfga, no drkg wtr. Fishing, hiking, horseback riding, biking.

Paradise FREE
Bitterroot National Forest
4 mi S of Darby on US 93; 14 mi W on CR 473; 37 mi W on FR 468; 11 mi N on FR 6223; at Selway River. Free. 6/15-

11/26; 10-day limit. 11 sites, 25-ft RV limit. Toilets, cfga, drkg wtr. Fishing, hiking, horseback riding, boating(l).

Raven Creek FREE
Bitterroot National Forest
4 mi S of Darby on US 93; 14 mi W on CR 473; 37 mi W on FR 468; 2 mi N on FR 6223; at Selway River. Free. 6/1-9/15; 14-day limit. 2 sites; 25-ft RV limit. Toilet, cfga, no drkg wtr. Fishing, hiking.

DEARY (N)

Little Boulder Creek $12
Clearwater National Forest
4 mi E of Deary on ID 8; 3 mi SE on CR 1963; at Potlatch River. $12 Mid May-Oct 14-day limit. 17 sites (35-ft RV limit). Toilets, tbls, drkg wtr, cfga. Fishing. Near Palouse River, hiking, biking.

DONNELLY (S)

Amanita $7.50
Boise National Forest
4.8 mi SW of Donnelly on CR 422. $7.50 with federal senior pass; others pay $15. Best Season 5/15-10/31; 14-day limit. 10 sites (RVs under 23 ft). Tbls, toilets, cfga, drkg wtr. Fishing, swimming, boating(l), waterskiing. Cascade Reservoir. Elev 5000 ft; 4 acres.

Kennally Creek $10
Payette National Forest
3 mi W of Donnelly on SR 55; 10 mi E on FR 388. $10 (double sites $15). 6/1-9/30; 18-day limit. 11 sites (26-ft RV limit). Tbls, toilet, cfga, drkg wtr, no trash service. Fishing, hiking, horseback riding. Horse unloading ramp, hitching rails. Elev 6000 ft.

Lakeside City Park $10
Half mi SW of Donnelly. $10. All year. 5 sites (RVs under 20 ft). Tbls, toilets, cfga, firewood, sanitary station, playground. Store nearby. Swimming, picnicking, fishing, boating (rd).

Rainbow Point $10
Boise National Forest
1.5 mi W of Donnelly on W. Roseberry Rd; 1 mi S on Norwood Rd; 1.5 mi E on Tamarack Falls Rd; 0.5 mi S on W. Mountain Rd; at W shore of Cascade Lake. $10 - $30. 14-day limit. 12 sites; 45-ft RV limit. Tbls, toilets, cfga, drkg wtr. Boating(l), fishing, swimming, waterskiing, canoeing. Elev 4800 ft.

DOWNEY (S)

Malad Summit Campground $10
Caribou National Forest
10 mi SW of Downey on CR 80N; 1.5 mi W on co rd; 1 mi W on FR 41. $10. MD-10/31; 16-day limit. 12 sites (60-ft RV limit). Tbls, toilets, cfga, drkg wtr. Fishing, hiking, horseback riding, biking. Elev 6200 ft.

DRIGGS (S)

Mike Harris $12
Targhee National Forest
13 mi SE of Driggs on SR 33; half mi S on FR 80330; at Harris Creek & Trail Creek jct. $12. 5/22-9/14; 14-day limit. 12 sites (typically 40 ft). Tbls, toilets, cfga, drkg wtr. Fishing, hiking trailhead. Elev 6200 ft; 5 acres.

Teton Canyon $12
Targhee National Forest
From Driggs, 0.5 mi E on Cemetery Rd; 3.5 mi NE on E. Ski Hill Rd, becoming Alta Rd/Targhee Rd in Wyoming for 2 mi; right at Teton Canyon Rd for 4.7 mi, then right qtr mi. $12. 5/15-9/15; 16-day limit. 22 sites (20-ft RV limit). Tbls, toilets, cfga, drkg wtr. Beginning of Teton Crest Trail into Jedediah Smith Wilderness. Fishing, hiking. Elev 6900 ft; 4 acres.

DUBOIS (S)

Webber Creek FREE
Targhee National Forest
25 mi NW of Dubois on CR A3; 2.3 mi W on FR 196. Free. Elev 7000 ft. 6/15-9/15. 4 sites on 5 acres (RVs under 16 ft). Toilet, cfga, no drkg wtr, no trash service. Hiking, fishing, horseback riding.

EASTPORT (N)

Copper Creek $6
Kaniksu National Forest
S of Eastport 2 mi to the Three Mile Jct (US 95 & US 2); N on US 95 to the Mount Hall Jct (US 95 & SR 1); right on US 95 for 13.5 mi; E on Copper Falls Rd (FR 2517) for half mi; at Moyie River. $6. Elev 2610 ft. 5/15-9/15; 14-day limit. 16 sites; 40-ft RV limit. Tbls, toilets, cfga, well drkg wtr. Fishing, berry picking, horseback riding. Copper Falls 1 mi. 8 acres.

Robinson Lake $8
Kaniksu National Forest
7 mi S of Eastport on US 95; 1 mi N on FR 448. $8. MD-LD; 14-day limit. 10 sites; 27-ft RV limit. Toilets, tbls, cfga, drkg wtr. Boating(l), fishing, swimming, hiking. 60-acre lake. Handicap access to 3 sites. Elev 2800 ft.

ELK CITY (N)

Bridge Creek FREE
Nez Perce National Forest
3 mi SW of Elk City on SR 14; 14 mi SE on FR 222; 12 mi NE of Red River Ranger Station (now closed) on FR 234. Free. May-Oct Elev 4800 ft. 6/1-10/31; 14-day limit. 5 sites (RVs under 16 ft). Tbls, toilets, cfga, firewood, no drkg wtr. Fishing, swimming, horseback riding. 1 mi from Red River Hot Springs.

Crooked River #3 & #4 FREE
Nez Perce National Forest
6 mi W of Elk City on SR 14; 3 mi S on FR 233. Free. May-Oct; 14-day limit. 5 undeveloped sites straddling Crooked River. Elev 3960 Toilet, cfga, no drkg wtr. N of campgrounds are historic dredgings from the gold rush days.

Ditch Creek FREE
Nez Perce National Forest
3 mi SW of Elk City on SR 14; 14 mi SE on FR 222; 4 mi NE on FR 234; at Red River. Free. Elev 4500 ft. 6/1-10/31; 14-day limit. 4 sites (RVs under 16 ft). Tbls, toilets, cfga, no drkg wtr. Berry picking, fishing, horseback riding. Stock-handling facilities. Red River Hot Springs at end of the road.

Five Mile Campground FREE
Nez Perce National Forest
7 mi W of Elk City on SR 14; 11 mi S on FR 233; at Crooked River & Five Mile Creek. Free. 5 undeveloped sites. Toilet, cfga, no drkg wtr. Nice swimming area, fish pond. Historic spots date from gold rush period.

French Gulch FREE
Nez Perce National Forest
6 mi S of Elk City on CR 1818; at Red River. Free. June-Oct; 14-day limit. 3 sites. Tbls, toilets, cfga, no drkg wtr. Fishing, hiking, ATV activity. Elev 4210 ft.

Granite Springs FREE
Nez Perce National Forest
3 mi SW of Elk City on SR 14; 15 mi SE on FR 222; 17 mi E on FR 468. Free. 7/15-10/15; 14-day limit. 4 sites (RVs under 16 ft). Piped drkg wtr, toilets, no tbls. Horseback riding, biking, hiking trails. 6700 ft; 4 acres. Primarily a developed hunters' camp. Stock-handling facilities. The Nez Perce used a trail through the camp for their migrations to reduce chances of meeting their enemies, the Blackfeet.

Halfway House FREE
Nez Perce National Forest
32 mi W of Elk City on SR 14; 5 mi SW on FR 233; 1.5 mi S on FR 311; at Crooked Creek. Free. 5/1-10/30; 14-day limit. 4 sites (RVs under 16 ft). Tbls, toilets, cfga, no drkg wtr. Fishing, horseback riding. Elev 5000 ft; 4 acres. Dixie Trailhead into Gospel-Hump Wilderness. Stock handling facilities available.

Legget Creek FREE
Nez Perce National Forest
14 mi W of Elk City on SR 14; across the road from the Clearwater River. Free. June-Oct; 18-day limit. 5 undeveloped sites. Toilets, cfga, no drkg wtr. Cutthroat & rainbow trout fishing.

Magruder Corridor FREE
Backcountry Byway Dispersed Sites
Nez Perce National Forest
S of Elk City to Red River Ranger Station, then E on FR

468; primitive road follows Nez Perce trail between Frank Church and Selway-Bitterroot Wilderness areas. May-Oct; 18-day limit. Primitive dispersed sites along the byway. No facilities except some toilets. Historical markers, ranger stations. Fishing, mountain biking, hiking.

Newsome Campground   FREE
Nez Perce National Forest
About 12 mi W of Elk City on SR 14; 5.5 mi N on FR 1858; at Newsome Creek. 6 sites for tents, pickup campers. Tbls, toilet, cfga, no drkg wtr. Fishing, hiking trails. Nearby are remains of historic Newsome townsite from gold rush era. Group camping free in the field across the road.

Orogrande Camp 1, 2, 3 & 4   FREE
Nez Perce National Forest
6 mi W of Elk City on SR 14; 12 mi S on FR 233; sites on both sides of rd, 1 on Crooked River. Free. 18-day limit. 11 undeveloped sites. Toilets, cfga, no drkg wtr. Near the Orogrande townsite, trading center for the Buffalo Hump mining town. Site's name means "course gold" from the ore found there.

Oxbow Campground   FREE
Nez Perce National Forest
12 mi W of Elk City on SR 14; 2 mi N on FR 1858; at Newsome Creek. Free. 18-day limit. 1 site. Toilet, cfga, no drkg wtr. Fishing, hiking, mountain biking.

Red River Campground $12
Nez Perce National Forest
3 mi SW of Elk City on SR 14; 14 mi SE on FR 222; 6 mi NE of Red River Ranger Station on FR 234. $12 year-round best May-Oct; 14-day limit. 16 sites (typically 50 ft, but limited access for large RVs; pre-view sites). Tbls, toilets, cfga, no drkg wtr or trash service. Berry picking, fishing, horseback riding, hiking, biking. Elev 4600 ft; 25 acres.

Sam's Creek   FREE
Nez Perce National Forest
32 mi W of Elk City on SR 14; 3 mi SW on Mackay Bar Rd (FR 233); 1 mi on FR 311. Free; at Crooked Creek & Sams Creek. Elev 5200 ft. Best May-October; 16-day limit. 3 sites (RVs under 16 ft). Tbls, toilets, cfga, no drkg wtr. Hiking, fishing. No horses.

Sing Lee Campground   FREE
Nez Perce National Forest
13 mi W of Elk City on SR 14; 4.5 mi N on FR 1858; at Newsome Creek. Free. Best May-Oct; 14-day limit. 4 sites. Fishing, hiking.

Table Meadows   FREE
Nez Perce National Forest
3 mi N of Elk City via CR 1854; 7 mi N FR 283 (Ericson Ridge Rd); 5.1 mi NW on FR 420. Best May-Oct; 18-day limit. 6 sites (RVs under 16 ft). Toilets, cfga, no drkg wtr.

Set up for horse camping. Berry picking, horseback riding. Elev 5220 ft; 7 acres. West fork American River adjacent to site.

FAIRFIELD (S)

Abbott Campground $6
Sawtooth National Forest
18 mi N of Fairfield on FR 094; 27 mi W on FR 337; at South Fork of Boise River. $6. Elev 4400 ft. 5/1-9/30; 14-day limit. 7 sites on 5 acres (RVs under 16 ft). Tbls, toilets, cfga, firewood, no drkg wtr. Picnicking, fishing, horseback riding.

Baumgartner $10
Sawtooth National Forest
NW of Fairfield on FR 227 (12 mi E of Featherville); at South Fork of Boise River. $10. 5/1-9/14; 14-day limit. 39 sites (typically 45 ft); also group camping. Tbls, flush toilets, cfga, drkg wtr. Hiking, fishing, 111-degree hot springs, nature trail.

Bird Creek $6
Sawtooth National Forest
18 mi N of Fairfield on FR 094; 24 mi W on FR 337; at South Fork of Boise River. $6. 5/15-10/31; 14-day limit. 5 sites (RVs under 22 ft). Tbls, toilets, cfga, firewood, no drkg wtr. Canoeing, fishing, horseback riding.

Bowns $6
Sawtooth National Forest
18 mi N of Fairfield on FR 094; 1 mi W on FR 337; at South Fork of Boise River. $6. 6/1-9/30; 14-day limit. 10 sites (typically 45 ft). Tbls, toilets, cfga, drkg wtr. Hiking, fishing.

Canyon Transfer Camp $6
Sawtooth National Forest
26 mi N of Fairfield on FR 094 and FR 227, past Big Smokey Guard Station at Big Smokey Creek. $6. 6/1-9/30; 14-day limit. 7 sites. Tbls, toilets, cfga, drkg wtr. Fishing, hiking trails.

Chaparral $6
Sawtooth National Forest
18 mi N of Fairfield on FR 094; 26 mi W on FR 227; at South Fork of Boise River. $6. Elev 4600 ft. 5/15-9/30; 14-day limit. 7 sites (RVs under 22 ft). Tbls, toilets, cfga, firewood, no drkg wtr. Picnicking, fishing.

Five Points   FREE
Sawtooth National Forest
5.9 mi N of FR 093; 11.4 mi N on FR 094; near Five Points Creek. Free. Elev 5900 ft. 6/1-9/30; 14-day limit. 5 sites (RVs under 16 ft). Tbls, toilets, cfga, firewood, no drkg wtr. Picnicking, fishing, horseback riding. Near hot springs.

Pioneer Campground — FREE
Sawtooth National Forest
11 mi N of Fairfield on FR 094 and FR 093 past soldier Mountain ski area. 5 sites. 6/1 - 9/30. Tbls, toilets, cfga, firewood, drkg wtr. Elev 5800 ft. Fishing, hiking horseback riding.

Skeleton Creek — $8
Sawtooth National Forest
18 mi N of Fairfield on FR 094; 16 mi W on FR 337; on South Fork of Boise River. $8 Elev 5300 ft. 6/1-9/30; 14-day limit. 5 undeveloped sites; no facilities. 4 acres. Picnicking, fishing, horseback riding, hiking trails.

Willow Creek — $6
Sawtooth National Forest
18 mi N of Fairfield on FR 094; 23 mi W on FR 337; at South Fork of Boise River. $6. Elev 4800 ft. 5/20-9/30; 14-day limit. 3 sites on 5 acres (RVs under 16 ft). Tbls, cfga, firewood, no drkg wtr. Fishing, swimming, horseback riding. Nearby Willow Creek Transfer Camp has 3 free sites (donations accepted) with corrals, stock loading ramps.

FREEDOM (WYOMING)
Pine Bar Campground — FREE
Caribou National Forest
1 mi N of Freedom on CR 34; 9.5 mi W on SR 34; on Tin Cup Creek. Free. 5/1-11/1; 14-day limit. 5 sites (30-ft RV limit). Tbls, toilets, cfga, no drkg wtr, firewood. Horseback riding, picnicking, fishing. Extensive hiking trail system.

Tincup Campground — FREE
Caribou National Forest
1 mi N of Freedom, Wyoming, on CR 111; 2.6 mi W on SR 34; at Tin Cup Creek. Free. 5/1-10/31; 14-day limit. 5 sites (16-ft RV limit). Toilet, no drkg wtr, cfga, tbls. Fishing, picnicking, extensive hiking trails, biking.

GARDEN VALLEY (S)
Boiling Springs — $7.50
Boise National Forest
2.5 mi W of Garden Valley on SR 17; 22 mi N on FR 698; at Middle Fork of Payette River. $7.50 with federal senior pass others pay $15. Elev 4053 ft. 5/9-10/20; 14-day limit. 9 sites (RVs under 30 ft). Tbls, toilets, cfga, drkg wtr. Non-campers pay $8 day use fee. Fishing, horseback riding.

Hardscrabble — $12
Boise National Forest
2.5 mi W of Garden Valley on SR 17; 14 mi N on FR 698; along Middle Fork Payette River. $12. Elev 3400 ft. 5/15-9/30. 6 sites; 30-ft RV limit. Tbls, toilets, cfga, no drkg wtr. Non-campers pay $5 day use fee. Picnicking, fishing, horseback riding.

Hot Springs — $8
Boise National Forest
2 mi E of Garden Valley on SR 17; at South Fork Payette River. $8 with federal senior pass; others pay $16 during 5/5-9/4; 14-day limit. 8 sites (35-ft RV limit). Non-campers pay $8 day use fee. Tbls, toilets, cfga, drkg wtr. Fishing.

Rattlesnake — $7.50
Boise National Forest
2.5 mi W of Garden Valley on SR 17; 18 mi N on FR 698; at Middle Fork of Payette River. $7.50 with federal senior pass others pay $15. Elev 3600 ft. MD-LD; 14-day limit. 11 sites on 7 acres (RVs under 36 ft). Group camping $110. Non-campers pay $8 day use fee. Tbls, toilets, cfga, drkg wtr. Fishing, horseback riding.

Silver Creek — $7.50
Boise National Forest
2.5 mi W of Garden Valley on SR 17; 19 mi N on FR 698; 7 mi NE on FR 671 (rebuilt in 2010). $7.50 with federal senior pass; others pay $15.5/15-11/1; 14-day limit. 57 sites; 50-ft RV limit. Non-campers pay $8 day use fee. Tbls, toilets, cfga, drkg wtr. Fishing, horseback riding, hiking.

Tie Creek — $7.50
Boise National Forest
2.5 mi W of Garden Valley on SR 17; 11 mi N on FR 698; at Middle Fork of Payette River. $7.50 with federal senior pass others pay $15. Elev 3200 ft. 5/1-10/20; 14-day limit. 8 sites RV limit 35 ft. Non-campers pay $8 day use fee. Tbls, toilets, cfga, firewood, well drkg wtr. Fishing, horseback riding.

Trail Creek — $12
Boise National Forest
2.5 mi W of Garden Valley on SR 17; 19 mi N on FR 698; at Middle Fork of Payette River. $12. Elev 3800 ft. 4/20-10/20; 14-day limit. 11 sites RV Limit 35 ft. Tbls, toilets, cfga, no drkg wtr. Picnicking, fishing, horseback riding. Non-campers pay $7 day use fee.

GEORGETOWN (S)
Summit View — $12
Caribou National Forest
2.4 mi E on CR 102; 6 mi N on FR 95 (Georgetown Canyon Rd). $12 during 5/24-LD, $6 LD-10/2, but no wtr. 14-day limit. 21 sites (32-ft RV limit). Tbls, toilets, cfga, drkg wtr, amphitheater. Hiking trail, biking, fishing, horseback riding, OHV activity. Elev 7200 ft.

GIBBONSVILLE (S)
Twin Creek — $10
Salmon National Forest
5 mi NW of Gibbonsville on SR 93; half mi NW on FR 449. $10. $10. 5/22-10/15; 14-day limit. 40 sites, 32-ft RV limit. Tbls, toilets, cfga, drkg wtr. No drkg wtr off-season. Nature trails, fishing, horse ramp.

IDAHO

GLENNS FERRY (S)

Three Island Crossing State Park $11
On W. Madison St, off I-84 at Glenns Ferry. $11 for seniors Mon-Thurs at 82 sites with elec/wt; others pay $22. All year; 15-day limit. No RV size limit. Tbls, flush toilets, cfga, drkg wtr, showers, dump. Swimming, fishing, hiking, guided walks, interpretive center, historical programs. Site of a key river crossing on the Oregon Trail. 513 acres; elev 2484 ft.

GOODING (S)

Little City of Rocks   FREE
Bureau of Land Management
Shoshone Field Office
W from SR 46 about 12.5 mi N of Gooding; dirt rd 1 mi. RV parking S of rock wall recommended. Free. All year; 14-day limit. Undeveloped primitive area; limited camping opportunities. No facilities, no wtr or trash service. Picnicking, hiking, rock climbing.

GRANGEVILLE (N)

Castle Creek $12
Nez Perce National Forest
1 mi E of Grangeville on SR 13; 10 mi SE on CR 17; 6 mi SE on SR 14; at South Fork Clearwater River. $12 (no wtr; 14-day limit. 8 sites (RVs under 26 ft). Toilets, cfga, tbls, drkg wtr. Dump at South Fork Campground. Hiking, swimming, fishing, picnicking.

Fish Creek Campground $12
Nez Perce National Forest
1 mi E of Grangeville on SR 13; 1 mi S on CR 17; 6.8 mi SE on FR 221. $12 year-round best summer and fall; 14-day limit. 11 sites on 3 acres (RVs under 24 ft). Tbls, toilets, cfga, drkg wtr, no trash service. Fishing, horseback riding, hiking trails. Camp free when wtr off.

Meadow Creek   FREE
Nez Perce National Forest
1 mi E of Grangeville on SR 13; 10 mi SE on CR 17; 9 mi SE on SR 14; between Meadow Creek & South Fork of Clearwater River. Free. All year; 14-day limit. 3 sites. Tbls, toilets, cfga, no drkg wtr. Hiking, fishing. Elev 2300 ft.

Sourdough Saddle Camp   FREE
Nez Perce National Forest
25 mi E of Grangeville on SR 14; 5 mi S on FR 212/1894; 15 mi W on FR 492. Sept-Oct; 14-day limit. Undeveloped area for 4 camping units. Toilets, tbls, cfga, no drkg wtr, no trash service. Hiking, horseback riding. Elev 6090 ft.

South Fork $12
Nez Perce National Forest
1 mi E of Grangeville on Hwy 13; 9.9 mi SE on CR 17; 6 mi SE on SR 14. $12. year-round best May-Oct 14-day limit. 8 sites (RVs under 25 ft); 1 multi-family picnic site. Toilets,

tbls, cfga, drkg wtr (May-Oct), dump. Fishing, swimming. Camp free when wtr shut off.

HAILEY (S)

Bridge Camp Dispersed Area $8
Sawtooth National Forest
2.6 mi N of Hailey on SR 75; 9 mi W on FR 097; at Deer Creek. $8. 5/15-10/15. 3 dispersed sites (no trailers). Tbls, cfga, no drkg wtr, no toilets. Fishing, horseback riding. Elev 5600 ft; 2 acres. Douglas fir seed production area.

Federal Gulch   FREE
Sawtooth National Forest
6.1 mi N of Hailey on SR 75; 11.5 mi E on FR 118; at East Fork of Wood River. Free. Elev 6790 ft. 5/1-10/15; 16-day limit. 3 sites (RVs under 22 ft). Tbls, toilets, cfga, firewood, piped drkg wtr. Hiking, fishing, horseback riding. 17 mi SE of Sun Valley. Trailhead to Pioneer Mountains.

Wolftone Dispersed Sites $8
Sawtooth National Forest
2.6 mi N of Hailey on SR 75; 8.1 mi W on FR 097; at Deer Creek. $8. Elev 5500 ft. 5/15-10/15. 3 dispersed sites. Tbls, toilets, cfga, firewood, no drkg wtr. Fishing, horseback riding, hiking trail. 126-degree Clarendon Hot Springs nearby.

HANSEN (S)

Lower Penstemon $8
Sawtooth National Forest
27 mi S of Hansen on CR G3 (Rock Creek Rd). $8. mid May-Oct; 14-day limit. 7 sites (16-ft RV limit). Tbls, toilets, cfga, no drkg wtr. Group camping available. Popular winter sports.

Upper Penstemon $8
Sawtooth National Forest
24 mi S of Hansen on CR G3 (Rock Creek Rd); near base of Magic Mountain. $8. All year; 14-day limit. 8 sties. Tbls, toilets, cfga, drkg wtr. Fishing, hiking, winter sports.

HARVARD (N)

Giant White Pine $8
Clearwater National Forest
8.5 mi N of Harvard on SR 6. $8. MD-LD; 14-day limit. 14 sites (RVs under 30 ft). Tbls, toilets, cfga, drkg wtr. Hiking trails, observation site. Camp may be open free until 11/1 after wtr is off.

Laird Park Campground $12
Clearwater National Forest
3 mi NE of Harvard on SR 6; 1 mi SE on FR 447; at Palouse River. $12. MD-LD; 14-day limit. 31 sites (35-ft RV limit). Tbls, toilets, cfga, drkg wtr. Fishing, nature trails, swimming beach, playground.

HAYDEN LAKE (N)

Mokins Bay $9
Coeur d'Alene National Forest
12 mi E of Hayden Lake on FR 3090; E at "Public Camp" sign. $9 with federal senior pass; others pay $18. MD-LD Peak; 14-day limit. 15 sites (RVs under 22 ft). Tbls, toilets, cfga, firewood, piped drkg wtr. Picnicking, fishing, boating, waterskiing. Nearest public boat launch 5 mi by rd at N end of lake.

HEADQUARTERS (N)

Aquarius $10
Clearwater National Forest
42 mi NE of Headquarters on Hwy 11; 25 mi NE on FR 247; at North Fork of Clearwater River. $10. May-Oct 14-day limit. 9 sites (RVs under 23 ft). Tbls, toilet, cfga, drkg wtr. (MD-Mid Seo) Fishing, boating, hiking, horseback riding Elev 1700 ft.

Grandad Campground FREE
Corps of Engineers
Dworshak Reservoir
From project office, 68 mi N on Silver Creek Rd & Musselman Rd (both gravel); no signs. Free. 10 primitive sites in undeveloped parking area. 14 day limit. Pit toilets, seasonal launch ramp, tbls, cfga, no drkg wtr. Fishing, boating(l).

HOWE (S)

Summit Creek Recreation Site FREE
Bureau of Land Management
Challis Field Office
41 mi NW on co rd; 9.5 mi NE on Summit Rd. (30 mi S of Patterson.) Free. Elev 7000 ft. All year; 16-day limit. 7 sites on 1 acre (30-ft RV limit). Tbls, toilets, cfga, no drkg wtr. Hiking, fishing. On Little Lost River.

IDAHO CITY (S)

Bad Bear $7.50
Boise National Forest
9.5 mi NE of Idaho City on SR 21; at Mores Creek. $7.50 with federal senior pass; others pay $15. 5/22-9/25; 14-day limit. 6 sites; 40-ft RV limit. Tbls, toilets, cfga, drkg wtr. Fishing, hiking. Elev 4900 ft.

Bald Mountain Camp FREE
Boise National Forest
1 mi N of Idaho City on SR 21; 6 mi SE on FR 304; 1 mi SE on FR 203. Free. 7/1-9/30; 14-day limit. 4 sites. Tbls, toilets, cfga, no drkg wtr or trash service. Hiking, mountain biking, horseback riding, OHV activities. Trail leads to Middle Fork of Boise River.

Black Rock $8
Boise National Forest
3 mi NE of Idaho City on SR 21; 18 mi E on FR 327. $8-$15. About 5/22-9/25. 14-day limit. 11 sites, most 45 ft. Tbls, toilets, cfga, drkg wtr. Fishing, horseback riding, hiking.

Adjacent to N fork of Boise River.

Bonneville $7.50
Boise National Forest
18 mi NE of Idaho City on SR 21; half mi N on FR 25. $7.50 with federal senior pass; others pay $15. MD-LD; 14-day limit. 22 sites (4 Tent); 55-ft RV limit. Non-campers pay $5 day use fee. Tbls, toilets, cfga, firewood, drkg wtr. Fishing, hiking, boating. Elev 4700 ft. Natural hot springs quarter mi upstream, Boating suitable for whitewater craft only on S fork of the Payette River.

Grayback Gulch $10
Boise National Forest
2.6 mi SW of Idaho City on SR 21. $10 5/18-9/25 14-day limit. 14 sites 45-ft RV limit. Tbls, toilets, cfga, drkg wtr. Fishing, swimming. Also group camping.

Ten Mile $7.50
Boise National Forest
9.3 mi NE of Idaho City on SR 21; near Mores Creek. $7.50 with federal senior pass; others pay $15. 6/1-10/15; 14-day limit. 16 sites RV Limit 23 ft.. Tbls, toilets, cfga, drkg wtr. Fishing. Hiking.

IDAHO FALLS (S)

Kelly Island Campground $10
Bureau of Land Management
Upper Snake Field Office
23 mi NE of Idaho Falls on US 26. $10 (double site $20). 5/15-9/30 14-day limit. 14 sites (RVs under 23 ft); some pull-through. Tbls, toilets, cfga, drkg wtr. Boating, fishing, hiking.

North Tourist Park FREE
Municipal Campground
NE on US 26-91 to Lincoln St. and N Yellowstone Hwy (US 26); paved access rds. Free. All year; 1-day limit. About 20 undesignated sites in pull-through areas. Toilets, near city golf course and large shopping center. Site of a Peter "Wolf" Toth Indian sculpture, carved from huge log.

South Tourist Park FREE
Municipal Campground
US 26-91 exit off I-15; 2.5 mi to Southside rest area at S Yellowstone. Free. All year; 1-day limit. 4 back-in sites; 30-ft RV limit. Tbls, toilets, cfga, drkg wtr, playground. Picnicking, fishing, boating (l). Snake River.

Tex Creek FREE
Wildlife Management Area
14 mi NE of Idaho Falls on US 26; just after milepost 350, turn right at Ririe Dam/Recreation Area sign; follow Meadow Creek Rd SE past the dam. Free. All year; 10-day limit. Primitive camping in designated areas; no facilities. Hunting, hiking, horseback riding.

IDAHO

JORDAN VALLEY (S)

North Fork Recreation Site   FREE
Bureau of Land Management
Owyhee Field Office
27 mi SE of Jordan Valley on Owyhee Uplands Backcountry Byway; at North Fork of Owyhee River. Free. 5/1-10/31; 7-day limit. 7 primitive sites. Toilet, cfga, no drkg wtr, no trash service. Biking, fishing, hiking, horseback riding.

Owyhee Uplands   FREE
National Backcountry Byway
Bureau of Land Management
Owyhee Field Office
Starting 5 mi SE of Jordan Valley, Oregon, or 3 mi from Grand View, ID, on Owyhee Byway along the Owyhee River. Free. Secluded primitive sites all along the road at riverside. Some are like the small, tree-shaded picnic area at Poison Creek near E end of byway. No facilities. Fishing, boating, hiking, horseback riding.

KAMIAH (N)

Lolo Creek Campground   FREE
Clearwater National Forest
21 miles NE of Kamiah, East on US 12 into MT right on FR 2170. 9 sites along Lolo and Eldorado Creeks. Toilets, no drk wtr, cfga, tbls. Minutes from Lewis & Clark Trail (#25) Hiking, OHV trail riding, fishingberry picking.

Riverfront City Park $5
At E end of town on US 12 by Clearwater River. $5 with elec; free without hookups. $5 All year; 3-day limit. 6 sites. Tbls, flush toilets, cfga, drkg wtr, elec, beach, covered barbecue bldg. Boating(l), fishing, swimming, waterskiing, nature trail, playground, badminton, horseshoes.

KETCHUM (S)

Baker Creek   FREE
Sawtooth National Forest
Sawtooth National Recreation Area
15 mi N of Ketchum on SR 75. Free. All year; 14-day limit. Primitive undeveloped sites (RVs under 32 ft). Tbls, toilets, firewood, no drkg wtr. Picnicking, fishing, swimming, snowmobile area.

Boundary Campground $10
Sawtooth National Forest
From Ketchum, go NE through Sun Valley about 4 mi on FR 408; at Trail Creek. Mid July-Labor Day; 14-day limit. 9 sites. Tbls, toilets, cfga, no drkg wtr, corrals. Hiking, horseback riding, fishing.

Cottonwood Campground   FREE
Sawtooth National Forest
6 mi W of Ketchum on FR 227; at Warm Springs Creek. Free. 5/15-10/15; 14-day limit. 1 site; no facilities, no drkg wtr, no trash service. Fishing. 124-degree Warfield Hot Springs 2 mi W.

Cougar Dispersed Area   FREE
Sawtooth National Forest
Sawtooth National Recreation Area
7 mi N on SR 75; 3 mi N on FR 146. Free. 6/15-10/1; 16-day limit. 10 sites; 5 acres. Toilets, cfga, tbls, no drkg wtr. Hiking, picnicking, fishing. Elev 6700 ft.

Easley $11
Sawtooth National Forest
Sawtooth National Recreation Area
14.5 mi N of Ketchum on SR 75; turn S at sign; at Big Wood River. $11. MD-LD; 10-day limit. 10 sites (40-ft RV limit). Tbls, toilets, cfga, drkg wtr. Swimming, fishing, hiking. Elev 6800 ft. Wtr system closed by flood damage; check current status before arrival.

East Fork Baker Creek   FREE
Sawtooth National Forest
Sawtooth National Recreation Area
15 mi N of Ketchum on SR 75; 3 mi S on FR 162. Free. 6/1-11/15; 14-day limit. 7 sites. Tbls, toilet, cfga, no drkg wtr. Fishing, hiking.

Murdock $8
Sawtooth National Forest
Sawtooth National Recreation Area
7 mi N of Ketchum on SR 75; 1 mi E on FR 146. $8 during about MD-9/30; free before & after season, but no wtr or services; 10-day limit. 11 sites on 60 acres (typically 55 ft). Tbls, toilets, cfga, drkg wtr. Picnicking, fishing, hiking trails. Visitor center with exhibits, interpretive programs, dump 2 mi down canyon at headquarters. Elev 6200 ft.

North Fork $8
Sawtooth National Forest
Sawtooth National Recreation Area
8.1 mi N of Ketchum on SR 75; at Big Wood River. $8 during about MD-LD; 9 sites free before & after season, but no wtr or services; 10-day limit. 29 sites (typically 40 ft). Tbls, toilets, cfga, drkg wtr. Fishing, hiking, biking. Visit center, exhibits, interpretive programs, dump are across SR 75 at recreation area headquarters. Elev 5900 ft; 40 acres.

Park Creek $10
Challis National Forest
12 mi NE of Ketchum on SR 75; 26 mi NE on Sun Valley Rd, becoming Trail Creek Rd. $10. 6/15-9/30; 14-day limit. 12 sites 32-ft RV limit. Tbls, toilets, cfga, drkg wtr. Hiking trails, fishing, horseback riding (corral just W on FR 141). Elev 7700 ft; 10 acres.

Phi Kappa $10
Challis National Forest
15 mi NE of Ketchum on SR 75; 23 mi NE on Sun Valley Rd,

becoming Trail Creek Rd. $10. 5/15-10/15; 14-day limit. 21 sites (32-ft RV limit). Tbls, toilets, cfga, drkg wtr (naturally rusty color). Hiking trails, fishing. Elev 7600 ft; 8 acres.

Prairie Creek   FREE
Sawtooth National Forest
Sawtooth National Recreation Area
18 mi N of Ketchum on SR 75. Free. All year; 16-day limit. Primitive undeveloped sites 32-ft limit. Tbls, toilets, cfga, no drkg wtr. Picnicking, swimming, fishing, cross-country skiing. 60 acres.

Starhope $10
Challis National Forest
20 mi NE of Ketchum on SR 75; 23.1 mi E on FR 135 (Sun Valley Rd/Trail Creek Rd); 13 mi SW on Copper Basin Rd; 9 mi on Copper Basin Loop Rd 138. $10. 5/30-9/30; 14-day limit. 21 sites 32-ft RV limit. Tbls, toilets, cfga, drkg wtr, hitching post. Fishing, hiking trails, horseback riding. Elev 8000 ft; 9 acres.

Wildhorse $10
Challis National Forest
20 mi NE of Ketchum on SR 75; 3 mi on FR 135; 6 mi S on FR 136. $10. 6/1-10/15; 14-day limit. 13 sites 44-ft RV limit. Tbls, toilets, cfga, drkg wtr. Hiking trails, fishing. Elev 7400 ft; 30 acres.

Wood River $8
Sawtooth National Forest
Sawtooth National Recreation Area
10 mi NW of Ketchum on SR 75; second camp on S side of hwy after passing NRA headquarters; at Big Wood River. $8 during about MD-LD; 10-day limit; 8 sites free off-season, but no wtr or services. 30 sites (22-ft RV limit). Tbls, flush toilets, cfga, drkg wtr. Hiking, fishing, swimming. Elev 6300 ft; 41 acres.

KINGSTON (N)
Bumblebee $9
Coeur d'Alene National Forest
7 mi NE of Kingston on FR 9; 3 mi NW on FR 209; on North Fork of Coeur d'Alene River. $9 with federal senior pass; others pay $18. MD-LD; 14-day limit. 25 sites; 30-ft RV limit. Tbls, toilets, cfga, drkg wtr. Fishing, hiking, kayaking. Elev 2200 ft. Renovated in 2010.

KOOSKIA (N)
CCC Camp   FREE
Nez Perce National Forest
23.5 mi E of Kooskia on US 12; 7 me SE on FR 223; at Selway River. Free. year-round best Apr-Oct; 14-day limit. 6 sites. Tbls, toilets (Apr-Oct), cfga, no drkg wtr. Swimming, fishing, horseback riding. Elev 1550 ft.

Johnson Bar $6
Nez Perce National Forest
23.5 mi E of Kooskia on US 12; 4 mi SE on FR 223; on Selway River. $6. MD-10/1; 7 undesignated sites (RVs under 22 ft). Tbls, toilets, cfga, drkg wtr (May-Sep), beach. Swimming, fishing, boating, rafting in spring. Elev 1600 ft. Visitor center (1 mi). Scenic. River.

Knife Edge River Portal   FREE
Dispersed Campground
Clearwater National Forest
1 mi N of Kooskia on Hwy 13; 33.5 mi E on US 12; at Lochsa River. Free. Year-round but may not be accessible in winter; 14-day limit. 5 sites; Toilet, no drkg wtr. Fishing, biking, boating, hiking. Undeveloped boat ramp. May be closed to camping in May & June for river running season.

Race Creek   FREE
Nez Perce National Forest
23.5 mi E of Kooskia on US 12; 20.5 mi SE on FR 223 (gravel rd for 13 mi); at upper Selway River. Free. MD-11/1; 14-day limit. 3 sites (RVs under 22 ft). Tbls, toilets, cfga, no drkg wtr. Hiking, fishing (Meadow Creek), boating, horseback riding, horse feedrack, hitching rails, horse loading ramp. Elev 1800 ft. At Bitterroot Wilderness Trailhead. End-of-rd facilities for Bitterroot Wilderness Portal.

Rackliff Campground $8
Nez Perce National Forest
22 miles E of Kooskia on US 12, 9 miles SE on FR223. $8. 6 sites. Year-round but might not be accessible due to snow. Toilet (Apr-Sep), No drk wtr, CFGA. Fishing, Hiking. Elev 1600.

Slims   FREE
Nez Perce National Forest
23.5 mi E of Kooskia on US 12; 21 mi SE on FR 223; 2 mi S on FR 290; at Meadow Creek. Free. MD-11/1; 14-day limit. 1 RV site (RV under 16 ft). Tbls, toilet, cfga, no drkg wtr. Equestrian facilities. Fishing, hiking, horseback riding. Trailhead for Meadow Creek Recreation Trail.

Twentymile Bar   FREE
Nez Perce National Forest
23.5 mi E of Kooskia on US 12; 10.5 mi SE on FR 223; at Selway River. Free. MD-11/1; 14-day limit. 2 unimproved sites (RVs under 22 ft). Tbls, toilet, cfga, no drkg wtr. Boating, swimming from sandy bar, fishing. Carry-down boat access.

Twentythreemile Bar   FREE
Nez Perce National Forest
23.5 mi E of Kooskia on US 12; 12 mi SE on FR 223; at Selway River. Free. MD-11/1; 14-day limit. 1 dispersed site; no facilities. Very steep access to river. Fishing, swimming, boating.

KUNA (S)

Celebration Park   FREE
Snake River Birds of Prey
National Conservation Area
Bureau of Land Management
Canyon County Parks & Recreation
4 mi W of Kuna on Kuna Rd; about 5 mi S on Robinson Blvd; at its end, right on Dickman Rd, 1 mi W to Can-Ada Rd (at Baseline, Can-Ada Rd jogs, so turn left on Baseline, then right onto Can-Ada); S to Victory Lane; right, into park (rough dirt rd last half mi). Free. All year; 3-day limit. Numerous primitive undesignated sites within state's only archaeological park; small RVs such as van campers, truck campers. Toilets, cfga, drkg wtr. Boating(l), interpretive displays, educational programs, hiking. Petroglyphs. Non-campers pay $2 day use fee. Annual pass $15; senior annual pass $5. Managed by county parks system.

LAVA HOT SPRINGS (S)

Big Springs $10
Caribou National Forest
10 mi N of Lava Hot Springs on Bancroft Hwy; 8 mi W on FR 036. $10. MD-9/30; 14-day limit. 29 sites (typically 45 ft). Tbls, toilets, cfga, drkg wtr. Fishing, hiking, biking, horseback riding, OHV activity. 3 equestrian sites; corrals.

Chesterfield Reservoir   FREE
Caribou County Park
E of Hot Springs on Hwy 30, then 10 mi N on Old Route 30; left on Kelly-Toponce Rd for 10 mi, then turn on Nipper Rd at sign for Chesterfield Reservoir. Free. 14-day limit. 3 primitive sites. Tbls, toilet, cfga, no drkg wtr. Boating, fishing.

LEADORE (S)

Big Eightmile   FREE
Salmon National Forest
6.7 mi W of Leadore on Lee Creek Rd; at second jct, bear left at Big Eightmile Creek on FR 097 for 7 mi. Free. 5/15-10/15. 10 sites, 25-ft RV limit. Tbls, toilet, cfga, drkg wtr; no trash service. Fishing, horseback riding. Elev 7608 ft.

Meadow Lake $10
Salmon National Forest
16.8 mi SE of Leadore on SR 28; 6 mi W on FR 002. $10. 6/25-9/15; free rest of year; 14-day limit. 18 sites, 23-ft RV limit. Tbls, toilets, cfga, drkg wtr (check status of spring, potable water may not be available). Fishing, swimming, boating, hiking. Scenic. No wtr during free period. Elev 9200 ft.

McFarland Campground $5
Bureau of Land Management
Salmon Field Office
10 mi NW of Leadore on SR 28. $5. 14-day limit. 5 sites (RV limit 28 ft); some pull-through. Toilets, tbls, cfga, drkg wtr.

Hiking, fishing. Elev 5370 ft; 6 acres.
Smokey Cubs Recreation Site   FREE
Bureau of Land Management
Salmon Field Office
4 mi E of Leadore off Hwy 28 South, on Railroad Canyon Rd. Free. All year; 14-day limit. 8 sites (28-ft RV limit). Tbls, toilets, cfga. Hiking, fishing, picnicking.

LEWISTON (N)

Blyton Landing   FREE
Corps of Engineers
Lower Granite Lake
20 mi W of Lewiston on CR 9000 (North Shore Snake River Rd) in Washington. Free. All year; 14-day limit. Primitive undesignated sites. Fire restrictions. Tbls, toilets, cfga, no drkg wtr. Boating(ld), fishing.

Lake Waha Campground   FREE
Bureau of Reclamation
Lewiston Orchards Irrigation District
5 mi S of Lewiston on Tammany Creek Rd; 10 mi S on Waha Rd to W shore of lake. Free. All year; 7-day limit. Primitive undesignated sites; limited facilities. Boating(l), fishing, swimming. 180-acre lake developed by Bureau of Reclamation, managed by irrigation district. Lake

McKay's Bend Recreation Site $9
Bureau of Land Management
Cottonwood Field Office
Idaho Dept. of Fish & Game
15 mi E of Lewiston on US 12; on N shore of Clearwater River. $9 with federal senior pass at 15 full hookups; others pay $18. $10 at 10 tent sites. All year; 14-day limit. Tbls, flush toilets, cfga, drkg wtr. Shelters($). Boating(l), fishing.

Nisqually John Landing   FREE
Corps of Engineers
Lower Granite Lake
15 mi W of Lewiston on CR 9000 (North Shore Snake River Rd) in Washington. Free. All year; 14-day limit. Primitive undesignated sites. Fire restrictions. Tbls, toilets, cfga, no drkg wtr. Boating(ld), fishing.

Offield Landing   FREE
Corps of Engineers
Lower Granite Lake
1 mi E of Lower Granite Dam on Lower Granite Lake, Snake River milepost 108, S shore in Washington; Free. All year; 14-day limit. Primitive undesignated sites. Pit toilets, cfga, no drkg wtr. Boating(l), fishing.

Soldiers Meadow Reservoir   FREE
Bureau of Reclamation
Lewiston Orchards Irrigation District
5 mi S of Lewiston Orchards on Tammany Creek Rd, then 14 mi S on Waha Rd, past the lake turnoff, then E on Sol-

diers Meadow Rd. All year; 7-day limit. Primitive camping on shore of 124-acre lake. Tbls, toilets, cfga, no drkg wtr. Boating(l), fishing, swimming, hiking. Lake built by Bureau of Reclamation; managed by irrigation district.

Wawawai Landing FREE
Corps of Engineers
Lower Granite Lake
28 mi W of Lewiston on North Shore Snake River Rd in Washington; on N shore of river. Or 19 mi W of Pullman, WA, on Wawawai Rd. Free. All year; 14-day limit. 9 sites; 24-ft RV limit. Fire restrictions. Tbls, toilets, cfga, no drkg wtr. Volleyball, hiking trails, fishing, boating(ld).

LOLO HOT SPRINGS (MT)
Hoodoo Lake FREE
Clearwater National Forest
11 mi SW of Lolo on US 12; 17 mi S on FR 111 & FR 360; in Idaho. Free. 6/15-9/15 or until inaccessible; 14-day limit. 4 sites. Tbl, toilet, cfga, no drkg wtr. Hiking, horseback riding. Elev 5756 ft.

Powell $7
Clearwater National Forest
18 mi W of Lolo Hot Springs on US 12, in Idaho at Lochsa River. $7 with federal senior pass others pay $14 base; $20 with elec ($10 with federal senior pass). MD-10/15; 14-day limit. 39 sites (32-ft RV limit). Tbls, flush toilets, cfga, drkg wtr. Fishing, hiking. Lewis & Clark passed through here on their way to the Pacific. Camp may be open free without wtr until about 11/1.

Wendover $7
Clearwater National Forest
22 mi W of Lolo Hot Springs on US 12, in Idaho at Lochsa River. $7 with federal senior pass others pay $14. MD-LD; 14-day limit. 27 sites (32-ft RV limit). Tbls, toilets, cfga, drkg wtr. Fishing, hiking & bridle trails. Elev 3280 ft.

White House $7
Clearwater National Forest
22 mi W of Lolo Hot Springs on US 12 in Idaho at Lochsa River and Whitehouse Pond. $7 with federal senior pass others pay $14. MD-LD; 14-day limit. 13 sites (32-ft RV limit). Tbls, toilets, cfga, drkg wtr. Fishing, hiking, horseback riding. Whitehouse Pond named for a member of the Lewis & Clark expedition; it was noted in his journal.

White Sand $7
Clearwater National Forest
22 mi W of Lolo Hot Springs on US 12; 1 mi S on Elks Summit Rd; in Idaho at Lochsa River. $7 with federal senior pass others pay $14. MD-LD or until inaccessible; 14-day limit. 6 sites (32-ft RV limit). Tbls, toilets, cfga, drkg wtr. Swimming, fishing, hiking.

LOWELL (N)
Apgar Creek $7
Clearwater National Forest
7 mi E of Lowell on US 12; at Lochsa River. $7 with national senior pass others pay $14. MD-LD 14-day limit. 7 sites (22-ft RV limit). Tbls, toilets, cfga, drkg wtr. Fishing, hiking, rafting.

Boyd Creek $8
Nez Perce National Forest
12 mi E of Lowell on Selway Rd 223; on Selway River. $8. year-round limited access due to snow; 14-day limit. 5 sites. Tbls, toilet Apr-Sep), cfga, no drkg wtr. Horse loading ramp & feed rack. Trailhead for East Boyd National Recreation Trail. Terrain very steep. Swimming, boating, fishing.

Glover Campground $8
Nez Perce National Forest
16 mi E of Lowell on Selway River Rd 223. $8. 5/15-10/31; 14-day limit. 7 sites (16-ft RV limit). Tbls, toilets, cfga, no drkg wtr. Hitching rail, horse loading ramp. Trailhead for Glover National Recreation Trail. Terrain very steep; limited maneuvering space for trailers.

O'Hara Bar $7
Nez Perce National Forest
At Lowell, 12.7 mi SE on CR 223; 1 mi S on FR 651; at Selway River. $7 with federal senior pass; others pay $14 5/15-10/1; 14-day limit. 32 sites; 45-ft RV limit. Tbls, cfga, drkg wtr, toilets. Swimming, boating, fishing. Permit (by lottery) needed to float river from Selway Falls to Lowell during 5/15-7/31.

Selway Falls $6
Nez Perce National Forest
21 mi E of Lowell on Selway River Rd 223; 1 mi S on FR 290; at Meadow Creek. $6. 5/1-9/30; 14-day limit. 7 sites. Tbls, toilets, cfga, no drkg wtr. Limited maneuvering space for trailers. Swimming, boating, fishing. Permit (by lottery) needed to float river from Selway Falls to Lowell during 5/15-7/31.

Slide Creek FREE
Nez Perce National Forest
11 mi E of Lowell on Selway Rd 223; at Selway River. Free. May-Oct. Unimproved camping area. Toilet, cfga, no drkg wtr. Sandy beach. Hiking, fishing, swimming, kayaking.

Twenty-five mile Bar FREE
Nez Perce National Forest
15 mi E of Lowell on Selway River Rd 223; at Selway River. year-round but limited during snow; 14-day limit. 3 Undeveloped sites at river bar. Toilet, cfga, no drkg wtr. Swimming, fishing. Carry-down boat access.

Wild Goose $7
Clearwater National Forest
2 mi W of Lowell on US 12; at Lochsa River. $7 with national senior pass others pay $14. May 15-LD; 14-day limit. 6 sites (22-ft RV limit). Tbls, toilets, cfga, drkg wtr. Hiking, fishing.

Wilderness Gateway $7
Clearwater National Forest
27 mi E of Lowell on US 12; at Lochsa River. $7 with national senior pass others pay $14. Fees reduced when water turned off late Sept. 5/22-11/1; 14-day limit. 91 sites; 50-ft RV limit. Tbls, flush & pit toilets, cfga, drkg wtr, dump. Fishing, hiking, swimming, rafting, horseback riding. Handicap access.

LOWMAN (S)

Barney's $12
Boise National Forest
36 mi NE of Lowman on SR 21; 28 mi W on FR 579; 7.5 mi S on FR 555; E side of Deadwood Reservoir. $12. All year; 14-day limit. 6 sites (22-ft RV limit). Tbls, toilets, cfga, drkg wtr, no trash service. Non-campers pay $6 day use fee. Fishing, boating(l), hiking. Sites large, but big RVs have difficulty navigating campground rds. Closed due to fires in 2016 check status before arrival.

Bear Valley FREE
Boise National Forest
36 mi NE of Lowman on SR 21; 1s mi N on FR 579 (Landmark-Stanley Rd); at Bear Valley Creek. Free. Elev 6390 ft. 6/15-9/30; 14-day limit. 10 sites; 20 acres (22-ft RV limit). Tbls, toilets, cfga, no drkg wtr or trash service. Fishing, horseback riding, hiking.

Bull Trout Lake $7.50
Boise National Forest
34 mi NE of Lowman on SR 21; 2 mi W on FR 250. $7.50 with federal senior pass; others pay $15 (double sites $30 during 7/1-9/30; free off-season; 14-day limit. 38 sites on 15 acres (60-ft RV limit), plus group sites. Toilets, drkg wtr, tbls, cfga, corrals. Boating (no motors), biking, canoeing, fishing, horseback riding, hiking, ATV trails, swimming. Historic sites along SR 21. Several other lakes nearby. Non-campers pay $5 day use fee. Elev 6900 ft.

Boundary Creek $10
Challis National Forest
34.8 mi NE of Lowman on FR 668 (Boundary Creek Rd); on Middle Fork of Salmon River. $10. 6/1-10/15; 14-day limit. 15 sites, 22-ft RV limit. Tbls, toilets, cfga, drkg wtr. Fishing, hiking, floating on Marsh Creek. Elev 5800 ft; 6 acres.

Cozy Cove $12
Boise National Forest
36 mi NE of Lowman on SR 21; 28 mi W on FR 579; 11 mi S on FR 555; at S end of Deadwood Reservoir. $12. 7/1-9/5;

14-day limit. 16 sites; 40-ft RV limit, but difficult navigating campground rds. Non-campers pay $6 day use fee. Tbls, toilets, cfga, firewood, drkg wtr, no trash service. Boating(d), fishing, waterskiing, horseback riding. Elev 5367ft; 15 acres.

Daggar Falls Campground $10
Challis National Forest
32 mi NE of Lowman on FR 082; N on FR 668 Boundary Creek Rd). $10 during 6/1-10/15; free rest of season; 14-day limit. 8 sites; 16-ft RV limit. Tbls, toilets, cfga, drkg wtr. Picnicking, fishing, hiking, horseback riding. Near the West and Middle Forks of Salmon River. Elev 6400 ft.

Deer Flat Campground FREE
Boise National Forest
36 mi NE of Lowman on SR 21; 22 mi E on Cape Horn Turn-off (Landmark-Stanley Rd/FR 579); at confluence of Deer Creek, North Fork & South Fork. Elev 6200 ft. Free. 7/1-9/30; 14-day limit. 5 sites (not recommended for trailers or large motorhomes). Tbls, toilets, cfga, firewood, no drkg wtr or trash service. Fishing, horseback riding.

Edna Creek $7.50
Boise National Forest
18 mi N of Lowman on SR 21. $7.50 with federal senior pass others pay $15, 5/22-9/25; 14-day limit. 9 sites; 40-ft RV limit. Tbls, toilets, cfga, drkg wtr. Fishing, hiking.

Fir Creek FREE
Boise National Forest
33 mi NE of Lowman on FR 082; 1 mi NE on FR 470. Free. 7/1-9/30; 14-day limit. 8 small dispersed sites. Tbls, toilets, cfga, no drkg wtr or trash service. Fishing (catch & release), horseback riding, hiking. Elev 6348 ft. Wilderness canoeing, kayaking, rafting on Bear Valley Creek.

Grandjean $8
Sawtooth National Forest
Sawtooth National Recreation Area
21 mi NE of Lowman on SR 21; 6 mi E on FR 524; left on FR 824 at Sawtooth Lodge. $8 with federal senior pass; others pay $13. MD-LD; 10-day limit. 31 sites, typically 60 ft). Non-campers pay $5 day use fee. Tbls, toilets, cfga, drkg wtr. Swimming, fishing, hiking. 10 sites allow horses, have hitchlines. Trailhead to Sawtooth Wilderness. On South Fork of Payette River. Natural hot springs 1.5 mi. Elev 5400 ft.

Helende Campground $7.50
Boise National Forest
11 mi E of Lowman on SR 21; near South Fork Payette River. $7.50 with federal senior pass; others pay $15. 5/15-9/30; 14-day limit. Free when wtr shut off. 6 small sites; 15-ft RV (trailer) limit. Tbls, toilets, cfga, firewood, drkg wtr. Fishing, horseback riding. Elev 3700 ft. Boating suitable for whitewater craft only.

Howers Campground $12
Boise National Forest
36 mi NE of Lowman on SR 21 to milepost 109.2; 28 mi W on FR 579; 7.5 mi S on FR 555; at E side of Deadwood Reservoir. $12. 7/1-9/5; 14-day limit. 10 sites (22-ft RV limit; difficult navigation). Non-campers pay $6 day use fee. Tbls, toilets, cfga, drkg wtr, no trash service. Fishing, boating(l), hiking trail, swimming beach.

Kirkham Hot Springs $7.50
Boise National Forest
5 mi E of Lowman on SR 21; at South Fork Payette River. $7.50 with federal senior pass; others pay $15. 5/1-9/30; 14-day limit. 16 sites; 50-ft RV limit. Non-campers pay $5 day use fee. Drkg wtr, pit toilets, cfga, laundry, dump, tbls. Boating, fishing, swimming, hiking. Natural hot springs on site.

Mountain View $7.50
Boise National Forest
Half mi E of Lowman on SR 21 at milepost 73.9 along South Fork Payette River. $7.50 with federal senior pass; others pay $15. About MD-LD 14-day limit. Non-campers pay $5 day use fee. 14 sites; 50-ft RV limit. Tbls, toilets, cfga, drkg wtr. Fishing, hiking.

Park Creek $12
Boise National Forest
3 mi N of Lowman on FR 582; at confluence of Park & Clear Creeks. $12. About MD-LD 14-day limit. 26 sites; RV limit 55-ft. Non-campers pay $6 day use fee. Group camping available. Tbls, toilets, cfga, drkg wtr. Fishing, hiking.

Pine Flats $7.50
Boise National Forest
5 mi W of Lowman on SR 17. $7.50 with federal senior pass; others pay $15 (double site $30). MD-LD; 14-day limit. Non-campers pay $5 day use fee. 26 sites up to 80 ft. Tbls, toilets, cfga, drkg wtr. Fishing, hiking trails, canoeing, biking. South Fork Payette River. Elev 3700 ft; 22 acres.

Riverside $12
Boise National Forest
36 mi NE of Lowman on SR 21 to milepost 104.2; 28 mi W on FR 579; 7 mi S on FR 555; at N end of Deadwood Reservoir. $12. 7/1LD; 14-day limit. 8 sites (RVs under 22 ft; difficult navigation). Non-campers pay $6 day use fee. Tbls, toilets, drkg wtr, cfga, no trash service. Fishing, boating(l), hiking, horseback riding, biking. Elev 5300 ft.

Willow Creek FREE
Boise National Forest
11 mi S of Lowman on SR 21; 23 mi E on FR 268. Free. 6/1-10/31; 14-day limit. 9 sites (16-ft RV limit). Tbls, toilets, cfga, firewood, no drkg wtr. Picnicking, fishing, horseback riding. At Arrowhead Lake's Boise River inlet.

MACKAY (S)

Broad Canyon Trailhead FREE
Challis National Forest
16 mi N of Mackay on US 93; left on Trail Creek Rd for 18 mi; left on Copper Basin Rd for 13 mi; right on Copper Basin Loop Rd for 7.5 mi; right on Broad Canyon Rd for half mi. Free. 6/1-9/30; 14-day limit. 8 primitive sites. Toilet, cfga, no drkg wtr. Hiking.

Fall Creek Trailhead FREE
Dispersed Camping Area
Challis National Forest
16 mi N of Mackay on US 93; left on Trail Creek Rd for 18 mi; left on Copper Basin Rd; keep to the right for 3.5 mi on Wildhorse Creek Rd; left on Fall Creek Rd for 1.5 mi. Free. 6/15-10/15; 14-day limit. 1 primitive undesignated site. Toilet, cfga, no drkg wtr or trash service. Elev 7200 ft.

Garden Creek Campground FREE
Bureau of Land Management
Challis Field Office
35 mi NW of Mackay on US 93; at Big Lost River. Free. 5/1-10/31; 14-day limit. 5 sites. Tbls, toilet, cfga, no drkg wtr. Hiking. No trash service.

Iron Bog $10
Challis National Forest
14 mi SE of Mackay on US 93; 10 mi SW on Antelope Creek Rd; 7.2 mi SW on FR 137. $10. 6/1-10/1; 14-day limit. 21 sites; 35-ft RV limit. Tbls, toilets, cfga, drkg wtr. Fishing, hiking trails. Elev 7200 ft; 30 acres.

Joseph T. Fallini Campground $10
Mackay Reservoir Recreation Site
Bureau of Land Management
Challis Field Office
5 mi NW of Mackay on US 93. $10 at 18 RV sites without hookups; $14 with wtr/elec ($7 with federal senior pass); double sites $16 ($4 surcharge for elec). 14-day limit. 26sites (28-ft RV limit). Tbls, toilets, cfga, drkg wtr, dump. Boating(l), fishing, hiking, picnicking, swimming. Elev 6000 ft; 80 acres.

Lake Creek Trailhead $5
Challis National Forest
16 mi N of Mackay on US 93; left on Trail Creek Rd for 18 mi; left on Copper Basin Rd for 18 mi to second turnoff to Copper Basin Loop Rd at Copper Basin guard station; right for 4 mi on Copper Basin Loop Rd. $5. 5/25-9/30 14-day limit. 4 primitive sites. Toilet, cfga, no drkg wtr, hitching rails, horse loading ramp. Hiking, horseback riding.

Mill Creek Trailhead $5
Challis National Forest
7 mi S of Mackay on US 93; left on Pass Creek Rd for 28 mi; left on Little Lost/Pahsimeroi Rd for qtr mi; right on

Sawmill Canyon Rd; right on Mill Creek Rd. $5. 5/20-9/30; 14-day limit. 6 primitive sites. Toilet, cfga, no drkg wtr. Fishing, hiking.

Timber Creek $5
Challis National Forest
7 mi S of Mackay on US 93; 28 mi NE on Pass Creek Rd (FR 122); 13 mi N on Sawmill Canyon Rd (FR 101); at Little Lost River. $5. 5/20-9/30; 14-day limit. 12 sites (32-ft RV limit). Tbls, toilet, cfga, drkg wtr. Hiking, fishing, horseback riding (horse loading ramp). Elev 7340 ft.

MACKS INN (S)
Big Springs $7.50
Targhee National Forest
4.5 mi S of Macks Inn on US 20; part of Island Park at Buffalo River, headwaters of Henrys Fork River. $7.50 with federal senior pass; others pay $15; $5 surcharge for elec. MD-9/30; 16-day limit. 15 sites (32-ft RV limit). Tbls, toilets, cfga, drkg wtr. Boating (1 mi), hiking. Elev 6400 ft; 8 acres. Big Springs Water Trail is 2-3 hour float or canoe trip to above Island Park Reservoir. Watch trout feed in springs.

Box Canyon Campground $7.50
Targhee National Forest
About 6 mi S of Macks Inn on US 20; right about 0.5 mi on CR A2 (Kilgore-Yale Rd); on canyon rim near Henrys Fork of Snake River. $7.50 with federal senior pass; others pay $15. MD-9/15; 16-day limit. 18sites; 35-ft RV limit. Tbls, toilets, cfga, drkg wtr. Fishing, boating, hiking. Non-campers pay $7.50 day use fee.

Buffalo Campground $7.50
Targhee National Forest
About 6 mi S of Macks Inn on US 20; left at campground sign; at Buffalo River. $7.50 base with federal senior pass; others pay $15 base without hookups. Elec sites $20 or $11.50 with senior pass. MD-10/1; 16-day limit. 121 sites (17 with elec); 60-ft RV limit; several pull-through. Tbls, flush toilets, cfga, drkg wtr, grey wtr stations. Fishing pier, boating, canoeing. Non-campers pay day use fee.

Flatrock $7.50
Targhee National Forest
W of US 20 at Macks Inn; on shore of Henry's Fork of Snake River (32 mi N of Ashton). $7.50 base with federal senior pass; others pay $15 base ($5 surcharge for elec). About 5/15-10/1; 16-day limit. 37 sites (32-ft RV limit). Tbls, toilets, cfga, drkg wtr. Swimming, fishing, canoeing, hiking. Non-campers pay $7.50 day use fee.

McCrea Bridge $7.50
Targhee National Forest
About 6 mi S of Macks Inn on US 20; 2.1 mi W on CR A2 (Kilgore-York Rd), then left at campground sign; on inlet

of Island Park Reservoir. $7.50 with federal senior pass; others pay $15. MD-9/30; 16-day limit. 23 sites; 45-ft RV limit. Tbls, toilets, cfga, drkg wtr, fish cleaning stations. Boating(l), fishing, waterskiing, canoeing. Non-campers pay $7.50 day use fee.

Upper Coffee Pot $7.50
Targhee National Forest
Qtr mi S of Macks Inn on US 20; 2 mi SW on FR 130; at Henry's Fork of Snake River. $7.50 base with federal senior pass; others pay $15 base ($5 surcharge for elec at 8 sites). MD-9/15; 14-day limit. 14 sites (16-ft RV limit); 5 pull-through. Tbls, toilets, cfga, drkg wtr (no wtr after LD). Swimming, fishing, hiking. Non-campers pay $7 day use fee.

MALAD CITY (S)
Curlew Campground $10
Curlew National Grasslands
24 mi W of Malad to Holbrook; 7.5 mi S on paved rd, then W for 1.7 mi to Curlew turnoff; right on gravel rd 0.5 mi; at Stone Reservoir. $10. 5/1-9/30; 14-day limit. 7 primitive sites. Tbls, toilets, cfga, drkg wtr. Hiking, birdwatching, fishing, swimming.

Dry Canyon Campground FREE
Caribou National Forest
3.5 mi N of Malad City on I-15; 17 mi E on Weston Hwy; 6 mi W on FR 53. Free. MD-9/30; 14-day limit. 3 sites. Tbls, toilet, cfga, no drkg wtr. Hiking, biking, horseback riding. Elev 5320 ft.

MALTA (S)
McClendon Spring FREE
Recreation Site
Bureau of Land Management
Burley Field Office
1.5 mi W of Malta on Hwy 77; N 3 mi to campground. Free. 4/15-10/31; 14-day limit. 2 sites (25-ft RV limit). Toilets, cfga, tbls, no drkg wtr. Hiking, picnicking.

Sublett Creek FREE
Sawtooth National Forest
20.8 mi E of Malta on FR 568; around N end of Sublett Reservoir at Sublett Creek. Free. Elev 5500 ft. 6/1-10/30; 14-day limit. 9 sites on 10 acres (RVs under 22 ft). Tbls, toilets, cfga, firewood, no drkg wtr or trash service. Picnicking, horseback riding, Fishing, swimming, boating(l). Creek

MCCALL (S)
Buckhorn Bar $10
Payette National Forest
39 mi NE of McCall on FR 48; 7.5 mi S on FR 674; at South Fork Salmon River. $10. 18-day limit. 9 sites; 30 & 45-ft RV limit. Tbls, toilets, cfga, piped drkg wtr. Horseback riding, fishing, hiking. Elev 3800 ft.

Camp Creek $10
Payette National Forest
39 mi NE of McCall on FR 48; 11.5 mi S on FR 674. $10.
May-Nov; 14-day limit. Tbls, toilet, cfga, no drkg wtr,
no trash service. Fishing, hiking, horseback riding. Elev
4500 ft.

Chinook $10
Payette National Forest
39 mi NE of McCall on FR 48 (Warren Wagon Rd). 8 mi NE
of Warren on FR 21; adjacent to Secesh River-Loon Lake
trailhead. $10 (double sites $15) during MD-9/30; free rest
of year but no wtr. 9 sites. Tbls, toilets, cfga, drkg wtr.
Horse trailer parking, horse unloading ramp, hitching rails.
Loon Lake Trail access. Elev 5700 ft; 10 acres.

Four Mile Creek $10
Payette National Forest
39 mi NE of McCall on FR 48, then S on FR 674; along
South Fork of Salmon River Rd. $10 during MD-9/30;
reduced fee off-season. 16-day limit. 4 sites. Tbls, cfga,
toilet, drkg wtr, no drkg wtr. Fishing, hiking trails.

Lake Fork $10
Payette National Forest
9.5 mi E of McCall on FR 48 (Lick Creek Rd); along North
Fork of Lake Fork River. $10. MD-9/30; 16-day limit. 9
sites (22-ft RV limit). Tbls, toilets, cfga, drkg wtr, no trash
service. Hiking, fishing. Elev 5600 ft.

Ponderosa $10
Payette National Forest
31 mi NE of McCall on FR 48 (Lick Creek Rd); at Secesh
River. $10. All year; 14-day limit. 14 sites (typically 35
ft). Tbls, toilets, cfga, drkg wtr, no trash service. Hiking,
fishing. Elev 4050 ft.

Poverty Flat $10
Payette National Forest
NE of McCall along Salmon River Rd. $10 during MD-9/30;
free rest of year if wtr is shut off. 16-day limit. 10 sites
(including 4 walk-in tent sites). Tbls, toilet, cfga, drkg wtr,
no trash service. Hitch rails. Fishing, hiking, horseback
riding.

Rapid Creek FREE
Payette National Forest
16 mi S of Mccall on Hwy 55; E of FR 388. Free. 7/1-10/1;
16-day limit. 2 primitive undesignated sites; 22-ft RV limit.
Tbls, toilets, cfga, no drkg wtr, no trash service.

Upper Payette Lake $10
Payette National Forest
18.5 mi N of McCall on FR 21 (Warren Wagon Rd); 1 mi
N on FR 495. $10 (double sites $15). 6/15-10/15; 18-day
limit. 19 sites; 50-ft RV limit. Tbls, toilets, drkg wtr, cfga,
no trash service. Fishing, swimming, boating(l).

MCCAMMON (S)

Goodenough Creek FREE
Bureau of Land Management
Pocatello Field Office
From McCammon, cross over I-15 & travel about 1 mi W to
fork; take left fork S for qtr mi, then right on Goodenough
Creek access rd for 2 mi; at foot of Bannock Range. Free.
6/1-10/31; 14-day limit. 13 primitive sites. Tbls, toilets,
cfga, no drkg wtr. Hiking trail, biking.

MONTPELIER (S)

Montpelier Canyon $8
Caribou National Forest
3.3 mi E of Montpelier on US 89. $8. 5/15-LD 14-day limit.
13 sites (32-ft RV limit). Tbls, toilets, cfga, no drkg wtr.
Fishing. Elev 6100 ft; 6 acres.

MOSCOW (N)

McCroskey State Park $10
30 mi N of Moscow on US 95 & Skyline Dr (an 18-mi gravel
rd that traverses the park). $10 at primitive sites; standard
sites without hookups $12. All year; 15-day limit. 9 devel-
oped sites, primitive and roadside camping areas; 25-ft
RV limit. Tbls, pit toilets, cfga, drkg wtr, no trash service.
Horseback riding, mountain biking, hiking. Drkg wtr at
milepost 8.25 on Skyline Dr.

Robinson Lake $10
Latah County Parks & Recreation
5 mi E of Moscow on Robinson Park Rd. $10. 5 RV sites
with elec plus overflow area, numerous tent spaces; $5
tents. 14-day limit Tbls, pit toilets, cfga, drkg wtr. Volleyball, horseshoes, ballfields. .

MOUNTAIN HOME (S)

Big Roaring River Lake $10
Boise National Forest
30 mi NE of Mountain Home on SR 20; 29 mi NE on FR 61;
1.5 mi NE on FR 172; 3 mi S on FR 129 (rd not recommended for RVs). $10. 7/15-10/15; 14 day limit. 12 sites (RVs
under 22 ft). Tbls, toilets, cfga, firewood, drkg wtr, no
trash service. Boating (no mtrs), fishing, hiking, horseback
riding. Elev 8200 ft. Four high alpine lakes nearby.

Big Trinity Lake $10
Boise National Forest
35 mi NE of Mountain Home on SR 20 to Pine/Feather-
ville exit; 29 mi N on SR 61; 15 mi NW on FR 172; 3 mi
S on FR 129 to Guard Station Junction. $10. 7/15-10/15;
14-day limit. 17 sites (RVs under 22 ft). Tbls, toilets, cfga,
firewood, drkg wtr. Boating (no mtrs), fishing, horseback
riding, hiking, no trash service. Elev 7900 ft. Four high
alpine lakes nearby.

Bruneau Dunes State Park $12
Off I-84 near Mountain Home; westbound exit 112 or
eastbound exit 90; Hwy 78 off SR 51. Seniors pay Seniors

receive 50% discount Mon-Thurs. Base Rates, Std site $12-$21, w/wtr or elec $20-$25. wtr and elec $24-$29 wtr, elec & sewer $26-$29. All year; 15-day limit. 35-ft RV limit. Tbls, flush toilets, cfga, drkg wtr, showers, dump, observatory, store. Hiking, horseback riding, boating(l), fishing, swimming, volleyball. 4,800 acres; elev 2470 ft.

C.J. Strike Parks $10
Idaho Power Company
Bureau of Land Management
Hwy 67 to Grandview from Mountain Home; SE on Hwy 78, turn left at high school, N to C.J. Strike Dam. $10 4/1-10/31, half price off season. Three parks. All year. 50 sites (40-ft RV limit). Tbls, toilets, cfga, drkg wtr, handicap sites, pull-through sites. Fishing, hiking, boating(l), horseback riding.

Castle Creek   FREE
Boise National Forest
24 mi NE of Mountain Home on SR 20; 5 mi NE on FR 134; 14 mi N on FR 113; at Anderson Ranch Reservoir. Free. 5/1-10/31; 14-day limit. 2 sites (RVs under 16 ft okay). Tbls, cfga, no drkg wtr, toilet destroyed by fire in. Fishing, boating, waterskiing. Elev 4300 ft.

Curlew Creek $5
Boise National Forest
35 mi NE of Mountain Home on SR 20; about 14 mi N on SR 61; at E side of Anderson Ranch Reservoir. $5 day use or camping. 6/1-9/30; 14-day limit. 9 sites. Tbls, toilets, cfga, drkg wtr. Fishing, hiking, boating(l), waterskiing.

Dog Creek   Closed
Boise National Forest
29 mi NE of Mountain Home on SR20; 13 mi NE on FR 163; 14 mi N on FR156. 13 sites $10 all year. Tbls, toilets, cfga, drkg. wtr. Fishing, hiking, horeseback riding. Closed in 2016 due to potentiol flooding or mudslides.

Elks Flat Campground $10
Boise National Forest
29 mi NE of Mountain Home on SR 20; 22 mi NE on FR 61; along East Fork Boise River. $10. MD-LD; 14-day limit. 36 sites; 50-ft RV limit. Tbls, toilets, cfga, drkg wtr. Fishing, hiking, boating(l), OHV activities, horseback riding, biking, hiking.

Evans Creek   FREE
Boise National Forest
24 mi NE of Mountain Home on SR 20; 5 mi NE on FR 134; 9 mi on FR 113. Free. All year; 14-day limit. 10 sites. Tbls, toilets, cfga, no drkg wtr. Picnicking, fishing, boating, waterskiing. Boat ramp at Fall Creek Campground.

Ice Springs   FREE
Boise National Forest
24 mi NE of Mountain Home on SR 20; 5 mi NE on FR 134;

9 mi NE on FR 113; 5 mi N on FR 125; at Fall Creek. Free. Elev 5000 ft. 6/1-10/31; 14-day limit. 4 sites, RV limit 16 ft. Tbls, toilets, cfga, no drkg wtr. Hiking, horseback riding, fishing.

Jack's Creek   FREE
Sportsman's Access Area
Idaho Power Company
State Wildlife Management Area
Hwy 67 to Grandview from Mountain Home; SE on Hwy 78; turn left at high school; N to C.J. Strike Dam. Free. 8/1-2/1; 10-day limit. 50 primitive sites in designated area. Toilet, cfga, no drkg wtr. Boating(l), fishing.

Little Roaring River Lake   FREE
Boise National Forest
29 mi NE of Mountain Home on SR 20; 29 mi N on FR 61; 15 mi NE on FR 172; 3 mi S on FR 129; between Upper Roaring River & Little Roaring River Lake. Free. 6/1-9/30; 14-day limit. 4 sites. Tbls, toilets, cfga, no drkg wtr or trash service. Fishing, horseback riding. Elev 7900 ft; 2 acres. No motor boats. 4 high alpine lakes nearby.

Pine RV Campground $10
Boise National Forest
35 mi NE of Mountain Home on US 20; about 20 mi N around Anderson Ranch Reservoir on SR 61 & FR 128. $10. 5/1-10/31; 14-day limit. 7 RV sites. Non-campers pay $5 day use fee Tbls, toilets, cfga, no drkg wtr. Fishing, boating(l), hiking. Non-campers pay $5 day use fee. Elev 4300 ft.

Spillway Campground   FREE
Boise National Forest
24 mi N of Mountain Home on US 20; 5 mi N on FRs 134 & 113; at Anderson Ranch Reservoir. Free. 5/1-10/31; 14-day limit. 3 sites. Tbls, toilets, cfga, no drkg wtr, no trash service. Fishing, boating(l). Elev 4200 ft.

MUD LAKE (S)
Birch Creek   FREE
Bureau of Land Management
Upper Snake Field Office
25 mi NW of Mud Lake on Hwy 28; no sign on SR 28, but access rd between mileposts 40 & 41. Free. 5/1-11/1; 14-day limit. 25sites (25-ft RV limit). Tbls, toilets, cfga, no drkg wtr. Fishing. Quiet.

MURPHY (S)
Silver City Ghost Town   FREE
Bureau of Land Management
Owyhee Field Office
From Hwy 78 near Murphy, turn off at Silver City sign; unpaved access rds. 6 primitive sites near the town. Free. 6/1-11/30; 14-day limit. Toilets, tbls, cfga, no drkg wtr. Biking, fishing, hiking, horseback riding. Jordan Creek may contain mercury.

NEWPORT (N)

Albeni Cove Campground $10
Corps of Engineers
Lake Pend Oreille
From Newport, SE on SR 41; 3 mi E (left) on Fourth St (part gravel); stay on the dirt road, veering left at the forks; directly across from dam. Rough access, not suitable for large RVs. $10 with federal senior pass at 10 non-elec RV/tent sites; others pay $20 Sites up to 40 ft. 5/14-9/10; 14-day limit. Tbls, flush toilets, cfga, drkg wtr, coin laundry, beach. Boating(l), fishing, birdwatching, canoeing, interpretive programs, kayaking, swimming. Visitor Center.

NEW MEADOWS (S)

Cold Springs   Closed
Payette National Forest
8 mi SW of New Meadows on US 95; 4 mi W on FR 089; 1 mi W on FR 091; near Lost Valley Reservoir. $10 (double sites $15) during 5/15-10/15; reduced fee off-season if wtr is off. 14-day limit. 32 single sites, 5 double sites. 30 & 50-ft RV limit. Tbls, toilets, cfga, drkg wtr, dump. Boating(l), fishing, waterskiing, berry picking, horseshoe pits. Elev 4820 ft. CLOSED for 2016 season check status before arrival.

Grouse $10
Payette National Forest
6 mi E of New Meadows on SR 55; 10.5 mi N on FR 257; half mi W on FR 273; .1 mi N on FR 278; at Goose Lake. $10; double sites $15. About 7/1-LD; 14-day limit. 22 sites; 45-ft RV limit. Tbls, toilets, cfga, drkg wtr, no trash service. Swimming, boating(no mtrs), fishing. Elev 6350 ft.

Hazard Lake $10
Payette National Forest
6 mi E of New Meadows on SR 55; 22 mi N on FR 257 (Goose Lake Mountain Rd); .1 mi E on FR 259. $10 (double sites $15). 7/1-9/30; 18-day limit. 12 sites; 35-ft RV limit. Tbls, toilets, cfga, drkg wtr. Fishing, boating (no mtrs), horseback riding, hiking. Elev 7100 ft. Scenic.

Last Chance Campground $10
Payette National Forest
SE of New Meadows (7 mi W of McCall) on SR 55; 2 mi N on FR 453. $10 (double site $15). 5/15-10/15; 18-day limit. 20 single sites, 3 double sites (40-ft RV limit). Tbls, toilets, cfga, drkg wtr, no trash service. Hiking, fishing. Elev 4650 ft.

NORTH FORK (S)

Spring Creek $10
Salmon National Forest
16.9 mi W of North Fork on Salmon River Rd (FR 30). $10. 3/1-11/1; 14-day limit. 5 sites & several undeveloped sites; 32-ft RV limit. Tbls, toilet, cfga, drkg wtr. Fishing, boating, swimming, floating.

OLA (S)

Antelope $7.50
Boise National Forest
10 mi NE of Ola on FR 618; 6.7 mi NE on FR 626; 2.3 mi NE on FR 614; at Sagehen Reservoir. $7.50 with federal senior pass; others pay $15. 5/15-LD; 14-day limit. Non-campers pay $8 day use fee. 14 sites (30-ft RV limit). Tbls, toilets, cfga, drkg wtr. Boating(l), fishing, swimming.

Hollywood Campground $8
Boise National Forest
10 mi NE of Ola on FR 618; 6.7 mi NE on FR 626; 4.5 mi E on FR 614; at Sagehen Reservoir. $8 with federal senior pass; others pay $16. 5/15-10/20; 14-day limit. 6 sites (22-ft RV limit). Non-campers pay $8 day use fee. Tbls, toilets, cfga, drkg wtr. Fishing, swimming, boating, hiking.

Sage Hen Creek $7.50
Boise National Forest
10 mi NE of Ola on FR 618; 6.7 mi NE on FR 626; 3.5 mi NE on FR 614; at Sagehen Reservoir. $7.50 with federal senior pass; others pay $15. 5/20-LD; 14-day limit. 9 sites (RVs under 32 ft). Non-campers pay $8 day use fee. Tbls, toilets, cfga, drkg wtr. Fishing, swimming, boating(l). 11 acres.

OROFINO (N)

Ahsahka Access $10
Clearwater River Recreation Area
Bureau of Land Management
From Orofino, 3.6 mi W on SR 7; at Clearwater River below Dworshak Dam. $10 Primitive undesignated sites. $18 wtr & elec.. All year; 30-day limit. Tbls, toilet, cfga, no drkg wtr, no trash service. Boating(l), fishing.

Canyon Creek   FREE
Corps of Engineers
Dworshak Reservoir
From Orofino, 11 mi NE off Elk River, Wells Bench & Eureka Ridge Rds (following signs) at Dworshak Lake. Steep, winding gravel rd. Free. Open unless closed by snow; 14-day limit. 17 primitive gravel sites (RVs under 22 ft). Toilets, tbls, cfga, no drkg wtr or trash service. Fishing, hiking, boating(l), swimming, waterskiing, hunting. Elev 1600-1650 ft.

Dam View Recreation Area   FREE
Corps of Engineers
Dworshak Reservoir
From Orofino, 5 mi S on SR 7 to Dworshak project entrance; follow signs 2 mi; turn on Big Eddy Rd. Free primitive sites. Open spring through fall; 14-day limit. Chemical toilets, cfga, tbls, no drkg wtr.

Dent Acres Campground $7
Corps of Engineers
Dworshak Reservoir
From Orofino, 20 mi NE on Elk River Rd via Wells Bench Rd, following signs. $7 with federal senior pass at 49 pull-through elec/wtr sites (50-amp) during 5/19-9/5; others pay $14. During 4/1-5/22 & 9/2-12/15, fee is $10 ($5 with senior pass). RV limit 35 ft. Tbls, flush toilets, cfga, drkg wtr, showers, dump, beach, playground, shelters, fish cleaning station (closed in winter). Fishing, boating(l), swimming, hiking.

Dworshak State Park $12
24 mi NE of Orofino, off US 12 on county rd (last 2 mi twisting, narrow 10% downgrade). Seniors receive 50% discount Mon-Thurs. Base Rates, Std site $12-$21, w/wtr or elec $20-$25. wtr and elec $24-$29 wtr, elec & sewer $26-$29. 46 std and 57 serviced sites. 5/15-9/10; 15-day limit. 50-ft site length. Tbls, flush toilets, cfga, drkg wtr, showers, dump, beach, playground, fish cleaning station. Boating(ld), horseshoes, volleyball, swimming, fishing, hiking. 850 acres; elev 1600 ft.

Pink House Recreation Site $10
Clearwater River Recreation Area
Bureau of Land Management
3 mi W of Orofino between US 12 & Clearwater River. $10 base; $18 for full hookups (30-amp elec) at 15 RV sites ($13 with federal senior pass). All year; 14-day limit. Large developed camping area. Tbls, toilets, cfga, drkg wtr. Fishing, hiking, boating(l).

OVID (S)
Emigration $7.50
Cache National Forest
Caribou National Forest
10.5 mi W of Ovid on SR 36. $7.50 with federal senior pass; others pay $15. 6/1-LD; 14-day limit. 25 sites; 40-ft RV limit. Tbls, flush toilets, cfga, drkg wtr. Hiking & biking trails, picnicking, horseback riding, OHV activity. Elev 7100 ft; 17 acres. In Cache NF, administered by Caribou NF.

PALISADES (S)
Calamity $12
Targhee National Forest
2.6 mi S of Palisades on US 26; 1.1 mi SW on FR 058; at N end of Palisades Reservoir. $12 during MD-LD; free LD-9/30, but no wtr; 14-day limit. 41 sites (45-ft RV limit). Tbls, toilets, cfga, drkg wtr. Boating(l), fishing, swimming, waterskiing. Non-campers pay $6 day use fee. Elev 5900 ft; 21 acres.

Palisades Creek $12
Targhee National Forest
2 mi E of Palisades on FR 255. $12. 6/25-LD; 14-day limit. 8 sites (25-ft RV limit). Tbls, toilets, cfga, drkg wtr,

handicapped facilities. Hiking trailhead, fishing, horse-back riding (stock loading ramp). Elev 5890 ft; 10 acres. Non-campers pay $6 day use fee.

PARIS (S)
Paris Springs $12
Caribou National Forest
Qtr mi S of Paris on US 89; 3.8 mi W on FR 421; 1 mi W on FR 427. $12 during 6/1-LD; $6 during LD-10/31. 14-day limit. 12 sites; 30-ft RV limit. Tbls, toilets, cfga, drkg wtr. Hiking trails, fishing, biking, horseback riding, OHV activity. Nearby ice cave filled with ice all year.

PARMA (S)
Fort Boise FREE
Wildlife Management Area
From SR 20/26 about 3 mi from Parma, follow Old Fort Boise Rd 2 mi W. Free. All year; 5-day limit. Primitive camping in designated areas, and pack-in tent camping No facilities. Fishing, boating(l), hunting, hiking.

PIERCE (87N)
Cedars FREE
Clearwater National Forest
Half mi S of Pierce on SR 11; NE on FR 250. Free. Elev 3800 ft. Open Year-round best 5/31-11/30 (or until inaccessible); 14-day limit. 5 sites (RVs under 16 ft). Tbls, toilets, cfga, no drkg wtr. Swimming, fishing, hiking, horseback riding, OHV activity. On upper North Fork of Clearwater River & Long Creek.

Hidden Creek $10
Clearwater National Forest
Half mi S of Pierce on SR 11; 58 mi NE on FR 250 (single-lane rd not suitable for big RVs. $10. Jun-Oct; 14-day limit. 13 sites (typically 45 ft). Tbls, toilets, cfga, drkg wtr, no trash service. Fishing (cutthroat trout). Elev 3400 ft; 5 acres. On North Fork Clearwater River. Wtr shut off mid Sept.

Kelly Forks $10
Clearwater National Forest
Half mi S of Pierce on SR 11; 49 mi NE on FR 250; at confluence of Kelly Creek & North Fork of Clearwater River. $10. June-Oct; 14-day limit. 14 sites (RVs under 33 ft). Tbls, toilets, cfga, drkg wtr, no trash service. Boating, fishing (catch & release cutthroat). Elev 2680 ft; 5 acres. Camp Wtr shut off Mid Sep.

Noe Creek $10
Clearwater National Forest
Half Mi S of Pierce on Hwy 11; 49 mi NE on FR 250; at North Fork of Clearwater River. $10. MD-10/31; 14-day limit. 6 sites (RVs under 23 ft). Tbls, toilets, cfga, drkg wtr(MD-Mid Sep). Fishing; hiking trails nearby.

Washington Creek $10
Clearwater National Forest
29 mi NE of Pierce on FR 250; 6 mi NW on FR 249. $10
MD-1-/24; 14-day limit. 23 sites (typically 55 ft). Tbls, toilets, cfga, drkg wtr (MD- Mid Sep). Fishing, hiking trails. On North Fork of Clearwater River. 8 acres. Elev 2100 ft. Camp may be free during LD-10/15, but no wtr.

Weitas Meadows   FREE
Clearwater National Forest
34 mi NE of Pierce on FR 250. Free. 5/15-10/31 or until inaccessible; 14-day limit. 6 sites. Tbls, toilets, cfga, firewood, no drkg wtr. Picnicking, fishing, berry picking, boating(d). Elev 2500 ft; 4 acres. Scenic. On North Fork of Clearwater River.

PLUMMER (N)
Heyburn State Park $12
Between Plummer & St. Maries on SR 5, off US 95; at S tip of Coeur d'Alene Lake. Seniors receive 50% discount Mon-Thurs. for Base rates: std site $12-$21, w/wtr or elec $20-$25. wtr and elec $24-$29 wtr, elec & sewer $26-$29. 4/1-10/31; 15-day limit. 73 std 56 serviced sites in 3 campgrounds; 55-ft RV limit. Tbls, drkg wtr, flush & pit toilets, cfga, showers, dump, playground, beach. Fishing, boating(ldr), swimming, volleyball, horseback riding, biking, hiking, guided walks, birdwatching, waterskiing. 8076 acres.

POCATELLO (S)
Scout Mountain $12
Caribou National Forest
10 mi S of Pocatello on CR 231; 3.8 mi SE on FR 1. $10. MD-10/15; 14-day limit. 25 sites; 45-ft RV limit. Tbls, toilets, cfga, drkg wtr. Hiking trails, biking, horseback riding, OHV activity. Crestline Cycle Trail starts just N of camp. Elev 6500 ft; 26 acres. Non-campers pay $5 day use fee.

PONDS LODGE (S)
Buttermilk $7.50
Targhee National Forest
2 mi N of Ponds Canyon on US 20; 2 mi NW on FR 30; 3.5 mi SW on FR 126. $7.50 base with federal senior pass; others pay $15 base ($5 surcharge for elec). 5/15-9/15; 16-day limit. 57 sites (32-ft RV limit). Tbls, toilets, cfga, drkg wtr, fish cleaning stations. Swimming, boating(l), fishing, waterskiing, canoeing. E arm of Island Park Reservoir. Group camping available by reservation. Elev 6300 ft.

POWELL JUNCTION (N)
Elk Summit   FREE
Clearwater National Forest
17 mi S of Powell Junction on FR 360. Free. 6/15-10/15; 14-day limit. 16 sites (many suitable for horse & stock use with hitching rails & wtr). Tbls, toilets, cfga, no drkg wtr, no trash service. Horseback riding, hiking. Trailhead to Selway Bitterroot Wilderness. Elev 5756 ft.

PRESTON (S)
Albert Moser $12
Caribou National Forest
4 mi SE of Preston on US 91; 10 mi NE on Cub River Rd; on Cub River. $12 during MD-9/15; $6 during 9/15-10/30 but no wtr; 14-day limit. 9 sites (RVs under 21 ft). Tbls, toilets, cfga, drkg wtr. Fishing, hiking trails, horseback riding, biking, OHV activity.

Marijuana Flat   FREE
Caribou National Forest
4.7 mi S of Preston on US 91; left for 4 mi on E. Cub River Rd. Free. All year; 14-day limit. 10 primitive dispersed sites. Toilet, cfga, no drkg wtr.

Willow Flat $7.50
Caribou National Forest
4 mi SE of Preston on US 91; 10 mi NE on Cub River Rd & FR 406; along North Fork of St. Charles Creek. $7.50 with federal senior pass during MD-9/15; others pay $15 14-day limit. 54 sites (typically 45 ft). Tbls, toilets, cfga, drkg wtr. Hiking trails, fishing, horseback riding, OHV activity. Elev 6000 ft; 30 acres. Non-campers pay $6 day use fee.

PRICHARD (N)
Big Hank $9
Coeur d'Alene National Forest
20 mi NW of Prichard on FR 208; 1 mi NE on FR 306; at Coeur d'Alene River. $9 with federal senior pass; others pay $18. MD-LD; 14-day limit. 30 sites; 40-ft RV limit. Tbls, toilets, cfga, drkg wtr. Hiking, fishing, kayaking, boating(l), rafting. 10 acres.

Devil's Elbow $9
Coeur d'Alene National Forest
14 mi NW of Prichard on FR 208. $9 with federal senior pass; others pay $18. MD-LD; 14-day limit. 20 sites; 20-ft RV limit except 2 pull-throughs at 87 & 100 ft. Tbls, portable toilets, cfga, drkg wtr. Boating(l), fishing, hiking. On Coeur d'Alene River.

Kit Price $9
Coeur d'Alene National Forest
11 mi NW of Prichard on FR 208. $9 with federal senior pass; others pay $18. MD-9/30; 14-day limit. 52 sites; 45-ft RV limit. Tbls, toilets, cfga, drkg wtr. Fishing, kayaking, rafting. On Coeur d'Alene River.

PRIEST RIVER (N)
Osprey Campground $9
Kaniksu National Forest
25 mi N of Priest River on SR 57; 2 mi NE on FR 237 at Priest Lake; 1 mi past Outlet Camp. $9 base with federal senior pass; others pay $18 base, $20 for premium locations ($10 with senior pass). 5/15-9/30; 14-day limit. 16 sites; 50-ft RV limit. Tbls, toilets, cfga, NO drkg wtr. Swim-

ming, hiking, fishing, boating(lr), beach, waterskiing. On W shore of Priest Lake. Carry-down boat access or launch at Kalispell Bay ramp.

Outlet $9
Kaniksu National Forest
25 mi N of Priest River on SR 57; 1 mi NE on FR 237. $9 base with federal senior pass; others pay $18 base, $20 for premium locations ($10 with senior pass). MD-LD, 14-day limit. 27 sites. Tbls, flush toilets, cfga, drkg wtr, beach. Fishing, boating(l), hiking, swimming. On W shore of Priest Lake. Carry-down boat access or launch at Kalispell Bay ramp.

Priest River Recreation Area $10
Corps of Engineers
Lake Pend Oreille
From Priest River at jct with SR 57, 1 mi E on US 2; turn right; at confluence of Priest & Pend Oreille Rivers. $10 with federal senior pass at 20 non-elec RV sites (8 pull-through); others pay $20. 5 bike-in tent sites $4. 5/10-9/7; 14-day limit. 60-ft RV limit. Tbls, flush toilets, showers (25 cents), dump, cfga, drkg wtr, playground, beach, shelters, amphitheater. Boating(l), fishing, swimming. No day use fees; dump, boat ramp, swimming areas, picnicking open to non-campers. Also known as Mudhole Campground.

Riley Creek Recreation Area $12.50
Corps of Engineers
Lake Pend Oreille
From Priest River Park, 9 mi E on US 2 to LaClede; 1 mi S on Riley Creek Rd. $12 with federal senior pass at 67 elec/wtr sites; others pay $25. 5/10-9/28; 14-day limit. 40-ft RV limit. Tbls, flush toilets, coin showers, cfga, drkg wtr, playground, beach, dump, amphitheater, information center, shelters. Boating, fishing, swimming, waterskiing, canoeing, interpretive programs, kayaking, play field, sand volleyball, horseshoe pits, birdwatching, trails. No day use fees; non-campers can use facilities.

RED RIVER (S)

Deep Creek Campground FREE
Bitterroot National Forest
55 mi E of Red River on FR 468. Free. 6/1-10/31; 14-day limit. 3 sites; 30-ft RV limit. Tbls, toilet, cfga, no drkg wtr. Fishing, hunting, hiking. Access point to Selway-Bitterroot and River of No Return Wilderness.

REXBURG (S)

Beaver Dick Park $5
Madison County Park
6 mi W of Rexburg on SR 33; at Henry's Fork of Snake River. $5 or 5 nights for $15. All year; 5-day limit. 9 RV/tent sites. Tbls, toilets, cfga, no drkg wtr, no elec, playground, shelters($). Boating(ld), fishing, swimming.

Twin Bridges Park $5
Madison County Park
12 mi SE of Rexburg on Archer Hwy; at South Fork of Snake River. $5 or 5 nights for $15. All year; 5-day limit. 21 RV/tent sites. Tbls, toilets, cfga, no drkg wtr, no elec, shelters($). Boating(l), fishing, swimming. 27 acres.

RIGGINS (N)

Papoose FREE
Nez Perce National Forest
1 mi S of Riggins on US 95; 5.4 mi on Papoose Creek Rd (FR 517) from mouth of Squaw Creek; rd not recommended for trailers or motorhomes. July-Oct; 18-day limit. 2 undeveloped spaces for small RVs. Tbls, toilet, cfga, no drkg wtr or trash service. Papoose Cave. Hiking, fishing. Near Hells Canyon National Recreation Area.

Seven Devils FREE
Hells Canyon National Recreation Area
Wallowa-Whitman National Forest
1.2 mi S of Riggins on US 95; 16.5 mi SW on FR 517 (Squaw Creek Rd); last 15 mi gravel & steep. Free. 6/30-10/1; 14-day limit. 10 sites for small RVs or tents. Tbls, toilets, cfga, no drkg wtr. Hiking, picnicking, fishing. Not recommended for large RVs because of parking space & steep, narrow access. Seven Devils Lake. Within Hells Canyon-Seven Devils Scenic Area. End of rd facility.

Shorts Bar/Island Bar FREE
Bureau of Land Management
Cottonwood Field Office
2 mi E of Riggins on Big Salmon Rd; along Lower Salmon River. Free. Developed site; No trash service. Fire plans required for camp & cooking fires. Tble, toilets, no drkg wtr. Fishing, boating, rafting, kayaking, swimming. Put-in spot for floating river.

Spring Bar $12
Nez Perce National Forest
1.5 mi S of Riggins on US 95; 11 mi E on FR 1614 (Salmon River Rd). $12 15 sites (accommodates most RVs). Tbls, toilets, cfga, firewood, piped drkg wtr(summer). Rock-hounding, fishing, boating(ld). Elev 1740 ft. River of No Return. Popular take-out point for float trips. Gold prospecting. Fall & spring steelhead fishing.

Windy Saddle Camp FREE
Wallowa-Whitman National Forest
15-20 mi SW of Riggins on FR 517 (very steep and narrow) off Hwy 95. Free. Open Late June. 14-day limit. 4 sites. Tbls, toilets, cfga, no drkg wtr or trash service. Fishing, horseback riding (horse ramps), hiking. Wilderness trailheads. In Seven Devils Mountains 2 mi from Heaven's Gate Vista Point.

RIRIE (S)

Juniper Campground $10
Ririe Reservoir
Bureau of Reclamation
Bonneville County Parks & Recreation
1 mi E of Ririe off Hwy 26, S on county rd to headquarters. $10 without hookups, $18 full hookups. $2 discount with federal senior pass. 5/15-10/15; 14-day limit. 49 sites (35-ft RV limit). Tbls, flush toilets, cfga, drkg wtr, showers, dump. Fishing, hiking, swimming, boating(l).

ROGERSON (1S)

Jarbridge River Recreation Area   FREE
Bureau of Land Management
Jarbridge Field Office
Follow Jarbridge Rd (Three Creek Rd) to Murphy Hot Springs. Free. All year; 14-day limit. Four Camping areas, Big Cottonwood 4 sites, River Launch Site 3 sites, Juniper Grove 4 sites, The Forks 4 sites. Toilet, cfga, tbls. Fishing, hunting, whitewater rafting.

Lud Drexler Park $5
Bureau of Land Management
Burley Field Office
8 mi W of Rogerson on Jarbridge Rd (Three Creek Rd); next to Salmon Falls Dam. $5 and free. All year; 14-day limit. 20 RV sites ($5); about 60 free RV spaces near high-water mark; 25-ft RV limit. Tbls, toilets, cfga, drkg wtr, dump. Boating(l), fishing, swimming, hiking, waterskiing. Elev 5000 ft.

RUPERT (S)

Lake Walcott State Park $12
11 mi NE of Rupert on SR 24 at Minidoka Dam; at NW end of Lake Walcott. Seniors receive 50% discount Mon-Thurs. Base Rates, Std site $12-$21, w/wtr or elec $20-$25. wtr and elec $24-$29 wtr, elec & sewer $26-$29. 18 std, 22 serviced sites. All year; 15-day limit. 60-ft sites. Tbls, flush toilets, cfga, drkg wtr, showers. Fishing, boating(l), horseshoes, disc golf. 65 acres; 20,700-acre lake.

Lake Walcott Campground $10
Bureau of Reclamation
7 mi E of Rupert on Hwy 24; 6 mi E on CR 400N; at Minidoka Dam. $10 base at primitive sites; $12 with wtr hookups; $18-$24 with elec hookups. Reduced fees with federal senior pass. All year; 14-day limit. 22 sites (60-ft RV limit). Tbls, flush toilets, cfga, drkg wtr, dump. Fishing, hiking, playground. In Minidoka National Wildlife Refuge.

SAINT ANTHONY (S)

Sand Creek   FREE
Wildlife Management Area
From St. Anthony, follow SR 20 (Business) E 1.5 mi; N at sportsman's access sign for 16 mi to Sand Creek ponds.

Free. All year; 10-day limit. Primitive designated camping areas; no facilities. Fishing, hunting, hiking, horseback riding.

SAINT CHARLES (S)

Bear Lake State Park $12
5 mi E of St. Charles off Hwy 89 to T, then S 5 mi. Seniors receive 50% discount Mon-Thurs. Base Rates, Std site $12-$21, w/wtr or elec $20-$25. wtr and elec $24-$29 wtr, elec & sewer $26-$29. 4/1-11/30; 15-day limit. 27 std and 27 serviced sites (sites 60 ft). Tbls, toilets, cfga, drkg wtr, dump. Swimming, boating(rl), fishing, waterskiing, volleyball, winter sports. 20-mile lake on Utah border; 2-mile beach on N; half-mi beach on E. Wildlife refuge.

Beaver Creek $10
Caribou National Forest
About 11 mi W of St. Charles on FR 11. $10. 5/15-9/15; 14-day limit. 5 sites. Tbls, toilets, cfga, drkg wtr. Fishing, hiking. Access to High Line National Recreation Trail.

Cloverleaf $7
Caribou National Forest
1.2 mi N of St. Charles on US 89; 7 mi W on FR 412. $7 with federal senior pass; others pay $14 (lower fees after LD, but no wtr). 6/6-9/7; 14-day limit. 18 sites (32-ft RV limit). Tbls, flush toilets, cfga, drkg wtr. Hiking, fishing, picnicking, mountain biking, horseback riding. Elev 6900 ft; 7 acres. Nearby Minnetonka Cave open for tours June-LD.

Porcupine $7
Caribou National Forest
1.2 mi N of St. Charles on US 89; 2.5 mi W on CR 312; 5 mi W on FR 412; at St. Charles Creek. $7 with federal senior pass; others pay $14 (reduced fees after LD but no wtr). 6/6-LD; 14-day limit. 15 sites (22-ft RV limit). Tbls, flush toilets, cfga, drkg wtr. Hiking, biking, fishing, picnicking, horseback riding, OHV activity. Elev 6800 ft; 4 acres.

SAINT. MARIES (N)

Camp 3   FREE
St. Joe National Forest
35 mi E of St. Maries on FR 50 to Marble Creek Historical Site; 15 mi S on FR 321 (Marble Creek Rd). Free. 4 sites; 20-ft RV limit. Tbls, toilets, cfga, no drkg wtr; horse loading ramp, no trash service. Fishing. Elev 3200 ft.

Huckleberry Campground $9
Bureau of Land Management
Coeur D'Alene Field Office
29 mi E of St. Maries on St. Joe River Rd. $9 base with federal senior pass; others pay $18 base, $4 surcharge for elec/wtr hookups. All year; 14-day limit. 33 sites (26-ft RV limit). Tbls, toilets, cfga, drkg wtr (no wtr during free period), dump. Fishing, swimming, hiking, boating, canoeing, rafting.

Shadowy St. Joe $6
St. Joe National Forest
1 mi E of St. Maries on US 3; 10 mi E on FR 50; at St. Joe River. $6. 5/15-9/30; 14-day limit. 14 sites; 40-ft RV limit. Tbls, toilets, cfga, drkg wtr. Fishing, swimming, boating(l), swimming. Elev 2150 ft.

SALMON (S)

Agency Creek Recreation Site FREE
Bureau of Land Management
Salmon Field Office
22 mi SE of Salmon on SR 28 to Tendoy; 10 mi E on co rd. Free. 6/1-9/30; 14-day limit. 4 sites. Tbls, toilets, cfga, no drkg wtr. Hiking, picnicking.

Cougar Point FREE
Salmon National Forest
5 mi S of Salmon on US 93; 12 mi W on FR 021. FREE. 6/1-10/15; 14-day limit. 18 sites 40-ft RV limit. Tbls, toilets, cfga, no drkg wtr. Elev 6800 ft; 15 acres. Hiking.

Iron Lake $4
Salmon National Forest
5 mi S of Salmon on US 93; 20 mi W on FR 021; 21 mi S on FR 020 (Salmon River Mountain Rd). $4. 14-day limit. 8 primitive sites, 20-ft RV limit) Tbls, toilets, cfga, drkg wtr, stock facilities. N Boating, fishing, horseback riding.

Morgan Bar Recreation Site $5
Bureau of Land Management
Salmon Field Office
3.2 mi N of Salmon on US 93; left on Diamond Creek Rd (at the Lemhi County Fairgrounds) for 1.5 mi; on Salmon River. $5. 5/1-9/31; 14-day limit 8 sites; 28-ft RV limit. Tbls, toilets, cfga, drkg wtr. Boating(l), fishing, swimming, horseshoe pits, volleyball.

Shoup Bridge Recreation Site $5
Bureau of Land Management
Salmon Field Office
5 mi S of Salmon on US 93; right just past Shoup bridge. $5. 4/1-10/31; 14-day limit. 5 sites; 28-ft RV limit. Tbls, toilets, cfga, drkg wtr. Fishing, hiking, boating(l). Primary river access.

Tower Rock Recreation Site $5
Bureau of Land Management
Salmon Field Office
10 mi N of Salmon on US 93. $5 ($3 with federal Senior Pass). 3/15-11/30; 14-day limit. 6 sites (some pull-through); 28-ft RV limit. Toilets, tbls, cfga, drkg wtr. Picnicking, hiking, boating(l), fishing. Primary river access site.

Wallace Lake $4
Salmon National Forest
3.2 mi N of Salmon on US 93; 14 mi NW on FR 023; 4 mi S

on FR 020 (rough, unpaved, not recommended for trailers). $4. 6/15-10/15, 14-day limit. 12 primitive sites, typically 35-ft RV limit. Tbls, toilets, cfga, drkg wtr. Fishing, boating (carry-down access). Elev 8800 ft; 11 acres.

Williams Lake Recreation Site $5
Bureau of Land Management
Salmon Field Office
4 mi SW on US 93, cross Shoup Bridge; 7 mi on forest rds, following signs. $5 during 5/1-10/31; free rest of year; 14-day limit. 11 sites (28-ft RV limit). Toilets, tbls, cfga, no drkg wtr. Hiking, boating, fishing, swimming. Access to forest service boat ramp.

SANDPOINT (N)

Garfield Bay $10
Bonner County Park
From Sandpoint, 7.5 mi S on Hwy 95; 7.5 mi E on Sagle Rd to town of Garfield; on edge of town at Pend Oreille Lake. $10. RV Sites $15 All year. 28 sites. Tbls, pit toilets, cfga, drkg wtr. Boating(l), fishing, swimming. Marina. 208-255/5681.

Green Bay Campground FREE
Kaniksu National Forest
From US 95 about 5 mi S of Sandpoint, 7.2 mi E on Sagle Rd to Garfield Bay; left on first rd past forest service picnic area for 0.75 mi; right on FR 532 for 1 mi; follow Green Bay Rd 2672 to site (rd not suitable for large RVs). Free. May-Sept; 14-day limit. 11 primitive sites. Tbls, toilets, cfga, beach, no drkg wtr. Also accessible by boat.

Sam Owen Campground $10
Kaniksu National Forest
From Sandpoint, 21 mi E on SR 200; right on Peninsula Rd (CR 1028) for 1 mi. $10 base with federal senior pass; others pay $20 base, $22 for premium locations ($11 with senior pass). About 5/15-9/30; 14-day limit. 80 sites; 60-ft RV limit. Tbls, flush toilets, cfga, drkg wtr, dump, beach, shelter. Group picnic area. Boating(ld), fishing, swimming. Non-campers pay $8 day use fee, $7 dump station, $8 boat launch.

Springy Point Recreation Area $10
Corps of Engineers
Lake Pend Oreille
From Sandpoint at jct with US 2, S on US 95 across long bridge; 3 mi W on Lakeshore Dr, N of rd. $10 with federal senior pass at 37 non-elec sites; others pay $20. 5/10-9/28; 14-day limit. Tbls, flush toilets, cfga, drkg wtr, coin showers, phone, beach, dump. Boating(l), fishing, swimming, interpretive programs.

SHOSHONE (S)

Hot Springs Landing   FREE
Magic Reservoir Recreation Area
Bureau of Land Management
Shoshone Field Office
18 mi N of Shoshone, then follow signs .8 mi S of US 20 on dirt rd. Free. All year; 14-day limit. Undesignated sites near reservoir. Tbls, cfga, toilets, no drkg wtr or trash service. Fishing (trout, perch), boating(ld), hiking. R

Lava Recreation Sites   FREE
Magic Reservoir Recreation Area
Bureau of Land Management
Shoshone Field Office
18 mi N of Shoshone on Hwy 75; 10 mi NW from SR 75 at Big Wood River, then follow co rd and signs E. Access difficult in winter or after rain. Free. 4/1-10/31; 10-day limit. 30 pull-through sites (RVs under 30 ft) and undesignated sites at lakeshore. Toilets, cfga, tbls, no drkg wtr or trash service. Boating (primitive launch), fishing. GGR

Magic City Boat Ramp   FREE
Magic Reservoir Recreation Area
Bureau of Land Management
Shoshone Field Office
18 mi N of Shoshone, then follow signs 5 mi W from SR 75. Free. All year; 14-day limit. Undesignated sites. No facilities, no drkg wtr. Boating(ld), fishing, hiking. R

Magic Dam   FREE
Magic Reservoir Recreation Area
Bureau of Land Management
Shoshone Field Office
18 mi N of Shoshone, then follow signs about 5 mi W from SR 75. Free. 4/1-10/31; 10-day limit. Undesignated sites. Tbls, toilets, no drkg wtr or trash service. Fishing, boating (primitive access), hiking. Stream fishing below dam.

Moonstone Recreation Site   FREE
Magic Reservoir Recreation Area
Bureau of Land Management
Shoshone Field Office
18 mi N of Shoshone, then follow signs half mi S of US 20 on dirt rd. Low level of use; plenty of solitude. Free. 4/1-10/31; 10-day limit. 5 sites & undesignated sites near reservoir (RVs under 30 ft). Tbls, cfga, toilets, no drkg wtr or trash service. Boating(l), fishing, hiking.

Myrtle Point Recreation Site   FREE
Magic Reservoir Recreation Area
Bureau of Land Management
Shoshone Field Office
18 mi N of Shoshone on Hwy 75; 9 mi NW on co rd; follow signs 2 mi E. Free. 4/1-10/31; 10-day limit. 30 pull-through sites (RVs under 30 ft) and undesignated sites at lakeshore. Toilets, cfga, no drkg wtr or trash service. Boating, fishing.

Richfield Diversion   FREE
Magic Reservoir Recreation Area
Bureau of Land Management
Shoshone Field Office
18 mi N of Shoshone on SR 75, then 2.5 mi W following signs. Last 1.5 mi rough, not suitable for RVs or passenger cars; area little used because of rough access. Free. All year; 14-day limit. Undesignated campsites. Primitive. Toilet, no drkg wtr. Fishing, hiking, boating.

Seagull Point   FREE
Magic Reservoir Recreation Area
Bureau of Land Management
Shoshone Field Office
18 mi N of Shoshone on SR 75, then NW 6 mi at Big Wood River and E 1.5 mi. Watch signs. Last 1.5 mi rough, not recommended for RVs; may be closed in spring to protect nesting waterfowl. Free. All year; 14-day limit. Parking area for self-contained RVs. No facilities, no trash service. Fishing, boating, bird watching.

Silver Creek South   FREE
Bureau of Land Management
Shoshone Field Office
33 mi NE of Shoshone on US 26/93; 2 mi W on Pacabo Cutoff Rd; BLM sign indicates a turn left off the highway; site is about 1 mi. Free. 4/15-11/30; 14-day limit. Primitive camping near the riparian zone along Silver Creek. Hiking, fishing. Silver Creek Preserve, a nearby fly-fishing hot spot, is operated by the Nature Conservancy.

SHOUP (S)

Corn Creek $10
Salmon National Forest
28.8 mi W of Shoup on FR 030 (Salmon River Rd). $10. 3/1-11/15; free rest of year; 14-day limit. 18 sites 40-ft RV limit. Tbls, toilets, cfga, drkg wtr, no trash service. Boating(l), fishing, swimming, hiking, horse ramp. No wtr off-season. Access to Salmon River, Frank Church-River of No Return Wilderness.

Horse Creek Hot Spring   FREE
Salmon National Forest
1.5 mi NE of Shoup on FR 030 (Salmon River Rd); 18 mi NW on FR 038 (Spring Creek Rd); 5 mi NW on FR 044 (rds unpaved, rough). Free. 6/15-10/15. 9 sites (RVs under 23 ft). Toilets, no drkg wtr. Horseback riding, fishing. Access to Frank Church-River of No Return Wilderness. Elev 6200 ft.

SODA SPRINGS (S)

Cold Springs   FREE
Caribou National Forest
9.1 mi S of Soda Springs on CR 425; 2 mi S on FR 425; at Eightmile Creek. Free. Elev 6100 ft. 5/25-10/30; 14-day limit. 6 sites (RVs under 22 ft). Tbls, toilets, cfga, firewood, no drkg wtr. Fishing, hiking.

Diamond Creek   FREE
Caribou National Forest
10.1 mi N of Soda Springs on SR 34; 14 mi E on CR 30C (Blackfoot River Rd); 11 mi SE on FR 102. Free. 6/1-10/31; 14-day limit. 12 rustic sites. Toilets, cfga, no tbls, drkg wtr. Hiking, fishing, picnicking.

Blackfoot Reservoir $5
Bureau of Land Management
Pocatello Field Office
11 mi N of Soda Springs on Hwy 34 at SW end of Blackfoot Reservoir. $5. 5/1-10/31; 14-day limit. 16 developed sites, 20 dispersed sites. Toilets, cfga, drkg wtr, tbls, dump, 2 elec hookups. Hiking, boating(l), fishing, picnicking.

Eightmile Canyon   FREE
Cache National Forest
Caribou National Forest
9.2 mi S of Soda Springs on Bailey Creek-Eightmile Rd; 4 mi S on FR 425. Free (fee for group sites). Elev 7200 ft. 6/1-9/30; 14-day limit. 7 sites on 5 acres (RVs under 16 ft). Tbls, toilets, cfga, firewood, no drkg wtr. Picnicking, fishing, hiking, horseback riding, OHV activity. Part of Cache NF, administered by Caribou NF.

Maple Grove Campground $5
Bureau of Land Management
Pocatello Field Office
S of Soda Springs on SR 34 to about 6 mi N of Preston; left for 3 mi on SR 36; left at sign that says "Oneida Narrows," and go N along Bear River to Redpoint & Maple Grove camps; at Oneida Narrows Reservoir. $5. 5/1-10/31; 14-day limit. 12 sites. Tbls, toilets, cfga. Fishing, boating(l), swimming, horseshoes.

Mill Canyon   FREE
Caribou National Forest
10.1 mi N of Soda Springs on SR 34; 11.4 mi E on Blackfoot River Rd; 7 mi on FR 99; at Blackfoot Narrows of Blackfoot River. Free. 6/1-10/15; 14-day limit. 10 sites (32-ft RV limit). Pull-through sites. Tbls, toilets, cfga, drkg wtr. Hiking, fishing.

Morgan's Bridge   FREE
Bureau of Land Management
Pocatello Field Office
11 mi N of Soda Springs on SR 34; 4 mi W on China Cap Rd; 14 mi NW on Government Dam Rd; 14 mi N on Corral Creek Rd & Trail Creek Rd; on Blackfoot River. Free. 5/1-10/31; 14-day limit. 5 primitive sites. Portable toilet, tbls, cfga. Floating, tubing, fishing.

Redpoint Recreation Site $5
Bureau of Land Management
Pocatello Field Office
S of Soda Springs on SR 34 to about 6 mi N of Preston; left for 3 mi on SR 36; left at sign that says "Oneida Narrows," and go N along Bear River to Redpoint & Maple Grove camps; at Bear River below Oneida Narrows Reservoir dam. $5. 5/1-10/31. 9 primitive sites. Tbls, toilets, cfga. Tubing, rafting, fishing, caving, horseshoe pits.

Trail Creek Bridge Camp   FREE
Bureau of Land Management
Pocatello Field Office
11 mi N of Soda Springs on SR 34; 4 mi W on China Cap Rd; 14 mi NW on Government Dam Rd; 20 mi N on Corral Creek Rd, Lincoln Creek Rd & Trail Creek Rd; at Blackfoot River. Free. 5/1-10/31; 14-day limit. 6 primitive sites. Tbls, toilets, cfga, no drkg wtr. Fishing, boating, hiking.

SPENCER (S)
Stoddard Creek $10
Targhee National Forest
3.5 mi N of Spencer on I-15 to exit 184; 1 mi NW on FR 002 (Stoddard Creek Rd). $10 (double site $20, group site $30). MD-9/15; 16-day limit. 22 sites (typically 45 ft). Tbls, toilets, cfga, drkg wtr. Hiking, fishing, biking, horseback riding. 6 acres.

STANLEY (S)
Alturas Inlet Campground $8
Sawtooth National Forest
Sawtooth National Recreation Area
21 mi S of Stanley on SR 75; 4 mi W on FR 205; at Alturas Lake. $8. About 6/1-9/15; 14-day limit. 28 sites (8 double); 40-ft RV limit. Tbls, toilets, cfga, drkg wtr, amphitheater. Canoeing, fishing, boating, mountain biking, swimming, fishing, interpretive programs.

Banner Creek $5
Challis National Forest
22 mi W of Stanley on SR 21. $5. 6/15-10/15; 16-day limit. 3 sites; 32-ft RV limit. Tbls, toilets, cfga, no drkg wtr. Horseback riding, picnicking, fishing in nearby streams. Elev 6500 ft.

Beaver Creek $10
Challis National Forest
17 mi NW of Stanley on SR 21; 3 mi N on Beaver Creek Rd (FR 008). $10. 6/1-10/15; 16-day limit. 8 sites (32-ft RV limit. Tbls, toilets, cfga, drkg wtr. Fishing, hiking, horseback riding. Elev 6700 ft.

Bench Creek $5
Challis National Forest
24 mi W of Stanley on SR 21. $5. 6/15-10/15; 16-day limit. 5 sites; 30-ft RV limit. Toilet, tbls, cfga, no drkg wtr. Fishing, horseback riding, hiking. Elev 6900 ft.

Blind Creek $5
Challis National Forest
14.9 mi NE of Stanley on SR 75; 1 mi N on Yankee Fork Rd;

in canyon of Yankee Fork of Salmon River. $5. 6/15-9/10; 16-day limit. 5 sites 32-ft RV limit. Tbls, toilets, cfga, no drkg wtr or trash service. Fishing, hiking. Interpretive & historical tours nearby.

Bonanza CCC Campground   FREE
Challis National Forest
15 mi E of Stanley on SR 75; 7 mi N on FR 013; near ghost town of Bonanza. Free family camping off-season; group camping by reservation rest of year. 12 sites; 32-ft RV limit. Tbls, toilets, cfga, drkg wtr (no wtr during free period of 9/2-5/31). Grey wtr drain station. Hiking, fishing, horseback riding.

Casino Creek Campground $8
Sawtooth National Forest
Sawtooth National Recreation Area
From jct with SR 21 at Stanley, 5 mi N on SR 75; right on FR 651 for qtr mi; on S side of Salmon River at Casino Creek. $8. 5/15-LD; 10-day limit. 19 sites (3 for equestrians with hitch rails); 35-ft RV limit. Tbls, toilets, cfga, no drkg wtr. Hiking, mountain biking, horseback riding, fishing.

Chinook Bay Campground $8
Sawtooth National Forest
Sawtooth National Recreation Area
1.5 mi S of Stanley on SR 75; about qtr mi S on FR 214; at Redfish Lake Creek. $8 with federal senior pass; others pay $16. About 5/15-9/30; 10-day limit. 13 sites, typically 45 ft. Tbls, toilets, cfga, drkg wtr. Fishing, boating, hiking.

Custer 1 $5
Challis National Forest
14.9 mi NE of Stanley on US 75; 8 mi N on FR 13; 4 mi NE on FR 070; near ghost town of Custer. $5. 7/1-9/30; 16-day limit. 6 sites 32-ft RV limit. Tbls, cfga, toilets, no drkg wtr. Fishing at Fivemile Creek, hiking, picnicking.

Deadwood Campground $7.50
Boise National Forest
21 mi W of Stanley on SR 21; 21 mi W on FR 579; 7 mi S on FR 555; at Deadwood River & South Fork of Payette River. $7.50 with federal senior pass; others pay $15. 4/20-10/20; 14-day limit. 6 sites; 15-ft RV limit. Non-campers pay $5 day use fee. Tbls, toilets, cfga, drkg wtr. Fishing, boating. (3 other camps on E side of lake: Riverside, Howers, Cozy Cove.) Closed in 2016 due to fires check status before arrival.

Eightmile   FREE
Challis National Forest
14.9 mi NE of Stanley on US 75; 3 mi N on FR 13; 6.5 mi NE on FR 70; at Eightmile Creek. Free. 6/15-9/10; 16-day limit. 2 sites 16-ft RV limit. Tbls, toilet, cfga, no drkg wtr. Fishing.

Flatrock $10
Challis National Forest
14.9 mi NE of Stanley on SR 75; 2 mi N on FR 013; at Yankee Fork of Salmon River. $10. 6/1-9/15; 16-day limit. 6 sites 32-ft RV limit. Tbls, toilet, cfga, drkg wtr. Fishing.

Glacier View Campground $8.5
Sawtooth National Forest
Sawtooth National Recreation Area
4.5 mi S of Stanley on SR 75; 2.5 mi S on FR 214; at N shore of Redfish Lake. $8.5 with federal senior pass; others pay $17. About 5/15-9/15 (Walk ins early May and Late Sep); 14-day limit. 8 sites; 50-ft RV limit. Tbls, flush toilets, cfga, drkg wtr, playgrounds. Canoeing, fishing, swimming, boating(l), swimming.

Iron Creek $8
Sawtooth National Forest
Sawtooth National Recreation Area
2 mi W of Stanley on SR 21; 4 mi S on FR 619. $8 during MD-9/15; free rest of year, but no wtr or services; 14-day limit. 9 sites (22-ft RV limit). Tbls, toilets, cfga, drkg wtr. Hiking, fishing for wild cutthroat. Elev 6600 ft; 35 acres.

Jerry's Creek   FREE
Challis National Forest
15 mi E of Stanley on US 93; 5 mi N on FR 013. Free. 6/1-9/15; 16-day limit. 3 sites 22-ft RV limit. Tbls, toilets, cfga, firewood, no drkg wtr. Picnicking, fishing.

Josephus Lake   FREE
Challis National Forest
17 mi N of Stanley on SR 21; 12 mi N on FR 008. Free. 7/1-9/30; 14-day limit. 3 sites. Tbls, toilets, cfga, no drkg wtr. Fishing, hiking. Elev 7200 ft.

Lake View $8
Sawtooth National Forest
Sawtooth National Recreation Area
5 mi N of Stanley on SR 21; 3.5 mi W on FR 455; at Stanley Lake. $8. About MD-9/15; 14-day limit. 6 sites (22-ft RV limit). Tbls, toilets, cfga, drkg wtr. Fishing, hiking, boating (ramp at Stanley Lake Inlet).

Lola Creek $10
Challis National Forest
17 mi NW of Stanley on SR 21; 2 mi NW on FR 083. $10. 6/15-9/15; 16-day limit. 21 sites; 35-ft RV limit. Tbls, toilets, cfga, drkg wtr. Fishing, hiking, horseback riding. Access to River of No Return Wilderness Area. Horse stalls & loading ramps.

Lower O'Brien $7.00
Sawtooth National Forest
Sawtooth National Recreation Area
16.9 mi E of Stanley on SR 75; 4 mi S on FR 454 (Robinson Bar Rd); at Stanley River. $7.00 with federal senior pass; others pay $14. About 5/15-8/15; 10-day limit. 10 sites

(typically 40 ft). Tbls, toilets, cfga, drkg wtr. Fishing, boating, hiking. Road narrow & crosses a narrow bridge. Elev 5800 ft; 4 acres.

Mormon Bend $7
Sawtooth National Forest
Sawtooth National Recreation Area
7 mi E of Stanley on SR 75; at Salmon River. $6.50 with federal senior pass; others pay $14. 5/15-LD. MD-10/31; 10-day limit. 15 sites (typically 45 ft). Tbls, toilets, cfga, drkg wtr. Fishing, boating. Designated river put-in site. Elev 6100 ft; 15 acres.

Mount Heyburn Campground $8
Sawtooth National Forest
Sawtooth National Recreation Area
4.5 mi S of Stanley on SR 75; 3 mi S on FR 214; near Redfish Lake. $8. About 6/1-9/15; 10-day limit. 20 sites, typically 40 ft. Tbls, toilets, cfga, drkg wtr, playgrounds. Canoeing, fishing, swimming, boating. Elev 6600 ft.

North Shore Campground $8
Sawtooth National Forest
Sawtooth National Recreation Area
21 mi S of Stanley on SR 75; 3 mi W on FR 205; at Alturas Lake. $8. 14 sites, typically 55 ft. About 6/15-9/30; 14-day limit. Tbls, toilets, cfga, drkg wtr. Hiking, horseback riding, interpretive programs, canoeing, fishing, boating (ramp at Smokey Bear Campground), swimming.

Outlet Campground $8.50
Sawtooth National Forest
Sawtooth National Recreation Area
4 mi S of Stanley on SR 75; W on FR 214, then right into campground; at Redfish Lake. $8.50 with federal senior pass; others pay $17. About 5/23-9/15; 10-day limit. 19 sites; 50-ft RV limit. Tbls, toilets, cfga, drkg wtr, playgrounds. Hiking, fishing, swimming, canoeing, boating(l). Elev 6600 ft

Pettit Lake $12
Sawtooth National Forest
Sawtooth National Recreation Area
From jct with SR 21 near Stanley, 18 mi S on SR 75 to sign for Petit Lake; right for 1.6 mi on FR 208, then right for 0.4 mi; near lake. 6/15-10/31; 14-day limit. $12. 12 sites, typically 48 ft. (RVs under 22 ft). Toilets, cfga, tbls, drkg wtr. Fishing, boating (no mtrs).

Point Campground $8.50
Sawtooth National Forest
Sawtooth National Recreation Area
1.5 mi S of Stanley on SR 75; 2.5 mi W on FR 214; at Redfish Lake. $8.50 with federal senior pass; others pay $17. 17 sites; 28-ft RV limit. About 5/23-9/15; 14-day limit. Tbls, toilets, cfga, drkg wtr, beach. Interpretive programs, boating, fishing, swimming.

Pole Flat $10
Challis National Forest
14.9 mi NE of Stanley on SR 75; 3 mi N on FR 013; in canyon of Yankee Fork of Salmon River. $10. 5/25-10/13; 16-day limit. 12 sites, 32-ft RV limit. Tbls, toilets, drkg wtr, cfga. Fishing, horseback riding. Elev 6300 ft; 8 acres.

Riverside $8
Sawtooth National Forest
Sawtooth National Recreation Area
6.8 mi E of Stanley on SR 75; on Salmon River. $6.50 with federal senior pass; others pay $13. About 5/15-LD; 10-day limit. 17 sites (typically 40 ft). Tbls, toilets, cfga, drkg wtr. Fishing, hiking, boating.

Salmon River $8
Sawtooth National Forest
Sawtooth National Recreation Area
5.1 mi E of Stanley on SR 75. $8. About 3/15-LD; 10-day limit. 30 sites (32-ft RV limit). Tbls, toilets, cfga, drkg wtr, coin laundry. Fishing, boating. Elev 6200 ft.

Smokey Bear $8
Sawtooth National Forest
Sawtooth National Recreation Area
From Stanley at jct with SR 21, 21 mi S on SR 75; right on FR 205 at Alturas Lake sign, 3 mi, left; at Alturas Lake. $8. 6/15-9/15; . Free rest of year, but no wtr or services; 10-day limit. 12 sites (typically 45 ft). Tbls, toilets, cfga, drkg wtr. Boating(l), fishing, hiking, swimming. Perkins Lake nearby.

Sockeye Campground $8
Sawtooth National Forest
Sawtooth National Recreation Area
4.5 mi S of Stanley on SR 75; 3 mi SW on FR 214; at end of rd on shore of Redfish Lake. $8. About 5/15-9/15; 10-day limit. 23 sites, typically 35 ft. Tbls, toilets, cfga, drkg wtr. Interpretive programs, swimming, fishing, boating(l), hiking, horseback riding. Elev 6600 ft,

Stanley Lake $7.50
Sawtooth National Forest
Sawtooth National Recreation Area
5 mi N of Stanley on SR 21; 3.5 mi W on FR 455. $7.50 with federal Senior Pass; others pay $15. About MD-LD; 10-day limit. 18 sites (45 ft). Tbls, toilets, cfga, drkg wtr. Swimming, fishing, boating, waterskiing, hiking. 12 acres.

Stanley Lake Inlet $7.50
Sawtooth National Forest
Sawtooth National Recreation Area
5 mi N of Stanley on SR 21; 6.5 mi W on FR 455. $7.50 with federal Senior Pass; others pay $15. About MD-10/30; free rest of year, but no wtr or services; 10-day limit. 14 sites (45 ft). Tbls, toilets, cfga, drkg wtr. Boating(l), fishing, swimming, waterskiing, hiking. 9 acres. Elev 6500 ft.

Sunny Gulch $8
Sawtooth National Forest
Sawtooth National Recreation Area
3.2 mi S of Stanley on SR 75; on Salmon River. $8 with federal senior pass; others pay $16 about MD-9/30; free rest of year, but no wtr or services; 10-day limit. 19 sites (typically 35 ft). Tbls, toilets, cfga, drkg wtr. Fishing, picnicking, hiking, horseback riding, boating, interpretive program, visitor center. Elev 6500 ft; 10 acres. Visitor center & horseback rides 3 mi at Redfish Lake; dump 1 mi at Stanley ranger station.

Thatcher Creek $10
Challis National Forest
15 mi NE of Stanley on SR 31. $10. MD-9/30; 16-day limit. 5 sites, 32-ft RV limit. Tbls, toilet, cfga, drkg wtr. Fishing. Marsh across the road often contains feeding moose, elk, birds.

Tin Cup FREE
Challis National Forest
12 mi NE of Stanley on US 93; 11 mi NW on FR 112; 20 mi N on FR 007 (narrow rd, so RVs over 16 ft not recommended); on Loon Creek. 7/1-10/1; 16-day limit. 13 sites 23-ft RV limit, Toilets, cfga, no drkg wtr or trash service. Rockhounding, picnicking, fishing, horseback riding. Elev 5600 ft; 4 acres.

Upper O'Brien $8
Sawtooth National Forest
Sawtooth National Recreation Area
16.9 mi E of Stanley on SR 75; 2 mi E on FR 054; at Salmon River. $8, 5/15-9/15; free rest of year, but no wtr or services; 10-day limit. 9 sites, 22-ft RV limit. Tbls, toilets, cfga, drkg wtr. Fishing. Boat ramp only for rafts, canoes, kayaks. 3 acres. Elev 5730 ft. Must cross narrow bridge to access site; not recommended for large RVs.

SWAN VALLEY (S)

Big Elk Campground $12
Targhee National Forest
1.5 mi E of Swan Valley on US 26; 1.4 mi E on FR 262; on narrow area of Palisades Reservoir. $12 during MD-9/12; free but no wtr during 9/13-MD; 14-day limit. 18 sites, typically 45 ft. Tbls, toilets, cfga, drkg wtr. Fishing, boating(l), swimming, waterskiing, hiking, horseback riding (horse loading ramp). Trailhead. Elev 5700 ft; 20 acres. Snake River. Non-campers pay $6 day use fee.

Blowout $12
Targhee National Forest
15 mi SE of Swan Valley on US 26. $12 during MD-LD; free LD-MD, but no wtr or services; 14-day limit. 15 sites, typically 45 ft. Tbls, toilets, cfga, drkg wtr. Fishing, boating(ld), swimming, waterskiing. Elev 5700 ft. Palisades Reservoir, Snake River. Non-campers pay $6 day use fee.

Falls Campground $12
Targhee National Forest
4 mi W of Swan Valley on US 26; 2.3 mi S on FR 058; at Snake River. $12 during 5/15-9/15; free 9/15-10/31, but no wtr; 16-day limit. 24 sites (no RV size limit); group & double sites available. Tbls, toilets, cfga, drkg wtr. Hiking, fishing, birdwatching, rafting, canoeing. Elev 5800 ft; 18 acres. Palisades Reservoir, Snake River. 60-ft Fall Creek Falls.

TENSED (N)

RV Milepost 382 $11
At 2nd & D Sts, Tensed. $11. All year. 11 sites. Tbls, toilets, cfga, drkg wtr. Unable to verify for 2017.

TWIN FALLS (S)

Bear Gulch FREE
Sawtooth National Forest
27 mi W & S of Twin Falls on US 93; 8 mi S on Foothills Rd; 9 mi N on FR 500 & FR 513. Free. Elev 4900 ft. 6/1-9/30; 14-day limit. 8 sites on 3 acres (RVs under 16 ft). Tbls, toilets, cfga, firewood, piped drkg wtr. Horseback riding (loading ramp), fishing, hiking trails. Near Shoshone Wildlife Pond.

Bostetter FREE
Sawtooth National Forest
8 mi E of Twin Falls on SR 50 & US 30; 39 mi S on Rock Creek Rd, FR 538 & FR 526. Free. 6/15-10/1; 14-day limit. 10 sites on 20 acres (typically 32 ft). Tbls, toilets, cfga, firewood, no drkg wtr, no trash service. Picnicking, fishing, horseback riding. Elev 7160 ft.

Diamondfield Jack $8
Sawtooth National Forest
8 mi E of Twin Falls on US 30; 29 mi S on Rock Creek Rd (CR G3/FR 515). $8. All year; 14-day limit. 8 sites (RVs under 32 ft). Toilets, tbls, cfga, no drkg wtr. Fishing, hiking. Winter sports activities. Elev 7000 ft.

Father and Sons FREE
Sawtooth National Forest
8 mi E of Twin Falls on SR 50 & US 30; 38 mi S on Rock Creek Rd, FR 538 & FR 526. Free. 6/1-9/15; 16-day limit. 12 sites. Tbls, toilets, cfga, firewood, piped drkg wtr. Picnicking, fishing, horseback riding. Elev 7320 ft; 13 acres. Stream.

Porcupine Springs $10
Sawtooth National Forest
8 mi E of Twin Falls on SR 50 & US 30; 30 mi S on Rock Creek Rd (CR G3/FR 515). $10 (double sites $14). 6/1-9/15. 12 sites (RVs under 31 ft). Tbls, toilets, cfga, firewood, piped drkg wtr. Picnicking, fishing, horseback riding. 6800 ft; 44 acres. Biking, hiking, horseback riding.

Schipper Campground $5

Sawtooth National Forest
8 mi E of Twin Falls on SR 50 & US 30; 16 mi S on CR G3/FR 515 (Rock Creek Rd); at Birch Creek. $5. 5/1-10/15; 14-day limit. 5 sites (limited RV space). Tbls, toilet, cfga, no drkg wtr. Fishing, hiking.

Steer Basin $5
Sawtooth National Forest
8 mi E of Twin Falls on SR 50 & US 30; 20 mi S on Rock Creek Rd (CR G3/FR 515); at Rock Creek. $5. 5/1-10/15; 14-day limit. 5 sites; limited RV space. Tbls, toilets, cfga, drkg wtr. Fishing, hiking, horseback riding.

VIRGINIA (S)

Hawkins Reservoir   FREE
Bureau of Land Management
Pocatello Field Office
10 mi W of Virginia on Hawkins Reservoir Rd. Free. May-Oct; 14-day limit. 10 sites. Tbls, toilets, cfga, no drkg wtr. Fishing, hiking, boating(l), fishing.

VICTOR (S)

Pine Creek $10
Targhee National Forest
5.3 mi W of Victor on SR 31; at Little Pine Creek. $10. 5/15-9/15; 16-day limit. 10 sites (32-ft RV limit). Tbls, toilets, cfga, no drkg wtr, no trash service. Hiking, fishing. Elev 7800 ft; 3 acres.

Trail Creek $12
Targhee National Forest
5.5 mi E of Victor on Sr 33; qtr mi S on SR 22, in Wyoming. $12. 5/15-9/15; 16-day limit. 11 sites (35-ft RV limit). Tbls, toilet, cfga, drkg wtr. Fishing, hiking. Elev 6600 ft; 7 acres.

WARREN (S)

Burgdorf $10
Payette National Forest
30 mi W of Warren on Warren Wagon Rd (FR 21) and FR 246; near Burgdorf Hot Springs. $10. 7/1-9/30; 14-day limit. 5 sites 21-ft RV limit. Tbls, toilet, cfga, no drkg wtr, no trash service. Hiking, fishing. Elev 6000 ft. Near private Burgdorf Hot Springs.

WEISER (S)

Justrite   FREE
Payette National Forest
12.5 mi N of Weiser on US 95; 11.5 mi N on CR 004; 3.2 mi N on FR 009; at Mann Creek. Free. 6/1-10/31; 16-day limit. 4 dispersed sites. Tbls, toilet, cfga, no drkg wtr. Fishing, horseback riding. Elev 4200 ft.

Mann Creek Campground $10
Bureau of Reclamation
Payette National Forest
18 mi N of Weiser on Hwy 94; at Mann Creek Reservoir. $10 single sites, $15 double sites. 5/15-10/30; 14-day limit. 13 sites (45-ft RV limit). Tbls, toilets, cfga, drkg wtr. Swimming, boating, fishing, hiking. 283-acre lake owned by Bureau of Reclamation; managed by Payette NF.

Spring Creek $10
Payette National Forest
12.5 mi N of Weiser on US 95; 14 mi N on FR 009. $10 (double sites $15) during 5/15-10/15; reduced fee off-season if wtr shut off; 16-day limit. 14 sites; 32-ft RV limit. Tbls, cfga, drkg wtr, toilet. Fishing, horseback riding. Elev 4800 ft.

Steck Recreation Site $8
Bureau of Land Management
Four Rivers Field Office
22 mi W of Weiser on SR 70 to Olds Ferry Rd; on Brownlee Reservoir. $8 for RVs, $5 tents. 4/15-10/31; 14-day limit. 45 RV sites (25-ft RV limit). Non-campers pay $2 day use fee. Tbls, toilets, cfga, drkg wtr, dump. Swimming, picnicking, fishing, boating(ld), hunting, hiking, waterskiing.

WHITE BIRD (1N)

Hammer Creek $10
Lower Salmon River Recreation Area
Bureau of Land Management
Cottonwood Field Office
1.5 mi S of White Bird on Hwy 95; 1.5 mi N on co rd; along Lower Salmon River. $10. All year; 14-day limit. 12 sites (24-ft RV limit). Tbls, toilets, cfga, drkg wtr, handicapped facilities. Swimming, boating(l), rafting, fishing. 20 acres; elev 1500 ft. Put-in spot for river floats.

North Fork Slate Creek   FREE
Nez Perce National Forest
11 mi S of White Bird on US 95; 10 mi E on FR 354. Free. Year-round but might not be reacable in winter. 5 sites for tents or pickup campers. Tbls, toilets, cfga, firewood, no drkg wtr. Fishing, horseback riding. Elev 3000 ft. Slate Creek Ranger Station (half mi S). Creek-side camping.

Pittsburg Landing $8
Hell's Canyon
National Recreation Area
Wallowa-Whitman National Forest
17 mi up Deer Creek Rd 493, off Hwy 95 S of White Bird. Access rough & slippery when wet. $8. 28 sites. Tbls, toilets, cfga, drkg wtr. Trailhead for Snake River National Recreation Trail. Boating(l), fishing, hiking.

Rocky Bluff   FREE
Nez Perce National Forest
11 mi S of White Bird on US 95; 14 mi NE on FR 233; 1 mi E on FR 641. Adjacent to Gospel Hump Wilderness. 6/1-10/1; 14-day limit. 4 sites. Tbls, toilets, cfga, no drkg wtr. Suitable for tents, pickup campers, mini motorhomes and small trailers; trailers longer than 16 ft have maneuvering difficulty. Fishing, Hiking.

Slate Creek Recreation Site $10
Bureau of Land Management
Cottonwood Field Office
8 mi S of White Bird on US 95. $10. All year; 14-day limit. 6
sites (26-ft RV limit). Tbls, toilets, cfga, drkg wtr, handicap
facilities. Boating(l), fishing, swimming. Fee for use of
dump station. 20 acres.

WINCHESTER (N)
Winchester Lake State Park $12
Qtr mi SW of Winchester, off US 95, following signs.
Seniors receive 50% discount Mon-Thurs. Base Rates,
Std site $12-$21, w/wtr or elec $20-$25. wtr and elec
$24-$29 wtr, elec & sewer $26-$29. All year; 15-day limit.
22 std and 46 serviced sites, up to 60 ft. Flush toilets,
cfga, drkg wtr, showers, dump. Fishing, hiking, biking,
boating(l), guided walks.

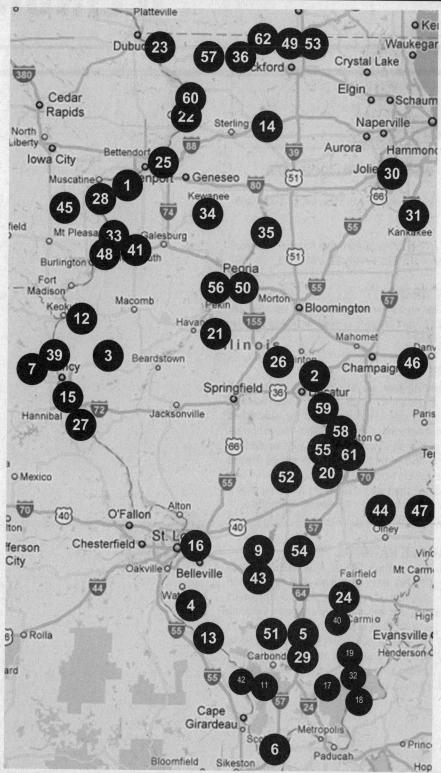

ILLINOIS

CAPITAL: Springfield
NICKNAME: Prairie State
STATEHOOD: 1818 – 21st State
FLOWER: Violet
TREE: White Oak
BIRD: Cardinal

WWW.ENJOYILLINOIS.COM

Toll-free number for travel information: 1-800-406-6418.

Dept. of Natural Resources, One Natural Resources Way, Springfield, IL 62702. 217-782-9175.

REST AREAS
Overnight stops are not permitted. Vehicles are allowed to park 24 hours at oases on Illinois Tollway; no facilities.

STATE PARKS
RV camping fees are $8-35. Maximum stay, 15 days; maximum RV length, 35 ft. Illinois residents 62 years or older are charged half the established rate (not including utilities fees) Mon-Thurs. Special rates also apply to state residents with disabilities. Class C sites with vehicular access are $8 (free to Illinois seniors Monday-Thursday). State parks that offer those sites are listed on the following pages. Department of Natural Resources, Springfield, IL 62702. 217/782-6752.

SHAWNEE NATIONAL FOREST
Located in southern Illinois, this national forest covers 261,592 acres spread between the Ohio and Mississippi Rivers. Forest features free dispersed camping all year, 205 miles of hiking trails, including 55 miles of the River to River Trail from Camp Cadiz to US Route 45; hunting, fishing, horseback riding and ATV use on designated routes. Forest supervisor, Shawnee National Forest, 50 Highway 145 South, Harrisburg, IL 62946. 618/253-7114.

ANDALUSIA (1)

Andalusia Slough　　　　　　　　　　FREE
Corps of Engineers
Mississippi River Public Use Area
Lock & Dam 12
2 mi W of Andalusia on IL 92, across river S of Davenport. All year; 14-day limit. Free from late Oct-5/15; $4 rest of year. 16 road-style primitive sites, some pull-through. Tbls, pit toilets, cfga, drkg wtr, fishing pier. Swimming, boating(l), fishing, picnicking. 10 acres. GPS: 41.4392, -90.7754.

ARGENTA (2)

Friends Creek Regional Park　　　　　　$12
Macon County Conservation
2 mi N of Argenta on CR 18; right for 1 mi; left on Friends Creek Park Rd for half mi. $12 for sites without hookups ($10 for county residents); elec sites $18 ($15 for county residents). 5/1-11/1. 36 sites on 526 acres. Tbls, flush toilets, cfga, drkg wtr, elec, showers. Hiking trails, fishing, playground nearby, nature programs. Restored historical school. GPS: 40.029688, -88.781583.

AUGUSTA (3)

Weinberg-King　　　　　　　　　　　$8
State Fish & Wildlife Area
3 mi E of Augusta; N of Rt 101. $8 for Class C primitive sites (free to Illinois seniors Mon-Thurs). All year; 15-day limit. Sites separate from equestrian area. Tbls, pit toilets, cfga, drkg wtr, dump. Horseback riding, fishing, hiking. 772 acres. GPS: 40.233398, -90.897705.

BALDWIN (4)

Kaskaskia　　　　　　　　　　　　$10
Lock & Dam Recreation Area
Corps of Engineers
Kaskaskia River Project
About 4 mi SE of Mococ on CR 7, then 2.4 mi S on Lock Dam Rd about three-fourths mi N of confluence of Kaskaskia River with Mississippi River. $10 at 15 elec 30/50-amp sites. All year; 14-day limit. Tbls, toilets, cfga, drkg wtr. Boating(l), fishing, shelter ($ or free if not reserved). GPS: 37.59011, -895617.

Kaskaskia River　　　　　　　　　FREE
State Fish & Wildlife Area
Baldwin Lake
4 mi N of Baldwin on 5th St, passing the Illinois Power generator; 1 mi W on Risdon School Rd to park entrance; turn left & follow sign. Free. All year. Camp along both sides of Kaskaskia River for 50 mi between Fayetteville and Mississippi River, E and W of Baldwin. Lake is E of Baldwin. Boat launch ramps at Fayetteville, on Hwy 154 W of Baldwin, at New Athens and at Evansville. Undesignated primitive camping areas adjacent to river. Fishing, boating. Baldwin Lake GPS: 38.21755, -89.86927.

BENTON (5)

Gun Creek　　　　　　　　　　　　$8
Corps of Engineers
Rend Lake
6 mi N of Benton on I-57 to exit 77; 0.2 mi W on SR 154, then S. $8 with federal senior pass; others pay $16. 3/15-11/30; 14-day limit. 99 elec sites; 65-ft RV limit. Tbls, toilets, cfga, drkg wtr, pavilion, amphitheater, playground, fishing pier, interactive programs. Handicap access. Fishing, boating(l), golf, tennis, trap shooting, biking,hiking. GPS: 38.07861, -88.93028.

North Sandusky Recreation Area　　　　$8
Corps of Engineers
Rend Lake
6 mi N of Benton on I-57 to from exit 77; 6 mi W on SR 154; S on Rend City Rd to stop sign, then continue S following signs. $8 base with federal senior pass at 118 elec/wtr sites; others pay $16 base, $24 for full hookups ($12 with senior pass). Group camping area $100. RV limit 65 ft. About 3/15-11/1; 14-day limit. Tbls, flush toilets, cfga, drkg wtr, showers, dump, coin laundry, playground, fishing pier, beach. Boating(l), fishing, hiking, golf, swimming, bike trail. GPS: 38.07888, -89.00556.

South Marcum Recreation Area　　　　$8
Corps of Engineers
Rend Lake
1 mi N of Benton on Hwy 37; 2 mi W to end of Main Dam. $8 base with federal senior pass at 146 elec/wtr RV sites; others pay $16 base, $24 for full hookups ($12 with senior pass). Walk-to tent sites $12. 4/1-10/30; 14-day limit. Tbls, flush toilets, cfga, drkg wtr, dump. Swimming, boating(l), fishing, playground, tennis court, sports field, hiking trails. Boat rentals, horseback riding nearby. 35 acres. GPS: 38.0375, -88.93611.

South Sandusky Campground　　　　　$8
Corps of Engineers
Rend Lake
2.5 mi W of Benton on SR 14; N on CR 900; 2.5 mi E; N on CR 850E following signs. $8 base with federal senior pass at119 elec/wtr sites; others pay $16 base, $24 full hookups ($12 with senior pass). Walk-to tent sites $12. 4/1-10/31; 14-day limit. Tbls, flush toilets, cfga, drkg wtr, showers, dump, playground, amphitheater, pavilion. Boating(lr), fishing, trap shooting, golf, motorcycle trails, hiking & biking trails. Boat rentals, horseback riding nearby. GPS: 38.06028, -89.00472.

CAIRO (6)

Horseshoe Lake　　　　　　　　　　$8
State Fish & Wildlife Area
7 mi NW of Cairo on SR 3; 2.5 mi E; at Olive Branch jct. $8 at 10 primitive Class C sites; $13 at 40 Class B sites with elec; $15 at 38 Class A sites (on Mon-Thurs, sites are free, $9 & $10, respectively, for Illinois seniors). All year; 14-day

limit. 178 sites. Tbls, flush & pit toilets, cfga, drkg wtr, dump, playground, store. Boating(lr), fishing, horseback riding, hunting, fishing, canoeing. Horse camp. Bald eagle observations. 10,200 acres with shallow, 2,400-acre lake.

CANTON (MISSOURI) (7)
Fenway Landing   FREE
Corps of Engineers
Mississippi River Public Use Area
4.5 mi N of Canton on MO 61; E on co rd over levee to campground. Free. All year; 14-day limit. 15 primitive sites. Tbls, toilets, cfga, drkg wtr. Picnicking, fishing, swimming, boating(l). GPS: 40.238281, -91.517334.

CARLYLE (9)
Boulder Recreation Area $8
Corps of Engineers
Carlyle Lake
8 mi E of Carlyle on US 50; 5 mi N on Boulder-Ferrin Rd; at E shore of lake. $8 base with federal senior pass at 84 elec sites; others pay $16 base, $24 for full hookups ($12 with senior pass). About 4/15-10/15; 14-day limit. RV limit in excess of 65 ft. Tbls, flush toilets, cfga, drkg wtr, dump, elec, showers, coin laundry, playground, fish cleaning station. Fishing, hiking, boating(l), waterskiing, picnicking, basketball. Fish cleaning station, amphitheater, pavilion. Boat rentals nearby. GPS: 38.69167, -89.23306.

Coles Creek Recreation Area $8
Corps of Engineers
Carlyle Lake
8 mi E of Carlyle on US 50; 3.5 mi N on Boulder Rd; look for signs & turn left on CR 1700N, following it around the curve; at E shore of lake. $8 base with federal senior pass at 119 elec sites; others pay $16 base, $24 for full hookups ($12 with senior pass). Tbls, flush toilets, cfga, drkg wtr, showers, dump, coin laundry, fish cleaning station, hookups, playground, fishing pier, amphitheater, picnic shelter ($30). Fishing, boating(l), basketball. GPS: 38.65444, -89.26722.

Dam West Recreation Area $12
Corps of Engineers
Carlyle Lake
1 mi N of Carlyle on CR 1800E; at S shore of lake. $12 at 30-amp elec sites; $14 at 50-amp elec; $18 at 50-amp elec/wtr premium sites; $24 full hookups. Seniors with federal senior pass pay $6, $7, $9 & $12. 4/1-10/31; 14-day limit. 109 elec sites; RV limit in excess of 65 ft. Tbls, flush toilets, cfga, drkg wtr, dump, beach, pavilion, fish cleaning station, showers, playground, coin laundry, amphitheater. Boating(l), horseshoes, basketball, tennis, hiking trails, golf, swimming, fishing. Boat rentals nearby. GPS; 38.62778, -90/35933.

Dam East Recreation Area $12
Corps of Engineers
Carlyle Lake
1 mi NE of Carlyle below dam on E side of river. $12 at elec sites ($6 with federal senior pass). Tbls, flush toilets, cfga, drkg wtr, picnic shelter ($3). Fishing. Dam GPS: 38.61839, -89.352856.

McNair Campground $10
Corps of Engineers
Carlyle Lake
1 mi E of Carlyle on US 50 within the Dam East Recreation Area. $10 at single non-elec sites if space not reserved by groups; $16 at elec sites ($5 & $8 with federal senior pass). 5/1-9/30; 14-day limit. 44 sites & 4 group camping areas. Tbls, flush toilets, showers, dump, cfga, drkg wtr, fish cleaning station. Boating, swimming, fishing, hiking, ranger programs. GPS: 38.630615, -89.29248.

CARTERVILLE (11)
Crab Orchard Camp $10
Crab Orchard
National Wildlife Refuge
8 mi W of I-57 toward Carterville on SR 13; S qtr mi at Pirates Cove Marina on Crab Orchard Lake. $10 base. 4/1-12/31. Base fee without elec; $15 for elec sites, $20 elec/wtr, $25 full hookups. 315 sites. Tbls, flush toilets, cfga, drkg wtr, dump, elec($), store. Boating(ldr), fishing, hiking, swimming, canoeing. Now a public campground. GPS: 37.62, -89.07.

Devils Kitchen Camp $10
Crab Orchard
National Wildlife Refuge
10 mi W of I-57 toward Carterville on SR 13; 8 mi S to Devils Kitchen Lake. $10 base. 3/1-Thanksgiving. Base fee for non-elec sites; $15 with elec, $20 elec/wtr, $25 full hookups. Federal America the Beautiful pass discounts apply. 65 sites. Tbls, toilets, cfga, drkg wtr, marina, hookups($), dump. Canoeing, fishing, boating(lr). Now operated as public campground. GPS: 37.6426, -89.1026.

CARTHAGE (12)
Carthage Lake Jaycee Park $10
Qtr mi W of Carthage on Hwy 136. $10 base. All year. 40 sites (no RV size limit). Tbls, toilets, cfga, drkg wtr, elec($), pool, play area. Swimming, fishing, basketball. Unable to verify fees for 2014. Lake GPS: 40.7975394, -91.0712553.

CHESTER (13)
Randolph County $8
State Recreation Area
4 mi N of Chester on county rd. $8 at 95 Class C primitive sites (free to Illinois seniors Mon-Thurs). All year; 14-day limit. Tbls, flush & pit toilets, cfga, drkg wtr, dump, playground, no elec, showers. Boating(lr), fishing, hunting, hiking, canoeing, horseback riding trails. Group camping available. 1,021 acres. GPS: 37.971808, -89.803104.

DIXON (14)

Green River $8
State Wildlife Area
10 mi S of Dixon (6 mi NW of Ohio village) on Hwy 26; follow signs on county rd. $8 at 50 Class C primitive sites (free for Illinois seniors Mon Thurs). All year; 14-day limit. Tbls, toilets, cfga, drkg wtr, dump, store, no elec, no showers. 35-ft RV limit. Horseback riding (5/1-8/31), hunting (9/1-2/28), hiking, birdwatching, trapshooting. Primarily a horse camp. GPS: 1.3756, -89.3057.

EAST HANNIBAL (15)

John Hay Recreation Area   FREE
Mississippi River Public Use Area
Corps of Engineers
On Hwy 106 near East Hannibal. Free. All year; 14-day limit. 8 primitive sites. Tbls, toilets, cfga, no drkg wtr. Boating(l), fishing.

EAST ST. LOUIS (16)

Horseshoe Lake State Park $8
5 mi NE of East St. Louis on Hwy 111. $8 at 48 primitive Class C sites (free for Illinois seniors Mon-Thurs). 5/1-10/31; 15-day limit. Tbls, pit toilets, cfga, drkg wtr, dump, no elec, no showers. Ski trails, boating(lr)m fishing, hunting, hiking, canoeing. 2,854 acres. Cahokia Mounds nearby. GPS: 38.6856053, -90.0942737.

EDDYVILLE (17)

Oak Point $12
Lake Glendale Recreation Area
Shawnee National Forest
8.5 mi S of Eddyville on SR 145; qtr mi E on FR 443; half mi S on FR 442 (21 mi S of Mitchellsville). $12 base. All year; 14-day limit. Base fee for single sites; $6 surcharge for elec. Seniors with federal senior pass pay $6 & $12. 57 sites; 31 with elec. No RV size limit. Double & triple sites $24 & $36. Tbls, flush & pit toilets, showers, cfga, drkg wtr, dump, beach, playground. Boating (lr), swimming($), fishing, hiking trails, volleyball. GPS: 37.245360, -88.394292.

Redbud $10
Bellsmith Springs Recreation Area
Shawnee National Forest
2.6 mi N of Eddyville on SR 145; 3.5 mi SW on FR 848. $10. 3/15-12/15; 14 day limit. 21 sites (32-ft RV limit). Tbls, toilets, cfga, drkg wtr. Swimming, fishing, hiking, nature trails. 37 acres. GPS: 37.31825, -88.392540.

ELIZABETHTOWN (18)

Tecumseh Lake   FREE
Shawnee National Forest
W on SR 145 from Elizabethtown to ranger station; 2 mi N, then 2 mi W following signs. Free. 4/1-12/15; 14-day limit. 3 sites. Tbls, no toilets, cfga, no drkg wtr. Boating(l), hiking, hunting. No trash service. GPS: 37.285924, -88.193222.

EQUALITY (19)

Saline County $8
State Fish & Wildlife Area
6 mi SW of Equality on access rd. $7. All year; 14-day limit. 250 primitive Class C sites (free to Illinois seniors Mon-Thurs). Tbls, flush & pit toilets, cfga, drkg wtr, dump, no elec, no showers. Boating(lr), hunting, hiking, fishing, canoeing, horseback riding. Horse camping. 1,248 acres. GPS: 37.702, -88.377.

FINDLAY (20)

Coon Creek $9
Lake Shelbyville
Corps of Engineers
2.8 mi S of Findlay, then qtr mi W on CR 1900; 1.7 mi S on CR 2075; on W shore of lake. $9 base with federal senior pass at 176 elec/wtr sites; others pay $18 base, $24 at 8 full-hookup sites ($12 with senior pass). RV limit in excess of 65 ft; 30 pull-through. 4/1-10/15; 14-day limit. Tbls, flush toilets, cfga, drkg wtr, showers, fish cleaning station, playground, beach, coin laundry, dump, fishing pier. Hiking, fishing, boating(l), basketball, swimming, horseshoes, nature trail. Non-campers pay $3 for boat ramp. GPS: 39.2712, -88.7625.

Eagle Creek $10
State Recreation Area
Lake Shelbyville
1.5 mi E of Findlay on CR 3; at W shore of Lake Shelbyville. $10 at primitive Class B sites with showers ($5 for Illinois seniors Mon-Thurs); $8 at Class D sites (free for Illinois seniors Mon-Thurs); $20 at 75 Class A elec sites ($15 for Illinois seniors Mon-Thurs). Tbls, flush toilets, showers, cfga, drkg wtr, playground, dump, fish cleaning station, shelter($25). Fishing, boating(ld), hiking trail, golf, horseshoes, interpretive exhibits, volleyball. Overlook platform. 2,200 acres. 217-756-8260. GPS: 39.49472, -88.71167.

Lone Point $8
Lake Shelbyville
Corps of Engineers
2.8 mi S of Findlay, then half mi E on CR 1785; 0.8 mi S on CR 1725; 0.5 mi S on CR 2175 (E of Coon Creek Rd). $8 with federal senior pass; others pay $16. 82 elec sites. About 5/15-LD; 14-day limit. RV limit in excess of 65 ft. Tbls, flush toilets, cfga, drkg wtr, playground, beach, fishing pier, fish cleaning station, dump, showers. Golf, tennis, swimming, fishing, boating(l), hiking. GPS: 39.2720, -88.441324.

FOREST CITY (21)

Sand Ridge State Forest $8
3 mi NW of Forest City (25 mi SW of Peoria). $8 at 27 Class C primitive sites (free for Illinois seniors Mon-Thurs). All year; 14-day limit. Tbls, pit toilets, cfga, drkg wtr, dump. Horseback riding (15 mi of trails), hunting, hiking, skiing, snowmobiling. State's largest forest at 7,112 acres. GPS: 40.411377, -89.866211.

FULTON (22)

Lock & Dam 13   **FREE**
Corps of Engineers
Mississippi River Public Use Area
2 mi N of Fulton on IL 84; W on Lock Rd, following sign. Free. All year; 14-day limit. 6 primitive sites. Tbls, toilets, cfga, shelter. Boating(l), fishing, hunting, canoeing. Observation deck. $3 for boat ramp during 5/1-11/30 ($1.50 with federal senior pass); free rest of year. GPS: 41.898438, -90.154297.

GALENA (23)

Blanding Landing   **$10**
Corps of Engineers
Mississippi River Public Use Area
From US 20 at Galena, S on county rd to Blanding, then W. $10 at 7 non-hookup sites; $14 at 30 elec sites ($5 & $7 with federal senior pass). No wtr hookups. 50-ft RV limit. About 5/15-10/25; 14-day limit. Tbls, toilets, cfga, drkg wtr, showers, dump, amphitheater. Fishing, boating(l). GPS: 42.28, -90.40

GOLCONDA

Golconda Marina   **$8**
State Recreation Area
In Golconda at 1 Marina Lane on W shore of Ohio River. $8 at primitive sites on bluff overlooking river (free for Illinois seniors Mon-Thurs). All year; 15-day limit. Tbls, toilets, cfga, drkg wtr. Fishing, boating(dlr), hiking trail. Concession-operated 274-acre marina with 206 boat slips. 618-683-5875.GPS: 37.370278, -88.481944.

GRANITE CITY

Horseshoe Lake State Park   **$8**
From I-55 exit 6 S of Granite City, half mi N on SR 111. $8 at 48 Class C sites (free for Illinois seniors Mon-Thurs). 5/1-10/31; 15-day limit. Tbls, pit toilets, cfga, drkg wtr, dump, no elec, no showers. Ski trails, boating(lr), fishing, hunting, hik67ing. 10,200 acres with 2,400-acre lake (not including Lake Michigan, the largest natural lake in Illinois, an oxbow or meander lake once part of the Mississippi River. Cahokia Mounds nearby. 618-931-0270. GPS: 38.6856053, -90.0942737.

GRAYVILLE (24)

Hilltop Public Campground   **$10**
1.5 mi N on SR 1 from I-64; 3 blks E on North St; qtr mi S on Water St; 1 blk E on Water St; qtr mi S on Oxford St, following signs; on Wabash River. $10. 4/1-11/1; 14-day limit. About 35 sites. Tbls, flush toilets, cfga, drkg wtr, showers, dump, elec/wtr, pool, playground, firewood. Fishing, swimming, boating(l), tennis.

HAMPTON (25)

Fisherman's Corner   **$8**
Corps of Engineers
Mississippi River Public Use Area
From Hampton (E of Davenport, IA), 1 mi N on SR 84. Or, from I-80, 1 mi S on SR 84; near Lock & Dam 14. $8 with federal senior pass at 29 elec 30-amp sites; others pay $16; 50-amp elec sites $18 ($9 with senior pass). RV limit in excess of 65 ft. About 4/9-10/24; 14-day limit. Tbls, toilets, cfga, drkg wtr, dump, elec($), playground, amphitheater. Fishing, boating, biking, horseshoes. GPS: 41.56972, -90.39.

Illiniwek Forest Preserve   **$9**
Rock Island County Forest District
From SR 84 N of Hampton, about 2 mi E on Hubbard Rd. $9 for seniors over 62 at primitive sites ($11 at river), others pay $11 ($14 at river); $14 for seniors at elec/wtr sites, others pay $15. Discounts for county residents. 25 primitive sites (17 at river) & 60 elec/wtr pads at 3 campgrounds. 4/1-10/31. Tbls, flush toilets, showers, cfga, drkg wtr. Boating(l), hiking, fishing, biking trails, scenic overlook, ball fields. GPS: 41.5584, -90.4037.

HAVANA (26)

Anderson Lake   **$8**
State Fish & Wildlife Area
About 10 mi S of Havana on Hwy 100. $8. 100 Class C sites (free for Illinois seniors Mon-Thurs). All year; 14-day limit. Tbls, flush & pit toilets, cfga, drkg wtr, dump no showers, fishing pier. Limited facilities in winter. Boating(lr), fishing, hunting, canoeing, picnicking. On backwater of Illinois River. 40.201434, -90.191787.

HULL (27)

Park-N-Fish Recreation Area   **FREE**
Corps of Engineers
Mississippi River Public Use Area
Three-fourths mi W of Hull on US 36; 6.2 mi S on paved rd; on Illinois side of Lock & Dam 22, off Hwy 106. All year; 14-day limit. 6 free primitive sites. Tbls, toilets, cfga, drkg wtr, picnic shelter. Fishing, swimming, picnicking, horseback riding. GPS: 91.1449, -39.3818.

ILLINOIS CITY (28)

Blanchard Island Recreation Area   **$4**
Corps of Engineers
Mississippi River Public Use Area
About 10 mi SW of Illinois City. From Muscatine at the Iowa bridge, 1.5 mi E on SR 92; 4 mi S on New Boston Rd, then second right past Copperas Creek Bridge; off the river's main channel. $4 during 5/15-10/15; free rest of year; 14-day limit. 34 primitive sites; 8 acres. Tbls, toilets, cfga, drkg wtr, dump. Picnicking, boating(l), fishing, waterskiing. Volunteer host. GPS: 41.3481, -91.0557.

Loud Thunder Forest Preserve   **$9**
Rock Island County Forest District
NE of Illinois City on CR 59; at N shore of White Oak Campground & S shore of Mississippi River. $9 for seniors at primitive sites ($10 riverfront); others pay $11 & $12. Seniors pay $14 at wtr/elec sites; others pay $16. Discount

for county residents. 4/1-10/31. 5 campgrounds with 111 sites, including equestrian sites. Tbls, flush toilets, showers, cfga, drkg wtr, playgrounds, dump. Boating(ldr), fishing, hiking trails, multi-use trails, bridle trail. 1,621 acres; 167-acre lake. GPS: 41.4319, -90.8208.

JOHNSTON CITY (29)
Arrowhead Lake $7
Public Campground
About 1 mi E of Johnston City on Broadway. $7 for seniors; others pay $13. 23 sites. Tbls, flush toilets, cfga, drkg wtr, dump, showers, elec/wtr, playground. Fishing, boating(l).

JOLIET (30)
Des Plaines $8
State Fish & Wildlife Area
10 mi S of Joliet on I-55; take Wilmington exit. $8 at 24 Class C primitive sites (free for Illinois seniors on Mon-Thurs). 4/15-10/15; 15-day limit. Tbls, pit toilets, cfga, drkg wtr, dump, no showers, no elec. Limited facilities in winter. Boating(l), fishing, hunting, archery range, trap-shooting. GPS: 41.358398, -88.200928.

KANKAKEE (31)
Chippewa Campground $8
Kankakee River State Park
7 mi NW of Kankakee on SR 102. $8 at Class C primitive sites (free for Illinois seniors Mon-Thurs). All year; 15-day limit. 150 sites on 3,932 acres. Tbls, flush & pit toilets, cfga, drkg wtr, dump, playground. Nature program, fishing, hiking, skiing, horseback riding(r), hunting, boating(l), canoeing (r), biking trails. Horse camping at equestrian camp off SR 113. GPS: 41.187988, -87.958984.

KARBERS RIDGE (32)
Camp Cadiz $10
Shawnee National Forest
2 mi E of Karbers Ridge on FR 17; 3 mi E on CR 4. $10. All year; 14-day limit. 11 sites (typically 40 ft). Toilets, tbls, cfga, drkg wtr. Hiking, fishing, ORV use, horseback riding (hitch rails). Remains of CCC camp. 4 acres. GPS: 37.344259, -88.143884.

Pharaoh $10
Gardens of the Gods Recreation Area
Shawnee National Forest
2 mi W of Karbers Ridge on FR 17; 1.5 mi N on FR 10; 1 mi W on FR 114. $10. All year; 14-day limit. 12 sites (22-ft RV limit). Tbls, toilets, cfga, drkg wtr. Biking, hiking, picnicking. 3 acres. Rock formations. GPS: 37.361423, -88.23741.

Pine Ridge $10
Pounds Hollow Recreation Area
Shawnee National Forest
5.3 mi NE of Karbers Ridge on FR 17; N on FR 134 to camp; at Pounds Hollow Lake. $10. 4/1-12/15; 14-day limit. 35 sites (22-ft RV limit). Tbls, toilets, cfga, drkg wtr,

showers($), beach with concession. Boating(rl), fishing, hiking trails, swimming, paddleboats(r). 24 acres. GPS: 37.365392, -88.162675.

KEITHSBURG (33)
Big River State Forest $8
4 mi N of Keithsburg on Oquawka-Keithsburg Rd. $8 at Class C sites (free for Illinois seniors Mon-Thurs). 104 sites. Tbls, flush & pit toilets, cfga, drkg wtr, dump. Boating(l), canoeing, fishing, hunting, hiking, horseback riding, waterskiing, skiing, trap shooting. 3,000 acres along Mississippi River. 1.5-mi Lincoln Hiking Trail. GPS: 41.049072, -90.938721.

KEWANEE (34)
Francis City Park $7
4 mi NE of Kewanee on US 34. $7 base. 3/15-10/15. Base fee for primitive sites; $11 for sites with elec. About 60 sites; 60-ft RV limit. Tbls, cfga, drkg wtr, flush toilets, elec($), dump. Hiking, biking, picnicking. Replica log cabin, historic home. GPS: 41.245657, -89.92637.

LACON (35)
Marshall $8
State Fish & Wildlife Area
Illinois Waterway
From Lacon at jct with SR 17, 5 mi S on SR 26, following brown highway signs; at E shore of Babb Slough pool of Illinois River. $8 at Class C sites without elec (free for Illinois seniors Mon-Thurs); $18 with elec ($14 for Illinois seniors Mon-Thurs). 15 sites plus canoe camping on islands. All year; 15-day limit. Tbls, toilets, cfga, drkg wtr, dump, fish cleaning station, pay phone. Boating(l), canoeing, fishing, hiking trail. 6,000 acres in 3 sections. GPS: 40.99472, -89.4325.

Woodford County $8
State Fish & Wildlife Area
12 mi S of Lacon at jct of SRs 17 & 26; on SR 26 E of Illinois River. $8 at 52 Class C primitive sites (free for Illinois seniors Mon-Thurs). 4/1-12/1; 15-day limit. 52 sites. Tbls, pit toilets, cfga, drkg wtr, dump, no showers, no elec. Boating(lr), fishing, hunting, canoeing. GPS: 40.885742, -89.45752.

LENA (36)
Lake Le-Aqua-Na $8
State Recreation Area
3 mi N of Lena on county rd. $8 at Class C sites, (free for Illinois seniors Mon-Thurs). All year; 15-day limit (dump, showers & flush toilets open 5/1-11/1). 178 sites. Tbls, flush & pit toilets, cfga, drkg wtr, dump, store, beach. Ski trails, hiking, swimming, fishing, downhill skiing, boating(lr), canoeing. 715 acres. GPS: 42.421143, -89.823975.

MARCELLINE (39)

Bear Creek   FREE
Corps of Engineers
Mississippi River Public Use Area
From Quincy, 12 mi N on SR 96 to Marcelline; 1.5 mi W on Bolton Rd; 3 mi W across the levee. Free. All year; 14-day limit. 40 primitive sites. Tbls, toilets, cfga, drkg wtr, dump, shelter. Swimming, picnicking, fishing, boating(l), horseback riding. 6 acres. GPS: 40.111816, -91.47949.

MCLEANSBORO (40)

Hamilton County $8
State Fish & Wildlife Area
8 mi SE of McLeansboro on SR 14; S on park access rd; at Dolan Lake. $8 at Class C primitive sites (free to Illinois seniors Mon-Thurs). All year; 14-day limit. Tbls, flush & pit toilets, cfga, drkg wtr, dump, no showers. Boating(lr), fishing, hiking, hunting, horseback riding. 1,683 acres. GPS: 38.056885, -88.395996.

MONMOUTH (41)

Henderson County $8
State Conservation Area
20 mi SW of Monmouth; 5 mi E of Mississippi River. $8 at for 25 primitive Class C sites (free for Illinois seniors Mon-Thurs). Tbls, toilets, cfga, drkg wtr, no showers, no dump, fishing pier. Boating(l), fishing. GPS: 40.852051, -90.979736.

MURPHYSBORO (42)

Lincoln Memorial Campground $10
Johnson Creek Recreation Area
Shawnee National Forest
8 mi W of Murphysboro on SR 149. $10 base. 5/15-10/31; 14-day limit. Base fee for single RV/tent sites; double sites $12; triple sites $15. 20 sites (typically 60 ft). Tbls, flush & pit toilets, cfga, no drkg wtr, dump, beach. Fishing, swimming, boating(l), hiking, hunting, horseback riding. Near Kincaid Lake. GPS: 37.502742, -89.305857.

Turkey Bayou   FREE
Shawnee National Forest
9 mi W of Murphysboro on SR 149; left on SR 3 for 6 mi; left on Oakwood Bottom Rd for 4.3 mi; along Big Muddy River. Free. All year; 14-day limit. 5 sites. Tbls, toilets, cfga, no drkg wtr. Boating(l), fishing. GPS: 37.68306, -89.4125.

NASHVILLE (43)

Washington County $8
State Conservation Area
4 mi S of Nashville on SR 127; 1 mi E. $8 at primitive Class C sites (free to Illinois seniors Mon-Thurs). All year; 15-day limit. Tbls, flush toilets, cfga, drkg wtr, playground. Boating(l), fishing, hunting, hiking. 1,440 acres. GPS: 38.283936, -89.3479.

NAUVOO

Nauvoo State Park $8
From Hwy 96 in Nauvoo, just E on Parley St to park entrance; on E shore of Mississippi River. $8 at primitive Class C sites (free for Illinois seniors Mon-Thurs); $10 at Class B sites with showers ($5 for Illinois seniors Mon-Thurs); $25 at Class A sites with elec & showers. All year; 15-day limit. 150 sites. Tbls, flush toilets, showers, cfga, drkg wtr, playground, dump, shelters($25). Hiking trail, fishing, boating, museum. 13-acre lake. GPS: 40.5425, -91.38444.

NEWTON (44)

Sam Parr State Park $8
3 mi NE of Newton on Hwy 33. $8 at primitive Class C sites (Free to Illinois seniors Mon-Thurs). All year; 15-day limit. Tbls, pit toilets, cfga, drkg wtr, dump, no elec, no showers. Fishing, horseback riding, hunting, boating(l), hiking. 1,133 acres. GPS: 39.023193, -88.12085.

OAKVILLE (IOWA) (45)

Ferry Landing   FREE
Corps of Engineers
Mississippi River Public Use Area
6 mi from N edge of Oakville on CR X71 to levee (follow signs). Free. All year; 14-day limit. 20 primitive sites. Tbls, toilets, cfga, drkg wtr, dump. Fishing, boating(l), hiking, picnic area. GPS: 41.161621, -91.007568.

OAKWOOD (46)

Middle Fork $6
State Fish & Wildlife Area
8 mi N of I-74 from Oakwood exit. $8 at primitive Class C sites (free to Illinois seniors Mon-Thurs). All year; 14-day limit. Tbls, toilets, cfga, drkg wtr, dump, fishing pier. Hunting, canoeing, archery, trapshooting, fishing, hiking trails, canoeing, skiing, snowmobiling, 35 mi of bridle trails. Horse camping. 2,778 acres. GPS:40.197754, -87.770752.

OBLONG (47)

Oblong Village Park $10
On SR 33 in town. $10. 4/1-10/31. Tbls, flush toilets, showers, elec, dump, wtr/elec hookup at each site. Fishing, sightseeing. Oil museum nearby. Lake GPS: 39.0045, -87.9014.

OQUAWKA (48)

Delabar State Park $8
1.5 mi E of Oquawka SR 164; 1 mi N on county rd, along Mississippi River. $8 at Class C primitive sites (free to Illinois seniors Mon-Thurs). All year; 15-day limit. Tbls, flush toilets, no showers, cfga, drkg wtr, dump. Boating(l), fishing, hiking, playground. 89 acres. Near Gladstone Lake in Henderson County Conservation Area. GPS: 40.962646, -90.939453.

PECATONICA (49)

Pecatonica River $10
Forest Preserve
Winnebago County Park
About 3 mi N of Pecatonica on Pecatonica Rd; 1 mi E on Brick School Rd; on Pecatonica River. $10 base ($8 for seniors). 4/15-11/15; 10-day limit. Base fee at non-hookup sites; $15 with elec ($13 seniors). 60 sites. Tbls, toilets, cfga, drkg wtr, dump ($10 for non-campers), elec($), playground, pay phone, playground. Fishing, boating(l), canoeing, 1.5-mi interpretive nature trail, ballfield. 466 acres. GPS: 42.361544, -89.321271.

Seward Bluffs Forest Preserve $10
Winnebago County Park
About 3 mi S of Pecatonica on Jackson Rd; qtr mi W on Comly Rd. $10 base ($8 for seniors). 4/15-11/15 (winter camping by permit); 10-day limit. Base fee for non-hookup sites; $15 with elec ($13 seniors). 50 sites. Tbls, pit toilets, cfga, drkg wtr, dump ($10 fee non-campers), elec($), playground, public phone. Fishing, horseshoes, hiking, ballfield. 202 acres.

PEORIA (50)

Jubilee College State Park $8
15 mi NW of Peoria on US 150, near Kickapoo (take Kickapoo exit from I 74). $8 at Class C sites (free to Illinois seniors Mon-Thurs). 4/15-11/1; 15-day limit. Tbls, flush toilets, cfga, drkg wtr, dump, playground, fishing pier, showers. Ski trails, bridle trails, hunting, hiking, fishing, downhill skiing. Horse camping. 3,500 acres. GPS: 40.816985, -89.78833.

PINCKNEYVILLE (51)

Pyramid State Park $8
5 mi S of Pinckneyville on SR 13 & 127. $8 at primitive Class C sites (free for Illinois seniors Mon-Thurs). All year; 15-day limit. 79 sites. Tbls, toilets, cfga, drkg wtr, no showers, no elec, dump. Boating, fishing, hiking, hunting, horseback riding, canoeing. Horse camp. 2,528 acres. GPS: 38.018066, -89.414551.

RAMSEY (52)

Ramsey Lake State Park $8
1 mi N of Ramsey on US 51; 1 mi W on county rd (N of Vandalia). $8 at primitive Class C sites; (free to Illinois seniors Mon-Thurs). All year; 15-day limit. Tbls, flush & pit toilets, cfga, drkg wtr, playground, dump, showers. Hunting, horseback riding, hiking, fishing, boating(lr), canoeing. Horse camping. 1,960 acres. GPS: 39.164551, -89.135742.

ROCKDALE

Hollywood Casino Camp $12
From I-80 at Rockdale, S on SR 7 (S. Larkin Ave), then about 2 mi W on US 6 (E. Eames St) & S on Hollywood Blvd. Formerly Empress Casino. $12 winter rate but no wtr; $34

in-season full hookups. Tbls, flush toilets, cfga, drkg wtr, elec, dump, showers, coin laundry.

ROCKTON (53)

Pine Tree Campground $12
Sugar River Forest Preserve
Winnebago County Park
W of Rockton on Rockton Rd. $12 base. 4/15-11/15; 10-day limit. Base fee at primitive area; $12 at non-hookup sites ($10 for seniors); $17 with elec ($15 seniors). 100 sites. Tbls, toilets, cfga, drkg wtr, dump ($10 for non-campers), elec($), playground, showers, public phone. Canoeing, hiking trail, fishing, ballfields. 524 acres. GPS: 42.2750, -89.1423.

Winnebago Indian Campground $10
Hononegah Forest Preserve
Winnebago County Park
2 mi SE of Rockton on Hononegah Rd; on N shore of Rock River. $10 base ($8 for seniors). 4/15-11/15; 10-day limit. Base fee at non-hookup sites; $15 with elec ($13 seniors). About 70 sites. Tbls, toilets, cfga, drkg wtr, dump ($10 non-campers), elec($), playground, public phone. Boating(l), fishing, horseshoes, hiking, canoeing. Preserve once a camping area of Stephen Mack, county's first permanent white settler, and his Winnebago wife, Hononegah. 228 acres. GPS: 42.436317, -89.045992.

SALEM (54)

Stephen A. Forbes State Park $8
15 mi NE of Salem on SR 37. $8 at Class C sites (free to Illinois seniors Mon-Thurs). All year; 15-day limit. Recently renovated sites. Tbls, flush toilets, cfga, drkg wtr, beach, dump. Swimming, boating(lr), fishing, hunting, hiking, waterskiing, canoeing, horseback riding. 3,095 acres; 585-acre lake. GPS: 38.726318, -88.765381.

SAVANNA

Mississippi Palisades State Park $10
3 mi N of Savanna on SR 84; on backwater pool of Mississippi River. $10 at 137 Class B/S sites ($5 for Illinois seniors Mon-Thurs); $20 at 108 Class A elec sites ($15 for Illinois seniors Mon-Thurs). All year; 15-day limit. Tbls, flush toilets & showers 5/1-10/31, cfga, drkg wtr, dump, playground, store, phone, shelters($). Hiking trails, boating(ld), fishing. 2,500 acres. GPS: 42.14056, -90.15556.

SHELBYVILLE (55)

Lithia Springs $9
Lake Shelbyville
Corps of Engineers
3.2 mi E of Shelbyville on SR 16; 2.1 mi N on CR 2200E; 1.4 mi W following signs. $9 base with federal senior pass at 104 elec sites; others pay $18 base, $22 for full hookups ($11 with senior pass). 4/15-10/30; 14-day limit. RV limit in excess of 65 ft; 4 pull-through sites. Tbls, flush toilets, showers, cfga, drkg wtr, dump, beach, fishing pier, coin

laundry, playground, amphitheater, fish cleaning station. Swimming, boating(l), fishing, horseshoes, tennis. GPS: 39.28253, -88.4537.

Opossum Creek $8
Lake Shelbyville
Corps of Engineers
3.4 mi N of Shelbyville on SR 128; 0.9 mi E on CR 1650N; 0.5 mi S on CR 1880E; 1.2 mi E on CR 1600N. $8 with federal senior pass for 55 elec RV/tent sites; others pay $16; 12 new full hookup sites, $24 ($12 with senior pass). RV limit in excess of 65 ft. About 5/15-LD; 14-day limit. Fish cleaning station, tbls, flush toilets, showers, cfga, drkg wtr, playground, fishing pier, dump. Boating(l), fishing. 39.2652, -88.4629.

ST. DAVID (56)
Fulton County $9
Camping & Recreation Area
1.5 mi SE of St. David on SR 100. $9 base; $12 with elec. 50 sites. Tbls, flush toilets, cfga, drkg wtr, showers, dump, elec($), playground. Boating(l), fishing. 309-668-2931. GPS: 40.4916, -90.0528.

STOCKTON (57)
Apple River Canyon $8
State Park
3 mi W of Stockton on US 20; 6 mi on county rd; S of Apple River village. $8. All year; 15-day limit. 47 Class C sites (free to Illinois seniors Mon-Thurs). Tbls, flush toilets, cfga, drkg wtr, dump, store, playground, no showers. Hiking, fishing. 298 acres. 42.446045, -90.052734.

STRASBURG (58)
Hidden Springs State Forest $8
3 mi S of Strasburg on SR 32; W on county rd. $8 at 28 primitive Class C sites (free for Illinois seniors Mon-Thurs). All year; 15-day limit. Tbls, toilets, cfga, drkg wtr, dump, no showers, no elec. Fishing, hiking, hunting, archery. 1,121 acres. Forest demo area. GPS: 39.316895, -88.689453.

SULLIVAN (59)
Forrest W. "Bo" Wood $9
Lake Shelbyville
Corps of Engineers
2.6 mi S of Sullivan on SR 32; half mi W at sign. $9 base with federal senior pass for 77 elec sites; others pay $18 base, $24 for full hookups ($12 with senior pass). About 4/15-10/30; 14-day limit. Tbls, flush toilets, cfga, showers, drkg wtr, playground, fishing pier, coin laundry, dump, fish cleaning station, amphitheater. Boating(l), fishing, hiking. GPS: 39.331206, -88.3646.

THOMSON (60)
Thomson Causeway $8
Corps of Engineers
Mississippi River Public Use Area
On W edge of Thomson, 4-5 blocks W on Main St; S on Lewis Ave, following signs; on island in river's backwater. During about 4/12-10/27, $8 base with federal senior pass at 131 30/50-amp elec sites; others pay $16 base, $18 for premium locations ($9 with senior pass). Off-season, $10 for primitive sites & no amenities. 14-day limit. RV limit in excess of 65 ft; 4 pull-through sites. Tbls, toilets, cfga, drkg wtr, dump, playground, showers. Fishing, swimming, hiking, canoeing, boating(l), hunting. New & renovated shower facilities, sewer lines added, dump station renovated in 2011. GPS: 41.95167, -90.11083.

WINDSOR (61)
Wolf Creek State Park $8
8 mi NW of Windsor on E shore of Lake Shelbyville. $8 at 78 primitive Class C sites (free to Illinois seniors Mon-Thurs). All year; 15-day limit. 1,967 acres. Tbls, flush & pit toilets, cfga, drkg wtr, dump, beach. Boating(l), fishing, hiking, horseback riding, hunting, swimming. Horse camping. GPS: 39.885742, -88.689209.

WINSLOW (62)
Winslow Community Park $5
On Hwy 73 in Winslow. $5 at wtr/elec sites; $6 with A/C; $3 tent sites. All year; 6-day limit. 30-ft RV limit. Tbls, toilets, cfga, drkg wtr, dump ($2 for non-campers). 815-367-5691.

WOLF LAKE (63)
Pine Hills $10
Shawnee National Forest
1 mi N of Wolf Lake on CR 13; half mi N on FR 336. $10. 3/16-12/14; 14-day limit. 13 sites (22-ft RV limit). Tbls, toilets, cfga, no drkg wtr. Fishing. 8 acres. GPS: 37.305697, -89.252013.

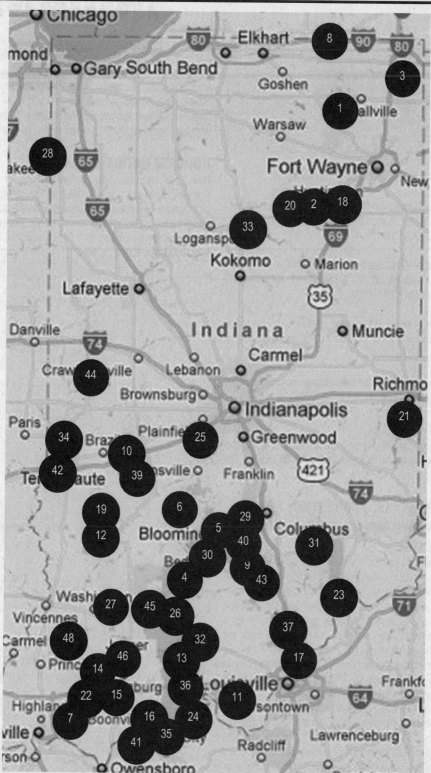

INDIANA

CAPITAL: Indianapolis
NICKNAME: Hoosier State
STATEHOOD: 1816 – 19th State
FLOWER: Peony
TREE: Tulip
BIRD: Cardinal

WWW.IN.GOV/TOURISM

Dept. of Commerce, Office of Tourism Development, State House, Suite 100, Indianapolis, IN 46204; 1-800-677-9800.

Dept. of Natural Resources, Fish and Wildlife Div., 402 W. Washington St., Room W273, Indianapolis, IN 46204. 317/232-4200.

Dept of Natural Resources, Division of Forestry, 402 W. Washington St, Room 296, Indianapolis, IN 46204. 317/232-4105.

Indiana State Chamber of Commerce, One N. Capitol, 2nd Floor, Indianapolis, IN 46204.

REST AREAS
Overnight camping is not permitted, but there are free provisions for self contained RVs at Indiana Toll Road Service Areas 1, 3, 5, 7, and 8.

STATE PARKS, RECREATION AREAS, FISH & WILDLIFE AREAS, STATE FORESTS
Campground fees are $10 to $40, depending upon when and where you camp and facilities used. Primitive sites (with table, fire ring, parking spur, central water supply and pit toilets) and backpack/canoe sites (located in remote areas with tables, fire rings and nearby water) are $10. Non-electric sites are $12 Sunday-Wednesday, $15 Thursday-Saturday. No other campsites at state-operated campgrounds qualify to be included in this book. Off-season rates are lower but vary from park to park.

State park and recreation area entry fees are $5 per vehicle for Indiana vehicles, $7 for non-Indiana vehicles. A $40 annual entrance permit is available to Indiana residents; non-residents pay $60. Indiana seniors can acquire annual permits for $20. For any-one planning to camp more than a few times in Indiana, we recommend paying the annual fee, thereby allowing base camping fees at state facilities to be kept quite low; fees listed in this book assume purchase of the annual permit. Maximum stay, 14 days. Dept. of Natural Resources, Div. of State Parks, 402 W. Washington St, W298, Indianapolis, IN 46204.

HOOSIER NATIONAL FOREST
Developed campgrounds charge $4-$23 per night. Camping in some areas is free in the off-season, but there is no water. Free backcountry camping is permitted anywhere in the forest. Forest Supervisor, Hoosier National Forest, 811 Costitution Ave., Bedford, IN 47421. 812/275-5987.

ALBION (1)

Chain O'Lakes State Park $10
5 mi S of Albion on SR 9. $10 at 33 primitive sites. All year; 14-day limit. $12 at 49 non-elec sites weekdays ($15 weekends). Also 331 elec sites. Tbls, flush & pit toilets, cfga, drkg wtr, elec($), showers, dump, playground, store. Swimming beach, boating(lrd - elec mtrs), canoeing(r), fishing, biking(r), ice skating, ski trails, nature program. 2,678 acres. GPS: 41.33310, -85.3805339.

ANDREWS (2)

Lost Bridge West $10
State Recreation Area
Salamonie Lake
10 mi S of Andrews on SR 105, then W on CR 400S; at Salamonie Lake. $10 at 38 primitive sites. All year; 14-day limit. Also 245 elec sites & horseman sites. Tbls, toilets, showers, cfga, drkg wtr, dump, picnic shelter, playground. Wtr services may be off in winter. Swimming beach, boating(lrd), fishing, winter sports, recreation program, hiking trail, cross-country & snowmobile trails, basketball, horseshoes, volleyball. GPS: 40.767822, -85.623047.

ANGOLA (3)

Pokagon State Park $12
1 mi off US 27 & I-69 on SR 727. $12 weekdays at 73 non-elec sites ($15 weekends). All year; 14-day limit. Also 200 elec sites. Flush & pit toilets, tbls, cfga, drkg wtr, dump, store, restaurant, nature center, saddle barn, beach. Boating (lrd), fishing, tennis court, winter sports, tobogganing, hiking trails, nature program, biking, horseback riding($), picnicking, ski rental. On Lake James. 1,203 acres. GPS: 41.7083836, -85.0219094.

BEDFORD (4)

Blackwell Horsecamp   FREE
Charles C. Deam Wilderness
Hoosier National Forest
5 mi E of Bedford on US 50; about 10 mi N on SR 446, then E on Tower Ridge Rd. Free. All year; 14-day limit. 100 primitive sites; no facilities, no trash service. 60 mi of bridle, hiking trails. Camping also permitted within 100 yds of Tower Ridge Rd between Hwy 446 and jct of Hickory Ridge Rd & Maumee Rd. GPS: 39.0142162, -86.3977695.

Bluegill Loop $8.50
Hardin Ridge Recreation Area
Hoosier National Forest
5 mi E of Bedford on US 50; about 11 mi N on SR 446; 2 mi E on Chapel Hill Rd, then right on Hardin Ridge access rd; Bluegill is 3rd campground on right past the gatehouse. Near E shore of Monroe Lake. $8.50 base with federal senior pass at non-elec sites; others pay $17 base, $22 for elec sites ($13.50 with senior pass); $25 for elec/wtr ($16.50 with senior pass). 4/15-10/15; 14-day limit. 51 sites (typically 40 ft). 19 acres. Non-campers pay $5 day use fee in-season. Tbls, flush toilets, cfga, drkg wtr, dump, showers, playground. Fishing, waterskiing, nature trails, swimming, boating(l), fishing pond. Visitor center. Hardin Ridge GPS: 39.019043, -86.451416.

Eads Loop $8.50
Hardin Ridge Recreation Area
Hoosier National Forest
5 mi E of Bedford on US 50; about 11 mi N on SR 446; 2 mi E on Chapel Hill Rd, then right on Hardin Ridge access rd; Eads is first campground on right past the gatehouse. Near E shore of Monroe Lake. $8.50 with federal senior pass at 23 non-elec sites; others pay $17. Non-campers pay $5 day use fee in-season. 4/15-10/15; 14-day limit. Sites 33-72 ft; 9 acres. Flush & pit toilets, cfga, drkg wtr, dump, tbls. Fishing, waterskiing, hiking, swimming, boating(l), nature trails. GPS: 39.014, -86.8310

Holland Loop $8.50
Hardin Ridge Recreation Area
Hoosier National Forest
5 mi E of Bedford on US 50; about 11 mi N on SR 446; 2 mi E on Chapel Hill Rd, then right on Hardin Ridge access rd; Holland is second campground on right past the gatehouse. Near E shore of Monroe Lake. $8.50 base with federal senior pass at non-elec sites; others pay $17 base, $22 for elec sites ($13.50 with senior pass), $25 for elec/wtr ($16.50 with senior pass). Non-campers pay $5 day use fee in-season. 4/15-10/15; 14-day limit. 13 sites 40-70 ft. Tbls, flush & pit toilets, cfga, drkg wtr, showers, elec($). Fishing, boating(l), waterskiing. GPS: 39.017822, -86.4367

Pine Loop $8.50
Hardin Ridge Recreation Area
Hoosier National Forest
5 mi E of Bedford on US 50; about 11 mi N on SR 446; 2 mi E on Chapel Hill Rd, then right on Hardin Ridge access rd; Pine is fifth campground on right past the gatehouse. Near E shore of Monroe Lake. $8.50 base with federal senior pass at non-sites without hookups; others pay $17 base, $20 for elec sites ($13.50 with senior pass), $25 for elec/wtr ($16.50 with senior pass). Non-campers pay $5 day use fee in-season. 4/15-9/15; 14-day limit. 40 sites 22-60 ft. Tbls, toilets, showers, cfga, drkg wtr, elec($), showers, store. Skiing, boating(l), hiking, fishing. GPS: 39.026611, -86.452148.

Southern Point Loop $8.50
Hardin Ridge Recreation Area
Hoosier National Forest
5 mi E of Bedford on US 50; about 11 mi N on SR 446; 2 mi E on Chapel Hill Rd, then right on Hardin Ridge access rd; Southern Point first campground on left past the work center & warehouses. Near E shore of Monroe Lake. During 4/15-9/30, $8.50 with federal senior pass at 60 non-elec sites; others pay $17. During off-season, sites

are $5 for self-service & no wtr. Non-campers pay $5 day use fee in-season. 14-day limit. Sites 30-75 ft. 32 acres. Tbls, toilets, cfga, dump, drkg wtr, showers. Fishing, waterskiing, nature trails, swimming, boating(l). GPS: 39.015137, -86.446045

White Oak Loop $8.50
Hardin Ridge Recreation Area
Hoosier National Forest
5 mi E of Bedford on US 50; about 11 mi N on SR 446; 2 mi E on Chapel Hill Rd, then right on Hardin Ridge access rd; White Oak is fourth campground on right past the gatehouse. Near E shore of Monroe Lake. $8.50 base with federal senior pass at non-elec sites; others pay $17 base, $22 for elec ($13.50 with senior pass); $25 for elec/wtr ($16.50 with senior pass). 4/15-10/15; 14-day limit. 17 sites 41-60 ft. Tbls, toilets, cfga, drkg wtr, dump, showers, elec($). Fishing, waterskiing, nature trails, swimming, boating(l). GPS: 39.0209, -86.4451

BELMONT (5)

Deckard Church Road   FREE
Hoosier National Forest
From SR 46, 1.5 mi S on Steele Rd to Gilmore Ridge Rd, then 1 mi S to Deckard Church Rd. Roadside Camping is permitted along Deckard Church Rd. Free. All year; 14-day limit. Numerous undesignated sites, no facilities.

BLOOMINGTON (6)

Hickory Ridge Rd   FREE
Mitchell Ridge Rd
Charles C. Deam Wilderness
Hoosier National Forest
From Jct SR 46 & Sr 46 Bus, 1 mi E on SR 46, then 12 mi S on SR 446 to Tower Ridge Rd (on L), 5 mi to Hickory Ridge Rd. Roadside camping is permitted anywhere along Hickory Ridge Road and adjacent Mitchell Ridge Rd. Free. All year; 14-day limit. Numerous undesignated sites, no facilities. Also, at Hickory Ridge trailhead is 20-site primitive equestrian camp with pit toilets, cfga, no drkg wtr except for stock. No roadside camping allowed on Tower Ridge Rd. GPS: 39.0217, -86.2117.

Paynetown $12
State Recreation Area
Monroe Lake
4 mi E of Bloomington on SR 46; 7 mi S on SR 446; just N of causeway, turn W on access rd; at Monroe Lake. $12 at 94 non-elec sites weekdays ($15 weekends). Also 226 elec sites. All year; 14-day limit. Tbls, toilets, cfga, drkg wtr, dump, beach, fishing pier, store, visitor center, wildlife exhibit, playground, picnic shelters, fishing cleaning station. Wtr services may be turned off in winter. Swimming, boating (ldr), fishing, winter sports, hiking trails, nature program, waterskiing, volleyball. 23,952 acres. GPS: 39.082764, -86.439453.

BRIGHTON (8)

Pigeon River   CLOSED
State Fish & Wildlife Area
3 mi SE of Brighton on Hwy 3 to Mongo, 1 mi E on CR 300N. This campground was closed in 2013 due to budget cuts.

BROWNSTOWN (9)

Jackson-Washington State Forest $10
3 mi SE of Brownstown on SR 250. $10 at 54 primitive sites. 4/28-11/3; 14-day limit. Tbls, toilets, cfga, seasonal drkg wtr, 6 shelterhouses, horseshoes, playgrounds, fishing pier. Archery range, basketball, boating (l - elec mtrs), fishing, hiking trails, 2 horseback trails, hunting, sightseeing, picnicking. 5 small fishing lakes. 18,000 acres. GPS: 38.844971, -86.052002.

CLOVERDALE (10)

Lieber State Recreation Area $12
Cagles Mill Lake
10 mi W of Cloverdale on SR 42. $12 weekdays at 96 non-elec sites ($15 weekends). 4/28/11/3; 14-day limit. Also 120 sites with elec. Tbls, flush toilets, cfga, drkg wtr, showers, dump. Wtr may be off during winter. Activity center, playground, basketball court, fishing (handicapped fishing trips available), hiking & fitness trails, horseshoes, picnicking, boating (r), swimming beach, waterskiing. 8,075 acres; 1,400-acre Cagles Mill Lake. State's largest waterfall, Cataract Falls, at E end of lake. GPS: 39.503174, -86.880371.

CORYDON (11)

Stagestop Campground $10
O'Bannon Woods State Park
Harrison-Crawford State Forest
From I-65 exit 105 at Corydon, S on SR 135, then W 7 mi on SR 62 and S on SR 462. $10 at 25 primitive sites. Also 281 elec sites & 47 non-elec horseman sites. All year; 14-day limit. Toilets, cfga, drkg wtr, dump. Fishing, hiking trails, hunting, nature center, picnicking, swimming pool, bridle trails, boating(l), canoeing(l). 2,000 acres. GPS: 38.179235, -86.305847.

DUGGER (12)

Greene-Sullivan State Forest $10
2 of Dugger on SR 159 at CR 250S. $10 at 100 primitive sites. All year; 14-day limit. Also 20 horseman campsites near Ladder Lake. Tbls, toilets, cfga, drkg wtr, dump. Boating(l - elec mtrs), fishing, horseback riding trails, hiking trails, fishing, hunting, archery range. 6,764 acres. Forest has more than 120 fishing lakes. Main camping area is at Reservoir 26. GPS: 38.986084, -87.243652.

ENGLISH (13)

Hemlock Cliffs Rec Area   FREE
Hoosier National Forest
From town, 4 mi S on SR 37 to CR 8, W 4.75 mi to CR 13,

then 0.75 mi to Hemlock Cliffs, a box canyon. Free. Camping allowed in the parking area; no camping in rock shelters. 14-day limit, no facilities. GPS: 38.1639, -86.3219.

FERDINAND (14)
Ferdinand State Forest $10
6 mi E of Ferdinand on SR 264. $10 at 77 primitive sites. All year; 14-day limit. Tbls, toilets, cfga, drkg wtr, dump, 5 picnic shelters, beach. Boating(rl - elec mtrs), swimming, fishing, horseback riding, hunting, hiking trails. 7,657 acres. Former 1934 CCC camp. GPS: 38.223145, -86.753174.

FRENCH LICK (15)
Springs Valley Recreation Area   FREE
Hoosier National Forest
2 mi S on SR 145, then 6 mi E on SR 145 following signs. Free. All year; 14-day limit. 10 sites; 47 acres at 140-acre lake. Toilets, no drkg wtr, tbls, cfga, shelter. Boating(elec motors only), boating(l), fishing. GPS: 38.4853, -86.5528.

GATCHEL (16)
Saddle Lake   FREE
Recreation Area
Hoosier National Forest
NW of Gatchel off SR 37 on FR 443. Free. All year; 14-day limit. Primitive camping. 13 sites. Tbls, toilets, cfga, no drkg wtr. Swimming, fishing, boating(l), hunting, hiking trail. GPS: 38.0639476, -86.6658187.

HENRYVILLE (17)
Clark State Forest $10
1 mi N of Henryville on US 31 (10 mi S of Scottsburg). $10 at 45 primitive sites. All year; 14-day limit. Also 26 primitive horseman sites. Tbls, toilets, cfga, drkg wtr, dump, 7 shelterhouses. Boating(l - elec mtrs), fishing, horseback & hiking trails, hunting, picnicking, gun range. 7 fishing lakes & nature preserve on 24,000 acres. GPS: 38.547607, -85.93335.

HUNTINGTON (8)
Roush Lake Fish & Wildlife Area $10
J. Edward Roush Lake
2 mi SE of Huntington on US 224; half mi S of Huntington dam. $10 at 67 primitive sites. All year; 14-day limit. Also 25 elec sites. Tbls, toilets, cfga, drkg wtr, beach, shelters, playground. Archery, basketball courts, boating(l), fishing, hiking trails, horseshoes, croquet, hunting, interpretive programs, picnicking, shooting range, swimming, volleyball, waterskiing. Radio-controlled model airplane port. Formerly called Huntington Lake. GPS: 40.8337, -85.4439.

JASONVILLE (19)
Shakamak State Park $12
3.5 mi W of Jasonville on SRs 48 & 59. $12 weekdays at 42 non-elec sites ($15 weekends). All year; 14-day limit. Also 122 sites with elec. Tbls, toilets, cfga, drkg wtr, dump, nature center, shelters, pool. Tennis, boating(lr - elec

mtrs), horseback riding (saddle barn), fishing, hiking trails, seasonal nature programs, picnicking, swimming. GPS: 39.165039, -87.231934.

LAGRO (20)
Salamonie River State Forest $10
3 mo S of Lagro on SR 524 (7 mi NE of Wabash to Lagro). $10 at 21 primitive sites. All year; 14-day limit. 15 horseman sites available. Tbls, toilets, cfga, drkg wtr, shelterhouse with ovens, playground. Boating(l - elec mtrs), fishing, 19 mi of bridle trails, hiking & cross-country ski trails, hunting, picnicking. 781 acres. GPS: 40.813477, -85.699219.

LIBERTY (21)
Whitewater Memorial State Park $12
State Park
2 mi S of Liberty on SR 101. $12 weekdays at 45 non-elec sites ($15 weekends). All year; 14-day limit. Also 37 primitive horseman sites and 236 elec sites. Tbls, toilets, cfga, drkg wtr, dump, saddle barn, store, shelters, beach. Boating(lr - elec mtrs), 7 mi of bridle trails, fishing, hiking trails, nature programs, biking(r), canoeing(r), swimming. 1,710 acres; 200-acre Whitewater Lake. GPS: 39.615049, -84.9652384.

LINCOLN CITY (22)
Lincoln State Park $10
Half mi W of Lincoln City on SR 162. $10 at 31 primitive sites; $12 at 88 non-elec sites weekdays, $15 weekends. Also 150 elec sites. All year; 14-day limit. Toilets, tbls, cfga, drkg wtr, dump, store, nature center, shelters, beach. Swimming, boating(lrd - elec mtrs), fishing, canoeing(r), hiking trails, nature program. 1,747 acres. GPS: 38.1042189, -86.9963853.

MADISON (23)
Clifty Falls State Park $12
1 mi W of Madison on SR 65 & 62. $12 weekdays at 63 non-elec sites, $15 weekends. All year; 14-day limit. Also 106 elec sites. Tbls, toilets, cfga, drkg wtr, dump, restaurant, nature center, shelters, pool. Swimming, waterslide, tennis court, hiking trails, nature program. Waterfalls nearby. GPS: 38.7595036, -85.4185697.

MAGNET (24)
Buzzard Roost Recreation Area   FREE
Hoosier National Forest
From Magnet on NW shore of Ohio River, 2mi N on Dexter-Magnet Rd, the left on CR 261; overlook of river. Free. All year; 14-day limit. 5 primitive sites. Tbls, portable toilets, no drkg wtr. GPS: 38.1215, -86.4639

MARTINSVILLE (25)
Mason Ridge Campground $10
Morgan-Monroe State Forest
6 mi S of Martinsville on SR 37; 2 mi E on Old SR 37; behind fire tower N of forest office. $10 at 35 primitive sites. All year; 14-day limit. Tbls, toilets, cfga, drkg wtr, dump, 5

shelterhouses. No wtr in winter. Boating(l - elec mtrs), fishing (4 small lakes), hiking trails (two 10-mile circular), tree identification trail. Pan for gold with permit. 24,443 acres. GPS: 39.359131, -86.461426.

MITCHELL (26)
Spring Mill State Park $10
3.5 mi E of Mitchell on SR 60. $10 at 36 primitive sites. All year; 14-day limit. Also 187 elec sites. Toilets, cfga, drkg wtr, tbls, dump, pool, store, restaurant, nature center, saddle barn. Boating(lr - elec mtrs), fishing, tennis, hiking trail, nature program, horseback riding, canoeing(r). 1,319 acres. GPS: 38.7333862, -86.4199891.

MONTGOMERY (27)
Glendale Fish & Wildlife Area $12
7.5 mi S of US 50E on CR 550E at Lake Dogwood. $12 weekdays at 54 non-elec sites, $15 weekends. Also 67 elec sites. All year; 14-day limit. Tbls, flush & pit toilets, showers, cfga, drkg wtr, elec($), dump. No wtr service 10/15-4/15; no showers & flush toilets 11/1-3/31. Fishing, boating(lrd), hunting. 8,060 acres. GPS: 38.551758, -87.043701.

MOROCCO (28)
Willow Slough $12
State Fish & Wildlife Area
4 mi W of Morocco on Hwy 114; 2 mi N. $12 weekdays at 50 non-elec sites during 5/1-9/15 ($15 weekends), $10 rest of year without showers. All year; 14-day limit. Tbls, flush toilets, showers, cfga, drkg wtr. Picnicking, fishing (J.C. Murphey Lake), boating(lr), hunting. 9,956 acres. GPS: 39.475098, -86.869385.

NASHVILLE (29)
Brown County State Park $12
2 mi SE of Nashville on SR 46; RVs use W gate; horseman entrance off 135 South. $12 weekdays at 28 non-elec sites ($15 weekends). All year; 14-day limit. Also elec & horseman sites. Tbls, flush toilets, cfga, drkg wtr, showers, dump, saddle barn, store, restaurant, nature center, shelters, pool, playground. Fishing, boating, 12 mi of hiking trails, 49 mi of bridle trails, nature programs, swimming, tennis. 15,545 acres. GPS: 39.1136605, -86.2647112.

Yellowood State Forest $10
5 mi W of Nashville on SR 46. $10 weekdays at 80 primitive sites. Also 12 horseman sites. All year; 14-day limit. Tbls, toilets, cfga, drkg wtr, visitor's center, shelterhouse. Wtr may be shut off in winter. Boating(rl - elec mtrs) fishing (3 lakes), playground, bridle trails, 5 hiking trails, hunting. Gold panning allowed with permit. 22,451 acres. 23,326 acres. GPS: 39.205078, -86.345703.

NORMAN (30)
Hickory Ridge Horse Camp   FREE
Hoosier National Forest
N of Norman on Hickory Ridge Rd. Free. All year; 14-day limit. 20 primitive sites; no facilities. 20 mi of trails for horseback riding, hiking & mountain biking. Also, roadside camping is permitted at obvious pull-offs along Hickory Ridge Rd. See Bloomington entries.

NORTH VERNON (31)
Muscatatuck $10
Jennings County Park
2 mi S on SR 7 from jct with US 50; at 325 North SR 7. $10 base. All year; 14-day limit (no wtr Nov-Apr). Base fee for 15 primitive sites; $16 for sites with elec; full hookups $23. 238 sites. Tbls, flush toilets, cfga, drkg wtr, showers, dump, playground, rec room. Horseshoes, fishing, hiking, volleyball, canoeing. GPS: 39.001041, -85.623600.

PAOLI (32)
Youngs Creek   FREE
Horse Camp
Hoosier National Forest
S of Paoli on SR 37, then W on county rd toward Springs Valley Recreation Area; N of Youngs Creek. Free. All year; 14-day limit. 50 primitive sites; no facilities except shelter, no wtr except for horses. 10 mi of trails for horseback riding, hiking, mountain biking. GPS: 38.4334, -86.5333.

PERU (33)
Miami $12
State Recreation Area
Mississinewa Lake
S of Peru on SR 19; E on CR 550S (Old Slocum Trail); N on CR 650E; on S side of lake. $12 weekdays at 57 non-elec sites ($15 weekends). All year; 14-day limit. Also 335 elec sites & 39 full hookups. Tbls, flush toilets, cfga, drkg wtr, showers, dump, hookups($). fishing pier, shelterhouse, playground, beach. Wtr may be off during winter. Swimming, boating(ldr), fishing, winter sports, hiking trails, disc golf, interpretive programs, waterskiing, volleyball. 3,210-acre lake on 14,386 acres. Primitive camping area closed due to budget cuts; Frances Slocum SRA also closed to camping. GPS: 40.70254, -85.93999.

ROCKVILLE (34)
Raccoon Lake $10
State Recreation Area
Cecil M. Hardin Lake
10 mi E of Rockville on US 36. $10 at 35 primitive sites; $12 weekdays at 37 non-elec sites ($15 weekends). All year; 14-day limit. Also 240 elec sites. Tbls, flush toilets, cfga, drkg wtr, dump, fishing pier, shelterhouses, store, playground, beach. Wtr may be off in winter. Basketball, volleyball, boating(lr), fishing, hiking trails, horseshoes, hunting, interpretive programs, picnicking, swimming, waterskiing, cross country skiing. 2,060-acre lake on 4,065 acres. GPS: 39.7495, -87.0764.

ROME (35)

German Ridge Horse Camp $4
Hoosier National Forest
Half mi W of Rome on co rd; 3.2 mi NW on SR 66; .7 mi N on CR 1002. $4. All year; 14-day limit. 20 sites (21-ft RV limit). Tbls, toilets, cfga, no drkg wtr except for horses. Swimming, fishing, picnicking, hiking, 24-mi horseback & mountain biking trails, nature trails. Visitor center. 8 acres. GPS: 37.951172, -86.589111.

ST. CROIX (36)

North Face Loop $8.50
Indian-Celina Lakes Recreation Area
Hoosier National Forest
1.5 mi S of St. Croix on Hwy 37; quarter mi W on FR 501. During 4/15-10/15, $8.50 base with federal senior pass at non-elec; others pay $17 base, $22 for elec ($13.50 with senior pass); double sites with senior pass are $15.50 non-elec, $22.50 elec. During 10/16-4/14, sites are $5 base & $8 for elec ($2.50 & $5.50 with senior pass), but no flush toilets or showers. Non-campers pay $5 day use fee. 14-day limit. 36 sites 37-60 ft. 23 acres. Tbls, toilets, cfga, drkg wtr, elec($). Boating(l), fishing, hiking (nature trails). GPS: 38.1970, -86.6062

South Slope Loop $11
Indian-Celina Lakes Recreation Area
Hoosier National Forest
1.5 mi S of St. Croix on Hwy 37; quarter mi W on FR 501. During 4/15-10/15, $11 with federal senior pass at 27 elec sites; others pay $22. During 10/16-1/5, sites are $5 base & $10 for elec ($2.50 & $5 with senior pass), but no flush toilets or showers. Non-campers pay $5 day use fee. Double sites available. 14-day limit. Sites 38-63 ft. Tbls, toilets, cfga, drkg wtr, elec($). Boating(l), fishing, hiking (nature trails). GPS: 38.1931, -86.6088

Dogwood Loop $8.50
Tipsaw Recreation Area
Hoosier National Forest
7 mi SW of St. Croix; 4.5 mi S on SR 37; 2.5 mi W on FR 503 to gatehouse. $8.50 base with federal senior pass at non-elec sites; others pay $17 base, $22 at 2 elec sites ($13.50 with senior pass). 4/1-10/15; 14-day limit. Non-campers pay $5 day use fee. 14 sites 36-52 ft. Tbls, flush toilets, cfga, drkg wtr, showers, elec($), recharge table for elec batteries, beach. Swimming, fishing, boating (l), hiking. 131-acre Tipsaw Lake. GPS: 38.115666, -86.35539

Jackpine Loop $8.50
Tipsaw Recreation Area
Hoosier National Forest
7 mi SW of St. Croix; 4.5 mi S on SR 37; 2.5 mi W on FR 503 to gatehouse. $8.50 base with federal senior pass at non-elec sites; others pay $17 base, $22 at elec sites ($13.50 with senior pass). Double sites available. 4/1-

10/15; 14-day limit. Non-campers pay $5 day use fee. 23 sites 43-57 ft. Tbls, flush toilets, cfga, drkg wtr, showers, elec($), recharge table for elec batteries, beach. Swimming, fishing, boating (l), hiking. 131-acre Tipsaw Lake. GPS: 38.11566, -86.35539

SCOTTSBURG (37)

Wooster Campground $10
Hardy Lake State Recreation Area
5 mi N of Scottsburg on I-65 to Austin exit; 5 mi E on SR 256E; 4 mi N on CR 400E. $10 at 18 primitive sites. All year; 14-day limit. Tbls, pit toilets, cfga, drkg wtr, playground. Wtr may be off during winter. Fishing, boating(l), hiking, swimming. Campers may moor boats overnight at Wooster Bay. GPS: 38.776611, -85.701904.

SHOALS (38)

Martin State Forest $10
4 mi NE of Shoals on US 50. $10 at 26 primitive sites. All year; 14-day limit. Tbls, toilets, drkg wtr, cfga. Wtr may be shut off in winter. Picnicking, hiking trails, fishing, hunting, boating (elec mtrs). 3 fishing lakes, 7,023 acres. GPS: 38.70166, -86.735596.

SPENCER (39)

McCormick's Creek State Park $10
2 mi E of Spencer on SR 46 (14 mi NW of Bloomington). $10 at 32 primitive sites. All year; 14-day limit. Also 189 elec sites. Tbls, toilets, cfga, drkg wtr, dump, restaurant, nature center, saddle barn, shelters, pool. Hiking trails, naturalist programs, picnicking, horseback riding, swimming, tennis. 1,833 acres. GPS: 39.2897675, -86.7266714.

Fish Creek Campground $10
Owen-Putnam State Forest
4.5 mi W of Spencer on Hwy 46; follow signs. $10 at 14 primitive sites. All year; 14-day limit. Tbls, toilets, cfga, drkg wtr. Fishing, bridle trails, hiking, picnicking, hunting. 6,205 acres. Several small ponds, Fish Creek. Horseman camp offers 15 large primitive sites, water trough. Forest GPS: 39.475098, -86.869385.

Rattlesnake Campground $10
Owen-Putnam State Forest
4.5 mi W of Spencer on Hwy 46; follow signs. $10 at 11 primitive sites. 4/15-11/1; 14-day limit. Tbls, toilets, cfga, drkg wtr. Fishing, bridle trails, hiking, picnicking, hunting. 6,205 acres. Several small ponds, Fish Creek. GPS: 39.399399, -86.856697

STORY (40)

Berry Ridge Rd.   FREE
Dispersed Camping Area
Wayne-Hoosier National Forest
SR 135. 2.25 mi E of Story to Mount Nebo Rd, then 1.5 mi to Berry Ridge Rd. Free. All year; 14-day limit. Numerous undesignated sites, no facilities.

TELL CITY (41)

Saddle Lake Recreation Area   FREE
Hoosier National Forest
9.5 mi NE on Hwy 37; 1 mi NW on FR 443. Free. All year; 14-day limit. 13 primitive sites (21-ft RV limit). Tbls, toilets, cfga, drkg wtr. Boating(l), fishing, hiking, swimming. 15 acres. Nature trails. No boat motors. GPS: 38.0607, -86.650

TERRE HAUTE (42)

Fowler Campground $12
Vigo County Park
7.2 mi S on US 41 from downtown Terre Haute; 0.8 mi E on Oregon Church Rd. $12 at primitive sites, $20 with elec; weekly & monthly rates available. 5/1-10/15. 81 sites (14 primitive). Tbls, flush toilets, cfga, drkg wtr, dump, playground, beach. Hiking, fishing, swimming, boating(l-rd), canoeing(r), horseshoe pits. Pioneer village. GPS: 39.3389, -87.3734

Hawthorn Campground $12
Vigo County Park
3 mi N on Hwy 46 from I-70; 1 mi E on US 40; half mi N on Stop 10 Rd; half mi W. $12 at 10 primitive sites; $20 at 75 elec sites; weekly & monthly rates available. 5/1-10/15. Tbls, flush toilets, cfga, drkg wtr, dump, playground, beach. Fishing, swimming, horseshoes, hiking. GPS: 39.2771, -87.1772

Prairie Creek Campground $12
Vigo County Park
From I-70 S of Terre Haute, 10 mi S on US 41; 4 mi W on West French Dr. $12 at primitive sites, $20 at elec sites; weekly & monthly rates available. 5/1-10/15. Tbls, flush toilets, showers, cfga, drkg wtr, dump, playground. Fishing pond, trails, ball diamond, multi-purpose court, tennis courts, horseshoe pits. GPS: 40.1462, -85.2933

VALLONIA (43)

Starve Hollow $10
State Recreation Area
3 mi S of Vallonia on SR 135. $10 at 20 primitive sites. Also 55 full hookup & 98 elec sites. Flush toilets, cfga, drkg wtr, showers, tbls, dump, nature center, shelterhouses, beach. Wtr may be off in winter. Swimming, boating(lr - elec mtrs), canoeing(r), fishing, hiking trails, picnicking, volleyball, softball, baseball. 300 acres; 145-acre lake. GPS: 38.81665, -36.07666.

WAVELAND (44)

Shades State Park $12
4 mi N of Waveland on SR 47 & SR 234 (17 mi SW of Crawfordsville). $12 weekdays at 105 non-elec sites ($15 weekends). All year; 14-day limit. Tbls, flush toilets, showers, cfga, drkg wtr, dump. Wtr service may be off in winter. Fishing, hiking trails, biking, playground, horseback riding, recreation program, shelters. 3,084 acres. GPS: 39.9417095, -87.0916766.

WEST BADEN SPRINGS (45)

Shirley Creek Horse Camp   FREE
Hoosier National Forest
From West Baden Springs, W on US 150, then N on forest rd toward village of Bonds; left following signs. Free. All year; 14 day limit. 40 primitive sites; no facilities. 16 mi of trails for horseback riding, hiking, mountain biking. GPS: 38.6494973, -86.5974927.

WICKLIFFE (46)

Newton-Stewart $10
State Recreation Area
Patoka Lake
On SR 164 N of Wickliffe. $10 at 45 primitive sites. Also 455 elec sites. All year; 14-day limit. Tbls, toilets cfga, drkg wtr, dump, shelterhouses, visitor center, beach. Wtr may be off in winter. Archery range, boating(l), cross-country skiing, fishing, disc golf, hiking & fitness trails, bike trails, hunting, interpretive programs, picnicking, swimming, waterskiing. 25,800 acres; 8,800-acre lake. GPS: 38.399902, -86.658447.

WINSLOW (48)

Pike State Forest $10
S of Winslow on SR 61; 4 mi E on SR 264. $10 at 11 primitive sites. Also 29 horseman sites. All year; 14-day limit. Tbls, toilets, cfga, drkg wtr, horse camp shelters. 7 mi of bridle trails, 15 mi of hiking trails, fishing, hunting, picnicking. 2,914 acres. GPS: 38.360352, -87.157471.

Northwood Otranto Stacyville
Saint Ansgar
Mitchell
Osage
Cresco Bluffton

Rock Falls
Mason City
Floyd Colwell Jerico Calmar
North Washington
Lawler
Rockwell Ionia New Hampton
Thornton Marble Rock Nashua Fredericksburg West Union Marquette
Sheffield Greene Hawkeye Elgin McGregor
Frederika
Plainfield Sumner Fayette Elkader Garnavillo
Clarksville Maynard Guttenberg
Hampton Dumont Shell Rock Waverly
Oelwein Strawberry Point
Hazleton Aurora Colesburg
Popejoy Ackley Parkersburg New Hartford Dunkerton
Alden Iowa Falls Cedar Falls Dubuque
Wellsburg Dike Evansdale Jesup Winthrop Manchester Dyersville
Steamboat Rock Quasqueton Delhi
Eldora Grundy Center
Reinbeck Brandon Cascade
New Providence Union Urbana Bellevue
Gladbrook Traer Vinton
Albion Anamosa
Viola Center Junction
Baldwin Maquoketa
Blairstown Mount Vernon
Baxter Toronto
Lowden Calamus Clinton
Newton Kellogg Solon Tipton Bennett Camanche
Mitchellville North Liberty
Iowa City
Montezuma Millersburg
Hills
South English Wellman Lone Tree
Pella Muscatine
Knoxville Oskaloosa Sigourney Fredonia
Washington
Ollie Wapello
Eddyville Brighton Coppock
Williamson Morning Sun Oakville
Chariton Albia Fairfield Kingston
Lockridge Mount Pleasant Dodgeville
Moravia Stockport Lowell Danville
Mystic Drakesville Keosauqua Augusta
Allerton Centerville Bloomfield Bonaparte
Cantril Farmington

IOWA

WWW.TRAVELIOWA.COM

Iowa Division of Tourism, Department of Economic Development, 200 E. Grand Ave., Des Moines, IA 50309. 515/725-3084 or 800-472-6035.

CAPITAL: Des Moines
NICKNAME: Hawkeye State
STATEHOOD: 1846 – 29th State
FLOWER: Wild Rose
TREE: Oak
BIRD: Eastern Goldfinch

STATE PARKS

Basic camping rates are $6 per night off-season (the Tuesday after Labor Day through the Sunday prior to Memorial Day) and $9 in-season for non-modern sites (those without flush toilets and showers) that do not have electricity. Other typical fees:

Non-modern sites (without flush toilets and showers) are $14 ($11 off-season) with electric.

Modern sites (flush toilets and showers) with electric are $16 ($13 off-season). Modern sites without electricity are $11 ($8 off-season).

Remember, sites with electricity are $5 higher, and the fee must be paid for electricity whether or not the service is used. A maximum of two weeks camping is allowed in an area. At 12 state parks, peak seasonal fees are in effect through Oct. 31 or until showers are closed for the season. Pets on leashes are permitted. Department of Natural Resources, 502 East 9th St, Des Moines, IA 50319. 515/281-5918.

COUNTY CONSERVATION PROGRAM

Of Iowa's 99 counties, 98 have created county conservation boards which are authorized to auire, develop and maintain areas devoted to conservation and public recreation. Parks, wildlife areas, river accesses, recreation areas and museums are included in this program. The conservation boards also serve as primary natural resource management agencies, help educate local residents about environmental issues and manage county wildlife conservation efforts. When traveling, watch for arrowhead signs which direct you to a county areas under jurisdiction of the Iowa Association of County Conservation Boards. Most of the county areas which offer free or low-cost camping are included in this book. Some do not make information about their facilities and fees readily avilable to the public, so some of those are not included here.

CORPS OF ENGINEERS

Although camping fees have changed dramatically at Corps of Engineers parks during the last couple of years, some new policies also benefit campers. All Corps of Engineers campgrounds are listed in this edition because even those with fees higher than $12 provide low-cost sites to older Americans who have federal America the Beautiful Senior Passes or Golden Age Passports. Corps of Engineers, Kansas City District, 700 Federal Bldg, Kansas City, MO 64106.

ACKLEY (E)

Prairie Bridges Municipal Park $10

In Ackley, from Hwy 20 (Sherman St) & CR S-56 (Franklin/
Wren), qtr mi N on S-56. $10 at primitive RV sites with
elec, no wtr; $15 with 30/50-amp elec/wtr; tent sites $7.
5/15-11/15. 30 basic sites, 120 total; some pull-through.
Tbls, flush toilets, cfga, drkg wtr, showers, dump ($5 for
non-campers). 120 total sites (32-ft RV limit). Biking/walk-
ing trails, fishing, canoeing, interpretive signs, boating(d),
new enclosed shelter.

ADEL (W)

Dallas County Fairgrounds $10
Dallas County Fair Association

On N side of Adel just off Hwy 169. $10 non-elec sites;
$14 with elec/wtr, $20 full hookups. 80 total hookups.
4/1-10/31 (closed to public 7/6-7/14). Flush toilets, tbls,
cfga, dump, showers, playground.

AFTON (W)

Three Mile Lake Recreation Area $10
Union County Conservation Board

From jct with US 169 just N of Afton, left (NW) 1 mi on
US 34; 2 mi N on Creamery Rd (CR P53); W on CR H33 to
access rd; at W shore of Three Mile Lake. $10 at non-elec
sites, $17 at 80 elec sites (20/30/50-amp). Two camp-
grounds (South & Mallard Point). All year. Tbls, flush toilets, cfga, drkg wtr, showers, dump, fish cleaning station,
beach. Fishing, boating(l), swimming. 24 mi of shoreline.

AKRON (W)

Akron City Park $10
Akron Parks & Recreation Department

On N side of Akron along SR 12; E on City Park Dr. $10. 5/1-
10/15; 7-day limit. 17 elec sites. Tbls, flush toilets, cfga,
drkg wtr (1 hydrant), 30-amp elec, showers at pool house.
Fishing, swimming, tennis, golf, hiking trail, horseshoes.

ALBIA (E)

Georgetown Rest Area FREE
Monroe County Conservation Board

9 mi W of Albia on US 34. Free. Primitive camping. Toilets,
tbls, cfga, no drkg wtr. Picnicking. 3 acres.

Miami Lake Park $11
Monroe County Conservation Board

6 mi N of Albia (5 mi E of Lovilia). $11 for sites with elec;
$16 full hookups; tents $6. 5/1-9/30; no wtr off-season.
65 sites. Tbls, flush toilets, cfga, drkg wtr, showers, dump,
shelters($). Picnicking, fishing, boating(ld), hunting. Out-
door education center 879 acres; 135-acre lake.

ALBION (E)

Timmons Grove Park $12
Marshall County Conservation Board

1 mi S of Albion on Hwy 330; both sides of Iowa River
(camping on S segment). $12 at 18 30-amp elec sites.
Tbls, toilets, cfga, drkg wtr, playground. Hiking trail, boat-
ing(l), fishing, shelter.

ALDEN (E)

Circle C Campground $12

On CR D20 between Iowa Falls and Alden, along the Iowa
River. $12 for elec/wtr; $14 full hookups. 27 sites. Tbls,
toilets, cfga, drkg wtr, dump. Fishing, canoeing, boating.

ALGONA (W)

Ambrose A. Call State Park $6

1.5 mi SW of Algona on SR 274. $6 base. All year; 14-day
limit. Base fee for 3 non-modern sites without elec
off-season ($9 rest of year); $11 for 13 non-modern sites
with elec off-season ($14 rest of year). Tbls, toilets, cfga,
drkg wtr, elec($5). Picnicking, hiking trails, interpretive
trail, playground. Enclosed group shelter (by reservation)
with elec, wtr, toilets, cookstoves, refrigerator. 130 acres.

ALLERTON (E)

Bobwhite State Park $10
Wayne County Conservation Board

1 mi W of Allerton on SR 40; at E shore of Bobwhite
Lake. $10. 4/1-12/1; 14-day limit. 30 elec/wtr sites ($150
monthly). Tbls, toilets, cfga, drkg wtr, elec($5). Picnicking,
swimming, fishing, hiking trails, interpretive trail, boat-
ing(l), shelter. 398 acres; 89-acre lake. Park now managed
by Wayne County.

ALTON (W)

Alton Roadside Park $10
Sioux County Park

Jct of Hwys 60 & 16 half mi N of Alton. $10. All year. 4 elec
sites. Tbls, flush toilets, cfga, drkg wtr, enclosed shel-
ter($), showers, dump. Picnicking, fishing, playground,
canoeing, disc golf. 11 acres; 5-acre lake.

ANAMOSA (E)

Wapsipinicon State Park $9

3.5 mi SW of Anamosa on US 151. $9 base. All year; 14-day
limit. Base fee for 12 modern sites without elec off-season; $11 rest of year; $13 for 14 modern sites with elec
off-season ($16 rest of year). Tbls, flush toilets, showers,
cfga, drkg wtr, no dump. Interpretive trail, hiking, boat-
ing(l), fishing, caving, golf. 390 acres.

ANDALUSIA (ILLINOIS)

Andalusia Slough $10
Corps of Engineers
Mississippi River Public Use Area
Lock & Dam 16

2 mi W of Andalusia off IL 92. $10 self-registration during
5/15-10/15; free rest of year. All year; 14-day limit. 16
road-style primitive sites.; some pull-through. Tbls, pit
toilets, cfga, drkg wtr. Swimming, boating(l), fishing,
picnicking. 10 acres.

ANITA (W)
Lake Anita State Park $8
Half mi S of Anita on SR 148. $8 base. All year; 14-day limit. Base fee for 52 modern sites without elec off-season ($11 rest of year); $13 for 52 modern sites with elec off-season ($16 rest of year); 40 sites have full hookups at $19. Tbls, flush toilets, cfga, drkg wtr, dump, shower. Interpretive trail, swimming, fishing (jetty), boating(l), playground. 182-acre lake.

ARMSTRONG (W)
Iowa Lake Wildlife Area $10
Emmet County Conservation Board
6 mi N of Armstrong on Hwy 15; W on 110th St. $10 (or $60 weekly). 4/1-11/1. Primitive camping at 16-acre area with 802-acre lake. Water hookups, cfga, tbls, toilets, fish cleaning station. Hiking trails, boating(ld), fishing.

ASHTON (W)
Ashton Pits Area FREE
Wildlife Management Area
Osceola County Conservation Board
NE edge of Ashton. Free. Undeveloped primitive camping. No facilities. Hiking trails, fishing, boating, hunting.

AUBURN (W)
Grant Park $12
Sac County Conservation Board
From US 71 at Auburn, 1.5 mi N on Xavier Ave; qtr mi W on 360th St to park entrance; at N shore of North Raccoon River. $12 base. 4/1-10/15; 14-day limit. Base fee for primitive sites; $17 at RV sites with any hookups (30/50-amp). 25 full-hookup sites & several primitive sites. Tbls, flush toilets, cfga, showers, drkg wtr hookups, elec($), dump. Hiking & bridle trails, playground, fishing, hunting, canoeing, horseshoe pits. Historic site. 98 acres.

AUGUSTA (E)
Sycamore Loop $8
Weiter Recreation Park
Lower Skunk River Area
Des Moines County Conservation Board
Half mi E of Augusta on Hwy 394 (Skunk River Rd). $8 for 6 primitive sites; $15 for 12 sites with elec. Seniors pay $5 for non-elec sites, $10 for elec. 4/1-11/1; 14-day limit. Tbls, toilets, cfga, drkg wtr, dump. Picnicking, hiking trails, fishing, boating, hunting, canoeing, horseshoes, volleyball. 86 acres. Non-campers pay $5 for dump station.

Cottonwood Loop $8
Weiter Recreation Park
Upper Skunk River Area
Des Moines County Conservation Board
1 mi NW of Augusta; along Skunk River. $8 at 6 primitive sites (seniors pay $5). Toilets, tbls, cfga, no drkg wtr. Dump at Sycamore Loop. Hiking trails, fishing, boating(l), canoeing, hunting. 16 acres.

Maple Loop $8
Weiter Recreation Park
Lower Augusta Sunk River Area
Des Moines County Conservation Board
In Augusta, on E edge along Skunk River. $8 at 10 primitive sites (seniors pay $5). Tbls, toilets, cfga, drkg wtr, no elec. Dump at Sycamore Loop. Hiking trails, fishing, boating, canoeing. 16 acres. On shore of Skunk River.

AURELIA (W)
Larson Lake $5
Cherokee County Conservation Board
From 2 mi N of Aurelia at jct with SR 2, 3 mi E on SR 3; 1.5 mi S on gravel 10th Ave; left on access rd to park. $5. 5/1-10/31. 5 primitive sites. Tbls, toilets, cfga, drkg wtr, shelters, playground. Picnicking, fishing, boating. 12 acres; 5-acre lake, former gravel pit.

AURORA (E)
Jakway Forest Area $12
Buchanan County Conservation Board
1.5 mi S of Aurora on CR W45; at Buffalo Creek. $12 without hookups, $18 with elec. 4/15-10/15, weather permitting; 14-day limit. 40 sites. Tbls, flush toilets, cfga, drkg wtr, showers, dump, elec($), playground, beach. Picnicking, swimming, boating, hiking trails, fishing, hunting, cross-country skiing. Historic site. 315 acres.

BALDWIN (E)
Eden Valley Refuge $10
Clinton County Conservation Board
2 mi S of Baldwin on 50th Ave; at Bear Creek. $10 at non-electric sites; $15 with elec. All year; 14-day limit. Also 30 free primitive sites for backpackers. Tbls, pit toilets, cfga, drkg wtr. Hiking, cross-country skiing, picnicking, hiking trails, nature center, observation tower, swinging bridge. 201 acres.

BATTLE CREEK (W)
Crawford Creek Recreation Area $12
Ida County Conservation Board
2 mi S of Battlecreek on CR L51. $12 without hookups; $17 at 37 sites with elec. 4/1-10/30; 14-day limit. 40-ft RV limit. Tbls, flush toilets, showers, cfga, drkg wtr, elec($), dump, playground, beach, shelters. Swimming, fishing, boating(ld), hunting. Facilities for handicapped. 260 acres. At N side of 62-acre Crawford Creek Lake.

BAXTER (E)
Ashton Wildwood Park $7
Jasper County Conservation Board
7 mi W of Baxter on CR F-17; S on W. 122nd St; entrance next to Ashton Chapel. $7. All year; 14-night limit in 17-day period. Self-contained RVs. Drkg wtr, cfga, toilets. Hiking trails, golf course, astronomy observatory. 113 acres.

BEDFORD (W)

Lake of Three Fires State Park $8
3 mi NE of Bedford on SR 49. $8 base off-season at 110 modern sites without elec ($11 rest of year); $13 off-season at 30 modern sites with elec ($16 rest of year). 22 equestrian sites, 8 with elec, available. Tbls, flush toilets, showers, cfga, drkg wtr, dump. Interpretive trail, hiking, horseback riding (15 holding pens), swimming, fishing, boating(l). 85-acre lake.

BELLEVUE (E)

Bellevue State Park $6
2.5 mi S of Bellevue on US 52. $6 base off-season at non-modern sites without elec ($9 rest of year); $11 off-season at non-modern sites with elec ($14 rest of year; $8 off-season at modern sites without elec ($11 rest of year); $13 at modern sites off-season with elec ($16 rest of year). 46 sites (31 with elec). Tbls, flush toilets, showers, cfga, drkg wtr, dump. Hiking, fishing, boating (lr), playground, nature center. 547 acres.

Pleasant Creek Recreation Area $12
Corps of Engineers
Mississippi River Public Use Area
Lock & Dam 12
3.5 mi S of Bellevue on US 52, following signs; on river's main channel. $12 during 5/15-10/15 ($6 with federal senior pass); free rest of year; 14 day limit. 55 primitive sites. Tbls, flush toilets, cfga, drkg wtr, dump. Boating(l), fishing, waterskiing. Self-registration. 32 acres.

BELMOND (W)

Pikes Timber FREE
Wright County Conservation Board
3 mi S of Belmond on US 69; 2 mi W on CR C25; 0.25 mi S on Quincy Ave; at W shore of Iowa River. Free. 4 primitive sites with elec. Tbls, toilets, cfga, well drkg wtr. Fishing, canoeing, picnicking. 46 acres.

Iowa River RV Park $10
Belmond City Park
In Belmond, 3 blocks S of Main St on US 69; at 312 River Ave South. $10 for wtr/elec, $12 full hookups; $8 tents. All year. 16 RV sites, 8 with full hookups; 5 pull-through. Tbls, flush toilets, cfga, showers, drkg wtr, dump.

BENNETT (E)

Bennett Park $7
Cedar County Conservation Board
2 mi E of Bennett on Hwy 130. $7 for primitive camping; $10 with elec. 20 sites. Tbls, toilets, cfga, drkg wtr, shelters, playground. Fishing, baseball field, winter sports, volleyball, hiking trails, horseshoes, picnicking, bluebird trail. 75 acres.

BLAIRSTOWN (E)

Hannen Park $10
Benton County Conservation Board
1 mi S of Blairstown on CR V56; 0.5 mi W on CR E68; 2.5 mi S on 20th Ave; 0.5 mi W on Benton Iowa Rd. $10 base, no hookups; $15 for sites with elec. Mar-Nov; 14-day limit; limited facilities in winter. 98 elec sites. Flush toilets, tbls, cfga, drkg wtr, dump, elec ($), handicapped facilities, store. Boating(lr), swimming beach, fishing, playground, swimming, winter sports. Restaurant. 180 acres; 50-acre lake.

BLENCOE (W)

Huff-Warner Access Area $12
Monona County Conservation Board
2.5 mi SW of Blencoe on Filbert Ave. 55 mi N of Council Bluffs on I-29, exit 105; 3 mi W, follow signs; at Missouri River. $12 without hookups, $15 elec. All year; 14-day limit. About 25 scattered sites on 5.6 acres. Tbls, cfga, drkg wtr, dump, pit toilets. Boating(l), fishing, picnicking, canoeing.

BLOCKTON (W)

Sand's Timber Recreation Area $5
Taylor County Conservation Board
About qtr mi W of Blockton on CR J55, then follow signs qtr mi N on Yellowstone Ave & W onto access rd. $5 at primitive sites, $10 at 7 modern sites. Tbls, toilets, cfga, drkg wtr. Fishing, boating, hiking trail, hunting. 76-acre lake.

BLOOMFIELD (E)

Lake Fisher City Park $10
2 mi NW of Bloomfield on Jaguar Tr, left on W. Lake Fisher Rd to park. $10 at 6 sites with elec; tent sites $5. Tbls, toilets, cfga, drkg wtr. Fishing, boating. 100-acre lake was built in 1936 as a WPA project.

Pioneer Ridge Nature Area $8
Wapello County Conservation Board
About 6 mi N of Bloomfield on US 63 (6 mi S of Ottumwa); right on access rd. $8 at 3 primitive sites (all 3 sites for group, $20); 9 elec sites $12. All year; 14-day limit. Tbls, flush toilets, cfga, drkg wtr, picnic shelter. Multi-use trails, nature center with interpretive displays & programs; 4 fishing ponds, bird observation blind.

BLUFFTON (E)

Chimney Rock Park FREE
Winneshiek County Conservation Board
2.5 mi N of Bluffton on gravel Chimney Rock Rd (10 mi NW of Decorah). Free. All year. Undeveloped primitive camping. Toilets, tbls, cfga no drkg wtr. Fishing, boating, picnicking, canoeing. 17 acres. Canoe-access camping for Upper Iowa River (one day downstream from Kendalville).

BONAPARTE (E)
Des Moines River Public Access   FREE
Van Buren County Conservation Board
3 mi SE of Bonaparte. Free. Undeveloped primitive camping on 8 acres. No facilities. Fishing, boating.

BOONE (W)
Ledges State Park $8
6 mi S of Boone on SR 164. $8 off-season at 42 modern non-elec sites ($11 rest of year); $13 off-season at modern sites with elec ($16 rest of year). Tbls, flush toilets, cfga, drkg wtr, showers, dump. Interpretive trail, hiking, fishing, playground. 176 acres.

BRADDYVILLE (W)
Ross Park   FREE
Page County Recreation Area
From Braddyville, 1 mi E on 320th St; 2 mi N on Teak Ave; 1.5 mi E on 300th St; at S shore of Buchanan Creek. Free. 4/15-10/15; 14-day limit. Primitive campsites. Cfga, toilets, no drkg wtr. Fishing, hiking, picnicking. Two 6 acre ponds on 76-acre reclaimed quarry.

BRANDON (E)
Lime Creek Area $8
Buchanan County Conservation Board
From jct with SR 283 just E of Brandon, 1 mi NE on Brandon Diagonal Blvd; at shore of Lime Creek. $8 base without hookups; $14 with elec. 4/15-10/1; 14-day limit. 25 sites. Tbls, toilets, cfga, drkg wtr, elec($), playground, beach, pool($). Picnicking, swimming, fishing, boating, hunting, biking. 45 acres.

BRIDGEWATER (W)
Mormon Trail Park $6
Adair County Conservation Board
1 mi S of Bridgewater on 280th St; right on Delta Ave to park. $6 base at 5 non-elec sites; $9 at 15 elec sites. 4/15 10/30; free rest of year, but no wtr; 14-day limit. 20 sites (15 with elec). Tbls, pit toilets, cfga, drkg wtr, playground, beach. Picnicking, fishing, boating(ld), swimming, hunting. Historic site. 35-acre lake on 170 acres.

BRIGHTON (E)
Brinton Timber Park   FREE
Washington County Conservation Board
3 mi W of Brighton on SR 78; 2 mi N on CR W21; in wildlife refuge along Skunk River. Free. Undeveloped primitive camping. Toilet, tbls, no other facilities. Hiking & bridle trails, fishing. 320 acres.

Lake Darling State Park $8
3 mi W of Brighton on SR 78. $8 base off-season at 36 modern sites without elec ($11 rest of year); $13 off-season at 66 modern sites with elec ($16 rest of year), 15 with full hookups ($19). Tbls, flush toilets, cfga, drkg

wtr, showers, dump, elec($5). Interpretive trail, hiking, swimming, fishing (jetty), boating(lr), hunting, playground, mountain biking.

McKain River Access   FREE
Washington County Conservation Board
36 mi W of Brighton on SR 78; 5 mi N on CR W21 at Skunk River. Free. All year. Primitive undesignated sites. Tbls, pit toilet, cfga, drkg wtr. Picnicking, fishing, boating, hunting. 10 acres.

CALAMUS (E)
Sherman Park $12
Clinton County Conservation Board
1.5 mi W of Calamus on SR 30; follow signs S to Wapsipinicon River. $12 primitive sites, $15 elec. 5/1-11/1; 14-day limit. 20 primitive sites; 8 new RV sites. Tbls, pit toilets, cfga, drkg wtr, playground. Fishing, boating(l), hiking, cross-country skiing, canoeing. 231 acres. Star-gazing events at observatory.

CALMAR (E)
Lake Meyer $10
Winneshiek County Conservation Board
2.5 mi SW of Calmar on SR 24; 1 mi W on gravel rd; at 2546 Lake Meyer Rd. $10 at 8 non-elec sites; $15 at 19 elec sites. 4/1-10/31. Tbls, flush toilets, cfga, drkg wtr, elec, dump, showers, shelters, playground. Cross-country & hiking trails, fishing, boating(dl), nature center, ball field, ranger programs, picnicking. 160 acres.

CAMANCHE (E)
Rock Creek Marina $10
Clinton County Park
2 mi S of Camanche on US 67, then E following signs; on at jct with Wapsipinicon River. $10 at 30 primitive sites, $15 at 38 elec sites ($18 at reserved elec sites). 5/1-11/15; 14-day limit. Tbls, flush & pit toilets, cfga, drkg wtr, elec($), dump, showers, fish cleaning station, coin laundry, playgrounds, store. Fishing, boating(rdl). Concession. 75 acres.

CANTRIL (E)
Waubonsie Trail Park $10
Municipal Campground
Just NW of downtown Cantril at jct of SR 2 & CR V64. $10 at primitive sites; $16 at elec/wtr sites; $18 at 11 full hookups. Apr-Nov. Tbls, flush toilets, cfga, drkg wtr, showers, playground, shelters. Hiking trails, disc golf. 25 acres; 3 covered bridges.

CARROLL (W)
Swan Lake State Park $10
Carroll County Conservation Board
1 mi S of Carroll on US 71; 1 mi E on 220th St. $10 at primitive sites; $16 elec/wtr; $19 full hookups. 4/15-10/30. 120 sites. Tbls, flush toilets, cfga, drkg wtr, showers, dump ($3

for non-campers), shelters, beach, store, wildlife areas, wireless Internet service. Boating(ldr), horseshoes, swimming, fishing, hiking trails (3.8 mi paved), cycle trails, naturalist programs, farmstead museum, Conservation Education Center. Sauk Rail Trail connects with Black Hawk State Park. 510 acres; 110-acre lake.

CASCADE (E)

Fillmore Recreation Area $12
Dubuque County Conservation Area
6 mi E of Cascade on US 151. All year; 14-day limit. $12 base for 25 primitive sites; $15 at 4 sites with 20-amp elec; $17 at 8 sites with 30-amp elec. 4/15-11/1; 14-day limit. 30-ft RV limit; 116 acres. Flush toilets, cfga, tbls, drkg wtr, elec($), showers, shelter, golf course, dump, playground. 9-hole golf, hiking trails, stream fishing, baseball field, horseshoes, restaurant. Non-campers pay $12 at dump station.

CASEY (W)

Abram Rutt Park & Campground $10
Casey Municipal Park
From I-89 exit 83 just S of Casey, 1 mi N on Antique Country Dr, becoming McPherson St; right on E. 3rd St, then right into park, following signs. $10 at RV sites with elec (one 30-amp, others 20-amp); tents $10. 5/1-9/15. About 6 undesignated sites; 2 for large rigs. Tbls, flush toilets, cfga, elec, playground. Drkg wtr, dump, showers at bath house.

CEDAR FALLS (E)

George Wyth State Park $8
At US 218 & SR 57 between Waterloo & Cedar Falls. $8 off-season at 22 modern sites without elec ($11 rest of year); $13 off-season at 46 modern sites with elec ($16 rest of year). Tbls, flush toilets, showers, cfga, drkg wtr, dump, elec($5). Interpretive trail, hiking, biking trails, swimming, fishing (pier), boating(lr), playground. 300-acre lake.

CENTER JUNCTION (E)

Central Park $10
Jones County Conservation Board
From jct with SR 38 just N of Center Junction, 1 mi W on 130th St; right on access rd. $10 base. 4/15-10/15 (primitive camping all year); 14-day limit. Base fee for primitive sites; $14 with elec; $16 elec/wtr; $18 full hookups. 100 sites. Tbls, flush toilets, cfga, drkg wtr, dump, phone, playground, dump ($2 fee). Horseshoes, hiking trails, volleyball, boating (I - elec mtrs), fishing, baseball, horseback riding, paddleboats(r), horseshoes, nature center, swimming beach. Historic site. 297 acres; 25-acre lake.

CENTERVILLE (E)

Lelah Bradley Preserve $12
Appanoose County Conservation Board
From SW edge of Centerville, W on Cottage St from S. Main

St; at 180-acre Centerville Reservoir. $12 without hookups; $15 with elec. All year; 14-day limit. 12 modern sites. Tbls, toilets, cfga, drkg wtr. Boating(l), fishing, picnicking, hiking. 43 acres; 180-acre lake.

Sharon Bluffs State Park $12
Appanoose County Conservation Board
2.5 mi E of Centerville on SR 2; 0.5 mi S on 248th Ave; E on access rd 520th St. $12 base. All year; 14-day limit. Base fee for primitive sites; $15 with elec. 8 sites; 40-ft RV limit. Tbls, pit toilets, cfga, drkg wtr, dump, elec($). Boating(l), fishing, hiking, nature center. 144 acres.

CHARITON (E)

Broadhead Woods   FREE
Lucas County Conservation Board
From Chariton, 1.5 mi W on US 34; 2 mi N on SR 23; 1 mi NW on 505th Lane, then right on 185th Trail into park; at White Breast Creek. Free. Primitive camping on 40 acres; no facilities. Hiking, hunting.

Red Haw State Park $8
1 mi E of Chariton on US 34. $8 off-season at 21 modern sites without elec ($11 rest of year); $13 off-season at 58 modern sites with elec ($16 rest of year). Tbls, flush toilets, showers, cfga, drkg wtr, dump, elec($5). Interpretive trail, hiking, swimming, fishing, boating(lr), playground. 72-acre lake.

CHEROKEE (W)

Silver Sioux Recreation Area $10
Cherokee County Conservation Board
5 mi S of Cherokee on US 59; 2 mi W on gravel Silver Sioux Rd; near confluence of Silver Creek & Little Sioux River. $10 for 11 primitive sites; $15 for 32 RV sites with 30-amp elec/wtr. 5/1-10/31. RVs under 25 ft. Tbls, toilets, cfga, drkg wtr, elec($), dump, shelters, playground. Picnicking, fishing, boating(l), hunting, cross-country ski & hiking trails. 160 acres.

CHURDAN (W)

Hyde Park $8
Greene County Conservation Board
5 mi W of Churdan on CR E19; 2 mi S on CR N65. $8 at primitive sites, $10 elec. All year. 28 elec sites (30-ft RV limit), unlimited primitive sites. Tbls, toilets, cfga, drkg wtr, dump, shelter, playground. Boating(l), fishing, picnicking. 57 acres at Raccoon River.

CLARINDA (W)

Nodaway Valley Park $6
Page County Conservation Board
From jct with SR 2 E of Clarinda, 2 mi N on US 71. $6 at 2 primitive sites; $12 at 4 pull-through sites with 30-amp wtr/elec; $15 at 8 sites with 50-amp elec/wtr. All year; 14-day limit (no wtr in winter). 56-ft RV limit. Tbls, toilets,

cfga, playground, dump. Multi-use trails, picnicking, fishing.

Pioneer Park $6
Page County Conservation Board
5.5 mi W of Clarinda on SR 2 (E of Shenandoah). $6 at 2 non-elec primitive sites; $15 at 10 elec/wtr 50-amp sites. All year; 14-day limit (no wtr in winter). Tbls, flush toilets, cfga, showers, shelter, playground. Picnicking, fishing. 22 acres; 2-acre pond.

CLARKSVILLE (E)
Heery Woods State Park $10
Butler County Conservation Board
On S edge of Clarksville (2.5 mi N on Hwy 188 from jct with Hwy 3); at Shell Rock River. $10 without hookups ($60 weekly); $12 at 30 sites with 30/50-amp elec ($72 week-ly). All year; 14-day limit. Tbls, flush toilets, cfga, drkg wtr, showers, playground. Picnicking, fishing, hiking & horseback trails, paved bike trail, interpretive trail. Nature Center. 380 acres. Camp free Wed nights.

CLEAR LAKE (W)
Clear Lake State Park $8
2 mi SW of Clear Lake on SR 107. $8 off-season at 8 mod-ern sites without elec ($11 rest of year); $13 off-season at 168 modern sites with elec ($16 rest of year). Tbls, flush toilets, showers, cfga, drkg wtr, dump, elec($5). Inter-pretive trail, biking trail, swimming, fishing, boating (lr), playground. 3,684-acre lake. 900-ft sandy beach.

McIntosh Woods State Park $8
2 mi W of Clear Lake on US 18; at Clear Lake. $8 off-sea-son at 4 modern sites without elec ($11 rest of year); $13 off-season at 45 modern sites with elec ($16 rest of year). Tbls, flush toilets, cfga, drkg wtr, showers, dump, elec($5), fish cleaning station. Swimming, hiking, interpretive trail, fishing (jetty), boating(lr), playground. 3,684-acre lake.

CLINTON (E)
Bulger's Hollow $12
Corps of Engineers
Mississippi River Public Use Area
Lock & Dam 13
3 mi N of Clinton on US 67; 1 mi E on 170th St; at widest point on the river. $12 during 5/15-10/15 ($6 with federal senior pass); some sites free rest of year; 14-day limit. 17 RV sites. Tbls, pit toilets, cfga, drkg wtr, dump, pavilion, playground, shelter($). Horseshoes, fishing, boating(l).

COLESBURG (E)
Twin Bridges $10
Delaware County Conservation Board
5 mi W of Colesburg on Hwy 3; at Elk Creek. $10 base. 4/15-10/15; 14-day limit. Base fee for no hookups; $14 with elec; $16 elec/wtr. 44 sites, 15 with elec, 29 elec/

wtr (30-ft RV limit). Tbls, toilets, cfga, drkg wtr, elec($), playground, handicapped facilities, shelter. Swimming, fishing, hiking trails, hunting, horseshoes. 144 acres.

COLWELL (E)
Colwell Park   FREE
Floyd County Conservation Board
2.5 mi W of Colwell on 140th St at Little Cedar River. May-Sept. Free. Primitive undesignated sites. Tbls, pit toilet, cfga, no drkg wtr, picnic shelter. 19 acres.

COON RAPIDS (W)
Riverside Park $10
Carroll County Conservation Board
On NE side of Coon Rapids off CR E63 on Walnut St just E of Riverside Park. $10 for primitive camping; $14 at 12 elec RV sites. 4/15-10/30; 14-day limit. 30 sites (24-ft RV limit). Tbls, flush toilets, cfga, well drkg wtr, showers, dump. 3-mi hiking/biking trail, picnicking, fishing. Part of park's 144 acres along Middle Raccoon River; scenic rock bluffs.

COPPOCK (E)
Coppock Acces   FREE
Just W of Coppock on SR 78 at Skunk River. Undeveloped primitive camping at river access. Formerly a Washington County property, but no longer maintained by anyone. No facilities, no drkg wtr. Fishing, boating, picnicking. GPS: 41.1652967, -91.7251676.

CORLEY (W)
Nishna Bend Recreation Area $12
Shelby County Conservation Board
From Corley, about 1 mi W on Street F58; 1 mi S on Maple Rd; E on access rd; at shore of West Nishnabotna River. $12 at 14 elec sites. Tbls, flush toilets, showers, cfga, drkg wtr. Hiking trail, hunting, fishing. Reclaimed mining ponds; 80 acres.

CORNING (W)
Lake Binder City Park $11
Corning Parks & Recreation Department
1.5 mi NE of Corning on CR N-53. $11 at primitive RV sites. 4/15-10/15; 14-day limit. Elec sites $16; tents $9. Tbls, toilets, cfga, drkg wtr, shelter. Boating(l), fishing, hiking. 50-Acre lake. Seasonal fees: $275 without elec ($425 with elec) moving every 2 weeks; seasonal without moving, $525 without elec, $675 with elec.

COUNCIL BLUFFS (W)
Lake Manawa State Park $8
1 mi S of Council Bluffs on SR 192. $8 off-season at 35 modern sites without elec ($11 rest of year); $13 off-sea-son at 37 modern sites with elec ($16 rest of year). Tbls, flush toilets, showers, cfga, drkg wtr (except in winter), dump, beach. Interpretive trail, swimming, fishing (pier), boating(lr), playground. 660 acres.

CRESCO (E)

Howard County $10
Fairgrounds Campground
On W edge of Cresco on W 7th St (turn N off Hwy 9 on W. 7th, following fairgrounds signs 2 blocks W); camp at NW corner of fairgrounds, self-register. $10 (or $50 weekly). Apr-Nov. 26 gravel RV sites (50-ft RV limit) & 18 grass sites. Tbls, cfga, drkg wtr, dump, 30/50-amp elec; no showers or toilets.

Kendallville Park $10
Winneshiek County Conservation Board
Off Hwy 139 between Cresco & Harmony, Minnesota; at Upper Iowa River. $10 at 10 sites without hookups; $15 at 28 elec sites. 4/1-10/31; 14-day limit. Tbls, flush & pit toilets, cfga, drkg wtr, dump, showers, shelters, playground. Canoeing, fishing.

CRESTON (W)

Green Valley State Park $8
3 mi N of Creston on CR P27; at Green Valley Lake. $8 off-season at 17 modern sites without elec ($11 rest of year); $13 off-season at 83 modern sites with elec ($16 rest of year), 18 with full hookups ($19). Tbls, flush toilets, showers, cfga, drkg wtr, dump, playground. Interpretive trail, hiking, swimming, fishing (jetty & pier), boating.

Cozy Campers Campground $12
McKinley City Parks & Recreation Department
1.5 mi W of Creston on US 34, at McKinley Lake. $12 with 30-amp elec/wtr; also primitive camping; tents $8-$10. All year; 14-day limit. 38 sites with elec. Toilets, cfga, drkg wtr, dump, no showers. Fishing, boating(ld), pool. No reservations.

CRYSTAL LAKE (W)

Crystal Lake $10
Hancock County Conservation Board
On E side of Crystal Lake at 1045 320th St. $10 at 30 primitive sites and off-season at 65 modern elec sites without wtr ($15 for elec/wtr during 4/15-10/15; 14-day limit. Tbls, flush toilets, cfga, drkg wtr, showers, beach, dump, playground, beach. Hunting, fishing, canoeing, boating, picnicking, swimming. 260-acre lake.

DANVILLE (E)

Geode State Park $8
4 mi SW of Danville off US 34. $8 off-season at 81 modern sites without elec ($11 rest of year); $13 off-season at 87 modern sites with elec ($16 rest of year). Tbls, flush toilets, showers, cfga, drkg wtr, dump. Interpretive trail, hiking, swimming, fishing, boating(lr), playground. 186-acre lake.

DAVIS CITY (W)

Nine Eagles State Park $8
6 mi SE of Davis City on county rd. $8 off-season at 39 modern sites without elec ($11 rest of year); $13 off-season at 28 modern sites with elec ($16 rest of year). Tbls, flush toilets, cfga, drkg wtr, dump. Hiking & bridle trails, swimming, fishing, boating. 67-acre lake at 1,119-acre park.

Slip Bluff Park $10
Decatur County Conservation Board
2 mi W of Davis City on CR J52; 1 mi N on access rd (N of Lamoni). $10 at non-elec sites, $15 at RV sites with elec. All year; 14-day limit. Tbls, flush toilets, cfga, drkg wtr, showers (closed in winter), shelter, playground. Picnicking, hiking trails, fishing, boating(I - elec mtrs). 400 acres; 16-acre lake. Grand River. No reservations.

DAWSON (W)

Sportsman Park $8
Dallas County Conservation Board
Half mi NE of Dawson on 130th St; at North Raccoon River. $8 at 6 primitive sites; $12 at 10 elec sites. 5/1-10/31 (weather permitting, camping permitted in Apr & Nov, but no wtr services). Tbls, flush toilets, cfga, drkg wtr. Picnicking, hiking, fishing. Pack out trash. Handicapped facilities. 40 acres. Self-registration.

DAYTON (W)

Oak Municipal Park $12
5 blocks S of downtown on Hwy 175, at golf course. $12. 4/1-10/30. 45 sites with full hookups. Tbls, flush toilets, cfga, drkg wtr, showers, playground, dump. Picnicking, golf.

DEFIANCE (W)

Manteno Park $10
Shelby County Conservation Board
From just W of Defiance, 2 mi N on US 59; about 5 mi W on R F16; 0.5 mi N on Fir Rd to park. $10 without hookups; $12 with elec. 4/1-10/15. Tbls, flush toilets, showers, cfga, drkg wtr, playground, 2 shelters. Hiking trails, fishing, canoeing, boating(l), picnicking, handicapped facilities. 75-acre nature area; 12-acre lake.

DELHI (E)

Turtle Creek Recreation Area $10
Delaware County Conservation Board
6 mi SW of Delhi on CR D5X; S on X-21 from Manchester. $10 base. 5/1 10/1; 14-day limit. Base fee at 5 sites without hookups; $14 at 24 elec sites; $16 elec/wtr. 29 sites. Tbls, toilets, cfga, drkg wtr, picnic shelter. Fishing, swimming, picnicking, boating(l). Snowmobile, biking, bridle & hiking trails. 200 acres; 450-acre lake. Above Delhi Dam at Maquoketa River.

DES MOINES (W)

Bob Shetler Campground $10
Corps of Engineers
Saylorville Lake
From I-35/80 N of Des Moines, exit 131 (Johnston/Saylor-

ville Rd), then 2.8 mi N on Merle Hay Rd through Johnston; at 4-way stop sign, turn left (NW) for 1 mi on Beaver Dr; at large concrete water storage tank on right, turn right for nearly 1 mi NW on 78th Ave; right at "T" intersection for half mi. $10 base with federal senior pass at 67 elec sites; others pay $20 base, $22 at premium locations ($11 with senior pass). RV limit in excess of 65 ft; 8 pull-through sites. 5/1-9/30; 14-day limit. Tbls, drkg wtr, flush toilets, cfga, showers, playground, fish cleaning station, shelters($). Ball field, waterskiing, biking, golf, hiking, fishing, boating(l).

Cherry Glen Campground $10
Corps of Engineers
Saylorville Lake
From I-35/80 exit 90 N of Des Moines, 2.4 mi on Hwy 160 to its end; continue N 4.1 mi on Hwy 415; at campground sign, use left turn lane, then half mi NW on 94th Ave. $10 base with federal senior pass at 125 elec sites; others pay $20 base, $24 at premium locations ($12 with senior pass). 4/15-10/15; 14-day limit. RV limit in excess of 65 ft. Fish cleaning station, showers, flush toilets, drkg wtr, tbls, cfga, dump, playground. Waterskiing, biking(r), hiking, fishing, boating(l), tennis, golf.

Prairie Flower Recreation Area $9
Corps of Engineers
Saylorville Lake
From I-35 exit 90 N of Des Moines, 2.4 mi on Hwy 160 to its end; continue 5.6 mi on Hwy 415; at campground sign, turn left, then qtr mi on NW Lake Dr. $9 base with federal senior pass at 153 elec sites; others pay $18 base, $20 for premium elec sites; $24 full hookups & 50-amp elec ($9, $10 & $12 with senior pass). 5/1-10/15; 14-day limit. RV limit in excess of 65 ft. 10 group camping areas. Tbls, flush toilets, cfga, drkg wtr, showers, dump, beach. Swimming, fishing, tennis, waterskiing, biking.

Yellow Banks Park $10
Polk County Conservation Board
From US 65 exit 77 SE of Des Moines (at town of Pleasant Hill), 2 mi SE on CR F70, then S on either 64th St or CR S14 to park; on bluff above N shore of Des Moines River. At non-elec sites, $10 for seniors except during holiday weekends (others pay $15). Elec sites $20 during 4/15-10/15; seniors pay $15. With online reservations, non-elec sites are $18, elec sites $23 (no senior discounts with reservations). All year. 12 primitive sites,, 48 elec sites, 5 backpacker sites. Tbls, flush toilets, cfga, drkg wtr, showers (4/15-10/15), shelters, dump, playground. Boating(l), fishing, hiking trails, ball fields. 552 acres; 5-acre pond.

DIAGONAL (W)

Kokesh Recreation Area $5
Ringgold County Conservation Board
1 mi S of Diagonal on SR 66; veer right onto 170th Ave access rd after crossing Grand River bridge. $5 at primitive sites, $10 with 20/30/50-amp elec. Gates open 3/15-11/15; walk in all year; 14-day limit. Tbls, pit toilets, cfga, shelter. Fishing. Pond renovated as water garden. 15 acres. At reserved sites, 2-day minimum stay required on weekends.

DIKE (E)

Grundy County Lake & Campground $10
Grundy County Conservation Board
Just S of Dike on CR T55; at North Fork Black Hawk River. $10 at 61 elec sites; $5 primitive camping. All year; 14-day limit. Tbls, flush toilets, cfga, drkg wtr, showers. Paved hiking/biking trail, fishing, boating. 225 acres; 40-acre lake.

Roadman Roadside Park   FREE
Grundy County Conservation Board
1.5 mi W of Dike on Hwy 20. Free. All year. Overnight camping in parking area of 10-acre roadside park. Tbls, toilets, cfga, drkg wtr, playground, shelter with elec. 2 fishing ponds, hiking trails, interpretive trail. GPS: 42.469867, -92.664591

DODGEVILLE (E)

Big Hollow Campground $8
Big Hollow Recreation Area
Des Moines County Conservation Board
2.5 mi W & half mi N of Dodgeville. $8 (seniors pay $5). 4/1-11/1; 14-day limit. 16 primitive sites. 32 new elec sites $15. Tbls, toilets, cfga, drkg wtr. Picnicking; cross-country ski, hiking and bridle trails; fishing; archery course; shooting range; handicapped facilities. 721 acres. Dump station, shower house planned.

DRAKESVILLE (E)

Drakesville Park $10
Davis County Conservation Board
NE end of Drakesville; newly developed campground. $10 with elec when camping 7 nights; $15 nightly with elec/wtr; tents $5. 12 elec 30/50-amp sites. 40 total sites; 70-ft RV limit. Tbls, toilets, cfga, showers, elect($), store, playground. Picnicking, fishing, horseback riding, hunting, shooting range. 12 acres. Most of Davis County's parks (Lake Fisher, West Grove, Pulaski, Troy & Floris) allow free primitive overnight camping.

Lake Wapello State Park $8
10 mi W of Drakesville on SR 273. $8 off-season at 36 modern sites without elec ($11 rest of year); $13 off-season at 42 modern sites with elec ($16 rest of year). Tbls, flush toilets, showers, dump, drkg wtr (except in winter). Interpretive trail, hiking, swimming, fishing (jetty & pier), boating, playground. 289-acre lake.

DUBUQUE (E)

Bankston Park $12
Dubuque County Conservation Board
18 mi NW of Dubuque on US 52, then S following signs

(6 mi SE of Holy Cross). $12. 4/15-11/1; 14-day limit. 25 primitive sites. Tbls, toilets, cfga, drkg wtr, playground, shelter. Picnicking, hiking, fishing, baseball, hunting. 120 acres.

Finley's Landing Park $12
Dubuque County Conservation Board
From Dubuque, 6 mi NW on SR 3/US 52 to Sageville; right for 0.24 mi on CR C9Y, becoming Sherrill Rd, then 5 mi NW through Sherill; 3 mi N on Finley's Landing Rd. $12 at 10 non-elec sites; 20 sites with elec, $17-23 (24 wtr hookups). 4/15-11/1; 14-day limit. 25-Ft RV limit. Tbls, toilets, cfga, drkg wtr, elec($), dump ($12 for non-campers), showers, playground. Nature trail, fishing, boating (ld), canoeing, hunting, ice fishing. 120 acres. Marina.

Grant River Recreation Area $10
Corps of Engineers
Mississippi River
E of Dubuque, across river in Wisconsin, N on US 61; W on SR 133 following signs. $10 base with federal senior pass at 30-amp elec sites; others pay $20 base, more for premium 50-amp elec sites ($10 with senior pass). 5/1-10/24; 14-day limit. 63 sites with 30-amp elec; 10 sites 50-amp; no wtr hookups. RV limit 55 ft. Tbls, flush toilets, cfga, drkg wtr, dump, playground, beach, shelter($), amphitheater. Boating(l$), fishing, swimming.

Massey Marina $12
Dubuque County Conservation Board
11 mi S of Dubuque on US 52, following signs to 9400 Massey Marina Lane. $12 base. 4/15-11/1; 14-day limit. Base fee for 14 non-elec sites; $16-$17 at 47 sites with elec (48 wtr hookups); 40-ft RV limit. Tbls, flush toilets, cfga, showers, drkg wtr, dump ($12 for non-campers), snack bar, playground, coin laundry, pavilion, store. Boating(ld), fishing, horseshoes, canoeing, waterskiing.

Miller Riverview City Park $12
At Dubuque, follow Greyhound Park Dr from US 151; left on Admiral Sheeley Dr to camp; on shore of Mississippi River adjacent to Mystique Casino. $12 for RV sites without hookups (elec sites $15); tents $10. 4/1-10/31; 14-day limit. 97 full hookups. Tbls, flush toilets, cfga, drkg wtr, showers, dump. Boating(l), fishing, trail, no swimming. Non-campers pay $2 for dump station.

Mud Lake Park $12
Dubuque County Conservation Board
6 mi N of Dubuque on US 52; follow signs N on Sageville Rd; 3 mi E on Mud Lake Rd. $12 base. 4/15-11/1; 14-day limit. Base fee for 32 non-elec sites; $17-$18 at 42 sites with elec/wtr; 40-ft RV limit. Tbls, flush toilets, showers, cfga, drkg wtr, elec($), dump ($12 for non-campers). Boating(ld), canoeing, fishing. Marina. 20 acres.

Swiss Valley Park $12
Dubuque County Conservation Board
6 mi SW of Dubuque on US 141, or 6 mi W on Hwy 20; 5 mi S on Swiss Valley Rd; half mi E on Whitetop Rd. $12 base. 4/15-11/1; 14-day limit. Base fee at 10 non-elec sites; $15-$18 at 60 sites with elec (54 wtr hookups). Flush toilets, cfga, tbls, drkg wtr, showers, elec($), dump ($12 for non-campers), playground. Hiking trails, horseshoes, nature program, volleyball, softball trout fishing in stream, cross-country skiing. 62 acres.

DUMONT (E)
Lake Considine Park FREE
Butler County Conservation Board
2 mi S of Dumont on Douglas Ave; 1.5 mi E on 230th St. All year; 14-day limit. Free primitive camping at lake & West Fork Cedar River. No facilities. Fishing.

South Fork Park FREE
Butler County Conservation Board
Half mi W of Dumont on SR 3; left on Cedar Ave; at South Fork of the West Fork River. Free. All year. Primitive undesignated sites on 20 acres. No facilities, no drkg wtr. Fishing, hunting. 3-acre lake.

DUNKERTON (E)
Siggelkov $7
Black Hawk County Conservation Board
5 mi N of Dunkerton on Hwy 281; at Wapsipinicon River. $7 base; $13 with elec. All year; 14-day limit. 50 sites. Tbls, toilets, cfga, drkg wtr, playground, dump, elec($), shelter. Canoeing, picnicking, fishing. 54 acres.

DYERSVILLE (E)
New Wine Park $12
Dubuque County Conservation Board
4 mi N of Dyersville on SR 136. $11 base. 4/15-11/1; 14-day limit. Base fee at 10 non-elec sites; $15-$17 at 27 sites with elec; 40-ft RV limit. Tbls, flush toilets, cfga, drkg wtr, elec($), showers, dump ($12 for non-campers), playground, baseball field, handicapped facilities. Fishing, volleyball, hiking & biking trails, picnicking. 168 acres.

EARLY (NW)
Reiff Park Wildlife Area $12
Sac County Conservation Board
1.5 mi S of Early on US 71. $12 base. 4/1-10/15. Base fee at primitive sites; $17 at 7 RV sites with 30-amp elec/wtr. Tbls, flush toilets, cfga, drkg wtr hookups, elec($), dump. Playground, hiking trails, canoeing, picnicking, fishing, hunting. 95 acres.

EDDYVILLE (S)
Hardfish Access FREE
Wildlife Management Area
Monroe County Conservation Board
Half mi SW of Eddyville; at Des Moines River. Free. Unde-

veloped primitive camping. Toilets, tbls, cfga, no drkg wtr. Fishing, boating(l), canoeing. 12 acres.

ELDORA (E)

Pine Lake State Park $8
E of Eldora on SR 57; N on SR 118. $8 off-season at modern sites without elec ($11 rest of year); $13 off-season at 123 modern sites with elec ($16 rest of year); 97 have 50-amp. Tbls, flush toilets, showers, cfga, drkg wtr, dump. Interpretive trail, hiking, swimming, fishing (jetty), boating(lr). 69 & 50-acre lakes. Iowa River Greenbelt nearby.

ELGIN (E)

Gilbertson Conservation Education Area $10
Fayette County Conservation Board
Eastern edge of Elgin on Agate Rd (CR B64); at Turkey River. $10 at 8 primitive sites, $15 at 28 elec sites. 4/1-11/1; limited facilities in winter. 36 sites (28 with elec) plus primitive equestrian camping, $10. Tbls, flush toilets, showers, cfga, drkg wtr, dump, playground. Canoeing(l), hiking & bridle & biking trails, fishing, nature center, seasonal petting zoo, fishing pond, historic site, nature programs, hunting, cross-country skiing. 565 acres. County park annual camping pass $350; 11 nights, $150.

ELKADER (E)

Frieden's Park $5
Clayton County Conservation Board
5.5 mi NW of Elkader on CR C1X; at W shore of Turkey River. $5. Undeveloped primitive camping. Toilets, cfga, tbls, no drkg wtr. Fishing, boating. Canoe access. 1 acre. Note: Closed in 2016; check with county conservation agency for current status before arrival.

Motor Mill Historic Park $5
Clayton County Conservation Board
From jct with SR 56 just S of Elkader, 2 mi S on SR 13; 3 mi SE on CR X3C; 2 mi NE on Galaxy Rd, veering right onto 293rd St to park; at shore of Turkey River. $5 at 8 primitive sites. May-Oct. Tbls, toilets, cfga, drkg wtr. Canoeing, hiking, horseback riding. Historic limestone mill, cooperage, ice house, stable. 155 acres.

ELKHART (W)

Chichaqua Bottoms Greenbelt $10
Polk County Conservation Board
From Elkhart, 4 mi E & NE on CR F22; 1 mi S on NE 80th St; left (E) into park; along Skunk River. At non-elec sites, $10 for seniors except on holiday weekends during about 4/15-10/15 (others pay $15). Elec sites $15 for seniors, $20 for others. With online reservations, non-elec sites are $18, elec sites $23 (no senior discounts with reservations). 12 elec sites, 28 primitive sites Tbls, flush toilets, cfga, drkg wtr, showers, dump. Fishing, canoeing(r), dog training area, bird observation blind, trap shooting range, flower trail, hiking trails.

ELK HORN (W)

Elk Horn Creek Recreation Area $10
Shelby County Conservation Area
1 mi S of Elk Horn SR 173; 1 mi W on 600th St; half mi S on Yellowwood Rd; at S shore of Elkhorn Creek. $12 at 7 sites with elec; $10 at non-elec & tent sites. 4/1-10/15; 14-day limit. Tbls, toilets, cfga, drkg wtr, shelter, playgrounds. Picnicking, fishing, hiking trails, bow hunting. 60 acres. Half-acre pond. Adjacent nature preserve.

EMERSON (W)

Bass Memorial Park FREE
Half mi S of Emerson on US 59. Free. All year; 14-day limit. Undeveloped primitive camping. Shady, grassy with pit toilets, cfga, ball field.

EMMETSBURG (W

Kearny State Park $10
City of Emmetsburg Recreation Department
From downtown Emmetsburg at jct with US 18, 9 blocks N on Lawler St. to park; at W shore of Five Island Lake. $10 at non-elec sites, $15 with elec. Tbls, flush toilets, showers, cfga, drkg wtr, playground, shelters, fish cleaning station. Boating(l), fishing, swimming, winter sports. No reservations.

ESTHERVILLE (W)

Fort Defiance State Park $6
2 mi W of Estherville on SR 9; 2 mi S on access rd. $6 off-season at 8 non-modern sites without elec ($9 rest of year); $11 off-season at 8 non-modern sites with elec ($14 rest of year). All year; 14 day limit. Tbls, pit toilets, cfga, drkg wtr, dump, playground. Picnicking, fishing, hiking trails, equestrian trails. Enclosed group shelter (by reservation) with elec, wtr, toilets, cookstoves, refrigerator. 191 acres.

Riverside City Park FREE
Estherville Parks & Recreation Department
W end of town 1 block N of SR 9 on First St; W side of river bridge at shore of West Fork Des Moines River. Free. 3-day limit. Tbls, toilets, cfga, drkg wtr. Very small park, tight spaces; not suitable for many RVs.

EVANSDALE (E)

Deerwood City Park $12
Evansdale Parks & Recreation Department
1 block N on River Forest Rd from I-380 exit 70; qtr mi W on access rd. $12 without hookups; $15 with elec/wtr (seniors pay $14); $19 full hookups (seniors pay $18). Weekly, monthly & seasonal rates available. 4/1-9/30. 86 elec sites. Tbls, flush toilets, cfga, drkg wtr, showers, dump, pavilion, playground. Hiking trails, horseshoes, swimming, boating(l), fishing, canoeing, bike trails.

FAIRFIELD (E)

Round Prairie Park $9
Jefferson County Conservation Board
9 mi SE of Fairfield on Glasgow Rd; 2 mi S on Tamarack Ave.
$9 without hookups; $12 with elec. All year; 14-day limit; wtr
may be off 11/1-4/20. 12 sites. Tbls, pit toilets, cfga, drkg
wtr, shelter. Hiking & bridle trails, fishing, boating, canoeing,
playground. Historic site; 101 acres.

FARMINGTON (E)

White Oak Campground $9
Donnellson Unit
Shimek State Forest
5 mi E of Farmington on IA 2 (paved access rds). $9 during
10/1-12/31 at 11 non-modern sites ($12 during 5/1-9/30).
All year. Spaces for self-contained RVs. Tbls, toilets, cfga.
Picnicking, hiking, walk-in fishing access & walk-in tent
sites at Shagbark Lake. Nature trails.

FAYETTE (E)

Klock's Island Municipal Park $8
In Fayette, half mi W on W. Water St from jct with SR 150
& SR 93. $8 without hookups; $10 with 30-amp elec. 10
non-elec sites, 25 with elec. 5/1-11/1. 30-ft RV limit. Tbls,
toilets, cfga, drkg wtr, dump($2). Fishing, playground,
recreation field. Volga River.

Volga River State Recreation Area $6
4 mi N of Fayette on SR 150, then 1 mi E. $6 base. All year;
14-day limit. Base fee at 50 non-modern sites off-season
($9 rest of year). Tbls, toilets, cfga, drkg wtr, no hookups.
Picnicking, fishing, boating(l), hunting, hiking trails, interpretive trail, equestrian trails. 5,422 acres.

FLOYD (E)

West Idlewild Campground $5
Floyd County Conservation Board
2 mi NW of Floyd on Quarry Rd. $5. About 30 undeveloped
primitive sites. Tbls, toilets, cfga, drkg wtr, shelter, playground. Picnicking, hiking trails, fishing, boating, hunting,
canoe access to Cedar River. 50 acres. Self-registration.
Owned by Iowa Department of Natural Resources; leased
by county.

FOREST CITY (W)

Pilot Knob State Park $8
5 mi E of Forest City on SR 9; 1 mi S. $8 off-season at 12
modern sites without elec ($11 rest of year); $13 off-season
at 48 modern sites with elec ($16 rest of year). Tbls, flush
toilets, cfga, drkg wtr, showers, dump. Hiking & bridle trails,
fishing, playground. 15-acre lake. During winter of 2013-14,
shower building was replaced.

Thorpe Park $8
Winnebago County Conservation Board
5.5 mi W of Forest City on CR B14; 1.5 mi N, then 1 mi W
to park. $8 for 2 non-elec sites, $12 for 13 sites with elec.
Apr-Nov; 14-day limit. Drkg wtr, pit toilets, cfga, shelter,
playground. Horseback riding, hunting, fishing, canoeing,
boating(l), hiking trails.

Winnebago Visitor Center FREE
From southbound US 69, turn W & north, then W at Rally
Grounds marquee; make immediate N turn on 4th St to
visitor center. Free for service customers only; 2-night
limit. Gravel parking lot with 30-amp elec for 32 sites,
dump. Tour Winnebago RV plant.

FREDERIKA (E)

Alcock Park $10
Bremer County Conservation Board
From CR C16 just SW of Frederika, qtr mi N on Midway Ave;
E on 118th St into park; on shore of Wapsipinicon River.
$10 without hookups, $15 with elec. 5/1-10/31. 70 sites
(50 with elec). Tbls, toilets, cfga, drkg wtr, shelters, dump
($2 for non-campers), showers ($2 for non-campers). Picnicking, fishing, boating(l), horseshoes, sand volleyball.
42 acres. Free camping on non-holiday Wed nights.

FREDERICKSBURG (E)

Brad Niewoehner Memorial Park $12
On Schult Ridge Rd. $12 (weeky, $75). All year. Tbls,
toilets, cfga, elec, drkg wtr, showers (during pool hours),
pool. Swimming, horseshoes.

Fredericksburg City Park FREE
3 blocks N of Hwy 18 (follow signs). Free. Get permit at
police station. All year. Spaces for self-contained RVs. Two
shelters, cfga. Shady, scenic park.

Split Rock Park $12
Chickasaw County Conservation Board
2.5 mi S of Fredericksburg on CR V48; 1 mi W on 300th
St; 0.5 mi S on Pembroke Ave to park entrance on left.
$12 base at 30 non-elec sites; $15 for 42 elec 20/30/50-
amp sites. 5/1-10/31; 14-day limit. Tbls, pit & flush toilets,
cfga, drkg wtr, 3 shelters, showers, playground. Fishing,
swimming beach, picnicking, hunting, canoeing, hiking,
cross-country skiing, volleyball. Facilities for handicapped.
80 acres; 10-acre lake.

FREDONIA (E)

River Forks Access FREE
Louisa County Conservation Board
From Fredonia, W on Main St. to E shore of Iowa River just
below confluence with Cedar River. Free primitive camping. No facilities. Boating(l), fishing.

FULTON (ILLINOIS)

Lock & Dam 13 FREE
Corps of Engineers
Mississippi River Public Use Area
2 mi N of Fulton on IL 84; W at sign. Free. All year; 14-day

limit. 6 primitive sites. Tbls, toilets, cfga. Boating(l), fishing, hunting, canoeing. Observation deck.

GARNAVILLO (E)
Buck Creek Park $5
Clayton County Conservation Board
3 mi NE of Garnavillo on US 52; at Buck Creek. $5 at two primitive sites. Toilets, cfga, no drkg wtr, no elec. Fishing, hunting. 103 acres.

GLADBROOK (E)
Union Grove State Park $6
5 mi S of Gladbrook on gravel rd. $6 off-season at non-modern sites without elec ($9 rest of year); $11 off-season at 25 non-modern sites with elec ($14 rest of year), 9 with full hookups ($19). All year; 14-day limit. Tbls, toilets, cfga, drkg wtr, elec($5). Picnicking, swimming, fishing, boating(rl), hiking trails. 172 acres.

GLENWOOD (W)
Pony Creek Park $10
Mills County Conservation Board
3 mi W of Glenwood on US 34; 2 mi N on Deacon Rd; . $10 without hookups; $12 at 6 RV sites with 30/50-amp elec (typically 30 ft). 4/1-11/1. Tbls, toilets, cfga, drkg wtr, playground, 2 shelters. Hiking trails, scenic overlook platform, restored prairie area, fishing, boating(l), canoeing. 53 acres.

GLIDDEN (W)
Dickson Timber Forest Preserve $10
Carroll County Conservation Board
2 mi E of Glidden on US 30; 3.5 mi N on Velvet Ave; at Dickson Timber County Park. $10 at primitive & equestrian sites; $12 at 12 elec RV sites & 8 equestrian elec sites. Equestrians pay $2 daily per person or $15 annually. 4/15-10/31; 14-day limit. 50 sites, including equestrian facilities. Tbls, pit toilets, cfga, well drkg wtr, shelter. Picnicking, playground, hiking, bridle & snowmobile trails; hunting. Corrals. 155 acres. At Dickson Branch North Raccoon River.

Merritt Access FREE
Carroll County Park
2 mi E of Glidden on US 30; 4 mi N on Velvet Ave, past Dickson Timber Park; E on access rd; at W shore of North Raccoon River. Free. All year; 14-day limit. 40 spaces for self-contained RVs on 68 acres (24-ft RV limit). Tbls, toilets, cfga, firewood, well drkg wtr. Picnicking, fishing, hiking, boating, bridle & snowmobile trails, hunting.

GOODELL (W)
Eldred Sherwood $10
Hancock County Conservation Board
3 mi E of Goodell on 110th St; 1 mi N on Vail Ave; left on 120th St to park entrance. $10 for primitive sites, $15 with elec. 4/15-10/15. 5 primitive sites, 40 sites with elec. Tbls,

flush toilets, cfga, drkg wtr, dump, showers, playground, beach. Swimming, fishing, boating (l - elec mtrs only), nature trail, cross country skiing. 100 acres; 25-acre lake.

GRANDVIEW (E)
Flaming Prairie $12
Louisa County Conservation Board
3 mi E of Grandview on CR X61 at Mississippi River. $12. All year; 14-day limit. 5 primitive sites & 17 sites with 20/30/50-amp elec (some pull-through). Tbls, toilets, cfga, drkg wtr (no wtr in winter), no trash service. Natural playground. Fishing, boating (l - elec mtrs), picnicking, canoeing, nature study. 71 acres.

GRANGER (W)
Jester Park $10
Polk County Conservation Board
From jct with SR 18 just E of Granger, 1 mi E on NW 110th St; 1 mi N on NW 121st St; 1 mi E on NW 118 St to park, following signs; at W. shore of Saylorville Lake. $10 at non-elec sites for seniors except holiday weekends during about 4/15-10/15 (others pay $15). Elec sites, $15 for seniors; others pay $20. With online reservations, non-elec sites are $18, elec sites $23 (no senior discounts with reservations). 168 sites, including 80 elec, 82 non-elec, 4 primitive walk-in & 2 reservable youth areas. Tbls, flush toilets, cfga, drkg wtr, showers, dump, playground, shelters. Golf, fishing, boating(l), 8 mi of hiking trails, nature programs. Bison & elk herds with education facility & observation deck. Equestrian center. 1,675 acres.

GREENE (E)
Camp Comfort $8
Butler County Conservation Board
4 mi SE of Greene on CR C23; 1 mi N on gravel Camp Comfort Rd at Shell Rock River. $8 at non-elec RV & tent sites ($48 weekly); $10 at 30 RV/tent sites with 30/50-amp elec ($60 weekly). 4/1-10/30; 14-day limit; 31-ft RV limit. Tbls, flush toilets, cfga, drkg wtr, no dump. Boating (l), fishing, hiking trails, canoeing. Free camping Wed nights.

Wunsch Memorial Park $8
Greene Recreation Area
Butler County Conservation Board
From Main St. & W. Rowley St. in Greene, 1 block NE on Rowley to park; at W shore of Shell Rock River. $8 at non-elec RV & tent sites ($48 weekly); $10 at 10 elec 20/30-amp RV/tent sites ($60 weekly). All year; 14-day limit; limited amenities off-season. Tbls, flush toilets, cfga, drkg wtr, shelter, playground, disc golf, showers, wireless connection, bike path. Fishing, boating (l), hiking, canoeing. Free camping Wed nights.

GREENFIELD (W)
Middle River Forest Park FREE
Adair County Conservation Board
8 mi E of Greenfield on SR 92; 2 mi N on CR P39; qtr mi E

on 200th St; right into park; at Middle River. Free. All year; 14-day limit. Small RVs camp free in 2 parking lots. Also walk-in primitive tent camping area. Tbls, toilets, cfga, no drkg wtr. Hiking trail, canoeing. 38 acres.

GRUNDY CENTER (E)
Wolf Creek Recreation Area $5
Grundy County Conservation Board
11 mi S of Grundy Center on CR 529 (1 mi S of Beaman). $5 at undesignated sites and primitive camping area; $10 at sites with elec. All year; 21-day limit; may be free during 11/15-4/15, but no services. 22 designated sites (11 with elec) plus primitive area. Tbls, toilets, cfga, drkg wtr, elec($). Fishing, hiking, hunting, picnicking.

GUTHRIE CENTER (W)
Springbrook State Park $8
8 mi N of Guthrie Center on SR 25; E on SR 384. $8 off-season at 39 modern sites without elec ($11 rest of year); $13 off-season at 81 modern sites with elec ($16 rest of year). Tbls, flush toilets, cfga, showers, drkg wtr, dump, beach. Interpretive center, hiking, swimming, fishing (jetty), boating, playground. 920 acres; 16-acre lake.

GUTTENBERG (E)
Frenchtown Park   FREE
Clayton County Conservation Board
Frenchtown Lake
About 3 mi N of Guttenberg following CR X56 (Great River Rd), then Mississippi Rd; at Mississippi River backwater area known as Frenchtown Lake. Free. All year; 14-day limit. 3 primitive sites. Tbls, toilets, cfga, no drkg wtr. Boating(l), fishing.

HAMBURG (W)
Waubonsie State Park $8
N of Hamburg on US 275; W on SR 2; SW on SR 239. $8 off-season at 16 modern sites without elec ($11 rest of year); $13 off-season at 24 modern sites with elec ($16 rest of year). Also 32-site equestrian area. Tbls, flush toilets, showers, cfga, drkg wtr (except in winter), dump. Interpretive trail, hiking & bridle trails. 1,990 acres.

HAMPTON (E)
Beeds Lake State Park $8
1 mi W of Hampton on SR 3; 3 mi N on county rd. $8 off-season at 45 modern sites without elec ($11 rest of year); $13 off-season at 99 modern sites with elec ($16 rest of year). Tbls, flush toilets, cfga, drkg wtr, showers, dump, fishing piers. Interpretive trail, swimming, fishing (jetty), boating(lr). 99-acre lake.

Robinson Park $12
Franklin County Conservation Board
From jct with SR 3 in downtown Hampton, 1 mi N on US 65; 1 mi E on 170th St; left (N) on Quail Ave, then W on access rd; at S shore of Otter Creek. $12. 4/1-11/30; 14-day limit.

30 sites with elec. Tbls, toilets, cfga, drkg wtr, elec. Hiking trails, fishing (Otter Creek), picnicking, shelter house. Handicapped facilities. 30 acres.

WKW Conservation Park $12
Franklin County Conservation Board
From jct with SR 3 in downtown Hampton, 1 mi N on US 65; 1 mi E on 170th St; right (S) on Quail Ave, then left into park; at shore of Otter Creek. $12. 4/1-11/30; 14-day limit. 8 sites with 20/30/50-amp elec (RVs under 32 ft). Tbls, toilets, cfga, firewood, playground, elec. Picnicking, fishing, horseback riding, hiking. River. Nature trails. Shelters. Located on heavily timbered ground. A 1.8-mi hiking, horseback, snowmobiling trail winds through the timber. 54 acres. Register at Robinson Park.

HANOVER (ILLINOIS)
Blanding Landing Recreation Area $7
Corps of Engineers
Mississippi River Public Use Area
W of US 20 onto first rd N of Apple River Bridge in Hanover; take first RR crossing. $7 at 7 non-elec sites with federal senior pass; others pay $14. $10 with senior pass at 30 elec sites (others pay $20). 5/1-10/25; 14-day limit. Tbls, toilets, cfga, drkg wtr, showers, dump. Horseback riding, picnicking, fishing, swimming, boating(l$), hiking, canoeing, hunting. Snow skiing nearby in winter.

HARLAN (W)
Prairie Rose State Park $8
4 mi E of Harlan; 4 mi S; 2 mi E; 1.5 mi N. $8 off-season at modern sites without elec ($11 rest of year); $13 off-season at 77 modern sites with elec ($16 rest of year), 8 full hookups ($19). Tbls, flush toilets, cfga, drkg wtr, showers, dump, elec($5). Interpretive center, swimming, fishing, hiking, boating(l).

HARTLEY (W)
City of Hartley Campground $12
Neeble Park
Hartley Parks & Recreation Department
From N side of Hartley on US 18, about 8 blocks S on Central Ave; 1 block W on 3rd St SW to park entrance; 6 small sites W of tennis courts, 4 larger 55-ft sites S of swimming pool. $12 at 10 sites with elec/wtr, CATV, WiFi. Tbls, flush toilets, cfga, drkg wtr, playground, picnic shelter.

HAWKEYE (E)
Gouldsburg Park $10
Fayette County Conservation Board
5 mi N of Hawkeye (W of West Union) on CR W14; left on park access rd. $10 at primitive sites, $15 at 26 elec sites. 4/1-11/1; 14-day limit. 48 sites (25 with elec); 36-ft RV limit. Tbls, flush toilets, cfga, drkg wtr, showers, dump. Picnicking, hiking trails, fishing, nature programs. 64 acres. Annual county park camping pass $350; 11 nights for $150. GPS: 43.010669, -91.959412

HAZLETON (E)
Fontana Park $12
Buchanan County Conservation Board
0.5 mi S of Hazleton on SR 150; right (W) on access rd.
$12 without hookups, $18 with elec. All year; 14-day limit.
80 sites. Tbls, toilets, cfga, drkg wtr, elec($), shelter,
playground, beach, dump. Hiking, swimming, fishing,
boating(d), canoeing. Historic site, nature center, wildlife
display. 134 acres. Dump at Hazleton City Shop. Reservations available, 319-636-2617.

HILLS (E)
Hills Access $10
Johnson County Conservation Board
On Iowa River, half mi E of Hills on 520th St. $10 at 5 sites
without hookups, $15 at 14 elec sites; 120-ft limit at 7
pull-throughs. Tbls, pit toilets, cfga, drkg wtr. Boating(l),
fishing. 40 acres.

HULL (W)
Westside City Park   FREE
On NW side of town, entrance on Birch St. Free 3 days; $5
thereafter. All year. 3 elec sites, 1 with wtr hookup. Tbls,
toilets, cfga, drkg wtr, elec, dump, pool, playground.

HUMBOLDT (W)
Frank A. Gotch State Park $10
Humboldt County Conservation Board
4 mi S of Humboldt on SR 169; follow signs 1 mi E on 260th
St, following signs; at Des Moines River. $10 base, $15 at
32 elec/wtr sites. Also seasonal sites. 4/1 10/30; 14-day
limit. Tbls, showers, flush toilets, cfga, drkg wtr, elec,
dump($), 2 shelters, WiFi($). Fishing, canoeing, biking/
hiking trail, picnicking, playground, boating(l), horseshoes. 67 acres.

Joe Sheldon Park $10
Humboldt County Conservation Board
1.5 mi W of Humboldt on SR 3; S on access rd; at West Fork
of Des Moines River. $10 without elec; $15 with 30/50-amp
elec/wtr. 4/1-10/31; 14-day limit. 60 sites (RVs under 31 ft).
Tbls, flush toilets, hot showers, cfga, drkg wtr, 2 shelters,
playground, WiFi($). Hiking trails, fishing, picnicking, boat-
ing(l), sand volleyball, disc golf. 81 acres.

IDA GROVE (W)
Cobb Memorial Park $10
American Legion Park
From just NW of Ida Grove at jct with SR 175, 1 mi E on
US 59, then S on access rd to park. $10. 45 sites (25
pull-through). Tbls, flush toilets, showers, cfga, drkg wtr,
30-amp elec hookups, playground, ball field, dump. Pond.

Ida Grove City Park $3
From US 59 on NE side of Ida Grove, 1 block S on Washington St. $3 at primitive sites, $8 with elec. Tbls, flush toilets, cfga, drkg wtr, playground, picnic shelter. No showers. Get camping permit from City Hall, Third & Main Sts.

Moorehead Pioneer Park $12
Ida County Conservation Board
Half mi NW of Ida Grove on Hwy 175. $12. About 20 prim-
itive undesignated sites. All year; 14-day limit. Tbls, pit
toilets, cfga, drkg wtr, no elec. Hiking, bridle trails, fishing,
boating(l), playground, hunting, winter sports. 258 acres
with 12-acre lake. Restored train depot serves as winter
warming house for sledders.

INDIANOLA (W)
Hickory Hills Park   FREE
Warren County Conservation Board
12 mi S of Indianola on Hwy 69. Free. All year. 6 primitive
sites. Tbls, toilets, cfga, drkg wtr. Hiking trails, fishing
ponds, picnicking. 160 acres.

Lake Ahquabi State Park $8
5.5 mi S of Indianola on Hwy 65 & 69; W on SR 349. $8
off-season at 30 modern sites without elec ($11 rest of
year); $13 off-season at 85 modern sites with elec ($16 rest
of year). Tbls, flush toilets, showers, cfga, drkg wtr, dump.
Interpretive trail, hiking & biking trails, swimming, fishing
(jetty & pier), boating(lr), playground. 130-acre lake.

IONIA (E)
Chickasaw County Park $5
Chickasaw County Conservation Board
2.5 mi W of Ionia on CR B57; on both sides of Little Cedar
River. $5. Undesignated primitive sites. All year; 14-day
limit. Tbls, pit toilets, cfga, drkg wtr, shelters. Picnicking,
fishing, hunting, canoeing, hiking, horseshoes. 33 acres.

Twin Ponds   FREE
Chickasaw County Conservation Board
2 mi S of Ionia on CR V14; 3 mi E on 250th St. Free. All
year; 14-day limit. Primitive undesignated sites along
Wapsipinicon River. Tbls, toilets, cfga, drkg wtr. Hiking,
fishing, hunting, canoeing. Two ponds. 157 acres. Site
of Twin Ponds Nature Center; educational displays, bird
blind, nature trails.

IOWA CITY (E)
Linder Point $8
Corps of Engineers
Coralville Lake
2 mi N of Iowa City on Hwy 66W to Coralville Lake turnoff;
right (N) 1 mi to lake on W side of dam. $8 base with
federal senior pass at non-elec RV/tent sites; others pay
$16. $10 with senior pass at 30-amp elec sites; others pay
$20; $13 with senior pass for full hookups; others pay $26.
4/15-10/14; 14-day limit. 26 sites (9 full hookups). RV limit
in excess of 65 ft. Tbls, showers, flush toilets, cfga, drkg
wtr, dump, beach. Swimming, boating(l), hiking trails,
fishing, picnicking, playground, snowmobile trails.

Tailwater East Campground $10
Corps of Engineers
Coralville Lake
2 mi N of Iowa City on SR W66; E at Coralville Lake sign. Follow signs across Coralville Dam, turn right; below dam on E side of outlet. $10 with federal senior pass at 30-amp elec sites; others pay $20. $11 with senior pass at 50-amp sites; others pay $22. $13 with senior pass for full hookups; others pay $26. RV limit in excess of 65 ft. 4/15-10/14; 14-day limit. 28 sites (22 30-amp elec, 5 are 50-amp). Tbls, cfga, flush toilets, drkg wtr, showers, beach. Boating(l), fishing, picnicking, boating, hiking, swimming.

Tailwater West Campground $10
Corps of Engineers
Coralville Lake
Follow directions to Tailwater East; below dam on W side of outlet. $10 with federal senior pass at 30-amp elec sites; others pay $20. $12 with senior pass at 50-amp sites; others pay $24. $13 with senior pass for full hook-ups; others pay $26. 4/15-10/15; 14-day limit. 30 sites (9 for tents, $14). Fish cleaning station, pavilion, tbls, toilets, cfga, drkg wtr, playground, dump, beach. Swimming, fishing, boating, golf, waterskiing.

West Overlook Campground $10
Corps of Engineers
Coralville Lake
Follow directions to Tailwater East, using signs; on W side of dam, N of dam access rd. $10 base with federal senior pass at 89 30-amp elec sites; others pay $20. $11 with senior pass for premium locations; others pay $22. 4/15-10/15; 14-day limit. Picnic shelter, cfga, dump, flush toilets, showers, tbls, fish cleaning station. Fishing, boating(l), swimming beach.

IOWA FALLS (E)

Eagle City Park   FREE
Hardin County Conservation Board
From Iowa Falls, 5 mi E on CR D15; 2 mi S on R Ave; 1.5 mi W on 145th St; 0.5 mi E on E on Ave; access via 160th St; on W shore of Iowa River. Free primitive sites. Tbls, pit toilets, cfga, drkg wtr, swing sets. Hiking trails, fishing, boating, hunting, canoeing. 172 acres.

Westside City Park   FREE
Iowa City Parks & Recreation Department
On US 20, W side of city. Free. 4/15-9/15. Primitive undesignated sites; 55-ft RV limit. Tbls, flush toilets, cfga, drkg wtr, playground. Fishing, hiking.

JEFFERSON (W)

Henderson Park $8
Greene County Conservation Board
1 mi S of Jefferson on SR 4; right into park at shore of North Raccoon River. $8 at primitive sites. 4/1-11/1;

14-day limit. Tbls, pit toilets, cfga, drkg wtr. Fishing, boating(l), canoeing, picnic shelter. Primarily a fishing camp. 39 acres.

Spring Lake Park $8
Greene County Conservation Board
7 mi E of Jefferson on US 30 (2 mi W of Grand Junction); 2.5 mi N on P33; half mi W on co rd. $8 base. All year; 14-day limit. Base fee for primitive sites; modern sites with elec, $15. 126 elec sites (30-ft RV limit). Tbls, toilets, cfga, drkg wtr, showers. Hiking trails, swimming beach, fishing, boating(r), canoeing, playground, handicapped facilities. 240 acres; 50-acre lake.

Squirrel Hollow Park $8
Greene County Conservation Board
3 mi E of Jefferson on CR E53; 4 mi S on CR P30; 1 mi S on Redwood Ave. (5 mi NW of Rippey). $8 primitive sites, $10 with elec. 4/1-11/1; 14-day limit. 20 sites with 30-amp elec plus equestrian camp with 10 elec sites. Tbls, toilets, cfga, drkg wtr. Hiking & bridle trails, fishing, boating(l), playground. 56 acres. Adjacent to 147-acre Squirrel Hollow Wildlife Area; at North Raccoon River.

JERICO (E)

Saude Recreation Area $5
Chickasaw County Park
5 mi E of Jerico on CR B22; half mi N on Stevens Ave (5 mi W of Protivin). $5. All year; 14-day limit. 20 primitive sites. Tbls, toilets, cfga, drkg wtr, playfield. Along Little Turkey River. Fishing, hunting, canoeing, baseball. 13 acres.

JESUP (E)

Cutshall Area   FREE
Buchanan County Conservation Board
4 mi N of Jesup on CR V65. All year; 14-day limit. Free. Undeveloped primitive camping at Wapsipinicon River. Tbls, cfga, no drkg wtr, shelter, pit toilets. Picnicking, fishing, boating (no motors), canoeing, hunting. 85 acres.

JOHNSTON (W)

Acorn Valley $10
Corps of Engineers
Saylorville Lake
From dam near Johnston, 1 mi W on NW 78th Ave; 2.5 mi NW on Beaver Dr, then E. $10 base with federal senior pass for 29 elec sites; others pay $20 base, $22 for premium elec sites ($11 with senior pass). About 5/1-9/6; 14-day limit. RV limit 65 ft. Tbls, flush toilets, cfga, drkg wtr, dump, showers, playground, interpretive center, recycle center, shelter($), recycle center, small pond. Hiking trails, fishing, boating(l), waterskiing, tennis, baseball, interpretive programs, shooting range, visitor center.

KELLOGG (E)

Rock Creek State Park $8
3 mi N of Kellogg on Hwy 218 & Hwy 61; 1.6 mi W. $8

off-season at 95 modern sites without elec ($11 rest of year); $13 off-season at 101 modern sites with elec ($16 rest of year). Tbls, flush toilets, cfga, drkg wtr, showers, dump. Hiking, swimming, fishing (jetty), boating(lr), playground. 602-acre lake.

KEOSAUQUA (E)

Austin Park   FREE
Van Buren County Conservation Board
2 mi E of Keosauqua on CR J40, across Des Moines River, then qtr mi N on 3rd St; turn right at intersection, then 2.5 mi N on Eagle Dr.; on W shore of river. Free. All year. Facilities removed from this park; now just primitive camping; no wtr or toilets. Boating(l), fishing.

Bentonsport River Side Park $7
Van Buren County Conservation Board
5 mi E of Keosauqua & 4 mi NW of Bonaparte. $7 for primitive sites, $12 with 30/50-amp elec. Apr-Oct. 23 sites. Tbls, flush toilets, cfga, drkg wtr. Historic town with antique & craft shops, Gothic picnic shelter($). Fishing, boating(l). Des Moines River.

Lacey-Keosauqua State Park $8
2 mi SW of Keosauqua off SR 1. $8 off-season at modern sites without elec ($11 rest of year); $13 off-season at 45 modern sites with 30-amp elec, 10 with 50-amp ($16 rest of year). Tbls, flush toilets, cfga, drkg wtr, showers, dump. Hiking, swimming, fishing, boating(lr). 22-acre lake.

Lake Sugema Recreation Area $12
Van Buren County Conservation Board
S of Keosauqua at SE side of Lake Sugema. $12 for primitive sites, $17 at 10 elec/wtr sites, $22 at 12 full hookups. All year. 22 sites. Tbls, flush toilets, cfga, drkg wtr, hookups, dump, showers, fish cleaning station, shelter. Boating(ld), fishing. 574-acre lake. In-season reservations.

KINGSTON (E)

4th Pumping Plant $8
Des Moines County Recreation Park
Des Moines County Conservation Board
6 mi N of Kingston on SR 99; 5 mi E; near Mississippi River. $8 for 24 primitive sites; $15 for 22 elec sites (seniors pay $5 & $10). 4/1-12/1; 14-day limit. 46 sites (22 with elec). Tbls, toilets, cfga, drkg wtr, dump. Fishing, boating(l). 17 acres. Non-campers pay $5 for dump station.

KNOXVILLE (E)

Elk Rock State Park $11
5 mi N of Knoxville on Hwy 14; at Lake Red Rock. $11 at 9 non-elec sites during 5/1-9/30 ($8 off-season); $16 at 21 elec sites in-season ($13 off-season). 57 equestrian sites $3 higher. Tbls, flush toilets, cfga, drkg wtr, showers, dump. Interpretive trail, multi-use trails, fishing, boating(l). 10,600-acre lake.

Marion County Park $12
Marion County Conservation Board
Half mi W of Knoxville on Hwy 5 & 92. $12 without elec; $16 for 30-amp elec; $20 for 50-amp elec/wtr; $25 full hookups. Seniors with federal America the Beautiful senior pass get $2 per night discounts. 4/1-11/15. 165 sites (10 without elec); RVs under 31 ft. Tbls, flush toilets, showers, drkg wtr, elec($), dump. Boating, playground, fishing, canoeing. Historic site. Handicapped facilities. 115 acres.

Whitebreast Campground $9
Corps of Engineers
Lake Red Rock
1.5 mi E of Knoxville on SR B-92; 2 mi N on CR S-71; on S side of lake. $9 with federal senior pass for 109 elec sites; others pay $18. About 4/25-9/30; 14-day limit. 60-ft RV limit. Fish cleaning station, tbls, flush toilets, showers, cfga, drkg wtr, dump, beach, playground, amphitheater, fish cleaning station. Fishing, boating(l), swimming, hiking. Non-campers pay day use fee.

LAKE CITY (W)

Mike Macke Campground $10
Michael Macke Memorial Park
From jct with SR 175 (W. Main St) in Lake City, 1 mi N & W on N. 37th St (becoming CR N35) to park at Lake Creek. $10 at 5 elec RV sites, $5 tents. Tbls, flush toilets, cfga, drkg wtr, showers, playground. Fishing.

Rainbow Bend $10
Calhoun County Park
Half mi W of S edge of Lake City; 2.5 mi S on Hwy 286; at the Raccoon River. $10. All year; 14-day limit. 10 sites. Tbls, pit toilets, cfga, firewood, well drkg wtr. Picnicking, fishing, boating(l). River. 19-acre park owned by state, managed by county. Raccoon River Wildlife Area connects with park by bridge over river; vehicle access from Iberia St S of Lake City.

LAKE MILLS (W)

Dahle Park $5
Winnebago County Park
About 4 mi NW of Lake Mills on CR A16; on Winnebago River. $5. All year. 8 sites with elec. Tbls, pit toilets, cfga, drkg wtr, shelter, playground. Canoe access, fishing, geocaching. 7 acres.

LAKE PARK (W)

Silver Lake City Park Campground $10
Lake Park Parks & Recreation Department
About 4 mi E of Lake Park on SR 9; 1.2 mi N on M-27; 2 blks E on Park Dr. $10 without elec; $25 with elec ($100 weekly, $250 monthly, $1,300 seasonal). 5/1-10/15. 40 sites. Tbls, toilets, cfga, drkg wtr, elec($), dump, pool, playground, showers, WiFi. Fishing, boating(l), swimming, sand volleyball, horseshoes, basketball.

Silver Lake South Shore Park $10
Lake Park Parks & Recreation Department
About 3 mi E of Lake Park on SR 9; qtr mi N on county
rd. $10 without elec; $25 with elec ($100 weekly, $225
monthly, $1,200 seasonal). 5/1-10/30. 15 sites. Tbls, toi-
lets, cfga, drkg wtr, elec($). Fishing, boating(ld).

LAKE VIEW (W)
Black Hawk State Park $8
E of Lake View on Black Hawk Lake. $8 base off-season
at 39 modern sites without elec ($11 rest of year); $13
off-season at 89 modern sites with elec ($16 rest of year).
Tbls, flush toilets, showers, cfga, drkg wtr, dump. Interpretive trail, hiking, swimming, fishing (pier), boating (lr),
playground. 925-acre lake.

LANESBORO (W)
Carroll County Park   FREE
Carroll County Conservation Board
1.5 mi S of Lanesboro on CR N47; 0.5 mi W on Voyager
Rd; at shore of North Raccoon River. Free. All year; 14-day
limit. Primitive undeveloped camping; no facilities. Fishing, hiking, boating, hunting, picnic area. 70 acres.

Hobbs Access   FREE
Carroll County Conservation Board
1 mi S of Lanesboro on CR N47; 1.2 mi W on 130th St; S on
access rd at N shore of North Raccoon River. Free. Undeveloped primitive camping. Tbls, toilets, cfga, well drkg
wtr. Fishing, boating, canoe access. 11 acres.

LARRABEE (W)
Martin Access Park $5
Cherokee County Conservation Board
From jct with US 59 just N of Larrabee, about 3.5 mi E on
CR C16; 1 mi S on Martin Access Rd; right into park; at
shore of Little Sioux River. $5 at 25 primitive sites; $15 at
11 full-hookup 50-amp sites. 5/1-10/31. Tbls, flush & pit
toilets, cfga, drkg wtr, showers, picnic shelters, dump,
playground. 5.3 mi of hiking trails, 5 mi equestrian trails,
canoeing, boating(l), fishing.

LAWLER (E)
Adolph Munson Park   FREE
Chickasaw County Conservation Board
3.5 mi NW of Lawler at 2749 170th St. Free primitive sites.
Tbls, toilets, cfga, drkg wtr, shelters. Picnicking. 3 acres;
historical site (cabin, school house, store).

LEHIGH (W)
Brushy Creek State Recreation Area $6
4 mi E of Lehigh on CR D46. $6 base. All year; 14-day limit.
Base fee off-season at non-modern sites without elec ($9
rest of year); $8 off-season at modern sites without elec
($11 rest of year); $11 off-season at non-modern sites
with elec ($14 rest of year); $13 off-season at modern

sites with elec ($16 rest of year). Tbls, toilets, cfga, drkg
wtr, elec($5), sewer/wtr hookups($3). Picnicking, fishing,
boating, hunting, hiking trails, equestrian trails. 6,500
acres.

Dolliver Memorial State Park $8
3 mi NW of Lehigh on SR 121; overlooks Des Moines River.
$8 base off-season at 2 modern sites without elec ($11
rest of year); $13 off-season at 33 modern sites with
elec ($16 rest of year). Tbls, flush toilets, cfga, drkg wtr,
showers, dump. Hiking, fishing, boating(l), playground,
canoeing.

LENOX (W)
Wilson Lake Park $5
Taylor County Conservation Board
3 mi SE of Lenox. From CR N64, 1 mi E on CR J20; 1.5 mi
S on Utah Ave. $5 at primitive undesignated sites, $10 at
developed sites. Tbls, toilets, cfga, drkg wtr. Picnicking,
fishing, canoeing, boating (elec mtrs only). 20-acre lake;
54 acres.

LEWIS (W)
Cold Springs Park $10
Cass County Conservation Board
2 mi S of Lewis on CR M56. $10 without hookups; $12 with
elec. 4/1-10/31; 14-day limit. 20 primitive sites, 26 with
elec. Tbls, flush toilets, cfga, drkg wtr, showers, dump.
Boating(l - elec mtrs), fishing, playground, hiking trails,
swimming. 104 acres.

LINN GROVE (W)
Buena Vista County Park $6
Buena Vista County Conservation Board
4 mi W of Linn Grove on CR C13 (S. River Rd); left on 440th
St. $6 at primitive sites; $12 at 18 elec 30-amp sites.
4/15-10/15 (primitive sites open all year); 14-day limit.
Numerous primitive sites around picnic shelters. Tbls,
flush toilets, hot showers, drkg wtr, dump, cfga. Picnicking, hiking, playground, bridle trails, cross-country skiing,
horseshoe pits. 308 acres. New campground planned with
19 elec/wtr hookups & restrooms.

Linn Grove Dam Area $6
Buena Vista County Conservation Board
On both shores of Little Sioux River in town of Linn Grove.
$6. Open spring-fall. Primitive open sites. Tbls, pit toilets,
cfga, drkg wtr, playground. Boating(l), fishing, canoeing.
12 acres.

LIVERMORE (W)
Lotts Creek Park $9
Humboldt County Conservation Board
Half mi W of Livermore on Hwy 222. $10 at primitive sites,
$12 with elec. 5/1-10/31; 14-day limit. 5 sites. Tbls, flush
toilets, cfga, drkg wtr, shelter. Picnicking, fishing, hiking,
canoeing, boating. 40 acres. Pack out trash.

LOCKRIDGE (E)
MacCoon Access $9
Jefferson County Conservation Board
2 mi N of Lockridge on CR W40, then from Four Corners, follow Willow Blvd 2 mi NE & E on access rd; at W shore of Skunk River. $9 without hookups; $12 with elec. All year; 14-day limit; no wtr off-season. 20 sites. Tbls, pit toilets, cfga, drkg wtr, playground, fish cleaning station, dump. Hiking trails, fishing, boating(l), hunting. 71 acres. Prone to flooding.

LOHRVILLE (W)
University "40"   FREE
Calhoun County Conservation Board
Half mi E of Lohrville on IA 175; 1 mi S on CR N65; qtr mi E to entrance; at Cedar Creek. Free. All year; 14-day limit. Primitive sites. Tbls, flush toilets, cfga, firewood, shelters, drkg wtr. Picnicking, fishing, hiking, canoeing, horseback riding, saddle club camping, winter sports. 40 acres. Previously owned by University of Iowa.

LONE TREE (E)
River Junction Access $10
Johnson County Conservation Board
6 mi W of Lone Tree on SR 22; qtr mi S on CR W66 or Middle St SE; along Iowa River. $10 at 12 primitive sites. Tbls, pit toilets, cfga, drkg wtr. Boating(l), fishing, picnicking.

LOWDEN (E)
Massillon Area Park $7
Cedar County Conservation Board
At N edge of Massillon on CR Y-24 (Washington Ave), 4 mi N of Lowden. $7. Primitive camping in 20-acre park on S shore of Wapsipinicon River. Tbls, toilets, cfga, drkg wtr. Hiking trails, canoeing, boating(l), fishing. Enclosed shelter, playground.

LOWELL (E)
Stephenson Park $10
Henry County Conservation Board
Just S of Lowell on CR X23; at N shore of Skunk River. $10 for primitive sites. Tbls, toilets, cfga, no drkg wtr. Fishing, boating, picnicking. 4 acres.

LUCAS (W)
Stephens State Forest $6
W of Lucas & E of Chariton on US 34. $6 base. All year; 14-day limit. Base fee for 80 non-modern sites off-season ($9 during 5/1-9/30). Tbls, toilets, cfga, drkg wtr, no elec. Picnicking, fishing, hunting, hiking trails, interpretive trail, equestrian trails. (Note: Some readers report sites are near a stagnant pond with swarms of flies.)

MACEDONIA (W)
Old Town Park   FREE
Pottawattamie County Conservation Board
1 mi W of Macedonia on CR G-66. Free. 10 primitive sites. Toilets, drkg wtr, tbls. Picnicking, fishing, hunting, tubing, canoeing. 8 acres. West Nishnabotna River. On the historic Mormon Trail. 9.5 acres.

MADRID (W)
Swede Point $11
Boone County Conservation Board
Saylorville Lake
1 mi W of Madrid on SR 210; 1 mi N on QM Ave; E on access rd; on upper Des Moines River leg of Saylorville Lake. $11 without hookups at 2 areas; $17 with elec at 24 sites. 4/15-10/15; 14-day limit. 40 sites. Tbls, showers, flush toilets, cfga, drkg wtr, dump. Picnicking, hiking trails, fishing. Handicap facilities. 128 acres leased from Corps of Engineers.

MANNING (W)
Great Western Park $10
Carroll County Conservation Board
1 mi W of Manning on SR 141; S on CR M66; at 12-acre Great Western pond. $10 at primitive sites, $12 at 8 elec/wtr sites. 4/15-10/31. Tbls, flush toilets, cfga, drkg wtr, dump ($ for non-campers), playground, group shelter. Boating(l), fishing, shooting range, walking trail.

MANCHESTER (E)
Bailey's Ford Recreation Area $10
Delaware County Conservation Board
4 mi SE of Manchester on CR D5X, changing to Jefferson Rd. $10 without hookups; $14 with elec; $16 with elec/wtr. 4/15-10/25; 14-day limit. 12 hookup sites, 35 with elec plus primitive area (30-ft RV limit). Tbls, toilets, cfga, drkg wtr, dump, firewood($), playground, showers. Boating(l), trout fishing, hiking trails, nature program, playground, volleyball, softball, horseshoes, shuffleboard. Nature center with raptors. 78 acres.

Coffins Grove Park $10
Delaware County Conservation Board
1 mi W of Manchester on 210th St (Old US 20); 2 mi NW on on Early Stagecoach Rd; at S shore of Coffins Creek. $10 for primitive sites; $14 with elec; $16 elec/wtr. 5/1-10/30; 14-day limit. 25 sites (30-ft RV limit). Tbls, toilets, cfga, drkg wtr, elec($), dump, handicapped facilities. Ball field, picnicking, hiking, fishing, swimming, softball, volleyball, horseshoes. 22 acres.

MAPLETON (W)
Grays Landing $12
Wildlife Management Area
Monona County Conservation Board
5 mi S of Mapleton on Hwy 175; at Maple River. $12 at non-elec sites; $15 with elec. All year; 14-day limit. Pit toilets, tbls, cfga, drkg wtr, shelter. Fishing. 43 acres.

MAQUOKETA (E)

Horseshoe Pond Municipal Park $12
From US 61 just S of Maquoketa, 0.5 mi N on 200th Ave; right on 22nd St or S. 2nd St; at shore of Prairie Creek. $12 at 20 elec sites (3 pull-through with 50-amp). Tbls, flush toilets, cfga, drkg wtr, dump, playground, showers. Fishing pond, volleyball.

Maquoketa Caves State Park $8
8 mi N of Maquoketa on US 61; W on SR 130. $8 base off-season at 12 modern sites without elec ($11 rest of year); $13 off-season at 17 modern sites with elec ($16 rest of year). Tbls, flush & pit toilets, elec($5) showers, cfga, drkg wtr, dump. Interpretive trail, hiking, playground, interpretive center. 272 acres.

MARBLE ROCK (E)

Ackley Creek $10
Floyd County Park
0.5 mi W of Marble Rock on CR B60; half mi S on West St (Indigo Ave). $10 at primitive sites; $15 with elec/wtr. 5/1-10/1. 10 primitive sites; 37 elec sites. Tbls, flush toilets, showers, cfga, drkg wtr, elec($), dump, playground. Hiking trails, picnicking, fishing. 40 acres.

Gates Bridge FREE
Floyd County Park
4 mi SE of Marble Rock at 2920 Kirdwoood Rd, Greene. Free. 6 undeveloped primitive sites. No facilities. Picnicking, fishing, boating. 4 acres.

Marble Rock City Park FREE
From SR 14 E of Marble Rock, go W 3 mi on B-60 to Marble Rock, then follow signs on Park Rd 1 block Free; donations accepted. All year; 3-day limit. Tbls, toilets, 6 sites, primitive tent/RV areas with elec, cfga, drkg wtr, playground, shelters, elec($1), dump. Tennis, fishing, boating(d).

MARCELLINE (ILLINOIS)

Bear Creek Recreation Area FREE
Corps of Engineers
Mississippi River Public Use Area
1.5 mi W of IL 96 in Marcelline on Bolton Rd; quarter mi on gravel rd; 3 mi W across the levee to the campground. Free. All year; 14-day limit. 40 primitive sites. Tbls, toilets, cfga, drkg wtr, dump. Swimming, picnicking, fishing, boating(l), horseback riding. 6 acres.

MARQUETTE (E)

Bloody Run Park $7
Clayton County Conservation Board
2 mi W of Marquette on US 18; at Bloody Run River. $7. All year; 14-day limit. 19 primitive sites at rear of park. Tbls, toilets, cfga, drkg wtr. Fishing, hunting. 135 acres.

Yellow River State Forest $6
10 mi N of Marquette on SR 76. $6 base. All year; 14-day limit. Base fee at 152 non-modern sites off-season ($9 rest of year). Tbls, toilets, cfga, drkg wtr, no elec. Picnicking, fishing, boating(l), hunting, hiking trails, equestrian trails. 76 acres.

MASON CITY (E)

Margaret MacNider City Park $12
In Mason City, 5 blks N on Kentucky Ave from US 18; 1 blk W on Birch Ave; on Winnebago River. $12 base. About 4/15-10/15; 14-day limit. Base fee for primitive & tent sites; $16 with wtr/elec; $25 full hookups. About 200 sites (125 with elec). Tbls, flush toilets, cfga, drkg wtr, showers, elec($), dump, pool, playground. Fishing, swimming, canoeing.

Shell Rock River Green Belt FREE
Cerro Gordo County Conservation Board
8 mi E of Mason City on 12th St NE (CR B25); left (N) on Yarrow Ave, then right (E) on 277th St & N on Yucca Ave. Primitive camping & picnicking in preserve section of the greenbelt between 290th & 280th Sts SE of Rock Falls (not to be confused with Wilkinson Pioneer Park at SE corner of Rock Falls -- a fee site). Free. 5/1-10/1; 14-day limit. 12 primitive sites. Toilets, tbls, cfga, drkg wtr. Swimming, fishing, picnicking, hunting, snowmobiling, hiking, bridle trails. 590 acres.

MAYNARD (E)

Twin Bridges Park $5
Fayette County Conservation Board
3 mi N of Maynard on CR W25; at Volga River. $5. 4/1-10/30; 14-day limit. Undesignated sites (35-ft RV limit). Tbls, pit toilets, cfga, drkg wtr, playground. Fishing, picnicking. 17 acres. Annual county parks camping pass $350.

MCGREGOR (N)

Pikes Peak State Park $11
3 mi S of McGregor on CR X56 (Great River Rd). $11 at non-elec sites during 5/1-9/30 ($6 off-season); $16 at elec sites in-season, $11 off-season. 70 sites (52 elec). Tbls, flush toilets, cfga, drkg wtr (except in winter), showers, dump, playground. Hiking/biking trails, boardwalk to Bridal Veil Falls. 970 acres.

MENLO (W)

Menlo City Park $12
2 mi N of I-80 exit 88; E to Sherman St; N 2 blocks; on N edge of Menlo by RR tracks. $12. All year; 14-day limit. 7 sites. Tbls, toilets, cfga, elec. Groceries, ice, restaurant. Picnicking, playground, adult room, basketball.

MILFORD (W)

Emerson Bay $8
State Recreation Area
2.5 mi N of Milford on SR 32; on West Okobji Lake. $8 base off-season at modern sites without elec ($11 base rest of year). $13 off-season at 82 modern sites with 52-amp elec ($16 rest of year), 23 with full hookups ($19). Tbls, flush toilets, cfga, drkg wtr (except in winter), showers, dump. Swimming, fishing, boating (lr), playground. 3,847-acre lake.

Gull Point State Park $8
Off SR 32, 3.5 mi N of Milford on SR 86; W side of West Okobji Lake. $8 base off-season at 52 modern sites without elec ($11 base rest of year); $13 off-season at 60 modern sites with elec ($16 rest of year). Tbls, flush toilets, cfga, drkg wtr (except in winter), showers, dump. Swimming, hiking, interpretive trail, fishing, boating, playground.

MILLERSBURG (E)

Lake Iowa Park $10
Iowa County Conservation Board
From Millersburg, about 5 mi N on CR V52; 1 mi W following signs, to 216th St, then N to park access rd. $10 during 10/16-4/14 at elec sites (5 with 50-amp), $7 tents but no wtr services; in-season fees $16 at elec sites, $10 tents. All year; 14-day limit. 120 sites. Tbls, flush toilets, cfga, drkg wtr, showers, dump, shelters, beach, fish cleaning station. Swimming, fishing, boating(l), hiking trails, naturalist programs. Nature center, butterfly garden, bird observation blind, disc golf. No reservations.

MISSOURI VALLEY (W)

Wilson Island State Recreation Area $8
3 mi W of Missouri Valley on US 30; 6 mi S (from sign) on gravel rd. $8 base. All year; 14-day limit. Base fee off-season at 72 modern sites without elec ($11 rest of year); $13 off-season at 62 modern sites with elec ($16 rest of year). Tbls, toilets, cfga, drkg wtr, sewer/wtr hookups($2), dump, playground. Picnicking, swimming, fishing, boating(l), hunting, hiking trails, interpretive trail. 577 acres.

MITCHELL (S)

Interstate Park $10
Mitchell County Conservation Board
On W edge of Mitchell on CR A43; at Cedar River. $10 without hookups; $18 at 40 undesignated sites with elec/wtr (with week's stay, 7th night free). 5/15-10/15; 14-day limit. 50 sites. Tbls, flush toilets, cfga, drkg wtr, showers, dump, beach. Canoeing, fishing, boating(ld), hiking trails, swimming, sand volleyball. 27 acres. Historic powerhouse & dam.

MITCHELLVILLE (E)

Thomas Mitchell Park $10
Polk County Conservation Board
From Mitchellville, 2 mi S on CR S27; 1 mi E on NE 46th Ave; S on NE 108th St to park entrance; at shore of Camp Creek. $10 at non-elec sites for seniors except on holiday weekends during 4/15-10/15 (others pay $15). Elec sites $15 in-season for seniors; others pay $20. With online reservations, non-elec sites are $18, elec sites $23 (no senior discounts with reservations). 23 elec sites, 28 primitive sites. Tbls, flush toilets, cfga, drkg wtr, showers, dump, playground, fishing pier. Fishing, canoeing, hiking trails, ball fields, basketball, fishing pond.

MONTEZUMA (E)

Diamond Lake $10
Poweshiek County Conservation Board
Half mi W of Montezuma on US 63. $10 base at primitive sites; $17 with elec. All year; 14-day limit. Free non-elec camping before & after regular season. 60 sites. Tbls, flush toilets, dump, cfga, drkg wtr, showers, fish cleaning station. Fishing, boating (elec mtrs), picnicking, biking/hiking trails, playground. 301 acres; 98-acre lake. Campground & sites were renovated 2012.

MORAVIA (E)

Bridgeview Campground $7
Corps of Engineers
Rathbun Lake
From SR 5 at Moravia, 10.4 mi W on SR 142; 1.2 mi S on SR 142; N of bridge. $7 with federal senior pass at 11 non-elec sites; others pay $14. $9 base with senior pass at 30-amp elec sites; others pay $18 base. $10 with senior pass at premium 50-amp sites; others pay $20. 100 elec sites, including 7 double sites. RV limit in excess of 65 ft; 6 pull-through. 5/1-9/30; 14-day limit. Tbls, flush toilets, cfga, drkg wtr, showers, dump, playground, fish cleaning station, pavilion, fishing pier. Boating(l), fishing.

Buck Creek Campground $9
Corps of Engineers
Rathbun Lake
From SR 5 at Moravia, 2 mi W on SR 142; 3 mi S on CR J5T; E end of lake. $9 base with federal senior pass for 42 elec sites; others pay $18 base, $20 at premium 50-amp elec sites ($10 with senior pass). RV limit in excess of 65 ft; 10 pull-through sites. 5/1-9/30; 14-day limit. Tbls, flush toilets, cfga, drkg wtr, pavilion, fish cleaning station, beach, showers, dump, playground, picnic shelter. Swimming, boating(l), fishing.

Honey Creek State Park $8
3.5 mi W of Moravia on SR 142; S on 185th Ave; at N shore of Rathbun Lake. $8 base off-season at modern sites without elec ($11 rest of year); $13 off-season at 75 modern sites with elec ($16 rest of year), 28 with full

hookups ($19). Tbls, flush toilets, cfga, drkg wtr, showers, dump, fish cleaning stations. Interpretive trail, hiking, swimming, fishing.

Prairie Ridge Campground $9
Corps of Engineers
Rathbun Lake
From SR 5 at Moravia, 4 mi W on SR 142; 3 mi S; at N side of lake. $9 with federal senior pass for 54 sites with 50-amp elec; others pay $18. 5/15-9/15; 14-day limit. RV limit in excess of 65 ft. Picnic shelter, fish cleaning station, tbls, flush toilets, cfga, drkg wtr, showers, dump, playground. Boating(l), fishing.

MORNING SUN (E)

Virginia Grove Recreation Area $12
Louisa County Conservation Board
3 mi NW of Morning Sun on CR X37; 1.2 mi W on 50th St; right on Q Ave, then left on 55th St into park. $12. All year; 14-day limit. 11 gravel sites with 20/30/50-amp elec; some pull-through. Tbls, toilets, cfga, drkg wtr. Hiking trails, fishing, hunting, canoeing. 1066 acres; 5-acre pond, historic schoolhouse.

MOUNT AYR (W)

Fife's Grove $5
Ringgold County Conservation Board
1 mi N of Mount Ayr on IA 169; E on SR 344. $5 at non-elec sites; $10 with elec. 3/15-9/15; 14-day limit. Primitive sites & 10 elec RV sites. Tbls, pit toilet, cfga, drkg wtr, playground. Picnic shelters, fishing, hiking. 52 acres, 1-acre pond.

Poe Hollow $5
Ringgold County Conservation Board
1.5 mi E of Mount Ayr on SR 2. $5 without hookups, $10 at 10 sites with elec. 3/15-11/15; 14-day limit. Tbls, pit toilets, cfga, drkg wtr, firewood, playground. Picnicking (2 shelters); hiking trails. 72 acres, 1-acre pond.

MOUNT PLEASANT SE)

Faulkner's Access FREE
Henry County Conservation Board
3 mi SW of Mt. Pleasant on CR H46; right on Hickory Ave for half mi; 1 mi E on 253rd St; 0.5 mi SE on 265th St; at E shore of Skunk River. Free. 4/15-10/1; 14-day limit. 5 primitive sites. Tbls, cfga, no toilets or drkg wtr. Fishing, boating(l), hunting. 27 acres.

Oakland Mills $10
Henry County Conservation Board
2 mi W of Mt. Pleasant on Washington St; 2 mi S on CR W55; on both sides of Skunk River. North Shore Campground open 4/15-10/15 with 10 primitive sites, $10. South Shore Campground also 4/15-10/15 with 11 primitive sites ($10) & 24 elec 30/50-amp sites, $15. Top-of-the-Hill Campground open all year with 6 sites & 4 new group sites. Tbls, toilets,

cfga, drkg wtr, elec($), shelters, fish cleaning station, dump ($2 for non-campers). Hiking trails, fishing, boating. Historic foot bridge. 104 acres.

Water Works Park $10
Henry County Conservation Board
2 mi W of Mount Pleasant on Washington St; 2 mi S on CR W55; right before river bridge into park; along E shore of Skunk River. $10 for 10 primitive sites; $15 for 20 elec sites. 4/15-10/15; 14-day limit. Tbls, toilets, cfga, drkg wtr. Boating(l), fishing. 16 acres.

MOUNT VERNON (E)

Palisades-Kepler State Park $8
3.5 mi W of Mount Vernon on SR 22; 1 mi N on CR P. $8 base off-season at 18 modern sites without elec ($11 base rest of year); $13 off-season at 26 sites with elec ($16 rest of year). Tbls, flush toilets, cfga, drkg wtr, showers, dump. Hiking, fishing, boating(l). 840 acres at Cedar River.

MURRAY (W)

Hopeville Square Park $10
Clarke County Conservation Board
7 mi S of Murray at Hopeville. $10. All year. 4 sites with elec/wtr by reservation (515-342-3960). Tbls, pit toilets, cfga, drkg wtr, playground, picnic shelters, sports court. 4 acres.

MUSCATINE (E)

Blanchard Island Recreation Area $12
Corps of Engineers
Mississippi River Public Use Area
Lock & Dam 17
From Muscatine bridge in Illinois, 1.5 mi E on IL 92; 4 mi S, then second right past Copperas Creek bridge; off the river's main channel. $12 during 5/15-10/15 ($6 with federal senior pass); free rest of year. 34 primitive sites. Tbls, toilets, cfga, drkg wtr, dump. Boating(l), fishing.

Clarks Ferry $10
Corps of Engineers
Mississippi River Public Use Area
Lock & Dam 16
From Muscatine, 15 mi E on SR 22 (W. 2nd St) following signs; along main river channel. $10 base with federal senior pass at 27 elec sites; others pay $20 base, $22 for 50-amp service ($11 with senior pass). 5/1-10/24; 14-day limit. Tbls, flush toilets, cfga, drkg wtr, dump, shelter($), amphitheater. Picnicking, boating(l$), fishing, waterskiing, horseshoe pits.

Fairport State Recreation Area $11
From Muscatine, 7 mi E on Hwy 22 at Fairport. $11 at 42 elec sites. All year; 14-day limit. Tbls, flush toilets, cfga, drkg wtr, showers, fish cleaning station, dump. Boating(ld), fishing, canoeing, horseshoes, playground. Fish hatchery nearby.

Shady Creek Recreation Area $10
Lock & Dam 16
Corps of Engineers
Mississippi River Public Use Area
From Muscatine, 10 mi E on SR 22 following signs. $10 with federal senior pass at 53 elec 50-amp sites; others pay $20. 5/1-10/22; 14-day limit. RV limit in excess of 65 ft. Tbls, flush toilets, cfga, drkg wtr, dump, showers, picnic shelter($). Boating(l$) fishing, horseshoes.

Shady Creek Campground $6
Wildcat Den State Park
11 mi E of Muscatine on SR 22; 1 mi N on CR P. $6 base. All year; 14-day limit. Base fee for 28 non-modern sites off-season ($9 rest of year). Tbls, toilets, cfga, drkg wtr (except in winter), no elec. Picnicking, fishing, hiking trails, interpretive trail. 423 acres.

MYSTIC (E)
Island View $9
Corps of Engineers
Rathbun Lake
1.8 mi N of Mystic on CR T-14; 2.6 mi E on CR J5T; half mi N. $9 with federal senior pass at 50-amp elec sites; others pay $18. 5/1-9/15; 14-day limit. 54 elec sites; RV limit in excess of 65 ft. Tbls, flush toilets, cfga, drkg wtr, showers, dump, playground, beach, pavilion($), fish cleaning station, ball field. Boating (l), fishing, swimming, basketball.

Rolling Cove Campground FREE
Corps of Engineers
Rathbun Lake
1.8 mi N of Mystic on CR T-14; 2.7 mi W on CR J5T; 4 mi N & E on CR RC-1. Formerly $12, now free. 5/1-9/15; 14-day limit. 31 non-elec sites; RV limit in excess of 65 ft. Tbls, toilets, cfga, drkg wtr, showers, dump, no elec, fishing pier, fish cleaning station. Fishing, boating(l).

NASHUA (E)
Howard's Woods $5
Chickasaw County Conservation Board
1 mi N of Nashua on Asherton Ave; 1 mi W on 260th St; along Cedar River at Cedar Lake. $5. All year. Primitive camping. Tbls, toilets, cfga, drkg wtr. Fishing, boating, hunting. 20 acres.

NEW HAMPTON (E)
Airport Lake Park $12
Chickasaw County Conservation Board
1 mi W of New Hampton on SR 18; 1 mi N on Kenwood Ave; left on 190th St to park entrance. $12 at 20 non-elec sites; $15 at 18 sites with 30/50-amp elec. 5/1 10/31. Tbls, toilets, cfga, drkg wtr, elec($), beach. Picnicking, swimming beach, fishing, hunting. Handicapped facilities. 57 acres; 10-acre lake. Pool nearby.

NEW HARTFORD (E)
West Fork Forest Access FREE
Butler County Conservation Board
N of New Hartford on CR T-55; at West Fork River. Free. All year. Primitive open camping on 108 acres; no facilities, no drkg wtr. Hunting, fishing, boating(l), canoeing. GPS: 42.6355, -92.653

NEW MARKET (W)
Windmill Lake $5
Taylor County Conservation Board
6 mi E of New Market on IA 2; 1 mi N on Highland Ave; W on 220th St to Franklin Ave. $5 at primitive area on W side of lake; $10 at 14 modern sites. All year; 14-day limit. Toilets, cfga, tbls, drkg wtr. Fishing, boating, hiking, horseback riding, canoeing. 61 acres, 20-acre lake.

NEW PROVIDENCE (E)
Reece Memorial Park FREE
Hardin County Conservation Board
1 mi S of New Providence on CR S57; 1 mi W on 310th St; on both sides of Honey Creek. Free. All year; 14-day limit. 12 sites. Tbls, toilets, cfga, drkg wtr, shelter. Picnicking, hiking, archery. Facilities for handicapped. 70 acres.

NEWTON (E)
Mariposa Recreation Area $7
Jasper County Conservation Board
2 mi E of Newton on US 6; 5 mi N on CR T-12. $7. All year; 14-day limit in 17-day period. Primitive non-elec sites. Tbls, toilets, cfga, drkg wtr. Fishing, hiking, winter sports. 151 acres; 17-acre lake.

NORTH LIBERTY (SE)
Sugar Bottom Par $10
Corps of Engineers
Coralville Lake
From North Liberty at jct with SR 965, 2.6 mi NE on CR F28 (Mahaffey Bridge Rd); cross bridge, then 1.3 mi S on access rd; at east-central shore of lake. $10 base with federal senior pass at 224 30-amp elec sites; others pay $20 base; $22 for 50-amp sites ($11 with senior pass); $24 for 50-amp elec/wtr ($12 with senior pass); $26 full hookups ($13 with senior pass). RV limit in excess of 65 ft. Tbls, flush toilets, cfga, drkg wtr, showers, dump, beach, playground, amphitheater, phone. Snowmobiling, boating(l), fishing, swimming, hiking trails, golf, horseshoes, disc golf, mountain biking trails.

NORTH WASHINGTON (E)
Haus Park FREE
Chickasaw County Conservation Board
From North Washington, E on Pine St, then N on CR B33, across Little Wapsipinicon River, then right into park. Free primitive camping. All year; 14-day limit. Tbls, toilets, cfga, drkg wtr. Picnicking, fishing, hunting, canoeing. 7 acres.

Ferry Landing Recreation Area   FREE
Corps of Engineers
Mississippi River Public Use Area
Lock & Dam 18
6 mi from N edge of Oakville on CR X71 to levee (follow signs); at mouth of Iowa River. Free. All year; 14-day limit. 22 primitive sites. Tbls, toilets, cfga, drkg wtr. Fishing, boating(l), hiking, picnic area.

NORTHWOOD (E)

Ochee Yahola Park $10
Worth County Conservation Board
1 mi W of Northwood on SR 105; 2.5 mi N on Mallard Ave; left at 495th St, then 100 yds. $10. 4/15-10/30; 14-day limit. 4 primitive sites. Tbls, pit toilet, cfga, 20-amp elec; no drkg wtr or trash pickup. Hiking, bridle & cross-country ski trails, fishing, picnicking, boating. 160 acres.

Silver Lake Park $10
Worth County Conservation Board
From Hwy 105 W of Northwood, N on either Wheelerwood Rd or Finch Ave; left on 500th St; park entrance 200 yds W of jetty; on N shore of Silver Lake. $10. 4/15-10/30; 14-day limit. 8 sites with 20-amp elec. Tbls, pit toilet, cfga, shelter, no drkg wtr or trash service. Picnicking, fishing, boating, hunting. 28 acres; 330-acre lake.

OAKVILLE (E)

Cappy Russell River Access   FREE
Louisa County Conservation Board
From Oakville at jct with Russell St, about 1 mi W & N on SR 99; left (W) on CR X71 to E shore of Iowa River. Free primitive camping; no facilities. Boating(l), fishing. Winter eagle watching.

OCHEYEDAN (W)

Ocheyedan Pits   FREE
County Recreation Area
Osceola County Conservation Board
2 mi S of Ocheyedan. Free. All year. Primitive, undeveloped camping in 33-acre park next to wildlife management area. Tbls, pit toilets, cfga, drkg wtr. Fishing, swimming, nature trails, mountain biking trail.

ODEBOLT (W)

Odebolt Memorial Walk $10
Municipal RV Park
From jct with SR 175 in Odebolt, 4 blocks S on SR 39; 3 blocks W to park at 6th St. & Willow St. $10 with elec. Tbls, flush toilets, cfga, drkg wtr.

OELWEIN (E)

Oelwein City Park Campground $8
Oelwein Parks & Recreation Department
Qtr mi W on Hwy 281 from jct with Hwy 150 near Oelwein. $8 base. 4/1 10/31. Base fee at primitive sites; $14 (or $75 weekly) with hookups (seniors pay $12 or $70 weekly). 30 modern sites plus primitive area. Tbls, toilets, cfga, drkg wtr, showers, playground, dump. Fishing, boating(ld), swimming, horseshoes, volleyball, tennis, waterskiing. 69 acres; 55-acre Lake Oelwein.

OGDEN (W)

Don Williams Recreation Area $11
Boone County Conservation Board
5 mi N of Ogden on CR P70; E on 162nd Lane. $11 base. 4/15-10/30. Base fee at 30 sites without hookups; 150 sites with 30-amp elec, $17. Tbls, showers, flush toilets, cfga, drkg wtr, dump. Picnicking, fishing, swimming beach, boating(l), biking, hiking, golf course, tennis court. 598 acres; 160-acre lake. Bait shop.

OLLIE (E)

Manhattan Bridge   FREE
Keokuk County Conservation Board
3 mi N of Ollie on CR V56 at Skunk River. Free. Undeveloped primitive camping. Toilets, tbls, playground, no drkg wtr. Picnicking, fishing, boating, canoeing. 1 acre.

ORIENT (W)

Lake Orient Recreation Area $9
Adair County Conservation Board
1 mi W of Orient on Hwy 25. $9 at 22 RV sites with 30-amp elec during 4/1-10/31; 14-day limit. Tent sites $6. Sites free off-season but no wtr or elec. 14-day limit. Tbls, toilets, cfga, drkg wtr. Picnicking, fishing, boating (ld), hunting, hiking. Historic site. 86 acres; 22-acre lake. County's dump station E in town, $2.

ORANGE CITY (W)

Veterans Memorial Park $5
Parks & Recreation Department
S entrance on 5th St. in Orange City; N entrance at 300 Iowa Ave SW. $5 without elec; $7.50 with elec; $10 full hookups. 16 sites, 12 full hookups Tbls, flush toilets & showers at nearby ball park, cfga, drkg wtr, playground. Sand volleyball.

ORLEANS (W)

Marble Beach State Recreation Area $8
2 mi NW of Orleans on SR 276. $8 base off-season at 124 modern sites without elec ($11 base rest of year); $13 off-season at 100 modern sites with elec ($16 rest of year). Tbls, flush toilets, cfga, drkg wtr (except in winter), showers, dump. Swimming, fishing, boating(ldr), hiking. 4,169-acre lake.

OSAGE (E)

Cedar Bridge Park $10
Mitchell County Conservation Board
Just W of Osage on SR 9. $10 at non-elec sites ($60 weekly); $18 at elec sites ($108 weekly). Also equestrian sites for $19 ($114 weekly). 18 elec sites. 5/15-10/15; 14-day limit. Tbls, flush toilets, cfga, drkg wtr, showers, dump.

Hiking, horseback riding, fishing, canoeing. Nature center, wildlife exhibit, museum.

Spring City Park $5
Osage Parks & Recreation Department
2 mi W of Osage on SR 9. $5, self-registration 5/1-11/1; 14-day limit. 26 sites; 45-ft RV limit. Tbls, toilets, cfga, drkg wtr. Playground, boating(l), fishing.

OSCEOLA (W)
East Lake $10
Clarke County Park
1 mi E of Osceola on Hwy 34. $10. All year. 4 sites with elec/wtr by reservation (515-342-3960). Tbls, toilets, cfga, drkg wtr, playgrounds, basketball court, volleyball courts, horseshoe pits. Fishing, hiking trails, fishing piers, 6 picnic shelters. 160 acres; 15-acre lake.

OSKALOOSA (E)
Lake Keomah State Park $8
5 mi E of Oskaloosa on SR 92; 1 mi S on SR 371. $8 base off-season at 24 modern sites without elec ($11 rest of year); $13 off-season at 41 modern sites with elec ($16 rest of year). Tbls, flush toilets, cfga, drkg wtr, showers, dump. Interpretive trail, hiking, swimming, fishing (jetties), boating. 84-acre lake.

OTRANTO (E)
Otranto Park $10
Mitchell County Conservation Board
Half mi E of Otranto on 480th St (4 mi N of Carpenter); at Cedar River. $10 without hookups; $18 at 20 undesignated elec sites. 5/15-10/15; 14-day limit. 16 sites. Tbls, toilets, cfga, drkg wtr, playground, shelter, showers, dump. Fishing, canoeing, boating(l). 5 acres. Camp 6 nights & get 7th night free.

PANORA (W)
Lenon Mills $10
Guthrie County Conservation Board
On S edge of Panora. From SRs 44 & 4, 3 blks S on East 3rd St, then W to Middle Raccoon River and N (right) just before river. $10 without elec; $15 with elec (free Thurs nights). All year; 14-day limit. 14 sites (8 for tents). Tbls, toilets, cfga, drkg wtr; dump nearby at museum area. Hiking trails, boating(l), canoeing, biking, fishing, picnicking. 32 acres.

PARKERSBURG (E)
Beaver Meadows $10
Butler County Conservation Board
On N edge of Parkersburg on Hwy 14; on N shore of Beaver Creek. $10 without hookups ($60 weekly); $12 at RV sites with elec ($72 weekly). 4/1-10/31; 14-day limit. About 50 sites (20 with elec); 55-ft RV limit. Tbls, toilets, cfga, drkg wtr. Picnicking, fishing, boating, canoeing, golf course. 32 acres. Formerly a state park. Camp free Wed nights.

PELLA (E)
Howell Station Recreation Area $10
Corps of Engineers
Lake Red Rock
From jct with SR 163 at Pella, 0.5 mi W on SR 28; 5 mi SW on CR T-15; E on Idaho; S on 198th Place, then S following signs; on shore of Des Moines River. $10 with federal senior pass at 143 elec sites; others pay $20. About 4/21-10/15; 14-day limit. RV limit in excess of 65 ft. Tbls, flush toilets, cfga, drkg wtr, dump, showers, playground, fish cleaning station. Biking, fishing, boating(l), hiking, amphitheater with weekend programs MD-LD. Boat launch fee for non-campers.

Ivan's Recreation Area $8
Corps of Engineers
Lake Red Rock
Below dam, SW side of outlet on Des Moines River. $8 with federal senior pass; others pay $16. About 4/30-10/1; 14-day limit. 21 sites; no fee booth (ranger collects fees). Fish cleaning station, tbls, flush toilets, showers, cfga, drkg wtr, elec, playground, fish cleaning station. Hiking & biking trails, fishing.

North Overlook Recreation Area $9
Corps of Engineers
Lake Red Rock
From jct with SR 163 at Pella, 0.5 mi W on SR 28; 3 mi SW on CR T-15; at N side of dam off T-15. $9 with federal senior pass at 54 elec sites; others pay $18. $10 at tent sites. 65-ft RV limit. About 4/25-10/1; 14-day limit. Pavilion, amphitheater, tbls, flush toilets, cfga, drkg wtr, elec, showers, dump, playground, beach (fee for non-campers). Weekend ranger programs, swimming, hiking, fishing.

Roberts Creek West Campground $12
Marion County Conservation Board
Lake Red Rock
From Pella, 7 mi W of Pella on CR G28; half mi N on Fillmore Dr; at N shore of lake along Robert Creek arm. $12 at non-elec sites; $16 with 30-amp elec; $20 with 50-amp elec/wtr; $25 full hookups. Seniors with federal senior pass get $2 per night discounts. About 4/25-10/25; 14-day limit. 85 sites. Tbls, flush toilets, showers, drkg wtr, playground, 2 picnic shelters, swimming beach. Boating(l), fishing, archery range, shuffleboard, disc golf. Adjoining Robert Creek West Campground has 50 sites with 30-amp elec, $14. 1,535-acre park.

Wallashuck Recreation Area $9
Corps of Engineers
Lake Red Rock
From Pella, 4 mi W on CR G-28; 2 mi S on 190th Ave. $9 with federal senior pass; others pay $18. About 4/25-9/30; 14-day limit. 83 elec sites (23 with 50-amp). Tbls, flush toilets, cfga, drkg wtr, showers, dump, playground,

amphitheater with campfire programs MD-LD, fish clean-ing station. Hiking, fishing, boating(l), campfire programs.

PLAINFIELD (E)

North Cedar $10
Bremer County Conservation Board
2 mi E of Plainfield on SR 188. $10 without hookups, $15 with elec. 5/1-10/31; 14-day limit. 58 sites (40 with elec). Tbls, toilets, cfga, drkg wtr, dump ($2 for non-campers), showers ($2 for non-campers). Picnicking, hiking trails, horseshoes, sand volleyball, fishing, boating(l), canoeing, hunting (11/1 1/10). 168 acres. Free camping on non-hol-iday Wed nights.

POCAHONTAS (W)

Little Clear Lake   FREE
Outdoor Recreation Area
Pocahontas County Conservation Board
9 mi W of Pocahontas on SR 3; 1 mi S on access rd; Free. Undeveloped primitive camping at W side of lake. Toilets, drkg wtr, tbls, cfga. Fishing, boating, hunting. 16 acres; adjacent to 7-acre Little Clear Lake Wildlife Area.

POMEROY (W)

Kelly Access   FREE
Calhoun County Conservation Board
2 mi S of Pomeroy on Marengo Ave; 9 mi W on CR D15; N into park at Big Cedar Creek. Free. Undeveloped primitive camping. Toilets, tbls, cfga, no drkg wtr. Picnicking, fish-ing, hunting. 7 acres.

POPEJOY (E)

Popejoy Conservation Park $5
Franklin County Conservation Board
From Popejoy, 0.5 mi W on CR S13; 0.75 mi S on CR S21 to park; at Iowa River. $5. 4/1-11/30; 14-day limit. About 30 undesignated sites. Tbls, toilets, cfga, drkg wtr, elec, shelter house, playground. Hiking & bridle trails, fishing, boating, 2 picnic areas. Historic site. Handicapped facili-ties. Winter sledding hill. 61 acres.

PRIMGHAR (W)

Tjossem Park $12
O'Brien County Conservation Board
1 mi S of Primghar on US 59; qtr mi E on 400th St. $12. 5/1-9/30; 14-day limit. 6 sites with elec/wtr. Tbls, pit toi-lets, cfga, drkg wtr, shelter. Fishing in ponds.

QUASQUETON (E)

Boies Bend Access Area   FREE
Buchanan County Park
From jct with CR D47 just S of Quasqueton, 1.5 mi W on 278th St, then N on park access rd; at S shore of Wapsipin-icon River. Free. All year; 14-day limit. Undeveloped primi-tive camping. Toilets, cfga, no drkg wtr. Picnic shelter with elec, fishing, hunting. 26 acres. Cranes Creek.

Troy Mills Wapsi Access Area   FREE
Buchanan County Conservation Board
SE of Quasqueton along Wapsipiinicon River (ask for directions locally). Free primitive camping on 63 acres. All year. Tbls, cfga, no toilets, no drkg wtr. Boating(l), fishing.

RALSTON (W)

Richey Campground $8
Carroll County Conservation Board
3 mi N of Ralston on Apple Ave (CR N58); at S shore of North Raccoon River. $8 at 12 elec RV sites; tents $6. All year; 14-day limit. 12 elec sites. Tbls, pit toilets, cfga, well drkg wtr. Fishing, canoeing.

RENWICK (W)

Oakdale Park   FREE
Wright County Conservation Board
2 mi S of Renwick on SR 17; 1 mi E on 175th St; at E shore of Boone River. Free. All year; 14-day limit. Primitive sites with elec, tbls, toilets, cfga, drkg wtr. Fishing, trapshoot-ing, hunting.

REINBECK (E)

Herbert Gutknecht Park   FREE
Grundy County Green Belt
Grundy County Conservation Board
3 mi W of Reinbeck on CR T-55 at SR 175. Free. 5 prim-itive sites. Tbls, pit toilets, cfga, well drkg wtr, shelter. Cross-country ski, snowmobile, hiking & bridle trails; fishing; hunting.

ROCK FALLS (E)

Wilkinson Pioneer Park $7
Cerro Gordo County Park
On SE edge of Rock Falls off CR B-20 on CR S62. $7 with-out hookups; $12 at 42 sites with 30-amp elec. 5/1-10/1; 14-day limit. 66 sites. Tbls, flush toilets, cfga, drkg wtr, dump, showers, playground. Canoeing, fishing, snowmo-biling, picnicking, hiking. 80 acres on Shell Rock River.

ROCKWELL CITY (W)

Featherstone Memorial Park $10
Calhoun County Conservation Board
7 mi N on CR N57 from jct with US 20 just W of Rockwell City on NW shore of North Twin Lake. $10 base at 50-plus primitive sites; $16 at 61 elec sites. Apr-Oct. Tbls, show-ers, flush toilets, cfga, wtr hookups, playground, 2 shel-ters, fishing pier. Swimming beach, fishing, boating(dl). 56 acres. 7-mi biking/hiking trail being built.

ROCKWELL (E)

Linn Grove Park $7
Cerro Gordo County Conservation Board
In Rockwell, just SE of US 65 & CR B-60; at Beaver Dam Creek. $7 without hookups, $12 at 30-amp elec sites. 5/1-10/1; 14-day limit. 66 elec sites. Tbls, flush toilets, show-

ers, cfga, drkg wtr, dump, playground, pool. Swimming, tennis, golf($), fishing. 38 acres.

RODNEY (W)

Peters Park $12
Rodney Pits Recreation Area
Monona County Park
1 mi E of Rodney. $12 at non-elec sites; $15 at 25 elec 20/30/50-amp site. All year; 14-day limit. Tbls, toilets, cfga, drkg wtr, dump. Picnicking, fishing, boating(l), hunting. 73-acre recreation area consists of 3 former gravel pits.

RUTHVEN (W)

Pleasant Creek State Recreation Area $8
5 mi N of Palo at Pleasant Creek Lake. $8 off-season at 26 modern sites without elec ($11 in-season); $13 at off-season at 41 modern sites with elec ($16 rest of year). All year; 14-day limit. Tbls, flush toilets, cfga, drkg wtr, showers, visitor center. Fishing, boating(l), hiking & biking trails, horseback riding, swimming.

SAC CITY (W)

Hagge Park $12
Sac County Conservation Board
1 mi S of Sac City on CR M54; qtr mi E on CR D42. $12 at primitive sites; $17 at 15 RV sites with 30-amp full hookups. 4/1-10/31; 14-day limit. Tbls, flush toilets, dump, drkg wtr hookups, elec($), showers, playground. A/C okay. Hiking & bridle trails, fishing, ranger programs. Sauk Rail Trail. Black Hawk Lake. 85 acres.

SANBORN (W)

Douma Park $12
O'Brien County Conservation Area
2 mi W of Sanborn on US 18; 2 mi S on Polk Ave. $12. 5/1-9/30; 14-day limit. 12 sites with wtr/elec. Tbls, cfga, playground, pit toilets shelters. Fishing lake, picnicking, hiking, swimming beach, boating (l - elec motors). 21 acres. 21-acre converted gravel pit.

SHEFFIELD (E)

Galvin Memorial City Park $10
1 mi W on county rd from US 65 following signs. $10 for RVs, $5 tents. May-Nov. 40 primitive sites; 40-ft RV limit. Tbls, toilets, cfga, drkg wtr, dump, playground, some elec. Fishing.

SHELL ROCK (E)

Shell Rock Recreation Area $10
Butler County Conservation Board
From downtown Shell Rock at jct with CR T63, N on W. Main St to park. $10 without hookups ($60 weekly); $12 with elec ($72 weekly). 4/1-10/30; 14-day limit. Undesignated primitive sites & 40 elec 30/50-amp RV sites. Tbls, flush toilets, cfga, drkg wtr, showers, playground. Hiking,

picnicking, fishing, boating(l), canoeing, nature trail. 67 acres. Camp free Wed nights.

SHENANDOAH (W)

Manti Memorial Park   FREE
Fremont County Conservation Board
2 mi S of Shenandoah on US 59; 1 mi W on CR J40; right into park. Free. Open primitive camping. Tbls, toilets, cfga, drkg wtr. Hiking trails.

Pierce Creek Park & Recreation Area $6
Page County Conservation Board
4 mi N of Shenandoah on Hwy 59; 1 mi E. $6 at 8 primitive sites, $15 at 12 elec/wtr 50-amp sites; equestrian sites $12-$17. 4/15-10/15; 14-day limit. Tbls, toilets, cfga, drkg wtr, shelter. Hiking trails, boating (l), archery range, fishing, shooting range. Handicapped facilities. 389 acres.

Pioneer Park $6
Page County Conservation Board
0.5 mi S of Shenandoah to SR 2, then 8 mi E to just past jct with CR M48. $6 at primitive sites; $15 at 10 elec 50-amp sites. Tbls, flush toilets, cfga, drkg wtr, 2 picnic shelters, playground. 2-acre pond. Boating, fishing.

Rapp Park & Recreation Area $6
Page County Conservation Board
2 mi NE of Shenandoah on SR 48; at B Ave. $6 at primitive sites; $15 at 12 sites with elec. All year; 14-day limit. Park still being developed in 2016; no drkg wtr, no modern restrooms. Tbls, pit toilets, picnic shelters, fishing pier. Fishing ponds, boating (l - no mtrs), nature trail. 270 acres.

SIDNEY (W)

Pinky's Glen Park   FREE
Fremont County Conservation Board
5 mi N of Sidney on US 275 through Tabor; 1 mi W on CR 10 Co Rd; 2 mi W of Tabor. Free. 3/1-11/30. Undesignated hillside sites. Tbls, toilets, cfga, firewood, dump, drkg wtr. Picnicking, fishing, horseback riding. No motorbikes. 48 acres & 15-acre lake. Camp is poorly maintained.

SIGOURNEY (E)

Checauqua River Access   FREE
Keokuk County Conservation Board
2 mi S of Sigourney; at North Skunk River. Free. Undeveloped primitive camping. No facilities. Picnicking, fishing, boating. 3 acres.

Lake Belva Deer Park $10
Keokuk County Conservation Board
From Sigourney, 2 mi W on SR 92; 3 mi N on 230th Ave; right on 192nd St, then left on 235th Ave before turning E on access rd into park. $10 at 11 primitive sites, $18 at 56 elec/wtr sites. Tbls, flush toilets, showers, cfga, drkg wtr, shelters. Hiking/bridle trails, fishing ponds. 1,669 acres; 260-acre lake.

Lake Yen-Ruo-Gis $10
Keokuk County Conservation Board
From Sigourney, 3 mi N of SR 92 & Main St on 208th Ave.
$10. All year; 14-day limit. About 30 primitive sites. Tbls,
toilets, cfga, firewood, no drkg wtr. Picnicking, fishing,
hunting, swimming, boating(l - elec mtrs), hiking. Beach.
76 acres; 17-acre lake, Sigourney written backward.

SIOUX CITY (W)
Stone State Park $6
4 mi NW of I-29 in Sioux City on SR 12. $6 base off-season
at 20 non-modern sites without elec ($9 base rest of year);
$11 off-season at 10 non-modern sites with elec ($14
rest of year). Tbls, flush toilets, cfga, drkg wtr, showers,
dump, playground. Hiking, swimming, fishing, boating (lr),
mountain biking, nature center. 22-acre lake.

SOLDIER (W)
Oldham Recreation Area $12
Monona County Park
1.5 mi NW of Soldier. $12 at non-elec sites, $15 with elec.
Tbls, toilets, cfga, drkg wtr, elec. Fishing, boating(l), picnick-
ing. 13 acres; 12-acre lake.

SOLON (E)
Lake MacBride State Park $6
4 mi W of Solon on SR 382. $6 base. All year; 14-day limit.
Base fee at 56 non-modern sites without elec off-season
($9 rest of year); $16 at modern elec sites (showers)
in-season ($13 off-season), with 10 of 38 sites offering full
hookups for $3 more. Tbls, toilets, cfga, drkg wtr, dump.
Picnicking, swimming beach, fishing, boating(lrd), multi-
use trails, interpretive trail. 2,180 acres; 812-acre lake.

Sandy Beach Campground $10
Corps of Engineers
Coralville Lake
2 mi NW of Solon on SR 382; .7 mi N on CR W6E; 3 mi W &
S on CR W4F to park; at N shore of lake. $10 with federal
senior pass at 48 elec sites; others pay $10. $12 with senior
pass 2 full-hookup sites; others pay $24. 5/1-9/30; 14-day
limit. RV limit in excess of 65 ft. Tbls, flush toilets, showers,
cfga, drkg wtr, dump, beach, shelter. 4WD trails, swimming,
biking, snowmobiling, swimming, boating(l), fishing, waterskiing, horseshoe pits.

SOUTH ENGLISH (E)
Coffman Wood FREE
Keokuk County Park
On N edge of South English. Free. Undeveloped primitive
camping. Toilets, no other facilities. 15 acres.

SPENCER (W)
East Leach Park Campground $13
Spencer Parks & Recreation Department
From jct with US 71 S of city, about 0.5 mi N on US 18; qtr

mi E on 4th St SE; at Little Sioux River. $13 at 20 non-elec
sites; $15 at 100 elec sites. 4/15-10/15. 40-ft RV limit (10
pull-throughs). Tbls, flush toilets, showers, cfga, drkg wtr.
Hiking trail, boating(l), fishing.

SPIRIT LAKE (W)
Vick's Corner $10
4 mi W of Spirit Lake at Hwys 9 & 86. $10 base. All year.
Base fee for primitive sites; $15 with elec; $20 full hookups. 69 RV sites. Tbls, toilets, cfga, drkg wtr, dump, beach,
store. Swimming, fishing. No sites on MD, LD or July 4.
One day free after 6 days.

SAINT ANSGAR (E)
Halvorson Park $10
Mitchell County Conservation Board
1.5 mi S of St. Ansgar on CR T26 (Foothill Ave); at W
shore of Cedar River. $10 without hookups; $18 at about
50 undesignated elec sites. 5/15-10/15; 14-day limit. 70
sites. Tbls, flush toilets, showers, cfga, drkg wtr, dump,
store, playground, beach, shelters. Fishing, boating(ldr),
swimming, canoeing(r). 11 acres. Camp 6 nights, get 7th
night free.

STACYVILLE (E)
Riverside Park $10
Mitchell County Conservation Board
Half mi E of Stacyville on CR A23; at E shore of Little Cedar
River. $10 without hookups; $18 with elec/wtr. Camp 6
nights & get 7th night free. All year; 14-day limit. 24 sites.
Tbls, pit toilets, cfga, drkg wtr, showers, dump. Boating(l),
fishing, hiking, hunting, canoeing, sand volleyball, softball
field. 12 acres.

STANTON (W)
Viking Lake State Park $8
4 mi E of Stanton on county rd. $8 base off-season at
26 modern sites with elec ($11 base rest of year); $13
off-season at 94 modern sites with elec ($16 rest of year),
22 full hookups ($19). Tbls, flush toilets, cfga, drkg wtr,
showers, dump. Interpretive trail, hiking, swimming, fishing, boating(lr), playground. 137-acre lake.

STEAMBOAT ROCK (E)
Pine Ridge Park $10
Hardin County Conservation Board
Half mi W of Steamboat Rock on CR D-35; N to park; at W
shore of Iowa River. $10 for primitive sites; $15 for elec/
wtr. All year; 14-day limit. 40 elec sites. Tbls, flush toilets,
cfga, drkg wtr, showers, group shelter. Hiking & bridle
trails, picnicking, fishing, boating(l), hunting, shooting
range. Handicap facilities. 131 acres.

Tower Rock Park FREE
Hardin County Conservation Board
Half mi S of Steamboat Rock on CR S56; right on access
rd; at S shore of Iowa River. Free. All year; 14-day limit. 20

primitive sites. Tbls, toilets, cfga, drkg wtr, firewood. Picnicking, fishing, boating(l), canoeing, hiking. Nature trails. Pioneer Keystone Bridge. Tower Rock. 65 acres.

STOCKPORT (E)
Morris Memorial Park $7
Van Buren County Conservation Board
From Stockport, 1 mi N on CR W30; at road's western curve, turn right, then E for 1.5 mi on 115th St; 1 mi N on Timber Rd, following signs. $7 for primitive sites, $12 with elec. 4/1-10/31; 14-day limit. 15 sites. Tbls, toilets, cfga, drkg wtr, shelter, playground. Fishing pond, horseshoes, hiking trails. 7-building museum with antiques.

STRAWBERRY POINT (E)
Backbone State Park $6
4 mi SW of Strawberry Point on SR 410. $6 base. All year; 14-day limit. Base fee for non-modern sites off-season ($9 rest of year); modern sites $11 without elec ($8 off-season); modern sites with elec $13 off-season ($16 rest of year). 125 sites, 49 with elec($5). Tbls, toilets, cfga, drkg wtr, sewer/wtr hookups($3), dump, playground. Picnicking, swimming, fishing (85-acre lake); boating(rl), hiking trails, interpretive trail. 1,780 acres.

STUART (W)
Nation's Bridge $10
Guthrie County Conservation Board
6 mi N of Stuart on CR P28; at S shore of South Raccoon River. $10 for primitive sites; $15 with elec (free Thurs nights). All year; 14-day limit. 60 elec sites and primitive area. Tbls, flush toilets, showers, dump, cfga, drkg wtr, elec($), shelters($). Hiking trails, fishing, horseshoes, playground, nature trail, disc golf. Historic site, museum. 81 acres.

SUMNER (E)
North Woods Park $10
Bremer County Conservation Board
2 mi N of Sumner on CR V-62. $10 without hookups, $15 with elec. 5/1-11/1. 45 sites. Tbls, pit toilets, cfga, drkg wtr. Picnicking, hiking trails, sand volleyball, horseshoes. 82 acres. Free camping Wednesday nights.

SWEA CITY (W)
Burt Lake Park $10
Kossuth County Conservation Board
8.5 mi N of Swea City on CR K; 4 mi W on CR A16; qtr mi N on 40th Ave, then N on access rd; lake is on Minnesota border. $10 at 12 sites with 20/30/50-amp elec; tent sites $6. 145 acres. Tbls, pit toilets, cfga, drkg wtr. Hiking, horseback riding, fishing, boating(l), canoeing, hunting.

THAYER (W)
Thayer Lake Park $8
Union County Conservation Board
From Thayer, about qtr mi S on 3rd Ave, then right (W) 1 mi on Thayer Lake Rd. $8 at primitive sites, $12 with elec. 16 total sites; 30-ft RV limit. Tbls, pit toilets, cfga, drkg wtr, shelters. All year. Fishing, boating(l). 10-acre lake, 47-acre nature area.

THOMSON (ILLINOIS)
Thomson Causeway $10
Corps of Engineers
Mississippi River Public Use Area
W edge of Thomson. $10 base with federal senior pass at 131 elec sites; others pay $20 base, $22 for premium 50-amp locations ($11 with senior pass). Tent sites $14. About 5/1-10/24; 14-day limit. RV limit in excess of 65 ft; 4 pull-through sites. Tbls, flush toilets, cfga, drkg wtr, dump, playground, elec($). Picnicking, fishing, swimming, hiking, boating, canoeing, hunting. In 2011, new & renovated shower facilities, sewer line added, dump station renovated.

THORNTON (E)
Ingebretson $7
Cerro Gordo County Conservation Board
From I-35 exit 180 at Thornton, 1.2 mi W on SR 107; right on CR S25 to park entrance. $7 without hookups, $12 at 23 sites with elec. 5/1-10/1; 14-day limit. 23 acres. Tbls, flush toilets, cfga, drkg wtr, dump, playground, showers. Golf, fishing, hiking, biking, disc golf. On Bailey Creek.

TIPTON (E)
Cedar Bluff Access $7
Cedar County Park
9 mi W of Tipton on CR F-28 (210th St). $7. Open primitive camping; no facilities. Canoeing, fishing, picnicking, boating(l). 17 acres.

Cedar Valley $7
Cedar County Park
7 mi SW of Tipton off CR X-40; along Cedar River. $7 base. All year; 14 day limit. Base fee for primitive sites; $10 with elec. 30 sites. Tbls, toilets, cfga, drkg wtr, enclosed & open shelters, playground. Hiking, fishing, boating(l), hunting, horseshoes, basketball, volleyball. 228 acres. Cedar River, rock quarries. No wtr during winter.

TORONTO (E)
Walnut Grove Prk $10
Clinton County Conservation Board
6 mi N on CR Y32 from jct with US 30; on E side of 118th Ave, both N & S of Wapsipinicon River. $10 for primitive sites; $15 with elec. All year; 14-day limit. 25 sites. Tbls, toilets, cfga, drkg wtr, playground, showers. Fishing, boating(l), canoeing. 24 acres.

TRAER (E)
T. F. Clark Park $5
Tama County Conservation Board
About 2 mi N of Traer on US 63; 2 mi E on 155th St

(becoming 150th St); at E shore of Wolf Creek. $5. 5/11-10/31; 14-day limit. 10 sites with elec; 3 non-elec sites. Tbls, playground, pit toilet, cfga, drkg wtr. Hiking, fishing. Remote park subject to vandalism. 79 acres.

UNION (E)

Brekke Memorial Park FREE
Hardin County Conservation Board
From Union, 1 mi W on CR D65; 7 mi S on CR D67 2 mi SE of Union. Free. Undeveloped primitive camping. All year; 14-day limit. Tbls, playground, toilets, no drkg wtr, no elec. Picnicking. 7 acres.

Daisy Long Memorial Park $10
Hardin County Conservation Board
1 mi E of Union on CR D65; at E shore of Iowa River. $10 for primitive sites; $15 for elec/wtr. All year; 14-day limit. 30 elec sites. Tbls, toilets, cfga, drkg wtr, elec. Fishing, swimming, boating (l), playground, volleyball court. 7 acres.

URBANA (E)

Wildcat Bluff Recreation Area $10
Benton County Conservation Board
2 mi S of Urbana on W26. $10 base. 5/1-11/1; 14-day limit; limited facilities in winter. Base fee for primitive sites; $15 with elec. 35 sites (no RV size limit). Tbls, toilets, cfga, drkg wtr. Boating(l), tobogganing, hiking, fishing, hunting, 18-hole disc golf. 131 acres.

VILLISCA (W)

Hacklebarney Woods Park $10
Montgomery County Conservation Board
4 mi N of Villisca on US 71; half mi E on US 34. $10 base without elec; $15 at 14 elec sites with 20/30/50-amp. 4/1-10/31. Equestrian camping area with 4 non-elec sites. Tbls, pit & flush toilets, showers cfga, drkg wtr, swing set. Hiking & bridle trails, boating(l - elec mtrs), fishing, hunting, canoeing. 230 acres; 10-acre lake; 2 ponds.

VINTON (E)

Benton City-Fry Area $10
Benton County Park
5 mi E of Vinton on E24; 1 mi on gravel rd; along Cedar River. $10 base. 5/1-11/1; 14-day limit; limited facilities in winter. Base fee at 5 primitive sites; $15 at 16 elec/wtr sites. No RV size limit. Tbls, toilets, cfga, elec($), drkg wtr, playground. Picnicking, fishing, boating(l), tobogganing. 39 acres.

Hoefle-Dulin Area $10
Benton County Park
4 mi E of Vinton on E14; 1 mi N on gravel rd; at Cedar River. $10 base. 5/1-11/1; 14-day limit; limited facilities in winter. Base fee at 4 primitive sites; $15 at 12 elec sites. No RV size limit. Tbls, toilets, cfga, drkg wtr, playground. Boating(dl), fishing, hunting, tobogganing. 62 acres.

Minne Estema $10
Benton County Park
5 mi N of Vinton on Hwy 101; 1 mi N on gravel rd; along Cedar River. $10 at 2 non-elec sites; $15 at 10 elec sites. 5/1-11/1; 14 day limit; limited facilities in winter. Tbls, toilets, cfga, drkg wtr. Picnicking, fishing, boating (ld), waterskiing, tobogganing. 63 acres.

Rodgers $10
Benton County Park
3 mi W of Vinton on Hwy 218; 1 mi N on V61. $10 base. 5/1-11/1; 14-day limit; limited facilities in winter. Base fee for primitive sites; $15 at 53 elec sites. 30-ft RV limit. Tbls, flush toilets, cfga, drkg wtr, elec($), playground, dump. Swimming beach, boating (ld), fishing. Historic site. Handicapped facilities. 122 acres; 21-acre lake.

VIOLA (E)

Matsell Bridge Natural Area $10
Linn County Conservation Board
1 mi NW of Viola on Prairie Chapel Rd; 1 mi N on Shaw Rd; 1.5 mi E on Merritt Rd, then N on Matsell Park Rd; at shore of Wapsipinicon River. $10 for primitive sites at main campground & at Mount Hope Public Use Area; $13 at equestrian camp. 4/15-10/15; 14-day limit. 70 primitive sites in 4 campgrounds. Tbls, toilets, cfga, drkg wtr, no elec. Hiking, bridle & cross-country ski trails, fishing boating, hunting, shooting range. 1,588 acres.

WAPELLO (E)

Snively's Campground $12
Odessa Lake
Louisa County Conservation Board
3 mi E of Wapello; on W shore of Odessa Lake. $12. All year. 30 sites with elec; tent sites $10. Tbls, toilets, cfga, drkg wtr. Hiking, fishing, boating, no swimming. 6 acres at 2,500-acre lake. Lake is site of Port Louisa National Wildlife Refuge & Odessa State Wildlife Management Area.

WASHINGTON (E)

Fern Cliff Access FREE
Washington County Conservation Board
6 mi S of Washington on CR W55; 3 mi E on 320th St; on Crooked Creek. Free. All year; 14-day limit. Sites with tbls, toilets, cfga, drkg wtr, shelter. Hiking & bridle trails, fishing, hunting. 56 acres.

Marr Park $10
Washington County Conservation Board
7 mi E of Washington on Hwy 92 at Ainsworth. $10 without hookups, $16 at 42 full hookups. All year; 14-day limit. Flush toilets, tbls, cfga, drkg wtr, elec, showers. Hiking & biking trails, fishing, hunting, playgrounds, shelter($). No wtr in winter. 125 acres.

Sockum Ridge Park   FREE
Washington County Conservation Board
4.5 mi S of Washington on CR W55; qtr mi E to park. Free. All
year; 14-day limit. Undeveloped primitive camping. Toilets,
no other facilities. Hiking & bridle trails, fishing, hunting.
213 acres. No trash service.

WASHTA (W)
Ranney Knob $5
Cherokee County Conservation Board
Half mi SW of Washta on CR C66. $5. 5/1-10/31; 14-day
limit. 3 primitive sites Tbls, toilets, cfga, drkg wtr. Fishing,
boating, canoeing hunting, swingset, shelter. Cross-country ski & hiking trails. 90 acres on Little Sioux River.

Stieneke Area $5
Cherokee County Conservation Board
1 mi W of Washta on CR C-66; on E side of Little Sioux
River. $5. 5/1-10/31; 14-day limit. 3 primitive sites. Tbls,
toilets, cfga, drkg wtr, no elec. Picnicking, canoeing, fishing, boating(l), hunting. 16 acres.

WAVERLY (E)
Cedar Bend $10
Bremer County Conservation Board
Half mi N of jct with SR 3 on US 218; half mi E on 210th St;
left on CR T27; right on CR T77; left onto access rd. $10 base
without hookups; $15 elec. 5/1-11/1. 60 sites. Tbls, flush
toilets, showers ($2 non-campers), cfga, drkg wtr, dump ($2
non-campers), shelters, amphitheater. Hiking trails, horseshoes, sand volleyball, fishing, boating, canoeing, hunting.
180 acres. Free camping on non-holiday Wed nights.

WELLMAN (E
English River Wildlife Area   FREE
Washington County Conservation Board
About 4 mi W of Wellman on SR 22, then 2 mi N on Birch
Ave; continue N on 120th St to English River. Free. All year.
Primitive camping on 782-acres. No facilities, no drkg wtr.
Hunting, fishing, hiking, horseback riding.

Foster Woods Park   FREE
Washington County Conservation Board
From Wellman, half mi W on 2nd St; 1 mi S on Fir Ave. Free.
All year. Primitive camping on 20 acres. Toilets, cfga, tbls,
no drkg wtr. Hiking, horseback riding, fishing, hunting.

WELLSBURG (E)
Stoehr Fishing Area   FREE
Grundy County Conservation Board
5 mi SE of Wellsburg on H Ave. Free. All year. Primitive
undesignated camping on 5 acres. Tbls, pit toilet, cfga, no
drkg wtr, fishing pier, shelter with elec. Fishing in 2 ponds.

WEST UNION (E)
Dutton's Cave Park $5
Fayette County Conservation Board
2.5 mi NE of West Union on US 18, then half mi N on
Ironwood Rd. $5 for primitive sites, $8 with elec. 4/1-11/1.
Undesignated sites (RVs under 25 ft); 2 elec sites. Tbls,
toilets, cfga, drkg wtr, playground. Hiking trails. 46 acres.
Camp free with $350 annual county park pass.

Echo Valley State Park $5
Fayette County Conservation Board
2 mi SE of West Union on Echo Valley Rd. $5. 4/1-11/1;
14-day limit. Undesignated primitive sites. Tbls, toilets,
cfga, no drkg wtr. Fishing, hiking trails. Camp free with
$350 annual county park pass. Built by CCC in 1930s.

Goeken $5
Fayette County Conservation Board
5 mi N of West Union on Hwy 150 (S of Eldorado). $5. 4/1-
11/1; 14-day limit. Undesignated sites (36-ft RV limit). Tbls,
toilets, cfga, drkg wtr, playground. 6.5 acres. Camp free with
$350 annual county park pass.

WHITTEMORE (W)
Siems Park $12
Kossuth County Conservation Board
0.5 mi S of Whittemore on CR W; 1 mi E on 200th St. $12 at
12 RV sites with 20/30/50-amp elec; tents $6. 4/15-11/1;
14-day limit. Tbls, flush toilets, cfga, drkg wtr, shelters,
playground, dump, showers. Fishing, horseshoe pits, fishing piers. 11-acre gravel pit lake; 41-acre park.

WILLIAMSON (E)
Williamson Pond   FREE
Lucas County Conservation Board
3 mi E of Williamson. Free. Primitive undesignated sites.
Tbls, cfga, no toilets, no drkg wtr. Fishing, canoeing,
hunting. 126 acres.

WINTERSET (W)
Criss Cove Park $12
Madison County Conservation Board
8 mi S of Winterset on US 169; at SW corner of jct with
CR G-61. $12 for 18 RV sites with 20/30/50-amp elec/wtr.
Spring-fall. Tbls, pit toilets, cfga, drkg wtr; no showers or
dump. Fishing, hiking, boating(l), canoeing. 9-acre pond.

WINTHROP (E)
Buffalo Creek Park   FREE
Buchanan County Conservation Board
1 mi E of Winthrop on Hwy 20; along Buffalo Creek. Free.
4/15-10/1. Primitive undesignated sites. Tbls, pit toilets,
cfga, no drkg wtr, shelter with elec. Fishing, picnicking,
hunting, disc golf. 80 acres.

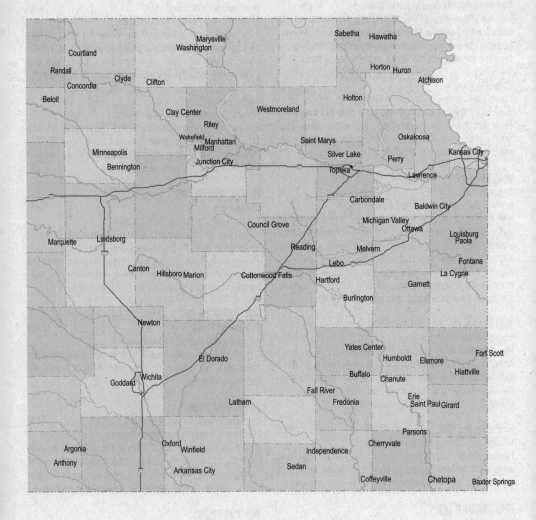

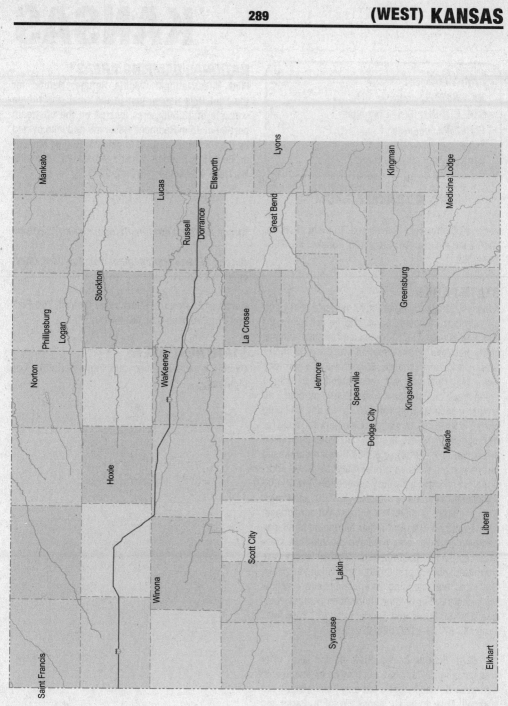

KANSAS

CAPITAL: Topeka
NICKNAME: Sunflower State
STATEHOOD: 1861 – 34th State
FLOWER: Sunflower
TREE: Cottonwood
BIRD: Western Meadowlark

WWW.TRAVELKS.COM

Dept. of Commerce, Travel and Tourism Division, 1000 S.W. Jackson St., Suite 100, Topeka, KS. 785-296-2009.

STATE PARKS

Kansas State Parks are among America's best value in overnight camping. Basic charge for overnight camping is only $10.00 in-season for sites without utility hookups. Prime-location sites are $2 more. State parks also charge $5 per vehicle per day entry fee. However, we recommend that anyone doing much camping in Kansas should purchase an annual vehicle permit for $25. A 14-day camping permit is $112.50. Annual camping permits, good for free camping all year, are $252.50 when purchased in-season (4/1 - 9/30) or $202.50 when purchased out of season. Sites with one utility are $9.00 additional; sites with two utility connections are $11.00 additional; with three utilities, $12.00 additional. Camping limit, 14 days. For purposes of our listings, we assume purchase of either an annual or 14-day camping permits, and we have included all state park camping without hookups. Pets on leashes are permitted, but are prohibited from bathing beaches. Unlimited tent camping is available, and overflow sites cost $6. For further information contact: Kansas Wildlife, Parks and Tourism, 512 SE 25th Ave., Pratt, KS 67124-8174; 620-672-5911.

State Fishing Lakes. State fishing lakes offer free camping; 7-day limit, but may be extended with approval. No sport boats, but only fishing boats are allowed. Pets on leash. Kansas Wildlife, Parks and Tourism, RR 2, Box 54A, Pratt, KS 67124. 620-672-5911.

NATIONAL CAMPING AREAS

Flint Hills National Wildlife Refuge. Named for the Flint Hills Region just to the west, the refuge consists of 18,500 acres located on the upstream portion of John Redmond Reservoir and land owned by the US Army Corps of Engineers. Refuge Manager, Flint Hills National Wildlife Refuge, P.O. Box 128, Hartford, KS 66854; 316-392-5553.

Kirwin National Wildlife Refuge, Kirwin, KS 67644.

Bureau of Land Management, P.O. Box 1828, Cheyenne, WY 82001.

Corps of Engineers, Kansas City District, 700 Federal Bldg, Kansas City, MO 64106.

STATE REST AREAS

Overnight self-contained camping is permitted one night only.

ANTHONY (E)

Anthony City Lake Park $5
1 mi N of Anthony on SR 2; W on access rd. $5 base for primitive unimproved areas; $15 for improved sites with elec. All year; 14-day limit. 47 sites. Tbls, flush toilets, cfga, drkg wtr, elec($), playground. Swimming, fishing, waterskiing, boating(l), horseshoes, gun club, go-cart track, bike trails, sand volleyball, driving range, walking trails. 153-acre lake; 416 acres. Self-pay stations.

ARGONIA (E)

Argonia River Park $10
S of US 60 at 210 S. Main St; half mi S of town at the Chikaskia River. $10 for RV sites with elec/wtr; $15 full hookups; $5 tents. All year. 14 RV sites. Tbls, flush toilets, cfga, drkg wtr, dump ($5). Walking trail, fishing.

ARKANSAS CITY (E)

Cowley State Fishing Lake   FREE
13 mi E of Arkansas City on US 166; in canyon of Panther Creek. Free. All year; 7-day limit. 10 sites; 84-acre lake. Tbls, toilets, cfga, drkg wtr. Picnicking, fishing boating(rld).

ATCHISON (E)

Atchison State Fishing Lake   FREE
3 mi N of Atchison on Hwy 7; then follow 318th Rd to Pawnee Rd access. Free. All year; 7-day limit. 15 sites; 66 acre-lake. Tbls, toilets, cfga, drkg wtr,no elec. Boating(l), picnicking, fishing.

Warnock Lake City Park $10
Dam 23
US 73 to Price Blvd; then right on gravel rd to park. $10 (seniors $8). All year; 7-day limit. 16 RV sites with elec; no RV slideouts. Drkg wtr, tbls, cfga, shelters, playground, toilets, dump. Fishing, picnicking, swimming, paddleboating, hiking on nature trail, playground. Dump station at NW corner of Hwy 59 & Woodlawn Ave.

BALDWIN CITY (E)

Douglas County   FREE
State Fishing Lake
1.5 mi N of Baldwin on CR 1055; 1 mi E on CR 150 to campground; on W side of lake. Free. All year; 7-day limit. 20 sites; 180-acre lake. Tbls, 3 pit toilets, cfga, firewood, drkg wtr, fish cleaning stations 2 floating docks, marina. Picnicking, fishing, hunting, boating(rl). 538 acres.

BAXTER SPRINGS (E)

Riverside City Park $10
On E edge of Baxter Springs, S side of Hwy 166 at Spring River. $10 for RV sites with elec; $5 without elec. All year; 30-day limit. Check in with Police Dept. Tbls, flush toilets, cfga, drkg wtr, showers. Fishing, boating(l).

BELOIT (E)

Chautauqua City Park   FREE
From Hwy 24 in Beloit, turn S on Hwy 14 through town to park sign on S side of town; at Solomon River. Free but donations solicited. Jan-Oct; 10-day limit. 30 sites with elec/wtr. Tbls, flush toilets, cfga, drkg wtr, elec (14 30-amp, 5 50-amp, the rest 20-amp), dump, playground, picnic shelters, pavilion($), pool with waterslide($). Boating(l), fishing, canoeing, golf, horseshoe pits, tennis courts, 18-hole disc golf, basketball. Nice, clean park.

Glen Elder State Park $10
11 mi W of Beloit on US 24 to Glen Elder (Waconda) Lake. $10 without hookups in-season ($7 during 10/1-3/31); $19-22 with hookups. All year; limited facilities in winter; 14-day limit. 420 sites at 12 campgrounds (107with elec). Tbls, flush toilets, cfga, drkg wtr, showers, elec, dump, fish cleaning station, showers, beach. Boating(lrd), fishing, hiking & biking trails, horseshoes, sand volleyball (at Osage area), softball, hunting, swimming. 13,250 acres with 12,500-acre lake. Here are campgrounds, all with some primitive sites:

Cheyenne -- Primitive sites near shore; 36 wtr/elec sites (19 w/50-amp); shower house & pit toilets.

Kanza -- 66 wtr/elec (38 w/50-amp), shade, shower house & pit toilets; on Manna Cove.

Kaw -- 18 wtr/elec (12 w/50-amp); shower house & pit toilets; pull-through

Comanche -- Primitive sites, shower house & pit toilets, under development.

Arickaree -- Primitive sites, low maintenance, no shade; shower house & pit toilets.

Osage -- Primitive sites near Osage boat ramp; little shade; shower house, pit toilets.

Sioux -- 20 Primitive sites 5/Elec near shore; shower house & pit toilets.

Pawnee -- Primitive sites near lake; no facilities.

BENNINGTON (E)

Ottawa State Fishing Lake   Free
5 mi N of Bennington and 1 mi E. All year; 14 day limit. Free, non-elec sites. 121 sites; 148 acres. Drkg wtr, toilets, store. Swimming, boat rental, boating (rl), fishing. 111-acre lake.

BLUE RAPIDS (E)

Riverside Park $10
Chamber of Commerce Park
On Hwys 77/99 in Blue Rapids. Camp free, but $10 donation for elec requested. 41 sites; 60-ft RV limit. Tbls, toilets, cfga, drkg wtr, dump, playground, pool. Basketball, baseball, swimming, croquet. Tennis courts nearby at 5th & East Aves.

BUFFALO (E)

Wilson State Fishing Lake   FREE
1.5 mi SE of Buffalo on US 75. Free. All year; 14-day limit.

20 sites; 110-acre lake. Tbls, toilets, cfga, no drkg wtr. Picnicking, fishing, boating(l).

BURLINGTON (E)
Damsite Area Campground $7.50
Corps of Engineers
John Redmond Lake
3 mi N of Burlington on US 75, 1 mi W on JR access rd. All year; 14-day limit. During 5/1-9/30, up to 22 sites with 30-amp elec available for $15 if not reserved for group camping ($7.50 with federal senior pass). Some sites free off-season but no amenities or services. Group camping by reservation. Tbls, flush & pit toilets, showers, cfga, dump, drkg wtr, group shelters, playground, shelter. Horseshoes, boating(ld), fishing, hiking,swimming (sandy beach), horseback riding, bridle/mountain biking trail.

Drake City Park $10
Burlington Dam
On E edge of Burlington along Neosho River. $10 Self Pay Stations have been installed. Sites include 8 new concrete pads. Tbls, flush toilets, cfga, drkg wtr, elec/wtr, showers, dump. Fishing, hiking.

Kelley City Park $10
On E edge of Burlington, 3rd St, a few blocks S of city dam on Neosho River. $10 Self Pay Stations have been installed. RV sites with tbls, flush toilets, showers, cfga, drkg wtr, playground, shelters, dump. 46 acres.

Riverside East Campground $7.50
Corps of Engineers
John Redmond Lake
3.5 mi N of Burlington on US 75; 1.5 mi W on Embankment Rd following signs. On Neosho River below dam. $7.50 with federal senior pass; others pay $15. 4/1-10/31; 14-day limit; 28 days with written permission. 53 gravel sites with 30-amp elec/wtr. 65-ft RV limit; 7 pull-through sites. Toilets, cfga, drkg wtr, tbls, showers, dump. Fishing, boating, hiking, interpretive trail, hiking/bike trail. Note: Ticks are a problem on the Rush Hill hiking trail.

Riverside West Campground $7
Corps of Engineers
John Redmond Lake
From Burlington, 3.5 mi N on US 75; 1.5 mi W on Embankment Rd, following signs; at W bank of Neosho River below dam. 5/1-9/30; 14-day limit. Campers with federal senior pass pay $7 at 6 non-elec sites, $7.50 at all elec sites (others pay $14-$15). 21 sites with 30-amp elec/wtr, 13 sites with 30/50-amp elec. RV limit in excess of 65 ft, 3 pull-through. Tbls, toilets, cfga, drkg wtr, showers, shelter, playground, dump. Boating(l), fishing, hiking, interpretive trail.

West Wingwall $7.50
Corps of Engineers
John Redmond Lake
From US 75, W approx 2.5 mi; left down ramp on back side of dam; left again for half mi; below dam at Neosho River. $7.50 with federal senior pass others pay $15. 4/1-10/31; 14-day limit. 125 sites wtr, elec avalilable. Tbls, toilets, cfga, drkg wtr. Fishing, boating. No day use fees with camping permit.

CANTON (E)
McPherson State Fishing Lake FREE
Maxwell State Wildlife Refuge
6 mi N of Canton on CR 304; 2.5 mi W on CR 1771. Free. All year; 7-day limit. 25 sites; 306 acres; 46-acre lake. Tbls, no drkg wtr, cfga, toilets, fishing piers. Picnicking, fishing, hiking, boating(l), nature trails. 260 acres; 46-acre lake.

CARBONDALE (E)
Osage State Fishing Lake FREE
3 mi S and half mi E of Carbondale on US 56; then half mi S. Free. All year; 7-day limit. 120 undesignated sites; 506 acres; 140-acre lake. Tbls, drkg wtr, cfga, toilets. Picnicking, fishing, hiking, boating(l).

CHANUTE (E)
Santa Fe City Park FREE
1 mi S of Chanute on US 169 at 35th & S. Santa Fe Sts. $10 with elec/wtr after 2 nights free. All year; 10-day limit. 40 sites; no RV size limit & several pull-through sites. Tbls, flush toilets, cfga, drkg wtr, elec (18 thirty-amp, some 50-amp), showers, playground, dump. Fishing, boating(l), horseshoes.

CHERRYVALE (E)
Cherryvale Campground $8.50
Corps of Engineers
Big Hill Lake
From Olive St on the W side of Cherryvale, 4.5 mi E on CR 5000 (becoming 1900 Rd); 2 mi N on Cherryvale Pkwy, following signs; NW of dam at W shore. During about 4/1-11/1 $8.50 base with federal senior pass at 9 sites with 30/50-amp elec; others pay $17 base. $20 at 11 full-hook-up 30/50-amp sites, $22 at premium locations ($10 & 11 with senior pass). During 11/1-3/31, elec sites $15, full hookups $18 with reduced services, no showers. All year; 14-day limit. RV limit in excess of 65 ft; 2 pull-through. Tbls, flush toilets, cfga, drkg wtr, showers, playground, beach. Fishing, boating(l), hiking, swimming.

Mound Valley North Campground $12
Corps of Engineers
Big Hill Lake
From Olive St. on W side of Cherryvale, 5 mi E on CR 5000 (becoming 1900 Rd); N on Mound Valley Pkwy, following signs; NE of dam at SE shore. $12 at 8 non-elec sites ($6 with federal senior pass). $8-$8.50 base with senior pass at 74 sites with 30-amp elec (others pay $16-$17 base);

$18-19 for premium locations ($9 & $9.50 with senior pass); $20 for 50-amp elec & 2 sites with 50-amp full hookups ($10 with senior pass). 4/1-11/1; 14-day limit. Closed off-season. Tbls, flush toilets, cfga, drkg wtr, dump, showers, beach with change house, shelter, pay phone. Boating(l), fishing, swimming, fishing pier, hiking & equestrian trails.

Timber Hill Campground $12
Corps of Engineers
Big Hill Lake
From Olive St on W side of Cherryvale, 5.5 mi E on CR 5000 (becoming 1900 Rd); 3 mi N on Elk Rd; W on gravel Timber Trail, following signs; on E shore of lake. About 4/1-11/1; 14-day limit. $12 at 20 non-elec sites, some pull-through. Free off-season, but no amenities. Tbls, toilets, cfga, drkg wtr, dump. Boating(dl), fishing, waterskiing, horseback riding trail.

CHETOPA (E)
East River City Park $10
At jct of Hwys 59 & 166 in Chetopa; along Neosha River E of bridge. 40 sites. $10 with elec/wtr. Tbls, toilets, cfga, drkg wtr, picnic shelters.

Elmore City Park $10
N of town on 3rd St to 4000 Rd, West. $10 at 26 sites with elec/wtr; tents $2. Tbls, toilets, cfga, drkg wtr, dump, shelter. Fishing, walking trail. .

CLAY CENTER (E)
Clay County Fairgrounds $12
At 205 S. 12th St in Clay Center. Free, but donations requested. 2 RV sites with elec, $12; 2 full hookups $15. Tbls, toilets, drkg wtr, dump. 3-day limit.

Huntress City Park   FREE
On W side of town on US 24, W of SR 15 (6th St.); E on Court St; N on B St; E on W. Dexter St; RV area on right. Free, but donations requested. 3-day limit. Six 30-amp elec/wtr. Tbls, flush toilets at pool, cfga, drkg wtr. Free dump station at Clay County Fairgrounds. .

Sportsman Wayside Park   FREE
On W side of town just W of Huntress City Park & E of football field, on S side of US 24 (low tree limbs at entry; best for small RVs). Free, but donations requested. 3-day limit. Two 15/20-amp elec sites. Tbls, toilets, cfga, drkg wtr. Free dump at Clay County Fairgrounds, 12th & Bridge Sts in SE part of town.

CLIFTON (E)
Berner Memorial City Park $8
W of junior high school in Clifton on N side of Hwy 9. $8 for 20-amp elec; $12 for 30-amp. 50 sites with hookups. Seasonal. Tbls, flush toilets, cfga, drkg wtr, playgrounds, dump. Ball fields, horseshoes, pool, tennis.

CLYDE (E)
Clyde City Park   FREE
From SR 9 at Clyde, N on N. Grant St, then W on Grand Ave to far W end of park; off N end of Perrier, to the right. Free, donations accepted. All year. Several 20 & 30-amp hookups, toilets, cfga, drkg wtr.2 bathrooms with showers at pool bathhouse. Beautiful park.

COFFEYVILLE (E)
Walter Johnson Park $8
On E side of Coffeyville off Hwys 169 & 166 just S of Verdigris River. $8 with elec/wtr at Woods Campground. All year. 56 sites. Tbls, flush toilets, cfga, drkg wtr, elec. Dump, showers. Fishing, recreation center, playground, horseshoe pits, fairground. Park named for noted baseball player who once resided in town. Rivercrest Campground at 600 Wood, has 62 full hookups, $15.

CONCORDIA (E)
Airport Park   FREE
Concordia City Campground
1.3 mi S of town on US 81 across from Wal-Mart. Donations solicited; camping free. All year; 7-day limit (register if longer than 24 hrs). 12 sites; 45-ft RVs. Elec (10 with 30 or 50-amp), wtr hookups, tbls, cfga, flush toilets, dump. Picnic shelter & play area next to campground. Pay phone in pilot's lounge behind park.

COTTONWOOD FALLS (E)
Chase State Fishing Lake   FREE
3 mi W of Cottonwood on gravel co rd on the left (runs between Cottonwood Falls and Elmdale). Free. All year; 7-day limit. 10 sites. Tbls, toilets, cfga, drkg wtr. Picnicking, fishing, swimming, boating(l). 109-acre lake.

COUNCIL GROVE (E)
Canning Creek Cove Campground $7
Corps of Engineers
Council Grove Lake
From SR 177 at Council Grove, 0.1 mi W on US 56; 1.4 mi NW on Mission St (becoming Lake Rd) to spillway, then 2 mi NW on Lake Rd & N on park access rd. During 4/1-10/31, $14 at 1 non-elec site ($7 with federal senior pass); free off-season but no amenities. With senior pass, $9 base at 4 sites with 20/30-amp elec; $9.50 at 32 sites with 20/30-amp elec/wtr; $11 for 50-amp elec sites at premium locations (others pay $18, $19 & $22). All year; 14-day limit. RV limit in excess of 65 ft; 5 pull-through. Tbls, flush toilets, cfga, drkg wtr, dump, playground, showers, beach, shelter. Swimming, fishing, boating(l), horseshoe pits, hiking & nature trails.

Kanza View Campground $10
Corps of Engineers
Council Grove Lake
2 mi N of Council Grove on SR 177; qtr mi W on dam rd;

KANSAS

at E end of dam. $10 during 4/1-10/31 at 5 small primitive sites; some sites free off-season, but get wtr from Neosha campground & project office area. All year; 14-day limit. Sites most suitable for tents, but van & truck campers okay. Tbls, toilets, cfga, no drkg wtr, free shelter. Fishing, boating (no ramp).

Kit Carson Cove $10
Corps of Engineers
Council Grove Lake
From Council Grove at jct with US 56, 2.5 mi N on SR 177/57, then W. $10 at 1 non-elec site; $8.50 with federal senior pass at 14 sites with 30-amp elec/wtr; $9.50 with senior pass at 1 full-hookup site (others pay $17 & $19). 5/1-9/30; 14-day limit. Gated closed off-season. No RV size limit. Tbls, flush toilets, cfga, drkg wtr. Boating(l), fishing, hiking trail, picnicking.

Marina Cove $11
Corps of Engineers
Council Grove Lake
From SR 177 at Council Grove, 0.1 mi W on US 56; 1.4 mi NW on Mission St (becoming Lake Rd) to spillway, then 1.5 mi W on Lake Rd; on right. All year; 14-day limit. During 4/1-10/31, $11 at 1 primitive site; $14 at 3 sites with 30-amp elec ($5 & $7 with federal senior pass). Off-season, some sites free without elec; after 11/1, no drkg wtr except at Neosho Campground & near project office. No RV size limit specified. Tbls, toilets, cfga, drkg wtr, fish cleaning station, marina. Boating(lr), fishing, waterskiing, swimming.

Neosho Campground $7
Corps of Engineers
Council Grove Lake
From SR 177 at Council Grove, 0.1 mi W on US 56; 1.4 mi NW on Mission St (becoming Lake Rd) to spillway, then 0.3 mi W; on right. $7 with federal senior pass at 7 sites with 30-amp elec; others pay $14. All year; 14-day limit; during 11/1-3/31, some sites free without elec, but wtr available all year from camp hydrant. Tbls, toilets, cfga, drkg wtr. Swimming, fishing, boating(l), picnicking.

Richey Cove $9
Corps of Engineers
Council Grove Lake
From Council Grove at jct with US 56, 2.8 mi on SR 56/177; on W side. During 4/1-10/31, campers with federal senior pass pay $9 at 14 RV/tent sites & 1 tent-only site with 30-amp elec; $10-$11 at 16 sites with 30-amp elec/wtr; $12.50 at 7 sites with 50-amp elec or premium locations & 1 full-hookup site (others pay $18, $20-$22 & $25. All year; 14-day limit. Wtr/elec off during 11/1-3/31; some sites free but reduced services. RV limit in excess of 65 ft, all back-in. 8-site group camping area with elec for up to 40 people. Tbls, flush toilets, cfga, drkg wtr, showers,

dump, beach access, playground. Boating(dl), fishing, swimming, hiking trail, horseshoe pits.

Richey Cove North Park $10
Corps of Engineers
Council Grove Lake
From Council Grove at jct with US 56, 3.5 mi N on SR 55/177, then W to park. $10. 5/1-9/30; 14-day limit; gated closed off-season. 8 small sites most suitable for tents, vans, pickup campers. Tbls, concrete pit toilets, cfga, drkg wtr. Picnicking, boating(l), fishing. Formerly named Custer Park.

Santa Fe Trail $11
Corps of Engineers
Council Grove Lake
From SR 17 at Council Grove, 0.1 mi W on US 56; 1.4 mi NW on Mission St (becoming Lake Rd) to spillway, then 2 mi W on Lake Rd; right on access rd. All year if weather permits; 14-day limit. During 4/1-10/31, campers with federal senior pass pay $7 at one non-hookup site; $9 at 3 sites with 30-amp elec (no wtr hookups); $11 at 11 sites with 30-amp elec/wtr and 14 sites with 50-amp elec/wtr and 3 full hookups (others pay $14, $18, $22). No drkg wtr after 11/1 until campground is gated closed. Group camping available. Tbls, flush & pit toilets, cfga, drkg wtr, showers, playground, beach. Boating(l), fishing, hiking, horseshoe pit, hiking, swimming. RV limit in excess of 65 ft, all back-in.

COURTLAND (E)
Larsen City Park FREE
Off SR 199 in Courtland near the water tower. S of US 36 on SR 199; 1 blk E of Main St. on Freedom St. Free courtesy overnight RV parking with two 20-amp elec/wtr. No RV size limit. Tbls, toilets, cfga.

DODGE CITY (W)
Ford County Lake FREE
State Fishing Lake
7 mi NE of Dodge City off US 283. Free. All year. Spaces for self-contained RVs at 45-acre lake. Fishing, boating(l).

DORRANCE (W)
Minooka Park $7
Corps of Engineers
Wilson Lake
From Dorrance at I-70 exit 199, 7 mi N on Dorrance Rd (200th Rd), following signs; on S side of lake. During 5/1-9/30, campers with federal senior pass pay $7 at 47 non-hookup sites, $9 at 66 sites with 30-amp elec (no wtr hookup), $10 at 52 sites with 30/50-amp elec/wtr (others pay $14, $18 & $20). Weather permitting, basic sites free off-season, $10 with wtr and/or elec but reduced services & amenities. Group camping available. RV limit in excess of 65 ft; 17 pull-through. Drkg wtr, showers, cfga, 2

dumps, tbls, playground, fish cleaning staton, picnic shelter, amphitheater, visitor center, beach access. Fishing, hiking trails, swimming, boating(ld), ranger programs, tennis, horseshoes, volleyball courts, jet skiing.

EL DORADO (E)
El Dorado State Park $10
5 mi E of El Dorado on SR 177; at El Dorado Reservoir. $10 without hookups in-season; $19-$22 with hookups. All year; limited facilities in winter; 14-day limit. About 1,100 sites at four campgrounds. Tbls, flush toilets, cfga, drkg wtr, showers, elec($), dump, 2 beaches, marina, amphitheater. Swimming, boating (ld), fishing, hiking & biking trails. 3,800 acres.

   Bluestem Point -- 233 primitive site; 197 wtr/elec sites 70 wtr/elec/swr sites.

   Shady Creek -- 71 primitive sites.

   Walnut River -- 8 primitive site; 63 wtr/elec sites 95 wtr/elec/swr sites.

   Boulder Bluff -- 124 primitive site; 24 wtr/elec sites.

ELKHART (W)
Cimarron Recreation Area $7
Cimarron National Grasslands
7.5 mi N of Elkhart on SR 27; 4 mi E on FR 700. $7. All year; 10-day limit. 14 sites (32-ft RV limit). Tbls, toilets, no open campfires, charcoal fires and gas camp stoves are permitted, drkg wtr. Fishing, hiking.

ELSMORE (E)
Bourbon State Fishing Lake   FREE
4 mi E of US 59 in Elsmore on co rd to campground. Free. All year; 7-day limit. 10 sites. Tbls, toilets, cfga, drkg wtr. Picnicking, fishing, boating(l). 103-acre lake.

ELLSWORTH (W)
Kanopolis State Park $10
21 mi SE of Ellsworth on SR 141. $10 without hookups $19-$22 with hookups. All year; limited facilities in winter; 14-day limit. Tbls, flush toilets, cfga, drkg wtr, showers, elec($), dump, beaches. Swimming, boating(ld), fishing, hiking trails, biking, horseback riding, volleyball, softball, hunting, nature trails. 3,500-acre lake; 12,500-acre wildlife area.

   Langley Point-- 105 primitive site; 31 wtr/elec sites 16 wtr/elec/swr sites.

   Horsethief -- 32 elec; 197 wtr/elec sites 70 wtr/elec/swr sites.

ERIE (E)
Erie City Park $10
In Erie, follow signs from US 59 to E on Third St. $10 for 4 RV sites with elec/wtr; tent camping free. Tbls, toilets, cfga, no drkg wtr, dump. Swimming, tennis.

FALL RIVER (E)
Damsite Recreation Area $6.50
Corps of Engineers
Fall River Lake
From W of Fall River on US 400, N at milemarker 344 on Z50 Rd for 0.9 mi; right (E), then NE 2.4 mi on Cummins Rd; right (S) on access rd into park. All year; 14-day limit. During 4/1-10/31 campers with federal senior pass pay $6.50 at 4 non-elec sites (40-85-ft spaces); $8.50 at 13 sites with 30-amp elec/wtr; $9 at 12 sites with 50-amp elec/wtr; $10.50 at 1 full-hookup 50-amp site (others pay $13, $17, $18 & $21). All open sites $10 off-season with drkg wtr but no showers or other amenities. Group camping available. RV limit in excess of 65 ft; 2 pull-through. Tbls, flush & pit toilets, cfga, drkg wtr, dump, showers, interpretive programs, picnic shelter, playground. Fishing, hiking, boating, jet skiing, nature trails, canoeing. 30 acres.

Rock Ridge North Campground $4.50
Corps of Engineers
Fall River Lake
From W of Fall River on US 400, at milemarker 344, 0.9 mi N on Z50 Rd; at split, continue straight on Twp Rd 534 about 1 mi into Fall River State Park area; left (W) on Twp Rd 50B, and follow its curves N & E to Rock Ridge Park at lakeshore. All year; 14-day limit. During 4/1-10/31, campers with federal senior pass pay $4.50 at 19 non-elec sites; $6.50 at 23 sites with 30-amp elec (others pay $9 & $13). Off-season, some sites open without utilities & reduced services for $10. Tbls, flush & pit toilets, cfga, drkg wtr, dump. Boating(l), fishing, hiking nature trail.

Whitehall Bay Campground $7.50
Corps of Engineers
Fall River Lake
From W of Fall River on US 400, N at milemarker 344 on Z50 Rd for 0.09 mi; right (E), then 2.4 mi NE on Cummins Rd; at split, veer left on CR 20 across dam, then left (N) 0.8 mi; left (W) 0.7 mi; right (N) 1.7 mi to low water crossing, then N 0.1 mi, W 0.4 mi & left (S) for 1.1 mi to park. All year; 14-day limit. During 4/1-10/31, campers with federal senior pass pay $7.50 at 15 sites with 30-amp elec (no wtr hookups); $8 at 9 sites with 50-amp elec/wtr. $10 off-season with limited amenities & services Group camping available. Tbls, flush & pit toilets, cfga, drkg wtr. RV limit in excess of 65 ft, all back-in. Tbls, flush & pit toilets, cfga, drkg wtr, beach, showers, dump, playground, shelter, beach. Swimming, boating(l), fishing, waterskiing, hiking, jet skiing, canoeing.

FONTANA (E)
Miami State Fishing Lake   FREE
2 mi N & E of Fontana on county rd (5 mi S of Osawatomie). Free. All year; 7-day limit. 14 primitive sites. Tbls, toilets, cfga, no drkg wtr, no trash service. Fishing, boating.

FORT SCOTT (E)

Gunn City Park $10
NW corner of Fort Scott; at Marmaton River. $10 for RVs with elec/wtr. Nov-Mar for RVs (wtr off rest of year). 14 RV sites. Tbls, toilets, cfga, drkg wtr, one 30-amp elec site. Boating(lr), canoeing(r), fishing, picnicking, playground, Frisbee golf. Dump at fairgrounds. 155 acres.

FREDONIA (E)

Fall River State Park $10
17 mi NW of Fredonia on SR 96; 3 mi N on Fall River Rd. $10 without hookups in-season $19-$22 with hookups. All year; limited facilities in winter; 14-day limit. 125 sites at 2 camps (45 with elec). Tbls, flush toilets, cfga, drkg wtr, showers, elec, dump. Swimming beach, boating(ld), canoeing, fishing, fitness trail, canoeing. 917 acres; 2,450-acre lake.

GARDEN CITY (W)

Concannon State Fishing Lake FREE
15 mi NE of Garden City. Free. All year; 7-day limit. Primitive camping at 60-acre lake. Tbls, toilets, cfga, no drkg wtr. Fishing, boating(l).

GARNETT (E)

Cedar Valley Reservoir $9
7 mi SW of Garnett at Kentucky & 1500 Rds on 705 acres surrounding the lake. $9 base. All year; 7-day limit. Base fee for non-residents at primitive sites; $14 with elec; $16 with elec/wtr. 12 sites with elec. Tbls, toilets, cfga, drkg wtr, hookups($). Fishing, boating. Register at police dispatch office, 131 W. 5th Ave. Boating(l), fishing, hiking, swimming.

North Lake City Park $9
Lake Garnett
North end of Garnett at Lake Garnett. $9 base. All year; 7-day limit. Base fee for non-residents at primitive sites; $14 with elec; $16 elec/wtr. 30 sites with hookups plus designated primitive area. Tbls, toilets, cfga, drkg wtr, hookups($), pool, playground. Fishing, boating(l), shooting range, tennis, basketball, swimming, horseshoes, sand volleyball, golf. 55-acre lake. Register at police dispatch office, 131 W. 5th Ave.

Veterans Memorial City Park $9
Crystal Lake
Just S of Garnett on US 59; camp on S side of Crystal Lake. $9 base for non-residents at primitive sites. 5 elec/wtr sites, $14-$16. Tbls, toilets, cfga, drkg wtr. Fishing, boating(l). Register at police dispatch office, 131 W. 5th Ave.

GIRARD (E)

Crawford State Park $10
10 mi N of Girard on SR 7. $10 without hookups in-season; $19-$22 with hookups. All year; limited facilities in winter; 14-day limit. 112 sites (83 with elec) at 6 campgrounds.

Tbls, flush toilets, cfga, drkg wtr, showers, dump, store, beach, marina. Swimming, boating (lrd), fishing, sand volleyball, horseshoes, interpretive nature trail, scuba diving. 439 acres; 150-acre lake.

GODDARD (E)

Lake Afton $8
Sedgwick County Park
3 mi S of Goddard on Goddard Rd; 3 mi W on 39th St. $8 base. 4/1-10/31; 14-day limit. Base fee for primitive sites ($7 for seniors); $12 with elec/wtr ($10 seniors); wtr at 16 sites, $1 extra. Weekly & monthly rates available. 180 sites (55-ft RV limit). Tbls, flush toilets, cfga, drkg wtr, elec, showers, 2 dumps, store, playgrounds, 3 fishing piers. Horseshoes, swimming, fishing, boating (ld), shooting range. Open ground fires prohibited. 725 acres; 258-acre lake. $3 recreational permit ($25 annual).

GREAT BEND (W)

Cheyenne Bottoms Inlet FREE
State Wildlife Area
6 mi NE of Great Bend. Free. All year; 3-day limit. Undesignated sites. No drkg wtr. Fishing. 2 acres.

GREENSBURG (W)

Kiowa State Fishing Lake FREE
NW corner of Greensburg. Free. All year; 7-day limit. 10 sites; 21 acres. Tbls, drkg wtr, cfga, toilets. Picnicking, fishing, boating(l).

HARTFORD (E)

Flint Hills National Wildlife Refuge FREE
On upstream portion of John Redmond Reservoir. Free. All year. Open camping. No facilities. Hiking, fishing, hunting, boating, waterskiing.

Hartford Recreation Area CLOSED
Corps of Engineers
John Redmond Lake
From CR 130 at Hartford, 0.5 mi E on gravel rd, following signs; NW of lake at Neosho river. Campsites removed; now lake access point.

HIATTVILLE (E)

Elm Creek Lake $3
Bourbon County Park
2 mi N of Hiattville on 130th St; 1 mi E on Fern Rd. $3 for primitive sites; $10 with elec. All year; 14-day limit. 10 sites at 106-acre lake. Tbls, toilets, cfga, drkg wtr; limited facilities in winter. Picnicking, boating(l), fishing, swimming.

HIAWATHA (E)

Brown State Fishing Lake FREE
7.5 mi E of Hiawatha on US 36; 1 mi S to campground. Free. All year; 7-day limit. 10 sites; 62-acre lake. Tbls, toilets, cfga, no drkg wtr, food. Picnicking, fishing, boating(rl).

HILLSBORO (E)

French Creek Cove Recreation Area $12
Corps of Engineers
Marion Reservoir
3 mi E of Hillsboro on US 56; 3 mi N on Limestone Rd; at S shore of lake's French Creek cove. Open 3/15-11/15; 14-day limit. During 4/10-10/15, $12 at 20 sites with 30-amp elec ($6 with federal senior pass); free rest of season but no amenities. No camping off-season. Tbls, toilets, cfga, drkg wtr. Boating(dl), fishing, waterskiing.

HOLTON (E)

Banner Creek Reservoir $6
Jackson County Campground
1.5 mi W of US 75 on SR 16. $9 without hookups; $16 with elec. All year. 130 sites. 14 day limit. Drkg wtr, cfga, tbls, flush toilets, showers, dump ($5 for non-campers). Boating, fishing, swimming, waterskiing, 5.2-mi hiking & biking trail. .

Nebo State Fishing Lake   FREE
8 mi E of Holton on SR 116; 1 mi S, then half mi W. Free; $5 with elec. All year; 7-day limit. Primitive designated camping area on shore of 38-acre lake. Toilets, cfga, tbls, no drkg wtr, no trash service. Hunting, fishing, boating(lr), picnic area, swimming.

Prairie Lake City Park $8
1.5 mi N & 3.5 mi W of Holton on CR 246. $8 base. All year; 14-day limit. $8 without elec; $10 with elec. 30 sites. Tbls, toilets, cfga, drkg wtr, elec. Boating(l), fishing, picnicking. Boating & fishing permits ($3.50-$7) needed.

HORTON (E)

Mission Lake City Park $8
1 mi N of Horton on US 73; follow signs to just W of fishing pond. $5 base for primitive sites ($175 for season); $15 with elec; free tent camping at nearby Little Mission Lake. All year; limited facilities in winter. 130 sites. Tbls, toilets, cfga, drkg wtr, dump, shelter, elec($ - permit needed). Boating(l), canoeing, fishing, wheel-chair accessible fishing dock, waterskiing. Seasonal rates available. 278 acres; 177-acre lake.

HOXIE (W)

Sheridan County Fairgrounds $10
From jct of SR 23 (Main St) & US 24 (Oak St), N on SR 23 past W side of Express Deli, then E into fairgrounds; sites are NE behind the building & the deli (no signs for camping). $10. About a dozen sites with 30-amp elec/wtr. Flush toilets, showers, dump.

Sheridan State Fishing Lake   FREE
12 mi E of Hoxie on US 24; .7 mi N. Free. All year. 12 sites. Tbls, toilets, cfga. Picnicking, fishing, boating(l), swimming. 263 acres; 67-acre lake.

HUMBOLDT (E)

Camp Hunter City Park $10
From Bridge St in Humboldt, 3 blocks S on First St to 806 S. 1st. $10. All year; 5-day limit. 17 RV sites with elec/wtr; no tents. Tbls, toilets, cfga, drkg wtr, dump, playground, Internet access, showers. Register at city hall or water plant after hours & weekends.

HURON (E)

Atchison County Lake $3
W of Huron on 326th Rd. $3 daily for 2 days; $1 each additional day; 10-day limit. Tbls, toilets, cfga, drkg wtr, no elec. Fishing, boating.

INDEPENDENCE (E)

Card Creek Recreation Area $8
Corps of Engineers
Elk City Lake
From SR 39 at Elk City, 7 mi S then E on US 160; 1.3 mi N on 2500 Rd; W then N on 4600 Rd; 1.7 mi W on 4800 Rd. During 4/1-10/31, $8 with federal senior pass at 15 RV/tent 30-amp elec sites (some pull-through) and 7 RV sites with 50-amp elec; others pay $16. Some sites free during 11/1-3/31 but no utilities & reduced services. All year; 14-day limit. Tbls, showers, flush toilets, cfga, drkg wtr, dump, playground, picnic shelter. Boating(ld), fishing, hiking.

Elk City State Park $10
5.5 mi NW of Independence on co rd. $10 without hookups; $19-$22 with hookups. All year; limited facilities in winter; 14-day limit. Primitive camping in wildlife area (no trash service). 65 elec/wtr sites; 120 elec/wtr/sewer. Tbls, flush toilets, cfga, drkg wtr, showers, elec($), dump, playground, fishing piers, beach. Swimming, basketball, sand volleyball, boating(ld), fishing, hiking (15-mi trail), 4-mi mountain biking trail, birdwatching. 857 acres; 4,500-acre lake.

Montgomery   FREE
State Fishing Lake
3 mi S and 1 mi E of jct of US 75 and US 160 (in Independence) on co rd to campground. Free. All year; 7-day limit. 60 sites; 408 acres; 92-acre lake. Tbls, toilets, cfga, firewood, no drkg wtr. Picnicking, fishing, swimming, boating(rl).

Outlet Channel Recreation Area $10
Corps of Engineers
Elk City Lake
From US 75 in Independence, about 3 mi W on Taylor Rd (becoming CR 4675); half mi N on CR 3525; 2 mi W on CR 4800; N on Table Mound Rd, then veer left at split onto 3300 Rd; NW on 3300 Rd; W on dam rd to W side of spillway, then NE (right) on access rd to campground. $10 at 13 non-elec RV/tent sites during 4/1-10/31; free off-season but no wtr & reduced services. $8 in-season with federal

senior pass at 7 sites with 30/50-amp elec; some sites free off-season but no utilities & reduced services (others pay $16). 14-day limit. Tbls, flush & pit toilets, cfga, drkg wtr, dump, playground, shelter, showers. Boating, fishing, hiking.

JETMORE (W)

Buckner Valley Park	FREE

Pawnee Watershed District
5 mi W of Jetmore on US 156. Free. Primitive sites. Tbls, toilets, cfga, drkg wtr, elec. Horseback riding, fishing, picnicking. At Buckner Creek.

Hodgeman State Fishing Lake	FREE

5 mi E of jct of US 156 and US 283 (in Jetmore); 2 mi S. All year; 7-day limit. Undesignated sites. Tbls, toilets, cfga, drkg wtr. Picnicking. 87 acres. Lake periodically dry; it is stocked with fish when water present.

Jetmore City Lake	$7

3 mi W & 1.5 mi S of Jetmore on Spring Creek. $7 for primitive & tent sites; 5 RV sites $15 with elec. 15 total sites. Tbls, toilets, cfga, drkg wtr, elec. Boating(l), fishing. $4 vehicle permit may apply.

JEWELL (W)

Jewell City Park	FREE

In Jewell, 2 blks E of SR 14 on SR 28 (Delaware St). Free primitive camping; $5 with four 30/50-amp elec, flush toilets, showers, dump (at NE corner of park), playground. 30-ft & 40-ft RV limit. Nice park (but 6 p.m. tornado test siren sounds).

JUNCTION CITY (E)

See entries at Milford and Wakefield

Curtis Creek	$7

Corps of Engineers
Milford Lake
2 mi NW of Junction City on SR 57 (N. Jackson St); W on SR 244 until it curves N, becoming Trail Rd; about 3 mi N on Trail Rd; at split, veer right on 3500 Ave about 1 mi to park access rd. Campers with federal senior pass pay $14 at 8 tent sites & 14 RV/tent sites without hookups, $9 at 26 sites with 30-amp elec (no wtr hookup), $10 at 41 sites with 30-amp elec/wtr (others pay $14, $18 & $20). 4/15-9/30; 14-day limit. 65-ft RV limit, all back-in. Drkg wtr, cfga, flush & pit toilets, tbls, dump, playground, showers, pay phone. Boating(l), fishing, swimming, 2 hiking trails, fishing pier, waterskiing.

Geary State Fishing Lake	FREE

8.5 mi S of Junction City on US 77. Free. All year; 7-day limit. 50 sites. Tbls, toilets, cfga, drkg wtr. Picnicking, fishing, boating(ld). 451 acres.

Milford State Park	$8.50

4 mi N of Junction City on US 77; 3 mi W on SR 57. $8.50 without hookups in-season ($7.50 off-season); $14.50-18.50 with hookups. All year; limited facilities in winter; 14-day limit. 5 campgrounds with 222 sites (see below). Tbls, flush toilets, cfga, drkg wtr, showers, hookups($), dump, beach, marina. Swimming, boating(lrd), fishing, hiking, nature trails. 16,000-acre lake.

Eagle Ridge Camp -- 21 full-hookup sites.
Eagle Ridge Shelter -- 4 wtr/elec sites.
Group Shelter -- 4 wtr/elec sites.
Hickory Hollow Camp -- 30 full-hookup sites & dump station.
Cedar Point Camp -- 7 primitive sites, 40 sites with elec/wtr; new shower building, dump.
Prairie View Camp--20 elec/wtr sites; portable toilets.
Sunset Ridge, 14 primitive sites.
Woodland Hills: 58 primitive sites, 29 sites with elec/wtr, 1 site wtr/elec/sewer.
Three Trees Cabin Shelter -- 3 primitive sites.
Walnut Grove Camp: 29 primitive sites, shower house, basketball court.

West Rolling Hills Campground	$7

Corps of Engineers
Milford Lake
2 mi NW of Junction City on SR 57 (N. Jackson St); about 4 mi W on SR 244; N on W. Rolling Hills Rd, following signs to campground; at lake's SE shore. Campers with federal senior pass pay $7 at 12 tent sites & 6 RV/tent sites without hookups, $10 at 40 sites with 30-amp elec/wtr, $10.50 at 16 sites with 50-amp elec/wtr. 4/15-9/30; 14-day limit. 60-ft RV limit except at 2 long pull-throughs. Flush & pit toilets, cfga, dump, tbls, drkg wtr, showers, fish cleaning stations, pay phone, playground. Boating(l), hiking, fishing, swimming.

KALVESTA (W)

Finney State Fishing Lake	FREE

8 mi N, 3 mi W, then 1 mi N of Kalvesta. Free. All year; 7-day limit. Primitive camping at 110-acre lake. Tbls, toilets, cfga, no drkg wtr. Fishing, boating(l).

KANSAS CITY (E)

Leavenworth State Fishing Lake	FREE

4 mi N of Kansas City on KS 16; 2 mi E on KS 90 to park (3 mi W and 1 mi N of Tonganoxie). Free. All year; 14-day limit. 20 sites; 175-acre lake. Toilets, tbls, cfga, drkg wtr, dump, playground. Fishing, hiking, boating(lr), swimming.

KINGMAN (W)

Kingman County Fairgrounds	$6

In Kingman at 110 W. 1st Ave, across from Riverside City Park. $6. All year. 90 RV sites (fee, plus $20 deposit for key to hookups). Tbls, toilets, cfga, drkg wtr, elec, dump. Contact Wyatts' Grocery Store, 838 E. D Ave (Hwy 54); 620-532-3851.

Kingman   FREE
State Fishing Lake
8 mi W of Kingman on US 54. Free. All year; 14-night limit.
60 primitive sites around the lake. Tbls, toilets, cfga, no
drkg wtr, no trash service. Picnicking, fishing, boating(l),
nature trail, hunting. 4,242 acres; 144-acre lake. Byron
Walker Wildlife Area.

Riverside City Park   FREE
E of town on US 54 across from fairgrounds at 100 W. 1st
Ave. Sign says "All night parking for tourists only." Contact
Wyatts' Grocery Store fpr leu tp elec. Free. Tbls, toilets,
cfga, drkg wtr, hookups, dump. Camping also at Champlin
Park, 600 E. D Ave; no services.

KINGSDOWN (W)
Clark State Fishing Lake   FREE
10 mi S of Kingsdown on SR 94; 1 mi W on co rd to
campground. Free. All year; 7-day limit. 65 sites; 1,243
acres. Tbls, toilets, cfga, no drkg wtr. Picnicking, fishing,
boating(lr).

LA CROSSE (W)
Grass City Park   25 cents
1 mi S of jct SR 4 & US 183 on US 183 in town. 25 cents
per hr for elec; primitive camping free. All year; 3-day
limit. 4 RV sites plus tent area. Tbls, flush toilets, cfga,
drkg wtr, elec($). Picnicking. Laundry, store nearby.

LA CYGNE (E)
LaCygne Lake $9
Linn County Park
On Lake Rd, E of Hwy 69; N of power plant. $9 without
hookups; $14 elec; $15 wtr/elec; $16 full hookups ($2
additional for 50 amp) All year. About 100 sites. Tbls, flush
toilets, showers, cfga, drkg wtr, elec($), playground, shel-
ter, pool, store, coin laundry, dump. Fishing, boating(l),
swimming. 2,600-acre lake.

LAKIN (W)
Beymer Water Recreation Park $10
Kearny County Park
2.5 mi S of Lakin on SR 25. $10 at elec/wtr sites. 5/1-10/1;
3-day limit. 8 sites. Tbls, flush toilets, drkg wtr, showers,
cfga, 30-amp elec. Fishing, swimming, picnicking, playground. Beautiful spot.

LATHAM (E)
Butler State Fishing Lake   FREE
2 mi W of Latham and 1 mi N on co rd to campground.
Free. All year; 7-day limit. 20 sites. Tbls, toilets, cfga, drkg
wtr. Picnicking, fishing, boating(l). 351 acres.

LAWRENCE (E)
Bloomington East Park
Corps of Engineers
Clinton Lake

From Lawrence, 4 mi W on Hwy 40 (6th St); 5 mi left on
CR 442 to Stull; 6 mi S (left) on CR 458; 4 mi NE (left) on
CR 6 through Clinton, then follow signs. Between the Rock
Creek & Wakarusa River arms of the lake. It contains Ash,
Cedar Ridge, Elm, Hickory/Walnut and Oak Campgrounds.
It also features Bloomington Beach picnic shelters, a
swimming beach, horseshoe pits, sand volleyball courts,
3 boat ramps, playgrounds, amphitheater, coin laundry
and a fishing pier. Clinton Lake Museum has historical
exhibits. Reservations through Hickory/Walnut camps.

Ash Group Campground in Bloomington East Park near
Hickory/Walnut Campgrounds is a group camping area,
primarily for tent groups of 10-75 people, $50. Also open
to small RVs such as folding trailers & pickup campers on
the gravel circle drive. No hookups. Picnic shelter, fish
cleaning station, horseshoe pits. Pit toilets; shower at
Hickory/Walnut Campground.

Cedar Ridge Campground, in Bloomington East Park.
5/1-9/30; 14-day limit. Campers with federal senior pass
pay $10 at 88 paved sites with 20/30-amp elec/wtr, $12
at 13 paved sites with 20/30-amp elec/wtr (others pay $20
& $24). 60-ft RV limit; 69 pull-through sites. Tbls, flush
toilets, cfga, drkg wtr, fish cleaning station, dump, coin
laundry, beach, showers, playground. NRRS

Elm Group Campground, in Bloomington East Park near
Hickory/Walnut Campgrounds. 5/1-9/30; 14-day limit.
Grassy, undesignated-site group camping area, $50.
Primarily for group tenting, but small RVs such as folding
trailers & pickup campers okay on grassy area. Tbls, flush
toilets, showers, cfga, drkg wtr, shelter. Volleyball court.
Pick up keys at the Walnut Creek Campground.

Hickory Campground, in Bloomington East Park. 5/1-
9/30; 14-day limit. Campers with federal senior pass pay
$7 at 47 non-elec sites, $8 at 53 gravel sites with 30-amp
elec (no wtr hookup), $9 at 1 site with 30-amp elec/wtr,
$12 at 3 sites with 50-amp elec/wtr (others pay $14, $16,
$18 & $24). Tbls, flush toilets, showers, cfga, drkg wtr,
dump, playground, beach, coin laundry, fish cleaning station. Boating(l), fishing, hiking, biking, swimming, volleyball. Sat evening programs. Group camping at Oak Creek
loop.

Walnut Campground, in Bloomington East Park. 5/1-
9/30; 14-day limit. Campers with federal senior pass pay
$7 at 53 gravel non-elec sites, $9 at 29 gravel sites with
20/30-amp elec (no wtr hookup), $10 at 6 gravel sites with
20/30-amp elec/wtr, $11 at 1 sites with 50-amp elec/wtr,
$24 at 3 sites with 20/30/50-amp full hookups. 60-ft RV
limpt; 5 pull-through. Tbls, flush & pit toilets, showers, cfga,
drkg wtr, coin laundry, amphitheater, fish cleaning station,
playground, beach. Biking, boating(l), fishing, hiking, swimming, volleyball.

Clinton State Park $10
4 mi W of Lawrence at Clinton Reservoir. $10 without
hookups in-season; $19-$22 with hookups. All year;
limited facilities in winter; 14-day limit. About 419 sites
(265 elec/wtr). Tbls, flush toilets, cfga, drkg wtr, showers,

dump, beach, playground, marina. Swimming, boating (lrd), fishing, winter sports, hiking & mountain biking trails, horseback riding, waterskiing.

Lone Star Lake $11
Douglas County Park
4 mi SW of Lawrence. $11 primitive sites; $16 with elec. 4/1-10/15. 62 sites. Tbls, flush toilets, cfga, drkg wtr, dump, showers, elec($). Boating(l), fishing, picnicking. Fees for boating & fishing.

Rockhaven Park Campground $12
Corps of Engineers
Clinton Lake
From just SW of Clinton, 2 mi SW on CR 458; 0.8 mi N on gravel CR 700E. 12 at 30 non-elec sites; $16 at 18 sites with 30-amp elec ($6 & $8 with federal senior pass). Sites 1-5 & 22-50 only for equestrians. 4/1-10/30; 14-day limit. 48 total sites. Flush & pit toilets, plus pit toilets just outside the campground for non-campers. New showers, picnic shelter, corral. Tbls, drkg wtr, cfga. Day use parking area for non-campers.

LEBO(E)
Sun Dance Park   FREE
Corps of Engineers
Melvern Lake
From just N of Lebo at I-35/US 50, 4.5 mi N on Fauna Rd NW (becoming S. Hoch Rd); right into park just S of Arvonia; at SW shore of lake. All year; 14-day limit. 25 free primitive gravel sites. Boating(l), fishing.

LIBERAL (W)
Arkalon City Park $5
10 mi NE of US 83 in Liberal on US 54; 2 mi N on county rd. $5 base; $10 with elec. 4/1-10/15; 14-day limit. 35 sites (27 with elec). Tbls, flush toilets, cfga, drkg wtr, elec($), dump, showers. Fishing, horseshoes, nature trails, birdwatching.

Seward County Fairgrounds $10
About 10 mi E of Liberal on US 54. $10 elec only. Sites with 20-amp or 30-amp elec; elec/wtr sites $15; 7 sites with 50-amp full hookups, $30. Open all year. Flush toilets, showers, drkg wtr, dump.

LINDSBORG (E)
Old Mill Museum Campground $5
McPherson County Park
Across the river on S First St from the Old Mill Museum, 120 Mill St. $5 for basic sites; $7 with elec. Check in at museum office. 24 sites. Tbls, flush toilets, cfga, drkg wtr at museum.. Fishing, canoeing.

LOGAN (W)
Logan City Lake / Logan City Park $10
Park is in town, the lake is 2 mi S of Logan. Camp $10. at both locations Tbls, toilets, cfga, elec (at lake). Picnicking, playground. Lake has fishing, boating(l),

LOUISBURG (E)
Louisburg-Middlecreek   FREE
State Fishing Lake
7 mi S of Louisburg on Metcalf Rd. Free. All year; 7-day limit. 5 sites. Tbls, toilets, cfga, no drkg wtr, no trash service. Boating(l), fishing, hunting. 280-acre lake.

LUCAS (W)
Lucas Park $7
Corps of Engineers
Wilson Lake
From Lucas, about 6 mi S on SR 232; just before curve, turn right (S) on 203 St for 2 mi to park; on N side of lake. During 5/15-9/15, campers with federal senior pass pay $7 at 34 non-elec sites, $9 at 54 sites with 30-amp elec (no wtr hookup), $10 at 16 sites with wtr/elec (others pay $14, $18 & $20). Weather permitting, during off-season, basic sites free, utility sites with wtr and/or elec, $10, but reduced amenities & services. Group camping available. rea with elec. RV limit in excess of 65 ft; 29 pull-through. Tbls, showers, flush & pit toilets, cfga, drkg wtr, playground, beach, pavilion, fish cleaning station. Picnicking, fishing, swimming, boating(ld), volleyball courts, 3-mi loop hiking trail, waterskiing, horseshoe pits.

Sylvan Park $7
Corps of Engineers
Wilson Lake
7 mi S of Lucas on SR 232, then over dam; left on Outlet Rd; below dam on N side of spillway; at Saline River. During 5/1-9/30, campers with federal senior pass pay $7 at 4 non-elec sites, $10 at 24 sites with 30 & 50-amp elec/wtr & full hookups (others pay $14 & $20). Off-season, basic sites free, utility sites with wtr and/or elec $10 but reduced amenities & services. Group camping available. All year, weather permitting; 14-day limit. RV limit in excess of 65 ft; most pull-through. Tbls, flush & pit toilets, cfga, drkg wtr, playground, shelter, visitor center, beach, dump, showers all year, beach, fishing pier. Hiking, boating(l), fishing, horseshoe pits, sand volleyball, swimming.

LYNDON (E)
Eisenhower State Park $10
5 mi S of Lyndon on US 75; 3 mi W on SR 278; at N shore of Melvern Lake. $10 without hookups in-season; $19-$22 with hookups. All year; limited facilities in winter; 14-day limit. 25 sites with full hookups, 118 sites with elec/wtr; 261 sites with elec, 35 primitive sites; 3 campgrounds. Tbls, flush toilets, cfga, drkg wtr, showers, elec, dump, beaches. Swimming, boating(rld), fishing, hiking trail, interpretive trail, horseshoes, volleyball, archery, hunting, horseback riding, naturalist programs. Equestrian camping at Cowboy Campground & N loop of Westpond Camp (4 sites have wtr; 10 have elec). 6,930-acre lake.

Carbolyn Park $7
Corps of Engineers
Pomona Lake
From Lyndon, 4.5 mi N on US 75; E on E. 217th St before Dragoon Creek bridge (signs), then left on access rd; at W side of lake on Dragoon Creek arm. 5/1-9/30; 14-day limit. $7 with federal senior pass at 3 primitive sites (others pay $14); $9 at about 30 elec/wtr sites (others pay $18). 50-ft RV limit; 2 pull-through. Tbls, flush & pit toilets, showers, cfga, drkg wtr, dump, playground, shelter. Fishing, boating(l), swimming, hiking.

LYONS (W)
Lyons Overnight FREE
Municipal Park
From jct US 56 & 96, half mi S on Hwy 96; half mi W at 500 W. Taylor St. Camp free 5 days; donations suggested. All year. 18 close sites. Tbls, toilets, cfga, drkg wtr, showers, 30-amp elec, dump. Picnicking, hiking. Check in at city hall or police station before camping.

MANHATTAN (E)
Pottawatomie County FREE
State Fishing Lake #2
2.5 mi E of Manhattan on US 24; 2 mi N; 2 mi NW to campground. Free. All year; 7-day limit. 25 sites. Tbls, toilets, cfga, no drkg wtr. Picnicking, fishing, boating(rl).

Tuttle Creek Cove Park $7
Corps of Engineers
Tuttle Creek Lake
From Manhattan at the Kansas River, about 8 mi N on US 24; right (N) on SR 13, then immediately left (NW) on Tuttle Cove Rd for 3 mi into park. $7 with federal senior pass at 17 non-elec sites; $10 with senior pass at 39 sites with 30/50-amp elec/wtr (others pay $14 & $20). During off-season, some sites free but no utilities & reduced amenities & services. All year; 14-day limit. Tbls, toilets, cfga, drkg wtr, beach, fishing pier, playground, dump, shelter. Boating (ld), fishing.

Tuttle Creek State Park $10
5 mi N of Manhattan on US 24; at base of dam. $10 without hookups, $19-$22 with hookups. All year; limited facilities in winter; 14-day limit. Park's 4 camping areas are outlined below. Tbls, flush toilets, cfga, wtr hookups, showers, dump, beach, playground, marina. Swimming, boating(lrd), fishing, waterskiing, 4-mi hiking & biking trail, waterskiing, windsurfing, sand & mud volleyball, 18-hole disc golf course, wildlife viewing blind. 12,200 acres; 15,800-acre lake.
South Randolph -- 50 primitive sites, 20 elec sites. Equestrian trails, horse pens, wash racks, covered picnic shelter; showers and toilets.
River Pond Park -- 514 acres below the dam. 540 primitivesites, 167 with wtr/elec (24 with 50 amp; 16 winterized with frost-free hydrants). 3 boat ramps, dump, 3 shower houses, 2 courtesy docks, playground, fishing pier, fish cleaning station, beach, nature trail.
Cedar Ridge -- 100 primitive sites, 4 lane boat ramp, marina, shower house, fish cleaning station.
Fancy Creek Park -- Secluded 372 acres at W side of N end of lake. 24 elec sites, 200 primitive sites, drkg wtr nearby, pit toilets, hiking trail, 2 high-water boat ramps, no showers.

MANKATO (W)
Jewell State Fishing Lake FREE
1 mi W on US 36; 6 mi S of Mankato on co rd; 2 mi W on co rd. Free. All year; 14-day limit. 10 sites; 57 acres. Tbls, toilets, cfga, drkg wtr. Picnicking, fishing, boating(l).

Lovewell State Park $10
4 mi E of Mankato on US 36; 10 mi N on SR 14; 4 mi E on co rd; 1 mi S on access rd. $10 without hookups in-season $19-$22 with hookups. All year; limited facilities in winter; 14-day limit. 4 campgrounds (1 for groups). Tbls, flush & pit toilets, cfga, drkg wtr, showers, elec, dumps, store, beach, playground, marina, lighted fish cleaning station with elec outlets. Swimming, boating(ld), fishing, archery range, sand volleyball, horseshoes, basketball courts. 1,126 acres; 3,000-acre lake.
Walleye Point -- 100 primitive sites, 28 elec sites, 6 wtr/elec sites, 4 full hookups.
Willow --100 primitive sites, 14 full hookups.
Cedar Point --100 primitive sites, 24 elec, 7 wtr/elec, 1 full hookup.
Cottonwood -- 100 primitive sites, 30 elec sites

Mankato City Park FREE
At W end of town, turn N on South McRoberts St; park on W side, loop rd. Free. All year. Mostly off-level sites with several prs of 15 & 20-amp elec outlets on 3 poles; space for 3-4 medium or large RVs on sides of driveway. Flush toilets, playgrounds, cfga, drkg wtr. Less appealing than other N Kansas parks.

MARION (E)
Cottonwood Point Camp $9
Corps of Engineers
Marion Lake
From Marion, 3 mi W on US 56; about 3.5 mi N on Quail Creek Rd; 2 mi W on 220th St; at E shore of lake. All year; 14-day limit. During 3/15-11/15, campers with federal senior pass pay $9 at 53 sites with 20/30-amp elec, $10.50 at 41 sites with 20/30/50-amp elec, $11.50 at 36 sites with 20/30/50-amp full hookups (others pay $18, $21 & $23). Some sites free off-season, but no utilities & reduced services. RV limit in excess of 65 ft; 11 pull-through. Group camping available. Tbls, flush & pit toilets, cfga, drkg wtr, showers, amphitheater, beach access, dump, shelters, playground, shelters. Swimming, fishing, boating(l), interpretive trails.

Hillsboro Cove Campground $9
Corps of Engineers
Marion Lake
From Marion, about 7 mi W on US 56; qtr mi N on Night-hawk Rd, then E on access rd to park; at SW shore of lake. All year; 14-day limit. During 4/10-10/15, campers with federal senior pass pay $9 at 21 sites with 20/30-amp elec; $9.50 at 31 sites with 20/30/50-amp elec (others pay $18 & $19). Sites open off-season are free but no amenities & reduced services. Group camping available. 50-ft RV limit; 8 pull-through. Tbls, flush & pit toilets, cfga, drkg wtr, showers, dump, beach, playground, sun shelters, picnic shelter, pay phone. Boating(ld), fishing, swimming, hiking.

Marion County Lake Park $6
2 mi E of Marion on US 256; 2 mi S on Airport Rd; half mi W on Lakeshore Dr. $6 for primitive camping permit; $14 elec/wtr. All year; 14-day limit. Primitive camping at Durham Cove and near spillway. Tbls, toilets, cfga, drkg wtr, dump ($6 for non-campers), showers, CATV ($1.75). Fishing, boating(ld), swimming.

Marion Cove Campground $12
Corps of Engineers
Marion Lake
3 mi W of Marion on US 56; 2 mi N on Quail Creek Rd; 2 mi W on 210th St; right on park access rd; at SE shore of lake. All year; 14-day limit. During 4/10-10/15, $12 at 20 primitive sites (14 tents). Free off-season but no amenities or services. Tbls, cfga, tbls, toilets, beach, no drkg wtr. Boating(l), fishing, picnicking, swimming.

MARQUETTE (W)
Riverside Campground $7
Corps of Engineers
Kanopolis Lake
From Marquette, about 6 mi W on SR 4; 3 mi N on SR 141; 0.5 mi E on Riverside Dr, following signs; at SE end of dam on Smoky Hill River. During 5/15-9/15, campers with federal senior pass pay $7 at 12 primitive sites and $10 at 16 elec/wtr sites (9 with 30-amp, 7 with 50-amp); others pay $14 & $20. Primitive ites free during 9/16-5/14 but no wtr; elec sites $6 utility charge($3 with senior pass). 60-ft RV limit; 2 pull-through. Tbls, flush & pit toilets, showers, cfga, drkg wtr, dump, playground. Handicap access. Fishing, boating, basketball court.

Venango Campground $7
Corps of Engineers
Kanopolis Lake
From Marquette, about 6 mi W on SR 4; 5 mi N on SR 141; on left, at NW end of dam. All year; 14-day limit. During 5/1-9/30, campers with federal senior pay $7 at 72 primitive sites (10 pull-through), $9 at 2 sites with 50-amp elec (no wtr hookup), $9 at 51 sites with 30-amp elec (no wtr hookup), $10 at 29 sites with 50-amp elec/

wtr. Off-season, primitive sites free; no elec or wtr service & reduced amenities. Primitive group camping area with shelter house, $60. 4 picnic shelters. RV limit in excess of 65 ft. Tbls, flush & pit toilets, cfga, drkg wtr, showers, dump. Fishing, boating(l), swimming beach, playground, motorcycle trail, ATV trail, nature trail.

Yankee Run Point   NO CAMPING
Corps of Engineers
Kanopolis Lake
From Marquette, about 6 mi W on SR 4; 1 mi N on SR 141; about 5 mi W on gravel Avenue T; 3 mi N on gravel 25th Rd; at E shore of lake. Camping discontinued; amenities removed; boat ramp available.

MARYSVILLE (E)
Marysville City Park   FREE
Just S of Hwys 36 on US 77 in Marysville. Free; 5-day limit. Tbls, flush toilets, cfga, drkg wtr, two 30/50-amp elec plus 20-amp, dump, playground, pool, gazebo, tennis. No camping May 12-14; no parking on grass. Historical exhibits.

MEADE (W)
Meade City Park   FREE
E side of Meade on KS 54E. Free. All year. 30 undesignated sites; no hookups. Tbls, flush toilets, cfga, drkg wtr, playground, pavilion, dump on W side near pool entry (flush wtr only). No wtr or toilets 11/15-4/1.
Meade State Park $10
13 mi SW of Meade on SR 23; at Lake Meade. $10 without hookups, $19-$22 with hookups. All year; limited facilities in winter; 14-day limit. 98 sites (42 wtr/elec). Tbls, flush toilets, cfga, drkg wtr, showers, elec, dump, beach, playground. Swimming, boating (ld), fishing, hiking, nature trail. 443 acres; 80-acre lake.

MEDICINE LODGE (W)
Barber State Fishing Lake   FREE
At jct of US 160 and US 281; on N edge of Medicine Lodge. Free. All year; 14-day limit. 20 sites. Tbls, toilets, cfga. Picnicking, fishing, boating(l). 77-acre lake.

MELVERN (E)
Arrow Rock Park $7
Corps of Engineers
Melvern Lake
From Melvern, 3 mi W on SR 31 (Melvern Rd); 3 mi S on US 75 to Olivet exit; 1.5 mi W on CR 276; 1 mi N on S. Fairlawn Rd; 1 mi W on Arrow Rock Pkwy; at S shore of lake. During 5/1-9/30, $7 with federal senior pass (others pay $14) at 24 sites without hookups, $10 at 19 sites with 30-amp elec/wtr (others pay $20). Off-season, some sites free; toilets & cfga only amenities available. RV limit typically 65 ft except at 3 pull-through sites. Tbls, flush & pit toilets, showers, cfga, drkg wtr, dump, playground, coin laundry, shelters, fish cleaning station. Fishing, boating(l), hiking, horseback riding trail.

Coeur d'Alene Park $7
Corps of Engineers
Melvern Lake
From Melvern, 3 mi W on SR 31 (Melvern Rd) to just past jct with US 75; 2 mi S on Melvern Lake Pkwy; 1 mi NW on Coeur D'Alene Pkwy access rd; at SE corner of lake. During 5/1-9/30, campers pay $7 at 22 non-elec sites, $9.50 at 34 sites with 30-amp elec (no wtr hookup), $10.50 at 1 handicap site with 50-amp elec/wtr. Some sites free off-season without hookups & reduced amenities (only toilets & cfga). All year; 14-day limit. 65-ft RV limit, but typical sites 50-5 ft, all back-in except 1 large pull-through. Tbls, showers, drkg wtr, flush & pit toilets, beach, dump, coin laundry, playgrounds, marina, picnic shelters, fish cleaning station. Boating(l), fishing, hiking, swimming, 2 nature trails, horseshoe pits. 450 acres.

Outlet Park $10
Corps of Engineers
Melvern Lake
From Melvern, 3 mi W on SR 31 (Melvern Rd) to just past jct with US 75; 0.3 mi W on Melvern Lake Pkwy; 0.3 mi W on Cutoff Rd; 0.5 mi N on River Pond Pkwy, below dam. During 4/1-10/31, campers with federal senior pass pay $10 at 61 sites in A Loop with 30-amp elec/wtr, $11 at 50-amp full hookups in B Loop, $12 in 50-amp full hookups in C Loop (others pay $20, $22 & $24). Some sites free off-season, but no utilities. Group camping available in A Loop; group shelter reservable for registered campers. RV limit typically 60 ft; 79 pull-through. Tbls, flush toilets, cfga, drkg wtr, showers, beach, dump, coin laundry, sewer hookups($), fish cleaning station, amphitheater, picnic shelter, pay phone. Fishing, boating(ld), hiking, swimming, pedestrian/biking trails, historic suspension bridge, 4 nature trails, volleyball, softball field, horseshoes, interpretive trail. Fish stocked in 90-acre pond, but gasoline engines prohibited.

Turkey Point Park $7
Corps of Engineers
Melvern Lake
From Melvern, 3 mi W on SR 31 (Melvern Rd); 2.5 mi N on US 75; about 5 mi W on SR 278 (past Eisenhower State Park); at "Y" jct with 293rd St, veer right (S) for 1 mi on SR 278 (S. Indian Hills Rd), then continue S on Indian Hills; follow Turkey Point Pkwy 0.5 mi into campground at N shore of lake. During 5/1-9/30, campers with federal senior pass pay $7 at non-elec sites, $10 at 16 sites with 30-amp elec/wtr, $10.50 at sites with 50-amp elec/wtr (others pay $14, $20 & $21). Some sites free off-season, but no utilities & reduced amenities. Group camping available. All year; 14-day limit. 65-ft RV limit; 3 pull-through. Tbls, cfga, flush & pit toilets, showers, drkg wtr, dump, playground, coin laundry, fish cleaning station. Boating(l), fishing, hiking, horseshoe pits.

MICHIGAN VALLEY (E)

110 Mile Park   FREE
Corps of Engineers
Pomona Lake
From Michigan Valley, 1 mi N on S. Michigan Rd; about 2.5 mi W on E. 205th St; 1 mi S on Lake Rd; 1 mi E on E. 209th St; 2 mi S on S. Paulen Rd; about 1 mi S into park, following signs. On tip of peninsula between lake's 110-Mile Creek & Wolf Creek arms. Free. All year; 14-day limit. 25 primitive sites. No wtr during 10/1-4/30. Tbls, toilets, cfga, drkg wtr (except in winter), playground. Picnicking, 33-mi bridle/hiking/biking trail, short walking trail, boating (dl), fishing, nature trail. Group horse camping available.

Cedar Park   FREE
Corps of Engineers
Pomona Lake
2 mi W of Michigan Valley on E. 213th St; 1 mi N on S. Shawnee Heights Rd; 3 mi W on 205th St, then follow signs; at NE side of lake. Or, 1 mi N of Michigan Valley on S. Michigan Rd, then W on 205th St to park. Free. All year; 14-day limit. 8 primitive sites. Tbls, pit toilet, cfga, drkg wtr. Picnicking, fishing, swimming, boating(l); rock boat ramp. 72 acres.

Michigan Valley Park $7
Corps of Engineers
Pomona Lake
1 mi S of Michigan Valley on S. Stubbs Rd; 1 mi W on E. 221st St; S on access rd; at NW side of dam. Campers with federal senior pass pay $7 base at 38 primitive sites, $8 at 25 non-elec developed sites, $9 at 33 sites with 30-amp elec/wtr, $10 at 8 prime-location pull-through sites with 50-amp elec/wtr, $11 at 9 sites with 50-amp full hookups. 5/1-9/30; 14-day limit. RV limit in excess of 65 ft. Group primitive camping area with beach, playground. Tbls, flush & pit toilets, cfga, drkg wtr, dump, playground, beach, amphitheater. Boating(l), fishing, swimming.

Outlet Area Park $8
Corps of Engineers
Pomona Lake
From Michigan Valley, 2 mi S on S. Stubbs Rd; 1.5 mi W on gravel E. 229th St, then left (SW) on access rd; below dam along 110 Mile Creek at S side of lake. During 4/1-10/31, $8 with federal senior pass at 34 sites with 30-amp elec/wtr (others pay $16); $10 at 8 sites with 50-amp elec/wtr (others pay $20). Elec sites may be available off-season without wtr services for $10, but we could not verify this for 2018. 55-ft typical RV limit. All year; 14-day limit. Tbls, flush toilets, cfga, drkg wtr, showers, amphitheater, dump, interpretive nature trail, shelters, playground, coin laundry. Hiking, interpretive trails, boating(l), fishing.

Wolf Creek Park $7
Corps of Engineers
Pomona Lake
From Michigan Valley, about 3 mi W on E. 213th St, then SW on Pomona Dam Rd to park; on W side of lake's Wolf Creek arm. Campers with federal senior pass pay $7 at 43 primitive sites (others pay $14); $10 at 54 sites with 30/50-amp elec/wtr (others pay $20). 5/1-9/15; 14-day limit. Typically 45-ft RV limit, all back-in. Group camping available. Flush toilets, tbls, drkg wtr, showers, dump, picnic shelter, group camp, playground, elec($). Fishing, baseball, boating(l), 18-hole disc golf course.

MILFORD (E)
Farnum Creek Park $7
Corps of Engineers
Milford Lake
From Milford at Houston Rd, about 2 mi S on US 77 across bridge, then left on access rd, following signs; pass Acorns Resort entry, then left into park; at S shore of bay, east-central part of lake. Campers with federal senior pass pay $7 at 30 sites without hookups, $10 at 41 sites with 30-amp elec/wtr, $10.50 at 5 sites with 50-amp elec/wtr (others pay $14, $20 & $21). 60-ft RV limit; 3 pull-through. 4/15-9/30; 14-day limit. Tbls, flush & pit toilets, cfga, drkg wtr, dump, playground, fish cleaning station, fishing pier. Boating(ld), fishing.

MINNEAPOLIS (W)
Markley Grove City Park $10
From Hwy 106 at Minneapolis, park is on left after crossing Solomon River bridge; 161 S. Mill. $10. Tbls, toilets, cfga, drkg wtr, elec, shelters, playground, pool, showers. Dump across street at fairgrounds. Fishing, swimming, hunting. Register at clerk's office, 218 N. Rock St or with police officer.

Ottawa Free
State Fishing Lake
7 mi E of Minneapolis on SR 93. Free primitive camping. All year; 14-day limit. 120 sites. Tbls, toilets, cfga, drkg wtr, elec($). Boating(l), fishing, hunting.

NEWTON (W)
Harvey County East Park $10
7 mi E of Newton. $10 without hookups; $20 with elec 3/1-9/30; 15-day limit. 66 sites. Tbls, flush toilets, cfga, drkg wtr, showers, dump, elec. Fishing, hiking, boating(l), swimming. Tent camping $10 at Camp Hawk Park, 4 mi SW of Newton.

Harvey County West Park $10
9 mi W of Newton on 12th St to Moundridge Rd. $10 without elec); $20with elec. 3/1-9/30; 15-day limit. 130 sites. Tbls, flush toilets, cfga, drkg wtr, showers, dump, elec, store, playground. Fishing, swimming, biking. 310 acres.

NORTON (W)
Norton State Wildlife Area FREE
3 mi SE of Norton off US 36. Free. All year; 14-day limit. Primitive camping in 6 designated areas (in conjunction with hunting and fishing activities). Tbls, toilets, cfga, no drkg wtr, no trash service. Boating(l), fishing, horseback riding & hiking trail, hunting.

Prairie Dog State Park $10
4 mi W of Norton on US 36; S on SR 261; at N shore of Sebelius Reservoir. $10 without hookups, $19-$22 with hookups. All year; limited facilities in winter; 14-day limit. About 105 primitive sites; 18 sites with elec, 46 sites with wtr/elec. Tbls, flush toilets, cfga, drkg wtr, showers, elec, dumps, beach. Swimming, boating(ld), fishing, hiking, hunting (in Norton Wildlife Area), 7.5-mi bridle trail. 1,150 acres; 2,000-acre lake.

OSKALOOSA (E)
Longview Park $7
Corps of Engineers
Perry Lake
5.5 mi W of Oskaloosa on SR 92; 2.1 mi S on Ferguson Rd; 1.5 mi W on 86th St; 1 mi S on Hamilton Rd into park; at E shore of lake. Campers with federal senior pass pay $7 at 13 basic RV/tent sites & 6 walk-to tent sites, $9 at 26 sites with 30-amp elec (no wtr hookup); otehrs pay $14 & $18. 5/1-9/30; 14-day limit. No off-season camping. RV limit in excess of 65 ft. Cfga, tbls, drkg wtr, dump, flush & pit toilets, showers, showers. Group camping available. Fishing, boating(ld), swimming, hiking trail, biking, 18-hole disc golf course. 316 acres.

Old Town Park $7
Corps of Engineers
Perry Lake
6 mi W of Oskaloosa on SR 92; on S side before bridge; at E side of lake. All year; 14-day limit. During 5/1-9,30, $7 with federal senior pass (others pay $14) at 31 non-elec sites; $9.50 with senior pass at 33 sites with 30-amp elec/wtr (others pay $19). Off-season, $12 at non-elec sites. All year; 14-day limit. 65-ft RV limit at back-in sites plus 2 long pull-through. Cfga, flush & pit toilets, drkg wtr, dump, playground, showers, tbls, picnic shelter. Boating(ld), fishing, swimming, hiking, biking.

OTTAWA (E)
Pomona State Park $10
14 mi W on SR 68; NW on SR 268; N on SR 368; at S shore of Pomona Reservoir. $10 without hookups, $19-$22 with hookups. All year; limited facilities in winter; 14-day limit. 93 sites with wtr/elec, 41 with wtr/elec/sewer; numerous primitive sites. Tbls, flush toilets, cfga, drkg wtr, showers, elec($), dump, beach, playground. Swimming, boating(rld), fishing, hiking, horseshoes, volleyball, nature trail. 490 acres.

OXFORD (E)
Cave Park   Free
From downtown Oxford, E on US 160 to W shore of Arkansas River. Free primitive camping. Restrooms open 4/15-10/15. Tbls, toilets, cfga, drkg wtr, playground, shelters. Boating(l), fishing.

Napawalla City Park $3
In Oxford (9 mi W of Winfield) off Hwy 160 at jct of W. Clark St & Napawalla Rd. $3.00 base. Restrooms open 4/15-10/15. $3 base fee for primitive sites; $10 with elec. Limited elec service (25 20/30-amp). Tbls, toilets, cfga, drkg wtr, playground, shelters. Basketball court.

PAOLA (E)
Hillsdale State Park $10
On W 255th St., Paola (25 mi SW of Kansas City) at Hillsdale Reservoir. $10 without hookups, $19-$22 with hookups. All year; limited facilities in winter; 14-day limit. About 320 reservable sites with 79 primitive, 180 wtr/elec, 61 full hookup. May be non reservable sites. Tbls, flush toilets, cfga, drkg wtr, showers, dump, shelters, 2 beaches. Boating(l), fishing, hunting, hiking, horseback riding trails, swimming, model airplane flying area. 4,500-acre lake.

Lake Miola City Park $12
At N edge of Paola at 299th St & Hedge Lane Rd. $12 base. 5/1-LD; 14-day limit. Base fee for primitive camping (non-residents); $5 daily elec fee, $2 sewer. 54 sites (25 with RV hookups). Tbls, toilets, cfga, drkg wtr, dump, elec($), playground, beach. Boating (l), fishing, swimming, 8 picnic areas, ATV use, volleyball, hiking trails. 725 acres.

PARSONS (E)
Marvel City Park $10
7 blocks E on US 160 from jct with US 59. $8 at primitive sites ($60 annually); $12 at 24 RV sites with 20-amp elec ($120 annually). Free camping in undesignated site area. 10-day limit Tbls, toilets, cfga, drkg wtr, showers, sports field, dump, shelters. Walking trail, horseshoes. 58 acres.

Lake Parsons City Park $10
2 mi N of Main St in Parsons on 32nd St; 3 mi W on county rd; 2 mi N, following signs. $10 without elec ($60 annual permit); $12 with elec ($120 annually); tents $5. 4/1-11/1; 10-day limit. 47 sites. Tbls, flush toilets, cfga, drkg wtr, showers, dump, playground, beach. Swimming, fishing, boating (ld). 1,000 acre park; 980-acre lake.

PERRY (E)
Rock Creek Park $7
Corps of Engineers
Perry Lake
2 mi N of US 24 on CR 1029, then 3 mi W on park rd; W side of lake just above dam. 5/1-9/30; 14-day limit. Campers with federal senior pass pay at 56 non-hookup RV/tent sites, $9.50 at 40 sites with 30-amp elec/wtr, $20 at 35 sites with 50-amp elec/wtr (others pay $14, $19 & $20). RV limit in excess of 65 ft; 6 pull-through. Drkg wtr, tbls, flush & pit toilets, showers, dump, fish cleaning stations, playground, shelter. Fishing, boating(ld), horseback riding, swimming, swimming, hiking.

Slough Creek Park $7
Corps of Engineers
Perry Lake
From Perry at jct with Hwy 24, 7 mi N on Ferguson Rd (CR 1029), crossing bridge over Slough Creek arm of lake; 1 mi S on Slough Creek Rd; on peninsula at NE shore. Campers with federal senior pass pay $7 at 138 non-elec RV/tent sites, $9 at 64 sites with 30-amp elec, $9.50 at 43 sites with 30-amp elec/wtr, $10 at 50-amp full-hookup sites (others pay $14, $18, $19 & $20). RV limit in excess of 65 ft; 10 pull-through sites. Tbls, flush & pit toilets, dump, showers, beach, fish cleaning station, playground. Fishing, boating (ld), swimming, 2.5-mi interpretive trail & 30-mi Perry Hiking Trail, horseback riding.

PHILLIPSBURG (W)
Phillipsburg City Campground $10
About 5 blocks W of US 183 on US 36 at W end of town, turn S on Ft. Bissel Ave & follow signs; small rigs can enter at next entrance. $10. May-Oct. 10 30-amp elec/wtr sites. Tbls, flush toilets, cfga, drkg wtr, showers, rec hall, playground, five 30-amp & six 15/20-amp elec/wtr, pool, dump with threaded flush wtr outlet in day-use section.

RANDALL (E)
Randall City Park   FREE
S on Main St behind grain elevator complex. Free. 2 sites. 3-day limit. No working elec at last report. Pit toilets in roofless, doorless bldg.

READING (E)
Lyon State Fishing Lake   FREE
5 mi W of Reading on KS 170; 1.5 mi N to campground. Free. All year; 7-day limit. About 100 sites. Tbls, toilets, cfga, firewood, no drkg wtr. Picnicking, boating(l), fishing, swimming. 582 acres; 135-acre lake.

RILEY (E)
Stockdale Park $10
Corps of Engineers
Tuttle Creek Lake
From Riley, about 4 mi E on US 24 to jct with US 27; 2.5 mi E on CR 396; on W shore of lake at Mill Creek arm. During 4/15-10/15, $10 with federal senior pass at 12 sites with 30/50-amp elec/wtr; others pay $20. Off-season, some sites free with reduced amenities & no utilities. RV limit in excess of 65 ft; 2 pull-through. Tbls, flush & pit toilets, cfga, drkg wtr, showers, dump, playground. Boating(l), fishing, ORV trails, biking, hiking. 188 acres.

KANSAS 306

RUSSELL (W)
Wilson State Park $10
20 mi E of Russell on I-70; 8 mi N on SR 232; at S side of
Wilson Lake. $10 without hookups $19-$22 with hookups.
All year; limited facilities in winter; 14-day limit. Reservable sites; 4 full hookups, 99 with wtr/elec, 37 elec, 90
primitive. Tbls, flush toilets, cfga, drkg wtr, showers, elec,
dumps, 2 beaches, store, marina. Swimming, boating(rld),
fishing, hiking & biking trails, volleyball, basketball, horseshoes, interpretive programs, mountain biking trail.

SABETHA (E)
Pony Creek Lake $5
From downtown Sabetha, 2 mi N on US 75. Free camping
with one-day or annual boat permit. $5 without hookups,
$12 elec, $7 with $30 annual camping permit. Primitive
undesignated sites. Tbls, toilets, cfga, drkg wtr. 171-acre
lake. Fishing, boating(l).

Sabetha City Lake $5
From downtown Sabetha, 1 mi N on N. 14th St; 5 mi W on
Berwick Rd; S on access rd to lake. $5 without hookups;
$12 elec, $7 with $30 annual camping permit. Primitive
undesignated sites. Toilet, cfga, no other facilities except
picnic shelter; no drkg wtr. Fishing at 114-acre lake.

SAINT FRANCIS (W)
St. Francis Sandpits State Fishing Area   FREE
1 mi W and 2 mi S of St. Francis. Free. All year; 7-day limit.
Primitive camping area. Tbls, toilet, cfga, no drkg wtr.

SAINT MARYS (E)
Riverside City Park $10
On US 24 NW of Topeka, S on 3rd or 6th St 4 blks W to S
side of the park; RV sites just E of beige shop bldg close
to 6th St. $10 5-day limit. 3 RV sites with 30/50-amp elec/
wtr. Pool, tennis, horseshoes. Dump at sewage plant on S
side of town.

SAINT PAUL (E)
Neosho State Fishing Lake   FREE
1 mi E of St. Paul on SR 57. Free. All year; 7-day limit. 5 RV
sites. Tbls, toilets, cfga, drkg wtr, no trash service. Fishing, boating(l), swimming, picnic area, hunting. 92-acre
lake adjacent to Neosho Wildlife Area.

SCOTT CITY (W)
Scott State Park $10
10 mi N of Scott City on US 83; 3 mi N on SR 95; at Lake
Scott. $10 without hookups $19-$22 with hookups. All
year; limited facilities in winter; 14-day limit. Reservable
sites; 7 full hoookup, 50 wtr/elec, 80 primitive. Additinal
primitive sites available. Tbls, flush toilets, cfga, drkg wtr,
showers, elec($), beach, playground, dump. Swimming,
boating (ld), canoeing(r), fishing, hiking, horseback riding,
nature trails. Buffalo & elk herds. 1,180 acres.

SEDAN (E)
Sedan City Park $10
5 mi N of Sedan on SR 99. $10. All year. 15 sites. Tbls,
toilets, cfga, drkg wtr, 20-amp elec, pool, playground.
Tennis, swimming.

SILVER LAKE (E)
Shawnee State Fishing Lake   FREE
7 mi N of US 24 in Silver Lake; 2 mi E to campground.
Free, but $5 with elec All year; 7-day limit. 50 sites; 135-
acre lake. Tbls, toilets, cfga, drkg wtr, dump. Fishing,
boating(l).

SPEARVILLE (W)
Hain State Fishing Lake   FREE
1 mi SW of Spearville on US 56, then right on county rd for
5 mi. Free. All year except during duck season; 7-day limit.
Primitive undesignated sites at 53acre lake. No facilities
except cfga, tbls; no trash pickup. Fishing, hunting.

STOCKTON (W)
Nicodemus National Historical Site   FREE
About 10 mi W of Stockton on US 24; on S side of hwy at
village of Nicodemus in front of the park. Free. 1-night
limit. Paved frontage rd with overnight parking. Drkg wtr,
pit toilets, cfga, tbls, 15-amp elec (long cords needed).
Site of the last remaining all-black settlements in Kansas.
Unable to verify in 2017

Rooks State Fishing Lake   FREE
Half mi S of Stockton on US 183; 2 mi W; 2 mi S to park.
Free. Apr-Oct; 7-day limit. 15 sites. Tbls, toilets, cfga, drkg
wtr, firewood. Picnicking, fishing, boating(l). 64 acres.
Periodically dry. Ltd facilities in winter.
Webster State Park $10
8 mi W of Stockton on US 24; S on access rd; split between
N & S shores of Webster Reservoir. $10 without hookups
$19-$22 with hookups. All year; limited facilities in winter;
14-day limit. Reservable sites; 1 full hookup, 82 wtr/elec,
10 elec, 155 primitive. May be additional sites. Tbls, flush
toilets, cfga, drkg wtr, showers, elec, dump, beach, playgrounds, fish cleaning station, 2 fishing piers. Swimming,
boating (ld), fishing, tennis, ball fields, volleyball, hiking
trail, horseshoes, nature trail, hunting.

Webster State Wildlife Area   FREE
8 mi W of Stockton off US 24. Free. All year; 14-day limit.
Primitive camping in 5 designated areas. Toilets, cfga, no
drkg wtr, no trash service. Fishing, hunting, boating(l),
hiking, horseback riding. Fish cleaning station on N shore;
pier at stilling basin. 5,500 acres surrounding 3,800-acre
lake.

SYRACUSE (W)
Hamilton State Fishing Lake   FREE
3 mi W of Syracuse on US 50; 2 mi N to campground. Free.

All year; 7-day limit. Undesignated sites; 432 acres. Tbls, toilets, cfga, no drkg wtr. Picnicking, fishing, boating(l).

TOPEKA (E)
Perry State Park $10
10 mi E of Topeka on US 24; 4 mi N; SW of Perry Lake. $10 without hookups. $19-$22 with hookups. All year; limited facilities in winter; 14-day limit. About 200 primitive sites and 104 with elec. Tbls, flush toilets, cfga, drkg wtr, showers, elec, dump, beach, playground. Swimming, boating(ld), fishing, hiking, hunting, mountain biking & equestrian trails, hunting. 1,597 acres.

TORONTO (E)
Cross Timbers State Park $10
From US 54, S on KS 105, left on W main street, right on S Point Rd in Toronto. $10 without hookups; $19-$22 with hookups. All year; Four camping areas; 50 wtr/elec sites, 16 full hookup sites and over 100 primitive sites. Toilets, showers, cfgs drkg wtr. Hiking, backpacking, fishing. Adjacent to the 4600 acre Toronto wildlife Area.

Woodson State Fishing Lake   FREE
From US 54, S on KS 105 to Toronto; 5 mi E on co rd. Free. All year; 14-day limit. 50 sites. Tbls, toilets, cfga, no drkg wtr, dump. Picnicking, fishing, boating(rl). 180-acre lake, also known as Lake Fegan; built during Depression by the CCC.

WAKEFIELD (E)
Timber Creek Park $10
Corps of Engineers
Milford Lake
From Wakefield, 1 mi E across lake bridge on SR 82, then S into park; at NE shore of lake. $10 during 4/15-9/30 ($5 with federal senior pass); some sites free off-season, but pit toilets & no services. 14-day limit. 36 sites (30-ft RV limit). Tbls, flush & pit toilets, cfga, drkg wtr, dump, playground. Fishing, boating(l), nature trail.

WAKEENEY (W)
Cedar Bluff State Park $10
8 mi SE of WaKeeney on I-70; 15 mi S on SR 147. $10 without hookups; $19-$22 with hookups. All year; limited facilities in winter; 14-day limit. 16 full hookup sites, 24 wtr/elec sites, numerous primitive sites and the state park system's only group campground. Tbls, flush toilets, cfga, drkg wtr, showers, elec($), dump, beach, 2 fishing piers. Swimming, boating(ld), fishing, hiking, horseshoes, sand volleyball, basketball, disc golf, interpretive programs, hunting. 6,000-acre lake.

WASHINGTON (E)
Rotary Park   FREE
Half mi E of Washington on KS 36. Free. All year. Undesignated sites. Tbls, no toilets, well drkg wtr. Picnicking. The

city's campground at 900 D St. has 20 sites with 30-amp elec, $15.

WICHITA (E)
Cheney State Park $10
20 mi W of Wichita on US 54; 5 mi N on SR 251; at Cheney Reservoir. $10 without hookups in-season $19-$22 with hookups. All year; limited facilities in winter; 14-day limit. 3 full hookup sites 222 wtr/elec sites, numerous primitive sites. Tbls, flush toilets, cfga, drkg wtr, showers, elec, 4 dumps, beach, marina. Swimming, boating (rld), fishing, hiking. 1,913 acres; 9,537-acre lake.

WINFIELD (E)
Winfield Fairgrounds $3
1 mi W of downtown Winfield on US 160; at Walnut River. $3 at primitive sites; $12 with elec. All year; 15-day limit. 600 sites with 20-amp elec plus limited 30-amp sites. Tbls, elec($), flush toilets, cfga, drkg wtr, dump (near horse barn). Fishing, boating(l). 10.2-acre primitive camping area; 6.5-acre developed area. Pecan Grove area has 44 acres of primitive camping & some electrical service. Pay park personnel or at on-site drop box or at city hall.

Tunnel Mill City Park $3
From jct with US 160 in Winfield, 10 blocks S on US 77; right (W) on 19th Ave to E shore of Walnut River. $3 at primitive sites on 11.3 acres. All year. Tbls, toilets, cfga, drkg wtr, no hookups. Fishing, boating(l).

Winfield City Lake Park $3
From Winfield at jct with US 77, 6 mi E on 82nd Rd (2 mi S of US 77/SR 15 jct). $3 at primitive sites; $12 with full hookups. Tbls, flush toilets, cfga, drkg wtr. Boating(l), fishing, canoeing, swimming.

YATES CENTER (E)
Yates Center Reservoir Park $10
3 mi S of Yates Center on Hwy 75; about 3 mi W on 80th RD or 4 mi W on Hwy 54, then 3 mi S on Indian Rd, following signs. $10. All year. Tbls, toilets, cfga, drkg wtr, elec, dump. Also primitive camping on 500 acres around the lake. Fishing, boating(l), hiking, hunting. $10 fees also at nearby South Owl Lake City Park, at Hwy 75 & 105th Rd (GPS: 37.867301, -95.74677). Yates Center Park.

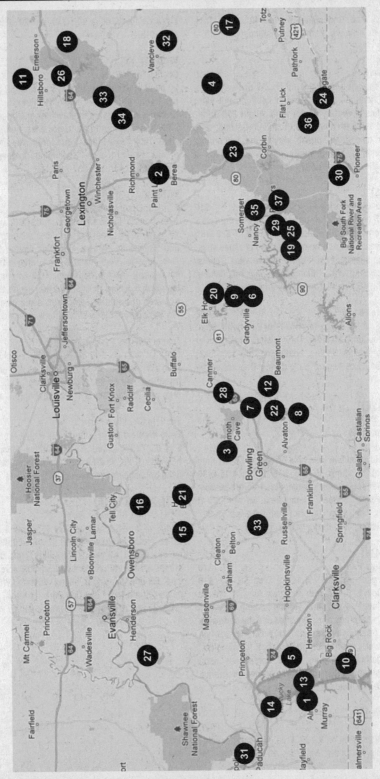

KENTUCKY

WWW.KENTUCKYTOURISM.COM

Kentucky Dept of Tourism, 500 Mero St, Frankfort, KY 40601; 502-564-4930.

REST AREAS
No overnight parking is permitted unless otherwise posted.

STATE PARKS
Camping fees have increased to the point that no state parks have overnight fees of $12 or less and no longer qualify for this guidebook. 800-255-PARK.

DANIEL BOONE NATIONAL FOREST
Primitive backcountry camping is permitted throughout the forest.The forest's two largest campgrounds, Grove and Holly Bay, now charge RVers a minimum of $16 (even with federal senior pass discounts) to camp. Daniel Boone National Forest, 1700 Bypass Rd., Winchester, KY 40391. 859/745-3100.

Cumberland Gap National Historical Park
See the Middlesboro entry. Reservations can be made up to 3 months in advance. P.O. Box 1848, Middlesboro, KY 40965. 606/248-2817.

Mammoth Cave National Park
The park is open year-round. The park headquarters is 32 miles northeast of Bowling Green on I-65, then 10 miles west. Mammoth Cave, KY 42259; 502-758-2328.

Corps of Engineers
For further information contact: Corps of Engineers, Louisville District, P.O. Box 59, Louisville, KY 40201-0059; or Corps of Engineers, Nashville District, PO Box 1070, Nashville, TN 37202-1070.

Land Between the Lakes
Three types of camping are available at the LBL area between Kentucky Lake and Lake Barkley: Family campgrounds are fully developed and offer sites from $12 to $19 per night; Lake Access Areas, which offer basic amenities such as tables, campfire grill areas, chemical toilets, drinking water, trash pickup and boat ramps; Backcountry Camping Areas, where facilities are more basic, including boat ramps and possibly pit toilets, tables and grill areas but no trash service. Lake Access areas have fees of $9 per night; Backcountry Camping areas are free after purchase of annual $20 per person or 3-day $5 per person camping permits. The LBL is operated by the National Forest Service, and federal discounts such as the America the Beautiful Senior Pass (formerly Golden Age Passport) are honored.

CAPITAL: Frankfort
NICKNAME: Bluegrass State
STATEHOOD: 1792 – 15th State
FLOWER: Goldenrod
TREE: Tulip Poplar
BIRD: Kentucky Cardinal

AURORA (1)

Boswell Landing   FREE
Backcountry Camping Area
Land Between the Lakes National Recreation Area
6 mi W of Aurora to The Trace; 23 mi S on The Trace
into Tennessee; 7 mi W on CR 230; 2 mi N on CR 233;
on Kentucky Lake. Camp free with 3-day $7 per person
backcountry permit or $30 per person annual backcoun-
try permit. All year; 14-day limit. 23 sites. Tbls, chemical
toilets, cfga, drkg wtr. Boating(l), fishing, waterskiing,
swimming. Future plans include adding more RV spaces.
GPS: 36.5173, -88.0264

Ginger Bay   FREE
Land Between The Lakes National Recreation Area
5 mi E of Aurora on US 68/80; 8 mi S on The Trace; 1 mi W on
CR 211; 1.5 mi on CR 206 into Tennessee; 1 mi on CR 212 to
Kentucky Lake. Camp free with 3-day $7 per person back-
country permit or $30 per person annual backcountry per-
mit. All year; 14-day limit. 13 primitive sites. No facilities, no
drkg wtr. Picnicking, fishing, boating(l), hiking, waterskiing.
Nearby: Homeplace 1850 and buffalo range. Future plans
include renovating camping areas. GPS: 36.6237, -88.0384

Ginger Ridge   FREE
Backcountry Camp
Land Between The Lakes National Recreation Area
5 mi E of Aurora on US 68/80; 8 mi S on The Trace; 2 mi W
on CR 112 (Ginger Creek Rd) through entrance to Rushing
Creek campground (in Tennessee, on E shore of Kentucky
Lake). Camp free with 3-day $7 per person backcountry
permit or $30 per person annual backcountry permit. All
year; 14-day limit. Undesignated backcountry sites. Boating, fishing. GPS: 36.6334, -88.0425

BEREA (2)

Primitive Sites   FREE
Daniel Boone National Forest
Get directions from district ranger's office in Berea for
primitive dispersed sites adjacent to Sheltowee Trace
National Recreation Trail. Reservations required. Free. All
year; 14-day limit. 2 primitive sites. Tbls, toilets, cfga, no
drkg wtr. Hiking, picnicking.

S-Tree Campground   FREE
Daniel Boone National Forest
5.5 mi E of Berea on KY 21; 11 mi SE on KY 421 to Sand-
gap; 5.5 mi S on CR 20; 3.5 mi SE on FR 20. Free. All year;
14-day limit. 20 sites (RVs under 22 ft). Tbls, toilets, cfga,
no drkg wtr, shelters. Pack out trash. Picnicking, horseback riding, hiking. Adjacent to Sheltowee Trace National
Recreation Trail. (Note: Heavy use by off-road vehicles;
noisy.) GPS: 37.386719, -84.074219

BROWNSVILLE (3)

Dog Creek $7.50
Corps of Engineers
Nolin River Lake
8 mi N of Brownsville on SR 259; 5 mi N on SR 1015.
$7.50 base with federal senior pass at 20 non-elec sites;
others pay $15 base, $19 for premium locations ($9.50
with senior pass). 50 elec/wtr sites: $11 with senior pass;
others pay $22. About 5/15-9/20; 14-day limit. RV limit in
excess of 65 ft. Tbls, toilets, cfga, drkg wtr, dump, beach
(campers only), picnic shelter, watchable wildlife area.
Boating(l), fishing, hiking, picnicking, swimming (beach
open only to campers). GPS: 37.3208, -86.12917

Houchins Ferry $12
Mammoth Cave National Park
2 mi E of Brownsville off SR 70 on Houchins Ferry Rd.
$12 ($6 with federal senior pass). All year; 14-day limit.
12 primitive sites. Tbls, chemical toilets, cfga, drkg wtr.
Boating(l), fishing. GPS: 37.202148, -86.237305

BUCKHORN (4)

Buckhorn $12
Corps of Engineers
Buckhorn Lake
S of Buckhorn on W side of Stilling Basin below the dam;
adjacent to Tailwater Recreation Area. $12 at 18 primitive
& overflow sites ($6 with federal senior pass. 31 elec/
wtr sites with optional CATV: $11 base with senior pass;
others pay $22; double sites $30. 5/1-9/30; 14-day limit.
RV limit 50 ft. Tbls, flush toilets, cfga, drkg wtr, showers,
coin laundry, beach. Boating(l), fishing, horseshoe pits,
swimming. 3-night minimum stay on holiday weekends.
GPS: 37.35083, -83.47278

CADIZ (5)

Bacon Creek   CLOSED
Backcountry Camping Area
Land Between the Lakes National Recreation Area
15 mi W of Cadiz on US 68; one-fifth mi S on The Trace;
7 mi E at sign to Lake Barkley. Camp free with 3-day $7
per person backcountry permit or $30 per person annual
backcountry permit. This site was closed in 2012 for
safety reasons.

Hurricane Creek $8
Corps of Engineers
Lake Barkley
From Cadiz, 7.5 mi N on SR 139; 0.3 mi N on SR 274, then W
on access rd following signs. $8 base with federal senior
pass at 51 elec/wtr sites for 30-amp, $11 for 50-amp, $11
at premium locations (others pay $16, $22 & $22). RV limit
in excess of 65 ft; 11 pull-through sites. About 4/25-10/30;
14-day limit. Tbls, flush toilets, cfga, drkg wtr, showers,
dump, playground, beach, fishing pier. Swimming, boating
(l), fishing. GPS: 36.92, -87.97583

CAMPBELLSVILLE (6)

Smith Ridge Campground $8.50
Corps of Engineers
Green River Lake
From Campbellsville, 1 mi E on Hwy 70; 3 mi S on SR 372; W (right) on County Park Rd (signs). $8.50 with federal senior pass at 18 non-elec sites; others pay $17. 62 elec sites: $11.50 with senior pass; others pay $23. About 5/15-9/15; 14-day limit. RV limit in excess of 65 ft. Tbls, flush toilets, cfga, drkg wtr, showers, beach, playground, dump. Boating(l), swimming, fishing, hiking, nature trail. 3-night minimum stay on holiday weekends. GPS: 37.29583, -85.31

CAVE CITY (7)

Mammoth Cave Camp $8.50
Mammoth Cave National Park
From jct with I-65 at Cave City, W on SR 70 (becoming Mammoth Cave Pkwy) into park; campground 0.25 mi from visitor center. $8.50 with federal senior pass; others pay $17. All year; 14-day limit (full service during 5/15-9/15). 105 sites. Tbls, toilets, cfga, drkg wtr, dump, showers ($). GPS: 37.1714, -86.0896

CEDAR SPRINGS (8)

Bailey's Point Campground $8.50
Corps of Engineers
Barren River Lake
From Cedar Springs at jct with US 231/31E, 2 mi N on SR 252; 1.5 mi E on CR 517 (signs). $8.50 base with federal senior pass at 53 non-elec sites; others pay $17 base, $18 for wtr hookup ($9 with senior pass). 150 elec sites: $11.50 with senior pass; others pay $23. About 4/15-10/25; 14-day limit. RV limit in excess of 65 ft. Tbls, flush toilets, cfga, drkg wtr, showers, dump, coin laundry, playground, beach, interpretive trail, coin laundry, amphitheater, shelter. Fishing, boating(l), hiking, swimming, basketball, sand volleyball. GPS: 36.89083, -86.09528

COLUMBIA (9)

Holmes Bend Campground $8.50
Corps of Engineers
Green River Lake
From Columbia at SR 206 exit 49, 1.2 mi N on SR 55; 1 mi NE on SR 551; 3.8 mi N on Holmes Bend Rd. $8.50 with federal senior pass at 23 primitive sites; others pay $17. 101 elec sites, 41 wtr hookups: $11.50 with senior pass; others pay $23. 4/15-10/30; 14-day limit. RV limit in excess of 65 ft. Tbls, flush toilets, cfga, drkg wtr, amphitheater, showers, dump, beach, playground, shelter. Hiking trail, fishing, boating(l), swimming, interpretive trail. GPS: 37.2138, -85.2666

DOVER, TENNESSEE (10)

Devils Elbow   CLOSED
Land Between the Lakes National Recreation Area
3 mi W of Dover on US 79 to The Trace; 31 mi N to US 68/80 in Kentucky; 4 mi E to Lake Barkley. Closed to camping; day use only. GPS: 36.791016, -87.988037

Gatlin Point $12
Lake Access Area
Land Between the Lakes National Recreation Area
5 mi W of Dover on US 79; 7 mi N on The Trace; 3.5 mi NE on CR 227, following signs in Tennessee. $12 at 19 basic sites. All year; 21-day limit. Tbls, chemical toilets, cfga, drkg wtr, no elec. Free dump at south welcome station. Boating(ld), fishing. On Kentucky Lake. Nearby Bards Lake (320 acres) has boat launch. GPS: 36.5566, -87.903809

Piney Campground $12
Land Between the Lakes National Recreation Area
12 mi W of Dover on US 79/SR 49; 2.5 mi NW on Fort Henry Rd; at Kentucky Lake in Tennessee. $12 at non-elec sites; $22 for 30-amp elec; $34 full hookups ($6, $16 & $30 with federal senior pass). 3/1-11/30; 21-day limit. In March & Nov, if wtr is off, lower fees may be charged. 369 sites any size RV or tent, some shelters. Tbls, flush toilets, cfga, drkg wtr, showers, dump, vending machines, beach, fishing pier. Boating(l), fishing, hiking trails, biking(r) trails, archery range, swimming, campfire theater, bike skills court. GPS: 36.487305, -88.034668

Rushing Creek $12
Lake Access Area
Land Between the Lakes National Recreation Area
3 mi W of Dover on US 79 to The Trace (Hwy 453); 3 mi N to Buffalo Range, then 3 mi W on Ginger Creek Rd; 1 mi N on Lake Ferry Rd; W on Rushing Creek & follow signs; on E shore of Kentucky Lake. $12 at 56 basic sites. All year; 21-day limit. Tbls, toilets, cfga, drkg wtr. Campground is in 2 sections -- one on Rushing Creek & one on Jones Creek. Rushing Creek section has showers, drkg wtr, flush toilets. Jones Creek has pit toilets, no drkg wtr & is primarily a tenter camp. Volleyball, basketball, boating(l), fishing, waterskiing, hiking. 250 acres. Elec hookups & new playground considered in future. GPS: 36.66626, -88.050049

FLEMINGSBURG (11)

Fox Valley Recreation Area $6
Fleming County Park
5.6 mi SE on SR 32 from S edge of Flemingsburg at jct with SR 11; 2 mi E on James Rd. $6 base. 3/15-10/31. Base fee for primitive sites; $15 full hookups. 44 sites. Tbls, flush toilets, cfga, drkg wtr, showers, hookups, playground, dump. Fishing ($5), boating(ldr), horseshoes. Fox Valley Lake. GPS: 38.35025, -83.553028

GLASGOW (12)

Beaver Creek Campground $12
Corps of Engineers
Barren River Lake
5 mi S of Glasgow on US 31E (Scottsville Rd); 3 mi W on SR 252, following signs; left on Beaver Creek Rd to lake. $12. About 4/15-10/25; 14-day limit. 12 primitive sites. Tbls, pit toilets, cfga, drkg wtr. Swimming, boating(l), fishing. GPS: 36.929932, -86.027344

KENTUCKY

Tailwater Campground $9.50
Corps of Engineers
Barren River Lake
2 mi S of Glasgow on US 31E; W on SR 252 to park below the dam. From jct of SRs 252/1533, N to entrance rd at S end of dam; follow signs. $9.50 with federal senior pass at 48 elec/wtr sites; others pay $19. 5/6-9/10; 14-day limit. Some primitive sites free off-season with reduced services & no utilities. RV limit in excess of 65 ft. Tbls, toilets, cfga, drkg wtr, picnic shelter, amphitheater. Boating(l), fishing, waterskiing; nature programs, playground, horseshoe pits. 3-night minimum stay on holiday weekends. GPS: 36.89444, -86.13306

GOLDEN POND (13)

Fenton Campground $12
Land Between the Lakes National Recreation Area
2.5 mi W of Golden Pond Visitor Center on US 68 to Kentucky Lake. $12 base; $22 with elec ($6 & $16 with federal senior pass). All year; 21-day limit. 29 sites. Tbls, chemical toilets, cfga, drkg wtr. Boating(ld), fishing. Campground expected to be redesigned. GPS: 36.776367, -88.109863

Neville Bay FREE
Backcountry Camping Area
Land Between the Lakes National Recreation Area
16 mi S on The Trace; .8 mi E on CR 214 to Lake Barkley in Tennessee. Camp free with 3-day $7 per person backcountry permit or $30 per person annual backcountry permit. All year; 14-day limit. 50 sites. Tbls, chemical toilets, no cfga, no drkg wtr. Boating(l), fishing, waterskiing. Camp expected to be upgraded with more tbls & cfga. GPS: 36.6126, -87.9167

Redd Hollow FREE
Backcountry Camping Area
Land Between the Lakes National Recreation Area
4 mi S of Golden Pond Visitors Center on The Trace; W on Redd Hollow Rd. Camp free with 3-day $7 per person backcountry permit or $30 per person annual backcountry permit. All year; 14 day limit. 39 sites. Tbls, toilets, cfga, drkg wtr. Boating(l), fishing. Future plans include allowing 24-hr generator use. GPS: 36.714, -88.069

Turkey Bay OHV Area $8
Land Between the Lakes National Recreation Area
2 mi S on The Trace; half mi E on SR 167. $8 at 18 primitive sites. All year; 21-day limit. Toilets, tbls, cfga, chemical toilets, drkg wtr. OHV trails, fishing, picnicking, boating. Primarily an off-highway vehicle use area with unloading ramps. Nearby: Golden Pond Visitors Center. GPS: 36.4500, -88.04190

GRAND RIVERS (14)

Birmingham Ferry $12
Lake Access Area
Land Between the Lakes National Recreation Area
9 mi S of Grand Rivers on The Trace (Hwy 453); 2 mi W on Old Ferry Rd. to Kentucky Lake. $12. All year; 21-Day limit. 29 primitive sites. Tbls, chemical toilets, cfga, drkg wtr. Boating(lr), fishing. GPS: 36.922363, -88.153564

Cravens Bay $12
Lake Access Area
Land Between the Lakes National Recreation Area
7.5 mi S of Grand Rivers on The Trace; 1 mi E on CR 117; 3 mi E on CR 118. On Lake Barkley. $12. All year; 21-day limit. 31 sites. Flush toilets, tbls, cfga, drkg wtr. Boating(l), fishing. Back section closed & gated during winter. GPS: 36.962646, -88.046875

Demumbers Bay FREE
Land Between The Lakes National Recreation Area
3.8 mi S of Grand Rivers on The Trace (Hwy 453); then 1.9 mi E on CR 108 to Lake Barkley. Camp free with 3-day $7 per person backcountry permit or $30 annual backcountry permit. All year; 14-day limit. 5 sites. Chemical toilets, no tbls, no other facilities; no drkg wtr. Picnicking, fishing, boating(l). Lake access. GPS: 36.97785, -88.15305

Energy Lake $12
Land Between the Lakes National Recreation Area
15.8 mi S of Grand Rivers on The Trace; 3 mi SE on Silver Rail Rd; 4.7 mi S on CR 134, then across Energy Dam to campground. $12 for non-elec sites, $22 for 30-amp elec ($6 & $16 with federal senior pass). 3/1-11/30; 21-day limit. Tbls, flush toilets, drkg wtr, cfga, beach, dump, showers, playground. Canoeing(r), swimming, hiking trails, archery range, campfire theater. GPS: 36.885742, -88.0354

Eureka Campground $8.50
Corps of Engineers
Lake Barkley
From just N of Grand Rivers on US 62/641, S on Hwy 810, then W on Hwy 1271; near spillway on E side of dam. $8.50 base with federal senior pass at 26 wtr/elec sites; others pay $17 base, $23 for premium locations ($11.50 with senior pass). About 4/25-LD; 14-day limit. RV limit in excess of 65 ft. Tbls, flush toilets, cfga, drkg wtr, showers, playground, coin laundry, beach, dump, group shelter. Biking & hiking trails, boating(l), fishing, swimming. 3-night minimum stay on holiday weekends. GPS: 37.02056, -88.22361

Hillman Ferry $12
Land Between the Lakes National Recreation Area
8.3 mi S of Grand Rivers on The Trace; 1 mi W on CR 110; on Kentucky Lake just N of Pisgah Point. $12 at non-elec sites, $22 for 30-amp elec, $24 for 50-amp elec, $28 for 30-amp elec/wtr, $32 for 50-amp elec/wtr, $34 for 30-amp full hookups, $40 for 50-amp full hookups. Basic sites $6 with federal senior pass; $6 discounts with senior pass for all hookups. 3/1-11/30; 21-day limit. 380 sites. Tbls, flush toilets, cfga, showers, drkg wtr, dump, store, fish cleaning

station. Boating(l), fishing, swimming, campfire theater, biking(r), archery range. GPS: 36.938232, -88.181152

Kuttawa Landing Dispersed Area FREE
Land Between the Lakes National Recreation Area
9 mi S of Grand Rivers on The Trace (Hwy 453); then 6 mi E on Old Ferry Rd (CR 117); half mi N on CR 126; 1.1 mi on CR 127. Camp free with 3-day $7 per person backcountry permit or $30 annual backcountry permit. All year; 14-day limit. About 4 primitive sites. No facilities, no drkg wtr; no trash service or maintenance. Picnicking, fishing, boating. Lake access. GPS: 37.06108, -88.10625

Nickell Branch Backcountry Camping Area FREE
Land Between the Lakes National Recreation Area
1 mi S of Grand Rivers on The Trace; 1 mi E on CR 102. On Lake Barkley. Camp free with 3-day $7 per person backcountry permit or $30 annual backcountry permit. All year; 14-day limit. 11 sites. Tbls, chemical toilets, cfga, no drkg wtr. Boating(l) fishing. GPS: 36.98762, -88.19988

Pisgah Point FREE
Land Between the Lakes National Recreation Area
6 mi S of Grand Rivers on The Trace; then 2 mi W on CR 111. Camp free with 3-day $7 per person backcountry permit or $30 annual backcountry permit. All year; 14-day limit. Undesignated sites. Chemical toilets, no other facilities; no drkg wtr. Picnicking, boating(l), fishing. Woodlands Nature Center located in the Environmental Education Area. In 2012, user-made rds along shoreline were closed & converted to tent-only camping. GPS: 36.940332, -88.168362

Smith Bay Backcountry Camping Area FREE
Land Between the Lakes National Recreation Area
6 mi S of Grand Rivers on The Trace; 1.5 mi W on Old Ferry Rd; half mi S on CR 116; on Kentucky Lake. Camp free with 3-day $7 per person backcountry permit or $30 annual backcountry permit. All year; 14-day limit. About 16 primitive sites. Tbls, chemical toilets, cfga, no drkg wtr. Boating(l), fishing. In 2012, site was downgraded to backcountry recreation site from lake access site. Boat ramp GPS: 36.90883, -88.14844

Star Backcountry Camp CLOSED
Land Between the Lakes National Recreation Area
5 mi S of Grand Rivers on The Trace; turn W at sign. Closed to camping; day use only.

Sugar Bay Backcountry Camping Area FREE
Land Between the Lakes National Recreation Area
14 mi S of Grand Rivers on The Trace; 2 mi W on CR 140 to Kentucky Lake. Camp free with 3-day $7 per person backcountry permit or $30 annual backcountry permit. All year; 14-day limit. 18 sites. Tbls, chemical toilets, cfga, no drkg wtr. Boating(l), fishing. GPS: 36.85633, -88.12713

Taylor Bay Backcountry Camping Area FREE
Land Between the Lakes National Recreation Area
13 mi S on The Trace; 5 mi E on Mulberry Flat Rd. On Lake Barkley. Camp free with 3-day $7 per person backcountry permit or $30 annual backcountry permit. All year; 14-day limit. 35 sites. Tbls, chemical toilets, cfga, no drkg wtr. Boating(l), fishing. Boat ramp. GPS: 36.8826, -88.0205

Twin Lakes Backcountry Camping Area FREE
Land Between the Lakes National Recreation Area
3.5 mi S on the Trace; half mi W on co rd. On Kentucky Lake. Camp free with 3-day $7 per person backcountry permit or $30 annual backcountry permit. All year; 14-day limit. 17 sites. Tbls, chemical toilets, cfga, no drkg wtr. Boating(l), fishing. Tbls & cfga added to Twin Lakes North in 2012; south area gated in winter and waterfront camping spaces closed to prevent further shoreline erosion; south tent camping allowed only on hilltop above boat ramp. GPS: 36.964198, -88.199273

HARTFORD (15)
Ohio County Park $6
2 mi N of Hartford on Hwy 69. $6 base. All year. Base fee for primitive sites ($36 weekly); $17 with elec/wtr ($15 seniors); $21 full hookup. Tbls, flush toilets, cfga, drkg wtr, dump, showers, shelters, playgrounds. Horse shoes, races, mud bogs, sprint car races, dog field trials, softball, dances, musical shows, trapshooting, archery, muzzleloading competition, mini golf, hiking, golf range, basketball, volleyball, putting greens, horseback riding. Non-campers pay $5 for dump station. GPS: 37.467110, -86.861880

HARNED (16)
Axtel Campground $8.50
Corps of Engineers
Rough River Lake
From Harned, 9 mi S on SR 259; 0.5 mi W on SR 79, on left. $8.50 with federal senior pass at 61 non-elec sites; others pay $17. 92 elec/wtr sites: $11 base with senior pass; others pay $22 base, $24 at premium locations ($12 with senior pass). About 3/25-10/31; 14-day limit. RV limit 45 ft. Tbls, flush toilets, showers, cfga, drkg wtr, dump, fishing pier, playground, beach, picnic shelter. Swimming, fishing, boating(l). Boat rentals nearby. GPS: 37.625, -86.44972

HAZARD (17)
Littcarr Campground $11
Corps of Engineers
Carr Creek Lake
From Hazard, about 20 mi E on SR 15, past entry to Carr Creek State Park, then 2.4 mi NE on SR 160; on NE side of lake, E of SR 160. About 4/25-10/1; 14-day limit. $11 with federal senior pass at 32 elec/wtr sites; $14 with senior pass at 14 full hookups; others pay $22 & $28. RV limit 50 ft. Tbls, flush toilets, cfga, drkg wtr, dump, beach, playground, picnic shelter, coin laundry, showers. Boating(l),

fishing, waterskiing, horseshoe pits. 3-night minimum stay on holiday weekends. GPS: 37.2375, -82.94972

HYDEN (18)

Trace Branch Campground $12
Corps of Engineers
Buckhorn Lake
6 mi N of Hyden on SR 257; E across Dry Hill Bridge near Confluence, then N 6 mi on Grassy Branch Rd. $12 at 13 paved primitive sites (8 along shoreline); $6 with federal senior pass. 15 elec/wtr sites: $11 with senior pass; others pay $22. 50-ft RV limit. 5/1-9/309; 14-day limit. Tbls, flush toilets, cfga, drkg wtr. Picnicking, fishing, swimming, boating(l), horseshoe pits, volleyball net. 9 acres. GPS: 37.24167, -83.37278

JAMESTOWN (19)

Kendall Recreation Area $10
Corps of Engineers
Lake Cumberland
From Jamestown, 10 mi S on US 127; right on Kendall Rd before crossing the dam, following signs. $10 base with federal senior pass at 115 wtr/elec sites; others pay $20 base, $22 for premium locations ($11 with senior pass). About 4/1-12/1; 14-day limit. RV limit in excess of 65 ft. Tbls, flush toilets, cfga, drkg wtr, showers, fish cleaning station, coin laundry, fishing pier, 2 playgrounds, dump. Basketball, fishing, boating(l), hiking trail, horseshoe pits, canoeing, biking. GPS: 36.86806, -85.1475

KNIFLEY (20)

Pikes Ridge Campground $7.50
Corps of Engineers
Green River Lake
From Knifley, 4.8 mi NW on SR 76; SW on Pikes Ridge Rd (signs). $7.50 with federal senior pass at 40 primitive sites; others pay $15. 19 elec/wtr sites: $10.50 with senior pass; others pay $21. 4/15-9/30; 14-day limit. RV limit in excess of 65 ft. Tbls, pit toilets, cfga, drkg wtr, shelter, beach, playground, dump. Interpretive trails, boating(l), fishing, hiking, horseback riding. 3-night minimum stay on holiday weekends. GPS: 37.28056, -85.29167

LEITCHFIELD (21)

Moutardier $7.50
Corps of Engineers
Nolin River Lake
From Leitchfield, 16 mi S on SR 259; 2 mi SE on SR 2067 (Moutardier Rd). $7.50 with federal senior pass at 86 non-elec sites; others pay $15 base, $19 for premium locations ($9.50 with senior pass). 81 wtr/elec sites: $10.50 with senior pass; others pay $21, $24 at premium locations ($12 with senior pass). About 5/15-9/30; 14-day limit. RV limit in excess of 65 ft. Tbls, flush toilets, cfga, showers, drkg wtr, hookups($), playground, beach, fishing pier, fish cleaning station. Picnicking, fishing, boating(rld), hiking & motorcy-cle trails, golf, horseshoe pits. 280 acres. 3-night minimum stay on holiday weekends. GPS: 37.31639, -86.23306

LUCAS (22)

The Narrows Campground $11.50
Corps of Engineers
Barren River Lake
From Lucas, 1.7 mi W on The Narrows Rd, following signs. $11.50 with federal senior pass at 89 elec/wtr sites; others pay $23. 5/6-9/10; 14-day limit. RV limit in excess of 65 ft. Tbls, flush toilets, cfga, drkg wtr, dump, showers, coin laundry, beach, playground, amphitheater, shelter. Fishing, boating(l), hiking, tennis, swimming, horseshoe pits, interpretive trail, marina. 3-night minimum stay on holiday weekends. NRRS. GPS: 36.90417, -86.07083

LONDON (23)

Rockcastle   FREE
Daniel Boone National Forest
16 mi W of London on SR 192; 5 mi S on SR 3497; at backwaters of Lake Cumberland at mouth of Rockcastle River, near London Dock Marina. Free. About 5/15-9/30; 14-day limit. 24 sites (16-ft RV limit). Tbls, toilets, cfga, drkg wtr. Boating(lr), fishing, hiking. 8 acres. Camp undergoing improvements. GPS: 36.965332, -84.345947

MIDDLESBORO (24)

Wilderness Road $10
Cumberland Gap National Historic Park
Just S of Middlesboro on US 25E to visitor center, then E on US 58 into Virginia. $10 with federal senior pass at RV sites with elec; others pay $20. All year; 14-day limit. 160 sites. Tbls, showers, flush toilets, cfga, drkg wtr. Hiking, fishing.

MONTICELLO (25)

Fall Creek Recreation Area $10
Corps of Engineers
Lake Cumberland
From Monticello, 0.4 mi NW on SR 92; 1.5 mi NE on SR 90; 6 mi N on SR 1275, then NW on access rd. $10 with federal senior pass at 10 elec/wtr sites (newly renovated); others pay $20. 5/1-10/30; 14-day limit. Tbls, flush toilets, cfga, drkg wtr, showers, dump, fishing pier, playground, picnic shelter. Boating(l), fishing, waterskiing, shelter. GPS: 36.943604, -84.847412

MOREHEAD (26)

Twin Knobs Recreation Area $12
Daniel Boone National Forest
8.5 mi SW of Morehead on US 60; 5.5 mi SE on SR 801; on Cave Run Lake. $12 with federal senior pass for non-elec sites; others pay $24. $5 surcharge for elec, $7 for full hookups. About 3/15-10/30; 14-day limit. 216 sites (32-ft RV limit). Tbls, flush toilets, cfga, drkg wtr, dump ($6 non-campers), showers, beach. Waterskiing, fishing, hiking trails, swimming, boating(l), interpretive programs,

horseshoes, basketball, windsurfing. Concessionaire-operated. 700 acres. GPS: 38.097412, -83.516602

MORGANFIELD (27)

Higginson-Henry   **FREE**
State Wildlife Management Area
6 mi E on KY 56; S and follow signs. On 80-acre Lake Mauzy & 2 small lakes. Free. All year; 14-day limit. 100 unimproved sites for tents only, no RVs. Tbls, pit toilets, grills. Picnicking, boating(l), fishing. 5,424 acres; 10 mi of hiking trails. GPS: 37.635647, -87.879523.

MUNFORDVILLE (28)

Wax Campground   **$7.50**
Corps of Engineers
Nolin Lake
From Munfordville, 20 mi W on SR 88. $7.50 base with federal senior pass at 24 non-elec sites; others pay $15 base, $19 for premium locations ($9.50 with senior pass). 86 elec/wtr sites: $11 base with senior pass; others pay $22 base, $24 at premium locations ($12 with senior pass). About 5/15-9/30; 14-day limit. RV limit in excess of 65 ft; 7 pull-through sites. Tbls, flush toilets, cfga, drkg wtr, showers, dump, playground, fishing pier, fish cleaning station, shelter. Boating(l), fishing, swimming beach, horseshoe pits. GPS: 37.32083, -86.12917

NANCY (29)

Cumberland Point Recreation Area   **$10**
Corps of Engineers
Lake Cumberland
From Nancy, 0.2 mi E on SR 80; 1 mi S on SR 235; 8 mi SE on SR 761; on peninsula off main channel at mouth of Faubush Creek. $10 with federal senior pass at 20 elec/wtr sites; others pay $20. Fees higher on holidays. About 5/10-9/15; 14-day limit. RV limit in excess of 65 ft. Tbls, flush toilets, cfga, drkg wtr, showers, dump, coin laundry, new playground, beach, amphitheater. Horseshoe pits, fishing, boating(l), swimming, waterskiing. GPS: 36.96556, -84.43222

ONEIDA, TENNESSEE (30)

Bandy Creek Campground   **$9.50**
Big South Fork National River and Recreation Area
18 mi W of Oneida on SR 297; 3 mi NW on Bandy Creek access rd. $9.50 with federal senior pass at non-elec sites; others pay $19. $11 with senior pass at 96 elec/wtr sites; others pay $22. 4/1-10/31; 14-day limit. Tbls, flush toilets, showers, drkg wtr, cfga, dump, pool. Fishing, boating(l), hiking, swimming. GPS: 36.48778, -84.69083

PADUCAH (31)

Canal Campground   **$8.50**
Corps of Engineers
Lake Barkley
From Paducah, E on I-24 to exit 31 jct with "The Trace" (at

Land Between the Lakes); 3 mi S on The Trace (SR 453), then E to lake, following signs. $8.50 base with federal senior pass at 110 wtr/elec sites; others pay $17 base; extra fees for 50-amp & premium locations. $29 full hookups ($14.50 with senior pass). Group camping area with shelter, $192. About 3/25-10/30; 14-day limit. RV limit in excess of 65 ft. Tbls, flush toilets, cfga, drkg wtr, showers, playground, coin laundry, fishing pier, beach, amphitheater. 3-night minimum stay on holiday weekends. GPS: 36.99556, -88.20972

PIKEVILLE (32)

Grapevine Recreation Area   **$10**
Corps of Engineers
Fishtrap Lake
From Pikeville, 9.5 mi E on US 119; 16 mi S on SR 194; on Grapevine Creek arm of lake. $10 at 18 primitive sites ($5 with federal senior pass). 10 elec/wtr sites: $10 with senior pass; others pay $20. MD-LD; 14-day limit. Drkg wtr, toilets, cfga, showers, dump, tbls, grocery, pavilions($). Boating(l), fishing, hiking, playground, scenic area, hunting. GPS: 37.4281, -82.4902

ROFF (33)

Cave Creek   **$8.50**
Corps of Engineers
Rough River Lake
From the dam, 2.9 mi S on SR 79, 0.8 mi E on SR 736. $8.50 with federal senior pass at 23 non-elec RV/tent sites; others pay $17. 34 elec/wtr sites: $11 with senior pass ; others pay $22. About 5/20-10/30; 14-day limit. 40-ft RV limit. Tbls, toilets, cfga, drkg wtr, elec($), dump, fishing pier, playground. Boating(l), fishing, hiking. 3-night minimum stay on holiday weekends. GPS: 37.575, -86.49167

Laurel Branch   **$8.50**
Corps of Engineers
Rough River Lake
From Roff, 3 mi S on SR 259; 1 mi W on SR 110, following signs. $8.50 with federal senior pass at 13 non-elec sites; others pay $17. 48 elec/wtr sites: $11 with senior pass; others pay $22. Off-season, some sites may be open at reduced rates & amenities. About 3/1-10/30; 14-day limit. RV limit 40 ft. Tbls, flush toilets, cfga, drkg wtr, playground, dump, beach, fishing pier. Fishing, boating(ld), hiking, swimming, waterskiing. GPS: 37.6083, -86.4583

North Fork   **$8.50**
Corps of Engineers
Rough River Lake
1.5 mi S of Roff on SR 259. $8.50 with federal senior pass at 56 non-elec sites; others pay $17. 48 elec/wtr sites: $11 with senior pass; others pay $22. About 5/1-9/15; 14-day limit. 60-ft RV limit. Tbls, flush toilets, cfga, showers, dump, drkg wtr, beach, playground, shelter, fishing

pier. Fishing, swimming, boating(rld), waterskiing. GPS: 37.63306, -86.44167

SALT LICK (33)

Clear Creek $12
Daniel Boone National Forest
4 mi S of Salt Lick on SR 211; 2.5 mi E on FR 129. $12 (double sites $18). About 4/10-10/30; 14-day limit. During 10/30-11029, fee reduced to $10 (double sites $14). 21 sites (22-ft RV limit). Tbls, toilets, cfga, drkg wtr, lantern poles. Boating(l - elec mtrs), fishing, hiking, picnicking. 25 acres. Pioneer Weapons Wildlife Area. GPS: 38.046143, -83.586182

White Sulphur Horse Camp $12
Daniel Boone National Forest
4 mi S of Salt Lick on SR 211; 2 mi E on FR 129. $12 during 4/9-10/29; $10 during 10/30-4/8. $6 day use fee. All year; 14-day limit. 40 sites. Toilets, cfga, no drkg wtr. Horse watering trough, horse trailer parking, picket lines. 25 mi of bridle trails, hiking. Near Sheltowee Trace National Recreation Trail & Pioneer Weapons Hunting Area. Equestrian camping only.

Zilpo Recreation Area $11
Daniel Boone National Forest
4 mi S of Salt Lick on SR 211; 2.5 mi E on FR 129; 8 mi NE on FR 918; at Cave Run Lake. $11 with federal senior pass; others pay $22; $5 surcharge for elec, $7 full hookups. About 4/10-10/15; 14-day limit. 156 sites on 335 acres. Tbls, flush toilets, cfga, drkg wtr, showers, dump($5 non-campers), store, beaches. Waterskiing, fishing, boating(l), swimming, interpretive programs. Concessionaire operated. GPS: 38.070557

SLADE (34)

Koomer Ridge $11
Daniel Boone National Forest
5 mi SE of Slade on SR 15. $11 with federal senior pass during 4/19-11/2; others pay $22. $3.50 with federal senior pass during 11/3-4/18; others pay $7. All year; 14 day limit. 53 sites (19 for RVs). Tbls, toilets, cfga, drkg wtr (except off-season), lantern posts, amphitheater. Hiking, picnicking, sightseeing. Near natural bridge, unusual rock formations. GPS: 37.786133, -83.629883

SOMERSET (35)

Bee Rock $8
Daniel Boone National Forest
1.5 mi NE of Somerset on SR 80; 17.2 mi SE on SR 192; half mi SE on FR 623; on Rockcastle River at bridge. $8 (double site $12). 4/10-10/25; 14-day limit. 28 sites (RVs under 22 ft). Tbls, toilets, cfga, drkg wtr. Fishing, picnicking, boating(ld - 1 mi). 42 acres. Boat ramp across river approx 500 yds foot travel. Scenic cliff-top overlook accessible by trails. GPS: 37.027588, -84.314453

Bee Rock East $8
Daniel Boone National Forest
1.5 mi NE of Somerset on Hwy 80; 17.2 mi SE on Hwy 192; half mi SE on FR 623 on SE side of Rockcastle River). $8 during 4/10-10/25; free rest of year; 14-day limit. 8 small sites. Tbls, toilets, cfga, no drkg wtr. Fishing, boating, hiking trail.

Fishing Creek Recreation Area $10
Corps of Engineers
Lake Cumberland
From Somerset at jct with US 27, 5.5 mi W on SR 80; exit prior to lake bridge, then 2 mi N on Hwy 1248 (signs). $10 with federal senior pass at 20 elec/wtr sites; others pay $20. About 5/10-9/15; 14-day limit. RV limit in excess of 65 ft. Tbls, flush toilets, cfga, showers, drkg wtr, dump, coin laundry, fishing pier, new playground, beach. Waterskiing, boating(l), fishing, swimming. GPS: 37.0497, -84.6833q

Little Lick FREE
Daniel Boone National Forest
13 mi SE of Somerset on KY 192; 3.3 mi S on CR 122; 1 mi S on FR 816; 2 mi S on FR 8163. Free. All year; 14-day limit. 8 sites (RVs under 22 ft). Tbls, toilets, cfga, well drkg wtr. Picnicking, hiking trail horseback riding trail. Elev 1100 ft. 3 acres. Corral, accommodations for horses. GPS: 36.96444, -14.39778

Waitsboro Recreation Area $10
Corps of Engineers
Lake Cumberland
From Somerset, 5 mi S on US 27, then W (right) on Waitsboro Rd, following signs. $10 with federal senior pass at 22 wtr/elec sites; others pay $20. Fees higher on holidays. About 5/1-10/31; 14-day limit. RV limit in excess of 65 ft. Tbls, flush toilets, cfga, drkg wtr, showers, fishing pier, coin laundry, playground, dump. Hiking, fishing, boating(l), waterskiing. GPS: 37.04972, -84.68333

STEARNS (36)

Bell Farm Horse Camp FREE
Daniel Boone National Forest
6 mi NW of Stearns on SR 92; S on SR 1263 for 12 mi to Bell Farm; left for half mile across bridge to camp. Equestrian camping only; no space for RVs to park. Free. All year; 14-day limit. 5 sites. Drkg wtr, tbls, toilets, cfga Hiking, horseback riding, picnicking. Horse corral; horse trailer space. Horse trails.

Blue Heron Campground $8.50
Big South Fork National Recreation Area
E of Stearns on SR 92, then right on SR 742. $8.50 with federal senior pass; others pay $17. 4/1-10/31; 14-day limit. 45 sites with elec/wtr. Tbls, flush toilets, cfga, drkg wtr, showers, dump. Fishing, boating, kayaking, canoeing, hiking, whitewater rafting. GPS: 36.67806, -84.51889

Great Meadows   FREE
Daniel Boone National Forest
6 mi W of Stearns on SR 92; 12 mi SW on SR 1363; 5 mi
SW on FR 137. Free. 4/1-11/1; 14-day limit. 12 tent sites,
2 RV sites (RVs under 22 ft). Toilets, drkg wtr, playground.
Trout fishing, nature trails. GPS: 36.627197, -84.724609

WHITLEY CITY (37)

Alum Ford $5
Big South Fork National River & Recreation Area
2 mi N of Whitley City on US 27; about 5 mi W on SR 700 to
E shore of Big South Fork River. $5. All year; 14-day limit.
6 primitive sites. Tbls, toilets, cfga, no drkg wtr. Fishing,
boating(l), hiking. GPS: 36.6737, -84.5468

Barren Fork Horse Camp $8
Daniel Boone National Forest
From N of Whitley City on US 27 at Stearns district office
of national forest, 1 mi E on FR 684. $8 for 1 day; $12 for 2
days; $100 annual camping permit. All year; 14-day limit.
41 back-in horse trailer sites. Toilets, cfga, no drkg wtr.
Ponds for watering horses. Built jointly by national forest,
Daniel Boone Distance Riders and Kentucky Horse Coun-
cil. Numerous loop trails, connection to Sheltowee Trace
National Recreation Trail. Day use fee for non-campers.
GPS: 37.0326, -85.8400

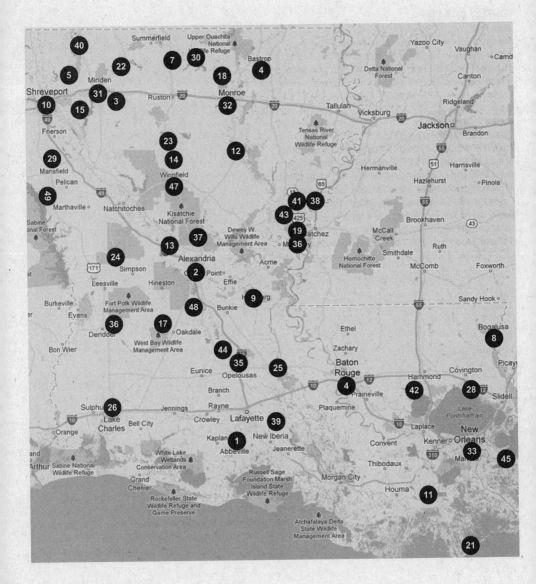

LOUISIANA

Office of Tourism, Dept of Culture, Recreation and Tourism, PO Box 94291, Baton Rouge, LA 70804-9291. 504-342-8119. 1-800-99-GUMBO.

Dept. of Wildlife and Fisheries, 2000 Quail Drive, Baton Rouge, LA 70808; 225/765-2800.

CAPITAL: Baton Rouge
NICKNAME: Pelican State
STATEHOOD: 1812 – 18th State
FLOWER: Magnolia
TREE: Bald Cypress
BIRD: Eastern Brown Pelican

REST AREAS
Overnight stops are not permitted. Most interstate highway rest areas provide RV sanitary dump stations.

STATE PARKS
Daily day-use entry fee are $2 per person (free for seniors); $80 annually for vehicles. Base camping fees are now $14 at unimproved sites (without water or electricity hookup); $22 in-season at wtr/elec sites ($18 off-season); $28 in-season at premium sites ($20 off-season). Louisiana, Arkansas & Maryland residents who have federal senior recreation site passes (Golden Age Passports or America the Beautiful Senior Passes) can camp at all Louisiana state parks for half price. Premium sites have either sewers, pull-through spaces or prime locations. Camping fees listed in this book assume purchase of an annual state park entry pass. Office of State Parks, PO Box 44426, Baton Rouge, LA 70804-4426. 888-677-1400.

KISATCHIE NATIONAL FOREST
Camping is permitted anywhere in the forest except for a few well-marked areas. 2500 Shreveport Hwy., Pineville, LA 71360-2009. Phone 318-473-7160.

ABBEVILLE (1)

Palmetto Island State Park $11
S of Abbeville on SR 82; left on SR 690, then right on Pleasant Dr. to park; at Vermilion River. $11 for LA, AR & MD seniors at 96 elec/wtr sites (others pay $22). $9 off-season for LA, AR & MD seniors (others pay $18). Tbls, flush toilets, cfga, drkg wtr, visitor center, dump, coin laundry. Fishing, boating (lr), canoeing. GPS: 29.52158, -92.091010.

ALEXANDRIA (2)

Bankston Camp FREE
Kisatchie National Forest
23 mi N of Alexandria on US 167; 4 mi E on SR 472; right on FR 145 for 2 mi. Free. All year; 14-day limit. Primitive undesignated camping area. Pit toilet, cfga, no drkg wtr. Hiking, hunting, picnicking. GPS: 31.698441, -92.511867.

Kincaid Lake $7.50
Kincaid Lake Recreation Complex
Kisatchie National Forest
12 mi W of Alexandria on SR 28; qtr mi SW on SR 121; 1 mi SE on FR 279; 1.5 mi on FR 282. $7.50 with federal senior pass; others pay $15 ($20 for double sites). All year; 14-day limit. 41 sites (33-ft RV limit) at two campgrounds (third one for primitive tent camping, $10). Tbls, flush toilets, showers, cfga, drkg wtr, elec, beach. Hiking/biking trails, fishing, boating(l), swimming, waterskiing. On 2,600-acre lake. GPS: 31.468262, -92.633301.

Rapides Coliseum $10
Alexandria-Pineville
Convention & Visitors Bureau
At Alexandria, 1 mi from I-49 on Hwy 28 W. $10 base. All year. Base fee for 200 sites with wtr/elec; $12 full hookups. 27 sites with full hookups. Tbls, flush toilets, cfga, drkg wtr, showers. GPS: 31.2955171, -92.5034185.

Valentine Lake $10
Kisatchie National Forest
16.7 mi W of Alexandria on SR 28; qtr mi SW on SR 121; 1 mi SE on FR 279; 1.5 mi on FR 282. $10. 4/1-10/31; 14-day limit. 14 RV/tent sites at north shore campground; south shore for walk-to tent camping. Tbls, flush toilets, cfga, drkg wtr, dump, showers. Fishing, hiking trails, swimming. Wild Azalea National Recreation Trail. GPS: 31.243408, -92.681396.

ARCADIA (3)

Sandy Hollow FREE
Wildlife Management Area
State Dept. of Wildlife & Fisheries
6 mi E of Arcola on SR 10; follow signs N on gravel rd. Free. All year. About one dozen open sites. Toilets, cfga, drkg wtr. No trash service. Picnicking, hunting. GPS: 30.829163, -90.40545.

BASTROP (4)

Chemin-A-Haut State Park $11
10 mi N of Bastrop on US 425; half mi E on Loop Park Rd; at Big Slough Lake. $11 for LA, AR & MD seniors at 26 elec/wtr sites (others pay $22); $9 off-season for LA, AR & MD seniors (others pay $18). All year; 14-day limit. Tbls, flush toilets, cfga, drkg wtr, showers, dump, playground, pool, coin laundry. Hiking, swimming, boating(l). 503 acres. GPS: 32.908447, -91.845703.

BELLEVUE (5)

Horse campground FREE
Corps of Engineers
Bayou Bodcau Dam
From Bellevue, about 4 mi N on Bodcau Dam Rd; at N end of dam near the spillway. Large groups should call for a permit and information. More than 50 miles of horse trails available. Free primitive camping. Open all year; 14-day limit.

South Abutment East $6
Recreation Area
Corps of Engineers
Bayou Bodcau Dam
From Bellevue, 2 mi N on Bodcau Dam Rd; just past Bodcau lookout tower near SE shore of Bodcau Bayou Reservoir; on upstream side of the dam. All year; 14-day limit. 12 primitive sites, $6 ($3 with federal senior pass). Toilet, cfga, no drkg wtr. Boating(l), fishing. GPS: 32.7022, -93.5079.

Tom Merrill Recreation Area $12
Corps of Engineers
Bayou Bodcau Dam
From Bellevue, 2 mi NE on Boacau Dam Rd, following signs. $12 ($6 with federal senior pass) at 20 elec/wtr sites; $6 at non-elec sits ($3 with senior pass). All year; 14-day limit. 2 pull-through sites. Durdin Hill Trail starts at campground and extends 6 mi for hikers & mountain bikers. Toilets, cfga, tbls, drkg wtr, pavilion($). Boating(l), fishing. GPS: 32.705779, -93.51692.

BERNICE (7)

Corney Lake (South Shore) FREE
Corney Lake Recreation Area
Kisatchie National Forest
1 mi N of Bernice on US 167; 12 mi NW on LA Alt. 2; 2.5 mi NE on LA 9; 2.3 mi SE on FR 900. Free. All year; 14-day limit. 8 sites (RVs under 22 ft); 4 acres. Tbls, toilets, cfga, firewood, piped drkg wtr. Fishing, waterfowl hunting, picnicking, boating(dr 1 mi). 2,300-acre Corney Lake. GPS: 32.906459, -92.745818.

BOGALUSA (8)

Ben's Creek FREE
Wildlife Management Area
State Dept of Wildlife & Fisheries
W of Bogalusa in Washington Parish. Free. All year; 14-day

limit. Primitive undesignated camping; no facilities. Hiking, hunting. 13,000 acres. GPS: 30.815427, -89.953344

BORDELONVILLE (9)
Grassy Lake   FREE
Wildlife Management Area
State Dept of Wildlife & Fisheries
18 mi N of Bordelonville. Free. All year; 14-day limit. Primitive sites in 3 camping areas. Tbls, toilets, cfga, no drkg wtr. Boating(l), fishing, hunting. 13,608 acres. GPS: 31.1335, -91.7626.

BOSSIER CITY (10)
Bodcau   FREE
Wiildlife Management Area
State Dept of Wildlife & Fisheries
About 10 mi E of Bossier City on I-20; 15 mi N on SR 7; half mi W on SR 160. Free. All year.; 14-day limit. Primitive sites. No facilities. Canoeing, fishing, hiking, boating(l), birdwatching, hunting. 37,000 acres. 32.77186, -93.470033.

Loggy Bayou   FREE
Wildlife Management Area
State Dept of Wildlife & Fisheries
Just NE of Bossier City in Bossier Parish. Free. All year; 14-day limit. Primitive designated sites. Tbls, toilets, cfga, no drkg wtr. Boating(l), fishing, hiking, hunting, birwatching. 6,381 acres. GPS: 32.281228, -93.434691.

BOURG (11)
Grand Bois Park $12
Terrebonne Parish
On SR 24 in Bourg. $12 base for RV sites, $9 tents. All year. 44 sites; 40-ft RV limit. Tbls, flush toilets, cfga, drkg wtr, showers, dump, elec($). Nature trails, playground. GPS: 29.553597, -90.561338.

COLUMBIA (12)
Boeuf   FREE
Wildlife Management Area
State Dept of Wildlife & Fisheries
1 mi S of Columbia on US 165; 3 mi E on SR 4. Free. All year; 14-day limit. Primitive sites at 3 designated camping areas. Tbls, toilets, cfga, no drkg wtr. Boating (10 boat launches), fishing, birdwatching, canoeing, hunting, hiking. GPS: 32.000944, -91.929468.

Ft. Necessity Recreation Area   FREE
Corps of Engineers
Ouachita Black River Navigation Project
From Columbia, about 7 mi E on SR 4; along Boeuf River. All year; 14-day limit. Free primitive sites in designated areas. Tbls, pit toilet, cfga, no drkg wtr. Boating(l), fishing, hikng trail. See Haile entry.

DERRY (13)
Lotus ORV Camp $3
Kisatchie National Forest
5 mi S on LA 119; 12 mi NW on FR 59. $3. All year. Undesignated sites for ORV riders only; 2 acres. Piped drkg wtr, toilets, cfga. Just outside W boundary of National Red Dirt Wildlife Mgmt. Preserve. GPS: 31.478797, -93.159281.

DODSON (14)
Cloud Crossing   FREE
Kisatchie National Forest
15 mi W of Dodson on LA 126; 2.5 mi S on LA 1233; 1 mi W on FR 513. Free. All year; 14-day limit. 13 sites (RVs under 22 ft). Tbls, toilets, cfga, firewood, well drkg wtr. Boating(lrd), picnicking, fishing. On Saline Bayou (national wild & scenic river). 7 acres. GPS: 32.083008, -92.905518.

DOYLINE (15)
Lake Bistineau State Park $11
On SR 163 near Doyline. $11 for LA, AR & MD seniors at 44 wtr/elec sites (others pay $22); $9 off-season for LA, AR & MD seniors (others pay $18). $10 off-season for LA, AR & MD seniors at 17 premium sites ($14 in-season); others pay $20 off-season, $28 in-sason. 14-day limit. Tbls, flush toilets, cfga, drkg wtr, dump, pools, beach, playgrounds. Boating(l), fishing, swimming, hiking/biking trail, nature trail, bridle trail, fishing pier. GPS: 32.444043, -93.3804489.

ELIZABETH (17)
West Bay   FREE
Wildlife Management Area
State Dept of Wildlife & Fisheries
4 mi S of Elizabeth on SR 112. Free. All year; 14-day limit. About 50 primitive open sites at 2 camping areas. Drkg wtr, cfga, no toilets, no trash service. Hiking, hunting. GPS: 30.796858,-92.797901.

FARMERSVILLE (18)
Lake D'Arbonne State Park $11
W of Farmersville on SR 2; left on Evergreen Rd for qtr mi. $11 for LA, AR & MD seniors at 51 elec/wtr sites (others pay $22; $9 off-season for LA, AR & MD seniors (others pay $18). $10 off-season for LA, AR & MD seniors at 7 premium sites ($14 in-season); others pay $20 off-season, $28 in-season. 14-day limit. Tbls, flush toilets, cfga, drkg wtr, showers, playground, fishing piers, dump, coin laundry, shelter. Biking, fishing, boating(lr), waterskiing, 4 hiking trails, fishing pier. GPS: 32.7765298, -92.4834789.

FERRIDAY (19)
Red River   FREE
Wildlife Management Area
State Dept of Wildlife & Fisheries
35 mi S of Ferriday in Concordia Parish. Free. All year; 14-day limit. Primitive sites at 3 maintained camping areas. Tbls, toilets, cfga, no drkg wtr. Hiking, fishing,

hunting, birdwatching. Nature trail. 35,000 acres. GPS: 31.239936,-91.705232.

GRAND ISLE (21)
Grand Isle State Park $10
At E end of Grand Isle; on Gulf of Mexico. $10 off-season for LA, AR & MD seniors at 49 pull-through premium elec/wtr sites ($14 in-season); others pay $20 off-season, $28 in-season. 14-day limit. Tbls, flush toilets, cfga, drkg wtr, dump, showers, beach, fishing pier, coin laundry. Swimming, crabbing, fishing, sunbathing, canoeing(r), nature trail. GPS: 29.2588382, -89.9547937.

HAILE
Finch Bayou Recreation Area   FREE
Corps of Engineers
Ouachita Black River Project
From Haile, 4 mi E on Hooker Hole Rd (PR 2204E); N on River Rd (PR 2293); within the Upper Ouachita National Wildlife Refuge at the Ouachita River. All year; 14-day limit. Free primitive sites in designated area. Tbls, pit toilet, cfga, drkg wtr. Boating(rl), fishing, hiking trail. Ouachita Black River Navigation Project is a 337-mile-long waterway through southern Arkansas & Louisiana, consisting of 4 locks and dams and several recreation areas.

HOMER (22)
Bucktail Hunter Camp   FREE
Kisatchie National Forest
1.2 mi N on LA 79; 5.8 mi NE on LA 520. Free. All year. Undesignated sites; 5 acres. Piped drkg wtr. Portable toilet only in hunting season. Picnicking, fishing (2 mi). Near middle fork of Bayou D'Arbonne. GPS: 32.9005068, -93.007718.

Lake Claiborne State Park $7
7 mi SE of Homer on SR 146. $7 for LA, AR & MD seniors at 2 unimproved sites witout hookups (others pay $14). $11 for LA, AR & MD seniors at 67 wtr/elec sites ($9 off-season); others pay $22 in-season, $18 off-season. $10 for LA, AR & MD seniors at 20 premium sites off-season ($14 in-season); others pay $20 off-season, $28 in-season. 14-day limit. Tbls, flush toilets, cfga, drkg wtr, coin laundry, beach, dump. Hiking trails, fishing, waterskiing, nature trail, boating(lr), swimming. GPS: 32.7232041, -92.920436.

Turkey Trot Hunter Camp   FREE
Kisatchie National Forest
6.2 mi N on SR 9; 4 mi N on CR 10; quarter mi N on FR 909. Free. All year; 14-day limit. Undesignated camping. Cfga, tbls, no trash service. Portable toilets only during hunting season. Hunting, fishing, picnicking. GPS: 32.892462, -92.950422.

JONESBORO (23)
Jimmie Davis State Park $11
12.8 mi E of Jonesboro on SR 4 to Lakeshore Dr., then S on SR 1209 & the park; at N shore of Caney Creek Lake. $11

for LA, AR & MD seniors at 64 elec/wtr sites (others pay $22); $9 off-season for LA, AR & MD seniors (others pay $18). $10 off-season for LA, AR & MD seniors at 9 premium elec/wtr sites ($14 in-season); others pay $20 off-season, $28 in-season. Tbls, flush toilets, cfga, drkg wtr, showers, fishing pier, coin laundry, beach, playground. Birdwatching, fishing, boating(l), swimming, waterskiing. GPS: 32.246822, -92.5204244.

KISATCHIE (24)
Cane Horse Camp $3
Kisatchie National Forest
About 8-mi N of Kisatchie on LA 117 to Longleaf Trail Scenic Byways; 4.1 mi E on forest rd. In National Red Dirt Wildlife Management Preserve. $3. All year; 14-day limit; designated horse camp, but anyone can camp there. Primitive camping. Flush toilets, cfga, drkg wtr, horse feeding tie poles. Hunting, hiking, picnicking. GPS: 31.485893, -93.131769.

Corral ORV Camp $3
Kisatchie National Forest
About 8 mi N of Kisatchie on LA 117 to Longleaf Trail Scenic Byways; .8 mi E on FR 311. In National Red Dirt Wildlife Management Preserve. $3. All year; 14-day limit; designated ORVcamp. Undesignated primitive camping. Pit toilets, cfga, no drkg wtr. Hunting, hiking, picnicking. GPS: 31.522405, -93.060092.

Coyote Hunter Camp   FREE
Kisatchie National Forest
About 8 mi N of Kisatchie on LA 117 to Longleaf Trail Scenic Byways; 9.5 mi E on forest rd; left qtr mi on FR K18E. In National Red Dirt Wildlife Management Preserve. Free. All year; 14-day limit; designated hunter camp 10/1-4/30, but open to anyone. Undesignated primitive camping. Pit toilets, cfga, no drkg wtr. Hunting, hiking, picnicking. GPS: 31.519767, -93.049832.

Custis Hunter Camp   FREE
Kisatchie National Forest
About 8 mi N of Kisatchie on LA 117 to Longleaf Trail Scenic Byways; 10.6 mi E on forest rd; left for 2.4 mi on FR 339; left again for half mi on FR 341. In National Red Dirt Wildlife Management Preserve. Free. All year; 14-day limit; designated hunter camp 10/1-4/30, but open to anyone. Undesignated primitive camping. No facilities except portable toilets during hunting season; no drkg wtr. Hunting, hiking, picnicking. GPS: 31.532358, -93.005038.

Dogwood   FREE
Kisatchie National Forest
3 mi N of Kisatchie on LA 117; camp is near jct of LA 117 with Longleaf Trail Scenic Byways. Free. All year; 14-day limit. 16 sites (RVs under 22 ft). Tbls, flush toilets, cfga, firewood, piped drkg wtr. Picnicking. Interpretive display on the forest. 6 scenic acres. 26 mi S of Natchitoches, oldest town in Louisiana Purchase. GPS: 32.942627, -93.32666

Oak Horse Camp   FREE
Kisatchie National Forest
About 8 mi N of Kisatchie on LA 117 to Longleaf Trail Scenic Byways; 8.7 mi on forest rd; left qtr mi on FR 311. In National Red Dirt Wildlife Management Preserve. Free. All year; 14-day limit; designated equestrian camp for riders only. Undesignated primitive camping. No facilities, no drkg wtr. Hunting, hiking, picnicking. GPS: 31.516932 -93.060841.

KROTZ SPRINGS (25)
Sherburne   FREE
Wildlife Management Area
State Dept of Wildlife & Fisheries
E of Krotz Springs on US 190, then 2 mi S on CR 975. Free. All year; 14-day limit. Primitive undesignated sites at 2 designated areas, one on S part of WMA & one on N, with wtr. Drkg wtr, cfga, no toilets, no trash service. Boating(l), fishing, hunting. Shooting range. GPS: 30.457972, -91.715114.

LAKE CHARLES (26)
Sam Houston Jones State Park $11
3.7 mi N of Lake Charles on US 171; 3.6 mi W on SR 378; at West Fork of Calcasieu river. $11 for LA, AR & MD seniors at 42 elec/wtr sites (others pay $22); $9 off-season for LA, AR & MD seniors (others pay $18). $10 off-season for LA, AR & MD seniors at 20 pull-through elec/wtr premium sites ($14 in-season); others pay $20 off-season, $28 in-season. Tbls, flush toilets, cfga, drkg wtr, showers, hookups, dump, playground. Boating(l), fishing, hiking trails. View nutrias. GPS: 30.3007594, -93.2640445.

MADISONVILLE (27)
Fairview-Riverside State Park $11
2 mi S of Madisonville on US 190; 3.3 mi W on SR 22; at Tchefuncte River. $11 for LA, AR & MD seniors at 59 elec/wtr sites (others pay $22); $9 off-season for LA, AR & MD seniors (others pay $18). $10 off-season for LA, Ar & MD seniors at 22 premium elec/wtr sites ($14 in-season); others pay $20 off-season, $28 in-season. 14-day limit. Tbls, flush toilets, cfga, drkg wtr, showers, dump, fishing pier, playground. Fishing, boating, canoeing, crabbing, hiking trail. Historic house tour($). GPS: 30.4107495, -90.1442451.

MANDEVILLE (28)
Fontainbleau State Park $7
3.5 mi SE of Mandeville on US 190; on N shore of Lake Ponchartrain. All year. $7 for LA, AR & MD seniors at 37 unimproved sites without hookups (others pay $14). $11 for LA, AR & MD seniors at 103 elec/wtr sites (others pay $22); $9 off-season for LA, AR & MD seniors (others pay $18). $10 for LA, AR & MD seniors off-season at 23 premium sites ($14 in-season); others pay $20 off-season, $28 in-season. Tbls, flush toilets, cfga, drkg wtr, hookups($), dump, pool, playground. Boating, fishing, swimming, hiking trails. GPS: 30.3371399, -90.0328521.

MANSFIELD (29)
Park Site 2, Oak Ridge $11.25
Toledo Bend Reservoir
Sabine River Authority
W of Mansfield on US 84; left on SR 191 for 3.5 mi; right at Sportsman's Corner; follow signs. $11.25 base for seniors at 40 elec/wtr RV sites (30/50-amp); others pay $15. Seniors pay $15 for full hookups; others, $20. Tent sites $10. Monthly rates available. All year; 14-day limit. Tbls, toilets, cfga, drkg wtr, dump ($5 non-campers), beach. Boating(l), fishing, swimming. Non-campers pay $2 day use and boat ramp fees. 117 acres. GPS: 31.897509, -93.895651.

MARION (30)
Union   FREE
Wildlife Management Area
State Dept of Wildlife & Fisheries
4 mi W of Marion. Free. All year; 14-day limit. Primitive sites on E side of WMA. Tbls, toilets, cfga, no drkg wtr. Hunting, hiking, birdwatching. 11,192 acres. GPS: 32.93337, -92.332023.

MINDEN (31)
Beaver Dam Campground $7.50
Caney Lakes Recreation Area
Kisatchie National Forest
N from Minden on SR 159; 2 mi W on Parish Rd 111; at shore of Upper Caney Lake. $7.50 with federal senior pass at elec/wtr sites; others pay $15. All year; 14-day limit; limited facilities in winter. 29 sites. Tbls, flush toilets, showers, cfga, drkg wtr, dump, elec/wtr. Fishing, swimming, boating(l), hiking. Sugar Cane National Recreation Trail. GPS: 32.673392, -93.292061.

Turtle Slide Campground $10
Caney Lakes Recreation Area
Kisatchie National Forest
N of Minden on SR 159; 2 mi W on Parish Rd 111; on shore of Lower Caney Lake. $10. All year; 14-day limit. 19 small sites. Tbls, flush toilets, cfga, drkg wtr, no hookups, dump, no showers. Fishing, swimming, boating(l), hiking. GPS: 32.671417, -93.305896.

MONROE (32)
Ouachita   FREE
Wildlife Management Area
State Dept of Wildlife & Fisheries
6 mi SE of Monroe. Free. All year; 14-day limit. 8-acre primitive camping area, undesignated sites. Tbls, toilets, cfga, drkg wtr. Fishing, hunting. 8,747 acres. GPS: 32.368123,-92.032217.

Russel Sage   FREE
Wildlife Management Area
State Dept of Wildlife & Fisheries
7 mi E of Monroe. Free. All year; 14-day limit. Primitive sites N of US 80. Tbls, toilets, cfga, no drkg wtr. Hiking,

hunting, birdwatching, fishing. 16,829 acres within Bayou Lafourche floodplain. GPS: 32.46552, -91.958801.

NEW ORLEANS (33)
Bayou Segnette State Park $10
From I-10 SW of New Orleans, follow I-310 S across the Luling Bridge over Mississippi River; exit E on US 90, which becomes Westbank Exprssway into town of Westwego. $10 off-season for LA, AR & MD seniors at 98 premium elec/wtr sites ($14 in-season); others pay $20 off-season, $28 in-season. Tbls, flush toilets, cfga, drkg wtr, showers, wave pool, playground. Boating(l), canoeing, nature study, swimming, fishing, hiking trail. GPS: 29.8838174, -90.1681304.

OIL CITY (34)
Earl G. Williamson $6
Caddo Parish Park
Just S of Oil City at 11425 SR 1. $6 for sites without elec; $12 with elec. 18 sites; 14-day limit. Tbls, flush toilets, showers, cfga, drkg wtr, dump($2 non-campers), elec($), fishing pier, playgrounds. Swimming, volleyball, ball field, tennis, boating, fishing, biking. 40 acres. GPS: 32.761942, -92.979511.

OPELOUSAS (35)
Opelousas South City Park $10
In Opelousas, 2 mi W on US 190 from I-49; at 1489 S Market St. $10. All year. 67 sites with elec/wtr; no tents. Tbls, flush toilets, cfga, drkg wtr, dump, playground, pool. Swimming, tennis, horseshoes, volleyball. GPS: 30.519234, -92.086981.

PITKIN (36)
Fullerton Lake $5
Kisatchie National Forest
6 mi W of Pitkin on LA 10; 3.5 mi NE on LA 399. $5. All year; 14-day limit. 9 sites (RVs under 22 ft). Tbls, toilets, cfga, firewood, piped drkg wtr. Trails. Hiking, picnicking, fishing, boating(d). 3 acres. Historic. GPS: 31.010628, -92.986239.

Hunter Camp   FREE
Kisatchie National Forest
8 mi W of Pitkin on SR 10; 4 mi NW on VP 443; difficult access. Free. All year; 14-day limit. Primitive undesignated sites; pit toilets, cfga, no drkg wtr, no trash service.. Hunting, hiking, horseback riding. GPS: 31.008382, -92.107909.

POLLOCK (37)
Stuart Lake Campground $5
Kisatchie National Forest
1.5 mi SW of Pollock on SR 8; 1.5 mi SW on FR 144. $5. All year; 14-day limit. 8 sites; half can handle large RVs. Tbls, flush toilets, cfga, drkg wtr, shelter. Fishing, hiking, interpretive & biking trails, swimming, hunting, boating (no mtrs). Renovated in 2009. GPS: 31.508578, -92.444018.

ST. JOSEPH (38)
Lake Bruin State Park $11
Just E of St. Joseph on SR 607; half mi N on SR 605; 7 mi E on SR 604; half mi SW on Lake Bruin St. $11 for LA, AR & MD seniors at 36 elec/wtr sites (others pay $22); $9 off-season for LA, AR & MD seniors (others pay $18). $10 off-season for LA, AR & MD seniors at 12 premium elec/wtr sites ($14 in-season); others pay $20 off-season, $28 in-season. 14-day limit. Tbls, flush toilets, cfga, drkg wtr, dump, beach, playground. Waterskiing, boating(lr), fishing, swimming. GPS: 31.9604359, -91.2012223.

ST. MARTINVILLE (39)
Lake Fausse Pointe State Park $11
3 mi NE of St. Martinville on SR 96; 4 mi E on SR 679; 4 mi E on SR 3083; 7.5 mi S on West Atchafalaya Basin Protection Levee Rd. $11 for LA, AR & MD seniors at 33 elec/wtr sites (others pay $22); $9 off-season for LA, AR & MD seniors (others pay $18). $10 off-season for LA, AR & MD seniors at 17 premium elec/wtr sites ($14 in-season); others pay $20 off-season, $28 in-season. Tbls, flush toilets, cfga, drkg wtr, dump, coin laundry. Hiking trails, canoe trail, fishing, boating(lr), nature center. GPS: 30.06470, -91.60758.

SEREPTA (40)
See Springhill listings
Bodcau Road Primitive Area   FREE
Corps of Engineers
Bayou Bodcau Dam
From Sarepta, 2 mi E on SR 2; turn right (S) for 2 mi on CR 529, then 2 mi E on improved gravel Bodcau Rd through wooded area to the bayou. Free primitive undesigned sites. All year; 14-day limit. No facilities, no drkg wtr. Boat ramp for hand launching. GPS: 32.8709, -93.4767.

Corner of the Old Field   FREE
Corps of Engineers
Bayou Bodcau Dam
About 3 mi S of Sarepta on US 371 to just W of Cotton Valley; 3 mi W on SR 160; S on Young Rd, then E through wooded area on improved gravel rd toOldField Rd. All year; 14-day limit. Free primitive camping at undesignated sites on rock parking lot. No facilities, no drkg wtr. Boat ramp. GPS: 32.7877, -93.4746.

Crow Lake Recreation Area   FREE
Corps of Engineers
Bayou Bodcau Dam
1 mi S of Serepta on US 371; 2 mi W pm Park Rd 238 (becoming Crow Lake Rd) to camping area. All year; 14-day limit. 2 free primitive sites, no facilities, no drkg wtr. Rock boat ramp. GPS: 32.8824, -93.4609.

Highway 160 Primitive Area   FREE
Corps of Engineers
Bayou Bodcau Dam
From Serepta, about 3 mi S on US 317 to just W of Cotton Valley; 2 mi W on SR 160, to bridge, then S on gravel rd to site. All year; 14-day limit. Free primitive camping at undesignated sites. No facilities, no drkg wtr. Concrete boat ramp. GPS: 32.8138, -93.4309.

Highway 2   FREE
Primitive Camping Area
Corps of Engineers
Bayou Bodcau Dam
From Sarepta, about 5 mi E on SR 2. All year; 14-day limit. Free primitive camping at undesignated sites. No facilities, no drkg wtr. Concrete boat ramp. GPS: 32.9049, -93.4829.

Ivan Lake Recreation Area   FREE
Corps of Engineers
Bayou Bodcau Dam
About 3 mi S of Serepta on US 371 to just W of Cotton Valley; about 5 mi E on SR 160; right (N) for 1 mi on Ivan Lake Rd (NE of Bellevue). Overlooks 520-acre Ivan Lake. All year; 14-day limit. Free. 4 primitive sites. Pit toilets, fire rings, no drkg wtr. Boat ramp nearby. GPS: 32.8317, -93.4931.

Pardee Calloway Primitive Area   FREE
Corps of Engineers
Bayou Bodcau Dam
About 3 mi S of Sarepta on US 371 to just W of Cotton Valley; about 5 mi E on SR 160; right (N) for 1 mi on Ivan Lake Rd (NE of Bellevue). Overlooks 520-acre Ivan Lake. All year; 14-day limit. Free primitivecamping at undesignated sites. No facilities, no drkg wtr. Rock boat ramp. GPS: 32.7726, -93.4622.

Wenk's Landing   FREE
Corps of Engineers
Bayou Bodcau Dam
From Sarepta, about 1 mi S on US 371; left (W) for half mi on Wenk's Landing Rd, following signs. All year; 14-day limit. Free primitive camping in designated areas only. Pit toilets, fire rings, no drkg wtr. Fishing, boating(l). GPS: 32.5206, -93.2655.

SICILY ISLAND (41)
Sicily Island Hills   FREE
Wildlife Management Area
State Dept of Wildlife & Fisheries
6 mi W of Sicily Island in Catahoula Parish. Free. All year; 14-day limit. 2 primitive camping areas. Tbls, toilets, cfga, no drkg wtr. Hiking, hunting, fishing. 7,524 acres. GPS: 31.855475, -91.763618.

SPRINGFIELD (42)
Tickfaw State Park $11
6 mi W of Springfield on SR 1037; 1.2 mi S on Patterson Rd; at Tickfaw River. $11 for LA, AR & MD seniors at 30 elec/wtr sites (others pay $22); $9 off-season for LA, AR & MD seniors (others pay $18). Tbls, flush toilets, cfga, drkg wtr, showers, coin laundry. Canoeing(lr), fishing, nature center, 4 hiking trails, guided boardwalk hikes. GPS: 30.3817, -90.6309.

SPRINGHILL (40)
See Sarepta listings
Della Field Primitive Area   FREE
Corps of Engineers
Bayou Bodcau Dam
2 mi W of Springhill on SR 157; about 2 mi S on Timothy Church Rd; turn right (W) on improved gravel rd for about 1 mi, then left (SW) on access rd for about 1 mi to bayou. All year; 14-day limit. Free primitive undesignated sites. No facilities, no drkg wtr. Boat ramp for hand launching. GPS: 32.9876, -95.5209.

Highway 157 Primitive Area   FREE
Corps of Engineers
Bayou Bodcau Dam
From Springhill, about 4 mi W on SR 157. Free primitive camping on rock parking lot. No facilities, no drkg wtr. Gravel boat ramp. All year; 14-day limit. GPS: 33.0188, -93.5214.

Rainey Wells Recreation Area   FREE
Corps of Engineers
Bayou Bodcau Dam
2 mi W of Springhill on DR 157; about 5 mi S on Timothy Church Rd; on N shore of Bodcau Bayou Reservoir. All year; 14-day limit. 2 free primitive sites. No facilities, no drkg wtr. Rock boat ramp. GPS: 32.9588, -93.5193.

Teague Lake   FREE
Primitive Camping Area
Corps of Engineers
Bayou Bodcau Dam
From Springhill, about 4.5 mi S on SR 157, past Highway 157 Primitive Area; right (N) on Oglee Rd about 2 mi, then 2 mi N on improved gravel Teague Rd to the bayou. All year; 14-day limit. Free primitive camping pad. No facilities, no drkg wtr. Gravel boat ramp. GPS: 33.0188, -93.5214.

VIDALIA (43)
Three Rivers   FREE
Wildlife Management Area
State Dept of Wildlife & Fisheries
50 mi S of Vidalia in Concordia Parish. Free. All year; 14-day limit. 3 primitive camping areas. Tbls, toilets, cfga, no drkg wtr. Hunting, fishing, birdwatching, boating(l). 26,295 acres. GPS: 31.080365, -91.646925.

VILLE PLATTE (44)
Chicot State Park $11
16.4 mi NW of Ville Platte on US 167; 7 mi N on SR 3042. $11 for LA, AR & MD seniors at 208 wtr/elec sites (others pay $22); $9 off-season for LA, AR & MD seniors (others pay $18). 14-day limit. Tbls, flush toilets, cfga, drkg wtr, showers, dump, playground, pool, pavilions, fishing pier. Boating(rl), canoeing(r), fishing, hiking trails, swimming. GPS: 30.8004732, -92.2798498.

VIOLET (45)
St. Bernard State Park $11
8.7 mi S of Violet on SR 47; 10.5 mi E on SR 39; at Mississippi River. $11 for LA, AR & MD seniors at 51 wtr/elec sites (others pay $22); $9 off-season for LA, AR & MD seniors (others pay $18). 14-day limit. Tbls, flush toilets, cfga, drkg wtr, showers, pool, dump. Swimming, fishing, canoeing, nature trail. Man-made lagoons. GPS: 29.8613171, -89.9008997.

WINNFIELD (47)
Gum Springs Campground $3
Kisatchie National Forest
8 mi W of Winnfield on US 84. $3. All year; 14-day limit. 16 sites. Tbls, toilets, cfga, drkg wtr. Hiking, biking, horseback riding. $3 horse camp nearby. GPS: 31.8971078, -92.7787641.

WOODSWORTH (48)
Loran/Claiborne $7
Trailhead Camp
Kisatchie Ntaional Forest
6 mi SW of Woodsworth on US 165; about 3.5 mi W on SR 112; 2 mi N on FR 258; difficult access. $7. All year; 14-day limit. Primitive undesignated sites; no facilities except toilets, cfga. Hunting, hiking/biking trail. Popular as ATV & motorcycle camp. GPS: 31.097801, -92.566609.

ZWOLLE (49)
Pleasure Point $11.25
Site #13
Sabine River Authority
W of Zwolle on SR 475 to SR 191; 34 mi S on SR 191 to SR 473; continue S another 4 mi & turn right between mileposts 5 & 6 on Pleasure Point Rd for 1.5 mi. Seniors pay $11.25 at 74 sites with elec/wtr (others pay $15) & $15 at 50 full-hookup sites (others pay $20). $10 for tent sites. Tbls, toilets, cfga, drkg wtr, dump, playground, beach, pay phone, fishing pier & jetty. Fishing, swimming, boating(l). Non-campers pay $2 day use and boat ramp fees. GPS: 31.243713, -93.578489.

Sabine FREE
Wildlife Management Area
State Dept of Wildlife & Fisheries
5 mi S of Zwolle. Free. All year; 14-day limit. Primitive sites on NW section. Tbls, toilets, cfga, no drkg wtr. Hunting, birdwatching. 14,780 acres. GPS: 31.561082, -93.586331.

North Toledo Bend State Park $11
Half mi W of Zwolle on SR 482; 4 mi W on SR 3229, then follow signs; on N shore of Toledo Bend Reservoir. $11 for LA, AR & MD seniors at 55 elec/wtr sites (others pay $22); $9 off-season for LA, AR & MD seniors (others pay $18). $10 off-season for LA, AR & MD seniors at for 5 premium-location elec/wtr sites ($14 in-season); others pay $20 off-season, $28 in-season. All year; 14-day limit. Tbls, flush toilets, cfga, drkg wtr, showers, dump, coin laundry, hookups($), pool, playground. Swimming, boating(l), fishing, waterskiing.

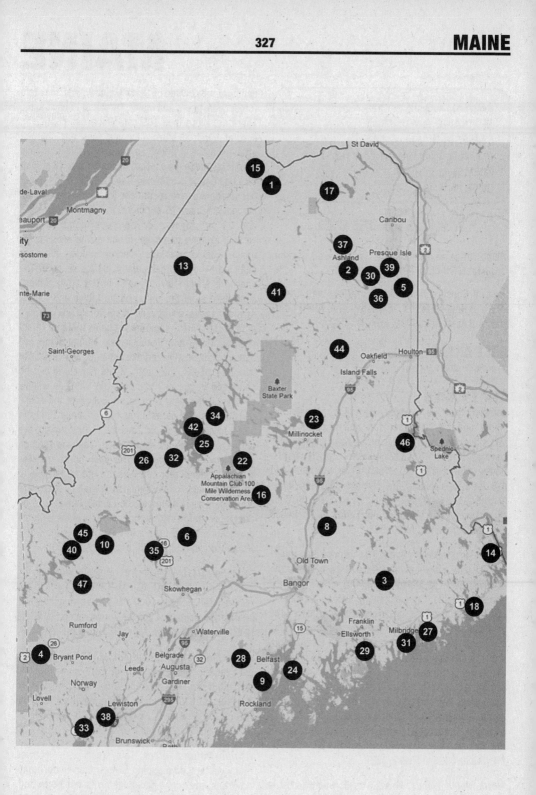

MAINE

CAPITAL: Augusta
NICKNAME: Pine Tree State
STATEHOOD: 1820 – 23rd State
FLOWER: White Pine Cone and Tassel
TREE: White Pine
BIRD: Chickadee

WWW.VISITMAINE.COM

Maine Office of Tourism, 59 State House Station, Augusta, ME 04333; 888-624-6345.

Dept. of Conservation, Bureau of Parks and Lands, 22 State House Station, 18 Elkins Lane, AMHI Complex, Augusta, ME 04333. 207-287-3821.

REST AREAS
Overnight stops are not permitted.

STATE PARKS
Camping fees are generally $14-15 for Maine residents and $8-$10 more for non-residents. Only Aroostook and Bradbury Mountain have regular-season fees (5/15-9/15) of $12 or less for state residents. However, off-season rates of $10 for residents and $18 for non-residents are charged between 9/15-5/15. Day-use park fees are charged. Dept. of Conservation, Bureau of Parks and Lands, State House Station 22, Augusta, ME 04333.

Bureau of Parks & Lands. The Bureau is a multiple-use land management agency responsible for the administration of Maine's 450,000 acres of Public Reserved Lands. Free camping, hiking and fishing in secluded locations are available on most of the 29 Public Reserved Lands units except those within the North Maine Woods area (such as Gero Island) and a few others that are managed in cooperation with neighboring landowners. Unpaved private roads provide access to many of these backcountry recreation areas, which range in size from 500 to 43,000 acres. Drivers are cautioned to yield the right-of-way to logging trucks at all times. Write or call the Bureau of Parks & Lands, State House Station #22, Augusta, ME 04330-0022. 207/287-3821.

North Maine Woods. This 2.5-million-acre forest is both privately and state-owned and administered. Camping and backcountry recreation are available at campgrounds owned by North Maine Woods, the state forest department and Maine Bureau of Public Lands. There are more than 100 camping areas containing several hundred sites. Camping fees are charged after payment of either an annual permit or a daily permit has been purchased. Anyone under 15 or over 70 years of age is admitted free. Daily fees are $6 per person for Maine residents and $10 for non-residents; camping fees are $8 per night, $10 for non-residents and $4 for seniors. For purposes of our listings, we will assume purchase of one of the seasonal or annual passes available, thereby making overnight camping $8 or $10 per person ($4 for seniors). The season is May 1-Nov. 30, with 14 day limits. Campsites have steel fire rings, picnic tables and toilets; at more rustic designated state forest service fire permit campsites, campfires require a Maine forest service fire permit. Because new campgrounds are opened occasionally and existing ones are closed for various reasons, the North Maine Woods should be contacted before any camping trip into this wilderness area. Camping permits are issued at the area's checkpoints; fire permits must be obtained from the state forest service in advance if designated fire permit campsites are to be used. Passage through any checkpoint before or after open hours requires a $20 additional fee; late fees are not acceptable at Canadian border checkpoints. Warning: There are no rangers or hookups at the campgrounds, and no drinking water, gasoline stations, tow trucks, stores or restaurants. For further information contact: North Maine Woods, PO Box 425, Ashland, ME 04732.

State Forests. Camping is free except for sites that are within the Maine North Woods. Campfire permits are required; call 800-750-9777. For a free map and further information contact: Dept. of Conservation, 22 State House Station, Augusta, ME 04333. 207-287-2791.

White Mountain National Forest. All campgrounds have tables, toilets, campfire grill areas and drinking water, but none has hookups. Daily fees generally are in excess of $10 per night. White Mountain National Forest, 719 N. Main St., Laconia, NH 03246. Call 603 528-8721 for information.

Acadia National Park. This small park receives many visitors, so camping is restricted to designated areas; overnight backpacking is not permitted. Superintendent, Acadia National Park, P.O. Box 177, Bay Harbor, ME 04609; 207-288-3338.

ALLAGASH (1)

Big Brook River $8
North Maine Woods
About 7 mi NE of Allagash on Hwy 151 to St. Francis checkpoint. S about 10 mi to Gardner Brook; take right fork S (not onto Maine Public Reserve Land) about 12 mi to Big Brook River bridge. $8 ($10 non-residents, seniors $4). Open 5/1-11/30; 14-day limit. Primitive developed sites; 28-ft RV limit. Tbls, toilets, cfga, no drkg wtr. Fishing, canoeing. Checkpoint open daily 5 a.m.-9 p.m. Access also from the S from Musquacook.

Gardner Pond $8
North Maine Woods
About 7 mi NE of Allagash on Hwy 161 to St. Francis checkpoint; S about 10 mi to Maine Public Reserve Land, then E to Gardner Pond. $8 ($10 non-residents, seniors $4). Open 5/1 11/30; 14-day limit. Primitive developed sites; 28-ft RV limit. Tbls, toilets, cfga, no drkg wtr. Fishing, boating(l). Checkpoint open daily 5 a.m. 9 p.m. GPS: 46.5745, -68.8875431.

Perch Pond $8
North Maine Woods
About 7 mi NE of Allagash on Hwy 161 to St. Francis checkpoint; S about 10 mi to Maine Public Reserve Land, then E along N shore of Togue Pond past Togue Pond camps to Perch Pond. $8 ($10 non-residents, seniors $4). Open 5/1-11/30; 14-day limit. Primitive developed sites; 28-ft RV limit. Tbls, toilets, cfga, no drkg wtr. Fishing, boating(l). Checkpoint open daily 5 a.m.-9 p.m. GPS: 46.938688,-68.861558.

Pushinger Pond $8
North Maine Woods
About 7 mi NE of Allagash on Hwy 161 to St. Francis checkpoint; S about 10 mi to Maine Public Reserve Land, then E along N shore of Togue Pond past Togue Pond camps, past Perch Pond, past Upper Pond; W to Pushinger Pond camp. $8 ($10 non-residents, seniors $4). Open 5/1-11/30; 14-day limit. Primitive developed sites; 28-ft RV limit. Tbls, toilets, cfga, no drkg wtr. Fishing, boating. Checkpoint open daily 5a.m.-9p.

State Forest Camp $8
About 11 mi SW of Allagash on Michaud Tote Rd; along Allagash River. $8 (non-residents $10, seniors $4). Primitive undeveloped camp; state fire permit required. Primitive facilities, cfga, no drkg wtr. Fishing, boating, hunting. Checkpoint open daily 5 a.m.-9 p.m.

Third Chase Pond $8
North Maine Woods
About 7 mi NE of Allagash on Hwy 161 to St. Francis checkpoint; S about 15 mi through Maine Public Reserve Land; continue S about 5 mi to Third Class Pond. $8 ($10 non-residents, seniors $4). Open 5/1-11/30; 14-day limit.

Primitive developed sites; 28-ft RV limit. Tbls, toilets, cfga, no drkg wtr. Fishing, boating(l). Checkpoint open daily 5 a.m.-9 p.m.

Togue Pond $8
North Maine Woods
About 7 mi NE of Allagash on Hwy 161 to St. Francis checkpoint; S about 10 mi to Maine Public Reserve Land, then E to NW shore of Togue Pond. $8 ($10 non-residents, seniors $4). Open 5/1-11/30; 14-day limit. 3 campgrounds with primitive developed sites; 28-ft RV limit. Tbls, toilets, cfga, no drkg wtr. Fishing, boating(l). Checkpoint open daily 5 a.m.-9 p.m. GPS: 46.935188, -68.89934.

Twin Brook I $8
North Maine Woods
About 5 mi SW of Allagash on Michaud Tote Rd; along Allagash River. $8 ($10 non-residents, seniors $4). Open 5/1-11/30; 14-day limit. Primitive developed sites; 28-ft RV limit. Tbls, toilets, cfga, no drkg wtr. Fishing, boating. Checkpoint open daily 5 a.m.-9 p.m.

Twin Brook II $8
North Maine Woods
About 6 mi SW of Allagash on Michaud Tote Rd; along Allagash River. $8 (non-residents $10, seniors $4). 5/1-11/30; 14-day limit. Primitive developed sites; 28-ft RV limit. Tbls, toilets, cfga, no drkg wtr. Fishing, boating. Checkpoint open daily 5 a.m.-9 p.m.

Upper Pond $8
North Maine Woods
About 7 mi NE of Allagash on Hwy 161 to St. Francis checkpoint; S about 10 mi to Maine Public Reserve Land, then E along N shore of Togue Pond past Togue Pond camps to Perch Pond then qtr mi to Upper Pond. $8 ($10 non-residents, seniors $4). Open 5/1-11/30; 14-day limit. Primitive developed sites; 28-ft RV limit. Tbls, toilets, cfga, no drkg wtr. Fishing, boating(l). Checkpoint open daily 5 a.m. 9 p.m. GPS: 45.5639, -68.5110.

ASHLAND (2)

East Shore Camp $8
Big Machias Lake
North Maine Woods
From Russell Crossing Camp, continue W 3 mi to SE shore of lake. $8 ($10 non-residents, seniors $4). Open 5/1-11/30; 14-day limit. Primitive developed sites; 28-ft RV limit. Tbls, toilets, cfga, no drkg wtr. Fishing, boating(l). Checkpoint open 24 hrs. Lake GPS: 46.681904, -68.793253.

Clayton Lake $8
North Maine Woods
From East Shore Camp, continue W about 2.7 mi, then N on primary rd; turn E for half mi on second rd to right to NW shore of Clayton Lake. $8 ($10 non-residents, seniors $4).

Open 5/1-11/30; 14-day limit. Primitive developed sites; 28-ft RV limit. Tbls, toilets, cfga, no drkg wtr. Fishing, boating(l). Checkpoint open 24 hrs. Note: Access to site also from Fish River Checkpoint. GPS: 46.4307, -68.4547.

Greenlaw Crossing State Forest Camp $8
From Greenlaw Stream Camp, continue 3 mi W on American Realty Tote Rd. $8 (non-residents $10, seniors $4). Open 5/1-11/30; 14-day limit. Primitive undeveloped sites; 28-ft RV limit; limited facilities (cfga, no drkg wtr). Hiking, hunting. Checkpoint open 24 hrs. GPS: 46.661708, -68.628101.

Greenlaw Stream $8
North Maine Woods
5 mi W of Ashland on American Realty Tote Rd to 6-Mile Checkpoint; continue 3 mi W to Greenlaw bridge. $8 ($10 non-residents, seniors $4). Open 5/1-11/30; 14-day limit. Primitive developed sites; 28-ft RV limit. Tbls, toilets, cfga, no drkg wtr. Fishing, canoeing. Checkpoint open 24 hrs. Stream GPS: 46.6114, -68.4898.

Moosehorn Stream $8
North Maine Woods
From Greenlaw Crossing Camp, continue 1 mi on American Realty Tote Rd to Moosehorn Stream bridge. $8 ($10 non-residents, seniors $4). Open 5/1-11/30; 14-day limit. Primitive developed sites; 28-ft RV limit. Tbls, toilets, cfga, no drkg wtr. Fishing, canoeing. Checkpoint open 24 hrs. Stream GPS: 46.652, -68.6203.

Number One Brook State Forest Camp $8
From Pratt Lake Camp, continue about 5 mi W to No 1 Brook bridge. $8 (non-residents $10, seniors $4). Open 5/1-11/30; 14-day limit. Primitive undeveloped sites; 28-ft RV limit; limited facilities (cfga, no drkg wtr). Hiking, hunting, canoeing. Checkpoint open 24 hrs; access also available from W via Musquacook Checkpoint. Brook GPS: 46.6095, -68.9687.

North Shore Camp $8
Big Machias Lake
North Maine Woods
From East Shore Camp, continue W 2 mi to lake's northeast shore. $8 ($10 non-residents, seniors $4). Open 5/1-11/30; 14-day limit. Primitive developed sites; 28-ft RV limit. Tbls, toilets, cfga, no drkg wtr. Fishing, boating(l). Checkpoint open 24 hrs. Lake GPS: 46.68278, -68.79222.

Pratt Lake $8
North Maine Woods
From North Shore Camp, continue about 8.7 mi W on American Realty Tote Rd. $8 ($10 non-residents, seniors $4). Open 5/1-11/30; 14-day limit. Primitive developed sites; 28-ft RV limit. Tbls, toilets, cfga, no drkg wtr. Fishing, boating(l). Checkpoint open 24 hrs. Note: Access to site also available from Musquacook Checkpoint about 15 mi W. GPS: 46.640784, -68.887296.

Pratt Lake Stream State Forest Camp $8
From North Shore Camp, continue about 8 mi W on American Realty Tote Rd. $8 (non-residents $10, seniors $4). Open 5/1-11/30; 14-day limit. Primitive undeveloped sites; 28-ft RV limit; limited facilities (cfga, no drkg wtr). Hiking, hunting, canoeing. Checkpoint open 24 hrs. Stream GPS: 46.6659, -68.8292.

Right Fork Camp $8
North Maine Woods
From Twentymile Brook Camp, continue N on secondary access rd about 4 mi to jct of Right Fork and Left Fork Brook. $8 ($10 non-residents, seniors $4). Open 5/1-11/30; 14-day limit. Primitive developed sites; 28-ft RV limit. Tbls, toilets, cfga, no drkg wtr. Fishing, canoeing. Checkpoint open 24 hrs.

Round Lake Camps $8
(Washington County)
Public Reserved Land
50 mi W of Ashland on American Realty Tote Rd, passing through 6 Mile Checkpoint of North Maine Woods, to Musquacook Checkpoint just S of Second Musquacook Lake; then 15 mi N on primary access rd along W shore of Lake to S shore of Round Pond (a wide section of Allagash River). $8 (non-residents $10, seniors $4). Open 5/1-11/30; 14-day limit. 1 drive-to primitive camp on S shore of lake, 3 boat-in or hike-in camps along lake's W shore. Limited facilities, no drkg wtr. Popular canoe camps as part of 20,000-acre area. Hunting, fishing, boating, canoeing, hiking. Lake GPS: 45.01995,-67.267479.

Russell Crossing $8
North Maine Woods
From Moosehorn Stream camp, continue W about 5 mi. $8 ($10 non-residents, seniors $4). Open 5/1-11/30; 14-day limit. Primitive developed sites; 28-ft RV limit. Tbls, toilets, cfga, no drkg wtr. Fishing, canoeing. Checkpoint open 24 hrs.

Twentymile Brook $8
North Maine Woods
From North Shore Camp, continue W about 2 mi; turn N on secondary access rd for about 3 mi. $8 ($10 non-residents, seniors $4). Open 5/1-11/30; 14-day limit. Primitive developed sites; 28-ft RV limit. Tbls, toilets, cfga, no drkg wtr. Fishing, canoeing. Checkpoint open 24 hrs. Brook GPS: 46.6875, -68.7867.

BAR HARBOR
Blackwoods Campground $10
Acadia National Park
5 mi S of Bar Harbor on Hwy 3. $10 with federal senior pass; others pay $20. All year; 14-day limit. Free to tent campers 12/1-3/31. 306 sites. Tbls, flush toilets, cfga, drkg wtr, showers nearby($).Hiking, campfire programs. GPS: 44.307, -68.205

BEDDINGTON (3)

Bracey Pond   FREE
Narraguagus River District State Forest Camp
10.5 mi N of ME 9 from Beddington on W side of CCC Rd.
Free. All year. Sites. Tbls, toilets, cfga, drkg wtr (should be
boiled). Free permit required for fires in non-designated
areas. Picnicking, fishing. GPS: 44.961866, -68.12244.

Deer Lake   FREE
Narraguagus River District State Forest Camp
13 mi N on ME 9 from Beddington on S side of CCC Rd. Free.
All year. Sites. Tbls, toilets, cfga, drkg wtr (should be boiled).
Free fire permit required for fires in non-designated areas.
Picnicking, fishing. Lake GPS: 44.995552, -68.130561.

BETHEL (4)

Crocker Pond $7
White Mountain National Forest
From Bethel at jct with SR 5, 5 mi W on Pattie Brook Rd.
$7 with federal senior pass; others pay $14. 5/15-10/15;
14-day limit. 7 primitive sites. Tbls, toilets, cfga, no
drkg wtr. Canoeing, boating(l), fishing. GPS: 44.31028,
-70.82389

BRIDGEWATER (5)

Number 9 Lake   FREE
Number Nine District State Forest Camp
14 mi W of Bridgewater on NE shore of Number 9 Lake.
Free. All year. Sites. Tbls, toilets, cfga, drkg wtr (should be
boiled). Free fire permit required for fires in non-designated areas. Picnicking, fishing. GPS: 46.416601, -68.046807.

BRIGHTON (6)

Smith Pond   FREE
Parling Pond District State Forest Camp
E side of ME 151; N of Brighton. Free. Sites. Tbls, toilets,
cfga, drkg wtr (should be boiled). Free fire permit required
for fires in non-designated areas. Picnicking, fishing. GPS:
45.062746,-69.71191.

BURLINGTON (8)

Duck Lake Preserve   ·FREE
Bureau of Public Lands
E (over rough private rds) off an extension of Route 188 out
of Burlington; from the S, off the Stud Mill Rd in T-34 or
T-35 MD. Free. All year. Open camping. No facilities. Fishing, boating (l), hiking, snowmobiling, swimming. 25,000
acres encompass Duck Lake, Unknown Lake, Gassabias
Lake & take in SW secion of Fourth Machias Lake. Best
spots are Longfellow Cove on Duck; on spit between
Middle & Lower Unknown; on S shore of Gassabias -- all
have tbls & cfga, with pit toilets nearby. Most excellent
for RVers. Fires only at authorized or permit campsites,
but self-contained stoves allowed. Good boat-in tent sites
along W shore of Duck & SE shore of Fourth Machias;
hike-in site on Upper Unknown by trail from parking area

near Middle Unknown. Gravel boat launch at Duck Lake
campground. Eastern Main Canoe Trail passes through
area, entering at Fourth Machias & exiting the Gassabias
Stream. Duck Lake GPS: 45.341051, -68.046433.

CAMDEN (9)

Camden Hills State Park $10
2 mi N of Camden on US 1. $10 during 9/15-5/15 ($18 for
non-residents); $15-37 rest of season. 107 sites. Tbls,
flush toilets, cfga, drkg wtr, dump($5 non-campers), show-
ers. Hiking, skiing, snowmobiling. GPS: 44.23, -69.047.

CARRABASSET (10)

Big Eddy   FREE
Dead River District State Forest Camp
15 mi N of Carrabasset on Spring Lake Rd; E shore of Dead
River. Free. Sites. Tbls, toilets, cfga, drkg wtr (should be
boiled). Free fire permit required for fires in non-designated areas. Picnicking, fishing.

Bigelow Preserve   FREE
Bureau of Public Lands
N on rough co rd off Hwy 27 in Carrabassett and by the
Long Falls Dam Rd from North New Portland. S of Flagstaff
& 40 mi N of Farmington in western Maine. Free. All year.
Open camping. No facilities. Snack bar. Boating, fishing,
swimming, picnicking. 35,027 acres. Hike Appalachian
Trail, other trails. Scenic. 21 mi of frontage on Flagstaff
Lake. 36,000 acres. GPS: 45.038606, -70.397954.

DAAQUAM (13)

Ninemile Bridge Camps $8
North Maine Woods
From St. John River Camps, continue 5 mi W, then N on
first primary access rd 5 mi; NW 3 mi on secondary access
rd to Ninemile Bridge area. 2 camps. $8 ($10 non-residents, seniors $4). Open 5/1-11/30; 14-day limit. Primitive
developed sites; 28 ft RV limit. Tbls, toilets, cfga, no drkg
wtr. Fishing, boating. Checkpoint open Mon 5 a.m.-1 p.m.;
Tues-Fri, 6 a.m.-2 p.m.

St. John River Camps $8
North Maine Woods
10 mi E of Daaquam on Daaquam River Rd to St. John
River bridge. Three drive-to camps, 2 boat-in camps. $8
($10 non-residents, seniors $4). Open 5/1-11/30; 14-day
limit. Primitive developed sites; 28-ft RV limit. Tbls, toilets,
cfga, no drkg wtr. Fishing, boating. Checkpoint open Mon
5 a.m.-1 p.m.; Tues-Fri, 6 a.m.-2 p.m.

DENNYSVILLE (14)

Cobscook Bay State Park $10
6 mi S of Dennysville on US 1. $10 during 9/15-5/15 ($18
for non-residents); $14-24 rest of year. 100 sites. Tbls,
pit toilets, cfga, drkg wtr, dump($5 non-campers), play-
ground. Boating(l), fishing, hiking, golf, snowmobiling.
GPS: 44.854, -67.153.

DICKEY (15)

Chimenticook $8
North Maine Woods
About 13 mi SW of Dickey on St. John River Rd near jct of river & Chimenticook Stream. $8 ($10 non-residents, seniors $4). Open 5/1-11/30; 14-day limit. Primitive developed sites; 28-ft RV limit. Tbls, toilets, cfga, no drkg wtr. Fishing, boating. Checkpoint open daily 5 a.m.-9 p.m.

Falls Pond $8
North Maine Woods
About 4 mi N of Dickey on Fall Brook Lake Rd; on S edge of lake. $8 ($10 non-residents, seniors $4). Open 5/1-11/30; 14-day limit. Primitive developed sites; 28-ft RV limit. Tbls, toilets, cfga, no drkg wtr. Fishing, boating. Checkpoint open daily 5 p.m.

Fox Brook $8
North Maine Woods
About 10 mi SW of Dickey on St. John River Rd at jct of river & Fox Brook. $8 ($10 non-residents, seniors $4). Open 5/1-11/30; 14-day limit. Primitive developed sites; 28-ft RV limit. Tbls, toilets, cfga, no drkg wtr. Fishing, boating. Checkpoint open daily 5 a.m.-9 p.m.

Fox Pond State Forest Camp $8
About 2 mi SW of Dickey on St. John River Rd; about 10 mi NW on major access rd; near jct with secondary rd toward Rocky Mountain; at Fox Pond lake. $8 (non-residents $10, seniors $4). Open 5/1-11/30; 14-day limit. Primitive undeveloped camping area; limited facilities; cfga, no drkg wtr. Fishing, boating. Checkpoint open daily 5 a.m.-9 p.m. GPS: 45.0952, 69.1710.

Little Black River State Forest Camp $8
About 12 mi NW of Dickey past Little Falls Pond; half mi SW to Little Black River. $8 (non-residents $10, seniors $4). Open 5/1-11/30; 14-day limit. Primitive undeveloped camping area; limited facilities; cfga, no drkg wtr. Fishing, boating. Checkpoint open daily 5 a.m.-9 p.m.

Little Falls Pond $8
North Maine Woods
About 7 mi N of Dickey to W shore of Little Falls Pond. $8 ($10 non-residents, seniors $4). Open 5/1 11/30; 14-day limit. Primitive developed sites; 28-ft RV limit. Tbls, toilets, cfga, no drkg wtr. Fishing, boating. Checkpoint open daily 5 a.m.-9 p.m. GPS: 47.181486, -69.10734.

Little Falls Pond State Forest Camp $8
About 7.5 mi N of Dickey to shore of Little Falls Pond. $8 (non-residents $10, seniors $4). Open 5/1-11/30; 14-day limit. Primitive undeveloped camping area; limited facilities; cfga, no drkg wtr. Fishing, boating. Checkpoint open daily 5 a.m.-9 p.m. GPS: 47.181486, -69.10734.

Ouelette Brook $8
North Maine Woods
About 11 mi SW of Dickey on St. John River Rd at jct of river & Ouelette Brook. $8 ($10 non-residents, seniors $4). Open 5/1-11/30; 14-day limit. Primitive developed sites; 28-ft RV limit. Tbls, toilets, cfga, no drkg wtr. Fishing, boating. Checkpoint open daily 5 a.m.-9 p.m.

Oxbow Brook State Forest Camp $8
About 12 mi NW of Dickey past Little Falls Pond; half mi SW to Little Black River Camp; 1 mi NW on secondary access rd to Oxbow Brook bridge. $8 (non-residents $10, seniors $4). Open 5/1-11/30; 14-day limit. Primitive undeveloped camping area; limited facilities; cfga, no drkg wtr. Fishing, boating. Checkpoint open daily 5 a.m.-9 p.m.

Poplar Island $8
North Maine Woods
About 3 mi W of Dickey on St. John River Rd. $8 ($10 non-residents, seniors $4). Open 5/1-11/30; 14-day limit. Primitive developed sites; 28-ft RV limit. Tbls, toilets, cfga, no drkg wtr. Fishing, boating. Checkpoint open daily 5 a.m.-9 p.m.

Rocky Mountain North State Forest Camp $8
About 2 mi SW of Dickey on St. John River Rd; about 10 mi NW on major access rd; past jct with secondary rd toward Rocky Mountain; first secondary access rd to right for half mi; N of Fox Mountain. $8 (non-residents $10, seniors $4). Open 5/1 11/30; 14-day limit. Primitive undeveloped camping area; limited facilities; cfga, no drkg wtr. Hiking. Checkpoint open daily 5 a.m.-9 p.m. Access also S from Estcourt at Canadian line.

DOVER-FOXCROFT (16)

Peaks-Kenny State Park $10
5 mi N of Dover-Foxcroft, off SR 153 on Sebec Lake. $10 during 9/15-5/15 ($18 for non-residents); $15-25 rest of year. 56 sites. Tbls, flush toilets, cfga, drkg wtr, showers, dump($5 non-campers), playground. Boating(l), fishing, hiking trails, swimming, snowmobiling. 839 acres. GPS: 42.26, -69.289.

EAGLE LAKE (17)

Eagle Lake Preserve FREE
Bureau of Public Lands
Access from Sly Brook Rd, which connects with SR 11 at Soldier Pond (Wallagrass) and with SR 161 in Fort Kent. Free. All year. Open camping. No facilities. Fishing, boating, hunting. 22,000 acres, including most of Eagle Lake and abutting square Lake to the E. Fish River outlet of Eagle Lake flows N to the St. John River. GPS: 46.819941, -68.476606.

EAST MACHIAS (18)

Rocky Lake Reserve   FREE
Bureau of Public Lands
N of East Machias 8 mi on SR 191, which passes through the area. Free. All year. Open camping. Tbls, cfga, toilet, no drkg wtr. Fishing, canoeing, boating, swimming, hiking. 8,800 acres. Rocky Lake coves & islands. Second Lake & Patrick Lake. East Cachias River canoeing, fishing, hunting, swimming. Gravel boat launch at Mud Landing; hand launch at South Bay. 10,000 acres. GPS: 44.984932, -67.677684.

EUSTIS (19)

Alder Stream   FREE
Dead River District State Forest Camp
4-1/2 mi N of Eustis on the W side of ME 27. Free. Sites. Tbls, toilets, cfga, drkg wtr (should be boiled). Free fire permit required for fires in non-designated areas. Picnicking, fishing.

Flagstaff Lake   FREE
Dead River District State Forest Camp
E of Eustis. Free. Sites. Tbls, toilets, cfga, drkg wtr (should be boiled). Free fire permit required for fires in non-designated areas. Picnicking, fishing. GPS: 45.212438, -70.365501.

Rock Pond   FREE
Dead River District State Forest Camp
20 mi W of ME 201; on N shore of Rock Pond. Free. Sites. Tbls, toilets, cfga, drkg wtr (should be boiled). Free fire permit required for fires in non-designated areas. Picnicking, fishing. GPS: 45.297569, -70.75489

FRYEBURG (20)

Basin Campground $10
White Mountain National Forest
15 mi N of Fryeburg, Maine, on Hwy 113; on S side of Basin Pond; in New Hampshire. $10 with federal senior pass; others pay $20. 5/15-10/15; 14-day limit. 21 sites (typically 65 ft). Tbls, flush toilets, cfga, drkg wtr. Hiking, fishing, boating. GPS: 44.269, -71.021

Cold River $9
White Mountain National Forest
15 mi N of Fryeburg, Maine, on Hwy 113; in New Hampshire. $9 with federal senior pass; others pay $18. 5/15-10/15; 14-day limit. 14 sites (12 for RVs, typically 60 ft). Tbls, toilets, cfga, drkg wtr. Hiking, fishing, boating(l). GPS: 44.265, -71.013

GILEAD (21)

Hastings Campground $8
White Mountain National Forest
3 mi S of Hwy 2 on Hwy 113 near Gilead. $8 with federal senior pass; others pay $16. 5/15-10/15; 14-day limit. 24 sites, typically 55 ft. Tbls, pit toilets, cfga, drkg wtr. Hiking, fishing, interpretive programs. GPS: 44.35228, -70.98396

Wild River Campground $8
White Mountain National Forest
0.4 mi W of Gilead on US 2; 3 mi S on SR 113; 5.5 mi SW on FR 12. $8 with federal senior pass; others pay $16. 5/15-10/15; 14-day limit. 12 sites (3 for RVs); 45-ft RV limit. Tbls, toilets, cfga, drkg wtr. Hiking, fishing. 4 acres. GPS: 44.1820, -71.0348

GREENVILLE (22)

Bear Brook   FREE
Moosehead District State Forest Camp
27 mi NE of Greenville on the S side of Ripogenus Dam Rd. Free. Tent sites. Tbls, toilets, cfga, drkg wtr (should be boiled). Free fire permit required for fires in non-designated areas. Picnicking, fishing. GPS: 45.4502, -69.2123.

Big Squaw   FREE
Moosehead District State Forest Camp
5 mi N of Greenville on ME 15. Free. Tent/RV sites. Tbls, toilets, cfga, drkg wtr (should be boiled). Free fire permit required for fires in non-designated areas. Picnicking, fishing, boating.

Lily Bay State Park $10
8 mi N of Greenville on Great Northern Paper Co. Rd; on Moosehead Lake. $10 during 9/15-5/15 ($18 for non-residents); $14-24 rest of year. 93 sites. Tbls, toilets, cfga, drkg wtr, no showers, dump($5 non-campers), playground. Fishing, snowmobiling, boating (l). 924 acres. GPS: 45.569, -69.542.

Little Squaw Reserve   FREE
Bureau of Public Lands
Just W of Greenville & Greenville Junction off SR 15; follow gravel rd W into reserve. Free. All year. Primitive undesignated camping on 15,000 acres. Includes numerous remote ponds with excellent fishing & hiking opportunities. In winter, cross-country skiing & snowmobiling popular. GPS: 45.704986,-69.337507.

Little Wilson Stream   FREE
Moosehead District State Forest Camp
1 mi N of Big Wilson Stream Bridge at end of road. Free. Sites. Tbls, toilets, cfga, drkg wtr (should be boiled). Free fire permit required for fires in non-designated areas. Picnicking, fishing.

Old Duck   FREE
Pond Storehouse
Moosehead District State Forest Camp
6 mi N of Ripogenus Dam, on Nesowad-nehunk Rd. Free. Sites. Tbls, toilets, cfga, drkg wtr (should be boiled). Free fire permit required for fires in non-designated areas. Picnicking, fishing.

Ragged Dam   FREE
Moosehead District State Forest Camp
30 mi NE of Greenville; N of Ripogenus Dam Rd; Ragged Lake. Free. Sites. Tbls, toilets, cfga, drkg wtr (should be boiled). Free fire permit required for fires in non-designated areas. Picnicking, fishing. Dam GPS: 45.786709, -69.332829.

GRINDSTONE (23)
Wassataquoik Preserve   FREE
Bureau of Public Lands
From just S of Grindstone N along both sides of East Branch of Penobscot River & Wassataquoik Stream. Free. Primitive streamside sites, accessed by boat & gravel rds. No facilities. Fishing, hunting, boating, snowmobiling.

ILESBORO (24)
Warren Island State Park $10
In Penobscot Bay, just S off Ilesboro Ferry Landing. $10 during 9/15-5/15 ($18 for non-residents); $14-24 rest of year. 10 tent sites. Tbls, pit toilets, cfga, drkg wtr. Fishing, boating(d). GPS: 44.260445, -68.952255.

KOKADJO (25)
Nahmakanta Reserve   FREE
Bureau of Public Lands
About 5 mi E of Kokadjo on Second Roach Pond Rd; 10 mi NE on Penobscot Pond Rd to SW boundary of preserve. Access also available from E off Hwy 11 via Church Pond Rd, but visitors must pay day-use fee at KI Jo-Mary checkpoint (207-435-6213). Free. All year. Primitive undesignated sites, many with vehicle access along shores of ponds & at hiking trailheads; most for pickup campers or tenters, but Musquash Field accommodates small RVs. 43,000 acres (largest reserve in state's syatem). Tbls, cfga, pit toilets. Hiking, fishing, backpacking, boating.

LAKE PARLIN (26)
Lone Jack   FREE
Parlin Pond District
State Forest Camp
E side Chain of Ponds, 10 mi S of ME 15 on Scott Paper Company. Rd is very narrow, rough, poorly maintained. Sites. Tbls, toilets, cfga, drkg wtr (should be boiled). Free fire permit required for fires in non-designated areas. Picnicking, fishing. 45.337326, -70.669075.

LAMOINE BEACH (27)
Lamoine State Park $10
On SR 184 at Lamoine Beach. $10 during 9/15-5/15 ($18 for non-residents); $15-25 rest of year. 61 sites. Tbls, flush toilets, cfga, showers, drkg wtr, fishing pier. Boating(ld), fishing, cross-country skiing. 55 acres. GPS: 44.454, -69.299.

LIBERTY (28)
Lake St. George State Park $10
1.5 mi W of Liberty on SR 3. $10 during 9/15-5/15 ($18 for non-residents); $15-25 rest of year. 38 sites. Tbls, flush toilets, cfga, drkg wtr, dump($5 non-campers), showers. Swimming, boating(rl), fishing, volleyball, hiking trails, snowmobiling. 1,017-acre lake. GPS: 44.399, -69.34.

MANSET (29)
Seawall Campground $10
Acadia National Park
2.5 mi S of Manset on SR 102A. $10 with federal senior pass at 214 sites; others pay $20. 5/15-9/30; 14-day limit. 35-ft RV limit. Tbls, flush toilets, cfga, drkg wtr, dump, showers nearby($). Boating, fishing, hiking, nature programs. GPS: 44.241, -68.306

MASARDIS (30)
Cold Spring   FREE
Number Nine District State Forest Camp
1.5 mi W of ME 11, on Oxbow Rd. Free. Sites. Tbls, toilets, cfga, drkg wtr (should be boiled). Free fire permit required for fires in non-designated areas. Picnicking, fishing. GPS: 46.2615, -68.2450.

MILBRIDGE (31)
McClellan Town Park $10
S of Milbridge on Wyman Rd. $10. Open 6/1-9/15; 40-ft RV limit. Primitive camping. 11 sites (2 for RVs). Tbls, toilets, cfga, drkg wtr. Swimming, fishing. Fee unverifed in 2014. GPS: 44.485, -67.859

MOOSEHEAD (32)
Indian Pond   FREE
Seboomook District State Forest Camp
N shore of Indian Pond at end of MEC RR r/w 9 mi SW of ME 15 at W outlet. Free. Sites. Tbls, toilets, cfga, drkg wtr (should be boiled). Free fire permit required for fires in non-designated areas. Picnicking, fishing. GPS: 45.524402, -69.80841.

Seven Mile Hill   FREE
Seboomook District State Forest Camp
S side of Seboomook Dam Rd. Free. Tent sites. Tbls, toilets, cfga, drkg wtr (should be boiled). Free fire permit required for fires in non-designated areas. Picnicking, fishing.

NAPLES (33)
Sebago Lake State Park $10
On US 302 near Naples. $10 during 9/15-5/15 ($18 for non-residents); $15-25 rest of year. 250 sites. Tbls, flush toilets, cfga, drkg wtr, dump($5 non-campers), showers, beach. Swimming, fishing, boating(l), nature program, snowmobiling. 1,300 acres. GPS: 43.913, -70.56.

NORTHEAST CARRY (34)

Allagash Pond $8
North Maine Woods
From Golden Rd (N of Northeast Carry) drive about 15 mi
N on Ragmuff Rd; 2 mi W on unimproved rd toward Loon
Lake, then N on paved rd about 10 mi to Caucomgomoc
checkpoint; continue about 10 mi N & NE on paved primary
rd to St. Francis Lake, then 11 mi N past Wadleigh Pond. $8
($10 non-residents, seniors $4). Open 5/1 11/30; 14-day
limit. Primitive developed sites; 28-ft RV limit. Tbls, toilets,
cfga, no drkg wtr. Fishing, boating. Checkpoint open daily
6 a.m.-8 p.m. GPS: 46.422136, -69.671195.

Avery Brook State Forest Camp $8
From Golden Rd (N of Northeast Carry) drive about 15 mi
N on Ragmuff Rd; 2 mi W on unimproved rd toward Loon
Lake, then N on paved rd about 10 mi to Caucomgomoc
checkpoint; continue about 7 mi N & NE toward St. Francis
Lake. $8 (non-residents $10, seniors $4). Open 5/1-11/30;
14-day limit. Primitive undeveloped camping; 28-ft RV
limit. Limited facilities; cfga, no drkg wtr. Fishing, boating.
Checkpoint open daily 6 a.m.-8 p.m.

Baker Lake State Forest Camp $8
From Golden Rd (N of Northeast Carry) drive about 15 mi
N on Ragmuff Rd; 2 mi W on unimproved rd toward Loon
Lake, then N on paved rd about 10 mi to Caucomgomoc
checkpoint; continue about 20 mi N & E on primary rd &
International Paper Rd past St. Francis Lake to N shore of
Baker Lake. $8 (non-residents $10, seniors $4). Open 5/1-
11/30; 14-day limit. Primitive undeveloped camping; limited
facilities; cfga, no drkg wtr. 28-Ft RV limit. Fishing, boating.
Checkpoint open daily 6 a.m.-8 p.m. Lake GPS: 45.53, -69.41

Baker Lake North $8
North Maine Woods
From Golden Rd (N of Northeast Carry) drive about 15 mi N
on Ragmuff Rd; 2 mi W on unimproved rd toward Loon Lake,
then N on paved rd about 10 mi to Caucomgomoc checkpoint; continue about 20 mi N & E on primary rd & International Paper Rd past St. Francis Lake to N shore of Baker
Lake. $8 ($10 non-residents, seniors $4). Open 5/1-11/30;
14-day limit. Primitive developed sites; 28-ft RV limit. Tbls,
toilets, cfga, no drkg wtr. Fishing, boating. Checkpoint open
daily 6 a.m.-8 p.m. GPS: 46.1717, -69.5548.

Baker Lake South $8
North Maine Woods
From Golden Rd (N of Northeast Carry) drive about 15 mi
N on Ragmuff Rd; 2 mi W on unimproved rd toward Loon
Lake, then N on paved rd about 10 mi to Caucomgomoc
checkpoint; continue about 20 mi N & E on primary rd &
International Paper Rd past St. Francis Lake; turn S (left)
on access rd along E shore of Baker Lake for 3 mi. $8 ($10
non-residents, seniors $4). Open 5/1-11/30; 14-day limit.
Primitive developed sites; 28-ft RV limit. Tbls, toilets, cfga,

no drkg wtr. Fishing, boating. Checkpoint open daily 6
a.m.-8 p.m. GPS: 46.1543, -9.5328.

Caucomgomoc Lake $8
North Maine Woods
From Golden Rd (N of Northeast Carry) drive about 15 mi
N on Ragmuff Rd; 2 mi W on unimproved rd toward Loon
Lake, then N on paved rd about 10 mi to Caucomgomoc
checkpoint; E to shore of lake. $8 ($10 non-residents,
seniors $4). Open 5/1-11/30; 14 day limit. Primitive devel-
oped sites; 28-ft RV limit. Tbls, toilets, cfga, no drkg wtr.
Fishing, boating. Checkpoint open daily 6 a.m.-8 p.m. Lake
GPS: 46.205221, -69.598763.

Caucomgomoc Dam $8
North Maine Woods
From Golden Rd (N of Northeast Carry) drive about 15 mi
N on Ragmuff Rd; 2 mi W on unimproved rd toward Loon
Lake, then N on paved rd about 10 mi to Caucomgomoc
checkpoint; continue 4 mi N, then 9 mi E past turnoff to
Round Pond, turning right at 2nd rd; 1 mi SE to dam. $8
($10 non-residents, seniors $4). Open 5/1-11/30; 14-day
limit. Primitive developed sites; 28-ft RV limit. Tbls, toilets,
cfga, no drkg wtr. Fishing, boating. Checkpoint open daily
6 a.m.-8 p.m. GPS: 46.194759, -69.55867.

Caucomgomoc River State Forest Camp $8
From Golden Rd (N of Northeast Carry) drive about 15 mi
N on Ragmuff Rd; 2 mi W on unimproved rd toward Loon
Lake, then N on paved rd about 10 mi to Caucomgomoc
checkpoint; continue 4 mi N, then 9 mi E past turnoff to
Round Pond, turning right at 2nd rd; half mi SE toward
dam, but turn left on secondary rd to river. $8 (non-res-
idents $10, seniors $4). Open 5/1-11/30; 14-day limit.
Primitive undeveloped camping; 28-ft RV limit. Limited
facilities; cfga, no drkg wtr. Fishing, boating. Checkpoint
open daily 6 a.m.-8 p.m.

Crescent Pond $8
North Maine Woods
From Golden Rd (N of Northeast Carry) drive about 15 mi
N on Ragmuff Rd; 2 mi W on unimproved rd toward Loon
Lake, then N on paved rd about 10 mi to Caucomgomoc
checkpoint; continue about 10 mi N & NE on paved primary
rd to St. Francis Lake, then 11 mi N past Wadleigh Pond;
just S of Allagash Pond, take right fork about 8 mi to N
shore of Crescent Pond; hike (or boat) qtr mi S to E lakeshore. $8 ($10 non-residents, seniors $4). Open 5/1-11/30;
14-day limit. Primitive developed tent sites. Tbls, toilets,
cfga, no drkg wtr. Fishing, boating. Checkpoint open daily
6 a.m.-8 p.m. Pond GPS: 46.425717, -69.609499.

Desolation Pond $8
North Maine Woods
From Golden Rd (N of Northeast Carry) drive about 15 mi
N on Ragmuff Rd; 2 mi W on unimproved rd toward Loon
Lake, then N on paved rd about 10 mi to Caucomgomoc

checkpoint; continue about 10 mi N & E on primary rd to St. Francis Lake, then 5 mi W on International Paper Rd; turn right at first rd W of St. Francis Lake & proceed NE about 8 mi to Desolation Pond. $8 ($10 non-residents, seniors $4). Open 5/1-11/30; 14-day limit. Primitive developed sites; 28-ft RV limit. Tbls, toilets, cfga, no drkg wtr. Fishing, boating. Checkpoint open daily 6 a.m.-8 p.m. Pond GPS: 46.384918, -69.74387.

Knowles Brook State Forest Camp $8
From Golden Rd (N of Northeast Carry) drive about 15 mi N on Ragmuff Rd; 2 mi W on unimproved rd toward Loon Lake, then N on paved rd about 10 mi to Caucomgomoc checkpoint; continue about 10 mi N & NE on paved primary rd to St. Francis Lake, then 11 mi N past Wadleigh Pond; just S of Allagash Pond, take left fork about 8 mi to Knowles Brook bridge. $8 (non-residents $10, seniors $4). Open 5/1 11/30; 14-day limit. Primitive undeveloped sites; 28-ft RV limit. Limited facilities; cfga, no drkg wtr. Fishing. Checkpoint open daily 6 a.m.-8 p.m.

Middle Branch State Forest Camp $8
Follow directions to Wadleigh Pond Camp; continue N 3 mi, then take right fork at Allagash Stream about 3 mi to Middle Branch. $8 (non-residents $10, seniors $4). Open 5/1-11/30; 14-day limit. Primitive undeveloped camping; no facilities except cfga; no drkg wtr. 28-Ft RV limit. Fishing, boating. Checkpoint open daily 6 a.m.-8 p.m.

Narrow Pond State Forest Camp $8
Follow directions to Middle Branch Camp; continue E about 5 mi to S shore of Narrow Pond. $8 (non-residents $10, seniors $4). Open 5/1-11/30; 14-day limit. Primitive undeveloped camping; no facilities except cfga; no drkg wtr. 28-Ft RV limit. Fishing, boating. Checkpoint open daily 6 a.m.-8 p.m. Pond GPS: 46.374514, -69.572911.

Round Pond Camps $8
(Piscataqios County)
North Maine Woods
From Golden Rd (N of Northeast Carry) drive about 15 mi N on Ragmuff Rd; 2 mi W on unimproved rd toward Loon Lake, then N on paved rd about 10 mi to Caucomgomoc checkpoint; continue 4 mi N on International Paper Rd, then 6 mi E toward Round Pond; 1 mi N to N shore of lake. $8 ($10 non-residents, seniors $4). Open 5/1 11/30; 14-day limit. Primitive developed sites at 2 campgrounds; 28-ft RV limit. Tbls, toilets, cfga, no drkg wtr. Fishing, boating. Checkpoint open daily 6 a.m.-8 p.m. Pond GPS: 46.407002, -69.355306.

State Forest Camp $8
From Golden Rd (N of Northeast Carry) drive about 15 mi N on Ragmuff Rd; 2 mi W on unimproved rd toward Loon Lake, then N on paved rd about 10 mi to Caucomgomoc checkpoint; continue about 24 mi N & E on paved primary rd & International Paper Rd past St. Francis Lake & Baker Lake. $8 (non-residents $10, seniors $4). Open 5/1-11/30;

14-day limit. Primitive undeveloped camping; limited facilities; cfga, no drkg wtr. 28-Ft RV limit. Fishing, boating. Checkpoint open daily 6 a.m.-8 p.m.

Wadleigh Pond $8
North Maine Woods
From Golden Rd (N of Northeast Carry) drive about 15 mi N on Ragmuff Rd; 2 mi W on unimproved rd toward Loon Lake, then N on paved rd about 10 mi to Caucomgomoc checkpoint; continue about 10 mi N & NE on paved primary rd to St. Francis Lake, then 4 mi N to Wadleigh Pond; camp on N shore. $8 ($10 non-residents, seniors $4). Open 5/1-11/30; 14-day limit. Primitive developed sites; 28-ft RV limit. Tbls, toilets, cfga, no drkg wtr. Fishing, boating. Checkpoint open daily 6 a.m.-8 p.m. Pond GPS: 45.744772, -69.188814.

NORTH NEW PORTLAND (35)
Dead River Preserve   FREE
Bureau of Public Lands
About 30 mi NW of North New Portland on Long Falls Dam Rd. Park land begins just W of Long Falls area & extends westward on both sides of unimproved access rd toward Dead River secton of Flagstaff Lake. Vehicle-accessible at Big Eddy on the river; lakeshore sites; boat-access sites and hike-in areas. Free. All year. No facilities. Swimming, boating(l), fishing, snowmobiling. 4,771 acres include several miles of Flagstaff lakeshore.

OXBOW (36)
Bartlett Pond State Forest Camp $8
About 5 mi W of Oxbow on Aroostook River Rd to Oxbow checkpoint; connect to westbound Pinkham Rd; about 8 mi W on Pinkham, then right on first primary rd; continue N about 5 mi to Bartlett Mtn area; take right fork about 2 mi, then N (left) 1.5 mi to S shore of Bartlett Pond. $8 (non-residents $10, seniors $4). Open 5/1-11/30; 14-day limit. Primitive undeveloped camping; limited facilities (cfga, no wtr); 28-ft RV limit. Fishing, boating, hunting. Checkpoint open daily 6 a.m.-10 p.m. (5-9 Oct/Nov). Pond GPS: 46.555272, -68.871721.

Brown Brook State Forest Camp $8
From Mooseleuk Stream Camp, continue 7 mi W on Pinkham Rd. $8 (non-residents $10, seniors $4). Open 5/1-11/30; 14-day limit. Primitive undeveloped camping; limited facilities (cfga, no wtr); 28-ft RV limit. Fishing, boating, hunting. Checkpoint open daily 6 a.m.-10 p.m. (5-9 Oct/Nov).

Chandler Deadwater Camp $8
North Maine Woods
About 5 mi W of Oxbow on Aroostook River Rd to Oxbow checkpoint; connect to westbound Pinkham Rd; about 10 mi W on Pinkham to area of Chandler Deadwater near Malcolm Branch Brook bridge. $8 ($10 non-residents, seniors $4). Open 5/1 11/30; 14-day limit. Primitive devel-

oped sites; 28-ft RV limit. Tbls, toilets, cfga, no drkg wtr. Fishing, boating, hunting. Checkpoint open daily 6 a.m.-10 p.m. (5-9 Oct/Nov). GPS: 46.422881, -68.740704.

Chase Lake Camp $8
North Maine Woods
From Mooseleuk Stream Camp, follow Pinkham Rd just W of camp, then turn N (right) on paved primary rd, following it as it curves to the E past Mooseleuk Mtn for about 15 mi to NE shore of Chase Lake. $8 ($10 non-residents, seniors $4). Open 5/1 11/30; 14-day limit. Primitive developed sites; 28-ft RV limit. Tbls, toilets, cfga, no drkg wtr. Fishing, boating(l). Checkpoint open daily 6 a.m. 10 p.m. (5-9 Oct/Nov). Lake GPS: 46.89024, -68.909479.

Devils Elbow $8
North Maine Woods
About 5 mi W of Oxbow on Aroostook River Rd to Oxbow checkpoint; continue 17 mi W to area near Isthmus Brook bridge. $8 ($10 non-residents, seniors $4). Open 5/1-11/30; 14-day limit. Primitive developed sites; 28-ft RV limit. Tbls, toilets, cfga, no drkg wtr. Fishing, boating, hunting. Checkpoint open daily 6 a.m. 10 p.m. (5-9 Oct/Nov).

Grand Lake Seboeis $8
North Maine Woods
Follow directions to Devils Elbow camp, but about 2 mi before reaching there, turn SE (left) just after crossing Isthmus Brook bridge; follow secondary rd about 14 mi to W shore of lake. $8 ($10 non-residents, seniors $4). Open 5/1-11/30; 14-day limit. Primitive developed sites; 28-ft RV limit. Tbls, toilets, cfga, no drkg wtr. Fishing, boating(l), hunting. Checkpoint open daily 6 a.m.-10 p.m. (5-9 Oct/Nov).

Jack Mountain Camp $8
North Maine Woods
From Machias River state forest camp, continue W on primary rd about 2 mi; just E of Jack Mountain. $8 ($10 non-residents, seniors $4). Open 5/1-11/30; 14-day limit. Primitive developed sites; 28-ft RV limit. Tbls, toilets, cfga, no drkg wtr. Fishing, canoeing, hunting. Checkpoint open daily 6 a.m.-10 p.m. (5-9 Oct/Nov).

LaPonkeag Stream Camp $8
North Maine Woods
About 5 mi W of Oxbow on Aroostook River Rd to Oxbow checkpoint; continue 10 mi W to area of LaPonkeag River bridge. $8 ($10 non-residents, seniors $4). Open 5/1-11/30; 14-day limit. Primitive developed sites; 28-ft RV limit. Tbls, toilets, cfga, no drkg wtr. Fishing, boating, hunting. Checkpoint open daily 6 a.m. 10 p.m. (5-9 Oct/Nov).

LaPonkeag Stream State Forest Camp $8
About 5 mi W of Oxbow on Aroostook River Rd to Oxbow checkpoint; continue 10 mi W to area of LaPonkeag River bridge. $8 (non-residents $10, seniors $4). Open 5/1-11/30;

14-day limit. Primitive undeveloped camping; limited facilities (cfga, no wtr); 28-ft RV limit. Fishing, boating, hunting. Checkpoint open daily 6 a.m.-10 p.m. (5-9 Oct/Nov).

Little Mooseleuk Stream State Forest Camp $8
About 5 mi W of Oxbow on Aroostook River Rd to Oxbow checkpoint; connect to westbound Pinkham Rd; about 14 mi W on Pinkham to bridge over Mooseleuk Stream; just W of Mooseleuk Stream camp, turn S (left) on paved primary rd for about 3 mi, then continue S & W 3 mi to Little Mooseleuk Stream bridge. $8 (non-residents $10, seniors $4). Open 5/1-11/30; 14-day limit. Primitive undeveloped camping; limited facilities (cfga, no wtr); 28-ft RV limit. Fishing, boating, hunting. Checkpoint open daily 6 a.m.-10 p.m. (5-9 Oct/Nov).

Little Munsungan Lake State Forest Camp $8
From Mooseleuk Stream Camp, continue W on Pinkham Rd about 4 mi; after crossing Brown Brook bridge, turn on 3rd rd to left; proceed 3 mi to NE shore of lake. $8 (non-residents $10, seniors $4). Open 5/1-11/30; 14-day limit. Primitive undeveloped camping; limited facilities (cfga, no wtr); 28-ft RV limit. Fishing, boating, hunting. Checkpoint open daily 6 a.m.-10 p.m. (5-9 Oct/Nov).

Lower Hudson Pond State Forest Camp $8
From McPherson Brook camp, continue N about 5 mi on secondary access rd; take left fork NW about 3 mi to S shore of Lower Hudson Pond. $8 (non-residents $10, seniors $4). Open 5/1-11/30; 14-day limit. Primitive undeveloped camping; limited facilities (cfga, no wtr); 28-ft RV limit. Fishing, boating, hunting. Checkpoint open daily 6 a.m.-10 p.m. (5-9 Oct/Nov). Pond GPS: 46.559079, -69.035622.

Lower LaPomkeag Lake State Forest Camp $8
About 5 mi W of Oxbow on Aroostook River Rd to Oxbow checkpoint; continue about 2.5 mi, then turn S (left) on secondary access rd at Fourmile Brook; 5 mi S to W shore of lake. $8 (non-residents $10, seniors $4). Open 5/1-11/30; 14-day limit. Primitive undeveloped camping; limited facilities (cfga, no wtr); 28-ft RV limit. Fishing, boating, hunting. Checkpoint open daily 6 a.m.-10 p.m. (5-9 Oct/Nov). Lake GPS: 46.374212, -68.599792.

Lower Munsungan Stream $8
North Maine Woods
Follow directions to Devils Elbow camp; continue W about 5 mi, then take right fork for 2 mi to Munsungan Stream bridge (near Libby Pinnacle). $8 ($10 non-residents, seniors $4). Open 5/1-11/30; 14-day limit. Primitive developed sites; 28-ft RV limit. Tbls, toilets, cfga, no drkg wtr. Fishing, boating(l). Checkpoint open daily 6 a.m.-10 p.m. (5-9 Oct/Nov). Note: Access also from the E, about 5 mi W of Little Mooseleuk Stream Camp.

Machias River Camps $8
North Maine Woods
From South Branch Camp, continue N on primary rd about 4 mi to Machias River; 3 campgrounds near bridge. $8 ($10 non-residents, seniors $4). Open 5/1-11/30; 14-day limit. Primitive developed sites; 28-ft RV limit. Tbls, toilets, cfga, no drkg wtr. Fishing, boating(l). Checkpoint open daily 6 a.m.-10 p.m. (5-9 Oct/Nov). Note: Access also available from 6-Mile Checkpoint W of Ashland.

Machias River State Forest Camp $8
From South Branch Camp, continue N on primary rd about 4 mi to Michias River; just before bridge, turn W (left) on primary rd for about 1 mi. $8 (non-residents $10, seniors $4). Open 5/1-11/30; 14-day limit. Primitive undeveloped camping; limited facilities (cfga, no wtr); 28-ft RV limit. Fishing, boating, hunting. Checkpoint open daily 6 a.m.-10 p.m. (5-9 Oct/Nov).

McPherson Brook State Forest Camp $8
Follow directions to Mooseleuk Lake North Shore Camp; McPherson camp is just to the N. $8 (non-residents $10, seniors $4). Open 5/1-11/30; 14-day limit. Primitive undeveloped camping; limited facilities (cfga, no wtr); 28-ft RV limit. Fishing, boating, hunting. Checkpoint open daily 6 a.m.-10 p.m. (5-9 Oct/Nov).

Middle Brook State Forest Camp $8
Follow directions to Mooseleuk Stream Camp; just W of camp, turn N (right) on paved primary rd for 1 mi, then right on secondary access rd for 2 mi to jct of Middle Brook & Mooseleuk Stream. $8 (non-residents $10, seniors $4). Open 5/1-11/30; 14 day limit. Primitive undeveloped camping; limited facilities (cfga, no wtr); 28-ft RV limit. Fishing, boating, hunting. Checkpoint open daily 6 a.m.-10 p.m. (5-9 Oct/Nov).

Mooseleuk Lake North Shore $8
North Maine Woods
Follow directions to Smith Brook Camp; continue N on secondary access rd for about 5 mi; at split, take left fork about 4 mi to NW shore of lake. $8 ($10 non-residents, seniors $4). Open 5/1-11/30; 14-day limit. Primitive developed sites; 28-ft RV limit. Tbls, toilets, cfga, no drkg wtr. Fishing, boating(l). Checkpoint open daily 6 a.m.-10 p.m. (5-9 Oct/Nov). Lake GPS: 46.511406, -68.908454.

Mooseleuk Lake South Shore $8
North Maine Woods
Follow directions to Smith Brook Camp; continue N on secondary access rd for about 5 mi; at split, take right fork about 2 mi to S shore of lake. $8 ($10 non-residents, seniors $4). Open 5/1-11/30; 14-day limit. Primitive developed sites; 28-ft RV limit. Tbls, toilets, cfga, no drkg wtr. Fishing, boating(l). Checkpoint open daily 6 a.m.-10 p.m. (5-9 Oct/Nov).

Mooseleuk Stream $8
North Maine Woods
About 5 mi W of Oxbow on Aroostook River Rd to Oxbow checkpoint; connect to westbound Pinkham Rd; about 14 mi W on Pinkham to bridge over Mooseleuk Stream. $8 ($10 non-residents, seniors $4). Open 5/1-11/30; 14-day limit. Primitive developed sites; 28-ft RV limit. Tbls, toilets, cfga, no drkg wtr. Fishing, boating(l). Checkpoint open daily 6 a.m.-10 p.m. (5-9 Oct/Nov).

Ragged Pond $8
North Maine Woods
From Mooseleuk Stream Camp, follow Pinkham Rd just W of camp, then turn N (right) on paved primary rd, following it as it curves to the E past Mooseleuk Mtn for about 12 mi; 2 mi N on secondary access rd, then take left fork 2 mi and follow Ragged Pond access rd 1 mi S to camp. $8 ($10 non-residents, seniors $4). Open 5/1-11/30; 14-day limit. Primitive developed sites; 28-ft RV limit. Tbls, toilets, cfga, no drkg wtr. Fishing, boating(l). Checkpoint open daily 6 a.m. 10 p.m. (5-9 Oct/Nov).

Salmon Pond $8
North Maine Woods
5 mi W of Oxbow on Aroostook River Rd to Oxbow checkpoint; continue 5 mi W. $8 ($10 non-residents, seniors $4). Open 5/1-11/30; 14-day limit. Primitive developed sites; 28-ft RV limit. Tbls, toilets, cfga, no drkg wtr. Fishing, boating. Checkpoint open daily 6 a.m.-10 p.m. (5-9 Oct/Nov). Pond GPS: 47.027819, -68.328371.

Smith Brook $8
North Maine Woods
Follow directions to Middle Brook Camp; continue N on secondary rd for 3 mi to Smith brook bridge. $8 ($10 non-residents, seniors $4). Open 5/1-11/30; 14-day limit. Primitive developed sites; 28-ft RV limit. Tbls, toilets, cfga, no drkg wtr. Fishing, canoeing, hunting. Checkpoint open daily 6 a.m.-10 p.m. (5-9 Oct/Nov).

South Branch Camp $8
North Maine Woods
About 5 mi W of Oxbow on Aroostook River Rd to Oxbow checkpoint; connect to westbound Pinkham Rd; about 8 mi W on Pinkham, then right on first primary rd; 3 mi N to Chandler Lake, then continue 5 mi N on primary rd to South Branch bridge. $8 ($10 non-residents, seniors $4). Open 5/1-11/30; 14-day limit. Primitive developed sites; 28-ft RV limit. Tbls, toilets, cfga, no drkg wtr. Fishing, canoeing, hunting. Checkpoint open daily 6 a.m.-10 p.m. (5-9 Oct/Nov).

Trout Brook $8
North Maine Woods
About 4 mi E of Oxbow on Aroostook River Rd at bridge over Trout Brook. $8 ($10 non-residents, seniors $4). Open 5/1-11/30; 14-day limit. Primitive developed sites; 28-ft

RV limit. Tbls, toilets, cfga, no drkg wtr. Fishing, boating. Checkpoint open daily 6 a.m.-10 p.m. (5-9 Oct/Nov).

Upper Munsungan Stream $8
North Maine Woods
From Brown Brook Camp, continue W 1.5 mi on Pinkham Rd. $8 ($10 non-residents, seniors $4). Open 5/1 11/30; 14-day limit. Primitive developed sites; 28-ft RV limit. Tbls, toilets, cfga, no drkg wtr. Fishing, canoeing, hunting. Checkpoint open daily 6 a.m.-10 p.m. (5-9 Oct/Nov).

PORTAGE (37)
Carr Pond $8
North Maine Woods
From Gleason Brook Camp, continue W on primary rd 8 mi, then S on first primary rd, past Freeman Ridge & North Ridge to W shore of Carr Lake. $8 ($10 non-residents, seniors $4). Open 5/1-11/30; 14-day limit. Primitive developed sites; 28-ft RV limit. Tbls, toilets, cfga, no drkg wtr. Fishing, canoeing, boating(l), hunting. Checkpoint open daily 6 a.m.-10 p.m. (5-9 Oct/Nov). Pond GPS: 46.76533, -68.728287.

Fish River State Forest Camp $8
From Mosquito Brook Camp, continue NE 4 mi to Fish River; access also available by driving 2 mi W from SR 11 N of Portage. $8 (non-residents $10, seniors $4). Open 5/1-11/30; 14-day limit. Primitive undeveloped sites; 28-ft RV limit; limited facilities (cfga, no wtr). Fishing, canoeing, hunting. Checkpoint open daily 6 a.m.-10 p.m. (5-9 Oct/Nov).

Fish River Camp $8
North Maine Woods
From Gleason Brook Camp, continue W on primary rd 5 mi, then turn N (right) on secondary access rd for 1.5 mi; bear left at fork for 3 mi to Fish River just S of Fish River Lake's Round Pond. $8 ($10 non-residents, seniors $4). Open 5/1-11/30; 14-day limit. Primitive developed sites; 28-ft RV limit. Tbls, toilets, cfga, no drkg wtr. Fishing, canoeing, boating(l), hunting. Checkpoint open daily 6 a.m.-10 p.m. (5-9 Oct/Nov).

Fish River Lake Camp $8
North Maine Woods
From Smith Brook Camp, continue N 2 mi on access rd; on NW shore of Fish River Lake. $8 ($10 non-residents, seniors $4). Open 5/1-11/30; 14-day limit. Primitive developed sites; 28-ft RV limit. Tbls, toilets, cfga, no drkg wtr. Fishing, canoeing, boating(l), hunting. Checkpoint open daily 6 a.m.-10 p.m. (5-9 Oct/Nov). Lake GPS: 46.825891, -68.779544

Gleason Brook $8
North Maine Woods
5 mi W of Portage to Fish River Checkpoint, then 2 mi beyond to camp. $8 ($10 non-residents, seniors $4). Open 5/1-11/30; 14-day limit. Primitive developed sites; 28-ft RV limit. Tbls, toilets, cfga, no drkg wtr. Fishing, canoeing, hunting. Checkpoint open daily 6 a.m.-10 p.m. (5-9 Oct/Nov).

Mosquito Brook State Forest Camp $8
At Gleason Brook Camp, turn N on primary access rd for 4 mi; take right fork for half mi, then second right fork onto secondary access rd for 3 mi to camp near Mosquito Brook. $8 (non-residents $10, seniors $4). Open 5/1-11/30; 14-day limit. Primitive undeveloped sites; 28-ft RV limit; limited facilities (cfga, no wtr). Fishing, canoeing, hunting. Checkpoint open daily 6 a.m.-10 p.m. (5-9 Oct/Nov).

North Branch Camp $8
North Maine Woods
From Gleason Brook Camp, follow primary access rd about 15 mi W (about 3 mi W of turnoff for Fish River Lake); at North Branch Fox River. $8 ($10 non-residents, seniors $4). Open 5/1-11/30; 14-day limit. Primitive developed sites; 28-ft RV limit. Tbls, toilets, cfga, no drkg wtr. Fishing, canoeing, hunting. Checkpoint open daily 6 a.m.-10 p.m. (5-9 Oct/Nov).

Rocky Brook State Forest Camp $8
From just N of Round Pond Camp at Fish River Lake, 10 mi N on secondary access rd to Rocky Brook bridge. $8 (non-residents $10, seniors $4). Open 5/1-11/30; 14-day limit. Primitive undeveloped sites; 28-ft RV limit; limited facilities (cfga, no wtr). Fishing, canoeing, hunting. Checkpoint open daily 6 a.m.-10 p.m. (5-9 Oct/Nov).

Round Pond of Fish River Lake $8
State Forest Camp
Follow directions to North Maine Woods's Fish River Camp; continue NW qtr mi to Round Pond camp. $8 (non-residents $10, seniors $4). Open 5/1-11/30; 14-day limit. Primitive undeveloped sites; 28-ft RV limit; limited facilities (cfga, no wtr). Fishing, canoeing, hunting, boating(l). Checkpoint open daily 6 a.m.-10 p.m. (5-9 Oct/Nov). Pond GPS: 46.762157, -69.26556.

Smith Brook State Forest Camp $8
From Gleason Brook Camp, continue W on primary rd about 8 mi; bear right at fork for 5 mi; cross Fish River bridge & continue W on primary access rd 1.5 mi, then N along W shore of Fish River Lake; bear right at fork onto secondary rd; follow it to camp. $8 (non-residents $10, seniors $4). Primitive undeveloped sites; 28-ft RV limit; limited facilities (cfga, no wtr). Fishing, canoeing, hunting, boating. Checkpoint open daily 6 a.m.-10 p.m. (5-9 Oct/Nov).

POWNAL (38)
Bradbury Mountain State Park $10
Half mi N of Pownal on SR 9. $10 for residents during 9/15-5/15 ($18 non-residents); rest of year, $11 for residents, $19 non-residents. All year; 14-day limit. 41 sites. Tbls, pit toilets, cfga, drkg wtr, playground. Nature trails. GPS: 43.902, -70.177.

PRESQUE ISLE (39)
Aroostook State Park $10
6 mi S of Presque Isle off US 1. $10 for residents during 9/15-5/15 ($18 non-residents); rest of year, $12 residents, $20 non-residents. All year; 14-day limit. 30 sites. Tbls, pit toilets, cfga, drkg wtr, no showers. Boating(lr), fishing, swimming, skiing, hiking, canoeing(r). GPS: 46.61, -68.003.

RANGELEY (40)
Cold Spring FREE
Rangeley District State Forest Camp
7 mi N of Rangeley on W side of ME 16; S branch of Dead River. Free. Sites. Tbls, toilets, cfga, drkg wtr (should be boiled). Free fire permit required for fires in non-designated areas. Picnicking, fishing.

Rangeley Lake State Park $10
4 mi S of Rangeley on SR 4; 4 mi W on S. Shore Dr. $10 during 9/15-5/15 ($18 for non-residents); $15-25 rest of year. 50 sites. Tbls, flush toilets, cfga, drkg wtr, showers, dump ($5 non-campers). Swimming, boating(ld), fishing, skiing, snowmobiling. GPS: 44.939, -70.72.

RIPOGENUS DAM (41)
Cliff Lake Campground $8
North Maine Woods
Follow directions to Pillsbury Pond; 2 mi N of Pillsbury Pond camp, take left "Y" & continue N & W for 10 mi to SE shore of Cliff Lake. $8 ($10 non-residents, seniors $4). Open 5/1-11/30; 14-day limit. Primitive developed sites; 28-ft RV limit. Tbls, toilets, cfga, no drkg wtr. Fishing, boating, hunting. Checkpoint open daily 6 a.m.-10 p.m. (5-9 Oct/Nov). Lake GPS: 46.393185, -69.24889.

Coffeelos Pond $8
North Maine Woods
2 mi E of Ripogenus Dam on Golden Rd; 13 mi N on Telos Rd to Telos checkpoint; 10 mi N to Chamberlain bridge, then about 3 mi S & E on unimproved secondary to S shore of Coffeelos Pond. $8 ($10 non-residents, seniors $4). Open 5/1-11/30; 14-day limit. Primitive developed sites; 28-ft RV limit. Tbls, toilets, cfga, no drkg wtr. Fishing, boating, hunting. Checkpoint open daily 6 a.m. 10 p.m. (5-9 Oct/Nov). Pond GPS: 46.163009, -69.142359.

Haymock Lake $8
North Maine Woods
2 mi E of Ripogenus Dam on Golden Rd; 13 mi N on Telos Rd to Telos checkpoint; 10 mi N to Chamberlain bridge; 5 mi NE on Telos Rd; about 10 mi after sharp curve to left, take right "Y" 2 mi to camp; on W shore of Haymock Lake. $8 ($10 non-residents, seniors $4). Open 5/1-11/30; 14-day limit. Primitive developed sites; 28-ft RV limit. Tbls, toilets, cfga, no drkg wtr. Fishing, boating(l), hunting. Checkpoint open daily 6 a.m.-10 p.m. (5-9 Oct/Nov). Lake GPS: 46.305245, -69.187686.

Indian Pond $8
North Maine Woods
2 mi E of Ripogenus Dam on Golden Rd; 13 mi N on Telos Rd to Telos checkpoint; 10 mi N to Chamberlain bridge; 5 mi NE on Telos Rd; about 4 mi after sharp curve to left, take second unimproved secondary rd E (left) about 5 mi (past Little Indian Pond) to E shore of Indian Pond Lake. $8 ($10 non-residents, seniors $4). Open 5/1-11/30; 14-day limit. Primitive developed sites; 28-ft RV limit. Tbls, toilets, cfga, no drkg wtr. Fishing, boating(l), hunting. Checkpoint open daily 6 a.m.-10 p.m. (5-9 Oct/Nov). Pond GPS: 45.524402, -69.80841.

Kellog Brook $8
North Maine Woods
2 mi E of Ripogenus Dam on Golden Rd; 13 mi N on Telos Rd to Telos checkpoint; 10 mi N to Chamberlain bridge, then 1 mi W on Telos Rd. $8 ($10 non-residents, seniors $4). Open 5/1-11/30; 14-day limit. Primitive developed sites; 28-ft RV limit. Tbls, toilets, cfga, no drkg wtr. Fishing, canoeing, hunting. Checkpoint open daily 6 a.m.-10 p.m. (5-9 Oct/Nov).

Leadbetter Pond State Forest Camp $8
Follow directions to Cliff Lake camp, but instead of turning off to Cliff Lake, take right "Y" & follow paved rd about 7 mi to Leadbetter Pond. $8 (non-residents $10, seniors $4). Open 5/1-11/30; 14-day limit. Primitive undeveloped camping; 28-ft RV limit. Limited facilities; cfga, no drkg wtr. Fishing, boating, hunting. Checkpoint open daily 6 a.m.-10 p.m. (5-9 Oct/Nov). Pond GPS: 46.237624, -69.259412.

Little Pillsbury Pond $8
North Maine Woods
Follow directions to Haymock Lake camp; proceed N for 2 mi, then turn right (E) on secondary unimproved rd for about 4 mi. $8 ($10 non-residents, seniors $4). Open 5/1-11/30; 14-day limit. Primitive developed sites; 28-ft RV limit. Tbls, toilets, cfga, no drkg wtr. Fishing, boating(l), hunting. Checkpoint open daily 6 a.m.-10 p.m. (5-9 Oct/Nov). Pond GPS: 46.327997, -69.152728.

Middle Elbow Pond State Forest Camp $8
Follow directions to Peaked Mountain Pond camp; continue N about 2 mi to S shore of Middle Elbow Pond. $8 (non-residents $10, seniors $4). Open 5/1-11/30; 14-day limit. Primitive undeveloped camp; limited facilities; cfga, no drkg wtr; 28-ft RV limit. Fishing, hunting, boating(l). Checkpoint open daily 6 a.m.-10 p.m. (5-9 Oct/Nov). Pond GPS: 46.527265, -69.073105.

Peaked Mountain Pond $8
North Maine Woods
Follow directions to Spider Lake, but about 1.5 mi before Spider Lake turnoff, turn right (N) on unimproved second-

ary rd for about 12 mi. $8 ($10 non-residents, seniors $4). Open 5/1-11/30; 14-day limit. Primitive developed sites; 28-ft RV limit. Tbls, toilets, cfga, no drkg wtr. Fishing, boating, hunting. Checkpoint open daily 6 a.m.-10 p.m. (5-9 Oct/Nov). Pond GPS: 46.507883, -69.088411.

Pillsbury Pond $8
North Maine Woods
Follow directions to Haymock Lake camp; proceed N about 5 mi. $8 ($10 non-residents, seniors $4). Open 5/1-11/30; 14-day limit. Primitive developed sites; 28-ft RV limit. Tbls, toilets, cfga, no drkg wtr. Fishing, boating, hunting. Checkpoint open daily 6 a.m.-10 p.m. (5-9 Oct/Nov). Pond GPS: 46.333852, -69.183536.

Pleasant Lake State Forest Camp $8
Follow directions to Spider Lake Camp, but instead of turning left to Spider Lake, continue half mi to Pleasant Lake camp on right. $8 (non-residents $10, seniors $4). Open 5/1-11/30; 14-day limit. Primitive undeveloped camp; limited facilities; cfga, no drkg wtr; 28-ft RV limit. Fishing, hunting, boating(l). Checkpoint open daily 6 a.m.-10 p.m. (5-9 Oct/Nov). Lake GPS: 46.473827, -69.178293.

Snake Pond State Forest Camp $8
2 mi E of Ripogenus Dam on Golden Rd; 13 mi N on Telos Rd to Telos checkpoint; 10 mi N to Chamberlain bridge; 5 mi NE on Telos Rd; after sharp curve to left, take unimproved secondary rd N about 5 mi to Snake Pond. $8 (non-residents $10, seniors $4). Open 5/1-11/30; 14-day limit. 2 primitive undeveloped camps; 28-ft RV limit. Limited facilities; cfga, no drkg wtr. Fishing, boating, hunting. Checkpoint open daily 6 a.m.-10 p.m. (5-9 Oct/Nov). Pond GPS: 46.251663, -69.122844.

Soper Brook State Forest Camp $8
Follow directions to Haymock Lake camp, but take left "Y" instead of right one; proceed about 12 miles to bridge over Soper Brook. $8 (non-residents $10, seniors $4). Open 5/1 11/30; 14-day limit. Primitive undeveloped camp; limited facilities; cfga, no drkg wtr; 28-ft RV limit. Fishing, hunting. Checkpoint open daily 6 a.m. 10 p.m. (5-9 Oct/Nov).

Spider Lake Camp $8
North Maine Woods
Follow directions to Leadbett Pond camp; continue about 4 mi to "T"; turn left for 2 mi, then left onto Spiker Lake access rd. $8 ($10 non-residents, seniors $4). Open 5/1-11/30; 14-day limit. Primitive developed sites; 28-ft RV limit. Tbls, toilets, cfga, no drkg wtr. Fishing, boating(l), hunting. Checkpoint open daily 6 a.m.-10 p.m. (5-9 Oct/Nov). Lake GPS: 46.449987, -69.211327.

Umbazooksus Stream $8
North Maine Woods
2 mi E of Ripogenus Dam on Golden Rd; 13 mi N on Telos Rd to Telos checkpoint; 10 mi N to Chamberlain bridge,

then 7 mi W on Telos Rd to Umbazooksus Stream bay of Chesuncook Lake. Campground on E & W shores of bay. $8 ($10 non-residents, seniors $4). Open 5/1-11/30; 14-day limit. Primitive developed sites; 28-ft RV limit. Tbls, toilets, cfga, no drkg wtr. Fishing, boating, hunting. Checkpoint open daily 6 a.m.-10 p.m. (5-9 Oct/Nov). Dam GPS: 45.5254, -69.1341.

Upper Elbow Pond State Forest Camp $8
Follow directions to Middle Elbow Pond; turn NW (left) from Middle Elbow camp for about 2 mi. $8 (non-residents $10, seniors $4). Open 5/1-11/30; 14-day limit. Primitive undeveloped camp; limited facilities; cfga, no drkg wtr; 28-ft RV limit. Fishing, hunting. Checkpoint open daily 6 a.m.-10 p.m. (5-9 Oct/Nov). Pond GPS: 46.532963, -69.086497.

ROCKWOOD (42)

Moosehead Lake Reserve   FREE
Bureau of Public Lands
Several access routes exist. For shoreline camping & hiking along NE shore of Moosehead Lake at North Bay, launch boat or canoe E from Rockwood. Or travel by road westward from down of Kakadjo. Or reach Sugar Island by boat or canoe either from Rockwood to the N or Lily Bay State Park from the E. Free. All yaer. Primitive, undesignated shoreline sites along North Bay shoreline; 3 more defined camps along N shore of Sugar Island. Reserve also includes Farm island. Boating, fishing, waterskiing, hiking.

ST. JUSTE DE BRETENIERES (QUEBEC, CAN) (43)

St. John River Camps $8
North Maine Woods
E of St. Juste de Bretenieres in Quebec for 5 mi, across border into U.S.; from St. Juste Checkpoint on Boise Cascade Rd, 10 mi E; just before river bridge, turn S for 1 mi on secondary rd. Two developed campgrounds on N shore of river. $8 ($10 non-residents, seniors $4). Open 5/1-11/30; 14-day limit. Primitive developed sites; 28-ft RV limit. Tbls, toilets, cfga, no drkg wtr. Fishing, boating, hunting. Checkpoint open 6 a.m.-5 p.m. weekdays. Written permission to enter Maine required from U.S. Customs at Daaquam or Jackman.

St. John River South Shore $8
State Forest Camp
Follow directions to St. John River Camps, but cross river bridge & continue E 1.5 mi; turn W (right) on secondary rd to S shore of river. $8 (non-residents $10, seniors $4). Open 5/1-11/30; 14-day limit. Primitive undeveloped camp; limited facilities; cfga, no drkg wtr; 28-ft RV limit. Fishing, hunting, canoeing. Checkpoint open 6 a.m.-5 p.m. weekdays. Written permission to enter Maine required from U.S. Customs at Daaquam or Jackman.

Southwest Branch State Forest Camp $8
E of St. Juste de Bretenieres in Quebec for 5 mi, across border into U.S.; from St. Juste Checkpoint on Boise Cascade Rd for 1 mi; S on first secondary access rd past checkpoint to Southwest Branch of St. John River. $8 (non-residents $10, seniors $4). Open 5/1-11/30; 14-day limit. Primitive undeveloped camp; limited facilities; cfga, no drkg wtr; 28-ft RV limit. Fishing, hunting, canoeing. Checkpoint open 6 a.m.-5 p.m. weekdays. Written permission to enter Maine required from U.S. Customs at Daaquam or Jackman.

SHIN POND (44)
Camp Colby   FREE
East Branch District State Forest Camp
At MFS camp, 5 mi N of Grand Lake Rd on Scraggly Lake Rd. Free. Sites. Tbls, toilets, cfga, drkg wtr (should be boiled). Free permit required for fires in non-designated areas. Picnicking, fishing.

Sawtelle Brook   FREE
East Branch District State Forest Camp
1.5 mi N of Grand Lake Rd on Scraggly Lake Rd. Sites. Free. Tbls, toilets, cfga, drkg wtr (should be boiled). Free permit required for fires in non-designated areas. Picnicking, fishing.

Scraggly Lake   FREE
East Branch District State Forest Camp
Half mi above outlet. Sites. Free. Tbls, toilets, cfga, drkg wtr (should be boiled). Free permit required for fires in non-designated areas. Picnicking, fishing, boating(l). Lake GPS: 46.237416, -68.756291.

Scraggly Lake Reserve   FREE
Bureau of Public Lands
About 20 mi N of Shin Pond on SR 159 extension & American Thread Rd. Free. All year. 12 primitive sites, most for self-contained RVs pm S shore; 4 boat-in tent sites; 1 hike-in site on W end of lake; 1 drive-to site on E shore of Green Pond. Tbls, cfga, nearby toilets, no drkg wtr. Also hike to Ireland Pond for open primitive tent camping. Boating(l), fishing, hiking, hunting, snowmobiling.

Sebqeis Stream   FREE
East Branch District State Forest Camp
E shore of Sebqeis Stream, 6 mi W of Shin Pond via the Grand Lake Rd. Free. Sites. Tbls, toilets, cfga, drkg wtr (should be boiled). Free permit required for fires in non-designated areas. Picnicking, fishing.

STRATTON (45)
Chain of Ponds Preserve   FREE
Bureau of Public Lands
Starting about 18 mi N of Stratton on SR 27; connected small lakes, beginning with Lower Pond, include Bag, Long, Natanis, and Round Ponds, all on W side of rd. Free. All yaer. Open shoreline camping; no facilities. Fishing, swimming, boating(l), hiking. GPS: 45.2043, 70.4050.

TOPSFIELD (46)
Clifford Lake   FREE
St. Croix District State Forest Camp
E shore of E arm of lake; W side of gravel rd from Princeton to Wesley; near Topsfield. Free. Sites. Tbls, toilets, cfga, drkg wtr (should be boiled). Free permit required for fires in non-designated areas. Picnicking, boating(l), fishing, swimming (beach).

Middle Oxhead Lake   FREE
St. Croix District State Forest Camp
Near Topsfield. Free. Sites. Tbls, toilets, cfga, drkg wtr (should be boiled). Free permit required for fires in non-designated areas. Picnicking, fishing, swimming, boating(l).

St. Croix River   FREE
St. Croix District State Forest Camp
At W shore of Loon Bay; near Topsfield. Free. Sites. Tbls, toilets, cfga, drkg wtr (should be boiled). Free permit required for fires in non-designated areas. Picnicking, fishing.

WELD (47)
Mount Blue State Park $10
8 mi from Weld. $10 during 9/15-5/15 ($18 for non-residents); $15-25 rest of year. 136 sites. Tbls, flush toilets, cfga, drkg wtr, dump($5 non-campers), showers. Boating(lr), nature program, fishing, snowmobiling, swimming, hiking, biking & bridle trails, canoeing(r). 5,021 acres. GPS: 44.681, -70.448.

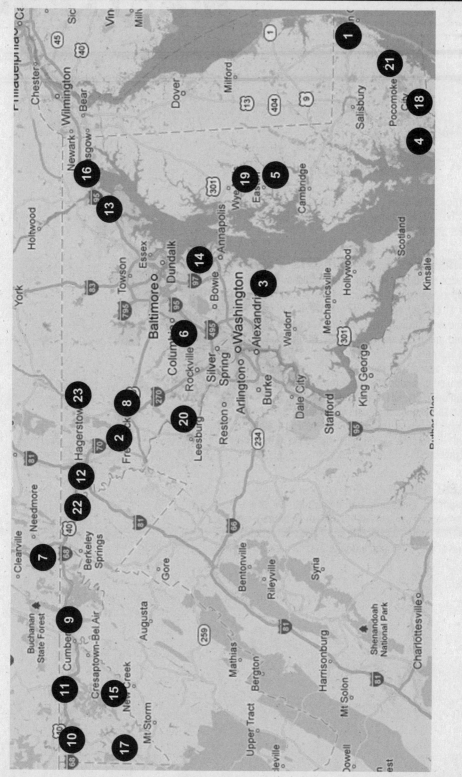

MARYLAND

CAPITAL: Annapolis
NICKNAME: Free State
STATEHOOD: 1788 – 7th State
FLOWER: Black-Eyed Susan
TREE: White Oak
BIRD: Baltimore Oriole

WWW.VISITMARYLAND.ORG

Office of Tourism Development, 401 East Pratt St, 14th Floor, Baltimore, MD 21202. 866-639-3526 or 866-MDWELCOME.

STATE PARKS AND FORESTS

Overnight camping fees at all state parks generally range from $16.49 for sites without hookups to $27.49 for electric sites. However, as part of a unique reciprocity agreement, residents of Maryland and Louisiana who are 62 or older can camp at half price during Sunday through Thursday nights after acquiring a free Maryland "Golden Age" pass. Similarily, senior Maryland residents can camp at half price at Louisiana's state parks.

Three state forest still offer camping for $10 per night. Maryland Department of Natural Resources, 580 Taylor Ave., Annapolis, MD 21401. 877-620-8367.

REST AREAS

Overnight stops are not permitted. RV sanitary stations are available at I-70 (South Mountain) Information Center, westbound on I-70 at milemarker 39, and at I-95 Information Center at milemarker 37.

BERLIN (1)

Bayside Campground $10
Assateague Island National Seashore
8 mi SE of US 113 on SR 376 and SR 611. $10 with federal senior pass during 4/15-10/15; others pay $20. $8 with senior pass rest of year; all others pay $16. All year; 7-day limit during 5/1-9/30. About 100 sites; 36-ft RV limit. Tbls, chemical toilets, cfga, drkg wtr, cold showers, dump. Nature program, hiking, boating, fishing, swimming, birdwatching, crabbing, ORV activities. Entry fee charged.

Oceanside Campground $10
Assateague Island National Seashore
8 mi SE of US 113 on SR 376 and SR 611. $10 with federal senior pass during 4/15-10/15; others pay $20. $8 with senior pass rest of year; others pay $16. All year; 7-day limit during 5/1-9/30. About 50 sites; 36-ft RV limit. Tbls, chemical toilets, cfga, drkg wtr, cold showers, dump. Fishing, swimming, boating(l), nature programs, crabbing, birdwatching. Entry fee charged.

BOONSBORO (2)

Greenbrier State Park $10.75
From Boonsboro, NE on SR 34 (Shephardstown Pk), becoming St. Paul St., becoming Boonsboro Mtn Rd; left on US 40 (National Pike) for 0.2 mi. $10.75 Sun-Thurs for MD & LA seniors at 125 non-elec sites; others pay $21.49. 40 elec sites, $27.49 ($13.75 Sun-Thurs for MD & LA seniors). 4/1-10/30; 14-day limit. Tbls, flush toilets, cfga, drkg wtr, showers, store, playground. Boating(r), fishing, mountain biking, hunting. GPS: 39.550855, -77.612734

BRANDYWINE (3)

Cedarville State Forest $9.25
SE of Brandywine toward Westwood on SR 381; W on Cedarville Rd, through Cedarville to Bee Oak Rd (park access rd) on the right. $9.25 Sun-Thurs for MD & LA seniors at non-elec sites; others pay $18.49. Elec sites $24.49 ($12.25 Sun-Thurs for MD & LA seniors). 4/1-10/30; 14-day limit; 2-night minimum stay MD-LD. Tbls, flush toilets, cfga, drkg wtr, showers. Hiking, horseback riding, fishing, hunting. GPS: 38.660019, -76.835733

CRISFIELD (4)

Janes Island State Park $10.74
From jct with SR 413 N of Crisfield, 1.5 mi E on Plantation Rd to park entrance (Alfred Lawson Dr); turn right. $10.74 Sun-Thurs for MD & LA seniors at 51 non-elec sites; others pay $21.49. 49 elec sites $27.49 ($13.74 for MA & LA seniors Sun-Thurs). 4/1-11/27; 14-day limit. Tbls, flush toilets, cfga, drkg wtr, showers, coin laundry, beaches, fish cleaning station. Fishing, swimming, boating(lr), crabbing, canoeing(r). GPS N 38.00490,75.50620

DENTON (5)

Martinek State Park $9.25
2 mi E of Denton off SR 404 on Deep Shore Rd at Choptank River & Watts Creek. $9.25 Sun-Thurs for MD & LA seniors at 33 non-elec sites; others pay $18.49; $24.49 at 30 elec sites ($12.25 for MD & LA seniors Sun-Thurs). 4/1-11/30; 14-day limit. Tbls, flush toilets, cfga, drkg wtr, showers, dump, playground, nature center. Fishing, boating(l), hiking trails. GPS: 38.865234, -75.83667

ELLICOTT CITY (6)

Hollofield Campground $9.25
Patapsco Valley State Park
From I-695 exit 15 (E of Ellicott City), 2 mi W on US 40 (Baltimore National Pike) to park entrance (RVs taller than 11 ft must use this entrance). $9.25 Sun-Thurs for MD & LA seniors at non-elec sites; others pay $18.49. Elec sites $24.49 ($12.25 for MD & LA seniors Sun-Thurs). 4/1-10/30; 14-day limit. 73 sites. Tbls, flush toilets, cfga, drkg wtr. Swimming, hiking trails, fishing. GPS: 39.2954, -76.7888

FARMINGTON, PENNSYLVANIA (7)

Forbes State Forest FREE
SW of Farmington, Pennsylvania, on SR 381. Primitive camping with free permit throughout forest except at Mt. Davis Natural Area; vehicle camping not allowed at Quebec Run Wild Area. Picnicking, hiking, fishing, hunting, snowmobiling. Six areas are designated for camping: two in forest section N of I-70; one just off SR 653 near Laurel Ridge SP; one E of Hwy 281 close to Mt. Davis, and two just N of Maryland state line S of US 40. Some are suitable for small RVs.

FREDERICK (8)

Gambrill State Park $9.25
In Frederick, W on SR 144 (E. Patrick St, becoming Baltimore National Pike); right on Gambrill Park Rd. $9.25 Sun-Thurs for MD & LA seniors at non-elec sites; others pay $18.49. Elec sites $24.49 ($12.25 Thurs-Sun for MD & LA seniors). 4/1-10/23; 14-day limit. 34 sites. Tbls, flush toilets, cfga, drkg wtr, dump, showers, playground. Fishing, hiking trails, nature center. GPS: 39.471461,-77.494206

FLINTSTONE (9)

Green Ridge State Forest $10
8 mi E of Flintstone off I-68 exit 64. $10. All year; 14-day limit. 100 primitive sites. Tbls, toilets, cfga, drkg wtr. Hiking & mountain biking trails, horseback riding, boating(l), fishing, hunting, shooting range. 46,000 acres. GPS: 39.65222, -78.47534179

Rocky Gap State Park $10.75
0.3 mi N of Flintstone on Murleys Branch Rd; 2nd left onto Flintstone Dr NE for 0.3. 4.6 mi W on I-68; exit 50 to Pleasant Valley Rd; E for 0.6 mi to park. $10.75 Sun-Thurs for MD & LA seniors at 248 non-elec sites; others pay $21.49. $7.49 at 30 elec sites ($13.75 for MD & LA seniors Sun-Thurs). 4/29-12/11; 14-day limit. Tbls, flush toilets, cfga, drkg wtr, showers, coin laundry, nature center, beach,

store dump, game room. Interpretive programs, nature hikes, crafts, campfire programs, hunting, boating(lr), fishing, hiking trails. GPS: 39.695936, -78.64961

FRIENDSVILLE (10)

Mill Run Recreation Area $6.50
Corps of Engineers
Youghiogheny River Lake
3.7 mi N of Friendsville off MD 53, on Mill Run Rd. $6.50 with federal senior pass during 5/1-9/8; others pay $13. Free for self-contained RVs rest of year, but no amenities. 30 sites without hookups; 8 sites for self-contained RVs during free period. 14-day limit. Tbls, toilets, drkg wtr, dump, playground, beach. Boating, swimming, fishing. GPS: 39.717285, -79.385742

GRANTSVILLE (11)

Elk Neck Camping Area $10
Savage River State Forest
5 mi S of US 40 on New Germany Rd, then E 1 mi on Westernport Rd. $10. All year; 14-day limit. 52 low-density roadside sites. Cfga, no wtr or toilets. Hiking trails. Hiking, fishing, hunting, cross-country skiing, boating, canoeing. Forest GPS: 39.68278, -79.20722

New Germany State Park $9.25
E of Grantsville on US 40 (National Pike); right on New Germany Rd for about 5 mi; right on Headquarters Lane to park. $9.25 Sun-Thurs for MD & LA seniors at 39 non-elec sites; others pay $18.49. 4/15-10/10; 14-day limit. Tbls, flush toilets, showers, cfga, drkg wtr. Boating(r), fishing, swimming beach, nature center, multi-use trails. GPS: 39.628928, -79.132854

Poplar Lick Camping Area $10
Savage River State Forest
6 mi S of US 40 on New Germany Rd, then 1.5 mi E on Poplar Lick Rd. $10. All year; 14-day limit. Low-density sites. Cfga, no wtr or toilets. Hiking trails. Hiking, fishing, hunting, cross-country skiing, boating, canoeing.

HAGERSTOWN (12)

Fort Frederick State Park $11.75
18 mi W of Hagerstown on I-70 to exit 12; S on SE on SR 56 to park; at Potomac River. $11.75 for 29 primitive sites (MD & LA seniors pay $5.88). Tbls, portable toilets, cfga, drkg wtr, store, playground, visitor center, playground. Boating(l), fishing, canoeing, hiking trail, interpretive programs. GPS: 39.613523, -78.006239

HAVRE DE GRACE (13)

Susquehanna State Park $10.75
3 mi NW of Havre de Grace off Hwy 155. $10.88 Sun-Thurs for MD & LA seniors at 63 non-elec sites; others pay $21.49. Six elec sites $27.49 ($13.75 Sun-Thurs for MD & LA seniors). 4/1-10/30; 14-day limit; 2-day minimum stay MD-LD. Tbls, flush toilets, cfga, drkg wtr, showers, play-

ground. Hiking trails, boating(l - $), canoeing, mountain bike & bridle trails, archery range, historical interpretation. Museum. GPS: 39.65833, -76.14861

LEXINGTON PARK (14)

Point Lookout State Park $10.75
About 20 mi S of Lexington Park on SR 235 to jct with SR 5; 10 mi S on SR 5. $10.75 Sun-Thurs for MD & LA seniors at 112 non-elec sites; others pay $21.49. 31 elec sites $33.49, full hookups $38.49 ($16.75 and $19.25 for seniors Sun-Thurs). 4/1-10/30; 14-day limit. Off-season RV camping available, but no restrooms. Tbls, flush toilets, cfga, drkg wtr, showers, dump, pet trail, playground. Museum, store, nature center, lighthouse. Boating(lr), fishing, campfire programs, hiking trails, canoeing, swimming. GPS: 38.050121, -76.322131

LUKE (15)

Big Run State Park $10
11 mi NW of Luke, 14 mi S of US 40 on Savage River Rd; near Savage River Dam. $10 ($5 Sun-Thurs for MD & LA seniors). All year; 14-day limit. 29 sites. Tbls, pit toilets, cfga, drkg wtr, no showers. Nature trails, fishing, boating(l), biking trails. GPS: 39.544678, -79.137939

NORTH EAST (16)

Elk Neck State Park $10.75
S of North East on SR 272; bear right at "Y" to park; on peninsula of Chesapeake Bay. $10.75 Sun-Thurs for MD & LA seniors at non-elec sites; others pay $21.49. Elec sites $27.49, full hookups $36.49 (MD & LA seniors pay $13.75 & $18.25 Sun-Thurs). 2/25-11/27; 14-day limit. 250 sites. Tbls, flush toilets, cfga, drkg wtr, showers, snack bar, store, playgrounds, nature center, beach. Historic lighthouse. Canoeing, kayaking, swimming, boating(l), crabbing, fishing, hunting. GPS: 39.493652, -75.974609

OAKLAND (17)

Potomac-Garrett State Forest $10
3.5 mi SE on Hwy 560, approx 3 mi E on Bethlehem Rd, E and N to forest hdqtrs. $10. All year; 14-day limit. 38 primitive sites; also primitive undeveloped sites along forest rds, $5. Tbls, toilets, cfga. Picnicking, fishing.

Swallow Falls State Park $10.75
NW of Oakland on W. Liberty Rd, passing Herrington Manor State Park & becoming Herrington Manor Rd; at "Y" intersection, veer left on Cranesville Rd, which runs through the park. The right leg of the "Y" becomes Swallow Falls Rd, which links to Maple Glade Rd, running the width of the park. $10.75 Sun-Thurs for MD & LA seniors at 62 non-elec sites; others pay $21.59. Three full-hookup sites $32.49 ($16.25 Sun-Thurs for MD & LA seniors). 4/15-12/15; 14-day limit. 2-night minimum stay on weekends. Tbls, flush toilets, cfga, drkg wtr, showers. Hiking trails. Waterfall. GPS: 39.49585, -79.435059

POCOMOKE CITY (18)

Milbun Landing Camp $9.25
Pocomoke River State Park
7 mi NE of Pocomoke City on SR 364; E on Nassawango Rd. $9.25 Sun-Thurs for MD & LA seniors at non-elec sites; others pay $18.49. Elec sites $24.49 ($12.25 for MD & LA seniors Sun-Thurs). 4/1-12/10; 14-day limit. Tbls, flush toilets, cfga, drkg wtr, showers, dump, playground, pool at Shad Landing ($3). Fishing, hiking. GPS: 38.1445, -75.4259

QUEEN ANNE (19)

Tuckahoe State Park $10.75
From jct with SR 404 just N of Queen Anne, N on SR 480, then immediate left on Eveland Rd, following signs to park. $10.75 Sun-Thurs for MD & LA seniors at 18 non-elec sites; others pay $21.49. 33 elec sites $27.49 ($13.75 for MD & LA seniors Sun-Thurs). 4/1-10/30; 14-day limit. Tbls, flush toilets, cfga, drkg wtr, showers, dump. Arboretum. Fishing, boating(l), canoeing(r). Multi-use trails. GPS: 39.00306, -75.91361

SHARPSBURG (20)

McCoy's Ferry   FREE
Chesapeake & Ohio Towpath
At mile 110.4. Access point, I-70 to Clear Springs exit; 5 mi SE on MD 68; W on MD 56; 3 mi on 4 Lock Rd. (From Big Spring, take MD 56 to McCoy Ferry Rd). Free. Memorial Day-Labor Day; 14-day limit. 14 primitive tent & RV sites. No drkg wtr. Tbls, toilets, cfga. Picnicking, fishing, hiking, boating(l). 2 acres.

Fifteen Mile Creek   FREE
Chesapeake & Ohio Towpath
At mile 140.9; access point, 2.5 mi W of Hancock on US 40; 10 mi S on Woodmont Rd. Free. Memorial Day-Labor Day; 14-day limit. 10 tent & RV sites. Drive-in area. Tbls, toilets, cfga, drkg wtr (except in winter). Picnicking, fishing, hiking, canoeing.

Spring Gap   FREE
Chesapeake & Ohio Towpath
At mile 173.3; access point, 11 mi E of Cumberland on MD 51. Free. 14-day limit. 17 primitive tent & RV sites. Tbls, toilets, cfga, no drkg wtr. Picnicking, fishing, hiking, boating(l).

SNOW HILL (21)

Shad Landing Campground $10.75
Pocomoke River State Park
3.5 mi S of Snow Hill on US 113; no on access rd. $10.75 Sun-Thurs for MD & LA seniors at non-elec sites; others pay $21.49. Elec sites $27.49 ($13.75 for MA & LA seniors Sun-Thurs). All year; 14-day limit. 175 sites. Tbls, flush toilets, cfga, drkg wtr, showers, coin laundry, dump. Boating(lr), fishing, playground, store, pool($3), nearby nature center. GPS: 38.1327, -75.4413

SWANTON (22)

Deep Creek Lake State Park $10.75
W of Swanton on Swanton Rd;first right onto Bittinger Rd/ SR 495 (if you reach Fox Hollow Rd, you've gone 0.25 mi too far); left on Glendale Rd (0.3 mi past Hunt Valley Rd); right on Toothpick Rd; continue right again on Toothpick; veer right on State Park Rd for 9.9 mi; park on right just past Brant Rd. $10.75 Sun-Thurs at 86 non-elec sites for MD & LA seniors; others pay $21.49. 26 elec sites $27.49 ($13.75 Sun-Thurs for MD & LA seniors). 4/15-12/15; 14-day limit. Tbls, flush toilets, cfga, drkg wtr, showers, dump. Boating(l), fishing, interpretive programs, hiking, hunting. GPS: 39.516464, -79.304221

THURMONT (23)

Manor Area Campground $10.75
Cunningham Falls State Park
3 mi S of Thurmont off US 15. $10.75 Sun-Thurs for MD & LA seniors at 15 non-elec sites; others pay $21.49. 8 elec sites $27.49 ($13.75 for MD & LA seniors). 4/1-10/30; 14-day limit; Tbls, flush toilets, cfga, drkg wtr, showers. Tbls, flush toilets, cfga, drkg wtr, showers, Swimming, hiking trails, fishing, canoeing, boating(l), hunting, interpretive programs. GPS: 39.586, -77.436

William Houck Campground $10.75
Cunningham Falls State Park
3 mi W of Thurmont on SR 77; just S of Catoctin Mountain NP. $10.75 Sun-Thurs for MD & LA seniors at 74 non-elec sites; others pay $21.49. Elec sites $27.49 ($13.75 for MD & LA seniors). MD-10/30; 14-day limit. Tbls, flush toilets, cfga, drkg wtr, showers, Swimming, hiking trails, fishing, canoeing, boating(l), hunting, interpretive programs. 78-ft waterfall. GPS: 39.625772, -77.463634

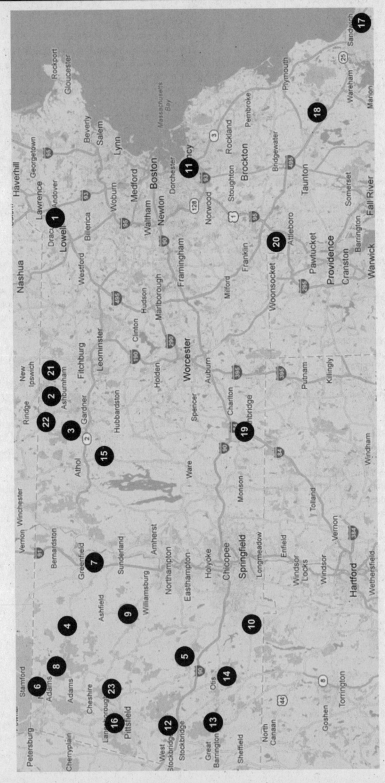

MASSACHUSETTS

WWW.MASSVACATION.COM

Massachusetts Office of Travel and Tourism, 10 Park Plaza, Suite 4510, Boston, MA 02116; 800-227-MASS or 617-973-8500. E-mail: Vacationinfo@state.ma.us

REST AREAS
Overnight stops are not permitted.

STATE PARKS AND FORESTS
Primitive camping fees, with pit toilets, are $6 for Massachusetts residents, $8 for non-residents. "Limited service campgrounds" are $10 for state residents, $8 for non-residents. Non-coastal campgrounds have fees of $12 for residents, $14 non-residents. Higher rates are charged at the state's four heavily used coastal campgrounds -- Horseneck Beach State Reservation, Nickerson State Park, Salisbury Beach State Reservation and Scusset Beach State Reservation. At campgrounds with utilities, campers pay $2 for water hookups, $3 for electricity, $2 for sewer. Daily vehicle entry fees are charged. No free backcountry camping is permitted at state forests. Dump station use by non-campers is now a whopping $15! Pets on leashes are permitted. Department of Conservation and Recreation, 251 Causeway St., Suite 900, Boston, MA 02114. 617-626-1250. E-mail mass.parks@state.ma.us.

CAPITAL: Boston
NICKNAME: Bay State
STATEHOOD: 1788 – 6th State
FLOWER: Mayflower
TREE: American Elm
BIRD: Chickadee

ANDOVER (1)

Harold Parker State Forest $12
From jct with SR 125 NE of Andover, about 8 mi SE on SR 114; right on Jenkins Rd to campground. $12 for state residents; $14 non-residents. MD-LD; 14-day limit. 89 sites; 40-ft RV limit. Tbls, flush toilets, cfga, drkg wtr, showers, dump, no hookups. Canoeing, fishing, hiking, swimming, horseback riding, mountain biking, hunting. 3,000 acres. GPS: 42.625244, -71.074951

ASHBY (2)

Willard Brook State Forest $8
From jct with SR 31 at Ashby, 0.5 mi E on SR 119. $8 for state residents; $10 non-residents. MD-LD; 14-day limit. 18 sites (folding trailers, pickup campers, tents. Tbls, flush toilets, cfga, drkg wtr, no showers, no hookups. Swimming, hunting, hiking, horseback riding, fishing, interpretive program, mountain biking. 2,597 acres. GPS: 42.666648, -71.774414

BALDWINVILLE (3)

Otter River State Forest $12
1 mi N of Baldwinville on US 202 (New Winchendon Rd). $12 for state residents; $14 non-residents. 5/55-10/15; 14-day limit. 75 sites; 20-ft RV limit. Tbls, flush toilets, cfga, drkg wtr, dump, showers, no hookups. Swimming, hiking, fishing, hunting, interpretive program, mountain biking. 2-acre pond GPS: 42.632779, -72.10376

CHARLEMONT (4)

Mohawk Trail State Forest $12
On SR 2 at W end of Charlemont. $12 for state residents; $14 non-residents. About 5/1-10/15; 14-day limit. 47 sites. Tbls, flush toilets, cfga, drkg wtr, showers, pavilion. Swimming, hunting, fishing, hiking, canoeing, interpretive program. Non-campers pay $5 day use 5/1-10/15. GPS: 42.641602, -72.941406

CHESTER (5)

Chester-Blandford State Forest FREE
About 4 mi E of Chester on US 20, following signs. Free. All year; 14-day limit. 20 primitive sites; 35-ft RV limit. Tbls, pit toilets, cfga, drkg wtr, no showers, no hookups. Hunting, fishing, hiking, horseback riding. 60-ft Sanderson Brook Falls. GPS: 42.254268, -72.933909

CLARKSBURG (6)

Clarksburg State Park $12
3 mi N of Clarksburg on SR 8. $12 for state residents; $14 non-residents. MD-LD; 14-day limit. 45 sites (30-ft RV limit). Tbls, flush toilets, cfga, drkg wtr, showers, no hookups. Hiking (3-mi loop trail), fishing, no swimming, canoeing, boating. 368 acres. Non-campers pay $5 day use fee. GPS: 42.740723, -73.081787.

ERVING (7)

Erving State Forest $12
From SR 2 in Erving, left at fire station onto Church St (becoming North St), then right for 1.5 mi on Swamp Rd, following signs. $12 for state residents; $14 non-residents. MD-LD; 14-day limit. 29 sites (16-ft RV limit). Tbls, flush toilets, cfga, drkg wtr, showers, no hookups, beaches. Swimming, boating(l), hunting, fishing, horseback riding, hiking, canoeing, walking trails, interpretive program, mountain biking. GPS: 42.613281, -72.399414

FLORIDA (8)

Savoy Mountain State Forest $12
From SR 2 in Florida, S on Central Shaft Rd & follow signs 3.7 mi past day use area parking. $12 for state residents; $14 non-residents. MD-10/15; 14-day limit. 45 sites (40-ft RV limit). Tbls, flush toilets, cfga, drkg wtr, showers, no hookups. Boating(l), fishing, hiking, hunting, swimming, biking, horseback riding. Non-campers pay $5 day use fee. GPS: 42.600098, -73.024658

GOSHEN (9)

DAR State Forest $12
From SR 9 just NW of Goshen, 0.7 mi N on SR 112. $12 for state residents; $14 non-residents. All year; 14-day limit. 51 sites (30-ft RV limit). Tbls, flush & pit toilets, showers (except off-season), cfga, drkg wtr, no hookups, beach. Swimming, boating(l), fishing, hiking trails, canoeing, mountain biking, bridle trails. 1,770 acres. Non-campers pay $5 day use fee MD-9/15. GPS: 42.460205, -72.792725

GRANVILLE (10)

Granville State Forest $12
About 2 mi W of Granville on SR 57; 2 mi S on unpaved W. Hartland Rd. $12 for state residents; non-residents $14. 5/22-LD; 14 day limit. 22 sites (35-ft RV limit). Tbls, flush toilets, cfga, drkg wtr, showers, no hookups. Swimming, hunting, fishing, hiking trails, bridle trails, mountain biking. 2,426 acres bordering Connecticut's 9,00-acre Tunxis State Forest. GPS: 42.053467, -72.968994

HINGHAM (BOSTON) (11)

Wompatuck State Park $12
7 mi N of Rt 3 on Rt 228; Free St. to Union St. $12 base for state residents; non-residents $14. About 5/15-10/15; 14-day limit. 262 sites (40-ft RV limit). Tbls, flush toilets, cfga, drkg wtr, showers, dump, 20-amp elec hookups($3), visitor center. Boating(l), hunting, fishing, hiking, paved biking trails, horseback riding. GPS: 42.218994, -70.866943

LEE (12)

October Mountain State Forest $12
From US 30 in Lee, 1 mi E on Center St (becoming Woodland Rd), then follow signs 1 mi to campground. $12 for state residents; non-residents $14. About 5/15-10/15;

14-day limit. 47 sites (50-ft RV limit). Tbls, flush toilets, cfga, drkg wtr, showers, dump. Hunting, hiking, boating, fishing, canoeing, mountain biking, ORV activities. 16,500 acres. GPS: 42.350098, -73.174561

MIDDLEBORO (20)

Massasoit State Park $12
From I-495 exit 5 W of Middleboro, S on SR 18 to flashing light, then right onto Taunton St (becoming Middleboro Ave) for about 2.5 mi to entrance. $12 base for state residents; non-residents $14 base. 4/15-10/10; 14-day limit. 120 sites (30-ft RV limit). Tbls, flush toilets, showers, cfga, drkg wtr, dump, 90 elec hookups ($3 surcharge), 24 wtr hookups ($2). Swimming, hiking, boating(l), horseback riding, biking, canoeing, hunting, interpretive program, mountain biking. GPS: 41.884521, -70.99585

MONTEREY (13)

Beartown State Forest $8
From Monterey, follow signs about 0.5 mi E on SR 23 (Blue Hill Rd) to forest. $8 for state residents; non-residents $10. MD-LD; 14-day limit. Reduced services & no wtr rest of year. 12 sites; 25-ft RV limit. Tbls, pit toilets, cfga, drkg wtr, no hookups. Fishing, hiking, hunting, horseback riding, boating(l), canoeing, mountain biking, swimming. 35-acre pond. GPS: 42.233398, -73.274658

OTIS (14)

Tolland State Forest $12
About 1 mi S of Otis on SR 8; left on W. Shore Rd & follow signs; at 1,065-acre Otis Reservoir. $12 for state residents; non-residents $14. MD-LD; 14-day limit. 92 sites (35-ft RV limit). Tbls, flush toilets, showers, cfga, drkg wtr, dump, no hookups. Swimming, boating(l), hiking, fishing, canoeing, hunting, interpretive program, ORV activities. GPS: 42.134277, -73.029541

PETERSHAM (15)

Federated Women's Club State Forest $6
W about 2 mi on SR 122 from Petersham, following signs about 1.7 mi S on State Forest Rd. $6 for state residents; non-residents $8. 6/16-9/4, 14-day limit; 9/10-10/8, Saturdays only. 83 wilderness sites on 984 acres. Tbls, pit toilets, cfga, drkg wtr, cold showers. Biking, equestrian trails, fishing, hunting, cross-country skiing, snowmobiling. Register at Erving State Forest before camping.

PITTSFIELD (16)

Pittsfield State Forest $8
4 mi NW of Pittsfield off US 20. $8 for state residents; non-residents $10. 5/5-10/9; 14-day limit. 31 sites; 35-ft RV limit. Tbls, flush & pit toilets, cfga, drkg wtr, no showers, no hookups. Swimming, hunting, hiking, boating, horseback riding, biking, canoeing, fishing. GPS: 42.480957, -73.301514

SANDWICH (17)

Shawme-Crowell State Forest $12
Half mi W of Sandwich on SR 6A; 1 mi S off SR 130, following signs. $12 for state residents; non-residents $14. All year; 14-day limit. 285 sites (30-ft RV limit); 25 self-contained RV sites off-season weekends (Thurs-Sat). Tbls, flush toilets, cfga, drkg wtr, dump, showers. Hiking, hunting, interpretive program, hunting, swimming. Historic site. GPS: 41.763184, -70.511719

SOUTH CARVER (18)

Myles Standish State Forest $12
3 mi E of South Carver on county rds. $12 for state residents; non-residents $14. 5/5-10/9; 14-day limit; 44 sites for self-contained RVs during off-season. 475 sites (30-ft RV limit); 5 campgrounds. Tbls, flush toilets, cfga, drkg wtr, showers, dump. Swimming, hiking trails, boating, horseback riding trails. GPS: 41.856689

STURBRIDGE (19)

Wells State Park $12
2 mi E on Rt 20 from Turnpike exit 9; 1 mi N on Rt 49; left on Walker Pond Rd. $12 for state residents; non-residents $14. About 5/5-10/10; 14-day limit. 60 sites (35-ft RV limit). Tbls, flush toilets, cfga, drkg wtr, dump, showers. Swimming, hunting, fishing, hiking, horseback riding, boating(l), canoeing, interpretive programs, mountain biking. 16 ponds. GPS: 42.145508, -72.068604

WEST TOWNSEND (21)

Pearl Hill State Park $12
From SR 119 in West Townsend, 1.5 mi S on New Fitchburg Rd. $12 for state residents; non-residents $14. 5/5-10/9; 14-day limit. 51 sites (35-ft RV limit); 2 pull-through. Tbls, flush toilets, cfga, drkg wtr, showers, no hookups. Hiking, swimming, fishing, horseback riding, interpretive program, mountain biking. 1,000 acres. GPS: 42.656982, -71.760498

WINCHENDON (22)

Lake Dennison $12
State Recreation Area
2 mi S of Winchendon on US 202; at 85-acre lake. $12 for state residents; non-residents $14. MD-LD; 14-day limit. 151 sites; 38-ft RV limit. Tbls, flush toilets, cfga, drkg wtr, showers, dump. Swimming, boating(l), hunting, fishing, hiking. GPS: 42.647949, -72.083496

WINDSOR (23)

Windsor State Forest   CLOSED
On county rd, off SR 9. $8 for state residents; non-residents $10. MD-LD; 14-day limit. 23 primitive sites. Tbls, pit toilets, cfga, drkg wtr, no showers, no hookups. Swimming, hunting, hiking. 1,743 acres. Note: Closed for 2014; check current status before arrival. GPS: 42.555908, -73.010254

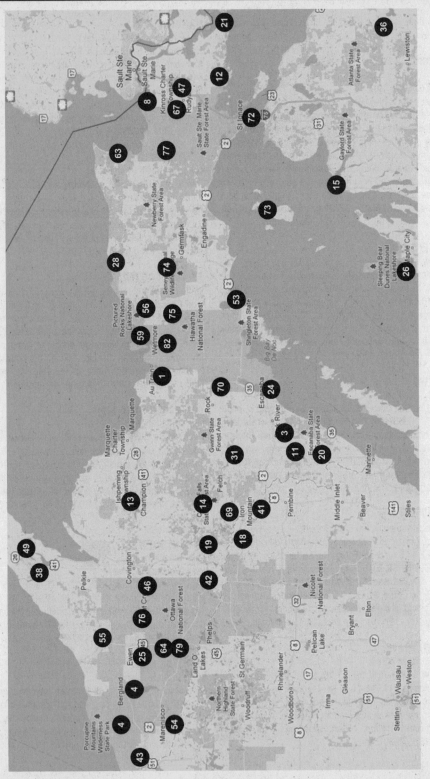

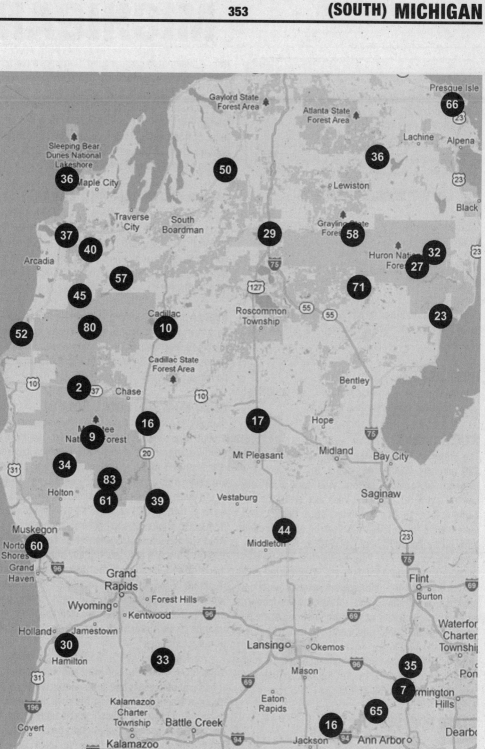

MICHIGAN

CAPITAL: Lansing
NICKNAME: Wolverine State
STATEHOOD: 1837 – 26th State
FLOWER: Apple Blossom
TREE: White Pine
BIRD: Robin

WWW.MICHIGAN.ORG

Toll-free number for travel information: 1-800-5432-YES.

Michigan Travel Bureau, PO Box 30226, Lansing, MI 48909.

Dept. of Natural Resources, Parks & Recreation Division, P.O. Box 30257, Lansing, MI 48909; 517-373-9900.

REST AREAS
Overnight stops are not permitted. No state rest areas have RV sanitary dump stations.

STATE PARKS
The entry fee is $8 ($6 for Michigan residents) or $29 annually ($24 for residents, $6 for Michigan seniors). Motorhome drivers who tow a vehicle pay an extra $6. Camping fees are $10-$33 per night with a 15-day maximum stay. Rustic sites (no showers, flush toilets or electric) are $12; sites with utility hookups begin at $16 at most parks. Horse camps are $17. Pets on leashes are permitted. Camping from April 1-Nov 1 is permitted only in designated sites. Modern sites have electrical hookups, flush toilets and showers; semi-modern lack either electricity or modern restrooms; rustic sites have pit toilets and centrally located water but no hookups. During the off-season, services are reduced. For further information contact: Dept of Natural Resources, Parks and Recreation Div, P.O. Box 30257, Lansing, MI 48909.

STATE FORESTS
Rustic camping at state forest campgrounds is now $13, so those sites have been deleted from this edition. Dispersed camping is allowed anywhere within the state forests at spots at least one mile from a designated campground. Campers must post a camp registration card at their sites; the cards are available from any DNR service center. The six Michigan state forests represent 3.9 million acres of land, 7,000 miles of canoeable streams and 13,000 miles of trout water. For information on state forests contact: Dept. of Natural Resources, Forest Mgt Div, P.O. Box 30425, Lansing, MI 48909-7952.

OTHER STATE CAMPING AREAS
State Game Areas. Camping from April 1-Nov 1 is permitted only in designated areas. From Nov 2-March 31 camping is permitted in all areas. For further information contact: Dept. of Natural Resources, Forest Mgt Div, P.O. Box 30028, Lansing, MI 48909.

Boat Launches. Camping is permitted in designated areas at many access sites, mostly in northern Michigan. For further information contact: Dept. of Natural Resources, Forest Mgt Div, P.O. Box 30028, Lansing, MI 48909.

HIAWATHA NATIONAL FOREST
Camping is permitted throughout the national forest, except where restrictions are posted. Most developed campgrounds provide full services between mid-May and mid-September, and a few of those are open free or at reduced rates during the rest of the year, although services are not provided and water is turned off. Permits are not required except at the Manistique "Inland Lakes" camping areas, for which permits costing $10 for one to three days (or $20 for 4-7 days) are issued. Daily charges are now made at all tent sites at the Grand Island National Recreaton Area. All single-track trails and roadless areas are closed to vehicles unless otherwise posted. Only dead wood may be used for campfires. Free permits to cut firewood for home use are available at ranger stations.

Au Train River. A 10-mi canoe route on the Au Train River winds through wild and scenic country. It has smooth rapids and turns and is portage-free. There is free camping along the river. Put in at the Forest Service boat launch and campsite on the southeast side of Au Train Lake, or at the bridge on FR 2276. The river flows to Lake Superior. For further information contact: Forest Supervisor, Hiawatha National Forest, 2727 N Lincoln Rd, Escanaba, MI 49829. 906/786-4062.

OTTAWA NATIONAL FOREST

Sylvania Wilderness Area. Thirty-four named, pristine lakes and virgin timber distinguish this 18,000-acre area, which is part of the National Wilderness Preservation System. Access is by foot or canoe only; motorized vehicles are prohibited. Primitive camping at 84 designated sites is by permit only; registration is at the visitor center at US 2 and 45 in Watersmeet or at the area's entrance on FR 535; a $20 annual entry fee is charged (or $5 daily). Daily camping permits, formerly free, are now $10 during 5/15-9/30. So for purposes of listings in this book, we are assuming anyone camping in the Sylvania Wilderness Area has already purchased a $20 annual permit, and therefore his per-day cost of camping is $10. Camping is free 10/1-5/14, but registration at the main entrance station or other trailheads is required. No more than 5 people may use 1 campsite. Because each camping area has only 1-3 sites, they are quickly filled, so reservations are suggested (they are another $10); Sylvania Visitor Center, 906-358-4724. When arriving to pick up passes, campers must view an orientation video a the Sylvania entrance station. Most campgrounds open by May 15 and close after Labor Day, although some remain open until December. The recreation area includes a day-use building, hot showers, boat launches, picnic areas, beach, parking areas and other facilities. Special fishing regulations apply to Sylvania lakes. Ottawa National Forest, 2100 E. Cloverland Dr., Ironwood, MI 49938; 906 932-1330 (800-562-1201 in Upper Peninsula).

HURON-MANISTEE NATIONAL FORESTS

These two forests are now enrolled in the national Recreation Fee Demonstration Program and have set aside areas that were formerly free as places where fees are collected for camping and watercraft. Within those areas, vehicle passes are required. They may be annual passes (available for $30), weekly passes ($15) or daily passes ($5). In addition, formerly free dispersed camping sites along the Au Sable River below the 4001 Bridge landing now cost $5 per night. For purposes of this book, we are assuming that anyone camping in that area has already purchased a $30 annual permit, and therefore his per-day cost for camping is just $5.

Huron National Forest. Includes 431,800 acres in northeastern part of the Lower Peninsula. It has 12 developed family campgrounds and four group campgrounds; most are on lakes or streams; all include picnic tables, tent spaces, campfire grill areas, water and toilets. Some sites are open off season, when full services are not provided; during those periods, reduced fees may be charged, or free camping allowed. Free dispersed camping is available outside developed recreation sites, areas designated as part of the fee demonstration program or areas specifically closed to camping; no facilities are provided.

Manistee National Forest. It consists of 531,700 acres in the northwestern section of the Lower Peninsula. It has 18 developed campgrounds, all with tables, campfire grill areas, drinking water and toilets. A few campgrounds are now operated by concessionaires. Fees listed her are for the summer recreation period when full services are provided; during the rest of the year, sites may be open at reduced charges and reduced services. Dispersed camping is available throughout the forest at no charge for up to 16 days.

Huron and Manistee National Forests, 1755 S Mitchell St, Cadillac, MI 49601. 616/775-2421; 800/821-6263.

PICTURED ROCKS NATIONAL LAKESHORE

The many old logging roads and established trails provide a wealth of hiking possibilities. The 42.8-mile Lakeshore Trail is a component of the North Country National Scenic Trail. Camping is permitted at designated backcountry campgrounds. A backcountry camping permit is available at visitor centers. No pets allowed in the backcountry. Camping fees are charged at the lakeshore's three drive-in campgrounds near Grand Marais and Melstrand and for backcountry camping permits (which were formerly free). To reach the area from the lower peninsula take I-75 to US 2, travel north to MI 77 and take MI 28 west to the lakeshore. For further information and a map contact: Pictured Rocks National Lakeshore, P.O. Box 40, Munising, MI 49862. 906/387-3700.

Corps of Engineers, Detroit District, P.O. Box 1027, Detroit, MI 48231.

AU TRAIN (1N)
Au Train Lake $8
Hiawatha National Forest
4.5 mi S of Au Train and 10 mi W of Munising off FR 2276; 1.5 mi N on FR 2596. $8 with federal senior pass; others pay $16. 5/15-10/1; 14-day limit. 37 sites (typically 35 ft). Tbls, toilets, cfga, drkg wtr. Swimming beach, boating(l), fishing, picnicking, waterskiing. 6 acres. Au Train Song Trail within campground; tape recording & field guide can be rented from local merchants to enhance the illustrated interpretive signs. GPS: 46.39167, -86.83806

BALDWIN (2S)
Bowman Bridge Campground $8
Manistee National Forest
Pere Marquette National Scenic River
5 mi W of Baldwin on Carrs Rd; along Pere Marquette River. $8 with federal senior pass; others pay $16. 5/9-10/15; 14-day limit. 20 RV sites (plus group sites), typically 40 ft. Tbls, toilets, cfga, drkg wtr. Swimming, boating, fishing, canoeing(r), hiking. Access to North Country Trail. Non-campers pay $6 day use fee. GPS: 43.889188, -85.944588

Claybanks Campground $5
Manistee National Forest
Pere Marquette National Scenic River
At Baldwin, qtr mi W on 52nd St; 0.5 mi S on Astor Rd; S on Claybanks Rd. $5 daily or $15 weekly, $40 annually. Non-campers pay $5 for day use fee. All year; 14-day limit. 9 sites; 25-ft RV limit. Tbls, toilets, cfga, no drkg wtr. Boating(l), fishing, canoing. GPS: 43.870053, 85.883319

Highbank Lake Campground $8
Manistee National Forest
S of Baldwin on M-37; W at Lilly on 15-Mile Rd; at 20-acre lake. $8 with federal senior pass; others pay $16. 5/15-9/22; 14-day limit. 9 sites 20-ft RV limit. Tbls, toilets, cfga, drkg wtr. Hiking, fishing. Near North Country Scenic Trail. GPS: 43.769991, -85.890555

Ivan's Campground & Cabins $12
1 mi S of Baldwin on M-37; at Pere Marquette River. $12 base. Summers. Base fee is minimum charge for $10 per person rate. Tbls, flush toilets, showers($), cfga, drkg wtr, elec($4), playground. Volleyball, horseshoes, canoeing(r). GPS: 42.14813, -84.518695

Old Grade Campground $8
Manistee National Forest
Little Manistee River
11 mi N of Baldwin on M-37, then right on FR 5190. $8 with federal senior pass; others pay $16. About 4/15-9/15; 14-day limit. 20 rustic sites (40-ft RV limit). Tbls, toilets, cfga, drkg wtr. Fishing good; boating & canoeing poor. Non-campers pay $6 day use fee. GPS: 44.060791, -85.85122

Sulak Campground FREE
Manistee National Forest
Pere Marquette National Scenic River
8.5 mi W of Baldwin on 52nd St; 2.5 mi N on South Branch Rd. Free. All year; 14-day limit (not maintained off-season). 12 sites; 25-ft RV limit. Tbls, toilets, cfga, no drkg wtr. Canoeing, fishing (qtr mi walk to river). GPS: 43.923778, -86-103254

Timber Creek Campground $10
Manistee National Forest
10 mi NW of Baldwin on US 10 (2 mi E of Branch village), then N on FR 5198; at Tank Creek. $10. All year; 14-day limit. Non-campers pay $5 day use fee, $15 weekly. 9 sites (50-ft RV limit). Tbls, toilets, cfga, drkg wtr. Hiking (trailhead for North Country Trail), berry picking. GPS: 43.9476, -85.996

Walkup Lake Campground $10
Manistee National Forest
10 mi S of Baldwin on SR 37; 1 mi W on 14 Mile Rd; 0.5 mi S on Bingham Rd; 2.5 mi W on Cleveland Dr. $10. 5/1-10/30; 14-day limit (not maintained off-season; no amenities). Tbls, toilets, cfga, drkg wtr. 12 sites; 35-ft RV limit. Fishing, boating(l). GPS; 43.73464, -85.905172

BANAT (3N)
Campsite #3 $10
WE Energies
Wilderness Shores Recreation Area
5 mi W of Banat; .7 mi N to campground (on Menominee River). $10. 5/1-9/30; 15-day limit. 4 primitive sites. Tbls, toilets, cfga, no drkg wtr. Picnicking, boating(l), fishing.

Campsite #4 $10
WE Energies
Wilderness Shores Recreation Area
5 mi W of Banat; 1.9 mi N to campground (on Menominee River). $10. 5/1-9/30; 15-day limit. 4 primitive sites. Tbls, toilets, cfga, no drkg wtr. Picnicking, boating(l), fishing.

BERGLAND (4N)
Bergland Township Park $10
In Bergland, S of M-64 & M-28 jct. $10 ($60 weekly). 5/1-9/30. 15 sites. Tbls, flush toilets, cfga, drkg wtr, elec, beach, dump, showers, playground, elec. Swimming, fishing, boating(l). GPS: 46.35328, -89.342355

BESSEMER (5N)
Black River Harbor Recreation Area $8
Ottawa National Forest
14 mi N of Bessemer on CR 513. $8 with federal senior pass; others pay $16. About 5/15-9/30; 14-day limit. 40 sites (32-ft RV limit). Tbls, flush toilets, cfga, drkg wtr, store, dump. Fishing, swimming, boating(lr). 150 acres. GPS: 46.66416323, -90.05190622

BIG RAPIDS (6S)

Hungerford Lake Trail Camp $7.50
Hungerford Recreation Area
Manistee National Forest
6 mi W of Big Rapids on Hwy 20; 1 mi NE on Co 5134; half mi W on FR 5955. $7.50 with federal senior pass; others pay $15. 4/15-11/1; 14-day limit. 50 sites; no RV size limit (also 2 free primitive sites at boat ramp). Toilets, cfga, drkg wt. Fishing, boating(ld), bridle trail, mountain biking trail. GPS: 43.701452, -85.622118

BRIGHTON (7S)

Brighton State Recreation Area $12
3 mi W of Brighton, then S on Chilson Rd. $12 base. 4/15-11/30; 15-day limit. Base fee at 25 rustic sites at Murray Lake & 25 at Appleton Lake (pit toilets, cfga, drkg wtr, tbls); $17 & $19 at horseman & modern sites with elec/wtr, flush toilets, showers, tbls, cfga. Shelter, playground, dump, beach, concession, stable. Swimming, hunting, fishing, boating(lr), canoeing(r), bridle trails (18 mi), hiking trails (7 mi), snowmobiling, cross-country skiing. GPS: 42.533936, -83.867676.

BRIMLEY (8N)

Monocle Lake $8
Hiawatha National Forest
6.3 mi NW of Brimley on CR 3150; .6 mi W on FR 3699. $8 with federal senior pass; others pay $16. About 5/15-9/15; 14-day limit. 39 sites (32-ft RV limit). Tbls, toilets, cfga, drkg wtr. Swimming beach, hiking trails, boating(l), fishing. 23 acres. Point Iroquois Lighthouse nearby with museum & book store. Non-campers pay $5 day use fee. GPS: 46.4750212, -84.63811

BROHMAN (9S)

Benton Lake Campground $8
Manistee National Forest
From M-37 in Brohman, travel W on Pierce Dr; at 33-acre lake. $8 with federal senior pass; others pay $16. 5/9-9/28; 14-day limit. 25 sites; 40-ft RV limit. Tbls, toilets, cfga, drkg wtr, beach, barrier-free fishing pier. Swimming, boating(ld), fishing, picnicking. Near North Country Scenic Trail, Loda Lake Wildflower Sanctuary and Mena Creek waterfowl area. Non-campers pay $5 day use fee. GPS: 43.669308, -85.88881

Indian Lake Campground $10
Manistee National Forest
Half mi S of Brohman on SR 37; W on Center Rd; left (S) 0.5 mi on Nagek Rd, veering left at split to end of rd at 34-acre lake. $10. 5/1-10/31; 14-day limit (free but not maintained in winter). 6 sites. Tbls, toilets, cfga. Minimal services and facilities provided. GPS: 43.671751, -85.822261

Nichols Lake South Campground $8
Manistee National Forest
2 mi N of Brohman on M-27; 4.25 mi W on 11-Mile Rd; at S side of lake. $8 with federal senior pass; others pay $16. 5/1-9/22; 14-day limit. 30 paved sites; 50-ft RV limit. Tbls, flush toilets, cfga, drkg wtr, beach, barrier-free fishing pier, lantern posts, showers. Swimming, boating(ld), hiking, waterskiing. North Country Trail trailhead. GPS: 44.19538, -86.00923

Shelly Lake Campground $10
Manistee National Forest
1 mi N of Brohman on M-37; 0.5 mi NE on FR 5450.; qtr mi W on access rd, which is narrow & winding, not for large RVs. $10. All year; 14-day limit; free off-season, but not maintained. About 8 primitive undesignated sites. Toilets, cfga, no drkg wtr, no trash service. Fishing, boating (carry-in launch). GPS: 43/811807, -85.807186

CADILLAC (10S)

Hemlock Campground $8
Manistee National Forest
5 mi W of Cadillac: 1 mi W on SR 55 from jct with SR 115 in Cadillac; 1.4 mi N on South Lake Mitchell Dr; at W end of 1,600-acre Lake Mitchell. $8 with federal senior pass; others pay $16; double sites $25 ($12.50 with senior pass). 5/9-9/15; 14-day limit. 19 sites; 25-ft RV limit. Tbls, toilets, cfga, drkg wtr. Boating(l), fishing. Non-campers pay $5 day use fee. GPS: 44.232153, -85.503651

Peterson Bridge South $9
Manistee National Forest
Pine National Scenic River
20 mi W of Cadillac on SR 55; 1.5 mi S on SR 37; on left after bridge. $9 with federal senior pass; others pay $18. About 5/9-9/15; 14-day limit. 20 RV sites (typically 40 ft). 10 walk-in or canoe-in tent sites, $6 per person. Tbls, flush toilets, cfga, drkg wtr. Canoeing, fishing, boating(l). 10 acres. On Pine River. Non-campers pay $4 day use fee. GPS: 44.202064, -85.797847

Ravine Campground $5
Manistee National Forest
10.2 mi W on Hwy 55; 1 mi S on FR 5181; 2.4 mi W on FR 5182; 1 mi S on FR 5334. $5. All year; 14-day limit. 4 sites (25 ft RV limit). Tbls, toilets, cfga, drkg wtr. Fishing, picnicking, hiking. GPS: 44.1803, -85.6572

CARNEY (11N)

Sturgeon Bend Township Park $5
12 mi W of Carney on G-18; N for 4 mi on Old State Rd at Nathan. $5. May-Oct. 11 primitive sites. Tbls, toilets, cfga, drkg wtr. Fishing, hiking trails, boating(l). 19-acre wilderness area on Menominee River.

CEDARVILLE (12N)

Dispersed Campsite 15 FREE
Search Bay
Hiawatha National Forest
W of Cedarville on SR 134 to Search Bay on Lake Huron.

Free. All year; 14-day limit. Two large open camp areas on the bay; no facilities. Boating(l), fishing, swimming. Bay GPS: 45.9875, -84.4995

CHAMPION (13N)

Craig Lake State Park $12
6 mi W of Champion on US 41; 12 mi N on Keewaydin Lake Rd, taking left fork after 5 mi; rocky road; high-clearance vehicles suggested. $12. All year; 15-day limit. 17 rustic sites. Fishing at 6 lakes & several small ponds, hiking, wildlife study, canoeing, boating(l). This remote park has 6,900 acres. GPS: 46.6, -88.1875

CHANNING (14N)

Campsite #13 $10
Michigamme Reservoir
WE Energies
Wilderness Shores Recreation Area
Half mi N of Channing on MI 95; quarter mi N on co rd; 5.6 mi W on Channing Rd; S half mi on co rd; 1.3 mi W to campground; on N shore of south bay, Michigamme Reservoir. $10. 5/1-9/30; 15-day limit. 4 primitive sites. Tbls, toilets, cfga, no drkg wtr. Picnicking, boating(l), fishing. Lake GPS: 46.17398, -88.225147.

Campsite #14 $10
Michigamme Reservoir
WE Energies
Wilderness Shores Recreation Area
Half mi N of Channing on MI 95; 1/5 mi N on co rd; 4.8 mi W on Channing Rd; 1.3 mi N on co rd; 1 mi W on co rd to campground; on E shore of Michigamme Reservoir. $10. 5/1-9/30; 15-day limit. 4 primitive sites. Tbls, toilets, cfga, no drkg wtr. Picnicking, boating(l), fishing.

Campsite #29 $10
Michigamme River
WE Energies
Wilderness Shores Recreation Area
3 mi N of Channing on MI 95; 3 mi NW on co rd to S shore of Michigamme River. $10. 5/1-9/30; 15-day limit. Open primitive camping. Toilets, cfga, no drkg wtr. Picnicking, boating(l), fishing.

CHARLEVOIX (15N)

Fisherman's Island State Park $12
3 mi SW of Charlevoix on US 31 & Bells Bay Rd; on Lake Michigan. $12. 4/22-11/20; 15-day limit. 81 rustic sites in two campgrounds. Tbls, pit toilets, cfga, drkg wtr, beach. Swimming, fishing, boating, hiking trails, hunting. 2,678 acres with 5 mi of undeveloped lake shoreline. GPS: 45.266, -85.361

CHELSEA (16S)

Green Lake Campground $12
Waterloo State Recreation Area
4 mi N of Chelsea off exit 159 from I-94. $12. 5/6-12/1; 15-day limit. 25 rustic sites (32-ft limit). Tbls, pit toilets,

cfga, drkg wtr. Fishing, hiking trails, horseback riding, swimming, playground, snowmobiling, ski trails, boating(l). Part of 20,000-acre recreation area -- largest park in the lower peninsula. Abundant wildlife. Other campgrounds have sites for $17-24. GPS: 42.367432, -84.070557

COMMONWEALTH (WISCONSIN) (18N)

Campsite #24 $10
WE Energies
Wilderness Shores Recreation Area
3.6 mi S of Commonwealth on CR N; 1.3 mi W on CR D; 3.5 mi S on co rd to Campsite #34 (on Pine River); cross dam to #24. $10. 5/1-9/30; 15-day limit.. 3 primitive sites. Tbls, toilets, cfga, no drkg wtr. Picnicking, boating(l), fishing. Lake GPS: 45.830873, -88.265708.

Campsite #34 $10
WE Energies
Wilderness Shores Recreation Area
3.6 mi S of Commonwealth on CR N; 1.3 mi W on CR D; 3.5 mi S on co rd to campground (on Pine River). $10. 5/1-9/30; 15-day limit. 3 primitive sites. Tbls, toilets, cfga, drkg wtr. Picnicking, boating(l), fishing. Lake GPS: 45.830, -88.2657

CRYSTAL FALLS (19N)

Dawson Lake $12
Mansfield Township Campground
10 mi E of Crystal Falls on M-69; 1 mi S on Dawson Lake Rd. $12. 10 sites. Tbls, toilets, cfga, no drkg wtr, beach. Swimming, fishing. GPS: 46.07583, -88.18333.

Runkle Lake Municipal Park $12
1 mi E of Crystal Falls from US 2 & M-69 jct. $12 with wtr/ elec ($70 weekly, $200 monthly); $20 full hookups ($100 weekly, $300 monthly). MD-LD. 57 sites. Tbls, flush toilets, cfga, drkg wtr, elec($), beach, showers, dump, playground, fishing pier. Swimming, tennis, basketball, volleyball, horseshoes boating (l). GPS: 46.10156, -88.306396

Campsite #9 $10
Peavy Falls Dam
WE Energies
Wilderness Shores Recreation Area
About 12 mi E of Crystal Falls on MI 69; 7 mi S on Camp Five Rd; 3 mi E on Upper Dam Rd; at Peavy Falls Dam, S of Peavy Falls Pond on Michigamme River. $10. 5/1-9/30; 15-day limit. 4 primitive sites. Tbls, toilets, cfga, drkg wtr. Picnicking, fishing, boating(l). Dam GPS: 45.990786, -88.208467.

Campsite #10 $10
Peavy Falls Pond
WE Energies
Wilderness Shores Recreation Area
3.9 mi E of Crystal Falls on MI 69; 4.9 mi S on Lake Mary Rd; SE on co rd; on N shore of Peavy Falls Pond. $10. 5/1-9/30; 15-day limit. 4 primitive sites. Tbls, toilets, cfga, drkg wtr. Picnicking, fishing, boating(l).

Campsite #19 $10
Michigamme Reservoir
WE Energies
Wilderness Shores Recreation Area
6.6 mi N of Crystal Falls on co rd; half mi NE on co rd to
campground (on SW shore of Michigamme Reservoir). $10.
5/1-9/30; 15-day limit. 20 primitive sites. Tbls, toilets,
cfga, drkg wtr. Picnicking, boating(rl), fishing.

Campsite #20 $10
Michigamme Reservoir
WE Energies
Wilderness Shores Recreation Area
15 mi NE of Crystal Falls off M-69 on Way Dam Rd; on S
shore of Michigamme Reservoir. $10 base, $12 at 10 pre-
mium sites. 5/1-9/30; 15-day limit. 22 total primitive sites.
Tbls, toilets, cfga, drkg wtr. Picnicking, fishing, boating(l).

Campsite #22 $10
Little Bull Dam
WE Energies
Wilderness Shores Recreation Area
3.9 mi E of Crystal Falls on MI 690; 3.6 mi S on co rd; 2 mi
W and SW on co rd to campground (on Peavy Falls Pond
overlooking Little Bull Dam of Paint River). $10. 5/1-9/30;
15-day limit. 3 primitive sites. Tbls, toilets, cfga, no drkg
wtr. Picnicking, fishing, boating(l).

Campsite #26 $10
Michigamme Reservoir
WE Energies
Wilderness Shores Recreation Area
8.8 mi E of Crystal Falls on M-69; about 8 mi N on Way
Dam Rd; on S shore of Michigamme Reservoir at mouth of
Michigamme River. $10. 5/1-9/30; 15-day limit.
Tbls, toilets, cfga, no drkg wtr. Picnicking, fishing, boat-
ing(l). Dam GPS: 46.160504, -88.239025.

Campsite #27 $10
Peavy Falls Pond
WE Energies
Wilderness Shores Recreation Area
3.9 mi E of Crystal Falls on MI 69; 7 mi S on Lake Mary Rd;
at NW shore of Peavy Falls Pond. $10. 5/1-9/30; 15-day
limit. 4 primitive sites. Tbls, toilets, cfga, drkg wtr. Picnicking, fishing, boating(l).

DAGGETT (20N)

Campsite #1 $10
WE Energies
Wilderness Shores Recreation Area
5.6 mi W on CR 358; 2 mi S on CR 577; 4.5 mi NW on CR
536 to campground (on Menominee River). $10. 5/1-9/30;
15-day limit. Tbls, toilets, cfga, no drkg wtr. Picnicking,
fishing, boating(l).

DE TOUR (21N)

Drummond Island Township Park $12
Take ferry from DeTour village to Drummond Island, then 5
mi E on SR 134; at Potagannissing Bay of Lake Huron. $12
tent & primitive sites; $14 with elec. 4/15-11/30. 48 sites;
31-ft RV limit. Tbls, toilets, cfga, drkg wtr, dump, elec($).
Boating(l), swimming, fishing, hunting, 3-mi nature trail.
GPS: 45.99771, -83.78702

EAST TAWAS (23S)

Monument Campground $7.50
Huron National Forest
River Road National Scenic Byway
14.2 mi NW of East Tawas on Monument Rd; right for 0.5
mi on River Rd. $7.50 with federal senior pass; others pay
$15. About 5/15-9/15; 14-day limit. 19 sites (2 double);
50-ft RV limit. Tbls, toilets, cfga, drkg wtr. Hiking, fishing. Scenic boardwalks, interpretive displays at visitor
center. Near Lumberman's Monument visitor center. GPS:
44.43425, -83.619952

Rollways Campground $7.50
Huron National Forest
River Road National Scenic Byway
From jct with M-55 about 6 mi W of East Tawas, 14.7 N on
M-65; qtr mi N on Rollway Rd. $7.50 with federal senior
pass; others pay $15. About 5/15-9/15; 14-day limit. 19
sites (most pull-through); 50-ft RV limit. Tbls, toilets, cfga,
drkg wtr, store. Fishing, boating(l), waterskiing, hiking.
GPS: 44.457734, -83.773784

Round Lake Campground $7
Huron National Forest
9 mi NW of East Tawas on Lathham Rd (5 mi from Indian
Lake Rd). $7 with federal senior pass; others pay $14;
double sites $25 ($12.50 with senior pass). About 5/21-
9/10; 14-day limit. 33 sites; 25-ft RV limit. Tbls, toilets,
cfga, drkg wtr, store. Fishing, boating(l), waterskiing. 14
acres; 89-acre lake. GPS: 44.343342, --83.661825

ESCANABA (24N)

Boney Falls Campground   FREE
Wells Township Park
3 mi N of Escanaba on US 2/41; N on CR 426 to Cornell;
N on CR 523 to Boney Falls. Free. All year. 8 sites. Tbls,
toilets, cfga, drkg wtr. Fishing, biking, boating. Owned by
Mead Paper Company; maintained by the township.

EWEN (25N)

Matchwood   FREE
Ottawa National Forest
5.5 mi W on MI 28; 5 mi S on co hwy; half mi S on FR
178. Free. 5/1-12/1; 14-day limit. 5 sites (RVs under 22
ft). Well drkg wtr, tbls, toilets, cfga, firewood. Picnicking,
berry picking, fishing (2 mi). Elev 1300 ft. 2 acres. Good
grouse & deer area. Popular hunting, camping area. GPS:
46.49667, -89.42778

Ely Lake Campground $12
Allegan County Park
About 5 mi S of Fennville on 57th St; 3 mi E on 116th Ave (between 51st St & 48th St), then S on access rd to Ely Lake; within the Allegan State Game Area. $12. All year, but roads not plowed in winter. 73 primitive sites. Toilets, tbls, cfga, no drkg wtr. Swimming beach, fishing, hiking, cross-country skiing, canoeing, boating (no motors). GPS: 42.574, -86.033

Pine Point Campground $12
Allegan County Park
About 4 mi S of Fennville on 57th St; about 7 mi E on 118th Ave; S on 44th St, following signs; within the Allegan State Game Area. $12. All year, but roads not plowed in winter. 33 primitive sites & 4 group sites. Tbls, toilets, cfga, no drkg wtr, beach. Swimming, fishing, boating(l) at Swan Creek Pond. Pond GPS: 42.552010, -85.978003

GLEN ARBOR (26N)
D.H. Day Campground $12
Sleeping Bear Dunes National Lakeshore
1.5 mi W of Glen Arbor on M-109. $12. 4/2-11/30; 14-day limit. 88 sites. Tbls, toilets, cfga, drkg wtr, dump. Fishing, swimming, hiking. Generators permitted at times. Park entrance fee. GPS: 44.8998926, -86.02002

GLENNIE (27S)
Alcona Park (priv) $12
From Glennie, W from M-65 on Bamfield Rd to jct with AuSable Rd; right on AuSable Rd; at AuSable River above Alcona Dam. $12 at primitive secluded sites; $14 at primitive waterfront sites. 4/15-12/1. 400 primitive sites with tbls, pit toilets, cfga, drkg wtr, playgrounds, coin laundry, showers. $20-26 with hookups. Swimming, fishing, boating(l), volleyball, basketball, hiking trails, canoeing(r). 1,100 acres. GPS: 44.45761, -81.698297

Gabions Campground $10
Huron National Forest
From Glennie at jct with SR 65, 3 mi W on Bamfield Rd; 4/9 mi N on Au Sable Rd; left on FR 3993 for 0.3 mi. $10 during 5/1-11/30; free rest of year but no amenities or services. 10 sites; 25-ft RV limit. Tbls, toilets, cfga, no drkg wtr. Non-campers pay $5 day use fee ($15 weekly, $30 annually). Hiking (Shore-to-Shore State Hiking Trail), canoeing, fishing. GPS: 44.620111, -83.845948

Horseshoe Lake Campground $7.50
Huron National Forest
3 mi N of Glennie on M-65; 1 mi W on FR 4124. $7.50 with federal senior pass; others pay $15. 5/1-11/30; 14-day limit (sites $10 when wtr is off). 9 sites (25-ft RV limit). Tbls, toilets, cfga, drkg wtr. Boating(l), fishing (16-acre trout lake). Foot trail. GPS: 44.6005691, -83.7655401

Pine River Campground $7.50
Huron National Forest
9 mi E of Glennie on CR F30; 2.2 mi S on FR 4121. $7.50 with federal senior pass; others pay $15. About 5/1-11/15; 14-day limit. 11 sites; 25-ft RV limit. Tbls, toilets, cfga, drkg wtr. Fishing, picnicking. On South Branch Pine River. Non-campers pay $5 day use fee. GPS: 44.563327, 83.599359

GRAND MARAIS (28N)
Hurricane River $7
Pictured Rocks National Lakeshore
From lower peninsula, take I-75 to US 2, N to M-77 to the national lakeshore; campground is 12 mi W of Grand Marais on CR H-58. $7 with federal senior pass at inland sites without hookups; others pay $14. $8 with senior pass at premium lakeside sites; others pay $16. 5/10-10/31; 14-day limit. 22 sites (36-ft RV limit). Tbls, toilets, drkg wtr, cfga. Picnicking, fishing, swimming, hiking, boating, hunting. Pets on leash except in backcountry. Bring insect repellent in summer. GPS: 46.42, -86.62

Twelvemile Beach $7
Pictured Rocks National Lakeshore
From lower peninsula, take I-75 to US 2, N to M-77 to the national lakeshore; campground 15 mi W of Grand Marais on CR H-58. $7 with federal senior pass; others pay $14. 5/10-10/30; 14-day limit. 36 sites (36-ft RV limit). Tbls, toilets, cfga, drkg wtr. Picnicking, fishing, swimming, hiking, boating, hunting. Pets on leash except in backcountry.

GRAYLING (29S)
Kneff Lake Campground $7.50
Huron National Forest
8 mi E of Grayling on SR 72; 1 mi S on Down River Rd. $7.50 with federal senior pass; others pay $15. 5/1-9/30; 14-day limit. 27 sites; 25-ft RV limit. Tbls, flush toilets, cfga, drkg wtr, beach. Boating, swimming, fishing. 30 acres. Non-campers pay $5 day use fee. GPS: 44.638488, -84.572071

Luzerne Horse Trail Camp   FREE
Huron National Forest
22 mi E of Grayling on SR 72; 2 mi S on Deeter Rd (CR F490); 1 mi S on Durfee Rd (FR 4551). Free. 4/1-11/14, but open all year without services; 14-day limit. 10 sites; no RV size limit. Tbls, toilets, cfga, no drkg wtr except for horses. Hiking, bridle trails. GPS: 44.586171, -84.288841

Meadows ORV Camp $10
Huron National Forest
22 mi E of Graying on SR 72; 2 mi S on Deeter Rd; 3 mi S on Durfee Rd (FR 4541). $10 (day use $5 daily, $15 weekly, $30 annually). 4/1-11/14; 14-day limit (free off-season, but no amenities or service). 16 sites (typically 35 ft). Tbls, toilets, cfga, drkg wtr. Trailhead for Meadows ORV Trail. GPS: 44.560817, -84.312315

HAMILTON (30S)

Silver Creek $12
Allegan County Park
Half mi S on MI 40, 4 mi E on 134th Ave; just S of Hamilton River at 38th St, in Hamilton. $12. All year; 15-day limit. 75 primitive, well-spaced sites. Tbls, toilets, cfga, well drkg wtr. Picnicking, playground. 320 acres. Separate horseman camping area with bridle trails. Caution: Don't follow camping signs W on 134th; it's a private campground. GPS: 42.6658619, -85.9269765

HARDWOOD (31N)

Stromberg Park Campground $10
Dickinson County Park
Hardwood Impoundment
From SR 69 at Hardwood, N & E on Fordville Rd to access rd to S shore; or, from W of Hardwood on SR 69, 1 mi N on Kime Backlund Rd, then E on N. Dam Rd. $10 non-residents. Primitive camping. Fishing, boating(l). 1,500-acre lake. GPS: 45.97611, -87.68333

HARRISVILLE (32S)

Jewell Lake $7.50
Huron National Forest
13.5 mi W of Harrisville on SR 72; 2 mi N on Sanborn Rd; 1 mi W on Trask Lake Rd.; left on FR 4601; near Barton City on E side of lake. $7.50 with federal senior pass; others pay $15. About MD-LD; 14-day limit. 32 sites (typically 45 ft). Tbls, toilets, cfga, drkg wtr, store. Swimming, fishing, boating(l), hiking, waterskiing. GPS: 44.677492, -83.597111

HASTINGS (33S)

Yankee Springs $12
State Recreation Area
19 mi W off SR 37 & 43 on Gun Lake Rd. $12 base. All year; 15-day limit. Base fee at 120 rustic sites at Deep Lake with pit toilets, cfga, tbls, drkg wtr; $17 at 25 horseman sites; $18-24 for 220 modern sites at Gun Lake. Shelter, playground, beach, dump. Cross-country ski trails, snowmobile trails, hiking trails (15.5 mi), bridle trails, boating(l), swimming, hunting. GPS: 42.645996, -85.337646

HESPERIA (34S)

Diamond Point $10
Manistee National Forest
7 mi S of Hesperia on M-120; 8 mi on Skeels Rd until it turns S into Nichols Rd; half mi on Nichols; right on Fruitville for 0.5 mi; right on Kops Rd for 0.5 mi, then continue on FR 9304; at White River. $10 during 4/1-11/30; free rest of year, but no services. 14-day limit. 2 sites; 20-ft RV limit. Tbls,toilets, cfga, no drkg wtr. Fishing, canoeing; important canoe landing. GPS: 43.473836, -86.21164

Minnie Pond Campground $10
Manistee National Forest
6 mi E of Hesperia on SR 20; 3 mi N on Luce Ave; half mi E

on 4 Mile Rd; 1.1 mi N on Alger Ave. $10 during 5/15-9/30 (free off-season, but no services); 14-day limit. 11 sites (RVs under 32 ft). Tbls, cfga, no toilets or wtr. Fishing, boating, hiking. 2 acres. Flat terrain, dense forest. Minimal facilities and services provided. Carry-in boat access. GPS: 43.627224, --85.898959

Pines Point $9
Manistee National Forest
2 mi W of Hesperia on M-20; left on 192nd Ave; right 3 mi on Garfield Rd; 2.5 mi left on 168th Ave (FR 5118). $9 with federal senior pass; others pay $18. 33 sites; 40-ft RV limit. 5/15-10/15; 14-day limit. Tbls, flush toilets, cfga, drkg wtr. Boating, canoeing(lr), fishing, tubing, picnicking. On White River. 20 acres. Non-campers pay $5 day use fee. GPS: 43.530254, -86.11699

HIGHLAND (35S)

Highland State Recreation Area $12
2 mi E of Highland on M-59. $12. Horseman camp also open to non-horsemen ($17 for campers with horses). 4/15-10/1; 15-day limit. Tbls, pit toilets, cfga, drkg wtr, playground, stable. Swimming, boating(l), fishing, ski trails, hiking trails, horseback riding, picnicking. 5,524 acres

HILLMAN (36N)

Emerick Municipal Park $12
Half block from SR 32 on State St. In Hillman; at Thunder Bay River. $12 at 4 primitive sites; $16 at 22 wtr/elec sites; $18 at 12 sites with full hookups. About 4/15-12/1; 15-day limit; weekly rates available. Tbls, flush toilets, cfga, drkg wtr, playground, dump, showers. Swimming, boating(l), fishing, golf. GPS: 46060791, -83.901611

HONOR (37S)

Platte River Campground $8
Sleeping Bear Dunes National Lakeshore
About 5 mi NE of Honor on Hwy 708 (Deadstream Rd). $8 with federal senior pass at 53 non-elec sites; others pay $16. At 96 elec sites, $10.50 with senior pass; others pay $21. All year; 14-day limit. Tbls, flush toilets, cfga, drkg wtr, camp sinks, showers($), dump. GPS: 44.713867, -86.104248

HOUGHTON (38N)

City of Houghton RV Park $5
Just W of town off SR 26 & US 41; access to waterway at base of hill; at 1100 W. Lakeshore Dr. $5 without hookups; ($15 motorhomes); $30 with hookups. 5/1-10/7. 24 RV sites up to 60 ft. Tbls, toilets, cfga, drkg wtr, beach, fishing pier, playground. Biking/jogging path, boating(l), fishing. GPS: 47.122072, -88560891

HOWARD CITY (39S)

Little Muskegon $5
Manistee National Forest
From M-82 exit of US 131, half mi W on M-82; 2.5 mi N on

Dagget Rd. to Little Muskegon River. $5 daily forest pass (or $15 weekly, $30 annually). Primitive undesignated camping area. Toilets, cfga, no drkg wtr. Fishing.

INTERLOCHEN (40S)

Interlochen State Park $12
1 mi S of Interlochen on SR 137 (15 mi SW of Traverse City); between Duck & Green Lakes. $12 base. 4/15-11/6; 15-day limit. Base fee at 52 rustic sites with tbls, cfga, drkg wtr, pit toilets; $21-23 at 428 modern sites. Playground, shelter, beach, store, dump. Nature trail, boating(lr), fishing, swimming. Interpretive display of 1890s logging era. GPS: 44.6277792, -85.7628551

IRON MOUNTAIN (41N)

Groveland Iron Ore Basin FREE
Department of Natural Resources
About 10 mi N of Iron Mountain on M-95; 3.7 mi E on M-69 (some maps show M-569); 1.7 mi S on Groveland Mine Rd, then SW into the area (unimproved roads rough, not recommended for large RVs. Free. All year; 14-day limit. Primitive undesignated camping; no facilities, no drkg wtr. Fishing, hunting, boating(l) on 5,000 acres with 4 ponds containing walleye, bass, perch, crappie.

IRON RIVER (42N)

Bates Township Park $10
Sunset Lake
1 mi E of Iron River on US 2; 4 mi NE on CR 651 to lake. $10. 13 sites. Tbls, toilets, cfga, drkg wtr. Boating (l), swimming, fishing. GPS: 46.129, -88.59

Blockhouse Campground FREE
Ottawa National Forest
9 mi NW of Iron River on CR 653 (Gibbs City Rd); at Gibbs City, road becomes FR 2130 (Ponozzo Rd); continue 4.5 mi N; right on FR 2180 for 4 mi; at the Paint River. Free. 5/1-11/30; 14-day limit. 2 sites (RVs under 60 ft). No drkg wtr, tbls, toilets, cfga. Picnicking, fishing. Elev 1400 ft. 3 acres. Canoe camp. Fishing. GPS: 46.24236480, -88.63176147

Golden Lake $7
Ottawa National Forest
13.2 mi W of Iron River on US 2; 1 mi N on FR 16. $7 with federal senior pass; others pay $14. 5/15-10/15; 14-day limit. 22 sites, typically 45 ft. Tbls, toilets, cfga, drkg wtr. Boating(l), fishing, hiking. 15 acres. GPS: 46.17160677, -88.88275779

Lake Ottawa Recreation Area $8
Ottawa National Forest
0.5 mi W of Iron River on US 2; .75 mi SW on SR 73; 4 mi W on Lake Ottawa Rd. $8 with federal senior pass; others pay $16. MD-10/1; 14-day limit. 31 sites, typically 60 ft. Tbls, flush toilets, cfga, drkg wtr, dump, beach. Boating(l), fishing, hiking, interpretive trail; archaeological dig, playground, swimming. GPS: 46.08076080, -88.76003616

Paint River Forks FREE
Ottawa National Forest
13 mi NW of Iron River on US 2, CR 653 (Gibbs City Rd), FR 2130 and FR 2180. Free. 5/1-12/1. 4 sites (RVs under 22 ft). Toilet, cfga, no drkg wtr. Picnicking, fishing boating(l), canoeing, hunting. 3 acres. Starting point for Paint River Forks Canoe Route. GPS: 46.23240559, -88.71756443

IRONWOOD (43N)

Curry City Park $10
On West US 2 near fairgrounds; E of Montreal River. $10 without elec; $15 with 20-amp elec; $20 at 9 full hookups. 5/15-10/1. 56 sites. Tbls, flush toilets, cfga, drkg wtr, dump ($10 for non-campers, $10 to fill water tank), visitor center, playground, coin laundry. GPS: 46.463623, -90.182861

ITHACA (44S)

Woodland Park FREE
Municipal Park
5 blocks W of US 27A on W. Center St. Free. 5/11-10/1; 1 or 2-night limit. 3 sites (25-ft RV limit). Tbls, toilets, drkg wtr, elect. Picnicking, hiking, shopping, sightseeing. GPS: 43.2928, -84.6161

KALEVA (45S)

Village Roadside Park $10
In town on CR 598 at High Bridge. $10 without hookups; $15 for wtr/elec ($75 weekly). All year; not plowed in winter; 7-day limit. 32 sites for self-contained units only (6 sites with elec); 42-ft RV limit. Wtr, elec (20 amp), tbls, cfga, playground, sports field. Picnicking. Restaurant a short walk. GPS: 44.370242, -86.018031

KENTON (46N)

Lower Dam FREE
Ottawa National Forest
Half mi SE of Kenton on FR 16; 5 mi E on Lake Thirteen Rd; 1 mi S on FR 3500. Free. 5/15-12/1; 14-day limit. 7 sites (22-ft RV limit). No facilities except cfga, no drkg wtr. Good trout fishing on small lake, boating(l), swimming. GPS: 46.45333, -88.78028

Sparrow Rapids Free
Ottawa National Forest
2 mi NW of Kenton on FR 1100. Free. 5/15-12/1; 14-day limit. 6 sites (22-ft RV limit). Toilet, cfga, no drkg wtr, no service. Fishing, hiking. GPS: 46.50477544, -88.94735023

Sturgeon River FREE
Ottawa National Forest
15 mi NE of Kenton on M-28 and FR 2200; on Sturgeon River. Free. 5/15-12/1; 14-day limit. 9 sites. Tbls, toilets, cfga, no drkg wtr, no trash service. Near North Country Scenic Trail and Sturgeon River Gorge Wilderness. Trout fishing. Too shallow for summer canoeing. GPS: 46.570096, -88.65636953

KINROSS (47N)

Kinross Township $12
RV Park East
From I-75 exit 378 east 2.5 mi to Tone Rd. $12 base for primitive sites; $19 with elec ($17 seniors); $20 full hookups (weekly & monthly rates available). 5/15-110/15. 64 developed back-in sites with 20/30-amp elec plus primitive area. Tbls, flush toilets, showers, cfga, drkg wtr, elec($), coin laundry. Horseshoes. GPS: 46.260254, -84.461426

Kinross Township $10
RV Park West
From I-75 exit 378 east qtr mi on Tone Rd to Fair Rd. $10 base at primitive sites; $17 with elec/wtr ($14 seniors); weekly & monthly rates available. 5/15-10/15. 52 elec/wtr sites plus primitive areas. Tbls, flush toilets, showers, cfga, drkg wtr, elec, playground. Horseshoes. GPS: 46.26636, -84.461426.

LAKE LINDEN (49N)

Lake Linden $10
Village Recreation Park
On M-26, shoreline of Torch Lake. $10 at 6 rustic sites. MD-9/30. $23 at 20 elec/wtr (30/50-amp) sites ($100 weekly. Tbls, flush toilets, cfga, drkg wtr, showers, dump, playground, CATV. Picnicking, boating(ld), swimming, fishing, nature trail, horseshoes, basketball, tennis, canoeing. Boat access to Lake Superior. GPS: 47.188655, -88.409407

MANISTEE (52S)

Lake Michigan Recreation Area $10.50
Manistee National Forest
13 mi S of Manistee (10 mi S of US 31 on M-55; 8 mi W on Forest Trail Rd, becoming FR 5629). $10.50 with federal senior pass; other spay $21. 5/9-9/15; 14-day limit; fees $10 off-season, but minimal amenities. 99 sites; 50-ft RV limit. Tbls, flush toilets, cfga, drkg wtr, beach, playground. Swimming, hiking trails. Nordhouse Dunes Wilderness Area. GPS: 44.116584, -86.42369

MANISTIQUE (53N)

Bear Lake $8
Hiawatha National Forest
20 mi W of Manistique on CR 442; 8 mi N on CR 437; W on FR 2436 to FR 2696; 0.5 mi S to 21-acre lake. $8 camping permit required. All year; 7-day limit. 1 undeveloped primitive site for small RV or tents. No facilities. Carry-in boat access. Swimming, fishing, boating, picnicking, hiking. Rustic, secluded; 14-day limit.

Camp Cook $8
Hiawatha National Forest
10.6 mi W of Manistique on CR 442; 7.8 mi W on FRs 2222 and 2231; 3.7 mi N on CR 13; 3.1 mi NE on CR 442;, then right (SE) on FR 2052B. $8 for camping permit. 5/15-9/15;

14-day limit. 4 sites (RVs under 32 ft). Toilets, well drkg wtr. Fishing, hiking, swimming, waterskiing, boating(ld 3 mi). 11 acres. CCC campsite from 1934.

Camp 7 Lake $12
Hiawatha National Forest
10 mi W of Manistique on CR 442; 8 mi N on CR 437; 5 mi W on CR 442. $12. 5/15-10/7; 14-day limit. 41 sites (typically 30 & 70 ft). Tbls, toilets, cfga, drkg wtr. Swimming beach, boating(l), hiking trails, fishing. Van Winkle Nature Trail. 60-acre lake. GPS: 46.0578, -86.5497

Carr Lake $8
Hiawatha National Forest
10 mi W of Manistique on CR 442; 8 mi N on CR 437; W 2 mi on FR 2436. $8 for camping permit. 1 primitive site in cleared, open area 70 x 40 ft; suitable for 2 families. No facilities, no drkg wtr, no toilets. Boat access via carry-in slide or rough rd by 4WD. Swimming not recommended. Secluded, private site. 14-day limit. 16-acre lake. GPS: 46.079875, -86.5059847

Crooked Lake $8
Hiawatha National Forest
28 mi N of Manistique on SR 94; E qtr mi on FR 2246 (Clear Lake Rd); qtr mi S on FR 2661 (hard-packed, sandy rd). 1 site (35x35 ft); level, suitable for 1 family. $8 for camping permit. Carry-in public boat access. No toilets or drkg wtr. Fishing for bluegill, crappie, northern pike, some bass & perch. 14-day limit. 190-acre lake. GPS: 46.2130174, -86.4195965

Gooseneck Lake $8
Hiawatha National Forest
10 mi W on CR 442; 7 mi N on CR 437; 4 mi W on CR 442; 1 mi N on FR 2218. $8 for camping permit. 3 primitive undeveloped camping areas. No facilities; no drkg wtr. Site #1 is N of the lake, has rough access from FR 2218E; suitable for 1 family. Site #4 on NE side of lake, also accessible from FR 2218E (good access); suitable for 2 families. Site #6 at SE side of lake, for 2 families; limited turning space, so large RVs discouraged; rd firm, but narrow with sharp turns. Swimming except at Site #1. Fishing (muskies, northern pike, walleye, largemouth & smallmouth bass, panfish). Unimproved boat accesses at Site #6 and between Sites #1 and #4. 14-day limit. 123-acre lake. Improved Camp & Campground 2 mi S of lake, with boat access and 3-mi guided interpretive trail (Van Winkle Nature Trail). GPS: 46.0683, -86.5485

Ironjaw Lake $8
Hiawatha National Forest
10 mi W on CR 442; 17 mi N on CR 437; 3 mi W on CR 440; 1 mi N on FR 2733. $8 for camping permit. 1 primitive undeveloped camping area 50x40 ft. No facilities; no drkg wtr. Site overlooks Ironjaw & Lake Nineteen; suitable for 1 RV family. (See Lake Nineteen entry.) Poor swimming,

excellent fishing (crappie, northern pike, largemouth bass, bluegill). Boat access down a steep, sandy hill with limited turning space at bottom (4WD recommended). 14-day limit. 62-acre lake. GPS: 46.1733, -86.5532

Lake Nineteen $8
Hiawatha National Forest
10 mi W of Manistique on CR 442; 17 N on CR 437; 3 mi W on CR 440; 1 mi N on FR 2733 (also see Ironjaw Lake entry). $8 for camping permit. 2 primitive undeveloped camping areas. No facilities; no drkg wtr. Site #3 is on E shore of lake & can be reached only by boat. Suitable for 1 family with tents; parking on W side of lake. Site #4 near end of access rd; narrow, pull-in site for 1 family with small trailer or pickup camper. Poor swimming. Fishing (rainbow trout). Unimproved boat access steep; firm rd, but 4DWD recommended. 14-day limit. 26-acre lake; GPS: 46.1018, -86.3243

Lyman Lake $8
Hiawatha National Forest
10 mi W of Manistique on CR 442; 7 mi N on CR 437; W on CR 442 to FR 2218 or FR 2436; access FRs 2880, 2700 and 2085 lead to lake sites. $8 for camping permit. 10 camping areas. No drkg wtr. Site #1: small 35 x 25 ft area with good rd access off FR 2700 at S end of lake; suitable for 1 family; lake access via steep bank. Site #4: level, 30 x 40 ft, suitable for 1 family; stairway to lake; access via FR 2880 on S side of lake. Site #5: SE end of lake via FR 2880 or 2700; open area suitable for 3 families with RVs; toilet. Site #6: Wooded site with space for 2 RV families but limited turn-around; E end of lake via FR 2700 or 2880; toilet shared with Site #7. Site #7: large area suitable for 3 families; good rd access from FRs 2700 or 2880. Site #8: large area, but sloping ground difficult for RVs; suitable for 2 families; access off FR 2085. Site #10: sloping ground suitable for 1 family; tents recommended; access off FR 2085. Site #11: Wooded, overlooking lake; level, suitable for 2 families; access off FR 2085. Site 13: wooded, 80 x 40 ft; on hill overlooking lake; level, suitable for 2 families; access off FR 2085. Site #14: 50 x 30 ft, isolated with separate access rd; suitable for 1 family; access via FR 2085. Swimming (best at Sites 4, 5 & 7). Fishing (northern pike, bluegill, largemouth bass). Trailered boat access between Sites #8 and #10; carry-in boat access at Sites #5, #6, #7. 14-day limit. 67-acre lake. GPS: 46.,0714, -86.5352

Mowe Lake $8
Hiawatha National Forest
10 mi W on CR 442; 17 mi N on CR 437; 5 mi W of CR 440 to FR 2692; three-fourths mi S. Rd narrow but capable of handling moderate-size RVs. $8 for camping permit. 2 primitive undeveloped camping areas. No drkg wtr; cfga, primitive toilet. Site #1 in semi-open space 60 x 40 ft; space for 1 family. Site #2 slightly smaller, for 1 family. Fishing (northern pike, bass, panfish). Unimproved boat access between sites; sand landing for small boats & trailers. 25-acre lake. GPS: 46.145, -86.5796

Steuben Lake $8
Hiawatha National Forest
25 mi N of Manistique on SR 94, just N of Steuben and S of Crooked Lake; quarter mi E on FR 2662 or FR 2247. $8 for camping permit. 4 primitive undeveloped camp areas. No drkg wtr; cfga, primitive toilet. Site #2 is 50 x 70 ft, suitable for 2 families; on W side of lake via FR 2662; steep, sandy bank to lake. Site #3 large 75 x 75 ft, suitable for 3 families with RVs; on W side of lake via FR 2247, then FR 2554. Sites #4 & #6 on SE corner of lake; each accommodates 2 RV families; access via FR 2247 to FR 2664. Fishing (stocked walleye; also northern pike, largemouth bass, perch, bluegill). Unimproved boat accesses. Swimming. 151-acre lake. Groceries, gas, supplies, ice, boat rentals 2 mi W on CR 437. GPS: 46.19907, -86.4213

Swan Lake $8
Hiawatha National Forest
10 mi W of Manistique on CR 442; 17 mi N on CR 437; 5 mi W on CR 440 to FR 2258; N to access rds FR 2725 or FR 2100; .7 mi to lake. $8 for camping permit. 4 primitive undeveloped camping areas. 3 primitive toilets, cfga, no drkg wtr, no facilities. Site #1: on W side of lake, access on FR 2100; single family; RVs not recommended unless set up in parking area at base of knoll. Site #2: on SE side of lake, 65 x 50 ft; level, suitable for 2 RV families; share toilet with Sites 3 & 5. Site #3: level area 65 x 35 ft for 2 RV families. Site #5: small site for 1 family; RVs not recommended; not level. Excellent swimming areas. Fishing (managed trout population, largemouth bass). Very good unimproved boat access with ample turn-around and parking space at Site #1; sandy access between Sites 3 & 5 not recommended for large boats or trailers. 14-day limit. 52-acre lake. Quiet, peaceful recreation opportunities in semi-private setting. Lake GPS: 46.15526, -86.57405

Triangle Lake #1 $8
Hiawatha National Forest
10 mi W of Manistique on CR 442; 18 mi N on CR 437, past CR 440 jct; W half mi on FR 2734. Good access. $8 for camping permit. 3 family sites. Toilet, no drkg wtr, no other facilities. Level, sandy site 100 x 30 ft suitable for 3 RVs. Excellent swimming area. Fishing (northern pike, smallmouth bass, crappie, bluegill, perch). Sandy boat access with limited turn-around at end of FR 2734. 169-acre lake; GPS: 46.1006, -86.3008

MARENISCO (54N)
Bobcat Lake $12
Ottawa National Forest
Half mi E of Marenisco on SR 64; 2 mi SE on FR 8500. $12 during 5/15-9/30; free rest of year, but no services; 14-day limit. 12 sites (22-ft RV limit). Tbls, toilets, cfga, drkg wtr, beach, change house. Boating(l), fishing (bass, pike), waterskiing, swimming. 10 acres. Lake Gogebic, excellent walleye fishing (7 mi). GPS: 46.35924047, -89.6729413

Henry Lake $12
Ottawa National Forest
6 mi S of Marenisco on SR 64; 4 mi NW on FR 8100. $12
during 5/15-9/30; free rest of year, but no services; 14-day
limit. 11 sites (22-ft RV limit). Most sites & boat pier handicap-accessible. Tbls, toilets, cfga, drkg wtr. Boating(l),
fishing (good bass, panfish), water skiing, swimming.
15 acres. Among many small lakes and streams. GPS:
46.33163728, -089.79004348

Langford Lake $12
Ottawa National Forest
2 mi NE of Marenisco on SR 64; 10 mi SE on US 2; 4.5 mi
S on CR 527; 1 mi NE on FR 118. $12 during 5/15-9/30;
free rest of year, but no services; 14-day limit. 11 sites
(22-ft RV limit). Tbls, toilets, cfga, drkg wtr. Swimming,
hunting, picnicking, fishing (walleye, bass, pike), waterskiing, boating(l). Good family fishing and picnicking. GPS:
46.27222492, -89.49279231

Pomeroy Lake $12
Ottawa National Forest
Half mi E on SR 64; 4 mi SE on FR 122; 5 mi S on FR 119;
2 mi NE on FR 118. $12 during 5/15-9/30; free rest of year,
but no services; 14-day limit. 17 sites (22-ft RV limit) Tbls,
toilets, cfga, drkg wtr. Boating(l), fishing (walleye, bass,
pike, musky), waterskiing. 17 acres. GPS: 46.28146596,
-89.57396769

MASS CITY (55N)
Bob Lake $7
Ottawa National Forest
2 mi NE of Mass City on M-26; 7.5 mi SE on M-38; 6 mi S on
CR 16; 2 mi W on co rd. $7 with federal senior pass; others
pay $14 during 5/20-10/15. Free or reduced fees rest of
year About MD-12/30; 14-day limit. 17 sites (typically 40
ft). Tbls, toilets, cfga, drkg wtr. Swimming, boating(l),
fishing (walleye, trout), hiking trails. Interpretive trail &
North Country Scenic Trail. 10 acres. GPS: 46.66230759,
-88.91411255

Courtney Lake $7
Ottawa National Forest
2.2 mi NE of Mass City on SR 26; 5.5 mi SE on SR 38.
$7 with federal senior pass; others pay $14. MD-10/15;
14-day limit. 21 sites (some quite large). Tbls, toilets, cfga,
drkg wtr. Swim-ming, boating(l), fishing (trout). 11 acres.
GPS: 46.75241443, -88.94030846

MELSTRAND (56N)
Little Beaver Lake $7
Pictured Rocks National Lakeshore
From lower peninsula, take I-75 to US 2, north to M-77 to
M-28, west to the national lakeshore; 5 mi NE of Melstrand
on CR H-58 and 3 mi N to campground. $7 with federal
senior pass; others pay $14. 5/10-10/31; 14-day limit. 8
sites (36-ft RV limit). Tbls, toilets, cfga, drkg wtr. Pic-

nicking, fishing, hiking, boating, canoeing, hunting. Pets
on leash except in backcountry. Bring insect repellent in
summer. GPS: 46.42, -86.62

MESICK (57S)
Seaton Creek $8
Manistee National Forest
4.5 mi S of Mesick on M-37; 3 mi W on 26 Mile Rd; veer
right at fork; right 0.4 mi on FR 5993. $8 with federal
senior pass; others pay $16 (double sites $25). 5/9-
9/15 (may be open & free off-season, but no amenities
or service); 14-day limit. 17 sites (typically 40 ft). Tbls,
toilets, cfga, drkg wtr. Boating(ld), fishing, hiking trails.
On Big Manistee River at upper end of Hodenpyle Dam
Pond. Non-campers pay $4 day use fee. GPS: 44.358069,
-85.81051

MIO (58S)
Au Sable Loop Campground $10
Huron National Forest
Au Sable National Scenic River
About 3 mi E of Mio on SR 72; 0.5 mi N on SR 33; 3 mi E on
McKinley Rd; turn right, following signs to site. $10. 4/15-
11/30; 14-day limit. Free off-season, but no amenities or
services. 5 sites; 25-ft RV limit. Non-campers pay $5 day
use fee (or $15 weekly, $30 annually). Tbls, toilets, cfga,
drkg wtr. Fishing, boating(l), canoeing. GPS: 44.651347,
--84.099365

Buttercup Campground   FREE
Huron National Forest
Au Sable National Scenic River
About 3 mi E of Mio on SR 72; 0.5 mi N on SR 33; E on
McKinley Dr; 0.1 mi S on E. River Dr; 1 mi E on Reed Rd (FR
4836). Free. All year; 14-day limit. 3 sites. Tbls, toilet, cfga,
no drkg wtr. Canoeing, fishing. GPS: 44.64083, -83.9138

Island Lake Campground $7.50
Huron National Forest
10 mi S of Mio on SR 33; 1 mi W on CR 486. $7.50 with fed-
eral senior pass; others pay $15. About 5/1-9/30; 14-day
limit. 17 sites; 25-ft RV limit. Tbls, toilets, cfga, drkg wtr,
beach. Hiking, fishing, swimming, boating (elec mtrs). 7
acres on Island Lake Nature Trail connecting Loon & Island
Lakes. Non-campers pay $5 day use fee, $15 weekly. GPS:
44.510199, -84.141461

Mack Lake ORV Camp $7.50
Huron National Forest
3.7 mi S of Mio on M-33; 4.2 mi E on CR 489. $7.50 with fed-
eral senior pass; others pay $15. About 5/15-12/1; 14-day
limit. 42 sites (25-ft RV limit). Tbls, toilets, cfga, drkg wtr,
beach. Swimming, boating, fishing. 5 acres. Access trail to
Bull Gap ORV Trail. Group camping available. Non-campers pay $5 day use fee, $15 weekly. GPS: 44.578778,
-84.064904

McKinley Trail Camp   FREE
Huron National Forest
7 mi E of Mio on CR 602; 1 mi N on FR 4004. Free, but
donations accepted. All year; 14-day limit (not maintained
in winter). Undesignated open camping; no RV size limits.
Tbls, drkg wtr (generator needed to power pump), toilets,
cfga. Fishing, hunting, swimming, boating. During some
weekends, camp may be occupied by horse groups. Parking
lot designed for trucks with horse trailers. Easy access to
Shore-to-Shore State Horse Trail. GPS: 44.6401, -83.97288

Wagner Lake $7.50
Huron National Forest
7 mi S of Mio on SR 33; 1 mi W on FR 4211 (West Wagner
Lake Rd), following signs. $7.50 with federal senior pass;
others pay $15. About 5/1-12/1; 14-day limit; may be
open & free off-season, but no amenities. 12 sites; 50-ft
RV limit. Tbls, toilets, cfga, drkg wtr, beach. Boating,
swimming, fishing. Non-campers pay $5 day use fee, $15
weekly. GPS: 44.554126, -84.147346

MUNISING (59N)
Bay Furnace $8
Hiawatha National Forest
4.7 mi NW of Munising on SR 28; S shore of Lake Superior.
$8 with federal senior pass; others pay $16. 5/15-10/1;
14-day limit. 50 sites up to 50 ft. Tbls, toilets, cfga, wtr
hookups, store, dump ($5 non-campers). Fishing, swim-
ming. GPS: 46.43833, -86.70833

Hovey Lake   FREE
Hiawatha National Forest
7.5 mi SW of Munising on M-94; 3.6 mi SE on CR 2254;
qtr mi S on FR 2473. Free. 5/30-9/15; 14-day limit. 5 sites
(16-ft RV limit). Well drkg wtr, tbls, toilets, cfga, firewood.
5 acres. Picnicking, boating, fishing. 99-acre lake. GPS:
46.29056, -86.70083

Island Lake $8
Hiawatha National Forest
7.5 mi SW of Munising on M-94; 6.3 mi SE on CR 2254;
one-third mi S on FR 2557. $8 with federal senior pass;
others pay $16. 5/15-9/8; 14-day limit. 23 sites (up to 80
ft). Tbls, toilets, cfga, drkg wtr. Boating, fishing. 11 acres;
32-acre lake. GPS: 46.2708, -86.6335

Pete's Lake $8
Hiawatha National Forest
3.5 mi E of Munising on M-28; right on FR 13; 15 mi S. $8
base with federal senior pass; others pay $16 base, $18
for premium locations, $21 double sites ($9 & $10.50 with
senior pass). 5/15-9/30; 14-day limit. 41 sites (typically
55 ft). Tbls, toilets, cfga, drkg wtr, accessible fishing pier.
Swimming beach, boating(l), fishing, picnicking, Bruno's
Run Hiking Trail (7-mi loop along Indian River & among
small lakes). GPS: 49.89111, -97.15361

MUSKEGON (60S)
Cedar Creek   FREE
Motorcycle Staging Area
Manistee National Forest
5 mi N of Muskegon on US 31; 6 mi N on M-120 to Twin
Lake; 2 mi E on Reyerson Rd.; follow signs. Free undes-
ignated camping area. Tbls, cfga, no toilets, no drkg wtr.
Staging area for motorcycle trail riders. Accessible to RVs.

NEWAYGO (61S)
Newaygo State Park $12
12 mi NE of Newaygo on M-37; W to 32nd & 36th Sts. $12.
4/15-10/23; 15-day limit. 99 rustic sites. Tbls, pit toilets,
cfga, drkg wtr, dump, playground. Boating(l), hiking trails,
fishing. GPS: 43.5025244, -85.5917121

PARADISE (63N)
River Mouth Unit $12
Tahquamenon Falls State Park
4.5 mi S of Paradise on SR 123; at mouth of Tahquamenon River. $12. 4/15-11/15; 15-day limit. 36 rustic &
semi-modern sites with pit & flush toilets, cfga, drkg
wtr, tbls ($16 at semi-modern sites). Shelter, dump.
Hunting, fishing, boating(l), hiking, snowmobiling, skiing.
Three other campgrounds have sites at $16-23. GPS:
46.5964062, -85.2084386

PAULDING (64N)
Bond Falls Park $10
Upper Peninsula Power Company
Ontonagon County Park
4 mi E of Paulding off US 45 on Bond Falls Rd. $10. Primi-
tive sites. Tbls, toilets, cfga, drkg wtr at concession stand.
Picnicking, hiking (well marked trail leads to Bond Falls;
below Bond Falls, 2 foot bridges permit scenic views of the
falls from all angles); hunting in season; fishing (brown and
rainbow trout fishing in the river north of the falls; panfish,
walleye, large northern pike in the 2200-acre flowage).
Bait & food at concession stand. All 50,000 acres open to
public for camping. GPS: 46.408338, -89.133218

Bruce Crossing $10
Stannard Township Campground
N of Paulding on US 45 to Bruce Crossing (jct with M-28);
just N of Settler Co-op. $10. 13 sites. Tbls, toilets, cfga,
drkg wtr, elec. GPS: 46.536987, -89.176871

Robbins Pond   FREE
Ottawa National Forest
One-fifth mi N of Paulding on US 45; 2.5 mi W on CR
527; 1.6 mi S on FR 181. Free. 5/1-12/1; 14-day limit.
3 sites (RVs under 22 ft). Tbls, toilets, cfga, well drkg
wtr. Picnicking, fishing, berry picking. Elev 1300 ft. 2
acres. Trout pond. Historic site; old lumbering town. GPS:
46.38512818, -89.17486451

PINCKNEY (65S)

Crooked Lake Campground $12
Pinckney State Recreation Area
4 mi SW of Pinckney. $12. 4/1-12/1; 15-day limit. 25 rustic sites. Tbls, toilets, cfga, drkg wtr. Shelter, playground, dump, beach, concession. Ski trails, backpacking trails, bridle trails, horseback riding (stable), boating(lr), canoeing(r), swimming, fishing. 11,000 acres. GPS: 42.2534, -83.58115

PRESQUE ISLE (66S)

Moosehead Lake $12
Ottawa National Forest
6 mi S of Presque Island on SR 64; 5 mi E on FR 8220; 3 mi SE on FR 6860; 2 mi S on FR 6862. $12 during 5/15-9/30; free rest of year, but no services; 14-day limit. 17 sites (some quite spacious). Tbls, toilets, cfga, drkg wtr. Boating(l), canoeing, fishing, swimming. 10 acres. GPS: 46.24162668, -089.60435854

RACO (67N)

Bay View $8
Hiawatha National Forest
8 mi W of Raco on M-28; 6.5 mi N on FR 3154; 2.3 mi SW on FR 3150. $8 with federal senior pass; others pay $16. About 5/15-10/15; 14-day limit. 24 sites, typically 20 ft. Tbls, toilets, cfga, drkg wtr. Fishing. 20 acres. GPS: 84.7794, -46.46

RANDVILLE (69N)

Campsite #8 $10
WE Energies
Wilderness Shores Recreation Area
2.6 mi S of Randville on CR 607; 7.4 mi W on co rd to campground (at Michigamme Falls on Michigamme River). $10. 5/1-9/30; 15-day limit. Open primitive camping. No drkg wtr; tbls, toilets, cfga. Picnicking, fishing, boating(l).

Campsite #9 $10
WE Energies
Wilderness Shores Recreation Area
2.3 mi S of Randville on CR 607; 5.6 mi W on co rd; 2.7 mi E on co rd to campground (at Peavy Falls on Michigamme River). $10. 5/1-9/30; 15-day limit. 4 primitive sites. No drkg wtr; tbls, toilets, cfga. Picnicking, fishing, boating(l).

RAPID RIVER (70S)

Flowing Well $12
Hiawatha National Forest
14 mi E of Rapid River on US 2 (1.5 mi E of Nahma Junction); 3 mi N on FR 13; at Sturgeon River. $12. 5/1-12/1; 14-day limit. 10 sites (22-ft RV limit). Tbls, toilets, cfga, drkg wtr. Fishing, picnicking, hiking trails. Flowing well is 1,160 ft deep. GPS: 45.9375, -86.60694

Haymeadow Creek   FREE
Hiawatha National Forest
1.6 mi E of Rapid River on US 2; 9.4 mi N on CR 509. Free. 4/15-12/1; 14-day limit. 15 large sites. Tbls, toilets, cfga, drkg wtr. Pack out trash. Hiking trails, fishing (brook trout in Haymeadow Creek). Bay de Noc-Grand Island National Recreation Area. Trail nearby. 1 mi scenic hike to waterfall. Creek GPS: 46.48, -85.97

Little Bay De Noc $12
Hiawatha National Forest
2 mi E of Rapid River on US 2; 5 mi S on CR 513. $12 base. 5/15-10/7; 14 day limit. Base fee for Oaks loop; $13 for premium North Maywood & Twin Springs areas. 36 sites, typically 40 ft. Tbls, toilets, cfga, drkg wtr. Boating(l), fishing, hiking, waterskiing, fishing. GPS: 45.84167, -86.98306

ROSE CITY (71S)

Rifle River State Recreation Area $12
4.7 mi E of Rose City on Rose City Rd. $10 base. 4/20-12/1; 15-day limit. Base fee for 101 rustic sites at 3 locations (pit toilets, cfga, drkg wtr, tbls); $19 at 75 modern sites. Dump, group camping area, playground. Fishing, hunting, swimming, boating(l), ski trails, hiking trails. GPS: 44.391113, -84.025146

ST. IGNACE (72N)

Brevoort Lake $9
Hiawatha National Forest
17 mi NW of St. Ignace on US 2; 1.5 mi N on FR 3108; half mi NE on FR 3473. $9 with federal senior pass; others pay $18. 5/7-9/13; 14-day limit. 70 sites, typically 45 ft. Tbls, flush toilets, cfga, drkg wtr, dump, store. Swimming, boating(lr), fishing, hiking, waterskiing. 21 acres. Non-campers pay $5 day use fee, $8 for dump station. GPS: 46.00722, -89.97222

Carp River $8
Hiawatha National Forest
7.7 mi N of St. Ignace on I-75; 5 mi N on CR 412 (Mackinac Trail). $8 with federal senior pass; others pay $16. About 5/7-10/15; 14-day limit. 44 sites. Tbls, toilets, cfga, drkg wtr. Fishing, biking, hiking, boating(l). 15 acres. GPS: 46.03306, -84.71916

Dispersed Campsite 1   FREE
Round Lake
Hiawatha National Forest
About 10 mi NW of St. Ignace on US 2; N on Hwy H-57; access on FR 3105 on S shore of Round Lake. Free. All year; 14-day limit. Primitive camping; no facilities, no drkg wtr. Boating(l), fishing, hiking. North Country Trail nearby.

Dispersed Campsite 6 — FREE
Carp River
Hiawatha National Forest
About 20 mi NW of St. Ignace on US 2; N on country rd, then N on two-track primitive rds; just N of Rock Rapids on Carp River. All year; 14-day limit. Primitive camping area; no facilities. Fishing (trout), hiking.

Dispersed Campsite 7 — FREE
Rock Rapids
Hiawatha National Forest
About 20 mi NW of St. Ignace on US 2; N on county rd, then N on two-track primitive rds to Rock Rapids. Free. All year; 14-day limit. Primitive camping area; no facilities, no drkg wtr. Fishing, hiking.

Dispersed Campsite 10 — FREE
Carp River Bridge
Hiawatha National Forest
About 20 mi NW of St. Ignace on US 2; N on county rd, then N on Nogi Rd (FR 3458); at bridge over Carp River. Free. All year; 14-day limit. Primitive undesignated sites; no facilities, no drkg wtr. Fishing, hunting.

Dispersed Campsite 12 — FREE
Hiawatha National Forest
7.7 mi N of St. Ignace on I-75; 5 mi N on CR 412 (Mackinac Trail) to Carp River Recreation Area (which offers camping for fee); E on two-track CR 500 to shore of Lake Huron. Free. All year; 14-day limit. Fishing, boating, swimming.

Foley Creek — CLOSED
Hiawatha National Forest
4 mi N of St. Ignace on I-75; 2.3 mi N on CR 412 (Mackinac Trail). GPS: 45.93278, -84.75

Lake Michigan Campground — $9
Hiawatha National Forest
16.5 mi NW of St. Ignace on US 2. $9 with federal senior pass; others pay $18. About 5/7-9/15; 14-day limit. 35 sites, typically 45 ft. Tbls, flush toilets, cfga, drkg wtr, store, dump($5 non-campers). Fishing, swimming, biking. 10 acres. Non-campers pay $5 day use fee. GPS: 45.98583, -84.97167

ST. JAMES (73N)

Bill Wagner Memorial Campground — $10
Peaine Township Park
Beaver Island
8 mi S of St. James on shore of Lake Michigan. $10. May-Oct. 22 rustic sites. Tbls, pit toilets, cfga, drkg wtr, no showers. Fishing, hiking, boating. GPS: 45.656326, -85.494658

St. James — $5
Peaine Township Campground
1 mi W of St. James on Donegal Bay Rd; on N end of Bea-

ver Island. $5. May-Oct. 12 rustic sites. Tbls, pit toilets, cfga, drkg wtr, no showers. Fishing, hiking, boating. GPS: 46.655273, -85.493652

SENEY (74N)

Seney Township Campground — FREE
Half mi N of Seney on School St (turn N at gs station in town); at the Fox River. Free. 25 sites, 15 with elec. Tbls, toilets, cfga, drkg wtr, metered elec, playground. 27-mi hiking trail. GPS: 46.353616, -85.962757.

SHINGLETON (75N)

Colwell Lake — $12
Hiawatha National Forest
10 mi S of Shingleton on SR 94; half mi NE on CR 2246. $12 base. About 5/15-10/7; 14-day limit. Base fee for non-elec RV/tent sites; $4 elec surcharge ($10 with federal senior pass at elec sites). Group sites $50. 35 sites, typically 40 ft. Tbls, toilets, cfga, drkg wtr, dump($4 non-campers). Swimming, boating(l), fishing, hiking, waterskiing. 145-acre lake. GPS: 46.22167, -86.4375

Indian River — $12
Hiawatha National Forest
14.5 mi S of Shingleton on SR-94. $12. About 5/15-10/7; 14-day limit. 5 sites (22-ft RV limit). Tbls, toilets, cfga, drkg wtr. Free or reduced fees after mid-Sept; limited facilities then. Boating, good fishing. GPS: 46.1557976, -86.4043174

Little Bass Lake — $12
Hiawatha National Forest
11.7 mi S of Shingleton on SR 94; 1.7 mi W on CR 437; 1.5 mi SE on FR 2213; 1 mi S on FR 2639. $12. About 5/15-10/10; 14-day limit. 12 sites. Tbls, toilets, cfga, drkg wtr. Picnicking, hiking, fishing, swimming. 84-acre lake. GPS: 46.1639, -86.4502

SIDNAW (76N)

Lake Sainte Kathryn — $7
Ottawa National Forest
8 mi S of Sidnaw on Sidnaw Rd. $7 with federal senior pass; others pay $14. Open 5/15-10/15; 14-day limit. 25 sites (22-ft RV limit). Tbls, toilets, cfga, drkg wtr. Free during early spring, but no facilities provided. Swimming, boating(l), fishing. 17 acres. GPS: 46.39317419, -88.72262918

Norway Lake — $7
Ottawa National Forest
6 mi S of Sidnaw on Sidnaw Rd; 2 mi E on FR 2400. $7 with federal senior pass; others pay $14. 5/15-10/15; 14-day limit. 27 sites (typically 40 ft). Tbls, toilets, cfga, drkg wtr. Swimming, boating(l), fishing, hiking trails. 20 acres. GPS: 46.41583408, -88.68205671

Perch Lake West $7
Ottawa National Forest
10.5 mi S of Sidnaw on Sidnaw Rd; 1.5 mi E on co rd. $7
with federal senior pass; others pay $14 during 5/15-10/15;
free rest of year but no services; 14-day limit. 20 sites
(22-ft RV limit). Tbls, toilets, cfga, drkg wtr. Swimming,
boating(l), fishing. 13 acres. GPS: 46.364325, -88.67442

STRONGS (77N)
Soldier Lake $8
Hiawatha National Forest
1 mi S of Strongs on FR 3159; 5.2 mi E on Hwy 28; three-
fourths mi S on FR 3138. $8 with federal senior pass;
others pay $16. About 5/15-10/15; 14-day limit. 44 sites
(32-ft RV limit). Tbls, toilets, cfga, drkg wtr. Swimming,
boating, fishing, hiking trails. 25 acres. Non-campers pay
$5 day use fee. GPS: 46.349184, -84.8695116

Three Lakes $8
Hiawatha National Forest
2 mi S of Strongs on CR 33142. $8 with federal senior
pass; others pay $16. About 5/15-10/15; 14-day limit. 28
sites (32-ft RV limit). Tbls, toilets, cfga, drkg wtr. Boating,
fishing. GPS: 46.3194597, -84.9775738

WATERSMEET (79N)
Burned Dam FREE
Ottawa National Forest
From Watersmeet, 6.1 mi E on Cr 208; 1.2 mi N on FR 169.
Free. 5/15-11/30; 14-day limit. 5 sites. Tbls, toilets, cfga,
no drkg wtr. Fishing, berry-picking, swimming, boat-
ing. 3 acres. Historical interest; site of early log drives.
Trout fishing on Middle Branch of Onotongon River. GPS:
46.31379535, -89.05313987.

Imp Lake $7
Ottawa National Forest
Half mi S of Watersmeet on US 45; 6 mi E on US 2; 1.5 mi
S on FR 3978. $7 with federal senior pass; others pay $14
during 5/15-9/15; free rest of year, but no services; 14-day
limit. 22 sites (typically 40 ft). Tbls, toilets, cfga, drkg wtr.
Boating(l), fishing (bass & trout), hunting, hiking trails.
GPS: 46.21766654, -89.070557

Marion Lake $7
Ottawa National Forest
Half mi S of Watersmeet on US 45; 3.7 mi E on US 2; 2.5 mi
E on FR 3980. $7 with federal senior pass; others pay $14
during 5/15-9/15; free rest of year, but no services; 14-day
limit. 39 sites (22-ft RV limit). Tbls, toilets, cfga, drkg wtr.
Swimming, boating(lr), fishing (walleye & trout), hunting,
group camping. Near Sylvania Recreation Area and Wilderness. 14 acres. GPS: 46.26834589, -89.09292218

Paulding Pond FREE
Ottawa National Forest
9 mi N of Watersmeet on US 45. Free. All year; 14-day

limit. 4 sites (60-ft RV limit). Tbls, toilets, cfga, no drkg
wtr. Fishing, boating. 2 acres. Trout pond. Carry-down
boat launch.

Sylvania (Clark Lake) Campground $8
Ottawa National Forest
Sylvania Recreation Area
4 mi W of Watersmeet on US 2; 5 mi S on CR 535; half
mi SW on FR 6360. On Clark Lake. $8 with federal senior
pass; others pay $16. About MD-9/15; free rest of year, but
no services; 14-day limit. 48 sites. Tbls, flush toilets, cfga,
drkg wtr, showers, dump. Hiking, hunting, swimming,
boating(l), fishing. Non-campers pay $5 day use fee (or
$20 annual permit). Note: Road to campground closed
during 2014. GPS: 46.24463410, -089.31003087

WELLSTON (80S)
Bear Creek $5
Manistee National Forest
2 mi W of Wellston on M-55; 3.2 mi N on High Bridge Rd; 6
mi W on River Rd. $5 daily forest pass (or $15 weekly; $30
annually). Primitive camping for self-contained RVs only.
Undesignated sites. Toilets, cfga, no drkg wtr. Fishing.

Bear Track $8
Manistee National Forest
3.9 mi S of Wellston on Seaman Rd, turning right on Seaman
just past store for 3 mi to Irons; right on 10.5 Mile Rd for
2.5 mi; right on Bass Lake Rd for 0.9 mi, then straight onto
11-Mile Rd, following signs for 2.5 mi; right on Riverside Dr
to campground above Little Manistee River. $8 with federal
senior pass; others pay $16 (double sites $26, or $13 with
senior pass). 5/9-9/30; free off-season, but no amenities or
service; 14-day limit. 20 sites up to 68 ft. Tbls, toilets, cfga,
drkg wtr. Scenic hiking, group camping, fishing, canoeing.
North Country National Scenic Trail. Non-campers pay $5
day use fee. GPS: 44.291727, -86.03068

Blacksmith Bayou $5
Manistee National Forest
Manistee National Recreation Area
2 mi W of Wellston on M-55; 2.8 mi N on High Bridge Rd;
half mi W on FR 5175; N on dirt rd. Follow signs. $5 daily
forest pass (or $15 weekly; $30 annually). All year; 14-day
limit; may be open & free off-season, but no services.
Self-contained RVs only. Undesignated camping; about
8 sites. Toilets, cfga, no drkg wtr. Fishing. GPS: 44.2617,
-86.0359

Driftwood Valley FREE
Manistee National Forest
Three-fourths mi W of Wellston on co rd; right on 10-Mile
Rd for half mi; left on 10.5-Mile Rd for 7.5 mi; left on Bass
Lake Rd for 1 mi; right on FR 5357 for 1 mi. Free primitive,
undesignated sites. No facilities, no drkg wtr. All year;
14-day limit. Decommissioned as campground & not
maintained. GPS: 44.220027, -86.310388

MICHIGAN

Government Landing   FREE
Manistee National Forest
Manistee National Recreation River
2 mi W of Wellston on SR 55; 6 mi N on High Bridge Rd; 3.5
mi E on Coates Hwy; 2.5 mi S on Dilling Rd; 2.5 mi NE on
Upper River Rd. Free. All year (no amenities or services in
winter); 14-day limit. 3 sites. Tbls, toilet, cfga, no drkg wtr.
Canoeing, fishing. GPS: 44.263275, -85.888673

High Bridge $5
Manistee National Forest
2 mi W of Wellston on M-55; 3 mi N on High Bridge Rd. $5
daily (or $15 weekly $30 annually). Camping for self-contained RVs only. Undesignated sites. Toilets, cfga, no drkg
wtr. Fishing.

Marzinski Horse Camp   FREE
Manistee National Forest
From Wellston at jct with Seaman Rd, 10.2 mi W on SR
56; left on Marzinski Rd for .25 mi; on the left. Free. All
year; 14-day limit. 21 sites (7 pull-through for large RVs);
typically 30-ft sites. Tbls, toilets, cfga, drkg wtr, no trash
service. Hitching posts, space for portable corrals. Hiking,
horseback riding. GPS: 44.22845, -86.15896

Pine Lake Campground $8
Manistee National Forest
1 mi SW of Wellston on Bosschem Rd; 3 mi E on Pine
Lake Rd. $8 with federal senior pass; others pay $16
during 5/7-9/19; free rest of year, but no amenities or
service; 14-day limit. 12 sites up to 74 ft. Tbls, toilets,
cfga, drkg wtr, beach. Boating(l), fishing, canoeing, picnicking. Non-campers pay $4 day use fee. GPS: 44.19538,
-83.599359

Red Bridge River Access Site   FREE
Manistee National Forest
Manistee National Recreation River
2 mi W of Wellston on SR 55; 6 mi N on High Bridge Rd;
8 mi E on Coates Hwy. Free. All year; 14-day limit (no
amenities or services in winter). 4 sites. Tbls, toilets, cfga,
no drkg wtr. Hiking, boating(l), fishing. GPS: 44.283943,
-85.861726

Sand Lake Recreation Area $10.50
Manistee National Forest
3.9 mi S of Wellston on Seaman Rd; just past grocery
store in Dublin, Seaman turns right for 0.5 mi; right on
Sand Lake Rd (FR 728) for 0.5 mi. $10.50 with federal
senior pass; others pay $21. 5/8-9/20; 14-day limit. 47
sites; 50-ft RV limit. Tbls, flush toilets, cfga, drkg wtr,
showers($), beach. Boating(l), fishing, swimming. GPS:
44.167, -85.93615

Sawdust Hole River Access $5
Manistee National Forest
Manistee National Recreation River
2 mi W of Wellston on SR 55; 6 mi N on High Bridge Rd; 3.5
mi E on Coates Hwy; 2 mi S on Dilling Rd; N on FR 8799.
$5 daily (or $15 weekly, $40 annually). All year; 14-day
limit (free but not maintained in winter). 8 sites. Tbls, toilets, cfga, no drkg wtr. Boating(l), fishing, canoeing. GPS:
44.269312, -85.951684

WETMORE (82N)
Widewaters Campground $8
Hiawatha National Forest
11.7 mi S of Wetmore on CR 13; .6 mi NW on FR 2262.
$8 with federal senior pass; others pay $16. 5/15-10/1;
14-day limit. 34 sites (typically 45 ft). Tbls, toilets, cfga,
drkg wtr. Boating(lr), fishing, Bruno's Run Hiking Trail
(7-mi look among small lakes & along Indian River). 12
acres. GPS: 46.21944, -86.62833

WHITE CLOUD (83S)
Brush Lake Campground $10
Manistee National Forest
2.5 mi N of White Cloud on SR 37; 6 mi E on Monroe St (Old
SR 20); 3.5 mi N on Poplar Ave; 1.5 mi E on 6 Mile Rd; S on
FR 5534 to site. $10. All year; 14-day limit (free in winter
but no amenities or services). Non-campers pay $5 day
use fee ($15 weekly, $30 annually). 7 sites; 35-ft RV limit.
Tbls, toilets, cfga, no drkg wtr. Fishing, boating(l). GPS:
43.638985, -85.689801.

Twinwood Lake $10
Manistee National Forest
4.5 mi S of White Cloud on M-37; E on 40th St; S on Bass-
wood Rd qtr mi to lake. $10. All year, but only partial ser-
vices during 11/1-5/1. Primitive camping; 5 undesignated
sites. Toilets, cfga, no drkg wtr. Fishing, boating. GPS:
43.4734, -86.7656.

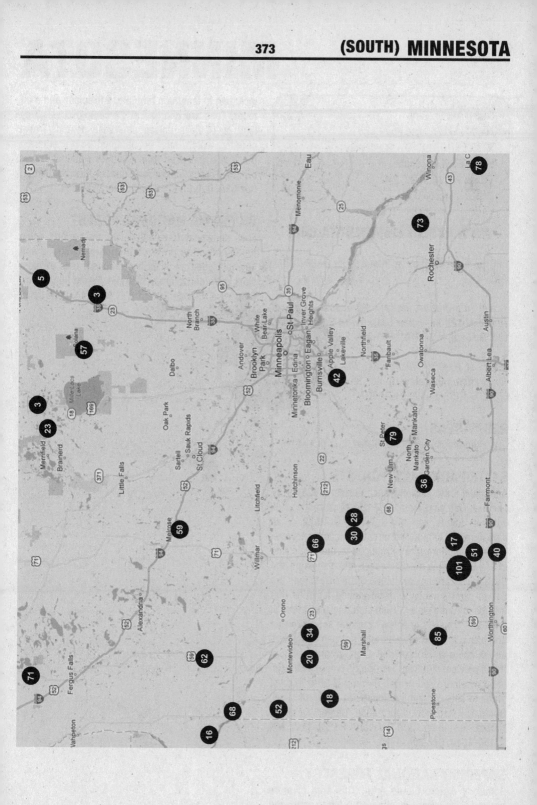

MINNESOTA

CAPITAL: St. Paul
NICKNAME: North Star State
STATEHOOD: 1858 – 32nd State
FLOWER: Lady Slipper
TREE: Red (Norway) Pine
BIRD: Common Loon

WWW.EXPLOREMINNESOTA.COM

Toll-free number for travel information: 1-888-TOUR-ISM.

Travel Information Center, Minnesota Office of Tourism, 121 7th Place East, Metro Square, Suite 100, St. Paul, MN 55101. 651-296-5029.

Dept. of Natural Resources, Div of Parks and Recreation, 500 Lafayette Rd., St. Paul, MN 55155. 651/296-6157 or 888-646-6367.

REST AREAS
Overnight stops are not permitted.

STATE PARKS AND FORESTS
An annual state park entrance permit is $25, or $7 per day. Camping fees are $12-$14 at rustic sites with pit toilets and no showers; $12-$22 at all campgrounds with modern restrooms and showers. The semi-modern rate is reduced to the rustic rate of $12-$14 during the off-season when showers and flush toilets are not available. State forest fees are $12 in campgrounds with developed facilities that include drinking water, trash containers and toilets. Each site consists of a level parking spur, fire ring and picnic table, with vault toilets, trash containers and drinking water provided. Campgrounds without those services are free. Electricity, where available, is $6 whether used or not. RV limit is 20 ft in most state forests. Maximum length of stay, 14 days. Outdoor Recreation Information Center, Dept. of Natural Resources, 500 Lafayette Rd, St. Paul, MN 55155-4040; 612-296-4776.

SUPERIOR NATIONAL FOREST
Boundary Waters Canoe Area. This area of more than 1 million acres has almost 2000 free, managed campsites. Most have simple camping facilities, including at least one tent site, a fireplace and a pit toilet. Fees are charged at 23 campgrounds. Stay limit is 14 days unless otherwise posted. Travel permits, which must be obtained before entering the BWCA, are free from Superior National Forest offices. Forest Supervisor, Superior National Forest, Box 338, Duluth, MN 55801; 218 720-5324.

CHIPPEWA NATIONAL FOREST
Fees shown at forest sites are for periods when full services are provided. During early spring and late fall when services are reduced, fees at most sites are reduced or not charged. Forest Supervisor, Chippewa National Forest, P.O. Box 244, Cass Lake, MN 56633. 218/335-8600.

ARGYLE (2N)
Old Mill State Park $12
12 mi E of Argyle on CR 4, then N 1 mi N on CR 4 to CR 39. $12 base at 26 standard non-elec sites; $16 at 10 elec sites. All year; 14-day limit. Flush toilets, tbls, cfga, drkg wtr, no showers. Shelter, playgrounds, historic grist mill, 67-ft RV rig limit. Volleyball, interpretive program, hiking trails, swimming, fishing, winter sports. 287 acres. GPS: 48.361364, -96.5703288

BADGER (4N)
Durgin Memorial Park $12
At SR 11 & CR 2 in Badger. $12 with elec; $8 no elec ($50 weekly, $150 monthly). May-Sept. Tbls, flush toilets, cfga, drkg wtr, elec, dump, shelter, playground. Connects with CanAm Wilderness Trail. GPS: 48.782574, -96.00999

BARNUM (5S)
Barnum City Park $10
Barnum City Park
From I-35 at Barnum, 0.75 mi on CR 6 (Main St); at Moosehorn River. $10 ($70 weekly) 5/1-9/30. 12 primitive sites. Playground, tbls, toilets, cfga, drkg wtr, shelters. Horseshoe pits, volleyball. No longer camping at county's Hanging Horn Access. GPS: 46.5031, -92.6914

BAUDETTE (6N)
Frontier Access   FREE
Koochiching County Park
17 mi E of Baudette on SR 11. Free primitive camping. 6 sites; 2 picnic sites. Tbls, toilets, cfga, drkg wtr, playground. Boating(l), fishing. Vicinity GPS: 48.3922, -94.1523

BEMIDJI (7N)
Coffee Pot Landing   FREE
Mississippi Headwaters State Forest
6 mi N on CR 2 from Lake Itasca to CR 40; E 2 mi; N half mi. Free. 5/5-9/9; 14-day limit. 2 sites, cfga, tbls, no drkg wtr. Fishing, canoeing, picnicking. On Mississippi River canoe route. Forest GPS: 47.4377313.

Legrande Landing   FREE
Mississippi Headwaters State Forest
S of Bemidji 10 mi on US 71; E on CR 16, past Guthrie 2 mi; S 2 mi to Steamboat River. Free. 5/5-9/9; 14-day limit. 2 sites, cfga, tbls, no drkg wtr. Canoeing, swimming, fishing on Steamboat River.

Pine Point Landing   FREE
Mississippi Headwaters State Forest
CR 3 N from Becida 3 mi to Stecker forest rd; N 2.5 mi. Free. 5/5-9/9; 14-day limit. 2 sites, cfga, tbls. No drkg wtr. Canoeing, picnicking, fishing. On Mississippi River canoe route.

Stumphges Rapids   FREE
Mississippi Headwaters State Forest
6 mi N from Lake Itasca on CR 2; E 2 mi on CR 40; N half mi to Coffee Pot Landing, then N 8 mi. Free. 5/5-9/9; 14-day limit. 2 sites, cfga, tbls, no drkg wtr, no toilets. Canoeing, fishing, picnicking. On Mississippi River canoe route.

Wannagan Landing   FREE
Mississippi Headwaters State Forest
4 mi N from Lake Itasca on CR 2; W 1.5 mi to landing on Mississippi River. 5/5-9/9; 14-day limit. 2 sites, cfga, tbls, no toilets, no drkg wtr. Canoeing, fishing, picnicking. Water access. On Mississippi River canoe route.

BENA (8N)
Tamarack Point $7
Chippewa National Forest
1.5 mi E of Bena on US 2; 5.5 mi NE on CR 9; 3.5 mi NW on FR 2163. $7 with federal senior pass; others pay $14. 5/1-7/6; 14-day limit. 31 sites (typically 50 ft). Tbls, toilets, cfga, drkg wtr. Swimming, fishing, boating(ld), hiking trails. GPS: 47.444, 94.121

BIG FALLS (9N)
Benn Linn Landing   FREE
Pine Island State Forest
1.5 mi N of Big Falls on CR 13; follow signs W 3.5 mi. Free. 5/5-9/9; 14-day limit. 3 sites, cfga, tbls, no drkg wtr. Fishing, canoeing, boating, picnicking. On Big Fork River canoe route. GPS: 48.12111, -94.1100.

Big Fork River Camp   FREE
Boise Cascade Corp
13.5 mi S of Big Falls on MN 6; half mi SW on gravel rd to river. Free. 5/1-11/15; 14-day limit. 3 sites. Tbls, toilets, cfga, drkg wtr, mechanical boat lift. Picnicking, fishing, hunting, hiking, boating(l). On marked river float trip route.

First River Access   FREE
Pine Island State Forest
13.5 mi S of Big Falls on MN 6; half mi SW on logging rd (watch for small sign at jct). Free. All year. 3 sites. Tbls, toilets, cfga. Picnicking, fishing, boating(l).

Johnson's Landing   FREE
Koochiching State Forest
10 mi S of Big Falls on SR 6; follow signs E 1 mi. Free. 5/5-9/9; 14-day limit. 2 sites, cfga, tbls, no drkg wtr. Canoeing, fishing, swimming, picnicking. On Big Fork canoe route.

Kueffner's Landing   FREE
Koochiching County Park
10 mi N of Big Falls on CR 13; 1 mi W; at Big Fork River. Free primitive camping. 2 sites. Tbls, toilet, no drkg wtr. Boating(l), fishing.

Sturgeon River Camp   FREE
Pine Island State Forest
CR 30 W 3.5 mi from Big Falls, then 1.5 mi N to Big Fork River. Free. 5/5-9/9; 14-day limit. 2 sites, cfga, tbls, no drkg wtr. Fishing, boating, canoeing, picnicking.

BIRCHDALE (11N)
Birchdale Access (Nelson Park)   FREE
Koochiching County Park
1 mi N of Birchdale. Free. 4/1-11/15. About 10 undesignated sites. Tbls, toilets, cfga, drkg wtr. Boating, fishing, hiking trail.

Franz Jevne State Park $12
3 mi NE of Birchdale on SR 11; along shore of Rainy River on Canadian border. $12. All year; 14-day limit. 18 rustic sites with pit toilets, tbls, cfga, drkg wtr, no showers; 1 elec site $16. 30-ft RV limit. Fishing, boating(l), hiking trail. 118 acres. GPS: 48.38527, -94.03755

BLACKDUCK (12N)
Webster Lake $7
Chippewa National Forest
7 mi S of Blackduck on SR 39; 1 mi E on FR 2207; 2 mi S on FR 2236. $7 with federal senior pass; others pay $14. 5/17-LD; 14-day limit. 15 sites (typically 45 ft). Tbls, toilets, cfga, drkg wtr. Boating(l), fishing, hiking. GPS: 47.3611, 94.3028

BLUE EARTH (13S)
Blue Earth $5
Faribault County Fairgrounds
2 blks N of US 169 & 16 on US 169; N edge of town (paved access rds). Free first night; $20 thereafter ($10 for tents). 4/1-11/30; 5-night limit. 9 sites. Tbls, toilets, cfga, drkg wtr, dump ($5), elec/wtr hookup. Ball fields, horseshoes, playground, walking/biking trail. GPS: 44.255086, -94.157616

BRIMSON (15NW)
Cadotte Lake $8
Superior National Forest
6 mi N of Brimson on CR 44; 1.5 mi W on CR 16 (FR 11); half mi N on FR 425; 1 mi SW on FR 778. $8 base with federal senior pass; others pay $16 base, $18 at premium locations ($9 with senior pass). About 5/1-9/30; 14-day limit. 27 sites up to 45 ft. Tbls, toilets, cfga, drkg wtr. Boating(l) fishing, swimming. GPS: 47.380420, -91.916634

BROWNS VALLEY (16S)
Browns Valley City Park $10
2 blocks S of Main Street on Hwy 28 in Browns Valley. $10 without elec, $15 with elec/wtr. 5/1-11/1. 50 sites. Tbls, toilets, cfga, drkg wtr. Store, food, laundry, gas, ice, bottled gas nearby. Picnicking, playground. 320-695-2110

Traverse County Park $10
6 mi N of Browns Valley on MN 27. $9 without hookups, $15 elec. All year. 25 sites. Tbls, toilets, cfga, firewood, drkg wtr, elec hookups. Picnicking, fishing, swimming, boating(l), playground, snow skiing nearby, snowmobile trails.

BUTTERFIELD (17S)
Voss Municipal Park $12
1 mi W of Butterfield on CR 2. $12 base. 5/1-10/1. Base fee for primitive sites. $13 with elec; $14 with full hookups. 110 sites. Tbls, toilets, cfga, drkg wtr, showers, elec($), A/C($), playgrounds, dump. Picnicking. GPS: 43.9632903, -94.8030381

CANBY (18S)
Lake Sylvan Park $10
Canby Municipal Park
Half mi S of jct of US 75 & SR 68 in Canby; turn on Haafager Ave to campsites. $10. 5/15-10/15. 6 sites. Tbls, flush toilets, cfga, drkg wtr, dump, playground, elec, showers. Tennis, wading pool, swimming pool($). 12 acres. GPS: 44.705633, -96.279422

Triangle Municipal Park $10
N of jct of US 75 & CR 3 in Canby. $10. 5/1-9/3. 20 sites. Tbls, flush toilets, cfga, drkg wtr, elec, dump. Picnicking. GPS: 44.718611, -96.255278

CASS LAKE (19N)
Cass Lake Campground $10.50
Norway Beach Recreation Area
Chippewa National Forest
3.7 mi E of Cass Lake on US 2; left for 0.2 mi at recreation area sign; left at second sign for 0.2 mi. $10.50 with federal senior pass; others pay $21. 5/11-MD; 14-day limit. 23 sites (typically 45 ft). Tbls, flush toilets, cfga, drkg wtr, dump, beach. Interpretive trails, swimming, biking trail, boating(l), fishing. Nearby Chippewa Campground is $26. GPS: 47.380859, -94.529

Knutson Dam $8
Chippewa National Forest
6 mi E of Cass Lake on US 2; 5.3 mi N on CR 10; .7 mi W on FR 2176; on N shore of Cass Lake. $8 with federal senior pass; others pay $16. 5/11-11/7; 14-day limit. 14 sites (typically 40 ft). Tbls, toilets, cfga, drkg wtr. Swimming, boating(lr), fishing. Canoe access to Mississippi River. GPS: 47.2645, 94.2858

Leech Lake Campground $12
Leech Lake
Corps of Engineers
From Cass Lake at jct with US 2, 8 mi S on Hwy 8; on SW side of dam. $12 with federal senior pass at 73 elec sites; others pay $24. 5/1-10/31; 14-day limit. RV limit in excess of 65 ft; 3 pull-through sites. Tbls, flush toilets,

cfga, drkg wtr, fish cleaning station, interpretive programs, marina, dump, coin laundry, playground, showers, picnic shelter. Basketball, baseball, boating(l), fishing, hiking, tennis, canoeing, horseshoes, nature trails. GPS: 47.24472, -94.231201

Norway Beach Campground $10.50
Norway Beach Recreation Area
Chippewa National Forest
3.7 mi E of Cass Lake on US 2; left on FR 2171 at recreation area sign for 0.6 mi. $10.50 with federal senior pass; others pay $21. MD-LD; 14-day limit. 55 sites; no RV size limit. Tbls, flush toilets, cfga, drkg wtr, visitor center, dump, beach. Swimming, interpretive trails, biking trail, boating(l), fishing. GPS: 47.37861, -94.52139

South Pike Bay $8
Chippewa National Forest
3 mi S of Cass Lake on Hwy 371; 2 mi E on FR 2137. $8 with federal senior pass; others pay $16. 5/11-9/7; 14-day limit. 24 sites, typically 35 ft. Tbls, toilets, cfga, drkg wtr. Boating(l), fishing, biking. GPS: 47.1948, -94.3506

Wanaki Campground $10.50
Norway Beach Recreation Area
Chippewa National Forest
3.7 E of Cass Lake on US 2; left on FR 2171 at recreation area sign for 1.2 mi. $10.50 with federal senior pass. MD-LD; 14-day limit. 46 sites (typically 60 ft). Tbls, flush toilets, cfga, drkg wtr, showers, dump, beaches. Interpretive trails, swimming, biking trail, boating(l), fishing. GPS: 47.37861, -94.52139

Winnie Campground $8
Chippewa National Forest
6 mi E of Cass Lake on US 2; qtr mi N on CR 10; 7 mi NE on FR 2171; 4 mi S on FR 2168; on E shore of Lake Winnibigoshish. $8 with federal senior pass; others pay $16. 5/11-9/7; 14-day limit. 35 sites; 40-ft RV limit. Tbls, toilets, cfga, drkg wtr. Boating(l), fishing. GPS: 47.2530, -94.1860

CLARKFIELD (20S)
North Park Municipal Park $5
N edge of Clarkfield at 15th Ave & Hwy 59. $5 without hookups; $10 elec/wtr. Tbls, flush toilets, cfga, drkg wtr, showers, elec, shelter, playground, pool. Tennis, swimming, softball, golf. GPS: 44.7963889, -95.8066667.

CRANE LAKE (22N)
Echo Lake Campground $10
Superior National Forest
S of Crane Lake on CR 24; 2 mi E on CR 116 (Echo Trail). Also accessible via Echo Trail from Orr. $10. May-Sept; 14-day limit. 24 sites (typically 60 ft). Tbls, toilets, cfga, drkg wtr, playground. Fishing, swimming, boating(ld). GPS: 48.17056, -92.49111

CROSBY (23S)
Cross Lake Campground $10
Pine River Dam, Mississippi River
Corps of Engineers
From Crosby at jct with SR 210, 12 mi N on SR 6; 6 mi W on CR 11; NE on CR 3. During 5/1-9/30, $10 with federal senior pass at 30 non-elec sites (others pay $20); at 73 elec sites, $13 with senior pass (others pay $26). During 4/1-4/30 & 10/1-10/31, fees at non-elec sites are $10 ($5 with senior pass); at elec sites, fees are $13 ($6.50 with senior pass). Also 6 tent sites. 14-day limit. Tbls, flush toilets, cfga, drkg wtr, showers, playground, beach, fish cleaning station, dump, coin laundry, shelter. Boating(l), fishing, swimming, tennis, biking. GPS: 46.673584, -94.113525

Portsmouth Campground $12
Cuyuna Country State Recreation Area
Just SW of Crosby off SR 210 on NW shore of Portsmouth Lake. $12. All year; 14-day limit. 17 rustic sites. Tbls, pit toilets, cfga, drkg wtr. Fishing, boating, canoeing, biking trails. Reclaimed former mining pits. GPS: 46.489808, -94.000676

DEER RIVER (24N)
Cut Foot Horse Camp $8
Chippewa National Forest
1 mi W of Deer River on US 2; about 20 mi N on SR 46 past Cut Foot Sioux Visitor Center; left on FR 2171 for 3 mi. $8 for seniors with Golden Age Passports; others pay $16. About 4/15-10/15; 14-day limit. 34 sites (typically 35 ft). Tbls, toilets, cfga, drkg wtr. Picket lines for tying horses; manure pits at sites. Bridle trails, hiking, fishing. GPS: 47.55833, -94.06639

Deer Lake Campgrounds $8
Chippewa National Forest
1 mi W of Deer River on US 2; 19.1 mi N on SR 46; 3.5 mi W on gravel Eagle Nest Rd; at W shore of Big Cut Foot Sioux Lake. $8 with federal senior pass; others pay $16. 5/1-11/24; 14-day limit. 48 sites at 2 campgrounds, typically 45 ft. Tbls, toilets, cfga, drkg wtr, beach. Fishing, hiking trail, boating(l), canoeing, swimming. GPS: 47.3051, -94.0621

East Seelye Bay $8
Chippewa National Forest
1 mi W of Deer River on US 2; 19.1 mi N on SR 46; 2.5 mi W on gravel Eagle Nest Rd; at E side of Seelye Point on shore of Big Cut Foot Sioux Lake. $8 with federal senior pass; others pay $16. 5/4-10/12; 14-day limit. 13 sites, typically 45 ft. Tbls, pit toilets, cfga, drkg wtr, beach. Boating(l), fishing, swimming, hiking trail. GPS: 47.523, -94.097

Mosmo Point $8
Chippewa National Forest
1 mi W of Deer River on US 2; 18.1 mi N on SR 46 to campground sign, then left half mile on gravel rd between Little

& Big Cut Foot Sioux Lakes. $8 with federal senior pass; others pay $16. 5/1-9/10; 14-day limit. 23 sites (typically 40 ft). Tbls, flush toilets, cfga, drkg wtr, fish cleaning station. Interpretive programs, hiking trail, biking, boating(ld), fishing, swimming. GPS: 47.517, -94.045

O-Ne-Gum-E Campground $10
Chippewa National Forest
1 mi W of Deer River on US 2; 17 mi N on SR 46 to campground sign; turn right. $10 with federal senior pass; others pay $20. 5/1-11/25; 14-day limit. 48 sites, typically 40 ft (11 sites along Little Cut Foot Sioux Lake). Tbls, flush toilets, cfga, drkg wtr, fish cleaning station. Boating(l), fishing, hiking trail, interpretive programs, swimming, biking. GPS: 47.511, -94.044

Schoolcraft State Park $12
5 mi E of Deer River on Hwy 2; 8 mi S on Hwy 6; half mi W on CR 28; 2 mi W on CR 65; N on CR 74; along Mississippi River. $12 at 28 rustic sites; 40-ft RV rig limit. 4/1-10/31; 14-day limit. Pit toilets, cfga, drkg wtr, tbls, no showers, no dump, no hookups. Hiking trail, fishing, boating(lr), canoeing(r). GPS: 47.224609, -93.80127

West Seelye Bay $7
Chippewa National Forest
1 mi W of Deer River on US 2; 19.3 mi NW on SR 46; 3 mi SW on CR 33; S on FR 3153; on Cut Foot Sioux Lake. $7 with federal senior pass; others pay $14 (double sites $24). 5/1-6/1; 14-day limit. 22 sites; 45-ft RV limit. Tbls, toilets, cfga, drkg wtr, store. Boating(lr), fishing, hiking, mountain biking, horseback riding. GPS: 47.524, -94.102

West Seelye Overflow $8
Chippewa National Forest
1 mi W of Deer River on US 2; 19.3 mi NW on SR 46; 3 mi SW on CR 33. $8. 5/15-6/15; 14-day limit. 60 sites. Tbls, toilets, cfga, no drkg wtr. Dump/visitor center (5 mi). This facility open only during periods when the other Seelye campgrounds are full; its fee is half the daily fee at East Seelye.

Williams Narrows Campground $8
Chippewa National Forest
1 mi W of Deer River on US 2; 15.4 mi N on SR 46; 1.8 mi W on CR 148 (Williams Narrows Rd). $8 with federal senior pass; others pay $16. 5/1-LD; 14-day limit. 17 sites (20-30 feet long). Tbls, toilets, cfga, drkg wtr, fish cleaning station, beach. Fishing, boating(l), swimming, nature trails, interpretive programs, canoeing. GPS: 47.504, -94.064

Winnie Dam Campground $9
Lake Winnibigoshish
Corps of Engineers
From Deer River, 1 mi W on US 2; 12 mi N on SR 46; 2 mi W (left) on CR 9, following signs. $9 & $11 with federal senior

pass at 22 elec sites; others pay $18 & $22. 5/1-10/31; 14-day limit. RV limit in excess of 65 ft. Tbls, flush toilets, cfga, drkg wtr, dump, fish cleaning station, playground. Fishing, boating(l). GPS: 47.43, -94.04917

EFFIE (25N)

Bass Lake Campground $10
Boise Cascade Corp
Itasca County Parks
12 mi E of Effie on MN 1; 2 mi S on logging rd. 5/15-11/15; 14-day limit. $10. 29 sites (5 for tents). Tbls, toilets, cfga, drkg wtr, dump, no elec. beach. Picnicking, hunting, hiking trails, boating, waterskiing, swimming. 663 acres. Lake GPS: 47.7083, -93.9605

ELY (27NW)

Bear Island Lake   FREE
Superior National Forest
10 mi SW of Ely on CR 21N. Free. All year; 14-day limit. 4 primitive dispersed sites; no facilities except cfga, no trash service. Fishing, boating(l). GPS: 47.777828, -91.946244

Big Lake Dispersed Sites   FREE
Superior National Forest
11 mi E of Ely on Hwy 169; left for 2 mi on CR 88; 18 m on CR 116 (Echo Trail); left on FR 1872 to lake. Free. 3 dispersed primitive sites outside boundary waters area; 1 site within BWCAW. Toilets, cfga, no drkg wtr, no trash service. Fishing, boating(l). GPS: 48.091749, -91.9915

Birch Lake $7.50
Superior National Forest
8 mi S of Ely on SR 1; 4 mi S on gravel FR 429. $7.50 with federal senior pass; others pay $15. 5/15-9/30; 14-day limit. 29 sites, typically 45-50 ft. Tbls, toilets, cfga, drkg wtr. Boating(l), fishing, hiking trail. 10 acres. GPS: 47.758383, -91.783572

Birch Lake Dispersed Sites   FREE
Superior National Forest
8 S of Ely on SR 1; 4 mi S on gravel FR 429. Free. 5/15-9/90; 14-day limit. 14 backcountry dispersed sites. Toilets, cfga, no drkg wtr, no trash service. Boating(l), fishing, hiking trail.

Circle Route Dispersed Sites   FREE
Superior National Forest
Access to dispersed sites from Echo Trail (CR 116) to Fenske Lake, Everett Lake, Little Long Lake, Burntside Lake. Free. 5/1-9/30; 14-day limit. 18 primitive dispersed sites; no facilities, no drkg wtr. Hike-in & canoe access to tent sites at other lakes. Fishing, boating, canoeing.

Fall Lake $9
Superior National Forest
5.3 mi E of Ely on SR 169 & CR 18; 1.8 mi NE on FR 551. $9 with federal senior pass; others pay $18. 5/1-9/30; 14-day limit. 64 sites (typically 35-40 ft). Tbls, flush toilets, showers, cfga, drkg wtr, dump, elec. Fishing, boating(lr), hiking trails, canoeing(r), playground, swimming beach, waterskiing. GPS: 47.952291, -91.717889

Fenske Lake $7.50
Superior National Forest
2 mi E of Ely on SR 169; 2.5 mi N on CR 88; 8.3 mi N on CR 116 (Echo Trail). $7.50 with federal senior pass; others pay $15. 5/15-9/30; 14-day limit. 15 sites (typically 45-50 ft). Tbls, toilets, cfga, drkg wtr. Swimming, boating(l), fishing, hiking trails, interpretive programs, canoeing(r). GPS: 47.995480, -91.914876

Johnson Lake Dispersed Site FREE
Superior National Forest
6 MI SW of Ely on CR 21N. Free. 1 primitive site near lake. No facilities except cfga, no drkg wtr. Fishing. Boat ramp on E side of lake. GPS: 47.8136, -91.8971

Sand Lake Dispersed Sites FREE
Superior National Forest
S of Ely off Hwy 1 on Hwy 2. Free. 2 primitive sites at boat ramp. Toilet, tbls, cfga, no drkg wtr, no trash service. Boating(l), fishing.

South Kawishiwi River $7.50
Superior National Forest
11 mi S of Ely on SR 1. $7.50 with federal senior pass; others pay $15. 5/15-9/30; 14-day limit. 31 sites up to 60 ft. Tbls, pit toilets, cfga, drkg wtr. Hiking, boating(l), swimming, fishing. Near Boundary Waters Canoe Area. 47.815712, -91.731646

Tofte Lake Dispersed Sites FREE
Superior National Forest
14.5 E on SR 169 (becoming Fernberg Rd); left for qtr mi on FR 1541 to boat ramp. Free. 4 primitive dispersed sites; no facilities. Fishing, boating(l). GPS: 47.962275, -91.57065q

FAIRFAX (28S)
Fort Ridgely State Park $12
7 mi S of Fairfax on Hwy 4. $12 base at 16 non-elec RV sites with pit toilets, tbls, cfga, drkg wtr, no showers; $16 at 15 elec sites with flush toilets, showers. Visitor center, shelters, playground, historic site, no dump, 60-ft RV rig limit. Interpretive center, hiking trails (10 mi), bridle trails (7 mi), fishing, winter sports. 584 acres. GPS: 44.4524621, -94.7308199

FINLAND (29N)
Fourmile Lake FREE
Superior National Forest
About 7 mi NE of Finland on CR 7; 10 mi NE on FR 357. Free. 5/15-9/30; 14-day limit. 2 small RV sites. Tbls, toilets, cfga, no drkg wtr, no trash service. Boating(l), fishing, hiking. Opportunity to view ospreys & their nests. GPS: 47.70, -90.963

Harriet Lake Camp FREE
Superior National Forest
About 9 mi NE of Finland on CR 7; W on access rd. Free. 5/15-9/30; 14-day limit. 2 RV sites. Tbls, toilet, cfga, no drkg wtr. Fishing, hiking, boating(l), canoeing, swimming. GPS: 47.6560, -91.1115

Kawishiwi Lake FREE
Superior National Forest
21 mi NE of Finland on CR 7; 3 mi NW on FR 354; at edge of Boundary Water Canoe Area Wilderness. Free. 5/15-9/30; 14-day limit. 5 RV sites. Tbls, toilet, cfga, no drkg wtr, no trash service. Hiking, hunting, boating(l - no mtrs), fishing. GPS: 47.8382, -91.1024

Toohey Lake Camp FREE
Superior National Forest
About 7 mi NE of Finland on CR 7; 12 mi NE on FR 357. Free. 5/15-9/30; 14-day limit. 5 RV sites. Tbls, toilet, cfga, no drkg wtr., no trash service Fishing, boating(l), hiking, swimming. Lake GPS: 47.7207, -90.9543

Whitefish Lake Camp FREE
Superior National Forest
About 7 mi NE of Finland on CR 7; 12 mi NE on FR 357. FREE. 5/15-9/30; 14-day limit. 3 RV sites & 11 scattered backcountry sites on 5 lakes. Tbls, toilets, cfga, no drkg wtr, no trash service. Fishing, boating, canoeing, hiking, swimming. Carry-down boat access. Part of Timber Frear Canoe Route including connecting Timber, Finger, Frear & Elbow Lakes. Lake GPS: 47.7017, -91.0393

Wilson Lake Camp FREE
Superior National Forest
About 7 mi NE of Finland on CR 7; 2 mi NE on FR 357; N on access rd to lake. Free. 5/15-9/30; 14-day limit. 4 RV sites. Tbls, toilets, cfga, no drkg wtr, no trash service. Hiking, hunting, boating(l), fishing. GPS: 47.671268, -91.074423

FRANKLIN (30S)
Franklin Campsites FREE
Municipal Park
In Franklin, off SR 19; camp at Rover boat landing or at city ball park. Free. 5/1t-10/27; 7-day limit at boat landing, 3-day at ball park. 12 total sites (RVs under 30 ft). Tbls, flush toilets, showers, cfga, dump at ball park; drkg wtr playground. Picnicking, boating(l), fishing, tennis, swimming nearby. Shelter house at boat dock.

GRAND MARAIS (32NE)
Ball Club Lake FREE
Superior National Forest
3.7 mi N of Grand Marais on CR 12 (Gunflint Trail); about

20 mi N on CR 8. Free. 4/15-9/30; 14-day limit. 1 site. Tbl, toilet, cfga, no drkg wtr, no trash service. Boating(l), fishing, hiking, swimming. Lake GPS: 47.912136, -90.486765

Birch Lake   FREE
Superior National Forest
About 65 mi N of Grand Marais on CR 12 (Gunflint Trail). Free. 5/15-9/30; 14-day limit. 1 site. Tbl, toilet, cfga, no drkg wtr. Fishing, boating, swimming, hiking. Carry-down boat access on SW side of lake. GPS: 48.066162, -90.518946

Cascade River   FREE
Superior National Forest
Half mi N of Grand Marais on CR 12; 4 mi W on CR 7; 9 mi NW on FR 158. Free. All year; 14-day limit. 1 RV site. Toilet, cfga, no drkg wtr, no tbls. Boating(l), fishing. GPS: 47.8335021, -90.5303904

Devil Track Lake $8
Superior National Forest
3.8 mi N of Grand Marais on CR 12 (Gunflint Trail); 1 mi W CR 6; 7.6 mi NW on CR 8. $8 with federal senior pass; others pay $16 during MD-LD; free rest of year but no amenities or services. 14-day limit. 16 sites; no RV size limit. Tbls, toilets, cfga, drkg wtr, store. Boating(lr - hand-carry), fishing. GPS: 47.830142, -90.467023

East Bearskin Lake $9
Superior National Forest
25.6 mi NW of Grand Marais on CR 12 (Gunflint Trail); 1.5 mi NE on FR 146. $9 with federal senior pass during MD-LD; others pay $18; free rest of year but no amenities or service; 14-day limit. 33 sites up to 60 ft. Tbls, toilets, cfga, drkg wtr, store. Fishing, boating(lr). Near Boundary Waters Canoe Area. GPS: 48.037392, -90.394175

Flour Lake Campground $9
Superior National Forest
27 mi N of Grand Marais on CR 12 (Gunflint Trail); 3 mi E on CR 66. $9 with federal senior pass; others pay $18 during MD-LD; free rest of year, but no amenities or services; 14-day limit. 37 sites; no RV size limit. Tbls, toilets, cfga, drkg wtr. Boating(l), fishing. GPS: 48.052527, -90.407926

Iron Lake Campground $8
Superior National Forest
37.7 mi NW of Grand Marais on CR 12. $8 base with federal senior pass; others pay $16 base, $18 for premium locations ($9 with senior pass). 6/1-9/15; 14-day limit. 7 sites (RVs under 22 ft). Tbls, toilets, cfga, drkg wtr. Boating, fishing, picnicking. GPS: 48.067712, -90.614884

Kimball Lake $8
Superior National Forest
12 mi N of Grand Marais on CR 12 (Gunflint Trail); 2 mi E on FR 140. $8 base with federal senior pass; others pay $16 base, $18 for lakefront sites ($9 with senior pass). 5/15-

9/30; 14-day limit. 10 sites up to 55 ft. Tbls, toilets, cfga, drkg wtr. Boating(l), fishing. GPS: 47.863259, -90.226835

Trails End Campground $8
Superior National Forest
57 mi NW of Grand Marais on CR 12 (Gunflint Trail) to the end of the Trail; at Seagull Lake. $8 base with federal senior pass; others pay $16 base, $18 for premium sites, $22 with wtr hookups ($9 & $11 with senior pass). Free 10/1-MD but no amenities or services; 14-day limit. 9 of 33 sites suitable for RVs (site lengths to 40 ft). Tbls, toilets, cfga, drkg wtr. Fishing, boating(l), swimming. GPS: 48.158848, -90.894719

Two Island Lake $8
Superior National Forest
3.8 mi N of Grand Marais on CR 12 (Gunflint Trail); 1 mi W on CR 6; 4.8 mi NW on CR 8; 4.5 mi NW on CR 27. $8 with federal senior pass; others pay $16. Fees about 5/15-LD; free or reduced fees rest of year, but no services; 14-day limit. 38 sites up to 50 ft. Tbls, toilets, cfga, drkg wtr. Boating(l), fishing. GPS: 47.88005, -90.444446

GRAND RAPIDS (33N)

Long Lake Dispersed Recreation Area   FREE
Itasca County Park
12 mi N of Grand Rapids on SR 38; 1 mi W on Cr 19. Free. Undesignated primitive site; no facilities, no trash service. 2-day limit. Boating(l), fishing. Lake GPS: 47.594749, -93.396402

Hartley Lake Dispersed Recreation Area   FREE
Chippewa National Forest
12 mi E of Grand Rapids on US 169 to Taconite; 22 mi N on CR 7; 1 mi N on CR 52; 2 mi E on CR 53; 1 mi S on Rd 336 to camp. Free. Undesignated primitive site; no facilities, no trash service. 2-day limit. Boating(l), fishing. Boat access on NE side of lake, off CR 53. Lake GPS: 47.5572, -93.3071

Pug Hole Lake   FREE
Chippewa National Forest
14 mi N of Grand Rapids on MN 38. All year. Spaces for self-contained RVs at wayside park. Fishing. GPS: 47.4117, -93.5917

Scooty Lake Dispersed Recreation Area   FREE
Itasca County Park
12 mi E of Grand Rapids on US 169 to Taconite; 22 mi N on CR 7; 1 mi N on CR 52; 2 mi E on CR 53; N on access rd. Free. Undesignated primitive site; no facilities, no trash service. 14-day limit. Fishing, boating(l). Lake GPS: 47.57971, -93.30033

Shingle Mill   FREE
Management Unit
Blandin Paper Company
Two main trails into the unit area; Shingle Mill Rd, running

S off CR 449; and Smith Creek Trail, 9.5 mi S of Grand Rapids on Hwy 169; both access rds are marked by signs. Free. All year. Spaces for self-contained RVs. Hiking, snowmobiling. Blandin's largest forest mgnt. unit containing 44,000 acres is located in SW corner of Itasca Co. 70-mi of snowmobile trails.

GRANITE FALLS (34S)
Memorial Municipal Park $9
1 mi SE of Granite Falls on SR 67. $9 for RV sites with elec ($7 primitive camping). 5/1-10/31. About 37 sites; 34-ft RV limit. Tbls, toilets, cfga, drkg wtr, elec($), dump nearby. Fishing, boating(l), golf, snowmobile trails, playground, museum. 97 acres. GPS: 44.8008333, -95.5383333

Upper Sioux Agency State Park $12
8 mi SE of Granite Falls on SR 67. $12 base. All year; 14-day limit. Base fee at rustic sites with pit toilets, cfga, drkg wtr, tbls, no showers; $16 base at sites with flush toilets, showers. Elec $4 at 14 sites (2 have 50 amp). 45-ft RV rig limit. Hiking trails (18 mi), horse trails (16 mi), fishing, boating(l), snowmobiling trails (16 mi). Visitor center, shelter, historic site. Horse camping permitted. 1,280 acres. GPS: 44.7380132, -95.4539039

HANSKA (36S)
Lake Hanska $9
Brown County Park
2.7 mi S of Hanska on CR 13; 2.5 mi W on CR 6; 1 mi N on CR 11; on E shore of lake. $9 for primitive sites; $20 for RV sites with hookups. 5/1-9/30. 22 sites (30-ft RV limit). Tbls, toilets, cfga, drkg wtr, elec ($), A/C or htr ($), playground, dump ($7 non-campers), beach. Boating(l), fishing, hiking & biking trails, swimming. Archaeological findings from 500 B.C.; old fort site & log cabin. GPS: 44.1222222, -94.5541667

HOLT (37N)
Holt City Park   FREE
In Holt at E side of SR 32. Free. All year. Primitive camping. Toilets, cfga, drkg wtr, playground, tbls. Hiking trail. GPS: 48.292, -96.193

HOVLAND (38NE)
Devilfish Lake   FREE
Superior National Forest
About 20 mi N of Hovland on CR 16; 2 mi W, then 3 mi N on CR 313; 1 mi W on FR; N on access rd to lake. Free. 5/15-9/30; 14-day limit. 1 primitive sites. Tbl, toilet, cfga, no drkg wtr, no trash service. Boating, fishing, canoeing, swimming, hiking. Carry-down boat access. Lake GPS: 47.9971, -90.1031

Swamp River #1   FREE
Grand Portage State Forest
11.5 mi N of Hovland on CR 16; 3 mi E on FR 8. 5/5-9/9; 14-day limit. Free. Undesignated campsites, tbls, cfga,

no drkg wtr. Fishing (many small northern pike), boating, picnicking.

Swamp River #2   FREE
Grand Portage State Forest
6 mi N of Hovland on CR 16; quarter mi E on river access rd. 5/5-9/9; 14-day limit. Undesignated campsites, tbls, cfga, no drkg wtr. Fishing (many small northern pike), boating, picnicking.

HOYT LAKES (38N)
Butterball Lake   FREE
Superior National Forest
From Hoyt Lakes, 4.5 mi SE on CR 110 (FR 11); 4 mi E on Skibo Rd/UT 9232 (becoming FR 120); right for 3.5 mi on Laird Creek Rd (FR 795) to boat ramp at S shore of lake. Free. 5/15-9/15; 14-day limit. Toilet, cfga, no drkg wtr, no trash service. Boating(l), fishing, canoeing on St. Louis River. GPS: 47.46141, -91.8684

ISABELLA (39N)
Divide Lake $7
Superior National Forest
5 mi E on of Isabella on FR 172. 5/15-10/31; 14-day limit. $7 with federal senior pass; others pay $14. About 5/15-9/30; 14-day limit. 3 RV sites. Tbls, toilet, cfga, drkg wtr. Fishing, boating, berry picking. GPS: 47.609981, -91.256434

Eighteen Lake   FREE
Superior National Forest
1 mi E of Isabella on FR 172; 2 mi N on FR 369; qtr mi E on access rd. Free. 5/15-9/30; 14-day limit. 3 RV sites. Tbls, toilet, cfga, no drkg wtr. Hiking, boating(l), fishing, swimming. GPS: Lake GPS: 47.6438, 91.3485

Hogback Lake Camp   FREE
Superior National Forest
10 mi E of Isabella on FR 172. All year; 14-day limit. 3 RV sites. Tbls, toilet, cfga, no drkg wtr, no trash service. Fishing, boating, canoeing, hiking trails. GPS: 47.644582, -91.135077

Little Isabella River $7
Superior National Forest
4 mi W of Isabella on SR 1. $7 with federal senior pass; others pay $14 during 5/10-10/1 (free rest of year but no amenities or service); 14-day limit. 11 sites (typically 45 ft). Tbls, toilets, cfga, drkg wtr. Hiking, fishing. GPS: 47.647586, -91.423983

McDougal Lake $7
Superior National Forest
11.6 mi W of Isabella on SR 1; .6 mi SE on FR 106. $7 with federal senior pass; others pay $14 during 5/10-10/1 (free or reduced fees rest of year, but no amenities or services);

14-day limit. 21 sites, typically 45 ft. Tbls, toilets, cfga, drkg wtr. Swimming, boating(l), fishing. 18 acres. GPS: 47.6390766, -91.5351499

JACKSON (40S)
Kilen Woods State Park $12
9 mi NW of Jackson & 10 mi N of Windom on CR 24, E off CR 17. $12 off-season at rustic sites with pit toilets, tbls, cfga, drkg wtr, no showers; $16 in-season. 50-ft RV rig limit. Shelter, dump, primitive group camping, playgrounds, no showers. Picnicking, hiking trails (5 mi), snowmobile trails, canoeing(r), boating(lr), fishing. Visitor center. 200 acres. GPS: 43.7266244, -95.0630473

Sandy Point Park $12
Jackson County Park
S of Jackson on US 71; W on 770th St to park. $12 without hookups, $16 with elec. 12 sites. Tbls, toilets, cfga, drkg wtr. Fishing. GPS: 43.598799, -95.143207

JACOBSON (41N)
Jacobson Campground $12
Aitkin County Park
At Jacobson, .8 mi N of SR 200 & half mi W of SR 65 on Great River Rd; W side of Mississippi River. $12. 5/3-10/21; 14-day limit. 10 rustic sites. Tbls, toilets, cfga, drkg wtr. Boating(l), fishing, hiking, ATV trail, snowmobiling. GPS: 47.0123, -93.1632

JORDAN (42S)
Minnesota Valley $12
State Recreation Area
4 mi SW of Jordan on US 169, then follow signs on CR 9 & CR 57. $12 at 25 rustic sites with pit toilets, cfga, drkg wtr, tbls, no showers. No elec. Shelter, historic site. 50-ft RV rig limit. Hiking trails (37 mi), biking (6 mi of trails), horseback riding (31 mi of trails), fishing, boating(l), winter sports. 8,000 acres. GPS: 44.663206, -93.701818

KARLSTAD (43N)
Moose City Park $5
On N edge of Karlstad on Hwy 59. $5. All year. 16 sites. Tbls, flush toilets, cfga, drkg wtr, elec/wtr hookups, dump, playground. Tennis, softball, picnicking. GPS: 48.578, -96./520

LAKE BRONSON (44N)
Lake Bronson State Park $12
2 mi E of Lake Bronson on US 59. $12 base. All year; 14-day limit. Base fee at rustic sites with pit toilets, tbls, cfga, drkg wtr, no showers; $16 base at sites with elec. Dump, playgrounds, shelter, 50-ft RV rig limit, fishing pier, lookout tower, snack bar. Volleyball, interpretive program, hiking trails (14 mi), biking (5 mi of trails), swimming, fishing, boating(lr), canoeing(r), winter sports. 2,983 acres. GPS: 48.7247004, -96.6033741

LANCASTER (46N)
Lancaster City Park $10
From US 59 just E of Lancaster, 4 blocks W on CR 4; 1 block N on Central Ave. $10 without hookups ($140 monthly), $15 with elec ($210 monthly). 28 sites on 287 acres. Tbls, flush toilets, cfga, drkg wtr, dump, playground. Interpretation programs, golf, hiking/biking trails. GPS: 48.8667, -96.79916

Scull Lake FREE
State Wildlife Area
E of Lancaster off CR 4. Free. Primitive sites on 7,500-acre refuge. No facilities, no drkg wtr. Hiking, fishing, hunting.

LIBBY (47N)
Sandy Lake Recreation Area $12
Corps of Engineers
Big Sandy Lake
Half mi E of SR 65 at Libby to lake outlet. $12 with federal senior pass at 48 elec sties; others pay $24. 4/1-10/31; 14-day limit. RV limit in excess of 65 ft; 8 pull-through sites. Some sites may have lower fees during Apr & Oct. Tbls, flush toilets, cfga, drkg wtr, showers, dump, playground, beach, interpretive display, fish cleaning station, museum, picnic shelters. Fishing, boating(l), swimming, hiking, horseshoes. GPS: 46.78833, -93.32833

LITTLE FORK (48N)
Dentaybow Highway 65 Access FREE
Koochiching County Park
13 mi S of Little Fork on SR 65; at Little Fork River. Free primitive camping. 1 site. Tbl, toilet, no drkg wtr. Boating(l), fishing.

LUTSEN (50NW)
Clara Lake FREE
Superior National Forest
.7 mi NE on MN 61; 10 mi N on CR 4; 4 mi NW on FR 339. Free. 5/15-9/30; 14-day limit. 3 sites (one suitable for small RV). Tbls, toilets, cfga, no drkg wtr, no trash service. Boating(l), fishing. Lake GPS: 47.4648, -90.4420

Poplar River FREE
Superior National Forest
.7 mi NE on SR 61; 8 mi N on CR 4; 5 mi W on FR 164; at Poplar River. Free. 5/15-9/30; 14-day limit. 4 sites (2 suitable for RVs). Tbls, toilets, cfga, no drkg wtr or trash service. Fishing, boating, canoeing, hunting. GPS: 47.7382281, -90.7779119

White Pine Lake FREE
Superior National Forest
.7 mi NE of Lutsen on SR 61; 8 mi N on CR 4; 4 mi W on FR 164. Free. 5/15-9/30; 14-day limit. 4 sites (2 suitable for RVs). Tbls, toilet, cfga, no drkg wtr or trash service. Fishing, boating(l), hiking. Barrier-free fishing pier. Lake GPS: 47.7527, -90.7549

MADELIA (51S)
Watona City Park $12
In SW corner of city next to golf course. $12 base for primitive sites; $17 with elec; $22 full hookups. 28 sites. 4/15-10/15. Tbls, flush toilets, cfga, drkg wtr, showers, playground, dump. Horseshoes, tennis. Next to pool, golf course, historical center. GPS: 44.0416269, -94.4238535

MARCELL (55N)
Clubhouse Lake Campground $8
Chippewa National Forest
Half mi NE of Marcell on SR 38; 5.2 mi E on CR 45; 1.5 mi N on FR 2181; 1.5 mi E on FR 3758; at W shore of lake. $8 with federal senior pass; others pay $16 (double sites $24). About 5/4-10/15; 14-day limit. 47 sites (20-40 ft long). Tbls, toilets, cfga, drkg wtr. Swimming, boating(l), fishing. Canoe route nearby. GPS: 47.610, 94.577

Crooked Lake Dispersed Recreation Area FREE
Itasca County Park
Half mi N of Marcell on SR 38; 5 mi E on gravel CR 45; 1 mi S on access rd. Free. Undesignated primitive site; no facilities. 2-day limit. Boating(l), fishing. Pack out trash. Lake GPS: 47.446373, -93.323263

Eagle Lake Dispersed Recreation Area FREE
Chippewa National Forest
Half mi N of Marcell on SR 38; 15 mi E on gravel CR 45 to Eagle Lake. Camp on S side of Rd. Free. Undesignated primitive site; no facilities. 2-day limit. Boating(l), fishing. Pack out trash. Lake GPS: 47.6097, -93.4777

North Star Campground $7
Chippewa National Forest
3.5 mi SE of Marcell on SR 38; E shore of lake. $7 with federal senior pass; others pay $14. About 5/4-10/15; 14-day limit. 38 sites up to 72 ft. Tbls, toilets, cfga, drkg wtr, beach. Boating(l), fishing, waterskiing, swimming. GPS: 47.557, 94.652

MARKHAM (56N)
Whiteface Reservoir $9
Superior National Forest
5 mi NW of Markham on CR 4; 6.7 mi E on CR 16; 3 mi S on FR 417; on Whiteface Reservoir. $9 base with federal senior pass; others pay $18 base, $20 for premium locations ($10 with senior pass). 24 elec sites, $5 surcharge. Also monthly sites ($350 non-elec, $457 elec). About 5/1-11/30; 14-day limit. 52 sites, typically 45 ft. Tbls, toilets, cfga, drkg wtr. Fishing, swimming, boating(lr). GPS: 47.332207, -92.144103

MCGRATH (57S)
Snake River $12
Aitkin County Campground
2 mi E of Hwy 65 on unimproved rd; on W bank of Snake River; 6 mi S of McGrath. $12. 5/3-10/21; 14-day limit. 12 sites. Tbls, toilets, cfga, drkg wtr, no elec. Hiking, fishing, boating(l), ATV trails. GPS: 46.1012, -93.1533

MCINTOSH (58N)
Roholt City Park $6
E end of McIntosh on US 2; at Hill River Lake. $6. 5/15-10/15. 10 sites. Tbls, flush toilets, cfga, drkg wtr, showers, elec, dump, CATV, playground. Picnicking, sightseeing. Handicap-accessible bathhouse. GPS: 47.63501, -95.883789

MELROSE (59S)
Sauk River City Park $9
From I-94 exit, N 5 blocks in Melrose to Main; E three blocks on Main, then N on 5th Ave 1 block; at Sauk River. $9 without hookups, $15 with elec/wtr. 8 RV sites with hookups. 5/1-10/1; 7-day limit. 28 gravel sites with tbls, flush toilets, cfga, drkg wtr, elec, shelter, playground, dump. Fishing, picnicking, volleyball, basketball, horseshoes. GPS: 45.67471, -94.806523

MIDDLE RIVER (60N)
Community Club City Campground $10
On W side of SR 32 at Hill Ave in Middle River. $10 ($50 weekly). 4/1-11/30. 12 elec/wtr sites. Dump, tbls, cfga, showers, playground. Fishing, hiking. No membership required. GPS: 48.434, -96.166

MORRIS (62S)
Pomme De Terre City Park $12
2.7 mi E of CR 10 in Morris; 1601 N. Jefferson. $12 without elec; $18 with elec ($65-90 weekly). 28 elec sites, numerous primitive. Canoeing, fishing, nature & biking trail, swimming beach, volleyball. GPS: 45.5725, -95.8875.

OLIVIA (66S)
Memorial City Park FREE
Hwy 212 and 71 in West Olivia, near Da Joint Dr. next to the Olivia Corn monument. Free. 4/1-10/30; 3-day limit. 6 primitive sites. Flush toilets, wtr at park shelter, dump. Swimming pool, 9-hole golf nearby. GPS: 44.775905, -95.006561

ORR (67N)
Lake Jeanette $10
Superior National Forest
2 mi S of Orr on US 53; about 30 mi NE on CR 23; 17 mi E on CR 116 (Echo Trail). $10 during 5/15-9/30; free off-season, but no amenities or service; 14-day limit. 12 sites, typically 45 ft. Tbls, toilets, cfga, drkg wtr. Fishing, boating(l), hiking. GPS: -92.144103, -92.296733

Meander Lake Dispersed Camping FREE
Superior National Forest
2 mi S of Orr on US 53; about 30 mi NE on CR 23; 37 mi E on CR 116 (Echo Trail); 2 mi NW on FR 457 to S shore of

lake. Free. 5/15-9/30; 14-day limit. 2 sites. Tbls, toilet, cfga, no drkg wtr, fishing pier. Boating(l), fishing, hiking, swimming. GPS: 48.0809, -92.0847

Myrtle Lake   FREE
Superior National Forest
2 mi S of Orr on US 53; 13 mi E on CR 23 to SE shore of lake. Free. 5/15-9/30; 14-day limit. 3 primitive sites. Tbls, toilets, cfga, no drkg wtr. Boating(l), fishing, hiking, swimming. GPS: 48.0816, -92.682.

Pauline Lake   FREE
Superior National Forest
2 mi S of Orr on US 53; about 30 mi NE on CR 23; 14 mi E on CR 116 (Echo Trail) to N shore of lake. Free. 1 site. Tbl, toilet, cfga, no drkg wtr. Boating, fishing, swimming, hiking, canoeing. Carry-down boat access. GPS: 48.1238, -92.3301

OUTING (69N)
Baker & White Oak Lake   FREE
Land O' Lakes State Forest
7 mi N of Outing on SR 6; 3.5 mi E on Draper Tower Rd. Free. All year; 14-day limit. 2 primitive sites. Tbl, cfga, no toilets or drkg wtr. Fishing, hiking. GPS: 46.900936, -93.880613.

PELICAN RAPIDS (71S)
Sherin Memorial Municipal Park $10
In Pelican Rapids; from US 59, qtr mi E on SR 108. $10 without hookups, $15 full hookups. 5/15-9/15. 30 sites (no RV size limit). Tbls, flush toilets, showers, cfga, drkg wtr, elec($), dump. Fishing, swimming, boating, picnicking, hiking. GPS: 46.570007, -96.082524

PLAINVIEW (73S)
Carley State Park $12
4 mi S of Plainview on CR 4. $12. All year; 14-day limit. 20 rustic sites (30-ft RV limit). Tbls, pit toilets, cfga, drkg wtr, no showers, no elec, playground, no dump, rustic group camping. Interpretive program, hiking trails (5 mi), fishing, cross-country ski trails (6 mi), winter sliding hill. 1,712 acres. On north branch of Whitewater River. GPS: 44.1166318, -92.1760002

REMER (75N)
Mabel Lake $7
Chippewa National Forest
7.4 mi W of Remer on SR 200; qtr mi N on FR 2104. $7 with federal senior pass; others pay $14. MD-11/25; 14-day limit. 22 sites; no RV size limit. Tbls, toilets, cfga, drkg wtr, sandy beach. Picnicking, boating(l), fishing, hiking, cross-country skiing, swimming. GPS: 47.050, 94.072

ROSEAU (77N)
Hayes Lake State Park $12
15 mi S of Roseau on SR 89; 9 mi E on CR 4; on N fork of Roseau River. $12 base. All year; 14-day limit. Base fee at rustic sites with pit toilets, cfga, drkg wtr, tbls, no showers; $16 at 18 elec sites. Dump, store, 40-ft RV rig limit. Hiking trails (12 mi), bridle trails (3 mi), swimming, fishing, boating(l), winter sports, fishing pier, winter sliding hill. GPS: 48.6233095, -95.5077539

RUSHFORD (78S)
Vinegar Ridge Camp   FREE
Dorer Memorial Hardwood State Forest
4 mi E of Rushford on Twp Rd 270; at New Root River. Free. All year; 14-day limit. 8 sites; 20-ft RV limit. Tbls, toilets, cfga, no drkg wtr. Fishing, hiking, bridle trails, nature trails. GPS: 43.7833, -91.6747

ST. PETER (79S)
St. Peter Riverside City Park $10
Turn off Hwy 169 at Nassau St (watch for sign); check in at police station. $10 base. All year. Base fee for primitive sites; $20 for sites with elec; numerous undesignated sites. Some cfga, showers, dump, flush toilets, shelter house, playground. Hiking & biking trails, boating(l), fishing.

SCHROEDER (81NW)
Ninemile Lake $7.50
Superior National Forest
One-tenth mi SW of Schroeder on US 61; 10 mi W on CR 1 & CR 8; 4 mi N on CR 7. $7.50 with federal senior pass; others pay $15 during 5/1-11/1; free off-season, but no amenities or services; 14-day limit. 26 sites, typically 45 ft. Tbls, toilets, cfga, drkg wtr. Boating(l), hiking, fishing. GPS: 47.578762, -91.074015

SILVERDALE (84N)
Samuelson   FREE
Koochiching County Park
3.5 mi S of Silverdale on SR 65; left (east) 2.5 mi on CR 75. Free primitive camping. 1 site; 2 picnic sites. Tbls, toilet, cfga, no drkg wtr. Boating, fishing.

SLAYTON (85S)
Lake Sarah West $12
Sundquist Park
Murray County Park
About 10 mi N of Slayton on US 59; 2 mi W on CR 16; 2 mi N on CR 30 to W side of Lake Sarah. $12. Campsites on 10 acres with elec, drkg wtr, cfga, flush toilets, playground, shelters, beach, dump. Boating(ld), fishing, swimming. GPS: 44.15246, -95.764217.

Swensen Park $12
Murray County Park
About 12 mi W of Slayton on SR 30; 14 mi N on SR 91; at E end of Current Lake. $12. 9 sites with elec on 10 acres. Tbls, flush toilets, cfga, drkg wtr, playground, dump. Boating(l), fishing. GPS: 44.166661, -95.939866

THIEF RIVER FALLS (89N)

Municipal Tourist Park $12
On Oakland Park Rd, qtr mi S of jct with SR 32; overlooking lower Red Lake River. $12 base at primitive sites ($72 weekly); $19 with elec ($114 weekly); $23 full hookups ($138 weekly). 5/4-10/15; 10-day limit. 84 sites. Tbls, toilets, cfga, cold showers, drkg wtr, elec($), dump. Fishing, playground, hiking trails. GPS: 48.11, -96.1852778

Thief Lake   FREE
State Wildlife Area
3 mi E of Thief River Falls on Hwy 1, then N on CR 20 (becoming CR 12); then 7 mi on CR 7; adjacent to Agassiz National Wildlife Refuge. Free. All year; 14-day limit. Primitive undesignated sites; no facilities, no drkg wtr. Summer nature interpretation program, fishing, hiking. GPS: 48.03918, -96.075015.

TOFTE (90NW)

Baker Lake   FREE
Superior National Forest
Half mi NE of Tofte on Hwy 61; 17 mi N on CR 2, 5 mi NE on FR 165, half mi N on FR 1272. Free. 5/15-9/30; 14-day limit. 5 sites (2 suitable for RVs under 16 ft). Tbls, toilets, cfga, drkg wtr, no trash service. Fishing, boating (dl). Pets. 2 acres. Entrance point to Boundary Waters Canoe Area. GPS: 47.846317, -90.816757.

Crescent Lake $9
Superior National Forest
Half mi NE of Tofte on US 61; 17 mi N on CR 2; 7 mi NE on FR 165. $9 with federal senior pass; others pay $18 during 5/10-10/11 (free off-season, but no amenities or services); 14-day limit. 33 sites, typically 45 ft. Tbls, toilets, cfga, drkg wtr. Fishing, swimming, boating(l), hiking. GPS: 47.832741, -90.774124

Sawbill Lake $9
Superior National Forest
Half mi NE of Tofte on US 61; 24 mi N on CR 2. $9 with federal senior pass; others pay $18 during 5/10-10/1; free off-season but no amenities or services; 14-day limit. 52 sites; no RV size limit. Tbls, toilets, cfga, drkg wtr. Fishing, swimming, boating (carry in), hiking. GPS: 47.866043, -90.885868

Silver Island Dispersed Site   FREE
Superior National Forest
About 2 mi SW of Tofte on SR 61; 6 mi N on Temperance Rd (past state park); left (W) on FR 166 (Six Hundred Rd) for 5 mi; right (N) on CR 7 about 9 mi past several jcts , then left on FR 369 for 2.5 mi to FR 921 (Silver Island access rd) for 1.5 mi. Free. 8 rustic RV/tent sites. Tbls, toilet, cfga, no drkg wtr, no trash service. Hike-in backcountry tent sites at lakeshore. Fishing, boating(l). GPS: 47.727389, -91.149167

Temperence River $9
Superior National Forest
About 10 mi N of Tofte on CR 2. $9 with federal senior pass; others pay $18. Apr-Nov; 14-day limit. 9 sites; 22-ft RV limit. Tbls, toilets, cfga, drkg wtr. Fishing, mountain biking, hiking. GPS: 47.718118, -90.878883

VIRGINIA (93N)

Big Rice Lake   FREE
Superior National Forest
From Virginia, 8 mi N on US 53; right (NE) for 1 mi on CR 131; 0.3 mi W on CR 68, veering right onto CR 405 (becoming UT8116); right on one-lane gravel FR 251 for 6 mi, then right for 1 mi onto FR 247 to site at NW shore of lake. Free. 5/15-9/15; 14-day limit. 3 small rustic sites. Toilet at boat ramp, cfga, no drkg wtr, no trash service. Fishing, boating(l). GPS: 47.704245, -92.498522

Pfeiffer Lake $12
Superior National Forest
22 mi Ne of Virginia on SR 169; 5 mi W on SR 1; 2 mi S on FR 256. $12. About 5/15-9/30; 14-day limit. 16 sites, typically 45 ft. Tbls, toilets, cfga, drkg wtr. Swimming, boating(l), hiking, swimming. GPS: 47.751646, -92.473852

WARROAD (97N)

Bemis Hill   FREE
Beltrami Island State Forest
12 mi S of Warroad on CR 5 to ranger station; 7 mi W on gravel rd. Free. 5/5-9/9; 14-day limit. 2 drive-to primitive sites (RVs under 20 ft); 4 equestrian sites $16. Tbls, toilets, cfga, drkg wtr (hand pump). Shelter. Picnicking, snowmobiling, hiking, toboggan slide, snow skiing. Shelter, ski slopes, horse corral & tie rails, access to Beltrami Island snowmobile trails. Forest GPS: 48.3302, -95.0915.

WASKISH (98N)

Waskish Campground   FREE
Red Lake State Forest
At Waskish, just S of bridge on SR 72. Free dispersed sites. 14-day limit. No facilities. Fishing, boating, canoeing, picnicking. On Tamarack River and Upper Red Lake. Forest GPS: 48.0208, -94.3319.

WILLIAMS (99N)

Zippel Bay State Park $12
10 mi NE of Williams on CR 8; on Lake of the Woods. $12 off-season at 57 rustic sites (50-ft RV limit); $16 in-season. Tbls, toilets, cfga, drkg wtr, dump, showers, shelter, group camping. Volleyball, hiking trails (6 mi), boating(l), fishing, swimming, winter sports. 2,946 acres. GPS: 48.8638742, -94.8593862

WINDOM (101S)

Island Municipal Park $10
Hwy 62 & 4th Ave in S end of Windom at Des Moines River. $10. 7/1-10/30; 3-day limit without authorization. 10 sites

with elec. Tbls, flush toilets, cfga, drkg wtr, shelter, dump ($10 non-campers). Softball, baseball, horseshoes, playground, swimming. GPS: 43.858888, -95.119089

WIRT (103N)
Noma Lake $7
Chippewa National Forest
1.8 mi NW of Wirt on CR 31. $7 with federal senior pass; others pay $14. 5/11-9/7; 14-day limit. 14 sites; no RV size limit. Tbls, toilets, cfga, drkg wtr. Fishing, boating, picnicking. GPS: 47.4505, 93.5758

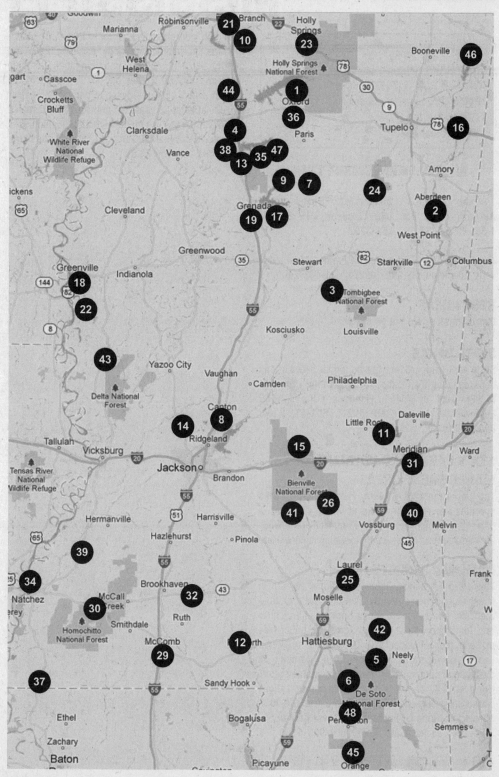

MISSISSIPPI

CAPITAL: Jackson
NICKNAME: Magnolia State
STATEHOOD: 1817 – 20th State
FLOWER: Evergreen Magnolia
TREE: Magnolia
BIRD: Mockingbird

WWW.VISITMISSISSIPPI.ORG

Tourism Division, Mississippi Development Authority, P.O. Box 849, Jackson, MS 39205; 1-866-SEE-MISS. 601/359-3297.

Dept of Wildlife, Fisheries and Parks, 1505 Eastover Dr, Jackson, MS 39211-6374; 601-432-2400.

REST AREAS
Overnight stops are not permitted.

STATE PARKS
State park campgrounds are no longer listed in this book because their campsite fees range from $13 to $24. Dept. of Wildlife, Fisheries & Parks, 1505 Eastover Dr, Jackson, MS 39211. 601-432-2400. 800-GOPARKS.

STATE LAKES AND WILDLIFE MANAGEMENT AREAS
The Department of Wildlife, Fisheries and Parks operates several state lakes at which camping is permitted. Camping is primitive and free at the Wildlife Management Areas where camping is permitted.

NATIONAL FORESTS
There are 1.1 million acres of national forests in Mississippi, represented by six individual forests -- Bienville, Delta, DeSoto, Holly Springs, Homochitto and Tombigbee. Most campgrounds are either free or have fees of under $10. Delta National Forest has no developed campgrounds, but camping is available at numerous undeveloped dispersed sites. However, a $7 permit is required to camp at those sites during 10/1-4/30; the sites are free 5/1-10/1. Mississippi National Forests: 100 West Capitol St., Suite 1141, Jackson, MS 39269. 601/965-4391.

Pat Harrison Waterway District serves a 15-county area and contains nine water parks with campgrounds. In addition to daily camping fees, the district also offers 30-day camping plans. Camping discounts include $1 per day for residents of the district and $1.50 per day per person for senior citizens at least 55 years old and/for 100% disabled persons. Charges are made for boat launching, lake use, picnic pavilions. PO Drawer 1509, Hattiesburg, MS 39401; 800-264-5951.

ABBEVILLE (1)

Graham Lake Campground　　　　　　FREE
Corps of Engineers
Sardis Lake
From Abbeville, 2 mi N on CR 201, then qtr mi N on SR 7; right (E) for 2 mi on CR 244; left (N) on CR 297 to Little Tallahatchie River. All year; 14-day limit. Free primitive sites, 6 picnic sites; toilets, cfga, no drkg wtr. Boating(l), fishing. GPS: 34.320, -89.232

Hurricane Landing　　　　　　　　　$9
Corps of Engineers
Sardis Lake
From Abbeville, 3.6 mi W on CR 214, becoming CR 108 (Hurricane Landing Rd); at south-central shore of lake. All year; 14-day limit. $9 with federal senior pass at 19 primitive sites; others pay $18. 20-ft RV limit. Tbls, flush & pit toilets, cfga, firewood, drkg wtr, playground. Picnicking, fishing, boating(l). GPS: 34.495605, -89.564951

ABERDEEN (2)

Blue Bluff Recreation Area　　　　　　$9
Corps of Engineers
Tennessee-Tombigbee Waterway
From Aberdeen at jct with Commerce St (Hwy 145), N on Meridian from center of town, cross RR tracks & bridge, then first right, following signs; S of Aberdeen Lake at river. $9 base with federal senior pass at 92 wtr/elec sites; others pay $18 base, $22 for full hookups & waterfront sites ($11 with senior pass). All year; 14-day limit. RV limit in excess of 65 ft. Tbls, flush toilets, showers, cfga, drkg wtr, beach, playground, fishing pier, fish cleaning station, coin laundry, amphitheater, picnic shelter. Waterskiing, boating(l), fishing, swimming, basketball, interpretive programs, information center, multi-use court, phone, wildlife viewing. GPS: 33.84444, -88.53222

Morgan Landing Access　　　　　　　$10
Columbus Lake City Park
2 mi E of Aberdeen on gravel rd. $10 for RVs with elec ($7 popups, $5 tents); seniors pay $7. Weekly $45 for elec. All year; 14-day limit. 14 sites. Tbls, toilets, drkg wtr, cfga. Boating(l), fishing. Non-campers pay $5 for dump station. GPS: 33.80194, -88.51667

ACKERMAN (3)

Choctaw Wildlife Management Area　　　FREE
SE of Ackerman on SR 15; in Tombigbee National Forest. Free. All year; 14-day limit. Primitive undesignated sites. No facilities. Hunting, hiking. Nature preserve. GPS: 33.25846, -89.11673

Jeff Busby Park　　　　　　　　　　FREE
Natchez Trace Parkway
National Park Service
12 mi NW of Ackerman; 2 mi S of Natchez Trace Parkway and SR 9 intersection. Free. All year; 15-day limit. 18 sites (9 pull-through for any size RV); 300 acres. Flush toilets, drkg wtr, cfga, tbls, groceries. Nature trails, hiking. GPS: 33.41626, -89.262207

BATESVILLE (4)

Oak Grove　　　　　　　　　　　　$9
Corps of Engineers
Sardis Lake
11 mi NE of Batesville on SR 35; below the dam on Lower Lake. $9 with federal senior pass at 82 elec/wtr sites; others pay $18. All year; 14-day limit. 40-ft RV limit. Tbls, toilets, cfga, drkg wtr, amphitheater, picnic shelter. Boating(l), fishing, hiking, swimming. GPS: 34.409424, -89.803711

Pats Bluff　　　　　　　　　　　　$8
Corps of Engineers
Sardis Lake
From Batesville at I-55 exit 243A, 9 mi on Hwy 6, then N on county rd; watch for signs. $8 ($4 with federal senior pass). 14 primitive sites (20-ft RV limit). Tbls, toilets, cfga, drkg wtr, playground. Boating(l), fishing, waterskiing. Note: in 2013, the campground was still closed for renovations & site upgrades with wtr & elec; check current status with lake office before arrival. 662-0563-4531. GPS: 34.4223, -89.7334

Sleepy Bend　　　　　　　　　　　$8
Corps of Engineers
Sardis Lake
From Batesville, N on I-55 to exit 246; E on SR 35 to Lower Lake below John Kyle State Park. $8 during 4/1-9/30 ($4 with federal senior pass); free 10/1-3/31; 14-day limit. 50 primitive sites (20-ft RV limit). Toilets, cfga, drkg wtr. Fishing, boating, waterskiing. GPS: 34.401367, -89.791504

BEAUMONT (5)

Cypress Creek Landing　　　　　　　$7
DeSoto National Forest
From jct with CR 301 at Janice, 0.25 mi N on Hwy 29; 3 mi E on FR 305; S on FR 305-B; on high bluff overlooking Black Creek. $7. All year; 14-day limit. 15 sites (no RV size limit). Tbls, toilets, cfga, no drkg wtr. Picnicking, fishing, canoeing, boating(ld). On Black Creek float trip. Non-campers pay $3 day use fee. GPS: 30.96547, -89.00477

Janice Landing　　　　　　　　　　FREE
DeSoto National Forest
From jct with CR 301 at Janice, 2.5 mi S on SR 29. Free. All year; 14-day limit. 5 sites. Tbls, chemical toilet, cfga, drkg wtr, shelter. Fishing, boating(l), hiking trail, canoeing. GPS: 30.9946, -89.0503

BROOKLYN (6)

Big Creek Landing　　　　　　　　　FREE
DeSoto National Forest
From just W of Brooklyn, 1 mi S on Old Hwy 49 E; after crossing Black Creek, turn W on CR 334 for 0.5 mi; 1.5 mi

W on CR 335; N on FR 335E to landing; at shore of Black Creek. Free. All year; 14-day limit. 1 site. Tbls, toilet, drkg wtr, cfga. Canoeing, fishing, hiking. GPS: 31.07084, -89.25416

Moody's Landing   FREE
DeSoto National Forest
From just W of Brooklyn, 6 mi E on CR 301 to landing at Black Creek. Free. All year; 14-day limit. Primitive sites. Tbls, chemical toilet, cfga, drkg wtr. Canoeing, fishing. GPS: 31.0568, -89.1185

BRUCE (7)
Calhoun County   FREE
Wildlife Management Area
SE of Bruce off Hwy 330. Free. All year. Primitive camping; no facilities. Hunting, hiking.

CANTON (8)
Pearl River   FREE
Wildlife Management Area
Just SE of Canton on SR 43. Free. All year. Primitive undesignated sites. Tbls, toilets, cfga, drkg wtr. Hunting, hiking, wildlife tours. GPS: 30.3940819, -89.7008957.

COFFEEVILLE (9)
Skuna-Turkey Creek   FREE
Corps of Engineers
Grenada Lake
4.5 mi SE of Coffeeville on SR 330; 2.1 mi S on CR 221; 3.8 mi SW on CR 229; W on CR 202 to NE shore of lake. Free. All year; 14-day limit. 6 primitive sites (20-ft RV limit). Tbls, pit toilets, cfga, drkg wtr. Picnicking, fishing, boating(lr). GPS: 33.5240, -89.4120

COLDWATER (10)
Dub Patton Recreation Area $9
Corps of Engineers
Arkabutla Lake
From Coldwater, 7 mi W on Arkabutla Rd; 5 mi N on Arkabutla Dam Rd, then across dam; on N side (signs). During 3/1-10/31, $9 base at 51 RV/tent elec sites; others pay $18 base, $20 for premium locations ($10 with senior pass). During 11/1-2/28, regular fees are $16 base, $18 for premium locations ($8 & $9 with federal senior pass). All year; 14-day limit. 50-ft RV limit. Tbls, flush toilets, cfga, drkg wtr, showers, dump, amphitheater, nature trails, picnic shelters. Boating(l), fishing, hiking. GPS: 34.77444, -90.11472

Hernando Point $9
Corps of Engineers
Arkabutla Lake
From Coldwater, 5 mi N on US 51; about 5 mi W on Wheeler Rd; follow signs into campground. During 3/1-10/31, $9 base with federal senior pass at 83 elec/wtr sites; others pay $18 base, $20 for premium locations ($10 with senior

pass). During 11/1-2/28, regular fees $16 base, $18 at premium locations ($8 & $9 with senior pass). 14-day limit. RV limit in excess of 65 ft. Tbls, flush toilets, showers, cfga, drkg wtr, hookups, dump, beach, playground, amphitheater, picnic shelter. Fishing, boating(l). GPS: 34.73361, -90.06889

Kelly's Crossing $5
Corps of Engineers
Arkabutla Lake
From Coldwater, 6.5 mi W on Arkabutla Rd; 3 mi N on Kelly Crossing Rd, following signs. $5 at 24 primitive sites during 5/1-9/30 ($2.50 with federal senior pass); free rest of year. 14-day limit. 20-ft RV limit. Drkg wtr, tbls, pit toilets, cfga. Swimming, boating(l), fishing. GPS: 34.4340, -90.618

South Abutment Campground $9
Corps of Engineers
Arkabutla Lake
From Coldwater, 7 mi N on Arkabutla Rd; 5 mi N on Arkabutla Dam Rd; just S of dam, following signs. All year; 14-day limit. During 3/1-10/31, $9 base with federal senior pass at 80 elec sites; others pay $18 base, $20 for premium locations. During 11/1-2/28, fees are $16 base, $18 at premium locations ($8 & $9 with senior pass). 60-ft RV limit. Tbls, flush toilets, showers, cfga, drkg wtr, elec, playground, beach, dump, picnic shelter. Boating(l), fishing, swimming. GPS: 34.74667, -90.1325

South Outlet Channel $6
Corps of Engineers
Arkabutla Lake
From Coldwater, 7 mi W on Arkabutla Rd; 4.5 mi N on Arkabutla Dam Rd; below dam (signs). All year; 14-day limit. $6 at 22 primitive sites during 5/1-9/30 ($3 with federal senior pass); free rest of year. 20-ft RV limit. Tbls, pit toilets, cfga, drkg wtr, pavilion. Picnicking, fishing, boating(l), playground, hiking trails. GPS: 33.4832, -89.4635

COLLINSVILLE (11)
Gin Creek Campground $8
Corps of Engineers
Okatibbee Lake
From Collinsville at jct with SR 19, 2.8 mi N on CR 17 (West Lauderdale School Rd) past "T"; 1 mile E on Martin-Center Hill/Causeway Rd; on right. $8 ($4 with federal senior pass). All year; 14-day limit. 7 primitive sites. Tbls, toilets, cfga, drkg wtr. Fishing, boating, canoeing, hunting. GPS: 32.52159, -87.81104

Twiltley Branch Campground $12
Corps of Engineers
Okatibbee Lake
From SR 19 at Collinsville, 1 mi E on CR 17; exit 1.7 mi E on Hamrick Rd W, then S on Hamrick Rd W, following signs. $12 at 12 non-elec RV/tent sites ($6 with federal senior

pass). 50 elec/wtr sites: $9 base with federal senior pass (others pay $18 base), $20 for premium locations ($10 with senior pass). 3 group camping area. RV limit in excess of 65 ft; 4 pull-through sites. Tbls, flush toilets, cfga, drkg wtr, beach, showers, coin laundry, picnic shelter. Boating(l), swimming, biking, hiking. GPS: 32.49583, -88.80972

COLUMBUS (12)

DeWayne Hayes Recreation Area $9
Columbus Lake
Corps of Engineers
Tennessee-Tombigbee Waterway
From Columbus, 4 mi N on US 45; 1.5 mi W on SR 373; 2 mi SW on Stinson Creek Rd; 0.5 mi left on Barton Ferry Rd; at Columbus Lake. $9 base with federal senior pass at 100 elec/wtr RV/tent sites; others pay $18 base, $20 for premium locations ($10 with senior pass). 25 full hookups, $24 ($12 with senior pass). RV limit in excess of 65 ft. Also 10 walk-to tent sites. Flush toilets, cfga, drkg wtr, tbls, beach, showers, dump, playground, fishing pier, coin laundry, pavilion, fish cleaning station, information center, interpretive programs, picnic shelter. Hiking trails, fishing, boating(l), swimming, interactive water sprayground, interpretive trail, guided interpretive walks, game courts. GPS: 33.60028, -88.47139

Town Creek $10
Columbus Lake
Corps of Engineers
Tennessee-Tombigbee Waterway
From Columbus at jct with US 45N, W on SR 50; 1 mi W of Tenn-Tom Bridge on SR 50; 1.5 mi N; right on J. Wither-spoon Rd; on Columbus Lake. $10 base with federal senior pass at 100 elec/wtr sites; others pay $20 base, $22 at premium locations ($11 with senior pass). Also 10 walk-to tent sites. All year (but campground was closed 12/1-3/1 during winter of 2010-11); 14-day limit. Tbls, flush toilets, cfga, drkg wtr, fish cleaning station, beach, coin laundry, playground, interpretive programs. Fishing, boating(l), hiking trails, motorcycle trails, swimming, guided inter-pretive walks. GPS: 33.60833, -88.50417

COMO (11)

Hayes Crossing Campground   FREE
Corps of Engineers
Sardis Lake
From Como, about 6 mi E on SR 310; 2 mi S on Fredonia Rd; 4 mi E on Simon Chapel Rd; 2 mi S on Farris Fonville Rd; 1 mi S on Hayes Crossing Rd to lake. All year; 14-day limit. Free primitive sites. 5 picnic sites. Tbls, toilets, cfga, no drkg wtr. GPS: 34.45, -89.76139

ENID (13)

Ford's Well Recreation Area $7
Corps of Engineers
Enid Lake
From I-55 exit 227 S of Enid, E on SR 32 to CR 557, then N to campground. $7 with federal senior pass at 12 elec/wtr

sites; others pay $14. Camp for horsemen using the 17-mi Spyglass Equestrian Trail. All year; 14-day limit. New in 2010, Ford's Well features hitching rails, horse wash station & overlook with hitching rails; joint effort involving Corps, state parks department & a private equestrian club. Gazebo, picnic shelter, fire rings, grills, drkg wtr, tbls. GPS: 34.1148331, -89.7973

Long Branch $6
Corps of Engineers
Enid Lake
From I-55 exit 227 S of Enid, 3.8 mi NE on SR 32; 1.9 mi N on CR 26. $6 during 3/1-10/31 ($3 with federal senior pass); $5 rest of year. All year; 14-day limit. 14 primitive sites; 20-ft RV limit. Tbls, pit toilets, cfga, drkg wtr, beach, playground. Picnicking, fishing, swimming, boating(lr). GPS: 34.121094, -89.843994

Persimmon Hill Park $9
Corps of Engineers
Enid Lake
From I-55 exit 233 near Enid, 1 mi E on CR 35 to dam; cross dam, turn NE on CR 34; at S end of dam (signs). All year; 14-day limit. During 3/1-10/31, $9 with federal senior pass at 72 elec sites; others pay $18. During off-season, sites $12 ($6 with senior pass). 65-ft RV limit; 2 pull-through sites. Tbls, flush toilets, showers, cfga, drkg wtr, elec, dump, playground, pavilion. Fishing, boating(l). GPS: 34.13556, -89.88611

Point Pleasant   FREE
Corps of Engineers
Enid Lake
From I-55 exit 227 S of Enid, 6.3 mi NE on SR 32; half mi N on CR 44; 3 mi NW on CR 41, then follow signs. Free. All year; 14-day limit. 3 primitive sites; 235 acres (20-ft RV limit). Tbls, pit toilets, cfga, drkg wtr. Picnicking, fishing, swimming, boating(l). GPS: 34.1376108, -89.834811

Wallace Creek $8
Corps of Engineers
Enid Lake
From I-55 exit 233 near Enid, 2.5 mi E on CR 36 to dam; cross spillway; on W side of dam. During 3/1-10/31, $8 base with federal senior pass at 101 elec/wtr sites; others pay $16 base, $18 at premium locations ($9 with senior pass). Off-season, sites are $10 base, $12 at premium locations ($5 & $6 with senior pass). 65-ft RV limit; 7 pull-through sites. Drkg wtr, tbls, flush toilets, elec, amphitheater, showers, playground, dump, fish cleaning station, picnic shelter. Hiking trail, interpretive trail, bik-ing, fishing, boating(l). GPS: 34.16111, -89.89167

FLORA (14)

Mississippi Petrified Forest $12
Campground (Priv)
Just W of Flora on SR 22, then nearly 2 mi S on paved rd

following signs. $12 for primitive sites; $22 full hookups. 4/1-11/30. 27 sites. Tbls, toilets, cfga, drkg wtr, dump, showers, hiking trails. GPS: 32.51505, -90.321888

FOREST (15)

Caney Creek — FREE
Wildlife Management Area
SW of Forest on county rds; in Bienville National Forest. Free. All year; 14-day limit. Primitive designated camping. No facilities. Hunting, hiking. Nature preserve. 28,000 acres.

Shockaloe Base Camp — $7
Bienville National Forest
4 mi W of Forest on US 80; qtr mi N on FR 513. $7. Apr-Nov; 14-day limit. 10 sites. Tbls, toilets, cfga, drkg wtr, hitching rails, shelter. Horseback riding, hiking. Adjacent to Shockaloe Horse Trail. No day use fee. GPS: 32.3657, -89.56229

FULTON (16)

John Bell Williams — FREE
Wildlife Management Area
NW of Fulton on county rds; along Tennessee-Tombigbee River. Free. All year. Primitive camping. Tbls, toilets, cfga, drkg wtr. Hunting, hiking.

Whitten Campground — $10
Fulton Pool
Corps of Engineers
Tennessee-Tombigbee Waterway
From jct with US 78 at Fulton, N on Hwy 25, then W on Main St to waterway & 2 mi N following signs; adjacent to City of Fulton at Fulton Pool. $10 base with federal senior pass at 60 elec/wtr sites; others pay $20 base, $22 for premium locations, some with 50-amp ($11 with senior pass). All year; 14-day limit. RV limit in excess of 65 ft; 3 pull-through sites. Tbls, flush toilets, cfga, drkg wtr, dump, coin laundry, showers, fishing pier, playground, amphitheater, beach. Swimming, waterskiing, boating(l), fishing, hiking, basketball, interpretive trail, nature trails, game courts. GPS: 34.28972, -88.41583

GORE SPRINGS (17)

Choctaw Campground — FREE
Corps of Engineers
Grenada Lake
From Gore Springs at SR 8, N on Graysport Crossing Rd across lake bridge, past North Graysport Campground; N (left) on Gums Crossing Rd; S (left) on Rounsville Church Rd; at "Y," veer right on Choctaw Landing Rd, following signs. Free. All year; 14-day limit. 5 primitive sites. Pit toilet, cfga, tbls, no drkg wtr. Boating(l), fishing. GPS: 33.8293, -89.6401

Gums Crossing Campground — FREE
Corps of Engineers
Grenada Lake
From Gore Springs at SR 8, N on Graysport Crossing Rd across lake bridge, past North Graysport Campground, then N on CR 221 (Gums Crossing Rd) to river. All year; 14-day limit. 14 free primitive sites. Pit toilet, cfga, no drkg wtr. GPS: 33.897949, -89.631592

North Graysport — $7
Corps of Engineers
Grenada Lake
From Gore Springs at jct with SR 8, 5.8 mi N on Graysport Crossing Rd, across bridge; on NE side of lake between rivers. $7 with federal senior pass at 50 elec/wtr sites; others pay $14. All year; 14-day limit. 55-ft RV limit. Pavilion, amphitheater, tbls, flush toilets, cfga, drkg wtr, showers, dump, elec, playground. Boating(l), fishing. GPS: 33.84417, -89.60361

Old Fort Campground — $6
Corps of Engineers
Grenada Lake
From Grenada, 2 mi NE on Scenic Loop Rd (Old Hwy 8), following signs; S of dam. $6 at 21 primitive sites ($3 with federal senior pass). All year; 14-day limit. 20-ft RV limit. Tbls, pit toilets, cfga, drkg wtr. Boating(l), hiking. GPS: 33.8003, -89.764297

GREENVILLE (18)

Warfield Point — $12
Washington County Park
From jct of SR 1 & US 82, W 3 mi on US 82. $12 for seniors with 20/30-amp elec/wtr; others pay $13, $15 full hookups. All year; monthly rates available. 52 sites. Tbls, flush toilets, showers, cfga, drkg wtr, elec, sewer, dump. Playground. Boating(l), fishing. GPS: 33.351709, -91.127614

GRENADA (19)

Bryant Campground — $12
Corps of Engineers
Grenada Lake
From I-55 exit 55 N at Grenada, NE on SR 7, then SE on CR 74 to campground. All year; 14-day limit. $12 at elec/wtr sites, $6 at wtr sites ($6 & $3 with federal senior pass). Pit toilet, tbls, cfga, drkg wtr. GPS: 33.921299, -89.698402

Malmaison — FREE
Wildlife Management Area
SE of Grenada on SR 7. Free. All year. Primitive undesignated camping; no facilities. Hunting, hiking. Nature preserve. GPS: 33.70012, -90.08342.

North Abutment Camp — $10
Corps of Engineers
Grenada Lake
From I-55 exit 55 N of Grenada, 5 mi NE on SR 7, then S on SR 333 past the primitive campground; at N end of dam. $10 with federal senior pass at 88 elec/wtr sites; others pay $20. All year; 14-day limit. 40-ft RV limit; 4 pull-through. Tbls, toilets, cfga, drkg wtr, pavilion, amphithe-

ater, fish cleaning station. Boating(l), fishing, picnicking, hiking, archery range. GPS: 33.84694, -89.77444

HERNANDO (21)

Pleasant Hill $5
Corps of Engineers
Arkabutla Lake
From Hernando, 5 mi W on SR 304; 5 mi S on Fogg Rd; right on access rd, following signs. All year; 14-day limit. $5 during 5/1-9/30 at 10 primitive sites ($2.50 with federal senior pass); free rest of year. 20-ft RV limit. Tbls, pit toilets, cfga, drkg wtr, beach, playground. Picnicking, fishing, swimming, boating(l). GPS: 34.783203, -90.091309

HOLLANDALE (22)

Leroy Percy   FREE
Wildlife Management Area
About 5 mi S of Hollandale on SR 12; W on CR 436. Free. All year. Primitive undesignated sites. Tbls, toilets, cfga, drkg wtr. Hiking, hunting.

HOLLY SPRINGS (23)

Chewalla Lake $7
Holly Springs National Forest
1.4 mi E of Holly Springs on Hwy 4; at Chewalla Lake sign, proceed left for about 6 mi; left for 1.3 mi on FR 611 (Chewalla Lake Rd). $7 at primitive sites; $20 with elec ($3.50 & $13 with federal senior pass) All year; 14-day limit. 36 sites up to 56 ft (9 with elec). Tbls, flush toilets, cfga, drkg wtr, showers, dump, playground. Swimming, boating(l), fishing. Fishing may be restricted. Non-campers pay $5 day use fee. GPS: 34.742676, -89.330566

HOUSTON (24)

Chickasaw   FREE
Wildlife Management Area
N of Houston off SR 15. Free. All year. Primitive camping in designated area & in the deer hunting area. No facilities, no drkg wtr. Hunting, hiking.

LAUREL (25)

Long Leaf Horse Trail   FREE
DeSoto National Forest
8 mi S of Laurel on SR 15; left at Long Leaf Horse Trail sign onto George Boswell Rd for 2 mi; right on FR 201 for 4.5 mi; right on FR 213 for half mi. Free. All year; 14-day limit. 11 sites up to 47 ft, each with hitching post. Tbls, toilets, cfga, no drkg wtr except for horses. Hiking, boating, biking, bridle trails.

LOUIN (26)

Tallahala   FREE
Wildlife Management Area
NW of Louin on county rds; in Bienville National Forest. Free. All year; 14-day limit. Primitive undesignated sites. Tbls, toilets, cfga, drkg wtr. Hiking, hunting. GPS: 32.1835, -89.3001.

MCCOMB (29)

Bogue Chitto Water Park $10
Pearl River Basin Development District
12 mi E of McComb on Dogwood Trail, off Hwy 98. $10 base. All year. Base fee for primitive camping; $16 at RV sites with elec/wtr ($14 for seniors 55 or older), $20 for full hookups. Tbls($), flush toilets, cfga, drkg wtr, showers, picnic area, pavilion, playgrounds, multi-use play court. Boating(l - $), tubing($), hiking trails, fishing, canoeing (r). 230 acres. 601-684-9568. GPS: 31.165417,-90.280409

MEADVILLE (30)

Clear Springs Campground $7
Homochitto National Forest
3.6 mi W of Meadville on US 84; left at national forest recreation area sign for 4.1 mi; steep roads in camping area. $7 at non-elec sites; $20 for 50-amp elec ($13 with federal senior pass). All year; 14-day limit. 44 sites up to 59 ft (22 with elec). Tbls, flush toilets, cfga, drkg wtr, showers, beach. Boating, fishing, swimming, hiking trail. Non-campers pay $5 day use fee. GPS: 31.425537, -90.990234

MERIDIAN (31)

Okatibbee   FREE
State Waterfowl Area
About 14 mi NW of Meridian on SR 19; W on county rd. Free. All year. Undesignated primitive sites. Tbls, toilets, cfga, drkg wtr. Hunting, hiking, fishing at Okatibbee Lake. GPS: 32.5668055, -88.8042159.

MONTICELLO (32)

Atwood Water Park $10
City of Monticello Park
At US 85 bridge over Pearl River on E side of Monticello. $10 for non-elec sites; $15 with wtr/elec; $25 full hookups. All year. 44 RV sites. Tbls, flush toilets, cfga, wtr hookups, showers, playground. Boating(l), fishing, tennis, hiking trails. GPS: 31.5238, -90.128

NATCHEZ (34)

Pipes Lake   FREE
Homochitto National Forest
Off SR 33 on FR 121-A; at 14-acre lake. Free. All year; 14-day limit. Primitive undesignated camping. Chemical toilets, cfga, tbls, no drkg wtr. Fishing, boating(l). GPS: 31.2235, -91.0953

OXFORD (36)

Clear Creek Campground $10
Corps of Engineers
Sardis Lake
From Oxford at jct with SR 7, 10.5 mi NW on SR 314, then 2 mi SW on CR 100. All year; 14-day limit. $10 at 52 elec/wtr sites ($5 with federal senior pass). 65-ft RV limit. Tbls, flush toilets, cfga, drkg wtr, dump, showers, beach,

playground, picnic shelter. Fishing, boating(l), swimming, 13-mi mountain biking trail. GPS: 34.02139, -87.26917

Puskus Lake $7
Holly Springs National Forest
1.5 mi N of Oxford on SR 7; 9.3 mi E on SR 30; 2.8 mi N on FR 838. $7 during Apr-Dec; free rest of year but no services or wtr; 14-day limit. 19 sites (22-ft RV limit). Tbls, toilets, cfga, drkg wtr. Fishing, boating(l), hiking, waterskiing, hunting. Non-campers pay $3 day use fee. GPS; 34.436768, -89.348633

Upper Sardis FREE
Wildlife Management Area
N of Oxford on SR 7, then W on county rds; in Holly Springs National Forest. Free. All year; 14-day limit. Primitive undesignated sites. Tbls, toilets, cfga, no drkg wtr. Hunting, hiking, fishing. Nature preserve.

PICKENSVILLE, AL (37)

Pickensville Recreation Area $9
Aliceville Lake
Tennessee-Tombigbee Waterway
Corps of Engineers
From AL 14 at Pickensville, 2.6 mi W on SR 86; across waterway bridge, on right at Aliceville Lake. $9 base with federal senior pass at 176 elec/wtr sites; others pay $18 base. Premium waterfront sites $22 ($11 with senior pass); some 50-amp, 29 full hookups. All year; 14-day limit. RV limit in excess of 65 ft. Tbls, flush toilets, showers, cfga, drkg wtr, fish cleaning station, interpretive programs, playground, beach, visitor center. Biking trail, guided interpretive walks, multi-use courts, boating(l), fishing. GPS: 33.226, -88.276

POPE (38)

Chickasaw Hill $7.50
Corps of Engineers
Enid Lake
8.8 mi SE of Pope, then 1.6 mi SW; on N side of lake. $7.50 with federal senior pass during 3/1-10/31 at 44 RV/tent sites; others pay $14. During off-season, regular fee $10 ($5 with senior pass). 65-ft RV limit. Tbls, flush toilets, showers, cfga, dump, drkg wtr, elec, beach, playground, amphitheater. Hiking, fishing, boating(l), swimming, picnic shelter. GPS: 34.16389, -89.82222

Plum Point Campground $6
Corps of Engineers
Enid Lake
From Pope, 5.3 mi SE on Pope Water Valley Rd; 3.7 mi SE on all-weather Plum Point Rd. All year; 14-day limit. $6 at 10 primitive sites during 3/1-10/31 ($3 with federal senior pass); $5 off-season ($2.50 with senior pass). 20-ft RV limit. Tbls, pit toilets, cfga, drkg wtr, playground, beach. Picnicking, fishing, swimming, boating(l), bridle trails. 30 acres. GPS: 34.162019, -89.854492

PORT GIBSON (39)

Rocky Springs FREE
Natchez Trace Parkway
17 mi NE of Port Gibson on parkway or 11 mi S of jct of MS 27 and parkway. Free. All year; 15-day limit. 22 sites; no size limit. Tbls, toilets, cfga, pull-through spaces, drkg wtr. Picnicking, hiking trails. In summer; Campfire program Fri/Sat evenings, organized walks Sat/Sun. 600 acres. GPS: 32.086182, -90.799805.

QUITMAN (40)

Mucatunna FREE
Wildlife Management Area
About 16 mi S of Quitman on US 45; E on county rds. Free. All year. Primitive undesignated sites. Hunting, hiking. Nature preserve.

RALEIGH (41)

Shongelo Lake Campground $5
Bienville National Forest
5 mi N of Raleigh on SR 35. $5. 4/15-10/15; 14-day limit. 4 sites. Tbls, flush toilet, cfga, drkg wtr, shelter. Hiking, fishing, boating, swimming, 7 picnic sites. Lake GPS: 32.0555, -89.3044

RICHTON (42)

Turkey Fork Recreation Area $7
DeSoto National Forest
12 mi E of Richton on Hwy 42 to Sandhill, then follow signs. $7 without hookups; $20 elec wtr (seniors with federal senior pass pay $14). All year; 14-day limit. 28 sites (20 with wtr/elec). Tbls, flush toilets, showers, drkg wtr, cfga, dump, fishing pier. Boating(l), hiking trail, fishing. Non-campers pay $5 day use fee. GPS: 31.341309, -88.703857

ROLLING FORK (43)

Barge Lake $7
Delta National Forest
7.5 mi E of Rolling Fork on SR 16; SW on FR 715. $7 camping permit 11/1-4/30; free rest of year; 14-day limit. Primitive undeveloped sites. Tbls, toilets, cfga, no drkg wtr. Fishing, picnicking. Lake GPS: 32.4938, -90.4837.

Blue Lake Recreation Area $7
Delta National Forest
7.5 mi E of Rolling Fork on SR 16; 3.5 mi SW on FR 715. $7 during 11/1-4/30; free rest of year; 14-day limit. 3 primitive, undeveloped sites; 28-ft RV limit. Tbls, toilets, cfga, no drkg wtr. Fishing, picnicking, hunting. GPS: 32.8209635, -90.8089882

Little Sunflower River $7
Delta National Forest
16.5 mi S of Rolling Forks; 4 mi E on SR 433. $7 during 11/1-4/30; free rest of year; 14-day limit. 3 primitive, undeveloped sites; 40-ft RV limit. No facilities. Parking

for 11 vehicles. Boating(l), fishing, canoeing, interpretive display. Reservations required.

Shipland Wildlife Management Area   FREE
About 13 mi S of Rolling Forks on US 61; about 11 mi W on SR 1 from Onward; at Lake Providence. Free. All year. Primitive undesignated sites; no facilities. Hunting, fishing, hiking, boating.

Sunflower Wildlife Management Area   FREE
About 16 mi S of Rolling Fork on US 61; E on county rds; in Delta National Forest. Free. All year; 14-day limit. Primitive undesignated sites. No facilities. Hunting, hiking, fishing.

SARDIS (44)
Beach Point $8
Corps of Engineers
Sardis Lake
From Sardis at jct with I-55 exit, 8 mi E of on SR 315. $8 during 4/1-9/30; free 10/1-3/31; 14-day limit. 14 primitive sites (20-ft RV limit). Tbls, flush & pit toilets, cfga, drkg wtr. Boating(l), fishing, swimming. GPS: 34.41816, -89.80898

Lower Lake Campground   FREE
Corps of Engineers
Sardis Lake
From Sardis, 3 mi SE on SR 315, across dam, following signs. All year; 14-day limit. Free primitive sites. 250 picnic sites. Tbls, toilets, cfga, drkg wtr, playground, beach. Fishing, boating(l). GPS: 34.2405, -89.4738

SAUCIER (45)
Airey Lake Recreation Area   FREE
DeSoto National Forest
From Saucier, about 3 mi E on Old Hwy 67, then 3 mi N on CR 412; at 3-acre lake. Free. All year; 14-day limit. 5 sites. Tbls, chemical toilets, cfga, drkg wtr. Hiking (Tuxachanie National Recreation Trail), fishing. GPS: 30.69047, -89.05865

Big Foot Horse Camp   FREE
DeSoto National Forest
From Saucier, about 3 mi E on Old Hwy 67, then 3 mi N on CR 412; 1 mi E on FR 440; at Tuxachanie Creek. Free. All year; 14-day limit. Primitive sites, primarily for equestrians. Tbls, toilets, cfga, hitching rails, no drkg wtr except for horses. Big Food Horse Trail (5-11 mi), fishing.

P.O.W. Lake Recreation Area   FREE
DeSoto National Forest
From Saucier, about 4 mi E on Old Hwy 76 (becoming Bethel Rd (CR 402); left on FR 420-E to S shore of 7-acre lake. Free. All year; 14-day limit. Primitive sites. No facilities except cfga, no drkg wtr. Fishing, hiking. GPS: 30.3821, -89.002

TISHOMINGO (46)
Piney Grove Recreation Area $11
Bay Springs Lake
Tennessee-Tombigbee Waterway
Corps of Engineers
From Tishomingo, 1 mi N on SR 25; about 6 mi W on SR 30 past town of Burton; left (SE) for 3 mi on CR 3501; right (E) on CR 3550, following signs; at W shore of Bay Springs Lake. $11 base with federal senior pass at 141 elec/wtr sites; others pay $22 base, $24 at premium locations ($12 with senior pass). All year-11/30; 14-day limit. RV limit in excess of 65 ft; 6 pull through. 10 free primitive boat-in tent sites (no drkg wtr). Tbls, flush toilets, showers, drkg wtr, cfga, dump, fish cleaning station, fishing pier, playground, beach, coin laundry, amphitheater, picnic shelters. Boating(l), waterskiing, hiking, fishing, basketball, swimming, interpretive trail. GPS: 34.56889, -88.32722

WATER VALLEY (47)
Bynum Creek Landing   FREE
Corps of Engineers
Enid Lake
From Water Valley at jct with SR 7, 8.3 mi NW on SR 315; 2.8 mi SW on Pope Water Valley Rd; 2.4 mi SE on all-weather Cliff Finch Rd; on NE shore of lake. All year; 14-day limit. 5 primitive sites, free. RV limit 20'. Pit toilets, tbls, cfga, drkg wtr. Boating(l), fishing, swimming beach. GPS: 34.1779, -89.7348

Water Valley Landing $7.50
Corps of Engineers
Enid Lake
From Water Valley at jct with SR 315, 2 mi S on SR 7; 5.3 mi W on SR 32; 3.2 mi NW; on S side of lake. 3/1-10/31; 14-day limit. $7.50 with federal senior pass a5 26 elec/wtr sites; others pay $15. 60-ft RV limit. Tbls, flush toilets, cfga, drkg wtr, showers, dump, playground, picnic shelter. Hiking, fishing, boating(l), swimming. GPS: 34.14306, -89.76389

WIGGINS (48)
Fairley Bridge Landing   FREE
DeSoto National Forest
6 mi NE of Wiggins on SR 29; 7 mi E on FR 374. Free. All year; 7-day limit. 3 sites. Tbls, chemical toilet, cfga, no drkg wtr. Fishing, boating(l), hiking, hunting, canoeing. Serves as end point for both Black Creek float trip & Black Creek National Hiking Trail. GPS: 30.9182, -88.9664

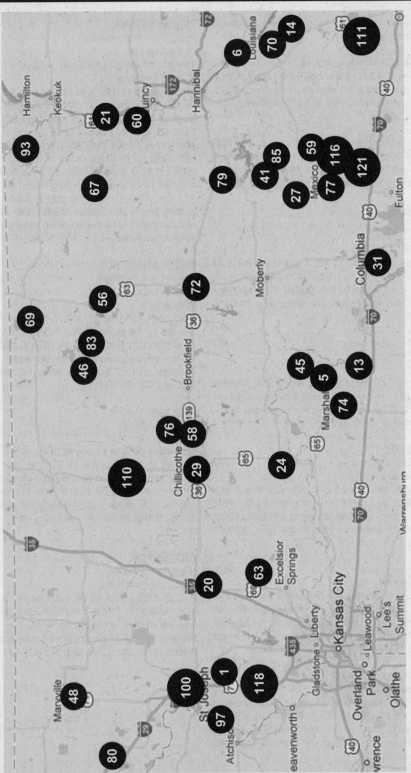

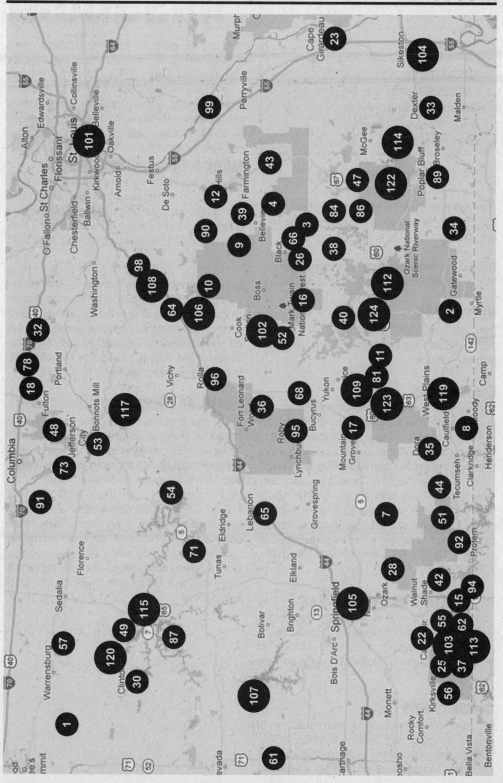

MISSOURI

CAPITAL: Jefferson City
NICKNAME: Show-Me State
STATEHOOD: 1821 – 24th State
FLOWER: Hawthorn
TREE: Flowering Dogwood
BIRD: Bluebird

WWW.VISITMO.COM

Missouri Division of Tourism, PO Box 1055, Jefferson City, MO 65102.For travel information by mail: 800-519-2100.

Dept of Conservation, 2901 W. Truman Blvd, Jefferson City, MO 65102. 314-751 4115. 800-392-1111

REST AREAS

Overnight stops are not permitted. No sanitary dump stations are provided at major interstate highway rest areas.

STATE PARKS

Camping fees are $13 in-season for basic sites, $12 off-season (October-March); seniors 65 or older pay $11 in-season, $10 off-season. All other campsite fees are above the $12-or-under guidelines for this book and are not included here. At "value parks," lower rates are offered to those who camp Sunday-Thursday. Basic sites are $10 or $12 Sunday through Thursday and nightly off-season (when open), $13 Friday and Saturday in-seaon. Seniors get $2 discounts all year at "value parks." Division of Parks, PO Box 176, Jefferson City, MO 65102, 800-334-6946.

OTHER STATE CAMPING AREAS

State Forests. Although there are not many developed facilities, primitive camping is permitted at many state conservation areas. Dept of Conservation, Forestry Division, PO Box 180, Jefferson City, MO 65102.

CANOE CAMPS

Canoeing down crystal-clear streams is one of Missouri's most popular outdoor activities. On several streams, particularly in the southern half of the state, canoe rentals have been established that provide overnight camping accommodations for their guests. Camping usually is at a very low rate, ranging from as little as $2 per person, and a few canoe rental outlets even offer free camping to those renting canoes. This book lists numerous canoe/camping locations and their fees. The majority of these camps cannot be found in any other campground directory.

MARK TWAIN NATIONAL FOREST

Camping and hiking are permitted anywhere without a permit. Campground fees are charged only during managed periods. Services are reduced during unmanaged season. Forest Supervisor, Mark Twain Forest, 401 Fairgrounds Rd, Rolla, MO 65401, 573-364-4621.

Ozark National Scenic Riverways, PO Box 490, Van Buren, MO 63965. 314 323-4236. Fees are charged all year for camping at all of the this agency's developed campgrounds, and all campgrounds are free off-season. Stays are limited to 14 days within any 30-day period. Primitive campsites (without facilities) on the riverways are free.

CORPS OF ENGINEERS

Due to budget issues of 2011-2014, the Little Rock District of Corps of Engineers intended to shift management of four Missouri campgrounds to the a non-profit agency -- Ozark Rivers Heritage Foundation; however, agreements between the Corps and the foundation were terminated in September 2013, and the status of those campgrounds for 2014 and beyond was unknown at presstime. Those campgrounds are Old Highway 86, Mill Creek, Baxter and Campbell Point Campgrounds. Seasonal operations at other campgrounds on the lake were cut back to 5/1-9/15. Check current status with the lake office before arrival.

AGENCY (1)

Agency State Conservation Area   FREE
Follow Hwy FF/H/MM south from Agency, then E on Rock Creek Rd. Free. All year; 14-day limit. Primitive designated camping area; no facilities, no drkg wtr. Hunting, fishing, hiking, nature study. GPS: 39.620028, -94.735514.

ALTON (2S)

Greer Crossing Recreation Area $10
Mark Twain National Forest
9 mi NE of Alton on SR 19; right on FR 3188; on Eleven Point National Scenic River. $10 (double sites $15). 5/15-9/30; free rest of year but no wtr or services; 14-day limit. 19 sites to 50 ft. Tbls, toilets, cfga, drkg wtr. Boating(l), hunting, canoeing, fishing, hiking (McCormack-Greer Trail). 6 acres. Canoe rentals nearby. 1-mi trail to Greer Spring. GPS: 36.7936672, -91.3293019.

ANNAPOLIS (3S)

Funk Branch Wilderness Site   FREE
Corps of Engineers
Clearwater Lake
From Annapolis, half mi W on SR K; 3 mi SW on CR 149, then S on CR 446 to site; along Funk Branch of Black River within Clearwater Lake project. Free primitive camping at undesignated sites with Corps permit from lake office. No amenities. Fishing, boating. GPS: 37.1815, -90.4639

Highway K Campground $7
Corps of Engineers
Clearwater Lake
From Annapolis, 5 mi SW on CR K; after bridge, on W side (signs); above lake on Back River. $7 with federal senior pass at 21 non-elec sites; others pay $14. 45 elec sites (some wtr hookups): $8 base with federal senior pass; others pay $16 base, $20 for 50-amp elec/wtr ($10 with senior pass). 4/1-10/31; 14-day limit. Some sites typically free off-season without utilities, but off-season camping eliminated in 2013 due to budget cuts. 60-ft RV limit; 2 pull-through sites. Tbls, flush toilets, cfga, drkg wtr, showers, dump, beach, playground, pavilion, pay phone. Swimming, boating, fishing, canoeing. GPS: 37.32417, -90.7667

ARCADIA (4S)

Marble Creek Recreation Area $10
Mark Twain National Forest
1.2 mi SW of Arcadia on SR 21; 12 mi SE on CR E. $10. 4/1-10/30; 14-day limit. 24 sites to 70 ft. Tbls, toilets, cfga, no drkg wtr. Hiking, fishing, hunting. 9 acres. Formerly a free camp operated by a volunteer group. GPS: 37.4511628, -90.5406745.

ARROW ROCK (5N)

Arrow Rock State Historic Site $12
13 mi N of I-70 on SR 41 (15 mi E of Marshall). $12 off-season (11/1-4/14) at 12 basic sites ($13 off-season); seniors pay $11 in-season, $10 off-season. Also 34 elec sites. All year; 15-day limit. 46 sites (30-ft RV limit). Tbls, flush toilets, cfga, drkg wtr, dump, elec($), showers, WiFi. Playground, museum (restored village). 139 acres. GPS: 39.065674, -92.942627

ASHBURN (6N)

DuPont Reservation   FREE
State Conservation Area
1 mi N of Ashburn on Hwy 79; campsites along 1.5 mi of Mississippi River. Free. All year; 14-day limit. 20 primitive sites. Camping also permitted on or adjacent to all parking lots but not along roadways. Toilet, cfga, no drkg wtr, no trash service. Fishing, boating(l), hunting, canoeing, hiking. 1,285 acres. GPS: 39.558064, -91.178502.

AVA (7S)

Rippee State Conservation Area   FREE
10 mi E of Ava on SR 14; 2 mi NE on CR 328; on Bryant Creek. Free. All year; 14-day limit. 15 RV sites. Tbls, toilets, cfga, no drkg wtr. Fishing, hunting, canoeing, swimming, hiking. 328 acres. GPS: 36.87351, -92.466596.

BAKERSFIELD (8S)

Udall Park $12
Corps of Engineers
Norfork Lake
9 mi W of Bakersfield on CR O (1.5 mi W of Udall); 0.7 mi on access rd. $12. 5/1-9/15; 14-day limit. 7 primitive sites. Tbls, pit toilets, cfga, drkg wtr, dump. Boating(lr), fishing. GPS: 36.544592, -92.285376

BELGRADE (9S)

Wild Boar Ridge $10
Council Bluff Recreation Area
Mark Twain National Forest
4 mi W of Belgrade on CR C; 7 mi S on CR DD. $10 during 4/4-10/3; 14-day limit. 55 sites including 7 double sites, 4 group sites ($25) & walk-in tent sites. 40-ft RV limit. Toilets, cfga, tbls, drkg wtr. Swimming, boating(l - $), fishing, hiking trails (3.5-mi lakeshore trail. Non-campers pay $3 day use fee or $20 annually. GPS: 37.7242136, -90.9426305

BERRYMAN (10S)

Berryman Recreation Area   FREE
Mark Twain National Forest
2 mi E of Berryman on SR 8; 1.5 mi N on FR 2266. Free. All year; 14-day limit. 8 sites (22-ft RV limit). Tbls cfga, toilets, no drkg wtr, no trash service. Hiking trails. GPS: 37.9298, -91.03252.

Brazil Creek   FREE
Mark Train National Forest
2 mi E of Berryman on MO 8; 4 mi NE on FR 2266; 3 mi NW on FR 2265; 1.5 mi NE on Hwy W. Free, but donations accepted. All year; 14-day limit. 8 sites (RVs under 22 ft). Tbls, toilets, cfga, no drkg wtr or trash service. Picnicking; hiking; horseback riding (1 mi). GPS: 37.9865, -91.0325

BIRCH TREE (11S)

Rymers $5
Ozark National Scenic Riverways
About 4.5 mi W of Birch Tree on US 60; 6 mi N on CR M to
Jacks Fork River. $5 during 4/15-10/15; free off-season;
14-day limit. Primitive undesignated sites. Tbls, toilets,
cfga, no drkg wtr. Fishing, boating, swimming, canoeing.
GPS: 37.06255, -91.56264.

BONNE TERRE (12S)

St. Francois State Park $12
4 mi N of Bonne Terre on US 67; on Big River. $12 base
off-season (11/1-3/31) at 47 basic sites ($13 rest of year);
seniors pay $11 in-season, $10 off-season. Also 63 elec
sites. All year; 15-day limit. 30-ft RV limit. Tbls, flush
toilets, cfga, drkg wtr, dump, showers, coin laundry (no
wtr service off-season), WiFi. Fishing, swimming, canoeing, hiking & bridle trails, playground. 2,735 acres. GPS:
37.9769963, -90.5184591

BOONVILLE (13N)

Taylors Landing Access   FREE
Department of Conservation
E of Boonville on Hwy 98; at Missouri River. Free. All year.
1 small primitive camping area near parking lot; no amenities, no drkg wtr, no trash service. Boating(l), fishing. GPS:
38.959387, -92.548438.

BOWLING GREEN (14N)

Ranacker State Conservation Area   FREE
9 mi N of Bowling Green on US 61; SW on CR RA. Free.
All year; 14-day limit. 6 primitive designated sites, also
on and adjacent to all parking areas except for shooting
range & along roadways. Toilet, cfga, no drkg wtr. Hunting,
shooting range, hiking. GPS: 39.453392, -91.293919.

BRANSON (15S)

Indian Point Park $8.50
Corps of Engineers
Table Rock Lake
From W of Branson at jct with SR 13, 3 mi W on SR 76;
2.8 mi S on Indian Point Rd; on White River arm of lake.
$8.50 with federal senior pass at 2 non-elec sites; others
pay $17. At 21 elec sites, $11 with senior pass; others pay
$22. At 54 elec/wtr sites, $11.50 with senior pass; others
pay $23. 5/1-9/15; 14-day limit. RV limit in excess of 65
ft. Non-campers pay $5 day use fee for boat ramp, dump,
station, picnicking, beach. Tbls, flush toilets, cfga, drkg
wtr, pavilion, beach, showers, dump, marina. Fishing, boat-
ing(ld), swimming. GPS: 36.63111, -93.34722

Table Rock State Park $12
5 mi W of SR 76 on SR 165. $12 off-season at 43 basic
sites ($13 in-season 3/1-11/30); seniors pay $11 in-season, $10 off-season. Also 78 elec sites. All year; 15-day
limit. 30-ft RV limit. Flush toilets, cfga, drkg wtr, showers,

tbls, dump, elec($), sewer($), WiFi. Swimming, boat-
ing(drl), fishing, playground. 356 acres. GPS: 36.5875633,
-93.3101832

BUNKER (16S)

Loggers Lake Recreation Area $8
Mark Twain National Forest
Qtr mi W of Bunker on CR A; 6.2 mi SW on FR 2221 (Lincoln
Ave); 1.3 mi SE on FR 2193. $8. About 4/1-10/31; 14-day
limit. 14 sites up to 50 ft. Tbls, toilets, cfga, drkg wtr.
Fishing, swimming beach, boating (l - elec mtrs), hiking
trails. 8 acres. Non-campers pay $2 day use fee. GPS:
37.3900463, -91.2640219

CALWOOD (18S)

Moores Mill Access   FREE
Department of Conservation
SE of Calwood on CR JJ; at Auxvasse Creek. Free. All
year; 14-day limit. Primitive designated camping area. No
facilities, no drkg wtr, no trash service. Fishing, canoeing,
hunting. GPS: 37.1731038, -91.291522.

CAMERON (20N)

Pony Express Lake State Conservation Area   FREE
9 mi E of Cameron on Hwy 36; N on Hwy 33, then 1 mi on Rt
RA (marked with a cantilever sign). Free. All year; 14-day
limit. 2 primitive camping areas. Toilets, cfga, tbls, drkg
wtr, fishing piers, fish cleaning station. Boating(lr), fishing,
hunting, hiking trails. GPS: 39.800718, -94.392494.

Wallace State Park $12
6 mi S of Cameron on US 69; E on SR 121. $12 base
off-season at 35 basic sites ($13 in-season 4/15-10/31);
seniors pay $11 in-season, $10 off-season. Also 42
elec sites. All year; 15-day limit. No RV size limit. Tbls,
flush toilets, showers, drkg wtr, dump, elec($), WiFi.
Horseshoes, swimming, boating, fishing, hiking trails,
playground. Club camping available. 502 acres. GPS:
39.6547258, -94.217722

CANTON (21N)

Fenway Landing Campground   FREE
Corps of Engineers
Mississippi River Lock & Dam 20
4.5 mi N of Canton on US 61 then E on CR 454; camping area
is just across the levee. Free. All year; 14-day limit. 15 sites.
Tbls, toilets, cfga, drkg wtr. Picnicking; fishing; swimming;
boating(l). 3 acres. GPS: 40.238281, -91.517334

CAPE FAIR (22S)

Cape Fair Park $8
Corps of Engineers
Table Rock Lake
1 mi SW of Cape Fair on CR 76/82, following signs; on
James River arm of lake. $8 with federal senior pass at
13 non-elec sites; others pay $16. At 23 elec sites, $10.50
with senior pass; others pay $21. At 46 elec, wtr sites, $11

with senior pass; others pay $22. 5/1-9/15; 14-day limit. RV limit in excess of 65 ft; 7 pull-through sites. Picnic shelter, tbls, flush toilets, cfga, drkg wtr, showers, dump, beach, playground. Non-campers pay $5 day use fee for boat ramp, dump, beach, picnicking. Swimming, fishing, boating(l), waterskiing. GPS: 36.7225, -93.53157

CAPE GIRARDEAU (23S)

Trail of Tears State Park $12
10 mi N of Cape Girardeau on SR 177. $12 off-season at 35 basic sites ($13 in-season 4/1-10/31); seniors pay $11 in-season, $10 off-season. Also 10 elec sites, 7 full-hookups. All year; 15-day limit. 30-ft RV limit. Tbls, flush toilets, showers, drkg wtr, dump, elec($), coin laundry. Swimming, boating (l), fishing, hiking trails, playground, bridle trails. 3,415 acres. GPS: 37.2658, -89.2833

CARROLLTON (24N)

Bunch Hollow State Conservation Area FREE
10 mi N of Carrollton on Hwy 65; 7 mi N on Rt Z; 2 mi W on CR 712. Free. All year; 14-day limit. 13 primitive designated sites; no facilities, no drkg wtr. Hiking & bridle trails, nature study, fishing, hunting. GPS: 39.583512, -93.593925.

CASSVILLE (25S)

Roaring River State Park $12
7 mi S of Cassville on SR 112. $12 off-season at 45 basic sites ($13 in-season 2/25-10/31); seniors pay $11 in-season, $10 off-season. Also 137 elec sites, 2 full hookups. All year; 15-day limit. 30-ft RV limit. Tbls, flush toilets, showers, drkg wtr, dump, elec($), coin laundry, WiFi. Pool, fishing (stream stocked frequently), playground, hiking trails, horseback riding. 3,403 acres. GPS: 36.5856239, -93.8157525

CEDARCREEK (92S)

Yocum Creek Recreation Area FREE
Corps of Engineers
Bull Shoals Lake
From town of Cedarcreek (about 8 mi NW of Protem), 2 mi S on SR M, then 1 mi W on Yocum Creek Rd to lake. Free primitive, undesignated sites; no facilities. Boating(l), fishing. GPS: 36.5259, -93.043

CENTERVILLE (26S)

Sutton Bluff Recreation Area $8
Mark Twain National Forest
2.3 mi NE of Centerville on SR 21; 7 mi NW on FR 2233; 3 mi S on FR 2236 (narrow); at West Fork of Black River. $8. About 4/1-10/31; 14-day limit. 34 sites to 48 ft. Flush toilets, cfga, drkg wtr, tbls, showers. Hiking (Sutton Bluff Trail), swimming, fishing, ORV trails, boating, canoeing. 10 acres. GPS: 37.475603, -91.0065134

CENTRALIA (27N)

Tri-City Community Lake FREE
Department of Conservation
W of Centralia on CR CC; 1 mi S on gravel Tri-City Rd, following signs. Free. All year; 14-day limit. 6 primitive sites; no amenities, no drkg wtr. Fishing, boating(l). GPS: 39.190041, -92.208511.

CHADWICK (28S)

Bar K Wrangler Camp FREE
Mark Twain National Forest
6 mi SE of Chadwick on SR 125 at Swan Creek. Free. All year. Open primitive sites. Tbls, toilets, cfga, no drkg wtr, no trash service. Swimming, fishing, hunting, hiking, mountain biking, horseback riding. GPS: 36.860298, -93.008499

Cobb Ridge Recreation Area $10
Mark Twain National Forest
1.2 mi S of Chadwick on MO 125; 2.5 mi SW on CR H; half mi W on FR 171. $10 base; $15 with elec ($5 & $10 with federal senior pass). All year; 14-day limit. 56 sites; 34-ft RV limit. Tbls, cfga, toilets, drkg wtr, showers. 5 acres. Serves Chadwick motorcycle area. GPS: 36.913251, -93.088768

CHILLICOTHE (29N)

Poosey State Conservation Area FREE
13 mi NW of Chillicothe on Hwy A, 1 mi W of Hwy W jct; area also marked with a cantilever sign on Hwy A, 1 mi E of Hwy U jct. Free. All year; 14-day limit. Self-contained RVs at 4 primitive sites, at 3 specified parking lots and in 17 parking areas during deer and spring turkey hunting seasons. Equestrian camping at parking lot 6 at Pikes Lake; tie rails provided. Toilets, tbls, cfga, no drkg wtr, fish cleaning station at Indian Creek Lake. Hiking, bridle & biking trails, fishing, canoeing on lake, hunting, boating(l). Archery & firearms shooting ranges. GPS: 39.923357, -93.689582.

CLINTON (30S)

Bucksaw Park $7
Corps of Engineers
Harry S Truman Lake
From Clinton, 7.8 mi W on SR 7; 3.3 mi S on CR U (signs); left on SE 803 for 3 mi; on Grand River arm of lake. During 4/15-10/15, $7 with federal senior pass at 178 non-elec sites; others pay $14. $8 regular fee rest of year, but reduced amenities. At 129 elec sites, $9 base with senior pass; others pay $18 base, $22 for 50-amp elec/wtr during 4/15-10/15. Off-season, elec site fees $8 & $22 but reduced services ($4 & $11 with senior pass). 14-day limit. RV limit in excess of 65 ft. Fish cleaning station, amphitheater, tbls, flush toilets, cfga, drkg wtr, showers, dump, elec($), playground, coin laundry, beach, change house. Golf, swimming, fishing, boating(l). GPS: 38.26, -93.60556

Haysler A. Poague State Conservation Area   FREE
Just W of Clinton on SR 7, then 1 mi N on CR NW 251. Free. Primitive designated camping area; no facilities, no drkg wtr. Boating(l), fishing, hunting. GPS: 38.414477, -93.837541.

Sparrowfoot Park $12
Corps of Engineers
Harry S Truman Lake
From Clinton, 6 mi S on SR 13; 1.5 mi E, following signs; near confluence of Grand River & Deepwater Creek. $12 base, $14 at premium locations, at 18 non-elec sites during 4/15-10/15 ($6 & $7 with federal senior pass); $8 rest of year, but reduced amenities. At 93 elec sites, $8 base with senior pass during 4/15-10/15; others pay $16 base, $18 at premium locations ($9 with senior pass). $8 off-season but no utilities ($4 with senior pass). 14-day limit. RV limit in excess of 65 ft; 3 pull-through sites. Picnic shelters, tbls, flush toilets, cfga, drkg wtr, showers, dump, playground, beach, change house, coin laundry, elec($). Fishing, boating(l), golf, ranger programs, horseshoes. Note: In 2013, the swimming beach was closed for budget cuts; check with lake office for current status before arrival. GPS: 38.29639, -93.72639

Talley Bend Park $12
Corps of Engineers
Harry S Truman Lake
17 mi S of Clinton on Hwy 13; 5 mi E on CR C (about 7 mi E of Lowry City); S side across bridge; on Osage arm of lake. During 4/15-9/30, $12 base, $14 at premium locations at 65 non-elec sites ($6 & $7 with federal senior pass); $8 off-season 9$4 with senior pass), but reduced amenities. At 109 elec sites, $9 with senior pass during 4/15-9/30; others pay $18 ($8 rest of year, but no utilities). 14-day limit. RV limit in excess of 65 ft; 8 pull-through sites. Tbls, flush toilets, cfga, drkg wtr, elec($), showers, dump, playground, coin laundry. Swimming, fishing, boating(l). Note: In 2013, Loop B sites were closed, and the number of other sites was reduced for budget cuts. GPS: 38.13778, -93.61722

Windsor Crossing Park $10
Corps of Engineers
Harry S Truman Lake
From Clinton, E on SR 7 to Rt PP (3.5 mi N of Tightwad); follow signs 4 mi N; at Tebo Creek arm of lake. During 4/15-9/30, $10 at 47 non-elec sites; $6 rest of year but reduced amenities ($5 & $3 with federal senior pass). 14-day limit. RV limit in excess of 65 ft; 6 pull-through sites. Tbls, cfga, drkg wtr, beach, toilets, playground. Fishing, swimming, boating(l), hiking. GPS: 38.36444, -93.545

COLUMBIA (31N)

Finger Lakes State Park $12
10 mi N of Columbia off Hwy 63. $12 off-season at 19 basic sites ($13 in-season 4/1-10/31); seniors pay $11 in-season, $10 off-season. Also 16 elec sites. All year; 15-day limit. Tbls, flush toilets, cfga, drkg wtr, elec($), showers, dump (no wtr or showers off-season), WiFi. Boating, fishing, swimming, playground, canoeing, OHV/ATV activities, mountain biking. 7 strip pits. GPS: 39.090595, -92.316569

Three Creeks State Conservation Area   FREE
5 mi S of Columbia on Hwy 63; 1.75 mi W on Deer Park Rd. Free. All year; 14-day limit. Open primitive camping; camping along roads & parking lots only by hunters during firearms deer season. No facilities, no drkg wtr. Hiking, biking & bridle trails, hunting, fishing. Turkey Creek interpretive trail. GPS: 38.834826, -92.287664.

DANVILLE (32S)

Danville State Conservation Area   FREE
SE of Danville on CR RB. Free. All year; 14-day limit. 6 primitive designated sites at Post Oak area with pit toilet, cfga; 3 camping areas with no amenities. No drkg wtr, no trash service. Hunting, hiking trails, poor fishing. GPS: 38.87171, -91.50544.

Graham Cave State Park $12
2 mi W of Danville on CR TT, off I-70. $12 Sun-Thurs & nightly off-season at 34 basic sites; $13 Fri-Sat in-season Apr-Oct. Seniors get $2 discounts all year. Also 18 elec sites. All year; 15-day limit. 30-ft RV limit. Tbls, flush toilets, showers, cfga, drkg wtr, dump, elec($), coin laundry. Off-season modern restrooms, showers & drkg wtr available. Playground, boating(l), fishing, hiking. Loutre River. 357 acres. Historic cave. GPS: 38.9067079, -91.57711

DEXTER (33S)

Otter Slough State Conservation Area   FREE
4 mi S of Dexter on SR 25; W on CR H to jct of CR ZZ, then follow signs 4 mi on gravel rd. Free. All year; 14-day limit. 2-4 primitive campsites in each of 3 areas: St. Francis River bridge, Cul-de-Sac & Pool 14; no amenities. Not recommended as camping destinations; used primarily by hunters & fishermen. Tbls, toilets at area headquarters & Cypress Lake; no drkg wtr. Fishing, boating (21 unimproved boat ramps), hunting, hiking trail, fishing dock. GPS: 36.722631, -90.107393.

DONIPHAN (34S)

Buffalo Creek   FREE
Mark Twain National Forest
18 mi W of Doniphan on US 160; 2 mi N on FR 3145. Free. All year; 14-day limit. 3 sites (RVs under 22 ft). Tbls, cfga, well drkg wtr. Picnicking; fishing; swimming. GPS: 36.6892243, -91.0567955

Camp Five Pond   FREE
Mark Twain National Forest
20 mi W on Doniphan on Hwy 160; 7 mi N on Rt J. Free. All year; 14-day limit. 3 sites. Pit toilets, tbls. Picnicking; fishing; hiking. GPS: 36.7664, -91.136

Deer Leap Recreation Area $12
Mark Twain National Forest
5 mi NW of Doniphan on SR Y; 1.5 mi W on FR 4349. $12.
Open 5/1-9/30; 14-day limit. 7 sites to 48 ft. Tbls, toilets,
cfga, drkg wtr, lantern posts. Boating(rl), fishing, swimming,
hiking, kayaking, canoeing. 10 acres. Non-campers pay $3
day use fee. Current River. GPS: 36.67561, -90.8854

Dunrovin Recreation Area   FREE
Mark Twain National Forest
4 mi W of Doniphan on Hwy 160; 1.1 mi on Hwy 160W,
then follow FR 4819 to camp. Free. All year; 14-day limit.
Tbls, toilets, cfga, no drkg wtr. Boating, canoeing, hiking,
picnicking. Site damaged by vandals in April 2014. GPS:
36.65347, -90.86165

Float Camp Recreation Area $12
Mark Twain National Forest
4.5 mi NW of Doniphan on SR Y; half mi W on FR 3210;
on E bank of Current River. $12 (double sites $18). About
4/24-10/1; 14-day limit. 20 sites, 8 with elec, $20 (double
sites $30); 40-ft RV limit. Seniors with federal senior pass
pay $6 base, $14 with elec. Tbls, toilets, cfga, no drkg wtr,
picnic shelter($). Fishing, boating(lr), hiking trail, swim-
ming, canoeing, kayaking. Non-campers pay $2 day use
fee. Newly renovated. GPS: 36.6676, -90.876

Fourche Creek State Conservation Area   FREE
11 mi W of Doniphan on Hwy 142; 7 mi S on Hwy P; at West
Fourche Creek. Free. All year; 14-day limit. Open primitive
camping. No facilities, no drkg area. Hunting, hiking, hunting, fishing. GPS: 36.510368, -91.03707

Fourche Lake Recreation Area   FREE
Mark Twain National Forest
18 mi W of Doniphan on US 160; 4 mi S on CR V; 2 mi E on
unpaved rd to lake. Free. All year; 14-day limit. 6 primitive
sites. Tbls, toilets, cfga, no drkg wtr. Boating(l - elec mtrs),
fishing. 49-acre lake. Lake GPS: 36.63839, -91.052906

Gooseneck (Hawes) $5
Ozark National Scenic Riverways
10 mi W of Doniphan on US 160; 15 mi N on Hwy C; 3 mi
E on gravel FR 3142 to the Current River. $5 during 4/15-
10/15; free off-season; 14-day limit. About 10 primitive
undesignated sites. Toilets, cfga, tbls, no drkg wtr. Boat-
ing(l), fishing, canoeing. GPS: 36.8211656, -90.946793

Little Black State Conservation Area   FREE
8 mi N of Doniphan on Hwy 21; E on Hwy NN. All year;
14-day limit. Undesignated open primitive camping; no
amenities, no drkg wtr. Fishing, hunting, hiking path,
archery range. GPS: 36.755009, -90.803218.

Mudpuppy State Conservation Area   FREE
6 mi E of Doniphan on Hwy 160; 4 mi N on Hwy BB. All year;
14-day limit. Primitive open camping; no facilities, no drkg

wtr. Hiking, fishing, hunting, canoeing. GPS: 36.721908,
-90.711714.

DORA (35S)

Patrick Bridge Access   FREE
Department of Conservation
S of Dora on CR H, at North Fork of White River (E of
Gainesville & 4 mi N of Hwy 160). Free. All year; 14-day
limit. 12 primitive sites. Tbls, toilets, cfga, no drkg wtr.
Fishing (trout & bass), canoeing, swimming, hunting. GPS:
36.643306, -92.226741.

Riverside Canoe Rental $9
9 mi S of Dora on Hwy H on North Fork of White River.
$9 per person for 1 night with boat rental or shuttle; $8
for 2 or more nights (children half price). Elec $8 extra.
Tbls, flush toilets, cfga, drkg wtr, showers, volleyball,
horseshoes. Canoeing, boating, fishing. GPS: 36.3331,
-92.14550

DUKE (36S)

Rich's Last Resort $7
At 33401 Windsor Lane on the Big Piney River. $7 per
person; $7 extra for elec. Apr-Nov. Tbls, toilets, cfga,
drkg wtr. Canoeing, float trips, fishing. GPS: 37.672977,
-92.051612

EAGLE ROCK (37S)

Big M Park $8
Corps of Engineers
Table Rock Lake
2 mi N of Eagle Rock on SR 86; 6 mi E on SR E; 2 mi S on
CR M; on White River arm of lake. $8 with senior pass at
37 non-elec sites; others pay $16. At 9 elec sites, $10 with
senior pass; others pay $20. 14 full hookups, $23 ($11.50
with senior pass). 5/1-9/15; 14-day limit. RV limit in excess
of 65 ft. Non-campers pay $4 day use fee for picnicking,
boat ramp, beach, dump station. Tbls, flush toilets, cfga,
drkg wtr, elec($), beach, showers, dump. Fishing, swim-
ming, boating(l), waterskiing. GPS: 36.55835, -93.67627

Eagle Rock $8
Corps of Engineers
Table Rock Lake
From Eagle Rock, 3 mi S on SR 86; right before bridge
(signs); on White River arm of lake. $8 with federal senior
pass at 37 non-elec sites; others pay $16. At 24 elec sites,
$10 with senior pass; others pay $20. 1 elec/wtr site &
1 full hookup site, $21 & $22 ($10.50 & $11 with senior
pass). 5/1-915; 14-day limit. RV limit in excess of 65 ft;
6 pull-through sites. Non-campers pay $4 day use fee
for boat ramp, dump station, picnicking, sand volleyball
court. Tbls, flush toilets cfga, drkg wtr, elec($), sewer($),
beach, showers, playground, dump. Fishing, swimming,
boating(l), waterskiing. GPS: 36.52722, -93.73

Viney Creek $8
Corps of Engineers
Table Rock Lake
8.5 mi SE of Eagle Rock on SR 86; 4 mi N on CR J; on White River arm of lake. $8 with federal senior pass at non-elec RV/tent sites; others pay $16. At elec sites, $10 with senior pass; others pay $20. At 24 elec/wtr sites, $10.50 with senior pass; others pay $21. 5/1-9/15; 14-day limit. 50-ft RV limit; 9 pull-through sites. Non-campers pay $4 day use fee for boat ramp, beach, dump station, picnicking. Tbls, flush toilets, cfga, drkg wt, elec($), showers, dump, beach. Fishing, swimming, boating(ld), waterskiing, basketball. GPS: 36.56611, -93.67583

ELLINGTON (38S)
Logyard $5
Ozark National Scenic Riverways
14 mi W of Ellington on Hwy 106; 6 mi S on CR HH to Current River. $5 during 4/15-10/15; free off-season; 14-day limit. 8 primitive undesignated sites. Pit toilets, cfga, no drkg wtr. Boating, fishing, canoeing, swimming. GPS: 37.0631, -91.0713

Webb Creek $7
Corps of Engineers
Clearwater Lake
2.6 mi SE of Ellington on SR 21; 10.3 mi SE on CR H. $7 with federal senior pass at 10 non-elec sites during 5/15-9/15; others pay $14. Some sites free off-season, but limited amenities. At 25 elec sites (some pull-through) $8 with senior pass during 5/15-9/15; others pay $16; some sites free off-season, but no utilities. Tbls, flush toilets, cfga, drkg wtr, elec($), showers, beach, playground, dump, store, picnic shelter, store. Overflow camping. Boating(lr), fishing, picnicking, swimming, waterskiing. GPS: 37.151123, -90.812756

ELVINS (39S)
St. Joe State Park $12
3 mi SE of Elvins on CR B (W of Farmington). $12 off-season at 35 basic sites ($13 in-season 4/1-10/31); seniors pay $11 in-season, $10 off-season. Also 40 elec sites. 15-day limit. 30-ft RV limit. Tbls, flush toilets, cfga, showers, drkg wtr, lantern posts, dump, elec($), beach, coin laundry, WiFi. Swimming, fishing, boating(l), playground, bridle trails, hiking, mountain biking, bike trail. Monsanto Lake. 8,238 acres. One campground has ORVs; one for equestrians, but everyone may camp. 2,000-acre area for ORV use. 5 free trailside tent sites. GPS: 37.8042177, -90.5170688

EMINENCE (40S)
Alley Spring $7
Ozark National Scenic Riverways
6 mi W of Eminence on SR 106. $7 with federal senior pass during 4/15-10/30; others pay $14; free off-season but no wtr. 14-day limit. 162 sites. Tbls, flush toilets, cfga, drkg wtr, showers($), dump, store, firewood, dump. Group camping available. Canoeing (r), fishing, boating, swimming, campfire programs, biking/walking trails. 417 acres. GPS: 37.1483824, -91.4498598

Horse Camp   FREE
Ozark National Scenic Riverways
3 mi W of Eminence on Hwy 106; N on access rd to Jacks Fork River. Free. All year; 14-day limit. Primitive undesignated sites; no facilities. Boating, fishing, swimming, canoeing. GPS: 37.1597709, -91.4162478.

Jack's Fork Canoe Rental/Campground $7.50
Qtr mi E of Eminence on SR 106; at Jack's Fork River. $7.50 per person base Sun-Thurs; $8.50 per person Fri-Sat; $8-10 per site for elec/wtr. 4/15-10/15. 95 sites (50 for tents). Tbls, flush toilets, cfga, drkg wtr, showers, hookups($), dump, playground, store, shelter. Boating, fishing, swimming, hiking, canoeing(r), tubing(r).

Jerktail Landing   FREE
Ozark National Scenic Riverways
7 mi N of Eminence on SR 19; 6 mi NE on access rd to Current River. Free. All year; 14-day limit. Primitive undesignated sites; no facilities. Fishing, boating, canoeing, swimming. GPS: 37.2306, -91.3085.

Keatons Campground $5
Ozark National Scenic Riverways
3 mi W of Eminence on Hwy 106; N on access rd, past Horse Camp to Jacks Ford River. $5 during 4/15-10/15; free off-season; 14-day limit. Primitive undesignated sites; tbls, toilets, cfga, no drkg wtr. Boating, fishing, swimming, canoeing. GPS: 37.1581044, -91.4109698

Powder Mill Campground $6
Ozark National Scenic Riverways
13 mi E of Eminence on SR 106. $6 with federal senior pass during 4/15-10/15; others pay $12; free rest of year but no wtr; 14-day limit. 8 sites. Tbls, toilets, cfga, drkg wtr. Canoeing, fishing, boating, swimming. 60 acres. GPS: 37.1811593, -91.1729077

Pulltite Campground $7
Ozark National Scenic Riverways
16 mi N of Eminence on SR 19; 4 mi W on CR EE. $7 with federal senior pass during 4/15-10/15; others pay $14. Free rest of year but no wtr; 14-day limit. 55 sites. 3 group sites by reservation Tbls, flush toilets, cfga, drkg wtr, store, firewood. Canoeing(r), swimming, fishing, boating, campfire programs, biking/walking trails, equestrian trails. 80 acres. GPS: 37.3350458, -91.479585

Round Spring Campground $7
Ozark National Scenic Riverways
13 mi N of Eminence on SR 19. $7 with federal senior pass during 4/15-10/15; free off-season but no wtr; 14-day

limit. 60 sites. Three group sites by reservation. Tbls, flush toilets, cfga, drkg wtr, coin laundry, dump, store, firewood, showers($). Canoeing(r), fishing, swimming, boating, campfire programs, biking/walking trails, equestrian trails. GPS: 37.2836574, -91.4065262

Shawnee Creek　　　　　　　　　　　　　　　　$5
Ozark National Scenic Riverways
About 7 mi E of Eminence on Hwy 106; N on access rd to Jacks Fork River. $5 during 4/15-10/15; free rest of year; 14-day limit. Primitive undesignated sites. Tbls, toilets, cfga, no drkg wtr. Fishing, boating, swimming, canoeing. GPS: 37.1731038, -91.291522

Sinking Creek Campground　　　　　　　　　　$5
Ozark National Scenic Riverways
12 mi N of Eminence on SR 19; at jct of Current River & Sinking Creek. $5 during 4/15-10/15; free rest of year; 14-day limit. Primitive undesignated sites; tbls, cfga, toilets, no drkg wtr. Boating(l), fishing, canoeing. GPS: Creek GPS: 37.3025, -91.4154

Two Rivers Campground　　　　　　　　　　　$7
Ozark National Scenic Riverways
4 mi E of Eminence on SR 106; 2 mi N on CR V. $7 with federal senior pass during 4/15-10/15; others pay $14. Free rest of year but no wtr; 14-day limit. 19 sites. Two group sites by reservation. Tbls, flush toilets, cfga, drkg wtr, showers($), dump, store, firewood. Canoeing(r), fishing, swimming, boating. GPS: 37.192, -91.2685

FLORIDA (41N)
Mark Twain State Park　　　　　　　　　　　$12
Half mi S of Florida on SR 107; on Mark Twain Lake. $12 Sun-Thurs & nightly off-season at 22 basic sites ($13 in-season 4/1-10/31, with 2-night minimum stay required. Seniors get $2 discounts all year. Also 75 elec sites. 15-day limit. 30-ft RV limit. Tbls, flush toilets, drkg wtr, showers, cfga, dump, elec($), coin laundry, beach. Fishing, playground, boating(l), swimming, interpretive programs. Cabin where Mark Twain was born at visitor's center. 2,771 acres. Mark Twain Historic Site museum. GPS: 39.2758, -91.4730

FORSYTH (42S)
Beaver Creek Campground　　　　　　　　　　$9
Corps of Engineers
Bull Shoals Lake
6.6 mi E of Forsyth on US 160 (2.5 mi S of Kissee Mills) on CR O. $9 base with federal senior pass at 34 elec sites; others pay $18 base, $19 for premium 50-amp sites ($9.50 with senior pass). 4/1-10/15; 14-day limit. 40-ft RV limit. Tbls, flush toilets, cfga, drkg wtr, elec, coin laundry, beach, playground, pavilion, dump, showers. Boating(l), fishing, swimming. GPS: 36.6433, 93.0322

River Run Campground　　　　　　　　　　$9.50
Corps of Engineers
Bull Shoals Lake
From Forsyth, E on SR 60 across bridge, then S following sign, then W; on upper end of lake. $9.50 base with federal senior pass; others pay $19 base, $20 at 10 premium 50-amp sites ($10 with senior pass). 4/1-9/30; 14-day limit. 32 elec sites; 40-ft RV limit. Tbls, flush toilets, cfga, drkg wtr, showers, coin laundry, playground, dump. Boating(l), fishing, waterskiing, biking. GPS: 36.679932, -93.101074

Shadow Rock City Park & Campground　　　　$12
At Hwys 160 & 76 in Forsyth; at Bull Shoals Lake. $12 for RV sites with elec/wtr hookups (50% discount for seniors); $15 full hookups ($12 for seniors). Apr-Oct; 14-day limit. 175 sites (50 for tents) at 2 campgrounds. Tbls, flush toilets, cfga, drkg wtr, hookups($), showers, coin laundry nearby, playground, dump. Boating(lr), canoeing(r), fishing, shuffleboard, tennis, horseshoes, volleyball, shuffleboard. 50 acres. GPS: 36.684156, -93.099288.

FREDERICKTOWN (43S)
Amidon Memorial State Conservation Area　　FREE
E of Fredericktown on Hwy J, then S on Hwy W & E on CR 208. Free. 10/1-12/31; 14-day limit. Primitive open camping at 1,600-acre natural area; also primitive walk-in camping all year 100 yds from all public rds, open fields & parking lots. Specified camping area accessible from S entrance off CR 248, through a private gate. No facilities, no drkg wtr. Hunting, horseback riding, hiking trail, hunting, fishing, canoeing. GPS: 37.545356, -90.156521.

Silver Mines Recreation Area　　　　　　　$10
Mark Twain National Forest
6.5 mi W of Fredericktown on SR 72; 3 mi SW on CR D. $10 without hookups; $17 elec ($5 & $12 with federal senior pass). About 3/15-10/15; 14-day limit. 61 sites (34-ft RV limit). Tbls, toilets, cfga, drkg wtr. Swimming, hiking, kayaking, fishing. 25 acres. Non-campers pay $2 day-use fee. GPS: 37.5619969, -90.4415086

GAINESVILLE (44S)
Tecumseh Park　　　　　　　　　　　　　　$11
Corps of Engineers
Norfork Lake
11 mi E of Gainesville on US 160 at Tecumseh on both sides of White River. $11 at 7 non-elec sites during 5/1-9/15 ($5.50 with federal senior pass); may be free rest of year, but no services or wtr. 7 sites. Tbls, pit toilets, cfga, drkg wtr. Fishing, boating(ld). 10 acres. GPS: 36.586587, -92.286826

GLASGOW (45N)
Stump Island City Park & Campground　　　$10
Half mi S on Old Hwy 87 from jct with Hwy 240; on Missouri River. $10 primitive sites; $20 with elec/wtr (6 full

hookups). 4/1-10/31. 14 sites. Tbls, flush toilets, cfga, drkg wtr, hookups($), dump, showers, playground. Boating(l), fishing, hiking, tennis, swimming. 10 acres. GPS: 39.217786, -92.84836

GREENCASTLE (46N)

Union Ridge State Conservation Area   FREE
2 mi N of Greencastle on Hwy D. Free. All year; 14-day limit. Primitive designated camping on & adjacent to 15 parking lots; also designated Dry Bridge camping area with toilets next to parking lot off Hwy D. No camping along roadways. Toilets, cfga, no drkg wtr. Fishing, hiking, hunting. Gravel boat ramp at Union Ridge Lake. 7,981 acres. GPS: 40.309044, -92.872675.

GREENVILLE (47S)

Greenville Recreation Area $7
Corps of Engineers
Wappapello Lake
2.5 mi S of Greenville on US 67; before bridge; follow signs. $7 with federal senior pass at 8 non-elec sites; others pay $14. At 98 elec sites (30-amp), $9 with senior pass; others pay $18. Overflow camping open when all public & private campgrounds in the area are full; $3 for primitive sites, no facilities. 3/29-11/25; 14-day limit. RV limit in excess of 65 ft. Tbls, flush toilets, cfga, drkg wtr, showers, dump, playground, fishing pier, amphitheater, historic trail, interpretive trail. Boating(l), hiking, horseshoes. GPS: 37.10278, -90.45833

Northern Primitive Camping Zone   FREE
Corps of Engineers
Wappapello Lake
Free primitive camping available on all Corps public lands S of Hwy 34 to PA 34 (access N of Greenville) on E side of the St. Francis River and all Corps land on the W side, N of where Hwy FF intersects with Hwy 67. All year; 14-day limit. No facilities, no drkg wtr. Camping prohibited in the state wildlife area.

St. Francis Parking Areas   FREE
Corps of Engineers
Wappapello Lake
S of Greenville, off Hwy F, Hwy D & Hwy BB, both sides of St. Francis River on Corps of Engineers land; camp within 100 feet of 19 designated parking areas S of US 67. No facilities, no drkg wtr. Fishing, hiking, boating. Also camp within 100 feet of the Ozark Trail in same area.

St. Francis River East Shore   FREE
Corps of Engineers
Wappapello Lake
N of Greenville on Hwy 67, using westbound access rds to E shore of St. Francis river S of Hwy 34 & N of Hwy 67's jct with Hwy FF. Free primitive camping zone all along river. All year; 14-day limit. No facilities, no drkg wtr. Boating, fishing, hiking.

St. Francis River West Shore   FREE
Corps of Engineers
Wappapello Lake
N of Greenville on Hwy FF, then N on CR 380, using eastbound access rds to W shore of St. Francis River. Free primitive camping zone all along river to Hwy 34. All year; 14-day limit. No facilities, no drkg wtr. Boating, fishing, hiking.

Sulphur Springs Campground   FREE
Corps of Engineers
Wappapello Lake
From Greenville, 1.3 mi S on US 67, 3.2 mi S on CR D, W on Corps Rd. 17. Free. All year; 14-day limit. 4 primitive sites at parking area. Pit toilets, cfga, no drkg wtr. Boating(l), fishing.

GUTHRIE (48S)

Dry Fork Recreation Area   FREE
Mark Twain National Forest
1 mi W of Guthrie on Hwy Y; 2 mi N on Hwy 361. Free, donations accepted. All year; 14-day limit. 8 sites on 15 acres plus small group area; 34-ft RV limit. Tbls, toilets, cfga, drkg wtr. Hitching posts at each site. Hiking, horseback riding. GPS: 38.7648, -92.163

Pine Ridge Recreation Area   FREE
Mark Twain National Forest
2 mi W of Guthrie on Hwy Y. Free but donations accepted. All year; 14-day limit. 20 acres. 8 sites; 34-ft RV limit. Tbls, toilets, cfga, drkg wtr. Hiking. GPS: 38.4535, -92.0852

HERMITAGE (49S)

Damsite Campground $12
Corps of Engineers
Pomme de Terre Lake
3 mi SE of Hermitage on SR 254, then half mi W at Carson's Corner. During 4/15-10/1, $12 base, $14 at premium locations at 22 non-elec RV/tent sites ($6 & $7 with federal senior pass). At 80 elec sites, $10 base with senior pass during 4/15-10/1; others pay $20 base, $22 with elec/wtr ($11 with senior pass). Sites free off-season, but no utilities & reduced amenities. All year; 14-day limit. 40-ft RV limit. Picnic shelters, amphitheater, tbls, flush toilets, cfga, drkg wtr, hookups($), dump, showers, coin laundry, playground. Boating(l), fishing, waterskiing, accessible fishing area. GPS: 37.90472, -93.30778

Nemo Landing $12
Corps of Engineers
Pomme de Terre Lake
3 mi SE of Hermitage on SR 254; 1 mi W from Carson's Corner before bridge. $12 base at 64 non-elec RV/tent sites during 4/16-10/15; $14 at premium sites ($6 & $7 with federal senior pass); some sites free during 10/16-4/15, but no wtr or services. At 41 elec sites, $8 base;

others pay $16 base, $18 for premium 30-amp/wtr sites ($9 with federal pass), $20 at premium sites with 50-amp elec/wt ($10 with senior pass). Some hookup sites may have lower fees & reduced amenities off-season. All year; 14-day limit. 60-ft RV limit. Picnic shelter, amphitheater, tbls, flush toilets, showers, cfga, drkg wtr, elec($), dump, playground, beach, coin laundry. Swimming, fishing, boating(ld), waterskiing, horseshoe pits. GPS: 37.86611, -93.27389

Outlet Park Campground $12
Corps of Engineers
Pomme de Terre Lake
3 mi SE of Hermitage on SR 254; 2 mi W from Carson's Corner; below dam on W side of outlet. During 4/15-10/15, $12 at 7 non-elec RV/tent sites ($6 with federal senior pass). At 14 elec/wtr sites, $11 with senior pass during 4/15-10/15; others pay $22. Off-season, some sites without hookups are free with reduced amenities. 14-day limit. 50-ft RV limit; 10 pull-through sites. Group camping available. Picnic shelter, tbls, toilets, cfga, drkg wtr, elec($), playground, no dump, no showers. Boating(l), fishing, waterskiing, basketball, tennis, horseshoe pits. 37.90278, -93.32917

ISABELLA (51S)
Theodosia Campground $7
Corps of Engineers
Bull Shoals Lake
From Isabella (sign), 3 mi W on US 160, across bridge, then S (left). Also 1 mi E of Theodosia on SR 160. $7 with federal senior pass at 2 non-elec sites; others pay $14. $9 with federal senior pass at 31 elec sites (double sites $17); others pay $18 (double sites $34). 4/1-10/31; 14-day limit. 45-ft RV limit. Tbls, toilets, cfga, drkg wtr, dump, group shelter, playground, elec, coin laundry, beach, showers. Swimming, picnicking, fishing, boating(ldr). Park was renovated in 2010. GPS: 36.57333, -92.65361

JADWIN (52S)
Cedar Grove State Conservation Area   FREE
3 mi S of Jadwin off Hwy K. Free. All year; 14-day limit. Primitive open camping area. No facilities, no drkg wtr. Hiking, hunting. GPS: 37.42819, -91.586272.

Jadwin Canoe Rental & Campground $4.28
Just N of Jadwin on Hwy K at Hwy ZZ. $4.28 base per person; $5.70 per site extra for elec. All year. Tbls, flush toilets, cfga, drkg wtr, elec($), dump, showers. Fishing, hiking, canoeing(r), swimming. Canoe trips. GPS: 37.486711, -91.570979

JEFFERSON CITY (53S)
Mari-Osa Access   FREE
Department of Conservation
6 mi E of Jefferson City on US 50; at Osage River. Free. All year; 14-day limit. Primitive designated camping area. Toilet, cfga, no drkg wtr. Boating(l), fishing. GPS: 38.492063,-92.01324.

KAISER (54S)
Lake of the Ozarks State Park $12
4 mi E on Hwy 42 from jct with US 54; 5 mi S on Hwy 134. $12 off season at 62 basic sites ($13 in-season 4/1-10/31); seniors pay $11 in-season, $10 off-season. Also 127 elec sites. 15-day limit. Tbls, flush toilets, cfga, drkg wtr, dump, elec($), showers, pool, beaches, coin laundry, WiFi, playground. Swimming, fishing, boating(lrd), canoeing(r), kayaking(r), mountain biking hiking, bridle trails, cave tours. 17,213 acres; 89 mi of shoreline. GPS: 38.0980899, -92.6168501

KIMBERLING CITY (55S)
Aunt's Creek $8
Corps of Engineers
Table Rock Lake
2 mi N of Kimberling City on SR 13; 2.7 mi W on SR OO & CR OO-9, following signs; on James River arm of lake. $8 with federal senior pass at 3 non-elec sites; others pay $16. At 52 elec sites, $10.50 with senior pass; others pay $21. 5/1-9/15; 14-day limit. RV limit in excess of 65 ft; 6 pull-through sites. Pavilion, tbls, flush toilets, cfga, drkg wtr, elec($), beach, showers, dump. Fishing, swimming, boating(l). Non-campers pay $4 day use fee for picnicking, boat ramp, beach, dump station. GPS: 36.67361, -93.45972

Mill Creek Park $10.50
Corps of Engineers
Table Rock Lake
3 mi S of Kimberling City on SR 13; 1 mi W on CR RB; on White River arm of lake. $10.50 with federal senior pass at 67 elec/wtr sites; others pay $21. (5/1-9/15; 14-day limit. 19 pull-through; RV limit in excess of 65 ft. Non-campers pay $5 day use fee for boat ramp, dump station, picnicking, beach. Picnic shelter, tbls, flush toilets, cfga, drkg wtr, showers, dump, beach, elec($). Swimming, fishing, boating, waterskiing. GPS: 36.59361, -93.44111

KIRKSVILLE (56S)
Montgomery Woods   FREE
State Conservation Area
18 mi W of Kirksville on Hwy 11; three-fourths mi S on Copper Trail. Free. All year; 14-day limit. Primitive camping on & adjacent to parking lots; no camping on roadways. No facilities, no drkg wtr. Hiking, hunting. GPS: 40.042805, -92.836519.

Sugar Creek State Conservation Area   FREE
4 mi W of Kirksville on Hwy 11; qtr mi S on Hwy N. All year; 14-day limit. Primitive camping on & adjacent to parking lots; no amenities. No camping along roadways. No drkg wtr. Hiking & bridle trail, hunting. Shooting range. GPS: 40.110087, -92.643744.

Thousand Hills State Park $12
4 mi W of Kirksville on SR 6. $12 off-season at 15 basic sites ($13 in-season 4/1-10/31); seniors pay $11 in-season, $10 off-season. Also 42 elec sites. All year; 15-day limit. 30-ft RV limit. Tbls, flush toilets, showers, drkg wtr, cfga, dump, elec($). Swimming, boating(rld), fishing, playground, hiking. 573-acre Forest Lake. 3,215 acres. GPS: 40.1750305, -92.642973

KNOB NOSTER (57S)
Knob Noster State Park $12
Off US 50 on Hwy 132; on Buteo Lake. $12 off-season at 27 basic sites ($13 in-season 4/1-10/31); seniors pay $11 in-season, $10 off-season. Also 41 elec sites. All year; 15-day limit. No RV size limit. Tbls, flush toilets, cfga, drkg wtr, showers, dump, elec($), coin laundry. Fishing, swimming, biking/hiking trails, playground, horseback riding. Group camping available. 3,549 acres. GPS: 38.7361239, -93.6046578

LACLEDE (58N)
Pershing State Park $12
3 mi W of Laclede on US 36; 2 mi S on SR 130. $12 off-season at 12 basic sites ($13 in-season 4/15-10/31); seniors pay $11 in-season, $10 off-season. Also 26 elec sites; 15-day limit. 30-ft RV limit. Tbls, flush toilets, cfga, drkg wtr, showers, dump, elec($), coin laundry. Fishing, swimming, playground, hiking/backpacking trails, interpretive programs. 2,909 acres. GPS: 39.7666903, -93.2168724

LADDONIA (59N)
Vandalia Community Lake FREE
Department of Conservation
4 mi E of Laddonia on CR K; follow signs 1.5 mi E on CR 100. Free. All year. 3 primitive designated sites; no amenities. No drkg wtr, no trash service. Fishing, boating(l). GPS: 39.236707, -91.538491.

LA GRANGE (60N)
Wakonda State Park $12
3 mi S of LaGrange off US 61. $12 off-season at 12 basic sites ($13 in-season 4/15-10/31); seniors pay $11 in-season, $10 off-season. Also 65 elec sites; 15-day limit. 30-ft RV limit. Tbls, flush toilets, cfga, drkg wtr, showers, dump, elec ($), coin laundry. Swimming, fishing, boating(rld), kayaking(r). 273 acres; 75-acre Wakonda Lake. GPS: 40.0064346, -91.5237664

LAMAR (61S)
Prairie State Park $12
16 mi W of Lamar, off Hwy 160, N on Hwy NN to Central Rd. $12 off-season for 2 basic sites ($13 in-season). Seniors pay $11 in-season, $10 off-season. All year; 15-day limit. Tbls, toilets, cfga, drkg wtr, interpretive programs, playground. 4,000 acres. State's largest remaining tallgrass prairie. GPS: 37.3044, -94.3418

LAMPE (62S)
Baxter Park $8
Corps of Engineers
Table Rock Lake
From Lampe at jct with SR 13, 4.8 mi W on CR H (signs); on White River arm of lake. $8 with federal senior pass at 29 non-elec sites; others pay $16. At 25 elec/wtr sites, $11 with senior pass; others pay $22. 5/1-9/15; 14-day limit. RV limit in excess of 65 ft. Non-campers pay $4 day use fee for boat ramp, dump station, picnicking, beach. Tbls, flush toilets, cfga, drkg wtr, elec($), dump, beach, playground, showers. Swimming, fishing, boating(ld). GPS: 36.67361, -93.45972

LAWSON (63N)
Watkins Mill State Park $12
3 mi N of Excelsior Springs on US 69 & 1 mi W on CR MM; at Watkins Woolen Mill. $12 off-season at 22 basic sites ($13 in-season 4/15-10/31); seniors pay $11 in-season, $10 off-season. Also 74 elec sites. 15-day limit. Tbls, flush toilets, cfga, drkg wtr, elec($), sewer($), showers, coin laundry, WiFi. No wtr or laundry services in winter. Swimming, boating(l), fishing, paved hiking & biking trail. 1,367 acres. GPS: 39.4011151, -94.2602223.

LEASBURG (64S)
Onondaga Cave State Park $12
On Rt H near Leasburg. $12 off-season at 19 basic sites ($13 in-season 4/1-10/31); seniors pay $11 in-season, $10 off-season. Also 47 elec/wtr sites; 15-day limit. No RV size limit. Tbls, flush toilets, cfga, drkg wtr, elec($), playground, showers, coin laundry; no showers or laundry off-season. Cave tours ($), fishing, boating(rl), swimming, nature programs, biking/hiking trail. Meramec River. 1,317 acres. GPS: 38.340, -91.1338

LEBANON (65S)
Bennett Spring State Park $12
12 mi W of Lebanon on SR 64. $12 off-season at 15 basic sites ($13 in-season 2/25-10/31); seniors pay $11 in-season, $10 off-season. Also 128 elec sites & 48 full-hookups. 15-day limit. 30-ft RV limit. Tbls, flush toilets, showers, drkg wtr, cfga, dump, elec($), sewer($), coin laundry; no wtr services off-season. Pool, hiking trails, playground, fishing, boating(rl), canoeing(r), rafting(r). Niangua River. 3,096 acres. Trout stocked daily. Interpretive center. GPS: 37.725595, -92.862404.

Ho-Humm Canoe Rental & Campground $5
On Rd 64-999 north of Lebanon; keep left. $5 base per person (children $3) with canoe rental, $7 without rental; $12 with elec. Apr-Oct. Open RV & tent sites on 15 acres. Tbls, flush toilets, cfga, drkg wtr, showers, 18 elec sites($), playground, store, WiFi. Boating(r), tubing(r), rafting(r), swimming, canoeing(r). GPS: 37.805976, -92.863338

Maggard Canoe and Corkery Campground $7
Follow Hwy 64 W from Lebanon; cross Niangua River bridge near Bennett Springs State Park, then right at Clyde's Store on Rt 64-152, following signs. $7 per person ($15 with elec). 2 nights free with canoe rental. All year. Tent & RV sites. Tbls, flush toilets, cfga, showers, drkg wtr, playground. Hiking, boating, canoeing(r), rafting(r), tubing(r), swimming, fishing. No pets. 888-546-9788. GPS: 37.48343, -92.52246

Redbeard's Ranch $6
NW of Lebanon on 12 mi SR 64 to Bennett Springs; just before crossing Niangua River bridge, turn right on Marigold Dr & follow signs. $6 per person for tents or self-contained RVs ($3 children 4-11); primitive sites. $22 full hookups. Tbls, flush toilets, cfga, drkg wtr, showers. Generators in designated areas. Boating, fishing, canoeing(r), kayaking(r), rafting(r). 295 acres. GPS: 37.781845, -92.853974

LESTERVILLE (66S)

Bearcat Campground $8.50
From Hwy 21 in Lesterville, turn onto Peola Rd at Lenny's Convenience Store; at sign indicating right turn, continue straight ahead onto gravel rd, watching for campground signs. $8.50 per person weekdays ($5 children); $12.50 per person weekends ($7.50 for children); $11 extra for elec. Flush toilets, tbls, cfga, drkg wtr, showers. Tubing(r), rafting(r), canoeing(r).

Johnson's Shut-ins State Park $12
8 mi N of Lesterville on CR N. $12 off-season at 14 basic sites ($13 in-season 4/1-10/31); seniors pay $11 in-season, $10 off-season. Also 21 elec sites, 20 full hookups. 15-day limit. Tbls, flush toilets, cfga, drkg wtr, elec, dump, showers, coin laundry, playground; no wtr services off-season. Hiking, fishing. 900 species of plants & wildflowers. 8,755 acres. GPS: 37.5372701, -90.8504011

Parks Bluff Campground $8
Just E of Lesterville on SR 21 near Black River forks. $8 per person ($4 children 6-12); $14 extra for elec/wtr, $15 full hookups. May-Oct. 30 sites. Tbls, flush toilets, cfga, drkg wtr, showers, elec($), dump, store. Boating, fishing, swimming, hiking, rafting, tubing(r), canoeing(r). 180 acres. GPS: 37.452407, -90.848438

LEWISTOWN (67N)

Deer Ridge State Conservation Area FREE
N of Lewiston & Midway on CR H & CR Y about 5 mi; on North Fabius River. Free. All year; 14-day limit. 4 primitive designated camping areas, including equestrian camp with tie rails, toilets & trailer parking space. Tbls, cfga, drkg wtr, toilets. Fishing, boating (l), hunting, canoeing, shooting ranges, archery range; hiking, biking & bridle trails. GPS: 40.202305, -91.841587.

LICKING (68S)

Boiling Springs Resort & Canoe Rental $7
3 mi S of Licking on Hwy 63; 8 mi W on Hwy BB; at Big Piney River. $7 per person base ($3 children); add $6 for elec, $10 full hookups. All year. Tbls, flush toilets, cfga, drkg wtr, showers, playground, dump, game room. Swimming, hiking, fishing, canoeing(r), tubing(r), boating(r). Canoe trips on Big Piney River. GPS: 37.462051, -91.986026.

LIVONIA (69N)

Rebel's Cove State Conservation Area FREE
2.5 mi N of Livonia on Rt N. All year; 14-day limit. 13 primitive sites; camping at & adjacent to parking lots. No camping along roadways. No facilities, no drkg wtr. Boating(l), canoeing, fishing. Chariton River. GPS: 40.557456, -92.703357.

LOUISIANA (70N)

Calumet Creek Access FREE
Department of Conservation
5 mi SE of Louisiana on SR 79; on Calumet Creek at Mississippi River. Free. All year; 14-day limit. Primitive undesignated sites at & adjacent to parking lots; no amenities, no drkg wtr, no trash service. Fishing, boating(l). GPS: 39.399421, -90.967282.

MACKS CREEK (71S)

Cedar Camp $6
At 891 Bannister Hollow Rd, on the Little Niangua River. $6 per person ($3 children); $6 extra with elec. Tbls, flush toilets, showers, cfga, drkg wtr. Hiking, fishing, canoeing(r). GPS: 37.96874,-92.966759.

MACON (72N)

Atlanta/Long Branch FREE
State Conservation Area
5 mi N of Macon on Hwy 63; 2 mi W on Hwy AX; 2.5 mi N on Jupiter Ave. All year; 14-day limit. 12 primitive designated camping areas; no facilities, no drkg wtr. Shooting range, fishing, boating, biking. 4,630 acres. Long Branch Lake & East Fork of Little Chariton River. GPS: 39.877234, -92.504941.

Long Branch State Park $12
From jct of US 60 & SR 5N (Mansfield-Hartville exit), S .8 mi, then 1 mi E on CR A. $12 off-season at 9 basic sites ($13 in-season 4/1-10/31); seniors pay $11 in-season, $10 off-season. Also 63 elec sites. 15-day limit. Tbls, flush toilets, cfga, drkg wtr, elec($), dump, showers, beach, marina, WiFi. Fishing, boating(lr), swimming, hiking. 1,834 acres. GPS: 39.770628, -92.526588

Thomas Hill Reservoir FREE
State Conservation Area
5.3 mi W of Macon on Hwy 36; 10 mi S on Hwy C to College Mound, then 2.4 mi W on Hwy T. Free. All year; 14-day

limit. 4 primitive designated camping areas plus 3 overflow areas. Highway T Campground has 10 concrete pads, cfga, toilets, covered shelters, tbls. No drkg wtr. Boating(ld), fishing, canoeing, hunting. GPS: 39.5514, -99.6444.

MARION (73S)

Marion Access   FREE
Department of Conservation
On E side of Marion off Hwy 179 at Missouri River. Free. All year; 14-day limit. Primitive designated camping area. Toilet, cfga, no drkg wtr, no trash service. Fishing (poor for bass), boating(l).

MARSHALL (74N)

Van Meter State Park $12
12 mi NW on SR 122 from SR 41. $12 Fri-Sat & off-season at 9 basic sites ($13 in-season 4/15-10/31, with 2-night minimum stay required). Seniors get $2 discount all year. Also 12 elec sites; 15-day limit. Tbls, flush toilets, cfga, drkg wtr, elec($), showers. Fishing, hiking trails, playground, interpretive programs. Fishing lake. Historic earthwork. 983 acres. GPS: 39.2647453, -93.2679838

MARYVILLE (75N)

Bilby Ranch Lake State Conservation Area   FREE
14 mi W of Maryville on Hwy 46. Free. All year; 14-day limit. Primitive camping in 7 designated, improved areas. Tbls, toilets, cfga, fish cleaning station, drkg wtr. Fishing, hunting, hiking, boating(l). Covered fishing pier. 5,000 acres. 110-acre lake & 14 ponds. GPS: 40.352582,-95.14842.

MEADVILLE (76N)

Fountain Grove State Conservation Area   FREE
5 mi S of Meadville on Hwy W; qtr mi S on Blackhorn Dr. Free. All year; 14-day limit. 5 primitive sites at Jo Shelby Lake. Tbls, toilets, cfga, drkg wtr. Also primitive camping at & adjacent to designated parking lots. Hiking trails (including boardwalk trail), fishing, hunting, boating(l), canoeing. GPS: 39.702669, -93.313712.

MEXICO (77N)

Lakeview Municipal Park $8
Hwy 54 S to Lakeview Rd, left 6 blocks then left on Fairground St, in Mexico. $8 for residents at RV sites, $10 non-residents. All year; 14-day limit. 12 sites. Flush toilets, showers, tbls, wtr hookups, elec, dump, shelter. Boating, fishing, hiking. 573-581-2100 or 581-8310. GPS: 39.153266, -91.894719

MINEOLA (78S)

Loutre Lick Access   FREE
Department of Conservation
SW of Mineola on CR N (3 mi S of I-70); three-fourths mi on CR 278; on Loutre River. Free. All year; 14-day limit. Primitive designated sites; no amenities, no drkg wtr, no trash service. Fishing, hiking, boating(l), hunting, canoeing. 163 acres. GPS: 38.87644, -91.587484.

MONROE CITY (79N)

Frank Russell Campground $9
Mark Twain Lake
Corps of Engineers
From US 36 at Monroe City, 4 mi E on US 24/36; 9 mi S on Rt J; 1 mi N of dam. $9 with federal senior pass; others pay $18. 4/15-10/10; 14-day limit. 65 elec sites; RV limit in excess of 65 ft. Tbls, flush toilets, cfga, drkg wtr, elec, showers, playground, amphitheater, horse corral & stalls. Horseback riding, fishing, boating, hiking, biking. Access to 32-mi Joanna Trail. GPS: 39.53556, -91.6475

Indian Creek Campground $8
Corps of Engineers
Mark Twain Lake
6 mi S of Monroe City on US 24; 1.7 mi S on Rt HH. $8 at 12 non-elec RV/tent sites & hike-in tent sites ($4 with federal senior pass). At 215 elec sites, $9 base with senior pass; others pay $18 base, $24 for full hookups ($12 with senior pass). 4/1-11/24; 14-day limit. RV limit in excess of 65 ft. Tbls, flush & pit toilets, cfga, drkg wtr, elec($), beach, showers, playground, dump, pavilion, amphitheater, fish cleaning station, marina, pay phone. Boating (l), hiking & biking trails, fishing, waterskiing, swimming, interpretive trail. Group camping available. GPS: 39.53917, -91.73306

MOUND CITY (80N)

Big Lake State Park $12
11 mi SW of Mound City on SR 111. $12 off-season at 18 basic sites ($13 in-season 4/15-10/31); seniors pay $11 in-season, $10 off-season. Also 57 elec sites; 15-day limit. 30-ft RV limit. Tbls, drkg wtr, cfga, flush toilets, showers, dump, elec($), coin laundry. Pool, playground, fishing, boating(rl), canoeing(r), kayaking(r), biking(r), horseshoes, birdwatching. 625-acre oxbow Big Lake. 407 acres. GPS: 40.537, -95.2112

MOUNTAIN VIEW (81S)

Blue Spring   FREE
Ozark National Scenic Riverways
1 mi E of Mountain View on US 60; 4 mi N on CR OO. Free. Primitive undesignated sites. Tbls, toilets, cfga, no drkg wtr. Fishing, boating, canoeing, swimming. Spring GPS: 37.0548, -91.6382

Twin Pines Campground $12
2 mi E of Mountain View on US 60; N on SR 17; 2 mi E on Hwy O. $12 without hookups; $10 wtr/elec. All year. 25 sites. Tbls, flush toilets, cfga, drkg wtr, showers, hookups($), dump, coin laundry, playground, pool. Swimming, hiking, nature trails. GPS: 36.988724, -91.716946

NOVINGER (83N)

Shoemaker State Conservation Area   FREE
7 mi N of Novinger on Hwy O; turn on Spring Creek Rd, then left on Stahl Rd. Free. All year; 14-day limit. Open primitive

camping on & adjacent to parking lot. No facilities, no drkg wtr. Hiking, hunting, fishing (rated poor). 200 acres. GPS: 40.287851, -92.800392.

PATTERSON (84S)

Sam A. Baker State Park $12
3 mi N of Patterson on SR 143. $12 off-season at 47 basic sites ($13 in-season); seniors pay $11 in-season, $10 off-season. Also 140 elec sites; 15-day limit. 30-ft RV limit. Tbls, flush toilets, showers, drkg wtr, cfga, dump, elec($), store, coin laundry, WiFi. Swimming, boating(lr), fishing, hiking trails, playground, canoeing, kayaking(r), rafting(r). Equestrian sites available but closed Dec-Feb. 5,168 acres. GPS: 37.2533842, -90.5262278

PERRY (85N)

John C. "Jack" Briscoe $9
Group Campground
Corps of Engineers
Mark Twain Lake
9 mi N of Perry on Hwy J; check in at Frank Russell Campground. $9 per site for seniors with federal senior pass; others pay $18. 3-site minimum required. About 4/20-9/24; 14-day limit. 20 sites; 60-ft RV limit. Tbls, flush toilets, cfga, drkg wtr, showers, elec, visitor center, playground. Horseshoes. GPS: 39.51889, -91.64583

Ray Behrens Recreation Area $9
Corps of Engineers
Mark Twain Lake
From Perry at jct with SR 154, 6.6 mi N on CR J, N side. $9 base with federal senior pass at 112 wtr/elec 30/50-amp sites; others pay $18 base, $24 for full hookups ($12 with senior pass). RV limit in excess of 65 ft. About 4/5-11/25; 14-day limit. Tbls, flush toilets, cfga, drkg wtr, dump, showers, fishing pier, playground, amphitheater. Boating(l), fishing, hiking, basketball. GPS: 39.51583, -91.66306

PIEDMONT (86S)

Bluff View $7
Corps of Engineers
Clearwater Lake
From Piedmont at jct with SR 34, 0.9 mi N on SR 49; 6.9 mi W on CR AA. $7 at 14 non-elec sites during 5/15-9/15 (others pay $14); free off-season, but no services. 41 elec sites: $8 base with senior pass ($10 for 50-amp elec); others pay $16 & $20; some sites free off-season but no utilities. 14-day limit. RV limit in excess of 65 ft. Tbls, flush toilets, showers, cfga, drkg wtr, elec($), store, beach, playground, dump, picnic shelter. Boating(lr), fishing, swimming, picnicking, hiking trails, waterskiing, nature programs, canoeing, interpretive trail, marina. GPS: 37.18194, -90.78944.

Clearwater Dam FREE
Corps of Engineers
Clearwater Lake
From Piedmont, W on SR HH to dam, then S on access rds to both shores of Black River below dam. Free primitive, undeveloped sites with permit from Corps project office. Tbls, toilet, cfga, no drkg wtr. Fishing, boating(l). Dam GPS: 37.18755, -90.81262

Piedmont Park $7
Corps of Engineers
Clearwater Lake
From SR 49 at Piedmont, half mi S on SR 34; 5.6 mi SW on CR HH; 1.5 mi NE on Lake Rd; on ridge above lake. $7 with federal senior pass at 8 non-elec sites during 4/15-9/30; others pay $14. Some sites free off-season, but limited amenities. At 69 elec sites (some wtr hookups), $8 base with senior pass; others pay $16 base, $20 for 50-amp elec/wtr ($10 with senior pass); some elec sites free off-season but no utilities. Group camping area. RV limit in excess of 65 ft; 7 pull-through sites. Tbls, flush toilets, cfga, drkg wtr, 2 pavilions, amphitheater, beach, showers, dump, playground. Boating(l), fishing, swimming, canoeing. Group camping available. GPS: 37.1425, -90.77028

River Road Campground $7
Corps of Engineers
Clearwater Lake
1.4 mi S of Piedmont on SR 34; 5.6 mi SW on CR HH; below dam on shore of Black River. $7 with federal senior pass at 4 non-elec sites during 3/15-10/31; others pay $14; some sites free off-season with limited amenities. At 84 elec sites (no wtr hookups), $8 base with senior pass; others pay $16 base & $20 with 50-amp elec ($10 with senior pass); some sites free off-season but no utilities. RV limit in excess of 65 ft; 11 pull-through sites. Tbls, flush toilets, cfga, drkg wtr, playground, dump, showers, interpretive trail, 3 picnic shelters. Canoeing, fishing pier, tennis, fishing, boating(l), hiking trail, basketball. GPS: 37.13361, -90.76694

Thurman Point Public Use Area FREE
Corps of Engineers
Clearwater Lake
From Piedmont, about 5 mi W on SR HH, across Clearwater Dam, then 3 mi N on CR RA; on W shore of lake. Free undeveloped camping. Pit toilet, cfga, no drkg wtr. Boating(l), fishing. GPS: 37.1465, -90.79567

PITTSBURG (87S)

Pittsburg Landing FREE
Corps of Engineers
Pomme de Terre Lake
From Pittsburg at jct with CR J, 1 mi S on SR 64; 3 mi E on CR RA; on Lindley Creek arm of lake. Free all year; 14-day limit. 40 undesignated primitive sites. Tbls, cfga, 2 pit toi-

lets, drkg wtr, fishing pier, picnic shelter. Boating(l), fishing, swimming, hiking, playground. 173 acres. GPS: 37.836949, -93.261612

Pomme De Terre State Park $10
5 mi N of Pittsburg on SR 64; on Pomme De Terre Lake. $10 Sun-Thurs & nightly off-season (Nov-March) at 41 basic sites ($13 in-season weekends, with 2-night minimum stay required). Seniors get $2 discounts all year. Also 192 elec sites & 20 elec/wtr sites; 15-day limit. Tbls, flush toilets, showers, drkg wtr, cfga, dump, elec($), coin laundry, marina, beaches (no dump, showers or wtr Nov-Mar). Boating(l-rd), fishing swimming, playground, hiking trails, interpretive programs. Marina. 734 acres. GPS: 37.87683, -93.31934

POPLAR BLUFF (89S)
Chaonia Campground $9
Wappapello Lake
Corps of Engineers
From Poplar Bluff at jct with US 67, 3.5 mi E on SR 172; 2 mi NE on CR W. $9 ($4.50 with senior pass). All year; 14-day limit. 12 primitive sites; 10 acres (22-ft RV limit). Tbls, toilets, cfga, drkg wtr, fishing pier, showers. Fishing, boating(l), waterskiing. GPS: 36.5823, -90.2136

Lake Wappapello State Park $10
12 mi N of Poplar Bluff on US 67; 9 mi E on SR 172. $10 at 4 basic sites Sunday-Thursday at Asher Creek Campground ($14 Fri & Sat, 2-night minimum stay required). Seniors get $2 discount. Apr-Oct; closed off-season; 15-day limit. Also 70 elec sites. 30-ft RV limit. Tbls, flush toilets, showers, drkg wtr, cfga, dump, elec($), coin laundry. Swimming, boating(lr), fishing, playground, hiking & backpacking trails, mountain biking. 8,600-acre Lake Wappapello. 1,854 acres. GPS: 36.9439418, -90.3309412

POTOSI (90S)
Hazel Creek Campground   FREE
Mark Twain National Forest
15 mi SW of Potosi on SR P; 4 mi W on SR C; 3.1 mi NW on SR Z; 1 mi W on FR 2392. Donations accepted, but camp free. All year; 14-day limit. About 11 undesignated dispersed sites (22-ft RV limit). Tbls, cfga, hitching posts, lantern posts, no drkg wtr, no tbls, no mowing or trash service. Fishing, hiking, horseback riding. GPS: 37.837546, -91.0168005

Red Bluff Recreation Area $11
Mark Twain National Forest
17 mi W of Potosi on SR 8; .1 mi W on CR C; 4.5 mi W on CR V (qtr mi E of Davisville); on Huzzah Creek. $11 base, $18 elec ($5.50 & $12.50 with federal senior pass). 4/15-10/15; 14-day limit. 55 sites; 34-ft RV limit. Tbls, toilets, cfga, drkg wtr. Fishing, hiking, hunting. 133 acres. Non-campers pay $2 day use fee. GPS: 37.8139348, -91.1693033

Washington State Park $12
14 mi NE of Potosi (9 mi from DeSoto) on SR 21; at Big River. $12 off-season at 26 basic sites ($13 in-season 4/1-10/31); seniors pay $11 in-season, $10 off-season. Also 24 elec sites. 15-day limit. No RV size limit. Tbls, flush toilets, showers, cfga, drkg wtr, dump, elec($), coin laundry. Pool, fishing, canoeing(r), tubing(r), kayaking(r), boating(lr), hiking trails, playground, interpretive programs. 1,417 acres. Rock carvings. GPS: 38.432, -90.4156

PRAIRIE HOME (91S)
Prairie Home State Conservation Area   FREE
W of Prairie Home on CR J; 2 mi S on CR W. Free. All year; 14-day limit. 5 primitive designated camping areas; no amenities, no drkg wtr, no trash service. Fishing pier. Fishing, hiking, bridle & biking trails, hunting. 13 ponds & lakes. GPS: 38.773937, -92.576769.

PROTEM (92S)
Buck Creek $7
Bull Shoals Lake
Corps of Engineers
6 mi SE of Protem on MO 125; in Arkansas. $7 with federal senior pass at 2 non-elec sites; others pay $14. $9 with senior pass at 36 elec sites; others pay $18. 4/1-9/30; 14-day limit. 40-ft RV limit. 68 acres. Tbls, flush toilets, cfga, drkg wtr, dump, showers, group shelter, playground, beach, marine dump station, change shelter. Swimming, picnicking, fishing, boating(ld), baseball. GPS: 36.48667, -92.7944.

Highway 125 Park $9
Corps of Engineers
Bull Shoals Lake
6 mi SE of Protem on SR 125; take free ferry across lake to Highway 125 Campground in Arkansas. $9 with federal senior pass at 38 elec sites; others pay $18. 4/1-10/31; 14-day limit. 45-ft RV limit. 303 acres. Tbls, flush toilets, cfga, drkg wtr, dump, showers, group shelter, playground, elec, beach, marine dump station. Swimming, picnicking, fishing, boating(ld), baseball. GPS: 36.48972, -92.77278.

REVERE (93N)
Battle of Athens State Historic Park $12
10 mi W of Revere on CR CC. $12 off-season at 14 basic sites ($13 rest of year); seniors pay $11 in-season, $10 off-season. Also 15 sites with elec. Toilets, cfga, drkg wtr, elec($). Fishing, swimming, hiking. Site of Civil War battle. 395 acres. GPS: 40.587626, -91.711371

RIDGEDALE (94S)
Long Creek Park $8
Corps of Engineer
Table Rock Lake
From US 65 N of Ridgedale, 3 mi W on SR 86; S on CR 86-50 prior to bridge (signs); on Long Creek arm of lake.

$8 with federal senior pass at 10 non-elec RV/tent sites; others pay $16. At 24 elec sites, $10 with senior pass; others pay $20. At 13 elec/wtr sites, $10.50 with senior pass; others pay $21. 5/1-9/15; 14-day limit. 55-ft RV limit; 2 pull-through sites. Picnic shelter, tbls, flush toilets, showers, cfga, drkg wtr, dump, beach. Non-campers pay $4 daily for boat ramp, dump, picnicking, beach, playground. Fishing, swimming, boating(l), waterskiing. GPS: 36.52056, -93.30417

Old Highway 86 Park $11
Corps of Engineers
Table Rock Lake
From Ridgedale at jct with US 65, 7.6 mi W on SR 86; N on CR UU; on White River arm of lake. $11 with federal senior pass at 77 elec/wtr sites; others pay $22. 5/1-9/15; 14-day limit. Tbls, flush toilets, cfga, showers, dump, drkg wtr, beach, playground. Sand volleyball, fishing, hiking, boating(ld), swimming. Non-campers pay $5 day use fee for boat ramp, sand volleyball court, dump station, picnicking. 36.55944, -93.31944

ROBY (95S)

Big Piney Trail Camp FREE
Mark Twain National Forest
2 mi N on MO 17; 5 mi NE on FR FH78. Free. 5/15-11/15; 14-day limit. 4 sites (RVs under 16 ft). Tbls, toilet, cfga, hitching posts, no drkg wtr. Hiking/bridle trail. Big Piney trailhead. GPS: 37.5658767, -92.0434926

Paddy Creek Recreation Area FREE
Mark Twain National Forest
1 mi NE of Roby on MO 17; NE on CR 7600; 2 mi S on FR 220. Free but donation accepted ($5 previously suggested). 4/1-12/1; 14-day limit. 23 sites; 34-ft RV limit. Tbls, toilets, cfga, no drkg wtr. Hiking, play field, fishing at Big Piney River. GPS: 37.5544879, -92.0412702

ROLLA (96S)

Lane Spring Recreation Area $8
Mark Twain National Forest
10 mi S of Rolla on US 63; 1.4 mi W on FR 1892 (5.5 mi SW of Vida); at Little Piney Creek. $8 base, $15 elec ($4 & $11 with federal senior pass). 4/1-10/30; 14-day limit. 18 sites; 34-ft RV limit. Tbls, toilets, cfga, drkg wtr. Hiking, fishing. GPS: 37.7964304, -91.8368236

RUSHVILLE (97N)

Lewis & Clark State Park $12
20 mi SW of Rushville on SR 45; on SW shore of Sugar Lake. $12 off season at 7 basic sites ($13 in-season 4/15-10/31); seniors pay $11 in-season, $10 off-season. Also 62 elec sites; 15-day limit. 30-ft RV limit. Tbls, flush toilets, cfga, drkg wtr, showers, dump, elec($), coin laundry. Swimming, boating(l), fishing, playground. 121 acres. GPS: 39.5377737, -95.0585779

ST. CLAIR (98S)

Robertsville State Park $12
Near jct of CRs O & N in Franklin County; along Meramec River. $12 Sun-Thurs & off-season at 12 basic sites ($13 Fri-Sat during Apr-Oct with 2-night minimum stay required). Seniors get $2 discounts all year. Also 14 elec sites; 15-day limit. Tbls, flush toilets, cfga, drkg wtr, showers, dump, elec($), coin laundry (no showers, dump or laundry off-season). Hiking, boating(l), fishing, interpretive programs, playground. 1,110 acres. GPS: 38.443684, -90.81153

STE. GENEVIEVE (99S)

Hawn State Park $12
14 mi SW of Ste. Genevieve on SR 32, then on co access rd. $12 off-season at 19 basic sites ($13 in-season 4/1-10/31); seniors pay $11 in-season, $10 off-season. Also 26 elec sites; 15-day limit. 30-ft RV limit. Tbls, flush toilets, showers, cfga, drkg wtr, dump, elec($), coin laundry, WiFi. Fishing, hiking trails, 10-mi backpacking trail. 3,271 acres. GPS: 37.8217191, -90.2362307

ST. JOSEPH (100N)

Bluffwoods State Conservation Area FREE
9 mi S of St. Joseph off Hwy 59. Free. All year; 14-day limit. 2 primitive designated camping areas. Toilets, tbls, cfga, no drkg wtr. Bridle & hiking trails, hunting, fishing (poor). 2,300-acre forest. GPS: 39.623952, -94.950675.

ST. LOUIS (101S)

Dr. Edmund A. Babler $12
Memorial State Park
20 mi W of St. Louis on SR 109, off CR CC. $12 off-season at 30 basic sites ($13 in-season 4/1-10/31); seniors pay $11 in-season, $10 off-season. Also 43 elec sites; 15-day limit. 30-ft RV limit. Tbls, flush toilets, showers, tbls, cfga, drkg wtr, elec($), riding stable, coin laundry, WiFi. Pool, tennis, biking/hiking trails, bridle trails, playground, interpretive programs. 2,439 acres. GPS: 38.6206086, -90.6959608

SALEM (102S)

Akers Ferry Canoe Rental $7.50
23 mi S of Salem at jct of Hwys K & KK. $7.50 per person base Sun-Thurs ($8.50 per person Fri-Sat); $10 per site elec. All year. Open primitive sites. Tbls, cfga, flush toilets, drkg wtr, store, elec($7.50 weekdays, $8.50 Fri & Sat), wtr hookups $1, sewer $2, showers, coin laundry, playground, dump, pool. Boating, canoeing (r), tubing(r), swimming, hiking, fishing. NPS concession of Ozark National Scenic Rivers. Float trips on Jacks Fork & Current Rivers. GPS: 37.22330, -91.33108.

Cedargrove Campground $5
Ozark National Scenic Riverways
21 mi SW of Salem on SR 119; 4 mi S on CR AY; 4 mi E on CR ZZ; on the Current River. $5 during 4/15-10/15; free

off-season; 14-day limit. About 15 primitive sites. Tbls, pit toilets, cfga, no drkg wtr. Canoeing, fishing, swimming, boating.

Indian Trail State Conservation Area   FREE
12 mi NE of Salem on Hwy 19. Free. All year; 14-day limit. 5 primitive designated camping areas and open camping space at 13,000-acre natural area. No amenities, but drkg wtr at Indian Trail shop. Hiking, hunting; no fish in ponds. Fish hatchery, shooting range. GPS: 37.726625, -91.356569

Montauk State Park $12
21 mi SW of Salem on SR 119; on Current River. $12 off-season at 31 basic sites ($13 in-season 2/25-10/31); seniors pay $11 in-season, $10 off-season. Also 123 elec sites. 15-day limit. 30-ft RV limit. Tbls, flush toilets, cfga, drkg wtr, showers, dump, WiFi elec($), coin laundry (no showers or laundry during Nov-Feb). Fishing, hiking trails, playground. 1,353 acres. GPS: 37.4550447, -91.681815

R. F. Clement Memorial   FREE
State Forest & Wildlife Area
N of Salem on Hwy 72, then 5 mi W on Hwy C; 2 mi N on Hwy O; 3.5 mi W on Hwy OO. Free. All year; 14-day limit. Open primitive camping on 520 acres. No facilities, no drkg wtr. Hiking, hunting. GPS: 37.750228, -91.780662.

Silver Arrow Campground/Canoe Rental $5
17 mi S of Salem on Hwy 19. $5 per person (children under 12 free); $6 extra per site for elec (50-amp $7). 4/1-10/15. Primitive sites. Tbls, flush toilets, cfga, drkg wtr, showers, elec($), shelters, store. Swimming, fishing, canoeing(r). Canoe trips on Current River. 800-333-6040. GPS: 37.509098, -91.465321.

SHELL KNOB (103S)
Big Bay Recreation Area   CLOSED
Mark Twain National Forest
1 mi SE of Shell Knob on SR 39; 3 mi SE on SR YY; 0.7 mi on FR 1083; on Table Rock Lake. GPS: 36.617432, -93.570313

Campbell Point Park $8
Corps of Engineers
Table Rock Lake
From Shell Knob at jct with CR 39-5, 5.1 mi SE on SR YY; on White River arm of lake. $8 with federal senior pass at 4 non-elec sites; others pay $16. At 28 elec sites, $10.50 with senior pass (others pay $21); $11 with senior pass at 42 elec/wtr sites (others pay $22). 1 full-hookup site $23 ($11.50 with senior pass). 5/1-9/15; 14-day limit. RV limit in excess of 65 ft; 4 pull-through sites. Non-campers pay $4 day use fee for dump station, beach, sand volleyball, picnicking, boat ramp. Tbls, flush toilets, cfga, drkg wtr, showers, dump, playground, beach, sports field, marina, picnic shelter. Fishing, boating(dl), swimming. Fishing pier. GPS: 36.59583, -93.55028

SIKESTON (104S)
General Watkins State Conservation Area   FREE
14 mi N of Sikeston on Hwy 61 (3 mi S of Benton). Free. All year; 14-day limit. Primitive designated camping area; about 5 defined camping areas. Tbls, cfga, gravel pads, no drkg wtr or toilets. Hiking trails, fishing, nature study. 1,038 acres. GPS: 37.066261, -89.620456.

SPRINGFIELD (105S)
Busiek State Forest & Wildlife Area   FREE
Department of Conservation
18 mi S of Springfield on Hwy 65. Free. All year; 14-day limit. 9 primitive designated sites. Tbls, cfga, no drkg wtr. Hiking, biking & bridle trails, fishing, hunting, canoeing, target shooting. 2,505 acres. Camping by permit only; call 417-895-6880. GPS: 36.86453, -93.235738.

STEELVILLE (106S)
Bass' River Resort $9.50
9.5 mi E of Steelville on SR 8; left on Butts Rd. $9.50 base per adult Sun-Thur; $11 Fri-Sat. $12 extra per site for wtr/elec hookups. All year (lower rates off-season). 212 sites (200 for tents). Tbls, flush toilets, cfga, drkg wtr, showers, hookups($), dump, equipment rental, cafe, store, coin laundry, playground, game room. Boating(r), fishing, canoeing(r), rafting(r), tubing(r), hayrides, hiking, swimming, horseback riding, hog roasts($). GPS: 37.991901, -91.175419.

Bird's Nest Lodge & River Resort $10
On Bird's Nest Rd., 4.5 mi S of I-44 off SR 19. $10 per adult; $10 extra per site for elec/wtr. All year; 14-day limit. 70 sites (50 for tents). Tbls, flush toilets, cfga, drkg wtr, showers, hookups($8), playground, restaurant, store. Boating(r), fishing, canoeing(r), swimming, hiking, rafting(r), weekend buffets. GPS: 37.999731, -91.3592.

Garrison's Canoe Rental, $7.50
Campground & RV Park
1.5 mi E of Steelville on SR 8; left for 2.5 mi on Hwy TT. $7.50 base per person ($3.30 kids 3-11); $6.60 per person 2 or more nights; $6.60 per site extra for elec; $8.80 extra full hookup. All year (Nov-Mar by reservation). 360 sites (200 for tents). Tbls, flush toilets, cfga, drkg wtr, showers($), hookups($), dump, playground, pool, cafe, store, coin laundry, shelters. Boating(r), fishing, swimming, hiking, canoeing(r), tubing(r), rafting(r), horseback riding. GPS: 38.014749, -91.319336

Huzzah State Conservation Area   FREE
SE of Leasburg on Hwy H & NE of Steelville on Hwy E. Free. 9/15-5/15; 14-day limit. Primitive camping at 6 designated locations. Tbls, toilets, cfga, no drkg wtr, no trash service. Horseback riding, fishing, hiking, berrypicking, hunting, shooting range on FR 2-23. Historic Scotia Furnace & Iron Works nearby. 6,144 acres. GPS: 38.030714, -91.188108.

Huzzah Valley Camping Resort $9.58
10 mi E of Steelville on SR 8; cross Huzzah, then turn at big
red barn. $9.58 per person Sun-Thurs; $11.71 per person
Fri-Sat; $12.78 extra for wtr/elec. Apr-Oct. Over 200 sites.
Tbls, flush toilets, cfga, drkg wtr, showers, hookups($),
dump, playground, cafe, store, coin laundry. Boating, fishing, swimming, hiking, canoeing(r), horseback trail rides,
cookouts($). Group rates available. 800-367-4516. GPS:
37.973694, -91.201065.

Indian Springs Resort $10
3 mi W of Steelville on SR 8 to sign; turn right. $8 base
per person; $15 extra for wtr/elec. 3/1 11/1. 238 sites
(220 for tents). Tbls, flush toilets, cfga, drkg wtr, showers,
hookups($), dump, playground, cafe, store, pool. Boat-
ing(r), tubing(r), rafting(r), fishing, swimming, hiking. GPS:
37.974, -91.428817

Lucky Clover River Resort $9
2 mi N of Steelville on SR 19 to Lucky Clover Rd. $9 per
person for primitive camping; $10 extra for RV sites with
elec/wtr. All year. 20 sites. Tbls, flush toilets, cfga, drkg
wtr, showers, elec & wtr, dump, playground, store, pool.
Boating(r), canoeing(r), rafting(r), tubing(r), fishing, swimming, hiking, volleyball, horseshoes, fee fishing. GPS:
37.994856, -91.383326.

Rafting Company Camping/RV Resort $9
From I-44 exit 208 at Cuba, 7 mi S on Hwy 19; 100 yds
beyond Meramec River bridge, right on McCormick Rd;
right at the "T" for half mi, then right on Waters Edge Rd.
$9 weekdays per adult ($4.50 per child); $10 adults & $5
children weekends; $9 extra for elec, $10 elec/wtr, $11 full
hookups. 4/1-10/31. 90 sites. Tbls, flush toilets, cfga, drkg
wtr, showers, dump, beach, playground, store. Rafting(r),
canoeing(r), trail rides($), swimming, cookouts($), fishing,
volleyball. Float trips. Weekday & off-season rates available. GPS: 37.983711, -91.376817

STOCKTON (107S)
Cedar Ridge Campground $12
Corps of Engineers
Stockton Lake
From Stockton, 2 mi N on SR 245 & SR RA from jct with
SR 215; 340-acre park on Little Sac arm of lake. All year;
14-day limit. $12 base at 33 non-elec sites during 4/16-
9/30; $14 at premium locations ($6 & $7 with federal
senior pass). Non-elec sites $5 during 3/15-4/15 & 10/1-
11/30; free rest of year but no flush toilets or showers. At
21 elec sites during 4/16-9/30, $7 base with senior pass;
others pay $14 base, $18 for premium locations & $20 for
50-amp elec ($9 & $10 with senior pass). During 3/15-4/15
& 10/1-11/30, elec sites are $9 ($4.50 with senior pass)
but reduced amenities. 14-day limit. 60-ft RV limit. Tbls,
flush & pit toilets, cfga, drkg wtr, dump, showers, beach,
fishing pier, pavilion, pay phone. Boating(l), fishing, swimming. GPS: 37.57556, -93.68139

Crabtree Cove Campground $12
Corps of Engineers
Stockton Lake
From Stockton at jct with SR 39, 3.5 mi E on SR 32, then
SW; 168-acre park on NW corner of lake. During 4/16-
9/30, $12 base at 32 non-elec sites; $14 at premium
locations ($6 & $7 with federal senior pass); non-elec sites
$5 during 3/15-4/15 & 10/1-10/31, but no wtr services.
During 4/16-9/30 at 32 elec sites, $8 base with senior
pass; others pay $16 base, $18 for premium locations ($9
with senior pass), $20 for 50-amp elec ($10 with senior
pass). Elec sites $9 during 3/15-4/15 & 10/1-11/30 ($4.50
with senior pass). Some sites free off-season but no wtr or
elec services. 14-day limit. 50-ft RV limit; 3 pull-through
sites; 2 handicap sites without elec; 1 handicap site with
elec; overflow sites. Tbls, flush & pit toilets, cfga, drkg
wtr, dump, showers, fishing pier, handicap accessible
fishing area. Boating(l), fishing. GPS: 37.66972, -93.75306

Hawker Point Campground $12
Corps of Engineers
Stockton Lake
From Stockton at jct with SR 32, 6.2 mi S on SR 39; 5.2
mi E on CR H; 518-acre park at N end of Big Sac arm of
lake. During 4/15-9/30, $12 base at 32 non-elec sites; $14
for premium locations ($6 & $7 with federal senior pass);
non-elec sites $5 during 3/15-4/15 & 10/1-11/30; free rest
of year, but reduced services & no wtr available. At 30 elec
sites, $8 base with senior pass during 4/15-9/30; others
pay $16 base, $18 for premium locations ($9 with senior
pass); elec sites $9 during 3/15-4/15 & 10/1-11/30 ($4.50
with senior pass). Some sites free off-season, but no
utilities & reduced amenities. 14-day limit. 60-ft RV limit.
Tbls, flush & pit toilets, cfga, drkg wtr, dump, showers.
Boating(l), fishing, horseback riding (equestrian trailhead),
golf. GPS: 37.60651, -93.7836

Masters Campground $12
Corps of Engineers
Stockton Lake
10 mi SE of Stockton on Hwy 32; 3.5 mi S on CR RA, then
W; 836-acre park on Little Sac arm of lake. During 3/15-
4/15, $12 base & $14 for premium locations at 66 non-
elec sites; sites $5 during 3/15-4/15 & 10/1-11/30 ($2.50
with senior pass); free rest of year, but no wtr services &
reduced amenities. 14-day limit. 60-ft RV limit. 8 overflow
sites. Tbls, flush & pit toilets, cfga, drkg wtr, dump, no
elec, beach, fishing pier, showers. Boating(l), fishing,
swimming. GPS: 37.59917, -93.68

Orleans Trail North & South $12
Corps of Engineers
Stockton Lake
From SE edge of Stockton, 0.5 mi E on CR RB; 0.5 mi
right on Blake St; 959-acre park on NW shore of lake.
$12 during 5/9-9/15 at 110 non-elec sites ($6 with federal senior pass); free off-season, but no wtr services

& reduced amenities. 14-day limit. 50-ft RV limit; 4 pull-through sites. 5 sites at equestrian trailhead. Group camping available. Tbls, flush & pit toilets, cfga, drkg wtr, dump, showers, beach, no elec, picnic shelter. Boating(l), fishing, swimming, hiking, golf. GPS: 37.6544, -93.78306

Ruark Bluff East Campground $12
Corps of Engineers
Stockton Lake
12 mi S of Stockton on Hwy 39; 4 mi E on CR 6; 1 mi S on CR H; turn right on park access rd & follow signs; on Big Sac arm of lake. During 4/15-9/30, $12 base, $14 for premium locations at 87 non-elec sites ($6 & $7 with federal senior pass); sites $5 during 3/15-4/15 & 10/1-11/30 ($2.50 with senior pass); free off-season, but no wtr services & reduced amenities. At 28 elec sites, $8 base with senior pass during 4/16-9/30; others pay $16 base, $18 for premium locations ($9 with senior pass); elec sites $9 during 3/15-4/15 & 10/1-11/30 ($4.50 with senior pass); some sites free off-season but no utilities & reduced amenities. 14-day limit. RV limit in excess of 65 ft; 4 pull-through sites. Tbls, flush & pit toilets, cfga, drkg wtr, dump, beach, playground, fishing pier, showers, handicap accessible fishing area. Boating(l), fishing, swimming. GPS: 37.52240, -93.80544

Ruark Bluff West $12
Corps of Engineers
Stockton Lake
12 mi S of Stockton on Hwy 39; 4 mi E on CR 6; 1 mi S on CR H; left on park access rd & follow signs; before bridge; on Big Sac arm of lake. 4/16-9/30; 14-day limit. $12 base, $14 for premium locations at 40 non-elec sites ($6 & $7 with federal senior pass). At 46 elec sites, $8 base with senior pass; others pay $16 base, $18 for premium locations ($9 with senior pass). Group camping available. 50-ft RV limit. Tbls, pit & flush toilets, cfga, drkg wtr, showers, dump, playground, beach, fishing pier. Boating(l), fishing, swimming. GPS: 37.52612, -93.80962

Stockton State Park $6
On S side of town on SR 215; on Stockton Lake. $6 off-season at 14 basic sites ($13 in-season, with 2-night minimum stay required). Seniors get $2 discount all year. Also 60 elec sites. 15-day limit. 30-ft RV limit. Tbls, flush toilets, drkg wtr, showers, cfga, dump, elec($), coin laundry. Swimming, boating(rdl), fishing, playground, horseshoes, interpretive programs. Stockton Lake. Marina. 2,176 acres. GPS: 37.6105961, -93.7488202

SULLIVAN (108S)
Meramec State Park $12
4 mi E of Sullivan on SR 185; along Meramec River. $12 off-season at 50 basic sites ($13 in-season 4/1-10/31); seniors pay $11 in-season, $10 off-season. Also 124 elec sites, 14 elec/wtr sites, 21 full hookups. 15-day limit. 32-ft RV limit. Tbls, flush toilets, cfga, drkg wtr, showers, dump,

elec($), sewer($), coin laundry, WiFi. Boating(lrd), fishing, playground, swimming, canoeing, nature center, cave tours. 6,785 acres. GPS: 38.18755, -91.06264

SUMMERSVILLE (109S)
Bay Creek $5
Ozark National Scenic Riverways
7 mi E of Summersville on Hwy 106; 10 mi SE on county rd to N shore of Jacks Fork River. $5 during 4/15-10/15; free rest of year; 14-day limit. Primitive undesignated sites; tbls, toilets, cfga, no drkg wtr. Fishing, boating, swimming, canoeing. GPS: 37.0723, -91.3007

TRENTON (110N)
Crowder State Park $12
2 mi W of Trenton on SR 6; 2 mi N on SR 128 & SR 146. $12 off-season at 10 basic sites ($13 in-season); seniors pay $11 in-season, $10 off-season. Also 31 elec sites; 15-day limit. 30-ft RV limit. Tbls, flush toilets, cfga, drkg wtr, showers, dump, elec($). Fishing, swimming, playground, boating. Crowder Lake. Group camping available. 673 acres. GPS: 40.094734, -93.6621642.

TROY (111N)
Cuivre River State Park $12
5 mi E of Troy on SR 47. $12 off-season at 41 basic sites ($13 in-season 4/15-10/31); seniors pay $11 in-season, $10 off-season. Also 20 elec sites, 31 full-hookups; 15-day limit. No RV size limit. Tbls, flush toilets, cfga, drkg wtr, showers, dump, elec ($), sewer($), coin laundry, WiFi. Also equestrian sites. Swimming, fishing, bridle & hiking trails (30 mi), playground, boating(l). Lake Lincoln. 6,271 acres. GPS: 39.033659, -90.9309694

William R. Logan FREE
State Conservation Area
10 mi N of Troy on US 61; W on CR E, then N on CR RA. Free. All year; 14-day limit. 3 designated primitive camping areas. Tbls, toilets, cfga, no drkg wtr or trash service. Pond fishing, hunting, shooting range. GPS: 39.152415, -91.032284.

VAN BUREN (112S)
Big Spring $12
Ozark Scenic Riverways
National Park Service
5 mi S of Van Buren on SR 103. $12 without elec during 4/15-10/30, $15 with elec; no non-elec sites open rest of year. 14-day limit. 123 sites. 3 group sites by reservation. Tbls, flush toilets, cfga, drkg wtr, showers, dump, firewood, shelters, playground. Canoeing(r), fishing, swimming, boating, hiking.

Big Tree $5
Ozark National Scenic Riverways
From Big Springs Lodge, Hwy Z S to sign for campground. $5 during 4/15-10/15; free off-season; 14-day limit. 7

primitive sites; 40-ft RV limit. Tbls, toilets, cfga, no drkg wtr. Fishing, swimming, archery.

Hickory Landing   FREE
Ozark National Scenic Riverways
17 mi E of Van Buren on US 60; about 5 mi S on SR 21; 3 mi E on CR E to Hickory Landing access rd; on Current River. Free. All year; 14-day limit. Primitive camping; no facilities. Boating, fishing, swimming. GPS: 36.8928, -90.9096.

Watercress Recreation Area $10
Mark Twain National Forest
Half mi N of Van Buren on FR 4282; downhill on Watercress Dr past ranger office; next to Current River. $10 during 5/1-10/1; free rest of year but no wtr or services; 14-day limit. 17 sites (double sites $15); 34-ft RV limit. Tbls, flush toilets, cfga, drkg wtr. Boating(l), fishing, hiking, canoeing(r), tubing. Historic Civil War gun trenches on Songbird Hiking Trail. GPS: 37.0028287, -91.0181826

VIOLA (113S)
Viola Park $8
Corps of Engineers
Table Rock Lake
5 mi S of Viola on SR 39; W on CR 39/48 (6 mi S of Shell Knob); on White River arm of lake. $8 with federal senior pass at 11 non-elec RV/tent sites; others pay $16. At 15 elec sites, $10 with senior pass; others pay $20. At 24 elec/wtr sites, $10.50 with senior pass; others pay $21. 5/1-9/15; 14-day limit. RV limit in excess of 65 ft; 2 pull-through sites. Non-campers pay $4 day use fee for boat ramp, dump station, beach, picnicking. Tbls, flush toilets, cfga, drkg wtr, dump, showers. Swimming, boating(l), fishing, waterskiing. GPS: 36.56167, -93.59472

WAPPAPELLO (114S)
Blue Springs Campground   FREE
Corps of Engineers
Wappapello Lake
From dam, 17 mi N on CR D, 1.8 mi S on CR BB, 1.5 mi W on CR 531. Free. 2 primitive sites. No facilities except cfga, no drkg wtr. Boating(l), fishing. GPS: 39.0038, -94.2056

Lost Creek Landing   FREE
Corps of Engineers
Wappapello Lake
From dam, 11 mi N on CR D; W on Corps Rd 9. Free. All year; 14-day limit 3 primitive sites in parking area. No facilities except cfga; no drkg wtr. Boating(l), fishing. GPS: 37.0223, -90.3065

Peoples Creek Recreation Area $8
Corps of Engineers
Wappapello Lake
From dam, 1.7 mi N on CR D, following signs. $8 base with federal senior pass at 57 elec sites; others pay $16 base,

$20 for full hookups & 50-amp elec ($10 with senior pass). 3/3-11/25; 14-day limit. RV limit in excess of 65 ft. 2-night minimum stay required at all sites on weekends. Tbls, flush toilets, cfga, drkg wtr, showers, beach, elec. Boating(l), fishing, swimming. GPS: 36.943604, -90.327879

Possum Creek Campground   FREE
Corps of Engineers
Wappapello Lake
From dam, 3 mi N on CR 3, 1.5 mi W on CR 521 & Corps Rd. 7. Free. All year; 14-day limit. 2 primitive sites at parking area. Pit toilet, cfga, no drkg wtr. Boating(l), fishing.

Redman Creek Recreation Area $10
Corps of Engineers
Wappapello Lake
From dam, 1 mi S on CR T, following signs. $10 base with federal senior pass at 30-amp elec sites; others pay $20 base, $24 for full hookups ($12 with senior pass). All year; 14-day limit. 2-night minimum stay required at all sites on weekends. Tbls, flush toilets, cfga, drkg wtr, showers, playground, beach, fishing pier, elec, fish cleaning station, visitor's center, picnic shelters. Boating(lrd), horseshoes, swimming, fishing, tennis, basketball, hiking trail, horseshoe pits, volleyball court. GPS: 36.92278, -90.2875

WARSAW (115S)
Berry Bend $7
Corps of Engineers
Harry S Truman Lake
From Warsaw, 4.4 mi W on SR 7; 3 mi W on CR Z; 1.8 mi S on Berry Bend Rd; on Osage arm of lake, a peninsula in bend of river; equestrian camp on the north. $7 with federal senior pass at 82 non-elec sites during 4/15-10/15; others pay $14; off-season regular fee $8 ($4 with senior pass), but reduced amenities. At 113 elec sites, $8 with senior pass during 4/15-10/15; others pay $16; off-season regular fee $8 ($4 with senior pass), but reduced amenities. 14-day limit. RV limit in excess of 65 ft; 4 pull-through sites. Picnic shelter, amphitheater, tbls, flush toilets, cfga, drkg wtr, elec($), showers, playground, dump, beach, change house, coin laundry. Boating(l), fishing, bridle trails, ranger programs, swimming, golf, horseshoe pits. GPS: 38.1997, -93.51

Berry Bend Equestrian Park $12
Corps of Engineers
Harry S Truman Lake
4.4 mi W of Warsaw on SR 7; 3 mi W on CR Z; 1.8 mi S on Berry Bend Rd; on Osage arm of lake, N of Berry Bend Park. Limited to horse campers; call 660-438-3912 for special rules on horses. $12 base at 65 non-elec sites, $14 for premium locations ($6 & $7 with federal senior pass). Some non-elec sites $8 ($4 with senior pass) during 10/16-4/14, but reduced amenities. At 24 elec sites during 4/15-10/15, $8 base with senior pass; others pay $16 base, $18 for premium locations ($9 with senior pass).

All year; 14-day limit. RV limit in excess of 65 ft. Tbls, drkg wtr, flush toilets, showers, cfga, playground, corrals, overhead tie posts all-season wtr hydrants. Bridle & hiker trails. Note: In 2013, Loop A sites & equestrian overflow sites were closed except as needed on holiday weekends. GPS: 38.19972, -93.51

Harry S Truman State Park $10
7 mi W of Warsaw on CR UU, off SR 7. $10 Sun-Thurs at 71 basic sites ($13 Fri-Sat, with 2-night minimum stay required). Off-season (Oct-Mar), $10 Sun-Thurs, $11 Fri-Sat. Seniors get $2 discount all year. Also 127 elec sites; 15-day limit. 32-ft RV limit. Tbls, flush toilets, cfga, drkg wtr, showers, dump, elec($), marina, coin laundry, Wi-Fi. Boating(rld), fishing, playground, swimming, interpretive programs, hiking trails. Marina. Truman Lake. GPS: 38.2791909, -93.4371505

Long Shoal Park $7
Corps of Engineers
Harry S Truman Lake
4.4 mi W of Warsaw on SR 7; on Grand River arm of lake. During 4/15-10/15, $7 with federal senior pass at 27 non-elec sites; others pay $14; regular fee $8 off-season ($4 with senior pass), but reduced amenities. At 95 elec sites, $9 with senior pass during 4/15-10/15; others pay $18; regular fee $8 off-season ($4 with senior pass), but no utilities. 14-day limit. RV limit in excess of 65 ft; 3 pull-through sites. Picnic shelter, fish cleaning station, tbls, flush toilets, cfga, drkg wtr, dump, showers, elec($), beach, change house, playground, coin laundry. Golf, fishing, boating(l), hiking, swimming. GPS: 38.27611, -93.46972

Osage Bluff Campground $7
Corps of Engineers
Harry S Truman Lake
From Warsaw at jct with SR 7, 3 mi S on US 65; 3 mi SW on SR 83, then 1 mi W on SR 295 following signs; at confluence of Osage & Pomme De Terre Rivers. During 4/15-10/15, $7 with federal senior pass at 27 non-elec sites; others pay $14; regular fee $8 off-season ($4 with senior pass), but reduced amenities. At 41 elec sites, $9 with senior pass during 4/15-10/15; others pay $18; regular fee $8 off-season ($4 with senior pass), but no utilities. 14-day limit. RV limit in excess of 65 ft. Tbls, flush toilets, cfga, drkg wtr, showers, dump, coin laundry, elec($), playground. Golf, boating(lr), fishing, swimming. GPS: 38.19056, -93.39333

Thibaut Point Park $7
Corps of Engineers
Harry S Truman Lake
4.3 mi N of Warsaw on US 65; 2.8 mi W on CR T, then 1 mi S on gravel CR 218; at confluence of Little Tebo & Starett Creeks. During 4/15-10/15, $7 with federal senior pass at 20 non-elec sites; others pay $14; regular fee $8 off-season ($4 with senior pass), but reduced amenities.

At 30 elec sites, $9 with senior pass during 4/15-10/15; others pay $18; regular fee $8 off-season ($4 with senior pass), but no utilities. 14-day limit. RV limit in excess of 65 ft. 4 concrete slabs for disabled, equipped with accessible grills, tbls, lantern holders (2 without elec); they are available to other campers if campground is full. Group camping was eliminated in 2013 due to budget cuts; 3 former group camping areas are now open to individual campers on a first-come basis. Tbls, flush toilets, cfga, drkg wtr, dump, beach, coin laundry, pavilion, change house, 2 picnic shelters. Swimming, boating (l), fishing, golf, horseshoe pits. GPS: 38.29639, -93.39639

WELLSVILLE (116N)
Diggs Access State Conservation Area   FREE
SW of Wellsville on CR ZZ; 2 mi W on CR RA. Free. All year; 14-day limit. 2 primitive sites; no amenities. Boating(l), fishing, hunting. GPS: 39.067475, -91.634788.

Wellsville Lake State Conservation Area   FREE
2 mi S of Wellsville on US 19, then W on CR 22 to Wellsville Lake. Free. All year; 14-day limit. Primitive designated camping area; no amenities, no drkg wtr, no trash service. Hunting, fishing, boating(l), hiking, shooting range. GPS: 39.033092, -91.577787.

WESTPHALIA (117S)
Painted Rock State Conservation Area   FREE
7 mi SW of Westphalia on Hwy 133. Free. All year; 14-day limit. 8 designated primitive sites. Toilet, cfga, no drkg wtr. Hiking trail, fishing, hunting. GPS: 38.400368, -92.108208.

WESTON (118N)
Weston Bend State Park $12
1 mi S of Weston on Hwy 45; along Missouri River. $12 off-season at 4 basic sites ($13 in-season 4/15-10/31); seniors pay $11 in-season, $10 off-season. Also 31 elec sites; 15-day limit. 40-ft RV limit Tbls, flush toilets, cfga, drkg wtr, showers, dump, elec($), coin laundry, playground, WiFi. Hiking, fishing, paved biking trail. 1,024 acres. GPS: 39.3905542, -94.8780183

WEST PLAINS (119S)
North Fork Recreation Area $10
Mark Twain National Forest
16 mi W of West Plains on CR CC; qtr mi SE on FR 805; on North Fork of White River. $10 base, $15 elec ($5 & $10 with federal senior pass). 5/15-12/1; 14-day limit. 20 sites (34-ft RV limit). Tbls, toilets, cfga, drkg wtr. Boating(l), fishing, canoeing (rentals nearby), hiking. 10 acres. Non-campers pay $2 day use fee. GPS: 36.7547818, -92.1526562

WHEATLAND (120S)

Lightfoot Landing $12
Corps of Engineers
Pomme de Terre Lake
9 mi S of Wheatland on SR 83 (2.3 mi S of Elkton); 3.4 mi E on CR RB. During 4/15-10/1, $12 base, $14 at premium locations at 6 non-elec RV/tent sites ($6 & $7 with federal senior pass). Free off-season but reduced amenities. At 29 elec/wtr sites, $11 with senior pass; others pay $22. All year; 14-day limit. RV limit in excess of 65 ft; 6 pull-through sites. Group camping available. Picnic shelter, heated fishing pier, tbls, flush toilets, cfga, drkg wtr, elec($), dump, showers, playground. Fishing, boating(l), waterskiing, horseshoe pits. Boat rentals nearby. GPS: 37.82611, -93.36139

Wheatland Park Campground $12
Corps of Engineers
Pomme de Terre Lake
From Wheatland at jct with US 54, 4.2 mi S on SR 83; 2 mi E on SR 254; 1 mi S on SR 205. During 4/16-10/15, $12 base at 15 non-elec RV/tent sites during; $14 at premium locations ($6 & $7 with federal senior pass); some sites free off-season with reduced amenities. At 26 elec sites, $8 with senior pass; others pay $16. At 41 elec/wtr sites, $11 with senior pass; others pay $22. 14-day limit. 35-ft RV limit; 8 pull-through sites. Picnic shelter, tbls, flush toilets, cfga, drkg wtr, beach, elec($), dump, showers, playground. Fishing, swimming, boating(dl), golf. GPS: 37.87556, -93.37444

WILLIAMSBURG (121S)

Whetstone Creek State Conservation Area   FREE
2 mi N of Williamsburg on gravel CR 1003. Free. All year; 14-day limit. 30 primitive designated sites. Big Lake Camping Area; also camping adjacent to shooting range parking lot. Toilets, cfga, no drkg wtr, no trash service. Hunting, fishing, boating(l), shooting range. GPS: 38.943963, -91.705232.

WILLIAMSVILLE (122S)

Markham Spring Recreation Area $10
Mark Twain National Forest
3 mi W of Williamsville on SR 49; half mi N on FR 2997 (23 mi W of Poplar Bluff); on Black River. $10 base, $15 elec ($5 & $10 with federal senior pass); double sites $15 & $30. 5/1-10/1; 14-day limit. 36 sites; 34-ft RV limit. Tbls, flush toilets, cfga, drkg wtr, dump, showers. Boating(rl), fishing, hiking, canoeing, volleyball. Non-campers pay $2 day use fee. GPS: 36.976563, -90.600586

WILLOW SPRINGS (123S)

Sugar Hill/Sycamore   FREE
Noblett Lake Recreation Area
Mark Twain National Forest
8 mi W of Willow Springs on SR 76; 1.5 mi S on SR 181; 3 mi SE on CR AP; 1 mi SW on FR 857 to Sugar Hill Loop;

1.8 mi to Sycamore Loop (Sycamore Loop has double & single sites). Free. 5/1-10/15; 14-day limit. 25 sites in two sections. Tbls, toilets, cfga, drkg wtr. Hiking, fishing, boating(l- elec mtrs). GPS: 36.9064452, -92.0973775.

WINONA (124S)

McCormack Lake Recreation Area   FREE
Mark Twain National Forest
14 mi S of Winona on Hwy 19; 2 mi SW on FR 3155. Free. All year; 14-day limit. 8 sites. Tbls, toilet, cfga, no drkg wtr or trash service. Boating (elec mtrs), fishing, hiking, picnicking, bridle trails. GPS: 36.8217224, -91.3526355.

Peck Ranch State Conservation Area   FREE
5 mi E of Winona on Hwy H; 7 mi E on gravel rd. Free. All year; 14-day limit. 25 primitive sites 5 designated areas. Tbls, toilets, cfga, no drkg wtr, viewing tower. Hiking trails, hunting, shooting range. 21,000 acres. GPS: 37.023613, -91.164097.

Roberts Field   FREE
Ozark National Scenic Riverways
8 mi NE of Winona on CR H; 5 mi NE on county rd to Current River at Rocky Creek. Free. All year; 14-day limit. Primitive undesignated sites; no facilities. Boating, canoeing, fishing, swimming. GPS: 37.1262, -91.1718.

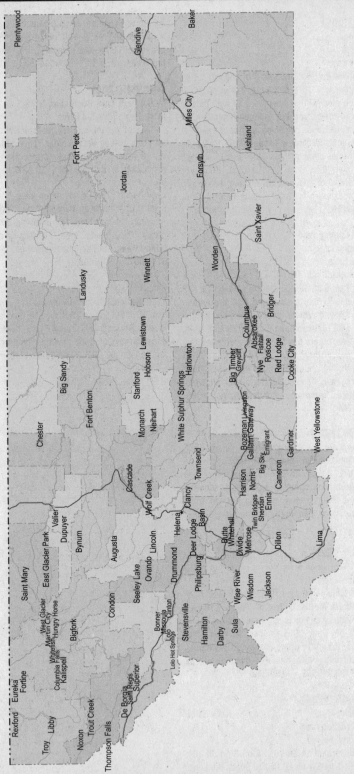

WWW.VISITMT.COM

Toll-free number for travel information: 1-800-847-4868.

Dept of Fish, Wildlife and Parks, 1420 E 6th Ave, Helena, MT 59620, 406-444-1200. At fishing access sites where fees are charged, the cost is $7 per night for campers with Montana fishing licenses, $12 per night for others. Montana seniors get special discounts: $6 fees for state residents without fishing licenses, $3.50 for state seniors with licenses.

Note: Montana campgrounds charge a state bed tax of 4.8%.

REST AREAS

Overnight stops are not permitted.

STATE PARKS

Although a few of the Montana state parks offer free primitive camping, in general, overnight camping fees are a minimum of $15 per night and threfore do not qualify for inclusion in this book any longer.

U.S. FOREST SERVICE - NORTHERN REGION

PO Box 7669, Missoula, MT 406/329-3511.

Beaverhead/Deerlodge National Forests. The main camping season is from Memorial Day through the Labor Day weekend. Although most campgrounds remain open later, water system are shut down to prevent freezing. Campers may not stay more than 16 days at each campground. At some, the limit is 14 days. 420 Barrett St., Dillon, MT 59725-3572. 406/683-3900.

Bitterroot National Forest
This forest in west-central Montana and east-central Idaho offers camping at 18 developed campgrounds. At campgrounds where fees are charged, free off-season camping is permitted. Forest supervisor, 1801 N. 1st St, Hamilton, MT 39840; 406/363-7100.

CAPITAL: Helena
NICKNAME: Treasure State
STATEHOOD: 1889 – 41st State
FLOWER: Bitterroot
TREE: Ponderosa Pine
BIRD: Western Meadowlark

Custer National Forest
Consisting of 1.2 million acres, this forest is scattered across eastern Montana and western North Dakota. Most campgrounds have occupancy periods of 10 days. Generally, its sites have recommended RV limits of about 30 feet. 1310 Main St, Billings, MT 59105. 406-657-6200.

Flathead Natioanal Forest
The official camping season is Memorial Day weekend through Labor Day weekend, although most campgrounds remain open to free camping after the regular season. However, water systems are shut down to prevent freeze damage, and trash collection is discontinued. 1935 3rd Ave East, Kallispell, MT 59901. 406/758-5204.

Gallatin National Forest
This forest has about three dozen very nice campgrounds. PO Box 130, Bozeman, MT 59771. 406/587-6701.

Helena National Forest
This small forest has only about a dozen developed campgrounds, all with overnight fees of $10 or less. 2880 Skyway Drive, Helena, MT 59601. 406/449-5201.

Kootenai National Forest
Many of the forest's 40 developed campgrounds are open all year, or when accessible, even though the managed period is generally from June through September. Free off-season camping is permitted in some of the campgrounds where fees are charged during the managed season. 1101 US Highway 2 West, Libby, MT 59923. 406/293-6211.

Lewis and Clark National Forest
1101 15th St. North, Great Falls, MT 59403. 406-791-7700. Camping fees are $10 and under.

Lolo National Forest, Building 24A, Fort Missoula, Missoula, MT 59801. 406/329-3750. Camping fees are $6 to $10.

BUREAU OF LAND MANAGEMENT
500 Southgate Dr, Billings, MT 59101. 406/896-5000. Camping at undeveloped sites is limited to 16 days; for developed sites, the limit is 14 days.

BUREAU OF RECLAMATION:
Many reclamation projects are managed for recreation by cooperating sister agencies. Pishkun and Willow Creek Reservoirs and Intake Diversion Dam are managed by the Montana Department of Fish, Wildlife and Parks. Gibson Reservoir and Hungry Horse Reservoir are managed by the U.S. Forest Service. Lake Sherburne at Glacier National Park and Bighorn Lake behind Yellowtail Dam are managed by the National Park Service.

BOR's Canyon Ferry Lake property had been administered by the state parks department, but the property and its various camping areas were returned to the a few years ago. The BOR now operates the campgrounds, charging camping fees with no entry fees.

The bureau also directly manages several projects, including Clark Canyon Reservoir and Barretts Park near Dillon; Tiber Reservoir (Lake Elwell) near Chester; Fresno Reservoir near Malta; Anita Reservoir near Pompeys Pillar, and the Huntley Diversion Dam on the Yellowstone River. All those reclamation-administered recreation sites are free for camping and day-use. Vault toilets are provided in all camping areas; drinking water is available at many, and all reservoirs are accessible by concrete boat ramps. Clark Canyon and Tiber feature public concessions that provide on-site gasoline, groceries and other amenities. Bureau of Reclamation, Montana Projects Office, PO Box 30137, Billings, MT 59107-0137; 406/657-6202. For details about camping at Canyon Ferry Lake, contact the Canyon Ferry field office, 7661 Canyon Ferry Rd, Helena, MT 59601.

ABSAROKEE

Buffalo Jump   **FREE**
Stillwater River State Fishing Access Site
21 mi SW of Absarokee on Secondary 419; at Stillwater River. Free. All year; 7-day limit. 3 primitive sites on 6 acres; 35-ft RV limit. Toilets, fire restrictins, no drkg wtr. Boating (no mtrs), fishing.

Castle Rock   **$12**
Stillwater River State Fishing Access Site
15 mi W of Absarokee on CR 420; at Stillwater River. $12 for licensed fishermen, $18 others; $6 unlicensed MT seniors, $3.50 licensed MT seniors.; All year; 7-day limit. 10 primitive sites on 80 acres; 35-ft RV limit. Tbls, toilets, fire restrictions, drkg wtr. Fishing, hiking, boating, swimming. Spectacular scenery, but difficult access.

Cliff Swallow   **FREE**
Stillwater River State Fishing Access Site
9 mi W of Absarokee on CR 420; at Stillwater River. All year; 7-day limit. 8 primitive sites on 160 acres; 32-ft RV limit. Toilets, fire restrictions, no drkg wtr. Fishing pier, boating (hand launch, no mtrs), swimming. Easy access.

Moraine   **FREE**
Stillwater River State Fishing Access Site
16.1 mi W of Absarokee on CR 420; at Upper Stillwater River. Free. All year; 7-day limit. 2 primitive sites on 60 acres. Toilet, tbls, fire restrictions, no drkg wtr. Fishing, swimming, boating (no mtrs). Difficult access.

Rosebud Isle   **FREE**
West Rosebud Creek State Fishing Access Site
3 mi S of Absarokee on SR 78; 3 mi SW on CR 419 to Fishtail; at West Rosebud Creek. Free. All year; 7-day limit. 8 primitive sites on 11 acres; 35-ft RV limit. Toilets, fire restrictions, no drkg wtr. Fishing, boating. Difficult access.

ANACONDA

Racetrack Campground   **FREE**
Deerlodge National Forest
3.1 mi E of Anaconda on MT 1; NW on FR 169. Free. 5/15-9/15; 16-day limit. 13 sites (RVs under 23 ft). Tbls, toilets, cfga, drkg wtr, no trash service. Fishing. Elev 5400 ft; 5 acres. Stream. Geological.

Spring Hill Campground   **$12**
Deerlodge National Forest
10.7 mi NW of Anaconda on MT 1. $12. 6/15-9/15; 16-day limit. 15 sites (RVs under 23 ft). Toilets, tbls, cfga, drkg wtr, no trash service. Fishing, hiking. Elev 6500 ft.

Stuart Mill Bay   **$12**
Georgetown Lake State Fishing Access Site
13 mi W of Anaconda on SR 1; about 1.5 mi SW on Georgetown Lake Rd. All year; 7-day limit. $12 for licensed fishermen, others pay $18; $6 unlicensed MT seniors, $3.50 licensed MT seniors. 16 sites; 30-ft RV limit. Tbls, toilets, cfga, no drkg wtr. Boating(l - shallow wtr), fishing.

ASHLAND

Blacks Pond Campground   **FREE**
Custer National Forest
0.75 mi E of Ashland on US 212, right on tonque river road for 8 mi; left on O'dell creek rd 7 mi to FR 4021 & FR 4131 intersection; right on FR 4921 .5 mi. Free. May-Nov 2 sites. Toilets, no drkg wtr.

Cow Creek FREE
Custer National Forest
4 mi E of Ashland on US 212; 20 mi S on CR 485; 5 mi W on FR 95; at Cow Creek. Free. 4/15-11/30; 10-day limit. 5 sites; 30-ft RV limit. Tbls, toilets, cfga, no drkg wtr. Hiking, hunting, horseback riding.

Holiday Springs   **FREE**
Custer National Forest
5 mi E of Ashland on US 212; 9.5 mi NE on FR 423; E on FR 777; at East Fork Otter Creek. Free. All year; 10-day limit. 3 primitive sites; 30-ft RV limit. Toilet, cfga, no drkg wtr. Hiking, horseback riding Elev 3120 ft.

Red Shale   **FREE**
Custer National Forest
6 mi E of Ashland on US 212; at East Fork Otter Creek. Free. MD-11/30; 10-day limit. 14 sites; 30-ft RV limit. Tbls, toilets, cfga, no drkg wtr or trash service. Hiking, horseback riding, fishing. Elev 3200 ft.

AUGUSTA

Bean Lake State Fishing Access Site   **$7**
15 mi S of Augusta on Hwy 435, then right on Dearborn Canyon Rd to site. $7 for licensed fishermen, $12 others; $6 unlicensed MT seniors, $3.50 licensed MT seniors. All year; 7-day limit. 8 sites. Tbls, toilets, fire restrictions, no drkg wtr. Boating(l), fishing.

Benchmark Campground   **$6**
Lewis and Clark National Forest
14 mi W of Augusta on CR 235; 16 mi SW on FR 235. $6. Open MD-11/30, but free & no wtr after LD; 14-day limit. 25 sites (35-ft RV limit). Tbls, toilets, cfga, drkg wtr, no trash service. Fishing, hiking. Trailhead for horsemen & backpackers to the Skapegoat Wilderness; feeding troughs , hitching posts. Elev 5200 ft; 19 acres.

Home Gulch Campground   **$6**
Lewis and Clark National Forest
4 mi W of Augusta on Manix St; 17 mi NW on Sun River Canyon Rd; 2 mi W on FR 108; at North Fork of Sun River. $6 during MD-LD; free LD-11/30 but no wtr or services after LD; 14-day limit. 15 sites, typically 45 ft. Tbls, toilets, cfga, drkg wtr, no trash service. Fishing, boating (l),

nature trails, swimming. Trail into Bob Marshall Wilderness. Grizzly bear country. Elev 4400 ft; 6 acres.

Mortimer Gulch $8
Lewis and Clark National Forest
4 mi W of Augusta on Manix St; 22 mi NW of Augusta on Sun River Canyon Rd; 4 mi W on FR 108; 3 mi N on FR 8984; near Gibson Reservoir. $8 during MD-LD; free LD-11/30 but no wtr or services; 14-day limit. 26 sites, typically 45 ft. Tbls, toilets, cfga, drkg wtr, no trash service. Hiking (trailhead to the Bob Marshall Wilderness). Swimming, boating (l), water skiing, fishing, horseback riding. Elev 5300 ft; 8 acres.

South Fork $8
Lewis and Clark National Forest
31 mi W of Augusta on Benchmark Rd (FR 235). $8. MD-11/30, but free & no wtr after LD; 14-day limit. 7 sites (35-ft RV limit). Tbls, toilet, cfga, drkg wtr, no trash service. Fishing, hiking & bridle trails into Bob Marshall Wilderness and Scapegoat Wilderness. Be wary of grizzly bears. Elev 5500 ft; 9 acres.

Wood Lake $6
Lewis and Clark National Forest
24 mi W of Augusta on FR 235 (Benchmark Rd). $6. Open MD-11/30, but free & no wtr after LD; 14-day limit. 9 sites; 22-ft RV limit. Tbls, toilet, cfga, drkg wtr. Fishing, swimming, hiking. GEkev 5500 ft.

BAKER

South Sandstone Reservoir FREE
State Fishing Access Site
3.5 mi S off US 12 near milepost 75; then 2.5 mi W on gravel county rd. Free. All year; 7-day limit. 11 primitive sites; 55-ft RV limit. Tbls, toilet, fire restrictions, no drkg wtr. Boating(l), fishing, swimming. Difficult access. 679 acres.

BASIN

Basin Canyon FREE
Deerlodge National Forest
5 mi N of Basin on I-15; 3 mi NW on FR 172. Free. Elev 5800 ft. MD-9/15; 16-day limit. 2 undeveloped sites (RVs under 17 ft). Tbls, toilets, cfga, firewood, no drkg wtr, no trash service. Fishing. On Basin Creek.

Galena Gulch FREE
Bureau of Land Management
Butte Field Office
From I-15 exit 16 (High Ore Rd) at Basin, 0.75 mi N on paved rd along I-15; E under I-15; cross Boulder River bridge to site. Free. All year; RV-limit 40 ft. 14-day limit. 10 sites. Tbls, toilets, cfga, no drkg wtr. Fishing.

Mormon Gulch FREE
Deerlodge National Forest
4 mi W of Basin on I-15; 2 mi W on FR 82. Free. About

6/20-9/15; 14-day limit. Elev 5500 ft. 16 sites on 10 acres (RVs under 17 ft). Tbls, toilets, cfga, firewood, no drkg wtr, no trash service.

Whitehouse Campground FREE
Deerlodge National Forest
4 mi W of Basin on I-15; 8 mi W on FR 82. Free. 6/15-12/10; 14-day limit. 5 sites (22-ft RV limit). Tbls, toilets, cfga, drkg wtr. Fishing, hiking trails. At Boulder River.

BIGFORK

Swan Lake Compound $7.50
Flathead National Forest
17 mi S of Bigfork on Hwy 83; E just N of milemarker 72; across rd from Swan Lake. $7.50 with federal senior pass; others pay $15. 5/15-9/30; 16-day limit. 36 sites (50-ft RV limit). Tbls, toilets, cfga, drkg wtr. Boating, fishing, swimming beach. Elev 3300 ft.

BIG SANDY

Paul F. Williams Memorial
Big Sandy City Park FREE
In Big Sandy on US 87. Free overnight. 4/1-11/1. pull in primitive sites, no hookups. 3 designated sites. Tbls, flush toilets, cfga, drkg wtr, no showers. Well maintained.

Judith Landing FREE
Bureau of Land Management
Lewiston Field Office
US 87 at Big Sandy, milepost 79; 44 mi S on SR 236. Free. 5/15-10/15; 14-day limit. 8 sites; 48-ft RV limit. Tbls, no drkg wtr, cfga, toilet. Fishing; hiking; boating(l).

BIG SKY

Greek Creek $7.50
Gallatin National Forest
3 mi E of Big Sky on SR 191S; 9.5 mi N on US 191 (31 mi S of Bozeman); at Gallatin River. $7.50 with federal senior pass others pay $15 5/15-9/15; 16-day limit. 15 sites; 45-ft RV limit. Tbls, toilets, cfga, drkg wtr, firewood($). Fishing, boating, rafting, kayaking, birdwatching, winter snowmobiling. Elev 5600 ft; 5 acres.

Moose Creek Flat $7.50
Gallatin National Forest
3 mi E of Big Sky on SR 191S; 7 mi N on US 191 (33 mi S of Bozeman). $7.50 with federal senior pass others pay $15. 5/15-9/15; 16-day limit. 13 sites (45-ft RV limit). Tbls, toilets, cfga, drkg wtr, firewood($). Fishing on Gallatin River. Elev 5700 ft; 6 acres.

Red Cliff $7.50
Gallatin National Forest
3 mi E of Big Sky on SR 191S; 6.5 mi S on US 191 (48 mi S of Bozeman). $7.50 base with federal senior pass others pay $15.00; $2.00 additional fo 26 elec sites; 5/15-9/15; 16-day limit. 40-ft RV limit. Tbls, toilets, cfga, drkg wtr.

Fishing, rafting, kayaking on Gallatin River. Elev 6400 ft; 49 acres.

Swan Creek $7.50
Gallatin National Forest
3 mi E of Big Sky on SR 191S; 8.5 mi N on US 191; 1 mi E on FR 481 (Swan Creek Rd); at confluence of Swan Creek & Gallatin River. $7.50 with federal senior pass; others pay $15. 5/15-9/24; 16-day limit. 13 sites; 35-ft RV limit. Tbls, toilets, cfga, drkg wtr. Fishing, hiking, kayaking, rafting. Scenic. Elev 5400 ft; 6 acres.

BIG TIMBER

Aspen Campground $5
Gallatin National Forest
25 mi S of Big Timber on SR 298; 8.5 mi S on CR 212; at Boulder River. $5. All year; 14-day limit; free 10/1-MD, but winter access may be limited by snow. 8 sites; 32-ft RV limit on access rd. Tbls, toilets, cfga, no drkg wtr. Fishing, hiking. Elev 4500 ft; 8 acres.

Big Beaver Campground   FREE
Gallatin National Forest
25 mi S of Big Timber on MT 298; 8 mi S on CR 212; at Boulder River. Free. Elev 5500 ft. All year; 15-day limit. Winter access may be limited by snow. 5 sites (32-ft RV limit on access rd). Tbls, toilets, cfga, no drkg wtr, no trash service. Fishing, horseback riding, hiking, birdwatching.

Big Rock   FREE
Boulder River State Fishing Access Site
4 mi S of Big Timber on Upper Boulder River (river mile 5.3). Free. All year; 7-day limit. Tbls, toilets, fire restrictions, no drkg wtr. Primitive camping on 76 acres. Boating, fishing. Difficult access.

Boulder Forks   FREE
Boulder River State Fishing Access Site
17 mi S of Big Timber off Hwy 298 on Upper Boulder River (stream mile 0.4). Free. All year; 7-day limit. Primitive camping on 72.4 acres. Toilets, fire restrictions, tbls, no drkg wtr. Fishing, boating. Difficult access. Popular.

Bratten $12
Upper Yellowstone River State Fishing Access Site
16 mi E of Big Timber on I-90; 2 mi E on frontage rd; at Yellowstone River (river mile 434.2). $12 with fishing license, $18 otherwise; $6 unlicensed MT seniors, $3.50 licensed MT seniors. All year; 7-day limit. 12 primitive sites on 436 acres; 25-ft RV limit. Tbls, toilets, fire restrictions no drkg wtr. Boating(l), fishing. Difficult site access, but good access to river for floating & fishing. "Clark on the Yellowstone" historic site.

Chippy Park Campground $5
Gallatin National Forest
25 mi S of Big Timber on MT 298; 9 mi S on FR 212; at

mouth of Boulder Canyon. $5. Elev 5500 ft. All year; 15-day limit. 7 sites (32-ft RV limit on access rd). Tbls, toilets, cfga, firewood, drkg wtr (MD-LD), no trash service. Rockhounding; fishing, hiking. Scenic view. Horseback riding nearby.

Grey Bear $7
Upper Yellowstone River State Fishing Access Site
E of Big Timber to I-90 exit 367, then N to frontage rd and 5 mi W to Yellowstone River; N on N. Yellowstone Tr. Rd for 0.5 mi. $7 for licensed fishermen, $12 for others; $6 unlicensed MT seniors, $3.50 licensed MT seniors. All year; 7-day limit. 11 developed sites at large, open 25.7 acres. Toilets, fire restrictions, tbls, no drkg wtr. Boating(l), fishing, hiking. Difficult access.

Halfmoon Campground $5
Gallatin National Forest
12 mi N of Big Timber on US 191; 8 mi W on CR 197; 2 mi W on FR 197; at Timber Creek. $5. All year; 15-day limit. Winter access limited by snow. 6 sites (32-ft RV limit on access rd). Tbls, toilets, cfga, drkg wtr MD-LD, no trash service. Fishing, mountain climbing. Crazy Mountain (only public access E side). Elev 6500 ft.

Hells Canyon   FREE
Gallatin National Forest
25 mi SW of Big Timber on SR 298; 14 mi S on CR 212. All year; 16-day limit. 11 sites (20-ft RV limit due to access rd). Tbls, toilets, cfga, no drkg wtr, no trash service. Fishing, hiking trails, rockhounding. Elev 6000 ft; 5 acres.

Hicks Park $5
Gallatin National Forest
25 mi SW of Big Timber on SR 298; 20 mi S on CR 212; near Boulder Creek. $5. All year; 15-day limit; free during LD-MD, but no drkg wtr; winter access limited by snow. 16 sites (RVs under 32 ft due to turns on access rd). Tbls, toilets, cfga, drkg wtr. Fishing, hiking trails. Elev 5500 ft; 5 acres.

Indian Fort $7
Yellowstone River State Fishing Access Site
E of Big Timber on I-90 to exit 392 at Reedpoint; across bridge to first left; at Yellowstone River. $7 for licensed fishermen; $12 for others. All year; 7-day limit. Primitive camping on 18.7 acres. Tbls, toilets, fire restrictions, no drkg wtr. Boating(l), fishing. Good access.

Otter Creek   FREE
Upper Yellowstone River State Fishing Access Site
2 mi N of Big Timber on Hwy 191; 1.5 mi E on Howie Rd; at Upper Yellowstone River mile 454. Free. All year; 7-day limit. 3 primitive sites on 29 acres. Tbls, toilets, fire restrictions, no drkg wtr. Boating(l), fishing.

West Boulder $5
Gallatin National Forest
16 mi SW of Big Timber on SR 298 to McLeod; 6.5 mi SW on CR 30; 8 mi SW on West Boulder Rd. $5. All year; 16-day limit. Free LD-MD, but no drkg wtr; winter access limited by snow. 10 sites (20-ft RV limit due to access rd turns). Tbls, toilets, cfga, drkg wtr, no trash service. Good fishing, hiking, horseback riding. Equestrian facilities next to camp.

BONNER
Clearwater Crossing $7
Clearwater River State Fishing Access Site
34 mi E of Bonner on SR 200; 1 mi W of Clearwater Junction (stream mile 3.4). $7 for licensed fishermen, $12 for others; $6 unlicensed MT seniors, $3.50 licensed MT seniors. All year; 7-day limit. 6 sites; 50-ft combined length limit. Tbls, toilets, cfga, no drkg wtr. Boating (no mtrs), fishing. Canoes can be hand-launched. 19 acres.

Corrick's River Bend $7
Blackfoot River State Fishing Access Site
25.5 mi E of Bonner on Hwy 200 to milepost 26; 7.5 mi W on Ninemile Prairie Rd (stream mile 23). $7 for licensed fishermen, $12 for others; $6 unlicensed MT seniors, $3.50 licensed MT seniors. All year; 7-day limit. 9 developed sites on 32 acres; 55-ft RV limit. Tbls, toilets, cfga, drkg wtr. Fishing, boating(l). Difficult access. No boat motors on Blackfoot River or tributaries.

Monture Creek $7
State Fishing Access Site
39 mi E of Bonner to milepost 39; at Monture Creek. $7 with fishing license, $12 otherwise; $6 unlicensed MT seniors, $3.50 licensed MT seniors. All year; 7-day limit. 3 primitive sites on 112 acres; 40-ft combined limit. Tbls, toilets, cfga, no drkg wtr. Fishing, boating (hand launch, no mtrs). Difficult access.

Ninemile Prairie $7
Blackfoot River State Fishing Access Site
26 mi E of Bonner on Hwy 200 to milepost 26; 4 mi W on Ninemile Prairie Rd (stream mile 25.1). $7 for licensed fishermen, $12 for others; $6 unlicensed MT seniors, $3.50 licensed MT seniors. All year; 7-day limit. 4 developed sites on 14 acres; 25-ft RV limit. Tbls, toilet, cfga, no drkg wtr. Fishing. Boat launching not advised. Difficult access; rough rds.

River Junction $7
Blackfoot River State Fishing Access Site
39 mi E of Bonner on Hwy 200 to milepost 39; 9 mi SE on county rd (stream mile 52.5). $7 with fishing license, $12 otherwise; $6 unlicensed MT seniors, $3.50 licensed MT seniors. All year; 7-day limit. 6 primitive sites on 224 acres; 25-ft RV limit. Tbls, toilets, cfga, no drkg wtr. Boating(l), fishing. Difficult access; rds very rough. Canoes can be hand-launched; no boat motors on Blackfoot River & tributaries.

Russell Gates Memorial $7
Blackfoot River State Fishing Access Site
35 mi E of Bonner on SR 200 to milepost 35 (stream mile 40.1). $7 for fishing license holders, $12 for others; $6 unlicensed MT seniors, $3.50 licensed MT seniors. All year; 7-day limit. 11 sites (45-ft combined limit). Tbls, toilets, cfga, drkg wtr (no wtr 5/1-9/30). Boating(I - no mtrs), canoeing, fishing. 41 acres.

Thibodeau $7
Blackfoot River State Fishing Access Site
10.3 mi E of Bonner on SR 200; 5.5 mi N of Johnsrud FAS (stream mile 17.7). $7 for licensed fishermen, $12 for others; $6 unlicensed MT seniors, $3.50 licensed MT seniors. All year; 14-day limit. 8 developed sites; 45-ft RV limit. Most Difficult Accessibility. Tbls, toilets, cfga, no drkg wtr. Fishing, no boat launch, no day use parking.

Upsata Lake $7
State Fishing Access Site
38 mi E of Bonner on Hwy 200 to milepost 38; 4 mi N on Woodworth Rd. $7 for licensed fishermen, $12 for others; $6 unlicensed MT seniors, $3.50 licensed MT seniors. All year; 7-day limit. 6 primitive sites; 40-ft combined limit. Toilets, tbls, cfga, no drkg wtr. Fishing, boating(l). Catch-and-release fishing for bass. Difficult access. 11 acres.

BOZEMAN
Battle Ridge FREE
Gallatin National Forest
21 mi NE of Bozeman on SR 89. Elev 6400 ft; in Bridger Mtns at Battle Ridge Pass. Free. 5/15-9/15; 16-day limit. 13 sites up to 30 ft. Toilets, cfga, tbls, no drkg wtr or trash service. Hiking. Elev 6500 ft.

Chisolm Campground $7.50
Gallatin National Forest
18 mi S of Bozeman on Hyalite Canyon Rd; Hyalite Reservoir. $7.50 with federal senior pass; others pay $15. 5/15-9/15; 16-day limit. 10 sites up to 60 ft. Tbls, toilets, cfga, drkg wtr. Fishing, hiking, mountain biking nearby, boating (hand launch).

Greycliff $7
Madison River State Fishing Access Site
23 mi W of Bozeman on SR 84; 6 mi N on Madison River Rd. $7 for licensed fishermen, $12 for others; $6 unlicensed MT seniors, $3.50 licensed MT seniors. All year but closed to camping 1/1-MD; 7-day limit. 12 sites; 25-ft RV limit. Tbls, toilets, fire restrictions, drkg wtr. Boating(l), fishing. Difficult access. 552 acres.

Hood Creek $7.50
Gallatin National Forest
17 mi S of Bozeman on CR 243; 10 mi SE on CR 62; at
Hyalite Reservoir. $7.50 with federal senior pass; others
pay $15. 5/22-9/30; 16-day limit. 25 sites (40-ft RV limit).
Tbls, toilets, cfga, drkg wtr. Pack out trash. Boating(l),
fishing, mountain biking, hiking. Hand boat launch. Elev
6800 ft; 5 acres.

Langohr Campground $7.50
Gallatin National Forest
8 mi S of Bozeman on CR 243; 5.5 mi SE on CR 62. $7 with
federal senior pass; others pay $15. 5/16-9/24; 16-day
limit. 19 sites to 32 ft. Tbls, toilets, cfga, drkg wtr. Boating,
fishing (handicap-accessible fishing trail), hiking. Wheelchair-accessible fishing trail & nature walk. Scenic. Elev
6100 ft; 5 acres.

BRIDGER
Sage Creek $5
Custer National Forest
3 mi S of Bridger on US 310; 22 mi SE on Pryor Mountain
Rd; half mi E on FR 50. $5 single sites, $10 double. Elev
5600 ft. MD-LD; 14-day limit. 12 sites; 30-ft RV limit.
Tbls, toilets, cfga, firewood, no drkg wtr. Rockhounding;
fishing. High-clearance vehicles recommended. Cave
exploring (permit needed). Pryor Mountains contain wild
horses, bighorn sheep.

BUTTE
Beaverdam $5
Deerlodge National Forest
7 mi W of Butte on I-90; 18 mi S on I-15; 6 mi W on FR 961.
$5. MD-LD; 16-day limit. 15 sites (50-ft RV limit). Tbls,
toilets, cfga, drkg wtr, no trash service. Fishing, hiking
trails. 6 acres.

Delmoe Lake $8
Deerlodge National Forest
17 mi NE on I-90 from Butte to Homestake Pass exit;
follow signs 10 mi on FR 222. $8. MD-9/15; 16-day limit.,
food storage required, 25 sites; 32-ft RV limit. Tbls, toilets,
cfga, drkg wtr. Swimming, fishing, hiking, boating.

Lowland Campground $5
Deerlodge National Forest
9 mi NE of Butte on I-15; 6 mi W on FR 442; left on FR 9485
for 1.5 mi. $5 during about MD-LD; free rest of yr, weather
permitting (but wtr shut off); 16-day limit. 12 sites (RVs
under 23 ft). Tbls, toilets, cfga, drkg wtr. Picnic area can
be reserved ($). Elev 6400 ft.

BYNUM
Bynum Reservoir State Fishing Access Site $12
7 mi W of Bynum on Blackleaf Rd. $12 for licensed fish-
ermen, $18 others; All year; 7-day limit. 4 sites. Trailer/

RV not reccommended. Tbls, toilet, cfga, no drkg wtr.
Boating(l), fishing.

CAMERON
Madison $14
Beaverhead National Forest
23.5 mi S of Cameron on SR 287; SW on CR 8381. $14.
MD-10/15; 16-day limit. 10 sites (32-ft RV limit). Tbls,
toilets, cfga, drkg wtr. Fishing. Mandatory food storage
3/1-12/1.

Ruby Creek Campground $8
Bureau of Land Management
Dillon Field Office
7 mi S of Cameron on US 287; cross McAttee bridge, continue 3 mi S on BLM rd; at Upper Madison River. $8 during
5/1-12/1; free rest of year but no wtr or services; 14-day
limit. Tbls, toilets, cfga, drkg wtr. Boating(l), fishing, rafting, canoeing.

CASCADE
Mountain Palace $7
Missouri River State Fishing Access Site
14 mi S of Cascade to Canyon Exit 244; 1 mi N on Recreation Rd; at Missouri River (river mile 2,180.6). $7 for
licensed fishermen, $12 for others; $6 unlicensed MT
seniors, $3.50 licensed MT seniors. All year; 14-day limit.
3 primitive sites on 2.8 acres. Toilets, tbls, cfga, no drkg
wtr. Boating(l), fishing. Difficult access.

CHESTER
Island Area   FREE
Lake Elwell (Tiber Reservoir)
Bureau of Reclamation
12 mi S of Chester on Rt 223; follow signs to site. Free.
All year; 14-day limit. Primitive undesignated camping
area. Toilets, drkg wtr, cfga, dump. Fishing, boating (l).
Summer concession nearby with gasoline, supplies, fee
campground, marina.

North Bootlegger   FREE
Lake Elwell (Tiber Reservoir)
Bureau of Reclamation
12 mi S of Chester on Rt 223; follow signs to site. Free.
All year; 14-day limit. Primitive undesignated camping
area. Toilets, no drkg wtr, cfga. Fishing, boating (primitive
launch). Summer concession nearby with gasoline, supplies, fee campground, marina.

Sanford City Park   DONATIONS
Sanford Lake Elwell (Tiber Reservoir)
Bureau of Reclamation
From US 2 on N edge of Chester, 3 blocks S on either 3rd
St or 2nd St. Donations. All year; 3-night limit. 32 non-elec
sites. 32x15 RV limit. Tbls, flush toilets, showers, no drkg
wtr, cfga, playground, shelter, gas barbecue, horseshoe
pits. Museum nearby.

Sanford Lake Elwell (Tiber Reservoir)   FREE
Bureau of Reclamation
12 mi S of Chester on Rt 223; follow signs to site. Free. All year; 14-day limit. Primitive undesignated camping area. Toilets, drkg wtr, cfga. Fishing, boating(l).

South Bootlegger   FREE
Lake Elwell (Tiber Reservoir)
Bureau of Reclamation
12 mi S of Chester on Rt 223; follow signs to site. Free. All year; 14-day limit. Primitive undesignated camping area. Toilets, drkg wtr, cfga. Fishing, boating (l). Summer concession nearby with gasoline, supplies, fee campground, marina.

VFW Campground   FREE
Lake Elwell (Tiber Reservoir)
Bureau of Reclamation
12 mi S of Chester on Rt 223; follow signs to site. Free. All year; 14-day limit. Primitive undesignated camping area. Toilets, no drkg wtr, cfga. Fishing, boating (l). Summer concession nearby with gasoline, supplies, fee campground, marina.

Willow Creek   FREE
Lake Elwell (Tiber Reservoir)
Bureau of Reclamation
12 mi S of Chester on Rt 223; follow signs to site. Free. All year; 14-day limit. Primitive undesignated camping area. Toilets, no drkg wtr, cfga. Fishing, boating (l). Summer concession nearby with gasoline, supplies, fee campground, marina.

CHOTEAU

Cave Mountain $6
Lewis and Clark National Forest
5 mi NW of Choteau on SR 89; 22 mi W on Teton Canyon Rd (FR 144). $6. MD-LD; 14-day limit. 18 sites; 35-ft RV limit. Tbls, toilets, cfga, drkg wtr. Fishing, hiking trails. 5 acres.

Choteau City Campground $8
From US 89 in downtown area, E on SR 222; cross railroad tracks, then right at city park. $8. 5/15-10/1; 3-day limit. 35 RV sites, 35 tent sites. Tbls, flush toilets, cfga, drkg wtr, dump, playground. Fishing, children's pond, access to river. Elev 4000 ft; 2 acres.

Elko Campground   FREE
Lewis and Clark National Forest
5.5 mi N of Choteau on US 89; 23 mi W on CR 144 (Teton Canyon Rd); 2.5 mi N on FR 144; at Teton River. Free. MD-Thanksgiving, but no services after LD; 14-day limit. 3 sites. Tbls, toilets, cfga, no drkg wtr, no trash service. Hiking, fishing.

Freezeout Lake   FREE
State Wildlife Refuge
10 mi S of Choteau on Hwy 89 (3 mi N of Fairfield). Free. All year; 14-day limit. Primitive undesignated camping on refuge; no facilities, no drkg wtr. Montana's primary staging area for snow geese & tundra swans in spring & fall.

Mills Falls   FREE
Lewis and Clark National Forest
5.5 mi N of Choteau on US 89; 19 mi W on CR 144 (Teton Canyon Rd); 9 mi S on CR 109 & W on FR 109; at South Fork of Teton River. Free. MD-LD; 14-day limit. 4 sites. Tbls, toilet, cfga, no drkg wtr, no trash service. Fishing, hiking trails.

CLANCY

Park Lake Campground $8
State Fishing Access Site
Helena National Forest
1 mi N of Clancy on CR 426; 5.5 mi W on FR 4000; 2.1 mi SW on FR 426.1; 5 mi W on FR 4009. $8. MD-9/15; 15-day limit. 22 sites (35-ft RV limit). Tbls, toilets, cfga, drkg wtr. Swimming, fishing, boating (no motors; primitive launch); canoeing, hunting, hiking. Elev 6400 ft; 10 acres. Free dispersed camping is available along the roadways nearby.

CLINTON

Bitterroot Flat $6
Lolo National Forest
4.9 mi SE of Clinton on I-90 to Rock Creek exit; 23 mi S on rough FR 102. $6 during 5/15-9/30; free rest of year, when accessible, but no drkg wtr; 14-day limit. 15 sites (32-ft RV limit, but rd quite narrow & rough for RVs). Tbls, toilets, cfga, firewood, well drkg wtr, no trash service. Fishing. Elev 4300 ft.

Dalles Campground $6
Lolo National Forest
4.9 mi SE of Clinton on I-90 to Rock Creek exit; 14.5 mi S on FR 102. $6 during 5/15-9/30; free rest of year, but no wtr or services; 14-day limit. 10 sites (RVs under 32 ft, but rd quite narrow & rough for RVs). Tbls, toilets, cfga, drkg wtr. Fishing. Elev 4200 ft.

Garnet Ghost Town   FREE
Bureau of Land Management
E of Clinton on I-90 to either the Drummond or Bearmouth exit; follow N side frontage rd to Bear Gulch Rd, about 10 mi W of Drummond or 5 mi E of Bearmouth for about 7.5 mi; take Cave Gulch Rd 4 mi. Camp free at dispersed sites around town; $3 per person fee for admission to ghost town. BLM & private preservation group maintain the town, which is Montana's most intact ghost town from the 1890s gold mining period.

Grizzly Campground $6
Lolo National Forest
4.9 mi SE of Clinton on I-90 to Rock Creek exit; 10.6 mi S on rough FR 102 (Rock Creek Rd); 1 mi SE on FR 88 (Ranch Creek Rd). Elev 4200 ft. $6 during 5/15-9/30; free rest

of year, but no wtr or services; 14-day limit. 9 sites (RVs under 32 ft, but rd rough & narrow for RVs). Tbls, toilets, cfga, drkg wtr, no trash service. Fishing, volleyball, horseshoes. Elev 4100 ft.

Harry's Flat $6
Lolo National Forest
4.9 mi SE of Clinton on I-90 to Rock Creek exit; 17.6 mi S on rough FR 102 (Rock Creek Rd). $6 during 5/15-9/30; free rest of year, but no wtr or services; 14-day limit. 15 sites (RVs under 32 ft, but rd rough & narrow for RVs). Tbls, toilets, cfga, piped drkg wtr, no trash service. Fishing. Elev 4300 ft.

Norton Campground $6
Lolo National Forest
4.9 mi SE of Clinton on I-90 to Rock Creek exit; 11 mi S on rough FR 102 (Rock Creek Rd). $6 during 5/15-9/30; free rest of year, but no wtr or services; 14-day limit. 13 sites (16 ft RV limit but rd rough & narrow for RVs). Tbls, toilets, cfga, drkg wtr, no trash service. Fishing, hiking trails. Elev 4100 ft; 5 acres.

Siria Campground FREE
Lolo National Forest
4.9 mi SE of Clinton on I-90; 29.2 mi S on FR 102 (rough rd); at Rock Creek. Free. All year; 14-day limit. 4 sites (RVs under 16 ft but rd rough & narrow for RVs). Toilet, cfga, firewood, no drkg wtr. Fishing. Elev 4500 ft; 5 acres.

COLUMBIA FALLS
Big Creek $7.50
Flathead National Forest
21 mi N of Columbia Falls on CR 486; at North Fork of Flathead River. $7.50 with federal senior pass during 5/9-9/30; others pay $14. 16-day limit. 22 sites (40-ft RV limit). Tbls, toilets, cfga, drkg wtr. Fishing, boating (I), hiking. 3 mi from Glacier National Park. Elev 3300 ft. Non-campers pay $5 day use fee.

Moose Lake Campground FREE
Flathead National Forest
20 mi N of Columbia Falls on CR 486; 17.5 mi W on FR 316 (Big Creek Rd); right on FR 315, then right on FR 5207; at Moose Lake. Free. All year; 14-day limit. 3 sites plus others along the road. Tbls, toilet, cfga, no drkg wtr or trash service. Fishing, canoeing, berry-picking, hiking.

Red Meadow Lake Campground FREE
Flathead National Forest
About 42 mi N of Columbia Falls on CR 486; 11.5 mi W on FR 115. Free. All year; 14-day limit. 6 sites; 32-ft RV limit. Tbl, toilet, cfga, no drkg wtr, no trash service. Fishing, hiking, canoeing. Elev 5500 ft.

Tuchuck Campground FREE
Flathead National Forest
53 mi N of Columbia Falls on FR 210; 10 mi W on FR 114 (4WD or high-clearance vehicles only on FR 114). Free. 6/15-9/1; 14-day limit. 7 sites (RVs under 22 ft). Tbls, toilets, cfga, firewood, no drkg wtr. Fishing. Hitch rails, loading ramp, feed bunks for horsemen. Elev 4500 ft; 2 acres.

COLUMBUS
Itch-Kep-Pe City Park FREE
S of Columbus on SR 78 (go right off I-90 milepost 408); at Yellowstone River (several sites along river). Free, but donations accepted. 4/1-10/31; 10-day limit. 48 sites (no RV size limit). Tbls, flush toilets, cfga, drkg wtr. Fishing, swimming. 406-322-4505.

Swinging Bridge FREE
Stillwater River State Fishing Access Site
5.3 mi SW of Columbus on Hwy 78; 1 mi S on gravel rd; at Stillwater River. All year; 7-day limit. Tbls, toilets, fire restrictions, no drkg wtr. 5 sites on 4 acres. Fishing, boating. Difficult access.

Whitebird $7
Stillwater River State Fishing Access Site
5.9 mi S of Columbus on Hwy 78; half mi NW on gravel rd; at Stillwater River (river mile 5.8). $7 for licensed fishermen, $12 otherwise; $6 unlicensed MT seniors, $3.50 licensed seniors. All year; 7-day limit. Tbls, toilets, fire restrictins, no drkg wtr. 10 primitive sites on 22.7 acres. Fishing, hiking, boating (I - no mtrs). Difficult access.

CONDON
Holland Lake $7.50
Flathead National Forest
9 mi SE of Condon on SR 83; 3 mi E on FR 44 (Holland Lake Rd). $7.50 with federal senior pass; others pay $15. About 5/15-9/30; 14-day limit. 39 sites (50-ft RV limit). Tbls, toilets, cfga, drkg wtr, dump ($3), beach. Fishing, boating(I), hiking trails, swimming.

COOKE CITY
Chief Joseph Campground $8
Gallatin National Forest
4.8 mi E of Cooke City on US 212. $8. 6/15-9/30; 16-day limit. 6 sites (42-ft RV limit on access rd). Tbls, toilets, cfga, drkg wtr. Hiking. Nearby trailhead to Absaroka-Beartooth Wilderness. Ranger programs. Elev 8000 ft. Less than 20 mi to Yellowstone NP. Note:

Colter Campground $8
Gallatin National Forest
2.3 mi E of Cooke City on US 212 in Wyoming. $8. 7/15-9/30; 16-day limit. 18 sites (48-ft RV limit); hard-sided RVs only due to bear danger. Tbls, toilets, cfga, drkg wtr, food storage boxes. Fishing, hiking trails along Lady of the Lake Creek. Elev 7900 ft; 15 acres.

Crazy Creek $10
Shoshone National Forest
10.5 mi SE of Cooke City on US 212 in Wyoming. Along Clarks Fork of Yellowstone River. $10. About MD-LD; 16-day limit. 16 sites (28-ft RV limit); no tents or folding trailers permitted due to bears. Tbls, toilets, cfga, drkg wtr. Fishing, hiking. Crazy Lakes trailhead to backcountry lakes in Absaroka-Beartooth Wilderness. Scenic walk to Crazy Creek Falls. Elev 6900 ft.

Fox Creek Campground $10
Shoshone National Forest
7.5 mi SE of Cooke City on US 212 in Wyoming. $10 base with federal senior pass; others pay $20 base. Elec sites $60 ($30 with senior pass). 6/15-9/23; 16-day limit. 33 newly remodeled sites; 32-ft RV limit. Tbls, toilets, cfga, drkg wtr. Fishing, hiking, boating. At Fox Creek and Clarks Fork of Yellowstone River. Elev 7100 ft.

Hunter Peak Campground $7.50
Shoshone National Forest
14.4 mi SE of Cooke City on US 212; 5 mi S on Hwy 296 in Wyoming. $7.50 with federal senior pass others pay $15 during May-Nov; free off-season but no wtr service. All year; 14-day limit. 10 sites (32-ft RV limit). Tbls, toilets, cfga, drkg wtr. Fishing, hiking. Clarks Fork Trailhead nearby has horse facilities. Elev 6500 ft.

Lake Creek $10
Shoshone National Forest
14.4 mi SE of Cooke City on US 212 in Wyoming. $10 during 6/1-9/30; free off-season but no wtr; 16-day limit. 6 sites (22-ft RV limit). Tbls, toilets, cfga, drkg wtr. Fishing, hiking, boating(l). Elev 6949 ft.

Soda Butte $9
Gallatin National Forest
1.2 mi E of Cooke City on US 212. $9. 7/1-9/30; 16-day limit. 27 sites; 48-ft RV limit on access rd. Tbls, toilets, cfga, drkg wtr, no trash service. Fishing, hiking. Elev 7500 ft; 10 acres.

DARBY

Alta Campground $8
Bitterroot National Forest
4 mi S of Darby on US 93; 21.5 mi S on CR 473; 6 mi S on CR 96. $8 during MD-LD; free rest of year; 14-day limit. 15 sites; 30-ft RV limit. Tbls, toilets, cfga, drkg wtr (no wtr during free period). Hunting, fishing, hiking, gold panning. On West Fork of Bitterroot River. Nearby Hughes Creek was site of early placer gold mining. Elev 5000 ft; 6 acres.

Bear Creek Pass Horse Camp Trailhead   FREE
Bitterroot National Forest
7.3 mi N of Darby on US 93; 1.4 mi W on co rd; 17 mi W on FR 429 (dirt mountain rd). High cleareance vehicles

reccommended. Free. 7/15-9/15; 14-day limit. 6 sites (RVs under 33 ft) & 4 hunter camps. Tbls, toilet, cfga, drkg wtr. Hunting; hiking; fishing(1 mi); boating(ld-3 mi). Elev 6200 ft; 2 acres. At the head of Lost Horse Creek. Access point for Selway-Bitterroot Wilderness. Stream.

Deep Creek   FREE
0 National Forest
4.3 mi S of Darby on US 93; 14.3 mi S on West ford Rd; 31 mi W on FR 468 (Nez Perce Rd, becoming Magruder Corridor); at Deep Creek. Free. All year; 14-day limit. 3 sites; 30-ft RV limit. Tbl, toilet, cfga, no drkg wtr, no trash service. Fishing, hiking.

Indian Creek   FREE
Bitterroot National Forest
4.1 mi S of Darby on US 93; 14.4 mi SW on CR 473; 36.5 mi W on FR 468; 5 mi N on FR 6223; at Selway River. Free. 6/15-11/30; 14-day limit. 2 sites; 25-ft RV limit. Tbls, toilet, cfga, no drkg wtr. Hiking, fishing.

Indian Trees $10
Bitterroot National Forest
4 mi S on US 93; 14 mi SW on CR 473; 37 mi W on FR 468; 5 mi N on FR 6223; at Eat Fork of Bitterroot River. $10. About 5/15-9/30; 14-day limit. 16 sites (50-ft RV limit). Tbls, toilets, cfga, drkg wtr. Hiking, fishing.

Lake Como $8
Como Lake Recreation Area
Bitterroot National Forest
4 mi N of Darby on US 93; 3 mi W on Lake Como Rd; N following signs. $8 with federal senior pass for 11 elec/wtr sites; others pay $16 (no surcharge for elec). MD-LD; 7-day limit. No RV size limit; 10 pull-through. Tbls, toilets, cfga, drkg wtr; Water system may be down due to presence of bacteria contact ranger station @406-821-3913. Swimming, boating(l), fishing, hiking, canoeing.

Logging Camp   FREE
Dispersed Camping Area
Lick Creek Demonstration Forest
Bitterroot National Forest
4 mi N of Darby on US 93; 3 mi W on Lake Como Rd to Lake Como Recreation Area, then N on Lick Creek Interpretive Auto Tour toward Lost Horse Creek; camp just past the Lick Creek bridge on left side of rd. Free. All year; 14-day limit. No facilities except cfga, no drkg wtr. Hiking, fishing.

Magruder Crossing   FREE
Bitterroot National Forest
4.1 mi S of Darby on US 93; 14.3 mi SW on West Fork Rd (CR 473); 37 mi W on Nez Perce Rd (FR 468). Free. All year; 14-day limit. 6 sites; 30-ft RV limit. Tbls, toilet, cfga, no drkg wtr. Fishing, horseback riding.

Observation Point　　　　　　　　　　FREE
Bitterroot National Forest
4.1 mi S of Darby on US 93; 14.3 mi S on West Fork Rd;
35 mi W on FR 468 (Nez Perce Rd, becoming Magruder
Corridor); 11.3 mi W on Magruder Corridor Rd to trailhead.
Free. All year; 14-day limit. 4 dispersed sites. Toilet, cfga,
no other facilities, no drkg wtr.

Paradise　　　　　　　　　　　　　FREE
Bitterroot National Forest
4.1 mi S of Darby on US 93; 14.4 mi SW on CR 473; 36.5 mi
W on FR 468; 11.4 mi N on FR 6223. All year; 14-day limit.
11 sites (RVs under 26 ft). Tbls, toilets, cfga, firewood, no
drkg wtr. Elev 3200 ft; 6 acres. Scenic. Whitewater float
trips down Selway River in June.

Raven Creek　　　　　　　　　　　FREE
Bitterroot National Forest
4.1 mi S of Darby on US 93; 14.4 mi SW on CR 473; 36.5
mi W on FR 468; 2.6 mi N on FR 6223. Free. 6/15-11/26;
14-day limit. 2 sites; 25-ft RV limit. Tbls, toilets, cfga, no
drkg wtr. Hiking; fishing. Elev 3800 ft; 1 acre. Mountains.
Dense forest. Raven Creek. In Selway Canyon.

Rock Creek Horse Camp　　　　　　　$8
Lake Como Recreation Area
Bitterroot National Forest
5 mi N of Darby on US 93; 1 mi SW on CR 550; 2 mi W on
forest rd. $8. Fee includes $4 for daily vehicle pass. 5/15-
9/15; 14-day limit. 11 sites (40-ft RV limit). Tbls, toilets,
cfga, no drkg wtr. Hitch rails, feed troughs. Fishing, hiking,
bridle trails, boating(l).

Rombo　　　　　　　　　　　　　$8
Bitterroot National Forest
4 mi S of Darby on US 93; 18 mi SW on CR 473; at West
Fork of Bitterroot River. $8 during MD-LD; no fees, wtr or
services off-season; 14-day limit. 15 sites (30-ft RV limit).
Tbls, toilets, cfga, drkg wtr. Fishing, hunting, hiking. Elev
4400 ft; 6 acres. Handicap toilet facilities.

Sam T. Billings Memorial　　　　　　FREE
Bitterroot National Forest
4 mi S of Darby on US 93; 13 mi SW on CR 473; 1 mi NW
on FR 5631. Free. All year; 14-day limit. 12 sites (30-ft RV
limit). Tbls, toilets, cfga, no drkg wtr. Hunting, fishing,
horseback riding, picnic area. Elev 4503 ft; 8 acres. Sel-
way/Bitterroot Wilderness Takeoff, half mi. Scenic.

Schumaker　　　　　　　　　　　FREE
Bitterroot National Forest
7.3 mi N of Darby on US 93; 2 mi W on CR 76; 16 mi W
on FR 429; 2.4 mi N on FR 5605. Free. 7/15-9/15; 14-day
limit. 16 sites; 55-ft RV limit. Tbls, toilets, cfga, no drkg
wtr. Fishing(1 mi); boating(l-1 mi). Elev 6600 ft. At Twin
Lakes. Access to Selway-Bitterroot Wilderness (1 mi,
unsurfaced rd).

Slate Creek　　　　　　　　　　　FREE
Bitterroot National Forest
4.1 mi S of Darby on US 93; 21.6 mi S on CR 473; 2 mi S
on CR 96. Free. Elev 4800 ft. 6/25-9/6; 10-day limit. 12
sites on 6 acres RV-Limit 30 ft. Tbls, toilets, cfga, no drkg
wtr. Fishing; boating(ld); waterskiing(1 mi). Adjacent to
700-acre Painted Rocks Lake on W fork of Bitterroot River.

Three Frogs Campground　　　　　　$8
Lake Como Recreation Area
Bitterroot National Forest
5 mi N of Darby on US 93; 1 mi SW on CR 550; follow signs.
$8 during MD-LD; free rest of year; 14-day limit. 16 small
RV sites (30-ft RV limit). Tbls, toilets, cfga, drkg wtr. Water
system may be down due to presence of bacteria contact
ranger station @406-821-3913. Boating(l), fishing, hiking,
cross-country skiing; no wtr during free period. Newly
reconstructed.

DE BORGIA
Cabin City Campground　　　　　　　$7
Lolo National Forest
3 mi SE of DeBorgia on I-90 (exit 22 at Henderson); 2.5 mi
NE on Camel's Hump Rd; qtr mi N on FR 353 (Twelvemile
Creek Rd). $7. MD-LD; 14-day limit. 24 sites (32-ft RV
limit). Tbls, toilets, cfga, drkg wtr. Fishing in Twelvemile
Creek, self-guided nature trail, beaver dams in area. Elev
3200 ft; 8 acres.

DEER LODGE
Powell County Fairgrounds　　　　　　$5
N end of Deer Lodge at 422 Fairgrounds Rd. $5 dry camp-
ing, $15 elec. Tbls, flush toilets, showers, cfga, drkg wtr.

Orofino Campground　　　　　　　FREE
Deerlodge National Forest
13 mi SE of Deer Lodge on FR 82 (Boulder Basin Rd) via
Champion Pass. Free. About 6/20-9/15; 16-day limit. 10
sites (RVs under 23 ft). Tbls, toilets, cfga, firewood, drkg
wtr, no trash service. Hiking, horseback riding. Elev 6500
ft; 3 acres.

DILLON
Barretts Park　　　　　　　　　　FREE
Clark Canyon Reservoir
Bureau of Reclamation
5 mi S of Dillon on I-15. Free. All year; 14-day limit. Prim-
itive undesignated camping area. Toilets, drkg wtr, cfga.
Fishing, boating (primitive launch). Concession nearby
with gasoline, supplies, fee campground, marina.

Beaverhead　　　　　　　　　　　FREE
Clark Canyon Reservoir
Bureau of Reclamation
S of Dillon, at reservoir off I-15. All year; 14-day limit.
Primitive undesignated camping area. Toilets, drkg wtr,

cfga. Fishing, boating (l). Concession nearby with gasoline, supplies, fee campground, marina.

Cameahwait   FREE
Clark Canyon Reservoir
Bureau of Reclamation
20 mi S of Dillon, at reservoir off I-15. Free. All year; 14-day limit. Primitive undesignated camping area. Toilets, drkg wtr, cfga. Fishing, boating. Concession nearby with gasoline, supplies, fee campground, marina.

Cattail Marsh   FREE
Bureau of Reclamation
S of Dillon on I-15 to exit 44 at Clark Canyon; follow Secondary Hwy 324 over the dam; turn right across cattle guard at river fishing access sign. Free. All year; 14-day limit. Tbls, toilets, cfga, drkg wtr. Hiking, fishing, birdwatching. View trout near large spring on W side of hiking trail.

Deadman Gulch   FREE
Bureau of Land Management
Dillon Field Office
55 mi S of Dillon on I-15; W at Dell exit. Free. All year; 14-day limit. Primitive undesignated sites. Gulch

Dinner Station   FREE
Beaverhead National Forest
12 mi N of Dillon on I-15; from Apex exit, 12 mi NW on Birch Creek Road. Free. 5/15-9/15; 16-day limit. 8 sites (16-ft RV limit). Toilets (handicapped facilities), cfga, drkg wtr. Fishing; boating; hiking. Multi-family picnic area can be reserved. Elev 7500 ft; 5 acres.

Fishing Access   FREE
Clark Canyon Reservoir
Bureau of Reclamation
S of Dillon, at reservoir off I-15. Free. All year; 14-day limit. Primitive undesignated camping area. Toilets, drkg wtr, cfga. Fishing, boating (l). Concession nearby with gasoline, supplies, fee campground, marina.

Glen   FREE
Big Hole River State Fishing Access Site
19 mi N of Dillon on I-15 to milepost 85, Glen exit; 6 mi S on frontage rd (stream mile 34.9). Free. All year; 7-day limit. 7 primitive sites on 9.4 acres; 30-ft RV limit. Toilets, cfga, tbls, no drkg wtr. Fishing, boating(l). Difficult access.

Grasshopper $8
Beaverhead National Forest
4 mi S of Dillon on I-15; 22 mi NW on MT 278; 13 mi N on Hwy 73 (Pioneer Mountain Scenic Byway); half mi N on FR 484. Elev 6900 ft. $8. MD-9/15; 16-day limit. 24 sites on 9 acres; 30-ft RV limit. Tbls, cfga, toilets, firewood, piped drkg wtr, no trash service. Horseback riding, fishing, boating(l).

Hap Hawkins   FREE
Clark Canyon Reservoir
Bureau of Reclamation
S of Dillon, at reservoir off I-15. Free. All year; 14-day limit. Primitive undesignated camping area. Toilets, drkg wtr, cfga. Fishing, boating. Concession nearby with gasoline, supplies, fee campground, marina.

Horse Prairie   FREE
Clark Canyon Reservoir
Bureau of Reclamation
S of Dillon, at reservoir off I-15. Free. All year; 14-day limit. Primitive undesignated camping area. Toilets, drkg wtr, cfga. Fishing, boating(l). Concession nearby with gasoline, supplies, fee campground, marina.

Lewis & Clark Camp   FREE
Clark Canyon Reservoir
Bureau of Reclamation
20 mi S of Dillon, at reservoir off I-15. Free. Primitive undesignated camping area. Elec sites $30 ($15 with federal senior pass) Toilets, drkg wtr, cfga. Fishing, boating. Concession nearby with gasoline, supplies, fee campground, marina.

Lonetree   FREE
Clark Canyon Reservoir
Bureau of Reclamation
20 mi S of Dillon, at reservoir off I-15. Free. All year; 14-day limit. Primitive undesignated camping area. Toilets, drkg wtr, cfga. Fishing, boating (primitive ramp). Concession nearby with gasoline, supplies, fee campground, marina.

Price Creek $8
Beaverhead National Forest
2.5 mi S of Dillon on I-15; from exit 58, right on Hwy 278 for 25.2 mi; right on Hwy 73 at Polaris for 16 mi; right on FR 2406 for qtr mi. $8. MD-9/30; 14-day limit. 28 sites; 30-ft RV limit. Tbls, toilets, cfga, drkg wtr, no trash service. Fishing, hiking. No cell phone service in this area.

Reservoir Lake $8
Beaverhead National Forest
19 mi S of Dillon on I-15; 16.8 mi W on MT 324; 10 mi NW on CR 1814; 5 mi N on FR 1813. Elev 7000 ft. $8. 6/1-9/15; 16-day limit. 16 sites up to1 6 ft. Tbls, toilets, cfga, firewood, well drkg wtr, no trash service. Swimming; fishing; boating(ld - no mtrs); horseback riding. Family picnic area can be reserved. Horse loading ramp. No cell phone service.

West Cameahwait   FREE
Clark Canyon Reservoir
Bureau of Reclamation
S of Dillon, at reservoir off I-15. Free. All year; 14-day limit. Primitive undesignated camping area. Toilets, drkg wtr,

cfga. Fishing, boating. Concession nearby with gasoline, supplies, fee campground, marina.

DIVIDE
Dickie Bridge   FREE
Big Hole River Recreation Area
Bureau of Land Management
Butte Field Office
10 mi W of Divide on Hwy 43. Free. All year; 14-day limit. 8 Sutes RVs; 24-ft RV limit. Toilets, cfga, no drkg wtr. Boating, fishing, hiking.

Divide Bridge $10
Big Hole River Recreation Area
Bureau of Land Management
Butte Field Office
2.5 mi W of Divide on SR 43. $6 during 5/15-9/15; free rest of year; 14-day limit. 22 sites 50-ft RV limit) Toilets (handicap-accessible), cfga, drkg wtr. Fishing, boating(l), hiking, backpacking trails. Elev 5400 ft.

Humbug Spires   FREE
Wilderness Study Area
Bureau of Land Management
I-15 S of Divide, Moose Creek exit; 3 mi NE on Moose Creek Rd. Free. All year; Undesignated sites 24-ft RV limit; 14-day limit. Tbls, toilets, no drkg wtr. Backpacking trails. 11,175-acre public lands area.

DRUMMOND
Drummond Campground $10
Municipal Park
From I-90 exit 153, S to Frontage Rd, then E to center of Drummond; S (left) on Old Hwy 10A, following signs for city park; cross bridge over Clark Fork River, then left to park entrance; next to fairground. $10 at 7 non-elec grass sites; 3 pull-through RV sites with wtr/elec, $15 ($75 & $85 weekly; $157 & $210 for 2 weeks; $257 & $325 monthly). 5/15-10/1. Tbls, toilets, cfga, drkg wtr, dump. Horseshoes, playground, fishing. Clark Fork River. Boating(l).

DUPUYER
William Jones   FREE
Memorial City Park
On W edge of town. Free. Primitive camping & picnic areas along Dupuyer Creek. Fishing, canoeing.

EAST GLACIER PARK
Summit Campground $10
Lewis and Clark National Forest
13 mi SW of East Glacier on US 2; adjacent to Glacier National Park. $10. MD-LD; 14-day limit. 17 sites (36-ft RV limit). Tbls, toilets, cfga, drkg wtr, no trash service. Elev 5200 ft. Roosevelt and Slippery Bill Morrison Memorials. Trailhead for Continental Divide National Scenic Trail. Fishing. Snowmobiles okay 7/1-4/1.

EMIGRANT
Dailey Lake State Fishing Access Site $7
1 mi E of Emigrant on Murphy Lane; 4 mi S on CR 540 (E. River Rd); 6 mi S on Six Mile Creek Rd (becoming Dailey Lake Rd); at E shore of lake. $7 for licensed fishermen, others $12; $6 unlicensed MT seniors, $3.50 licensed MT seniors. All year; 7-day limit. 18 sites. Tbls, toilets, cfga, no drkg wtr, fishing pier. Boating(ld), fishing.

ENNIS
Bear Creek FREE
Beaverhead National Forest
10 mi S of Ennis on Hwy 287; 10 mi E on Bear Creek Rd. Free. 6/15-11/30; 16-day limit. 12 sites; 28-ft RV limit. Tbls, toilets, cfga, drkg wtr (spring & summer), no trash service. Hiking, horseback riding. Elev 6350 ft. No cell phone reception.

Ennis $7
Madison River State Fishing Access Site
Qtr mi SE of Ennis on US 287 at Madison River. $7 for licensed fishermen, $12 for others; $6 unlicensed MT seniors, $3.50 licensed MT seniors. 4/1-11/30; 7-day limit. 18 sites (25-ft RV limit). Tbls, toilets, cfga, drkg wtr. Boating(l), fishing. Elev 5406 ft; 76.8 acres. Difficult access.

Meadow Lake   FREE
State Fishing Access Site
6 mi N of Ennis on US 287 to milepost 55; 2 mi E on county rd. Free. All year; 7-day limit. Primitive undesignated sites; 25-ft RV limit. Tbls, toilets, fire restrictions, no drkg wtr. Fishing, boating(l). 5.5 acres.

Palisades Recreation Area $8
Bureau of Land Management
Dillon Field Office
26 mi S of Ennis on US 287; 1 mi W on access rd; on Upper Madison River. $8 during 5/1-12/1; free rest of year but no wtr or services; 14-day limit. 10 sites. Tbls, toilets, cfga, drkg wtr, food storage boxes. Boating(l), fishing, canoeing, rafting.

Riverview $12
Beaverhead National Forest
34 mi S of Ennis on Hwy 287; at the Madison River. $12 for tent sites $14 for RV. during MD-10/15; 16-day limit. 21 sites; 30-ft RV limit. Tbls, toilets, cfga, drkg wtr (spring & summer). Fishing, hiking Elev 6000 ft. No cell phone reception.

Valley Garden $7
Madison River State Fishing Access Site
Half mi S of Ennis on US 287 to milepost 48, 2 mi N on co rd to Madison River (river mile 48.5). $7 for licensed fishermen, $12 for others; $6 unlicensed MT seniors, $3.50 licensed MT seniors. 4/1-11/30; 7-day limit. 8 sites (25-ft

RV limit) on 143 acres. Tbls, toilets, fire restrictions, no drkg wtr. Fishing, boating(l). Moderate access.

Varney Bridge $7
Madison River State Fishing Access Site
9 mi S of Ennis on US 287; 2 mi W on co rd to Madison River (river mile 59.9). $7 for licensed fishermen, $12 for others; $6 unlicensed MT seniors, $3.50 licensed MT seniors. All year; 7-day limit. 8 sites (20-ft RV limit). Tbls, toilets, fire restrictions, no drkg wtr. Boating(l), fishing, hiking. Elev 5400 ft; 220 acres. Easy access.

EUREKA
Big Therriault Lake $5
Kootenai National Forest
7 mi SE of Eureka on US 93; 3.2 mi NE on CR 114; 10.6 mi NE on FR 114; 12 mi W on FR 319; 16 S on graded dirt Therriault Lakes Rd 319 (4 mi S of Canadian border). $5 during 7/1-9/10; free rest of season (without wtr), but snowed in about 12/15-5/30); 14-day limit. 10 sites on 5 acres (32-ft RV limit). Tbls, toilets, cfga, drkg wtr. Boating (small boat launch); fishing; hiking. Scenic. Trailhead to Ten Lakes Scenic Area (1.5 mi). Elev 5700 ft.

North Dickey Lake $10
Kootenai National Forest
13 mi SE of Eureka on US 93; 0.1 mi on access rd. $10. 4/15-9/30 (free but no wtr or services before MD & after LD); 14-day limit. 25 sites (32-ft RV limit). Tbls, toilets, cfga, drkg wtr. Swimming beach, fishing. Elev 4483 ft; 8 acres.

Riverside City Park $10
From downtown Eureka at 3rd St, 3 blocks S on US 93; right on Dewey Ave to park; at shore of Tobacco River. $5 at RV/tent sites. All year. Tbls, toilets, cfga, drkg wtr, showers, dump.

Rocky Gorge $9
Kootenai National Forest
24 mi SW of Eureka on SR 37; at Lake Koocanusa. $9 ($12 Canadian) during 5/15-9/15; free rest of year when accessible, but no wtr or services; 14-day limit. 60 sites; 32-ft RV limit. Tbls, toilets, cfga, drkg wtr. Fishing, boating(l), hiking trails, cross-country & downhill skiing, water skiing. Elev 2470 ft; 25 acres.

FISHTAIL
Emerald Lake $9
Custer National Forest
1 mi W of Fishtail on CR 419; 6 mi SW on CR 425 (West Rosebud Rd); 12 mi S on rutted FR 72. $9 during MD-LD; 14-day limit. Free off-season, weather permitting, but no wtr or services. 32 sites; 30-ft RV limit. Tbls, toilets, cfga, drkg wtr. Fishing (rainbow trout), boating (no mtrs), hiking. Elev 6400 ft.

Pine Grove $9
Custer National Forest
1 mi W of Fishtail on CR 419; 6 mi SW on CR 426; 8 mi S on rough FR 72. $9 during MD-9/15; 10-day limit. Free off-season, weather permitting, but no wtr or services. 46 sites, including large group site; 30-ft RV limit. Tbls, toilets, cfga, drkg wtr. Along West Rosebud Creek. Fishing, hiking trail.

FORSYTH
Rosebud County Fairgrounds $10
From I-94 exit 95 at Forsyth, N across railroad tracks, then left on Main St; right on 15th Ave to 4-H campground or on 16th Ave to main gate. $10 for primitive sites at 4-H area, $20 elec/wtr sites. Tbls, flush toilets, cfga, drkg wtr.

FORT BENTON
Coal Banks Landing FREE
Missouri River Waterway
Bureau of Land Management
Lewistown Field Office
N of Fort Benton, milepost 67, on US 87; 8 mi S on co rd, following signs. Free. 5/1-10/1; 14-day limit. 5 sites; 24-ft RV limit. Toilets, tbls, cfga, drkg wtr (5/1-10/31). Boating(l), fishing.

FORT PECK
Bonetrail Recreation Area FREE
Fort Peck Lake
Corps of Engineers
From Fort Peck, about 3 mi NW on SR 24; left (W) for 60 mi on Maxness Rd, becoming gravel Willow Creek Rd (impassable when wet; dirt last 30 mi); at N shore of lake. All year; 14-day limit. 6 primitive sites (16-ft RV limit). Toilets, cfga, no drkg wtr, picnic shelter. Boating(l), fishing, swimming. Nearest dump station, 60 mi.

Downstream Campground $9
Fort Peck lake
Corps of Engineers
From Fort Peck, 1 mi E on Judith Rd; W of spillway below dam on Missouri River. $9 with federal senior pass, base at 62 elec sites for 30-amp; others pay $18 base, $20 for 50-amp ($10 with senior pass). No wtr hookups. Group camping area, $184. About 4/25-10/14; 14-day limit. RV limit in excess of 65 ft. Tbls, flush toilets, showers, cfga, drkg wtr, dump, fish cleaning station, interpretive center, playground. Boating(l), hiking trails, fishing pond, interpretive trail.

Duck Creek Recreation Area FREE
Fort Peck Lake
Corps of Engineers
From Fort Peck at W end of dam on SR 24, 4 mi S following signs on paved rd to park. Free. All year; 14-day limit. 9 primitive sites; 40-ft RV limit. Toilets, cfga, no drkg wtr, picnic shelter. Boating(l), fishing.

Flat Lake Recreation Area   FREE
Fort Peck Lake
Corps of Engineers
From Fort Peck, 5.7 mi E on SR 24. Free. All year; 14-day limit. 3 primitive sites. Toilets, tbls, cfga, no drkg wtr. Boating(l), fishing. Nearest dump station 6 mi.

Floodplain Recreation Area   FREE
Fort Peck Lake
Corps of Engineers
From Fort Peck, N on SR 117 (Yellowstone Rd) near jct with Judith Rd; on the right just before C.M. Russell National Wildlife Refuge office. Free. All year; 14-day limit. 5 primitive sites; 50-ft RV limit. Tbls, toilets, cfga, drkg wtr. Boating(l), fishing.

McGuire Creek   FREE
Fort Peck Lake
Corps of Engineers
From dam at Fort Peck, 37 mi SE on SR 24; about 6 mi W on access rd; at W side of McGuire Creek arm of lake. Free. All year; 14-day limit. 10 primitive sites (16-ft RV limit). Toilets, cfga, no drkg wtr. Boating(l - primitive), fishing. Nearest dump station 45 mi.

Nelson Creek   FREE
Fort Peck Lake
Corps of Engineers
From dam at Ft. Peck, 44 mi SE on SR 24; 7 mi W on all-weather gravel Nelson Creek Rd, following signs; at tip of Big Dry arm of lake within Hell Creek Geological Formation, called the badlands. Free. All year; 14-day limit. 16 primitive sites (40-ft RV limit). Tbls, toilets, cfga, drkg wtr, fishing pier, picnic shelter. Fishing, boating(l). Nearest dump station 45 mi.

Rock Creek   FREE
Fort Peck Lake
State Fishing Access Site
30 mi S of Fort Peck on SR 24; 7 mi W on county rd; at Fort Peck Lake. Free. All year; 7-day limit. Primitive undesignated sites. Tbls, toilets, fire restrictions, no drkg wtr, fish cleaning station. Boating(l), fishing. 5 acres. Moderate access.

Roundhouse Point   FREE
Fort Peck Lake
Corps of Engineers
From Ft. Peck, N of dam on SR 117, right following signs. Free. All year; 14-day limit. 3 primitive sites. Toilets, cfga, no drkg wtr, walkway, fishing pier. Boating(l), fishing, swimming. Nearest dump station 2 mi.

The Pines Recreation Area   FREE
Fort Peck Lake
Corps of Engineers
From near Ft. Peck at jct with SR 117, 4 mi W on SR 24; 12

mi SW on all-weather gravel Willow Creek Rd, then 15 mi S on gravel Pines Rd. Free. All year; 14-day limit. 30 primitive sites; 30-ft RV limit. Pit toilets, tbls, cfga, no drkg wtr, fishing pier, fish cleaning station, playground, picnic shelter with elec & grill. Swimming, boating(l), fishing. Limited facilities in winter. 200 acres. Nearest dump station 33 mi.

West End Recreation Area $9
Fort Peck Lake
Corps of Engineers
2 mi off SR 24 on Duck Creek Rd; overlooking lake at W side of dam. $9 with senior pass at 13 elec sites; others pay $18 MD-LD; 14-day limit. Primitive camping may also be availalble. 35-ft RV limit. Flush toilets, cfga, drkg wtr, tbls, showers. Boating(l), fishing, swimming. 350 acres. Nearest dump station 3 mi.

FORTINE
Grave Creek Campground   Free
Kootenai National Forest
3 mi NE of Fortine on US 93, right on CR 114 (Grave Creek Rd) for about 3 mi, right on 7062 (Stoken Road) .6 miles to campground on left. Free. 4 sites, 20' RV-Limit. Toilets, tbls CFGA. Fishing Elev 3022 Ft.

Little Therriault Lake $5
Kootenai National Forest
2.8 mi NW of Fortine on US 93 to milepost 169.34; 3.2 mi NE on CR 114 (Grave Creek Rd); 13.2 mi W on FR 319; veer right (S) on FR 7085 for 0.71 mi. $5 ($7 Canadian) during about 6/1-LD; free rest of year when accessible, but no wtr; 14-day limit. 6 sites (32-ft RV limit). Tbls, toilets, cfga, firewood, drkg wtr. Boating (hand launch); horseback riding; fishing(d); hiking. Elev 5520 ft. Trailhead to Ten Lakes Scenic Area(1 mi).

GALLATIN GATEWAY
Spire Rock Campground $11
Gallatin National Forest
11.4 mi S of Gallatin Gateway on US 191; 3.3 mi E on FR 1321 (Squaw Creek Rd); at Squaw Creek. $11. 5/21-9/15; 16-day limit. 18 sites up to 50 ft. Tbls, toilets, cfga, no drkg wtr. Fishing. Elev 5600 ft; 5 acres.

GARDINER
Bear Creek Campground   FREE
Gallatin National Forest
5 mi NE of Gardiner on Jardine Rd; 5.5 mi NE on Bear Creek Rd (FR 493 at Upper Bear Creek. Free. 6/15-10/31; 16-day limit. 31 dispersed primitive sites; 21-ft RV limit on access rd. Tbls, toilets, cfga, no drkg wtr or trash service. Hiking, fishing, horseback riding, hunting.

Canyon Campground $7
Gallatin National Forest
18 mi N of Gardiner on US 89; at Yellowstone River. $7. All year; 16-day limit. 18 sites; 48-ft RV limit. Tbls, toilets,

cfga, no drkg wtr, no trash service. Fishing, boating. Less than 20 mi from Yellowstone NP. Boat ramp at nearby Yankee Jim Canyon.

Carbella Recreation Site FREE
Bureau of Land Management
Butte Field Office
20 mi N of Gardiner on US 89; 1 mi W at Miner on Tom Miner Rd. Free. All year; 14-day limit. 10 sites (RVs under 35 ft). Tbls, toilets, cfga, no drkg wtr. Boating (primitive launch), fishing.

Eagle Creek Campground $7
Gallatin National Forest
3 mi NE of Gardiner on FR 493 (Jardine Rd); along Yellowstone River. $7. All year; 14-day limit. 16 sites up to 40 ft. Cfga, tbls, toilets, corral, horse facilities, no drkg wtr or trash service. Fishing, hiking horseback riding. 2 mi from Yellowstone NP. Elev 6200 ft.

Timber Camp FREE
Gallatin National Forest
5 mi NE of Gardiner on Jardine Rd; 4 mi NE on FR 493; at Upper Bear Creek (4 mi NE of Jardine). Free. 6/15-10/31; 16-day limit. Dispersed primitive sites between Yellowstone NP and the Absaroka-Beartooth Wilderness; 35-foot RV limit. Toilets, cfga, no drkg wtr. Fishing, hiking, horseback riding.

Tom Miner Campground $7
Gallatin National Forest
16 mi NW of Gardiner on US 89; 12 mi SW on CR 63; 3.5 mi SW on FR 63. $7. 6/1-10/31; 16-day limit. 16 sites (35-ft RV limit). Tbls, toilets, cfga, drkg wtr, no trash service. Petrified forest, hiking, fishing. Elev 6640 ft. Near the remote NW corner of Yellowstone NP.

GLENDIVE
Intake Dam $7
Lower Yellowstone River State Fishing Access Site
16 mi N of Glendive on SR 16; 3 mi S on county rd; difficult access. $7 for licensed fishermen, $12 for others; $6 unlicensed MT seniors, $3.50 licensed MT seniors. All year; 7-day limit. 15 primitive sites in open area. Tbls, toilets, cfga, drkg wtr (except 10/1-5/5). Fishing, boating(l). 93 acres.

Jaycee West Municipal Park FREE
Glendive exit from I-94, to town; at 100 W Towne St. Free. 5/1-10/1; 2-day limit. 20 sites (RVs under 25 ft). Pool, wading pool, 4 tennis courts, playground, no drkg wtr. Grocery, cafe nearby. Boating(l) nearby. Quiet, next to Yellowstone River.

GREYCLIFF
Pelican FREE
Upper Yellowstone River State Fishing Access Site
From I-90 exit 392 to North Frontage Rd, then 12.2 mi W;

0.3 mi N on Lower Sweet Grass Rd; at Yellowstone River. Free. All year; 7-day limit. 3 primitive sites. Toilet, fire restrictions, no drkg wtr. Boating(l), fishing.

HAMILTON
Black Bear FREE
Bitterroot National Forest
3 mi S of Hamilton on US 93; 12.9 mi E on MT 38; at Skalkaho Creek. Free. 6/1-9/15; 14-day limit. 6 sites (50-ft RV limit). Tbls, toilets, cfga, firewood, no drkg wtr. Hunting, hiking, fishing.

Blodgett Campground FREE
Bitterroot National Forest
5 mi NW of Hamilton. 5/15-9/15; 5-day limit. 7 sites (45-ft RV limit). Tbls, toilets, cfga, no drkg wtr. Fishing, swimming, rock climbing at Blodgett Canyon.

Hannon Memorial $7
Bitterroot River State Fishing Access Site
20 mi S of Hamilton on Hwy 93 to milepost 27 (stream mile 81.8). $7 for licensed fishermen, others pay $12; $6 unlicensed MT seniors, $3.50 licensed MT seniors. All year; 7-day limit. 5 primitive sites on 47 acres; 25-ft RV limit. Toilet, cfga, tbls, no drkg wtr. Boating(l), fishing. One of two areas; second is day use only.

HARLOWTON
Chief Joseph City Park $12
From jct with US 191, 6 blocks E on US 12; right on B Ave NW into park, following signs. $12.00 for tent sites, $14 for RV sites with no elec; $20 with elec. 4/1-10/31. 8 RV sites; unlimited tent camping. Tbls, flush toilets, cfga, drkg wtr, no showers. Hiking trails, fishing pond, picnic shelters, playground. Dump avaialble 5 blocks in Harlowton.

Deadman's Basin Reservoir FREE
State Fishing Access Site
20 mi E of Harlowton on US 12 to milepost 120; 1 mi N on co rd. Free. All year; 7-day limit. Undesignated sites. Tbls, toilets, fire restrictions, no drkg wtr. Boating (l), fishing. 101 acres. Difficult access, but popular site.

Selkirk FREE
Musselshell River State Fishing Access Site
19 mi W of Harlowton on Hwy 13; at Musselshell River (river mile 338.7). Free. All year; 7-day limit. 6 sites on 265 acres. Tbls, toilets, fire restrictions, no drkg wtr. Fishing, boating (primitive launch). Moderate access.

HARRISON
Potosi FREE
Beaverhead National Forest
7 mi W of Harrison on Pony Rd; at Pony, go 10 mi S on South Willow Creek Rd. Free. MD-9/15; 16-day limit. 15 sites (22-ft RV limit). Tbls, toilets, cfga, firewood, drkg wtr,

no trash service. Horseback riding; fishing. Elev 6200 ft; 3 acres. Scenic. South Willow Creek drainage. Stream. No cell phone reception.

HAVRE (51)

Bearpaw Lake $7
State Fishing Access Site
21mi S of Havre on Hwy 234; at Beaver Creek county Park. $7 for licensed fishermen; others pay $12; $6 unlicensed MT seniors, $3.50 licensed MT seniors. All year; 7-day limit. Toilets, tbls, cfga, no drkg wtr. Primitive sites on 185 acres. Fishing, hiking, boating (no motors of any type), fishing pier. Easy access.

Beaver Creek $10
Hill County Park
From Havre, 10 mi S on Fifth Ave (becoming CR 234), then S on Beaver Creek Rd, following signs. $10 daily or $45 for non-residents of county. All year; 14-day limit. 254 sites. Tbls, toilets, cfga, drkg wtr, dump, rec room, dump. Boating(l), fishing, horseback riding & hiking trails, swimming, canoeing, winter sports. 2 lakes. 10,000 acres along N slope of Bear Paw Mtns; said to be among the nation's largest county parks. Unable to verify rates for 2017

Fresno Beach   FREE
Fresno Reservoir
Bureau of Reclamation
W of Havre on US 2; 2 mi N on co rd; follow signs to site at reservoir. Free. All year; 14-day limit. Primitive undesignated camping area. Toilets, no drkg wtr, cfga. Fishing, boating(l), swimming.

Fresno Tailwater   FREE
Milk River State Fishing Access Site
11 mi W of Havre on Hwy 2; 1 mi N on Fresno Rd; at Milk River. All year; 7-day limit. 3 primitive sites on Bureau of Reclamation land adjacent to the fishing site. Tbls, toilets, cfga, no drkg wtr, fishing pier. Boating(l), fishing. 35.6 acres.

Kiehns Campground   FREE
Fresno Reservoir
Bureau of Reclamation
W of Havre on US 2; 2 mi N on co rd; follow signs to site at reservoir. Free. All year; 14-day limit. Primitive undesignated camping area. Toilets, no drkg wtr, cfga. Fishing, boating, swimming.

Kremlin Campground   FREE
Fresno Reservoir
Bureau of Reclamation
W of Havre on US 2; 2 mi N on co rd; follow signs to site at reservoir. Free. All year; 14-day limit. Primitive undesignated camping area. Toilets, no drkg wtr, cfga. Fishing, boating, swimming.

River Run Campground   FREE
Fresno Reservoir
Bureau of Reclamation
W of Havre on US 2; 2 mi N on co rd; follow signs to site at reservoir. Free. All year; 14-day limit. Primitive undesignated camping area. Toilets, no drkg wtr, cfga. Fishing, boating, swimming.

HELENA

Canyon Ferry $10
Bureau of Reclamation
Bureau of Land Management
10 mi E of Helena on US 12/287; 8 mi N on CR 284. $10 & $15. Formerly state park; now returned to BOR. 5/1-9/30; 10-day limit. 233 sites at 12 developed camping areas (some free) with 3 commercial marinas, 7 boat docks, 2 boat access areas. Tbls, flush & pit toilets, cfga, drkg wtr. Swimming, boating(), fishing, water skiing. Elev 3800 ft; 9,000 acres.

Chinaman's Gulch Rec. Area $10
Bureau of Reclamation
Bureau of Land Management
9 mi E of Helena, milepost 55, on US 287; 10 mi NE on CR 284. $10. 5/1-9/30; 10-day limit. 45 sites. Flush toilets, tbls, cfga, drkg wtr, dump. Boating(l); fishing; swimming. Elev 3800 ft.

Court Sheriff Recreation Area $7.50
Bureau of Reclamation
Bureau of Land Management
9 mi E of Helena, milepost 55, on US 287; 9 mi NE on CR 284. $7.50 with federal senior pass; others pay $15 5/1-9/30; 10-day limit. 49 sites. Toilets, drkg wtr, tbls, cfga, picnic shelters. Swimming; boating (4WD launch).

Cromwell-Dixon Campground $8
Helena National Forest
17 mi SW of Helena on US 12. $8. MD-9/15; 15-day limit. 15 sites (35-ft RV limit). Toilets, tbls, cfga, drkg wtr. Fishing, hiking trails. Replica Frontier Town nearby. On the continental divide.

Devil's Elbow Recreation Area $7.50
Bureau of Land Management
Butte Field Office
At Helena, from I-15 exit 193 (Cedar St), follow Washington St past airport entrance; right on Canyon Ferry for 0.5 mi; left on York Rd about 12 mi through Lakeside to Devil's Elbow sign; at Hauser Lake. $7.50 with federal senior during 5/15-10/15; others pay $15. Free rest of year but no wtr or services. 45 sites. Tbls, toilets, cfga, drkg wtr, fish cleaning station. Swimming, boating(l), fishing. Non-campers pay $5 day use fee (or $40 seasonal pass).

Fish Hawk $10
Bureau of Reclamation
Bureau of Land Management
9 mi E of Helena on US 287; 8 mi NE on Hwy 284 to Yachat Basin; 1 mi S on West Shore Rd. $10. All year; 10-day limit. Undesignated sites. Tbls, toilets, cfga, no drkg wtr. Fishing, boating, swimming.

Hellgate Recreation Area $10
Bureau of Reclamation
Bureau of Land Management
9 mi E of Helena, milepost 55, on US 287; 18 mi NE on CR 284. $10. All year; 10-day limit. 130 sites. Toilets, drkg wtr, picnic shelters. Boating(l); swimming.

Jo Bonner $10
Bureau of Reclamation
Bureau of Land Management
9 mi E of Helena on US 287; 12 mi NE on Hwy 284. $10. All year; 14-day limit. About 28 undesignated sites (no RV size limit). Tbls, toilets, cfga, drkg wtr. Boating(l), fishing.

Kading Campground $8
Helena National Forest
23.3 mi W on MT 12; 4 mi S on CR 227; 9 mi SW on FR 227; at Little Blackfoot River. $8 during MD-10/15; free rest of year, but no drkg wtr; 15-day limit. 11 sites (30-ft motorhome limit; 16-ft trailer limit). Tbls, toilets, cfga, firewood, piped drkg wtr. Berry picking; fishing; boating; hiking; horseback riding (corral); hunting. Elev 6100 ft.

Moose Creek $5
Helena National Forest
10 mi W of Helena on US 12; 4 mi SW on Rimini Rd; at confluence of Tenmile Creek & Moose Creek. $5. MD-9/15; 14-day limit. 9 sites (32-ft RV limit). Tbls, toilet, cfga, drkg wtr, no trash service. Fishing, hiking trails. Elev 5100 ft; 4 acres.

Overlook FREE
Bureau of Reclamation
Bureau of Land Management
E of Helena, milepost 55, on US 287; NE on CR 284 to yacht basin; 1 mi S. Free. All year; 10-day limit. Undesignated sites. Toilets, no drkg wtr.

Ponderosa Recreation Area $10
Bureau of Reclamation
Bureau of Land Management
9 mi E of Helena, milepost 55, on US 287; 9 mi NE on CR 284. $10. All year; 14-day limit. 49 sites (no RV size limit). Toilets, tbls, cfga, drkg wtr. Boating; swimming.

Riverside Recreation Area $7.50
Bureau of Reclamation
Bureau of Land Management
9 mi E of Helena, milepost 55, on US 287; 9 mi NE on CR 284 to Canyon Ferry Village; 1 mi NW on FR 224 toward power plant. $7.50 with federal senior pass; others pay $15. All year; 14-day limit. 38 sites. Toilets, drkg wtr. Boating(l), fishing.

Vigilante Campground $8
Helena National Forest
E on Custer Ave 1.3 mi from jct with Montana Ave in Helena; bear left at Y onto York Rd for 24.3 mi; at Trout Creek. $8 during MD-9/15; free rest of year but no wtr or services; 14-day limit. 12 sites (16 ft RV lilmit). Tbls, toilets, cfga, drkg wtr, no trash service. Hiking trail, fishing, horseback riding, mountain biking.

White Earth Recreation Area $8
Bureau of Reclamation
Bureau of Land Management
32 mi SE of Helena to Winston, milepost 64, on US 287; 5 mi E on co rd. $8. All year; 14-day limit. 38 sites (no RV size limit). Toilets, drkg wtr. Boating(l), fishing.

White Sandy Recreation Site $7.50
Bureau of Land Management
Butte Field Office
From Lincoln Rd exit of I-15 about 7 mi N of Helena, E to"T" jct, then left (N) on gravel Hauser Dam Rd to White Sandy access at Hauser Lake. $7.50 with federal senior pass; others pay $15 during 5/15-9/30; free off-season, but no wtr or services. 32 sites. Tbls, toilets, cfga, drkg wtr, fish cleaning station, shelters. Hiking trails, boating(ld), fishing. Non-campers pay $5 day use fee.

York Bridge $7
Hauser Reservoir State Fishing Access Site
7 mi N of Helena on I-15; 5 mi E on Secondary 453; 4 mi S on Lake Helena Dr; 5 mi E on York Rd (CR 280); easy access; at Hauser Reservoir. $7 for licensed fishermen, $12 others; $6 unlicensed MT seniors, $3.50 licensed MT seniors. All year; 7-day limit during 30-day period. 14 sites (30-ft RV limit). Tbls, toilets, fire restrictions, drkg wtr. Boating(l), fishing. 10 acres.

HOBSON

Hay Canyon Campground FREE
Lewis and Clark National Forest
12 mi W on MT 239; 11.8 mi SW on co rd; 4.4 mi SW on FR 487. Free. Elev 5300 ft. 6/15-LD; 16-day limit. 7 sites (30-ft RV limit). Tbls, toilets, cfga, firewood, no drkg wtr. Fishing, 4WD activities, hunting, rockhounding for Yogo sapphires.

Indian Hill Campground FREE
Lewis and Clark National Forest
12 mi W of Hobson on MT 239; 11.8 mi SW on co rd; 3.1 mi SW on FR 487; at South Fork of Judith River. Free. 6/15-LD; 14-day limit. 7 sites (20-ft RV limit). Tbls, toilets, cfga, firewood, no drkg wtr. Fishing; horseback riding, rockhounding for Yogo sapphires.

HUNGRY HORSE

Abbot Bay Boat Launch · · · · · · · · · · · · FREE
Flathead National Forest
Half mi E of Hungry Horse on US 2; 5 mi S along E side of Hungry Horse Reservoir on FR 38; about 1 mi W on Abbot Bay Rd (FR 5301). Free camping only before & after 5/15-9/30; 14-day limit. Toilet, cfga, no drkg wtr or trash service. Boating(l), fishing, hiking. Elev 3600 ft. Bay

Beaver Creek · · · · · · · · · · · · FREE
Flathead National Forest
Half mi E of Hungry Horse on US 2, then follow signs for E side of Hungry Horse Reservoir, following FR 38 (Abbot Bay Rd) 54 mi S, then 8.5 mi E on FR 568; at Spotted Bear River. Free. MD-10/1, but open all year if accessible; 14-day limit. 6 sites; 32-ft RV limit. Tbls, toilets, cfga, no drkg wtr, no trash service; no cell phone service. Fishing, hiking, horseback riding, hunting. Stock loading ramp. Food storage requirements.

Canyon Creek Boat Ramp · · · · · · · · · · · · FREE
Flathead National Forest
Half mi E of Hungry Horse on US 2; 26 mi S along E side of Hungry Horse Reservoir off FR 38 (Abbot Bay Rd) on FR 9801A. Free. MD-10/1; 14-day limit. Dispersed primitive camping. Toilet, cfga, no drkg wtr. Fishing, boating(l).

Crossover Boat Ramp · · · · · · · · · · · · FREE
Flathead National Forest
Half Mi E of Hungry Horse on US 2; about 45 mi S along E side of Hungry Horse Reservoir on FR 38. Free. MD-10/1; 14-day limit (maintained 7/1-9/15). Primitive, undeveloped small RV sites near boat launch. Toilets, no drkg wtr or tbls; no cell phone service. Fishing, boating(l). Elev 3600 ft. Food storage requirements.

Doris Creek Campground · · · · · · · · · · · · $11
Flathead National Forest
From U.S. Highway 2 at milepost 144 and follow the W Side of Hungry Horse Reservoir FR 895 across the Hungry Horse Dam, 3 miles south of the Dam. $11 May 13-Sep 24. 16-day limit. 10 sites all over 40ft. Tbls, toilets, cfga, no drkg wtr. Fishing, boating(l), canoeing, beach access.

Devil's Corkscrew Campground · · · · · · · · · · · · FREE
Flathead National Forest
Half mi E of Hungry Horse on US 2; about 37 mi S along E side of Hungry Horse Reservoir on FR 38. Free. MD-10/1; 14-day limit. 4 primitive sites; 43-ft RV limit. Toilet, cfga, no drkg wtr. Boating(l), fishing, hiking, mountain biking. Trapper's grave.

Graves Bay Campground · · · · · · · · · · · · FREE
Flathead National Forest
35 mi SE of Hungry Horse on FR 895; near W shore of

Hungry Horse Reservoir. Free. 6/15-9/30; 14-day limit. 10 sites; 22-ft RV limit. Toilets, cfga, no drkg wtr. Fishing, boating, hiking. Boat access at Lost Johnny Point.

Lakeview Campground · · · · · · · · · · · · FREE
Flathead National Forest
24 mi SE of Hungry Horse on FR 895; near W shore of Hungry Horse Reservoir. Free. 6/15-9/30; 14-day limit. 5 sites (RVs under 23 ft). Tbls, toilets, cfga, firewood, no drkg wtr or trash service. Fishing. Elev 3600 ft. Use boat ramp at Lost Johnny Point.

Lid Creek · · · · · · · · · · · · $12
Flathead National Forest
15 mi SE of Hungry Horse on FR 895; on W shore of Hungry Horse Reservoir. $12 during MD-9/17; free off-season but no wtr or services; 16-day limit. 23 sites (32-ft RV limit). Tbls, toilets, cfga, no drkg wtr or trash service. Boating, swimming, fishing, water skiing, berry picking.

Lost Johnny Campground · · · · · · · · · · · · $6.50
Flathead National Forest
8.5 mi SE of Hungry Horse on FR 895; near W shore of Hungry Horse Reservoir. $6.50 with federal senior pass; $13 during 5/6-9/30; free rest of yr, but no wtr or services; 16-day limit. 5 sites (50-ft RV limit). Tbls, toilets, cfga, drkg wtr, no trash service. Fishing, boating (primitive launch). Elev 3570 ft. 27,750-acre lake.

Lost Johnny Point · · · · · · · · · · · · $7.00
Flathead National Forest
8.5 mi SE of Hungry Horse on FR 895; near W shore of Hungry Horse Lake. $6.50 with federal senior pass; others pay $13 during 5/26-9/24; 16-day limit. 21 sites (40-ft RV limit). Tbls, toilets, cfga, drkg wtr, no trash service. Swimming, fishing, boating(l). Elev 3600 ft; 6 acres.

Peters Creek · · · · · · · · · · · · FREE
Flathead National Forest
Half mi E of Hungry Horse on US 2; about 41 mi S along E side of Hungry Horse Reservoir on FR 38. Free. 5/15-10/1; 14-day limit. 6 sites; 30-ft RV limit. Toilet, cfga, no drkg wtr or trash service; no cell phone service. Fishing, boating, hiking. Elev 3600 ft.

JACKSON

North Van Houten · · · · · · · · · · · · FREE
Beaverhead National Forest
1.5 mi S of Jackson on Hwy 278; 10.5 mi S n Bloody Dick Rd (FR 181). Free. MD-LD; 16-day limit. 3 sites; 20-ft RV limit. Tbls, toilets, cfga, no drkg wtr, no trash service. Fishing, swimming, canoeing.

South Van Houten · · · · · · · · · · · · FREE
Beaverhead National Forest
1.5 mi S of Jackson on Hwy 278; 10 mi S on Bloody Dick Rd (FR 181); on S shore of Van Houten Lake. MD-LD; 16-day

limit. 3 sites; 30-ft RV limit. Tbls, toilets, cfga, no drkg wtr, no trash service. Swimming, fishing, hiking, canoeing.

JORDAN

Devils Creek Recreation Area   FREE
Fort Peck Lake
Corps of Engineers
From Jordan, at jct with SR 200, NW on gravel Brusett Rd, following signs through badlands of Hell Creek Geological Formation to S shore of lake. Free. All year; 14-day limit. 6 primitive sites; 16-ft RV limit. Picnic shelter, pit toilets, cfga, tbls, no drkg wtr. Nearest dump station, 50 mi. Boating(l), fishing.

KALISPELL

Ashley Lake North   FREE
Flathead National Forest
7 mi W of Kalispell on US 2; 7 mi NW on county rd; 5 mi W on FR 912 to first forest campground on N shore of Ashley Lake (just W of the state fishing lake site). Free. MD-9/15; 14-day limit. 5 primitive sites; 25-ft RV limit. Toilet, cfga, no drkg wtr. Boating, fishing.

Lions Bitterroot Camp $8
5 mi N of Marion at 1650 Pleasant Valley Rd. $8. 5/15-9/30. 14 RV sites; no hookups; 35-ft RV limit. Tbls, toilets, cfga, showers, coin laundry. Swimming area, playground.

McGregor Lake $12
Kootenai National Forest
32 mi SW of Kalispell on US 2. $12 during MD-LD; free rest of year when accessible, but no wtr or services; 14-day limit. 27 sites (32-ft RV limit). Tbls, toilets, cfga, drkg wtr. Boating(l), fishing, water skiing, cross-country & downhill skiing, hiking trails. Elev 3900 ft; 10 acres.

LANDUSKY

Montana Gulch $8
Bureau of Land Management
Drive approx 4.5 mi N on SR 376 from its jct with SR 191; turn right on gravel country rd toward Landusky for approx 3 mi; turn left at sign to Montana Gulch Campground; qtr mi on BLM graded rd. $8. 5/1-10/31; 14-day limit. 10 sites. Tbls, toilets, cfga, no drkg wtr. Hiking, mountain climbing, snowmobiling.

LEWISTOWN

Crystal Lake $10
Lewis and Clark National Forest
9 mi W of Lewistown on US 87; 16 mi S on county rd; 8.5 mi S on FR 275. $10. 6/15-LD; 16-day limit. 28 sites; 22-ft RV limit. Tbls, toilets, cfga, drkg wtr. Fishing, hiking, nature trails. Elev 6800 ft. Day use fee.

East Fork Dam Municipal Park   FREE
About 11 mi SE of Lewistown on SR 238 near the US Gypsum plant at Heath. Free. Primitive sites. All year; 14-day

limit. Tbls, toilets, cfga, drkg wtr. Boating(l), fishing.

Jack Pine Flats   FREE
Kootenai National Forest
9 mi SE of Trout Creek on Hwy 200; right on Beaver Creek Rd for about 10 mi (just 3.5 mi from Idaho state line). All year; 14-day limit. Small dispersed camp. Toilet, cfga, no drkg wtr. Hiking, fishing.

James Kipp Recreation Area $12
Bureau of Land Management
Lewiston Field Office
65 mi NE of Lewistown on US 191. $12 without dump use ($6 seniors); $15 with dump use ($10 seniors); $60 seasonal without dump ($30 seniors). All year, but wtr during 4/1-11/15; 14-day limit. 34 sites (15 for groups) plus 1 floater's tent site. Tbls, toilets, cfga, drkg wtr, fish cleaning station, dump ($10 fee), no trash service. Boating(l), fishing, hiking. Public phone.

LIBBY

Alexander Creek   FREE
Lake Koocanusa
Corps of Engineers
From Libby, about 12 mi E on SR 37; 3.5 mi N on Big Bend Rd, becoming gravel FR 228. On W shore of Kootenai River below dam at mouth of Alexander Creek. Free. All year; 14-day limit. 2 primitive sites. Tbls, toilets, cfga, no drkg wtr. Boating(l), fishing.

Barron Creek Boating Site   FREE
Kootenai National Forest
13.6 mi E of Libby on SR 37; 12.4 mi N on FR 228; right on FR 4849 access rd; at W shore of Lake Koocanusa. Free. All year, but serviced 5/15-9/10; 14-day limit. 7 dispersed sites (40-ft RV limit). Tbls, toilets, cfga, no drkg wtr, no trash service. Boating(l), fishing, swimming, canoeing.

Blackwell Flats Campground   FREE
Lake Koocanusa
Corps of Engineers
From Libby, about 12 mi E on SR 37; 3.5 mi N on gravel FR 228; on W side of Kootenai River, 3.5 mi below dam. Free. All year; 14-day limit. 7 primitive sites, some pull-through. Tbls, toilets, cfga, no drkg wtr. Fishing, boating(l).

Downriver Camping Area   FREE
Lake Koocanusa
Corps of Engineers
From Libby, about 14 mi E on SR 37, across David Thompson Bridge over Kootenai River; at E shore of river below bridge. Free. All year; 14-day limit. 2 primitive sites; third site above gravel boat ramp near wildlife ponds. Tbls, cfga, toilets, no drkg wtr. Bridge

Dunn Creek Flats Campground   **FREE**
Lake Koocanusa
Corps of Engineers
From Libby, about 14 mi E on SR 37, across David Thompson Bridge over Kootenai River, then 2 mi N; at E shore of river about 3 mi below dam. Free. All year; 14-day limit. 13 primitive sites, some pull-through. Tbls, toilets, cfga, no drkg wtr, small amphitheater. Fishing, boating(l). Footpath from ramp to wildlife ponds.

Fireman Memorial Municipal Park
W end of city on S side of US 2 at Mahoney Rd beside cemetery & behind chamber of commerce office. $10 for RV sites. MD-10/1; 5-day limit. 15 sites, 28 ft RV limit. Drkg wtr, flush toilets, tbls, dump (donation), shelters, playground.

Howard Lake Campground   **$8**
Kootenai National Forest
12 mi S of Libby on US 2; 14 mi W on FR 231 to camp sign at FR 4779. $8. MD-LD (free but no wtr after LD); 14-day limit. 10 sites; 20-ft RV limit; 3 pull-through. Tbls, toilets, cfga, no drkg wtr, beach. Fishing, swimming, boating(l), winter sports, hiking trails. Cabinet Mountain Wilderness Area 3 mi. Elev 4000 ft. Libby Gold Panning Area nearby.

Lake Creek   **FREE**
Kootenai National Forest
24.7 mi S of Libby on US 2 to milepost 56.7; 6.4 mi SW on FR 231; right on Bramlet Creek Rd (FR 2332) for 0.72 mi. Free. All year; 14-day limit. 4 sites (32-ft RV limit) & 4 dispersed sites. Tbls, toilets, cfga, firewood, piped drkg wtr. Berry picking (huckleberries); fishing (trout). Elev 3400 ft; 9 acres. Nice stream. Scenic. Trailhead to Cabinet Mountain Wilderness Area.

Libby Creek   **FREE**
Recreational Gold Panning Area
Kootenai National Forest
13 mi S of Libby on US 2; 10 mi up Libby Creek Rd (FR 231) to panning area. Free dispersed camping areas. All year; 14-day limit. Toilets, cfga, no drkg wtr, no trash service. Hiking, swimming. Developed Howard Campground is 1 mi south. Gold panning area open for recreational panning. Former site of major gold mining operations.

Loon Lake Campground   **FREE**
Kootenai National Forest
Half mi N of Libby on MT 37; right (N) for 17.9 mi on FR 567; 2.9 mi W on FR 371 (Seventeen Mile Rd). Free. All year; 14-day limit. 4 sites (20-ft RV limit). Tbls, toilet, cfga, no drkg wtr. Boating (hand launch), fishing. Elev 3600 ft.

McGillivray   **$10**
Kootenai National Forest
13.6 mi E of Libby on SR 37; 10 mi N on FR 228; at W side of Lake Koocanusa. $10. MD-LD; 14-day limit. 33 sites (40-ft RV limit). Also group sites. Tbls, toilets, cfga, drkg wtr, fish cleaning station. Boating(l), fishing, water skiing, swimming beach, winter sports, rock climbing, horseshoe pits. Elev 2500 ft; 50 acres.

LIMA

East Creek   **FREE**
Beaverhead National Forest
7.5 mi SW of Lima on CR 179; half mi S on FR 3929; 1.1 mi SE on FR 3930. Free. Elev 6600 ft. 5/15-10/1; 16-day limit. 4 sites (RVs under 17 ft). Tbls, toilets, cfga, firewood, no drkg wtr, no trash service, no cell phone reception. Hiking.

LINCOLN

Aspen Grove   **$8**
Helena National Forest
7.1 mi E of on Lincoln on SR 200; qtr mi SE on FR 1040; near Blackfoot River. $8 (group sites $30). MD-LD; 14-day limit. 20 sites (50 ft RV Limit). Tbls, toilets, cfga, drkg wtr. Fishing, excellent birdwatching along river. Elev 4800 ft; 8 acres.

Copper Creek   **$8**
Helena National Forest
6.5 mi E of Lincoln on SR 200; 8.5 mi NW on FR 330; near Snowbank Lake. $8. MD-LD; 14-day limit. 17 sites (typically 40 ft). Tbls, toilets, cfga, drkg wtr. Fishing, hiking, mountain biking, horseback riding. Trailhead to Scapegoat Wilderness. Bear-safe food storage required. Elev 5300 ft; 3 acres.

Reservoir Lake   **FREE**
Dispersed Camping Area
Helena National Forest
1 mi W of Lincoln on SR 200; 9 mi N on FR 4106. Free. 6/15-9/15; 14-day limit. Primitive undeveloped sites; 16-ft RV limit. Tbls, toilets, cfga, no drkg wtr; some equestrian facilities. Boating(l), fishing, hiking trail.

LIVINGSTON

Carbella Recreation Site   **FREE**
Bureau of Land Management
Butte Field Office
34 mi S of Livingston on US 89; right on Tom Miner Rd about 100 yds, then right to site; at Upper Yellowstone River. Free. All year; 14-day limit. Primitive camping, undesignated sites. Tbls, toilets, cfga, no drkg wtr. Boating(l), fishing.

Loch Leven   **$7**
Upper Yellowstone River State Fishing Access Site
9 mi S of Livingston on US 89 to milepost 44; 2 mi E & 4 mi S on CR 540; at Yellowstone River $7 for licensed fishermen, $12 for others; $6 unlicensed MT seniors, $3.50 licensed MT seniors. All year; 7-day limit. 10 sites (no RV size limit). Tbls, toilets, cfga, drkg wtr. Boating(l), fishing. Good access. 76 acres. Possible fire restrictions.

Mallard's Rest $7
Upper Yellowstone River State Fishing Access Site
13 mi S of Livingston on US 89 to milepost 42; at Yellowstone River. $7 for licensed fishermen, $12 for others; $6 unlicensed MT seniors, $3.50 licensed MT seniors. All year; 7-day limit. 8 primitive sites; 30-ft RV limit. Tblets, cfga, drkg wtr. Boating (l), fishing. Moderate access; steep rd into site. Possible fire restrictions.

Paradise   FREE
Upper Yellowstone River State Fishing Access Site
9 mi S of Livingston on US 89 to milepost 44; 2 mi E, then 4.5 i S on Secondary Hwy 540; at Yellowstone River. Free. All year; 7-day limit. 3 primitive sites on 2.5 acres; 20-ft RV limit. Toilet, cfga, tbls, no drkg wtr. Boating(l), fishing. Difficult access. Possible Fire Restrictions.

Pine Creek $7.50
Gallatin National Forest
9 mi S of Livingston on US 89; 2 mi W on CR 540; 2.5 mi W on FR 202 (narrow, steep). $7 with federal senior pass; others pay $15. MD-LD; 16-day limit. Closed to vehicles Dec-May to protect wildlife habitat. 25 sites; 45-ft RV limit. Group sites available. Tbls, toilets, cfga, drkg wtr. Fishing (brook trout), hiking, nature trails. Trailhead for Absaroka-Beartooth Wilderness. Elev 6000 ft; 25 acres.

Shields River   FREE
Gallatin National Forest
28 mi N of Livingston on US 89 to Wilsall; NE on Shields River Rd 24 mi. Free. MD-9/30; 14-day limit. About 4 primitive dispersed sites; 22-ft RV limit. Tbls, toilets, cfga, no drkg wtr, no trash service. Hiking, fishing.

Snowbank $7.50
Gallatin National Forest
15 mi S of Livingston on US 89; 12 mi SE on CR 486 (Mill Creek Rd); at Mill Creek. $7.50 with federal senior pass; others pay $15. MD-LD; 16-day limit. Free in fall until 11/31, but reduced services; closed Dec-May to protect wildlife habitat. 10 sites up to 35 ft. Tbls, toilets, cfga, drkg wtr. Fishing, hiking. Elev 5800 ft; 5 acres.

LOLO

Chief Looking Glass $7
Bitterroot River State Fishing Access Site
6.5 mi S of Lolo on Hwy 93; E on Chief Looking Glass Rd (stream mile 21.4). $7 for licensed fishermen, others pay $12; $6 unlicensed MT seniors, $3.50 licensed seniors. 5/1-11/30; 7-day limit. 17 sites on 13 acres; 28-ft RV limit. Tbls, toilets, cfga, drkg wtr. Boating (no motors), fishing. Canoes & rafts can be hand launched.

Lee Creek $10
Lolo National Forest
26 mi W of Lolo on US 12; at Lee & Lolo Creeks. $10 during MD-9/30; free but no wtr or services until 11/1; 14-day limit. 22 sites (34-ft RV limit). Tbls, toilets, cfga, drkg wtr. Fishing, hiking trails, interpretive trail. Elev 4200 ft; 6 acres. Segment of historic Lolo Trail nearby.

Lolo Creek Campground and Picnic area $10
Lolo National Forest
15 mi W of Lolo on US 12; at Lolo Creek. $10 during 5/15-9/30; free but no wtr or services until 11/1. 17 sites; 30-ft RV limit. Tbls, toilets, cfga, drkg wtr, interpretive site. Fishing, boating

LOLO HOT SPRINGS

Hoodoo Lake   FREE
Clearwater National Forest
11 mi SW of Lolo on US 12; 17 mi S on FR 111 & FR 360; in Idaho. Free. 6/15-9/15 or until inaccessible; 14-day limit. 4 sites. Tbl, toilet, cfga, no drkg wtr. Hiking, horseback riding.

Powell $7
Clearwater National Forest
18 mi W of Lolo Hot Springs on US 12, in Idaho at Lochsa River. $7 with federal senior pass others pay $14 base; $20 with elec ($10 with federal senior pass). MD-10/15; 14-day limit. 39 sites (32-ft RV limit). Tbls, flush toilets, cfga, drkg wtr. Fishing, hiking. Lewis & Clark passed through here on their way to the Pacific. Camp may be open free without wtr until about 11/1.

Wendover $8
Clearwater National Forest
22 mi W of Lolo Hot Springs on US 12, in Idaho at Lochsa River. $7 with federal senior pass others pay $14. MD-LD; 14-day limit. 27 sites (32-ft RV limit). Tbls, toilets, cfga, drkg wtr. Fishing, hiking & bridle trails. Elev 3280 ft.

White Sands $7
Clearwater National Forest
22 mi W of Lolo Hot Springs on US 12; 1 mi S on Elks Summit Rd; in Idaho at Lochsa River. $7 with federal senior pass others pay $14. 6/1-9/15 or until inaccessible; 14-day limit. 7 sites (32-ft RV limit). Tbls, toilets, cfga, drkg wtr. Swimming, fishing, hiking.

Whitehouse $7
Clearwater National Forest
22 mi W of Lolo Hot Springs on US 12 in Idaho at Lochsa River and Whitehouse Pond. $7 with federal senior pass others pay $14. MD-LD; 14-day limit. 13 sites (32-ft RV limit). Tbls, toilets, cfga, drkg wtr. Fishing, hiking, horseback riding. Whitehouse Pond named for a member of the Lewis & Clark expedition; it was noted in his journal. .

MALTA

Camp Creek Recreation Area $10
Bureau of Land Management
Malta Field Office
40 mi SW of Malta on US 191; 7 mi W on county rd. $10. 20

sites (24-ft RV limit). Tbls, toilets, cfga, drkg wtr. Hunting, hiking. 20 acres.

Fourchette Bay FREE
Corps of Engineers
Fort Peck Lake
From Malta at jct with SR-2, 60 mi S on gravel rds (last 20 mi impassable when wet). S of Malta on Hwy 365, then 0.4 mi E; S on Content Rd, through Content; right (S) on Sun Prairie Rd to Reynolds Rd, then S on Reynolds to site. At N shore of Rorchette Creek arm of lake. Free. All year; 14-day limit. 44 primitive sites (20-ft RV limit). Tbls, pit toilets, cfga, no drkg wtr, fishing pier, picnic shelters. Fishing, boating(l), swimming.

Nelson Reservoir FREE
Bureau of Reclamation
State Fishing Access Site
18 mi E of Malta on US 2; 2 mi N on co rd. Free. All year; 7-day limit. About 9 undesignated sites. Tbls, toilets, cfga, drkg wtr, 3 picnic areas. Fishing, boating (l), swimming. Managed by BOR.

Trafton Municipal Park $3
From jct of Hwys 2 & 191, N in Malta to park; at Milk River. $3. All year, but limited facilities in winter; 7-day limit. 25 sites (no RV size limit). Tbls, toilets, cfga, drkg wtr, playground, no showers, dump. Basketball, volleyball, horseshoes, fishing. 6 acres. Also dumps ($) at Westside Conoco & Greens Exxon in town.

MARTIN CITY
Emery Bay Campground $7
Flathead National Forest
6 mi SE of Martin City on FR 38. $7 with federal senior pass during 5/9-9/30; others pay $14; free off-season, but no wtr or services; 16-day limit. 26 sites; 32-ft RV limit. Tbls, toilets, cfga, drkg wtr, no trash service. Boating(l), fishing, swimming.

Murray Bay Campground $7
Flathead National Forest
22 mi SE of Martin City on FR 38; at E side of Hungry Horse Reservoir. $7 with federal senior pass; others pay $14 during 5/5-9/30; free off-season, but no wtr or services; 16-day limit. 20 sites (32-ft RV limit). Tbls, toilets, cfga, drkg wtr, no trash service. Boating(l), fishing, swimming. Elev 3570 ft; 19 acres. Food storage requirements.

Riverside Campground (Boating Site) $12
Flathead National Forest
South on Hwy 2. This road becomes the East Side Reservoir Road. About 20 miles to the campground. $12. 3 sites (2 are dble) renovated in 2014. 5/15-9/18. 50ft RV-limit. No drkg wtr, toilets, CGFA, TBLS no trash service. Fishing, boating(l), wildlife viewing, swimming, food storage locker.

Spotted Bear $10
Flathead National Forest
55 me SE of Martin City on FR 38 (rough rds); at confluence of Spotted Bear River & North Fork of Flathead River. $10 during 5/15-9/30; 14-day limit. 13 sites (32-ft RV limit). Tbls, toilets, cfga, drkg wtr (only MD-LD). Fishing, boating, hiking trails. Elev 3700 ft.

MELROSE
Browne's Bridge FREE
Big Hole River State Fishing Access Site
6 mi S of Melrose on I-15's frontage rd (stream mile 32). Free. All year; 7-day limit. 5 primitive sites on 10.4 acres; 20-ft RV rig limit. Tbls, toilets, fire restrictions, no drkg wtr. Boating(l), fishing. Historic interpretation of bridge. Easy access.

Canyon Creek FREE
Beaverhead National Forest
From S of Melrose on US 91, 10.2 mi W on FR 187; 4.5 mi SE on FR 7401 (poor rds). Free. 6/15-9/15; 16-day limit. 3 sites; 18-ft RV limit. Tbls, toilets, cfga, no drkg wtr, no trash service. Hiking, fishing, horseback riding. Horse loading ramp.

Salmon Fly $7
Big Hole River State Fishing Access Site
I-15 at Melrose, milepost 93; 6 mi W & N on co rd (stream mile 38.3). $7 for licensed fishermen, others pay $12; $6 unlicensed MT seniors, $3.50 licensed MT seniors. All year; 7-day limit. 6 primitive sites on 12 acres. Tbls, toilets, fire restrictions, no drkg wtr. Fishing, boating(l). Difficult access.

MILES CITY
Twelve Mile Dam FREE
Tongue River State Fishing Access Site
12 mi S of Miles City on Hwy 59; 1 mi SW of Tongue River Rd (Hwy 332). Free. All year; 7-day limit. 8 primitive sites; 20-ft RV limit. Toilet, tbls, fire restrictions, no drkg wtr. Boating, fishing.

MISSOULA
Big Pine FREE
Fish Creek State Fishing Access Site
W of Missoula on I-90 at exit 66, then 4.5 mi S on Fish Creek Rd (stream mile 2.5). Free. All year; 7-day limit. 5 primitive sites; 23-ft RV limit due to tight corner on entry rd. Tbls, toilets, cfga, no drkg wtr. Fishing, no boat launch. Difficult access. 19 acres. Site of huge ponderosa pine.

Forest Grove $7
Clark Fork River State Fishing Access Site
W of Missoula on I-90 to Tarkio exit 61; 4 mi W on frontage rd to Clark Fork River (river mile 154.8). $7 for licensed fishermen, $12 for others; $6 unlicensed MT seniors, $3.50 licensed MT seniors. All year; 7-day limit. 4 devel-

oped sites on 5.6 acres; 20-ft RV limit. Tbls, toilets, cfga, no drkg wtr. Boating(l), fishing. Difficult access.

Forks   FREE
West Fork Fish Creek State Fishing Access Site
W of Missoula off I-90 at exit 60, then S & W about 10 mi on Fish Creek Rd. Free. All year; 7-day limit. 5 sites; 25-ft RV limit. Tbls, toilets, cfga, no drkg wtr. Fishing. Difficult access. 5.8 acres.

Kreis Pond   FREE
Lolo National Forest
About 20 mi NW of Missoula on I-90; from Exit 82 at Ninemile, take SR 10 W to Remount Rd; 2.5 mi N to Ninemile Ranger Station, then 3.5 mi NW via Edith Peak & Butler Creek Loop Rds. Free. 4/1-10/31; 14-day limit. 7 sites. Tbls, toilets, cfga, no drkg wtr. Boating, fishing, mountain biking.

MONARCH
Logging Creek $10
Lewis and Clark National Forest
3 mi N of Monarch on MT 89; 10 mi E on FR 839. $10 during MD-9/15; free 9/16-11/30, but no wtr; 14-day limit. 25 sites (typically 50 ft but access rds not suitable fro large RVs). Tbls, toilets, cfga, well drkg wtr, no trash service. Fishing. Elev 4600 ft; 8 acres. Scenic. Access rds not suitable for large RVs.

NEIHART
Aspen Campground $10
Lewis and Clark National Forest
6 mi N of Neihart on US 89; in canyon of Belt Creek. $10 during about MD-10/15; 14-day limit. 6 sites (22-ft RV limit). Tbls, toilet, cfga, drkg wtr, no trash service. Fishing (brook trout), hiking trails. Elev 5200 ft; 5 acres.

Kings Hill Campground $10
Lewis and Clark National Forest
9 mi S of Neihart on US 89. $10 during 6/15-9/15; free but no wtr or services until 11/30. 14-day limit. 18 sites; 22-ft RV limit. Tbls, toilets, cfga, drkg wtr, no trash service. Fishing, biking, hiking trails. Winter snowmobiling, skiing. Elev 8000 ft; 9 acres.

Many Pines Campground $10
Lewis and Clark National Forest
4 mi S of Neihart on US 89; at Belt Creek. $10 during MD-9/15; free 9/15-Thanksgiving weekend but no wtr or services; 14-day limit. 24 sites; 22-ft RV limit. Tbls, toilet, cfga, drkg wtr. Fishing, hiking trails, biking. Elev 6000 ft; 15 acres.

NORRIS
Harrison Lake $7
Willow Creek Reservoir State Fishing Access Site
10 mi N of Norris on US 287 to Harrison; 5 mi E on co rd; at Willow Creek Reservoir. $7 for licensed fishermen, $12 others; $6 unlicensed MT seniors, $3.50 licensed MT seniors. All year; 7-day limit. 15 sites (no RV size limit). Tbls, toilets, cfga, no drkg wtr. Boating (4WD launch), fishing. 39 acres.

Red Mountain Campground $8
Bureau of Land Management
Dillon Field Office
9 mi E of Norris on SR 84; right at Beartrap Canyon Recreation Areas sign to the camp. $8 during 5/1-12/1; free rest of year, but no wtr. All year; 14-day limit. 17 sites (35-ft RV limit). Tbls, toilets, cfga, firewood, store, drkg wtr. Hunting, fishing, hiking, rockhounding, flat boating, mountain climbing. Elev 4485 ft; 20 acres. Madison River. Beartrap Wilderness Area, 3 mi S on BLM rds. Bike trails. High winds & lack of trees make tents inadvisable at times.

NOXON
Bull River Campground $10
Kootenai National Forest
6 mi NW of Noxon on US 200 to milepost 11.2, then 0.7 mi E. $10. Open 4/15-12/1, but wtr & services available only MD-LD (free when water is off); 14-day limit. 26 sites (40-ft RV limit). Also group camping. Tbls, flush & pit toilets, cfga, drkg wtr, fish cleaning station. Hiking, water skiing, boating(l), fishing, swimming. Access to Cabinet Gorge Reservoir. Next to Bull River, near Cabinet Mountains Wilderness and Lake Koocanusa. Bike trails, beach. Elev 2200 ft; 13 acres.

NYE
Woodbine Campground $8.50
Custer National Forest
8 mi SW of Nye on SR 419; at Stillwater River. $8.50 with federal senior pass; others pay $17. About 5/15-9/15; 10-day limit. 44 sites in 3 loops; 40-ft RV limit. Tbls, toilets, cfga, drkg wtr. Fishing, boating (2-hp motor limit) hiking (trail to Woodbine Falls). Horse loading ramp. Elev 5300 ft; 30 acres. Non-campers pay $6 day use fee.

OVANDO
Big Nelson   FREE
Lolo National Forest
8 mi E of Ovando on SR 200; 11 mi NE on FR 500 (North Fork Blackfoot Rd). 6/15-9/15; 14-day limit. 4 sites (RVs under 17 ft). Tbls, toilets, cfga, no drkg wtr. Boating (cartop boats), fishing, hiking trails, picnic area. 3 acres on Coopers Lake. Elev 4500 ft.

Harry Morgan $7
North Fork Blackfoot River State Fishing Access Site
4 mi S of Ovando on SR 272; at North Fork of Blackfoot River. $7 for licensed fishermen, others pay $12; $6 unlicensed MT seniors, $3.50 licensed MT seniors. All year; 7-day limit. 4 primitive sites on 65 acres; 45-ft combined-limit. Tbls, toilets, cfga, no drkg wtr. Boating(l - no mtrs), fishing. Difficult access.

Monture Creek   FREE
Lolo National Forest
8.9 mi N on Monture Rd (FR 89). Free. 6/15-9/30; 14-day limit. 5 site (RVs under 22 ft). Tbls, toilets, cfga, firewood, no drkg wtr. Rockhounding, hiking, fishing, horseback riding. Elev 4100 ft; scenic.

PHILIPSBURG

Cable Mountain $11
Deerlodge National Forest
12.8 mi S of Philipsburg on SR 1; left at "Ski Area" sign for 0.8 mi, then veer left at split onto North Fork Flint Creek Rd & right for qtr mi; at North Fork of Flint Creek. $11. About MD-9/15; 14-day limit. 11 sites (22-ft RV limit). Tbls, toilets, cfga, drkg wtr. Fishing, biking, rockhounding, boating. Elev 6500 ft; 5 acres. Historic. Near Georgetown Lake & Echo Lake.

Copper Creek   FREE
Deerlodge National Forest
6.5 mi S of Philipsburg on SR 1; right on SR 38 (Skalkaho Hwy) for 8.5 mi, then 10 mi S on FR 5106 (Middle Fork Rd); qtr mi on FR 80. Free. 6/15-9/30; 16-day limit. 7 sites (22-ft RV limit). Tbls, toilets, cfga, drkg wtr, no trash service. Fishing, hiking.

Crystal Creek   FREE
Deerlodge National Forest
6.5 mi S of Philipsburg on SR 1; 24.5 mi SW on SR 38 (Skalkaho Hwy), following signs. Free. 6/15-9/30; 16-day limit. 3 sites (RVs under 17 ft). Tbls, toilets, cfga, firewood, no drkg wtr, no trash service, no cell phone reception. Rockhounding, fishing, hiking. Elev 7000 ft; 1 acre. Historic.

East Fork Campground   FREE
Deerlodge National Forest
6 mi S of Philipsburg on SR 1; 6 mi SW on SR 38 (Skalkaho Hwy); 5 mi SE on FR 3; 1 mi SE on FR 9349. Free. 6/15-9/30; 16-day limit. 7 sites (22-ft RV limit). Toilets, cfga, tbls, drkg wtr. Fishing. Elev 6000 ft. Access to Anaconda-Pintlar Wilderness Area. On East Fork Creek.

Flint Creek Campground   FREE
Deerlodge National Forest
7.7 mi S of Philipsburg on SR 1; qtr mi SE on Power House Rd. Free. 5/1-9/30; 16-day limit. 16 sites (RVs under 13 ft). Tbls, toilets, cfga, firewood, no drkg wtr, no trash service. Rockhounding, fishing. Elev 5800 ft; 3 acres. Historic.

Lodgepole Campground $6.50
Deerlodge National Forest
10.7 mi S of Philipsburg on SR 1; left into camp, across hwy from Georgetown Lake. $6.50 with federal senior pass others pay $13.00; free but no wtr or services off-season; 14-day limit; roads not plowed in winter. 31 sites; 32-ft RV limit. Tbls, toilets, cfga, drkg wtr. Fishing,

hiking, water skiing, biking, nature trails, boating(l). Elev 6400 ft; 14 acres.

Philipsburg Bay $7.50
Deerlodge National Forest
9 mi S of Philipsburg on SR 1; 1.5 mi SW on FR 402 following sign; half mi SE on FR 9460; at Georgetown Lake. $7.50 with federal senior pass others pay $15. About MD-9/15 (opening depends on snow conditions); 14-day limit. 69 sites; 32-ft RV limit. Tbls, toilets, cfga, drkg wtr. Water skiing, biking, fishing, swimming, boating(l). Elev 6400 ft; 29 acres.

Piney Campground $7.50
Deerlodge National Forest
9 mi S of Philipsburg on SR 1; 2 mi SW on FR 402; at Georgetown Lake. $7.50 with federal senior pass others pay $15 about 5/20-9/15; 14-day limit; free rest of year, weather permitting, but no wtr or trash service (interior rd not plowed). 48 sites (32-ft RV limit). Tbls, toilets, cfga, drkg wtr. Boating(l), fishing, swimming, water skiing. Elev 6400 ft; 14 acres.

Spillway Campground   FREE
Deerlodge National Forest
6.6 mi S of Philipsburg on SR 1; 6.2 mi SW on SR 38; 5.1 mi SE on FR 672 (East Fork Rd); 0.5 mi S on access rd; at East Fork Reservoir. Free. 5/1-11/1; 14-day limit. 13 sites (22-ft RV limit). Tbls, toilets, cfga, drkg wtr, no trash service. Boating, fishing, swimming.

Stony Campground   FREE
Deerlodge National Forest
From Philipsburg, qtr mi N on SR 1; left on SR 348 for 14.m (pavement ends); right on dirt FR 102 (Rock Creek Rd) for 4.8 mi; left onto FR 241 (Stony Creek Rd) to camp. Free. 4/15-10/30; 14-day limit. 10 sites; 32-ft RV limit. Tbls, toilet, cfga, drkg wtr, no trash service. Fishing, hiking.

PLENTYWOOD

Bolster Dam Campground   FREE
Municipal Park
On N edge of Plentywood. Free, but $10 suggested donation for RVs. All year. 18 back-in RV & tent sites. Tbls, pit toilets, cfga, 30-amp elec, drkg wtr. Boating(l), fishing, canoeing. Dump near town. Elev 2075 ft.

RED LODGE

Basin Campground $8
Custer National Forest
1 mi S of Red Lodge on US 212; 7 mi W on FR 71 (West Fork Rd); at West Fork of Rock Creek near Wild Bill Lake. $8 with federal senior pass; others pay $16. MD-LD; 10-day limit. 30 sites; 30-ft RV limit. Tbls, toilets, cfga, drkg wtr fire wood. Fishing, hiking, mountain biking. Non-campers pay $6 day use fee. Elev 6800 ft. 2-night minimum stay required on weekends.

Bull Springs **FREE**
Rock Creek State Fishing Access Site
5.3 mi N of Red Lodge on Hwy 212; 0.4 mi E on Fox/E.
Bench Rd, then N on Two Mile Bridge Rd. Free. All year;
7-day limit. Tbls, toilets, fire restrictions, no drkg wtr. 1
primitive site on 32 acres. Fishing. Very difficult access.

Cascade Campground **$12**
Custer National Forest
1.5 mi S of Red Lodge on US 212; 9.5 mi W on FR 71 (West
Fork Rd); at West Fork of Rock Creek. $12. 6/1-LD; 10-day
limit. 30 sites; 30-ft RV limit. Tbls, toilets, cfga, drkg wtr
firewood ($5). Fishing, hiking. Elev 7600 ft. On primary
access route into the Absaroka-Beartooth Wilderness.
Non-campers pay $6 day use fee. 2-night minimum stay
required on weekends.

Greenough Lake **$8**
Custer National Forest
12 mi SW of Red Lodge on US 212 (Beartooth Scenic
Byway); 1 mi SW on FR 421 (Rock Creek Rd); at 5-acre
Greenough Lake. $8 with federal senior pass; others
pay $16. MD-LD; 10-day limit. 18 sites; 45-ft RV limit.
Tbls, toilets, cfga, drkg wtr firewood ($5). Fishing, nature
trails. Trail leads to popular fishing area (rainbow trout).
Non-campers pay $6 day use fee. 2-night minimum stay
required on weekends. Elev 7300 ft; 8 acres.

Horsethief Station **FREE**
Rock Creek State Fishing Access Site
5.3 mi N of Red Lodge on Hwy 212; 0.4 mi E on Fox/E.
Bench Rd; 3 mi S on Two Mile Bridge Rd; at Rock Creek.
Free. All year; 7-day limit. 2 primitive sites on 84 acres.
Tbls, toilets, fire restrictions, no drkg wtr. Fishing. Difficult
access. Dump station at local visitor center picnic area,
Hwys 78 & 212.

Limber Pine **$8**
Custer National Forest
12 mi SW of Red Lodge on US 212; 1 mi SW on FR 421
(Rock Creek Rd); at Rock Creek. $8 with federal senior
pass; others pay $16. 5/15-LD; 10-day limit. 13 sites;
45-ft RV limit. Tbls, toilets, cfga, drkg wtr firewood ($5).
Non-campers pay $6 day use fee. Fishing (rainbow trout),
hiking. Elev 7200 ft; 16 acres.

M-K Campground **FREE**
Custer National Forest
12 mi S of Red Lodge on US 212; 3.5 mi SW on FR 421; on
a ridge above Rock Creek. Free. MD-LD; 10-day limit. 10
sites (20-ft RV limit). Tbls, toilets, cfga, firewood, no drkg
wtr, no trash service. Rockhounding; fishing. Elev 7500
ft. Scenic.

Palisades Campground **FREE**
Custer National Forest
1.5 mi S of Red Lodge on US 212; 1 mi W on FR 71; 1.5 mi
W on CR 3010; half mi NW on FR 3010; at Willow Creek.
Free. Elev 6300 ft. MD-LD; 10-day limit. 6 sites (16-ft RV
limit). Tbls, toilets, cfga, no drkg wtr or trash service.
Rockhounding; fishing; horseback riding.

Parkside Campground **$8**
Custer National Forest
12 mi SW of Red Lodge on US 212; half mi SW on FR 421
(Rock Creek Rd). $8 with federal senior pass; others pay
$16 during 5/15-9/30; free rest of year, weather permit-
ting; 10-day limit. 28 sites; 40-ft RV limit. Tbls, toilets,
cfga, drkg wtr. Fishing, hiking. Non-campers pay $6 day
use fee. 2-night minimum stay required on weekends.
Elev 7200 ft.

Ratine Campground **$7.50**
Custer National Forest
8 mi S of Red Lodge on US 212; 3 mi SW on FR 379 (East Side
Rd). MD-LD; $7.50 with federal senior pass others pay $15.
Free rest of year, weather permitting; 10-day limit. 6 sites;
20-ft RV limit; no turn-around for large rigs. Tbls, toilets,
cfga, drkg wtr firewood ($5). Fishing, hiking. Non-campers
pay $6 day use fee. Elev 6836 ft.

Sheridan Campground **$7.50**
Custer National Forest
5 mi SW of Red Lodge on US 212; 2 mi SW on FR 379 (East
Side Rd); at Rock Creek. 5/15-LD; $7.50 with federal senior
pass others pay $15. Free rest of year, weather permitting;
10-day limit. 8 sites; 16-ft RV limit. Tbls, toilets, cfga, drkg
wtr. Non-campers pay $6 day use fee. Fishing, hiking.
Elev 6300 ft.

REXFORD

Camp 32 Campground **FREE**
Kootenai National Forest
2.5 mi S of Rexford on Hwy 37; 2 mi SE on FR 856; 1.5 mi
SW on FR 7182. Free. 4/15-11/15; 14-day limit. 8 sites;
20-ft RV limit. Tbls, toilets, cfga, no drkg wtr. Fishing. On
Pinkham Creek. Pinkham Falls nearby--hike upstream.

Caribou Campground **FREE**
Kootenai National Forest
1 mi SW on MT 37; 20.4 mi W on FR 92; at East Fork Yaak
River at Caribou Creek. Free. 4/15-11/15; 14-day limit. 3
sites; 32-ft RV limit. Tbls, toilets, cfga, firewood, no drkg
wtr or trash service. Fishing, hiking. Elev 3500 ft. Watch
for logging trucks.

Peck Gulch Campground **$9**
Kootenai National Forest
Half mi NE & 16 mi SW of Rexford on SR 37; at Lake Koocanusa. $9 during 5/15-9/15 ($12 Canadian); free earlier
& later, but no wtr or services; 14-day limit. 22 sites (32-
ft RV limit). Tbls, toilets, cfga, drkg wtr (wtr turned off
during free period). Fishing, boating(l), biking, swimming.
Handicapped facilities. Nearby is Stone Hill climbing area.

Rexford Bench Complex $8
Kootenai National Forest
7 mi SW of Rexford on SR 37. $8 base. 6/1-10/1. Base fee for camping at Kamloops Terrace Regular campground, $12; 80 sites open 5/15-9/15; 32-ft RV limit. Tbls, toilets, cfga, drkg wtr, dump ($2 for non-campers), beach. Swimming, boating(l), fishing, water skiing, biking, hiking. Elev 2500 ft; 120 acres.

Tobacco River   FREE
Kootenai National Forest
2 mi E of Rexford on SR 37 to river; half mi W on forest rd; at Tobacco River. Free. All year; 14-day limit. 6 sites; 20-ft RV limit due to rd conditions. Tbls, toilets, cfga, no drkg wtr. Fishing, hiking, boating.

ROSCOE

East Rosebud Lake $9
Custer National Forest
7 mi SW of Roscoe on CR 177; 6 mi SW on FR 177 (East Rosebud Rd). $9 during MD-9/15; 14-day limit. Free 9/16-5/31, but no wtr or trash service. 14 sites (RV limit 20 ft). Tbls, toilets, cfga, piped drkg wtr. Boating(ld); hiking; water skiing; fishing; mountain climbing. Elev 6200 ft; 14 acres. Scenic. Hiking and riding trail into Beartooth Primitive Area; adjacent to East Rosebud Trailhead.

Jimmy Joe Campground   FREE
Custer National Forest
7 mi SW of Roscoe on CR 177; 3 mi SW on FR 177 (East Rosebud Rd. Free. Elev 5600 ft. MD-LD; 10-day limit. 10 sites on 4 acres (RVs under 30 ft). Tbls, toilets, cfga, no drkg wtr or trash service. Rockhounding; fishing. 4 acres.

SAINT MARY

Cut Bank Campground $10
Glacier National Park
15 mi S on US 89; 4 mi W on dirt Cut Bank Rd; at E side of park. $10. MD-LD; 14-day limit (7-day 7/1-8/31). 14 primitive sites (22-ft RV limit; not recommended). Tbls, toilets, cfga, drkg wtr. Hiking, fishing, backpacking. Elev 5500 ft; 2 acres.

St. Mary Lake $11.50
Glacier National Park
1 mi W of St. Mary on Going-to-the-Sun Rd; E side of Glacier NP. $11.59 with federal Senior Pass; others pay $23 during 6/1-9/30; 7-day limit. $10 off-season primitive camping 4/1-5/20 and 9/18-11/1. Free winter camping 11/1-3/30. 148 sites; 3 with 40-ft RV limit, 22 with 35-ft RV limit. Tbls, flush toilets, cfga, drkg wtr, dump. Fishing, hiking (paved trail). Elev 4500 ft; 5 acres.

SAINT REGIS

Cascade Campground $10
Lolo National Forest
16 mi E of St. Regis on SR 135; at Clark Fork River. $10

(group site $14). MD-10/1; 14-day limit. 10 sites (20-ft RV limit). Tbls, toilets, cfga, drkg wtr, boating (hand launch), fishing, hiking trails, swimming. Extra charge for pets. Cascade National Recreation Trail. Elev 2500 ft.

Slowey Campground $10
Lolo National Forest
7 mi SE of St. Regis on I-90 or US 10; 3 mi W on Dry Creek Rd. On Clark Fork River. $10. About MD-LD; 14-day limit. 16 sites plus 10 pull-through RV sites, typically 60 ft. Tbls, toilets, cfga, drkg wtr. Fishing, horseback riding, volleyball, horseshoe pits, sandbox, horse camp facilities. Elev 2800 ft; 14 acres.

SAINT XAVIER

Mallard's Landing   FREE
Bighorn River State Fishing Access Site
5.5 mi N of St. Xavier on Hwy 313, then 1.8 mi W (stream mile 62.9). Free. All year; 7-day limit. 1 primitive site / undesignated camping on 43 acres. Toilet, tbl, fire restrictions, no drkg wtr. Fishing, boating(l).

SEELEY LAKE

Big Larch $10
Lolo National Forest
1.3 mi NW of Seeley Lake on SR 83; half mi W on FR 2199; on E side of lake. $10 during MD-LD; free rest of year, but no drkg wtr or services; 14-day limit. 48 sites; 40-ft RV limit. Tbls, toilets, cfga, drkg wtr, pay phone. Boating(l), fishing, swimming, cross-country ski trails, birdwatching, nature & interpretive trails. Near Bob Marshall Wilderness. Elev 3993 ft; 17 acres.

Harpers Lake $7
State Fishing Access Site
13 mi S of Seeley Lake on SR 83. $7 for licensed fishermen, $12 for others; $6 unlicensed MT seniors, $3.50 licensed MT seniors. All year; 7-day limit. 14 sites; 50-ft combined limit. Tbls, toilets, cfga, no drkg wtr, fishing pier. Fishing, boating (l - no mtrs). Elev 4000 ft; 100 acres.

Hidden Lake   FREE
Lolo National Forest
4 mi S of Seeley Lake on SR 83; 7 mi E on FR 349; 1 mi N on unimproved dirt rd. Free. 6/15-9/15; 14-day limit. 5 primitive sites; no facilities, no drkg wtr. Fishing, swimming. No signs to indicate campsites; be careful not to trespass on private land. Lake

Lake Alva $10
Lolo National Forest
13 mi NW of Seeley Lake on Hwy 83; at N end of Lake Alva. $10 during MD-LD; free rest of year, but no wtr or services; 14-day limit. 39 sites plus 2 small group camping areas (12 vehicles maximum, $25 & $35). Tbls, toilets, cfga, drkg wtr. Boating(concrete launch), fishing, swimming. Reservations accepted for small groups. Elev 4100 ft.

Lake Inez   FREE
Lolo National Forest
9 mi NW of Seeley Lake on SR 83; at N end of Lake Inez.
Free. All year (when snow-free); 14-day limit. 5 primitive
open sites plus group site ($14). Toilet, cfga, tbls, no drkg
wtr, no trash service. Boating(l), fishing, swimming, hiking, water skiing. Elev 4100 ft.

Lakeside Campground $7
Lolo National Forest
10 mi N of Seeley Lake on SR 83; on W side at N end of
Lake Alva. $7 with federal senior pass; others pay $14
during MD-LD; free off-season but no wtr or services. 5
sites plus group site ($14). Tbls, toilet, cfga, drkg wtr, no
trash service. Fishing, boating.

Lindbergh Lake Campground   FREE
Flathead National Forest
18 mi N of Seeley Lake on SR 83; about 4 mi W on FR 79;
at Lindbergh Lake. Free. 6/15-9/15; 14-day limit. 11 sites;
20-ft RV limit. Toilets, cfga, no drkg wtr. Boating(l), fishing, hiking, canoeing, mountain biking, hunting.

Owl Creek Packer Camp   FREE
Flathead National Forest
21 mi N of Seeley Lake on SR 83; about 3.5 mi S on FR 44;
at S side of Holland Lake. Free. 5/15-9/15; 14-day limit. 8
sites. Tbls, toilet, cfga, drkg wtr, corrals. Hiking, horseback riding. Horse feed stations. Beware of grizzly bears.

River Point $10
Lolo National Forest
3 mi S of Seeley Lake on SR 209; 2 mi NW on CR 70; on W
side of lake. $10. MD-LD; 14-day limit. 26 sites, typically
48 ft. Tbls, toilets, cfga, drkg wtr. Swimming, fishing,
canoeing on Clearwater River; boating (l-1 mi), 8 picnic
sites, horseshoes, sand volleyball. Elec 4000 ft; 8 acres.

Seeley Lake $10
Lolo National Forest
.3 mi S of Seeley Lake on SR 83; 3 mi NW on CR 70; on
W side of lake. $10. All year; 14-day limit. 29 sites; 32-ft
RV limit. Tbls, flush toilets, cfga, drkg wtr, pay phone.
Boating(l), swimming, water skiing, fishing. Elev 4000 ft;
11 acres.

SHERIDAN
Cottonwood   FREE
Beaverhead National Forest
10 mi SE of Sheridan on SR 287, then 12 mi S of Alder
on CR 248; 11 mi SE on CR 142; 2 mi S on FR 100. Free.
MD-11/30; 16-day limit. 10 sites (28-ft RV limit). Tbls,
toilets, cfga, no drkg wtr, no trash service, no cell phone
reception. Fishing, hunting.

Mill Creek   FREE
Beaverhead National Forest
7 mi E of Sheridan on Mill Creek Rd. Free. MD-LD; 16-day
limit. 10 sites (RVs under 23 ft). Tbls, toilets, cfga, drkg
wtr, food storage required, no trash service. Hiking.

STANFORD
Dry Wolf Campground $5
Lewis and Clark National Forest
20 mi SW of Stanford on co rd; 6 mi SW on FR 251, following signs; at Dry Wolf Creek. $5. MD-LD; 16-day limit. 26
sites (32-ft RV limit). Tbls, toilets, cfga, drkg wtr, no trash
service. Hiking trails, fishing. Marine fossils in nearby
Bandbox Mtns. Elev 5900 ft. Camp built in 1930 as a
Kiwanis Club project; it was improved in 1937 by the WPA
& by the NFS in the 1960s.

Thain Creek $5
Lewis and Clark National Forest
15 mi N of Stanford on US 87 to Geyser; turn right & follow
signs 25 mi. $5 during MD-LD; free rest of year but no wtr
or services; 14-day limit. 12 sites (22-ft RV limit). Tbls,
toilets, cfga, drkg wtr, no trash service. Fishing, hiking
trails. Elev 4700 ft.

STEVENSVILLE
Charles Waters $10
Bitterroot National Forest
2 mi NW of Stevensville on CR 269; 4 mi N on US 93; 2 mi
W on CR 22; 1 mi W on FR 1316; on Bass Creek. $10 during
MD-9/30; free rest of year, but no wtr or services; 14-day
limit. 26 sites; no RV size limit; 4 pull-through; 1 bicycle
site, 1 double site. Drkg wtr, toilets, cfga, tbls. Handicapped facilities. Hiking trails, fishing, hunting, physical
fitness trail. Historical area at Stevensville (St. Mary's
Mission and Fort Owen, Montana's first white settlement).
Access point to Selway-Bitterroot Wilderness. Elev 3200
ft; 12 acres.

Gold Creek   FREE
Bitterroot National Forest
Half mi S of Stevensville on CR 269; 10.4 mi SE on CR 372;
3.8 mi S on FR 312. Free. 6/1-9/15; 14-day limit. 4 sites;
25-ft RV limit. Tbls, toilets, cfga, firewood, no drkg wtr.
Hiking; fishing; hunting. Elev 4800 ft; 3 acres. Poor rd up
Burnt Fork Creek.

SULA
Crazy Creek $8
Bitterroot National Forest
4.8 mi NW of Sula on US 93; 1 mi SW on CR 100; 3 mi SW
on FR 370; on Warm Spring Creek. $8 during 6/1-9/15; free
rest of yr but no wtr or services; 14-day limit. 7 sites (RVs
under 27 ft); the lower sites are for horse camping with tie
racks, watering trough. Tbls, toilets, cfga, firewood, well
drkg wtr, no trash service. Hiking; fishing. Elev 5000 ft; 9

acres. Trailhead to Warm Springs Area. Upper loop open to use by hunters; lower loop closed to hunters.

Jennings Camp FREE
Bitterroot National Forest
1 mi W of Sula on US 93; 10 mi NE on CR 472. Free. 6/15-9/15; 14-day limit. 4 sites (RVs under 21 ft). Tbls, toilets, cfga, firewood, well drkg wtr. Hunting; hiking; fishing (1 mi). On E Fork of the Bitterroot River.

Martin Creek $10
Bitterroot National Forest
1 mi N of Sula on US 93; 4 mi NE on CR 472; 12 mi NE on FR 80. Elev 5400 ft. $10 during 6/15-9/15; free rest of yr, but no wtr or services; 14-day limit. 7 sites (50-ft RV limit). Tbls, toilets, cfga, firewood, well drkg wtr. Hunting; hiking; fishing (1 mi). On Moose and Martin Creeks.

Spring Gulch $12
Bitterroot National Forest
3 mi NW of Sula on US 93. $12. 5/15-12/1; 14-day limit. 10 sites & 1 biking group site; 50-ft RV limit. Tbls, toilets, cfga, drkg wtr. Fishing, hunting, hiking, swimming.

Warm Springs $8
Bitterroot National Forest
4.7 mi NW on US 93; 1 mi SW on CR 100. $8. 5/1-9/30; 14-day limit. 14 sites; 26-ft RV limit. Tbls, toilets, cfga, drkg wtr, picnic area. Fishing, swimming, hiking. Elev 4400 ft; 7 acres.

SUPERIOR

Quartz Flat $10
Lolo National Forest
10 mi SE of Superior on I-90 (at rest area); most RVs can negotiate tunnel to site. $10. About 5/15-9/30; 14-day limit. 77 sites; 7 pull-through, typically 45-50 ft. Tbls, flush toilets, cfga, drkg wtr. Dump $2 for non-campers. Short walk to Clark Fork River. Self-guided nature trail. Fishing. Elev 2900 ft; 40 acres.

Trout Creek $6
Lolo National Forest
5 mi SE of Superior on SR 269; 3 mi SW on FR 257 (Trout Creek Rd). $6 during MD-LD; free rest of year, but no drkg wtr; 14-day limit. 12 sites (30-ft RV limit). Tbls, toilets, cfga, drkg wtr, no trash service. Fishing, boating(l). 6 acres.

THOMPSON FALLS

Copper King FREE
Lolo National Forest
5 mi E of Thompson Falls on MT 200; 4 mi NE on FR 56 (Thompson River Rd); at Thompson River. Free. 6/1-10/15; 14-day limit. 5 sites (RVs under 16 ft). Tbls, toilets, cfga, no drkg wtr. Fishing. Access rd not suitable for long RVs.

Fishtrap Lake FREE
Lolo National Forest
5 mi E of Thompson Falls on MT 200; 13 mi NE on FR 56; 14.7 mi NW on FR 516; 1.8 mi W on FR 7593. Free. All year; 14-day limit. 13 sites (some pull-through; 32-ft RV limit). Tbls, toilets, cfga, drkg wtr (MD-9/25). Berry picking, rockhounding, boating (ld, qtr mi).

Gold Rush Campground FREE
Lolo National Forest
9 mi S of Thompson Falls on FR 352 (E fork of Dry Creek Rd). Free. All year; 14-day limit. 7 sites (32-ft RV limit). tbls, toilets, cfga, drkg wtr (MD-9/25). Fishing. Motor vehicles not permitted on trails 12/1-5/15 to reduce wildlife disturbance.

West Fork Fishtrap Creek FREE
Lolo National Forest
5 mi E of Thompson Falls on MT 200; 13 mi NE on FR 56 (Thompson River Rd); 15 mi NW on FR 516 (Fishtrap Creek Rd); 2 mi W on FR 6593. Free. All year; 14-day limit. 4 sites (32-ft RV limit). Tbls, toilets, cfga, well drkg wtr (MD-9/25). Fishing, boating(l). Elev 3900 ft.

TOWNSEND

Gipsy Lake Campground $10
Helena National Forest
2 mi E of Townsend on US 12; 10 mi N on SR 284; about 15 mi E on Duck Creek Rd (FR 139); 2 mi S on FR 8961. $10. MD-9/15; 14-day limit. 5 sites; 16-ft RV limit. Toilets, cfga, no drkg wtr, no trash service. Hiking, boating (hand launch), fishing (rainbow trout). Historic gold mines nearby. Lake

Indian Road Recreation Area FREE
Bureau of Reclamation
N of Townsend, milepost 75, on US 287 at bridge. All year, 14-day limit. 25 sites (no RV size limit). Drkg wtr, tbls, toilets, cfga. Boating; boating(l), fishing.

Silos Recreation Area $10
Bureau of Reclamation
Bureau of Land Management
7 mi N of Townsend on US 287, milepost 70; 1 mi E on county rd. $10. All year; 14-day limit. 80 sites. Drkg wtr, shelters, tbls, cfga. Boating(l); fishing;

Skidway Campground $10
Helena National Forest
23 mi E of Townsend on US 12; turn right at milemarker 22; 2 mi S on FR 4042 (paved but tough access). $10. 5/15-10/30; 14-day limit. 13 sites; 35-ft RV limit. Tbls, toilets, cfga, firewood, tank drkg wtr. Fishing, hiking trails. Elev 6000 ft.

Toston Dam   FREE
Bureau of Land Management
Butte Field Office
13 mi S of Townsend on US 287; E to Toston Dam. All year; 14-day limit. 2 locations, with 5-10 sites each, 24-ft RV limit. Tbls, cfga, toilets, no drkg wtr. Boating(l), fishing.

TROUT CREEK

Big Eddy   FREE
Kootenai National Forest
N of Trout Creek on SR 200; on N side of Cabinet Reservoir. Free. All year; 14-day limit. 5 sites; 30-ft RV limit. Tbls, toilets, cfga, no drkg wtr. Boating(l), fishing. Creek

Marten Creek   FREE
Kootenai National Forest
7 mi NW of Trout Creek on Marten Creek Rd. All year; 14-day limit. 6 sites (32-ft RV limit). Tbls, toilets, cfga, no drkg wtr or trash service. Boating(l), fishing, hiking. At Marten Creek Bay on Noxon Reservoir. Creek

North Shore $10
Kootenai National Forest
2.5 mi NW of Trout Creek on SR 200; half mi E on co rd. $10 during MD-LD; free earlier & later, but no wtr or services; 14-day limit. 16 sites (40-ft RV limit, 3 pull-through). Tbls, toilets, cfga, drkg wtr. Swimming; fishing; hiking; horse-back riding; boating(ld). Elev 2200 ft. On N shore of Noxon Rapids Reservoir.

Sylvan Lake   FREE
Kootenai National Forest
1 mi W of Trout Creek on Hwy 200; 17 mi N on FR 154 (Vermilion River Rd). 5/15-10/15; 14-day limit. 5 primitive sites; 32-ft RV limit. Tbls, toilets, cfga, no drkg wtr or trash service. Boating(l), fishing.

Willow Creek   FREE
Kootenai National Forest
19.4 mi E of Trout Creek on FR 154. Free. All year; 14-day limit. 6 sites (40-ft RV limit). Tbls, toilets, cfga, firewood, no drkg wtr. Fishing; hiking; boating(l).

TROY

Bad Medicine $10
Kootenai National Forest
3 mi E on US 2; 18 mi S on SR 56. $10 during MD-LD; free earlier & later, but no wtr or services. 14-day limit. 18 sites (32-ft RV limit). Tbls, toilets, cfga, drkg wtr, 6 picnic sites. Fishing, boating(ld), swimming, hiking trails. Elev 2367 ft; 15 acres.

Dorr Skeels $7
Kootenai National Forest
3 mi SE of Troy on US 2; 12.5 mi S on SR 56; W on FR 1117 to camp; on Bull Lake. $7 during MD-LD; free earlier & later, but no wtr or services; 14-day limit. 2 RV sites, 5 for tents; 32-ft RV limit. Tbls, toilets, cfga, drkg wtr, beach. Fishing, boating(l), water skiing, swimming, biking, water skiing.

Kilbrennen Lake   FREE
Kootenai National Forest
2.7 mi NW of Troy on US 2; 9.8 mi NE on FR 2394. Free. All year; 14-day limit. 7 sites (32-ft RV limit). Tbls, toilet, cfga, no drkg wtr or trash service. Boating(l), fishing.

Pete Creek Campground $7
Kootenai National Forest
9.5 mi NW of Troy on US 2; 12.8 mi NE on SR 508; 14 mi NE on FR 92; at confluence of Yaak River & Pete Creek. $7 ($9 Canadian) during MD-LD; free earlier & later, but no wtr or services; 14-day limit. 13 sites (32-ft RV limit). Tbls, toilets, cfga, drkg wtr. Fishing (trout). Elev 3000 ft; 8 acres.

Red Top Creek   FREE
Kootenai National Forest
10.2 mi NW on US 2; 12.8 mi NE on MT 508; 3 mi N on FR 92; at Yaak River. Free. All year; 14-day limit. 3 sites (32-ft RV limit). Tbls, toilet, cfga, no drkg wtr. Fishing. Watch for logging trucks.

Spar Lake $8
Kootenai National Forest
2.5 mi SE of Troy on US 2; 8 mi S on Lake Creek Rd; 12 mi on Spar Lake RD (FR 384). $8 during MD-LD; free earlier & later, but no wtr or services; 14-day limit. 13 sites; 28-ft RV limit. Tbls, toilets, cfga, drkg wtr. Fishing, boating(l), hiking, biking, ATV activity.

Whitetail Creek Campground $7
Kootenai National Forest
9.5 mi NW of Troy on US 2; 12.8 mi NE on SR 508; 10 mi NE on FR 92; at Yaak River. $7 during MD-LD; free rest of year, but no wtr or services; 14-day limit. 12 sites (32-ft RV limit). Tbls, toilets, cfga, drkg wtr. Fishing, boating, hiking trails, mountain biking. Elev 2913 ft; 8 acres.

Yaak Falls   FREE
Kootenai National Forest
10 mi NW of Troy on US 2; 6.5 mi NE on MT 508. Free. All year; 14-day limit. 7 sites (32-ft RV limit). Tbls, toilet, cfga, firewood, no drkg wtr. Hiking; fishing. Adjacent to scenic Yaak River Falls; easy trail.

Yaak River $10
Kootenai National Forest
7.5 mi NW of Troy on US 2. $10 during MD-LD; free rest of year, but no wtr or services; 14-day limit. 44 sites (7 pull-through); 32-ft RV limit. Tbls, toilets, cfga, drkg wtr. Hiking, fishing, boating, swimming. Yaak & Kootenai Rivers.

TWIN BRIDGES

Notch Bottom   FREE
Big Hole River State Fishing Access Site
4 mi S of Twin Bridges on SR 41; 10 mi W on Biltmore
Rd/Ziegler Hot Springs Rd (stream mile 17.9 of Big Hole
River). Free. All year; 7-day limit. Primitive camping on
12.3 acres; 20-ft RV limit. Toilets, tbls, cfga, no drkg wtr.
Boating(l), fishing. Difficult access; not an all-weather rd.

Ruby Reservoir Recreation Site   FREE
Bureau of Land Management
Dillon Field Office
S of Twin Bridges on SR 287 to Alder; S to E shore of Ruby
River Reservoir. Free. All year; 14-day limit. 10 sites (35-
ft RV limit). Tbls, toilets, no drkg wtr. Boating(l), fishing
(trout), swimming, rockhounding for garnets along shore.

VALIER

Lake Frances City Park $10
2 mi E of Valier just off US 44 on Teton Ave (becoming Lake
Frances Rd). $10 at primitive sites, $20 at 50 sites with
elec; full hookups $35 ($25 off-season). Tbls, toilets, cfga,
drkg wtr, playground, dump, beach, fish cleaning station.
Boating(ld), swimming, fishing, sailing. Dam

WEST GLACIER

Apgar $10
Glacier National Park
2 mi W of West Glacier near park headquarters on Going-
to-the Sun Rd. $10 in-season with federal Senior Pass;
others pay $20. $10 for primitive camping off-season
during 4/1-5/3 and 10/15-11/30; free winter camping
12/1-3/31. 194 sites (40-ft RV limit). Tbls, flush toilets,
cfga, drkg wtr, store, dump. Wtr shut off; self-contained
RVs only during winter. Hiking, fishing, boating(rl), water
skiing. America the Beautiful pass or entry fee.

Avalanche Campground $10
Glacier National Park
NE of West Glacier on Going to the Sun Rd; at Lake McDonald. $10 in-season with federal senior pass; others pay
$20. 6/11-9/6; 7-day limit. 87 sites; 26-ft RV limit. Tbls,
flush toilets, cfga, drkg wtr. Fishing, hiking.

Bowman Lake $7.50
Glacier National Park
32 mi NW of West Glacier on North Fork Rd; 6 mi on dirt
rd. $7.50 in-season with federal Senior Pass; others pay
$15. $10 for primitive camping off-season prior to 5/25 &
after 9/14. All year; 14-day limit (7-day during 7/1-8/31).
48 primitive sites.22-ft RV limit; RVs not recommended.
Tbls, toilets, cfga, drkg wtr. Boating(l), fishing. 5 acres.
America the Beautiful pass or entry fee.

Devil Creek $6.50
Flathead National Forest
45 mi SE of West Glacier on US 2; near Middle Fork of
Flathead River. $6.5 with federal senior pass all others
pay $13.00 during 5/26-9/30; free rest of year, but no wtr
or services; 16-day limit. 12 sites; 40-ft RV limit. Tbls,
toilets, cfga, drkg wtr. Fishing, horseback riding, hiking.
Elev 4360 ft. Between Glacier National Park and Great
Bear Wilderness.

Kintla Lake $7.50
Glacier National Park
47 mi N of West Glacier on North Fork Rd. $7.50 in-season
with federal Senior Pass; others pay $15. $10 off-season
for primitive camping prior to 5/25 & after 9/14. 14-day
limit (7-day 7/1-8/31). 13 sites, 18-ft RV limit, not recommended. Tbls, toilets, cfga, drkg wtr. Boating(l), hiking.

WEST YELLOWSTONE

Baker's Hole Campground $8
Gallatin National Forest
3 mi NW of West Yellowstone on US 191; at Madison River.
$8 base with federal senior pass at 40 non-elec sites;
others pay $16; 33 elec sites $23 ($15 with federal senior
pass). 5/15-9/15; 16-day limit. 73 total sites up to 75 ft.
Tbls, toilets, cfga, drkg wtr, fishing platform. Fishing.

Beaver Creek Campground $7.50
Gallatin National Forest
8 mi N of West Yellowstone on US 191; 17.3 mi W on US
287; at E end of Earthquake Lake. $7.50 with federal
senior pass; others pay $15. 6/10-9/10; 16-day limit. 65
sites; 45-ft RV limit. Tbls, toilets, cfga, drkg wtr. Boat-
ing(l), fishing; boat ramp half mi W on US 287; excellent
birdwatching. Earthquake site. Elev 6400 ft; 9 acres.

Cabin Creek $7.50
Gallatin National Forest
8 mi N of West Yellowstone on US 191; 14 mi W on US
287; on E end of Earthquake Lake along Madison River.
$7.50 with federal senior pass; others pay $15. 16-day
limit. 15 sites (22-ft RV limit). Tbls, toilets, cfga, drkg wtr.
Fishing, boating. Hiking, boating, fishing; boat launch near
Beaver Creek Camp. Excellent birdwatching W of camp.
Elev 6140 ft.

Cherry Creek   FREE
Gallatin National Forest
8 mi W of West Yellowstone on US 20; 6 mi N on Hebgen
Lake Rd; at Hebgen Lake. Free. MD-10/15; 16-day limit.
7 primitive dispersed sites. Toilets, cfga, no drkg wtr, no
trash service. Fishing, mountain biking on old logging
roads winding through forest to the west.

Cliff Point Campground $7.50
Beaverhead National Forest
8 mi N of West Yellowstone on US 191; 27 mi W on US
287; 6 mi SW on FR 241. $7.50 with Federal Senior Pass
others pay $15 during MD-9/15; 14-day limit. 6 sites 16-ft
RV-Limit. Tbls, toilets, cfga, firewood, well drkg wtr.

Hiking; good trout fishing; water skiing; boating (rld-1 mi). Elev 6400 ft. Botanical. Nature trails. Cliff Lake.

Hilltop Campground $7.50
Beaverhead National Forest
8 mi N of West Yellowstone on US 191; 27 mi W on US 287; 6 mi SW on FR 241. $7.50 with Federal Senior Pass others pay $15 5/15-9/15; 16-day limit. 18 sites 22-ft RV Limit. Tbls, toilets, cfga, firewood, piped drkg wtr. Horseback riding; sailing; fishing; water skiing; boating. Elev 6400 ft; 8 acres. Scenic. Botanical. Wade and Cliff Lakes.

Lonesomehurst Campground $8
Gallatin National Forest
8 mi W of West Yellowstone on US 20; 4 mi N on Hebgen Lake Rd; at small arm of 13,000-acre Hebgen Lake. $8 base with federal senior pass; others pay $16. Elec addutuibak $7. 5/15-9/30; 16-day limit. 27 sites; 40-ft RV limit. Tbls, toilets, cfga, drkg wtr, fishing pier. Fishing, swimming, boating, canoeing.

Raynolds' Pass FREE
Madison River State Fishing Access Site
31 mi NW of West Yellowstone on US 287 to milepost 8; half mi S to bridge (river mile 97.7); also walk-in area on E side of US 287. Free. May-Oct; 7-day limit. 6 primitive sites on 162.5 acres; 25-ft RV limit. Tbls, toilets, fire restrictions, no drkg wtr. Boating(l), fishing. Difficult access.

Rainbow Point $8
Gallatin National Forest
5 mi N of West Yellowstone on US 191; 3 mi W on Rainbow Point Rd (FR 6954); 2 mi N on Rainbow Point Rd after intersection. $8 with federal senior pass others pay $16. at 58 non-elec sites, 26 elec sites additional $7.. 5/15-9/30; 16-day limit. Tbls, toilets, cfga, drkg wtr. Fishing, boating(l).

Spring Creek FREE
Gallatin National Forest
8 mi W of West Yellowstone on US 20; N on Hebgen Lake Rd 9 mi; at Hebgen Lake. MD-10/15; 16-day limit. Undeveloped primitive camping area. No facilities except toilet, cfga, no trash service. Fishing, boating.

Wade Lake $7.50
Beaverhead National Forest
8 mi N of West Yellowstone on US 191; 27 mi W on US 287; 6 mi SW on FR 5721. $7.50 with Federal Senior Pass others pay $15 during MD-10/15; 16-day limit. $16 double occupancy. 30 sites 30-ft RV limit. Tbls, toilets, cfga, firewood, piped drkg wtr. Fishing; water skiing; sailing; boating(lr). Elev 6200 ft; 5 acres. Good trout fishing at lake.

WHITEFISH
Sylvia Lake FREE
Flathead National Forest
10 mi N of Whitefish on US 93; 23 mi W on FR 538 & FR 113, then about 3 mi S on FR 538B; near scenic Sylvia Lake. Free. 5/15-11/15; 14-day limit. About 3 very small, primitive undesignated sites; 20-ft RV limit. Toilet, cfga, no drkg wtr, no trash service. Fishing, hiking, biking. Lake

Tally Lake $7.50
Flathead National Forest
6 mi W of Whitefish on US 93; 15 mi W on FR 113. $7.50 with federal senior pass; others pay $15. 5/15-9/30; 16-day limit. 40 sites; 40-ft RV limit. Tbls, toilets, cfga, drkg wtr, dump. Fishing, boating(l), swimming, hiking trails, volleyball court, horseshoe pits. Elev 3400 ft; 23 acres.

Upper Stillwater Lake FREE
Flathead National Forest
23 mi N of Whitefish on US 92; about 1 mi S on FR 10354. Free. 5/6-9/15; 14-day limit. 5 small sites near the lake and Stillwater River. Toilets; 25-ft RV limit. Toilet, cfga, no drkg wtr, no trash service. Boating, fishing, biking. Boat access to river about 1 mi N at state's Spring Creek. Lake

WHITEHALL
Toll Mountain Campground FREE
Deerlodge National Forest
15 mi W of Whitehall on SR 2; 3 m N on FR 240. Free. All year; 14-day limit. 5 sites; 22-ft RV limit. Tbls, toilet, cfga, no drkg wtr, no trash service. Fishing, hiking.

WHITE SULPHUR SPRINGS
Camp Baker Smith River State Park FREE
Smith River State Fishing Access Site
17 mi W of White Sulphur Springs on Hwy 360; 9.6 mi N on Smith River Rd. Free. All year; 14-day limit. Primitive camping on 49 acres. Tbls, toilets, cfga, no drkg wtr. Fishing, boating(l). Put-in point for Smith River floats. Difficult access.

Grasshopper Creek Campground $8
Lewis and Clark National Forest
7 mi E of White Sulphur Springs on US 12; 4.2 mi S on FR 211. $8 Elev 6000 ft. 6/1-10/15; 14-day limit. 12 sites (22-ft RV limit). Tbls, toilets, cfga, firewood, well drkg wtr, no trash service. Fishing, hiking trails. Elev 5700 ft.

Jumping Creek $10
Lewis and Clark National Forest
22 mi NE of White Sulphur Springs on US 89; at jct of Sheep Creek & Jumping Creek. $10 during MD-10/1; free after MD, but no wtr; 14-day limit. 10 sites (22-ft RV limit). Tbls, toilets, cfga, drkg wtr. Fishing, hiking trails. Elev 5700 ft.

Moose Creek $10
Lewis and Clark National Forest
18 mi N of White Sulphur Springs on US 89; 5.5 mi W on
FR 119; 3.2 mi N on FR 204. $10. 6/1-9/15. 6 sites 22-ft RV
limit. Tbls, toilets, cfga, firewood, well drkg wtr. Fishing,
mountain biking, ATV activities, hiking trail.

Richardson Creek   FREE
Lewis and Clark National Forest
7 mi E of White Sulphur Springs on US 12; 5 mi S on FR 211.
Free. Elev 5500 ft. 6/1-10/15; 14-day limit. 3 sites; 16-ft RV
limit. Toilet, cfga, no tbls, no drkg wtr.

Smith River State Park   FREE
Fort Logan State Fishing Access Site
17 mi NW of White Sulphur Springs; 2 mi N on Smith River
Rd. Free. All year; 14-day limit. Primitive undesignated
sites on 215 acres. Tbls, toilets, cfga, no drkg wtr. Fishing. 59-mile river corridor between Camp Baker & Eden
Bridge; float permits by lottery.

Spring Creek $7
Lewis and Clark National Forest
26.3 mi E of White Sulphur Springs on US 12; 4.1 mi N on
FR 274 (Spring Creek Rd); right for qtr mi at campground
sign. $7. MD-12/1; 14-day limit. 10 sites; 22-ft RV limit.
Tbls, toilets, cfga, drkg wtr. Fishing; hiking, bridle & biking
trail. No horses in camp.

WINNETT

Crooked Creek Recreation Area   FREE
Fort Peck Lake
Corps of Engineers
From Winnett, N on all-weather gravel Dovetail Valentine Rd
(also called Drag Ridge Trail); 0.5 mi E on 79 Trail Rd; N (left)
on Crooked Creek Rd to site (signs). Free. All year; 14-day
limit. 20 primitive sites; 25-ft RV limit. Toilets, tbls, cfga,
drkg wtr, boating(l). Marina nearby.

WISDOM

Fishtrap Creek $7
Big Hole River State Fishing Access Site
23 mi N of Wisdom on SR 43 (stream mile 81.4). $7 with
fishing license, $12 otherwise; $6 unlicensed MT seniors,
$3.50 licensed MT seniors. All year; 7-day limit. 20 sites
on 82 acres; 28-ft RV limit. Toilets, tbls, cfga, drkg wtr.
Boating(l), fishing. Difficult access.

May Creek $7
Beaverhead National Forest
17 mi W of Wisdom on SR 43. $7. 6/20-LD; 16-day limit.
21 sites (30-ft RV limit). Tbls, toilets, cfga, drkg wtr, no
trash service. Fishing, hiking trails. Elev 6200 ft; 10 acres.

Miner Lake $7
Beaverhead National Forest
19 mi S of Wisdom at Jackson on SR 278; 7 mi W on CR

182; 3 mi W on FR 182. $7. 6/20-LD; 16-day limit. 18 sites
(20-ft RV limit). Tbls, toilets, cfga, drkg wtr, no trash
service. Fishing, boating(l--no motors), hiking trails. Elev
7000 ft; 10 acres. 54-acre lake.

Mussigbrod $7
Beaverhead National Forest
1.1 mi W of Wisdom on MT 43; 7 mi NW on Lower North
Fork Rd; 8.1 mi W on co rd; 2.8 mi NW on FR 573 (rutted
gravel access). $7. About 6/20-LD; 16-day limit. 10 sites
(30-ft RV limit). Tbls, toilets, cfga, firewood, drkg wtr, no
trash service. Boating(l); fishing (no power boats), hiking,
horseback riding. 102-acre lake.

Pintler Campground   FREE
Beaverhead National Forest
1.1 mi W on MT 43; 14 mi N on co rd; 4.1 mi N on FR 185.
Free. 6/15-9/15; 16-day limit. 2 sites (18-ft RV limit). Tbls,
toilets, cfga, firewood, no drkg wtr. Fishing; boating;
hiking. Elev 6300 ft; 3 acres. Mountains. Lake. Narrow
access rd. Within 4 mi of Anaconda-Pintlar Wilderness.
Pintler Lake (36 acres).

Steel Creek Campground $7
Beaverhead National Forest
Quarter mi N on MT 43; 4 mi E on CR 3; 1.3 mi E on FR
90. $7. Elev 6200 ft. About 6/15-LD; 16-day limit. 9 sites
(22-ft RV limit). Tbls, toilets, cfga, well drkg wtr, no trash
service. Fishing, hiking.

Twin Lakes Campground $7
Beaverhead National Forest
6.8 mi S of Wisdom on MT 278; 7.8 mi W on CR 1290 (Bris-
ton Lane Rd); 4.8 mi W on CR 1290; 4.8 mi S on FR 945;
5.8 mi SW on FR 183. $7. 6/20-LD; 16-day limit. 21 sites
on 13 acres (RVs under 26 ft). Tbls, toilets, cfga, firewood,
well drkg wtr. Boating(ld); water skiing, fishing (no power
boats). 75-acre lake. Elev 7200 ft.

WISE RIVER

Boulder Creek $8
Beaverhead National Forest
12 mi SW of Wise River on Pioneer Mtns Scenic Byway
(Hwy 73). $8 during MD-LD; free rest of year, but no drkg
wtr or trash service; 16-day limit. 13 sites (30-ft RV limit).
Tbls, toilets, cfga, drkg wtr. Fishing, hiking.

Fourth of July $8
Beaverhead National Forest
12 mi SW of Wise River on Pioneer Mtns Scenic Byway
(Hwy 73). $8 during 6/15-9/30; 16-day limit; free rest of
year, but no wtr or trash service. 5 sites (30-ft RV limit).
Tbls, toilets, cfga, drkg wtr. Hiking.

Little Joe   Campground $8
Beaverhead National Forest
19.6 mi SW of Wise River on Hwy 73 (Pioneer Mtns Scenic

Byway). $8 during 6/15-9/30; 16-day limit; free rest of year, weather permitting, but no drkg wtr or trash service. 5 sites; 28-ft RV limit. Tbls, toilets, cfga, drkg wtr. Fishing. Elev 7000 ft; 2 acres. River.

Lodgepole Campground $8
Beaverhead National Forest
12.9 mi SW of Wise River on Hwy 73 (Pioneer Mtns Scenic Byway). $8 during MD-LD; 16-day limit; free rest of year, but no drkg wtr or trash service. 10 sites (30-ft RV limit). Tbls, toilets, cfga, drkg wtr. Fishing (brook trout). Elev 6400 ft; 2 acres. Scenic.

Mono Creek Campground $8
Beaverhead National Forest
22.8 mi SW of Wise River on Hwy 73 (Pioneer Mtns Scenic Byway). $8 during MD-LD; 16-day limit; free rest of year, but no drkg wtr or trash service. 5 sites (18-ft RV limit). Tbls, toilets, cfga, drkg wtr. Fishing. Torrey & Schultz Lakes. Elev 6800 ft.

Pettengill Campground $8
Beaverhead National Forest
10 mi S of Wise River on Hwy 73 (Pioneer Mtns Scenic Byway). $8 during MD-LD; 16-day limit; free rest of year, but no services. 3 sites; 24-ft RV limit. Tbls, toilets, cfga, no drkg wtr, no trash service. Fishing.

Seymour Creek FREE
Beaverhead National Forest
11.2 mi W of Wise River on MT 43; 4 mi N on CR 274; 8 mi NW on FR 934. Free. All year (no wtr or services after LD); 16-day limit. 17 sites (18-ft RV limit). Tbls, toilets, cfga, firewood, no drkg wtr. Hunting; hiking; fishing. Elev 6700 ft; 7 acres. Stream. Trailhead into Anaconda-Pintlar Wilderness.

Willow Campground $8
Beaverhead National Forest
13.4 mi SW of Wise River on FR 484 (Pioneer Mtns Scenic Byway). $8 during 6/15-9/30; 16-day limit; free rest of year, weather permitting, but no drkg wtr or services. 5 sites (26-ft RV limit). Tbls, toilets, cfga, drkg wtr, no trash service. Fishing (good brook trout). Scenic area on Wise River. Elev 6600 ft; 3 acres.

WOLF CREEK
Departure Point $7.50
Holter Lake Recreation Area
Bureau of Land Management
Butte Field Office
3 mi N of Wolf Creek on Recreation Rd; 8 mi SE on county rd; E side of Missouri River. $7.50 with federal senior pass; others pay $15 (sites at dam $10) during about 5/15-10/15; free off-season but no wtr or services; 14-day limit. 50 sites (50-ft RV limit). Tbls, toilets, cfga, no drkg wtr.

Boating (hand launch), fishing, hiking. Non-campers pay $5 day-use fee or $40 seasonally.

Holter Lake $7.50
Holter Lake Recreation Area
Bureau of Land Management
Butte Field Office
2 mi N of Wolf Creek on Recreation Rd; cross bridge; 3 mi E on co rd. $7.50 with federal senior pass; others pay $15 (sites at dam $10). About 5/15-10/15; 14-day limit. 50 sites. Tbls, toilets, cfga, drkg wtr. Swimming, fishing, hiking, boating(ld), water skiing. Elev 3560 ft; 22 acres. Non-campers pay $5 day-use fee or $40 seasonally.

Log Gulch $7.50
Holter Lake Recreation Area
Bureau of Land Management
3 mi E of Wolf Creek on paved rd to gravel rd; 8 mi on E side of Missouri River. $7.50 with federal senior pass; others pay $15. About 5/15-10/15; 14-day limit. 70 sites 50-ft RV limit. Tbls, toilets, cfga, drkg wtr. Beach, swimming, boating(l), fishing. Non-campers pay $5 day-use fee or $40 seasonally.

Sleeping Giant FREE
Wilderness Study Area
Bureau of Land Management
From I-15 exit 234 at Wolf Creek, follow frontage rd to BLM Wood Siding Gulch Rd. Free. All year; 14-day limit. About 40 primitive sites scattered along the Holter Lake shoreline, and dispersed camping is permitted throughout the WSA. No facilities, no drkg wtr. Hiking, horseback riding, hunting. 11,000 acres.

WORDEN
Voyagers Rest FREE
Middle Yellowstone River State Fishing Access Site
1.5 mi E of Worden on US 312, then 1.5 mi N on 18th Rd. $7 with fishing license, $12 otherwise; $6 unlicensed MT seniors, $3.50 licensed MT seniors. All year; 7-day limit.. 5 primitive sites on 20 acres. Tbls, toilet, cfga, no drkg wtr. Boating(l), fishing. Difficult access.

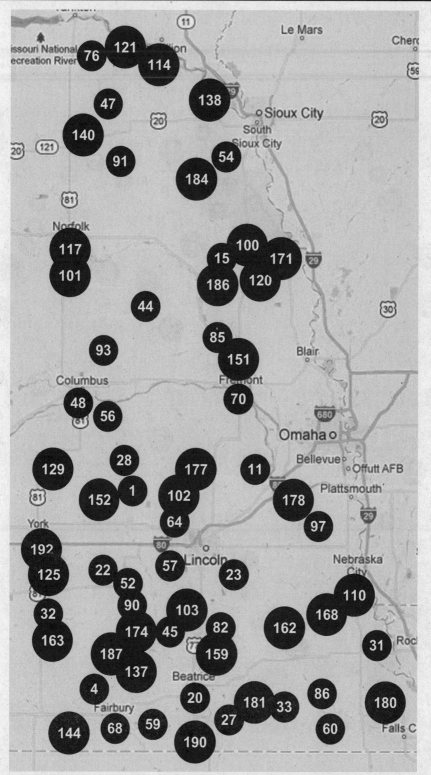

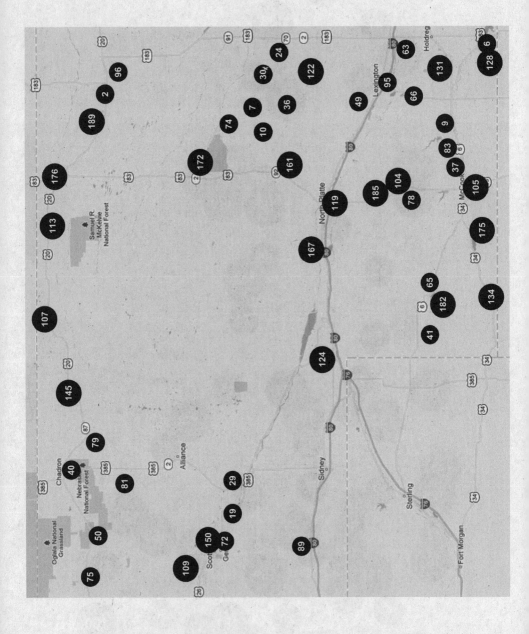

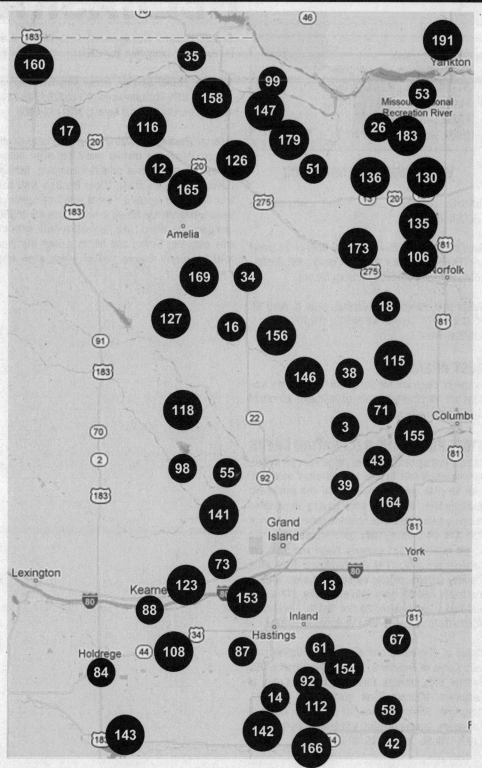

NEBRASKA

WWW.VISITNEBRASKA.GOV

Toll-free numbers for travel information: 1-877-NEBRASKA.

Dept of Economic Development, Division of Travel and Tourism, PO Box 94666, Lincoln, NE 68509-4666. E-mail: tourism@visitnebraska.org

Game and Parks Commission, 2200 N 33rd St, PO Box 30370, Lincoln NE 68503. 402/471-0641 or 800/826-PARK.

REST AREAS
Overnight stops are not permitted. RV sanitary stations are not provided at any of the major interstate highway rest areas.

STATE PARKS AND RECREATION AREAS
Basic primitive campsite fees range from $8 to $20, varying according to the tyes of sites available, with $8 sites generally being open and somewhat undesignated and $13 sites having designated camping pads. Sites with hookups generally start at $20 ($14 off-season). Daily park entrance fees are $5 per vehicle or $25 annually. Water and restroom services are shut off at the developed SRAs after the May-October regular season, and sites without electricity cost $8; sites with electricity, $16. Game and Parks Commission, PO Box 30370, Lincoln, NE 68503-0370. 402-471-0641 or 800/826-PARK.

Corps of Engineers. For further information contact: Corps of Engineers, Kansas City District, 700 Federal Bldg, Kansas City, Mo, 64106; Corps of Engineers, Missouri River District, PO Box 103, Downtown Station, Omaha, NE 68101; or Corps of Engineers, Omaha District, USPO and Court House, 215 N 17th St, Omaha, NE 68102.

Bureau of Land Management, 2515 Warren Ave, PO Box 1828, Cheyenne, WY 82001.

National Forest Service, Rocky Mountain Region, 11177 W. 8TH St., Lakewood, CO 80225; 303/234-4185. Nebraska National Forest, 308-432-0300.

Natural Resources Districts: Lower Platte South Natural Resources District maintains eight public access lakes with free primitive camping, fishing, hiking and wildlife study. Upper Big Blue NRD has four developed recreation areas with free camping, fishing, boating and hiking. Lower Platte North NRD manages Czechland Lake Recreation Area, with its free camping, fishing and hiking. Lower Big Blue NRD has eight reserves, all of which allow free camping.

AGNEW (1E)

Meadowlark Lake   FREE
Lower Platte South Natural Resources District
4 mi W of Agnew, then 1 mi N & 1 mi W. Free. All year; 14-day limit. Primitive open camping at 320-acre reserve with 55-acre lake. No facilities except cfga, no drkg wtr. Boating(l), fishing, hiking, hunting. GPS: 41.031673, -96.91419

AINSWORTH (2W)

Ainsworth East City Park $7
From US 20 at E end of Ainsworth, S on N. Richardson Dr; park on E side. $7 without hookups; $10 for 30/50-amp elec/wtr. May-Oct; 14-day limit. 30 sites (14 with 30-amp elec); 30-ft RV limit. Flush toilets, dump($5), showers, drkg wtr, cfga. Swimming, picnicking. Alternative is Rock County Fairgrounds in Bassett. GPS: 42.5486103, -99.8448457

Keller Park State Recreation Area $8
From Ainsworth, 4 mi E on US 20; about 8 mi N on US 183; at Bone Creek. $8 at 10 non-elec sites; $17 at 25 sites with 20/30-amp elec ($14 during 9/16-5/14 but no wtr services). Tbls, pit toilets, cfga, drkg wtr. Boating (elec mtrs), fishing at 5 ponds.

Willow Lake Wildlife Management Area   FREE
20 mi S of Ainsworth on Hwy 181, then 12.5 mi W on Elsmere Rd & 1 mi N. Free. All year; 14-day limit. Primitive camping. Fishing, boating(l). GPS: 42.14217, -100.04.603.

ALBION (3C)

Albion Campground $10
Fuller Municipal Park
From jct with SR 91 in Albion, about 7 blocks S on S. 11th St to Fairview. $10 ($60 weekly). 4/1-10/15. 14 full hookups, 12 elec/wtr; tents $6. Tbls, flush toilets, cfga, drkg wtr, dump, showers, elec, playground, adjoining pool. Swimming, picnicking. Register at city hall, 420 W. Market. No year-round camping available at adjacent fairground. GPS: 41.682789, -98.006728

ALEXANDRIA (4E)

Alexandria State Recreation Area $8
From Alexandria at jct with SR 53, 3 mi E on North St (becoming 719th Rd); 1 mi S on 560th Ave; at Alexandria Lakes. $8 without elec, $15 with 20/30-amp elec. All year; 14-day limit. 46 sites. Tbls, flush toilets, cfga, drkg wtr, playground, shelters, dump. Fishing, mtn biking, boating (nonpower or elec mtrs). 55 acres with 2 lakes. GPS: 40.23253, -97.33354

ALMA (6W)

Methodist Cove Park $12
Corps of Engineers
Harlan County Lake
From Alma at jct with US 183, 2.5 mi W on South St; near W end of lake. $12 & $14 at 82 non-elec site during 5/1-9/30 ($6 & $7 with federal senior pass), $8 during Oct, Nov

& April ($4 with senior pass). At 48 elec sites, $10 base with senior pass during 5/1-9/30; others pay $20 base, $24 at premium locations ($12 with senior pass). During Oct, Nov & April, elec sites $12 ($6 with senior pass). RV limit in excess of 65 ft. Two group camping areas, $50. Tbls, flush toilets, showers, cfga, drkg wtr, dump, playground, fish cleaning station with grinder. Group camping available. Non-campers pay $3 day use fee for boat ramp. Boating(l), fishing, swimming, picnicking. GPS: 40.08694, -99.31556

ANSELMO (7W)

Victoria Springs State Recreation Area $8
From Anselmo at jct with Hwy 2, six mi E on Hwy 21A. $8 at 60 non-elec sites during 9/16-5/14 but no wtr services ($13 in-season); $20 at 21 elec sites ($14 off-season but no wtr). Tbls, flush toilets, cfga, drkg wtr, showers, shelter, dump. 5-acre fishing pond. GPS: 41.6094483, -99.7526196

ARCADIA (9W)

Arcadia Garden Club   Donations
Village Wayside Park
W edge of village on Hwy 70. Donations requested, but camping free. All year; "reasonable" stay limit. 6 RV sites with elec. Drkg wtr, elec, pit toilets, cfga, dump, playground. Fishing, swimming. GPS: 41.423271, -99.130491

ARNOLD (10W)

Arnold Lake State Recreation Area $6
Village of Arnold Park
0.6 mi S of Arnold on SR 40; at South Loup River. $6 at 60 primitive sites; $10 at 20 elec (30-amp) sites. All year; 14-day limit. Tbls, pit toilets, cfga, drkg wtr, playground, dump. Fishing, hiking, biking, boating (nonpower or elec mtrs). 10 acres; 22-acre lake. Managed by village. GPS: 41.24.754, -100.11.672

ASHLAND (11E)

Memphis State Recreation Area $8
8 mi NW of Ashland on SR 63, then 1 mi W on CR D. $8. All year; 14-day limit. 150 primitive sites; 163 acres, 48-acre lake. Tbls, pit toilets, cfga, dump, playground, picnic shelters. Fishing, boating(l - elec mtrs), hiking. GPS: 41.10326, -96.4456

ATKINSON (12C)

Atkinson Mill Race City Park $7
City of Atkinson City Park
Half mi W of jct with US 20 on 5th St; N on access rd; at 14-acre lake on Elkhorn River. $7 at 20 primitive sites; $12 at 8 elec (20/30-amp) sites. All year; 14-day limit. 54 acres. Tbls, pit toilets, cfga, playground, shelters, drkg wtr. Swimming, fishing, boating (nonpower or elec mtrs). Sites need blocking. Half mi bluebird trail. Former state recreation area now managed by city. GPS: 42.5386, -99.00032

AURORA (13C)

Streeter Municipal Park   Donations
N side of Aurora on NE 34 (3 mi N of I-80, exit 332). Donations solicited, but camp free. All year (weather permitting); 3-day limit. 20 sites; 18 with hookups (trailers under 27 ft) plus primitive camping area. Tbls, flush toilets, drkg wtr, dump, hookups. Picnicking; swimming (pool nearby), playground, horseshoes. GPS: 40.8730679, -98.003110

AYR (14C)

Crystal Lake Recreation Area $7
Village of Ayre
Little Blue Natural Resources Area
1.5 mi N of Ayr on US 281; at Little Blue River. $7 at 50 primitive sites; $13 at 12 sites with 20/30-amp elec. All year; 14-day limit. Tbls, pit toilets, cfga, drkg wtr, shelters, beach, playground. Picnicking, fishing, swimming, boating (elec mtrs). 33 acres; 30-acre lake. Former state recreation area; now jointly managed by town & resources district. GPS: 40.45544, -98.43981

BANCROFT (15E)

Bancroft Village Park $10
4 blocks S of 1st National Bank & 2 blocks W; on W edge of Bancroft Park. $10. 5/1-10/15. 4 elec/wtr sites. Drkg wtr, tbls, cfga, flush toilets, dump, showers, playground. GPS: 42.0094394, -96.5753101

BARTLETT (16C)

Pibel Lake Recreation Area   FREE
Lower Loup Natural Resources District
9 mi S and 1 mi E of Bartlett on US 281. Free. All year; 14-day limit. About 30 undesignated primitive sites around the lake; 72 acres; 24-acre lake. Tbls, pit toilets, cfga, drkg wtr, playground. Picnicking, fishing, boating (dl--5-hp mtr limit); hunting, hiking. District took ownership from state in 2012. GPS: 41.75817, -98.53155

BASSETT (17C)

Bassett City Park   FREE
On W Hwy 20. Camp free, but donations requested. All year. 17 RV sites with elec. Coin laundry, tbls, cfga, pool, shelters, playground, dump, flush toilets, showers. Swimming. GPS: 42.577976, -99.540793

Rock County Fairgrounds   FREE
SW of city on Hwy 20. 1 block W of US 183 to fairground entrance. Free or donations. All year. 50 RV & tent sites. Flush & pit toilets, cfga, drkg wtr, showers, most 30-amp elec (one 50-amp), dump. Swimming, picnicking. GPS: 42.5775, -995421

BATTLE CREEK (18C)

Municipal Park   Donations
6 blocks S of Main St, E side of Hwy 121. Camp free, but donations encouraged. 5/1-10/15; 3-day limit or prearranged. 1 open RV site. Flush toilet, cfga, tbl, elec, dump, drkg wtr, playground. Swimming, picnicking. River. Field report says this park hard to find. GPS: 41.992854, -97.00043

BAYARD (19W)

Oregon Trail Wagon Train $10
S of Bayard off Hwy 28. $10 without hookups; $20 full hookups. 10 RV sites, 60 tent sites. Tbls, flush toilets, cfga, drkg wtr, showers. Canoeing(r).

BEATRICE (20E)

Bear Creek Wildlife Management Area   FREE
Lower Big Blue Natural Resources District
4 mi N of Beatrice, then 2.5 mi E. Free. All year; 14-day limit. Open primitive camping on 94-acre reserve at 24-acre lake. No facilities, no drkg wtr. Fishing, hunting, hiking. GPS: 40.321454, -96.695138

Rockford Lake State Recreation Area $8
From Beatrice at jct with US 77, 8 mi E on US 136; 2 mi S on S. 94th Rd; 1 mi E on Lilac Rd; 0.5 mi S on S. 108 Rd; at E shore of 150-acre lake. $8 at 77 primitive sites; $17 at 30 elec (30/50-amp) sites ($14 off-season but no wtr services). All year; 14-day limit. 40-ft RV limit. Tbls, pit toilets, cfga, playground, drkg wtr, beach. Swimming, fishing, boating(l), hiking. 436 acres. GPS: 40.22091, -96.58174

BEAVER CROSSING (22E)

Beaver Crossing City Park   FREE
E Elk St and Martin Ave in Beaver Crossing (2 blocks S & 1 block E of post office); after entering park, curve E, then S around E side of baseball field to area near Army tank. Donations requested, but camp free. All year; 3-day limit. 4 designated RV sites with 30-amp elec & one 50-amp site, but numerous other undesignated sites. Elec hookups, flush toilets, cfga, drkg wtr, tbls, playground. Swimming. 402-532-3925. GPS: 40.584, -97.16579

BENNET (23E)

Bennet City Park   FREE
In town off SR 43. Free overnight during summer. Undesignated sites; no hookups. Tbls, toilets, cfga, drkg wtr, playground, sand volleyball, shelter. 1.6 acres.

BLOOMFIELD (26C)

Bloomfield City Park $5
On W Park St in Bloomfield. $5 without hookups, $10 with elec ($50 weekly, $150 monthly). All year. 6 elec/wtr sites. Flush toilets, cfga, drkg wtr, showers, playground equipment. Horseshoes, basketball, playground. GPS: 42.59351, -97.64754.

Knox County Fairgrounds $10
On E edge of town at 612 E. Main. $10 (weekly rates available). 4/1-11/1. 30 sites. Tbls, flush toilets, cfga, drkg wtr, elec, showers. Owned by City of Bloomfield. GPS: 42.599736, -97.652711

BLUE SPRINGS (27E)

Feits Memorial City Park   FREE
N at W end of Blue River Bridge, at 104 E Broad St at River
Rd in Blue Springs. Free. All year; 3-day limit. 5 RV sites & 10
tent spaces. Cfga, drkg wtr. Swimming, fishing, boating(dl).
GPS: 40.1411122, -96.6600231

BRAINARD (28E)

Timber Point Lake   FREE
Lower Platte South Natural Resources District
1 mi E, 1 mi S & 1 mi E from S edge of Brainard. Free.
Primitive open camping on 160-acre reserve at 29-acre
lake. 3 designated sites. Tbls & portable toilets (Apr-Oct),
cfga, no drkg wtr, picnic area. Boating(l), fishing, hunting.
GPS: 41.1611, -96.9653

BRIDGEPORT (29W)

Bridgeport State Recreation Area $8
Just NW of Bridgeport. From jct of US 385, about 10 blocks
W on US 26; NW on Recreation Rd to park; along S shore
of North Platte River. $8. All year; 14-day limit. About 130
undesignated primitive sites; 197 acres. Tbls, pit toilets,
cfga, drkg wtr, dump, playground, beach, shelters. Fishing, swimming, boating(ld), hiking. 4 sand pit lakes. GPS:
41.68015, -103.11064

BROKEN BOW (30W)

Milburn Dam Wildlife Management Area   FREE
20 mi N off SR 2. Free. All year. 10 sites; 537 acres. Tbls,
toilets, cfga, drkg wtr. Picnicking, boating, fishing. GPS:
41.75, -99.77.

BROWNVILLE (31E)

Indian Cave State Park $8
10 mi S of Brownville on SR 67; 5 mi E on S-64E Rd. $8
during 9/16-5/14 at primitive sites (no wtr services); $13
in-season. Sites with elec $20 in-season, $14 off-season.
14-day limit. Tbls, flush toilets, cfga, drkg wtr, showers,
dump, coin laundry. Fishing, trail rides, hiking trails, summer programs. GPS: 40.264, -95.56964

BRUNING (32E)

Bruning Dam Wildlife Management Area   FREE
Little Blue Natural Resources District
2 mi E of Bruning; 1 mi N; .7 mi E; in Fillmore County. Free.
All year. Undesignated primitive sites. Tbls, toilets, cfga,
no drkg wtr. Boating(l), fishing, hunting, picnicking. 250-
acre lake. GPS: 40.3486, -97.51

BURCHARD (33E)

Burchard Lake Wildlife Management Area   FREE
3 mi E of Burchard, then half mi N on NE 65 or 4. Free. All
year; 14-day limit. 15 sites. Tbls, toilets, cfga, drkg wtr.
Picnicking; swimming; fishing; boating(l). Area closed
during waterfowl season except at face of dam. GPS:
40.168589, -96.303055.

BURWELL (34C)

Burwell City Park $5
5 blocks N of City Square on 7th Ave; turn E at pool. $5.
All year; 3-day limit. 8 unmarked RV sites. Tbls, pit toilets,
drkg wtr, elec, cfga, dump, playground. No wtr in winter.
Fishing, swimming. GPS: 41.7883, -99.1331

Calamus Reservoir State Recreation Area $8
6 mi NW of Burwell on SR 96. $8 for primitive camping
in open areas of Hannaman Bayou, Valleyview & Nunda
Shoals; facilities there include pit toilets, cfga, drkg
wtr. 122 modern sites up to $20 at Homestead Knolls
Campground & Nunda Shoals (or $14 during 9/15-5/15
with limited amenities); those have flush toilets, showers
(except at Nunda), tbls, drkg wtr, elec, dump. Swimming,
boating(ld), fishing, winter sports. 11,720 acres at reservoir. Calamus State Fish Hatchery below dam, open for
free tours. GPS: 41.87433, -9928328
  Homestead Knolls on lake's N shore has 83 hard-sur-
face RV pads with hookups, bathhouse, 2 boat ramps,
beach.
  Valleyview Flat offers primitive camping, with only vault
toilets and water pump. GPS: 41.9111155, -99.3017737
  Hannamon Bayou is popular with anglers due to its
boat ramp and primitive camping, with drinking water, pit
toilets, tbls, cfga. GPS: 41.9222264, -99.3309415.
  Nunda Shoal, midway along the lake's S shore, has
developed sites, pit toilets, drkg wtr (no showers), boat
ramp. GPS: 41.8658383, -99.2698274.

BUTTE (35C)

Butte City Park   FREE
From SR 12, W on Butte St or Center St, on E edge of
town; sites at NW corner of park on Eugene St. Camp free,
but $5 donation suggested, but no donation box. All year.
Undesignated tent & 2 back-in sites for medium-size RVs.
Drkg wtr, portable & pit toilets, tbls, cfga, 30-amp elec/
wtr, store, LP-gas. GPS: 42.913057, -98.840648

Hull Lake State Wildlife Management Area   FREE
3 mi S of Butte, and 2 mi W via US 281 or SR 11. Free.
Open all year; 14-day limit. 10 sites. Toilets, cfga, no
drkg wtr. Swimming, fishing. Picnicking. GPS: 42.867402,
-98.881073.

CALLAWAY (36W)

Morgan City Park $5
Morgan & Adams Sts. $5. All year; 7-day limit. 30 sites (6
with elec). Tbls, flush & pit toilets, cfga, drkg wtr, showers. Fishing, swimming, playground. GPS: 41.292423,-
99.922586.

CAMBRIDGE (37W)

Cambridge City RV Park   Donations
E edge of Cambridge on Hwy 6 at shore of Medicine Creek.
Donations. All year; 3-day limit. 11 pull-through sites for

self-contained RVs. 20/30/50-amp wtr/elec hookups, portable toilets, drkg wtr, showers, cfga, store, dump. Fishing, swimming. Showers & flush toilets at nearby at adjoining McKinley Park. GPS: 39.963673,-83.040576

Medicine Creek State Recreation Area $8
2 mi W of Cambridge on US 6/34; 10 mi N on Harry Strunk Lake Rd. $8 in open primitive areas (about 240 sites); 8 non-elec pads $13 (or $8 during 9/16-5/14 with no wtr services); $20 at 68 elec sites ($14 off-season). All year; 14-day limit. Tbls, flush toilets, cfga, showers, dump, playground, 2 fish cleaning stations, beach. Boating(lrd), fishing, picnicking, swimming. At Harry Strunk Lake. GPS: 40.37917, -100.21194

CEDAR RAPIDS (38C)
Mel's Landing Municipal Park $5
On N edge of Cedar Rapids, on Hwy 52; at Cedar River. $5, All year. 6 RV sites; 10 tent sites. 1 elec hookup. Toilets, tbls, cfga, drkg wtr (shut off in winter), playground. Fishing, swimming, boating(l), canoeing. GPS: 41.564457, -98.147564

CENTRAL CITY (39C)
Lone Tree Wayside Area   FREE
1 mi W of Central City on S side of SR 30. Free. All year; 1-night limit. Spaces for self-contained RVs. Tbls. Picnicking. GPS: 41.1058476, -98.0008914

CHADRON (40W)
Chadron State Park $8
9 mi S of Chadron on US 385. $8 during 9/16-5/14 at 18 non-elec sites (no wtr services); $13 in-season. 30-amp elec sites, $20 in-season, $14 off-season but no wtr. 14-day limit; 65-ft RV limit. Tbls, flush toilets, cfga, drkg wtr, showers, dump, shelters, pool, playground. Trail rides, swimming, fishing, boating(r), hiking, evening programs, tennis, sand volleyball, mountain biking(r). GPS: 42.7088593, -103.0174069

Roberts Tract Trailhead $8
Nebraska National Forest
Pine Ridge National Recreation Area
8 mi W of Chadron on Hwy 20; 7 mi S on Eleson Rd; 1.5 mi E on Bethel Rd. $8 during 5/15-11/15; free rest of year, but no wtr. 3 tent sites, 1 RV site. Tbls, toilet, cfga, drkg wtr, corrals. Hiking, horseback riding, mountain biking. GPS: 42.6785801, -103.1513028

CHAMPION (41W)
Champion Lake State Recreation Area $8
Half mi W of Champion off 2nd St. $8. All year. 14-day limit. 7 primitive sites. Tbls, pit toilets, cfga, drkg wtr. Fishing, boating (elec mtrs), hiking. At Frenchman Creek. 14 acres. GPS: 40.47155, -101.75244

CHESTER (42C)
Chester City Park   FREE
1 blk W of jct of SRs 81/8, on SR 8 in Chester. Low fee after one free night. 4/15-10/31. 2 RV sites & tent spaces. Flush toilets, cfga, drkg wtr, tbls, elec. Basketball, horseshoes, tennis, sand volleyball, golf, ball fields, shelter. GPS: 40.015871, -97.619899.

CLARKS (43C)
Mormon Trail   FREE
State Wayside Park
1.5 mi S of Clarks on NE 30; 3 mi W on NE 92. Free. All year; 2-day limit. Undesignated sites. Tbls, toilets, cfga, drkg wtr. Picnicking; fishing; hiking. GPS: 41.13, -97.50.

CLARKSON (44E)
Clarkson City Park $8
101 mi N of Clarkson on Hwy 91 Spur (121 Bryan St.). $8 non elec; $18 for elec/wtr. 5/1-10/1; 14-day limit. 20 RV sites with elec, 6 with sewer; 20 tent sites. Tbls, flush toilets, cfga, drkg wtr, showers, dump. Swimming pool, lighted tennis court, playground, museum. 5 acres. GPS: 41.7272295, -97.1169822

CLATONIA (45E)
Clatonia Public Use Area   FREE
Lower Big Blue Natural Resources District
1 mi N of Clatonia. Free. All year; 14-day limit. Primitive open camping on 115-acre reserve at 40-acre lake. Tbls, toilets, cfga, drkg wtr. Fishing, hiking, hunting.

COLERIDGE (47E)
Coleridge Village Park $5
NW corner of Coleridge on Nebraska St. $5 donation requested. All year. 4 RV sites with elec, dump, flush toilets, drkg wtr, cfga, playground. GPS: 42.5061111, -97.2036635

COLUMBUS (48E)
Lake North   FREE
Loup Power District
4 mi N of jct of US 30 and 18th Ave in Columbus on 18th Ave (Monastery Rd). Paved access rds. Free. 5/1-11/1; 7-day limit in 30-day period. 100 tent, 25 RV sites (12 with elec). Tbls, toilets, cfga, playground, drkg wtr. Picnicking; fishing; swimming; boating(l); waterskiing. Sites need blocking. More than 2 mi of beaches at 200-acre lake. GPS: 41.4964, -97.355874

Loup Park   FREE
Loup Power District
4 mi N of Columbus on 18th Ave; 1.5 mi W on Lakeview Dr (paved access rds). On N & W shores of Lake Babcock. Free. 5/1-11/1; 7-day limit during 30-day period. 120 tent sites, 50 RV sites (28 with elec). Tbls, pit toilets, cfga, drkg wtr, elec hookups, playground. Picnicking; fishing, swimming, boating(l). 40 acres. GPS: 41.498218, -97.374616

Powerhouse Park   FREE
Loup Power District
Half mi E of city limits on US 30; 1.5 mi N on 18th Ave.
Free. All year; 7-day limit in 30-day period. 20 tent sites,
6 RV sites (32-ft RV limit). Tbls, pit toilets, cfga, drkg wtr.
Picnicking; fishing in Loup Canal; playground. Adjacent to
Columbus Powerhouse (free tours available). 4 acres. GPS:
41.465038, -97.331909

Southgate Campground $12
At Hwys 81 & 30 S, Columbus. $12. All year. 22 sites with
full hookups (elec only during Dec-Mar). Tbls, toilets, cfga,
drkg wtr. GPS: 41.4100122, -97.3669867. Unable to verify
fees for 2014.

Tailrace Park   FREE
Loup Power District
3 mi E of Columbus on 8th St Rd; 1.5 mi S on co rd. Free.
5/1-11/1; 7-day limit during 30-day period. 20 tent, 6 RV
sites. Tbls, pit toilets, cfga, drkg wtr, playground. Picnicking; fishing. Scenic; heavily wooded. Elec lights illuminate
park areas at night. GPS: 41.401956, -97.284206

COZAD (49W)
Gallagher Canyon State Recreation Area $8
About mi S of Cozad on SR 21 on US 30; 2 mi E on CR
755; 2 mi S on CR 442; 1 mi W on access rd; at N shore
of 424-acre Johnson Lake, formed by irrigation canal. $8.
All year; 14-day limit. 72 primitive sites. Tbls, pit toilets,
cfga, drkg wtr, playground. Fishing, boating(ld). 424-acre
Johnson Lake. GPS: 40.73485, -99.97898

Muny City Park $10
14th & O Sts, Exit 222. $10. All year. 18 RV sites. Drkg
wtr, elec, dump, flush toilets, showers, playground, pool.
Swimming, ball fields, exercise trail, horseshoes, volleyball, Frisbee golf. No swimming or showers in winter. GPS:
40.8661184, -99.9970667

CRAWFORD (50W)
City Park Campground   FREE
From US 20, follow Main St W through town to park
entrance; curve right (N) after crossing White Creek in
park; elec on power pole near restrooms. Free. All year;
3-night limit. 10 sites. Flush toilets, tbls, drkg wtr, cfga,
dump. Picnicking, fishing, swimming pool, playground,
tennis, walking trail & bridle trail to state park. Watch for
low tree limbs. GPS: 42.686614

Fort Robinson State Park $8
3 mi W of Crawford on US 20. During 5/15-9/15, $8 at 25
non-elec sites during 9/16-5/14 (no wtr services or showers); $13 in-season. About 100 sites with 30/50-amp elec,
$20 in-season, $14 off-season without wtr. 14-day limit;
60-ft RV limit. Tbls, flush toilets, cfga, drkg wtr, showers,
dump, shelters, coin laundry, playground, pool. Trail rides,
swimming, boating (elec mtrs), fishing, hiking. 22,000

acres. Museum, restored fort buildings, restaurant. GPS:
42.6844122, -103.5110374

Soldier Creek Trailhead $8
Nebraska National Forest
3.5 mi W of Crawford on US 20; 6 mi N on Soldier Creek Rd.
$8 during 5/15-11/15; free rest of year, but no wtr & limited
service. 14-day limit. 4 primitive sites. Toilets, cfga, drkg
wtr, tbls, corrals. Fishing, hiking trails, hunting, horseback
riding trails. GPS: 40.1438, -111.0468

Toadstool Campground $5
Nebraska National Forest
Toadstool Geologic Park
4.5 mi N of Crawford on SR 71; 12 mi W on CR 904; left on
CR 902 for 1 mi. $5 during 5/19-11/17; free rest of year,
but pack out trash; 14-day limit. 6 sites. Tbls, toilets,
cfga, no drkg wtr. Hiking, explore rock formations, longest
known mammal trackway from Oligocene period. Sod
homestead replica. Non-campers pay $5 day use fee. GPS:
42.857746, -103.5838147

CREIGHTON (51C)
Bruce Municipal Park $10
Main St and Douglas Ave in Creighton (W edge of town on
Hwy 59). $10. 4/1-10/1. 7 spaces for self-contained RVs.
Elec hookups, flush toilets, cfga, drkg wtr, dump. Swim-
ming, boating. GPS: 42.4638928, -97.9136784

CRETE (52E)
Tuxedo Municipal Park $10
Approaching Crete from the W on SR 33, turn N on CR
2150, then E on CR F; N & E on Idaho Ave to side of fairgrounds. $10. 4/1-10/15; 10-day limit. 10 RV sites; unlim-
ited tent sites. Tbls, flush toilets, cfga, drkg wtr, 30-amp
elec, dump, showers, playground. Fishing, picnicking.
Note: Bridges over Big Blue River have 3-ton limits. GPS:
40.37814 -96.58392

Walnut Creek Wildlife Management Area   Closed
Lower Big Blue Natural Resources District
2.5 mi NE of Crete. Closed to camping. GPS: 40.665, -96.926

CROFTON (53C)
Bloomfield Campground $8
Lewis and Clark State Recreation Area
From Crofton, 0.5 mi W on SR 12; about 5 mi W on C-54
Rd; 1 mi N on State Recreational Rd, following signs; at S
shore of lake. $8 at primitive sites; $20 at 20/30/5-amp
elec sites ($14 during 9/16-5/14 but no wtr services). 50-ft
RV limit. All year, 14-day limit. Tbls, flush & pit toilets,
cfga, drkg wtr, playground, beach. Fishing, boating(l),
swimming. GPS: 42.838888, -97.6383977

Deep Water Campground $8
Lewis and Clark State Recreation Area
From Crofton, 0.5 mi W on SR 12; about 8 mi N on SR 121;

1 mi W on C-54 Rd; 1 mi N on Park Dr, following signs; at S shore of lake. $8. All year; 14-day limit. Spaces for self-contained RVs. Tbls, toilets, cfga, drkg wtr. Fishing, boating, hiking. GPS: 42.8352766, -97.5325635

Miller Creek Campground $8
Lewis and Clark State Recreation Area
From Crofton, 0.5 mi W on SR 12; about 8 mi N on SR 121; about 5.5 mi W on C-54 Rd; at split following turnoff to Bloomfield Campground, veer right onto 895 Rd about 1 mi to campground on S shore of lake. $8. All year; 14-day limit. Primitive undesignated sites. Tbls, pit toilets, cfga, drkg wtr. Fishing, boating (lrd), waterskiing, hiking trail overlooking camping area of the 1804 Lewis and Clark expedition. Low-water boat ramp. GPS: 42.8299993, -97.6622866

Weigand-Burbach Campgrounds $8
Lewis and Clark State Recreation Area
From Crofton, 0.5 mi W on SR 12; about 3 mi W on C-54 Rd; 0.5 mi N on State Recreational Rd; W on Park Rd to campgrounds. $8 at primitive undesignated sites; non-elec sites with gravel pads $13; sites with 30/50-amp elec $20 ($14 during 9/16-5/14 but no wtr services). 50-ft RV limit. All year; 14-day limit. Tbls, flush toilets, cfga, drkg wtr, phone, dump, coin showers, store, playground, beach, marina, fish cleaning station, boat slips, marine fuel, boat pump-out station. Swimming, fishing, boating(dl), waterskiing; hiking. Nature trails. GPS: 42.8347211, -97.5683972

DAKOTA CITY (54E)
Cottonwood Cove Municipal Park $10
13th & Hickory Sts in Dakota City at Missouri River. $10 without elec; $18 with elec/wtr/CATV. 5/1-10/1; 14-day limit. 16 sites (10 for RVs). Tbls, flush toilets, cfga, drkg wtr, elec, dump($1 for non-campers). Fishing, boating(lr), canoeing(r), playground, hiking trails, ball fields, soccer, horseshoes. 45 acres. GPS: 42.4116605, -96.4016965

DANNEBROG (55C)
Village Park $10
In town. $10 for 4 elec sites. 5/1-9/30, weather permitting. Tbls, flush toilets, cfga, elec, dump (no wtr hookups), playground. Hiking, picnicking, biking, game court. On Oak Creek. Register with village office in Howard County Bank building on Mill St or Kerry's Grocery (after 12:30 pm). GPS: 41.1183, -98.5459

DAVID CITY (56E)
David City Campground $10
On S end of David City, Hwy 15 south (camp on NE section of park). $10. 4/1-10/31; 14-day limit. 12 RV sites with elect. Tbls, cfga, flush toilets, dump. Swimming, boating(dl), fishing. Pond, playground, sport field, rec room. 85 acres; 2 lakes. Expansion of the park planned, including pool,

running track, lake renovation, trail. Park listed on National Register of Historic Places. GPS: 41.2452907, -97.1258705

DENTON (57E)
Conestoga State Recreation Area $8
The main N shore campground is 2 mi N of Denton on SR S-55A, then 1 mi W on W. Pioneer Blvd & S on SW 98th St; the S shore campground is 1.5 mi N of town on SW 98th St. $8 at 24 primitive undesignated sites, $13 at 8 designated non-elec pads; $15 at 25 sites with 30/50-amp elec. All year; 14-day limit. All non-elec sites $8 during 9/16-5/14 but no wtr services; elec sites $14 off-season but no wtr. 40-ft RV limit. Tbls, pit toilets, cfga, drkg wtr, picnic shelters, dump, fish cleaning station. Fishing, hiking, mountain biking, boating (ld). 486 acres, 230-acre lake. GPS: 40.76431, -96.86019

Yankee Hill FREE
State Wildlife Management Area
2.5 mi E & 1 mi S of Denton. Free. All year; 14-day limit. Primitive undesignated sites; limited facilities. Fishing, boating(l), hunting. GPS: 40.728943, -96.790011.

DESHLER (58C)
City Park FREE
From US 136 N of town, S on First St, then E on Park St to 4th St; Eat 4th & Park into the park's newest 10 sites; 6 other sites E over small bridge with 8-ton limit or N on 4th St, E on Elm & S on 6th past E side of pool. Free; donations accepted. All year; 3-day limit. 16 RV sites (11 with 30-amp elec, 5 with 50-amp. Wtr hookups, flush toilets, cfga, drkg wtr, cfga, tbls, showers, dump (at 3rd & Railway, 4 blocks N). Picnicking, boating, swimming pool, tennis, sand volleyball, playground. 10 acres. GPS: 40.08172, -97.43372.

DILLER (59E)
Diller Municipal Campground $9.95
In Diller. $9.95 ($19.95 for 3 days, $39.95 for 30 days. All year. 7 full-hookup RV sites. Tbls, flush toilets, cfga, drkg wtr, hookups, dump, new playground equipment, WiFi. Basketball, tennis, picnic shelter. GPS: 40.1094471, -96.9350288

DU BOIS (60E)
Iron Horse Trail Lake $12
Nemaha Natural Resources District
Half mi N & 2 mi W of DuBois, following signs, in Pawnee County. $12. All year; 14-day limit. 11 elec sites on W shore; primitive sites free, but $5 for 2-day permit required or $12 annual permit for all NNRD parks.. Pit toilets, tbls, cfga, drkg wtr, beach, playground, beach, sand volleyball. Fishing, boating(dl), hiking, swimming, sand volleyball, nature trails. 85-acre lake. GPS: 40.2638888, -96.5627982

EDGAR (61C)

WPA South Park $10

At 300 N. C St. (at Maple) in Edgar. $10. All year. 4 RV/tent sites. Tbls, flush toilets, cfga, drkg wtr, elec, sewer, dump, playground, shelters. Tennis, basketball. Rock shelter was built in 1937 by WPA. GPS: 40.366728, -97.9700928

ELM CREEK (63W)

Sandy Channel State Recreation Area   FREE

From Elm Creek exit of I-80, about 1.5 mi S on US 183; at Platte River. Free. All year; 14-day limit. About 30 undesignated primitive sites on 134 acres. Pit toilets, cfga, no drkg wtr. 47 acres of ponds. Fishing, boating (elec mtrs). GPS: 40.66825, -99.37529

EMERALD (64E)

Pawnee State Recreation Area $8

From Emerald, 1.5 mi W on US 6; 2 mi N on NW 112th St; at E shore of Pawnee Lake. $8 at 97 sites in open primitive areas; $13 at 34 designated non-elec sites ($8 during 9/16-5/14 but no wtr services); $20 at 68 sites with 30/50-amp elec ($14 off-season, no wtr). All year; 14-day limit. Flush toilets, showers, dump, playground, fish cleaning station, 2 beaches. Boating(drl), swimming, fishing, hiking/biking trails. 2,540 acres; 740-acre lake. Blue rock area. GPS: 40.84961, -96.88159

ENDERS (65W)

Center Dam Campground $7

Enders Reservoir State Recreation Area

Half mi S of Enders at US 6 & SR 61; W 100 ft on US 6. $7 at open primitive areas; $17 at 32 sites with 20/30-amp elec ($14 during 9/16-5/14 but no wtr services). All year; 14-day limit. Dump, flush toilets, cfga, drkg wtr, coin showers, fish cleaning station. Fishing, boating(l), picnicking. GPS: 40.44166, -101.52738

Church Grove Campground $8

Enders Reservoir State Recreation Area

0.5 mi S of Enders on main city street, then 2 mi W on county rd & 1 mi S on access rd. $8 at primitive sites; $17 with elec ($14 during 9/16-5/14 but no wtr services). All year; 14-day limit. About 160 sites. Tbls, flush toilets, cfga, coin showers, drkg wtr, dump, playground, horseshoes, fish cleaning station. Fishing, boating(lrd), swimming, picnicking. 3.278 acres in recreation area; 1,707-acre lake. GPS: 40.4306, -101.5841

EUSTIS (66W)

Eustis Municipal Park   FREE

From SR 23, S on Hale St, W on Railroad St; S on Main St between 2 huge silos and Kinder Park, cross RR track, then E on Allison St. Free; no stay limit. Primitive camping & full hookups. Tbls, toilets, cfga, drkg wtr, dump. Tennis, picnicking. GPS: 40.66036, -100.02673

EXETER (67C)

Gilbert's Village Park RV $10

From jct with US 81, 7.7 mi E on US 6; right (S) on Exeter Ave in town for 2 blocks; sites on SE corner by pool. $10. All year; 14-day limit. 2 RV sites on concrete pads with 20/50-amp elec (no 30-amp); 33-ft RV limit. Tbls, flush toilets, cfga, drkg wtr, playground. Swimming, horseshoe pits, ball fields, basketball, tennis. GPS: 38.326, -97.26997

FAIRBURY (68E)

Crystal Springs Municipal Park $10

1.5 mi SW of town. From US 136, follow Maple St S, following blue camping sign to W. 3rd St & Park Rd; SW of Frontier Fun Park, continue S on Frederick St (CR 2880, then W on Crystal Springs (CR 2880), then N into park. $10 with elec. 5/1-10/15; 14-day limit. 60 sites. Tbls, flush toilets, cfga, drkg wtr, 30-amp wtr/elec, dump, showers, playground. Fishing, swimming, boating. Very pretty park with several lakes, trees, ducks, pelicans. GPS: 40.1291693, -97.203092

Rock Creek Station $8
State Recreation Area

From Fairbury, 1 mi SE on SR 8; about 5 mi E on 710th Rd to camping area adjacent to Rock Creek Station State Historical Park. $8 at 10 non-elec sites during 9/16-5/14 but no wtr services ($13 in-season); $20 in-season ($14 off-season) at 25 elec 20/30/50-amp sites. All year; 14-day limit. Tbls, flush toilets, cfga, drkg wtr, dump, showers, playground. Visitor center, exhibits, covered wagon rides, hiking & nature trails. Site of Pony Express station. James Butler Hickok got his name "Wild Bill" there when he killed station agent D.C. McCanless in 1861. GPS: 40.11483, -97.06183

FREMONT (70E)

Fremont Lakes State Recreation Area $12

From just W Fremont on US 30, 2 mi W to recreation area at sandpit lakes. $8 at 600 non-elec sites during 9/16-5/14 but no wtr services ($13 in-season); $20 at 212 sites with 20/30-amp elec ($14 off-season but no wtr). All year; 14-day limit. Tbls, toilets, showers, dump, beaches, coin showers. Swimming, boating(ld), fishing. 666 acres. 20 sandpit lakes. GPS: 41.44169, -96.55833

Luther Hormel Memorial Park   FREE
Fremont Parks & Recreation Department

Half mi SW of Fremont. Free. Primitive camping on river; canoe stopover. Tbls, toilets, cfga, drkg wtr, shelter, nature trail. 167 acres. GPS: 41.4105556, -96.5130811.

GENOA (71C)

Genoa City Park   FREE

3 blocks S of SRs 22 and 39 in Genoa (310 South Park St). Free 2 nights; $10 thereafter; 14-day limit. Apr-Nov. 4 RV sites with elec (20-amp). Tbls, toilets, cfga, playground, drkg wtr, showers, dump, coin laundry. Picnicking; ten-

nis; softball, shuffleboard, fishing, swimming pool. Extra charge for a/c. GPS: 41.44627, -97.73466

Headworks Park   FREE
Loup Power District
6 mi W of Genoa on SR 22. Free. 5/1-11/1; 7-day per month limit. 12 sites with elec; 25 other RV sites; 25 tent sites. Tbls, toilets, cfga, drkg wtr, playground. Picnicking, boating(l), fishing (in small lake in park or at the Loup Canal nearby). River. Adjacent to entrance of Loup Power District Headquarters, the beginning of the Loup Canal. GPS: 41.399357, -97.792954

GERING (72W)
Wildcat Hills State Recreation Area $8
10 mi S of Gering on NE 71; entry rd not accessible for large RVs. $8. All year; 14-day limit. About 30 undesignated sites on several grass parking areas and along interior trail roads; 705 acres. Tbls, toilets, cfga, drkg wtr, playground, shelters, nature center. Picnicking; hiking; fishing; hunting. Sites need blocking. Nature trails. Game refuge with buffalo, elk. 41.70257, -103.67166

GIBBON (73C)
Windmill State Recreation Area $8
At NE corner of Gibbon exit from I-80. $8 at 20 primitive sites during 9/16-5/14 but no wtr ($13 in-season); $20 at 69 elec sites in-season ($14 during 9/16-5/14 but no wtr). All year; 2-day limit. Tbls, flush toilets, showers, cfga, drkg wtr, coin laundry, dump, coin showers, shelters, beach. Boating, swimming, fishing. Park features an assortment of antique windmills. GPS: 40.70704, 98.83886

HALSEY (74W)
Bessey Campground $8
Nebraska National Forest
2 mi W of Halsey on SR 2. $8 base; $11 for 15-amp elec sites. All year; 10-day limit. 40 sites, 18 with elec; 30-ft RV limit. Flush toilets, cold showers, cfga, wtr hookups, dump, elec($), pool. No wtr 10/15-MD. Swimming($), boating, canoeing, biking, hiking trails, nature programs, cross-country skiing, hunting, tennis, softball. 3 acres. Group camping available. GPS: 41.8999997, -100.2976362

Natick Horse Camp $8
Nebraska National Forest
W of Halsey on SR 2 & W of 4-H Camp. $8. All year; 14-day limit. 7 sites. Tbls, toilets, cfga, no drkg wtr, corrals. Hiking, mountain biking, horseback riding.

Whitetail Campground $8
Nebraska National Forest
W of Halsey on SR 2 near Dismal River. $8. All year; 14-day limit. 10 sites. Tbls, toilets, cfga, no drkg wtr, corrals. Hiking, mountain biking, horseback riding.

HARRISON (75W)
Gilbert-Baker Wildlife Management Area   FREE
6 mi N of Harrison on access rd near the Wyoming border. Free. All year; 14-day limit. Undesignated sites. Tbls, toilets, cfga, drkg wtr. Picnicking, fishing, hunting. GPS: 42.763629, -103.925777.

HARTINGTON (76E)
City Camper Court   FREE
In Hartington at jct of Broadway & Felber. Camp free, but donations suggested. 4/15-10/15. 6 RV sites. Tbls, wtr/elec/sewer hookups, cfga, drkg wtr, dump. GPS: 42.624628, -97.264601

HAYES CENTER (78W)
Hayes Center Wildlife Management Area   FREE
12 mi NE of Hayes Center on SR 25; at S end of Camp Hayes Lake. Free. All year. 10 sites. Tbls, toilets, cfga, drkg wtr. Boating, swimming, fishing, picnicking. 119 acres. No boat motors. GPS: 40.35.049, -100.55665.

HAY SPRINGS (79W)
Metcalf State Wildlife Management Area   FREE
E edge of Hay Springs, 7 mi N of Hwy 20 on county rd. Free. All year; 14-day limit. Primitive hike-in tent camping in pine forest area. No facilities; no drkg wtr. No vehicles. GPS: 42.836999, -102.678812.

Walgren Lake State Recreation Area $8
2 mi S of Hay Springs on SR 87; 3 mi E on county rd; 0.5 mi N on Walgren Lake Rd. $8 at 40 primitive sites. All year; 14-day limit. Closed during waterfowl season. 80 acres; 50-acre lake. Tbls, pit toilets, cfga, drkg wtr, picnic shelters, playground, handicap fishing pier. Fishing, boating(ld) GPS: 42.63765, -102.62868

HEMINGFORD (81W)
Box Butte State Recreation Area $8
9.5 mi N of Hemingford on SR 2. $8 at 40 undesignated primitive sites; $15 at 14 sites with 30/50-amp elec. All year; 14-day limit. 2,212 acres; 1,600-acre lake. Tbls, toilets, cfga, drkg wtr, shelters, playground. Swimming, fishing, boating(ld). GPS: 42.45567, -103.11284

HICKMAN (82E)
Stagecoach State Recreation Area $8
1 mi S of Hickman on S. 68th St; half mi W on Panama Rd; at W shore of 195-acre Stagecoach Lake. $8 at 50 undesignated primitive sites; $17 at 22 sites with 30/50-amp elec ($14 off-season but no wtr). All year; 14-day limit. Tbls, flush toilets, cfga, drkg wtr, fishing piers. Boating(ld), fishing. GPS: 40.59685, -96.64191

Wagon Train State Recreation Area $8
2 mi E of Hickman on either Hickman Rd or Wagon Train Rd, following signs. $8 at 80 primitive sites; $17 at 28 sites with 30/50-amp elec ($14 off-season but no wtr). All year;

14-day limit. Tbls, pit toilets, cfga, drkg wtr, playground, beach, dump. Fishing, swimming, boating(ld - 5 hp motor limit). GPS: 40.63625, -96.58482

HOLBROOK (83W)

Holbrook Public Park   FREE
W edge of town on Hwys 6 & 34, exit 237. Free but donations accepted. All year; 7-day limit. 5 RV sites. Drkg wtr, pit toilets, cfga, tbls, elec. Picnicking, playground. GPS: 40.3047287, -100.010129

HOLDREGE (84C)

City Campground $5
202 S East Ave at 2nd St in Holdrege. From eastbound US 6 from center of town, S (right) on East St, cross RR tracks to park. $5. All year; 3-night limit. 8 level but short RV back-in sites (40-ft RV limit) on concrete pads. 30/50-amp elec hookups, flush toilets, showers, cfga, dump, drkg wtr, tbls. Picnicking, fishing. Nice small park, but passing trains are noisy. Visitor reports toilets were locked. GPS: 40.26095, -99.22182

HOOPER (85E)

Hooper Memorial City Park   FREE
6 blocks N of Hwy 275 at 415 N. Main St. Free, but donation requested. All year; 1-night limit. 3 sites. Flush toilets, cfga, drkg wtr/elec hookups, tbls. Picnicking, swimming, playground, fishing. GPS: 41.6155533, -96.5489151

HUMBOLDT (86E)

Humboldt Lake City Recreation Park $10
1 mi S from jct of Hwys 105 & 4; at 1st & Long Branch Sts on N side of lake. $10. Apr-Sept; 2-day limit. 12 sites with elec hookups. Tbls, flush toilets, cfga, drkg wtr, elec, showers, pool($). Free public dump, 2 blocks. Fishing, swimming, tennis, boating(l), horseshoes, playground. GPS: 40.1594448, -95.9474985

Kirkman's Cove Recreation Area $12
Nemaha Natural Resources District
3 mi NW of Humboldt. $12. All year. $12 at 16 elec sites. Free primitive sites, but $5 for 2-day entry permit, $12 annual permit for all NRRD parks. Toilets, cfga, drkg wtr, tbls, beach, playground, outdoor chapel. Fishing, swimming, boating(dl), ball fields, sand volleyball, nature trails, golf. 510-acre area with 160-acre lake. GPS: 40.1808,-95.992299

JUNIATA (87C)

Prairie Lake Recreation Area   FREE
Little Blue Natural Resources District
3 mi S & qtr mi E of Juniata. Free All year. Primitive undesignated sites. Toilets, cfga, drkg wtr, tbls. Fishing, boating, archery. 124 acres; 36-acre lake. GPS: 40.534275,-98.488362

Roseland Lake Wildlife Management Area   FREE
Little Blue Natural Resources District
4.5 mi W & 2.2 mi S of Juniata. Free. All year; 14-day limit. About 7 primitive undesignated sites. Toilets, tbls, drkg wtr. Fishing, picnicking. GPS: 40.5542, -98.5859

KEARNEY (88C)

Fort Kearney State Recreation Area $8
From I-80 exit 279 E of Kearney, about 2.5 mi S on SR 10; 3 mi W on SR 50A, past Fort Kearney SP entrance; 1 mi N on 29 Rd; E into recreation area around 8 sand pits & S of Platt River. $8 at 25 non-elec sites during 9/16-5/14 but no wtr services ($13 in-season with wtr); $20 at 75 sites with 30/50-amp elec in-season ($14 off-season, no wtr services). 14-day limit. Tbls, flush toilets, cfga, drkg wtr, coin showers, dump, shelters, beach. Swimming, fishing at 8 sandpit lakes, boating(no mtrs), nature trail, hiking/biking trail. GPS: 40.654625, -98.994937

KIMBALL (89W)

Gotte Municipal Park   FREE
On US 30 in city limits; E edge of Kimball. From I-80 exit 20, 1 mi N on SR 71 (S. Chestnut) to center of town traffic light, then E about half mi on US 30 (E. Third St) past Dairy Queen to marked park entrance. Free. Open seasonally; 1-day limit. 10 RV sites (most sites are level), but no signs about RV parking. Tbls, flush toilets, cfga, drkg wtr, pool, playground. Picnicking; horseshoes, swimming, tennis, skateboard area. GPS: 41.2352583, -103.6493852

Oliver Reservoir State Recreation Area $8
8 mi W of Kimball on US 30. $8 at 175 primitive sites (75 at camping pads). All year; 14-day limit. 1,187 acres. Pit toilets, tbls, cfga, drkg wtr, beach. Fishing, boating(dl), swimming. GPS: 41.22453, -103.82729

KRAMER (90E)

Merganser Lake   FREE
Lower Platte South Natural Resources District
0.5 mi N of Kramer on SW 114th St; 1 mi E on W. Panama Rd; 0.5 mi N on SW 100th St. Free. All year; 14-day limit. Primitive open camping on 103-acre reserve at 41-acre lake. Drkg wtr, cfga, no toilets or tbls. Boating(l), fishing. GPS: 40.60139, -96.855

Olive Creek State Recreation Area $8
SE of Kramer at 3 campgrounds. For Area 1, 0.5 mi S of Kramer on SW 114th St; 1 mi E on Olive Creek Rd; 0.5 mi S on SW 100th St; E on access rd. For Area 3, 0.5 mi N of Kramer on SW 114th St; 2 mi E on W. Panama Rd; 1 mi S on SW 86th St, then W on W. Olive Creek Rd to lake's E shore. For Area 2, follow directions or Area 3 but turn W on access rd about 0.25 mi before W. Olive Creek Rd. $8 at 50 undesignated primitive RV/tent sites. All year; 14-day limit. Tbls, pit toilets, cfga, drkg wtr, playground. Fishing, boating (ld - 5 hp limit). 175-acre lake. GPS: 40.57679, -96.84611

Tanglewood Lake   FREE
Lower Platte South Natural Resources District
0.5 mi N of Kramer on SW 114th St; 1 mi W on W. Panama
Rd; 0.5 mi S on SW 128th Rd. Free. All year; 14-day limit.
Primitive open camping on 68-acre reserve at 33-acre
lake. No facilities except cfga, no drkg wtr. Fishing. GPS:
40.5894, -96.8984

Wild Plum Lake   FREE
Lower Platte South Natural Resources District
1.5 mi N of Kramer on SW 114th St; 0.5 mi W on W. Stagecoach Rd. Free. All year; 14-day limit. Primitive open
camping on 35-acre reserve at 16-acre lake. No facilities
except cfga, no drkg wtr. Boating(l), fishing. GPS: 40.6144,
-96.9025

LAUREL (91E)
Laurel City Park $5
In Laurel at 3rd & Cedar. $5. All year. 7 RV sites. Tbls, flush
toilets, cfga, drkg wtr, dump, showers, elec. Swimming,
playground. GPS: 42.4277783, -97.087826

Laurel Lions Club Municipal Park   Donations
600 Wakefield St, at 6th St, on the S edge of Laurel.
Donations appreciated; camp free. 4/1-10/1; 14-day limit.
5 sites. Elec/wtr hookups, flush toilets, cfga, drkg wtr,
showers, pool. Swimming, tennis. GPS: 42.4294449,
-97.0897704

LAWRENCE (92C)
Liberty Cove Recreation Area $5
Little Blue Natural Resources District
2 mi W; 2 mi S; qtr mi W of Lawrence on Hwy 4; in Webster
County. $5. All year; 14-day limit. Primitive undesignated
sites. Toilets, cfga, elec, drkg wtr, tbls. Boating(dl), fishing, swimming, 2.5 mi of hiking trails, bridle trail, arboretum. 247 acres. GPS: 40.267875, -98.306107

LEIGH (93E)
Centennial Park $5
Main St to dead end; right half mi. $5 at primitive sites,
$15 elec/wtr Apr-Oct. 14 RV sites with elec, drkg wtr,
flush toilets, showers, cfga, tbls, playground equipment,
dump. Fishing, boating(l), swimming, horseshoes, sand
volleyball, pool. GPS: 41.7055647, -97.246151

LEXINGTON (95W)
Johnson Lake State Recreation Area $8
7 mi S of Lexington on US 283. $8 at 94 non-elec sites during
9/16-5/14 but no wtr services ($13 in-season with wtr); $20
at 113 sites with 20/30/50-amp electric ($14 off-season but
no wtr). 14-day limit. Tbls, flush toilets, coin showers, cfga,
drkg wtr, dump, shelters, beach, 2 fish cleaning stations.
Swimming, boating(dl), fishing. 3 locations: main area on
SE side of lake has gravel pads with elec, showers, flush
toilets, dump, fish cleaning station, beach; across the lake,
South Side Inlet also has gravel pads, elec hookups, modern

restrooms, fishing pier, boat ramp, fish cleaning station;
North Side Inlet offers primitive sites, fishing pier, drkg wtr,
pit toilets. All areas leased from Central Nebraska Public
Power & Irrigation District. GPS: 40.68463, -99.82957

LONG PINE (96W)
Long Pine State Recreation Area $8
1 mi N of Long Pine on US 20; at Long Pine Creek. $8 at 20
undesignated primitive sites; $11 at 8 designated primitive
camping pads. All year; 14-day limit. Short sites most
suitable for small RVS & pickup campers. Tbls, pit toilets,
cfga, drkg wtr. Fishing, hiking. GPS: 42.54651, -99.7109

LOUISVILLE (97E)
Louisville State Recreation Area $12
Half mi NW of Louisville on SR 50; at S shore of Platte
River. $12 at 47 primitive undesignated sites; $13 at 13
non-elec camping pads ($8 during 9/16-5/14 but no wtr
services); $20 at 223 sites with 30/50-amp elec ($14
during 9/16-5/14 but no wtr). 14-day limit Tbls, flush toilets, solar showers, cfga, drkg wtr, dump, shelters, beach.
Swimming, boating (elec mtrs), fishing, hiking, biking. 142
acres. GPS: 41.00583, -96.17064

LOUP CITY (98C)
Bowman Lake State Recreation Area $8
Half mi W of Loup City on SR 92; at Loup River. $8. All year;
14-day limit. 10 primitive sites; 23 acres. Tbls, pit toilets,
cfga, drkg wtr, playground, shelters. Fishing, boating
(l - elec mtrs). 20-acre lake. GPS: 41.275635, -98.991455

Sherman State Recreation Area $7
Main camping area 2 mi E of Loup City on county rd; 1 mi
N to Thunder Bay area at S shore of Sherman Reservoir;
other areas off Trails 1, 2, 3, 8, 10 & 11. $8. All year; 14-day
limit. 360 primitive sites around 2,845-acre lake. Dump,
tbls, flush toilets, cfga, drkg wtr, playground, shelters,
coin showers, fish cleaning stations. Fishing, boating(ld).
GPS: 41.31469, -98.90856

LYNCH (99C)
Lynch RV Park & Campground $10
From SR 12 at E end of Lynch,1 block N on 4th St. to city
park. $10 for 6 diagonal 50-ft back-in RV sites with 30/50-
amp elec/wtr ($4 for 10 tent sites). Flush toilets, cfga, drkg
wtr, dump, playground. Swimming, fishing, boating(l).
GPS: 42.829238, -98.466183

LYONS (100C)
Island Park Municipal Campground $12
1 mi W on Main St in Lyons from jct with US 77. $12.
4/15-10/15. 16 RV sites. Tbls, flush toilets, showers, elec,
dump, cfga, wtr hookups, shelter, pool, play field. Swimming, fishing, tennis, sand volleyball, horseshoes. GPS:
41.9361041, -96.4808622

MADISON (101E)

Memorial Municipal Park $9
5 blocks N of Hwy 32 on Main St. $9-10. All year; 14-day limit. 9 RV sites, 4 tent sites. Tbls, flush toilets, cfga, drkg wtr, hookups, showers, dump. Park was once in poor condition, full of old, long-term RVs & not recommended; no recent field inspections made. If you stop there, let us know. GPS: 41.8350067, -97.4569927

Taylor Creek RV Park (Private) $10
501 W. 6th St. N. $10. All year (weather permitting). 8 RV sites. Tbls, flush toilets, hookups, cfga, drkg wtr, showers, dump. GPS: 41.8388955, -97.4583818

MALCOLM (102E)

Areas 10, 11 & Campgrounds $8
Branched Oak State Recreation Area
From Malcolm, 4 mi N on Malcolm Rd, becoming NW 112th St; 3 mi NE on W. Raymond Rd around E side of lake before becoming NW 91st St (then W access rd into Area 12); W on W. Davey Rd, then S into Areas 10 & 11 at NE shore of lake. $8. Primitive sites in open area. All year; 14-day limit. Tbls, toilets, cfga, drkg wtr, showers, dump, fishing pier. Fishing, boating, pay phone, shelters. Boating(l), fishing.

Middle Oak Campground (Area 4) $8
Branched Oak State Recreation Area
From Malcolm, 1 mi NW on Malcolm Rd, then left (W) for 2 mi on W. Bluff Rd; about 4 mi N on CR 140; 2 mi E on W. Branched Oak Rd to campground on W shore of lake. $8 at primitive undesignated sites; $13 at non-elec pads ($8 during 9/16-5/14 but no wtr); $20 at 20/30/50-amp elec sites ($14 off-season but no wtr); $26 at 12 full-hookup sites. All year; 14-day limit. Tbls, toilets, cfga, drkg wtr, showers, dump, playground, pay phone, fish cleaning station, shelters, beach. Boating(ld), fishing, hiking, swimming. Area 3 Campground entry is S off W. Branched Oak Rd before Middle Oak Camp; Area 5 Campground entry is N off W. Branched Fork after passing Middle Oak; Area 3 Campground is accessed by turning N on N-126th St just before reaching Area 4; all have primitive sites for $8; Area 3 offers equestrian sites with drkg wtr, toilets & cfga. GPS: 40.9711, -96887

South Shore Campground (Area1) $8
Branched Oak State Recreation Area
From Malcolm, 4 mi N on Malcolm Rd, becoming NW 112th St; at S shore of lake. $8 for primitive undesignated sites; $13 at designated non-elec pads ($8 during 9/16-5/14 but no wtr services); $20 at 20/30/50-amp elec sites ($14 off-season but no wtr). All year; 14-day limit. Tbls, toilets, cfga, drkg wtr, showers, dump, fish cleaning station, pay phone. Fishing, boating(l), hiking, horseback riding, mountain biking (3-mi multi-use trail). Area 2 Campground with primitive sites is W of South Shore; N off W. Raymond Rd GPS: 40.9586, -96.8724

Wildwood Lake FREE
Lower Platte South Natural Resources District
1 mi N of Agnew (NW if Branched Oak Lake) on SR 79; W. on Little Salt Rd. Free. All year; 14-day limit. Primitive open camping at 491-acre reserve at 103-acre lake. Toilets, cfga, no drkg wtr. Boating(l), hiking trails, hunting. GPS: 41.03806, -96.83889

MARTELL (103E)

Cottontail Lake Recreational Use Area FREE
Lower Platte South Natural Resources District
1 mi N of Martell on SW 29th St. Free. All year; 14-day limit. Open primitive camping on 148-acre reserve at 29-acre lake. No facilities except cfga, no drkg wtr. Boating(l), fishing. GPS: 40.603212, -96.854532

MAYWOOD (104W)

Maywood Village Park $5
From US 83, about 1 mi E on SR 23 to center of town; N (left) on Commercial for 2 blocks; park on right at end of 2nd block. $5. Open 5/15-9/15; 5-day limit. 3 undesignated RV sites, 3 tent sites. Tbls, flush toilets, cfga, drkg wtr, elec, dump. No fee signs, no silent ranger. On-street parking; need extension cord to reach elec box. GPS: 40.654956, -100.619327

MCCOOK (105W)

Karrer Municipal Park Donations
At the E edge of McCook on SRs 6/34. 4/1-11/1; 3-day limit. Donations appreciated. 7 RV sites (trailers under 30 ft). Tbls, toilets, 20-amp elec, cfga, drkg wtr, dump, showers, pay phone. Picnicking; golf nearby. GPS: 40.197507, -100.601895

Red Willow Reservoir State Recreation Area $8
11 mi N of McCook on US 83; W on access rds around the reservoir (also called at Hugh Butler Lake). $8 at 110 sites in open primitive areas; $13 at 50 developed non-elec sites ($8 during 9/16-5/14 but no wtr services); $20 at 45 sites (Willow View Campground) with 20/30-amp elec ($14 during 9/16-5/14 but no wtr); 14-day limit. Tbls, flush & pit toilets, cfga, drkg wtr, dump, beach, store, playground, coin showers, fish cleaning station. Boating(ld), fishing, swimming. Longhorn cattle display; prairie dog town near Spring Creek. GPS: 40.35979, -100.66351

MEADOW GROVE (106C)

Millstone State Wayside City Park DONATION
Half mi E of Meadow Grove on US 275. Camp free, but donations solicited. All year; 7-day limit. 3 undesignated RV sites. Tbls, pit toilets, cfga, drkg wtr, 15-amp elec, playground, picnic shelters. Picnicking; hiking. Old millstones.

MERRIMAN (107W)

Cottonwood Lake State Recreation Area $8
Half mi E of Merriman on US 20; half mi S on gravel Park

Rd. $8. All year; 14-day limit. 30 primitive undesignated sites. Tbls, pit toilets, cfga, drkg wtr, playground, shelters. Fishing; boating(ld). Most sites level. Adjacent to Arthur Bowring Sandhills Ranch State Historic Park. GPS: 42.91593, -101.67505

Shady Spot RV Camp (Priv.) $12
1 block N of Hwy 20 on Hwy 61 at Merriman; follow signs. $12 base (weekly rates available). 5/1-10/1. 6 RV sites. Hookups, drkg wtr, dump. GPS: 42.9197225, -101.7007033

MINDEN (108C)
Bassway Strip Wildlife Management Area   FREE
At I-80, Newark-Minden Interchange. Free. All year. 10 sites. Primitive camping. Drkg wtr, no shower. Swimming, boating, no motors; fishing. GPS: 40.68, -98.94.

MITCHELL (109W)
Scotts Bluff County Fairground $10
W on US 26 to 22nd Ave; S to 13th St, then right. $10 without hookups, $15 with elec/wtr. All year except fair time (about 8/10-8/17). About 80 RV sites, about 14 tent sites. Tbls, flush toilets, cfga, drkg wtr, elec ($), showers, dump. GPS: 41.940388, -103.818526

Ziegler Municipal Park $5
12th Ave & 12th St in town. $5. All year; 5-day limit. 4 elec RV sites. Tbls, cfga, drkg wtr, elec. GPS: 41.939168, -103.805894.

NEBRASKA CITY (110E)
Riverview Marina State Recreation Area $12
Access via US 75B & SR 2 just NE of Nebraska City; on Missouri River. $12 at 30 non-elec sites; $19 at 16 sites with 20/30-amp elec ($14 during 9/16-5/14 but no wtr). All year; 14-day limit. Tbls, flush toilets, cfga, drkg wtr, showers, shelter. Fishing, boating(dl). GPS: 41.69202, -95.85046

NELSON (112C)
Harbine Park $10
From SR 14 (Main St), W on W. 8th St to Denver St at NW corner of football field; park is on S side of football field; some low tree limbs. $10; 3-day limit (doesn't seem to be observed by squatters). 2-4 30-amp full hookup RV sites. Tbls, flush toilets, cfga, drkg wtr, showers, dump. Swimming. Veteran RVer recommends trying other nearby community parks. GPS: 40.11767, -98.04334

NENZEL (113W)
Steer Creek $5
Samuel R. McKelvie National Forest
19 mi S of Nenzel on NE S16F. $5. All year; 14-day limit. 23 sites, typically 57 ft. Tbls, toilets, cfga, firewood, drkg wtr. Picnicking; fishing, hunting. 10 acres. GPS: 42.6894484, -101.1537631

NEWCASTLE (114E)
Buckskin Hills Wildlife Management Area   FREE
2 mi W, 3 mi S & half mi W of Newcastle in Dixon County. Free. All year; 14-day limit. Undesignated primitive camping at 75-acre lake. Toilets, cfga, no drkg wtr. Boating(l), fishing. GPS: 42.62, -96.92.

NEWMAN GROVE (115C)
Newman Grove City Park $10
E end of Park Ave in Newman Grove. $10. Apr-Oct; no stay limit. 10 RV sites, full hookups. Tbls, flush toilets, cfga, drkg wtr, elec, pool, dump. Swimming, tennis, sand volleyball, playground. GPS: 41.7522318, -97.7786661

NEWPORT (116C)
Spring Valley Park   FREE
0.25 mi W of Newport on Hwy 20. Free. All year; 1-day limit. Primitive overnight camping. Tbls, toilets, cfga, drkg wtr. Among the oldest rest stops in Nebraska. GPS: 42.594449, -99.3337195

NORFOLK (117E)
Elkhorn Wayside   FREE
1 mi N of Norfolk on US 81 (paved access rds). Free. All year; 2-day limit. Undesignated sites. Tbls, toilets, cfga, drkg wtr, shelters. LP, flush toilets, showers, ice nearby. Picnicking, hiking. Game and Parks Commission District Office. Most sites are level. GPS: 42.02889, -97.73361

Ta-ha-zouka Municipal Park $12
S of viaduct on US 81 at Norfolk; at 22034 S. 13th St; near Elkhorn River. $12 without hookups; $18 with elec ($12 during 10/16-4/15 along rd outside campground). 4/15-10/15; 7-night limit. 13 sites with 20/30/50-amp elec. Tbls, flush toilets, cfga, drkg wtr, showers, dump WiFi. Recently renovated. GPS: 42.0058381, -97.4239405

NORTH LOUP (118E)
Davis Creek Recreation Area   FREE
Lower Loup Natural Resources District
From North Loup, 0.5 mi S on SR 11; 5.5 mi S on Ashton Hwy; left on access rd to SW shore of Davis Creek Reservoir. Free. All year. Primitive sites. Tbls, toilets, cfga, drkg wtr, fishing pier. Nature trails, boating(dl), fishing. GPS: 35.1647, -84.09555

NORTH PLATTE (119W)
Buffalo Bill Ranch State Recreation Area $8
From North Platt, N on US 83; 1.7 mi W (left) on Hwy 30; 1 mi N (right) on Buffalo Bill Ave to Scout's Rest Ranch Rd; left 0.25 mi, then right on gravel rd for 0.75 mi; along Platte River & adjacent to Buffalo Bill Historical Park. $8 at 6 primitive sites; $15 at 23 elec (50-amp) sites ($8 during 9/16-5/14 but no wtr). All year; 14-day limit. Tbls, toilets, cfga, drkg wtr, shelter. Hiking, fishing. GPS: 41.16219, -100.79494

Cody Municipal Park $5
3 mi N of I-80 on Hwy 83, exit 177. $5. 5/1-10/15; 7-day
limit during 30-day period. 39 RV sites. Tbls, flush toilets,
cfga, drkg wtr, dump, playground. Swimming, fishing,
boating(l). GPS: 41.1494424, -100.760979

Lake Maloney State Recreation Area $8
5 mi S of North Platte on US 83; half mi W on access rd. $8
at 200 sites in open primitive areas; $17 at 56 modern sites
with 20/30-amp elec ($14 during 9/16-5/14 but no wtr ser-
vices). All year; 14-day limit. Tbls, pit toilets, cfga, drkg wtr,
dump, showers, 2 fish cleaning stations, 2 beaches. Swimming, fishing, boating(dl), playground. GPS: 41.048, -100.699

OAKLAND (120E)
Oakland City Park   DONATIONS
SW edge of Oakland on SR 32. Donations, but $15 sug-
gested. 4/1-11/1. 6 RV sites. Wtr/elec hookups, flush
toilets, cfga, drkg wtr, showers, dump. Swimming pool,
picnicking, tennis, basketball, sand volleyball, playground.
Large, shady park. 40-acre park contains century-old
maple tree, flower garden, picnic areas, shelter. GPS:
41.8319379, -96.4780823

OBERT (121E)
Obert City Park   Donations
S side of Hwy 12 in Obert at Main St. Donations requested; camp free. All year. 2 primitive RV/tent sites. Tbls, pit
toilets, cfga, drkg wtr, elec. GPS: 42.6897205, -97.028101

OCONTO (122W)
Pressey State Wildlife Management Area   FREE
5 mi N of Oconto on NE 21. Free. All year; 14-day limit. 15
undesignated sites. Tbls, toilets, cfga, elec hookups, playground. Picnicking; fishing; swimming. GPS: 41.189599,
-99.709811.

ODESSA (123C)
Union Pacific State Recreation Area $8
At Odessa interchange of I-80; 2 mi N. $8. All year; 14-day
limit. 5 undesignated primitive sites on 26 acres. Flush
toilets, tbls, cfga, drkg wtr. Limited facilities in winter.
Boating (elec mtrs), fishing. GPS: 40.67777, -99.25293

OGALLALA (124W)
Arthur Bay Campground $8
Lake McConaughy State Recreation Area
1.5 mi W of jct SR 92/61, 2 mi W of dam on N side of lake
(Gate 2) on Shoreline Rd. $8. All year; 14-day limit. Open
camping. Toilets, tbls, cfga, drkg wtr. 600 undesignated
sites. Toilets, cfga, tbls, drkg wtr, coin showers, dump,
beaches. Boating(l), fishing, swimming, waterskiing. GPS:
41.2513789, -101.7204528

Cedar Vue Campground $8
Lake McConaughy State Recreation Area
13 mi W of jct of with SR 61 on SR 92 (Shoreline Rd) just W

of Otter Creek, Gate 13. $8 at primitive sites in open areas;
$20 at modern sites with elec ($14 during 9/16-5/14 but no
wtr services). All year; 14-day limit. 117 sites. Toilets, tbls,
showers, cfga, dump, beach, fish cleaning station, beach.
Boating(ld), fishing, swimming, waterskiing, playground.
GPS: 41.2952661, -101.9282349

Eagle Canyon Campground $8
Lake McConaughy State Recreation Area
15 mi W on US 26 from jct with SR 61; 5 mi N on access
rd; on S side of lake. $8. All year; 14-day limit. About 100
undesignated primitive sites. Popular among fishermen.
Pit toilets, cfga, drkg wtr, tbls. Boating(l), fishing, swimming, waterskiing. GPS: 41.271952, -101.968973

Lake Ogallala State Recreation Area $8
9 mi N of Ogallala on SR 61. $8 at 180 primitive sites;
$13 at 20 non-elec sites ($8 during 9/16-5/14 but no wtr
services); $20 at 62 elec sites ($14 during 9/16-5/14, but
no wtr services). All year; 14-day limit. Flush & pit toilets,
cfga, tbls, drkg wtr, dump, showers, fish cleaning station.
Boating(ld), fishing, swimming, playground, hiking trails.
320-acre lake. GPS: 41.226074, -101.662842

Lakeview Campground $8
Lake McConaughy State Recreation Area
7 mi W of Ogallala on US 26 from jct with SR 61. $8. All
year; 14-day limit. Open primitive camping. Toilets, cfga,
drkg wtr, showers. Boating, swimming, fishing, picnicking, waterskiing. GPS: 41.2383229, -101.848233

LeMoyne Bay Campground $8
Lake McConaughy State Recreation Area
7 mi W of dam on SR 92; on N shore. $8. All year;
14-day limit. Open camping; about 200 undesignated
primitive sites. Pit toilets, cfga, drkg wtr, tbls. Boating(l-
rd), swimming, fishing, waterskiing. GPS: 41.2824891,
-101.8098991

Little Thunder Campground $8
No Name Bay
Lake McConaughy State Recreation Area
On W side of No Name Bay, which is on Nor shore along
Shore Line Rd just W of Martin Bay. $8 at primitive sites;
$13 at pads without elec ($8 during 9/16-5/14, but no
wtr services); $20 at 34 modern sites with elec; $26 at 8
sites with full hookups (elec sites $14 during 9/16-5/14,
but no wtr services). All year; 14-day limit. Tbls, flush &
pit toilets, cfga, drkg wtr, coin showers. Boating, fishing,
swimming. GPS: 41.251098, -101.711799

Lone Eagle Campground $8
Lake McConaughy State Recreation Area
Jct SR 92/61 at Sandy Beach area on N shore of lake. $8 at
primitive sites; $13 at developed non-elec sites ($8 during
9/16-5/14 but no wtr services); $20 at 54 30-amp and 14
50-amp elec sites; $26 at 16 full-hookup sites. Elec sites

$14 during 9/16-5/14, but no wtr services. All year; 14-day limit. Tbls, flush & pit toilets, coin showers, cfga, drkg wtr, dump. Boating, fishing. GPS: 41.25526, -101.69071

Martin Bay Campground $8
Lake McConaughy State Recreation Area
N end of Kingsley Dam. $8. All year; 14-day limit. 600 undesignated sites. Toilets, dump, picnic shelter, drkg wtr cfga, tbls, beach, fish cleaning station, playground. Boating(ld), fishing, swimming, waterskiing. Lake's most popular camping area. GPS: 41.251379, -101.6990634

No Name Bay Campground $8
Lake McConaughy State Recreation Area
On W shore along Shoreline Rd (first bay W of Martin Bay). $8. All year; 14-day limit. Open primitive camping. Tbls, flush toilets, showers, cfga, drkg wtr, playground, dump. GPS: 41.1502, -101.4227

North Shore Campground $8
Lake McConaughy State Recreation Area
About 5 mi W of dam on SR 92 (Gate #5); follow gravel W to site. $8. Open primitive camping at undesignated sites. Tbls, toilets, cfga, no drkg wtr. GPS: 41.2666561, -101.8004544

Ogallala Beach $8
Lake McConaughy State Recreation Area
5 mi N of Ogallala & 2.5 mi N of Hwy 26/61 jct. $8. All year; 14-day limit. Open primitive camping. Toilets, no drkg wtr, tbls, cfga, beach. Boating, fishing, swimming, picnicking, waterskiing. GPS: 41.2055465, -101.7240636

Omaha Beach Campground $8
Lake McConaughy State Recreation Area
15 mi W of jct of SR 92/61 on Hwy 92; on NW side of lake. $8. All year; 14-day limit. Open camping; about 30 undesignated primitive sites. Toilets, cfga, drkg wtr, cfga, playground. Boating(l), fishing, swimming, picnicking, waterskiing. GPS: 41.298877, -101.9685135

Otter Creek Campground $8
Lake McConaughy State Recreation Area
11 mi W of jct of SR 92/61 on SR 92. $8. All year; 14-day limit. Open camping; about 400 undesignated primitive sites. Toilets, cfga, drkg wtr, cfga, dump, fish cleaning station, playground. Boating(ld), fishing, swimming, waterskiing. Regarded as a fisherman's headquarters. GPS: 41.2972105, -101.9246237

Sand Creek $8
Lake McConaughy State Recreation Area
10 mi W of jct of SR 92/61. $8. All year; 14-day limit. Open primitive camping. No facilities except toilets. Boating(l), fishing. GPS: 41.2880443, -101.8743449

Sandy Beach Campground $8
Lake McConaughy State Recreation Area
Jct SR 92/61. $8. All year; 14-day limit. Open camping. About 400 primitive sites. Toilets, drkg wtr, tbls, cfga. Boating, fishing, swimming, waterskiing. GPS: 41.2591564, -101.774065

Spring Park Campground $8
Lake McConaughy State Recreation Area
9 mi W of jct of SR 92/61 on access rd 9. $8. All year; 14-day limit. Open camping; about 150 undesignated sites. No facilities except toilets, cfga, playground equipment. Boating(l), fishing, swimming, picnicking. GPS: 41.2930443, -101.8735116

Theis Bay Campground $8
Lake McConaughy State Recreation Area
Along Shoreline Rd between Sandy Beach & Arthur Bay. $8. All year; 14-day limit. Open primitive camping at undesignated sites. Toilets, cfga, drkg wtr.

OHIOWA (125E)
Ohiowa Village RV Park $7
From jct with SR 74 N of town, S on SR 30C (becoming Main St) through Ohiowa; on NE corner of S. Main St & Stang St, under W side of city water tower. $7 ($150 monthly). 4/1-11/1. 6 RV sites with 30-amp elec/wtr/ sewer, 3 tent sites. Tbls, flush toilets, cfga, drkg wtr, dump. GPS: 40.24645, -97.27183

O'NEILL (126C)
Carney Municipal Park   Donations
In the S part of O'Neill on NE 281; or, as you come from the E or W on NE 20, turn S at the stop light (only one in town); go 4 blks; park is approx half blk past the railroad tracks, on the W side of the rd. 4/1-12/1. Donations requested; after 1 week, $11.40 per night. 18 RV sites, 4 tent sites. Wtr & elec hookups (15 amps), flush toilets, drkg wtr, cfga, dump, showers. Fishing in pond, horseshoes, sports field, playground, biking, sand volleyball. GPS: 42.4513922, -98.6448093

Goose Lake State Wildlife Management Area   FREE
22 mi S of O'Neill on US 281; 4 mi E to campground. Free. All year; 14-day limit. 10 sites on 349 acres. Tbls, toilets, cfga. Picnicking; fishing; swimming, boating(l). GPS: 42.118448, -98.573661.

ORD (127C)
Bussell Municipal Park $10
On 24th & G Sts in town; sites at N end of park. $10 at primitive sites; $15 at elec sites. All year; 5-day limit (longer with permission). 7 concrete RV sites plus tent area. Tbls, pit & flush toilets, drkg wtr, cfga, dump, 30-amp elec/wtr (one 50-amp), showers, playgrounds. No wtr in winter. Swimming pool, tennis, basketball, sand volley-

ball, nature trail, fishing pond, disc golf, golf. Beautifully maintained, patrolled. City's Anderson Island Park free for primitive sites. GPS: 41.6072, -98.9394

ORLEANS (128W)
Orleans City RV Park   FREE
2 mi S of Orleans on Hwy 136 at Harlan Ave. Free for 1 night per month, then $15 per night. All year. 10 RV sites. Tbls, drkg wtr, cfga, dump, full hookups. Picnicking, fishing. GPS: 40.133511, -99.453194

OSCEOLA (129E)
City Park   FREE
In town on US 81, across from Terry's Drive-In, go N on State St, then E immediately N of RR tracks to sites; main park with restrooms is farther N. Free. 3-day limit. All year. Undesignated sites & two 35-ft back-in sites with 30-amp elec. Wtr, flush toilets, cfga, tbls, shelter. Tennis, pool, sand volleyball, tennis, playground, ball fields. GPS: 41.183336, -97.545489.

OSMOND (130C)
Grove Lake State Wildlife Management Area   FREE
W of Osmond on US 20, then 2 mi N in Royal (paved access rds). Free. All year; 14-day limit. 15 sites; 1,600 acres. Tbls, toilets, cfga. Picnicking; fishing; hunting; boating(l); hiking (trails). 5 hp limit. GPS: 42.371369, -98.118764.

OXFORD (131W)
George R. Mitchell Municipal RV Park   FREE
In Oxford at Clark & Central (1 block S of US 136 on Central, then 1 block W on Clark, following camping signs). Free first night, $8 thereafter. All year. 10 sites with elec/wtr (2 with 50-amp). Tbls, pit toilets nearby, cfga, drkg wtr, dump, playground. Fishing (bass, crappie, catfish), disc golf. Park empty during field check; town not thriving. GPS: 40.247041, -99.636704

PARKS (134W)
Rock Creek Lake State Recreation Area $8
From Parks, 2 mi N on Avenue 327; 2 mi NW on county rd to Rock Creek Lake impoundment of Rock Creek. $8. All year; 14-day limit. 43 primitive sites on 54 acres. Pit toilets, tbls, cfga, drkg wtr. Fishing, boating (ld - elec mtrs). GPS: 40.46954, -101.52792

PIERCE (135C)
Gilman Municipal Park $10
1 block N of Main St in Pierce, on Mill St (Hwy 89). $10. 3/1-11/1; 5-day limit (longer with permission). 4 RV sites with 30-amp elec; unlimited tent space. Tbls, flush toilets, cfga, drkg wtr, elec, showers (at nearby pool during MD-8/15), shelter, pool. Boating(l), swimming, fishing, sand volleyball, horseshoes. Museum, 14-acre arboretum. GPS: 42.2008366, -97.5217246

Willow Creek State Recreation Area $8
Lower Elkhorn Natural Resources District
2 mi SW of Pierce. $8 at 18 non-elec sites during 9/16-5/14 but no wtr services ($13 in-season with wtr). $20 in-season at 84 elec sites ($14 during 9/16-5/14 but no wtr). All year; 14-day limit. Tbls, flush toilets, cfga, drkg wtr, coin laundry, showers, dump, beach. Swimming, fishing, horseback/hiking trail, archery, fishing pier. GPS: 42.17531, 097.57205

PLAINVIEW (136C)
Chilvers Municipal Park   FREE
1 block N of Hwy 20 at Maple. All year. 3 nights free, but $10 donation suggested. 4 RV sites with elec. Flush toilets, tbls, drkg wtr, showers, pool. Swimming, picnicking, tennis, playground. GPS: 42.3513933, -97.7906202

PLYMOUTH (137E)
Cub Creek Recreation Area   FREE
Lower Big Blue Natural Resources District
3 mi W of Plymouth, then 4.5 mi S. Free. All year; 14-day limit. Primitive camping on 85-acre reserve at 40-acre lake. Tbls, toilets, drkg wtr, cfga, shelter. Boating(l), fishing, hiking, hunting. GPS: 42.826, -99.916

Leisure Lake Wildlife Management Area   FREE
Lower Big Blue Natural Resources District
3 mi S of Plymouth. Free. All year; 14-day limit. Primitive open camping on 47-acre reserve at 38-acre lake. No facilities, no drkg wtr. Fishing, hunting, hiking.

PONCA (138E)
Ponca State Park $8
2 mi N of Ponca on SRs 9 & 12. During 5/15-9/15, $8 at 75 non-elec sites during 10/20-4/9 but no wtr services ($13 in-season wit wtr); $20 in-season at 92 elec (30/50-amp) sites ($14 off-season with no wtr). All year; 14-day limit. Tbls, flush toilets, showers, cfga, drkg wtr, dump, pool, shelters. Hiking trails, swimming, horseback trail rides, playground. GPS: 42.6024973, -96.7147589

RANDOLPH (140E)
Randolph City RV Park   DONATIONS
In Randolph, 5 blocks S of Hwy 20 & Main St, then 1 block E. Donations requested. All year. 6 RV sites. Elec, wtr, dump. Adjacent to Veteran's Memorial Park with playground, tbls, shelter, sand volleyball, ball fields, pool. GPS: 42.378613, -97.357

RAVENNA (141C)
Buffalo County Recreation Area   FREE
0.5 mi S of Ravenna on SR 61; 1 mi E on SR 2; NE on Buffalo Lake access rd. Free. All year. Primitive undesignated sites. Tbls, toilets, cfga, drkg wtr, playground. Boating(l), fishing. About 100 acres. State parks department plans to renovate & improve this park in the future as Ravenna State Recreation Area.

RED CLOUD (142C)

Bell's Sleepy Valley RV Park $12
Three-fourths mi N of Hwy 136 on US 281 near Red Cloud. $12. All year. 6 RV sites, 3 tent sites. All year. Hookups, tbls, flush toilets, drkg wtr, coin laundry, showers. GPS: 40.1027913, -98.5192272

REPUBLICAN CITY (143C)

Cedar Point/Patterson Harbor Park $10
Corps of Engineers
Harlan County Lake
From Republican City at jct with US 136, 5 mi S on CR A; at dam on the S side. During 5/15-9/15, $10 at 30 non-elec sites ($5 with federal senior pass); some sites open & free off-season. 14-day limit. 30-ft RV limit. Pit toilets, drkg wtr, cfga, picnic shelter, changehouse, beach, playground. Picnicking, hiking, boating(l), snowmobiling, motor bike trail, fishing, swimming. GPS: 40.045, -99.224

Gremlin Cove Park $12
Harlan County Lake
Corps of Engineers
From Republican City at jct with US 136, 1.2 mi S on CR A (Berrigan Rd) to the dam, on N side. During 5/15-9/15, $12 at 70 primitive gravel sites ($6 with federal senior pass). Some sites open & free off-season but reduced amenities. All year; 14-day limit. No RV size limit. Tbls, showers, flush & pit toilets, cfga, drkg wtr, beach, playground, changehouse, picnic shelter, beach. Fishing, swimming, boating(l), volleyball. GPS: 40.0852895, -99.2145362

Hunter Cove $7
Harlan County Lake
Corps of Engineers
From Republican City at jct with US 136, 1 mi S on Berrigan Rd; 0.5 mi W on CR B; on N side, E end of lake. During 5/1-9/30, $7 with federal senior pass at 47 non-elec RV/ tent sites; others pay $14; non-elec sites $12 in Oct, Nov & Apr ($6 with senior pass). In-season at 84 elec sites: $16 base, $20 at premium locations ($8 & $10 with senior pass); elec sites $12 in Oct, Nov & Apr ($6 with senior pass). RV limit in excess of 65 ft; 19 pull-through sites. Tent sites $12 in-season. Tbls, flush toilets, cfga, drkg wtr, showers, dump, fish cleaning station, playground, coin laundry, amphitheater, picnic shelters, beach. Swimming, boating(rl), fishing. Boat rentals at North Shore Marina. 275 acres. Non-campers pay $3 day use fee for boat ramp. GPS: 40.08306, -99.2277

North Outlet Park $10
Harlan County Lake
Corps of Engineers
From Republican City, 2 mi S on CR A, below dam on N side of the outlet. All year; 14-day limit. $10 at 30 non-elec sites during 5/15-9/15 ($5 with senior pass); some sites open & free off-season with reduced amenities & no wtr.

Tbls, pit toilets, cfga, drkg wtr, picnic shelter, playground. Hiking trails, fishing, boating, basketball. GPS: 40.072998, -99.210205

South Outlet Park $10
Harlan County Lake
Corps of Engineers
From Republican City, 2 mi S on CR A; 1 mi N on CR 1; below the dam. $10 at 30 non-elec sites during 5/15-9/15; some sites open & free off-season, but no wtr & reduced amenities. No RV size limit. 14-day limit. Tbls, pit toilets, cfga, drkg wtr. Fishing, boating, picnicking. 78 acres. GPS: 40.070313, -99.208984

REYNOLDS (144E)

Buckley Creek Recreation Area $5
Little Blue Natural Resources District
1 mi E & half mi N of Reynolds; in Jefferson County. All year. $5. Primitive undesignated sites. 4 hookups, tbls, toilets, cfga, drkg wtr. Boating(l), golf. Arboretum. 78 acres. This is considered the second-muddiest lake in the world, the mud composed of volcanic ash; no fish can live in it. GPS: 40.168073, -97.179026.

RUSHVILLE (145W)

Rushville Service Center (Private) $10
On W end of town, N side of Hwy 20 & S of RR tracks; at E side of the business. $10 base. All year. 6 sites with hookups, 5 tent sites. Tbls, toilets, cfga, drkg wtr, sewer, dump. Monthly rates available. GPS: 42.43107, -102.28172

Smith Lake State Wildlife Management Area   FREE
23 mi S of Rushville on NE 250. All year; 14-day limit. 15 primitive sites; 640 acres. Tbls, toilets, cfga, playground. Picnicking; swimming; fishing; boating (5 hp motor limit). GPS: 42.408098, -102.443850.

ST. EDWARD (146C)

St. Edward City Park $6
3rd & Clark St (1 blk N of SR 39). $6. Apr-Oct; 7-day limit. 3 RV sites with elec. All year. Drkg wtr, dump, tbls, flush toilets, playground, shelters. Swimming pool, sand volleyball, horseshoe pits, tennis. GPS: 41.5709, -97.8655

SANTEE (147C)

Mnisose Wicot (Wandering River)   FREE
Municipal Park
In center of town on Veteran's Memorial Dr. Free, but donations accepted. All year. Tbls, flush toilets, cfga, drkg wtr, dump. Fishing. 40-acre park along Missouri River.

SCOTTSBLUFF (150W)

Lake Minatare State Recreation Area $8
5 mi N of Scottsbluff on SR 71; 6 mi E on gravel CR F. $8 at 110 primitive sites in open camping areas around the lake; $13 at 49 developed non-elec sites ($8 during 9/16-5/14 but no wtr services); $20 at 52 gravel 20/30-amp elec

sites ($14 during 9/16-5/14 but no wtr services). All year; 14-day limit. Tbls, toilets, cfga, drkg wtr, dump, shelters, showers, 3 fish cleaning stations, coin laundry, beach, playground. Fishing, swimming, boating(ld), waterskiing. GPS: 41.943359, -103.516357

Riverside City Campground $10
1 mi W of Broadway on S. Beltline Hwy. $10 without hookups; $15 elec/wtr; $20 full hookups ($60, $90 & $120 weekly; $200, $300 & $400 monthly). 5/1-9/30. 43 pull-through RV sites, 50 tent sites. Tbls, flush toilets, cfga, drkg wtr, showers, dump ($5), elec. Fishing, playground, zoo($), hiking. GPS: 41.861221, -103.69505

SCRIBNER (151E)
Dead Timber State Recreation Area $8
4 mi N of Scribner on US 275; 1.5 mi E on CR B; 0.5 mi S on 12 Blvd; at Elkhorn River. $8 at 25 primitive sites; $17 at 17 sites with 20/30-amp elec ($14 during 9/16-5/14 but no wtr services. All year; 14-day limit. Tbls, pit toilets, cfga, drkg wtr, playground, shelter. Pack out trash due to budget cuts. Boating (nonpowered or elec mtrs), fishing, canoeing. 200 acres. GPS: 41.71698, -96.69138

Powderhorn State Wildlife Management Area   FREE
4 mi N of Scribner on US 275; adjoins Dead Timbers SRA; on the Elkhorn River (state canoe trail access). All year; 14-day limit. Primitive undesignated camping. Toilets, cfga, no drkg wtr. 289 acres. Hunting, fishing, canoeing. GPS: 41.71, -96.69.

SEWARD (152C)
Blue Valley Municipal Campground $10
Half mi S of Seward on SR 15. $10 for RV sites ($7 seniors), $7 tents. 4/1-11/1; 14-day limit. 16 RV sites, 100 tent sites. Tbls, pit toilets, cfga, drkg wtr, elec hookups, dump, playground. Fishing, playground. GPS: 40.9022307, -97.097534

SHELTON (153C)
War Axe State Recreation Area $8
4 mi S of Shelton on SR 10D, at Shelton Rd I-80 Interchange, Exit 291. $8. All year; 14-day limit. 8 primitive sites. Tbls, flush toilets, cfga, drkg wtr, shelters. Fishing, boating (elec mtrs). GPS: 40.72391, -98.63473

SHICKLEY (154C)
Shickley South Park   CLOSED
At 101 N. Market St. near downtown Shickley on N. Railroad St. No longer exists. New campground coming in late 2015.

SILVER CREEK (155C)
Silver Creek Park   FREE
In town with entrances on First St & Vine St, off Hwy 39. From US 30, 1.25 blks on SR 39 (Vine St). Free. May-Oct. Undesignated RV sites; 4 double 15-amp elec outlets on 2

posts. Tbls, flush toilets, cfga, drkg wtr, playground. Ball fields, horseshoes. Low-cost camping also available at Fisher's Cove private camp S of town. GPS: 41.3150, -97.6621.

SPALDING (156C)
City Park   Donations
2 blocks S of post office next to ballfield in SE corner of town. Donations suggested; camp free. All year; 2-day limit (longer with permission). 4 RV sites. Drkg wtr, cfga, tbls, 30-amp elec, flush toilets, dump, playground. Swimming, fishing. GPS: 41.6871, -98.3593

Spalding Dam Site   Donations
Almost 1 mi S of Spalding on Cedar River. Donations suggested; camp free. All year; 2-day limit (longer with permission). 4 RV sites, 15 tent sites. Hookups, pit toilets, cfga, drkg wtr. Fishing, boating(l), swimming. GPS: 41.6889002, -98.363404

SPENCER (158C)
City Park $3
Boyd County Fairgrounds
On Logan St (W edge of town). From SR 12, 3 blocks W on Main St, then N on Logan to first fairground entrance. $3 dry camping; $8 with wtr or elec. 4/15-10/1; 8 RV sites plus primitive sites (one 50-amp site, two 20-amp, one 30-amp). Drkg wtr, flush toilets, cfga, showers. Swimming, picnicking. GPS: 42.8738877, -98.7014753

SPRAGUE (159E)
Bluestem State Recreation Area $8
2.5 mi W of Sprague on W. Sprague RD at 325-acre Bluestem Lake. $8. All year; 14-day limit. 219 primitive sites, 19 with pads. Tbls, pit toilets, cfga, drkg wtr, dump, beach. Fishing, swimming, boating(l), archery range. GPS: 40.63915, -96.80171

SPRINGVIEW (160C)
Cub Creek Lake   FREE
State Fishing Access Lake
8.5 mi W of Springview in Keya Paha County (3 mi N of Jansen). Free primitive camping. Toilets, cfga, no drkg wtr. Boating(ld), fishing, swimming.

STAPLETON (161W)
Stapleton Village Park   FREE
1.5 blks W of Main St on NE 92 or 3rd St in Stapleton (from US 83, W on SR 92/3rd St into town); enter with RV from G St E of park entrance because of trees, then N & W across grass. Free but donations suggested. All year. About 4 undesignated sites. Flush toilets, 30-amp elec/wtr, drkg wtr, cfga, tbls, playground, dump. Picnicking. GPS: 41.28.841, -100.30886

STERLING (162E)
Sterling Village Park   Donations
Corner of Iowa & Lincoln Sts (NE corner of town). Dona-

NEBRASKA

476

tions suggested; camp free. 4/15-11/1; 1-day limit. 2 RV sites & tent spaces. Tbls, flush toilets, cfga, elec, drkg wtr, playground, shelter. Tennis courts, sand volleyball, ball field. GPS: 40.4591663, -96.3775136.

STRANG (163E)
Strang City Park — FREE
On Main St between Sharon & Racine Sts at S end of Strang. Free. Tbls, pit toilets, cfga, drkg wtr, no elec available during field inspection.

STROMSBURG (164C)
Buckley Municipal Park — FREE
S edge of Stromsburg on US 81; between confluence of Big Blue River & Prairie Creek; N of city park at camping sign, just S of the RR line. Free for 2 nights; donations suggested. 4/1-10/15; 2-day limit (longer with permission--$8 thereafter); no wtr or restrooms during 10/15-5/1. Twelve 20/30/50-amp elec sites, 11 30-amp, 11 20-amp. Tbls, showers, flush toilets, dump, drkg wtr, firewood, playgrounds. Food, ice, laundry, store nearby. Swimming pool, picnicking, tennis, softball, sports field, sand volleyball, horseshoe complex, trails. Sites on N & W of loop are 30-ft back-ins; 3 sites on E loop handles 45-ft back-ins. GPS: 41.106681, -97.5994961

STUART (165C)
Stuart Municipal Park — $10
1 mi N of Stuart's Main St off US 20. $10 (weekly rates available). Mar-Nov; 14-day limit. 20 RV sites; no RV size limit. Tbls, flush toilets, cfga, drkg wtr, elec/wtr/sewer, showers, dump, playground. GPS: 42.5991677, -99.1426014.

SUPERIOR (166C)
Lincoln Park Municipal Campground — FREE
From W of town on SR 14, follow camping signs on W. Fourth St. Donations suggested, but camp free. All year; 3-day limit (see city clerk for extension, $5 per day for 14 days). 20 concrete RV sites with 30-amp elec/wtr. Tbls, flush toilets, cfga, drkg wtr, dump, playground. Horseshoes, sand volleyball. Note: 3-ton bridge weight limit on 4th St from center of town. GPS: 40.020569, -98.082822

SUTHERLAND (167W)
Sutherland Reservoir State Recreation Area — $8
2 mi SW of Sutherland on SR 25. $8. All year; 14-day limit. 85 primitive sites (50 designated with pads). Pit toilets, cfga, drkg wtr, fish cleaning station, beach. Swimming, fishing, boating(ld). 3,017-acre lake. GPS: 41.10646, -101.13099

SYRACUSE (168E)
Syracuse South Park — $10
Municipal Campground
3rd & Midland Sts on S end of Syracuse. $10 for 40 sites with elec/wtr; $16 for 5 sites with full hookups ($100 per

week). 5/1-10/15; 14-day limit. Drkg wtr, cfga, tbls, flush & pit toilets, dump, elec. Sand volleyball, horseshoes, playground, ball field, batting cage. GPS: 40.6572236, -96.1863975

TAYLOR (169C)
City RV Tourist Park — $6
(Hoops Municipal Park)
From US 281, 2 blocks W on Broadway St (SR 91) to 5th St. $6 base with elec; $12 with full hookups. 4/1-11/15. Six small 30-amp full-hookup RV sites (no tents). Drkg wtr, elec. Restrooms at city park 1 block E. GPS: 41.7708, -99.3823

TEKAMAH (171E)
Pelican Point State Recreation Area — $10
4 mi E of Tekamah on CR GA; 4 mi N on CR 45; right (E) 1 mi on CR KL to park; at W shore of Missouri River. $10. All year; 14-day limit. 6 non-elec sites on 36 acres. Pit toilets, cfga, tbls, drkg wtr. Fishing, boating(ld). River boat access. GPS: 41.83667, -96.111084

Summit Lake State Recreation Area — $8
1 mi S of Tekamah on US 75, 3 mi W on CR EF. $8 at 22 undesignated primitive sites; $9 at 15 designated non-elec sites; $17 at 30 sites with 50-amp elec ($14 during 9/16-5/14 but no wtr services). All year; 14-day limit. Tbls, pit toilets, cfga, drkg wtr, beach, fish cleaning station. Fishing, boating(dl), swimming. 190-acre lake. GPS: 41.7597, -96.29503

Tekamah Memorial Park — $10
1 block N of S St. on US 75 in Tekamah. $10. All year. 8 sites with 20/30-amp elec/wtr. Tbls, toilets, cfga, drkg wtr, sewer, dump. Swimming, playground, tennis, basketball. Pool nearby.

THEDFORD (172W)
Thedford City Park — FREE
From US 83 & SR 2, W through Thedford to city park sign on E side of town, S side of SR 2 (access park just past baseball field to avoid low-hanging tree limbs. Free, but donations requested. All year. About 4 back-in RV sites with 15/20/30-amp elec. Tbls, drkg wtr, no dump, no restrooms. GPS: 41.58642, -100.34942

TILDEN (173C)
Tilden Sunrise Park — DONATIONS
From US 275 in Tilden, S on Elm St, then E on 2nd St between Walnut & East St. Donations. 4/1-11/1; 14-day limit in 30-day period. 4 short back-in RV sites, one for big rigs. Flush toilets, 30-amp elec/wtr hookups, cfga, dump (hard to use). Fishing. Sign in at city clerk office. Park is maintained by Girl Scouts. Formerly called East City Park. GPS: 42.046879, -97.827388

TOBIAS (174E)

Swan Lake Recreation Area   FREE
Lower Big Blue Natural Resources District
4 mi E of Tobias and 6 mi N. Free. All year; 14-day limit.
Open primitive camping on 195-acre reserve at 95-acre
lake. Tbls, toilets, cfga, drkg wtr, shelter. Boating(l), fishing, hiking, hunting. GPS: 40.30596, -97.152595

TRENTON (175W)

Swanson Reservoir $8
State Recreation Area
2 mi W of Trenton on US 34. $8 at 150 primitive sites in
open camping areas around the lake; $20 at 54 sites with
20/30-amp elec in two modern campgrounds ($14 during
9/16-5/14 but no wtr services). All year; 14-day limit. Tbls,
flush toilets, cfga, drkg wtr, dump, playground, fish cleaning stations. Boating(lrd), fishing, swimming. 4,794-acre
lake at the Republican River. GPS: 40.15677, -101.06213

VALENTINE (176W)

Ballards Marsh Wildlife Management Area   FREE
20 mi S on SR 83. Free. All year. 10 sites; 939 acres. Primitive camping. Pit toilets, tbls, cfga. Picnicking, hiking.
GPS: 42.35.693, -100.539516.

Big Alkali Lake Wildlife Management Area   FREE
12 mi S on US 83, 3 mi W on SR 483. Free. All year; 14-day
limit. 10 sites; 880 acres. Primitive camping. Pit toilets,
tbls, cfga. Swimming, boating(l), fishing. Primarily a fishing camp. GPS: 42.63, -100.60.

Merritt Reservoir State Recreation Area $8
25 mi SW of Valentine on SR 97. $8 at 190 undesignated
primitive sites; $17 at 28 sites with 30/30-amp elec ($14
during 9/16-5/14 but no wtr services). All year; 14-day
limit. Tbls, flush toilets, cfga, drkg wtr, shelters, dump,
showers, 2 fish cleaning stations. Fishing, boating(d).
GPS: 42.60175, -100.88588

Valentine City Park $5
1 mi N of Valentine on NE 20; follow Main St N toward the
pine-covered hills and down into the valley. $5. All year;
5-day limit. About 32 undesignated sites; no RV size limit.
Tbls, flush toilets (in-season), cfga, showers (in-season),
wtr, sewer, playground, free dump at baseball field (N on
Green St from fairgrounds, E on Bias St). Picnicking, fishing,
horseshoes. A natural park on the banks of Minnechaduza
Creek. (Note: A reader said no showers provided during
visit. Nice wooded park with stream.) GPS: 42.531, -100.327

VALPARAISO (177E)

Red Cedar Lake Recreation Area   FREE
Lower Platte South Natural Resources District
6 mi N & 2 mi W of Valparaiso. Free. All year; 14-day limit.
Primitive open camping on 175-acre reserve at 51-acre
lake. Portable toilets Apr-Oct, cfga, no drkg wtr. Boat-
ing(l), fishing.

VENICE (178E)

Two Rivers State Recreation Area $8
1 mi S & 1 mi W of Venice on SR 92. $8 at 10 primitive
sites; $13 at 106 designated non-elec sites; $20 at 113
sites with 20/30-amp elec, $22 with elec/wtr hookups.
MD-LD; 14-day limit. 5 camping areas. Tbls, flush toilets,
showers, cfga, drkg wtr, dump, shelters, 2 fish cleaning
stations, beach. Swimming, boating, biking(r), fishing,
hiking trail. GPS: 41.219238, -96.353516

VERDIGRE (179C)

Wildwood Acres Municipal Park $11
From jct of Hwys 14 & 84, W on SR 84, then S into park at
camping sign. $11 (tents, $9). All year. 27 RV sites (many
short, back-in). Tbls, flush toilets, cfga, drkg wtr, 30-amp
& 15/20-amp elec, showers, pool. Swimming, tennis,
basketball, sand volleyball, playground. GPS: 42.5938914,
-98.0281257

VERDON (180E)

Verdon State Recreation Area $8
Half mi W of Verdon on US 73. $8. All year; 14-day limit. 20
primitive sites. Tbls, pit toilets, cfga, drkg wtr, playground.
Fishing, boating (nonpower or elec mtrs). GPS: 40.14742,
-95.72422

VIRGINIA (181E)

Wolf-Wildcat Wildlife Management Area   FREE
Lower Big Blue Natural Resources District
6 mi S of Virginia. Free. All year; 14-day limit. Open primitive camping on 160-acre reserve at 42-acre lake. No
facilities, no drkg wtr. Fishing, hiking, hunting.

WAUNETA (182W)

Wauneta RV Park $10
At Wauneta on US 6. $10. All year. 32 RV sites. Tbls, toilets,
cfga, drkg wtr, elec, sewer. Swimming, playground.

WAUSA (183C)

Gladstone City Park   Donations
From jct with SR 121, 2 blocks N on N. Vivian St; right
into park. Camp free; donation encouraged. 4/15-10/1. 7
RV sites. Tbls, flush toilets, cfga, drkg wtr, dump, elec.
Swimming, playground. GPS: 42.5027802, -97.5431181

WAYNE (184E)

Henry Victor Municipal Park $7
Wayne Public Works Department
From jct of SR 15 & 35, 1 mi S on SR 15. $7. All year;
5-day limit (longer on request). 20 RV sites with tbls,
flush toilets, cfga, drkg wtr, elec, dump, playground. GPS:
42.2261143, -97.0183792

Lions RV Park $10
1.5 mi E of Wayne on SR 35 at airport. $10. 4/1-10/31. 10
RV sites; 4 acres. Dump, tbls, cfga, drkg wtr, phone, pit
toilets, playground. GPS: 42.2361141, -96.9892119

WELLFLEET (185W)

Wellfleet Lake   FREE
State Wildlife Management Area
Half mi SW of Wellfleet. Free. All year. Primitive camping at 50-acre lake. Toilets, tbls, cfga. Fishing, boating(l); no motors. GPS: 40.75, -100.74.

WEST POINT (186E)

Neligh City Park $10
3 blocks W of West Point on Hwy 275; at 400 W. Bridge St. $10. 4/1-10/1. 8 RV sites with 50-amp elec/wtr (30-ft RV limit); numerous tent spaces. Tbls, flush toilets, cfga, drkg wtr, dump ($2), elec, showers during pool hours($). Picnicking, sand volleyball, horseshoe pits, fishing, swimming. GPS: 41.8427772, -96.7161433

WESTERN (187E)

Village Park   FREE
Half block E of Main St on Sumner St. in Western. Camp free, but donations suggested. All year; 7-day limit. 2 sites with 20/30/50-amp elec; 4 sites no elec. Tbls, flush toilets, cfga, drkg wtr, dump, showers, store. GPS: 40.3930, -97.19615

WOOD LAKE (189W)

Wood Lake City Park   Donations
3 blks N of SR 20 on Main St, 1 blk E in Wood Lake. Free, but donations requested (no donations box, though). 5/1-9/30; 2-day limit at hookup sites. 2 sites with wtr/elec hook-ups (one 30-amp, one 50-amp). No parking inside park except next to 2 wtr/elec hookups. Toilets, pit tbls, cfga, drkg wtr. Not recommended; inconvenient elec, foul toilets during field trip. GPS: 42.6386118, -100.2381825

WYMORE (190E)

Big Indian Recreation Area   CLOSED
Lower Big Blue Natural Resources Dist.
6 mi S of Wymore on US 77; 2 mi W on Hwy 8. Closed to camping. GPS: 40.056567, -96.692517

YANKTON, SOUTH DAKOTA (191C)

Cottonwood Recreation Area $8
Lewis & Clark Lake
Corps of Engineers
From Yankton, South Dakota, 4 mi W on SR 52, then S on Dam Toe Rd; E of dam on the downstream side. About 4/21-10/16; 14-day limit. $8 base with federal senior pass at 77 elec (30/50-amp) sites; others pay $16 base, $18 at premium locations ($9 with senior pass). During off-season, some sites open & free, but no wtr services & reduced amenities. RV limit in excess of 65 ft. Tbls, flush toilets, cfga, drkg wtr, fish cleaning station, shelter, dump, playground, showers. Boating(l), fishing, tennis. GPS: 4.85861, -97.4825

Nebraska Tailwaters Rec. Area $12
Lewis & Clark Lake
Corps of Engineers
From Yankton, South Dakota, 2 mi S on US 81, then 4 mi W on Nebraska SR 121; E of the dam on S side of river off Rt 121. $12 at 11 non-elec sites ($6 with federal senior pass); $8 with senior pass at 31 elec (30/50-amp) sites; others pay $16. About 5/15-10/15; 14-day limit. RV limit in excess of 65 ft. Tbls, flush toilets, cfga, drkg wtr, fish cleaning station, shelter, dump, showers, picnic shelters. Golf, hiking, boating(l), fishing. GPS: 42.84889, -97.47028

YORK (192E)

Overland Trail Recreation Area   FREE
Upper Big Blue Natural Resources Dist.
2 mi E & 1.5 mi S of York. Free. All year; 14-day limit. Primitive camping in designated areas; no facilities, no drkg wtr. 14.5-acre lake. Hiking, boating(l), fishing.

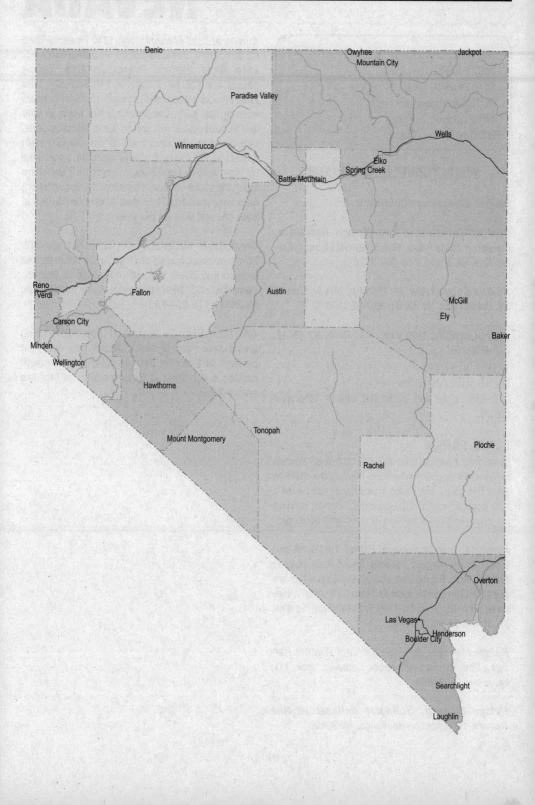

Denio
Owyhee
Mountain City
Jackpot
Paradise Valley
Wells
Winnemucca
Elko
Spring Creek
Battle Mountain
Reno
Verdi
Fallon
Austin
McGill
Ely
Carson City
Baker
Minden
Wellington
Hawthorne
Mount Montgomery
Tonopah
Pioche
Rachel
Overton
Las Vegas
Henderson
Boulder City
Searchlight
Laughlin

NEVADA

CAPITAL: Carson City
NICKNAME: Silver State
STATEHOOD: 1864 – 36th State
FLOWER: Sagebrush
TREE: Single-Leaf Pinon
BIRD: Mountain Bluebird

WWW.TRAVELNEVADA.COM

Toll-free information: 800/NEVADA-8.

Dept of Conservation and Natural Resources, Division of State Parks, 901 S. Stewart Street, Carson City, NV 89710. 775-884-2770.

Nevada Commission on Tourism, 401 N. Carson St., Carson City, NV 89701. 800-NEVADA-8.

Dept of Wildlife, 1100 Valley Rd., Reno, NV 89512. 775-688-1500.

REST AREAS
Overnight stops are permitted unless otherwise posted.

STATE PARKS
Base daily camping fees are $17, although Nevada seniors (65 or older) who have lived in the state at least five years can camp free after purchase of a $30 annual "senior citizen permit." Permit holders are charged $10 for utilities at sites with hookups.

Humboldt-Toiyabe National Forest. This combined forest is the largest national forest area outside Alaska, with 6.3 million acres. Sections of it are scattered through Nevada and into California; it features 40 campgrounds. 1200 Franklin Way, Sparks, NV 89431. 775-331-6444.

Refuge Manager, Sheldon National Wildlife Refuge, Sheldon-Hart Mountain Complex, Box 111, Lakeview, OR 97630.

Refuge Manager, Stillwater National Wildlife Refuge, 1000 Auction Rd, Fallon, NV 89406.

Bureau of Land Management, 1340 Financial Blvd, PO Box 12000, Reno, NV 89520. 775-861-6400
Lake Mead National Recreation Area. Vehicle passes are $20 for 7 days or $40 annually. User fees also are assessed against motorized boats entering the park. Campgrounds are open all year and feature restrooms, water, dump stations, grills, tables and shade. Fees are $20 per site ($10 with federal Senior Pass). Primitive camping, accessible by boat, foot or horseback, is permitted anywhere along the shore outside of developed areas or where otherwise prohibited by signs, limited to 30 days at each site and 90 days per year.

Great Basin National Park. Campsites are $12. Primitive campgrounds are free. An RV dump station is open just inside the park from May to October. Dump fee is $5. 100 reat Basin National Park, Baker, NV 89311. 775-234-7331.

CASINO PARKING. Several of Nevada's gaming towns have casinos which permit free overnight parking. In Laughlin, for example, free overnight parking is permitted at 10 casino lots. No facilities are available.

AUSTIN

Big Creek Campground FREE
Toiyabe National Forest
About 1.5 mi W of Austin on US 50, then 11 mi S on Big Creek Rd; FR 002). Free. 5/15-11/1; 14-day limit. 6 sites along the creek; 35-ft RV limit. Fee for group camping. Tbls, toilets, cfga, no drkg wtr. OHV activities, hiking, fishing.

Bob Scott Campground $10
Toiyabe National Forest
About 6 mi E of Austin on US 50; on left. $10. 5/15-10/31; 14-day limit. 10 sites; 35-ft RV limit. Tbls, flush & pit toilets, cfga, drkg wtr. Also group camping $25. Hiking, fishing, biking trails.

Columbine Campground FREE
Toiyabe National Forest
1.5 mi W of Austin on US 50; 7 mi SW on SR 722; left on SR 21 to Yomba Indian Reservation; 10 mi E on FR 119. Free. 5/15-10/31; 14-day limit. 5 sites; 35-ft RV limit. Tbls, toilets, cfga, no drkg wtr. Hiking, horseback riding, fishing, biking.

Hickison Petroglyph Recreation Site FREE
Bureau of Land Management
24 mi E of Austin on US 50, then gravel access rd, in Central Nevada. Free. All year; 14-day limit. 16 primitive sites (RVs under 55 ft). Tbls, toilets, cfga, picnic shelters, no drkg wtr. Hunting, hiking. Elev 6500 ft; 40 acres. Most sites are level pull-through spaces. No fishing. Petroglyphs in the area.

Kingston Campground FREE
Toiyabe National Forest
12 mi E of Austin on US 50; 15 mi S on SR 376; 6 mi NW on FR 20012 (improved gravel rds). Free. 5/15-10/15; 14-day limit. 11 sites (RVs under 36 ft). Tbls, toilets, cfga, no drkg wtr. Fishing, hiking, hunting. Elev 7000 ft; 12 acres. Adjacent to fish and game reservoirs. Trailhead for Toiyabe Crest National Recreation Trail. No off-season camping.

Toquima Cave Campground FREE
Toiyabe National Forest
E of Austin on US 50 to SR 376; S on SR 376 about 1 mi, watching for Nevada state shaped road sign; turn right onto next rd for about 12 mi. Free. 5/15-10/31; 14-day limit. 2 sites (1 for RV up to 25 ft) Tbls, 1 toilet, cfga, no drkg wtr. Explore caves with petroglyphs. Hiking.

BAKER

Baker Creek $12
Great Basin National Park
5 mi W of Baker on SR 488; 3 mi S on Baker Creek Rd. $12. 5/15-10/30; 14-day limit. 38 sites (16-ft RV limit). Tbls, flush toilets, cfga, drkg wtr. Fishing, hiking trails. Elev 8000 ft; 30 acres.

Lower & Upper Lehman Creek $12
Great Basin National Park
5 mi W of Baker on SR 488, following signs. $12. All year; 14-day limit. 33 total sites (30-ft RV limit). Tbls, toilets, cfga, drkg wtr. Hiking. Elev 7300 ft.

Shoshone Primitive Area FREE
Great Basin National Park
Within the park, at end of Snake Creek Rd. Free. May-Oct; 14-day limit. 3 primitive sites. Tbls, toilets, cfga, no drkg wtr. Fishing, hiking.

Snake Creek Primitive Area FREE
Great Basin National Park
Within the park, along Snake Creek Rd. Free. May-Oct; 14-day limit. 12 primitive sites along the rd. Tbls, toilets, cfga, no drkg wtr. Fishing, hiking.

Strawberry Creek Primitive Area FREE
Great Basin National Park
Within the park, along Strawberry Creek Rd. Free. May-Oct; 14-day limit. 8 primitive sites along the road. Tbls, toilets, cfga, no drkg wtr. Fishing, hiking. Closed by fire 2017.

Wheeler Peak $12
Great Basin National Park
5 mi W of Baker on SR 488; 12 mi W on FR 10446. $12. 6/1-9/30; 14-day limit. 37 sites (RVs under 17 ft). Tbls, toilets, cfga, drkg wtr. Hiking trails, nature programs. Elev 9900 ft. 22 acres.

BATTLE MOUNTAIN

Mill Creek Recreation Area FREE
Bureau of Land Management
24 mi S of Battle Mountain on US 305; 4 mi on gravel rd. Free. All year; 14-day limit. 11 RV/tent sites, 3 RV sites; suitable for RVs under 30 ft. Tbls, toilets, cfga, no drkg wtr. Fishing, hiking (half-mi interpretive trail). Site developed by CCC in 1930s.

BOULDER CITY

Boulder Beach $10
Lake Mead National Recreation Area
6 mi NE of Boulder City on SR 166. $10 with federal senior pass; others pay $20. All year; 30-day limit. 154 sites, full hookups. Flush toilets, cfga, drkg wtr, coin laundry, dump. Fishing, boating(ldr), waterskiing. 33 acres. Elev 1200 ft.

Temple Bar Campground $10
Lake Mead National Recreation Area
From Boulder City, about 15 mi S on US 93; left (N) about 15 mi on Temple Bar Rd to S shore of Lake Mead. $10 with federal senior pass at 153 full-hookup RV sites; others pay $20. All year; 30-day limit. Tbls, flush toilets, cfga, drkg wtr, coin laundry, dump. Fishing, hiking, boating(l).

CARSON CITY

Indian Creek $10
Bureau of Land Management
From Carson City, W on US 395 to Hwy 88; right on Hwy 88 across state line into California; at Woodfords, S on Hwy 89 toward Markleeville; follow signs. $10 with federal senior pass at RV sites; others pay $20. 5/5-10/9; 14-day limit. 19 RV sites; 30-ft RV limit. Tbls, flush toilets, cfga, drkg wtr, showers, dump($10), bear lockers. Boating(l), fishing, hiking, biking, interpretive trail.

DENIO

Big Spring Reservoir FREE
Sheldon National Wildlife Refuge
In the refuge W of Denio off Hwy 140. Free. All year. 12 sites. Toilets, tbls, cfga, no drkg wtr, showers, no trash service. Fishing, hiking, boating. Popular fishing spot.

Onion Valley Reservoir FREE
Bureau of Land Management
9 mi W of Denio on US 140; S 8 mi from Knott Creek turn-off. Free. 6/15-10/15; 14-day limit. 6 primitive sites (RVs not recommended except for pickup campers, folding trailers). Tbls, toilets, cfga, no drkg wtr. Hunting, boating, canoeing, fishing, sailboating. Jeep & hiking trails lead to Blue Lake & Little Onion Lake.

Sheldon Antelope Refuge FREE
National Wildlife Refuge
27 mi W of Denio on NV 140; 3 mi on gravel rd (Denio is on the Nevada-Oregon border, 87 mi N and slightly W of Winnemucca, NV). Free. Season for camps, except Virgin Valley, depends on weather & road conditions. From May-Oct, most roads usually accessible. Virgin Valley Camp available all year. 14-day limit. 15 designated campgrounds. All camps, except Virgin Valley Camp, are primitive (RVs under 25 ft). No facilities. Natural spring wtr at most campgrounds, restroom facilities and wtr at Virgin Valley Camp. Hunting during seasons; rockhounding (max 7 lbs per person. Map of camping from Sheldon Antelope Refuge, PO Box 111, Lakeview, OR 97630; or from Refuge Headquarters. Campfires permitted during times of low fire hazard. Inquire at refuge sub-headquarters for current regulations.

Virgin Valley Campground FREE
Sheldon National Wildlife Refuge
In the refuge W of Denio off SR 140. Free. All year; 14-day limit. 12 sites. Tbls, toilets, cfga, no drkg wtr, no trash service, spring-fed showers, hot springs (pooling at 90 degrees). Hiking, tour opal mines, fishing.

ELKO

Jack Creek Campground FREE
Humboldt National Forest
27 mi N of Elko on NV 225; 33 mi NW on NV 226; 1.4 mi NE on CR 732. Elev 6500 ft. All year (depending on weather); 14-day limit. 3 RV/tent sites on 4 acres; 30-ft RV limit. Tbls, toilet, cfga, no drkg wtr or trash service. Hunting (sites full during season); fishing.

North Wildhorse Reservoir Recreation Site $6
Bureau of Land Management
68 mi N of Elko on SR 225. $5 during 5/15-11/15; free rest of year but no wtr; 14-day limit. 18 sites (RVs under 25 ft). Tbls, toilets, cfga, drkg wtr, dump. Fishing, boating(ld), swimming, horseback riding. Elev 6500 ft; 40 acres. Ice fishing in winter.

South Fork Canyon Recreation Area FREE
Bureau of Land Management
5 mi S of Elko on SR 227; 5 mi S on SR 228; W to recreation area. Free. All year; 14-day limit. Primitive camping in canyon along river NW of reservoir; no facilities, no drkg wtr. Popular rafting area.

South Fork of Owyhee River FREE
Bureau of Land Management
110 mi NW of Elko via SR 225 & 226 to river. Free. 4/1-6/15; 14-day limit. Undesignated primitive sites. No facilities. Kayaking, rafting, hiking, climbing. Check in at Petan Ranch for permission to launch.

Wilson Reservoir $4
Bureau of Land Management
27 mi N of Elko on SR 225; 40 mi W on Hwy 226; at Wilson Reservoir. $4. All year; 14-day limit. 15 sites. Tbls, toilets, cfga, drkg wtr, dump, fishing dock. Boating(l - $2) fishing, hiking.

Zunino/Jiggs Reservoir $2
Recreation Management Area
Bureau of Land Management
7 mi E of Elko on SR 227; 23 mi S on SR 228. $2 use fee. Open dispersed camping on N & S shores plus 9 sites (30-ft RV limit). All year; 14-day limit. Tbls, toilets (in day-use area), cfga, no drkg wtr. Fishing, picnicking, boating, wind-surfing, ice fishing Dec-Feb. Elev 5600 ft.

ELY

Cherry Creek FREE
Humboldt National Forest
24 mi S of Ely on US 6; 46 mi S on SR 318 to Sunnyside, then 44 mi W on improved gravel & dirt rd; NW on FR 410. Free. Apr-Oct depending on weather; 14-day limit. 4 undesignated dispersed sites; 20-ft RV limit. Toilet, cfga, no drkg wtr. Hiking, fishing, biking.

Cleve Creek Campground FREE
Bureau of Land Management
30 mi SE on US 50; 12 mi N on NV 893; 4 mi W on FR 1043. Elev 6400 ft. 5/16-9/30; 14-day limit. 12 sites; 24-ft RV limit; also dispersed camping along the creek; 20 acres. Tbls, toilets, cfga, firewood, no drkg wtr. Fishing; hiking.

Currant Creek   CLOSED
Humboldt National Forest
45 mi SW of Ely on US 6. Decomissioned as a campground
and closed.

Garnet Hill Campground   FREE
Bureau of Land Management
6.4 mi W of Ely on US 50; 1.7 mi E on graded rd; from right
fork, 1.4 mi S & W; near Garnet Hill. Free. All year; 14-day
limit. 2 primitive areas for tents, small RVs, primarily for
rockhounds. Tbls, toilet, cfga, no drkg wtr. Hiking, biking.
Find dark red garnets nearby. View open-pit copper mine.
Elev 7280 ft.

Goshute Creek   FREE
Bureau of Land Management
45 mi N of Ely on US 93 to MP 98.56; 6.9 mi W on Hwy 489;
11 mi N on county rd to sign, then W 1.5 mi (high-clearance vehicles recommended). Free. All year; 14-day limit.
About 20 primitive sites (20-ft RV limit) in 3 areas. Tbls,
cfga, no drkg wtr, no toilets. Hunting, fishing, hiking,
mountain climbing, caving. Bristlecone pine forests, limestone formations. Elev 6230 ft.

Illipah Reservoir Recreation Area   FREE
Bureau of Land Management
37 mi W of Ely on Hwy 50; 1 mi SE on dirt rd. Free. All
year; 14-day limit. 17 primitive sites; no RV size limit. Tbls,
toilets, cfga, no drkg wtr. Fishing, boating(l).

Rest Area & Elk Viewing   FREE
Bureau of Land Management
10 mi S of Ely on US 60/50. Free. Tbls, toilets, cfga, no drkg
wtr. View migrating elk herds.

Ward Mountain Campground $8
Humboldt National Forest
7 mi SW of Ely on US 6; half mi S on FR 10439. $8. About
5/15-9/30; 14-day limit. 29 sites (typically 40 ft). Tbls,
toilets, cfga, drkg wtr. Hiking, horseback riding, hunting,
biking, volleyball, baseball, swing set. Elev 7400 ft; 6
acres. Renovated 2012.

FALLON

Churchill County Fairgrounds $7
Churchill County Regional Park
From jct with US 50 at Fallon, about 1 mi S on US 95; W
side. $7 without hookups, $15 elec/wtr. Events camping,
$10 with elec, $5 without hookups. All year. 88 RV fairground sites. Primitive area in equestrian section; drkg
wtr & dump for a fee. Flush toilets, showers; drkg wtr &
dump for a fee.

Sand Mountain Recreation Area $40
Bureau of Land Management
25 mi E of Fallon on US 50; at Sand Springs Pony Express

Station and desert study area; camp at base of mountain
in open desert (follow signs). 4x4 recommended (Sand
Mtn is 2 mi long, 600 ft high). $40 weekly permit, $90
annual pass (holders of federal senior pass pay $20 &
$45); free Tues/Wed. 4/1-10/31; 14-day limit. 100 primitive
sites, most for tents or self-contained RVs. Tbls, toilets,
cfga, no drkg wtr, no wood for campfire. OHV activity,
hiking. Self-guided tours of 1860s express station.

Stillwater Wildlife Management Area   FREE
Anaho Island & Fallon National Wildlife Refuges
5 mi E of Fallon on US 50; 13 mi on Stillwater Rd. Free. All
year. Primitive camping & boating facilities in 24,000-acre
WMA. No facilities. Birdwatching, fishing, boating.

HAWTHORNE

Sportsman's Beach $4
Walker Lake Recreation Area
Bureau of Land Management
16 mi N of Hawthorne on Hwy 95, on W shore of Walker
Lake. $4 for primitive sites; $6 developed sites. All year;
14-day limit. About 30 developed sites (30-ft RV limit),
plus primitive camping at the Cove, East Shore, Tamarack
& Twenty-Mile Beach. Tbls, toilets, cfga, drkg wtr. Fishing,
hiking, boating (l), waterskiing, swimming beach. Walker
Lake has 38,000 acres of water, 15 mi long.

Tamarack Point Recreation Site   FREE
Bureau of Land Management
18 mi N of Hawthorne on US 95 (W shore of Walker Lake).
All year; 14-day limit. 10 sites (RVs under 31 ft). Tbls,
toilets, cfga, no drkg wtr. Boating, picnicking, fishing,
swimming, hiking, horseback riding, sailing, rockhounding, hunting. Elev 4500 ft. Gillis Range is E of lake. Wassuk
Range, with Mount Grant (11,239 ft), is W.

HENDERSON

Callville Bay $10
Lake Mead National Recreation Area
22 mi NE of Henderson on SR 147. $10 with federal senior
pass; others pay $20. All year; 30-day limit. 80 full-hookup
sites. Tbls, flush toilets, cfga, drkg wtr, coin laundry. Boat-
ing(l), fishing, waterskiing.

Las Vegas Bay $10
Lake Mead National Recreation Area
8 mi NE of Henderson on SR 166 (13 mi NW of Boulder
City). $10 with federal senior pass; others pay $20. All
year; 30-day limit. 85 full-hookup sites. Tbls, flush toilets,
cfga, drkg wtr. Fishing, boating(lr), hiking, waterskiing.

JACKPOT

Salmon Falls Creek Recreation Area   FREE
Bureau of Land Management
Two access points: 1 mi & 2 mi S of Jackpot. Free. All year;
14-day limit. Primitive dispersed camping along Salmon

Falls Creek; no facilities, no drkg wtr. Fishing, hiking, boating. Best floating is late Apr through June.

LAS VEGAS

Hilltop Campground $11.50
Spring Mountains National Recreation Area
Toiyabe National Forest
From Las Vegas at Centennial Pkwy exit 91, 4.1 mi N on US 95; right on SR 157 for 4.6 mi to campground sign; right at sign. $11.50 with federal senior pass; others pay $23 (double/triple sites available). MD-10/9; 14-day limit. 34 RV/tent sites; 35-ft RV limit. Tbls, flush toilets, coin showers.

Red Rock Campground $7.50
Red Rock Canyon National Conservation Area
Bureau of Land Management
18 mi W of Las Vegas strip via W. Charleston Blvd. $7.50 with federal senior pass; others pay $15. About 9/1-5/30; 14-day limit. 71 sites (including 10 group sites & 24 walk-in tent sites). Also free primitive camping in several backcountry locations. Tbls, pit toilets, cfga, drkg wtr. Also group sites. Hiking, rock climbing, 13-mile scenic loop drive, mountain biking trails, horseback riding, hunting, caving. Visitor center with desert tortoise exhibit. Wild burros nearby. $7 entry fee; free with senior pass.

LAUGHLIN

Telephone Cove FREE
Lake Mohave National Recreation Area
From Laughlin, 4.4 mi W on mi N on SR 163; 4.3 mi NE on Telephone Cove Rd to W shore of lake. Free. 7-day limit; closed 10/15-3/15. Toilets, cfga, no other facilities. Fishing, boating, swimming. Desert scenery.

MCGILL

Berry Creek FREE
Humboldt National Forest
5 mi N of McGill on US 93; 1 mi E on SR 496; 3 mi E on FR 1067 (not fore low-clearance vehicles). Free. About MD-10/31; 14-day limit. 3 scattered primitive sites. Toilets, cfga, no drkg wtr. OHV activity, hiking, fishing, biking.

East Creek $4
Humboldt National Forest
5 mi N of McGill on Hwy 93; 4 mi E on SR 486; turn at East Creek sign, then 1 mi NE on FR 427; 3.5 mi E on FR 56. $4. 5/15-9/30; 14-day limit. 26 primitive sites; 20-ft RV limit. Tbls, toilets, cfga, no drkg wtr. Fishing, hiking, biking.

Kalamazoo Campground FREE
Humboldt National Forest
5 mi N of McGill on US 93; 4 mi E on SR 486 to East Creek turnoff, then 4 mi on FR 1054 (high clearance vehicles); at Kalamazoo Creek. Free dispersed area. June-Sept; 14-day limit. 5 sites. Tbls, cfga, no drkg wtr or toilets. Fishing, hiking, hunting, biking. Elev 6900 ft.

Timber Creek $8
Humboldt National Forest
5 mi N of McGill on US 93; 8 mi E on SR 486; 4 mi E on Timber Creek Rd. $6. 6/1-9/30; 16-day limit. 6 sites; 20-ft RV limit. Tbls, flush toilets, cfga, drkg wtr. Hiking, fishing. Elev 8200 ft. N of Cave Lake State Park.

MINDEN

Crystal Springs Campground $9
Toiyabe National Forest
From Minden at jct with US 395, 15.5 mi W on SR 88 into California; left at sign. $9 with federal senior pass; others pay $18. About 4/15-9/30; 14-day limit. 19 RV sites (35-ft RV limit). Tbls, toilets, cfga, drkg wtr. Fishing, hiking. West Fork of Carson River. Elev 6000 ft.

Hope Valley Campground $11
Toiyabe National Forest
From Minden at jct with US 395, 22.3 mi W into California on SR 88; left at campground sign on Blue Lakes Rd for 1.5 mi. $11 with federal senior pass; others pay $22. 6 double sites $40. About 5/15-9/30; 14-day limit. 22 single sites (22-ft RV limit). Tbls, toilets, cfga, drkg wtr. Fishing, hiking. Elev 7300 ft. Renovated 2011.

Kit Carson Campground $9
Toiyabe National Forest
From Minden at jct with US 395, 18.4 mi W into California on SR 88. $9 with federal senior pass; others pay $18. About 5/15-9/15; 14-day limit. 8 RV/tent sites (30-ft RV limit). Tbls, toilets, cfga, drkg wtr. West Fork of Carson River. Fishing, hiking. Elev 6900 ft.

MOUNTAIN CITY

Big Bend $8
Humboldt National Forest
18 mi S of Mountain City on SR 225; 10.5 mi E on CR 745. $8. About 5/10-10/15; 14-day limit. 15 sites & 2 group sites; 25-ft RV limit. Tbls, toilets, cfga, no drkg wtr. Fishing, hiking. Elev 6900 ft; 8 acres.

Wildhorse Crossing Campground $5
Humboldt National Forest
10 mi SE of Mountain City on SR 225; at Owyhee River. $5. About 5/10-11/15; 14-day limit. 20 sites (plus 1 group site). Tbls, toilets, cfga, no drkg wtr. Fishing. Elev 5900 ft; 12 acres. 5 mi N of Wildhorse Reservoir.

MOUNT MONTGOMERY

Fish Lake Valley Hot Well FREE
Esmeralda County Park
From Mount Montgomery, about 5 mi E on US 6; 5 mi SE on SR 264 to jct with SR 773; continue 6 mi S on SR 264, then 7 mi E on gravel rd to camping area, called "The Crossing" on some maps. Dispersed primitive camping; no facilities. Hot geothermal spring area, popular OHV

activity spot. Nearby Boundary Peak, Nevada's highest point at 13,140 ft elev.

OVERTON

Echo Bay Campground $10
Lake Mead National Recreation Area
30 mi S of Overton on SR 167. $10 with federal senior pass; others pay $20. All year; 30-day limit. 166 full-hook-up sites. Flush toilets, tbls, cfga, drkg wtr. Boating(lr), fishing, hiking, waterskiing. Elev 1200 ft.

OWYHEE

Lake Billy Shaw $6
Duck Valley Indian Reservation
Shoshone-Paiute Tribes Fish, Wildlife & Parks Dept.
From just S of Owyhee on US 225, 3 mi W on paved SR 11 (China Town Rd) to fork; continue straight W for 4 mi to lake. $6 at primitive sites around lakeshore; no hookups. Fishing permit $15 ($17.50 with two fishing rods); children $3. Annual fishing/camping permit $85 for all reservation fisheries (family permit $150). Fly fishing, boating(l).

Sheep Creek Reservoir $6
Duck Valley Indian Reservation
Shoshone-Paiute Tribes Fish, Wildlife & Parks Dept.
From just S of Owyhee on US 225, 3 mi W on paved SR 11 (China Town Rd) to fork; veer left for 5 mi on SR 11 (Sheep Creek Rd) to Sheep Creek Reservoir. $6 at primitive sites around lakeshore; no hookups. Fishing permit $15 ($17.50 with two fishing rods); children $3. Annual fishing/camping permit $85 for all reservation fisheries (family permit $150). Fly fishing, boating(l).

PARADISE VALLEY

Lye Creek Campground $8
Humboldt National Forest
18 mi N of Paradise Valley on SR 792; 2 mi W on FR 087. $8 (double sites $10). 6/1-10/15; 14-day limit. 14 sites (RVs under 25 ft). Tbls, toilets, cfga, drkg wtr (June-Oct). Fishing, hunting. No trash service. Elev 7400 ft.

PIOCHE

Pioche City Park FREE
S end of town, just off US 93 E of courthouse. From US 93, W on Main St, then right on 4th North behind courthouse. Free overnight camping; donations accepted. 10 RV sites with wtr/sewer, no elec. Toilets, drkg wtr, showers at public pool. Playground, recreation area, swimming.

RACHEL

Little A'Le'Inn FREE
On SR 375 (the Extraterrestial Hwy) at Rachel (between US 6 & US 93 NW of Las Vegas). Free primitive camping at motel geared to alien-investigating tourists. 1 non-elec site; 3 sites with elec, $20, no other facilities.

RENO

Lookout Campground $6
Toiyabe National Forest
9 mi W of Reno off I-80 in Dog Valley (gravel entrance rd). $6. 6/1-10/15; 14-day limit. 22 sites (22-ft RV limit). Tbls, toilets, cfga, no drkg wtr. Hiking, horseback riding, hunting, rockhounding (crystals) & fishing nearby.

Mt. Rose Campground $11
Toiyabe National Forest
S of Reno on US 395 to exit 56; 15.6 mi W on SR 431 to campground sign, on left. $11 with federal senior pass; others pay $22. About 6/10-9/15; 14-day limit. 18 RV/tent sites; 35-ft RV limit. Double, triple sites available. Tbls, flush toilets, cfga, drkg wtr, bear lockers. Renovated 2012.

SEARCHLIGHT

Cottonwood Cove $10
Lake Mohave National Recreation Area
14 mi E of Searchlight on SR 164; on Lake Mohave. $10 with federal senior pass; others pay $20. All year; 30-day limit. 145 sites. Tbls, flush toilets, cfga, drkg wtr, coin laundry, store, full hookups. Fishing, boating(ldr), hiking, waterskiing. 3 acres.

SONORA JUNCTION

Obsidian Campground $12
Toiyabe National Forest
4 mi S of Sonora Junction off Hwy 395; 4 mi on gravel Little Walker Rd (FR 66). $12. About 6/1-10/15; 14-day limit; 30-ft RV limit. 10 sites; 35-ft RV limit. Tbls, toilets, cfga, no drkg wtr or trash service. Hiking, fishing. Elev 7840 ft. Poorly maintained at last report.

SPRING CREEK

Thomas Canyon $8.50
Humboldt National Forest
From Spring Creek at jct with SR 228, 12.2 mi E on SR 227; left for 7.5 mi on Lemoille Canyon Rd to campground sign. $8.50 with federal senior pass; others pay $17. All year; 14-day limit. 40 sites; 40-ft RV limit. Tbls, toilets, cfga, drkg wtr. Hiking trail.

TONOPAH

Barley Creek FREE
Toiyabe National Forest
W of Tonopah to SR 376, then 12 mi N; 42 mi N on CR 82, then follow FR 005 to its end at the edge of the wilderness area. Free. Open primitive camping. May-Oct. Tbl, toilet, cfga, no drkg wtr. Hiking, fishing, biking.

Miller's Rest Area FREE
10 mi W of Tonopah on US 95. Free. All year; 18-hr limit in 14-day period. Designated overnight area at end of circle rd. Tbls with canopies, flush toilets, cfga, drkg wtr, dump.

Peavine Campground   FREE
Toiyabe National Forest
5 mi E of Tonapah on US 6; 40 mi N on SR 376; left (W) at campground turnoff for 9 mi; at Peavine Creek. Free. 5/1-10/31; 14-day limit. 10 sites in open area; 35-ft RV limit. Tbls, toilets, cfga, no drkg wtr. Fishing, hiking, horseback riding, hunting, rockhounding. Elev 6700; 6 acres. No off-season camping. Near desert big horn sheep habitat.

Pine Creek Campground   FREE
Toiyabe National Forest
5 mi E of Tonopah on US 6; 13 mi NE on SR 376; 15 mi NE on CR 82; 2.5 mi W on FR 009 (30 mi of improved gravel rd). Free. 5/1-10/31 or until closed by weather; 14-day limit. 21 sites (35-ft RV limit). Tbls, toilets, cfga, drkg wtr. Horseback riding, picnicking, fishing (trout), hunting, rockhounding, hiking. On E side of Toquima Range next to Pine Creek. Trailhead portal to Mt. Jefferson Natural Area. Elev 7600 ft; 20 acres.

Saulsbury Wash   FREE
Toiyabe National Forest
State Rest Area & Campground
30 mi E of Tonopah on US 6. Free. Elev 5800 ft. All year. 6 sites (RVs under 32 ft). Tbls, toilets, cfga, no drkg wtr. Rockhounding; picnicking. Basically a roadside rest area.

VERDI
Hunting Camp #1   FREE
Toiyabe National Forest
3 mi NW on FR 027. Free. All year; 14-day limit. Undesignated primitive area, undeveloped. Toilet, cfga, no drkg wtr. Horses permitted. Primarily a hunter's camp.

Hunting Camp #2   FREE
Toiyabe National Forest
3.5 mi NW on FR 027. Free. 4/1-11/1; 14-day limit. Undesignated primitive area, undeveloped. Toilet, cfga, no drkg wtr. Horses permitted. Primarily a hunter's camp.

Hunting Camp #4   FREE
Toiyabe National Forest
NW of Verdi on FR 027. Free. 4/1-11/1; 14-day limit. Undesignated primitive area, undeveloped. Toilet, cfga, no drkg wtr. Primarily a hunter's camp.

WELLINGTON
Desert Creek   FREE
Toiyabe National Forest
3 mi SW of Bridgeport, California, on SR 338; 7 mi S on FR 027 (Desert Creek Rd); near Desert Creek. Free. All year; 14-day limit. 13 sites; 18-ft RV limit. Tbls, toilets, cfga, no drkg wtr or trash service. Fishing, hiking. Also numerous primitive dispersed sites along the creek.

Wilson Canyon Dispersed Campsites   FREE
Bureau of Land Management
NE of Wellington on SR 208 along the West Walker River. Free. All year; 14-day limit. Pull-out areas along W end of canyon. Undesignated primitive sites; no facilities. Hiking, fishing. Dump ($3) at Bybee's store in Smith.

WELLS
Angel Creek $7.50
Humboldt National Forest
From Wells at jct with Humboldt Ave, 3.7 mi W on Angel Lake Rd; left at Angel Creek sign for 0.7 mi. $7.50 with federal senior pass; others pay $15. 5/15-10/31; 14-day limit. 18 sites; 35-ft RV limit. Tbls, toilets, cfga, drkg wtr.

Angel Lake Campground $8
Humboldt National Forest
From Wells at jct with Humboldt Ave, 11.6 mi W on Angel Lake Rd; right at campground sign. $8 with federal senior pass; others pay $16. 6/15-9/15; 14-day limit. 25 sites, typically 30 ft. Tbls, toilets, cfga, drkg wtr. Hiking, fishing.

South Ruby Campground $7.50
Humboldt National Forest
Ruby Mountains Recreation Area
S of Wells on US 93 & SR 229. $7.50 with federal senior pass; others pay $15. 5/15-10/31; 14-day limit. 35 sites, typically 45 ft. Tbls, toilets, cfga, drkg wtr, dump ($5), fish cleaning station (MD-LD). Boating, fishing, hunting, picnicking. Adjacent to Ruby Lake Wildlife Refuge.

Tabor Creek $2
Bureau of Land Management
30 mi N of Wells on US 93 7 gravel rds. $2 use fee. About 4/15-11/15; 14-day limit. 10 sites. Toilets, cfga, no drkg wtr. Picnicking, fishing, hiking, mountain biking.

WINNEMUCCA
Winnemucca Events Complex $12
(Formerly Humboldt County Fairgrounds)
From I-80 exit 178 at Winnemucca, S on SR 289, then SE on Fairgrounds Rd. $10 for sites without hookups; $20 at 30-amp elec sites. Non-hookup camping at several locations & limited number of other spaces with elec; sites available only to those participating in an event or activity at the complex. Reservations required; 775-623-2220. All year. 225 sites with 30/50-amp elec; wtr & dump available.

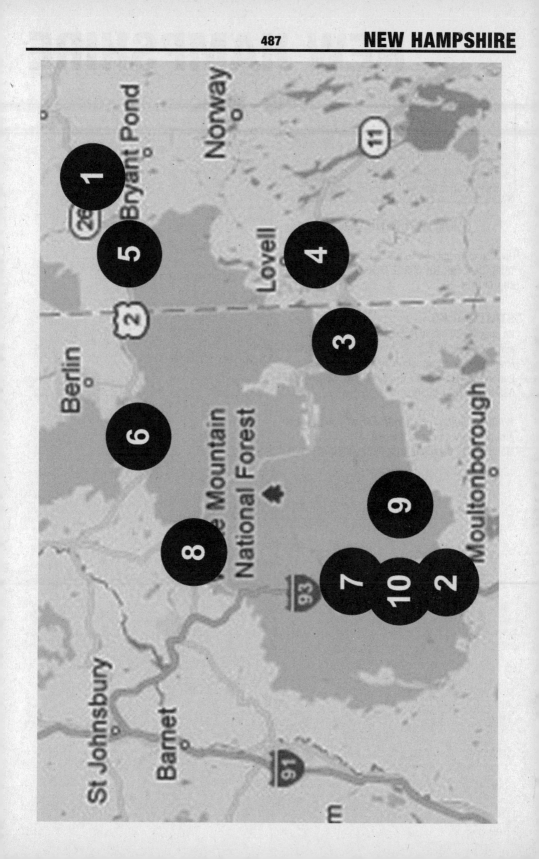

NEW HAMPSHIRE

CAPITAL: Concord
NICKNAME: Granite State
STATEHOOD: 1788 – 9th State
FLOWER: Purple Lilac
TREE: White Birch
BIRD: Purple Finch

WWW.VISITNH.GOV

Division of Travel and Tourism Development, PO Box 1856, Concord, NH 03302-1856. 603/271-2665 or 800-FUN-IN-NH.

STATE PARKS

No specific RV facilities exist at state parks; RVs are admitted only if they fit into existing tent spaces. Maximum length of state is 14 days. Division of Parks and Recreation, PO Box 1856, Concord, NH 03302. 603/271-3556.

White Mountain National Forest. Most campgrounds now charge fees of $16-20. 71 White Mountain Dr, Campton, NH 03223. 603/536-6100.

BETHEL, (MAINE) (1)

Crocker Pond $7

White Mountain National Forest

From Bethel at jct with SR 5, 5 mi W on Pattie Brook Rd. $7 with federal senior pass; others pay $14. 5/15-10/15; 14-day limit. Free-off-season without amenities or services. 7 primitive sites. Tbls, toilets, cfga, no drkg wtr. Canoeing, boating(l), fishing. GPS: 44.31028, -70.82389.

CAMPTON (2)

Campton Campground $11

White Mountain National Forest

1 mi E of Campton on SR 49 (Mad River Rd). $11 with federal senor pass; others pay $22. 5/15-10/15; 14-day limit. 58 sites; no RV size limit. Tbls, flush toilets, cfga, drkg wtr, coin showers. Hiking, fishing, boating interpretive & nature programs. GPS: 43.873779, -71.626953

CONWAY (3)

Blackberry Crossing $11

White Mountain National Forest

6 mi W of Conway on Hwy 112. $11 with federal senior pass; others pay $22. 5/1-11/1; 14-day limit. 26 sites up to 60 ft (20 for RVs). Tbls, pit toilets, cfga, drkg wtr. Hiking, canoeing, fishing, interpretive programs. Remains of CCC center. GPS: 43.9992373, -71.2256268

Covered Bridge $11

White Mountain National Forest

6 mi W of Conway on Hwy 112, then W on Dugway Rd (7-ft, 9-inch bridge height restricts passage of large RVs). $11 with federal senior pass; others pay $22. 5/15-10/15; 14-day limit. 49 sites; no RV length limit. Pit toilets, cfga, drkg wtr, cfga. Mountain biking, hiking trails, fishing. Accessible fishing pier nearby. GPS: 44.0039595, -71.231738

Jigger Johnson $12

White Mountain National Forest

12.5 mi W of Conway on Hwy 112. $12 with federal senior pass; others pay $24. About 5/22-10/15; 14-day limit. 76 sites; no RV length limit. Tbls, flush toilets, coin showers, drkg wtr, cfga. Hiking, fishing, interpretive programs. Near historic house. GPS: 43.9139606, -71.3334059

Passaconaway Campground $11

White Mountain National Forest

15 mi W of Conway on Hwy 112; at Swift River. $11 with federal senior pass; others pay $22. 5/15-10/15; 14-day limit. 33 sites; no RV size limit. Tbls, pit toilets, cfga, drkg wtr (solar). Hiking, fishing. GPS: 43.9970141, -71.3709072

White Ledge Campground $8

White Mountain National Forest

6 m S of Conway on Hwy 16. $8 with federal senior pass; others pay $16. 5/15-9/15; 14-day limit. 28 sites; no RV size limit. Tbls, cfga, toilets, drkg wtr. Hiking, fishing, mountain biking. GPS: 43.9547938, -71.2139596.

FRYEBURG (MAINE) (4)

Basin Campground $10

White Mountain National Forest

15 mi N of Fryeburg, Maine, on Hwy 113; on S side of Basin Pond; in New Hampshire. $10 with federal senior pass; others pay $20. 5/15-10/15; 14-day limit. 21 sites (typically 65 ft). Tbls, flush toilets, cfga, drkg wtr. Hiking, fishing, boating (l - no mtrs). GPS: 44.269, -71.021

Cold River $9

White Mountain National Forest

15 mi N of Fryeburg, Maine, on Hwy 113; in New Hampshire. $9 with federal senior pass; others pay $18. 5/15-10/15; 14-day limit. 14 sites (12 for RVs, typically 60 ft). Tbls, toilets, cfga, drkg wtr. Hiking, fishing, boating(l). GPS: 44.265, -71.013

GILEAD (MAINE) (5)

Hastings Campground $8

White Mountain National Forest

3 mi S of Hwy 2 on Hwy 113 near Gilead. $8 with federal senior pass; others pay $16. 5/10-10/15; 14-day limit. 24 sites, typically 55 ft. Tbls, pit toilets, cfga, drkg wtr. Hiking, fishing, interpretive programs. GPS: 44.3522852, -70.9839625

Wild River $8

White Mountain National Forest

0.4 mi W of Gilead on US 2; 3 mi S on SR 113; 5.5 mi SW on FR 12. $8 with federal senior pass; others pay $16. 5/10-10/15; 14-day limit. 12 sites (3 for RVs); 45-ft RV limit. Tbls, toilets, cfga, drkg wtr. Hiking, fishing. 4 acres. GPS: 44.1820, -71.0348

GORHAM (6)

Barnes Field Campground $10

White Mountain National Forest

6 mi S of Gorham on Hwy 6; 0.75 mi left on Dolly Copp Rd; near Peabody River. $10 for individual campers in winter; serves as group campground in-season. All year; 14-day limit. Tbls, toilet, cfga, drkg wtr. Hiking trails, fishing. GPS: 44.33886, -71.218392

Dolly Copp Campground $11

White Mountain National Forest

6 mi S of Gorham on Hwy 6; left half mi on Dolly Copp Rd. $11 with federal senior pass; others pay $22. 5/15-10/15; 14-day limit. 177 sites; no RV size limit. Tbls, flush toilets, cfga, drkg wtr, trash recycling. Fishing, hiking, nature trails, interpretive programs. Largest campground in the national forest system. GPS: 44.3325632, -71.2184082

LINCOLN (7)

Big Rock Campground $11

White Mountain National Forest

6.5 mi E of Lincoln on FR 112. $11 with federal senior pass; others pay $22. 5/15-10/15; 14-day limit. 28 sites; no RV size limit. Tbls, toilets, cfga, drkg wtr. Hiking, fishing. GPS: 44.0486785, -71.560634

Hancock Campground $12
White Mountain National Forest
5 mi E of Lincoln on the Kancamagus Hwy; at East Branch of Pemigewasset River. $12 with federal senior pass; others pay $24. All year, but no wtr in winter; 14-day limit. 56 sites (35-ft RV limit). Tbls, flush & pit toilets, cfga, drkg wtr. Fishing, hiking. Swimming hole known as Upper Lady's Bath. GPS: 44.0653447, -71.5903571

Wildwood Campground $8
White Mountain National Forest
7 mi W of Lincoln on Hwy 112. $8 with federal senior pass; others pay $16. 5/15-12/15; 14-day limit. 26 sites; no RV size limit. Fishing, hiking. Picnic pavilion built by the CCC in the 1930s. GPS: 44.0758991, -71.7934177

TWIN MOUNTAIN (8)
Sugarloaf Campground I $10
White Mountain National Forest
3 mi E of Twin Mountain on SR 302; half mi S on Zealand Rd. $10 with federal senior pass; others pay $20. 5/15-10/15; 14-day limit. 29 sites; no RV size limit. Tbls, flush toilets, cfga, drkg wtr. Hiking, fishing, biking. GPS: 44.2578418, -71.503691

Sugarloaf Campground II $8
White Mountain National Forest
3 mi E of Twin Mountain on SR 302; half mi S on Zealand Rd. $8 with federal senior pass; others pay $16. 5/15-10/15; 14-day limit. 32 sites; no RV size limit. Pit toilets, cfga, drkg wtr, cfga. Hiking, fishing, biking. GPS: 44.25809, -71.50393

Zealand Campground $8
White Mountain National Forest
2 mi E of Twin Mountain on SR 302; along Ammonoosuc River. $8 with federal senior pass; others pay $16. 5/15-10/15; 14-day limit. 11 sites; 45-ft RV limit. Pit toilets, cfga, drkg wtr. Fishing, hiking, biking. GPS: 44.2645083, -71.4950797

WATERVILLE VALLEY (9)
Osceola Vista $8
White Mountain National Forest
10 mi E of Waterville Valley on Hwy 49; left on Tripoli Rd, pass Waterville Campground entrance sign for 1.5 mi, then bear right at the Mt. Tecumseh sign for 1.6 mi. $8 with federal senior pass; others pay $16. 5/15-10/15; 14-day limit. 11 sites. Tbls, toilets, cfga, drkg wtr. Fishing, hiking. Group camping available. GPS: 43.9678, -71.5158

Waterville Campground $8
White Mountain National Forest
10 mi E of Waterville Valley on Hwy 49; left on Tripoli Rd for qtr mi. $8 with federal senior pass; others pay $16. 5/15-10/15; 14-day limit. 27 sites; 45-ft RV limit. Tbls, drkg wtr, toilets, cfga. Hiking, fishing, horseback riding. GPS: 43.9425696, -71.5092428

WOODSTOCK (10)
Russell Pond $12
White Mountain National Forest
3.7 mi E of I-93 exit 31 on Tripoli Rd at Woodstock. $12 with federal senior pass; others pay $24. 5/15-10/15; 14-day limit. 86 sites; no RV size limit. Flush toilets, cfga, drkg wtr, coin showers, fishing pier. Boating(ld); fishing, swimming, hiking, interpretive programs. GPS: 44.0119444, -71.651111

Tripoli Road Dispersed Sites $12
White Mountain National Forest
On Tripoli Rd E of I-93 exit 31; camp along roadway from Russell Pond Rd to Osceola Vista Campground & all ungated spur rds & parking areas. $12 for weekday pass, good for entire mid-week; $16 for weekend pass, good for Fri-Sat. Holders of federal senior pass pay $6 & $8. Primitive undesignated camping; no facilities, no drkg wtr. MD-Columbus Day; 14-day limit. Permits issued & monitored by concessionaire from booth on Tripoli Rd near Russell Pond Rd.

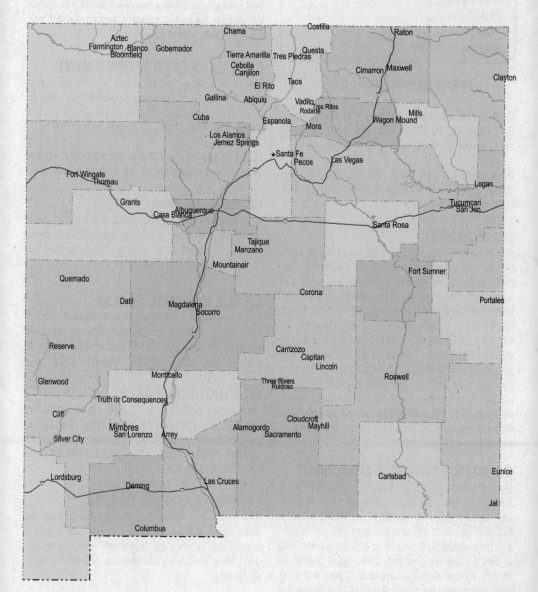

NEW MEXICO

CAPITAL: Santa Fe
NICKNAME: Land of Enchantment
STATEHOOD: 1912 – 47th State
FLOWER: Yucca
TREE: Pinon
BIRD: Roadrunner

WWW.NEWMEXICO.ORG

Dept of Tourism, Lamy Building, 491 Old Santa Fe Trail, Santa Fe, NM 87501. 800-545-2070; 505-827-7400. enchanntment@newmexico.org.

Dept of Game and Fish, Villagra Bldg, PO Box 25112, Santa Fe, NM 87504. 505-827-7911 & 827-7880 or 800-275-3474.

STATE PARKS

The overnight camping fee is $8 for primitive sites, $10 for a developed site with a $4 charge for electricity and $4 for sewer; water hookups are free when available. Primitive sites offer only a cleared space, although some may have trash cans, chemical toilets or parking. Annual camping permits are $180 for state residents ($100 for seniors or disabled); $225 for non-residents; with an annual permit, non-hookup sites are free, and with electric or sewage, they are $4; sites with electric and sewer are $8. Daily entrance fee is $5 ($40 annual). 14-day camping limit. Pets on leashes are permitted. State Parks Division, 1220 Sout St. Francis Dr., Santa Fe, NM 87505. 888-NMPARKS.

BANDELIER NATIONAL MONUMENT

Most of Bandelier's 29,661 acres are open to backcountry camping all year. Required but free backcountry permits are available at the visitor center in Frijoles Canyon. 7-day entry fees of $20 per vehicle, $15 for motorcycle (2 riders) or $10 per person. (aily or $40 annual are charged. Camping at the monument's Juniper Campground is $12, plus entry fee. Superintendent, Bandelier National Monument, Los Alamos, NM 87544. 505-672-3861

CHACO CULTURE NHP

The Chaco Culture National Historic Park offers rugged all-year camping among the fallen boulders and cliffs of Gallo Wash. Sites are $15 by reservation ($7.50 with a federal senior pass).

GILA CLIFF DWELLINGS NM

This secluded national monument offers free camping at four areas but charges entry fees. All four campgrounds have RV spaces.

BUREAU OF LAND MANAGEMENT

The BLM in New Mexico offers a wide variety of free and low-cost camping opportunities. Bureau of Land Management, PO Box 27115, Santa Fe, NM 87505. 505/438-7400.

Corps of Engineers, Albuquerque District, PO Box 1580, Albuquerque, NM 87103. 505-342-3464.

CARSON NATIONAL FOREST

Most formerly free campgrounds now have $5 overnight fees, but several undeveloped camping areas are still available at no charge. 208 Cruz Alta Rd, Taos, NM 87571. 505-758-6200.

CIBOLA NATIONAL FOREST

Many developed campgrounds in this forest also are free, and where fees are charged, they are generally between $5 and $10. 2113 Osuna Rd NE, Suite A, Albuquerque, NM 87113-1001; 505-346-3900.

GILA NATIONAL FOREST

This forest contains 3,321,000 acres (including 614,200 of the Apache National Forest). Most of its campgrounds are free, and fees are between $6 and $10. 3005 E. Camino del Bosque, Silver City, NM 88061. 505-388-8201.

LINCOLN NATIONAL FOREST

The forest has fewer free campgrounds than the other New Mexico national forests, but it has a significant number of dispersed camping areas. 1101 New York Ave., Alamogordo, NM 88310. 505-434-7200.

SANTA FE NATIONAL FOREST

Santa Fe NF offers free camping at about half of its developed campgrounds. 1474 Rodeo Rd, Santa Fe, NM 87505. 505-438-7840.

ABIQUIU

Riana Recreation Area $12
Corps of Engineers
Abiquiu Dam
6 mi NW of Abiquiu on US 84; 1 mi SW on SR 96; N on access rd; at bluff overlooking SE shore of lake near dam. $12 at 24 non-elec RV sites; $16 at 15 elec/wtr sites ($6 and $8 with federal senior pass). 4/15-10/15; closed off-season; 65-ft RV limit. Tbls, flush & pit toilets, cfga, firewood, drkg wtr, amphitheater. Boating(l), waterskiing, new swimming beach (at Cerrito Recration Area), hunting (waterfowl), picnicking, fishing, waterskiing, wind-surfing. Visitor center.

ALAMOGORDO

Oliver Lee $10
Memorial State Park
12 mi S of Alamogordo on US 54, then 4 mi E on Dog Canyon Rd. $10 base. All year; 14-day limit. 44 developed sites (1 with handicap access, 15 with elec); 48-ft RV limit. Tbls, elec($4), cfga, drkg wtr, tbls, showers, flush toilets, dump, beach. Nature trails, picnicking. Historical exhibits; restored 19th Century ranch house. Elev 4400 ft.

ALBUQUERQUE

Cochiti Recreation Area $12
Corps of Engineers
Cochiti Lake
From Albuquerque, NE on I-25 to exit 259; N on SR 22 through Pena Blanca to project office & campsits. $12 at 32 non-elec sites, $20 at 48 elec sites, some wtr hookups ($6 & $10 with federal senior pass). 4/15-11/30; 14-day limit. 45-ft RV limit; 16 pull-through sites. Tbls, flush & pit toilets, cfga, drkg wtr, showers, beach, dump, fishing pier, covered shelters. Fishing, boating(l), hiking, swimming, interpretive trails. Visitor Center.

Tetilla Peak Recreation Area $12
Corps of Engineers
Cochiti Lake
From Albuquerque, NE on I-25 to exit 264; about 6 mi NW on SR 16, then right (NE) at Tetilla Peak turnoff to recreation area at S shore of lake. $12 at 9 non-elec sites, $20 at 36 elec sites (no wtr hookups); seniors with federal senior pass pay $6 & $10. 4/1-10/30; 14-day limit. 45-ft RV limit; 11 pull-through sites. Tbls, flush & pit toilets, cfga, drkg wtr, showers, dump, shelters. Boating(dl), fishing, hiking.

ANTONITO (COLORADO)

Los Pinos Campground   FREE
Carson National Forest
15 mi SW of Antonito, in New Mexico, on US 285. Free. May-Sept; 14-day limit. 4 sites (16-ft RV limit) plus dispersed camping. Toilets, tbls, cfga, no drkg wtr. Excellent trout fishing at state fishing area nearby. Elev 8000 ft.

Rio de Los Pinos   FREE
State Wildlife & Fishing Area
10 mi SW of Antonito on CR C (becomes FR 284 in New Mexico). Free. All year; 14-day limit. Developed & dispersed sites. Toilets, cfga, no drkg wtr. Fishing, hiking trails, hunting. 850 acres with 1.5 mi of stream trout fishing.

ARREY

Arrey RV Park $10
1 mi S of I-25 from milemarker 59 on Hwy 187 to milemarker 19; near Caballo Lake. $10 plus elec cost at RV sites with hookups ($52 weekly plus elec cost); tents $5. 22 sites. Tbls, flush toilets, cfga, drkg wtr, tbls, showers, dump.

AZTEC

Ruins Road RV Park $10
At 312 Ruins Rd, Aztec. $10 for primitive sites; $20 (30 amp) & $25 (50 amp) with full hookups. All year. 30 sites. Tbls, toilets, cfga, drkg wtr, hookups($).

Pine Rivers Area $10
Navajo Lake State Park
13 mi E of Aztec on SR 173; 10 mi E on SR 511. $10 base. All year; 14-day limit. Base fee for about 150 developed sites; 50-ft RV limit. Tbls, flush toilets, cfga, drkg wtr, dump, elec($4), playground. Fishing, canoeing, hunting, hiking, boating(ld). Visitor center, exhibits, marina.

San Juan Area $8
Navajo Lake State Park
17 mi E of Aztec on SR 173. $8 base. All year; 14-day limit. Base fee for primitive sites; developed sites (50-ft RV limit), $10 base. Tbls, flush toilets, cfga, drkg wtr, elec($4), dump. Fishing, hunting, boating. Handicap access sites.

BLANCO

Buzzard Park   FREE
Carson National Forest
43 NE of Blanco on US 64; 17 mi N on FR 310 (rds treacherous when wet). All year; 14-day limit. 4 sites (32-ft RV limit) plus dispersed camping. Toilets, no drkg wtr. Elev 7300 ft. W of Jicarilla Apache Reservation.

BLOOMFIELD

Angel Peak Campground   FREE
Bureau of Land Management
About 10 mi SE of Bloomfield on SR 44 in NW New Mexico; 4 mi E on CR 7175. Free. All year (weather permitting); 14-day limit. 9 sites (35-ft RV limit); 200 acres. Tbls, toilets, cfga, shelters, no drkg wtr. Hiking, rockhounding, picnicking. Elev 6400 ft.

Gallo Wash Campground $7.50
Chaco Culture National Historic Park
27 mi S of Bloomfield on SR 44; 29 mi S on SR 57 to N entrance of the monument. Visitor center is 7 mi beyond entrance. Campground is 1 mi from visitor center. $7.50 with federal senior pass (others pay $15), plus $20 entry fee for 7 days (free with senior pass). All year. 14-day limit. 49 sites; 35-ft RV limit. Group sites available. Tbls, flush toilets, cfga, drkg wtr at visitor center parking area, no showers. Picnicking, hiking. Call the monument. 505-988-7627, about dirt road conditions during stormy weather. Pets in campgrounds but not on trails. 34,000 acres. Limited facilities in winter. 34,000 acres.

CANJILON

Lower Canjilon Lakes $5
Carson National Forest
7 mi E of Canjilon on SR 110; 4 mi N on FR 129. $5. MD-LD; 14-day limit. 11 sites; 22-ft RV limit. Tbls, toilets, cfga, drkg wtr. Boating(l), fishing, hiking. Closed 2017 for tree clearance; 2018 opening uncertain.

Middle Canjilon Lakes $5
Carson National Forest
7 mi E of Canjilon on SR 110; 4 mi N on FR 129. $5. MD-9/30; 14-day limit. 32 sites (22-ft RV limit). Tbls, toilets, cfga, drkg wtr. Boating, fishing, hiking. Elev 9900 ft. Closed 2017 for tree clearance; 2018 uncertain.

Upper Canjilon Lakes   FREE
Carson National Forest
12 mi NE of Canjilon on FR 559 & FR 129. Free. Primitive, undesignated camping area (22-ft RV limit). Tbls, toilets, no drkg wtr. Picnicking, fishing. Elevation 10,100 ft. Closed 2017 for tree clearance; 2018 uncertain.

CAPITAN

Baca Campground   FREE
Lincoln National Forest
About 10 mi E of Capitan on US 380; left on FR 57 for about 7 mi. Free sites on left side of rd for RVs & tents. All year; 14-day limit. Toilets, cfga, sometimes piped spring wtr, but not dependable. Once a CCC camp. 33.53876, -105.359283

CARLSBAD

Brantley Lake State Park $8
12 mi N of Carlsbad on US 285, then 4.5 mi E on CR 30. $8 base. All year; 14-day limit. Base fee for primitive sites; 51 developed sites (48 wtr/elec, 36 with shelters), $10 base (no RV limit). Tbls, flush toilets, cfga, drkg wtr, elec ($4), dump, showers, playground. Picnicking, boating(ld), fishing, hiking trails, canoeing, birdwatching, waterskiing, sailing. Visitor center with Wild West town of Seven Rivers. Elev 3300 ft; 3,000 acres. Southernmost lake in New Mexico. Food must be secured due to bears.

Dog Canyon Campground $8
Guadalupe Mountains National Park
10 mi N of US 285; 60 mi SW on SR 137, in Guadalupe Mountains National Park. $8. All year; 14-day limit. 4 RV sites. Limited facilities in winter. Drkg wtr, flush toilets, cfga, tbls, no showers. Also group sites. Nature trails. Park entry fee $5 for 7 days or $20 annual pass.

Pine Springs Canyon $8
Guadalupe Mountains National Park
Frijoe information station is located 55 mi SW of Carlsbad on US 62-180. The campground is 1.5 mi W of the information station. $8. All year; 14-day limit. 19 paved sites for self-contained RVs; 20 tent sites. Tbls, flush toilets, drkg wtr, no cfga or showers. Also group sites. Hiking, picnicking. Park entry fee $5 for 7 days ($20 annually).

CARRIZOZO

Three Rivers $6
Lincoln National Forest
24 mi S of Carrizozo on US 54 (18 mi N of Tularosa); turn E on FR 579 at sign that says "Three Rivers Petroglyphic Site and Campground" for 13 mi, follow signs. $6. All year; 14-day limit. 12 sites (RVs under 26 ft). Tbls, toilets, cfga, firewood, drkg wtr. Hiking, mountain climbing, picnicking, fishing, horseback riding. Elev 6400 ft; 10 acres. Good cool-weather campground. Trailhead into White Mountain Wilderness. Scenic. Horse corrals. Popular hunting camp.

Valley of Fires Recreation Area $12
Bureau of Land Management
Roswell Field Office
4 mi W of Carrizozo on SR 380 (NW of Alamogordo). $12 base. All year; 14-day limit. Base fee at RV sites without hookups; $18 for elec sites ($9 with federal senior pass). 19 sites (14 with elec); tents $7. Tbls, flush toilets, cfga, drkg wtr, dump ($15), showers. Hike past 1,000-yr-old lava flow. Visitor center. Elev 6300 ft.

CASA BLANCA

Dancing Eagle Casino RV Park $10
Laguna Pueblo Indian Reservation
From I-40 exit 108, about 2 mi S on SR 23/22. $10 at 34 full-hookup sites, 5 pull-through (20/30/50-amp). Flush toilets, coin laundry, store.

CEBOLLA

Trout Lakes   FREE
Carson National Forest
1 mi S of Cebolla on US 84; 9.5 mi NE on FR 125 (primitive rd). 6/1-9/30. 14-day limit. 5 primavige sites (15-ft RV limit). Tbls, toilets, cfga, no drkg wtr. Picnicking, fishing, horseback riding, hiking, biking. 4 acres. Scenic. Primitive rd, not recommended for large RVs. Elev 9300 ft.

CHAMA

Chama Basin Trailhead   FREE
Rio Grande National Forest
4.6 mi SW on SR 17; 7 mi N on FR 121. Free. 5/13-11/15. Undesignated dispersed sites. Tbls, cfga, toilets. Hiking, fishing, picnicking. GPS: 37.03497326, -106.5533922

CIMARRON

Cimarron Canyon State Park $8
Colin Neblett Wildlife Area
11 mi W of Cimarron on Hwy 64. $8 base. All year; 14-day limit. Base fee for primitive sites; 94 developed sites, $10 base; 30-ft RV limit. Tbls, flush toilets, no elec, cfga, drkg wtr, dump. Picnicking, fishing, hiking trails, winter sports. Elev 8000 ft; 400 acres, part of the 33,116-acre Colin Neblett Wildlife Area.

McCrystal $12
Carson National Forest
From Cerrososo Canyon (off US 64 about 5 mi NE of Cimarron), 20 mi along canyon ; 7 mi on FR 1950. $12 until wtr system is repaired. MD-10/31; 14-day limit. 60 sites (40-ft RV limit), including 1 group site & 6 sites for equestrians. Toilets, tbls, cfga, no drkg water. Horse facilities at 6 sites. Bridle & hiking trails, hunting, fishing.

CLAYTON

Clayton Lake State Park $8
12 mi N of Clayton on SR 370. $8 base. All year; 14-day limit. Base fee for primitive sites; 26 developed sites with shelters (7 with wtr/elec), $10. 70-ft RV limit. Tbls, flush toilets, cfga, drkg wtr, showers, elec($4), no dump, playground. Boating(dl) (ramp may be closed for low water), fishing, hiking trails, swimming, sailing. Trail overlooks rare 100-million year-old dinosaur trackway. Elev 5040 ft; 417 acres.

CLIFF

Bill Evans Wildlife Area   FREE
State Fishing Lake
3 mi S of Cliff on US 180; 5 mi SW on FR 809 (Bill Evans Rd); left 0.2 mi on access rd. Free. All year; 14-day limit. Primitive designated camping areas. Tbls, toilets, cfga, no drkg wtr. Boating(l), fishing. No shade. GPS: 32.866214, -108.57948

CLOUDCROFT

Apache Campground $10
Lincoln National Forest
1.2 mi E of Cloudcroft on US 82; 1.5 mi NW on SR 244; 1 mi S on FR 24G. $10 with federal senior pass; others pay $20. 5/15-LD; 14-day limit. 25 sites (30-ft RV limit). Tbls, toilets, cfga, drkg wtr ($ after 5 gal), gray water sumps, trash service ($ daily). Showers & dump at Silver CG ($5). Interpretive trails nearby. Elev 8900 ft; 6 acres.

Deerhead Campground $10
Lincoln National Forest
From W side of Cloudcroft, 1 mi S on SR 130 to jct with US 82; on the right. $10 with federal senior pass; others pay $20. About 5/15-LD; 14-day limit. 20 paved sites; 30-ft RV limit. Tbls, toilets, cfga, drkg wtr ($ after 5 gal), gray water sumps; trash service($ daily). Dump & showers at Silver CG ($5). Hiking (trailhead of 21-mi Rim Trail). Elev 8700 ft; 10 acres.

Pines Campground $10
Lincoln National Forest
1.2 mi E of Cloudcroft on US 82; half mi NW on SR 244. $10 with federal senior pass; others pay $20 (double sites $25, triple $32, quad-site $38). About 5/15-LD; 14-day limit. 24 sites; 40-ft RV limit. Tbls, toilets, cfga, drkg wtr ($ after 5 gal), gray water sumps, trash service ($ daily). Showers & dump at Silver CG ($5). Hiking trail access.

Saddle Campground $10
Lincoln National Forest
1.2 mi E of Cloudcroft on US 82; 1.5 mi NW on SR 44; half mi S on FR 24G. $10 with federal senior pass; others pay $20. About 5/15-9/15; 14-day limit. 16 sites (30-ft RV limit). Tbls, toilets, cfga, drkg wtr ($ after 5 gal), gray water sumps at each site (garden hose needed), trash service ($ daily). Showers & dump at Silver CG ($5). Interpretive trails. Elev 9000 ft; 6 acres.

Silver Campground $10
Lincoln National Forest
1.2 mi E of Cloudcroft on US 82; 1.5 mi NW on SR 244; half mi S on FR 24G. $10 with federal senior pass; others pay $20. 4/15-10/15; 14-day limit. 30 sites; 30-ft RV limit. Tbls, toilets, cfga, drkg wtr ($ after 5 gal), gray water sumps at each site (garden hose needed), dump ($5 per use), showers ($5), trash service ($ daily). Interpretive trail. Weekend ranger programs at amphitheater. Elev 9000 ft.

Silver Overflow $8
Lincoln National Forest
1.2 mi E of Cloudcroft on US 82; 1.5 mi NW on SR 244; qtr mi S on FR 24G. $8 with federal senior pass; others pay $16. About 5/1-10/15; 30-day limit. 52 sites (no RV length limit). Tbls, toilets, cfga, drkg wtr ($ after 5 gal), grey water sumps, trash service ($ daily). Showers & dump $5 at Silver Camp. Hiking, interpretive trails.

Sleepy Grass Campground $8
Lincoln National Forest
1.4 mi S of Cloudcroft on SR 130; veer left onto FR 24B. $8 with federal senior pass; others pay $16 (double sites $25, triple sites $32). About 5/15-LD; 14-day limit. 15 sites (8 for RVs); 30-ft RV limit. Tbls, toilets, cfga, drkg wtr. Hiking trail for blind & sighted.

COLUMBUS

Pancho Villa State Park $8
On S edge of Columbus on SR 11. $8 base. All year; 14-day
limit. Base fee for primitive sites; 79 developed sites with
shelters 75 elec, $10 base; 48-ft RV limit. Tbls, flush toi-
lets, cfga, drkg wtr, dump, elec($4), showers. Picnicking,
hiking. Historical exhibit, desert botanical garden. Visitor
center, historic buildings. Elev 4000 ft; 60 acres.

CORONA

Red Cloud   FREE
Cibola National Forest
9.5 mi SW of Corona on US 54; 1.5 mi W on FR 161. 6.5 mi
NW on FR 399. 4/1-10/31; 14-day limit. 5 sites (RVs under
22 ft). Tbls, toilet, no drkg wtr. Picnicking. Elev 7600 ft. 2
acres. Primitive forest environment.

COSTILLA

Cimarron   Campground $9
Carson National Forest
30 mi SW of Costilla on SR 196; E on FR 1950 past Valle
Vidal Unit line to jct with FR 1900; 10 mi S on FR 1950 to
FR 1910, then 1 mi to camp. $9 with federal senior pass;
others pay $18. MD-10/23; 14-day limit. 36 sites (38-ft RV
limit); horse camping facilities at 11 sites. Tbls, toilets,
cfga, no drkg wtr, corrals. Fishing, hunting, hiking, horseback riding. Elev 9400 ft.

CUBA

Cabezon Peak Recreation Area   FREE
Bureau of Land Management
Rio Puerco Field Office
20 mi SW of Cuba via CR 279. Free. All year; 14-day limit.
Primitive undesignated camping. No facilities except cfga;
no drkg wtr. Biking, hiking, hunting.

Clear Creek $10
Santa Fe National Forest
11.2 mi E of Cuba on SR 126; at th Rio de las Vacas River.
$10. 5/30-10/1, depending on snow; 14-day limit. 12 sites
(16-ft trailer limit; 30-ft motorhome limit). Tbls, toilets,
cfga, firewood, drkg wtr. Picnicking, fishing, hiking trails.
Elev 8500 ft.

Rio de las Vacas $10
Santa Fe National Forest
12.7 mi E of Cuba on SR 126. $10. 5/30-11/1; 14-day limit.
15 sites; 16-ft RV limit. Tbls, toilets, cfga, firewood, drkg
wtr (but treat it before drinking to be safe). Fishing, hiking.
Elev 8200 ft. 2 acres. Stream.

DATIL

Datil Well Campground $5
Bureau of Land Management
Socorro Field Office
.4 mi W of US 60 near Datil in western New Mexico. $5.

All year (weather permitting); 7-day limit. 22 sites. Tbls,
toilets, cfga, drkg wtr, recreation hall, no trash service.
Picnicking, hiking. Elev 7400 ft. 680 acres. Interpretive
display. Nature trails. Fee increase to $10 expected.

DEMING

City of Rocks State Park $10
22 mi NW of Deming on US 180; 5 mi E on SR 61. $10.
All year; 14-day limit. 52 developed sites (10 with elec, 2
with sewer); no RV size limit. Tbls, flush toilets, cfga, drkg
wtr, showers, elec($4), sewer($4), no dump. Hiking trails.
Volcanic rocks, cactus gardens, interpretive exhibits. Elev
5200 ft; 680 acres.

Rockhound State Park $10
14 mi SE of Deming on SR 11 and Rd 549. $10 base. All
year; 14-day limit. 29 developed sites (23 with elec); 40-ft
RV limit. Tbls, flush toilets, cfga, drkg wtr, elec($4), show-
ers, dump. Picnicking, hiking, playground, rockhounding
for agates, opals & quartz. Visitor center. Elev 4500 ft;
250 acres.

EL RITO

El Rito Creek   FREE
Carson National Forest
5.3 mi NW of El Rito on FR 129. Free. Elev 7600 ft. 4/15-
10/15; 14-day limit. 11 sites (RVs under 22 ft). Firewood,
tbls, cfga, toilets, no drkg wtr. Picnicking, fishing, horseback riding, biking. Crowded in summer.

ESPANOLA

Santa Cruz Lake Recreation Area $7
Bureau of Land Management
Taos Field Office
13 mi E of Espanola on SR 4 & SR 76. $7 for primitive sites
at Overlook Campground; $9 for developed sites at North
Lake. All year; 14-day limit. 30 sites (no RV size limit). Tbls,
toilets, cfga, drkg wtr. Fishing, boating (l), hiking.

EUNICE

Eunice Municipal Recreation Area   FREE
4 mi W of Eunice on SR 176; at Eunice Lake. Free 3 days
with pass from city hall. About 10 sites. Flush toilets,
sheltered picnic units, elec/wtr, dump, playground. Tennis,
picnicking, fishing (stocked lake), baseball fields, croquet
courts, horseshoes, golf nearby, basketball, nature trails.
GPS: 32.4642912, -103.2335266

FARMINGTON

McGee County Park $10
San Juan County Fairgrounds
From jct with SR 516 near downtown Farmington, about 6
mi E on US 64; S on Road 5568 to park. $10 at 100 sites
without hookups; $30 at 574 elec/wtr sites. Tbls, flush
toilets, cfga, drkg wtr, showers, pay phones, dump. Volleyball, basketball, tennis, convention center, classrooms.
Park hosts equestrian events.

FORT SUMNER

Sumner Lake State Park $8
16 mi N of Fort Sumner on US 84. $8 base. All year; 14-day limit. Base fee for primitive sites; 50 developed sites (18 with elec) with shelters, $10 base. 45-ft RV limit. Tbls, flush toilets, elec($), cfga, drkg wtr, dump, playground, showers, beach. Swimming, boating(l), fishing, waterskiing, sailing, hiking, biking. Elev 4300 ft; 6,667 acres.

FORT WINGATE

McGaffey Canyon Campground $10
Cibola National Forest
7 mi S of Fort Wingate on SR 400. $10 base ($5 with senior pass). 5/9-9/15; 14-day limit. Base fee for 22 tent & RV sites without hookups; $5 surcharge at 7 RV sites with elec/sewer hookups. 5/15-9/30; 14-day limit. 29 sites; 22-ft RV limit. Flush toilets, cfga, tbls, drkg wtr, showers. Group sites by reservation. Fishing, hiking, boating (very small, shallow lake). Elev 8000 ft; 46 acres.

Quaking Aspen $5
Cibola National Forest
6 mi S of Fort Wingate on SR 400. $5. 5/15-9/30; 14-day limit. 20 sites (22-ft RV limit). Tbls, toilets, cfga, drkg wtr. Hunting, fishing, hiking trail. Elev 7600 ft.

GALLINA

Resumidero Campground FREE
Santa Fe National Forest
2.5 mi SE of Gallina on Hwy 96; 6.5 mi S on FR 103; 2 mi W on FR 93. Free. All year; 14-day limit. 6 RV sites & 15 dispersed sites; suitable for large RVs. Tbls, portable toilets, cfga, no drkg wtr, no trash service. Hiking, fishing.

GLENWOOD

Bighorn Campground FREE
Gila National Forest
On N edge of Glenwood at US 180. Free. All year; 14-day limit. 5 sites. Tbls, toilet, cfga, no drkg wtr. Elev 4800 ft.

Pueblo Park FREE
Gila National Forest
25 mi N of Glenwood on US 180; 5.6 mi W on CR 13 (18 mi SW of Reserve). Apr-Nov; 15-day limit. 10 sites. Tbls, toilets, cfga, no drkg wtr, no trash service. Hiking, rock-hounding, horseback riding. Corrals. Elev 6150 ft.

GOBERNADOR

Sims Mesa Area $8
Navajo Lake State Park
N of Gobernador on Hwy 527. $8 base. All year; 14-day limit. Base fee for primitive sites; developed sites $10 base; 35-ft RV limit. Tbls, flush toilets, cfga, drkg wtr, dump, showers, playground, elec($4), store. Fishing, waterskiing, boating(ldr), birdwatching, hunting, swimming.

GRANTS

Bluewater Lake State Park $8
28 mi W of Grants via I-40 and SR 412. $8 base. All year; 14-day limit. Base fee for primitive sites; 149 developed sites, $10 base (14 with elec). 45-ft RV limit. Elec($4), tbls, flush toilets, cfga, drkg wtr, dump, playground, store, no showers. Nature trails, fishing, waterskiing, boating(lrd), swimming. Elev 7500 ft; 2,104 acres. Visitor center.

Coal Mine Canyon Campground $5
Cibola National Forest
10 mi NE of Grants on SR 547. $5 campsites & day use. About 5/15-9/15; 14-day limit. 17 sites; 22-ft RV limit. Tbls, flush toilets, cfga, no drkg wtr. Hiking, nature trail. Elev 7400 ft.

Joe Skeen Campground FREE
El Mapais National Conservation Area
Bureau of Land Management
Rio Puerco Field Office
E of Grants on I-40 to exit 89, then 11 mi S on Hwy 117. Free. All year; 14-day limit. 10 sites plus dispersed camping area. Tbls, flush toilets, cfga, drkg wtr. Hiking, climbing, biking. El Mapais National Monument nearby (no camping at the monument).

El Morro National Monument Free
42 mi SW of Grants on Hwy 53 at Ramah. Free all year; for 7 days. Wtr is off in winter. 9 sites. 27fr RV-Limit. Tbls, toilets, cfga, drkg wtr. Hiking, museum, visitor center. .

JAL

Jal Lake City Park FREE
From jct with SR 128, 1 mi S through town on SR 205; park at jct with Whitworth Dr. Free. All year; 3-day limit. 5 sites; no RV size limit. Tbls, pit toilets, cfga, elec/wtr, dump. Fishing lake, tennis courts, playground, basketball. GPS: 32.0987, -103.19.

JEMEZ SPRINGS

Calaveras Campground FREE
Seven Springs Fish Hatchery
7.5 mi N of Jemez Springs on Hwy 4; left on Hwy 126 for 12 mi. Free. May-Nov. Primitive undesignated sites for about 5 RVs. Tbls, toilets, cfga, no drkg wtr. Hiking, hunting, fishing. Fish hatchery about half mi. GPS: 35.9297, -106.7092

Jemez Falls Campground $10
Santa Fe National Forest
15 mi NE of Jemez Springs on NM 4; 1 mi S on FR 133 (primitive roadway). $10. 4/15-11/15; 14-day limit. 52 sites (40-ft trailer limit, 45-ft motorhome limit). Tbls, toilets, cfga, drkg wtr. Hiking, fishing. Elev 7900 ft; 2 acres. National Recreation Trailhead. Trail access to scenic Jemez Falls & nearby hot springs.

Redondo Campground $10
Santa Fe National Forest
11.3 mi NE of Jemez Springs on SR 4. $10. 4/15-11/15, weather permitting; 14-day limit. 59 sites (30-ft trailer limit, 45-ft motorhome limit). Tbls, toilets, cfga, no drkg wtr, amphitheater. 4 hiking trails, nature trail. Elev 8200 ft.

San Antonio Campground $10
Santa Fe National Forest
9 mi NE of Jemez Springs on SR 4; 1.5 mi N on SR 126. $10 at non-elec sites, $15 at 6 wtr/elec sites ($5 & $12.50 with federal senior pass). About 5/1-10/15; 14-day limit. 21 sites (35-ft RV limit). Tbls, toilets, cfga, drkg wtr (may be limited). Swimming, fishing, hiking. Wheelchair access; group sites available. Elev 7800 ft; 10 acres.

Vista Linda Campground $10
Santa Fe National Forest
5 mi S of Jemez Springs on SR 4; near James River in scenic San Diego Canyon. $10. All year; 14-day limit. 13 pull-through sites; 40-ft RV limit. Tbls, toilets, cfga, drkg wtr. Charcoal-only fires. Hiking, fishing.

LAS CRUCES

Aguirre Spring Campground $7
Organ Mountains-Desert Peaks National Monument
Bureau of Land Management
Las Cruces Field Office
5 mi S of US 70 and 17 me E of Las Cruces. $7. All year; 14-day limit. 57 sites (RVs under 22 ft). Tbls, toilets, cfga, shelters, no drkg wtr. Also group camping. Hiking, picnicking, horseback riding. Interpretive trails and facilities. Elev 6400 ft; 160 acres.

Leasburg Dam State Park $8
15 mi N of Las Cruces on I-25; from exit 19, W on SR 157; at Radium Springs. $8 base. All year; 14/-day limit. Base fee for primitive sites; 31 developed sites (10 with elec) with shelters, $10 base; 36-ft RV limit. Tbls, flush toilets, cfga, drkg wtr, elec($4), dump, showers, playground. Fishing, hiking trails, kayaking, canoeing. Visitor center. Fort Selden State Monument nearby. Elev 4000 ft; 140 acres.

LAS VEGAS

E.V. Long Campground $8
Santa Fe National Forest
16.2 mi NW of Las Vegas on SR 65; .1 mi SW on FR 156; at El Porvenir Creek. $8. Elev 7500 ft. 5/1-11/15; 14-day limit. 14 sites (typically 32 ft). Tbls, toilets, cfga, no drkg wtr. Fishing, hiking, climbing, hunting.

El Porvenir $8
Santa Fe National Forest
17 mi NW of Las Vegas on SR 65; .7 mi W on FR 261. $8. About 4/10-1/5; 14-day limit. 13 sites; 32-ft RV limit. Tbls, toilets, cfga, no drkg wtr. Fishing, hiking.

Storrie Lake State Park $8
4 mi N of Las Vegas on SR 518. $8 base. All year; 14-day limit. Base fee for primitive sites; 45 developed sites with shelters (22 with elec), $10 base; 35-ft RV limit. Tbls, flush toilets, cfga, drkg wtr, showers, elec($4), playground. Windsurfing, waterskiing, boating(l), fishing. Visitor center with historical displays. Elev 6591 ft; 82 acres.

Villanueva State Park $10
23 mi S of Las Vegas on I-25 to exit 323; 15 mi S on SR 3. $10 base. All year; 14-day limit. 33 developed sites (19 with shelters, 12 with elec); 40-ft RV limit. Tbls, flush toilets, cfga, drkg wtr, elec($4), showers, dump, playground. Fishing, spring canoeing & rafting, nature trails. Visitor center. Old ranching ruins. Elev 6000 ft; 1,679 acres.

LINCOLN

Fort Stanton Recreation Area FREE
Bureau of Land Management
W of Lincoln via US 380 & SR 214. Free . All year; 14-day limit. Primitive undesignated sites. $5 for RV Hookups. Toilets, tbls, cfga no drkg wtr. Hiking (Rio Bonito Petroglyph Trail), horseback riding, biking, caving, fishing.

LOGAN

Ute Lake State Park $8
3 mi W of Logan on SR 540; on Canadian River. $8 base. All year; 14-day limit. Base fee at primitive sites; 142 developed sites (77 with elec) with shelters, $10 base; 45-ft RV limit. Tbls, flush toilets, elec($4), cfga, drkg wtr, dump, showers, playground, beach. Swimming, boating(l-rd), fishing, nature trails, waterskiing. 2 handicap-access sites. Visitor center.

LORDSBURG

Lower Gila Box FREE
Bureau of Land Management
2 mi NW of Lordsburg on US 70; 14 mi N on Hwy 464; 3.5 mi W on CR A027, then 4.5 mi N on CR A024 from the steel storage tank; camp area not marked. Free. About 12 primitive undesignated sites; no facilities, no trash service. Hiking, canoeing, fishing. Gila River.

LOS ALAMOS

Camp May $10
Los Alamos County Parks Division
2 mi W of Los Alamos on SR 501; 2 mi NW on Camp May Trail above Pajariot ski area. $10 at refurbished 27-acre park). 5/1 (weather permitting) - 10/31. 25-ft RV limit; mainly tent spaces. Tbls, toilets, cfga, drkg wtr. Horseback riding, hiking trail. County camping permit required.

Fenton Lake State Park $10
35 mi W of Los Alamos on Hwy 4. $10 base. All year; 14-day limit. 37 developed sites (2 handicap access; 15 sites with elec); 32-ft RV limit. Tbls, flush toilets, cfga, drkg wtr, elec($4), playground. Fishing, picnicking, boat-

ing(ld), hiking trails, skiing, wheelchair-accessible fishing platforms. Elev 7978 ft; 700 acres.

MAGDALENA
Bear Trap Campground   FREE
Cibola National Forest
13 mi SW of Magdalena via US 60; 13 mi S & Old SR 52 (FR 549); just N of Hughes Mill CG. Free. May-Oct; 14-day limit. 4 sites (20-ft RV limit). Toilets, cfga, no drkg wtr. Hiking, hunting, horseback riding. Elev 8500 ft.

Hughes Mill   FREE
Cibola National Forest
13 mi SW of Magdalena via US 60 & 13 mi S on Old SR 52 (FR 549). Free. May-Oct; 14-day limit. 2 sites (20-ft RV limit) and dispersed camping with trailhead. Toilet, cfga, no drkg wtr. Hiking trail. Elev 8100 ft.

Water Canyon   FREE
Cibola National Forest
9 mi SE of Magdalena on US 60; 7 mi SW on FR 235 (Water Canyon Rd). Free. All year; 14-day limit. 4 sites (22-ft RV limit); 11 picnic sites. Tbls, toilets, cfga, no drkg wtr. Hiking, biking trail. Elev 6800 ft.

MANZANO
New Canyon   FREE
Cibola National Forest
2 mi SW of Manzano on SR 131; SW on FR 253. Free. Apr-Nov; 14-day limit. 10 sites (22-ft RV limit). Tbls, toilet, cfga, no drkg wtr. Hiking, picnicking, hunting. Elev 7800 ft

Red Canyon $7
Cibola National Forest
2 mi SW of Manzano on SR 131; SW on FR 253 past New Canyon CG. $7. Apr-Nov; 14-day limit. 38 sites; 22-ft limit (camp recently refurbished). Tbls, toilets, cfga, drkg wtr. Hiking, hunting, horseback riding. Elev 8000 ft.

MAXWELL
Lake 13 Campground   FREE
Maxwell National Wildlife Refuge
1 mi N of Maxwell on Hwy 455; 2.5 mi W on Hwy 505, then 2 mi N to lake. Free. 3/1-10/31; 3-day limit. Primitive undesignated sites. Tbls, toilets, no drkg wtr, no fires. Fishing, birdwatching, boating(l).

MAYHILL
Bear Canyon & Dam Dispersed Area   FREE
Lincoln National Forest
S of Mayhill on SR 130, then S on SR 24; after crossing the Rio Penasco, keep to the right onto FR 621 to switchback. Free. All year; 14-day limit. Primitive undeveloped RV area. Caution: No space at Bear Canyon Dam for RVs to turn around. No facilities, no drkg wtr. Hiking, hunting.

Burnt Canyon Dispersed Area   FREE
Lincoln National Forest
2 mi E of Mayhill on US 82; 3 mi N on FR 607 (Car Gap Rd); turn right to the curve. Free. All year; 14-day limit. Primitive undeveloped area for 4-5 RVs. Hiking.

Hoosier Canyon Dispersed Area   FREE
Lincoln National Forest
S of Mayhill on SR 130, then SE on SR 24; W on FR 521 through Weed & Sacramento to FR 64; follow FR 64 about 6 mi to Hoosier Canyon (FR 5959). Free. All year; 14-day limit. Primitive undeveloped flat camping areas; no facilities, no drkg wtr. Hiking, hunting.

James Canyon Campground   FREE
Lincoln National Forest
2 mi NW of Mayhill on US 82. Apr-Nov; 14-day limit. 5 sites; 16-ft RV limit. Tbls, toilet, cfga, no drkg wtr, 1 group ramada. Picnicking, fishing. Elev 6800 ft. GPS: 32.904688, -105.505055

Miller Flats Road Dispersed Area   FREE
Lincoln National Forest
1.5 mi S of Mayhill on SR 130; left onto Miller Flats Rd (FR 212) for about 2 mi; on left is sign for Bible Canyon; on right is flat, grassy area for free primitive camping. No facilities, no drkg wtr. Hiking.

Prestridge Hill/Hay Canyon   FREE
Dispersed Area
Lincoln National Forest
S of Mayhill on SR 30, past SR 24 turnoff for about 4 mi; S onto FR 164 for half mi from sign for Wills Canyon; S on FR 541 over Prestridge Hill, intersecting with FR 257 at Hay Canyon. Free. All year; 14-day limit. Primitive undesignated camping in flat areas among trees. No facilities, no drkg wtr. Hiking, hunting.

Top of Denny Hill Dispersed Area   FREE
Dispersed Area
Lincoln National Forest
S of Mayhill on SR 130 to southbound SR 24; ascend Denny Hill; cross cattle guard to pull-off. Free. All year; 14-day limit. Primitive undeveloped camping; no facilities, no drkg wtr. Hiking.

MILLS
Mills Canyon   FREE
Kiowa National Grassland
Cibola National Forest
10 mi SW of Mills, off Hwy 39 on FR 600. Rd is poor for RVs; high clearance vehicles only. Free. All year; 14-day limit. 12 rebuilt sites. Tbls, toilets, cfga, drkg wtr. Fishing, hiking, rockhounding. Located in a very scenic canyon in the middle of flat plains; excellent spot for watching cliff-dwelling birds & Barbury sheep. Elev 5160 ft.

MIMBRES

Bear Canyon Reservoir   FREE
State Fishing Area
State Game & Fish Department
Gila National Forest
2 mi N of Mimbres, then W on forest rd; dispersed sites along shore of lake. Toilets, cfga, tbls, no drkg wtr. Fishing, boating(l).

Mesa Campground $10
Gila National Forest
3 mi from Mimbres Ranger station at Lake Roberts (30 mi NE of Silver City via SRs 15 & 35). $10 base, $15 at 12 elec/wtr sites ($10 with federal senior pass). All year; 15-day limit. 24 sites, typically 45 ft. Tbls, flush toilets (remodeled 2012), cfga, drkg wtr. Fishing, boating, hiking.

Rocky Canyon   FREE
Gila National Forest
4 mi NW of Mimbres on Hwy 35; 13 mi N on FR 150 (high-clearance vehicles suggested). Free. 4/1-11/30; 30-day limit. 2 sites (17-ft RV limit). Tbls, toilet, cfga, no drkg wtr. Hiking, fishing. Favored as fall hunting camp. Elev 7300 ft.

Sapillo Group Camp   FREE
Gila National Forest
9.8 mi NW of Mimbres on SR 61; 6.6 mi W on SR 35; half mi S on FR 606. Free. All year; 15-day limit. 8 dispersed group sites. Toilets, cfga, no tbls, no drkg wtr. Hiking, horseback riding, fishing. Elev 6100 ft; 5 acres. Scenic.

Upper End $10
Lake Roberts Recreation Area
Gila National Forest
12 mi NW of Mimbres on SR 35. $10 during MD-LD; free rest of yr, but no wtr; 14-day limit. 12 sites (32-ft RV limit). Tbls, toilet, cfga, drkg wtr. Fishing, boating(lr nearby), hiking. Elev 6000 ft; 13 acres.

MONTICELLO

Luna Park Campground   FREE
Cibola National Forest
8 mi N of Monticello on CR 34, becoming Luna Park Rd (FR 139). High clearance vehicles only. Free. Apr-Nov; 14-day limit. 3 sites (20-ft RV limit). Toilet, cfga, no drkg wtr. Hiking, horseback riding, hunting. Odd volcanic rock formations give moon-like appearance to this site. Elev 7400 ft.

MORA

Coyote Creek State Park $8
17 mi N of Mora on SR 434. $8 base. All year; 14-day limit. Base fee at primitive sites; 47 developed sites (12 with shelters, 19 with elec), $10; 35-ft RV limit. Tbls, flush toilets, cfga, drkg wtr, elec($4), showers, playground, dump. Fishing, picnicking, hiking trails. Visitor center. Elev 7700 ft. Recent expansion added 382 acres to 80-acre park.

Morphy Lake State Park $10
4 mi S of Mora on SR 94; 4 mi W on newly paved rd. $10 at 24 developed sites. 4/1-10/31; 14-day limit. No drkg wtr. Tbls, toilets, cfga. Picnicking, boating (elec mtrs), fishing. Elev 7840 ft; 18 acres.

MOUNTAINAIR

Manzano Mountains State Park $10
16 mi NW of Mountainair on SR 55. $8 base. About 4/15-10/31; 14-day limit. 23 developed sites (5 with shelters, 9 with elec), $10 base; 30-ft RV limit. Elec($4), tbls, flush toilets, cfga, drkg wtr, playground, no showers. Nature trails, birdwatching, cross-country skiing. Salinas National Monument nearby. Elev 7200 ft.

PECOS

Mora Campground   FREE
State Game & Fish Department
14 mi N of Pecos on Hwy 63; at Mora & Pecos Rivers. Free. All year; 14-day limit. About 40 primitive undesignated sites. Tbls, toilets, cfga, no drkg wtr. Fishing.

Field Tract Campground $8
Santa Fe National Forest
9 mi N of Pecos on SR 63. $8. 5/1-11/15; 14-day limit. 15 sites (typically 45 ft). Tbls, flush & pit toilets, cfga, drkg wtr. Fishing, hiking. Elev 7400 ft; 5 acres.

Holy Ghost Campground $8
Santa Fe National Forest
13.2 mi N of Pecos on SR 63; 2.2 mi NW on FR 122; at Holy Ghost Creek. $8. 5/1-11/15 but closed 7/21-9/30; 14-day limit. 24 sites (32-ft RV limit). Tbls, toilets, cfga, no drkg wtr in 2017. Fishing. 20 acres.

Iron Gate Campground $4
Santa Fe National Forest
18.8 mi N of Pecos on SR 63; 4.2 mi NE on FR 223; rough rd, poor access. $4. Elev 9400 ft. 5/1-10/31; 14-day limit. 14 sites (RV rigs under 31 ft). Tbls, toilets, cfga, no drkg wtr. Hiking, picnicking, fishing, horseback riding (4 corrals). Pecos Wilderness.

Jacks Creek Horse Camp $10
Santa Fe National Forest
18 mi N of Pecos on SR 63 to Cowles; 1 mi N on FR 555. $10. 5/1-11/15; 14-day limit. 39 sites; 40-ft RV limit. Also 8 equestrian sites with 5 corrals. Tbls, toilets, cfga, no drkg wtr, corrals, horse trailer parking. Hiking, fishing, horseback riding.

Terrero Campground   FREE
Bert Clancy Fish & Wildlife Area
N of Pecos on SR 63 along the Pecos River. Free. All year; 14-day limit. 10 primitive sites. Tbls, toilets, cfga, drkg wtr. Fishing, wildlife study, hiking. 2,166 acres. GPS: 35.742, -105.675

PORTALES

Oasis State Park $8
7.5 mi NE of Portales off SR 467. $8 base. All year; 14-day limit. Base fee for primitive sites; 29 developed sites (13 with shelters), $10 base. 65-ft RV limit. Tbls, flush toilets, cfga, drkg wtr, dump, elec($4), showers, playground. Picnicking, fishing, hiking trails, birdwatching. Elev 4030 ft; 196 acres; 3-acre pond.

QUEMADO

Armijo Springs Campground   FREE
Gila National Forest
20 mi S of Quemado on Hwy 32; left on FR 854 for 6 mi. Free. All year; 14-day limit. About 5 primitive undesignated sites for tents or self-contained RVs. Tbls, toilet, cfga, no drkg wtr or trash service. Horseback riding, hunting.

El Caso Campgrounds   FREE
Gila National Forest
20 mi S of Quemado on Hwy 32; 4 mi E on Hwy 103; just past E end of Quemado Lake on FR 13. Free. All year; 15-day limit. 22 small primitive dispersed sites along rd in 3 areas for RVs under 20 ft. Tbls, toilets, cfga, no drkg wtr. Boating(l), fishing at lake. Part of Apache National Forest. 2017; some areas closed due to hazardous trees.

Juniper Campground $10
Gila National Forest
Quemado Lake Recreation Area
W of Quemado on US 60; S on SR 32; E on FR 13; on N side of Quemado Lake. $10 without hookups (double site $16); $15 for elec ($10 with federal senior pass). 5/1-9/30; 14-day limit. 36 sites; 30 to 42-ft RV limit. Tbls, toilets, cfga, drkg wtr. Boating(l), fishing.

Pinon Campground $10
Gila National Forest
W of Quemado on US 60; S on SR 32; E on FR 13; on N side of Quemado Lake one-third mi E of Juniper camps. $10. 5/1-9/30; 15-day limit. 22 sites; 40 ft RV limit. Tbls, toilets, cfga, drkg wtr, dump ($5). Fishing, boating(l). Elev 8000 ft.

Valle Tio Vinces   FREE
Gila National Forest
9 mi E of Quemado on Hwy 60; 19 mi S on FR 214. All year; 15-day limit. 4 sites. Tbls, cfga, no drkg wtr, no toilets. Wtr, troughs & corrals for horses. Bridle trails, hunting. Primarily a horse camp.

QUESTA

Big Arsenic Springs $7
Wild Rivers Recreation Area
Bureau of Land Management Taos Field Office
3 mi N of Questa on Hwy 522; left on Hwy 378, follow signs. $7 (two RVs, $10). All year; 14-day limit. $5 for hike-in tent sites along river. 6 developed sites and designated primitive hike-in river sites. Tbls, toilets, cfga, drkg wtr. Fishing, hiking, mountain biking. Visitor center exhibits.

Cabresto Lake   FREE
Carson National Forest
6 mi NE of Questa on FR 134; 2 mi NE on FR 134A (poor access rd); overlooking 15-acre lake. Elev 9500 ft. 5/15-10/1; 14-day limit. 9 sites for tents, pop-ups, vans or pickup campers (no larger RVs due to winding rd). Tbls, toilet, cfga, drkg wtr. Boating (no motors in lake), picnicking, fishing.

Cebolla Mesa   FREE
Carson National Forest
8 mi SW of Questa on NM 3 & FR 9 (hazardous, muddy when wet). Free. May-Oct; 14-day limit. 5 sites (32-ft RV limit). Toilets, tbls, cfga, no drkg wtr. Fishing, hiking. Trailhead. Elev 7300 ft.

Columbine Campground $9
Carson National Forest
5 mi E of Questa on SR 38. $9 with federal senior pass; others pay $18. MD-10/1; 14-day limit. 26 sites (40-ft RV limit). Tbls, toilets, cfga, drkg wtr. Fishing, hiking, rockhounding, horseback riding. Non-campers pay Columbine Creek, Red River. Elev 7900 ft; 22 acres.

El Aguaje Campground $7
Wild Rivers Recreation Area
Bureau of Land Management Taos Field Office
3 mi N of Questa on Hwy 522; left on Hwy 378, follow signs. $7. All year; 14-day limit. $5 for hike-in tent sites along river. 6 developed sites. Tbls, toilets, cfga, drkg wtr. Fishing, hiking.

Goat Hill $7
Carson National Forest
4 me E of Questa on NM 38; roadside camping with access to Red River. $7. 5/15-10/31; 14-day limit. 5 sites (32-ft RV limit). Toilet, no drkg wtr. Fishing. Elev 7500 ft.

La Bobita $7
Carson National Forest
6.1 mi E of Questa on NM 38. $7. All year as needed; 14-day limit. Primitive overflow camp open by concessionaire when others nearby are full. Group sites $50. Tbls, cfga, no toilets, no drkg wtr.

La Junta Campground $7
Wild Rivers Recreation Area
Bureau of Land Management Taos Field Office
3 mi N of Questa on Hwy 522; left on Hwy 378, follow signs. $7. All year; 14-day limit. $5 for hike-in tent sites along river. 6 developed sites. Tbls, toilets, cfga, drkg wtr. Fishing, hiking.

Little Arsenic Spring $7
Wild Rivers Recreation Area
Bureau of Land Management Taos Field Office
3 mi N of Questa on Hwy 522; left on Hwy 378, follow signs. $7. All year; 14-day limit. $5 for hike-in tent sites along river. 4 developed sites. Tbls, toilets, cfga, drkg wtr. Fishing, hiking.

Montoso Campground $7
Wild Rivers Recreation Area
Bureau of Land Management Taos Field Office
3 mi N of Questa on Hwy 522; left on Hwy 378, follow signs. $7. All year; 14-day limit. $5 for hike-in tent sites along river. 2 developed sites. Tbls, toilet, cfga, drkg wtr. Fishing, hiking.

Red River State Trout Hatchery   FREE
Carson National Forest
6 mi S of Questa on US 522; W on Hwy 515; sites along road at tbls, shelters, cfga. Free. Drkg wtr & toilets at hatchery. Fishing. Tour hatchery. Open all year. Unable to verify status for 2018.

RATON

Sugarite Canyon State Park $10
10 mi NE of Raton on SR 526. $10 base. All year; 14-dayimit. 40 developed sites (10 with shelters, 8 with elec); 40-ft RV limit. Tbls, elec($4), flush toilets, cfga, drkg wtr, showers, dump. Boating(ld), canoeing, fishing, winter sports, hiking trails. Historical, nature exhibits; visitor center. Elev 7000 ft; 3,600 acres

RESERVE (68)

Ben Lilly   FREE
Gila National Forest
5 mi S of Reserve on SR 435; 28.5 mi SE on FR 141; 12.5 mi SW on SR 78; 1 mi W on FR 507. Free. 4/1-11/30; 15-day limit. 7 sites (RVs under 18 ft). Tbls, toilets, cfga, no drkg wtr. Picnicking, fishing, horseback riding. Elev 8012 ft. At N edge of Gila Wilderness.

Dipping Vat $5
Gila National Forest
6 mi S of Reserve on SR 435; 23.5 mi SE on FR 141; 9.5 mi SW on FR 78; 7 mi E on FR 142; at W side of Snow Lake. $5 for primitive sites during 5/1-11/15; free rest of yr at lower loop, but no wtr; 14-day limit. 40 sites RV limit 19-ft. Tbls, toilets, cfga, drkg wtr. Fishing (trout), boating(l - elec mtrs only), hiking. Elev 7300 ft; 17 acres.

Dutchman Spring   FREE
Gila National Forest
9 mi N of Reserve on SR 12; 13 mi SE of Apache Creek on FR 94. Free. All year; 14-day limit. Undesignated dispersed camping along FR 94; no facilities, no drkg wtr. Hunting, hiking, horseback riding. Spring GPS: 33.738, -108.4745

Head-of-the-Ditch   FREE
Gila National Forest
4 mi W of Luna (NW of Reserve) on Hwy 180 on San Francisco River. Free. Apr-Nov; 14-day limit. 12 primitive sites (30-ft RV limit at 3 sites). Tbls, toilets, cfga, no drkg wtr, no trash service. Rockhounding for agates, fishing, horseback riding. Elev 7187 ft.

Snow Lake   FREE
Gila National Forest
5 mi S of Reserve on Hwy 435; 28.5 mi E on FR 141; 9.5 mi SW on FR 28; 7 mi E on FR 142. All year; 30-day limit. Undesignated dispersed sites near Snow Lake along FR 142. No facilities, no drkg wtr, no trash service. Use facilities at lake. Boating (no mtrs), fishing, hiking. Lake

Willow Creek   FREE
Gila National Forest
5 mi S of Reserve on SR 435; 28.5 mi SE on FR 6141; 12.5 mi SW on SR 78. Free. 4/1-11/30; 14-day limit. 9 sites (RVs under 18 ft). Tbls, toilets, cfga, no drkg wtr. Hiking, picnicking, fishing (trout), horseback riding. Elev 8000 ft; 2 acres. At northern edge of Gila Wilderness. 2017 opening delayed to MD due to road repairs.

RODARTE

Hodges Campground   FREE
Carson National Forest
3 mi E of Rodarte on SR 73; 3 mi S on FR 2116; half mi S on FR 2702. Free. 5/1-10/31; 14-day limit. 14 dispersed sites (RVs under 22 ft). Tbls, toilets, cfga, firewood, no drkg wtr or trash service. Fishing, horseback riding, hiking, biking, hunting. Elev 8000 ft. GPS: 36.114, -105.639

Santa Barbara $8
Carson National Forest
2 mi E of Rodarte on SR 73; 6.3 mi E on FR 21162. $8 with federal senior pass; others pay $16. 5/15-9/25; 14-day limit. 22 sites (32-ft RV limit). Tbls, toilets, cfga, drkg wtr. Fishing, hiking, horseback riding. Corral.

ROSWELL

Bottomless Lakes State Park $10
16 mi SE of Roswell on US 380 & SR 409. $10 base. 2/1-11/30; 14-day limit. Park is actually seven small lakes bordered by red bluffs. 37 developed sites (9 with shelters, 32 with elec). No RV size limit. Tbls, flush toilets, cfga, drkg wtr, elec($4), dump, showers, playground. Boating(lr), fishing, nature trails, picnicking, swimming, scuba diving. Visitor center. Elev 2617 ft; 1,400 acres.

Haystack Mountain OHV Recreation Area $5
Bureau of Land Management
Roswell Field Office
W of Roswell via US 380. Free camping, but $5 vehicle entry fee. All year; 14-day limit. Primitive undesignated camping in pull-outs next to sun shelters & in gravel

parking lot; also hike-in tent sites. No facilities except cfga. Small mound in flat 1,500-acre area attracts OHV enthusiasts. Hunting, biking.

Mescalero Sands $5
North Dunes OHV Area
Bureau of Land Management
35 mi E of Roswell via US 380. Free camping, but $5 vehicle entry fee. All year; 14-day limit. Primitive undesignated camping in 3 separate OHV parking areas; 610 acres. Tbls, toilets, cfga, no drkg wtr. Hiking, OHV activity.

RUIDOSA

Argentine/Bonito Trailhead   FREE
Lincoln National Forest
18 mi NW of Ruidoso via SR 48; left on FR 107 to its end, about 5 mi past turnoff to South Fork Camp (rough rd). Free. All year; 14-day limit. No developed sites. Toilets, cfga, no drkg wtr. Corrals, wilderness area. Horseback riding, hiking trails. Elev 7800 ft. Primarily a horse camp.

Eagle Creek Dispersed Area   FREE
Lincoln National Forest
4 mi N of Ruidoso on SR 48; 3 mi W on SR 532; N on FR 127; free dispersed camping along the creek for a couple mi. All year; 14-day limit. No facilities; no drkg wtr. Fishing, hiking.

Oak Grove Campground $6
Lincoln National Forest
4 mi N of Ruidoso on SR 48; 5 mi W on SR 532. Not recommended for RVs over 18 ft due to grades & curves of access rds. $6. About 5/15-9/15; 14-day limit. 30 sites. Tbls, cfga, toilets, no drkg wtr. Elev 8400 ft; 6 acres. Scenic. Quiet mountain setting.

Philadelphia Canyon   FREE
Lincoln National Forest
Follow Hwy 48 to Hwy 37, to Bonita Lake turnoff; watch for signs. Free. All year; 14-day limit. Primitive undesignated sites. No facilities except cfga; no drkg wtr. Hiking, fishing, horseback riding. Corrals.

Pennsylvania Canyon   FREE
Lincoln National Forest
Follow Hwy 48 to Hwy 37, then to Bonita Lake turnoff; watch for signs. Near Nogal Canyon. Free. All year; 14-day limit. Primitive undesignated sites; no facilities except cfga; no drkg wtr. Fishing, hiking. Beautiful site not often visited.

Skyline Campground   FREE
Lincoln National Forest
4 mi N of Ruidoso on SR 48; 1 mi W on SR 532; 4 mi NW on gravel FR 117(last 2 mi rough). Free. About 5/1-11/1; 14-day limit. 17 sites (RVs under 17 ft). Tbls, toilets, cfga, firewood, no drkg wtr or trash service. Hiking. Elev 9000 ft; 4 acres. Panoramic views of Eagle Creek Drainage.

South Fork Campground $10
Lincoln National Forest
9 mi NW of Ruidosa on SR 48; 1.5 mi W on SR 37; 5 mi SW on FR 107 (pass Bonito Lake, then turn left, continuing 1 mi). $10. 5/15-9/15; 14-day limit. 60 sites (35-ft RV limit). Tbls, flush toilets, cfga, drkg wtr. Wheelchair access. Hiking, fishing, horseback riding. Trail to White Mountain Wilderness. Closed in 2014 due to fire damage; still closed during 2017.

SACRAMENTO

Alamo Peak Road Dispersed Area   FREE
Lincoln National Forest
W of Sacramento on Scenic By-Way 6563, then follow Alamo Peak Rd. Free. All year; 14-day limit. Several undeveloped primitive camping areas along the rd. No facilities, no drkg wtr.

Bailey Canyon Dispersed Area   FREE
Lincoln National Forest
Access S of US 82 on FR 206 at Bailey Canyon; steep rd, not suited to low-clearance vehicles or those towing trailers; several undeveloped camping areas along FR 206. No facilities, no drkg wtr. Restrictions on ORVs.

Bluff Springs Dispersed Area   FREE
Lincoln National Forest
W of Sacramento on Scenic By-Way 6563, then 4 mi on FR 164. Free. All year; 14-day limit. Primitive undeveloped camping. Toilet, cfga, no drkg wtr. Small waterfall; spring nearby. Popular area.

Dry Canyon Dispersed Area   FREE
Lincoln National Forest
NW of Sacramento on US 82; between mileposts 5 & 6, turn S on steep rd to top of Horse Ridge. Free. All year; 14-day limit. Primitive undeveloped camping. Hiking, target shooting.

Horsebuckle Hill Dispersed Area   FREE
Lincoln National Forest
On ridge W of Sacramento River on West Side Rd (FR 90). Free. All year; 14-day limit. Primitive undeveloped sites; no facilities, no drkg wtr. Spring 1 mi W below rd. Hiking trails.

Sacramento River Dispersed Area   FREE
Lincoln National Forest
Along the Sacramento River from Thousandmile Canyon to Scott Able Canyon, accessible from FR 537. Marshy Sacramento Lake is near mouth of Thousandmile Canyon, surrounded by numerous undeveloped camping sites; 16-ft RV limit. Some good spots for equestrian camping. Free. No facilities, no drkg wtr. Fishing, horseback riding.

West Side Road Dispersed Area   FREE
Lincoln National Forest
W of Sacramento to FR 90 (West Side Rd) between US 82 at High Rolls and FR 537 at Hornbuckle Hill (distance of 30.1 mi); N half of rd is gravel, S half is rough & muddy after rains. Free. All year; 14-day limit. Numerous primitive undeveloped campsites along the rd. No facilities, but some drkg wtr sources. Popular in hunting season. Elev 7000 ft.

Wills Canyon Road Dispersed Area   FREE
Lincoln National Forest
Follow Wills Canyon Rd (FR 169) WSW from FR 164, W of its jct with SR 130 (NW of Sacramento); rd can be muddy during winter & after rain. Free. All year; 14-day limit. Numerous primitive, undeveloped sites; several good spots for equestrian camping. No facilities, no drkg wtr. Hiking, horseback riding. Riparian area closed in 2014 to protect jumping mouse habitat.

SAN JON

San Jon Municipal Park   FREE
Qtr mi S of I-40 exit 356 on W side of SR 469. Free overnight RV parking. No hookups. Tbls, flush toilets, cfga, drkg wtr. Volleyball & tennis courts, basketball, swing set.

SAN LORENZO

Iron Creek   FREE
Gila National Forest
12 mi W of Kingston via SR 152. Free. 4/1-11/30; 14-day limit. 15 sites RV limit 17-ft. Tbls, cfga, toilets, no drkg wtr. Hiking. Elev 7200 ft; 7 acres. Nature trails. On scenic route between I-25 and US 180.

SANTA FE

Aspen Basin Campground   FREE
Santa Fe National Forest
From Santa Fe, quarter mi N on SR 22; 16 mi NE on SR 475. Free. All year; 14-day limit. 10 RV/tent sites. Tbls, toilet, cfga, no drkg wtr. Hiking. Elev 10,300 ft; 5 acres. Scenic. Stream. Pegono Wilderness. Pecos Wilderness jump-off, Trail 254. Area may be closed due to flood danger at certain times of year. Check with visitor center.

Backcountry Camping $12
Bandelier National Monument
16 mi N of Santa Fe on US 84/285; 12 mi W on SR 502; 8 mi SW on SR 4. $12 for 7-day entry fee; camp free. All year; 14-day limit. Get free backcountry permit & directions from visitor center. No facilities. Elev 7000 ft.

Black Canyon Campground $10
Santa Fe National Forest
7 mi NE of Santa Fe on Hwy 475 to Hyde Park Rd; tight turn into camp for RVs. $10. 5/1-10/14; 14-day limit. 36 sites (32-ft RV limit). Tbls, toilets, cfga, no drkg wtr. Hiking &

biking trail, horseback riding. State dump station at nearby Hyde Memorial State Park ($5).

Borrego Mesa Campground   FREE
Santa Fe National Forest
N of Santa Fe and 20 mi E of Espanola. SR 76 from Espanola to Chimayo; SR 4 toward Santa Cruz Lake. E on FR 306, from this intersection, 10 mi of unsurfaced rd to campground (rd muddy if wet). Free. All year; 14-day limit. 8 dispersed sites (RVs under 32 ft) with corrals. No drkg wtr or toilets. Tbls, cfga. Hiking, fishing. Elev 8400 ft. 3 acres. Stream in canyon (half mi, steep access). Campground on mesa. Pacos Wilderness boundary 4.3 mi by good trail.

Hyde Memorial State Park $10
7.5 mi NE of Santa Fe on SR 475. $10 base. All year; 14-day limit. Base fee for 50 developed sites (7 with 30-amp elec). 42-ft RV limit. Elec($4), tbls, flush toilets, cfga, drkg wtr, dump, no showers, playground, 3 shelters. Hiking trails (4.2 mi), volleyball, winter sports, meeting room, visitor center. Elev 8600 ft; 350 acres.

Juniper Campground $12
Bandelier National Monument
16 mi N of Santa Fe on US 84/285; 12 mi W on SR 502; 8 mi SW on SR 4. $12 (plus entry fee $20/ vehicle for 7 days); $6 to camp with federal senior pass. 94 sites, 40ft RV-limit. Must secure all food due to bears. Tbls, flush toilets, cfga, drkg wtr, dump, showers. All year; 14-day limit. Hiking, visitor center, interpretive programs, backpacking.

North Lake Campground   Closed
Santa Cruz Lake Recreation Area
Bureau of Land Management Taos Field Office
20 mi N of Santa Fe on US 84; 13 mi E on Rt 503; right on Rt 596. $9 for developed sites. All year; 14-day limit. 5 sites. Tbls, toilets, cfga, drkg wtr. Boating(l), fishing, hiking. Closed indefinitely for construction.

Overlook Campground $7
Santa Cruz Lake Recreation Area
Bureau of Land Management Taos Field Office
20 mi N of Santa Fe on US 84; 9 mi E on Rt. 503. $7. All year; 14-day limit. 5 sites. Tbls, toilets, cfga, drkg wtr. Fishing, hiking.

SANTA ROSA

Santa Rosa State Park $8
7 mi N of Santa Rosa on access rd via 2nd St. $8 base. All year; 14-day limit; limited facilities in winter. Base fee for 8 primitive sites; 75 developed sites (25 with elec) with shelters, $10 base. 80-ft RV limit. Elec($4), tbls, flush toilets, cfga, drkg wtr, showers, dump. Boating(l), fishing, waterskiing, nature trails, winter sports. Historical & nature exhibits; visitor center. Elev 4650 ft; 500 acres.

SILVER CITY

Cherry Creek   FREE
Gila National Forest
13.2 mi NW of Silver city on SR 15. Free. Elev 7400 ft. 4/1-10/31; 15-day limit. 9 primitive sites RV limit 17-ft, . Tbls, toilet, cfga, no drkg wtr.

Forks Campground   FREE
Gila Cliff Dwellings National Monument
44 mi N of Silver City on SR 15; located near the main Gila Bridge. SR 15 is a 2-lane blacktop that only recently was a rough, winding trail. The trip through this mountainous terrain takes about 2 hrs because of the rd condition; RVs more than 20 ft long should use SR 35 through the scenic Mimbres Valley instead of SR 15. SR 35 is reached from SR 61, N from San Lorenzo, 19 mi E of Silver City on SR 90. Free, but park entry fee charged (free with federal senior pass). All year (except during flood conditions). 7 sites (RVs under 22 ft). 14 day limit. Toilets, cfga, no drkg wtr. Hiking, picnicking, fishing nearby. Cliff dwellings nearby (100-400 A.D.).

Grapevine Campground   FREE
Gila Cliff Dwellings National Monument
44 mi N of Silver City on SR 15; located at main Gila Bridge. Because of rd conditions, RVs more than 20 ft should use SR 35 through the scenic Mimbres Valley instead of SR 15. SR 35 is reached from SR 61, N from San Lorenzo, 19 me E of Silver City on SR 90. Free, but park entry fee charged (free with federal senior pass0. All year (except during flood conditions). 20 sites (RVs under 22 ft). Toilets, cfga, no drkg wtr. Hiking, picnicking, fishing nearby. Cliff dwellings nearby.

Lower Scorpion   FREE
Gila Cliff Dwellings National Monument
Gila National Forest
44 mi N of Silver City on SR 15 between cliff dwellings & visitor center (see other entries for alternative route). Free, but park entry fee charged. All year (except during flood conditions); 14-day limit. 7 tent sites (paved parking area for RVs). Tbls, flush toilets, cfga, dump. Wtr available at trailer dump site except during winter months. Picnicking, hiking, fishing, horseback riding (r, 5 mi). Elev 5700 ft; 5 acres. Access to Gila National Forest Wilderness and Primitive Area. Cliff Dwellings nearby.

McMillan Campground   FREE
Gila National Forest
14.7 mi NE of Silver City on SR 15; at Cherry Creek. Free. 4/1-10/31; 15-day limit. 3 sites; 17-ft RV limit. Tbls, toilets, cfga, no drkg wtr. Picnicking, hiking. Elev 6950 ft.

Upper Scorpion   FREE
Gila Cliff Dwellings National Monument
Gila National Forest
45 mi N of Silver City via SR 15. Free but park entry fee charged (free with federal senior pass). All year; 14-day limit. 10 sites; paved area for RVs. Tbls, toilets, cfga, drkg wtr. Hiking, horseback riding, biking, caving, climbing, hunting, fishing. Half mi from Gila Cliffs.

SOCORRO

San Lorenzo Canyon Recreation Area   FREE
Bureau of Land Management
Socorro Field Office
NE of Socorro, accessed from Lemitar exit via frontage & county rds. Free. All year; 14-day limit. Primitive dispersed camping throughout east-west canyon. No facilities, no drkg wtr. Sandy arroyo requires caution with vehicles in all weather. Hiking.

TAJIQUE

Tajique   FREE
Cibola National Forest
5 mi W of Tajique via NM 55 & FR 55. Free. Apr-Oct; 14-day limit. 6 sites (no trailers), 2 picnic sites. Tbls, toilet, cfga, no drkg wtr. Fishing, hiking, hunting. Elev 6800 ft. . Closed in 2014 by flood damage; check current status before arrival. R

TAOS

Capulin Campground $6
Carson National Forest
About 5 mi E of Taos on US 64. $6. MD-LD; 14-day limit. 11 sites; 30-ft RV limit. Tbls, toilets, cfga, no drkg wtr, no trash service. Fishing, hunting, hiking. Elev 7,800 ft.

Cuchilla Campground   FREE
Carson National Forest
16.6 mi NE of Taos on SR 522 & 150. Free. May-Oct; 14-day limit. 3 primitive sites; RV-limit 22 ft. Tbls, toilet, cfga, no drkg wtr. Fishing, hunting, hiking.

Cuchillo del Medio   FREE
Carson National Forest
13 mi N of Taos on NM 230 & 150. Free. May-Sept; 14-day limit. 3 sites RV-Limit 22 ft. Toilet, no drkg wtr. Fishing, hiking, biking. Elev 7800 ft.

Las Petacas $6
Carson National Forest
4.3 mi SE of Taos on US 64. $6 camping & day use fee. MD-LD; 14-day limit. 8 sites (RVs under 16 ft). tbls, toilet, cfga, firewood, no drkg wtr or trash service. Picnicking, fishing. Elev 7400 ft; 2 acres. Historic. Visitor center 4 mi.

Lower Hondo   FREE
Carson National Forest
12 mi N of Taos via SR 522 & 150. Free. May-Sept; 14-day limit. 4 sites (22-ft RV limit). Toilets, no drkg wtr. Fishing, hiking, hunting. Elev 7700 ft.

Orilla Verde Recreation Area $7
Bureau of Land Management
Taos Field Office
12 mi S of Taos on SR 68; W on SR 570, following signs; at Rio Grande River. $7 base ($10 two vehicles). All year; 14-day limit. Base fee for non-elec sites; elec/wtr hookups $15 ($7.50 with federal senior pass). Numerous designated primitive sites & 24 developed sites at 5 campgrounds. Tbls, toilets, cfga, drkg wtr (at developed sites), shelters, handicapped fishing pier. Campgrounds are Taos Junction (4 sites), Petaca (5 sites), Arroyo Hondo (5 sites), Orilla Verde (10 sites) and Pilar (12 sites, 9 w/hookups.) Boating, fishing, hiking, nature programs. Swimming not recommended. Petroglyphs. Elev 6000 ft.

Twining Campground FREE
Carson National Forest
20 mi N of Taos on NM 3 & 150. Free. May-Sept; 14-day limit. 4 sites (22-ft RV limit). Tbls, cfga, no toilet, no drkg wtr. Fishing, hiking, horseback riding, biking. Elev 9300 ft.

THOREAU
Ojo Redondo FREE
Cibola National Forest
24.5 mi SE of FR 178; 3.2 mi E on FR 480. Free. About 6/1-9/15; 14-day limit. 15 sites (2 for RVs under 23 ft). Tbls, toilet, cfga, no drkg wtr, no trash service. Picnicking. Elev 8900 ft. Isolated site.

THREE RIVERS
Three Rivers Petroglyph Site $7
Bureau of Land Management
Las Cruces District Office
5 mi E of Three Rivers off SR 54 on gravel co rd. $7 at primitive sites; $18 for 2 sites with hookups ($3.50 & $9 with federal senior pass). All year; 14-day limit. 6 sites. Tbls, toilets, cfga, picnic shelters, drkg wtr (available at picnic sites). Hiking, picnicking. 120 acres. Area has extensive interpretive displays. Carvings made with stone tools (900-1400 A.D.). Site contains more than 500 petroglyphs.

TIERRA AMARILLA
El Vado Lake State Park $8
17 mi SW of Tierra Amarilla on SR 112. $8 base. All year; 14-day limit. Base fee at primitive sites; 80 developed sites (18 with shelters, 19 with elec), $10 base; 40-ft RV limit. Elec($4), tbls, flush toilets, cfga, drkg wtr, playground, showers, dump. Boating(ld), fishing, swimming, waterskiing, sailing. 5.5-mi scenic trail along Rio Chama River connects with Heron Lake. Elev 6845 ft; 1340 acres.

Heron Lake State Park $8
11 mi W of Tierra Amarilla on US 64 & SR 95. $8 base. All year; 14-day limit. Base fee at primitive sites. 250 developed sites (54 with elec), $10 base; 35-ft RV limit. Elec($4), tbls, flush toilets, cfga, drkg wtr, dump, showers.

Swimming, boating(l), fishing, nature trails, winter sports, sailing. No-wake boating. 5.5 mi-scenic trail along Rio Chama River connects with El Vado Lake State Park. Elev 7105, 1900 acres. Low Lake levels may cause launch closure.

TRES PIEDRAS
Hopewell Lake $8
Carson National Forest
20 mi NW of Tres Piedras on US 64. $8 with federal senior pass; others pay $16. MD-LD; 14-day limit. 32 sites (16-ft RV limit) plus primitive dispersed sites. Toilets, tbls, cfga, no trash service, drkg wtr. Fishing, boating (electric mtrs only) on 19-acre lake, hiking, biking, horseback riding. Elev 9800 ft.

Laguna Larga FREE
Carson National Forest
25 mi N of Tres Piedras on US 285, FR 87 & FR 78 (primitive rd can be very muddy). Free. May-Oct; 14-day limit. 4 sites and dispersed camping around the lake. No facilities, no drkg wtr. Fishing, boating, hiking, hunting, horseback riding. Elev 9000 ft.

Lagunitas FREE
Carson National Forest
10 mi N of Tres Piedras on US 285; 26 mi NW on FR 87; .8 mi NW on FR 87B. Free. 6/1-10/15; 14-day limit. 12 sites (RVs under 17 ft). Tbls, toilet, cfga, no drkg wtr. Picnicking, fishing, hiking, horseback riding, hunting, biking. Elev 10,400 ft; 5 acres. Scenic. Rd poor during rainy season; beautiful when dry.

TRES RITOS
Duran Canyon $11
Carson National Forest
2 mi NE of Tres Ritos on Hwy 51; 2 mi on FR 76. $11. MD-LD; 14-day limit. 12 sites RV-limit 16 ft. Tbls, toilets, cfga, drkg wtr. Fishing, hiking, motorcycling, mountain biking, hunting, OHV activity. Non-campers pay $5 day use fee. Duran Creek. Elev 9000 ft.

TRUTH OR CONSEQUENCES
Caballo Lake State Park $8
16 mi S of Truth or consequences on I-25, at Caballo Lake. $8 base. All year; 14-day limit. Base fee at primitive sites; 170 developed sites 108 elec, 7 full hookup. $10 base. Tbls, flush toilets, showers, dump, cfga, drkg wtr, elec($4), beach, playground, store, beach. Boating (dlr) fishing, picnicking, hiking, waterskiing, swimming. Visitor center, cactus gardens. Bald & golden eagles nest here in winter. Park has 2 cactus gardens. Elev 4180 ft; 5,326 acres.

Elephant Butte Lake State Park $8
5 mi N of Truth or Consequences on I-25. $8 base. All year; 14-day limit. Base fee for numerous primitive sites; 173

developed sites (86 with shelters, 144 with wtr/elec. 8 full hookup), $10 base; 40-ft RV limit. Elec($4), tbls, flush toilets, dump, cfga, drkg wtr, playground, showers. Boating(ldr), fishing, hiking, swimming, waterskiing, nature trails. Interpretive exhibits; visitor center. Elev 4407 ft; 24,520 acres.

Percha Dam State Park $10
21 mi S of Truth or Consequences on I-25; near Arrey. $10 base. All year; 14-day limit. 50 developed sites, 30 with elec; no RV size limit. Tbls, flush toilets, cfga, drkg wtr, playground, showers, elec($4), no dump. Picnicking, fishing, hiking. Along Rio Grande River. Elev 4447 ft; 84 acres.

TUCUMCARI
Conchas Lake State Park $8
32 mi NW of Tucumcari on SR 104. $8 base. All year; 14-day limit. Base fee at primitive sites; 105 developed sites (40 with elec) with shelters, $10 base; 45-ft RV limit. Elec($4), tbls, flush toilets, cfga, drkg wtr, dump, showers, playground, marina. Swimming, boating(lrd), fishing, waterskiing, sailing. Visitor center. Elev 4230 ft; 600 acres.

VADITO
Agua Piedro $8
Carson National Forest
3 mi E of Vadito on SR 75; 7 mi E on SR 3. $8 with federal senior pass; others pay $16. MD-LD; 14-day limit. 44 sites; RV-limit 36 ft. Tbls, flush toilets, cfga, drkg wtr (wtr tastes of sulfur), horse facilities. Hiking, fishing, biking, hunting, horseback riding, OHV activity. National Recreational Trail available (23 mi long)

Comales Campground $10
Carson National Forest
3 mi E of Vadito on SR 75; 2.5 mi E on SR 3. $10. Elev 7800 ft. MD-LD; 14-day limit. 13 sites RV-Limit 36 ft. Toilet, no cfga, no drkg wtr, no tbls. Hiking, picnicking, fishing, horseback riding, mountain biking.

Upper La Junta $11
Carson National Forest
3 mi E of Vadito on SR 75; 8.5 E on SR 3; 4 mi N on FR 2761. $11. Elev 9400 ft. MD-LD; 14-day limit. 11 RV sites on 8 acres (RVs under 16 ft). Tbls, toilets, cfga, firewood, drkg wtr. Hiking, picnicking, fishing. Parking lot for fishermen.

WAGON MOUND
Charette Lakes   FREE
Fishing & Waterfowl Area
State Game & Fish Department
From I-25 about 16 mi N of Wagon Mound, 13 mi W of Colmor exit on Hwy 569. Free. 3/1-10/31; 14-day limit. Primitive undesignated sites at lower lake. Tbls, toilets, cfga, no drkg wtr, no trash service. Fishing, hunting, boating(l), birdwatching.

EAST

WEST

WWW.VISITNC.COM

Toll-free number for travel information: 1-800-VIS-IT-NC. In state: 919/733-4172.

REST AREAS
Overnight stops are not permitted.

STATE PARKS
Fees are a minimum of $13 per night for primitive sites, and therefore no state park campgrounds are listed in this edition. Division of Parks and Recreation, 1615 MSC, Raleigh, NC 27699, 919 733-4181.

NATIONAL CAMPING AREAS
National forest trails, wilderness areas, landing and other areas are open year-round. Free primitive camping is allowed without a permit throughout forests unless otherwise posted. National Forests in North Carolina: 160 Zillicoa St. Suite A, Asheville, NC 28801. 828-257-200.

CROATAN NATIONAL FOREST
Located on the coast of North Carolina, the name of this 157,000-acre forest was derived from the Algonquin word for the "Council Town" that was located in the area. Fees are charged at only three campgrounds -- Cedar Point, Oyster Point and Neuse River; all others are free.

NANTAHALA NATIONAL FOREST
The name means "noon day sun" in Cherokee and refers to the fact that the sun penetrates the bottom of the Nantahala Gorge only at noon. The forest is 516,000 acres. It features several free primitive campgrounds and low fee camps with fees ranging from $5 to $15.

PISGAH NATIONAL FOREST
Consisting of 495,000 acres, it nestles in the mountains of western North Carolina. It is named for the mountain from which Moses saw the promised land. It features an outdoor museum and forestry monument called the Cradle of Forestry in America complex -- formerly a part of George Washington Vanderbilt's estate. Besides several free campgrounds, the forest contains camps with overnight fees ranging from $8 to $30. Some campgrounds managed by Cradle of Forestry Interpretive Association.

CAPITAL: Raleigh
NICKNAME: Tar Heel State
STATEHOOD: 1789 – 12th State
FLOWER: Dogwood
TREE: Pine
BIRD: Cardinal

UWHARRIE NATIONAL FOREST
The smallest of the state's national forests at just 46,000 acres, most of its activities are centered just east of Badin Lake. The forest has several free campgrounds as well as four large campgrounds with moderate fees.

GREAT SMOKY MOUNTAINS NATIONAL PARK
The park service maintains two developed campgrounds in North Carolina -- Smokemont and Caaloochee. 107 Park Headquarters Rd., Gatlinburg, TN 37738.

The Blue Ridge Parkway has five North Carolina campgrounds.

ASHEVILLE (1)

Lake Powhatan Campground $11
Pisgah National Forest
From I-26E exit 2 near Asheville, 4 mi S on SR 191; right on FR 806 for 3 mi. $11 with federal senior pass; others pay $22. Surcharges: wtr/sewer, $3; elec, $6; full hookups, $9. 97 sites; 40-ft RV limit. 4/1-10/31; 14-day limit. Tbls, flush toilets, cfga, drkg wtr, dump, showers, fishing pier. Hiking, fishing, swimming beach, boating. Non-campers pay $2 day use ($30 annually), $10 for dump station. GPS: 35.4817783, -82.62984

Mount Pisgah $8
Blue Ridge Parkway
National Park Service
SW of Asheville on SR 191; 15 mi SW on parkway to Milepost 408.6. $8 with federal senior pass; others pay $16. 5/13-10/30; 21-day limit. With reservations, fees are $8 with federal senior pass during 5/13-5/19 & 10/24-10/30 (others pay $16); $9.50 with federal senior pass during 5/20-10/21 (others pay $19), plus $9 reservation fee. 137 sites (30-ft RV limit). Tbls, flush toilets, cfga, drkg wtr, dump, no showers or elec. Nature program. GPS: 35.40278, -82.75667.

North Mills River $11
Pisgah National Forest
13.3 mi S of Asheville on SR 191; 5 mi W on FR 478. $11 with federal senior pass during 4/1-10/31; others pay $13; regular fee $11 off-season ($5.50 with senior pass) but no wtr services (pit toilets). 1 full-hookup site, $25. 14-day limit. 31 sites, typically 50 ft. Group camping, $40. Tbls, flush toilets, cfga, drkg wtr, dump, showers. Hiking, fishing, biking. 8 acres. Non-campers pay $3 day use fee ($30 annually), $10 dump station. GPS: 35.40625, -82.64624

BLOWING ROCK (2)

Julian Price Campground $8
Blue Ridge Parkway
National Park Service
3 mi N of Linn Cove Information Center near Blowing Rock at Milepost 297. With reservations, fees are $8 with federal senior pass during 5/13-5/19 & 10/24-10/30 (others pay $16); $9.50 with senior pass during 5/20-10/21 (others pay $19). 21-day limit. 197 sites (68-ft RV limit). Tbls, flush toilets, cfga, drkg wtr, dump, no showers. Nature program. Canoeing(r), boating(l), fishing, hiking. GPS: 36.13889, -81.73111.

BREVARD (3)

Davidson River $11
Pisgah National Forest
1 mi N of Brevard on US 276; at Davidson River. $11 with federal senior pass; others pay $22; elec & wtr/sewer available at $6 & $9 surcharges. All year; 14-day limit. 161 sites; no RV size limit. Tbls, flush toilets, cfga, drkg wtr, dump, showers. Fishing, hiking. Generators 8-8 daily. GPS: 35.268865, -82.733887

BRYSON CITY (4)

Tsali Recreation Area $7.50
Nantahala National Forest
9 mi S of Bryson City on US 19; 5.5 mi W on SR 28; 1.5 mi N on FR 521; at Fontana Lake. $7.50 with federal senior pass; others pay $15. 4/1-10/31; 14-day limit. 42 sites to 47 ft. Tbls, flush toilets, cfga, drkg wtr, showers. Horseback riding, hiking, fishing, biking. GPS: 35.408426, -83.5884988.

BURNSVILLE (5)

Black Mountain $11
Black Mountain Recreation Area
Pisgah National Forest
5 mi E of Burnsville on US 19E; 12 mi S on SR 80; 3 mi E on FR 472; at South Toe River. $11 with federal senior pass; others pay $22; 2 elec sites, $7 surcharge for 30/50-amp. 4/15-11/1; 14-day limit. 43 sites to 84 ft. Tbls, flush toilets, cfga, drkg wtr, coin showers. Dump 1 mi. Hiking, trout fishing. GPS: 35.7528959, -82.221231

Carolina Hemlock $11
Black Mountain Recreation Area
Pisgah National Forest
5 mi E of Burnsville on US 19E; 9 mi S on SR 80; at South Toe River. $11 with federal senior pass; others pay $22. 4/15-10/31; 14-day limit. 31 primitive sites, typically 55 ft. Tbls, flush toilets, cfga, drkg wtr, picnic shelters($). Fishing, swimming, tubing, hiking & biking trails. Non-campers pay $5 day use fee ($25 annual). GPS: 35.804443, -82.204346

CASHIERS (6)

Ralph J. Andrews $12
Jackson County Park
At Lake Glenville between Sylva & Cashiers. $12 base. Apr-Oct. Base fee for primitive sites. $14 for elec/wtr. 44 sites. Tbls, flush toilets, cfga, showers, dump, coin laundry, hookups ($). Fishing, boating(l), horseshoe pits. GPS: 35.191732, -83.14672

CHEROKEE (7)

Smokemont Campground $10
Great Smoky Mountains National Park
About 6 mi N of Cherokee off US 441. $10 with federal senior pass; others pay $20. All year; 14-day limit. 140 sites; 27-ft RV limit. Tbls, flush toilets, cfga, drkg wtr, dump. Fishing, hiking, interpretive programs. GPS: 83.3086, -35.5533

FONTANA VILLAGE (8)

Cable Cove Recreation Area $10
Nantahala National Forest
4.7 mi E of Fontana Village on Hwy 28; left on FR 520 for 1.4 mi. $10. 4/15 10/1; 14-day limit. 26 sites to 74 ft. Tbls, flush toilets, cfga, drkg wtr. Fishing, boating(l), swimming, nature trail. On Fontana Lake. GPS: 35.4328671, -83.7521176

FRANKLIN (9)

Deep Gap   FREE
Nantahala National Forest
18.9 mi SW of Franklin on US 64; 4.5 mi S on FR 711. Elev 4400 ft. Free. 5/24-10/15; 14-day limit. 4 sites. Tbls, toilets, cfga, no drkg wtr. Fishing, berry picking, hiking. Adjacent to Appalachian Trail. GPS: 35.040925, -83.551826

Hurricane Creek $6
Nantahala National Forest
13.6 mi SW of Franklin on US 64; 5 mi S on FR 67. $6. 3/15-12/31; 14-day limit. Open camping, undesignated sites. Toilet, cfga, no drkg wtr, stalls. Fishing, hiking, horse camping. GPS: 35.0635, -80.0537

Standing Indian $8
Nantahala National Forest
9 mi W of Franklin on US 64; left & follow signs on Old US 64. $8 with federal senior pass; others pay $16. 4/1-12/1; 30-day limit. 78 sites (35-ft RV limit). Tbls, flush toilets, cfga, drkg wtr, showers. Hiking, fishing, swimming. Near Appalachian Trail. 22 acres. GPS: 34.99975, -83.46777

HAVELOCK (10)

Siddie Fields   FREE
Croatan National Forest
4.7 mi E of Havelock on SR 101; 3.2 mi N on Ferry Rd; right on Pine Cliff Rd, then left on gravel FR 167 & bear left. Free. All year; 14-day limit. Undeveloped undesignated sites; no facilities, no drkg wtr. Fishing, canoeing. GPS: 34.55807, -76.47476

HAYESVILLE (11)

Bristol Fields Horse Camp $5
Nantahala National Forest
From Hayesville, follow SR 1301 for 3 mi to SR 1300, then 5.7 mi to SR 1344 (FR 340) & follow signs; on Fires Creek. $5. All year; 14-day limit. 7 sites; primarily a horseman camp. Tbls, pit toilets, cfga, drkg wtr, tethering posts. Hiking, horse trails, fishing. GPS: 35.1045333, -83.818787

Fires Creek Recreation Area   FREE
Nantahala National Forest
5.7 mi NW of Hayesville on NC 1300; 1.1 mi N on NC 1344. All year; 14-day limit. 15 sites (RVs under 22 ft). Toilets, no drkg wtr. Hiking trails; berry picking; trout fishing. Elev 1800 ft. Scenic. GPS: 35.0875877, -83.8682339

Huskins Branch Hunter Camp   FREE
Nantahala National Forest
5.7 mi NW of Hayesville on NC 1300; about 1 mi N on NC 1344; access via FR 442. Free. All year; 14-day limit. Primitive undesignated sites; no facilities. Hiking, fishing, berry picking. GPS: 35.087, -83.8663

Jackrabbit Mountain $7.50
Nantahala National Forest
6.2 mi E of Hayesville on US 64; right on SR 175 for 2.5 mi, then right on SR 1155. $7.50 with federal senior pass; others pay $15. 5/1-19/30; 14-day limit. 101 sites to 56 ft. Tbls, flush toilets, cfga, drkg wtr, showers, dump. Boating(l), swimming, fishing, hiking. Seasonal evening programs. GPS: 35.0112019, -83.7726719.

HIGHLANDS (12)

Ammons Branch   FREE
Nantahala National Forest
4.9 mi SE of Highlands on FR 1603; 1.2 mi SE on FR 1100. Free. All year; 14-day limit. 4 primitive dispersed sites. Tbls, toilets, cfga, no drkg wtr, no trash service. Fishing (1 mi). Elev 2600 ft. GPS: 35.0228672, -83.1454278

Blue Valley Dispersed   FREE
Nantahala National Forest
6.2 mi S of Highlands on NC 28; 2.1 mi W on NC 1618; about 22 dispersed sites along the road. Free. All year; 14-day limit. Toilet, cfga, tbls no drkg wtr. Rockhounding, fishing. Elev 2700 ft; 3 acres. Stream. GPS: 35.0120337, -83.2298749

Vanhook Glade $8.50
Nantahala National Forest
4 mi W of Highlands on US 64; right at sign; at Cliffside Lake. $8.50 with federal senior pass; others pay $17. About 4/1-10/31; 14-day limit. 18 primitive sites; small RVs. Tbls, flush toilets, cfga, drkg wtr, dump, showers, shelters($). Hiking, swimming, fishing. Near Dry Falls & Cullasaja Gorge. Non-campers pay $4 day use fee. GPS: 35.0773143, -83.2482073

HOT SPRINGS (13)

Harmon Den Horse Camp $7.50
Black Mountain Recreation Area
Pisgah National Forest
7 mi S of Hot Springs on SR 209; right on SR 1175 (Meadowfork Rd) for 6 mi; right on SR 1181 (Little Creek Rd) for 0.75 mi; right (SW) on FR 148 (Cold Springs Rd) for 3 mi to jct with Fall Branch Rd (FR 3526); half mi to site. $7.50 with federal senior pass; others pay $15. 5/1-10/31; 14-day limit. Camp by reservation only (877-444-6777) 4 days in advance. 10 sites; no RV size limit. Tbls, toilets, cfga, drkg wtr. Horse stalls, watering tank, manure station. Bridle trails. GPS: 35.75861, -82.97667

Rocky Bluff $8
Hot Springs Recreation Area
Pisgah National Forest
3 mi S of Hot Springs on SR 209. $8. MD-LD; 14-day limit. 15 sites (typically 45 ft). Tbls, flush toilets, cfga, drkg wtr. Fishing, hiking, tubing on Spring Creek; whitewater on French Broad River. Site of former logging camp. Spring Creek Nature Trail. 13 acres. GPS: 35.861816, -82.8457

LENOIR (15)

Boone Fork $3
Pisgah National Forest
7 mi NW of Lenoir on SR 90; 4.7 mi NW on SR 1368 (Mulberry Creek Rd); 2 mi NE on FR 2055 (Boone Fork Rd). $3. MD-LD; 14-day limit. 14 sites; no RV size limit. Tbls, toilets, cfga, drkg wtr. Nature trails, fishing. GPS: 36.009766, -81.608887.

Mortimer $10
Pisgah National Forest
SR 90W to SR 1337; N on gravel rd 1328 at Collettsville; continue SW on 1337; N on gravel SR 1328. $10. 4/1-10/30; 14-day limit. 23 sites, typically 45 ft. Tbls, flush toilets, cfga, drkg wtr, showers. Fishing, hiking. GPS: 36.000, -81.770264.

LINVILLE FALLS (16)

Linville Falls $8
Blue Ridge Parkway
National Park Service
1 mi N of Linville Falls & US 221 on parkway; at Milepost 316.3. With reservations, fees are $8 with federal senior pass during 5/13-5/19 & 10/24-10/30 (others pay $16); $9.50 with federal senior pass during 5/20-10/21 (others pay $19). 21-day limit. 75 sites (30-ft RV limit). Tbls, flush toilets, cfga, drkg wtr, dump, amphitheater, information station, interpretive programs. No showers or elec. Hiking trails. On 3,900 acres. Generators 8 a.m. to 9 p.m. GPS: 35.94889, -81.92694.

MAGGIE VALLEY (17)

Cataloochee Campground $100
Great Smoky Mountains National Park
US 276 exit off I-40 to Cove Creek Rd turnoff. $10 with federal senior pass; others pay $20. 3/12-11/1; 7-day limit. 27 sites (31-ft RV limit). Tbls, flush toilets, cfga, drkg wtr, no showers, no elec. Hiking, fishing. GPS: 35.631592, -83.086914

MAYSVILLE (18)

Catfish Lake   FREE
Croatan National Forest
S on SR 58 from Maysville; left on SR 1105; left on FR 158. Free. All year; 14-day limit. Primitive undesignated sites; no facilities. Boating(l), fishing, canoeing. Shallow lake. GPS: Lake GPS: 34.5559, -77.0616

Cedar Point Campground $7.50
Croatan National Forest
East of Maysville on SR 58; right on SR 1114; left on FR 153-A. $7.50 at non-elec sites with federal senior pass; others pay $15; $7 elec surcharge. Fees increase to $20 in 2016 with $7 elec surcharge. Double sites $30, increasing to $40 in 2016 with $14 elec surcharge. All year; 14-day limit. 40 sites with elec (typically 60 ft). Tbls, flush toilets, drkg wtr, showers, dump ($15 for non-campers). Fishing, hiking, boating(l). GPS: 34.69306, -77.08222

Great Lake   FREE
Croatan National Forest
SR 58 S of Maysville; left on Fr 126. Free. All year; 14-day limit. Primitive undesignated sites. No facilities. Boating(l), fishing, canoeing. GPS: 34.8596, -77.0522.

Long Point   FREE
Croatan National Forest
S of Maysville on SR 58; right on FR 120. Free. All year; 14-day limit. 2 primitive sites. Toilet, cfga, no drkg wtr. Fishing, canoeing, boating(l). GPS: 34.7982, -77.17788

MT. GILEAD (19)

River Access Camping   FREE
Progress Energy
Free camping along shores of Pee De River near town. Free. No facilities, no drkg wtr. Warning: River rises & falls 2-3 feet during certain times of day.

MURPHY (20)

Hanging Dog Recreation Area $8
Nantahala National Forest
5 mi NW of Murphy on SR 1326. $8. All year; 14-day limit (30 days in winter); 5 sites free in winter, but no wtr. 68 sites (22-ft RV limit). Tbls, flush toilets, cfga, drkg wtr. Boating(l), fishing, hiking trails, waterskiing. Overlooks Hiwassee Lake. Closed in 2014 at last report; check current status before arrival. GPS: 35.107422, -84.080566

NEW BERN (21)

Neuse River Campground $12
Croatan National Forest
S of New Bern on US 70 about 12 mi; 1.5 mi E on SR 1107. $12 without elec, $17 with elec ($6 & $11 with federal senior pass). 3/1-11/30; 14-day limit. About 40 sites, 14 with elec; 50-ft RV limit. Tbls, flush toilets, cfga, drkg wtr, cold showers, dump ($5 for non-campers). Fishing, swimming, hiking. GPS: 34.9817, -76.948502

NEWPORT (22)

Oyster Point Campground $8
Croatan National Forest
E of Newport on SR 1154 to FR 181, then turn right to Oyster Point at Newport River estuary. $8. All year; 14-day limit. 15 sites; 50-ft RV limit. Tbls, toilets, cfga, drkg wtr. Hiking, boating, fishing. GPS: 34.761, -76.761597

OLD FORT (23)

Curtis Creek $5
Pisgah National Forest
From jct with US 70 near Old Fort, proceed N on SR 1227, then E on FR 482. $5. 4/1-11/30; 14-day limit. 19 sites, typically 40 ft. Tbls, toilets, cfga, drkg wtr. Fishing, hiking. GPS: 40.33959, -82.11571

ROBBINSVILLE (24)

Cheoah Point Recreation Area $7.50
Nantahala National Forest

7 mi NW of Robbinsville on US 129; left at sign for .8 mi. $7.50 with federal senior pass at 17 non-elec sites (others pay $15); 6 elec sites $20 ($12.50 with federal senior pass). Open 4/15 10/31; 14-day limit. 22-ft RV limit. Tbls, flush toilets, cfga, drkg wtr. Swimming, boating(lr), fishing, hiking trails. On Santeelah Lake. 10 acres. GPS: 35.3703645, -83.8718459

Horse Cove $10
Nantahala National Forest

2 mi N of Robbinsville on US 129; 3 mi W on SR 1116; 10 mi N on SR 1127. $10. 4/15-10/30; 14-day limit. Some sites open in winter but no amenities or drkg wtr. 18 sites (25-ft RV limit). Tbls, flush toilets, cfga, drkg wtr. Fishing, hiking trails. 4 acres. GPS: 35.3648079, -83.9199039

Wolf Laurel Hunter Camp FREE
Nantahala National Forest

1 mi N of Robbinsville on US 129; 3 mi W on Hwy 116; 7 mi N on Hwy 1127; W & N 11 mi on FR 81, quarter mi from end of Wolf Laurel Rd. Free. All year; 14-day limit. 6 sites (RVs under 22 ft). Tbls, toilets, cfga, no drkg wtr. Fishing, hiking. Near Joyce Kilmer-Slickrock Wilderness.

SPRUCE PINE (25)

Crabtree Meadows $8
Blue Ridge Parkway
National Park Service

6 mi S of Spruce Pine; 9 mi S on parkway to Milepost 339.5. $8 with federal senior pass; others pay $16. 5/14-10/31; 14-day limit. 93 sites (30-ft RV limit). Tbls, flush toilets, cfga, drkg wtr, no showers. Nature program. 253 acres. GPS: 35.815918, -82.141602

TAPOCO (26)

Indian Grave Branch FREE
Cherokee National Forest

1.2 mi SE of Tapoco on NC 129; 2 mi SW on FR 445. Free. All year; 14-day limit. 1 site (no RVs). Toilets, cfga, firewood, no drkg wtr. Fishing; hiking. Elev 2000 ft; 1 acre. Primitive shelter on gravel rd.

TROY (27)

Arrowhead Campground $7.50
Uwharrie National Forest

N of Troy on Hwy 109; just past Macedonia Church, turn left on Mullinix Rd, past horse camp; right on FR 544 for 1.8 mi; left on FR 597 for half mi; right on FR 597B. $7.50 base for non-elec sites with federal senior pass; others pay $15; elec surcharge $5. Base fee $18 in 2016, with elec surcharge at $7. Double sites $30, increasing to $36 in 2016. All year; 14-day limit. 50 sites; 40-ft RV limit. Tbls, flush toilets, cfga, showers, drkg wtr, lantern post, laun-

dry sink, dump. Bike path, boating(l), swimming, fishing, hiking, OHV trail. GPS: 35.43972, -80.075

Badin Lake Campground $12
Uwharrie National Forest

10 mi NW of Troy on SR 109; qtr mi S on SR 1153; 3 mi W on FR 576; bear left on FR 544; 1 mi N on FR 597; 1 mi W on FR 597A. $12; double sites $24 ($6 & $12 with federal senior pass). All year; 14-day limit. 34 sites (32-ft RV limit). Tbls, flush toilets, cfga, drkg wtr, showers, dump. Boating(l), fishing, swimming, hiking, mountain biking, hunting. 8 acres. GPS: 35.4484734, -80.0786621

Canebrake Horse Camp $7.50
Uwharrie National Forest

11 mi N of Troy on SR 109; 2 mi W on Mullinex Rd to "T" jct; right on FR 554 for qtr mi. $7.50 with federal senior pass at non-elec sites (others pay $15); elec surcharge $5. Base fee $18 in 2016, with elec surcharge at $7. All year; 14-day limit. 28 sites, typically 50 ft. Tbls, flush toilets, cfga, drkg wtr, showers, dump, lead lines, lantern poles, horse showers. Bridle trails, boating, swimming, fishing, OHV trail. GPS: 35.4394, -80.0486

East Morris Mountain FREE
Uwharrie National Forest

3 mi NW on SR 109; 4 mi N on CR 509. Free. All year; 14-day limit. Primitive undesignated sites. No facilities, cfga, no drkg wtr. Picnicking, hiking. GPS: 35.4398618, -79.9586576

Uwharrie Hunt Camp $5
Uwharrie National Forest

9 mi N of Troy on Sr 109; left on SR 1153. $5. All year; 14-day limit. 8 primitive sites. Tbls, toilets, cfga, no drkg wtr, no trash service. Hunting. GPS: 35.4314097, -80.023272

West Morris Mountain Camp $5
Uwharrie National Forest

8 mi NW on SR 109; 1.5 mi N on CR 1303. $5 ($10 group sites). All year; 14-day limit. 14 primitive sites, typically 55 ft. Toilets, lampposts, cfga, tbls, no drkg wtr. Nature trails. Hiking, biking. GPS: 35.4295844, -79.9944932

Woodrun Hunt Camp FREE
Uwharrie National Forest

10 mi SW on Hwy 24; 1 mi N on FR 517. Free. All year; 14-day limit. 8 primitive sites (RVs under 16 ft). Tbls, toilets, cfga, no drkg wtr. Hiking, hunting.

Yates Place FREE
Uwharrie National Forest

5 mi NW on NC 109; 3 mi S on CR 1147. Free. All year; 14-day limit. 2 primitive sites (RVs under 32 ft). Tbls, toilets, cfga, no drkg wtr. Hiking, biking, hunting. GPS: 35.3645857, -79.988662

WAYNESVILLE (28)

Sunburst Campground $7.50
Pisgah National Forest
7 mi E of Waynesville on US 276; 8 mi S on SR 215 (a Natural Scenic Byway). $7.50 with federal senior pass; others pay $15. 4/1-10/31; 14-day limit. 9 primitive sites up to 51 ft. Tbls, flush toilets, cfga, drkg wtr. Fishing, hiking trails. Adjacent to Shining Rock Wilderness. Elev 3000 ft; 3 acres. Non-campers pay $3 day use fee ($30 annual). GPS: 35.375488, -82.941895

WILKESBORO (29)

Bandits Roost $11
Corps of Engineers
W. Kerr Scott Lake
From US 421 at Wilkesboro, 5.5 mi W on SR 268, then N on CR 1141; at S side of lake. $11 base with federal senior pass at 85 elec/wtr RV sites; others pay $22 base, $24 for premium sites ($12 with senior pass). RV limit in excess of 65 ft; 5 pull-through sites. 4/1-10/31; 14-day limit. Picnic shelter, amphitheater, tbls, flush toilets, cfga, drkg wtr, showers, dump, elec, fishing pier, playground, beach. boating(l), swimming, basketball, hiking, fishing. GPS: 36.11972, -81.24528

Doughton Park $8
Blue Ridge Parkway
National Park Service
20 mi N of North Wilkesboro on SR 18; 9 mi N on parkway to Milepost 241.1. $8 with federal senior pass; others pay $16. Open 5/1-10/31; 14-day limit. 136 sites (30-ft RV limit). Tbls, flush toilets, cfga, drkg wtr, dump, no showers or elec. Fishing, nature program. 6,430 acres. GPS: 36.406006, -81.174316

Fort Hamby Campground $12
Corps of Engineers
W. Kerr Scott Lake
From Wilkesboro, 5 mi N on US 421; 1.5 mi S on Recreation Rd; at N side of lake. $12 with federal senior pass at 33 elec sites; others pay $24. RV limit in excess of 65 ft. 4/15-10/31; 14-day limit. Tbls, toilets, cfga, drkg wtr. Fishing, swimming, playground, boating(l), amphitheater, horseshoe pits. Group camping area with elec, $125. GPS: 36.13833, -81.27111

Warrior Creek $10
Corps of Engineers
W. Kerr Scott Lake
From Wilkesboro, 8 mi W on SR 268, across bridge, then N on access rd; at S side of lake. $10 base with federal senior pass at 61 elec/wtr sites; others pay $20 base, $24 at premium locations ($12 with senior pass). 4/15-10/15; 14-day limit. RV limit in excess of 65 ft. Pavilion, tbls, flush toilets, cfga, drkg wtr, dump, beach, fishing pier, playground, showers, elec. Swimming, hiking, fishing, baseball, boating. 3 group camping areas with elec, $85. GPS: 36.11056, -81.30944

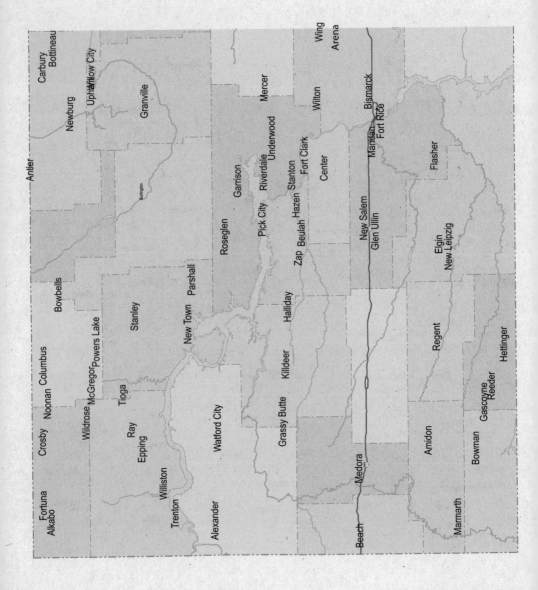

NORTH DAKOTA

WWW.NDTOURISM.COM

Toll-free number for travel information: 800-435-5663. Home page: http://www.ndtourism.com

Game and Fish Dept, 100 North Bismarck Expressway, Bismarck, ND 58501. 701/328-6300. E-mail: ccmail.ndgf@ranch.state.nd.us

---

CAPITAL: Bismarck
NICKNAME: Sioux State
STATEHOOD: 1889 – 39th State
FLOWER: Wild Prairie Rose
TREE: American Elm
BIRD: Western Meadowlark

REST AREAS
Overnight stops are not permitted.

STATE PARKS
Camping fees are $12 without hookups at Little Missouri and Sully Creek Parks; sites without hookups at other parks are $12 off-season, $17 in-season. Most sites with hookups are $20-25 off-season, $25-30 in-season. A $5 daily entrance fee is charged at all parks ($25 annually; $20 for North Dakota seniors). Non-campers pay $5 for showers. Parks and Recreation Dept, PO Box 5594, Bismarck, ND 58506; 701/328-5357.

STATE FORESTS
Camping fees are $10 per night in developed campgrounds without hookups -- Turtle Mountain and Homen Forests. Equestrian campers pay an additional $5 per horse at Twisted Oaks Equestrian camp in Turtle Mountain Forest. Sites have 14-day limits. No developed campgrounds are available in the Sheyenne Valley, Tetrault or Mouse River State Forests, but free backcountry camping is permitted in all state forests.

NATIONAL GRASSLANDS
Unlike in other states west of the Mississippi, the federal government operates national grasslands in North Dakota instead of national forests. Free dispersed camping is permitted virtually anywhere in the grasslands, but ten developed campgrounds ar provided in he Little Missouri National Grasslands. Small camping fees of $6 are charged. Dakota Prairie Grasslands, 240 W. Century Ave., Bismarck, ND 58503. 701-250-4443.

THEODORE ROOSEVELT
NATIONAL MEMORIAL PARK
A $25 per vehicle entry fee (good for 7 days) is charged; free entry with a federal senior pass. Camping is $14 per day, $7 off-season. Backcountry camping is permitted with a free permit, available at the park's north or south unit ranger stations. PO Box 7, Medora, ND 58645; 701/623-4466.

ADAMS (E)

Adams City Park $10
From CR 11A, N on Park St to Third Ave. $10. 2 RV sites with hookups, drkg wtr, tbls, cfga, dump, flush toilets, showers. Museum, playground, pioneer log cabin.

ALEXANDER (W)

First Responders Park   FREE
Alexander Municipal Campground
On ND 85 in Alexander across street from village park, Manning & Elk St. Free but donations requested. 5/1-9/30; 1-night limit. Policed. 4 primitive sites. Tbls, toilets, cfga, playground. Restrooms removed after vandalism.

Sather Lake $6
Little Missouri National Grasslands
16 mi SW of Alexander on Hwy 68. $6 during 5/1-10/15; free rest of year but no services; 14-day limit. 18 sites (typically 50 ft) on W & E sides of dam. Tbls, 2 toilets, cfga, no drkg wtr (wtr supply has high levels of fluoride). Swimming, boating(ld), fishing (trout & bass in lake).

ALKABO (W)

Writing Rock State Historic Site   FREE
5 mi S of Alkabo on CR 5; 1 mi E. Free; donations welcome. 5 RV sites. All year. Tbls, toilets, cfga, drkg wtr, playground. Free admission to see inscribed rocks with thunderbird figures.

AMIDON (W)

Burning Coal Vein   FREE
Little Missouri National Grasslands
2 mi W of Amidon on US 85; 12 mi NW on CR 742; 1.4 mi E on FR 772. Free. All year; 14-day limit. 5 sites. Tbls, toilets, cfga, well drkg wtr. Hiking, berry picking, swimming, boating, fishing. Burned coal vein (no longer burning) & columnar juniper tree area nearby. Trailhead for Maah Daah Hey Trail.

ANTLER (W)

Antler Memorial Park   FREE
1 mi N of Antler off 4th Ave. Pop. 47. Free. 5/1-11/30; 3-day limit. Primitive sites with tbls, pit toilets, cfga, drkg wtr, elec. Tours of historic school. 701-267-3370.

ARENA (W)

Arena   FREE
Wildlife Management Area
1 mi S & half mi E of Arena in Burleigh County. Free primitive camping. All year; 10-day limit. No facilities. Hunting, fishing. 800 acres.

ARTHUR (E)

Arthur City Park   FREE
From SR 18, E on 5th Ave to ballfields; between 4th & 5th Aves. Free. 4 RV sites with pair of 15/20-amp elec hookups. Drkg wtr, flush toilets, cfga, tbls. Tennis courts, horseshoes.

ASHLEY (E)

Ashley Wildlife Management Area   FREE
8 mi NE of Ashley in McIntosh County. Free primitive camping. All year; 10-day limit. No facilities. Hunting. 80 acres.

Coldwater Lake Park $10
McIntosh County Park
16 mi E Ashley on SR 11; 1 mi S on 64th Ave SE; 1 mi W on 9th St SE. $20 with hookups; $10 primitive sites. 5/15-10/15. 6 sites for dry camping; 15 sites with elec/wtr. Toilets, tbls, cfga, drkg wtr, fish cleaning station. Fishing, boating(ld).

BALTA (E)

Balta Dam   DONATIONS
Municipal Recreation Area
1 mi S of Balta (pop. 65) on 27th Ave NE; at Sheyenne River. All year. Donations. 20 sites. Tbls, toilets, cfga, elec. Picnicking; fishing; swimming, boating(l). No trash service. 99-acre lake.

Balta Wildlife Management Area   FREE
Half mi S of Balta in Pierce County. Free primitive camping. All year; 10-day limit. No facilities. 105 acres.

BARTLETT (E)

Black Swan Wildlife Management Area   FREE
6 mi S of Bartlett in Nelson County. Free primitive camping. All year; 10-day limit. No facilities. Fishing, boating, hunting. 854 acres.

BEACH (W)

Camel's Hump Lake   FREE
North Dakota Fish & Game Department
Fish Management Area
8.6 mi E of Beach on I-94 to exit 10 (N of Sentinel Butte); left 0.3 mi to Camel's Hump Rd; N on Camel's Hump Rd (CR 1711) to lake. Free. All year; 10-day limit. Tbls, 1 toilet, cfga, no drkg wtr. Boating(l - no mtrs), fishing.

Elkhorn Campground $6
Little Missouri National Grasslands
From jct with I-94 at Beach, 29.5 mi N on SR 16; 15 mi E on gravel Blacktail Rd; turn left after campground sign for 0.9 mi. $6 during 5/15-11/15; free rest of year but no wtr or services. 9 sites (typically 60 ft). Tbls, toilet, cfga, drkg wtr. Hitching rails. Horseback riding.

Odland Dam   FREE
State Fish Management Area
7 mi N of Beach on SR 16 N. Free. Primitive sites. Tbls, toilets, cfga, no drkg wtr. Boating(l), fishing.

Wannagan Campground $6
Little Missouri National Grasslands
8.6 mi E of Beach on I-94 to exit 10 (N of Sentinal Butte); left 0.3 mi to Camel's Hump Rd (CR 1711); right on Camel's Hump Rd 0.5 mi to intersection, then straight on 160 Ave SW for 2.5 mi (rd changes into 30th St SW) & continue 4.1 mi; left at sign onto Wannagan Creek Rd for 9.1 mi; follow signs to campground. $6 during 5/15-11/15; free rest of year but no wtr or services; 14-day limit. 10 sites, typically 50 ft (4 pull-through). Tbls, toilets, cfga, drkg wtr. Multi-use trails.

BELCOURT (E)

Belcourt Lake $1.50
Turtle Mountain Indian Reservation
1 mi N of Belcourt. $1.50 at 7 RV sites, (4 with elec). 6/15-9/15; 14-day limit. Undesignated & designated sites. Tbls, toilets, cfga, drkg wtr. Picnicking; swimming; fishing; boating(l). Fess for recreation.

Jarvis Lake Access   FREE
Turtle Mountain Indian Reservation
7 mi N of Belcourt, 5 mi W to campground. Free. 5 sites. Tbls, toilets, cfga, drkg wtr. Picnicking; fishing; boating(l). Reservations accepted.

Lake Gordon $1.50
Turtle Mountain Indian Reservation
6 mi N and 1 mi W of Belcourt. $1.50 at 5 RV sites. 6/15-9/15; 14-day limit. Undesignated & designated sites. Tbls, toilets, cfga, drkg wtr, showers, coin laundry. Picnicking; swimming; fishing; boating(l). Fee for activities.

BEULAH (W)

Beulah Bay Park $10
Beulah Park District
From jct of SR 49 & 200, N 15 mi on SR 49; follow signs 1 mi; on S shore of Lake Sakakawea. $10 primitive sites; $20 & $25 with elec; full hookups $25. 5/15-9/15; 7-day limit; 21-day rates available. 117 sites with elec (no RV size limit). Tbls, flush toilets, cfga, drkg wtr, elec ($), shelters, dump, store, new showers, fish cleaning station, horseshoe pits. Swimming, fishing, boating (ld), playground, bocce ball, croquet.

Beulah Eagles RV Park $10
Beulah Park District
At 1101 SR 49, S side of Beulah at Knife River. $10 primitive sites; $15 with elec ($90 weekly, $300 monthly). 12 RV sites with elec/wtr; tent sites. Tbls, toilets, cfga, drkg wtr, dump.

Riverside Park $10
Beulah Park District
On S side of Beulah E of SR 49 at S shore of Knife River. $10 for primitive sites; $15 for RV sites with elec. 4/1-11/1; 7-day limit. 15 RV sites with elec; tent sites. Tbls, flush toilets, cfga, drkg wtr, showers. Canoeing, fishing, hiking, horseshoes, disc golf. Permit required from parks department, city hall.

BINFORD (E)

Centennial Municipal Park $5
3 blocks W of Main St in Binford (pop. 183). $5 base for primitive sites; $15 with elec/wtr. May-Nov. 6 RV sites. Drkg wtr, flush toilets, elec ($), cfga, tbls, dump. Biking, picnicking.

BISMARCK (W)

Kimball Bottoms Recreation Area   FREE
Lake Oahe
Burleigh County Park
From Bismarck, 9 mi S on SR 1804, then go S on Desert Rd; at E shore of lake. Free. Primitive undesignated sites; 14-day limit. Drkg wtr, cfga, no toilets. Boating(l), fishing. Formerly Corps of Engineers park.

Eagles City Park $9
Bismarck Parks & Recreation
9 mi N of Pioneer Park on River Rd. $8 (3-day rates available). 25 primitive sites. Tbls, toilets, cfga, drkg wtr, shelter, playground. Boating(l), fishing, walking trail.

BOTTINEAU (W)

Black Lake Wildlife Management Area   FREE
7 mi N of Bottineau; 2 mi W. Free primitive camping. All year; 10-day limit. No facilities. Fishing, boating, hunting. 180 acres.

Carbury Dam   FREE
State Fishing Access Site
4 mi W of Bottineau on Hwy 5; 5 mi N on Hwy 14 (1 mi W of Carbury). Free. All year. 10 primitive sites. Elec hookups, cfga, tbls, toilets, shelter. Boating(l), fishing.

Hahn's Bay Recreation Area $10
Turtle Mountain State Forest
14 mi N of Bottineau on Lake Metigoshe Rd; half mi N; on W side of Lake Metigoshe. $10. MD-LD; 14-day limit. 35 sites (RVs under 26 ft). Tbls, pit toilets, cfga, drkg wtr, fishing pier. Boating(l), fishing, swimming, paved hiking/biking trail, winter sports. 150 acres.

Lake Metigoshe State Park $12
14 mi NE of Bottineau. $12 primitive sites; $17 in-season; $20-$25 at 30-amp elec sites. All year; 14-day limit. Tbls, toilets, cfga, drkg wtr, dump, showers, playground. Boating(l), fishing, ice skating, picnicking, swimming beach, hiking trails, cross-country ski trails, nature programs, amphitheater, snowmobile trails. 1,551 acres.

Long Lake   FREE
State Fishing Access Site
1 mi E of Bottineau; 11 mi N; 4 mi E; 1 mi S; 1 mi W. Free. All year; 10-day limit. Primitive undesignated sites; no facilities. Boating, fishing.

Pelican Lake   FREE
State Fishing Access Site
1 mi E of Bottineau; 11 mi N; 6 mi E; 1 mi SW. Free. All year; 10-day limit. Primitive undesignated sites; no facilities. Boating, fishing.

Pelican Lake/Sandy Lake Rec. Area $10
Homen Mountain State Forest
11 mi N of Bottineau on Lake Metigoshe Rd; 12 mi E on SR 43. $10. 5/1-10/31; 14-day limit. 10 RV sites; tent sites. Tbls, toilets, cfga, drkg wtr. Fishing, boating(l), swimming. 4,500 acres.

Strawberry Lake Recreation Area $10
Turtle Mountain State Forest
From jct of SR 14 & SR 5 near Bottineau, N 9.5 mi; 2.5 mi E on SR 43. $10. 5/1-10/31; 14-day limit. 25 sites (RVs under 29 ft). Tbls, toilets, cfga, drkg wtr. Swimming, boating(l), fishing, hiking, horseback riding, swimming, winter sports, canoeing. 7,500 acres.

Twisted Oaks Recreation Area $10
Turtle Mountain State Forest
9.5 mi N of jct of ND 14 and ND 5; 1.5 mi E on ND 43. $10 plus $5 per horse. All year. 15 sites. Tbls, toilets, cfga, drkg wtr. Corrals, bridle trails, horse trailer parking, hitching rails. Observation tower. Picnicking, hiking, horseback riding, canoeing.

BOWBELLS (W)
Bowbells City Park   FREE
Campground and RV Park
Park 2 blocks from downtown Bowbells (pop. 336) at Main St & Third Ave, 3 free sites but donations accepted. 3-day limit; 5/1-9/30. RV park at Railway St no longer exists. Tbls, toilets, cfga, drkg wtr, playground. 701-377-2608.

BOWDON (E)
Bowdon RV Campground $10
Half mi N of ND 200 in Bowdon. $10 without hookups, $20 at 6 RV sites with full hookups (30 or 50-amp). All year. Tbls, flush toilets, cfga, drkg wtr, showers, dump, playground. Fishing, boating.

BOWMAN (W)
Bowman Haley Campground $5
Bowman Dam Marina County Park
11 mi S of Bowman on US 85; 8 mi E & 2 mi S; on N shore of Bowman lake. $5 for primitive lakeshore camping; $15 for 51 sites with elec. Tbls, cfga, drkg wtr. Toilets, show-

ers for a fee at marina. Boating(l), fishing. Proceeds used by Bowman Haley Anglers Association for conservation, fishing improvement. 7,000 acres of primitive camping. Lake built by Army Corps of Engineers.

Bowman Lions Park   DONATION
Bowman Parks & Recreation
In Bowman at 506 Third Ave SE & Hwy 12 beside fairground. Free but donations requested. Primitive sites. Tbls, flush toilets, cfga, drkg wtr, dump, no elec. Horseshoes.

BRADDOCK (E)
Braddock Dam City Park   FREE
2 mi S & half mi W of Braddock (pop. 21). All year. Free primitive camping. Toilets, cfga, no drkg wtr. Camping also on grounds of South Central Threshing Bee during the bee. Boating(l), fishing. 701-332-6632.

CARBURY (W)
Carbury Dam   FREE
State Fishing Access Site
1 mi S & 1 mi W of Carbury to dam. Free. All year; 10-day limit. Primitive undesignated sites; no facilities. Fishing, boating.

Carbury Lake Recreation Area   FREE
Bottineau County Park
3.2 mi N of SR 5 on SR 14; 1 mi W on access rd. Free 5/1-9/30. 10 sites. Tbls, toilets, cfga, drkg wtr, elec. Boating(l), fishing, swimming. 111-acre lake. 701-228-2225.

Dalen Recreation Area   FREE
Turtle Mountain State Forest
7.7 mi N of Carbury on ND 14; 4 mi E to campground. Free. All year. 10 sites (28-ft RV limit). Tbls, toilets, cfga, drkg wtr. Picnicking; snowmobiling.

Homen State Forest   FREE
6 mi E of Lake Metigoshe; encompasses Pelican and Sandy Lakes ($10 fee area). Free. All year. Primitive undesignated camping in 4,184-acre forest. Tbls, toilets, cfga, drkg wtr. Birdwatching, fishing, canoeing, hunting.

Strawberry Lake   FREE
State Fishing Access Site
4 mi N of Carbury on SR 14; 2.5 mi E; half mi S. All year; 10-day limit. Primitive undesignated sites; no facilities. Boating (elec mtrs only), trout fishing.

CENTER (W)
Klein Municipal Park $10
On E edge of city, E of jct SR 25 & 48. $10 base (monthly $400). 5/1-10/15. 20 sites with full hookups (some phone & CATV). Tbls, flush toilets, drkg wtr, cfga, dump. Fishing. Indoor pool nearby.

Ball Park City RV Park　　　$10
On S side of town on SR 25. $10. 5/1-10/15. 10 sites with elec (no sewer or wtr hookups). Tbls, toilets, cfga, drkg wtr. Dump at Betty Hagel Memorial Civic Center (N on Hwy 48 from Hwy 25).

Nelson Lake Campground　　　FREE
Oliver County Park
5 mi E on SR 25; 2 mi S on 33rd Ave SW; 1 mi SW on 24th St SW. Free primitive camping. Tbls, toilets, cfga, no drkg wtr.

COLUMBUS (W)

Columbus City Park　　　$5
Parks & Recreation Department
In Columbus (pop. 133), E on 4th St from Main by golf course. $5 base; $10 with elec. 4/15-10/15. 2 RV sites. Toilets, cfga, drkg wtr, tbls. Golf course, tennis courts, ball diamond, playground, picnic area. Unable to verify current status for 2017.

Short Creek Dam Municipal Park　　　$5
6 mi N of town. $5 base; $10 full hookups. 40 RV sites with elec, tbls, pit toilets, cfga, drkg wtr, shelter, beach, fish cleaning station. Boating(dl), fishing, swimming. Unable to verify current status for 2017.

COOPERSTOWN (E)

City Park　　　$10
At 10th & Foster in Cooperstown. $10 without hookups; $20 full hookups ($100 weekly, $300 monthly). 5/31-9/30. 10 RV sites, several tent sites. Tbls, flush toilets, cfga, showers, drkg wtr, elec($), dump, store, pool, playground. Swimming, biking, picnicking, horseshoes, playground. 701-797-3613.

CROSBY (W)

Fairgrounds Campsite　　　FREE
Divide County Fairgrounds
In Crosby at 107 W. Central Ave. Free but donations requested. 5/1-9/1. Primitive RV parking (some elec). 7-day limit. 7 RV sites with hookups, other elec sites & tent sites. Showers, flush toilets, dump, drkg wtr. Patrolled. 965-6029.

Pioneer Village Camping Area　　　FREE
Divide County Historical Society
On SE side of Crosby. Free without hookups $10 with elec/wtr. 5/1-9/15. 30 RV sites with hookups; open tent sites. Tbls, flush toilts, cfga, drkg wtr, showers. 9-hole greens course, tennis, ball diamonds, outdoor pool. 19 historic buildings represent frontier life. Patrolled. 3-day threshing show 3rd weekend in July.

DEVILS LAKE (E)

Grahams Island State Park　　　$12
9 mi W of Devils Lake on Hwy 19, then 6 mi S. $12 at primitive sites off-season, $17 in-season; $20-$25 with elec. All year;14-day limit. Tbls, toilets, cfga, drkg wtr, dump, showers, playground. Showers at bait shop all year. Marina, Boating(l), swimming beach, fish cleaning station, store, hiking trails, shelters. 1,122 acres.

DRAKE (E)

City Park Campground　　　$8
In Drake at Lake & 6th St. $8 without hookups, $10 for elec/wtr. 20 sites (12 with elec). Tbls, elec($), drkg wtr, flush toilets, tbls, playground, shelter, DUMP. Picnicking, biking.

DRAYTON (E)

Drayton Dam　　　FREE
Pembina County Recreation Area
2 mi N of Drayton, then E 1 mi to dam of Red River. Free. 5/1-9/30. 12 primitive sites; tent sites. Tbls, toilets, cfga, drkg wtr. Fishing, picnicking.

DRISCOLL (E)

Driscoll Sibley County Park　　　FREE
Burleigh County Parks
Exit 41 from I-94, 1 mi S to old Rt 10; 1.5 mi W to park. Free. All year; 14-day limit. Small park, tbls, drkg wtr, toilets.

ELGIN (W)

Sheep Creek Dam　　　FREE
Grant County Water Resources District
From jct of ND 49 and ND 21, 4 mi S on Elgin Rd; 0.5 mi W on 74th St SW; at dam on Cannonball River. Free, donations welcomed. 5/1-10/1; 5-day limit, 14 days per season. 10 sites (RVs under 26 ft). Tbls, toilets, cfga, drkg wtr, some elec, dump, playground, fishing pier. Picnicking; swimming; fishing, boating(l).

Heart Butte Dam　　　$10
Lake Tschida Recreation Area
Bureau of Reclamation
Tri-Cities Joint Job Development Authority
15 mi N of Elgin on Hwy 49. 3/1-11/30; 14-day limit in 30-day period. $10 primitive sites at all 10 campgrounds (Rattlesnake Point, Sled Creek, Schatz Point, Hawebesl, Koehlers Point, Southside, Crappie Creek, Rimrock and Downstream. Two campgrounds (Rimrock and Downstream also offer elec sites for $20. Boy Scout Reserve may be open when not used by Scouts. Tbls, toilets, cfga, drkg wtr, dump, shelters. Boating(l), fishing, swimming, fish cleaning station. Online reservations ($7 fee) available for all sites. 2-day minimum stay required on weekends at Rimrock during MD-LD; $4 daily vehicle pass (or $14 annually) also required at Rimrock. 701-584-2201. 7,575-acres, 3,400-acre lake owned by BOR; recration areas are managed by job development authority.

ELLENDALE (E)

Johnson Gulch   FREE
Wildlife Management Area
13 mi W on Ellendale on SR 11; 3 mi N on SR 56; 4 mi W & 0.75 mi N. All year; 10-day limit. Primitive camping. Toilets, cfga, no drkg wtr. 1,400 acres at largest & best known of several glacial ravines. Hiking, wildlife study.

Oster Park $10
N end of Ellendale, 4 blocks E of Hwy 281 on Hwy 11 at Fifth Ave N. $10. 4/15-10/15; 1-night limit. 3 RV sites with elec; tent sites. Tbls, toilets, cfga, drkg wtr. Dump nearby. Disc golf. Unable to verify status for 2017.11

Pheasant Lake   FREE
Dickey County Park
7 mi W of Ellendale on SR 11. Free primitive sites with elec. Tbls, toilets, cfga, no drkg wtr, beach. Boating(l), fishing. Not verified for 2017.

Whitestone Battlefield   FREE
State Historic Site
13 mi W of Ellendale on SR 11; 3 mi N on SR 56; 4 mi E on 88th St SE; 2 mi N on 73rd Ave SE. Free. 10 primitive RV sites with elec.

Wilson's Dam   FREE
Dickey County Park
13 mi W of Ellendale on Hwy 11; 10 mi N on SR 56; 1 mi E; 0.25 mi N. Free primitive sites with elec. Tbls, toilets, cfga, no drkg wtr. Boating(l), fishing. Not verified for 2017.

EPPING (W)

Epping/Springbrook Dam $5
Williams County Water Resources District
8.5 mi W of Epping on CR 6 (58th St NW). $5 at primitive sites, $10 at six 20/30/50-amp elec sites. Tbls, toilets, cfga, drkg wtr. Dump at city park in Epping. 128-acre lake.

ENDERLIN (E)

Enderlin Campground $10
Patrick Pierce City Park
NE corner of Enderlin. $10 at 6 RV sites; 13 tent sites. 5/1-11/1. Tbls, flush toilets, cfga, drkg wtr, dump, no elec. Fishing, boating.

ESMOND (E)

Buffalo Lake Campground   FREE
Benson County Recreation Area
5 mi W of Esmond on SR 19; 2 mi S. Donations suggested; camp free. All year. Open primitive camping; 9 RV sites. Toilets, drkg wtr, cfga, elec, playground, showers. Picnicking, swimming, boating(ld), fishing.

Randy Marthe Memorial Park $5
4 blocks S of SR 19 in Esmond; at W side of school (430 Hwy 19 SW). $5 without hookups; $7.50 with wtr/elec

($50 weekly). Apr-Oct. Tbls, flush toilets, cfga, drkg wtr, showers. Esmond also has small camping area with 3 elec hookups, but it is usually occupied by traveling farm workers. 701-249-3493 or 249-3531.

FLASHER (W)

Nygren Dam   FREE
Morton County Park
6 mi N of Flasher on CR 84; 1 mi E on 60th St; 3 mi N on CR 136. Free. All year; 10-day limit. Primitive camping. Tbls, pit toilet, cfga, no drkg wtr. Boating(l), fishing pier. 19.2 acres. Note: The nearby city of Flasher clearly does not want RVing travelers stopping at its park and spending money in the town. The city refused to provide us with current camping fee information about its park, so it has been deleted from this book. We strongly recommend against stopping overnight in this town.

FORDVILLE (E)

Fordville Dam Recreation Area $10
Grand Forks, Walsh & Nelson County Watershed Boards
Grand Forks County Water Resources District
Half mi S of Fordville; 2 mi E; 1 mi S (N of US & SR 18). $10 at 24 primitive sites with wtr; $20 with hookups. Weekly camping pass $100, monthly $250, annual $900. 24 primitive sites with wtr, 19 with full hookups. Tbls, flush toilets, showers, cfga, drkg wtr, dump. Swimming, boating(l), fishing, horseshoes, playground. Non-campers pay $5 day use fee ($25 annual). 2,185-acre pool 701-360-0515.

R & J's RV Park (Priv.) $10
At 120 Walsh St. N in Fordville. $10 for RVs up to 25 ft; $12 for 26 ft or more ($70 weekly, $270 monthly). Tbls, toilets, cfga, 30/50-amp elec, coin laundry.

FORMAN (E)

Forman City Park & Campground $10
On Hwy 32 at Forman. $10 for RV sites, $5 tents. 4/15-10/15. 4 RV sites with elec; tent sites. Toilets, cfga, drkg wtr, dump, playground, tbls, shelter.

FORT CLARK (W)

Arroda Lake   FREE
Wildlife Management Area
1 mi E of Fort Clark in Oliver County. Free primitive camping. All year; 10-day limit. No facilities. Fishing, boating, hunting. 384 acres.

FORT RICE (W)

Fort Rice Boat Ramp   FREE
Morton County Park
At SR 1806 & 63rd St at Missouri River/Lake Oahe. Free. 10 primitive sites. All year; 10-day limit. Tbls, pit toilet, cfga, no drkg wtr, fish cleaning station. Boating(ld), fishing.

Fort Rice Campground $8
Morton County Park
S of Fort Rice on Hwy 1806. $8 at 25 primitive sites, $18 at 10 RV sites with elec. All year; 10-day limit. Tbls, flush toilets, cfga, drkg wtr, dump. Walking trail. Access to Fort Rice State Historic Site. Former Corps of Engineers facility.

FORTUNA (W)
Skjermo Lake Municipal Park   FREE
7 mi W of town. Free. Primitive undesignated sites. Swimming, picnicking, fishing (perch), boating(l). Length of stay limits to be considered in 2017.

GARRISON (W)
Audubon   FREE
Wildlife Management Area
8 mi E of Garrison in McLean County. Free primitive camping. All year; 10-day limit. No facilities. Fishing, boating, hunting. 11,285 acres. Leased from Corps of Engineers.

Douglas Creek   FREE
State Fishing Access Site
11 mi W of Garrison, then 5 mi S & 4 mi E. Free. All year; 10-day limit. Primitive camping. Tbls, toilets, cfga, drkg wtr. Boating(ld), fishing. 1,980-acre wildlife area.

Douglas Creek Recreation Area   FREE
Corps of Engineers
Lake Sakakawea
From Garrison, about 12 mi W on SR 37 (through Emmet) to jct with US 83, then 7 mi SE on gravel rds; at Douglas Creek Bay section of lake. Free. 20 primitive sites (25-ft RV limit). All year; 14-day limit. Drkg wtr, pit toilets, cfga, tbls. Picnicking, boating(l), fishing, hiking, horseback riding.

East Totten Trail Recreation Area $8
Corps of Engineers
Lake Sakakawea
6 mi E of Garrison on SR 37; 2.5 mi S (N on US 83 from Coleharbor, then qtr mi E). $8 with federal senior pass at 30 elec sites; others pay $16. $12 at 10 primitive sites. 5/15-9/15; 14-day limit. 25-ft RV limit. Tbls, pit toilets, cfga, drkg wtr, elec, fish cleaning station, dump. Wheelchair access. Boating(l), fishing.

Fort Stevenson State Park $12
3 mi S of Garrison on N shore of Lake Sakakawea. $12 without hookups off-season; $17 in-season; $20-$25 elec, $25-$30 full hookups. All year; 14-day limit. Tbls, flush toilets, cfga, drkg wtr, dump, showers, marina, playground, restaurant, store, fish cleaning station, visitor center. Picnicking, boating(lrd), swimming, fishing, hiking, cross-country ski trails, snowmobiling. North Dakota Fishing Hall of Fame nearby. 549 acres.

Sportsmen's Centennial Park $12
McLean County Park
5 mi E & 3 mi S of Garrison. $12 without hookups. 5/1-10/30. Base fee for primitive sites; $20 with elec. 71 primitive sites plus 54 with elec. 5/1-10/30. Tbls, toilets, cfga, drkg wtr, store, playground, bait store, fish cleaning station, showers. No dump. Swimming, fishing, boating(ld), hiking trail, volleyball, trout pond nearby. Adjacent to de Trobriand Wildlife Management Area.

Steinke Bay   FREE
De Trobriand Wildlife Management Area
3 mi E & 2 mi S of Garrison. Free primitive camping. All year; 10-day limit. Toilets, cfga, no drkg wtr. Boating(ld), fishing.

GASCOYNE (W)
Gascoyne Lake Park   FREE
Quarter mi W of Gascoyne on US 12; 1/4 mi N. Free. All year. 10 sites (no hookups). Tbls, toilets, cfga. Picnicking; swimming; fishing; boating(l). 187-acre lake. No longer a city park.

GLENFIELD (E)
Glenfield City Park   FREE
At SW Jct SR 20 & 200. Free. All year; 1-night limit. 16 sites; 4 acres. Tbls, toilets, cfga, drkg wtr. Elec at 5 sites. Tennis court; playground, horseshoes, volleyball, softball.

GLEN ULLIN (W)
Danzig Dam/Storm Creek   FREE
Morton County Park
NW of Glen Ullin on SR 49 to I-94; about 10 mi E on I-94 to exit 120; 3 mi N on CR 86; W to dam at Storm Creek Lake. Free. Primitive undesignated sites. All year; 10-day limit. Toilet, tbls, cfga, no drkg wtr. Boating(ld), fishing.

GOODRICH (E)
Goodrich City Park   Donations
Just off SR 200 in town (pop. 98). Donations suggested; camp free. 6/1-10/15; 7-day limit. 3 sites with 20-amp elec. Tbls, toilets, cfga, drkg wtr, elec, dump, showers. Picnicking, tennis.

GRAND FORKS (E)
Turtle River State Park $12
22 mi W of Grand Forks, off US 2. $12 without elec off-season, $17 in-season); $20-$25 with elec. All year; 14-day limit. 125 sites. Tbls, flush toilets, cfga, drkg wtr, dump, showers, playground, store, shelters. Fishing, swimming, snowmobiling, sledding, ice rink, hiking trails, cross-country ski trails, horseback riding. 784 acres.

GRANVILLE (W)
Buffalo Lodge Lake   FREE
McHenry County Park
3 mi N of Granville on 12th Ave N, 2 mi E on 86th Ave NE,

1 mi N. Free. All year. Primitive undesignated sites. Tbls, toilets, cfga, no drkg wtr. Boating(ld), fishing.

Granville City Park   FREE
In Granville, 4 blocks W of Main St. on 6th Ave. Camp free, but $10 donation requested. 20 RV sites with wtr/elec. Drkg wtr, toilets, tbls, cfga. Ball fields, rodeo arena, playground, sand volleyball, ball fields, tennis. Patrolled.

GRASSY BUTTE (W)
Bennett Campground $6
Little Missouri National Grasslands
7.5 mi N of Grassy Butte on US 85 to Bennett Camp sign; 4 mi W on gravel 6th St SW toward Bennett Creek to "T" intersection; 1 mi S on Rd 824 across green cattle guard, then W to camp; steep access. Badlands terrain. $6 during 5/15-11/15; free rest of year but no wtr or services. 14-day limit. 13 sites (4 pull-through); no RV size limit. Hitching posts. Multi-use trail.

Grassy Butte Community Park $10
McKenzie County Parks & Recreation Department
On Hwy 85 S, about 38 mi S of Watford City. $10 at primitive sites; $15 with elec. About 25 RV sites with elec; 35-ft RV limit. Tbls, pit toilets, cfga, drkg wtr, playground, dump. Horseshoe pits, volleyball nets.

Magpie Campground $6
Little Missouri National Grasslands
About 13 mi S of Grassy Butte on US 85; 15.5 mi W on gravel Rd 712 (Magpie Rd); 0.25 mi N on access rd past day use parking lot. $6 during 5/15-11/15; free rest of year but no wtr or services. All year; 14-day limit. 11 sites; 60-ft RV limit. Tbls, toilets, cfga, drkg wtr. Hitching rails. Multi-use trail.

Summit Campground   FREE
Little Missouri National Grasslands
10 mi N of Grassy Butte on US 85, then W on gravel rd at campground sign. Free. 6/1-10/31; 14-day limit. 5 sites (30-ft RV limit, some pull-through). Tbls, toilets, cfga, no drkg wtr. Rockhounding. 4 mi S of N Unit of Theodore Roosevelt National Memorial Park.

HAGUE (E)
Hague City Park $11
On Main St in Hague. $11. 4 RV sites with hookups; tent area. Toilets, showers, tbls, cfga, drkg wtr, dump, playground, shelter. Basketball, horseshoe pits.

HALLIDAY (W)
Charging Eagle Bay   FREE
Fort Berthold Indian Reservation
Lake Sakakawea
14 mi N of Halliday on ND 8; 4 mi W and 4.5 mi NW to campground. 4/1-10/31. Undesignated sites. Tbls, toilets, cfga, firewood, dump, well drkg wtr, showers, store, elec

hookup. Swimming; picnicking; fishing; boating(rl; fuel and storage facilities).

Twin Buttes Recreation   FREE
Three Affiliated Tribes
Fort Berthold Indian Reservation
15 mi N of Halliday on ND 8; 6 mi E of Twin Buttes School. Free. 5/1-9/30; 14-day limit. 200 sites (RVs under 32 ft). Tbls, toilets, cfga, firewood, drkg wtr. Boating(l); picnicking; fishing; swimming nearby.

HANKINSON (E)
American Legion Campground $8
Lake Elsie City Park
From I-29 exit 8, W on SR 11; 1.5 mi S on 3rd Ave SE (167 1/2 Ave SE), then W to Lake Elsie. $8. Primitive sites. Tbls, flush toilets, cfga, drkg wtr, beach. Boating(l), swimming, fishing.

Dakota Magic Casino $10
From I-29 exit 1 just across SD/ND border, E to casino entrance; RV sites in rear, NW corner. $10 summer rates, $5 winter but no wtr. 25 sites with 30/amp elec/wtr/sewer up to 52 ft, pull-through. Tbls, flush toilets, cfga, drkg wtr. Closed in 2016 for 2 years for repair & updating.

Hankinson City Park $10
From I-29 exit 8, 4 mi W on SR 11/Sixth St along S side of town; S on 2nd Ave for 1 block, then right (W) on 7th St SW into park. RV sites on S side, payment box on N side. $10. 8 RV sites with elec; tent area. Drkg wtr, tbls, cfga, toilets. Ball diamonds, playground, lighted tennis & basketball courts, lighted skating rink, 2-mi hiking/biking/jogging trail, railroad museum, horseshoe pits.

Hankinson Hills Campground $6
Sheyenne National Grasslands
From Hankinson at jct with Main St, 1.4 mi W on SR 11; 1.4 mi N on 166th Ave SE; 2.1 mi E on unidentified rd at intersection; right on FR 1250 (Hankinson Hills Rd) for 1.8 mi. $6 during 5/15-11/15; free rest of year but no wtr or services. 15 sites (6 equestrian); no RV size limit. Tbls, toilets, cfga, drkg wtr. 8-mi multi-use trail, hunting. 10 acres.

HANNAFORD (E)
CAB City Park $12
(Clinton A. Brown Memorial Park)
0.25 mi E of Hannaford on SR 1 at Bald Hill Creek. $12 with elec, $15 full hookups ($75 weekly). MD-LD. 5 RV sites with utilities. Tbls, flush toilets, cfga, drkg wtr, showers, playground. Fishing, swimming, biking & walking trails.

HARVEY (E)
Lone Tree   FREE
State Wildlife Management Area
13 mi S of Harvey. Free. All year; 10-day limit. 3 primitive campgrounds. Tbls, toilets, cfga, drkg wtr, corrals. Hunting on 33,000 acres, fishing in Sheyenne River.

HASTINGS (E)
Clausen Springs   FREE
State Fishing Access Site
Just N of Hastings on SR 1, then 1 mi E & half mi N. All year; 10-day limit. Primitive undesignated sites. Recreation area, fishing pier. Boating, fishing.

HAVANA (E)
Williamson City Park   FREE
In town (pop 148) at end of E Main St. All year. Donations accepted. Undesignated sites; 2 RV sites, 1 with elec, 1 with wtr. Tbls, toilets, cfga, drkg wtr. Playground.

HAZELTON (E)
Badger Bay Recreation Area   FREE
Corps of Engineers
Lake Oahe
From Hazelton, 13 mi W on gravel 63rd St SW to Livona, then 1 mi S on SR 1804; W following signs. Free. 6 primitive sites. Pit toilets, cfga, no drkg wtr. Boating, fishing. Nearest dump station 23 mi.

Hazelton Recreation Area $12
Corps of Engineers
Lake Oahe
13 mi W of Hazelton on gravel 63rd St SW to Livona, then 1 mi N on SR 1804; at E shore of lake. $12 at 18 primitive sites ($6 with federal senior pass); $16 at 12 elec sites ($8 with senior pass). 4/1-10/31; 14-day limit. 30-ft RV limit. Toilets, tbls, cfga, no drkg wtr, fish cleaning station, playground. Boating(l), fishing, horseshoe pits.

HAZEN (W)
Hazen Bay $10
City Recreation Area
15 mi N on CR 27; on Lake Sakakawea. $10 for primitive sites; $15 with elec; $19 wtr/elec; $21 full hookups. MD-10/31. 120 sites (6 primitive, 7 with elec, 32 wtr/elec, 69 full hookups). Monthly, seasonal & group sites available. Drkg wtr, toilets, tbls, cfga, playgrounds, fish cleaning station, 60-ft dock, shelter. Boating (ld), fishing, swimming, hiking, golf, group camping area.

John Moses Memorial Park $10
Just E of Hazen High School near city pool. $10 primitive sites, $15 with elec. Tbls, toilets, cfga, drkg wtr.

HETTINGER (W)
Grand River Dispersed   FREE
Grand River National Grasslands
SE of Hettinger, S of Hwy 12. Free. 6,700-acre mixed-grass prairie. Primitive dispersed camping permitted, but no developed sites. Wildlife & wildflower photo. Mule, antelope, bird, upland game hunting.

HILLSBORO (E)
Woodland Municipal Park
N end of 3rd St NE; at Goose River. Camping no longer permitted.

JAMESTOWN (E)
Parkhurst Park $10
Pipestem Lake
Stutsman County Park Board
4 mi N of Jamestown on ND 281; 1 mi W on gravel road to campground. $10. All year; 14-day limit. 6 primitive sites (RVs under 24 ft). Tbls, toilets, cfga, firewood, drkg wtr, store. Equestrian facilities: corrals, tethers. Swimming; picnicking; fishing; boating(ld); mountain biking/hiking.

KILLDEER (W)
Little Missouri Bay $12
Primitive State Park
18 mi N of Killdeer on SR 22; 2 mi E on twp rd. $12 at primitive sites, $15 with elec. 5/15-11/1; 14-day limit. 30 sites (10 with elec). Tbls, vault toilets, cfga, drkg wtr, no showers, group shelters. Horseback riding($), corral, hiking & bridle trails, hiking trails picnicking. 5,748 acres.

LAMOURE (E)
Lake LaMoure Campground $11
LaMoure County Memorial Park
5 mi S of LaMoure on 102nd Ave SE. 5/15-fall. $11. $600 for summer at 50 RV sites with 30/50-amp elec; 15 tent sites. Tbls, toilets, cfga, drkg wtr, dump. Fishing, boating. 701-883-5856.

James River Dam Site
Municipal Park
Half mi W of LaMoure on ND 13. Camping no longer allowed.

LANGDON (E)
Mt. Carmel Dam Recreation Area $11
Cavalier County Water Resources Board
9 mi N of Langdon, then 2 mi E; 2 mi N; 1 mi E; on South Fork of Little Pembina River. $11 for primitive sites; $15 with elec/wtr ($55 & $75 weekly). 5/15-9/15. 200 RV sites, 7 with full hookups; 45-ft RV limit. Tbls, toilets, cfga, drkg wtr, fish cleaning station. Fishing, swimming, boating(ld). Daily entry fee $3; $20 seasonal. 322-acre lake. 701-256-3964.

LAWTON (E)
Centennial City Park   FREE
In Lawton (pop. 30). Free. 1 RV site with elec; tent area. Nearby Lawton City Park has 3 free RV sites with elec. For info, 701/655-3641.

LEEDS (E)

Fireman's Memorial Park   FREE
From US 2 in town, N on 2nd St to Main St, then W (left) to the park between 1st Ave SW & 2nd Ave SW. Free. 10 sites. 6/1-9/15. 12 sites (8 with 4 pr of 15-amp elec). Tbls, flush toilets, cfga, drkg wtr, playground, shelter, sand volleyball.

LEMMON (SOUTH DAKOTA)

North Lemmon Lake   FREE
State Fishing Access Site
Five mi N of Lemmon, in North Dakota. Free. All year; 10-day limit. Primitive undesignated sites; no facilities. Fishing.

LINTON (E)

Beaver Creek Recreation Area $8
Corps of Engineers
Lake Oahe
From Linton, 16 mi W on SR 13; 1 mi S on SR 1804; on N side of Beaver Bay. $8 peak-season at 16 non-elec sites with federal senior pass; others pay $16 ($7 & $14 off-season). $10 peak-season with federal senior pass at 45 elec sites; others pay $20 ($8 and $16 off-season). Some pull-through. 5/1-9/30; 14-day limit. Tbls, toilets, cfga, drkg wtr, playground, dump, showers, picnic shelter, fish cleaning station. Boating(l), fishing, sand volleyball, nature trail.

LISBON (E)

Sheyenne National Grasslands   FREE
E of Lisbon on Hwy 27. 70,000-acre grassland. Primitive camping; no developed sites. Canoeing & fishing on Sheyenne River. Largest population in U.S. of prairie chicken; western white-fringed orchid.

Sheyenne State Forest   FREE
10 mi NW of Lisbon on CR 13. Free. All year; 14-day limit. Primitive undesignated camping. No facilities except cfga. Hiking trail, hunting, cross-country skiing. Only documented waterfall in North Dakota.

MANDAN (W)

Breien Centennial Park   FREE
Morton County Park
About 33 mi S of Mandan on Hwy 6 at Breien. Free. Primitive undesignated sites. 10-day limit. Tbls, toilet, cfga, no drkg wtr, shelter. Popular during hunting seasons.

Crown Butte Dam   FREE
Morton County Park
Off I-94 exit 147; W on county rd to lake. Free. Primitive undesignated sites. 10-day limit. Tbls, pit toilets, cfga, drkg wtr, shelter, fishing pier. Boating(ld), fishing.

Fort Abraham Lincoln State Park $12
7 mi S of Mandan on SR 1806. $12 at primitive off-season, $17 in-season); $20-$25 with elec. 14-day limit. 95 sites.

Tbls, flush toilets, cfga, drkg wtr, dump, showers, amphitheater, playground. Picnicking, shoreline fishing, hiking, snowmobiling, cross-country ski trails. Visitor center, reconstructed Indian village & infantry post; interpretive & cultural programs. 1,006 acres.

Graner Park Campground $8
Morton County Park
17 mi S of Mandan on SR 1806; at Lake Oahe. $8 for primitive camping; $18 with elec. All year; 10-day limit. 46 elec sites plus primitive sites. Tbls, pit toilets, cfga, drkg wtr, dump, playground, fish cleaning station. Boating(l), fishing, hiking. Former Corps of Engineers park.

Harmon Lake Recreation Area $8
Morton County Park
Morton County Water Resource District
8 mi N of Mandan at Hwy 1806 & CR 140. $8 at primitive sites, $18 at 23 new RV pads with elec. All year; 10-day limit. Tbls, pit toilets, cfga, drkg wtr, 2 beaches, playground. Under development as a multi-use recreation area. 8-mi hiking/biking trail. Plans include visitor center, bath houses, horseback riding area.

Little Heart Bottoms   FREE
(Schmidt Bottoms)
Morton County Park
13 mi S of Mandan on Hwy 1806 at Schmidt Bottoms Rd. Free. 15 primitive sites. All year; 10-day limit. Toilet, cfga, tbls, no drkg wtr. Boating(ld), fishing.

Sweet Briar Lake   FREE
Morton County Park
20 mi W of Mandan on I-94 to exit 134. Free. All year; 14-day limit. Numerous primitive sites around lake. All year; 10-day limit. Tbls, pit toilets, cfga, drkg wtr, 8 fishing piers. Boating(l), fishing, hunting.

MARION (E)

City Park Campground   FREE
On E side of Marion (pop 214). Free. All year. Undesignated sites with drkg wtr, elec, flush toilets, tbls, cfga, shelters, playground.

MARMARTH (W)

Marmarth City Park   FREE
7 mi E of the MT/ND state line on US 12 (Second Ave W at Fourth St S). Camp free, but $5 for elec. 5/1-10/30; 1-day limit. 10 sites. Tbls, flush toilets, cfga, drkg wtr, firewood, playground. Fishing, swimming nearby.

MAYVILLE-PORTLAND (E)

Willowood Campground $8
Mayville Park District
1 mi W of downtown area on Hwy 200 to 427-599 3rd St SW. $8. 20 RV sites; 25 tent sites. May-Oct. Drkg wtr,

16 elec hookups, 20 picnic tbls, 4 cfga, showers, toilets, shelter, dump, sewer. Swimming, fishing, boating. Unable to verify status for 2017.

MCCLUSKY (E)

Hoffer Lake Recreation Area $5
Bureau of Reclamation
Sheridan County Parks and Recreation
2 mi N of McClusky on 5th Ave NE; W on 7th St NE to lake. $10 at primitive sites, $20 with elec/wtr. All year; 14-day limit. 27 RV sites. Tbls, toilets, cfga, fishing pier, drkg wtr, no trash service. Boating(l), fishing.

MCGREGOR (W)

McGregor Dam Park $10
Williams County Water Resources District
1.5 mi S of McGregor on CR 21A/SR 50; W on access rd (16 mi N of Tioga). $10 at primitive sites, $15 with elec. Tbls, toilets, cfga, drkg wtr, fishing pier. Boating(l), fishing.

MEDORA (W)

Buffalo Gap $6
Little Missouri National Grasslands
7 mi W of Medora on I-94; N on CR 7263; 1 mi W on FR 726A. Two loops separated by tall hill. $6 during 5/15-11/15; free rest of year but no services or wtr. MD-LD; 14-day limit. 37 sites (no RV size limit). Tbls, flush toilets, cfga, drkg wtr, coin showers. Hiking/biking trails, fishing. Prairie dog town. 40 acres. Some traffic noise at Hidatsa loop from I-94.

Cottonwood Campground $7
South Unit
Roosevelt National Park
6 mi N of I-94 & Medora on paved rd. $7 with federal senior pass during about 5/1-9/30 ($3.50 rest of year); others pay $14 or $7 off-season. All year; 14-day limit. 76 sites, some pull-through. Tbls, flush toilets, cfga, drkg wtr. Nature program, visitor center. Limited service in winter. Museum. Entry fee $14 for 7 days; free with federal senior pass.

South Buffalo Gap Lake FREE
Little Missouri National Grasslands
7 mi W of Medora on I-94 to exit 18 (Buffalo Gap exit), then three-fourths mi S, 1 mi E, half mi N to lake. Free. Primitive dispersed camping; no facilities, no drkg wtr. Fishing, boaiting.

Sully Creek State Park $12
2.5 mi SE of Medora on gravel rd. $12. 5/15-12/1; 14-day limit. 33 primitive sites. Tbls, vault toilets, cfga, drkg wtr, corrals, coin showers, dump. Horseback riding($), canoeing, fishing, hiking trails. Corrals. 80 acres.

MERCER (W)

Blue Lake FREE
Wildlife Management Area
5 mi N of Mercer, then 2.5 mi W & half mi S in McLean County. Free primitive camping. All year; 10-day limit. Fishing. 13 acres.

MICHIGAN (E)

Michigan City Park FREE
From US 2, follow South St if arriving from the E or SR 35 from the W; N on SR 35/Jeanette Ave; W (left) on 3rd St (sign to park), pass red sandstone Catholic church to park; RV sites just E of fenced tennis courts. Free but donations encouraged to pay for elec. All year; no stay limit. 4 RV sites. Tbls, flush toilets, cfga, dump, sewer hookup, elect, playground, tennis court.

MONANGO (E)

City Park $10
In town (pop. 36). $10. 3 sites & tenting area. 1-night limit. Tbls, flush toilets, cfga, drkg wtr, elec, playground. Biking, volleyball, picnicking, playfield.

MOORETON (E)

City Park FREE
In town (pop 197) at 7876-7898 170th Av. Free primitive sites with drkg wtr, toilets, tbls, cfga, playground.

NAPOLEON (E)

Beaver Lake State Park $12
17 mi SE of Napoleon. $12 at primitive sites off-season. $17 in-season); $20-$25 with elec. 14-day limit. Tbls, flush toilets, cfga, drkg wtr, dump, showers, playground. Picnicking, fishing, swimming beach, hiking. 200 acres.

NEWBURG (W)

Newburg City Park
In town (pop 110) N of school. Closed for camping. Nearby Tommy Turtle City Park $20 with hookups.

NEW LEIPZIG (W)

City Campground $12
S side of Main in New Leipzig. $12 full hookups ($50 weekly, $175 monthly). 11 RV sites with 30/50-amp elec; tent camping area. Tbls, toilets, cfga, drkg wtr, dump. Volleyball, picnic area, golf area.

NEW ROCKFORD (E)

Archie & Jesse Campbell
Memorial Park & Campground $12
New Rockford Park District
N side of New Rockford at jct of SR 15 & US 281; at James River. $12 ($70 weekly). 5/1-9/30. 22 sites, 13 with elec. Tbls, flush toilets, cfga, drkg wtr, elec, pool, playground, showers. Tennis, fishing, boating, swimming. Formerly Kiwanis Park.

Eddy County Fairgrounds $10
SW of town. 701-947-2429. $10 for full hookups. Tbls, flush toilets, showers, drkg wtr. 701-947-2084.

NEW SALEM (W)
North Municipal Park $12
Half mi N of New Salem, three-fourths mi S of I-94, exit 27. $12. 5/15-9/30; 7-day limit. 16 sites (6 with elec). Tbls, flush toilets, cfga, drkg wtr. Picnicking, playground, golf nearby. Future planning includes updating to 12 elec/wrt sites, with fees of $15.

Fish Creek Dam   FREE
State Fishing Access Site
6 mi E of New Salem on CR 139; 10.5 mi S on CR 84; E on 46th St & S on 37th Ave to dam. Free. All year; 14-day limit. Primitive camping at 55-acre Fish Creek Lake. Pit toilets, cfga, no drkg wtr. Boating(l), fishing.

NEW TOWN (W)
4 Bears Casino RV Park   FREE
Three Affiliated Tribes
Fort Berthold Reservation
4 mi W of New Town on Hwy 23. Free primitive camping, $25 at 115 full-hookup sites ($550 monthly). 5/15-10/15. Drkg wtr, flush toilets, showers, store, dump. Swimming, boating(l), fishing.

Antelope Creek   FREE
Wildlife Management Area
12 mi NW of New Town in McKenzie County. Free primitive camping. All year; 10-day limit. No facilities. Boating, fishing, hunting. 964 acres. Leased from Corps of Engineers.

Bear Den Recreation Area   FREE
Three Affiliated Tribes
Fort Berthold Reservation
W of New Town on ND 23 to jct with ND 22; 12 mi S on ND 22. Free. 5/1-9/30; 14-day limit. 150 sites (RVs under 32 ft). Tbls, cfga, firewood, no drkg wtr. Boating(l); fishing; picnicking; swimming nearby.

Little Beaver Bay Recreation Area $10
Williams County Water Resources District
32 mi NW of New Town on SR 1804; 3 mi S to site (20 mi SE of Tioga); on N shore of Lake Sakakawea. $10 without elec, $15 with elec. 48 elec sites, 11 primitive sites. Tbls, toilets, cfga, drkg wtr, dump, fish cleaning station, shelter. Boating(l), fishing. 701-577-4500.

Pouch Point Bay and Recreation Area $10
Three Affiliated Tribes
Fort Berthold Reservation
16 mi S of New Town on SR 1804. $10. 11 RV sites with elec; tent camping area. 5/1-10/1. Tbls, cfga, drkg wtr, flush toilets, showers, dump, playground. Fishing, swimming, boating(ld). Unable to verify fees for 2017.

White Earth Bay $11
Montrail County Park
28 mi NW of New Town on Hwy 1804; 2 mi S, 1 mi E, 3 mi S, 3 mi E. $11 at 14 sites without hookups; $16 at 18 elec sites, $20 elec/wtr; $26 full hookups. Tbls, toilets, cfga, drkg wtr, playground. Boating(ld), fishing. Former Corps of Engineers park.

NIAGARA (E)
Niagara City Park   FREE
In SE corner of Niagara (pop 73). Free. 4 overnight RV sites with elec. Picnic shelter, ballpark. Historic Fort Totten Trail marker 4 mi E on Hwy 2. At field report, no businesses open except garage.

NOONAN (W)
Baukol-Noonan Campground   FREE
Divide County Recreation Area
3 mi E of Noonan on SR 5; 1 mi S on 102nd Ave NW; half mi W on 101st St NW. Donations suggested; camp free. 10 RV sites with elec; open tent area. Toilets, tbls, cfga, no drkg wtr, no trash service. Fishing, swimming, hiking, boating(ld). Unable to verify status for 2017.

Noonan Lions Campground $10
In town at 500 Main St. $10 ($50 weekly; $200 monthly). 5/15-10/15. 10 RV sites with elec; tent camping area. Tbls, toilets, cfga, drkg wtr, dump. Unable to verify status for 2017.

NORTHWOOD (E)
D. L. Campbell City Park $10
From Hwy 15, follow Raymond St to park on S end of town at 404 Old Hwy 15. $10 ($60 weekly). 5 RV sites with 20/30-amp & 50-amp elec/wtr (typically 65 ft). Tbls, flush toilets, cfga, drkg wtr, dump, shelters, pool, playground, dump, arboretum. Tennis, volleyball, swimming, sand volleyball. Tree identification on walking path. 20 acres.

OBERON (E)
City Park   FREE
In town (pop 105). Free primitive sites. Tbls, drkg wtr. Playground, shelter.

PARK RIVER (E)
Homme Dam $10
Walsh County Park
Follow signs 2 mi W of Park River on SR 17; at S branch of Park River near dam. $10 at 8 sites without elec; $15 at 15 elec sites, $25 full hookups. 4/1-11/1. Tbls, flush toilets, cfga, drkg wtr, showers, dump, fishing pier, beach. Boating(l), fishing, canoeing, waterskiing, swimming, biking/walking path. 200-acre lake. Non-campers pay $5 day use fee ($25 annual).

PARSHALL (W)

North City Park　　　　　　　　　　　　CLOSED
Qtr mi S of downtown on Hwy 37, just N of Rock Museum in town. Now closed to camping.

Parshall Bay Campground　　　　　　　　$11
Montrail County Recreation Area
2 mi S of SR 23 on SR 37; 10 mi W & S on winding county rd; at Lake Sakakawea. $11 at up to 50 sites without elec, $16 at 50 sites with elec ($20 elec/wtr, $24 full hookups). Weekly rates available. Tbls, flush toilets, cfga, drkg wtr, dump, fish cleaning station, showers. Boating(dl), fishing, playground, swimming.

PEKIN (E)

Pioneer City Park　　　　　　　　　　　$10
On NE side of Pekin (pop 80) at SRs 1 & 15, N on 2nd St for 2 blocks. $10 daily or $50 weekly. All year. 10 RV sites with elec; tent sites. Elec, drkg wtr, cfga, tbls, shelters. Boating & fishing nearby. Unable to verify fees for 2017.

PETTIBONE (E)

City Park　　　　　　　　　　　　　　$10
From SR 36 N of town, 1 mi S on 46th Ave SE, then E (right) on 3rd Ave North E to park. $10 donation requested without hookups; $15 with elec/wtr. All year; 14-day limit. Tent & 4 RV sites; 25-ft RV limit. Tbls, flush toilets, showers, cfga, drkg wtr, shelter. Boating, fishing.

PICK CITY (W)

Lake Sakakawea State Park　　　　　　　$12
1 mi N of Pick City. $12 at primitive sites off-season, $17 in-season; $20-$25 with elec. 14-day limit. 192 sites. Tbls, flush toilets, cfga, drkg wtr, dump, showers, marina, store, playgrounds, shelters, beach, amphitheater. Boating(ldr), fishing, picnicking, swimming. Knife River Indian Village National Historic Site nearby.

POWERS LAKE (W)

Lake Park Campground　　　　　　　　$6-8
1 mi E & qtr mi E of town a t lake. Donations of $6-8 suggested, $12.50 at lakeside. 5/1-10/1; 3-day limit. 5 RV sites elec($), and several tent sites. Drkg wtr, tbls, flush toilets, cfga, elec($), dump. Swimming, fishing, boating(l), tennis, basketball. Patrolled.

Lone Tree Municipal Park Campround　　$10
1 mi E of Powers Lake on SR 50; 1 mi S on access rd. $10. 5/1-10/1. 38 sites, 12 with elec. Tbls, toilets, cfga, drkg wtr, elec. Boating(l), swimming, fishing.

Smishek Dam City Park　　　　　　　　$8
Just NW of town off SR 50. $8. 5/1-10/1; 3-day limit. 30 primitive sites, 30 RV sites with elec. Tbls, toilets, cfga, drkg wtr, fishing pier. Boating(dl), fishing, swimming.

RAY (W)

Kota Ray Dam Campsite　　　　　　　　$10
Williams County Water Resources District
7 mi S of Ray on CR 17 (13th Drive NW). $10 at primitive sites; $15 with elec. 20 sites with 20/30-amp elec. Tbls, toilets, cfga, drkg wtr, fishing pier. Boating(l), swimming, fishing.

REEDER (W)

Reeder City Campground　　　　　　　　$8
From US 12, 4 blocks S on 3rd Ave E. From northbound SR 22, cross RR tracks & turn right on 2nd St; on SE side of Reeder. $8 for 11 RV sites with wtr/sewer; 3 poles with 50-amp elec. 5/1-10/1. Tbls, flush toilets, cfga, drkg wtr. Tennis, golf, playground.

REGENT (W)

Indian Creek Dam　　　　　　　　　　FREE
Hettinger County Park
State Wildlife Management Area
1.5 mi W of Regent, then 2 mi S, 2 mi W, 3 mi S. Free. Primitive undesignated camping Thurs-Mon; closed to camping Tues-Wed. Toilets, cfga, no drkg wtr. Fishing, hiking, swimming, boating(l). 196 acres.

RIVERDALE (W)

Deepwater Recreation Area　　　　　　FREE
Corps of Engineers
Lake Sakakawea
From Jct US 83, W on SR 37 (17 mi S of Parshall). Free. 4/1-9/30; 14-day limit. 30 primitive sites. Drkg wtr, pit toilets, tbls, cfga, pavilion. Picnicking, boating(l), pier, fishing.

Downstream Campground　　　　　　　$10
Corps of Engineers
Lake Sakakawea
Near Riverdale, below dam, W side of spillway. $10 with federal senior pass at 101 elec sites; others pay $20. 16 primitive tent sites, $14. 5/15-9/15; 14-day limit. RV limit in excess of 65 ft. Tbls, flush toilets, cfga, drkg wtr, showers, shelter, amphitheater, fish cleaning station. Wheelchair access. Fishing, boating(l), interpretive programs, playground, horseshoe pits.

Wolf Creek Recreation Area　　　　　　$12
Corps of Engineers
Lake Sakakawea
2 mi E of Riverdale on Hwy 200; 3 mi N on gravel rd, following signs. $12. 5/15-9/15; 14-day limit. 67 primitive sites. Tbls, pit toilets, cfga, drkg wtr, dump, fish cleaning station. Boating(l), fishing, horseshoe pits, volleyball.

ROCKLAKE (E)

Rocklake City Park　　　　　　　　　FREE
In town (pop 101) 8 primitive sites, 1 with elec. All year. Cfga, drkg wtr, 2 shelters, tbls, playground, pit toilets.

ROLETTE (E)

Rolette Municipal RV Park $12
At W side of town next to airport on SR 66. $12 with full hookups ($200 monthly). 8 sites. Tbls, toilets, cfga, drkg wtr, CATV, phone. Swimming pool. Reservations 246-3511.

ROLLA (E)

Armourdale Lake   FREE
Wildlife Management Area
9 mi E & 1.5 mi N of Rolla in Towner County. Free primitive camping. All year; 10-day limit. No facilities. Fishing, boating, hunting. 23 acres.

ROSEGLEN (W)

White Shield Recreation Area   FREE
Three Affiliated Tribes
Fort Berthold Reservation
8 mi S of Roseglen on CR 7. Free. 4/1-10/31. About 200 undesignated campsites; 2 elec sites. Tbls, pit & flush toilets, cfga, drkg wtr, kitchen shelter. Picnicking, hiking, playground. No attendance. Indian ceremonies held in area.

RUGBY (E)

Pierce County Fairgrounds   FREE
From US 2, N on state route 0.75 mi, past RR tracks, then E (right) on 1st St NE & N (left) on 2nd Ave NE; E (right) on 2nd St NE to arched fairground entrance. Free. All year. Policed. 25 sites with 20/30-amp elec, some 50-amp. 2-night limit. Tbls, flush toilets, cfga, drkg wtr, playground, shower.

SAINT JOHN (E)

Dion Lake   FREE
State Game & Fish Department
11 mi W of St. John on Hansboro Rd; 2 mi N just past access to Streitzel Lake; 2 mi E on 108th St NE. In Turtle Mountains. Free. Undesignated sites; 14-day limit. Toilets, tbls, cfga, no drkg wtr. Swimming, fishing, boating (l). 82-acre lake.

Gravel Lake   FREE
State Game & Fish Department
5 mi W of St. John on SR 43; 1 mi N to lake; in Turtle Mountains. Free. Undesignated primitive sites; 14-day limit. Toilets, tbls, cfga, fishing pier. Swimming, fishing, boating(l - elec mtrs).

Hooker Lake   FREE
Wakopa Wildlife Management Area
State Game & Fish Department
9 mi W of St. John on SR 43; N, then E on secondary rds to lake. Free. Primitive, undeveloped campsites. All year; 10-day limit. Toilets, tbls, cfga, no drkg wtr. Trout fishing, canoeing, swimming, boating(l); idle boat speed only. Secluded.

Lake Upsilon   FREE
State Game & Fish Department
8 mi W of St. John in Turtle Mountains. Free. All year; 10-day limit. Undesignated primitive sites. Toilets, tbls, no drkg wtr. Fishing, boating, swimming.

SAINT THOMAS (E)

Hager Municipal Park   FREE
St. Thomas Park Board
In town (pop 528) 2 blocks W of Main St. Free overnight at last report for unlimited tent & self-contained RV camping, 6 full-hookup sites for $200 monthly, $1,500 annual rates. Tbls, toilets, cfga, drkg wtr, shelters. Lighted ball diamonds, playground, tennis, horseshoes, recreation hill. Unable to verify overnight fee status for 2017.

SHEYENNE (E)

Hendrickson Municipal Park   FREE
1.5 mi W of Sheyenne (pop 204). Free overnight at last report. All year. 6 elec RV sites. Tbls, toilets, cfga, drkg wtr, playground. Unable to verify status for 2017.

Warsing Dam   FREE
Wildlife Management Area
E of Sheyenne on Sheyenne River. Free primitive camping. All year; 10-day limit. No facilities. Boating, fishing. 86 acres.

STANLEY (W)

Stanley Campground $10
On US 2 across from the courthouse, at N edge of Stanley. $10 for RVs without hookups ($60 weekly); $15 with elec ($100 weekly); $6 tents ($31 weekly). 13 total sites (12 with elec). 5/1-10/1; 7-day limit. Policed. Tbls, flush toilets, cfga, firewood, dump, drkg wtr, showers, playground. Lake. Picnicking; fishing; swimming; golf nearby; 2 tennis courts.

STANTON (W)

Sakakawea Park $8
On E side of Stanton at Knife River. $8 without hookups, $15 at 8 elec RV sites; also primitive camping area. Drkg wtr, elec, flush toilets, cfga, tbls, dump, showers. Swimming, fishing, boating, fish cleaning station. Park with playground, horseshoes, tennis nearby. Fish cleaning station, RV dump & fresh wtr on W side of town.

STEELE (E)

Steele Municipal Park   CLOSED
3 mi W of Steele (pop. 715) on old US 10; S of I-94 Interchange. Now closed to overnight camping.

STRASBURG (E)

Cattail Bay Recreation Area   FREE
Corps of Engineers
Lake Oahe
From Strasburg, about 12 mi W on gravel 89th St SE; 0.5

mi S on Main Ave; 6 mi W on 90th St SW; 2 mi S on SR 1804; 3 mi W on 91st St SW; at SE shore of lake's Cattail Bay. Free. All year; 14-day limit. 6 primitive sites. Pit toilets, cfga, tbls, no drkg wtr. Nearest dump station 15 mi. Boating(l), fishing.

TAPPEN (E)

Alkaline Lake   FREE
Wildlife Management Area
11 mi S & 1 mi E of Tappen in Kidder County. Free. All year; 10-day limit. Primitive camping. No facilities. Boating, fishing. 47 acres.

TIOGA (W)

Tioga City Park $10
3 mi N of US 2 on ND 40, in Tioga; on NE edge of town. $10 primitive sites, $17 elec, $20 elec/wtr; 8 full hookups $25. All year; 7-day limit. Policed. 25 sotal RV sites, undesignated tent sites. Tbls, flush toilets, cfga, firewood, drkg wtr, playground, showers, dump. Swimming; picnicking; fishing; golf nearby. 701-664-2158.

Tioga Dam   FREE
State Fishing Access Site
1 mi N & W of Tioga off Hwy 10. Free primitive camping at 4 sites with elec. Tbls, toilets, cfga, fishing pier. Boating(l), fishing.

TOLNA (E)

Tolna Dam   FREE
1 mi S of Tolna (pop. 166) on CR 23A; 2 mi E on SR 15. Free but donations requested. 10 primitive RV sites; some elec. Tbls, cfga, toilets. Boating(ld), fishing.

Tolna City Park $10
In town on Lee Ave. $10 (or $25 for 3-day weekend, $40 weekly). RV sites with elec. Tbls, toilets, cfga, drkg wtr. Reservations: 701-230-0356.

TOWNER (E)

Towner City Park   FREE
2 mi N of town. Free. Spring-fall. 4 free RV sites with elec/wtr & primitive tent sites. Drkg wtr, tbls, cfga, elec, toilets, dump, playground, shelters. Tennis, sand volleyball.

Towner Recreation Area   FREE
Mouse River State Forest
2 mi N of Towner on paved co rd. Free. All year. 8 undesignated sites. Tbls, toilets, cfga, firewood, dump, drkg wtr, playground. Fishing; boating; picnicking; golf nearby.

Vagabond Recreation Area   FREE
Mouse River State Forest
10 mi N of Towner on paved co rd. Free. All year. Undesignated sites. Tbls, toilets, cfga, firewood, drkg wtr. Snowmobiling; picnicking; fishing.

TRENTON (W)

Trenton Lake Recreation Area $10
Williams County Parks
In Trenton just off Hwy 1804. $10 without hookups, $15 with full hookups. MD-LD. Tbls, flush toilets, cfga, drkg wtr, playground, fishing pier, fish cleaning station, beach. Fishing, boating(l), volleyball, horseshoes, swimming.

UNDERWOOD (W)

Pioneer City Park   FREE
Inquire locally for directions; on E side of town, CR 14. Free. All year. Policed. Undesignated RV sites; 50 tent sites. Tbls, toilets, cfga, playground, no elec. Picnicking, swimming, fishing, boating.

McLean County Fairgrounds $10
In Underwood on US 83. $10 at RV sites with 30-amp elec. Tbls, flush toilets, showers, drkg wtr. 442.5481.

UPHAM (W)

Upham Municipal Park   Donations
S of Upham (pop. 130) business district at 111 C Ave S. Camp free, but donations of $10 requested to cover elec costs. 4 RV sites with full hookups, 6 with elec/wtr. Drkg wtr, toilets, tbls, cfga. Playgrounds. J. Clark Salyer National Wildlife Refuge nearby. 701-263-7798.

VALLEY CITY (E)

Lake Ashtabula   FREE
Baldhill Dam
State Fishing Access Site
10 mi N of Village City. Free. All year; 10-day limit. Primitive undesignated sites; no facilities. Boating(rl), fishing.

Moon Lake   FREE
State Fishing Access Site
2 mi W of Valley City to SR 1. 5.5 mi S on SR 1; 4 mi W; 2 mi N. Free. All year; 10-day limit. Primitive undesignated sites; no facilities. Fishing for trout, smallmouth bass, catfish.

WALHALLA (E)

Tetrault Wood State Forest   FREE
Half mi S of Walhalla on W side of Hwy 32. Free. All year. Dispersed camping in the forest. No facilities. Pembina River.

WATFORD CITY (W)

CCC Campground $6
Little Missouri National Grasslands
14 mi S of Watford City on US 85; 1 mi W on Rd 842 just S of Long X bridge over Little Missouri River. $6 during 5/15-11/15; free rest of year but no wtr or services. Badlands terrain. All year; 14-day limit. 38 gravel sites; some pull-through; no RV size limit. Tbls, toilets, cfga, drkg wtr, trash service. Hunting, horseback riding. Newly remodeled & expanded camp. Multi-use trails.

Juniper Campground $10
North Unit
Roosevelt National Park
15 mi S of Watford City on Us 85; 6 mi W (4 mi from North Unit park entry). $7 with federal senior pass during 5/1-9/30 ($3.50 rest of year but no wtr services); others pay $14 in-season, $7 rest of year. All year; 14-day limit. 50 sites, some pull-through. Tbls, flush toilets, cfga, drkg wtr, dump. Limited facilities in winter. Hiking, scenic drive, nature program. Entry fee $14 for 7 days, free with federal senior pass.

WILDROSE (W)
Municipal Park $10-12
On S. Main St in Wildrose. $10-$12. 6 RV sites. Drkg wtr, toilets, cfga, tbls, elec, dump. Nearby historic school with golf, tennis, horseshoes. In 2017 all sites rented to oil pipeline workers.

WILLISTON (W)
Blacktail Dam Campsite $10
Blacktail Dam Association
Williams County Water Resources District
17 mi N of Williston on Hwy 85, 5.5 mi W on CR 10; 1 mi N on access rd. $10 without elec, $15 with elec. 5/1-9/1. 32 RV sites with elec. Tbls, flush toilets, cfga, drkg wtr, dump, playground, coin laundry. Swimming boating(l), fishing.

Lewis & Clark State Park $12
19 mi SE of Williston on Hwy 1804; at Lake Sakakawea. $12 at primitive sites off-season, $17 in-season); $20-$25 with elec. 14-day limit. 80 sites. Tbls, flush toilets, cfga, drkg wtr, dump, showers, shelters, marina, store, beach, amphitheater, fish cleaning station. Nature trail, picnicking, boating(ldr), swimming, fishing, cross-country skiing, snowmobiling. New concession store.

WILLOW CITY (W)
Willow City Campground FREE
In town on Hwy 60 (pop 163). Free. May-Oct. 2 RV sites with elec. Tbls, toilet, cfga, drkg wtr.

WILTON (W)
Wilton City Park $7
Wilton Park Board
On Burleigh Rd, E across RR tracks. $7 without hookups, $12 with elec. All year (no wtr 11/1-3/31). Policed. Undesignated sites, 8 sites with 20/30-amp elec/wtr. Tbls, toilets, cfga, dump, drkg wtr, playground.

WING (W)
Lake Mitchell
Burleigh County Park Donations
1 mi W of Wing on SR 36; 2 mi N. Donations suggested; camp free. Open primitive camping area; 14-day limit. Tbls, toilets, drkg wtr, cfga, beach, fishing pier. Boating, fishing, swimming.

WOODWORTH (E)
Woodworth City Park $5
In center of Woodworth (pop. 50); follow signs; on N. Main St. $5. 5/1-10/30. 15 tent sites; 3 RV sites (1 with elec). Tbls, toilets, cfga, drkg wtr, showers.

YORK (E)
Village Park FREE
From US 2, N on Main St to park; on left across from post office. Free. 2 sites with elec that did not work during field check. Tbls, cfga, drkg wtr, showers, flush toilets, playground. Picnicking. Pop. 26.

ZAP (W)
Beaver Creek Bay Recreation Area $7
Lake Sakakawea
Zap Park Board
Corps of Engineers
12 mi N of Zap. $7. All year; 14-day limit. Primitive camping. Tbls, toilets, cfga, no drkg wtr. Boating(ld), fishing. Managed by city; owned by corps of engineers.

Beaver Creek FREE
Wildlife Management Area
12 mi N of Zap in Mercer County. Free primitive camping. No facilities. Fishing, boating, hunting. 298 acres. Leased from Corps of Engineers.

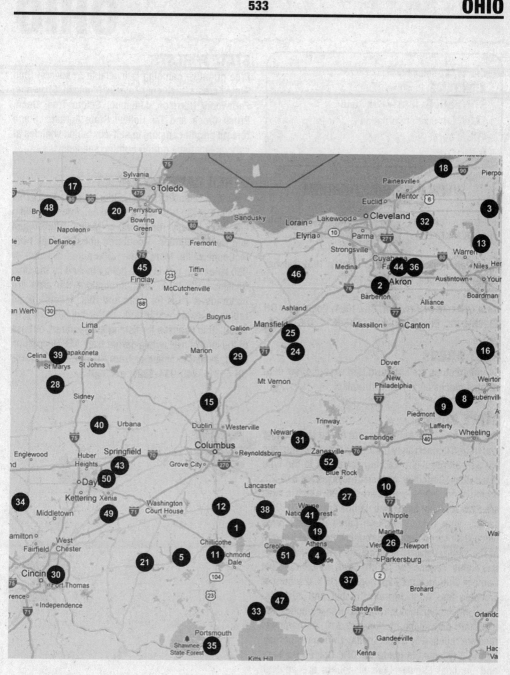

OHIO

> **CAPITAL:** Columbus
> **NICKNAME:** Buckeye State
> **STATEHOOD:** 1803 – 17th State
> **FLOWER:** Scarlet Carnation
> **TREE:** Buckeye
> **BIRD:** Cardinal

WWW.OHIO.GOV/TOURISM

Toll-free numbers for travel information: 1-800-BUCKEYE.

Ohio State Parks Information Center, 1952 Belcher Dr, C-3, Columbus, OH 43224-1386.

Ohio Division of Tourism, Box 1001, Columbus, OH 43266-0101. Phone 800-BUCKEYE. 614-466-8844.

REST AREAS
Overnight stops are not permitted except at six designated places on the Ohio Turnpike.

STATE PARKS
No entry fees are charged except at the Muskingum Watershed Conservancy District parks. Camping fees are $18-39 per night, varying according to the type of services. Generally, non-electric sites are $19-23; premium non-electric sites are $19-26; electric sites are $23-30; most horsemen camps are $18-20. Ohio seniors with Golden Buckeye cards pay half price when they camp Sunday through Thursday; holders of the card receive 10% discounts Friday and Saturday nights. Anyone can purchase an annual Cardinal Camper Club membership, good for 15% discount of camping fees April through October and 20% discount November through March. Non-campers can use state park dump stations for $10. All campsite fees are reduced by $1 on Sunday through Thursday, and that discount is made BEFORE Golden Buckeye and Cardinal Camper Club discounts are applied. Thus, a $20 site, reduced to $19 on weekdays, costs seniors (60 or older) with the Golden Buckeye card $9.50 per night. RV limit, 35 ft. Limit 14-day stay. Where there is camping year-round, winter fees are reduced by $2. Pet camping is now permitted in designated areas of 36 state park campgrounds and in most horseman camps.

STATE FORESTS
Free primitive camping is available at several Ohio State Forests, including Zaleski, Mohican, Shawnee, Fernwood, Harrison, Maumee, Scioto Trail, Dean, Brush Creek and Tar Hollow State Forests. Some forests permit camping in self-contained vehicles at various locations during hunting seasons.

OTHER CAMPING AREAS
American Electric Power Recreation Land. This consists of 30,000 acres of lakes, forests, rolling hills and grassy meadows in Meigs, Muskingum and Noble Counties -- centered about 8 miles from McConnelsville. More than 1,500 acres of water or 350 lakes and ponds have been stocked by the Ohio Division of Wildlife, and throughout the area are hundreds of sites for tents and RVs. Toilets, picnic tables, drinking water and shelter houses are provided. Ohio licenses for fishing are required, but use of the land is free with a permit from AEP Recreation Land, available online or from PO Box 158, Beverly, OH 45715. 740-984-2321, ext 3902.

ADELPHI (1)

Tar Hollow State Park　　　　　$10.50
10 mi S of Adelphi off SR 327 on Tar Hollow Rd. $10.50 Golden Buckeye fee weekdays for non-elec sites ($12 for elec). Others pay $22 & $25 weekends; $2 lower off-season (no showers 1/1-3/31); 14-day limit. 11 non-elec sites, 71 elec. Tbls, showers, pit toilets, cfga, drkg wtr, dump, beach. Fishing, hunting, hiking trails, bridle trails, mountain biking trails, backpacking trails, mini golf, swimming, nature center, boating (lr), volleyball, basketball, horseshoes, playground, game room. GPS: 39.215338, -82.4694

AKRON (2)

Portage Lakes State Park　　　　　$10.50
15 mi S of SR 619. $10.50 Golden Buckeye fee weekdays at 68 non-elec sites (others pay $21 weekdays, $22 weekends); fees $2 lower in winter. All year at 20 non-elec sites; 14-day limit. Tbls, pit toilets, cfga, drkg wtr, dump, no showers, shelter, beach. Hiking trails (5 mi), winter sports, boating(rdl), fishing, hunting, swimming, volleyball, horseshoes, basketball. GPS: 40.581579, -81.3229

ANDOVER (3)

Pymatuning State Park　　　　　$10.50
2 mi E of Andover on SR 85; 3 mi S on Pymatuning Lake Rd. $10.50 Golden Buckeye fee weekdays at 21 non-elec sites (others pay $21 weekdays, $22 weekends); $12 Golden Buckeye fee weekdays at 331 elec sites, $13 at premium sites. (all others pay $21 & $24). 4/1-10/31; 14-day limit. Flush toilets, cfga, drkg wtr, tbls, showers, coin laundry, beach, nature center, playgrounds. Swimming, boating(rdl), fishing, hiking trails, basketball, volleyball. GPS: 41.344989, -80.295846

ATHENS (4)

Strouds Run State Park　　　　　$9
3 mi E of Athens off US 33 on CR 20. $9 Golden Buckeye fee weekdays at 78 non-elec sites (others pay $18 weekdays, $19 weekends); fees $2 lower in winter. All year; 14-day limit. Tbls, cfga, drkg wtr, pit toilets, dump, waste drains, beach. Hiking trails (13 mi), boating(lrd), fishing, hunting, swimming, scuba diving. Pet camping area. Dow Lake. GPS: 39.211707, -82.211743

BAINBRIDGE (5)

Pike Lake State Park　　　　　$10
6 mi S of US 50 on Pohs Hill Rd. $10 Golden Buckeye fee weekdays at elec sites (others pay $20 weekdays, $21 on weekends); fees $2 lower in winter. All year; 14-day limit. 80 sites with elec. Tbls, pit toilets, cfga, drkg wtr, dump, store, nature center, beach, concessions. Hiking trails (3.5 mi plus 3 mi of Buckeye Trail), boating(lr), canoeing(r), fishing, swimming, nature programs, basketball, horseshoes, disc golf. Pet camping sites. 13-acre lake. GPS: 39.936, -83.1360

BLOOMINGDALE (8)

Hidden Hollow Camp　　　　　FREE
Fernwood State Forest
SE of Bloomingdale on CR 25 and CR 26; two camping areas. Free. All year; 14-day limit. 22 sites. Tbls, pit toilets, cfga, drkg wtr. Hunting, fishing, hiking (3 mi), nature trail, trap shooting, 3 shooting ranges. 3,023 acres. GPS: 40.334, -80.764.

CADIZ (9)

Harrison State Forest　　　　　FREE
3 mi N of Cadiz, E of SR 9; 2 primitive camps. Free. All year; 14-day limit. 7 sites at Ronsheim family camp; 20 sites at Trailriders horse & family camp. Tbls, toilets, cfga, drkg wtr. Fishing ponds, hunting, bridle trails (4 mi), hiking trails (4 mi), rifle range, trap shooting, shooting range. 1,345 acres of restored strip mine area. GPS: 39.1531132, -84.7532817.

CALDWELL (10)

Wolf Run State Park　　　　　$9.50
4 mi N of Caldwell on SR 821. $9.50 Golden Buckeye fee weekdays at 67 non-elec sites, $10 weekdays at non-elec premium locations, $11.50 weekdays at elec sites (others pay $19, $20 & $23 weekdays; $20, $21 & $24 weekends). Fees $2 lower in winter. All year; 14-day limit (54 elec sites open in winter). Tbls, pit toilets, cfga, drkg wtr, showers, dump, coin laundry, shelter, beach. Hiking (2.5 mi of the Buckeye Trail), winter sports, boating(ld), fishing, hunting, scuba diving, swimming. Pet camping area. GPS: 39.473607, -81.322443

CHILLICOTHE (11)

Great Seal State Park　　　　　$9
US 23 N of Chillicothe to Delano Rd; E to Marietta Rd; S to park. $9 Golden Buckeye fee weekdays at 15 primitive non-elec sites (others pay $18 weekdays, $19 on weekends. 3/1-11/30; 14-day limit. Tbls, pit toilets, cfga, drkg wtr. Bridle trails (17 mi), hiking & biking trails, cross-country skiing, hunting, volleyball, basketball, horseshoes, disc golf. Pet camping area. GPS: 39.225907, -82.56175

Scioto Trail State Park　　　　　$9
9 mi S of Chillicothe on US 23; half mi E on SR 372. $9 Golden Buckeye fee weekdays at 15 non-elec RV sites, $11 weekdays at 40 elec sites (others pay $18 & $22 weekdays, $19 & $23 on weekends); fees $2 lower in winter. All year; 14-day limit. Pit toilets, cfga, drkg wtr, tbls, dump, no showers. Fishing, hiking, boating(l), canoeing, winter sports, basketball, horseshoes, volleyball. GPS: 39.13178, -82.554536

Tar Hollow State Forest　　　　　FREE
E of Chillicothe on Charleston Pk, then S on Poe Run Rd to horseman camp. Free. All year; 14-day limit. 48 sites. Tbls, toilets, cfga, no drkg wtr. Hiking & bridle trails. 16,120 acres. GPS: 39.2103, -82.4618

CIRCLEVILLE (12)

A.W. Marion State Park $9

6 mi NE of Circleville off US 22 & SR 122. $9 Golden Buckeye fee weekdays at 29 non-elec sites; $11 weekdays at 29 sites with elec (others pay $18 & $22 weekdays, $19 & $23 on weekends). 3/26-11/1; 14-day limit. Tbls, pit toilets, cfga, drkg wtr, dump, no showers, playground. Hiking trails (6 mi), boating(ldr), hunting, fishing, volleyball, basketball, horseshoes. Pet camping area. 145-acre Hargus Lake. GPS: 39.373771, -82.524414

CORTLAND (13)

Mosquito Lake State Park $10

2 mi S of Cortland on SR 5; 2.5 mi W on SR 305; on S shore of Mosquito Lake. Golden Buckeye weekday fees are $10 at 16 non-elec sites, $12 at 218 elec sites (others pay $20 & $24 weekdays, $21 & $25 on weekends); fees $2 less in winter at 27 elec sites, 8 non-elec. All year; 14-day limit. Tbls, flush & pit toilets, showers (closed 11/1-4/1), cfga, drkg wtr, dump, playground. Boating(ldr), hiking trails, hunting, swimming, fishing, horseshoes, volleyball. GPS: 41.21653, -80.445453

DEERFIELD (14)

Mill Creek $7
Corps of Engineers
Berlin Lake

From I-76 exit 54, 5.5 mi S on SR 534; 2 mi E on US 224; 0.8 mi S on Bedell Rd. $7 base with federal senior pass at 241 non-elec sites; others pay $14 base, $18 for premium locations ($9 with senior pass). At 107 elec sites, $10 base with senior pass, $12 for 50-amp elec; others pay $20 & $24. MD-LD; 14-day limit. RV limit in excess of 65 ft. Tbls, flush toilets, cfga, drkg wtr, dump, showers, beach, playground, picnic shelter, amphitheater. Swimming, boating(l), fishing, interpretive programs, canoeing, kayaking. GPS: 41.00694, -80.99806

EAST LIVERPOOL (16)

Beaver Creek State Park $9

11 mi N of East Liverpool on SR 7; half mi E. $9 Golden Buckeye fee weekdays at 44 non-elec sites (others pay $18 weekdays, $19 on weekends); fees $2 lower in winter at 50 non-elec sites. All year; 14-day limit; limited facilities in winter. Tbls, pit toilets, cfga, drkg wtr, dump, playground, no elec or showers. Pet camping area. Hunting, fishing, canoeing(r), horseshoes, hiking, bridle trails. Reconstructed pioneer village. GPS: 40.425352, -80.355998

FAYETTE (17)

Harrison Lake State Park $9

5 mi SW of Fayette off US 20. $9 Golden Buckeye fee weekdays at 21 non-elec sites (others pay $18 weekdays, $19 on weekends); fees $2 lower in winter, but no showers or dump 11/1-4/1; 14-day limit. Tbls, flush toilets, showers, cfga, drkg wtr, dump, coin laundry,

beach. Canoeing, sailing, boating(l), hiking trails (4 mi), nature programs, volleyball, basketball, horseshoes, winter sports, fishing, swimming. Pet camping area. GPS: 41.382682, -84.221795

GENEVA (18)

Geneva State Park $10

2 mi N of Geneva on SR 534; 1 mi E on SR 531; at 4499 Padanarum Rd in Geneva-on-the-Lake. $10 Golden Buckeye fee weekdays at non-elec sites (others pay $20 weekdays, $21 on weekends). Fees $2 lower in winter, but showers closed 11/1-4/15. 7 non-elec sites. Elec sites $29 weekends. Tbls, flush toilets, showers, cfga, drkg wtr, coin laundry, fish cleaning station, beach. Swimming, boating(l), fishing, hiking trails, basketball, sand volleyball. Pet camping area. GPS: 41.5176, -80.583459

GLOUSTER (19)

Burr Oak Cove $6.50
Wayne National Forest

4 mi N of Glouster on SR 13; half mi E on CR 107; at NW tip of Burr Oak Reservoir. $6.50 with federal senior pass during 5/15-9/30 (others pay $13); $5 with senior pass rest of year but no drkg wtr (others pay $10). 14-day limit. 19 primitive sites; no RV size limit. Tbls, toilets, cfga, drkg wtr. Hiking trails. GPS: 39.3235, -82.0320

Burr Oak State Park $9.50

4 mi N of Glouster on SR 13; 2.5 mi E on county rd. $9.50 Golden Buckeye fees weekdays at 78 non-elec sites (others pay $10 weekdays, $20 on weekends). $11.50 Golden Buckeye fee weekdays at elec sites (others pay $23 weekdays, $24 weekends). $12.50 Golden Buckeye fees weekdays at elec sites; others pay $23 weekdays, $24 weekends. Open 4/1-10/31; 14-day limit. Tbls, flush toilets, showers, cfga, drkg wtr, dump, coin laundry, nature center, beach, concession. Bridle trails (8 mi), backpack trails (29 mi), hiking trails (10 mi), boating(ld), hunting, fishing, swimming, nature programs. GPS: 39.322993, -82.21588

GRAND RAPIDS (20)

Mary J. Thurston State Park $9

W of Grand Rapids on SR 65. $9 Golden Buckeye fee weekdays at non-elec sites, $10 weekdays at premium non-elec sites (others pay $18 & $20 weekdays, $19 & $21 on weekends); fees $2 lower in winter at non-elec sites. All year; 14-day limit. 16 RV sites without elec. Tbls, toilets, cfga, drkg wtr, no showers. Boating(ld), hiking trails, fishing, winter sports, horseshoes. GPS: 41.244296, -83.53041

HILLSBORO (21)

Rocky Fork State Park $10.50

5 mi E of Hillsboro on SR 124; on W shore of Rocky Fork Lake. Golden Buckeye fees are $10.50 weekdays at non-elec sites ($12 at premium locations); others pay $21 & $24 weekdays, $22 & $25 on weekends. Golden

Bucky fees $12 weekdays at elec sites; others pay $24 weekdays, $25 on weekends. 4/1-12/5; 14-day limit. Tbls, flush toilets, showers, cfga, drkg wtr, dump, coin laundry, playgrounds, beach. Pet camping sites. Hunting, hiking trails, mountain biking trails, swimming, boating(ldr), volleyball, winter sports, mini golf, tetherball, basketball, horseshoes. GPS: 39.111139, -83.292492

IRONTON (22)

Iron Ridge Campground $6.50
Lake Vesuvius Recreation Area
Wayne National Forest
Half mi off SR 93 about 10 mi NE of Ironton; on E side of lake. $6.50 at non-elec sites with federal senior pass (others pay $13); $11.50 with senior pass at elec sites (others pay $18). 4/15-11/1; 14-day limit. Free during deer hunting season, but no utilities. 34 sites up to 45 ft. Tbls, pit toilets, cfga, drkg wtr, beach. Horseback riding, backpack trail, hiking trails, boating(ldr), swimming, fishing. GPS: 38.61448 -82.62440

LOUDONVILLE (24)

Mohican State Park $10
5 mi SW of Loudonville off SR 97. Golden Buckeye fees are $10 weekdays at 33 non-elec sites, $12.50 at premium non-elec sites (others pay $20 & $25). Fees $2 lower in winter, but no showers 11/1-4/1; 14-day limit. 35 non-elec sites. Tbls, pit & flush toilets, cfga, drkg wtr, showers, dump, coin laundry, store, restaurant, shelters, nature programs, pool. Hiking trails (9 mi), tubing, canoeing(r), fishing, swimming, biking(r), volleyball, basketball, horseshoes. Waterfall, sandstone rock shelter, covered bridge. GPS: 40.361363, -82.1748

LUCAS (25)

Malabar Farm State Park $9
10 mi SE of Mansfield on SR 603. $9 Golden Buckeye fees weekdays at 15 non-elec sites (others pay $18 weekdays, $19 on weekends). 3/31-11/30; 14-day limit. Tbls, pit toilets, cfga, drkg wtr, no showers, no dump. Bridle trails (12 mi), hiking trails (4 mi), winter sports, fishing, nature programs. Pet camping area; Malabar Inn restaurant. GPS: 40.384279, -82.23019

MARIETTA (26)

Haught Run Campground FREE
Wayne National Forest
Covered Bridge Scenic Byway
17 mi NE of Marietta on SR 26, then right at covered bridge & follow camping signs right again. Free. All year; 14-day limit. 4 sites. Tbls, toilets, cfga, drkg wtr. Fishing, canoeing on Little Muskingum River. Sites were closed temporarily in 2014; check current status before arrival. GPS: 39.53422, -81.22319

Hune Bridge Campground FREE
Wayne National Forest
Covered Bridge.Scenic Byway
14 mi NE of Marietta on SR 26, then right at covered bridge. Free. All year; 14-day limit. 3 sites just below bridge. Tbls, toilets, cfga, drkg wtr, no drkg wtr. Fishing & canoeing in Little Muskingum River, hiking trails. GPS: 39.5105, -81.2506

Lane Farm Campground FREE
Wayne National Forest
Covered Bridge Scenic Byway
5 mi NE of Marietta on SR 26. Free. All year; 14-day limit. 4 sites. Tbls, toilets, cfga, no drkg wtr. Fishing & canoeing at Little Muskingum River (canoe access pond). GPS: 39.4358, -81.3588

Leith Run Recreation Area $7.50
Recreation Area
Wayne National Forest
18 mi N of Marietta on SR 7; at Ohio River. $7.50 with federal senior pass at non-elec sites (others/ pay $15); $12.50 with senior pass at elec sites (others pay $21). 4/1-9/15; 14-day limit. 17 RV/tent sites (no RV size limit); undesignated tent sites. Tbls, flush toilets, showers, cfga, drkg wtr, dump, lantern posts. Boating(ld), wildlife study area. GPS: 39.4463, -81.1521

Ring Mill Campground FREE
Wayne National Forest
Covered Bridge Scenic Byway
22 mi NE of Marietta on SR 26, then follow signs to the right. Free. All year; 14-day limit. 3 primitive undesignated sites. Tbls, toilets, cfga, shelter, no drkg wtr. Fishing & canoeing on Little Muskingum River. GPS: 39.6082, -81.1224

MCCONNELSVILLE (27)

Parksite #A Hook Lake FREE
American Electric Power
Approx 10.5 mi NE of McConnelsville on OH 78; approx half mi N on OH 284; approx 2.3 mi NE on OH 83; entrance on right side of rd. Free. All year; 14-day limit. Sites. Toilets, drkg wtr, shelter house, parking area. Boating; picnicking; fishing; hiking; hunting; trapping. No swimming or scuba diving. Get free camping permit & map online from Ohio Power Co. GPS: 39.133754,-77.890482.

Parksite #B FREE
American Electric Power
Approx 1.7 mi SW of Reinersville on OH 78; approx half mi N on paved, all-weather rd. Free. All year; 14-day limit. Sites. Toilets, firewood, drkg wtr. Fishing; boating; hiking; hunting; trapping. No swimming or scuba diving. Free camping permit required.

Parksite #C Sand Hollow   FREE
American Electric Power
Approx 10.5 mi NE of McConnelsville on OH 78; approx 2.5 mi N on OH 284; qtr mi NE on unpaved all-weather rd. Free. All year; 14-day limit. Sites. Tbls, drkg wtr, shelter house, firewood, cfga. Boating; picnicking; fishing; hiking; hunting; trapping. No swimming or scuba diving. Free camping permit required.

Parksite #D Sawmill Road   FREE
American Electric Power
Approx 10.2 mi NE of McConnelsville on OH 78; approx half mi N on OH 284; approx 3.5 mi NE on OH 83; .8 mi S on Haul Rd. Free. All year; 14-day limit. Sites. Toilets, shelter house, drkg wtr. Boating; picnicking; fishing; hiking; hunting; trapping. No swimming or scuba diving. Free camping permit required.

Parksite #F R.V. Crews   FREE
American Electric Power
Approx 10 mi NE of McConnelsville on OH 78; on left side of rd. Free. All year; 14-day limit. Sites. Tbls, toilets, cfga, shelter house, information center, parking area, firewood, drkg wtr. Boating; picnicking; fishing; hiking; hunting; trapping. Free camping permit required.

Parksite #G Magpie Grove   FREE
American Electric Power
Approx 10.2 mi NE of McConnelsville on OH 78; approx half mi N on OH 284. Free. All year; 14-day limit. Sites. Tbls, toilets, cfga, drkg wtr, parking area, firewood. Boating; picnicking; fishing; hiking; hunting; trapping. No swimming or scuba diving. Free camping permit required.

Parksite #H Woodgrove   FREE
American Electric Power
Approx 2 mi SW of Reinersville on OH 78; approx 3.2 mi N on Haul Rd (parallel to railroad tracks). Free. All year; 14-day limit. Sites. Toilets, drkg wtr, parking area, firewood. Fishing; boating; hiking; hunting; trapping. Free camping permit required.

Parksite #L   FREE
American Electric Power
Approx 10.5 mi NE of McConnelsville on OH 78; approx half mi N on OH 284; approx half mi NE on OH 83; approx 1.1 mi SE on unpaved, all-weather rd. Free. All year; 14-day limit. Sites. Tbls, toilets, cfga, firewood, drkg wtr. Boating; picnicking; fishing; hiking; hunting; trapping. No swimming or scuba diving. Free camping permit required.

Parksite #N Keffler Kamp   FREE
American Electric Power
Approx 10.2 mi NE of Mcconnelsville on OH 78; approx half mi N on OH 284; approx 4 mi NE on OH 83; approx 1.24 mi S on CR 27. Free. All year; 14-day limit. Sites. Tbls, toilets, cfga, firewood, parking area. Hiking; picnicking; fishing;

boating; trapping; hunting. No swimming or scuba diving. Free camping permit required.

Parksite #Q   FREE
American Electric Power
Approx 10.5 mi NE of McConnelsville on OH 78; approx half mi N on OH 284; approx 3.5 mi NE on OH 83; approx .7 mi NW on Haul Rd. Free. All year; 14-day limit. Sites. Toilets, drkg wtr, firewood. Boating; fishing; hiking; hunting; trapping. No swimming or scuba diving. Free camping permit required.

Parksite #R   FREE
American Electric Power
Approx 2 mi SW of Reinersville on OH 78; approx half mi NE on Ual Rd; approx half mi N on Haul Rd, which turns into unpaved, all-weather rd. Free. All year; 14-day limit. Sites. Drkg wtr, toilets, firewood, cfga. Fishing; boating; hiking; hunting; trapping. No swimming or scuba diving. Free camping permit required.

MINSTER (28)
Lake Loramie State Park $10
3 mi SE of Minster on SR 362. Golden Buckeye fees are $10 weekdays at non-elec sites, $11 at premium locations (others pay $20 & $22 weekdays, $21 & $23 on weekends). Golden Buckeye fees are $12 weekdays at elec sites (others pay $24 weekdays, $25 on weekends). Fees reduced $2 in winter, but no showers11/10-4/1; 14-day limit. 15 non-elec sites, 115 with elec. Tbls, flush toilets, cfga, drkg wtr, showers, dump, shelters, beach. Hiking trails, winter sports, boating(ld), fishing, hunting, swimming, nature programs. GPS: 40.2218, -84.2029

MT. GILEAD (29)
Mt. Gilead State Park $10.50
Just E of Mt. Gilead on SR 95. Golden Buckeye fees are $10.50 weekdays at 59 elec sites (others pay $21 weekdays, $22 on weekends); fees $2 lower in winter. 4 primitive sites also available (no fee specified). All year; 14-day limit. Tbls, pit toilets, cfga, drkg wtr, waste drains. Pet camping sites. Boating(ldr), nature programs, hiking trails, fishing, winter sports, fishing. GPS: 40.32517, -82.48449

MT. REPOSE (30)
Stonelick State Park $9.50
10 mi E of Mt. Repose on SR 727 (Woodville Pike); half mi S on Newtonsville Rd. Golden Buckeye fees are $9.50 weekdays at 6 non-elec sites, $11.50 weekdays at 108 elec sites (others pay $19 & $23 weekdays, $20 & $24 on weekends); fees $2 lower in winter, but showers closed 11/1-4/1; 14-day limit. Tbls, flush toilets, cfga, drkg wtr, showers, dump, playground. Pet camping sites. Boating(l), fishing, hunting, hiking trails, swimming beach, volleyball, basketball, horseshoes, tetherball, biking(r). GPS: 39.13632, -84.4011

NASHPORT (31)
Dillon State Park $9
2 mi S of Nashport off SR 146. Golden Buckeye fees are $9 weekdays at 12 non-elec sites (others pay $18 weekdays, $19 on weekends); $12 at elec sites (others pay $24 weekdays, $25 on weekends; fees $2 less in winter, but showers closed 12/7-4/9; 14-day limit. Tbls, flush toilets, showers, cfga, drkg wtr, dump, coin laundry, store, shelter, beach, sports center. Hiking & bridle trails, boating(rdl), waterskiing, hunting, fishing, swimming, trap & skeet shooting, rifle & pistol ranges, indoor firing range, winter sports, basketball, volleyball, tennis, nature center, shuffleboard. Pet camping area. GPS: 40.12001, -82.73816

NEWBURY (32)
Punderson State Park $10.50
2 mi E of Newbury on SR 87. $10.50 for Ohio seniors with Golden Buckeye cards at 12 non-elec sites; others pay $21 weekdays, $22 on weekends; fees $2 less in winter. All year; 14-day limit. Tbls, drkg wtr, flush toilets, showers, cfga, dump, nature center. Hiking trail, swimming beach, winter sports, golf, boating(ldr), fishing, basketball, volleyball, horseshoes, shuffleboard. GPS: 41.2724, -81.1238

OAK HILL (33)
Jackson State Park $10.50
2 mi W of Jackson, following signs. $10.50 Golden Buckeye fee weekdays at 34 sites with 30/50-amp elec (others pay $20 weekdays, $22 on weekends); fees $2 lower in winter at 2 sites. All year; 14-day limit. Tbls, cfga, drkg wtr, dump (closed in winter), playground, beach. Boating(lr), fishing, volleyball, horseshoes. GPS: 38.541725, -82.35545

OXFORD (34)
Hueston Woods State Park $9.50
5 mi NW of Oxford on SRs 732 & 177; at Acton Lake. Golden Buckeye fees are $9.50 weekdays at 236 non-elec sites with pit toilets & $11.50 weekdays at elec sites (others pay $19 & $24 weekdays, $20 & $25 on weekends). Fees $2 lower in winter, but showers closed 12/1-4/1; 14-day limit. Tbls, toilets, cfga, drkg wtr, dump, coin laundry, nature center, beach, concession, pool. Bridle trails, hiking trails, canoeing, winter sports, golf, boating(ldr), fishing, swimming, nature programs, horse rental, mountain biking, volleyball, mini golf, horseshoes, fossil hunting. Pet camping sites. GPS: 39.342332, -84.443619

PORTSMOUTH (35)
Shawnee State Park $9
8 mi SW of Portsmouth on US 52; 6 mi on SR 125. Golden Buckeye fees are $9 weekdays at non-elec sites & $11.50 weekdays at 107 sites with elec (others pay $18 & $23 weekdays, $19 & $24 on weekends); fees $2 lower in winter. All year; 14-day limit. Tbls, showers, flush toilets, cfga, drkg wtr, dump, shelters, beach, concession. Hiking trails(5 mi), boating(ldr), hunting, fishing, swimming,

nature programs, golf, volleyball, basketball, horseshoes, tennis. Pet camping area. A 58-site horse camp is nearby at Bear Lake on state forest land. GPS: 38.4601, -83.1344

RAVENNA (36)
West Branch State Park $11
About 6 mi E of Ravenna on SR 5; 1 mi S on access rd; on N shore of Michael Kirwin Reservoir. Golden Buckeye fees are $11 weekdays at 14 non-elec sites; (others pay $22 weekdays, $23 on weekends; fees $2 lower in winter, but showers closed11/15-4/1; 14-day limit. Flush toilets, showers, cfga, drkg wtr, tbls, coin laundry, playground, dump, beach. Hunting, fishing, boating(ldr), hiking & bridle trails, swimming, nature programs, volleyball, winter sports. GPS: 41.8388, -81.81982

REEDSVILLE (37)
Forked Run State Park $9
3 mi SW of Reedsville on SR 124. Golden Buckeye fees are $9 weekdays at 64 non-elec sites, $11 weekdays at 81 elec sites (others pay $18 & $22 weekdays, $19 & $23 on weekends). Fees $2 lower in winter, but showers closed 12/7-4/1; 14-day limit. Tbls, flush toilets, cfga, drkg wtr, 50-amp elec($), showers, dump, coin laundry, beach. Hiking trails, disc & mini golf, volleyball, horseshoes, winter sports, boating(lr), hunting, fishing, swimming. Pet camping area. GPS: 39.61116, -81.4728

ROCKBRIDGE (38)
Hocking Hills State Forest FREE
S of Rockbridge on SR 374 & forest rds; primitive campground off Laurel Twp. Rd 231. Free. All year; 14-day limit. 23 primitive sites at horseman's camp. Tbls, toilets, cfga, no drkg wtr (except for horses). Hiking & bridle trails, rock climbing. 9,267 acres. GPS: 39.4306225, -82.5387701.

ST. MARYS (39)
Grand Lake $10.50
St. Marys State Park
2 mi W of St. Marys on SR 703. Golden Buckeye fees are $10.50 weekdays at 28 non-elec sites (others pay $21 weekdays, $22 on weekends). Fees $2 lower in winter, but showers closed 11/10-4/1; 14-day limit. Tbls, flush toilets, cfga, drkg wtr, showers, dump, coin laundry, beach, shelters. Hiking & horseback riding at canal towpath (40 mi). Snowmobiling, boating(ldr), swimming, mini golf, basketball, volleyball, horseshoes, hunting, waterskiing, fishing, nature programs. GPS: 40.3137, -84.2815

ST. PARIS (40)
Kiser Lake State Park $9
2 mi W of St. Paris on US 236; 6 mi N on SR 235. $9 Golden Buckeye fee weekdays at 108 non-elec sites & $11 weekdays at 10 elec sites (others pay $18 & $22 weekdays, $19 & $23 on weekends); fees $2 lower in winter for 10 elec sites, 79 non-elec. All year; 14-day limit. Tbls, pit toilets, cfga, drkg wtr, dump, no showers, shelters, beach, fishing

piers. Hiking trails, winter sports, boating(lrd), sailing, hunting, fishing, swimming, volleyball, basketball, horseshoes. GPS: 40.111, -83.57487

SHAWNEE (41)

Stone Church Horse Camp $7
Wayne National Forest
About 5 mi N of Shawnee on SR 93; E on access rd. $7 with federal senior pass; others pay $14. 4/15-12/15; 14-day limit. 8 sites (up to 45 ft) with covered paddock, cfga. Toilets, tbls, drkg wtr. Tent camping also available at Stone Church Trailhead; it has portable toilet & trash cans. Hiking, horseback riding. GPS: 39.60980, -82.24123

SPRINGFIELD (43)

Buck Creek State Park $11
About 2 mi E of Springfield on Hwy 40; 2 mi N on North Bird Rd; 1 mi E on Buck Creek Lane; on W shore of C.J. Brown Lake. Golden Buckeye fees are $11 weekdays at 22 non-elec sites (others pay $22 weekdays, $23 on weekends). Fees $2 lower in winter, but showers closed 11/17-4/1; 14-day limit. Tbls, flush toilets, showers, cfga, drkg wtr, dump, fishing pier, beach. Pet camping areas. Boating(l), fishing, hunting, hiking trail, snowmobile & bridle trails, swimming, nature center, biking(r), volleyball, basketball, tetherball, horseshoes, shuffleboard. GPS: 39.58756, -83.43538

STOW (44)

Silver Springs $12
Stow Municipal Park
From SR 8, right on Graham Rd, left on Darrow Rd (Rt 91), right on Stow Rd, right on Call Rd, then left on Young Rd to campground. $12 ($10 for local residents). 4/15-10/31; 10-day limit. 27 sites. Tbls, flush toilets, cfga, drkg wtr, showers, dump, playground, shelters. Swimming($), fishing, hiking, fitness trail, paddleboats(r), tubing(r), volleyball, biking trail, museum.

VAN BUREN (45)

Van Buren State Park $9
1 mi SE of Van Buren off US 25. Golden Buckeye fees are $9 weekdays at 19 non-elec sites & $10.50 weekdays at 10 elec sites (others pay $18 & $21 weekdays, $19 & $22 on weekends). The same fee structure applies for 28 non-elec & 3 elec sites at horseman camp. Fees $2 lower in winter. All year; 14-day limit. Tbls, pit toilets, cfga, drkg wtr, no showers, dump. Bridle trails, hiking trails, boating, fishing, hunting, nature center, volleyball, horseshoes. GPS: 41.7598, -83.381716

WELLINGTON (46)

Findley State Park $11
5 mi S of Wellington on SR 58; E on access rd. $11 weekdays for Ohio seniors with Golden Buckeye cards at 181 non-elec sites (others pay $22 weekdays, $23 on weekends). Fees $2 lower in winter, but showers closed

11/3-4/11; 14-day limit. Tbls, flush toilets, showers, dump, drkg wtr, cfga, game room, beach, playground. Hiking trail, hunting, boating(lr), fishing, swimming, nature center, basketball, volleyball. GPS: 41.1269982, -82.2068238.

WELLSTON (47)

Lake Alma State Park $9
1 mi N of Wellston on Hwy 93; 1 mi NE on Hwy 349. Golden Buckeye fees are $9 weekdays at 10 non-elec sites & $11 weekdays at 71 elec sites (others pay $18 & $22 weekdays, $19 & $23 on weekends); fees $2 lower in winter. All year; 14-day limit. Tbls, flush toilets, cfga, drkg wtr, showers, dump, beach, playground. Fishing, swimming, boating(lr), horseshoes, paved biking(r) & walking trail, volleyball, basketball. GPS: 39.83939, -82.305464

WEST UNITY (48)

Indian Meadow Plaza   FREE
Turnpike Commission
On I-80, W to milepost 21. Free. All year; 1-night limit. 10 spaces for self-contained RVs (RVs under 30 ft). Tbls, flush toilets, dump, food, phone, drkg wtr, gas, dump station. Picnicking. Open 4pm to 10am. Stone-surfaced parking area. Hardees restaurant.

WILMINGTON (49)

Cowan Lake State Park $11
10 mi S of Wilmington on US 68; 2 mi W on SR 350; 1 mi N on access rd; on SE shore of Cowan Lake. Golden Buckeye fees are $11 weekdays at 17 non-elec sites (others pay $22 weekdays, $23 on weekends); fees $2 lower in winter, but showers closed 11/10-3/31. Tbls, flush toilets, showers, drkg wtr, cfga, dump, coin laundry, beach. Pet camping sites. Boating(ldr), fishing, hunting, hiking, swimming, biking(r), basketball, volleyball, mini golf. GPS: 39.23026, -83.54005

YELLOW SPRINGS (50)

John Bryan State Park $9
2 mi E of Yellow Springs on SR 343 & SR 370. Golden Buckeye fees are $9 weekdays at 50 non-elec sites & $11 weekdays at 10 elec sites (others pay $18 & $22 weekdays, $19 & $23 on weekends); fees $2 lower in winter. All year; 14-day limit. Tbls, pit toilets, cfga, drkg wtr, dump, shelters. Hiking trails (10 mi), fishing, nature programs, hunting, canoeing, rock climbing. Clifton Gorge State Nature Preserve nearby. GPS: 39.472616, -83.511875

ZALESKI (51)

Lake Hope State Park $9
3 mi NE of Zaleski on SR 278. Golden Buckeye fees are $9 weekdays at 141 non-elec sites & $11 weekdays at 46 sites with elec (others pay $18 & $22 weekdays, $19 & $23 on weekends); fees $2 lower in winter, but showers closed 1/15-4/1. All year; 14-day limit. Tbls, pit toilets, cfga, drkg wtr, showers, dump, coin laundry, shelter, nature center,

beach, concession. Hiking trails (13 mi; Zaleski State Forest backpack trailhead), winter sports, boating(l), fishing, swimming, nature programs. Pet camping area. GPS: 39.2022, -82.2119

Zaleski State Forest   FREE
E of Zaleski on forest rds, this 26,000-acre forest has several camping areas -- a seasonal hunter's camp, a 16-site primitive horseman's camp & 10 remote back-country sites. Headquarters on SR 278 near Zaleski. Free. All year; 14-day limit. Tbls, toilets, cfga. Bridle & hiking trails, shooting range. GPS: 39.1534, -82.2357.

ZANESVILLE (52)
Blue Rock State Park $8
6 mi SE of Zanesville off SR 60; on CR 45. Golden Buckeye fees are $8 weekdays at 97 non-elec sites (others pay $16 weekdays, $17 on weekends). 5/22-11/2; 14-day limit. Tbls, pit toilets, cfga, drkg wtr, showers, dump, shelter, beach. Hiking trails (3 mi), boating(l), fishing, swimming. Pet camping area. GPS: 39.485897, -81.505579

Muskingum River Parkway $8
Lock & Dam 11
State Park
27 mi N of Zanesville on CR 49; off SR 60 at Ellis Lock. $8 Golden Buckeye fee weekdays at 20 primitive sites without elec & $8.50 weekdays for premium locations (others pay $16 & $17 weekdays, $17 & $18 on weekends). 4/1-12/15; 14-day limit (fees $2 lower in winter). Tbls, pit toilets, cfga, drkg wtr. Boating(l), fishing, hiking trails. Pet camping area. GPS: 39.37566, -81.5138

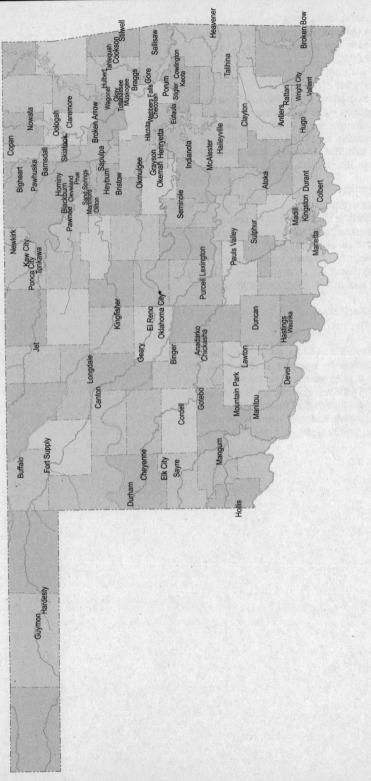

OKLAHOMA

WWW.TRAVELOK.COM

Toll-free number for travel information: 800-652-6552.

Tourism and Recreation Department, PO Box 52002, Oklahoma City, OK 73152. 405-230-9400 or 800-652-6552.

Dept of Wildlife Conservation, 1801 N Lincoln, Oklahoma City, OK 73152; 405-521-3851.

REST AREAS
Overnight stops in self-contained RVs are permitted.

STATE PARKS
RV camping without hookups at a low cost no longer is available at Oklahoma's state parks. Fees of $12 for primitive sites apply only to tent camping; RV sites are much higher. Dept of Tourism and Recreation, 800/654-8240.

Oklahoma Department of Wildlife Conservation properties
Camping (free) is limited to 14 days except at areas open only to hunter camping for special season. Camping on those areas is limited to two days longer than the period which the hunter/camper is authorized to hunt. Camping is permitted only in areas listed in this chapter. All camping on these properties is primitive; no facilities are provided. Camping areas are meant to accommodate fishermen and hunters using the properties.

Salt Plains National Wildlife Refuge, Route 1, Box 76, Jet, OK 73749.

Tishomingo National Wildlife Refuge, PO Box 248, Tishomingo, OK 73460.

Bureau of Indian Affairs, Eastern Oklahoma Development District, PO Box 1367 , Muskogee, OK 74401; or Bureau of Indian Affairs, Anadarko Area Office, PO Box 368, Anadarko, OK 73005.

OUACHITA NATIONAL FOREST
Camping is available without cost except in developed campgrounds. All camping areas are on a

CAPITAL: Oklahoma City
NICKNAME: Sooner State
STATEHOOD: 1907 – 46th State
FLOWER: Mistletoe
TREE: Redbud
BIRD: Scissor-Tailed Flycatcher

first-come, first-served basis, with a 14-day limit. 501-321-5202.

CORPS OF ENGINEERS
In the Tulsa District, camping fees are charged according to three classifications of campgrounds: Class A sites are those having flush toilets, showers, paved roads, sanitary dump stations, designated tent or RV spaces, trash containers and potable water; Class B areas have similar facilities except flush toilets or showers are not provided; Class C areas have basic sanitary facilities, designated tent or RV spaces, trash containers and potable water. Campers are exempt from $5 day-use charges.

For the best information available about Corps of Engineers campgrounds, contact us for your own cop of *Camping With the Corps of Engineers* ($17.95 plus $5 shipping), 800-272-5518.

ANADARKO

Randlett City Park $10
From jct with US 281 in Anadarko, W on US 62 (becoming westbound EW 1340 Rd); 1 block N on SW 8th St, then W on SW Oklahoma Ave to park; at Washita River. $10 ($5 for seniors). All year; 21-day limit. 35 sites, 14 with elec. Tbls, toilets, cfga, drkg wtr, playground, elec, dump. Fishing, horseshoes. GPS: 35.0745062, -98.2606076

ANTLERS

Lake Ozzie Cobb FREE
State Fishing Lake
Department of Wildlife Conservation
About 10 mi E of Antlers on SR 3 to just past Rattan; 2 mi N on Cloudy Rd; 1 mi N on gravel rd to lake. All year. Primitive camping at 116-acre lake. 30-ft RV limit. Toilets, tbls, cfga, no drkg wtr. Fishing, boating(l).

ATOKA

Atoka Rest Area FREE
Confederate Memorial Museum
1 mi N of Atoka on Hwy 69; near museum. All year; 1-night limit. Free. Primitive undesignated sites for self-contained RVs. Tbls, drkg wtr.

Fred's Fish Camp FREE
Municipal Park
5 mi N of Atoka on US 69, past Stringtown; half mi W on access rd. Free. Primitive, undeveloped camping area; no facilities. Boating (l), fishing.

Lake Atoka
Wildlife Management Area FREE
12 mi N of Atoka on US 69. Free. All year. 1 designated primitive area; no facilities. At 6,000-acre lake. Fishing, hiking, waterskiing, boating(l).

Old 43 Landing Municipal Park FREE
8 mi N of Atoka on US 69, past Stringtown; 2 mi W on SR 43, across lake; qtr mi SE on access rd. Free. Primitive, undeveloped camping area; no facilities. Boating(l), fishing, swimming beach. Lake Atoka.

BARNSDALL

Birch Cove A Recreation Area $10
Corps of Engineers
Birch Lake
From Barnsdall at jct of SR 11 & 8th St, 3.1 mi S on 8th St (becoming CR 2409), across spillway, then 0.7 mi W on Birch Cove Rd, following signs. $10 with federal senior pass at 85 elec sites (no wtr hookups); others pay $20. 4/1-10/31; 14-day limit. RV limit in excess of 65 ft; 5 pull-through sites. Tbls, flush toilets, cfga, drkg wtr, dump, beach, fishing pier, amphitheater, change house, handicap fishing area, playground, showers, 2 picnic shelters. Boating(l), fishing, swimming.

Birch Cove B Recreation Area $10
Corps of Engineers
Birch Lake
From Barnsdall at jct of SR 11 & 8th St (becoming CR 2409), across spillway, then 0.7 mi W on Birch Cove Rd, following signs. $10 with federal senior pass at 12 elec/wtr sites; others pay $20. All year; 14-day limit. Tbls, pit toilets, cfga, drkg wtr, showers, dump, beach, playground. Hiking, fishing, swimming, hiking, boating(l). Fishing pier, bech, showers, flush toilets, playground at Birch Cove A open to registered campers.

Candy Creek FREE
State Wildlife Management Area
6 mi SE of Barnsdall on SR 11 to just S of Wolco; E on co rd to WMA entrance. Two parking areas on northbound access rds, and one 1.5 mi from entrance. South entrance E on SR 11 from Avant, then N on CR N3908. Free. Primitive camping for fishermen and hunters only in designated areas; 14-day limit. Stream fishing. 3,658 acres.

Twin Cove Recreation Area $10
Corps of Engineers
Birch Lake
From Barnsdall, 1.5 mi S on 8th St (becoming CR 2409); right on lake access rd before spillway. $10. Open 4/1-9/30; 14-day limit. 11 non-elec sites. Tbls, pit toilets, cfga, drkg wtr, beach, playground, change house. Boating(dl), fishing pier, hiking, waterskiing, swimming, nature trail, picnic shelters($).

BIGHEART

Whippoorwill Unit FREE
Hulah Lake State Wildlife Management Area
N of Bigheart on SR 99 to WMA's headquarters; E on access rds. 2 camping areas: one near mouth of Birch Creek, the second at mouth of Cotton Creek, with public boat launch nearby at wildlife development unit. Free. Only fishermen/hunter primitive camping permitted in designated areas; 14-day limit. Lake is 3,600 acres, 62-mi shoreline; WMA is 16,141 acres. Deer & waterfowl hunting excellent. Big catfish.

BINGER

Fort Cobb FREE
State Wildlife Management Area
Fort Cobb Lake
4 mi SW of Binger on SR 142; 4 mi S on SR 146 to Albert; W on co rds. Free. Only fishermen & hunter primitive camping is permitted in designated areas; 14-day limit. 2,623-acre lake and 3,500-acre WMA boast of some of the best hunting areas in state and excellent fishing. Deer, quail, rabbit, turkey abound, and up to 20 million crows descend on area each winter. Game refuge attracts 60,000 nesting ducks. Boat ramps at Lemmons Area, Fort Cobb State Park and West Side Area.

BLACKBURN

Blackburn Section   FREE
Keystone Lake
State Wildlife Management Area
Arkansas River
4 mi E of Blackburn on co rds to WMA entrance on Arkansas River W shore NW of Keystone Lake. Free. Hunter & fisherman primitive camping is permitted only within 50 yds of public use rds. WMA is 16,537 acres.

BRAGGS

Pumpkin Center Camp   FREE
Camp Gruber Public Hunting Area
Gruber State Wildlife Management Area
N of Braggs on SR 10 to WMA entrance; 4 mi E on Hilltop Rd; 4 mi S on North South Rd to camp near Pumpkin Center Pond. Free. Only primitive hunter camping permitted. Camp only in designated areas during open hunting season; 14-day limit. Well known for top deer yields. Fishing at nearby Greenleaf Lake. Combined Gruber & Cherokee Wildlife Management Areas 55,515 acres.

BRISTOW

(See Heyburn listing)
Northeastern Section   FREE
Lake Heyburn
State Wildlife Management Area
9 mi N of Bristow on SR 43; 2 mi E on SR 33; 1 mi S on access rd to WMA entrance (just W of Heyburn State Park). Free. Only fishermen & hunter primitive camping permitted in designated areas; 14-day limit. 1,070-acre lake noted for bass, catfish, sunfish & crappie fishing. The 4,615-acre WMA is popular for duck, goose, quail and squirrel hunting.

Western Section   FREE
Lake Heyburn State Wildlife Management Area
7 mi N of Bristow on sR 43; 2 mi E on access rd to WMA entrance. Ask directions to camping area. Free. Only hunter & fishermen primitive camping in designated areas; 14-day limit. Boat ramps at Heyburn State Park, Heyburn Recreation Area & Sheppards Point.

BROKEN ARROW

Bluff Landing Campground $7
Corps of Engineers
Newt Graham Lake
Arkansas River Lock & Dam #18
From Broken Arrow, 12.7 mi E on 71st St; left (N) on 3695th E Ave to S shore of Verdigris River oxbow. $7 with federal senior pass at 7 non-elec sites; others pay $14; 25 elec/wtr sites, $9 with senior pass for 30-amp, $10 for 50-amp (others pay $18 & $20). All year; 14-day limit. During 11/1-3/31, some sites available at same rates. Tbls, flush toilets, cfga, drkg wtr, dump. Boating(l), fishing.

BROKEN BOW

Broken Bow   FREE
State Wildlife Management Area
About 21 mi N of Broken Bow on US 259; 3 mi E on co rds from Herman (just S of Bethel) to lake. WMA is along E shore of Mountain Fork River arm of Broken Bow Lake, adjacent to W edge of McCurtain County Wilderness Area. Free. Hunter & fishermen camping only within 50 yds of designated public rds; 14-day limit. Noted for largemouth bass. Boat ramp at nearby Holly Creek.

BUFFALO

Doby Springs City Park $10
W of Buffalo on Hwy 64 at municipal golf course. $10 for seniors with elec; others pay $15. 18 RV sites. Tbls, toilets, cfga, drkg wtr, hookups, playground, grey wtr dump. Fishing pond, golf, nature trails.

CANTON

Beaver Dam Camps   FREE
Canton Lake State Wildlife Management Area
2 mi W of Canton on SR 51; 4 mi N on co rd; 3 mi N on co rd; 1 mi N to camp, on S bank of North Canadian River near its entry into Canton Lake. Second camp is 1 mi farther W; third camp is 2 mi W. Free. Only fishermen and hunter primitive camping is permitted. 14-day limit.

Big Bend Recreation Area $8.50
Corps of Engineers
Canton Lake
1.8 mi W of Canton on SR 51; 4 mi N on paved N2460 Rd; 0.1 mi right (E) on E0620 Rd, then left (N) into campground at W shore of lake. 2 camping areas. At Loop A, primitive sites $8.50 with federal senior pass; others pay $17. Loop A elec/wtr sites $11 with senior pass for 30-amp, $12 for 50-amp; others pay $22 & $24. At Loop B, primitive sites $8.50 with senior pass; others pay $17. Loop B's 42 elec/wtr sites $11 with senior pass; others pay $22. 4/1-10;31; 14-day limit. During Nov & early March, some sites may be open & free without amenities. 45-ft RV limit. Tbls, flush & pit toilets, cfga, drkg wtr, dump, playground, shelter($). Fishing, boating(ld), waterskiing. Non-campers pay self-deposit $5 day use fees for boat ramps.

Blaine Park $10
Corps of Engineers
Canton Lake
Three-fourths mi W of Canton on SR 51; 1.7 mi N on SR 58A, below dam. $10 at 16 primitive sites ($5 with federal senior pass). 4/1-10/31; 14-day limit. Some sites open & free off-season but no utilities (pit toilets). Tbls, flush & pit toilets, cfga, drkg wtr, playground, no showers. Boating(l), fishing, swimming, hiking, ball field. Note: During 2013, park was closed for work on auxiliary spillway; still closed in 2017, expected open 2018; check current status with lake office before arrival; 580-886-2989.

Canadian Recreation Area $10.50
Corps of Engineers
Canton Lake
0.7 mi W of Canton on SR 51; 1.5 mi N on SR 58A; 0.8 mi W on secondary rd. Loop B, $10.50 with federal senior pass during 4/15-10/31 at 56 elec (no wtr hookups) sites; others pay $21; lower rates rest of year but no wtr services (pit toilets). At 21 elec/wtr sites, $12 with federal senior pass during 4/15-10/31; others pay $24; lower rates off-season but no wtr services (pit toilets). 10 sites have 50-amp elec in-season. 2 group camping areas with elec. RV limit in excess of 65 ft. Non-campers pay day use fee for boat ramp. Tbls, flush toilets, cfga, drkg wtr, showers, dump, elec($), picnic shelter. Boating(dl), fishing. 2-night minimum stay required on peak weekends. Note: 10 Loop B sites closed until March 31, 2018, due to auxiliary spillway work.

Eastern Dam Camp   FREE
Canton Lake State Wildlife Management Area
4 mi N of Canton on SR 58; 2 mi W on SR 58A to designated camp below dam. Free. Only fishermen and hunter primitive camping is permitted; 14-day limit. Sandy Cove Recreation Area (Corps of Engineers) nearby.

North Canadian River Camp   FREE
Canton Lake State Wildlife Management Area
17 mi NW of Canton on co rds; N to camp on S bank of North Canadian River. Free. Only fishermen & hunter primitive camping is permitted; 14-day limit.

Sandy Cove Recreation Area $10
Corps of Engineers
Canton Lake
From Canton, 0.7 mi W on SR 51; 5 mi N on SR 58A; left (N) on access rd; at SE shore of lake, North Canadian River. $10 with federal senior pass at 35 elec sites (no wtr hookups); others pay $20. 4/15-10/31; 14-day limit. Not open off-season. 40-ft RV limit. Tbls, flush toilets, cfga, drkg wtr, showers, beach, playground, picnic shelter. Swimming, fishing, swimming.

Western Dam Camp   FREE
Canton Lake State Wildlife Management Area
Half mi W of Canon on SR 51; 2.2 mi N & NW on SR 58A, then S of Canton dam to camp on E side of Canadian River. Free. Only hunter & fishermen primitive camping permitted; 14-day limit. Nearby Blaine Park has boat ramp, picnic area, toilets.

CHATAUQUA (KANSAS)
Hog Pen Units   FREE
Hulah Lake State Wildlife Area
3 mi S of Chatauqua on R 99; W on co rds to 7 camping areas. Their general locations are on Caney River arm near Caney River Park; at the mouth of Pond Creek; on Caney River arm at Boulanger Landing; at the state line E of Cedar Creek; at the state line W of Cedar Creek; on Caney Creek arm half mi W of Cedar Creek mouth, and on Caney Creek arm at the mouth of Buck Creek. Free. Only fishermen & hunter primitive camping permitted in designated areas; 14-day limit. Lake is 3,600 acres; 62-mi shoreline; WMA is 16,141 acres. Deer & waterfowl hunting excellent. Big catfish.

Turkey Creek Unit   FREE
Hulah Lake State Wildlife Area
2 mi S of Chatauqua on SR 99; 4 mi SE to Turkey Creek arm of Hulah Lake; cross bridge, camp on the right, on E shore of arm. Free. Only fishermen & hunter primitive camping is permitted in designated areas; 14-day limit. Boat launch at Turkey Creek Public Use Area at mouth of Turkey Creek.

CHECOTAH
Belle Starr Recreation Area $9.50
Corps of Engineers
Eufaula Lake
From I-40 S of Checotah, 7 mi S on US 69 to SR 150 jct; 2 mi E Texanna Rd (E1140 Rd); 2 mi S on N4200 Rd (Belle Starr Rd), following signs; on right. $9.50 base with federal senior pass at 111 elec/wtr sites; others pay $19 base, $22 for 50-amp elec ($11 with senior pass). 4/1-9/30; 14-day limit. RV limit in excess of 65 ft; 36 pull-through sites. Tbls, flush toilets, cfga, drkg wtr, beach, change house, dump, fishing pier, showers, picnic shelters. Boating(l), fishing, hiking, swimming, fishing pier.

Gentry Creek Recreation Area $7
Corps of Engineers
Eufaula Lake
9 mi W of Checotah on US 266; S to lake following signs. $7 with federal senior pass at 11 primitive RV/tent sites; others pay $14. At 14 elec sites, $9.59 with senior pass; others pay $19. 50-ft RV limit; 3 pull-through sites. 4/1-10/31; 14-day limit. Flush toilets, tbls, cfga, drkg wtr, showers, dump, beach. Boating(l), fishing, swimming.

CHEYENNE
Dead Indian Lake   FREE
Black Kettle National Grasslands
11 mi N of Cheyenne on SR 47; left to lake; at 80-acre national grasslands area. Free. All year; 14-day limit. 12 primitive sites. Tbls, toilets, cfga, drkg wtr, fishing pier. Boating(l), fishing, swimming, wildlife study, nature trail. Lake now named Dead Warrior Lake.

Black Kettle Campground   FREE
Black Kettle National Grasslands
From Cheyenne at jct with SR 83, 9.9 mi N on US 283 to Black Kettle Recreation Area sign; left to site. Free. All year; 14-day limit. 12 sites, typically 35 ft, several pull-through. Tbls, toilets, cfga, drkg wtr. Boating(l), fishing, hiking.

Skipout Lake Campground   FREE
Black Kettle National Grasslands
10 mi W of Cheyenne at 60-acre national grasslands area; 5 mi E of Reydon on SR 47 to lake sign; left on RMNS 175 for half mi. Free. All year; 14-day limit. 2 RV sites; no RV size limit. Tbls, toilet, cfga, drkg wtr. Boating(l), hunting, fishing, swimming, wildlife study.

CHICKASHA

Lake Burtschi   FREE
State Fishing Lake
Dept. of Wildlife Conservation
11 mi SW of Chickasha on SR 92. Free primitive camping. Tbls, toilets, cfga, no drkg wtr. Fishing, boating(l), picnicking.

Lake Chickasha $10
Chickasha Parks Department
From jct with US 81 just W of Chickasha, 4 mi W on US 62 to town of Verden; 3 mi N on NS 2750 Rd; 2 mi W on E1300 Rd; half mi N on N2730 Rd; at E shore of lake. $10 without hookups, $15 at 50 elec/wtr sites (18 pull-through); 35-ft RV limit. All year. Tbls, flush toilets, cfga, drkg wtr, showers, dump, playground. Swimming, fishing, boating(l). No camping on W shore. $5 boating permit ($30 annually).

CLAREMORE

Blue Creek Recreation Area $8
Corps of Engineers
Oologah Lake
From Claremore, 12 mi N on SR 66 to settlement of Foyil; 4 mi W on EW400 Rd; 1.2 mi N on NS4180 Rd; 1.5 mi W on gravel EW390 Rd, following signs; at SE shore of lake. $8 with federal senior pass at 36 non-elec sites (others pay $16). At 22 elec sites (no wtr hookups), $10 with senior pass; others pay $20. 4/1-9/30; 14-day limit. RV limit in excess of 65 ft. Tbls, flush toilets, cfga, drkg wtr, showers, dump, picnic shelter. Boating(l), fishing, bridle trail (horses allowed in one loop).

Spencer Creek Recreation Area $8
Corps of Engineers
Oologah Lake
From Claremore, 12 mi N on SR 66 to settlement of Foyil; 6 mi N on NS4200 Rd; 2 mi W on EW350 Rd; 1 mi N on NS4180 Rd, then left (W) on access rd, following signs. $8 with federal senior pass at 22 non-elec sites (others pay $16). At 29 elec sites (30-amp, no wtr hookups), $10 with senior pass; others pay $20. 4/1-9/30; 14-day limit. RV limit in excess of 65 ft. Tbls, flush toilets, cfga, drkg wtr, dump, showers, picnic shelter. Fishing, boating(l), picnicking.

CLAYTON

Nanih Waiya Lake   FREE
Gary Sherer State Wildlife Management Area
NW of Clayton on Sardis Lake Rd, past Sardis Cove Public Use Area, N across bridge; 10 mi W on CR D1606 to village of Counts; 1 mi N of Counts on CR D4170 to WMA entrance; 1.5 mi E on dirt rd to camp area. Free. Camping permitted only during open hunting season, and only within 50 yds of public use rds; 14-day limit. 4 primitive camp locations along Bolen Creek. Fishing, picnicking, boating(l), drkg wtr, toilets. 1,280 acres.

Potato Hills Central Recreation Area $9
Corps of Engineers
Sardis Lake
From Clayton at jct with US 271, 3.3 mi N on SR 2; W into campground on access rd; at E shore of lake. $9 with federal senior pass at 80 elec/wtr sites; others pay $18. 4/1-10/31; 14-day limit. RV limit in excess of 65 ft. Tbls, flush toilets, cfga, drkg wtr, showers, dump, fishing pier, playground. Hiking, nature trail, fishing, boating(l).

Potato Hills South Recreation Area $12
Corps of Engineers
Sardis Lake
From Clayton at jct with US 271, 2.5 mi N on SR 2; 0.5 mi W on CR 1625, then N on access rd; at E shore of lake. $12. 4/1-10/31; 14-day limit. 18 primitive sites; 65-ft RVs. Tbls, toilets, showers, cfga, drkg wtr, fishing pier, beach, change house. Fishing, boating(ld), swimming, nature trail.

Pushmataha   FREE
State Wildlife Management Area
SE of Clayton on US 271, pass Clayton Lake State Park, then W following signs. Free. All year; 14-day limit. Primitive camping in designated areas only during hunting seasons. Hunting, hiking.

Sardis Cove Recreation Area $12
Corps of Engineers
Sardis Lake
From N of Clayton at jct with SR 2, 8.3 mi W on SR 43. $12 for 23 non-elec sites; $16 at 22 elec sites ($8 with federal senior pass). 4/1-10/31; 14-day limit. Toilets, cfga, drkg wtr, tbls, dump, fishing pier. Fishing, boating(lr), picnicking.

CLEVELAND

Cleveland Section   FREE
Keystone State Wildlife Management Area
Arkansas River
2 mi N of Cleveland on SR 99, across bridge to WMA entrance on Arkansas River east shore NW of Keystone Lake. Free. Hunter & fisherman primitive camping is permitted only within 50 yds of public-use rds. Within Osage Indian Reservation. WMA is 16,537 acres.

Feyodi Creek City Park $11
Keystone Lake
Cleveland Parks & Recreation Department
2 mi S of Cleveland on US 64; at W shore of Keystone Lake. $11 for self-contained RVs with elec/wtr ($300 monthly); $6 tents; $15 full hookups ($300 monthly). 3/1-11/30; 14-day limit. 37 primitive sites; 16 30-amp elec/wtr; 19 full hookups. Tbls, flush toilets, cfga, drkg wtr, showers, dump. Hiking trails, swimming, fishing, boating(l), horseshoes, paddleboats(r). Former state park. GPS: 36.2781272, -96.4330756

COLBERT

Burns Run East Camp $10
Corps of Engineers
Lake Texoma
4 mi W of Colbert on SR 75A to Cartwright, then W on Main St & SW on Boat Club Rd, following signs; at E shore of Burns Run Cove just NW of Denison Dam. $10 base with federal senior pass at 44 elec/wtr sites; others pay $20 base, $24 for premium locations ($12 with senior pass). During 10/1-3/31, 25 elec sites $12 without wtr hookups ($6 with senior pass); payment by honor deposit; wtr at frost-free hydrant near park entrance; no showers or bathroom facilities. All year; 14-day limit. RV limit in excess of 65 ft. Toilets, tbls, cfga, drkg wtr, dump, showers, shelter. Swimming, boating(l), fishing, nature trail.

Burns Run West CAMP $10
Corps of Engineers
Lake Texoma
From Colbert, 4 mi W on SR 75A to Cartright, then 1 mi W on Main St; 2 mi N on Boat Club Rd; 3 mi W & S on West Burns Run Rd; at SE shore of lake, W of Burns Run Cove. 4/1-9/30 (not open off-season); 14-day limit. At 105 elec/wtr sites, $10 base with federal senior pass; others pay $20 base, $24 at premium locations ($12 with senior pass). 5 group camping areas. RV limit in excess of 65 ft; 43 pull-through sites. Tbls, flush toilets, cfga, drkg wtr, dump, showers, 2 shelters, beach, playground. Boating(l), fishing, swimming, hiking.

Dam Site North Area
Corps of Engineers
Lake Texoma
From Colbert, 5 mi W (through Cartwright) & S on SR 75A; at Oklahoma side of dam, 5 mi N of Denison, TX. Camping no longer permitted.

COPAN

Post Oak Recreation Area $10
Corps of Engineers
Copan Lake
From just S of Copan on US 75, 3 mi W (over dam) on SR 10; 1.2 mi N on SR 10, then E on access rd. $10 base with federal senior pass at 17 back-in elec/wtr sites (30-amp); others pay $20 base, $22 for 2 full-hookup handicap sites

($11 with senior pass). 4/1-10/31; 14-day limit. RV limit in excess of 65 ft. Tbls, flush & pit toilets, cfga, drkg wtr, showers, dump, new playground. Hiking, fishing.

Skull Creek Campground   FREE
State of Oklahoma
Hulah Lake
10 mi W of Copan on SR 10; 1.5 mi N; 1.5 mi W; half mi N on co rds. Free. All year; 14-day limit. 22 sites (no RV size limit). Tbls, toilets, cfga, drkg wtr. Fishing.

Washington Cove $10
Corps of Engineers
Copan Lake
From NW corner of Copan, 0.3 mi W on W 800 Rd; 1 mi N on N3970 Rd; left on access rd, following signs; at SE shore of lake. $10 with federal senior pass at 101 elec/wtr sites (30-amp); others pay $20. 4/1-10/31; 14-day limit. RV limit in excess of 65 ft. Tbls, flush toilets, cfga, drkg wtr, showers, dump, playground, fishing pier. Boating(l), fishing, hiking, horseback riding, baseball.

COOKSON

Chicken Creek Recreation Area $9
Tenkiller Ferry Lake
Corps of Engineers
From Cookson, 4 mi S on SR 100; 1.5 mi NW (right) on Chicken Creek Rd, following signs. All year; 14-day limit. 101 elec/wtr sites. During 4/1-9/30, $9 with federal senior pass for 30-amp elec, $9.50 with senior pass for 50-amp; others pay $18 & $19. During 10/1-3/31, 30-amp sites $16, 50-amp sites $17 ($8 & $8.50 with senior pass). RV limit in excess of 65 ft. Tbls, flush toilets, showers, cfga, drkg wtr, beach, playground, fishing pier, dump. Fishing, boating(l), swimming. Note: Some years, campground is closed for the winter on 12/1 due to budget.

Cookson Bend $7
Corps of Engineers
Tenkiller Ferry Lake
2 mi W of Cookson on W. Cookson Bend Rd, following signs; at E shore of lake. $7 with federal senior pass at 65 primitive sites during 4/1-10/31 (others pay $14); $12 during 10/1-11/30 ($6 with senior pass). At 45 elec sites (no wtr hookups) & 17 elec/wtr sites, $9 with senior pass for 30-amp, $9.50 with senior pass for 50-amp elec; others pay $18 & $19. During 11/1-3/31, some elec sites are $16 & $17 ($8 & $8.50 with senior pass); no wtr hookups, showers or flush toilets off-season. RV limit in excess of 65 ft. Shelters, tbls, flush toilets, cfga, drkg wtr, dump, beach, showers. Boating(lr), fishing, swimming.

Elk Creek Landing Recreation Area $7
Corps of Engineers
Tenkiller Lake
From Cookson, 4 mi N on SR 100; left (W) before Illinois River bridge on access rd; at N end of lake, E shore.

$7 with federal senior pass at 23 non-elec sites during 5/1-9/30 (others pay $14); $12 during 10/1-3/31 ($6 with senior pass). At 18 elec sites (no wtr hookups), $18 during 5/1-9/30 ($9 with senior pass), $16 during off-season ($8 with senior pass). No showers, flush toilets or wtr services off-season. RV limit in excess of 65 ft. Tbls, toilets, cfga, drkg wtr, dump, beach, shelters. Fishing, boating(ldr), swimming.

Standing Rock Landing Rec. Area
Corps of Engineers
Tenkiller Lake
From Cookson, 1 mi N on S. Molly Brown Mountain Rd; 2 mi N on S550 Rd to park; at E shore of lake. Camping no longer permitted.

CORDELL

Cordell City Park $10
From jct with SR 52 in downtown Cordell, about 6 blocks N on US 183 (N. Glenn L. English St) to park on right. $10 at sites with elec. All year; 3-day limit. Tbls, flush toilets, showers, cfga, drkg wtr, dump.

Cordell Reservoir $5
State Fish & Wildlife Conservation Area
Along I-40, SR 152 & Hwy 183 near Cordell; 3 mi N & half mi E of Dill City. $5 daily or $50 annually for entrance fee (with key) and general use permit. Primitive sites. Tbls, toilets, cfga, drkg wtr. Fishing, hiking, wildlife study, picnicking.

COWLINGTON

Short Mountain Cove $9.50
Corps of Engineers
Robert S. Kerr Reservoir
Arkansas River Lock & Dam 15
From Cowlington (12 mi S of Sallisaw), 0.5 mi E on CR 42; 1 mi N on CR N4630, following signs; at SE shore of lake. $9.50 with federal senior pass for 30-amp at 42 elec/wtr sites, $10 for 50-amp; others pay $19 & $20. All year; 14-day limit. 55-ft RV limit. Tbls, toilets, cfga, drkg wtr, dump, picnic shelter. Boating(l), fishing, hiking, swimming, nature trail.

DEVOL

Comanche Red River Casino   FREE
From I-44 exit 5, 1 mi W on US 70; 1 mi S on SR 36. Free at 5 RV sites next to casino hotel; elec/wtr hookups, no dump or restroom facilities.

DENISON (TEXAS)

Dam Site South $7.50
Corps of Engineers
Lake Texoma
From Denison, 5 mi N on SR 91; turn right on Denison Dam Rd; below dam on S side of Red River. $7.50 with federal senior pass at 9 non-elec sites; others pay $15. At 21 elec/

wtr sites, $10 with senior pass; others pay $20. During 11/1-3/31, some sites open with $12 fees & reduced amenities (elec & 1 frost-free faucet available). RV limit in excess of 65 ft. Tbls, flush toilets, showers, cfga, drkg wtr, dump. Boating(l), fishing.

DUNCAN

Clear Creek Lake $7
Municipal Campground
N of Duncan on US 81; 6 mi E on Plato Rd; 5 mi N on Clear Creek Rd. $7 without elec, $17 with elec ($9 seniors). All year; 21-day limit. 102 sites. Tbls, flush toilets, cfga, showers, drkg wtr, dump, store, snack bar. Swimming, boating (ld), fishing (enclosed dock), waterskiing. 380-255-9538 for all campgrounds.

Duncan Lake $7
Municipal Campground
7 mi E of Duncan on Bois D'Arc; 2 mi N on Duncan Lake Rd. $7 without elec, $17 with elec ($8 seniors). All year; 21-day limit. 44 sitesat 550-acre lake. Tbls, flush toilets, cfga, drkg wtr, showers, dump, elec, playground. Boating, fishing(l), waterskiing, swimming, picnicking.

Fuqua Lake $7
Municipal Campground
10 mi N of Duncan on US 81; 18 mi E on SR 29; 3 mi S. $7 without elec, $17 with elec ($9 seniors). All year; 21-day limit. 54 sites at 1,500-acre lake. Tbls, flush toilets, cfga, drkg wtr, showers, dump, elec. Fishing, swimming, boating(ld).

Humphrey's Lake $7
Municipal Campground
N of Duncan on US 81; 4 mi E on Osage Rd; 3 mi N; .7 mi W. $7 without elec, $17 with elec ($9 seniors). All year; 21-day limit. 44 sites at 840-acre lake. Tbls, flush toilets, cfga, drkg wtr, dump, store. Boating(ld), fishing (fishing dock).

DURANT

Johnson Creek $10
Corps of Engineers
Lake Texoma
From Durant, 10 mi W on US 70, N side of road before causeway. $10 with federal senior pass at 53 elec/wtr sites; others pay $20. During 10/1-3/31, 20 elec sites (no wtr hookups) are $12 ($6 with senior pass); payment by honor deposit; shower & bathroom facilities closed; wtr from frost-free hydrant near park entrance. All year; 14-day limit. RV limit in excess of 65 ft. Non-campers pay day use fee for dump station, boat ramp. Flush toilets, cfga, tbls, drkg wtr, elec, dump, showers, fishing pier. Boating(l), fishing, hiking.

Lakeside Campground $10
Corps of Engineers
Lake Texoma
From Durant, 10 mi W on US 70; 4 mi S on Streetman Rd. $10 base with federal senior pass at 133 elec/wtr sites; others pay $20 base, $22 for premium locations ($11 with senior pass). During 11/1-3/31, 23 elec sites (no wtr hookups) are $12 ($6 with senior pass); payment by honor deposit; shower & bathroom facilities closed; wtr from frost-free hydrant near B Area entrance. All year; 14-day limit. RV limit in excess of 65 ft. Non-campers pay day use fee for boat ramp, dump station. Flush toilets, cfga, tbls, showers, playground, dump, picnic shelter, fishing pier. Boating(l), fishing, hiking, waterskiing, bridle trail.

Platter Flats Campground $12
Corps of Engineers
Lake Texoma
From Durant, 5 mi S on US 75; 6 mi W on Platter Rd; 1 mi SW on Trail Ride Rd; on NE shore of lake at Rock Creek Cove. During 4/1-9/30, $12-$15 at 20 equestrian non-elec sites ($6-$7.50 with federal senior pass). At 36 equestrian & 26 non-equestrian elec/wtr sites, $10 base with senior pass; others pay $20 base, $22 at premium locations ($11 with senior pass). During 10/1-3/31, 58 elec sites (no wtr hookups) are $12 ($6 with senior pass); payment by honor deposit; shower & bathroom facilities closed; wtr from frost-free hydrant near park entrance. 14-day limit. Equestrian sites open to campers without horses. RV limit in excess of 65 ft. Picnic shelters, tbls, flush toilets, cfga, drkg wtr. Fishing, boating (l), swimming, horseback riding, equestrian trails.

DURHAM
Spring Creek Lake Campground FREE
Black Kettle National Grasslands
2 mi S, 4 mi E, 3 mi SE of Durham. 4/11-11/15; 7-day limit. 5 sites (RVs under 25 ft). Tbls, toilet, cfga, drkg wtr. Fishing; swimming; hiking; canoeing; rockhounding.

EL RENO
Lucky Star Casino FREE
Cheyenne-Arapaho Tribes of Oklahoma
From I-40 exit 125 S of El Reno, N on I-40B into El Reno, then about 3.5 mi N on US 81. Free hookups at 6 elec/wtr RV sites in small second of casino parking lot. No restrooms or showers.

ELK CITY
Elk City Lake Park FREE
About 3 mi S of Elk City on Washington St; left off access D1137 Rd on N side of lake. Free. All year; 4-night limit in 30-day period. 5 elec/wtr sites; no wtr in winter. Tbls, playground, toilets, cfga, beach. Boating(l), fishing, picnicking, golf, swimming. 750 acres; 250-acre lake.

EUFAULA
Brooken Cove Recreation Area $9.50
Corps of Engineers
Eufaula Lake
From the settlement of Enterprise (12 mi E of Eufaula), 5 mi N on SR 71 toward dam, then NW following signs on either W Bk 800 Rd or E 1200 Rd. $9.50 base with federal senior pass at 73 30-amp elec sites (no wtr hookups); others pay $19 base, $20 for 50-amp elec ($10 with senior pass). 4/1-9/30; 14-day limit. 60-ft RV limit; 8 pull-through sites. Tbls, flush toilets, cfga, drkg wtr, dump, showers, playground, beach, fishing pier, picnic shelters. Boating(l), fishing, swimming.

Damsite East Recreation Area $7.50
Corps of Engineers
Eufaula Lake
From settlement of Enterprise (12 mi E of Eufaula), 7 mi N on SR 71; cross dam, then follow SR 71 curving SE; right (S) on second rd into small campground; below dam near N shore of Canadian River. $7.50 with federal senior pass during 4/1-10/31 at 10 elec sites (others pay $15). 14-day limit. Some sites open & free off-season, but no amenities. Tbls, flush toilets, cfga, drkg wtr. Boating, fishing.

Gaines Creek FREE
Corps of Engineers
Eufaula Lake
From Eufaula, S across lake bridge on US 69; 1.5 mi E on SR 9A, then S on McNally Rd & W on Lake Access Rd. Free. All year; 14-day limit. 10 primitive sites without facilities or drkg wtr. Hiking; boating(l); picnicking; fishing; waterskiing. Managed by State of Oklahoma as part of Eufaula Wildlife Management Area.

Highway 9 Landing Recreation Area $10
Corps of Engineers
Eufaula Lake
From Eufaula at jct with US 69, 9 mi SE on SR 9 across 2 bridges, then N on access rd. $10 base at 15 non-elec sites, $14 at premium locations ($5 & $7 with federal senior pass). At 65 elec sites, $15 base, $20 at premium locations ($7.50 & $10 with senior pass). 4/1-9/30; 14-day limit. Tbls, toilets, cfga, drkg wtr, dump, playground, beach, fishing pier, picnic shelter. Swimming, boating(l), fishing.

Ladybird Landing Recreation Area $12
(formerly Dam Site South)
Corps of Engineers
Eufaula Lake
From settlement of Enterprise (12 mi E of Eufaula), 7 mi N on SR 71 (across dam from Damsite East), then W following signs. $12 at 8 primitive RV/tent sites & 5 tent sites ($6 with federal senior pass). At 44 elec sites (no wtr hookups), $9.50 base with senior pass; others pay $19

base, $20 at premium locations ($10 with senior pass). 4/1-9/30; 14-day limit. 55-ft RV limit. Picnic shelter($), tbls, flush toilets, cfga, drkg wtr, showers, beach, dump, change house, fishing pier, playground. Fishing, boating(l), swimming, hiking trails.

Mill Creek Bay Recreation Area $10
Corps of Engineers
Eufaula Lake
From Eufaula at jct with US 69, 6 mi W on SR 9; 2 mi S on CR N4110; just N of lake bridge, turn right into campground. $10. 3/1-10/31; 14-day limit. 12 primitive sites. Picnic shelter, tbls, pit toilets, cfga, drkg wtr. Boating(l), fishing.

Mill Creek Unit FREE
Eufaula State Wildlife Management Area
3 mi W of Eufaula on SR 9; 1 mi S, 1 mi E & 1 mi S on co rds. Free. On Mill Creek arm of Eufaula Lake. WMA encompasses the N & S shores of the Mill Creek arm. Lake noted for bass & catfish. Only hunter & fishermen primitive camping permitted in designated areas; 14-day limit. The Mill Creek Bay facility operated by the U.S. Army Corps of Engineers is nearby, also offering free camping and boat ramps. Mill Creek WMA Unit connects with the South Canadian River Unit of Eufaula WMA, where free primitive camping also available to hunters and fishermen in designated areas. That area can best be reached by co rds from Indianola.

Oak Ridge Recreation Area $10
Corps of Engineers
Eufaula Lake
From Eufaula at jct with US 69, 6 mi S to just across Canadian River bridge, then turn NE on SR 9A into campground on right. $10 at 5 primitive sites; $15 at 8 elec sites (no wtr hookups), $7.50 with federal senior pass. Fees charged 3/1-10/31; 14-day limit. Off-season, some sites may be open & free, but no wtr or amenities. Tbls, toilets, cfga, drkg wtr. Fishing, boating(ld), fishing pier.

FORT SUPPLY

Crappie Cove Section $9
Beaver Point Campground
Corps of Engineers
Fort Supply Lake
From E edge of Fort Supply at US 270, 2 mi S on N1930 Rd; 1 mi SE across dam to Crappie Cove section. $9. 4/1-10/31; 14-day limit. 16 primitive sites ($4.50 with federal senior pass). Tbls, pit toilets, cfga, shelters, no drkg wtr. Fishing, boating(l), hiking, swimming. Rest of Beaver Point and all of Wolf Creek Public Use Areas are for day use & lake access; camping prohibited.

Supply Park Campground $8.50
Corps of Engineers
Fort Supply Lake
From E edge of Fort Supply at US 270, 2 mi S on N1930

Rd; at 4-way stop, turn left on access rd (E0320 Rd; along lakeshore W of dam. All year; 14-day limit. $8.50 with federal senior pass at 16 non-elec sites; others pay $17. At 94 elec sites, $11 with senior pass for 30-amp elec, $12 with senior pass for 50-amp; others pay $22 & $24. Off-season fees paid by self-deposit; showers & waterborne restrooms closed until 4/1; pit toilets open. RV limit in excess of 65 ft; 14 pull-through sites. Non-campers pay day use fee (self-deposit) for boat ramp, beach. Non-camper fee also for using dump station. Tbls, flush toilets, cfga, drkg wtr, showers, dump, playground, fishing berm, picnic shelter. Boating(ld), fishing, swimming.

Western Wolf Creek FREE
Fort Supply State Wildlife Management Area
4 mi S of Fort Supply on co rd (or N on co rd from Airport Rd W of Woodward). Free. 5 primitive camping areas W of Wolf Creek. Only hunter & fishermen primitive camping permitted in designated areas; 14-day limit. Hunting; shooting range; fishing in river & Fort Supply Lake; boat launch at state park, Cottonwood Point & Supply Park. Picnic areas on E & W sides of lake. Lake has 26-mile shoreline; WMA is 5,550 acres.

GEARY

American Horse Lake FREE
State Fishing Lake
Dept of Wildlife Conservation
1 mi N of Geary on US 270/281; 12 mi W; 1 mi S. Free primitive camping. Toilets, tbls, cfga, drkg wtr. Fishing, boating(l), picnicking. 100 acres.

GORE

Gore Landing City Park $8
Robert S. Kerr Lake
2 mi E on US 64; 1 mi N. $8 without hookups, $15 with wtr/elec (seniors with federal senior pass pay $4 without elec, $7.50 with hookups). 3/1-LD; 14-day limit. 24 sites (no RV size limit). Tbls, toilets, cfga, drkg wtr. Fishing, boating(l). Formerly a Corps of Engineers park.

Snake Creek Cove $9
Corps of Engineers
Tenkiller Ferry Lake
From Gore, 15 mi N on SR 100, then W (left) on access rd; at Snake Creek Cove. All year; 14-day limit. 111 elec sites. $9 base with federal senior pass for 30-amp sites; $9.50 with senior pass at five 50-amp sites; $10 with senior pass at 4 full-hookup sites; others pay $18, $19 & $20 during peak season. Reduced fees off-season, but no wtr hookups, showers or flush toilets. RV limit in excess of 65 ft. Non-campers pay day use fee for boat ramp, dump station, beach. Tbls, flush toilets, cfga, drkg wtr, showers, beach, playground, dump, fishing pier. Boating(l), fishing, swimming.

Strayhorn Landing $9
Corps of Engineers
Tenkiller Ferry Lake
From Gore, 7 mi NE on SR 100; 1.5 mi N on SR 10A; 0.3 mi E (right) at sign on access road. All year; 14-day limit. At 40 elec sites, $9 base with federal senior pass during 4/1-9/30 (others pay $18 base); $10 with senior pass at premium locations (others pay $20). During 10/1-3/31, elec sites are $16 & $18 ($8 & $9 with senior pass); no wtr hookups, flush toilets or showers off-season. RV limit in excess of 65 ft. Tbls, flush & pit toilets, showers, cfga, drkg wtr, dump, playground, beach, picnic shelters. Boating(l), fishing, hiking, swimming.

Summers Ferry City Park $8
Robert S. Kerr Lock & Dam
From I-40 exit 287 at Gore, 1.5 mi N on SR 100; cross Arkansas River bridge & turn left; at E shore of Arkansas River. $8 without hookups, $15 with wtr/elec (seniors with federal senior pass pay $4 without elec, $7.50 with hookups). 3/1-LD; 14-day limit. Tbls, portable toilets, cfga, drkg wtr, dump. Fishing, boating(l).

GOTEBO
Lake Vanderwork FREE
State Fishing Lake Park
5 mi N & 2 mi E of Gotebo. All year. Primitive undesignated sites; no facilities. Boating, fishing. 135 acres. 580-529-2795.

GRAYSON
Deep Fork Unit FREE
Eufaula Wildlife Management Area
3 mi S of Grayson on SR 52; 1 mi SW on co rd. Only fishermen & hunter primitive camping permitted in designated areas; 14-day limit. WMA encompasses both N & S shorelines of Deep Fork River just W of Eufaula Lake and the Deep Fork arm of Eufaula.

GUYMON
Beaver River FREE
State Wildlife Management Area
About 15 mi W of Guymon on US 64; S on co rds to management area. Headquarters located on E side of area on N shore of Beaver River. Free. Primitive camping; camp only in designated areas; 14-day limit. Fishing, hunting. 15,600 acres.

No Man's Land Regional Park FREE
On SR 3 just E of US 54/64; RV parking in lot NE of behind visitor center or behind on grass. Free. All year; 1-night limit. Tbls, flush toilets, cfga, drkg wtr, showers, dump, no elec. Hiking, playground. Don't confuse this park with the day-use Centennial Park at the jct of US 54 & US 412/SR 3.

HAILEYVILLE
Gaines Creek Unit FREE
Eufaula State Wildlife Management Area
Follow co rds N from Haileyville to Gaines Creek arm of Lake Eufaula and US 270 W 1 mi to Brushy Creek arm. Free. Only fishermen & hunter primitive camping permitted in designated areas; 14-day limit. Hickory Point Recreation Area (Corps of Engineers) E of McAlester also offers free camping, boat launch & toilets at mouth of Gaines Creek.

HARDESTY
Optima Lake FREE
State Wildlife Management Area
3 mi NE of Hardesty on SR 3; 6 mi N on SR 94; turn right just across bridge over North Canadian River. Free. 4 primitive camping areas within 2 mi of WMA's entrance. On N shore of Optima Lake. Only fishermen & hunter primitive camping permitted in designated areas; 14-day limit. Boat ramps, Hooker Point & Prairie Dog Point. Lake, at jct of Coldwater Creek & Beaver River, is 600 acres with good hybrid striper & walleye fishing. WMA is 3,400 acres, known for deer, quail & pheasant hunting.

HASTINGS
Chisholm Trail Ridge Recreation Area $7
Waurika Lake
Corps of Engineers
From Hastings, 5.2 mi E on SR 5; merge onto gravel county rd, then 3 mi N on Advent Rd & 0.9 mi W on Chisholm Trail Rd. $7 base with federal senior pass at 95 elec/wtr sites; others pay $14 base, $18 for premium locations ($9 with senior pass). 5/1-9/30; 14-day limit. 60-ft RV limit; 14 pull-through sites. Tbls, flush toilets, cfga, drkg wtr, dump, beach, change house, playground, fishing pier. Nature trail, boating(l), fishing, swimming.

Kiowa Recreation Area $7
Waurika Lake
Corps of Engineers
From Hastings, 1.2 mi E on SR 5; 3 mi N on County N240 Rd; 1.5 mi E on Kiowa Park Rd (E1900 Rd); at W shore of lake. $7 base with federal senior pass at 164 elec/wtr sites; others pay $14 base, $18 at premium locations ($9 with senior pass). 60-ft RV limit; 47 pull-through sites. 5/1-10/31; 14-day limit Flush toilets, tbls, showers, cfga, drkg wtr, dump, playground, fishing pier, beach, change house, nature trail. Boating(l), fishing, hiking, swimming.

HEAVENER
Billy Creek Recreation Area $8
Ouachita National Forest
6 mi W of Heavener (W of Bena, Ark) on SR 63; 3 mi N on FR 22. $8. All year; 14-day limit. 11 sites (small RVs). Tbls, toilets, cfga, drkg wtr. Hiking trail, fishing.

Cedar Lake Equestrian Camp $6
Ouachita National Forest
Winding Stair National Recreation Area
10 mi S of Heavener on US 270; 3 mi W on CR 5; 1 mi N on
FR 269. $6 for primitive, undesignated sites with no facili-
ties in original campground; $12 for non-elec sites in new
section. All year; 14-day limit. Elec/wtr sites $17 ($10 with
federal senior pass); double elec/wtr sites $23. 53 sites
(47 with wtr/elec), typically 50 ft. Also about 100 primitive
& overflow sites. Tbls, flush toilets, cfga, firewood, piped
drkg wtr, showers, dump, hitching posts, accessible
mounting stand. Hiking; fishing; swimming; boating(ld-1
mi), 75 mi of equestrian trails. 3 acres.

Cedar Lake Family Camp $10
Ouachita National Forest
Winding Stair National Recreation Area
10 mi S of Heavener on US 270; 3 mi W on CR 5; a mi N
on FR 269. $10 at non-elec sites. $10 with federal senior
pass at elec sites; others pay $15. $12 with senior pass
at full-hookup sites; others pay $17. Group sites $21-25
before discounts. All year; 14-day limit. 71 sites, typically
40 ft. Tbls, toilets, cfga, drkg wtr, dump. Swimming, boat-
ing(l), fishing, boating (l), hiking trails.

Wister Lake FREE
State Wildlife Management Area
2 mi S of Heavener on US 59. Free. WMA encompasses
Poteau River below Wister Lake. Hunter & fishermen primitive camping permitted only within 50 yds of public-use
rds. Boat dock 3 mi W of US 59 off co rds.

HENRYETTA
Jim Hall Lake $6
Municipal Park Campground
Just S of Henryetta, with entry from Main St (SR 52), E on
New Lake Rd, following signs. $6 at primtive sites; $7.48
at 4 sites with wtr and/or elec hookups. Tbls, toilets, cfga,
drkg wtr. Boating(l), fishing, fishing piers. 660 acres; 450-
acre lake. Formerly named Lake Henryetta Park. Camping
& boating permits at city hall. 918-652-3348.

Nichols Lake FREE
Municipal Park Campground
2 mi S of Henryetta on Main St (SR 52); E on lake rd,
following signs. Free. 7 primitive sites. Tbls, toilets,
cfga, drkg wtr, covered shelters, playgrounds. Ball fields,
volleyball, walking trails, boating(l), swimming, fishing.
Municipal golf & tennis nearby. Gates are locked each
evening. 225 acres. 918-652-3348.

HEYBURN
Heyburn Campground $10
Heyburn Lake
Corps of Engineers
From SR 66 just W of Heyburn, 3 mi N on S273rd Ave

W; 0.5 mi W on W151st St; at W side of dam. 4/1-10/31;
14-day limit. At 45 elec/wtr sites, $10 with federal senior
pass; others pay $20. 10 pull-through sites. Group camp-
ing area, $100. Non-campers pay day use fee for beach,
boat ramp, dump. Tbls, flush toilets, cfga, drkg wtr, showers, dump, playground, beach, fishing pier, picnic shelter,
change house. Boating(l), fishing, swimming.

Sunset Bay Campground $10
Corps of Engineers
Heyburn Lake
From SR 77 just E of Heyburn, 3 mi N on S257th Ave;
right (W) on Heyburn Lake Rd; at NE side of dam (6 mi
W of Kellyville). All year; 14-day limit. $10 at 14 primitive
sites ($5 with federal senior pass). No RV size limit. Tbls,
toilets, cfga, drkg wtr, beach, dump. Boating(ld); swimming; fishing.

HITCHITA
Headquarters Area FREE
Deep Fork Unit
Eufaula State Wildlife Management Area
1 mi S of Hitchita on co rd; 1 mi W on US 266 to headquarters. Get directions to camping areas. Free. Only
fishermen & hunter primitive camping permitted in designated areas; 14-day limit. WMA encompasses both N & S
shorelines of most Deep Fork River just W of Eufaula Lake
and the Deep Fork arm of Eufaula.

HOLLIS
Lake Hall FREE
State Fishing Lake
Dept of Wildlife Conservation
11 mi N of Hollis on SR 30; 1 mi W on E. 1510 Rd; 1 mi N on
N. 1705 Rd; in Harmon County. Free primitive camping. No
facilities. Boating, fishing(l). 36 acres.

HOMINY
Bull Creek Peninsula Campground $10
Corps of Engineers
Skiatook Lake
From NE edge of Hominy, about 8.5 mi E on CR 2130,
across lake bridge, following signs. $10. All year; 14-day
limit. 41 non-elec sites. Tbls, toilets, cfga, no drkg wtr.
Limited facilities in winter. Boating(ld), fishing.

Hominy Section FREE
Keystone State Wildlife Management Area
Arkansas River
7 mi S of Hominy on SR 99; W on co rds along N shore of
Arkansas River. 3 WMA entrances in Boston Pool area of
Arkansas River E shore NW of Keystone Lake. Free. Hunter
& fisherman primitive camping is permitted only within 50
yds of public-use rds. Within Osage Indian Reservation.
WMA is 16,537 acres.

Boar Creek Branch   FREE
Skiatook Lake State Wildlife Management Area
5 mi E of Hominy on SR 20 to WMA entrance on Boar Creek arm of Skiatook Lake. Free. Only fishermen & hunter primitive camping is permitted in designated areas; 14-day limit.

Buck Creek Branch   FREE
Skiatook Lake State Wildlife Management Area
5 mi E of Hominy on SR 20; 1.5 mi S on CR D3541; 2 mi E on CR D0451 to WMA's entrance on Buck Creek arm of Skiatook Lake. Free. Only fishermen/hunter primitive camping permitted in designated areas; 14-day limit.

Bull Creek Branch   FREE
Skiatook Lake State Wildlife Management Area
7 mi E of Hominy on CRs D0410 & D0400 to Bull Creek arm of Skiatook Lake. Free. Only fishermen & hunter primitive camping permitted in designated areas; 14-day limit.

HUGO
(See Rattan entry)
Hugo Lake   FREE
State Wildlife Management Area
N of Hugo on SR 93. (Wildlife refuge portion, immediately N of lake & encompassing Kiamichi River, is closed to camping.) Free. Only hunter & fishermen primitive camping permitted in designated areas; 14-day limit. Hugo Lake has 13,250 acres and 110 mi of shoreline; WMA has 18,196 acres. Boat lanes provided in uncleared upper half of lake. Noted Florida bass & blue catfish angling. Duck, geese, squirrel, quail, deer and rabbit hunting. Boat ramps at Frazier Point & Rattan Landing.

Kiamichi Park $7
Corps of Engineers
Hugo Lake
6.8 mi E of Hugo on US 70; 1 mi N on county rd, following signs; at S shore of lake near Hugo Lake State Park. $7 with federal senior pass at 24 primitive sites (others pay $14). At 37 elec sites (no wtr hookups), $9 with senior pass; others pay $18. At elec/wtr sites, $20; 5 full hookups $22 ($10 & $11 with senior pass). 4/1-9/30; 14-day limit. RV limit in excess of 65 ft. One camping loop remains open in winter for archery deer hunters. Tbls, picnic shelters, flush toilets, cfga, drkg wtr, dump, showers, beach, playground, change house. Fishing, boating (l), swimming, equestrian trail, nature trail, archery range.

Virgil Point Campground $8.50
Corps of Engineers
Hugo Lake
From just E of Hugo on US 70, 2 mi N SR 147, then W on access rd; at SE shore of lake. $8.50 base at 52 elec/wtr sites; others pay $17 base, $19 for premium sites ($9.50 with senior pass). All year; 14-day limit. 55-ft RV

limit. Tbls, flush toilets, showers, cfga, drkg wtr, dump. Boating(l), fishing.

HULBERT
Wildwood Campground $9
Fort Gibson Lake
Corps of Engineers
From Hulbert, 5 mi W on SR 80. All year; 14-day limit. $9 with federal senior pass for 30-amp sites and 30 elec/wtr sites; $10 with senior pass for 50-amp sites; others pay $18 & $20. Fees not reduced off-season. RV limit in excess of 65 ft; 9 pull-through sites. Tbls, pit & flush toilets, cfga, drkg wtr, dump, showers, shelter($). Boating(l), fishing.

INDIANOLA
South Canadian River Unit   FREE
Eufaula State Wildlife Management Area
E & W of Indianola on co rds to south shore of South Canadian River arm of Eufaula Lake. WMA encompasses the N & S shorelines of the lake arm. Free. Lake noted for bass & catfish. Only fishermen & hunter primitive camping permitted in designated areas; 14-day limit. The Mill Creek Bay facility operated by the U.S Army Corps of Engineers is nearby (in the next lake arm north, by boat), also offering free camping and boat ramps. The Mill Creek Unit of the WMA connects with the South Canadian River Unit and also offers free primitive camping to hunters and fishermen in designated areas. That area can best be reached by SR 9 and co rds from Eufaula. Public boat access is available just E of Indianola.

JET
Jet Recreation Area   FREE
Salt Plains National Wildlife Refuge
3 mi N of Jet on OK 38. Free. 4/1-10/15; 7-day limit. 20 sites (RVs under 20 ft). Tbls, toilets, cfga, firewood, drkg wtr. Hiking; waterskiing; boating(l); swimming; picnicking; fishing. No off-road vehicles. The Salt Plains is a flat expanse of mud, completely devoid of vegetation. 9,300-acre dam has 41-mile shoreline. Crystal digging 4/1-10/15. Nature trails.

KAW CITY
Sarge Creek Cove Recreation Area $9
Corps of Engineers
Kaw Lake
From Kaw City, 2.8 mi E on SR 11 across bridge, then S on access rd, following signs; at Sarge Creek arm on east-central section of lake. $9 with federal senior pass at 51 elec/wtr sites; others pay $18. 3/1-11/30; 14-day limit. RV limit 60 ft. Sites 1-7 with horse pens for equestrians. Group camping area, $100. Shelter, amphitheater, tbls, flush toilets, cfga, drkg wtr, showers, dump, fishing pier, playground. Equestrian trail, ATV trail, boating(l), fishing.

Washunga Bay Recreation Area $7
Corps of Engineers
Kaw Lake
From Kaw City, 2.6 mi E on SR 11 across bridge; 0.6 mi NE on county rd; 4.5 mi W on E. Ferguson Rd, across a second bridge, then right into park, following signs; at SW mouth of Washunga Bay section of lake. $7 with federal senior pass at 11 non-elec sites (others pay $14). At 24 elec/wtr sites, $9 base with federal senior pass; others pay $18. 5/1-9/30 (also open periods during hunting season, with wtr when cold weather permits); 14-day limit. RV limit 60 ft. Tbls, flush toilets, cfga, drkg wtr, showers, dump, beach, playground, fishing pier. Boating(l), fishing, hiking, swimming, hiking.

HUGO

Kiamichi Park $7
Corps of Engineers
Hugo Lake
From Hugo, 6.8 mi E on US 70; 1 mi N on CR N4285, then left on access rd, following signs; at S. shore of lake near Hugo Lake State Park. 3/1-12/31; 14-day limit. 24 non-elec sites, $14 ($7 with federal senior pass); 37 elec sites (no wtr hookups), $18 ($9 with senior pass); 62 elec/wtr sites, $20 ($10 with senior pass); 5 full hookups, $22 ($11 with senior pass). RV limit in excess of 65 ft. Tbls, flush toilets, cfga, drkg wtr, showers, dump, playground, change house, beach, two picnic shelters($). Nature trail, equestrian trail, archery range, paved biking/hiking trail, waterskiing. One camping loop remains open in winter for archery deer hunters.

Virgil Point Campground $8.50
Corps of Engineers
Hugo Lake
From just E of Hugo on US 70, 2 mi N on SR 147; right on E2040 Rd, then immediate left (S) on access rd; at SE shore of lake. All year; 14-day limit. 52 elec/wtr sites, $8.50 base with federal senior pass; others pay $17 base, $19 at premium locations ($9.50 with senior pass). 55-ft RV limit. Tbls, flush toilets, cfga, drkg wtr, showers, dump. Boating(l), fishing, hiking, biking, waterskiing.

KEOTA

Cowlington Point $7
Corps of Engineers
Robert S. Kerr Reservoir
Arkansas River Lock & Dam 15
From Keota, 2.5 mi E on SR 9; 3 mi N on N. Star Rd to town of Star; 2 mi E on E1175 Rd (becoming D1171 Dr); left (N) into park, following signs; at SE shore of lake. $7 with federal senior pass at 6 primitive sites ($3.50 with federal senior pass). At 32 elec/wtr sites, $9.50 with senior pass for 30-amp, $10 for 50-amp; others pay $19 & $20. All year; 14-day limit. RV limit 60 ft. Tbls, flush toilets, shelter($), cfga, drkg wtr, beach, dump. Boating(l), fishing.

KINGFISHER

Elmer Lake FREE
State Fishing Lake
Dept of Wildlife Conservation
1 mi N of Kingfisher on US 81; 2 mi W on E. 0780 Rd; S on access rd. Primitive camping at 60-acre lake. Toilets, cfga, drkg wtr, tbls, shelters. Fishing, boating(l).

KINGSTON

Buncombe Creek Campground $8
Corps of Engineers
Lake Texoma
4 mi W of Kingston on SR 32; 7 mi S on SR 99; 2 mi E on Willis Beach Rd, following signs; at N side of lake along E shore of Buncombe Creek Cove. $8 base with federal senior pass at 52 elec/wtr sites; others pay $16 base, $20 for premium locations ($10 with senior pass). All year; 14-day limit. During 10/1-3/31, park is closed; nearest off-season Corps camping & boat launch facilities at Juniper Point West or Caney Creek. RV limit 45 ft. Tbls, flush toilets, cfga, drkg wtr, elec, showers, dump. Boating(l), fishing, hiking, nature trail.

Caney Creek Campground $7.50
Corps of Engineers
Lake Texoma
3 mi S of Kingston on Donahoo St (Rock Creek Rd); 2 mi E on E. Lasiter Rd; 2 mi S on Muncrief Rd; on N shore of lake at mouth of Caney Creek Cove. All year; 14-day limit. $7.50 with federal senior pass at 10 primitive sites; others pay $15. At 42 elec/wtr sites, $10 base with senior pass; others pay $20 base, $22 for premium locations ($11 with senior pass). During 10/1-3/31, elec sites $12 without wtr hookups ($6 with senior pass); payment by honor deposit; wtr at frost-free hydrant near park entrance. RV limit in excess of 65 ft. Non-campers pay day use fee for dump station. Tbls, flush toilets, cfga, drkg wtr, showers, beach, playground, dump. Hiking, fishing, boating(l), swimming. Note: New 50-amp elec service planned.

LAWTON

Collier Landing Municipal Park $8
12 mi NE of Lawton on I-44 to Elgin exit; 1 mi W on SR 277; 3.5 mi NE on Tony Creek Rd; left after crossing Tony Creek bridge; follow signs to park on E shore of Lake Ellsworth. $8 at sites without hookups; $17 base for RV sites with elec ($13 for seniors); $20 for premium locations. 6 sites with shelters. Tbls, toilets, cfga, drkg wtr, elec, showers. Boating(l), fishing, swimming. 580-529-2663 for all city parks.

Doris Campground $10
Wichita Mountains
National Wildlife Refuge
12 mi N of Cache. $8 base. All year; 14-day limit. Base fee at 47 non-elec sites; $20 at 23 elec/wtr sites ($5 and $10 with federal senior pass). All year. Tbls, flush toilets, cfga,

drkg wtr, showers, dump. Wildlife viewing, boating(ld), fishing, hiking, rock climbing, biking. Open range is home to buffalo, elk, deer, Texas longhorn cattle. Visitor center with interactive displays, theater.

Fisherman's Cove City Park $8
12 mi NE of Lawton on I-44 to Elgin exit; 0.5 mi W on US 277; 1 mi N on NE Tony Creek Rd; 1 mi W on NE Fishermans Cove Rd; at E shore of Lake Ellsworth. $8 at sites without hookups; $17 for RV sites with elec ($13 for seniors); $20 for premium locations. 30 sites with shelters. Tbls, toilets, cfga, drkg wtr, elec, showers. Boating(l), fishing, swimming.

Lake Ellsworth City Park $8
W of Lawton on I-44 to exit 53; 4 mi W on US 277; right (N) 1 mi on NE Bonafield Rd; at S shore of lake. $8 at sites without hookups; $17 for RV sites with elec ($13 for seniors); $20 for premium locations. All year (limited services off-season). 41 sites; 55-ft RV limit. Tbls, flush toilets, cfga, drkg wtr, showers, dump, store, playground. Marina. Boating(dl), fishing, swimming.

Lake Lawtonka Municipal Park $8
8 mi N of Lawton on I-44; 3.7 mi W on SR 49; 2 mi N on SR 58 to park at Lake Lawtonka, following signs. $8 at sites without hookups; $17 for RV sites with elec ($13 for seniors); $20 for premium locations. 60 sites with shelters; 55-ft RV limit; pull-through. All year. Tbls, toilets, cfga, drkg wtr, elec, showers, pavilion, playground, dump. Boating(lrd), fishing, canoeing, swimming. Marina.

LEXINGTON
Dahlgren Lake FREE
Lexington State Wildlife Management Area
4 mi N of Lexington on US 77 to Slaughterville; 6 mi E on co rd to WMA's entrance and main camping area. SE on co rd to 30-acre Dahlgren Lake. Free. Hunter & fishermen primitive camping permitted only within 50 yds of public-use rds. Boating(l), fishing, hunting. Heisel, Little Buckhead Creeks; Conklin Lake. 9,433 acres. Playground, shelters.

LONGDALE
County Line Camp FREE
Canton Lake State Wildlife Management Area
2 mi N of Longdale on SR 58; 5 mi W on co rd to Dewey/ Blaine co line; qtr mi S to camp. On N shore of Canton Lake. Free. Only fishermen & hunter primitive camping permitted in designated areas; 14-day limit. Boating, fishing, hunting.

Headquarters Camp FREE
Canton Lake State Wildlife Management Area
2 mi N of Longdale on SR 58; 6 mi W on co rd into Dewey County; qtr mi S to camp, near WMA headquarters. On N shore of Canton Lake. Free. Only fishermen & hunter primitive camping permitted in designated areas; 14-day limit. Boating, fishing, hunting.

Longdale Camp FREE
Canton Lake State Wildlife Management Area
1.5 mi W of Longdale on Blaine County rd; just NE of Longdale Recreation Area. Free. Only fishermen & hunter primitive camping permitted in designated areas; 14-day limit. Boating (launch at Longdale RA), fishing, hunting.

Longdale Recreation Area $6.50
Corps of Engineers
Canton Lake
From Longdale at jct with SR 58, 2 mi W on paved E0610 Rd; at E shore of lake. $6.50 with federal senior pass at 35 primitive non-elec sites during 3/15-10/31 (others pay $13); free off-season but no amenities (pit toilets) or drkg wtr. All year; 14-day limit. 40-ft RV limit. Toilets, tbls, cfga, drkg wtr, playground, shelter, no elec. Fishing, hiking, boating(ld), fishing pier.

Northwest Shore Camps FREE
Canton Lake State Wildlife Management Area
2 mi N of Longdale on SR 58; 6.5 mi W on co rd; qtr mi S to camp. Second camp three-fourths mi farther S & qtr mi W. Free. Only fishermen & hunter primitive camping is permitted in designated areas; 14-day limit. Boating, fishing, hunting.

Unwins Cutoff Lake Camps FREE
Canton Lake State Wildlife Management Area
2 mi W of Longdale on SR 58; 11-13 mi W on co rd to 3 camps N of Canadian River at cutoff lake. Free. Only fishermen & hunter primitive camping permitted in designated areas; 14-day limit. Boating, fishing, hunting.

MADILL
Juniper Point $10
Corps of Engineers
Lake Texoma
From Madill, 17 mi S on SR 99, across lake bridge, then E; in Texas. $10 base with federal senior pass at 14 wtr/elec 30-amp sites; $11 with senior pass at 14 elec/wtr 50-amp sites; others pay $20 & $22. All year; 14-day limit. During 10/1-3/31, East Juniper area is closed, but West Juniper open; elec/wtr sites $20 in Oct; elec with 1 frost-free faucet $12 (those sites $10 & $6 with senior pass). Tbls, flush toilets, cfga, drkg wtr, showers, dump. Boating(l), fishing, hiking.

MANITOU
Lake Frederick Campground $9
Tillman County Park
From jct with US 183 in Manitou, 5 mi E on SR 5C (Baseline Rd); 0.5 mi N on N2290 Rd; E to park following signs. $9 for seniors at 40 wtr/elec sites; others pay $15. 40-ft RV limit (10 pull-through). All year; 14-day limit. Tbls, flush toilets, cfga, drkg wtr, showers, dump, playground. Boating(l), fishing, swimming.

MANGUM

Sandy Sanders   FREE
State Wildlife Management Area
W of Mangum on SR 9. Free. All year. Primitive, undesignated sites, but in designated areas; no facilities. On 19,000 acres. Hunting, fishing ponds, hiking, bridle trails, mountain biking. 45 mi of unpaved rds.

MANNFORD

House Creek Branch   FREE
Cimarron River
Keystone State Wildlife Management Area
W of Mannford on SR 51 to SR 48; N on sR 48 across Keystone Lake bridge, then W on co rd to WMA entrance on N shore of House Creek. Free. Hunter & fishermen primitive camping is permitted only within 50 yds of public rds.

Keystone Ramp Recreation Area   FREE
Keystone Lake
Corps of Engineers
From Mannford, about 3 mi E on SR 15, then N on Tower Rd (becoming Coyote Trail), following signs. Free. All year; 14-day limit. 6 primitive, undesignated sites. Pit toilets, cfga, no drkg wtr.

New Mannford Ramp $10
Keystone Lake
Mannford City Park
Half mi N of Mannford on county rd; half mi E on access rd. $10 at 12 primitive sites. 44 RV sites with elec, $11 during 11/1-4/1 off-season ($8 for seniors), $17 in-season. Tbls, flush toilets, cfga, drkg wtr, flush toilets, dump, elec($). Boating(l), fishing. This is a former Corps of Engineers park now operated by the city.

Salt Creek Cove North Recreation Area
Corps of Engineers
Keystone Lake
From Mannford, 1 mi E across lake bridge on SR 51, then left (N) on access rd, following signs. Now operated by City of Mannford as a Jellystone Park.

Waterfowl Development Unit   Free
Cimarron River
Keystone State Wildlife Management Area
W of Mannford on SR 51 across 1st Keystone Lake bridge just W of SR 48; N & W on access rd to WMA entrance on S shore of Cimarron River, W of main lake. Free. Hunter & fishermen primitive camping is permitted only within 50 yds of public-use rds.

MARIETTA

Hickory Creek   FREE
State Wildlife Management Area
1.5 mi E of Marietta on SR 32; 6 mi N on SR 77S; 1.5 mi E on county road. Controlled hunt campground. Other entrances to the WMA are on CR D3370, W of Enville; on CR D3352, W of Enville, and NE of Marietta on CR D2038. In those areas, ask for directions to the designated campsites. Free. Only fishermen & hunter primitive camping is permitted in designated areas; 14-day limit. Hickory Creek Public Use Area, with campsites, boat ramps, picnic tables and toilets, is at the mouth of Hickory Creek just outside the WMA, on SR 32. The WMA encompasses the Hickory Creek arm of Lake Texoma.

Love Valley   FREE
State Wildlife Management Area
E of Marietta on SR 32; along N shore of Lake Texoma, NE of where I-35 crosses into Oklahoma from Texas; near point where Hickory Creek empties into the lake at SR 32. Includes Brown's Spring, Crow Bottom, Hog Pen areas. Free. Hunter & fishermen primitive camping permitted only within 50 yards of public-use rds.

MCALESTER

Elm Point Recreation Area $10
Corps of Engineers
Eufaula Lake
From McAlester at jct with US 69, 12 mi NE on SR 31, then NW on Elm Point access rd following signs. $10 at 3 primitive sites; $15 at 17 elec sites (no wtr hookups); $5 & $7.50 with federal senior pass. 3/1-10/31; 14-day limit. Sites $9 off-season, but no utilities or restrooms. No RV size limit. Tbls, flush toilets, cfga, drkg wtr, beach. Fishing, boating(l), swimming.

Hickory Point Recreation Area   FREE
Corps of Engineers
Eufaula Lake
From McAlester at jct with US 69, 4 mi E on SR 31; 6 mi E on Adamson Rd, then N before bridge on N4180 Rd. Free. All year; 14-day limit. 10 primitive sites; no facilities, no drkg wtr. Fishing, boating(l), swimming. Managed by State of Oklahoma as part of Eufaula Wildlife Management Area.

MOUNTAIN PARK

Mountain Park   FREE
State Wildlife Management Area
Tom Steed Reservoir
10 mi N of Mountain Park on US 183; qtr mi E to camp. Second camp 1 mi farther on US 183; half mi W on co rd; half mi S on co rd. Free. Only fishermen & hunter primitive camping permitted in designated areas; 14-day limit. Great Plains State Park nearby. Tom Steed Reservoir is 6,400 acres & 31-mi of shoreline. Bluegill, channel catfish & bass fishing. WMA is 5,000 acres, with hunting for waterfowl & dove.

MUSKOGEE

See Tullahassee entry
Spaniard Creek Campground $7
Corps of Engineers
Webbers Falls Reservoir

Arkansas River Lock & Dam 16

From Muskogee at jct with Muskogee Turnpike & SR 10, 3 mi S on SR 64; 4 mi E on 103rd St (Elm Grove Rd), then 0.5 mi S following signs across S 65th St E bridge & right into campground.on access rds, following signs. During 4/1-10/31, $7 with federal senior pass at 1 non-elec site (no wtr hookup); others pay $14. At 35 elec/wtr sites, $9 with senior pass (others pay $18) for 30-amp, $9.50 & $19 for 50-amp. All year; 14-day limit; no reduced fees off-season. Tbls, flush toilets, cfga, drkg wtr, showers, dump. Boating(l), fishing.

NEWKIRK

Kaw State Wildlife Management Area   FREE

9 mi E of Newkirk on co rd; 2 mi s; 3 mi 3 to two Little Beaver Creek entrances. Continue 4 mi E to another east branch (Beaver Creek) entrance. 3 mi W of Newkirk on co rd to western branch (Arkansas River) entrance. East branch encompasses Little Beaver Creek & Beaver Creek; W branch encompasses Arkansas River N of Kaw Lake & Bear Creek arm. Free. Only fishermen & hunter prim. Camping permitted in designated areas; 14-day limit. New lake has 17,000 acres & 169-mi shoreline; Kaw WMA has 16,254 acres. Excellent fishing & hunting. Duck, deer, geese, wild turkey. Free camping area at Traders Bend has boat ramp within Arkansas River section; Bear Creek Cove camp area also has ramp.

Bear Creek Cove Recreation Area $8

Kaw Lake

Corps of Engineers

From Newkirk, 7 mi E on Peckham Rd (E. River Rd); 3 mi S on Bear Creek Rd to area where Bear Creek enters lake along E shore. $8 with federal senior pass at 22 wtr/elec sites; others pay $16. 3/1-11/30; 14-day limit. RV limit 40 ft. Tbls, flush toilets, showers, cfga, drkg wtr, dump, fishing pier, picnic shelter. Boating(l), fishing.

Southwind Casino   FREE

Kaw Nation of Oklahoma

From Newkirk, 1 mi N on US 77; 1 mi E on E. Earth Rd; 0.5 mi N on La Cann Rd. RV sites with free elec hookups at casino.

NOWATA

Big Creek Ramp Campground   FREE

City of Nowata Park

Oologah Lake

5.1 mi E of Nowata on US 60; 2 mi N on CR N4190; on left at Verdigris River N of lake. Free. All year; 3-day limit. 16 primitive sites; 40-ft RV limit. Tbls, pit toilets, cfga, drkg wtr. Boating(l), picnicking, fishing. Corps of Engineers property now managed by City of Nowata.

OILTON

Oilton/Lagoon Creek Sections   FREE

Keystone State Wildlife Management Area

Cimarron River

1 mi N of Oilton on SR 99; turn E just across bridge to WMA's western entrance on N shore of Cimarron River. Or, continue 2 mi N on SR 99, then E on co rd to parking area on N shore of Lagoon Creek. Free. Hunter and fishermen primitive camping permitted only within 50 yds of public-use rds.

OKAY

Damsite Campground $9

Fort Gibson Lake

Corps of Engineers

From Okay, 6 mi E on SR 251A; S on access rd below dam on W side of outlet. $9 base with federal senior pass for 30-amp elec at 48 elec/wtr sites; others pay $18 base, $20 for 50-amp locations ($10 with senior pass). All year; 14-day limit. Fees not reduced off-season. RV limit in excess of 65 ft. Tbls, flush toilets, cfga, drkg wtr, showers, dump, pay phone, shelters($). Boating(l), fishing. Note: During 2017, sites were walk-in only due to flood damage; check current status before arrival.

Wahoo Bay Recreation Area   FREE

Fort Gibson Lake

Corps of Engineers

From Okay at jct with SR 16, 0.5 mi E on SR 251A; 2 mi N on Sequoyah Bay Rd; 1 mi E on 100th St N; 0.5 mi S on S340 Rd, then E to bay on SW shore of lake. All year; 14-day limit. Free. Primitive designated sites. Pit toilets, cfga, no drkg wtr. Boating(l), fishing.

OKEMAH

Okemah City Lake $11

From SR 56 at Okemah, 5 mi N on North 3770 Rd; 1 mi W on East 1040 Rd; NW on North 3760 Rd to park; at E shore of lake. $11 at 15 primitive sites ($9 for seniors); elec/wtr sites $21 (monthly $400 off-season, $18 seniors daily). All year. 18 RV sites. Tbls, cfga, drkg wtr, toilets, showers, dump, playground. Handicap access. Picnicking, boating(ld), fishing, swimming. Free primitive camping at Jaycee Point-swimming beach area.

OKLAHOMA CITY

Lake Stanley Draper Park & Marina $8

Lake with 34-mi shoreline is in city, extending S from SE 74th St to SE 134th St. From Oklahoma City, E on I-240 to exit 8 (Sooner Rd), then 2 mi S on Sooner Rd (Hwy 77H); 2 mi E to lake on 104th St. $8. All year. 50 primitive lakefront sites (RV park planned). Tbls, toilets, cfga, drkg wtr. Boating(ldr), fishing, OHV activity, canoeing(r), paddle boating(r). No swimming. N shore park with picnic area, playground, volleyball courts, fishing pier, boat ramp. 2,900-acre lake. Marina. Boating permit required (from area vendors).

OKMULGEE

Okmulgee FREE
State Wildlife Management Area
Deep Fork River
1 mi W of Okmulgee on co rd to WMA's E entrance. Second entrance from there, 2 mi N & 1 mi W on co rds to WMA's northern headquarters. S headquarters & entrances at Lions Point area off SR 56. Free. Camp only in the public hunting portion of WMA N & E of the Deep Fork River. Only fishermen & hunter primitive camping permitted in designated areas; 14-day limit. 9,700 acres.

OOLOGAH

Hawthorn Bluff Recreation Area $8
Oologah Lake
Corps of Engineers
From Oologah at jct with US 169, 1.5 mi E on SR 88; right on access rd, following signs. $8 with federal senior pass at 15 non-elec sites; others pay $16. At 41 elec sites (30-amp, no wtr hookups), $10 with senior pass; others pay $20. 4/1-10/31; 14-day limit. RV limit in excess of 65 ft. Amphitheater, beach, change house, showers, tbls, flush toilets, cfga, drkg wtr, dump, playground, fishing pier, group shelters. Hiking trail, interpretive trail, swimming, boating(l), fishing.

Redbud Bay Recreation Area $8
Oologah Lake
Corps of Engineers
From Oologah, 3.2 mi E on SR 88; at E side of dam. $8 with federal senior pass at 12 wtr/elec sites; others pay $16. 4/1-10/31; 14-day limit. Tbls, toilets, cfga, drkg wtr, fishing pier, marine dump station, concessionaire services. Boating(l), fishing.

Sunnyside Ramp $4
Oologah Lake
City of Talala Park
From Talala (town is N of Oologah on US 169), 4 mi E on East 340 Rd to W shore of lake. $4. All year; 14-day limit. 8 primitive sites. Tbls, toilets, cfga, drkg wtr. Hunting, waterskiing, fishing, swimming, picnicking, boating(l). Leased by Corps of Engineers to City of Talala, 918-275-4203.

Verdigris River Recreation Area $12
Oologah Lake
Corps of Engineers
From Oologah at jct with US 169, 3.1 mi E on SR 88, below the dam, then right (S) on access rd; at Verdigris River. $12. All year; 14-day limit. 8 non-elec sites ($6 with federal senior pass). Tbls, toilets, cfga, drkg wtr. Boating(l), fishing.

PAULS VALLEY

Lake R.C. Longmire $12
Pauls Valley Parks & Recreation
11 mi E of Pauls Valley on Hwy 19; 3 mi S non N3340 Rd.

$10 at 12 elec RV sites; $15 full hookups; tents $5. $2 senior discount. All year; 14-day limit. Primitive camping. Tbls, toilets, cfga, drkg wtr, showers, dump. Fishing, boating(l), hunting, swimming. 935-acre lake. Favored winter nesting place for bald eagles. Boating, fishing fees.

Pauls Valley City Lake $12
Pauls Valley Parks & Recreation
1.5 mi E of Pauls Valley on Hwy 19; half mi N; half mi W. $12 with elec/wtr; $15 full hookups ($2 seniors discount). All year; 14-day limit. No tents around pavilion. 8 full-hookup sites; 12 with wtr/elec. Tbls, flush toilets, showers, drkg wtr, cfga, dump, pavilion. Picnic areas, boating(ld), fishing, fishing dock. 750-acre lake.

PAWNEE

Pawnee City Lake $12
1 mi N of Pawnee on SR 18. $12 at 5 sites with hookups. All year. 20 total sites. Tbls, flush toilets, cfga, drkg wtr, elec, shelter, showers, beach. Boating(l), fishing, swimming, waterskiing. Pistol range, archery, 9-hole golf, picnic area. 250-acre lake.

PAWHUSKA

Bluestem Lake City Park $6
Pawhuska Parks Department
2.5 mi W of Pawhuska on US 60; 2 mi N on CR 4275; at N side of dam. $6 at non-elec sites ($25 weekly); $15 with elec. All year. 15 primitive sites, 4 sites with elec. Tbls, toilets, cfga, drkg wtr. Boating(ld), fishing. 762-acre lake. Boating fee.

Lake Pawhuska Campground $6
Pawhuska Parks Department
2 mi W of Pawhuska on US 60, then 2 mi S. $6 at 6 primitive sites ($25 weekly). Tbls, toilets, cfga, drkg wtr, handicap dock, dump. Boating(ld), fishing (state trout license required). Boating fee.

PONCA CITY

Coon Creek Cove Recreation Area $7
Corps of Engineers
Kaw Lake
4 mi N of Ponca City on US 77; 6 mi E on SR 11; 1 mi N on Rocky Ridge Rd; at W shore where Coon Creek enters lake. $7 with federal senior pass at 12 primitive sites (others pay $14). At 54 elec/wtr sites, $8 base with senior pass; others pay $16 base, $18 for premium locations ($9 with senior pass). 3/1-11/30; 14-day limit. 55-ft RV limit. Tbls, flush toilets, cfga, drkg wtr, fishing pier, showers, dump. Boating(l), fishing.

Lake Ponca Recreation Area $12
Ponca City Park & Recreation Department
From US 77 in Ponca City, 2 mi E on Lake Rd; qtr mi N on Kygar Rd; E on L.A. Cann Dr to park, turning W into park; campground behind East Lake Ponca on E. Dam Rd. $12

at 30 sites, 12 with 30/50-amp elec/wtr; 3 pull-through. Primitive camping $8. All year except 11/1-1/31; 14-night limit. Tbls, flush toilets, showers, cfga, drkg wtr, dump, shelters, playground. Boating(l), fishing, swimming, golf.

McFadden Cove Recreation Area $7
Corps of Engineers
Kaw Lake
From Ponca City at US 77, 7 mi E on Lake Rd; after curve to S, left (E) on access rd; at SE shore of lake, N side of dam. $7 with fedreal senior pass; others pay $14. 5/1-9/30 (with open periods during hunting season, with wtr when cold permits); 14-day limit. 15 non-elec sites. Tbls, toilets, cfga, drkg wtr, picnic shelter. Fishing, boating(l).

Osage Cove Recreation Area $9
Corps of Engineers
Kaw Lake
From Ponca City at US 77, 9 mi E on Lake Rd, across dam on Kaw Dam Rd; 0.5 mi E on E 20th Rd; 2 mi N on Osage Cove Rd; 1 mi W on Osage Park Rd to SE shore of lake. $9 with federal senior pass at 94 elec sites (no wtr hookups); others pay $18. 3/1-11/30; 14-day limit. RV limit 60 ft. Tbls, flush toilets, cfga, drkg wtr, dump, showers, fishing pier, playground, amphitheater, picnic shelter. Nature trail, biking, horseback riding, boating(l), fishing.

Sandy Park $8
Corps of Engineers
Kaw Lake
From Ponca City at US 77, 9 mi E on Lake Rd, across dam on Kaw Dam Rd; 0.5 mi below dam on E side. $8 with federal senior pass; others pay $16. 4/1-10/31 (closed off-season); 14-day limit. 12 elec sites. Tbls, toilets, cfga, drkg wtr, beach. Swimming, fishing, boating(l).

PORUM
Dutchess Creek Unit FREE
Eufaula State Wildlife Management Area
NW of Porum on SR 2 and co rds to Dutchess Creek section of Eufaula Lake. Southbound co rds lead to camping areas inside the WMA. Free. Only fishermen & hunter primitive camping permitted in designated areas; 14-day limit. WMA encompasses the N and most of the S shorelines of the Dutchess Creek arm.

Porum Landing Recreation Area $7
Corps of Engineers
Eufaula Lake
From Porum, 7 mi W on Texanna Rd, following signs. $7 with federal senior pass at 4 non-elec sites; others pay $14. At 45 elec sites, $19 base, $20 at premium locations ($9.50 & $10 with senior pass). 4/1-9/30; 14-day limit. 60-ft RV limit; 6 pull-through sites. Tbls, flush toilets, cfga, drkg wtr, showers, beach, pavilion, dump, fishing pier. Boating(l), swimming, fishing, golf.

PRUE
Walnut Creek Park $8
Corps of Engineers
Kaystone Lake
From town of Prue (NW of Tulsa), 2 mi W on CR 1200; 2 mi S on CR 1521 to park on N shore of lake. 4/1-10/30; 14-day limit. $8 base with federal senior pass; others pay $16 base, $17 at premium locations ($8.50 with senior pass). 140 sites, including 8 full hookups & 71 with elec/wtr. Tbls, flush toilets, cfga, drkg wtr, beaches, showers, shelter. Boating(ld), fishing, swimming, ball fields, volleyball, horseback riding, hiking, nature trail, mountain biking. Closed in 2014 as state park, currently operated by Corps of Engineers.

PURCELL
Chandler City Park $12
Purcell Parks & Recreation Department
From I-35 exit 91, qtr mi N on SR 74; left (W) at traffic light for 0.5 mi on Chandler Park Rd; at Purcell City Lake. $12 without hookups, $20 at 22 full hookups (10 pull-through); no RV size limit. All year. Tbls, flush toilets, cfga, drkg wtr, showers, playground, dump. Boating(l), fishing, swimming. Pool($).

RATTAN
Rattan Landing Campground $7
Corps of Engineers
Hugo Lake
From Rattan, 4 mi W on SR 3/7, then S on access rd before bridge; at E shore of Kiamichi River above lake. $7 with federal senior pass; others pay $14. All year; 14-day limit. 13 elec/wtr sites. Tbls, flush toilets, cfga, drkg wtr. Boating(l), fishing.

SALLISAW
Applegate Cove Recreation Area $9.50
Corps of Engineers
Robert S. Kerr Reservoir
Arkansas River Lock & Dam 15
From I-40 at Sallisaw, 1 mi S on US 59; 3.5 mi W on Drake Rd; 4 mi S on Dwight Mission Rd; right into park, following signs. $9.50 with federal senior pass at 27 elec/wtr sites; others pay $19. All year; 14-day limit. 50-ft RV limit. Tbls, flush toilets, showers, cfga, drkg wtr, beach, fishing pier, dump. Boating(l), fishing.

SAND SPRINGS
Appalachia Bay Campground $10
Corps of Engineers
Keystone Lake
From Sand Springs, 10.1 mi W on US 64; 2 mi SW on Appalachia Bay Rd. $10. All year; 14-day limit. 28 very primitive sites (no RV size limit); $4 with federal senior pass. Tbls, toilets, cfga, drkg wtr, beach. Boating (l), fishing, swimming, ATV activities (trail $5).

Brush Creek Campground $7.50
Corps of Engineers
Keystone Lake
From Sand Springs, 8 mi W on US 64; 0.25 mi S on SR 151; right (SE) on W. Wekiwa Rd, then left (S) into campground; below dam, N side of spillway at Brush Creek. $7.50 base at 5 elec sites with federal senior pass; others pay $15 base, $20 at 15 premium elec/wtr sites ($10 with senior pass). All year; 14-day limit. Flush toilets, tbls, cfga, drkg wtr, dump. Fishing, boating.

Cowskin Bay South FREE
Corps of Engineers
Keystone Lake
13 mi NW of Sand Springs on US 64; 1 mi NW on Old Keystone Rd (Old US 64) past town of Westport. Free. All year; 14-day limit. 30 primitive undesignated sites (no RV size limit). Tbls, toilets, cfga, drkg wtr, dump. Boating(l), fishing.

Washington Irving South $12
Corps of Engineers
Keystone Lake
From Sand Springs, 10.1 mi W on US 64, across lake bridge to Bears Glen exit; left at stop sign onto Frontage Rd for 1 block; right at first paved rd for 2 mi to park entrance at W shore of lake. $12 at 2 primitive sites ($6 with federal senior pass). At 39 elec sites (no wtr hookups), $10 with senior pass; others pay $20. 4/1-10/31; 14-day limit. 65-ft RV limit. Tbls, flush toilets, cfga, drkg wtr, beach, dump, showers, playground. Boating(l), fishing, hiking, swimming, nature trail.

SAPULPA

Lake Sahoma Campground $12
Sapulpa City Parks
From I-44 exit 215 at Sapulpa, 2 mi N on SR 97; 1 mi W on W. 86th St South; right at S. 145th Ave W; left (S) to bait store & campground at NE shore of 340-acre lake. $12 RV sites (seniors $10); $6 tents. All year; monthly rates available. Tbls, toilets, cfga, drkg wtr, playground, heated fishing pier. Boating(lr), fishing.

Sheppard Point $10
Corps of Engineers
Heyburn Lake
From I-44 exit 211 just W of Sapulpa, about 7 mi E on SR 33; 2 mi S on 305th Ave; 1 mi E on W141st St S, then right (S) on access rd; at N side of lake. 4/1-10/31; 14-day limit. At 21 elec/wtr RV/tent sites, $10 with federal senior pass; others pay $20. RV limit in excess of 65 ft. Tbls, flush toilets, cfga, drkg wtr, showers, dump, playground, beach, 2 picnic shelters. Fishing, boating(l), swimming, nature trail.

SAWYER

Lake Schooler FREE
State Fishing Lake
Dept of Wildlife Conservation
7 mi N of Sawyer. Primitive camping on 35-acre lake. No facilities. Fishing, boating(l).

SAYRE

Sayre City R.V. Park $12
Half mi S from city stoplight on SR 66. $12. All year. 80 RV sites with hookups, some pull-through. Tbls, flush toilets, cfga, drkg wtr, elec, showers, dump, playground. 3 stocked fishing ponds surrounded by lighted walking trail; mini-golf, volleyball, ball fields, tennis, pool. Picnic areas.

SEMINOLE

Sportsman Lake Recreation Area $8
Seminole City Parks
From jct with US 377 at downtown Seminole, 4 mi E on SR 9; 2 mi S on NS 360 Rd; 2 mi E on EW 124 Rd. $8 at 29 primitive sites; $15 for 20/30/50-amp wtr/elec sites ($12 seniors). All year; 14-day limit during 3/1-10/31. 10 full hookups, 11 RV sites with 50-amp, 19 RV sites with 30-amp, 12 equestrian sites with 20/30-amp elec/wtr. Tbls, flush toilets, showers, cfga, drkg wtr, dump, playground, beach, group shelters, fishing pier. Boating(l), fishing, swimming, hiking trails, equestrian trails. 354-acre lake. Boating fee. Monthly camping fees available.

SKIATOOK

Tall Chief Cove Campground $10
Corps of Engineers
Skiatook Lake
From Skiatook, 2 mi W on SR 20; 1.7 mi S on W.C. Rogers Blvd; 3 mi S on Lake Rd, following signs; right (W) on Tall Chief Cove Rd. $10 with federal senior pass at 50 wtr/elec sites; others pay $20. 5/1-10/31; 14-day limit. RV limit in excess of 65 ft. Amphitheater, tbls, flush toilets, cfga, drkg wtr, showers, dump, beach, playground. Interpretive trail, swimming, hiking, fishing, boating(l).

Twin Points Campground $10
Corps of Engineers
Skiatook Lake
From Skiatook, about 10 mi W on SR 20, across main lake bridge, then right (N) on access rd, following signs. $10 with federal senior pass at 49 elec/wtr sites; others pay $20. 5/1-10/31; 14-day limit. RV limit in excess of 65 ft. Tbls, flush toilets, showers, cfga, drkg wtr, dump, playground, fishing pier, beach. Hiking, boating(l), swimming.

STIGLER

Lake John Wells City Park $5
From jct with SR 9 (E. Main St) in Stigler, 1 mi SE on E. Old Military Rd; 1 mi S on Airport Rd, then SW on S. City Lake Rd to park; at W shore of 220-acre lake. $5 at 10 RV sites

with elec; also 10 primitive sites. All year. Tbls, toilets, cfga, drkg wtr. Boating(l), fishing, swimming.

STILLWELL

Stillwell Adair Park $12
Adair County Parks
From jct with US 59 in Stillwell, 0.5 mi E on SR 59; 1 mi N on park rd; formerly a state park, now operated by county. $12 at 20 primitive sites, $20 at 7 elec/wtr sites (30/50-amp); some pull-through. Tbls, flush toilets, cfga, showers, drkg wtr. Fishing pond, picnicking. 25 acres.

SULPHUR

Arbuckle Public Hunting Area Free
State Recreation Area
1 mi W of Sulphur on OK 7; 3 mi S on Point Rd. Free. All year; 1-night limit. Primitive sites. Fishing; hunting.

Buckhorn Campground $8
Chickasaw National Recreation Area
6 mi S of Sulphur on Hwy 177; 3 mi W following signs. $8 with federal senior pass at non-elec sites (others pay $16); $11 with senior pass at 41 elec/wtr sites (others pay $22); $12 with senior pass at premium elec/wtr sites May-Sept (others pay $24). All year; 14-day limit. 134 sites, typically 45 ft. Tbls, flush toilets, cfga, drkg wtr, store, dump. Fishing, swimming. Handicap access.

Cold Springs $7
Chickasaw National Recreation Area
1 mi E of Sulphur on Hwy 7, following signs. $7 with federal senior pass; others pay $14. 5/1-9/30; 14-day limit. 63 small non-elec sites (suitable for pop-up, truck & van campers. Tbls, flush toilets, cfga, drkg wtr, coin laundry, store, restaurant. Swimming, fishing, hiking.

Guy Sandy $7
Chickasaw National Recreation Area
3 mi SW of Sulphur on Hwy 7, following signs. $7 with federal senior pass; others pay $14. 5/8-9/8; 14-day limit. 40 primitive sites; 40-ft RV limit. Tbls, pit toilets, cfga, drkg wtr. Swimming, fishing.

The Point Campground $8
Chickasaw National Recreation Area
6 mi SW of Sulphur on Hwy 7, following signs. $8 with federal senior pass at non-utility sites (others pay $16); $11 with senior pass at 21 50-amp elec sites (others pay $22). All year; 14-day limit. 55 sites; 40-ft RV limit. Tbls, flush toilets, cfga, drkg wtr; dump nearby. Fishing, swimming, hiking.

Rock Creek $7
Chickasaw National Recreation Area
2 mi W of Sulphur on Hwy 7, following signs. $7 with federal senior pass at primitive sites (others pay $14); $11 with senior pass at utility sites (others pay $22). All year;

14-day limit. 106 small sites. Tbls, flush toilets, cfga, drkg wtr, dump, coin laundry, store. Swimming, fishing.

TAHLEQUAH

Buck Ford FREE
Public Access Area
Oklahoma Scenic Rivers Commission
32 mi N of SR 51/US 62 bridge on SR 10; at Illinois River. Free primitive camping. Toilets, drkg wtr. Boating(l), fishing. Canoe access at about 28-mi pt on Illinois Wild & Scenic River.

Carters Landing Recreation Area $10
Corps of Engineers
Tenkiller Ferry Lake
From Tahlequah, 4 mi SE on US 62; 6.6 mi S (left) on SR 82; 2 mi NE (left) on E. Carters Landing Rd; on shore of upper Illinois River, about 2.5 mi from lake. $10 at 15 non-elec sites; $14 at 10 elec/wtr sites ($5 & $7 with federal senior pass). All year (fees may be reduced in winter); 14-day limit. 30-ft RV limit. Tbls, toilets, cfga, firewood, drkg wtr. Swimming; picnicking; fishing; boating(rld).

Cherokee FREE
State Wildlife Management Area
5 mi S of Tahlequah on US 62 to Zeb; S on co rd to Zeb entrance to Cherokee Public Hunting Area; S on Burnt Cabin Rd 5 mi to camp (3.5 mi S of WMA headquarters). Free. Only fishermen & hunter primitive camping permitted; camp only in designated areas; 14-day limit. No camping in game management (refuge) portion. Combined Cherokee and Gruber WMA is 55,515 acres. Fishing at nearby Greenleaf Lake.

Chewey Bridge FREE
Public Access Area
Oklahoma Scenic Rivers Commission
36 mi N of SR 51/US 62 bridge on SR 10; 2 mi E on Chewey Rd to bridge. Free primitive camping. Toilets, drkg wtr. Boating(l), fishing. Canoe access at about 20-mi pt on Illinois Wild & Scenic River.

Echota FREE
Public Access Area
Oklahoma Scenic Rivers Commission
2 mi N of SR 51, US 62 bridge on SR 10. Free primitive camping. Toilets, drkg wtr. Boating (l), fishing. Canoe access at 50-mi marker on Illinois Wild & Scenic River.

No Head Hollow FREE
Public Access Area
Oklahoma Scenic Rivers Commission
3 mi N of SR 51, US 62 bridge on SR 10. Free primitive camping. Toilets, drkg wtr. Boating(l), fishing. Canoe access at 50-mi marker on Illinois Wild & Scenic River. Note: 10 mi of river between No Head & Echota Public Access Areas are only about 1 mi apart by road.

Peavine Hollow FREE
Public Access Area
Oklahoma Scenic Rivers Commission
30 mi N of SR 51/US 62 bridge on SR 10. Free primitive camping. Toilets, drkg wtr. Canoe access at about 40-mi point on Illinois Wild & Scenic River. Boating (l), fishing.

Pettit Bay Recreation Area $7
Corps of Engineers
Tenkiller Ferry Lake
4 mi S of Tahlequah on US 64; 4.6 mi S (left) on SR 82; 2 mi S (right) on Indian Rd; 1 mi SE (left) on W870 Rd. Pettit Bay was operated as two parks with a marina between them; now it is a single park with 2 camping areas: Pettit I is on the N side of the recreation area; it has non-reservable non-elec & elec sites; Pettit II is on the S and has reservable sites, all with hookups. $7 with federal senior pass at 14 non-elec sites during 4/1-9/30 (others pay $14); $10 during 10/1-3/31 ($5 with senior pass). At 72 elec sites (7 wtr hookups), during 4/1-9/30, 30-amp sites $18, 50-amp sites $19, full hookups $20 ($9, $9.50 & $10 with federal senior pass). Off-season, 30-amp elec is $16, 50-amp elec is $17 ($8 & $8.50 with senior pass). No wtr hookups, showers or flush toilets off-season. RV limit in excess of 65 ft. Picnic shelters, tbls, flush toilets, cfga, drkg wtr, showers, dump, beach, elec($). Wheelchair access. Boating (l), fishing, swimming.

Riverside Park FREE
Public Access Area
Oklahoma Scenic Rivers Commission
Just S of SR 51/US 62 bridge on W side of Illinois River. Free primitive camping. Toilets, drkg wtr. Canoe access at about 52-mi point on Illinois Wild & Scenic River. Boating(l), fishing.

Round Hollow FREE
Public Access Area
Oklahoma Scenic Rivers Commission
34 mi N of SR 51/US 62 bridge on SR 10. Free primitive camping. Toilets, drkg wtr (not recommended). Boating(l), fishing. Canoe access at about 26-mi pt on Illinois Wild & Scenic River. Heavy nighttime use of pay phone by travelers. Summer campfire programs on Sat.

Sizemore Landing Recreation Area $8
Corps of Engineers
Tenkiller Ferry Lake
From Tahlequah, 4 mi SE on US 62; 4.6 mi S (left) on SR 82; 3.5 mi S (right)on Indian Rd; 1 mi left at sign on Sizemore Rd. $8 at 32 primitive sites; 30-ft RV limit. All year; 14-day limit. Reduced fees in winter. Non-campers pay day use fee for boat ramp. Tbls, toilets, cfga, no drkg wtr. Boating(l), fishing.

Stunkard FREE
Public Access Area
Oklahoma Scenic Rivers Commission
33 mi N of SR 51/US 62 bridge on SR 10. Free primitive camping. Toilets, drkg wtr. Boating(l), fishing. Canoe access at about 27-mi pt on Illinois Wild & Scenic River.

Todd FREE
Public Access Area
Oklahoma Scenic Rivers Commission
From SR 51/US 62 bridge, E on SR 51 2 mi; N on access rd to Todd PAA. Or, boat/canoe access downstream from No Head Hollow Public Access Area, or upstream from Echota Public Access. Free primitive camping. Toilets, drkg wtr. Boating (l), fishing. Canoe access at about 48 mi point on Illinois Wild & Scenic River.

Turner Ford FREE
Public Access Area
Oklahoma Scenic Rivers Commission
6 mi S of SR 51/US 62 bridge. Free primitive camping (no facilities). Boating(l), fishing.

Watts Public Access Area FREE
Oklahoma Scenic Rivers Commission
36 mi N of SR 51/US 62 bridge on SR 10; about 10 mi E on Chewey Rd to US 59; N on US 59 to Watts bridge (adjacent to Lake Frances Resort). Free primitive camping. Toilets, drkg wtr. Boating(l), fishing. Canoe access at beginning of Illinois Wild & Scenic River canoe route.

TALIHINA

Emerald Vista FREE
Ouachita National Forest
7.2 mi NE of Talihina on US 271; E on Hwy 1. Primitive dispersed camping. Tbls, toilets (except in winter), cfga, no wtr.

Homer L. Johnson Sector FREE
Ouachita State Wildlife Management Area
4 mi E of Talihina on SR 1; 9-12 mi NE & E on FR 1005. Free. 7 camps. Primitive camping within 50 yds of public-use rds; follow rules of Ouachita National Forest when camping outside this sector in the WMA.

Lake Nanih Waiya FREE
State Fishing Access Site
12 mi S of Talihina on US 271; 2 mi W following signs. All year. Primitive undesignated sites; 30-ft RV limit. Tbls, toilets, cfga, no drkg wtr. Boating(l), fishing, hiking.

Winding Stair Campground $10
Ouachita National Forest
Winding Stair National Recreation Area
7.2 mi NE of Talihina on US 271; 18 mi E on Hwy 1. $10 (fee reduced to $8 when wtr not available; double sites $14). 3/1-12/1; 14-day limit. 23 sites, typically 50 ft. Tbls, flush

toilets, showers, cfga, drkg wtr (not available 2017). Fishing, boating, swimming.

TONKAWA

Ray See City Park   FREE
From S end of Tonkawa on US 77, left (W) into park just N of river bridge; at E shore of Salt Fork Arkansas River. Free. Get 3-day permit at police station. Tbls, toilets, cfga, drkg wtr, dump.

TULLAHASSEE

Tullahassee Loop Recreation Area   FREE
Corps of Engineers
Chouteau Pool
Arkansas River Lock & Dam 17
From Tullahassee, 1 mi W on SR 51B; about 4 mi N on 477th E Ave to oxbow loop of Verdigris River. Free. All year; 14-day limit. Primitive designated sites. Pit toilets, cfga, toilets, drkg wtr. Boating(l), fishing.

VALLIANT

Pine Creek Cove Park $7
Corps of Engineers
Pine Creek Lake
From just N of Valliant at jct with Old State Hwy 98, 8 mi N on Pine Creek Rd, following signs; on SW shore of lake near dam. $7 with federal senior pass at 1 primitive site; others pay $14. At 40 elec/wtr sites, $9.50 with senior pass for 30-amp elec, $11 with senior pass for 50-amp elec, $11.50 with senior pass for premium locations; others pay $19, $22 & $23. All year; 14-day limit. RV limit in excess of 65 ft. Group camping with elec, $65. Tbls, toilets, cfga, drkg wtr, nature trails, dump, beach, showers, playground, ball field. Fishing, boating(l), hiking, swimming.

WAGONER

Afton Landing Recreation Area $10
Corps of Engineers
Chouteau Pool
Arkansas River Lock & Dam 17
5 mi W of Wagoner on SR 51; left (S) on access rd before Verdigris River bridge about 2 mi (signs); at N shore of river loop & W shore of main river. Now a Corps "Class B" park without showers or flush toilets. $10 at 2 non-elec sites; 22 elec/wtr sites, $14 for 30-amp, $18 for 50-amp ($7 & $9 with federal senior pass). All year; 14-day limit. Tbls, pit toilets, cfga, drkg wtr, dump, shelter($). Boating(l), fishing.

Blue Bill Point Campground $11
Corps of Engineers
Fort Gibson Lake
From SR 51 at Wagoner, 6 mi N on US 69; 3 mi E/NE on E680 Rd & E670 Rd, following signs; at shore of lake's Flat Rock Bay. All year; 14-day limit. $11-$14 at 3 primitive sites ($5.50-$7 with federal senior pass). At 40 elec/wtr sites, $8 with senior pass for 30-amp elec, $10 with senior pass for 50-amp; others pay $16 & $20. Fees not reduced off-season. RV limit in excess of 65 ft. Tbls, flush toilets, cfga, drkg wtr, showers, dump, picnic shelter($). Fishing, boating(ld).

Flat Rock Creek Campground $7
Fort Gibson Lake
Corps of Engineers
From Wagoner, 8 mi N on US 69; 3 mi E on E660 Rd; 2 mi S on S320 Rd; 1 mi W on E670 Rd. $7 with federal senior pass at 2 primitive sites during 4/1-11/30; others pay $14; free off-season. $9 base for 30-amp with federal senior pass at 36 elec/wtr sites during 4/1-11/30; others pay $18 base, $20 for 50-amp elec ($10 with senior pass); rest of year, some sites may be open & free without utilities. 14-day limit. RV limit in excess of 65 ft. Tbls, flush toilets, showers, cfga, drkg wtr, dump. Boating(l), fishing.

Jackson Bay Recreation Area   FREE
Corps of Engineers
Fort Gibson Lake
From Wagoner, about 3.5 mi S on SR 16; 4 mi E on 100th St N; 2 mi N on S340 Rd; left on access rd. All year; 14-day limit. Free primitive sites near lakeshore. Tbls, pit toilets, cfga, no drkg wtr. Boating(l), fishing.

Mission Bend Recreation Area   FREE
Fort Gibson Lake
Corps of Engineers
From Wagoner, 11.5 mi N on US 69 (to just S of Mazie settlement); 4 mi E on W630 Rd; 1 mi N on S433 Rd (Rocking Rd); 1.5 mi E on W620 Rd (Mission Bend Rd); 1 mi N on S4345 Rd; right on access rd, following signs; at W shore of Neosho River. All year; 14-day limit. Free designated sites. No toilets or no drkg wtr. Boating(l), fishing.

Rocky Point Campground $7
Corps of Engineers
Fort Gibson Lake
From Wagoner at jct with SR 51, 5 mi N on US 69; 1.8 mi E on SR 251D Rd; 1 mi N on N4310 Rd, following signs. All year; 14-day limit. $7 with federal senior pass at 3 primitive sites; others pay $14. At 57 elec/wtr sites, $9 with senior pass for 30-amp elec, $10 with senior pass for 50-amp elec; others pay $18 & $20. No reduced fees off-season. RV limit in excess of 65 ft. Shelter($), tbls, flush & pit toilets, showers, drkg wtr, cfga, dump, beach, change house. Boating(l), fishing, swimming, fishing pier.

Taylor Ferry South Campground $7
Corps of Engineers
Fort Gibson Lake
From Wagoner at jct with US 69, 8 mi E on SR 51; S before bridge on access rd. All year; 14-day limit. $7 with federal senior pass at 6 primitive sites; others pay $14. At 85 elec/wtr sites, $8 with senior pass for 30-amp elec, $10 with

senior pass for 50-amp; others pay $16 & $20. Fees not reduced off-season. RV limit in excess of 65 ft. Tbls, flush toilets, cfga, drkg wtr, showers, beach, nature trail, picnic shelters. Swimming, boating(l), fishing.

WAURIKA

Lake Jap Beaver	FREE

State Fishing Lake
Dept of Wildlife Conservation
4.5 mi NW of Waurika in Jefferson County. Free primitive camping at 65-acre lake. Toilets. Fishing, boating(l).

Moneka Park	$10

Corps of Engineers
Waurika Lake
From Waurika, 6 mi N on SR 5; 0.8 mi N on County N2780 Rd, then left on Dam Access Rd; just E of dam at E shore of Beaver Creek. 35 primitive sites, $10; 3 elec sites, $14 ($7 with federal senior pass). 3/1-10/31; 14-day limit. 38 primitive sites. Tbls, toilets, cfga, no drkg wtr. Boating, fishing, swimming, nature trail.

Wichita Ridge Recreation Area	$12

Corps of Engineers
Waurika Lake
From just E of Hastings at jct with SR 5, 4 mi N on County N2740 Rd (Corum Rd); at NW shore of lake. All year; 14-day limit. 16 sites without hookups & 1 site with wtr, $12 ($6 with federal senior pass); 10 elec sites (2 wtr hookups), $14 ($7 with senior pass). Self-deposit fee system. No RV size limit. Toilets, drkg wtr, cfga, tbls, dump, picnic shelter($). Boating(ld), fishing, nature trail, equestrian trail, swimming, hiking.

WEBBERS FALLS

Brewers Bend Recreation Area	$7

Corps of Engineers
Webbers Falls Reservoir
Arkansas River Lock & Dam 16
2 mi W of Webbers Falls on US 64; 3 mi N & 2 mi NW on N4410 Rd; right (E) into park, following signs. $7 with federal senior pass at 8 basic non-elec sites (others pay $14). At 34 elec/wtr sites, $9 with senior pass (others pay $18); no reduced fees off-season. Tbls, toilets, cfga, drkg wtr, beach, dump, picnic shelter, amphitheater. Boating(l), fishing, swimming.

WRIGHT CITY

Little River Park	$7

Corps of Engineers
Pine Creek Lake
From Wright City, 6 mi N on Old State Hwy 98; 8.5 mi W on SR 3 across bridge, then SE on Little River Park Rd, following signs; on W shore of lake. $7 with federal senior pass at 25 primitive sites (others pay $14). At 62 elec/wtr sites, $9 with federal senior pass at 30-amp sites; $11 with senior pass at 21 50-amp sites; $11.50 with

senior pass at 12 full-hookup sites; others pay $18, $22 & $23. All year; 14-day limit. RV limit in excess of 65 ft; 4 pull-through sites. Group camping area with elec, $65. Picnic shelter, tbls, flush toilets, cfga, drkg wtr, showers, playground, dump, beach. Baseball, hiking, fishing, boating(l), nature trail.

Lost Rapids Park	$12

Corps of Engineers
Pine Creek Lake
From Wright City, 6 mi N on SR 98; 6 mi W on SR 3, then S before causeway following signs; at E shore of lake. $12 at 14 non-elec sites ($6 with federal senior pass). At 16 elec sites, $8.50 with senior pass; others pay $17. All year; 14-day limit. RV limit in excess of 65 ft. Tbls, flush toilets, cfga, drkg wtr, dump, playground. Boating(l), fishing.

Turkey Creek Park	$12

Corps of Engineers
Pine Creek Lake
At town of Ringold on N end of lake. From Little River Park at jct with SR 3, 1 mi W on SR 3; 0.5 mi E on E1950 Rd to Burwell; about 3 mi N of Burwell on County Line Rd (N4430 Rd); 1.5 mi E on Pine Creek Park Rd, following signs. $12 at 20 non-elec sites. At 10 elec/wtr sites, $8.50 with federal senior pass; others pay $17. All year; 14-day limit. RV limit in excess of 65 ft. Tbls, toilets, cfga, drkg wtr, dump, playground. Boating(l), fishing.

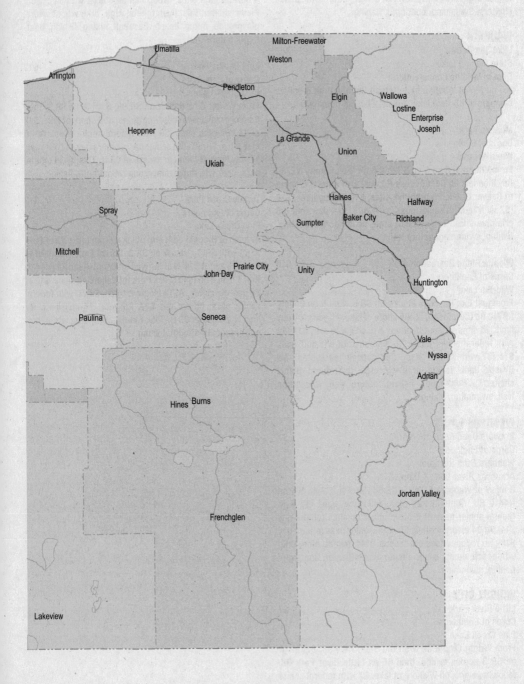

Arlington
Umatilla
Milton-Freewater
Weston
Pendleton
Elgin
Wallowa
Lostine
Enterprise
Joseph
Heppner
La Grande
Union
Ukiah
Haines
Halfway
Spray
Sumpter
Baker City
Richland
Mitchell
Prairie City
Unity
John Day
Huntington
Paulina
Seneca
Vale
Nyssa
Adrian
Hines Burns
Jordan Valley
Frenchglen
Lakeview

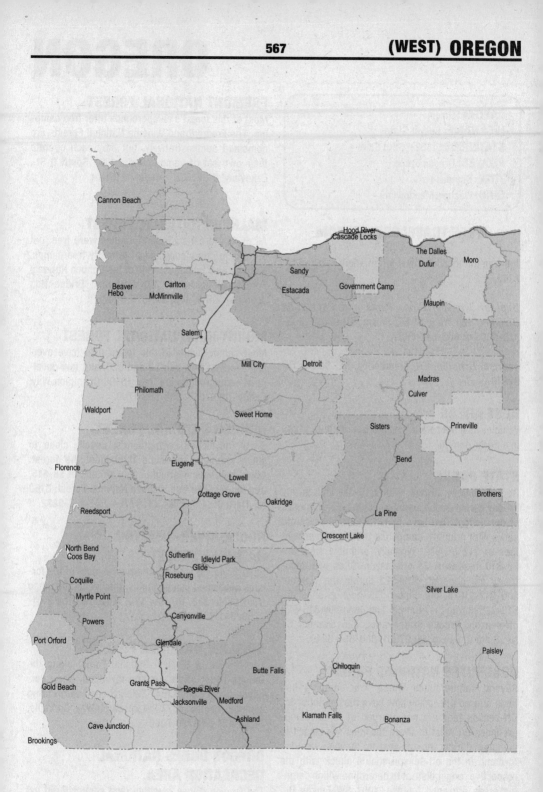

Cannon Beach

Hood River
Cascade Locks

The Dalles
Dufur   Moro

Sandy   Government Camp
Beaver   Carlton   Estacada
Hebo   McMinnville   Maupin

Salem

Mill City   Detroit   Madras
Philomath   Culver

Waldport   Sweet Home   Sisters   Prineville

Eugene   Bend
Florence   Lowell
                        Cottage Grove
Reedsport   Oakridge   Brothers

North Bend   La Pine
Coos Bay   Sutherlin   Idleyld Park
                Glide   Crescent Lake
Coquille   Roseburg

Myrtle Point   Silver Lake

Powers   Canyonville

Port Orford   Glendale
                                                                    Paisley

Gold Beach   Grants Pass   Butte Falls   Chiloquin
                Rogue River
                Jacksonville Medford
Cave Junction   Ashland   Klamath Falls   Bonanza

Brookings

OREGON

CAPITAL: Salem
NICKNAME: Beaver State
STATEHOOD: 1859 – 33rd State
FLOWER: Oregon Grape
TREE: Douglas Fir
BIRD: Western Meadowlark

WWW.TRAVELOREGON.COM

Toll free number for travel information: 1-800-547-7842.

Dept of Transportation, Parks and Recreation Division, 525 Trade St SE, Salem, OR 97310. 503-378-6305 or 800-542-5687.

Tourism Division, 775 Summer St. NE, Salem, OR 97310.

REST AREAS

Vehicles may not park in rest areas more than 14 hrs in a 24-hr period.

STATE PARKS

RV limit usually 30 feet, with a 10-day limit in any 14-day period during summer months. For purposes of our listings, we have included only those state parks with primitive campsites that have overnight fees of $12 or less. Typically, primitive sites are $8-$10 in-season, $5 off-season. Sites with electricity are generally $16-$23 during the summer and $12-$16 in the winter. Full-hookup sites are $18-$25 during the summer and generally $15-$20 off-season. Oregon State Parks, 725 Summer ST NE, Suite C, Salem, OR 97301. 800-551-6949.

DESCHUTES NATIONAL FOREST

Several campgrounds where free camping had been offered previously now have fees of about $6. Off-season fees are not charged at forest campgrounds, but most of those facilities are closed to camping during the off-season. Anyone desiring to camp in the off-season should check with the respective ranger district to determine which camping areas are open for use. 1001 SW Emkay Dr., Bend OR 97702. 541-383-5300.

FREMONT NATIONAL FOREST

Most of this forest's campgrounds offer free camping. The Fremont and Winema National Forests are combined administratively, but they each operate their own set of campgrounds. 1301 South G St., Lakeview, OR 97630. 541-947-2151.

MALHEUR NATIONAL FOREST

All of this forest's 23 campgrounds were free, but $8 fees are now collected at formerly free camps. Malheur also manages some of the Ochoco National Forest campgrounds. 431 Patterson Bridge Rd., John Day, OR 97845. 541-575-3000.

MOUNT HOOD NATIONAL FOREST

Most campgrounds in this forest now have overnight fees of between $8 and $20, and few developed campgrounds are free. 16400 Champion Way, Sandy, OR 97055. 503-668-1700.

OCHOCO NATIONAL FOREST

Small, developed campgrounds, usually close to small streams, are found throughout the forest. About half have overnight camping fees of $8-$15, and the rest are free. Ochoco National Forest, 3160 NE Third St., Prineville, OR 97754. 541-475-9272.

ROGUE RIVER-SISKIYOU NATIONAL FOREST

Small camping fees are charged at most of the forest's developed campgrounds; they generally range from $6 to $10. PO Box 520, Medord, OR 97501-0209. 541-858-2200.

SIUSLAW NATIONAL FOREST

The section of Siuslaw National Forest along the Oregon coast offers exciting diversion. Cape Perpetua Visitor Center (547-3289) is open daily during summer months. 4077 SW Research Way, Corvallis, OR 97339. 541-750-7000.

OREGON DUNES NATIONAL RECREATION AREA

The Oregon Dunes is within (and administered by) Siuslaw National Forest. The dunes area stretches along 40 miles of Oregon's Central Coast and has about a dozen federal campgrounds open for winter use. All have fees higher than $12.

UMATILLA NATIONAL FOREST
The forest has several campgrounds with low-cost sites available, as well as hundreds of primitive, undeveloped sites for which overnight camping fees are not charged. 2517 SW Hailey, Pendleton, OR 97801. 541-278-3716.

UMPQUA NATIONAL FOREST
Low-cost camping is available at several developed campgrounds, with fees ranging from $6 to $12 per night. Some of those campgrounds are completely closed during the off-season, but others are open without drinking water and services. There are no fees during the off-season for those that are open. 2900 Stewart Pkwy, Roseburg, OR 97470. 541-672-6601.

WALLOWA-WHITMAN NATIONAL FOREST
The forest's campsite fees are generally $8-14. PO Box 907, Baker City, OR 97814. 541-523-6391.

WILLAMETTE NATIONAL FOREST
Many of the forests developed campgrounds are now operated by concessionaires. Camping fees range from $16 to $20. 3106 Pierce Parkway, Springfield, OR 97477. 541-225-6300.

WINEMA NATIONAL FOREST
The Fremont and Winema National Forests are combined Fees at Winema's 12 developed campgrounds are generally $6-$13, but about half of the campgrounds are free. 1301 South G St., Lakeview, OR 97630. 541-947-2151.

BUREAU OF LAND MANAGEMENT
The North Umpqua River area is considered by many outdoorsmen to be one of the finest steelhead and trout angling rivers in the nation. The river is restricted to fly fishing upstream form the fish hatchery intake at Rock Creek. RV and tent campers have numerous opportunities for free and low-clst camping.

BLM's Prineville District manages almost 50 per cent of the landin the Lower Deschutes River

National Backcountry Byway corridor. Along the path are numerous free and low -cost campgrounds (see entries under Maupin and Madras).

The Lower Crooked River National Backcountry Byway is within the ceded lands of the Confederated Tribes of the Warm Springs Indian Reservation. Fires are prohibited June 1-Oct. 15 and, during the rest of the year, fire rings are prohibited.

U.S. ARMY CORPS OF ENGINEERS
Low-cost camping is available at Cottage Grove Lake, Dorena Lake and Fall Creek Lake, while free camping is offered at Fall Creek, Lake Umatilla, Lake Wallula and Lost Creek Lake. For the best information available about Corps campgrounds nationally, contact us for your own copy of *Camping With the Corps of Engineers* ($17.95 plus $5 shipping from Thw Wright Guide at 800-275-5518.

ADRIAN (E)

Slocum Canyon Camp   FREE
Bureau of Land Management
Vale District
8 me S of Adrian on Hwy 201, following Leslie Gulch/Succor Creek National Back Country Byway signs; rd steep & narrow, not recommended for large RVs. Free. 4/1-11/1; 14-day limit. 12 primitive undesignated sites along Owyhee Reservoir. Toilets, cfga, no drkg wtr. Fishing, boating(l), swimming, waterskiing.

Succor Creek State Natural Area   FREE
About 6 mi S of Adrian on SR 201; right (S) for 15 mi on rough gravel Succor Creek Rd to natural area. Free. All year; 14-day limit. 8 primitive sites & pit toilet on W side of creek; 15 walk-in tent sites on E side. Tbls, cfga, no drkg wtr. Fishing, hiking.

ARLINGTON (E)

Port of Arlington RV Park/Marina $9
City of Arlington
From I-84 exit 137 at Arlington, follow Cottonwood Ave to its end; park at 475 Shane Dr. $9 without hookups; $30 full hookups; weekly & monthly rates available. All year. 35 sites. Tbls, flush toilets, showers, cfga, drkg wtr, phones, coin laundry, pool. Swimming, hiking.

ASHLAND (W)

Beaver Dam $8
Rogue River National Forest
25 mi NE of Ashland on Dead Indian Hwy; 1.5 mi N on FR 37; at Beaver Dam Creek. $8. 5/7-11/15; 14-day limit. 4 sites; 16-ft RV limit. Tbls, toilets, cfga, no drkg wtr or trash service. Fishing, hiking. Elev 4500 ft.

Daley Creek $8
Rogue River National Forest
25 mi NE of Ashland on FR 25 (Dead Indian Hwy); 1.6 mi N on FR 37. $8. 5/7-11/15; 14-day limit. 3 RV sites; 19-ft limit. Tbls, toilets, cfga, no drkg wtr or trash service. Fishing, hiking. At Beaver Dam & Daley Creeks. Elev 4500 ft.

Hyatt Lake Recreation Area $12
Cascade-Siskiyou National Monument
Bureau of Land Management
Medford District
17.5 mi SE of Ashland on SR 66; 5 mi E of Hyatt Rd. $12 on Mon-Thurs; $15 Fri-Sun; $10 equestrian; $7 at Wildcat Campground (with 12 sites, 1.5 mi past main campground). About 5/1-9/30. 14-day limit. 47 RV sites (40-ft RV limit). Tbls, flush & pit toilets, cfga, drkg wtr, showers, dump, fish cleaning station. Fishing, swimming, boating(ld), volleyball, horseshoes, playground, horseback riding (corrals). Elev 5070 ft.

Mount Ashland   FREE
Klamath National Forest
12.1 mi SE of Ashland on I-5; 1.1 mi W on CR 993; 9.1 mi W on CR 1151; 4.8 mi W on FR 40S01. Free. 7/1-10/31. 6 sites (RVs under 16 ft). Tbls, toilets, cfga, no drkg wtr or trash service. Mountain climbing; hiking. Elev 6600 ft. Mountain summit (1.5 mi). Maintained by Rogue River National Forest.

Surveyor Mountain Campground   FREE
Bureau of Land Management
Lakeview District
From jct with SR 66 at SE side of Ashland, about 10 mi E on Dead Indian Memorial Rd; right (SE) on Keno Access Rd for 4 mi to site; on right. Free. 5/1-10/31; 14-day limit. 5 RV/tent sites. Tbls, toilets, cfga, drkg wtr. Wheelchair access.

BAKER CITY (E)

Lake Fork Campground $6
Hells Canyon Nat. Recreation Area
Wallowa-Whitman National Forest
4 mi N of Baker City on I-84; 62 mi E on Hwy 86; 8 mi N on FR 39; left on access rd; at Lake Fork Creek. $6. 6/1-11/30; 14-day limit. 10 sites; 22-ft RV limit. Tbls, toilets, cfga, no drkg wtr. Fishing, hiking, boating.

McCully Forks Campground $6
Wallowa-Whitman National Forest
33 mi SW of Baker City on SR 7 & SR 220 (just past Sumpter). $6. MD-10/15; 14-day limit. Toilet, tbls, cfga, no drkg wtr. 7 RV/tent sites. Primarily a hunting camp. Fishing, hiking, biking, horseback riding.

Millers Lane Campground $10
Wallowa-Whitman National Forest
24 mi SW of Baker City on SR 7; just past Phillips Lake, go 2 mi S on Hudspath Lane, then 3.5 mi SE on FR 2220 (gravel); on S shore of Phillips Lake. $10. 5/1-11/15; 14-day limit. 11 RV/tent sites (20-ft RV limit). Tbls, toilets, cfga, no drkg wtr. Boating(l), fishing, hiking, swimming.

Southwest Shore Campground $10
Wallowa-Whitman National Forest
24 mi SW of Baker City on SR 7; just past Philips Lake, go 2 mi S on Hudspath Lane, then 2.5 mi SE on FR 2220 (gravel); on S shore of Phillips Lake. $10. 5/1-11/15; 14-day limit. 16 RV/tent sites (24-ft RV limit). Tbls, toilets, cfga, no drkg wtr, no trash service. Fishing, boating(l), swimming, waterskiing, hiking.

BEAVER (W)

Nestucca River Backcountry Byway $7.50
Bureau of Land Management
Salem District
About 16 mi E of Beaver on Blaine Rd to Bible Creek Rd for W access to loop route. $7.50 with federal senior pass; others pay $15. Designated sites at four BLM locations

along route. Tbls, toilets, cfga, drkg wtr. Fishing, OHV activities.

Rocky Bend Campground   FREE
Siuslaw National Forest
13 mi SE of Beaver (S of Tillamook) via CR 858 (Blaine Rd); at the Nestucca River. Free. All year; 14-day limit. 6 sites (RVs under 16 ft). Toilet, tbls, cfga, no drkg wtr, no trash service. Hiking, fishing, clamming, swimming. Fee expected in 2017.

BEND (W)
Big River Campground $10
Deschutes National Forest
17 mi S of Bend on US 97; 5 mi W on CR 42. $10 ($30 groups). 4/15-10/31; 14-day limit. 9 RV sites, 3 for groups (26-ft RV limit). Tbls, toilet, cfga, no drkg wtr. Boating(l), fishing. On Deschutes River. Elev 4150 ft.

Bull Bend $10
Deschutes National Forest
26.8 mi S of Bend on US 97; 8 mi W on CR 43; 2 mi S on FR 4370. $10. 4/15-10/31; 14-day limit. 12 sites; 30-ft RV limit. Tbls, toilets, cfga, no drkg wtr. Fishing, boating(l), swimming, canoeing, rafting. On the Deschutes River. Elev 4300 ft.

Cinder Hill $9
Newberry National Volcanic Monument
Deschutes National Forest
23.5 mi S of Bend on Hwy 97; 17.6 mi E on CR 21; half mi N on FR 2100-700; at East Lake. $9 with federal senior pass; others pay $18. MD-10/31; 14-day limit. 110 sites; 40-ft RV limit. Tbls, pit & flush toilets, cfga, drkg wtr, dump. Boating(l), fishing, hiking, swimming, birdwatching, biking, canoeing. Forest pass required for trailhead parking. Non-campers pay $10 at dump station.

Cow Meadow $10
Deschutes National Forest
44.7 mi SW of Bend on CR 46; half mi E on FR 40 to Cow Meadow sign; 1 mi S on gravel FR 970, then right at "T" for 0.5 mi; on N end of Crane Prairie Reservoir at Deschutes River. $10. Open 5/18-9/15; 14-day limit. 18 sites (30-ft RV limit). Tbls, toilets, cfga, drkg wtr. Fishing, boating(l - small boats only). Elev 4500 ft.

Cultus Corral Horse Camp $7
Deschutes National Forest
43 mi SW on CR 46 (Cascade Lakes Hwy); right on FR 4635 for 1 mi, then left on FR 4630 for 1 mi; right at sign. $7 with federal senior pass; others pay $14. About MD-9/30; 14-day limit. 11 RV sites; 40-ft RV limit. Tbls, toilets, cfga, drkg wtr, horse corral, stalls. Fishing, boating, hiking, horseback riding. Near Cultus Lake. Elev 4450 ft.

Cultus Lake Campground $9
Deschutes National Forest
43.5 mi SW of Bend on CR 46 (Cascade Lakes Hwy); 2 mi W on FR 4635. $9 with federal senior pass; others pay $18. About MD-9/30; 10-day limit. 55 RV/tent sites; 36-ft RV limit. Tbls, toilets, cfga, drkg wtr. Swimming, boating(rl), fishing, waterskiing. Elev 4700 ft; 7 acres.

Deschutes Bridge   CLOSED
Deschutes National Forest
39 mi SW of Bend on CR 46 (Cascade Lakes Hwy); half mi E on FR 4270. Campground closed permanently.

East Lake Campground $9
Newberry National Volcanic Monument
Deschutes National Forest
23.5 mi S of Bend on Hwy 97; 16.6 mi E on CR 21; at SE shore of East Lake. $9 with federal senior pass; others pay $18. 6/15-10/15; 14-day limit. 29 sites; 40-ft RV limit. Tbls, flush & pit toilets, cfga, drkg wtr. Boating(l), fishing, hiking, swimming, biking, birdwatching.

Elk Lake Campground $7
Deschutes National Forest
33.1 mi W of Bend on CR 46 (Cascade Lakes Hwy); on N end of Elk Lake. $7 with federal senior pass; others pay $14. About 6/15-9/30; 14-day limit. 23 sites (36-ft RV limit). Tbls, toilets, cfga, drkg wtr. Swimming, boating(lr), fishing, hiking trails. Elev 4900 ft; 7 acres.

Fall River Campground $10
Deschutes National Forest
17.3 mi S of Bend on US 97; 12.2 mi SW on CR 42. $10. 4/15-10/31; 14-day limit. 10 sites (40-ft RV limit). Toilets, cfga, no drkg wtr, tbls. Fishing, boating(no mtrs), hiking. Elev 4000 ft. Fishing.

Lava Lake Campground $8
Deschutes National Forest
38.4 mi SW of Bend on CR 46 (Cascade Lakes Hwy); 1 mi E on FR 500. $8 with federal senior pass; others pay $16 ($30 multi-site). About 5/25-10/9; 14-day limit. 43 sites (40-ft RV limit). Tbls, toilets, cfga, drkg wtr, showers, dump. Fishing, boating(ldr), hiking trails. Elev 4800 ft.

Little Cultus Lake $8
Deschutes National Forest
44.5 mi SW of Bend on CR 46 (Cascade Lakes Hwy); 1 mi NW on FR 4635; 2 mi SW on FR 4630; 1 mi W on FR 4636. $8 with federal senior pass; others pay $16. About MD-9/30; 14-day limit. 31 sites; 40-ft RV limit. Tbls, toilets, cfga, drkg wtr. Swimming, fishing, boating(l), waterskiing.

Little Fawn Campground $8
Deschutes National Forest
35.5 mi SW of Bend on CR 46 (Cascade Lakes Hwy); 2 mi SE on FR 4625; at Elk Lake. $8 with federal senior pass;

others pay $16 ($12 until wtr service restored). About 6/15-9/10; 14-day limit. About 20 sites plus group camping; 30-ft RV limit. Tbls, toilets, cfga, drkg wtr. Boating, fishing, hiking, windsurfing.

Little Lava Lake Campground $7
Deschutes National Forest
38.4 mi SW of Bend on CR 46 (Cascade Lakes Hwy); 0.7 mi E on FR 4600; 0.4 mi E on FR 4600-520; on Little Lava Lake. $7 with federal senior pass; others pay $14 ($26 double sites, $50 groups). About MD-10/10; 14-day limit. 12 sites (36-ft RV limit). Tbls, toilets, cfga, drkg wtr. Boating (rentals, dock, launch nearby), fishing, hiking, nature trails.

Mallard Marsh Campground $10
Deschutes National Forest
33 mi W of Bend on CR 46; 1.9 mi N on FR 4625; on Hosmer Lake. $10. 6/15-9/30; 14-day limit. 15 sites (40-ft RV limit). Tbls, toilets, no drkg wtr. Fishing, boating(l), nature trails. Elev 4900 ft.

North Twin Lake Campground $7
Deschutes National Forest
17.5 mi S of Bend on US 96; 19 mi W on CR 42; 2 mi SW on FR 4260. $7 with federal senior pass; others pay $14. 4/20-10/31; 14-day limit. 29 sites; 36-ft RV limit. Tbls, toilets, cfga, no drkg wtr, dump. Fishing, boating, swimming.

Point Campground $7
Deschutes National Forest
33 mi SW of Bend on CR 46 (Cascade Lakes Hwy); at Elk Lake. $7 with federal senior pass; others pay $14 ($26 multi-site). 6/15-9/25; 14-day limit. 9 sites (36-ft RV limit). Tbls, toilets, cfga, drkg wtr. Fishing, hiking, boating(l).

Quinn Meadow Horse Camp $7
Deschutes National Forest
30 mi W of Bend on CR 46 (Cascade Lakes Hwy); qtr mi SE on FR 450. $7 with federal senior pass at sites with 2-horse corrals; $9 with senior pass at sites with 4-horse corrals; others pay $14 & $18. MD-9/30; 14-day limit. 26 sites (60-ft RV limit). Tbls, toilets, cfga, drkg wtr, horse stalls. Horseback riding trails, hiking trails, fishing. Elev 5100 ft; 5 acres.

Reservoir Campground $10
Deschutes National Forest
57 mi W of Bend on CR 46; 2 mi E on FR 44 (gravel rd sometimes rough). $10. About 5/19-9/30; 14-day limit. 28 sites (30-ft RV limit). Tbls, toilets, cfga, no drkg wtr. Fishing, boating(l), hiking. Elev 4400 ft. On S shore of Wickiup Reservoir.

Sand Springs Campground   FREE
Deschutes National Forest
21.2 mi E of Bend on US 20; 18.6 mi SE on CR 23. Free.

Elev 5100 ft. 5/15-10/30. 3 sites on 3 acres (RVs under 31 ft). Toilets, cfga, no tbls, no drkg wtr; site not maintained.

Sheep Bridge Campground $12
Deschutes National Forest
26.8 mi S of Bend on US 97; 11 mi W on CR 43; 4.6 mi SW on FR 42; half mi W on FR 4260. $12 (group site $30). About 4/20-10/31; 14-day limit. 23 sites; 40-ft RV limit. Tbls, toilets, cfga, drkg wtr. Fishing, boating (l). On Deschutes River at entrance to Wickiup Reservoir.

Soda Creek Campground $10
Deschutes National Forest
26.2 mi W of Bend on CR 46; at Sparks Lake. $10. 5/1-10/15; 14-day limit. 7 RV/tent sites; 36-ft RV limit. Tbls, toilets, cfga, no drkg wtr. Hiking, fly fishing, boating (no mtrs), hiking trails. Closed in 2017 for road work & stream restoration.

South Campground $12
Deschutes National Forest
35.5 mi W of Bend on CR 46; 1.2 mi N on FR 4625. $12. 6/15-9/30; 14-day limit. 23 sites (100-ft RV limit). Tbls, toilets, cfga, no drkg wtr. Fishing, boating (l), nature trails. Elev 4900 ft.

Swamp Wells Camp   FREE
Deschutes National Forest
4 mi S of Bend on US 97; 5.4 mi SE on CR 18; 5.8 mi S on FR 1810; 3.2 mi SE on FR 1816 (last mi rough rd). Free. 5/15-10/30; 14-day limit. 5 primitive sites (30-ft RV limit). Tbls, cfga, toilets, no drkg wtr. Hiking trails, horseback riding. Nearby Arnold Ice Cave lava tubes.

Todd Creek $5
Trailhead & Horse Camp
Deschutes National Forest
24 mi W of Bend on CR 46; 0.6 mi S on FR 4600-390. $5 daily or $30 annual forest pass. Primitive undesignated camping area. Toilets, cfga, no drkg wtr. Horseback riding, hiking, mountain biking.

Wyeth Campground $10
Deschutes National Forest
26 mi S of Bend on US 97; 8 mi W on FR 43; 0.3 mi S on FR 4370; at Deschutes River below Wickiup Reservoir. $10. About 4/20-10/31; 14-day limit. 5 sites; 40-ft RV limit. Tbls, toilet, cfga, no drkg wtr, horse facilities. Fishing, horseback riding, boating(l). Elev 4300 ft.

BONANZA (W)

Gerber Reservoir Campground $7
Bureau of Land Management
Lakeview District
16 mi E of Bonanza on gravel East Longell Valley Rd to site (or, S on gravel rd from Bly). $7 during 5/15-9/15; limited

services off-season; 14-day limit. 50 sites at two areas (30-ft RV limit). Tbls, toilets, cfga, drkg wtr, dump, fish cleaning station. Boating(dl), fishing, swimming, hiking. 80 acres. Free primitive & dispersed camping at surrounding BLM and NFS lands with toilets, cfga, tbls, no drkg wtr or trash service.

BROOKINGS (W)

| First Camp Campground | FREE |

Siskiyou National Forest

5.6 mi SE of Brookings on US 101; 6.3 mi NE on CR 896; E on FR 1107 just before Winchuck Campground; at Winchuck River. Free. 5/15-9/30; 14-day limit. Small primitive dispersed sites. Tbls, cfga, toilets, no drkg wtr or trash service. Fishing, swimming, floating, hiking trail.

| Little Redwood Dispersed Site | FREE |

Siskiyou National Forest

Half mi S of Brookings on US 101; 7.5 mi NE on CR 784; 6 mi NE on FR 1376. On the Cheto River. Free. 5/15-9/30; 14-day limit. 12 sites (16-ft RV limit). Tbls, no toilets, cfga, no drkg wtr, no trash service. Fishing (good trout), swimming, hiking trail. 2 acres. Closed as a developed campground in 2010; call ranger office before arrival (541-247-3600).

| Ludlum Campground | $10 |

Siskiyou National Forest

5.6 mi SE of Brookings on US 101; 6.3 mi NE on CR 896; 1 mi E on FR 1107, then 2 mi on FR 1108; at Wheeler Creek & Winchuck River. $10. 4/21-12/1; 14-day limit. 7 sites. Tbls, flush toilets, cfga, drkg wtr. Hiking, swimming, fishing.

| Miller Bar Dispersed Camping | $10 |

Siskiyou National Forest

Half mi S of Brookings on US 101; 7.5 mi NE on CR 784 (becomes FR 1376); 2 mi past forest boundary; at the Cheto River. Operated as a dispersed site, but with fee. $10. 5/15-10/15; 14-day limit. Small undesignated RV/tent sites. Tbls, toilets, cfga, no drkg wtr. Trash service MD-LD. Fishing, swimming, floating.

| Nook Bar Dispersed Camp | $10 |

Siskiyou National Forest

Half mi S of Brookings on US 101; 7.5 mi NE on CR 784 (becomes FR 1376); 3 mi past forest boundary; at the Cheto River. Operated as dispersed site but with fee. $10. 5/15-10/15; 14-day limit. Small undesignated RV/tent sites. Tbls, toilet, cfga, no drkg wtr. Trash service MD-LD. Fishing, swimming, floating.

| Redwood Bar Dispersed Camping | $10 |

Siskiyou National Forest

Half mi S of Brookings on US 101; 7.5 mi NE on CR 784 (becomes FR 1376); 6 mi past forest boundary, just past Little Redwood Camp; at the Cheto River. Operated as dispersed site but with fee. $10. 5/15-10/15; 14-day limit.

Small undesignated RV/tent sites. Tbls, toilet, cfga, no drkg wtr (but planned). Trash service 5/15-9/15. Fishing, swimming, floating, hiking.

| South Fork Dispersed Camping | $10 |

Siskiyou National Forest

Half mi S of Brookings on US 101; 7.5 mi NE on CR 784 (becomes FR 1376); 8 mi past forest boundary, just past Redwood Bar Camp; at the South Fork of Cheto River. Operated as dispersed site but with fee. $10. 5/15-10/15; 14-day limit. Upper & Lower South Fork Campgrounds. Small undesignated RV/tent sites. No facilities or trash service, no drkg wtr; portable toilet. Fishing, swimming, floating, hiking.

BROTHERS (W)

| Pine Mountain | FREE |

Deschutes National Forest

10 mi W on US 20; 7 mi S on FR 2017. Free, but donations accepted for observatory. 5/15-10/30. 3 sites (RVs under 31 ft). Tbls, toilets, cfga, no drkg wtr. Birdwatching. Elev 6200 ft; 2 acres. Qtr mi S of Pine Mountain Observatory at mountain summit.

BURNS (E)

| Alder Springs Camp | FREE |

Malheur National Forest

From Burns, S on Hwy 395 to CR 127; N to FR 41, then NE to site. Free. All year; 14-day limit. 3 rustic sites. Tbls, toilet, cfga, no drkg wtr or trash service. Primarily a hunting camp.

| Chickahominy Reservoir Campground | $8 |

Bureau of Land Management

Burns District

34 mi W of Burns on US 20 (5 mi W of Riley) to milepost 100; N on entrance rd. Some free or variable rates during Oct-Mar; $8 rest of year; 14-day limit. 28 sites; 35-ft RV limit. Tbls, toilets, cfga, drkg wtr. Boating(ld), fishing, fish cleaning station. No wtr during off-season. Elev 4300 ft; 20 acres. Wild horse herds around Palomino Buttes E of river; in Smoky Hollow S of reservoir; W of Malheur Lake. Ice fishing in winter. Dump at Sage Hen rest area. Dispersed camping also near dam.

| Harney County Fairgrounds | $10 |

From jct with SR 78 in downtown Burns, 6 blocks W on US 20, then 7 blocks S on Egan Ave & right into fairgrounds. Egan in Burns. $10 without hookups, $15 full hookups. All year. 32 sites. Tbls, toilets, cfga, drkg wtr, showers, elec, dump.

| Idlewild Campground | $10 |

Malheur National Forest

17 mi N of Burns on US 395. $10. 5/15-10/15; 14-day limit. 26 sites (20-ft RV limit). Tbls, toilets, cfga, drkg wtr, grey

wtr stations. Fishing. Elev 5300 ft. 18 acres. Excellent stop for US 395 travelers.

Joaquin Miller Horse Camp $8
Malheur National Forest
20 mi N of Burns on US 395. $8. All year; 14-day limit. 8 sites; 20-ft RV limit. Tbls, toilet, cfga, drkg wtr, corrals, hitch rails. Horseback riding, hiking.

Mann Lake Recreation Site FREE
Bureau of Land Management
Burns District
65 mi SE of Burns on SR 78; 24 mi S on Fields-Denio Rd (Harney CR 201); at Mann Lake. Free. All year; 14-day limit. Primitive undesignated sites; no facilities except cfga; 35-ft RV limit. Fishing, boating, swimming, hiking, rockhounding. Tents not recommended because of high winds. Wild mustangs. Elev 4200 ft.

Rock Springs Campground $6
Malheur National Forest
From Burns, N on US 395, the E on FR 17. $6. All year; 14-day limit. 12 sites. Tbls, toilet, cfga, no drkg wtr or trash service. Horseback riding, hiking.

Yellowjacket $10
Malheur National Forest
1 mi S of Burns on US 20; 32 mi NW on FR 47; 4 mi E on FR 37; half mi S on FR 3745. $10. 5/15-10/15; 14-day limit. May be open off-season, but no wtr. 20 sites (typically 45 ft). Tbls, toilets, cfga, drkg wtr. Hunting, fishing, boating(l; no motors), beach. Elev 4800 ft. Adjacent to Yellowjacket Reservoir.

BUTTE FALLS (W)
Abbott Creek Campground $7
Rogue River National Forest
From Prospect (15 mi N of Butte Falls), 6.7 mi N on SR 62; 3.7 mi NW on FR 68. $7 with federal senior pass; others pay $14. 5/15-10/15; 14-day limit. 25 sites, typically 50 ft. Tbls, toilets, cfga, no drkg wtr, grey wtr stations. Fishing. 7 acres. Elev 3100 ft.

Farewell Bend Campground $11.50
Rogue River National Forest
From jct with 1st St in Prospect (15 mi N of Butte Falls), 0.3 mi N on Mill Creek Dr; 11 mi E on SR 62; left at campground sign. $11.50 with federal senior pass; others pay $23. 5/1-10/15; 14-day limit. 61 sites; 40-ft RV limit. Tbls, flush toilets, cfga, drkg wtr, grey wtr stations, playground. Hiking trail, fishing.

Fourbit Ford Campground $7
Rogue River National Forest
9.3 mi SE of Butte Falls on CR 30; 1.2 mi NE on FR 3065. $7 with federal senior pass; others pay $14. 5/15-10/1; 14-day limit. 7 sites; 16-ft RV limit. Tbls, toilets, cfga,

drkg wtr (at Whiskey Springs), no trash service. Fishing. Secluded, at Fourbit Creek.

North Fork Campground $7
Rogue River National Forest
From Butte Falls, about 12 mi SE on Fish Lake Rd (CR 821/ FR 37); right (W) on SR 140 for 0.25 mi, then left (S) on FR 35 for 1 mi to entrance on right; at North Fork of Little Butte Creek. $7 with federal senior pass; others pay $14. 5/15-11/15; 14-day limit. 9 sites (3 for RVs with 24-ft RV limit). Tbls, cfga, toilets, drkg wtr. Swimming, boating, fishing. Showers($) at Fish Lake Resort.

Hamaker Campground FREE
Rogue River National Forest
From Prospect (15 mi N of Butte Falls), 12 mi N on SR 62; 11 mi N on SR 230; half mi SE on FR 6530; half mi S on FR 900. Now free. 10 primitive sites (30-ft RV limit). Tbls, toilets, cfga, no drkg wtr or trash service. Fishing, hiking trails. Elev 4000 ft; 3 acres.

Huckleberry Mountain FREE
Rogue River National Forest
From Prospect (15 mi N of Butte Falls), 6 mi N on SR 62; right on FR 60 for 12 mi; near Crawford Creek. Free. 5/15-10/30; 14-day limit. 12 RV/tent sites; 16-ft RV limit. Tbls, toilets, cfga, no drkg wtr or trash service. Hiking trails.

Imnaha Campground $10
Rogue River National Forest
From Prospect (15 mi N of Butte Falls), 2.7 mi SE on co hwy; 8 mi SE on FR 3317. $10. Elev 3800 ft. 5/15-10/31. 4 sites; 16-ft RV limit. Tbls, toilets, cfga, drkg wtr, no trash service. Fishing. Some structures built by CCC in the 1930s.

Mill Creek Campground $8
Rogue River National Forest
From Prospect (15 mi N of Butte Falls), 2 mi N on Hwy 62; 1 mi E on FR 30. $8. 5/15-10/15; 14-day limit. 10 sites, typically 40 ft. Tbls, toilets, cfga, no drkg wtr or trash service, grey wtr station. Fishing, hiking, hunting.

Natural Bridge Campground $10
Rogue River National Forest
From Prospect (15 mi N of Butte Falls), 9.9 mi N on OR 62; 1 mi W on FR 3106; at Upper Rogue River. $10. 5/15-10.15; 14-day limit. 17 sites (RVs under 31 ft). Tbls, toilets, cfga, no drkg wtr or trash service. Fishing. Elev 2900 ft.

Parker Meadows Campground $10
Rogue River National Forest
9 mi E of Butte Falls on Hwy 821; 10 mi S on FR 37; near Parker Creek. $10. Jul-Oct; 14-day limit. 5 RV sites; 16-ft RV limit. Tbls, toilets, cfga, drkg wtr, no trash service. Historic shelter, fishing, berry picking. Elev 5000 ft.

River Bridge Campground $8
Rogue River National Forest
From Prospect (15 mi N of Butte Falls), 4 mi N on Hwy 62; 1 mi N on FR 6210. $8. 5/15-10/15; 14-day limit. 11 sites; 25-ft RV limit, sites typically 50 ft. Tbls, toilets, cfga, no drkg wtr or trash service. Fishing, hiking (Upper Rogue River Trail passes site).

South Fork Campground $10
Rogue River National Forest
1 mi E of Butte Falls on Hwy 821; 9 mi N on Hwy 992; right on FR 34 for 8 mi; near South Fork Rogue River. $10. 5/15-10/30; 14-day limit. 6 sites (16-ft RV limit). Tbls, toilets, cfga, no drkg wtr or trash service. Fishing, hiking. Trails east to Sky Lakes Wilderness Area. Elev 4000 ft.

Union Creek Campground $10.50
Rogue River National Forest
From Prospect (15 mi N of Butte Falls), 10.7 mi N on SR 62; at jct of Union Creek with Rogue River. $10.50 with federal senior pass; others pay $21. About 5/10-10/15; 14-day limit. 74 sites; 30-ft RV limit. Tbls, toilets, cfga, drkg wtr, community kitchen, grey water sumps. Fishing, hiking trails (Upper Rogue River Trail nearby). Elev 3200 ft; 14 acres. Concessionaire.

Whiskey Springs Campground $8
Rogue River National Forest
9.3 mi SE of Butte Falls on CR 30; qtr mi E on FR 3317. $8 with federal senior pass; others pay $16. 5/15-10/30; 14-day limit. 34 sites (30-ft RV limit). Tbls, toilets, cfga, drkg wtr. Fishing, hiking trails. Elev 3200 ft; 40 acres.

CANNON BEACH (W)

Saddle Mountain State Natural Area $11
E from Cannon Beach on US 26 to Necanicum Junction; 8 mi N on park entrance rd. $11 for primitive & overflow sites during 5/1-9/30 ($5 off-season). 10-day limit in any 14-day period. RVs restricted to parking area. Tbls, flush toilets, cfga, drkg wtr. Hiking trail. 2,922 acres.

CANYONVILLE (W)

Ash Flat Campground $10
Umpqua National Forest
From Tiller (20 mi E of Canyonville), quarter mi SE on SR 227; 18 mi NE on CR 46 (becoming S. Umpqua Rd); at South Umpqua River & Ash Creek. $10. All year; 14-day limit. 4 sites; 35-ft RV limit. Tbls, toilet, cfga, no drkg wtr. Fishing, swimming.

Boulder Creek $10
Umpqua National Forest
From Tiller (20 mi E of Canyonville), quarter mi SE on OR 227; 6.2 mi NE on CR 46; 7.7 mi NE on FR 28. $10. 5/1-10/31; 14-day limit. 7 sites (22-ft RV limit). Tbls, toilets, cfga, drkg wtr, grey wtr stations. Fishing, swimming, hiking. Along picturesque section of South Umpqua River.

Camp Comfort $10
Umpqua National Forest
From Tiller (20 mi E of Canyonville), quarter mi SE on OR 227; 6.2 mi NE on CR 46; 17.9 mi NE on FR 28; 2 mi NE on FR 2739. $10. 5/1-10/31; 14-day limit. 5 sites; 22-ft RV limit. Tbls, toilet, cfga, open shelter, no drkg wtr. Swimming, fishing, hiking. Trail from CCC Shelter to confluence of Black Rock Fork & Castle Rock Fork (beginnings of South Umpqua River).

Cover Campground $10
Umpqua National Forest
From Tiller (20 mi E of Canyonville), qtr mi SE on CR 1; 5 mi NE on CR 46; 11.8 mi E on FR 29. Along Jackson Creek. $10. 5/20-10/31; 14-day limit. 7 sites; 22-ft RV limit. Tbls, toilet, cfga, drkg wtr, grey water stations. Fishing, hiking. Only developed campsites on Jackson Creek.

South Umpqua Falls $10
Umpqua National Forest
From Tiller (20 mi E of Canyonville), qtr mi SE on SR 227; 6.2 mi E on CR 46; NE on FR 28 to South Umpqua Falls; no camping at picnic area, but at undeveloped area just downstream & across rd. $10. All year; 14-day limit. 19 sites; 35-ft RV limit. Tbls, toilets, cfga, grey wtr stations, no drkg wtr.

Three C Rock Campground $10
Umpqua National Forest
From Tiller (20 mi E of Canyonville), qtr mi SE on SR 227; 4 mi NE on CR 46; at South Umpqua River boat ramp. $10. All year; 14-day limit. 5 sites; 35-ft RV limit. Tbls, toilet, cfga, no drkg wtr. Hiking trail to waterfall, horseback riding. Named for a CCC camp built there in 1930s. Waterfall upstream from boat ramp.

Threehorn Campground $10
Umpqua National Forest
From Tiller (20 mi E of Canyonville), 12.7 mi SE on CR 1. $10. All year; 14-day limit. 5 sites (RVs under 22 ft). Tbls, toilets, cfga, no drkg wtr. Hiking.

CARLTON (W)

Alder Glen $7.50
Bureau of Land Management
Salem District
Nestucca Back Country Byway
21 mi W of Carlton on Nestucca access rd; or, off US 101, 18 mi NE of Alder Glen. $7.50 with federal senior pass; others pay $15. About 4/6-11/30; 14-day limit. 11 sites (RVs under 27 ft). Tbls, toilets, cfga, drkg wtr. Fishing.

Dovre Campground $7.50
Tillamook Resource Area
Bureau of Land Management
Salem District
Nestucca Back Country Byway

14 mi W of Carlton on Nestucca access rd. $7.50 with federal senior pass; others pay $15. About 4/6-11/30; 14-day limit. 10 sites (RVs under 25 ft. Tbls, toilets, cfga, drkg wtr, shelter. Swimming, fishing.

Fan Creek Campground $7.50
Bureau of Land Management
Tillamook Resource Area
Salem District
Nestucca Back Country Byway
16 mi W of Carlton on Nestucca access rd. All year; 7-day limit. $7.50 with federal senior pass; others pay $15. 11 sites (RVs under 25 ft). Tbls, toilets, cfga, drkg wtr. Swimming, fishing.

CASCADE LOCKS (W)

Eagle Creek $7.50
Columbia River Gorge National Scenic Area
2 mi W of Cascade Locks on I-84; from Bonneville exit, under hwy, up hill through picnic area. $7.50 with federal senior pass; others pay $15. About 5/1-10/1; 14-day limit. 17 sites (typically 45 ft, but 20-ft RV limit). Tbls, flush toilets, cfga, drkg wtr. Swimming, fishing, hiking (Eagle Creek Trail to Wahtum Lake, connects to Pacific Crest Trail), biking. 5 acres. Built in 1945, this is considered the first forest service campground in America. Features first restroom with flush toilets built by forest service. However, flush toilets inoperable in 2017, replaced with pit or portable facilities.

Herman Creek Horse Camp $10
Columbia River Gorge National Scenic Area
1.5 mi E of Cascade Locks on I-84. $10. About 5/1-10/1; 14-day limit. 7 sites (22-ft RV limit). Tbls, toilets, cfga, drkg wtr. Horse facilities. Dump & showers nearby. Hiking, fishing, boating, biking.

Wyeth Campground $10
Columbia River Gorge National Scenic Area
7 mi E of Cascade Locks on I-84 to Wyeth exit; half mi W on county rd. $10 with federal senior pass; others pay $20. 5/1-10/1; 14-day limit. 13 sites (30-ft RV limit). Flush toilets, tbls, cfga, drkg wtr. Swimming, hiking, fishing. 18 acres. Site of CCC camp in 1930s.

CAVE JUNCTION (W)

Bolan Lake Campground $5
Siskiyou National Forest
Half mi S of Cave Junction on US 199 to O'Brien; 8 mi SE on CRs 5560; 7 mi SE on FR 48; 6 mi E on FR 48. $5. Elev 5400 ft. 6/15-LD; 14-day limit. 12 dispersed sites on 3 acres (RVs under 16 ft). Tbls, toilets, cfga, no drkg wtr or trash service. Swimming, fishing, boating(ld), hiking trail to Bolan Lake Trail.

Cave Creek Campground $10
Siskiyou National Forest
Oregon Caves National Monument & Preserve
16 mi E of Cave Junction on SR 46; 1 mi S on FR 4032 (narrow, curving rd not recommended for large RVs). $10. MD-LD; 14-day limit. 18 primitive sites, typically 37 ft but 16-ft RV limit. Tbls, toilets, cfga, drkg wtr or trash service. Oregon Caves National Monument 4 mi. Hiking, fishing. Elev 2900 ft; 10 acres. GPS: 42.11792, -123.435791. Temporarily closed in 2014, now managed by National Park Service for visitors to Oregon Caves NM.

Grayback Campground $10
Siskiyou National Forest
12 mi E of Cave Junction on SR 46 (Oregon Caves Hwy); at Sucker Creek. $10. MD-9/30; 14-day limit. 39 sites; 26-ft RV limit. Tbls, toilets, cfga, drkg wtr. Swimming, fishing, hiking (1-mi loop trail), horseshoe pits, volleyball, picnic shelter. Built by CCC in 1930s.

Josephine Campground   FREE
Siskiyou National Forest
N of Cave Junction on Hwy 199 to FR 5240; W on FR 5240, then 3 mi on FR 4201; above Illinois River. Free. Spring-fall; 14-day limit. 6 sites. Tbls, toilet, cfga, no drkg wtr or trash service. Fishing, swimming, hiking.

CHILOQUIN (W)

Jackson F. Kimball $11
State Recreation Site
From Chiloquin, about 5 mi W on SR 422; right (N) on SR 62 (Crater Lake Hwy) about 7 mi, veering right (N) onto CR 623 to park entrance. $11 for 10 primitive sites during 5/15-11/15 ($5 off-season). All year; 10-day limit in 14-day period. 45-ft RV limit. Tbls, toilets, cfga, no drkg wtr. Near Wood River. Hiking, fishing, canoeing.

Scott Creek Campground   FREE
Winema National Forest
From 1 mi S of Chiloquin at jct with US 97, about 13 mi N on SR 62 toward Fort Klamath, veering right at jct with CR 623 (Sun Mountain Rd); continue N on CR 623 about 10 mi; left on FR 2310 about 3 mi; right on FR 2310110 to campground at shore of Scott Creek. Free all year; maintained 5/15-10/15; reduced services off-season; 14-day limit. 6 rustic sites. Toilet, tbls, cfga, no drkg wtr. Hiking. Elev 4700 ft.

Williamson River Campground $10
Winema National Forest
5.5 mi N of Chiloquin on US 97; 1 mi NE on FR 9730. $10 during 5/15-10/15; reduced services off-season; 14-day limit. 19 sites (32-ft limit). Tbls, toilets, cfga, drkg wtr. Good trout fishing, interpretive areas. Coin laundry.

COOS BAY (W)

Nesika Campground　　　　　　　　　$10
Coos County Park
From town of Eastside (across bay from City of Coos Bay), 2 mi E on Coos River Rd, across Coos River bridge, then 11 mi NE on Coos River Hwy 241 (past county's Rooke Higgins Park) to campground (about 5 mi W of Gold and Silver Falls State Natural Area); at East Fork of Millicoma River. $10. 5/16-9/30; 10-day limit. 20 primitive sites. Toilets, cfga, no drkg wtr (tbls in picnic area). Fishing, swimming, hiking. 77 acres. Unable to verify fees for 2017.

Rooke Higgins　　　　　　　　　　　$10
Coos County Park
From town of Eastside (across bay from City of Coos Bay), 2 mi E on Coos River Rd, across Coos River bridge, then 6 mi NE on Coos River Hwy 241 to park; along North Fork of Coos River at Millicoma River. $10. 5/16-9/30; 10-day limit. 20 primitive sites. Toilets, cfga, no drkg wtr. Swimming, boating(l), fishing. 26 acres. Unable to verify fees for 2017.

COQUILLE (W)

Bear Creek　　　　　　　　　　　CLOSED
Bureau of Land Management
Coos Bay District
26 mi SE of Coquille on OR 42. Free. Closed as campground in 2015.

Frona　　　　　　　　　　　　　　$10
Coos County Park
From Coquille, 9 mi NE on Coquille-Fairview Rd to Fairview; 9 mi E on Coos Bay Wagon Rd; at East Fork of Coquille River. $10. 5/16-9/30; 10-day limit. 15 primitive sites (scattered). Toilets, tbls, cfga, no drkg wtr. Fishing, rockhounding. 77 acres. Unable to verify fees for 2017.

Ham Bunch-Cherry Creek　　　　　　$10
Coos County Park
9 mi NE of Coquille to Fairview; 7 mi E on Coos Bay Wagon Rd; at Cherry Creek. $10. 5/16-9/30; 10-day limit. 10 primitive sites. Tbls, toilets, cfga, no drkg wtr. Fishing, wading pool, rockhounding. Unable to verify fees for 2017.

LaVerne　　　　　　　　　　　　　$11
Coos County Park
From Coquille, 9 mi NE on Coquille-Fairview Rd to Fairview, then 5 mi N on that rd to the park; at North Fork of Coquille River. $11 without hookups, $16 with hookups during 5/1-9/30 ($2 extra Thurs-Sat); all sites $15 off-season. All year; 10-day limit. 76 sites (30 non-elec). Tbls, flush toilets, cfga, drkg wtr, showers($), portable dump, elec($). Swimming, playground, fishing, volleyball, horseshoes, hiking trails. 350 acres.

Park Creek Campground　　　　　　FREE
Bureau of Land Management
Coos Bay District
24 mi E of Coquille on Middle Cove Rd. Free. All year; 14-day limit. 15 shaded sites; 8 acres. Tbls, toilets, cfga, drkg wtr. Fishing; hunting; berry picking. Park Creek & Middle Creek. Myrtlewood grove.

COTTAGE GROVE (W)

Cedar Creek　　　　　　　　　　　$8
Umpqua National Forest
From Culp Creek (10 mi SW of Cottage Grove), 4.3 mi SE on CR 2400; 4.6 mi SE on CR 2470; .1 mi N on FR 448. $8. All year but services 4/15-11/30; 14-day limit. 9 sites (16-ft RV limit). Tbls, toilet, cfga, no drkg wtr, 3 gray water stations. Hiking, fishing, swimming, gold panning, swimming. Brice Creek. Gold panning. Hiking on Crawfish Trail (1 mi E).

Emerald Pool Dispersed Area　　　　FREE
Umpqua National Forest
From Culp Creek (10 mi SW of Cottage Grove), 4.3 mi SE on CR 2400; 2.4 mi SE on CR 2470 (Brice Creek Rd); right on FR 2200-124 for 1.5 mi. Free. All year; 21-day limit. Primitive camping areas along rd near swimming hole known as Emerald Pool. No facilities except cfga. Swimming, fishing. 50 acres.

Hobo Camp Campground　　　　　　FREE
Umpqua National Forest
From Culp Creek (10 mi SW of Cottage Grove), 4.3 mi SE on CR 2400; 7.5 mi SE on CR 2470 (Brice Creek Rd); on both sides of rd. Free. All year; 14-day limit. 2 undeveloped areas for 2-4 RVs; 16-ft RV limit. Tbl, toilet, cfga, no drkg wtr or trash service. Hiking. Above Brice Creek, used by day-use swimmers & picnickers, gold panning.

Lund Park Campground　　　　　　　$8
Umpqua National Forest
From Culp Creek (10 mi SW of Cottage Grove), 4.3 mi SE on CR 2400 (Row River Rd); 6.3 mi E on CR 2470 (Brice Creek Rd). $8 during 5/15-11/15; free off-season but no services; 14-day limit. 10 sites on 6 acres & 2 dispersed sites (RVs under 16 ft). Tbls, toilets, cfga, no drkg wtr. Swimming, fishing. Brice Creek.

Mineral Camp Campground　　　　　FREE
Umpqua National Forest
From I-5 exit 174 at Cottage Grove,13 mi E on Row River Rd (CR 2400); 12 mi S on Sharps Creek Rd (CR 2460), bearing E when rd becomes gravel. Free. 3/15-9/15; 14-day limit. 3 dispersed sites along Sharps Creek. Tbls, cfga, toilet, no drkg wtr or trash service. Fishing, hiking, horseback riding, mountain biking, motorcycling.

Pine Meadows $10
Corps of Engineers
Cottage Grove Lake
From downtown Cottage Grove, 2 mi S on S. 6th St; 3 mi SE on London Rd, then left (SE) on Cottage Grove Reservoir Rd for about 2 mi; on NE shore of lake. $10 with federal senior pass; others pay $20. 5/20-9/11; 14-day limit. 85 non-elec sites; RV limit in excess of 65 ft; 26 pull-through sites. Amphitheater, tbls, flush & pit toilets, cfga, drkg wtr, playground, beach, dump, showers, fishing pier. Swimming, boating(l), fishing.

Pine Meadows Primitive Camp $7
Corps of Engineers
Cottage Grove Lake
Primitive area is approx 0.25 mi S of Pine Meadow Campground. $7 with federal senior pass at 15 primitive sites (others pay $14). Tbls, pit toilets, fire rings, no hookups or showers. MD-LD; 14-day limit.

Rujada Campground $12
Umpqua National Forest
From Culp Creek (10 mi SW of Cottage Grove), 4.3 mi SE on CR 202; 2 mi NE on FR 2143; .1 mi S on FR 2148; on terrace above Laying Creek. $12. 5/19-LD; 14-day limit. 15 sites (RVs under 23 ft). Tbls, flush & pit toilets, cfga, elec in restrooms, drkg wtr, grey wtr stations. Swimming, fishing, horseshoe pits. Elev 1200 ft; 9 acres.

Schwarz Campground $9
Corps of Engineers
Dorena Lake
From below dam at jct with Row River Rd, 0.2 mi SE on Shoreline Dr, then E near outlet. $9 with federal senior pass; others pay $18. 4/28-9/11; 14-day limit. 82 non-elec sites; 65-ft RVs; 3 pull-through sites. Six group camping areas without hookups. Dump, drkg wtr, solar hot showers, flush toilets. Fishing, swimming, boating, hiking trails.

Sharps Creek Campground $7.50
Bureau of Land Management
Eugene District
From Culp Creek (10 mi SW of Cottage Grove), 5 mi S on Sharps Creek County Rd. From southbound I-5 exit 174, left 4 mi on Row River Rd; straight for 6.5 mi on Shoreview Dr until it rejoins Row River; merge right onto Row River for 4 mi to Sharps Crest Rd; right for 3 mi. $7.50 with federal senior pass; others pay $15. 5/15-10/15; 14-day limit. 10 sites. Tbls, toilets, cfga, drkg wtr. Swimming, fishing, hiking, gold panning. Covered bridges in area. 1200 acres. Site fees to be $20 in 2019 ($10 with senior pass).

CRESCENT LAKE (W)

Boundary Springs Dispersed Camp FREE
Deschutes National Forest
From settlement of Crescent (10 mi W of Crescent Lake), 2 mi S on US 97; 6 mi E on FR 9768; 1 mi S on FR 600; at base of Walker Rim. Free. All year; 14-day limit. 4 primitive sites; 50-ft RV limit. Toilet, cfga, no tbls, no drkg wtr, no trash service.

Contorta Flat Campground $12
Deschutes National Forest
From settlement of Crescent (10 mi W of Crescent Lake), at jct with US 97, 11.9 mi W on Crescent Cut-off Rd; at "T" intersection, W on SR 58 for 3.4 mi to Crescent Lake sign; left on FR 60 for 2.5 mi; right at sign for campground & boat launch for 7.6 mi; left on FR 280 at Contorta Flat sign. $12. 5/25-9/30; 14-day limit. 18 sites; 40-ft RV limit. Tbls, toilets, cfga, no drkg wtr. Boating(l), hiking, windsurfing, fishing.

Crescent Creek Campground $7
Deschutes National Forest
From just W of Crescent Lake, 1 mi S on SR 58 (Williamette Hwy); 1.5 mi E on CR 61/CR 1351 (Crescent Cut-off Rd). $7 with federal senior pass; others pay $14. 5/25-9/25; 14-day limit. 9 sites (40-ft RV limit). Tbls, toilets, cfga, drkg wtr. Boating(lr), fishing, swimming. Elev 4500 ft. Note: No wtr in 2017 awaiting pump repair.

Crescent Lake $9
Deschutes National Forest
2.7 mi SW of Crescent Lake on FR 60. $9 with federal senior pass during 5/1-9/30 (others pay $18); $7 with senior pass during 10/1-4/30 (others pay $12). 14-day limit. 43 sites (23 pull-through); 36-ft RV limit Tbls, toilets, cfga, drkg wtr (except off-season), grey water stations. Swimming, boating(ld), fishing, waterskiing, hiking trail into Diamond Peak Wilderness and to Odell Lake.

Cy Bingham FREE
Klamath County Park
Half mi W of Crescent settlement (10 mi W of Crescent Lake) on CR 61 (Crescent Cutoff Rd). Free. 3/1-10/31; 14-day limit. 10 sites. Tbls, toilets, cfga, drkg wtr. 2.5 acres.

East Davis Lake Campground $12
Deschutes National Forest
From just W of Crescent Lake, 1 mi S on SR 58 (Williamette Hwy); 1 mi E on CR 61/CR 1351 (Crescent Cut-off Rd); 7.7 mi N on CR 1352/CR 46; 2.6 mi W on FR 4600-850; at E shore of Odell Creek at East Davis Lake. $12. 4/27-9/25; 14-day limit. 29 sites (26 pull-through); 40-ft RV limit. Tbls, toilets, cfga, drkg wtr. Hiking, fly fishing, boating, swimming.

Lava Flow North FREE
Deschutes National Forest
From just W of Crescent Lake, 1 mi S on SR 58 (Williamette Hwy); 1 mi E on CR 61/CR 1351 (Crescent Cut-off Rd); 10 mi N on CR 46/CR 1352; 0.25 mi S on FR 4600-850. Free. All year; 14-day limit. 6 sites up to 60 ft. Tbls, toilets, cfga,

no drkg wtr, no trash service. Boating(l), fishing. Future plans are to develop area into a 25-site campground with fees.

Lava Flow South — FREE
Deschutes National Forest
From just W of Crescent Lake, 1 mi S on SR 58 (Williamette Hwy); 1 mi E on CR 61/CR 1351 (Crescent Cut-off Rd); 7.7 mi N on CR 46; 1.8 mi N on FR 4600-850. Free. Open only 9/1-12/31 for wildlife protection, although a few sites at N end are not in the closure area; 14-day limit. 6 undesignated sites (40-ft RV limit). Tbls, toilets, cfga, no drkg wtr, no trash service. Boating(l), fishing, bird watching, waterskiing, windsurfing, swimming, sailing. On E shore of Davis Lake. Lava formation. Elev 4400 ft.

Odell Creek — CLOSED
Deschutes National Forest
1.5 mi NW of Crescent Lake on SR 58; half mi SW on FR 2317. Decommissioned as a forest campground; now under private ownership.

Princess Creek Campground — $7
Deschutes National Forest
5.5 mi NW of Crescent Lake on SR 58; at E shore of Odell Lake. $7 with federal senior pass; others pay $14. 6/8-9/10; 14-day limit. Free in fall before weather closes access. 32 sites (9 pull-through); 32-ft RV limit. Tbls, toilets, cfga, no drkg wtr. Fishing, swimming, waterskiing, boating.

Rock Creek Campground — $8
Deschutes National Forest
From just W of Crescent Lake, 1 mi S on SR 58 (Williamette Hwy); 1 mi E on CR 61/CR 1351 (Crescent Cut-off Rd); left (N) on CR 46/CR 1352 about 18 mi to site; on SW shore of Crane Prairie Reservoir. $8 with federal senior pass; others pay $16 (multi-site $26). 5/15-9/30; 14-day limit. 30 sites; 40-ft RV limit. Tbls, toilets, cfga, drkg wtr, fish cleaning station. Boating(l), fishing.

Spring Campground — $9
Deschutes National Forest
8 mi SW of Crescent Lake on FR 60; NE on FR 260; at S shore of Crescent Lake. $9 with federal senior pass; others pay $18 (multi-site $34). 6/25-10/31; 14-day limit. Free in fall before weather closes access. 68 sites; 40-ft RV limit. Tbls, toilets, cfga, drkg wtr. Swimming, fishing, waterskiing, hiking, biking.

Summit Lake Campground — FREE
Deschutes National Forest
12.2 mi SW of Crescent Lake on CR 61; 3.5 mi N on Hwy 58; 7.2 mi W on CR 60; 6.5 mi W on FR 6010 (high-clearance vehicles suggested, RVs not recommended); at N shore of Summit Lake. Free. 7/1-9/30; 14-day limit. 3 sites (RVs under 22 ft). Tbls, toilets, cfga, no drkg wtr or trash

service. Swimming, fishing, boating, hiking. Elev 5600 ft. Access to Pacific Crest Trail (200 yds).

Sunset Cove Campground — $8
Deschutes National Forest
2.5 mi NW of Crescent Lake on SR 58; at SE shore of Odell Lake. $8 with federal senior pass; others pay $16 (double sites $30). 5/4-10/31; 14-day limit. Free in fall before weather closes access. 21 sites; 40-ft RV limit. Tbls, toilets, cfga, drkg wtr, fish cleaning station. Boating(rl), fishing, hiking, windsurfing.

Trapper Creek Campground — $8
Deschutes National Forest
7 mi NW of Crescent Lake on Hwy 58; 1.7 mi SW on FR 5810; at E shore of Odell Lake. $8 base with federal senior pass; others pay $16 base, $18 for premium lakeside sites ($9 with senior pass). Double sites $30 & $34. 6/8-10/31; 14-day limit. Free in fall before weather closes access. 30 sites; 40-ft RV limit. Tbls, toilets, cfga, drkg wtr. Fishing, boating, swimming, hiking.

CULVER (W)

Monty Campground — $7
Deschutes National Forest
20 mi W of Culver on CR 63; 10 mi W on CR 64 (rough rd for RVs); at Metolius River. $7 with federal senior pass; others pay $14. 6/6-9/10; 14-day limit. 34 sites (20-ft RV limit). Tbls, toilets, cfga, no drkg wtr. Fishing, hiking, boating at Lake Billy Chinook. Elev 2000 ft; 10 acres. No access to campground 1/1-5/15 to protect bald eagles. Campground closed 10/1-5/15 because canoer noises can cause nesting failures.

DETROIT (W)

Big Meadows Horse Camp — $7
Willamette National Forest
27 mi SE on SR 22; left for 2 mi on FR 2267 (Big Meadows Rd); left 1 mi on FR 2257. $7 with federal senior pass; others pay $14. About 7/1-9/15; 14-day limit. 9 sites; 36-ft RV limit. Tbls, toilets, cfga, drkg wtr, horse corrals, loading ramp, stock water trough. Horseback riding, hiking.

Breitenbush Lake Campground — $8
Willamette National Forest
10 mi NE of Detroit on FR 46. $8 with federal senior pass; others pay $16 (double sites $30). About 5/25-9/15; 14-day limit. 30 sites (24-ft RV limit). Tbls, toilets, cfga, drkg wtr. Fishing, swimming, hiking.

Cove Creek Campground — $11
Willamette National Forest
2.5 mi E of Detroit on SR 22; right on Blowout Rd 3.5 mi; right at sign. $11 with federal senior pass; others pay $22. 5/19-9/15; 14-day limit. 65 sites: 30-ft RV limit. Tbls, flush toilets, cfga, drkg wtr, grey wtr stations, coin showers. Boating(ld), fishing.

Hoover Campground $11
Willamette National Forest
2.5 mi E of Detroit on SR 22; right on Blowout Rd for 0.5 mi. $11 with federal senior pass; others pay $22. 5/5-9/16; 14-day limit. 37 sites; 30-ft RV limit. Tbls, flush toilets, cfga, drkg wtr, amphitheater, interpretive trail, nature trail, fishing platform, grey wtr stations. Boating(ld), fishing, hiking.

Humbug Campground $8
Willamette National Forest
5 mi NE of Detroit on FR 46. $8 with federal senior pass; others pay $16. 5/19-9/16; 14-day limit. 21 sites (30-ft RV limit). Tbls, toilets, cfga, drkg wtr. Fishing, hiking. On Breitenbush River. 15 acres. May-June, rhododendrons are spectacular.

Marion Forks Campground $10
Willamette National Forest
16 mi SE of Detroit on SR 22. $10. All year; 14-day limit. 15 sites (24-ft RV limit). Tbls, toilets, cfga, drkg wtr, grey wtr stations. Fishing, hiking. On Marion Creek. Marion Forks Fish Hatchery nearby.

Riverside Campground $8
Willamette National Forest
13 mi SE of Detroit on SR 22. All year; 14-day limit. $8 with federal senior pass; others pay $16. 5/13-9/10; 14-day limit. 32 sites (24-ft RV limit). Tbls, toilets, cfga, drkg wtr. Fishing, hiking. North Santiam River.

Santiam Flats Campground $8
Willamette National Forest
2 mi E of Detroit on Hwy 22. $8 with federal senior pass; others pay $16. 5/5-9/24; 32 sites; 30-ft RV limit. All year; 14-day limit. Tbls, toilets, cfga, drkg wtr. Fishing, swimming, boating.

Southshore Campground $10
Willamette National Forest
2.8 mi E of Detroit on SR 22; right for 4.3 mi on Blowout Rd. $10 with federal senior pass; others pay $20. 5/25-9/8; 14-day limit. 32 sites; 30-ft RV limit. Tbls, toilets, cfga, drkg wtr, grey wtr stations. Boating(l), fishing. 3500-acre Detroit Lake.

Whispering Falls Campground $8
Willamette National Forest
7 mi E of Detroit on SR 22. $8 with federal senior pass; others pay $16. About 5/19-9/9; 14-day limit. 16 sites; 30-ft RV limit. Tbls, flush toilets, cfga, drkg wtr. Hiking, fishing.

DUFUR (W)

Eightmile Campground $7.50
Mount Hood National Forest
12 mi SW of Dufur on CR 1; 4.3 mi W on FR 44; half mi N on FR 4430. $7.50 with federal senior pass; otehrs pay $15. 5/15-10/15; 14-day limit. 21 sites (30-ft RV limit). Tbls, toilets, cfga, no drkg wtr, grey wtr stations. Fishing, hunting. Elev 4200 ft.

Fifteenmile Campground FREE
Mount Hood National Forest
2 mi S of Dufur on OR 197; 14 mi W on CR 118; 9 mi W on FR 205. Free. Elev 4600 ft. 6/1-9/10. 3 sites (RVs under 17 ft). Tbls, toilet, cfga, no drkg wtr.

Knebal Springs Campground $12
Mount Hood National Forest
12 mi SW of Dufur on CR 1; 4.3 mi SW on FR 44; 4 mi NW on FR 105; 1 mi SW on FR 16. $12. 5/15-9/15; 14-day limit. 8 sites; 22-ft RV limit. Tbls, toilet, cfga, no drkg wtr. Horseback riding, hiking.

Lower Eightmile Crossing $7.50
Mount Hood National Forest
12 mi SW of Dufur on CR 1; 4 mi W on FR 44; 1 mi N on FR 167. Elev 3800 ft. $7.50 with federal senior pass; others pay $15. 5/15-10/15; 10-day limit. 3 sites; 16-ft RV limit. Tbls, toilet, cfga, no drkg wtr. Hunting; fishing.

Pebble Ford Campground $12
Mount Hood National Forest
12 mi SW of Dufur on CR 1; 5 mi W on FR 44; half mi S on FR 131; between Eightmile & Ramsey Creeks. $12. 5/15-10/15; 14-day limit. 3 sites; 16-ft RV limit. Tbls, toilet, cfga, no drkg wtr. Hunting. Elev 4000 ft. 1 acre.

ELGIN (E)

Minam State Recreation Area $10
15 mi NE of Elgin off SR 82; at Wallowa River. $10 for 22 primitive sites during 5/1-9/30; $5 off-season but not wtr services. No RV size limit. All year; 10-day limit. Tbls, toilets, cfga, drkg wtr, coinless pay phone. Boating(l), fishing, trails.

ENTERPRISE (E)

Coyote Campground FREE
Wallowa-Whitman National Forest
14 mi N of Enterprise on SR 3; right (E) on FR 46 for 13 mi; left (N) on Crow Creek Rd for 1 mi; right (NE) on CR 46 for 12.5 mi & into campground on FR 4650. Free. 5/15-11/30; 10-day limit. 8 RV/tent sites (22-ft RV limit). Tbls, toilets, cfga, no drkg wtr. Space available for large groups.

Dougherty Campground FREE
Hells Canyon National Recreation Area
Wallowa-Whitman National Forest
14 mi N of Enterprise on OR 3; 13 mi NE on FR 56; left 1 mi on Crow Creek Rd; right on Chesnimus Creek Rd (becoming FR 4625 for 6.5 mi; left on FR 4670 for 9.5 mi toward

Billy Measdows; after Billy Meadows guard station, right on FR 46 for 1.8 mi; left on FR 583 to campground. Free. Elev 5100 ft. 6/1-12/1; 14-day limit. 4 RV/tent sites (RVs under 22 ft). Tbls, toilets, cfga, no drkg wtr. Self-service sites. Berrypicking.

Vigne Campground $6
Wallowa-Whitman National Forest
14 mi N of Enterprise on OR 3; 13 mi NE on FR 56; left 1 mi on Crow Creek Rd; right on Chesnimus Creek Rd (becoming FR 4625 for 11.5 mi to camp entry sign; entrance on right; at Cesnimus Creek. $6. 4/15-11/30; 14-day limit. 6 sites (22-ft RV limit). Tbls, toilets, cfga, drkg wtr. Fishing. Elev 3500 ft.

ESTACADA (W)

Armstrong Campground $9
Mount Hood National Forest
About 15 mi E of Estacada on SR 224. $9 with federal senior pass; others pay $18. All year; 14-day limit. Free Nov-June, but no services or wtr. 12 sites, typically 35 ft, but 18-ft limit. Tbls, toilets, cfga, drkg drkg wtr. Fishing, rafting.

Carter Bridge Campground $8
Mount Hood National Forest
About 15 mi SE of Estacada on SR 224; at Clackamas River. $8 with federal senior pass; others pay $16. 5/15-LD; 14-day limit. 15 sites; 28-ft RV limit. Tbls, toilets, cfga, no drkg wtr. Fishing (catch & release steelhead & salmon), hiking.

Fish Creek Campground $10
Mount Hood National Forest
About 15 mi SE of Estacada on SR 224; at Clackamas River. $10 with federal senior pass; others pay $20. 5/15-9/15; 14-day limit. 24 sites; 16-ft RV limit. Tbls, toilets, cfga, drkg wtr. Fishing, hiking.

Hideaway Lake Campground $9
Mount Hood National Forest
27 mi SE of Estacada on Hwy 224; 7.5 mi E on FR 57; 3 mi N on FR 58; 5.5 mi NW on FR 5830. $9 with federal senior pass; others pay $18. 6/15-9/15; 14-day limit. 9 sites; 16-ft RV limit. Tbls, toilets, cfga, no drkg wtr. Hiking, fishing. Elev 4500 ft.

Horseshoe Lake Campground $7.50
Mount Hood National Forest
27 mi SE of Estacada on OR 224; 21.8 mi S on FR S46; 8.2 mi SE on FR S806; 8.3 mi S on FR 4220 (rough rd). $7.50 with federal senior pass; others pay $15 ($20 for premium sites). 6/15-9/20; 14-day limit. 6 sites (16-ft RV limit). Tbls, toilet, cfga, no drkg wtr. Fishing, hiking, boating (rl-3 mi; no mtrs).

Kingfisher Campground $10.50
Mount Hood National Forest
29 mi E of Estacada on SR 224; right at Bagby Hot Springs sign on FR 36; at "Y," bear right for 3.3 mi; right at second Bagby sign for 1.6 mi on FR 70. $10.50 base with federal senior pass; others pay $21 base, $23 for premium locations ($11.50 with senior pass). 5/15-9/15; 14-day limit. 23 sites; 36-ft RV limit. Tbls, toilets, cfga, drkg wtr, grey wtr stations. Fishing.

Lake Harriet Campground $8
Mount Hood National Forest
24.7 E of Estacada on SR 224; after passing Ripplebrook Guard Station, 2.9 mi N on FR 4631; bear right at "Y"; 3.1 mi on FR 4630; on E end of Lake Harriet. $8 with federal senior pass; others pay $16. All year; 14-day limit. Some sites open & free after 9/15, but no wtr or services. 13 sites; 30-ft RV limit. Tbls, toilets, cfga, drkg wtr. Fishing, swimming, boating. Non-campers pay $5 day use fee or $30 annually. GPS: 45.07360, -121.95911

Lazy Bend Campground $10.50
Mount Hood National Forest
9.6 mi E on SR 224; at Clackamas River. $10.50 with federal senior pass; others pay $21. 4/15-10/8; 14-day limit. 21 sites; 24-ft RV limit. Tbls, flush toilets, cfga, drkg wtr. Fishing, rafting.

Little Fan Creek Campground $7
Mount Hood National Forest
27 mi SE of Estacada on OR 224; S on FR 46; bear right at "Y" onto FR 63 to site on Collawash River. $7 with federal senior pass; others pay $14. 5/15-9/15; free off-season but no services; 14-day limit. 3 sites; 16-ft RV limit. Tbls, toilet, cfga, no drkg wtr. Fishing, hiking.

Lockaby Campground $10.50
Mount Hood National Forest
14.4 mi E of Estacada on SR 224; at Clackamas River. $10.50 with federal senior pass; others pay $21. 5/15-9/10; 14-day limit. 30 sites, typically 37 ft, but 16-ft RV limit. Tbls, toilets, cfga, drkg wtr. Fishing, rafting.

Lower Lake Campground $7.50
Mount Hood National Forest
27 mi SE of Estacada on OR 224; 21.8 mi S on FR S46; 8.2 mi SE on FR S806; 4.5 mi S on FR 4220. $7.50 base with federal senior pass; others pay $15 base, $20 for premium sites. 6/15-9/20; 14-day limit. 8 sites; 16-ft RV limit. Tbls, toilets, cfga, firewood, no drkg wtr. Horseback riding; boating(rl); fishing (1 mi). Elev 4600 ft; 2 acres.

North Arm Campground $10
Mount Hood National Forest
SE of Estacada on Hwy 224, past Indian Henry & Alder Flat Camps to FR 57; E on FR 57; N on FR 58 past FRs 5830, 5850 & 5860; S on FR 5890, then S on 5890-012;

at Timothy Lake. $10 with federal senior pass; others pay $20. MD-9/16; 14-day limit. 8 RV sites; 16-ft RV limit. Tbls, toilet, cfga, drkg wtr. Boating, fishing, hiking. Elev 3200 ft.

Olallie Meadows Campground $7.50
Mount Hood National Forest
27 mi SE of Estacada on OR 224; 21.8 mi S on FR S46; 8.2 mi SE on FR S806; 1.4 mi S on FR 4220. $7.50 base with federal senior pass; others pay $15 base, $20 at premium sites. 5/15-10/31; 14-day limit. 7 sites (16-ft RV limit). Tbls, no toilets, cfga, no drkg wtr. Berry picking; boating (rld-4 mi); fishing (1 mi). Elev 4500 ft; 1 acre. Spring.

Paul Dennis Campground $7.50
Mount Hood National Forest
27 mi SE of Estacada on SR 224; 21.7 mi S on FR 46; 8.2 mi SE on FR 4690; 6.3 mi S on FR 4220. $7.50 base with federal senior pass; others pay $15 base, $20 at premium sites. 7/1-10/15; 14-day limit. 17 sites (16-ft RV limit). Tbls, toilets, cfga, drkg wtr. Boating (lr -- no motors), fishing, hiking. Elev 5000 ft; 4 acres.

Peninsula Campground $7.50
Mount Hood National Forest
27 mi SE of Estacada on SR 224; 21.7 mi S on FR 46; 8.2 mi SE on FR 4690; 6.5 mi S on FR 4220; at Olallie Lake. $7.50 base with federal senior pass; others pay $15 base, $20 for premium sites. 7/1-10/15; 14-day limit. 35 sites (24-ft RV limit). Tbls, toilets, cfga, drkg wtr. Fishing, boating(lr -- no motors), swimming, hiking. Elev 4900 ft.

Rainbow Campground $9
Mount Hood National Forest
27 mi SE of Estacada on SR 224. $9 with federal senior pass; others pay $18. 5/19-9/10; 14-day limit. 17 sites; 30-ft RV limit. Tbls, toilets, cfga, drkg wtr. Swimming, hiking, fishing. 3 acres.

Ripplebrook Campground $9
Mount Hood National Forest
26.5 mi SE of Estacada on SR 224. $9 with federal Senior Pass; others pay $18. MD-LD; 14-day limit. 13 sites, typically 40 ft, but 16-ft RV limit. Tbls, toilets, cfga, drkg wtr. Fishing, hiking. On Oak Grove Fork of Clackamas River.

Riverford Campground $9
Mount Hood National Forest
27 me SE of Estacada on SR 224; 3.5 mi S on FR 46. $9 with federal senior pass; others pay $18. About 5/20-LD; 14-day limit. 10 sites; 16-ft RV limit. Tbls, toilet, cfga, no drkg wtr (get wtr at Two Rivers Picnic Area). Rockhounding, fishing.

Riverside Campground $9
Mount Hood National Forest
28.1 mi SE of Estacada on SR 224; right on FR 46; at Clackamas River. $9 with federal senior pass; others pay

$18. 5/19-9/10; 14-day limit. 16 sites; 24-ft RV limit. Tbls, toilets, cfga, drkg wtr. Fishing, rafting.

Roaring River Campground $9
Mount Hood National Forest
17 mi SE of Estacada on SR 224; at Clackamas River. $9 with federal senior pass; others pay $18. 5/15-9/15; 14-day limit. 14 sites; 16-ft RV limit. Tbls, toilets, cfga, drkg wtr. Fishing, rafting.

Shellrock Creek Campground $9
Mount Hood National Forest
27 mi SE of Estacada on SR 224; 7.5 mi E on FR 57; half mi N on FR 58. $9 with federal senior pass during 6/1-LD; others pay $18; free rest of year, but no services; 14-day limit. 8 sites; 16-ft RV limit. Tbls, toilets, cfga, no drkg wtr, no trash service. Fishing, hiking, hunting. Elev 2200 ft.

Sunstrip Campground $10
Mount Hood National Forest
21 mi SE of Estacada on SR 224. $10 with federal senior pass; others pay $20. 4/7-9/10; 14-day limit. 9 sites up to 60 ft, but 16-ft RV limit. Tbls, toilets, cfga, drkg wtr. Fishing.

Triangle Lake Horse Camp $7.50
Mount Hood National Forest
27 mi SE of Estacada on SR 224; 21.7 mi S on FR 46; 8.2 mi SE on FR 4690; S on FR 4220. $7.50 base with federal senior pass; others pay $15 base, $20 for premium sites. 5/15-9/15; 14-day limit. 8 sites; 30-ft RV limit. Tbls, toilets, cfga, no drkg wtr. Horseback riding, hiking.

EUGENE (W)

Hult Reservoir Dispersed Campsites FREE
Bureau of Land Management
Eugene District
28 mi NW of Eugene (5 mi N of Horton) off SR 36 on gravel rd. All year; 14-day limit. Primitive undesignated sites along S & W shores of Hult Reservoir. Free. Tbls, portable chemical toilets in summer, tbls, cfga, no drkg wtr. Fishing, hiking, boating (no motors). Primitive boat launch. Within the Upper Lake Creek Special Recreation Management Area (15,000 acres acquired from Willamette Industries in 1995). Primitive dispersed camping permitted throughout the area off poorly defined rds (access to many only by horse, hiking or biking).

FLORENCE (W)

Alder Dune $12
Siuslaw National Forest
6 mi N of Florence on US 101; W side at Dune Lake. $12 with federal senior pass; others pay $24. All year; 14-day limit. 39 sites; 62-ft RV limit. Tbls, flush toilets, cfga, drkg wtr. Fishing, swimming, hiking trails.

Baker Beach $6.50
Siuslaw National Forest
About 6 mi N of Florence at end of Baker Beach Rd. $6.50 with federal senior pass; others pay $13. All year; 14-day limit. 4 rustic sites primarily for equestrian campers. Tbls, toilet, cfga, no drkg wtr. Hiking & bridle trails to beach & forest; fishing.

Carter Lake Campground $11
Siuslaw National Forest
Oregon Dunes National Recreation Area
7.5 mi S of Florence on US 101; right at campground sign for 1 mi on Transpacific Lane; right across RR tracks; right on Horsfall Beach Rd for 1.3 mi; at Carter Lake. $11 with federal senior pass; others pay $22. 5/1-9/30; 14-day limit. 23 sites, typically 45 ft. Tbls, flush toilets, cfga, drkg wtr. Swimming, fishing.

Clay Creek Recreation Site $7.50
Bureau of Land Management
Eugene District
From Mapleton (10 mi E of Florence), 15 mi SE on SR 126, then 16 mi S on Siuslaw River Rd; follow signs. $7.50 with federal senior pass; others pay $15. 5/15-10/1; 14-day limit. 21 sites; 32-ft RV limit. Tbls, toilets, cfga, drkg wtr. Hunting, fishing, swimming beach, horseshoes, interpretive trail. Site fees $20 in 2019 ($10 with senior pass).

Lagoon Campground $11
Oregon Dunes National Recreation Area
7.1 mi S of Florence; right on Beach Access Rd for 1 mi; near Silcoos River. $11 with federal senior pass; others pay $22. All year; 14-day limit. 41 sites up to 88 ft, typically 45 ft (9 pull-through). Flush toilets, tbls, cfga, drkg wtr. Hiking, beachcombing.

Sutton Campground $12
Siuslaw National Forest
2.3 mi N of Florence on US 101; left at campground sign on FR 794 for 0.8 mi; right at sign. $12 with federal senior pass at 55 non-elec sites; others pay $24; $16 with senior pass at 22 elec sites; others pay $29. All year; 14-day limit. 24-72 ft & 3 group areas. Flush toilets, tbls, cfga, drkg wtr, grey wtr stations.

Tahkenitch Campground $12
Oregon Dunes National Recreation Area
12.5 mi S of Florence on US 101; right at sign. $12 with federal senior pass; others pay $22. 5/1-9/30; 14-day limit. 9 RV sites, typically 50 ft. Flush toilets, tbls, cfga, drkg wtr. Fishing, hiking.

Tahkenitch Landing Campground $11
Siuslaw National Forest
Oregon Dunes National Recreation Area
12.1 mi S of Florence on US 101; left into campground. $11 with federal senior pass; others pay $22. All year; 14-day limit. 28 sites, typically 33 ft. Pit toilets, cfga, tbls, drkg wtr. Fishing, boating(l).

Tyee Campground $11
Siuslaw National Forest
Oregon Dunes National Recreation Area
5.6 mi S of Florence on US 101; left on Pacific Ave. $11 with federal senior pass; others pay $22. 5/1-9/30; 14-day limit. 14 sites, typically 35 ft. Tbls, pit toilets, cfga, drkg wtr. Fishing.

Waxmyrtle Campground $11
Siuslaw National Forest
Oregon Dunes National Recreation Area
7.1 mi S of Florence on US 101; 1 mi E on Beach Access Rd; left at campground sign. $11 with federal senior pass; others pay $22. 5/1-9/30; 14-day limit. 55 sites, typically 55 ft (19 pull-through). Flush toilets, tbls, cfga, drkg wtr. Fishing, beachcombing, hiking trails, interpretive trail.

Whittaker Creek Recreation Site $7.50
Bureau of Land Management
Eugene District
From Mapleton (10 mi E of Florence), 15 mi SE on SR 126; 5 mi S on Siuslaw River Rd. $7.50 with federal senior pass; others pay $15. 5/15-9/30; 14-day limit. 31 sites; 32-ft RV limit. Tbls, toilets, cfga, drkg wtr. Boating(l), fishing, swimming, hunting, hiking. 10 acres; elev 1300 ft. Site fees $20 in 2019 ($10 with senior pass).

FRENCHGLEN (E)

Fish Lake Campground $8
Bureau of Land Management
Burns District
From Hwy 205 at Frenchglen, 17 mi E on Steens Mountain Loop Rd (gravel). $8 during 6/10-10/31; free rest of year; 14-day limit. 23 sites (35-ft RV limit). Tbls, toilets, cfga, drkg wtr. Swimming, fishing, hunting, hiking, birdwatching, boating(ld), mountain biking, horseback riding (corral). 25 acres. Limited parking for large RVs; average site 20 ft, but 3 up to 35 ft. Dump station at nearby Steen Mountain Resort.

Hot Springs Campground FREE
Hart Mountain National Wildlife Refuge
From settlement of Frenchglen, about 3 mi S on SR 205; right (W) about 12 mi on Rock Creek Rd, becoming Frenchglen Rd inside wildlife refuge; continue SW to refuge station, then to campground. Free. 5/1-10/31; 14-day limit. 12 primitive sites (20-ft RV limit). Tbls, toilets, cfga, drkg wtr. Fishing, hiking.

Jackman Park Campground $6
Bureau of Land Management
Burns District
From Hwy 205 at Frenchglen, 19 mi E on Steens Mountain Loop Rd (gravel); 2 mi E of Fish Lake camp. $6. 6/10-11/1;

14-day limit. 6 sites (35-ft limit, but RVs not recommended). Tbls, toilets, no drkg wtr, cfga. Fishing, hiking, hunting, birdwatching, mountain biking. Dump at nearby Steen Mountain Resort. See mustangs at nearby Kiger Gorge Overlook. Elev 8100 ft.

Page Springs Campground $8
Bureau of Land Management
Burns District
From Hwy 205 at Frenchglen, SE 3 mi on Steens Mountain Loop Rd (gravel); at Blitzen River. $8 during May-Oct; free rest of year; 14-day limit. 36 sites (35-ft RV limit). Tbls, toilets, cfga, drkg wtr. Fishing, hiking, hunting, nature trail, birdwatching, mountain biking. Horse herd at SW end of loop rd. Elev 4200 ft; 8 acres. Dump at nearby Steen Mountain Resort.

South Steens Campgrounds $6
Bureau of Land Management
Burns District
10 mi S of Frenchglen on SR 205; 18 mi E on Steens South Loop Rd (Steens Mountain Back Country Byway). $6 during 5/20-11/1; free rest of year; 14-day limit. 36 sites at family sites & 15 at equestrian camp; 35-ft RV limit. Tbls, toilets, cfga, drkg wtr, hitch bars at 15 sites. Hiking, fishing, horseback riding, mountain biking. Horse herd S of camp.

Willow Creek Hot Springs FREE
Bureau of Land Management
Vale District
From Frenchglen, about 10 mi SE on SR 205 to settlement of Fields; continue 3 mi SE on SR 205; left (NE) on White Horse Ranch Rd, then 2.5 mi S on gravel rd. Free. Undeveloped primitive area with hot spring; 4 sites. No facilities except cfga; no drkg wtr or trash service. All year; 14-day limit. Wilderness camping in Pueblo Mountains. Hunting, fishing, hiking.

GLENDALE (W)

Devils Flat Campground $10
Umpqua National Forest
From I-5 at Azalea (6 mi N of Glendale, 18.2 mi E on CR 36 (Cow Creek Rd). Alternative route: From ranger station at Tiller, 1.5 mi S on CR 1 to Callahan Rd 3230, then 7 mi to FR 32; turn right for 2 mi to campground. FR 32 becomes CR 36 the last mi. $10. 5/1-10/31; 14-day limit. 3 sites; 22-ft RV limit. Tbls, toilet, cfga, no drkg wtr. Hiking. Elev 2100 ft; 2 acres. Cow Creek Falls Trail makes qtr mi loop along Cow Creek Falls. Site of 1915 ranger cabin & horse barn.

Skull Creek Campground FREE
Bureau of Land Management
Medford District
W of Glendale on Brown Rd, becoming Reuben County Rd, then BLM 33-7-2 in town of Reuben; continue 6 mi W to Skull Creek turn-off, on left. Free. All year; 14-day limit.

5 sites. Tbls, toilets, cfga, no drkg wtr or trash service. Rockhounding.

Tucker Flat Campground FREE
Bureau of Land Management
Medford District
20 mi W of Glendale on Cow Creek Rd; 5 mi W on Mule Creek Rd; 14 mi SW on Marial Rd. Free. 5/1-10/31; 14-day limit. 6 small primitive sites. Tbls, firewood, cfga, toilets, no drkg wtr. Swimming; fishing nearby. River permit needed if floating 5/15-10/15. Remote. Roads are one lane, curvy, not recommended for RVs.

GLIDE (W)

Beaver Pond Dispersed Camp FREE
Dispersed Camp
Umpqua National Forest
From North Umpqua Ranger Station at Glide, 23 mi E on Hwy 138; Steamboat Creek Rd 38 for 9 mi; FR 3816 for 4 mi; FR 3816-200 S for 4 mi. Free. Primitive dispersed camping area at 2-acre pond; no facilities. Rainbow & eastern brook trout fishing. Rds 38 & 3816 often have heavy logging traffic.

Bradley Ridge Trailhead FREE
Umpqua National Forest
24 mi E of North Umpqua Ranger Station at Glide to FR 4713 (on left about half mi E of Island Campground); follow FR 4713 (Jack Creek Rd) 3.5 mi; 3 mi on FR 4713-100; 3 mi on FR 120; 1 mi on FR 130 to trailhead. Free. Undeveloped camping areas. Trail (1.75 mi) open to foot, horse, bicycle and motorcycle traffic. Rock overhang where Umpqua Indians lived; Dog Creek Indian caves. Trail borders & enters Limpy Rock Research Natural Area.

Cavitt Creek Falls Recreation Site $7
Bureau of Land Management
Roseburg District
7 mi E of Glide on Little River Rd; 3 mi S on Cavitt Creek Rd. $7 with federal senior pass; others pay $14. About 5/15-9/30; 14-day limit. 10 sites (20-ft RV limit) & 14 picnic sites. Tbls, toilets, cfga, drkg wtr. Swimming (at base of 10-ft waterfall), fishing.

Cavitt Lake Dispersed Camp FREE
Umpqua National Forest
From North Umpqua Ranger Station at Glide, qtr mi W on Hwy 138; Little River Rd 17 for 2.6 mi; New Bridge Rd (Cavitt Creek Rd) FR 25 to FR 763 & follow 763 to its end. Sign on Cavitt Creek Rd points way. Total distance, 21 mi. Free. Dispersed primitive camping area; no facilities. Lake just being formed. Fishing.

Cinderella Springs Dispersed Camp FREE
Umpqua National Forest
From North Umpqua Ranger Station at Glide, qtr mi W on Hwy 138; Little River Rd 17 for 28 mi; FR 2715 for 2.5 mi;

FR 4720 for 1.5 mi. Free. Dispersed primitive camping area. Log tbls, cfga, flat area for RVs, no toilet, no drkg wtr (spring wtr may be boiled). Wildlife & flowers plentiful. Fishing, hunting, berry-picking.

Coolwater Campground $10
Umpqua National Forest
15.5 mi SE of Glide on CR 17. Along Little River. $10 during 5/20-10/31; free off-season but no services or wtr; 14-day limit. 7 sites (24-ft RV limit). Tbls, toilets, cfga, drkg wtr. Fishing, hiking, swimming. Waterfall nearby.

Grassy Ranch Dispersed Camp   FREE
Umpqua National Forest
From North Umpqua Ranger Station at Glide, 23 mi E on Hwy 138; Steamboat Creek 38 for 9 mi; FR 3817 for 3 mi; FR 3850 for 9 mi; right on FR 3810 for 0.7 mi; right on Spur 370 for qtr mi. Free. Undeveloped dispersed camp on W side of Boulder Creek drainage. No facilities. Berrypicking, hunting, hiking, photography.

Hemlock Lake $10
Umpqua National Forest
16.5 mi E of Glide on CR 17; 15.5 mi E on FR 27; half mi S on FR 495. $10. 6/1-10/31; 14-day limit. 13 sites (RVs under 36 ft). Tbls, toilets, cfga, no drkg wtr. Swimming, boating(l), fishing, hiking trail. 28-acre lake. Elev 4400 ft.

Hi Si Pond Dispersed Area   FREE
Umpqua National Forest
From North Umpqua Ranger Station at Glide, 23 mi E on Hwy 138; 3 mi on Steamboat Creek Rd 38; left for 8 mi on FR 3806. Free. Spring-fall; 14-day limit. Primitive undesignated sites. No facilities. Fishing, hunting. GPS: 43.126069, -123.249236.

Illahee Flat Dispersed Area   FREE
Umpqua National Forest
From North Umpqua Ranger Station at Glide, 29 mi E on Hwy 138; left on FR 4760 for 2 mi; qtr mi on Spur 039 to gazebo. Free. Spring-fall; 14-day limit. Primitive undesignated camping near covered gazebo. No facilities except cfga. Hiking.

Lake in the Woods $10
Umpqua National Forest
17 mi E of Glide on CR 17; 11 mi E on FR 27. $10. MD-10/1; 14-day limit. 11 sites (35-ft RV limit). Tbls, flush & pit toilets, cfga, no drkg wtr. Fishing, hiking, boating. On 4-acre Lake in the Woods. Hike to Yakso or Hemlock Falls.

Limpy Sump Dispersed Area   FREE
Umpqua National Forest
From North Umpqua Ranger Station at Glide, qtr mi W on Hwy 138; 28 mi on Little River Rd 17; 1.5 mi on FR 2715; 154 mi on FR 4720, then either follow FR 200 or continue on FR 2715 past FR 4720 and left on FR 210. Free. Sum-

mer-fall; 14-day limit. Primitive undesignated site. Tbl, cfga, no toilet, no drkg wtr. Youtkut Pillars rock formation about half mi S on FR 2715. Hiking, fishing, hunting, berrypicking. GPS: 43.1260699, -123.249236.

Millpond Recreation Site $7
Bureau of Land Management
Roseburg District
4 mi E of Glide on Hwy 138; 5 mi N on Rock Creek Rd. $7 with federal senior pass; others pay $14. About 5/15-10/1; 14-day limit. 12 sites (30-ft RV limit). Tbls, flush & pit toilets, cfga, drkg wtr. Swimming, horseshoes, hiking (nature trail), playground. 20 acres. Free fish hatchery nearby.

Rock Creek Recreation Site $7
Bureau of Land Management
Roseburg District
4 mi E of Glide on Hwy 138; 8.5 mi N on Rock Creek Rd. $7 with federal senior pass; others pay $14. About 5/15-9/30; 14-day limit. 16 sites (30-ft RV limit). Tbls, toilets, cfga, drkg wtr. Fishing (at North Umpqua River), rafting, hiking. 12 acres. Free fish hatchery nearby.

Susan Creek $10
Bureau of Land Management
Roseburg District
11 mi E of Glide on Hwy 138. $10 with federal senior pass; others pay $20. About 4/1-15/10/28; 14-day limit. 29 sites (35-ft RV limit). Tbls, flush toilets, showers, cfga, drkg wtr. Fishing on North Umpqua Wild and Scenic River, hiking, rafting, kayaking.

White Creek Campground $10
Umpqua National Forest
13.1 mi E of Glide on CR 17; 4 mi E on FR 27; 2 mi E on FR 2792; at Little River. $10. 5/20-9/30; 14-day limit. 4 sites (1 for RV). Tbls, toilets, cfga, well drkg wtr. Fishing; swimming (no lifeguards); hiking. Sandy beach. Elev 1600 ft; 1 acre. Mountains. White Creek. Central parking area with walk-in sites. Grotto Falls Trail, Overhang Trail. Limited parking for RVs. Excellent sandy swimming beach for children. Grotto Falls Trail, Overhang Trail.

Willow Flat Sump Dispersed Camp   FREE
Umpqua National Forest
From North Umpqua Ranger Station at Glide, qtr mi W on Hwy 138; Little River Rd 17 for 16.5 mi to Coolwater Campground; left onto FR 2703 for 7.9 mi; FR 4711 qtr mi; FR 4711-750 for 3.3 mi; right at FR 4711-835 for half mi. Free. May-Sep; 14-day limit. Undeveloped primitive camping area. Toilet, log tbl, cfga, no drkg wtr or trash service. 2-acre trout lake. Hunting, fishing, swimming, hiking, berry-picking, photography.

Wolf Creek Campground $7.50
Umpqua National Forest
12 mi SE of Glide on CR 17. $7.50 with federal senior pass;

others pay $15. 5/20-9/30; 14-day limit. 8 sites (30-ft RV limit). Tbls, flush toilets, cfga, drkg wtr, gray water sumps. On Little River. Fishing, horseshoes, volleyball, swimming.

GOLD BEACH (W)

Elko Dispersed Camping — FREE
Siskiyou National Forest
SE of Gold Beach on CR 635, then follow FR 3680 and FR 11503 (10 mi total); near Hunter Creek. Free. All year; 14-day limit. 3 small sites. No facilities, no drkg wtr or trash service. Elev 3000 ft.

Foster Bar Campground — $10
Siskiyou National Forest
30 mi E of Gold Beach on Agness-Gold Beach Rd; right on Illahe-Agness Rd for 3 mi. $10. All year; 14-day limit. 4 RV sites. Tbls, flush toilets (portable toilets Nov-May), cfga, drkg wtr, drinking fountain, trash service Apr-Nov. Hiking, boating(l), fishing & tubing in Rogue River. Former dispersed site is now a developed campground. Site of final battle in Rogue River Indian wars.

Game Lake Dispersed Camping — FREE
Siskiyou National Forest
Follow CR 635 from Gold Beach, then FR 3680 to camp. 5/1-11/1; 14-day limit. 3 small, primitive undesignated sites. Toilet, cfga, no drkg wtr or trash service. Fishing, hiking.

Huntley Park — $12
Port of Gold Beach
From US 101 at N end of Gold Beach, 7 mi E on CR 595 (Jerry Flats Rd); at S shore of Rogue River. $12 at 70 primitive sites ($77 weekly). All year; 30-ft RV limit. Tbls, flush toilets, showers, cfga, drkg wtr, no elec. Hiking & mountain biking trails, fishing, boating.

Lobster Creek Campground — $10
Siskiyou National Forest
4.2 mi NW of Gold Beach on CR 375; 5.6 mi NW on FR 333; at Rogue River. $10. All year; 14-day limit. 4 RV sites (22-ft RV limit). Tbls, toilets, cfga, no drkg wtr. Boating(l), fishing, swimming, rockhounding. Scenic.

Oak Flat Dispersed Campground — FREE
Siskiyou National Forest
Follow CR 545 E from Gold Beach along Rogue River, then S on CR 450 to camp. Free. 5/1-11/1; 14-day limit. 15 small primitive dispersed sites. Toilet, cfga, no drkg wtr or trash service. Horse corral. Hiking, horseback riding. Access to Illinois River Trail 1161. Elev 3000 ft.

Quosatana Campground — $7.50
Siskiyou National Forest
1 mi N of Gold Beach on US 101; 4.2 mi NE on CR 595; 10 mi NE on FR 33. $7.50 with federal senior pass; others pay $15. All year; 14-day limit. 43 sites (32-ft RV limit).

Tbls, flush toilets, cfga, drkg wtr, dump, grey wtr stations, fish cleaning station. Boating(l), fishing, hiking trail. On Rogue River.

Wildhorse Meadows Dispersed Camp — FREE
Siskiyou National Forest
Follow CR 595 E along Rogue River, then FR 3318 to camp. Free. 5/1-11/1; 14-day limit. 3 primitive undesignated sites. Toilet, tbls, cfga, no drkg wtr or trash service. Fishing, hiking. Solitude. Scenic.

GOVERNMENT CAMP (W)

Alpine Campground — $10
Mount Hood National Forest
From US 26 just E of Government Camp, 4.3 mi N on FR 173 following signs to Timberline Lodge. $10 with federal senior pass; others pay $20. 6/1-MD; 14-day limit. 16 sites, typically 33 ft, but 16-ft RV limit. Tbls, portable toilets, cfga, drkg wtr.

Barlow Creek Campground — $11
Mount Hood National Forest
2 mi E of Government Camp on US 26; 4.5 mi N on Hwy 35; 4.2 mi SE on FR 3530. $11. Elev 3100 ft. 5/1-10/1; 14-day limit. 3 sites. Tbls, toilet, cfga, no drkg wtr. Hunting; fishing; horseback riding & hiking (1 mi).

Barlow Crossing Campground — $11
Mount Hood National Forest
2 mi E of Government Camp on US 26; 4.5 mi N on OR 35; 5.2 mi SE on FR 3530 (dirt rd). $11. Elev 3100 ft. 5/15-10/1; 14-day limit. 6 sites. Tbls, toilet, cfga, no drkg wtr. Fishing; horseback riding (1 mi); hiking (2 mi).

Bonney Crossing Campground — $11
Mount Hood National Forest
From Wamic (about 30 mi W of Government Camp), 6 mi W on CR 226/FR 2710 (Dodson Rd); at Badger Creek. $11 during MD-LD; free off-season but no services; 14-day limit. 8 sites; 16-ft RV limit. Tbls, toilet, cfga, no drkg wtr. Boating, fishing. Elev 2200 ft.

Bonney Meadow Campground — FREE
Mount Hood National Forest
From Government Camp, 3 mi W on US 26; 4.5 mi NE on SR 35; right (S) on FR 48 for 6.8 mi; left (N & S) for 3.6 mi on FR 4890; at 4-way intersection, continue N onto unimproved FR 4891 (high-clearance vehicles suggested) for 4 mi; site on right near Bonney Creek. Free. 6/1-9/10; 14-day limit. 6 dispersed sites (16-ft RV limit). Tbls, toilet, cfga, no drkg wtr. Berry-picking, fishing.

Camp Creek Campground — $9
Mount Hood National Forest
5 mi W of Government Camp on US 26. $9 base with federal senior pass; others pay $18 base, $20 for premium sites ($10 with senior pass). MD-LD; 14-day limit. 25 sites,

typically 40 ft, but 22-ft RV limit. Tbls, toilets, cfga, drkg wtr, grey wtr stations. Hiking/bridle trail, fishing.

Clackamas Lake Campground $10
Mount Hood National Forest
11.2 mi E of Government Camp on US 26; at sign for Timothy Lake, turn right on Skyline Rd (FR 42) for 8.2 mi; bear left at "Y", then left at campground sign. $10 with federal senior pass; others pay $20. MD-9/17; 14-day limit. 46 sites; 32-ft RV limit. Tbls, toilets, cfga, drkg wtr. Fishing, hiking trails.

Clear Lake Campground $10.50
Mount Hood National Forest
9.2 mi E of Government Camp on US 26; 1 mi S on FR 2630; at E shore of Clear Lake. $10.50 with federal senior pass; others pay $21 ($14 in overflow). 6/15-9/30; 14-day limit. 26 sites; 32-ft RV limit. Tbls, toilets, cfga, drkg wtr. Boating(l), fishing, swimming, fishing.

Devils Half Acre   FREE
Mount Hood National Forest
2 mi E of Government Camp on US 26; 4.5 mi N on OR 35; 1 mi E on FR 3530 (dirt rd). Free. 5/15-10/1; 14-day limit. 2 small dispersed sites. No amenities, no drkg wtr. Horseback riding, hiking.

Forest Creek Campground $11
Mount Hood National Forest
From Wamic (about 30 mi W of Government Camp), 1 mi SW on Wamic Market Rd, becoming Rock Creek Rd for 6 mi, becoming FR 48 within forest; follow FR 48 SE for 12.5 mi; 1 mi SE on FR 4885; qtr mi S on FR 3530. $11 during MD-LD; free pre-season & post-season while rds open; 14-day limit. 8 sites (16-ft RV limit). Tbls, toilet, cfga, no drkg wtr. Hiking, fishing.

Frog Lake Campground $10.50
Mount Hood National Forest
6.7 mi E of Government Camp on US 26; left, then immediate right on paved single-lane rd for 0.25 mi; right at campground sign, then immediate left; N end of Frog Lake. $10.50 with federal senior pass; others pay $21. 6/15-9/30; 14-day limit. 33 sites, typically 40 ft, but 22-ft RV limit. Tbs, toilets, cfga, drkg wtr, grey wtr stations. Boating(l), hiking, fishing.

Gone Creek Campground $10
Mount Hood National Forest
11.2 mi E of Government Camp on US 25; right at Timothy Lake sign (FR 42) for 8.2 mi across Warm Springs Indian Reservation & back into national forest; bear right at "Y" for 1.5 mi on FR 57. $10 with federal senior pass; others pay $20. MD-9/16; 14-day limit. 50 sites; 32-ft RV limit. Tbls, toilets, cfga, drkg wtr, grey wtr stations. Fishing, hiking, swimming, boating(l).

Green Canyon Campground $10
Mount Hood National Forest
From Government Camp, 8 mi E on US 26 to village of Zigzag, then 4.6 mi S on Salmon River Rd (FR 2618). $10 with federal senior pass; others pay $20. 5/15-9/15; 14-day limit. 15 sites, typically 40 ft, but 22-ft RV limit. Tbls, toilets, cfga, drkg wtr. Fishing, hiking trails.

Grindstone Campground   FREE
Mount Hood National Forest
2 mi E of Government Camp on US 26; 4.5 mi N on OR 35; 3 mi SE on FR 3530 (dirt rd). Free. 5/15-10/1; 14-day limit. 3 primitive sites. Tbls, toilet, cfga, no drkg wtr. Fishing. On Barlow Creek.

Hoodview Campground $10
Mount Hood National Forest
11.2 mi E of Government Camp on US 26; 8.2 mi S on Skyline Rd (FR 42); bear right at "Y" for 2.5 mi on FR 57; at Timothy Lake. $10 with federal senior pass; others pay $20. MD-9/30; 14-day limit. 43 sites; 32-ft RV limit. Tbls, toilets, cfga, drkg wtr, grey wtr stations. Fishing, hiking trails, boating(l).

Little Crater Lake Campgroiund $10
Mount Hood National Forest
11.2 mi E of Government Camp on US 26; right at Timothy Lake sign for 4.1 mi on Skyline Rd (FR 42); right after campground sign for 2.3 mi on FR 58. $10 with federal senior pass; others pay $20. MD-LD; 14-day limit. 16 sites; 22-ft RV limit. Tbls, toilets, cfga, drkg wtr. Hiking trail, fishing, boating(l).

Lost Creek Campground $10
Mount Hood National Forest
From Government Camp, 8 mi E on US 26 to village of Zigzag, then 4.1 mi N on E. Lolo Pass Rd (CR/FR 18); right at "Campgrounds/Trailheads" sign for 2.75 mi on FR 1825. $10 with federal senior pass; others pay $20. MD-9/10; 14-day limit. 16 sites, typically 40 ft, but 22-ft RV limit. Tbls, toilets, cfga, drkg wtr. Fishing, hiking trail.

McNeil Campground $8
Mount Hood National Forest
From Government Camp, 8 mi E on US 26 to village of Zigzag; 4.7 mi NE on CR/FR 18 (Lolo Pass Rd); E on FR 1825 (Muddy Fork Rd). $8 with federal senior pass; others pay $16. MD-LD; 14-day limit. 34 sites, typically 45 ft, but 22-ft RV limit. Tbls, toilets, cfga, no drkg wtr. Hiking, fishing, mountain biking.

Oak Fork Campground $10
Mount Hood National Forest
11.2 mi E of Government Camp on US 26; right at Timothy Lake sign for 8.2 mi on Skyline Rd (FR 42); bear right at "Y" for 1.3 mi on FR 57. $10 with federal senior pass; others pay $20. MD-9/30; 14-day limit. 47 sites; 32-ft

RV limit. Tbls, toilets, cfga, drkg wtr, grey wtr stations. Fishing, hiking trails, swimming, boating(l).

Pine Point Campground $10
Mount Hood National Forest
11.2 mi E of Government Camp on US 26; right at Timothy Lake sign for 8.2 mi on Skyline Rd (FR 42); bear right at "Y" for 3.2 mi on FR 57; on SW side of Timothy Lake. $10 with federal senior pass; others pay $20. 5/22-LD; 14-day limit. 21 sites; 32-ft RV limit. Tbls, toilets, cfga, drkg wtr, grey wtr stations. Boating(l), fishing, hiking trails.

Post Camp Campground   FREE
Mount Hood National Forest
From Wamic (about 30 mi W of Government Camp), 6 mi SW on CR 226; 11 mi SW on FR 408; 2 mi NW on FR 339; .7 mi W on FR 468. Free (NW Forest Pass may be required). 5/15-9/15; 14-day limit. 4 sites (RVs under 17 ft). Tbls, toilets, cfga, firewood, no drkg wtr. Fishing.

Rock Creek Reservoir Campground $10
Mount Hood National Forest
From Wamic (about 30 mi W of Government Camp), 1 mi SW on Wamic Market Rd, becoming Rock Creek Rd for 5.4 mi W to campground sign, then right for 0.25 mi on FR 4820; N at sign on FR 4810; at Rock Creek Lake. $10 base with federal senior pass; others pay $20 base, $22 for premium sites ($11 with senior pass). 4/1-9/10 (free off-season but no services); 14-day limit. 28 RV/tent sites; 35-ft RV limit. Tbls, toilets, cfga, drkg wtr. Fishing, boating, hiking.

Still Creek Campground $10.50
Mount Hood National Forest
0.5 mi E of Government Camp on SR 26;turn right at campground sign for 0.4 mi. $10.50 with federal senior pass; others pay $21. 6/9-9/10; 14-day limit. 27 sites, typically 37 ft, but 16 ft RV limit. Tbls, toilets, cfga, drkg wtr, grey wtr stations. Fishing, hiking trails.

Summit Lake Campground $8
Mount Hood National Forest
15 mi SE of Government Camp on SR 26; 13 mi S on FR 42; 1 mi SE on FR S601; 1 mi W on FR 141. $8 with federal senior pass; others pay $16. 6/9-9/4; 14-day limit. 5 sites; 16-ft RV limit. Tbls, toilets, cfga, no drkg wtr. Boating; swimming. Elev 4000 ft; 3 acres.

Lost Creek Campground $10
Mount Hood National Forest
From Government Camp, 8 mi E on US 26 to village of Zigzag, then 4.1 mi N on E. Lolo Pass Rd (CR/FR 18); right at "Campgrounds/Trailheads" sign for 2.75 mi on FR 1825. $10 with federal senior pass; others pay $20. MD-9/10; 14-day limit. 16 sites, typically 40 ft, but 22-ft RV limit. Tbls, toilets, cfga, drkg wtr. Fishing, hiking trail.

McNeil Campground $8
Mount Hood National Forest
From Government Camp, 8 mi E on US 26 to village of Zigzag; 4.7 mi NE on CR/FR 18 (Lolo Pass Rd); E on FR 1825 (Muddy Fork Rd). $8 with federal senior pass; others pay $16. MD-LD; 14-day limit. 34 sites, typically 45 ft, but 22-ft RV limit. Tbls, toilets, cfga, no drkg wtr. Hiking, fishing, mountain biking.

Trillium Lake Campground $9
Mount Hood National Forest
1.7 mi E of Government Camp on SR 26; right at sign for 1.3 mi on FR 2656. $9 with federal senior pass; others pay $18. 5/19-10/1; 14-day limit. 56 sites; 40-ft RV limit. Tbls, toilets, cfga, drkg wtr, grey wtr stations. Boating(l), fishing, hiking trail.

White River Station Campground $7
Mount Hood National Forest
2 mi E of Government Camp on US 26; 4.5 mi N on OR 35; 7 mi NE on FR 3530. $7 with federal senior pass; others pay $14. 5/15-10/1; 14-day limit. 5 sites; 32-ft RV limit. Tbls, toilets, cfga, no drkg wtr. Fishing.

GRANTS PASS (W)
(Note: All campgrounds are via steep, narrow rd, not recommended for trailers.)

Bear Camp Pasture Dispersed Camp   FREE
Siskiyou National Forest
From 35 mi NW of Grants Pass on I-5; take Merlin exit 61, follow Merlin-Galice Rd to Bear Camp Rd 23; then 19 mi to camp. Free. About 5/15-9/30; 1-day limit. Primitive undesignated sites. Tbls, toilets, cfga, no drkg wtr or trash service.

Big Pine Campground $5
Siskiyou National Forest
3.4 mi N of Grants Pass on I-5; 12.4 mi NW on Merlin-Galice Rd; 12.8 mi SW on FR 25. $5. MD-Oct; 14-day limit. 12 sites, typically 42 ft but 20-ft RV limit. Tbls, toilets (handicap access), cfga, firewood, Elev 2400 ft; 15 acres. 12.5 mi SW of Rogue River. Fishing, hiking, play field, blind interpretive trail. Site of the world's tallest Ponderosa pine tree. Closed temporarily in 2017 due to hazardous trees.

Briggs Creek Campground   FREE
Siskiyou National Forest
SW of Grants Pass on US 199 to Selma; 6 mi W on FR 4103; 11 mi N & W on FR 4105; 3 mi W on FR 152; on Illinois River. Free. Spring-fall; 14-day limit. 3 sites. No facilities, no trash service. Fishing, hiking.

Meyers Camp Dispersed Campsites   FREE
Siskiyou National Forest
From 35 mi NW of Grants Pass on I-5, take Merlin exit 61; follow Merlin-Galice Rd 12 mi; W on FR 25 for 11 mi. Free.

All year; 14-day limit. 2 primitive undesignated sites. Tbls, toilet, cfga, no drkg wtr or trash service.

Sam Brown Campground $5
Siskiyou National Forest
3.4 mi N of Grants Pass on I-5; 12.4 mi NW on Merlin-Galice Rd; 13.7 mi SW on FR 25. $5. MD-LD; 14-day limit. 19 sites (24-ft RV limit). Tbls, toilets, cfga, no drkg wtr, solar shower, shelter. Hiking & horseback trails, fishing.

Sam Brown Horse Camp   FREE
Siskiyou National Forest
3.4 mi N of Grants Pass on I-5; 12.4 mi NW on Merlin-Galice Rd; 13.7 mi SW on FR 25. Free. May-Oct; 14-day limit. 7 sites. Tbls, toilets, cfga, no drkg wtr or trash service; corrals. Hiking, horseback riding, fishing.

Secret Creek Campground   FREE
Siskiyou National Forest
35 mi NW of Grants Pass, exit 61 off I-5 to Merlin-Galice Rd for 19 mi (from Hwy 199 on FR 25, Onion Mt. Lookout Rd, it is about 37 mi). Free. All year; 14-day limit. 4 sites. Tbls, toilet, cfga, no drkg wtr or trash service.

Spalding Pond Campground   FREE
Siskiyou National Forest
15 mi SW of Grants Pass on US 199; 7 mi NW on FR 25; 5 mi W on FR 2524. Free. May-Oct; 14-day limit. 4 sites. Tbls, cfga, toilet, no drkg wtr or trash service. Fishing, swimming, hiking. Near historical mill site; pond stocked with trout.

Store Gulch Campground $10
Siskiyou National Forest
SW of Grants Pass on US 199 to Selma; connect to Illinois River Rd 4301 for 9 mi, passing Store Gulch day use area & guard station, then left into campground; on Illinois River. $10. May-Oct; 14-day limit. 4 sites (2 walk-in). Tbls, toilet, cfga, no drkg wtr or trash service. Fishing.

HAINES (E)

Anthony Lake Campground $7
Anthony Lakes Recreation Area
Wallowa-Whitman National Forest
17 mi NW of Haines on SR 411; 7 mi W on FR 73. $7 with federal senior pass at 37 RV/tent sites; others pay $14. 7/1-10/31; 14-day limit. Tbls, toilets, cfga, drkg wtr, grey wtr dumps. Fishing, hiking (trailhead), boating, swimming. Elev 7100 ft.

Grande Ronde Lake Campground $10
Anthony Lakes Recreation Area
Wallowa-Whitman National Forest
17 mi NW of Haines on SR 411; 8.5 mi W on FR 73; half mi NW on FR S438; qtr mi W on FR S438B. $10. 7/1-9/15; 14-day limit. 8 sites (16-ft RV limit). Multi-family site $18 ($9 with senior pass). Tbls, toilets, cfga, drkg wtr. Boat-

ing(ld), trout fishing, swimming. Elev 6800 ft. Trail to site of Aurelia Mine.

Mud Lake Campground $8
Anthony Lakes Recreation Area
Wallowa-Whitman National Forest
17 mi NW of Haines on SR 411; 7.3 mi W on FR 73. $8. 7/1-9/15; 14-day limit. 7 sites (16-ft limit). Tbls, toilets, cfga, no drkg wtr. Swimming, boating(rl), hiking trails, trout fishing. Group camping available. Elev 7100 ft.

HALFWAY (E)

Copperfield Park $8
Idaho Power Company
From just E of Halfway at jct with Pine Creek Hwy, about 12 mi NE on SR 86 to campground on W shore of Snake River. Hwy 71 from Cambridge to Oxbow, Oregon; right on OR 86. $8 for RV sites Nov-Mar ($16 Apr-Oct). All year; 14-day limit. 62 elec sites (50-ft RV limit). Tbls, flush toilets, cfga, drkg wtr, dump, showers. Hiking, fishing. Seniors over 60 pay $2 less in summer, $1 less in winter.

Fish Lake Campground $6
Wallowa-Whitman National Forest
5 mi N of Halfway on CR 733; 18.6 mi N on FR 66. $6. 7/1-10/31; 10-day limit. 21 sites; 25-ft RV limit. Tbls, toilets, cfga, piped drkg wtr. Swimming; fishing; boating(ld). Elev 6600 ft; 12 acres. Stream. Self-service site.

McBride Campground   FREE
Wallowa-Whitman National Forest
6 mi NW of Halfway on Hwy 413; 2.5 mi W on FR 7710. Free. 5/15-10/31; 10-day limit. 6 sites (16-ft RV limit). Tbls, toilet, cfga, no drkg wtr. Fishing, hiking. Brooks Ditch.

Tunnel Launch   FREE
Bureau of Land Management
Vale District
23 mi NE of Halfway on SR 86. Free. All year; 14-day limit. Undeveloped camping area. No facilities, no drkg wtr. Rockhounding, boating(l), fishing. GPS: 44.76523, -117.67692.

HEBO (W)

Hebo Lake Campground $9
Siuslaw National Forest
Qtr mi E of Hebo on Hwy 22; 5 mi E on FR 14. $9 with federal senior pass; others pay $18. 4/1-11/1; 14-day limit. 12 sites, typically 40 ft. Tbls, toilets, cfga, no drkg wtr. Boating (no mtrs), 5 fishing platforms, hiking (loop trail).

South Lake Dispersed Area   FREE
Siuslaw National Forest
13 mi off Hwy 22 at Little Hebo/Coast Range Summit. Travel FR 2234 to FR 2282, then N to FR 2210 & FR 14 jct; left on FR 14 to FR 1428 & follow signs. Free. All year, weather permitting; 14-day limit. Primitive sites. Toilets, cfga, no drkg wtr, no trash service.

HEPPNER (E)

Anson Wright Memorial $12
Morrow County Park
26 mi S of Heppner on Hwy 207; at Rock Creek. $12 for primitive sites ($72 weekly); $15 wtr hookups ($90 weekly); $18 elec/wtr hookups ($108 weekly); $21 full hookups ($126 weekly). 5/1-11/30; 10-day limit. 45 sites (42-ft RV limit). Tbls, flush toilets, coin showers, cfga, drkg wtr, dump ($10), playground. Fishing pond, hiking trails, rock-hounding, horseshoe pits. The only public park within 25 miles, it is often full. Elev 3400 ft; 15 acres.

Bull Prairie Lake Campground $7
Umatilla National Forest
32 mi SW of Heppner on SR 207; 3.5 mi E on FR 2039; at S shore of lake. $7 with federal senior pass; others pay $14; double sites $19, $28 group. MD-10/15; free off-season but no wtr or services; 14-day limit. 30 sites (32-ft RV limit). Tbls, toilets, cfga, drkg wtr, dump. Boating(l), fishing, swimming, hiking. Elev 4000 ft.

Coalmine Hill $8
Umatilla National Forest
22 mi SE of Heppner on CR 678 (Willow Creek Rd). $8. All year; 14-day limit. 6 sites. Toilet, cfga, tbls, no drkg wtr or no trash service. Hiking, horseback riding.

Cutsforth Forest $12
Morrow County Park
20 mi SE of Heppner on Willow Creek County Rd. $12 for primitive sites ($72 weekly; $15 wtr hookups ($90 weekly); $18 for elec/wtr hookups ($108 weekly); $21 full RV hookups ($126 weekly). 5/15-11/30; 10-day limit. 52 sites (36-ft RV limit). Tbls, flush toilets, coin showers, cfga, drkg wtr, dump ($10). Fishing pond, playground, hiking & equestrian trails. Horse pens. Elev 4000 ft; 15 acres.

Morrow-Grant OHV Park $12
Morrow County Park
22 mi SW of Heppner on SR 207. $12 for primitive sites ($72 weekly); $15 wtr hookups ($90 weekly); $18 elec/wtr hookups ($108 weekly); $21 full RV hookups ($126 weekly). 5/15-10/30; 10-day limit. 9,000-acre park with trails geared to OHV activities. Tbls, toilets, cfga, drkg wtr, dump ($10), playground, fishing ponds, restaurant. Hiking trails, OHV trails.

Penland Lake Campground   FREE
Umatilla National Forest
From Heppner, 0.7 mi S on SR 207; left (E) on Willow Creek Rd (CR 678) for 22.4 mi past Cutsforth Park, up Coalmine Hill & past Coalmine Hill Campground & continuing on FR 53/CR678 for qtr mi; left on FR 2103 (Penland Lane/CR 849) for 2 mi; left (E) on FR 2103-030 for qtr mi to W shore of lake. Free all year; maintained MD-11/15; 14-day limit. 3 RV/ten sites. Tbls, toilets, cfga, no drkg wtr or trash service. Hunting, fishing, boating, swimming. Elev 4950 ft. Note: With wtr service, fee is $8.

HINES (E)

Buck Spring Campground $6
Ochoco National Forest
1 mi S of Hines on US 20; 12 mi NW on CR 127; 26.5 mi NW on FR 41; SW of Delintment Lake off FR 4545. $6. 5/15-9/15; 14-day limit. About 8 primitive undesignated sites; 20-ft RV limit. Tbls, cfga, toilet, no drkg wtr. Managed by Malheur NF.

Delintment Lake Campground $10
Ochoco National Forest
1 mi S of Hines on US 20; 12 mi NW on CR 127; 26.5 mi NW on FR 41; 5 mi W following signs; at W side of Delintment Lake. $10. 5/15-9/15; 14-day limit. 29 sites (20-ft RV limit). Tbls, toilets, cfga, drkg wtr, fishing pier. Swimming, boating(l), fishing. Elev 5600 ft. 11 acres. Managed by Malheur NF.

Doe Springs   FREE
Ochoco National Forest
1 mi S of Hines on US 20; 12 mi NW on CR 127; 26.5 mi NW on FR 41; SW of Delintment Lake off FR 4515. Free. 5/15-9/15; 14-day limit. 5 primitive undesignated sites. Tbls, cfga, toilets, no drkg wtr. Elev 5276 ft. Managed by Malheur NF.

Donnelly Camp   FREE
Ochoco National Forest
1 mi S of Hines on US 20; 12 mi NW on CR 127; 26.5 mi NW on FR 41; E of Delintment Lake off FR 45. Free. 5/15-9/15; 14-day limit. Primitive undesignated sites. Tbls, cfga, toilets, no drkg wtr. Managed by Malheur NF.

Emigrant $8
Ochoco National Forest
1 mi S of Hines on US 20; 20 mi NW on CR 127; 9.7 mi W on FR 43; left on FR 4340 then turn on FR 4340-050; along Emigrant Creek. $8. 6/1-10/15; 14-day limit. 6 sites (20-ft RV limit). Tbls, toilet, cfga, no drkg wtr. Swimming, fly fishing. Elev 5400 ft. Managed by Malheur NF.

Falls Campground $8
Ochoco National Forest
1 mi S of Hines on US 20; 25 mi NW on CR 127; 8.5 mi W on FR 43; half mi NW on FR 4300-50. $8. 5/8-9/15; 14-day limit. 6 sites (30-ft RV limit). Tbls, toilets, cfga, drkg wtr, no trash service. On Emigrant Creek. Fishing, hunting, swimming, hiking. Waterfalls nearby. Elev 5300 ft. Managed by Malheur NF.

Pendleton Springs Forest Camp   FREE
Ochoco National Forest
1 mi S of Hines on US 20; 12 mi NW on CR 127; 26.5 mi NW on FR 41; NE of Delintment Lake off FR 43. Free. 5/15-9/15;

14-day limit. Primitive undesignated sites. Tbls, cfga, toilets, no drkg wtr. Managed by Malheur NF.

Tip Top Campground $6
Ochoco National Forest
1 mi S of Hines on US 20; 12 mi NW on CR 127; 26.5 mi NW on FR 41; near Delintment Lake off FR 41. $6. 5/15-9/15; 14-day limit. 4 sites. Tbls, cfga, toilets, no drkg wtr. Fishing, hiking, swimming. Managed by Malheur NF. Newly renovated from a dispersed site.

HOOD RIVER (W)
Kingsley Reservoir $10
Hood River County Parks & Building Department
From US 30 in Hood River, S on 13th St, then onto 12th St, becoming Tucker Rd; 2 mi S on Tucker Rd; 3.5 mi W on Portland Dr, past Oak Grove County Park, then W on Binns Hill Dr to park. At NE shore of upper Green Point Lake (Kingsley Reservoir). $10 at 20 primitive sites. 4/1-10/31; 7-day limit. Toilet, tbls, cfga, no drkg wtr. Fishing, boating(l), biking & hiking trails. Elev 3200 ft.

Nottingham Campground $7.50
Mount Hood National Forest
25.7 mi S of Hood River on SR 35; at East Fork Hood River. $7.50 with federal senir pass; others pay $15. MD-9/30; 14-day limit. 23 sites; 32-ft RV limit. Tbls, toilets, cfga, no drkg wtr.

Routson Park   CLOSED
Hood River County Parks & Building Department
From Hood River, about 3 mi S on SR 35 to jct with Baseline Rd 35 just E of Parkdale, then continue about 7 mi S to park at East Fork Hook River & Ash Creek. Closed permanently in 2016.

Sherwood Campground $12
Mount Hood National Forest
From Hood River, about 3 mi S on SR 35, passing town of Parkdale, then continue 11 mi S to site at E shore of East Fork Hood River. $7.50 with federal senior pass; others pay $15. MD-9/30; 14-day limit. 14 sites, typically 35 ft, but 16-ft RV limit. Tbls, toilets, cfga, drkg wtr. Fishing, hiking (East Fork & Tamanawas Falls Trails). Elev 3000 ft; 4 acres.

Wahtum Lake Campground $7.50
Mount Hood National Forest
About 25 mi SW of Hood River. From Hood River, SW on FR 13 (also named Tucker Rd, then Dee Hwy before becoming Lost Lake Rd near village of Dee); at split, merge right for about 1 mi past NF boundary; follow crooked FR 13 NW to site just S of lake. $7.50 with federal senior pass; others pay $15. 5/15-9/15; 14-day limit. 5 sites. Tbls, toilets, cfga, no drkg wtr. Swimming, fishing, boating. Be wary of rock falls on rd.

HUNTINGTON (E)
Bassar Diggins Camp   FREE
Bureau of Land Management
Vale District
From I-84 exit 345 at Huntington, 10 mi N on I-84 to exit 335; follow Sisley Creek Rd, then Lookout Mountain Rd about 25 mi toward Big Lookout Mountain, following signs; at Sisley Creek (dirt rds). Free. 5/1-11/1; 14-day limit. About 3 primitive undesignated sites. Toilets, cfga, tbls, no drkg wtr or trash service. Rockhounding, fishing. Primarily a hunter camp.

Spring Recreation Site $5
Bureau of Land Management
Vale District
6 mi NE of Huntington on co rd from I-84 exit 5; at Brownlee Reservoir. $5 during 4/1-10/30; free off-season 14-day limit. 35 undesignated sites (30-ft RV limit). Tbls, toilets, cfga, drkg wtr, fish cleaning station. Boating(l), fishing, hunting. 20 acres.

IDLEYLD PARK (W)
Apple Creek Campground $10
Umpqua National Forest
22.5 mi E of Idleyld on Hwy 138; near North Umpqua River. $10. 5/20-10/31; 14-day limit. 8 sites (RVs under 23 ft). Tbls, toilets, cfga, no drkg wtr, gray water sump. Hiking on segments of North Umpqua National Recreation Trail. Whitewater boating.

Bogus Creek Campground $7.50
Umpqua National Forest
On SR 138 near Idleyld Park; at North Umpqua Wild & Scneic River. $7.50 with federal senior pass; others pay $15. 5/20-10/15; 14-day limit. 15 sites; 35-ft RV limit. Tbls, flush toilets, cfga, drkg wtr, gray water sump. Fishing, rafting, hiking. Major launch site for whitewater boaters.

Boulder Flat Campground $10
Umpqua National Forest
31.7 mi E of Idleyld Park on SR 138. $10. 5/1-10/15; 14-day limit. 9 sites, typically 45 ft. Tbls, toilets, cfga, no drkg wtr, gray water sump. Boating, good fly fishing, hiking. At North Umpqua River & Boulder Creek. Adjacent to major launch point for whitewater boaters.

Bunker Hill Campground $10
Umpqua National Forest
49.4 mi E of Idleyld Park on Hwy 138; 5 mi N on FR 2610 (Lemolo Lake Rd) across dam; right on FR 2610-999 for half mi; on NW shore of Lemolo Reservoir. $10. 5/15-10/31; 14-day limit. 8 sites; 22-ft RV limit. Tbls, toilets, cfga, no drkg wtr, limited trash service. Hiking trails.

Canton Creek Campground $10
Umpqua National Forest
18 mi E of Idleyld Park on SR 138; half mi NE on FR 38.

$10. 5/20-10/15; 14-day limit. 5 sites (24-ft RV limit). Tbls, toilets, cfga, drkg wtr, gray water sump, no trash service. Swimming, hiking trails. At jct of Canton & Steamboat Creeks; no fishing.

Clearwater Falls Campground $10
Umpqua National Forest
46.2 mi E of Idleyld Park on Hwy 138; qtr mi E on FR 4785. $10. 6/1-10/31; 14-day limit. 12 sites (25-ft RV limit). Tbls, toilets, cfga, no drkg wtr or trash service. Along Rogue-Umpqua Scenic Byway corridor. Whitehorse Falls viewpoint.

Eagle Rock Campground $10
Umpqua National Forest
30 mi E of Idleyld Park on SR 138 (14 mi SE of Steamboat). $10. 5/20-9/15; 14-day limit. 25 sites (30-ft RV limit). Tbls, toilets, cfga, drkg wtr, gray water sump. Fishing, hiking.

East Lemolo Campground $10
Umpqua National Forest
49.4 mi E of Idleyld Park on Hwy 138; 3.2 mi N on FR 2610; 2.3 mi NE on FR 400. $10. 5/15-10/30; 14-day limit. 15 sites, typically 44 ft. Tbls, toilets, cfga, no drkg wtr or trash service. Fishing, swimming, boating, waterskiing, hiking trails.

Horseshoe Bend Campground $7.50
Umpqua National Forest
About 35 mi E of Idleyld Park on SR 138 (10 mi E of Steam-boat). $7.50 with federal senior pass; others pay $15. 5/20-9/30; 14-day limit. 25 sites (35-ft RV limit). Tbls, flush toilets, cfga, drkg wtr, gray water sump. Fishing, rafting, hiking. Major launch point for whitewater boating near camp entry.

Inlet Campground $10
Umpqua National Forest
49.5 mi E of Idleyld Park on Hwy 138; 3.2 mi N on FR 2610; 2.7 mi NE on FR 2610-400; at Lemolo Reservoir. $10. 5/15-10/30; 14-day limit. 14 sites (RVs under 26 ft). Tbls, toilets, cfga, no drkg wtr, limtited trash service. Swimming, boating, fishing, waterskiing. Elev 4160 ft.

Island Campground $10
Umpqua National Forest
19.3 mi E of Idleyld Park on SR 138. Along Umpqua River. $10. 5/1-10/31; 14-day limit. 7 sites (RVs under 25 ft). Tbls, toilets, cfga, no drkg wtr or trash service, gray water sump. Fly fishing (steelhead), boating, rafting, swimming, rafting, hiking.

Kelsay Valley Trailhead $10
Umpqua National Forest
50.4 mi E of Idleyld Park on SR 138; 4.7 mi NE on FR 60; qtr me E on FR 6000-958. $10. 5/15-9/30; 14-day limit.

16 sites (RVs under 21 ft). Tbls, toilets, cfga, no drkg wtr, limited trash service. Hiking, hunting. Elev 430 ft; 1 acre. Mountains, stream. Primitive hunter camp near Lemolo Lake. Camp accommodates horse riders, serves as trail-head for North Umpqua Trail, connecting to Lucille Lake Trail, Tolo Creek Trail, Pacific Crest Trail.

Poole Creek $7.50
Umpqua National Forest
4.5 mi N of Idleyld Park on FR 2610 (Lemolo Lake Rd) from Hwy 138; at mouth of Poole Creek on W shore of Lemolo Lake. $7.50 with federal senior pass; others pay $15 (double sites $20). 5/15-9/30; 14-day limit. 59 sites (35-ft RV limit). Tbls, toilets, cfga, drkg wtr, beach. Swimming, boating(l), fishing. NW forest pass needed for boat ramp.

Scaredman Creek $10
Bureau of Land Management
Roseburg District
39.5 mi NE of Idleyld Park on OR 138 to Steamboat; 3 mi N on Canton Creek Rd. $10 (formerly free; closed 2013-16). 5/1-10/31; 14-day limit. 15 sites (RVs under 40 ft). Tbls, toilets, cfga, drkg wtr. Swimming. 10 acres. Motorbikes prohibited. Site named by hunters afraid of the quantity of wolves. Popular fall hunting site. No fishing at Canton Creek. Elev 1360 ft.

Steamboat Falls $10
Umpqua National Forest
18 mi NE of Idleyld Park on OR 138; 5.5 mi NE on FR 232; half mi SE on FR 2432. $10. 6/1-12/1; self-service 12/2-5/31; 14-day limit. 10 sites, typically 50 ft, but 20-ft RV limit. Tbls, toilets, cfga, no drkg wtr. Swimming. Elev 1400 ft; 4 acres. Steamboat Creek; stream closed to all fishing. View steelhead trout jump falls in summer. Wtr 6 mi W at Canton Creek Campground.

Toketee Lake $10
Umpqua National Forest
35.2 mi E of Idleyld Park on SR 138; 1.5 mi NE on FR 34. $10. All year; 14 day limit. 33 sites (RVs under 31 ft). Tbls, toilets, cfga, no drkg wtr, limited trash service. Swimming, boating(l), fishing. 6 acres.

Whitehorse Falls $10
Umpqua National Forest
42.4 mi E of Idleyld Park on Hwy 138. Along Clearwater River. $10. 6/1-10/31; 14-day limit. 5 sites; 25-ft RV limit. Tbls, toilets, cfga, no drkg wtr or trash service.

JACKSONVILLE (W)
French Gulch Boat Ramp FREE
Rogue River National Forest
8 mi SW of Jacksonville on SR 238 to Ruch; left on Upper Applegate Rd (CR 859) for 15 mi to Applegate Lake; left on CR 959, across dam, then .3 mi to boat ramp. Free. All year; 14-day limit. 2 RV sites. No facilities, but toilets at adjacent

French Gulch Trailhead. Site of decommissioned French Gulch campground. Boating(l), fishing.

Hart-Tish Campground $10
Rogue River National Forest
8 mi SW of Jacksonville on SR 238; 16 mi SW on CR 859 (Upper Applegate Rd), about 0.5 mi S of dam. $10 with federal senior pass; others pay $20. 4/21-9/10; 14-day limit. Open space for self-contained RVs, 8 lakeside RV sites. Group camping $40. Tbls, flush toilets, cfga, drkg wtr, fish cleaning station. Boating(l), fishing, swimming, hiking. Elev 2000 ft. On Applegate Lake. Concessionaire.

Jackson Campground $10
Rogue River National Forest
8 mi SW of Jacksonville on SR 238; 7 mi SW on CR 859 (Upper Applegate Rd); 1 mi SW on FR 1095; across the river from decommissioned Flumet Flat Campground. $10 with federal senior pass; others pay $20 (group site $40). 5/1-9/30; 14-day limit (reduced rates rest of year). 12 sites (trailers not recommended due to tight corners & short sites). Tbls, flush toilets, cfga, drkg wtr. Fishing, boating, hiking. Concessionaire.

JOHN DAY (E)

Canyon Meadows Campground FREE
Malheur National Forest
10 mi S of John Day on US 395; 9 mi SE on FR 15; 5 mi NE on FR 1520. Free. 5/15-10/30; 14-day limit. 5 sites (15-ft RV limit). Tbls, cfga, toilet, drkg wtr or trash service. Fishing, hiking. Elev 5100 ft. Lake doesn't hold water. Closed in 2017; check current status before arrival.

Wickiup Campground $6
Malheur National Forest
10 mi S of John Day on US 395; 8 mi SE on CR 65/FR 15. $6. 4/1-11/1; 14-day limit. 6 sites (16-ft RV limit). Tbls, toilets, cfga, no drkg wtr. Fishing in Wickiup Creek. Elev 4300 ft.

JORDAN VALLEY (E)

Antelope Reservoir FREE
Bureau of Land Management
Vale District
10 mi SW of Jordan Valley on US 95; follow signs 1 mi SE to site. Free. All year; 14-day limit. 4 sites. Tbls, toilets, cfga, no drkg wtr. Boating(l), fishing. Elev 4318 ft.

Birch Creek Historic Ranch FREE
Bureau of Land Management
Vale District
8 mi N of Jordan Valley, then W on Cow Creek Rd, following Jordan Craters signs; follow BLM's Owyhee River access signs 28 mi; high-clearance vehicles recommended; rd may be impassible when wet. Free. All year (depending on rd conditions); 14 day limit. 5 primitive sites. Toilets, tbls, cfga, no drkg wtr. River floating, hiking, hunting, fishing.

Cow Lakes Campground FREE
Bureau of Land Management
Vale District
5 mi S of Jordan Valley on US 95; follow signs NW on Danner Loop Rd to site. Free. All year; 14-day limit. 10 sites. Tbls, toilets, cfga, no drkg wtr or trash service. Boating(l), fishing, hiking. Elev 4338 ft. Lava flows at nearby Jordan Crater.

Rome Launch FREE
Bureau of Land Management
Vale District
32 mi SW of Jordan Valley on US 95; S at Owyhee River & BLM boat launch sign. Free. 3/1-12/1; 14-day limit. 5 sites. Tbls, toilets, cfga, drkg wtr (no firewood). Boating(l), fishing, hiking.

Three Forks Campground FREE
Bureau of Land Management
Vale District
15 mi SW of Jordan Valley on US 95; 35 mi S on Three Forks Rd; high-clearance vehicles suggested; rd may be impassible when wet. Free. All year; 14-day limit. Undeveloped camping area; 4 very small sites. Toilet, cfga, tbls, no drkg wtr. Fishing, hiking, canoeing, floating.

JOSEPH (E)

Blackhorse Campground $8
Hells Canyon National Recreation Area
Wallowa-Whitman National Forest
7.5 mi E of Joseph on Hwy 350; 29 mi S on FR 39; at Imnaha River. $8. 5/15-10/31; 14-day limit. 16 sites; 30-ft RV limit. Tbls, toilets, cfga, no drkg wtr (available at nearby Ollokot Camp), grey wtr dumps. Fishing, boating, swimming.

Coverdale Campground $6
Wallowa-Whitman National Forest
1 mi S of Joseph on SR 82; 7.3 mi E on Hwy 350; 28.8 mi SE on FR 39; 4 mi S on FR 3960. $6. 6/15-11/15; 14-day limit. 2 RV/tent sites (32-ft RV limit). Tbls, toilets, cfga, no drkg wtr. Fishing, hiking. Elev 4300 ft; 4 acres.

Ollokot Campground $8
Hells Canyon National Recreation Area
Wallowa-Whitman National Forest
7.5 mi E of Joseph on Hwy 350; 30 mi S on FR 39; at Imnaha River. $8. 5/15-10/31; 14-day limit. 12 RV/tent sites; 30-ft RV limit. Tbls, toilets, cfga, drkg wtr. Fishing, hiking, boating.

Evergreen Group Camp CLOSED
Hells Canyon National Recreation Area
Wallowa-Whitman National Forest
1 mi S of Joseph on Hwy 82; 7.7 mi E on Hwy 350; 28.8 mi S on FR 39; 8 mi SW on FR 3960. Decomissioned and closed permanently.

Hidden Campground $6
Hells Canyon National Recreation Area
Wallowa-Whitman National Forest
7.5 mi E of Joseph on Hwy 350; 29 mi S on FR 39; at Imnaha River. $6. 5/15-10/31; 14-day limit. 10 sites. Tbls, toilets, cfga, drkg wtr. Fishing, boating, hiking.

Hurricane Creek Campground $6
Wallowa-Whitman National Forest
11 mi N of Joseph on OR 82; 1.9 mi W on Co Hwy 774; qtr mi SW on FR S218A. $6. 5/15-10/31; 10-day limit. 3 RV/tent sites (RVs under 16 ft). Tbls, toilets, cfga. Self-service site. Fishing. Elev 4800 ft. S end of camp rd not recommended for low-clearance vehicles.

Indian Crossing Campground $6
Wallowa-Whitman National Forest
Hells Canyon National Recreation Area
1 mi S of Joseph on SR 82; 7.3 mi E on SR 350; 28.7 mi S on FR 39; 8.7 mi SW on FR 3960. On Imnaha River. $6. 6/15-11/15; 14-day limit 10 RV/tent sites (32-ft RV limit). Tbls, toilets, cfga, drkg wtr. Fishing, hiking trails, horseback riding. Horse facilities.

Lick Creek Campground $6
Hells Canyon National Recreation Area
Wallowa-Whitman National Forest
7.5 mi E of Joseph on Hwy 350; 15 mi S on FR 39; at Lick Creek. $6. 6/1-11/30; 14-day limit. 5 RV/tent sites; 30-ft RV limit. Tbls, toilets, cfga, drkg wtr. Fishing, boating, hiking.

KLAMATH FALLS (W

Aspen Point Campground $10
Winema National Forest
From jct with US 97 at Klamath Falls, 31.8 mi W on SR 140 to campground sign; left on FR 3704, follow signs; at NW shore of Lake of the Woods. $10 with federal senior pass; others pay $20. 5/1-10/1; 14-day limit. 55 RV sites, typically 50 ft. Tbls, flush toilets, cfga, drkg wtr, dump, grey wtr stations. Boating(l), fishing, hiking trails.

Doe Point Campground $10
Rogue River National Forest
From jct with US 97 at Klamath Falls, 38.8 mi W on SR 140; left at campground sign for 0.4 mi on FR 810, then right, following sign; at N shore of Fish Lake. $10 with federal senior pass; others pay $20. 5/15-10/30; 14-day limit. 24 paved RV/tent sites up to 48 ft. Tbls, flush toilets, wash basins, cfga, drkg wtr, grey wtr sumps. Hiking trails, fishing.

Eagle Ridge FREE
Klamath County Park
15 mi W of Klamath Falls off Hwy 140; at 17300 Eagle Ridge Rd; at Upper Klamath Lake, on W side at Shoalwater Bay. Free. All year. 6 sites. Tbls, toilets, cfga, drkg wtr. Boating(l), fishing, boating(l). 635 acres. Elev 4139 ft.

Fish Lake Campground $11.50
Rogue River National Forest
From jct with US 97 at Klamath Falls, 38.1 mi W on SR 140; left at Fish Lake sign for 0.5 mi. $11.50 with federal senior pass; others pay $23. About 5/1-10/15; 14-day limit. 17 RV/tent sites; 40-ft RV limit. Tbls, flush toilets, cfga, drkg wtr, grey wtr stations. Fishing, hiking trail, boating(l).

Fourmile Lake Campground $7.50
Winema National Forest
Bureau of Reclamation
33 mi NW of Klamath Falls on SR 140; 5.5 mi N on FR 3661. $7.50 with federal senior pass during 5/1-LD; others pay $17; free off-season but no wtr or services; 14-day limit. 29 sites (9 for equestrians), typically 50 ft. Tbls, toilets, cfga, drkg wtr. Swimming, boating(l), fishing. Elev 5800 ft; 14 acres.

Hagelstein FREE
Klamath County Park
9 mi N of Klamath Falls on US 97. Free. 4/15-11/30; 14-day limit. 10 RV/tent sites. Tbls, flush toilets, cfga, wtr. Swimming; fishing; boating(l); waterskiing; hiking. 3.5 acres on Upper Klamath Lake. Elev 4139 ft.

Hunter Camp Development FREE
Klamath County Parks
The county has set 28 pit toilets at free hunter campsites throughout the county, and cfga have been established by the users. No other facilities, no drkg wtr. Fishing.

Jackson Creek Campground FREE
Winema National Forest
About 50 mi N of Klamath Falls on US 97; 22.1 mi NE on CR 676 (Silver Lake Rd); 5.3 mi SE on FR 49. Free all year; maintained 5/15-10/15; reduced services off-season; 14-day limit. 12 scattered rustic sites (RVs under 22 ft). Tbls, toilets, cfga, firewood, no drkg wtr or trash service. Fishing. Elev 4600 ft.

Keno Reservoir Recreation Area $10
Pacific Power Company
From jct with US 97 S of Klamath Falls, 11 mi W on SR 66. $10. MD-9/15; 14-day limit. 25 sites. Tbls, flush toilets, cfga, drkg wtr, public phone, dump. Fishing, boating(ld), hiking, horseshoes.

Klamath River Recreation Site FREE
Bureau of Land Management
Lakeview District
16 mi E of Klamath Falls on SR 66 through settlement of Keno; about qtr mi before bridge over John C. Boyles Reservoir, make right (N) for 1 mi on rough gravel rd to site near Boyles dam. Free. 5/15-10/15; 14-day limit. 4 primitive sites. Toilets, cfga, no drkg wtr. Boating(l), fishing.

Odessa Campground FREE
Winema National Forest
21.5 mi NW of Klamath Falls on SR 140; 1 mi NE on FR 3639. Free all year; maintained 5/15-10/15; reduced services off-season; 14-day limit. 6 sites. Tbls, toilet, cfga, no drkg wtr. Fishing, boating(l).

Sunset Campground $10
Lake of the Woods Recreation Area
Winema National Forest
From jct with US 97 at Klamath Falls, 31.8 mi W on SR 140; left at sign on FR 3704 for 1.3 mi to "T" intersection; right 1 mi, then right for 0.2 mi; at Lake of the Woods. $10 with federal senior pass; others pay $20. 5/1-10/1; 14-day limit. 64 RV sites, typically 48 ft. Tbls, flush toilets, cfga, drkg wtr, grey wtr stations. Dump at Aspen Point Campground. Boating(l), fishing, swimming, hiking trail.

Topsy Campground $7
Bureau of Land Management
Lakeview District
16.5 mi E of Klamath Falls on SR 66 through settlement of Keno; just before bridge over John C. Boyles Reservoir, turn right (S) for 1 mi on gravel Topsy Grade Rd to site at S shore of lake. $7 if wtr is available; free if no water. All year; 14-day limit. 13 accessible sites (no RV size limit). Toilets, drkg wtr, gray water dump. Fishing, swimming, hiking, boating(ld), waterskiing, hunting. Elev 3800 ft.

LA GRANDE (E)
Bird Track Springs Campground $5
Wallowa-Whitman National Forest
W of LaGrande on I-84 to exit 252; 6 mi W on Hwy 244. $5. 6/1-10/15; 14-day limit. 22 RV/tent sites. Tbls, toilets, cfga, no drkg wtr. Nature study, hiking trails, birdwatching, fishing (poor).

Buck Creek Forest Camp $5
Wallowa-Whitman National Forest
24 mi Se of LaGrande on SR 203; 8 mi NE on FR 7785, FR 7787 & FR 150. $5 or NW Forest Pass. MD-10/15; 14-day limit. 4 sites, typically 60 ft pull-through. Tbls, toilet, cfga, no drkg wtr (or wtr for stock). Hiking, horseback riding.

Fox Hill Campground FREE
Mount Emily Recreation Area
Union County Public Works Department
From LaGrande, follow Second St N to Black Hawk Trail Lane; left on Black Hawk (becoming Fox Hill Rd); rd becomes gravel & 17% grade is very steep for big RV rigs. Free. All year; 14-day limit. 4 primitive pull-through RV sites & 4 back-in spaces; numerous tent sites. Tbls, toilets, cfga, drkg wtr. Boating(l), fishing, windsurfing. Campground is trailhead for motorized OHV access area. Eastern half of MERA limited to non-motorized use with hiking, biking, bridle trails.

Frog Heaven Forest Camp FREE
Wallowa-Whitman National Forest
9 mi NW of LaGrande on I-84; 21 mi SW on SR 244; 6 mi W on FR 21. Free. May-Sept; 14-day limit. About 6 primitive, dispersed sites; no facilities, no drkg wtr, no maintenance. Fishing.

Hilgard Junction State Park $10
8 mi W of LaGrande on Starkey Rd; at Grande Ronde River. $10 for 18 primitive sites during 4/18-10/12; $5 off-season. All year; 10-day limit in 14-day period. 30-ft RV limit. Tbls, toilets, cfga, drkg wtr, dump. Oregon Trail interpretive display. Rafting, boating, fishing, hiking.

Moss Springs Campground $5
Wallowa-Whitman National Forest
2 mi NE of Lagrande on SR 82; at Island City, go13 mi on SR 237 (Cove Hwy); at Cove, right on Union Cove Hwy, then left on Hill St to 2nd St (which becomes Mill Creek Rd) for about 8 mi (last 10 mi steep, narrow & gravel). $5. June-Dec; 14-day limit. 8 small RV/tent sites. Tbls, toilet, cfga, no drkg wtr (except for horses), no trash service, natural history exhibits. Popular with horse campers. Hiking, horseback riding.

North Fork Catherine Creek FREE
Wallowa-Whitman National Forest
24 mi SE of LaGrande on Hwy 203 (past Union); 4 mi E on FR 7785 (last 6 mi gravel); sites over 1 mi area from Buck Creek Rd to the North Fork Catherine Creek trailhead. Free. 6/1-10/15; 14-day limit. 7 sites. Tbls, cfga, no drkg wtr or toilets. Fishing, hiking, horseback riding.

Red Bridge State Wayside $10
8 mi W of LaGrande on US 30, then 7.5 mi SW on SR 244; turn right into wayside just after crossing Grande Ronde River bridge. $10 at 10 primitive RV sites 4/18-10/13; $5 off-season. All year; 14-day. Tbls, flush toilets, cfga, drkg wtr. Fishing, horseshoe pits.

Spool Cart Campground $5
Wallowa-Whitman National Forest
8.1 mi NW of LaGrande on I-84; 13 mi SW on Hwy 244; 7 mi S on FR 51. $5. MD-9/30; 14-day limit. 12 sites, typically 33-45 ft. Tbls, toilets, cfga, no drkg wtr. Fishing, hiking. Grande Ronde River.

Umapine Campground FREE
Wallowa-Whitman National Forest
8 mi N of LaGrande on I-84 to exit 252; 23 mi W on Hwy 244; left on FR 5160 for 8 mi. Free. May-Oct; 14-day limit. 8 sites (including 3 for groups). Tbls, toilet, cfga, no drkg wtr. Staging area for OHV trails.

West Eagle Meadow Campground $5
Wallowa-Whiteman National Forest
46 mi SE of LaGrande on Hwy 203, FR 77 & FR 7755. $5.

5/15-11/15; 14-day limit. 5 small RV/tent sites. Tbls, toilets, cfga, no drkg wtr (except for horses). Fishing, hiking, horseback riding.

LA PINE (W)

Cabin Lake Campground FREE
Deschutes National Forest
From just S of La Pine at jct with US 97, 26 mi E on FR 22; about 5 mi S on FR 18 (China Hat Rd); at old guard station area. Free. 5/1-10/15; 14-day limit. 14 sites (RVs under 31 ft). Tbls, no toilets, no drkg wtr, cfga. Birdwatching. Elev 4550 ft. Toilets were vandalized and will not be replaced. This seldom-used, secluded campground will be allowed to deteriorate.

Chief Paulina Horse Camp $7
Newberry National Monument
Deschutes National Forest
5 mi N of La Pine on US 97; 13 mi E on CR 21. $7 with federal senior pass at sites with 2-horse stalls; $9 with federal senior pass at sites with 4-horse stalls; others pay $14 & $18. MD-9/30; 14-day limit. 14 equestrian sites; 40-ft RV limit. Tbls, toilets, cfga, no drkg wtr. Bridle trails, hiking. Near Paulina Lake in Newberry National Volcanic Monument. Elev 6400 ft. Monument entry fee.

China Hat Campground FREE
Deschutes National Forest
From just S of La Pine at jct with US 97, 26 mi E on FR 22; 6 mi N on FR 18. N of Fort Rock on FR 18 (China Hat Rd). Free. Elev 5100 ft. 5/1-10/15; 14-day limit. 14 sites (RVs under 31 ft). Tbls, toilets, drkg wtr, cfga. Hiking, birdwatching, OHV activity.

Corral Springs Campground FREE
Winema National Forest
About 27 mi S of La Pine (2.7 mi N of Chemult) on US 97; 1.9 mi W on FR 9774 (Corral Springs Rd). Free all year; maintained 5/15-10/15; reduced services off-season; 14-day limit. 6 sites (RVs up to 50 ft). Tbls, toilets, cfga, firewood, no drkg wtr. Mountain biking, hunting. Elev 4900 ft; 2 acres. Mosquitoes abound. Historic (explorer John C. Fremont probably camped there).

Crane Prairie $8
Deschutes National Forest
2.5 mi NW of LaPine on US 97; 20 mi W on FR 42; 4 mi N on FR 4270. $8 with federal senior pass; others pay $16 ($30 double sites). About 4/19-10/31; 14-day limit. 146 sites; 30-ft RV limit. Tbls, toilets, cfga, drkg wtr. Boating(lr), fishing, hiking. Fish cleaning station. On Crane Prairie Reservoir. Elev 4400 ft; 10 acres. Group sites.

Digit Point Campground $12
Winema National Forest
About 29 mi S of La Pine (1 mi N of Chemult) on US 97; 12 mi W on FR 9772 (Miller Lake Rd). $12 during 5/15-10/15;

reduced services off-season; 14-day limit. 64 RV sites; no RV size limit. Tbls, flush & pit toilets, cfga, drkg wtr, dump. Swimming, fishing, boating(l), hiking, waterskiing. On Miller Lake. Elev 5600 ft; 10 acres.

Gull Point $8
Deschutes National Forest
2.5 mi W of LaPine on CR 42; S on FR 4262; at N shore of Wickiup Reservoir. $8 with federal senior pass; others pay $16 (double sites $30). About 4/19-10/31; 14-day limit. 81 sites; 36-ft RV limit. Tbls, flush & pit toilets, cfga, drkg wtr, gray wtr disposals, fish cleaning station, dump. Boating (ldr), fishing, hiking, swimming, waterskiing.

Little Crater Campground $9
Deschutes National Forest
5 mi N of LaPine on US 97; 14.5 mi E on FR 21; 0.5 mi N on FR 2100-570. $9 with federal senior pass; others pay $18. 6/8-10/31; 14-day limit. 49 sites; 40-ft RV limit. Tbls, toilets, cfga, drkg wtr, grey wtr stations, dump ($10). Fishing, hiking, swimming, biking.

McKay Crossing Campground $10
Deschutes National Forest
5 mi N of LaPine on US 97; 5 mi E on CR 21; 2.7 mi E on FR 2120; at Paulina Creek. $10. About 5/18-9/30; 14-day limit. 16 sites; 26-30 ft RV limit. Tbls, toilets, cfga, no drkg wtr. Hiking, fishing, boating. Elev 4750 ft.

North Davis Creek Campground $10
Deschutes National Forest
2.5 mi W of LaPine on US 97; 11 mi W on CR 42; 9 mi W on CR 42; 4 mi S on CR 46 (Cascade Lakes Hwy). $10. About 4/8-9/10; 14-day limit. 14 sites; 40-ft RV limit. Tbls, toilets, cfga, drkg wtr. Boating(ld), fishing, hiking. At Wickiup Reservoir.

Paulina Lake Campground $9
Newberry National Volcanic Monument
Deschutes National Forest
5 mi N of La Pine on US 97; 12.9 mi E on CR 21; at Paulina Lake. $9 base with federal senior pass (others pay $18 base); $10 with senior pass at premium lakeside sites (others pay $20). 6/8-10/31; 14-day limit. 69 sites; 40-ft RV limit. Tbls, flush & pit toilets, cfga, drkg wtr, fish cleaning station, dump nearby ($10). Boating(l), fishing, hiking, swimming, birdwatching, biking. 3-day monument entry fee; free with federal senior pass.

Prairie Campground $7
Deschutes National Forest
5 mi N of La Pine on US 97; 3 mi SE on CR 21; at Paulina Creek. $7 with federal senior pass; others pay $14. 5/11-9/25; 14-day limit. 17 sites; 40-ft RV limit. Tbls, toilets, cfga, drkg wtr. Fishing, biking, hiking trails, horseback riding. Elev 4300 ft.

Pringle Falls Campground $10
Deschutes National Forest
2.4 mi NE of La Pine on US 97; 7.2 mi W on CR 43; three-fourths mi NE on FR 4330-500; at Deschutes River below Wickiup Reservoir. $10. 4/20-10/31; 14-day limit. 7 sites; 30-ft RV limit. Tbls, toilets, cfga, no drkg wtr. Fishing, canoeing on Deschutes River. Pringle Falls nearby. Elev 4300 ft.

Quinn River Campground $7
Deschutes National Forest
2.5 mi NE of LaPine on US 97; 10 mi W on CR 43; 10 mi W & 4 mi N on CR 46 (Cascade Lakes Hwy); at Crane Prairie Reservoir. $7 with federal senior pass; others pay $14. 5/18-9/10; 14-day limit. 41 sites; 40-ft RV limit. Tbls, toilets, cfga, drkg wtr. Hiking, fishing, boating(l). Elev 4400 ft; 20 acres.

Rosland Campground $12
LaPine Parks & Recreation District
From LaPine, 3 mi N on SR 97 (or 3 mi N on scenic Huntington Rd), then W on CR 43, across river bridge & left (S) on access rd; at W shore of Little Deschutes River. $12 at 10 primitive sites, $15 at one elec site, $18 at one elec/wtr site. May-Aug. Tbls, pit toilets, cfga, drkg wtr. Fishing, hiking, swimming.

South Twin Lake Campground $9
Deschutes National Forest
2.5 mi N of LaPine on US 97; 11 mi W on CR 43; 5 mi W on CR 42; 2 mi S on FR 4260; on South Twin Lake. $9 with federal senior pass; others pay $18 (double site $30). 4/20-10/9; 14-day limit. 21 sites; 40-ft RV limit. Tbls, flush toilets, cfga, drkg wtr, dump. Boating(l), hiking trails, fishing, swimming, biking.

West South Twin $7
Deschutes National Forest
2.5 mi N of LaPine on US 97; 11 mi W on CR 43; 5 mi W on CR 42; 1.5 mi S on FR 4260; at Wickiup Reservoir. $7 with federal senior pass; others pay $14. 4/20-9/25; 14-day limit. 24 sites; 40-ft RV limit. Tbls, flush toilets, cfga, drkg wtr, horse facilities, dump. Fishing, boating(ldr), hiking, horseback riding, waterskiing.

Wickiup Butte CLOSED
Deschutes National Forest
2.5 mi NE of LaPine on US 97; 10 mi W on CR 43; 3.5 mi SW on FR 4380; 2.3 mi SW on FR 4260. Campground closed.

LAKEVIEW (E)

Can Springs Campground FREE
Fremont National Forest
2.5 mi N of Lakeview on Hwy 395; 8 mi E on Hwy 140; left on FR 3615 for 11.5 mi; right on FR 3720 for 4 mi. Free all year; maintained 5/15-10/15; 14-day limit. 3 primitive sites. Tbls, cfga, toilet, no drkg wtr or trash service.

Birdwatching, hiking, mountain biking, horseback riding. Elev 6300 ft.

Clear Springs Forest Camp FREE
Fremont National Forest
3 mi W of Lakeview on Hwy 140; right on CR 2-16 for 5 mi; left on CR 2-16A (becomes FR 28) for 19 mi; after crossing Dairy Creek, left on FR 047 for 4 mi to pull-off marked "Clear Springs." Free all year; maintained 5/15-10/31; 14-day limit. 2 primitive undeveloped sites. Tbl, cfga, toilet, no drkg wtr or trash service. Fishing, hiking.

Corral Creek Forest Camp FREE
Fremont National Forest
17 mi NE of Lakeview (toward Bly) on SR 140; right (N) on FR 366 (Campbell Rd) for 13 mi; right on FR 34 for one-eighth mi, then left on FR 212 to camp. Free all year; maintained 5/15-10/15; reduced services off-season; 14-day limit. 6 sites. Tbls, toilet, cfga, no drkg wtr or trash service. Box-style horse stalls. Birdwatching, hiking, horseback riding, fishing.

Cottonwood Recreation Area $6
Fremont National Forest
24 mi W of Lakeview on SR 140; 8 mi NE on FR 3870 (surfaced rd); at N shore of Cottonwood Meadow Lake. $6 during 5/15-10/15; reduced services off-season; 14-day limit. 22 RV/tent sites (RVs under 32 ft). Tbls, toilets, cfga, drkg wtr, no trash service. Good fishing, hiking, boating(no motors), birdwatching, swimming, horseback riders, mountain biking. 12 mi of trails. Popular among fishermen. Elev 6100 ft.

Dead Horse Creek Forest Camp FREE
Fremont National Forest
3 mi W of Lakeview on Hwy 140; right on CR 2-16 for 5 mi; left on CR 2-16A (becomes FR 28) for 19 mi; after crossing Dairy Creek, left on FR 047 for 3 mi; just past Deadhorse Creek is unmarked rd to campsites. Free. Apr-Nov; 14-day limit. 4 primitive sites. Toilets, cfga, no drkg wtr, no trash service. Fishing in Dairy Creek. Elev 5400 ft.

Deep Creek Forest Camp FREE
Fremont National Forest
5.4 mi N of Lakeview on US 395; 6.5 mi E on SR 140; 6.1 mi S on FR 3915. Free all year; maintained 5/15-10/15; 14-day limit. 4 primitive sites. Tbls, toilet, cfga, no drkg wtr or trash service. Fishing, hunting. Elev 5600 ft. Good rds.

Dog Lake Campground $6
Fremont National Forest
5 mi W of Lakeview on OR 140; 7 mi S on CR W60; 13 mi W on gravel FR 4017. $6 during 5/15-10/15; reduced services off-season; 14-day limit. 15 sites (RVs under 16 ft). Tbls, toilets, cfga, no drkg wtr or trash service. Hunting; fishing; boating(l). Elev 5100 ft; 4 acres. Good gravel rds.

Dismal Creek Forest Camp   FREE
Fremont National Forest
3 mi N of Lakeview on Hwy 395; right on Hwy 140 for 8 mi; right on FR 3615 for half mi, then right on Old Hwy 140 for 1.4 mi; left on FR 3915 for 15 mi; left at jct with FR 4015, staying on FR 3915 for 1 mi. Free. Decommissioned as campground; facilities removed. All year; 14-day limit. 3 primitive sites. Fishing, birdwatching, hiking. Elev 5600 ft.

Drews Creek Campground   FREE
Fremont National Forest
10 mi W of Lakeview on SR 140; 4.5 mi S on CR 1-13 & 1-11; 4 mi W on CR 1-13; right on CR 1-11D & FR 4017 for 6 mi. Free all year; maintained 5/15-10/15; reduced services off-season; 14-day limit. 3 sites. Tbls, toilets, cfga, no drkg wtr or trash service. Fishing, hiking, horseshoes. Elev 4900 ft.

Holbrook Reservoir Campground   FREE
Fremont National Forest
25 mi W of Lakeview on Hwy 140; left on FR 3715 for 6 mi; right on FR 3817 to picnic area entrance. Free all year; maintained 5/15-10/15; reduced services off-season; 14-day limit. 4 designated sites & about 8 primitive dispersed sites without amenities. Tbls, toilets, cfga, no drkg wtr. Boating(l), fishing, birdwatching, swimming. Elev 5400 ft.

Horseglade Trailhead   FREE
Fremont National Forest
From settlement of Bly (30 mi NW of Lakeview on SR 140) continue 3.5 mi NW, then turn right (N) on CR 1257 (Ivory Pine Rd) for 12 mi to its split into FR 27 & FR 30; veer left for 1.5 mi W on FR 27; trailhead at Five Mile Creek. Free all year; maintained 5/15-10/15; reduced services off-season; 14-day limit. 2 dispersed sites. Tbls, toilets, cfga, no drkg wtr. Birdwatching, fishing, hiking.

Lake County Fairgrounds $5
From jct with US 395 at Lakeview, 0.5 mi W on SR 140. $5 at primitive sites; $18 at 10 sites with RV hookups in summer, $12 in winter. Flush toilets, drkg wtr, elec($). Dump $5.

Lofton Reservoir Campground $6
Fremont National Forest
17 mi NE of Lakeview (toward Bly) on SR 140; 7 mi S on FR 3715; 1.3 mi NE on FR 013. $6 during 5/15-10/15; reduced services off-season; 14-day limit. 26 sites (typically 45 ft). Tbls, toilets, cfga, drkg wtr, gray water sump, fishing pier. Boating(l; no mtrs), fishing, swimming. Little Lofton Lake. Elev 6200 ft.

Mud Creek Campground   FREE
Fremont National Forest
2.5 mi N of Lakeview on US 395; 6.5 mi E on SR 140; 6.1 mi N on FR 3615. Free all year; maintained 5/15-10/15; reduced services off-season; 14-day limit. 7 large sites. Tbls, toilet, drkg wtr, cfga. Hunting, good fishing. Elev 6600 ft. Scenic drive.

Overton Reservoir Forest Camp   FREE
Fremont National Forest
2.5 mi N of Lakeview on US 395; 6.5 mi E on SR 140; 12.5 mi N on FR 3615; left on FR 3624 for 2 mi; right on FR 011 to trout pond. Free. All year; 14-day limit. Primitive undesignated sites. No amenities or trash service. Fishing. Elev 6600 ft.

Twin Springs Campground   FREE
Fremont National Forest
2.5 mi N of Lakeview on Hwy 395; 8 mi E on SR 140; half mi N on FR 3615; right on Old Hwy 140 for 1.4 mi; left on FR 3915 for 3 mi; left on FR 3910 for 2 mi to camp entrance sign. Free all year; maintained 5/15-10/15; reduced services off-season; 14-day limit. 3 sites. Tbls, toilet, cfga, no drkg wtr or trash service. Hiking, birdwatching. Elev 6300 ft.

Willow Creek Campground   FREE
Fremont National Forest
5.5 mi N of Lakeview on US 395; half mi E on SR 140; 10 mi S on FR 391. Free all year; maintained 5/15-10/15; reduced services off-season; 14-day limit. 8 sites (22-ft RV limit). Tbls, cfga, toilets, no drkg wtr, no trash service. Fishing. Elev 5800 ft; 5 acres on E shore of Willow Creek.

LOSTINE (E)

Shady Campground $5
Wallowa-Whitman National Forest
7 mi S of Lostine on CR 551; 10.1 mi S on FR 8210. $5. Elev 5400 ft. 6/15-11/1; 10-day limit. 7 RV/tent sites, typically 42 ft. Tbls, toilets, cfga, firewood, no drkg wtr. Self-service sites. Swimming; fishing. On Lostine River.

Turkey Flat Forest Camp $5
Wallowa-Whitman National Forest
7 mi S of Lostine on Lostine River Rd; 9 mi on FR 8210; at Lostine River. $5. 6/1-10/15; 14-day limit. 4 small RV/tent sites. Tbls, toilet, cfga, no drkg wtr. Fishing, hiking.

Two Pan Campground $5
Wallowa-Whitman National Forest
7 mi S of Lostine on CR 551; 10.8 mi S on FR 8210. On Lostine River. $5. Elev 5600 ft. 6/15-11/1; 10-day limit. 5 RV/tent sites (RVs under 16 ft). Tbls, toilets, cfga, no drkg wtr. Self-service site. Swimming; berry picking; horseback riding (2 mi).

Walla Walla Forest Camp $5
Wallowa-Whitman National Forest
7 mi S of Lostine on Lostine River Rd; 6 mi S on FR 8210; at Lostine River. $5. 6/1-10/15; 14-day limit. 4 small RV/tent sites. Tbls, toilet, cfga, no drkg wtr. Fishing, hiking, horseback riding.

Williamson Campground $6
Wallowa-Whitman National Forest
7 mi S of Lostine on CR 551; 4 mi S on FR 8210. On Lostine
River. $6. Elev 5000 ft. 6/15-11/1; 10-day limit. 8 RV/tent
sites (RVs under 16 ft). Tbls, toilet, cfga, no drkg wtr.
Self-service sites. Swimming, fishing.

LOWELL (W)
Bedrock Campground $7.50
Willamette National Forest
2 mi N of Lowell on CR 6220; 10 mi E on CR 6240; 4 mi
on Fall Creek Rd (FR 18); at Fall Creek. $7.50 with federal
senior pass; others pay $15 (double sites $28). 4/28-
9/10; 14-day limit. 21 sites (24-ft RV limit). Tbls, toilets,
cfga, no drkg wtr. Swimming, fishing, hiking. Access
to Fall Creek National Recreation Trail and Jones Trail.

Big Pool Campground $6.50
Willamette National Forest
2 mi N of Lowell on CR 6220; 10 mi E on CR 6240; 1.5 mi
on FR 18 (Fall Creek Rd). $6.50 with federal senior pass;
others pay $13. 4/28-9/10; 14-day limit. 5 sites (14-ft RV
limit). Tbls, toilets, cfga, grey wtr station, no drkg wtr.
Swimming, fishing, hiking.

Broken Bowl Campground $8.50
Willamette National Forest
1 mi N of Lowell on Jasper-Lowell Rd, then N on Unity Rd;
at crossroads near covered bridge, right onto FR 6240;
bear left (E) at "Y" onto FR 18. $8.50 with federal senior
pass; others pay $17. 4/21-9/24; 14-day limit. 16 sites;
20-ft RV limit. Tbls, flush toilets, cfga, drkg wtr. Hiking,
fishing.

Ivan Oakes Campground $7
Corps of Engineers
Lookout Point Lake
From Lowell, 6.3 mi E on West Boundary Rd (North Shore
Dr) & on gravel rd along N shore of lake to park. $7 with
federal senior pass; others pay $14. MD-LD; 14-day limit.
24 sites. Tbls, pit toilets, cfga, drkg wtr. Boating(l), fishing.

Puma Campground $7.50
Willamette National Forest
2 mi N of Lowell on CR 6220; 10 mi E on CR 6240; 6.5 mi E
on FR 18. $7.50 with federal senior pass; others pay $15.
4/28-9/10; 14-day limit. 11 sites (20-ft RV limit). Tbls,
toilets, cfga, drkg wtr. Swimming, fishing, hiking trails.

Winberry Campground   CLOSED
Willamette National Forest
2 mi N of Lowell on CR 6220; half mi E on CR 6240; 5.8 mi
SE on CR 6245; 3.5 mi SE on FR 191. Decommissioned as
campground; amenities removed & site closed.

MADRAS (W)
Haystack Reservoir Campground $7.50
Ochoco National Forest
Crooked River National Grasslands
9.3 mi S of Madras on US 97; 3.3 mi SE on Jericho Lane;
half mi N on FR 9605; at E shore of lake. $7.50 with federal
senior pass; others pay $15. 4/1-10/31; 14-day limit. 24
sites (32-ft RV limit). Tbls, flush toilets, cfga, drkg wtr.
Fishing, swimming, waterskiing, hiking, boating(l). Elev
2900 ft; 5 acres. Rehabilitation of campsites planned.

Haystack West Shore Campground $12
Ochoco National Forest
Crooked River National Grasslands
9.3 mi S of Madras on US 97; 1.25 mi SE on Jericho Lane;
right on Springer Rd (FR 96) for 2 mi to W shore of Haystack Reservoir. $12. 3/18-10/31; 14-day limit. 14 sites;
32-ft RV limit. Tbls, cfga, toilets, no drkg wtr. Boating(l),
fishing, swimming.

Jefferson County RV Park $12
Jefferson County Fairgrounds
In town at Madison & M Sts. $12 without hookups ($62
weekly); $20 full hookups with 30-amp ($140 weekly); $23
full hookups with 50-amp ($161 weekly). All year; 14-day
limit. 660 sites (65 with full hookups); 55-ft RV limit. Tbls,
flush toilets, cfga, drkg wtr, elec($), sewer($), wtr hookups
($), showers.

Mecca Flat Campground $8
Lower Deschutes River System
Bureau of Land Management
Prineville District
From Madras at jct with US 97, 8 mi N on US 26 toward
Warm Springs Indian Reservation; 1 mi N on Mecca Rd to
site along E shore of Desschutes River (poor access). $8
Sun-Thurs & off-season; $12 Fri & Sat during 5/15-9/15.
Group sites $15 on Sun-Thurs, $30 Fri & Sat in-season
($7.50 & $15 with federal senior pass). All year; 14-day
limit. 10 sites (2 pull-through). Tbls, toilets, cfga, no drkg
wtr. Fishing, hiking, boating.

Skull Hollow Camp & Trailhead $10
Ochoco National Forest
Crooked River National Grasslands
SE of Madras on Hwy 26; right on Lone Pine Rd for 2.5 mi,
then right on FR 1395 to camp; poor access. $10. 3/15-
10/31; 14-day limit. 28 primitive sites. Toilets, no drkg wtr,
tbls, cfga. Hiking, mountan biking, horseback riding, SE of
Haystack Reservoir. Elev 3000 ft. Note: Dispersed camping in nearby area closed in 2017 to prevent over-use.

South Junction Campground $8
Bureau of Land Management
Prineville District
Lower Deschutes Wild & Scenic River System
29 mi N of Madras on US 97; left on gravel rd near inter-

section of US 97 & US 197 at sign, "BLM Recreation Site." Sign's GPS: 44.780121, -120.965805. $8 Sun-Thurs & off-season; $12 Fri-Sat during 5/15-9/15. All year; 14-day limit. 11 sites. Tbls, toilets, cfga, no drkg wtr. Hunting, boating(l), fishing, rafting, swimming. Elev 2900 ft.

Trout Creek Campground $8
Bureau of Land Management
Prineville District
Lower Deschutes Wild & Scenic River System
3 mi N of Madras on US 97; 7 mi NW on gravel rd; E side of Deschutes River. $8 Sun-Thurs & off-season; $12 Fri-Sat during 5/15-9/15. All year; 14-day limit. 21 sites (35-ft RV limit). Tbls, toilets, cfga, no drkg wtr. Fishing, hiking, rafting, boating(l), hunting, summer interpretive programs. 11 acres.

MAUPIN (W)
Bear Springs Campground $8
Mount Hood National Forest
25 mi W of Maupin on SR 216 through part of Warm Springs Indian Reservation (24 mi SE of Government Camp) at Indian Creek near US 26. $8 with federal senior pass; others pay $16 during 5/19-10/1; free off-season but no services. 14-day limit. 21 sites (32-ft RV limit). Tbls, toilets, cfga, drkg wtr. Fishing, hiking.q

Beavertail Recreation Site $8
Bureau of Land Management
Prineville District
Lower Deschutes River System
17 mi NE of jct of Hwy 216 and Deschutes River Rd at Sherars Falls. All year; 14-day limit. $8 Sun-Thurs & off-season; $12 Fri & Sat during 5/15-9/15. 17 sites (28-ft RV limit). Tbls, toilets, cfga, drkg wtr, cold showers. Boating(l), fishing, rafting, hiking. Co-managed with Confederated Tribes of Warm Springs Indian Reservation.

Blue Hole Campground $8
Bureau of Land Management
Lower Deschutes River System
Prineville District
From US 197 in Maupin, N on paved Lower Access Rd along Lower Deschutes River; pass Oasis CG & Grey Eagle day-use area. $8 Sun-Thurs & off-season; $12 Fri & Sat during 5/15-9/15. All year; 14-day limit. 1 site. Tbls, toilets, cfga, no drkg wtr. Boating, fishing, swimming, rafting. Wheelchair-accessible fishing ramp & toilets. Reservations available for physically handicapped individuals or groups (395-2270).

Clear Creek Crossing $11
Mount Hood National Forest
25 mi W of Maupin on Hwy 216; 3 mi NW on FR 2130. $11 during MD-LD; free off-season but no services; 14-day limit. 7 sites; 16-ft RV limit. Tbls, toilet, cfga, no drkg wtr. Fishing; horseback riding/hiking (1 mi).

Devil's Canyon Campground $8
Bureau of Land Management
Prineville District
Lower Deschutes River System
N into Maupin on US 197, first left on gravel Upper Access Rd for 4 mi; pass Wapinitia, Harpham Flat & Long Bend camps. $8 Sun-Thurs & off-season; $12 Fri & Sat during 5/15-9/15. All year; 14-day limit. 4 sites. Tbls, toilets, cfga, no drkg wtr. Boating, swimming, fishing, hunting. Elev 980 ft.

Harpham Flat Campground $8
Warm Springs Reservation
Bureau of Land Management
Lower Deschutes River System
Prineville District
3.5 mi N of Maupin along Lower Deschutes River on gravel Lower Access Rd. (RVs not recommended on rough rd). $8 Sun-Thurs & off-season; $12 Fri & Sat during 5/15-9/15. All year; 14-day limit. 9 sites. Tbls, toilets, cfga, drkg wtr. Fishing, boating(l), rafting. Owned by Confederated Tribes of the Warm Springs Indian Reservation; operated by BLM. Upgrading of site planned.

Jones Canyon Campground $8
Bureau of Land Management
Prineville District
Lower Deschutes Wild & Scenic River System
NE of Maupin on Deschutes River Rd (Upper Access Rd) from jct with Hwy 216; pass Oasis, Blue Hole, White River, Twin Springs & Oakbrook camps; at Jones Canyon Creek. $8 Sun-Thurs & off-season; $12 Fri & Sat during 5/15-9/15. All year; 14-day limit. 10 sites; 28-ft RV limit. Tbls, toilets, cfga, no drkg wtr (available at Beavertail CG). Boating (l), fishing, rafting, hiking. Co-managed with Confederated Tribes of Warm Springs Indian Reservation.

Little Badger Campground FREE
Mount Hood National Forest
From Maupin, 6 mi NW on US 197 to just past Tygh Valley; right (S) on Lawrence Ave (becoming westbound Fairgrounds Rd/CR 27, then FR 27/Badger Creek Rd) for 8 mi; left on FR 2710 for 1 mi. Free. 5/15-9/15; 14-day limit (free off-season, but no wtr or services). 3 sites; 16-ft RV limit. Tbls, toilet, cfga, no drkg wtr. Fishing, hiking, horseback riding.

Longbend Campground $8
Bureau of Land Management
Prineville District
Lower Deschutes Wild & Scenic River System
N into Maupin on US 197, first left on gravel Upper Access Rd for 4 mi; pass Wapinitia & Harpham Flat camps. $8 Sun-Thurs & off-season; $12 Fri & Sat during 5/15-9/15. All year; 14-day limit. 4 sites. Tbls, toilets, cfga, no drkg wtr. Boating(l), swimming, fishing, hunting. Elev 980 ft.

Macks Canyon Recreation Site $8
Bureau of Land Management
Prineville District
Lower Deschutes Wild & Scenic River System
24 mi NE of Maupin on Deschutes River Rd. (Upper Access Rd) from jct with Hwy 216. $8 Sun-Thurs & off-season; $12 Fri & Sat during 5/15-9/15. All year; 14-day limit. 17 sites (28-ft RV limit). Tbls, toilets, cfga, drkg wtr, cold showers. Boating(l), fishing, rafting, hiking. Co-managed with Confederated Tribes of Warm Springs Indian Reservation.

McCubbins Gulch $11
Mount Hood National Forest
24.5 mi NW of Maupin on OR 216; 1 mi E on FR 2110. $11 during 5/19-9/10; free off-season but no services. 14-day limit. 15 sites (RVs under 26 ft). Tbls, toilet, cfga, firewood, no drkg wtr. Primitive 10 acres. Fishing, ORV use. 4-site overflow camp nearby, $11 in-season.

Oak Springs Campground $8
Bureau of Land Management
Prineville District
Lower Deschutes Wild & Scenic River System
From US 197 in Maupin, N on paved Lower Access Rd along Lower Deschutes River; pass Oasis & Blue Hole camps. $8 Sun-Thurs & off-season; $12 Fri & Sat during 5/15-9/15. All year; 14-day limit. 7 sites. Tbls, toilets, cfga, no drkg wtr. Boating, fishing, swimming, rafting.

Oasis Flat Campground $8
Bureau of Land Management
Prineville District
Lower Deschutes Wild & Scenic River System
From US 197 in Maupin, N on paved Lower Access Rd along Lower Deschutes River. $8 Sun-Thurs & off-season; $12 Fri-Sat during 5/15-9/15. All year; 14-day limit. 10 sites and 2 group sites (16 or 24-person capacities). Tbls, toilets, cfga, no drkg wtr. Boating, fishing, swimming, rafting.

Rattlesnake Canyon Campground $8
Bureau of Land Management
Prineville District
Lower Deschutes Wild & Scenic River System
About 22 mi NE of Maupin on Deschutes River Rd (Upper Access Rd) from jct with Hwy 216; pass Oasis, Blue Hole, White River, Twin Springs, Oakbrook, Jones Canyon & Gert Canyon camps. $8 Sun-Thurs & off-season; $12 Fri & Sat during 5/15-9/15. All year; 14-day limit. 11 sites; 28-ft RV limit. Tbls, toilets, cfga, no drkg wtr (available at Beavertail CG). Boating, fishing, rafting, hiking. Co-managed with Confederated Tribes of Warm Springs Indian Reservation.

Twin Springs Campground $8
Bureau of Land Management
Prineville District
Lower Deschutes Wild & Scenic River System

NE of Maupin on Deschutes River Rd (Upper Access Rd) from jct with Hwy 216; pass Oasis, Blue Hole, White River camps & cross Elder Creek. $8 Sun-Thurs & off-season; $12 Fri & Sat during 5/15-9/15. All year; 14-day limit. 7 sites; 28-ft RV limit. Tbls, toilets, cfga, no drkg wtr (available at Beavertail CG). Boating, fishing, rafting, hiking. Co-managed with Confederated Tribes of Warm Springs Indian Reservation.

Wapinitia Campground $8
Bureau of Land Management
Prineville District
Lower Deschutes Wild & Scenic River System
N into Maupin on US 197, first left on gravel Upper Access Rd for 3 mi. $8 Sun-Thurs & off-season; $12 Fri & Sat during 5/15-9/15. All year; 14-day limit. 6 sites. Tbls, toilets, cfga, no drkg wtr. Boating(l), swimming, fishing, hunting. Elev 2900 ft.

White River Campground $8
Warm Springs Reservation
Bureau of Land Management
Lower Deschutes Wild & Scenic River System
From US 197 in Maupin, N on paved Lower Access Rd along Lower Deschutes River; pass Oasis CG, Grey Eagle day-use area, Blue Hole & Oak Springs camps. $8 Sun-Thurs & off-season; $12 Fri & Sat during 5/15-9/15. All year; 14-day limit. 3 sites. Tbls, toilets, cfga, no drkg wtr. Boating, fishing, swimming, rafting. Site owned by Confederated Tribes of Warm Springs Reservation, managed by BLM's Prineville District.

MC MINNVILLE (W)
Yamhill County Fairgrounds $10
From downtown McMinnville (N of Salem) at jct with 2nd St, 3 blocks N on SR 99W; about 7 blocks E on NE 5th St, then 1.5 mi NE on Lafayette St to fairgrounds (just past Wortman City Park). $10 at 40 non-elec sites, $15 at 34 elec sites (no wtr hookups). Flush toilets, showers, drkg wtr. All year weekdays & events.

MEDFORD (W)
Willow Prairie Horse Campground $10
Rogue River National Forest
31.5 mi E on SR 140; 1.5 mi N on FR 37; 1 mi W on FR 3738. $10. 5/15-10/31; 14-day limit. 10 RV sites, typically 55 ft; 4 corrals at each site. Tbls, toilets, cfga, drkg wtr, horse troughs, stalls. Primarily a horse camp, in use since the 1950s. Fishing, boating, 19 mi of bridle trails.

MILL CITY (W)
Fishermen's Bend Recreation Site $10
Bureau of Land Management
Salem District
2 mi W of Mill City on Hwy 22; on S side of rd. New fees: $10 with federal senior pass at non-elec sites; others pay $20. Elec sites $26, full hookups $30. 5/1-10/31 by reservation;

14-day limit. 39 sites (40-ft RV limit). Tbls, flush toilets, cfga, drkg wtr, group shelter, 12 picnic sites, showers. 162 acres. Boating(l), fishing, rafting, hiking trails, swimming. Adjacent to North Santiam River. Visitor center.

Shady Cove Campground $8
Opal Creek Scenic Recreation Area
Willamette National Forest
From Mehama (6 mi W of Mill City) at jct with SR 22 next to Oregon Department of Forestry building, 15.3 mi NE on Little North Fork Rd, continuing NE 1.3 mi on FR 2209; right on FR 2207 for 1.9 mi to site at Battle Creek & Scenic Creek. $8. All year; 7-day limit. 13 sites; 16-ft RV limit. Tbls, toilet, cfga, no drkg wtr. Fishing, swimming, hiking.

MILTON-FREEWATER (E)

Bone Spring Campground FREE
Umatilla National Forest
9.2 mi S of Milton-Freewater on SR 11; 17.5 mi E on SR 204; 16.3 mi E on FR 64 (Kendall Skyline Rd); 0.5 mi NE on FR 360. Free. Primitive, undeveloped area, popular as hunting camp. Usually free of snow from July through October. No facilities except pit toilet. GPS: 45.8834726, -117.9407682

MITCHELL (E)

Barnhouse Campground FREE
Ochoco National Forest
13 mi E of Mitchell on US 26; 5 mi S on FR 12. Free. All year; 14-day limit. 6 sites; 25-ft RV limit. Tbls, toilet, cfga, no drkg wtr. Hiking trail.

Big Spring Rustic Camp FREE
Ochoco National Forest
13 mi E of Mitchell on US 26; 18 mi S on FR 12; 8 mi W on FR 4270; cattle guard at camp entrance. Free. All year; 14-day limit. 5 primitive sites. Tbls, toilet, cfga, no drkg wtr.

Cottonwood Campground FREE
Ochoco National Forest
From Mitchell, 13 mi E on US 26; 14 mi S on Buck Point Rd (becoming FR 12); left on FR 200 to site; near Cottonwood Spring. Free. All year; 14-day limit. 7 sites. Tbls, toilet, cfga, no drkg wtr. Elev 5700 ft.

Cottonwood Pit Campground FREE
Ochoco National Forest
13 mi E of Mitchell on US 26; 15 mi S on FR 12; qtr mi W to access rd, FR 4274-080. Free. 5/1-9/15; 14-day limit. 3 sites. Tbls, toilet, cfga, no drkg wtr.

MORO (W)

Sherman County RV Park $10
Sherman County Parks
From US 97 in Moro (NW of Spray), qtr mi SE on 1st St

(becoming Lone Rock Rd); adjacent to county fairgrounds. $10 without hookups, $20 with 30-amp elec, $25 with 50-amp full hookups. All year; weekly & monthly rates available. 65-ft RV limit, 19 pull-throughs. Tbls, flush toilets, cfga, drkg wtr, coin laundry, dump, showers, Wi-Fi.

Tollgate Campground $10
Mount Hood National Forest
From Government Camp, 6 mi E on US 26; on left at Zigzag River. $10 with federal senior pass; others pay $20. 5/15-9/15; 14-day limit. 15 sites, typically 32 ft but 16-ft RV limit. Tbls, toilets, cfga, drkg wtr. Hiking trail, fishing. Non-campers pay day use fee.

MYRTLE POINT (W)

Bennett $10
Coos County Park
1 mi N of Myrtle Point on SR 42; 7 mi NE on N. Fork Lake (becoming Sitkum Rd); left on Gravelford Lane to park; along North Fork Coquille River. $10. 5/1-10/31. 18 primitive sites. Tbls, toilets, cfga, wading pool. Rockhounding, hiking, fishing. 4 acres.

NORTH BEND (W)

Bluebill Campground $11
Siuslaw National Forest
Oregon Dunes National Recreation Area
2 mi N of North Bend on US 101; left at sign for Horsfall Dune; bear right at "Y" for 1.7 mi, then left at campground sign. $11 with federal senior pass; others pay $22. 5/1-9/30; 14-day limit. 19 sites 32-85 ft, typically 45 ft. Tbls, pit toilets, cfga, drkg wtr. Hiking, beachcombing.

Eel Creek Campground $11
Siuslaw National Forest
Oregon Dunes National Recreation Area
12.6 mi N of North Bend on US 101. $11 with federal senior pass; others pay $22. All year; 14-day limit. 53 sites, typically 60 ft. Flush toilets, cfga, tbls, drkg wtr. Fishing.

Horsfall Beach Campground $11
Siuslaw National Forest
Oregon Dunes National Recreation Area
2 mi N of North Bend on US 101; left on Transpacific Lane for 1 mi; right across RR tracks for 100 ft, then right on Horsfall Beach Rd for 3 mi. $11 with federal senior pass; others pay $22. All year; 14-day limit. OHV campground with direct access to OHV dunes. 34 sites, typically 50 ft. Tbls, flush toilets, cfga, drkg wtr. Temporarily closed by flooding in 2017; check current status before arrival.

Horsfall Campground $11
Siuslaw National Forest
Oregon Dunes National Recreation Area
2 mi N of North Bend on US 101; left on Transpacific Lane for 1 mi; right across RR tracks for 100 ft, then right on Horsfall Beach Rd. $11 with federal senior pass; others

pay $22. All year; 14-day limit. OHV campground with direct access to OHV dunes. 70 sites up to 52 ft. Tbls, flush toilets, showers, cfga, drkg wtr. Horse loading ramp.

North Spit Recreation Area　　　　　　　　　FREE
Bureau of Land Management
Coos Bay District
Northbound from North Bend on US 101, just N of McCullough Bridge outside North Bend, watch for signs to "Oregon Dunes/Horsfall Beach); use left lane at base of incline & follow Transpacific Hwy; cross rail tracks near Weyerhaeuser plant, then bear right over second sent of tracks; turn left past Horsfall Beach rd & on to the BLM boat ramp (ramp is 6 mi from Hwy 101 on Transpacific Hwy). Southbound on US 101, look for rd heading W through the waters of the Bay as you approach North Bend. All year; 14-day limit. Undesignated sites. Tbls, flush toilets, cfga, drkg wtr, info exhibits, phone. Boating(l), fishing, clamming, crabbing, beachcombing, hiking. Sand dunes, wetlands. Watch commercial ships from strip of land between ocean & the bay. Three 4WD sand rds open to public.

NYSSA (E)

Cow Hollow Park　　　　　　　　　　　　　$5
Malheur County Parks Department
Cow Hollow Park & Recreation Associations
From Nyssa, 5 mi S on SR 201; 2 mi W on Ivanhoe Ave; 0.3 mi S on Jefferson Dr; 1 mi W on Janeta Ave to park access rd. $5 without hookups, $10 with elec, $15 full hookups at 21 sites. 3/1-12/31. Flush toilets, tbls, cfga, drkg wtr, playground, showers. Fishing, mountain biking, tennis court, baseball fields, basketball, hunting. Site of Nyssa Japanese-American Internment Camp in 1942. Owned by county parks department, operated by a non-profit corporation.

OAKRIDGE (W)

Black Canyon Campground　　　　　　　　$10
Willamette National Forest
6 mi W of Oakridge on SR 58. $10 with federal senior pass; others pay $20 (double site $38). 5/19-10/1; 14-day limit. 75 sites (38-ft RV limit). Tbls, toilets, cfga, drkg wtr. Swimming, boating(l), fishing, hiking, interpretive trails. On Middle Fork of Willamette River. Lookout Point Lake nearby.

Blue Pool Campground　　　　　　　　　$8.50
Willamette National Forest
8.7 mi SE of Oakridge on SR 58. $8.50 with federal senior pass; others pay $17. 5/19-9/24; 14-day limit. 24 sites (20-ft RV limit). Tbls, flush & pit toilets, cfga, drkg wtr. Fishing, swimming in Salt Creek. Picnic area at creek has 5 stoves built by CCC in 1930s. Half mi to public hot springs (no facilities). Elev 2000 ft.

Campers Flat Campground　　　　　　　$6.50
Willamette National Forest
2.2 mi SE of Oakridge on OR 58; .5 mi SE on CR 360; 20 mi S on FR 21. $6.50. MD-9/17; 14-day limit. 5 sites (RVs under 19 ft). Tbls, toilets, cfga, well drkg wtr. Fishing, hiking trails. On Middle Fork of Willamette River.

Gold Lake Campground　　　　　　　　$9.50
Willamette National Forest
28 mi E of Oakridge on SR 58; left on Gold Lake Rd for 2 mi. $9.50 with federal senior pass; others pay $19. MD-10/9; 14-day limit. 21 sites; 24-ft RV limit. Tbls, toilets, cfga, drkg wtr. Boating(l), fishing, hiking trails.

Hampton Campground　　　　　　　　CLOSED
Willamette National Forest
10 mi W of Oakridge on SR 58 on E shore of Lookout Point Lake on Middle Fork of Willamette River. $10. About MD-9/15; 14-day limit. 4 sites; 36-ft RV limit. Tbls, toilets, cfga, drkg wtr. Boating(l), fishing, hiking. Closed in 2015 for dam repair; still closed 2017.

Harralson Horse Camp　　　　　　　　　$5
Willamette National Forest
25 mi SE of Oakridge on SR 58 to Waldo Lake Rd (FR 5897), then 10.5 mi on FR 5897. $5 daily or $30 annual pass. July-Sept when snow-free. 6 sites; 24-ft RV limit. Toilet, cfga, tbls, no drkg wtr; dump near Islet camp. Tether horses at North Waldo Campground; water them near there off Waldo Lake Trail. Hiking, horseback riding.

Islet Campground　　　　　　　　　　$11
Willamette National Forest
25 mi E of Oakridge on SR 58; left on Waldo Lake Rd (FR 5897) for 12 mi; at "T" jct, left on FR 5898. $11 with federal senior pass; others pay $22 (double site $40). 6/9-9/24; 14-day limit. 55 sites; 24-ft RV limit. Tbls, toilets, cfga, drkg wtr, grey wtr stations, 2 beaches. Swimming, boating(l), fishing, hiking trail.

Kiahanie Campground　　　　　　　　$10
Willamette National Forest
2 mi E of Oakridge on SR 58; 19.3 mi N of Westfir on FR 19 (Aufderheide Scenic Byway). $10. 5/18-10/10; 14-day limit. 19 sites (24-ft RV limit). Tbls, toilets, cfga, drkg wtr. Fishing, hiking. 15 acres.

North Waldo Campground　　　　　　　$11
Willamette National Forest
25 mi E of Oakridge on SR 58; left on Waldo Lake Rd (FR 5897) for 11 mi; right on FR 5898 for 0.3 mi; left on FR 5895. $11 with federal senior pass; others pay $22. 6/9-10/9; 14-day limit. 58 sites; 30-ft RV limit. Tbls, toilets, cfga, drkg wtr, beach. Swimming, fishing, boating(l), hiking trails.

Packard Creek Campground $9
Willamette National Forest
2.2 mi SE of Oakridge on SR 58; half mi SE on CR 360; 7 mi SE on FR 21; at Hills Creek Reservoir. $9 with federal senior pass; others pay $18 (double sites $34). 4/21-9/24; 14-day limit. 37 sites; 32-ft RV limit. Tbls, toilets, cfga, drkg wtr, gray water sumps. Swimming, boating(ld), fishing, playground.

Sacandaga Campground $8
Willamette National Forest
2.2 mi SE of Oakridge on SR 58; half mi SE on CR 360; 23 mi S on FR 21. $8. 6/15-10/10; 14-day limit. 17 sites (24-ft RV limit). Tbls, toilets, cfga, drkg wtr. Hiking, fishing, hunting. On Middle Fork of Willamette River.

Salmon Creek Falls Campground $7.50
Willamette National Forest
1 mi SE of Oakridge on SR 58; 4 mi NE on FR 24. $7.50 with federal senior pass; others pay $15. 4/21-9/5; 14-day limit. 14 sites (20-ft RV limit). Tbls, toilets, cfga, drkg wtr. Fishing (Salmon Creek); next to Salmon Creek Waterfall.

Sand Prairie Campground $6.50
Willamette National Forest
2.2 mi SE of Oakridge on SR 58; half mi SE on CR 360; 12 mi S on FR 21. $6.50 with federal senior pass; others pay $13. 5/26-9/17; 14-day limit. 21 sites (28-ft RV limit). Tbls, flush & pit toilets, cfga, no drkg wtr. Fishing, hiking (along 40-mi Middle Fork Trail). Middle Fork of Willamette River. 14 acres.

Secret Campground $6.50
Willamette National Forest
2.2 mi SE of Oakridge on SR 58; half mi SE on CR 360; 19 mi S on FR 21; at Middle Fork of Willamette River. $6.50 with federal senior pass; others pay $13. About MD-9/17; 14-day limit. 6 sites; 24-ft RV limit. Tbls, toilets, cfga, no drkg wtr. Fishing, hiking, biking.

Shadow Bay Campground $11
Willamette National Forest
22 mi E of Oakridge on SR 58; left on Waldo Lake Rd (FR 5897) for 6.7 mi; left on FR 5896 for 1.6 mi. $11 with federal senior pass; others pay $22 (multiple sites $40). About 7/1-10/1; 14-day limit. 47 sites, 32-ft RV limit. Tbls, toilets, cfga, drkg wtr, grey wtr stations, beach. Swimming, fishing, hiking trails, boating(l).

Timpanogas Campground $8
Willamette National Forest
2.2 mi SE of Oakridge on OR 58; half mi SE on CR 360; 38.4 mi SE on FR 211; 3 mi S on FR 250. $8. 6/30-10/10; 14-day limit. 10 sites (RVs under 25 ft). Tbls, toilets, cfga, well drkg wtr. Swimming; fishing; boating(d; no mtrs); hunting; hiking. Elev 5200 ft; 7 acres.

PAISLEY (E)

Campbell Lake Campground $6
Fremont National Forest
1 mi W of Paisley on SR 31; left on Mill St, which becomes FR 33 at the Y; 22.6 mi W on FR 33; stay right at the T & follow FR 28 for 11 mi; left on FR 33 for 2 mi. $6 during 5/15-10/15; reduced services off-season; 14-day limit. 18 sites, typically 40 ft. Tbls, toilets, cfga, no drkg wtr. Fishing, boating(l; no mtrs), hunting, swimming. Elev 7200 ft; 4 acres. Trails to Dead Horse Lake. Camp usually full holidays & weekends.

Chewaucan Crossing Campground FREE
Fremont National Forest
1 mi W of Paisley on SR 31; left on Mill St (becomes FR 33 at "Y"); stay to left for 8.5 mi to trailhead sign; unmarked sites just past cattle guard. Free all year; maintained 5/15-10/15; reduced services off-season; 14-day limit. 5 sites. Tbls, toilet, cfga, no drkg wtr or trash service. Hiking (accesses Fremont National Recreation Trail 160 along Chewaucan River), fishing, birdwatching.

Dairy Point Campground FREE
Fremont National Forest
1 mi W of Paisley on SR 31; left on Mill St to Y; 20 mi W on CR 28 & FR 33; 2 mi S on FR 28; SE on FR 3428; along Dairy Creek. Free. 4/15-10/15 (maintained 5/15-10/31); 14-day limit. 5 sites (some suitable for groups). Tbls, toilet, cfga, drkg wtr. No trash service. Fishing (rainbow trout), horseshoes, birdwatching. Full holidays & most weekends.

Dead Horse Lake Campground $6
Fremont National Forest
1 mi W of Paisley on SR 31; left on Mill St to Y, then 20 mi W on FR 33; 11 mi S on FR 28; left on gravel FR 033 for 3 mi. $6 during 5/15-10/15; free rest of year but no wtr or services; 14-day limit. 9 sites (22-ft RV limit); 7 group sites. Tbls, toilets, cfga, drkg wtr, no trash service. Boating (l; no mtrs), good fishing; hiking loop trails connect with Deadhorse Rim & Campbell Lake & accesses Dead Cow Trail, Lakes Trail system. Elev 7400 ft; 9 acres. Grassy & pebble beaches. Full most holidays & weekends.

Hanan/Coffeepot Trailhead FREE
Fremont National Forest
1 mi N of Paisley on SR 31; left on Mill St to Y, then continue on FR 3315 for 18 mi; Hanan Trail directional sign is on the W side of the rd just past milepost 18; turn W into trailhead. Free all year; maintained 6/15-9/15; reduced services off-season; 14-day limit. Rustic undesignated sites; no facilities except toilet, no drkg wtr, no trash service. Adequate RV turn-around. Birdwatching, hiking on historic trail.

Happy Camp Campground — FREE
Fremont National Forest
1 mi N of Paisley on SR 31; left on Mill St to Y, then 20 mi SW on FR 33; 2.4 mi S on FR 28; 1 mi W on FR 047; along Dairy Creek. Free all year; maintained 5/15-10/15; reduced services off-season; 14-day limit. 9 sites, some pull-through. Tbls, toilets, cfga, drkg wtr, no trash service. Trout fishing, horseshoe pits, birdwatching. Elev 5200 ft. Three 1930s-era CCC-built picnic shelters.

Jones Crossing Forest Camp — FREE
Fremont National Forest
Half mi N of Paisley on SR 31; left on Mill St to Y; 9 mi farther on FR 33; along Chewaucan River. Free all year; maintained 5/15-10/15; reduced services off-season; 14-day limit. 8 large primitive sites. Tbls, cfga, toilet, no drkg wtr, no trash service. Fishing, birdwatching. Elev 4810 ft. Park 100 ft from river's edge.

Lee Thomas Campground — FREE
Fremont National Forest
1 mi N of Paisley on SR 31; left on Mill St to Y, then right on FR 3315 for 18 mi; right on FR 28 for half mi; right on FR 3411 for 5 mi; along North Fork of Sprague River. Free all year; maintained 5/15-10/15; reduced services off-season; 14-day limit. 7 sites (16-ft RV limit). Tbls, toilet, cfga, drkg wtr, no trash service. Hunting, fishing, birdwatching. Elev 6200 ft; 3 acres. Good to fair rds. Popular fall hunt camp.

Marster Spring Campground — $6
Fremont National Forest
1 mi W of Paisley on Hwy 31; 7.1 mi S on Mill St, which becomes FR 33 at the Y (stay to the left; good gravel rd). $6 during 5/15-10/15; free off-season but no wtr or services; 14-day limit. 10 large sites, typically 32 ft. Tbls, toilets, cfga, drkg wtr, no trash service. Fishing, birdwatching, hunting. Elev 4700 ft; 4 acres.

Pike's Crossing Forest Camp — FREE
Fremont National Forest
12 mi N of Paisley on SR 31; left on FR 29 (Government Harvey Rd) for 10 mi to jct with FR 2910 & Summer Lake viewpoint; stay on FR 29 for 2 more mi; at T with FR 28, stay to the right for 3.6 mi; stay left at Y jct with FR 30 for 3 mi on FR 30 to sign for Pike's Crossing; along Paradise Creek & Sycan River. Free all year; managed 5/15-10/15; no services off-season; 14-day limit. 4-6 sites. Toilet, cfga, no drkg wtr, no tbls, no trash service. Fishing, birdwatching. Quiet, secluded.

Rock Creek Forest Camp — FREE
Fremont National Forest
11 mi N of Paisley on SR 31; left on FR 29 (Government Harvey Rd) for 10 mi to jct with FR 2901 & Summer Lake viewpoint; stay on FR 29 for 2 more mi; at T jct with FR 28, go left for half mi; along Sycan River. Also, for 3

mi on FR 28 after Rock Creek turnoff, there are several dispersed camping areas in meadows & trees along river. Free. 5/15-10/15; 14-day limit. 4-6 primitive sites. Toilets, cfga, no tbls, no drkg wtr, no trash service. Trout fishing, birdwatching, mountain biking. Hanan/Sycan Trailhead nearby. Quiet, secluded.

Sandhill Crossing Campground — FREE
Fremont National Forest
1 mi W of Paisley on Hwy 31; left on Mill St to the Y; right on FR 3315 for 18 mi; 1 mi S on FR 28; 8 mi W on FR 3411. Free all year; maintained 5/15-10/15; reduced services off-season; 14-day limit. 5 sites (16-ft RV limit). Tbls, toilet, cfga, drkg wtr, no trash service. Fishing, swimming (Sprague River), hiking, birdwatching. Elev 6100 ft.

Upper Jones Forest Camp — FREE
Fremont National Forest
Half mi N of Paisley on SR 31; left on Mill St to Y; stay to left on FR 33 for 9.5 mi; unmarked sites in trees, off to left, along Chewaucan River. Free. 4/15-11/1; 14-day limit. 2 dispersed sites. No facilities except cfga, toilet; no drkg wtr, no trash service. Rainbow & brook trout fishing, birdwatching.

PAULINA (E)

Frazier Campground — FREE
Ochoco National Forest
3.5 mi E on CR 112; 2.2 mi N on CR 113; 10 mi E on CR 135; 6.3 mi E on FR 58; 1.1 mi NE on FR 5800-500; cattle guard at entrance. Free. All year (closed only by snow, maintained MD-11/15); 14-day limit. 10 sites (RVs under 22 ft). Tbls, toilet, cfga, firewood, nearby drkg wtr. Horseback riding (1 mi). Elev 5000 ft. Campground reconstructed in 2010.

Mud Springs Horse Camp/Trailhead — FREE
Ochoco National Forest
Take left fork 3 mi E of Paulina to FR 58. 6/1-9/15; 14-day limit. 11 equestrian sites. Tbls, toilets, cfga, no drkg wtr. 9 steel horse pens Hiking, bridle trails.

Sugar Creek Campground — $8
Ochoco National Forest
3.5 mi E of Paulina on CR 380; 6.5 mi N on CR 113; 1.7 mi E on FR 58. $8. 5/1-10/28; 14-day limit. 17 sites (32-ft RV limit). Tbls, toilets, cfga, drkg wtr. Swimming, fishing, hiking. Half mi loop trail along Sugar Creek. Elev 4100 ft. Seasonal closures possible due to roosting bald eagles.

Wolf Creek Campground — $6
Ochoco National Forest
3.5 mi E of Paulina on CR 380; 6.5 mi N on CR 113; 1.5 mi N on FR 42; W on Bull Springs rd; sites on both sides of rd. $6. 5/1-10/28; 14-day limit. 16 sites, typically 45 ft. Tbls, toilets, cfga, drkg wtr. Fishing. Elev 4100 ft; 3 acres.

Wolf Creek Industrial Campground FREE
Ochoco National Forest
3.5 mi E of Paulina on CR 380; 6.5 mi N on CR 113; N on FR 42 to first left after Rd 3810 jct (Bull Springs Rd, not signed); E of Wolf Creek bridge. $6. 5/1-10/28; 14-day limit. 6 sites; 20-ft RV limit. Tbls, toilets, cfga, no drkg wtr. Now managed as part of nearby Wolf Creek Campgournd.

Wolf Creek Overflow Dispersed Sites FREE
Ochoco National Forest
3.5 mi E of Paulina on CR 380; 6.5 mi N on CR 113; 1.5 mi N on FR 42, then half mi on FR 3810 to camp's access, FR 3810-541 (not signed); S of Wolf Creek sites above. Free. 3 sites; 20-ft RV limit. Tbls, toilet, cfga, no drkg wtr. GPS: 44.2497, -119.8268

PENDLETON (E)
Umatilla Forks $10
Umatilla National Forest
32 mi E of Pendleton on CR N32; half mi SE on FR 32; access via Hwy 11 & I-84; between South Fork & North Fork of Umatilla River. $10. 5/18-10/15; 10-day limit. 6 RV/tent sites (RVs under 23 ft). Tbls, toilets, cfga, drkg wtr. Fishing, nature trails, hunting, horse trail, trail bikes, wilderness access. 5 acres.

PHILOMATH (W)
Alsea Falls Recreation Site $10
Bureau of Land Management
Salem District
From just W of Philomath at jct with US 20, 9 mi SW on SR 34 to settlement of Alaea; turn left (S) for 1 mi on SR 501 (Alsea Deadwood Hwy), then left (E) again for 7 mi on South Fork Alsea Rd to site. New fees: $10 with federal senior pass at basic RV sites; others pay $20 (non-senior tent sites $15, group sites $50). 5/1-10/30; 14-day limit. 16 sites (30-ft RV limit). Tbls, toilets, cfga, drkg wtr. Fishing, hunting, rockhounding, swimming, hiking. 40 acres.

Mary's Peak Campground $12
Siuslaw National Forest
3 mi SW of Philomath on SR 34; right (NW) for 4 mi on FR 30; 3 mi N on FR 3010. $12. 5/1-10/1; 14-day limit. 6 sites (small RVs & tents only). Tbls, toilet, cfga, no drkg wtr. Hiking. Elev 4,097 ft.

PORT ORFORD (W)
Butler Bar Campground FREE
Siskiyou National Forest
3 mi N of Port Orford on US 101; 7.4 mi SE on CR 208; 11.2 mi SE on FR 5325; at Elk River. Free. All year; 14-day limit. 7 sites (RVs under 16 ft). Tbls, toilet, cfga, firewood, no drkg wtr or trash service. Swimming; fishing; berry picking, hiking. Elk River Fish Hatchery (11 mi W). Signed for user management; infrequently serviced.

Edson Creek Campground $8
Bureau of Land Management
Coos Bay District
4.4 mi N of Port Orford on Hwy 101; 4.5 mi E on Sixes River Rd; bear S just before Edson bridge; at confluence of Edson Creek & Sixes River. $8. MD-9/30; 14-day limit. 27 primitive sites along creek & 5 group sites ($10-$25). Tbls, toilets, cfga, drkg wtr. Swimming, fishing, boating(l).

Laird Lake Campground FREE
Siskiyou National Forest
3 mi N of Port Orford on US 101; 7.5 mi SE on CR 208; 15.5 mi SE on FR 5325. All year; 14-day limit. 4 primitive sites. Toilet, tbls, cfga, no drkg wtr or trash service. Fishing, birdwatching. Infrequently serviced.

Sixes River Recreation Site $8
Bureau of Land Management
Coos Bay District
4.4 mi N of Port Orford on US 101; 11 mi E on Sixes River Rd (gravel). $8. All year; 14-day limit. 19 sites (RVs under 30 ft). Tbls, toilets, cfga, dump, no drkg wtr, firewood. Elev 400 ft; 20 acres. Trout fishing in river. Sluice for gold by permit. Non-campers pay $2 day use fee.

Sunshine Bar Campground FREE
Siskiyou National Forest
19 mi E of Port Orford on FR 5325; at Elk River. Free. All year; 14-day limit. 6 sites. Tbls, toilets, cfga, no drkg wtr or trash service. Fishing, swimming. Infrequently serviced.

POWERS (W)
Buck Creek Campground FREE
Siskiyou National Forest
About 30 mi SE of Powers via FRs 3300 & 3348. Free. All year; 14-day limit. 2 primitive sites. Tbls, toilet, cfga, no drkg wtr or trash service. Recently refurbished. On Powers-Glendale bike route.

Daphne Grove Campground $6
Siskiyou National Forest
4.2 mi SE of Powers on CR 219; 10.5 mi S on FR 333. $6 during MD-LD; free rest of year but no wtr or services; 14-day limit. 14 RV sites (30-ft RV limit). Tbls, toilets, cfga, drkg wtr, grey wtr stations, trash service MD-LD. Fishing, swimming, hiking trails. On South Fork of Coquille River. Near Azalea Lake (1-mi hike). 11 acres.

Eden Valley Campground FREE
Siskiyou National Forest
33 mi SE of Powers via FRs 3300 & 3348. Free. All year; 14-day limit. 11 small sites along Powers-Glendale bike route. Tbls, toilets, cfga, no drkg wtr or trash service. Biking. Dispersed camping nearby.

Island Campground $6
Siskiyou National Forest
17 mi S of Powers on FR 3300; at South Fork of Coquille River. $6 during MD-10/30; free rest of year; 14-day limit. 5 sites. Tbls, toilet, cfga, no drkg wtr, trash service MD-10/30. Swimming, fishing. Dispersed camping nearby.

Lockhart Campground   FREE
Siskiyou National Forest
22 mi SE of Powers via FRs 3300 & 3348; on Powers-Glendale bike route. Free. All year. 1 primitive site. Toilet, cfga, tbl, no drkg wtr or trash service. Fishing, biking.

Myrtle Grove Campground   FREE
Siskiyou National Forest
4.2 mi SE of Powers on CR 90; 4.5 mi S on FR 33; at South Fork Coquille River. All year; 14-day limit. 5 sites. Tbls, toilet, cfga, no drkg wtr or trash service. Signed for user management. Swimming; fishing.

Peacock Campground   FREE
Siskiyou National Forest
22 mi SE of Powers via FRs 3300, 3348 & 3358; on Powers-Glendale bike route. Free. All year; 14-day limit. 1 primitive site. Toilet, cfga, tbl, no drkg wtr or trash service. Fishing, biking.

Pioneer Campground   FREE
Siskiyou National Forest
28 mi SE of Powers via FRs 3300, 3348 & 5000; on Powers-Glendale bike route. Free. All year; 14-day limit. 1 primitive site. Toilet, cfga, tbl, no drkg wtr or trash service. Fishing, biking.

Powers County Park $11
Coos County
Half mi N of downtown Powers on CR 219 (Powers Hwy); 18 mi S of Myrtle Point. $11 without hookups, $16 with hookups during 5/1-9/30 ($2 extra Thurs-Sat); all sites $15 off-season. 10-day limit. 70 sites. Tbls, flush toilets, showers($), elec($), wtr hookups($), cfga, portable dump. Fishing, boating(l -- no motors), swimming, canoeing, tennis courts, horseshoes, volleyball, basketball, softball field, hiking trails, playground. Covered shelters, coin-operated stoves. Near South Fork of Coquille River. 93 acres.

Sru Lake Campground   FREE
(Formerly Squaw Lake)
Siskiyou National Forest
4.2 mi SE of Powers on CR 90; 12.6 mi S on FR 33; 4.6 mi SE on FR 321; 1 mi E on FR 3348-080. Free. All year; 14-day limit. 6 sites (21-ft RV limit). Tbls, toilet, cfga, no drkg wtr or trash service. Fishing platform. Elev 2200 ft; 2 acres. Stream. Coquille River Falls National Recreation Area nearby.

Wooden Rock Creek Campground   FREE
Siskiyou National Forest
About 30 mi SE of Powers via FRs 3300, 3348 & 5000; on Powers-Glendale bike route. Free. All year; 14-day limit. 1 site. Tbl, toilet, cfga, no drkg wtr or trash service. Fishing.

PRAIRIE CITY (E)

Bates State Park $11
About 5 mi E of Prairie City on US 26 to Austin Juntion; 1 mi N on SR 7; NW on CR 20, then W on access rd, following signs; at Bates Pond & Middle Fork John Day River. $11 during 5/1-10/31; $5 off-season. 28 primitive RV/tent sites. Tbls, pit toilets, cfga, drkg wtr, picnic shelter. Hiking trails, TransAmerica Bicycle Trail nearby, fishing.

Crescent Campground   FREE
Malheur National Forest
17 mi SE of Prairie City on CR 62; on right at John Day River. Free. All year; 14-day limit. 4 sites. Tbls, toilets, cfga, no drkg wtr. Fishing, hiking. Elev 5200 ft.

Dixie Campground $8
Malheur National Forest
7 mi SE of Prairie City on US 26; half mi N on FR 1220. $8. MD-11/1; 14-day limit. 11 sites; 30-ft RV limit. Tbls, toilets, cfga, no drkg wtr. Hunting, berry-picking. Elev 5300 ft at Dixie Summit. Bridge Creek nearby.

Elk Creek Campground   FREE
Malheur National Forest
8.3 mi SE of Prairie City on CR 14; 16 mi SE on FR 130; 1.3 mi S on FR 16. Free. 5/15-11/15. 5 sites (RVs under 32 ft). Toilets, cfga, no drkg wtr. Fishing. Elev 5100 ft; 1 acre. North Fork Malheur River.

Lower Camp Creek $6
Malheur National Forest
From Prairie City, 3 mi W on US 26; right (NW) on CR 18 for 9 mi; right on FR 36 for 11 mi; on left. $6. Elev 3700 ft. 4/15-11/1; 14-day limit. May be open & free off-season. 6 primitive undeveloped sites (RVs under 32 ft). Toilets, cfga, no drkg wtr, no trash service. Fishing.

Magone Lake Campground $6.50
Malheur National Forest
3 mi W of Prairie City on US 26; 12 mi NW on CR 18; 2 mi S on FR 3620; 1 mi W on FR 3618; at N shore of Magone Lake. $6.50 with federal senior pass during MD-LD; others pay $13. Free off-season, but no amenities. 21 sites, typically 45 ft. Tbls, toilets, cfga, piped drkg wtr, changehouse. Swimming; fishing; boating (ld); hiking. Elev 5100 ft. Geological.

Middle Fork Campground $8
Malheur National Forest
11.5 mi NE of Prairie City on SR 26; 5 mi NW on CR 20. $8. 4/1-11/1; 14-day limit. 10 sites; 32-ft RV limit. Tbls, toilets,

cfga, no drkg wtr. Fishing at Middle Fork of John Day River. Elev 4200 ft.

North Fork Malheur Campground   **FREE**
Malheur National Forest
8.3 mi SE of Prairie City on CR 14; 16 mi SE on FR 13; 2 mi S on FR 16; 2.7 mi S on FR 1675; rd rough & muddy after rain. Free. 4/1-11/15; 14-day limit. 5 sites. Tbls, toilet, cfga, no drkg wtr. Fishing. Elev 4900 ft.

Slide Creek Campground   **FREE**
Malheur National Forest
6.6 mi S of Prairie City on CR 60; 2.1 mi FR 1428. 4/1-11/15. 3 sites (RVs under 22 ft). Tbls, toilets, cfga, no drkg wtr. Fishing; hiking; hunting; horseback riding (corral).

Strawberry Campground   **$8**
Malheur National Forest
6.5 mi S of Prairie City on CR 60; 4.5 mi S on FR 6001. $8. MD-10/15; 30-day limit. 10 sites (22-ft RV limit). Tbls, toilet, cfga, drkg wtr. Boating, fishing, hiking trails. Strawberry Mountain Wilderness nearby. Elev 5700 ft. On Strawberry Lake, near Strawberry Falls.

Trout Farm Campground   **$8**
Malheur National Forest
8.3 mi SE of Prairie City on CR 14; 6.9 mi S on FR 14. $8. 5/1-11/15; 14-day limit. 6 sites (21-ft RV limit). Tbls, toilets, cfga, drkg wtr. Good trout fishing pond.

PRINEVILLE (W)

Allen Creek Horse Camp   **FREE**
Ochoco National Forest
25 mi E of Prineville on US 26 to Ochoco Ranger Station; 19 mi NE on Rd 22; just past Walton Lake. Free. All year; 14-day limit. 5 sites. Tbls, toilets, cfga, no drkg wtr except for stock. Corrals, 16 stalls. Hiking & bridle trails.

Antelope Flat Reservoir Campground   **$8**
Ochoco National Forest
29 mi SE of Prineville on SR 380; 9 mi S on FR 17; 1.3 mi S on FR 1700. $8. 5/1-10/28; 14-day limit. 24 sites (32-ft RV limit). Tbls, toilets, cfga, drkg wtr. Swimming, boating(l), fishing, canoeing. Elev 4600 ft. 20 acres.

Biggs Springs Campground   **FREE**
Ochoco National Forest
25 mi E of Prineville on US 26 merging right onto Ochoco Ranger Rd; 14 mi SE on FR 42; 5 mi S on FR 4215; right on FR 150 to camp near headwaters of North Fork Crooked River. Free. All year; 14-day limit. 3 sites. Tbls, toilet, cfga, no drkg wtr.

Castle Rock Campground   **$8**
Bureau of Land Management
Prineville District
Lower Crooked Wild & Scenic River System
12 mi S of Prineville on SR 27 (Crooked River Hwy); along Crooked River below Prineville Reservoir. $8 during 4/1-11/30; free rest of year; 14-day limit. 6 sites. Tbls, toilets, cfga, no drkg wtr. Boating, swimming, fishing. Elev 2960 ft.

Chimney Rock Recreation Site   **$8**
Bureau of Land Management
Prineville District
Lower Crooked Wild & Scenic River System
14 mi S of Prineville on SR 27 (Crooked River Hwy). $8 during 4/1-11/30; free rest of year; 14-day limit. 16 sites. Tbls, toilets, cfga, drkg wtr. Fishing, hiking. Elev 3100 ft; 10 acres.

Cobble Rock Campground   **$8**
Bureau of Land Management
Prineville District
Lower Crooked Wild & Scenic River System
14.5 mi S of Prineville on SR 27 (Crooked River Hwy). $8 during 4/1-11/30; free rest of year; 14-day limit. 15 sites. Tbls, toilets, cfga, no drkg wtr. Fishing, hiking, boating.

Cyrus Horse Camp   **FREE**
Ochoco National Forest
Crooked River National Grassland
16 mi NE of Prineville on US 26; left (W) on FR 96 (Laurel Lane) for 2 mi; just before cemetery, left on FR 5750 for half mi, then right, staying on FR 5750 at jct with Hagman Rd; 1.5 mi SE on SE Hagman Lane to camp. All year; 14-day limit. 5 sites. Tbls, toilet, cfga, no drkg wtr. 8 horse corrals, stock wtr seasonally, 2 hitching racks, water trough, manure pit. Bridle trails.

Deep Creek Campground   **$8**
Ochoco National Forest
16.7 mi E of Prineville on US 26; 8.5 mi NE on CR 123; 23.6 mi SE on FR 42; .1 mi S on FR 42G; at N Fork of Crooked River. $8. Elev 4200 ft. 5/1-10/28; 14-day limit. 14 sites on 2 acres, typically 48 ft. Tbls, toilets, cfga, firewood, drkg wtr. Fishing.

Devil's Post Pile   **$8**
Bureau of Land Management
Prineville District
Lower Crooked Wild & Scenic River System
14 mi S of Prineville on SR 27 (Crooked River Hwy); along Crooded River below Prineville Reservoir. $8 during 4/1-11/30; free rest of year; 14-day limit. 7 sites. Tbls, toilets, cfga, no drkg wtr. Fishing, hiking, boating.

Double Cabin Campground   **FREE**
Ochoco National Forest
48 mi SE of Prineville on Hwy 380 to FR 17; left on FR 16; left on FR 1600-350. Free. All year; 14-day limit. 5 sites (equestrian camping allowed); tight turnaround. Tbls, toilet, cfga, no drkg wtr. Fishing, hiking, horseback riding.

Dry Creek Horse Camp FREE
Ochoco National Forest
17 mi NE of Prineville on US 26; left on Mill Creek Rd; 2.5 mi on FR 3370 to FR 3370-200. Free. 4/5-11/28. 5 sites; 20-ft RV limit. Tbls, toilet, cfga, no drkg wtr except for stock. 18 horse corrals, stalls. Hiking & horseback riding trails. Roads not suitable for large RVs.

Elkhorn Campground FREE
Ochoco National Forest
37 mi SE of Prineville on Hwy 380 to FR 16; NW of Antelope Reservoir. Free. All year; 14-day limit. 5 sites. Tbls, toilet, cfga, no drkg wtr.

Lone Pine Campground $8
Bureau of Land Management
Prineville District
Lower Crooked Wild & Scenic River System
13 mi S of Prineville on SR 27 (Crooked River Hwy). $8. during 4/1-11/30; free rest of year; 14-day limit. 8 sites. Tbls, toilets, cfga, no drkg wtr. Fishing, hiking, boating.

Lower Palisades Campground $8
Bureau of Land Management
Prineville District
Lower Crooked Wild & Scenic River System
13.5 mi S of Prineville on SR 27 (Crooked River Hwy). $8 during 4/1-11/30; free rest of year; 14-day limit. 15 sites. Tbls, toilets, cfga, no drkg wtr. Fishing, hiking, boating.

Ochoco Divide Campground $6.50
Ochoco National Forest
30.8 mi NE of Prineville on US 26; .1 mi SE on access rd. $6.50 with federal senior pass during 5/15-10/1; others pay $13; free off-season, weather permitting; 14-day limit. 28 sites (32-ft RV limit). Tbls, toilets, cfga, no drkg wtr. Rockhounding; fishing (2 mi). Elev 4700 ft; 10 acres.

Ochoco Forest Campground $7.50
Ochoco National Forest
15 mi E of Prineville on US 26; right on CR 123 for 7 mi; left on FR 2610; cross Ochoco Creek to site on right. $7.50 with federal senior pass; others pay $15. 5/1-10/1; 14-day limit. 5 sites. Tbls, toilet, cfga, drkg wtr, grey wtr sump. Fishing, hiking. Elev 4000 ft.

Poison Butte Campground $8
Bureau of Land Management
Prineville District
Lower Crooked Wild & Scenic River System
14.5 mi S of Prineville on SR 27 (Crooked River Hwy); along Crooked River below Prineville Reservoir. $8 during 4/1-11/30; free rest of year; 14-day limit. 5 sites. Tbls, toilets, cfga, no drkg wtr. Fishing, hiking, boating. Rds rough & narrow, not recommended for RVs.

Salters Cabin Horse Camp FREE
Ochoco National Forest
SE of Prineville on SR 380 to CR 112, then 3.5 mi to CR 113 (Beaver Creek Rd); turn at left fork onto CR 113 for 7.5 mi; 1.2 mi on FR 42 to camp sign & access rd 4200-865. Free. All year; 14-day limit. Tbls, toilet, cfga, no drkg wtr. 1 horse corral. Hiking, horseback riding.

Scotts Campground FREE
Ochoco National Forest
27 mi E of Prineville on US 26; right on FR 2630 for 3 mi; right on FR 2210 for 2 mi; left on FR 22 for 13 mi; make sharp left onto FR 150 for 2 mi to camp; on left across from gravel pit. Free. All year; 14-day limit. 3 sites. Tbls, toilet, cfga, drkg wtr.

Stillwater Campground $8
Bureau of Land Management
Prineville District
Lower Crooked Wild & Scenic River System
12.5 mi S of Prineville on SR 27 (Crooked River Hwy); along Crooked River below Prineville Reservoir. $8 during 4/1-11/30; free rest of eyar; 14-day limit. 10 sites. Tbls, toilets, cfga, no drkg wtr. Fishing, hiking, boating.

Walton Lake Campground $7.50
Ochoco National Forest
15 mi E of Prineville on US 26; 8.5 mi NE on CR 123; 15 mi NE on FR 22 to lake; site on left. $7.50 with federal senior pass; others pay $15 during about 5/15-9/14; free rest of year (weather permitting); 14-day limit. 27 sites (RVs under 32 ft). Tbls, toilets, cfga, drkg wtr, beach, fishing pier, grey wtr stations. Rockhounding, boating(l), hiking, swimming. Elev 5000 ft; 15 acres. Newly renovated.

Whistler Campground FREE
Ochoco National Forest
30 mi NE of Prineville on Main St/McKay Creek Rd (becoming FR 33; at split, veer left onto FR 27 for 12 mi; at FR 2745, veer right again on FR 27 for 4 mi along wilderness boundary, then right (S) on FR 200 into campgrounds (roads very rough; large RVs not recommended). Free. All year; 14-day limit. 4 undefined sites. Tbls, toilet, cfga, no drkg wtr. Corrals. Hiking & bridle trails. Also known as Whistler Spring.

White Rock Campground FREE
Ochoco National Forest
25 mi E of Prineville on US 26; left on FR 3350 for 5 mi, then right on FR 300 (White Rock Spring Rd) to end. Free. All year; 14-day limit. 3 primitive undesignated sites (1 for RVs, which are not recommended). Tbls, toilet, cfga, no drkg wtr. Hiking. Horse camping allowed.

Wildcat Campground $7.50
Ochoco National Forest
9.2 mi E of Prineville on US 26; 11 mi NE on FR 33; E on

access rd. $7.50 with federal senior pass; others pay $15. 5/1-9/15; 14-day limit. 17 sites; 20-ft RV limit due to tight loops. Tbls, toilets, cfga, drkg wtr, grey wtr stations. Fishing, hiking trails. On E fork of Mill Creek; trailhead to Mill Creek Wilderness. 11 acres; elev 3700 ft.

Wildwood Campground FREE
Ochoco National Forest
20 mi E of Prineville on US 26; 8 mi E on FRs 22 & 2210 (Old Ochoco Hwy). Free. All year; 14-day limit. 5 sites; tight RV turn-around. Tbls, toilet, cfga, no drkg wtr. Hiking, hunting.

Wiley Flat Campground FREE
Ochoco National Forest
34 mi SE of Prineville on Hwy 380; 9.8 mi S on FR 16 (Drake Creek Rd); 1 mi W on FR 400. Free. All yea but not maintained regularlyr. 5 sites (large RVs okay). Tbls, toilet, cfga, no drkg wtr. Fishing (2 mi); horseback riding (1 mi). Elev 500 ft; 3 acres.

REEDSPORT (W)

Fawn Creek Dispersed Camping FREE
Bureau of Land Management
Coos Bay District
Qtr mi N of Reedsport on US 101; 25 mi E on Smith River Rd; no sign at site, just old rd that parallels main rd along river. Free. All year; 14-day limit. Primitive dispersed camping (small RVs) at boat ramp area below falls. Tbls, cfga, no toilets or drkg wtr. Undeveloped setting along river with small boat ramp for access to confluence of Fawn Creek & Smith River. Boating, fishing, hiking, swimming.

Loon Lake Recreation Site $9
Bureau of Land Management
Coos Bay District
20 mi E of Reedsport on SR 38; follow signs 7 mi S on CR 3. $9 with federal senior pass; others pay $18. 5/22-9/30; 14-day limit. 61 sites. Tbls, toilets, cfga, drkg wtr (limited supply), playground. Boating(l), fishing, hiking, swimming, ranger-led programs. Non-campers pay $5 day use fee.

Smith River Falls Campground FREE
Bureau of Land Management
Coos Bay District
Qtr mi N of Reedsport on US 101, 28 mi NE on Smith River Rd. Free. All year; 14-day limit. 8 sites. Tbls, toilets, cfga, dump, no drkg wtr. Berry picking; swimming; fishing.

Vincent Creek FREE
Bureau of Land Management
Coos Bay District
Qtr mi N of Reedsport on US 101; 35 mi NE on Smith River Rd just prior to Smith River Falls area at mouth of Vincent Creek. Free. All year; 14-day limit. Primitive area; 6 sites. Toilets, cfga, tbls, no drkg wtr. 1-day limit. Swimming, hiking, berry picking, hunting.

RICHLAND (E)

Eagle Forks Campground $5
Wallowa-Whitman National Forest
10 mi NW of Richland on FR 7735 (gravel). $5. 6/1-10/15; 14-day limit. 7 RV/tent sites (21-ft RV limit). Tbls, toilets, cfga, drkg wtr. Fishing, hiking, gold panning.

ROGUE RIVER (W)

Elderberry Flat Campground FREE
Bureau of Land Management
Medford District
20 mi NE of Rogue River on East Fork Evans Creek Rd; 8 mi N on West Fork Evans Creek Rd. Free. Elev 3000 ft. 5/15-10/31; 14-day limit. 11 sites (4 next to creek); 40-ft RV limit. Toilets, cfga, no drkg wtr. Fishing; hunting; berry picking; swimming in creek. ATV & motorcycle trails.

ROSEBURG (W)

Broken Arrow $7.50
Umpqua National Forest
80 mi E on SR 138 from I-5 exit 120 at Roseburg; FR 4795 to camp on S shore of Diamond Lake. $7.50 with federal senior pass; others pay $15 (double sites $20). 5/15-9/15; 14-day limit. 134 sites; 32-ft RV limit. Tbls, flush toilets, showers, drkg wtr, dump, grey water sumps. Swimming, fishing, hiking, biking, boating(rld). Crater Lake National Park, Mount Thielsen Wilderness, Mount Bailey nearby. Elev 5200 ft.

Clearwater River Dispersed Camp FREE
Umpqua National Forest
About 60-75 mi E of Roseburg on SR 138. Free undesignated sites along Clearwater River, Lemolo Lake & Diamond Lake. All year; 14-day limit. No facilities, no drkg wtr, no trash service. Fishing, hiking. Elev 4,000-5,000 ft.

Diamond Lake Campground $8
Umpqua National Forest
78 mi E on SR 138 from I-5 exit 120 at Roseburg; turn at sign for Diamond Lake Resort & follow rd to campground. $8 base with federal senior pass; others pay $16 base, $22 for premium lakeshore sites ($11 with senior pass); double sites $21 & $27 ($10.50 & $13.50 with senior pass). 5/15-9/15; 14-day limit. 238 sites (35-ft RV limit). Tbls, flush toilets, showers, cfga, drkg wtr, dump, grey wtr sumps, amphitheater, fish cleaning station. Boating(lrd), fishing, hiking, swimming.

Hemlock Meadows Campground $10
Umpqua National Forest
About 16 mi E of Roseburg on SR 138; 32 mi SE on Little River Rd (CR 17); at E arm of Hemlock Lake. $10. 6/1-10/31; 14-day limit. 4 dispersed primitive sites; 35-ft RV limit. Tbls, toilet, cfga, no drkg wtr or trash service. Fishing, hiking, boating (no mtrs), horseback riding, biking.

Thielsen View Campground $7.50
Umpqua National Forest
80 mi E on SR 138 from I-5 exit 120 at Roseburg; S on FR 4795; on W shore of Diamond Lake. $7.50 with federal senior pass; others pay $15 (double sites $20 or $10 with senior pass). 5/15-9/31; 14-day limit. 60 sites (35-ft RV limit). Tbls, toilets, cfga, drkg wtr. Boating(ldr), fishing, waterskiing. Scenic view of Mt. Thielsen. Access to Pacific Crest National Scenic Trail.

SALEM (W)

Elkhorn Valley Recreation Site $9
Little North Santiam Recreation Area
Bureau of Land Management
Salem District
25 mi E of Salem on SR 22; 9 mi NE on Elkhorn Rd. New fees: $10 with federal senior pass; others pay $20. 5/15-9/25; 14-day limit. 24 sites (18-ft RV limit). Tbls, toilets, cfga, drkg wtr. Swimming, hiking, fishing.

SANDY (W)

Camp Ten Campground $7.50
Mount Hood National Forest
E of Sandy on Hwy 26, then S on FR 42, across part of Warm Springs Indian Reservation, and S on FR 4220 to camp; at Olallie Lake. $7.50 base with federal senior pass; others pay $15 base, $20 for premium site. 6/19-9/30; 14-day limit. 10 sites; 16-ft RV limit. Tbls, toilet, cfga, no drkg wtr. Fishing, hiking. Elev 5000 ft.

SENECA (E)

Big Creek Campground $8
Malheur National Forest
20.5 mi E of Seneca on FR 16; half mi N on FR 1600. $8. 5/15-11/15; 14-day limit. 15 sites (RVs under 31 ft). Tbls, toilets, cfga, well drkg wtr. Fishing. Elev 5100 ft; 4 acres. On edge of Logan Valley.

Murray Campground $8
Malheur National Forest
21 mi W of Seneca via FR 16, then N on FR 924. $8. 5/15-11/30; 30-day limit. 5 sites. Tbls, toilets, cfga, no drkg wtr. Fishing, hiking, hunting.

Parish Cabin Campground $8
Malheur National Forest
12 mi E of Seneca on FR 16. $8 during MD-LD; free off-season but no wtr or services. 14-day limit. 16 sites (32-ft RV limit). Tbls, cfga, toilets, drkg wtr, grey wtr dumps. Fishing at Little Bear Creek.

Starr Campground $6
Malheur National Forest
9 mi N of Seneca on US 395. $6. 5/10-11/1; 30-day limit. 10 sites (25-ft RV limit). Tbls, toilets, cfga, no drkg wtr. Elev 5100 ft. 7 acres.

SILVER LAKE (W)

Alder Springs Forest Camp   FREE
Fremont National Forest
Half mi W of Silver Lake on SR 31; left on CR 4-11 (becoming FR 27) for 13 mi; right on FR 021 for 1.5 mi. Free. 6/1-12/1; 14-day limit. 3 sites. Toilets, cfga, no drkg wtr or tbls, no trash service. Hunting. Historic, tiered water troughs made from dug out logs.

Antler Horse Camp   FREE
Fremont National Forest
Half mi W of Silver Lake on SR 31; left on CR 4-11 (becoming FR 27) for 9 mi; right on FR 2804 for 2.5 mi; left on FR 7645 for 5 mi; left on FR 036 about 2.3 mi; right on FR 038 for half mi. Free all year; maintained 6/15-9/15; reduced services off-season; 14-day limit. 5 large sites. Tbls, toilet, cfga, no drkg wtr, corrals, hitching rails. Hiking, horseback riding, mountain biking.

Bunyard Crossing Forest Camp   FREE
Fremont National Forest
6 mi S of Silver Lake on CR 4-12 (becoming FR 28); 1 mi on FR 28; right on FR 2917 for 1 mi (W); right on FR 413 just before bridge. Free. 5/1-12/1; 14-day limit. 3 primitive sites. Tbl, toilet, cfga, no drkg wtr or trash service. Hiking, birdwatching, fishing at Silver Creek. Wildflowers in season.

Duncan Reservoir Campground   FREE
Bureau of Land Management
Lakeview District
5 mi E of Silver Lake on OR 31; S 1 mi on rough Lake County RD 4-14; 4 mi S on BLM 6197; at W side of lake. Free. All year, subject to winter closure. 4 sites plus group area below dam. Toilets, no drkg wtr or trash service. Fishing, swimming, hiking, boating(l). Ice fishing in winter, but access variable.

East Bay Campground $10
Fremont National Forest
From forest's office at Silver Lake, qtr mi E on Hwy 31; right on FR 28 for 13 mi; right on FR 014. $10 during 5/15-10/15; reduced services off-season; 14-day limit. 18 sites, typically 45 ft. Drkg wtr, tbls, toilets, cfga, drkg wtr, fishing pier. Boating(l), fishing, hiking, swimming, birdwatching.

Green Mountain Campground   FREE
Bureau of Land Management
Lakeview District
From Silver Lake, 1 mi E on SR 31; 1 mi N on CR 5-14, continuing E on CR 5-14 about 5 mi through settlement of Christmas Valley; left N on Crack in the Ground Rd about 8 mi, following signs; near Green Mountain summit. All year; 14-day limit. About 4 primitive undesignated sites. Tbls, cfga, toilet, no drkg wtr or trash service. Rockhounding, OHV activities. Elev 5100 ft.

Lower Buck Creek Forest Camp FREE
Fremont National Forest
1 mi N of Silver Lake on SR 31; 10 mi W on CR 4-10; left on FR 2804 for 2 mi; after second cattle guard, left on FR 015 for 1 mi. Free all year; maintained 5/15-10/15; reduced services off-season; 14-day limit. 5 sites. Tbls, toilet, cfga, no drkg wtr or trash service. Fishing. Elev 5000 ft.

Silver Creek Marsh Campground $6
Fremont National Forest
1 mi W of Silver Lake on SR 31; left on CR 4-11, then 9.7 mi S on FR 27; qtr mi SW on FR 2919. $6 during 5/15-10/15; reduced services off-season; 14-day limit. 15 sites; no RV size limit. Tbls, toilet, cfga, drkg wtr, no trash service. Fishing, hiking, horseback riding, mountain biking, bird-watching. Quiet, secluded. Elev 5000 ft. On Thompson Reservoir. Overflow area for Thompson camp. Corrals, hitching rails, watering troughs.

Thompson Reservoir Campground $6
Fremont National Forest
1 mi W of Silver Lake on SR 31; left on CR 4-11, then 13.6 mi S on FR 287; 1 mi E on FR 3204. $6 during 5/15-10/15; reduced services off-season; 14-day limit. 19 sites, typically 42 ft. Tbls, toilets, cfga, drkg wtr. Swimming, boating(l), fishing. 8 acres. 2,179-acre lake.

Trapper Spring Forest Camp FREE
Fremont National Forest
NW of Silver Lake on SR 31; 10 mi W on CR 4-10; 4 mi N on FR 2516; left on FR 2780 for 8 mi; left on FR 146 at Trapper Spring sign. Free. 5/15-10/31; 14-day limit. 2 primitive sites. Tbl, cfga, toilet, no drkg wtr or trash service.

Upper Buck Creek Forest Camp FREE
Fremont National Forest
NW of Silver Lake on SR 31; 10 mi W on CR 4-10; left on FR 2804 for 4 mi. 5/1-12/1; 14-day limit. 5 primitive sites. Tbls, toilets, cfga, no drkg wtr or trash service. Fishing, wildflower viewing, birdwatching.

SISTERS (W)

Allen Springs Campground $8
Deschutes National Forest
9.6 mi NW of Sisters on US 20; 11.1 mi N on FR 14 (bear right at "Y"). $8 with federal senior pass; others pay $16. During 10/1-4/30, sites are $12 ($6 with senior pass). 7 RV sites; 30-ft RV limit. Tbls, toilets, cfga, no drkg wtr. Fishing, hiking trails.

Allingham Campground $8
Deschutes National Forest
9.6 mi NW of Sisters on US 20; 6.1 mi N on FR 14; 1 mi N on FR 1419. $8 with federal senior pass; others pay $16. 4/20-12/31; 14-day limit. 10 sites; 40-ft RV limit. Tbls, toilets, cfga, drkg wtr, grey wtr stations. Hiking trails, fishing.

Big Lake Campground $11
Willamette National Forest
From Sisters, 15 mi W on US 20 toward Santiam Pass; 3 mi S on Big Lake Rd (FR 2690); at NW shore of lake. $11 with federal senior pass; others pay $22. 5/26-10/9; 14-day limit (2017 opening delayed by snow until 6/15). 49 sites; 35-ft RV limit. Tbls, flush & pit toilets, cfga, drkg wtr. Fishing, hiking trails, boating(l), swimming, waterskiing. Nearby Big Lake West Campground is a tent-only facility.

Black Pine Springs Dispersed Camp FREE
Deschutes National Forest
8.2 mi S of Sisters on FR 16. Free. 6/15-10/15; 14-day limit. About 4 sites (RVs under 16 ft). All facilities removed; no drkg wtr or trash service. Elev 4350 ft.

Blue Bay Campground $9
Deschutes National Forest
13.2 mi NW of Sisters on US 20; 1 mi W on FR 2070; at Suttle Lake. $9 with federal senior pass; others pay $18 (double sites $34). About 5/18-9/10; 14-day limit. 25 sites; 50-ft RV limit. Tbls, toilets, cfga, drkg wtr, fish cleaning station, grey wtr stations. Fishing, boating(l), hiking trails.

Box Canyon Horse Camp FREE
Willamette National Forest
About 30 mi W of Sisters on SR 242; left (W) on SR 126, through settlement of McKenzie Bridge about 4 mi; S on Aufderheide Dr (FR 19), taking right at Y to the top of Cougar Reservoir; continue S on FR 19 past the lake for 31 mi to horse camp on W side of rd at top of the pass. Free. All year, but FR 19 not maintained; 14-day limit. 13 sites (RVs under 31 ft). Tbls, toilets, cfga, no drkg wtr except for stock, no trash service. Corrals, wtr troughs, trails. Hiking, horseback riding. Open to non-equestrians.

Camp Sherman $9
Deschutes National Forest
9.6 mi NW of Sisters on US 20; 6.1 mi N on FR 14; 0.50 mi N on FR 1419. $9 with federal senior pass during 5/1-10/1; others pay $18. During off-season, fee reduced to $14 ($7 with senior pass). 14-day limit. 15 sites; 40-ft RV limit. Tbls, toilets, cfga, drkg wtr, shelter, grey wtr stations, shelter. Fishing, hiking trails.

Candle Creek Campground $12
Deschutes National Forest
From Sisters at jct with SR 242, 12.4 mi NW on US 20; 12.3 mi N on FR 12; 1.6 mi E on FR 1200-980; on Candle Creek at Metolius River. $12. About 5/8-9/10; 14-day limit. 9 RV/tent sites; 18-ft RV limit, but RVs not recommended). Tbls, toilets, cfga, no drkg wtr. Fly fishing; hiking trails. Elev 2600 ft.

Cold Springs Campground $7
Deschutes National Forest
4 mi W of Sisters on SR 242. $7 with federal senior pass;

others pay $14. 5/5-10/31; 14-day limit. 23 sites; 50-ft RV limit. Tbls, toilets, cfga, drkg wtr. Hiking, fishing. Elev 3400 ft; 12 acres.

Cold Water Cove Campground $10
Willamette National Forest
From jct with SR 242 at Sisters, 20 mi W on US 20, pass Santiam Junction, then left (S) on SR 126 for 3 mi to SW shore of Clear Lake; left (NE) for 0.5 mi on FR 770 access rd on SE shore. $10 with federal senior pass; others pay $22 (multiple site $38). MD-10/9; 14-day limit. 34 sites; 30-ft RV limit. Tbls, toilets, cfga, drkg wtr. Fishing, interpretive trail, boating(l).

Cougar Creek Trailhead $8
Willamette National Forest
Bureau of Land Reclamation
About 30 mi W of Sisters on SR 242; left (W) on SR 126, through settlement of McKenzie Bridge about 4 mi; S on Aufderheide Dr (FR 19), keeping left; from stop sign, go 1.5 mi on FR 411, then turn right; make immediate right into camp. $8. 5/19-9/11; 14-day limit. 2 sites. Tbls, toilets, cfga, no drkg wtr. Fishing, hiking. Elev 1200 ft. Trailhead might be closed to camping by new forest restrictions.

Cougar Crossing Campground $7
Cougar Recreation Area
Willamette National Forest
About 30 mi W of Sisters on SR 242; left (W) on SR 126, through settlement of McKenzie Bridge about 4 mi; S 9.5 mi on Aufderheide Dr (FR 19). $7 with federal senior pass; others pay $14. All year, but managed 5/5-9/8; reduced fees & services off-season. 14-day limit. 11 sites; 40-ft RV limit. Tbls, portable toilets, cfga, no drkg wtr. Hiking, swimming, fishing. At jct of South Fork of McKenzie River & S end of Cougar Reservoir.

Cow Camp Horse Camp FREE
Deschutes National Forest
1.7 mi W of Sisters on Hwy 242. Free. 6/15-10/15; 14-day limit. 5 sites; 40-ft RV limit. Tbls, toilet, cfga, no wtr except for horses. Corrals. Hiking & bridle trails. Open only to horse campers.

Delta Campground $9
Cougar Recreation Area
Willamette National Forest
About 30 mi W of Sisters on SR 242; left (W) on SR 126, through settlement of McKenzie Bridge about 4 mi; qtr mi S on FR 19, then FR 400 to camp; at McKenzie River. $9 with federal senior pass; others pay $18 ($34 double sites). About 4/15-10/9; 14-day limit. 38 sites (40-ft RV limit). Tbls, toilets, drkg wtr, cfga, gray water sumps. Fishing, hiking.

Driftwood Campground $7
Deschutes National Forest
17 mi S of Sisters on rough, rocky FR 16 (Elm St); at Three Creek Lake. $7 with federal senior pass; others pay $14. 6/28-10/9; 14-day limit. 5 RV sites, 12 tent sites; not good sites for RVs, but 30-ft RV limit. Tbls, toilets, cfga, drkg wtr, store. Fishing, hiking, boating (elec mtrs). Elev 6600 ft.

French Pete Campground $8
Cougar Recreation Area
Willamette National Forest
About 30 mi W of Sisters on SR 242; left (W) on SR 126, through settlement of McKenzie Bridge about 4 mi; S on FR 19, on right side of dam. $8 with federal senior pass; others pay $16. 4/4-9/8; 14-day limit. 14 RV/tent sites (30-ft RV limit). Tbls, toilets, cfga, drkg wtr, gray water sumps.

Frissell Crossing Campground $7
Willamette National Forest
About 30 mi W of Sisters on SR 242; left (W) on SR 126, through settlement of McKenzie Bridge about 4 mi; 23 mi S on FR 19; at South Fork of McKenzie River. $7 with federal senior pass; others pay $14. About 5/5-9/8; 14-day limit. 12 sites (36-ft RV limit). Tbls, toilets, cfga, drkg wtr. Built 1934 by CCC. Elev 2600 ft.

Gorge Campground $8
Deschutes National Forest
9.6 mi NW of Sisters on US 20; 6.1 mi N on FR 14; 2 mi N on FR 1419; at Metolius River. $8 with federal senior pass; others pay $16 during 5/15-9/30; $12 ($6 with senior pass off-season) 14-day limit. 18 sites; 40-ft RV limit. Wtr available at nearby Arlington, Smiling River or Camp Sherman campgrounds. Tbls, toilets, cfga, no drkg wtr (available at guard station), grey wtr stations. Fishing, hiking trails, biking.

Graham Corral Horse Camp $8
Deschutes National Forest
4.2 mi W of Sisters on Hwy 242; 2 mi N on FR 1012; 0.8 mi NW on FR 1012-300. $8 with federal senior pass; others pay $16. 5/5-10/31; 14-day limit. 13 sites; 40-ft RV limit. Tbls, toilets, cfga, no drkg wtr in early 2017, horse stalls, corral. Bridle trails, hiking trails. Open only to horse campers.

Homestead Campground FREE
Willamette National Forest
About 30 mi W of Sisters on SR 242; left (W) on SR 126, through settlement of McKenzie Bridge about 4 mi; 22 mi S on FR 19; on South Fork of McKenzie River. Free. All year; 14-day limit. 7 sites; 32-ft RV limit. Tbls, toilets, cfga, no drkg wtr, no trash service. Fishing, swimming, boating, hunting. Near Cougar Reservoir.

Ice Cap Creek Campground $8
Willamette National Forest
From jct with SR 242 at Sisters, 20 mi W on US 20, pass Santiam Junction, then left (S) on SR 126 for 4 mi; right at Ice Cap/Koosah Falls sign, then follow signs on access rd; N of Carmen Reservoir. $8 with federal senior pass; others pay $16. MD-9/10; 14-day limit. 22 sites; 30-ft RV limit. Tbls, toilets, cfga (no firewood), no drkg wtr. Fishing, hiking, biking.

Indian Ford Campground $12
Deschutes National Forest
5 mi NW of Sisters on US 20. $12. 5/5-10/31; 14-day limit. 25 sites; 40-ft RV limit. Tbls, toilets, cfga, no drkg wtr. Fishing (Indian Ford Creek), birdwatching, biking. Elev 3200 ft; 9 acres. Note: 12 sites closed in 2016 for bridge work.

Jack Creek Campground $12
Deschutes National Forest
From Sisters at jct with SR 242, 12.4 mi NW on US 20; 4.5 mi N on FR 12; 0.6 mi N on FR 1230. $12. 5/4-10/31; 14-day limit. 20 sites (40-ft RV limit). Tbls, toilets cfga, no drkg wtr. Fishing, hiking trail. Elev 3100 ft.

Link Creek Campground $9
Deschutes National Forest
13.2 mi NW of Sisters on US 20; 2.3 mi W on FR 2070; at W end of Suttle Lake. $9 with federal senior pass; others pay $18. 5/1-9/30; 14-day limit. 29 sites; 40-ft RV limit. Tbls, toilets, cfga, drkg wtr, fish cleaning station, grey wtr stations, fish cleaning station. Boating(l), fishing, hiking trails, swimming.

Limberlost Campground $6.50
Willamette National Forest
About 28 mi W of Sisters on SR 242; right (N) on access rd. $6.50 with federal senior pass; others pay $13. 5/5-9/17; 14-day limit. 12 sites; 16-ft RV limit. Tbls, toilets, cfga, no drkg wtr. Fishing.

Lookout Campground $7
Willamette National Forest
About 30 mi W of Sisters on SR 242; left (W) on SR 126, through settlement of McKenzie Bridge about 6 mi (2.5 mi E of Blue River settlement); 3 mi N on FR 15. $7 with federal senior pass; others pay $14. All year; 14-day limit. 20 sites; 40-ft RV limit. Tbls, toilets, cfga, drkg wtr, gray wtr sump. Boating(l), fishing. On NE shore of Blue River Reservoir.

Lost Lake Campground $8
Willamette National Forest
About 15 mi W of Sisters on US 20 toward Santiam Junction; right (N) on FR 835. $8. About 7/1-10/15 (depending on snow); 14-day limit. 16-ft RV limit (trailers not recommended). Tbls, toilets, cfga, no drkg wtr. Fishing.

Lower Bridge Campground $8
Deschutes National Forest
9.6 mi NW of Sisters on US 20; 13.6 mi N on FR 14. $8 with federal senior pass; others pay $16 during 5/1-9/30; 14-day limit. 12 sites; 30-ft RV limit. Tbls, toilets, cfga, drkg wtr, grey wtr stations. Fishing, hiking trails.

Lower Canyon Creek $12
Deschutes National Forest
From Sisters at jct with SR 242, 9.9 mi NW on US 20; 2.7 mi N on FR 14; 2 mi N on FR 1419; 3.4 mi N on FR 1420 & follow signs to campground; on W side of Metolius River at Canyon Creek. $12. 4/5-9/10; 14-day limit. 6 sites; 40-ft RV limit. Tbls, toilets, cfga, no drkg wtr. Fly fishing, hiking, kayaking.

McKenzie Bridge Campground $9
Willamette National Forest
About 30 mi W of Sisters on SR 242; left (W) on SR 126, past settlement of McKenzie Bridge about 1 mi. $9 with federal senior pass; others pay $18. 4/14-9/17; 14-day limit. 13 sites (35-ft RV limit). Tbls, toilets, cfga, drkg wtr. Boating(l), fishing, hiking. Elev 1400 ft.

Mona Campground $9
Willamette National Forest
About 30 mi W of Sisters on SR 242; left (W) on SR 126, through settlement of McKenzie Bridge about 6 mi (2.5 mi E of Blue River settlement); 4 mi N on FR 15, past Lookout Campground; left (W & S) for 1 mi on FR 120 to site on NW shore of Blue River Reservoir. $9 with federal senior pass; others pay $18 (double sites $34). 5/19-9/9; 14-day limit. 23 sites; 36-ft RV limit. Tbls, flush toilets, cfga, drkg wtr, grey wtr stations. Boating(l), fishing, hiking.

Olallie Campground $9
Willamette National Forest
From jct with SR 242 at Sisters, 20 mi W on US 20, past Santiam Junction, then left (S) on SR 126 for 12 mi; site on left near jct of Olallie Creek & McKenzie River. $9 with federal senior pass; others pay $18. 4/14-10/9; 14-day limit. 16 sites (40-ft RV limit). Tbls, toilets, cfga, drkg wtr. Fishing, hiking, horseback riding. Pacific Crest Trail & Olallie Lake nearby. Elev 4500 ft; 11 acres.

Paradise Campground $11
Willamette National Forest
About 30 mi W of Sisters on SR 242; left (W) on SR 126, through settlement of McKenzie Bridge for about 4 mi; N side at McKenzie River. $11 with federal senior pass; others pay $22. 5/5-10/15; 14-day limit. 64 sites: 40-ft RV limit. Tbls, flush & pit toilets, cfga, drkg wtr, amphitheater. Fishing, boating(l). Originally built by CCC in 1930s.

Perry South Campground $9
Deschutes National Forest
5 mi NW of Sisters on US 20; 20.8 mi N on FR 11; 5 mi E on FR 1170; 2.6 mi NW on FR 64 (last 7 mi rough, rocky with

switchbacks; not recommended for large RVs); at Lake Billy Chinook. $9 with federal senior pass; others pay $18. 5/18-9/18; 14-day limit. Free off-season, but no amenities or services. 64 RV sites (recommended 30-ft RV limit due to rds). Tbls, toilets, cfga, drkg wtr, fish cleaning station. Boating(l), fishing, swimming.

Pioneer Ford Campground $9
Deschutes National Forest
9.6 mi NW of Sisters on US 20; 12.6 mi N on FR 14. $9 with federal senior pass; others pay $18. 5/4-9/10; 14-day limit. 20 RV sites; 40-ft RV limit. Tbls, toilets, cfga, drkg wtr, grey wtr stations. Hiking trails, fishing.

Round Lake Dispersed Camp FREE
Deschutes National Forest
12.4 mi NW of Sisters on Hwy 20; 1 mi N on FR 12; 5.5 mi W on FR 1210; at Suttle Lake. Free. All year; 14-day limit. 4 sites. No facilities except cfga, no drkg wtr. Fishing, boating. All facilities were removed after the camp was severely damaged by fire. Dispersed camping is still available.

Scout Lake $9
Deschutes National Forest
12.4 mi NW of Sisters on US 20; 1 mi W on FR 2070; 1 mi S on FR 2066. $9 with federal senior pass; others pay $18. Formerly a group campground, now offers 1 single site (40-ft RV limit). 5/17-9/10; 14-day limit. 9 double or triple sites for $34-$44; 40-ft RV limit. Tbls, toilets, cfga, drkg wtr, beach. Boating, fishing, swimming, nature trails.

Sheep Springs Horse Camp $8
Deschutes National Forest
12.4 mi NW of Sisters on US 20; 7 mi N on FR 12; 1.1 mi W on FR 1260; 1 mi N on FR 1260-200. $8 with federal senior pass; others pay $16. 5/4-10/9; 14-day limit. 11 sites; 40-ft RV limit. Tbls, toilets, cfga, drkg wtr, horse stalls. Horseback riding, hiking trails.

Slide Creek Campground $8
Cougar Recreation Area
Willamette National Forest
About 30 mi W of Sisters on SR 242; left (W) on SR 126, through settlement of McKenzie Bridge about 4 mi; S on Aufderheide Dr (FR 19), turning right at the Y & on to the top of Cougar Reservoir; continue S on FR 19 for 8 mi; left on FR 500 for 1.5 mi; at E side of Cougar Reservoir. $8 with federal senior pass; others pay $16 (double sites $30). 4/21-9/8; 14-day limit. 16 sites (40-ft RV limit). Tbls, toilets, cfga, drkg wtr. Boating, fishing, hiking. 3 acres.

Smiling River Campground $9
Deschutes National Forest
9.6 mi NW of Sisters on US 20; 6.1 mi N on FR 14; 1 mi N on FR 1419. $9 with federal senior pass; others pay $18 during 5/1-9/30; $14 ($7 with senior pass) off-season;

14-day limit. 36 sites; 40-ft RV limit. Tbls, toilets, cfga, drkg wtr, grey wtr stations. Hiking trails, fishing, biking, boating(l).

South Shore Campground $9
Deschutes National Forest
13.2 mi NW of Sisters on US 20; 1.5 mi W on FR 2070. $9 with federal senior pass; others pay $18. About 5/11-9/10; 14-day limit. 38 sites; 40-ft RV limit. Tbls, toilets, cfga, drkg wtr, fish cleaning station, grey wtr stations. Fishing, boating(l), hiking trails, swimming.

Sunnyside Camp $7
Cougar Recreation Area
Willamette National Forest
About 30 mi W of Sisters on SR 242; left (W) on SR 126, through settlement of McKenzie Bridge about 4 mi; S on Aufderheide Dr (FR 19), turning right at the Y & on to the top of Cougar Reservoir; continue S on FR 19 for 8 mi; left on FR 500 for 0.5 mi; on SE side of Cougar Reservoir. $7 with federal senior pass; others pay $14. About 5/10-9/9; 14-day limit. 13 sites; 36-ft RV limit. Tbls, toilets, cfga, no drkg wtr. Fishing, boating, hiking. Steep entrance rd; large RVs not recommended.

Three Creek Lake $7
Deschutes National Forest
18 mi S of Sisters on FR 16. $7 with federal senior pass; others pay $14. 6/28-10/9; 14-day limit. 11 sites; 30-ft RV limit. Tbls, toilets, cfga, no drkg wtr. Swimming, boating(l - for canoes; no mtrs), fishing, hiking. On SE shore of Three Creek Lake. 6 acres; elev 6400 ft.

Three Creek Meadow Horse Camp $7
Deschutes National Forest
17 mi S of Sisters on FR 16 (Elm St); N of Three Creek Lake. $7 with federal senior pass; others pay $14. 6/20-10/9; 14-day limit. 11 non-equestrian sites, 9 equestrian sites (4 stalls per site); 30-ft RV limit. Tbls, toilets, cfga, no drkg wtr. Fishing, swimming, horseback riding.

Trail Bridge Campground $10
Willamette National Forest
From jct with SR 242 at Sisters, 20 mi W on US 20, past Santiam Junction, then left (S) 12 mi on SR 126; right on FR 730, across river bridge, then S to site; at W shore of McKenzie River. $10. About 4/20-10/15; 14-day limit. 46 sites, including 19 RV sites; (45-ft RV limit). Tbls, toilets, cfga, drkg wtr. Boating, fishing platform, boating(l). Elev 2000 ft; 19 acres. Note: Closed for renovations 2017-2021.

Whispering Pine Horse Camp $8
Deschutes National Forest
6 mi W of Sisters on SR 242; 5 mi S on FR 1018; 3 mi on FR 1520. $8 with federal senior pass; others pay $16. 5/25-10/31; 14-day limit. 9 sites (4 box stalls per site);

30-ft RV limit. Tbls, toilets, cfga, no drkg wtr. Fishing, horseback riding.

SPRAY (E)

Big Bend Campground $5
Bureau of Land Management
Prineville District
John Day River System
From Kimberly (6 mi SE of Spray), at jct with SR 19, 7.4 mi E on Long Creek Hwy (CR 402). $5. MD-LD; 14-day limit. 4 sites. Tbls, toilets, cfga, no drkg wtr. Fishing, boating, hiking. Along North Fork of John Day River.

Fairview Campground FREE
Umatilla National Forest
2.5 mi E of Spray on Hwy 19; 11.5 mi N on Hwy 207; half mi W on FR 400. Free all year, but maintenance during 5/1-10/30; 14-day limit. 5 sites (RVs under 17 ft). Tbls, toilets, cfga, no drkg wtr. Hunting.

Lone Pine Campground $8
Bureau of Land Management
Prineville District
John Day River System
From Kimberly (6 mi SE of Spray), 1 mi E o Long Creek Hwy (CR 402); at N shore of Big Pine Creek. $8. All year; 14-day limit. 8 sites. Group site $16. Tbls, toilets, cfga, no drkg wtr. Fishing, hiking, boating. Along North Fork of John Day River.

Muleshoe Campground $5
Bureau of Land Management
Prineville District
John Day Wild & Scenic River System
5 mi E of Spray along SR 207/19; at N shore of John Day River. $5. All year; 14-day limit. 10 sites. Tbls, toilets, cfga, no drkg wtr. Fishing, hiking, boating.

Spray Riverfront Municipal Park $12
From jct with SR 19 in Spray, 2 blocks S on Main St, then right on Old Parish Creek Rd & right again on park access rd; at shore of John Day River. $12 at 8 primitive sites. Tbls, toilets, cfga, drkg wtr. Fishing, boating(l - $5).

SUMPTER (E)

Union Creek Campground $12
Wallowa-Whitman National Forest
8 mi SE of Sumpter on SR 7; on N shore of Phillips Lake. $12 base at primitive sites. $13 with senior pass at wtr/elec sites (others pay $20); $15 with senior pass for full hookups (others pay $22); double sites full hookups $34 ($25 with senior pass); double sites $34; group sites $60. 5/15-10/15; 14-day limit. 74 RV/tent sites; no RV size limit. Tbls, flush toilets, cfga, drkg wtr, showers, dump, grey wtr stations. Fishing, hiking, boating(l), swimming, waterskiing.

SUTHERLIN (W)

Tyee Recreation Site $7
Bureau of Land Management
Roseburg District
11 mi W of Sutherlin on SR 138; turn across Bullock Bridge; then right half mi. $7 with federal senior pass; others pay $14. About 3/11-11/30; 14-day limit. 15 sites (25-ft RV limit), 11 picnic sites. Tbls, toilets, cfga, drkg wtr, shelter. Fishing. 15 acres, on main stem of Umpqua River.

SWEET HOME (W)

Fernview Campground $7.50
Willamette National Forest
Linn County Parks & Recreation
23 mi E of Sweet Home on US 20; at Boulder Creek & Santiam River. $7.50 with federal senior pass; others pay $15. 5/1-9/30; 14-day limit. 11 sites (22-ft RV limit). Tbls, toilets, cfga, drkg wtr. Fishing, hiking trails. 5 acres. Managed by county park system.

House Rock Campground $7.50
Willamette National Forest
Linn County Parks & Recreation
26.5 mi E of Sweet Home on US 20; SE on FR 2044; at Sheep Creek & South Santiam River. $7.50 with federal senior pass; others pay $15. 5/6-9/25; 14-day limit. 17 sites; 22-ft RV limit, but tight turn-around space for motorhomes. Tbls, toilets, cfga, drkg wtr, grey wtr stations. Hiking (loop trail), fishing, swimming. Historic House Rock & Old Santiam Wagon Road. Managed by county park system.

Lost Prairie Campground $7.50
Willamette National Forest
Linn County Parks & Recreation
40 mi E of Sweet Home on US 20. $7.50 with federal senior pass; others pay $15. About MD-10/15; 14-day limit. 10 sites (24-ft RV limit). Tbls, toilets, cfga, drkg wtr, grey wtr stations. Fishing, hiking. Elev 3300 ft; 5 acres on Hackleman Creek. Managed by county parks system.

Trout Creek $7.50
Willamette National Forest
Linn County Parks & Recreation
18.6 mi E of Sweet Home on US 20. $7.50 with federal senior pass; others pay $15. 5/5-9/23; 14-day limit. 24 sites (32-ft RV limit). Tbls, toilets, cfga, drkg wtr. Fishing, hiking, interpretive trail, swimming. On Santiam River. 14 acres. Operated by Linn County Parks system.

Yellowbottom Recreation Site $7.50
Bureau of Land Management
Salem District
From U.S. 20 just E of Sweet Home, 22 mi NE on Quartzville Rd. New fees: $7.50 with federal senior pass; others pay $15. 5/1-9/30; 14-day limit. 22 sites; 28-ft RV limit.

Tbls, toilets, cfga, drkg wtr. Fishing, hiking, nature trail. On Quartzville Creek. 15 acres. Operated by Linn County Parks.

Yukwah Campground　　　　　　　　　　　$7.50
Willamette National Forest
Linn County Parks & Recreation
19 mi E of Sweet Home on US 20. $7.50 with federal senior pass; others pay $15. 5/5-9/23; 14-day limit. 13 sites (32-ft RV limit). Tbls, toilets, cfga, drkg wtr, grey wtr stations. Fishing, hiking. Santiam River. 15 acres. Managed by county park system.

THE DALLES (W)

Deschutes River State Recreation Area　　　　$10
12 mi E of The Dalles on I-84; exit 97 to Celio, then 5 mi S on Hwy 206. $10 for 25 primitive sites during 5/1-9/30 ($5 off-season with 24-ft RV limit); $22 at 34 sites with elec/wtr (no wtr services in winter). All year; 10-day limit in 14-day period. 30-ft RV limit. Tbls, flush toilets, cfga, drkg wtr, showers. At Deschutes River near Columbia River. Fishing, rafting, boating(l), hiking, bridle trail, biking trail.

Giles French Park　　　　　　　　　　　　FREE
Lake Umatilla
Corps of Engineers
Below dam of Lake Umatilla, on Oregon side. From I-84 exit 102, N toward river on John Day Dam Rd, then left into park. Free. Primitive undesignated sites. All year; 14-day limit. Tbls, toilets, cfga, drkg wtr. Boating(l), fishing.

LePage Park　　　　　　　　　　　　　　$11
Lake Umatilla
Corps of Engineers
From John Day dam, 9 mi E on I-84 to exit 114, then S on access rd; at confluence of John Day & Columbia Rivers. $11 with federal senior pass at 22 elec sites; others pay $22 (overflow sites $15). 4/1-10/31; 14-day limit. RV limit 55 ft; 8 pull-through sites. Non-campers pay $5 day use fee for dump station, $3 for boat ramp. Tbls, toilets, cfga, drkg wtr, showers, dump, beach. Fishing, boating(l).

Quesnel Park　　　　　　　　　　　　　FREE
Lake Umatilla
Corps of Engineers
From about 6 mi E of Arligton to I-84 exit 151 (3 mi E of LePage Park). Free primitive camping. All year; 14-day limit. Pit toilets, cfga, tbls, no drkg wtr. Boating(l), fishing, windsurfing. Also known as Three Mile Canyon Park. Windsurfing.

UKIAH (E)

Bear Wallow Creek Campground　　　　　　$8
Umatilla National Forest
10 mi E of Ukiah on Hwy 244. $8. All year (closed only by snow, maintained MD-11/15; free off-season but not maintained & no services; 14-day limit. 8 sites (RVs under

32 ft). Tbls, toilets, cfga, no drkg wtr. Hunting, fishing. Qtr mi interpretive trail.

Big Creek Meadows Campground　　　　　FREE
Umatilla National Forest
22 mi SE of Ukiah on CR 1475 (becoming FR 52); right (S) on FR 5225 for short distance, then right on FR 5225020 for half mi across bridge; left into site. Free all year, but not maintained in winter; 14-day limit. 3 sites. Tbls, toilets, cfga, no drkg wtr. Hunting, fishing, hiking, wilderness access. ATV trails nearby. Elev 5100 ft.

Divide Well Campground　　　　　　　　FREE
Umatilla National Forest
From Ukiah, W on SR 244 (becoming FR 53), past US 395 for 9 mi; left (S) on FR 5312 for 7 mi; right (W) on FR 5320 for 1.5 mi to site, on right. Free (formerly $8). All year (closed only by snow, maintained MD-11/15); 14-day limit. 11 sites. Tbls, toilets, cfga, no drkg wtr. Hunting, trail bike riding. Popular among elk hunter groups. Elev 4700 ft.

Drift Fence Campground　　　　　　　　FREE
Umatilla National Forest
7 mi SE of Ukiah on CR 1475 (becoming FR 52); right on rought access rd FR 500. Free all year, but not maintained after 11/15; 14-day limit. 6 small sites. Tbls, toilets, cfga, no drkg wtr. Hunting. Improvements planned. Elev 4250 ft.

Driftwood Campground　　　　　　　　　$8
Umatilla National Forest
From SR 395 at Ukiah, 15 mi S toward Dale, 5 mi NE on FR 55; on shore of North Fork of John Day River. $8 during MD-11/15; free but not maintained off-season; 14-day limit. 6 sites; 45-ft RV limit (one site downhill with tight turn-around). Tbls, toilets, cfga, no drkg wtr or trash service. Fishing, hiking, boating. Elev 2500 ft.

Four Corners Campground　　　　　　　FREE
Umatilla National Forest
From SR 395 at Ukiah, 15 mi S toward Dale; 0.5 mi E on FR 55; right (SE) 26 mi on FR 10. Free. All year; 14-day limit. 2 dispersed sites eighth mi E of snow park area. Tbls, no toilet, cfga, no drkg wtr or trash service. Permits required for snow park 11/15-4/30. Hiking, hunting.

Frazier Campground　　　　　　　　　　$10
Umatilla National Forest
18 mi E of Ukiah on SR 244; half mi S on FR 5226; qtr mi E on FR 20. $10 during 6/1 through hunting season; free but not maintained after 11/15; 14-day limit. 20 sites (32-ft RV limit). Tbls, toilets, cfga, no drkg wtr. Popular big-game hunting site. Fishing, trail bikes. Elev 4300 ft; 10 acres.

Gold Dredge Campground　　　　　　　$8
Umatilla National Forest
From SR 395 at Ukiah, 15 mi S toward Dale; 7 mi E on FR 55 past Driftwood CG; right (SE) on FR 5506; at North Fork

of John Day River. $8 ($25 groups) during MD-11/15; free but not maintained off-season; 14-day limit. 7 sites; 40-ft RV limit. Tbls, toilet, cfga, no drkg wtr or trash service. Hunting, fishing, trail bikes. Elev 4300 ft.

Lane Creek Campground $8
Umatilla National Forest
10.5 mi E of Ukiah on Hwy 244. $8 from MD through hunting season ($25 group); free but not maintained after 11/15; 14-day limit. 7 sites (RVs under 45 ft). Tbls, toilets, cfga, no drkg wtr or trash service. Hunting, fishing.

North Fork John Day Campground $8
Umatilla National Forest
36 mi S of Ukiah on FR 52 (Blue Mountain Scenic Byway; access via Hwy 244; on North Fork John Day River. $8 from MD through hunting season ($25 group); free but not maintained after 11/15; 14-day limit. 20 sites, typically 48 ft. Tbls, toilets, cfga, no drkg wtr; horse handling facilities at adjacent trailhead. Hunting, fishing, wilderness access.

Olive Lake Campground $12
Umatilla National Forest
From Ukiah, 5 mi S on CR 1475, becoming FR 52 & continuing 48.5 mi to town of Granite; right (SE) for 3.5 mi on CR 24/FR 10 to end of pavement, then follow gravel FR 10 up hill to the right for 9 mi; left on FR 1000480 about qtr mi to site near E shore of lake. $12 during MD-11/15; free off-season but not maintained; 14-day limit. 21 RV/tent sites; 40-ft RV limit. Tbls, toilets, cfga, no drkg wtr or trash service. Fishing, boating(ld), swimming, 2-mi hiking trail. Elev 6000 ft; 11 acres. Closed in 2017 for hazardous tree removal; check current status before arrival.

Pearson Woods Camp   CLOSED
Umatilla National Forest
22 mi NE of Ukiah on FR 5400, off Hwy 244. Site decommissioned & closed.

Tollbridge Campground $8
Umatilla National Forest
17 mi S of Ukiah on FR 10; at Desolation Creek. $8. All year (closed only by snow, maintained MD-11/15; free rest of year); 14-day limit. 5 sites; 40-ft RV limit. Tbls, toilet, cfga, no drkg wtr or trash service. Fishing, hiking, swimming, rafting. Elev 3800 ft.

Ukiah-Dale Forest $10
State Scenic Corridor
SW of Ukiah on US 395 about 3 mi; at Camas Creek. $10 at 27 primitive sites during 5/1-9/30; $5 off-season. 10-day limit in 14-day period. 27 primitive sites; 40-ft RV limit. Tbls, flush toilets, cfga, drkg wtr. Elev 3000 ft.

Welch Creek Campground $8
Umatilla National Forest
From SR 395 at Ukiah, 15 mi S toward Dale; 1 mi E1 mi

N on FR 55; right (SE) on FR 10 for 12 mi to site on right. $8 during MD-11/15; free off-season but not maintained; 14-day limit. 6 sites; 35-ft RV limit. Tbls, toilet, cfga, no drkg wtr or trash service. Fishing, hunting. Desolation Creek. Elev 4200 ft.

Winom Campground $10
Umatilla National Forest
22 mi SE of Ukiah off FR 52; access rd too narrow, winding for large RVs. $10 MD through hunting season; free but not maintained after 11/15; 14-day limit. 10 sites; 3 group sites $25. 2 shelters, toilets, cfga, no drkg wtr or trash service. Primarily an OHV & equestrian camp; staging area for S end of an OHV complex. Built as joint effort by state dept. of transportation, Umatilla NF and Northwest Trailriders.

UMATILLA (E)
Paterson Park   FREE
Lake Umatilla
Corps of Engineers
From Umatilla, about 3 mi W on US 730 (Columbia River Hwy) to Irrigon; 2 mi W on S. Main Ave becoming CR 971, then N on Paterson Ferry Rd (CR 930) about 0.75 mi to park. Free. 5/15-915; 7-day limit. Primitive undesignated sites. Toilet, cfga, no drkg wtr. Boating(l), fishing.

Sand Station Recreation Area   FREE
Lake Wallula
Corps of Engineers
10.5 mi E of Umatilla on US 730. Free. All year; 14-day limit. About 20 undesignated primitive sites, 5 for RVs. Group camping by permit only May-Sept (541-922-2268). Tbls, pit toilets, cfga, no drkg wtr. Beach. Swimming, boating, fishing. 8 acres.

UNION (E)
Boulder Park Campground   FREE
Wallowa-Whitman National Forest
From Union at jct with SR 237, 15 mi SE on SR 203 to settlement of Medical Springs; right (SE) on Big Creek Rd 1.5 mi, then veer left on FR 67 for 14 mi; left on FR 77 for 0.5 mi; right on FR 7755 for 3.5 mi; along Eagle Creek (gravel last 14 mi). Free. 6/1-11/1; 14-day limit. 7 RV/tent sites. Tbls, toilet, cfga, no drkg wtr. Fishing, hiking, horseback riding. Corrals.

Catherine Creek State Park $10
8 mi SE of Union on SR 203. $10 for 20 primitive sites during 4/18-10/11; ($5 off-season). 10-day limit in 14-day period. 50-ft RV limit. Tbls, flush toilets, cfga, drkg wtr. Fishing, horseshoe pits, hiking trail. 160 acres.

Pilcher Creek Reservoir   FREE
Union County Public Works Department
Powder Valley Water Control District
From I-84 exit 285 SW of Union, about 7 mi W on North

Powder River Lane; right on Tucker Flat Rd about 2 mi, then right on park access rd; at N shore of Pilcher Creek Reservoir. Free. All year; 14-day limit. 17 primitive sites. Pit toilets, cfga, tbls, drkg wtr. Fishing, boating(ld), windsurfing. Lake owned & operated by Powder Valley Water Control District, maintained by Union County Public Works Dept.

Tamarack Campground $6
Wallowa-Whitman National Forest
From Union at jct with SR 237, 15 mi SE on SR 203 to settlement of Medical Springs; right (SE) on Big Creek Rd for 1.5 mi, then veer left onto FR 67 for 14 mi; right on FR 77, looping back south for 0.7 mi; on the right near Eagle Creek (gravel last 14 mi). $6. 6/1-10/31; 10-day limit. 12 RV/tent sites (22-ft RV limit). Tbls, toilets, cfga, drkg wtr. Fishing, hiking.

Thief Valley Reservoir FREE
Union County Public Works Department
Powder Valley Water Control District
From I-84 exit 285 SW of Union, E through town of North Powder on SR 237 (LaGrande-Baker Hwy), aka Telocaset Lane; veer left (N) at rail tracks near Telocaset, then veer right onto Thief Valley Rd. Alternative access from Union, about 3 mi S on SR 237 to Thief Valley Rd. Free. All year; 14-day limit. 10 primitive sites. Pit toilets, cfga, drkg wtr. Boating(l), fishing, swimming windsurfing. Beware of rattlesnakes in summer. Lake owned by Bureau of Reclamation, operated by Powder Vally agency, maintained by Union County.

Two Color Campground FREE
Wallowa-Whitman National Forest
From Union at jct with SR 237, 15 mi SE on SR 203 to settlement of Medical Springs; right (SE) for 1.5 mi, then veer left onto FR 67 for 14 mi; left on FR 77 for 0.5 mi, then right onto FR 7755 for 0.5 mi; site on right (gravel last 14 mi). Free. 6/15-9/30; 10-day limit. 11 RV/tent sites (22-ft RV limit). Tbls, drkg wtr, cfga, toilets. Fishing. Elev 4800 ft. 4 acres.

UNITY (E)

Eldorado Forest Camp FREE
Wallowa-Whitman National Forest
11 mi E of Unity on Hwy 26; 1 mi SW on FR 16. Free. 6/1-11/15; 14-day limit. 10 sites (28-ft RV limit). Tbls, toilets, cfga, no drkg wtr. Fishing, hiking. East Camp Creek. Self-service.

Elk Creek Campground $5
Wallowa-Whitman National Forest
5.5 mi SW of Unity on US 26; W about 7 mi on South Fork Burnt River Rd (becoming FR 6005 for about 2 mi; at N shore of South Fork Burnt River at Elk Creek. $5. Elev 4400 ft. 6/1-9/15; 14-day limit. 6 RV/tent sites. Tbls, toilet,

cfga, no drkg wtr. Fishing, OHV activity, mountain biking. Self-service.

Long Creek Forest Camp FREE
Wallowa-Whitman National Forest
9 mi S of Unity on FR 1680 & FR 1692. Free. 5/1-9/15; 14-day limit. Primitive undesignated sites (28-ft RV limit). Tbls, toilets, cfga, no drkg wtr. Fishing, hiking. Long Creek Reservoir. Self-service. GPS: 44.3568282, -118.1613203

Mammoth Springs FREE
Wallowa-Whitman National Forest
9 mi W of Unity on Hwy 600, FR 6005 & FR 2640 (gravel last 5 mi). 5/1-10/15; 14-day limit. 2 dispersed sites (28-ft RV limit). Tbls, toilet, cfga, no drkg wtr. Fishing, hiking. Self-service.

Oregon Campground $5
Wallowa-Whitman National Forest
10.5 mi NW of Unity on US 26; right side. $5. 4/28-9/15. 8 RV/tent sites (28-ft RV limit). Tbls, toilets, cfga, wtr. Hiking, fishing. Elev 5000 ft. Self-service.

South Fork Campground $5
Wallowa-Whitman National Forest
5.5 mi SW of Unity on Hwy 26; left on CR 600 (South Fork Burnt River Rd) for 7 mi (becoming FR 6005); 1 mi SW on Fr 6005. $5. 5/28-9/15; 10-day limit. 12 RV/tent sites (28-ft RV limit, some pull-through). Tbls, toilets, cfga, drkg wtr. Self-service. OHV activity, fishing, hiking.

Steven's Creek Campground $5
Wallowa-Whitman National Forest
7 mi SW on CR 6005; at South Fork of Burnt River. $5. 6/1-9/15; 14-day limit. 7 undesignated sites. Tbls, toilets, cfga, firewood, no drkg wtr. Berry picking. Self-service.

Wetmore Campground $5
Wallowa-Whitman National Forest
8.2 mi NW of Unity on US 26; right side. 5/28-9/15; 14-day limit. $5. 12 RV/tent sites (28-ft RV limit). Tbls, toilets, cfga, drkg wtr. Hiking (nature trails), fishing. Yellow Pine Handicap Trail.

Yellow Pine $5
Wallowa-Whitman National Forest
10.5 mi NW of Unity on US 26; right side. $5. 5/28-9/15. 21 RV/tent sites (28-ft RV limit). Tbls, toilets, cfga, drkg wtr, firewood. Hiking (nature trails); fishing. Yellow Pine Handicap Trail.

VALE (E)

Chukar Park Recreation Site $5
Bureau of Land Management
Vale District
From E of Juntura (35 mi W of Vale) on US 20, 3 mi NW on Beulah Reservoir Rd. $5. All year; 14-day limit. 18 sites

(28-ft RV limit). Tbls, toilets, cfga, drkg wtr (May-Oct). Hunting, fishing. On North Fork of Malheur River. 80 acres.

Twin Springs Campground FREE
Bureau of Land Management
Vale District
3.5 mi W of Vale on US 20; 34 mi S on Dry Creek Rd; high-clearance vehicles only. Free. 5/1-10/30; 14-day limit. Open only during dry road conditions. 5 primitive sites. Tbls, toilets, cfga, no drkg wtr. Fishing, hiking, rockhounding.

WALDPORT (W)

Blackberry Campground $12
Siuslaw National Forest
18 mi E of Waldport on SR 34; right at sign; Alsea River. $12 with federal senior pass; others pay $24. All year; 14-day limit. 32 sites, typically 50 ft. Tbls, toilets, cfga, drkg wtr, grey wtr stations. Boating(l), fishing.

WALLOWA (E)

Lions RV Park FREE
From downtown Wallowa, N on SR 82, then left on N. Bear Creek Rd. Free, but donations accepted. Spring-fall. Undesignated sites. Tbls, toilets, cfga, drkg wtr, dump. Operated by Lions Club.

WESTON (E)

Jubilee Lake Campground $8.50
Umatilla National Forest
19.8 mi E on SR 204; left at sign on FR 64 for 10.9 mi; right at campground sign for 0.4 mi (dirt & gravel last 7.5 mi). $8.50 with federal senior pass; others pay $17 (double sites $24). 7/1-10/15. 50 sites, typically 50 ft. Tbls, flush & pit toilets, cfga, drkg wtr. Boating(l), fishing, hiking trail.

Mottet Campground $8
Umatilla National Forest
19.8 mi E of Weston on SR 204; 11 mi NE on FR 64. $8 during 7/1-10/17 (free through 10/30); 14-day limit. 6 sites. Tbls, toilet, cfga, drkg wtr, grey wtr. Hiling trail, mountain biking, horseback riding, motorcycling.

Target Meadows Campground $12
Umatilla National Forest
17.5 mi E of Weston on SR 204; one-third mi E on FR 64; 22 mi N on FR 6401; 0.6 mi NE on FR 50. $12 during 7/1-10/15; free off-season but no services or wtr; 14-day limit. 20 sites, typically 45 ft. Tbls, toilets, cfga, drkg wtr (turned off 9/30), grey wtr stations. Nature trails, hunting. Elev 5100 ft; 20 acres.

Woodland Campground $8
Umatilla National Forest
17.5 mi E of Weston on Hwy 204. $8 during 7/1-10/17 (free through 10/30); 14-day limit. 7 sites (RVs under 23 ft). Tbls, toilet, cfga, no drkg wtr. Hunting. Elev 5200 ft.

Woodward Campground $12
Umatilla National Forest
17.5 mi E of Weston on SR 204. $12. 7/1-9/30; 14-day limit. 15 sites, typically 40 ft. Tbls, toilets, cfga, drkg wtr, dump. Hiking, trail bikes. No public access to adjoining private Langdon Lake.

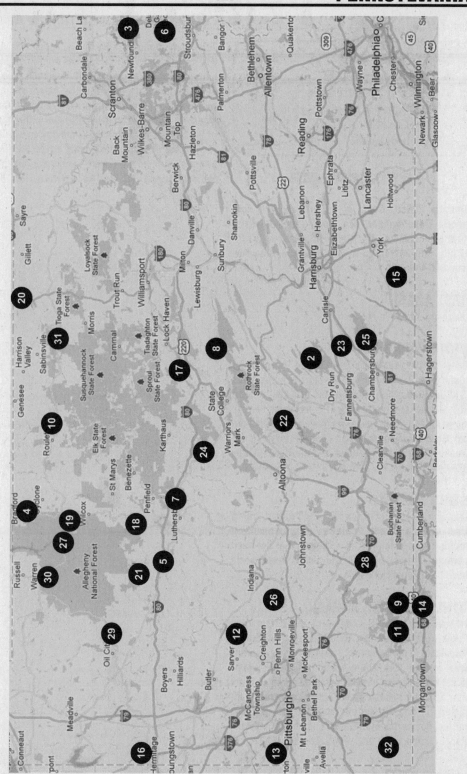

PENNSYLVANIA

CAPITAL: Harrisburg
NICKNAME: Keystone State
STATEHOOD: 1787 – 2nd State
FLOWER: Mountain Laurel
TREE: Hemlock
BIRD: Ruffed Grouse

WWW.VISITPA.COM

Tourism Office, Dept. of Community and Economic Development, 4th Floor, Commonwealth Keystone Building, 400 North St., Harrisburg, PA 17120. 800-237-4363 or 717-787-5453. Information: 800-VISIT-PA.

REST AREAS

Overnight stops are not permitted.

STATE PARKS

Base camping rates are $15 Sunday-Thursday for rustic sites without electricity by state residents ($17 non-residents). Seniors 62 or older receive 35% discounts, and therefore Pennsylvania seniors camp for $10.50 on weekdays (non-resident seniors pay $12.50 weekdays). Extra charges are made for weekend camping, hookups and showers.PO Box 8767, Harrisburg, PA 17105-8767. 888-PA-PARKS.

STATE FORESTS

Camping in some state forests is permitted with a free camping permit. Primitive campers spending no more than one night at a campsite do not need permits. Permits are available online. Five forests have designated campsites.

OTHER CAMPING AREAS

HAMMERMILL PAPER COMPANY. The Hammermill Paper Company owns 170,000 acres of hardwood forestland in northwestern Pennsylvania and southwestern New York. There are no designated campsites, but campers in self-contained camping units may use any suitable area. Activities include picnicking, hiking, fishing and hunting. Pets are permitted. For further information contact Hammermill Paper Company, PO Box 14400, Erie, PA 16533.

Allegheny National Forest. The forest has about 600 campsites as well as 126 free boat-in dispersed sites alongside the Allegheny Reservoir and five developed boat-access, primitive campgrounds on the lake. Campfire permits are not required. Camping is not permitted on the shores and within 1500 ft of the timberline around the Allegheny and Tionesta Reservoirs, except in designated areas. For further information contact Forest Supervisor, Allegheny National Forest, PO Box 847, Warren, PA 16365. 814/723-5150.

ANSONIA (1)

Colton Point State Park $10.50
6 mi S of Ansonia off US 6; on W rim of Pennsylvania Grand Canyon. $10.50 for PA seniors at rustic sites on weekdays; $12.50 for non-resident seniors; others pay $15 & $17. About 4/15-10/15; 14-day limit. 25 sites (some walk-in); 30-ft RV limit. Tbls, pit toilets, cfga, drkg wtr, dump, pavilion($), playground. Hiking & snowmobile trails, skiing, fishing, hunting. 386 acres. GPS: 41.699707, -77.458496

BLAIN (2)

Fowlers Hollow State Park $10.50
7 mi SW of Blain on SR 274; 3 mi E on Upper Buckridge Rd. $10.50 base PA seniors at rustic sites on weekdays; $12.50 for non-resident seniors; others pay $15 & $17. 4/15-12/15; 14-day limit. Tbls, toilets, cfga, drkg wtr, dump, elec($). 12 RV sites; 35 ft RV limit. Fishing, hiking. 104 acres. GPS: 40.2725841, -77.5797108

Tuscarora State Forest   FREE
5 mi SE of Blain on Hwy 274. Free. Camp only in designated areas with free permit. A favorite is Campsite 22, a pull-off on West Licking Creek Dr along West Licking Creek. No facilities, no drkg wtr. Hiking, fishing, ATV trails, snowmobile trails, naturalist programs at Messing Nature Center on Marshall Creek Rd, self-guided nature trail through Tarkill Forest Demonstration Area, fishing & picnicking at Pecks Pond. GPS: 40.3611927, -77.5555447

BLOOMING GROVE (3)

Delaware State Forest   FREE
4 mi S of Blooming Grove on SR 402. Free. All year. Vehicle camping allowed off the rds. Backpack camping permitted throughout the forest except where posted or near ponds & along trails. The following are designated sites:
   S1, Snow Hill Campsite, 4/12-12/13, no facilities. On Laurel Run Rd just N of Hwy 447.
   E1, Edgemere Campsite, on Silver Lake Rd just E of Meadow Rd, 5 mi E of Hwy 402, just past the ranger station. Site suitable for truck camper & small horse trailer. Seasonal toilet, cfga, no drkg wtr.
   01, Owego Campsite, on Fire Tower Rd N of I-84. No facilities, no drkg wtr. Suitable for truck camper & small horse trailer. GPS: 41.1234, -75.1663

BRADFORD (4)

Tracy Ridge Recreation Area $12
Allegheny National Forest
From Bradford, about 12 mi W on SR 346; 4 mi S on SR 321, then right into camp. $12. About 4/1-12/15; 14-day limit (no winter maintenance). 119 sites (40-ft RV limit). Group camping $50 by reservation. Tbls, toilets, cfga, drkg wtr, dump. Hiking trails. GPS: 41.94417, -78.87611

Willow Bay Recreation Area $9
Allegheny National Forest
15 mi W of Bradford on SR 346, just S of the NY state line; at S shore of Willow Bay arm of Allegheny Reservoir. $9 base with federal senior pass; others pay $18 base, $21 for premium waterfront locations ($10.50 with senior pass). $5 surcharge for elec hookups. All year; 14-day limit. 102 sites up to 56 ft. Tbls, flush toilets, cfga, drkg wtr, showers, dump. Fishing, boating(ld), hiking. GPS: 41.98778, -78.91056

BROOKVILLE (5)

Clear Creek State Park $10.50
12 mi N of Brookville on SRs 36 & 949. $10.50 for PA seniors at rustic sites on weekdays; $12.50 for non-resident seniors; others pay $15 & $17. About 4/15-12/15; 14-day limit. 53 tent & RV sites (6 with 50 amps). Toilets, tbls, cfga, drkg wtr, dump, no showers, elec($), beach. 9-hole disc golf, basketball, canoeing, hunting, swimming, hiking trails, fishing. GPS: 41.3289516, -79.0914271

CANADENSIS (6)

Promised Land State Park $10.50
10 mi N of Canadensis on SR 390. $10.50 for PA seniors at rustic sites on weekdays; $12.50 for non-residents seniors; others pay $17 & $17. About 4/1-12/15; 14-day limit. Tbls, toilets, cfga, drkg wtr, dump, beach. 487 sites. Swimming, boating(rld), fishing, 30 mi of hiking trails, 6.5-mi bike trail, access to bridle trails, seasonal interpretive programs, snowmobile trails. 3,000 acres. GPS: 41.315368, -75.198789

CLEARFIELD (7)

S.B. Elliott State Park $10.50
10 mi NW of Clearfield on SR 153. $10.50 for PA seniors at rustic sites on weekdays; $12.50 for non-resident seniors; others pay $15 & $17. About 4/15-10/15; 14-day limit. 25 sites. Tbls, flush toilets, cfga, drkg wtr, playground. No showers or hookups. Hiking trails, hike-in fishing. Wilderness campground. 318 acres within Moshannon State Forest. GPS: 41.1083921, -78.5328013

COBURN (8)

Poe Paddy State Park $10.50
2 mi SE of Coburn; 4 mi E of Poe Valley State Park. $10.50 for PA seniors at rustic sites on weekdays; $12.50 for non-resident seniors; others pay $15 & $17. About 4/15-10/15; 14-day limit. 38 sites. Tbls, pit toilets, cfga, drkg wtr. Dump at nearby Poe Valley State Park. Hiking trails, fishing, hunting. GPS: 40.8335, -77.418

CONFLUENCE (9)

Outflow Campground $6.50
Corps of Engineers
Youghiogheny Lake
From Confluence, 0.7 mi SW on SR 281; at lake. $6.50 with federal senior pass at 15 non-elec sites during 4/10-5/15 & 9/8-10/6; others pay $13. During peak season of 5/15-9/8, 15 non-elec RV/tent sites are $9 with senior pass, $18 for others; 36 elec sites are $11 with senior

pass, $22 for others. During about 10/7-4/9, sites free for self-contained RVs but no wtr, elec or amenities. 14-day limit. 2 group camping areas. Flush toilets, cfga, tbls, drkg wtr, showers, dump, playground, shelter, amphitheater, fishing pier. 4,350 acres. Swimming, boating(rl), biking(r) trail. GPS: 39.805, -79.36694

Tub Run Campground $9
Corps of Engineers
Youghiogheny Lake
7 mi SW of Confluence on SR 281; 1.5 mi S on Tub Run Rd. $9 base with federal senior pass at 59 non-elec sites; others pay $18 base, $19 for premium locations ($9.50 with senior pass). 30 elec sites $11 with senior pass; others pay $22. About 5/15-9/5; 14-day limit. RV limit 55 ft. Tbls, flush toilets, cfga, drkg wtr, coin laundry, showers, dump, pay phone. Biking, boating(l), swimming. GPS: 39.77083, -79.40194

COUDERSPORT (10)
Cherry Springs State Park $10.50
16 mi SE of Coudersport on US 6 & SR 44. $10.50 for PA seniors at rustic sites on weekdays; $12.50 for non-resident seniors; others pay $15 & $17. About 4/15-12/15; 14-day limit. 30 sites. Tbls, pit toilets, lantern hangers cfga, drkg wtr, no showers, dump, playground. Hiking & biking trails. 48 acres surrounded by the 262,000-acre Susquehannock State Forest. GPS: 41.6628445, -77.8230494

FARMINGTON (11)
Forbes State Forest   FREE
SW of Farmington on SR 381. Primitive camping with free permit throughout forest except at Mt. Davis Natural Area; vehicle camping not allowed at Quebec Run Wild Area. Picnicking, hiking, fishing, hunting, snowmobiling. Six areas are designated for camping: two in forest section N of I-70; one just off SR 653 near Laurel Ridge SP; one E of Hwy 281 close to Mt. Davis, and two just N of Maryland state line S of US 40. Some are suitable for small RVs. GPS: 40.1295, -79.1875

FORD CITY (12)
Crooked Creek $10
Corps of Engineers
Crooked Creek Lake
From Ford City, 5 mi S on SR 66; 0.1 mi E on SR 2019 to park manager's office. $10 ($5 with federal senior pass). About 5/15-LD; 14-day limit. 46 non-elec sites. Group camping area. Tbls, flush toilets, cfga, drkg wtr, dump. Playground, hiking, boating(l), fishing, interpretive programs. Non-campers pay $4 day use fee for boat ramp, beach. GPS: 40.707275, -79.497803

FRANKFORT SPRINGS (13)
Raccoon Creek State Park $10.50
Rustic Sioux Campground
About 2 mi N of Frankfort Springs on SR 18. $10.50 for PA seniors at rustic sites on weekdays; $12.50 for non-resident seniors; others pay $15 & $17. All year; 14-day limit. Pit toilets, tbls, cfga, drkg wtr. Also 172 modern sites with showers, hookups. Dump. Hunting, boating(rld), interpretive programs, hiking. GPS: 40.5078448, -80.4361767

FRIENDSVILLE (MARYLAND) (14)
Mill Run Campground $6.50
Corps of Engineers
Youghiogheny Lake
From I-68 exit 4 at Friendsville, Maryland, 5 mi N on SR 53; S of Mill Run Reservoir just W of SR 381. $6.50 with federal senior pass during 5/1-9/8; others pay $13. Free rest of year for self-contained RVs. 14-day limit. 30 non-elec sites. Tbls, toilets, drkg wtr, dump, playground, beach. Limited facilities during free period. Boating, swimming, fishing. GPS: 39.7161, -79.384

HANOVER (15)
Codorus State Park $10.50
3 mi SE of Hanover along SR 216. $12 base at modern sites, $10.50 for PA seniors at basic sites on weekdays; $12.50 for non-resident seniors; others pay $15 & $17. About 4/15-11/1; 14-day limit. 198 sites; 50-ft RV limit. Tbls, flush toilets, showers($), cfga, drkg wtr, elec($), pool. Swimming, fishing, boating(l), hiking trails, hunting. GPS: 39.7701008, -76.9363681

HERMITAGE (16)
Shenango Recreation Area $9.50
Corps of Engineers
Shenango River Lake
From Hermitage at jct with US 62, 4.6 mi N on SR 18; 0.8 mi W on Lake Rd, then S; at N shore of lake. $9.50 base with federal senior pass at 215 non-elec sites; others pay $19 base, $34 for premium locations ($17 with senior pass). At 110 elec sites, $12 with senior pass; others pay $24. MD-LD; 14-day limit. RV limit in excess of 65 ft; 4 pull-through sites. Tbls, cfga, drkg wtr, flush toilets, showers, dump, playground, pay phone, coin laundry, fishing pier, beach, amphitheater, picnic shelter. Fishing, boating(ldr), swimming, horseshoes, interpretive trails, volleyball, horseshoe pits. GPS: 41.28889, -80.43833

HOWARD (17)
Primitive Camping Area $10.50
Bald Eagle State Park
I-80 eastbound exit 23, follow Rt 150 N 10 mi; westbound exit 26, N on Hwy 220 to Rt 50; at Sayers Reservoir. $10.50 for PA seniors at rustic sites on weekdays; $12.50 for non-resident seniors; others pay $15 & $17. 4/15-12/15; 14-day limit. 35 rustic RV sites. Tbls, pit toilets, cfga, drkg

wtr, no showers, dump. Swimming, hiking trails, boating(l-rd), waterskiing, hunting. GPS: 41.0417311, -77.6030495

JOHNSONBURG (18)

East Branch Recreation Area $7.50
Corps of Engineers
East Branch Lake
From Johnsonburg, 5 mi N on US 219 to Wilcox; 5 mi SE on Glen Hazel Rd; exit E (left) past resource mgr's office to campground. $7.50 with federal senior pass at 16 non-elec sites; others pay $15. $10 with senior pass at 16 elec sites; others pay $20. About 4/15-10/15; 14-day limit. Shelter, tbls, toilets, cfga, drkg wtr, dump, playground. Fishing, boating(ld), canoeing, sailing, hunting, waterskiing. GPS: 41.564209, -78.594727

KANE (19)

Dewdrop Recreation Area $8.50
Allegheny National Forest
10 mi NW of Kane on SR 321; 9 mi N on Longhouse Scenic Byway (FR 262); at Kinzua Point on the W shore of Kinzua Bay branch of Allegheny Reservoir. $8.50 base with federal senior pass; others pay $17 base, $19 for waterfront sites ($9.50 with senior pass. MD-LD; 14-day limit (no winter maintenance). 74 sites; no RV size limit. Tbls, flush toilets, cfga, drkg wtr, dump, showers, play area. Boating(l), fishing, hiking. GPS: 41.83194, -78.95944

Kiasutha Recreation Area $9.50
Allegheny National Forest
10 mi NW of Kane on SR 321; 1 mi N on Longhouse Scenic Byway (FR 262); on W shore of Kinzua Bay. $9.50 base with federal senior pass; others pay $19 base, $21 for premium waterfront sites ($10.50 with senior pass). $3 surcharge for elec, $6 surcharge full hookups. MD-LD; 14-day limit (no winter maintenance). 116 sites up to 75 ft. Tbls, flush toilets, cfga, drkg wtr, showers, dump, beach, playground. Fishing, hiking, boating(ld), interpretive trail, swimming. GPS: 41.785, -78.9025

Red Bridge Recreation Area $9
Allegheny National Forest
9 mi NW of Kane along SR 321; on E shore of Kinzua Bay branch of Allegheny Reservoir. $9 base with federal senior pass at non-elec sites; others pay $18 base, $20 for waterfront sites ($10 with senior pass). $5 surcharge for elec, $12 surcharge full hookups. 4/3-12/15; 14-day limit. 67 sites, typically 60 ft. Tbls, pit & flush toilets, cfga, drkg wtr, dump, play area, showers. Hiking, fishing. GPS: 41.77694, -78.88611

Red Mill Campground FREE
Allegheny National Forest
From Kane, about 7 mi S on SR 66; left on SR 948, then right on FR 143; along Big Mill Creek. Free. All year; 14-day limit. No facilities except cfga; no drkg wtr. Fishing.

Twin Lakes Recreation Area $8
Allegheny National Forest
8 mi SE of Kane on SR 321; right on FR 191. Warning: 10-ft railroad underpass & small sites restrict this campground to use by large RVs. $8 base with federal senior pass; others pay $16 base at non-elec sites. $5 surcharge for elec. 4/1-10/19; 14-day limit. 48 sites; 28-ft RV limit. Tbls, flush toilets, cfga, drkg wtr, showers, dump, elec($), beach, playground. Fishing, boating(l), hiking, interpretive trail. GPS: 41.61222, -78.76083

KELLETTVILLE (29)

Kellettville Recreation Area $10
Corps of Engineers
Tionesta Lake
        (See Tionesta entry)
From Kellettville at jct with SR 666, SW across bridge on FR 127 (17 mi upstream from dam). $10 during 4/15-10/30 ($5 with federal senior pass); free during 11/11-12/15; 14-day limit. 20 primitive sites. Drkg wtr, low-volume flush toilets & dump in season; vault toilets off-season. Fishing, boating(l), swimming. 5 acres. GPS: 41.541016, -79.541016

LAWRENCEVILLE (20)

Tompkins Campground $10
Corps of Engineers
Cowanesque Lake
5 mi W of Lawrenceville on Bliss Rd, then S (W of the town of Nelson); on N shore of lake. $10 with federal senior pass at 24 non-elec sites; others pay $20. 34 elec/wtr sites & 52 full-hookup sites, $32 & $34, respectively. 5/15-9/29; 14-day limit. RV limit 55 ft. Group camping area available. Tbls, flush toilets, cfga, drkg wtr, dump, showers, beach, hookups($), amphitheater, fish cleaning station, picnic shelters. Baseball, fishing, boating(l), hiking trail, swimming, interpretive trail. GPS: 40.2734186, -77.4163747

MARIENVILLE (21)

Beaver Meadows Recreation Area CLOSED
Allegheny National Forest
5 mi N of Marienville on North Forest St, becoming FR 128. $12. About 4/15-10/15; 14-day limit. 38 sites (40 ft RV limit). Tbls, pit toilets, cfga, drkg wtr, playground. Boating(l - elec mtrs), fishing, hiking. Note: Campground was closed for 2013 & 2014; check current status with forest office before arrival (814-723-5150). GPS: 41.52361, -79.11278

Kelly Pines Campground FREE
Allegheny National Forest
From Marienville, about 4.5 mi E on FR 130 (Lamonaville Rd); 2 mi N on FR 131 (Rd T327); at shore of Wolf Run. Free. All year; 14-day limit. 5 equestrian sites with tie-down stalls & 2 family sites. Toilet, wtr for horses, no drkg wtr. Manure bin. Horseback riding, fishing.

Loleta Recreation Area $7.50
Allegheny National Forest
6 mi S of Marienville on SR 27027. $7.50 base with federal senior pass at non-elec sites; others pay $15 base, $20 at premium locations ($10 with senior pass). $5 surcharge for elec. 4/1-10/19; 14-day limit. 38 sites; 50-ft RV limit. Tbls, flush & pit toilets, cfga, drkg wtr, beach, showers at beach bathhouse. Swimming, fishing, hiking trails. Non-campers pay $5 swimming fee. GPS: 41.40167, -79.08333

MC CONNELSTOWN (22)

Seven Points Campground $11.50
Corps of Engineers
Raystown Lake
1.2 SW of McConnelstown on SR 26; 2 mi SE past Hesston & S of administration building. $11.50 with federal senior pass at five 30-amp elec/wtr sites & 8 sites at group camping area when not in use; others pay $23. Elec/wtr sites are $25 & $30. 4/1-10/31; 14-day limit. Reservations required during 5/14-9/1. RV limit in excess of 65 ft. Visitor center, marina, amphitheater, flush toilets, cfga, drkg wtr, showers, central dump, playground, beach, picnic shelter. Hiking, boating(l), fishing, swimming, golf, interpretive trail, boat & kayak rentals. GPS: 40.38306, -78.07833

Susquehannock $12
Corps of Engineers
Raystown Lake
From Seven Points campground, I mi NE past the administration building, then SE. $12 base at 36 non-elec sites, $17 at premium waterfront sites ($6 & $8.50 with federal senior pass). About 5/22-10/30; 14-day limit. RV limit in excess of65 ft, but many primitive sites most suitable for folding trailers or pickup campers. Tbls, toilets, cfga, drkg wtr; showers & day use at Seven Points. Hiking. GPS: 40.3875, -78.05

NEWVILLE (23)

Colonel Denning State Park $10.50
9 mi N of Newville on SR 233. $10.50 for PA seniors at rustic sites on weekdays; $12.50 for non-resident seniors; others pay $15 & $17. About 4/15-12/15; 14-day limit. Tbls, pit toilets, cfga, drkg wtr, dump, no showers. Swimming, nature program, hiking trails, fishing. 273 acres with 3.5-acre pond. GPS: 40.2734186, -77.4163747

PHILIPSBURG (24)

Black Moshannon State Park $10.50
9 mi E of Philipsburg on SR 504. $10.50 for PA seniors at rustic sites on weekdays; $12.50 for non-resident seniors; others pay $15 & $17. 74 sites. Tbls, flush toilets, cfga, drkg wtr, coin laundry, showers($), dump, elec($). Boating(lrd), biking, trout fishing, swimming, hiking. Nature boardwalk. 3,394 acres surrounded by 43,000-acre Moshannon State Forest. GPS: 0.8983914, -78.0563965

PINE GROVE FURNACE (25)

Pine Grove Furnace State Park $10.50
On SR 233; SE of I-81, Newville exit. $10.50 for PA seniors at rustic sites on weekdays; $12.50 for non-resident seniors; others pay $15 & $17. All year; 14-day limit. 70 sites. Tbls, pit toilets, cfga, drkg wtr, dump, showers($), dump. Nature program, hiking trails, fishing, boating(rl), biking(r), skiing. 696 acres. GPS: 40.0234248, -77.2913725

RIDGEWAY

Bear Creek Dispersed Recreation Area   FREE
Allegheny National Forest
From Ridgeway, about 9 mi W on SR 949; mi N on Arroyo-Portland Rd (FR 138) to Owls Nest area; 2 mi E on FR 135 to shore of Bear Creek. Free. No facilities except cfga, no drkg wtr, scattered toilets. Trout fishing, hunting.

Clarion River Campsites   FREE
Clarion Wild & Scenic River
Allegheny National Forest
From Ridgeway, W on SR 949 along S shore of Clarion River from Irwin Run to Millstone Creek. Also 6 sites on Millstone Creek between the Clarion & pipeline below Loleta Campground. Signs at Irwin Run canoe launch, Robin Island & mouth of Millstone. Toilet at Irwin Run; 2 more planned for Millstone Creek & Robin Island. Camp only at numbered sites; cfga but no tbls or drkg wtr. Fishing, hiking.

SALTSBURG (26)

Bush Recreation Area $8
Corps of Engineers
Loyalhanna Lake
S of Saltsburg, S on SR 981 past dam; 1 mi S on Bush Rd; at E side of lake. $8 with federal senior pass at 39 primitive sites; others pay $16. $11 with senior pass at 10 elec/wtr sites; others pay $22. 5/15-9/15; 14-day limit. 35-ft RV limit. Tbls, flush toilets, cfga, drkg wtr, elec($) dump, playground, beach, coin showers, playground, picnic shelter. Boating(l), swimming, fishing, canoeing, waterskiing, sailing, interpretive programs. GPS: 40.427988, -79.433105

SHEFFIELD (27)

Minister Creek $12
Allegheny National Forest
15 mi SW of Sheffield on SR 666. $12 about 4/1-12/15; free rest of year but no maintenance or wtr; 14-day limit. 6 sites. Tbls, toilets, cfga, drkg wtr. Hunting, fishing, hiking. GPS: 41.37280, -79.09244

SOMERSET (28)

Kooser State Park $10.50
11 mi W of Turnpike exit 10; 9 mi E of Turnpike exit 9 on SR 31. $10.50 for PA seniors at rustic sites on weekdays; $12.50 for non-resident seniors; others pay $15 & $17. 4/15-10/15; 14-day limit. 35 sites (30 with elec). Tbls,

flush toilets, cfga, drkg wtr, dump, no showers, elec($). Swimming, hunting, nature program, fishing, skiing. 250 acres. GPS: 40.0603526, -79.2300316

TIOGA (31)

Ives Run Recreation Area $10
Hammond Lake
Corps of Engineers
From Tioga, 5 mi S on SR 287; exit E, following signs; on E shore of Hammond Lake. $10 with federal senior pass at 56 non-elec sites during peak season of 5/15-10/30; others pay $20. During 11-1-12/11, 32 non-elec sits are $10 ($5 with senior pass), self-registered. 131 elec/wtr sites cost $32 & $34. Camping by reservation only through National Recreation Reservation Service (ReserveAmerica/recreation.gov) during 4/20-5/14 and 10/1-10/31. At reserved sites, 2-night minimum stay required on weekends, 3 night on holiday weekends. RV limit in excess of 65 ft. Tbls, flush toilets, cfga, drkg wtr, showers, dump, coin laundry, playground, beach, fish cleaning station, amphitheater. Waterskiing, hiking, archery, fishing, boating(l), swimming. GPS: 41.880835, -77.20

TIONESTA (29)

(See Kellettville entry)
Outflow Recreation Area $8
Corps of Engineers
Tionesta Lake
Half mi S of Tionesta on SR 36, then SE. $8 during 4/15-5/20 ($4 with federal senior pass); $12 during about 4/12-10/31 ($6 with senior pass) with flush toilets & showers; free rest of year, pit toilet, no wtr. 14-day limit. 39 non-elec sites; 35-ft RV limit. Tbls, toilets, cfga, drkg wtr, dump, picnic shelter. Boating(l), fishing. Note: Nearby Tionesta Recreation Area has 78 full-hookup sites for $28 (see our Camping With the Corps of Engineers book). GPS: 39.80404, -79.36748

WARREN (30)

Buckaloons Recreation Area $9
Allegheny National Forest
6 mi from Warren on US 6W, S of jct with Hwy 62. At confluence of Allegheny River, Brokenstraw Creek & Irvine Run. $9 with federal senior pass at non-elec sites; others pay $18. $5 surcharge for elec. 5/1-10/31; 14-day limit; no winter maintenance. 57 sites (43 with elec); 40-ft RV limit. Tbls, flush & pit toilets, cfga, drkg wtr, dump, showers, playground, store. Hiking, boating(l), fishing. On site of former Indian village at Allegheny River. GPS: 41.8397, -79.2564

Hearts Content Recreation Area $12
Allegheny National Forest
11 mi S of Warren on Pleasant Dr; 4 mi SE on gravel rd. $12 ($6 with federal senior pass). 5/1-10/1; 14-day limit; no winter maintenance. 26 sites (40-ft RV limit). Tbls, toilets, cfga, drkg wtr, dump, playground. Hunting, fishing, hiking. 16 acres. GPS: 41.692627, -79.25415

WIND RIDGE (32)

Ryerson Station State Park $10.50
1.5 mi S of Wind Ridge off SR 21. $10.50 for PA seniors at rustic sites on weekends; $12.50 for non-resident seniors; others pay $15 & $17. All year; 14-day limit. 46 rustic sites, 22 with elec. Tbls, pit toilets, cfga, drkg wtr, dump, no showers, pool. Swimming, boating(lr), fishing, hiking trails, snowmobiling. 1,164 acres. GPS: 39.8820223, -80.4442381

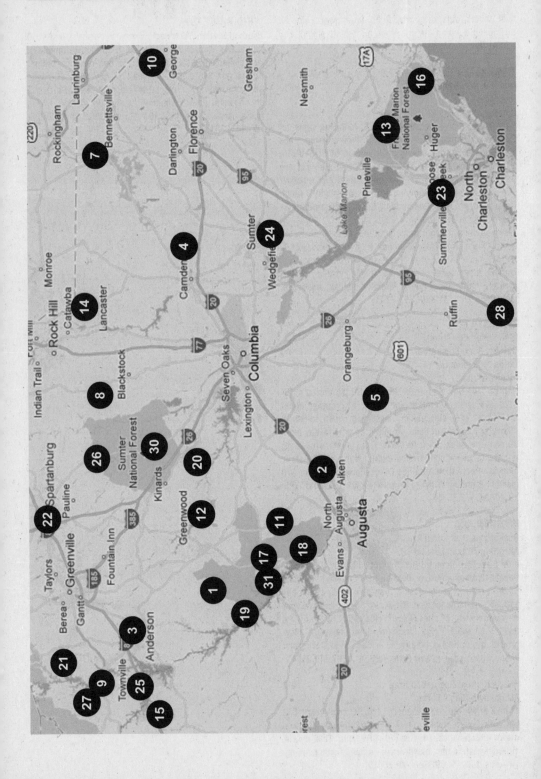

WWW.DISCOVERSOUTHCAROLINA.COM

Department of Parks, Recreation and Tourism, 1205 Pendleton St., Columbia, SC 29201; 803 734-1700.

Forestry Commission, PO Box 21707, Columbia, SC 29221.

Dept of Wildlife and Marine Resources, PO Box 167, Columbia, SC 29202; 803-734-3886.

REST AREAS
Overnight stops are not permitted.

STATE PARKS
Most base camping fees with electric and water hookups are $16-$21, but at some others, fees range from $18 to $22. South Carolina seniors receive 35% discounts on camping fees, and the parks where fees are $12 or less after those discounts are listed here. State Parks Division, 1205 Pendleton St., Columbia, SC 29201; 803-734-1700.

SUMTER NATIONAL FOREST
Most formerly free campgrounds are now considered to be "seasonal camps" and have fees of $5 per night, $50 per month or $150 per season. National Forest Service, 4931 Broad River Rd, Columbia, SC 29212. 803-561-4000.

ARMY CORPS OF ENGINEERS
Campgrounds are managed by two impoundments in South Carolina -- the 56,000-acre Hartwell Lake and 70,000-acre J. Strom Thurmond Lake (once known as Clark Hill).

Management of five Thurmond campgrounds was scheduled to be turned over to the non-profit Lake Thurmond Campgrounds agency for five years, but in 2013 that agreement was terminated because the Corps learned it did not have authority to make it. The agreement included Petersburg, Ridge Road, Raysville and Winfield Campgrounds in Georgia and Modoc Campground in South Carolina. Later in 2013, the Corps announced it would close Leroys Ferry and Mt. Carmel Campgrounds in South Carolina for the 2014 camping season as well as Raysville, Broad River, Clay Hill and Hesters Ferry Campgrounds in Georgia. Check current status of those facilities with the lake office before arrival. Resource Manager, J. Stom Thurmond Lake, Rt. 1, Box 12, Clarks Hill, SC 29821-9701. 864-333-1100/800-533-3478.

CAPITAL: Columbia
NICKNAME: Palmetto State
STATEHOOD: 1788 – 8th State
FLOWER: Carolina Yellow Jessamine
TREE: Palmetto
BIRD: Carolina Wre

ABBEVILLE (1)

Fell Hunt Camp $5
Sumter National Forest
8 mi SE of Abbeville on SC 33; 1.5 mi SE on SC 47. $5 daily, $50 monthly or $150 seasonal forest pass (9/14-1/4). All year; 14-day limit. 66 sites (RVs under 32 ft). Toilets, cfga, firewood, no drkg wtr, no tbls. Berry picking, hunting, fishing (3 mi). 40 acres. Non-campers pay $3 day use fee. GPS: 34.092041, -82.288574

Parsons Mountain Recreation Area $7
Sumter National Forest
2.2 mi SW of Abbeville on SR 72; 2 mi S on SR 28; 1.3 mi SE on SR 251; .7 mi S on FR 514. $7. 5/1-11/15; 14-day limit. 23 sites; no RV size limit. Tbls, flush toilets, cfga, drkg wtr, showers, dump. Hiking, fishing, hunting, swimming, boating (elec mtrs). 28-acre lake. Non-campers pay $3 day use fee. GPS: 34.101074, -82.356445

AIKEN (2)

Aiken State Park $9.10
16 mi E of Aiken between US 78 & SR 215. $9.10 for SC seniors in-season; others pay $14. All year; 14-day limit. 25 elec/wtr sites; 35-ft RV limit most sites. Tbls, flush toilets, cfga, drkg wtr, showers, dump, elec, playground. Boating(r), fishing, nature trails, swimming, fishing piers, canoeing(r). GPS: 33.5507016, -81.4903834

ANDERSON (3)

Sadlers Creek State Park $9.75
10 mi SE of Anderson on US 29; 1 mi N on SR 187; 1 mi W on access rd; at Lake Hartwell. $9.75 base for SC seniors in-season at 52 elec/wtr RV sites; others pay $15 base. 40-ft RV limit. All year; 14-day limit. Tbls, flush toilets, cfga, drkg wtr, showers, dump. Boating(l), fishing, swimming, nature trails. GPS: 34.4251043, -82.8276392

BISHOPVILLE (4)

Lee State Park $9.75
3 mi NE of Bishopville on US 15; 4 mi S at signs. $9.75 base for SC seniors in-season; others pay $15 base. All year; 14-day limit. 25 elec/wtr sites; 36-ft RV limit. Tbls, flush toilets, cfga, wtr/elec, dump, playground. Nature trails, swimming, fishing, pedalboats(r), horseback riding (bridle trails & stable). GPS: 34.2057105, -80.1967376

BLACKVILLE (5)

Barnwell State Park $9.10
3 mi SW of Blackville on SR 3. $9.10 for SC seniors at elec/wtr sites; others pay $14; $10.40 for SC seniors at 50-amp full-hookup sites; others pay $16. All year; 14-day limit. 17 elec/wtr sites, 8 full hookups; 36-ft RV limits. Tbls, flush toilets, cfga, showers, playground, dump. Swimming, nature trails, fishing, boating(r), pedalboats(r). 307 acres. Park was built by CCC in 1930s. GPS: 33.32944, -81.30278

CARLISLE

Herbert Campground $5
Sumter National Forest
1.3 mi E of Carlisle on SR 7; qtr mi SW on FR 404. $5 daily, $50 monthly or $150 seasonal pass (9/14-1/4); 14-day limit. 16 sites; 16-ft RV limit. Pit toilets, drkg wtr. Hunting. GPS: 34.5734728, -81.4589884

CHERAW (7)

Cheraw State Park $11.05
4 mi S of Cheraw on US 52; at Lake Juniper. $11.05 in-season for SC seniors at 17 elec/wtr sites; others pay $17. 40-ft RV limit. Tbls, flush toilets, showers, cfga, drkg wtr, dump. Boating(l), fishing, bridle & hiking trails, golf. GPS: 34.6284896, -79.9292314

CHESTER (8)

Chester State Park $9.10
3 mi SE of Chester on SR 72. $9.10 in-season for SC seniors at 25 elec/wtr sites; others pay $14. All year; 14-day limit. 33-ft RV limits; 5 pull-through sites. Tbls, flush toilets, cfga, drkg wtr, showers, dump, playground. Fishing, boating(r), nature trails, archery. 523 acres with 160-acre lake. Built by CCC in 1930s. GPS: 34.6776393, -81.2400907

Woods Ferry Recreation Area $7
Sumter National Forest
12 mi SW of Chester on SR 72; 2 mi N on SR 25; 3.5 mi N on SR 49; 3.5 mi NW on SR 574. $7. 4/1-10/31; 14-day limit. 23 sites up to 49 ft. Tbls, toilets, cfga, drkg wtr, showers, 7 sites with horse stalls. 2 group sites. Boating(l), fishing, waterskiing, nature trails, bridle trails. Broad River unsafe for swimming. GPS: 34.7006923, -81.4506528

CLEMSON (9)

Twin Lakes Campground $12
Hartwell Lake
Corps of Engineers
5.5 mi SE of Clemson on US 76; 3 mi SW on CR 56, following signs; at N end of lake. $12 base with federal senior pass at 30-amp elec/wtr sites; others pay $24 base, $26 for 50-amp elec ($13 with senior pass). 4/1-11/30; 14-day limit. Some sites open all year. 102 elec sites (89 waterfront); 60-ft RV limit. Drkg wtr, flush toilets, cfga, hookups, showers, beach, playground, dump. Fishing, boating(l). GPS: 34.62806, -82.86556

DILLON (10)

Little Pee Dee State Park $10.40
12 mi SE of Dillon between SRs 9 & 57. $10.40 in-season for SC seniors at 32 elec/wtr sites; others pay $16. All year; 14-day limit. Tbls, flush toilets, cfga, drkg wtr, showers, elec & wtr, dump, playground. Swimming, nature trails, boating(r). 835 acres with 54-acre Lake Norton. GPS: 34.3287722, -79.2692113

EDGEFIELD (11)

Lick Fork Recreation Area $7
Sumter National Forest
8.3 mi W of Edgefield on SR 23; qtr mi S on SR 230. $7.
5/1-11/15; 14-day limit. 9 sites plus walk-in tenting; no
RV size limit. Tbls, flush toilets, cfga, drkg wtr, showers,
dump. Boating(l), fishing, hiking, canoeing, hunting, biking, swimming. Non-campers pay $3 day use fee. GPS:
33.73062, -82.0401

GREENWOOD (12)

Lake Greenwood State Park $11.70
17 mi E of Greenwood on SR 702. $11.70 base in-season
for SC seniors at 125 elec/wtr sites; others pay $18 base.
All year; 14-day limit. 40-ft RV limit. All year; 14-day
limit. Playground, store, fishing, hiking. 914 acres with
212 mi of shoreline. Built 1938 by CCC. GPS: 34.1945733,
-81.9506714

Midway Seasonal Camp
Sumter National Forest
6.8 mi W of Greenwood on SR 72; 0.5 mi S on co rd. $5
daily, $50 monthly or $150 seasonally (9/14-1/4). 14-day
limit. 10 sites; 32-ft RV limit. Well drkg wtr, toilets, no tbls.
Hiking, hunting.

LANCASTER (14)

Andrew Jackson State Park $11.70
8 mi from Lancaster on US 521. $11.70 in-season for SC
seniors at RV sites with elec/wtr sites; others pay $18.
All year; 14-day limit. 25 sites; 36-ft limit; 5 pull-through
sites. Tbls, flush toilets, cfga, showers, dump, playground.
Nature trail, fishing, boating(r), nature programs, museum. 360 acres. GPS: 34.839592, -80.80507

LAVONIA, (GEORGIA) (15)

Lake Hartwell State Park $10.40
From I-85's Lavonia exit, 6 mi N on SR 11. $10.40 base
in-season for elec/wtr sites; others pay $16 base. All year;
14-day limit. 115 paved RV sites; 40-ft RV limit. Tbls, flush
toilets, cfga, drkg wtr, showers, dump, coin laundry, store.
Boating(l), fishing, hiking, nature programs. 14 mi of lake
shoreline. GPS: 34.500026, -83.040165

MCCORMICK (17)

Hawe Creek $12
Corps of Engineers
J. Strom Thurmond Lake
From US 221 in McCormick, half mi SW on US 378, past jct
with SR 439, then 4 mi S on Chamberlains Ferry Rd. $12
with federal senior pass at 30-amp elec/wtr sites (others
pay $20); $13 with senior pass at 50-amp elec/wtr sites
(others pay $26). 4/1-9/30; 14-day limit. 45-ft RV limit; 6
pull-through sites. Flush toilets, cfga, drkg wtr, hookups
at all sites, showers, dump, tbls. Golf, boating(l), fishing.
GPS: 33.8361, -82.3386

Morrows Bridge Seasonal Camp $5
Sumter National Forest
2.3 mi NW of McCormick on SC 28; .8 mi SW on CR 39.
$5 daily, $50 monthly or $150 seasonal forest pass
(9/14-1/4); 14 day limit. 11 sites (RVs under 32 ft); toilets,
firewood, well drkg wtr, no tbls.

MODOC (18)

Modoc Campground $9
Corps of Engineers
J. Strom Thurmond Lake
1 mi S of Modoc on US 221, then E following signs. $9 with
federal senior pass at 1 non-elec site; others pay $18. At
69 wtr/elec sites, most 30/50-amp, $11 base with senior
pass; others pay $22 base, $26 at premium locations ($13
with senior pass). 4/1-11/30; 14-day limit 69 sites; 45-ft
RV limit; 29 pull-through sites. Tbls, flush toilets, cfga,
drkg wtr, showers, dump, playground, picnic shelter. Fishing, boating(l), hiking. GPS: 33.71917, -82.22417

MOUNT CARMEL (19)

Mount Carmel Campground $9
Corps of Engineers
J. Strom Thurmond Lake
About 0.5 mi SW of Mount Carmel on SR S-33-331; continue SW on SR S-33-91, SR S-33-333 & SR S-33-337
to park. $9 with federal senior pass at 5 non-elec sites;
others pay $18. At 39 elec/wtr 30/50-amp sites, $12 base
with senior pass; others pay $24 base, $26 at premium
locations ($13 with senior pass). 4/1-9/6; 14-day limit.
40-ft RV limit; 12 pull-through sites. Shelter, fish cleaning
station, tbls, flush toilets, cfga, drkg wtr, showers, dump,
playground. Fishing, boating (dl). Note: This campground
was closed for 2014 season (boat ramp open) due to
budget cuts. See explanation under "Corps of Engineers"
heading at beginning this chapter; check current status
with lake office before arrival GPS: 33.95833, -82.53944

NEWBERRY (20)

Rocky Branch Seasonal Camp $5
Sumter National Forest
18 mi NW of Newberry on SR 34; 2 mi N on FR 412. $5
daily, $50 monthly or $150 seasonal forest pass. 10/1-
3/1; 14-day limit. 10 sites (22-ft RV limit). Drkg wtr,
toilets, cfga, no tbls. Berry picking, hunting. 2 acres. GPS:
33.5223, -84.1046

PICKENS (21)

Keowee-Toxaway State Park $10.40
18 mi NW of Pickens off SR 11 at Lake Keowee. $10.40
in-season for SC seniors at elec/wtr RV sites; others
pay $16. All year; 14-day limit. 10 sites; 40-ft RV limit.
Tbls, toilets, cfga, drkg wtr, dump. Fishing, hiking &
nature trails, museum. 1,000 acres. GPS: 34.9298248,
-82.8840312

Table Rock State Park $11.70
12 mi N of Pickens on SR 11. $11.70 base in-season for SC
seniors at elec/wtr RV sites; others pay $18 base. All year;
14-day limit. 94 RV sites; 35-ft RV limit. Tbls, flush toilets,
cfga, drkg wtr. Fishing, hiking. 3,083 acres. Park built by
CCC in 1930s. GPS: 35.0370627, -82.7073531

SPARTANBURG (22)
Croft State Park $9.10
3 mi SE of Spartanburg off SR 56. $9.10 in-season for
SC seniors at wtr/elec RV sites; others pay $14. All year;
14-day limit. 25 RV sites with 30/50-amp elec; 40-ft RV
limits. Tbls, flush toilets, cfga, showers, dump, playground, pool, equestrian facilities. Tennis, swimming,
nature trails, fishing, boating(rl), horseback riding. Former
World War II training camp. 7,054 acres. GPS: 34.875961,
-81.8373239

SUMMERVILLE (23)
Givhans Ferry State Park $9.10
16 mi W of Summerville on SR 61. $9.10 in-season for
SC seniors at wtr/elec RV sites; others pay $14. All year;
14-day limit. 25 sites; 40-ft RV limit. Tbls, flush toilets,
cfga, showers, dump, playground. Nature trails, fishing,
boating, canoeing. Park built by CCC in 1930s. On Edisto
River Canoe & Kayak Trail. GPS: 33.0318353, -80.3875986

SUMTER (24)
Poinsett State Park $11.70
18 mi SW of Sumter on SR 763; 2 mi W; on Wateree
Swamp. $11.70 in-season for SC seniors at elec/wtr RV
sites; others pay $18. All year; 14-day limit. 24 RV sites;
40-ft RV limit. Tbls, flush toilets, cfga, elec/wtr, showers, dump, playground. Nature & recreation programs,
hiking, fishing, boating(r). CCC built park in 1930s. GPS:
33.8079356, -80.5392521

TOWNVILLE (25)
Coneross Campground $7
Corps of Engineers
Hartwell Lake
1.4 mi N of Townville on SR 24; right (E) on Coneross
Creek Rd, following signs; at Senaca River arm of lake.
$7 base with federal senior pass at 12 primitive sites;
others pay $14 base, $18 at premium locations. At 94 wtr/
elec 30/50-amp sites, $10 base with senior pass; others
pay $20 base, $24 at premium locations ($12 with senior
pass). 5/1-9/30; 14-day limit. 104 sites; RV limit in excess
of 65 ft; 36 pull-through, 1 handicap. Tbls, flush toilets,
cfga, drkg wtr, showers, dump, beach, playground, fishing
pier. Boating(ld), fishing, swimming. Nearby Oconee Point
Campground has 70 elec sites for $26; Springfield Camp-
ground's lowest fees are now $26. See our "Camping With
the Corps of Engineers" book. GPS: 34.59111, -82-89722

UNION (26)
Sedalia Hunt Camp $5
Sumter National Forest
8 mi SW of Union on SC 49; 1.9 mi SE on SR 481; quarter
mi NE on co rd. $5 daily, $50 monthly or $150 seasonal
forest pass (10/1-1/4). 13 sites; 16-ft RV limit. All year;
14-day limit Toilets, well drkg wtr, no tbls. Store, ice, gas
(2 mi). Hunting; hiking; fishing (2 mi). Elev 600 ft; 8 acres;
primitive hunt camp. GPS: 34.631524, -81.6289907

WALHALLA (27)
Cherry Hill Recreation Area $10
Sumter National Forest
8 mi NW of Walhalla on SR 28; 8 mi N on SR 107. $10. 4/1-
10/31; 14-day limit. 29 sites up to 42 ft. Tbls, flush toilets,
cfga, showers, drkg wtr, dump. Hiking, nature programs.
GPS: 34.946045, -83.084961

Oconee State Park $10.40
12 mi NW of Walhalla on SR 107. $10.40 base in-season for
SC seniors at wtr/elec RV sites; others pay $16 base. All
year; 14-day limit. 140 RV sites; 35-ft RV limit. Coin laundry, flush toilets, showers, drkg wtr, store, playground.
Museum, summer rec program, canoeing(r), hiking, boat-
ing(r), pedalboats(r), carpet golf, archery. 1,165 acres,
developed in 1935 by CCC. GPS: 34.867592, -83.1026521

Whetstone Horse Camp $12
Sumter National Forest
4.9 mi W of Walhalla on SR 28; 4.9 mi S on SR 193, past
4-way stop & onto Earls Ford Rd for 2.7 mi; left at campground sign. $12. All year; 14-day limit. 19 sites up to 63
ft Tbls, toilets, cfga, drkg wtr. Bridle & hiking trails. GPS:
34.88944, -83.25306

WALTERBORO (28)
Colleton State Park $9.75
12 mi N of Walterboro on US 15; on Edisto River. $9.75
in-season for SC seniors at elec/wtr RV sites; others pay
$15. All year; 14-day limit. 25 sites; 40-ft RV limit. Tbls,
flush toilets, cfga, elec/wtr, showers, dump. Hiking, fishing, canoeing, kayaking. 35-acre park built in 1930s by
CCC. GPS: 33.0637765, -80.615655.

WESTMINSTER
Woodall Shoals Dispersed Area   FREE
Sumter National Forest
18 mi NW of Westminster on US 76; W on Orchard Rd, then
right on Woodall Shoals Rd. All year; 14-day limit. Primitive
open sites near Chattooga River. Some tbls, cfga, no drkg
wtr or toilets. Fishing, swimming, whitewater rafting. GPS:
34.7984, -83.3127

WHITMIRE (30)

Brick House Campground $5
Sumter National Forest
6.2 mi SW of Whitmire on SR 66; .3 mi S on FR 358. $5 daily, 50 monthly or $150 seasonal forest pass (Sept-Dec). Open all year; 14-day limit. 23 sites up to 49 ft. Tbls, toilets, cfga, drkg wtr. Some sites have hitching stalls. Picnicking, hiking, hunting, boating, OHV trail, bridle trail. GPS: 34.446289, -81.707031

Collins Creek Hunt Camp $5
Sumter National Forest
3.2 mi NE of Whitmire on Hwy 121; 4.2 mi SE on Hwy 45; half mi SW on FR 393. $5 daily, $50 monthly or $150 seasonal forest pass (10/1-1/4); 14-day limit. 40 sites (22-ft RV limit). Toilets, drkg wtr, cfga, no tbls. Hunting, hiking. 8 acres. GPS: 34.4726402, -81.5253806

WILLINGTON (31)

Leroys Ferry Recreation Area $6
J. Strom Thurmond Lake
Corps of Engineers
2 mi SW of Willington on SR S-33-135, following signs; 2 mi S on Leroys Ferry Rd. $6 paid on honor system. All year; 14-day limit. About 10 sites. Tbls, toilets, cfga, drkg wtr. Boating(l), fishing, swimming. Note: This campground was closed for 2014 season due to budget cuts (boat ramp open). See details under "Corps of Engineers" heading at beginning of this chapter. Check current status with lake office before arrival. GPS: 33.921143, -82.489746

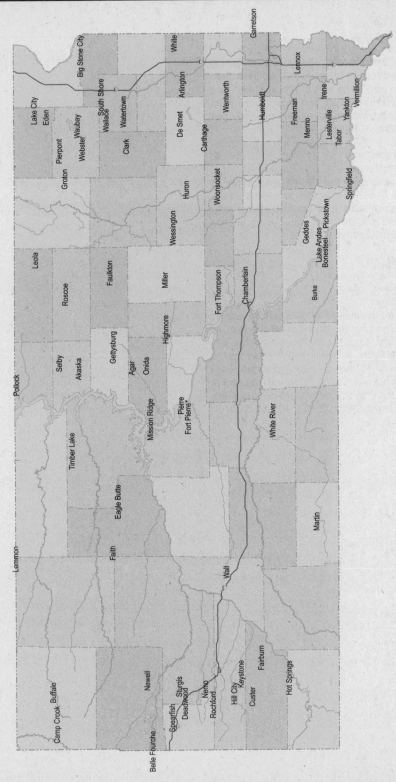

SOUTH DAKOTA

WWW.TRAVELSD.COM

Toll-free number for travel information: 1-800-S-DA-KOTA.

Dept of Tourism, Capitol Lake Plaza, Pierre, SD 57501-5070; 605-773-3301. E-mail: SDINFO@state.sd.us

Division of Parks and Recreation, 523 East Capitol, Pierre, SD 57501; 605-773-3391. Reservations, 800-710-2267 or www.campsd.com.

REST AREAS
Overnight stops are not permitted.

STATE PARKS
Overnight are $13 to $19 at most state parks for basic campsites, and most parks no longer qualify to be included in this guidebook. Some camping fees are reduced when water systems and comfort stations are winterized; self-registration may be required at such times. Pets on leashes are permitted. Fees listed here do not include entry fees. For further information contact Dept of Game, Fish & Parks, 523 E. Capitol, Pierre, SD 57501; 605-773-3391.

LAKESIDE USE AREAS
Approximately 40 state-operated LUAs provide easy access to lakes and rivers. Nearly all have boat ramps & docking facilities, and most offer picnicking and primitive camping facilities. Camping is free at some sites, but basic camping fees, and in some cases entry fees, are charged at many of them. At about a dozen LUAs, both $11 camping fees and state park permits are required, and at some, just the $6 entry permits are necessary.

BLACK HILLS NATIONAL FOREST
Camping is permitted throughout the national forest outside of developed campgrounds, except at signed locations around Pactola, Sheridan, Roubaix, Bismark and Deerfield Lakes. Open fires are not permitted in the South Dakota portion of the forest. Fires must be built in grates in campgrounds and picnic area; or built safely in a stove, charcoal grill or other similar container. At forest service-operated campgrounds, fees are charged from the end of May through about Labor Day. During the off-season, fees are not collected at most of those camps, but drinking water is shut off and trash pickup is not provided; pack out your own trash. No free off-season periods are offered at the campgrounds operated by concessionaires.

CAPITAL: Pierre
NICKNAME: Mt. Rushmore State
STATEHOOD: 1889 – 40th State
FLOWER: American Pasqueflower
TREE: Black Hills Spruce
BIRD: Ring-Necked Pheasant

AGAR

Sutton Bay Lakeside Use Area   FREE
12 mi W and 4 mi NW of Agar on SR 1804. Free. All year. Primitive undesignated sites. Pit toilet, tbls, shelters, cfga, no drkg wtr. Picnicking, boating(l), fishing. 18 acres. Former Corps of Engineers facility.

AKASKA

LeBeau Lakeside Use Area   FREE
4 mi S of Akaska on 303rd Ave; 7 mi W on 146th St to E shore of Lake Oahe. Free. All year; 5-day limit. Primitive camping. Toilets, cfga, no drkg wtr. Fishing.

Walth Bay Lakeside Use Area $11
1 mi W of Akaska on Swan Creek Rd; 3 mi N on 303rd Ave; 2.5 mi W on 139th St; 4 mi N on 300th Ave; 4 mi W on SR 1804; 1.5 mi S on 294th Ave; on E shore of Lake Oahe. $11. 15 primitive sites. Non-campers pay $6 daily entry fee (or $30 annually). Cfga, toilets, no drkg wtr. Boating(l), fishing.

ARLINGTON

Maxwell Park   FREE
From US 81, NW 4 blocks on US 14 (Elm St); right (N) on Main St to dirt access rd into park, then left at park entrance to sites. Free without hookups; $10 with elec (pay at city hall). 5/30-9/14. 12 sites, 4 with 50-amp elec. Flush toilets, tbls, firewood, wtr/elect hookups, dump (W of laundromat). Noisy from traffic, freight trains.

Nordland City Park   FREE
At lake, jct of US 81 & US 14 in Arlington. Free without hookups, $10 with 30/50-amp elec. 5/30-9/14. Flush toilets, tbls, cfga, drkg wtr.

BELLE FOURCHE

Bearlodge Campground $7
Black Hills National Forest
W of Belle Fourche on SR 34, connecting to Wyoming SR 24; between Aladdin & Hulett, WY. $7 with federal senior pass; others pay $14. All year; 10-day limit. 8 sites; 25-ft RV limit. Tbls, toilet, cfga, no drkg wtr. Fishing, hiking.

BIG STONE CITY

Rearing Ponds Water Access Site   FREE
4 mi N of Big Stone City off SR 109. Free. All year. Primitive camping. Toilets, cfga, no drkg wtr. Boating(l), fishing.

BONESTEEL

South Scalp Creek Lakeside Use Area $11
4 mi S of Bonesteel on US 18; 11 mi NE on gravel rd. $11. All year; 14-day limit. Primitive sites (RVs under 26 ft). Tbls, cfga, drkg wtr, shelters. Boating(l); picnicking, fishing. Fish cleaning table. Former Corps of Engineers campground.

Whetstone Bay Lakeside Use Area $11
7 mi NE of Bonesteel on SR 1806; 1.7 mi E on access rd at Lake Francis Case. $11. Non-campers pay $6 day use fee or $30 annual entry pass. All year; 14-day limit. 30 primitive sites; 25-ft RV limit. Toilets, drkg wtr, cfga. Boating(l), fishing. Fish cleaning table. Formerly free Corps of Engineers park.

BUFFALO

Picnic Springs   FREE
Custer National Forest
26 mi NE of Buffalo on US 85; 4.2 mi W on CR 7330; 2 mi S on co rd; 1.6 mi W on FR 114. Free. 5/1-11/15; 10-day limit. 15 sites (RVs under 31 ft); tbls, toilets, cfga, firewood, piped drkg wtr. Picnicking, hiking. Elev 3300 ft; 3 acres. Campground in the scenic north cave hills. Eagles, falcons, hawks in rimrocks.

Reva Gap   FREE
Custer National Forest
1 mi S of Buffalo on US 85; 19 mi E on SD 20. Free. 5/1-11/15; 14-day limit. 8 sites (RVs under 30 ft); tbls, toilet, cfga, firewood, drkg wtr. Store/gas (4 mi). Picnicking. Elev 3600 ft; 13 acres. Colorful castle rock formations nearby.

BURKE

Burke City Park $10
From N of the SR 47 & US 18 jct in Burke, 3 blocks N on CR 23 following City Park sign; entrances on CR 23 & 7th St.. $10. All year, 7-day limit. 5 RV sites with 30-amp elec/wtr; 40-ft RV limit; back-in sites. Tbls, flush toilets, showers, playground. Elec, wtr, sewer hookups. Dump at convenience store. Horseback riding; picnicking; swimming, fishing, golf nearby. Lake.

Burke Lake State Recreation Area $11
2 mi E of Burke off US 18. $11. All year; 14-day limit. 15 basic sites. Tbls, pit toilets, cfga, drkg wtr, playground, beach; no hookups, no dump. Limited facilities in winter. Picnicking, fishing, swimming, boating(l), hiking, canoeing. 25-acre lake.

CAMP CROOK

Lantis Spring Campground   FREE
Custer National Forest
3 mi W of Camp Crook, on gravel SR 20 extension (SE of Ekalaka, Montana); 2.8 mi N on Capitol Rock Rd; 1.7 mi E on CR 3049; right at fork for 1.2 mi. In Montana. Free. 5/15-9/30; 14-day limit. 5 undesignated sites (RVs under 30 ft). Tbls, toilet, cfga, drkg wtr. Hiking.

Wickham Gulch Campground   FREE
Custer National Forest
3 mi W of Camp Crook on SR 20 gravel extension; 3 mi N on Capitol Rock Rd (CR 3049); 1.5 mi on CR 3060; in Montana. Free. 5/15-9/30; 14-day limit. 2 primitive sites; 16-ft RV limit. Tbls, toilet, cfga, drkg wtr, no trash service. Hunting, hiking, mountain biking. Near Capitol Rock National Natural Area.

CARTHAGE
Lake Carthage Lakeside Use Area $11
Half mi NE of Carthage on NE side of lake. $11 for primitive sites; $15 for 13 sites with elec. Tbls, toilets, cfga, shelters, drkg wtr, beach. Swimming, picnicking, fishing, boating(ld), playground, waterskiing.

CHAMBERLAIN
Elm Creek Lakeside Use Area   FREE
From Chamberlain, I-90, exit 265, 18 mi S of Chamberlain; at Lake Francis Case. Free. 21 primitive sites. May-Oct; 14-day limit. Toilets, cfga, no drkg wtr. Boating(l), fishing. This park was a Corps of Engineers facility; now managed by the state.

CLARK
Bailey Lake Lakeside Use Area   FREE
From jct with US 212 W of Clark, 9 mi N on CR 2; 2 mi E on CR 22; half mi S on CR 55. Free. All year. Free primitive camping. Tbls, toilets, cfga, no drkg wtr. Picnicking, boating, fishing.

CUSTER
Comanche Park Campground $8
Black Hills National Forest
5.2 mi W of Custer on US 16; left at sign. $8 with federal senior pass; others pay $16. About 5/15-9/15; 14-day limit. 34 sites; no RV size limit. Tbls, pit toilets, cfga, drkg wtr.

DEADWOOD
Roubaix Lake Campground $9.50
Black Hills National Forest
13.5 mi S of Deadwood on US 385; right at sign for 0.5 mi. $9.50 with federal senior pass; others pay $19. All year; 14-day limit. 56 sites (13 open through winter), typically 55 ft. Tbls, flush toilets, cfga, drkg wtr. Fishing, swimming.

DE SMET
Washington City Park $8
Third St & Harvey Dunn Ave in DeSmet. $8 base; $9 with elec. 40 sites. Tbls, flush toilets, showers, cfga, drkg wtr, elec($), showers. Sand volleyball, horseshoes, 9-hole golf, playground; Father DeSmet Memorial. Patrolled. 605/854-3731. Reservations okay.

EAGLE BUTTE
Foster Bay Lakeside Use Area   FREE
3 mi W of Eagle Butte on US 212; 22 mi S on SD 63; at Lake Oahe. Free. All year; 14-day limit. 20 primitive sites (RVs under 30 ft); tbls, no toilets, cfga, drkg wtr. Picnicking, fishing, swimming, boating(l). Former Corps of Engineers park; now managed by the state.

EDEN
Buffalo South Lakeside Use Area   FREE
6.5 mi E of Eden on 122nd St; half mi S to Buffalo Lakes.
Free. All year. Primitive camping. Toilets, cfga, no drkg wtr. Boating(ld), fishing.

FAIRBURN
French Creek Camp   FREE
Buffalo Gap National Grasslands
10.5 mi E of Fairburn on US 79. Free. 5/30-9/15. 8 primitive sites. Tbls, toilet, cfga, no drkg wtr. Picnicking.

FAITH
Durkee Lake City Park $10
3 mi S of Faith on SD 73. Free. All year. 50 sites, some elec. Tbls, toilets, cfga, dump, firewood, drkg wtr. Swimming, picnicking, fishing, boating(l); golf nearby. Lake.

Faith City Park $10
On Main St in Faith. $10. All year. 12 sites with shared elec/wtr; 38-ft RV limit. Tbls, flush toilets, cfga, drkg wtr, elec, dump, playground.

FAULKTON
Lake Faulkton Lakeside Use Area   FREE
2.5 mi W of Faulkton on US 212; half mi S. Free. All year; 5-day limit. 4 undeveloped campsites, but camping is allowed. Toilets, cfga, drkg wtr, shelters, playground, dump, covered picnic tbls. Picnicking, fishing, boating(ld).

FORT PIERRE
Fischer's Lilly City Park $10
From SE 83, E on Cedar St; left on Casey Tibbs; right on Ash; on S side of Bad River. $10. May-Nov weather permitting; no stay limit. 12 RV sites with wtr/elec. Tbls, flush toilets, cfga, drkg wtr, no showers, basic dump (no flush water), playground, pool. This park was site of the Lewis & Clark expedition's first encounter with the Teton Sioux. Boating(l), fishing.

FORT THOMPSON
Left Tailrace Campground $7
Lake Sharpe
Corps of Engineers
From Fort Thompson, 3 mi S on SR 47; below dam on S side of spillway. May-Sept; 14-day limit. $7 with federal senior pass at primitive sites; others pay $14. $9 with senior pass at 81 elec sites; others pay $18. All year; 14-day limit. 81 elec sites; 35-ft RV limit. Tbls, flush toilets, cfga, drkg wtr, dump (half mi), playground, amphitheater, fish cleaning station, fishing pier, coin laundry, showers. Boating(l), fishing, swimming, basketball. Note: Campground re-opened in 2013 after being closed in 2011 by flooding.

Old Fort Thompson   FREE
Lake Sharpe
Corps of Engineers
1 mi SW of Fort Thompson on SR 47; at Old Fort Thompson

Rs below dam on E side of spillway. Free. All year; 14-day limit. 13 primitive sites. Pit toilets, showers, drkg wtr, tbls, playground, picnic shelter. Dump station half mi. Boating(l), fishing.

North Shore Recreation Area   FREE
Lake Sharpe
Corps of Engineers
From SW of Fort Thompson at jct with SR 47, 1.5 mi NW on BIA Rd 8, past the project office. Free. All year; 14-day limit. 24 primitive sites. Pit toilets, tbls, cfga, drkg wtr, playground, shelter, fish cleaning station, beach. Dump 1 mi. Boating(l), fishing, swimming, basketball.

FREEMAN
Freeman City Park $10
From US 81, exit W on N. County Rd or 278th St about qtr mi W to Wipf St, then S 1 block on Parkway St. $10. 7 sites. Tbls, toilets, cfga, drkg wtr, showers, shelters, tennis, pool.

GARRETSON
Split Rock City Park $10
NW end of Garretson on SR 11; along Split Rock River. $10 at 16 primitive sites (9 tent only); $16 at 11 elec RV sites. WPA-built park. Tbls, toilets, cfga, drkg wtr, playground. Dump nearby. Canoeing, fishing, volleyball, boating(l).

GEDDES
North Wheeler State Recreation Area $11
7 mi W of Geddes on paved rd; 8 mi S on gravel rd to Lake Francis Case. $11 for basic sites; $15 with elec. 25 elec sites; 25-ft RV limit. Pit toilets, cfga, drkg wtr, tbls, fish cleaning station. Fishing, boating(l). Formerly a Corps of Engineers park; now managed by the state.

GETTYSBURG
Gettysburg City Park   FREE
On Main St, 5 blocks S of SD 212 in Gettysburg. Free; donations accepted. 5/1-10/31; 3-day limit. 15 sites; tbls, flush toilets, cfga, showers, drkg wtr, 6 elec hookups. Store, food, dump nearby. Swimming, picnicking, golf nearby.

Dodge Draw Lakeside Use Area   FREE
5 mi W of Gettysburg on US 212; 9 mi N on US 83; 10 mi NW off US 83. Free. All year. Primitive undesignated sites. Toilets, cfga, no drkg wtr. Boating(l), fishing. 25 acres.

East Whitlock Lakeside Use Area $10
12 mi W & 3 mi N of Gettysburg on Old US 212. $10. All year; 7-day limit. Primitive camping; undesignated sites. Toilets, cfga, drkg wtr. Boating (ld), fishing. Self-registration. Non-campers pay $6 day use fee or $30 annually.

Forest City Lakeside Usa Area   FREE
19 mi W of Gettysburg on US 212, on W side of Lake Oahe. Free. All year; 14-day limit. 7 primitive undesignated sites (RVs under 30 ft); tbls, toilets, cfga, firewood, no drkg wtr. Picnicking, fishing, boating(ld).

GROTON
Amsden Dam Lakeside Use Area $11
6 mi E of Groton on US 12; 5.5 mi S; 1 mi E to campground. $11. All year; 5-day limit. 11 primitive sites. Tbls, toilets, cfga, drkg wtr. Swimming, picnicking, fishing, boating(l).

HIGHMORE
East City Park $8
In the center of Highmore off US 14. $8. 4/1-10/15. 10 sites, 6 with elec. Toilets, tbls, cfga, drkg wtr, playground.

HILL CITY
Custer Trail $8
Black Hills National Forest
12 mi NW of Hill City on CR 17 to NW shore of Deerfield Lake; right (S) on FR 417 to end. $8 with federal senior pass; others pay $16. MD-LD; 10-day limit; 16 sites, typically 50-ft. Tbls, toilets, cfga, drkg wtr. Fishing, boating(ld), swimming, hiking, bridle trail, mountain biking.

Ditch Creek Campground $10
Black Hills National Forest
12 mi NW of Hill City on CR 17; 7 mi W on CR 110; 4 mi S on FR 291. $10 with federal senior pass; others pay $10. All year; 10-day limit. 13 sites; 50-ft RV limit. Tbls, toilets, cfga, drkg wtr. Fishing, hiking, mountain biking.

Dutchman Campground $7.50
Black Hills National Forest
About 14 mi W of Hill City on CR 17; 2 mi S on FR 607; near Deerfield Reservoir. $10 with federal senior pass; others pay $20. All year; 14-day limit. Limited services after LD & before MD. 44 sites, typically 50 ft. Tbls, pit toilets, cfga, drkg wtr. Fishing, boating(l), hiking trails.

Oreville Campground $9.50
Black Hills National Forest
6 mi S of Hill city on US 385; left at sign. $10 with federal senior pass; others pay $20. About 5/20-9/15; 14-day limit. 26 sites, typically 65 ft. Tbls, flush toilets, cfga, drkg wtr.

Whitetail Campground $10
Black Hills National Forest
About 16 mi W of Hill City on CR 17; 1 mi N on FR 421; at Deerfield Reservoir. $10 with federal senior pass; others pay $20. All year; 14-day limit. Limited services after LD & before MD. 17 sites, typically 55 ft. Tbls, pit toilets, cfga, drkg wtr. Fishing, hiking trails.

HOT SPRINGS

Cold Brook Campground $10
Cold Brook Lake
Corps of Engineers
From Hot Springs, 0.5 mi N on Germond St. $10 ($5 with federal senior pass) during 5/15-9/15; free rest of year with reduced amenities. Group camping area. Picnic shelters, tbls, toilets, cfga, drkg wtr, beach, playground, fishing pier. Boating(l), fishing, hiking, swimming, archery range, basketball court.

Cottonwood Springs $10
Cottonwood Springs Lake
Corps of Engineers
From Hot Springs, 5 mi W on SR 18, then 2 mi N on CR 17. $10 ($5 with federal senior pass). 5/15-9/15; 14-day limit. 18 sites; 30-ft RV limit. Tbls, toilets, cfga, drkg wtr, playground. Boating(l), fishing, hiking.

Elk Mountain $9
Wind Cave National Park
10 mi N of Hot Springs on US 385. $9 with federal senior pass during 5/15-9/15 (others pay $18); $9 rest of year, but no wtr & reduced services ($4.50 with senior pass). 14-day limit (no RV size limit at Loop B). 75 sites; 25 pull-through. Tbls, flush toilets, cfga, drkg wtr, visitor center, no showers. No wtr during free period. Picnicking, hiking, nature trails, cave tours($), nature programs.

HUMBOLDT

Larry Pressler City Park   FREE
From I-90, exit 379, N 100 yds on Hwy 19, E on paved rd to water tower, 4 blks S. Free. Spring-fall. Primitive undesignated site at outer perimeter of park, flush toilets, tbls, cfga, pavilion, drkg wtr. Basketball hoop, tennis courts, playground, horseshoes.

HURON

James River Unit #1 Lakeside Use Area   FREE
14 mi N of Huron on SR 37; 1 mi W on CR 6; half mi N. Free. All year; 5-day limit. Undeveloped camping; 4 primitive sites. Tbls, cfga. Fishing, picnicking.

James River Unit #2 Lakeside Use Area   FREE
14 mi N of Huron on SR 37; 1 mi W on CR 6; half mi N. Free. All year; 5-day limit. Undeveloped camping; 4 primitive sites. Tbls, toilets, cfga. Fishing, boating(ld), picnicking.

Lake Byron Northwest Lakeside Use Area   FREE
15.5 mi N of Huron on SD 37, then E to lake. Free. All year; 5-day limit. All year; 5-day limit. Undeveloped camping. Tbls, toilets, cfga, drkg wtr. Fishing, boating(ld), swimming, picnicking.

Spink County Dam Lakeside Use Area   FREE
21 mi N of Huron on SR 37; 1 mi W. Free. All year; 5-day limit. Undeveloped camping; 4 sites. Tbls, toilets, cfga. Fishing, boating(ld), picnicking.

IRENE

Marindahl Lake Lakeside Use Area   FREE
4 mi W of Irene on SR 46; 3 mi S on 447th St; half mi W. All year. Free primitive camping. No facilities. Boating (l), fishing.

KEYSTONE

Hanna $9
Black Hills National Forest
8 mi SW of Keystone on US 85; 2.2 mi S on FR 17. $9 with federal senior pass; others pay $18. About 5/20-LD; 10-day limit. 13 sites, typically 55-ft. Tbls, toilets, cfga, drkg wtr. Elev 5600 ft; 3 acres. Near Spearfish Canyon.

LAKE ANDES

White Swan Lakeside Use Area $11
About 4 mi W of Lake Andes on SR 50; 6 mi S on 376th Ave to Lake Francis Case. $11. Primitive undesignated sites. May-Oct; 14-day limit. Toilets, tbls, cfga, no drkg wtr, shelters. Picnicking, boating (ld), fishing. Formerly a Corps of Engineers park, this facility now is operated by the state.

LAKE CITY

Clear Lake Lakeside Use Area   FREE
4 mi E of Lake City of SD 10. Free. All year; 5-day limit. No developed campsites, but camping is allowed. Tbls, toilets, cfga, no drkg wtr. Swimming, picnicking, fishing, boating(ld).

Four-Mile/Bullhead Water Access Area   FREE
2.5 mi W of Lake City on SR 10; 1 mi S on 438th Ave; half mi W on 115th St. All year. Free primitive camping. Toilets, cfga, no drkg wtr. Boating(l), fishing. Roy Lake.

LEMMON

Hugh Glass Lakeside Use Area   FREE
14 mi S of Lemmon on SR 73; 3 mi SW on winding secondary rd to site; opposite shore of Shadehill Reservoir from Shadyhill SRA, where sites are $16. Free. All year. 13 primitive sites. Tbls, toilets, cfga, no drkg wtr. Fishing, boating(l). 5,000-acre lake.

LEOLA

Lundquist Dam Campground   FREE
Leola City Park
From jct of SR 10 & SR 45 in Leola, half mi N on CR 19; at Lundquist Dam. Free first night; $7 daily thereafter. All year. 12 sites; limited elec hookups; tbls, portable toilets, cfga, well drkg wtr. Picnic shelter, boating(l), fishing. Flush toilets & showers planned.

LENNOX

Westerman City Park $11
From I-29 exit 64, W 4.5 mi on SR 44; 1 mi N on SR 17/44

(S. Pine St), then left (W) on SR 44, past Main St; right on Elm; 1 block N to Park Dr access. $11 or 7 consecutive nights for $66. Reservations accepted (605-647-2286). 5/1-9/30. 16 20/30-amp elec back-in sites. Tbls, flush toilets, cfga, drkg wtr, dump($), showers. Brochure online.

LESTERVILLE

Lesterville Lakeside Use Area   FREE
9.5 mi S of Lesterville on 430th Ave; 3.5 mi E on SR 52/ SR 50; from split of SR 52/50, 3.5 mi S on SR 52; abut 4 mi W on Gavins Point Rd; at Lewis & Clark Lake. All year. Free primitive camping. Tbls, toilets, cfga, no drkg wtr. Boating(l), fishing, picnicking.

MARTIN

Brooks Memorial Municipal Park   FREE
At 602 First Ave in Martin. Donations accepted; camp free. Primitive open sites. Tbls, flush toilets, cfga, drkg wtr, elec. Swimming, biking.

MENNO

Frederick P. Huber Memorial Campground   FREE
Lake Menno Recreation Area
1 mi W, 1.5 mi N & half mi W of Menno on lake built in 1995. Free, but $5 donation is suggested; 7-day limit. 9 sites. Elec, toilets, tbls, drkg wtr. Panfish fishing, boating at 40-acre lake. Boat ramp, picnic shelters.

Menno City Park $10
On Park St, S of US 18 on W side of town. $10 with elec/wtr at 4 RV sites with 20/30/50-amp, N end of park; 10-day limit. Tbls, toilets, cfga, drkg wtr, bathhouse new 2015. Picnic shelters. Dump at S end of Park St near football field.

MILLER

Crystal City Park   FREE
On 7th St W of SD 14 in Miller. Free, but donations accepted. 5/1-9/30; 3-day limit. RV sites with elec; tbls, flush toilets, cfga, drkg wtr, dump, playground. Picnicking. Tenters allowed in the more primitive area. 20 acres.

MISSION RIDGE

Minneconjou Park Lakeside Use Area   FREE
From Mission Ridge, NW on gravel 262nd Ave/Minneconjou Rd; at Lake Oahe. Free primitive undesignated sites. No toilets, cfga, no drkg wtr. Boating(l), fishing. Former Corps of Engineers Park; now managed by the state.

NEMO

Boxelder Forks Campground $9
Black Hills National Forest
About 1.5 mi W of Nemo on FR 140 (Boxelder Forks Rd). $9 with federal senior pass; others pay $18. All year; 14-day limit. 14 sites, typically 55 ft. Tbls, pit toilets, cfga, drkg wtr. Fishing, hiking trail.

Dalton Lake Campground $9
Black Hills National Forest
About 4 mi N of Nemo on FR 26; 5 mi E on FR 224. $9 with federal senior pass; others pay $18. 5/15-9/15; 14-day limit. 10 sites. Tbls, pit toilet, cfga, drkg wtr. Hiking, fishing.

NEWCASTLE (WYOMING)

Beaver Creek Campground $8
Black Hills National Forest
18 mi N of Newcastle on US 85; 6 mi E on FR 811. $8 with federal senior pass; others pay $16. May be free during LD-MD, but no wtr or trash service; 10-day limit. 8 sites (45-ft RV limit). Tbls, toilet, cfga, drkg wtr. Fishing, picnicking.

Moon Campground   FREE
Black Hills National Forest
10 mi SE of Newcastle on US 16; 15 mi N on FR 117. Free but donations accepted. Elev 6400 ft. 6/1-11/30; 10-day limit. 3 sites (RVs under 30 ft); tbls, toilets, cfga, no drkg wtr.

Redbank Spring Campground $8
Black Hills National Forest
14 mi NE of Newcastle. $8 with federal senior pass; others pay $16. All year; 10-day limit. 4 sites (40-ft RV limit). Tbls, toilets, cfga, no drkg wtr. Fishing. Elev 6600 ft.

NEWELL

Newell Lake Lakeside Use Area   FREE
8 mi N of Newell on SR 79; 2 mi E on Newell Lake Rd. Free. All year; 14-day limit. Primitive undesignated sites. Toilets, cfga, no drkg wtr, no trash service. Fishing, boating(l), swimming.

ONIDA

Bush's Landing Lakeside Use Area $6
About 11 mi W of Onida on SR 1804/Onida Rd; 3 mi N on 291st Ave; 9 mi W on 182nd St. 24 mi N of Oahe Dam on SR 1804; on E shore of Lake Oahe just N of Big Bend area. Camp free, but $6 daily or $30 annual entry permit required. All year; 14-day limit. Toilets, cfga, no drkg wtr. Boating(l), fishing.

Little Bend Lakeside Use Area $6
17.5 mi W of Onida on SR 1804/Onida Rd; from point where SR 1804 turns S, continue W, then NW about 13 mi on gravel rds toward Fort Sully game preserve. Camp free, but $6 daily (or $30 annual) entry permit. All year; 14-day limit. 13 sites. Tbls, toilets, cfga, no drkg wtr. Boating(l), fishing, swimming, waterskiing. 365 acres.

PICKSTOWN

South Shore Lakeside Use Area $10
Fort Randall Dam, Lake Francis Case
3 mi W of Pickstown on US 181/18; no to site. $10. May-

Sep; 14-day limit. 10 primitive sites; 25-ft RV limit. Tbls, toilets, cfga, drkg wtr. Fishing, boating(l). Formerly free Corps of Engineers park.

Spillway Lakeside Use Area $6
At Pickstown, half mi below dam of Lake Francis Case. Camp free but $6 daily (or $30 annual) entry permit. May-Sept; 14-day limit. 6 primitive sites. Tbls, toilets, cfga, no drkg wtr. Boating(l), fishing. This park formerly managed by Corps of Engineers; now operated by the state. Also known as Ft. Randall Lakeside Use Area.

PIERPONT
Pierpont Lake City Park   FREE
2 mi S of Pierpont at NW shore Lake Pierpont on SD 27. Free. All year. 50 sites; tbls, toilets, cfga, drkg wtr, dump. Picnicking. Very rustic.

PIERRE
Chantier Creek Lakeside Use Area   FREE
6 mi N of Pierre on SR 1806, then 15 mi NW of Oahe Dam, continung on SR 1806; 1.5 mi E on Chantier Creek Rd; on W shore of Lake Oahe. Free. All year; 14-day limit. Primitive camping; no facilities, no drkg wtr. Boating(l), fishing.

DeGrey Lakeside Use Area   FREE
20 mi E of Pierre on SD 34; 1 mi S to campground. Free. All year; 14-day limit. 10 primitive sites (RVs under 25 ft); tbls, toilets, cfga, firewood, no drkg wtr. Picnicking, boating(ld), fishing.

East Shore Lakeside Use Area $5
About 3 mi N of Oahe Dam on SR 1804. Camp free, but $5 daily or $20 annual entry permit required. All year; 14-day limit. Toilets, cfga, no drkg wtr. Boating(l), fishing.

Joe Creek Lakeside Use Area   FREE
20 mi E of Pierre on SR 34; 10 mi S on co rds. Free. All year; 14-day limit. Camping area (about 6 sites) with shelters, tbls, drkg wtr, cfga, toilets. Boating(l), fishing, picnicking.

North Bend Lakeside Use Area   FREE
31 mi E of Pierre on SD 34; 4 mi S. Free. All year. 10 sites. Pit toilets, tbls, cfga, no drkg wtr. Picnicking, boating(l), fishing.

West Shore Lakeside Use Area $6
From Pierre, NW on SR 1806, N near the dam at Lake Oahe. Camp free, but $6 daily or $30 annual entry permit required. All year; 14-day limit. Primitive undesignated sites. No toilets, cfga, no drkg wtr. Boating(l), fishing. Former Corps of Engineers camp; now managed by state.

POLLOCK
Lake Pocasse City Park $5
Follow SR 1804 qtr mi E of Pollock. $5. May-Sept; 14-day

limit. 13 primitive sites; 32-ft RV limit. Toilets, pit tbls, cfga, drkg wtr, dump, playground. Fishing, boating.

Shaw Creek Lakeside Use Area   FREE
From Pollock, 6 mi S on SR 1804, 2 mi W on Point of View Rd; at "Y," bear left (S) 1 mi; at Lake Oahe. Free. All year; 14-day limit. Primitive undesignated sites. Toilets, cfga, no drkg wtr. Boating(l), fishing. Former Corps of Engineers park; now managed by the state.

ROCHFORD
Black Fox Campground $8
Black Hills National Forest
6 mi W of Rochford on FR 231; roads closed to vehicles 12-15-3/31 for snowmobile trail. $8 with federal senior pass; others pay $16. 10-day limit. 9 sites (50-ft RV limit). Tbls, toilets, cfga, no drkg wtr. Fishing, hiking. Elev 5900 ft.

Castle Peak Campground $8
Black Hills National Forest
3.5 mi SW of Rochford on FR 17; 1 mi S on FR 187; 8 mi E on FR 181 (rough & narrow); at Castle Creek. $8 with federal senior pass; others pay $16. All year; 10-day limit. 9 sites (RVs under 40 ft). Tbls, toilets, cfga, drkg wtr. Fishing, picnicking, hiking, mountain biking.

ROSCOE
Roscoe City Park   FREE
On Third Avenue North in Roscoe. Donations suggested; camp free. 5/15-10/1; 3-day limit. Tbls, flush toilets, cfga, drkg wtr, dump, elec, playground. Picnicking.

SELBY
Lake Hiddenwood State Recreation Area $11
2 mi E of Shelby; 3 mi N on US 18/83. $11 at non-elec sites; $15 with elec. All year; 14-day limit. 13 basic sites (7 with elec). Tbls, pit toilets, cfga, drkg wtr, playground, shelter, no showers, no dump, beach. Fishing, boating(l), hiking trails, swimming.

SOUTH SHORE
Round Lake Lakeside Use Area   FREE
1 mi E of South Shore on SR 20; 0.25 mi N on access rd; on S shore. Free. All year; 5-day limit. Undeveloped camping; 6 sites. Tbls, toilets, cfga. Fishing, boating(ld), picnicking.

SPEARFISH
Rod and Gun Campground $9
Black Hills National Forest
1 mi E of Spearfish on US 14A; 13 mi S on US 14; 2.5 mi SW on FR 222; at Spearfish Creek. $9 with federal senior pass; others pay $18. MD-LD; 10-day limit. 7 sites p to 50 ft. Tbls, toilets, cfga, drkg wtr (no wtr during free off-season period). Fishing, picnicking, hiking. Elev 5500 ft. Stream. Site of "Dancing With Wolves" movie.

Timon Campground $9
Black Hills National Forest
1 mi E of Spearfish on US 14A; 13 mi S on US 14; 4 mi SW on FR 222. $9 with federal senior pass; others pay $18. MD-LD; 10-day limit. 7 sites up to 60 ft. Tbls, toilets, cfga, drkg wtr (no wtr during free period). Fishing, hiking trails, mountain biking trail. Elev 6000 ft. Stream. In Spearfish Canyon at Little Spearfish Creek.

SPRINGFIELD
Sand Creek Lakeside Use Area $11
1 mi N of Springfield on SR 37; 3 mi E on Apple Tree Rd. $11. All year; 7-day limit. 10 primitive sites. Toilets, cfga, drkg wtr, shelter. Boating(ld), fishing. 45 acres.

STURGIS
Alkali Creek Trailhead $6
Bureau of Land Management
Fort Meade Recreation Area
3 mi SW of Sturgis. $6. 5/15-9/30; 14-day limit. 6 sites. Tbls, toilets, cfga, drkg wtr. Fishing, hiking. 15 acres. Closed for 3 weeks during Sturgis motorcycle rally.

Alkali Creek Horse Camp $8
Bureau of Land Management
Fort Meade Recreation Area
3 mi SW of Sturgis; follow signs from exit 34 of I-90 about 1 mi. $8. 5/15-9/30; 14-day limit. 6 sites. Tbls, toilets, cfga, drkg wtr. Equestrian use only. Closed during Sturgis motorcycle rally. 11 acres.

Bear Butte State Park $11
4 mi E of Sturgis on SR 34/79; 3 mi N on SR 79. $10. All year; 14-day limit. 15 primitive sites ($13 at 4 equestrian sites). Tbls, pit toilets, cfga, drkg wtr, no showers, no elec, no dump, playground, shelter. Bridle trail, boating, fishing, hiking trail, interpretive program.

SUNDANCE (WYOMING)
Cook Lake Recreation Area
Black Hills National Forest $9
20 mi N of Sundance on US 16 and FRs 838, 841, 843 & 842. $9 with federal senior pass; others pay $18. Fees $10 off-season 9/15-5/15 ($5 with senior pass). All year; 10-day limit. 32 sites; 45-ft RV limit. Tbls, toilets, cfga, drkg wtr. Boating, fishing, mountain biking, hiking, canoeing. Elev 4400 ft. Non-campers pay $4 day use fees.

Reuter Campground $7
Black Hills National Forest
5 mi NW of Sundance. 2 mi W on US 14; 3 mi on FR 838. $7 with federal senior pass; others pay $14. $10 during 9/15-5/15 but no wtr or trash service. All year; 10-day limit. 24 sites; 45-ft RV limit. Tbls, toilets, cfga, drkg wtr. Boating, fishing, hiking.

Sundance Horse Camp $7
Black Hills National Forest
0.5 mi E of Sundance on US 14; left on CR 249 (Government Valley Rd) for 3 mi, then left. $7 with federal senior pass; others pay $14 during 5/15-9/15 (fees $10 off-season); 14-day limit. 10 sites; no RV size limit. Tbls, pit toilets, cfga, drkg wtr, corrals, loading dock. Hiking, biking, bridle trail.

TABOR
Tabor Lakeside Use Area $11
3 mi S of Tabor on SR 52; 0.25 mi E on SR 52; 2.5 mi S on Tabor Recreation Rd; at N shore of Lewis & Clark Lake. $11. All year; 7-day limit. 10 primitive sites. Tbls, cfga. Fishing, boating (ld). 221 acres.

TIMBER LAKE
Little Moreau State Recreation Area   FREE
6 mi S of Sturgis off SR 20. Free. All year; 14-day limit. 6 primitive sites. Toilets, tbls, firewood, drkg wtr. Limited facilities in winter. Boating(l), fishing, swimming, playground, shelter, canoeing. On Cheyenne River Indian Reservation. Lots of wildlife. 160 acres.

VERMILLION
Lions City Park   FREE
On Princeton at SD 50, on W side of Vermillion. Free. 4/1-11/1; 3-night limit ($5 thereafter by permission). 15 sites, 5 with wtr/elec, tbls, flush toilets, cfga, firewood, dump, showers($). Tennis, softball, picnicking; swimming, fishing, golf nearby.

WALL
Cedar Pass Campground $11
Badlands National Park
8 mi S of I-90 on SR 240 Badlands Loop; westbound exit 131 Cactus Flat; 30 mi E of I-90 on SR 240. $11 with federal senior pass without hookups; others pay $22 ($37 with elec). Reduced rates in winter. All year; 14-day limit. 96 sites. Tbls, flush toilets, cfga, drkg wtr, dump($1), visitor center. Nature program, museum. Park entry fee charged, good for 7 days.

Sage Creek Primitive $10
Badlands National Park
12 mi W of Pinnacles Ranger Station (on US 16A) on Sage Creek Rd. Camp free, but $10 park entry permit for 7 days. All year; 14-day limit. 15 sites (20-ft RV limit). Toilets, cfga, tbls, no drkg wtr. Hiking trails.

WATERTOWN
Dakota Sioux Casino   FREE
From I-29 exit 185 N of Watertown, 4.5 mi W on CR 6 (164th St); just inside reservation land. Free. All year. 9 20/30-amp elec sites (six pull-through). Self-contained RVs only; no tents. Dump. Check in at Guest Services. 877-250-2121.

Northwest Pelican Lake Lakeside Use Area   FREE
4 mi W of Watertown on US 212; 2 mi S on 450th Ave; E
on access rd. Free. All year; 7-day limit. 6 primitive sites.
Toilets, cfga, drkg wtr. Boating(ld), fishing. 50 acres.

WAUBAY
Southside Blue Dog Lake   FREE
City Park Campground
2 campgrounds half mi apart on the S side of Blue Dog
Lake. Free. All year. 20 sites, toilets, cfga, pumped wtr,
some elec hookups, shelters. Boating(ld), fishing, playground, sports field, swimming.

Enemy Swim Water Access Site   FREE
From US 12 just E of Waubay, 5 mi N on CR 1; 1 mi E on
CR T-500 (135th St); N on access rd; on S shore of Enemy
Swim Lake. All year. Free primitive camping. Toilets,
cfga, no drkg wtr. Boating(ld), fishing. GPS: 45.429584,
-97.2823.

South Blue Dog Lakeside Use Area   FREE
From Waubay at jct with Main St, half mi E on US 12; 1
block N on Wayland St; 0.25 mi E on E. Lakeshore Dr; on
S shore of Blue Dog Lake. Free primitive camping. Tbls,
toilets, cfga, drkg wtr. Picnicking, swimming, boating(ld),
fishing. Shelters, playground.

WEBSTER
Webster Overnight City Campground   FREE
In Webster at jct SR 25 & US 12. Free, donations accepted.
All year. Drkg wtr, 4 elec hookups, dump, cfga. Picnicking,
7 RV sites with fulll hookups, $15 ($75 weekly, $200
monthly) at nearby RV park. Permits at city hall or liquor
store.

WENTWORTH
West Brant Lakeside Use Area   FREE
5 mi S of Wentworth on SR 34. All year. Free primitive
camping; 5-day limit. Toilets, no drkg wtr. Boating(l),
fishing.

WESSINGTON
Rose Hill Lakeside Use Area   FREE
9 mi S of Wessington, then 3 mi W on gravel rd following
signs (S & E of Vayland); on N shore of Rose Hill Lake.
Free. All year; 41-day limit. Primitive undesignated sites.
Tbls, toilets, cfga, drkg wtr. Boating(l), fishing, swimming,
hunting.

WHITE
Lake Hendricks Lakeside Use Area   FREE
9 mi E of White on SR 30, 2 mi N on CR 29; 0.5 mi E on
201st St; N on access rd; on S shore of lake. Free. All year;
5-day limit. Undeveloped camping; 15 sites. Tbls, toilets,
cfga, drkg wtr. Fishing, boating(ld).

WHITE RIVER
White River Municipal Park   FREE
On S side of town off US 83; from US 83, 4 blks E on S. 4th
St; S on Brock St; E on S side of ballfield. Free. All year;
14-day limit. 12 narrow back-in sites on a circular drive;
48-ft RV limit. Best side for large rig is in far SE corner,
allowing easy back-in. All sites bordered by phone pole
stumps that could block slideouts. Best RV parking in
W section by ballfield. Tbls, toilets, cfga, drkg wtr. Fairgrounds, ball park, fishing.

White River Rest Area Park   FREE
About 11 mi N of White River city on E side of US 83 along
bank of White River. Free. All year. Tbls, 2 pit toilets, cfga,
no drkg wtr. Unlevel sites.

WOONSOCKET
Twin Lakes Lakeside Use Area   FREE
From jct with SR 34 about 1 mi W of Woonsocket, 6.4 mi
S on 394th Ave; at NW shore of Twin Lakes. Free. All year;
5-day limit. Undeveloped camping; 8 primitive sites. Tbls,
toilets, drkg wtr, cfga. Fishing, boating(ld), picnicking,
swimming.

YANKTON
Kelley's Cove Lakeside Use Area   FREE
3 mi N of Yankton on US 81; 2 mi E on 303rd St; N on CR
102 (NE Jim River Rd); site is NE of jct with 302nd St. All
year. Free primitive camping. No facilities. Fishing. GPS:
43.016179, -97.351656.

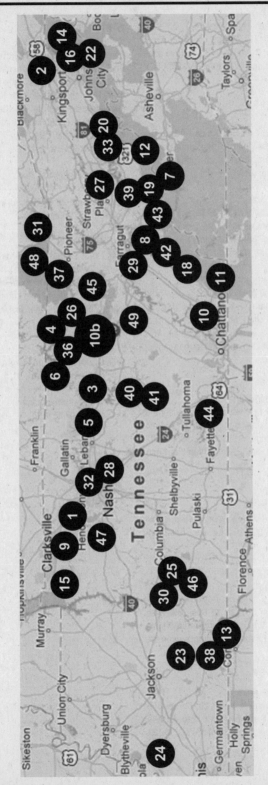

TENNESSEE

WWW.TNVACATION.COM

Tennessee Department of Tourist Development. Vacation guide: 800-462-8366 or info@tnvacation. com

Division of State Parks, 701 Broadway, Nashville, TN 37243; 615-742 6667.

> **CAPITAL:** Nashville
> **NICKNAME:** Volunteer State
> **STATEHOOD:** 1796 – 16th State
> **FLOWER:** Iris
> **TREE:** Tulip Poplar
> **BIRD:** Mockingbird

REST AREAS
Overnight stops are not permitted.

STATE PARKS
Among the state's 35 state parks with camping, the most developed have overnight fees of $20-25; all others range from $12 or $13 for primitive sites with water hookup available nearby, to $20 for sites with electricity and water hookups. Tennessee senior citizens receive discounts, with amounts varying by park. Park dump stations are available for non-campers at $3-5 fees. Some parks have been close by budget cuts. Pets on leashes are permitted. For further information contact Division of State Parks, 7th Floor, L & C Tower, 401 Church St., Nashville, TN 37243-0446. 800/TN-PARKS.

CHEROKEE NATIONAL FOREST
Tennessee's only national forest hosts more than 9 million visits per year. Backcountry camping without permits is allowed in most areas. Developed camping is available at 29 campgrounds with 685 sites. For further information contact: Forest Supervisor, Cherokee National Forest, PO Box 2010, Cleveland, TN 37320. 615/476-9700.

GREAT SMOKY MOUNTAINS NATIONAL PARK. Free backcountry permits for groups of up to 8 are available at all visitor centers and ranger stations. Stays at campsites are limited to 7 consecutive nights in-season and 14 days off-season. The park service maintains developed campgrounds at 10 locations: Abrams Creek, Balsam Mountain, Big Creek, Cades Cove, Cataloochee, Cosby, Deep Creek, Elkmont, Look Rock & Smokemont. Each has restrooms with running water and flush toilets but no showers or water/electric hookups. Great Smoky Mountains National Park, 107 Park Headquarters Rd., Gatlinburg, TN 37738.

LAND BETWEEN THE LAKES
Three types of camping are available at the LBL area between Kentucky Lake and Lake Barkley: Family campgrounds are fully developed and offer sites from $12 to $19 per night; Lake Access Areas, which offer basic amenities such as tables, campfire grill areas, chemical toilets, drinking water, trash pickup and boat ramps; Backcountry Camping Areas, where facilities are more basic, including boat ramps and possibly pit toilets, tables and grill areas but no trash service. Lake Access areas have fees of $9 per night; Backcountry Camping areas are free after purchase of annual $20 per person or 3-day $5 per person camping permits. The LBL is operated by the National Forest Service, and federal discounts such as the America the Beautiful Senior Pass (formerly Golden Age Passport) are honored.

TENNESSEE VALLEY AUTHORITY
TVA operates about 100 public recreation areas throughout the Tennessee Valley, including campgrounds, day-use areas and boat launching ramps. Federal America the Beautiful Passes are honored at all most campgrounds where fees are charged. Corporate headquarters, 400 W. Summit Hill Dr., Knoxville, TN 37902. 865-632-2101. tvainfo@ va.com

Corps of Engineers, Nashville District, PO Box 1070, Nashville, TN 37202; or Corps of Engineers, Memphis District, Clifford David Federal Bldg, Memphis, TN 38103 (615) 251-5115. Camping areas in Tennessee that have been closed in recent years include Indian Creek at Cordell Hull Reservoir; Poole Knob and Cooks Campground at J. Percy Priest Lake; Cove Creek at Dale Hollow and five parks at Center Hill Lake -- White County, Cave Hollow, East Shore, Davies Island and Holmes Creek.

ASHLAND CITY (1)

Harpeth River Bridge $12
Corps of Engineers
Cheatham Lake
From Ashland City, about 10 mi W on SR 49 to Harpeth River Bridge. $12 (or $6 with federal senior pass). 4/30-10/15; 14-day limit. 15 elec sites; tbls, cfga, toilets, drkg wtr, playground. Fishing, boating, waterskiing, canoeing. GPS: 36.28418, -87.118164

Lock A Recreation Area $9.50
Corps of Engineers
Cheatham Lake
From Ashland City, 8 mi W on SR 12 to hamlet of Cheap Hill; 4 mi SW (left) on Cheatham Dam Rd; at right bank of lake just upstream from dam. $9.50 base with federal senior pass at 45 elec/wtr sites; others pay $19 base, $23 for premium locations ($11.50 with senior pass). 4/1-10/30; 14-day limit. Tbls, flush toilets, cfga, drkg wtr, playground, showers, beach, fish cleaning station, dump, coin laundry, picnic shelter. Horseshoe pits, tennis, basketball, hiking trails, interpretive trail, boating(l), fishing, volleyball, waterskiing. GPS: 36.31583, -87.18694

BRISTOL (2)

Jacobs Creek Recreation Area $12
Cherokee National Forest
12 mi S of Bristol on US 421; 2 mi NW on FR 32 (Denton Valley Rd); E shore of Holston Lake. $12 during 4/15-10/15; reduced fee 3/11-4/15; 14-day limit. 27 sites (30-ft RV limit). Tbls, flush toilets, cfga, drkg wtr, showers, dump, beach. Fishing, swimming, boating(l), hiking. Non-campers pay $2 day use fee. GPS: 36.565701, -82.009204

Little Oak Campground $12
Cherokee National Forest
12 mi E of Bristol on US 421; 7 mi SW on FR 87 (Camp Tom Howard Rd); on South Holston Lake. $12 during 4/18-9/30; $10 3/1-4/17 & Oct-Dec with limited amenities & no wtr; 14-day limit. 68 sites; 30-ft RV limit. Tbls, flush & pit toilets, cfga, drkg wtr, showers, dump. Hiking, fishing, waterskiing, boating(l), interpretive trails. GPS: 36.519538, -82.060816

BUFFALO VALLEY (3)

Long Branch Recreation Area $10
Corps of Engineers
Center Hill Lake
From I-40 exit 268 at Buffalo Valley, 5 mi W on SR 96; 2 mi W on Center Hill Dam Rd; 1 mi N on SR 141, on right (signs); below dam on Caney Fork River. $10 base with federal senior pass for elec/wtr sites; others pay $20 base, $22 for full hookups, $24 at premium locations ($11 & $12 with senior pass). 4/1-10/30; 14-day limit. 60 elec sites: 57 are 30-amp, 3 50-amp. RV limit in excess of 65 ft. Tbls, flush toilets, cfga, dump, drkg wtr, showers, playground, fish cleaning station, coin laundry. Hiking, boating(l), fishing.

Note: in 2013, SR 96/141 across dam was one lane due to dam foundation work. GPS: 36.09903, -85.83176

BYRDSTOWN (4)

Obey River Recreation Area $7.50
Corps of Engineers
Dale Hollow Lake
3 mi S of Byrdstown on SR 111, following signs; on S side of Obey River arm of lake. 131 total sites. 21 non-elec RV/tent sites, $15 base, $21 at premium locations; 68 elec/wtr sites, $21 base, $24 for 50-amp ($7.50, $10.50 & $12 with federal senior pass). Tent sites also available. About 4/15-10/15; 14-day limit. RV limit 55 ft. Tbls, flush toilets, cfga, drkg wtr, showers, dump, beach, playground, coin laundry, pay phone. Boating(l), volleyball, hiking, swimming, fishing, basketball. GPS: 36.53083, -85.16944.

CARTHAGE (5)

Defeated Creek $7.50
Cordell Hull Lake
Corps of Engineers
4 mi W of Carthage on SR 25; 2 mi N on SR 80 (Pleasant Shade Hwy); 2 mi E on SR 85 (Turkey Creek Hwy), then S on Marina Lake, following signs. $7.50 base with federal senior pass at 155 elec/wtr sites; others pay $15 base, $18 at premium locations, $26 full hookups ($9 & $13 with senior pass). $1 additional fee may be charge don weekends & holidays. RV limit in excess of 65 ft; 35 pull-through sites. About 3/15-11/1; 14-day limit. Tbls, flush toilets, showers, dump, drkg wtr, coin laundry, playground, beach, pay phone, picnic shelters. Tennis, volleyball, biking & hiking trails, swimming, boating(l), fishing. GPS: 36.29972, -85.90889

Salt Lick Creek $7.50
Cordell Hull Lake
Corps of Engineers
4 mi W of Carthage on SR 25; 2 mi N on SR 80 (Pleasant Shade Hwy); about 7 mi E on SR 85 to Gladice; right (SE) for 1 mi on Smith Bend Rd, then 1 mi SE on Carl Dixon Lane, following signs; at N shore of lake. $7.50 base with federal senior pass at 145 wtr/elec sites; others pay $15 base, $26 fir full hookups ($13 with senior pass). $1 additional fee may be charged on weekends & holidays. RV limit in excess of 65 ft; 15 pull-through sites. About 4/15-10/15; 14-day limit. Tbls, flush toilets, cfga, drkg wtr, showers, playground, beach, dump, coin laundry, fishing pier, picnic shelter, visitor center. Fishing, boating(l), swimming. Non-campers pay $3 day use fee. GPS: 36.32278, -85.80861

CELINA (6)

Dale Hollow Dam Campground $8.50
Dale Hollow Lake
Corps of Engineers
From Celina, 2 mi NE on SR 53; 1 mi SE (right) on Dale Hollow Dam Rd, then 2nd right on Campground Rd, following

signs; on N shore of Obey River below spillway. $8.50 at 1 non-elec site; others pay $17. At 6 elec sites, $9 with senior pass; others pay $18. At 46 elec/wtr sites, $10.50 with senior pass; others pay $21. At 24 premium sites, $12 with senior pass; others pay $24. RV limit 60 ft; 16 pull-through sites. 4/1-10/31; 14-day limit. Tbls, flush toilets, cfga, drkg wtr, coin laundry, showers, dump, fishing piers, fish cleaning stations, picnic shelters, pay phone. Boating(l), hiking trails, fishing, volleyball, basketball, bike & walking trails. Dale Hollow National Fish Hatchery. GPS: 36.53778, -85.4575

CHEROKEE (NORTH CAROLINA) (7)
Balsam Mountain Campground $7
Great Smoky Mountain National Park
From the Oconaluftee Visitor Center near Cherokee, NC, half mi S on Newfound Gap Rd; left on Blue Ridge Pkwy for 10 mi; left on Heintooga Ridge Rd for 8 mi. $7 with federal senior pass; others pay $14. 5/14-10/11; 7-day limit. 46 sites; 30-ft RV limit. Tbls, flush toilets, cfga, drkg wtr. GPS: 35.564674, -83.174805

CHILHOWEE (8)
Abrams Creek Campground $7
Great Smoky Mountains National Park
6 mi N of Chilhowee off SR 129. $7 with federal senior pass; others pay $14. 3/12-10/31; 7-day limit. 16 sites; RVs limited to pop-up & truck campers. Tbls, flush toilets, cfga, drkg wtr, no showers or dump. Hiking, fishing. GPS: 35.617188, -83.92334

Chilhowee/Tellico Lakes   FREE
Dispersed Sites
Cherokee National Forest
Along Hwy 129, both E & W of Chilhowee. Free. All year; 14-day limit. Primitive undesignated camping along the highway at gravel pull-offs. No facilities, no drkg wtr & lots of hwy noise. Boating, fishing.

Look Rock Campground $7
Great Smoky Mountains National Park
67 mi N of Chilhowee off SR 129. $7 with federal senior pass; others pay $14. 5/14-10/31; 7-day limit. 68 sites; 35-ft RV limit. Tbls, flush toilets, cfga, drkg wtr, dump. Fishing, hiking. GPS: 35.639404, -83.933594

CLARKSVILLE (9)
Bumpus Mills Campground $8.50
Corps of Engineers
Lake Barkley
From Clarksville, 20 mi W on US 79; 10 mi NW on SR 120 through Bumpus Mills; W on Tobaccoport Rd (sign); 1 mi on gravel rd (continue straight at "Y" and sign, down hill). $8.50 base with federal senior pass; others pay $17 base, $20 for premium locations ($10 with senior pass). About 5/3-9/3; 14-day limit. 15 elec/wtr sites; 65-ft RV limit; 2 pull-through. Tbls, flush toilets, cfga, drkg wtr, showers, dump, coin laundry, playground. Fishing, boating(l). GPS: 36.6197, -87.8831

CLEVELAND (10)
Chilhowee Recreation Area $12
Cherokee National Forest
17.3 mi E of Cleveland on US 64; 7.5 mi NW on FR 77; on 7 Acre Lake. $12 at non-elec sites, $20 with elec ($14 with federal senior pass). 4/15-10/31 (16 sites open off-season with reduced amenities); 14-day limit. 78 sites up to 73 ft. Tbls, flush & pit toilets, cfga, drkg wtr, dump, beach. Swimming, hiking & biking trails, fishing, swimming. Non-campers pay $3 day use fee. GPS: 35.153751, -84.609120

Outdoor Adventure Rafting $5
About 9 mi E of Cleveland on US 74, rd narrows to 2 lanes; 3 mi farther, cross a bridge, then turn left on Welcome Valley Rd for 1 mi. $5 per person for regular sites; $8 per person for riverside sites. 42 primitive sites. Toilets, tbls, cfga, drkg wtr, showers. Rafting, tubing, fishing on Oconee River. GPS: 35.128238,-84.668366

Sylco Campground   FREE
Cherokee National Forest
12.5 mi E of Cleveland on US 64; 3 mi SE on CR 75; 7.5 mi SE on FR 55. Free. All year; 14-day limit. 12 sites (22-ft RV limit). Tbls toilets, cfga, no drkg wtr. Hiking trails. 4 acres. GPS: 35.02694, -84.60139

Thunder Rock $12
Cherokee National Forest
28.5 mi E of Cleveland on US 64; qtr mi S on FR 45; at Oconee River. $12 at 37 non-elec sites, $20 at 1 elec site; group site $15 ($6, $14 & $7.50 with federal senior pass). 4/1-11/30 (3 sites open off-season with reduced amenities & no wtr); 14-day limit. (seniors with GA Passports pay $6) during 4/1-10/31; 3 sites free Nov-Mar, but no flush toilets or showers. 14-day limit. 42 total sites, typically 58 ft. Tbls, flush & pit toilets, cfga, drkg wtr, lantern posts. Swimming, hiking & biking trails, fishing, volleyball, rafting. 4 acres. GPS: 35.076168, -84.485148

COOKEVILLE (10B)
Cane Creek Recreation Area   FREE
Center Hill Lake
Corps of Engineers
From Cookeville, 6 mi S on SR 135 (Burgess Falls Rd); right across Burgess Falls Dam; 2 mi S on CR 2214; 0.5 mi W on Browntown Rd; continue 1 mi W on Wildcat Rd, then right (NW) on Cane Hollow Rd to Falling Water River arm of lake. All year; 14-day limit. Free. Primitive, undesignated sites, free with camping permit from lake office. Toilet, tbls, cfga, drkg wtr. Boating(l), fishing. GPS: 36.032501, -85.6203

TENNESSEE 648

COPPERHILL (11)

Tumbling Creek   **FREE**
Cherokee National Forest
1.8 mi NW of Copperhill on TN 68; 4.9 mi W on CR 5496; 2.1 mi N on FR 221. Free. All year; 14-day limit. 8 sites (RVs under 22 ft); tbls, toilets, cfga, piped drkg wtr. Fishing, picnicking. Rds may be closed in winter. GPS: 35.017410, -84.467306

COSBY (12)

Cosby Campground   **$7**
Great Smoky Mountain National Park
About 3 mi SE of Cosby on SR 32, then 2 mi S on Cosby Cove Rd. $7 with federal senior pass; others pay $14. 3/12-10/31; 7-day limit. 157 sites; 25-ft RV limit. Tbls, flush toilets, cfga, drkg wtr, dump. Trout fishing in Little Cosby Creek, nature programs, hiking trail. GPS: 35.751709, -83.210449

COUNCE (13)

Pickwick Dam   **$8.50**
Tailwater Campground
Tennessee Valley Authority
From jct of Hwy 57 & Hwy 128 near Counce, 1.5 mi N on Hwy 128 across dam, then W below dam. $8.50 base with federal senior pass at non-elec sites, $11 for elec/wtr, $13 full hookups; others pay $17, $22 & $26. 3/18-12/12; 14-day limit. 100 sites (92 with elec/wtr). Flush toilets, showers, cfga, drkg wtr, tbls, dump. Shoreline fishing in Tennessee River. GPS: 35.066897, -88.260402

Bruton Branch Recreation Area   **$12**
Pickwick Landing State Park
From jct with Hwy 57 near Counce, about 4 mi N on Hwy 128, across dam; about 12 mi E on Pyburns Dr; 1 mi SE on Bruton Rd; right on Bruton Branch Rd to site; on N shore of Pickwick Dam, opposite main section of state park. $12 (TN seniors pay $8). Apr-Oct; 14-day limit. 43 primitive sites. Tbls, flush toilets, cfga, drkg wtr, playground. Boating(l), fishing. GPS: 35.07077, -88.188886.

DAMASCUS (14)

Backbone Rock Recreation Area   **$10**
Cherokee National Forest
5 mi SW of Damascus on Hwy 133. $10. About 5/6-10/15; 14-day limit. 9 sites; 28-ft RV limit). Tbls, portable & pit toilets, cfga, picnic shelters, no drkg wtr (system being repaired in 2014). Hiking trails built by CCC in 1930s, fishing. GPS: 36.594706, -81.814374

DOVER (15)

Bacon Creek   **CLOSED**
Land Between the Lakes
National Recreation Area
3 mi W of Dover on US 79 to the Trace; 30 mi N to CR 165 in Kentucky; E 6 mi to CR 166, then 1.5 mi on CR 166 to Lake Barkley. Camp free with 3-day $7 per person backcountry permit or $30 per person annual backcountry permit. This site was closed in 2012 for safety reasons.

Boswell Landing   **FREE**
Land Between the Lakes
National Recreation Area
9.5 mi W of Dover on US 79; 5 mi N on Fort Henry Rd; follow signs. Camp free with 3-day $7 per person backcountry permit or $30 per person annual backcountry permit ($3.50 & $15 for seniors with federal senior pass). All year; 14-day limit. 23 sites. Tbls, chemical toilets, cfga, drkg wtr (dump at Piney Campground). Picnicking, fishing, boating (l), waterskiing. On Kentucky Lake. Future plans include adding more RV spaces. GPS: 36.5173, -88.0264.

Devils Elbow   **CLOSED**
Land Between the Lakes
National Recreation Area
3 mi W of Dover on US 79 to The Trace; 31 mi N to US 68/80 in Kentucky; 4 mi E to Lake Barkley. Closed to camping; day use only. GPS: 36.791016, -87.988037.

Gatlin Point   **$12**
Land Between the Lakes
National Recreation Area
5 mi W of Dover on US 79; 7 mi N on The Trace; 3.5 mi NE on CR 227, following signs. $12 at 19 basic sites. All year; 21-day limit. Tbls, chemical toilets, cfga, drkg wtr, no elec. Free dump at south welcome station. Picnicking, fishing, boating(l). On Kentucky Lake. Nearby Bards Lake (320 acres) has boat launch. GPS: 36.556641, -87.903809.

Ginger Bay   **FREE**
Land Between The Lakes
National Recreation Area
3 mi W of Dover on US 79 to The Trace; 11.5 mi N to CR 211; 1 mi to CR 206; 1.5 mi to CR 212; 1 mi to Kentucky Lake. Camp free with 3-day $7 per person backcountry permit or $30 per person annual backcountry permit ($3.50 & $15 with federal senior pass). All year; 14-day limit. 13 primitive sites. No facilities, no drkg wtr. Picnicking, fishing, boating(l), hiking, waterskiing. Nearby: Homeplace 1850 and buffalo range. Future plans include renovating camping areas. GPS: 36.6237, -88.0384.

Ginger Ridge   **FREE**
Backcountry Camp
Land Between The Lakes
National Recreation Area
3 mi W of Dover on US 79 to The Trace; 13 mi N to Buffalo Range, then 3 mi W on Ginger Creek Rd to E shore of Kentucky Lake. Camp free with 3-day $7 per person backcountry permit or $30 per person annual backcountry permit ($3.50 & $15 with federal senior pass). All year; 14-day limit. Undesignated backcountry sites; no facilities. Boating, fishing. GPS: 36.6334, -88.0425.

Neville Bay   FREE
Backcountry Camping Area
Land Between the Lakes
National Recreation Area
3 mi W of Dover on US 79 to The Trace; 10 mi N to CR 214; 2.5 mi E to Lake Barkley. Camp free with 3-day $7 per person backcountry permit or $30 per person annual backcountry permit ($3.50 or $15 with federal senior pass). All year; 14-day limit. 50 sites. Tbls, toilets, cfga, drkg wtr. Boating(l), fishing, waterskiing. Camp expected to be upgraded with more tbls & cfga. GPS: 36.6126, -87.9167.

Piney Campground $12
Land Between the Lakes
National Recreation Area
About 11 mi W of Dover on US 79/SR 49; 2.5 mi NW on FR 230; 1 mi N on Fort Henry Rd to campground entrance; on E shore of Kentucky Lake. $12 for basic sites; $22 for 30-amp elec; $34 full hookups (seniors with federal senior pass pay $6, $16 & $30). 3/1-11/30; 21-day limit. In March & Nov, if wtr is off, lower fees may be charged. 369 sites any size RV or tent; some shelters. Tbls, flush toilets, showers, cfga, drkg wtr, vending machines, fish cleaning stations, coin laundry, fishing pier. Boating(l), fishing, hiking trails, biking(r) trails, archery range, swimming, campfire theater, bike skills court. GPS: 36.487305, -88.034668.

Rushing Creek Campground $12
Land Between the Lakes
National Recreation Area
3 mi W of Dover on US 79 to The Trace (Hwy 453); 3 mi N to Buffalo Range, then 3 mi W on Ginger Creek Rd; 1 mi N on Lake Ferry Rd; W on Rushing Creek & follow signs; on E shore of Kentucky Lake. $12 at 56 basic sites. All year; 21-day limit. Tbls, toilets, cfga, drkg wtr. Campground is in 2 sections -- one on Rushing Creek & one on Jones Creek. Rushing Creek section has showers, drkg wtr, flush toilets. Jones Creek has pit toilets, no drkg wtr & is primarily a tenter camp. Volleyball, basketball, boating(l), fishing, waterskiing, hiking. 250 acres. Elec hookups & new playground considered in future. GPS: 36.66626, -88.050049.

Turkey Bay OHV Area $8
Land Between the Lakes
National Recreation Area
3 mi W of Dover on US 79 to The Trace (Hwy 453); 25 mi N to Turkey Creek Rd into Kentucky; 1 mi W to OHV Area. $8 for 18 primitive sites ($4 for seniors with federal senior pass). All year; 21-day limit. Toilets, tbls, cfga, chemical toilets, drkg wtr. OHV trails, fishing, picnicking, boating. Primarily an off-highway vehicle use area with unloading ramps. Nearby: Golden Pond Visitors Center. GPS: 36.4500, -88.04190.

ELIZABETHTON (16)

Watauga Dam $8.50
Tailwater Campground
Tennessee Valley Authority
5 mi W of Elizabethton on Siam Rd, following signs. $8.50 base with federal senior pass at non-elec sites, $11 for sites with elec (all others pay $17 & $22). 3/18-11/14; 14-day limit. 29 sites with elec/wtr. Flush toilets, showers, cfga, drkg wtr, tbls. Boating(l), fishing, canoeing(l), hiking trail, walking trail, wildlife viewing area. Campground closed to tent camping due to bear activity. GPS: 36.347424, -82.134269

ETOWAH (18)

Gee Creek Campground
Hiwassee-Oconee $12
Scenic River State Park
6 mi S of Etowa on US 11 at Spring Creek Rd. $12 ($10 Tennessee seniors). All year; 14-day limit. 47 primitive sites & overflow area. Tbls, cfga, drkg wtr, showers, flush toilets. Free tent camping along most of the John Muir Trail above the Appalachia Powerhouse in the Cherokee National Forest. Nature walks, horseback riding, hiking, rafting, fishing. GPS: 35.242461, -84.557138

Lost Creek Campground   FREE
Cherokee National Forest
7 mi S of Etowah on US 411; 6 mi SE on SR 30; 7.2 mi E on FR 103. Free. All year, but limited facilities in winter; 14-day limit. 15 sites (22-ft RV limit). Tbls, toilets, cfga, no drkg wtr. Fishing. 5 acres. GPS: 35.160012, -84.467883

Quinn Springs $12
Cherokee National Forest
7 mi S of Etowah on US 411; 1.6 mi SE on SR 30; turn right at Quinn Springs campground sign. $12. All year; 14-day limit. 25 sites (22-ft RV limit). Tbls, flush & pit toilets, cfga, drkg wtr, showers. Fishing, hiking, interpretive trail. Note: Campground closed during 2014; check current status before arrival. GPS: 35.228673, -84.548208

GATLINBURG (19)

Elkmont Campground $8.50
Great Smoky Mountains National Park
9 mi W of Gatlinburg on SR 73; 1 mi S on Elkmont Rd. $8.50 base with federal senior pass; others pay $17 base, $23 with hookups. 3/12-11/30; 7-day limit. 220 sites; 32-ft trailer limit, 35-ft motorhome limit. Tbls, flush toilets, cfga, drkg wtr, dump. Hiking, fishing in Jakes Creek & Little River. GPS: 35.65918, -83.585693

GREENEVILLE (20)

Horse Creek Recreation Area $10
Cherokee National Forest
9 mi E of Greeneville on SR 107; 3 mi S on FR 94. $10. 4/15-11/15; 14-day limit. 15 sites (7 walk-in); 50-ft RV

limit. Tbls, flush & pit toilets, cfga, drkg wtr, lantern posts. Swimming, fishing, hiking trails. 4 acres. GPS: 36.109331, -82.657283

Paint Creek Campground $10
Cherokee National Forest
12 mi S of Greeneville on SR 70; 1.5 mi W on FR 13; 1.5 mi S on FR 31. $10. 4/15-11/15; 14-day limit. 18 sites (60-ft RV limit). Tbls, toilets, cfga, drkg wtr. Swimming, fishing, hiking trails. 6 acres. GPS: 35.978395, -82.844506

HAMPTON (22)
Cardens Bluff Campground $12
Cherokee National Forest
3 mi NE of Hampton on US 321; at 6,430-acre Watauga Lake. $12. Open 4/15-10/15; 14-day limit. 43 sites; 30-ft RV limit at 3 sites. Tbls, flush toilets, cfga, drkg wtr. Boating, fishing, hiking. GPS: 36.312045, -82.116459

Dennis Cove Recreation Area $10
Cherokee National Forest
1 mi E of Hampton on US 321; 7 mi SE on FR 50; at Laurel Fork Creek. $10. About 4/15-10/15; 14-day limit. 12 sites (30-ft RV limit). Tbls, toilets, cfga, drkg wtr. Swimming, picnicking, fishing. Elev 2600 ft; 2 acres. Within Laurel Fork Wildlife Management Area. Near Appalachian Trail. GPS: 36.256833, -82.110220

HENDERSON (23)
Cages Bend Campground $10
Corps of Engineers
Old Hickory Lake
5.5 mi NE of Henderson on SR 31E; follow signs SE on Benders Ferry Rd. $10 base with federal senior pass; others pay $20 base, $24 for premium locations ($12 with senior pass). 4/1-10/31; 14-day limit. 43 elec/wtr sites; RV limit in excess of 65 ft; 1 pull-through site. Tbls, flush toilets, cfga, drkg wtr, showers, dump, playground, fishing pier, coin laundry, marina, pay phone. Waterskiing, fishing, boating(l), hiking. GPS: 36.30389, -86.51528

HENNING (24)
Fort Pillow $8
State Historic Area
US 51N to Hwy 87; 17 mi W to SR 207, then N. $8 at 38 primitive sites meant for tents, but available to small RVs such as tent-campers, van-campers and pickup-campers. TN seniors pay $7. All year; 14-day limit. Tbls, flush toilets, cfga, drkg wtr, no hookups, visitor center, coin laundry, playground. Hiking, boating(l), fishing, volleyball, horseshoes. Interpretive center & museum. 1,642 acres. GPS: 35.6361906, -89.8423058.

HOHENWALD (25)
Meriwether Lewis Campground   FREE
Natchez Trace Parkway
Near TN 20. Free. All year; 15-day limit. 32 sites; tbls,

toilets, cfga, drkg wtr. Picnicking. The site of Grinder's Inn, where Lewis died of gunshot wounds; park monument contains his remains. Pets.

JAMESTOWN (26)
Pickett State Rustic Park $10
15 mi NE of Jamestown following SR 154 from US 127; on Arch Lake. $10 for TN seniors; others pay $13. All year; 14-day limit. 32 sites with elec/wtr. Tbls, flush toilets, cfga, drkg wtr, dump, playground, rec room. Swimming, boating(r), fishing, nature trails. 14,000 acres in remote area of Cumberland Mountains. Caves, natural bridges. Trail to home of Alvin York. GPS: 36.542969, -84.822266.

JEFFERSON CITY (27)
Cherokee Dam Campground $11
Tennessee Valley Authority
1.5 mi W of Jefferson City on US 11E, then follow signs 4.5 mi N to dam. $11 with federal senior pass; others pay $22. 3/18-11/14; 14-day limit. 42 sites with elec/wtr. Flush toilets, showers, pay phone, play area, tbls, cfga, beach. Paved walking trail, boating(l), fishing, hiking, swimming. GPS: 36.15917, -83.509788

LAVERGNE (28)
Poole Knobs $9
Corps of Engineers
J. Percy Priest Lake
From Lavergne, SE on US 41, then 2 mi N on Fergus Rd; 4 mi NE on Jones Mill Rd. $9 base with federal senior pass at 55 elec/wtr 30/50-amp sites; others pay $18 base, $24 for premium locations ($12 with senior pass). 5/1-9/30; 14-day limit. RV limit in excess of 65 ft; 56 pull-through sites. Group camping area, $50. Picnic shelter, tbls, flush toilets, cfga, drkg wtr, elec($), showers, dump, beach, coin laundry. Swimming, fishing, boating(l), hiking trails. GPS: 36.0508, -86.5103

LENOIR CITY (29)
Melton Hill Dam Campground $8.50
Melton Hill Reservoir
Tennessee Valley Authority
From I-40 exit 364 N of Lenoir City, 2 mi N on Hwy 95, then follow signs E to dam. $8.50 with federal senior pass at non-elec sites, $11 at elec/wtr sites, $13 at full-hookup sites; others pay $17, $22 & $26. 3/18-11/14; 14-day limit. 13 non-elec sites, 33 wtr/elec, 8 full hookups. Flush toilets, cfga, beach, showers, dump, tbls, drkg wtr. Boating(l), fishing, swimming, hiking. GPS: 35.873042, -84.298696

LINDEN (30)
Mousetail Landing State Park $12
12 mi W of Linden on Hwy 412; 2.7 mi NE on Hwy 50; on E shore of Tennessee River. $12 at non-elec sites ($10 for Tennessee seniors). $16 at 19 elec/wtr sites. All year; 14-day limit. 24 sites; 20-ft RV limit; 21 sites at Spring

Creek Campground. Tbls, flush toilets, cfga, drkg wtr, showers, dump, no hookups, pool, playground, coin laundry, store. Horseshoes, swimming, fishing, boating(ld), hiking trails (one for overnight with 2 screened shelters & beds), archery range, volleyball, nature programs, nature hikes. 1,247 acres. GPS: 35.6681235, -88.0069757.

MIDDLESBORO (KENTUCKY) (31)

Wilderness Road $7
Cumberland Gap National Historic Park
Just S of Middlesboro on US 25E to visitor center, E on US 58 into Virginia. $7 with federal senior pass at non-elec sites (others pay $14), $20 with elec ($10 with senior pass). All year; 14-day limit. 160 sites. Tbls, showers, flush toilets, cfga, drkg wtr. Hiking, fishing. GPS: 36.605225, -83.634277

NASHVILLE (32)

Anderson Road $7
Corps of Engineers
J. Percy Priest Lake
From Nashville, 5 mi E on I-40 to exit 219; 5 mi S on Ferry Pike (becoming Bell Rd); 1 mi E on Smith Spring Rd; 1 mi N on Anderson Rd. $7 base with federal senior pass at 26 primitive sites; others pay $14, $16 for premium locations ($8 with senior pass). At 10 new 30/50-amp elec/wtr sites, $12 with senior pass; others pay $24. 5/15-9/30; 14-day limit. RV limit in excess of 65 ft; 14 pull-through sites. Tbls, flush toilets, cfga, drkg wtr, coin laundry, beach, playground, dump. Fishing, boating(l), swimming, hiking. Non-campers pay day use fees for boat ramp, picnicking, dump station, beach. GPS: 36.10611, -86.60389

Cedar Creek Campground $10
Corps of Engineers
Old Hickory Lake
From jct with CR 109, 6 mi W on US 70, then N, following signs to lake. $10 base with federal senior pass; others pay $20 base, $24 for premium locations ($12 with senior pass). 4/1-10/31; 14-day limit. 59 elec/wtr sites; RV limit in excess of 65 ft. Tbls, flush toilets, cfga, drkg wtr, showers, dump, playground, coin laundry, fishing pier, marina, pay phone, picnic shelter. Hiking, fishing, waterskiing, swimming, boating(l). GPS: 36.27861, -86.50861

Seven Points $10
Corps of Engineers
J. Percy Priest Lake
From I-40 exit 221B at Nashville, S (right) on Old Hickory Blvd (sign), then E (left) on Bell Rd; 1 mi S (right) on New Hope Rd; 1 mi E (left) on Stewarts Ferry Pike, following signs; at mouth of North Creek arm of lake. $10 base with federal senior pass; others pay $20 base, $24 for premium locations ($12 with senior pass). 4/1-10/30; 14-day limit. 58 wtr/elec sites; RV limit in excess of 65 ft; 4 pull-through, 6 handicap sites. Tbls, flush toilets, cfga, drkg wtr, dump, showers, beach, playground, fishing pier,

coin laundry, 2 picnic shelters. Fishing, boating(l), hiking, swimming. GPS: 36.1331, -86.5703

NEWPORT (33)

Houston Valley Recreation Area $7
Cherokee National Forest
7 mi SE of Newport on US 25; 5 mi NE on SR 107. $7. 4/15-11/1; 14-day limit. 8 sites (22-ft RV limit). Tbls, toilets, cfga, drkg wtr, lantern posts. Fishing, hiking trails, volleyball. GPS: 35.963383, -82.944489

Round Mountain Campground $7
Cherokee National Forest
7 mi SE of Newport on US 25; 13 mi SE on SR 107. $7. Open 4/15-11/15; 14-day limit. 14 sites (2 walk-in); 35-ft RV limit). Tbls, toilets, cfga, drkg wtr, lantern posts. Hiking trails 6 acres. GPS: 35.839554, -82.952863

OAKLEY (36)

Lillydale Recreation Area $10.50
Corps of Engineers
Dale Hollow Lake
From Oakley (a small town 5 mi N of SR 111 on SR 294, Willow Grove Rd), 1.5 mi N on Lilly Dale Rd; at S shore of lake (across from Dale Hollow State Resort Park). $10.50 with federal senior pass at 16 elec/wtr 30-amp sites; others pay $21. $12 with senior pass at 58 elec/wtr 50-amp sites; others pay $24. About 4/25-9/15; 14-day limit. 65-ft RV limit; 3 pull-through sites. Picnic shelter, amphitheater, tbls, flush toilets, cfga, drkg wtr, showers, dump, playground, 2 volleyball courts. Basketball, swimming (2 beaches), 7.5-mi hiking trail, boating(l), fishing. GPS: 36.6044, -85.2997

Willow Grove $7.50
Corps of Engineers
Dale Hollow Lake
From Oakley, 10 mi N & W on SR 294 (Willow Grove Rd); at S shore of lake. 83 sites. 21 basic tent sites, $15, $18 at premium locations; 62 wtr/elec RV sites (all 30/50-amp), $18 base, 28 sites at premium locations for $24 ($7.50, $9 & $12 with federal senior pass). About 5/15-9/1; 14-day limit. Tbls, flush toilets, pavilion, amphitheater, cfga, drkg wtr, showers, dump, beach, playground. Swimming, boating(l), fishing, hiking. GPS: 36.5894, -85.34528

ONEIDA (37)

Bandy Creek Campground $9.50
Big South Fork National River and Recreation Area
18 mi W of Oneida on SR 297; 3 mi NW on Bandy Creek access rd. $9.50 with federal senior pass at non-elec sites, $11 for hookups; others pay $19 & $22. 4/1-10/31; 14-day limit. 100 sites with elec; 50 tent sites. Tbls, flush toilets, showers, drkg wtr, cfga, dump, pool. Fishing, boating(l), hiking, swimming. GPS: 36.47672, -84.68093

SELMER (38)

Big Hill Pond State Park $10
15 mi S of Selmer on Hwy 57 following signs; at Travis McNatt Lake. $10 for Tennessee seniors. Sites regularly $13. All year; 14-day limit. Tbls, flush toilets, cfga, drkg wtr. Fishing, boating(l), hiking, interpretive programs, horseback riding. Dismal Swamp boardwalk. 5,000 acres. GPS: 35.04583, -88.73472

SEVIERVILLE (39)

Douglas Dam $8.50
Headwaters Campground
Tennessee Valley Authority
About 5 mi N of Sevierville on SR 66; 2 mi NW on SR 338 (Old SR 66), then N to dam. $8.50 with federal senior pass at non-elec sites, $11 for wtr/elec; others pay $17 & $22. 3/18-12/12; 14-day limit. 65 sites (61 with elec). Tbls, flush toilets, cfga, drkg wtr, showers, dump, pay phone, beach. Boating(l), fishing, walking trail, wildlife viewing area. Trotter Bluff Small Wild Area. GPS: 35.948263, -83536231

Douglas Dam $11
Tailwaters Campground
Tennessee Valley Authority
About 5 mi N of Sevierville on SR 66; 5 mi NW on SR 338 (Old SR 66) to campground below the dam. $11 with federal senior pass at 62 elec/wtr sites; others pay $22. 3/18-12/12; 14-day limit. Flush toilets, showers, play equipment, drkg wtr, cfga, tbls, fishing pier, pay phone. Boating(l), fishing, wildlife viewing area. GPS: 35.95834, -83552002

SILVER POINT (40)

Floating Mill Park $8
Center Hill Lake
Corps of Engineers
From I-40 exit 273 at Silver Point, 3.5 mi S on SR 56; right at store on Floating Mill RD, following signs. $8 with federal senior pass at 9 non-elec RV sites; others pay $16. At 44 elec sites (30-amp), $10 with senior pass; others pay $20; At 13 elec/wtr 50-amp sites, $11 with senior pass; others pay $22 or $24 at premium locations ($12 with senior pass). About 4/15-10/15; 14-day limit. 60-ft RV limit. Tbls, flush toilets, cfga, drkg wtr, showers, fish cleaning station, dump, playground, beach, coin laundry, picnic shelter, amphitheater. Swimming, waterskiing, fishing, boating(l), hiking, interpretive trail, boating(l). Recent improvements include new elec/wtr hookups, renovating 9 sites, enlarging 4 sites & adding 50-amp service, improving 5 lakefront sites & adding wtr/elec service. GPS: 36.04489, -85.76347

SMITHVILLE (41)

Ragland Bottom Campground $10
Corps of Engineers
Center Hill Lake
From Smithville, 7.1 mi NE on US 70, across lake bridge, left on Ragland Bottom Rd for 1.1 mi (signs). $10 with federal senior pass at 10 premium elec/wtr RV/tent sites & 20 elec/wtr RV sites; others pay $20. $11 base with senior pass at 9 full-hookup 50-amp RV sites; others pay $22, $24 for premium locations ($12 with senior pass). 4/20-10/15; 14-day limit. RV limit in excess of 65 ft. Tbls, flush toilets, cfga, drkg wtr, elec($), showers, dump, coin laundry, beach, picnic shelter. Boating(l), fishing, waterskiing, hiking, interpretive trail, swimming. GPS: 35.9774, -85.72087

TELLICO PLAINS (42)

Big Oak Cove Campground $10
Cherokee National Forest
About 5 mi W of Tellico Plains on SR 165; qtr mi S on FR 35; left on FR 210 for 7 mi; at Tellico River. $10. 3/15-10/15; 14-day limit. 11 sites. Tbls, toilets, cfga, drkg wtr. Fishing, hiking. GPS: 35.264307, -84.086853

Birch Branch Campground $10
Cherokee National Forest
About 5 mi W of Tellico Plains on SR 165; right on FR 210 for 15 mi. $10. All year; 14-day limit. 7 sites. Tbls, toilet, cfga, no drkg wtr. Fishing. GPS: 35.281624, -84.098535

Davis Branch Campground $10
Cherokee National Forest
4 mi E of Tellico Plains on SR 165; 14 mi SW on FR 210; at Tellico River. $10. All year; 14 day limit. 6 sites. Tbls, toilets, cfga, drkg wtr. Fishing, hiking, hunting. GPS: 35.278783, -84.096582

Holder Cove Campground $10
Cherokee National Forest
About 5 mi W of Tellico Plains on SR 165; right on FR 210 for 16 mi. $10. All year; 14-day limit. 7 sites. Tbls, toilets, cfga, no drkg wtr. Fishing. GPS: 35.270982, -84.086226

Holly Flats $6
Cherokee National Forest
1 mi E of Tellico Plains on SR 68; 5 mi E on SR 165; 15 mi E on FR 210; 6 mi SE on FR 126. $6. All year; 14-day limit. 15 small sites (22-ft RV limit). Tbls, toilets, cfga, drkg wtr. Fishing, hiking trails. 6 acres. GPS: 35.285413, -84.177571

Jake Best Campground $6
Cherokee National Forest
1 mi E of Tellico Plains on Hwy 68; 15 mi NE on Hwy 165; 9.4 mi NE on FR 35 at Citico Creek. $6. All year; 14-day limit. 7 sites (22-ft RV limit). Tbls, toilets, cfga, drkg wtr. Fishing. GPS: 35.446513, -84.112355

North River Campground $8
Cherokee National Forest
1 mi E of Tellico Plains on SR 68; 5 mi E on SR 165; 10.5 mi E on FR 210; 2.5 mi E on FR 217; on North River. $8. All year; 14-day limit. 11 sites up to 60 ft. Tbls, pit toilets, cfga, drkg wtr. Swimming, fishing. GPS: 35.323394, -84.127577

Spivey Cove Campground $6
Cherokee National Forest
1 mi E of Tellico Plains on SR 68; 5 mi E on SR 165; 13.7
mi E on FR 210. $6. Open 4/1-12/15; 14-day limit (winter
rd conditions may close camp earlier). 16 sites (22-ft RV
limit). Tbls, toilets, cfga, drkg wtr. Fishing, hiking trails.
GPS: 35.303901, -84.113143

TOWNSEND (43)
Cades Cove $8.50
Great Smoky Mountain National Park
About 4 mi W of Townsend on SR 73; S on Laurel Creek Rd,
becoming Cades Cove Loop Rd. $8.50 base with federal
senior pass; others pay $17 base, $20 for premium sites
($10 with senior pass). All year; 7-day limit. 159 sites;
35-ft RV limit. Tbls, flush toilets, cfga, drkg wtr, dump, pay
phone. Biking(r), hiking, horseback riding, fishing (Abrams
Creek), nature programs. GPS: 35.603516, -83.777344

TRACY CITY (44)
Foster Falls Campground   CLOSED
Tennessee Valley Authority
7.5 mi SE of Tracy City on US 41; half mi W on access
rd. Campground & bath house closed. GPS: 35.18457,
-85.676025

WARTBURG (45)
Frozen Head State Park $10
A2 mi E of Wartburg on Hwy 62; left on Flat Fork Rd for
4 mi to park. $10 for TN seniors; others pay $13. All year;
14-day limit. 20 rustic, scattered sites at Big Cove camping area. Tbls, flush toilets, showers, cfga, drkg wtr. No
hookups. 11 backcountry sites by permit. 6.9-mi mountain biking trail, nature programs, fishing, hiking, visitor
center, bridle trail, volleyball, basketball, horseshoe pits.
36.115453, -84.464534

Rock Creek Campground $7
Obed Wild & Scenic River National Park
About 7 mi SW of Wartburg on Catoosa Heidel Rd; just
across the Obed River bridge, turn right to the campground. $7 ($3.50 with federal senior pass). All year;
14-day limit. 11 undeveloped, primitive sites. Tbls, cfga,
portable toilets, no drkg wtr. Boating, rafting, climbing,
fishing, hiking, hunting, interpretive programs, nature
walks, swimming. GPS: 36.0753, -84.6497

WAYNESBORO (46)
Topsy Turvy $5
Canoe Rental and Campground
About 15 mi N of Waynesboro on SR 99; at Hwy 412 on Buf-
falo River. $5 per person base. All year. Primitive sites for
tents or self-contained RVs. Tbls, flush toilets, showers,
cfga, drkg wtr. Canoeing(r), boating, fishing, swimming.
GPS: 35.451602, -87.698673

WHITE BLUFF (47)
Montgomery Bell $8.45
State Resort Park
4 mi W of White Bluff on US 70. $8.45 for Tennessee
seniors for non-hookup sites; $11.25 all others; $10.75
during 11/1-3/31 for resident seniors at sites with elec
($12.95 rest of year). Sites with elec are regularly $17.25
($14.25 off-season). Also free backcountry camping by
permit. 120 sites; 35-ft RV limit. Tbls, flush toilets, cfga,
drkg wtr, showers, dump, hookups, playground, store,
snack bar. Boating(l), fishing, nature trails, golf, tennis,
backpacking, canoe floats, volleyball, horseshoes. 3,782
acres. GPS: 36.0900599, -87.2733423.

WHITLEY CITY (KENTUCKY) (48)
Alum Ford $5
Big South Fork National River & Recreation Area
2 mi N of Whitley City on US 27; about 5 mi W on SR 700 to
E shore of Big South Fork River. $5. All year; 14-day limit.
6 primitive sites. Tbls, toilets, cfga, no drkg wtr. Fishing,
boating(l), hiking. GPS: 36.6737, -84.5468

Blue Heron Campground $8.50
Big South Fork National River & Recreation Area
2 mi S of Whitley City on US 27; 1 mi W on SR 92 just past
hamlet of Stearns; 1 mi S on SR 1651; 3 mi W on SR 782 to
E shore of river. $8.50 with federal senior pass; others pay
$17. 5/1-10/31; 14-day limit. 45 sites. Tbls, flush toilets,
drkg wtr, cfga, elec/wtr hookups, showers. Boating(l),
fishing, hiking. GPS: 36.67806, -84.51889

YATESTOWN (49)
White County Access   FREE
Center Hill Lake
Corps of Engineers
From Yatestown at jct with SR 136 (Old Kenton Rd), about
6 mi W on Three Island Rd (through village of Center Hill);
at E shore of Caney Fork River below Center Hill Lake.
Free. All year; 14-day limit. Primitive undesignated sites;
camping with permit from lake office.

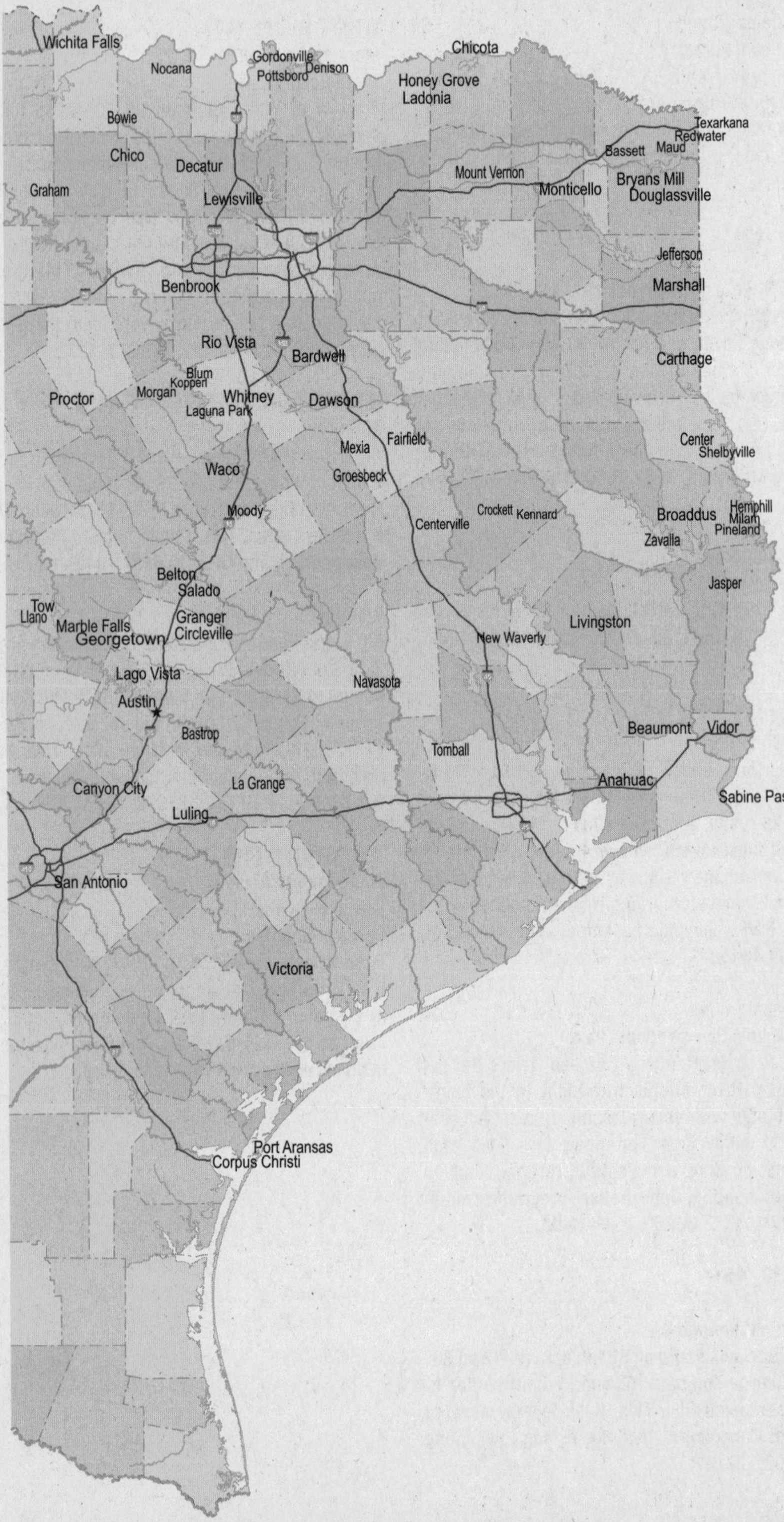

Wichita Falls

Nocana

Gordonville
Pottsboro Denison

Chicota

Honey Grove
Ladonia

Bowie

Texarkana
Redwater
Bassett Maud

Chico

Decatur

Mount Vernon

Bryans Mill
Monticello Douglassville

Graham

Lewisville

Jefferson

Benbrook

Marshall

Rio Vista

Bardwell

Carthage

Blum
Koppen

Morgan

Whitney
Laguna Park

Dawson

Proctor

Center
Shelbyville

Waco

Mexia
Groesbeck

Fairfield

Moody

Crockett Kennard
Centerville

Broaddus

Hemphill
Milam
Pineland

Zavalla

Belton
Salado

Jasper

Tow
Llano

Granger
Circleville

Livingston

Marble Falls
Georgetown

New Waverly

Lago Vista

Navasota

Austin

Bastrop

Tomball

Beaumont Vidor

Canyon City

La Grange

Anahuac

Sabine Pass

Luling

San Antonio

Victoria

Port Aransas
Corpus Christi

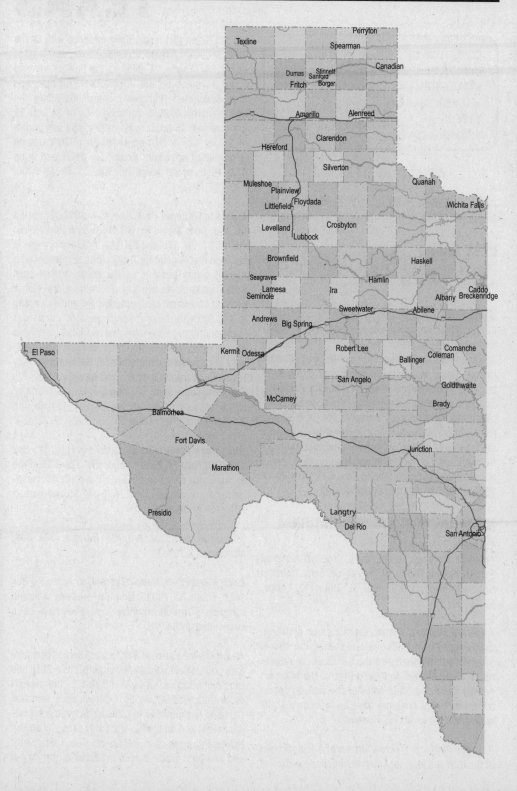

TEXAS

CAPITAL: Austin
NICKNAME: Lone Star State
STATEHOOD: 1845 – 28th State
FLOWER: Bluebonnet
TREE: Pecan
BIRD: Mockingbird

WWW.TRAVELTX.COM

Parks and Wildlife Dept, 4200 Smith School Rd, Austin, TX 78744. 1-800-792-1112 or 512-389-4800.

REST AREAS
One-day overnight parking is permitted at Texas state picnic areas and rest areas; no tents.

STATE PARKS
Camping fees have been changed with a new, higher fee schedule implemented. $2 to $7 per person entrance fees (or $70 annual pass good at all state parks). Texas residents 65 years and older, after being issued a special Texas Parklands Passport, pay 50% of the park entry fees. Pets on leashes are permitted. Generally, RV camping fees are $8-$12 for primitive sites; $10-$12 if water is at or near the site, and higher with water and electricity or full hookups. For further information contact: Parks and Wildlife Dept, 4200 Smith School Rd, Austin, TX 78744. 512-389-8950 or 800/792-1112.

NATIONAL FORESTS AND NATIONAL PARKS
Angelina National Forest, Davy Crockett National Forest, Sabine National Forest or Sam Houston National Forest, 415 S. First St, Suite 110, Lufkin, TX 75901.

Angelina National Forest has numerous primitive, undeveloped campsites scattered along the shores of Lake Sam Rayburn and the banks of the Angelina, Neches, Attoyac and Ayish Rivers. The sites are heavily used at various times of the year by fishermen. The forest does not have an inventory of the sites and their locations, however.

Amistad National Recreation Area, A joint project of the U.S. and Mexico, Amistad impounds waters of the Rio Grand just below its confluence with Devils River It covers 64,900 acres and extends 74 miles up the Rio Grande, 24 miles up the Devils River and about 14 miles up the Pecos River. Amistad has four designated primitive campgrounds along the lake's shoreline. Daily camping fees of $4 and $8 are charged. All boats must have a lake use permit of $4 per day or $40 annually. Shoreline camping is permitted anywhere except for developed aras. 4121 Highway 90 West, Del Rio, TX 78840-9350. 830-775-7491.

Big Bend National Park. Access from Marathon via US 385, from Alpine via SR 118, and from Presidio via US 67, FM 170 and SR 118. A $25 entry fee is charged that is good for 7 days (free admission with federal senior pass or similar card); annual pass $50. Camping fees are $14 ($7 with federal senior pass) at developed campgrounds. Primitive camping is $12 ($6 with federal senior pass) at numerous backcountry roadside sites and available by permit; all are listed in this edition. No showers are available at developed campgrounds, but campers may use coin-operated showers and laundry at the Rio Grande Village Store. Campgrounds and primitive areas are usually full during holiday periods. Big Bend National Park, Texas 79834; 432-477-2251.

Guadalupe Mountains National Park, HC 60, Box 400, Salt Flat, TX 79847-9400; 915/828-3251. Free backcountry camping by permit; developed campgrounds are $8 per night. A 7-day $5 per person entry fee is charged.

Muleshoe National Wildlife Refuge, Box 549, Muleshoe,TX 79347.

Lake Meredith National Recreation Area, PO Box 1460, Fritch, TX 79036. No entry fees are charged; camping is free at primitive sites. Fees have been suspended until 2018.

Padre Island National Seashore. There is primitive camping on North, South, Malaquite, Little Shell and Big Shell beaches. Little Shell and Big Shell beaches are accessible only by 4-wheel drive vehicles. Camping is prohibited in grasslands (watch for rattlesnakes) and on dunes. Most areas have chemical toilets and trash cans. Malaquite Beach has water and showers; water is also available at the ranger station. A $10 entry fee is charged, good for 7 days (or $20 annually). Padre Island National Seashore, PO Box 181300, Corpus Christi, TX 78480-1300. 361-949-8173.

Corps of Engineers, Fort Worth District, PO Box 17300, Fort Worth, TX 76102. Recreation areas such as campground have been operated jointly at some lakes by the Corps of Engineers and a non-profit agency -- the Our Land and Waters Foundation. The future of that relationshi is in question after an internal legal review determined the Corps does not have authority to allow cooperating agencies to retain user fees Following that review the Fort WorthDistrict re-assumed operation of the parks. At presstime, it appeard possible campgrounds in the Fort Worth District could be closed -- or their operating seasons shortened -- if the joint management agreement is dissolved and the district's funds are insufficient to pay for the parks' operations. Texas Corps campgrounds potentially affected include all those at Benbrook Lake and Sam Rayburn Reservoir, allong with the following: Lavon Lake's Lavonia Park, Lakeland Park, Clearlake Park, East Ford, Ticky Creek and Avalon day use; Lewisville Lake's Westlake, Oakland and Hickory Creek Parks. For 2014 and beyond, check with lake offices for status of those parts before arrival.

Bureau of Land Management, USPO and Federal Bldg, PO Box 1449, Santa Fe, NM 87501.

ABILENE (W)

Abilene State Park $12
19 mi S of Abilene on US 83; 8 mi W on FM 613 to Buffalo Gap; 5 mi SW on FM 89. $12 at 35-site overflow area with elec/wtr; no privacy screening, no tbls or cfga ($72 weekly). All year; 14-day limit. Developed sites with elec/wtr $15-$18. 40-ft RV limit. Tbls, flush toilets, showers, cfga, drkg wtr, dump, playground, pool, concessions. Picnicking, swimming, fishing, boating, hiking trail. State longhorn cattle herd. Lake Abilene nearby.

Johnson City Park   FREE
From I-20, Farm 600 N 6.6 mi; Farm 1082 E 6 mi. On Lake Fort Phantom Hill. All year; 3-day limit. 5 sites. Flush toilets, tbls, cfga, no drkg wtr. Fishing, boating (l at E end of dam). 37 acres.

Seabee City Park   FREE
From I-20, Farm 600 N 3.2 mi; E on Seabee Park Rd. On Elm Creek at SW end of Lake Fort Phantom Hill. All year; 3-day limit. 4 sites. Flush toilets, no drkg wtr, cfga, tbls. Fishing, boating(l). 40 acres.

ALANREED (W)

Lake McClellan Campground $10
McClellan Creek National Grassland
From Alanreed, 6.5 mi W on I-40 to exit 128; right on FM 2477 for 5.6 mi to RV section, following signs. $10 without elec, $15 with elec ($5 & $10 with federal senior pass). All year; 14-day limit. 23 sites, typically 45 ft. Tbls, flush & pit toilets, cfga, drkg wtr. Fishing, boating(l), ATV trails. 300-acre lake. Non-campers pay $3 day use fee, $5 for ATV on trail. Nearby East Bluff Campground for tenters.

ALBANY (W)

Fort Griffin State Historic Site $10
Texas Historical commission
15 mi N of Albany on US 283. $10 at primitive area; $15 elec/wtr; $22 full hookups. 28 sites & five acres for primitive camping. All year; 14-day limit. Tbls, toilets, cfga, drkg wtr, showers, dump, playgrounds, interpretive displays, picnic areas, historic buildings, amphitheater (weekend programs in summer), group shelter, longhorn herd. Ruins of frontier fort. No longer a state park, this facility is operated by the Texas Historical Commission. $4/day entry fees also charged.

AMARILLO (W)

Texas Welcome Center   FREE
Off I-40 exit 76 at Hwy 468 (Airport Blvd) in Amarillo, following signs. Free. All year; 1-night limit. Tbls, flush toilets, showers, cfga, drkg wtr, dump, interpretive displays, travel counseling, video theater, Internet access.

Rosita Flats Cycle Area   FREE
Lake Meredith National Recreation Area
N of Amarillo on US 87/287 to Canadian River Bridge; E on dirt rd designated for off-road vehicles and motorcycle use. Free camping, but $4 boat launch fee. All year; 14-day limit. Primitive undesignated sites. No toilets, tbls or drkg wtr. Horseback riding, OHV use.

ANAHUAC (E)

Cedar Hill   FREE
Chambers County Park
4 mi N of I-10 on FM 563 to Lake Charlotte Rd. Free at 15 primitive sites for self-contained RVs. Permit required. All year; 3-night limit. Pit toilets, cfga, no drkg wtr. Nature trail. Formerly operated by Corps of Engineers.

Double Bayou $5
Chambers County Park
From I-10 near Anahuac, 4 mi S on SR 61; 7 mi S on FM 562; half mi W on Eagle Ferry Rd; on East Fork of Double Bayou. $5 at primitive sites, $10 with elec. All year; 3-night limit, self-contained RVs only. 30-acre open camping area. Flush toilets, tbls, cfga, drkg wtr, playground, ball field. Fishing. Trees filled with Spanish moss.

East Galveston Bay   FREE
Anahuac National Wildlife Refuge
10 mi S of Anahuac on SR 61 & CR 562; 3 mi E on co rd to gravel wildlife refuge entry rd; half mi SW on Cross Rd; 5 mi S on Windmill Rd. Free. All year; 3-night limit. Camp only along shore of East Galveston Bay & at bayshore pull-offs on Frozen Point Rd to facilitate night fishing. No facilities except toilets. Camping is not encouraged by wildlife service. Wildlife observation, fishing, waterfowl hunting, hiking. Poisonous snakes, fire ants, alligators, mosquitoes. Refuge

Fort Anahuac $5
Chambers County Park
From I-10 near Anahuac, S 4 mi on SR 61; then 7 mi on Farm 562; half mi on Eagle Ferry Rd. At Trinity Bay on East Fork of Double Bayou. $5 for primitive sites; $10 with wtr & elec. All year; 3-night limit. 8 hookup sites; 40-acre primitive area. Self-contained RVs only. Flush toilets, concrete tbls, shelters, 3 ball fields, lighted fishing pier. Swimming, fishing, boating(l), playground; golf nearby; crabbing; birdwatching. Judge Oscar Nelson Boardwalk on E bank of Trinity River. R

Job Beason Park   Free
Chambers County Park
From I-10 at Anahuac, 11 mi S on FM 563; 4.7 mi S on Eagle Rd; half mi W on Bayshore Rd; on Double Bayou. Free All year; 3-night limit. 12-acre open camping area, self-contained RVs only. Tbls, flush toilets, cfga, drkg wtr, playground. Boating(l), fishing.

White Memorial   FREE
Chambers County Park
From I-10 at Anahuac, .1 mi S on SR 61; on White's &
Turtle Bayous. Free primitive sites; $10 with elec. All
year; 3-day limit. 15 sites & open 85-acre camping area;
self-contained RVs only. Flush toilets, cfga, drkg wtr, tbls,
shelters, elec, cold showers. Hiking trails, swimming,
fishing, boating (l), crabbing.

Winnie-Stowell $5
Chambers County Park
From I-10 at Anahuac, 1 mi S on SR 124; .1 mi E on LeBlanc
Rd. $5 base. All year; 3-night limit. Base fee for primitive
sites; $10 with wtr/elec. 10 RV sites & 30-acre open
camping area. Self-contained RVs only. Flush toilets, tbls,
cfga, drkg wtr, elec, playground, pavilion, ball field, dump.
Approximate

ANDREWS (W)
Prairie Dog Town   FREE
Chamber of Commerce RV Park
In Andrews, on TX 115/176; 7 blks W of US 385; behind
Chamber offices by memorial. All year; 3-day limit. 6 RV
sites with elec/wtr hookups. Tbls, toilets, cfga, dump, drkg
wtr. Swimming; fishing; golfing. Prairie dog town. Internet
access at Chamber office.

AUSTIN (E)
Grelle Recreation Area $12
Lower Colorado River Authority
From I-35 S of Austin, travel W on SR 71; 1 mi N on Spur
191 to Spicewood; right on CR 404 1 mi; left on CR 412
(gravel) for half mi; on upper S side of Lake Travis, E of
Starcke Dam. $12 at designated sites. Daily or annual
entry permit required. All year; 5-day limit. Primitive
camping at metal fire rings; 400 acres. Toilet, no other
facilities; no drkg wtr or trash service. Hiking trail, fishing.

Muleshoe Bend $10
Primitive Recreation Area
Lower Colorado River Authority
From I-35 S of Austin, travel W on SR 71; 4.5 mi N on CR
404; right on CR 414 for 1.5 mi; right just prior to Ridge
Harbor entrance for 1 mi; after pavement ends, continue
.3 mi to entrance; on upper S shore of Lake Travis, E of
Starcke Dam. $10. Daily or annual entry fee. All year;
5-day limit. Primitive camping at metal fire rings. Toilets,
tbls. Bridle & hiking trail, fishing, 6.5-mi mountain biking
trail. 1,000 acres.

BALLINGER (W)
Concho Park $5
O.H. Ivie Reservoir
Colorado River Municipal Water District
S of Ballinger on US 83 toward Paint Rock; E on FM 1929
(Ray Stoker Hwy) about 17 mi; left on dirt access rd to
lake. $5 daily pass for primitive sites ($60 annually or

$10 for seniors); $12 with elec; $16 elec/wtr; $20 at 30
full hookups. All year; 7-day limit. 50 sites. Tbls, flush
toilets, showers (for RVs), cfga, drkg wtr, dump. Boating(l),
fishing.

BALMORHEA (W)
Balmorhea State Park $11
Qtr mi N of Balmorhea on FM 3078. $11 base. All year;
14-day limit. Base fee for 6 sites with wtr; $14 for 16
sites with wtr/elec, $17 for 12 sites with wtr/elec & cable
TV. Tbls, flush toilets, cfga, drkg wtr, showers, dump,
playgrounds, pool, concessions. Fishing, group trips.
Park built by CCC in 1930s; features a 77,000-square-foot
artesian spring pool with constant 72-76 degree temperatures; ideal for swimming, scuba diving.

BARDWELL (E)
High View Park $7
Corps of Engineers
Bardwell Lake
From Bardwell, 1.7 mi NE on SR 34, then SW prior to lake
bridge on High View Marina Rd; on SW side of lake. $7
with federal senior pass at 18 wtr/30-amp elec sites;
others pay $14. $8 with senior pass at 21 wtr/50-amp
elec sites; others pay $16. All year; 14-day limit. 65-ft RV
limit. Night-time exit provided. Tbls, flush toilets, cfga,
drkg wtr, showers, dump, fishing pier. Boating(l), fishing,
swimming. $4 fee for non-campers to use dump station;
$3 for boat launch; $4 per vehicle to swim, picnic.

Mott Park $7
Corps of Engineers
Bardwell Lake
From Bardwell, 1 mi NE on SR 34, then SE (right) 1.4 mi
on FM 985, then NE on access rd; at SE shore of lake. $7
with federal senior pass at 7 non-elec sites; others pay
$14. $8 with senior pass at 31 wtr/elec sites; others pay
$16. 4/1-9/30; 14-day limit. 65-ft RV limit; 12 pull-through
sites. Night exit provided. Tbls, flush toilets, cfga, drkg
wtr, showers, dump, playground, fishing pier. Boating(l),
fishing, swimming. Non-campers pay day use fees: boat
launch, $3; swimming $4 per vehicle, dump station $4.

Waxahachie Creek Park $7
Corps of Engineers
Bardwell Lake
From Bardwell, 1.2 mi NE on SR 24; 1.6 mi NW (left) on
Bozek Lane, then right (NE) on Brightwater Lane; at NW
shore of lake. $7 with federal senior pass at 7 primitive
sites; others pay $14, At 69 elec/wtr 30-amp sites, includ-
ing 4 equestrian sites, $8 base with senior pass; others
pay $16 base, $18 for premium locations ($9 with senior
pass). All year; 14-day limit. 65-ft RV limit; 14 pull-through
sites. Group camping available. Tbls, flush toilets, showers, cfga, drkg wtr, dump. Boating(l), fishing, horseback
riding, nature trail, bridle trail. $3 boat ramp, $3 equestrian trail, $4 dump station.

BASSETT(E)

Bassett Creek & Glenns Mill   FREE
Corps of Engineers
Wright Patman Lake
From Bassett, 1 mi NE on US 67; 1 mi S on CR 4223; on N side of Bassett Creek. All year; 14-day limit. Free. Primitive camping at 2 camping areas. No tbls, toilets or drkg wtr.

Blue Lake Campground   FREE
Corps of Engineers
Wright Patman Lake
From Bassett, half mi SW on US 67; 1 mi SE on CR 4269; at shore of Mudd Lake. Free. All year; 14-day limit. Primitive, undesignated camping; cfga, no other amenities. Fishing.

BASTROP (E)

Buescher State Park $12
10 mi SE of Bastrop on SR 71; NE on FM 153. $12 base at 25 sites with wtr; $17 at 32 wtr/elec sites. All year; 14-day limit. Tbls, flush toilets, cfga, drkg wtr, dump, 4 screened shelters, picnic areas, playgrounds, pavilion, recreation hall, showers, store. Hiking trails, fishing, swimming, boating (no motors). 1,000 acres. $7 per person activity fee.

BEAUMONT (E)

Big Thicket National Preserve   FREE
NW of Beaumont on US 69/287 to visitor center. Free primitive backcountry camping in designated areas & on sandbars by permit. Hiking, fishing, canoeing, ranger programs.

BELTON (E)

Cedar Ridge Park $12
Corps of Engineers
Belton Lake
From jct with SR 317 N of Belton, 2 mi NW on SR 36; 2 mi SW on Cedar Ridge Park Rd. $12 with federal senior pass at wtr/elec 30/50-amp RV sites; others pay $24. All year; 14-day limit. 64 elec/wtr sites; 2 pull-through; RV limit in excess of 65 ft. Tbls, flush toilets, cfga, drkg wtr, showers, playground, beach, coin laundry, dump, 2 picnic shelters, lighted fishing pier, free wireless at activity bldg. Boating(l), fishing, hiking, basketball, swimming. Non-campers pay $5 vehicle day use fee for picnicking, beach, dump station; $5 for boat ramps. Park access codes provided to campers for late entry.

Dana Peak Campground $12
Corps of Engineers
Stillhouse Hollow Lake
From jct with US 190 SW of Belton, 0.3 mi S on Simmons Rd; 5 mi W on FM 2410; 5 mi S on Comanche Gap Rd; at N shore of lake. $12 with federal senior pass at 20 elec/wtr RV sites; others pay $24. 2 double elec/wtr sites $40 ($36 with senior pass). All year; 14-day limit. RV limit in excess of 65 ft. Tbls, flush toilets, cfga, drkg wtr, showers, dump, fishing pier, beach, picnic shelter. Hiking, boating(l), fishing, horseback riding, biking, swimming. Non-campers pay $5 day use fees for dump station, picnicking, beach; $5 for boat ramp.

Iron Bridge Park   FREE
Corps of Engineers
Belton Lake
From jct with SR 317 NW of Belton, 10 mi NW on SR 36, crossing lake bride; 0.5 mi E on Deer Ridge Rd; 2 mi NE on gravel Iron Bridge Park Rd, following sign; at NE shore of lake. Free. All year; 14-day limit. 30-acre camping area. 5 primitive sites. Toilets, cfga, shelters, tbls, no drkg wtr. Boating(l), fishing, swimming. Temporarily closed 2017, road being repaired.

Live Oak Ridge Park $10
Corps of Engineers
Belton Lake
From N of Belton at jct with SR 317, 1.7 mi NW on FM 2305 (W. Adams Ave); left (S) on FM 2271 (Morgans Point Rd); adjacent to dam & spillway. $10 base with federal senior pass at wtr/30-amp elec sites with covered tbls; others pay $20 base, $24 for 50-amp sites ($12 with senior pass). All year; 14-day limit. RV limit in excess of 65 ft. Tbls, flush toilets, showers, cfga, drkg wtr, fishing pier, dump, wireless access at activity bldg, amphitheater. Boating(l), fishing, hiking. Non-campers pay $5 vehicle day use fee for picnicking, dump station; $5 for boat ramps.

Owl Creek Park   FREE
Corps of Engineers
Belton Lake
From jct with SR 317 NW of Belton, 6.5 mi NW on SR 36, across lake bridge; 1.1 mi W on Owl Creek Rd; right on access rd. Free. All year; 14-day limit. About 20 sites undesignated primitive sites on 47 acres. Toilets, tbls, cfga, no drkg wtr. Swimming, fishing, boating(l). Temporarily closed 2017, road being repaired.

Westcliff Park $12
Corps of Engineers
Belton Lake
From jct with SR 317 N of Belton, 3.7 mi NW on FM 439 (Lake Rd); 0.2 mi NW on Sparty Rd, then NE on Westcliff Park Rd; at SE shore of lake. $12 with federal senior pass at 25 wtr/elec sites; others pay $24. All year; 14-day limit. 65-ft RV limit; 19 pull-through; sites have covered tbls, grills, lantern poles. Tbls, flush toilets, cfga, drkg wtr, showers, dump, beach, picnic shelters. Boating(l), fishing, swimming. Non-campers pay $5 vehicle day use fee for picnicking, beach, dump station; $5 for boat ramps.

White Flint Park $12
Corps of Engineers
Belton Lake
From jct with SR 317 NW of Belton, 5.5 mi NW on SR 36, across bridge, then right into park. $12 with federal senior pass; others pay $24. All year; 14-day limit. 13 elec/wtr 30/50-amp sites; 60-ft RV limit. Toilets, covered tbls, cfga, no drkg wtr. Swimming, fishing, boating(l). Non-campers pay $5 vehicle day use fee for picnicking, $5 for boat ramp. Access codes provided to registered campers for late night entry

Winkler Park $7
Corps of Engineers
Belton Lake
From jct with SR 317 NW of Belton, 7.5 mi NW on SR 36; exit right (SE) 2 mi past White Flint Park on Deer Ridge, then 3.5 mi SE to park; at NW shore of lake. $7 with federal senior pass others pay $14. All year; 14-day limit. 14 semi-primitive sites with wtr hookups Tbls, toilets, cfga, shelter, no elec. Swimming, fishing, boating(l). 128 acres. Register at nearby White Flint Park. Non-campers pay $5 vehicle day use fee for picnicking, $5 for boat ramp.

BENBROOK (E)

Mustang Park $7
Mustang Point Campground
Corps of Engineers
Benbrook Lake
From N side of Benbrook at jct with I-20, 6.4 mi SW on US 377; 1.4 mi SE on FM 1187; 2.6 mi NW on CR 1042; follow signs into Mustang Point; adjacent to Bear Creek Campground at Mustang Park. $7 with federal senior pass at primitive areas; others pay $14. No designated sites; 9 areas have covered tbls, but shoreline also open for RVs & tents. 4/1-9/30; 14-day limit. Toilets, cfga, drkg wtr, beach, dump. $2 for use of showers at other campgrounds.

Rocky Creek $7
Corps of Engineers
Benbrook Lake
From Benbrook, S on US 377; 7 mi SE on FM 1187; 3.6 mi N on CR 1089; at jct with CR 1150, exit S to park. $7 with federal senior pass at 11 sites with covered tbls, cfga, nearby wtr, flush toilets, dump; others pay $14. All year; 14-day limit. Boating(l), fishing.

Mustang Park $7
Westcreek Circle
Bear Creek Campground
Corps of Engineers
Benbrook Lake
From N side of Benbrook at jct with I-20, 6.4 mi SW on US 377; 1 mi SE on FM 1187; SE 1 mi to Ben Day-Murrin Rd (CR 1025), then E 1 mi to the park. Free primitive camping along Bear Creek shoreline, including equestrian camping

(future equestrian facilities planned). 1 pit toilet, no drkg wtr, $2 for showers at other campgrounds. Fees for dump, boat launch, beach at Bear Creek camp. Trailhead to 14 mi of hiking & equestrian trails.

BIG SPRING (W)

Moss Creek Lake City Park $9
7.2 mi E of US 87 on I-20; 2.9 mi S & 2.7 mi E on Moss Lake Rd. $9 base (includes entrance fee). Base fee primitive sites; $12 for elec/wtr; $15 full hookups ($100 annually). All year; closed 12/15-1/15. 15 RV sites with elec. Tbls, flush toilets, cfga, drkg wtr, playground. Hiking, fishing, boating(ld), fishing piers. Non-campers pay $3 entry fee.

BLUM (E)

Kimball Bend Park $10
Corps of Engineers
Whitney Lake
From NW of Blum at jct with FM 933, 6 mi SW on SR 174 across bridge, then NW into park; N of lake on W side of Brazos River. $10 with federal senior pass others pay $20. All year; 14-day limit. 35 sites plus 129-acre open area. Toilet, tbls, cfga, drkg wtr. Swimming, fishing, boating(l).

BORGER (W)

Huber City Park FREE
On S. Matin St at SR 207 in Borger. Free. All year; 3-day limit. 10 sites. Tbls, flush toilets, cfga, wtr, dump, elec. Golf, swimming, fishing, boating(r); horseback riding/rental; tennis. 17 acres.

BOWIE (E)

Selma City Park $10
3.5 mi SW of Bowie on TX 59; 3.6 mi on FM 2583; on W side of Amon Carter Lake. $10 for RVs with elec at 29 sites; $15 for elec/wtr. All year. 28 sites with elec/wtr. $5 for tent camping. 7 day limit. Tbls, flush toilets, cfga, dump, drkg wtr, showers, shelters. Boating(lr); picnicking; fishing. Park host on site from April to Sep.

BRADY (W)

Richards City Park $5
Follow US 87 in Brady to Memory Lane; on Brady Creek. $5 for primitive camping, $20 at 14 full-hookup sites. All year; 10-day limit. 295 sites. Tbls, flush toilets, cfga, drkg wtr, hookups($), dump nearby, pavilion, playground, rodeo arena, concession stand. Tennis, soccer, biking trails, disc golf.

BRECKENRIDGE (W)

Hubbard Creek Lake Dam FREE
West Central Texas Municipal Water District
From US 180 Breckenridge, turn N at Wal-Mart on FM 3099, then follow WDR 277 to Prater Ramp. Free primitive camping at dam. Tbls, toilets, cfga, no drkg wtr. Boating(l), fishing, swimming, waterskiing.

Lake Daniel City Park   FREE
6 mi S of Breckenridge on Hwy 183; right on paved rd; at Lake Daniel. Free. All year. Primitive undesignated sites. Tbls, cfga, no hookups, toilets or wtr. Boating(l), fishing, picnicking, no swimming. 950-acre lake.

BROADDUS (E)

Townsend Park $4
Angelina National Forest
San Augustine County Park
4 mi SE of Broaddus on Hwy 103; 3 mi S on SR 1277; 1 mi W on FR 2923. $4 at Cedar Loop near lake, $2 for other loops. All year; 14-day limit. 19 sites. Tbls, cfga, portable toilets, no drkg wtr. Boating(l), fishing, waterskiing. On Sam Rayburn Lake. $2 day use fee (or $25 annually) for boat launch, fishing, boating, picnicking, hiking. All national forest permits honored. Dump($) at nearby Jackson Hill Park.

BROWNFIELD (W)

Coleman   FREE
Terry County Park
From jct US 62 & Reppto St., 1 blk E on Reppto; 1 blk S on First St. Watch for park entry signs off First & Second Sts. Donations accepted, but camp free. All year; 4-day limit. 12 sites. Elec, wtr, flush toilets nearby, dump, cfga. Swimming pool, tennis court nearby.

BRYANS MILL (E)

Thomas Lake Park   FREE
Corps of Engineers
Wright Patman Lake Area
From Bryans Mill at jct with FM 1766, about 1.5 mi NE on CR 2472; at "Y," veer right for 1 mi, then left 1 mi to shore of Thomas Lake (just W of Wright Patman Lake). Free. All year; 14-day limit. Primitive undeveloped camping area. No facilities except tbls; no drkg wtr. Boating(l), fishing.

CADDO (W)

Possum Kingdom State Park $12
18 mi N of Caddo on Park Rd 33 off US 180. $12 at 55 sites with wtr hookups (some shared); $20 at 40 elec/wtr sites ($25 premium locations). All year; 14-day limit. Tbls, flush toilets, cfga, no drkg wtr due to high salt content, showers, dump, playgrounds, picnic areas, store, longhorn herd fish cleaning facilities. Boating (ldr), fishing (lighted pier), swimming, waterskiing, canoeing (r), paddleboating (r), biking. 19,800-acre lake.

CANADIAN (W)

Canadian Fairgrounds $10
Hemphill County Recreation Complex
N side of town, E side of US 60 just S of river bridge. $10. All year; 5-day limit. 26 RV sites with elec/wtr (8 with 50-amp). Flush toilets, tbls, dump.

Lake Marvin $10
Black Kettle National Grasslands
Half mi N of Canadian on US 83; 11 mi E on FM 2266 (Formby Rd). $10 with federal senior pass; others pay $20. All year; 14-day limit. 12 RV sites with elec. Tbls, toilets, cfga, drkg wtr. Birdwatching, hiking, fishing, boating.

Lake Marvin RV & Camping $10
FM2266 12 miles East on Lake Marvin Road. $10. All year; Primitive Camping and sites with elec/wtr available around the lake. No reservations. R

Old Military Road Camp   Free
Black Kettle National Grasslands
From jct of US 60/US 83 at Canadian, 0.25 mi W to Lake Marvin Recreation Area sign, then 11 mi E on FM 2266 (Formby Rd); right at recreation area sign, then right at next "Y" for 1 mi. Free primitive camping. All year; 14-day limit. 14 sites, typically 40 ft. Tbls, portable toilets, cfga, drkg wtr. Boating(l), fishing, hiking

CANYON CITY (E)

Canyon Park $12
Corps of Engineers
Canyon Lake
3.2 mi NW of Canyon City on FM 306, then SW (right) on Canyon Park Rd; at NW shore of Canyon Lake. $12 at 150 primitive sites ($6 with federal senior pass). 4/1-9/30; 14-day limit. Tbls, pit toilets, cfga, drkg wtr, dump, beach, picnic shelters. Handicap access. Fishing, boating(l), swimming. Non-campers pay $4 day use fee for dump station, beach; $3 boat ramp.

North Park $12
Corps of Engineers
Canyon Lake
From Canyon City, 1.2 mi NW on FM 306, then 1 mi SE of North Park Rd; near dam. Open only Fri & Sat nights during 4/1-9/30. $12 ($6 with federal senior pass). 19 primitive sites. Tbls, toilets, cfga, drkg wtr. Fishing, boating (no ramp).

CARTHAGE (E)

Dotson Road Crossing $5
Panola County Park
9 mi W of Carthage on Hwy 315; 3 mi S on FM 1971. Free. Primitive sites. Wtr/Elec $15-$20 ($16 for seniors)Tbls, cfga, drkg wtr. Fishing, boating(ldr).

CENTER (E)

Boles Field $6
Sabine National Forest
4 mi S of Center on SR 87; 8 mi E on FM 2694. $6. All year; 14-day limit. 20 sites with 30-amp elec; 24-ft RV limit. Tbls, flush toilets, cfga, showers, drkg wtr, elec. Hiking, horseback riding. Camp built by CCC in 1930s.

Ragtown Recreation Area $5
Sabine National Forest
Sabine River Authority of Texas
13 mi SE of Center on SR 87; 6.5 mi E on SR 139; E 4 mi on SR 3184; 1.5. mi E on FR 132. $5 (double sites $8). 4/1-12/15; 14-day limit. 24 sites up to 50 ft but 24-ft RV limit. Tbls, flush toilets, cfga, drkg wtr, dump, showers. Boating(l--open all yr), fishing, hiking trails. Non-campers pay $2 day use fee.

CHICO (E)
Wise County Park $5
1 mi W of Chico on FM 1810; 3 mi S on FM 2952; 1 mi W on County Park Rd. $5 for primitive sites; $20 with hookups. All year. 100 sites. Tbls, toilets, cfga, drkg wtr, dump ($5 non-campers), cold showers. Fishing, swimming, boating(l).

CHICOTA (E)
Pat Mayse East $7.50
Corps of Engineers
Pay Mayse Lake
From Chicota, 0.8 mi W on FM 197; S on CR 35850. $7.50 with federal senior pass; others pay $15. All year; 14-day limit. 26 wtr/elec 30-amp sites. Tbls, flush toilets, cfga, drkg wtr, beach, dump. Boating(l), fishing, swimming. Non-campers pay day use fee for boat ramp, beach, dump station.

Pat Mayse West $12
Corps of Engineers
Pay Mayse Lake
2.3 mi W of Chicota on FM 197; 1 mi S on gravel CR 35810, then E & S on Pat Mayse W Park Rd. $12 at 5 primitive sites with wtr hookups ($6 with federal senior pass). At 83 wtr/elec 30-amp sites, $9 with senior pass; others pay $18. 5 pull-through; RV limit in excess of 65 ft. All year; 14-day limit. Tbls, flush toilets, cfga, drkg wtr, beach, dump. Fishing, swimming, boating(l). Limited facilities in winter. Non-campers pay use fees for boat ramp, dump station.

Sanders Cove $9
Corps of Engineers
Pay Mayse Lake
From Chicota, 3.2 mi E on FM 906, then S on entrance rd. At 85 elec/wtr sites, $9 base with senior pass; others pay $18 base, $22 for 50-amp sites ($11 with senior pass). All year; 14-day limit. Tbls, picnic shelter, flush toilets, beach, showers, dump, cfga, drkg wtr. Fishing, swimming, boating(l). Limited facilities in winter. Non-campers pay day use fees for boat ramp, dump station, beach.

CIRCLEVILLE (E)
Taylor Campground $11
Corps of Engineers
Granger Lake
From Circleville at jct with SR 95, about 5 mi NE on FM

1331, then qtr mi N on Granger Dam Rd & NW on Fox Park Rd to park. $11 with federal senior pass at 48 elec/wtr sites others pay $22 & $26. 50-ft RV limit. all year; 14-day limit. Tbls, flush toilets, showers, cfga, drkg wtr, dump, beach. Hiking trail, fishing, boating(l), swimming. Non-campers pay $4 day use fee for boat ramp, beach, picnicking, hiking, horseback riding, dump station.

Wilson H. Fox Campground $11
Corps of Engineers
Granger Lake
From Taylor Park, 1 mi NE on FM 1331, then NW; adjacent to S side of dam. All year; 14-day limit. 49 wtr/elec sites, including 5 screened shelters. $11-$18 with federal senior pass others pay $22-$36. 50-ft RV limit. Tbls, flush toilets, cfga, drkg wtr, fish cleaning station, dump, beach, playground, showers. Non-campers pay $4 day use fees for boat ramp, beach, picnicking, hiking, horseback riding, fishing, dump station.

CLARENDON (W)
Lakeside Marina $12
Greenbelt Lake
Greenbelt Municipal and Industrial Water Authority
3 mi N of Clarendon on SR 70; left on CR N; at SE shore of lake. $12. All year; 14-day limit. 55 RV sites, $12 with elec (wtr available) at Sandy Beach area; $12 with elec/wtr at Kincaid Park. Tbls, flush toilets, cfga, drkg wtr. Boating(l), fishing, hiking, waterskiing. $5 per person access fee charged daily; boat access $3. Lake

Kincaid Park $12
Greenbelt Lake
Greenbelt Municipal and Industrial Water Authority
From US 287 at Clarendon, 4 mi N on SR 70. $12. All year; 14-day limit. 25 RV sites with elec/wtr. Tbls, cold showers, pit & chemical toilets, cfga, drkg wtr, dump, playground. Fishing, boating(l), swimming, volleyball, basketball, horseshoes, nature trail.

Primitive Shoreline Camping $5
Greenbelt Lake
Greenbelt Municipal and Industrial Water Authority
3 mi N of Clarendon on SR 70; camp in undesignated areas around the lake. Camp free, but $5 per person daily permit required. Tbls, cfga, toilets, no drkg wtr. Boating(l), fishing.

COLEMAN (W)
Flat Rock I & II Park $8
Corps of Engineers
Hords Creek Lake
From Coleman, 8.7 mi E on Hwy 153; S across dam on Hords Creek Rd, then W on Flat Rock Park Rd, following signs; on S shore of lake. $8 with federal senior pass at 44 wtr/30-amp elec sites; others pay $16. At 6 elec/wtr

50-amp sites, $10 base with senior pass; others pay $20 base, $22 for premium locations ($11 with senior pass); $32 double site. At 16 full-hookup sites, $11 with senior pass; others pay $22. Other sites with screened shelters at higher rates; also group camping areas. All Year; 14-day limit. RV limit in excess of 65 ft; 10 pull-through sites. Tbls, flush toilets, cfga, drkg wtr, showers, dump, beach, fishing pier, fish cleaning station. Tennis, boating(l), fishing, swimming.

Kennedy Recreation Area $5
Colorado River Municipal Water District
6 mi S of Coleman on SR 206; 4.5 mi W on US 67; 13.8 mi S on FM 503; 6.5 mi W on FM 1929; on O.H. Ivie Reservoir. $5 daily pass for primitive sites ($60 annually or $10 for seniors); All year; 7-day limit. Base fee for primitive camping. 70-acre primitive area. Tbls, flush & pit toilets,cfga, drkg wtr, dump, bait, snack bar, store. Swimming, fishing, boating(l). Annual permit available.

Lakeside I & II Park $8
Corps of EngineersHords Creek Lake
From Coleman, 8 mi W on Hwy 153 past Friendship Park, then S on Lakeside Rd, following signs; at N shore of lake. $8 base with federal senior pass at 39 wtr/30-amp elec sites; others pay $16 base, $20 for premium locations ($10 with senior pass). At 20 wtr/50-amp elec sites, $10 base with senior pass; others pay $20, $22 for premium locations. At full-hookup sites, $11 with senior pass; others pay $22. Also group camping areas. All year; 14-day limit. RV limit in excess of 65 ft; 18 pull-through sites. Tbls, flush toilets, cfga, drkg wtr, fish cleaning station, showers, beach, dump. Hiking, tennis, boating(l), fishing, swimming, horseshoe pits, fishing pier, handicap fishing area.

Padgitt Recreation Area $5
Colorado River Municipal Water District
6 mi N of Coleman on SR 206; 4.6 mi W on US 67; 11 mi S on FM 503; 7 mi W on FM 2134; on O.H. Ivie Reservoir. $5 daily pass for primitive sites ($60 annually or $10 for seniors). All year; 7-day limit. 15 primitive sites. Tbls, toilets, cfga, no drkg wtr. Boating(l), fishing, swimming.

COMANCHE(W)
(Promontory Campground $8
Corps of Engineers
Proctor Lake
From Comanche at jct with US 377, 12 mi N on SR 16; 5 mi E on FM 2318; at NW side of lake. $8 at 16 primitive sites ($4 with federal senior pass). At 52 elec/wtr 30-amp sites, $8 with senior pass; others pay $16 (double sites $32). At 5 premium elec/wtr 50-amp sites, $10 with senior pass; others pay $20. Also sites with screened shelters & 3 group camping areas. 4/1-9/30; 14-day limit. RV limit in excess of 65 ft; 4 pull-through sites. Picnic shelter, tbls, cfga, drkg wtr, flush toilets, dump, showers, shelters. Boating(ld), fishing.

CORPUS CHRISTI (E)
Bird Island $5
Padre Island National Seashore
SE of Corpus Christi on Hwy 358 to headquarters; SE on Park Rd 22, then W to campground; at Laguna Madre. Camp free, but $5 daily or $10 annual use fee ($2.50 or $5 with federal senior pass) plus park entrance fee. All year; 14-day limit. Primitive sites; tbls, chemical toilets, cfga, no drkg wtr. Fishing, swimming, beachcombing. GPS: 27.466, -97.313

Labonte City Park   FREE
Exit I-37 at Nueces River Park exit; follow signs. Park was renamed in 2001. Camp free for 3 days (except for Easter Weekend). Primitive sites, no hookups. Tbls, toilets, cfga, drkg wtr, visitor center. Fishing, hiking. Vicinity

Lake Corpus Christi State Park $10
35 mi NW of Corpus Christi on I-37; 4 mi S on SR 359; N on FM 1068. $10 for 60 sites with wtr hookups; $20 for 23 sites with elec/wtr; $25 full hookups. All year; 14-day limit. Tbls, flush toilets, cfga, drkg wtr, showers, dump, playgrounds, picnic areas, pavilion, fish cleaning shelters. Fishing (lighted piers), boating(rd), canoeing(r), birdwatching, swimming. 21,000-acre lake.

Malaquite Beach $8
Padre Island National Seashore
SE of Corpus Christi on Hwy 538 to headquarters; SE on Park Rd 22 to visitor center area. $8 (or $4 with federal senior pass). All year. 48 rustic sites. Tbls, flush toilets, cfga, drkg wtr, cold rinse showers, dump, wtr refill station. Swimming, fishing, beachcombing, shelling. $10 weekly entry fee or $20 annually.

North Beach   FREE
Padre Island National Seashore
SE of Corpus Christi on Hwy 358 to headquarters; SE on Park Rd 22 to beach access rd. Camp free, but $10 weekly entry fee or $20 annually. All year. 45 undesignated primitive sites; 14-day limit. Tbls, cfga, no drkg wtr or toilets (but use cold showers & flush toilets at Malaquite visitor center). Swimming, fishing, beachcombing, shelling, picnicking. RV generators okay except between 10 p.m. & 6 a.m.

South Beach   FREE
Padre Island National Seashore
SE on Hwy 358 from Corpus Christi to headquarters; SE on Park Rd 22 to end. Camp free, but $10 weekly entry fee or $20 annually. All year. 45 sites. Tbls, portable toilets, cfga, no drkg wtr (flush toilets & rinse showers at Malaquite visitor center). Swimming, fishing, beachcombing, shelling, picnicking.

CROCKETT (E)

Mission Tejas State Park $9
21 mi NE of Crockett & 12 mi W of Alto on SR 21; entrance in Weches from Park Rd 44. $9 for 2 sites with wtr hookups; $13 for 10 RV sites with wtr/elec ($78 weekly); $15 for 5 sites with full hookups ($90 weekly). All year; 14-day limit. Tbls, flush toilets, cfga, drkg wtr, showers, playgrounds, pavilion, picnic areas, dump. Historical features. Hiking trails, biking, fishing, nature trail.

Ratcliff Lake $7.50
Davy Crockett National Forest
20 mi NE of Crockett on SR 7; half mi N on FR 520 (1 mi W of Ratcliff). $7.50 with federal senior pass at non-elec sites; others pay $15. Elec & full-hookup sites $20 ($10 with senior pass for elec, $15 full hookups). All year; 14-day limit. 76 sites (30 with 20/30-amp elec); no RV size limit. Tbls, flush toilets, showers, cfga, drkg wtr, dump, amphitheater, shelter, beach, snack bar, fishing piers. Swimming, picnicking, fishing, boating(l--elec mtrs), hiking, canoeing(r). Trailhead to 20-mile 4-C Hiking Trail. Forest's only developed campground. Non-campers pay $3 day-use fee & for dump station. Fee increases proposed.

White Rock Horse Camp $10
Davy Crockett National Forest
11 mi E of Crockett on Hwy 7; 10 mi S on FR 514, then access to amp on FR 514-D. $10 use fee (or $50 annually). Primitive undesignated sites. Toilet, cfga, no drkg wtr. Hiking, horseback riding trails.

CROSBYTON (W)

Campground #1 $7
White River Municipal Water District
13.5 mi S of US 82 on FM 651; 8.6 mi E & S on FM 2794; on White River Lake. $7 at primitive sites plus $7 per person daily entry permit. 20 primitive sites; 25-ft RV limit. All year; 7-day limit. Tbls, flush toilets, cfga, drkg wtr. Fishing, boating(l), swimming. Boat launch fee.

Campground #2 $7
White River Municipal Water District
13.5 mi S of US 82 on FM 651; 8.6 mi E & S on FM 2794; 1.5 mi NE on local rd; on White River Lake. $7 at primitive sites plus $7 per person daily entry fee. 25 sites (added fee for elec at 10 sites). 25-ft RV limit. All year; 7-day limit. Tbls, flush toilets, cfga, drkg wtr. Fishing, boating, swimming. Boat launch fee.

Campground #3 $7
White River Municipal Water District
13.5 mi S of US 82 on FM 651; 7.2 mi E & S on FM 2794; N on Lake Rd; on White River Lake. $7 at primitive sites plus $7 per person entry fee. 25 primitive sites; 25-ft RV limit. All year; 7-day limit. Tbls, flush toilets, cfga, drkg wtr. Fishing, boating(l), swimming. Boat launch fee.

Campground #4 $7
White River Water Authority
13.5 mi S of US 82 on FM 651; 7.2 mi E & S on FM 2794; N on Lake Rd 5 mi past Campground #3; on White River Lake. $7 at primitive sites plus $7 per person entry fee. Primitive undesignated sites; no facilities. All year; 7-day limit. Fishing, boating, swimming.

City Park   FREE
Crosbyton Overnite RV Parking
Crosbyton Chamber of Commerce
US 82 at E city limit, corner of Main and East Aspen. Free. All year; 2-day limit; $10 thereafter. 8 sites full hookup. Toilets, drkg wtr, cfga. Pool($), playground. Restrooms closed in winter. Make arrangements at City Office.

DAWSON (W)

Liberty Hill Campground $9
Corps of Engineers
Navarro Mills Lake
From Dawson at jct with SR 31, 4 mi NW on FM 709, on right; at S shore of lake. All year; 14-day limit. $9 with federal senior pass at 3 primitive sites during 3/1-10/31; others pay $18; sites $14 off-season ($7 with senior pass). $20-$40 ($10-$20 with senior pass) in season. Off season ; 11/1-12/31 $16-$32 ($8-$16 with senior pass) at 92 elec/wtr sites, 14 wuth full hookups. Double sites and group sites also available. RV limit in excess of 65 ft. Tbls, flush toilets, cfga, drkg wtr, showers, beach, fishing pier, dump, playground, picnic shelter, fishing pier. Boating(l), fishing, swimming, handicap fishing area. Non-campers pay $4 at dump station, $3 at boat launch, $1 per person at beach.

Oak Campground $10
Corps of Engineers
Navarro Mills Lake
From Dawson, 4.3 mi NE on SR 31, 1.5 mi N on FM 667, on left; on NE shore of lake. All year; 14-day limit. $10-$12 with federal senior pass at 48 elec/wt sites during 3/1-10/31 (others pay $20-$24); during 11/1-12/31, elec/wtr sites are $16 ($8 with senior pass). RV limit in excess of 65 ft. Tbls, flush toilets, cfga, drkg wtr, showers, playground, beach, fishing pier, handicap accessible fishing area, dump, picnic shelter. Boating(l), fishing, swimming, handicap fishing area.

Pecan Point $12
Corps of Engineers
Navarro Mills Lake
3.5 mi NE of Dawson on SR 31; 3.2 mi N on FM 667; 2 mi SW on FM 744; 2 mi SE on FM 1578 right on CR 3360 Rd to park entrance on right; to park on N shore of lake. $12 at 30 non-elec sites; $14 at 5 elec/wtr 30/50-amp sites ($6 & $7 with federal senior pass). 11 pull-through sites; RV limit in excess of 65 ft. 4/1-9/30; 14-day limit. Picnic shelter, tbls, toilets, cfga, drkg wtr, dump. Boating (l), fishing, hiking.

Wolf Creek Campground $8
Corps of Engineers
Navarro Mills Lake
From Dawson, 3.5 mi NE on SR 31; 3.2 mi N on FM 667; 2.5 mi W on FM 639, then 1 mi S on NW 3140 Rd into park;; at N shore of lake. $8 with federal senior pass at 20 non-elec sites; others pay $16. 2 non-elec double sites $30 ($15 with senior pass). At 50 elec/wtr 30/50-amp sites, $9 with senior pass; others pay $18. RV limit in excess of 65 ft; 12 pull-through. 4/1-9/30; 14-day limit. Picnic shelter, tbls, flush toilets, cfga, drkg wtr, showers, dump, fishing pier. Boating(l), fishing.

DECATUR (E)

Black Creek Lake Park $2
Caddo/LBJ National Grasslands
From US 380 at Decatur, 6 mi N on FM 730; left on CR 2360 for 2 mi; right on CR 2461 for qtr mi, then left on FR 902; at NE shore of Black Creek Lake. $2 use fee. All year; 14-day limit. Open camping on 2 acres (about 7 small sites). Toilets, cfga, no drkg wtr. Fishing, boating(l); no swimming or shooting. Lake

Tadra Point Trailhead Camp $4
Caddo/LBJ National Grasslands
From US 380 at Decatur, 9 mi on FM 730; left on CR 2461, then right onto CR 2560 for 2.4 mi; left at sign on gravel FR 900 for 1.8 mi. $4 day use fee. 23 primitive undesignated sites. All year; 14-day limit. Pit toilets, cfga, tbls, no drkg wtr. Bike & bridle trails, boating(l), fishing.

DEL RIO (W)

Amistad National Recreation Area
3 mi N of Del Rio on US 90 W to National Park Service headquarters bldg. Camping restricted to 5 designated areas along shoreline below maximum flood pool level. Boating; fishing; swimming; scuba diving; waterskiing; hunting. Dump & drkg wtr at Diablo East. Headquarters bldg (also has wtr) open M-F, 8 am to 5 pm, all year; 9 am to 6 pm weekends (Nov-Mar, 8 am to 5 pm). Interpretive programs; schedules available at headquarters. Donation boxes are provided at the free camping areas, with funds earmarked for education and facilities improvements. $4 daily use fee (or $10 for 3 days, $40 annually) charged; $2, $5 & $20 with federal senior pass).

Devils River State Natural Area $10
43 mi N of Del Rio on US 277; 22 mi W on rough Dolan Creek Rd. $10. 7 primitive sites for self-contained RVs, by reservation only. No facilities, no trash service; drkg wtr nearby. Pictographs, hiking trail, guided hikes & tours($). 19,988 acres. Nearest service station, 25 mi. No entry fee.

Governor's Landing $8
Amistad National Recreation Area
9 mi E of Del Rio on US 90 to Amistad Dam; N on dirt rd.

Follow rd along railroad. Go under Hwy 90 bridge to campground. $8 ($4 with federal senior pass). All year; 15-day limit. 15 sites (RVs under 28 ft). Tbls, toilets, cfga, drkg wtr. Store. Dump nearby. Fishing, swimming, boating, waterskiing, scuba diving. Very popular. Has roped off swim area, fishing docks, and amphitheater. Only Amistad NRA campground with drkg wtr.

North Highway 277 $4
Amistad National Recreation Area
9 mi N of Del Rio on US 277. 3.5 mi on Hwy 90 W to US 277; turn off, travel N over San Pedro Bridge 1 mi; turn right to campground. $4. All year; 15-day limit. 17 sites. Group camping also available. Toilets, covered tbls, cfga, no drkg wtr. Dump nearby. Picnicking; fishing; swimming; boating; waterskiing.

Rock Quarry Organized Campground $2
Amistad National Recreation Area
By reservation only. $2 per person per day (15 person minimum.) All year; 7-day limit. Tbls, cfga, toilets, 1 large site with a shelter. Within 5 miles, Diablo East Marina, Ranger Station. Dump, water, gas supplies. Fina station on Hwy 90 W. Picnicking; fishing; swimming; hiking; waterskiing; boating; canoeing; rockhounding; scuba diving. Pets on leash. This campground has to be reserved. Designated for at least 32 persons. Reserve by calling 830-775-7491 or in person at park headquarters on Hwy 90 at Del Rio.

Rough Canyon Camp $4
Amistad National Recreation Area
About 15 mi N of Del Rio on US 277, cross lake bridge; 11 mi W on Recreation Rd 2, becoming Rough Canyon Rd 2. $4. All year; 14-day limit. 4 sites. Covered tbls, cfga, toilets, no drkg wtr. Boating, fishing.

San Pedro Flats $4
Amistad National Recreation Area
6 mi W of Del Rio on US 90 to Spur 454, N on dirt rd. $4. All year; 14-day limit. 35 sites (RVs under 29 ft). Tbls, toilets, cfga, no drkg wtr. Within 5 mi: Diablo East sanitary dump, Diablo East Marina. Picnicking; fishing; swimming; boating; waterskiing. Boats can be launched when lake is up.

San Pedro Organized Camp $2
Amistad National Recreation Area
By reservation only. $2 per person per day (15 person minimum.) All year; 7-day limit. Tbls, cfga, toilets, 1 large site with shelter. Within 5 mi: Diablo East Marina, Ranger Station. Water, dump. Picnicking; fishing; swimming; hiking; waterskiing; boating; canoeing. Available for groups of 20-plus. Reserve by calling 830-775-7491 or in person at park headquarters on Hwy 90 at Del Rio.

Seminole Canyon State Historical Park $8
42 mi NW of Del Rio on US 90; E of Pecos River (9 mi W of Comstock). $8 at 15 primitive sites; $14 at 8 sites with

wtr nearby; $20 at 23 elec/wtr sites. All year; 14-day limit. Tbls, flush toilets, cfga, drkg wtr, dump, showers, interpretive displays, canyon tours, store. Picnicking, hiking trail. Indian pictographs, mountain biking. Judge Roy Bean Visitor Center at Langtry.

Spur 406 $4
Amistad National Recreation Area
20 mi W of Del Rio on US 9; 4 mi S on Spur 406. $4. All year; 14-day limit. 6 sites (RVs under 29 ft). Toilets, covered tbls, no drkg wtr, dump, cfga. Fishing; swimming; boating; waterskiing; boat ramp. This campground is more isolated than the others.

DENISON (E)
Burns Run East $10
Corps of Engineers
Lake Texoma
8 mi N of Denison on SR 75A, across bridge, then 3 mi W; in Oklahoma. $10 base with federal senior pass at 44 elec/wtr sites; others pay $20 base, $24 for full hookups ($12 with senior pass). During 11/1-3/31, 25 elec sites $12 without wtr hookups ($6 with federal pass); payment by honor deposit; wtr at frost-free hydrant near park entrance; no showers or bathroom facilities. All year; 14-day limit. RV limit in excess of 65 ft; 43 pull-through sites. Non-campers pay day use fee for boat ramp, dump station. Tbls, flush toilets, cfga, drkg wtr, dump, showers, pavilion, beach, playground. Boating(l), fishing, swimming, hiking, nature trail.

Burns Run West $10
Corps of Engineers
Lake Texoma
8 mi W of Denison on SR 75A, across dam, W side; in Oklahoma. 4/1-9/30 (not open off-season); 14-day limit. At 44 elec/wtr sites, $10 base with federal senior pass; others pay $20 base, $24 for premium locations ($12 with senior pass). 1 group camping area. RV limit in excess of 65 ft. Non-campers pay day use fee for boat ramp, dump station. Flush toilets, tbls, cfga, drkg wtr, dump, showers, pavilions. Swimming, picnicking, boating(l), fishing, hiking.

Dam Site North Area $7
Corps of Engineers
Lake Texoma
5 mi N of Denison on SR 75A; on S side of dam in Oklahoma. $7 at 6 primitive sites. All year; 14-day limit. Tbls, cfga, drkg wtr, pit toilets, picnic shelter. Boating(l), fishing.

Dam SiteSouth $7.50
Corps of Engineers
Lake Texoma
From Denison, 5 mi N on SR 91; turn right on Denison Dam Rd; below dam on S side of Red River in Texas. $7.50 with federal senior pass at 9 non-elec sites; others pay $15. $10 with senior pass at 21 wtr/elec sites; others pay $20.

Some sites open during 11/1-3/31 with $12 fees & reduced amenities (elec & 1 frost-free faucet available). RV limit in excess of 65 ft. Tbls, flush toilets, showers, cfga, drkg wtr, dump. Boating(l), fishing.

DOUGLASSVILLE (E)
Jackson Creek   FREE
Corps of Engineers
Wright Patman Lake
From SR 8 at Douglassville, 4.1 mi E on SR 77; 1.5 mi N on FM 2791; 3 mi N on CR 2116: at S shore of lake at Poorboy Landing. Free. All year; 14-day limit. 10 primitive sites (25-ft RV limit). Tbls, pit toilet, cfga, drkg wtr. Fishing, boating (l).

DUMAS (W)
Blue Creek Bridge Public Use Area   Free
Lake Meredith National Recreation Area
S of Dumas on US 87/287; E 15.6 mi on Farm 1913; E 2.5 mi on local rd. Camp free, but $4 daily boat fee. All year; 14-day limit. Undeveloped backcountry camping area. Toilets, cfga, no drkg wtr. Boating, fishing, horseback riding. Off-road vehicles okay.

Blue West Public Use Area   Free
Lake Meredith National Recreation Area
S of Dumas on US 87/287; E 15.6 mi on Farm 1913; E. 2.6 mi on local rd. Camp free, but $4 daily boat fee. All year; 14-day limit. Undeveloped canyon rim camping area; about 40 sites. Toilets, cfga, no drkg wtr, shelters, dump. No firewood. Boating(l), fishing, picnicking.

Chimney Hollow Public Use Area   Free
Lake Meredith National Recreation Area
S of Dumas on US 87/287; 15.6 mi E on FM 1913; E 2 mi on local rd. Camp free, but $4 daily boat fee. All year; 14-day limit. Undeveloped shoreline camping. Toilets, cfga, tbls, no drkg wtr. Fishing, boating. Dump, boat ramp at nearby Blue West PUA.

Plum Creek   Free
Lake Meredith National Recreation Area
Approx 19 mi on TX 152 from Dumas; 3 mi on TX 1913 to Plum Creek Rd. Camp free, but $4 daily boat fee. All year; 14-day limit. 15 primitive backcountry sites. Tbls, toilets, no drkg wtr. Dump. Hunting; picnicking; fishing; boating(ld); waterskiing; bank fishing. Shallow-wtr launching ramp. Horse rails, pens.

Texhoma City Park   FREE
500 W First Street in Dumas (US 87 N). Free 1 night, but donation accepted. Spring-fall. 24 RV open, undesignated sites, some without hookups. Tbls, cfga, toilets, elec, wtr, dump. Picnicking; swimming; biking, rec hall.

EL PASO (W)

Franklin Mountains State Park $8
In El Paso, N on US 84 from I-10; left on Loop 375. $8 at 5 self-contained RV sites; no hookups. All year; 14-day limit. Shaded tbls, pit toilets, cfga, drkg wtr, store, charcoal cfga; no ground fires. Hiking & bridle trails, rock climbing, ranger tours($).

Hueco Tanks State Historical Park $12
35 mi NE of El Paso on US 62 & US 180; 8 mi N on Ranch Rd 2775, following signs. $12 at 4 sites with wtr hookups; $16 at 16 sites with 50-amp wtr/elec. All year; 14-day limit. Tbls, flush toilets, drkg wtr, showers, dump, amphitheater, picnic areas. Rock climbing, trails, guided weekend tours. 3500 Indian pictographs. Solid fuels prohibited; only containerized fuel cooking permitted. No activity fee. Non-campers pay $5 for dump station.

FAIRFIELD(E)

Fairfield Lake State Park $12
6 mi NE of Fairfield on FM 488; E on FM 2570; access on Park Rd 64. $12 at 35 sites with wtr hookups during 3/1-12/12 ($72 weekly); 96 elec/wtr sites $18 ($106 weekly) open all year; overflow sites $7. 14-day limit. Tbls, flush toilets, cfga, drkg wtr, showers, dump, playgrounds, picnic areas, amphitheater, dining hall. Fishing (lighted pier), boating(l), nature program, waterskiing, swimming, nature trail. 1,460 acres.

FLOYDADA (W)

Wayne Russell FREE
Municipal RV Park
In town at First St (US 70) and Taft St on N side of Floydada. Camp free 3 nights; $10 thereafter. 10 sites. Tbls, flush toilets & showers at pool house, cfga, drkg wtr, dump, pool($). Swimming, tennis, baseball, playground.

FORT DAVIS (W)

Overland Trail Campground $12
1 mi S of jct of Hwys 17 & 118 on Main St. $12 base for primitive sites; $16 for vans & cabovers with hookups; $25 full hookups. 27 sites. Tbls, flush toilets, cfga, drkg wtr, CATV($), showers, coin laundry. Veterans discount.

FRITCH (W)

Bates Canyon Public Use Area Free
Lake Meredith National Recreation Area
6 mi W & SW of Fritch on TX 136; 3 mi on Alibates Rd to jct; right fork to camping area. Camp free, but $4 daily boat fee. All year; 14-day limit. Primitive shoreline camping. Tbls, toilets, cfga, no drkg wtr. Boating(l), fishing.

Cedar Canyon Free
Lake Meredith National Recreation Area
6 mi NE of Fritch and 3 mi W of Sanford; take marked co rds from either Fritch or Sanford. Camp free, but $4 daily boat fee. All year; 14-day limit. Semi-developed with random shoreline camping. Flush toilets, cfga, dump, drkg wtr. Boating; waterskiing; hunting. courtesy dock. Opportunity for camping varies with the lake level.

Fritch Fortress Public Use Area Free
Lake Meredith National Recreation Area
E of Fritch on Eagle Blvd; N on co rd to campground; difficult shoreline access. Camp free, but $4 daily boat fee. All year; 14-day limit. 10 undeveloped canyon rim sites. Tbls, shelters, toilets, drkg wtr. No firewood. Fishing; boating(ld); waterskiing; hunting. Deep wtr launching ramp, courtesy dock.

Harbor Bay Free
Lake Meredith National Recreation Area
2 mi NW of Fritch on TX 136. Camp free, but $4 daily boat fee. All year; 14-day limit. Undeveloped primitive shoreline camping, some developed sites back from old shoreline; dump nearby. Tbls, toilets, cfga, shelters, dump. Boating. Hiking trail

McBride Canyon Free
Lake Meredith National Recreation Area
6 mi W & SW of Fritch on TX 136; 3 mi on Alibates Rd to jct; left-hand fork to undeveloped backcountry camping area. Camp free, but $4 daily boat fee. All year; 14-day limit. Tbls, toilets, cfga, no drkg wtr. Dump. Hunting; fishing; waterskiing. No lake access.

Mullinaw Creek Free
Lake Meredith National Recreation Area
6 mi W & SW of Fritch on TX 136; 3 mi on Alibates Rd to undeveloped backcountry camping area. Camp free, but $4 daily boat fee. All year; 14-day limit. Tbls, toilets, cfga, no wtr. Dump at McBride Canyon. Fishing, waterskiing, horseback riding (corrals).

Sanford-Yake Public Use Area Free
Lake Meredith National Recreation Area
1 mi E of Fritch on TX 136; 4 mi N on TX 687; W to campground. Camp free, but $4 daily boat fee. All year; 14-day limit. 40 sites, some with shade shelters. Flush toilets, tbls, cfga, drkg wtr, snack bar, dump. Boating, waterskiing, fishing. Deep wtr launching ramp and courtesy dock, dry land boat storage.

GEORGETOWN (E)

Jim Hogg Campground $11
Lake Georgetown
Corps of Engineers
From just S of Georgetown at jct with I-35, about 7 mi SE on FM 2338; 2 mi N on Jim Hogg Rd; at SW shore of lake opposite Cedar Breaks Park. $11-$18 base with federal senior pass; others pay $22 -$36. 140 sites All year; 14-day limit. 55-ft RV limit. Tbls, flush toilets, cfga, drkg wtr, showers, dump, fishing pier. Hiking, boating(l), fishing. Night exit provided.

Russell Park $12
Lake Georgetown
Corps of Engineers
From SE of Georgetown at jct with I-35, 7.5 mi SE on FM 2338, past exit to Jim Hogg Park; 0.7 mi E on FM 3405; 2 mi N on CR 262. $12 at 17 non-elec sites ($6 with federal senior pass). Also 10 non-elec screened shelters containing bunks (no mattresses), $12 with senior pass; others pay $24. All year; 14-day limit. Tbls, toilets, cfga, drkg wtr, picnic shelter. GPS: 30.6775, -97.75917

GOLDTHWAITE (W)
Goldthwaite City Park FREE
At US 183 & SR 16 in Goldthwaite. All year. 6 sites. Tbls, flush toilets, cfga, drkg wtr, playground, pool. Swimming, lighted sand volleyball court, washer pitching court. 50-ft deep lake was hand-dug in 1885 to provide wtr for railroad. Unable to verify rates for 2017

GORDONVILLE (E)
Juniper Point East Campground $10
Corps of Engineers
Lake Texoma
From just W of Gordonville at jct with FM 901, about 4 mi N on US 377; before Willis Bridge over lake, turn right on access rd, following signs; at S shore of lake. Base fee $10 at 14 elec/wtr 30-amp sites; others pay $20; $11 with senior pass at 17 elec/wtr 50-amp sites; others pay $22. Open 4/1-9/30; 14-day limit. Off-season, camp at nearby Juniper Point West. Tbls, flush toilets, showers, cfga, drkg wtr, picnic shelter, dump, fishing pier, beach. Fishing, boating(l), swimming.

Juniper Point West Campground $11
Corps of Engineers
Lake Texoma
From just W of Gordonville at jct with FM 901, about 4.2 mi N on US 377; just past Juniper Point East turnoff before Willis Bridge over lake; turn left on access rd, following signs; at S shore of lake. $11 at 13 elec/wtr 30/50-amp sites; others pay $22. All year; 14-day limit. During 10/1-3/31, all elec sites open, but shower & restroom facilities closed, and no wtr hookups after 11/1; fill fresh wtr tanks from frost-free hydrant near park entrance. Off-season fee $12 ($6 with senior pass). Cross Timbers Hiking Trail begins at Juniper Point West and follows the lake's S shoreline about 15 mi; free wilderness tent camping along trail, but no wtr.

GRAHAM (E)
Kindley City Park $10
7 mi NW of Graham on US 380 at Lake Graham Bridge; on Lake Graham. $10. All year; 5-day limit. 10 RV sites. Tbls, flush toilets, cfga, wtr, 30-amp elec. Swimming; picnicking; fishing; boating (l). Lake

Lake Eddleman City Park $12
1.6 mi N of Graham on US 380 from SR 16. On Lake Eddleman. $12. All year; 14-day limit. 12 RV sites. Tbls, flush toilets, cfga, drkg wtr, 30/50-amp elec, lighted fishing pier, dump. Fishing, picnicking, bike trails, boating(l). Lake

GRANGER (E)
Willis Creek Campground $10
Corps of Engineers
Granger Lake
From Granger at jct with Hwy 95, 0.8 mi E on FM 971; 4 mi SE on CR 348; NE on CR 346. $10 at 10 primitive sites (5 for equestrians). At 23 elec/wtr sites, $11-$13 with senior pass; others pay $22-$26. Equestrian & horse trailer sites near bridle trail. All year; 14-day limit. 50-ft RV limit. Tbls, flush toilets, cfga, drkg wtr, showers, dump, fishing pier. Hiking, horseback riding, boating(l), fishing. Non-campers pay $4 day use fees for boat ramp, beach, hiking, horseback riding, fishing, dump station.

GROESBECK (E)
Public Use Area #2 FREE
Brazos River Authority
Limestone County Parks
11.3 mi SE of SR 164 on Farm 937; 3.6 mi N & E on Farm 3371 to W side of Lake Limestone. Free. All year; 14-day limit. Primitive 17-acre camp area. Tbls, toilets, cfga, no drkg wtr. Fishing, boating(l).

Public Use Area #3 FREE
Brazos River Authority
Limestone County Parks
11.3 mi SE of SR 164 on Farm 937; 5 mi N & E on Farm 3371 to E side of Lake Limestone. Free. All year; 14-day limit. Tbls, cfga, no drkg wtr. Primitive 17-acre camp area. Fishing, boating(l)

Public Use Area #5 FREE
Brazos River Authority
6.7 mi N of US 79 on Farm 1146; local rd 1.8 mi W to E end of dam. On Lake Limestone. Free. All year; 14-day limit. Primitive 10-acre camp area. Tbls, flush toilets, cfga, fishing pier, no drkg wtr. Fishing, boating(l). Dam

HAMLIN (W)
City Park FREE
5 blocks W from center of town on S. Central Ave; 6 blocks SW on 5th St; 1 block E on SW Ave. Free first night; $12 afterward. All year; 7-day limit. 13-acre primitive camp area, undesignated sites. Drkg wtr, cfga, 30-amp elec. Playground, ball field, pool, tennis courts, volleyball court.

HASKELL (W
Haskell City RV Park FREE
At Haskell, 6 blocks S of US 380 on Ave C. First night free; $16 thereafter. All year. 36 sites (32-ft RV limit). Tbls, flush toilets, full hookups (30/50-amp), cold showers,

cfga, dump, pool, playground. Swimming, tennis, fishing. 24 acres. Vicinity

HEMPHILL (E)

Indian Mounds $4
Sabine National Forest
Sabine River Authority of Texas
8 mi E of Hemphill on SR 83; 3.5 mi S on FM 3382; 1 mi E on FR 130. $4. 3/1-10/15; 14-day limit. 25 sites up to 60 ft, but 24-ft RV limit. Tbls, toilets, cfga, drkg wtr. Boating(l), fishing. On shore of Toledo Bend Lake. Non-campers pay $2 day use fee.

Lakeview Campground $3
Sabine National Forest
Sabine River Authority of Texas
9 mi S of Hemphill on SR 87; 5 mi NE on SR 2928 to end of paved rd & follow signs 3.5 mi to Lakeview. $3. 3/1-10/15; 28-day limit on select sites. 10 primitive sites up to 43 ft, but 24-ft RV limit. Tbls, toilets, cfga, drkg wtr. Boating, fishing. 20 acres. On shore of Toledo Bend Lake. Trailhead for Trail-Between-the-Lakes. Boat ramp in poor condition.

HEREFORD (W)

Hereford RV Sites FREE
In town at Herford Aquatic Center; from US 385, 4 blks E at 400 E. 15th St. Free, but donations encouraged. All year; 3-night limit. 5 sites. Tbls, toilets, cfga, drkg wtr, 20-amp elec/wtr hookups, dump nearby. Pond, walking track, YMCA nearby.

HONEY GROVE (E)

Bois-D'Arc Trail Head $6
Caddo/LBJ National Grasslands
10 mi N of Honey Grove on FM100; within the national grasslands. $6. All year; 14-day limit. 20 campsites. Toilets, drkg wtr, cfga hitching rails. Hunting, fishing, hiking, horseback riding.

East Coffee Mill Lake Park $4
Caddo/LBJ National Grasslands
10.5 mi N from US 82 on Farm 100; 3.5 mi W on local rd. $4 ($2 with federal senior pass). All year; 14-day limit. 2-acre primitive camping area, 13 sites. Toilets, cfga, drkg wtr. Fishing, boating(l), waterfowl hunting, hiking No swimming. Non-campers pay $2 day use fee.

West Lake Crockett Campground $4
Caddo/LBJ National Grasslands
From US 82 near Honey Grove, 10.5 mi N on FM 100; 2 mi W on FM 409; at NW shore of Lake Crockett. $4. All year; 14-day limit. 12 sites, typically 40 ft. Toilets, drkg wtr. Fishing, waterfowl hunting, boating(l), no swimming, hiking. Non-campers pay $2 day use fee. Tent-only camping at East Lake Crockett Recreation Area.

IRA (W)

Bull Creek Park $5
Colorado River Municipal Water District
4.9 mi W of Ira on FM 1606; 2.6 mi W on FM 2085; 1.9 mi N on FM 1298; 3.2 mi W on FM 1610; 2 mi S on local rd; on Lake J.B. Thomas. $5 daily pass for primitive camping ($60 annually or $10 for seniors). All year; 7-day limit. Primitive camping. Tbls, toilets, cfga, no drkg wtr. Swimming, fishing, boating(l).

Sandy Beach Park $5
Colorado River Municipal Water District
4.9 mi W of Ira on FM 1606; 4 mi W on FM 2085; on Lake J.B. Thomas. $5 daily pass for primitive camping ($60 annually or $10 for seniors); $12 with hookups. All year; 7-day limit. Primitive open area. Tbls, toilets, cfga, no drkg wtr. Swimming, boating, fishing, picnicking.

South Side Park $5
Colorado River Municipal Water District
4.9 mi W of Ira on FM 1606; 2.6 mi W on FM 2085; .6 mi W & 1.8 mi S on FM 1298; on Lake J.B. Thomas. $5 daily pass for primitive camping ($60 annually or $10 for seniors). All year; 7-day limit. 100-acre primitive camping area. Tbls, toilets, cfga, no drkg wtr. Swimming, fishing, boating(l), picnicking.

White Island Park $5
Colorado River Municipal Water District
From FM 2085 west of Ira, 3.1 mi S on FM 1298; 2.2 mi W on local rd; on Lake J.B. Thomas. $5 daily pass for primitive camping ($60 annually or $10 for seniors). All year; 7-day limit. 5-acre primitive area. Tbls, toilets, cfga, no drkg wtr. Swimming, fishing, boating(l), picnicking.

JASPER (E)

Ebenezer Park $7
Corps of Engineers
Sam Rayburn Lake
From Jasper, 12 mi N on US 96; 8 mi W on Recreation Rd 255 across dam, then N; on CR 49; at S shore of lake. $7 at 17 non-elec sites; others pay $1; all year; 14-day limit. $15-$28 ($7-$14 with federal senior pass) at 13 equestrian sites, all with elec 3 have wtr hookup, 7 have 30-amp elec, 6 with 50-amp; each site includes hitching posts, tbl, fire ring; corral provided. 1.5 mi of Corps equestrian trail, 20 mi of national forest trails nearby. 50-ft RV limit. Tbls, toilets, cfga, drkg wtr, dump, beach, coin laundry. No boat ramp. Fishing, swimming, horseback riding.

Sandy Creek $10
Corps of Engineers
B.A. Steinhagen Lake
From Jasper, 10 mi W on US 190; 1.3 mi S on FM 777; 2.5 mi W on CR 155; at SE shore of lake. $10 at 8 primitive sites ($5 with federal senior pass). At 34 elec/wtr 30-amp

sites, $8 with senior pass; others pay $16. At 35 elec/wtr 50-amp sites, $9 with senior pass; others pay $18. At 2 elec/wtr 30-amp sites having screened shelters, $12.50 with senior pass; others pay $25. All year; 14-day limit. RV limit in excess of 65 ft. Tbls, toilets, cfga, drkg wtr, dump, picnic shelter, beach. Boating(l), volleyball, fishing, swimming. Non-campers pay $4 for dump station, swimming beach; $2 showers.

Twin Dikes Park $7
Corps of Engineers
Sam Rayburn Lake
From Jasper, 13 mi N on US 96; 5 mi W on FM 255, then N; on S shore of lake. $7 with federal senior pass at 24 non-elec sites; others pay $14. At 6 elec/wtr 30-amp sites, $13 with senior pass; others pay $26. At 4 elec/wtr 50-amp sites & 6 full-hookup 30-amp sites, $14 with senior pass; others pay $28. All year; 14-day limit. Other sites with screened shelters. 60-ft RV limit. Picnic shelter, tbls, flush toilets, cfga, drkg wtr, dump, fishing pier. Boating(l), fishing, swimming. Non-campers pay $4 for dump station.

JEFFERSON (E)

Alley Creek $13
Corps of Engineers
Lake O' the Pines
From Jefferson, 4 mi NW on SR 49; 12 mi W on FM 729 across 3 lake bridges; after third bridge, turn S on Alley Creek Rd, following signs. At RV sites, $13 with federal senior pass; others pay $26. Group camping & double sites available. 3/1-9/30; 14-day limit. RV limit in excess of 65 ft. Tbls, flush toilets, cfga, drkg wtr, beach, dump, showers, fishing pier. Boating(ld), fishing, swimming, hiking. Non-campers pay day use fees: $3 for boat ramps, $4 for dump stations, picnicking, beaches.

Brushy Creek $13
Corps of Engineers
Lake O' the Pines
From Jefferson, 4 mi NW on SR 49; 3.5 mi W on FM 729; 4.8 mi SW on FM 726 past dam, then right following signs; at SE shore of lake. $13 base with federal senior pass at elec RV sites; others pay $26 base, Up to $42 for premium locations (1/2 price with senior pass). 3/1-11/30; 14-day limit. RV limit in excess of 65 ft. Tbls, flush toilets, cfga, drkg wtr, showers, beach, dump, playground. Boating(l), swimming, fishing, hiking. Non-campers pay day use fees: $3 for boat ramps, $4 for dump stations, picnicking, beaches.

Buckhorn Creek $13
Corps of Engineers
Lake O' the Pines
From Jefferson, 4 mi NW on SR 49; 3.5 mi W on FM 729; 2.4 mi SW on FM 726, on right (sign) before the dam. $13 base with federal senior pass at RV sites; others pay $26

base, Up to $42 for premium locations (1/2 price with senior pass). RV limit in excess of 65 ft. Tbls, flush toilets, cfga, drkg wtr, dump, showers, playground, fishing pier. Fishing, hiking, boating(l), swimming. Non-campers pay day use fees: $3 for boat ramps, $4 for dump stations, picnicking, beaches.

Cedar Springs Campground   FREE
Corps of Engineers
Lake O' The Pines
16 mi NW of Jefferson on SR 49 to Avinger; 4 mi SW on SR 155, across lake, then left; at NW shore of lake. Free. All year; 14-day limit. 28 primitive sites; 48 acres. Tbls, pit toilets, cfga, drkg wtr. Picnicking; fishing; boating(l), hunting during season in undeveloped areas. Historical site.

Hurricane Creek   FREE
Corps of Engineers
Lake O' The Pines
From Jefferson, 4 mi NW on SR 49; 4 mi W on FM 729 past FM 726, then S following signs; at E shore of Hurricane Creek arm of lake. Free. All year (limited facilities during winter); 14-day limit. 23 primitive sites (camp only in designated areas). Tbls, pit toilets, cfga, drkg wtr. Swimming; picnicking; fishing; hunting in the undeveloped areas during hunting season. No firearms in developed public use areas.

Johnson Creek $13
Corps of Engineers
Lake O' the Pines
From Jefferson, 4 mi NW on SR 49; 8.5 mi W on FM 729, on left after crossing bridge over Johnson Creek; at NE shore of lake. At 63 elec RV sites, $13 base with federal senior pass; others pay $26 base, $30 for premium locations ($15 with senior pass). All year; 14-day limit. RV limit in excess of 65 ft. Group camping with 12 elec sites. Picnic shelter, amphitheater, tbls, flush toilets, cfga, drkg wtr, beach, dump, showers, playground, fish cleaning station. Boating (ld), fishing, hiking, swimming. Non-campers pay day use fees: $3 for boat ramps, $4 for dump stations, picnicking, beaches.

JUNCTION (W)

Schreiner City Park   FREE
From I-10 exit 457 E of Junction, SW on FM 2169; right on SR 481; first right after crossing bridge; on SW shore of South Llana River. Free up to 3 days. All year. 15-acre primitive camping area, undesignated sites. Flush toilets, cfga, tbls, drkg wtr, playground, pool, ball field. Swimming, fishing, boating(l). Sightseeing (scenic views).

KENNARD (E)

Piney Creek Horse Camp $10
Davy Crockett National Forest
From W of Kennard on SR 7, 2.5 mi S on CR 514; right for half mi on CR 4625. $10 for camping or using bridle trail

($50 annually). All year; 14-day limit. 15 primitive sites. Tbls, pit toilet, cfga, drkg wtr, hitching posts, stock pond. Hiking trails, horseback riding.

KERMIT (W)
Winkler County Park $10
10 mi NE of Kermit on SR 115 to RR-874. $10 (pay to treasurer at courthouse). All year; 10-day limit. Tbls, toilets, cfga, drkg wtr, elec, pool. Very popular dune buggy and OHV site. Former Corps of Engineers park.

KOPPERL (E)
Plowman Creek Park $7
Corps of Engineers
Whitney Lake
From downtown Kopperl, 2 blocks SE; 0.5 mi W & S on CR 1242 to park; at W shore of Brazos River N of lake. $7-$8 with federal senior pass, others pay $14-$16 45-ft RV limit.Equestiran sites available. Toilets, cfga, drkg wtr, tbls, showers, dump. Fishing, boating(l). Boat ramp fee for non-campers.

LADONIA (E)
Ladonia Unit FREE
State Wildlife Management Area
Caddo National Grasslands
4 mi W of Ladonia on SR 34. Within the national grasslands. Free. All year; 14-day limit. No permits or registration required. Primitive undesignated camping on 16,150 acres. Hunting, fishing, hiking, horseback riding.

LAGO VISTA (E)
Turkey Bend Primitive Recreation Area $12
Lower Colorado River Authority
8 mi W of Lago Vista on FM 1431 (NW of Austin); 1.8 mi S on Shaw Dr; on N side of Lake Travis, E of Starcke Dam. $12 at undesignated primitive area. Daily or annual entry fee. All year; 5-day limit. Tbls, cfga, portable toilet, no drkg wtr or trash pickup. 400 acres. Horseback/hiking trail; trailhead parking; boating, fishing. 2 mi of shoreline.

LA GRANGE (E)
Park Prairie Park $12
Fayette Power Project
Lower Colorado River Authority
9 mi E of SR 71 on Fayette Power Project Lake. $12 for primitive sites. All year; 5-day limit. 2 acres of primitive camping & 12 unimproved sites. Tbls, toilets, cfga, drkg wtr, showers, beach, fishing pier. Fishing, boating(ld), swimming, volleyball, horseback riding, bike trail, nature trail. Lake

LAGUNA PARK (E)
Walling Bend Park FREE
Corps of Engineers
Whitney Lake
From N of Laguna Park at jct with SR 22, 2 mi NW on FM 56; 2.5 mi NE on FM 2841; at W shore of lake. Free. All year; 14-day limit. 6 primitive camping/picnic sites. Tbls, pit toilet, cfga, drkg wtr, picnic shelter. No drkg wtr Nov-March. Swimming, fishing; boating(l). GPS: 31.897557, -100.739791

LAMESA (W)
City RV Parking Area FREE
Forrest Park
Lamesa Parks & Recreation Department
.5 mi S of US 180 on TX 137; at 9th St & Bryan Ave. Free camping up to 4 days; $20 thereafter. All year; 12-day limit. 8 sites with 30-amp elec (2 pull-through). Toilets, drkg wtr, dump. Softball; playground.

LANGTRY (W)
Judge Roy Bean FREE
Visitor Center Camping Area
Verde County Ghost Town
On Hwy 50, about 50 mi W of Del Rio. Free, but donations requested. Undesignated sites; no facilities. At visitor center adjoining Jersey Lilly Saloon.

LEVELLAND (W)
Levelland R.V Park FREE
Levelland Parks Department
1 mi S of Levelland on US 385 next to municipal airport. Free. All year; 3-night limit; $25 thereafter for 7 more days. 7 paved sites. Drkg wtr, elec/wtr hookups, dump. Picnicking.

LEWISVILLE (E)
Lake Park Campground $8
Lewisville Parks & Leisure Services Department
Near Lewisville, 3 mi E on FM 407E (Lake Park Rd) from US 35E, following signs. $8 for seniors with federal senior pass at wtr/elec sites ($16 for all others); $9 for seniors at premium sites ($18 for others). All year; 14-day limit. 119 sites. Tbls, flush toilets, cfga, drkg wtr, showers, dump, coin laundry, WiFi, free day park admission. Fishing, boating (ld), swimming. On land leased from the Corps of Engineers.

LITTLEFIELD (W)
Waylon Jennings RV Park FREE
At US 385 & 15th St (1 mi N of Hwy 84) in Littlefield. Free. All year; 4-day limit. $20 thereafter. 8 small RV sites & 1 longer space. Tbls, drkg wtr, dump. Picnicking; horseshoes; baseball; golf nearby. Donations accepted.

LIVINGSTON (E)
Lake Livingston State Park $10
1 mi S of Livingston on US 59; 4 mi W on FM 1988; half mi N on FM 3126; access on Park Rd 65. $10 at 16 sites with wtr hookups; $18 at 26 elec/wtr sites; $21-$24 full hookups. All year; no length-of-stay limit. Tbls, flush toilets, cfga, drkg wtr, dump, showers, playgrounds, picnic areas, amphithe-

ater, store, pool, observation tower. Fishing, boating(d), swimming, hiking & nature trails. 635 acres on 84,000-acre lake. $4 daily activity fee.

LLANO (E)
Black Rock Park $12
Lower Colorado River Authority
From SR 16 near Llano, 3 16.1 mi on SR 29; 4 mi N on SR 261. On Lake Buchanan. $12 at 21 primitive sites; $25 at 15 sites with 30/50-amp elec/wtr. All year; 14-day limit. Tbls, flush toilets, cfga, drkg wtr, dump, playground, cold showers. Fishing, boating(l), hiking, wading. Scenic. 2 sites & toilets for handicapped. Note: Park sometimes reaches vehicle capacity and closes on weekends.

LUBBOCK (W)
Samuel W. Wahl City Recreation Area $9
About 60 mi S of Lubbock on US 84, through Justiceburg; exit on FM 2458, then E on FM 3519 to Lake Alan Henry and 2 mi W of the John T. Montford Dam. $9 for non-residents Mon-Thurs; $12 Fri-Sun. Park also charges $8-$10 daily entry fee or $50 annually ($30 for seniors). All year. Primitive undeveloped camping area on 580 acres. 50 sites, 32 with concrete pads. Tbls, cfga, toilets, no drkg wtr. Hiking, boating(l), fishing, picnicking. Future plans include RV sites with hookups. 2,880-acre lake. Lake

LULING (E)
Palmetto State Park $12
6 mi S of Luling off US 183; 2 mi W on Park Rd 11 (21 mi SE of Lockhart). $12 at 19 sites with wtr hookups ($72 weekly); $18-20 for sites with multiple hookups. All year; 14-day limit. Tbls, flush toilets, cfga, drkg wtr, showers, dump, playgrounds, picnic areas, rec hall, fishing pier, store. Birdwatching, canoeing, fishing, tubing, rafting, biking. Numerous wildlfowers & plants. San Marcos River. $3 activity use fee.

MARATHON (W)
Chisos Basin $7
Big Bend National Park
69 mi S of Marathon on US 385; 3 mi W on park rd; 7 mi SW (15% grade into campground). $7 with federal senior pass; others pay $14. All year; 14-day limit. 60 sites (20-ft trailer limit, 24-ft motorhome limit). Tbls, flush toilets, cfga, drkg wtr, dump, shelters. Horseback riding, hiking, nature programs. $25 weekly entry fee (free with senior pass).

Cottonwood Campground $7
Big Bend National Park
69 mi S of Marathon on US 385; 13 mi W on park rd; 22 mi SW to Castolon; half mi W. On Rio Grande River. $7 with federal senior pass; others pay $14. All year; 14-day limit. 14 sites. Tbls, pit toilets, cfga, drkg wtr, no dump. No generators. Fishing, picnicking, hiking trails. $25 weekly entry fee (free with senior pass).

Rio Grande Village Campground $7
Big Bend National Park
69 mi S of Marathon on US 385; 20 mi SE. $7 with federal senior pass; others pay $14. All year; 14-day limit. 100 sites, typically 45 ft. Tbls, flush toilets, cfga, drkg wtr, dump, coin laundry. Fishing, hiking. Note: full hookups at higher fees available from concessionaire. $25 weekly entry fee (free with senior pass).

Backcountry Camping $12
Big Bend National Park
70 mi S of Marathon on US 385. All year; 14-day limit. $12 for primitive camping at numerous backcountry roadside sites on improved dirt roads, usually accessible to all vehicles except after rain (then many require high-clearance or 4x4 vehicles). No facilities or services at most sites. Obtain backcountry permit from visitor centers. Showers($), coin laundry at Rio Grande Village Store at SE side of park. Park entry fee $25 weekly 9free with senior pass) plus $12 backcountry permit ($6 with federal senior pass). The following backcountry sites are accessible by vehicle, listed by access roads:

Access via Old Ore Rd, 27-mile backcountry road along western flank of Dead Horse Mountains; recommended for high-clearance vehicles.
Candelilla Primitive Roadside Campsite $12
Big Bend National Park
On Old Ore Rd, 1.1 mi from its S end near Rio Grande Village or 25.4 mi from the Dagger Flat Auto Trail; 0.1 mi W of Old Ore Rd. $12 permit required. 2 sites for 8 persons. High-clearance vehicles usually recommended, RVs & cars okay if rd is in good condition. 4x4 needed following rains, however. No shade. Small cul-de-sac site.

Campe de Leon Primitive Roadside Campsite $12
Big Bend National Park
On Old Ore Rd, 3.6 mi from main paved rd to Rio Grande Village; $12 permit required. 1 site for 6 persons no horses. High clearance recommended, 4x4 needed after rain. RVs & cars okay if rd is in good condition. Fantastic panoramic views.

Ernst Basin Primitive Roadside Campsite $12
Big Bend National Park
On Old Ore Rd, 10 mi from main paved rd to Rio Grande Village; 16.4 mi from N end at the Dagger Flat Auto Trail; no rock sign, so watch for turn-off S of Willow Tank turn-off. High clearance recommended, 4x4 needed after rain because several washes mush be crossed. Access rd usually good. $12 permit. 1 site for 2 vehicles; no horses. Poor shade; protection from N by low hill. 8-mi hike to ruins of an ore discharge terminal.

Ernst Tinaja Primitive Roadside Campsite $12
Big Bend National Park
Site is 4.5 mi from paved rd & on qtr mi access rd; 21.5

mi from Dagger Flat Auto Trail. $12 1 site. 2 vehicles or10 people; No horses permitted. High-clearance vehicle highly recommended. No shade, Do not swim or bathe in nearby tinajas; water not potable.

McKinney Spring $12
Primitive Roadside Campsite
Big Bend National Park
On Old Ore Rd, 7.3 mi from Dagger Flat Auto Trail (19 mi from main paved rd and 2 mi N of Roy's Peak Vista campsite); 50-yd access rd. High clearance highly recommended, 4x4 after rain. $12. 1 site for 2 vehicles, 6 persons; no horses. No shade. Excellent scenery. In a valley near McKinney Spring creek bed. Easy cul-de-sac turn-around.

La Noria Primitive Roadside Campsite $12
Big Bend National Park
On Old Ore Rd, 4.9 mi from main paved rd to Rio Grande Village (half mi past Ernst Tinaja turn-off); 21 mi from Dagger Flat Auto Trail. High clearance recommended, 4x4 after rain. $12. 2 sites for 6 persons each; no horses. No shade, but both sites protected by low hills. Good scenery. Warning: Wash N of the Ernst Tinaja turn-off is sandy & deep. After rain, a tinaja 2 mi N in a ravine collects wtr & attracts wildlife; wtr not potable.

Roy's Peak Vista $12
Primitive Roadside Campsite
Big Bend National Park
On Old Ore Rd, 9.3 mi from Dagger Flat Auto Trail (17 mi from main paved rd to Rio Grande Village); short, rutted access rd on W side is quite rough. High clearance recommended, 4.4 needed after rain. $12. 1 large site for 2 vehicles & 6 persons; no horses. On cul-de-sac with good turn-around. No shade, some protection by low hills surrounding site. Old ranch site remains nearby.

Telephone Canyon $12
Primitive Roadside Campsite
Big Bend National Park
On Old Ore Rd, 14 mi from main paved rd to Rio Grand Village; 12.5 mi from Dagger Flat Auto Trail. Very rough qtr-mi access rd on E side of Old Ore Rd. High-clearance highly recommended; 4x4 may be needed following rain. $12. 2 sites for 3 vehicles & 18 persons; no horses permitted. Exposed sites, no shade. Primitive Telephone Canyon hiking trail from Site #2 through Dead Horse Mtns.

Willow Tank Primitive Roadside Campsite $12
Big Bend National Park
On Old Ore Rd, 10.1 mi from the main paved rd to Rio Grande Village (16.3 mi from Dagger Flat Auto Trail); on W side of short access rd. $12. High clearance vehicle recommended, 4x4 after rain. 1 vehicle, 6 persons, no horses. No shade in winter; scrub shade in summer, but not for parking or tents. Near natural spring. Good wildlife site.

Access via River Road, a remote 51-mile route that parallels the park's southern boundary & the U.S. border. Parts of roadway follow the Rio Grande, but most is some distance from the river, especially near Mariscal Mountain. The western end of the road is quite rough and much of it impassable following a rain. Easy access to the Rio Grande at end of rd; soft sand & gravel at launch may mire some vehicles. River can be accessed at end of the rd; boats must be carried a short distance. Approximate driving time between Castolon and Rio Grand Village is 5-7 hours:

Black Dike Primitive Roadside Campsite $12
Big Bend National Park
Via River Rd, 10.7 mi from W end near Castolon or 43.3 mi from E end near Rio Grande Village; high-clearance vehicle required, 4x4 after any rain; short access rd. $12. 1 site for 2 vehicles & 10 persons; no horses permitted. Good shade. River access by 1-minute walk by trail through heavy brush. Good fishing. Secure belongings while asleep or absent. Area frequented by passers-by and Mexican residents.

Buenos Aires Primitive Roadside Campsite $12
Big Bend National Park
Via River Rd, 4.4 mi from W end near Castolon or 49.6 mi from E end near Rio Grande Village; qtr mi access rd. High-clearance vehicle required, 4x4 after any rain. $12. Site for 2 vehicles & 10 persons; 4 horses permitted. On small hill overlooking Rio Grande floodplain, but no river access. Secure belongings when sleeping or absent. Area frequented by passers-by.

Dominguez Trailhead $12
Primitive Roadside Campsite
Big Bend National Park
Via River Rd, 22.7 mi from W end near Castolon or 31.3 mi from E end near Rio Grande Village. High-clearance vehicles required, 4x4 after any rain. $12. 1 sites for 2 vehicles, 8 persons; 4 horses permitted. No shade, but site protected from wind by low hills. No access to river. Vehicles may be parked at nearby Dominguez Spring trailhead; from there, 10-mile rugged trail leads into Sierra Quemada toward a rock house & several unreliable springs. Secure valuables while sleeping or absent.

Elephant Tusk Primitive Roadside Campsite $12
Big Bend National Park
Via River Rd 21 mi from its E end & 29 mi from W end; take Black Gap Rd for 3 mi N. High-clearance vehicle required, 4x4 after any rain. Black Gap Rd is not maintained and is very rough. $12. 1 small site near E side of rd across from Elephant Tusk trailhead. 1 vehicle, 6 persons, no horses. Gravel ground cover, no shade. Scenic. Secure all belongings while sleeping or absent.

Fresno Primitive Roadside Campsite $12
Big Bend National Park
Via River Road East, 18.6 mi from jct with main park rd; watch for Fresno turnoff to the N; it's easy to miss. High-clearance vehicles required, 4x4 after any rain. Access rd usually in good condition. Gravel base, no shade. $12. 2 vehicles & 8 persons; no horses. Good views of Sierra del Carmen Mtns in Mexico and historic Mariscal Mine. Secure belongings while sleeping or absent.

Gauging Station Primitive Roadside Campsite $12
Big Bend National Park
Via River Rd, 14.2 mi from W end near Castolon or 38.8 mi from E end near Rio Grande Village; NW 0.5 mi on Gauging Station access rd. High-clearance vehicles required, 4x4 after any rain. $12. 1 site for 6 persons, no horses. Excellent shade. River access by short trail through heavy brush. Fishing popular. Secure belongings while sleeping or absent. Area frequented by passers-by.

Gravel Pit Primitive Roadside Campsite $12
Big Bend National Park
Via River Road East, 1.8 mi from jct with main park rd to Rio Grande Village; 1.4 mi access rd; high clearance vehicles required. $12. Sites 1 & 2, 2 vehicles & 10 persons each; no horses. Site 3, 2 vehicles & 12 persons; no horses. Sites 1-3 have gravel base, no shade; Riverbank steep, accessible by foot, but boat launch difficult. Safeguard belongings while asleep or away from site.

Johnson Ranch Primitive Roadside Campsite $12
Big Bend National Park
Via River Rd, 15.6 mi from W end near Castolon or 38.4 mi from E end near Rio Grande Village; qtr mi access rd. High-clearance vehicles required, 4x4 after any rain. $12. 2 sites for 4 vehicles & 18 persons; 6 total horses permitted. Scenic 5-minute walk to Johnson house ruins. River access by following cow trails through thick riverside brush; best access from Site 2. Secure belongings while asleep or absent. Nearby remnants of historic structures. In 1929, Army Air Corps developed landing field; no artifact collecting permitted.

La Clocha Primitive Roadside Campsite $12
Big Bend National Park
Via River Road East, 2.6 mi from jct with main park rd; 0.7-mi access rd. High-clearance vehicle required, 4x4 after any rain. $12. 2 sites for 2 vehicles & 10 persons & 4 horses permitted at Site #1, 2 vehicles & 8 persons permitted at Site 2. Partial shade, sandy base at Site 2; no shade, gravel base at Site 1. River access by foot from Site 1; boat launching possible from Site 2. Secure belongings while sleeping or absent.

Loop Camp Primitive Roadside Campsite $12
Big Bend National Park
Via River Rd, 23 mi from W end near Castolon or 31 mi from E end near Rio Grande Village; sites just off Loop Camp access rd. High clearance vehicles required, 4x4 after any rain. $12. 2 sites for 5 vehicles & 20 persons; 4 horses permitted each site. Sites just above river, with foot trail access down a steep bluff. Minimal shade. Secure belongings while sleeping or absent; area frequented by passers-by

Solis Primitive Roadside Campsite $12
Big Bend National Park
Via River Road East, 13.7 mi from jct with main park rd. Sites 1-2 along access rd. High clearance vehicles required, 4x4 after any rain. $12. Space for 5 vehicles & 27 persons. Gravel base at sites. Boating, fishing, hiking. Secure belongings while sleeping or absent.

Talley Primitive Roadside Campsite $12
Big Bend National Park
Via River Road East, 23.2 mi from jct with main park rd. High clearance required, 4x4 after any rain. Site 1 is close to River Rd; other sites about 6 mi on access rd. $12. 2 sites, each for 2 vehicles & 8 persons; no horses. Sites 1-2 have gravel base, no shade. Excellent scenery. Theft a recurring problem, so safeguard valuables & take precautions against vehicle damage. Primitive Mariscal Rim hiking trail starts here.

Access via Glenn Springs Road, which begins 5 mi E of Panther Junction and skirts the E side of the Chison Mtns toward Pine Canyon and Juniper Canyon before bouncing over a rough section to the tiny desert oasis of Glenn Springs. Glenn Springs Rd and all campsite rds are rough & rutted, recommended for high-clearance vehicles only, and after a rain, road conditions can deteriorate fast. Many arroyos to cross, requiring 4x4. Five camping areas available:

Glenn Springs Primitive Roadside Campsite $12
Big Bend National Park
Via Glenn Spring Rd, 8.8 mi from jct with the main park rd to Rio Grande Village; S of Juniper Canyon Rd, Glenn Spring Rd is extremely rough for half mi over solid bedrock; caution & slow speed are critical. Site 1 is qtr mi along the very rough Black Gap Rd, which is not maintained; Site 2 is on the Glenn Spring Rd just past the historic area. $12. 2 sites for 2 vehicles each & 8 persons; no horses. Nearby historic remains of Glenn Springs community from early 1900s; brochure available at park headquarters. Glenn Springs.

Nugent Mountain $12
Primitive Roadside Campsite
Big Bend National Park
Via Glenn Springs Rd, 1.1 mi from jct with the main park rd to Rio Grande Village; qtr mi access rd. $12. 1 site for 3 vehicles & 20 persons; 4 horses permitted at each site. No shade, minimal ground cover. Scenic.

Pine Canyon Primitive Roadside Campsite $12
Big Bend National Park
Via Glenn Springs Rd, 2.6 mi from jct with the main park rd; 4.4 mi access rd, ending at Site #4. $12. 5 sites. Sites 1,2,4 & 5 sccommodate 2 vehicles, 6 persons each. Site 3 1 vehicle & 4 persons. No horses at any site. No shade. Good view of Chisos Mtns; very scenic area. From Site 4, trail continues up-canyon, ending at high pour-off that becomes a beautiful waterfall following rains. No river access. Hikers using Pine Canyon Trail often park near Site 4. Secure valuables while sleeping or absent.

Rice Tank Primitive Roadside Campsite $12
Big Bend National Park
Via Glenn Springs Rd, 4.3 mi from jct with the main park rd; sites along E side of rd. No shade, no river access. $12. 2 vehicles, 6 persons, no horses. Sites adjoin old earthen tank used in the 1920s to hold wtr for livestock; also old corral and loading chute.

Access via Paint Gap Hills Rd, which is about 6 mi W of the Panther Junction Visitor Center. Road is generally in good condition and accessible all year by all vehicles. One camping area:

Paint Gap Hills Primitive Roadside Campsite $12
Big Bend National Park
Site 1 is 1 mi from pavement; Sites 2-3 are about 2 mi; Site 4 is within the gap about 2.5 mi from pavement. High-clearance vehicle needed for access to Site 3. $12. 4 sites for 6 vehicles & 20 persons; no horses permitted at Site 1. Poor to moderate shade, no river access. Dripping Spring and an old ranch site at end of rd beyond Paint Gap.

Access via Old Maverick Road, a 13-mi improved gravel rd connecting the park's western entrance and the Santa Elena Canyon Trailhead. Although sometimes bumpy, the road is generally well maintained and accessible all year to all vehicles. Two sites in the middle of beautiful desert scenery:

Rattlesnake Mtn Primitive Roadside Campsite $12
Big Bend National Park
Located on west side of Old Maverick Road, turnoff may be difficult to spot. $12. 1 site for 1 vehicle, 6 persons, no horses. Not reccommended when heavy rain is forcast, check with rangers as rain can wash out access to campsite.

Ocotillo Grove Primitive Roadside Campsite $12
Big Bend National Park
Via Old Maverick Rd 3 mi from the southern end near Santa Elena Canyon or 20 miles from northern end near the Maverick Entrance Station. Site is onnorth side of road on the way to Terlingua Abajo. 1 site for 2 vehicles, 8 persons no horses. Road may become rutted after heavy ranis and require high clearance or 4-wheel drive. No shade. Secure belongings when away from site. Site not reccommended when heavy rain is forecast as rean can wash out access.

Terlingua Abajo Primitive Roadside Campsite $12
Big Bend National Park
Via Old Maverick Rd, 2.8 mi from S end & 10 mi from N end; 1.7 mi on access rd, which can wash out during rain. $12. 3 sites for 2 vehicles & 8 people per site; no horses permitted. No shade. Excellent views of Mesa de Anguila and desert scrub terrain. Easy 5-minute access to Terlingua Creek for fishing; wtr not potable. Ruins of old farming community nearby.

Access via Grapevine Hills Rd, which begins 3.3 mi W of the Panther Junction Visitor Center. One camping area.

Grapevine Hills Primitive Roadside Campsite $12
Big Bend National Park
Via Grapevine Hills Rd (improved rd 3.3 mi W of Panther Junction); some rough spots, but rd is accessible to Sites 2-3; Site 1 (Government Spring) is 0.3 mi on dirt rd. Adjoining sites 2-3 are 3.8 mi down dirt rd. Sites 4-5 are 7.2 mi at end of access rd. $12. 5 sites for 7 vehicles & 32 persons; no horses. No shade. Government Spring near Site 1; Grapevine Spring near Sites 4-5.

Access via Croton Springs Rd, which is 9 mi W of Panther Junction Visitor Center. Road is generally in good condition and accessible all year to all vehicles. Road is closed beyond the camping area due to erosion. One camping area:

Croton Springs Primitive Roadside Campsite $12
Big Bend National Park
1 mi dirt rd access from Croton Springs Rd. $12. 2 adjoining sites for 4 vehicles & 6 persons; no horses permitted. No shade. Good scenery. Croton Spring & Wash are short walk from sites. Spring is reliable source of wtr for wildlife.

Access via Panther Junction. Roads are genarally well-maintained and accessible to all passenger vehicles. Following rains, the roads may become very rutted and high-clearance vehicles may be necessary.

Hanold Draw Primitive Roadside Campsite $12
Big Bend National Park
Located 4.8 mi N of Panther Junction on Rte 11 (toward Persimmon Gap). Short, .25 gravel access road leads to campsite area. The turnoff is not marked so watch your odometer. $12 1 site for 3 vehicles, 20 people, corral for up to 8 horses. Suitable for several tents or a large RV. Secure all food in vehicle, including coolers as Javelina frequent this area. View of Chisos Mtns to the North and the Sierra delCarmen range is visibel in teh tistant east.

K-Bar Primitive Roadside Campsite $12
Big Bend National Park
K-Bar road id 2 miles east of the Panther Junction Visitor Center along the road to Rio Grande Village. KB-1 is one mile from the pavement, KB-2 is at the far end of the road. Each site accommodates 2 vehicles and 6 persons. Site 2 can have 4 horses. Secure all food in vehicle, including coolers as Javelina frequent this area. Primitive hking route to Banta Shut-in begins near site 2.

Nine Point Draw Primitive Roadside Campsite $12
Big Bend National Park
ocated near the Persimmon Gap Entrance Station, 22 miles north of Panther Junction. The short access road is on the east side of the main park road. $12. 1 site for 2 vehicles, 8 persons and 4 horses. No shade. Closest site to Persimmon Gap Visitor Center. Adequate turnaround space for RCs. Allows acess to hiking in Dog Canyon and canyoneering route through Devil's Den

MARBLE FALLS (E)

Camp Creek Primitive Recreation Area FREE
Lake Travis
Lower Colorado River Authority
About 6 mi E of Marble Falls on FM 1431; 1 mi W on CR 343 to N shore of Lake Travis (gravel rd may be impassable when wet). Free. All year; 10-day limit. Primitive camping in 5-acre waterfront park operated by Burnet County and in larger conservation area (by permit). Tbls, cfga, 1 toilet, no drkg wtr. Trash service. Boating(l), fishing, hiking trails. Info center. 500 acres.

Shaffer Bend Primitive Recreation Area $12
Lake Travis
Lower Colorado River Authority
About 7 mi E of Marble Falls on FM 1431 to Smithwick community; 1 mi S on CR 343A to N shore of Lake Travis. $12. All year; 10-day limit. Primitive camping; prime spots with metal fire rings. 1 toilet, cfga, tbls. No drkg wtr or trash service. Boating, fishing.

MARSHALL (E)

Caddo Lake State Park $12
15 mi NE of Marshall on SR 43; 1 mi E on FM 2198 (1 mi N of Karnack). $12 at 19 sites with wtr hookups for small trailers, pop-ups, truck & van campers, no motorhomes ($72 weekly). $18-$20 for multiple hookups. All year; 14-day limit. Tbls, flush toilets, cfga, drkg wtr, showers, dump, screened shelters, playgrounds, picnic areas, interpretive displays, rec hall. Hiking & nature trails, fishing (pier), boating(lr), canoeing(r), swimming, waterskiing.

MAUD (E

Malden Lake Park $11
Corps of Engineers
Wright Patman Lake
From Maud at jct with US 67, 4.8 mi S on SR 8; before bridge, on left. $11 with federal senior pass at 29 elec/wtr 30-amp sites; others pay $22. $13 with senior pass at 10 elec/wtr 50-amp sites; others pay $26; double sites $48. All year; 14-day limit. 55-ft RV limit. Tbls, toilets, cfga, drkg wtr. Limited facilities in winter. Fishing, boating (l), swimming in designated areas. Coded gate locks provided for late entry by registered guests.

MCCAMEY (W)

Santa Fe City Park FREE
Jct of Hwy 385 & US 67, 5 blocks E. All year. 4 sites. Tbls, toilets, cfga, wtr & elec hookups, dump, playground. Picnicking. Rare pecan & elm trees in camp. Obtain permit from city hall.

MEXIA (E)

Fort Parker State Park $12
7 mi S of Mexia on SR 14; access on Park Rd 28; on Navasota River. $12 at 10 sites with shared wtr & 5 overflow sites; $20 at 25 sites with elec/wtr. Tbls, flush toilets, cfga, drkg wtr, dump, showers, playgrounds, picnic areas, pavilion, store. Hiking trail, nature trails, swimming, canoeing(r), fishing, boating(lrd). Reconstructed fort. Old Fort Parker State Historical Park (1 mi S).

MILAM (E)

Red Hills Lake Recreation Area $6
Sabine National Forest
From SR 21 near Milam, 3 mi N on SR 87; 1 mi E on FR 116; on Red Hills Lake. $6 base. 5/1-LD; 14-day limit. Base fee for primitive sites; $10 with 30-amp elec ($7 with federal senior pass). 22 sites; 35-ft RV limit. Tbls, flush toilets, cfga, cold showers, drkg wtr, shelter, dump, elec($), bathhouse. Swimming($), fishing, hiking, biking trails, nature trails. Non-campers pay $3 day use fee.

MONTICELLO (E)

Monticello Campground $10
Titus County Park
1.3 mi SE on US 271 from jct with I-30; 8 mi SW on FM 127; 1.4 mi SE on FM 21; between Monticello Lake and Lake Bob Sandlin. $10 with elec/wtr, plus $2 per person entry fee. All year; 14-day limit. 28 RV sites plus primitive area. Flush toilets, cfga, drkg wtr, dump, showers, dump. Fishing, boating(l).

MOODY (E)

Mother Neff State Park $12
1.5 mi S of Moody on SR 236; access via Park Rd 14; at Leon River. $12 at 15 sites with wtr nearby; $25 at 6 20 full hookup sites. All year; 14-day limit. Tbls, flush toilets, showers, cfga, drkg wtr, dump, playground, picnic areas, pavilion, rec hall. Hiking, fishing & canoeing (Leon River). Tabernacle. First Texas state park. Only limited camping available at last report due to flood damage; no full-service restrooms or showers, but portable toilets available; check status before arrival if full service is required.

MORGAN (E)

Steele Creek Park   FREE
Corps of Engineers
Whitney Lake
7 mi E of Morgan on FM 927; 1 mi S on FM 56; 0.3 mi E on
CR 1295, then right (E) on CR 1304. All year; 14-day limit.
Free. 21 camping/picnic sites with tbls, ground cookers,
central wtr, 2 pit toilets. No drkg wtr Nov-March. Swim-
ming, fishing, boating(l).

MOUNT VERNON (E)

Dogwood Park $10
Franklin County Water District
From I-30, S 1 mi on SR 37; 7.8 mi SE on FM 21; 2.5 mi S
on FM 3007. $10 for undeveloped primitive sites. All year;
14-day limit. Flush toilets, cfga, drkg wtr. 10-acre park on
S side of 3,400-acre Lake Cypress Springs dam. Swimming, fishing (big bass & catfish), boating(l). Lake

Harris RV Park $11
From jct of Hwy 37 & Hwy 21 near Mount Vernon, follow
Hwy 21 to CR 4110; turn left on CR 4110 at Glade Branch
Baptist Church for 200 yds. $11 ($40 weekly, $150 month-
ly) for RV sites with elec. Tbls, flush toilets, cfga, drkg wtr,
hookups($), coin laundry, pool, showers. SKP discount. R

Overlook Park $10
Franklin County Water District
Lake Cypress Springs
From jct with I-30, S 1 mi on SR 37; 3.2 mi SE on FM 21;
4.6 mi on FM 2723. $10. All year; 14-day limit. Primitive
camping. Drkg wtr, flush toilets. 16-acre area. Fishing,
swimming, boating(l).

MULESHOE (W)

Muleshoe National Wildlife Refuge   FREE
20 mi S of Muleshoe on TX 214; 2.25 mi W on Caliche Rd
to headquarters. Free overnight primitive campsites in the
recreation area. Tbls, toilets, cfga, drkg wtr. Register at
refuge headquarters. Hiking, nature trail. No hunting or
boating. One of a chain of refuges in the Central Flyway, a
wintering area for migratory waterfowl. GPS: 33.962246,-
102.770981.

NAVASOTA (E)

City of Navasota RV Park $10
W of Navasota on SR 105; 0.2 mi S on Fairway Dr (on
left, hard to see). $10. All year; 14-day limit. 10 sites with
full hookups. Tbls, flush toilets, showers, cfga, pavilion,
dump. Non-campers pay $5 for dump station.

NEW WAVERLY (E)

Double Lake Recreation Area $10
Sam Houston National Forest
From I-45 at New Waverly, 25mi E on SR 150; 0.5 mi S on
FM 2025; left at Double Lake. $10 with federal senior pass
at non-elec sites; others pay $20. Elec/wtr sites about

$14-$20 with senior pass; others pay $28-$40. 65 sites
up to 56 ft. Tbls, flush toilets, cfga, drkg wtr, showers,
fishing piers,beach. Swimming, boating(l), fishing, hiking,
mountain biking.

Stubblefield Lake Recreation Area $7.50
Sam Houston National Forest
9 mi W of New Waverly on SR 1375; 3 mi NW on FR 215.
$7.50 with federal senior pass; others pay $15. All year;
14-day limit. 30 sites; 28-ft RV limit. Tbls, flush toilets,
cfga, drkg wtr, cold showers, shelter. Boating, fishing, hiking trails, designated motorcycle areas. N of Lake Conroe.

NOCONA (E)

Boone Park   FREE
North Montague County Water Supply District
5 mi N of Nocona on TX 103; 3 mi on FM 2634; 3.9 mi N
on FM 2953 to Oak Shores; 0.4 mi S to sign, "Public boat
ramp"; turn right on nameless rd; half mi to park (rough
rds). On Lake Nocona. Free. All year; 15-day limit. Undesignated RV & tent sites. Tbls, toilets, cfga. Swimming,
picnicking; fishing; boating (l). Reader says toilets at all
these camps quite dirty. Lake

Joe Benton Park   FREE
North Montague County Water Supply District
From FM 103, E 3 mi on FM 2634; 1.2 mi NE on FM 2953.
Free. All year; 21-day limit. Open RV & tent camping. Toi-
lets, tbls, shelters, cfga, no drkg wtr. Swimming, fishing,
boating(ld). On 1,470-acre Lake Nocona.

Weldon Rob Memorial Park   FREE
North Montague County Water Supply District
From FM 103, E 3 mi on FM 2634; three-fourths mi SE to
sites. Free. All year; 21-day limit. Open RV & tent camping.
Toilets, cfga, tbls, shelters, no drkg wtr. Also new section
with 10 full hookups, $20. On Lake Nocona. Swimming,
fishing, boating(l), playground.

ODESSA (W)

Goldsmith City Park $10
16 mi N of Odessa on SR 866, then to N side of small town
of Goldsmith on Avenue H. $10. All year. 4 sites with elec/
wtr. Tbls, toilets, cfga, drkg wtr, pool, playground.

PERRYTON (W)

Whigham City Park   FREE
In town at US 83 and Farm 377. Free. All year; 2-day limit.
5 sites. 30-amp elec/wtr hookups. Tbls, flush toilets, cfga,
dump. Tennis & basketball courts, playground. Check in
at Police Dept.

PINELAND (E)

Moore Plantation Wildlife Management Area   FREE
Sabine National Forest
E of Pineland on FM 1, then 3 mi E on FM 2426; info
station on N side of rd. Free. Oct-Jan; 14-day limit; in

Sabine National Forest. Primitive designated campsites; no facilities, no drkg wtr. Primarily a hunter camp. Fishing, hunting, hiking, horseback riding, biking.

Rayburn Park $7
Corps of Engineers
Sam Rayburn Lake
From Pineland at jct of US 96, 10 mi N on FM 83; 11 mi S on FM 705; 1.5 mi W on FM 3127; on N shore of lake. $7 with federal senior pass at 21 non electric sites. At 16 back-in 30-amp elec/wtr sites, $13 with senior pass; others pay $26. At 8 pull-through 50-amp elec sites, $14 with senior pass; others pay $28. All year; 14-day limit. RV limit in excess of 65 ft. Pit & flush toilets, shelters, showers, drkg wtr, cfga, dump, playground. Fishing, boating(l).

PLAINVIEW (W)
Ollie Liner Center RV Park $10
Hale County Park
At Plainview, 6 mi S of Columbia St from I-27; half block E at 2000 S. Columbia St. $10 for seniors; others pay $15 for sites with 30/50-amp elec/wtr. All year; 7-day limit. 44 sites. Tbls, toilets, cfga, drkg wtr, dump, elec. No tents.

PORT ARANSAS (E)
Mustang Island State Park $10
14 mi S of Port Aransas on SR 361 (formerly Park Rd 53). $10 at 50 primitive beach sites (chemical toilets, drkg wtr & rinse showers); $20 at 48 RV sites with wtr/elec, showers, site shelters. Tbls, flush toilets, cfga, drkg wtr, dump, showers, store. Swimming, fishing, mountain biking, birdwatching, hiking. 3,703 acres.

Port Aransas Beach Municipal Park $12
Port Aransas Parks & Recreation Department
Park along the beach on Mustang Island from the south jetty through Port Aransas Beach to the Kleberg County line S of Bob Hall pier. Free with the purchase of a $12 annual vehicle sticker from city hall (710 W. Avenue A). All year; 3-day limit. About 30 sites. Toilets, cfga, no other facilities except trash cans.

I.B. Magee Beach Park $12
Nueces County Coastal Parks
From SR 361 ferry landing in Port Aransas, take Cotter St. to park at tip of Mustang Island. $12 for primitive beach sites; $25 at RV sites with wtr/elec. 75 RV sites & primitive open beach camping (with cold rinse shower). All year; 3-day limit. Flush toilets, showers ($1), bathhouse, dump ($4), drkg wtr. Swimming, fishing (lighted pier). Patrolled.

POTTSBORO (E)
Preston Bend Recreation Area $10
Corps of Engineers
Lake Texoma
9 mi N of Pottsboro on SR 120; on peninsula between lake's main channel & Little Mineral Creek arm. $10 with

federal senior pass at 26 elec/wtr 30-amp RV sites; others pay $20. 4/1-9/7; 14-day limit. RV limit in excess of 65 ft. Tbls, flush toilets, cfga, drkg wtr, dump, beach, showers, picnic shelter. Fishing, boating(l), swimming. Note: Some roads and campsites under construction; campground will be walk in only in 2017, reservations will resume in 2018.

PRESIDIO (W)
Big Bend Ranch State Park $5
4 mi SE of Presidio to Fort Leaton State Historical Park for area N of gravel FM 170; or just E of Lajitas at Barton Warnock Environmental Education Center for area S of FM 170. $5 at numerous backcountry sites along roads within park; $8 at front-country primitive sites & 5 equestrian sites. Pit toilets at Madera Canyon & Grassy Banks; no other facilities, no wtr. Fishing, swimming, hiking, interpretive programs, birdwatching. Botanical gardens, museum. 268,495 acres. Waterfalls, pictographs. Park rd along Rio Grande River. Pay user fees at the education center, at Fort Leaton SP (4 mi E of Presidio on FM 170), or at park's Sauceda headquarters.

PROCTOR (E)
Copperas Creek Park $8
Corps of Engineers
Proctor Lake
From Proctor at jct with FM 1476, 5.5 mi S, through Hasse on US 377; 2.5 mi N on FM 2861 (CR 410). $8 base with federal senior pass at 67 wtr/30-amp elec sites; others pay $16 base, $20 for 2 premium 50-amp sites ($10 with senior pass); double sites $32. 2 group camping areas. All year; 14-day limit. RV limit in excess of 65 ft. Tbls, flush toilets, cfga, drkg wtr, showers, fishing pier, dump.

Sowell Creek Park $8
Corps of Engineers
Proctor Lake
From Proctor at jct with US 377, 2 mi W on FM 1476; S before dam on recreation road. $8 base with federal senior pass at 60 wtr/30-amp elec sites; others pay $16 base, $20 at 11 premium 50-amp sites ($10 with senior pass). 14 full hookups, $26; double elec/wtr sites $32 ($13 & $16 with senior pass). Also 2 group camping areas. All year; 14-day limit. RV limit in excess of 65 ft. Tbls, flush toilets, cfga, drkg wtr, playground, showers, dump, fishing pier. Boating(l), fishing, swimming.

QUANAH (W)
Copper Breaks State Park $10
13 mi S of Quanah on SR 6. $10 at 7 sites with wtr hookups & 7 equestrian sites with wtr; 24 elec/wtr sites $20. All year; 14-day limit. Tbls, flush toilets, cfga, drkg wtr, showers, dump, playgrounds, picnic areas, amphitheater (June productions), fishing pier, beach, store. Swimming, nature trail, hiking trail, equestrian trail, interpretive displays, boating(ld), fishing, paddleboats(r). Equestrian area has 2 tying rails. Longhorn herd.

REDWATER (E)

Clear Springs $12
Corps of Engineers
Wright Patman Lake
4 mi NE of Redwater on US 67; 3 mi S on FM 2148; 2 mi W on park rd; at NE shore of lake. $12 with federal senior pass at 25 elec/wtr 30-amp sites; others pay $24. $13 with senior pass at 19 elec/wtr 50-amp sites; others pay $26. $14 at 3 premium elec/wtr 50-amp deck sites; others pay $28. Also 12-site group camping area with screened shelter. All year; 14-day limit. RV limit in excess of 65 ft. Tbls, flush toilets, cfga, drkg wtr, picnic shelter, beach, playground, dump, showers. Fishing, boating(l), swimming, horseshoe pits, nature trail.

RIO VISTA (E)

Hamm Creek Park $10
Johnson County Park
From SR 174, SW 8.4 mi on FM 916. On Brazos River. $10 at non-elec sites; $20 with wtr/elec; $24 full hookups. 33 primitive sites, 30 RV sites with 30/50-amp elec/wtr (5 full hookups). All year; 14-day limit. Drkg wtr, flush toilets, cfga, tbls, dump ($6), showers ($4). Swimming, fishing, boating (l - $5). Park dramatically renovated by Corps of Engineers for the county. Former Corps park. Non-campers pay $6 vehicle fee

ROBERT LEE (W)

Lakeview Park $5
Colorado River Municipal Water District
NW of Robert Lee to E.V. Spence Lake Dam; camp on N shore of lake above dam. $5 daily pass for primitive camping ($60 annually or $10 for seniors). All year; 7-day limit. Primitive camping in open area. Tbls, toilets, cfga, no drkg wtr. Swimming, boating(l), fishing. Lake

Paint Creek Recreation Area $5
Colorado River Municipal Water District
From Robert Lee, 7.8 mi W of SR 208 on SR 158; half mi N & E on local rd; on E.V. Spence Reservoir. $5 daily pass for primitive camping ($60 annually or $10 for seniors); elec sites $12; elec/wtr $16; full hookups $20. All year; 7-day limit. 28 sites with hookups($). 100-acre primitive area. Tbls, flush & pit toilets, cfga, drkg wtr, dump, bait, shelters, marina. Swimming, boating(l).

Rough Creek Park $5
Colorado River Municipal Water District
About 6 mi NW of Robert Lee on SR 208; S & W on access rd. On E.V. Spence Reservoir. $5 daily pass for primitive camping ($60 annually or $10 for seniors). All year; 7-day limit. Primitive open area on 50 acres. Tbls, toilets, cfga, no drkg wtr. Swimming, boating(l), fishing.

Wildcat Creek Recreation Area $10
Colorado River Municipal Water District
From Robert Lee, 4.5 mi W of SR 208 on SR 158; .6 mi N & E on local rd; on E.V. Spence Reservoir. $10 at non-elec RV sites; $15 with elec; $18-$22 full hookups. Also $5 daily pass or $60 annually ($10 annually for seniors). All year; 7-day limit. Pavilions($), shelters($), tbls, flush toilets, cfga, drkg wtr, showers($), bait, store, snack bar. Swimming, boating(l), fishing

SABINE PASS (E)

Sea Rim State Park $10
10 mi W of Sabine Pass on SR 87 (20 mi SW of Port Arthur); hwy closed between Sea Rim & High Island). $10. All year; 14-day limit. Primitive beach camping. $20 at 8 sites with wtr/elec. Tbls, portable toilets, cfga, no drkg wtr. Observation blinds, interpretive displays. Nature trail, boating(l), canoeing(r), beachcombing, nature trail, kayaking, birdwatching, swimming, fishing.

SALADO (E)

Union Grove Campground $12
Corps of Engineers
Stillhouse Hollow Lake
From N of Salado at jct with I-35, 0.8 mi W on FM 2484; 1 mi N on Union Grove Park Rd; at S shore of lake. $12 with senior pass at 30 elec/wtr sites; others pay $24; double sites $40 ($20 with senior pass). Also 3 screened overnight shelters. All year; 14-day limit. RV limit in excess of 35 ft; 4 pull-through sites. Tbls, flush toilets, cfga, drkg wtr, showers, beach, playground, dump, fishing pier. Fishing, boating(l), horseback riding, swimming, biking. Non-campers pay $5 day use fees for dump station, beach; $5 for boat ramp.

SAN ANGELO (W)

Middle Concho Municipal Park $12
4 mi S of San Angelo on Hwy 584; 4 mi S & W on Red Bluff Rd; on Lake Nasworthy. $12. All year; 14-day limit. Primitive camping area. Tbls, pit toilets, cfga, drkg wtr. Swimming, fishing, boating(ld). 600 acres. Non-resident non-campers pay $6 entry fee on weekends. Lake

Spring Creek City Park $12
Follow Knickerbocker Rd from San Angelo to lake bridge; turn on Fisherman's Rd. $12 non-residents during about 3/7-LD; 14-day limit. All year; 14-day limit. Primitive sites. Pit toilets, cfga, drkg wtr, dump. Tennis, volleyball. Non-resident non-campers pay $6 entry fee on weekends.

Twelve-Mile Recreation Area $12
Twin Buttes Reservoir
12 mi W of San Angelo on Hwy 67, then E to lake; at 12-Mile boat ramp. $12 annual public use permit. Primitive camping; no facilities. Boating(ld), fishing.

SAN ANTONIO (W)

Calaveras Lake Park $8
CPS Energy
About 17 mi S of San Antonio on US 181, then 3 mi NE on Loop 1604. $8 for dispersed primitive camping; $24 full

hookups (reservations required). Tbls, toilets, cfga, drkg wtr, store, fishing piers. Boating(lr), fishing, hiking, nature trail. Entrance fees charged. Lake

Victor Braunig Lake $8
San Antonio River Authority
About 17 mi S of San Antonio; take exit 130 from I-37. $8 for dispersed primitive camping; $24 full hookups (reservations required). Tbls, toilets, cfga, drkg wtr, store, fish cleaning station. Boating(l), fishing. 1,350-acre lake. Entrance fees charged.

SANFORD (W)
Bugbee Canyon Free
Lake Meredith National Recreation Area
Take TX 687 from Sanford across Sanford Dam to Bugbee Rd; on Bugbee Rd to campground (difficult access). Camp free, but $4 daily boat fee. All year; 14-day limit. Semi-developed shoreline sites. Tbls, toilets, no drkg wtr. Hunting; waterskiing; fishing. Nestled within a narrow canyon. Opportunity for camping varies with the lake level.

SEAGRAVES (W)
Seagraves FREE
Chamber of Commerce RV Park
On US 385 in Seagraves. Free for 3 nights at 5 full-hookup sites; $5 thereafter.

SEMINOLE (W)
Seminole City Park FREE
From US 180 (W. Avenue A) in Seminole, 3 blocks N on NW 4th St; left on Ave D; park on left. Free. All year; 3-night limit. 6 sites with full hookups; 30-ft RV limit. Tbls, toilets, cfga, drkg wtr.

SHELBYVILLE (E)
Haley's Ferry FREE
Sabine National Forest
Sabine River Authority of Texas
12 mi E of Shelbyville on FM 2694; 1 mi on FM 172; 2 mi E on FM 100-A. On Toledo Bend Reservoir. Free. All year; 14-day limit. Undeveloped primitive area with 4 tbls, boat ramp. No camping in the parking area, but numerous dispersed spots nearby. Toilet at boat ramp. Day-use parking fee at boat ramp, $2.

SILVERTON (W)
Lake Mackenzie Park $5
Mackenzie Municipal Water Authority
4 mi W of Silverton on SR 86/207; 7 mi N on SR 207. $5/person base. All year. Base fee for primitive sites; 25 RV sites with elec/wtr $20. 18 sites. Tbls, flush toilets, cfga, drkg wtr, cold showers, elec/wtr hookups, playground, shelter, dump, store. Nature trail, fishing, boating(l - $2), swimming, waterskiing, store. Lake

SPEARMAN (W)
Palo Duro Reservoir $5
Palo Duro River Authority
N of Spearman on Hwy 15; furn on FM 3214 across the dam to N entrance. $5 base. All year; 14-day limit. Base fee for primitive sites (includes $2 per person entry fee); $20 for sites with elec (including entry fee). Two campgrounds, one with 26 RV sites with hookups, the other with 11 hookups. Tbls, toilets, cfga, drkg wtr. Fishing, boating(l), hiking. $2 boat ramp fee ($30 annually). Lake

STINNET (W))
Stinnet City Park FREE
On Broadway Street, 1 block W of TX 136 and TX 2097, in Stinnet. Free. All year; 3-day limit. 4 sites wtr/elec; Permits at city hall. $10 after 3 days. Toilets, cfga, pool, playground, elec, dump. Ice, groceries. Tennis, volleyball, swimming.

SWEETWATER (W)
Lake Sweetwater Municipal Park $6
From I-20 near Sweetwater, 3.6 mi S on FM 1856; half mi E on FM 2035; at Lake Sweetwater. $6 at non-hookup sites; $10 at 32 elec/wtr sites. Visitors also pay for $2 daily or $3 weekend recreation permit ($10 annually). Tbls, flush toilets, cfga, drkg wtr, playground, dump. Fishing, boating(l), swimming. Nearby Pappy's Bait & Grill charges $10 at non-elec sites, $20 for elec/wtr

Lake Trammell FREE
Nolan County Park
From I-20, S 4 mi on SR 70; 2.8 mi W on FM 1809; 1.2 mi S to camp; on Lake Trammell. 3 nights Free, $10 additional nights. All year. Primitive 300-acre camping area. Flush toilets, cfga, drkg wtr, tbls. Biking & bridle trail, fishing, boating(l), nature trails. Park operated by the City of Sweetwater. Lake

TEXARKANA (E)
Piney Point Park $12
Wright Patman Lake
Corps of Engineers
From Texarkana, 12 mi S on US 59; first right past Sulphur River bridge, following signs; just N of Rocky Point Park at SE shore of lake. $12 with federal senior pass at 42 wtr/30-amp elec sites; others pay $24. $13 with senior pass at 6 wtr/50-amp elec sites; others pay $26. 3/1-11/30; 14-day limit. 55-ft RV limit. Tbls, flush toilets, cfga, drkg wtr, showers, dump, fishing pier, picnic shelter. Boating(l), fishing, hiking, nature trail.

Rocky Point Park $12
Wright Patman Lake
Corps of Engineers
Just S of Piney Point campground, S of dam. $12 with federal senior pass at 77 wtr/30-amp elec sites; others pay $24. $13 with senior pass 29 elec/wtr 50-amp sites;

others pay $26. $13 with senior pass at 9 full-hookup or 29 50-amp sites; others pay $26. All year; 14-day limit. RV limit in excess of 65 ft. Tbls, flush toilets, cfga, drkg wtr, showers, dump, fishing pier, playground, beach, coin laundry, fish cleaning station, amphitheater. Ball field, boating(l), fishing, swimming, hiking, tennis,interpretive trails.

TEXLINE (W)

Thompson Grove   FREE
Cibola National Forest
15 mi NE of Texline. Free. May-Oct. Primitive undesignated area (22-ft RV limit). 10 picnic sites. Tbls, toilets, cfga, drkg wtr.

TOMBALL (E)

Spring Creek Park   FREE
Harris County Park
From jct with FM 2920 just W of Tomball, N on SR 249, then 0.8 mi W on Brown Rd to park. Free. All year. 8 RV sites with elec/wtr & primitive camping area. Tbls, flush toilets, cfga, drkg wtr, showers, dump, playground. Fishing, sand volleyball, tennis, basketball, skateboarding. Reservations required: 281-353-4196.

TOW (E)

Cedar Point Primitive Recreation Area   FREE
Lake Buchanan
Lower Colorado River Authority
Just E of Tow on FM 3014; at Lake Buchanan. Free. All year; 10-day limit. Primitive undeveloped camping. Toilet, cfga, no drkg wtr, no tbls. Boating(l), fishing, birdwatching, hiking trails.

VICTORIA (E)

Victoria City RV Park $12
At NW Victoria, 2 mi N on Vine St from Red River jct. $12 ($60 weekly). All year; 7-day limit. 18 pull-through RV sites. Tbls, no toilets, cfga, drkg wtr, hookups, dump. Boating(l), fishing. Guadalupe River. Next to Riverside Park with hiking & biking trails, zoo.

VIDOR (E)

Claiborne West $3
Orange County Park
Sabine River Authority
From I-10 near Vidor, exit 864 to N access rd, then 2 mi E; on Cow Bayou. $3 for primitive camping. All year. 433 acres. Tbls, flush toilets, cfga, drkg wtr, playground, amphitheater. Tennis, canoeing, softball, nature trails, exercise trail, fishing pond, picnicking (shelters). Cypress totem pole. Bayou

WACO (E)

Airport Park $12
Waco Lake
From I-35 exit 339 (Lake Shore Dr), W on Lake Shore (FM 3051); cross FM 3051 & FM 1637, then right (NW) on Air-

port Rd; left on Skeet Eason Rd to park (just W of regional airport); on NE shore of lake. $12 with federal senior pass at 25 elec/wtr sites; others pay $24. $14 with senior pass at 22 full-hookup sites; others pay $28. Also group camping area. All year; 14-day limit. RV limit in excess of 65 ft. Floating restaurant at nearby marina. Tbls, flush toilets, cfga, drkg wtr, showers, dump, beach. Biking, hiking, boating(l), swimming. Non-campers pay day use fees of $4 for beach, boat ramp, picnicking, dump station.

Midway Park $12
Corps of engineers
Waco Lake
From Waco & I-35 exit 330, 5 mi W on SR 6; exit on Fish Pond Rd and circle under SR 6, then stay on access road; on E shore of South Bosque River. $12 with federal senior pass at 22 wtr/30-amp elec sites; others pay $24. $14 with senior pass at 11 full-hookup sites; others pay $28. All year; 14-day limit. RV limit in excess of 65 ft. Tbls, flush toilets, cfga, drkg wtr, showers, dump, playground. Boating(l), fishing. Non-campers pay day use fees of $4 for boat ramps, picnicking, dump stations.

Reynolds Creek Park $10
Corps of Engineers
Waco Lake
From Waco & I-35 exit 330, 7 mi W on SR 6 across lake; 1 mi NE on Speegleville Rd, pass 4-way stop sign; approximately 1 mi on right; on W shore of lake. $10 with federal senior pass at 34 std elec and 10 Ewuestrian sites (some 50-amp). All year; 14-day limit. Tbls, flush toilets, showers, cfga, drkg wtr, dump, playground, picnic shelter. Boating(l), hiking, fishing, interpretive programs. Non-campers pay day use fees of $4 for boat launch, picnicking, dump station. IN 2017 Reynolds Creek is closed until further notice due to flood damage.

Speegleville Park $12
Corps of engineers
Waco Lake
From Waco & I-35, 6 mi N on SR 6; after crossing lake on Twin Bridges, exit left on access rd, past Twin Bridges Park about 0.25 mi; continue on Overflow Rd to park entrance; on W shore of lake. $12 with federal senior pass at 30 elec/wtr sites; others pay $24 All year; 14-day limit. Tbls, flush toilets, cfga, drkg wtr, showers, dump, playground. Boating(l), fishing, hiking. Non-campers pay day use fees of $4 for boat launch, picnicking, dump station.

WHITNEY (E)

Cedar Creek   FREE
Corps of Engineers
Whitney Lake
From Whitney, 5.5 mi NW on FM 933; 2.2 mi SW & SE on FM 2604; on E side of lake. Free. All year; 14-day limit. 20 primitive sites. Tbls, 1 toilet, cfga, drkg wtr, picnic shelter. Boating (l), fishing.

Cedron Creek Park $8
Corps of Engineers
Whitney Lake
From Whitney, 2.4 mi NW on FM 933; 6 mi SW on FM 1713 across Katy Bridge on left, following signs; at W side of lake. $8 with federal senior pass at 65 wtr/30-amp elec sites; others pay $16. Also group camping area. 45-ft RV limit. Tbls, flush toilets, cfga, drkg wtr, showers, dump. Boating(l), fishing, horseshoe pits.

Lofers Bend East $12
Corps of Engineers
Whitney Lake
From Whitney, 5.7 mi S on SR 22, then W on access rd, following signs; at SE shore of lake. $12 at 6 non-elec with wtr during 10/1-2/28, $12 during peak period of 3/1-9/30, $10 rest of year ($6 & $5 with federal senior pass). At 60 elec/wtr 30-amp sites, $8 with senior pass during 3/1-9/30; others pay $16; off-season, sites are $14 ($7 with senior pass). 45-ft RV limit. Also group camping area. Tbls, flush toilets, cfga, drkg wtr, beach, playground, showers, dump. Fishing, boating(l), swimming.

Lofers Bend West $12
Corps of Engineers
Whitney Lake
Adjacent to Lofers Bend East; on main stem of Brazos River. $12 at 22 wtr-only sites ($6 with federal senior pass). At 39 elec/wtr 30-amp sites, $8 with senior pass; others pay $16. At 6 elec/wtr 50-amp sites, $10 with senior pass; others pay $20. 4/1-9/30; 14-day limit. 45-ft RV limit. Tbls, flush toilets, cfga, drkg wtr, showers, dump, playground. Boating, fishing.

McGown Valley Park $12
Corps of Engineers
Whitney Lake
2.4 mi NW of Whitney on FM 933; 4 mi SW on FM 1713 (becoming CR 1241); at E shore of lake. $12 at 7 wtr hook-up sites during peak season of 3/1-9/30; $10 off-season ($6 & $5 with federal senior pass). At 14 elec/wtr 50-amp sites & 20 elec equestrian sites, $10 with senior pass in-season (others pay $20 in-season); $9 with senior pass off-season (others pay $18 off-season). 50-ft RV limit. Also camping cabins with & without RV hookups. Tbls, flush toilets, cfga, drkg wtr, beach, playground, showers, dump, picnic shelter. Boating(l), fishing, swimming, horseshoe pits, equestrian trails.

Riverside Park   FREE
Corps of Engineers
Whitney Lake
From Whitney, 5 mi S on SR 22; facilities on both sides of Brazos River, but camping only on SW shore, downstream from Whitney Dam. Free. All year; 14-day limit. 5 primitive camping/picnicking sites. Tbls, pit toilet on E side, cfga, no drkg wtr, fishing platform on W side. Fishing, boating.

Soldier Bluff   FREE
Corps of Engineers
Whitney Lake
6.5 mi S of Whitney on SR 22, then NW into park; at SE shore of lake just W of dam. Free. All year; 14-day limit. 14 primitive camping/picnic sites, some with wtr. Tbls, 1 portable toilet, cfga, drkg wtr, picnic shelter. No drkg wtr Nov-March. Swimming; picnicking; fishing.

WICHITA FALLS (E)

Lake Arrowhead State Park $10
8 mi S of Wichita Falls on US 281; 6 mi E on FM 1954. $10 at 19 sites with wtr nearby; 48 elec/wtr sites and 4 equestrian sites $20. All year; 14-day limit. Tbls, flush toilets, cfga, drkg wtr, showers, dump, playgrounds, equestrian area, picnic areas, pavilion, store, fish cleaning shelters. Waterskiing, fishing, boating (dl), swimming. 13,500-acre lake. 300-acre horseback area with wtr & toilets.

Magnolia Ridge $10
Corps of Engineers
B.A. Steinhagen Lake
From Woodville, 11 mi E on US 190; 1.5 mi NW on FM 92, then NE on park entrance rd. $10 at 4 non-electric sites ($5 with federal senior pass). 33 elec/wtr 30-am sites, $16 base, $18 at premium locations ($8 & $9 with senior pass). 1 elec/wtr site with screened shelter, $25 ($12.50 with senior pass). All year; 14-day limit. RV limit in excess of 65 ft. Tbls, flush toilets, cfga, drkg wtr, showers, dump, picnic shelter. Boating(l), fishing, hiking, children's fishing pond, handicap fishing area.

ZAVALLA (E)

Bouton Lake   FREE
Angelina National Forest
7 mi E of Zavalla on Hwy 63; 7 mi S on FR 303 to Bouton Lake. Free. All year; 14-day limit. 7 primitive sites. Tbls, toilets, cfga, no drkg wtr; dump at Caney Creek Camp. Fishing, boating, hiking on Sawmill Trail. W end of lake privately owned. 12-acre lake.

Boykin Springs Recreation Area $6
Angelina National Forest
11 mi E of Zavalla on SR 63; 2.5 mi S on FR 313. $6. All year; 14-day limit. 17 sites with tent pads; 9 sites up to 24-ft RV limit. Tbls, flush toilets, cfga, drkg wtr, showers, beach. Fishing, boating (no motors), hiking trails. Trout lake. 5

Caney Creek Recreation Area $6
Angelina National Forest
From US 69 at Zavalla, 4.8 mi E on SR 63; 5.2 mi E on FM 2743; 1 mi N on FR 336; on Sam Rayburn Lake. $6. All year; 14-day limit. 26 sites, typically 48 ft, but 24-ft RV limit. Tbls, flush toilets, cfga, drkg wtr, showers, shelter, campfire theater. Fishing, boating(l), swimming, waterskiing. Non-campers pay $3 day use fee.

Sandy Creek   FREE
Angelina National Forest
17.5 mi SE of Zavalla on SR 63; 3 mi N on FR 333. Free
primative, undesignated sites. All year; . Tbls, cfga, drkg
wtr, flush toilets. Boating(l), fishing, swimming.

ZWOLLE, LOUISIANA
Pleasure Point, Site #15 $11.25
Sabine River Authority
W of Zwolle, Louisiana, on SR 475 to SR 191; 34 mi S on
SR 191 to SR 473; continue S another 4 mi & turn right
between mileposts 5 & 6 on Pleasure Point Rd for 1.5 mi.
Seniors pay $11.25 at 74 sites with elec/wt (others pay
$15) & $15 at 50 full-hookup sites (others pay $20). $10 for
tent sites. Tbls, toilets, cfga, drkg wtr, dump, playground,
beach, pay phone, fishing pier & jetty. Fishing, swimming,
boating(l).

Garden City
Smithfield
Logan
Laketown
Hyrum
Mantua
Woodruff
Huntsville
Farmington
Salt Lake City
Oakley
Kamas
Woodland
Grantsville
Heber City
Manila
Dutch John
Clover
Pleasant Grove
Orem
Provo
Springville
Mapleton
Spanish Fork
Payson
Hanna
Whiterocks
Altonah
Lapoint
Vernal
Roosevelt
Myton
Duchesne
Vernon
Eureka
Nephi
Fairview
Price
Levan
Freedom
Oak City
Delta
Ephraim
Huntington
Cleveland
Manti
Orangeville
Ferron
Salina
Vermillion
Kanosh
Glenwood
Richfield
Moab
Marysvale
Koosharem
Milford
Loa
Hanksville
Beaver
Junction
Bicknell
Teasdale
Torrey
Antimony
Panguitch
Boulder
Escalante
Monticello
Cedar City
Enterprise
Blanding
Pine Valley
Virgin
Saint George
Kanab
Mexican Hat

UTAH

CAPITAL: Salt Lake City
NICKNAME: Beehive State
STATEHOOD: 1896 – 45th State
FLOWER: Sego Lily
TREE: Blue Spruce
BIRD: California Gull

WWW.UTAH.COM

Dept of Natural Resources, Division of Parks and Recreation, 1594 W. North Temple, Salt Lake City, UT 84114; 801-322-3770.

Utah Office of Tourism, Council Hall, Capitol Hill, Salt Lake City, UT 84114; 801-538-1900. Offers information about accommodations, campgrounds, rockhounding, fall color, hiking, nightlife and culture. 800-200-1160.

REST AREAS
Overnight stops are not permitted.

STATE PARKS
Primitive sites at state parks are now $10-$14, and developed sites with hookups begin at $16-$18. Daily entry fees are charged, and annual day use passes are $75 ($35 for Utah seniors). Dept of Natural Resources, Division of Parks and Recreation, 1594 W. North Temple, Salt Lake City, UT 84116; 801-538-7220.

Ashley and Wasatch-Cache National Forests. Camping is permitted throughout the forests. Ashley National Forest, Ashton Energy Center, 355 North Vernal Ave., Vernal, UT 84078 (435-789-1181); or Wasatch National Forest, 3285 East 3300 South, Salt Lake City, UT 84109 (801-4666411).

Ashley National Forest has numerous undeveloped areas that are available for free camping. Fees at many developed sites are terminated when water systems are closed to prevent freezing; timings on those closing dates vary from year to year. After the water is turned off, the sites remain open free until they are not accessible because of weather conditions. Flaming Gorge National Recreation Area is in the northeast part of the forest on Flaming Gorge Reservoir, which extends almost 90 miles into Wyo-

ming. A Flaming Gorge recreation pass is required except at developed campgrounds. Visitor centers are at Red Canyon and Flaming Gorge Dam.

Wasatch-Cache National Forest. At campsites where seasonal fees are charged, free off-season camping is permitted following the managed season until snowfalls block access.

Fishlake and Manti-LaSal National Forests. Permits are not required for camping and hiking. Forest Supervisor, Fishlake National Forest, 115 E. 900 North, Richfield, UT 84701 (435-896-9233); or Forest Supervisor, Manti-LaSal National Forest, 599 W Price River Dr, Price, UT 84501 (435-637-2817).

Dixie National Forest, 1789 Wedgewood Lane, Cedar City, UT 84721 (435-865-3700). The largest national forest in the state, it occupies almost 2 million acres.

Uinta National Forest, 88 W. 100 North, PO Box 1428, Provo, UT 84601 (801-342-5100). Most of the forest's campgrounds now have camping fees of $20-$21 ($10-$10.50 for seniors with American the Beautiful Senior Passes.

Arches National Park. Entrance fee $25 per vehicle or $10 per person for 7 days. Annual passes, $50 (good for entry to Arches, Canyonlands, Hovenweep & Natural Bridge). Located 25 miles south of I-70 just off US 191 and five miles north of Moab, it features the greatest concentration of natural stone arches in the world -- more than 1,800. A 21-mile paved road leads visitors to major points of interest. Camping is $25 per night in summer ($12.50 with the federal senior pass). PO Box 907, Moab, UT 84532 (435-719-2299). *NOTE: Devils Garden Campground closed in 2017 for construction.*

Bryce Canyon National Park. Entrance fee $30 per vehicle or $15 per person for 7 days or $35 annually. Campiing is $20 - $30 per night ($10 - $15 with federal senior pass). Bryce Canyon NP, PO Box 640201, Bryce, UT 84764-0201.

Canyonlands National Park. Entrance fee $25 per vehicle for 7 days or $50 for annual pass (good for entry to Arches, Canyonlands, Hovenweep & Natural Bridge); camping is $15-$20 ($7.50 -$10 with federal senior pass). 36 miles northwest of Moab via SR 313. Canyonlands NP, Moab, UT 85432 (435-719-2313).

Capitol Reef National Park, HC 70, Box 15, Torrey, UT 84775 (435-425-3791). Entrance fee, $5 per vehicle for 7 days. Capitol Reef charges $10 at Fruita Campground in the park, but free camping is permitted along the Fremont River outside the eastern boundary of the park on Hwy 24. On Scenic Byway SR 24 two hours southwest of Green River. Hiking trails lead to natural bridges, hidden canyons and ancient Indian petroglyphs.

Zion National Park, Springdale, UT 84767 (435-772-3256). Entrance fee $25 per vehicle for 7 days; $40 for annual pass. Camping is $16 (free at Lava Point). Due to growing number of visitors and limited road system, RVs entering the east or south entrances are charged $15 for escort service through the narrow Long Tunnel.

Cedar Breaks National Monument, 2390 W. Hwy 56, Suite 11, Cedar City, UT 84720. 435-586-9451. Entrance fee $4 per person for 7 days. Campground fees $14 late May through mid-October, free off-season.

Dinosaur National Monument, 4545 Highway 40, Dinosaur, CO 81610 (970-374-3000). Two campgrounds are located near the visitor center. Park entry fees are $20 per vehicle for 7 days, $40 annually; camping fees are free to $12.

Natural Bridges National Monument, HC 60, Box 1, Lake Powell, UT 84533 (435-692-1234). Visitor center and primitive campground are open all year. Entrance fee $6 per vehicle. Annual passes for Natural Bridges, Canyonlands and Arches are accepted; they are $25.

Glen Canyon National Recreation Area. Fee collections are lake-wide, with entrance and boating fees collected at Lees Ferry, Wahweap, Bullfrog, Halls Crossing and Hite. Entry fees (for 7 days) are $25 per vehicle and $30 per boat. Camping fees are $14 - $20 ($7 - $10 with federal senior pass.) Shoreline camping outside designated campgrounds is free, but campers must have self-contained RVs or portable toilets.

Utah State Office, Bureau of Land Management, 324 S. State, Salt Lake City, UT 84111 (801-539-4001).

ALTONAH

Bridge Campground $8
Ashley National Forest
12 mi NW of Altonah on CR 119; 2.6 mi N on FR 119. $8.
5/15-10/1; 14-day limit. 5 sites; 15-ft RV limit. Tbls, toilets,
cfga, drkg wtr. Fishing, horseback riding and rental(1 mi).
Elev 7700 ft; 2 acres.

Reservoir Campground $5
Ashley National Forest
12 mi NW of Altonah on CR 119; 5.4 mi N on FR 119; near
Yellowstone Reservoir & Yellowstone River. $5. 5/15-10/1;
14-day limit. 5 sites on 3 acres; 15-ft RV limit. Tbls, toilets,
cfga, drkg wtr. Fishing, hiking.

Swift Creek Campground $8
Ashley National Forest
12 mi NW of Altonah on CR 119; 7.5 mi N on FR 119; at jct
of Swift Creek & Yellowstone River. $8. 5/15-10/1; 14-day
limit. 13 sites. Tbls, toilet, drkg wtr, cfga. Fishing. Elev
8100 ft; 15 acres.

ANTIMONY

Otter Creek Reservoir   FREE
Recreation Area
Bureau of Land Management
Richland Field Office
4 mi NW of Antimony on SR 22. Free. All year; 14-day
limit. Dispersed camping scattered around reservoir; RV
limit 25-ft. No facilities, no drkg water. Fishing, boating, OHV
activities. Elev 6400 ft.

BEAVER

Anderson Meadow Recreation Site $7
Fishlake National Forest
Qtr mi N of Beaver on US 91; 10 mi E on SR 153; 8 mi SE on
FR 137. $7 with federal senior pass others pay $14. 6/15-
LD; 14-day limit. 10 sites (30-ft RV limit). Tbls, toilets,
cfga, drkg wtr. Fishing, boating, hiking, horseback riding,
ATV activities.

Big Flat #2   FREE
Dispersed Camping Area
Fishlake National Forest
20 mi E of Beaver on SR 153 to gravel rd; continue 2 mi.
Free. All year; 14-day limit. Primitive undesignated sites;
no facilities, no drkg wtr (wtr at Big Flat guard station).
Hiking, ATV activities.

Indian Creek Dispersed Site   FREE
Fishlake National Forest
7 mi N of Beaver on paved rd through Manderfield; 10 mi E
on FR 119. June Oct; 16-day limit. Primitive undesignated
sites along Indian Creek and at Manderfield Reservoir.
Toilet, cfga, no drkg wtr. Hiking, fishing. Elev 6500-7500
ft. 2017: FR 119 may be closed due to failing culverts,
check conditions.

Kents Lake Recreation Site $7
Fishlake National Forest
Qtr mi N of Beaver on US 91; 10 mi E on SR 153; 5 mi SE
on gravel FR 137. $7 with federal senior pass others pay
$14. 6/1-10/31; 14-day limit. 31 sites; 60-ft RV limit. Tbls,
toilets, cfga, drkg wtr. Boating(l), fishing (50-acre lake),
hiking (no trails).

LeBaron Lake Campground $10
Fishlake National Forest
29 mi SE of Beaver on SR 153; 3 mi SE on gravel FR 137.
$10. 6/15-10/1; 14-day limit. 13 sites. Toilet, cfga, tbls, no
drkg wtr. Fishing, hiking, OHV activity, biking, boating.
Elev 9900 ft.

Little Cottonwood Recreation Site $8
Fishlake National Forest
6 mi E of Beaver on SR 153. $7 with federal senior pass;
others pay $14. MD-LD; 14-day limit. 14 sites (2 handi-
cap-access); 40-ft RV limit. Tbls, flush toilets, cfga, drkg
wtr. Fishing (accessible fishing walkway), bridle trail
nearby.

Little Reservoir Recreation Site $12
Fishlake National Forest
Quarter mi N of Beaver on US 91; 10 mi E on Hwy 153. $12.
5/1-10/30; 14-day limit. 8 sites (40-ft RV limit). Tbls, toilets,
cfga, drkg wtr. Swimming, fishing, boating. 1 handicap-ac-
cess site. 3-acre Little Reservoir.

Lousy Jim Dispersed Site   FREE
Fishlake National Forest
About 15 mi E of Beaver on SR 153; W on FR 124. Free.
June-Oct; 16-day limit. Primitive undesignated sites in
about 3 areas. Toilet, no other facilities; no drkg wtr. Near
Merchant Valley Dam. Elev 8800 ft.

Mahogany Cove Recreation Site $10
Fishlake National Forest
12 mi E of Beaver on UT 153. $10. 5/1-10/30; 14-day limit.
7 sites (RVs under 25 ft). Tbls, toilets, cfga, firewood, drkg
wtr. Fishing, hunting. Elev 7700 ft. Whole campground can
be reserved for $60.

Merchant Valley Dispersed Sit   FREE
Fishlake National Forest
About 16 mi E of Beaver on SR 153; at jct of Merchant
Creek & Three Creeks. Free. June-Oct; 16-day limit.
Primitive undesignated sites. No facilities, no drkg wtr.
Fishing in nearby Beaver River, Merchant Valley Dam,
Three Creeks Reservoir.

Timid Springs/Big Flat   FREE
Dispersed Camping Area
Fishlake National Forest
About 24 mi E of Beaver on SR 153; 0.25 mi E on FR 129
to trailhead (just N of Big Flat dispersed area). June-Oct;

16-day limit. Primitive undesignated RV sites. Toilet, cfga, drkg wtr 1 mi S near Big Flat Ranger Station.

Tushar Lake Recreation Site $12
Fishlake National Forest
From Beaver, 10 mi E on SR 153; right on FR 137 for 4 mi. $12 for individuals when not occupied by groups; $2 per person for groups; $220 for whole 22-site campground. All year; 14-day limit.

BICKNELL
Sunglow Recreation Site $12
Fishlake National Forest
.7 mi SE of Bicknell on CR 24; 1.3 mi NE on FR 1431. $12. 5/15-10/30; 14-day limit. 6 sites. Tbls, flush toilet, cfga, firewood, piped drkg wtr. Hiking, rockhounding, mountain biking, nature trails. Elev 7200 ft.

BLANDING
Devils Canyon $10
Manti-LaSal National Forest
9.5 mi NE of Blanding on US 191. $10. 5/4-9/30 16-day limit. 42 sites (30-ft RV limit). Tbls, toilets, cfga, drkg wtr (winter shut off in winter). Hiking.

Farley Canyon $12
Glen Canyon National Recreation Area
4.4 mi S on Hwy 95 from the Hite jct. $12. All year; 14-day limit. Primitive sites. Toilets, cfga, no drkg wtr. Swimming, fishing, boating(l). Entry fee (free with federal senior pass). Canyon

Hite Campground $12
Glen Canyon National Recreation Area
60 mi W of Blanding on UT 95. $12. All year; 14-day limit. 6 sites (RVs under 20 ft). Tbls, toilets, cfga, boat sanitary station at marina. Store, food nearby. Swimming; fishing; boating(lr). Entry fee (free with federal senior pass).

Nizhoni $10
Manti-LaSal National Forest
18 mi N of Blanding on Johnson Creek-Dry Wash Rd. $10. About 5/18-10/1; 16-day limit. 21 sites; 40-ft RV limit. Tbls, toilets, cfga, drkg wtr. Swimming. Relatively new wheelchair-accessible sites. Trail to Anasazi cliff dwellings.

Natural Bridges National Monument $10
38 mi W of Blanding via UT 95 and UT 275 (paved rds). $10 (plus daily or annual entry fee). All year (but snow not cleared in winter); 14-day limit. 13 sites RV limit 26-ft. Tbls, cfga, toilets, drkg wtr at visitor center (quarter mi from campground). Campfire circle with ranger-led slide programs from MD-9/15. Entrance fee to national monument from mid-May to mid-Oct; federal senior pass honored. Pets (not on trails).

BOULDER
Deer Creek Campground $10
Bureau of Land Management
Grand Staircase/Escalante National Monument
6 mi SE of Boulder on Burr Trail. $10 during 5/1-11/30; free rest of year. 14-day limit. 7 sites. Tbls, toilets, cfga, no drkg wtr. Fishing, hiking, biking. Elev 5800 ft.

CEDAR CITY
Cedar Canyon Campground $8.50
Dixie National Forest
13 mi E of Cedar City on SR 14. $8.50 with federal senior pass; others pay $17 Managed about MD - LD; 14-day limit. 13 single sites; 24-ft RV limit. Tbls, toilets, cfga, drkg wtr. Hiking. Elev 8100 ft. Cedar Breaks NM nearby.

Duck Creek Campground $8.50
Dixie National Forest
28 mi E of Cedar City on SR 14. $8.50 with federal senior pass; others pay $17. MD-LD; 14-day limit. 84 single sites (45-ft RV limit). Tbls, flush & pit toilets, cfga, drkg wtr. Hiking, fishing, summer interpretive programs. Visitor center. Elev 8600 ft.

Navajo Lake Campground $8.50
Dixie National Forest
25 mi E of Cedar City on SR 14; 2.5 mi S & W on Navajo Lake Rd. $8.50 with federal senior pass; others pay $17. 12 single RV sites; 24-ft RV limit. 6/11-LD; 14-day limit. Tbls, flush toilets, cfga, drkg wtr. Swimming, boating(l-$2), fishing, hiking, waterskiing. Dump station 2 mi W. Elev 9200 ft; 21 acres.

Spruces Campground $8.50
Dixie National Forest
25 mi E of Cedar City on SR 14; 3 mi SW on FR 33; at Navajo Lake. $8.50 with federal senior pass; others pay $17 at 24 RV/tent sites. 24-ft RV limit. MD-LD; 14-day limit. Tbls, flush toilets, cfga, drkg wtr. Swimming, fishing, boating (l), waterskiing.

Te-Ah Campground $8.50
Dixie National Forest
25 mi E of Cedar City on SR 14; 4.5 mi S on Navajo Lake Rd; near Navajo Lake. $8.50 with federal senior pass; others pay $17. MD-LD; 14-day limit. 42 sites (24-ft RV limit). Tbls, flush & pit toilets, cfga, drkg wtr, dump. Swimming, boating(l), fishing, waterskiing, hiking. Elev 9200 ft; 12 acres.

CLEVELAND
San Rafael Bridge Recreation Site $10
Bureau of Land Management, Price Field Office
25 mi SE of Cleveland on co rd. $10. All year; 14-day limit. 4 sites (RVs under 36 ft). Tbls, toilets, cfga, no drkg wtr. Fishing, hiking, horseback riding, hunting, OHV activity,

biking. Also free dispersed camping at San Rafael Swell Recreation Area nearby.

CLOVER

Clover Spring Campground $12
Bureau of Land Management, Salt Lake Field Office
5 mi W of Clover off Hwy 199. $12 (group site $45. All year (usually closed Feb-Dec due to snow); 14-day limit. 10 sites (24-ft RV limit). Tbls, toilets, cfga, no drkg wtr. 1 group site. Horse troughs, tie-ups, unloading ramps. Popular trailhead for hikers, equestrians. Fishing, hiking. Elev 6000 ft.

DELTA

House Range Recreation Area FREE
Bureau of Land Management, Fillmore Field Office
40 mi W of Delta on US 50. Free. Primitive dispersed camping throughout the area. No facilities, no drkg wtr. Rockhounding at Antelope Springs trilobite beds, biking, caving, hiking, horseback riding, hunting, OHV activity.

DUCHESNE

Avintaquin Campground $5
Ashley National Forest
31.5 mi SW of Duchesne on SR 33; 1.2 mi W on FR 147. $5. MD-LD; 16-day limit. 13 sites; 16-ft RV limit. Also group site $20. Tbls, toilets, cfga, no drkg wtr. Hunting. Elev 8800 ft; 15 acres.

Riverview Campground $10
Ashley National Forest
21 mi N of Duchesne on SR 87, then follow FR 119 about 10 mi to camp; on Yellowstone River. $10 during about 5/15-9/15; free rest of year, but no wtr after 11/1. 19 sites; 20-ft RV limit. Tbls, cfga, toilets, drkg wtr. Fishing, hiking.

Starvation Lake State Park $12
4 mi NW of Duchesne on US 40. $12-$15 at primitive sites. Hookups availableAll year; 14-day limit. 74 sites; 40-ft RV limit. Tbls, flush toilets, cfga, drkg wtr, showers, dump, fish cleaning station. Fishing, boating, swimming. 3,500-acre lake.

Upper Stillwater Campground $10
Ashley National Forest
N of Duchesne on SR 87 to Mountain Home, then 19 mi NW on local rd which becomes FR 134. $10.-$16 5/26-9/4 16-day limit. 19 sites; 16-ft RV limit. Tbls, flush toilets, cfga, drkg wtr. Fishing, hiking.

DUTCH JOHN

Antelope Flat Campground $8
Ashley National Forest
Flaming Gorge National Recreation Area
5.5 mi NW of Dutch John on US 191; 4.9 mi NW on FR 145; half mi W on FR 343. $9 with federal senior pass; others pay $18. About 5/15-9/15; 16-day limit. Parking lot open for camping until wtr turned off. 45-ft RV limit. Toilets, cfga, tbls, drkg wtr, dump ($6). Swimming, boating(l), fishing. Day use/boat ramp fee $5.

Bridge Hollow $5
Browns Park Recreation Mgt. Area
Bureau of Land Management, Vernal Field Office
7 mi N of Dutch John on US 191 at Wyoming line; 10 mi E on Clay Basin Rd; 5 mi S in Jessee Ewing Canyon; 1 mi W; follow signs to Browns Park at Green River. $5. All year; 14-day limit. 15 sites. Tbls, toilets, cfga, drkg wtr. Rafting, hiking, fishing. Raft ramp.

Canyon Rim Campground $10
Ashley National Forest
Flaming Gorge National Recreation Area
From just W of Dutch John, about 8 mi S on US 191; 3.5 mi W on SR 44; 1.5 mi N on Red Canyon Rd (FR 95); above Flaming Gorge Reservoir near Greens Lake. $10 with federal senior pass; others pay $20. mid May-Mid Sep 16-day limit. 7 RV sites up to 65 ft.; 9 tent sites. Tbls, toilets, cfga, drkg wtr. Hiking, fishing, birdwatching. Elev 7400 ft.

Browns Park FREE
CO State Wildlife Area
E of Dutch John along Green River to Colorado line, then SE on CO 318 to CR 10; W to Beaver Creek Unit. To reach Cold Spring Mountain Unit, continue on CR 318 to CR 110; W to access rd; S to property. Free. All year; 14-day limit during 45-day period. Primitive campsites. No facilities. Big-game hunting, fishing. Elev 8700 ft. 2 mi of Beaver Creek.

Cold Spring Mountain Area FREE
Bureau of Land Management
Little Snake Field Office
E of Dutch John along Green River to Colorado line, then SE on CO 318 to CR 10N and CR 72. Lower portion of mountain accessible in Browns Park. Follow signs to camping areas. Free. All year; 14-day limit. Primitive camping at 5 camp areas. Pit toilets; 3 areas have fire rings. Hunting, hiking, backpacking, photography, fishing in Beaver Creek. Top of mountain wet until mid-June, restricting vehicle use.

Crook Campground FREE
Browns Park
National Wildlife Refuge
E of Dutch John along Green River to Colorado line, then SE on CO 318, nearly to access rd to Lodore Hall National Historic Site; turn right on gravel tour rd 1 mi. Free. All year; 14-day limit during 28-day period. 20 sites for tents of self-contained RVs. No facilities or drkg wtr. Wtr nearby at Subheadquarters and refuge headquarters. Hiking, hunting, fishing, sightseeing. Swing bridge across Green River. Bridge under capacity for RVs; okay for cars & light trucks.

Diamond Breaks   FREE
Wilderness Study Area
Bureau of Land Management
Little Snake Field Office
E of Dutch John along Green River to Colorado line, then
SE on CO 318 and W of Browns Park National Wildlife
Refuge. Free. All year; 14-day limit. Primitive camping; no
facilities. Photography, nature study, viewing wildlife, day
hikes, backpacking. Scenic mountainous area. Solitude.
Adjacent to north end of Dinosaur National Monument.
Spectacular views into Canyon of Lodore. 36,000 acres.

Douglas Mountain   FREE
Bureau of Land Management
Little Snake field Office
E of Dutch John along Green River to Colorado line, then
SE on CO 318 to CR 12 and CR 10 (through Greystone) and
CR 116 (Douglas Mountain Blvd dirt, poorly maintained).
Free. All year; 14-day limit. Primitive camping. No facili-
ties. Deer & elk hunting, sightseeing, hiking, backpacking,
horseback riding. Good views to north from Douglas
Mountain Blvd. High-clearance vehicles recommended.
Scenic: pine forests, red sandstone outcrops.

Dripping Springs Campground $9
Ashley National Forest
Flaming Gorge National Recreation Area
From just N of Dutch John on US 191, 3 mi E on Little Hole
Rd (FR 075); near Green River. $9 -$18 with federal senior
pass (others pay $18-$36;) All Year. 22 sites up to 50 ft
(1 95-ft pull-through). Tbls, flush & pit toilets, tbls, cfga,
drkg wt (in-season), shelters. Hiking trails, fishing, biking.

Firefighters Memorial Campground $11
Ashley National Forest
Flaming Gorge National Recreation Area
From just W of Dutch John, about 6 mi S on US 191; left into
campground. $11 with federal senior pass; others pay $22.
About 5/15-9/15; 16-day limit. 94 sites, typically 40 ft. Tbls,
flush toilets, cfga, drkg wtr, dump, fish cleaning stations,
amphitheater. Hiking/biking/bridle trails.

Gates of Lodore $10
Dinosaur National Monument
E of Dutch John along Green River to Colorado line, then
SE on CO 318 and 4 mi SW on unpaved rds. $10 during
4/15-10/15; $6 rest of year, but no wtr; 15-day limit. 19
sites RV limit 30-ft. Tbls, toilets, cfga, wtr faucets. Boating
(concrete launch--whitewater running craft only; special
rafting permit required); fishing; no swimming (cold water
& dangerous currents). Elev 5600 ft; 6 acres. River. N
portal to Lodore Canyon. Pets on leash. Park entry fee.

Greendale Campground $10
Ashley National Forest
Flaming Gorge National Recreation Area
From W of Dutch John, 7 mi S on US 191; left on Green

Dale Rd. $10 with federal senior pass; others pay $20.
5/15-9/7; 16-day limit. 8 sites up to 65 ft (3 pull-through).
Tbls, pit toilets, cfga, drkg wtr.

Greens Lake Campground $10
Ashley National Forest
Flaming Gorge National Recreation Area
From just W of Dutch John, about 8 mi S on US 191; 3.5
mi W on SR 44; 0.5 mi N on Red Canyon Rd (FR 95); 0.5 mi
NE on FR 371 at S shore of Greens Lake. $10 with federal
senior pass; others pay $20. 5/15-9/15; 16-day limit. 5/15-
9/15; 16-day limit. 20 sites, typically 40 ft. Tbls, toilets,
cfga, drkg wtr. Fishing, boating.

Indian Crossing $5
Browns Park Recreation Mgt. Area
Bureau of Land Management, Vernal Field Office
7 mi N of Dutch John on US 191 at Wyoming line; 22 mi
E on Clay Basin Rd (graded, steep dirt rd); at Green River.
$5. All year; 14-day limit. 22 sites. Tbls, toilets, cfga, drkg
wtr, dump. Swimming, boating(l), fishing, hiking, biking,
hunting. Historic homesteader buildings. Elev 5700 ft.

Irish Canyon   FREE
Bureau of Land Management
Little Snake Field Office
E of Dutch John along Green River to Colorado line, then
SE on CO 318, then 4 mi N through Irish Canyon on Moffat County Rd 10N (gravel rd) for 8 mi. Free. 4/15-9/30;
14-day limit. 6 sites (30-ft RV limit). Tbls, cfga, toilet, no
drkg wtr. Wildlife viewing, hunting, hiking, sightseeing.
14,400 acres.

Lodgepole Campground $9
Ashley National Forest
Flaming Gorge National Recreation Area
From just W of Dutch John, about 13 mi S on US 191.
$9 with federal senior pass; others pay $18. 5/15-9/15;
16-day limit. 35 sites, typically 42 ft. Tbls, flush toilets,
cfga, drkg wtr, dump ($6 non-campers), grey wtr stations.
OHV activities.

Red Canyon $10
Visitor Center & Campground
Ashley National Forest
Flaming Gorge National Recreation Area
From W of Dutch John, 7 mi S on US 191 to Greendale
Junction; 4 mi W on SR 44; 3 mi N on Red Canyon Rd. $10
with federal senior pass; others pay $20. 8 sites, typically
22 ft. 5/15-9/15; 16-day limit. Tbls, toilets, cfga, drkg wtr.
Biking, mountain biking, hiking, horseback riding, fishing.
Visitor center with nature trail, exhibits.

Rocky Reservoir Recreation Site   FREE
Bureau of Land Management, Little Snake Field Office
E of Dutch John along Green River to Colorado line, then
SE on CO 318; left on SR 10N for about 15 mi; left (W) on

CR 72; follow signs. Free. All year; 14-day limit. 3 primitive RV sites. Toilet, fire rings, no drkg wtr, no tbls. Hunting, hiking, sightseeing.

Skull Creek Campground $12
Ashley National Forest
Flaming Gorge National Recreation Area
From just W of Dutch John, about 8 mi S on US 191; 2.5 mi W on SR 44, then right into camp. $12. 17 sites; 30-ft RV limit. 5/15-9/15; 16-day limit. Tbls, toilets, cfga, drkg wtr. Hiking, mountain biking, horseback riding.

Swinging Bridge Camp FREE
Browns Park National Wildlife Refuge
E of Dutch John along Green River to Colorado line, then SE on CO 18 almost to access to Lodore Hall National Historic Site and access rd to Crook campground; right on gravel tour 2 mi. Free. All year. 15 sites for tents or self-contained RVs. Cfga, shade trees; no drkg wtr or other facilities. Wtr nearby at Subheadquarters and refuge headquarters. Hiking, hunting, fishing, sightseeing. Next to swinging bridge across Green River. Bridge under capacity for RVs, okay for cars and trucks. Boating on Butch Cassidy pond (no motors) & Green River.

West Cold Spring FREE
Wilderness Study Area
Bureau of Land Management
E of Dutch John along Green River to Colorado line, then SE on CO 318 to N side of Browns Park. Free. All year; 14-day limit. Primitive undesignated camping. No facilities. Hunting, backpacking, scenic viewing, fishing, trail hiking. Beaver Creek Canyon. 17,000 acres.

ENTERPRISE
Honeycomb Rocks Campground $13
Dixie National Forest
5 mi W of Enterprise on CR 120; 5 mi SW on FR 6; at Enterprise Reservoir. $13. 5/4-9/16 (may open earlier if weather permits); 14-day limit. 21 RV sites; 24-ft RV limit. Tbls, cfga, toilets, drkg wtr (high sodium content). Swimming, fishing, boating(l), waterskiing, rafting, kayaking. Elev 5700 ft.

EPHRAIM
Lake Hill Campground $10
Manti-LaSal National Forest
8.5 mi SE of Ephraim on SR 29. $10. 6/1-9/25; 16-day limit. 11 sites; 30-ft RV limit. When group sites #1 & #2 are not reserved, they are available for $15 ($7.50 with federal senior pass). Tbls, toilets, cfga, drkg wtr (no wtr after 9/15), no trash service. Fishing, hiking trails.

ESCALANTE
Barker Recreation Area $11
Dixie National Forest
From Escalante, 5 mi W on SR 12; right North Creek Lakes

sign between mileposts 55 & 56; cross Escalante River; right on FR 149 at Barker Campground sign for 16 mi (last 2 mi rough, not recommended for large RVs). $11 5/1-10/31; 14-day limit. 13 sites; 30-ft RV limit. Tbls, toilets, cfga, drkg wtr MD-LD). Hiking, horseback riding, mountain biking, canoeing.

Blue Spruce Campground $9
Dixie National Forest
From SR 12 at E end of Escalante 0.5 mi N on 300E St to fork; veer right to northbound Pine Creek Rd (becoming FR 153; after 13.6 mi, veer right at fork & follow signs for Hells Backbone Bridge; at 18 mi, turn left on FR 145 to camp. $9. MD-LD; 14-day limit. 5 small sites; 18-ft RV limit. Tbls, toilets, cfga, drkg wtr. Fishing. Elev 7800 ft.

Calf Creek $7.50
Bureau of Land Management
Grand Staircase/Escalante National Monument
15 mi E of Escalante on SR 12. $7.50 with federal senior pass; others pay $15. 4/15-11/30; 14-day limit. 14 sites (25-ft RV limit). Tbls, toilets, cfga, drkg wtr. Fishing, 3-mi trail to scenic 125-ft waterfall. Elev 5400 ft; 22 acres. Non-campers pay $5 day use fee.

Pine Lake Recreation Area $7.50
Dixie National Forest
E of Escalante to jct at Bryce Canyon Resort, then 14 mi N on CR 1660 (Johns Valley Rd); right on FR 132 (Clay Creek Rd) toward Pine Lake for 5.5 mi. $7.50 with federal senior pass others pay $15. 5/20-9/17; 14-day limit. 33 sites (45-ft RV limit). Tbls, toilets, cfga, drkg wtr, no trash service. Swimming, boating(l), fishing, waterskiing, hiking.

Posey Lake Campground $11
Dixie National Forest
From SR 12 at E side of Escalante, 0.7 mi N on 300E St; veer right at fork, then N on FR 153 (gravel); at 13.6 mi, veer left at fork & follow signs to lake. $11. 5/19-9/9; 14-day limit. 21 sites & 1 group site; 24-ft RV limit. Tbls, toilets, cfga, drkg wtr, fish cleaning station, no trash service. Fishing, hiking, canoeing, boating(ld). Elev 8600 ft.

EUREKA
Sand Mountain Campground $9
Little Sahara Recreation Area
Bureau of Land Management
Fillmore Field Office
19 mi S of Eureka on US 6; right on BLM rd, following signs. $9 with federal senior pass; others pay $18; or annual $120 Little Sahara pass. All year; 14-day limit. 300 sites at 3 paved loops; 40-ft RV limit. Tbls, flush toilets (pit toilets in winter), cfga, drkg wtr. Popular off-road vehicle camp.

EVANSTON, WYOMING

Bear River Campground $8
Wasatch National Forest
27.5 mi S of Evanston on SR 150; at the Bear River near FR 58 in Utah. $8 with federal senior pass others pay $16. during May-Oct; free off-season, but Mirror Lake vehicle pass required all year: $6 for 3 days, $12 weekly or $45 annually. 14-day limit. 4 sites; 16-ft RV limit. Tbls, toilets, cfga, drkg wtr in-season. Fishing.

Beaver View Campground $9
Wasatch National Forest
34.1 mi S of Evanston on SR 150; left at campground sign. In Utah. $9 with federal senior pass; others pay $18 during 6/15-10/15; free off-season but Mirror Lake vehicle pass required all year: $6 for 3 days, $12 weekly or $45 annually. No wtr after LD; 14-day limit. 17 sites; 22-ft RV limit. Tbls, toilets, cfga, drkg wtr. Fishing, hiking trails. Elev 9000 ft. Non-campers pay $7 day use fee.

Christmas Meadows $9
Wasatch National Forest
32 mi S of Evanston on SR 150 into Utah; 4 mi E on Christmas Meadows Rd. $9 with federal senior pass during 6/2-9/3 others pay $18. Free off-season but Mirror Lake vehicle pass required all year: $6 for 3 days, $12 weekly or $45 annually. No wtr after LD. 14-day limit. 11 sites; 45-ft RV limit. Tbls, toilets, cfga, drkg wtr. Hiking, fishing, horseback riding. Horse loading facilities. Trailhead to High Uintas Wilderness.

East Fork Bear River $8
Wasatch National Forest
27 mi S of Evanston on SR 150 into Utah; at East Fork Bear River. $8 with federal senior pass during June-Oct; others pay $16. Free off-season but Mirror Lake vehicle pass required all year: $6 for 3 days, $12 weekly or $45 annually. 14-day limit. 7 sites; 20-ft RV limit. Tbls, toilets, cfga, drkg wtr in-season. Fishing, hiking.

Hayden Fork Campground $8
Wasatch National Forest
33 mi S of Evanston on SR 150 into Utah; at Hayden Fork of the Bear River. $8 with federal senior pass; others pay $16 during 6/15-9/15; free off-season, but Mirror Lake vehicle pass required all year: $6 for 3 days, $12 weekly or $45 annually. 14-day limit. 9 sites (26-ft RV limit). Tbls, toilets, cfga, drkg wtr in-season. Fishing, hiking.

Stillwater Campground $9
Wasatch National Forest
32 mi S of Evanston on SR 150 into Utah; on E side of hwy. $9 with federal senior pass during 6/2-LD; others pay $18. Free off-season, but Mirror Lake vehicle pass required all year: $6 for 3 days, $12 weekly or $45 annually. 14-day limit. 17 sites, typically 42 ft. Toilets, cfga, tbls, drkg wtr in-season. Fishing, biking/hiking trail. Elev 8500 ft.

Sulphur Campground $9
Wasatch National Forest
39 mi S of Evanston on SR 150 into Utah; on W side of hwy. $9 with federal senior pass; others pay $18 during 6/15-10/15; free off-season, but Mirror Lake vehicle pass required all year: $6 for 3 days, $12 weekly or $45 annually. 14-day limit. 21 sites; 22-ft RV limit. Drkg wtr, toilets, cfga, toilets; no wtr after LD. Fishing, hiking trails. Elev 9000 ft.

Wolverine ATV Trailhead $7
Wasatch National Forest
37 mi S of Evanston on SR 150 into Utah; SE on FR 057 & FR 323; near Stillwater Fork of Bear River. $7 with federal senior pass; others pay $14 during June-Oct; 14-day limit. Free off-season, but Mirror Lake vehicle pass required all year: $6 for 3 days, $12 weekly or $45 annually. 6 dispersed sites; 16-ft RV limit. Tbls, toilets, cfga, no drkg wtr. Fishing, hiking, biking, horseback riding, ATV activity.

FAIRVIEW

Flat Canyon Campground $10
Manti-LaSal National Forest
12 mi E on SR 31; 4 mi E on SR 26. $10. 6/21-LD; 16-day limit. 13 sites (30-ft RV limit); if group site not reserved, it is $5. Tbls, toilets, cfga, drkg wtr. Boating(l), fishing, hiking. Elev 8900 ft.

Gooseberry Reservoir Campground $10
Manti-LaSal National Forest
9 mi E of Fairview on SR 31. $10. 6/1-9/26; 16-day limit. 16 sites. Tbls, toilets, cfga, drkg wtr. Fishing, hiking. Just to S are 10 more $10 sites & group camping at Gooseberry Campground; 25-ft RV limit.

FARMINGTON

Bountiful Peak Campground $8
Wasatch National Forest
Half mi N of Farmington on co rd; 8.8 mi E on FR 007 (narrow, steep, winding route; trailers over 24 ft not recommended). $8 with federal senior pass; others pay $16. 7/1-9/15; 7-day limit. 39 sites; RV limit 20-ft. Tbls, toilets, cfga, drkg wtr. Hunting, fishing.

FERRON

Ferron Reservoir Campground $7
Manti-LaSal National Forest
28 mi W of Ferron on FR 22. $7. 6/9-10/31; 16-day limit. 32 sites up to 99 ft. Tbls, toilets, cfga, drkg wtr. Fishing, boating(l), nature trails, mountain biking, canoeing. Elev 9500 ft; 17 acres.

Twelve Mile Flat Campground $7
Manti-LaSal National Forest
11 mi W of Ferron on FR 022. $7-$12. 6/16-10/31; 16-day limit. 16 sites; 35-ft RV limit. Tbls, toilets, cfga, drkg wtr (no wtr after 9/15). Wtr system can run dry if more than

5 gallons used at once. Biking, hiking. Farther W, FR 022 becomes a 4x4 rd into Grove of the Aspen Giants Scenic Area. Non-campers pay $3 day use fee.

FREEDOM

Maple Canyon Campground $8
Manti-LaSal National Forest
W of Freedom on Maple Canyon Rd (last 2 mi quite rough, not recommended for large RVs). $8. When group site #1 is not reserved, it is $15 ($7.50 with federal senior pass). MD-10/31; 16-day limit. 12 sites, typically 30 ft. Tbls, toilets, cfga, no drkg wtr, no trash service. Hiking, biking.

GARDEN CITY

Sunrise Campground $8.50
Cache National Forest
From jct with SR 30 in Garden City, 6.3 mi SW on US 89; left at sign to SW shore of Bear Lake. $8.50 with federal senior pass; others pay $17. 6/22-10/15; 7-day limit. 26 sites, typically 45 ft. Tbls, toilets, cfga, drkg wtr. Fishing, hiking/biking trails, OHV activity.

GLENWOOD

Big Lake Dispersed Site   FREE
Fishlake National Forest
From Main St in Glenwood, E on Center St to fish hatchery; 3 mi S on county rd; 8 mi E on FR 068 (Monroe Mountain Rd) to Big Lake. Free. Jun-Oct; 16-day limit. Primitive undesignated sites. Cfga, no toilet, no drkg wtr, no trash service. Fishing, hunting, boating.

GRANTSVILLE

Boy Scout Campground $7
Wasatch National Forest
Quarter mi W of Grantsville on US 40; 4.7 mi S on Hwy 138; 3.5 mi SW on CR 45; 1.8 mi SW on FR 171. $7 with federal senior pass; others pay $14 during 5/1-10/1 ($45 for entire campground); free rest of yr when access open; 7-day limit. 7 sites; RV limit 20-ft. Tbls, toilets, cfga, no drkg wtr. Fishing.

Cottonwood Campground $7
Wasatch National Forest
Quarter mi W of Grantsville on US 40; 4.7 mi S on SR 138; 3.5 mi SW on CR 45; 3.5 mi W on FR 171. $7 with federal senior pass; others pay $14 during 5/1-10/15; free rest of yr when access open; 7-day limit. 2 single primitive sites, 1 triple; RV limit 20-ft. Tbls, toilets, cfga, no drkg wtr. Fishing, hunting.

Loop Campground $7
Wasatch National Forest
Quarter mi W of Grantsville on US 40; 4.7 mi S on CR 138; 3.5 mi SW on CR 45; 3.8 mi SW on narrow, winding dirt FR 80171. Elev 7800 ft. $7 with federal senior pass; others pay $14 during 5/15-10/15; free rest of yr when access open. 7-day limit. 12 small sites. Tbls, toilets, cfga, no

drkg wtr. Rockhounding, hunting, fishing. Archaeological interest.

HANKSVILLE

Starr Springs $4
Bureau of Land Management, Richfield Field Office
25 mi S of Hanksville on SR 95; 17.5 mi S on SR 276; right on co rd, following signs; not recommended for large RVs. $4. 4/1-10/31; 14-day limit. 27 sites. Tbls, toilets, cfga, drkg wtr. Hiking trails. 37.8494327, -110.6615362

HANNA

Aspen Campground $10
Ashley National Forest
From Hanna, about 8 mi N on SR 35; 2.5 mi N on FR 144 (North Fork Rd); at North Fork of Duchesne River. $10 (double sites $16, group $30). About MD-LD. 28 sites; 16-ft RV limit. Tbls, toilets, cfga, drkg wtr. Hiking, horseback riding, fishing.

Hades Campground $10
Ashley National Forest
8 mi NW of Hanna on SR 35; 6 mi NW on FR 144 (North Fork Rd); at North Fork Duchesne River. $10 (double sites $16). MD-LD. 17 sites; 16-ft RV limit. Tbls, toilets, cfga, drkg wtr. Fishing. Elev 7100 ft; 15 acres.

Iron Mine Campground $10
Ashley National Forest
8 mi NW of Hanna on SR 35; 7.5 mi NW on FR 144 (North Fork Rd). $10 (double sites $16, group site $25); near North Fork Duchesne River. MD-LD. 27 sites. Tbls, toilets, cfga, drkg wtr. Fishing. Elev 7200 ft.

Yellowpine Campground $10
Ashley National Forest
1 mi N of Hanna on SR 35; 0.5 mi E on 42750W Rd; 18 mi NE on Blindside Rd, becoming FR 134 & Rock Creek Rd to camp E of Upper Stillwater Reservoir. $10 during MD-LD; 14-day limit ($16 double sites, $30 group). 29 sites; 16-ft RV limit. Tbls, flush toilets, cfga, drkg wtr. Fishing, paved interpretive trail along Rock Creek.

HEBER CITY

Aspen Grove Campground $10
Uinta National Forest
32 mi SE of Heber on US 40; 5 mi S on FR 090; past dam, at E arm of Strawberry Reservoir. $10 with federal senior pass; others pay $20. 5/5-10/15; 7-day limit; 2-day minimum stay required on weekends, 3 days holiday weekends. 42 sites; 40-ft RV limit. Flush toilets, cfga, drkg wtr, tbls, fish cleaning station. Boating(lr), fishing, hiking, horseback riding, biking.2017 be aware of road construction on HWY 40.

Currant Creek Campground $10
Uinta National Forest
41 mi SE of Heber on US 40 to Currant Creek Junction; 17 mi N on FR 083; at SW side of Currant Creek Reservoir. $10 with federal senior pass; others pay $20. MD-LD; 7-day limit; 2-day minimum stay required on weekends, 3 days holiday weekends. 99 sites; 40-ft RV limit. Flush toilets, tbls, cfga, drkg wtr, playground, fishing pier, fish cleaning station, dump. Boating(l), fishing, mountain biking, bridle trails, hiking. Managed jointly with Bureau of Reclamation. 2017 be aware of road construction on HWY 40.

Lodgepole Campsite $10
Uinta National Forest
18 mi SE of Heber City on US 40; at W side of rd. $10 with federal senior pass; others pay $20. MD-LD; 7-day limit. 51 sites; RV limit 70-ft. Tbls, flush toilets, cfga, drkg wtr, dump. Nature trail, mountain biking. Store, restaurant. 2017 Road construction may cause travel delays.

Renegade Point Campground $10
Uinta National Forest
23 mi SE of Heber City on US 40; about 8 mi S on FR 131 to its end; at Strawberry Reservoir. $10 with federal senior pass; others pay $20. 5/12-11/1; 7-day limit; 2-day minimum stay on weekends. 66 sites; 40-ft RV limit. Tbls, flush toilets, cfga, drkg wtr. Fishing, boating(l), hiking, biking. 2017 be aware of road construction on HWY 40.

Soldier Creek Campground $10
Uinta National Forest
Bureau of Reclamation
33 mi SE of Heber City on US 40; 3.5 mi S on FR 480; at Strawberry Reservoir. $10 with federal senior pass; others pay $20. 5/12-10/30; 7-day limit; 2-night minimum stay on weekends. 160 sites; RV limit 62-ft. Flush toilets, cfga, drkg wtr, tbls, marina, store, fish cleaning station, dump. Boating(lr), fishing, interpretive programs. Managed jointly with Bureau of Reclamation. 2017 be aware of road construction on HWY 40.

Strawberry Bay Campground $10
Uinta National Forest
23 mi SE of Heber City on US 40; about 5 mi S on FR 131; at Strawberry Reservoir. $10 base with federal senior pass; others pay $20 base; $11 surcharge for 26 full hookups. May-Oct for most sites; all year with elec; 14-day limit. 295 single sites; 40-ft RV limit. Tbls, flush & pit toilets, cfga, drkg wtr, dump (fee for non-forest campers), fish cleaning station, marina, store. Fishing, boating(ldr), biking, hiking. Visitor center nearby. 2017 be aware of road construction on HWY 40.

HUNTINGTON

Forks Of Huntington Canyon $10
Manti-LaSal National Forest
Huntington Canyon Recreation Area
18 mi NW of Huntington on Hwy 31. $10. 6/1-9/15; 16-day limit. 5 sites (RVs under 21 ft). Tbls, toilets, cfga, drkg wtr, no trash service. Fishing, bridle trail, hiking trail.

Old Folks Flat $10
Manti-LaSal National Forest
Huntington Canyon Recreation Area
22 mi NW of Huntington on Hwy 31. $10. MD-LD; 16-day limit. 9 sites; 35-ft RV limit. Tbls, flush toilets, cfga, drkg wtr, no trash service. Fishing, hiking. Ghost town.

HUNTSVILLE

Anderson Cove Campground $12
South Fork Recreation Complex
Cache National Forest
2.5 mi SW of Huntsville on SR 39; at SW shore of Pineview Reservoir. $12 with federal senior pass; others pay $24. 5/12-9/30; 7-day limit. 58 sites; RV limit 35-ft. Tbls, toilets, cfga, drkg wtr, dump, beach. Fishing, swimming, boating(l), canoeing, horseback riding, mountain biking. $13 boat ramp.

Botts Campground $10
South Fork Recreation Complex
Cache National Forest
6 mi E of Huntsville on SR 39 on bend of South Fork Ogden River. $10 with federal senior pass; others pay $20 during 6/1-9/30; free off-season, but no wtr or services. 7-day limit. 8 sites; 20-ft RV limit. Tbls, toilets, cfga, no drkg wtr. Fishing, hiking, swimming, tubing.

Jefferson Hunt Campground $10
Cache National Forest
2 mi S of Huntsville on SR 39; at South Fork of Ogden River & SE shore of Pinewood Reservoir. $10 with federal senior pass; others pay $20. 6/1-9/30; 7-day limit. 29 sites RV Limit 40-ft. Tbls, toilets, cfga, drkg wtr, dump. Fishing, boating, waterskiing, hiking. Handicap access. Elev 5000 ft; 9 acres.

Lower Meadows Campground $10
Cache National Forest
South Fork Recreation Complex
8 mi E of Huntsville on SR 39; cross bridge, then right at top of hill; at South Fork Ogden River. $10 with federal senior pass; others pay $20. 5/15-10/31; 7-day limit. 19 sites; 25-ft RV limit. Tbls, toilets, cfga, drkg wtr. Fishing, hiking, tubing.

Magpie Campground $10
Cache National Forest
South Fork Recreation Complex
6 mi E of Huntsville on SR 39; at South Fork Ogden River. $10 with federal senior pass; others pay $20. 5/15-9/15 & through big-game hunting season; 7-day limit. 14 sites RV limit 40-ft. Tbls, toilets, cfga, drkg wtr. Swimming, fishing, hiking.

Perception Park Campground $10
Cache National Forest
South Fork Recreation Complex
About 7.5 mi E of Huntsville on SR 39; at South Fork Ogden River. $10 with federal senior pass; others pay $20. 5/15-10/31; 7-day limit. 24 sites; RV limit 45-ft. Tbls, toilets, cfga, drkg wtr, playground. Fishing, hiking, tubing, horseshoe pits.

South Fork Campground $10
Cache National Forest
South Fork Recreation Complex
About 7.2 mi E of Huntsville on SR 39; at South Fork Ogden River. $10 with federal senior pass; others pay $20. 5/15-9/10; 7-day limit. 35 sites; RV limit 35-ft. Tbls, toilets, cfga, drkg wtr. Hiking, tubing, fishing.

Upper Meadows Campground $10
Cache National Forest
South Fork Recreation Complex
8 mi E of Huntsville on SR 39; at South Fork Ogden River. $10 with federal senior pass; others pay $20. 5/15-10/31; 7-day limit. 9 sites RV limit 25-ft . Tbls, toilets, cfga, drkg wtr. Fishing, hiking, tubing. Elev 5200 ft.

Willows Campground $10
Cache National Forest
South Fork Recreation Complex
8 mi E of Huntsville on SR 39; at South Fork Ogden River. $10 with federal senior pass; others pay $20. About 5/5-9/15; 7-day limit. 14 sites RV limit 25-ft. Tbls, toilets, cfga, drkg wtr. Swimming, hiking, fishing. Elev 5300 ft; 6 acres.

HYRUM

Friendship Campground $10
Cache National Forest
8.4 mi E of Hyrum on SR 101; 3.5 mi NE on gravel FR 245. $10 during 5/15-9/15; free rest of yr when access open; 7-day limit. 5 rustic sites RV limit 20-ft. Tbls, toilets, cfga, no drkg wtr. Fishing, hiking.

Pioneer Campground $8.50
Cache National Forest
8 mi E of Hyrum on US 101; turn at sign for Pioneer Camp; at Blacksmith Fork River. $8.50 with federal senior pass; others pay $17. 5/17-9/10; 7-day limit. 18 sites, typically 35 ft; Tbls, toilets, cfga, drkg wtr. Mountain biking, fishing.

JUNCTION

City Creek Recreation Site FREE
Fishlake National Forest
.1 mi N on US 89; 5.3 mi NW on UT 153; 1 mi NE on FR 131. Elev 7600 ft. 5/21-10/30; 14-day limit. 5 sites on 3 acres; 24-ft RV limit. Tbls, toilets, cfga, piped drkg wtr. Hiking trails, bridle trails, fishing; hunting, mountain biking.

KAMAS

Butterfly Lake Campground $9
Wasatch National Forest
14 mi NE of Kamas on SR 150; at Butterfly Lake. $9 with federal senior pass; others pay $18. About 7/1-10/15; 7-day limit. Mirror Lake vehicle pass may be required all year: $6 for 3 days, $12 weekly or $45 annually. 20 sites RV Limit 30-ft. Tbls, toilets, cfga, drkg wtr, horse loading ramp at trailhead. Fishing, hiking. Elev 10,300 ft; snow possible in summer.

Cobblerest Campground $9
Wasatch National Forest
19.5 mi E of Kamas on SR 150; at Provo River canyon. $9 with federal senior pass; others pay $18. MD-LD; 7-day limit. 18 sites (30-ft RV limit). Tbls, toilets, cfga, drkg wtr. Fishing. Elev 8500 ft.

Lilly Lake Campground $10
Wasatch National Forest
From jct with SR 32 in Kamas, 27 mi E on SR 150 (Mirror Lake Scenic Byway) to campground sign, then right. $10 with federal senior pass; others pay $20. 7/15-LD; 7-day limit. Mirror Lake vehicle pass may be required all year: $6 for 3 days, $12 weekly or $45 annually. 14 sites; 30-ft RV limit. Tbls, toilets, cfga, drkg wtr. Fishing, hiking.

Lost Creek Campground $10
Wasatch National Forest
From jct with SR 32 in Kamas, 27.2 mi E on SR 150 (Mirror Lake Scenic Byway) to campground sign, then right. $10 with federal senior pass; others pay $20. 7/15-LD; 7-day limit. Mirror Lake vehicle pass may be required all year: $6 for 3 days, $12 weekly or $45 annually. 35 sites; RV limit 40-ft. Tbls, toilets, cfga, drkg wtr. Fishing, hiking, canoeing.

Lower Provo River Campground $8
Wasatch National Forest
12 mi SE of Kamas on SR 150; near Provo River. $8 with federal senior pass; others pay $16. Mirror Lake vehicle pass may be required all year: $6 for 3 days, $12 weekly or $45 annually. MD-LD & through deer season; 7-day limit. 10 sites; RV limit 30-ft. Tbls, toilets, cfga, drkg wtr. Hiking, fishing, mountain biking. Elev 7400 ft.

Mirror Lake Campground $10
Wasatch National Forest
From jct with SR 32 in Kamas, 31.8 mi E on SR 150 (Mirror Lake Scenic Byway) to campground sign, then right for 0.5 mi. $10 with federal senior pass; others pay $18. 79 sites; 80-ft RV limit. 7/15-LD; 14-day limit. Mirror Lake vehicle pass may be required all year: $6 for 3 days, $12 weekly or $45 annually. 7-day limit. Tbls, toilets, cfga, drkg wtr, amphitheater. Boating(l), fishing, hiking trails, canoeing, nature trail.

Moosehorn Lake Campground $10
Wasatch National Forest
From jct with SR 32 in Kamas, 31.1 mi E on SR 150 (Mirror Lake Scenic Byway) to campground, sign; on the right. $10 with federal senior pass; others pay $20. 33 sites; 80-ft RV limit. Tbls, toilets, cfga, drkg wtr not reliable, bring your own. Hiking, fishing.

Shady Dell Campground $10
Wasatch National Forest
17 mi E of Kamas on SR 150; at Provo River. $10 with federal senior pass; others pay $20. MD-LD & through deer season; 7-day limit. Mirror Lake vehicle pass may be required all year: $6 for 3 days, $12 weekly or $45 annually. Non-campers also pay $8 day use fee. 20 sites; 45-ft RV limit. Tbls, toilets, cfga, drkg wtr. Fishing. Elev 8040 ft.

Shingle Creek ATV Campground $8
Wasatch National Forest
9.5 mi E of Kamas on SR 150. $8 with federal senior pass; others pay $16. MD-LD & through deer season; 7-day limit. Mirror Lake vehicle pass may be required all year: $6 for 3 days, $12 weekly or $45 annually. Non-campers also pay $8 day use fee. 21 sites RV limit 25-ft. Tbls, toilets, cfga, drkg wtr. Hiking, fishing. Elev 7400 ft.

Soapstone Campground $10
Wasatch National Forest
From jct with SR 32 in Kamas, 16 mi E on SR 150 (Mirror Lake Scenic Byway) to campground sign, then right. $10 with federal senior pass; others pay $20. About MD-9/17; 7-day limit. Mirror Lake vehicle pass may be required all year: $6 for 3 days, $12 weekly or $45 annually. 29 single sites; 45-ft RV limit. Tbls, toilets, cfga, drkg wtr systems are old, carry your own water. Hiking trail.

Taylors Fork ATV Campground $8
Wasatch National Forest
7.5 mi E of Kamas on SR 150. $8 with federal senior pass; others pay $16. MD-LD & through deer season; 7-day limit. This site now with Shingle Creek Campground.

Trial Lake Campground $10
Wasatch National Forest
From jct with SR 32 in Kamas, 25.9 mi E on SR 150 (Mirror Lake Scenic Byway) to Trial Lake sign; left, bearing right at "Y" to site. $10 with federal senior pass; others pay $20. About 7/15-LD; 7-day limit. Mirror Lake vehicle pass may be required all year: $6 for 3 days, $12 weekly or $45 annually. 60 sites; RV limit 45-ft. Tbls, toilets, cfga, drkg wtr systems failing carry your own water. Fishing.

Washington Lake Campground $10
Wasatch National Forest
25 mi E of Kamas on SR 150, then N to Washington Lake. $10 with federal senior pass; others pay $20. 7/1-LD; 7-day limit. Mirror Lake vehicle pass required all year:

$6 for 3 days, $12 weekly or $45 annually. Non-campers also pay $8 day use fee. 41 single sites; no RV size limit. Tbls, toilets, cfga, drkg wtr. Fishing, boating(l), hiking, horseback riding.

Yellow Pine Campground $8
Wasatch National Forest
6 mi E of Kamas on SR 150. $8 with federal senior pass; others pay $16. MD-LD & through deer season; 7-day limit. Mirror Lake vehicle pass may be required all year: $6 for 3 days, $12 weekly or $45 annually. 33 sites; RV limit 25-ft. Tbls, toilets, cfga, no drkg wtr. Fishing, hiking trails. 11 acres.

KANAB

Ponderosa Grove Campground $5
Bureau of Land Management
Kanab Field Office
8 mi N of Kanab on US 89; about 7 mi W on Hancock Rd; just N of Coral Pink Sand Dunes. $5. May-Nov; 14-day limit. 9 primitive sites; 24-ft RV limit. Tbls, toilets, no drkg wtr.

KANOSH

Adelaide Recreation Site $12
Fishlake National Forest
6 mi E of Kanosh on FR 106; at Corn Creek. $12. 5/15-9/15; 14-day limit. 8 sites. Tbls, flush toilets, cfga, drkg wtr, amphitheater, no trash service. Fishing, hiking, hunting. Elev 5500 ft.

KOOSHAREM

Box Creek Lakes Dispersed Sites   FREE
Fishlake National Forest
About 5 mi S of Koosharem on SR 62, then 1 mi N of Greenwich, turn W onto dirt rd toward Box Creek Canyon; follow FR 069 away from the creek up the mountain to Upper & Lower Box Lakes. Free primitive, undesignated sites. No facilities, no drkg wtr. All year; 14-day limit; vehicle access during summer & fall. Fishing, hiking. Lake

LAKETOWN

East Side Unit $12
Bear Lake State Park
10 mi N of Laketown on N. Cisco Rd; on E side of lake. $12. All year; 14-day limit. 4 primitive campgrounds (fees at South Eden $15) with pit toilets, cfga, drkg wtr (at South Eden Camp), tbls. Boating(l), fishing, swimming. Elev 5900 ft.

LAPOINT

Paradise Park Campground $5
Ashley National Forest
8.8 mi NW on FR 104 from CR 121 near LaPoint. $5 during 7/1-9/25; free rest of year. 16-day limit. 15 sites (25-ft RV limit). Tbls, toilets, cfga, no drkg wtr. Fishing, boating(l). Paradise Park Reservoir.

LEVAN
Chicken Creek Campground   FREE
Manti-LaSal National Forest
6 mi SE of Levan on Chicken Creek Canyon Rd (FR 101). Free. 6/1-LD; 16-day limit. 12 sites. Tbls, toilets, cfga, drkg wtr. Fishing. This site is in Uinta NF, administered by Manti-LaSal NF.

LOA
Elk Horn Recreation Site $8
Fishlake National Forest
12.5 mi NE of Loa on SR 72; 7.5 mi SE at Elkhorn cutoff (FR 062). 6/15-10/31; $8, 14-day limit. 6 sites; 22-ft RV limit (group sites $35). Tbls, toilets, cfga, drkg wtr. Hunting, fishing, hiking, horseback riding, OHV activity, mountain biking. Elev 9300 ft.

Frying Pan Recreation Site $7.50
Fishlake National Forest
13 mi NW of Loa on SR 24; 16 mi NE on SR 25; 3 mi N of Fish Lake. $7.50 with federal senior pass; others pay $15. MD-9/30; 14-day limit. 11 sites (22-ft RV limit). Group sites $65. Tbls, toilets, cfga, drkg wtr. Fishing, OHV activity, hunting, horseback riding, hiking, mountain biking, waterfowl viewing. Elev 8900 ft.

Paiute Recreation Site $10
Fishlake National Forest
13 mi NW of Loa on SR 24; 15 mi NE on SR 25; qtr mi W of Johnson Reservoir. $10. MD-9/30; 60-day limit. 47 pull-through RV sites in open setting. Toilets, cfga, no drkg wtr, no tbls; showers at Mackinaw Camp. Boating(l), fishing, hiking trails, OHV trails nearby, horseback riding.

LOGAN
Bridger Campground $8.50
Cache National Forest
7.6 mi E of Logan on US 89; right into site. $8.50 with federal senior pass; others pay $17. 5/17-9/10.; 7-day limit. 10 sites, typically 45 ft. Tbls, toilets, cfga, drkg wtr. Fishing. Elev 5000 ft.

Guinavah-Malibu Campground $9.50
Cache National Forest
8 mi E of Logan on US 89. $9.50 with federal senior pass; others pay $19. 5/18-10/9; 7-day limit. 34 single sites, typically 38 ft. Tbls, flush toilets, cfga, drkg wtr. Hiking, fishing. Elev 5200 ft; 38 acres.

Lewis M. Turner Campground $8.50
Cache National Forest
18.4 mi N of Logan on US 89; half mi W on FR 141. $8.50 with federal senior pass; others pay $17. 5/30-9/15; 7-day limit. 10 sites, typically 38 ft. Tbls, flush toilets, cfga, no drkg wtr. Elev 5900 ft; 6 acres.

Lodge Campground $8.50
Cache National Forest
11.7 mi E of Logan on US 89; 1.2 mi SE on FR 047; in right fork of Logan Canyon. $8.50 with federal senior pass; others pay $17. 5/15-10/15; 7-day limit. 10 sites RV limit 20-ft. Tbls, toilets, cfga, drkg wtr. Fishing.

Preston Valley Campground $8.50
Cache National Forest
9 mi E of Logan on US 89; at Logan River. $8.50 with federal senior pass; others pay $17. 5/17-9/10; 7-day limit. 9 sites; RV limit 20-ft. Tbls, flush toilets, cfga, drkg wtr. Fishing.

Red Banks Campground $8.50
Cache National Forest
From jct with SR 30 in Logan, 17.4 mi S on US 89; at Logan River. $8.50 with federal senior pass; others pay $17. 5/30-10/15; 7-day limit. 12 sites, RV limit 20-ft. Tbls, toilets, cfga, drkg wtr. Fishing.

Spring Hollow Campground $9.50
Cache National Forest
6.6 mi NE of Logan on US 89; at Logan River. $9.50 with federal senior pass; others pay $19. 5/15-10/15; 7-day limit. 12 sites, typically 38 ft. Tbls, cfga, toilets, drkg wtr. Fishing, hiking, interpretive trail. Elev 5100 ft.

Tony Grove Lake Campground $9.50
Cache National Forest
18.4 mi S of Logan on US 89; 6.8 mi W on FR 003. $9.50 with federal senior pass; others pay $19. 7/15-9/30; 7-day limit. 32 sites, typically 35 ft. Tbls, flush & pit toilets, cfga, dno rkg wtr. Hiking, horseback riding, boating, fishing.

Wood Camp Campground $8.50
Cache National Forest
12.4 mi NE of Logan on US 89 (Logan Canyon Scenic Byway). $8.50 with federal senior pass; others pay $17. All year; 7-day limit. 6 sites RV-limit 21-ft. Tbls, toilets, cfga, no drkg wtr. Fishing.

LONETREE (WYOMING)
Henry's Fork Trailhead   FREE
Wasatch National Forest
8 mi S of Lonetree, WY, on Cedar Basin Rd; 15 mi W on FR 58 to jct with FR 77 at Henry's Fork Creek. 6/1-10/15; 14-day limit. 7 sites; 20-ft RV limit. Toilets, cfga, no drkg wtr. Hunting, horse trails, hiking trails, fishing. Elev 9600 ft.

MANILA
Browne Lake Campground $7
Ashley National Forest
Flaming Gorge National Recreation Area
14 mi S of Manila on UT 44; 3 mi W on FR 218; half mi

W on FR 364; 3 mi W on FR 221. $7 with federal senior pass; others pay $14 at developed sites; free in dispersed areas (group sites $60). 5/15-9/15; 16-day limit. 20 sites; large RVs okay. Tbls, toilets, cfga, firewood, no drkg wtr, no trash service. Boating(d); fishing; hunting. Elev 8200 ft; 4 acres.

Carmel Campground $12
Ashley National Forest
Flaming Gorge National Recreation Area
3 mi S of Manila on SR 44. $12. 5/15-9/15; 16-day limit. 13 sites, typically 55 ft. Tbls, toilets, cfga, no drkg wtr. Fishing. Visitor center with interpretive displays.

Deep Creek Campground $12
Ashley National Forest
Flaming Gorge National Recreation Area
14 mi S of Manila on SR 44; 3 mi W on FR 218; 4.5 mi SE on FR 539. $12. All year; 16-day limit. 17 sites; 30-ft RV limit. Tbls, toilets, cfga, no drkg wtr, no trash service. Fishing. 8 acres. Carter Creek. Ute Tower.

Lucerne Campground $10
Ashley National Forest
Flaming Gorge National Recreation Area
From Manila, about 3 mi NE on SR 44 (becoming SR 530 in Wyoming); 4 mi E on Lucerne Valley Rd; in Utah at shore of Flaming Gorge Reservoir's Linewood Bay. $10-$14 with federal senior pass; others pay $20-$28. 5/15-9/30; 16-day limit. 45 non-elec sites, 75 elec; 45-ft RV limit. Tbls, flush toilets, cfga, drkg wtr, dump ($5 non-campers). Fishing, boating(l).

Manns Campground $10
Ashley National Forest
Flaming Gorge National Recreation Area
From Manila, 6.4 mi S on SR 44; at S shore of Sheep Creek, on left. $12. About 4/25-10/31; 16-day limit. Primitive sites. Tbls, toilets, cfga, no drkg wtr. Fishing.

Sheep Creek Bay Campground $10
Ashley National Forest
Flaming Gorge National Recreation Area
From Manila, about 7.5 mi S & E on SR 44; left on FR 92 to SW shore of Flaming Gorge Reservoir's Sheep Creek Bay. $10. 5/1-9/30; 16-day limit. RVs only in dispersed camping area. Boating(l), fishing.

Spirit Lake Campground $7
Ashley National Forest
Flaming Gorge National Recreation Area
14 mi S of Manila on SR 44; 3 mi W on FR 218; half mi W on FR 364; 14 mi W on FR 221. $7 with federal senior pass other pay $14. 6/1-10/1; 16-day limit. Open free after managed season to accommodate hunters. 24 sites (30-ft RV limit). Tbls, toilets, cfga, no drkg wtr, no trash service. Fishing, boating(r), hiking. 11 acres. Elev 10,000 ft.

Willows Campground $12
Ashley National Forest
Flaming Gorge National Recreation Area
From Manila, about 6 mi S on SR 44; near Sheep Creek. $12. About 5/1-10/31; 16-day limit. Primitive sites managed by concessionaire. Tbls, toilet, cfga, no drkg wtr. Fishing, hiking.

MANTI
Manti Community Campground $10
Manti-LaSal National Forest
7 mi E of Manti on Manti Canyon Rd (FR 045). $10. MD-10/31; 16-day limit. 9 sites; 30-ft RV limit. Tbls, toilets, cfga, drkg wtr. Fishing, biking, hiking. When group site #1 is not reserved, it is available for $15 ($7.50 with federal senior pass).

MANTUA
Box Elder Campground $9.50
Cache National Forest
4 mi E of Brigham City on US 89/91 near town of Mantua; at Mantua River. $9.50 with federal senior pass; others pay $19. 5/15-10/15; 7-day limit. 25 single sites, RV limit) 25-ftTbls, flush toilets, cfga, drkg wtr. Fishing. Elev 5200 ft; 11 acres.

MAPLETON
Whiting Campground $10
Uinta National Forest
4 mi E of Mapleton, up Maple Canyon on FR 025. $10 with federal senior pass; others pay $20. 5/1-11/1; 7-day limit. 26 sites (3 equestrian); RV limit 45-ft. Tbls, flush toilets, cfga, drkg wtr, cfga (no wtr after LD). Hiking, mountain biking trails, horseshoe pits, bridle trails,. Elev 5400 ft.

MARYSVALE
Piute State Park $8
12 mi S of Marysvale on US 89; 1 mi E. $8. All year; 14-day limit. Primitive undesignated sites on 40 acres. Tbls, pit toilets, cfga, no drkg wtr. Fishing, hiking, boating(ld), swimming. On N shore of 3,360-acre Piute Reservoir.

MEXICAN HAT
Goosenecks State Park $10
Located 4 mi N of Mexican Hat on Hwy 261; 3 mi SW. $10, All year; 14-day limit. 8 sites; 30-ft RV limit. Tbls, toilets, cfga, no drkg wtr. OHV & mountain biking trails nearby.

Johns Canyon   FREE
Slickhorn Canyon
Bureau of Land Management
Dirt rd along N rim of San Juan River from Goosenecks State Reserve, off SR 261. Or, by dirt rd off SR 261 to upper end. Free. All year; 14-day limit. Informal camping along access rds. Drkg wtr scarce; spring wtr in tributary of Trail Canyon. Hiking, fishing. 60,710 acres.

MILFORD

Rock Corral Campground FREE
Bureau of Land Management
Cedar City Field Office
Qtr mi from Milford on Hwy 21, follow signs on local rd for about 9 mi. Free. 5/1-10/31; 14-day limit. 3 sites. Tbls, toilet, cfga, no drkg wtr. Hiking, climbing, hunting. Elev 7000 ft.

MOAB

Big Bend Recreation Site $7.50
Colorado River Recreation Area
Bureau of Land Management, Moab Field Office
2 mi N of Moab on US 191; 6 mi NE on SR 128; at Colorado River. $7.50 with federal senior pass; others pay $15. All year; 14-day limit. 23 sites (space for large RVs). Tbls, toilets, cfga, no drkg wtr, beach. Fishing, swimming, boating.

Dewey Bridge $7.50
Colorado River Recreation Area
Bureau of Land Management, Moab Field Office
2 mi N of Moab on US 191; 28.7 mi N on SR 128; at Colorado River. $7.50 with federal senior pass; others pay $15. All year; 14-day limit. 7 sites. Tbls, toilets, cfga, no drkg wtr. Fishing, boating(l).

Diamond Canyon & Flume Canyon FREE
Bureau of Land Management
N of I-70 about 10 me W of Colorado border; take improved rd N along Westwater Creek. 4WD access routes farther S. Free. All year; 14-day limit. Undesignated campsites on access rds. No facilities. Hiking, backpacking.

Drinks Canyon Camping Area $7.50
Colorado River Recreation Area
Bureau of Land Management, Moab Field Office
2 mi N of Moab on US 191; 6.2 mi N on SR 128; at Colorado River. $7.50 with federal senior pass; others pay $15. All year; 14-day limit. 17 primitive sites. Tbls, toilets, cfga, no drkg wtr. Hiking & biking trails. Elev 4000 ft.

Echo Camping Area $7.50
Bureau of Land Management, Moab Field Office
From US 191 N of Moab, 8 mi N on Kane Creek Rd. $7.50 with federal senior pass; others pay $15. All year; 14-day limit. 9 sites. Tbls, toilets, cfga, no drkg wtr. Biking, hiking climbing. Elev 4100 ft. Petroglyphs, natural bridge nearby.

Goldbar Campground $10
Colorado River Recreation Area
Bureau of Land Management, Moab Field Office
2 mi N of Moab on US 191; 10.2 mi N on SR 128. $10. All year; 14-day limit. 10 primitive sites. Tbls, toilets, cfga, no drkg wtr. Elev 4000 ft.

Goose Island $7.50
Colorado River Recreation Area
Bureau of Land Management, Moab Field Office
2 mi N of Moab on US 191; 1.4 mi N on SR 128; at Colorado River. $7.50 with federal senior pass; others pay $15. All year; 14-day limit. 18 developed sites; 36-ft RV limit. Tbls, toilets, cfga, no drkg wtr. Fishing.

Hal Canyon $7.50
Colorado River Recreation Area
Bureau of Land Management, Moab Field Office
2 mi N of Moab on US 191; 6.6 mi N on SR 128; at Colorado River. $7.50 with federal senior pass; others pay $15. All year; 14-day limit. 11 sites; 24-ft RV limit. Tbls, toilets, cfga, no drkg wtr. Fishing.

Hamburger Rock $10
Bureau of Land Management, Monticello Field Office
S of Moab on US 191 to Needles section of Canyonlands National Park entrance rd SR 211, then about 20 mi W to Lockhart Rd; camp is just up the rd to the right. $10. All year; 14-day limit. 10 sites. Toilet, cfga, no drkg wtr. Biking, hunting, OHV activity.

Hittle Bottom $7.50
Colorado River Recreation Area
Bureau of Land Management, Moab Field Office
2 mi N of Moab on US 191; 22.5 mi N on SR 128. $7.50 with federal senior pass; others pay $15. All year; 14-day limit. 12 sites. Tbls, toilets, cfga, no drkg wtr. Fishing, boating(l). Elev 4000 ft.

Hunters Canyon/Spring Camping Area $7.70
Bureau of Land Management, Moab Field Office
From US 191 N of Moab, 7.8 mi N on Kane Creek Rd; at Colorado River. $7.50 with federal senior pass; others pay $15. All year; 14-day limit. 13 sites (including 4 walk-in sites). Tbls, toilets, cfga, no drkg wtr. Hiking, biking.

Ken's Lake Camp $7.50
Bureau of Land Management, Moab Field Office
7 mi S of Moab on US 191, then left 3 mi, following signs. $7.50 with federal senior pass; others pay $15. All year; 14-day limit. 31 sites; no RV size limit. Tbls, toilets, cfga, no drkg wtr. Hiking & bridle trails, boating. Lake

Kings Bottom Camping Area $7.50
Colorado River Recreation Area
Bureau of Land Management, Moab Field Office
From US 191 N of Moab, 2.8 mi N on Kane Creek Rd; at S side of Colorado River. $7.50 with federal senior pass; others pay $15. All year; 14-day limit. 21 primitive sites, most on river. Tbls, toilets, cfga, no drkg wtr. Hiking, biking. Vicinity .

Oak Grove $7.50
Colorado River Recreation Area
Bureau of Land Management, Moab Field Office
2 mi N of Moab on US 191; 6.9 mi N on SR 128. $7.50 with federal senior pass; others pay $15. All year; 14-day limit. 7 sites; 3 for RVs. Tbls, toilets, cfga, no drkg wtr. Fishing.

Sand Flats Recreation Area $7.50
Bureau of Land Management, Moab Field Office
Grand County Parks
3 mi E of Moab on Sand Flat Rd. $7.50 with federal senior pass; others pay $15. All year; 14-day limit. 124 sites at 9 campgrounds. Tbls, toilets, cfga, no drkg wtr. Mountain biking on 10-mi Moab Slickrock Bike Trail & 4x4 trails. 7,240 acres. $5 day use fee or $10 weekly.

Squaw Flat (Needles) $10
Canyonlands National Park
40 mi S of Moab on US 163; 45 mi W on UT 211 (paved rds). $10 with federal Senior Pass; others pay $20. 26 sites (RVs under 28 ft). Tbls, toilets, cfga, drkg wtr (available off-season at the ranger station about 3 mi from the campground). Rock climbing, hiking, interpretive talks, biking, horseback riding.

Warner Lake Campground $10
Manti-LaSal National Forest
6.5 mi SE of Moab on US 191; 7.3 mi SE on Ken's Lake/ LaSal Mountain Loop Rd to end of pavement; 7 mi NE on FR 062; 5 mi NE on FR 063. $10. 5/18-10/1; 16-day limit. 20 sites (25-ft RV limit). 2017 season water will be turned OFF. Tbls, toilets, cfga, drkg wtr, no trash service. Fishing, hiking. Elev 9400 ft; 10 acres.

MONTICELLO

Buckboard $10
Manti-LaSal National Forest
6.5 mi W of Monticello on FR 105. $10. 5/15-10/1; free rest of year, but no wtr; 16-day limit. 13 sites; 25-ft RV limit. Tbls, toilets, cfga, drkg wtr. Fishing, horseback riding, biking, OHV activity.

Dalton Springs Campground $10
Manti-LaSal National Forest
5 mi W of Monticello on FR 105. $10. 5/15-10/30; 16-day limit. 16 sites; no RV size limit. Tbls, toilets, cfga, drkg wtr. Fishing, swimming, hunting. 5 acres. Elev 8200 ft.

Hatch Point Campground $7.50
Canyon Rims Recreation Area
Bureau of Land Management, Moab Field Office
22 mi N of Monticello on US 191 to Canyon Rims entrance, then 25 mi on gravel rd toward Anticline Overlook. $7.50 with federal senior pass; others pay $15 during 4/15-10/15; 14-day limit. 10 sites (25-ft RV limit). Tbls, drkg wtr in season, toilets, cfga. Hiking, biking, wildlife viewing. Nearby Needles Overlook offers spectacular view of Can-

yonlands National Park; Anticline Overlook; Island in the Sky & Colorado River; 4WD trails.

Newspaper Rock CLOSED
Bureau of Land Management, Monticello Field Office
13 mi N of Monticello on US 191; 13 mi W on SR 211; across the road from Newspaper Rock State Park. Free. All year; 14-day limit. 14 sites. Tbls, toilets, cfga, no drkg wtr. Biking, climbing. Indian rock panel writing nearby. 2017 CLOSED destroyed in a flash flood.

Windwhistle Campground $7.50
Canyon Rims Recreation Area
Bureau of Land Management, Moab Field Office
22 mi N of Monticello on US ;191 to Canyon Rims entrance, then 6 mi on gravel rd toward Anticline Overlook. $7.50 with federal senior pass; others pay $15 during 4/15-10/15; 14-day limit. 15 sites; RV limit 30-ft. Tbls, drkg wtr (May - Sep), toilets, cfga. Hiking, wildlife viewing, biking. Nearby Needles Overlook offers spectacular view of Canyonlands National Park; Anticline Overlook; Island in the Sky & Colorado River; 4WD trails.

MOUNTAIN VIEW (WYOMING)

Bridger Lake Campground $9
Wasatch National Forest
7 mi SW of Mountain View on Wyoming SR 410; 16.5 mi S on CR 283 (becoming FR 72); half mi on FR 126. $9 with federal senior pass; others pay $18. 6/1-10/15, but no wtr after LD; 14-day limit. 28 sites; RV Limit 45-ft. toilets, cfga, drkg wtr. Fishing, hunting, hiking trails, canoeing, biking

China Meadows Campground $7
Wasatch National Forest
7 mi SW of Mountain View on WY 410; 18.4 mi S on CR 283 (becoming FR 72); S of China Lake. $7 with federal senior pass; others pay $14. About 7/1-10/15, but no wtr after LD; 14-day limit. 9 sites; RV limit 20-ft. Toilets, cfga, no drkg wtr. Fishing, hunting, boating(l). Elev 10,000 ft.

East Fork of Blacks Fork Trailhead
Wasatch National Forest FREE
S of Evanston on SR 410; SW on FR 073 past Meeks Cabin Lake to end of rd at Blacks Fork Trail on branch of Blacks Fork River. 8 sites; RV limit 20-ft. Tbls, toilets, cfga, no drkg wtr, horse loading ramps. Hiking, fishing, horseback riding.

Hoop Lake Campground $8
Wasatch National Forest
26.6 mi SE of Mountain View on Hwy 414; 3.2 mi S on CR 264; 6.5 mi SE on FR 58. $8 with federal senior pass; others pay $16. 6/15-10/30, but no wtr after LD; 14-day limit. 44 sites RV limit 25-ft. Tbls, toilets, cfga, drkg wtr (no wtr after LD). Fishing, boating(l), hiking, horseback riding.

Little Lyman Lake Campground $7
Wasatch National Forest
12.9 mi S of Mountain View on WY 410; left at Blacks Fork Access sign on CR 271 for 13.1 mi; rd becomes FR 058 for 5.9 mi; at "Y," bear right on FR 058 for 2.4 mi; right at next jct, still on FR 058, then left on FR 070 for half mi to Little Lyman access rd. $7 with federal senior pass; others pay $14. MD-LD; 14-day limit. 10 sites; RV limit 16-ft . Tbls; toilets, cfga, drkg wtr. Mountain biking, fishing.

Marsh Lake Campground $9
Wasatch National Forest
7 mi SW of Mountain View on WY 410; 17.8 mi S on FR 72. $9 with federal senior pass; others pay $18. 6/1-10/15, but no wtr after LD; 14-day limit. 40 single sites in 2 areas; 45-ft RV limit. Toilets, cfga, drkg wtr. Hiking, hunting, horse trails, fishing, canoeing. Elev 9400 ft.

Meeks Cabin Campground $8
Wasatch National Forest
S of Mountain View on SR 410; W on FR 073. $8 with federal senior pass; others pay $16 during 6/15-10/30. Free rest of year, but no drkg wtr after LD; 14-day limit. 24 sites; 40-ft RV limit. Tbls, toilets, cfga, drkg wtr. Swimming, fishing. Elev 8700 ft; 12 acres. Non-campers pay $7 day use fee.

Stateline Campground $9
Wasatch National Forest
7 mi S of Mountain View on WY 410; 8.2 mi on Uinta CR 283; 5.5 mi on FR 072. $9 with federal senior pass; others pay $18. 5/15-10/15; 14-day limit. 41 sites; 30-ft RV limit. Tbls, toilets, cfga, drkg wtr. Fishing, boating, hiking trails, biking trails, canoeing, bridle trails, swimming.

MYTON

Desolation Canyon/Gray Canyon FREE
Bureau of Land Management
42 mi S of Myton on local rds to Sand Wash Ranger Station; camp along Green River. Free. All year; 14-day limit. Open camping; no facilities. Permits required within Uintah & Ouray Indian Reservations.

Pariette Wetlands FREE
Bureau of Land Management, Vernal Field Office
1 mi W of Myton on US 40 to Sand Wash-Green River access turnoff; 1.7 mi S to Nine Mile-Sand Wash jct; left & follow signs 23 mi (slippery in wet weather). Free. Mar-Nov; 14-day limit. Dispersed camping around ponds complex; no facilities, no drkg wtr. Hiking, fishing, hunting, boating, canoeing in wetlands. Elev 4700 ft.

Sand Wash Recreation Area FREE
Bureau of Land Management, Vernal Field Office
1 mi W of Myton on US 40 to Sand Wash-Green River access turnoff; 1.7 mi S of Nine Mile-Sand Wash jct; left for 18 mi (slippery when wet). Free. Mar-Nov; 14-day limit. Primitive sites for Green River floaters in Labyrinth Canyon.

NAF (IDAHO)

Clear Creek FREE
Sawtooth National Forest
5.9 mi S of Naf on FR 60006, in Utah (4WD recommended). Free. 6/1-9/30; 7-day limit. 12 sites RV limit 24 ft. Tbls, toilets, cfga, drkg wtr. Fishing, hiking, horseback riding, motorcycling.

NEPHI

Cottonwood Campground FREE
Uinta National Forest
6 mi E of Nephi on UT 11; 6 mi N on FR 015. 5/15-10/31; 7-day limit. 18 primitive, undeveloped sites. No facilities, no drkg wtr. Hunting; fishing; horseback riding. Elev 6400 ft; 9 acres. Located near Mt Nebo. Site not recommended for tourist use.

Jericho Campground $9
Little Sahara Recreation Area
Bureau of Land Management, Fillmore Field Office
22 mi W of Nephi on US 6 & 50; 3 mi W of visitor center; 5 mi SW of visitor center on BLM rd. $9 with federal senior pass; others pay $18; or annual $120 Little Sahara pass. All year; 14-day limit. 41 sites. Tbls, flush toilets, cfga, drkg wtr. Nature program. Free camping Nov-Apr, but no wtr except at visitor center.

Oasis Campground $9
Little Sahara Recreation Area
Bureau of Land Management, Fillmore Field Office
22 mi W of Nephi on US 6 & 50; 3 mi W to visitor center; 5 mi SW of visitor center. $9 with federal senior pass; others pay $18; or annual $120 Little Sahara pass. All year; 14-day limit. 115 sites (40-ft RV limit). Tbls, flush toilets, cfga, drkg wtr. Nature program. Elev 5000 ft; 42 acres. Popular off-road vehicle camp.

Ponderosa Campground $9
Uinta National Forest
5 mi E of Nephi on SR 132, then about 3 mi N on Mount Nebo Loop Rd. $9 with federal senior pass; others pay $18. 5/15-11/1; 7-day limit. 23 sites; 45-ft RV limit. Tbls, toilets, cfga, drkg wtr (no wtr after LD). Fishing, hiking, horseback riding.

White Sands $9
Little Sahara Recreation Area
Bureau of Land Management, Fillmore Field Office
22 mi W of Nephi on US 6 & 50; 3 mi W to visitor center; 1 mi N of visitor center on BLM rd. $9 with federal senior pass; others pay $18; or annual $120 Little Sahara pass. All year; 14-day limit. 99 sites (40-ft RV limit). Tbls, flush toilets, cfga, drkg wtr. Nature program. 37 acres. No wtr Nov-Apr except at visitor center.

OAK CITY

Oak Creek Recreation Site $12
Fishlake National Forest
3.5 mi SE on SR 135; 1 mi E on FR 089. $12. 6/15-9/15; 14-day limit. 19 family sites, 4 group sites. Tbls, flush toilets, cfga, drkg wtr, shelter, amphitheater, no trash service. Fishing, hiking, horseback riding, biking. Groups can reserve whole campground.

OAKLEY

Oak Creek Campground $10
Fishlake National Forest
From jct with SR 32 at Oakley, 11.9 mi E on Weber Canyon Rd; right at Smith and Morehouse Recreation area sign for 3.9 mi. $10 with federal senior pass; others pay $20. About 5/20-10/31; 7-day limit. 73 sites; 30-ft RV limit. Tbls, toilets, cfga, drkg wtr. Hiking/bridle trail. Unable to verify rates in 2017

Smith and Morehouse $10.50
Fishlake National Forest
From jct with SR 32 at Oakley,11.9 mi E on Weber Canyon Rd; right at Smith and Morehouse Recreation Area sign for 1.8 mi; left into camp. $10.50 with federal senior pass; others pay $21. About 5/20-MD; 14-day limit. 34 sites; 45-ft RV limit. Tbls, toilets, cfga, drkg wtr. Fishing, boating(l).

ORANGEVILLE

Indian Creek Group Campground $3
Manti-LaSal National Forest
7.2 mi NW of Orangeville on SR 29; 12.2 mi N on FR 040. $3 single sites if not reserved by groups. 6/30-9/15; 16-day limit. 29 sites; 40-ft RV limit. Tbls, toilets, cfga, drkg wtr. Fishing. Elev 9000 ft; 43 acres.

Joes Valley Campground $10
Joes Valley Recreation Area
Manti-LaSal National Forest
17.5 mi NW of Orangeville on SR 29. $10 (double sites $18). 5/11-10/1; 16-day limit. 46 sites (45-ft RV limit). Tbls, flush toilets, cfga, drkg wtr. Fishing, waterskiing, boating(l). Managed jointly with Bureau of Reclamation.

OREM

Mount Timpanogos Campground $10.50
Uinta National Forest
NE of Orem on US 189, then left on SR 92 turnoff to Sundance ski area for about 3 mi. $10.50 with federal senior pass; others pay $21. MD-10/30; 7-day limit. 27 sites; RV limit 20-ft; 30-ft RV limit on SR 92; Tbls, toilets, cfga, drkg wtr. Hiking trails. Elev 6800 ft. Three-day $6 recreation passes also required ($12 for 7 days, $45 annually), available at entrance stations.

PAGE (ARIZONA)

Lee's Ferry Campground $10
Glen Canyon National Recreation Area
25 mi S of Page on US 89; 14 mi N (right on Hwy 89A; cross Colorado River & pass Navajo Bridge Interpretive Center (right); NRA entrance on right. $10 with federal senior pass others pay $20. All year; 14-day limit, entry fee. 54 developed sites with toilets, cfga, drkg wtr. Fishing, boating.

Lone Rock Campground $7
Glen Canyon National Recreation Area
13 mi N of Page on US 89. $7 with federal senior pass others pay $14, plus entry fee (no entry fee with federal senior pass). All year; 14-day limit. Undesignated primitive sites (RVs under 20 ft). 25 acres. Tbls, toilets, cfga, outdoor cold shower, dump. Swimming, fishing, picnicking.

Stateline Campground   FREE
Bureau of Land Management
Arizona Strip District
34 mi W of Page on US 89; pass BLM ranger station & rd to White House trailhead; left on House Rock Valley Rd (dirt) for 9.3 mi. Free. All year; 14-day limit. 4 sites (1 for tents). Tbls, toilets, cfga, no drkg wtr.

White House Trailhead $5
Bureau of Land Management
Kanab Field Office
34 mi W of Page on Hwy 89. $5. 4/1-11/1; 14-day limit. 5 primitive sites; 22-ft RV limit; 3 tent sites. Tbls, toilets, cfga, no drkg wtr. On Paria River. Elev 4600 ft.

PANGUITCH

King Creek $7.50
Dixie National Forest
7 mi S of Panguitch on US 89; E on SR 12 to town of Tropic, then continue E 7.6 mi; left at Kings Creek sign on gravel East Fort Rd 087 for 7 mi; left at campground sign onto access rd. $7.50 with federal senior pass others pay $15. 5/15-LD; 14-day limit. 37 sites; 45-ft RV limit. Tbls, flush toilets, cfga, drkg wtr, dump ($). Swimming, boating(l), fishing, hiking trails, waterskiing, ATV trail. Elev 8000 ft; 18 acres. Tropic Reservoir & East fork of Sevier River.

North Campground $10
Bryce Canyon National Park
7 mi S of Panguitch on US 89; 13 mi E on SR 12; 2 mi S on SR 63; just E of park headquarters. $10 with federal senior pass; others pay $20 for tent sites, $15 with federal senior pass others pay $30 for RV sites All year; 14-day limit. 107 sites. Tbls, flush toilets, cfga, drkg wtr, dump (showers at Sunset Point). Hiking, horseback riding. Entry fee.

Panguitch Lake North Campground $8.50
Dixie National Forest
16 mi SW of Panguitch on SR 143. $8.50 with federal senior pass; others pay $17. 6/11-LD; 14-day limit. 39 single sites (35-ft RV limit). Tbls, flush toilets, cfga, drkg wtr, dump, coin laundry. Hiking, fishing, boating, swimming. Elev 8400 ft.

Red Canyon Campground $9
Dixie National Forest
10 mi SE of Panguitch on Hwy 12. $9 with federal senior pass; others pay $19. 5/15-10/1; 14-day limit. 37 sites (45-ft RV limit. Tbls, flush & pit toilets, cfga, drkg wtr, coin showers, dump. Hiking trails, ATV activity, horseshoes, volleyball. Visitor center. Elev 7240.

Sunset Campground $10
Bryce Canyon National Park
7 mi S of Panguitch on US 89; 13 mi E on SR 12; S on SR 63 to park headquarters, then 2 mi S. $10 with federal senior pass; others pay $20 for Tent sites, $15 with federal senior pass others pay $30 for RV sites 4/15-11/30; 14-day limit. 111 sites. Tbls, flush toilets, cfga, drkg wtr (showers at Sunset Point; dump at North Campground). Hiking, horseback riding. Entry fee.

White Bridge Campground $8.50
Dixie National Forest
12 mi SW of Panguitch on SR 143; at Panguitch Creek. $8.50 with federal senior pass; others pay $17. MD-LD; 14-day limit. 27 sites (24-ft RV limit). Tbls, flush & pit toilets, cfga, drkg wtr, dump. Hiking, fishing, swimming, biking. Elev 7900 ft.

PAYSON
Blackhawk Campground $10
Uinta National Forest
16 mi SE of Payson on Nebo Loop Rd (FR 015); 2 mi S on FR 015. $10 with federal senior pass; others pay $20. M-11/1; 7-day limit. 15 sites equipped for horses; 45-ft RV limit. Tbls, toilets, cfga, drkg wtr (no wtr after LD), dump, horse loading ramp, corrals. Bridle & hiking trails, mountain biking, fishing.

Maple Bench Campground $9
Uinta National Forest
5 mi E of Payson on Nebo Loop Rd. $9 with federal senior pass; others pay $18. MD-10/1; 7-day limit. 10 sites RV limit 35-ft. Tbls, toilets, cfga, drkg wtr. Fishing, hiking trail. Handicap access. Half mi N of tiny Maple Lake (canoeing, fishing).

Payson Lakes Campground $10.50
Uinta National Forest
12 mi SE of Payson on Nebo Loop Rd, then SW following signs. $10.50 with federal senior pass; others pay $21. MD-11/1; 7-day limit. 98 single sites; 45-ft RV limit. Tbls, flush toilets, cfga, drkg wtr (no wtr after LD), corrals, beach. Paved loop nature trail among 3 lakes. Horseback riding, fishing, swimming, hiking, nature trails, swimming, biking/jogging path.

PINE VALLEY
Crackfoot Campground $8.50
Dixie National Forest
Pine Valley Recreation Area
From Pine Valley, 3 mi E to Pine Valley Recreation Area & follow signs; E of reservoir at Santa Clara River. $8.50 with federal senior pass; others pay $17. 5/15-9/30; 14-day limit. 15 single sites. Tbls, toilets, cfga, drkg wtr, no trash service. Biking, hiking, horseback riding, fishing.

Dean Gardner Campground $8.50
Dixie National Forest
Pine Valley Recreation Area
From Pine Valley, 3 mi E to Pine Valley Recreation Area & follow signs; new campground at shore of Pine Valley Reservoir. $8.50 with federal senior pass; others pay $17. 5/15-9/30; 14-day limit. 21 single sites; 45-ft RV limit. Tbls, toilets, cfga, drkg wtr (MD-LD), no trash service. Horseback riding, fishing, hiking, canoeing.

Ebenezer Bryce Campground $8.50
Dixie National Forest
Pine Valley Recreation Area
From Pine Valley, 3 mi E to Pine Valley Recreation Area & follow signs; renovated site previously called Blue Springs Campground. $8.50 with federal senior pass; others pay $17. 11 single sites; 45-ft RV limit. Tbls, toilets, cfga, drkg wtr MD-LD, no trash service. 5/15-9/15; 14-day limit. Hiking, fishing, horseback riding.

Equestrian Campground $8.50
Dixie National Forest
Pine Valley Recreation Area
2 mi E of Pine Valley; near Pine Valley Reservoir. $8.50 with federal senior pass at equestrian sites; others pay $17. MD-9/30; 14-day limit. 11 sites; 45-ft RV limit. Tbls, flush & pit toilets, cfga, drkg wtr, 4-way corral, horse stalls. Dump 5 mi. Fishing, horseback riding, ATV activities. Good turn-around for large RVs.

Yellow Pine Loop $8.50
Dixie National Forest
Pine Valley Recreation Area
From Pine Valley, 3 mi E to Pine Valley Recreation Area & follow signs; E of reservoir at Santa Clara River. $8.50 with federal senior pass at new camping area; others pay $17. 5/15-9/15; 14-day limit. 5 single sites. Tbls, toilets, cfga, drkg wtr (MD-LD), no trash service. Hiking trail, fishing.

PLEASANT GROVE
Granite Flat Campground $10.50
Uinta National Forest

14 mi NE of Pleasant Grove on SR 144, up American Fork Canyon, then FR 85 (North Fork Rd) past Tibble Fork Reservoir to camp. $10.50 with federal senior pass; others pay $21. MD-9/30; 7-day limit. 44 single sites; RV limit 45-ft. Tbls, flush toilets, cfga, drkg wtr. Horse transfer station & loading ramps nearby. Fishing, horseback riding, hiking, hunting, baseball, canoeing, horseshoe pits. Three-day user permits $6 ($12 for 7 days, $45 annually).

Little Mill Campground $10.50
Uinta National Forest
10 mi NE of Pleasant Grove on SR 92; at American Fork River. $10.50 with federal senior pass; others pay $21. 5/15-10/30; 7-day limit. 34 sites; RV limit 60-ft. Tbls, flush toilets, cfga, drkg wtr. Fishing, hiking. Visitor center nearby. Three-day user permits $6 ($12 for 7 days, $45 annually).

Timpooneke Campground $10.50
Uinta National Forest
14.1 mi NE of Pleasant Grove on SR 92. $10.50 with federal senior pass; others pay $21. MD-10/30; 7-day limit. 27 sites; RV limit 30-ft. Tbls, toilets, cfga, drkg wtr. Hiking trail, horseback riding, hunting, mountain biking. Three-day user permits $6 ($12 for 7 days, $45 annually).

PRICE
Price Canyon Recreational Area $8
Bureau of Land Management, Price Field Office
9 mi N of Price on US 50/6; turn left at entrance sign; 3 mi up mountain to site. Avoid open, exposed areas, as lightning frequently strikes ridge tops. $8. Free mid-Oct to mid-Apr; 14-day limit. 18 sites, RV limit 35-ft. Tbls, toilets, cfga, drkg wtr. Wildlife viewing, Price Canyon overlook, Bristlecone Ridge Hiking Trail.

PROVO
Hope Campground $10.50
Uinta National Forest
6 mi N of Provo on US 189 to Squaw Peak Rd; 5 mi S on FR 027. $10.50 with federal senior pass; others pay $21. MD-10/31; 7-day limit. 24 sites RV limit 40-ft. Tbls, toilets, cfga, no drkg wtr.

Tinney Flat Campground $10
Uinta National Forest
S of Provo on I-15 to exit 248 at Santaquin, then E on FR 014 about 9 mi (rd steep & narrow, not recommended for large RVs; at Santaquin River. $10 with federal senior pass; others pay $20. MD-11/1; 7-day limit. Toilets, cfga, drkg wtr (no wtr after LD), cfga. 13 sites; no RV size limit. Fishing, hiking trails, volleyball, mountain biking, horseshoe pits.

RICHFIELD
Castle Rock Campground $6.50
Fremont Indian State Park

21 mi SW of Richfield on I-70. $6.50 with federal senior pass; others pay $13. All year; 14-day limit. 31 sites; 30-ft RV limit. Tbls, flush toilets, cfga, drkg wtr, no showers, no dump. Horseback riding, museum of Anasazi Indian culture, boating, fishing. In Fishlake National Forest, managed by state. Visitor center & museum. 889 acres; elev 5900 ft.

ROOSEVELT
Uinta Canyon $5
Ashley National Forest
9.5 mi N of Roosevelt on Hwy 121; 12 mi NW on co rd; 2.5 mi NW on FR 118; at Uinta River. $5. 5/15-10/1; 14-day limit. 24 sites (22-ft RV limit). Tbls, toilets, no drkg wtr, cfga. Fishing. Elev 7600 ft; 15 acres.

ST. GEORGE
Baker Reservoir Dam $6
Bureau of Land Management, St. George Field Office
24 mi N of St. George on Hwy 18; right on Baker Dam Reservoir Rd for half mi. $6 single sites, $12 at four double sites. 16 sites, some for big rigs. All year; 14-day limit. 10 sites; 24-ft RV limit. Tbls, toilets, cfga, no drkg wtr. Fishing, hiking.

Red Cliffs Campground $7.50
Red Cliffs Recreation Area
Bureau of Land Management, St. George Field Office
15 mi NE of St. George (4.5 mi SW of Leeds) on I-15; 1.5 mi W on Frontage Rd & BLM rd. $7.50 with federal senior pass; others pay $15. All year; 14-day limit. 11 sites (25-ft RV limit). Tbls, toilets, cfga, drkg wtr.

Virgin River Gorge Camp $8
Bureau of Land Management
Arizona Strip District
20 mi SW of St. George on I-15, in Arizona, at Cedar Pockets interchange. Adjacent to the Virgin River and Arizona's Cedar Pockets Rest Area. All year; no time limit. $8 ($90 monthly). 75 sites, several pull-through. Toilets, drkg wtr, cfga, tbls. Scenic overlook, interpretive trail, 2 river access trails. Fishing, hiking.

SALINA)
Clear Creek Dispersed Site   FREE
Fishlake National Forest
34 mi E of Salina on I-70 to Exit 89; 1.5 mi W on frontage rd; S on FR 016 to Clear Creek. Free. May-Oct; 16-day limit. Primitive undesignated sites. Some cfga, no other facilities, no drkg wtr, no trash service. Hunting, fishing.

Gooseberry Reservoirs   FREE
Dispersed Recreation Sites
Fishlake National Forest
7.5 mi SE of Salina on I-70; 12 mi S on Gooseberry Rd; take numerous spur rds to various locations: Twin Ponds, Cold Spring, Salina Reservoir, Farnsworth Reservoir, Harves

River Reservoir, Browns Hole, Niotche Creek, Oak Ridge; Gooseberry Rd is quite rough. May-Oct; 16-day limit. Free. Primitive undesignated sites. Some cfga; toilets at Twin Ponds, Cold Spring, Oak Ridge & Salina Reservoir; no drkg wtr, no trash service. Trout fishing, hunting, boating, hiking trails (part of Great Western Trail) open to OHVs & horses.

Lost Creek Reservoir   FREE
Dispersed Recreation Site
Fishlake National Forest
7.5 mi SE of Salina on I-70; 20 mi S on Gooseberry Rd; 1 mi W on FR 058 to Lost Creek Reservoir; numerous pullouts & spur rds for camping. Free. May-Oct; 16-day limit. Some cfga, no other facilities, no drkg wtr, no trash service. Fishing, hunting, boating (no mtrs), hiking, horseback riding, mountain biking, OHV use. Area is a plateau at 9800 ft.

Maple Grove Recreation Site $7.50
Fishlake National Forest
11 mi NW of Salina on Hwy 50; 3 mi W on FR 101. $7.50 with federal senior pass; others pay $15. 5/15-9/15; 14-day limit. 20 sites RV limit 22-ft. Tbls, drkg wtr, toilets, cfga. Fishing, hunting, hiking trails, mountain climbing. Scenic; elev 6400 ft.

Old Woman Plateau   FREE
Dispersed Recreation Site
Fishlake National Forest
34 mi SE of Salina on I-70 to Exit 89; 4 mi W on frontage rd to FR 011 (Old Woman Plateau Rd); N under freeway to site. Free. May-Oct; 16-day limit. Primitive undesignated sites. Some cfga, no other facilities, no drkg wtr, no trash service. Hunting. Area is seldom used.

Red Creek Dispersed Site   FREE
Fishlake National Forest
34 mi SE of Salina on I-70 to Exit 89; 2.5 mi W on frontage rd; S on FR 141 to Red Creek. Free. May-Oct; 16-day limit. Primitive undesignated sites. Some cfga, no other facilities, no drkg wtr, no trash service. Hunting.

Rex Reservoir Dispersed Site   FREE
Fishlake National Forest
7.5 mi SE of Salina on I-70; 4 mi S on Gooseberry Rd; 1 mi W on FR 037 (Soldier Canyon Rd); 6 mi S on FR 050 (Rex Reservoir Rd). Free. May-Oct; 16-day limit. Primitive undesignated sites. Some cfga, no other facilities, no drkg wtr, no trash service. Fishing at Rex Reservoir & nearby Lost Creek, Little Lost Creek, Lost Creek Reservoir, Sevenmile Creek, Johnson Reservoir, Fish Lake & Gooseberry Reservoir; hunting; boating; hiking. Elev 7200 ft.

Salina Creek Dispersed Site   FREE
Fishlake National Forest
18 mi SE of Salina on I-70; from exit 71, qtr mi E on paved rd, then turn N on FR 009 to Salina Creek bottom area. Free. May-Oct; 16-day limit. Some cfga, no other facilities, no drkg wtr, no trash service. Trout fishing in lower sections of Salina Creek, hunting, hiking trails, horseback riding. Access to Salina Flats roadless area with its 26,000 sq acres of non-motorized walk-in camping. Note: better access than Gooseberry Reservoirs; view of a wide area of beaver ponds.

Water Hollow Dispersed Site   FREE
Fishlake National Forest
10.5 mi SE of Salina on I-70 (5 mi past Gooseberry Rd exit) to turnoff (not a formal exit) signaled by break in guard rail; turn sharply, reversing directions, through gate, then N under freeway; many sites after about 4 mi. Free. May-Oct; 16-day limit. Primitive undesignated sites. Some cfga, no other facilities, no drkg wtr, no trash service. Hunting, hiking trails, horseback riding.

Willow Creek Dispersed Site   FREE
Fishlake National Forest
3 mi N of Salina on US 89; 7 mi E on gravel rd to forest boundary. Free. May-Oct; 16-day limit. Primitive undesignated sites. Some cfga, tbls; no other facilities; no drkg wtr or trash service. Trout fishing, hunting, hiking trails, horseback riding.

SALT LAKE CITY
Rockport State Park $12
45 mi E of Salt Lake City on SR 32, near Wanship. $12 for primitive sites at 5 campgrounds; $24 for developed sites at Juniper Campground; 40-ft RV limit. Tbls, toilets, cfga, drkg wtr, showers. Hiking, biking, fishing, swimming, boating.

SMITHFIELD
Smithfield Canyon Campground $8.50
Wasatch National Forest
5 mi NE of Smithfield on co rd. $8.50 with federal senior pass; others pay $17. 5/15-9/15; 7-day limit. 7 sites, RV limit 25-ft. Tbls, toilets, cfga, drkg wtr. Fishing, hiking.

SPANISH FORK
Diamond Campground $9
Uinta National Forest
10 mi S of Spanish Fork on Hwy 89; 6 mi NE on FR 029; at Diamond Creek. $9 with federal senior pass; others pay $18. 4/1-11/1; 7-day limit. 38 single sites, 22 double RV limit 75-ft. Tbls, toilets, cfga, drkg wtr. Fishing, biking & hiking trails, nature trails.

SPRINGVILLE
Balsalm Campground $10
Uinta National Forest
About 12 mi E of Springville on SR 79, which becomes FR 058, to end of pavement; at Right Fork of Hobble Creek. $10 with federal senior pass; others pay $20. MD-LD;

7-day limit. 24 sites; RV limit 30-ft. Flush toilets, tbls, drkg wtr, cfga. Fishing, hiking trails, mountain biking trails, bridle trails.

Cherry Campground $10
Uinta National Forest
About 6 mi E of Springville on SR 79, which becomes FR 058; at Right Fork of Hobble Creek. $10 with federal senior pass; others pay $20. MD-11/1; 7-day limit. 24 single sites; RV limit 50-ft. Flush toilets, tbls, no drkg wtr, cfga (no wtr after LD). Fishing, hiking trails, biking trails, horseshoe pits, volleyball court. 2017 no water in campground.

TEASDALE
Lower Bowns Campground $12
Fishlake National Forest
22 mi SE of Teasdale on SR 12; at Lower Bowns Reservoir. $12. All year; 14-day limit. Primitive open camping near 37-acre Lower Bowns Reservoir. Toilet, cfga, no drkg wtr, no trash service.

Oak Creek Campground $10
Fishlake National Forest
20 mi SE of Teasdale on SR 12. $10. 5/15-10/31; 14-day limit. 8 sites; 25-ft RV limit. Tbls, toilets, cfga, drkg wtr. Fishing. Elev 8800 ft.

Pleasant Creek Campground $12
Fishlake National Forest
18 mi SE of Teasdale on SR 12. $12. MD-9/15; 14-day limit. 19 sites (25-ft RV limit). Tbls, toilets, cfga, drkg wtr. Fishing.

Singletree Campground $12
Fishlake National Forest
14 mi SE of Teasdale on SR 12. $12 base. 5/15-10/31; 14-day limit. 16 sites, RV limit 25-ft. Tbls, flush & pit toilets, cfga, drkg wtr, dump, WiFi ($5). Fishing, hiking trail.

TORREY
Cathedral Valley Campground $10
Capitol Reef National Park
36 mi from park's visitor center on Cathedral Valley Loop Rd. Camp free, but $10 entry fee. All year; 14-day limit. 6 sites. Tbls, toilets, cfga, no drkg wtr

Cedar Mesa Campground $10
Capitol Reef National Park
35 mi S of park's visitor center on Notom-Bullfrog Rd. Camp free, but $10 entry fee. All year; 14-day limit. 5 sites. Tbls, toilets, cfga, no drkg wtr.

Fruita Campground $10
Capitol Reef National Park
11 mi E of Torrey on U-24; 1.4 mi S of U-24. $10 with federal senior pass others pay $20, during 4/1-11/30; free rest of year. 71 sites. Tbls, drkg wtr, cfga, toilets. Visitor center

nearby. Hiking. Museum, historical schoolhouse and other exhibits nearby. Hiking trails. Scenic drive. Pets on leash. Restrooms during the fee season, pit toilets during the free season.

VERMILLION
Koosharem Reservoir   FREE
Bureau of Land Management, Richfield Field Office
30 mi S of Vermillion on SR 24. Free. All year; 14-day limit. Primitive undesignated sites. Tbls, toilets, cfga, no drkg wtr. Fishing, boating, hiking, OHV activity. Elev 7000 ft.

VERNAL
Book Cliffs Recreation Area   FREE
Bureau of Land Management
Access from I-70 or 60 mi S of Vernal on paved & gravel rds. Free. All year; 14-day limit. Primitive undesignated sites. No facilities, no drkg wtr. Fishing, hiking, horseback riding, hunting, OHV activities, biking, climbing. 455,000-acre wild area. Elev 5000-8200 ft.

Bull Canyon, Willow Creek   FREE
Skull Creek
Wilderness Study Areas
Bureau of Land Management
E of Vernal on US 40 into Colorado; N on co rds. Areas N of highway, S of Dinosaur National Monument. Free. All year; 14-day limit. Accessible earlier and later in spring & fall than higher-elevation areas. Primitive backcountry camping; no facilities. Scenic viewing, hiking, backpacking, viewing wildlife, photography, horseback riding. 39,000 acres in the three areas. Colorful canyons, sandstone cliffs, rock outcrops. Archaeological sites (protected by law). Bull Canyon WSA can be viewed from Dinosaur Monument's Plug Hat picnic area.

Cliff Ridge   FREE
Hang Gliding Area
Bureau of Land Management
30 mi E of Vernal on US 40; N at Dinosaur NM headquarters near Dinosaur, Colorado; at the Blue Mountain Plateau. Free. May-Sept; 14-day limit. Primitive campground; no facilities, no drkg wtr. Hang gliding, biking, hiking, horseback riding, OHV activity, hunting. Exhibits.

Dry Fork Canyon   FREE
Bureau of Land Management
15 mi NW of Vernal in Dry Fork Canyon. 4/1-11/1; 14-day limit. Free. Primitive undesignated camping area; 5 small sites & dispersed camping. Tbls, cfga, no drkg wtr, no facilities.

East Park Campground $12
Ashley National Forest
Flaming Gorge National Recreation Area
20 mi N of Vernal on US 191; 4.5 mi NW on FR 018 (Red Cloud Loop Rd); right on FR 020 (East Park Campground

Rd) for 7 mi; at East Park Reservoir. $12 during 6/15-9/15; free rest of year, but no wtr. 21 sites; 25-ft RV limit. Tbls, toilets, cfga, drkg wtr. Fishing, hiking.

Green River Campground $9
Dinosaur National Monument
13.4 mi W of Vernal on US 40; 6.5 mi N from Jensen on SR 149 to Quarry Visitors Center, then 5 mi E. $9 with federal senior pass others pay $18. 4/15-10/15; 14-day limit. About 100 sites; RV limit 35-ft. Tbls, flush & pit toilets, cfga, drkg wtr. Hiking trails. Entry fee. In off-season, use Split Mountain Campground.

Long Park Reservoir   FREE
Ashley National Forest
About 22 mi N of Vernal on Taylor Mountain Rd (N2500W, becoming FR 237/044, then FR 018) to turnoff for Oaks Park Reservoir; veer right onto FR 043 for about 5 mi to lake. Free dispersed primitive camping. Toilet, cfga, no drkg wtr, no trash service. Boating(l), fishing.

Oaks Park Campground   FREE
Ashley National Forest
About 22 mi N of Vernal on Taylor Mountain Rd (N2500W, becoming FR 237/044, then FR 018) to FR 025 turnoff (right) for Oak Park Reservoir; veer right onto campground rd/FR 024. Free. 6/1-9/15; 14-day limit. 11 rustic sites. Tbls, toilet, cfga, no drkg wtr (pump wtr on W shore). Fishing, boating, canoeing, hiking. At S shore of Oaks Park Reservoir. Elev 9200 ft.

Pelican Lake Recreation Area   FREE
Bureau of Land Management, Vernal Field Office
15 mi SW of Vernal on US 40; 7 mi S on SR 88; turn right on rd marked for Bandlett, for 2 mi; turn left on marked rd toward boat ramp & camping. Free. All year; 14-day limit. 13 informal sites, some with tbls. Toilets, no drkg wtr; 25-ft RV limit. Boating(l), fishing. No swimming. 840 acres of water.

Split Mountain Camp $6
Dinosaur National Monument
13.4 mi E of Vernal on US 40; 6.5 mi N from Jensen on SR 149 to Quarry Visitors Center, then 4 mi E on SR 149. $6 for individual camping in winter but no wtr; 4 group sites; Group camping only in-season ($40). All year; 14-day limit. 35-ft RV limit. Tbls, 1 pit toilet in winter, cfga, drkg wtr, showers. Boating(l), fishing, rafting, nature trail. Entry fee.

Stateline Cove Campground $12
Ashley National Forest
Flaming Gorge National Recreation Area
From Manila, 6 mi E on SR 43, then WY SR 530 to shore of Flaming Gorge Reservoir (about 25 mi S of Green River, WY). $12 at primitive dispersed sites. 5/15-9/15; 16-day limit. Tbls, pit & portable toilets, cfga, no drkg wtr. Fishing, boating.

VERNON

Simpson Springs $7.50
Bureau of Land Management, Salt Lake Field Office
30 mi W of Vernon on gravel co rd (30 mi W of Faust). $7.50 with federal senior pass others pay $15. All year; 14-day limit. 20 sites on 40 acres RV limit 20-ft Tbls, toilets, cfga, no drkg wtr. Fishing. Corral & horse wtr qtr mi W; no horses in campground.

Vernon Reservoir   FREE
Uinta National Forest
From Vernon, 0.5 mi S on SR 36; right at Benmore sign for 5 mi on dirt rd; left at "T" & follow signs 2 mi to site; along shore of Vernon Reservoir. Free. All year; 14-day limit. 11 small RV sites. Toilets, tbls, cfga, no wtr. Fishing.

VIRGIN

Lava Point Primitive Camp   FREE
Zion National Park
Approx 35 mi(last 2 mi are gravel rds) from park's S entrance on UT 9, just E of Virgin. Approx 20 mi N on Kolob Reservoir Rd (last mi is gravel); right at Lava Point Rd; 1.5 mi to campground. Camp free, but $30 entry fee for 7 days. Late May through late Oct, depending on snow conditions; 14-day limit. 6 sites; 19-ft RV limit. No drkg wtr. Hiking Area is inaccessible by vehicle during winter. Pets, but not on trails or in bldgs.

South Cammpground $10
Zion National Park
Approx 1/2 mi from park's S entrance on UT 9, just E of Virgin. $10 with federal senior pass others pay $20. Park Entry fee $30 for 7 days.. 117 sites, no hookups, dump, wtr.

WHITEROCKS

Pole Creek Lake Campground $5
Ashley National Forest
8 mi N of Whiterocks on CR 121; 13.5 mi NW on FR 117. $5. Elev 10,200 ft. 7/1-9/10; 16-day limit. 18 sites; 22-ft RV limit. Tbls, toilet, cfga, firewood, no drkg wtr. Hunting; fishing; horseback riding (1 mi). Elev 10,200 ft.

Whiterocks Campground $8
Ashley National Forest
7 mi N of Whiterocks on CR 121; 2.5 mi E at sign; 5.2 mi N on FR 492. $8 during 5/15-9/15; free rest of year; 16-day limit. 21 sites (RVs under 26 ft). Tbls, toilets, cfga, drkg wtr. Fishing. Elev 7400 ft; 13 acres.

WOODLAND

Mill Hollow Campground $9
Uinta National Forest
12 mi SE of Woodland on SR 35; S on FR 054; at Mill Hollow Reservoir. $9 with federal senior pass; others pay $18. 6/15-9/15; 7-day limit. 26 sites; RV limit 40-ft. Tbls, toi-

lets, cfga, drkg wtr. Fishing, boating (no mtrs), hiking (loop trail), canoeing, horseshoe pits. Late or early snowfall may shorten season. 2-night minimum stay on weekends. drkg wtr systems failing carry your own water.

WOODRUFF

Birch Creek   FREE
Bureau of Land Management, Salt Lake Field Office
10 mi W of Woodruff on US 39. Free. 5/1-11/1; 14-day limit. 4 walk-in tent sites, plus dry RV camping in parking lot. Tbls, toilets, cfga, no drkg wtr. Fishing, hiking, boating.

Little Creek Campground $12
Bureau of Land Management, Salt Lake Field Office
10 mi N of Woodruff on SR 16 to Randolph; about 3 mi W of Randolph on FR 058 to N side of 25-acre Little Creek Reservoir. $12 All year; 14-day limit. 10 sites. Tbls, toilets, cfga, drkg wtr, ramadas. Boating, fishing, snow sports, hunting, biking. Elev 6380 ft.

Monte Cristo Campground $10
Cache National Forest
20 mi E of Woodruff on Walton Canyon Rd. $10 with federal senior pass; others pay $20. 7/1-9/15; 7-day limit. 45 single sites; RV limit 25-ft. Tbls, toilets, cfga, drkg wtr. Hunting, snowmobile trails. Elev 8400 ft.

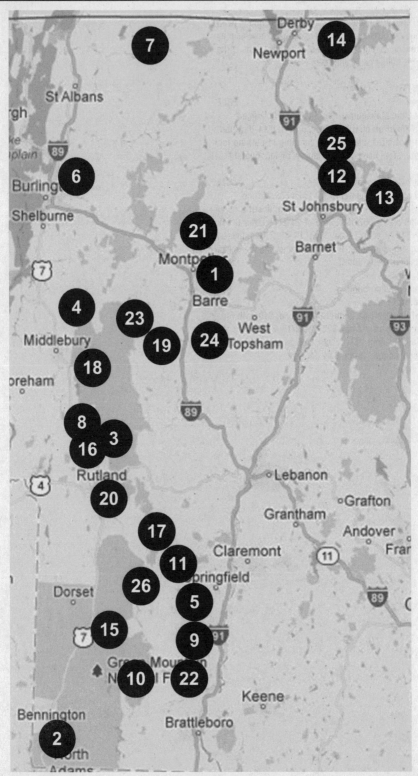

VERMONT

WWW.VERMONTVACATION.COM

Department of Tourism and Marketing, One National Life Dr., 6th Floor, Montpelier, VT 05620. 800-VERMONT.

Green Mountain National Forest, 231 North Main St, Rutland, VT 05701; 802/747-6700.

CAPITAL: Montpelier
NICKNAME: Green Mountain State
STATEHOOD: 1791 – 14th State
FLOWER: Red Clover
TREE: Sugar Maple
BIRD: Hermit Thrush

REST AREAS
Overnight stops are not permitted.

STATE PARKS
Overnight fees are $16-$20, with the higher fee charged for campgrounds that are near water and have high occupancy rates. None of the parks has hookups. Day use fees also are charged. Pets on leashes are permitted, except in picnic areas and on beaches. For further information contact: Vermont State Parks, 103 S. Main St, Waterbury, VT 05671-0601. 802-241-3655.

State Forests and Wildlife Management Areas. Small groups and individuals may camp in primitive areas at most state forests. Groups of 11 or more require a permit. Camping in wildlife management areas is usually not permitted except during deer hunting season. For further information contact: Fish and Wildlife Dept, Waterbury, VT 05671.

GREEN MOUNTAIN NATIONAL FOREST
Bristol Cliffs Wilderness. Primitive woodland covers most of this area's 3740 acres. There are no highly developed campsites, trail shelters, trails or parking facilities. Permits are not required.

Corps of Engineers, Ball Mountain Lake, RFD Box 372, Jamaica, VT 05343 9713.

BARRE (1)

L. R. Jones State Forest   FREE
NE of Barre on Reservoir Rd to East Hill Rd, then to Spruce Mountain Rd. Free. All year. Primitive undeveloped camping on 642 acres adjacent to Groton State Forest. No facilities, no drkg wtr. Established in 1909, features Bald Hill & Potter Brook. Fishing, hunting, hiking. Groton SF is popular for its boating, fishing, mountain biking & wildlife viewing (moose, black bear, otter, beaver). GPS: 44.227839, -72.370379.

BENNINGTON (2)

Red Mill Brook $10
Green Mountain National Forest
10.5 mi E of Bennington on SR 9; .7 mi N on FR 72 (narrow). $10. All year; 14-day limit. 31 sites; 22-ft RV limit). Tbls, toilets, cfga, no drkg wtr. Fishing, boating, swimming. 14 acres. GPS: 42.5359, -73.0237

BRANDON (3)

Chittenden Brook $10
Green Mountain National Forest
11.2 mi E of Brandon on SR 73; 2 mi S on FR 45. $10. MD-LD; 14-day limit. 17 sites (18-ft RV limit). Tbls, toilets, cfga, no drkg wtr. Hiking, fishing. GPS: 43.8256207, -72.9098309

BRISTOL (4)

Downingville   FREE
Dispersed Camping Area
Green Mountain National Forest
From Hwy 116 N of Bristol, turn right on Lincoln Gap Rd at Rocky Dale; follow New Haven River to Lincoln Village; bear left at the village store about 1 mi, then right on Downingville Rd for 1.5 mi; bear right across bridge onto FR 291 for qtr mi, then take middle of a 3-fork rd to a yellow tubular steel gate; continue for half mi to small clearing. Free. All year; 14-day limit. No facilities, no drkg wtr. Fishing, hiking.

CHESTER (5)

Dorand State Forest   FREE
SE of Chester on SR 103; right on Cambridge Port Rd. Free. All year. Primitive undeveloped camping on 518 acres. No facilities, no drkg wtr. Wildlife viewing (beaver), hiking, fishing, hunting. Nearby covered bridges. GPS: 43.203132, -72.552868

COLCHESTER (6)

Colchester Pond Natural Area   FREE
Winooski Valley Park District
Access via Colchester Pond Rd just N of the pond's dam in Colchester. Primitive undeveloped camping on 700 acres. No facilities. Hiking, fishing (smallmouth bass, panfish), boating, ice skating, cross-country skiing. No hunting. GPS: 44.553251, -73.119161.

ENOSBURG FALLS (7)

Brookside Campground North $12
3 mi E of Enosburg Falls on Hwy 105; 6 mi S on Boston Post Rd. $12 base; $16 full hookups. 5/1-10/1. 35 sites; 40-ft RV limit. Large tent area. Tbls, flush toilets, cfga, drkg wtr, hookup($), dump, coin laundry, playground. Horseshoes, volleyball, fishing. GPS: 44.846157, -72.752258

FORESTDALE (8)

Fay's Meadow   FREE
Dispersed Camping Area
Green Mountain National Forest
1.6 mi N of Forestdale on Hwy 73; qtr mi N on FR 32; bear left across cement bridge, then immediately left again on Town Rd to an open meadow (don't drive on the meadow). Free. All year; 14-day limit. Primitive undesignated sites; no facilities, no drkg wtr. Hiking, fishing.

Romance Header   FREE
Dispersed Camping Area
Green Mountain National Forest
1.6 mi N of Forestdale on Hwy 73; qtr mi N on FR 32; bear left across cement bridge for 2 mi; at next jct, turn right, then the first left on FR 224; at rd's end, past the Blueberry Management Area & a yellow steel gate, in a large meadow camping area. Free. All year; 14-day limit. Primitive undesignated sites; no facilities, no drkg wtr. Hiking, fishing.

GRAFTON (9)

C.C. Putnam State Forest   FREE
2 mi NW of Grafton on SR 121. Free. All year. Primitive undeveloped camping. No facilities, no drkg wtr. Hunting, hiking, fishing. GPS: 44.423426, -72.622864.

Grafton State Forest   FREE
W of Grafton on Hinkley Brook Rd, changing to Howellville Rd just before reaching forest; on W shore of Saxton River. Free. All year. Primitive undeveloped camping on 203 acres. No facilities, no drkg wtr. Hiking, fishing, cross-country skiing. GPS: 42.0945, -72-6392594.

Williams River State Forest   FREE
N of Grafton on SR toward Chester; W on Popple Dungeon Rd several mi, following South Branch Williams River; forest begins just after Ethan Allen Rd. Free. All year. Primitive undeveloped camping on 108 acres. No facilities, no drkg wtr. Primarily a hunting & wildlife viewing area. Fishing, hiking. GPS: 43.233299, -72.669811.

JAMAICA (10)

Winhall Brook Camp $9
Ball Mountain Lake
Corps of Engineers
From Jamaica, 1.5 mi NW on SR 30/100; 2 mi NW on Ball Mountain Lane; NW of dam & project offices. $9 with federal senior pass at 88 non-elec sites; others pay $18.

$11 with senior pass at 23 elec/wtr sites; others pay $22. About 5/15-10/15; 14-day limit. 60-ft RV limit. Tbls, flush toilets, cfga, showers, drkg wtr, dump, playground, beach. Swimming, fishing, hiking, tennis, interpretive programs, biking trail. Non-campers pay day use fee. GPS: 43.16333, -72.80972

LUDLOW (11)

Okemo State Forest   **FREE**
Just N of Ludlow on SR 103/100; left on Okemo Mountain Rd. Free. All year. Small primitive campground. Tbls, toilets, cfga, drkg wtr. Hiking trails, skiing, snowboarding. Lake Rescue, Lake Ninevah & Echo Lake nearby. GPS: 43.378487, -72.751092.

LYNDONVILLE (12)

Mathewson State Forest   **FREE**
N of Lyndonville off I-89 & Union House Rd. From Mathew Hill Rd N of Wheelock, pass Hoffman Rd, then turn left onto unmarked rd, which leads to S side of forest. Free. All year. Primitive undeveloped camping on 795 acres. No facilities, no drkg wtr. Hiking, fishing in Mathewson Brook. GPS: 44.609775, -72.068987.

NORTH CONCORD (13)

Victory State Forest   **FREE**
N of North Concord on forest rd that bisects the forest; near Burke Mtn. Free. All year. Primitive undeveloped camping on 15,826 acres. No facilities, no drkg wtr. Fishing, hiking, canoeing, hunting. GPS: 44.547916, -71.827697.

NORTON (14)

Black Turn Brook State Forest   **FREE**
1 mi N of Norton along SR 114 on the Canadian Border; just NE of Bill Sladyk WMA. Free. All year. Primitive undeveloped camping along the Coaticook River. No facilities. No drkg wtr. Trout fishing, hunting, hiking. GPS: 45.000364, -71.81749

PERU (15)

Hapgood Pond Recreation Area   **$10**
Green Mountain National Forest
1.8 mi NE of Peru on FR 3. $10. MD-LD; 14-day limit. 28 sites; 50-ft RV limit. Tbls, flush toilets, cfga, drkg wtr, showers, accessible fishing pier. Swimming, nature trails, boating (hand launch), fishing. 8 acres. Non-campers pay $4 day use fee. GPS: 43.2531305, -72.8892668

PITTSFORD (16)

Kettle Brook   **FREE**
Dispersed Camping Area
Green Mountain National Forest
From Hwy 7 in Pittsford, turn on rd across from Pittsford Elementary School that is marked for Holden Fish Hatchery; about 100 yds past hatchery, turn left on Furnace Brook Rd for 2.75 mi, then bear right at fork to a small

meadow at end of the rd. Free. All year; 14-day limit. Primitive undesignated sites; no facilities, no drkg wtr.

New Boston Turnout   **FREE**
Dispersed Camping Area
White Mountain National Forest
E off US 7 in Pittsford directly opposite a gas station & the jct with SR 3 (a very sharp left turn from the N) for 3.2 mi to center of Chittenden; turn left at the Civil War statue for 1.75 mi; just past the Mountain Top Inn, take the right fork & follow signs to the New Boston Trailhead; camp at large turnaround area near tubular steel gate. Free. All year; 14-day limit. Primitive undesignated sites; no facilities, no drkg wtr.

PLYMOUTH (17)

Coolidge State Forest   **FREE**
W of Plymouth on SR 100. Free. Undeveloped primitive camping. No facilities, no drkg wtr. Historical area includes restored village with birthplace of 30th President Calvin Coolidge. Fishing ponds, trout streams, down hill skiing. GPS: 43.507605, -72.768823.

RIPTON (18)

Goshen Brook Rd   **FREE**
Dispersed Camping Area
Green Mountain National Forest
3.1 mi E of Ripton on Hwy 125, past Breadloaf campus; right on FR 67 (Goshen Brook Rd) to open area just beyond the turn-around at FR 67's end. Free. All year; 14-day limit. Undesignated sites; no facilities, no drkg wtr. Hike half mi along old logging rd to fish at Sugar Hill Lake.

Moosalamoo Campground   **$10**
Green Mountain National Forest
.7 mi SE of Ripton on SR 125; 3 mi S on FR 32; half mi W on FR 24. $10. MD-LD; 14-day limit. 19 sites; no RV size limit. Tbls, toilets, cfga, drkg wtr. Fishing, hiking, play field, hunting, interpretive trail. 15 acres. GPS: 43.9192295, -73.0281689

New Haven River   **FREE**
Dispersed Camping Area
Green Mountain National Forest
From near the post office at Ripton, bear left from eastbound Hwy 125 on FR 59 (Stream Mill Rd) for 3.5 mi; left on FR 54 for 4 mi; right just before cement bridge on FR 201 for half mi; at New Haven River & the Emily Proctor and Cooley Glen trailhead. Free. All year; 14-day limit. Primitive undesignated sites; no facilities, no drkg wtr. Hiking trails to Long Trail shelters. Fishing & swimming in river pools upstream.

Sparks Landing   **FREE**
Dispersed Camping Area
Green Mountain National Forest
From near the post office at Ripton, bear left from east-

bound Hwy 125 on FR 59 (Stream Mill Rd) for 3.5 mi; left on FR 54 for half mi, then bear left onto FR 233 for short distance; campsites on the left about 100 ft down an old rd in a small meadow; at Sparks Brook. Free. All year; 14-day limit. Primitive undesignated sites; no facilities, no drkg wtr. Fishing, hiking.

Steam Mill Clearing FREE
Dispersed Camping Area
Green Mountain National Forest
2.8 mi E of Ripton on Hwy 125, then half mi past the Robert Frost Wayside; left on FR 59 for 3.5 mi to a large open field on both sides of the rd, where Skylight Pond Trail begins and leads to the Long Trail, Skyline Lodge Shelter (see above) and a high-elevation pond. Free. Primitive undesignated sites; no facilities, no drkg wtr. Hiking, fishing.

ROXBURY (19)
Roxbury State Forest Camp FREE
S of Roxbury on SR 12A (SW of Montpelier & Northfield). Free. All year. Primitive, undeveloped camping on 5,500 acres in foothills of the Northfield Mountain range. No facilities, no drkg wtr. Mixed forest with creeks & nearby ponds. Fishing, hunting, snowmobiling, hiking. Forest GPS: 44.055896, -72.729554

RUTLAND (20)
George D. Aiken FREE
Wilderness Camp
Green Mountain National Forest
Access off Notch Rd a few mi S of Rutland. Free. All year; 14-day limit. Primitive undesignated camping along plateau at 2,300 ft elev. No facilities except scattered cfga. Area also features primitive camping at Aitken State Forest and West Rutland State Forest. Hiking, fishing, hunting.

STOWE (21)
Mt. Mansfield FREE
State Forest Camp
Access via SR 108, which bisects the forest NW of Stowe, or Nebraska Ville Rd off SR 100 S of Stowe. Free. All year. Primitive, undeveloped camping near Vermont's tallest mountain. No facilities, no drkg wtr. Trout fishing, hiking, backpacking, snowmobiling, downhill skiing. Forest features Cantilever Rock jutting 60 feet above ground. 4 state parks are nearby -- Little River, Underhill, Waterbury Center & Smuggler's Notch. GPS: 44.4918, -72.818594.

TOWNSHEND (22)
Bald Mountain Campground
Townshend State Forest FREE
About 3 mi S of Townshend on SR 30; right on State Forest Rd; forest is at the foot of Bald Mtn on the West River. Free. All year. Primitive undeveloped camping. No facilities, no drkg wtr. Hiking, fishing, hunting, swimming, cross-country skiing. 95-acre Townshend Lake is nearby, as is Townshend State Park. GPS: 43.039322, -72.675699.

WARREN (23)
Austin Brook Rd FREE
Dispersed Camping Area
Green Mountain National Forest
Turn on FR 25 from Hwy 100 in Warren. Free. All year; 14-day limit. 3 primitive sites along the rd within qtr mi of Hwy 100. No facilities except cfga; no drkg wtr.

WASHINGTON (24)
Washington State Forest FREE
About 7 mi S of Washington on Corinth Rd. Free. All year. Primitive, undeveloped camping on 430 acres. Forest primarily a timber resource with few recreational opportunities. Hiking trails, fishing in Cookeville Brook. Washington Wildlife Management Area is just south, accessible from Riders Corner. GPS: 44.042287, -72.378987.

WEST BURKE (25)
Willoughby State Forest FREE
About 5 mi N of West Burke on SR 5A, which bisects E side of forest. Free. All year. Primitive undeveloped camping around Willoughby Cliffs, Bald Mountain & CCC Camp areas; no camping at South End area. No facilities, no drkg wtr. No camping within 100 ft of lake, ponds or streams. Natural swimming beach at S end of Lake Willoughby along SR 5A. Six small fishing ponds. Boating, hunting, hiking. GPS: 44.703662, -72.113711.

WESTON (26)
Greendale Campground $10
Green Mountain National Forest
2 mi N of Weston on SR 100; 3.2 mi NW on FR 18. $10. MD-LD; 14-day limit. 11 sites; 25-ft RV limit. Tbls, toilets, cfga, no drkg wtr. Hunting, fishing, picnicking, 4-mi hiking loop. 2 acres. GPS: 43.3509063, -72.8217658

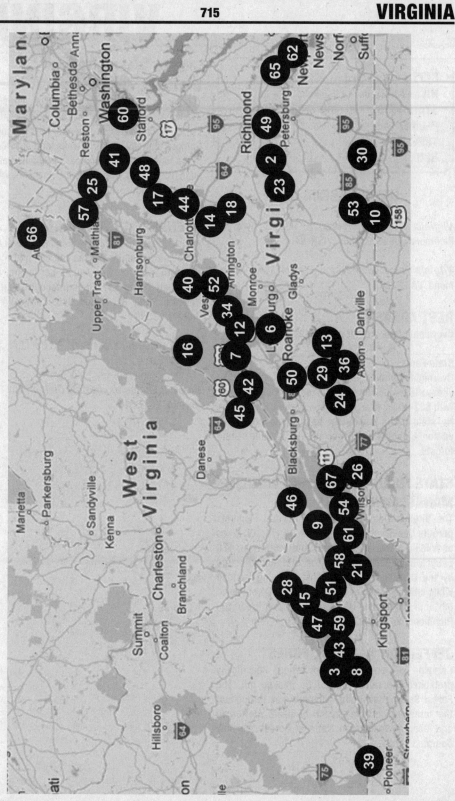

VIRGINIA

CAPITAL: Richmond
NICKNAME: The Old Dominion
STATEHOOD: 1788 – 10th State
FLOWER: American Dogwood
TREE: Dogwood
BIRD: Cardinal

WWW.VIRGINIA.ORG

Virginia Tourism Corporation, 901 E. Byrd St, Richmond, VA 23219. 800-VISIT VA.

Virginia Game Commission, PO Box 11104, Richmond, VA 23230.

REST AREAS
Overnight stops are not permitted.

State Parks
Overnight camping fees are $13-15 for primitive sites, $16-24 for developed sites without hookups, with $22-30 for sites with water & electric hookups. No state parks qualify for being included in this edition. Camping is NOT permitted in Virginia's state forests.

STATE FISHING LAKES AND WILDLIFE MANAGEMENT AREAS
The Virginia Commission of Game and Fisheries permits free primitive camping on its 170,000 acres of Wildlife Management Areas and at its nearly 30 publicly owned fishing lakes (the latter administered by the Division of Parks). Most camping is done while either hunting or fishing. Virginia Commission of Game and Inland Fisheries, 4010 West Broad St., Richmond, VA 23230. 804/367-1000.

JEFFERSON NATIONAL FOREST
Camping is permitted except where specifically prohibited. All refuse should be packed out. The Forest Service maintains campgrounds throughout the forest to serve all types of users. Jefferson and George Washington National Forest are now operated jointly.

GEORGE WASHINGTON NATIONAL FOREST
The forest has more than 1 million acres of land available for free primitive camping. Visitors are invited to camp beside streams, next to roads, next to more than 950 miles of trails, and anywhere else in the forest unless specifically prohibited and posted. 5162 Valleypointe Parkway, Roanoke, VA 24019. 540-265-5100.

SHENANDOAH NATIONAL PARK
A park entry fee is charged. Seniors federal America the Beautiful Senior Passes can camp at the park's campgrounds for $7.50-8.50 per night. Non-seniors pay $15 or $17. Superintendent Shenandoah National Park, Rt 4, Box 348, Luray, VA 22835. 540/999-3500.

Prince William Forest Park, PO Box 209, Triangle, VA 22172.

Corps of Engineers, Norfolk District, 803 Front St, Norfold, VA 23510.

ABINGDON (1)
Hidden Valley Lake   FREE
Wildlife Management Area
Between Lebanon and Abingdon on Rt 690, N of US 19.
Free. All year. Primitive undeveloped camping. No facilities. 61-acre lake. 6,400 acres. Hiking, hunting. Fishing.
GPS: 38.807957, -122.558315.

AMELIA COURT HOUSE (2)
Amelia Wildlife Management Area   FREE
10 mi NE of Amelia. Free. All year. Primitive undeveloped camping. No facilities. 2,727 acres. Hiking, hunting. GPS: 37.467448, -77.911032.

APPALACHIA (3)
Keokee Lake State Fishing Lake   FREE
Jefferson National Forest
1 mi SW of Appalachia on Alt. US 58; 7 mi W on SR 68, becoming SR 606; continue 2 mi on SR 606; right on SR 623 for 1 mi. Free. All year. Primitive, undeveloped camping. No facilities. 100-acre lake. Boating(l); fishing. GPS: 36.849157, -82.864399.

BACK BAY (4)
Pocahontas-Trojan   FREE
Wildlife Management Area
Shoreline and island areas of Back Bay. Free. All year. Primitive undeveloped camping. No facilities. 1,148 acres. Hiking, hunting. GPS: 37.431573, -78.656894.

BEDFORD (6)
Peaks of Otter $8
Blue Ridge Parkway
National Park Service
Milepost 85.9 on Parkway, W of Bedford. $8 with federal senior pass; others pay $16. All year; 21-day limit. 53 RV sites (30-ft RV limit). Drkg wtr, flush & chemical toilets, cfga, tbls, dump; limited facilities in winter. Fishing, hiking trails, shuttle bus to Sharp Top Mountain, visitor center. GPS: 37.44315, -79.60471

BIG ISLAND (7)
Otter Creek $8
Blue Ridge Parkway
National Park Service
Milepost 60.8 on Parkway, 5 mi N of Big Island, half mi N of SR 130 (NW of Lynchburg). $8 with federal senior pass; others pay $16. 5/1-10/31; 14-day limit. 24 RV sites (30-ft RV limit). Drkg wtr, flush & chemical toilets, cfga, tbls, dump. 6 picnic sites. Hiking trail; fishing; visitor center, restored canal lock. GPS: 37.574463, -79.338623

BIG STONE GAP (8)
Cave Springs Recreation Area $12
Jefferson National Forest
2.5 mi W of Big Stone Gap on US 58A; 6 mi on SR 621. $12 base; $17 with elec ($6 & $11 with federal senior pass).

5/15-9/15; 14 day limit. 40 sites, typically 53 ft. Tbls, flush toilets, showers, cfga, drkg wtr, beach, dump. Swimming, hiking. Non-campers pay $3 day use fee (or $30 annually). GPS: 36.856445, -82.862061

BLAND (9)
Walnut Flats   FREE
Jefferson National Forest
12 mi NE of Bland on VA 42; 1 mi NW on VA 606; 3.5 mi NE on FR 201. Free. 4/1-12/7; 14-day limit. 5 sites (RVs under 22 ft). Tbls, toilets, cfga, firewood, well drkg wtr. Fishing. Elev 2400 ft. GPS: 37.1982, -80.8859

BOYDTON (10)
(See Clarksville listings)
Ivy Hill Park   CLOSED
Corps of Engineers
John H. Kerr Reservoir
10 mi W of Boydton on SR 58 to Clarksville; 7 mi S on US 15 to NC SR 1501; 6 mi S on SR 1501 to SR 825, then 2 mi N on SR 825. Campsites closed due to budget cuts.

North Bend Campground $9
Corps of Engineers
John H. Kerr Reservoir
From Boydton, 5 mi E on US 58; 6 mi S on SR 4 (Buggs Island Rd); right at the dam for 200 yds on Mays Chapel Rd; at NE shore of lake. During 4/1-10/31, $9 with federal senior pass at 106 non-elec sites (others pay $18); $2.50 with senior pass off-season (others pay $5). At 138 elec/wtr sites, $12 with senior pass during 4/1-10/31 (others pay $24); $5 with senior pass off-season (others pay $10). No wtr services & reduced amenities off-season. Group camping available. RV limit in excess of 65 ft. Tbls, flush toilets, cfga, drkg wtr, showers, dump, beach, fishing pier, playground, amphitheater, visitor center. Boating(l), fishing, swimming, hiking. Non-campers pay $4 day use fee for boat launch, picnicking, fishing pier, swimming beach, dump station. GPS: 36.58833, -78.32483

Rudds Creek Recreation Area $9
Corps of Engineers
John H. Kerr Reservoir
From Boydton, 3 mi W on US 58; on S side of road before lake bridge; at Roanoke River. $9 with federal senior pass at 24 non-elec sites; others pay $18. At 75 elec/wtr sites, $12 with senior pass; others pay $24. 4/1-10/31; 14-day limit. No longer open off-season. RV limit in excess of 65 ft. Tbls, flush toilets, cfga, drkg wtr, showers, dump, beach, some sewer hookups, playground, amphitheater, fishing pier. Boating(l), fishing, swimming. GPS: 36.65528, -78.44028

BRANDYWINE (WEST VIRGINIA) (11)
Brandywine Recreation Area $8
Geo. Washington National Forest
2 mi E of Brandywine on US 33. $8 with federal senior

pass during about 5/15-10/15; others pay $16. During about 10/16-12/10, regular fees $5, but no wtr services ($2.50 with federal senior pass). 14-day limit. 34 sites up to 55 ft. Tbls, flush toilets, cfga, drkg wtr, showers, dump, store. Fishing, swimming hiking trails. 10 acres. Non-campers pay $5 day use fee (or $30 annually). GPS: 38.599609, -79.200928

BUCHANAN (12)

North Creek $10
Jefferson National Forest
2 mi NE of Buchanan on I-81; 3 mi SE on Hwy 614; 2.5 mi E on CR 59. $10. 3/15-11/30; 14-day limit. 14 sites up to 57 ft. Tbls, toilets, cfga, drkg wtr, dump nearby. Fishing, hiking trail. GPS: 37.52417, -79.579834

CALLANDS (13)

Lake Burton State Fishing Lake   FREE
6 mi N of Callands on Rt 800. Free. All year. Primitive, undeveloped camping. No facilities. 76-acre lake. Boating(l); fishing. GPS: 36.867165, -79.533999.

CHARLOTTESVILLE (14)

Albemarie Lake State Fishing Lake   FREE
12 mi W of Charlottesville on RT 675. Free. All year. Primitive, undeveloped camping. No facilities. Boating(l), fishing. GPS: 38.093754, -78.629944.

CLARKSVILLE (10)

(See Boydton listings)
Buffalo Park $9
Corps of Engineers
John H. Kerr Reservoir
From Carksville, 8 mi W on US 58 past jct with SR 49, across bridge, then 3 mi N on CR 732 (Buffalo Springs Rd) and E on CR 869 (Carters Point Rd) to its end; at W shore of lake. $9 with federal senior pass at 19 non-elec sites; others pay $18. $10 with senior pass at elec/wtr sites; others pay $20. 5/1-9/30; 14-day limit. RV limit in excess of 65 ft. Tbls, flush toilets, cfga, drkg wtr, dump, beach, playground, showers, beach. Boating (ld), fishing, swimming. GPS: 36.66194, -78.63139

Longwood Park $9
Corps of Engineers
John H. Kerr Lake
From Clarksville at jct of US 58/15, 2 mi S on US 15; on the W side at Beaver Pond Creek arm of lake. $9 with federal senior pass at 32 non-elec sites; others pay $18. At 34 elec/wtr sites, $12 with senior pass; others pay $24. 4/1-10/31; 14-day limit. No longer open off-season. RV limit in excess of 65 ft. Non-campers pay $4 day use fee for boat launch, picnicking, swimming, dump station. Tbls, flush toilets, showers, cfga, drkg wtr, beach, some sewer hookups($), playground, dump, shelter. Boating(l), fishing, swimming, tennis. GPS: 36.57722, -78.55139

CLINTWOOD (15)

Cranesnest Areas #1 & #2 $12
John W. Flannagan Lake
Corps of Engineers
2.5 mi SE of Clintwood on SR 83;, then N to lake; at Cranesnest River. $12 at 24 non-elec sites ($6 with federal senior pass). About 5/17-9/2; 14-day limit. Tbls, flush toilets, cfga, drkg wtr, showers, dump, playground, picnic shelter, amphitheater. Boating(l), fishing, swimming, waterskiing. GPS: 36.974, -82.4724

Cranesnest Area 3 $12
John W. Flannagan Lake
Corps of Engineers
From Cranesnest #1 & #2, 1 mi NE. $12 at non-elec sites; $14 for elec ($6 & $7 with federal senior pass). About 5/17-9/2; 14-day limit. 11 elec sites. Toilets, drkg wtr, cfga, tbls. Boating, fishing.

Pound River $7
John W. Flannagan Lake
Corps of Engineers
From Clintwood, 0.2 mi W on SR 83; 2 mi N on SR 631; 1.2 mi E on SR 754. $7 with federal senior pass at non-elec sites; others pay $14. $8 at elec sites; others pay $16. About 5/17-9/2; 14-day limit. 27 sites, some pull-through. Tbls, showers, toilets, cfga, drkg wtr, dump. Boating(l), fishing. GPS: 37.23389, -82,34327

COVINGTON (16)

Morris Hill Campgrounds $9
Geo. Washington National Forest
3 mi N of Covington on US 220; 6 mi NW on SR 687; 3 mi W on SR 641; 5 mi N on SR 666, then N on SR 605; near Lake Moomaw. $9 with federal senior pass: others pay $18. 5/1-11/1; 14-day limit. 55 sites on 370 acres; no RV size limit. Tbls, flush toilets, cfga, drkg wtr, showers, dump. Boating(l), swimming, fishing, waterskiing, hiking trails. GPS: 37.94528, -79.95917

T.M. Gaithright Wildlife Management Area   FREE
10 mi N of Covington. Free. All year. Primitive undeveloped camping. No facilities. 13,428 acres. Hiking, hunting. GPS: 38.020124, -79.943669.

CULPEPPER (17)

Rapidan Wildlife Management Area   FREE
25 mi SW of Culpepper on Rapidan River. Free. All year. Primitive undeveloped camping. No facilities. 9,373 acres. Hunting. GPS: 38.369661, -78.509288.

CUNNINGHAM (18)

Fluvanna Ruritan Lake State Fishing Lake   FREE
W of Cunningham on Rt 619; N on access rd. Free. All year. Primitive, undeveloped camping. No facilities. Boating(l), fishing. 50-acre lake. 37.891424, -78.373557.

DAMASCUS (19)

Beartree Recreation Area $10.50
Jefferson National Forest
7.6 mi E of Damascus on US 58; about 1 mi S following sign to entrance for Beartree Gap Trail Recreation Area, then 3.9 mi farther. $10.50 with federal senior pass; others pay $21. 4/15-10/31; 14-day limit. 84 sites up to 75 ft. Tbls, toilets, cfga, drkg wt, grey water stations, showers, beach. Swimming, horseback riding, fishing. 10-acre lake. Non-campers pay $5 for dump station, $4 for showers, $5 day use ($30 annually). GPS: 36.68472, -81.64722

DAYTON (20)

Hone Quarry $5
Geo. Washington Nation Forest
11 mi NW of Dayton on SR 257. $5. All year; 14-day limit. 10 sites up to 50 ft. Tbls, toilets, cfga, no drkg wtr. Nature trails, fishing, boating, hiking. GPS: 38.2812, -79.0835

DUNGANNON (21)

Hunters Ford Island $8
Just E of Dungannon on SR 65 next to the Clinch River bridge; on island in the river. $8 for pop-up trailers. 10 sites. Tbls, toilets, cfga, drkg wtr, showers, no elec. Fishing, boating, horseshoes, volleyball.

EDINBURG (22)

Camp Roosevelt Recreation Area $10
Geo. Washington National Forest
9 mi SE of Edinburg on SR 675. $10. About 5/1-10/15; 21-day limit. 10 sites, typically 38 ft. Tbls, flush toilets, cfga, drkg wtr, dump, playground. Fishing. Site of nation's first CCC camp. GPS: 38.731689, -78.516846

Wolf Gap Recreation Area FREE
Geo. Washington National Forest
12.1 mi NW on VA 675; in West Virginia. Free. All year; 14-day limit. 9 sites (22-ft RV limit). Tbls, toilets, cfga, well drkg wtr, no trash service. Hiking. Elev 2200 ft. 2-mi hike to Big Schloss Lookout. GPS: 38.92456, -78.68798

FARMVILLE (23)

Briery Creek Wildlife Management Area FREE
7 mi S of Farmington off Rt 15. Free. All year. Primitive undeveloped camping. No facilities. 27,775 acres. Hiking, hunting.

FLOYD (24)

Rocky Knob $8
Blue Ridge Parkway
National Park Service
8 mi S of Floyd; 2 mi off SR on the parkway at Milepost 167.1. $8 with federal senior pass; others pay $16. 5/14-10/1; 14-day limit. 28 RV sites (30-ft RV limit). Tbls, flush toilets, cfga, drkg wtr, dump, no showers, visitor center. Nature program, fishing, nature trails. GPS: 36.805176, -80.338867

FRONT ROYAL (25)

Mathews Arm Campground $7.50
Shenandoah National Park
S of Front Royal at milepost 22.1 of Skyline Drive. $7.50 with federal senior pass; others pay $15. About 5/15-10/31. 179 sites, typically 45 ft. Tbls, toilets, cfga, drkg wtr, dump. Hiking trails, fishing, hiking, horseback riding. GPS: 38.76389, -78.2925

Big Meadows Campground $8.50
Shenandoah National Park
S of Front Royal at milepost 51.3 of Skyline Drive. $8.50 with federal senior pass; others pay $17 ($20 when on reservation system). May-Oct. 217 sites. Tbls, toilets, cfga, showers, drkg wtr, dump. Hiking trails, fishing, hiking, horseback riding. GPS: 38.526611, -78.438965

Lewis Mountain Camp $7.50
Shenandoah National Park
S of Front Royal at milepost 57.5 of Skyline Drive. $7.50 with federal senior pass; others pay $15. May-Oct. 31 sites. Tbls, toilets, cfga, drkg wtr, dump, showers. Hiking trails, fishing, hiking, horseback riding. GPS: 38.436279, -78.477051

Loft Mountain Campground $7.50
Shenandoah National Park
S of Front Royal at milepost 79.5 of Skyline Drive. $7.50 with federal senior pass; others pay $15. About 5/15-10/31; 14-day limit. 219 sites, typically 50 ft. Tbls, toilets, cfga, drkg wtr, dump, showers. Hiking trails, fishing, hiking, horseback riding. GPS: 38.26056, -78.65528

GALAX (26)

Crooked Creek Wildlife Management Area FREE
3 mi SE of Galax. Free. All year. Primitive undeveloped camping. No facilities. 1,659 acres. Hiking, hunting. GPS: 36.675720, -80.813865.

HARRISONBURG (27)

Lake Shenandoah State Fishing Lake FREE
About 3 mi SE of Harrisonburg on US 33; 3 mi S on CR 687 to N shore of lake. Free. All year. Primitive, undeveloped camping. No facilities. Boating(l), fishing. 36-acre lake. Walking trail around upper end of lake.

HAYSI (28)

Lower Twin Branch Area $12
John W. Flannagan Lake
Corps of Engineers
From Haysi, 6 mi NW on SR 63; 3 mi N on SR 739; 3 mi W on SR 611; exit SE on SR 683. $12 at 18 non-elec sites, $14 at 15 elec sites ($6 & $7 with federal senior pass). About 5/17-9/2; 14-day limit. Tbls, flush toilets, cfga, drkg wtr, showers, playground, dump, elec($). Boating(l), fishing, waterskiing, hiking trail. GPS: 37.231934, -82.340332

HENRY (29)

Horseshoe Point Campground $10
Corps of Engineers
Philpott Lake
From Henry (NW of Martinsville off US 220, 2 mi W on Henry Rd (CR 605); about 3 mi W on Horseshoe Point Rd, following signs; at E shore of lake. $10 with federal senior pass at 34 non-elec sites; others pay $18. $12.50 with senior pass at 15 elec/wtr & waterfront sites; others pay $25. 5/1-9/30; 14-day limit. 40-ft RV limit. Picnic shelter, tbls, flush toilets, cfga, drkg wtr, showers, elec($), dump, beach, playground. Boating(l), fishing, swimming. Non-campers pay $4 day use fee for boat launch, courtesy dock, swimming area, playground, dump station. GPS: 36.83416, -80.07235

Jamison Mill Campground $10
Corps of Engineers
Philpott Lake
From Henry (NW of Martinsville off US 220), 5 mi NW on CR 605 (Henry Rd); 2 mi S on CR 778 (Nicholas Creek Rd); right on Jamison Mill Rd, following signs; at NE shore of lake near Nicholas Creek Arm. $10 with federal senior pass at 7 non-elec & overflow area (others pay $20); $12.50 with senior pass at 5 elec/wtr sites (others pay $25). 4/1-10/31; 14-day limit. Some pull-through sites. Tbls, flush toilets, showers, cfga, drkg wtr, dump. Boating(l), fishing. GPS: 36.84954, -80.70395

Salthouse Branch Park $10
Corps of Engineers
Philpott Lake
From Henry (NW of Martinsville off US 220), 3 mi W on CR 605 (Henry Rd); 2 mi SW on CR 798 (Knob Church Rd), then left (S) on CR 603 (Salthouse Branch Rd), following signs. All year; 14-day limit. During 4/1-10/31, $10 with federal senior pass at 14 non-elec sites (others pay $20); $12.50 with senior pass at 43 elec/wtr sites (others pay $25). Off-season, elec sites $20 ($10 with senior pass); no wtr hookups, but heated restrooms & showers. Some pull-through sites. Tbls, flush toilets, cfga, drkg wtr, showers, dump, fishing pier, picnic shelter, beach, amphitheater. Hiking, boating(l), fishing, swimming, interpretive trail. No day use fees. GPS: 36.81021, -80.05916

LAWRENCEVILLE (30)

Brunswick County State Fishing Lake FREE
E of Lawrenceville on Rt 638. Free. All year. Primitive, undeveloped camping. No facilities. 150-acre lake. Boating(l), fishing.

LENNING (31)

Lake Conner State Fishing Lake FREE
5 mi E of Lenning on Rt 624. Free. All year. Primitive, undeveloped camping. No facilities. 111-acre lake. Boating(l); fishing.

LEXINGTON (32)

Goshen-Little North Mountain FREE
Wildlife Management Area
12 mi W of Lexington. Free. All year. Primitive undeveloped camping. No facilities. 33,666 acres. Hiking, hunting.

LOST CITY (WEST VIRGINIA) (33)

Trout Pond Recreation Area $9.50
George Washington National Forest
10 mi N of Lost City on Hwy 259, then right on SR 259/55 for 6 mi; right on FR 500 about 1 mi. $9.50 with federal senior pass at non-elec sites during peak season of 5/1-9/10; others pay $19. Off-season fee with federal senior pass, $7.50 during 4/16-5/15 & 9/11-12/2; others pay $15. $3 surcharge for elec hookup. Double sites available. 50 sites (13 with elec), up to 55 ft. Tbls, flush toilets, showers, drkg wtr, dump, playground, beach. Boating (no motors), swimming, hiking trails, fishing, interpretive programs. Non-campers pay day use fees for fishing, picnicking, swimming. Trout Pond is West Virginia's only natural lake. GPS: 78.7347, -39.9528

LOVINGSTON (34)

James River Wildlife Management Area FREE
15 mi SE of Lovington on SR 56. Free. All year. Primitive undeveloped camping. No facilities. 671 acres. Hiking, hunting.

LYNDHURST (35)

Meadow Loop (Loop C) $8
Blue Ridge Parkway
National Park Service
7.3 mi SW of Lyndhurst on SR 664; 2 mi W on FR 91. $8 with federal senior pass; others pay $16. 4/1-10/31; 14-day limit. 18 sites (5 for tents). Tbls, flush toilets, cfga, drkg wtr, dump, showers. Swimming, boating, fishing, hiking.

Sherando Lake Recreation Area $10
George Washington National Forest
S of Lyndhurst on SR 664 about 6 mi. $10 with federal senior pass at non-elec sites; others pay $20; $15 with senior pass at elec sites; others pay $25. 4/1-10/31; 14-day limit. 65 sites (30 with elec), typically 30 ft. Tbls, flush toilets, showers, cfga, drkg wtr, elec($), phones, vending, play area, beach, dump. Hiking, fishing, swimming, boating. Camp built by CCC in 1930s. Non-campers pay $8 day use fees. GPS: 37.91978, -79.01006

MARTINSVILLE (36)

Fairy Stone Wildlife Management Area FREE
15 mi NW of Martinsville. Free. All year. Primitive undeveloped camping. No facilities. 5,321 acres. Hiking, hunting.

Goose Point $10
Corps of Engineers
Philpott Lake
From Martinsville, N on US 220, 11 mi N on SR 57; access on CR 822 (winding access roads). All year; 14-day limit. During 4/1-10/30, $10 with federal senior pass at 10 non-elec sites (others pay $20); $5 with senior pass off-season (others pay $10). During 4/1-10/30, $12.50 with senior pass at 53 elec/wtr sites (others pay $25); off-season fees $10 with senior pass (others pay $20). No wtr hookups but heated restrooms/showers off-season. 60-ft RV limit. Tbls, amphitheater, pavilion, flush toilets in-season, cfga, drkg wtr, showers, dump, beach, picnic shelter, fishing pier. Hiking, fishing, swimming, boating(l). Non-campers pay $4 day use fee for boat launch, swimming area, playground, dump station. GPS: 36.80422, -80.05816

MIDDLESBORO (KENTUCKY) (37)
Wilderness Road $10
Cumberland Gap National Historic Park
Just S of Middlesboro on US 25E to visitor center, E on US 58 into Virginia. $10 with federal senior pass at elec RV sites; others pay $20. All year; 14-day limit. 160 sites. Tbls, showers, flush toilets, cfga, drkg wtr. Hiking, fishing. GPS: 36.605225, -83.634277

MILLBORO SPRINGS (38)
Bubbling Springs   FREE
Geo. Washington National Forest
Follow signs SE from Millboro Springs through Millboro on SR 633; must ford creek repeatedly to reach camp. Free. All year; 14-day limit. Undesignated primitive sites. Tbls, toilets, cfga, no drkg wtr. Hiking, fishing, picnicking. GPS: 3.9242, -79.625.

MONTEREY (39)
Laurel Fork   FREE
Special Management Area
Geo. Washington National Forest
About 15 mi NW of Monterey on US 250, into West Virginia, then 8 mi farther to Thornwood; 6 mi NE (right) on SR 28; at FR 106, follow signs for Locust Springs Recreation Area. Primitive undesignated sites at Locust Spring picnic area. Tbls, toilets, cfga, drkg wtr. Also, dispersed tent camping anywhere along 28 mi of hiking trails. Trout fishing. GPS: 38.7403897, -79.6933909

NATURAL BRIDGE STATION (40)
Cave Mountain Lake $7.50
Jefferson National Forest
Qtr mi E of Natural Bridge Station on Rt 130; 3.3 mi on Rt 759; 1 mi on Rt 781. $7.50 with federal senior pass for seniors with GA Passports (all others pay $15). 5/1-11/1; 21-day limit. 42 sites up to 56 ft. Tbls, flush toilets, cfga, drkg wtr, showers, swimming beach, dump. Swimming, fishing. Non-campers pay $5 day use fees (or $30 annually). GPS: 37.57583, -79.53417

NEW BALTIMORE (41)
Lake Brittle State Fishing Lake   FREE
E of New Baltimore off Rt 675. Free. All year. Primitive undeveloped camping. No facilities. 77-acre lake. Boating(rl), fishing. GPS: 38.752555, -77.69441.

NEW CASTLE (42)
The Pines Campground   FREE
Jefferson National Forest
5 mi NE of New Castle on VA 615; 4.9 mi W on VA 611; 5.5 mi NE on VA 617. Free. 4/1-12/7; 14-day limit. 17 sites (RVs under 17 ft). Tbls, toilets, cfga, well drkg wtr. Fishing, horseback riding, hiking, caving. Horse corral & ramps. GPS: 37.605, -80.07667

NORTON (43)
High Knob Recreation Area $10
Jefferson National Forest
3.8 mi S of Norton on SR 619 (steep with switchbacks); left on FR 238 for 1.5 mi. $10. 5/15-9/15; 14-day limit. 14 sites up to 42 ft. Tbls, flush toilets, cfga, drkg wtr, dump, showers, beach. Swimming, hiking, lookout tower. Circa 1930s bathhouse built by CCC. Non-campers pay $3 day use fee (or $30 annually). GPS: 36.887695, -82.614014

ORANGE (44)
Orange County Lake State Fishing Lake   FREE
8 mi E of Orange off Rt 20. Free. All year. Primitive undeveloped camping. Tbls, cfga. 124-acre lake. Boating(rl), fishing. Lake produced world record white bass of 6 pounds, 13 ounces, in 1989; species never stocked there.

PAINT BANK (45)
Steel Bridge   FREE
Jefferson National Forest
.1 mi N of Paint Bank on VA 311; 3.5 mi NE on VA 18. Free. 4/1-12/7; 14-day limit. 12 sites up to 65 ft. Tbls, toilets, cfga, firewood, no drkg wtr. Fishing, swimming, hiking. GPS: 37.606689, -80.213135

PEARISBURG (46)
White Rocks $4
Jefferson National Forest
3.8 mi E of Pearisburg on US 460; 17 mi NE on Hwy 635; .8 mi S on Hwy 613; 1 mi E on FR 645. $4. 5/1-12/7; 14-day limit. 34 sites up to 51 ft. Tbls, flush toilets, cfga, drkg wtr, dump. Fishing, hiking on the Appalachian Trail. Waterfall & historic site nearby. GPS: 37.429443, -80.491455

POUND (47)
Cane Patch $12
Jefferson National Forest
6.5 mi W of Pound on SR 671; at Pound Lake. $12 at non-elec sites, $17 elec ($6 & $11 with federal senior pass). 5/15-9/15; 14-day limit. 34 sites (32-ft RV limit). Tbls, flush & pit toilets, showers, cfga, drkg wtr, playground, dump, amphitheater. Fishing, basketball. GPS: 37.10376, -82.62598

REMINGTON (48)

C.F. Phelps Wildlife Management Area   FREE
3 mi S of Remington. Free. All year. Primitive undeveloped camping. No facilities. 4,540 acres. Hiking, hunting. GPS: 38.452924, -77.75093.

RICHMOND (49)

Hog Island Wildlife Management Area   FREE
65 mi W of Richmond on Rt 650. Free. All year. Primitive undeveloped camping. No facilities. 2,864 acres. Hiking, hunting. GPS: 37.431573, -78.656894.

Powhatan Wildlife Management Area   FREE
33 mi W of Richmond at Powhatan Lake. Free. All year. Primitive undeveloped camping. No facilities. 4,148 acres. 66-acre lake. Hiking, boating(l), hunting. GPS: 37.54927, -77.990995.

ROANOKE (50)

Havens Wildlife Management Area   FREE
10 mi W of Roanoke. Free. All year. Primitive undeveloped camping. No facilities. 7,149 acres. Hiking, hunting.

Roanoke Mountain $8
Blue Ridge Parkway
National Park Service
Milepost 120.5 on Parkway S of Roanoke. $8 with federal senior pass; others pay $16. May-Nov; 14-day limit. 30 RV sites (30-ft RV limit). Drkg wtr, flush & chemical toilets, cfga, tbls, dump. Visitor center. GPS: 37.288086, -79.851807

SALTVILLE (51)

Clinch Mtn. Wildlife Management Area $9
From Saltville, follow SR 634 to SR 613, then 5 mi W of Saltville on SR 613; 6 mi N on SR 747 (gravel). $9. Apr-Sept; 14-day limit. 16 primitive sites. Tbls, toilets, cfga, drkg wtr, no showers, store, concession. $3 extra for pets. Fishing($), canoeing, hunting. Waterfalls. GPS: 36.994062, -81.736994.

SCOTTSVILLE (52)

Hardware River Wildlife Management Area   FREE
Off Rt. 6 near Scottsville. Free. All year. Primitive undeveloped camping. No facilities. 1,034 acres. Hiking, hunting. GPS: 37.752216, -78.415503.

SOUTH HILL (53)

Elm Hill Wildlife Management Area   FREE
16 mi SW of South Hill on Rt 664 at Lake Gordon. Free. All year. Primitive undeveloped camping. No facilities. 1,012 acres. 157-acre Lake Gordon. Hiking, hunting, fishing. Lake GPS: 36.693807, -78.214147.

SPEEDWELL (54)

Comers Rock Recreation Area $5
Jefferson National Forest
Mount Rogers National Recreation Area
5 mi S of Speedwell on US 21; 2 mi W on FR 57. $5. All year; 14-day limit. 10 sites (32-ft RV limit). Tbls, toilets, cfga, drkg wtr (no wtr services during reduced fee period). Fishing, hiking, hunting. GPS: 36.763428, -81.223389

Raven Cliff Recreation Area $5
Jefferson National Forest
Mount Rogers National Recreation Area
7 mi E of Speedwell on SR 469; at Cripple Creek. $5. All year; 14-day limit. 20 sites (32-ft RV limit). Tbls, toilets, cfga, drkg wtr (no wtr services during reduced-fee period). Fishing, hiking. GPS: 36.836426, -81.058594

STAUNTON (55)

Highland Wildlife Management Area   FREE
30 Mi W of Staunton off Rt 250. Free. All year. Primitive undeveloped camping. No facilities. 13,978 acres. Hiking, hunting. GPS: 38.324022, -79.571582.

North River Campground $5
Geo. Washington National Forest
20 mi W of Staunton on US 250; 9 mi N on SR 715; 1 mi NE on FR 95; 1 mi SW on FR 95B. $5. 3/1-12/3; 21-day limit. 16 undesignated sites; no RV size limit. Tbls, toilets, cfga, drkg wtr. Fishing. GPS: 38.33944, -79.2075

STOKESVILLE (56)

Todd Lake Recreation Area $8
Geo. Washington National Forest
2.5 mi W on Hwy 730 from jct with Hwy 731 at Stokesville; 1 mi NW on Hwy 718; 3.1 mi W on FR 95. $8 with federal senior pass; others pay $16. 5/15-10/20; 21-day limit. 20 sites; no RV size limit. Tbls, flush toilets, cfga, drkg wtr, showers, dump. Fishing, swimming, boating, hiking trails. Non-campers pay $5 day use fee GPS: 38.365723, -79.21167

STRASBURG (57)

Elizabeth Furnace Recreation Area $7
Geo. Washington National Forest
5 mi E of Strasburg on SR 55 to Waterlick, then 5 mi S on SR 678. $7 with federal senior pass during about 5/1-9/30; others pay $14. Fee $10 off-season ($5 with senior pass) but no wtr. 30 sites; no RV size limit. Tbls, flush toilets, cfga, drkg wtr, dump, showers. Hiking trails, fishing. Site of 150-year-old iron furnace named the "Elizabeth." Non-campers pay $5 (or $30 annually) day use fee. GPS: 38.9289999, -78.3269482

Little Fort Campground   FREE
George Washington National Forest
5 mi E of Strasburg on SR 55 to Waterlick, then about 8 mi S on SR 678 to small village of Seven Fountains; continue

1.2 mi SW on VA 678, then 2.5 mi NW on VA 758. All year; 14-day limit. 9 sites. Tbls, toilets, cfga, firewood, no drkg wtr. Picnicking; fishing, hiking. Near scenic observation tower on Rt 758. No RVs with holding tanks allowed. GPS: 38.8670569, -78.4433408

SUGAR GROVE (58)

Hurricane Campground $8
Jefferson National Forest
Mount Rogers National Recreation Area
5 mi S of Sugar Grove; right on Rt 650 for 2 mi. $8 with federal senior pass; others pay $16. 4/15-10/31; 14-day limit. 26 sites, typically 45 ft. Tbls, flush toilets, cfga, drkg wtr, showers (fee for non-campers). Fishing, hiking. GPS: 36.722168, -81.497559

Raccoon Branch Campground $7
Jefferson National Forest
Mount Rogers National Recreation Area
2 mi S of Sugar Grove on SR 16. $7 with federal senior pass during 4/15-10/31; others pay $14. During 11/1-12/2, regular fees $8 ($4 with federal senior pass), but no wtr services. Sites with elec, $19 in peak season, $12 off-season ($11 & $8 with senior pass). 19 sites (6 with elec/wtr), typically 40 ft. Tbls, flush & pit toilets, cfga, drkg wtr, dump (fee for non-campers). Hiking, biking. Non-campers pay $5 day use fee or $30 annually. GPS: 36.75333, -81.43639

TACOMA (59)

Bark Camp Lake State Fishing Lake   FREE
From Tacoma, 4.1 mi S on SR 706 (Stone Mountain Rd); left at Bark Camp Lake sign to lake. Free. All year. Primitive, undeveloped camping. No facilities. Boating (l); fishing. Concession. GPS: 36.865655,-82.523657.

Bark Camp Lake Recreation Area $12
Jefferson National Forest
From Tacoma, 4.1 mi S on SR 706 (Stone Mountain Rd); left at Bark Camp Lake sign for 0.3 mi, then right on Bark Camp Rd for 1.8 mi; right at sign for 0.7 mi. $12 at non-elec sites. Elec sites $17 ($11 with federal senior pass). 5/15-9/15; 14-day limit. 21 sites up to 65 ft. Tbls, flush toilets, cfga, drkg wtr, showers. Swimming, fishing, hiking trails. Non-campers pay $3 day use fee. GPS: 36.8683, -82.5208

TRIANGLE (60)

Oak Ridge Campground $10
Prince William Forest National Park
1 mi W of Triangle on Rt 619; qtr mi W of I-95 exit 150. $10 with federal senior pass; others pay $20. All year; 14 day limit. 100 sites (26-ft trailer limit, 32-ft motorhome limit). Tbls, flush toilets, cfga, drkg wtr, no showers. Ranger programs, hiking trails, fishing, backpacking, biking, visitor center. Entry fee. GPS: 38.59917, -77.41611

TROUTDALE (61)

Fox Creek Horse Camp $5
Jefferson National Forest
Mount Rogers National Recreation Area
.5 mi N of Troutdale on Va 16; 3.5 mi W on VA 603. $5. 4/1-1/1; 14-day limit. 31 sites; no RV size limit. Portable toilets, cfga, tbls, no drkg wtr except for horses. Hiking, fishing, horseback riding. Visitor center. Serves Virginia Highlands equestrian trail. GPS: 36.69833, -81.50417

Grindstone Recreation Area $10.50
Jefferson National Forest
Mount Rogers National Recreation Area
8 mi W of Troutdale on SR 603. $10.50 base with federal senior pass; others pay $21 base. $6 surcharge for 60 elec/wtr hookups. 4/15-11/30; 14-day limit. 108 sites; no RV size limit. Tbls, flush toilets, cfga, drkg wtr, showers, dump, amphitheater, wading pool, playground. Interpretive programs, volleyball, hiking. Non-campers pay $4 for showers, $5 for dump station, $3 day use fee. GPS: 81.54111, -35.68694

WAKEFIELD (62)

Airfield Lake State Fishing Lake   FREE
6 mi E of Wakefield on Rt 628. Free. All year. Primitive, undeveloped camping. No facilities. Boating(l), fishing. GPS: 36.907489, -77.032698.

WARM SPRINGS (63)

Bath County $10
Pumped Storage Station Lake
Virginia Power Recreation Area
12 mi W of Warm Springs on SR 39; 8 mi N on CR 600. $10 & $2 primitive camping. 4/15-10/31. 30 sites. Tbls, toilets, cfga, drkg wtr. Swimming, fishing, boating. 325 acres. GPS: 38.1137, -79.4835

Blowing Springs Campground $12
Geo. Washington National Forest
9 mi W of Warm Springs on SR 39. $12. 3/15-12/8; 21-day limit. 22 sites (22-ft RV limit). Tbls, toilets, cfga, drkg wtr, dump. Swimming, fishing. GPS: 38.069092, -79.884521.

Bolar Mountain Campground 1 $9
Bolar Mountain Recreation Area
Geo. Washington National Forest
11.4 mi W of Warm Springs on SR 39; 1 mi E of Mountain Grove, turn left on SR 600 for 7.8 mi; on NW shore of Lake Moomaw. $9 base with federal senior pass at non-elec sites; others pay $18 base, $23 at premium locations ($12.50 with senior pass). Elec sites $16 with federal pass; others pay $25; full hookups $21 with senior pass; others pay $30. About 4/1-LD; 21-day limit. 41 sites, typically 50 ft. Tbls, flush toilets, cfga, drkg wtr, showers, dump. Fishing, boating(lr), hiking trails. Non-campers pay $5 day use fee for beach, picnicking, boat ramp. GPS: 37.98361, -79.96694

Bolar Mountain Campground 2 $9
Bolar Mountain Recreaton Area
Geo. Washington National Forest
11.4 mi W of Warm Springs on SR 39; 1 mi E of Mountain Grove, turn left on SR 600 for 7.8 mi; on NW shore of Lake Moomaw. $9 with federal senior pass at non-elec sites; others pay $18. Elec sites $16 with federal pass; others pay $25. About 5/15-LD; 21-day limit. 17 sites, typically 48 ft. Tbls, flush toilets, cfga, drkg wtr, showers, dump. Fishing, boating(lr), hiking trails.

Bolar Mountain Campground 3 $9
Bolar Mountain Recreaton Area
Geo. Washington National Forest
11.4 mi W of Warm Springs on SR 39; 1 mi E of Mountain Grove, turn left on SR 600 for 7.8 mi; on NW shore of Lake Moomaw. $9 with federal senior pass at non-elec sites; others pay $18. Elec sites $16 with senior pass; others pay $25. About 5/15-LD; 21-day limit. 29 sites; no RV size limit. Tbls, flush toilets, cfga, drkg wtr, showers, dump. Fishing, boating(lr), hiking trails.

Hidden Valley Recreation Area $10
Geo. Washington National Forest
From jct with US 220 at Warm Springs, 3 mi W on SR 39; 1 mi N on SR 621 (McGuffin Rd); left at campground sign on Hidden Valley Rd for 1.5 mi. $10. MD-12/1; 14-day limit. 30 sites, typically 40 ft. Tbls, toilets, cfga, drkg wtr, dump. Fishing, hiking trails. GPS: 38.099365, -79.8900268

Hidden Valley   FREE
Dispersed Camping Area
Geo. Washington National Forest
1.5 mi W on SR 39; 1 mi N on SR 621; 1.7 mi N on FR 241. Free. All year; 14-day limit. Dispersed undesignated sites. Toilets, cfga, no drkg wtr. Hiking (20 mi of trails), fishing.

Poor Farm Campground   FREE
Geo. Washington National Forest
9.5 mi N of Warm Springs on Hwy 220; 2.3 mi W (left) on SR 623. Free. All year; 14-day limit. Primitive undesig-nated sites. Toilets, cfga, no drkg wtr. Fishing in Jackson River, hiking, hunting.

WAVERLY (64)
State Game Refuge Public Fishing Lake   FREE
4 mi E of Waverly on Rt 602. Free. All year. Primitive, undeveloped camping. No facilities. 40-acre lake. Fishing. Concession.

WILLIAMSBURG (65)
Chickahominey Wildlife Management Area   FREE
Wildlife Management Area
12 mi NE of Williamsburg off Rt 5. Free. All year. Primitive undeveloped camping. No facilities. 4,790 acres. Hiking, hunting. GPS: 37.318759, -76.903853.

WINCHESTER (66)
G.R. Thompson   FREE
Wildlife Management Area
SE of Winchester on US 17. Free. All year. Primitive undeveloped camping. No facilities. 4,084 acres. Hiking, hunting. GPS: 38.964583, -78.002413.

WYTHEVILLE (67)
Stony Fork Campground $12
Jefferson National Forest
8 mi N of Wytheville on Hwy 52; qtr mi E on Rt 717. $12 for non-elec sites, $18 elec hookups, $22 elec/wtr ($6, $12 & $16 with federal senior pass). 4/1-12/1; 14-day limit. 49 sites, typically 60 ft. Tbls, flush toilets, cfga, drkg wtr, dump, showers. Fishing, hiking, mountain biking, nature trails, horseshoe pits. GPS: 37.00972, -81.18167

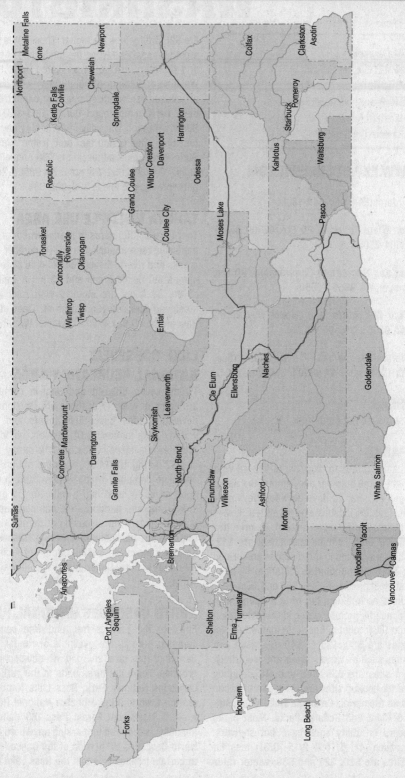

Metaline Falls
Northport
Ione
Newport
Chewelah
Colfax
Clarkston
Asotin
Kettle Falls
Colville
Pomeroy
Springdale
Starbuck
Harrington
Kahlotus
Waitsburg
Republic
Wilbur Creston
Davenport
Odessa
Grand Coulee
Pasco
Coulee City
Moses Lake
Tonasket
Riverside
Conconully
Okanogan
Winthrop
Twisp
Entiat
Naches
Goldendale
Cle Elum
Ellensburg
Skykomish
Leavenworth
North Bend
Concrete Marblemount
Darrington
White Salmon
Granite Falls
Enumclaw
Wilkeson
Ashford
Morton
Yacolt
Woodland
Camas
Sumas
Anacortes
Bremerton
Vancouver
Port Angeles
Sequim
Shelton
Elma
Tumwater
Hoquiam
Long Beach
Forks

WASHINGTON

CAPITAL: Olympia
NICKNAME: Evergreen State
STATEHOOD: 1889 – 42nd State
FLOWER: Pink Rhododendron
TREE: Western Hemlock
BIRD: Eastern Goldfinch

WWW.EXPERIENCEWA.COM

For travel information: 800-544-1800.

Washington State Tourism, PO Box 42500 Olympia, WA 98504-2500.

State Parks and Recreation Commission, PO Box 42650, Olympia, WA 98504-2650.

Dept of Fish & Wildlife, 600 Capitol Way North, Olympia, WA 98501. 360-902-2200.

Dept of Natural Resources, Public Lands Office, PO Box 47001, Olympia, WA 98504. 360-902-1004.

REST AREAS

Overnight stops are not permitted.

STATE PARKS

Overnight camping fees for 2007 were $12-40 with a 10-day limit in the summer and, among the parks that are open all year, 20 days between November and March. Pets on leashes are permitted. Lower fees are charged off-season except at primitive sites. Primitive sites (without amenities) are $12. All other sites are ranked in three stages and priced according to their popularity. "Standard" sites (available at most parks) are $25, $30 or $35 in-season; they have no hookups but offer a campstove, picnic table, nearby running water, sink waste, trash disposal and flush toilets; most accommodate RVs. "Utility" sites are $30, $35 or $40 in-season and offer hookups such as water, sewer and electricity. Full-hookup sites are $35, $40 and $45. Slightly lower rates for hookup sites are charged at Beacon Rock, Brooks Memorial, Columbia Hills, Conconully, Lewis & Clark and Schafer Parks. Most parks with standard or utility sites have hot showers. Shoulder-season (4/1-5/14 & 9/15-10/31) fees for standard sites are $20, $25 and $30; winter rates are $20. Utility fees are higher. These rates have put most state parks beyond the guidelines of this book and therefore are no longer listed here. However, Washington seniors (62 and older) who buy a $75 off-season senior citizen pass can camp free at any open park campground during 10/1-3/31 and on Sunday through Thursday in April; they pay just $10 for utility sites during that time frame. Washington State Parks' park admission is $30 annually or $10 daily. PO Box 42650, Olympia, WA 98504-2650. The park information line is 360-902-8844.

TAHUYA MULTIPLE USE AREA

There are 33,000 acres of state-owned land in this peninsula recreational area with a number of lakes, creeks and rivers. Eleven recreational sites offer 61 camps, 20 picnic areas and 13 mi of trails. Many of the 68 lakes are stocked with rainbow trout, steelhead and sea run cutthroat. Dept of Natural Resources, PO Box 47001, Olympia, WA 98504.

LAKE ROOSEVELT
NATIONAL RECREATION AREA

Twenty-seven drive-to and boat-in campgrounds are open all year; 17 of those are developed; most developed sites have flush toilets and drinking water during summers. Off-season, pit toilets are provided. Developed sites are $18 during 5/1-9/30 and $9 during 10/1-4/30. Fees are not charged for shoreline camping, which is permitted in undeveloped areas at least half a mile from a developed area -- marina, parking area, campground or boat launch. Devices for disposing of human waste are required for backcountry camping. Disposal must be at a concession marine pump-out facility or an RV dump station. Generator use is allowed 6am to 10pm.

NORTH CASCADES NATIONAL PARK

Entry to the park is free and free backcountry camping permits are available at ranger stations. Camping fees are charged at developed campgrounds. There are three units to the park -- North Cascades National Park, Ross Lake National Recreation Area and Lake Chelan National Recreation Area. A Northwest Forest Pass ($5 daily or $30 annually) is required for parking anywhere along the North Cascades NP portion of the Cascade River or at certain trailheads within the Ross Lake NRA. For further information contact: Superintendent, North Cascades National Park, 810 State Route 20, Sedro Woolley, WA 98284.

LAKE CHELAN NATIONAL RECREATION AREA

About 2,000 acres of this 55-mile-long lake are in the recreation area. There are 20 free camping areas (ask the park ranger for a map and detailed directions). Boaters using docks on Lake Chelan must purchase a dock site pass for $5 daily or $40 annually. Superintendent, Lake Chelan National Recreation Area, North Cascades National Park, 810 State Route 20, Sedro Woolley, WA 98284.

ROSS LAKE NATIONAL RECREATION AREA

Vehicles can reach this area from the north, through Canada to Hozomeen, which is 40 miles west of Hope, British Columbia, on Silver-Skagit Rd. Access to Ross Lake from the south is limited to trail and water routes. There is boat and trail access from the dam to specific sites along Ross Lake. There are 122 camping sites, including 15 boat-access camping areas on Ross Lake, many of which have docking facilities. Pets are not allowed. Drinking water is piped and treated. There are no RV hookups or dump stations. Pit toilets and tables are provided. Boat launching ramps are provided. All refuse should be packed out. Superintendent, Ross Lake National Recreation Area, North Cascades National Park, 810 State Route 20, Sedro Woolley, WA 98284. 360-856-5700.

Olympic National Park, 600 E Park Ave, Port Angeles, WA 98362; 360-565-3130. Entry fees are now collected at Elwha, Heart O' the Hills, Hurricane Ridge, Hoh, Sol Duc and Staircase entrance stations from May through September or later. Although most campgrounds have 21-ft RV length limits, the major campgrounds each have a few sites which will accommodate larger RVs. Backcountry permits are required for all trail and beach camping.

Lake Roosevelt National Recreation Area, 1008 Crest Drive, Coulee Dam, WA 99116; 509-633-9441. This park has 25 campgrounds scattered around Roosevelt Lake, with a total of more than 600 sites. Some are accessible only by boat. Fees are now charged at nearly all campgrounds accessible by vehicle, even during the off-season.

Mount Rainier National Park, 55210 238th Ave East, Ashford, WA 98304. Five developed campgrounds offer nearly 600 campsites. In addition, the park has numerous backcountry trailside camping area, accessible by free permit after payment of 7-day ($15) or annual ($30) entry fees.

Corps of Engineers, Seattle District, PO Box C-3755, Seattle, WA 98124, 206/764-3440; or Corps of Engineers, Walla Walla District, Bldg 602, City-County Airport, Walla Walla, WA 99362, 509/522-6717.

Bureau of Land Management, Spokane District Office, East 4217 Main Ave., Spokane, WA 99202.
Colville National Forest. Although the forest participates in the Recreational Fee Demonstration Program, northwest forest passes are not needed at any campgrounds, and only at four trailheads and one boat launch. However, several campgrounds that had been free now have $6 fees assigned. 765 S. Main St., Colville, WA 99114. 509/684-7000.

Gifford Pinchot National Forest
Fee campgrounds are usually left open for free camping after the managed season ends. However, services are discontinued, and campers must pack out their trash and leave a clean camp. The forest has almost unlimited camping opportunities for dispersed camping throughout the forest. Camping in the same developed campground for more than 14 consecutive days is prohibited; at dispersed sites, a 21-day limit is enforced, and staying at any combination of developed or dispersed sites longer than 45 days in a calendar year is prohibited. About half of the forest's campgrounds now have fees of $15-18 but are listed in this book because seniors with America the Beautiful federal pass can camp at half price. Gifford Pinchot National Forest, 10600 NE 51st St., Vancouver, WA 98668; 360-891/5000.

Mount Baker-Snoqualmie National Forests
38 developed campgrounds operate from Memorial Day through Labor Day weekends. Most charge fees of $12-$18. Some campgrounds remain open through September, and a few are open until mid-October. Overnight camping is not permitted at developed picnic sites. Free dispersed camping is permitted anywhere else in the forest, but user fees of $5 per day (or $30 annually) per vehicle are charged at various trailheads, picnic areas and three rustic areas. 21905 64th Avenue West,

Mountlake Terrace, WA 98043. 425-775-9702 or 800-627-0062.

Okanogan National Forest

Fees are now charged for overnight parking and camping on land west of the Okanogan River. A one-night or annual pass is necessary for camping outside many developed sites, parking at most trailheads and camping at developed campgrounds. Those passes replace fees formerly charged in developed campgrounds and convert formerly free campgrounds into fee sites. The northwest forest passes are $5 per night or $30 annually. Purchase of a season's pass permits the holder to camp without charge in the specified areas. 1240 South Second Ave., Okanogan, WA 98841.

Olympic National Forest

Coho Campground (not listed her due to its high fees) is the only forest camp with an RV waste disposal station. It is 38 miles north of Montesano. Be watchful of logging traffic on forest roads. All of the forest's 14 developed campgrounds have fees; free rustic camps have limited facilities, with water usually not available. Northwest forest passes are required at many locations; they are $5 daily or $30 annually. Olympic National Forest, 1835 Black Lake Blvd, SW, Olympia, WA 98512-5623. 360-956-2402.

UMATILLA NATIONAL FOREST has hundreds of primitive, undeveloped sites available to campers without charge as well as several campgrounds with low-cost sites, most in Oregon. 541/278-3716.

Wenatchee National Forest

Good free, dispersed camping opportunities (outside established campgrounds) are available at lower elevations in the Naches Ranger District; no facilities are available at those locations. Dispersed campers may travel established roads and camp in established camp spots; all litter must be removed. Throughout the forest, more than 150 campgrounds and picnic sites are provided. All campgrounds in the Chelan District are for tent camping; no RVs permitted. A totally new fee structure was implemented in that district a few years ago. Ten developed campgrounds which formerly were free now have fees of up to $12 per night. Also, $5 daily fees ($30 annually) northwest forest pass fees are now charged for formerly free dispersed camping

in the South Fork Tieton area and in the peninsula area between Tieton Road 1200 and Rimrock Lake. Wenatchee, like the other national forests of the Northwest, is participating forest-wide in the national Recreation Fee Demonstration Program. 215 Melody Lane, Wenatchee, WA 98801. 509/664-9200.

ANACORTES

Moran State Park $12
Ferry from Anacortes to Orcas Island, then 11 mi on Horse-shoe Hwy. $12 for 151 primitive sites. WA seniors with $75 off-season pass camp free during 10/1-3/31 & Sun-Thur in April. 45-ft RV limit. Tbls, flush toilets, showers, drkg wtr, cfga, dump, pay phone. 5 freshwater lakes, 30 mi of hiking trails, 4 waterfalls. Cascade Lake offers fishing, swimming, boating(lr), windsurfing(r), picnic area, shelter, interpretive display. Mountain Lake has good trout fishing, boating(rl), group camping. 5,000 acres of forest; 1,800 ft of shoreline. Store, golf, horseback riding/rental & trails, hiking & biking trails, mountain biking, interpretive trail.

ASOTIN

Fields Spring State Park $12
13.5 mi N of Asotin SR 129. $12 base at 20 primitive RV/tent sites; 30-ft RV limit. All year; 10-day limit. Limited facilities in winter (20-day limit). 20 standard sites at $25 base); 20 primitive RV/tent sites $12. 30-ft RV limit. WA seniors with $75 off-season pass camp free during 10/1-3/31 & Sun-Thurs in April. Tbls, cfga, drkg wtr, flush toilets, showers, dump. Hiking & biking trails, amphitheater, mountain biking, softball, horseshoe pits, volleyball. 825 acres.

Heller Bar Water Access Site $10
Department of Fish & Wildlife
21 mi SE of Asotin on Lower Snake River Rd at W shore of river (just N of Rogersburg). $10 daily or $30 annual Discover Pass. Primitive camping. All year; 14-day limit. Tbls, toilets, cfga, no drkg wtr. Boating(l), fishing. Primary take-out spot for rafters & primary launch site for power boats into Hells Canyon. GPS: 46.0855625, -116.093076

ASHFORD

Big Creek Campground $9
Gifford Pinchot National Forest
2 mi E of Ashford on SR 706; right on FR 52 for 1.8 mi. $9 with federal senior pass; others pay $18 (double sites $30). 5/22-9/15; 14-day limit. 27 sites up to 40 ft. Tbls, toilets, cfga, drkg wtr, grey wtr stations. Hiking trail, fishing, mountain biking.

Cougar Rock Campground $10
Mount Rainier National Park
14 mi E of Ashford on SR 706 (Paradise Rd); at SW area of park. $10 with federal senior pass; others pay $20. May-late Sept; 14-day limit. 173 sites; 35-ft motorhome limit, 27-ft trailer limit. Tbls, flush & pit toilets, cfga, drkg wtr, dump, amphitheater. Educational programs, hiking. Elev 3180 ft.

BREMERTON

Camp Spilman State Recreation Site $10
Tahuya State Forest
Department of Natural Resources
S of Bremerton 10 mi on SR 3 to Belfair, then 3.5 mi SW on SR 300; right on Belfair-Tahuya Rd for 1.9 mi; right on Elfendahl Pass Rd for 2.6 mi; left on Goat Ranch Rd for .7 mi. All year; 7-day limit. $10 daily or $30 annual state Discover Pass required. 6 small primitive sites. Tbls, toilets, cfga, drkg wtr, group shelter. Hiking trails; horseback trails; fishing; motorcycle trails; mountain biking. On Tahuya River.

Kammenga Canyon Campground $10
Tahuya State Forest
Department of Natural Resources
10 mi SW of Bremerton on SR 3 to Belfair, then 3.5 mi SW on SR 300; right on Belfair-Tahuya Rd for 1.9 mi; right on Elfendahl Pass Rd for 2.3 mi to Elfendahl Pass Staging Area; half mi farther N on Elfendahl Pas Rd, then left to camp; near Hood Canal. $10 daily or $30 annual Discover Pass required. All year; 7-day limit. 2 sites. Tbls, toilets, cfga, no drkg wtr, no trash service. Motorcycling, mountain biking, horseback riding. GPS: 47.417963, -122.911890

Tahuya River Horse Camp $10
Tahuya State Forest
Department of Natural Resources
10 mi SW of Bremerton on SR 3 to Belfair, then 3.5 mi SW on SR 300; turn right on Belfair-Tahuya Rd for 3.2 mi, then right on Spillman Rd for 2.1 mi; left 1 mi to camp; near Hood Canal. $10 daily or $30 annual state Discover Pass required. MD-LD; 7-day limit. 8 sites. Tbls, sites, cfga, no drkg wtr, horse facilities. Hiking, horseback riding.

Tunerville Campground $10
Tahuya State Forest
Department of Natural Resources
10 mi SW of Bremerton on SR 3 to Belfair, then 3.5 mi SW on SR 300; turn right on Belfair-Tahuya Rd for 1.9 mi, then right on Elfendahl Pass Rd 2.3 mi; pass jct with Goat Ranch Rd; camp on left; near Tahuya River. $10 daily or $30 annual state Discover Pass required. All year; 7-day limit. 4 sites. Tbls, toilets, cfga, no drkg wtr, corrals. Hiking trails; motorbike trails; horse trails mountain biking. GPS: 46.422232, -123.615943. Note: Due to bridge safety concerns, use alternate route, expecting steep grades: Turn right (S) onto 5910 Rd for 0.9 mi; left on 5920 Rd for 2.2 mi; left on 5970 Rd for 0.5 mi; right on 5900 Rd to campground.

CAMAS

Dougan Creek Campground   FREE
Yacolt Burn State Forest
Department of Natural Resources
From SR 14 at Camas, N on SR 140 about 5 mi to Wash-ougal River Rd; right 7.5 mi; bear left, then right next 1.3 mi; at Y, bear left for 6 mi to camp. Free but state Discover Pass required. 4/1-10/31; 14-day limit. 7 sites; 20-ft RV limit. Tbls, toilets, cfga, drkg wtr. Hiking, fishing, mountain biking, swimming. Waterfall.

CHEWELAH

Gifford Campground $9
Lake Roosevelt National Recreation Area
From settlement of Gifford (25 mi W of Chewelah), 2 mi S on SR 25. $9 with federal senior pass; others pay $18 during 5/1-9/30; $4.50 & $9 off-season; 14-day limit. 42 sites (20-ft RV limit). Tbls, toilets, cfga, drkg wtr, dump. Boating, fishing, swimming, waterskiing. On Franklin Roosevelt Lake. Flush toilets operate about 4/15-10/15.

CLARKSTON

Blyton Landing FREE
Lower Granite Lake
Corps of Engineers
From Clarkston at jct with US 12, N on SR 193 across Snake River bridge, then 20 mi W on Wawawai River Rd (Old Hwy 193). Free. All year; 14-day limit. Primitive undesignated sites. Tbls, pit toilets, cfga, no drkg wtr. Boating(ld), fishing. No wood fires 6/10-10/10. 3 acres.

Nisqually John Landing FREE
Corps of Engineers
From Clarkston at jct with US 12, N on SR 193 across Snake River bridge, then 15 mi W on Wawawai River Rd (Old Hwy 193). Free. All year; 14-day limit. Primitive undesignated sites. Pit toilets, tbls, cfga, no drkg wtr, shade shelter. Boating(ld), fishing. 8 acres. No wood fires 7/10-10/10.

Offield Landing FREE
Corps of Engineers
Lower Granite Lake
1 mi E of Lower Granite Ram on Wawawai Ferry Rd; at Lower Granite Lake, Snake River milepost 108, S Shore. Free. All year; 14-day limit. Primitive RV/tent camping at undesignated sites. Pit toilets, cfga, tbls, no drkg wtr, shade shelter. Boating(ld), fishing. 10 acres.

Wawawai Landing FREE
Corps of Engineers
Lower Granite Lake
28 mi W of Clarkson on CR 9000 (North Shore Snake River Rd) or 19 mi SW of Pulman on Wawawai Rd. Free. All year; 14-day limit. Primitive camping at about 9 undesignated sites. Pit toilets, cfga, no drkg wtr, shade shelters. Boating(ld), fishing, hiking. 3 acres.

CLE ELUM

29 Pines Campground $10
Teanaway Community State Forest
Department of Natural Resources
From I-90 exit 85, 6.9 mi E on SR 970; left on Teanaway Rd for 12.9 mi, then left into camp. All year; not plowed in winter; 10-day limit. $10 daily or $30 annual Discover Pass. 59 long RV/tent sites. Tbls, toilets, cfga, no drkg wtr. Biking, fishing, hiking trails. More dispersed sites farther along Teanaway River Rd.

Beverly Campground $8
Wenatchee National Forest
8.5 mi SE of Cle Elum on SR 970, turning E/NE; left (N) for 13 mi on Teanaway Rd & North Fork Teanaway; 4 mi NW on FR 9737 at North Fork Teanaway River to end of pavement; veer right onto FR 9737 for 4 mi; at left. $8 during 5/15-9/30; free 10/1-5/15 but typically snowbound early Dec through early May; 14-day limit. 16 sites (RVs under 22 ft). Tbls, toilets, cfga, no drkg wtr or trash service. Fishing, hiking; horseback riding (1 mi). Horse and motorcycle trail nearby.

Cle Elum River Campground $9
Wenatchee National Forest
15 mi NW of Cle Elum on SR 903, becoming Salmon la Sac Rd; at E shore of river at head of Lake Cle Elum. $9 with federal senior pass; others pay $18. MD-9/15; free off-season but no wtr or trash service; 14-day limit. 23 sites, typically 45 ft. Tbls, toilets, cfga, drkg wtr. Fishing, hunting, hiking.

Icewater Creek Campground $9
Wenatchee National Forest
12 mi SE of Cle Elum on I-90 to exit 93; .25 mi N from Thorp exit; right on Thorpe Prairie Rd about 3.5 mi; turn right & cross over I-90 onto W. Taneum Rd/FR 33 for 8.5 mi. $9 with federal senior pass; others pay $18. 5/15-10/30; free off-season but no services or trash pickup; 14-day limit. 15 sites, typically 27 ft. Tbls, toilets, cfga, no drkg wtr. Fishing, hunting, horseback riding, hiking, motorcycling.

Indian Camp State Recreation Site $10
Teanaway Community State Forest
Department of Natural Resources
From Exit 85 of I-90 at Cle Elum, 6.9 mi E on SR 970; left on Teanaway Rd for 7.3 mi; left on West Fork Teanaway Rd for half mi; right on Middle Fork Teanaway Rd for 3.9 mi; along Middle Fork Teanaway River. $10 daily or $30 annual Discover Pass. All year; 14-day limit. 6 sites. Tbls, toilets, cfga, no drkg wtr, hitching rails. Horseback riding, hiking, mountain biking.

Ken Wilcox Horse Camp $5
(Haney Meadows)
Wenatchee National Forest
12 mi NE of Cle Elum on SR 970; N on US 97 to Swauk Pass; 4 mi S on FR 9716, then right (E) about 4 mi on FR 9712. Camp free with $30 annual NW forest pass; $5 daily otherwise. 6/15-10/31. 19 sites. Tbls, toilets, cfga, no drkg wtr except for stock. Horse tethers, council area, horse loading ramps. Hunting, hiking, horseback riding.

Liberty Recreation Site FREE
Bureau of Land Management
12 mi NE of Cle Elum on SR 970; N on US 97 to Swauk Pass; E on Liberty Rd near Williams Creek. Free. All year; 14-day limit. 15 primitive dispersed sites in cottonwood grove on right side of rd (surrounded by forest service ORV

trails). No facilities except 2 toilets, cfga; no trash service. Fishing, hiking, ORV activities.

Mineral Springs Campground $9
Wenatchee National Forest
12 mi E of Cle Elum on US 970; 6 mi N on US 97. $9 with federal senior pass; others pay $18. 5MD-LD; free off-season but no services. 14-day limit. 7 sites (22-ft limit). Tbls, toilet, cfga, no drkg wtr. Fishing, berry-picking, hunting. Rockhounding nearby. Elev 2700 ft.

Red Mountain $7
Wenatchee National Forest
19.5 mi NW of Cle Elum on WA 903 & Cle Elum Valley Rd. 903, about 1 mi N of Cle Elum Lake at Cle Elum River. $7 with federal senior pass; others pay $14. MD-10/15, weather permitting; free off-season but no services; 14-day limit. 10 sites on 2 acres, typically 35 ft. Tbls, toilet, cfga, no drkg wtr. Berry picking, fishing; horseback riding (2 mi); swimming.

Red Top Dispersed Sites FREE
Wenatchee National Forest
10 mi E of Cle Elum on SR 970; 8 mi N on US 97; about 8 mi NW on FR 9702 (to nearly end of rd). All year; 14-day limit. 3 dispersed sites (22-ft RV limit). No amenities escept user-built cfga. Decommissioned as a campground. Hiking, hunting. Fire lookout.

South Fork Meadows Dispersed Site FREE
Wenatchee National Forest
From Cle Elum, take I-90 E and Thorp Prairie Rd 14 miles to Forest Road 33 / W Taneum Rd. Follow Forest Road 33 for 13 miles. Decommissioned & closed as campground, now a dispersed site & trailhead. Toilet, no other amenities, no wtr except for stock at creek. Horseback riding, hiking.

Swauk Campground $9
Wenatchee National Forest
10 mi E of Cle Elum on SR 970; 17 mi N on US 97; at N shore of Swauk Rver. $9 with federal senior pass; others pay $18. MD-LD; free off-season but no services; 14-day limit. 21 sites (22-ft RV limit). Tbls, toilets, cfga, no drkg wtr, community kitchen, swings. Horseshoes, baseball, hiking trail, hunting, fishing, group sports.

Tamarack Springs Campground FREE
Wenatchee National Forest
12 mi SE of Cle Elum on I-90; .75 mi S from Thorp exit; 12.5 mi on CR/FR 31 past Taneum Campground; 5 mi S on FR 3100; 1.5 mi E on FR 3120; at forest boundary. Free dispersed camping. All year, weather permitting; 14-day limit. 3 sites; no facilities, no drkg wtr except for horses. Hunting, hiking, horseback riding, motorcycling.

Taneum Campground
Wenatchee National Forest
12 mi SE of Cle Elum on SR 970; .qtr mi N, then right on Thorp Prairie Rd for 3.5 mi; right on E. Taneum Rd & cross over I-90, then W on W.Taneum Rd, becoming FR 33 for 6 mi; on left. $9 with federal senior pass; others pay $18. MD-LD, free off-season but no services or drkg wtr. 14-day limit. 11 sites. Tbls, toilets, cfga, drkg wtr. Near site of former CCC camp; picnic shelter built by CCC. Fishing, hiking.

Taneum Junction Campground $5
Wenatchee National Forest
12 mi SE of Cle Elum on I-90 to exit 93 at Elk Heights/Taneum Creek; qtr mi N, then right on Thorp Prairie Rd for 3.5 mi; right on E. Taneium Rd & cross over I-90, then right on W. Taneum Rd, becoming FR 33 for 9.5 mi to end of pavement; left across bridge, veering left into campground. Free with $30 annual NW pass; otherwise $5 daily. About 5/15-11/15 or until weather prevents access.14-day limit. Improved dispersed camping area for groups or individuals; about 15 vehicle capacity. Tbls, toilets, cfga, no drkg wtr. Fishing, hunting, motorcycling, horseback riding.

COLFAX

Illia Landing FREE
Corps of Engineers
Lake Bryan
From S. Main St in Colfax, 12 mi S on W. Almota Rd, becoming SR 194 for 5 mi to settlement of Almota; 2 mi SE on Lower Granite Rd (along Snake River) & across Lower Granite Dam, then 3 mi W on Almota Ferry Rd. Free. All year; 14-day limit. Primitive, undesignated sites. Tbls, toilet, cfga, drkg wtr, fishing pier. Boating(ld), fishing.

Lambi Dam FREE
Corps of Engineers
Lake Bryan
From S. Main St in Colfax, 12 mi S on W. Almota Rd, becoming SR 194 for 5 mi to settlement of Almota; 2 mi SE on Lower Granite Rd (along Snake River) & across Lower Granite Dam, then 5 mi W on Almota Ferry Rd. Free. All year; 14-day limit. Primitive undesignated sites. Tbls, toilet, cfga, no drkg wtr. Boating, fishing.

COLVILLE

Big Meadow Lake FREE
Colville National Forest
1 mi E of Colville on SR 20; 19.4 mi N on Aladdin Rd; 6 mi E on Meadow Creek Rd; slight right onto Settlers Way to camp. Free. MD-LD (reduced services off-season); 14-day limit. 17 sites. Tbls, toilets, cfga, no drkg wtr or trash service. Boating(l), interpretive trails (wheelchair access), fishing.

Douglas Falls Grange Park $10
Department of Natural Resources
From SR 20 on E side of Colville, N 1.9 mi on Aladdin Rd; left for 3 mi on Douglas Falls Rd, then left into park. $10 daily or $30 annual Discover Pass. All year; 14-day limit. 8 sites; 6 picnic sites. Tbls, toilets, cfga, drkg wtr. Baseball field, horseshoes, scenic waterfalls. Mill Creek.

Gillette Campground $9
Colville National Forest
20 mi E of Colville on Hwy 20; half mi E on FR 200 (Pend Oreille Lake Rd). $9 with federal senior pass; others pay $18. MD-LD (reduced services off-season); 14-day limit. 30 sites, typically 50 ft. Tbls, toilets, cfga, drkg wtr, bear-proof trash service. Boating(l), fishing, hiking.

Sherry Creek Campground $10
Little Pend Oreille State Forest
Department of Natural Resources
From jct with US 395 at Colville, 23.8 mi E on SR 20; right for half mi on gravel rd near Little Pend Oreille Lakes & Sherry Creek. $10 daily or $30 annual Discover Pass. 4/24-10/15; 10-day limit. 2 sites. Tbls, toilets, cfga, no drkg wtr. Fishing, hiking, ORV riders.

Starvation Lake State Campground $10
Little Pend Oreille State Forest
Department of Natural Resources
From jct with US 395 at Colville, 10.5 mi E on SR 20; right on gravel rd for qtr mi; left at next jct for half mi. $10 daily or $30 annual Discover Pass. 4/15-10/15; 14-day limit. 13 sites. Tbls, toilets, cfga, no drkg wtr, fishing pier. Fishing catch & release during late Apr through May), boating (hand launch, no mtrs). Moose sighted frequently.

CONCONULLY

Cold Springs Campground $10
Loomis State Forest
Department of Natural Resources
From settlement of Loomis (20 mi N of Conconully), 2.1 mi N of Loomis grocery on Loomis-Oroville Rd (CR 9425); left on Toats Coulee Rd for 5.6 mi to upper Toats Coulee Camp; then OM-T-1000 Rd 2.1 mi; turn right on gravel Cold Creek Rd for half mi; stay right; go 1.8 mi; stay left; go 2.3 mi to picnic area then half mi to camp. $10 daily or $30 annual Discover Pass. All year; 10-day limit. 5 sites. Toilets, tbls, cfga, no drkg wtr. Horse facilities. Hiking trails, horse trails, mountain biking.

Cottonwood Campground $8
Okanogan National Forest
2.1 mi NW of Conconully on CR 2361/FR 38; along North Fork Salmon Creek. $8. May-Oct; 14-day limit. 4 sites (22-ft RV limit). Tbls, new toilets, cfga, no drkg wtr. Fishing.

Kerr Campground $8
Okanogan National Forest
2 mi NW of Conconully on FR 2361; 2 mi NW on FR 38; at North Fork Salmon Creek. $8. All year; 14-day limit. 13 sites (22-ft RV limit) & 2 group sites. Tbls, toilets, cfga, no drkg wtr or trash service. Fishing, swimming, boating. Elev 3100 ft.

Long Swamp Campground $5
Okanogan National Forest
From settlement of Loomis (18 mi N of Conconully), 2.1 mi N on Loomis-Oroville Rd (CR 9425); 21 mi N & W on CR 4066 & FR 39. All year; 14-day limit. Free with $30 annual NW forest pass; $5 daily pass otherwise. 2 sites; 1 acre. Tbls, toilet, cfga, no drkg wtr. No trash service in winter. Stream. Hiking & horse trails. trailhead. Adopted & maintained by the Backcountry Horsemen.

North Fork Nine Mile Campground $10
Loomis State Forest
Dept of Natural Resources
From settlement of Loomis (20 mi N of Conconully) 2.1 mi N of Loomis grocery on Loomis-Oroville Rd (CR 9425); left on Toats Coulee Rd for 5.6 mi to upper Toats Coulee Camp; then OM-T-1000 Rd 2.5 mi. $10 daily or $30 annual Discover Pass. 4/15-11/30; 10-day limit. 11 sites. Tbls, toilets, cfga, drkg wtr.

Oriole Campground $8
Okanogan National Forest
2.6 mi NW of Conconully on CR 2361/FR 38; left 1 mi on FR 3008-025; along North Fork Salmon Creek. $8. All year; 14-day limit. 10 sites (22-ft RV limit). Tbls, toilet, cfga, no drkg wtr or trash trash service. Fishing, hiking.

Palmer Lake Campground $10
Loomis State Forest
Department of Natural Resources
From settlement of Loomis (20 mi N of Conconully), 8.5 mi N of Loomis grocery (keep right) on Loomis-Oroville Rd (CR 9425); on N shore of 2,100-acre lake. $10 daily or $30 annual Discover Pass. All year; 10-day limit. 7 lakeside sites. Toilets, tbls, cfga, no drkg wtr. Fishing, hiking, boating (hand launch), rockhounding, beach access. View cougar, bighorn sheep, eagles. Watch for rattlesnakes.

Salmon Meadows Campground $8
Okanogan National Forest
8.5 mi NW of Conconully on CR 2361, becoming FR 38. $8. All year; 14-day limit. 9 sites (22-ft RV limit). Tbls, toilets, cfga, no drkg wtr or trash service, community kitchen. Hiking trails, horseback riding (corral), birdwatching, historical exhibit. Campground, its gazebo & registration booth built 1937 by CCC.

Sugarloaf Campground $8
Okanogan National Forest
From Conconully, N on Main St to CR 4015 on right; 5 mi E on CR 4015, past Conconull Lake to campground on left. $8. All year; 14-day limit. 4 sites. Tbls, toilets, cfga, no drkg wtr or trash service. Fishing, boating, hiking.

Tiffany Springs FREE
Okanogan National Forest
From Conconully, 3 mi SW on CR 2017/FR 42 around Conconully Reservoir; 21 mi NW on FR 37 (becoming FR 39); right (NE) for 8 mi on FR 39 (rough roads). All year; 14-day limit. Free. 6 sites (RVs under 16 ft). Tbls, toilets, cfga, no drkg wtr or trash service. Fishing, bridle trails, hiking. Near Tiffany Lake.

Touts Coule Campground $10
Loomis State Forest
Department of Natural Resources
From settlement of Loomis (20 mi N of Conconully), 2.1 mi N from Loomis grocery on Loomis-Oroville Rd; left on Toats Coulee Rd for 5.5 mi to lower camp; continue .1 mi to upper camp; at Toats-Coulee Creek. $10 daily or $30 annual Discover Pass. 4/15-11/30. 9 sites. Tbls, toilets, cfga, game racks, no drkg wtr.

CONCRETE

Boulder Creek Campground $7
Mt. Baker-Snoqualmie National Forest
9.5 mi N of Concrete on CR 25; 5.5 mi N on CR 11. $7 with federal senior pass; others pay $14. 5/26-9/26; 14-day limit. 9 sites (24-ft RV limit). Tbls, toilets, cfga, no drkg wtr. Fishing, berrypicking, boating, hiking, horseback riding. 5 acres.

Horseshoe Cove Campground $9
Mt. Baker-Snoqualmie National Forest
5.1 mi W of Concrete on SR 20; right on Baker Lake Rd for 15.2 mi; right after campground sign on FR 1118 for 1.7 mi; on W shore of Baker Lake. $9 with federal senior pass; others pay $18 (double sites $30). 5/18-9/24; 14-day limit. 38 sites; no RV size limit. Tbls, flush & pit toilets, cfga, drkg wtr. Boating(l), fishing, swimming beach.

Panorama Point Campground $8
Mt. Baker-Snoqualmie National Forest
5.1 mi W of Concrete on SR 20; right on Baker Lake Rd for 19.2 mi; at W shore of Baker Lake. $8 with federal senior pass; others pay $16 (double sites $30). 5/18-9/24; 14-day limit. 15 sites, typically 33 ft. Tbls, pit toilets, cfga, drkg wtr. Boating(l), fishing.

Park Creek Campground $12
Mt. Baker-Snoqualmie National Forest
9.5 mi N of Concrete on CR 25; 7.4 mi NE on FR 11; .1 mi NW on FR 1144. $12. 5/18-9/10; 14-day limit. 12 sites (22-ft

RV limit). Tbls, toilets, cfga, no drkg wtr. Fishing, boating nearby on Baker Lake. Hiking trails.

Sauk Park Campground $7
Skagit County Parks & Recreation
From Concrete, 7 mi SE on SR 20 to settlement of Rockport; right S on SR 530 for about 8 mi, then cross Sauk River on Lower Government Bridge (about 8 mi N of Darrington); 0.5 mi after crossing river, turn right (N) on Christian Camp Rd, veering right onto S. Concrete Sauk Rd for 2.5 mi, then right into park on Sauk River Park Rd. $7. 3/1-10/31; 14-day limit. Self-contained RVs only rest of year. 15 primitive sites at 40-acre park. Tbls, cfga, portable toilets, no drkg wtr. Hiking. Self-registration.

Shannon Creek Campground $7
Mt. Baker-Snoqualmie National Forest
5.1 mi W of Concrete on SR 20; right on Baker Lake Rd for 23.4 mi; at NW shore of Baker Lake. $7 base with federal senior pass; others pay $14 base, $16 for premium locations ($8 with senior pass); double sites $26. 5/18-9/10; 14-day limit. 19 sites; 36-ft RV limit. Tbls, toilets, cfga, drkg wtr. Boating(l), fishing.

COULEE CITY

Banks Lake Fish Camp $10
Columbia Basin Wildlife Area
State Department of Fish & Wildlife
On US 2 at end of Banks Lake Dam just past turnoff for Rt 17. $10 daily or $30 annual Discover Pass. About 15 undesignated sites on large, flat gravel area (no size limit); in addition, designated sites are provided at Barker Canyon, Lena Lake, Million Dollar sites and Osborne Bay. Tbls, toilets, cfga, no drkg wtr. Boating(l); hunting. Beach.

CRESTON

Hawk Creek Campground $9
Lake Roosevelt National Recreation Area
14 mi NE of Creston on Miles-Creston Rd. $9 with federal senior pass; others pay $18 during 5/1-9/30; $4.50 and $9 off-season; 14-day limit. 21 sites (RVs under 16 ft). Tbls, toilets, cfga, drkg wtr. Boating(ld); fishing. Near Roosevelt Lake.

DARRINGTON

Bedal Campground $7
Mt. Baker-Snoqualmie National Forest
22 mi S of Darrington on FR 20; along Sauk River. $7 with federal senior pass; others pay $14 (double sites $26). 5/24-9/210 14-day limit. 21 sites (22-ft RV limit); 6 acres. Tbls, toilets, cfga, no drkg wtr. Fishing, hiking.

Buck Creek Campground $7
Mt. Baker-Snoqualmie National Forest
7.5 mi N of Darrington on SR 530; 15.2 mi SE on FR 26 along Suiattiei River. $7 with federal senior pass; others

pay $14. MD-LD; 14-day limit. 29 sites (30-ft RV limit). Tbls, toilets, cfga, no drkg wtr. Nature trails, fishing.

Clear Creek Campground $7
Mt. Baker-Snoqualmie National Forest
2.3 mi SE of Darrington on FR 20; quarter mi SE on FR 3205; on Sauk River at jct with Clear Creek. $7 with federal senior pass; others pay $14. 5/26-9/26; 14-day limit. 13 secluded sites, typically 40 ft. Tbls, toilets, cfga, firewood, no drkg wtr, no trash pickup. Hunting; hiking; fishing. 4 acres. Frog Lake Trailhead.

French Creek FREE
Mount Baker-Snoqualmie National Forest
8.1 mi W of Darrington on WA 530; .8 mi S on FR 2010; near Icicle & French Creeks. Free. 5/1-9/30; 14-day limit. Undeveloped primitive dispersed sites. No facilities. Fishing (2 mi). Elev 700 ft.

DAVENPORT
Fort Spokane Campground $9
Lake Roosevelt National Recreation Area
25 m N of Davenport on SR 25. $9 with federal senior pass; others pay $18 during 5/1-9/30; $4.50 & $9 off-season; 14-day limit. 67 sites (26-ft RV limit). Tbls, flush toilets, cfga, drkg wtr, dump, amphitheater. Boating(ld), fishing, playground, swimming. 22 acres.

Porcupine Bay Campground $9
Lake Roosevelt National Recreation Area
19 mi N of Davenport on SR 25. $9 with federal senior pass; others pay $18 during 5/1-10/30; $4.50 & $9 off-season; 14-day limit. 31 sites (20-ft RV limit). Tbls, flush toilets, cfga, drkg wtr, beach, dump, fish cleaning station. Swimming, boating(ld), fishing, volleyball.

ELLENSBURG
Big Pines Campground $7.50
Bureau of Land Management
19 mi S of Ellensburg on Hwy 821 (Canyon Rd); at milepost 10. $7.50 with federal senior pass; others pay $15. All year; 7-day limit (free about 9/15-5/15). Recently renovated with 41 paved pads, pedestrian sidewalks. Tbls, toilets, cfga. Hiking, boating(l), fishing.

Lmuma Creek Campground $7.50
Bureau of Land Management
13 mi S of Ellensburg on SR 821; along Yakima River. $7.50 with federal senior pass; others pay $15. All year; 7-day limit. 12 sites. Tbls, toilets, cfga, no drkg wtr. Boating(l), fishing, canoeing, rafting, hiking, hunting, horseback riding. Formerly named Squaw Creek.

Manastash Campground $5
Wenatchee National Forest
From I-10 Exit 101 NW of Ellensburg near Thorp, 2 mi SE on Thorp on Thorp Hwy; right (S) on Cove Rd for 4 mi; right on Manastash Rd, becoming FR 31, for 19 mi; right on FR 3104 to camp on right. Camp free with annual $30 NW forest pass; $5 daily otherwise. All year; 14-day limit. About 14 primitive undesignated sites, plus improved dispersed area for groups. Tbls, toilet, cfga, no drkg wtr except for horses, hitching posts. Hiking, horseback riding. This camp replaces the old Buck Meadows camp.

Quartz Mountain Dispersed Free
Wenatchee National Forest
33 mi W of Ellensburg on CR/FR 3100; near end of rd. Free dispersed camping; former developed campground decommissioned. No facilities except user-built cfga. GPS: 47.0767, -121.08

Riders Camp Dispersed Area $5
Wenatchee National Forest
From I-90 exit 101 NW of Ellensburg, 2 mi SE on Thorpe Hwy; right on Miller Rd to jct with Robinson Canyon Rd, where Miller becomes Cove Rd; follow Cove Rd to jct with Manastash Rd; right on Manastash to end of pavement & continue on FR 3100 to spur rd 114 to trailhead; near South Fork Manastash Creek. Camp free with annual $30 NW forest pass; $5 daily otherwise. All year; 14-day limit. Improved primitive dispersed area. Toilet, user-built cfga, no drkg wtr or trash service. Wtr for stock at creek. Hiking, horseback riding, OHV activity. GPS: 47.0291, -120.936

Roza Campground $7.50
Bureau of Land Management
18 mi S of Ellensburg on SR 821; along Yakima River at milepost 7. $7.50 with federal senior pass; others pay $15. All year; 7-day limit. 7 primitive sites. Tbls, toilets, cfga, no drkg wtr. Fishing, boating(l), horseback riding, canoeing, rafting, hiking, hunting.

Umtanum Campground $7.50
Bureau of Land Management
9 mi S of Ellensburg on SR 821; along Yakima River. $7.50 with federal senior pass; others pay $15. All year; 7-day limit. Primitive undesignated sites. Toilets, cfga, no drkg wtr. Boating(l), fishing, canoeing, hiking, rafting, kayaking, horseback riding, hunting.

ELMA
Porter Creek Campground $10
Capitol State Forest
Dept of Natural Resources
From jct with SR 8 in Elma, 6 mi S on US 12; 3.4 mi NE on Porter Creek Rd (becomes C-1100 Rd); at 4-way intersection, continue straight on B-Line Rd for 0.6 mi. $10 daily or $30 annual Discover Pass. 5/1-10/1; 10-day limit. 16 sites. Toilets, cfga, drkg wtr, no tbls, horse ramps. Hiking & horse trails; motorcycle trails; fishing.

ENTIAT

Cottonwood Campground $10
Wenatchee National Forest
1.5 mi S of Entiat on US 97; just before Entiat River bridge, right (W, curving NW) on CR 19 (Entiat River Rd), becoming CR 19; pavement ends after 34 mi & becomes FR5100; continue for total of 37 mi past Cottonwood Cabin to campground on left. $10 during MD-10/15; camp free withoug amenties in fall after wtr is shut off; 14-day limit. 25 small RV sites; 9 still closed due to 2014 wildfire; 3 open ot hardened gravel areas; 2 more being repaired for opening in 2017; 28-ft RV limit. Tbls, toilets, cfga, drkg wtr. Fishing, hiking & horseback trails. Departure point for Glacier Peak Wilderness.

Fox Creek Campground $10
Wenatchee National Forest
1.5 mi S of Entiat on US 97; just before bridge, right (W, curving NW) on Entiat River Rd (CR 19), becoming FR 51 for 26.7 mi to campground on left. $10 during MD-LD; camp free in fall without amenities after wtr is shut off; 14-day limit. 16 sites, typically 42 ft, but 28-ft RV limit. Tbls, toilets, cfga, drkg wtr. Fishing, hiking. Elev 2300 ft. 8 sites closed in 2017 due to effects of wildfires upstream.

Lake Creek Campground $10
Wenatchee National Forest
1.5 mi S of Entiat on US 97; just before bridge, right (W, curving NW) on CR 19 (Entiat River Rd), becoming FR 51, for 27.4 mi to campground on left. $10 during MD-LD; camp free without amenities in fall after wtr is shut off; 14-day limit. $10. 18 sites, typically 38 ft but 25-ft RV limit. Tbls, toilets, cfga, drkg wtr. Fishing, hiking trails, horseback riding.

Shady Pass Dispersed Camp FREE
Wenatchee National Forest
1.5 mi S of Entiat on US 97; just before bridge, right (W, curving NW) on CR 19 (Entiat River Rd), becoming FR 51, for 25.2 mi; 9 mi NE on Shady Pass Rd (FR 5900). Free. 7/15-9/30; 14-day limit. Primitive undesignated sites. Tbls, cfga, no toilet, no drkg wtr.

Silver Falls Campground $12
Wenatchee National Forest
1.5 mi S of Entiat on US 97; just before bridge, right (W, curving NW) on CR 19 (Entiat River Rd), becoming FR 51, for 29.5 mi to campground. $12 during MD-10/15; free without amenities in fall after wtr isshut off; 14-day limit. 31 sites (28-ft RV limit). Tbls, toilets, cfga, drkg wtr. Fishing, hiking trails. At Silver Creek & Entiat River. Half-mi hike to Silver Falls.

ENUMCLAW

Evans Creek Campground $5
Mount Baker-Snoqualmie National Forest
4 mi W of Enumclaw on SR 410 to Buckley; N on SR 165 toward Wilkeson; entrance to ORV area on left. Camp free with $30 annual NW Forest Pass; $5 daily otherwise. All year; 14-day limit. 23 sites. Tbls, toilets, cfga, drkg wtr. 40 mi of 4WD & ORV trails.

Sand Flats Trailhead FREE
Mount Baker-Snoqualmie National Forest
33 mi SE of Enumclaw on Hwy 410; left on FR 7190 (Crystal Mountain Blvd) for 4 mi, then right on FR Spur 510. Free but $5 daily or $30 annual NW Forest Pass required.. All year; 14-day limit. Undesignated sites, used primarily by horse campers. Tbls, toilets, cfga, no drkg wtr except for horses. Hitching rails. Hiking, horseback riding.

Silver Springs Campground $10
Mount Baker-Snoqualmie National Forest
32 mi E of Enumclaw on SR 410 (1 mi W of Mt. Ranier NP); at White River. $10 with federal senior pass; others pay $20. 5/24-9/24; 14-day limit. 56 sites up to 45 ft. Tbls, toilets, cfga, drkg wtr. Fishing.

The Dalles Campground $9
Mount Baker-Snoqualmie National Forest
26 mi E of Enumclaw on SR 410 (7 mi W of Mt. Ranier NP); at White River. $9 base with federal senior pass; others pay $18 base, $20 for premium locations ($10 with senior pass). 5/24-9/10; 14-day limit. 45 sites; 40-ft RV limit. Tbls, toilets, cfga, drkg wtr. Hiking trails.

White River Campground $10
Mount Rainier National Park
43 mi SE of Enumclaw on SR 410 in NE corner of park. $10 with federal senior pass; others pay $20. Late June to late Sept; 14-day limit. 112 sites; 27-ft motorhome limit, 18-ft trailer limit. Tbls, flush toilets, cfga, drkg wtr. Hiking, fishing, recreation program. Elev 4400 ft; 25 acres.

FORKS

Bear Creek Campground $10
Olympic Experimental State Forest
Department of Natural Resources
NW of Forks on US 101 at milepost 206, along Sol Duc River, just outside Olympic National Forest. $10 daily or $30 annual Discover Pass. All year; 7-day limit. 16 sites. Toilets, tbls, cfga, no drkg wtr or trash service. Hiking, fishing.

Coppermine Bottom Campground $10
Olympic Experimental State Forest
Department of Natural Resources
From milepost 147 on US 101 S of Forks, go N on Hoh-Clearwater Mainline Rd (paved) 12.6 mi; then right 1.5 mi on gravel, 1-lane C-1010. Camp on left along Clearwater River. $10 daily or $30 annual Discover Pass. All year; 7-day limit. 9 sites. Toilets, tbls, cfga, no drkg wtr or trash service. Hand boat launch, fishing.

Cottonwood Recreation Site $10
Olympic Experimental State Forest
Department of Natural Resources
From between mileposts 177 & 178 S of Forks, go W off US 101 on Oil City Rd (paved) 2.3 mi; left on gravel H-4060, then 1 mi to camp; at Hoh River. $10 daily or $30 annual Discover Pass. 7-day limit. 9 sites. Toilets, tbls, cfga, no drkg wtr or trash service. Boating, fishing, hiking. Hand boat launch.

Hoh Oxbow State Campground $10
Olympic Experimental State Forest
Department of Natural Resources
From between mileposts 176 and 177 S of Forks, go E off US 101 between rd and river. Free. 7-day limit during 30-day period at all regional campgrounds. 8 sites. Toilets, tbls, cfga, no drkg wtr, no trash service. Hand boat launch, fishing. On Hoh River. GPS: 47.8114695, -124.2501998.

Hoh Rain Forest Campground $10
Olympic National Park
14 mi S of Forks; 1.8 m N on Hoh River Bridge, 17.9 mi E on paved rd along Hoh River. Narrow, winding rds (watch out for logging trucks). $10 with federal senior pass; others pay $20. All year; 14-day limit. 88 sites (35-ft RV limit, 21-ft recommended). Tbls, toilets, cfga, drkg wtr, animal-proof lockers. Nature program, hiking trails, fishing. Roosevelt elk in vicinity of trails. Hoh River Trail (18 mi)leads to climb of Mount Olympus (highest peak in Olympic region). Ranger station provides information and backcountry use permits all year. Rd passes through one of the finest examples of rain forest. 35 acres.

Kalaloch Campground $11
Olympic National Park
From settlement of Queets (30 mi S of Forks), 2 mi N on US 101; on bluff overlooking Pacific Ocean. $11 with federal senior pass during 6/15-LD; others pay $22. Lower fees off-season. 170 sites; 35-ft RV limit (21-ft recommended). Tbls, toilets, cfga, drkg wtr, dump($10). Hiking trails.

Klahanie Campground $10
Olympic National Forest
1 mi N of Forks on US 101; 5 mi E on paved FR 29; at South Fork Calawa River. $10. All year; 14-day limit. 8 sites; 21-ft RV limit. Toilet, cfga, no drkg wtr or trash service. Hiking, fishing, biking.

Klahowya Campground $8.50
Olympic National Forest
20 mi NE of Forks on US 101. $8.50 with federal senior pass; others pay $17. 5/15-10/15; 14-day limit. 55 sites; 40-ft RV limit. Tbls, flush & pit toilets, cfga, drkg wtr. Fishing, boating(l), biking trails. 32 acres. On Soleduck River. Site name means "welcome" in Chinook.

Minnie Peterson I $10
Bert Cole State Forest
Department of Natural Resources
From between mileposts 178 & 179 S of Forks, 5 mi E of US 101 at Hoh Rain Forest Rd; camp on left. $10 daily or $30 annual Discover Pass. All year; 7-day limit. 8 sites. Tbls, toilets, cfga, no drkg wtr or trash service. Fishing.

Ozette Campground $10
Olympic National Park
From settlement of Clallam Bay (about 20 mi N of Forks), 5 mi NW on SR 112 through village of Sekiu; left (SW) on Hoko Ozette Rd for 15 mi to settlement of Ozette, then S on access rd to camp at N shore of Ozette Lake. $10 with federal senior pass; others pay $20. All year; 14-day limit. 15 sites; 21-ft RV limit. Tbls, toilets, cfga, drkg wtr. Boating, fishing, hiking.

Queets Campground $7.50
Olympic National Park
From Forks, 30 mi S on US 101 past settlement of Clearwater & onto Quinault Indian Reservation; continue E on US 101, then left (N) for 13.5 mi on gravel Queets River Rd (open all year; RVs not recommended) to campground. $7.50 with federal senior pass; others pay $15. All year but may close in winter; 14-day limit. 20 sites (15-ft RV limit, suitable for van & truck campers). Tbls, pit toilets, cfga, no drkg wtr. Fishing (no license required in park). Elev 290 ft. No park entrance fee. Roosevelt elk often seen in abandoned homestead fields in Rain Forest. Queets Campground Trail. Queets ranger station (1.5 mi) provides information and backcountry use permits summer and fall; closed winter. Note: In 2017, accessible from Upper Queets River Rd due to mudslide at primary access.

Mora Campground $10
Olympic National Park
2 mi N of Forks on US 101; 12 mi W (rd to campground paved but narrow; open all year) on LaPush Rd, then Mora Rd. Follow signs. $10 with federal senior pass; others pay $20. All year; 14-day limit. 94 sites (35-ft RV limit, 21-ft recommended). Tbls, flush toilets, cfga, drkg wtr, dump. 7 hiking trails, fishing (salmon, no license required in park); observation of sea and bird life; nature programs. Elev, sea level. Boat launch at public fishing access, 3 mi W. Hiking to Lake Ozette on the N. Wilderness Beach (18.5 mi), but check with ranger regarding tide tables, as some portions can be crossed only at low tide. 40 acres.

South Fork Hoh Campground $10
Olympic Experimental State Forest
Department of Natural Resources
From milepost 176 at US 101 S of Forks, E on Hoh Mainline Rd (paved) 6.6 mi, then left on H-1000 Rd (two lanes paved, then gravel 1 lane) for 7.4 mi; camp first rd on right past South Fork Hoh bridge; along South Fork Hoh

River. $10 daily or $30 annual Discover Pass. All year; 7-day limit. 3 sites. Tbls, toilets, cfga, no drkg wtr or trash service. Fishing.

Upper Clearwater Campground $10
Clearwater Corridor Natural Resources Cons. Area
Department of Natural Resources
From milepost 147 on US 101 S of Forks, 12.9 mi N on paved Hoh-Clearwater Mainline Rd; right 3.2 mi on gravel 1-lane C-3000 Rd to camp entrance on right. $10 daily or $30 annual Discover Pass. All year; 7-day limit. 9 sites. Toilets, no drkg wtr, tbls, cfga, shelter, no trash service. Hand boat launch, fishing.

Willoughby Creek $10
Yahoo Lake Campground
Olympic Experimental State Forest
Department of Natural Resources
From between mileposts 178 & 179 S of Forks, 3.5 mi E of US 101 on Hoh Rain Forest Rd; right 6.1 mi on C-3100 Rd. $10 daily or $30 annual Discover Pass. All year; 7-day limit. 3 small, rustic sites. Toilet, tbls, cfga, no drkg wtr or trash service. Fishing. On Hoh River.

GOLDENDALE

Bird Creek Campground $10
Ahtanum State Forest
Department of Natural Resources
From post office in settlement of Glenwood (30 mi NE of Goldendale), qtr mi W to Bird Creek Rd, then 0.9 mi N, left over cattle guard on Bird Creek Rd (K-3000) for 1.2 mi, then right on gravel S-4000 Rd for 1.3 mi; left on K-4000 rd, staying left for 2 mi; site on left, E side of Mount Adams Wilderness Area. $10 daily or $30 annual Discover Pass. All year; 7-day limit. 8 sites. Toilets, tbls, cfga, no drkg wtr.

Cliffs Park   FREE
Lake Umatilla
John Day Lock & Dam
Corps of Engineers
From Goldendale, 10 mi S on US 97 toward Maryhill; right (W) about 4 mi on SR 14; S on John Day Rd by old aluminum plant; follow until paved rd becomes gravel. Free. All year. Primitive undesignated sites. Tbls, toilet, cfga, no drkg wtr. Fishing, boating(l).

Island Camp State Recreation Site $10
Department of Natural Resources
Follow directions to Bird Creek Recreation Site, but continue on K-3000 Rd 1.4 mi; left on K-4200 Rd for 1.1 mi; left qtr mi to camp. All year; 7-day limit. Tbls, toilet, cfga, no drkg wtr or trash service. Elplore lava tubes.

Sundale Park   FREE
Lake Umatilla
John Day Lock & Dam
Corps of Engineers

From Goldendale, 10 mi S on US 97; left (E) for 35 mi on SR 14 to milepost 128; right at sign. Free. All year; 14-day limit. Primitive undesignated sites; no facilities except toilets, no drkg wtr. Boating(l), fishing.

GRAND COULEE

Spring Canyon $9
Lake Roosevelt National Recreation Area
3 mi E of Grand Coulee on SR 174. $9 with federal senior pass; others pay $18 during 5/1-9/30; $4.50 & $9 off-season; 14-day limit. 87 sites; 26-ft RV limit. Tbls, flush & pit toilets, cfga, drkg wtr, fish cleaning station, dump. Swimming area, boating(dl), waterskiing, fishing, nature trails, hiking trails. 7 acres.

Steamboat Rock State Park $12
12 mi S of Grand Coulee on Hwy 155; at N end of Banks Lake. $12 base. All year; 10-day limit. 44 primitive sites at Jones Bay (no wtr available, closed for winter 9/30); 36 primitive sites (no wtr) at Osborn Bay. 100 utility sites with full hookups available; 50-ft RV limit. WA seniors with $75 off-season pass camp free without hookups ($10 with hookups) during 10/1-3/31 & Sun-Thurs in April. Tbls, toilets, cfga, drkg wtr, dump, showers, playground. Swimming, boating(lr), fishing, hiking trails, waterskiing, volleyball, basketball, mountain biking; store; horse trails in nearby Northup Canyon. 3,523 acres.

GRANITE FALLS

Chokwich Dispersed Camp   FREE
Mt. Baker-Snoqualmie National Forest
30.1 mi E of Granite Falls on CR 92/FR 7; 4.6 mi NE on FR 20. Free. 5/30-9/10; 14-day limit. Undeveloped primitive sites; no facilities. Fishing. GPS: 48.0731637, -121.3987222

Gold Basin Campground $11
Mt. Baker-Snoqualmie National Forest
12.1 mi E of Granite Falls on Mountain Loop Rd. $11 with federal senior pass; others pay $22 (doubles $35). 5/12-9/26; 14-day limit. 78 sites; 40-ft RV limit. Tbls, flush toilets, cfga, drkg wtr, showers ($2 non-campers). Fishing, hiking trail, boardwalk & wildlife viewing platform, salmon fry viewing area. Non-campers pay $5 day use fee. GPS: 48.07820833, -121.7342028. Note: Campround closed in 2016-2017 until further notice, pending geological studies.

Red Bridge Campground $7
Mt. Baker-Snoqualmie National Forest
18.1 mi E of Granite Falls on CR 92/FR 7. $7 with federal senior pass; others pay $14 during 5/16-9/24 or until closed by snow; 14-day limit. 15 sites 32-ft RV limit. Tbls, toilets, cfga, no drkg wtr, no trash service. Fishing. On South Fork of Stillaguamish River.

Turlo Campground $8
Mt. Baker-Snoqualmie National Forest
9.6 mi E of Granite Falls on Mountain Loop Rd. $8 with
federal senior pass; others pay $16. 5/9-9/18; 14-day
limit. 18 sites; 40-ft RV limit. Tbls, toilets, cfga, no drkg
wtr. Fishing.

Verlot Campground $9
Mt. Baker-Snoqualmie National Forest
9.8 mi E of Granite Falls on Mountain Loop Rd. $9 with fed-
eral senior pass during 5/9-9/18; others pay $18 (doubles
$30). About 5/1-11/30; 14-day limit. 25 sites, typically 30-60
ft. Tbls, flush toilets, cfga, drkg wtr. Fishing.

HARRINGTON
Coffeepot Lake Recreation Site   FREE
Bureau of Land Management
From SR 28 in Harrington, 12 mi W on Coffee Pot Rd to
site's gravel access, on left. Free. All year; 14-day limit.
Primitive undesignated sites on 900 acres. Tbls, toilets,
cfga, no drkg wtr. Fishing, boating, hiking, horseback
riding.

Twin Lakes Campground   FREE
Bureau of Land Management
From SR 28 in Harrington, 12 mi W on Coffee Pot Rd;
right for 1.5 mi on Highline Rd; right at recreation area's
entrance for 2 mi; at Upper and Lower Twin Lakes.
Free. All year; 14-day limit. Primitive undesignated sites
between lakes. Tbls, toilets, cfga, no drkg wtr. Fishing,
boating(l), hiking, horseback riding, hunting. Part of
14,000-acre Channeled Scablands.

HOQUIAM
Campbell Tree Grove   FREE
Olympic National Forest
From settlement of Humptulips (20 mi N of Hoquiam), 8 mi
N on FR 22; 14 mi N on FR 2204; on W. Fork of Humptulips
Rd; along West Fork Humptulips River. Free. 5/15-12/15;
14-day limit. 11 sites (16-ft RV limit). Toilets, tbls, cfga, no
drkg wtr. Fishing, hiking, hunting, berry-picking.

Graves Creek Campground $10
Olympic National Park
39 mi N of Hoquiam on US 101 to just S of Lake Quinault;
18.6 mi NE on S. Shore Rd; 1st 7 mi paved, then gravel
rd (gravel portion may be closed in winter by snow;
narrow). No RVs due to road conditions (vans & pickup
campers okay). $10 with federal senior pass; others
pay $20. All year; 14-day limit. 30 sites (21-ft RV limit).
Tbls, toilets, cfga, drkg wtr May-Oct. Fishing (no license
required in park), boating, swimming, hiking. Trails. Rd
passes through town of Quinault and US Forest Service
Lake Quinault Recreation Area; rd winds up valley to a
dense stand of rain forest that begins beyond point where
Quinault river branches.

North Fork Campground $7.50
Olympic National Park
39 mi N of Hoquiam on US 101 to just S of Lake Quinaul;
about 8 mi NE on S. Shore Rd; 1st 7 mi paved, then gravel;
left over Quinault River bridge to campground; rds closed
in winter by snow; narrow, not suitable for large RVs,
especially trailers (vans & pickup campers okay). $7.50
with federal senior pass; others pay $15. All year; 14-day
limit. 9 sites (RVs under 22 ft). Toilets, cfga, no wtr. Hiking
trails; fishing (WA State license and Indian Reservation
Fishing Permit required). Rain forest beyond upper level
of Lake Quinault.

IONE
Edgewater Campground $9
Colville National Forest
1 mi S of Ione on SR 31; qtr mi E on CR 9345 (Sullivan Lake
Rd); 2 mi N on CR 3669; left on FR 1130 to camp at E shore
of Pend Oreille River. $9 with federal senior pass; others
pay $18. About 5/15-LD; 14-day limit. 19 sites (1 double);
no RV size limit. Toilets, cfga, drkg wtr, tbls. Boating(l),
fishing, waterskiing, hiking.

Lake Thomas Campground $9
Colville National Forest
S of Ione on Hwy 31 to settlement of Tiger; 11 mi SW on SR
20; 1 mi E on FR 200 (Pend Oreille Rd); at lake's E shore.
$9 with federal senior pass; others pay $18. 5/15-9/15;
14-day limit. 16 sites (16-ft RV limit). Tbls, toilets, cfga,
drkg wtr, bear-proof trash service. Swimming, biking,
boating, fishing, waterskiing, hiking trails. Elev 3200 ft.

Little Twin Lakes Campground   FREE
Colville National Forest
From Ione, S on SR 31 to SR 20, then 12.1 mi E; 1.7 mi N on
Black Lake Rd, becoming FR 4939 for 3.2 mi; N to site on
FR 150; both sides of lake. All year; 14-day limit (reduced
service LD-MD). 7 sites. Tbls, toilets, cfga, no drkg wtr or
trash service. Boating(l), fishing, ATV use.

Noisy Creek Campground $9
Colville National Forest
Half mi S of Ione on Hwy 31; 8.2 mi NE on Sullivan Lake Rd
(CR 9345); at S end of Sullivan Lake. $8 with federal senior
pass; others pay $18. About 5/12-9/15. Primitive overflow
meadow open all year; no fee, no services. 14-day limit. 19
sites; no RV size limit. Tbls, toilets, cfga, drkg wtr. Swimming area, boating(l), trailhead. Elev 2600 ft.

KAHLOTUS
Devils Bench   FREE
Corps of Engineers
Lake Herbert G. West
Lower Monument Dam
6 mi S of Kahlotus on SR 263 (Devils Canyon Rd); left on
access rd; at N shore of lake just above dam. Free. All

year; 14-day limit. 6 primitive designated sites. Toilets, cfga, tbls, no drkg wtr. Fishing, boating(ld).

Windust Park FREE
Corps of Engineers
Lake Sacajawea
From Kahlotus, 4 mi SW on Pasco-Kahlotus Rd; 5.2 mi SE on Burr Canyon Rd; at N shore of Snake River. Free primitive camping with services about 5/15-LD; free camping without services & portable toilets off-season. 14-day limit. 24 grass sites & boat camping. Covered sun shelters, picnic shelter available. 40-ft RV limit. Tbls, flush toilets, cfga, drkg wtr, dump. Fishing, swimming, boating(ld).

KETTLE FALLS

Canyon Creek Campground $6
Colville National Forest
3.7 mi NW of Kettle Falls on US 395; 7.7 mi W on SR 20; quarter mi S on FR 136 (Bangs Mountain Rd). $6 during MD-LD; free with reduced services off-season; 14-day limit. 12 sites (RVs under 32 ft). Tbls, toilets, cfga, firewood, no drkg wtr or trash service. Hiking, fishing. Elev 2200 ft. Interpretive center nearby.

Colville River FREE
Lake Roosevelt National Recreation Area
.8 mi W of Kettle Falls on US 395; 3.7 mi S on SR 25. Access rd is unmarked; watch on right for gravel rd located just before white guard rail. Rough, narrow, steep, but short (approx 200 yards) access rd. Free. All year; 14-day limit. Undesignated sites; room for 10 RVs. No facilities. Hunting; fishing (in Roosevelt Lake). Large area amidst a grove of evergreens.

Davis Lake Campground FREE
Colville National Forest
From Kettle Falls, 11.5 mi N of Kettle Falls (0.5 mi S of Boyds) on US 395; 3 mi W on CR 460; 4 mi N on CR 465; 5 mi W & N on CR 480/FR 80. Free. MD-LD; 14-day limit. 4 sites. Tbls, toilets, cfga, no drkg wtr or trash service. Fishing, boating(l), canoeing.

Evans Campground $9
Lake Roosevelt National Recreation Area
1 mi S of Evans on SR 25; on Roosevelt Lake. $9 with federal senior pass; others pay $18 during 5/1-9/30; $4.50 & $9 off-season; 14-day limit. 43 sites (26-ft RV limit). Tbls, flush toilets, cfga, drkg wtr, dump. Boating(l), fishing, hiking, swimming, waterskiing. 16 acres.

Haag Cove Campground $9
Lake Roosevelt National Recreation Area
12 mi W of Kettle Falls on CR 3. $9 with federal senior pass; others pay $18 during 5/1-9/30; $4.50 & $9 off-season; 14-day limit. 16 sites (RVs under 26 ft). Tbls, toilets, cfga, drkg wtr. Boating(d), swimming, fishing.

Kettle Falls Campground $9
Lake Roosevelt National Recreation Area
3 mi W of Kettle Falls on US 395. $9 with federal senior pass; others pay $18 during 5/1-9/30; $4.50 & $9 off-season; 14-day limit. 76 sites; 26-ft RV limit Tbls, flush toilets, cfga, drkg wtr, dump. Playground, fishing, boating(ld), swimming, waterskiing. 22 acres.

Kettle River Campground $9
Lake Roosevelt National Recreation Area
13 mi NW of Kettle Falls, on US 395. $9 with federal senior pass; others pay $18 during 5/1-9/30; $4.50 & $9 off-season; 14-day limit. 13 sites. Tbls, flush toilets, cfga, drkg wtr, marina, store. Fishing, swimming area.

Lake Ellen Campgrounds $6
Colville National Forest
3.7 mi NW of Kettle Falls on US 395; 4.1 mi S on SR 20; 4.5 mi SW on CR 3 (Inchellium Kettler Falls Rd); right (W) on Mary Ellen Rd for 1.3 mi; left (S) on CR 412 for about 2 mi to S shore of lake. $6. MD-LD; 14-day limit. 11 sites at eastern campground, 5 sites at western camp, typically 40 ft. Tbls, toilets, cfga, no drkg wtr or trash service. Fishing; boating(ld), swimming. 75-acre lake.

Marcus Island $9
Lake Roosevelt National Recreation Area
4 mi N of Kettle Falls, on WA 25. $9 with federal senior pass; others pay $18 during 5/1-9/30; $4.50 & $9 off-season; 14-day limit. 27 sites (RVs under 20 ft). Tbls, pit toilets, cfga, drkg wtr. Store nearby. Swimming; fishing, boating(d). On Roosevelt Lake.

North Gorge Campground $9
Lake Roosevelt National Recreation Area
20 mi N of Kettle Falls on WA 25; at Franklin Roosevelt Lake. $9 with federal senior pass; others pay $18 during 5/1-9/30; $4.50 & $9 off-season; 14-day limit. 12 sites. Tbls, toilets, cfga, drkg wtr. Fishing, boating(ld).

Pierre Lake Campground $6
Colville National Forest
Form settlement of Orient (15 mi N of Kettle Falls), 3.8 mi E on CR 4134; 3.2 mi N on CR 4013 (Pierre Lake Rd); at W shore of lake. $6 (free LD-MD, but no services). All year; 14-day limit. 15 sites on 8 acres (RVs under 32 ft). Tbls, toilets, cfga, no drkg wtr. Hiking; fishing; swimming; waterskiing; boating(ld).

Snag Cove Campground $9
Lake Roosevelt National Recreation Area
7 mi N of Kettle Falls on US 395; right on Northpoint-Flat Creek Rd for 7.5 mi. $9 with federal senior pass; others pay $18 during 5/1-9/30; $4.50 & $9 off-season; 14-day limit. 9 sites. Tbls, toilets, cfga, drkg wtr. Boating(ld), fishing.

Trout Lake   FREE
Colville National Forest
3.7 mi NW of Kettle Falls on US 395; 5.2 mi W on SR 20;
5.1 mi N on FR 020 (Trout Lake Rd). Free. All year; 14-day
limit; reduced services LD-MD. 5 small sites. Tbls, toilets,
cfga, no drkg wtr or trash service. Boating (I - no mtrs),
swimming, fishing pier, hiking trails.

LEAVENWORTH

Alpine Meadows Campground $7
Wenatchee National Forest
15.9 mi NW of Leavenworth on US 2; 4.4 mi N on SR 207;
0.8 mi E on CR 22; 21 mi NW on Chiwawa River Rd 6200
(last 11 mi very rough dirt & gravel; not recommended for
low-clearance vehicles); along Chiwawa River. $7 with
federal senior pass; others pay $14. 6/15-10/15; 14-day
limit. 8 sites; 20-ft RV limit. Tbls, toilets, cfga, no drkg
wtr. Fishing, hiking.

Atkinson Flat Campground $7
Wenatchee National Forest
15.9 mi NW of Leavenworth on US 2; 4.4 mi N on WA 207;
0.8 mi E on CR 22; 15 mi NW on FR 6100/62/311(Chiwawa
River Rd); last 5 my very roug gravel & dirt. At Chiwawa
River. $7 with federal senior pass; others pay $14. 6/15-
10/15; 14-day limit. 11 sites (RVs under 31 ft). Tbls, toilets,
cfga, no drkg wtr. Mountain climbing; fishing.

Blackpine Horse Camp $8
Wenatchee National Forest
Half mi SW of Leavenworth on US 2; left on Icicle Rd for
18 mi (rd becomes gravel FR 7600after 13 mi & turns left
to cross Icle Creek); camp on left. $8 with federal senior
pass; others pay $16 during 5/1-10/15; free off-season but
no amenities; 14-day limit. 10 sites; 60-ft RV limit. Tbls,
toilets, cfga, drkg wtr (solar pump), horse facilities. Trailhead into Alpine Lakes Wilderness. Horse trails, fishing. At
Black Pine Creek near Icicle Creek.

Bridge Creek Campground $9.50
Wenatchee National Forest
Half mi SE of Leavenworth on US 2; left on Icicle Rd (FR
7600) for about 10 mi; on the left at confluence of Bridge
& Icicle Creeks. $9.50 with federal senior pass; others pay
$19. 4/15-10/31; 14-day limit (road gated off-season). 6
sites (19-ft RV limit). Tbls, toilet, cfga, drkg wtr. Fishing,
hiking.

Chatter Creek Campground $9
Wenatchee National Forest
Half mi SE of Leavenworth on US 2; left on Icicle Rd (FR
7600) for 16 mi. $9 with federal senior pass; others pay
$18. 5/1-10/31; 14-day limit. 12 sites (22-ft RV limit). Tbls,
toilet, cfga, drkg wtr. Fishing, hiking. Along Icicle and
Chatter Creeks.

Chiwawa Horse Camp $7
Wenatchee National Forest
15.9 mi NW of Leavenworth on US 2; 4.4 mi N on SR 207;
right for 0.5 mi E on Chiwawa Loop Rd; stay right at jct &
take 2nd left for 13 mi NW on FR 6100/62/311 (Chiwawa
River Rd). $7 with federal senior pass; others pay $14.
5/1-10/15; 14-day limit. 21 sites (7 large pull-through
spurs). Tbls, toilets, cfga, drkg wtr, horse facilities. Hiking,
fishing, horseback riding.

Deep Creek Campground   FREE
Wenatchee National Forest
15.9 mi NW of Leavenworth on US 2; about 4 mi N on SR
207; right at state park toward Midway; left on FR 6100
for 4 mi; 2 mi SE on FR 6200. Free. 5/1-10/1; 14-day limit.
3 dispersed sites (30-ft RV limit). No amenities, no drkg
wtr or trash service. Hiking, fishing. GPS: 47.8198462,
-120.6339821

Deer Camp Campground   FREE
Wenatchee National Forest
15.9 mi NW of Leavenworth on US 2; about 4 mi N on SR
207; right at state park toward Midway; left on FR 6100 for
4 mi; 2 mi SE on FR 6200; left for 2 mi on FR 2722. Free.
5/1-10/1; 14-day limit. 3 dispersed sites (30-ft RV limit); no
amenities, not maintained. GPS: 47.808125, -120.594134

Eightmile Campground $11
Wenatchee National Forest
Half mi SE of Leavenworth on US 2; 2.9 mi S on CR 71;
4 mi NW on FR 7600 (Icicle Rd). $11 with federal senior
pass; others pay $22. 4/15-10/15; free off-season, but no
amenities; no access when road gated in winter; 14-day
limit. 45 sites (50-ft RV limit). Tbls, toilets, cfga, drkg wtr.
Fishing, hiking. Along Icicle & Eightmile Creeks.

Finner Creek Campground $7
Wenatchee National Forest
15.9 mi NW of Leavenworth on US 2; 4 mi N on WA 207;
1 mi E on CR 22; 15 mi NW on FR 6100/62/311 (Chiwawa
River Rd); along Finner Creek near Chiwawa River. $7 with
federal senior pass; others pay $14. 5/1-10/15; 14-day
limit. 3 sites (30-ft RV limit). Tbls, toilet, cfga, drkg wtr, no
trash service. Fishing, hiking.

Glacier View Campground $9
Wenatchee National Forest
15.9 mi NW of Leavenworth on US 2 to Coles Corner; 3.6
mi N on SR 207; left for 0.3 mi W on Cedar Brae Rd, then
continue 4.8 mi on FR 1600 to end of rd at SW shore of
Lake Wenatchee. $9 with federal senior pass; others pay
$18. 5/1-10/15; 14-day limit. 23 sites (no RVs except van
& truck campers). Tbls, toilets, cfga, drkg wtr. Boating(I),
fishing, swimming, waterskiing, hiking.

Goose Creek Campground $7
Wenatchee National Forest
15.9 mi NW of Leavenworth on US 2W; right on SR 207N for 4.3 mi; take slight right onto Chiwawa Loop Rd for 1.2 mi, then left on Chiwawa River Rd for 3.2 mi; right on FR 6208 for 423 ft & right on FR 6100 to campground on right; along Goose Creek near Chiwawa River. $7 with federal senior pass; others pay $14. 5/15-11/1; 14-day limit. 29 sites (no RV size limit). Tbls, toilets, cfga, drkg wtr. Fishing. Motorcycle trail access.

Grasshopper Meadows Campground FREE
Wenatchee National Forest
15.9 mi NW of Leavenworth on US 2; 10.5 mi N on WA 207; 8 mi NW on FR 6400 (White River Rd). Free. 5/1-10/31; closed off-season; 14-day limit. 5 sites (30-ft RV limit). Tbls, toilets, cfga, firewood, no drkg wtr. Berry picking, fishing. Elev 2000 ft. At White River.

Ida Creek Campground $9.50
Wenatchee National Forest
From Leavenworth, 0.8 mi S on US 2W; left onto Icicle Rd (FR 7600) for 12.5 mi to camp; at Ida Creek & Icicle Creek. $7 with federal senior pass; others pay $14. 5/1-10/15; 14-day limit. 10 sites; 30-ft RV limit. Tbls, toilets, cfga, drkg wtr. Fishing, hiking.

Johnny Creek Campground $9.50
Wenatchee National Forest
From Leavenworth, 0.8 mi S on US 2W; left onto Icicle Rd (FR 7600) for 12.5 mi to camp; at confluence of Johnny & Icicle Creeks. Upper campground: $9.50 with federal senior pass; others pay $19. Lower campground $11 with senior pass; others pay $22. 4/20-10/15; free off-season, but no amenities; 14-day limit. 65 sites; 50-ft RV limit. Tbls, toilets, cfga, drkg wtr. Fishing, hiking.

Lake Creek FREE
Wenatchee National Forest
15.9 mi NW of Leavenworth of US 2; 8.4 mi N on Hwy 207; 10.5 mi W on FR 6500/6504; at Little Wenatchee River. Free. 5/1-11/1; 14-day limit. 8 sites; no RV size limit. Tbls, toilets, cfga, no drkg wtr. Fishing, berry-picking. GPS: 47.8756702, -121.0134327.

Little Wenatchee Ford Trailhead FREE
Wenatchee National Forest
15.9 mi NW of Leavenworth of US 2; 8.4 mi N on SR 207; 15.5 mi W on FR 6500/6504. Free, but no amenities. All year; 14-day limit. Former developed campground decommissioned and closed, now available as dispersed site. Horseback riding, hiking. GPS: 47.9177, -121.087

Meadow Creek Campground FREE
Wenatchee National Forest
From Leavenworth, 15.9 mi NW on US 2; 4.4 mi NE on SR 207; 1.2 mi E on CR 22 (Chiwawa Loop Rd), keeping right

at intersection; take 2nd left (NE) onto Chiwawa River Rd for 2.4 mi; left on Meadow Creek Rd (FR 6300) for 2.4 mi; along Chiwawa River. Free. 5/1-10/31; 14-day limit (closed off-season). 4 sites (30-ft RV limit); 1 acre. Tbls, no toilets, cfga, no drkg wtr. Fishing.

Napeequa Crossing Campground FREE
Wenatchee National Forest
15.9 mi NW of Leavenworth on US 2; 10.5 mi N on SR 207; 5 mi NW on FR 6400 (White River Rd). Free. 5/1-10/31; 14-day limit; closed off-season. 5 sites; 30-ft RV limit. Tbls, toilets, cfga, no drkg wtr. Hiking; berry picking; fishing. User operated. Elev 2000 ft; 2 acres. Entrance to Glacier Peak Wilderness. Twin Lakes Trail.

Nineteen Mile Campground $7
Wenatchee National Forest
From Leavenworth 15 mi NW on US 2; right (N) for 4.3 mi on SR 207; 1.2 mi E on CR 22 (Chiwawa Loop Rd, stayin-gright at intersection; take second left (NW) on Chiwawa River Rd (FR 6200) for 18 mi; along Chiwawa River (last 10 mi very rough gravel & dirt, not recommended for low-clearance vehicles. $7 with federal senior pass; others pay $14. 6/15-10/15; 14-day limit. 4 sites (30-ft RV limit). Tbls, toilet, cfga, no drkg wtr, no trash service. Fishing, hiking.

Phelps Creek Campground $7
Wenatchee National Forest
15.9 mi NW on US 2; 4 mi N on WA 207; 1 mi E on CR 22; 21 mi NW on FR 6100/62/311; near confluence of Phelps Creek & Chiwawa River. $7 with federal senior pass; others pay $14. 6/1-10/15; 14-day limit; no access off-season. 7 sites plus 6 sites in equestrian section; 30-ft RV limit. Tbls, toilets, cfga, horse unloading ramp, corral, parking, no drkg wtr. Mountain climbing; fishing; horseback riding. Elev 2800 ft. Entrance to Glacier Peak Wilderness. Closed 2017 due to wilderness fire.

Rainy Creek FREE
Wenatchee National Forest
From Leavenworth, 15.9 mi NW on US 2; right on SR 207N for 10.5 mi; continue onto Little Wenatchee River Rd for 6.1 mi, then left 1 mi on FR 6701 (Rainy Creek Rd). Free. All year; 14-day limit. 30-ft RV limit. Tbls, toilet, cfga, no drkg wtr.

Riverbend Campground $7
Wenatchee National Forest
15.9 mi NW of Leavenworth on US 2; 4.4 mi N on SR 207; 1 mi E (right) on CR 22 (Chiwawa Loop Rd), staying right at the intersection, then take 2nd left on Chiwawa River Rd (FR 6200) for 14 mi; along Chiwawa River. $7 with federal senior pass; others pay $14. 5/1-10/15; free off-season, but no amenities; 14-day limit. 6 sites (30-ft RV limit). Tbls, toilet, cfga, no drkg wtr, no trash service. Hiking, fishing.

Rock Creek Campground $7
Wenatchee National Forest
15.9 mi NW of Leavenworth on US 2; 4.4 mi N on SR 207; 1 mi E (right) on CR 22 (Chiwawa Loop Rd), staying right at the intersection, then take 2nd left on Chiwawa River Rd (FR 6200) for 14.6 mi; along Rock Creek at Chiwawa River, next to Chiwawa Horse Camp. $7 with federal senior pass; others pay $14. 5/1-10/15; 14-day limit. 4 sites; 30-ft RV limit. Tbls, toilets, cfga, no drkg wtr, no trash service. Fishing, hiking.

Rock Island Campground $9
Wenatchee National Forest
Half mi NW of Leavenworth on US 2; left on Icicle Rd about 8.5 mi, continuing straight on FR 7600 anotehr 8 mi; take slight right onto FR 7609; camp on left near Boggy Creek & Icicle Creek. $9 with federal senior pass; others pay $18 during 5/1-10/15; free off-season but no amenities; 14-day limit. 10 RV sites (22-ft limit). Tbls, toilets, cfga, drkg wtr. Fishing, hiking trails, berry-picking. Elev 2900 ft.

Schaefer Creek Campground $7
Wenatchee National Forest
15.9 mi NW of Leavenworth on US 2; 4.4 mi N on SR 207; 1 mi N (right) on CR 22 (Chiwawa Loop Rd), staying right at intersection, then taking 2nd left onto Chiwawa Loop Rd (FR 6200) about 15 mi; along Chiwawa River. $7 with federal senior pass; others pay $14. 5/1-10/115; 14-day limit. 10 sites (30-ft RV limit). Tbls, toilet, cfga, no drkg wtr. River. Fishing.

White Pine Campground   FREE
Wenatchee National Forest
15.9 mi NW of Leavenworth on US 2; half mi W on FR 266 (White Pine Rd). Free. 5/1-10/31; 14-day limit. 5 RV/tent sites; no RV size limit. Tbls, toilets, cfga, firewood, no drkg wtr or trash service. Berrypicking; fishing; horseback riding.

LONG BEACH
Snag Lake Recreation Site $10
Department of Natural Resources
From jct with SR 401 at settlement of Naselle (E of Long Beach & S of Loomis Lake), NW on SR 4 to milepost 3; 1 mi N on C-Line (a 2-lane gravel rd that goes uphill while right fork goes to Naselle Youth Camp); turn right on C-4000 Rd for 1.4 mi, then left on C-2600 Rd (gravel, 1-lane) for .6 mi; right on C-2620 Rd for qtr mi. $10 daily or $30 annual Discover Pass. All year; 10-day limit. 4 primitive sites. Tbls, toilet, cfga, no drkg wtr. Hiking, fishing piers.

MARBLEMOUNT
Cascade Islands Campground   FREE
Mt. Baker-Snoqualmie National Forest
From Marblemount, 0.5 mi E on SR 20; continue stright over bridge on Cascade River Rd at 10 mi until 1 mi after it curves S; right on unpaved FR 1550 Rd about 1 mi N parallel to Cascade River; right (E) on campground access

rd just after gravel pit; at W shore of river. Free dispersed primitive sites. No facilities, no drkg wtr. Fishing. GPS: 48.525676, -121.390681

Colonial Creek $8
Ross Lake National Recreation Area
North Cascade National Park
From Newhalem (13 mi N of Marblemount), about mi E on SR 20; left on Diablo Rd. $8 with federal senior pass; others pay $16 (free about 10/1-5/1 or until rds closed by snow. 142 sites (18 open all year); 14-day limit. 32-ft RV limit. Tbls, flush toilets, cfga, drkg wtr, dump; no wtr during free period. Boating, hiking, fishing, nature walk, fishing pier. No park entry fee. At N shore of Diablo Lake.

Goodell Creek $8
Ross Lake National Recreation Area
North Cascade National Park
From Newhalem (13 mi N of Marblemount), half mi W on SR 20; on left at N shore of Skagit River. $8 with federal senior pass; others pay $16. Main campground 5/26-9/6; 14-day limit. 19 sites (22 ft RV limit). Tbls, toilets, cfga, drkg wtr. Fishing, boating, hiking, rafting. 4 acres.

Marble Creek Campground $7
Mt. Baker-Snoqualmie National Forest
8 mi E of Marblemount on CR 3528; 1 mi S on FR 1530 (.6 mi of access rd is narrow and winding). $7 with federal senior pass; others pay $14 (doubles $20). 5/24-9/24; 14-day limit. 23 sites; 32-ft RV limit. Tbls, toilets, cfga, firewood, no drkg wtr. Mountain climbing; hunting; hiking; fishing. Elev 900 ft. Adjacent to Cascade River.

Mineral Park Campground $12
Mount Baker-Snoqualmie National Forest
15 mi E of Marblemount on CR 3528 (Cascade River Rd); campground is on the right; quarter mi farther on the right, across the bridge, is more of the same campground (narrow and winding rd). $12 (doubles $22). 5/24-9/10; 14-day limit. 22 sites up to 60 ft. Tbls, toilets, cfga, no drkg wtr. Hiking; mountain climbing; fishing. Elev 1400 ft; 7 acres. Scenic.

Newhalem Creek $8
Ross Lake National Recreation Area
North Cascade National Park
From Newhalem (13 mi N of Marblemount), W on SR 20 to milepost 120; at shore of Skagit River. $8 with federal senior pass; others pay $16. 5/19-9/18; 14-day limit. 51 RV tent sites (Loop C closed for 2017); 45-ft RV limit. Tbls, flush toilets, cfga, drkg wtr, dump. Visitor center. Fishing, boating, hiking, interpretive trail. 22 acres.

METALINE FALLS
Backcountry Camping   FREE
Pend Oreille River Canyon
Bureau of Land Management

N of Metaline Falls to Boundary Dam on both sides of Pend Oreille River; free primitive camping only on BLM lands. All year; 14-day limit. No facilities. Boating, fishing, hiking.

Cliffs Park FREE
Lake Umatilla
John Day Lock & Dam
Corps of Engineers
From Goldendale, 10 mi S on US 97 toward Maryhill; right (W) about 4 mi on SR 14; S on John Day Rd by old aluminum plant; follow until paved rd becomes gravel. Free. All year. Primitive undesignated sites. Tbls, toilet, cfga, no drkg wtr. Fishing, boating(l).

East Sullivan Campground $9
Colville National Forest
From just N of Metaline Falls on SR 31, 12.9 mi E on CR 9345 (Sullivan Lake Rd); 1 mi E on FR 22 (Sullivan Creek Rd); at NE end of Sullivan Lake. $9 with federal senior pass; others pay $18. About 5/15-9/30; 14-day limit. 38 sites (55-ft RV limit). Tbls, toilets, cfga, drkg wtr, dump. Swimming beach & dock, boating(l), interpretive trail, fishing. Public airstrip; pilots & passengers may camp free at edges of airstrip in return for maintaining strip/fence; tbls, cfga provided.

Mill Pond Campground $9
Colville National Forest
From just N of Metaline Falls on SR 31, 3.9 mi E on CR 9345 (Sullivan Lake Rd); 1 mi NW of ranger station. $9 with federal senior pass during MD-LD; others pay $18. Fee is $9 LD-10/31, but no wtr or trash service ($4.50 with senior pass). 10 sites, typically 42 ft. Tbls, drkg wtr, cfga, toilets. Boating(carry-in access; no gas mtrs). Handicap interpretive trail, 1.5-mi hiking trail, fishing.

West Sullivan Campground $9
Colville National Forest
From just N of Metaline Falls on SR 31, 12 mi E on CR 9345 (Sullivan Lake Rd); 1 mi S on FR 22 (Sullivan Creek Rd); at N end of Sullivan Lake across rd from ranger station. $9 with federal senior pass during MD-9/15; others pay $18. Fee is $9 during 9/16-10/31 with reduced services ($4.50 with senior pass). 14-day limit. 10 sites (25-ft RV limit). Tbls, flush & pit toilets, cfga, drkg wtr, dump (at East Sullivan). Picnic shelter, swimming change house, swimming beach, boating(l), hiking trails, fishing. Public airstrip; pilots & passengers may camp free at edges of airstrip in return for maintaining strip/fence; tbls, cfga provided.

MORTON

Adams Fork Campground $8
Gifford Pinchot National Forest
From settlement of Randle (14 mi E of Morton) at jct with US 12, 0.9 mi S on SR 131; bear left at "Y" on FR 23 for 17.7 mi; at next "Y," bear left on FR 21 for 4.6 mi; right after

campground sign onto FR 56. $8 with federal senior pass; others pay $16. 6/15-9/10; 14-day limit. 22 sites; 22-ft RV limit. Tbls, toilets, cfga, drkg wtr. Hiking, mountain biking, bridle trails.

Elbe Hills ORV Campground $10
Elbe Hills State Forest
Department of Natural Resources
From settlement of Elbe (20 mi N of Morton), 6.3 mi E on SR 706; before reaching village of Ashford, left on paved & gravel Stoner Rd (278 Ave E) for 3.7 mi (keep right); left 0.1 mi to trailhead. $10 daily or $30 annual Discover Pass. All year; 10-day limit. 20 sites. Toilet, cfga, tbls, no drkg wtr. Group shelter, motorized trails. ORV trailhead.

Blue Lake Creek Campground $12
Gifford Pinchot National Forest
From settlement of Randle (14 mi E of Morton) at jct with US 12, 0.9 mi S on SR 131; bear left at "Y" on SR 23 (Cispus Rd) for 15.2 mi. $12. 5/22-9/24; 14-day limit. 11 sites; 22 to 30-ft RV limit. Tbls, toilets, cfga, no drkg wtr. Hiking, mountain biking, horseback riding trails. Closed in 2017 due to flood-damaged rds.

Chain-of-Lakes $12
Gifford Pinchot National Forest
From settlement of Randle (14 mi E of Morton) at jct with US 12, 3.1 mi S on SR 131; 28.9 mi SE on FR 23; 1.2 mi N on FR 2329; 1 mi N on FR 022. $12. 6/22-9/10; 14-day limit. 3 sites (RVs under 17 ft). Tbls, toilets, cfga, firewood, no drkg wtr. Fishing; boating; swimming; hiking; canoeing. Elev 4400 ft; 3 acres. Rolling hills. Lake. 3 mi N of Mount Adams Wilderness Area. Trailhead for Trail 116 to Keenes Horse Camp. Non-campers pay $5 day use fee. Closed in 2014 due to restroom damage; still closed 2017. Check current status before arrival (360-497-1100).

Horseshoe Lake $12
Gifford Pinchot National Forest
From settlement of Randle (14 mi E of Morton) at jct of US 12, 3.1 mi S on SR 131; 28.9 mi SE on FR 23; 6.8 mi NE on FR 2329; 1.3 mi NW on FR 078. $12. 6/22-9/10; 14-day limit. 12 poorly defined sites (RVs under 16 ft). Tbls, toilet, cfga, no drkg wtr. Boating(d-elec mtrs), fishing, berry picking, swimming, hiking. Elev 4200 ft; 3 acres, picturesque. 2 mi NW of Mount Adams. About 12 mi of gravel rd to camp; some access unusuable due to flooding in 2017; check status before arrival (360-497-1100).

Iron Creek Campground $10
Gifford Pinchot National Forest
From settlement of Randle (14 mi E of Morton) at jct with US 12, 0.9 mi S on SR 131; bear right at "Y" on FR 25 for 7.6 mi, then left, staying on FR 25 for 1 mi; on left; along Cispus River. $10 with federal senior pass; others pay $20 (double sites $38). 5/18-9/10; 14-day limit. 98 sites; 40-ft RV limit. Tbls, toilets, cfga, drkg wtr. Fishing, hiking trail.

Keenes Horse Camp $7
Gifford Pinchot National Forest
From settlement of Randle (14 mi E of Morton) at jct with US 12, 3.1 mi on SR 131; 28.9 mi SE on FR 23; 6 mi SE on FR 2329; qtr mi W on FR 073; at Spring Creek. $7 with federal senior pass; others pay $14. 6/22-9/10; 14-day limit. 13 scattered sites; 40-ft RV limit. Old loop limited to small trailers & pickup campers, larger rigs in new loop. Toilets, tbls, cfga, no drkg wtr. Mountain climbing; horseback riding; fishing. Elev 4300 ft. 2.4 mi NW of Mount Adams Wilderness. Corral, wtr for horses. Limited access due to flood damage; check current status at 360-497-1100.

Killen Creek Campground $12
Gifford Pinchot National Forest
From settlement of Randle (14 mi E of Morton) at jct with US 12, 3.1 mi S on SR 131; 28.9 mi SE on FR 23; 7 mi SE on FR 2329; qtr mi W on FR 073. $12. 6/22-9/10; 14-day limit. 9 sites (RVs under 22 ft). Tbls, toilets, cfga, no drkg wtr. Mountain climbing; hiking; fishing; berrypicking. Elev 4400 ft; 4 acres. Trailhead for climbing Mount Adams N face. Stream. In 2017, some rds my be unusable due to flooding; call 360-497-1100 for current status.

North Fork Campground $9
Gifford Pinchot National Forest
From settlement of Randle (14 mi E of Morton) at jct with US 12, 0.9 mi S on SR 131; bear left at "Y" onto FR 23 for 10.9 mi; site on left. $9 with federal senior pass; others pay $18. 5/18-9/24; 14-day limit. 32 sites; 32-ft RV limit. Tbls, toilets, cfga, drkg wtr. Hiking, biking trails. Section of camp decommissioned in 2017 due to hazardous trees.

Olallie Lake $12
Gifford Pinchot National Forest
From settlement of Randle (14 mi E of Morton) at jct with US 12, 3.1 mi S on SR 131; 28.9 mi SE on FR 23; 1 mi SW on FR 2334. $12. 6/22-9/24; 14-day limit. 5 sites (RVs under 23 ft). Tbls, toilet, cfga, firewood, no drkg wtr. Boating(no mtrs); fishing; berry picking. Elev 3700 ft; 3 acres. Scenic. Excellent view of Mount Adams. Canyon Ridge Trail. In 2017, some rds may be unusable due to flooding; call 360-497-1100 for current status.

Sahara Creek Horse Camp $10
Elbe Hills State Forest
Department of Natural Resources
From settlement of Elbe (15 mi N of Morton), 5.3 mi E on SR 706; left to camp. $10 daily or $30 annual Discover Pass. All year; 10-day limit. 20 sites. Tbls, toilets, cfga, drkg wtr, horse facilities. Horseback riding, mountain biking, hiking on 50 mi of trails.

Takhlakh Lake Campground $9
Gifford Pinchot National Forest
From settlement of Randle (14 mi E of Morton) at jct with US 12, 0.9 mi S on SR 131; bear left at "Y" on FR 23 for 17.7

mi; bear right at second "Y," following Takhlakh Lake sign on FR 23 for 12.8 mi (rough washboard gravel); left after next lake sign for 0.7 mi on paved FR 2329; continue right on FR 2329 at intersection for 0.7 mi to site; at lake's N shore. $9 with federal senior pass; others pay $18. 6/25-9/24; 14-day limit. 53 sites; 22-ft RV limit. Tbls, toilets, cfga, grey wtr stations, no drkg wtr. Fishing, boating, hiking trails. In 2017, some rds may be unusable due to flooding; call 360-497-1100 for current status.

Tower Rock Campground $9
Gifford Pinchot National Forest
From settlement of Randle (14 mi E of Morton) at jct with US 12, 0.9 mi S on SR 131; bear right at "Y" on FR 25 for 7.6 mi, then left, staying on FR 25 for 1.1 mi; left on FR 76 for 5.5 mi, then right, staying on FR 76 (Cispus Rd) for 0.7 mi; left at campground sign; at Cispus River. $9 with federal senior pass; others pay $18. 5/18-9/24; 14-day limit. 21 sites; 22-ft RV limit. Tbls, toilet, cfga, drkg wtr. Fishing.

Walupt Lake Campground $9
Gifford Pinchot National Forest
From settlement of Randle (14 mi E of Morton) at jct with US 12, 0.9 mi S on SR 131; bear left at "Y" on FR 23 (Cispus Rd) for 17.7 mi; bear left at second "Y" onto FR 21 for 6.5 mi; bear right at third "Y" on gravel FR 21 for 6 mi; right at Walupt Lake sign on paved FR 2160 for 4.6 mi. $9 with federal senior pass; others pay $18. 6/22-9/24; 14-day limit. 44 sites; 22-ft RV limit. Tbls, toilets, cfga, drkg wtr. Boating(l), fishing, hiking & bridle trails. In 2017, some rds may be unusable due to flooding; call 360-497-1100 for current status.

Winston Creek State Recreation Site $10
Department of Natural Resources
10 mi W of Morton on US 12 between mileposts 82-83; S 3.6 mi on Winston Creek Rd; left on Longbell Rd 1 mi (portions of rd are rough). $10 daily or $30 annual Discover Pass. 4/15-12/15; 10-day limit. 12 sites. Tbls, toilets, cfga, drkg wtr. Hiking, hunting.

MOSES LAKE
Potholes State Park $12
25 mi SW of Moses Lake on Hwy 170. $12 base. All year; 10-day limit. Base fee for 61 primitive RV/tent sites; utility sites $25 base (50-ft RV limit). WA seniors with $75 off-season pass camp free without hookups ($10 with hookups) during 10/1-3/31 & Sun-Thurs in April. Primitive sites have cfga, nearby drkg wtr & toilets; utility sites have campstove, drkg wtr, cfga, tbls, trash disposal, flush toilets, showers, ump. Boating(ld), fishing, waterskiing, volleyball, horseshoe pit, swimming, waterskiing. 640 acres.

NACHES
American Forks Campground $10
Wenatchee National Forest
From settlement of Cliffdell (20 mi NW of Naches), 7

mi W on SR 410 to milepost 88.4; left at Bumping Lake Recreation Area sign on Bumping River Rd (FR 1800); cross bridge, then left at sign; at confluence of Bumping & American Rivers. $10. About MD-LD; free off-season, but no services; toilets & wtr at nearby Cedar Springs Campground. 14-day limit. 12 sites; 30-ft RV limit. Tbls, toilets, cfga, no drkg wtr. Fishing, hiking.

Bumping Lake Campgrounds　　　　　　　　$9
Bumping Lake Recreation Area
Wenatchee National Forest
From settlement of Cliffdell (20 mi NW of Naches), 7 mi W on SR 410; left at Bumping Lake Recreation Area sign for 11.2 mi on FR 1800 (Bumping River Rd); right at campground sign; at S shore of lake (upper section first right; lower section is at end of road on left). $9 with federal senior pass; others pay $18 at 23-site lower camp; $10 with senior pass at 45-site upper camp; others pay $20. 5/22-9/24; Free off-season but no services or drkg wtr; wtr at nearby Cedar Springs Campground. 14-day limit. 50-ft RV limit in lower campground, 30-ft limit upper campground. Tbls, toilets, cfga, drkg wtr. Fishing, hiking.

Bumping Crossing　　　　　　　　　　CLOSED
Wenatchee National Forest
4.3 mi W of Naches on US 12; 28.5 mi N on SR 410; 10 mi S on FR 2000; at Bumping River. Decommissioned as campground and closed permanently. No vehicles on Bumping River shoreline.

Cedar Springs Campground　　　　　　　$8
Wenatchee National Forest
From settlement of Cliffdell (20 mi NW of Naches) 7 mi W on SR 410; left at Bumping Lake Recreation Area sign for 0.5 mi on FR 1800 (Bumping Lake Rd). $8 with federal senior pass; others pay $16. 5/24-9/10; 14-day limit. 14 single sites (some pull-through); 22-ft RV limit. Tbls, toilets, cfga, drkg wtr. Fishing, hiking.

Clear Lake North Campground　　　　　$10
Wenatchee National Forest
31 mi W of Naches on US 12; left (S) for .9 mi on CR 1200 (Tieton Reservoir Rd); left for half mi FR 740; below Clear Lake Dam between Clear Lake & Rimrock Lake. $10. 5/1-10/31; 14-day limit. 34 sites on 33 acres (RVs under 23 ft). Tbls, toilets, cfga, drkg wtr at Clear Lake boat launch. Fishing, rafting, boating(l-1 mi; r-3 mi). Elev 3100 ft.

Clear Lake South & Boat Landing　　　$10
Wenatchee National Forest
31 mi W of Naches on US 12; left (S) 0.5 mi S on FR 1200 (Tieton Reservoir Rd); left (S) 1 mi on FR 740. $10 at campground just beyond Clear Lake Dam crossing. Some dispersed sites available that were previously free but now are $5 daily or $30 annually. 5/1-10/31; 14-day limit. 22 sites (RVs under 22 ft). Tbls, toilets, cfga, drkg wtr. Fishing; boating(l). Elev 3100 ft.

Cottonwood Campground　　　　　　　　$8
Wenatchee National Forest
From settlement of Cliffdell (20 mi NW of Naches), 2.8 mi W on SR 410 to milepost 99.5; at Naches River; S side of rd. $8 with federal senior pass; others pay $16. 5/10-9/24; 14-day limit. 16 sites (some pull-through); 22-ft trailer limit. Tbls, toilets, cfga, drkg wtr. Fishing.

Cougar Flat Campground　　　　　　　　$8
Wenatchee National Forest
From settlement of Cliffdell (20 mi NW of Naches), 7 mi W on SR 410 to milepost 88.4; left at Bumping Lake Recreation Area sign for 5.9 mi on FR 1800 (Bumping Lake Rd). $8 with federal senior pass; others pay $16. 5/24-9/10; 14-day limit. 12 sites up to 40 ft; 20-ft trailer limit. Tbls, toilet, cfga, drkg wtr. Fishing, hiking trails.

Crow Creek Campground　　　　　　　　$10
Wenatchee National Forest
4.3 mi W of Naches on US 12W; continue onto SR 410 for 24.2 mi N; right (NW) on FR 19 for 3.2 mi; half mi W on FR 1902; near Little Naches River. $10. About 5/15-LD; 14-day limit. 15 sites; 30-ft RV limit. Tbl, toilets, cfga, no drkg wtr. OHV activities, hiking, fishing, hunting.

Dog Lake Campground　　　　　　　　　$8
Wenatchee National Forest
36.6 mi W of Naches on US 12 (past Rimrock Lake) nearly to forest's W boundary (or 22 mi NE of Packwood). $8. 6/16-11/1; 14-day limit. 8 sites; 20-ft trailer limit, 24-ft motorhome limit. Tbls, toilets, cfga, no drkg wtr. Boating(l.), fishing, hiking.

Halfway Flat Campground　　　　　　　$10
Wenatchee National Forest
4.4 mi W of Naches on US 12; continue onto SR 410 for 20.9 mi NW; left (NW) for 2.5 mi on FR 1704 (Old River Rd); at Naches River. $10. 5/15-11/15; 14-day limit. 11 sites for large RVs. Tbls, toilets, cfga, drkg wtr. Hiking, fishing, OHV activities.

Halfway Flat Dispersed Camp　　　　　$8
Wenatchee National Forest
4.4 mi W of Naches on US 12; continue onto SR 410 for 20.9 mi W; left on FR 1704 (Old River Rd) for 2.5 mi; just ouside Halfway Flat Campground. $8. No tbls, toilets or drkg wtr. Hiking, fishing.

Hause Creek Campground　　　　　　　　$9
Wenatchee National Forest
From jct with Naches Ave in Naches, 4.4 mi W on US 12; at jct with SR 410, continue 16.8 mi SW on US 12; at Tieton River below Rimrock Lake Dam. $9 with federal senior pass; others pay $18. 5/24-9/25; 14-day limit. 42 sites (some pull-through); 30-ft RV limit. Tbls, flush toilets, cfga, drkg wtr, grey wtr stations. Fishing. Note: Open after being closed in 2016; no wtr available in 2017.

Hells Crossing Campground $7
Wenatchee National Forest
From settlement of Cliffdell (20 mi NW of Naches), 11.8 mi W on SR 410 at milepost 83.4; along American River. $7 with federal senior pass; others pay $14. 5/24-9/24; 14-day limit. 18 sites up to 60 ft (some pull-through), but 20-ft trailer limit. Tbls, toilets, cfga, drkg wtr at W end only. Hiking trails (Pacific Crest Trail), fishing.

Indian Creek Campground $10
Wenatchee National Forest
From jct with Naches Ave in Naches, 4.4 mi W on US 12; at jct with SR 410, continue 25.9 mi SW on US 12; at N side of Rimrock Lake. $10 with federal senior pass; others pay $20. 5/26-9/10; 14-day limit. 39 sites; 32-ft RV limit. Tbls, toilets, cfga, drkg wtr. Fishing, boating.

Indian Creek Recreation Area FREE
Dispersed Camping Sites
Wenatchee National Forest
From jct with Naches Ave in Naches, 4.4 mi W on US 12; at jct with SR 410, continue 25 mi SW on US 12; 1 mi SW on FR 1200 (Tieton Reservoir Rd); qtr mi S on FR 740, then left (NE) on FR 746; just E of Indian Creek Campground; near N side of Rimrock Lake.

Jayhawk Flat Dispersed Areas FREE
Wenatchee National Forest
22 mi W of Naches on US 12; about 9 mi SW on FR 12 (just past South Fork Camp). Free. All year; 14-day limit. No facilities except cfga; no drkg wtr. Note: Numerous dispersed, free camping areas exist in the area.

Kaner Flat Campground $12
Wenatchee National Forest
4.4 mi W of Naches on SR 12; continue straight NW for 24.2 mi on SR 410; Right for 2.5 mi on FR 19 (Little Naches Rd); near Little Naches River. $12. About 5/15-11/20; 14-day limit. 41 sites (includes 6 double sites, 1 triple); 30-ft RV limit. Tbls, toilets (1 flush), cfga, drkg wtr. Old campsite for wagon trains traveling Old Naches Trail. Fishing, hiking trails. Near Little Naches River. Popular motorcycle area. Elev 2678 ft.

La Wis Wis Campground $10
Gifford Pinchot National Forest
From Packwood (30 mi W of Naches) at jct with Skate Rd, 6.6 mi E on US 12; left at campground sign. $10 with federal senior pass; others pay $20 (double site $38). 5/18-9/24; 14-day limit. 115 sites; 40-ft RV limit. Tbls, pit & flush toilets, cfga, drkg wtr. Hiking trails, fishing.

Little Naches Campground $7
Wenatchee National Forest
From settlement of Cliffdell (20 mi NW of Naches), 3.3 mi W on SR 410; right on FR 19 (Little Naches Rd) for 0.25 mi; on left at Naches River. $7 with federal senior pass; others

pay $14. 5/26-9/19; 14-day limit. 21 sites up to 50 ft; 32-ft trailer limit. Tbls, toilets, cfga, drkg wtr. Fishing.

Lodgepole Campground $9
Wenatchee National Forest
From settlement of Clifdell (20 mi NW of Naches), 18.7 mi W on SR 410 to milepost 75.8; at American River. $9 with federal senior pass; others pay $18. 5/26-9/10; 14-day limit. 33 sites up to 42 ft (some pull-through), but 20-ft trailer limit. Tbls, toilets, cfga, drkg wtr. Fishing, rafting, hiking.

Longmire Meadow Campground $5
Wenatchee National Forest
4.4 mi W of Naches on US 12; continue straight for 24.2 mi NW on SR 410; right on Little Naches Rd (FR 19) for 4 mi; on the left. Free with $30 annual NW pass; otherwise $5 daily. Developed & dispersed sites. Toilets, tbls, cfga, no drkg wtr (available at nearby Kaner Flat). Hiking, OHV staging area, motorcycle trails nearby.

Peninsula Campground $8
Wenatchee National Forest
22 mi W of Naches on US 12; left (S) at Lost Lake Rd onto FR 12 (Tieton Reservoir Rd) for 3 mi; 1.5 mi W on FR 711; at E shore of Rimrock Lake. $8. 4/15-11/15; 14-day limit. 19 dispersed sites. Toilets, cfga, no drkg wtr. Boating(l), fishing, swimming, hiking.

Peterson Prairie Campground $8
Gifford Pinchot National Forest
From settlement of Trout Lake (15 mi N of White Salmon), 5.5 mi SW SR 141 to forest boundary; continue 2.5 mi W on FR 24; on left. $8 with federal senior pass; others pay $16. 6/12-9/10; 14-day limit. 27 sites; 32-ft RV limit. Tbls, toilets, cfga, drkg wtr. Huckleberry fields.

Pleasant Valley Campground $8
Wenatchee National Forest
From settlement of Cliffdell (20 mi NW of Naches), 15.2 mi W on SR 410; on S side. $8 with federal senior pass; others pay $16. 5/26-9/10; 14-day limit. 16 sites; 32-ft RV limit. Tbls, toilets, cfga, drkg wtr. Hiking trails, fishing.

Ponderosa Camp $5
Wenatchee National Forest
4.4 mi W of Nacheson US 12; continue NW on SR 410 for 24.2 mi; right on Little Naches Rd (FR 19) for 3 mi; right for 1 mi on FR 1903. Free with $30 annual NW pass; otherwise $5 daily. All year; 14-day limit. Hiking, OHV activities.

Sawmill Flat Campground $9
Wenatchee National Forest
From settlement of Cliffdell (20 mi NW of Naches), 2.2 mi W on SR 410 to milepost 93.2; at Naches River. $9 with federal senior pass; others pay $18. 5/24-9/24; 14-day

limit. 24 sites up to 38 ft (some pull-through), but 24-ft trailer limit. Tbls, toilet, cfga, drkg wtr. Fishing.

Soda Springs Campground $9
Wenatchee National Forest
From settlement of Cliffdell (20 mi NW of Naches), 7 mi W on SR 410 to milepost 88.4; left at Bumping Lake Recreation Area sign for 4.8 mi on FR 1800 (Bumping Lake Rd); at Bumping River. $9 with federal senior pass; others pay $18. 5/24-9/24; 14-day limit. 26 sites (some pull-through); 30-ft RV limit. Tbls, toilets, cfga, drkg wtr. Fishing, hiking trail.

South Fork Bay Dispersed Camping $8
Wenatchee National Forest
22 mi W of Naches on US 12; about 8 mi SW on FR 12 (in same vicinity as South Fork of Tieton River); near Rimrock Lake. $8. About 5/15-9/15; 14-day limit. 15 dispersed sites. Toilets, cfga, no drkg wtr. Fishing, swimming. Note: Numerous dispersed camping opportunities in locale.

South Fork Tieton River $8
Wenatchee National Forest
22 mi W of Naches on US 12; about 8 mi SW on FR 12 (Tieton Reservoir Rd); on South Fork of Tieton River. $8. About 5/15-9/15; 14-day limit. 15 dispersed sites. Toilets, cfga, no drkg wtr. Fishing, swimming. Note: Numerous dispersed camping opportunities are in the vicinity.

Summit Creek FREE
Gifford Pinchot National Forest
From Packwood (30 mi W of Naches), 8.9 mi NE on US 12; 2.1 mi N on FR 45 & FR 4510. Free. 6/15-9/5; 14-day limit. 6 primitive tent or pickup camper sites. Tbls, toilet, cfga, no drkg wtr. Fishing. Elev 2400 ft; 2 acres. Rough driveway into campground.

Tieton Pond Campground $8
Wenatchee National Forest
From Naches, W on US 12 to milepost 152; W on FR 1304 to campground; on Tieton Pond. $8. MD-LD; 14-day limit. Tbls, toilet, cfga, no drkg wtr. Hiking, fishing. GPS: 46.691925, -121.075770

White Pass Lake $8
Wenatchee National Forest
About 50 mi W of Naches on US 12 (past Rimrock Lake) nearly to forest's W boundary; right on FR 498 to Leech Lake's NE shore (19 mi NE of Packwood). $8 for camping & day use. 6/1-11/15; 14-day limit. 16 sites; 20-ft RV limit. Tbls, toilets, cfga, no drkg wtr. Boating(l), fly fishing, hiking. Closed in 2017 due to hazardous trees; check current status before arrival.

Willows Campground $7
Wenatchee National Forest
From jct with Naches Ave in Naches, 4.4 mi W on US 12;

at jct with SR 410, continue 15 mi SW on US 12; at Tieton River. $7 with federal senior pass; others pay $14. 5/21-9/18; 14-day limit. 16 sites up to 35 ft, but 20-ft trailer limit. Tbls, toilets, cfga, drkg wtr. Fishing.

Windy Point Campground $7
Wenatchee National Forest
From jct with Naches Ave in Naches, 4.4 mi W on US 12; at jct with SR 410, continue 8 mi SW on US 12; at Tieton River. $7 with federal senior pass; others pay $14. 5/20-9/26; 14-day limit. 15 sites up to 35 ft, but 22-ft trailer limit. Tbls, toilets, cfga, drkg wtr. Fishing.

NEWPORT
Browns Lake Campground $8
Colville National Forest
From Newport, 15 mi N on SR 20 to settlement of Usk; right on 5th St, then cross Pend Oreille River; 14 mi NE on CR 3389 (Kings Lake Rd); E on FR 128 to camp on S shore of lake. $8 with federal senior pass; others pay $16 during MD-LD; fees $8 during LD-10/31 with reduced services ($4 with senior pass). 14-day limit. 18 sites (24-ft RV limit). Tbls, toilets, cfga, no drkg wtr. Boating(l- no motors), fly fishing, mountain bike trail, hiking trails. 22 acres.

Panhandle Campground $9
Colville National Forest
From Newport, 15 mi N on SR 20 to settlement of Usk; right on 5th St, across Pend Oreille bridge, then 15 mi N on LeClerc Rd (CR 9325); at N shore of Pend Oreille River. $9 with federal senior pass; others pay $18. 5/20-LD; 14-day limit. 13 sites (32-ft RV limit. Tbls, toilets, cfga, drkg wtr, beach. Swimming, boating(l), fishing. On Pend Oreille River. 20 acres.

Pioneer Park Campground $9
Colville National Forest
From downtown Newport, 0.75 E on US 2; immediately after crossing Pend Oreille River bridge, left (N) on LeClerc Rd for 2 mi to campground. $9 with federal senior pass; others pay $18. MD-LD; 14-day limit. 17 sites; no RV size limit. Tbls, toilets, cfga, drkg wtr. Boating(l), fishing, waterskiing, interpretive trail.

Pend Oreille County Park $10
Pend Oreille County Parks & Recreation
15 mi W of Newport on US 2; W of Rt 211 turnoff for Sacheen Lake. $10. MD-LD weekends; may be open earlier & later, depending on weather. 17 sites. Tbls, flush toilets, cfga, drkg wtr. Hiking & bridle trails. Plans include future equestrian group camping area.

South Skookum Lake Campground $8
Colville National Forest
From Newport, 15 mi N on SR 20 to settlement of Usk; right on 5th St, across Pend Oreille briddge, then 7.5 mi NE on Kings Lake Rd (CR 3389); 0.5 mi on FR 5032350 to W

shore of lake. $8 with federal senior pass; others pay $16. MD-LD; 14-day limit. 25 sites (32-ft RV limit). Tbls, toilets, cfga, drkg wtr. Boating(l), fishing, hiking, swimming, waterskiing. 15 acres.

NORTH BEND

Denny Creek Campground $10
Mt. Baker-Snoqualmie National Forest
From jct with North Bend Way, 0.7 mi SW on SR 202; 16.2 mi E on I-90 to exit 47; left on Tinkham Rd, then right on Denny Creek Rd, continuing left at next intersection for 2.1 mi; at Snoqualmie River. $10 with federal senior pass at 23 non-elec sites; others pay $20 (doubles $38); 8. $12 with senior pass at 8 elec sites; others pay $24. 6/4-9/24; 14-day limit. Tbls, flush & pit toilets, cfga, drkg wtr. Hiking trail. Non-campers pay $5 day use fee.

Middle Fork Campground $7
Mt. Baker-Snoqualmie National Forest
From jct with North Bend Way, 0.7 mi SW on SR 202; 4 mi E on I-90 to exit 34; left on 468th Ave SE for 0.3 mi; right on SE Middle Fork Rd, bearing left at "Y" for 1.2 mi, then left on Lake Dorothy Rd for 9.7 mi; at Middle Fork of Snoqualmie River. $7 with federal senior pass; others pay $14 (doubles $26). 5/26-9/24; 14-day limit. 36 sites, typically 37 ft. Tbls, pit toilets, cfga, drkg wtr. Hiking trails.

Mine Creek Recreation Site   FREE
Dept of Natural Resources
From I-90 Exit 34 E of North Bend, N half mi on 468 Ave SE; right on SE Middle Fork Rd (paved & gravel) for 4 mi, then left to camp. Free. All year; 14-day limit. 13 sites; 3 picnic sites. Toilets, cfga, tbls, no drkg wtr.

Tinkham Campground $7
Mt. Baker-Snoqualmie National Forest
From jct with North Bend Way, 0.7 mi SW on SR 202; 11.2 mi E on I-90 to exit 42; right on Tinkham Rd for 1.5 mi; at South Fork of Snoqualmie River. $7 base with federal senior pass; others pay $14 base, $16 for premium locations ($8 with senior pass). 5/24-9/24; 14-day limit. 47 sites, typically 48 ft. Tbls, toilets, cfga, drkg wtr. Hiking trail.

NORTHPORT

Sheep Creek Campground $10
Dept of Natural Resources
1 mi N of Northport on SR 25 (cross Columbia River); left on gravel Sheep Creek Rd for 4.3 mi; right into campground. $10 daily or $30 annual Discover Pass. 5/15-10/31; 10-day limit. 11 sites; 8 picnic sites. Toilets, tbls, drkg wtr, cfga, group shelter. Fishing, hiking. Interpretive site, stream viewing platform.

ODESSA

Pacific Lake   FREE
Lakeview Ranch Recreation Area
Bureau of Land Management

2.5 mi N of Odessa on SR 21; 4.5 mi W on Lakeview Ranch Rd; at dry Pacific Lake. Free. All year; 14-day limit. 5 sites. Tbls, toilets, cfga, no drkg wtr, corrals. Horseback riding, hiking, mountain biking, fishing, boating. 5300 acres.

Odessa Tourist Park   FREE
From SR 28 in downtown Odessa, 1 block N on 1st or 2nd St; right on E. Marjorie Ave to park. Free. Small park with primitive overnight sites; 3-day limit. Hiking, bridle trails, pool nearby. Do not confuse with Odessa Golf & RV on SR 28.

OKANOGAN

American Legion City Park $10
On Hwy 20 N of town. $3 base. Motorized vehicles, $10. All year; 72-hr limit. 35 sites (no RV size limit); no hookups. Tbls, flush toilets, cfga, drkg wtr, coin showers, Wi-Fi. Fishing, boating. On Okanogan River, next to Okanogan County Historical Museum. Dump nearby at River Ave & Tyee St by boat lanch. Farmers market Saturdays spring-fall.

Leader Lake Campground $10
Loup Loup State Forest
Department of Natural Resources
From US 97 at Okanogan, W 8.4 mi on SR 20 to Leader Lake Rd (paved, one lane); turn right, half mi to camp; at Leader Lake. $10 daily or $30 annual Discover Pass. All year; 10-day limit. 16 sites. Tbls, toilets, cfga, no drkg wtr, fishing platform. Boating(l), fishing.

Rock Creek Campground $10
Loup Loup State Forest
Department of Natural Resources
From jct with US 97 at Okanogan, W 9.8 mi on SR 20 to Loup Loup Canyon Rd (dirt, 2 lanes), then 3.9 mi and left into camp. On Loup-Loup Creek. $10 daily or $30 annual Discover Pass. All year; 10-day limit. 6 sites. Toilets, tbls, cfga, drkg wtr, shelter. Closed in 2017 due to wildfire damage; check current status before arrival.

Rock Lakes Campground $10
Loup Loup State Forest
Department of Natural Resources
From jct with US 90 at Okanogan, W 9.8 mi on SR 20 to Loup Loup Canyon Rd (dirt, 2 lanes) for 4.7 mi; left on Rock Lakes Rd for 5.8 mi, then left qtr mi to camp. On Rock Lakes, near Buck Mountain. $10 daily or $30 annual Discover Pass. All year; 10-day limit. 8 sites. Toilets, tbls, cfga, no drkg wtr. Hiking trail; fishing.

Sportsman's Camp $10
Loup Loup State Forest
Department of Natural Resources
From jct with US 97 at Okanogan, 14.9 mi W on SR 20; right on Sweat Creek Rd for 1 mi. $10 daily or $30 annual Discover Pass. All year; 10-day limit. 6 sites. Tbls, toilets, cfga, no drkg wtr, shelter.

PASCO

Ayer Boat Basin   FREE
Corps of Engineers
Lake Herbert G. West
Lower Monument Dam
From just N of the Burbank settlement (6 mi SE of Pasco), 26 mi E on SR 124; 24 mi N on Lyon's Ferry through Clyde & Pleasant View, N on Ayre Rd to Ayer, then 0.5 mi SW at river mile 51. Free. All year; 14-day limit. About 20 primitive undesignated sites (40-ft RV limit). Toilets, covered tbls, cfga, no drkg wtr. Boating(ld), fishing.

Charbonneau Park $12
Corps of Engineers
Lake Sacajawea
From just N of the Burbank settlement (6 mi SE of Pasco), 8.3 mi E on SR 124; 1.5 mi N on Sun Harbor Dr; left on Charbonneau Rd. $12 base with federal senior pass at 25 50-amp elec sites; others pay $24 base, $26 for 12 premium shoreline sites ($13 with senior pass). At 15 full-hookup sites, $15 with senior pass; others pay $30. 15 primitive overflow sites without amenities, $10 ($5 with senior pass). Fees half price Mon-Thur: Elec sites $12; elec at shoreline $13; full hookups $15 (senior discounts still apply). 4/1-10/31; 14-day limit. 60-ft RV limit. Tbls, flush toilets, cfga, drkg wtr, dump, showers, marine dump station, sun shelters, picnic shelters, pay phone, playground. Boating(dl), fishing, waterskiing, swimming, volleyball. 34 acres.

Fishhook Park $12
Corps of Engineers
Lake Sacajawea
From just N of the Burbank settlement (6 mi SE of Pasco), 16 mi E on SR 124; 4 mi N on Fishhook Park Rd. $12 base with federal senior pass at 39 wtr/50-amp elec sites; others pay $24 base, $26 for 10 premium shoreline sites ($13 with senior pass), $30 for full hookups ($15 with senior pass). 1 primitive shoreline non-elec site $18 ($9 with senior pass). Fees half price Mon-Thur: Elec sites $12, elec at shoreline, $13, full hookups $15 (senior discounts still apply). Also walk-to tent sites & boat camping. 5/24-9/12; 14-day limit. 45-ft RV limit. Picnic shelter, marine dump station, tbls, flush toilets, cfga, drkg wtr, dump, showers, beach, playground, pay phone, visitor center. Fishing, boating(ld), waterskiing, swimming. 29 acres. 2017 drkg water alert: high nitrate levels; provide your own wtr.

Hood Park Campground $12
Corps of Engineers
Lake Wallula
From Pasco, 3 mi S on US 12/395 to jct with SR 124 E of Burbank (W end of SR 124); turn on Hood Park Rd immediately E of roundabouts. $12 with federal senior pass at non-shoreline 30/50-amp elec sites (others pay $24); $13 with senior pass at 20 elec 30/50-amp shoreline sites (others pay $26). Fees half price Mon-Thur:

$12 at non-shoreline sites, $13 at shoreline sites (senior discounts still apply). 5/19-9/5; 14-day limit. 65-ft RV limit. Picnic shelter, amphitheater, horseshoe pits, beach, playground, showers, flush toilets, tbls, cfga, drkg wtr, dump. Basketball court, swimming, campfire programs, fishing, boating(l).

Matthews Park   FREE
Corps of Engineers
Lake Sacajawea
From just N of the Burbank settlement (6 mi SE of Pasco), 26 mi E on SR 124; 8.6 mi N on Lyons Ferry Rd to village of Clyde; left 15.2 mi on Lower Monument Rd; left 1 mi before the dam, then 1 mi E; on S shore of Snake River. All year; 14-day limit. Free. Primitive undesignated camping in parking area. Tbls, pit toilets, cfga, no drkg wtr. Boating(dl), fishing.

McNary Habitat Management Area $10
State Department of Fish & Wildlife
5 mi S of Pasco on US 395; 2 mi E on US 2; 3 mi E on E. Humorist Rd. $10 daily or $30 annual Discover Pass. All year; 14-day limit. 24 primitive sites; no facilities. Fishing in Columbia River or at wildlife refuge; hunting, hiking, boating(l). Adjoins McNary National Wildlife Refuge between Walla Walla and Snake Rivers. Refuge GPS: 46.198531, -118.955626

Paradise Park   FREE
Lake Umatilla
John Day Lock & Dam
Corps of Engineers
From the settlement of Plymouth (35 mi S of Pasco at shore of Columbia River), W on Christie Rd, then S on access rd to river. Free. About 5/15-9/15; 7-day limit. Primitive undesignated sites. Tbls, toilets, cfga, no drkg wtr. Boating(l), fishing.

Plymouth Park $12
Lake Umatilla
John Day Lock & Dam
Corps of Engineers
From McNary Dam on SR 14 (35 mi S of Pasco), 1.2 mi W below the dam on the N side. $12 with federal senior pass at wtr/elec sites; others pay $24. $13.50 with senior pass at full-hookup sites; others pay $27. 4/1-10/31; 14-day limit. 40-ft RV limit; 29 pull-through sites. Tbls, flush & pit toilets, cfga, drkg wtr, dump, showers, beach, coin laundry, playground. Boating(ld), fishing, swimming, waterskiing.

Walker Habitat Management Area   FREE
Corps of Engineers
Lake Sacajawea
From just N of the Burbank settlement (6 mi SE of Pasco), 26 mi E on SR 124: 8.6 mi N on Lyons Ferry Rd to village of Clyde; left, then 4 mi NW on Lower Monumental Rd; left 1 mi

before the dam, then 1 mi E; on S shore of Snake River. Free. All year; 14-day limit. Primitive undesignated sites. Tbls, pit toilets, cfga, no drkg wtr. Boating(dl), fishing, hunting.

POMEROY

Big Springs   FREE
Umatilla National Forest
10 mi S of Pomeroy on Hwy 128; at fork, continue straight to FR 40; pass the forest boundary & continue 9 mi to Clearwater lookout tower, then left on FR 42 for 3 mi; left on FR 4225 to camp. Free. 5/15-11/15; 14-day limit. 5 RV sites. Tbls, toilets, cfga, no drkg wtr (get wtr at Clearwater tower). Hiking, hunting. Fees during hunting season.

Teal Spring Campground   FREE
Umatilla National Forest
10 mi S of Pomeroy on Hwy 128; at fork, continue straight to FR 40 within the forest & on 9 mi to Clearwater lookout tower; camp's turnoff is half mi on right. Free. 6/1-11/15; 14-day limit. 7 sites. Tbls, toilets, cfga, no drkg wtr. Camp popular with OHV enthusiasts. Hunting season fees.

Tucannon Campground $8
Umatilla National Forest
17 mi S of Pomeroy on CR 101; 4 mi SW on FR 47; S on FR 160 to camp. $8. 5/15-11/15; 14-daylimit. 13 sites; 16-ft RV limit. Tbls, toilets, cfga, no drkg wtr. Fishing; hiking; hunting. Elev 1600 ft; 11 acres. River. Site also accessible via country road from Dayton. Very popular camp.

Wickiup Campground   FREE
Umatilla National Forest
10 mi S of Pomeroy on Hwy 128; at fork, continue straight to FR 40 for about 17 mi; at Troy Junction, turn on FR 44 for 3 mi to jct with FR 43. Free. 6/15-10/15; 14-day limit. 7 sites; 16-ft RV limit. Tbls, toilet, cfga, no drkg wtr. Hiking, hunting. Fees during hunting season.

PORT ANGELES

Altaire Campground $10
Olympic National Park
9 mi W of Port Angeles on US 101; 4 mi S on Olympic Hot Springs Rd. $10 with federal senior pass; others pay $20. May-Sept; 14-day limit. 30 sites, suitable for small RVs (35-ft RV limit, 21-ft recommended). Portions of rd closed by snow in winter. Tbls, flush toilets, cfga, drkg wtr. Fishing (no license required), hiking. Mountain goats & elk can sometimes be seen on rocks across river in late winter & early spring. Note: Campground closed 2017 due to shift of Elwha River after dam removals; closing probably permanent.

Elwha Campground $10
Olympic National Park
9 mi W of Port Angeles on US 101; 3 mi S on Olympic Hot Springs Rd; rd suitable for small RVs; part of rd closed in winter. $10 with federal senior pass; otehrs pay $20. All year; 14-day limit. 40 sites (35-ft RV limit, 21-ft recommended). Tbls, flush toilets, cfga, drkg wtr, picnic shelter, naturalist program. Fishing (no license required), hiking. Mountain goats & elk can sometimes be seen on rocks across river in late winter & early spring. Note: Campground closed indefinitely due to flood damage.

Fairholme Campground $10
Olympic National Park
17.9 mi W of Port Angeles on US 101; 10.7 mi N on North Shore Rd; .1 mi to campground; rds are steep; at W shore of Lake Crescent. $10 with federal senior pass; others pay $20. All year; 14-day limit. 87 sites; 21-ft RV limit. Tbls, flush toilets, cfga, drkg wtr, nature program, nature trails, store. Swimming, boating(l), fishing (no license required), hiking. Lake Crescent nestled between high, forested peaks and is the largest lake in the park. 35 acres.

Lyre River State Recreation Site $10
Department of Natural Resources
4 mi W of Port Angeles on WA 101, to jct with WA 112; 14.7 mi N to campground sign, right half mi to fork in rd; left fork (gravel rd) to campground. $10 daily or $30 annual Discover Pass. All year; 7-day limit (no wtr or trash services in fall/winter; 1 toilet). 11 sites (RVs under 22 ft). Tbls, toilets, cfga, drkg wtr, shelter. Hiking, Fishing. On Lyre River. Secluded sites.

Heart o' The Hills $10
Olympic National Park
From US 101 at Race St., .8 mi inside E city limits of Port Angeles, 5.4 mi S on Hurricane Ridge Rd (paved, often closed by snow in winter). $10 with federal senior pass; others pay $20. All year; 14-day limit. 105 sites (35-ft RV limit, 21-ft recommended). Tbls, flush toilets, cfga, drkg wtr, animal-proof containers. Hiking trails, nature program. Elev 1807. Trail to Mount Angeles (6400 ft). Elev 1807 ft; 35 acres.

REPUBLIC

Beth Lake Campground $8
Okanogan National Forest
From Rebublic, about 14 mi W through village of Wauconda on SR 20; N at exit to Bonapaarte Recreation Area (CR 4953, becoming FR 32 for 7 mi); 1.5 mi N on Chesaw Rd (CR 9480) to SW shore of lake. $8. All year; 14-day limit. 15 sites in 2 loops (32-ft RV limit). Tbls, pit toilets, cfga, drkg wtr. Boating, swimming. Hiking trails on Clackamas Mtn & Fir Mtn areas.

Bonaparte Lake Campground $12
Okanogan National Forest
From Republic, about 14 mi W through village of Wauconda on SR 20; 5 mi N on CR 4953; half mi N on FR 32; at S end of Bonaparte Lake. $12. All year; 14-day limit. 30 sites (32-ft RV limit). May-Oct; 14-day limit. Tbls, Pit & flush toilets, cfga, drkg wtr. Swimming, boating(l), fishing, hiking.

Deer Creek Campground $5
Colville National Forest
N of Republic on SR 21 to Curlew; right on CR 602 (Deer Creek Hwy) for 10 mi, then on left at Boulder Deer summit up short access rd. $5. MD-LD; 14-day limit. 9 sites plus 2 group areas. Tbls, toilets, cfga, no drkg wtr, no trash service. Fishing, hiking trails. Closed 2017 due to tree hazards.

Ferry Lake Campground $6
Colville National Forest
7 mi S of Republic on SR 21; 6 mi SW on FR 53 (Scatter Creek Rd); 1 mi N on FR 5330; N on FR 5330-100 to camp; at E shore of lake. $6. 5/15-9/15; 14-day limit. 9 sites (22-ft RV limit). Tbls, toilets, cfga, no drkg wtr. Trout fishing, boating(ld).

Long Lake Campground $8
Colville National Forest
7 mi S of Republic on SR 21; 7 mi SW on FR 53; 0.75 mi S on FR 5300-400. $8. 5/15-9/15; 14-day limit. 12 sites; 36-ft RV limit. Tbls, toilets, cfga, drkg wtr. Swimming, boating(l), fly fishing, hiking trail.

Lost Lake Campground $12
Okanogan National Forest
From Republic, about 14 mi W through village of Wauconda on SR 20; 5 mi N on CR 4953; 4 mi NE on FR 32; 6 mi NW on FR 33. $12. All year; 14-day limit. 18 sites (32-ft RV limit). Tbls, flush & pit toilets, cfga, drkg wtr. Boating(l), swimming, fishing, amphitheater.

Sherman Pass Overlook $6
Colville National Forest
Half mi E of Republic on SR 21; 20 mi E on SR 20. $6. 5/25-9/30; 14-day limit. 10 sites (24-ft RV limit). Tbls, toilets, cfga, drkg wtr, no trash service. Near highest pass in Washington. Hiking. GPS: 48.6054483, -118.4633461. Campground closed in 2014; still closed 2017.

Swan Lake Campground $10
Colville National Forest
6.8 mi S of Republic on SR 21; 7.3 mi SW on FR 53; slight left at Old Scatter Creek Rd for 0.2 mi; at E shore of lake. $10. All year, but wtr & services during MD-10/1; 14-day limit. 21 sites (32-ft RV limit). Tbls, toilets, cfga, drkg wtr. Swimming, boating(l), fishing, nature trails, hiking.

Ten Mile Campground $6
Colville National Forest
10 mi S of Republic on SR 21. $6 MD-LD; 14-day limit. 8 sites (both sides of rd); 21-ft RV limit. Tbls, cfga, no drkg wtr, toilets, no trash service. Hiking, fishing. Closed 2017 by storm damage.

Thirteen Mile Trailhead FREE
Colville National Forest
13 mi S of Republic on SR 21. Free. MD-LD; 14-day limit.

2 sites. Tbls, toilets, cfga, no drkg wtr, no trash service. Hiking, fishing.

RIVERSIDE

Crawfish Lake Campground FREE
Okanogan National Forest
17.7 mi E of Riverside on CR 9320 (becomes FR 30 for 2 mi); right 1 mi on FR 3000-100 access rd. Free. 5/15-9/15; 14-day limit. 19 sites (32-ft RV limit) & 4 group sites. Tbls, toilets, cfga, no drkg wtr (boil wtr from Balanced Rock Spring), no trash service. Boating(l), fishing, swimming.

SEQUIM

Dungeness Forks Campground $7
Olympic National Forest
From Sequim, about 5 mi E on US 101 to Sequim Bay State Park; left across from park on Louella Rd for 1 mi; left on Palo Alto Rd for 4 mi; right for 1 mi on FR 2880; at shore of Dungeness River. Trailers & motorhomes not recommended dueto steep one-lane unpaved access rd. $7 with federal senior pass for truck/van campers & tents; others pay $14. 10 sites. Tbls, toilet, cfga, no drkg wtr. Fishing.

Falls View Campground $10
Olympic National Forest
From Sequim, 16 mi SE on US 101 (N of Quilcene settlement); W side. $10. 5/15-9/15; 14-day limit. 30 sites; 35-ft RV limit.. Tbls, toilets, cfga, no drkg wtr. Hiking, fishing. 6 acres. Closed in 2017 due to root disease.

Lake Leland Campground
Jefferson County Park
About 6 mi N of Quilcene on Hwy 101. All year; 7-day limit. Closed to camping; budget problems.

Quilcene Campground
Jefferson County Park
In Quilcene next to the Quilcene Community Center on Hwy 101. Closed to camping. Budget problems.

SHELTON

Big Creek $10
Olympic National Forest
From settlement of Hoodsport (18 mi N of Shelton), 9 mi NW on SR 119; .1 mi W on FR 24. $10 with federal senior pass; others pay $20. 5/15-9/15; 14-day limit. 25 sites (36-ft RV limit). Tbls, toilets, cfga, drkg wtr, dump. Swimming nearby, boating (l), hiking trails, fishing. Near Lake Cushman. 30 acres.

Brown Creek Campground $7
Olympic National Forest
7.5 mi N of Shelton on US 101; 5.3 mi NW on Skokomish Valley Rd; 8.7 mi N on FR 23; cross bridge on FR 2353 to FR 2340, then qtr mi E. $7 with federal senior pass; others pay $14. All year; 14-day limit. 20 sites (21-ft RV limit).

Tbls, toilets, cfga, drkg wtr except off-season. Swimming, fishing, hiking trails. 6 acres.

Collins Campground $7
Olympic National Forest
From Brinnon (30 mi N of Shelton), 2 mi S on US 101; 4.7 mi W on FR 2510. $7 with federal senior pass; others pay $14. 5/15-9/15; 14-day limit. 10 RV/tent sites (21-ft RV limit). Tbls, toilets, cfga, no drkg wtr. Swimming, fishing, hiking trails. 4 acres on Duckabush River. Berries in Jul.

Hamma Hamma $7
Olympic National Forest
From settlement of Eldon (23 mi N of Shelton), 1.7 mi N on US 101; 6.5 mi W on FR 25; at E shore of Hamma Hamma River. $7 with federal senior pass; others pay $14. 5/15-9/15; 14-day limit. 15 RV sites (21-ft limit); 3 tent sites. Tbls, toilets, cfga, no drkg wtr. Swimming, fishing, hiking trails.

LeBar Creek Horse Camp $10
Olympic National Forest
6 mi N of Shelton on US 101; left on Skokomish Valley Rd for 5.6 mi; at FR 23 "Y," bear right for 9.5 mi; bear right at FR 2353 "Y" for half mi, then left at next "Y" for three-fourths mi. $10. All year; 14-day limit. 13 sites; 28-ft RV limit. Tbls, toilet, cfga, no drkg wtr or trash service. Horse facilities. Hiking, fishing, horseback riding. Camp built by volunteers, reserved for horsemen.

Lena Creek Campground $7
Olympic National Forest
From Eldon (23 mi N of Shelton), 1.7 mi N on US 101; 8 mi W on FR 25; N shore of Hamma Hamma River. $7 with federal senior pass; others pay $14. 5/15-9/15; 14-day limit. 13 sites (21-ft RV limit). Tbls, toilets, cfga, drkg wtr. Swimming, fishing, hiking trails (to Lena & Upper Lena Lakes). 7 acres.

Seal Rock Campground $9
Olympic National Forest
From settlement of Brinnon (30 mi N of Shelton), 2 mi N on US 101; on Hood Canal at famous Seal Rock. $9 with federal senior pass; others pay $18. Early Apr to mid-Oct. 41 sites (21-ft RV limit). Tbls, flush toilets, cfga, drkg wtr. 100 ft of beachfront. Swimming, fishing, nature trails, clamming, oyster gathering, shrimping offshore in spring.

Staircase Campground $10
Olympic National Park
From Hoodsport (18 mi N of Shelton), 16 mi NW on Skokomish River Rd. $10 with federal senior pass; others pay $20. All year; 14-day limit. 49 sites (35-ft RV limit, 21-ft recommended). Flush & pit toilets, cfga, drkg wtr May-Sept, tbls, animal lockers. Hiking trails, fishing. On Staircase Rapids of North Fork Skokomish River near Lake Cushman. Trails to backcountry.

SKYKOMISH

Beckler River Campground $8
Mt. Baker-Snoqualmie National Forest
1 mi E of Skykomish on US 2 to just W of milepost 50; 1.5 mi N on Beckler River Rd 65. $8 with federal senior pass; others pay $16 (doubles $30). 5/24-9/10; 14-day limit. 27 sites; 30-ft RV limit. Tbls, toilets, cfga, drkg wtr. Non-campers pay $5 day use fee.

Money Creek Campground $9
Mt. Baker-Snoqualmie National Forest
2.5 mi W of Skykomish on US 2; left at campground sign. $9 base with federal senior pass; others pay $18 base (double sites $34), $20 for premium locations ($10 with senior pass). 5/24-9/24; 14-day limit. 25 small sites (typically 25 ft). Tbls, toilets, cfga, drkg wtr, grey wtr stations. Fishing, swimming.

San Juan Campground $8
Mt. Baker-Snoqualmie National Forest
1 mi E of Skykomish on US 2 to just W of milepost 50; 15 mi N on Beckler Rd 65; 2 mi W on North Fork Skykomish Rd 63. $8 with federal senior pass; others pay $16. MD-LD; 14-day limit. Tbls, toilet, cfga, no drkg wtr. Fishing. Camp inaccessible in 2017; roads closed.

SPRINGDALE

Hunters Campground $9
Lake Roosevelt National Recreation Area
From SR 25 just N of Hunters settlement (30 mi W of Springdale), 2 mi E on Hunters Campground Rd. $9 with federal senior pass; others pay $18 during 5/1-9/30; $4.50 & $9 off-season; 14-day limit. 39 sites (26-ft RV limit). Tbls, flush toilets, cfga, drkg wtr, dump, outside shower station. Boating(ld), fishing, swimming, waterskiing. 12 acres on E shore of Franklin Roosevelt Lake.

STARBUCK

Little Goose Dam FREE
Corps of Engineers
Lake Bryan
From just NW of Starbuck on SR 261, 10 mi NW & then NE on Little Goose Dam Rd; at Snake River mile 70. All year; 14-day limit. Free primitive camping on N & S shores W of dam; undesignated sites. Tbls, toilets, drkg wtr at visitor center (features fish viewing room), fish cleaning station.

Little Goose Landing FREE
Corps of Engineers
Lake Bryan
From just NW of Starbuck on SR 261, 9 mi NW & then NE on Little Goose Dam Rd; 1 mi E of Little Goose Dam. All year; 14-day limit. Free primitive camping area, undesignated sites. Toilets, tbls, cfga, no drkg wtr, fishing pier. Boating(l), fishing.

Riparia Campground   FREE
Corps of Engineers
Lake Herbert G. West
Lower Monument Dam
From just NW of Starbuck on SR 261, 14 mi NW & then NE on Little Goose Dam Rd about qtr mi S of jct with Rivaria Rd, then right (S) on access rd to N shore of Snake River (about 3 mi W of Little Goose Dam). Free. All year; 14-day limit. Undesignated sites; 40-ft RV limit. Tbls, toilet, cfga, no drkg wtr. Fishing, boating(l).

Texas Rapids Campground   FREE
Corps of Engineers
Lake Herbert G. West
Lower Monument Dam
From just NW of Starbuck on SR 261, 16 mi NW & then NE on Little Goose Rd (2 mi W of Little Goose Dam); at S shore of Snake River. Free. All year; 14-day limit. Primitive undesignated sites. Pit toilets (flush toilets in summer), cfga, no drkg wtr, shade shelters, tbls. Boating(l), fishing.

Willow Landing   FREE
Corps of Engineers
Lake Bryan
From Starbuck, 7 mi E on SR 261; about 8 mi E on US 12; left (N) on SR 127 about 10 mi; 4 mi E on Deadman Rd; 5 mi N on Hastings Hill Rd. All year; 14-day limit. Free primitive camping area. Undesignated sites. Tbls, toilet, cfga, no drkg wtr, fishing pier. Boating(l), fishing. 74 acres.

SUMAS

Douglas Fir Campground $9
Mt. Baker-Snoqualmie National Forest
From the settlement of Glacier (30 mi SE of Sumas), 2.5 mi E on SR 542; on W after crossing North Fork Nooksack River near milepost 35. $9 base with federal senior pass; others pay $18 base, $20 for premium locations ($10 with senior pass). 5/16-9/24; 14-day limit. 29 sites; 36-ft RV limit. Tbls, pit toilets, cfga, drkg wtr. Hiking trail.

Hannegan Pass Campground $5
Mt. Baker-Snoqualmie National Forest
From the settlement of Glacier (30 mi SE of Sumas), 12.4 mi E on SR 542; 4 mi E on FR 32. Free with $30 annual NW pass or $5 daily. 5/15-9/15; 14-day limit. Undeveloped primitive camping area; toilet, cfga, no drkg wtr. Hiking, fishing. Trailhead to Mt Baker Wilderness. On Ruth Creek.

Silver Fir Campground $8
Mt. Baker-Snoqualmie National Forest
From the settlement of Glacier (30 mi SE of Sumas), 14 mi E on SR 542; on W just after crossing North Fork Nooksack River near milepost 46. $8 with federal senior pass; others pay $16 (doubles $30). 5/18-9/24; 14-day limit. 20 sites; 40-ft RV limit. Tbls, toilets, cfga, drkg wtr. Fishing.

THE DALLES, OREGON

Rock Creek Park   FREE
Lake Umatilla
John Day Dam
Corps of Engineers
From The Dalles, OR, 3 mi N on US 179, across river into Washington; 35 mi E on SR 14; left on Rock Creek Rd 1.5 mi, then left into park. Free. All year; 14-day limit. Primitive undesignated sites. Tbls, portable toilets Apr-Sept, cfga, no drkg wtr. Boating(l), fishing.

Roosevelt Park   FREE
Lake Umatilla
John Day Dam
Corps of Engineers
From The Dalles, OR, 3 mi N on US 197, across river into Washington, then 50 mi E on SR 14, following signs; on Columbia River. Free. All year; 14-day limit. Primitive, undesignated sites; park RVs on asphalt near lawns. Pit toilets all year, flush toilets during 4/1-9/30. Tbls, cfga, picnic sites, beach, shelters. Boating(l), fishing.

TONASKET

Beaver Lake Campground $8
Okanogan National Forest
24 mi E of Tonasket on SR 20; 5.5 mi NE on CR 4953 becoming FR 32; 3.3 mi NW on FR 32. $8. May-Oct; 14-day limit. 9 small sites (22-ft RV limit). Tbls, toilet, cfga, no drkg wtr. Boating(l - small boats), fishing, swimming, hiking, hunting.

Lyman Lake Campground   FREE
Okanogan National Forest
12.6 mi E of Tonasket on WA 20; 13 mi SE CR 9455; 2.4 mi S on FR 3785; qtr mi NW on FR 500 access rd; at lake. Free. 5/15-9/15; 14-day limit. 4 sites (RVs under 32 ft). Tbls, toilets, cfga, no drkg wtr or trash service. Fishing.

TUMWATER

Fall Creek Campground $10
Capitol State Forest
Department of Natural Resources
From Littlerock (12 mi S of Tumwater), NW on Waddell Creek Rd; continue NW (left) on Sherman Valley Rd SW turn right for 1.4 mi, then left fork (C-Line Rd) about 2 mi; turn left onto C-6000 Rd for 2.5 mi, then right after qtr mi to camp; at Fall Creek. $10 daily or $30 annual Discover Pass. 5/1-11/30; 10-day limit. 8 sites. Drkg wtr, toilets, cfga, horse facilities, no trash service. Fishing; 80 mi of horse, hiking, mountain biking & horseback riding trails.

Margaret McKenny Campground $10
Capitol State Forest
Department of Natural Resources
From Littlerock (12 mi S of Tumwater), 3 mi NW on Waddell Creek Rd to Mima Mound Natural Area entrance, then

continue 1.6 mi to campground. $10 daily or $30 annual Discover Pass. 5/1-11/30; 10-day limit. 24 sites. Toilets, tbls, cfga, no drkg wtr. Horse ramp. Hiking trails, fishing; 80 mi of horse trails, mountain biking.

Middle Waddell Campground $10
Capitol State Forest
Department of Natural Resources
From Littlerock (12 mi S of Tumwater), follow directions to Margaret McKenny Campground,then continue W on Waddell Creek Rd 1.2 mi; left to site at Waddell Creek. $10 daily or $30 annual Discover Pass. 5/1-11/30; 10-day limit. 24 sites. Toilets, tbls, cfga, drkg wtr. Motorcycle, mountain biking, horse and hiking trails, fishing.

Mima Falls Trailhead $10
Capitol State Forest
Department of Natural Resources
From Littlerock (12 mi S of Tumwater), 1 0.5 mi W on 128th Ave SW; left (S) at Mima Rd for 1.3 mi; right on Bordeaux Rd for 0.7 mi; right on Marksman Rd for 0.9 mi, then left qtr mi to site. $10 daily or $30 annual Discover Pass. 5/1-11/30; 10-day limit. 5 sites. Toilets, cfga, tbls, drkg wtr, no trash service. Horse ramp. Horse trails, mountain biking, hiking trails; trail to scenic Mima Falls.

TWISP
Black Pine Lake Campground $8
Okanogan National Forest
From Twisp, 10 mi W on Twisp River Rd (CR 9114); S on FR 43m crossing Buttermilk bridge over Twisp River; stay left on FR 43 about 8 mi; left into camp on N end of lake. Poorman Creek route very narrow, not recommended for RVs. Libby Creek 4300 Rd muddy with debris slides. $8 with federal senior pass; others pay $16. About 5/15-10/31; 14-day limit. 23 sites; 30-ft RV limit. Tbls, toilets, cfga, drkg wtr in summer. Boating(l), fishing, 2 floating docks, paved nature trail, swimming, hiking.

Foggy Dew Campground $8
Okanogan National Forest
From Carlton (9 mi S of Twisp), 4 mi S on SR 153; 1.1 mi S on CR 1029 (Gold Creek Loop); 1 mi W on CR 1043, becoming FR 4340 for 4 mi; at confluence of North Fork Gold Creek & Foggy Dew Creek. $8. All year; 14-day limit. 13 sites (no size limit). Tbls, toilets, cfga, no drkg wtr. No trash service in winter. Fishing, hiking, biking trails, winter sports. Access to motorbike use area. Watch for rattlesnakes. GPS: 48.2051427, -120.1920267. Closed in 2014 by area wildfires; check current status before arrival.

J.R. Campground $8
Okanogan National Forest
11.5 mi E of Twisp on SR 20; at left side. $8. All year; 14-day limit. 6 sites (25-ft RV limit). Tbls, toilets, cfga, no drkg wtr (no trash service in winter). Fishing, hunting,

hiking, biking, winter sports, picnic area. On Frazier Creek. GPS: 48.38798, -119.9006. Note: Access from SR 20 closed in early 2017 by road wash-out.

Loup Loup Campground $12
Okanogan National Forest
12.5 mi E of Twisp on SR 20; 1 mi N on FR 42. $12. 5/15-10/31; 14-day limit. 25 sites; 36-ft RV limit, sites typically 48 ft. Tbls, toilets, cfga, drkg wtr. Biking, hiking, horse trails, hunting, group picnic area, access to mountain-bike trails. Elev 4200 ft. 20 acres. Winter sports activity. Good location for large groups; picnic area. GPS: 48.3957025, -119.9025714. Note: Access from SR 20 closed in early 2017 by road wash-out.

Mystery Campground $8
Okanogan National Forest
10.8 mi W of Twisp on CR 9114; 7.2 mi NW on FR 44 (Twisp River Rd). $8. All year; 14-day limit. 4 sites; 30-ft RV limit. Tbls, toilets, cfga, no drkg wtr or trash service. Fishing, hiking, biking. On North Ford of Twisp River.

Poplar Flat Campground $12
Okanogan National Forest
10.7 mi W of Twisp on CR 9114; 9.5 mi NW on FR 44 (becoming FR 4440). $12. All year; 14-day limit. No wtr or trash service in winter. 16 sites; 30 ft RV limit, sites typically 41 ft. Tbls, toilets, cfga, drkg wtr, community kitchen. Fishing, bike & hiking trails. On Twisp River. Trails to small backcountry lakes & to Lake Chelan National Recreation Area.

Roads End Campground $8
Okanogan National Forest
10.8 mi W of Twisp on CR 9114; 14.4 mi NW on FR 44 (Twisp River Rd) & FR 4440; at Twisp River. $8. All year; 14-day limit. 4 sites; 16-ft RV limit. Tbls, toilets, cfga, firewood, no drkg wtr or trash service. Fishing. Elev 3600 ft; 2 acres. Gilbert Historical Site (1 mi E). Trailhead to backcountry & North Cascades National Park.

South Creek $8
Okanogan National Forest
10.8 mi W of Twisp on CR 9114; 11.3 mi NW on FR 44 (Twisp River Rd); off gravel FR 4440 by river. $8. All year; 14-day limit. 4 small sites up to 30 ft. Tbls, toilet, cfga, firewood, no drkg wtr or trash service. Fishing; horseback riding. On North Fork of Twisp River. Trailhead to Lake Chelan National Recreation Area & North Cascades National Park.

Twisp River Horse Camp $5
Okanogan National Forest
22.6 mi NW of Twisp via FR 4420, 4430 and 4435 to its end. All year; 14-day limit. Free with $30 annual NW forest pass; $5 daily otherwise. 12 sites up to 30 ft. Tbls, toilets, cfga, no drkg wtr or trash service. Primarily a horse camp;

loading ramp, hitch rails, feed stations. Access to Twisp River, South Creek & Scatter Creek trails. Site maintained by horseman club.

War Creek Campground $8
Okanogan National Forest
10.8 mi W of Twisp on CR 9114; 3.3 mi W on FR 44; near confluence of War Creek & Twisp River. $8. All year; 14-day limit. No wtr or trash service in winter. 10 sites; 25-ft RV limit. Tbls, toilets, cfga, drkg wtr. Fishing, hiking trails. Trailheads nearby. Picnic area. Rattlesnakes.

VANCOUVER
Paradise Point State Park $12
20 mi N of Vancouver off US 99 & I-5. $12 base. All year; 10-day limit. Limited facilities in winter (20-day limit). $12 base for primitive sites; $25 base for standard sites; $30 base at 20 utility sites with hookups (40-ft RV limit). WA seniors with $75 off-season pass camp free without hook-ups ($10 with hookups) during 10/1-3/31 & Sun-Thurs in April. Primitive sites have cfga, nearby drkg wtr & toilets; standard sites have campstove, drkg wtr, cfga, tbls, trash disposal, flush toilets, showers. Beach, dump, amphitheater. Swimming, boating(l), fishing, nature trails. East Fork Lewis River. 88 acres.

WAITSBURG
Lewis & Clark Trail State Park $12
4 mi E of Waitsburg on US 12 (24 mi E of Walla Walla); at Touchet River. $12 base. 5/1-9/30; 10-day limit. $12 for 15 primitive sites; $25 base for 24 standard sites; 28-ft RV limit. WA seniors with $75 off-seaon pass camp free without hookups ($10 with hookups) during Oct & Sun-Thurs in April Tbls, flush toilets, showers, cfga, drkg wtr, dump, beach. Swimming, fishing, hiking trails. 37 acres.

WHITE SALMON
Beaver Campground $10
Gifford Pinchot National Forest
From Carson (15 mi W of White Salmon) at jct with SR 14, 12 mi N on Wind River Hwy (FR 30); along W shore of Wind River. $10 with federal senior pass; others pay $20 (double sites $34). 5/18-9/21; 14-day limit. 23 sites; 40-ft RV limit. Tbls, pit & flush toilets, cfga, drkg wtr. Fishing, hiking.

Crest Camp/Trailhead FREE
Gifford Pinchot National Forest
From Carson (15 mi W of White Salmon), 4.9 mi N on Wind River Hwy (FR 30); right (E) at Panther Creek Rd (sign for Panther Creek Campground); it becomes FR 65; follow FR 65 about 11 mi, then right on FR60 for 1.7 mi to camp. No loop rd, so 1 RV must back in & others park on rd. Free. 6/15-9/30; 14-day limit. 1 back-in RV site & four sites along rd. Tbls, toilet, cfga, no drkg wtr. Hiking; horseback riding. Trailhead for Cascade Crest Trail.

Cultus Creek Campground $10
Gifford Pinchot National Forest
From settlement of Trout Lake (15 mi N of White Salmon), 5.5 mi SW on SR 141 to forest boundary; 12.5 mi NW on FR 24 (most of it gravel) past Peterson Prairie Campground; continue N (for 9 mi) on FR 24 past Little Goose Camp to Cultus Creek. $10. Open after snow melt, about 7/15-10/15; 14-day limit. 51 level gravel sites; 32-ft RV limit. Tbls, toilets, cfga, no drkg wtr. Fishing, nature trails, hiking, berry picking. Elev 4000 ft; 28 acres. Lightly used except during huckleberry season.

Falls Creek Horse Camp FREE
Gifford Pinchot National Forest
From Carson (15 mi W of White Salmon), 5 mi N on Wind River Hwy (FR 30); right on FR 65 (Old State Rd), then left on FR 65 (Panther Creek Rd) about 13 mi to camp. In 2017 summer, part of FR 65 N of camp was washed out, inaccessible by vehicles. Free. 6/15-9/30; 14-day limit. 4 small sites (RVs under 16 ft); poor turnaround. Tbls, toilet, cfga, no drkg wtr. Berry picking; fishing; horseback riding. Stream, hiking trailhead. In 2017, part of FR 65 N of camp was washed out, not accessible for vehicles.

Forlorn Lakes Campground $10
Gifford Pinchot National Forest
From settlement of Trout Lake (15 mi N of White Salmon), 5.5 mi SW on SR 141; to forest boundary; 6.5 mi W on FR 24 past Peterson Prairie Campground; at jct with FR 60 continue straight on FR 60, then right at FR 66, turn right (W) on FR 60 & follow signs for Goose Lake about 1.5 mi; right at sign for Forlorn Lakes onto FR 6040 (7 mi of gravel rd). $10. Open after snow melt, about 7/15-10/15; 14-day limit. Series of small camping areas near isolated, picturesque lakes; 8 defined sites, 25 total; 18-ft RV limit most sites; 3 sites for larger RVs. Tbls, toilets, cfga, no drkg wtr. Poor fishing (lakes quite shallow), boating. Very popular, crowded on weekends. Closed part of 2017 for hazardous tree removal; call 509-395-3400 for current status.

Government Mineral Springs $5
Gifford Pinchot National Forest
From Carson (15 mi W of White Salmon), 13.5 mi N of on Wind River Hwy (FR 30); just past fish hatchery, take left fork of V onto FR 3065 (narrow & rough) about 1 mi. $5. Open 5/15 until closed by snow; 14-day limit. 5 small sites; 18-ft RV limit. Toilet, tbls, cfga, no drkg wtr. Hiking, fishing.

Little Goose Campground FREE
Gifford Pinchot National Forest
From settlement of Trout Lake (15 mi N of White Salmon), 5.5 mi SW on SR 141 to forest boundary; N on FR 24 to just past Peterson Prairie Campground to jct with SR 60; continue N on FR 24 (Twin Buttes Rd) about 6 mi to camp off spur rd 161. Free. Open about 5/15 until closed by snow. 6

sites; 24-ft RV limit. Tbls, toilet, cfga, no drkg wtr. Hiking/bridle trails, fishing.

Little Goose Horse Camp   FREE
Gifford Pinchot National Forest
From settlement of Trout Lake (15 mi N of White Salmon), 5.5 mi SW SR 141 to forest boundary; 10.1 mi NW on FR 24; access rough, not recommended for large RVs. Free. 7/1-10/31; 14-day limit. 2 primitive sites (RVs under 25 ft). Tbls, toilet, cfga, no drkg wtr. Fishing; horseback riding. Sites next to dusty gravel rd. Elev 4000 ft.

Moss Creek Campground $8
Gifford Pinchot National Forest
From White Salmon, 8.7 mi W on SR 14; right after White Salmon Recreation Area sign on Cook-Underwood Rd for 5.1 mi; left on Willard Rd for 2.4 mi. $8 with federal senior pass; others pay $16. 5/18-9/10; 14-day limit. 17 sites; 32-ft RV limit. Tbls, toilets, cfga, drkg wtr.

Oklahoma Campground $8
Gifford Pinchot National Forest
From White Salmon, 8.7 mi W on SR 14; right after White Salmon Recreation Area sign on Cook-Underwood Rd for 5.1 mi; left on Willard Rd for 8.9 m (through settlement of Willard); continue about 1 mi on Oklahoma Rd/FR 18. $8 with federal senior pass; others pay $16. 5/18-9/10; 14-day limit. 17 sites; 22-ft RV limit. Tbls, toilets, cfga, drkg wtr. Hiking trail, fishing.

Panther Creek Campground $9
Gifford Pinchot National Forest
From Carson (15 mi W of White Salmon) at jct with SR 14, 4 mi N on Wind River Hwy (FR 30); right on FR 65 (Panther Creek Rd for 3.5 mi to camp W of Panther Creek. $9 with federal senior pass; others pay $18 (double sites $34). 5/18-9/10; 14-day limit. Tbls, toilets, cfga, drkg wtr. 32 sites; 40-ft RV limit. Tbls, toilet, cfga, drkg wtr.

Paradise Creek Campground $9
Gifford Pinchot National Forest
From Carson (15 mi W of White Salmon) at jct with SR 14, 14 mi N on Wind River Hwy (FR 30) to forest boundary, then 6 mi N on FR 30. $9 with federal senior pass; others pay $18. 5/18-9/10; 14-day limit. 42 sites; 25-ft RV limit. Tbls, toilets, cfga, drkg wtr. Hiking.

Peterson Prairie Campground $8
Gifford Pinchot National Forest
From settlement of Trout Lake (15 mi N of White Salmon), 5.5 mi SW SR 141 to forest boundary; continue 2.5 mi W on FR 24; on left. $8 with federal senior pass; others pay $16. 6/12-9/10; 14-day limit. 27 sites; 32-ft RV limit. Tbls, toilets, cfga, drkg wtr. Huckleberry fields.

Trout Lake Creek Campground $10
Gifford Pinchot National Forest
From settlement of Trout Lake (15 mi N of White Salmon), about 1.5 mi N on SR 141; right (N) on Trout Lake Creek Rd to forest boundary; continue N on FR 88 about 1 mi; right on FR 8810 (sign) to bottom of hill, across bridge, then right onto spur rd (FR 8810-010) to camp next to Trout Lake Creek. $10. All year; 14-day limit. 17 sites (large RVs not recommended). Tbls, toilets, cfga, no drkg wtr. Fishing, hiking.

WILBUR

Jones Bay Campground $9
Lake Roosevelt National Recreation Area
Half mi NW of Wilbur on SR 174; right for 6.2 mi; just before milepost 99, right on unmarked rd for 2 mi; veer left on Gollehon Rd for 2 mi, then veer left again on Hanson Harbor Rd for 3.5 mi; right at Y for 3 mi. $9 with federal senior pass; others pay $18 during 5/1-9/30; $4.50 & $9 off-season. 9 sites. Pit toilets, tbls, cfga, no drkg wtr. Fishing, boating(l).

WILKESON

Evans Creek ORV Camp $5
Mt. Baker-Snoqualmie National Forest
3.5 mi SE of Wilkeson on Hwy 165 & FR 7920. Free with $30 annual NW forest pass; $5 daily otherwise. 6/15-11/15; 14-day limit. 34 sites. Tbls, toilets, cfga, drkg wtr. No fishing. Take-off point for off-road vehicle trails.

WINTHROP

Ballard Campground $8
Okanogan National Forest
13.2 mi NW of Winthrop on SR 20; 7.5 mi NW on paved CR 1163 (Lost River Rd); 1.5 mi NW on gravel FR 5400; at West Fork Methow River. $8 during 5/15-9/15; free rest of year but no services; 14-day limit. 7 sites (28-ft RV limit). Toilets, tbls, cfga, no drkg wtr or trash service. Fishing, hiking. Access to Robinson Creek, West Fork Methow & Lost River/Monument Creek trails.

Buck Lake Campground $8
Okanogan National Forest
6.6 mi N of Winthrop on W. Chewuch Rd (CR 1213); left on Eightmile Rd (FR 5130), then left on Buck Lake Rd (FR 5130-100 for 1.5 mi; at N shore of Buck Lake.$8 during 5/15-9/15; free rest of year; 14-day limit. 9 sites (25-ft RV limit). Tbls, toilets, cfga, no drkg wtr or trash service. Fishing, boating (l - small boats), hiking, mountain biking. Good fishing early in year; lake stocked.

Camp Four Campground $12
Okanogan National Forest
6.6 mi N of Winthrop on W Chewuch Rd (CR 1213); 11.3 mi N on FR 51; along Chewuch River. $12. 5/15-10/15; free off-season but no services. 14-day limit. 5 sites up to 16 ft

on 2 acres (2 for small RVs such as pickup or van campers, but trailers not recommended). Tbls, toilets, cfga, no drkg wtr. River. Fishing. Access rd groomed for snowmobiles in winter, closed to vehicles 12/1-4/1.

Chewuck Campground $12
Okanogan National Forest
6.6 mi N of Winthrop on W Chewuch Rd (CR 1213); 8.6 mi NE on FR 51; along W shore of Chewuch River. $12. 5/15-9/15; free off-season but not services; 14-day limit. Open, undeveloped area with 16 sites (2 with 35-ft RV limit). Tbls, toilets, cfga, no drkg wtr, no trash pickup. Hunting, fishing, hiking. Elev 2200 ft. Watch for rattlesnakes.

Early Winters Campground $8
Okanogan National Forest
15 mi W of Winthrop on SR 20; along Early Winters Creek. $8 during 5/15-9/15; free rest of year but no wtr or services; 14-day limit. 12 sites; 32-ft RV limit. Tbls, toilets, cfga, drkg wtr. Fishing (prohibited at creek), hiking (trail S to Cedar Falls), interpretive trail.

Falls Creek Campground $8
Okanogan National Forest
6.6 mi N of Winthrop on CR 1213 (W. Chewwuch Rd); 11 mi N on paved FR 51; at Falls Creek & Chewuch River. $8. All year; 14-day limit. 7 sites (3 with 18-ft RV limit). Tbls, toilets, cfga, drkg wtr, no trash service. Fishing, swimming. Near Pasayten Wilderness. Hike qtr mi to scenic falls.

Flat Campground $8
Okanogan National Forest
6.6 mi N of Winthrop on W Chewuch Rd (CR 1213); 2.8 mi N on FR 51; 3.5 mi NW on FR 383 & FR 5130 (Eightmile Rd); at W shore of Eightmile Creek; easy access for RVs. $8 during 5/15-9/15; free rest of year; 14-day limit. 12 sites (36-ft RV limit; lower level is dead-end). Tbls, toilets, cfga, no drkg wtr or trash service. Fishing, mountain biking, hiking. Elev 2858 ft. Be wary of logging trucks weekdays.

Honeymoon Campground $8
Okanogan National Forest
6.6 mi N of Winthrop on W Chewuch Rd (CR 1213); 2.8 mi N on FR 51; 8.9 mi NW on FR 383 & FR 5130 (Eightmile Rd); at Eightmile Creek & Honeymoon Creek. $8 during 4/15-11/15; free rest of year but no services; 14-day limit. 5 sites up to 22 ft. Tbls, toilets, cfga, no drkg wtr. Fishing. Named after honeymoon spot of forest ranger & wife.

Klipchuck Campground $12
Okanogan National Forest
14.5 mi W of Winthrop on SR 20; 1.2 mi NW on FR 300. $12 during 4/15-11/15; 14-day limit. 46 sites (5 with 34-ft RV limit). Tbls, toilets, cfga, drkg wtr. Fishing, hiking. Elev 3000 ft; 20 acres. Rattlesnakes. Group camping.

Lone Fir Campground $12
Okanogan National Forest
27 mi W of Winthrop on SR 20; left onto access rd. $12 during 6/1-10/30; free rest of year but no services; 14-day limit. 27 sites (5 with 36-ft RV limit). Tbls, toilets, cfga, drkg wtr. Fishing, hiking. Elev 3640 ft. Along Early Winters Creek (fishing prohibited) near Cutthroat Lake trailhead.

Nice Campground $8
Okanogan National Forest
6.6 mi N of Winthrop on W. Chewuch Rd (CR 1213); 2.8 mi N on FR 51; 3.8 mi NW on FR 5130 (Eightmile Rd - beware of logging trucks weekdays); along Eightmile Creek near beaver pond. $8 during 5/1-11/15; free rest of year but no services; 14-day limit. 3 sites (35-ft RV limit; no turn-around). Tbls, toilets, cfga, no drkg wtr or trash service. Fishing. Good spot for group camping.

River Bend Campground $8
Okanogan National Forest
13.2 mi NW of Winthrop on SR 20; 6.9 mi NW on CR 1163; 2.5 mi NW on FR 5400; half mi W on FR 060; at West Fork Methow River. $8 during 5/1-11/15; free rest of year; 14-day limit. 5 sites (30-ft RV limit). Tbls, toilets, cfga, no drkg wtr. No trash service in winter. Fishing, hiking trails.

Ruffed Grouse $8
Okanogan National Forest
6.6 mi N of Winthrop on W. Chewuch Rd (CR 1213); 2.8 mi N on FR 51; 8.9 mi NW on FR 383 & FR 5130 (Eightmile Rd - beware of logging trucks weekdays); at Eightmile Creek. $8 during 5/15-11/15; free rest of year but no wtr or services; 14-day limit. 4 sites; 35-ft RV limit. Tbls, toilets, cfga, drkg wtr, no trash service. Fishing, hiking, biking. Good area for group camping.

WOODLAND

Rock Creek Campground $10
Yacolt Burn State Forest
Department of Natural Resources
From I-5 exit 9 S of Woodland, follow 179th St E 5.5 mi; right on SR 503 for 1.5 mi, then left on NE 159th St for 3 mi; right on 182nd Ave for 1 mi; left on NE 139th (L-400 Rd) about 8 mi; left on L-1000 Rd for 3.2 mi; left 1.3 mi; left on L-1200 Rd for qtr mi. Camp on right. $10 daily or $30 annual Discover Pass. All year; 7-day limit. 19 sites. Toilets, tbls, cfga, drkg wtr, group shelter. Horse facilities, horse trails, hiking trails, fishing. 20 acres.

YACOLT

Lewis River Horse Camp $5
Gifford Pinchot National Forest
From Yacolt, 4 mi N on N.E. Amboy Rd to settlement of Amboy; about 11 mi NW on SR 503 to settlement of Cougar; about 16 mi E on FR 90 (past Swift Reservoir & Lower Lewis Falls, continuing NE on FR 90 about 20 mi,

then left (N) on FR 93 (15 mi of gravel rd) for one-eighth mi to horse camp on right. $5. 5/15-9/30; 14-day limit. 9 poorly defined sites. Tbls, toilet, cfga, firewood, no drkg wtr. Horseback riding, fishing, swimming. Elev 1500 ft; 2 acres. On Upper Lewis River. Self-service. Waterfalls.

Lower Falls Recreation Area $7.50
Mt. St. Helens National Volcanic Monument
Gifford Pinchot National Forest
From Yacolt, 4 mi N on N.E. Amboy Rd to settlement of Amboy; about 11 mi NW on SR 503 through settlements of Chelatchie & Cougar; continue 33 mi E on SR 503, becoming FR 90 (rough rd); campground on right just past mile marker 28 (following signs). $7.50 with federal senior pass; others pay $15. 5/20-10/16; 14-day limit. 44 sites; 60-ft RV limit. Tbls, toilets, cfga, drkg wtr. Hiking, catch-and-release fishing, mountain biking.

Sunset Falls Campground $12
Gifford Pinchot National Forest
Mt. St. Helens National Volcanic Monument
From jct with Yacolt Rd at Yacolt, 2.4 mi S on Railroad Ave; left at Sunset sign on NE Sunset Falls Rd (becoming SR 42) for 7.3 mi; at Lewis River. $12. All year; 14-day limit. 18 sites; 22-ft RV limit; 10 pull-through. Tbls, toilets, cfga, drkg wtr. Hiking trail.

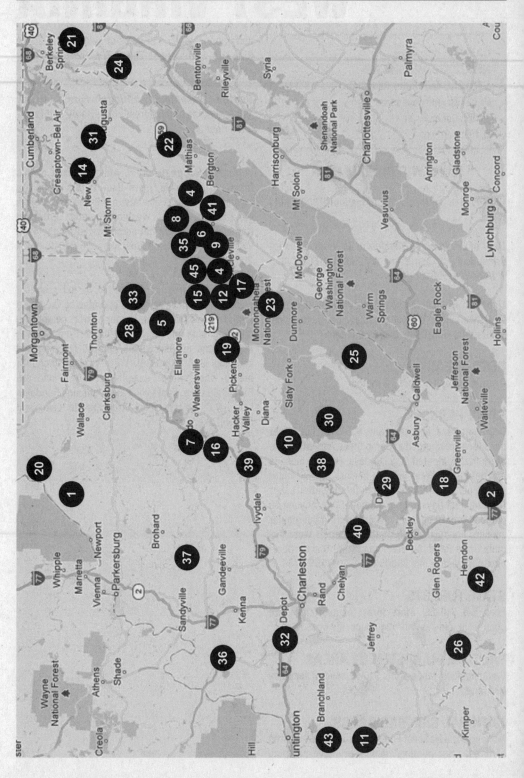

WEST VIRGINIA

CAPITAL: Charleston
NICKNAME: Mountain State
STATEHOOD: 1863 – 35th State
FLOWER: Rhododendron
TREE: Sugar Maple
BIRD: Cardinal

WWW.WVTOURISM.COM

Toll-free number for travel information: 1-800-CALL-WVA.

Dept of Commerce, Division of Tourism, 90 MacCorkle Ave SW, Charleston, WV 25303. 1-800-CALL-WVA or 304-558-2200.

Dept of Natural Resources, Wildlife Resources Office, State Capitol Complex, Charleston, WV 25305. 304-558-0660. www.wvdnr.gov

REST AREAS
Overnight stops are not permitted.

STATE PARKS
Overnight fees are generally $15-$19, but lower base fees are charged at Camp Creek and Bluestone State Parks. Limited stay, 14 days. Pets on leashes are permitted. West Virginia seniors 62 and older get 50 per cent discounts from the day after Labor Day until four days prior to Memorial Day. Anyone 60 or older gets 10 per cent discount during the regular season. For further information contact: West Virginia State Parks & Recreation, State Capitol Complex, Charleston, WV 25305 0314. 304/558-2764.

STATE FORESTS
Fees are $10-22. State forest campgrounds are open from mid-April through deer rifle season.

WILDLIFE MANAGEMENT AREAS
Camping fees range from $10 at several facilities to $14.

NATIONAL CAMPING AREAS
Monongahela National Forest. Nearly 900,000 acres of forest offer hunting, fishing, primitive camping and approximately 850 miles of hiking trails. USDA Bldg, 200 Sycamore St, Elkins, WV 26241; 304-636-1800.

George Washington National Forest. Nearly 100,000 acres of this forest are in Hardy and Pendleton Counties.

Jefferson National Forest. Although most of this forest is in Virginia, more than 18,000 acres are located in Monroe County on Potts and Peters Mountains. George Washington and Jefferson National Forests are not administered jointly. 5162 Valleypointe Parkway, Roanoke, VA 24019. 540-265-5100

U.S. Army Corps of Engineers. A full range of campgrounds developed and operated by the Corps is thoroughly reported in our sister guidebook, Camping With the Corps, available from Cottage Publications for just $17.95 plus $5 shipping and handling (800-272-5518). West Virginia impoundments where Corps camping can be found are Burnsville Lake, East Lynn Lake, Jennings Randolph Lake, R.D. Bailey Lake, Summersville Lake and Sutton Lake.

ALMA (1)

Conaway Run Lake $10
Wildlife Management Area
10 mi SE of Middlebourne off SR 18. $10. All year; 14-day limit. 10 primitive sites on 630 acres. Tbls, toilets, cfga, drkg wtr. Boating(l), fishing, hunting, shooting range. GPS: 39.424644, -80.855768.

ATHENS (2)

Short Mountain $10
Wildlife Management Area
From US 50 at Augusta, 8 mi S on CR 7; left at WMA sign. $10. All year; 14-day limit. 74 primitive sites at 6 camping areas (18-ft RV limit); 8,000 acres. Toilets, cfga, no other facilities. Hunting, fishing, hiking. Camping primarily for hunters. GPS: 39.196847, -78.673912.

BAILEYSVILLE (3)

Guyandotte Campground $8
R.D. Bailey Lake
Corps of Engineers
From the dam, 1.1 mi to US 52, then 2.2 mi S; 5.8 mi S on SR 97 toward Baileysville. Camping is in 2 areas along the Guyandotte River, the first being Reedy Creek about 3 mi from the campground entrance, with 31 elec 50/amp sites, 6 full hookups. The other camping area after 1 more mi along the river is Locust Branch, with 63 sites. Each camping areas has showers & comfort stations. 2 other camping areas were closed. $8 base with federal senior pass at 94 paved 50-amp elec sites; others pay $16 base, $24 for 6 full hookups ($12 with senior pass). 5 pull-through sites. Free primitive camping area open during pre-season & post-season periods, closed Jan & Feb. Tbls, flush toilets, cfga, drkg wtr, showers, dump, playground, marina, coin laundry, beach. Boating(rl), fishing, waterskiing, swimming. GPS: 37.59082, -81.719238

BARTOW (4)

Island Campground CLOSED
Monongahela National Forest
3 mi NE of Bartow on US 250; 2.7 mi NE of WV 28; qtr mi NW on FR 36. Closed to RVs due to bridge safety. Walk-in only.

Lake Buffalo FREE
Dispersed Camping
Monongahela National Forest
2 mi NE of Bartow on SR 54, then 4 mi SE. Free. 4/15-12/1; 14-day limit. Primitive, undesignated sites. Tbls, toilets, cfga, at boat ramp area. Hunting, fishing, boating(l), hiking. 22-acre lake. GPS: 38.531413, -79.701830

BELINGTON (5)

Teter Creek $10
Wildlife Management Area
From SR 92 at Meadowview, 3 mi E on CR 9. $10. All year; 14-day limit. 20 sites. Tbls, toilets, cfga, drkg wtr, play-ground, dump. Fishing, hunting, picnicking, boating(ld), horseshoes. GPS: 39.108424, -79.876583.

BRANDYWINE (6)

Brandywine Lake $8
Geo. Washington National Forest
2 mi E of Brandywine on US 33. $8 with federal senior pass during about 5/15-10/15; others pay $16. During about 10/16-12/10, regular fees $5, but no wtr services ($2.50 with federal senior pass). 14-day limit. 34 sites, not suitable for large RVs . Tbls, flush toilets, cfga, drkg wtr, showers, dump, store. Fishing, swimming hiking trails. 10 acres. Non-campers pay $5 day use fee (or $30 annually). GPS: 38.599609, -79.200928.

BURNSVILLE (7)

Riffle Run Campground $8
Corps of Engineers
Burnsville Lake
From Burnsville at I-79 exit 79, 3 mi E on SR 5. $8 with federal senior pass at 6 primitive sites (others pay $16); $13 with senior pass at 54 full-hookup sites (others pay $26). About 4/20-12/1; 14-day limit. Tbls, flush toilets, cfga, drkg wtr, showers, hookups($), dump, playground, amphitheater, coin laundry, picnic shelter. Boating(l), hiking, hunting, fishing, horseshoe pits, ball fields. GPS: 38.5029, -80.3655

CABINS (8)

Red Creek $11
Monongahela National Forest
4.5 mi S of Cabins on SR 28; 1 mi N on SR 4; 6 mi W on FR 19; 7 mi N on FR 75. $11 ($5.50 for seniors with GA Passport). About 4/15-12/1; 14-day limit. 12 sites (22-ft RV limit). Tbls, pit toilets, cfga, drkg wtr, no showers. Nature trail. Near Dolly Sods Wilderness. GPS: 39.032260, -79.315940

CHERRY GROVE (9)

Spruce Knob Lake Campground $7
Monongahela National Forest
Spruce Knob-Seneca Rocks National Recreation Area
2.5 mi SW of Cherry Grove on SR 28; 9 mi NW on CR 10; .7 mi NE on FR 112 (rough rd); half mi SW on FR 1. $7 with federal senior pass at 28 RV sites; others pay $14. (double sites $26). 4/15-10/11; 14-day limit. Tbls, toilets, cfga, drkg wtr (solar powered pump). Boating, fishing, hiking trails, hunting, no swimming. 38.707380, -79.588260

COWEN (10)

Williams River Sites $5
Monongahela National Forest
From Cowen, follow SR 46 to Williams River Rd (FRs 86 & 216). 30 numbered campsites are scattered along the river from the Three Forks area nearly to the river's headwaters. $5. 3/28/11/30; 14-day limit. Each site has a parking spur, a tbl, cfga, waste receptacle & lantern hanger. Vault

toilets are all along the rd. Trout fishing in the Williams River. Hiking & biking trails. GPS: 38.34584, -80.23642

DUNLOW (11)

Tick Ridge Campground $12
Cabwaylingo State Forest
I-64 exit 8; 4 mi off Rt 152, 10 mi off US 52. $12 for 10 rustic sites ($6 for WV seniors off-season, $12.60 non-resident seniors). 4/1-10/31; 14-day limit. 30-ft RV limit. Tbls, flush toilets, cfga, drkg wtr, showers, dump. Swimming, hiking, volleyball, horseshoes, fishing, hunting. 8,123 acres. Forest GPS: 37.968414, -82.361463.

DUNMORE (12)

Seneca State Forest $7
4 mi SW of Dunmore on SR 11; at Greenbrier River. $7 for WV seniors between 4/1 & 4 days before MD, then between day after LD until campground closes. Others pay $14. 4/1-early Dec; 14-day limit. 10 rustic sites; no RV size limit. Tbls, toilets, cfga, drkg wtr, picnic shelter, showers($), playground, volleyball court. Boating(r), hiking & biking trails, fishing, hunting, canoeing(r). 11,684 acres with 4-acre fishing lake. GPS: 38.327637, -79.935303

EDINBURG (VIRGINIA) (13)

Wolf Gap Recreation Area FREE
Geo. Washington National Forest
12.1 mi NW of Edinburg on VA 675; in West Virginia. All year; 14-day limit. 9 sites (22-ft RV limit). Tbls, toilets, cfga, firewood, well drkg wtr, no trash service. Hiking. Elev 2200 ft; 5 acres. Mountains. Hardwood forest. 2-mi hike to Big Schloss Lookout. GPS: 38.92456, -78.687988

ELK GARDEN (14)

Robert W. Craig Campground $9
Jennings Randolph Lake
Corps of Engineers
From Elk Garden, 5 mi NE on SR 46; exit N at sign. $9 with federal senior pass at 9 non-elec sites (others pay $18); $11 with senior pass at 73 elec sites (others pay $22). 5/1-10/11; 14-day limit. 55-ft RV limit Flush toilets, cfga, drkg wtr, elec($), showers, dump, tbls, beach, playground, store, amphitheater. Boating(l), fishing, swimming, horseshoes, waterskiing, hiking trail, interpretive trail. GPS: 39.41677, -79.11611

ELKINS (15)

Bear Heaven Recreation Area $5
Monongahela National Forest
About 10 mi E of Elkins on US 33; 3 mi N on FR 91 (Stuart Memorial Dr). $5 ($2.50 with federal senior pass). 4/15-12/1; free late fall & winter, but FR 91 not plowed; 14-day limit. 8 small sites. Tbls, toilets, cfga, drkg wtr; no wtr during free period. Hiking, hunting, picnicking. GPS: 38.929825, --79.730878

FLATWOODS (16)

Bulltown Campground $10
Burnsville Lake
Corps of Engineers
From I-79 exit 67 at Flatwoods, 10 mi N on US 19 through Flatwoods & Napier, across lake bridge; on left at signs. $10 with federal senior pass at 22 wtr/30-amp elec sites (others pay $20); $11 with senior pass at 48 wtr/50-amp elec sites (others pay $22); $13 with senior pass at 134 full-hookup 50-amp sites; others pay $26. About 4/20-12/1; 14-day limit. RV limit in excess of 65 ft. Tbls, flush toilets, cfga, drkg wtr, elec, showers, dump, beach, playground, coin laundry, horseshoe pits, picnic shelter. Waterskiing, boating(l), fishing, volleyball, horseshoe pits, interpretive trail, hiking, biking & bridle trails. GPS: 38.79167, -80.56639

FROST (17)

Bird Run Campground FREE
Monongahela National Forest
1.5 mi E of Frost on WV 84. Free. All year, but no services or wtr in winter; 14-day limit. 9 rustic sites (RVs under 32 ft). Tbls, toilets, cfga, firewood, well drkg wtr, no trash service. Hunting. Elev 2700 ft; 7 acres. Camp founded by CCC in 1935. Very primitive area. GPS: 38.27167, -79.85361.

HINTON (18)

Bluestone Lake $12
State Wildlife Management Area
1 mi NE of Hinton on SR 20. $12. Seniors pay $10.80; WV seniors pay $6 from day after LD until 4 days before MD. All year; 14 day limit. 330 primitive sites. Toilets, drkg wtr, cfga. Hunting, fishing, boating. 17,632 acres. GPS: 38.597626, -80.454903

Old Mill Campground $7
Bluestone State Park
4 mi S on Hinton on SR 20. $7 at primitive sites for WV seniors during early spring until 4 days before MD, then from day after LD until campground closes; others pay $14. All seniors pay $12.60 in-season (early May until late October). 14-day limit. Tbls, toilets, cold showers, cfga, tbls, drkg wtr, dump. Swimming, boating(lr), canoeing(r), croquet, horseshoes, shuffleboard, fishing, hunting, nature program, movies. GPS: 37.618164, -80.9360

Sandstone Falls FREE
New River Gorge National River
On River Rd (Hwy 26) off Hwy 20 in Hinton. Free. All year; 14-day limit. Primitive designated camping area. No facilities except cfga, no drkg wtr. Boating, swimming, fishing, canoeing, birdwatching. Falls GPS: 37.4530, -80.5419

HUTTONSVILLE (19)

Mill Creek Campground $7
Kumbrabow State Forest
7 mi S of Huttonsville on US 219 to Elkwater; W to state

forest. $7 for WV seniors between 4/15 & 4 days before MD, then between day after LD until campground closes. Others pay $14. 4/15-12/31; 14-day limit. 12 sites; 30-ft RV limit, but most sites meant for 20-ft RVs. Tbls, pit toilets, cfga, drkg wtr, playground, showers($), coin laundry. Hunting, fishing, hiking. Forest GPS: 38.639623, -80.087015.

JACKSONBURG (20)

Lewis Wetzel Wildlife Management Are $10
1 mi S of Jacksonburg on Buffalo Run Rd (CR 82). $10. 4/30-11/1; 14-day limit. 20 primitive sites. Toilets, tbls, cfga, drkg wtr. Hunting, fishing, hiking. 13,000 acres. GPS: 39.506967, -80.64934.

JONES SPRINGS (21)

Sleepy Creek Wildlife Management Area $10
5 mi W of Jones Springs. $10. All year; 14-day limit. 75 primitive sites (18 ft RV limit suggested due to roads). 22,000 acres. Toilets, drkg wtr, tbls, cfga. Fishing, hunting, boating(l - no mtrs), rifle range. GPS: 39.501963, -78.157868.

LOST CITY (22)

Trout Pond Recreation Area $9.50
George Washington National Forest
10 mi N of Lost City on Hwy 259, then right on SR 259/55 for 6 mi; right on FR 500 about 1 mi. $9.50 with federal senior pass at non-elec sites during peak season of 5/1-9/10; others pay $19. Off-season fee with federal senior pass, $7.50 during 4/16-5/15 & 9/11-12/2; others pay $15. $3 surcharge for elec hookup. Double sites available. 50 sites (13 with elec), up to 55 ft. Tbls, flush toilets, showers, drkg wtr, dump, playground, beach. Boating (no motors), swimming, hiking trails, fishing, interpretive programs. Non-campers pay day use fees for fishing, picnicking, swimming. Trout Pond is West Virginia's only natural lake. GPS: 78.7347, -39.9528

MARLINTON (23)

Day Run Campground $8
Monongahela National Forest
4 mi S of SR 150, following FR 86 to FR 216; 1 mi S on FR 216; along the upper Williams River. $8. 4/1-11/30; 14-day limit. 12 sites (32-ft RV limit). Tbls, toilets, cfga, drkg wtr. Fishing, hiking. Elev 3100 ft; 8 acres. GPS: 38.288360, -80.214940

Handley Wildlife Management Area $10
3.5 mi W of Marlinton on 219; 7 mi W on SR 17 to WMA sign, bear to right on gravel FR 86 (Williams River Rd) 1 mi. $10. All year; 14-day limit. 13 primitive sites. Tbls, pt toilets, cfga, drkg wtr. Boating (elec motors only), fishing, hunting. 784 acres; 5 acre lake. GPS: 38.307783, -80.195875.

Pocahontas $8
Monongahela National Forest
11 mi E of Marlinton on SR 39; 6 mi S on SR 92. $8 during 4/1-11/30; 14-day limit. 8 sites; no RV size limit. Tbls, toilets, cfga, drkg wtr. Hunting, hiking trails, mountain biking. GPS: 38.101630, -79.967850

Tea Creek $10
Monongahela National Forest
4 mi N of Marlinton on Hwy 219; 12 mi W on Hwy 17; 3 mi NW on FR 86; at jct of Tea Creek & Williams River. $10. 4/1-11/30; 14-day limit. 28 sites up to 64 ft. Tbls, toilets, cfga, drkg wtr. Fishing, hiking. GPS: 38.343270, -80.231860

MONTEREY (VIRGINIA) (24)

Laurel Fork   FREE
Special Management Area
Geo. Washington National Forest
About 15 mi NW of Monterey, Virginia, on US 250, into West Virginia, then 8 mi farther to Thornwood; 6 mi NE (right) on SR 28; at FR 106, follow signs for Locust Springs Recreation Area. Free. Primitive undesignated sites at Locust Spring picnic area. Tbls, toilets, cfga, drkg wtr. Also, dispersed tent camping anywhere along 28 mi of hiking trails. Good fishing for native trout in the Back River. GPS: 38.7403897, -79.6933909

NEOLA (25)

Blue Bend Campground $10
Blue Bend Recreation Area
Monongahela National Forest
9 mi N of Neola on SR 92; 2.6 mi W on CR 16; 1.2 mi W on CR 21. $10 during 5/15-9/30; fees & services reduced 4/1-5/15 & 9/30-11/30. 14-day limit. 21 sites up to 52 ft. Tbls, flush & pit toilets, cfga, drkg wtr (no wtr off-season). Fishing, picnicking, swimming, hiking & biking trails. Recreation area was built by the CCC in the 1930s. GPS: 37.920240, -80.269030

Meadow Creek $7
Lake Sherwood Recreation Area
Monongahela National Forest
11 mi NE of Neola on Hwy 14 (Lake Sherwood Rd), following signs for the recreation area. $7 with federal senior pass; others pay $14. 5/15-LD; 14-day limit. 36 sites up to 50 ft. Tbls, flush & pit toilets, cfga, showers, dump, drkg wtr. Swimming, boating(rl), fishing, sailing, hiking, canoeing(r). Non-campers pay $3 day use fee. GPS: 38.006836, -80.010254

Pine Run Campground $7
Lake Sherwood Recreation Area
Monongahela National Forest
11 mi NE of Neola on Hwy 14 (Lake Sherwood Rd); at Lake Sherwood. $7 with federal senior pass; others pay $14. 5/15-LD; 14-day limit. 34 sites up to 50 ft. Tbls, flush toilets, cfga, drkg wtr, dump, showers. Boating(lr), swim-

WEST VIRGINIA

ming, fishing, sailing, hiking, canoeing(r). Non-campers pay $3 day use fee. GPS: 38.006836, -80.010254

West Shore Campground $8
Lake Sherwood Recreation Area
Monongahela National Forest
11 mi NE of Neola on Lake Sherwood Rd. $8 with federal senior pass; others pay $16. 3/5-11/30; 14-day limit. 23 sites up to 78 ft. Tbls, flush & pit toilets, cfga, drkg wtr, dump, showers (except in winter). Swimming, boating(lr), fishing, canoeing(r), volleyball, hiking trails. Non-campers pay $3 day use fee. GPS: 38.012451, -80.005371

PANTHER (26)
Panther $11.70
State Wildlife Management Area
From post office in Panther, left at WMA sign for 3.5 mi to entrance. $11.70 for seniors; WV seniors pay $6.50 between 4/15 and 4 days before memorial day, then between day after LD until campground closes. 4/15-10/15; 14-day limit. 6 sites with elec. Tbls, pit toilets, cfga, drkg wtr. Swimming, fishing, hunting, hiking trails. 7,810 acres. GPS: 37.415192, -81.879365

PHILIPPI (28)
Pleasant Creek $10
Wildlife Management Area
10 mi N of Philippi on US 119 & 250. $10. 5/1-11/1; 14-day limit. About 40 primitive sites. Tbls, toilets, cfga, drkg wtr, no showers. Boating(l), fishing, swimming, canoeing, hunting, hiking, archery, horseshoes, shooting range. 2,769 acres. GPS: 39.248502, -80.029739.

PRINCE (29)
Army Camp FREE
New River Gorge National River
On unmarked dirt rd off Hwy 41 near Prince; from Beckley, it is first left after crossing New River bridge. Free. All year; 14-day limit. Primitive designated camping area; no facilities except cfga, no drkg wtr. Fishing, boating, swimming, hiking, canoeing, birdwatching.

Glade Creek FREE
New River Gorge National River
At end of Glade Creek Rd, off Hwy 41 near Prince.; well-marked turn before crossing New River bridge. Free. All year; 14-day limit. Primitive designated camping area; no facilities except cfga, no drkg wtr. Fishing, boating, swimming, hiking, birdwatching, canoeing.

Grandview Sandbar FREE
New River Gorge National River
On Glade Creek Rd, off Hwy 41 near Prince; well-marked turn before crossing New River bridge. Free. All year; 14-day limit. Primitive designated camping area; no facilities except cfga, no drkg wtr. Boating, fishing, hiking, swimming, canoeing.

RICHWOOD (30)
Big Rock Campground $10
Monongahela National Forest
6.2 mi N of Richwood on FR 76; at the Cranberry River. $10. 3/28-11/30; 14-day limit. 5 sites (24-ft RV limit). Tbls, toilets, cfga, drkg wtr. Fishing, hiking, hunting. GPS: 38.296059, -80.523888

Bishop Knob Campground $8
Monongahela National Forest
9 mi NE of Richwood on FR 76; left for 2.5 mi on FR 101. $8. 3/28-11/30; 14-day limit. 61 sites; 40-ft RV limit. Tbls, toilets, cfga, drkg wtr. District ranger station. Hiking & biking trails, trout fishing, hunting. GPS: 38.337760, -80.489680

Cranberry Campground $10
Monongahela National Forest
9 mi NE of Richwood on FR 76; right 1.3 mi on FR 101; along Cranberry River. $10. 3/28-11/30; 14-day limit. 30 sites (40-ft RV limit). Tbls, toilets, cfga, drkg wtr. Fishing, hunting, hiking. Generators allowed 6 a.m. until 10 p.m. GPS: 38.325180, -80.441710

Cranberry River Sites $5
Monongahela National Forest
9 mi NE of Richwood on FR 76; right 1.3 mi on FR 101. 13 individual, numbered sites dispersed along Cranberry River between Cranberry Campground & Big Rock Campground. $5. All year; 14-day limit. Tbls, lantern posts, trash cans, no wtr; toilets near site & near sites #15-19. Hiking, biking, fishing. 3 self-service pay tubes. GPS: 38.295470, -80.516070

Summit Lake Campground $10
Monongahela National Forest
6 mi E of Richwood on SR 39; 2 mi N on CR 39. $10. 3/28-11/30; 14-day limit. 33 sites; no RV size limit. Tbls, toilets, cfga, drkg wtr. Hiking, fishing, hunting, boating(l), swimming. 47-acre lake. GPS: 38.248730, -80.44480

ROMNEY (31)
Edwards Run $10
Wildlife Management Area
From US 50 at Capon Bridge, 2 mi N on SR 15. $10. All year; 14-day limit. 6 primitive sites on 397 acres. Pit toilets, cfga, no drkg wtr. Hunting, fishing. GPS: 39.318457,-78.446064.

Nathaniel Mountain $10
Wildlife Management Area
From US 50 just E of Romney, 8 mi S on CR 10 (Grassy Lick Rd) to access rd. $10. All year; 14-day limit. 75 primitive sites at 8 camping areas (18-ft RV limit). 8,875 acres. Toilets, tbls, cfga, drkg wtr. Fishing, hunting, hiking. GPS: 39.190669, -78.821275.

ST. ALBANS (32)
St. Albens   FREE
Municipal Roadside City Park
At end of St. Albens exit from I-64, turn right onto Hwy
35 to stop light; left on Hwy 60 about 3 mi. Donations
encouraged, but camp free. All year; 2-night limit. 4 RV
sites. Tbls, toilets, cfga, drkg wtr, dump, playground.
Boating(l), fishing.

ST. GEORGE (33)
Horseshoe Recreation Area $7.50
Monongahela National Forest
3 mi E of St. George on SR 1; 4 mi NE on SR 7. $7.50 with
federal senior pass at 5 non-elec sites (others pay $15);
$12.50 with senior pass at 13 elec sites (others pay $20).
MD-LD; 14-day limit. 50-ft RV limit. Tbls, flush toilets,
cfga, drkg wtr. Swimming, fishing, volleyball, hiking; rafting & canoeing on Cheat River. 3 acres. Built by the CCC in
1930s. GPS: 39.180240, -79.601810

SENECA ROCKS (35)
Seneca Shadows Campground $9.50
Monongahela National Forest
Spruce Knob-Seneca Rocks National Recreation Area
1 mi S of Seneca Rocks on US 33. $9.50 with federal
senior pass at non-elec sites (others pay $19); $15.50
with senior pass at elec sites (others pay $25). 4/1-10/24;
14-day limit. 25 RV sites (13 with elec), up to 38 ft. Tbls,
flush toilets, cfga, drkg wtr, showers, dump, grey wtr
stations, visitor center. Nature trails, fishing. Many sites
have view of 900-ft Seneca Rocks. GPS: 38.829430,
-79.383850

SOUTHSIDE (36)
Chief Cornstalk $10
Wildlife Management Area
From US 35 near Southside, W on Nine Mile Rd. $10. All
year; 14-day limit. 15 primitive sites. Tbls, toilets, cfga,
drkg wtr. Fishing, horseback riding, hunting, rifle range.
10,466 acres. GPS: 38.722302, -82.046162.

SPENCER (37)
Charles Fork Lake $7
Municipal Park
From Spencer, S on US 119; left on Hwy 36 & follow signs.
$7 without hookups, $14 with elec. All year. Primitive,
undesignated camping. Toilet, cfga, no drkg wtr. Fishing,
mountain biking & hiking trails, canoeing. 25 mi of trails
developed & maintained by local mountain bikers, Friends
of Charles Fork Lake. Lake GPS: 38.77182,-81.343207

SUMMERVILLE (38)
Battle Run Recreation Area $12
Corps of Engineers
Summerville Lake
From S of Summerville at jct with US 19, 3.4 mi W on SR
129 across dam, then N (right) at sign. $12 with federal

senior pass at 110 30-amp elec sites; others pay $24.
5/1-Columbus Day; 14-day limit. RV limit in excess of 65 ft.
Tbls, flush toilets, cfga, drkg wtr, elec, showers, coin laundry, beach, picnic shelter, playground, handicap accessible
swimming pier & fishing area. Boating(l), fishing, waterskiing, biking, swimming, basketball, hiking, horseshoe pits.
GPS: 38.22167, -80.90972

SUTTON (39)
Baker's Run Campground $8
Sutton Lake
Corps of Engineers
From exit 62 of I-79, 2 mi NE to Sutton; 4 mi S on old US 19
(CR 19/40); 12 mi E on CR 17. $8 with federal senior pass
at non-elec sites (others pay $16); $12 with senior pass
at elec sites (others pay $22). About 4/20-10/15; 14-day
limit. 79 sites, some pull-through; 58-ft RV limit. Tbls,
flush toilets, showers, drkg wtr, dump, playground, beach,
fishing pier. Fishing, boating(l), waterskiing, swimming,
basketball, horseshoe pits, volleyball, biking trails. GPS:
38.63501, -80.547951

Bee Run Campground $8
Corps of Engineers
Sutton Lake
From near Sutton on I-79, at exit 67, 1 mi E on SR 4; 1.2
mi E on SR 15; turn right. $8 ($4 with federal senior pass).
About 4/1-12/6; 14-day limit. 12 primitive pull-through
sites; 20-ft RV limit. No shoreline camping. Tbls, toilets,
cfga, no drkg wtr. Store/ice/food nearby. Boating(rl);
picnicking; swimming & fishing nearby. GPS: 38.666992,
-80.678467

Gerald R. Freeman Campground $8
Corps of Engineers
Sutton Lake
From near Sutton at I-79 exit 67, 1 mi S on SR 4; 12 mi E
on SR 15. $8 base with federal senior pass at 48 non-elec
sites; others pay $16 base, $18 at premium locations ($9
with senior pass) at 110 elec sites, $9 base with senior
pass; others pay $18 base, $26 at premium locations ($13
with senior pass). About 4/23 until close of deer hunting
season; 14-day limit. Tbls, flush toilets, showers, cfga,
dump, drkg wtr, elec($), playground, beach, coin laundry.
Biking, hiking trail, boating(l), swimming, basketball,
waterskiing, horseshoe pits, ball courts. GPS: 38.68,
-80.54694

THURMOND (40)
Stone Cliff Beach   FREE
New River Gorge National River
Off Hwy 25 near Thurmond; follow Stone Cliff signs. Free.
All year; 14-day limit. Primitive designated camping area;
no facilities except cfga, no drkg wtr. Fishing, hiking,
boating, swimming, canoeing, birdwatching.

UPPER TRACT (41)

Big Bend $10

Monongahela National Forest

1.5 mi N of Upper Tract on US 220; 8.5 mi N on CR 2; on South Branch of Potomac River. $10 base with federal senior pass; others pay $20 base, $21 for premium sites ($10.50 with senior pass). 4/1-10/25; 14-day limit. 30 standard sites, 11 premium location, up to 66 ft. Tbls, flush & pit toilets, cfga, drkg wtr, dump. Fishing, boating, rafting, hiking. GPS: 38.88961, -79.238060

WARRIORMINE (42)

Berwind Lake $11

Wildlife Management Area

From I-77 exit 9 at Princeton, W on Hwy 460 to Tazwell, Virginia; from exit 2, N on SR 16 to Warriormine; at city limits, turn left across bridge & follow signs 3 mi. $11 for rustic sites; $16 with elec/wtr. 6 rustic sites, 2 with elec/wtr. WV seniors pay $5.50 for rustic sites & $8 for elec/wtr sites during day after LD until 4 days before MD. All year; 14-day limit. Tbls, cfga, lantern posts, toilets, drkg wtr, fishing pier. Hunting, fishing (20-acre lake), boating(l), swimming pool, hiking trails. 18,00 acres. Lake GPS: 37.260672, -81.702276

WAYNE (43)

East Fork Campground $9

East Lynn Lake

Corps of Engineers

19 mi S of Wayne on SR 37 (about 10 mi E of dam at East Fork of Twelvepole Creek. $9 base with federal senior pass at 166 elec sites; others pay $18 base, $22 for premium locations ($11 with senior pass). About 5/10-10/18; 14-day limit. RV limit in excess of 65 ft; some pull through sites. Tbls, flush toilets, dump, showers, cfga, elec, coin laundry, beach, playground. Boating(l), fishing, hiking, swimming. GPS: 38.04421, -82.18566

WYMER (45)

Laurel Fork $8

Monongahela National Forest

12 mi S of Wymer on FR 14 (gravel); 2 mi S on FR 423. $8 (seniors with GA Passports pay $4). 4/15-12/1; 14-day limit. 14 sites up to 80 ft. Tbls, toilets, cfga, drkg wtr. Hiking, fishing, mountain biking. GPS: 38.740270, -79.692320

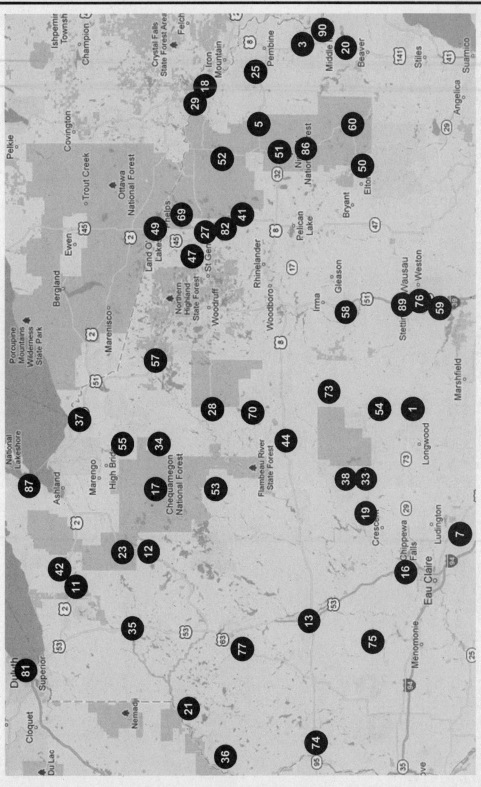

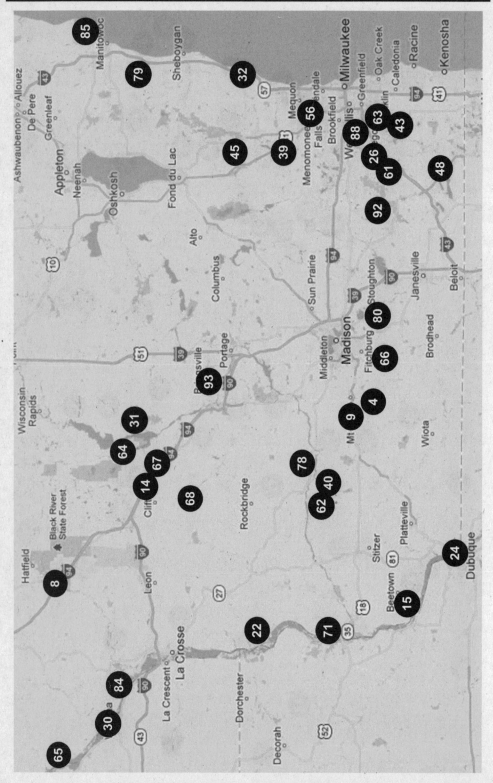

WISCONSIN

WWW.TRAVELWISCONSIN.COM

CAPITAL: Madison
NICKNAME: Badger State
STATEHOOD: 1848 – 30th State
FLOWER: Wood Violet
TREE: Sugar Maple
BIRD: Robin

Toll-free number 800-432-8747.

Wisconsin Department of Tourism Development, PO Box 8690, Madison, WI 53708; 608-266-2161.

Dept of Natural Resources, Box 7921, Madison, WI 53707. 608-266-2621.

STATE PARKS

Admission sticker ($10 daily, $35 annually for non-residents; $7 daily, $25 annually for residents) required on all vehicles in addition to camping fees. A resident senior admission annual sticker is $10; daily admission, $3.   Base campground fees without hookups are $12-15 for residents of Wisconsin; $14-17 for non-residents. Electricity is $5. Sites with views of water are $3 extra.

Northern state forest campgrounds are $7-10 for Wisconsin residents, $9-12 for non-residents. Electrical hookups are $5 extra.

COUNTY PARKS

Some of the best values in camping can be found at numerous county parks. Several county park systems have campgrounds.

Chequamegon-Nicolet National Forest, 500 Hanson Lake Rd, Rhinelander, WI 54501. 715/362-1300.

Nicolet National Forest in northern Wisconsin has 3,000 miles of backroads and hundreds of clear lakes and streams. In its 661,000 acres are 23 developed campgrounds with 460 sites. Although a few campgrounds are free, most have fees of $12 to $14 ($6 to $7 with federal America the Beautiful Senior Pass.

ABBOTSFORD (1N)

Red Arrow City Park   FREE
W side of town just S of high school; at 407 W. Hemlock St. Free. Tbls, toilets, cfga, drkg wtr. Playground, volleyball, disc golf.

Shortener City Park   FREE
Just N of Abbotsford at 100 Shortner Park Way. Free. Primitive camping on 40 acres. Tbls, cfga, drkg wtr, toilets. Shelter, playground, volleyball, 2 large fishing ponds.

AMBERG (3N)

Campsite #2 $10
We Energies
6.9 mi E of Amberg on CR K; half mi N; 2 mi E; 1.2 mi NE to campground. $10. On Menominee River. 5/1-9/30; 15-day limit; Primitive sites. Tbls, toilets, cfga, drkg wtr. Hunting in season, picnicking, fishing, ice fishing, cross-country skiing.

Campsite #32 $10
We Energies
6.9 mi E on CR K; half mi N on co rd; 2 mi E on co rd; 1.9 mi S on co rd (8 mi SW of Banat, MI). $9. 5/1-9/30; 15-day limit. 12 primitive sites. Tbls, toilets, cfga, drkg wtr. Picnicking, boating(l), fishing, hunting in season, ice fishing, cross-country skiing.

ARGYLE (4S)

Yellowstone Lake State Park $12
8 mi SW of Argyle on CR F. $12 base weekdays ($14 non-residents). 128 sites (38 with elec; 11 in winter). All year; 21-day limit. Tbls, pit toilets, cfga, drkg wtr, elec($5), dump, store. Fishing, swimming, boating(l), canoeing, waterskiing, hiking & cross-country ski trails. Adjoins wildlife area. 968 acres; 455-acre Yellowstone Lake. Bats roost in 31 bat houses in the park. GPS: 42.759277, -89.987305

ARMSTRONG CREEK (5N)

Laura Lake $12
Nicolet National Forest
2 mi W of Armstrong Creek on US 8; 4.3 mi N on FR 2163. $12. 5/1-10/15; 14-day limit. 41 sites, typically 45 ft. Tbls, toilets, cfga, drkg wtr. Swimming, boating(l), fishing. GPS: 45.705322, -88.508545

AUGUSTA (7N)

Harstad Park $11
Eau Claire County Campground
4 mi NW of Augusta on US 12; 2 mi E off CR HH; on Eau Claire River. $11 ($55 per week) during 5/15-9/15, $6 with limited facilities off-season. 14-day limit. 27 sites. Tbls, pit toilets, cfga, drkg wtr, playground. Canoeing, snowmobiling, fishing, mountain biking. 43 acres. GPS: 44.7374605, -91.1695979

BLACK RIVER FALLS (8S)

Castle Mound State Recreation Area $12
Black River State Forest
1.5 mi SE of Black River Falls on US 12. $12 base ($14 non-residents). All year; 21-day limit. 35 sites; 5 with elec (28-ft RV limit). Tbls, flush toilets, cfga, drkg wtr, elec($5), showers, dump. Horseshoes, playground, fishing, nature trail. 44.2799612, -90.8220856.

East Fork State Recreation Area $12
Black River State Forest
8 mi E of Black River Falls on SR 54; 7 mi N on CR K forest rd. $12 ($15 non-residents). Spring through Nov; 21-day limit. 24 sites. Tbls, pit toilets, cfga, drkg wtr, no elec. Canoeing, fishing. 15 acres. GPS: 44.4213508, -90.674306.

Pigeon Creek Area $12
Black River State Forest
12 mi SE of Black River Falls on US 12; 4 mi NE on CR O & North Settlement Town Rd (2 mi NE of Millstone). $12 ($14 non-residents). All year; 21-day limit. 38 sites. Tbls, pit toilets, cfga, drkg wtr, beach, no elec. Swimming, boating, fishing, playground, interpretive trail, bike trail. Forest GPS: 44.280762, -90.824707.

BLUE MOUNDS (9S)

Blue Mound State Park $12
1 mi NW of Blue Mounds off US 18 & 151. $12 ($14 non-residents). All year; 21-day limit. 89 wooded sites (15 with elec). Tbls, flush & pit toilets, cfga, drkg wtr, elec($5), dump, showers, playground. Swimming pool($), hiking trails, observation tower, cross-country skiing, nature center. 1,153 acres. No RV camping in winter. GPS: 43.026682, -89.852842.

BRULE (11N)

Bois Brule Campground $12
Brule River State Forest
1 mi S off US 2. $12 for residents; $14 non-residents. 5/1-10/31; 21-day limit. 17 RV sites (26-ft RV limit). Tbls, pit toilets, cfga, drkg wtr. Canoeing, fishing, hiking & nature trails, cross-country skiing, snowmobiling. 20 acres; part of 40,000-acre forest. GPS: 46.5275, -91.6126.

Copper Range Camp $12
Brule River State Forest
5 mi N of US 2 at Brule on CR H; W on park rd. $12 for residents; $14 non-residents. 5/1-10/31; 21-day limit. 15 sites (26-ft RV limit). Tbls, toilets, cfga, drkg wtr. Boating, canoeing, fishing, hiking trails, snowmobile trails, ski trails. Trout stream. 20 acres; part of 40,000-acre forest. GPS: 46.3632, -91.3454.

CABLE (12N)

Namekagon Lake $7
Chequamegon National Forest
11 mi E of Cable on CR M; 5.5 mi N on CR D; qtr mi SW on FR 209. $7 with federal senior pass; others pay $14. 5/1-11/1; 14-day limit. 34 sites; 45-ft RV limit. Tbls, toilets, cfga, drkg wtr. Hiking, fishing, swimming, boating(l), waterskiing. 23 acres. GPS: 46.244629, -91.08667

CAMERON (13N)

Veterans Memorial Park $10
Barron County Park
1 mi S of Cameron on CR SS; three-fourth mi E; at NE corner of Prairie Lake. $10 base for primitive sites; $15 with 20/30/50-amp elec. 5/1-10/31. 28 sites (21 elec). Tbls, toilets, cfga, drkg wtr, elec($), dump ($5 campers, $8 non-campers). Swimming, boating (l), fishing, playground, shelter, nature trail, view bald eagles. 160 acres. 2 nearby county parks have higher fees. GPS: 45.3885702, -91.7171138

CAMP DOUGLAS (14S)

Mill Bluff State Park $12
3 mi NW of Camp Douglas on US 12. $12 base ($14 non-residents). MD-9/30; 21-day limit. 21 rustic sites (6 with elec). Tbls, pit toilets, cfga, drkg wtr, dump, beach, no showers, elec($5). Swimming, hiking. Scenic rock formations, high bluffs (stone steps, observation deck). GPS: 43.9410774, -90.3190198.

CASSVILLE (15S)

Nelson Dewey State Park $12
1 mi NW of Cassville on CR V. $8 base ($14 non-residents). All year; 21-day limit. 45 sites (16 with elec). Tbls, toilets, cfga, drkg wtr, elec($5). Hiking trails. Nearby canoeing, boating, fishing. 755 acres. Home of first governor; reconstructed 1890s village. Mississippi River overlook. GPS: 42.7349922, -91.0190169.

CHIPPEWA FALLS (16N)

Lake Wissota State Park $12
8 mi NE of Chippewa Falls off SR 29; entrance on county rd. $12 base ($14 non-residents). All year; 21-day limit 116 sites (58 with elec). Tbls, flush & pit toilets, cfga, drkg wtr, showers, dump, accessible fishing pier with fish attractors, elec($5). Boating, fishing, swimming, waterskiing, canoeing(r), hiking trails, bridle trails, snowmobiling, self-guided wildflower trail, mountain biking, interpretive & evening programs. 6,300-acre lake created by Wisconsin Minnesota Light & Power in 1918. GPS: 44.97194, -91.29833.

CLAM LAKE (17N)

Day Lake Campground $7
Chequamegon National Forest
1 mi N of Clam Lake on CR GG; three-fourth mi W on FR 1298. $7 with federal senior pass; others pay $14. 5/1-10/31; 14-day limit. 52 sites (45-ft RV limit). Tbls, toilets, cfga, drkg wtr, fishing pier, beach. Swimming, boating(rl), fishing, hiking trails. 40 acres; 632-acre lake. 6 sites are barrier-free with paved trails to fishing pier. GPS: 46.1818973, -90.9043499

East Twin Lake Campground $12
Chequamegon National Forest
Qtr mi NW of Clam Lake on CR M; 3.5 mi NE on CR GG; half mi SE on FR 190; qtr mi S on FR 249. $12. 5/1-10/31; 14-day limit. 10 sites (30-ft RV limit). Tbls, toilets, cfga, drkg wtr, fishing pier. Boating(l), fishing, swimming. 8 acres; 110-acre lake. GPS: 46.1924527, -90.8590716

Moose Lake Campground $12
Chequamegon National Forest
12.2 mi W of Clam Lake on SR 77; 1 mi SE on FR 176; 5 mi S on FR 174; 1 mi W on FR 1643. $12. 5/1-10/31; 14-day limit. 15 sites (RV limit 40 ft). Tbls, toilets, cfga, drkg wtr, beach. Swimming, boating(l), fishing. 15 acres. GPS: 46.0155103, -91.0221227

COMMONWEALTH (18N)

Campsite #24 $10
We Energies
3.6 mi S of Commonwealth on co rd; 1.3 mi W on co rd; 3.5 mi S on co rd to Campsite #34 (on Pine River); cross dam to #24. $10. 5/1-9/30; 15-day limit. 3 primitive sites. Tbls, toilets, cfga, no drkg wtr. Picnicking, boating(l), fishing, hunting in season (whitetail deer, ruffled grouse); ice fishing and cross-country skiing in season. Lake GPS: 45.830873, -88.265708.

Campsite #34 $10
We Energies
3.6 mi S of Commonwealth on co rd; 1.3 mi W on co rd; 3.5 mi S on co rd to campground (on Pine River). $10. 5/1-9/30; 15-day limit. 3 primitive sites. Tbls, toilets, cfga, drkg wtr. Picnicking, boating(l), fishing, hunting in season (whitetail deer, ruffled grouse); ice fishing and cross-country skiing in season. Lake GPS: 45.830873, -88.265708.

CORNELL (19N)

Brunet Island State Park $12
1 mi N off SR 27 & 64; on island between Chippewa & Fisher Rivers. $12 base ($14 non-residents); $15 for water view sites ($17 non-residents). All year; 21-day limit. 69 sites; 24 with elec. Tbls, flush & pit toilets, showers, cfga, drkg wtr, elec($5), dump. Hiking trails, swimming, canoeing, boating(ld), fishing, ski trails. GPS: 45.1819104, -91.1559774

CRIVITZ (20N)

Veterans Memorial $10
Marinette County Park
12 mi W of Crivitz on CR W; 3 mi N on Parkway Rd at Thun-

der River. $10. About 5/1-11/15; 14-day limit. 15 rustic sites. Tbls, toilets, cfga, drkg wtr, playground, dump ($5 non-campers). Fishing, hiking. Waterfall with bridge over it. 320 acres. GPS: 45.2691382, -88.2098278.

DANBURY (21N)

Boulder Campground $12
Governor Knowles State Forest
3 mi W of Danbury on SR 77; cross St. Croix River bridge into Minnesota (on Hwy 48); just across bridge, turn N on CR 173 for 5 mi; 5 mi E on Tamarack Forest Rd. $12 ($14 non-residents). 21 sites; 20-ft RV limit. Tbls, toilets, cfga, drkg wtr. Swimming, hiking, fishing. Managed by Minnesota's St. Croix State Park. GPS: 46.0347, -92.2545.

Tamarack River Equestrian Camp $12
Governor Knowles State Forest
3 mi W of Danbury on SR 77; cross St. Croix River bridge into Minnesota (on Hwy 48); just across bridge, turn N on CR 173 for 5 mi; 3 mi E on Tamarack Forest Rd; left for 2 mi. $12 ($14 non-residents). 55 sites. Tbls, toilets, cfga, no drkg wtr. Primarily an equestrian camp with corrals, bridle trails, loading ramp, picket lines. Also nature trails. Managed by Minnesota's St. Croix State Park. GPS: 46.0638, -92.3855.

DE SOTO (22S)

Blackhawk Park $9
Corps of Engineers
Mississippi River Lock & Dam 9
Lake Winneshiek
From DeSoto, 3 mi N on SR 35, then SW on CR B1. $9 with federal senior pass at 100 non-elec sites; others pay $18. $12 with senior pass at 73 elec sites; others pay $24. 4/1-10/31; 14-day limit. RV limit 65 ft. Tbls, flush toilets, cfga, drkg wtr, dump, elec($), showers($), playground, beach, fishing dock, picnic shelters. Swimming, fishing, boating(l), interpretive programs, weekend movies, volleyball, horseshoes. GPS: 43.4608, -91.2231

Naga-Waukee $12
Waukesha County Park
Half mi N of Hwy 94 on Hwy 83; between Nagawicka Lake & Pewaukee Lake. $12 base. 4/15-11/1; 7-day limit. Base fee for vehicles with annual entry permit; $16 with no permit. 4/1-11/7; 7-day limit. 34 sites; 20-ft RV limit. Tbls, pit toilets, cfga, drkg wtr, beach. Boating(l), sailboating(l), fishing, nature trails, waterskiing, swimming, golf. GPS: 43.0594444, -88.3511111.

DRUMMOND (23S)

Perch Lake $12
Chequamegon National Forest
6 mi N of Drummond on FR 35. $12. 5/1-10/1; 14-day limit. 16 sites (35-ft RV limit). Tbls, toilets, cfga, drkg wtr. Boating(l), fishing, hiking. 23 acres; 72-acre lake. GPS: 45.9344013, -88.4948524

Two Lakes Campground $9.50
Chequamegon National Forest
S of Drummond on FR 213, then follow FR 214 (about 5 mi total); between 1,323-acre Lake Owen & 59-acre Bass Lake. $9.50 with federal senior pass; others pay $19. 5/1-10/10; 14-day limit. 90 sites; 50-ft RV limit. Tbls, toilets, cfga, drkg wtr, pay phone, fishing pier, 2 beaches, dump. Hiking, swimming, boating(lr), fishing, canoeing(r). North Country National Scenic Trail nearby. $8 boat launch, $10 dump fee for campers ($25 non-campers). GPS: 46.2921739, -91.1935214

DUBUQUE (IOWA) (24S)

Grant River Recreation Area $8
Corps of Engineers
Mississippi River
From Dubuque, Iowa, E across river, then N on US 61; 2 mi W on SR 133, following signs (2 mi S of Potosi). $8 base with federal senior pass at 63 30-amp elec sites; others pay $16 base, $18 for premium 50-amp sites ($9 with senior pass). 4/1-10/24; 14-day limit. Self pay. 55-ft RV limit. No wtr hookups. Tbls, flush toilets, cfga, drkg wtr, dump, playground, beach, picnic shelter, amphitheater. Boating(l), fishing, swimming. GPS: 42.6594, -90.7097

DUNBAR (25N)

Twelve-Foot Falls $10
Marinette County Park
About 2 mi W of Dunbar on US 8; 2 mi S on Lily Lake Rd; half mi W on Twin Lake Rd; S on Twelve Foot Falls Rd; on North Branch of Pike River. $10. 5/1-11/15; 14-day limit. 6 rustic sites. Tbls, toilets, cfga, drkg wtr. Hiking, boating(l), fishing. Waterfalls (including Eight-Foot Falls). GPS: 45.5799613, -88.1353961.

EAGLE (26S)

Horseriders Campground $12
Kettle Moraine State Forest
W of Eagle on Hwy 59 to Palmyra, then S on Third St. $12 ($14 non-residents. 4/1-12/1; 21-day limit. 55 equestrian sites (20 pull-through). Tbls, toilets, cfga, drkg wtr. Flush toilets & shower building planned in future. Hiking, horseback riding, fishing. GPS: 42.859985, -88.568126.

Ottawa Lake Recreation Area $12
Kettle Moraine State Forest
8 mi N of Eagle on CR ZZ. $12 base ($14 non-residents); $15 base for shoreline sites ($17 non-residents). All year; 21-day limit; 21-day limit. 100 sites, 49 with elec. Tbls, flush toilets (pit toilets in winter), cfga, drkg wtr, elec($5), showers, dump, beach. Swimming, boating (l), fishing. GPS: 42.5885988, -88.2794542.

EAGLE RIVER (27N)

Anvil Lake Campground $12
Nicolet National Forest
8 mi E of Eagle River on SR 70. $12. About 5/1-10/15;

14-day limit. 18 sites, typically 48 ft. Tbls, toilets, cfga, drkg wtr. Boating(l), swimming, fishing, waterskiing, hiking. GPS: 45.9366231, -89.0606844

Franklin Lake Campground $7.50
Nicolet National Forest
7 mi E of Eagle River on SR 70; 2 mi S on FR 2178; 6.3 mi NE on FR 2181. $7.50 with federal senior pass; others pay $15. 5/1-10/15; 14-day limit. 77 sites, typically 50 ft. Tbls, flush & pit toilets, cfga, drkg wtr. Swimming, boating(l), fishing, hiking, waterskiing. 881-acre lake. GPS: 45.9246795, -89.0081829

Kentuck Lake Campground $12
Nicolet National Forest
14.8 mi E of Eagle River on SR 70; 2.5 mi N on FR 2176; qtr mi W on FR 2203. $12 base, $15 for lakeshore sites ($6 & $7.50 with federal senior pass). 5/1-10/15; 14-day limit. 31 sites, typically 55 ft. Tbls, pit toilets, cfga, drkg wtr. Boating(l), fishing, swimming, hiking, waterskiing. GPS: 45.9924567, -88.9804072

Luna White Deer Campground $12
Nicolet National Forest
14.8 mi E of Eagle River on SR 70; 4.5 mi S on FR 2167; 1 mi NW on FR 2188. $12 base, $15 for lakeshore sites ($6 & $7.50 with federal senior pass). 5/1-10/15; 14-day limit. 37 sites, typically 55 ft. Tbls, pit toilets, cfga, drkg wtr, dump. Swimming, boating, hiking trails. GPS: 45.899958, -88.9620701

Windsor Dam Campground $5
Nicolet National Forest
17 mi E of Eagle River on SR 70; 3 mi S on FR 2174. Camp free, but $5 daily parking fee required. 5/1-12/2; 14-day limit. 8 sites (RVs under 22 ft). Tbls, toilets, cfga, drkg wtr. Swimming, boating, trout fishing. GPS: 45.9296804, -88.8606813

FIFIELD (28N)

Sailor Lake Campground $12
Chequamegon National Forest
7.5 mi E of Fifield on SR 70; 3 mi S on FR 139; 1 mi SW on FR 138. $12. 5/1-10/1; 14-day limit. 20 sites (45-ft RV limit). Tbls, toilets, cfga, drkg wtr, shelter. Fishing, boating(l), swimming, hunting, hiking. Trail spur to Flambeau ATV Trails (open to horses, hikers, bikers). GPS: 45.8431, -90.2772

Smith Rapids Campground
Chequamegon National Forest $12
12.5 mi E of Fifield on SR 70; 1.7 mi N on FR 148. $12. 5/1-10/1; 14-day limit. 11 sites; 40-ft RV limit. Tbls, toilets, cfga, drkg wtr, shelter. Fishing, boating (carry-in access), hiking, swimming, horseback riding, canoeing. Nine sites designed to accommodate horse trailers (long spurs & hitching rails). Smith Rapids Covered Bridge. GPS: 45.9116169, -90.1723811.

Twin Lakes Campground $12
Chequamegon National Forest
16.1 mi E of Fifield on SR 70; 5 mi NW on FR 144; 2.4 mi NE on FR 142; three-fourths mi N on FR 1177. $12. 5/1-10/31; 14-day limit. 17 sites up to 52 ft. Tbls, toilets, cfga, drkg wtr. Boating(l), fishing, hiking. GPS: 45.9646717, -90.0721033

FLORENCE (29N)

Campsite #5 $10
We Energies
6.8 mi SE of Florence on US 1/141; 4.3 mi S on co rd to campground. On Pine River. $10. 5/1-9/30; 15-day limit. Primitive sites. Tbls, toilets, cfga, drkg wtr. Hunting, fishing, boating(l), ice fishing, cross-country skiing.

Lost Lake Campground $12
Nicolet National Forest
16.5 mi W of Florence on SR 70; 1 mi S on FR 2450; 3 mi SE on FR 2156. $12. 5/1-10/15; 14-day limit. 27 sites on 12 acres; no RV size limit. Tbls, toilets, cfga, drkg wtr. Boating(l), fishing, hiking. GPS: 45.8838469, -88.5584597

West Bass Lake Campground $8
Florence County Park
About 10 mi S of Florence on SR 101; about 5 mi E on CR C, watching for signs, then 1 mi N on Fire Lane Rd; at E shore of West Bass Lake. $8 without elec. 15 sites. Pit toilets, cfga, drkg wtr, tbls, beach. GPS: 45.777337, -88.335147.

FOUNTAIN CITY (30S)

Merrick State Park $12
2 mi NW of Fountain City off SR 35; at Mississippi River. $12 base ($14 non-residents); $15 for waterfront sites ($17 non-residents). 5/1-10/31; 21-day limit. 69 sites; 22 with elec. Tbls, flush & pit toilets, cfga, drkg wtr, elec($5), fishing pier. Swimming, boating(l), fishing, waterskiing, hiking trails, birdwatching, canoeing. 320 acres. GPS: 44.1516302, -91.748208.

FRIENDSHIP (31S)

Roche-A-Cri State Park $12
3 mi N of Friendship on SR 13. $12 ($14 non-residents); $17 with elec ($19 non-residents). 5/1-10/15; 21-day limit. 33 rustic sites, 4 elec sites (25-ft RV limit). Tbls, pit toilets, cfga, drkg wtr, dump, no elec, no showers. Hiking trails, ski trails, playground, fishing in Carter Creek, nature programs. 605 acres. 300-ft rock outcropping with stairway to top. Petroglyphs, pictographs. GPS: 44.0016365, -89.8179042.

FREDONIA (32S)

Waubedonia Park $10
Ozaukee County Park
S of CR A near Hwy I on W edge of village; on the Milwaukee River. $10. May-Oct; 3-day limit. Rustic sites with cfga, tbls,

flush toilets but no drkg wtr or elec. Fishing, hiking. GPS: 43.4683329, -87.9678691.

GILMAN (33N)

Gilman Municipal Campground $5
In Gilman, just W of CR B on Riverside Dr at Yellow River. $5 (formerly free). 4/1-11/1. 10 undesignated sites. Tbls, toilets, cfga, drkg wtr. Swimming, fishing, biking, canoeing. GPS: 45.161473, -90.808901

GLIDDEN (34N)

Stockfarm Bridge Campground $12
Chequamegon National Forest
11 mi SW of Glidden: W on CR D; S on FR 166; E on FR 164; on Chippewa River. $12. 8 sites. Tbls, toilets, cfga, drkg wtr, no trash service. Boating(l), fishing, canoeing.

GORDON (35N)

Mooney Dam $10
Douglas County Park
12 mi E on CR Y from jct with US 53. $10. 5/15-9/15. 11 sites. Tbls, toilets, cfga, drkg wtr, no elec. Fishing, boating(l), canoeing, swimming. On Lower Eau Claire Lake. Two other county parks (Lucius Woods & Gordon Dam) offer sites for $15-$18. GPS: 46.2588334, -91.5690787.

GRANTSBURG (36N)

Crex Meadows State Wildlife Area   FREE
6 mi N on CR F from jct with SR 70; 4 mi E on N. Refuge Rd. Free. All year; 10-day limit. 10 sites. Tbls, toilets, cfga, drkg wtr. GPS: 43.78444,-88.787868

St. Croix Campground $12
Governor Knowles State Forest
About 8 mi W of Grantsburg on Hwy 70; at St. Croix River. $12 for Wisconsin residents ($14 non-residents) All year; 21-day limit. 30 rustic sites. Tbls, toilets, cfga, drkg wtr. Fishing, boating, hiking. GPS: 45.7631, -92.7847.

Trade River Campground $12
Governor Knowles State Forest
20 mi S of Grantsburg on SR 87; just before Bass Lake, half mi W on 270th Ave; half mi S on 255th St; about 8 mi W on Evergreen Ave to Cowan Creek. $12 for Wisconsin residents ($14 non-residents). All year; 21-day limit. 40 primitive equestrian sites. Toilets, cfga, no drkg wtr, no trash service. Hiking, horseback riding, fishing. Bridle trail.

GURNEY (37N)

Potato River Falls   FREE
Iron County Park
About 1 mi S of Gurney on SR 169, then 1.5 mi W on Potato Falls Rd. Free. Primitive camping near the falls. Tbls, toilets, cfga, no drkg wtr. Hiking, trout fishing. Waterfall. Falls GPS: 46.461059, -90.529071.

HANNIBAL (38S)

Chippewa Campground $12
Chequamegon National Forest
1 mi S of Hannibal on SR 73; 5 mi E on CR M; then FR 1417 to camp. $12 base; $18 at premium sites. About 5/15-LD; 14-day limit. Base fee for sites with pit toilets & drkg wtr; $18 for sites with hot showers & flush toilets ($6 & $9 with federal senior pass). Group sites available. 78 sites; 35-ft RV limit. Tbls, toilets, cfga, drkg wtr, showers, dump, fish cleaning station. Boating(l), fishing, hiking, nature programs, swimming. Newly renovated. 27-site Loop 4 open for gun-deer season, but no facilities or wtr. GPS: 45.220459, -90.704102

HARTFORD (39S)

Pike Lake Campground $12
Kettle Moraine State Forest
2 mi E of Hartford on SR 60; S into forest. $12 base ($14 non-residents). 4/15-10/15; 21-day limit 32 sites (11 with elec). Tbls, flush toilets, cfga, drkg wtr, showers, dump ($3 non-campers), elec($5). Swimming, boating (ramps nearby), fishing, hiking (Ice Age Trail), cross-country & snowmobile trails, nature programs. GPS: 43.3200021, -88.3148181

HIGHLAND (40S)

Blackhawk Lake Recreation Area $12
State Dept. of Natural Resources
Blackhawk Lake Commission
About 10 mi S of Highland on SR 80; 2 mi E on CR BH. $12 base with $24 annual pass or $6 daily permit; $18 with elec. 150 sites (78 with elec). Tbls, flush toilets, cfga, drkg wtr, playground, dump, fish cleaning station. Hiking/biking trails, volleyball, horseshoes, swimming, boating(l), fishing. GPS: 43.0199932, -90.2890123.

HILES (41N)

Pine Lake Campground $12
Nicolet National Forest
Qtr mi S of Hiles on SR 32; 2.5 mi SW on FR 2185. $12. 5/1-10/15; 14-day limit. 12 sites (22-ft RV limit). Tbls, toilets, cfga, drkg wtr. Swimming, boating(l), waterskiing, fishing. GPS: 45.6871826, -88.985119

IRON RIVER (42N)

Bladder Lake Campground   CLOSED
Chequamegon National Forest
About 10 mi NE of Iron River via US 2, FR 242 & FR 849. No camping; converted to day use area in 2011.

Brule River Campground $10
Nicolet National Forest
1.5 mi NE of Iron River on SR 55. $10. About 4/25-10/1; 14-day limit. 11 sites, typically 50 ft. Tbls, toilets, cfga, drkg wtr. Swimming, canoeing, fishing. 5 acres. GPS: 46.028564, -88.796387

Horseshoe Lake Campground $12
Chequamegon National Forest
About 10 mi E of Iron River on US 2 to village of Ino; 9.6 mi N on FR 236; left at campground sign. $12. 5/10-11/3; 14-day limit. 11 equestrian sites with hitching posts, pickett line. Horseback riding, canoeing, hiking. 12-mi bridle trail. GPS: Lake GPS: 46.642456, -91.178754

Wanoka Lake Campground $12
Chequamegon National Forest
7 mi SE of Iron River on US 2; 1.5 mi SW on FR 234; .7 mi N on FR 243. $12. 5/1-11/31; 14-day limit. 20 sites (35-ft RV limit). Tbls, toilets, cfga, drkg wtr. Fishing, boating (carry-in access), hiking (Tri-County Corridor Trail nearby). GPS: 46.543457, -91.279785

KANSASVILLE (43S)
Richard Bong State Recreation Area $12
1 mi W of Hwy 142 & Hwy 75 jct. $12 base ($14 non-residents). All year; 21-day limit. 217 sites; 54 with elec. Flush & pit toilets, elec($5), cfga, drkg wtr, showers, visitor center, beach. Horseback riding, hiking, swimming, fishing, motorcycling, hunting, interpretive programs, snowmobiling, sled dog training, hang gliding, model airplane area, canoeing. GPS: 42.63306, -88.125.

KENNAN (44N)
Big Falls $10
Price County Forestry
From Hwy 8 at Kennan, 10 mi S on CR N; W on Big Falls Rd, follow signs 1 mi; at W11337 Big Falls Rd. 12 mi S of Kennan at South Fork Jump River. $10. All year; 14-day limit. 6 sites. Tbls, toilets, cfga, drkg wtr (hand pump), swing set. Hiking trail, canoeing, fishing, hunting, horseshoe pits. Dump at Solberg Lake County Park. GPS: 45.401969, -90.606891.

KEWASKUM (45S)
Long Lake Recreation Area $12
Kettle Moraine State Forest
1.5 mi N of Kewaskum on SR S; 6.5 mi on CR G; 1.5 mi E on CR F, then 1 mi N on County Line Rd. $12 WI residents ($14 non-residents). 5/15-9/30; 21-day limit. 200 sites. Tbls, pit & flush toilets, cfga, drkg wtr, dump, showers, no elec, fishing pier. Boating(l), fishing, swimming. 43.6630503, -88.1648193.

Mauthe Lake Recreation Area $12
Kettle Moraine State Forest
4.5 mi N of Kewaskum on CR S; 1 mi N on SR SS. $12 WI residents ($14 non-residents). 137 sites; 51 with elec. All year; 21-day limit Tbls, flush & pit toilets, cfga, drkg wtr, showers, elec($5), fishing pier. Swimming, boating(l), fishing, horseback riding. GPS: 43.6005513, -88.1781521.

New Prospect Horseriders Camp $12
Kettle Moraine State Forest
1.5 mi N of Kewaskum on SR S; 4 mi N on CR G; 1 mi E on CR SS. $12 ($14 non-residents). About 5/7-10/25; 21-day limit. Entry limited to persons with horses. 22 sites, Tbls, pit toilets, cfga, drkg wtr. Horseback riding, hiking. On forest's 33-mi bridle trail. 24-stall horse shelter building available; some sites have pipe corrals. Recently renovated. Forest GPS: 43.60139, -88.18417.

LAC DU FLAMBEAU (47N)
Emily Lake Campground $12
Chequamegon National Forest
3.5 mi W on FR 142 from Lac du Flambeau; 1 mi N on FR 1178. $12 ($5 with federal senior pass). 5/1-10/26; 14-day limit. 11 sites; no RV size limit. Tbls, toilets, cfga, drkg wtr. Fishing, canoeing, swimming, waterskiing, boating(l). 6 acres; 26-acre lake. GPS: 45.9641165, -90.0146019

LAKE GENEVA (48S)
Big Foot Beach State Park $12
Half mi S of Lake Geneva on SR 120. $12 base ($14 non-residents). 5/15-11/1; 21-day limit. 100 sites, 14 with elec; 30-ft RV limit. Tbls, showers, pit toilets, cfga, drkg wtr, elec($5), no wtr hookups, beach, dump. Swimming, fishing, playground, canoeing, hiking trails. 272 acres on Lake Geneva. GPS: 42.5697394, -88.4234297.

LAND O'LAKES (49N)
Lac Vieux Desert Campground $12
Nicolet National Forest
2 mi S of Land O'Lakes on US 45; 3 mi E on CR 3; 1.7 mi N on FR 2205. $12. 5/1-10/15; 14-day limit. 31 sites (22-ft RV limit). Tbls, toilets, cfga, drkg wtr. Boating(l), fishing, swimming, hiking. GPS: 46.1357848, -89.1531919

LANGLADE (50N)
Boulder Lake Campground $7.50
Nicolet National Forest
7 mi SE of Langlade on Hwy 55; half mi E on CR WW; 1.5 mi N on FR 2166. $7.50 with federal senior pass at non-elec sites; others pay $15. $12.50 with senior pass at elec sites; others pay $20. 5/1-10/30; 14-day limit. 89 sites; 45-ft RV limit. Tbls, flush & pit toilets, cfga, drkg wtr, dump, beach, amphitheater. Fishing, boating, swimming, hiking. GPS: 45.140252, -88.628439

LAONA (51N)
Bear Lake Campground $12
Nicolet National Forest
4 mi S of Laona on US 8; 3 mi E on CR R; half mi N on CR H; 4 mi E on FR 2136. $12. 5/1-11/30; 14-day limit. 27 sites; no RV size limit. Tbls, toilets, cfga, drkg wtr. Fishing, boating (l), swimming. GPS: 45.5110752, -88.5317787

LONG LAKE (52N)
Morgan Lake Campground $10
Nicolet National Forest
3.5 mi S of Long Lake on SR 139; 8 mi E on FR 2161. $10. About 5/15-10/15 & for deer season (about 11/15-11/30);

14-day limit. 18 sites, typically 50 ft. (Group sites $30.) Tbls, toilets, cfga, drkg wtr. Boating(l), fishing, swimming, canoeing. GPS: 45.7721815, -88.5440103

Stevens Lake Campground $12
Nicolet National Forest
Half mi N of Long Lake on SR 139; 1 mi W on Long Lake Rd; 7 mi N on Stevens Lake Rd. $12. About 5/1-11/30; 14-day limit. 6 sites. Tbls, toilets, cfga, drkg wtr. Boating(l), fishing. 300-acre lake. GPS: 45.9241253, -88.7120694

LORETTA (53N)

Black Lake Campground $12
Chequamegon National Forest
8.8 mi N of Loretta on FR 32; 4 mi W on FR 172; half mi N on FR 173; half mi NE on FR 1666. $12. 5/1-10/31; 14-day limit. 26 sites (45-ft RV limit). Tbls, toilets, cfga, drkg wtr, beach. Hiking (4-mi interpretive trail), swimming, fishing, boating(l). GPS: 45.9877328, -90.9298971

MAIDEN ROCK

Maiden Rock Village Park $10
From SR 35 in Maiden Rock, SW on Chestnut St, then NW on Park St; at Lake Pepin. $10 primitive sites, $15 with elec. 12 sites. Tbls, toilets, cfga, drkg wtr. Boating(ld), biking, fishing. 715-448-2205. City's GPS: 44.561295, -92.309563

MEDFORD (54N)

Eastwood Campground $12
Chequamegon National Forest
15 mi N of Medford on SR 13; 6.7 mi W on CR D; 1.5 mi S on FR 104; half mi W on FR 1590; on E side of Mondeaux Flowage. $12. 5/1-10/31; 14-day limit. 22 sites (32-ft RV limit). Tbls, toilets, cfga, drkg wtr, dump. Swimming, boating(lr), fishing, hiking trails. 11 acres. GPS: 45.3319147, -90.4448671

Kathryn Lake Campground $12
Chequamegon National Forest
4 mi W of Medford on SR 64; 15 mi W on CR M; half mi S on FR 121 (half mi S of Perkinstown). $12. 5/1-10/31; 14-day limit. 8 sites (32-ft RV limit). Tbls, toilets, cfga, drkg wtr, beach. Swimming, boating(l), fishing. 4 acres; 63-acre lake. GPS: 45.2010837, -90.6204151

North Twin Lake Campground $12
Chequamegon National Forest
4 mi N of Medford on Hwy 13; 7 mi W on CR M; 6 mi N on CR E; 1 mi E on FR 102; 1 mi S on FR 566; .1 mi E on FR 1504; on S end of Mondeaux Flowage. $12. About 5/1-10/31; 14-day limit. 5 sites (30-ft RV limit). Tbls, toilets, cfga, drkg wtr, beach, fishing pier. Boating, fishing, swimming. GPS: 45.2802489, -90.4445885

Spearhead Point Campground $12
Chequamegon National Forest
4 mi N of Medford on SR 13; 7 mi W on CR M; 8.5 mi E on

CR E; 1 mi E on FR 1563; E on FR 106; on W shores of Mondeaux Flowage. $12 for standard site; $14 premium locations ($6 & $7 with federal senior pass. About 5/1-10/31; 14-day limit. 27 sites (several with docks). Tbls, cfga, toilets, drkg wtr. Hiking, boating(l), fishing. Ice Age National Scenic Trail access. GPS: 45.3277481, -90.444867

Westpoint Campground $12
Chequamegon National Forest
16 mi N of Medford on SR 13; 6.7 mi W on CR D; 1 mi S on FR 104; 3 mi W on FR 106; on W shore of Mondeaux Flowage. $12. About 5/1-10/13; 14 day limit. 15 sites (32-ft RV limit). Tbls, toilets, cfga, drkg wtr. Boating(l), fishing, hiking trails. GPS: 45.3171925, -90.4365336

MELLEN (55N)

Beaver Lake Campground $12
Chequamegon National Forest
7.7 mi SW of Mellen on CR GG; 3 mi NW on FR 187; 2 mi SW on FR 198; half mi N on FR 1800. $12. 5/1-10/31; 14-day limit. 10 sites (30-ft RV limit). Tbls, toilets, cfga, drkg wtr. Boating(l), fishing, hiking (spur trail connects to North Country National Scenic Trail. 7 acres; 35-acre trout lake. GPS: 46.30127, -90.897705

Lake Three Campground $12
Chequamegon National Forest
7.7 mi SW of Mellen on CR GG; 3.7 mi NW on FR 187; qtr mi NW on FR 1297. $12 ($6 with federal senior pass). 5/1-10/26; 14-day limit. 8 sites (30-ft RV limit). Tbls, toilets, cfga, drkg wtr. Fishing, boating. GPS: Lake GPS: 46.319144, -90.850515

Mineral Lake Campground $12
Chequamegon National Forest
8.7 mi SW of Mellen on CR GG; half mi NW on FR 1412. $12. 5/1-10/31; 14 day limit. 12 sites (30-ft RV limit). Tbls, toilets, drkg wtr, cfga. Swimming, boating(l), fishing, eagle watching. Lake GPS: 46.293536, -90.829211

MENOMONEE FALLS (56S)

Menomonee Park $12
Waukesha County Parks
1.3 mi N of Hwy 74 on CR V in Menomonee Falls & Lannon. $12 base. 4/15-11/1; 7-day limit. Base fee for vehicles with annual entry permit; $16 with no permit. 33 sites; 20-ft RV limit. Tbls, pit toilets, cfga, drkg wtr, shelter, playfield. Scuba diving, swimming, hiking, fishing, archery, bridle paths. 394 acres; 16-acre quarry lake. GPS: 43.155177, -88.183695.

MERCER (57N)

Shay's Dam   FREE
Iron County Park
2.5 mi E of Mercer on CR J; 3.6 mi N on Beaver Lodge Circle Rd; pass Beaver Lake Rd, then right for 1.5 mi on Fisher Lake Rd. to dam's access rd (following sign). Free.

All year. 5 primitive sites. Tbls, toilets, cfga, no drkg wtr. Boating(l), fishing. 15-ft Shay's Dam Waterfall. GPS: 46.236397, -89.993634.

MERRILL (58N)

Camp New Wood $10
Lincoln County Park
7 mi N of Merrill on SR 107; on Wisconsin River. $10. All year; 14-day limit. 7 sites. Tbls, pit toilets, cfga, drkg wtr, playground. Boating(l), fishing, ice-age hiking trail. Former CCC camp; about 80 acres. GPS: 45.2899669, -89.7917983.

Otter Lake Recreation Area $10
Lincoln County Park
17 mi N of Merrill (12 mi SE of Tomahawk) on US 51; 3.5 mi E & N on CTH S; 1.5 mi E on Stevenson Rd; qtr mi N on Grundy Rd; 2 mi E & N on Bear Trail Rd; 1 mi N on Otter Lake Rd. $10. All year; 14-day limit. 25 sites. Tbls, toilets, cfga, drkg wtr. Boating(l), fishing, swimming, hiking trails, winter sports. 50 acres. GPS: 45.4377386, -89.5434622.

Underdown Campground $10
Underdown Recreation Area
Lincoln County Campground
13 mi NE of Merrill on Copper Lake Ave. $10. All year; 14-day limit. 11 primitive sites. Tbls, toilets, cfga, drkg wtr. Horseback riding, mountain biking, hiking, fishing.

MOSINEE (59N)

Big Eau Pleine $11
Marathon County Park
5.5 mi W of Mosinee on Hwy 153; 2.5 mi S on Eau Pleine Park Rd; on N shore of Big Eau Pleine Reservoir. $11 without elec ($13 lakeside); $15 for sites with elec ($17 lakeside). 5/1-10/31; 14-day limit. 106 sites, 80 with elec. Tbls, toilets, cfga, drkg wtr, dump, beach, playground, elec($). Swimming, boating(l), fishing, hiking trails. Self registration. GPS: 44.7449661, -89.8434586.

Burma Road Unit   FREE
Marathon County Forest
N lot: about 4 mi NW of Mosinee on CR B; 2.4 mi W on Burma Rd; qtr mi S on access rd. S lot: 4 mi W of Mosinee on SR 153. Free. All year. RVs camp in parking lots; walk-in tent camping anywhere in forest. No facilities except toilets at N lot. 11 mi of ATV trails in 1,480-acre forest (trails closed Oct, Nov & Apr). Hunting, hiking, biking. Camping permit required.

Kronenwetter Unit   FREE
Marathon County Forest
S lot: About 15 mi E of Mosinee on SR 153; parking lot on N side of hwy. N lot: 8 mi E of Mosinee on SR 153; 2 mi N on CR X; 3 mi E on North Rd; 8 mi N on Creek Rd; 2 mi E on Martin Brothers Rd. 3 other parking lots around perimeter of forest. Free. All year. RVs camp only at parking lots; walk-in tent camping anywhere in forest. No facilities except toilets at N lot. Hunting, hiking, biking, fishing. 4,999 acres. Camping permit required. N lot near Sampson Creek.

Leather Camp Unit   FREE
Marathon County Forest
N lot: About 15 mi E of Mosinee on SR 153; parking lot on S side of highway. Other lots on Leather Camp Rd, CR C, Hunter's Rd & Guenther Rd. Free. All year. RVs camp only at parking lots; walk-in tent camping anywhere in forest. No facilities, no drkg wtr. Fishing, hunting, hiking, biking. 4,804 acres. Camping permit required.

Nine-Mile Unit   FREE
Marathon County Forest
Half mi NW of Mosinee on CR B; 5 mi N on CR KK to Springbrook Rd & S end of forest boundary. 5 parking lots around perimeter of forest; RVs camp only at lots; walk-in tent camping anywhere in forest. Free. All year. No facilities, no drkg wtr. Hiking trails, fishing, hunting, biking. Duane L. Corbin Shooting Range Park at S end of forest. 4,755 acres. Camping permit required.

MOUNTAIN (60N)

Bagley Rapids Campground $12
Nicolet National Forest
2 mi S of Mountain on SR 32; half mi W on FR 2072. $12. 5/1-10/31; 14-day limit. 30 sites, typically 42 ft. Tbls, pit toilets, cfga, drkg wtr. Swimming, rafting, fishing, canoeing. GPS: 45.1588649, -88.4659378

MUKWONAGO (61S)

Mukwonago Campground $12
Waukesha County Park
On Hwy 99, 3 mi W of Hwy 83. $12 base. 4/15-11/1; 7-day limit. Base fee for vehicles with annual entry permit; $16 fee with no permit. 30 sites; 20-ft RV limit. Tbls, pit toilets, cfga, drkg wtr, shelter, playfield. Swimming, hiking, fishing. 222 acres. GPS: 42.8627909, -88.3881513.

MUSCODA (62S)

Victoria Riverside City Park $10
On E River Rd., N side of Muscoda; on Wisconsin River. $10 without elec, $25 with elec. 5/1-10/1; 14-day limit. 36 sites. Tbls, flush toilets, cfga, drkg wtr, showers($), hookups($), dump, pool, playground, store, coin laundry. Swimming, boating(ld), walking path. GPS: 43.196533,-90.440531.

MUSKEGO (63S)

Muskego Campground $12
Waukesha County Park
1 mi W of CR Y on CR L near Muskego. $12 base. 4/15-11/1; 7-day limit. Base fee for vehicles with annual entry permit; $16 with no permit. 24 sites; 20 ft RV limit. Tbls, toilets,

cfga, drkg wtr, shelter, playfield. Hiking, fishing, tennis, swimming, bridle paths. 160 acres. GPS: 42.8972368, -88.1664786

NECEDAH (64S)

Buckhorn State Park $12
7 mi S of Necedah on SR 80; 3 mi S on CR Q; W across Castle Rock Lake bridge on CR G. $12 ($14 non-residents), $17 with elec ($19 non-residents). All year; 21-day limit. 11 RV sites (1 elec). Tbls, pit & portable toilets, cfga, drkg wtr. Boating(l), fishing, swimming, hiking, hunting, canoeing, cross-country skiing, playground, planned activities. 3,500-acre peninsula. GPS: 43.9416359, -89.9992944

NELSON (65S)

Tiffany Bottoms State Wildlife Area FREE
About 3 mi N of Nelson on Hwy 25. Free. All year. Primitive camping with DNR permit from Buffalo County Courthouse in Alma. Toilets, cfga, no drkg wtr. 14 public boat ramps are along the hwy. Fishing, hiking & walking trails.

NEW GLARUS (66S)

New Glarus Woods State Park $12
2 mi S of New Glarus on SR 69. $12 ($14 non-residents). All year; 21-day limit. 18 RV sites. Tbls, pit toilets, cfga, drkg wtr, no showers, no elec. Hiking trails (access to 23-mi Sugar River State Trail), playground, interpretive programs. 411 acres. GPS: 42.7872259, -89.6298438.

NEW LISBON (67S)

Kennedy Park Forest Recreation Area FREE
Juneau County Park
From I-90/94, W to US 12/16; 1 mi NW on CR M; 3 mi N; at Lemonweir River. Free. 5/1-9/30. 12 sites (24-ft RV limit). 30-day limit. Tbls, toilets, cfga, drkg wtr, elec hookups. Swimming, fishing, picnicking. 200 acres. GPS: 43.9121903, -90.1720737

ONTARIO (68S)

Wildcat Mountain State Park $12
3 mi E of Ontario on SR 33; at Kickapoo River. $12 ($14 non-residents). 4/1-10/31; 21-day limit. 30 sites plus 24-site equestrian area with corral, hitching posts, loading ramp. Tbls, flush & pit toilets, cfga, drkg wtr, showers, no elec, nature center. Playground, trout fishing, horseback riding, hiking & cross-country ski trails, canoeing, ski trails, interpretive programs. 3,526 acres; state's highest sand dunes. GPS: 43.7005266, -90.5615197.

PHELPS (69N)

Spectacle Lake Campground $12
Nicolet National Forest
1.8 mi E of Phelps on SR 17; 2.5 mi S on CR A; 2.5 mi SE on FR 2196; 1.5 mi E on FR 2572. $12 base, $15 for lakeshore sites ($6 & $7.50 with federal senior pass). MD-LD; 14-day limit. 34 sites. Tbls, pit toilets, cfga, drkg wtr.

Swimming, boating(l), fishing, waterskiing, hiking trails. GPS: 46.0088451, -89.0098524

PHILLIPS (70N)

Connors Lake Campground $12
Flambeau River State Forest
20 mi W of Phillips on CR W; 1 mi S on CR M; qtr mi N on access rd; on S shore of Connors Lake. $12 for WI residents, ($14 non-residents). MD-LD; 21-day limit. 29 sites. Tbls, toilets, cfga, drkg wtr, dump. Swimming, fishing, boating(rld). 10 acres. Lake GPS: 45.750923, -90.735551.

Lake of the Pines Campground $12
Flambeau River State Forest
20 mi W of Phillips on CR W; 2 mi N on Lower Hill Rd; on N shore of Lake of the Pines. $12 WI residents; $14 non-residents. 5/1-10/31; 21-day limit. 30 sites. Tbls, toilets, cfga, drkg wtr, dump. Swimming, fishing, boating(ldr). 10 acres. GPS: 45.7758333, -90.7113889.

PRAIRIE DU CHIEN (71S)

Wyalusing State Park $12
7 mi S of Prairie Du Chien on US 18; W on CR C. $12 base ($14 non-residents). All year; 21-day limit. 109 sites (34 with elec, some in winter). Tbls, flush & pit toilets, cfga, drkg wtr, elec($5), showers, dump, playground, store. Birdwatching, boating(l), fishing, skiing, biking, hiking trails, canoe trail, nature program. View wild turkeys, vultures, eagles. Indian burial mounds, waterfalls. 2,628 acres. GPS: 42.991652, -91.1223512.

RIB LAKE (73N)

Camp 8 Campground FREE
Taylor County Park
2 mi E of Rib Lake on SR 102; where SR 102 turns N, continue 3.5 mi E on Wilderness Ave, then half mi S on Camp 8 Rd to Camp 8 Flowage. Free. Primitive camping near lake. Tbls, toilets, cfga, drkg wtr. Boating(l), hiking, fishing. GPS: 45.317855, -90.055733.

Wood Lake FREE
Taylor County Park
2 mi NE of Rib Lake on SR 102; 3 mi E on Wood Lake Rd. Free. MD-LD. 5 sites. Tbls, toilets, cfga, drkg wtr. Boating(l), fishing, swimming, hiking, hunting. GPS: 45.33749, -90.08646.

ST. CROIX FALLS (74N)

Interstate State Park $12
On Hwy 36, 1 mi S of US 8; along St. Croix River. $12 base ($14 non-residents); $15 for lakeshore sites ($17 non-residents). 5/1-10/31; 21-day limit. 85 sites. Tbls, flush & pit toilets, cfga, drkg wtr, showers, no elec, playground, interpretive center. Nature trails, boating, hiking trails, fishing, swimming, canoeing. Ice Age Interpretive Center. Oldest state park. GPS: 45.3891289, -92.6574292.

SAND CREEK (75N)

Myron Campground $10
Dunn County Park
3 mi N of Sand Creek on CR I; at Red Cedar River. $10 base.
5/1-10/1; 17-day limit. Base fee for primitive sites; $15 with
elec. 45 sites (28 with elec). Tbls, flush toilets, cfga, drkg
wtr, elec, shelters, dump, playground. Hiking trails, swimming, canoeing, fishing, boating(l). GPS: 45.1921, -91.7032

SCHOFIELD (76N)

Ringle Unit   FREE
Marathon County Forest
3 mi E of Schofield on CR JJ; 3-5 mi S on CR J to parking
lots (one E on Sportsman's Rd, one E on Timber Ridge Rd.
Third lot on SE edge of forest; RVs camp only at lots; walk-
in tent camping anywhere in forest. Free. All year. No facilities, no drkg wtr. Trails for hiking, biking, snowmobiling;
fishing, hunting. 2,016 acres. Camping permit required.

SPOONER (77N)

Sawmill Lake Campground $8
Washburn County Forest
15 mi E of Spooner on Hwy 70; 2 mi S on CR B; 5 mi SE on
Birchwood fire lane. $8. 5/15-10/15. 25 sites (28-ft RV limit).
Tbls, pit toilets, cfga, drkg wtr, no hookups. Swimming, boat-
ing(l), fishing, hiking trails. GPS: 45.753971, -91.556388.

SPRING GREEN (78S)

Tower Hill State Park $12
3 mi SE of Spring Green on US 14 & Hwy 23. $12 ($14
non-residents). 5/15-11/1; 21-day limit. 11 primitive sites.
Tbls, toilets, cfga, drkg wtr, no elec. Fishing, boating,
canoeing, hiking. Visit unique 1880s shot tower & melting
house; film, displays. GPS: 43.1527704, -90.044846.

White Mound $5
Sauk County Park
20 mi N of Spring Green on SR 23; 2 mi W on CR GG; 2 mi
N on White Mound Dr; on shore of 104-acre White Mound
Lake. $5 per person, plus $1 daily vehicle entry fee; $5
per vehicle for elec. Apr-Nov. 59 sites (38 with elec).
Tbls, flush toilets, cfga, drkg wtr, showers($), elec($4).
Equestrian camping at N end of the park has toilets, tbls,
hitching posts, trailer parking, cfga & drkg wtr. Fishing,
boating(l), hiking, swimming, horseback riding. 1,100
acres. GPS: 43.422848, -90.11306.

SPRING VALLEY (79S)

Highland Ridge $7
Eau Galle Recreation Area
Corps of Engineers
Eau Galle Lake
From Spring Valley, 2 mi NE on SR 29; 2 mi E on 10th Ave; 1
mi S on CR NN; at NE shore of lake. $7 with federal senior
pass at 10 non-elec equestrian sites, $9 with senior pass at
3 non-elec RV sites; others pay $14 & $18. At 35 elec sites,
$10 with senior pass; others pay $20. 4/1-10/22; 14-day limit.

RV limit 65 ft. Tbls, flush toilets, cfga, drkg wtr, dump, beach,
elec($), playground, interpretive center, showers, pay phone,
ice machines. Swimming, hiking trails, fishing, boating(l),
canoeing, golf, horseshoe pits, free weekend movies or interpretive programs, ski trails, fishing dock, interpretive trail,
horseback riding. 150-acre fishing lake. GPS: 44.86, -92.244

STOUGHTON (80S)

Lake Kegonsa State Park $12
4 mi SW of I-90, Hwy N south; W on Koshkonong Rd; S on
Door Creek Rd. $12 base ($14 non-residents). 5/1-10/31;
21-day limit. 96 sites, 29 with elec($5). Tbls, flush & pit
toilets, cfga, drkg wtr, showers, playground. Swimming
beach, fishing, boating(r), waterskiing. Mysterious earth-
en effigy mounds along White Oak Nature Trail. 3,209-
acre lake. GPS: 42.9786109, -89.2348386.

SUPERIOR (81N)

Amnicon Falls State Park $12
3 mi E of Superior on US 2; qtr mi N on CR U. $12 ($14
non-residents). All year; 21-day limit. 36 RV sites. Tbls, pit
toilets, cfga, drkg wtr, no elec, no showers, no dump. Fishing, nature trails. Waterfalls & rapids on Amnicon River.
Covered bridge. 825 acres. GPS: 46.607666, -91.888428.

THREE LAKES (82N)

Boot Lake Campground $7.50
Nicolet National Forest
5.5 mi SW of Townsend on CR T. $7.50 with federal senior
pass; others pay $15. 5/1-11/30; 14-day limit. 34 sites,
typically 65 ft. Tbls, pit toilets, cfga, drkg wtr. Swimming, boating(l), fishing, waterskiing. 263-acre lake. GPS:
45.2685794, -88.6456619

Laurel Lake Campground $12
Nicolet National Forest
5 mi E of Three Lakes on SR 32. 2.5 mi NW on FR 2100.
$12. 5/1-10/15; 14-day limit. 12 sites, typically 32 ft. Tbls,
pit toilets, cfga, drkg wtr. Boating(l), fishing, waterskiing,
nature trails. GPS: 45.8155128, -89.1092927

Sevenmile Lake Campground $10
Nicolet National Forest
5.5 mi E of Three Lakes on SR 32; 4 mi N on FR 2178; 2.5 mi
NE on FR 2435. $10. MD-LD;14-day limit. 27 sites (30-ft RV
limit). Tbls, pit toilets, cfga, drkg wtr. Hiking trails, waterskiing, fishing, boating(l). GPS: 45.878013, -89.0426264

TREMPEALEAU (84S)

Perrot State Park $12
2 mi NW of Trempealeau off SR 35. $12 base ($14 non-residents); $15 base for waterfront sites ($17 non-residents).
All year; 21-day limit. 102 sites, 38 with elec (some open
in winter). Tbls, flush & pit toilets, cfga, drkg wtr, showers,
dump, elec($5). Boating(l), fishing, hiking, cross-country
skiing, canoeing, nature center. 1,400 acres at jct of Trempealeau & Mississippi Rivers. GPS: 44.0177408, -91.4657.

TWO RIVERS (85S)

Point Beach State Forest $12
4 mi N of Two Rivers on state forest rd; on Lake Michigan. $12 base ($14 non-residents). All year; 21-day limit 127 sites; 70 with elec (5 in winter). Tbls, flush & pit toilets, cfga, drkg wtr, elec($5), no showers, store, beach. Nature program, hiking trails, fishing, swimming, beachcombing. Rawley Point Lighthouse. GPS: 44.1647181, -87.5395246

WABENO (86N)

Ada Lake Campground $12
Nicolet National Forest
1 mi W of Wabeno on SR 32; 7 mi SW on SR 52; qtr mi S on FR 2357. $12. 5/1-10/15; 14-day limit. 19 sites, typically 50 ft. Tbls, pit toilets, cfga, drkg wtr. Swimming, boating(l), fishing. GPS: 45.3694115, -88.7317749

Richardson Lake Campground $12
Nicolet National Forest
.8 mi W of Wabeno on SR 32. $12. 5/1-11/30; 14-day limit. Free in Dec, but no services. 26 sites, typically 50 ft. Tbls, pit toilets, cfga, drkg wtr. Swimming, boating(l), fishing. GPS: 45.4416331, -88.7137203

WASHBURN (87N)

Big Rock $12
Bayfield County Park
2 mi W of Washburn on CR C; 1 mi W on Town Rd; on Sioux River. $12. 5/1-10/31. 13 rustic sites. Tbls, toilets, cfga, drkg wtr. Fishing, boating. GPS: 46.705697, -90.925503.

Birch Grove Campground $12
Chequamegon National Forest
1.7 mi S of Washburn on SR 13; 8 mi W on Wannebo Rd (FR 251); 2.5 mi N on FR 252; 1 mi E on FR 435; between 22-acre East Twin & 16-acre West Twin Lakes. $12. 5/1-11/30; 14-day limit. Reduced services & no wtr 10/16-11/30. 16 sites (35-ft RV limit). Tbls, toilets, cfga, drkg wtr, fishing pier. Boating(l), fishing, hiking, interpretive trail. Valhalla Trail nearby for ATV, horses, mountain biking, hiking. 8 acres. GPS: 46.686035, -91.060547

WAUKESHA (88S)

Minooka Park $12
Waukesha County Parks
About 2 mi SE of Waukesha at jct of Racine Ave & Sunset Dr. $12 for vehicles with annual entry permit; $16 without permit. All year; 7-day limit. Tbls, pit toilets, cfga, drkg wtr. Fishing, swimming, archery, horseback riding. 580 acres; 5-acre pond. GPS: 42.9811239, -88.1917579.

WAUSAU (89N)

Dells of the Eau Claire $11
Marathon County Park
15 mi E of Wausau on Hwy 52; 2 mi S on CR Y; along Eau Claire River. $11 for non-elec sites, $14 elec. 4/22-10/311;

14-day limit. 27 sites (16 with elec). Tbls, toilets, cfga, drkg wtr, elec($), playground, refuse/recycling center, pay phones. Swimming beach, hiking trails, fishing. Self-registration. Segment of Ice Age Trail. Nearby Marathon Park's fees are $14 non-elec, $18 elec. GPS: 45.0035799, -89.3428938.

WAUSAUKEE (90N)

Evergreen City Park $10
Entering town from the S on Hwy 141, just N of the bridge, turn right (E) on North Ave for qtr mi; campground is on the S side of street. $10 without elec; $15 with elec. Tbls, flush toilets, cfga, drkg wtr, no showers, playground, dump. Tennis, basketball. GPS: 45.3808036, -87.950667.

Goodman $10
Marinette County Park
About 20 mi W of Wausaukee on CR C; 9 mi N on Parkway Rd; 2 mi NW on Goodman Park Rd; at Peshtigo River at Silver Cliff. $10. 5/1-11/15; 14-day limit. 15 rustic sites. Tbls, toilets, cfga, drkg wtr, playground. Fishing, hiking trail. Waterfall. GPS: 45.5202399, -88.3376148.

McClintock $10
Marinette County Park
About 20 mi W of Wausaukee on CR C; 5 mi N on Parkway Rd (4 mi S of Goodman Park); on Peshtigo River. $10. 5/1-11/15; 14-day limit. 10 rustic sites. Tbls, toilets, cfga, drkg wtr. Fishing. GPS: 45.477633, -88.327156.

Old Veterans Lake Campground $10
Peshtigo River State Forest
About 6 mi S of Wausaukee on US 141 to Middle Inlet; 11 mi W on CR X; 3.5 mi N on Parkway Rd on Old Veteran's Lake & High Falls Lake. $10 ($14 non-residents). 5/1-11/15; 14-day limit. 15 rustic sites. Tbls, toilets, cfga, drkg wtr. Boating, fishing. GPS: 45.3480241, -88.2009421.

WHITEWATER (92S)

Whitewater Lake Campground $12
Kettle Moraine State Forest
2 mi SE of Whitewater on US 12; 4 mi S on CR P. $12 ($14 non-residents). 5/1-10/15; 21-day limit. 63 sites. Tbls, pit toilets, cfga, drkg wtr, dump, trash recycling station, no showers (available at Pinewoods & Ottawa Lake), beach, play area, no elec. Swimming, fishing. GPS: 42.4707546, -40.24272

WISCONSIN DELLS (93S)

Rocky Arbor State Park $12
1.5 mi N of Wisconsin Dells on US 12. $12 base ($14 non-residents). MD-LD; 21-day limit. 89 sites; 18 with elec. Tbls, flush & pit toilets, cfga, drkg wtr, elec($5), showers, dump. Hiking. GPS: 43.642201, -89.8081805.

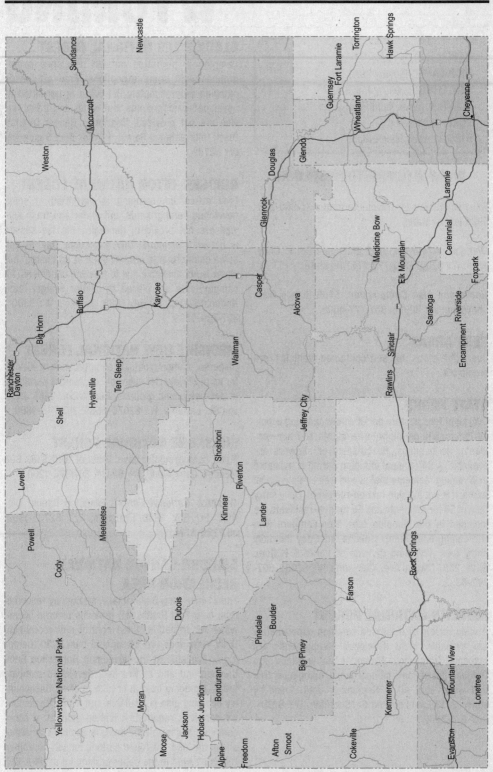

WYOMING

CAPITAL: Cheyenne
NICKNAME: Equality State
STATEHOOD: 1890 – 44th State
FLOWER: Indian Paintbrush
TREE: Cottonwood
BIRD: Western Meadowlark

WWW.WYOMINGTOURISM.ORG

Toll-free number for travel information: 1-800-225-5996 (out of state).

Division of Tourism, 1520 Etchepare Circle, Cheyenne, WY 82007: 307-777-7777 (in state).

Game and Fish Commission, 5400 Bishop Blvd, Cheyenne, WY 82006. 307-777-4600.

REST AREAS
Overnight stops by self-contained vehicles are prohibited.

STATE PARKS
Overnight fees at state parks where camping is permitted are $10 per night for residents, $17 non-residents; no hookups, flush toilets or showers are available. A $40 annual camping permit is available to Wyoming residents that allows free camping in all parks; it is not avilable for non-residents. Daily entry fees of $4 for residents and $6 for non-residents are included in the camping fees. Non-campers who use campground dump stations must pay the daily entry fees. Wyoming Division of Parks & Historic Sites, 2301 Central Ave., Cheyenne, WY 82002. 307-777-6323.

BIGHORN NATIONAL FOREST
A wide variety of dispersed camping opportunities are available. Most developed campgrounds are managed from about Memorial Day weekend into October, but at some campgrounds, camping is free and water shut off in September until closed by snow: 2013 Eastside 2nd St, Sheridan, WY 82801. 307-674-2600.

BLACK HILLS NATIONAL FOREST
Camping is permitted outside developed campgrounds with some exceptions. Free off-season camping (approximately 9/1-5/30) is permitted at developed campgrounds, but water and trash service are not provided. Bearlodge Ranger District, Black Hills National Forest, PO Box 680, Sundance, WY 82729.

BRIDGER-TETON NATIONAL FOREST
Free off-season camping is permitted at some developed campgrounds, but water and trash service are not provided; generally, the fee season is between Memorial Day and Labor Day. In fall, some campgrounds are left open at no charge, but water is not available due to freezing conditions. All campgrounds are closed by winter Bridger-Teton National Forest, PO Box 1888, Jackson, WY 83001. 307-739-5500.

MEDICINE BOW NATIONAL FOREST
Dispersed camping outside campgrounds is allowed for up to 21 days. No overnight camping is permitted at day-use picnic grounds. Supervisor, 2468 Jackson St., Laramie, WY 82070-6535. 307/745-2300.

SHOSHONE NATIONAL FOREST
Most campgrounds have fees of $10-$15. 808 Meadow Lane, Cody, WY 82414. 307/578-1200.

Wasatch National Forest, Evanston Ranger District, PO Box 1880 Evanston, WY 82731-1880. 307/789-3194.

BIGHORN CANYON NATIONAL RECREATION AREA
The 71-mile-long Bighorn lake, created by Yellowtail Dam near Fort Smith, MT, provides electric power, water for irrigation, flood control and recreation. Daily entry fees are $5; annual pass, $30. Camping is available at the developed Horseshoe Bend Campground and at five less developed camping areas, including boat-in or hike-in sites. Backcountry camping also is available, but a free backcountry permit is required. A limited amount of shore camping, accessible by boat, is available at either end of the lake. Overnight parking for self-contained RVs is allowed in the upper parking lot at Ok-A-Beh

and in the parking lot above the boat ramp at Barry's Landing. Summer activities include campfire campgrounds at Afterbay Campground in Montana and the Horseshoe Bend Campground amphitheater in Wyoming; topics include Indian culture, early settlers, geology, recreation and wildlife. Visitor center, 20 Highway, 14A East, Lovell, WY 82431; 307/548-2251.

Flaming Gorge National Recreation Area, Ashley National Forest PO Box 278, Manila, UT 84046; 801/784-3445.

YELLOWSTONE NATIONAL PARK
The park has 420 backcountry campsites. A $25 per vehicle park entrance fee is charged, valid for 7 days; or buy a $50 annual pass. Camping fees are $15-25. Yellowstone National Park, PO Box 168, Yellowstone National Park, WY 82190. 307/344-7381.

Bureau of Land Management, 2515 Warren Ave, PO Box 1828, Cheyenne, WY 82003; 307/775-6256.

Bureau of Land Management, Casper District, 1701 East E St., Casper, WY 82601.

Bureau of Land Management, Rawlins District, PO Box 670, 1300 3rd St, Rawlins, WY 82301.

Bureau of Land Management, Rock Springs District, P.O. Box 1869, Rock Springs, WY 82902-1170. Most of the district is open to unconfined camping, with requirements of keeping vehicles on existing roads and trails, packing out all trash and limiting camping to 14 days.

Bureau of Land Management, Worland District, PO Box 119, Worland, WY 82401.

AFTON

Swift Creek Campground $10
Bridger National Forest
1.5 mi E on county rd; qtr mi E on FR 10211. $10 during 5/1-LD; free rest of yr when accessible, but no drkg wtr; 16-day limit. 8 sites, typically 34 ft. Tbls, toilets, cfga, drkg wtr. Fishing, hiking. Periodic Springs geyser nearby.

ALCOVA

Pete's Draw FREE
Bureau of Land Management Casper Field Office
From Alcova, go east .6 miles east on Highway 220 to County Road 412 and turn right on County Road 412. Travel for two miles and take a right and continue for .1 miles to the camp. FREE 6 sites Tbls, toilets, cgfa. Hiking,wildlife viewing, fishing, boating.

ALPINE

Alpine Campground $12
Caribou-Targhee National Forest
3 mi NW of Alpine on US 26; at SE shore of Pallsades Reservoir. $12. MD-LD; 14-day limit. 17 sites (32-ft RV limit). Tbls, toilets, cfga, drkg wtr. Fishing, hiking, horseback riding. Palisades Reservoir. Snake River, Yellowstone & Grand Teton National Parks. Elev 5600 ft

Forest Park Campground $10
Bridger National Forest
.8 mi SE of Alpine on US 89; half mi SE on CR 1001; 35.3 mi SE on FR 10138. $10 during 5/1-9/30 free rest of yr, but no drkg wtr or services; 16-day limit. 13 sites (30-ft RV limit). Tbls, toilets, cfga, drkg wtr. Fishing. At Greys River. Elev 7000 ft; 8 acres.

McCoy Creek Campground $10
Caribou-Targhee National Forest
5 mi S of Alpine on US 89; 7 mi NW on FR 87 at S end of Pallsades Reservoir. Base $10 during MD-LD; free LD-10/31, but no wtr or services; 14-day limit. 17 sites (32-ft RV size limit). Tbls, flush toilets, cfga, drkg wtr. Boating(l), swimming, canoeing, fishing, waterskiing. Elev 5600 ft; 4 acres.

Moose Flat Campground $10
Bridger National Forest
.7 mi SE of Alpine on SR 89, .5 mi SE on CR 1001, 22.5 mi SE on FR 10138. $10 during 5/1-9/30 free off-season but no services; 16-day limit. 10 sites; RV limit 30 ft. Vault toilets, drkg wtr, cfga, tbls. Fishing. Along Greys River. Elev 6400 ft; 11 acres.

Murphy Creek Campground $10
Bridger National Forest
.8 mi SE of Alpine on US 89; 11.2 mi SE on FR 10138. $10. 5/1-9/30; 16-day limit. 10 sites (30-ft RV limit except 1 70 ft pull through.) Vault toilets, cfga, drkg wtr. Fishing. Elev 6300 ft; 12 acres.

ASHTON, (IDAHO)

Cave Falls Campground $10
Caribou-Targhee National Forest
5 mi N of Ashton on SR 47; 7 mi E on CR 36; half mi S of Yellowstone National Park. IN WYOMING. $10. 6/1-10/1; 16-day limit. 23 sites (22-ft RV limit). Tbls, toilets, cfga, drkg wtr. Swimming, fishing. Elev 6200 ft; 16 acres.

BELLE FOURCHE (SOUTH DAKOTA)

Bearlodge Campground $10
Black Hills National Forest
W of Belle Fourche on SR 34, connecting to Wyoming SR 24; between Aladdin & Hulett, WY. $10. All year; 10-day limit. 8 sites; 25-ft RV limit. Tbls, toilet, cfga, no drkg wtr. Fishing, hiking.

BIG PINEY

Middle Piney Lake Campground FREE
Bridger National Forest
20 mi W of Big Piney on SR 350; 4.3 mi W on FR 10046; . Free. 7/1-9/30; 16-day limit. 5 sites. 1 Vault toilet, no drkg wtr, no trash service. Fishing, hiking.

New Fork River Campground FREE
Bureau of Land Management.
12 mi E of Big Piney on Hwy 351. Free. All year; 14-day limit. 2 sites. Tbls, no drkg wtr, toilets. Fishing; boating. Names Hill, a "registry" for immigrants, is nearby.

Sacajawea Campground $7
Bridger National Forest
20 mi W of Big Piney on SR 350; 4.3 mi W on FR 10046; 1.2 mi W on FR 10024. $7. 6/1-9/1; 16-day limit. 26 sites, typically 40 ft. Tbls, toilets, cfga, drkg wtr. Fishing, hiking trails. On Middle Piney Lake. Elev 8200 ft; 5 acres.

BIG HORN

East Fork Campground $7.00
Bighorn National Forest
9.3 mi SW of Big Horn on CR 335; 8 mi SW on FR 26; half mi S on FR 293. RVs not recommended on FR 26 from Big Horn (steep, dirt). $7.00 with federal senior pass others pay $14.00 during 6/1-LD; free in fall but no services. 14-day limit. 11 sites (45-ft RV limit). Tbls, toilets, drkg wtr, cfga. Fishing, hiking. On East Fork of Big Goose Creek. Trails to Cloud Peak Wilderness. Elev 7500 ft; 6 acres.

Ranger Creek Campground $7.50
Bighorn National Forest
9.3 mi SW of Big Horn on CR 335; 10 mi SW on FR 26 (steep grades; RVs not recommended). $7.50 with federal senior pass others pay $15. June-Sept; free in fall but no services; 14-day limit. 11 sites (40-ft RV limit). Tbls, toilets, cfga, drkg wtr. Fishing, hiking. On Ranger Creek. Trails to Twin Lakes and Cloud Peak Wilderness. Elev 7700 ft; 5 acres.

BONDURANT
Kozy Campground $12
Bridger- Teton National Forest
8 mi NW of Bondurant on US 189; at Hoback River. $12. MD-LD; 10-day limit. 8 sites (30-ft RV limit). Tbls, toilet, cfga, no drkg wtr. Fishing, hunting. Elev 6500 ft.

BOULDER
Big Sandy Campground $7
Bridger-Teton National Forest
13.5 mi E of Boulder on SR 353; 15.5 mi E on Big-Sandy-Elkhorn Rd; 3.5 mi N on BLM Rd 4113; 6.5 mi N on FR 850. $7. 6/15-9/15; 10-day limit. 12 sites; 16-ft RV limit. Tbls, toilets, cfga, no drkg wtr, corrals. Hiking, horseback riding, fishing, mountain biking.

Boulder Lake North FREE
Bureau of Land Management
Pinedale Field Office
8.5 mi N of Boulder on BLM Rd 5106; on S shore of Boulder Lake. Free. 6/1-10/1; 14-day limit. 4 sites. Tbls, toilets, cfga, no drkg wtr. Fishing, boating, hunting. Lake

Boulder Lake Campground $7
Bridger-Teton National Forest
2 mi E of Boulder on SR 353; 9.75 mi on Boulder Lake Rd & FR 780; at E end of lake near Boulder Creek. $7. About 5/25-9/15; 10-day limit. 15 sites, typically 45 ft. Tbls, toilets, cfga, no drkg wtr. Hiking, horseback riding, mountain biking, fishing, boating(l).

Scab Creek Trailhead FREE
Bureau of Land Management
Pinedale Field Office
7 mi E of Boulder on SR 353; N of Scab Creek Rd, then bear left (north) onto BLM 5423 for 7.5 mi. Free. 6/1-10/15; 14-day limit. 10 sites. Tbls, toilets, cfga, no drkg wtr. Fishing, hiking, horseback riding, hunting, climbing.

BUFFALO
Circle Park Campground $7.50
Bighorn National Forest
12.5 mi W of Buffalo on US 16; 2.5 mi W on FR 20. $7.50 with federal senior pass others pay $15. 6/1-LD; 14-day limit. 10 sites, typically 25 ft. Tbls, toilets, drkg wtr, cfga. Nature trails; trailhead to Cloud Peak Wilderness Area. Elev 7900 ft; 5 acres.

Doyle Campground $7.50
Bighorn National Forest
26 mi W of Buffalo on US 16; 5.5 mi SW on FR 32. $7.50 with federal senior pass others pay$15. 6/1-LD or as snow allows; 14-day limit. 18 sites (40-ft RV limit). Tbls, toilets, cfga, drkg wtr. Fishing. Elev 8100 ft; 8 acres.

Hunter Campground $10
Bighorn National Forest
13 mi W of Buffalo on US 16; 3 mi NW on FR 19. $10. June-Sept; 14-day limit. Free during off-season but limited services. 11 sites (30-ft RV limit) for horse camping only. Tbls, toilets, cfga, drkg wtr. Hiking, horseback riding. Elev 7965 ft. Trailhead for Cloud Peak Wilderness.

Lost Cabin Campground $8
Bighorn National Forest
26 mi SW of Buffalo on US 16. $8.00 with federal senior pass; others pay $16. June-Sept 30-day limit. 19 sites (45-ft RV limit). Tbls, toilets, cfga, drkg wtr. Fishing. Along Muddy Creek. Elev 8200 ft; 5 acres.

Middle Fork Campground $8
Bighorn National Forest
13.5 mi SW of Buffalo on US 16. $8 with federal senior pass; others pay $16. Jun-Sept; 14-day limit. 9 sites (60-ft RV limit). Tbls, toilets, cfga, drkg wtr. Fishing. Elev 7400 ft; 3 acres.

South Fork Campground $8.50
Bighorn National Forest
15 mi W of Buffalo on US 16; 1.6 mi E on FR 21. $8 with federal senior pass; others pay $17. June-Sept 14-day limit. 9 RV sites (35-ft RV limit). Tbls, toilets, cfga, drkg wtr. Fishing, hiking trails nearby. Elev 7800 ft; 4 acres. Along South Fork of Clear Creek.

Tie Hack Campground $8.50
Bighorn National Forest
15 mi W of Buffalo on US 16; left for half mi on FR 21. $8.50 with federal senior pass; others pay $17. June-Sept; 14-day limit. 20 sites; 60-ft RV limit. Tbls, toilets, cfga, drkg wtr. Hiking, canoeing, fishing.

CASPER
Adams Archery Range $10
Casper Mountain County Park
Natrona County Park Board
About 6 mi S of Casper on SR 251 (Casper Mountain Rd); at crest of mtn after passing Broken Spur Cafe, veer right toward Hogadon Ski Resort; left on Micro Rd about 1 mi, then left before small housing area for qtr mi; right at "T" intersection, then 0.5 mi to archery range parking lot. $10 at undesignated primitive sites. Toilets, cfga, no drkg wtr. Two target ranges for archers.

Beartrap Campground $10
Beartrap Meadow County Park
Natrona County Park Board
9 mi S of Casper on SR 251 (Casper Mountain Rd), right on Beartrap Rd (Circle Dr) just before & just past jct with CR 506. $10. MD-LD; 10-day limit. Limited facilities in winter. About 35 RV sites & undesignated tent spaces. Tbls, toilets, cfga,

drkg wtr, shelters. Hiking, horseback riding, biking. Site of summer music festival.

Bishops Point Campground $10
Pathfinder Reservoir County Park
Natrona County Parks Board
Bureau of Reclamation
32 mi SW of Casper on SR 220; 3 mi S on CR 409; 2 mi W on Bishops Point Rd; at NE shore of Pathfinder Reservoir. $10. MD-LD; 10-day limit. 25 primitive designated sites. Tbls, toilets, cfga no drkg wtr, shelter. Boating(l), fishing. Park visitor center at dam. Interpretive trail, museum.

Black Beach Campground $10
Alcova Reservoir County Park
Natrona County Park Board
23 mi SW of Casper on SR 220; right on CR 407 (Kortas Rd); about 0.5 mi after crossing river bridge, right on Black Beach Rd to campground on NE shore of lake. $10. MD-LD; 10-day limit. 10 designated primitive sites. Tbls, toilets, cfga, shelter, fishing pier, no drkg wtr. Fishing, hiking, boating. 2,470-acre lake.

Cottonwood Campground $10
Alcova Reservoir County Park
Natrona County Park Board
23 mi SW of Casper on SR 220; right on CR 407 (Kortas Rd); about 4 mi S on CR 407, then 1 mi N on Cottonwood Creek Rd; at E shore of lake. $10. MD-LD; 10-day limit. 5 sites. Tbls, toilets, cfga, no drkg wtr, shelter. Boating(l), fishing, hiking. Dinosaur interpretive trail near Cottonwood Creek Beach.

Deer Haven Campground $10
Casper Mountain County Park
Natrona County Park Board
8 mi S of Casper on SR 251 (Casper Mountain Rd); left at Doe Trail into campground. $10. MD-LD; 10-day limit. 11 sites. Tbls, toilets, cfga, drkg wtr. Hiking, horseback riding, biking.

Diabase Campground $10
Pathfinder Reservoir County Park
Natrona County Parks Board
Bureau of Reclamation
32 mi SW of Casper on SR 220; 7 mi S on CR 409, past Sage & Weiss Campgrounds to lakeshore W of dam. $10. MD-LD; 10-day limit. About 14 designated primitive sites with sheltered tbls, cfga, toilets, no drkg wtr. Near marina. Boating(l), fishing. Park visitor center at dam. Interpretive trail, museum.

Elkhorn Springs Campground $10
Casper Mountain County Park
Natrona County Park Board
About 7 mi S of Casper on SR 251 (Casper Mountain Rd); right on Lemmers Rd into campground; at shore of Elkhorn Creek. $10. MD-LD; 10-day limit. 5 designated sites. Tbls, toilets, cfga, no drkg wtr. Fishing, hiking, horseback riding, biking.

Fremont Canyon Campground $10
Alcova Reservoir County Park
Natrona County Park Board
24 mi SW of Casper on SR 220; right on CR 406, becoming Lakeshore Dr along W shore of lake; camp at end of rd at lake's SW side. $10. MD-LD; 10-day limit. 20 RV/tent sites. Tbls, toilets, cfga, shelters, no drkg wtr or other services. Boating(l), fishing, hiking.

Gray Reef Reservoir Campground $10
Natrona County Park Board
Bureau of Reclamation
About 21 mi SW of Casper on SR 220; right on CR 412 for 0.5 mi; at W shore of North Platte River below reregulating dam. $10. LD-MD; 10-day limit. 24 RV/tent sites; 35-ft RV limit. Tbls, toilets, cfga, shelters, no drkg wtr, fishing pier. Fishing, boating(l), canoeing. Elev 5500 ft; 43 acres.

Lodgepole Campground $7
Muddy Mountain Environmental Education Area
Bureau of Land Management
9 mi S of Casper on Casper Mountain Rd; 6 mi to Muddy Mountain. $5 during 6/15-10/31; 14-day limit. 22 sites. Tbls, toilets, cfga, drkg wtr (at dam). Hunting, hiking trails. 200 acres. Non-campers pay $3 day use fee.

Miracle Mile Area FREE
Kortes Reservoir
Bureau of Reclamation
54 mi SW of Casper on US 220, then on CR 407 & CRs 291 & 351; Miracle Mile stretches about 5.5 mi from Kortes Dam to Pathfinder National Wildlife Refuge. Free. All year; 14-day limit. 11 primitive camping areas. Tbls, toilets, drkg wtr, cfga, fishing pier. Hiking, fishing.

Okie Beach Campground $10

Alcova Reservoir County Park
Natrona County Park Board
24 mi SW of Casper on SR 220; right on CR 406, becoming Lakeshore Dr; Okie Beach is first campground on W shore of lake. $10. MD-LD; 10-day limit. 16 sites, & open camping. Tbls, toilets, cfga, shelter, no drkg wtr. Boating(l), fishing, hiking.

Rim Campground $5
Muddy Mountain
Environmental Education Area
Bureau of Land Management
9 mi S of Casper on Casper Mountain Rd; 6 mi to Muddy Mountain. $5. 6/15-10/31; 14-day limit. 8 RV sites; tent spaces. Toilets, tbls, no drkg wtr except at Lodgepole Camp. Hunting, nature trails. Primarily a fall hunting camp. Non-campers pay $3 day use fee.

Sage Campground $10
Pathfinder Reservoir County Park
Natrona County Parks Board
Bureau of Reclamation
32 mi SW of Casper on SR 220; 6 mi S on CR 409 to lakeshore W of dam, just past Weiss Campground. $10. MD-LD; 10-day limit. Primitive designated sites with sheltered tbls, cfga, toilets, no drkg wtr. Boating(l), fishing, hiking. Park visitor center at dam. Interpretive trail, museum.

Tower Hill Campground $10
Casper Mountain County Park
Natrona County Park Board
8 mi S of Casper on SR 251 (Casper Mountain Rd); left on CR 506 (East End Rd), then veer right on Tower Hill Park Rd to campground. $10. MD-LD; 10-day limit. 11 designated sites. Tbls, toilets, cfga, no drkg wtr. Fishing, hiking, horseback riding, biking.

Weiss Campground $10
Pathfinder Reservoir County Park
Natrona County Park Board
Bureau of Reclamation
32 mi SW of Casper on SR 220; 5 mi S on CR 409; campground closest to Pathfinder Dam's museum & interpretive trail complex. $10. MD-LD; 10-day limit. 15 primitive designated sites. Tbls, toilets, cfga, no drkg wtr, dump. Fishing, boating(l), hiking. Dam

Westside Campground $10
Alcova Reservoir Park
Natrona County Park Board
24 mi SW of Casper on SR 220; right on CR 406, becoming Lakeshore Dr along W shore of lake; campground between marina & ski club. $10. MD-LD; 10-day limit. 19 RV & tent sites. Tbls, toilets, cfga, drkg wtr. Fishing, swimming, boating. Elev 5500 ft. Little Sandy Beach & RV Area just N of Westside Camp provides playground, swimming beach & sand volleyball as well as dump station and 12 reservable full-hookup RV sites for $35.

CENTENNIAL

Aspen Campground $10
Libby Creek Recreation Area
Medicine Bow National Forest
2 mi NW of Centennial on Hwy 130; qtr mi W on FR 351; at Libby Creek. $10. MD-9/30; 14-day limit. Free dry camping off-season. 8 sites (22-ft RV limit). Tbls, toilet, cfga, no drkg wtr. Fishing. Elev 8,600 ft.

Brooklyn Lake Campground $10
Medicine Bow National Forest
9.5 mi NW of Centennial on FR 317. $10. 7/15-LD; 14-day limit. 19 sites (22-ft RV limit). Tbls, toilets, cfga, drkg wtr. Fishing, boating (hand launch), hiking trails. Elev 10,581

ft; 7 acres. Trail to alpine lakes.

Nash Fork Campground $10
Medicine Bow National Forest
8 mi NW of Centennial on SR 130; N on FR 317. $10. 7/1-LD; 14-day limit. 27 sites; 22-ft RV limit. Tbls, toilets, cfga, drkg wtr. Fishing. Elev 10,385 ft; 16 acres.

North Fork Campground $10
Medicine Bow National Forest
3.5 mi NW of Centennial on SR 130; 1.7 mi NW on FR 101; at Little North Fork of Little Laramie River. $10. 7/1-9/30; 14-day limit. 10 sites (50 others closed in 2014 due to hazardous trees); 30-ft RV limit. Tbls, toilets, cfga, drkg wtr. Fishing, hiking trail, mountain biking. Elev 8600 ft.

Pine Campground $10
Libby Creek Recreation Area
Medicine Bow National Forest
2.3 mi NW of Centennial on Hwy 130; half mi NW on FR 351; at Libby Creek. $10. 5/15-9/30; 14-day limit. 6 sites (20-ft RV limit). Tbls, toilet, cfga, drkg wtr. Fishing. Elev 8639 ft.

Spruce Campground $10
Libby Creek Recreation Area
Medicine Bow National Forest
2.4 mi NW of Centennial on Hwy 130. $10. 5/15-9/30; 14-day limit. 8 sites (16-ft RV limit). Tbls, toilet, cfga, drkg wtr. Fishing. Elev 9555 ft.

Sugarloaf Campground $10
Medicine Bow National Forest
13 mi NW of Centennial on SR 130; 1 mi N on FR 346. $10. 7/15-LD; 14-day limit. 16 sites (RVs under 23 ft). Tbls, toilet, cfga, drkg wtr. Boating, fishing, hiking trails to alpine lakes. Elev 10,797 ft; 4 acres.

Willow Campground $10
Libby Creek Recreation Area
Medicine Bow National Forest
2 mi NW of Centennial on Hwy 130; half mi W on FR 351. $10. MD-9/30; 14-day limit. 16 sites (22-ft RV limit). Tbls, toilets, cfga, no drkg wtr. Fishing. Elev 8799 ft.

CHEYENNE

Curt Gowdy State Park $10
25 mi W of Cheyenne on Happy Jack Rd. to SR 210, then W to park. $10 residents ($17 non-residents). All year, but most wtr shut off after 10/1; 14-day limit. 145 sites; no RV length limit. Tbls, toilets, cfga, drkg wtr, dump, playgrounds. Boating(l), fishing, hiking, fishing pier, snowmobiling, beach (no swimming), birdwatching, ice fishing. Archery range. Elev 7,200 ft; 1,635 acres. Crystal and Granite Reservoirs; waterskiing. Natural area.

CODY

Big Game Campground $10
Shoshone National Forest
28.6 mi W of Cody on US 14/16/20. $10. 6/7-LD; 16-day
limit. 16 sites (32-ft RV limit). Tbls, toilets, cfga, drkg wtr.
Stream fishing. Poor cell phone reception. Elev 5900 ft; 10
acres. 25 mi from Yellowstone NP entrance.

Elk Fork Campground $10
Shoshone National Forest
29.2 mi W of Cody on US 14/16/20. $10 during 5/15-9/30;
16-day limit (free off-season but no wtr or services). 13
sites (22-ft RV limit). Tbls, toilets, cfga, drkg wtr. Stream
fishing; trailhead; public corrals. Trail along Elk Creek into
Washaki Wilderness. Elev 6000 ft; 4 acres.

Hogan and Luce Campground   FREE
Bureau of Land Management
Cody Field Offices
18 mi north of Cody off SR 120; left on Park County Rd
7RP, approx five miles; look for the Hogan-Luce Trailhead
sign and take a left onto the one-mile-long access road
to the site. 5 sites; Toilet, tbls, cfgr, Food Storage Boxes,
Hiking, Fishing. Horse trailer parking, stanchions and
hitching rails.

North Fork Campground $10
Buffalo Bill State Park
14 mi W of Cody on US 14/20/16 (North Fork Hwy). $10
WY residents ($17 non-residents). All year; 14-day limit;
limited facilities 10/1-4/30. 56 pull-through RV sites. Tbls,
toilets, cfga, drkg wtr, dump. Boating(l), fishing, swimming, hunting, waterskiing, windsurfing, biking, hiking.
Trout Creek Nature Trail.

North Shore Bay Campground $10
Buffalo Bill State Park
9 mi W of Cody on US 14/20/16 (North Fork Hwy). $10
WY residents ($17 non-residents). All year; 14-day limit;
limited facilities 10/1-4/30. 37 RV sites (29 pull-through, 3
backi-in, 5 tent only). Tbls, toilets, cfga, drkg wtr, dump.
Boating(l), fishing, swimming, hunting, waterskiing, windsurfing, biking, hiking.

Sunlight State Wildlife Management Area   FREE
13 mi N of Cody on SR 120; 25 mi W on FR 101 (Chief
Joseph Hwy). Free. 5/1-12/15; 14-day limit. Developed
campground with undesignated sites. Toilets, cfga, no
drkg wtr. Fishing, hiking, hunting, wildlife study. Area
inhabited by grizzly bears; store all food.

Threemile Campground $7.50
Shoshone National Forest
48.6 mi W of Cody on US 14/16/20. $7.50 with federal
senior pass others pay $15 7/1-LD; 16-day limit. 21 RV
sites; no tents or pop-ups due to bear danger; 32-ft RV
limit. Tbls, toilets, cfga, drkg wtr. Stream fishing, North

Fork of Shoshone River. Hiking trails nearby. Elev 6700
ft; 9 acres.

Wapiti Campground $7.50
Shoshone National Forest
29 mi W of Cody on US 14/16/20; at Shoshone River. $7.50
with federal senior pass others pay $15 at non-elec sites;
$20. 5/15-10/30; 16-day limit. 41 sites up to 50 ft. Tbls,
toilets, cfga, drkg wtr. Stream fishing, nearby hiking trails.
Elev 6000 ft; 20 acres. GPS: 44.46608, -109.62279

COKEVILLE

Cokeville City Park   FREE
In Cokeville on S side of Main St between 2nd St & Front
St; along RR track. Free (donation). All year; 1-day limit.
Tbls, toilets, cfga, drkg wtr, playground, pavilion. Golf.
307-279-3227.

Hams Fork Campground $7
Bridger National Forest
12 mi N of Cokeville on SR 232; 4 mi NE on county rd; 13 mi
E on FR 10062. $7. 5/1-9/1; 16-day limit. 13 sites, typically
45 ft. Tbls, toilets, cfga, drkg wtr. Nature trails, fishing.
Elev 8000 ft; 7 acres.

Hobble Creek Campground $7
Bridger National Forest
12.6 mi N of Cokeville on SR 232; bear right at "Y" onto FR
10062 for 8.4 mi; at second "Y," bear right for 4.9 mi; left
at Alice Lake sign for 9.1 mi. $7. 7/1-11/1; 16-day limit. 14
sites; 30-ft RV limit. Tbls, toilets, cfga, drkg wtr. Fishing,
hiking.

COOKE CITY (MONTANA)

Colter Campground $8
Custer Gallatin National Forest
2.3 mi E of Cooke City on US 212 in Wyoming. $8. 7/1-9/7;
16-day limit. 18 sites (48-ft RV limit); hard-sided RVs only
due to bear danger. Tbls, toilets, cfga, drkg wtr. Fishing,
hiking trails along Lady of the Lake Creek. Elev 7900 ft;
15 acres.

Crazy Creek Campground $10
Shoshone National Forest
10.5 mi SE of Cooke City on US 212. Along Clarks Fork
of Yellowstone River. $10. MD-LD; 16-day limit. 16 sites
(28-ft RV limit). No tents or folding trailers permitted due
to bears. Tbls, toilets, cfga, drkg wtr. Fishing, hiking.
Crazy Lakes trailhead to backcountry lakes in Absaroka-Beartooth Wilderness. Scenic walk to Crazy Creek
Falls. Elev 6900 ft.

Dead Indian Campground $10
Shoshone National Forest
40 mi SE of Cooke City, MT, on WY 296 (Chief Joseph
Scenic Hwy). $10 during MD-LD; free rest of year but no
services. All year; 16-day limit. 10 sites (RVs under 32 ft).

Tbls, toilets, cfga, no drkg wtr, no trash service. Fishing, hunting, hiking. Adjacent to Dead Indian Trailhead. 42 mi from Yellowstone. Elev 6100 ft; 11 acres.

Fox Creek Campground $10
Shoshone National Forest
7.5 mi SE of Cooke City on US 212 into Wyoming; at Fox Creek & Clarks Fork of Yellowstone River. $10 base with federal senior pass; others pay $20 base. Elec sites $60 ($30 with senior pass). 6/15-9/23; 16-day limit. 33 sites; 32-ft RV limit. Tbls, toilets, cfga, drkg wtr. Fishing, hiking, boating. Elev 7100 ft.

Hunter Peak Campground $7.50
Shoshone National Forest
14.4 mi SE of Cooke City on US 212; 5 mi S on Hwy 296. $7.50 with federal senior pass others pay $15; All year; 16-day limit. 10 sites (32-ft RV limit). Tbls, toilets, cfga, drkg wtr. Fishing, hiking. Elev 9600 ft.

Lake Creek Campground $10
Shoshone National Forest
14.4 mi SE of Cooke City on US 212. $10. 6/24-LD; 16-day limit. 6 sites (22-ft RV limit). Tbls, toilets, cfga, no drkg wtr. Fishing, hiking. Elev 6940 ft.

Little Sunlight Campground   FREE
Shoshone National Forest
In Sunlight Basin, 47 mi SE of Cooke City, MT, on WY 296 (Chief Joseph Scenic Hwy) & 13 mi on FR 101. Free; donations accepted. All year; 16-day limit. 5 dispersed sites (32-ft RV limit). Toilet, no drkg wtr, tbls & bear boxes. Horse corrals & hitchrails. Fishing, hiking, horseback riding.

DAYTON

Dead Swede Campground $8
Bighorn National Forest
34 mi SW of Dayton on US 14; 4 mi SE on FR 26. $8 with federal senior pass; others pay $16. June-Sept 14-day limit. 21 sites (40-ft RV limit). Tbls, toilets, cfga, drkg wtr. Fishing; on the South Tongue River; hiking. Elev 8500 ft; 10 acres.

North Tongue Campground $8
Bighorn National Forest
29 mi SW of Dayton on US 14; 1 mi N on FR 15. $8 with federal senior pass; others pay $16. June-Sept free in fall but no wtr or services; 14-day limit. 12 sites (60-ft RV limit). Tbls, toilets, cfga, drkg wtr. Store, dump nearby. Some handicap sites. Fishing. Elev 7800 ft; 4 acres.

Owen Creek Campground $8
Bighorn National Forest
34 mi SW of Dayton on US 14; qtr mi on FR 236. $8 with federal senior pass; others pay $16. June-Sept 14-day limit. 8 sites (45-ft RV limit). Tbls, toilets, cfga, drkg wtr. Fishing. Elev 8500 ft; 3 acres.

Prune Creek Campground $8.50
Bighorn National Forest
26 mi SW of Dayton on US 14. $8.50 with federal senior pass; others pay $17 June-Sept 14-day limit. 21 sites (60-ft RV limit); some handicap sites. Tbls, toilets, cfga, drkg wtr. Store nearby. Fishing, hiking. On South Tongue River at Prune Creek. Elev 7650 ft; 8 acres.

Sibley Lake Campground $8.50
Bighorn National Forest
25 mi SW of Dayton on US 14. $8 with federal senior pass at non-elec sites; others pay $16. $13 with senior pass at 15 elec sites; others pay $21. June-Sept; non-elec sites open & free in fall but no wtr or services; 14-day limit. 24 sites (60-ft RV limit). Tbls, toilets, cfga, drkg wtr. Fishing, boating(lr - no motors), hiking. Elev 7950 ft; 7 acres.

Tie Flume Campground $8.50
Bighorn National Forest
34 mi SW of Dayton on US 14; 2 mi E on FR 26. $8.50 with federal senior pass; others pay $17. June-Sept; some sites open & free in fall but no services or wtr; 14-day limit. 24 sites (60-ft RV limit). Tbls, toilets, cfga, drkg wtr. Fishing; hiking trails are nearby. Elev 7950 ft; 10 acres.

DOUGLAS

Ayres Natural Bridge   FREE
Converse County Park
12 mi W of Douglas on I-25 to exit 151; 5 mi S on CR 13. Camp free, but donations suggested. 4/1-11/1; 3-day limit. 5 sites (30-ft RV limit). Tbls, toilets, cfga, drkg wtr. Fishing, horseshoes, playground. Elev 5300 ft; Scenic mountain drives. Natural bridge. Reader says park open only 8-8 daily. Bridge

Campbell Creek Campground $10
Medicine Bow National Forest
2 mi S of Douglas on SR 94; right on Chalk Buttes Rd for 3 mi; left on SR 91 for 25 mi; continue S on unpaved Converse CR 24 for 14 mi. $10. 5/15-10/15. 6 sites; 22-ft RV limit. Tbls, Toilet, cfga, drkg wtr. Fishing, hiking. Elev 6800 ft.

Curtis Gulch Campground $10
Medicine Bow National Forest
20 mi W & S of Douglas on SR 91; 14 mi S on CR 16; 1 mi NE on FR 658 (gravel rds 25 mi from Douglas); at LaBonte Canyon. $10. 5/15-10/15; 14-day limit. 6 sites; 22-ft RV limit. Tbls, toilets, cfga, drkg wtr. Fishing, hiking. Elev 6800 ft. Note: also numerous dispersed campsites along FR 658 between Curtis Gulch & forest boundary along LaBonte Canyon.

Esterbrook Campground $10
Medicine Bow National Forest
16.4 mi S of Douglas on SR 94; bear left at "Y," Esterbrook Rd, for 10.8 mi; at second "Y," follow FR 633 qtr mi

through small town; at third "Y," bear left, staying on FR 633 for 3 mi. $10. 6/1-10/15; 14-day limit. 12 sites; 22-ft RV limit. Tbls, toilets, cfga, drkg wtr. Hiking, fishing.

Friend Park Campground $10
Medicine Bow National Forest
17 mi S of Douglas on SR 94; 11 mi S on CR 4; 15 mi SW on FR 653; 2 mi SE on FR 633. $10. 5/15-10/15; 14-day limit. 11 sites; 22-ft RV limit. Tbls, toilets, cfga, drkg wtr. Fishing, hiking.

Riverside City Park   FREE
Downtown Douglas on North Platte River; half mi E of I-25 from exit 140, cross river. Free. All year; 2-day limit. About 20 undesignated sites. Tbls, flush toilets, cfga, drkg wtr, showers, dump. Boating(l), fishing, hiking. Can be crowded in summer.

DRIGGS, (IDAHO)
Pine Creek Campground $10
Caribou-Targhee National Forest
5.3 mi W of Victor on SR 31. $10. 6/1-9/30; 16-day limit. 9 sites (32-ft RV limit). Tbls, toilets, cfga, no drkg wtr, no trash service. Hiking, fishing. Elev 7800 ft; 3 acres.

Teton Canyon Campground $12
Caribou-Targhee National Forest
6 mi E of Driggs on CR 009; 4.5 mi S on FR 009; in Wyoming. $12. 5/15-9/15; 14-day limit. 20 sites (30-ft RV limit). Tbls, toilets, cfga, drkg wtr. Beginning of Teton Crest Trail into Jedediah Smith Wilderness. Fishing, hiking. Elev 6900 ft; 4 acres.

Trail Creek Campground $12
Caribou-Targhee National Forest
5.5 mi E of Victor on SR 33; one-third mi S on SR 22. $12. 5/15-9/15; 14-day limit. 10 sites (32-ft RV limit). Tbls, toilets, cfga, drkg wtr. Fishing, hiking. Near Jedediah Smith Wilderness. Elev 6600 ft; 7 acres.

DUBOIS
Brooks Lake Campground $10
Shoshone National Forest
30 mi W on Hwy 287 from Dubois (gravel last 5 mi). $10. 6/15-9/30; 16-day limit. 13 sites (32-ft RV limit). NO drkg wtr, toilets, cfga, tbls. Fishing, hiking, boating(l). Elev 9200 ft; 9 acres.

Double Cabin Campground $7.50
Shoshone National Forest
28 mi N of Dubois on FRs 508 and 285 (hazardous when wet). $7.50 with federal senior pass others pay $15. MD-LD; 16-day limit. 14 sites (32-ft RV limit). Tbls, toilets, cfga, drkg wtr. Fishing, hiking. Elev 8053 ft; 8 acres. On edge of Washakie Wilderness area.

Falls Campground $7.50
Shoshone National Forest
25 mi NW of Dubois on US 26/287.$7.50 with federal senior pass others pay $15. $10 with senior pass at elec sites; others pay $20. 6/5-9/30; 16-day limit. 54 sites (32-ft RV limit). Tbls, toilets, cfga, drkg wtr. Fishing, hiking. Brooks Lake Creek Falls nearby. Elev 8000 ft; 18 acres.

Horse Creek Campground $7.50
Shoshone National Forest
12 mi N of Dubois on FRs 508 & 285 (hazardous when wet). $7.50 with federal senior pass others pay $15. 5/22-LD; 16-day limit. 9 sites (32-ft RV limit). Tbls, toilets, cfga, drkg wtr food storage required. Fishing, hiking. Trails to secluded lakes. Elev 7500 ft.

Pinnacles Campground $7.50
Shoshone National Forest
23 mi NW of Dubois on US 26/287; 15 mi N on FR 515. $7.50 with federal senior pass others pay $15. 6/26-LD; 16-day limit. 21 sites (32-ft RV limit). Tbls, toilets, cfga, drkg wtr food storage required. Fishing, hiking, boating. Elev 9200 ft; 14 acres.

ELK MOUNTAIN
Wick/Beumee Wildlife Management Area   FREE
Along I-80, 6 mi SE of Elk Mountain. Free. 4/1-11/30; 14-day limit. Primitive undesignated camping. Toilets, cfga, no drkg wtr (wtr available at Wagonhound interchange rest area). Fishing, hiking, hunting, wildlife study.

ENCAMPMENT
Bottle Creek Campground $10
Medicine Bow National Forest
5.8 mi SW of Encampment on SR 70; left at Hog Park Reservoir sign onto FR 550, then right at campground access. $10. MD-10/31; 14-day limit. No fees, wtr or services after 10/15. 16 sites; 16-ft RV limit. Tbls, toilets, cfga, well drkg wtr. Hiking, fishing. Elev 8700 ft; 4 acres.

Encampment River Canyon Trailhead $10
Bureau of Land Management
Rawlins Field Office
1 mi W of Encampment on SR 70; 1 mi S on CR 353; 1 mi on BLM rd. $10. 6/1-11/15 (weather permitting, free winter camping); 14-day limit. 8 sites; 25-ft RV limit. Tbls, toilets, cfga, no drkg wtr. Fishing; swimming; hiking; horseback riding; rockhounding; kayaking. Trail access to BLM Encampment River Canyon Wilderness WSA & USFS Encampment Wilderness Area. Free primitive camping also allowed anywhere within canyon; best sites with first 9 mi of trail.

Lost Creek Campground $10
Medicine Bow National Forest
17.3 mi SW of Encampment on SR 70. $10. 6/15-10/31; 14-day limit. 13 sites (22-ft RV limit). Tbls, toilets, cfga,

well drkg wtr. Hiking, fishing, rockhounding. Elev 8700 ft; 8 acres.

Six Mile Campground $10
Medicine Bow National Forest
24.6 mi SE of Encampment on SR 230; 2 mi SE on FR 492. $10. 5/15-10/31; 14-day limit. Free but no wtr or services off-season. 3 sites; 32-ft RV limit. Tbls, toilet, cfga, drkg wtr, no trash service. Fishing, boating, hiking. Elev 7800 ft.

EVANSTON

Bear River Campground $8
Wasatch National Forest
27.5 mi S of Evanston on SR 150; at the Bear River near FR 58 in Utah. $8 with federal senior pass; others pay $16.00 during May-Oct; free off-season, but Mirror Lake vehicles pass required all year: $6 for 3 days, $12 weekly or $45 annually. 14-day limit. 4 sites; 16-ft RV limit. Tbls, toilets, cfga, drkg wtr in-season. Fishing. Non-campers pay $7 day use fee.

Beaver View Campground $9
Wasatch National Forest
34.1 mi S of Evanston on SR 150; left at campground sign. In Utah. $9 with federal senior pass; others pay $18 during 6/15-10/15; free off-season but Mirror Lake vehicle pass required all year: $6 for 3 days, $12 weekly or $45 annually. No wtr after LD; 14-day limit. 17 sites; no RV size limit. Tbls, toilets, cfga, drkg wtr. Fishing, hiking trails. Elev 9000 ft. Non-campers pay $7 day use fee.

Christmas Meadows Campground $9
Wasatch National Forest
32 mi S of Evanston on SR 150 into Utah; 4 mi E on Christmas Meadows Rd. $9 with federal senior pass during 6/15-10/30; others pay $18. Free off-season but Mirror Lake vehicle pass required all year: $6 for 3 days, $12 weekly or $45 annually. No wtr after LD. 14-day limit. 11 sites, typically 40 ft. Tbls, toilets, cfga, drkg wtr. Hiking, fishing, horseback riding. Horse loading facilities. Trailhead to High Uintas Wilderness. Non-campers pay $7 day use fee.

East Fork Bear River Campground $8
Wasatch National Forest
27 mi S of Evanston on SR 150 into Utah; at East Fork Bear River. $8 with federal senior pass during June-Oct; others pay $16. Free off-season but Mirror Lake vehicle pass required all year: $6 for 3 days, $12 weekly or $45 annually. 14-day limit. 7 sites; 20-ft RV limit. Tbls, toilets, cfga, drkg wtr in-season. Fishing, hiking. Non-campers pay $7 day use fee.

Hayden Fork Campground $8
Wasatch National Forest
33 mi S of Evanston on SR 150 into Utah; at Hayden Fork of

the Bear River. $8 with federal senior pass; others pay $16 during 6/15-9/15; free off-season, but Mirror Lake vehicle pass required all year: $6 for 3 days, $12 weekly or $45 annually. 14-day limit. 9 sites (26-ft RV limit). Tbls, toilets, cfga, drkg wtr in-season. Fishing, hiking.

Stillwater Campground $9
Wasatch National Forest
32 mi S of Evanston on SR 150 into Utah; on E side of hwy. $9 with federal senior pass during MD-LD; others pay $18. Free off-season, but Mirror Lake vehicle pass required all year: $6 for 3 days, $12 weekly or $45 annually. 14-day limit. 21 single sites, typically 42 ft. Toilets, cfga, tbls, drkg wtr in-season. Fishing, biking/hiking trail. Elev 8500 ft. Non-campers pay $7 day use fee.

Sulphur Campground $9
Wasatch National Forest
39 mi S of Evanston on SR 150 into Utah; on W side of hwy. $9 with federal senior pass; during 6/15-10/15; others pay $18. Free off-season, but Mirror Lake vehicle pass required all year: $6 for 3 days, $12 weekly or $45 annually. 14-day limit. 21 sites, typically 45 ft. Drkg wtr, toilets, cfga, toilets; no wtr after LD. Fishing, hiking trails. Elev 9100 ft. Non-campers pay $7 day use fee.

Wolverine ATV Trailhead $7
Wasatch National Forest
37 mi S of Evanston on SR 150 into Utah; SE on FR 057 & FR 323; near Stillwater Fork of Bear River. $7.00 with federal senior pass others pay $14 June-Oct; 14-day limit. Free off-season, but Mirror Lake vehicle pass required all year: $6 for 3 days, $12 weekly or $45 annually. 6 dispersed sites; 16-ft RV limit. Tbls, toilets, cfga, no drkg wtr. Fishing, hiking, biking, horseback riding, ATV activity. Non-campers pay $7 day use fee.

FARSON

Big Sandy Recreation Area FREE
Bureau of Reclamation
8 mi N on US 191; 2 mi E on co rd. Free. 6/1-10/1; 14-day limit. 12 primitive sites. Tbls, toilets, cfga, no drkg wtr. Swimming, boating(l), fishing. Not well patrolled. Elev 6490 ft; 6190 acres.

FORT LARAMIE

Ft. Laramie City Park FREE
SW of town. From Ft Laramie, 1 m W on US 26, 1 blk S of jct US 85/26 on Ft. Laramie Ave; near RR track. Free but donations accepted. All year; 3-day limit. 25 non-elec sites. Tbls, toilets, cfga, drkg wtr, playground. Hunting, fishing. Elev 4200 ft; 3 acres. Lake Guernsey. Old Ft. Laramie. Register Cliff. Sunrise Mine.

FOXPARK

Bobbie Thomson Campground $10
Medicine Bow National Forest

7 me NW of Foxpark on FR 512; 5 mi on FR 542, cross Douglas Creek bridge and bear right. $10. 6/1-10/15; 14-day limit. 16 sites (32-ft RV limit); 2 pull-through. Tbls, toilet, cfga, drkg wtr. Fishing. Rob Roy Reservoir nearby. Elev 8710 ft.

Lake Owen Campground $10
Medicine Bow National Forest
7 mi NE of Foxpark on FR 517; 3 mi S on FR 540. $10. 5/15-9/30; 14-day limit. 35 sites (22-ft RV limit). Tbls, toilets, cfga, drkg wtr. Fishing, boating (launch nearby). Elev 8965 ft.

Miller Lake Campground $10
Medicine Bow National Forest
1 mi S of Foxpark on FR 512; at Evans Creek. $10. 5/15-19/30; 14-day limit. 7 sites (22-ft RV limit). Tbls, toilet, cfga, drkg wtr. Fishing, boating. Elev 9059 ft.

FREEDOM
Pinebar Campground   FREE
Caribou-Targhee National Forest
1 mi N of Freedom on CR 34; 9.5 mi W on SR 34. Free. 5/1-11/15; 14-day limit. 5 sites (30-ft RV limit). Tbls, toilets, cfga, no drkg wtr, firewood. Horseback riding, fishing, extensive hiking trail system.

Tin Cup Campground   FREE
Caribou-Targhee National Forest
1 mi N of Freedom on CR 111; 2.6 mi W on SR 34; at Tin Cup Creek. Free. 5/1-10/31; 14-day limit. 5 sites (16-ft RV limit). Toilet, no drkg wtr, cfga, tbls. Fishing, extensive hiking trails, biking

GLENDO
Glendo State Park Campground $10
3.5 mi E of Glendo on county rd; in state park. $10 WY residents ($17 non-residents). All year; limited facilities 10/1-4/1. 435 sites. Toilets, tbls, drkg wtr, cfga, dump. Hiking, canoeing, fishing, boating(l), playground. Elev 4700 ft; 9930 acres. Full-service marina nearby.
   Red Hills Area: About 30 sites; close to lake; ground not level.
   Reno Cove: About 30 sites; boat ramp; protected bay; ground not level, windy.
   Custer Cove, Soldier Rock and Colter Bay: About 40 sites; protected bay; some level sites.
   Whiskey Gulch and Sagebrush: About 100 sites; S side of large bay; many level sites.
   Two Moon: About 200 sites; largest & best camping area; on bluff overlooking lake; most sites level.
   Sandy Beach: Beach camping permitted, but no protection from wind; swimming; can be crowded in summer. Renovated in 2005; no RVs on beach, but tents okay.
   Elk Horn: About 20 sites, close to lake; boat ramp seasonal.

GLENROCK
Glenrock South   FREE
City Recreational Complex
From Birch St in Glenrock, 2 mi S on Mormon Canyon Rd (CR 18); right after going under I-25; at Deer Creek. Free, but fees for elec during events. 5-day limit. Tbls, toilets, cfga, drkg wtr, dump, playground. Ball fields, rodeo arena, fishing, paintball court. 307-436-9294.

GUERNSEY
Guernsey State Park $10
3 mi N of Guernsey, E on Hwy 26 from I-25 about 15 mi. $10 WY residents ($17 non-residents). All year; 14-day limit. Limited facilities 10/1-4/30. 240 sites at 7 campgrounds, including Fish Canyon on E side off Lakeshore Dr (good secluded tenting); Skyline on S end off Skyline Dr (best for large RVs). Tbls, toilets, cfga, drkg wtr, dump, beach. Fishing, boating (ld), hunting, hiking, waterskiing, windsurfing. Visitor center; museum open 10-6 daily 5/1-10/1. Oregon Trail wagon wheel ruts; Register Cliff. On 2,375-acre Guernsey Reservoir. Elev 4300 ft; 6,227 acres.

HAWK SPRINGS
Hawk Springs State Recreation Area $10
Off Hwy 85, 3 mi E on dirt rd. $10 WY residents ($17 non-residents). All year; 14-day limit; limited facilities 10/1-MD. 24 sites. Tbls, toilets, cfga, drkg wtr, beach, no dump. Boating(l), fishing, lake swimming, waterskiing, windsurfing. Elev 4400 ft; 50 acres. Blue heron rookery. POSSIBLE ROAD CLOSURES contact Goshen County 307 532-3879

HOBACK JUNCTION
East Table Creek Campground $7.50
Bridger-Teton National Forest
11 mi S of Hoback Junction on US 26/89; at Snake River. $7.50 with federal senior pass others pay $15. 5/1-9/1; 10-day limit. 17 sites, 28ft RV limit. Bear food storage required. Tbls, toilets, cfga, drkg wtr. Interpretive programs, boating(l), fishing, hiking, horseback riding. Overflow camp across hwy from Snake River, 17 sites, same fees.

Granite Creek Campground $7.50
Bridger-Teton National Forest
10 mi E of Hoback Junction on US 189/191; 6 mi N on FR 30500. $7.50 with federal senior pass others pay $15. 5/1-9/1; 10-day limit. 51 sites (28 ft RV limit) Tbls, toilets, cfga, drkg wtr. Thermal spring swimming, hiking, fishing, horseback riding, mountain biking and OHV riding.

Hoback Campground $7.50
Bridger-Teton National Forest
8 mi E of Hoback Junction on US 189/191; at Hoback River. $7.50 with federal senior pass others pay $15. 5/15 - 9/30; 10-day limit. 13 sites; 28-ft RV limit. Tbls, toilet, cfga, drkg wtr. Fly fishing, hiking.

Station Creek Campground $7.50
Bridger-Teton National Forest
14 mi S of Hoback Junction on US 26/89; at Snake River.
$7.50 with federal senior pass others pay $15. 5/15-9/10;
10-day limit. 16 sites, typically 45 ft but not suitable for
large RVs. Tbls, toilets, cfga, drkg wtr. Boating(l), fishing,
hiking trail.

Wolf Creek Campground $7.50
Bridger-Teton National Forest
7 mi S of Hoback Junction on US 26/89; at Snake River.
$7.50 with federal senior pass others pay $15. 5/15-9/1
10-day limit. 20 sites, typically 30 ft, a few larger pull
through. Tbls, toilets, cfga, drkg wtr. Fishing, rafting.

HYATTVILLE

Medicine Lodge $10
State Archaeological Site
6 mi NE of Hyattville off Hwy 31; about 4.5 mi N on Cold
Springs Rd; left at park sign on travel CR 268A. $10 WY
residents ($17 non-residents). 5/15-11/1; 14-day limit. 25
sites. Tbls, toilets, cfga, drkg wtr, playground, no dump.
Fishing, hunting, hiking, birdwatching, nature trail, rockhounding, mountain biking, 4-wheeling. Interpretive center. One of America's major digs; prehistoric petroglyphs
& pictographs on cliff walls.

JACKSON

Atherton Creek Campground $12
Bridger-Teton National Forest
2 mi N of Kelly on FR 30340; 5.2 mi E on FR 3040 (narrow
rd with sharp curves). $12. 5/1-9/1; 10-day limit. 20 sites
(30-ft RV limit). Bear food storage required. Tbls, toilets,
cfga, drkg wtr, fish cleaning station. Fishing, hunting,
boating (l), swimming. Lower Slide Lake. Elev 7250 ft.

Crystal Creek Campground $10
Bridger-Teton National Forest
2 mi N of Kelly on FR 30340; 10.5 mi E on FR 30400 (5 mi
of dirt rd); at Gros Ventre River. $10 during 5/15-9/10; free
in fall but no wtr or trash service; 10-day limit. 6 sites;
30-ft RV limit. Bear food storage required. Toilets, drkg
wtr, cfga. Fishing, hunting, hiking. Elev 7300 ft.

Curtis Canyon Campground $12
Bridger-Teton National Forest
1 mi E of Jackson on CR 25; 5 mi NE on FR 25; 3 mi E
on FR 98 (6 mi of dirt rd; small RVs only). $12. MD-LD;
10-day limit. 11 sites (24-ft RV limit). Bear food storage
required. Tbls, toilets, cfga, drkg wtr, firewood. Elev 6600
ft; 11 acres.

JEFFREY CITY

Cottonwood Campground $6
Bureau of Land Management
Lander Field Office
6 mi E of Jeffrey City on US 287; 8 mi S on Green Mountain

BLM Rd. $6. 6/1-10/31; 14-day limit. Free off-season. 18
sites. Tbls, toilets, cfga, drkg wtr. Hunting, fishing, hiking,
mountain biking. Elev 7800 ft; 320 acres along Cottonwood Creek.

KAYCEE

Kaycee Town Park   Donations
Just off I-25 and US 87; half block off Main St in Kaycee.
Donations. All year; 2-day limit. 15 pull-through sites (RVs
under 31 ft); 15 tent sites. Tbls, toilets, cfga. Store, food,
ice, laundry nearby. Hunting, fishing. Hole-in-the-Wall
Outlaw Cave. Historical tours. Q

KEMMERER

Fontenelle Creek Recreation Area $7
Bureau of Land Management
32 mi NE of Kemmerer on SR 189. $7. 5/20-10/15; 14-day
limit. 55 sites. Tbls, flush toilets, cfga, drkg wtr, dump
($3), fish cleaning station. Boating(l), playground, fishing.

Names Hill   FREE
Bureau of Land Management
34 mi N of Kemmerer on Us 189. Free. All year; 14-day
limit. Primitive undesignated sites. Tbls, cfga, no drkg wtr,
no toilets. Thousands of westward immigrants passed
near here and carved their names on the cliff faces;
among them was trapper Jim Bridger.

Slate Creek Campground   FREE
Bureau of Land Management
Kemmerer Field Office
From Kemmerer, take US 189 east 25 miles to WY 372. Go
8.4 miles and turn left onto Fontenelle Road. Located on
the west side of the Green River, approximately four miles
south of Fontenelle Reservoir. Gravel access roads within
campground, two ADA accessible 8 total sites vault toilets,
Tbls, CGFA. Fishing, Birdwatching

Tailrace Campground   FREE
Bureau of Land Management/Bur. of Reclamation
Kemmerer Field Office
25 mi E of Kemmerer on Hwy 189, then 8.4 mi on SR 372;
left onto County Line Rd; below Fontenelle Reservoir,
cross dam; along the Green River. Primitive rds. Free. 5/1-
11/30 (limited access in winter); 14-day limit. 3 sites. Tbls,
1 toilet, cfga, no drkg wtr. Canoeing, rafting (good river
access), birdwatching, fishing. Former gathering site of
mountain men during their annual rendezvous.

Weeping Rock Camp   FREE
Bureau of Land Management/Bur. of Reclamation
Kemmerer Field Office
25 mi E of Kemmerer on Hwy 189, then 8.4 mi on SR 372;
left onto County Line Rd for 5 mi at the Fontenelle Reservoir dam. Primitive rds. Free. All year; 14-day limit. 10
sites. Tbls, 1 toilet, no drkg wtr. Canoeing, rafting (good
river access), birdwatching, fishing.

KINNEAR

Morton Lake   FREE
Bureau of Reclamation
1 mi N of Kinnear. Free. All year; 14-day limit. 12 primitive sites. Tbls, toilets, cfga, drkg wtr. Boating, fishing, swimming.

LANDER

Atlantic City Campground $6
Bureau of Land Management
Lander Field Office
30 mi S of Lander on SR 28; 1 mi on Atlantic City Rd. $6. 6/1-10/31; 14-day limit. Free off-season when free of snow, but no wtr. 18 sites. Tbls, toilets, drkg wtr, cfga. Hunting, fishing, historical sites, mountain biking, rock climbing. Elev 8100 ft; 40 acres.

Big Atlantic Gulch Campground $6
Bureau of Land Management
Lander Field Office
30 mi S of Lander on SR 28; 1 mi on Atlantic City Rd. $6. 6/1-10/31; 14-day limit. Free off-season depending on snow, but no wtr. 10 sites. Tbls, toilets, drkg wtr, cfga. Hunting, fishing, historical area, mountain biking, rock climbing. Elev 8000 ft; 40 acres.

Fiddlers Lake Campground $7.50
Shoshone National Forest
8.7 mi SW of Lander on SR 131; 14.7 mi SW on FR 300, Loop Rd. $7.50 with federal senior pass others pay $15. 7/1-9/15; 16-day limit. 20 sites (40-ft RV limit). Tbls, toilets, cfga, drkg wtr. Boating(l), fishing, hiking. Elev 9400 ft; 4 acres.

Louis Lake Campground $10
Shoshone National Forest
8.7 mi SW of Lander on Hwy 701; 21.4 mi SW on FR 308. $10. 7/1-9/15; 16-day limit. 9 sites; 24-ft RV limit. Tbls, toilets, cfga, No drkg wtr. Boating(l), fishing, hiking. Elev 8600 ft.

Sinks Canyon Campground $7.50
Shoshone National Forest
8 mi SE of Lander on US 287. $7.50 with federal senior pass others pay $15. 5/1-10/31; 16-day limit. 5 RV sites (20-ft RV limit). Tbls, toilets, cfga, drkg wtr. Stream fishing, Middle Fork of Popo Agie River. Elev 6850 ft.

Sinks Canyon State Park $10
6 mi SW of Lander on SR 131. $10 WY residents ($17 non-residents). All year; 14-day limit; limited facilities 11/1-5/1. 29 sites; 40-ft RV limit. Tbls, toilets, cfga, drkg wtr, dump. Visitor center (MD-LD), nature program, fishing, trout display, hiking trails, fishing pier, birdwatching, rock climbing. River vanishes into a large cavern, then reappears in trout pool. Elev 6400 ft; 600 acres.

Sweetwater River Campgrounds   FREE
Bureau of Land Management
Rock Springs Field Office
33 mi S of Lander (1 mi S of the South Pass rest area) on SR 28; 23 mi W on CR 453, then about 8 mi on BLM 4105 to two camping areas (Guard Station and Bridge). Free. All year; 14-day limit. Primitive undesignated sites. Toilets, cfga, tbls, no drkg wtr. Fishing, hiking.

Worthen Meadow Campground $7.50
Shoshone National Forest
18 mi SW of Lander on SR 131.$7.50 with federal senior pass others pay $15. 7/1-10/15; 16-day limit. 28 sites (24-ft RV limit). Tbls, toilets, cfga, drkg wtr. Boating(l), fishing, hiking. Trails to Popo Agie Wilderness. Elev 8800 ft.

LARAMIE

Pelton Creek Campground $10
Medicine Bow National Forest
40 mi SW of Laramie on SR 230; 8 mi NW on FR 898. Along Douglas Creek. $10. 6/15-10/15; 14-day limit. 16 sites; only 9 sites open, typically 40 ft but 16-ft RV limit. Tbls, toilets, cfga, drkg wtr. Fishing, hiking trails.

Rob Roy Campground $10
Medicine Bow National Forest
22 mi W of Laramie on SR 130; 11 mi SW on Hwy 11; 9 mi W on FR 500. $10. 5/15-10/1; 14-day limit. 65 sites (35-ft RV limit), but only lower loop near boat ramp open. Tbls, toilets, cfga, no drkg wtr. Fishing, boating(l), hiking. At 500-acre Rob Roy Reservoir. Elev 9559 ft; 8 acres.

Tie City Campground   10
Medicine Bow National Forest
20 mi SE of Laramie; i-80 E 9.6 mi exit 323 WY 210 E/ Happy Jack Rd (Follow signs to Happy Jack Recreation area); 1.3 mi to FR 723. $10 6/1-9/30; Free when services unavailable; Interior road is narrrow and rough in places. Tbls, toilets, cfga, drkg wtr. Nearby corrals and mountain bike trails. Elev 8580.

Sybille/Johnson Creek State Access Area   FREE
14 mi N of Laramie on US 30/287; 18 mi E on SR 34; near Johnson Reservoir. Free. All year; 14-day limit (visitor center open spring-fall). Developed campground; primitive sites. Toilets, cfga, no drkg wtr. Fishing, hiking, hunting, wildlife study, exhibits, interpretive programs. Facility manages endangered wildlife, including breeding the Wyoming toad.

Vedauwoo Campground $10
Medicine Bow National Forest
19 mi SE of Laramie on I-80; 1 mi E on FR 722. $10. 6/1-9/30; 14-day limit. 28 sites (32-ft RV limit). Tbls, toilets, cfga, drkg wtr. Rock climbing, hiking trails. Unusual rock formation. Elev 8257 ft; 5 acres.

Yellow Pine Campground $10
Medicine Bow National Forest
12.3 mi SE of Laramie on I-80; 3 mi E on FR 722. $10.
MD-9/30; 14-day limit. 19 sites (32-ft RV limit). Tbls,
toilets, cfga, no drkg wtr. Fishing, hiking. Elev 8349 ft;
2 acres.

LONETREE

Henry's Fork Trailhead   FREE
Wasatch National Forest
8 mi S of Lonetree on Cedar Basin Rd; 15 mi W on FR 58
to jct with FR 77 at Henry's Fork Creek. Free. 6/1-10/15;
14-day limit. 7 sites; 20-ft RV limit. Toilets, cfga, no drkg
wtr. Hunting, horse trails, hiking trails, fishing. Elev 9600
ft.

LOVELL

Afterbay Campground $10.00
Bighorn Canyon National Recreation Area
42 mi S of Hardin on SR 313; 1 mi NE of Yellowtail Dam.
$5 entrance fee; $10 camping. All year; 14-day limit. 28
sites (20-ft RV limit); 12 more sites (no wtr) on N shore of
Afterbay. Tbls, toilets, dump, cfga, drkg wtr. Boating(l),
fishing, visitor center, recreational program, nature trails,
swimming.

Bald Mountain Campground $8
Bighorn National Forest
33 mi E of Lovell on US 14A. $8 with federal senior pass;
others pay $16. Juune-Sept free in fall but no wtr or
services; 14-day limit. 15 sites (55-ft RV limit); some
handicap sites. Tbls, toilets, cfga, drkg wtr. Fishing. Elev
9200 ft; 4 acres.

Barry's Landing Campground $5
Bighorn Canyon National Recreation Area
2 mi E of Lovell on US 14A; 24 mi N on SR 37 into Montana.
$5. Free, but entry fee charged. All year; 14-day limit.
15 sites, 5 are tent only. Tbls, toilets, cfga, no drkg wtr.
Boating(l), fishing, hiking.

Five Springs Falls $7
Bureau of Land Management
Cody Field Office
22 mi E of Lovell on Hwy 14A; 2 mi N on steep, narrow
access rd. $7. All year (but closed by snow); 14-day limit.
19 sites (25-ft RV limit on access rd). Tbls, toilets, cfga,
drkg wtr. Hiking trails, nature program, hunting, bird
watching.

Horseshoe Bend $10
Bighorn Canyon National Recreation Area
National Park Service
2 mi E of Lovell on US 14A to Jct 37; 14 mi N. $5 entry fee;
$10 at primitive sites, $20 utility fee at 19 elec sites (no
discount for federal senior pass). All year no utilities Sept-

May; 14-day limit. 48 sites. Tbls, toilets, cfga, drkg wtr,
dump. Fishing, boating(r), hiking, campfire talks. Pryor
Mtn Wild Horse Range.

Lovell Camper Park   FREE
On Quebec Avenue in Lovell. Camp free, but donations
encouraged. 5/1-9/30; 3-day limit. 15 sites. Flush toilets,
showers, drkg wtr, cfga, tbls, dump, wtr refill station. Store,
laundry, ice, food nearby. Swimming, fishing, golf, playground. Bighorn Canyon NRA nearby.

Porcupine Campground $8
Bighorn National Forest
33 mi E of Lovell on US 14A; 1.6 mi N on FR 13. $8 with
federal senior pass; others pay $16. June-Sept free in fall
but no wtr or services; 14-day limit. 14 sites (60-ft RV limit);
some handicap sites. Tbls, toilets, cfga, drkg wtr. Fishing.
Elev 8900 ft; 5 acres.

Trail Creek Campground $10
Bighorn Canyon National Recreation Area
2 mi E of Lovell, WY via US 14A, 24 mi N on HWY 37. $5
NRA entry fee; $10 canping. Open all year; 14-day limit.
4 RV/tent sites, 16 tent sites (16-ft RV limit). Tbls, toilets,
cfga, no drkg wtr. Swimming; boat ramp; fishing.

Yellowtail State Wildlife Management Area   FREE
6 mi E of Lovell on US 14A. Free. All year; 14-day limit.
Primitive undesignated camping; no facilities, no drkg wtr.
Fishing, hiking, hunting, boating, wildlife study.

MEDICINE BOW

Prior Flat Campground   FREE
Bureau of Land Management
22 mi N of Medicine Bow on SR 487; 9 mi NW on SR 77; 10
mi W on CR 102; left on Shirley Mtn Loop Rd about 3/4 mi.
Free. 6/1-11/15; 14-day limit. 15 sites. Tbls, toilets, cfga,
no drkg wtr. Hunting, mountain biking. Note: Dispersed
camping is permitted throughout the adjacent Shirley
Mountains.

MEETEETSE

Brown Mountain Campground   FREE
Shoshone National Forest
5 mi SW of Meeteetse on Hwy 290; 15.8 mi SW on county
rd; 3.2 mi W on FR 200. Camp free, but donations encouraged. 5/13-10/31; 16-day limit. 7 sites (16-ft RV limit & 1
40-ft site). Tbls, toilets, cfga, no drkg wtr, no trash service. Fishing, hiking. No cell phone service. Elev 7600 ft.

Jack Creek Campground   FREE
Shoshone National Forest
10 mi W of Meeteetse on Hwy 290; 20 mi W on FR 208.
Camp free, but donations encouraged. All year; 16-day
limit. 7 sites (RVs under 33 ft). Tbls, toilets, cfga, no drkg
wtr. Fishing. Access to Washakie Wilderness. No cell phone
service. Elev 7600 ft.

Wood River Campground FREE
Shoshone National Forest
5 mi SW of Meeteetse on Hwy 290; 15.8 mi SW on county rd; 0.7 mi W on FR 200. Camp free, but donations encouraged. 5/13-9/30; 16-day limit. 5 sites (30-ft RV limit). Tbls, toilets, cfga, no drkg wtr, no trash service. Fishing, hiking. Elev 7300 ft.

MOORCROFT
Keyhole State Park $10
12 mi E of Moorcroft on I-90; 6 mi N on paved co rd from Pine Ridge exit. $10 WY residents ($17 non-residents). All year; 14-day limit. 283 sites at 9 campgrounds overlooking lake (large RVs okay). Tbls, toilets, cfga, drkg wtr, dump, amphitheater, beach, playground. Fishing, boating(l), swimming, hunting, windsurfing, waterskiing. Limited facilities 10/1-5/1. Elev 4100 ft; 6256 acres.

Wind Creek Area: On W side of Pine Haven, accessed from I-90 at Moorcroft. 15 undeveloped sites, tbls, restrooms, no drkg wtr.

Coulter Bay Area: Next to the town of Pine Haven. 15 developed sites (half are walk in), tbls, restrooms, shelters, boat ramp.

Pat's Point Area: Next to park headquarters & marina. 33 sites, tbls, restrooms, shelters, playground, boat ramp.

Pronghorn Area: Next to park headquarters & marina. 36 sites, tbls, restrooms, playground.

Arch Rock Area: Next to park headquarters & marina. 14 sites, tbls, restrooms.

Homestead Area: Past park headquarters. 40 sites, restroom, tbls.

Cottonwood Area: Past park headquarters. 31 sites, restrooms, tbls, playground, shelters.

Rocky Point Area: Near the dam. 16 undeveloped sites, tbls, restrooms.

Tatanka Area; reservation only 5/15-9/15; 33 sites with wtr and elec hookups.

MOOSE
Signal Mountain Campground $12
Grand Teton National Park
18 mi N of Moose on Teton Park Rd. $12 with federal senior pass; others pay $24 std site. Elec site $47 or $35 with federal senior pass. 5/6-10/16; 14-day limit. 81 sites; 30-ft RV limit. Tbls, flush toilets, cfga, drkg wtr, dump, shore, no showers. Recreation program, boating(lrd), fishing, hiking. Entry fee.

MORAN
Hatchet Campground $10
Teton National Forest
8 mi E of Moran on US 26 (qtr mi W of Buffalo Ranger Station). $10 during 5/15-9/30, $5/ night through Oct, free rest of yr when accessible, but no wtr; 14-day limit. 8 sites (18-ft RV limit, 1 site 24-ft). Tbls, toilets, cfga, drkg wtr, food storage boxes. Hunting. Within Grizzly Recovery Area. Elev 8000 ft. Camp hosts.

Lizard Creek Campground $12
Grand Teton National Park
17 mi N of Moran on US 89. $12 with federal senior pass; others pay $24. About 6/10-LD; 14-day limit. 60 sites; 30-ft RV limit. Tbls, flush toilets, cfga, drkg wtr, dump. Fishing, swimming, boating. On Jackson Lake.

Pacific Creek Campground $10
Bridger-Teton National Forest
About 8 mi NE of Moran Junction on US 287 (access through Grand Teton NP), then N on Pacific Creek Rd (access rough). $10 during 5/15-10/31; free rest of yr when accessible, no wtr; 14-day limit. 8 sites; 38-ft RV limit. Tbls, toilets, cfga, bear-resistant food storage boxes, corral, hitchrails. Fishing, hunting, horseback riding. Elev 7000 ft. Camp hosts.

Sheffield Campground $5
Bridger-Teton National Forest
1 mi E off Hwy 89/287, 1 mi S of Flagg Ranch & across Sheffield Creek; high-clearance vehicles recommended. $5 during 5/15-9/1; free in fall but no services; 14-day limit. Tbls, toilets, cfga, no drkg wtr. Fishing, hiking. Elev 8200 ft.

Turpin Meadow Campground $10
Bridger-Teton National Forest
About 13 mi E of Moran Junction on US 287 (access through Grand Teton NP); N on FR 30050 (Buffalo Valley Rd). $10 during 5/15-9/1; free in fall but no wtr or trash service; 16-day limit. 18 sites; 30-ft RV limit. Tbls, toilets, cfga, drkg wtr, bear-resistant food storage boxes, corral, hitchrails at sites. Fishing, hunting. Stream. Elev 7300 ft. Primary access point for Teton Wilderness. Camp hosts.

MOUNTAIN VIEW
Bridger Lake Campground $9
Wasatch National Forest
7 mi SW of Mountain View on Wyoming SR 410; 16.5 mi S on CR 283 (becoming FR 72); half mi on FR 126. $9 with federal senior pass; others pay $18. 6/1-10/15, but no wtr after LD; 14-day limit. 28 sites; 45-ft limit. toilets, cfga, drkg wtr. Fishing, hunting, hiking trails, canoeing, biking Elev 9400 ft.

China Meadows Campground $7
Wasatch National Forest
7 mi SW of Mountain View on WY 410; 18.4 mi S on CR 283 (becoming FR 72); S of China Lake. $7.00 with federal senior pass others pay $14. About 7/1-10/15, but no wtr after LD; 7-day limit. 9 sites; 20-ft RV limit. Toilets, cfga, no drkg wtr. Fishing, hunting, boating(l). Elev 10,000 ft

East Fork of Black Forks Trailhead FREE
Wasatch National Forest
S of Evanston on SR 410; SW on FR 073 past Meeks Cabin

Lake to end of rd at Blacks Fork Trail on branch of Blacks Fork River. 8 sites; 20-ft RV limit. Tbls, toilets, cfga, no drkg wtr, horse loading ramps. Hiking, fishing, horseback riding.

Hoop Lake Campground $8
Wasatch National Forest
26.6 mi SE of Mountain View on Hwy 414; 3.2 mi S on CR 264; 6.5 mi SE on FR 58. $8 with federal senior pass; others pay $16. 6/15-10/30, 14-day limit. 44 sites (25-ft RV limit). Tbls, toilets, cfga, drkg wtr (no wtr after LD). Fishing, boating(l), hiking, horseback riding.

Little Lyman Lake Campground $7
Wasatch National Forest
12.9 mi S of Mountain View on WY 410; left at Blacks Fork Access sign on CR 271 for 13.1 mi; rd becomes FR 058 for 5.9 mi; at "Y," bear right on FR 058 for 2.4 mi; right at next jct, still on FR 058, then left on FR 070 for half mi to Little Lyman access rd. $7.0 with federal senior pass others pay $14. MD-LD; 14-day limit. 10 sites; 16-ft RV limit. Tbls, toilets, cfga, drkg wtr. Mountain biking, fishing.

Marsh Lake Campground $9
Wasatch National Forest
7 mi SW of Mountain View on WY 410; 17.8 mi S on FR 72. $9 with federal senior pass; others pay $18. 6/1-10/15, but no wtr after LD; 14-day limit. 40 single sites in 2 areas; 45-ft RV limit. Toilets, cfga, no drkg wtr. Hiking, hunting, horse trails, fishing, canoeing. Elev 9400 ft.

Meeks Cabin Campground $8
Wasatch National Forest
S of Mountain View on SR 410; W on FR 073. $8 with federal senior pass; others pay $16 during 6/15-10/30. Free rest of year, but no drkg wtr after LD; 14-day limit. 24 sites; 45-ft RV limit. Tbls, toilets, cfga, drkg wtr. Swimming, fishing. Elev 8700 ft; 12 acres. Non-campers pay $7 day use fee.

Stateline Campground $9
Wasatch National Forest
7 mi S of Mountain View on WY 410; 8.2 mi on Uinta CR 283; 5.5 mi on FR 072. $9 with federal senior pass; others pay $18. 5/15-10/15; 14-day limit. 41 sites; 30-ft RV limit. Tbls, toilets, cfga, drkg wtr. Fishing, boating, hiking trails, biking trails, canoeing, bridle trails, swimming.

NEWCASTLE

Beaver Creek Campground $10
Black Hills National Forest
18 mi N of Newcastle on US 85; 6 mi E on FR 811; camp is just past forest boundary. $10 during MD-LD; free rest of year; 10-day limit. 8 sites; 45-ft RV limit. Tbls, toilet, cfga, drkg wtr. Fishing. Elev 6500 ft.

Redbank Spring Campground $10
Black Hills National Forest
14 mi NE of Newcastle. $10. All year; 10-day limit. 4 sites (40-ft RV limit). Tbls, toilets, cfga, no drkg wtr. Fishing. Elev 6600 ft.

PINEDALE

Fremont Lake Campground $12
Bridger-Teton National Forest
1 mi NE of Pinedale on SR 187; 2.5 mi NE on CR 111; one mi E on Hwy 187 (interior rd narrow & rough). $12, MD-LD; 10-day limit. 56 sites, typically 45 ft. Tbls, toilets, cfga, drkg wtr, firewood. Boating(l), fishing, waterskiing. Elev 7600 ft; 77 acres.

Green River Lake Campground $12
Bridger National Forest
5 mi N of Pinedale on US 191; 28.5 mi E on SR 352; At "Y," bear right on FR 650 for 16 mi; at Lower Green River Lake. $12. 7/1-9/15; 10-day limit. 39 sites, typically 50 ft. Tbls, toilets, cfga, drkg wtr. Swimming, fishing, horseback riding. Elev 8000 ft; 19 acres.

Half Moon Lake $7
Bridger-Teton National Forest
From jct with US 191 at Pinedale, 7 mi N on Fremont Lake Rd; bear right at Half Moon Resort sign for 1.2 mi, then right at campground sign; at NE shore of lake. $7. 6/1-9/15; 10-day limit. 19 sites, typically 43 ft. Tbls, toilets, no drkg wtr. Fishing, swimming, boating (launch, docks nearby).

Narrows Campground $12
Bridger-Teton National Forest
5.5 mi NW of Pinedale on US 191; 13.5 mi N on SR 352; right on FR 730 for 5.5 mi; near NW corner of Lower New Fork Lake at strait between upper & lower lakes. $12. 6/1-9/15; 10-day limit. 19 sites (30-ft RV limit). Tbls, toilets, cfga, drkg wtr, firewood. Swimming, fishing, boating(l), waterskiing. Elev 7800 ft.

New Fork Lake Campground $7
Bridger-Teton National Forest
5.5 mi NW of Pinedale on US 191; 13.5 mi N on SR 352; 3.2 mi E on FR 730. $7. 6/1-9/15; 10-day limit. 15 sites, typically 30 ft. Tbls, toilets, cfga, no drkg wtr. Fishing, boating(l), mountain biking, hiking.

Soda Lake State Wildlife Management Area FREE
5 mi N of Pinedale on Willow Lake Rd. Free. 5/10-11/15; 14-day limit. Primitive campground; no facilities, no drkg wtr. Fishing, hiking, wildlife study.

Stokes Crossing FREE
Bureau of Land Management
22 mi N of Pinedale on US 171. Free. All year; 14-day limit.

2 sites. Tbls, toilets, cfga, no drkg wtr. Fishing, hunting. Elev 7300 ft.

Trails End Campground $12
Bridger-Teton National Forest
3 mi N of Pinedale on Fremont Lake Rd; 9 mi N on FR 740. $12. 6/1-9/15; 10-day limit. 8 sites (20-ft RV limit). Tbls, toilets, cfga, drkg wtr. Trail entrance to wilderness area.

Upper Green River Recreation Area FREE
Bureau of Land Management
24 mi N of Pinedale on Hwy 191 to Warren Bridge; 2 mi NE to site. Free. 6/1-10/31; 14-day limit. 12 sites (RVs under 33 ft). Tbls, toilets, cfga, no drkg wtr, information kiosk, dump. Floating, fishing.

Warren Bridge Campground $10
Bureau of Land Management
Pinedale Field Office
20 mi N of Pinedale on US 191. $10. 5/1-10/31; 14-day limit. 16 sites (30-ft RV limit). Tbls, toilets, cfga, drkg wtr, dump($5). Boating, fishing, hiking, nature program. 20 acres on Green River. Elev 7600

Whiskey Grove Campground $7
Bridger-TetonN ational Forest
5.5 mi W of Pinedale on US 191; 24 mi N on WY 352; along Green River. $7 when wtr available; free when no wtr. 6/15-9/15; 10-day limit. 9 sites. Tbls, toilets, cfga, drkg wtr. Fishing.

Willow Lake Campground FREE
Bridger-Teton National Forest
0.5 mi W of Pinedale on US 191; 8.5 mi N on Willow Lake Rd; 1.4 mi W on FR 751; on S shore of lake. Free. 6/1-9/15; 16-day limit. 7 sites. Tbls, toilets, cfga, no drkg wtr. Hiking, mountain biking, fishing, swimming, boating(l).

POWELL (51)
Homesteader Park FREE
Park County
Hwy 14A, E city limits. Free. 4/15-10/31; 2-day limit. 25 RV sites, unlimited tent camping. Tbls, toilets, cfga, drkg wtr, dump. Sightseeing. Renovated in 2010.

RANCHESTER
Connor Battlefield State Historic Site $11
2 blocks off Hwy 14 at Ranchester; in oxbow of Tongue River. $11. 5/1-10/1; 14-day limit. 20 sites. Tbls, toilets, cfga, drkg wtr, playground, no dump. Fishing, horseshoes, beach. Site of 1865 expedition against Arapaho village.

RAWLINS
Teton Reservoir FREE
Bureau of Land Management
Rawlins Field Office
15 mi S of Rawlins on SR 71/CR 401. Free. All year; 14-day

limit. 5 sites. Tbls, toilets, cfga, no drkg wtr. Fishing, hunting, boating(l).

RIVERSIDE
Bennett Peak $10
Bureau of Land Management
Rawlins Field Office
4 mi E of Riverside on SR 230; 12 mi E on French Creek Rd; 7 mi S on Bennett Peak Rd. $10. Free off-season but no wtr. 6/1-11/15; 14-day limit. 11 sites. Tbls, toilets, drkg wtr, cfga. Fishing, floating, canoeing, hunting, boating (l), nature trails. On North Platte River.

Corral Creek FREE
Bureau of Land Management
Rawlins Field Office
4 mi E of Riverside on SR 230; 12 mi E on French Creek Rd (CR 660); left for 7 mi on Bennett Peak Rd. Free. 6/1-11/15; 14-day limit. 6 sites. Tbls, toilets, cfga, no drkg wtr. Hiking trail, fishing, hunting. Popular big-game hunting site. Elev 7200 ft.

RIVERTON
Ocean Lake State Wildlife Management Area FREE
17 mi NW of Riverton on US 26; dispersed primitive camping around the lake. Free. All year; 14-day limit. Toilets, cfga, tbls, no drkg wtr. Fishing, hiking, hunting, boating(l). Developed day-use facilities managed by Bureau of Reclamation. Nesting habitat for sandhill & whooping cranes, other waterfowl. Several thousand pheasants released each year for hunters.

ROCK SPRINGS
Three Patches FREE
Bureau of Land Management
Rock Springs Field Office
S of Rock Springs on SR 130, then 10 mi S on Aspen Mountain Rd; near top of Aspen Mountain. Free. May-Oct; 14-day limit. Primitive undesignated sites, popular for picnicking. Tbls, toilets, cfga, no drkg wtr. Hiking.

SARATOGA
Bow River Campground $10
Medicine Bow National Forest
20.1 mi E of Saratoga on SR 130; left at North Brush Creek Rd (FR 100) for 19.8 mi; right at campground sign. $10 during 6/1-9/30; free off-season but no wtr or services; 14-day limit. 13 sites (32-ft RV limit). Tbls, toilets, cfga, well drkg wtr. Fishing. Elev 8600 ft; 6 acres. Good wildlife viewing.

Deep Creek Campground $10
Medicine Bow National Forest
20.1 mi E of Saratoga on SR 130; 20 mi N on FR 100 (Brush Creek Rd); bear right on FR 101 at "Y" for 9.8 mi. $10. 7/1-10/1; 14-day limit. 11 sites (1 RV pull-through), typically 40

ft, but 22-ft RV limit. Tbls, toilets, cfga, drkg wtr. Boating (hand launch), fishing, hiking trails. Elev 10000 ft;.

French Creek Campground $10
Medicine Bow National Forest
24 mi E of Saratoga on SR 130; 4.5 mi S on FR 225; right on FR 225 for 6.4 mi; right on FR 206 for 3.7 mi. $10 during MD-10/15; free off-season but no wtr or services; 14-day limit. 11 sites (32-ft RV limit). Tbls, toilets, cfga, drkg wtr. Fishing, hiking.

Jack Creek Campground $10
Medicine Bow National Forest
16 mi W of Saratoga on CR 500; 5 mi S on CR 405/FR 452. $10 during MD-10/31; free off-season but no wtr or services; 14-day limit. 16 sites (4 pull-through), typically 43 ft, but 22-ft RV limit. Tbls, toilets, cfga, well drkg wtr, fishing, hiking. Elev 8400 ft; 5 acres.

Lincoln Park Campground $10
Medicine Bow National Forest
20.2 mi SE of Saratoga on SR 130; 2.6 mi NE on FR 100. $10. 6/1-10/1; 14-day limit. 12 sites; 32-ft RV limit. Tbls, toilets, cfga, drkg wtr. Fishing. Elev 7800 ft.

Ryan Park Campground $10
Medicine Bow National Forest
8 mi SE of Saratoga on SR 130; 12 mi E on SR 130. $10. June-Sept; 14-day limit. 48 sites (32-ft RV limit); 13 pull-through. Tbls, toilets, cfga, well drkg wtr. Fishing, hiking. Elev 8900 ft; 18 acres. GPS: 41.32570107, -106.492524389

Saratoga Lake Campground $10
Municipal Park
1 mi N of Saratoga on Hwy 230; 1 mi E on Saratoga Lake Rd. $10 at 24 non-elec RV sites, $15 at 25 elec sites; $7 tents. May-Sept. Tbls, toilets, cfga, drkg wtr, dump, playground. Swimming, boating(ld), fishing, horseshoes.

Treasure Island Public Fishing Area FREE
9 mi S of Saratoga on Hwy 230; E on dirt rd, following signs. Free. All year; 14-day limit. Primitive undesignated sites at public access to North Platte River. Toilets, tbls, cfga, no drkg wtr. Fishing, boating(l).

SHELL

Lower Paintrock Lake Campground $7.50
Bighorn National Forest
15.7 mi NE of Shell on US 14; 25.7 mi SE on FR 17. $7.50 with federal senior pass others pay $15. June-Sept; free off-season but no wtr or services; 14-day limit. 5 sites; 60-ft RV limit. Tbls, toilets, cfga, drkg wtr. Fishing, boating(l), hiking. Elev 9300 ft.

Medicine Lodge Lake Campground $7.50
Bighorn National Forest
15.7 mi NE of Shell on US 14; 25 mi SE on FR 17. $7.50

with federal senior pass others pay $15. June-Sept; free off-season but no wtr or services; 14-day limit. 13 sites (45-ft RV limit). Tbls, toilets, cfga, drkg wtr. Boating, fishing, hiking trails. Elev 9300 ft; 5 acres.

Shell Creek Campground $8
Bighorn National Forest
15.7 mi NE of Shell on US 14; 1.2 mi S on FR 17. $8 with federal senior pass; others pay $16 June-Sept; free off-season but no wtr or services; 14-day limit. 12 sites (60-ft RV limit). Tbls, toilets, cfga, drkg wtr. Fishing, hiking trails; riding stable nearby. Elev 7500 ft; 7 acres.

SHOSHONI

Boysen State Park $10
12 mi NW of Shoshoni on US 20. Access also from Hwy 26 S of lake. $10 WY residents ($17 non-residents). All year; 14-day limit; limited facilities 10/1-3/31. 279 sites at 11 campgrounds (9 around lake). Tbls, toilets, cfga, drkg wtr, dump, group shelters, beach, playgrounds. Swimming, boating(ldr), fishing, hunting, waterskiing, windsurfing. Wind River Canyon. Elev 4820 ft; 19,560 acres.

SINCLAIR

Seminoe State Park $10
30 mi N of Sinclair on Seminoe Rd. $10 WY residents ($17 non-residents). All year; 14-day limit. 84 sites in 4 areas (35-ft RV limit). Tbls, toilets, drkg wtr, cfga, dump. Limited facilities 9/15-5/15. Swimming, boating(l), fishing. Seminoe Dam, sand dunes, North Platte River. Travel difficult Dec 1-Apr 15; snow; 4WD may be needed. Elev 6350 ft; 3821 acres.

The Dugway Recreation Site FREE
Bureau of Land Management
Rawlins Field Office
8 mi N of Sinclair on CR 351 (Seminoe Rd) to North Platte River. Free. All year, depending on weather and accessibility; 14-day limit. 5 sites. Tbls, toilets, cfga, no drkg wtr. Hunting, fishing, canoeing, boating. Take-out for canoes & kayaks.

SMOOT

Allred Flat Campground $10
Bridger-Teton National Forest
15.5 mi S of Smoot on US 89; qtr mi N on FR 10131; at Little White Creek. $10. 5/1-9/1; 10-day limit. 32 sites, typically 30 ft. Tbls, toilets, cfga, drkg wtr. Hiking, fishing. Elev 7000 ft; 8 acres. Beaver ponds, bird watching.

Cottonwood Lake Campground $10
Bridger-Teton National Forest
1 mi S of Smoot on US 89; 1.1 mi E on CR 153; 6.7 mi E on FR 10208. N end of Cottonwood Lake. $10. MD-LD; 10-day limit. 18 sites; 30-ft RV limit, 6 sites w/hitching posts. Tbls, toilets, cfga, drkg wtr. Boating, fishing, canoeing, ATV trails.

SUNDANCE

Cook Lake Recreation Area $9.00
Black Hills National Forest
20 mi N of Sundance on US 16 and FRs 838, 841, 843 & 842. $9.00 with federal senior pass; others pay $18 during 5/15-9/15. Off-season fees $10 ($5 with federal senior pass). All year; 10-day limit. 32 sites; 45-ft RV limit. Tbls, toilets, cfga, drkg wtr. Boating, fishing, mountain biking, hiking, canoeing. Elev 4800 ft.

Reuter Campground $10
Black Hills National Forest
5 mi NW of Sundance. 2 mi W on US 14; 3 mi on FR 838. $10. All year; 10-day limit. 24 sites; 45-ft RV limit. Tbls, toilets, cfga, drkg wtr. Boating, fishing, hiking.

TEN SLEEP

Boulder Park Campground $8
Bighorn National Forest
20 mi NE of Ten Sleep on US 16; half mi W on FR 27; 1.5 mi S on forest rd. $8 with federal senior pass; others pay $16. June-Sept; 30-day limit. 32 sites (40-ft RV limit). Tbls, toilets, cfga, drkg wtr. Store. Fishing, hiking. On Tensleep Creek. Elev 8000 ft; 10 acres.

Castle Garden Scenic Area FREE
Bureau of Land Management
1 mi W of Ten Sleep on Hwy 16/20 to Castle Garden Turn-off; left on unpaved Two Mile Hill Rd for 6 mi. Free. 6/1-10/31; 14-day limit. 2 sites (RV under 18 ft). Tbls, toilets, cfga, no drkg wtr. Hunting.

Deer Park Campground $8
Bighorn National Forest
20 mi NE of Ten Sleep on US 16; 6 mi N on FR 27. $7.50 with federal senior pass; others pay $16. June-Sept; 14-day limit. 7 sites (35-ft RV limit). Tbls, toilets, cfga, drkg wtr. Hiking, fishing. Trails to East Tensleep Lake and Cloud Peak Wilderness. Elev 8900 ft; 3 acres.

Island Park Campground $8
Bighorn National Forest
20 mi NE of Ten Sleep on US 16; 4 mi N on FR 27. $8 with federal senior pass; others pay $16. June-Sept 14-day limit. 10 sites (40-ft RV limit). Tbls, toilets, cfga, drkg wtr. Fishing, hiking. Along Tensleep Creek. Elev 8600 ft; 4 acres.

Lake View Campground $8.50
Bighorn National Forest
24 mi NE of Ten Sleep on US 16. $8.50 with federal senior pass; others pay $17. June-Sept; 14-day limit. 12 sites; 30-ft RV limit. Tbls, toilets, cfga, drkg wtr. Boating(lr), fishing, hiking. On NE shore of Meadowlark Lake. Elev 8300 ft.

Leigh Creek Campground $7.50
Bighorn National Forest
8 mi NE of Ten Sleep on US 16; 1 mi N on FR 18. $7.50 with federal senior pass others pay $15 with June-Sept; 14-day limit. 6 sites; 45-ft RV limit. Tbls, toilets, cfga, drkg wtr. Fishing in Leigh and Tensleep Creeks for brook trout. Elev 5400 ft; 5 acres.

Middle Fork of Powder River FREE
Bureau of Land Management
S of Ten Sleep on SR 434 to Big Trails, then E on BLM Dry Farm Rd. to Hazelton Rd., then S to the camp. Free. 6/1-10/31; 14-day limit. 5 sites. Toilets, cfga, drkg wtr, no trash service. Hunting. S of here on Arminto Rd is Hole in the Wall, where Butch Cassady & gang hid out.

Sitting Bull Campground $8.50
Bighorn National Forest
23 mi NE of Ten Sleep on US 16; 1 mi N on FR 432. $8.50 with federal senior pass; others pay $17. June-Sept; 14-day limit. 42 sites, typically 70 ft. Tbls, toilets, cfga, drkg wtr. Boating, fishing, hiking & nature trails. Elev 8600 ft; 21 acres.

West Tensleep Lake Campground $8
Bighorn National Forest
20 mi NE of Ten Sleep on US 16; 7.5 mi N on FR 27. $8 with federal senior pass; others pay $18. June-Sept; free off-season but no wtr or services; 14-day limit. 9 sites (35-ft RV limit). Tbls, toilets, cfga, drkg wtr. Fishing, hiking. Trail to Cloud Peak Wilderness. Elev 9100 ft; 4 acres.

TORRINGTON

Pioneer Municipal Park $10
At W 15th Ave & West E St, Torrington. $10 for elec sites at S end of park. 5/1-9/30; 10-day limit. 30-35 sites. Tbls, flush toilets, no open fires; grills ok, drkg wtr, dump. Picnic area.

WALTMAN

Buffalo Creek FREE
Bureau of Land Management
Casper Field Office
From Waltman (W of Casper on US 20/26), 12 Mi N on Buffalo Creek Rd to Arminto, then NW 8.5 mi on Big Horn Mountain Rd. Free. All year; 14-day limit. Undesignated primitive sites. Toilets, no drkg wtr. Hunting, fishing.

Grave Springs FREE
Bureau of Land Management
Casper Field Office
From Waltman (W of Casper on US 20/26), 12 mi N on Buffalo Creek Rd to Arminto, then NW 11.5 mi on Big Horn Mountain Rd. Free. All year, but limited access in winter; 14-day limit. 10 sites. Toilets, no drkg wtr. Hunting, fishing.

WESTON
Weston Hills Recreation Area   FREE
Bureau of Land Management
6 mi S of Weston on SR 59; just W of Thunder Basin National Grassland segment. Free. All year; 14-day limit. Primitive undesignated sites; no facilities, no drkg wtr. Hiking, horseback riding, hunting, OHV activity. 2-mi ATV trail open 10/16-9/14 but closed during hunting season. Dispersed camping permitted throughout the area and the grassland.

WHEATLAND
Festo Lake   FREE
Platte County Campground
Near Wheatland; follow signs. Free. Primitive undesignated camping; no facilities. Fishing, boating. Lake

Rock Lake Campground   FREE
Platte County Park
Next to Wheatland Reservoir #1. Free. All year; 5-day limit. Primitive undesignated sites. Fishing, boating.

Wheatland Reservoir #1, #2, #3   FREE
Platte County Park
Near Wheatland. Free. All year; 5-day limit. Primitive undesignated sites. Fishing, boating. Lake

Wheatland Campground   FREE
Lewis City Park
From I-25, E on any primary street (Walnut, Cole, South St) to 8th St; park is on 8th between Cole & Walnut on SE edge of town. Donations accepted, but camp free. All year; 3-day limit. 10 back-in 20/30-amp RV sites; 5 tent sites. Tbls, cfga, toilets, drkg wtr, hookups, elec, showers($) at pool, dump, wtr refill station. 307-322-2962.

YELLOWSTONE NATIONAL PARK
Bridge Bay Campground $11.75
30 mi E of Yellowstone entrance near Yellowstone Lake. $11.75 with federal senior pass; others pay $23.50. About 5/20-9/5 14-day limit. 432 sites; 40-ft RV limit. Tbls, flush toilets, cfga, drkg wtr, food storage boxes. Coin showers & laundry within 4 mi. Fishing, hiking, evening ranger programs June-Sept.

Indian Creek Campground $7.50
7.5 mi S of Mammoth Hot Springs Junction on the Mammoth-Norris Rd. $7.50 with federal senior pass others pay $15. About 6/10-9/12; 14-day limit. 70 sites, some pull-through; 10 @ 35ft 35 @ 30ft RV limit. Tbls, toilets, cfga, drkg wtr. No generators. Fishing. Elev 7300 ft.

Lewis Lake Campground $7.50
10 mi S of W Thumb Junction, on Lewis Lake. $7.50 with federal senior pass others pay $15. 6/15-11/6, 14-day limit. 85 sites; 25-ft RV limit. Tbls, toilets, cfga, drkg wtr. Fishing. Elev 7800 ft.

Madison Campground $11.75
14 mi E of West Yellowstone entrance & 16 mi N of Old Faithful near jct of Gibbon, Madison & Firehole Rivers. $11.75 with federal senior pass; others pay $23.50. 270 sites; 40-ft RV limit. 4/29-10/16; 14-day limit. Tbls, flush toilets, cfga, drkg wtr, food storage boxes, dump. Generators 8am-8pm. Evening ranger programs. Elev 6800.

Mammoth Campground $10
5 mi from N entrance. $10 with federal senior pass; others pay $20. All year; 14-day limit. 85 sites, most pull-through; 75-ft RV limit. Tbls, flush toilets, cfga, drkg wtr. Generators 8am-8pm. Fishing, hiking, evening ranger programs. Elev 6200 ft.

Norris Campground $10
On W side of park, 21 mi S of Mammoth Hot Springs & 12 mi W of Canyon. $10 with federal senior pass; others pay $20. 5/20-9/26; 14-day limit. More than 100 sites; 30 to 50-ft RV limits. Tbls, flush toilets, cfga, drkg wtr. Generators 8am-8pm. Fishing, hiking. Near Norris Geyser Basin. Elev 7500

Pebble Creek Campground $7.50
9 mi E of Northeast Entrance of Yellowstone NP. $7.50 with federal senior pass others pay $15. 6/15-9/26; 14-day limit. 27 sites. Tbls, toilets, cfga, drkg wtr. Food Storage Boxes available. Elev 6900 ft. No generators. Hiking, fishing.

Slough Creek Campground $7.50
5 mi E of Tower Junction; at Slough Creek. $7.50 with federal senior pass others pay $15. 6/13-10/27; 14-day limit. 23 sites; 30-ft RV limit. Tbls, toilets, cfga, drkg wtr. Fishing. Elev 6250 ft. Evening interpretive programs, hiking, fishing.

Tower Fall Campground $7.50
5 mi SE of Tower Junction; near Tower Creek. $7.50 with federal senior pass others pay $15. 6/15-10/7; 14-day limit. 31 sites; 30-ft RV limit. Tbls, pit toilets, cfga, drkg wtr. Food Storage Boxes. No Generators/. Fishing, hiking horseback riding. Store. Elev 6600 ft.